THE HISTORY OF PARLIAMENT

THE HOUSE OF COMMONS 1820–1832

Already published:

The House of Commons, 1386–1421, ed. J. S. Roskell,
Linda Clark and Carole Rawcliffe (4 vols., 1992)

The House of Commons, 1509–1558, ed. S. T. Bindoff
(3 vols., 1982)

The House of Commons, 1559–1603, ed. P. W. Hasler
(3 vols., 1981)

The House of Commons, 1660–1690, ed. B. D. Henning
(3 vols., 1983)

The House of Commons, 1690–1715, ed. E. Cruickshanks,
S. Handley and D.W. Hayton
(5 vols., 2002)

The House of Commons, 1715–1754, ed. Romney Sedgwick
(2 vols., 1970)

The House of Commons, 1754–1790, ed. Sir Lewis Namier
and John Brooke (3 vols., 1964)

The House of Commons, 1790–1820, ed. R. G. Thorne
(5 vols., 1986)

In preparation:

The House of Commons, 1422–1504
The House of Commons, 1604–1629
The House of Commons, 1640–1660
The House of Commons, 1832–1868
The House of Lords, 1660–1832

John Charles Spencer, Viscount Althorp
by Charles Turner, 1832 (National Portrait Gallery, London)

THE HISTORY OF PARLIAMENT

THE
HOUSE OF COMMONS
1820–1832

D. R. Fisher

VII
MEMBERS
S–Y

PUBLISHED FOR THE HISTORY OF PARLIAMENT TRUST
BY CAMBRIDGE UNIVERSITY PRESS
2009

CAMBRIDGE UNIVERSITY PRESS

Cambridge, New York, Melbourne, Madrid, Cape Town, Singapore, São Paulo, Delhi

Cambridge University Press
The Edinburgh Building, Cambridge CB2 8RU, UK

Published in the United States of America by Cambridge University Press, New York

www.cambridge.org
Information on this title: www.cambridge.org/9780521193146

First published 2009

Printed in the United Kingdom at the University Press, Cambridge

A catalogue record for this publication is available from the British Library

ISBN 978-0-521-19317-7 Volume 1 hardback
ISBN 978-0-521-19320-7 Volume 2 hardback
ISBN 978-0-521-19322-1 Volume 3 hardback
ISBN 978-0-521-19325-2 Volume 4 hardback
ISBN 978-0-521-19328-3 Volume 5 hardback
ISBN 978-0-521-19331-3 Volume 6 hardback
ISBN 978-0-521-19334-4 Volume 7 hardback
ISBN 978-0-521-19314-6 7-volume set hardback

Contents

Contributors

S.R.B.	Stephen Bairstow
M.P.J.C.	Martin Casey
R.B.C.	Richard Cockett
M.M.E.	Margaret Escott
S.M.F.	Stephen Farrell
D.R.F.	David Fisher
S.R.H.	Simon Harratt
R.M.H.	Robin Healey
T.A.J.	Terry Jenkins
S.K.	Sharman Kadish
P.J.S.	Philip Salmon
H.J.S.	Howard Spencer

Editorial note

A raised asterisk (*) following a name denotes a Member of the House of Commons during the period covered by these volumes, where such inference is not apparent from the surrounding text. A raised dagger (†) against a name indicates a Member sitting outside the period and for whom an entry is to be found in earlier or later volumes. Where two (or more) Members bear exactly the same name and style they have been differentiated by the addition of roman numerals according to when they first entered Parliament, for instance John Fane I, John Fane II. This numbering is specific to this section of the *History* only, and does not reflect a Member's seniority by age or within his family. For other conventions concerning the arrangement and content of biographies, the reader should refer to the section on 'Method' in Volume I (pp. xxi–xxvi).

Abbreviations

In addition to standard and self-explanatory abbreviations, the following abbreviations are used in this volume.

In the preliminary paragraphs:

abp.	archbishop
adn.	archdeacon
adv.	advocate
att.-gen.	attorney-general
Bar.	Baron
bp.	bishop
called	called to the bar
c.bar. exch.	chief baron of the exchequer
cdr.	commander
ch.	child, children
chan.	chancellor
c.j.	chief justice
coh.	coheir(ess)
commn.	commission
commr.	comissioner
c.p.	common pleas
cr.	created
ct.	court
cttee.	committee
dep.	deputy
d.s.p.	died *sine prole* (without issue)
d.v.p.	died *vita patris* (in the lifetime of his father)
e.	elder, eldest
E.I.	East Indies, East India
exch.	exchequer
f.m.	field marshall
Ft.	Foot regiment
g.s.	grammar school
[GB]	Great Britain

h.	heir(ess)
h.s.	high school
[I]	Ireland, Irish
jt.	joint
k.b.	king's bench
l.c.b.	lord chief baron of exchequer
l.c.j.c.p.	lord chief justice of common pleas
mq.	marquess
o.	only
posth.	posthumous
preb.	prebend, prebendary
q.m.g.	quartermaster general
q. sess.	quarter sessions
rect.	rector
recvr.	receiver
res.	resigned
ret.	retired
[S]	Scotland, Scottish
SCJ	Senator of the College of Justice
s.p.	*sine prole* (without issue)
s.p.m.	(without male issue)
suc.	succeeded
treas.	treasurer
[UK]	United Kingdom
vic.	vicar
vol.	volunteer
w.	wife
W.I.	West Indies, West Indian
wid.	widow
yr.	younger

In the endnotes:

Add.	Additional manuscripts, British Library
AHR	*American Historical Review*
Al. Cant.	*Alumni Cantabrigienses* ed. Venn
Al. Ox.	*Alumni Oxonienses* ed. Foster
Althorp Letters	*Letters of Lord Althorp* (private, 1929)
Ann. Reg.	*Annual Register*
AO	Archive(s) Office
Arbuthnot Corresp.	*The Correspondence of Charles Arbuthnot* ed. A. Aspinall (Camden ser. 3, lxv, 1941)
Arbuthnot Jnl.	*The Journal of Mrs. Arbuthnot, 1820–1832* ed. F. Bamford and the Duke of Wellington, 2vv (1950)

Argyll Mems.	8th Duke of Argyll, *Autobiography and Memoirs* ed. Dowager Duchess of Argyll, 2vv (1906)
Arniston Mems.	*The Arniston Memoirs. Three Centuries of a Scottish House* ed. G.W.T. Omond (1887)
Arnould, *Denman*	Sir J. Arnould, *Memoirs of Thomas, Lord Denman*, 2vv (1873)
AS	Archive Service
Ashley, *Palmerston*	Evelyn Ashley, *The Life of Henry John Temple, Viscount Palmerston*, 2vv (3rd edn. 1877)
Bagot, *Canning and Friends*	*George Canning and his Friends* ed. J. Bagot, 2vv (1909)
Balfour, *Aberdeen*	Lady Frances Balfour, *The Life of George, 4th Earl of Aberdeen*, 2vv (1922)
Baring Jnls.	*Journals and Correspondence of Francis Thornhill Baring, Baron Northbrook, 1808–1852* ed. Earl of Northbrook, 2vv (private, Winchester, 1905)
Bentham Coresp.	*The Correspondence of Jeremy Bentham* ed. T.L.S. Sprigge *et al*, 5vv (1968–81)
Berry Jnls.	*Extracts from the Journals and Correspondence of Miss [Mary] Berry, 1783–1852* ed. Lady Theresa Lewis, 3vv (1866)
BIHR/HR	*Bulletin of the Institute of Historical Research/ Historical Research*
Bk.	*Book*
BL	British Library
Blakiston, *Lord William Russell*	Georgiana Blakiston, *Lord William Russell and his Wife, 1815–1846* (1972)
Bodl.	Bodleian Library, Oxford
Borthwick	Borthwick Institute of Historical Research, York
Brougham, *Life and Times*	*The Life and Times of Henry, Lord Brougham, written by Himself*, 3vv (1871)
Broughton, *Recollections*	Lord Broughton, *Recollections of a Long Life* ed. Lady Dorchester, 6vv (1909–11)
Buckingham, *Mems. Geo. IV*	Duke of Buckingham and Chandos, *Memoirs of the Court of George IV, 1820–1830*, 2vv (1859)
Bulwer, *Palmerston*	Sir Henry Lytton Bulwer, *The Life of Henry John Temple, Viscount Palmerston*, 3vv (1870–4)
Bunbury Mem.	*Memoir and Literary Remains of Sir Henry Edward Bunbury* ed. Sir C.J.F. Bunbury (private, 1868)
Burke Coresp.	*The Correspondence of Edmund Burke* ed. various, 10vv (Cambridge, 1958–78)
Burke LG	*Burke's Landed Gentry*
Burke PB	*Burke's Peerage and Baronetage*
Buxton Mems.	*Memoirs of Sir Thomas Fowell Buxton* ed. C. Buxton (1848)

Cam. Soc.	Camden Society
Canning's Ministry	*The Formation of Canning's Ministry, February to August 1827* ed. A. Aspinall (Camden ser. 3, lix, 1937)
Canning Official Corresp.	*Some Official Correspondence of George Canning* ed. E.J. Stapleton, 2vv (1887)
Castlereagh Corresp.	*Correspondence, Despatches, and Other Papers of Viscount Castlereagh* (ser. 3) ed. Marquess of Londonderry, 4vv (1853)
CB	*Complete Baronetage*
CITR	*Calendar of Inner Temple Records*
CJ	*Journals of the House of Commons*
Cockburn Jnl.	*Journal of Henry Cockburn, 1831–1854*, 2vv (Edinburgh, 1874)
Cockburn, *Jeffrey*	Lord Cockburn, *Life of Lord Jeffrey*, 2vv (Edinburgh, 1850)
Cockburn Letters	*Letters Chiefly Connected with the Affairs of Scotland, from Henry Cockburn to Thomas Francis Kennedy, 1818–1852* (1874)
Cockburn Mems.	Henry Cockburn, *Memorials of His Time* ed. K.F.C. Miller (Chicago, 1974)
Colchester Diary	*The Diary and Correspondence of Charles Abbot, Lord Colchester* ed. Lord Colchester, 3vv (1861)
Countess Granville Letters	*Letters of Harriet, Countess Granville, 1818–1845* ed. F. Leveson Gower, 2vv (1894)
Cowley Diary	*The Diary and Correspondence of Henry Wellesley, First Lord Cowley, 1790–1846* ed. F.A. Wellesley (1930)
CP	*Complete Peerage*
Crabb Robinson Diary	*Diary, Reminiscences and Correspondence of Henry Crabb Robinson* ed. T. Sadler, 2vv (3rd edn. 1872)
Creevey Pprs.	*The Creevey Papers* ed. Sir Herbert Maxwell, 2vv (2nd edn. 1904)
Creevey's Life and Times	*Creevey's Life and Times* ed. J. Gore (1937 edn.)
Croker Pprs.	*The Correspondence and Diaries of John Wilson Croker* ed. L.J. Jennings, 3vv (1884)
CUL	Cambridge University Library
D. Am. B.	*Dictionary of American Biography*
Disraeli Letters	*Benjamin Disraeli Letters* ed. various, 7vv (Toronto, 1982–2004)
DNB	*Dictionary of National Biography*
DWB	*Dictionary of Welsh Biography*
Dyott's Diary	*Dyott's Diary, 1781–1845* ed. R.W. Jeffery, 2vv (1907)

EcHR	*Economic History Review*
Edgeworth Letters	*Maria Edgeworth. Letters from England, 1813–1844* ed. C. Colvin (Oxford, 1971)
Eg.	Egerton mss, British Library
EHR	*English Historical Review*
Ellenborough Diary	Lord Ellenborough, *A Political Diary, 1828–1830* ed. Lord Colchester, 2vv (1881)
Farington Diary	*The Diary of Joseph Farington* ed. various, 16vv (Yale, 1978–84)
Fox Jnl.	*The Journal of Henry Edward Fox, 1818–1830* ed. Lord Ilchester (1923)
Gen. Mag.	*Genealogist's Magazine*
Gent. Mag.	*Gentleman's Magazine*
Geo. IV Letters	*The Letters of King George IV* ed. A. Aspinall, 3vv (Cambridge, 1938)
GL	Guildhall Library
Gladstone Diaries	*The Gladstone Diaries* ed. M.R.D. Foot and H.G.C. Matthew, 14vv (Oxford, 1994)
Glenbervie Diaries	*The Diaries of Sylvester Douglas (Lord Glenbervie)* ed. F. Bickley, 2vv (1928)
Glenbervie Jnls.	*The Glenberve Journals* ed. W. Sichel (1910)
Greville Mems.	*The Greville Memoirs* ed. L. Strachey and R. Fulford, 8vv (1938)
Gronow Reminiscences	*The Reminiscences and Recollections of Captain Gronow*, 2vv (1900 edn.)
Heber Letters	R.H. Cholmondeley, *The Heber Letters, 1783–1832* (1950)
HEHL	Henry E. Huntington Library, San Marino, California
Heron, *Notes*	Sir Robert Heron, *Notes* (2nd edn. 1851)
Highland Lady	*Memoirs of a Highland Lady* ed. Lady Strachey (1911)
HJ	*Historical Journal*
HLB/HLQ	*Huntington Library Bulletin*, later *Huntington Library Quarterly*
HLRO	House of Lords Record Office (Parliamentary Archives)
HMC	*Historical Manuscripts Commission*
Hobhouse Diary	*The Diary of Henry Hobhouse (1820–1827)* ed. A. Aspinall (1947)
Holland, *Further Mems.*	Lord Holland, *Further Memoirs of the Whig Party, 1807–1821* ed. Lord Stavordale (1905)
Holland, *Mems. Whig Party*	Lord Holland, *Memoirs of the Whig Party during My Time* ed. Lord Holland, 2vv (1852)

Abbreviations	
Holland House Diaries	*The Holland House Diaries* ed. A.D. Kriegel (1977)
Horner Pprs.	*The Horner Papers* ed. K. Bourne and W.B. Taylor (Edinburgh, 1994)
Howard Sisters	*Three Howard Sisters* ed. Lady Leconfield and J. Gore (1955)
HP	*History of Parliament*
Huskisson Pprs.	*The Huskisson Papers* ed. L. Melville (1931)
IGI	International Genealogical Index
IHR	Institute of Historical Research
IR	Death duty registers
JBS	*Journal of British Studies*
JEH	*Journal of Ecclesiastical History*
JMH	*Journal of Modern History*
JRL	John Rylands University Library, Manchester
Lady Holland Jnl.	*The Journal of Elizabeth, Lady Holland (1791–1811)* ed. Lord Ilchester, 2vv (1908)
Lady Holland to Son	*Elizabeth, Lady Holland to her Son, 1821–1845* ed. Lord Ilchester (1946)
Lady-in-Waiting	Lady Charlotte Bury, *The Diary of a Lady-in-Waiting* ed. A.F. Steuart (1908)
Lady Lyttelton Coresp.	*Correspondence of Sarah Spencer, Lady Lyttelton, 1787–1870* ed. Mrs. Hugh Wyndham (1912)
Lady Palmerston Letters	*Letters of Lady Palmerston* ed. T. Lever (1957)
Later Corresp. Geo. III	*The Later Correspondence of George III* ed. A. Aspinall, 5vv (Cambridge, 1962–70)
Le Marchant, *Althorp*	Sir Denis Le Marchant, *Memoir of John Charles, Viscount Althorp, Third Earl Spencer* (1876)
Leveson Gower Coresp.	*Lord Granville Leveson Gower. Private Correspondence, 1781 to 1821* ed. Countess Granville, 2vv (1916)
Lieven Letters	*Letters of Dorothea, Princess Lieven, during her residence in London, 1812–1834* ed. L.G. Robinson (1902)
Lieven-Palmerston Coresp.	*The Lieven-Palmerston Correspondence, 1828–1856* ed. Lord Sudeley (1943)
Lieven-Grey Coresp.	*Correspondence of Princess Lieven and Earl Grey* ed. G. Le Strange, 2vv (1890)
Life of Campbell	*Life of John, Lord Campbell* ed. Mrs. Hardcastle, 2vv (1881)
Life of Wilberforce	R.I. and S. Wilberforce, *Life of William Wilberforce* (1838)
LJ	*Journals of the House of Lords*
LMA	London Metropolitan Archives

Macaulay Letters	*The Letters of Thomas Babington Macaulay* ed. T. Pinney, 6vv (Cambridge, 1974–81)
Malmesbury Letters	*A Series of Letters of the First Earl of Malmesbury, his Family and Friends, from 1745 to 1820* ed. Lord Malmesbury, 2vv (1870)
Malmesbury Mems.	Earl of Malmesbury, *Memoirs of an Ex-Minister*, 2vv (1884)
Martin, *Lyndhurst*	Sir Theodore Martin, *A Life of Lord Lyndhurst* (1883)
Martineau Letters	*Harriet Martineau. Selected Letters* ed. V. Sanders (Oxford, 1990)
Maxwell, *Clarendon*	Sir Henry Maxwell, *The Life and Letters of George William Frederick, Fourth Earl of Clarendon*, 2vv (1913)
Melbourne's Pprs.	*Lord Melbourne's Papers* ed. L.C. Sanders (1889)
Melville, *Cobbett*	L. Melville, *The Life and Letters of William Cobbett*, 2vv (1913)
MI	Monumental Inscription(s)
Mill Works	*Collected Works of John Stuart Mill* ed. various, 33vv (Toronto, 1963–91)
Misc. Gen. et Her.	*Miscellanea Genealogica et Heraldica*
Monypenny and Buckle, *Disraeli*	W.F. Monypenny and G.E. Buckle, *The Life of Benjamin Disraeli, Earl of Beaconsfield*, 6vv (1910–20)
Moore Jnl.	*The Journal of Thomas Moore* ed. Wilfrid S. Dowden, 6vv (Newark, Delaware, 1983–91)
Moore Mems.	*Memoirs, Journal and Correspondence of Thomas Moore* ed. Lord John Russell, 8vv (1853–6)
Morley, *Gladstone*	J. Morley, *The Life of William Ewart Gladstone*, 3vv (1903)
Mus.	Museum
NAI	National Archives of Ireland
N and Q	*Notes and Queries*
NAS	National Archives of Scotland
n.d.	no date
NLI	National Library of Ireland
NLS	National Library of Scotland
NLW	National Library of Wales
NLWJ	*National Library of Wales Journal*
NMM	National Maritime Museum
n.s.	new series
O'Connell Coresp.	*The Correspondence of Daniel O'Connell* ed. M.R. O'Connell, 8vv (Dublin, 1972–80)
OIOC	Oriental and India Office Collections, British Library

Oldfield, *Rep. Hist.*	T.H.B. Oldfield, *Representative History of Great Britain and Ireland*, 6vv (1816)
Oldfield, *Key* (1820)	T.H.B. Oldfield, *Key to the House of Commons* (1820)
OR	*Official Return of Members of Parliament* (1878–91)
Overstone Corresp.	*The Correspondence of Lord Overstone* ed. D.P. O'Brien, 3vv (Cambridge, 1971)
Oxford DNB	*Oxford Dictionary of National Biography*
Palmerston-Sulivan Letters	*The Letters of the Third Viscount Palmerston to Laurence and Elizabeth Sulivan, 1804–1863* ed. K. Bourne (Camden ser. 4, xxiii, 1979)
P and P	*Past and Present*
par.	parish
Parker, *Graham*	C.S. Parker, *Life and Letters of Sir James Graham*, 2vv (1907)
Parker, *Peel*	C.S. Parker, *Sir Robert Peel from his Private Papers*, 3vv (1891)
Parl. Deb.	*Hansard's Parliamentary Debates*
Peel Letters	*The Private Letters of Sir Robert Peel* ed. G. Peel (1920)
Peel Mems.	*Memoirs of Sir Robert Peel* ed. Lord Stanhope and E. Cardwell, 2vv (1856)
Pellew, *Sidmouth*	G. Pellew, *The Life and Correspondence of Henry Addington, First Viscount Sidmouth*, 3vv (1847)
PH	*Parliamentary History*
Phipps, *Plumer Ward Mems.*	E. Phipps, *Memoirs of the Political and Literary Life of Robert Plumer Ward*, 2vv (1850)
PP	*Parliamentary Papers*
Prince of Wales Corresp.	*The Correspondence of George, Prince of Wales, 1770–1812* ed. A. Aspinall, 8vv (1963–71)
PROB	Probate Records: wills, administrations and valuations
PRO NI	Public Record Office of Northern Ireland
Raikes Jnl.	*A Portion of the Journal kept by Thomas Raikes from 1831 to 1847*, 4vv (1856–7)
Reid, *Lord Durham*	S.J. Reid, *Life and Letters of the First Earl of Durham*, 2vv (1900)
Reid, *Monckton Milnes*	T.W. Reid, *The Life, Letters and Friendships of Richard Monckton Milnes, First Lord Houghton*, 2vv (1890)
RO	Record Office
Romilly Mems.	*Memoirs of the Life of Sir Samuel Romilly, written by himself; with a Selection from his Correspondence*, 3vv (1840)

Russell Early Corresp.	*Early Correspondence of Lord John Russell, 1805–40* ed. R. Russell, 2vv (1913)
Russell Later Corresp.	*The Later Correspondence of Lord John* Russell ed. G.P. Gooch, 2vv (1925)
Russell Letters	*Letters to Lord G. William Russell*, 3vv (private, 1915–20)
Russell, *Recollections*	Earl Russell, *Recollections and Suggestions* (1875)
Scott Jnl.	*The Journal of Sir Walter Scott* (Edinburgh, 1950 edn.)
Scott Letters	*The Letters of Sir Walter Scott: 1878-1828* ed. H.J.C. Grierson, 10vv (1932-6)
Scottish Electoral Politics	*Papers on Scottish Electoral Politics, 1832–1854* ed. J.I. Brash (Scottish Hist. Soc. ser. 4, xi, Edinburgh, 1974)
ser.	series
Shelley Diary	*The Diary of Frances, Lady Shelley* ed. R. Edgcumbe, 2vv (1912)
SHR	*Scottish Historical Review*
Smith Letters	*The Letters of Sydney Smith* ed. N.C. Smith, 2vv (Oxford, 1953)
Somerset Letters	*Letters, Remains, and Memoirs of Edward Adolphus Seymour, Twelth Duke of Somerset* ed. W. Mallock and Lady G. Ramsden (1893)
Spencer-Stanhope Letter-Bag	A.M.W. Stirling, *The Letter-Bag of Lady Elizabeth Spencer Stanhope, 1806–1873* (1913)
Stirling, *Coke of Norf.*	A.M.W. Stirling, *Coke of Norfolk and his Friends* (1912 edn.)
Taylor Autobiog.	*Autobiography of Henry Taylor, 1800–1875*, 2vv (1885)
Taylor Pprs.	*The Taylor Papers: being a Record of Certain Reminiscences, Letters and Journals in the Life of Sir Herbert Taylor* ed. E. Taylor (1913)
TCD	Trinity College, Dublin
Three Diaries	*Three Early Nineteenth Century Diaries* ed. A. Aspinall (1952)
TNA	The National Archives
Torrens, *Melbourne*	W.M. Torrens, *Memoirs of William, 2nd Viscount Melbourne*, 2vv (1878)
Trans.	*Transactions*
TRHS	*Transactions of the Royal Historical Society*
Twiss, *Eldon*	H. Twiss, *The Public and Private Life of Lord Chancellor Eldon*, 3vv (1844)
Two Brothers	*Correspondence of Two Brothers: Edward Adolphus, Eleventh Duke of Somerset, and his brother, Lord*

	Webb Seymour, 1800–1819 and after ed. Lady G. Ramsden (1906)
Two Duchesses	*The Two Duchesses: Georgiana, Duchess of Devonshire, Elizabeth, Duchess of Devonshire. Family Correspondence, 1777–1859* ed. V. Foster (1898)
UCL	University College, London
UCNW	University College of North Wales (now Bangor University)
VCH	*Victoria County History*
Victoria Letters (ser. 1)	*The Letters of Queen Victoria: a selection from Her Majesty's Correspondence between the years 1837 and 1861* ed. A.C. Benson and Lord Esher, 3vv (1907–11)
Victoria Letters (ser. 2)	*The Letters of Queen Victoria, 1862–1885* ed. G.E. Buckle, 3vv (1926–8)
Victoria Letters (ser. 3)	*The Letters of Queen Victoria, 1886–1901* ed. G.E. Buckle, 3vv (1930–2)
Vis.	*Visitation*
Von Neumann Diary	*The Diary of Philipp Von Neumann, 1819–1850* trans. and ed. E. Beresford Chancellor, 2vv (1928)
Walpole, *Russell*	S. Walpole, *Life of Lord John Russell*, 2vv (1889)
Ward, *Llandaff Letters*	*Letters to the Bishop of Llandaff by the Earl of Dudley* ed. E. Coplestone (1840)
Ward, *Letters to 'Ivy'*	*Letters to 'Ivy' from the First Earl of Dudley* ed. S.H. Romilly (1905)
WCA	Westminster City Archives
Wellesley Mems.	R.R. Pearce, *Memoirs and Correspondence of Richard, Marquess Wellesley*, 3vv (1846)
Wellesley Pprs.	*The Wellesley Papers: Life and Correspondence of Marquess Wellesley*, 2vv (1914)
Wellington and Friends	*Wellington and his Friends* ed. 7th Duke of Wellington (1965)
Wellington Despatches	*Despatches, Correspondence and Memoranda of the Duke of Wellington* ed. 2nd Duke of Wellington, 8vv (1867–80)
Wellington Pol. Corresp.	*The Prime Ministers' Papers: Wellington Political Correspondence I: 1833–November 1834* ed. J. Brooke and J. Gandy (1975); *II: November 1834–April 1835* ed. R.J. Olney and J. Melvin (1986)
WHR	*Welsh History Review*
Wilberforce Corresp.	*The Correspondence of William Wilberforce* ed. R.I. and S. Wilberforce, 2vv (1840)
Wilberforce Priv. Pprs.	*Private Papers of William Wilberforce* ed. A.M. Wilberforce (1897)

William IV-Grey Corresp.   *Correspondence of Earl Grey with King William IV*
                                 ed. Lord Grey, 2vv (1867)
Williams Wynn Corresp.   *Correspondence of Charlotte Grenville, Lady*
                                 Williams Wynn, and her Three Sons, Sir Watkin
                                 Williams Wynn, Charles Williams Wynn, and Sir
                                 Henry Williams Wynn ed. R. Leighton (1920)

MEMBERS
S–Y

SADLER, Michael Thomas (1780–1835), of 25 Albion Street, Leeds, Yorks.[1]

NEWARK	6 Mar. 1829–1831
ALDBOROUGH	1831–1832

b. 3 Jan. 1780, yst. s. of James Sadler (*d*. ?1800) of Old Hall, Doveridge, Derbys. and Frances, da. of Rev. Michael Ferrebee, rect. of Snelston, Staffs. *educ*. by Mr. Harrison of Doveridge. *m*. 30 Apr. 1816, Anne, da. of Samuel Fenton of Leeds, 7 ch. *d*. 29 July 1835.

Ensign, Yorks. (W. Riding) vols. 1804; capt. Leeds light inf. 1820; common councilman, Leeds.

Sadler, whose paternal ancestors were minor Derbyshire squires, while his mother was of Huguenot descent, was largely self-taught and developed an early interest in mathematics and theology. At the age of 17 he wrote his first 'stinging' pamphlet, *An Apology for the Methodists*, with whom his parents, though members of the Church of England, were in sympathy. Mary Howitt of Uttoxeter recalled him as a youth of 'gentlemanly bearing, handsome dress, intelligent face, and pleasant voice'.[2] He settled in business in Leeds in the firm of his elder brother Benjamin, and in 1810 they went into partnership with the widow of Samuel Fenton, as Irish linen importers. Six years later he married the Fentons' eldest daughter, thereby allying himself with one of Leeds's foremost Anglican dynasties. He took an active part in the intellectual life of the town, read papers to the Philosophical Society, which he helped to found in 1819, and became chairman of the library committee. Privately, he wrote poetry and metrical versions of the Psalms. He was actively engaged in philanthropic work, and knew Richard Oastler and the Reverend George Stringer Bull.[3] Drawn into political activity, he contributed to the Tory *Leeds Intelligencer*, became a prominent member of the local Pitt Club and delivered a speech against Catholic claims at a public meeting in 1813. Four years later he published his *First Letter to a Reformer*, a reply to Walter Fawkes's[†] advocacy of parliamentary reform.[4] His prominence in Leeds politics was well established by 1825, when a correspondent of Lord Milton* drew attention to his 'very considerable oratorical and poetical talents'.[5] In 1827, following the formation of Canning's ministry, he corresponded with the former home secretary Peel, reporting the temper of West Riding politics, applauding Peel's resignation and rejoicing that, locally, the 'loyal party' had prevailed decisively over a motley crew of Catholics, radicals, Whigs, Jacobins and liberals, 'or to give them a generic name ... all the Canningites'.[6] His political philosophy was greatly influenced by his Evangelical piety. He told a Leeds Tory gathering in 1826 that he wished 'to extend the utmost possible degree of human happiness to the greatest possible number of human beings'. He lectured on the poor laws, defending them in opposition to the views of political economists. He investigated the principles of demography, and in 1828 published an anti-Malthusian essay on *Ireland; its Evils and their Remedies*, in which he argued for the establishment of poor laws there. He detested the *laissez-faire* economics and individualism then in vogue, which he believed were destroying traditional society.[7] He was appalled by the new industrialism, particularly the factory system, 'calling infant existences into perpetual labour' and depraving morals.[8]

When his Member Clinton resigned his seat for Newark because he felt unable to oppose the Wellington ministry's concession of Catholic emancipation in February 1829, the 4th duke of Newcastle offered to bring in Sadler 'as a bulwark of the Protestant cause'.[9] Sadler accepted and declared his candidature as a supporter of the 'Protestant Ascendancy', rational economy, free trade if 'mutually beneficial' and 'practical reforms' that did not 'destroy the integrity of the constitution'. After a hard-fought contest with the common lawyer Serjeant Wilde*, brought forward to oppose the ducal interest, he was returned.[10] Meeting Sadler in London, 8 Mar., Newcastle found him 'full of energy and a most intelligent man', and gave him

> what he considered to be most useful advice as to his parliamentary proceedings so as to gain the favour of the House and to obtain a willing hearing; his Yorkshire dialect is rather broad, but that is the only thing against him.[11]

He took his seat the following day, and presented and endorsed several petitions against emancipation, 11 Mar. In a long and emotional maiden speech, 17 Mar., when he 'was listened to at least with attention', he challenged Parliament's authority to proceed 'in this work of counter-revolution' without making a fresh appeal to the people, dismissed the notion that emancipation would pacify Ireland and condemned Peel's apostacy.[12] The anti-Catholic Lord Lowther* reported that although he was

> nervous and unused to the tact of the House ... it was admitted even by his opponents that he displayed great force, power and energy of mind. He gave Peel a great dressing and in good taste. If he is not too old to learn to accommodate himself to the etiquette or forms of the House he will be a prominent debater.[13]

The poet Robert Southey*, who had long admired Sadler's politics and talents, thought he had 'answered my expectations'.[14] Henry Bankes*, another sympathizer, reckoned the speech was 'very powerful and able'; and even the Whig Lord Howick* admitted that his effort, which had been 'amazingly cried up by his party', did 'show some power of speaking'.[15] The backbencher Hudson Gurney thought he spoke 'in the tone of a Methodist preacher'.[16] Newcastle believed that Sadler's 'striking and eloquent speech' had 'astonished the House and astounded his antagonists'; but the cabinet minister Lord Ellenborough noted that 'he made some good hits, but will never have power'.[17] Sadler divided against the second reading of the relief bill, 18 Mar., and next day vouched for the genuineness of the London and Westminster anti-Catholic petition. He voted against a clause of the bill, 23 Mar., and on the 24th ironically observed that rather than continue to exclude Catholics from a few offices of state 'we ought to abandon the entire constitution' to them. His vehement speech against the third reading, 30 Mar., evidently did not enhance his reputation. The Whig Henry Howard* told his mother that Sadler, 'the most perfect specimen of a canting Methodist I ever saw', was 'awfully fallen off' and 'cheered but little by his own party'; while another Whig, James Abercromby*, thought he 'failed completely'.[18] Gurney decided that he was 'no great matter after all and ... will very soon preach to the winds'.[19] Sadler supported inquiry into

the silk trade, 13 Apr., when he castigated ministers for their blind adherence to free trade, and 1 May 1829, when he voted to that effect. On 7 May he presented and endorsed a petition for the introduction of poor laws to Ireland and, having been called to account by Wilmot Horton for certain allegations respecting the emigration committee in his tract on Ireland, he objected to government 'wasting its resources in so fruitless and anti-national, and practically so cruel, an attempt as that of lessening the population' and advocated cultivation of wastes at home. On 4 June he again rejected that 'modern metaphysical jargon, miscalled political economy' and clashed with Wilmot Horton over the interpretation of demographic statistics. He protested against the passage of the anatomy regulation bill, which would operate 'almost exclusively upon the poor', 19 May. He presented and endorsed the Blackburn petition complaining of manufacturing distress, 12 June, and deplored ministers' decision to adjourn Parliament without attending to the problem. At the postponed celebratory election dinner at Newark, 24 July, he expounded his political philosophy at length: he denounced Catholic relief as 'a base compromise' and advocated the encouragement of domestic industry and care for the 'just rights and essential interests' of every rank of society 'and above all, the labouring classes ... whose prosperity is the foundation of that of all others'. Newcastle reflected that Sadler had accomplished much to their mutual benefit in the borough.[20] In late July Sir Richard Vyvyan*, writing to Newcastle on the state of parties, named Sadler as a potentially 'powerful' recruit for the Ultras. A month later he asked Sadler whether he was prepared to take office in a putative coalition ministry, noting that the *Morning Journal* had already listed him as vice-president of the board of trade in one such. In his reply, from the 'obscure sea-bathing village' of Redcar, where he was pursuing his anti-Malthusian studies (the result was his *Law of Population* (1830)), Sadler said he had 'no objection to form part of a ministry founded upon such principles as you and I mutually adopt'. At the same time, Vyvyan was told by his coadjutor Sir Edward Knatchbull* that notwithstanding Sadler's 'great talents and great information', he would 'never be a minister, assuredly not under George IV'. But Vyvyan insisted that Sadler was 'a man of vast force and information', that 'the manufacturing interest look on him as one of themselves' and that, though lacking in social polish, he was 'as much a gentleman as Peel, if not in outward appearance and manners, at least in nobleness of mind'.[21] In October 1829 Vyvyan duly listed Sadler as one of the 'Tories strongly opposed to the present government'.

In September he had addressed a meeting of the shipping interest at Whitby on the state of the country and the evils of free trade.[22]

Sadler voted for Knatchbull's amendment to the address, 4 Feb. 1830, and next day took exception to 'the extraordinary levity' with which some Members treated the economic condition of the country, criticized absentee Irish landlords, blamed the resumption of cash payments for adding to the cost of government and called for stringent retrenchment. When in early February he and Clinton Fynes Clinton, Newcastle's Member for Aldborough, decided 'forcibly to take up the cause of the liberty of the press as connected with the late *ex-officio* prosecutions for libel', Newcastle had no doubt that their 'temperately though spiritedly managed' campaign would 'produce considerable effect'.[23] Having called for information on the prosecutions, particularly that of the editor of the Ultra *Morning Journal*, 11 Feb., Sadler on 2 Mar. gave notice of his intention to try to amend the law of libel, but he did not follow it up. He voted against the transfer of East Retford's seats to Birmingham, 11 Feb. When the Newark petition seeking to prevent renewal of the duke of Newcastle's crown leases at Newark came before the House, 1 Mar., he opposed referring it to a committee and defended his patron against the charge of boroughmongering and exercising 'undue' electoral influence; he was a teller for the majority against inquiry. Newcastle was pleased with his speech, which he thought as 'prudent and highly principled, as it was beautiful'; but John Cam Hobhouse* thought he had '*floored* Sadler' in his reply.[24] Sadler presented a petition from aggrieved landowners against the Leeds and Selby railway bill, 4 Mar., and immediately opposed its second reading, urging caution on railway development. Later that day he argued that pluralism in 'the civil establishments of the country' was more alarming than in the church. On 16 Mar. he presented and endorsed the Leeds manufacturers and operatives' petition complaining of distress and condemned government's economic policy. He voted to abolish the Bathurst and Dundas pensions, 26 Mar., and against Jewish emancipation, 5 Apr., 17 May. He presented and supported a licensed victuallers' petition against the proposal to open the beer trade, 8 Apr., spoke and voted against the second reading of the sale of beer bill, 4 May, and voted for Knatchbull's amendment to it, 21 June. He was added to the committees on the truck and population bills, 3 May. He supported Yorkshire petitions for protection of the shipping interest, 6 May, contending that without reduced taxation, free trade and competition were 'worse than a fallacy'. He voted to reduce the salary of the assistant secretary of the treasury, 10 May, and for inquiry into privy councillors' emoluments, 14 May. Entrusted with the Macclesfield petition against the administration of justice bill, 27 May, he endorsed its opposition to reform of the palatinate jurisdiction of Chester; he voted against going into committee on the bill, 18 June. He presented a petition from Westmeath for an Irish poor law, 28 May, and on 3 June spoke at length on his own scheme for such legislation. Unwilling to divide a hostile House, he withdrew his proposal but gave notice of his intention to renew it should the current select committee not recommend a system of poor laws for Ireland. He voted for reduction of the South American consular grant and abolition of the death penalty for forgery, 7 June, and divided for economies in other areas of the consular and colonial services, 11, 14 June. He presented and endorsed a Newark petition against the employment of juvenile chimney sweeps, 10 June, and next day presented Irish petitions against the increased stamp duties and for poor laws. He took exception to the petition presented on behalf of Richard Carlile against the civil disabilities of Jews on the ground that its substance contradicted the New Testament, 16 June 1830.

Sadler stood for Newark at the general election of 1830 and was returned in second place ahead of Wilde.[25] In the July *Edinburgh Review* (li. 297-321) Macaulay savaged his *Law of Population*, especially its crucial 'blunder in mathematical nomenclature'. Sadler published a *Refutation* in November, but Macaulay got the better of him.[26] Ministers listed him among the 'violent Ultras', and he voted against them in the division on the civil list which brought them down, 15 Nov. 1830. On the appointment of Brougham as lord chancellor he was rumoured to have received an invitation to stand for Yorkshire.[27] He endorsed the prayer of the Whitby petition to abolish the duty on seaborne coal, 13 Dec., and supported Littleton's bill to end truck payments, 14 Dec., when he again attacked the 'dry and barren generalities' of free trade and ridiculed Hume's reasoning on wage settlements. On 20 Dec. 1830 he presented petitions from Newbury for increased duties on foreign flour and from Ireland for equalization of the Galway franchise between Catholics and Protestants. He spent part of the Christmas recess furthering his investigation into the condition of 'the poor, and poor labouring peasantry' in the agricultural districts; and on 4 Jan. 1831 he told Stanley Giffard that 'very much may be accomplished in their behalf, by means at once simple and efficacious'.[28] On 3 Feb., however, he deferred his proposal to introduce a bill to better the condition of the labouring poor. That day he opposed the bill to abolish the oath of abjuration. Deploring the reduction of the barilla duties, 7 Feb., he dismissed the 'pernicious notions misnamed political economy', but said he would support the Grey ministry 'whenever I can do so consistently with my principles'. He gave his view of their budget to Giffard, 11 Feb.:

It was I believe ... felt on all hands to be a failure ... and above all cheerless in its general aspect as affording little or no surplus, and consequently little prospect of meeting any additional demands without fresh *impositions* or of reducing taxation much below its present amount in future. It was, however, the budget of political economy.[29]

He warmly welcomed Hobhouse's bill to regulate and restrict child factory labour, 15 Feb. On the 16th he argued that distress was attributable to a cause other than overpopulation and pressed for the development of uncultivated land. Next day he opposed the proposed levy on steamboat passengers, which would hit poor Irish migrant labourers and allow Irish landlords to 'continue without restraint their culpable system of absenteeism'. On 18 Feb. he declared that only 'wise and graduated poor laws' could rescue Ireland from recurrent famine and distress. He condemned Howick's Malthusian emigration scheme and pledged himself to produce a 'practical plan for the relief of the people', 22 Feb. He favoured the immediate committal of the calico duties repeal bill, 8 Mar. Having attended the public meeting convened by merchants and ship owners of London, he endorsed their petition against relaxation of the timber duties, 15 Mar. Requested to support the kelp growers' petition, 16 Mar., he affirmed that the reduction of duties on imported barilla would cause great hardship and that in parts of Scotland 'the people are hardly able to obtain the means of subsistence'. On 18 and 30 Mar. he again maintained that Irish distress would only be alleviated by the introduction of poor laws and dismissed the government's relief proposals as 'utterly inadequate'. He voted against the second reading of the reform bill, 22 Mar., questioned the alleged enthusiasm of the people for it, 28 Mar., and disputed the crown's right to suspend writs, 30 Mar. According to Mrs. Arbuthnot, the Ultras were 'voting with Mr. O'Connell, who sits whispering with Mr. Sadler all night, and Sir F. Burdett, with the object of breaking down the government'.[30] He was put up to second Gascoyne's wrecking amendment, 18 Apr., but by all accounts his speech fell flat, and against the background of a noisy and inattentive House, Spring Rice reported that Sadler had 'given us extracts from all imaginable books to prove the rotten boroughs are the salvation of England'.[31] He duly divided in the majority, 19 Apr. He later received the freedom of Dublin for 'his able and eloquent resistance to the reform bill', but at Newark his effigy was burnt and 'thrown hissing hot into the Trent'. On the advice of his agents Newcastle withdrew him from Newark and at the ensuing general election put him up for Aldborough, where he came in unopposed.[32] He was nominated without his consent at Norwich and got 977 votes. He wrote to his son on the eve of the new session:

It is calculated that the ministers will have a majority in the Commons of above 100, but that they will be in a minority in the Peers, except a large batch is made. Time alone will show ... Yesterday I was at a grand party of the opposition at which there were many dukes and nobles ... It was a party ... of all the Tories and we all shook hands. The duke of Newcastle and Sir Robert Peel were reconciled ... Its being supposed that I am true to my principles and have employed my abilities be they what they may in furthering them ... was the consideration that moved the duke of Newcastle to promote me to a seat; but if the constitution is destroyed, neither he nor anyone will have it in his power to countenance men these distinctions, many years.[33]

On the address, 21 June 1831, he called for more decisive action to relieve distress in Ireland, and by his own account 'was listened to and much cheered in what I said'.[34] Next day he announced his intention to renew his proposed measure of relief, clashed with the Irish secretary Smith Stanley and urged the House to force absentee landlords to bear some responsibility for the relief of the poor. On 28 June he took issue with Robert Slaney over the poor laws, and on the following day declared that the House ought to compensate individuals for legislation affecting their livelihoods. Presenting an Irish petition against the Beer Act, 30 June, he reiterated his plea for relaxation of the malt duty. He then spoke and voted in the minority of 13 for reductions in public salaries. Initially embarrassed by his mistaken belief that government intended to reduce the import duty on wax, 1 July, he welcomed its retention as a safeguard to cottage industry. He also advocated replacing the duty on printed calicoes with a tax on raw cotton, because the poor would bear the brunt of the new levy. On 8 July he approved the employment of criminals in the reclamation of uncultivated land, as opposed to detaining them in penitentiaries. Addressing a weary House, 11 July, he deemed it harsh to increase the tax on Cape wines while lowering that on wines generally consumed by the wealthy. He presented petitions concerning poor rates and emigration, 13, 18 July 1831. Sadler voted against the second reading of the reintroduced reform bill, 6 July, and for the adjournment, 12 July. At this time Greville noted that all concerted opposition by the Tory party seemed to have ceased, but that 'there is still a rabble of opposition, tossed about by every wind of folly and passion, and left to the vagaries and eccentricities' of, among others, Sadler.[35] On 15 and 21 July he drew attention to the inconsistent application of the disfranchisement criteria. Maintaining that Yorkshire was 'inadequately represented', 22 July, he argued that 'if you purpose to destroy our ancient institutions, it is the more necessary that those you erect on their ruins should be based upon some intelligible principles, either of property or population'. He condemned the bill's 'iniquitous levelling system of qualification', 27 July, when he briefly protested on his constituents' behalf against the disfranchisement of Aldborough and spoke and voted for Chippenham's retention of two Members. He spoke against the enfranchisement of Gateshead, 5 Aug., objected to urban freeholders having votes in counties, 24 Aug., and was in a minority of 38 for preserving freemen's voting rights, 30 Aug. He divided against the passage of the bill, 21 Sept. 1831.

On 29 Aug. 1831, after many frustrating delays, he brought on his motion for an Irish poor law, but although a number of Members spoke in its support, it was rejected by 64 votes to 52. Yet Sadler told Oastler that 'even the ministers themselves, acknowledge [the division] to be a defeat'; and *The Times*, hitherto disparaging of his endeavours, remarked that 'his speech ... was able and eloquent, nor are we among those who consider it a defect, that he treated the subject broadly'.[36] He presented further petitions for Irish poor laws, 2, 3 Sept. He brought up petitions from Galway to equalize voting rights between Catholics and Protestants, 13 July, 2 Sept., 18 Oct., and paired against the Maynooth grant, 26 Sept. He objected to the grant for New South Wales because colonization was redundant in the face of English agriculture's dependence on Irish labour, 25 July. On Sabbath observance, he stressed the need for rest on humanitarian grounds, 2 Sept., when he presented and endorsed petitions from Lancashire cotton weavers for a protective export duty on cotton yarn. On 11 Oct. he moved a resolution for improving the condition of the rural poor in England, principally through the provision of better housing and the allocation of allotments. He introduced and had printed a bill to effect this, 18 Oct. 1831.

Commenting on the distressed condition of the glove trade, 15 Dec. 1831, he warned government that 'people are not to be fed by abstract notions of political economy'. He objected to the anatomy bill that day, presented a hostile petition, 2 Feb., and spoke against its third reading, 11 May 1832. He voted against the second reading of the revised reform bill, 17 Dec. 1831, and its committal, 20 Jan. 1832. He criticized the £10 householder qualification, 2 Feb., voted against the enfranchisement of Tower Hamlets, 28 Feb., and divided against the third reading, 22 Mar., and the second reading of the Irish reform bill, 25 May. He endorsed the Leeds petition to reform the Irish tithes system and establish poor laws there, 23 Jan., when he also spoke in favour of inquiry into the condition of the country as a whole. He supported a petition for investigation of the state of the silk trade, 21 Feb. He backed the call for the accurate registration of births and deaths, 23 Mar. On 19 June he proposed to make permanent provision for the Irish poor by taxing absentees, but was defeated by 77-58. He divided against government on the Russian-Dutch loan, 26 Jan., 12 July, and was in the minority of 16 against the Greek loan, 6 Aug. He spoke in favour of remission of the death penalty for forgery, 31 July, and presented petitions for relaxation of the criminal code, 2 Aug. On 7 Aug. 1832 he alleged that he had been excluded from the silk trade select committee as a notorious advocate of protection and called for abolition of the redundant board of trade. Next day he drew unfavourable comparisons between the conditions of colonial slaves and factory children, opposed the civil list payments bill and moved to reduce the lord chancellor's salary by £2,000; he was a teller for the minority of six.

Sadler had become increasingly aware of the need for decisive action to regulate child factory labour. In correspondence with Oastler in September 1831 he wrote:

> I not only concur with Mr. Hobhouse's factory bill; but, as I have expressed to him over and over again, I go much beyond it. Had he not taken it up this session, I should have done so, as my views and feelings are very strong upon that subject.

When Hobhouse withdrew the measure in the face of strong opposition, Sadler assumed the lead in Parliament, despite Hobhouse's warning to Oastler that if he persisted in his determination to limit working hours to ten, he would 'not be allowed to proceed a single stage with any enactment' and would 'only throw an air of ridicule and extravagance over this kind of legislation'. This was not a view shared by Oastler, who suggested that when the reform bill became law, Sadler should contest the new parliamentary borough of Leeds in order to make factory reform an electioneering issue. In November 1831 Sadler told Oastler:

> The question of factory labour never has been taken up with sufficient energy in Parliament; and the law, as at present carried, is not only nothing, but actually worse

than nothing ... I am persuaded, and all I hear and read confirms me in conviction, that TEN hours can never be receded from by those who love children, or who wish to obtain the approbation of Him who was indeed their friend and lover. I am sorry, therefore, to see that Sir John Hobhouse has not only conceded his bill, but his very views and judgement to the political economists, who in this, as in many other things, are the pests of society and the persecutors of the poor ... *I had rather have no bill, than one that would legalize and warrant their excessive labour*.[37]

He introduced his bill to regulate the labour of children and young persons in mills and factories on 17 Jan. 1832: it prohibited the employment of children under nine, limited those under 18 to ten hours daily work and banned night work for those under 21. He presented numerous petitions in favour of factory reform throughout February, echoing the fervour of Oastler's extra-parliamentary campaign in support of the ten hours bill. On 6 Feb. he met the duke of Sussex and persuaded him to present favourable petitions to the Lords.[38] Countering a hostile petition, 7 Mar., he said that workers were 'entitled, from their extreme poverty and helplessness, to the protection of Parliament', and presented numerous supportive petitions, including those endorsed by public meetings at Leeds and Manchester. He presented several more petitions, 14 Mar. In a passionate, moving and graphically illustrated speech of three hours (subsequently published), 16 Mar., he moved the second reading of his bill. On government's insistence that further inquiry was necessary, it was referred to a select committee, which, under Sadler's painstaking chairmanship, met 43 times and heard 87 witnesses between 12 Apr. and 7 Aug. He told his wife, 17 Mar.:

I spoke last night and I believe pretty well. Old Mr. Marshall [John Marshall*] was under the gallery ... but I made a piece fly at his son Billy [William Marshall*] who *smiled* while I was describing the misery of a factory child. Lord Althorp proposed him on the committee but I said I could not allow it and would divide the House upon it. I said I would not have one factory man upon the list and he yielded. The great physician here Mr. Blundel was under the gallery and said that all I said physiologically was quite correct. The House after all did not like it, I am persuaded; but the country is up, and will not have [children] to be worked 12 hours a day for a cotton lord in the land.[39]

He continued to present petitions in favour of reform throughout the rest of March, and on the 26th he derided those which purported to endorse the existing factory system. According to Macaulay, there was 'a strong and general feeling in the House of Commons, that something ought to be speedily done for the protection of children', but 'also ... a general feeling that

the details of Mr. Sadler's bill have not been well considered'.[40] Despite illness, he addressed the York meeting called 'to break the yoke of infantile slavery', 24 Apr.[41] He steadily presented favourable petitions and spoke for reform in June and July. On 30 July he complained of the subsequent victimization of witnesses who had given evidence before the inquiry. On 8 Aug. 1832, after much arduous work, he presented the select committee's report to the House. Its shocking revelations had a profound effect on public opinion.[42] A month earlier Sadler had explained something of his current political philosophy in a letter to Giffard:

I repeat perhaps too little in accordance with the views of some whom I highly respect and revere, but they are such as can alone give our party in the north the slightest chance, and restore it to the affections and surround it by the power of the people though I hope I did not take them up for that purpose, but from a thorough belief and conviction that the grounds of our political adherence being smitten from under us, by the rascally Whigs, it better suited the principles as well as being the only policy of the true Tories to check for themselves some intelligible principles of actions, rather than to fight their battles in defending the fragments of the system which they have left us. In a word I lean to the people, not indeed to the mob ... but to the neglected, abused and deserted people, whose principles we may form and whose affections we may [win] if we think fit, but without whom we shall be found as powerless as our enemies could wish us ... I have then stated that in some few of the large towns, I would have given the operative classes some direct political influence, that though averse from *short*, I am not the defender of *septennial* parliaments ... as to the ballot they may fight about it that please. It is I know Lord Brougham's 'security'. I despise it as such, and I think it would be quite as favourable to the higher as to the lower classes, and in fact do neither good nor harm to either.[43]

Sadler stood for Leeds at its first parliamentary election in December 1832 but, after a bitter contest, which revolved largely around the principles of social reform, he was defeated by his old adversary Macaulay and John Marshall, son of the eminent flax manufacturer. He remained active in the factory movement, and in late 1833 accepted an invitation to contest a by-election at Huddersfield, but was defeated. Too ill to take up a renewed offer to stand for Leeds following Macaulay's resignation in February 1834, he played some part in the extra-parliamentary opposition to the Poor Law Amendment Act that year, but withdrew to Ireland, where he had business interests, settling at New Lodge, Belfast. He was invited to contest Birmingham and South Durham in 1835, but the breakdown of his health as a consequence of over-exertion made a public life impossible, and he died of heart failure in July. According to an obituary, it was generally understood that his 'severe study and great anxiety' had hastened his early death.[44] No will or administration has been found.

[1] See R.B. Seeley, *Mems. of Life of Sadler* (1842); R.V. Taylor, *Biographia Leodiensis*, 354-62; J.T. Ward, 'Michael Thomas Sadler', *Univ. of Leeds Rev.* vii (1960-1), 152-60; K. Lawes, *Paternalism and Politics* (2000); *Oxford DNB*. [2] *Oxford DNB*. [3] E. Kitson Clark, *Hist. Leeds Phil. Soc.* 14, 24, 36; C.H. Driver, *Tory Radical*, 20-21. [4] Seeley, 17, 29. [5] Fitzwilliam mss, Tottie to Milton, 6 June 1825. [6] Add. 40394, f. 86. [7] Seeley, 41-42, 49-81. [8] *Popular Movements* ed. J. T.Ward, 61. [9] Nottingham Univ. Lib. Newcastle mss Ne2 F3/1/100; Notts. Archives, Tallents mss, Newcastle to Tallents, 28 Feb. 1829. [10] *Nottingham Jnl.* 7, 14 Mar. 1829. [11] Newcastle mss Ne2 F3/1/114. [12] *The Times*, 18 Mar. 1829. [13] Lonsdale mss, Lowther to Lonsdale, 17 Mar. 1829. [14] *New Letters of Southey* ed. K. Curry, ii. 334. [15] Dorset RO, Bankes jnl. 166; Grey mss, Howick jnl. 17 Mar. [1829]. [16] Gurney diary, 17 Mar. [1829]. [17] Newcastle mss Ne2 F3/1/128; *Ellenborough Diary*, i. 397. [18] Cumbria RO, Howard mss D/HW8/481/14; Brougham mss, Abercromby to Brougham [31 Mar. 1829]. [19] Gurney diary, 30 Mar. 1829. [20] *Full Report of Newark Dinner, 24 July 1829*, pp. 5-13; Newcastle mss Ne2 F3/1/161. [21] Cornw. RO, Vyvyan mss, Vyvyan to Newcastle, 20 July, reply, 15 Aug., Vyvyan to Sadler, 22 Aug., reply, 26 Aug., Knatchbull to Vyvyan, 26 Aug., reply, 31 Aug. 1829. [22] *The Times*, 23 Sept. 1829. [23] Newcastle mss Ne2 F3/1/203. [24] Ibid. F3/1/210; Add. 56554, f. 70. [25] *Nottingham Jnl.* 7, 14 Aug. 1830. [26] *Macaulay Letters*, i. 275, 284-5, 312, 315, 318. [27] *Nottingham Jnl.* 27 Nov. 1830. [28] Add. 56359, f. 69. [29] Ibid. f. 71. [30] *Arbuthnot Jnl.* ii. 332. [31] Add. 51569, Ord to Lady Holland [18 Apr.]; 51573, Spring Rice to Holland [18 Apr.]; 51655, Mackintosh to Lady Holland [19 Apr. 1831]. [32] *Nottingham Jnl.* 30 Apr.; Newcastle mss NeC 4527; Tallents mss, Newcastle to Tallents, 23 Apr.; *The Times*, 2 May 1831. [33] LSE Lib. Archives, Coll. Misc. 62 I 13, Sadler to son [30 June 1831]. [34] Ibid. Sadler to son [21 June 1831]. [35] *Greville Mems.* ii. 165. [36] Alfred [S.H.G. Kydd], *Factory Movement*, 127-8; *The Times*, 31 Aug. 1831. [37] Alfred, 127-31; Driver, 93. [38] J.T. Ward, *Factory Movement*, 56. [39] LSE Coll. Misc. 62 I 7. [40] *Macaulay Letters*, ii. 117. [41] *Poor Man's Advocate*, 135. [42] *Oxford DNB*; Seeley, 379. [43] Add. 56369, f. 80. [44] *The Times*, 29 July 1835.

S.R.H.

ST. CLAIR ERSKINE, James Alexander, Lord Loughborough (1802–1866).

Dysart Burghs	1830–1831
Great Grimsby	10 Aug. 1831–1832

b. 15 Feb. 1802, 2nd but 1st surv. s. of Sir James St. Clair Erskine[†], 6th bt., of Alva, Clackmannan, 2nd earl of Rosslyn, and Henrietta Elizabeth, da. of Hon. Edward Bouverie[†] of Delapré Abbey, Northants. *educ.* Eton 1814. *m.* 10 Oct. 1826, Frances, da. of William Wemyss[†] of Wemyss, Fife, 2s.(1*d.v.p.*) 1da. *styled* Lord Loughborough 1805-37. *suc.* fa. as 3rd earl of Rosslyn 18 Jan. 1837. *d.* 16 June 1866.

Cornet 9 Drag. 1819, lt. 1820; lt. 47 Ft. 1821, capt. Mar. 1823; capt. 9 Drag. May 1823, maj. 1826, lt.-col. (half-pay) 1827; lt.-col. 9 Drag. 1828; col. 1841, half-pay 1842; maj-gen. 1854; lt.-gen. 1859; col. 7 Drag. 1864-d.; gen. 1866.

Master of the buckhounds Sept. 1841-July 1846, Feb.-Dec. 1852; PC 14 Sept. 1841; under-sec. state for war Mar.-June 1859.

Maj. 1 Fife mounted rifles

Loughborough's great-uncle Alexander Wedderburn[†], 1st earl of Rosslyn, was lord chancellor under Pitt. When he died in 1805 his peerage and half of his estates passed to his nephew, this Member's father, Sir James St. Clair Erskine. A career soldier and a Whig (as was his wife (*d.* 1810), a granddaughter of the 1st Viscount Folkestone), from 1796 until his removal to the Upper House he represented Dysart Burghs, where, in alliance with his partisan William Ferguson of Raith, he established a controlling interest. From 1806, he grudgingly acquiesced in the return there of Ferguson's second son Ronald Craufurd Ferguson.[1] Loughborough followed a military career, joined Brooks's, 13 Feb. 1822, and, taking the first opportunity after coming of age, he tested the ground in Dysart Burghs when a dissolution was anticipated in September 1825. His father's refusal to authorize his candidature there at the general election of 1826 infuriated him, and although he canvassed to safeguard his family's influence over the council of Dysart, he dissociated himself personally and politically from Ferguson, whose allegiance to Joseph Hume* he deplored.[2] He seconded the nomination for Fifeshire of his future brother-in-law James Wemyss*, 23 June 1826, and praised his 'independent and unbigoted support for Lord Liverpool's ministry'.[3] Rosslyn eschewed the duke of Wellington's offer of a seat in the cabinet in 1828, but he and Loughborough were promoted in the duke's regiment that year and Rosslyn accepted the privy seal in June 1829, his loyalty to his commanding officer proving stronger than his Whig politics. He gave Ferguson notice, 30 June 1830, of Loughborough's candidature for the Burghs at the general election.[4] His unopposed return at Dysart, where he spoke out against reform and praised the Wellington ministry's retrenchment, commercial and agricultural policies, was belied by a local campaign on Ferguson's behalf and the deliberate absence of the Kinghorn delegate and town clerk Thomas Barclay, who afterwards publicly denounced him and closely scrutinized his parliamentary conduct.[5]

Ministers of course listed Loughborough among their 'friends', but he was one of four sons of peers in the cabinet, with seats in the Commons, who, although in town, failed to speak or vote with government on the civil list when they were brought down, 15 Nov. 1830.[6] Rosslyn became one of the active organizers of the new Tory opposition. After some public wrangling in the press, Loughborough presented Kinghorn's petition for Scottish burgh reform, 17 Nov., and anti-slavery ones from Burntisland, Dysart and Kirkcaldy, 23 Nov. He received two weeks' leave 'on the public service' that day to return to his regiment.[7] He presented, as requested, a Kirkcaldy petition for burgh and parliamentary reform, including the ballot, 23 Dec. 1830, but dissented from its prayer and called for a 'measure ... unfettered by the pledges of any party whatever'.[8] He supported the London petition against any alteration in the timber duties on his constituents' behalf, and argued that their abolition would lead to the 'total annihilation of that trade', 15 Mar. 1831. Responding to the vice-president of the board of trade Poulett Thomson's criticism (earlier in the debate) of the self-serving landed interest, he maintained that they looked to the 'prosperity of every class of the community as the only means by which it can thrive'. He brought up a similar petition from Kirkcaldy and one from Dysart for parliamentary reform, 16 Mar. He voted against the second reading of the Grey ministry's reform bill, 22 Mar. Speaking for Gascoyne's wrecking amendment, 18 Apr., he asked why England and Scotland were treated differently, declared that the bill's only principle was that of 'change and revolution' and predicted that it would lead to universal suffrage, voting by ballot and annual parliaments. He maintained that it was his duty, 'careless of what my constituents may think', to oppose it in the wider interests of the country and asserted that if the proposals for Scotland were passed, the Act of Union would be violated and eventually dissolved. Justifying his majority vote on 19 Apr. to Barclay, 22 Apr., he hinted at support for Scottish parliamentary reform (excluding disfranchisements).[9] His decision to circulate copies to the burghs of the radical Henry Hunt's speeches highlighting the bill's inadequacies had already made his position as their Member untenable, and at the general election in May 1831 he was replaced by the reformer Robert Ferguson of Raith, Sir Ronald's elder brother.[10] He later recalled: 'On the dissolution, I went down again ... and they broke my head and kicked me out'.[11] He also vainly canvassed the Stirling Burghs.[12]

Loughborough was not without a seat for long. In August 1831 he successfully contested Great Grimsby, where the return of two Tories at the general election had been voided, with his partisan Henry Fitzroy. On the hustings he said it was evident that the reform bill would pass the Commons, but it was in the Lords, where his father sat, that the real struggle would be made, and they might 'fairly hope to obtain a reversion of the case of Grimsby', which was set to lose a Member. He claimed that he was not opposed to all

reform but 'decidedly hostile' to the ministerial bill.[13] In the House, 24 Aug., Loughborough criticized the proposed £10 householder voting qualification as unfairly discriminatory, as rentals for similar properties differed between large and smaller towns, predicted that it would cause a 'fictitious value [to be] given to property vested in the lower classes', and suggested making it £5 for schedule B boroughs. He was in a minority of only ten for Hunt's 'no taxation without representation' clause, 25 Aug. Defending the vote next day, he explained that he thought it an improvement on the £10 clause, but said he did not think his name should be 'connected with the views [Hunt] generally takes', and branded the bill as a 'most republican measure'. He voted to preserve the rights of non-resident freemen for their lives, 30 Aug., and divided against the bill's passage, 21 Sept. He voted against government on the Dublin election controversy, 23 Aug., and to deal with bribery at Liverpool, 5 Sept. He voted against the revised bill at its second reading, 17 Dec. 1831, and committal, 20 Jan., against enfranchising Tower Hamlets, 28 Feb., and the third reading, 22 Mar. 1832. When Grimsby's place in schedule B was considered, 23 Feb., he unavailingly maintained that no case could be made for its disfranchisement as a corrupt or a nomination borough, cited his own and Fitzroy's election as proof of the freemen's independence and stressed that the borough was growing in prosperity. He deliberately refrained from voting on the Scottish reform bill at its second reading, 21 May, but criticized it as inconsistent with the English measure and with the articles of the Union. Arguing that reform would not be the panacea its advocates predicted, he highlighted the disparity in county representation that provided one Member for 94,000 people in Scotland and one for 64,000 in England and said that he rejected it 'wholly'. He paired against the second reading of the Irish bill, 25 May.[14] He divided against government on the Russian-Dutch loan, 26 Jan., 20 July, and the Greek loan, 6 Aug., but with them for the malt drawback bill, 2 Apr. 1832.

Loughborough announced his candidature for Grimsby as a Conservative, 3 Oct. 1832, before joining his regiment in Ireland, but, as he had anticipated, he faced powerful opposition and was defeated at the general election in December.[15] He did not stand for Parliament again. After succeeding his father to the peerage, he held office under Peel, whom he supported in repealing the corn laws, and later under Lord Derby.[16] He died at his London home in Lower Belgrave Street in June 1866, predeceased in 1851 by his elder son James Alexander George, and in 1858 by his wife, and was succeeded in his titles and estates by his second son Francis Robert (1833-90).[17] Lord Ribblesdale recalled him as a 'fine horseman, and a great judge of a horse, or indeed any animal'.[18] A member of Benjamin Disraeli's[†] early coterie, he was supposedly the model for Lord Rambrooke in *Coningsby*.[19]

[1] *HP Commons, 1790-1820*, ii. 596-7; iii. 83-84. [2] Creevey mss, Creevey to Miss Ord, 6 Sept.; *Caledonian Mercury*, 8 Oct. 1825; NAS GD164/1770/3; 1782/1, 3. [3] *Caledonian Mercury*, 1 July 1826. [4] Creevey mss, Sefton to Creevey, 2 July 1830. [5] *Caledonian Mercury*, 12 July, 26, 28, 30 Aug. 1830. [6] Add. 40401, f. 292. [7] *Fife Herald*, 25 Nov.; *The Times*, 1 Dec. 1830. [8] *Fife Herald*, 25 Nov., 30 Dec. 1830. [9] Ibid. 28 Apr. 1831. [10] Ibid. 7 Apr.; *Caledonian Mercury*, 28 Apr., 2, 16 May 1831. [11] *Grimsby Pollbook* (Aug. 1831, Drury), 14. [12] *Caledonian Mercury*, 2 May 1831. [13] *Lincoln, Rutland and Stamford Mercury*, 19 May 1831. [14] *The Times*, 29 May 1832. [15] NAS GD164/1779/13; *Grimsby Pollbook* (1832, Palmer), 8. [16] *Raikes Jnl*. iv. 181. [17] *The Times*, 18 June 1866. [18] T. Lister, *Queen's Hounds*, 240. [19] *Disraeli Letters*, iii. 956; *Gent. Mag.* (1866), ii. 257-8.

M.P.J.C./M.M.E.

ST. JOHN MILDMAY, Paulet (1791–1845), of Hazlegrove, Som. and Farley Chamberlayne, Hants.

WINCHESTER	1818–1834
WINCHESTER	1837–1841

b. 8 Apr. 1791, 3rd but 2nd surv. s. of Sir Henry Paulet St. John Mildmay[†], 3rd bt. (*d.* 1808), of Dogmersfield Park, Hants and Jane, da. and coh. of Carew Mildmay of Shawford House, Hants. *educ.* Winchester 1803-5. *m.* 12 Mar. 1813, Anna Maria Wyndham, da. of Hon. Bartholomew Bouverie*, 4s. 3da. *suc.* fa. to Hazlegrove 1808. *d.* 19 May 1845.
Ensign 2 Ft. Gds. 1807, lt. and capt. 1811-12; lt. Dogmersfield yeoman cav. 1813.

St. John Mildmay was one of 15 children, who, according to an account of 1804, were 'all very handsome, and bear a strong resemblance to each other'.[1] At the 1818 general election he had replaced his dandified elder brother Henry St. John Carew St. John Mildmay as Member for Winchester on the interest controlled by their mother. Much of the family property had remained in her hands after the death of her husband in 1808, though St. John Mildmay was heir by settlement to Hazlegrove in Somerset, an estate of nearly 4,000 acres, which had originally descended from his maternal great-great-uncle Carew Hervey Mildmay, Member for Harwich, 1714-15. A token cash bequest was the only direct benefit he derived from his father's personalty, which was sworn under £60,000.[2] Curiously, a radical publication of 1831 identified him as a merchant, an assertion repeated in early editions of Dod's *Parliamentary Companion*. But from the lack of corroborative evidence, this seems

likely to have been a case of confusion with his younger brother Humphrey St. John Mildmay (1794-1853), Member for Southampton, 1842-7, and a partner in the merchant banking house of the Baring brothers from 1823.[3]

At the 1820 general election St. John Mildmay was returned again for Winchester unopposed. His hustings speech contained no political professions, though he dissented by implication from his Grenvillite colleague's support for the Six Acts.[4] A very lax and mostly silent attender, inaccurately 'supposed to vote with government' by a radical commentary of 1825, when present he gave general support to the Whig opposition to the Liverpool ministry on most major issues, including economy, retrenchment and reduced taxation.[5] He voted for Catholic relief, 28 Feb. 1821, 1 Mar., 21 Apr., 10 May 1825. On 5 Mar. 1821 he was a steward at a Winchester ball in honour of the duke of Wellington.[6] No trace of parliamentary activity has been found for 1822 or 1823, though he was present at the election of the mayor of Winchester in September 1823.[7] He contributed briefly to a debate on the game laws, 1 Apr., and welcomed Stuart Wortley's attempt to reform them, 31 May 1824.[8] On 20 Dec. 1824 his gun burst while shooting on the duke of Buckingham's property near Winchester, causing an injury to his left hand in which he 'lost the whole of the thumb, and the fingers are much torn'. That Christmas he distributed wool jackets to the poor of Winchester, having furnished them with gifts of money and coal on earlier occasions.[9] He presented a Winchester petition for repeal of the assessed taxes, 14 Feb. 1825.[10] He divided to allow the Catholic Association a hearing at the bar of the House, 18 Feb. 1825. He voted against the Jamaican slave trials, 2 Mar 1826. As a teller, he helped to defeat the Berkshire and Hampshire canal bill at its report stage by 48-38, 6 Apr. He voted for a revision of the corn laws, 18 Apr. He obtained returns of the number of persons imprisoned under the game laws and admitted to hospitals following injury from spring guns, 21 Mar., and was a majority teller against the third reading of a bill to outlaw their use, 27 Apr. 1826.[11]

At the 1826 general election he offered again for Winchester and at his unopposed return declared his unequivocal support for Catholic relief, observing that 'it was very easy to raise the cry of "No Popery", but they might just as well say "No Chinese"'. Responding to comments about the paucity of his contributions to debate, he urged the electors not to forget 'the not unimportant body of listeners' and insisted that he gave 'many hours of anxious attention' to the arguments deployed.[12] Perhaps stirred by this criticism, he spoke against the reintroduced bill to ban spring guns, 23 Mar., and offered a few words in defence of the siting of St. James's Palace, 11 May 1827.[13] He voted for Catholic relief, 6 Mar. 1827, 12 May 1828. No other recorded activity has been found until 1829, when he railed against the 'base and infamous' use of the king's name by petitioners against Catholic claims, in support of which he claimed a shift of opinion had taken place among his constituents, 27 Feb. He presented two petitions for the Wellington ministry's concession of emancipation, 6 Mar., and voted accordingly that day, when he clashed with Buckingham's son Lord Chandos over the timing of the division, and 30 Mar. He defended Sir Thomas Lethbridge from a charge that he had failed to represent the anti-Catholic sentiments of his Somerset constituents, 9 Mar. On 22 Oct. 1829 he attended a Winchester charity dinner.[14] He was among the opposition Members who voted against the amendment to the address, 4 Feb. 1830, when he warned ministers against complacency, but hoped that the 'holders of liberal opinions' who had hitherto supported them would not abandon this line for 'a mere quibble about words'. He voted against Lord Blandford's parliamentary reform scheme, 18 Feb., but was in the opposition minorities for military economies, 19 Feb., 22 Mar., and a reduction in the grant for public buildings, 3 May. He spoke at a Hampshire county meeting on agricultural distress, 10 Mar., when in an apparent response to further criticism of his silence in the House, he invited his audience to 'look to votes, and not to speeches'.[15] He could not discern 'a rag or a remnant of an argument' in the speeches against Jewish emancipation, for which he was a minority teller, 17 May. He presented Winchester petitions against the sale of beer bill, 27 Apr., 4 May, and against its provisions permitting on-consumption, 21 June 1830.

At the 1830 general election he was again returned unopposed. On the hustings he predicted that in the new Parliament 'there would be less occasion than ever to oppose the measures of government'.[16] Yet he was reckoned one of the 'bad doubtfuls' by ministers and was absent from the division on the civil list that brought them down, 15 Nov. 1830. By his own account in the House (21 July 1831), he was not personally affected by the 'Swing' disturbances then occurring across much of southern England, though according to a press report he was expected to command a corps of volunteer infantry in Winchester.[17] He pleaded ignorance to explain his absence from a meeting of the aldermen and inhabitants in favour of parliamentary reform, 17 Feb., and presented and endorsed their

petition, 28 Feb. 1831, when he applauded Winchester corporation's willingness to surrender its exclusive privileges but cautioned against any 'visionary schemes, which are calculated to overthrow the constitution'.[18] He was granted ten days' leave on account of ill health, 14 Mar., and excused himself on the same grounds from a Hampshire county meeting three days later, when his message of support for the ministerial reform proposals was greeted with cheers.[19] He had recovered sufficiently to present further constituency petitions in favour of the measure, 21 Mar., and to vote for its second reading next day and against Gascoyne's wrecking amendment, 19 Apr. 1831.

The contest in Winchester at the ensuing general election was not aimed at St. John Mildmay, and his profession of support for the reform bill in its entirety was warmly received. But he embroiled himself in controversy by giving a plumper to the anti-reform candidate, the son of his former colleague East. His effigy was burnt in the street and he was called to account for himself at a meeting, 4 May, when he confessed that his conduct had been dictated by a long standing electoral agreement. For this he was publicly censured, following which he 'left the city within an hour of the meeting, evidently in very dejected spirits', though his subsequent address of thanks ascribed his hurried departure to an anxiety to assist the cause of reform in Somerset, where he had privately promised Edward Sanford* 'to secure for you every vote I can influence'.[20] In the House, 21 July, 22 Sept. 1831, he sprang to the defence of William Bingham Baring*, the reform candidate at Winchester whose chances he had effectively blighted, who with his cousin Francis Thornhill Baring* had been charged with assault in the discharge of his magisterial duties during the 'Swing' disturbances. He presented a Winchester petition in their support and, with the object of demonstrating the falsity of the allegations, was in the minority for a select committee to investigate the incident, 27 Sept. He divided for the second reading of the reintroduced reform bill, 6 July, and gave generally steady support to its details, though he was in the opposition minority against giving urban freeholders the right to vote in counties, 17 Aug., and spoke and divided for the enfranchisement of £50 tenants-at-will, 18 Aug., as a balance to the increased influence given to commercial and manufacturing interests. He was in the minority for the complete disfranchisement of Saltash, on which ministers failed to offer a clear lead, 26 July. He was appointed to the select committee to investigate ways to make the Commons 'more commodious, and less unwholesome', 8 Aug. On 23 Aug. he was in the ministerial majorities on the Dublin election controversy. He divided for the passage of the reform bill, 21 Sept., and Lord Ebrington's motion of confidence in ministers, 10 Oct. In an apparent mark of forgiveness, he received a vote of thanks from Winchester's reformers, 27 Sept., but his attempt to address the Hampshire county reform meeting, 27 Oct. 1831, was drowned out by cries of 'a rat'.[21]

St. John Mildmay voted for the second reading of the revised reform bill, 17 Dec. 1831, again gave general support to its details, and divided for its third reading, 22 Mar. 1832. He was listed as absent 'in country' for the division on the motion for an address asking the king to appoint only ministers who would carry the bill unimpaired, 10 May, around which time he was reported to be canvassing Winchester in anticipation of a dissolution.[22] He voted with ministers on the Russian-Dutch loan, 26 Jan., 12, 16 July, and relations with Portugal, 9 Feb. He voted for Alexander Baring's bill to exclude insolvent debtors from Parliament, 27 June 1832. That month he was mentioned as a candidate for Hampshire on the appointment of Sir James Macdonald to an overseas posting.[23] No more was heard of this, and he came in again for Winchester at the general election later that year, topping the poll in a three-way contest. He was described as a 'moderate reformer', and was one of the readily discernible figures in Hayter's depiction of the new House.[24] In 1835 he was squeezed out by his former Conservative colleague, but he bounced back in 1837, according to a jaundiced report by unscrupulous use of 'different language to different parties'. He retired at the 1841 dissolution.[25]

St. John Mildmay died in May 1845 at his mother's seat at Dogmersfield. The cause was tetanus, which set in after his leg was broken in an altercation with an angry mare, with whose foal his pony had tangled while he was riding in the park. An obituarist praised his 'urbane, charitable and kind' character and cited the length of the tenancies on his Somerset estate as evidence of his generosity.[26] By his single-sentence will, composed six days before his death and presumably just after his accident, he left all his disposable property and personal estate to his wife.[27] Hazlegrove House passed to his three elder sons in turn, while his minor Hampshire estate at King's Somborne was partially sold off. His property at Farley Chamberlayne, near Winchester, had been disposed of in 1830.[28]

[1] H.A. St. John Mildmay, *Mem. Mildmay Fam.* 214. [2] Ibid. 195, 220, 230; IR26/144/187. [3] [W. Carpenter], *People's Bk.* (1831), 326; R.W. Hidy, *House of Baring in American Trade*, 43, 70. [4] *Hants Chron.* 13 Mar. 1820. [5] *Black Bk.* (1823), 177; *Session of Parl. 1825*, p. 476. [6] *Salisbury Jnl.* 26 Feb., 12 Mar. 1821. [7] Ibid. 22 Sept. 1823. [8] *The Times*, 2 Apr., 1 June 1824. [9] *Salisbury Jnl.* 5 Jan. 1821, 22 Dec. 1823, 3 Jan. 1825. [10] Ibid. 15 Feb. 1825. [11] *The Times*, 22 Mar.

1826. [12] *Hants Chron.* 19 June 1826. [13] *The Times*, 12 May 1827. [14] *Salisbury Jnl.* 26 Oct. 1829. [15] Ibid. 15 Mar. 1830. [16] *Hants Telegraph*, 2 Aug. 1830. [17] *Salisbury Jnl.* 14 Feb. 1831. [18] *The Times*, 23 Feb. 1831. [19] Ibid. 18 Mar. 1831. [20] *Portsmouth Herald*, 24 Apr., 8 May; *Salisbury Jnl.* 9 May 1831; Som. RO, Sanford mss DD/SF/4550/56. [21] *Salisbury Jnl.* 3 Oct.; *Hants Advertiser*, 29 Oct. 1831. [22] *Salisbury Jnl.* 14 May 1831. [23] *Hants Telegraph*, 4 June 1832. [24] *Dod's Parl. Companion* (1833), 2nd edn. 140; Mildmay, 215. [25] *The Times*, 17 July 1837. [26] *Sherborne, Dorchester and Taunton Jnl.* 22, 29 May; *Western Flying Post*, 24 May 1845. [27] PROB 8/238 (11 Sept. 1845); PROB 11/2024/724. [28] *VCH Hants*, iv. 444, 471-2.

H.J.S./P.J.S.

ST. PAUL, Henry Heneage (1777–1820), of Ewart Park, Belford, Northumb.

BERWICK-UPON-TWEED	1812–1820
BERWICK-UPON-TWEED	13 July 1820–1 Nov. 1820

b. 16 Mar. 1777, 2nd s. of Horace St. Paul (*d.* 1812) of Ewart Park, Count St. Paul of the Austrian Empire, and Anne, da. of Henry Weston of Chertsey and West Horsley Place, Surr.; bro. of Sir Horace David Cholwell St. Paul, 1st bt.* *educ.* Eton 1793. *unm. d.* 1 Nov. 1820.

Ensign 60 Ft. 1802; lt. 96 Ft. 1803, half-pay 1803; lt. 78 Ft. 1804, capt. 1805, half-pay 1806; capt. 3 Drag. Gds. 1807, half-pay 1807-*d.*

Maj. Cheviot Legion 1799, lt.-col. 1801, 1803; lt.-col. commdt. Northumb. militia 1808-*d.*

In 1820 St. Paul, a former personal private secretary to his father's friend Sylvester Douglas[†] as Irish secretary, who preferred managing his family's Northumberland and Staffordshire estates to his intended military career, fought his third consecutive contest for the venal and open borough of Berwick-upon-Tweed, where he could rely on the 3rd duke of Northumberland's interest.[1] Defeated by a surge of out-voter support for Sir David Milne*, a fellow anti-Catholic ministerialist opposed to parliamentary reform, St. Paul was disliked by the Whig leader Lord Grey, but was locally popular and had Milne's election voided on petition, 3 July 1820.[2] His unopposed return at the ensuing by-election was facilitated by his supporters' prompt execution of the writ and his own poor health, which encouraged his declared opponents to bide their time.[3] He died intestate at his Northumberland home in November 1820 without taking his seat and eighteen years before his mother, by whose death he had been due to inherit a quarter share of the Ewart estate.[4] His obituarist commended his personal qualities and eulogized him as a Member who 'attended to his duty with undeviating regularity, conscientiously supporting those measures which to him appeared most conducive to the prosperity of his country'.[5]

[1] *HP Commons, 1790-1820*, v. 92; G.G. Butler, *Col. St. Paul*, vol. i. p. clxxi; *Berwick in Parliament* ed. Sir L. Airey, A. Beith, D. Brenchley, J. Marlow and T. Skelly, 24, 93-94; NAS GD51/1/200/43. [2] Grey mss, Grey to Sir R. Wilson, 13 Mar.; *Edinburgh Advertiser*, 14 Mar. 1820; D.L. Stoker, 'Elections and Voting Behaviour: A Study of Elections in Northumb., co. Dur., Cumb. and Westmld. 1760-1832' (Manchester Univ. Ph.D. thesis, 1980), 153, 194, 328; *The Times*, 4 July 1820. [3] *Edinburgh Advertiser*, 11, 18 July 1820. [4] *Newcastle Chron.* 4 Nov. 1820; PROB 11/1638/42. [5] *Gent. Mag.* (1820), ii. 469.

M.M.E.

ST. PAUL, Sir Horace David Cholwell, 1st bt. (1775–1840), of Ewart Park, Belford, Northumb.; Willingsworth Hall, Staffs., and 10 Chapel Street, Grovesnor Square, Mdx.

Bridport	1812–1820
Bridport	20 June 1820–1832

b. 6 Jan. 1775, in Paris, 1st s. of Horace St. Paul of Ewart Park and Anne, da. of Henry Weston of Chertsey and West Horsley Place, Surr.; bro. of Henry Heneage St. Paul*. *educ.* Houghton le Spring; Eton 1783. *m.* 14 May 1803, Anna Maria, 'da.' and h. of John Ward[†], 2nd Visct. Dudley and Ward, 1s. 5da. *suc.* fa. 1812 as count of the Austrian Empire, title recogn. in this country by grant of the regent, 7 Sept. 1812; *cr.* bt. 17 Nov. 1813. *d.* 8 Oct. 1840.[1]

Ensign 1 Ft. 1793, lt. 1794; cornet 1 Drag. Gds. Mar. 1794, lt. July 1794, capt. 1798; maj. 5 Ft. 1802, brevet lt.-col. 1811, col. (half-pay) 1820.

At the general election of 1820 St. Paul, who had a pension of £600,[2] for the second time contested the venal borough of Bridport, where his unopposed return in 1818 had cost him about £2,500. After a four-day poll, he was defeated by the Whigs James Scott and Christopher Spurrier, but he petitioned against the latter (on 3 May) and was seated on 20 June, at the cost of at least another £2,500.[3] He was an inactive ministerialist and no trace of parliamentary activity has been found for that session.[4] In May he urged his brother Charles Maximilian, another soldier, to enter Parliament, but he replied that he had no private fortune out of which to pay the necessary expenses.[5] His other brother, Henry Heneage, Member for Berwick, died in November 1820. St. Paul voted against condemning the Liverpool ministry's conduct towards Queen Caroline, 6 Feb., repeal of the additional malt duty, 3 Apr., and parliamentary reform, 9 May 1821. He divided against Catholic relief, 28 Feb. 1821, and the Catholic peers bill, 30 Apr. 1822. He was listed with government against limiting the sinking fund to the real surplus of revenue, 13 Mar., repeal of the Foreign Enlistment Act, 16 Apr., and inquiry into the legal proceedings against the Dublin Orange

rioters, 22 Apr. 1823. He presented an anti-slavery petition from Wooler, near Ewart Park, 26 Mar. 1824.[6] Named as a defaulter on the Catholic question, 28 Feb., he paired against relief, 1 Mar., 21 Apr., 10 May 1825. He travelled in France from May to July that year, and from October 1825 until August 1826 made a tour of the continent, during which, as an Austrian count, he was received by Francis I in Vienna.[7] Despite a rumour that he had resigned his interest in the borough and his absence abroad, he was returned unopposed with the radical Henry Warburton for Bridport at the general election of 1826.[8]

He voted against Catholic relief, 6 Mar. 1827, 12 May, and repeal of the Test Acts, 26 Feb. 1828. He divided against reducing the salary of the lieutenant-general of the ordnance, 4 July 1828. In February 1829 he was listed by Planta, the Wellington ministry's patronage secretary, as likely to be 'opposed to the principle' of the government's Catholic emancipation bill. In presenting and endorsing an anti-Catholic petition from Tipton, 18 Feb., he declared that relief would 'lay the axe to the root of that constitution under which we have long enjoyed greater blessings than any other people in the world'. He was absent from the call of the House, 5 Mar., and on the 10th Sir John Brydges, who brought up the Bridport anti-Catholic petition on his behalf that day, explained that illness had prevented St. Paul voting in 'the glorious minority' on the 6th. In fact his name was included in the anti-Catholic list that day, as it was in the minorities against emancipation, 18, 27, 30 Mar. 1829. He voted against transferring East Retford's seat to Birmingham, 11 Feb., and the enfranchisement of Birmingham, Leeds and Manchester, 23 Feb. 1830. He divided in the minority for Knatchbull's amendment to prevent the sale of beer for on-consumption, 21 June 1830. Although there were rumours of a third candidate, he was returned unopposed at the general election that summer.[9]

He was listed by ministers among their 'friends', but was absent from the division on the civil list, 15 Nov. 1830, which led to their resignation. He supported prohibition of the truck system 'as a friend to the people', 13 Dec. 1830, and, in reply to Hume, who took him to task for this phrase, preposterously asserted that 'the course which I have pursued has been, I believe, as useful to the people and has tended as much to improve their comforts as that of the honourable Member'. He voted against the second reading of the Grey ministry's reform bill, 22 Mar., and for Gascoyne's wrecking amendment, 19 Apr. At the ensuing general election, when another possible challenge proved abortive, he was returned for Bridport as a professed moderate reformer who opposed the planned removal of one seat from the borough.[10] He divided against the second reading of the reintroduced reform bill, 6 July, and, according to the Dorset newspaper, on the motions to adjourn consideration of it on the 12th 'voted on this, as on other divisions, against the ministers'.[11] He divided for using the 1831 census to determine the boroughs in schedules A and B, 19 July, and to postpone consideration of the partial disfranchisement of Chippenham, 27 July, when he presented and endorsed the Bridport petition against its inclusion in schedule B. He divided against the passage of the bill, 21 Sept., but was named as a defaulter on Lord Ebrington's confidence motion, 10 Oct. 1831, presumably because he was in Dorset, where he voted for the anti-reformer Lord Ashley* in the county by-election.[12]

He voted against the second reading of the revised reform bill, 17 Dec. 1831, the enfranchisement of Tower Hamlets, 28 Feb., and the third reading, 22 Mar. 1832. He vindicated the conduct of the yeomanry in the protection of private property, 23 Feb. Illness prevented his siding against ministers on the Russian-Dutch loan, 26 Jan.,[13] but he did so on 12 July, his last known vote. By then, despite strong Conservative support, he judged that he had no chance of re-election in the reprieved borough of Bridport.[14] At the general election of 1832 he started for the newly enfranchised single Member constituency of Dudley, where his wife had considerable property. He was promised the support of her deranged kinsman the 1st earl of Dudley, who hoped that 'we shall make a good fight against the Jacobins'.[15] But he stood no chance against the Whig lawyer John Campbell II*, who, despite the efforts that were made against him, noted that 'I was told, and I believe told truly, that St. Paul could not buy five votes in the borough, for that any man suspected of taking money would be infamous'.[16] On the hustings St. Paul claimed that his principles had 'ever been of practical economy' and independence, but he resigned on the third day, when he trailed by 90 out of the total of 540 electors polled.[17] He is not known to have sought another seat in Parliament. St. Paul, who came into further property on the deaths of his wife (26 Jan. 1837) and mother (5 Aug. 1838), died in October 1840.[18] By his will, dated 22 Dec. 1838, he made provision for his daughters and left the bulk of his estate, including personalty sworn under £90,000 in the province of Canterbury and under £18,000 in that of York, to his only son Horace (1812-91), Conservative Member for Worcestershire East, 1837-41, who succeeded him in the titles of count and baronet.[19]

[1] HP Commons, 1790-1820, v. 92, following G.G. Butler, Col. St. Paul, i. pp. clxx, clxxxiv, wrongly states 10 Oct. 1840 as St. Paul's death date, whereas the 8th is given in the death duty register (IR26/1589/73) and is confirmed by Newcastle Jnl. 17 Oct. 1840. [2] Black Bk. (1820), 75. [3] Northumb. RO, St. Paul Butler mss ZBU C1/8/1, 4; Western Flying Post, 28 Feb.; Salisbury Jnl. 13, 20 Mar., 5, 26 June 1820. [4] Black Bk. (1823), 191; Session of Parl. 1825, p. 484. [5] Butler, i. pp. clxxiii-iv. [6] The Times, 27 Mar. 1824. [7] St. Paul Butler mss C1/10/1-5; Butler, i. pp. clxix-xx. [8] Dorset Co. Chron. 8, 15 June 1826. [9] Ibid. 1, 15 July, 5 Aug. 1830. [10] Ibid. 28 Apr., 5 May 1831. [11] Ibid. 21 July 1831. [12] St. Paul Butler mss B7/7; Dorset Pollbook (Sept.-Oct. 1831), 11. [13] Dorset Co. Chron. 9 Feb. 1832. [14] Ibid. 21 June; Sherborne Jnl. 5 July 1832. [15] Butler, i. p. clxxix; St. Paul Butler mss C1/9. [16] Life of Campbell, ii. 13-25. [17] Worcester Herald, 15 Dec. 1832. [18] Gent. Mag. (1837), i. 333; (1838), ii. 565; (1841), i. 202-3. [19] PROB 11/1941/143; IR26/1589/73.

S.M.F.

SANDERSON, Richard (?1783–1857), of 52 Upper Harley Street, Mdx. and 23 Lombard Street, London.

COLCHESTER	20 Apr. 1829–1830
COLCHESTER	1832–1847

bap. 4 Jan. 1784, yr. s. of Thomas Sanderson of Armthorpe, nr. Doncaster, Yorks. and Sarah, da. of John Cromack of Doncaster.[1] *m.* 12 Feb. 1833, Charlotte Matilda, da. of Charles Manners Sutton*, at least 6s. 4da. *d.* 28 Oct. 1857.

Sanderson came from an old south Yorkshire family, but little is known of his antecedents. His father may have been the son of John and Margaret Sanderson who was baptized at Armthorpe on 16 Apr. 1751. His parents married at Doncaster on 27 June 1775 and his brother Thomas was baptized at Armthorpe on 13 June 1779.[2] He may have had a Quaker upbringing, and as a young man he became a clerk in the London bill broking firm of Richardson, Overend and Company of 23 Lombard Street, in which the Norfolk Quaker Samuel Gurney was a partner.[3] By 1827 Sanderson was operating on his own account as a bill broker at 32 Lombard Street, while Gurney's business had become known as Overend, Gurney and Company. These two firms, together with those of the Alexanders and James Bruce, dominated the London bill broking market in the late 1820s.[4]

Sanderson, by now a very wealthy man, was taken up by the anti-Catholic and Tory corporation of Colchester in April 1829 to replace their member Sir George Smyth when he resigned his seat in disgust at the Wellington ministry's concession of Catholic emancipation. He was returned after a token challenge had come to nothing, and declared that he wished to promote 'the education of the poor' and help to 'put an end to the traffic in human blood'.[5] He took his seat on

28 Apr. According to a Colchester newspaper, he voted against allowing Daniel O'Connell to take his seat for Clare without swearing the oath of supremacy, 18 May.[6] At a Colchester dinner to celebrate his return, 17 July 1829, he said that although 'nothing of great importance' had so far 'come under discussion' in the House, he was ready when required to 'stand forward in support of those principles which he had publicly avowed'.[7] He divided with government against the transfer of East Retford's seats to Birmingham, 11 Feb., Lord Blandford's parliamentary reform scheme, 18 Feb., and the enfranchisement of Birmingham, Leeds and Manchester, 23 Feb. 1830. He was erroneously reported to have voted in the minority for reduction of the salary of the assistant secretary to the treasury, 10 May.[8] He is not known to have spoken in debate in this period, but on 11 May he presented Colchester and Harwich petitions against the sale of beer bill. As a businessman, he petitioned the Commons (14 May) for abolition of the death penalty for forgery; and he voted in that sense, 7 June 1830.

Sanderson offered for Colchester at the general election the following month but he had to withdraw at the last minute when one of his agents was detected in an act of bribery.[9] At the 1831 general election he stood, with corporation backing, in an attempt to prevent the return of two uncompromising reformers. When he went to canvass Colchester out-voters at Harwich, an angry mob forced his carriage into a pond. On the hustings he professed to accept

> the necessity of parliamentary reform ... Approving ... much of the [Grey ministry's reform bill] ... I doubt the ... necessity of some of its provisions. Agreeing in the extension of the franchise to large and populous places, yet I cannot see the wisdom and justice of seizing on the property and charters of unoffending towns and depriving them of their rights.

While he polled very respectably, he finished third.[10] At the general election of 1832 he had a resounding victory; and by dint of his wealth he sat for Colchester, as a Conservative who opposed the Maynooth grant and repeal of the corn laws, until his defeat at the 1847 general election.[11] In 1833 he married the Speaker's daughter, with whom he had a large family. By 1837 he had moved his business premises to 83 King William Street. The firm had to suspend payment in September 1847, but was able to resume trading early the following year.[12] Sanderson died at Hazlewood, Hertfordshire, in October 1857. Two weeks later his business, known since 1850 as Sanderson, Sandeman and Company, failed irrevocably with liabilities of £5,299,006.[13] By his brief will, dated 26 Sept. 1854,

he left £3,000 to his wife, who lived until 1898, and divided the residue of his property equally among his children. His son Thomas Henry Sanderson (1841-1923) was a stalwart of the foreign office for 47 years and was created Lord Sanderson in 1905.[14]

[1] IGI (Yorks.). [2] Ibid. [3] *Essex Rev.* viii (1899), 238. [4] Sir J. Clapham, *Bank of England,* ii. 142-3. [5] *Colchester Gazette,* 11, 25 Apr. 1829. [6] Ibid. 30 May 1829. [7] Ibid. 18 July 1829. [8] Ibid. 15 May; *The Times,* 17 May; *Kent and Essex Mercury,* 18 May 1830. [9] *Colchester Gazette,* 10, 31 July 1830. [10] Ibid. 30 Apr., 7 May; Gurney diary, 3 May; *The Times,* 6 May 1831. [11] A.F.J. Brown, *Colchester,* 84, 87, 120; Add. 40406, f. 93. [12] Clapham, ii. 204; *The Times,* 15, 16, 20, 21 Sept., 13 Oct., 11 Dec. 1847. [13] *Gent. Mag.* (1857), ii. 687; *Overstone Corresp.* ii. 762-3, 779-80, 783-5, 787, 799, 810, 814, 819. [14] *Oxford DNB; The Times,* 22 Mar. 1923.

D.R.F.

SANDON, Visct. *see* **RYDER, Dudley**

SANFORD, Edward Ayshford (1794–1871), of Nynehead Court, Wellington, Som. and 41 Grosvenor Street, Mdx.

SOMERSET	1830–1832
SOMERSET WEST	1832–1841

b. 23 May 1794, o.s of William Ayshford Sanford of Nynehead and Lynton, Devon and Mary, da. of Rev. Edward Marshall of Breage, Cornw. *educ.* Eton 1808-13; Brasenose, Oxf. 1813. *m.* (1) 4 Nov. 1817, Henrietta (*d.* 24 Aug. 1836), da. of Sir William Langham, 8th bt., of Cottesbrooke, Northants., 5s. (2 *d.v.p.*) 2da.; (2) 22 June 1841, Lady Caroline Anna Stanhope, da. of Charles Stanhope, 3rd earl of Harrington, *s.p. suc.* fa. 1833. *d.* 1 Dec. 1871.
Sheriff, Som. 1848-9.

Sanford, whose family had been established in Somerset since about 1600, 'made the tour of Europe' after leaving university and returned to play a leading role in the magistracy of his county.[1] He inherited his father's Whig politics and joined Brooks's Club, 18 June 1817. He made his maiden public speech at the Wellington meeting, 1 Jan. 1821, when he supported an address for the removal of ministers, condemning their 'unjust and unconstitutional' treatment of Queen Caroline and commenting on the 'impoverished state of all classes' caused by excessive taxation. In January 1822 he chaired the public meeting on agricultural distress at Taunton, which agreed a petition demanding economy and retrenchment. He signed the requisition for a county meeting on relief for the landed interest, held at Wells in January 1823, when he seconded the proposed petition, declaring that the 'overgrown' civil and military establishments must be cut; he also supported the call for a second meeting to consider parliamentary reform.[2] In the autumn of 1829 he announced his intention of offering for the county at the next general election, stating that he was 'unconnected with any party' and would abstain from making any specific promises. It was assumed that he would 'receive good countenance from the leading Whigs, which he merits as being a thorough gentleman'.[3] Despite rumours that some of the 'populous districts' were not satisfied with him and wanted another candidate, he was returned unopposed at the election of 1830 after the retirement of the Tory sitting Member Sir Thomas Lethbridge. He professed his loyalty to the constitution of 1688, the king, the established church and the rights and liberties of the people, particularly religious liberty, and reportedly 'had the soul of integrity legible in his countenance'. He also 'thought a further decrease of our national burthens could be effected'.[4] Addressing his supporters at a series of post-election dinners, he assured them that he would be 'no holiday Member' and would 'go into Parliament an independent man'. He revealed his support for reform, arguing that 'towns, when they have arrived at a certain degree of eminence, should have a share in the representation', and welcoming the recent events in France.[5]

The Wellington ministry regarded him as one of their 'foes'. In the debate on the address, 3 Nov. 1830, he maintained that they did not 'understand the feelings and sentiments of the people', as was shown by their dismissive attitude towards calls for reform and their apparent inclination to interfere in French affairs. He voted against them in the crucial civil list division, 15 Nov. He presented several anti-slavery petitions that month and supported the Sussex juries bill, hoping that its provisions would be extended to all counties, 9 Nov. 1830. He pronounced a 'decided negative' on Hunt's motion for an address asking the king to pardon the agricultural labourers convicted by the recent special commissions, 8 Feb. 1831, as 'the source of mercy is ... properly fixed in the crown and ... Parliament cannot ... constitutionally interfere in the exercise of that prerogative'. He presented but did not concur in two petitions against reduction of the coal duties, 23 Feb. He presented numerous petitions for reform in February and March but dissented from those which demanded the ballot. He divided for the second reading of the Grey ministry's reform bill, 22 Mar. He sent a letter to the Somerset county reform meeting, 28 Mar., expressing his 'cordial support' for the bill and explaining that he felt obliged to remain in London to attend the debate on slavery.[6]

He paired against Gascoyne's wrecking amendment, 19 Apr. 1831, 'being totally unable to attend from a distressing affliction'.[7] His eye complaint prevented him from canvassing at the ensuing general election, but he managed to attend the nomination meeting where, 'labouring under considerable indisposition', he declared that the vital question was 'whether the people would answer the appeal made to them by their king or suffer themselves to be rode over, roughshod, by an usurped oligarchy'. He was returned unopposed and free of expense, after two other candidates withdrew. He subsequently claimed that on being elected the previous year he had 'found an administration whom I wished to support', but that Wellington's declaration against reform had disappointed him.[8]

He introduced an Enclosure Acts titles bill, to remedy defects in the titles to land, 29 June 1831; it passed but did not reach the Lords. He suffered from 'renewed inflammation in his eyes' and paired for the second reading of the reintroduced reform bill, 6 July.[9] He generally supported its details, and spoke in favour of the enfranchisement of Frome, 'one of the most populous and thriving towns in Somerset', 5 Aug. However, he voted for separate representation for Merthyr Tydvil, 10 Aug., against the division of counties, 11 Aug., and for the Chandos amendment to enfranchise £50 tenants-at-will, 18 Aug., as he was 'most desirous to extend the principle of the bill'. He divided for its third reading, 19 Sept., its passage, 21 Sept., the second reading of the Scottish bill, 23 Sept., and Lord Ebrington's confidence motion, which was necessary to 'allay the excitement that prevails out of doors', 10 Oct. He voted for the second reading of the revised bill, 17 Dec. 1831, and its details. He declared that there 'never was a more gross ... foul [and] calumnious imputation' than that made by Hunt against his friend Edward Portman, Member for Dorset, concerning the alleged coercion of tenants at the general election, 27 Jan. 1832. He supported the provision restricting the interval between nomination and election in county contests to two days, 11 Feb., as this was the period when 'the great struggle is made' and 'very unworthy means' were occasionally resorted to; two days was 'quite sufficient for all honest purposes'. He divided for the third reading, 22 Mar., and Ebrington's motion for an address asking the king to appoint only ministers committed to carrying an unimpaired measure, 10 May. He presented Frome and Chard petitions for withholding supplies until reform was carried, 22 May. He voted for the second reading of the Irish bill, 25 May, and against increased representation for Scotland, 1 June 1832.

He presented petitions for amendment of the Sale of Beer Act, 22 July, 28 Sept. 1831, 7 May 1832, when he observed that 'much evil has arisen from the indiscriminate manner in which these licenses are granted'. He presented and approved of petitions for abolition of the death penalty for offences against property, 22 July, 16 Dec. 1831. He voted to print the Waterford petition for disarming the Irish yeomanry, 11 Aug. He voted to punish only those guilty of bribery at the Dublin election and against censuring the Irish administration, 23 Aug. He presented a Wells petition for tithes reform, in which 'I most cordially concur', 28 Sept., when he argued that tradesmen's bills for repairs and alterations to Windsor Castle must be paid. Next day he defended the proposal to reduce the salary of the president of the board of control and supported the 'highly beneficial' labourers' house rent bill, preventing the payment of cottage rents from the poor rate. Between October 1831 and May 1832 he presented numerous petitions against the general register bill, on which there was strong feeling in Somerset, and he argued unsuccessfully for it to be considered by a committee of the whole House, 22 Feb. He sympathized with petitions complaining of distress in the glove trade, 19 Jan., and voted for inquiry, 31 Jan., 3 Apr. He presented, without comment, petitions against the importation of foreign silks, 20, 24 Jan., 9 Feb. He voted against the second reading of the Vestry Act amendment bill, 23 Jan. He divided with ministers on the Russian-Dutch loan, 26 Jan., 12, 16, 20 July, and relations with Portugal, 9 Feb. However, he voted for Hunt's motion for information regarding military punishments, 16 Feb. He supported the conservators of the River Tone in their opposition to the Bridgwater and Taunton Canal bill and was a minority teller against the second reading, 27 Feb. He favoured the addition of Edward Bainbridge, Member for Taunton, to the committee on Sadler's factories regulation bill, 16 Mar., warning that it would do 'incalculable mischief' if carried in its present form, although he was not against it in principle. He presented a Somerset manufacturers' petition against the bill, 9 Apr., and a Somerset and Dorset silk manufacturers' petition for exemption from its provisions, 7 May. He voted for the navy civil departments bill, 6 Apr. He presented Wellington and Taunton petitions against the government's plan for Irish education, 9 Apr., 7 May, but believed it was 'calculated to lead to harmony and good will amongst the people of that country'. He voted for Buxton's anti-slavery motion, 24 May. He secured the postponement of the Exeter improvement bill to ascertain the real views of the inhabitants, 30 May. He was granted ten days' leave

to attend the quarter sessions, 28 June. He supported the Somerset coroners' petition against the coroners bill, 9 July 1832, when he had 'great pleasure' in presenting a Martock petition for restoration of the Polish constitution.

At the general election of 1832 Sanford offered for the new Western division of Somerset, so that he might 'support those future measures of reform in the institutions of our country ... which are so essential to their preservation, and which of necessity must arise where the people are truly represented'. He was anxious to address the problem of abuses in the church, believing that 'a national reformed church [is] the corner stone of national religion'. He was comfortably returned at the head of the poll and sat, representing 'Whig principles', until his retirement in 1841.[10] On his father's death in 1833 he inherited all his leasehold property and was the residuary legatee.[11] He died in December 1871 and left his estates to his eldest son, William Ayshford Sanford (1818-1902).

[1] *Taunton Courier*, 30 June 1830. [2] Ibid. 3 Jan. 1821, 2, 16 Jan. 1822; *Bristol Mirror*, 11, 25 Jan. 1823. [3] *Bristol Mirror*, 3 Oct.; Dorset RO, Fox Strangways mss D/FSI, box 332, Phelips to Ilchester, 31 Sept. 1829. [4] Fox Strangways mss D/FSI, box 332, Phelips to Ilchester, 19 June, 4 July; *Bristol Mirror*, 3 July, 7, 14 Aug.; *Keenes' Bath Jnl.* 9 Aug. 1830. [5] *Taunton Courier*, 25 Aug.; *Bristol Mirror*, 11, 18 Sept. 1830. [6] *Bristol Mirror*, 2 Apr. 1831. [7] *The Times*, 21 Apr. 1831. [8] *Bristol Mirror*, 23, 30 Apr., 7, 14 May; *Taunton Courier*, 18 May 1831. [9] *Bristol Mirror*, 16 July 1831. [10] *Taunton Courier*, 20 June, 5, 26 Dec. 1832; *Dod's Parl. Companion* (1833), 157. [11] The personalty was sworn under £4,000: PROB 11/1819/474; IR26/1336/369.

T.A.J.

SAUNDERSON, Alexander (1783–1857), of Castle Saunderson, co. Cavan.

Co. CAVAN 1826–1831

b. 22 July 1783, 1st s. of Francis Saunderson[†], MP [I], of Castle Saunderson and Anne Bassett, da. of Stephen White of Miskin, Glam. *m.* 18 Mar. 1828, Sarah Juliana, da. of Rev. Henry Maxwell (later 6th Bar. Farnham [I]), vic. of Templemichael, co. Longford, 5s. (1 *d.v.p.*) 2da. *suc.* fa. 1827. *d.* 28 Nov. 1857.
Sheriff, co. Cavan 1818-19.
Col. co. Cavan militia 1838.

Saunderson's father Francis, whose great-great-grandfather Robert Sanderson (as the name was then spelt) had sat for the same county about a century earlier, was Member for Cavan at Dublin and London from 1788 to 1806, when he withdrew after falling out with the Maxwells, whose dominant interest was headed by Lord Farnham.[1] Despite being an opposition Whig, he was firmly anti-Catholic, and it is supposed by the family's historian that he had an eldest son, William de Bedick Saunderson, whom he apparently disinherited for marrying the Catholic daughter of one of the lodge keepers at Castle Saunderson.[2] Whatever the truth of this, it was Alexander who was groomed to emulate him in Cavan, where he was sheriff during the 1818 election. He offered on his father's principles at the general election two years later, but withdrew after receiving insufficient support and backed the sitting Members on the hustings, where he was claimed as a sympathizer to the Catholic cause.[3] He was considered a potential candidate on a vacancy in the summer of 1823, but he supported the 5th Baron Farnham's nephew Henry Maxwell*.[4] Yet by October 1824 he was canvassing on the basis that his father 'has enabled me to promise to stand should I be so fortunate as to have a good prospect of success', and some credence seemed to have been given to his supposed pro-Catholic views by his controversially refusing to drink the toast to William III at a dinner.[5]

He duly offered in place of the anti-Catholic Nathaniel Sneyd at the general election of 1826, when he at first courted the independent interest. But, amid allegations that he had bartered his suspected views for a seat, he united with Maxwell on a staunchly anti-Catholic ticket, which secured him the votes of many hitherto sceptical country gentlemen. The target of a vitriolic Catholic campaign, he was shouted down on nomination day, when his father walked out of the hall in disgust, and, having received a blow on the head from a stone during the week-long poll, was too overcome by emotion and exhaustion to speak on being declared elected in second place behind Maxwell.[6] He attended the Cavan dinner in honour of the defeated Protestant Member for county Waterford Lord George Beresford, 30 Aug. 1826, but was careful to maintain an ambiguous stance, suggesting that relief was impracticable rather than undesirable as such, and at the county meeting on 25 Jan. 1827 he insisted that he would reserve his own opinion for the Commons.[7] However, he presented the ensuing hostile petition from Cavan, 2 Mar., and voted against relief, 6 Mar.[8] He objected to the spring guns bill, 23 Mar. He voted with Canning, the prime minister, against the disfranchisement of Penryn, 28 May, but divided in the Tory minorities against the third readings of the Penryn bill, 7 June, and the Coventry magistracy bill, 18 June 1827.

Saunderson succeeded to the family estates on the death of his senile father that year and early in 1828 he married Maxwell's sternly pious sister Sarah, whose father was an absentee clergyman.[9] Assuring Peel, the home secretary, that 'I feel it a duty I am most anxious to perform, to give every support in my power to the [Wellington] administration of which you are a member', he informally sought permission to absent himself on account of his nuptials.[10] Apart from again dividing against Catholic relief, 12 May, his only other known votes that session were against inquiry into chancery administration, 24 Apr., and reduction of the salary of the lieutenant-general of the ordnance, 4 July. At the Cavan meeting to establish a Brunswick Club, 13 Oct., he stated that he had always wished to treat the Catholics sympathetically, but would follow the revered memory of his Orangeman father and give the Protestants his backing. Elected president of the Belturbet branch, he attended the first meeting of the Brunswick Club of Ireland in Dublin, 4 Nov. 1828, when he admitted that he had hesitated to join, but had been persuaded to do so by the extremism of the Catholics.[11] Yet Saunderson, hiding behind the notion that Members should be allowed to go to Parliament unpledged, again made an equivocal speech at the Protestant county meeting, 21 Jan. 1829.[12] Although he was listed by Planta, the patronage secretary, as 'opposed to the principle' of the emancipation bill, he voted for it, 6 Mar., and explained on the 9th that he did so only because ministers had become persuaded that it was essential, though he added that they would need to accompany it with a higher franchise. Having been careful that day to sympathize with his Protestant constituents' righteous indignation, he brought up (but dissented from) their hostile petition, 11 Mar. He divided for raising the qualification from £10 to £20, 26 Mar., but for the third reading of the bill, 30 Mar. Unusually, in May Peel accepted a request for ecclesiastical patronage from Saunderson, who 'gave us his cordial support and has incurred the displeasure of many of his constituents and of Lord Farnham in particular'.[13] He accepted the need for the temporary renewal of the Irish Arms Act, but argued that emancipation had already calmed the turbulent Catholic population, 2 June 1829. Later that year the Ultra leader Sir Richard Vyvyan* listed him among 'those who voted in favour of the third reading but whose sentiments' towards a putative coalition ministry were 'unknown'.

Saunderson took a month's leave to attend the assizes, 8 Mar. 1830. He voted against Jewish emancipation, 17 May, the Galway franchise bill, 25 May, and (unless this was Richard Sanderson, Member for Colchester) reduction of the grant for South American missions, 7 June. Assured of government support, he was again returned at the general election that summer, when, despite having 'ratted', he was backed by those Protestant gentlemen who valued him above the interloper Sir William Young, and by the liberal electors, whose candidates withdrew before the contest.[14] So concerned was he about disturbances in Cavan that autumn that he contemplated raising a sort of yeomanry force among his own tenants for their mutual protection.[15] He was listed by ministers among their 'friends', but having been granted leave because of illness in his family, 15 Nov. 1830, he was absent from the division on the civil list that day. He again obtained leave for three weeks to attend the assizes, 4 Mar., and paired for the second reading of the Grey ministry's reform bill, 22 Mar. 1831. He presented a petition from Cavan borough requesting that it be granted its own Member, 12 Apr., and divided against Gascoyne's wrecking amendment, 19 Apr. 1831. Fatigued by his parliamentary duties, he announced his retirement at the ensuing dissolution, when he nominated the reformer Robert Henry Southwell, explaining that his pro-reform views were unwelcome to his main supporters.[16] He signed the reform declaration in county Cavan late that year, but declined the invitation to stand at the general election of 1832 and never sat in Parliament again.[17]

A conscientious landlord, Saunderson shut up the Castle and remitted his tenants' rents during the Famine, declaring in March 1847 that 'I feel as part of a crew of a sinking ship'. By that time, devastated by the death of his eldest son Francis and incapacitated by the loss of a leg, which had to be amputated after a riding accident, he moved abroad and lived as a recluse.[18] Remembered on his estates as 'the Old Colonel', he died at Nice in November 1857. Latterly under the influence of his strong-willed wife, he had disinherited their crippled son Alexander and his rebellious brother Somerset, so the bulk of the property passed to their fourth son Colonel Edward James Saunderson (1837-1906), Member for Cavan, 1865-74, and North Armagh, 1885-1906, who led the Liberal Unionist resistance to Gladstone's home rule bill.[19]

[1] Hist. Irish Parl. vi. 244-7; HP Commons, 1790-1820, ii. 631; v. 96-97. [2] H. Saunderson, Saundersons of Castle Saunderson, 53-55. [3] Dublin Evening Post, 26 Feb., 9 Mar.; Enniskillen Chron. 6 Apr. 1820. [4] NLI, Farnham mss 18602 (1), Clements to Farnham, 30 July; (2), Saunderson to same, 19 Aug. 1823. [5] PRO NI, Richardson mss D2002/C/27/1; PRO NI, Morley mss T3530/2/12/47, 49. [6] Dublin Evening Post, 10, 20 June, 1, 4 July; Impartial Reporter, 15, 29 June, 3 July; Farnham mss 18602 (22), Irvine to Maxwell, 16 June, Chambers to same, 17 June; (24), Saunderson to same, 19 June; (28), to same, 30 June 1826; Rev. T. P. Cunningham, '1826 General Election in Co. Cavan', Breifne, ii (1962), 16-17, 22-23, 27, 30. [7] Westmeath Jnl. 7 Sept. 1826; Enniskillen Chron. 1 Feb. 1827;

Cunningham, 38-39. [8] The Times, 3 Mar. 1827. [9] Roscommon and Leitrim Gazette, 8 Dec. 1827; Saunderson, 52, 56-58. [10] Add. 40395, f. 188. [11] Impartial Reporter, 23, 30 Oct.; 6, 13 Nov. 1828. [12] Enniskillen Chron. 29 Jan. 1829. [13] Add. 40336, f. 275. [14] NAI, Leveson Gower letter bks. M738, Leveson Gower to Planta, 11 July; Enniskillen Chron. 29 July, 5, 19 Aug.; Impartial Reporter, 19 Aug.; Farnham mss 18602 (41), Southwell to Maxwell, 12 Aug., Saunderson to same, 14 Aug. 1830. [15] Add. 40313, f. 114. [16] Dublin Evening Post, 26, 28 Apr.; Enniskillen Chron. 19 May 1831. [17] Enniskillen Chron. 1 Dec. 1831; Cunningham, 39. [18] Saunderson, 58-59; A. Jackson, Col. Edward Saunderson, 168-9, 174-7, 183, 185-6. [19] Dublin Evening Post, 5 Dec. 1857; Saunderson, 56, 58-60; Jackson, 27-28, 177-8.

S.M.F.

SAVILE, Albany (?1783–1831), of Sweetlands and Oaklands, nr. Okehampton, Devon.

OKEHAMPTON   1807–9 June 1820

b. ?1783, o. legit. s.[1] of Christoph of 3 Park Street, Mdx. and Hill Hall, Hales, Norf. and 2nd w. Jane, da. and coh. of John Savile, linen draper, of Clay Hill, Enfield, Mdx. *educ.* Christ Church, Oxf. 11 May 1802, aged 18; L. Inn 1804, called 1817. *m.* 7 Mar. 1815,[2] Eleanora Elizabeth, da. of Sir Bourchier Wrey, 7th bt., of Tawstock Court, Barnstaple, Devon, 8s. 5da. *suc.* fa. 1819. *d.* 26 Jan. 1831.
    Recorder, Okehampton 1807-*d.*
    Capt. E. Devon militia 1820.

Savile, who had inherited all of his father's estate in 1819, including personalty sworn under £60,000,[3] made a fleeting final appearance in the House in this period. Markedly independent in his politics before 1820, at the general election he returned himself and a supporter of Lord Liverpool's ministry for Okehampton, where his property gave him complete control. However, some seven weeks after the new Parliament met he made way for Lord Glenorchy, a Whig and fellow member of Brooks's Club. He continued to return paying guests for his borough, apparently without reference to their political leanings. He did not live to see it disfranchised by the Reform Act, dying in January 1831 from 'an inflammatory affection which ... ran its course with a rapidity baffling all medical assistance'.[4] The bulk of his estate, including the property in Okehampton, passed to his eldest son, Albany Bourchier Savile, a minor; his personalty was sworn under £25,000.[5]

[1] Robert Farrand* was his father's illegitimate son. [2] The Times, 15 Mar. 1815; Burke LG states 2 Mar. [3] PROB 11/1616/245; IR26/800/408. [4] Trewman's Exeter Flying Post, 27 Jan. 1831. [5] PROB 11/1790/543; IR26/1273/579.

D.R.F.

SAVILE, John, Visct. Pollington (1783–1860), of
Methley Park, nr. Leeds, Yorks. and 33 Dover
Street, Mdx.

PONTEFRACT	1807–1812
PONTEFRACT	22 Dec. 1812–1826
PONTEFRACT	1831–1832

b. 3 July 1783, o.s. of John Savile†, 2nd earl of
Mexborough [I], and Elizabeth, da. and h. of Henry
Stephenson of East Burnham, Berks. and Cox Lodge, nr.
Newcastle-upon-Tyne, Northumb. *educ.* Eton c. 1797;
Trinity Coll. Camb. 1801. *m.* 29 Aug. 1807, Lady Anne
Yorke, da. of Philip Yorke†, 3rd earl of Hardwicke, 6s. (2
d.v.p.) 1da. *suc.* fa. as 3rd earl of Mexborough [I] 3 Feb.
1830. *d.* 25 Dec. 1860.
   Capt. Pontefract vols. 1803, 2nd maj. 1806, lt.-col.
commdt. 1808; lt. S. regt. W. Riding yeoman cav. 1811,
capt. 1824.

Pollington, who had sat for the open and venal
borough of Pontefract with one brief interruption
since 1807, was returned there in second place in 1820.
Although he had previously acted with the Whig opposition to Lord Liverpool's ministry, he had exhibited a growing conservatism at the close of the 1818
Parliament. His changing political allegiance did not
help endear him to Robert Peel*, who had a 'particular dislike' of him and found him 'a most singular character with an apparent horror of truth'. Writing to his
wife during a visit to Lord Hertford's, Peel noted that
Pollington had been 'invited here to crow like a cock for
the amusement of the party after dinner'.[1] He was a very
lax attender, who gave silent support to government
when present. He was granted three weeks' leave for
private business, 2 June, and returned to divide against
economies in tax collection, 4 July 1820. He voted in
defence of ministers' conduct towards Queen Caroline,
6 Feb. 1821. He divided against repeal of the additional
malt duty, 3 Apr., and was allowed another two weeks'
leave for private business, 7 May 1821. He voted against
abolition of one of the joint-postmasterships, 13 Mar.,
and relieving Catholic peers of their disabilities, 30 Apr.
1822. He presented a Pontefract petition against the
hawkers and pedlars bill, 22 Feb. 1823, his only known
parliamentary activity for that session.[2] He divided
against the motion condemning the prosecution of
the Methodist missionary John Smith in Demerara,
11 June 1824. As in the past, he voted against Catholic
relief, 1 Mar., 21 Apr., 10 May 1825. It was said of him
at this time that he 'appeared to attend seldom and to
vote with ministers'.[3] In February 1826, at his father's
request, he announced his intention of retiring at the
next dissolution; the reasons for this are unclear.[4]

In February 1830 he succeeded his father as 3rd
earl of Mexborough, inheriting the Methley estate,
£14,000, an unspecified amount in government stock
and the residue of personalty which was sworn under
£33,000.[5] At the general election that summer he
offered for Lincoln, where his kinsman Lord Monson
had a powerful interest, but he withdrew before the
poll because of what he considered to be a scurrilous
and vexatious opposition to him.[6] He stood again for
Pontefract at the general election of 1831, in place of
Sir Culling Eardley Smith, the retiring anti-reformer.
When challenged on the hustings he maintained that
he was 'friendly to reform', but he declined to pledge
support for the Grey ministry's bill, observing that
this would be 'like requiring a man who dined at your
table to eat a certain dish, the whole dish, and nothing
but the dish'. He declared that he would 'most willingly vote for retrenchment and for lightening the
burdens of the people by making the rich bear a greater
proportion of the taxes', but he 'would not engage to
support a measure, the extent of the consequences
of which he believed ministers did not see'. He was
returned unopposed with a reformer, and immediately
left for Cambridge to 'vote for [William] Peel* and
[Henry] Goulburn*' in the University election.[7] He
divided against the second reading of the reintroduced
reform bill, 6 July, for use of the 1831 census in determining the disfranchisement schedules, 19 July, and
against the bill's passage, 21 Sept. 1831. His application next day for three weeks' leave to attend to urgent
private business was objected to by Daniel O'Connell,
who did not consider it a 'sufficient excuse'; the House
nevertheless agreed to it, 23 Sept. He voted against
the second reading of the revised reform bill, 17 Dec.
1831, the enfranchisement of Tower Hamlets, 28 Feb.,
and the third reading, 22 Mar. 1832. He presented a
petition from Leeds clergymen against the proposed
Irish education reforms, 9 July. He divided against
ministers on the Russian-Dutch loan, 12 July 1832. He
had hoped to retain his seat at the general election later
that year, but reportedly 'shuddered at being drawn
into expense' and abandoned it.[8]

Mexborough wrote to Peel in March 1835 requesting that he be given an English peerage, which he
claimed George IV had wished to see conferred on his
father; the application was refused.[9] Between 1830 and
1836 much building work was carried out at Methley,
and its cost may have contributed to his 'pecuniary difficulties' later in life. He spent his last few years living
in a small house on his estate, leaving the hall empty
and eventually leasing it to Titus Salt, the Bradford
industrialist.[10] He died in December 1860 and was succeeded by his eldest son, John Charles George Savile*.

[1] *Peel Letters*, 57, 61, 62. [2] *The Times*, 23 Feb. 1823. [3] *Session of Parl. 1825*, p. 481. [4] Add. 40385, f. 217. [5] PROB 11/1768/187; IR26/1231/51. [6] *Leeds Intelligencer*, 14, 29 July 1830. [7] *Leeds Mercury*, 7 May 1831. [8] Lonsdale mss, Beckett to Lowther, 4 Dec. 1832. [9] Add. 40416, ff. 288, 290. [10] N. Pevsner, *Buildings of England: W. Riding of Yorks.* 366; R.V. Taylor, *Biographia Leodiensis*, 490; *Gent. Mag.* (1861), i. 229.

M.P.J.C.

SAVILE, John Charles George, Visct. Pollington (1810–1899), of Methley Park, nr. Leeds, Yorks.

GATTON	1831–1832
PONTEFRACT	1835–1837
PONTEFRACT	1841–1847

b. 4 June 1810, 1st s. of John Savile*, 3rd earl of Mexborough [I], and Lady Anne Yorke, da. of Philip Yorke†, 3rd earl of Hardwicke. *educ.* Eton c. 1821-6; Trinity Coll. Camb. 1827-8. *m.* (1) 24 Feb. 1842, Lady Rachel Katherine Walpole (*d.* 21 June 1854), da. of Horatio Walpole*, 3rd earl of Orford, 1s.; (2) 27 July 1861, Agnes Louise Elizabeth, da. of John Raphael of Kingston, Surr., 2s. 2da. *styled* Visct. Pollington 1830-60; *suc.* fa. as 4th earl of Mexborough [I] 25 Dec. 1860. *d.* 17 Aug. 1899.

Savile had been renowned for his classical scholarship at Eton, from where comes a story of a pugilistic encounter in which he 'strutted about the ring, spouting Homer' between rounds.[1] He assumed the courtesy title of Lord Pollington on his father's succession to the earldom of Mexborough in 1830, and was returned for Gatton at the general election the following year on the interest of his cousin the 5th Baron Monson. Though under age at the time of his election, he had attained his majority by the time the House assembled.

Like his father, Pollington divided against the second reading of the Grey ministry's reintroduced reform bill, which proposed to disfranchise Gatton, 6 July 1831. He voted five times for adjournment motions, 12 July, for use of the 1831 census to determine the disfranchisement schedules, 19 July, and against the partial disfranchisement of Chippenham, 27 July. He divided against the bill's third reading, 21 Sept., and the second reading of the Scottish bill, 23 Sept. He voted to censure the Irish administration for its conduct during the Dublin election, 23 Aug. He was in the minority of seven for Waldo Sibthorp's motion complaining of a breach of parliamentary privilege by *The Times*, 12 Sept., when he voted for safeguards for the West Indian sugar trade. In his only recorded contribution to debate, 22 Sept., he declined to press his father's request for leave when the excuse of 'urgent

private business' was queried by Daniel O'Connell. He paired in favour of ending the Maynooth grant, 26 Sept. He divided against the second reading of the revised reform bill, 17 Dec. 1831, its passage into committee, 20 Jan., the enfranchisement of Tower Hamlets, 28 Feb., and the third reading, 22 Mar. 1832. Next day he was in the minority for Waldo Sibthorp's amendment regarding the freeholders of Lincolnshire, where his patron Monson owned large estates.[2] He voted against the second reading of the Irish reform bill, 25 May. He divided against ministers on the Russian-Dutch loan, 26 Jan., 12 July 1832.

With the disfranchisement of Gatton by the Reform Act, Pollington apparently made no attempt to find a new seat. Instead, he embarked on an adventurous variant of the grand tour, covering Russia, Persia and India. His experiences, which he set down in a journal, excited his interest in the Orient, and in 1834 he accompanied his school friend Alexander Kinglake† on an expedition through the Ottoman empire. This is chronicled in Kinglake's novel *Eothen*, in which Pollington (thinly disguised as 'Methley') is depicted as a formidable classical scholar who nonetheless possessed 'the practical sagacity of a Yorkshireman'.[3] He was obliged to return to England early in 1835 for his election at Pontefract, after which his father anticipated that he would offer Sir Robert Peel 'every support in his power'. He retired in 1837 but sat for the borough again in the 1841 Parliament, and was unsuccessfully nominated in his absence by the Protectionists at a by-election in 1851.[4] A friend of Benjamin Disraeli†, he and his 'very wild and gay' first wife are featured as Lord and Lady Gaverstock in *Coningsby*.[5] He succeeded to his father's title and estates in 1860, and later adopted the Roman Catholic faith of his second wife.[6] He died in August 1899, the last survivor of the unreformed Parliament, and was succeeded by the son from his first marriage, John Horatio Savile (1843-1916).

[1] W. Tuckwell, *Alexander Kinglake*, 10. [2] R.J. Olney, *Rural Soc. in 19th Cent. Lincs.* 24. [3] G. de Gaury, *Travelling Gentleman*, 9, 22-24, 28. [4] Add. 40413, f. 199; *The Times*, 2 Jan., 15 Feb. 1851. [5] *Disraeli Letters*, iv. 80; *Lady Holland to Son*, 219. [6] *VCH Surr.* iii. 463.

H.J.S.

SCARLETT, James (1769–1844), of Abinger Hall, Dorking, Surr. and New Street, Mdx.[1]

PETERBOROUGH	10 Feb. 1819–25 Nov. 1822
PETERBOROUGH	12 Feb. 1823–1830
MALTON	1830–26 Mar. 1831
COCKERMOUTH	1831–1832
NORWICH	1832–1834

b. 13 Dec. 1769, in Jamaica, 2nd s. of Robert Scarlett of Duckett's Spring, St. James, Jamaica and Elizabeth, da. of Col. Philip Anglin of Paradise, Jamaica, wid. of John Wright. *educ.* privately at home until 1785; I. Temple 1785, called 1791; Trinity Coll. Camb. 1785. *m.* (1) 23 Oct. 1792, Louise Henrietta (*d.* 8 Mar. 1829), da. of Peter Campbell of Kilmory, Argyll, 3s. 2da.; (2) 28 Sept. 1843, Elizabeth, da. of Lee Steere Steere (formerly Witts) of Jayes-in-Wotton, Surr., wid. of Rev. Henry John Ridley of Ockley, rect. of Abinger, *s.p.* kntd. 30 Apr. 1827; *cr.* Bar. Abinger 12 Jan. 1835. *d.* 7 Apr. 1844.

KC 8 Mar. 1816; bencher, I. Temple 1816; solicitor-gen. co. pal. of Dur. 1816, att.-gen. 1825-34; king's att. and sjt. co. pal. of Lancaster 1819-27; att.-gen. Apr. 1827-Jan. 1828, June 1829-Nov. 1830; c. bar. exch. 1834-*d.*; PC 15 Dec. 1834; sjt.-at-law 24 Dec. 1834.

Commr. on co. pal. of Lancaster cts. 1829-34.

Scarlett, who in this period acquired a Falstaffian girth, so that 'his belly projects to an unusual extent, even for a corpulent man', apparently wore 'a perpetual smile, blended with an air of joviality'.[2] As the leading *nisi prius* lawyer of his day, with an impressive record of success and fees to match, he had plenty to feel smug about. George Philips* of Sedgley, with whom he used to stay when attending Manchester sessions, wrote of him:

> No man was vainer than he, but he never let his vanity interfere with the interest of his clients. He ... never attempted any flights of eloquence, to which he was incompetent, though he did not think so. [Henry] Brougham* said ... no man in any age had such a talent for gaining verdicts ... [As a judge, he was] ... unpopular at the bar. He was accused of being supercilious, and of deciding *ex cathedra* upon the justness of any observation made to him.[3]

His professional reputation and a brilliant Commons debut in February 1819 as Member for the 2nd Earl Fitzwilliam's borough of Peterborough quickly propelled him into the second rank of the Whig opposition, but in the end he fell short of expectations. He was overshadowed by Brougham, whom he habitually got the better of in the courts, but who 'paid him off ... in the House of Commons', where his laconic and languid conversational style did not go down well.[4] One observer wrote that

when speaking in the ... Commons [Scarlett] was always above the common place ... His speeches frequently partook of the quality called special pleading. When it suited his purpose, no one could be more clear: when it served his object to mystify, there were few in the House who could do so with better effect. In both cases he appeared equally sincere. His manner was highly seductive ... He was always cool and collected ... [He had] no pretensions to the character of an orator, for which his manner is much too cold and quiet.[5]

At the general election of 1820 he was again returned for Peterborough, where an earlier report of trouble came to nothing.[6] Less than a fortnight later he had the 'delicate task', as attorney-general of the northern circuit, of leading the prosecution at York assizes of Henry Hunt* and others over the Peterloo incident, having condemned the massacre in the House in late 1819. Personally, however, he had no doubt that the meeting had been illegal and intimidatory. Hunt was convicted, but other defendants were acquitted; and one Tory observer reckoned that while Scarlett had been 'earnest in the cause notwithstanding his votes and speeches', he seemed to have 'mismanaged the prosecution, and not to have brought forward all that he was capable of doing'.[7] In the Commons, where he normally sat next to the opposition leader Tierney on the front bench,[8] he divided with his friends on the civil list, 5, 8 May, and against the appointment of an additional baron of exchequer in Scotland, 15 May 1820. He was named to the select committee on the criminal laws, 9 May. He dismissed an inmate's complaint of ill-treatment in Lancaster gaol, 31 May, and agreed that it was inconvenient that Welsh judges should double as counsel, 1 June, when he voted against the aliens bill. He opposed as inadequate the government's bill to relieve the superior courts of trivial business, 20 June. He declined an approach to act as counsel for Queen Caroline and on 21 June clashed with Brougham, her attorney-general, over the best way to proceed.[9] Next day he voted against Wilberforce's compromise resolution, as he did the ministerial proposal for a secret committee, 26 June, when, in what his friend Sir James Mackintosh* considered 'a very animated and rather violent attack on the ministers', he accused them of risking 'revolution' by defying public opinion on this issue.[10] After denouncing the 'tyrannical' aliens bill, 10 July, he stood by his description of the ministry as 'weak' in the face of angry personal attacks on him. He voted for economies in revenue collection, 4 July. On 17 Oct. 1820, soon after his future son-in-law John Campbell II* had noted that if ministers fell Scarlett, 'the best man the party furnishes since [Samuel] Romilly's[†] death', would become attorney-general, perhaps even lord chancellor, he condemned the bill of pains and penalties as a 'disgrace'.[11]

In late December 1820 he wrote to Fitzwilliam's son Lord Milton*:

I cannot imagine how the ministry can stand without [George] Canning* unless the plans of opposition are founded on folly or betrayed by treachery. Whatever is violent and extravagant on our part must give strength to ministers, and they are and will be safe if it becomes the fashion with us to be so candid as to admit that we had not the means of forming an administration. It is my honest conviction that a *total* change of ministers is essential to prevent a revolution, and that every man who has any property, not depending on the patronage of the present administration, has an immediate interest in effecting its dissolution ... I think it highly important that Lord Grey should be in town some days before the 23rd [of January], and that there should be a deliberate and concerted plan of the approaching campaign ... I dread the operations of the Mountain in the House of Commons. Grey's presence and counsels may bring it to order.[12]

He was involved in pre-session deliberations with Tierney and Brougham.[13] His part in the abortive parliamentary campaign on behalf of the queen was inconspicuous and undistinguished. A young Whig spectator thought his speech on the liturgy question, 26 Jan. 1821, was 'dull'; while the 'Mountaineers' Henry Grey Bennet and Thomas Creevey respectively deemed it 'a powerless, miserable' effort and 'rum'.[14] After the failure of the attack Campbell noted that Scarlett, who 'insinuated that if he had defended the queen he would have turned out the ministers' and had 'fully expected ere now to have been James, Lord Abinger' and chancellor, was disappointed, but 'affects to say that a man's happiness depends upon the state of his digestion, and not the station he fills'.[15] Grey Bennet approved his argument that the Langholme presbytery's loyal address was a breach of privilege, 1 Feb.[16] He was named to the select committees on the report of the Irish judicial commission, 26 June 1821, 19 Mar. 1823. Before leaving for the circuit in mid-March he voted in condemnation of the Allies' suppression of the liberal regime in Naples, 21 Feb., divided for reception of Davison's petition complaining of his treatment by Justice William Best† but spoke circumspectly on the case, 23 Feb.; paired for Catholic relief, 28 Feb.; supported Milton's proposal to give Leeds a ratepayer franchise if it received Grampound's seats, 2 Mar, and voted in the opposition minority on the revenue, 6 Mar. On his return from York assizes, where he resumed his rivalry with Brougham,[17] he voted for the disfranchisement of ordnance officials, 12 Apr., Lambton's parliamentary

reform scheme, 18 Apr., and Russell's general reform motion, 9 May. That day he obtained leave to introduce a bill to amend the poor laws, which he said operated 'as a premium for poverty, indolence, licentiousness and immorality'. He proposed to impose a maximum on rate assessments, to do away with relief for single able-bodied men and to end the power of justices to remove paupers to their place of birth. The measure had a mixed reception (and was publicly mocked by Sydney Smith in the autumn), and on 2 July Scarlett abandoned it for the session, complaining that 'many inflammatory and calumnious misrepresentations had gone abroad'.[18] He tried again in 1822, but the bill was thrown out on its second reading, 31 May, by 82-66. On Chetwynd's plan to amend the vagrancy laws, 24 May 1821, he pointed to the 'absurdity' of sending miscreants to their place of settlement to be punished. He divided sporadically for economy and said it was 'the only resource', 14 June; but in a review of the session Grey Bennet noted that Scarlett and Mackintosh 'took every occasion to separate themselves from the few combatants who fought on the third bench for public economy'.[19] He voted silently for mitigation of the punishment for forgery offences, 23 May, 4 June. He had no doubt that the proceedings of the Constitutional Association were illegal, 30 May, but was opposed to interference by Parliament, 3 July. He spoke and was a minority teller against Martin's bill to curb the ill-treatment of cattle, 1 June. He spoke and voted against Thomas Frankland Lewis's* inclusion in the Irish revenue commission, 15, 26 June. He divided in minorities of 28 to condemn the Holy Alliance, 20 June, and of 35 for intervention to preserve liberalism in Sicily next day. He said that the queen's right to be crowned was 'a matter of custom and law', 30 June 1821.

Scarlett voted for the amendment to the address, 5 Feb., more extensive tax reductions, 11, 21 Feb., and gradual remission of the salt tax, 28 Feb. 1822. On 5 Mar. he presented and endorsed a constituency petition ascribing agricultural distress largely to the resumption of cash payments. He divided against the Irish habeas corpus suspension bill, 7 Feb., in protest against Sir Robert Wilson's* dismissal from the army, 13 Feb., and for inquiry into the Scottish burghs, 20 Feb. He believed that Hunt's complaints about his treatment in Ilchester gaol were justified, 4 Mar. He voted again for reform, 25 Apr., 3 June. He was a fairly regular though silent supporter of economy, retrenchment and reduced taxation after his return from the circuit. He was in Ricardo's minority of 25 for a 20s. duty on imported wheat, 9 May. He joined in the successful opposition to the Salford Hundred court bill,

13 May, and called for reform of the 'defective' Welsh judicial system, 23 May. He voted for inquiry into the government of the Ionian Islands, 14 May, in support of Brougham's motion on the increasing influence of the crown, 24 June, and to condemn the lord advocate's dealings with the Scottish press, 25 June. He voted for Mackintosh's motion for criminal law reform, 4 June. Next day he spoke against the 'unjust, tyrannical and unnecessary' aliens bill, which he doggedly resisted thereafter; he was a teller for the minority of 13 for his own amendment, 10 July. Opposing the ill-treatment of cattle bill once more, 7 June 1822, he remarked that if its principle was admitted there would be 'punishment affixed to the boiling of lobsters, or the eating of oysters alive'.

From Lancaster assizes, 22 Aug. 1822, Scarlett, optimistically speculating on the imminent 'dissolution' of the ministry after Lord Londonderry's* suicide and the possibility of a Whig alliance in government with Canning, urged Lord Lansdowne to delay his continental holiday to be 'within reach of any call that may be made upon you':

> I am persuaded that for some years past the part of opposition has been much more agreeable in Parliament than that of the ministry. But notwithstanding my habits, which are almost inveterate, I cannot but entertain some fears that a long continued and a powerful opposition may become too factious, and that the determined exclusion of a very considerable portion of the rank and wealth of the nation from any share in the government may at length drive them to seek their just place even by revolution. On this account I sincerely wish for some change that may soften the fury of the Mountain by contact with the Court.[20]

Had the Whigs come in, he would have been made attorney-general, perhaps even lord chancellor.[21] In October he entertained Canning, now foreign secretary, at his Surrey home at Abinger, having originally invited him there to say his farewells when he was expected to go to India. 'Greatly puzzled to know' how Canning could act with his reactionary colleagues, he anticipated a 'turbulent' next session, and hoped 'we shall be rid of the sinking fund and the assessed taxes at the least'.[22] At the end of the month he declared his candidature for a vacancy for Cambridge University, where a division in the ministerial interest promised success, having obtained Fitzwilliam's permission to vacate Peterborough and an assurance that he could come in again if necessary. He finished a distant third behind an anti-Catholic Tory and fell back on Peterborough in February 1823, when he was returned after a token contest. Whishaw had commented to Lady Holland, 27 Nov. 1822:

> I am sorry for Scarlett, who has rashly involved himself in a great difficulty by an overweening confidence in himself ... It seems that the representation of Cambridge was an old object of ambition with him ... But he has acted his part very well, and, from whatever motive, has made great personal sacrifices to the Whig cause, for which I hope he will have due honour from the leaders of the party.[23]

Scarlett voted silently for parliamentary reform, 20 Feb., 24 Apr., 2 June 1823. He divided against the national debt reduction bill, 28 Feb., 6 Mar., and the ministerial plan to contract for naval and military pensions, 14, 18 Apr. He voted for repeal of the Foreign Enlistment Act, 16 Apr. On the 15th he questioned the 'constitutionality' of the Irish attorney-general's *ex-officio* informations in the case of the Dublin Orange rioters, and he was in the majority for inquiry (during which he examined witnesses), 22 Apr. He objected to any interference with mercantile law, 12 May, and was named to the select committee on this subject, 15 May. He spoke and voted for Mackintosh's motion for abolition of the death penalty for larceny, 21 May, and welcomed the conciliatory attitude of Peel, the home secretary. He approved the principle of Lord Althorp's small debts bill, 27 May, and of Colonel Wood's plans to amend the laws of settlement, 4 June. He voted in censure of the lord advocate, 3 June. He spoke and voted for inquiry into chancery arrears, 5 June, and divided for investigation of the coronation expenses, 9, 19 June, but he voted against inquiry into the currency, 12 June. He tried unsuccessfully to secure postponement of consideration of the case of the Irish judge O'Grady, 13, 17 June, and on 9 July was a majority teller for his own motion to drop proceedings. He was in small minorities against the beer duties bill, 13, 17 June, and voted in favour of the Irish Catholics' petition complaining of the administration of justice, 26 June, for the introduction of jury trial to New South Wales, 7 July, and against trying capital offences in the Indian army by courts martial, 11 July 1823. At Brighton in October Tierney was pleased to find him 'with the air and manner of a man with whom the world goes smoothly'; and soon afterwards he went with his two eldest sons to Italy, travelling as far as Florence and calling on the de Broglies en route.[24]

Scarlett strongly supported the complaint of breach of privilege against lord chancellor Eldon, 1 Mar. 1824. Later that month his sudden death on the circuit was convincingly but falsely reported in the press.[25] In the previous November Whishaw had wondered whether 'Canning's friendship' might soon secure him a senior judicial place. Two months later Canning apparently urged his claim to be made solicitor-general, and at the end of March 1824 warmly recommended him to Lord Liverpool as a radical but sound choice as lord chief justice of the common pleas, pointing to 'the singular ability, temper, firmness and *good faith*' with which he had conducted Hunt's prosecution, and the fact that he had 'never gone into violent politics'. The premier would have none of it, given that Scarlett, though 'never ... the advocate or supporter of jacobinical or dangerous opinions', was still 'systematically opposed' to government in the Commons. When he heard of this Scarlett, according to Campbell, said he would have declined the offer.[26] He supported the Scottish juries bill, 4 May. He voted for inquiries into the Irish church establishment, 6 May, and the state of Ireland, 11 May, for proper use of Irish first fruits revenues, 25 May, to end Irish church pluralities, 27 May, and, in a minority of 14, against the Irish insurrection bill, 18 June. He divided for repeal of the assessed taxes, 10 May, and was in Hume's small minority against naval impressment, 10 June. He condemned the exterior of the new Westminster courts as 'a disgrace to the national taste', 21 May, and on the 24th opposed Althorp's county courts bill. On 1 June he called for the adoption of some middle course on the case of the Methodist missionary John Smith, being unwilling, as Brougham proposed, to condemn outright his prosecution in Demerara; he paired against this motion, 11 June.[27] He disliked Peel's transportation bill, 4 June, but welcomed his 'very useful' juries empanelling bill, 18 June 1824.

Scarlett voted against the Irish unlawful societies bill, 15, 25 Feb., and supported Brougham's bid to permit the Catholic Association to state its legal case, 18 Feb. 1825. He divided silently for Catholic relief, 1 Mar., 21 Apr., 10 May, and presented a favourable petition from members of the English bar, 19 Apr. He argued that Hume's precipitate repeal of the Combination Acts had only created new problems, 4 May. He said that the proposed salary of £10,000 for the lord chief justice was too low, 16 May, and on the 27th tried unsuccessfully to increase it by £2,000. He would not support Brougham's amendment to deduct £500 from puisne judges' salaries, but later that day spoke and voted for his motion to make them immoveable. He divided against the duke of Cumberland's grant, 27, 30 May, 6 June. He supported inquiry into the Jamaican deportations, 16 June. He spoke and voted for the spring guns bill, 21 June, attacked the Scottish partnerships bill, 22 June, and ranted at length against the law of merchants bill, but did not divide the House, 28 June 1825. He apparently approved of the ministerial plan to restrict the circula-

tion of small bank notes in February 1826.[28] He did not think the case of William Kenrick[†] need concern the Commons, 17 Feb. On 1 Mar. he professed support for amelioration of the condition of West Indian slaves, but wanted the owners to be conciliated and not coerced. He divided against the proposed separate salary for the president of the board of trade, 10 Apr., for reform of Edinburgh's representation, 13 Apr., and general reform, 27 Apr., and for revision of the corn laws, 18 Apr. He reckoned the new chancery court building was a 'contemptible' waste of money, 17 Apr., when he made some comments on the criminal justice bill. He was not convinced by George Lamb's argument in favour of introducing defence by counsel to felony trials, 25 Apr., but remained open to persuasion and so voted for his bill. He was in Hume's minority for inquiry into the state of the nation, 4 May. Next day he presented and endorsed Daniel O'Connell's[*] petition for the removal of the aged Lord Norbury from the Irish bench. He favoured investigation of James Silk Buckingham's[†] grievances over infringement of press freedom in India, 9 May. He was in the majority for Russell's resolution condemning electoral bribery, 26 May 1826.

At the general election the following month he came in unopposed again for Peterborough. Later that summer he evidently sent Lady Holland a favourable report of economic conditions in the north; but the duke of Bedford was sceptical:

> A lawyer, leading on the circuit, thinks of little beyond filling his bags with briefs, and his pockets with money; and provided these do not fail, he thinks there can be no distress, and knows and sees but little of the sufferings of the manufacturer at the loom, or the labourer in the field.[29]

Scarlett believed that 'the pretext and probably the cause' of the early summoning of Parliament was the corn laws, though he suspected also that ministers were in 'great embarrassment' on the subject of Ireland.[30] He doubted the worth of Lord Althorp's resolutions against electoral bribery, 22 Nov. 1826, but supported them as 'a step towards a very desirable object'. He secured an adjournment of the confused debate on the same subject, 26 Feb. 1827. That month he stayed away from the discussions on the duke of Clarence's grant, of which he approved.[31] He voted for Catholic relief, 6 Mar., having earlier communicated to Peel Burdett's wishes as to the timing of his motion.[32] He defended the Wakefields against the charge of abduction at Lancaster assizes in March, when his illness caused the trial to be put back a day.[33] On his return to London in April he argued in favour of the Whigs supporting Canning in his bid to form a new ministry, to which he was touted as a potential recruit.[34] On 20 Apr. Canning offered him the attorney-generalship. He consulted Lansdowne and Lord Holland, who, as Canning's enemy Mrs. Arbuthnot put it, gave him 'leave to *rat*'; but he felt obliged to give Fitzwilliam the last and deciding word. Fitzwilliam initially gave 'a frank recommendation not to accept', while indicating his own determination to support Canning's ministry; and Milton, who distrusted Canning and had reservations about Scarlett's reliability as a Whig, was discouraging, arguing that joining Canning, especially when Lansdowne's stipulations about the composition of the Irish executive had been rejected, would not advance the Catholic cause. Scarlett, who was desperate for the office, even though it would materially diminish his income, contended that politicians must deal in practicalities, that 'an immediate adhesion to Canning's government' would 'shortly lead to a complete Whig government' and that Canning was 'at this moment the only bridge over which we can pass to that most desirable end of all, the emancipation and tranquillity of Ireland'. On 24 Apr. Fitzwilliam relented and not only gave his blessing, but promised him a secure re-election for Peterborough; and the following day Milton wrote that 'if you think that by accepting office, the Catholic question will be advanced, you are not only justified, but called upon to accept'. This he did, with great glee, according to Campbell, who believed that the appointment would 'give great satisfaction' to the profession.[35] 'On the wing for Peterborough', where he was quietly re-elected, 9 May, Scarlett urged Lansdowne to adopt 'some more distinct outward and visible sign of an union between you and the government than the mere support by speaking and voting in Parliament', perhaps by taking his place in the cabinet immediately: 'I hope it would set in motion ... the spirit which exists in the country but which cannot be called into action by a provisional government, not understood by the people'.[36] In his first speech as an official man, 18 May, he had a slight brush with Brougham on the Penryn corruption inquiry and welcomed in principle Peel's criminal justice bill. He now opposed Taylor's plan to separate bankruptcy from chancery administration, 22 May, when Brougham had some harsh words for him; but Brougham was more conciliatory towards him when he replied for the government against Hume's call for repeal of the Blasphemous Libels Act, 31 May.[37] He was in the ministerial minority against the disfranchisement of Penryn, 28 May. He opposed Hume's frivolous arrests bill and made fun of his legal ignorance, 1 June, endorsed the Coventry magistracy bill,

18 June 1827, and on the 20th approved Peel's small debts bill.

Scarlett was 'very much affected' by Canning's death, as he told Lady Holland:

> It has for many years been the first of my political wishes to see him in a position in which his just and liberal principles might be applied by his great and *practical* talents for the benefit of country and of mankind ... To look upon the possible consequences of his loss in the return of all the barbarous policy and prejudices which it has been his glory to combat ... to anticipate rebellion in Ireland, the bitterness of civil dissensions at home, a national bankruptcy, an irritated population and new laws of coercion to restrain them – all these fill me with horror and despair.

He initially expected to be 'turned out', but in the event he was retained by Lord Goderich, nothing having come of rumours that he was to replace Lord Lyndhurst as lord chancellor.[38] In late 1827 Scarlett, who had had a cool but civil encounter with Grey at Fitzwilliam's in September, apparently proposed to the cabinet repeal of the Foreign Enlistment and Libels Acts.[39]

When the duke of Wellington came to power in January 1828 Scarlett took a gloomy view of the likely political consequences, anticipating a return to Tory reaction.[40] He was told by William Huskisson, to whom he had looked 'as his leader since Canning's death', that he and his principal associates might well join the ministry; and Huskisson thought there was 'a very fair prospect' of persuading him to continue as attorney-general, which the king certainly wished him to do, so that he might handle some pending duchy legal business.[41] Aware that a proposal to stay in was likely to be made to him and conscious of the awkwardness which it would entail, he sounded Milton in general terms and sought and received from Huskisson assurances that Canning's domestic and foreign policies would be maintained, 'more especially with regard to the real neutrality of the government' on the Catholic question. Campbell encapsulated his dilemma:

> He cannot stay without a rupture with Lord Fitzwilliam and the whole of the Whig party. He will go *sine spe redeundi*, and with the certainty of seeing young and obscure men put over his head ... All that could be said is that Scarlett was not put in by Lansdowne and the Whigs, but by Canning, and that he is therefore justified in acting with Canning's friends. He says, I believe sincerely, that he would be well pleased to hear that he was dismissed.[42]

When he was formally invited, through Lyndhurst, to continue, he consulted Fitzwilliam and Milton:

Considering me as a mere party man, there can be no doubt what ought to be my decision; but ought I to consider myself so much of a party man as to make the duties of party paramount to all others in my case?

Both, being 'furious against the present government', were adamant that he should resign, though Brougham and Lansdowne encouraged him to stay (the former to keep him away from the circuit). He duly stood down after amicable explanations with Lyndhurst and Wellington.[43] The king wanted him to retain the lead in his duchy cases, but the new attorney-general Sir Charles Wetherell* refused to give him precedence.[44] Scarlett voted for repeal of the Test Acts, 26 Feb., presented a pro-Catholic petition, 31 Mar., and divided for relief, 12 May 1828. He was named to the select committees on parochial settlements, 21 Feb., and the poor laws, 22 May. On Brougham's motion for a commission on the common law, 29 Feb., he welcomed Peel's receptive attitude but denied the need for radical change and 'jealous', so it was said, 'that Brougham should run away with all the honour ... sneered at the length and infinite extent of Brougham's speech'. He 'rather shabbily' left the chamber before the 'furious' Brougham replied.[45] He spoke and voted against Taylor's renewed motion for chancery reform as a 'mere abstract proposition', 24 Apr. He 'entirely' approved the financial provision for Canning's family, 14, 22 May. He presented and endorsed attorneys' petitions calling for improvements to judges' chambers at Serjeants' Inn, 16 July, and to the new Westminster courts, 8 July 1828.

That autumn he was made cautiously optimistic by indications that Wellington 'intends to do something decisive for the Catholics': if so, he told his son, he would be 'ready to forget all "untoward events" and support his government de bon coeur', for he regarded the duke as 'the only man in the present crisis who can carry this question in *Court* and Parliament'.[46] Ministers were considering removing the troublesome Wetherell to the bench, but their general opinion was that it would not be politically expedient to replace him with Scarlett. He remained in their minds, however, as the Catholic emancipation furore broke and Wetherell defiantly opposed the concession.[47] Scarlett, who had reluctantly bowed to the king's express wish that he should head the commission of inquiry into the duchy courts,[48] and had lost his wife on 8 Mar, voted silently for emancipation, 6, 30 Mar., and presented and supported the English bar's favourable petition, 25 Mar. 1829. He called the new Westminster king's bench court 'a disgrace', 13 Apr. As the Whig Member George Agar Ellis saw it, he 'spoke for' but 'voted

against' O'Connell being allowed to take his seat unhindered, 18 May; he had left the House without voting on the 15th.[49] Wetherell had been dismissed, and once the emancipation dust had settled Scarlett was offered his place. Having already gathered that Grey, Fitzwilliam and 'the general wish of the party' favoured his acceptance, he took it without hesitation. He was at the same time offered government support for the vacancy for Cambridge University, but on Milton's insistence he continued at Peterborough.[50] The day after his formal acceptance of the office he received from Milton, who acquiesced in rather than approved of it, a letter requesting him to come to an understanding with Wellington that he was to remain free to support parliamentary reform. In reply Scarlett, who insisted that he had 'not been asked to abandon any principle or pledge as the condition of office', sought to clarify his views, and particularly to set out

the limits beyond which I should be very unwilling practically to go, however I might be disposed whilst in opposition to give a general vote as a testimony of my good will ... I have never yet heard propounded any uniform system of election which I could prefer to the present ... I never can approve of any system of representation that takes from property the power and influence necessary to protect it ... I am an advocate for all the improvements of which the present system is susceptible as occasions may suggest and above all disposed to take every fair opportunity of diverting the representation from the small towns, which do not want it, to the large towns which cry aloud for it.

Milton acknowledged that they were in broad agreement.[51] His appointment gave general cross-party 'satisfaction', though Tierney supposedly remarked that he would be 'of little use' to government in debate.[52] A hint of future trouble came in the shape of a letter from Milton, 14 June, threatening to boycott his re-election for Peterborough unless ministers 'disavowed' the support which Lyndhurst and others were giving to the anti-Catholic George Bankes* against a Whig in the Cambridge University by-election.[53] According to Grey's son Lord Howick*, 'it had been a matter of doubt' whether Scarlett and Lord Rosslyn, another recent recruit to the government, would dine with the Whigs at their Fox dinner, 27 June 1829, or opt for the ministerial fish dinner with which it clashed; but in the event Scarlett chose the Whig gathering.[54]

He discussed mitigation of the punishment for forgery with Peel during the recess and put to the cabinet plans for reform of the Welsh judicature.[55] He severely damaged himself in the eyes of most leading Whigs by 'engaging', as Abercromby had it, 'in a single-handed war against the press' by means of *ex-officio* informations for libel. In particular, his speech at the trial of Alexander of the *Morning Journal* in December 1829, when he lamented the unchecked licentiousness of the press for the past ten years, thereby implying that his predecessors had been negligent, caused great offence. Howick commented in his diary that Scarlett 'may call himself a Whig, but his conduct and speeches could not have been in a worse spirit had he been a pupil of Castlereagh himself'; while Althorp wondered 'what had happened to Scarlett's sanity'.[56] Privately, Scarlett was unrepentant, telling his son that he had been misreported and misrepresented and that he had done his 'duty' and was 'not afraid', for 'the liberty of the press does not consist in the power of publishing slander with *impunity*'.[57] Lord John Russell* thought on the eve of the 1830 session that he might 'feel his situation disagreeable', but he defiantly defended himself in the House against Wetherell's vindictive attack, 2 Mar., 'very well', as Howick conceded, but 'without ... at all clearing himself from what was really blameable in his conduct'.[58] He voted for the transfer of East Retford's seats to Birmingham, 1 Feb., but against Lord Blandford's reform scheme, 18 Feb. He endorsed Peel's proposed law reforms, 18 Feb., and the illusory appointments bill, 24 Feb. On 9 Mar. he obtained leave to bring in the administration of justice bill to assimilate the Welsh and Chester palatine jurisdictions into the English. He introduced it on 22 Mar. and saw it through the House, eventually conceding modifications to meet a plethora of objections. On the third reading, 7 July, he successfully opposed Hume's attempt to reduce the judges' salaries; and when proposing adoption of the Lords' amendments, which according to Lord Ellenborough, a member of the cabinet, had made him 'very angry indeed',[59] he called it 'the most important measure which has been submitted to Parliament for many years'. It received royal assent on 23 July 1830 (11 Geo. IV & 1 Gul. IV, c. 70). He saw no reason to resist reception of Drogheda's petition for repeal of the Union, 22 Mar. He supported the principle of Poulett Thomson's usury laws repeal bill, 26 Apr., but pointed out the need to establish a fixed rate of interest, and approved the principle of Brougham's plan to establish local judicatures, 29 Apr. He was suspicious of O'Connell's proposal to put Catholic charitable bequests on the same footing as those of Protestant Dissenters, 4 May, and on the 12th resisted his attack on John Doherty*, the Irish solicitor-general, over the Cork conspiracy trial. He voted against Jewish emancipation, 17 May. Next day he said that he could not force the abolition of arrest for debt on mesne process on a reluctant House and

persuaded Lord Morpeth to withdraw his motion for a bill to end banishment for a second libel offence so that he could introduce a measure of his own. He steered this (which Ellenborough considered 'a poor weak inoperative thing, ridiculous and unconciliating')[60] through the House, though Morpeth carried an amendment to it, 6 July. He secured one of his own to increase recognizances, 9 July.[61] He explained the bill brought in to deal with the four-and-a-half per cent duties, defended the grant for the annual law charges and replied to renewed criticism of his *ex-officio* prosecutions, 4 June. He apparently 'lost his temper' as he 'fell amongst thieves', and the cabinet, according to Ellenborough, thought he 'did ill'.[62] He was in the ministerial majority for the grant for South American missions, 7 June. He endorsed the bill to create an additional chancery judge, 24 June. 'Suffering under some degree of indisposition', he put the ministerial case on the regency issue, 6 July 1830.

In late March 1830 he had told Brougham that Wellington was 'more firmly entrenched than ever with the people, Parliament and the Court'; but a week before the death of George IV in June he informed his son, to whom he complained that he was 'worn out in the House of Commons' by constant late nights, that he was 'not sure' that the ministry would 'last long'.[63] Soon afterwards he was told through Lord Dundas that as Milton intended to give up his Yorkshire seat at the impending general election he was required to make way for him at Peterborough. He confirmed his acquiescence in a subsequent friendly conversation with Milton, who assured him that their now being on opposite sides in the Commons was not behind the move, and began negotiations through government for an alternative seat. On 12 July, however, he received from Fitzwilliam an unsolicited offer to return him for Malton, which he readily accepted, although he had received the same day an offer from Lord Cleveland.[64] Milton endorsed the arrangement, but wanted Scarlett to continue to support, as far as he conscientiously could, reform and revision of the corn laws. Scarlett had no problem with this, but a week before the Malton election he got from Brougham a letter informing him that his sitting as an office-holder under the aegis of men who were determinedly opposed to the administration was 'a subject of general disapprobation'. While the devious Brougham, who was nettled because he had wanted the Malton seat for his own brother, professed to be warning Scarlett 'as a friend', he had maliciously put it about that he had 'had the baseness' to solicit the seat from Fitzwilliam. Howick, for one, was taken in by Brougham's lie. Scarlett tried to set the record straight with Brougham and Milton, who concurred in the accuracy of his statement.[65] Scarlett, who also had to ask Holland to explain a reported recent public criticism of his abandonment of his past principles on the libel issue (Holland said that he had been mischievously misreported), decided to go to Malton, though he told his son that he would probably have to surrender the seat 'soon after Parliament meets'.[66] On the hustings, in what Carlisle heard was 'rather a dextrous speech', he promised to back 'any well considered reform that in my judgement is not calculated to affect the stability of the throne, or the just and useful authority of either House'; to support the abolition of slavery by 'such means as may be consistent with safety' to the negroes, and to continue to be 'a zealous advocate of retrenchment, and economy in the public service'. Of the elections in general he remarked to his son that 'public opinion was never so decided against the Tories', although he felt that it was in favour of Wellington and Peel as ministers.[67] In his pamphlet reviewing the elections the vindictive Brougham highlighted Fitzwilliam's 'unaccountable measure' of returning Scarlett for Malton and predicted that 'he *cannot*, he *will* not, for his honour's sake, he *dares* not to continue so to sit'.[68]

Scarlett, who was aware of the intensity of Brougham's malevolence, and was now also required to explain and justify to Milton his conduct on the libel law repeal, claiming that his hands had been tied by the cabinet, had an audience of the new king at Brighton on 29 Sept. 1830. To Milton he expressed his 'dread' of 'the consequences of the intemperate zeal of some who may second without intending it the attack which is made by the greater part of the press at this moment on property and rank and station, the natural objects of envy and hatred to the ignorant multitude'.[69] When press libels were discussed a month later Ellenborough noted that Scarlett who, with the solicitor-general, advised the cabinet against prosecution 'without the sanction of Parliament', appeared to be 'quite cowed by opposition and the press'.[70] He presented a Malton Dissenters' petition for the abolition of slavery, 5 Nov. Brougham's notice of a reform motion made his personal 'situation ... very painful'; and Campbell felt he should 'vote for the resolution, and receive his dismissal if the duke thinks fit'.[71] He and Peel were reckoned to have 'licked' Brougham in a clash on the civil list, 12 Nov., when Scarlett said that 'irregularity ... [was] a part of his hereditary claims'.[72] He was in the ministerial minority in the division on the civil list which brought the government down, 15 Nov. With some embarrassment, he introduced and rushed through a bill to remedy a technical defect which had made the Administration of Justice Act inoperable, 19

Nov. 1830. For a few days his fate was uncertain. He did not immediately resign, told Milton that he had foreseen the collapse of the ministry and, alarmed by the continuing 'terror' of the `Swing' disturbances, professed to perceive 'something like the beginning of that servile war which I predicted as the natural result of the system of poor laws which I endeavoured ineffectually to correct'. He heard nothing from Grey, the new premier, or Brougham, who had been appointed lord chancellor, until he was dismissed for Thomas Denman*.[73] He was 'much mortified' to be cast aside 'without a kind word from anybody', and bridled under the resulting 'supposition that I have done anything to forfeit the esteem of my friends or to make it proper that they should eject me from their party'. He later admitted that he had considered himself entitled to be afforded at least the chance to refuse the place of chief baron of the exchequer, which was given to Lyndhurst.[74] Scarlett, who dined with opposition party managers and ex-ministers at Ellenborough's, 11 Dec.,[75] took charge of the five law reform bills which had come from the Lords, 13 Dec., and approved the principle of his son-in-law's general registry bill, 16 Dec. 1830.

That month Arbuthnot urged Holland, his successor as chancellor of the duchy of Lancaster, to get Scarlett, who 'seems to feel that he has not been kindly treated by his old friends the Whigs', to complete the report on the palatine courts as soon as possible.[76] When sending Holland a partially finished report, Scarlett deplored the 'rage of the day' against the hereditary revenues of the crown, which he saw as 'a rapid stride' towards republicanism:

> Although I am not driven yet to be a Tory, I am really upon principle attached to the monarchy, being satisfied that under a republic the tyranny of the many would be more oppressive and the extravagance of the government just as great ... I hope that the new government will by the wisdom and moderation of their measures bring Europe as well as our own country into such a state of repose that I may soon find some corner of France or Italy in which to pass the remainder of my years or days in tranquillity and sunshine, undisturbed by frost or law or politics. At present I am terrified by the Hunts and the Cobbetts and the Humes and the O'Connells of the day ... and I find no place even in my own country to rest the soles of my unblessed feet.[77]

Soon afterwards Russell, one of the authors of the Grey ministry's reform bill, to whom Scarlett had evidently applied for some patronage, asked Milton if he thought he would 'support an extensive plan of reform'; and four days after the details of the measure had been revealed, 1 Mar. 1831, Holland wrote to

Grey: 'Should not Milton ascertain distinctly whether Scarlett means to vote against us, as his language occasionally indicates? If he does, a hint, and a broad one, should be given to him'.[78] Scarlett, who was horrified by the sweeping and radical nature of the bill, had told Russell that he did not think he would be able to support it; but on 6 Mar. he received a note from Milton urging him to try to do so. In reply that day he said that 'if the bill does not come out in a very different shape from the committee, I cannot support it', and in effect tendered the resignation of his seat. Milton, though disappointed, was unwilling to force him to vote for the bill and did not ask him to go out.[79] On 22 Mar. Scarlett, despairing of any prospect of the bill, which he felt would establish 'an entire new construction of the whole constitution and government of the country', being modified, spoke at length and voted against the second reading. Next day, finding that Milton had gone to the country, he wrote to him resigning his seat. In the House, 24 Mar., he presented, 'with cheerfulness', a petition in favour of the bill from Malton, and in what he later called a 'funeral dirge', announced that he was about to resign. He wrote to his son, 25 Mar.:

My speech ... [on the 22nd] met with more attention than *The Times* represents ... The game is ... up with the constitution. You must not state to any person, however, that I express a strong opinion upon it, as I made a moderate speech without any party feeling. There must be some sort of convulsion, I fear, whatever happens ... I am full of uneasiness about our home affairs.

In a curious incident that evening, he turned up, apparently uninvited, at Grey's drawing room, but departed abruptly when the premier 'received him ... coldly'. When he got Milton's reply the following morning he immediately took the Chiltern Hundreds. He commented to his son:

I have taken leave of Parliament, where I have never yet been in a desirable position between a party seat and moderate opinions ... I have lost my seat by an adherence to the same opinions upon which I came into Parliament, upon the question of reform, which opinions have never varied or been concealed.[80]

Scarlett, who received 'a very kind letter from the duke of Wellington ... regretting the loss of my seat', was angered by 'more persecution from the Whigs': he and Milton publicly refuted a revival of 'the old lie' that he had applied to Fitzwilliam for the Malton seat and been turned out for breaking a pledge on reform.[81] Four days before the reform bill's defeat on Gascoyne's amendment, 19 Apr., he wrote to his son:

It is said by many persons that most thinking men are against it ... Those who are for it are the radicals, the ultra Whigs, and a certain active and restless class that belongs to every government ... They have persuaded the people that it will give them cheap bread, abundant work, and exemption from taxes ... I ought to add to the supporters the vast class of journalists whose importance will be increased by it. Nevertheless I fear it will be carried. Fear will make men vote for it who actually disapprove of it ... We are altogether in a strange disjointed state. I am not upon the whole sorry to be out of Parliament at this moment.[82]

A few days later he had a conversation with Holland about his apparent 'proscription and exclusion' by the Whigs. Holland mentioned this to Grey and in writing assured Scarlett that there was 'nothing of the kind' and that once reform had been secured they would be happy to resume a political connection with him and give fair, unprejudiced consideration to his claims to professional advancement. Yet at Grey's behest he warned Scarlett that reform was the touchstone and that it was impossible now to give him 'any positive or implicit promise with respect to a specified place on the bench in the contingency of a vacancy', more especially as the claims of others would almost certainly be enhanced by their support for reform. In reply Scarlett, distressed to be thought to have been angling for promotion, reviewed his political conduct since 1801 and particularly since 1827; admitted his grievance over the way he had been unceremoniously ditched and discountenanced by the new ministry; claimed that he had been anxious to support the reform bill but could not honestly do so, and hinted at his belief that Brougham's personal malice lay behind the vendetta against him. He later wrote that Holland's assertion that 'the reform bill was the vital question of the Whig party' was what prompted him to accept the unbending Tory Lord Lonsdale's offer of a seat for Cockermouth (preferring this to one offered by Alexander Baring*) at the impending general election, 'in order that I might in the most authentic form indicate my resolution to be no longer a Whig'. In Campbell's words, he thereby 'openly leagued with the Tories'.[83] After his return, free and *in absentia*, Scarlett, who had his eye on Guildford for the future, having earlier declined to vote for reform to secure his return there, told his son:

I shall now take my part firmly in Parliament and meet my fate ... without dismay. The bill or something like it must be carried. I doubt if this was the original intention, but the ministers have excited a tumult which is still raging, and which if it continues much longer will force them to the ballot and universal suffrage ... The Whigs will keep the government for some time; indeed, their bill is intended to crush the Tory party in Parliament, and it will succeed. But the party will exist in the country, and, if it becomes factious, I think the Whigs will be very intolerant, and very unpopular before long.[84]

Scarlett voted silently against the second reading of the reintroduced reform bill, 6 July, and at least once for an adjournment, 12 July 1831. He voted for use of the 1831 census to determine the disfranchisement schedules, 19 July, when he argued that Appleby deserved a reprieve, as he did of Bere Alston next day. When he tried to make capital of the London livery's censure of their Member Thompson for opposing a detail of the bill, 22 July, Waithman, one of the other City Members, wiped the floor with and humiliated him.[85] He voted to postpone consideration of the partial disfranchisement of Chippenham, 27 July, and spoke against that of his own constituency, 28 July, and of Guildford, 29 July. He had the 'greatest possible objection' to the appointment of boundary commissioners 'to do that which the framers of the bill have not done themselves, nor empowered the House to do', 5 Aug. He made technical observations on the £10 householder and copyholder franchises, 17 Aug., and on the registration clause, 19 Aug., sarcastically thanked ministers for giving lawyers such potentially lucrative work. Supporting his son-in-law's attempt to deprive weekly rent-payers of the vote, 25 Aug., he declared, 'I am not ... never was ... and never will be a radical reformer'. He argued, 18 July, for referral of William Long Pole Wellesley's* case to the committee of privileges, where he 'of course took an active part against Brougham'; he was apparently miffed when his 'special pleading' for Wellesley was 'disregarded'.[86] He dismissed the Deacles' charges against William Bingham Baring* as 'utterly devoid of foundation', 21 July, and opposed an inquiry, 22 Sept. On 23 Aug. he spoke and voted in favour of censuring the Irish government over the Dublin election affair. He was supposed to open the debate for opposition against the motion for the third reading of the reform bill, 19 Sept., but 'from want of attention' failed to rise in time to prevent the Speaker putting the question, which led to a premature division. Opposition managers, especially Billy Holmes*, were 'very angry'; and Scarlett sought to make amends with a long harangue against the ensuing motion for the passage of the bill.[87] He was in the minority in both divisions. During the riots sparked by the bill's defeat in the Lords he commented to Sir Robert Wilson, another renegade Whig (who had helped to engineer his return for Cockermouth) that 'the king, the ministers, the press and the mob all combine to intimidate poor common sense out of its

propriety' and that 'it is plain the radicals and the press are at work to frighten the ministers from any departure from the bill'.[88]

He voted against the second reading of the revised bill, 17 Dec. 1831. He scored a technical point against O'Connell on the regulations governing the appointment of returning officers, 24 Jan., and on the £10 householder clause, 3 Feb., he argued for an increase to £20, predicting that in Manchester, for example, the bill as it stood would 'throw the whole representation into the hands of persons without education, or property of any kind'. He again put the case for reprieving Appleby, 21 Feb., voted against the enfranchisement of Tower Hamlets, 28 Feb., and protested against the transfer of a seat from Monmouthshire to Merthyr, 14 Mar. He divided against the third reading of the bill, 22 Mar. He saw no need for Campbell's proposal to add a clause to the fines and recoveries bill for the compensation of displaced officials, 20 Jan. He spoke and voted against government on the Russian-Dutch loan, 26 Jan., and voted silently in the same sense, 12 July. He was contemptuous of Hunt for raking over the ashes of Peterloo, 15 Mar., 17 May. He recommended delay on the Norfolk assizes bill, 23 May, and carried by 43-18 a motion to adjourn proceedings on Campbell's 'very objectionable' dower bill, 8 June. He approved the ministerial proposal to advance £1,000,000 to West Indian colonies to cover losses sustained in recent hurricanes, which would help to 'conciliate the angry feelings of the colonists', 29 June 1832.

In November 1832, to his chagrin, his old friend and professional junior Denman was made lord chief justice, not long after they had clashed publicly and heatedly, in a row over politics provoked by Scarlett, during the trial of the mayor of Bristol for negligence during the 1831 riots. Holland commented that while Scarlett 'may be a more subtle lawyer', it was a 'triumph of simplicity and honesty' over 'artifice [and] cunning', and that Scarlett 'really deserves all the mortification he feels'.[89] Scarlett told his son:

I have lost friends and perhaps made enemies, but ... my conscience is clear of offence, and I know of no reason in the world why I should be abandoned by those who once made such strong professions of kindness to me, and considered me entitled, in spite of adverse politics, to the honours of the profession. I am doing my best ... to prove that I still continue to deserve what I never shall attain ... At no period in my life have I been more engaged in business ... If I should get into Parliament and abuse the Whigs very much, they will perhaps propose to do something for me. I never got anything from their friendship.[90]

At the general election of 1832 he stood for Norwich and was returned in second place. He was later depicted during the new Parliament as a morose and largely silent figure, a living 'illustration of the homely aphorism of falling between two chairs'; but he reaped his reward for his apostacy when Peel came to power in 1834 and gave him a choice of the attorney-generalship and the chief barony of exchequer. Even now Brougham tried to thwart him, but he opted for the judgeship, though it would lose him £7,000 a year, and took a peerage.[91] He was not very active in the Lords and, being dictatorial and partial, was less successful on the bench than at the bar.[92] In 1843, when almost 74, he took a second wife who was 32 years his junior. He died at Bury St. Edmunds in April 1844, five days after suffering a stroke. Campbell remembered him for his 'good qualities', which 'made all his children most tenderly attached to him. He was likewise kind and attentive to all depending upon him, and very steady in his early friendships'.[93] By his brief will, dated 28 Sept. 1843 and in which he neglected to name an executor, he provided his wife with a life annuity of £400 and an additional £157 a year from the rent of two London houses and canal share dividends. He left all the rest of his property to his eldest son Robert Campbell (1794-1861), his successor in the peerage, a barrister and Conservative Member for Norwich, 1835-8, and Horsham, 1841-4.[94] His second son James Yorke (1799-1871), Conservative Member for Guildford, 1837-41, commanded the heavy brigade at Balaclava; and his youngest, Peter Campbell (1804-81), had a successful diplomatic career.

[1] See P.C. Scarlett, *Mem. of James, Lord Abinger* (1877). [2] [J. Grant], *Random Recollections of Lords* (1836), 196-7. [3] Warws. RO, MI 247, Philips mems. i. 96-97, 100. [4] Ibid. i. 97. [5] Grant, 194-6. [6] Wentworth Woodhouse mun. WWM F49/58. [7] Ibid. F52/56; *The Times*, 18, 20, 22, 25, 27, 28 Mar. 1820; *Colchester Diary*, iii. 126. [8] *Life of Campbell*, i. 375. [9] Torrens, *Melbourne*, i. 154; *Brougham and Early Friends*, iii. 23; *Geo. IV Letters*, ii. 831. [10] Add. 52444, f. 177. [11] *Life of Campbell*, i. 385. [12] Fitzwilliam mss 102/2. [13] Grey mss, Tierney to Grey, 13 Jan. 1821; *Creevey Pprs*. ii. 2. [14] Castle Howard mss, G. Howard to Lady Morpeth, 28 [Jan. 1821]; HLRO, Hist. Coll. 379, Grey Bennet diary, 6; *Creevey's Life and Times*, 136. [15] *Life of Campbell*, i. 394. [16] Grey Bennet diary, 9. [17] *Smith Letters*, i. 377. [18] Grey Bennet diary, 74, 88, 114; J. Wasson, *Whig Renaissance*, 113; Philips mems. i. 101-2; *Edinburgh Rev.* xxxvi (1821-2), 110-19. [19] Grey Bennet diary, 82. [20] Lansdowne mss. [21] Bessborough mss, Brougham to Duncannon [4 Sept.]; Grey mss, Grey to Holland, 9 Sept. 1822. [22] Scarlett, 105; Fitzwilliam mss, Scarlett to Milton. 10 Oct. 1822. [23] Add. 51659. [24] Add. 51586, Tierney to Lady Holland [Oct]; 51659, Whishaw to same, 3 Nov. 1823; Scarlett, 98, 102-3. [25] *The Times*, 27, 29 Mar.; Add. 51668, Bedford to Lady Holland [28 Mar. 1824]; Scarlett, 103; *Life of Campbell*, i. 419. [26] *Hobhouse Diary*, 108; Add. 40311, ff. 60, 64; 51659, Whishaw to Lady Holland, 29 Nov. 1823; *Life of Campbell*, i. 420-1. [27] Brougham mss, Wilberforce to Brougham, 6 June 1824. [28] Fitzwilliam mss 124/8/1. [29] Add. 51669, Bedford to Lady Holland, 28 Aug. [1826]. [30] Add. 51813, Scarlett to Lady Holland, 5 Sept. 1826. [31] Add. 51784, Holland to C.R. Fox,

17 Feb. 1827. [32] Add. 40392, f. 109. [33] *Macaulay Letters*, ii. 218. [34] Fitzwilliam mss, Scarlett to Milton [18 Apr.]; Bagot, *Canning and Friends*, ii. 387; *Canning's Ministry*, 150; *Life of Campbell*, i. 440. [35] *Life of Campbell*, i. 441, 443, 445; *Arbuthnot Jnl*. ii. 108; *Canning's Ministry*, 199, 200, 204, 232, 240, 244, 255-6, 258; *Geo. IV Letters*, iii. 1320; Grey mss, Grey to Fitzwilliam, 22 Apr.; Wentworth Woodhouse mun. G15/1, 3-6; Fitzwilliam mss 731, pp. 121, 125, 127. [36] *Canning's Ministry*, 295. [37] NLS, Ellice mss, Grey to Ellice, 31 May 1827; *Geo. IV Letters*, iii. 1341. [38] *Life of Campbell*, i. 447-8; Add. 51813, Scarlett to Lady Holland [?13 Aug. 1827]; *Arbuthnot Corresp*. 86; *Croker Pprs*. i. 392. [39] Add. 51586, Tierney to Lady Holland [19 Sept. 1827]; E. Herries, *Mem. John Charles Herries*, ii. 55. [40] Fitzwilliam mss, Scarlett to Milton, 15 Jan. 1828. [41] Add. 40395, ff. 18, 20, 21; Southampton Univ. Lib. Broadlands mss PP/GMC/26; *Wellington Despatches*, iv. 200; *Colchester Diary*, iii. 540. [42] Fitzwilliam mss, Scarlett to Milton [19 Jan. 1828]; Add. 38754, ff. 188, 190, 202; 40395, f. 26; *Life of Campbell*, i. 452. [43] Fitzwilliam mss, Scarlett to Milton, 22 Jan., reply, 24 Jan.; Add. 38754, f. 282; 40395, ff. 127, 129; *Wellington Despatches*, iv. 216-17, 222; *Life of Campbell*, i. 453-4; Devon RO, Sidmouth mss, Pearse to Sidmouth, 25 Jan. 1828; *Greville Mems*. ii. 148; *Creevey Pprs*. ii. 148. [44] *Geo. IV Letters*, iii. 1489, 1491, 1495-7; *Wellington Despatches*, v. 179. [45] *Croker Pprs*. i. 407-8. [46] Brougham mss, Scarlett to Brougham, 26 Sept. [late 1828]; Scarlett, 114; Fitzwilliam mss, Scarlett to Fitzwilliam [30 Oct. 1828]. [47] *Wellington Despatches*, v. 179, 192, 203, 217-18; *Ellenborough Diary*, ii. 285, 355, 388, 401; *Arbuthnot Jnl*. ii. 260; Lonsdale mss, Lowther to Lonsdale, 24 Mar. [1829]. [48] Scarlett, 101. [49] Northants. RO, Agar Ellis diary, 18 May; Dorset RO D/BKL, Bankes jnl. 167 (15 May 1829). [50] Scarlett, 139-40; Add. 40399, ff. 227, 229; *Ellenborough Diary*, ii. 28, 44, 49; *Arbuthnot Jnl*. ii. 277. [51] Scarlett, 141-3; Fitzwilliam mss, Scarlett to Milton 29 May 1829. [52] *Lady Holland to Son*, 105; *Arbuthnot Jnl*. ii. 278, 286-7; *Cockburn Letters*, 218; *Greville Mems*. i. 295, 298-9. [53] Fitzwilliam mss 731, p. 167. [54] Grey mss, Howick jnl. 27 June [1829]. [55] Add. 40399, ff. 312, 415; *Ellenborough Diary*, ii. 162. [56] Brougham mss, Abercromby to Brougham, 26 Dec.; Add. 51580, Carlisle to Lady Holland, 31 Dec. [1829]; 76369, Althorp to Brougham, 30 Dec. 1829; Grey mss, Durham to Grey, 1 Jan. 1830; *Greville Mems*. i. 346; Howick jnl. 25 Dec. [1829]. [57] Scarlett, 116-17. [58] Brougham mss, Russell to Brougham, 30 Jan.; *Life of Campbell*, i. 465; Howick jnl. 2 Mar.; Keele Univ. Lib. Sneyd mss, Littleton to Sneyd, 3 Mar. 1830. [59] *Ellenborough Diary*, ii. 312. [60] Ibid. ii. 247-8, 251. [61] Add. 40401, f. 28. [62] *Ellenborough Diary*, ii. 263. [63] Brougham mss, Scarlett to Brougham [27 Mar. 1830]; Scarlett, 117-18. [64] Scarlett, 119-20, 144-5; Wentworth Woodhouse mss G2/7; G83/110. [65] Scarlett, 145-7; Chatsworth mss 6DD/1960; Brougham mss, Scarlett to Brougham [26 July]; Fitzwilliam mss, same to Milton, 26 July; 732, p. 9, reply, 28 July; Howick jnl. 27 July [1830]; Nottingham Univ. Lib. Ossington mss OsC 75. [66] Scarlett, 119-20; Add. 51813, Scarlett to Holland, 26 July, reply, 27 July [1830]. [67] Scarlett, 120-2, 126; Add. 51580, Carlisle to Lady Holland, 25 Aug. 1830. [68] *Result of General Election* (1830), 9. [69] Wentworth Woodhouse mun. G83/111, 112; *Life of Campbell*, i. 47. [70] *Ellenborough Diary*, ii. 407-8. [71] *Life of Campbell*, i. 485. [72] *Ellenborough Diary*, ii. 431. [73] *Life of Campbell*, i. 488-91; Fitzwilliam mss, Scarlett to Milton [17 Nov. 1830]. [74] Fitzwilliam mss, Scarlett to Milton, 11 Dec. 1830; Add. 51813, same to Holland [25 Apr. 1831]; *Three Diaries*, 94. [75] *Three Diaries*, 32. [76] Add. 51835, Arbuthnot to Holland, 7, 14, 15 Dec. 1830. [77] Add. 51813, Scarlett to Holland, 15 Dec. [1830]. [78] Fitzwilliam mss, Russell to Milton, 28 Dec. [1830]; Grey mss, Holland to Grey [5 Mar. 1831]. [79] Scarlett, 148-50; *Life of Campbell*, i. 507. [80] Scarlett, 124, 127; *Life of Campbell*, i. 509; *Creevey Pprs*. ii. 225-6; Fitzwilliam mss 732, p. 21. [81] Scarlett, 128; *Sun*, 28 Mar.; *The Times*, 12 Apr. 1831. [82] Scarlett, 128-9. [83] Add. 51813, Holland to Scarlett and reply, 24 Apr. [1831], Abinger to Lady Holland, 14 Feb., 5 Apr. 1841; Scarlett, 130-8; *Life of Campbell*, i. 513. [84] Scarlett, 151-2. [85] Hatherton diary, 22 July; Creevey mss, Creevey to Miss Ord, 23 July 1831. [86] Hatherton diary, 20, 26 July [1831]. [87] *Arbuthnot Corresp*. 150; Hatherton diary, 19 Sept. [1831]. [88] Sir James Graham

mss (IHR microfilm XR 80), Wilson to Graham, 31 May 1831; Add. 30115, f. 51. [89] *Greville Mems.* ii. 329-30; Add. 51786, Holland to C.R. Fox, 8 Nov. 1832. [90] Scarlett, 155-6. [91] Grant, 192; Add. 30115, f. 54; 40405, f. 259; 40408, ff. 131, 175; 40409, ff. 44, 46, 73, 74; *Creevey Pprs.* ii. 298, 300-1; *Disraeli Letters* ii. 373. [92] *Oxford DNB*; E. Foss, *Lives of Judges*, ix. 260. [93] *Life of Campbell*, ii. 189-90; *Gent. Mag.* (1844), i. 648; Scarlett, 209-11. [94] PROB 11/1996/266; *Gent. Mag.* (1844), ii. 652.

D.R.F.

SCHONSWAR, George (1775–1859), of Ferriby, Yorks. and 18 Adam Street, Adelphi, Mdx.

KINGSTON-UPON-HULL	1830–1832

b. 15 July 1775, 1st s. of Robert Schonswar of Ellerker, Yorks. and Janet, da. of Thomas Lundlie of Glassel, Forfar. *m.* Sept. 1801, Lydia, da. and h. of James Smith of Kingston-upon-Hull, Yorks., 3s. 1da. *suc.* fa. 1801. *d.* 19 Jan. 1859.

Alderman, Kingston-upon-Hull, sheriff 1808, mayor 1811-12, 1817-18.

Schonswar's grandfather, a resident of Friesland in the Netherlands, had come to England with William III in 1688 and after military service settled in Hull. His son Robert, George's father, was one of the elder brethren of Trinity House, and in his capacity as a joiner was one of the craftsmen who built the new Trinity House in 1753. George and his brother Henry initially traded as East India merchants and later as wine merchants in Hull, where, according to a local historian, they built the block of property called 'Schonswar Square' in 1801.[1] During 1812-13 Schonswar became actively involved in the outports' campaign against the London monopoly on East India trade, serving as chairman of the United Deputation who campaigned against the privilege.[2] In 1818, while serving as mayor of Hull, he presided over the scrutiny of the election there.[3]

At the 1830 general election Schonswar, 'a very gentlemanly man, rather stout', with a walk 'as bolt upright as a turkey-cock', proposed John Broadley, a local merchant, as a third candidate for Hull at a large meeting of the freemen. In declining Broadley suggested that Schonswar would make a better Member, to unanimous agreement. Schonswar initially hesitated, but next day accepted a requisition inviting him to stand without pecuniary obligations, a situation unprecedented in Hull. In his address he cited his local residence and support for the abolition of slavery and retrenchment, and promised to safeguard the shipping interest. He was returned at the head of the poll with the support of the corporation, amidst 'enthusiastic acclamations of joy among all classes'.[4]

Schonswar was listed by the Wellington ministry as one of the 'good doubtfuls', who they believed would be 'generally friends', but he voted against them in the crucial division on the civil list, 15 Nov. 1830. He presented constituency petitions for the abolition of slavery, 12, 18, 25 Nov., repeal of the coal tax, 19 Nov., and the stamp duties, 2 Dec. 1830. That day he endorsed one for the easier recovery of small debts. On 9 Feb. 1831 he welcomed a petition for reform from Hull, which, although 'disgraced by practices at elections' in the past, had 'voluntarily and fairly restored their mode of election to what it was originally designed'. He brought up and endorsed a constituency petition against the proposed levy on merchant seamen towards Greenwich Hospital, and secured a pledge from ministers for a bill to facilitate their access to its facilities, 28 Mar. He expressed concerns about the proposed increase of duties on timber, fearing it would 'force ships out of business', 14 Feb., and again, 22 Feb., 15 Mar. He welcomed a Yorkshire petition for reform and the secret ballot, 20 Feb., and the Grey ministry's reform scheme, which he had initially viewed 'with the greatest caution', fearing it to be 'a measure of sweeping reform', but which he now saw contained 'so much that was just and true' that he would give it his full support, 9 Mar. He brought up favourable petitions, 19, 30 Mar., and divided for the second reading of the reform bill, 22 Mar., and against Gascoyne's wrecking amendment, 19 Apr. 1831. At the ensuing general election he offered again, explaining:

> When I first went to Parliament if I had any partiality, it was a wish that those who then held the reins of government might continue to hold them. But when I got to London, and saw how the affairs of the country were, in my opinion, ill conducted ... then I thought that those who held the reins ... ought to hold them no longer.

He promised to support ministers if they fulfilled their pledges and declared that reform was 'entitled to the support of every honest man and lover of his country', although he would defend the existing freemen's rights. He was returned unopposed.[5]

He called for the exemption of Hull and Yorkshire from the general register bill, 30 June, and brought up constituency petitions in these terms, 7 Dec. 1831, 2 Feb. 1832. He presented another against the East India monopoly, 1 July 1831. He voted for the second reading of the reintroduced reform bill, 6 July, initially supported its details, but was absent from all recorded divisions between 26 July and 7 Dec., during which time he was granted a month's leave due to 'severe indisposition', 13 Sept. He voted for the second reading of the revised reform bill, 17 Dec. 1831, and gave steady and occasionally vocal support to its details. He welcomed the enfranchisement of Whitby, as shipping required 'another voice in the House', 9 Mar. 1832. He divided for the bill's third reading, 22 Mar., the address calling on the king to appoint only ministers who would carry it unimpaired, 10 May, the second reading of the Irish measure, 25 May, and against a Conservative amendment to increase Scottish county representation, 1 June. He voted with ministers on the Russian-Dutch loan, 26 Jan., 12, 16 July, and relations with Portugal, 9 Feb. He spoke in support of Sadler's petition for restricting the hours of child workers in factories, 9 Feb., and his subsequent bill, 16 Mar. He divided with ministers on the navy civil departments bill, 6 Apr. He presented and endorsed a Hull petition condemning the Russian intrusion in Poland and demanded retaliation, 24 May, and endorsed others in similar terms, 28 June. He voted against Alexander Baring's bill to exclude insolvent debtors from Parliament, 6 June, and spoke in support of a petition from the Hull and Sculcoates Political Union condemning the bill, 20 June. He called for more consistent sentencing for sheep stealing, believing that death was too severe but a year's imprisonment too lenient, 7 July 1832.

That September he was declared bankrupt, but he had already decided not to seek re-election. The bankruptcy was annulled in March 1833, only for his joint business venture with his brother to be declared bankrupt the same day.[6] His wife succeeded to her father's estate in 1835 and the same year he retired to Cheltenham, where he died, leaving an estate valued under £800, in January 1859.[7]

[1] *White's Hull Dir.* (1821), 73; (1831), pp. xxxvi, 120; *VCH Yorks. E. Riding,* i. 406; *Hull Celebrities* ed. W.A. Gunnell, 452. [2] C.H. Philips, *E.I. Co.* 182. [3] *Hull Advertiser,* 27 June 1818. [4] Ibid. 30 July, 6 Aug. 1830. [5] Add. 40401, f. 187; *Hull Advertiser,* 29 Apr. 1831. [6] *The Times,* 8 Sept. 1832, 20 Mar. 1833; *Hull Advertiser,* 27 July 1832. [7] *Gent. Mag.* (1859), i. 329.

M.P.J.C.

SCOTT, Sir Edward Dolman, 2nd bt. (1793–1851), of Barr Hall, Great Barr, Staffs.

LICHFIELD   1831–1837

b. 22 Oct. 1793, 1st s. of Sir Joseph Scott[†], 1st bt., of Great Barr and Margaret, da. and coh. of Edward Whitby of Shut End, Staffs. *educ.* Westminster 1808-10; Oriel, Oxf. 1812. *m.* (1) 14 Feb. 1815, Catherine Juliana (*d.* 4 Aug. 1848), da. and coh. of Sir Hugh Bateman, 1st bt., of Hartington Hall, Derbys., 3s. (1 *d.v.p.*); (2) 8 Nov. 1848, Lydia, da. of Rev. Thomas Gisborne of Yoxall Lodge, Staffs., wid. of Rev. Edmund Robinson of Thorpe

Green, Yorks. *s.p., suc.* fa. as 2nd bt. 17 June 1828. *d.* 27 Dec. 1851.
    Sheriff, Staffs. 1847-8.

Scott's father, Whig Member for Worcester, 1802-6, was the largest landowner in Great Barr, where the family had settled in the reign of Edward I, and was created a baronet by the Grenville ministry, 30 Apr. 1806. Scott was tutored by the Rev. Thomas Harwood, presumably at Lichfield Grammar School, where he was headmaster, 1791-1813, before attending Westminster and Oxford. He succeeded his father in 1828 and by the 1840s had added industrial lime-works in the neighbouring township of Aldridge to the family's estates.[1] At the general election of 1830 he agreed to contest Lichfield at the request of the independents, whose initial invitation he had declined, in an 'attempt to compel the relinquishment of one seat' by the dominant interest of Lord Anson. After three days of polling he withdrew, having secured a pledge from his opponent George Vernon that he would retire at the next dissolution in his favour.[2] At the 1831 general election Vernon duly stood down and Scott came in unopposed, claiming to be 'perfectly free and unfettered' and declaring that 'the reform bill before the country should have his support'. 'No question', however, was 'ever asked him, what his political opinions were: though a general idea seemed to prevail that he was a moderate and liberal, not going to the extreme lengths of any party, and therefore not likely to offend any'.[3]

Scott, who like his father was mostly a silent Member, voted for the second reading of the reintroduced reform bill, 6 July, and gave general support to its details, although he was in the minority for giving two Members to Stoke, 4 Aug. 1831. He presented a Lichfield petition for extending the residence requirement to 'all persons claiming a right to be registered as voters for any city or borough, by reason of owning or occupying any freehold or tenement', 13 July, and next day an individual's petition for the disfranchisement of burgage tenants and the transfer of urban freehold and annuitant voters to the counties. He joined Brooks's, 17 Aug., sponsored by Sir John Wrottesley* and Sir Ronald Ferguson*, but next day divided in favour of Lord Chandos's amendment to enfranchise £50 tenants-at-will. He voted for the reform bill's passage, 21 Sept., the second reading of the Scottish bill, 23 Sept., and Lord Ebrington's confidence motion, 10 Oct. He divided with government on the Dublin election controversy, 23 Aug. He voted for the second reading of the revised reform bill, 17 Dec. 1831, and again gave steady support to its details.

On 24 Jan. 1832 he presented and endorsed a petition from Lichfield praying that 'the provision of the last reform bill, with respect to enforcing the residence of the voters, might be followed up'. He gave notice that day that he would move for the words 'a knight or knights of the shire' to be replaced by 'any Member' in clause 18, which set out occupational requirements for freeholders, but failed to do so. He divided for the bill's third reading, 22 Mar. He voted against ministers on the Russian-Dutch loan, 26 Jan., but with them on the issue, 12, 16, 20 July (as a pair). He was in the minority for reduction of the Irish registrar of deeds's salary, 9 Apr. He voted for the address calling on the king to appoint only ministers who would carry the reform bill unimpaired, 10 May, the second reading of the Irish bill, 25 May, and against a Conservative amendment to the Scottish bill, 1 June. He divided for a tax on Irish absentee landowners, 19 June, but against Hume's proposal to disqualify the recorder of Dublin from sitting in Parliament, 24 July 1832.

Scott was returned for Lichfield at the 1832 general election and sat as a Whig until the dissolution of 1837, when he retired. He canvassed again in 1841, but declined 'before the weight of the Anson influence'.[4] He was appointed sheriff of Staffordshire in 1847. He died at his seat in December 1851. Under the terms of his will, dated 5 June 1850, his second wife received a £600 life annuity. The family estates passed to his eldest son and successor in the title Sir Francis Edward Scott (1824-63), who had inherited his maternal grandfather's baronetcy at his birth. Scott's second son and namesake Edward Dolman (1826-1905), to whom the baronetcy eventually passed in 1884, received property in Bryanston Square, Marylebone and an annuity of £1,000.[5]

[1] *Lichfield Mercury*, 30 July 1830; *VCH Staffs.* xvii. 191. [2] *Staffs. Advertiser*, 17, 24, 31 July; *Lichfield Mercury*, 16, 30 July 1830. [3] *Lichfield Mercury*, 6 May 1831; Bodl. GA Staffs. b.6, election posters. [4] *Dod's Parl. Companion* (1833), 157; J.C. Wedgwood, *Staffs. Parl. Hist.* iii. 107. [5] *Gent. Mag.* (1852), i. 298; PROB 11/2148/159; IR26/1945/114.

P.J.S.

SCOTT, James (?1776–1855), of Rotherfield Park, nr. Alton, Hants and Manor House, Shepperton and 22 Grafton Street, Mdx.

BRIDPORT   1820–1826

b. ?1776, 2nd s. of William Scott (*d.* 1785) of Grosvenor Place, Mdx. *m.* (1) 6 Oct. 1797,[1] Martha (*d.* 16 May 1815),[2] da. of Thomas Bradbury Winter of Shenley, Herts., 9s. at least (2 *d.v.p.*) 3da. at least; (2) 29 Jan. 1819,[3] Margaret, da. of William Snell of Salisbury Hall, Herts., 1s. *suc.* uncle Thomas Scott[†] 1816. *d.* 28 Feb. 1855. Sheriff, Hants 1820-1.

Scott, whose family origins are obscure, was a grandson of Thomas Scott, brickmaker, of Fulham, Middlesex.[4] He had numerous children, several of whom were presumably the offspring of Thomas and Elizabeth Scott recorded as having been baptized at St. Alban, Wood Street, London.[5] He died in October 1748, and by his will, dated 1 Oct. 1748, he bequeathed to his sons John and Thomas (1723-1816) his estates in Fulham and elsewhere to be divided between his surviving children.[6] The business, in which several family members were presumably involved, traded as John Scott and Company of North End, Fulham. It may have been linked to other brickmaking firms listed in the London directories, such as John Scott of Hoxton and Islington.

Thomas Scott's fourth son, William, who was baptized on 11 Dec. 1732, died in 1785.[7] By his will, dated 6 June 1783, he left £8,000 in trust to his wife for the care of their infant sons William, James and George, who, with any other surviving children, were eventually to inherit equal shares in his estate.[8] It was apparently James, this Member, who took the leading role in the family concern, which in the late 1810s was listed as James and George Scott of Shepherd's Bush. From this he must have derived considerable wealth, as in 1808 he purchased the country estate of Rotherfield Park from the 13th marquess of Winchester, and made improvements to it, especially in the village of East Tisted. For this he received the praise of the radical William Cobbett[†], who wrote in 1823 that Scott was 'well known as a brickmaker at North End, Fulham, and who has, in Hampshire, supplanted a Norman of the name of Powlett'. He added, with characteristic hyperbole, that

> had there been no debt created to crush liberty in France and to keep down reformers in England, Mr. Scott would not have had bricks to burn to build houses for the Jews and jobbers and other eaters of taxes; and the Norman Powlett would not have had to pay in taxes, through his own hands and those of his tenants and labourers, the amount of the estate at Tisted, first to the Jews, jobbers and tax-eaters, and them by then to be given to 'Squire Scott' for his bricks.[9]

However, Scott continued to live in Hammersmith, where his first wife died in 1815.[10] On the death in 1816 of his uncle Thomas, who had been Member for Bridport, 1780-90, he inherited the bulk of his property, which included an estate at Shepperton and a house in Grafton Street, shares in the *London Tavern* and personalty sworn under £140,000.[11] He again became connected to a Hertfordshire gentry family when, in 1819, he remarried at Windlesham, Surrey, where his new wife's brother Thomas Snell was the rector.[12]

Scott, who was appointed a justice of the peace for Alton in 1818, was made sheriff of Hampshire in February 1820.[13] At the general election the following month he was brought forward for a seat beyond the county boundary in Dorset. As in the case of his uncle, his introduction to Bridport was probably on the interest of the Sturt family, who had a say in the choice of one of the Members. It was also intended to fill the vacancy created by the retirement of Henry Charles Sturt, whose conduct had failed to impress the radicals among the dominant independent Dissenting interest. After a fierce four-day contest, he was returned by a comfortable majority over the other two candidates, and his seat was unaffected by the successful petition of Sir Horace St. Paul against the other Whig Member, Christopher Spurrier.[14] Scott oversaw the uncontested Hampshire county election and the county meeting to agree an address of condolence and congratulation to George IV.[15] He sided with the Whigs on the civil list, 5 May, and against the appointment of an additional baron of exchequer in Scotland, 15 May, and thereafter was a regular but unobtrusive member of the opposition. He was granted a week's leave on urgent private business, 20 June 1820.

He presided at the Hampshire county meeting on the Queen Caroline affair, 12 Jan. 1821, when he was congratulated by Alexander Baring* for his impartiality in preventing an attempt to obstruct the requisition for the meeting.[16] He divided for reinstating Caroline's name in the liturgy, 23, 26 Jan., 13 Feb., and to condemn ministers' conduct towards her, 6 Feb. He attended the Friends of Reform dinner at the *London Tavern*, 4 Apr. 1821.[17] He voted steadily in the opposition campaign for economies and reduced taxes during the following session, speaking for repeal of the salt duties on 28 June; but he was 'shut out' on Hume's motion for inquiry into the government of the Ionian Islands, 14 May 1822. He voted for parliamentary reform, 25 Apr. 1822, 24 Apr. 1823, 27 Apr. 1826, and against the current influence of the crown, 24 June 1822. He divided for alteration of the Scottish representative system, 2 June 1823, and reform of the representation of Edinburgh, 26 Feb. 1824, 13 Apr. 1826. He voted in condemnation of the trial of the Methodist missionary John Smith in Demerara, 11 June 1824. He divided against the Irish unlawful societies bill, 15, 21 Feb. 1825, and, as he had on 28 Feb. 1821, for Catholic relief, 1 Mar., 21 Apr., 10 May 1825. He was listed in

the majority in favour of the second reading of the St. Olave tithe bill, 6 June 1825, and sided with opposition for inquiry into the treasurership of the navy, 7 Apr. 1826.

Scott, who was said in 1825 to have 'attended regularly, and voted with the opposition',[18] retired at the dissolution of 1826, when he recommended the radical Henry Warburton* to the corporation of Bridport as his successor.[19] Having reconstructed the Manor House at Shepperton, Scott appears to have taken up residence there, leaving Rotherfield Park to his eldest son and heir James Winter Scott (1799-1873), who became a local magistrate in 1824, married a Clarke Jervoise in 1828 and served as Liberal Member for Hampshire North, 1832-7.[20] It may have been this son, not he, who was elected to Brooks's in February 1830. Scott died, 'aged 78', in February 1855, leaving many surviving children (including a Septimus); his only son with his second wife (d. 3 Jan. 1850), was John Aubrey Scott (1821-78), rector of West Tytherley, Hampshire.[21]

[1] *Gent. Mag.* (1797), ii. 980. [2] Ibid. (1815), i. 569. [3] Ibid. (1819), i. 178. [4] *Burke LG* (1937), 2013. [5] IGI (London). [6] PROB 11/774/328. [7] IGI (London). [8] PROB 11/1138/58. [9] *VCH Hants*, iii. 30; iv. 424; *Cobbett's Rural Rides* ed. G.D.H. and M. Cole, i. 187. [10] IGI (London); *Gent. Mag.* (1815), i. 569. [11] PROB 11/1585/541; IR26/691/924; *VCH Mdx.* iii. 5; *Hist. Our Village ... Shepperton* (1867), 26-27. [12] IGI (Surr.); R. Clutterbuck, *Herts.* i. 483. [13] Hants RO, q. sess. recs. Q22/3/15, 204. It has sometimes been wrongly assumed that the sheriff in 1820 was Scott's eldest son James Winter Scott, who was then barely of age; e.g., R. Foster, *Politics of County Power*, 22-23, 163. [14] *Western Flying Post*, 28 Feb.; *Salisbury Jnl.* 13, 20 Mar. 1820. [15] *Hants Telegraph*, 13, 20 Mar. 1820. [16] *The Times*, 13 Jan. 1821. [17] Ibid. 5 Apr. 1821. [18] *Session of Parl. 1825*, p. 484. [19] Add. 51659, Whishaw to Lady Holland, 4 June; *Dorset Co. Chron.* 8 June 1826. [20] *VCH Mdx.* iii. 6; Hants q. sess. recs. Q22/3/237. [21] *Gent. Mag.* (1850), i. 228; *Hants Chron.* 10 Mar. 1855; IGI (London, Surr.).

S.M.F.

SCOTT, John, Visct. Encombe (1805–1854), of 109 Piccadilly, Mdx.

TRURO	6 Mar. 1829–1832

b. 10 Dec. 1805, o.s. of Hon. John Scott† (1st s. of John Scott†, 1st earl of Eldon) and Henrietta Elizabeth, da. of Sir Matthew White Ridley†, 2nd bt., of Blagdon and Heaton, Northumb. *educ.* Westminster 1821-3; New Coll. Oxf. 1824. *m.* 1 Oct. 1831, Hon. Louisa Duncombe, da. of Charles Duncombe*, 1st Bar. Feversham, 1s. 6da. *styled* Visct. Encombe 1821-38. *suc.* grandfa. as 2nd earl of Eldon 13 Jan. 1838; cos. Mary Anne Scott, Viscountess Sidmouth, to Stowell Park, Glos. 1842. *d.* 29 Sept. 1854.

Scott's father died when he was two weeks old, leaving him heir to the peerage of his redoubtable grandfather lord chancellor Eldon, who became his guardian. In 1811 his mother married James William Farrer of Ingleborough, Yorkshire; Eldon disapproved, but subsequently appointed Farrer a master in chancery. The chancellor, who regarded his grandson 'with all the affection of a father', was determined that he should attend a public school ('no considerable man can be formed in a private one') and supervised his education, impressing on him the importance of ensuring that 'a great stock of information is laid in the mind, and a great stock of virtuous and religious feeling is implanted in the heart'.[1] Scott witnessed the trial of Queen Caroline in the House of Lords in 1820. When Eldon accepted an earldom the following year, he sought a ruling from the college of heralds on his grandson's right to adopt the courtesy title which would have belonged to his father. On establishing that it was in order for him to do so, Eldon advised Encombe (as he was henceforth styled):

> If a peer does not do credit to his titles, his titles will confer no credit upon him ... Your time ... must be well spent and carefully husbanded. Dissipation of every kind must be anxiously avoided ... Acquire knowledge and practice virtue.

The reply, Eldon told his daughter, could not have given him 'greater satisfaction'. In 1824 Encombe went up to Oxford to experience, as Eldon put it, 'the most critical period of your life':

> If your time is not *well* spent there, it cannot but be *ill* employed ... The proper companions at Oxford are your books, and such students as love books, having, also, their minds stored with sound moral and religious principles.

When he came of age in 1826 his grandfather wrote to him with obvious affection, thanking him for his past exemplary conduct. Early in 1828 he was set up in his own London establishment at 109 Piccadilly.[2] That spring Lady Londonderry secured him membership of Almack's Club, and a slightly bemused Eldon noted that 'John, the dancer' was 'a constant attendant' and had 'grown an amateur entirely of the employment, which it was but a little while ago that he spoke of with contempt, if not with disgust'.[3] On 28 May 1828 he accompanied his grandfather for the first time to the annual Pitt Club dinner. About this time, the duke of Newcastle was willing to nominate him for East Retford, if a new writ was issued. In February 1829, while he was in residence in Oxford for the purposes of his Master's degree, he expressed his readiness to stand against the leader of the Commons, Peel, who was seeking re-election after announcing his conversion to Catholic emancipation; in the event

he was passed over for a more experienced candidate. Meantime, Eldon declined on his behalf an offer from Newcastle to bring him in for Newark, explaining that there had been

> a question whether, if you came into Parliament, you would immediately begin a vigorous and active *attack* and *leading conduct* as to the Catholic business. I thought that though you would be very zealous upon that and other points, it required not only abilities, but great experience, to manage such attack and conduct, that it would be dangerous to attempt it, that failure at first in Parliament is generally the effect of not waiting to learn by the experience which observation furnishes: and nine persons out of ten ... fail by such early attempts, and after failure never recover. I was clear therefore that this could not do.[4]

Yet a fortnight later Encombe was returned for Truro by Lord Falmouth, a connection of Eldon by his daughter's marriage, who had turned out the sitting Members for refusing to oppose the Wellington ministry's emancipation bill.[5]

Encombe took his seat on 9 Mar. and duly voted against emancipation, 18, 27, 30 Mar. 1829. When presenting a hostile petition, 24 Mar., he expressed his conviction that 'no further concessions can be granted to the Roman Catholics with safety to the constitution', and he cited Wellington as his authority for this view. He divided against the government on the silk bill, 1 May, and the issue of a new writ for East Retford, 2 June. In September 1829 the duke of Cumberland sent Eldon 'a pretty *correct list*' of 'the state of the House of Commons', as perceived by the Ultra leader Sir Richard Vyvyan*, and observed that '*we* are tolerably strong and probably will be stronger if Encombe is with you'. Cumberland wished Encombe to be shown the list, but 'say not from whom I have got it; he may perhaps *also* have his ideas respecting our strength'.[6] The following month Vyvyan listed him among the 'Tories strongly opposed to the present government'. He voted for Knatchbull's amendment to the address on distress, 4 Feb., and for many of the retrenchment motions that session in which the Ultras combined with the other opposition groups, including the successful one against the Bathurst and Dundas pensions, 26 Mar. 1830. He divided for Lord Palmerston's motion condemning British interference in the affairs of Portugal, 10 Mar. However, unlike some of the disaffected Tories, he had no truck with parliamentary reform and voted against the enfranchisement of Birmingham, Leeds and Manchester, 23 Feb. He divided against Jewish emancipation, 5 Apr., 17 May, and the administration of justice bill, 18 June. He raised some objections to the Wareham road bill, which affected Eldon's Dorset property, 17 Mar. Although he claimed to have no qualms about the new metropolitan police while they remained under Peel's control, 28 May 1830, he felt they had 'too much of a military character'. He was returned for Truro at the general election that summer, after an attempt to open the borough failed; he survived a subsequent petition.

The ministry listed him as one of the 'violent Ultras' and he duly voted against them in the crucial civil list division, 15 Nov. 1830. He divided against the second reading of the Grey ministry's reform bill, which proposed partially to disfranchise Truro, 22 Mar. 1831. Three days later he said he was 'anxious to let the inhabitants' of Truro know that it was 'his wish to represent their interests', as well as those of the corporation 'which sent me here'. He argued that the borough's population ought properly to include the residents of two neighbouring parishes and was big enough to justify its retention of two seats. He complained that the 'corrected' population returns were still full of errors, 12 Apr., and voted for Gascoyne's wrecking amendment, 19 Apr. 1831. He came in again for Truro at the ensuing general election, after another token contest. He was actively involved in the contest for Dorset, and was so again at the by-election that autumn.[7] He divided against the second reading of the reintroduced reform bill, by which Truro had its other seat restored, 6 July 1831. Although Eldon now spoke of his 'entire union' with Wellington, Lord Ellenborough still identified Encombe as one of the 'Ultras'.[8] He voted for use of the 1831 census to determine the disfranchisement schedules, 19 July, and later that day maintained, unsuccessfully, that Appleby was entitled to the same treatment as Truro. He attacked the Calcrafts and their Member Wood for abandoning Wareham to its fate, 26 July. He divided against the partial disfranchisement of Chippenham next day, and was in the ministerial minority against the Chandos clause to enfranchise £50 tenants-at-will, 18 Aug. He voted against the bill's passage, 21 Sept., and the second reading of the Scottish reform bill, 23 Sept. His honeymoon caused him to miss the division on Lord Ebrington's confidence motion, 10 Oct., when a call of the House was enforced, but his defalcation was passed over with 'a good humoured laugh'.[9] He divided for the motion to censure the Irish administration for its conduct during the Dublin election, 23 Aug., and against the issue of a new writ for Liverpool, 5 Sept. He voted against the second reading of the revised reform bill, 17 Dec. 1831, and entering committee, 20 Jan. 1832. Soon afterwards John Croker*, reflecting that 'the Ultra Tories' were 'but a hollow support' to the opposition leaders, named Encombe

and Eldon among a faction who, 'though they vote with us, are evidently a different party, and will never, I think, be reconciled to Peel unless ... he should swear allegiance to the duke of Cumberland'.[10] He divided against the enfranchisement of Tower Hamlets, 28 Feb., the third reading of the reform bill, 22 Mar., and the second reading of the Irish bill, 25 May. He voted against ministers on the Russian-Dutch loan, 26 Jan. He divided in the minorities for a tax on Irish absentee landlords, 19 June, and against the Irish education grant, 23 July 1832. He did not seek election to the reformed Parliament, and became instead 'a retired country gentleman'.[11]

In 1834 Eldon gave Encombe the money to buy a property at Shirley, near Croydon, but in his cantankerous last years he came to regret his generosity, for its effect was to deter his grandson from dancing attendance on him in London during the winters.[12] On Eldon's death in January 1838 Encombe succeeded to his title, his estates in Dorset and county Durham, his London house in Hamilton Place and the residue of his personalty, which was sworn under £100,000. On the death of Lady Sidmouth, the only surviving child of his great-uncle Lord Stowell, in 1842, he also came into possession of Stowell Park, Gloucestershire.[13] As a peer he was not particularly active in politics. He sponsored his half-brother James Farrer's unsuccessful attempt on South Durham at the general election of 1841 (Farrer later won the seat), was president of the Pitt Club the following year and opposed repeal of the corn laws in 1846.[14] He devoted much of his time between 1838 and 1844 to furnishing Horace Twiss* with material for the biography of his grandfather, whose memory he venerated.[15] He provided £4,000 in 1842 to enable Oxford University to purchase the remaining Michaelangelo and Raphael drawings from the Lawrence collection.[16] In June 1851 he became mentally ill and incapable of conducting his own affairs. His affliction manifested itself as 'a partial dementia, exhibited in great incoherence of conversation, occasional evanescent delusion, and considerable excitement'. Lady Eldon cared for him and managed his property, but after her death in November 1852 it became necessary to subject him to a commission of lunacy, which declared him insane, 15 Jan. 1853.[17] He died in September 1854 and was succeeded by his only son John Scott (1845-1926). Ironically, his eldest grandson John became a Roman Catholic in 1897.

[1] *Farington Diary*, xiv. 4995; Twiss, *Eldon*, i. 500-4; ii. 243, 287, 341-2, 502. [2] Twiss, ii. 383-4, 435-6, 442, 514-16, 578-80; iii. 34. [3] Ibid. iii. 46. [4] Ibid. iii. 47, 66-70; *Unhappy Reactionary* ed. R.A. Gaunt (Thoroton Soc. Rec. Ser. xliii, 2003), 54-55, 57. [5] *The Times*,

3, 10 Mar.; *West Briton*, 13 Mar. 1829. [6] Eldon mss, Cumberland to Eldon, 25 Sept. 1829. [7] See DORSET. [8] *Three Diaries*, 94; B.T. Bradfield, 'Sir Richard Vyvyan and the Country Gentlemen', *EHR*, lxxxiii (1968), 732-4. [9] Twiss, iii. 142-3. [10] *Croker Pprs.* ii. 151. [11] Bodl. MS Risley C. I. 2/14/12. [12] Twiss, iii. 236, 257-8, 293. [13] Ibid. iii. 258-9, 316; *Gent Mag.* (1838), i. 319-20. [14] Add. 34574, ff. 237, 240; *Gent. Mag.* (1854), ii. 622. [15] Add. 34572, ff. 393, 414; 34574, ff. 432, 481; 34575, ff. 160, 173, 180, 190, 260. [16] Add. 34574, f. 518. [17] *The Times*, 17 Jan. 1853.

D.R.F.

SCOTT, Samuel (1772–1849), of Sundridge Park, nr. Bromley, Kent.

MALMESBURY	1802–1806
CAMELFORD	1812–1818
WHITCHURCH	1818–1832

b. 29 Apr. 1772, o.s. of Claude Scott[†], corn dealer, of Sundridge Park and Lytchett Minster, Dorset and Martha, da. and h. of John Eyre of Stepney, Mdx. *m.* 4 Feb. 1796, Anne, da. and h. of Edward Ommanney of Bloomsbury Square, Mdx., 2s. 2da. *suc.* fa. as 2nd. bt. 27 Mar. 1830. *d.* 30 Sept. 1849.

Vol. London and Westminster light horse 1798, cornet 1805, lt. 1805, capt. 1818.

Scott's father had made his fortune as a government grain contractor during the French Wars and took his only son into partnership before 1795, when both signed the London merchants' loyal declaration. From 1811 the firm traded as Scott, Garnett and Palmer, corn merchants, at 12 Aldermanbury, and from 1840 until the year of this Member's death as Scott and Garnett, at 2 Moorgate Street. Scott was said by his father to be worth no less than £300,000 in 1813, though this probably owed more to a fortunate marriage than to business success.[1] On his death two years previously, his father-in-law Edward Ommanney had left a personal estate of about £250,000, of which Scott's wife was the principal beneficiary. Scott, who was the will's executor, made the most of his good fortune and in partnership with his father, who had been given a baronetcy in 1821, established the London bank of Sir Claude Scott and Company in 1824.[2] With premises at 26 Holles Street, Marylebone, they were well placed to take on 'a considerable remnant' of the business of Marsh, Sibbald and Company of Berners Street, which had failed after a partner's conviction for forgery. In 1827 the firm moved the short distance to 1 Cavendish Square.[3] On the death of his father in 1830, Scott received his share in the bank (on condition that he remained a member of the company) and succeeded to the Sundridge estate where he had resided since about 1810. Sir Claude Scott's personal estate

was sworn under £80,000, and the Lytchett Minster property, where he had latterly settled, was sold to provide an income for his wife, with partial remainder to his son.[4]

According to Oldfield, Scott's original return for the pocket borough of Whitchurch in 1818 was on the interest of the 4th Viscount Midleton. Scott sat undisturbed throughout this period and by 1831 had bought the patron out.[5] A lax and mostly silent attender, when present he continued to support the Liverpool ministry.[6] He voted in defence of their conduct towards Queen Caroline, 6 Feb., and in their majorities against repeal of the additional malt duty, 3 Apr., and motions calling for economy and retrenchment, 27 June 1821, and greater tax reductions, 11, 21 Feb. 1822. He divided against Catholic relief, 28 Feb. 1821, and removal of the disabilities of Catholic peers, 30 Apr. 1822. It was probably James Scott, Member for Bridport, who voted for a return of military estimates, 27 Feb., and a reduction of the salt duties, 28 Feb., and who then asserted that there were 'no just grounds' for continuing the tax, 28 June 1822.[7] It also seems unlikely that this Member was the 'Mr. Scott' who presented a petition from 'certain Unitarian Dissenters' for repeal or modification of the Marriage Act, 10 May 1822.[8] He divided against inquiry into chancery delays, 5 June 1823. No trace of parliamentary activity has been found for 1824 and thereafter his attendance appears to have become even more sporadic. In his only positively identified speech of this Parliament, 17 Mar. 1825, he spoke 'in a low tone' to deny the complicity of 'the firm with which he was connected' in fraudulent corn returns made at Ipswich.[9] He made no mark at all in 1826. He was granted a month's leave on account of ill health, 19 Feb., and secured another fortnight for the same reason, 3 Apr. 1827. His first recorded vote of the Parliament was against Catholic relief, 12 May 1828. In late February 1829 Planta, the Wellington ministry's patronage secretary, predicted that he would vote 'with government' for the concession of Catholic emancipation, but he divided against the measure, 6 Mar., and in favour of an amendment to prevent Catholics from sitting in Parliament, 23 Mar. 1829. He voted against Jewish emancipation, 17 May 1830.

Following the 1830 general election he was listed by ministers among their 'friends' and he duly voted with them on the civil list, 15 Nov. 1830. Thomas Gladstone* deemed him 'too ministerial' to present a petition he had prepared against the return for Queenborough, but noted that Scott had promised to attend for the select committee ballot, which took place, 30 Nov. 1830.[10] He divided against the second reading of the Grey ministry's reform bill, 22 Mar., and in favour of Gascoyne's wrecking amendment, 19 Apr. On the hustings at Whitchurch, which was scheduled for complete disfranchisement, he told the nominal electorate that he 'always had and always would oppose the ministerial plan of reform ... a measure he was convinced would be the cause of anarchy and confusion throughout the country'.[11] He voted against the second reading of the reintroduced reform bill, 6 July, and was in the minority for use of the 1831 census to determine the borough disfranchisement schedules, 19 July. On 26 July he spoke against the disfranchisement of Whitchurch, declaring that 'no borough in the kingdom possesses a better, a more honest, or respectable constituency'. He divided against ministers on the Dublin election controversy, 23 Aug., and against the passage of the reform bill, 21 Sept. He apparently missed the division on the second reading of the revised bill, 17 Dec. 1831, but he voted against the enfranchisement of Tower Hamlets, 28 Feb., and the bill's third reading, 22 Mar. 1832. He voted against government on the Russian-Dutch loan, 26 Jan., 12 July. The reformer Sir Edward Dolman Scott was probably the 'Sir W. Scott' listed in the majority for making coroners' inquests public, 20 June 1832.

Scott's Commons career ended with the extinction of Whitchurch as a parliamentary borough by the Reform Act. At the 1835 election for West Kent he gave a plumper to the Conservative candidate Sir William Geary†.[12] He died at Amiens in September 1849. By the terms of his will, dated 18 Aug. 1849, Sundridge passed to his younger son Samuel Scott (1807-69), who also received a three-fifths share of his stake in the family banking house, which had been styled Sir Samuel Scott and Company from 1847. The remainder went to Claude Edward Scott (1804-80), the heir to the baronetcy for whom his grandfathers had made ample provision. Scott followed his father's example by offering his sons a financial incentive for their continued involvement in the bank. To his two daughters he left income from £50,000 worth of bonds in the Republic of Chile and the Royal Agricultural and Commercial Corporation of Cuba. His personal estate was sworn under £700,000.[13]

[1] *Farington Diary*, xii. 4344. [2] PROB 11/1519/82; IR26/168/161. [3] F.G. Hilton Price, *London Bankers*, 48. [4] *Farington Diary*, xii. 4344; J. Hutchins, *Dorset* (1861), iii. 360; PROB 11/1771/337; IR26/1240/212. [5] Oldfield, *Key* (1820), 17; *The Times*, 11 Aug. 1831. [6] *Black Bk.* (1823), 191; *Session of Parl. 1825*, p. 484. [7] *The Times*, 28 Feb., 7 Mar. 1822. [8] Ibid. 11 May 1822. [9] *The Times*, 18 Mar. 1825. [10] St. Deiniol's Lib. Glynne-Gladstone mss 196, T. to J. Gladstone, 27 Oct., 1 Nov. 1830; *CJ*, lxxxvi. 134 [11] *Portsmouth Herald*, 8 May 1831. [12] *W. Kent Pollbook* (1835), 32. [13] *Gent. Mag.* (1850), i. 85; PROB 11/2101/796; IR26/1851/810; Hilton Price, 48.

H.J.S./P.J.S.

SCOTT, Hon. William (1794–1835), of 11 Grafton Street, Piccadilly, Mdx.

GATTON   1826–1 Mar. 1830

b. 23 Mar. 1794, 2nd but o. surv. s. of Sir William Scott*, 1st Bar. Stowell (*d.* 1836), and 1st w. Anna Maria, da. and h. of John Bagnall of Erleigh Court, nr. Reading, Berks. *educ.* Eton 1808-11; Univ. Coll. Oxf. 1812. *unm. d.v.p.* 26 Nov. 1835.

Scott, who was described by Joseph Farington in 1817 as 'a heavy indolent young man ... who would lay in bed for a fortnight',[1] never threatened to emulate his distinguished father, a judge in the admiralty court, who was created Lord Stowell in 1821. He was in Scotland when a relative on Newcastle corporation nominated him for his father's native borough at the 1820 general election, and he arrived on the scene half an hour after his name had been withdrawn, following one day's polling.[2] He was returned unopposed for Sir Mark Wood's† pocket borough of Gatton in 1826. He made no mark in the House, where he is not known to have contributed to debate. It is unclear whether it was he or his cousin William Henry John Scott, lord chancellor Eldon's son, who divided against Catholic relief, 6 Mar. 1827. He voted against repeal of the Test Acts, 26 Feb., and Catholic relief, 12 May 1828. In January 1829 Planta, the Wellington ministry's patronage secretary, suggested him as a possible mover or seconder of the address.[3] The following month Planta listed him as being 'opposed to the principle' of Catholic emancipation, and he voted accordingly, 6, 18, 27, 30 Mar. He was in the minority for the issue of a new writ for East Retford, 2 June 1829. His name does not appear in the lists compiled by the Ultra Tory leader Sir Richard Vyvyan* that autumn. It is uncertain whether it was he or his cousin who voted for Knatchbull's amendment to the address on distress, 4 Feb. 1830. He vacated his seat soon afterwards.

Although Scott was the heir to his father's considerable fortune, their relationship was 'unexceptionable' and Stowell 'would not make him a sufficient allowance to enable him to marry'. His congenitally 'intemperate habits increased under the disappointment', and his health eventually collapsed. By October 1835 he was 'in a hopeless state', while Stowell was now *non compos mentis* and oblivious to his plight. On 25 Nov. Lord Sidmouth, the second husband of Scott's only sister Marianne, told Eldon that 'the vital powers are nearly exhausted and not likely ... to hold out another day'. He died *v.p.* in November 1835, and Stowell remained 'unconscious of what has passed' until his own death two months later, when the title became extinct.[4] Administration of Scott's effects, which were sworn under £40,000, was granted to Sidmouth and another of Stowell's executors, 12 Mar. 1836. This grant was revoked by interlocutory decree after there came to light a 'small piece of paper', dated 1 Feb. 1821, on which Scott had devised all his property to his sister in the event of his death 'before marriage and without children'; administration was duly granted to Lady Sidmouth, 22 July 1837. She also inherited the bulk of Lord Stowell's estate.[5]

[1] *Farington Diary*, xiv. 4995. [2] *Newcastle Pollbook* (1820), pp. vii-ix. [3] Add. 40398, f. 87. [4] W.E. Surtees, *Lords Stowell and Eldon*, 143; Twiss, *Eldon*, iii. 251-2; *Gent. Mag.* (1836), i. 430. [5] PROB 6/212/185; 11/1859/190; 1882/567; Twiss, iii. 254-5.

D.R.F.

SCOTT, Sir William (1745–1836), of Doctors' Commons and Erleigh Court, nr. Reading, Berks.[1]

| DOWNTON | 1790–13 Mar. 1801 |
| OXFORD UNIVERSITY | 23 Mar. 1801–17 July 1821 |

b. 17 Oct. 1745, 1st s. of William Scott, coal-fitter, of Newcastle-upon-Tyne, Northumb. and 2nd w. Jane, da. of Henry Atkinson of Newcastle; bro. of Sir John Scott[†]. *educ.* Newcastle g.s.; Corpus, Oxf. 1761, BA 1764; fellow, Univ. Coll. Oxf. 1765-81, tutor 1765-76, MA 1767, BCL 1772, DCL 1779; Camden reader of ancient hist. 1773-85; M. Temple 1762, called 1780. *m.* (1) 7 Apr. 1781, Anna Maria (*d.* 4 Sept. 1809), da. and h. of John Bagnall of Erleigh Court, 2s. *d.v.p.* 1da.; (2) 10 Apr. 1813, Lady Louisa Catherine Howe, da. and coh. of Richard Howe[†], 1st Earl Howe, wid. of John Denis Browne, 1st mq. of Sligo [I], *s.p. suc.* fa. 1776; kntd. 3 Sept. 1788; *cr.* Bar. Stowell (of Stowell Park, Glos. which he bought for £165,000 in 1811 from the legatee of the 4th Bar. Chedworth) 17 July 1821. *d.* 28 Jan. 1836.

Adv. Doctors' Commons 1779; admiralty adv. 1782-8; registrar, ct. of faculties 1783-90; king's adv. 1788-98; judge of consistory ct. of London and vicar-gen. of province of Canterbury 1788-1821; master of faculties Apr. 1790-*d.*; bencher M. Temple 1794, reader 1799, treas. 1807; judge, ct. of admiralty Oct. 1798-Feb. 1828; PC 31 Oct. 1798; member, bd. of trade 1798-*d.*; charity commr. 1818-28; commr. for building new churches 1818.

Maj. L. Inn vols. 1799.

Scott, the elder brother of lord chancellor Eldon, had, from his entrance to the Commons in 1790,

pursued a brilliant and lucrative career as an advocate specializing in civil and maritime law, alongside a fairly unremarkable course in Parliament as a supporter of successive Tory governments. Widowed for a second time in 1817, he was a witty and companionable man, who was rarely without an invitation to dinner. He was noted for his scruffy appearance and, despite his great wealth, his stinginess. George Canning* once likened the 'waddling' Scott to 'a conceited Muscovy duck'.[2] A fortnight after George III's death in January 1820 he was reported to have expressed 'apprehension' that the Liverpool ministry might resign, to precipitate 'a general sweep' in government.[3] Three weeks later he was again returned unopposed for his university (where he had been a distinguished academic before turning to the more lucrative profession of the law) at the age of 74. His name appears in none of the surviving ministerial division lists of this period. On 21 Apr. 1820 he proposed the re-election of Manners Sutton as Speaker. He was perturbed by the implications of Henry Brougham's scheme of June 1820 to establish a more effective national system of education for the poor. Writing to the headmaster of Shrewsbury, Dr. Butler, whose hostile pamphlet he had admired, he deplored the possibility of 'education ... descending into the hands of writing masters, accountants [and] excisemen ... of whose principles we know nothing, and little of their literature beyond the multiplication table'.[4] On 7 July he brought in a bill designed to clarify the law relating to offences at sea. On its second reading, 10 July, he argued that 'recent circumstances' had shown the necessity of extending the punishment for offences committed on land to those committed at sea.[5] The bill became law on 24 July 1820. At this time he was prematurely tipped for elevation to the peerage.[6] He was at first alarmed at the prospect of the trial of Queen Caroline, but came to hope that 'all may pass off tolerably quietly', believing that the government had a strong case.[7] After the abandonment of the prosecution he wrote to a friend:

> I shall be very glad to hear of ... loyal addresses coming up. We want to be reinforced in our spirits by friendly declarations from respectable bodies and individuals. The Whigs appear too much disposed to a coalition with the radicals, in order to compel the king to dismiss the ministers, and that coalition is of itself a sufficient reason for a firm resistance to their admission into power; for they will be compelled to make very unpleasant concessions to their new allies, at the expense of the constitution.[8]

Scott paired against Catholic relief, 28 Feb. 1821. He presented petitions against it from Oxford University, 12 Mar., and the archdeaconry of Essex, 16 Mar.[9]

Opposing the second reading of the relief bill later that day, he objected to the alterations which Plunket proposed to make in his original bill and insisted that the House be given further details of the revisions and sufficient time in which to consider them. In committee, 23 Mar., he condemned any tinkering with the oath of supremacy, maintaining that by unambiguously denying the pope's authority it had effectively protected the nation from foreign influence. The anti-Catholic Member Henry Bankes wrote that 'more was expected from ... Scott than he performed: he was out of health and feeble, and fell far short of his former exertions in the same cause'.[10] The 'Mountaineer' Henry Grey Bennet dismissed his speech as 'tiresome and dull', as he did his effort when he led the opposition to the third reading (after presenting a hostile petition from the authorities of Canterbury cathedral), 2 Apr.[11] On 12 Apr. 1821 he was granted a fortnight's leave of absence because of ill health. He was made a coronation peer in July 1821, but rarely appeared in the Lords and took little part in debate.

He retired from the admiralty bench in 1828, having been handicapped for several years by failing eyesight and powers of speech. It was falsely rumoured before he stood down that he was trying to extort a pension from the tottering Goderich ministry. The Whig Sir James Mackintosh*, who aspired to replace him, commented that this was 'a shameless proposal from a man of 82 with a fortune of near half a million'.[12] He was a great civil lawyer, whose judgments laid the basis of modern admiralty law and the international law of war.[13] He lapsed into senility in about 1833 and remained oblivious to the death of his only surviving son, William Scott*, to whom he had devised the bulk of his property, in November 1835. He died two months later, leaving a personal fortune of some £230,000 and real estate worth £12,000 a year. His only surviving child Mary Anne, the second wife of the 1st Viscount Sidmouth, took a life interest in the whole property. On her death in 1842 the Gloucestershire estates passed to Scott's great-nephew John Scott*, 2nd earl of Eldon, and the personal estate was distributed among the children of his niece Mary Forster of Seaton Burn.[14]

[1] See H.J. Bourgignon, *Sir William Scott, Lord Stowell* (1987); *Oxford DNB*. [2] J.G. Lockhart, *Life of Scott* (1838), vii. 135; Hatherton diary, 17 Mar. 1836. [3] Buckingham, *Mems. Geo IV*, i. 8. [4] Add. 34585, f. 53. [5] *The Times*, 8, 11 July 1820. [6] Buckingham, i. 51. [7] Add. 51659, Whishaw to Lady Holland, 4, Aug.; 51679, Lord J. Russell to same, 14 [Aug. 1820]. [8] Twiss, *Eldon*, ii. 410-11. [9] *The Times*, 13, 17 Mar. 1821. [10] Dorset RO D/BKL, Bankes jnl. 126. [11] HLRO, Hist. Coll. 379, Grey Bennet diary, 43, 48; *The Times*, 3 Apr. 1821. [12] Add. 52447, f. 140. [13] *Oxford DNB*. [14] Twiss, iii. 251-2, 254-5; *Gent. Mag.* (1836), i. 430; PROB 11/1859/190.

R.M.H./D.R.F.

SCOTT, Sir William, 6th bt. (1803–1871), of Ancrum, nr. Jedburgh, Roxburgh.

CARLISLE	18 Feb. 1829–1830
ROXBURGHSHIRE	1859–Feb. 1870

b. 26 July 1803, 2nd. but o. surv. s. of Sir John Scott, 5th bt., of Ancrum and Harriet, da. of William Graham of Gartmore, Perth. *m.* 9 June 1828,[1] Elizabeth, da. and h. of David Anderson of Balgay, Forfar, 4s. (1 *d.v.p.*) 3da. *suc.* fa. as 6th bt. 24 Dec. 1812. *d.* 12 Oct. 1871.

Ensign 51 Ft. 1822; cornet 2 Ft. Gds. 1824; half-pay capt. unattached 1826; ret. 1836.

The Scotts of Ancrum, like their wealthier namesakes the dukes of Buccleuch, were descendants of the twelfth century Scottish warrior Lord Uchtred Scott, and their 2,000-acre estate in the Vale of Teviot had been the scene of many Border skirmishes. Scott's father, Lieutenant-General John Scott of Craigentinny, Edinburgh, had succeeded his uncle Sir William Scott to Ancrum and the baronetcy in 1769 and died in December 1812, having been predeceased by his elder son John. Scott, as 6th baronet, became an officer in the Life Guards and returned to Scotland on coming of age in 1824 to claim his inheritance. He went on half-pay with the rank of captain in October 1826, was appointed a deputy lieutenant of Roxburghshire in March 1827 and added a new wing to Ancrum Castle. He also let it be known that he was prepared to spend to enter Parliament.[2] Posing as a liberal Canningite and also as a Tory, he sounded both parties and 'flirted a little' with the electors of Carlisle at the by-election occasioned by the death of the sitting Tory in July 1827.[3] However, the Whig Blues disavowed him and the Tory Lord Lowther* dissuaded his father Lord Lonsdale from promoting a man who 'is a Member of Brooks's and the best construction put upon his politics would be trimming and uncertain'.[4] He married the heiress of David Anderson of Balgay at Dundee in June 1828 and, before consulting either party, declared again for Carlisle directly the sitting Whig Sir James Graham vacated in December. He hired Lowther agents and in February 1829 defeated the Whig Henry Aglionby* in a four-day poll, which cost him an estimated £30,000. He refused to give his views on the Catholic question, East India Company monopolies and the corn laws, but said he was for retrenchment and free trade and 'friendly' towards the Wellington ministry, 'as I conceive they intend to carry through the same liberal measures [as Canning]'. The Lowthers had no wish to retain him at a general election and declined further association with him.[5]

Scott, who made no reported speeches as Member for Carlisle, took his seat on 4 Mar. 1829. Despite press reports to the contrary, confusing him with 'Hon. W. Scott', Member for Gatton, he did not divide with the Lowthers against Catholic emancipation, 6, 18 Mar., and he voted for the measure when they abstained, 30 Mar. He was in the minority for amending the Irish freeholders bill to permit voter registration, 20 Mar.[6] He divided against Lord Blandford's parliamentary reform proposals, 18 Feb., and the Galway franchise bill, 25 May, and was probably in the majority against Jewish emancipation, 17 May 1830. At the general election in July he 'wisely' avoided a 'second *plucking*' at Carlisle, where he declined to 'play the anti-Catholic card', was refused the Buccleuch interest in Roxburghshire, and fell prey to the electioneering schemes of the attorney John Stanbury at Tregony, where defeat by Lord Darlington's nominees cost him 'thousands'.[7] He took no part in the subsequent petitioning.

Now convinced of the need for parliamentary reform, Scott headed the heritors' requisition for a county meeting, 25 Jan. 1831, and subsequently championed the cause at public meetings in Roxburghshire.[8] To the annoyance of the reformer Sir William Francis Eliott of Stobbs, he declared his candidature there at the dissolution precipitated by the defeat of the Grey ministry's English reform bill in April, and promised to support it outright, avoiding 'everything allied to party or faction' on other issues.[9] He was defeated *in absentia* and without his apparent collusion at Tregony, 30 Apr.;[10] and after corresponding with the sitting anti-reformer Hepburne Scott, whose return for Roxburghshire he had approved in 1826, on 11 May he made way for and agreed 'a very awkward coalition' (Sir Walter Scott) with Eliott, whose candidature posed less of a threat to the Tories than his own. He also nominated Eliott on the 18th.[11] He spoke for the reformers at the Haddington Burghs election at Jedburgh, 23 May, and the county meeting on 6 Dec. 1831.[12] The Conservatives regarded him as a 'turncoat, not to be trusted, though ... no doubt to be purchased by flattery', and from 1832 he chaired the Liberal committee at Roxburghshire elections.[13] He declined the nomination in 1837, when there was no prospect of success, but came in unopposed in 1859 as a declared supporter of Gladstone, opposed to the Derby ministry's reform bill.[14] He retired through ill health in

February 1870, having outpolled the Conservative Lord Schomberg in 1868, when his son Harry Warren Scott was the defeated Liberal at Dundee.[15] He died at Ancrum in October 1871, survived by his widow (*d.* 1878) and six of their seven children.[16] His titles and estates worth £3,201 a year passed to his eldest son William Monteath Douglas Scott (1829-1902), on whose death without surviving male issue the baronetcy lapsed. In December 1873 a fire at Ancrum Castle, which was insured for £36,000, caused £30,000 worth of damage, destroying Scott's art collection and most of the family papers.[17]

[1] IGI (Angus). [2] A. Jeffrey, *Hist. and Antiqities of Roxburghshire* (1864), ii. 356-60, 365-6. [3] Lonsdale mss, Lowther to Lonsdale, 23, 25 July 1827; Brougham mss, Scott to J. Brougham, 28 Dec. 1828. [4] Lonsdale mss, Lowther to Lonsdale, 26, 31 July 1827; J.R. McQuiston, 'Lonsdale Connection and its Defender', *Northern Hist.* xi (1975), 170-3. Scott was not admitted to Brooks's until 31 Mar. 1852. [5] Reading Univ. Lib. Carlisle election handbills, ff. 115-130; Lonsdale mss, Lowther to Lonsdale, 25 Jan., 4, 7, 10, 16, 18, 21, 24, 25 Feb.; bdle. on Carlisle election, 1829. [6] *Cumb. Pacquet*, 10, 24 Mar., 7 Apr. 1829; *Gent. Mag.* (1829), i. 365. [7] *Carlisle Jnl.* 10, 17, 24 July; *Cumb. Pacquet*, 20 July; *West Briton*, 6 Aug.; *R. Cornw. Gazette*, 14 Aug. 1830; NAS GD224/580/3/1/3-5. [8] *Kelso Mail*, 17, 27 Jan., 17 Mar.; *Caledonian Mercury*, 27 Jan.; NAS GD157/3010, draft, Hepburne Scott to Lothian, 15 Mar.; *Scotsman*, 26 Mar.; *The Times*, 28 Mar. 1831. [9] NAS GD157/2978/11-13; *Scotsman*, 27 Apr.; *Kelso Mail*, 28 Apr.; Brougham mss, Sir W. Eliott to Brougham, 3, 27 May 1831. [10] *West Briton*, 6 May; *R. Cornw. Gazette*, 7 May 1831. [11] *Glasgow Herald*, 9, 27 May; *Caledonian Mercury*, 14 May 1831; NAS GD157/2962/16; 2978/2-6, 14; 2980/25; 2981/8; *Scott Jnl.* ii. 170. [12] *Scotsman*, 28 May; *Kelso Mail*, 28 Nov., 8 Dec.; *The Times*, 12, 14 Dec. 1831. [13] NAS GD224/580/3/1/17, 18. [14] *The Times*, 19 Jan. 1835, 14 July 1837; *Hawick Advertiser*, 16 Apr., 7, 14 May 1859. [15] *The Times*, 5 Aug., 5, 12, 22 Sept., 23 Nov. 1868. [16] *Jedburgh Gazette*, 14 Oct.; *Hawick Advertiser*, 21 Oct. 1871. [17] *The Times*, 4 Dec. 1873.

M.M.E.

SCOTT, Hon. William Henry John (1795-1832), of 126 Park Street, Grosvenor Square, Mdx.

HEYTESBURY	1818–1820
HASTINGS	1820–1826
NEWPORT I.o.W.	1826–1830

b. 25 Feb. 1795, 4th but 2nd surv. s. of Sir John Scott†, 1st Bar. Eldon, of Bedford Square and Elizabeth, da. of Aubone Surtees, banker, of Newcastle-upon-Tyne, Northumb. *educ.* Eton; Univ. Coll. Oxf. 1813; M. Temple 1810, called 1816. *unm. d.v.p.* 6 July 1832.

Commr. of bankrupts 1816-21; recvr. of fines 1816-*d.*, sec. of decrees and injunctions 1816-21, clerk of patents and registrar of affidavits, ct. of chancery 1819-*d.*; cursitor and commr. of lunacy 1821-*d.*

Scott, described to Farington in 1817 as 'a young man of no promise', was a disappointment to his redoubtable father lord chancellor Eldon, who prayed in 1829 that he would be led to 'right ways of thinking, and by them, to that happiness which no man ever wished a son to enjoy more than I have'. Yet, as Horace Twiss* noted, his 'eccentricities seem not to have abated his father's interest in him'; and 'his agreeable qualities and natural talents rendered him an especial favourite' with Eldon, who indulged him.[1] Scott's elder brother had died in 1805, but left an infant son as heir to Eldon's peerage. The chancellor compensated William Henry with a clutch of chancery sinecures worth about £2,800 a year, and with the reversions to the 3rd Earl Bathurst's clerkship of the crown and the office of bankruptcy patentee after the lives of Edward, 2nd Baron Thurlow, and his brother the Rev. Thomas Thurlow. These were conservatively estimated at about £1,000 and £4,500 respectively, but the latter was a dubious prospect, as Thomas Thurlow was only seven years older than Scott.[2]

At the general election of 1820 he was returned for the treasury borough of Hastings at a reputed cost of 4,000 guineas. The Whig lawyer John Campbell II* later wrote that although he was 'disqualified for steady application to business by his sinecures', he had 'much natural cleverness' and 'a considerable share of dry humour':

> He once told me that, while a Member of the House of Commons, he made it a rule to be always present at the *division*, and never at the debate; adding, 'I regularly read the arguments on both sides in the newspapers next morning, and it is marvellous that I uniformly find I have been right in my votes'.[3]

Certainly he made no mark in the House, where he continued, when present, to give apparently silent support to his father's ministerial colleagues.[4] He voted in defence of their conduct towards Queen Caroline, 6 Feb., and presented a petition from Hastings 'complaining of agricultural distress', 22 Feb. 1821.[5] He voted against Catholic relief, 28 Feb. 1821, 30 Apr. 1822, 1 Mar., 21 Apr. 1825. He mustered for the divisions on the revenue, 6 Mar., repeal of the additional malt duty, 21 Mar., 3 Apr., the army estimates, 11 Apr., and the disfranchisement of ordnance officials, 12 Apr. 1821. He divided against mitigation of the penal code, 23 May, for the duke of Clarence's grant, 18 June, and against retrenchment, 27 June 1821. In his capacity as a baron of the Cinque Ports he was a canopy bearer at the coronation of George IV, by whom he had been 'quite graciously received' the previous year. Eldon reported that he cut 'a capital figure' in the uniform, 'looked amazingly well, and performed his duty well'.[6] His attendance seems to have fallen away during the

following sessions of the 1820 Parliament. He voted against reduction of the salt duties, 28 Feb., abolition of one of the joint-postmasterships, 13 Mar. 1822, inquiries into the legal proceedings against the Dublin Orange rioters, 22 Apr., and chancery delays, 5 June, the Scottish juries bill, 20 June 1823, and parliamentary reform, 26 Feb. 1824. He divided for the Irish unlawful societies bill, 25 Feb., against the Irish franchise bill, 26 Apr., and for the duke of Cumberland's annuity, 30 May, 10 June 1825. Three months later Brougham was told that Scott had 'made himself ill by perpetual hard living', but 'would be well enough if he would keep himself sober'.[7]

At the general election of 1826 he came in for Newport on the Holmes interest. It is not clear whether it was he or his cousin William Scott who voted against Catholic relief, 6 Mar. 1827. His father's long tenure of the great seal ended with the formation of Canning's ministry the following month. He divided against repeal of the Test Acts, 26 Feb. 1828, and was one of the steadfast opponents of Catholic emancipation in 1829. He was in the minority in favour of issuing a new writ for East Retford, 2 June 1829. Like his father, Scott was alienated from the Wellington ministry by their concession of emancipation, and in 1830 he acted with the disaffected Ultras in opposition to them. It is uncertain whether it was he or his cousin who divided for Knatchbull's amendment to the address, 4 Feb., but he definitely voted against government in favour of economy and retrenchment, 12, 22, 29 Mar., 7, 11 June. He divided against Jewish emancipation, 17 May. His last recorded votes were against the sale of beer bill, 1 July, and the libel law amendment bill, 9 July 1830. He left the House at the ensuing dissolution, though he had been rumoured as a candidate for Maidstone.[8]

In 1825 Eldon had reported that 'W.H.J. seems in good spirits, but not quite well', being 'plagued' by hostile comments on his sinecures, which grossly exaggerated their value to £10,000 a year.[9] By the Bankruptcy Act of 20 Oct. 1831, Thomas Thurlow's patentee office was abolished and replaced with an annuity of £11,734, with reversion to Scott. The following year it was alleged that Scott, who had so far received over £3,600 in compensation for his loss of fees as a cursitor incurred by the Act of 5 July 1825, and was 'entrenched chin-deep in sinecures and reversions', would have 'an income of £14,000 a year *for doing nothing*' if he survived Thurlow.[10] In the Commons, 6 Mar. 1832, Spring Rice, the Grey ministry's secretary to the treasury, responded to an opposition attack on the Irish lord chancellor Plunket's avaricious nepotism by comparing it favourably with Eldon's, making particular reference to the six sine-cures which he had bestowed on Scott. Eldon was 'much irritated' and on 12 Mar. 1832 replied indignantly in the Lords to his critics, pointing out that contrary to the 'wicked and diabolical' story that his son was currently in receipt of £12,000 a year from the bankruptcy patent, he had as yet derived nothing from the reversions and was unlikely ever to do so.[11] Scott was now terminally ill, and he died intestate and *v.p.* at his London house in July 1832, to the considerable grief of Eldon, who survived him by almost six years.[12] His effects were valued for administration under £30,000.[13] Twiss wrote that

> death had thrown his failings into the shade and brought his virtues into relief, in the view of his sorrowing father. 'Well', said Lord Eldon, 'I must say of him, that whatever faults he had, and however unfortunate they were for me, he had the best heart of any man I ever knew in my life' ... In society he indulged a sly humour, of which the effect was much heightened by a handsome countenance, and an appearance of shyness, under which however he maintained the most complete self-possession.[14]

[1] *Farington Diary*, xiv. 4995; Twiss, *Eldon*, iii. 94. [2] *Black Bk.* (1820), 37; (1823), 191-2. [3] Campbell, *Lives of Lord Chancellors*, vii. 588. [4] *Black Bk.* (1823), 191; *Session of Parl. 1825*, p. 484. [5] *The Times*, 23 Feb. 1821. [6] Twiss, ii. 363-4, 428. [7] Brougham mss, J. Smith to Brougham, 6 Sept. 1825. [8] *Maidstone Gazette*, 25 May 1830. [9] Twiss, ii. 556. [10] *Extraordinary Black Bk.* (1832), 331, 529, 568-9, 577. [11] Twiss, iii. 170-1; Campbell, vii. 555-7. [12] Twiss, iii. 185-6, 272-3. [13] PROB 6/208/220. [14] Twiss, iii. 185-6.

D.R.F.

SCOTT *see also* **HEPBURNE SCOTT**

SCOTT BENTINCK *see* **CAVENDISH SCOTT BENTINCK**

SCOURFIELD, William Henry (1776–1843), of Robeston Hall, Robeston West and New Moat, Pemb.

| HAVERFORDWEST | 1818–1826 |
| HAVERFORDWEST | 1835–1837 |

b. 1776, o.s. of Henry Scourfield of New Moat and Robeston Hall and Elizabeth, da. of Rt. Rev. John Ewer, DD, bp. of Bangor. *educ.* New Coll. Oxf. 3 July 1793, aged 17. *m.* (1) 27 Oct. 1804, Maria (*d.* 2 Aug. 1835), da. of Lt.-Col. Edward Goate of Brent Eleigh Hall, Suff., 1s. *d.v.p.*; (2) 28 Dec. 1837, Louisa Sarah, da. of Richard Bowen of Manorowen, Pemb., *s.p. suc.* fa. 1810. *d.* 31 Jan. 1843.

Sheriff, Pemb. 1812-13.
Capt. Pemb. militia 1795, maj. 1798, lt-col. 1798; capt.-commdt. Haverfordwest fusiliers 1803.

Scourfields had owned The Moat, near Haverfordwest, since the reign of Edward I and had long participated in the administration of Pembrokeshire, but Scourfield, whose 12,000 acres included valuable coal workings, was the first of the family to sit in Parliament, where his precise political allegiance baffled politicians.[1] He owed his return for Haverfordwest in 1818 to the reluctance of its principal patron, the ailing Baron Milford, to see the sitting Whig Lord Kensington make the seat his own, for it was designated for Milford's heir Richard Bulkeley Philipps Grant, who would not come of age until 1822; and it was on the understanding that 'any heir to the Picton Castle estate would have prior claim' that Scourfield was brought in in 1818 and again in 1820.[2] Milford claimed in a patronage application to the prime minister Lord Liverpool, 20 June 1820: 'Although *I myself* have no seat in either House ... Mr. Scourfield the Member for Haverfordwest (who votes with the administration) owes his election to my support'.[3]

Scourfield made no reported parliamentary speeches and continued to spend much time in Pembrokeshire, where he patronized local causes and was renowned as a huntsman and for his pack of harriers. His politics, though nominally Blue or Whig, were generally determined by local factors.[4] He signed requisitions for the county meeting of 17 Apr. 1820 which petitioned for agricultural protection and repeal of the coastwise coal duties, but he played no part in current petitioning on reform, or on the future of the Welsh judicature and courts of great sessions, which the county's Blues, led by the 1st Lord Cawdor, wanted to see abolished.[5] He received a month's leave on urgent private business, 28 June 1820. News that Queen Caroline's prosecution had been abandoned arrived in Haverforwest during the hunt week and Scourfield joined in the town's celebrations.[6] He voted to include her name in the liturgy, 23, 26 Jan., but divided with ministers against censuring their handling of her case, 6 Feb. 1821.[7] *Seren Gomer* criticized his failure to vote for Catholic relief, 28 Feb., repeal of the agricultural horse tax, 5 Mar., economies, 6 Mar., and retrenchment, 27 June; but praised his anti-government votes for repeal of the additional malt duty repeal, 21 Mar., 3 Apr.[8] On 12 Apr. he received a fortnight's leave on account of the tragic death of his young nephew, Henry Joshua Rowley.[9] He divided against parliamentary reform, 9 May 1821. Agricultural distress was rife and distraints a problem on his estates, when Scourfield cast a critical vote on the government's relief proposals, 21 Feb., and voted to reduce the salt duties, 28 Feb., and to abolish one of the joint-postmasterships, 2 May 1822.[10] According to *Seren Gomer*, he also voted against restoring their privileges to Catholic peers, 30 Apr., but he is not included in the usual lists.[11] In November, concerned at the implications for Pembrokeshire should the Irish packet service be lost, he joined the Members for the county and Pembroke Boroughs (Sir John Owen and John Hensleigh Allen) in lobbying the home secretary Peel for its continuation.[12] Possibly on account of poor health, for which he was granted a fortnight's leave, 25 Apr. 1823, his parliamentary attendance lapsed.[13] He was considered but passed over for the lord lieutenancy of Haverforwest, vacant by Milford's death in November 1823, in favour of the latter's heir, who had come of age and taken the name of Philipps.[14] *Seren Gomer* praised his vote in condemnation of the indictment in Demerara of the Methodist minister John Smith, 11 June 1824, but again he is not named in the surviving lists.[15] He voted to outlaw the Catholic Association, 25 Feb., and against Catholic relief, 1 Mar., 21 Apr., 10 May, and the attendant franchise bill, 21 Apr. 1825. A radical publication that session noted that he 'attended occasionally and voted sometimes with and sometimes against ministers'.[16] He had granted new leases on his estates in 1824, and in March 1825 became a director with Owen and others of the new Pembrokeshire Slate, Lime and Iron Company, an enterprise chaired by John Jones* and persevered in 'at great expense and without any prospect of success'.[17] Reports in October 1825 that he and Philipps were rival bidders for Lord Cawdor's estate and borough of Wiston, a contributory of Pembroke, were unfounded, and he made way for Philipps as expected at the dissolution in 1826.[18]

Scourfield remained a prominent figure in Pembrokeshire, where at public and magistrates' meetings he generally voiced the opinions of the Blues reluctant to toe the political line set by Cawdor and Allen. He remained a committed opponent of Catholic emancipation in 1829 and criticized Cawdor's proposal for hearing Pembrokeshire cases in Carmarthen, so depriving Haverfordwest of its assize town status, when the courts of great sessions and Welsh judicature were abolished.[19] He also addressed the Pembrokeshire reform meeting, 5 Apr. 1831, but his speech that day was inadequately reported.[20] He kept a low profile at the general election in May when the Blue nominee, Robert Fulke Greville of Castle Hall, first challenged Owen for the county seat, but he seconded Greville's nomination at the second election in October and

subscribed generously to his cause.[21] He was elected mayor of Haverfordwest in November 1831, and was foreman of the special jury which in March 1832 indicted the Carmarthen attorney George Thomas for insulting John Jones at the May 1831 election.[22] Scourfield seconded Philipps's nomination for the new Haverfordwest District of Boroughs in December 1832 and defeated the moderate Conservative Jonathan Peel of Cotts to come in there himself in 1835 when Philipps retired to avoid a poll.[23] Although returned as a Liberal 'on the reform interest', he was deemed to be 'a rank and uncompromising Tory' and in 1837 he lost his seat to Philipps, who accused him of 'misrepresenting the opinions of his constituents'.[24] His first wife had died in 1835, and in December 1837 he remarried, settling his Dewisland estate on his bride, to whom it reverted on his death in January 1843.[25] He also left her the lease of his London house in Charles Street, Berkeley Square, and an annuity. Family heirlooms, however, were entrusted to his brother-in-law, the Rev. Joshua Rowley, and passed with The Moat in 1862 to his nephew John Henry Philipps (1808-76) of Williamston, who assumed the name and arms of Scourfield. He represented Haverfordwest Boroughs as a Conservative, 1852-68, and was created a baronet shortly before his death in 1876.[26]

[1] *HP Commons, 1790-1820*, v. 115-16; R.G. Thorne, 'Pemb. and National Politics, 1815-1974', *Pemb. Co. Hist*. iv. ed. D. Howell, 233. [2] D.A. Wager, 'Welsh Politics and Parl. Reform, 1780-1835' (Univ. of Wales Ph.D. thesis, 1972), 235-6; Carm. RO, Cawdor mss 1/225; *Carmarthen Jnl*. 10, 17 Mar. 1820. [3] Add. 38285, f. 282. [4] Add. 40359, f. 184; NLW, Lucas mss 1833-8, 3380; *Cambrian*, 26 June 1824, 2 Feb. 1828; *Carmarthen Jnl*. 4 Apr. 1823, 1 Feb., 14 Nov. 1828. [5] *Carmarthen Jnl*. 14 Apr., 19 May 1820. [6] Ibid. 17 Nov. 1820. [7] *Seren Gomer*, iv (1821), 92-93. [8] Ibid. 124-5, 252. [9] *Gent. Mag*. (1821), i. 369; *Carmarthen Jnl*. 20 Apr. 1821. [10] *Seren Gomer*, v (1822), 124-5; Lucas mss 99, 414-18. [11] *Seren Gomer*, v. 187. [12] Add. 40352, f. 74. [13] *Carmarthen Jnl*. 4 Apr. 1823. [14] PROB 11/1681/96; *Carmarthen Jnl*. 5, 12 Dec. 1823; Add. 40359, ff. 100, 184-6, 205; NLW, Picton Castle mss 4728, 4731, 4793. [15] *Seren Gomer*, vii (1824), 224. [16] *Session of Parl. 1825*, p. 484. [17] Lucas mss 3621-3; *Cambrian*, 26 June 1824, 7 Mar. 1825; Bodl. Clarendon dep. C.372, bdle. 3, Harvey to Foster Barham, 9 June, 7 July 1827; C.374, bdle. 2, *passim*. [18] Clarendon dep. C.372, bdle. 2, Harvey to Foster Barham, 19 Oct. 1825; Cawdor mss 2/209; *Carmarthen Jnl*. 26 May, 2 June; *Cambrian*, 27 May; *The Times*, 30 May 1826. [19] *Carmarthen Jnl*. 13 Mar. 18, 25 Sept., 9 Oct.; *Cambrian*, 21 Mar., 10 Oct. 1829. [20] *Carmarthen Jnl*. 1, 8 Apr., 27 May, 3 June; *Cambrian*, 9 Apr. 1831. [21] *The Times*, 17 Oct. 1831; NLW, Eaton Evans and Williams mss 5121. [22] *Carmarthen Jnl*. 3 Dec. 1831; *Welshman*, 16, 23 Mar. 1832. [23] *Carmarthen Jnl*. 14 Dec. 1832, 12, 19, 26 Dec.; *Welshman*, 19, 26 Dec. 1834; *The Times*, 6 Jan. 1835. [24] Pemb. RO D/RTP/5/34; *Welshman*, 30 June, 7, 14 July; *The Times*, 5, 12, 13 July 1837; Lucas mss 44-98. [25] Lucas mss 3380; *Welshman*, 3 Feb. 1843. [26] PROB 11/1980/358; IR26/1657/349; Lucas mss 3301-3; Thorne, 247.

M.M.E.

SCUDAMORE, Richard Philip (1762–1831), of Kentchurch, Herefs. and Caroline Place, Regent's Park, Mdx.

HEREFORD	1 May 1805–1818
HEREFORD	21 Sept. 1819–1826

b. 30 June 1762, 2nd s. of John Scudamore I[†] (*d.* 1796) of Kentchurch and Sarah, da. and h. of Daniel Westcombe of Enfield, Mdx.; bro. of John Scudamore II[†]. *educ.* I. Temple 1778. *unm. d.* 5 Mar. 1831.
    Capt. Wormelow and Greytree vols. 1803.

By the death in 1805 of his brother John, Scudamore became trustee to the Kentchurch estate during the minority of his nephew John Lucy Scudamore (1798-1875) and Member for Hereford, which his family had represented since 1764 on their own and the Whig 11th duke of Norfolk's interest. Continuing the family tradition, he attended the House regularly, supported reform, retrenchment and Catholic relief and became a silent but uncompromising opponent of the Liverpool government. He was defeated by a Tory at Hereford in 1818 (at the first election following Norfolk's death), but regained his seat at a by-election the following year.[1] A 'stand-off' between the parties left him unopposed at the general election of 1820, when he confirmed his attachment to the Whig opposition and apologized for his recent absences from the House 'through severe indisposition'.[2]

Until 1822, when his health deteriorated and Kentchurch went into receivership, leaving his finances in disarray, Scudamore, as a radical publication of 1825 noted, 'attended frequently and voted with opposition'; he was fêted accordingly at the Hereford Whig dinner for Joseph Hume*, 7 Dec. 1821.[3] He backed the 1820-1 parliamentary and extra-parliamentary campaigns on behalf of Queen Caroline and presented supportive addresses to her from Hereford.[4] He divided unstintingly for retrenchment, paired for Catholic relief, 28 Feb. 1821, voted to permit Catholic peers to sit in the Lords, 30 Apr.,[5] and divided for parliamentary independence, 31 May 1821, and reform, 25 Apr. 1822. Affected by litigation brought on following the death in 1820 of the lunatic dowager duchess of Norfolk, and by his nephew's coming of age and marriage in October 1822 to the eldest daughter of Sir Harford Jones of Boultibrooke (who was confirmed as heir to Kentchurch in 1826 and took the name Brydges), Scudamore spent much of the next three years abroad.[6] He remained entitled to £4,000 under his father's settlement and £1,000 from his late mother, but he had unpaid debts of £3,200 and £300-400.[7] Naming Edward Bolton Clive* of Whitfield as

his political heir, he announced in December 1823 that he would retire at the dissolution.[8] He divided for Catholic relief, 10 May 1825.

He died childless and unmarried at his London home in March 1831 worth £450-600, having bequeathed his entire estate to 'Mary Webb, otherwise Prescott', who resided with him and was required to repay his debts.[9]

[1] *HP Commons, 1790-1820*, ii. 197-9; iv. 116-17; *Oxford DNB sub* Scudamore fam. 1500-1820; Herefs. RO, Kentchuch Court mss AL40/2036-40. [2] *Hereford Jnl.* 23 Feb., 15 Mar.; Herefs. RO AS53, E.B. Clive to S. Brooks, 17 Mar. 1820. [3] *Session of Parl. 1825*, p. 484; *Hereford Jnl.* 12, 19 Dec. 1821. [4] *Hereford Jnl.* 22 Nov.; *The Times*, 19 Dec. 1820, 30 Jan., 2 Mar. 1821. [5] *Seren Gomer*, v (1822), 187. [6] TNA C13/783/9; *The Times*, 7 Apr. 1824. [7] Kentchurch Court mss 1906. [8] Herefs. RO, Pateshall mss A95/V/EB/443. [9] PROB 11/1783/181; IR26/1271/145.

M.M.E.

SEBRIGHT, Sir John Saunders, 7th bt. (1767-1846), of Beechwood Park, nr. Hemel Hempsted, Herts. and Besford, Worcs.

HERTFORDSHIRE	1807–1834

b. 23 May 1767, 1st s. of Sir John Sebright[†], 6th bt., of Beechwood and Besford and Sarah, da. of Edward Knight of Wolverley, Worcs. *educ.* Westminster 1778. *m.* 6 Aug. 1793, Harriet, da. and h. of Richard Croftes[†] of West Harling, Norf. and Saxham, Suff., 1s. 8da. (5 *d.v.p.*). *suc.* fa. as 7th bt. 23 Feb. 1794. *d.* 15 Apr. 1846.
    Ensign 1 Ft. Gds. 1785, lt. and capt. 1792, ret. 1794.
    Sheriff, Herts. 1797-8; capt. Herts. yeoman cav. 1798.

Sebright's eccentricities made him one of the minor characters of the House. A quirky, opinionated, blunt, irascible man, fond of the sound of his own voice, he gloried in and frequently boasted of his independence, disclaiming all party connection.[1] Yet he was no buffoon, as Maria Edgeworth discovered in January 1822, when she was his guest, with a group of prominent scientists of both sexes, at Beechwood, a 'fine looking' but 'very cold and straggling large house with endless passages'. Sebright welcomed her with 'the most gracious countenance that his eyebrows would permit' – they were 'prodigious natural curiosities' in 'colour, size and projection' – and proved himself to be 'certainly a clever man and entertaining when he does not talk *all*':

> He is very clever, very vain, very odd, full of fancies and paradoxes and with abilities to defend them all. He has ... [a great] variety and range of acquirement in literature and science, an excellent chemist, mineralogist, horseman, huntsman, breeder of horses and dogs and pigeons whom he breeds and educates on philosophical

principles ... His maxim is that no violence should ever be used to animals, that all we need do is teach by gentle degrees the language of signs which tells them what we want them to do ... But, alas, notwithstanding his philosophical tenderness principles about dogs and horses I am afraid he has been violent with his children. He has treated his daughters like dogs perhaps and his dogs like children. Certainly they all look under abject awe of him and scarcely speak above their breath when he is within hearing. They have all dogs' faces, dogs' mouths ... There does not seem to be any communication between the sisters. They do not seem to live happily together and in the midst of luxuries and fine house and park this perception chills their guests ... Sir John, however, amused me incessantly. He is quite a new character – strong head and warm heart and oddity enough for ten.

She later commented that if Sebright, 'as arbitrary as the Grand Turk' in domestic matters, was to bid his gangling, ugly daughters to '*lie down*, he should expect to see the Miss Sebrights fall flat at their long lengths, sprawling motionless, crouching like spaniels'.[2]

Sebright, a steady supporter of religious toleration and parliamentary reform and a critic of excesses in public expenditure, had more often than not acted with the Whig opposition to the Liverpool ministry before 1820, though they could not implicitly rely on him for support, especially on questions of law and order. When he stood for Hertfordshire for the fourth time at the general election of 1820 as 'the independent representative of independent constituents', there was no opposition.[3] He voted against government on the civil list, 8 May, and the additional Scottish baron of exchequer, 15 May 1820. When presenting a local petition for relief from agricultural distress, 17 May, he wished it to be understood that he was 'not pledging himself to any opinion upon the subject'.[4] On 17 Oct. 1820 he dismissed Hume's attempt to implicate ministers in the dissemination of seditious literature:

The government ... was excessively unpopular ... But ... he was sorry to believe, that in such a state of feeling as existed, the people would be satisfied with no government whatever. The ministers had given reason for discontent; but all possible means had been employed to foment it.

Two months later he was reported in government circles as saying that in the 'merry session' which approached, he wished 'to impeach ministers and hang the opposition' for their respective parts in the Queen Caroline affair.[5] In the event, he voted silently for the restoration of her name to the liturgy, 23, 26 Jan. (he was shut out of the division of 13 Feb.), and to censure ministers, 6 Feb. 1821. He voted against them on the Allies' suppression of the liberal movement in Naples, 21 Feb. He presented a Hertfordshire agriculturists'

petition complaining of distress, 23 Feb.[6] He voted for Catholic relief, 28 Feb. He divided for army reductions, 14 Mar., 6 Apr., repeal of the additional malt duty, 21 Mar., 3 Apr., admiralty economies, 4 May, and against the Barbados defence fund pensions, 24 May. He voted for Russell's parliamentary reform proposals, 9 May, and denounced the Constitutional Association as 'illegal and unconstitutional', 30 May. He seconded his county neighbour Lord Cranborne's unsuccessful motion for inquiry into the 'absurd' and 'unjust' game laws, 5 Apr. He presented a Royston petition for amelioration of the criminal code, 1 May,[7] and voted for the forgery punishment mitigation bill, 4 June. He voted for inquiry into the administration of justice in Tobago, 6 June, and to omit the payment of arrears from the grant to the duke of Clarence, 18 June, 2 July; on 25 June 1821 he declared that this aspect of it was 'most improper' and 'a waste of public money'.

It was reported in December 1821 that Sebright would have no truck with any opposition attempt to make an issue of Sir Robert Wilson's* dismissal from the army and that he had 'already told Lord Londonderry that if he (Sir John) attacks ministers on that subject, it will be by complaining that they did not dismiss him some years ago'.[8] He had nothing to say on the subject in the House. At the Hertfordshire county meeting called to consider agricultural distress, 1 Feb. 1822, he agreed that the burden of taxation was oppressive, though he pointed out that the whole of Europe was paying the price of an expensive war. Replying to radical criticism of his failure to support enough of Hume's motions for economy, he defended his record on retrenchment, declined to enlist as the 'servile adherent' of Hume or any other man and argued that much as he admired Hume's pertinacity, his practice of constantly and vexatiously dividing the House was counter productive. He informed his audience that 'he could not surrender his own opinions absolutely: he was their representative, not their delegate'.[9] He nevertheless voted for Hume's amendment to the address, 5 Feb., when he urged on ministers 'the paramount necessity which at present existed of enforcing a system of economy in every branch of the public expenditure'. Although he did not vote for the opposition motions calling for more extensive tax reductions, 11, 21 Feb. (when he presented the petition from the county meeting),[10] he joined, on his own terms, in the ensuing campaign for economy, retrenchment and reduced taxation. Supporting repeal or reduction of the salt duties, 28 Feb., he called on the country gentlemen to act 'if they did not wish to see their rents unpaid, their tenantry ruined, their lands uncultivated, and their labourers reduced to beggary and want'. Miss

Edgeworth, a spectator in the ventilator, thought he was 'by far the best' of the country gentlemen who 'seemed to be speaking to please their constituents only'; 'he was as much at his ease as at Beechwood in his own drawing room'.[11] He spoke and voted for admiralty reductions, 1 Mar., but declared that 'so far from being actuated by any hostility' to ministers, 'he rather wished them to retain their places'. He supported abolition of one of the joint-postmasterships, 13 Mar., 2 May, calling on the first occasion for 'every reduction of the public expenditure that was consistent with the safety of the state'. He voted in favour of paying military pensions from the sinking fund, 3 May, 3 June, and for inquiry into diplomatic expenditure, 15 May; but on 18 May he declined to support Davies's motion for massive tax reductions, ostensibly because it had nothing to do with the question before the House. He returned to the fold to speak and vote for repeal of the salt duties, 3 June, and divided for abolition of the lottery tax, 1 July. He voted for parliamentary reform, 25 Apr. He presented a Hitchin petition for relaxation of the criminal code, 30 Apr., and voted for progress in this area after presenting a similar petition from Royston, 4 June.[12] On 6 May he deplored the present system of public house licensing. Later that day, on the report of the inquiry into agricultural distress, he stated that farmers had told him that 'legislative interference with the corn trade must ... be productive of harm'. He was in the minority of 37 for Wyvill's amendment for large tax remissions, 8 May, but on 18 May he welcomed the government's proposals to revise the corn laws as an improvement on the existing regulations, and he agreed with ministers that Canning's proposed clause to permit the grinding of foreign wheat would be 'fatal to the agricultural interest', 10 June. He was in the minority against the Irish constables bill, 7 June 1822.

At the Hertfordshire county meeting called to petition for parliamentary reform, 8 Feb. 1823, Sebright declared his personal preference for the moderate scheme propounded by his erstwhile colleague Thomas Brand (now Lord Dacre) in 1810, and his hostility to a radical amendment for taxpayer suffrage and annual parliaments. He condemned both the extremists who had 'made the question obnoxious to the country at large' and the reactionaries who would resist all change:

> I am a true friend to reform, but not such a reform as would altogether overturn the present state of things. I would amend, but not destroy; and I do not go hand in hand with those who would annihilate everything. I am a practical man, and a friend to practical reform; such a reform as should unite the House of Commons with the people of England.[13]

He voted for inquiry into the franchise, 20 Feb., but, for reasons unknown, was not in the minority for Russell's major reform motion, 24 Apr. 1823. He claimed that he would have voted for reform of the Scottish county representation, 2 June, had he not been accidentally locked out of the division. His only other known votes in that session were with opposition for inquiries into the prosecution of the Dublin Orange rioters, 22 Apr., chancery arrears, 5 June, and the expense of the coronation, 9 June; with ministers against currency reform, 12 June; and for Onslow's unsuccessful attempt to repeal the usury laws, 27 June, for which he also spoke.[14] He seconded Cranborne's motion for inquiry into the game laws, which 'affected the moral character of a vast body of the population', 13 Mar., and was named to the resulting select committee. When presenting a petition from Sir John Sinclair[†] against repeal of the protecting duties on foreign wool, 14 May, Sebright explained that he had rejected Sinclair's suggestion that he should lay a piece of British cloth on the table, but had agreed to wear a coat of the finest domestic wool, which he invited interested Members to inspect at close quarters in the lobby. He presented petitions from Royston for the abolition of slavery, 22 May, and from his own parish of Flamstead for the imposition of a duty on the importation of Leghorn hats, 10 July 1823.[15]

Sebright continued his support for repeal or reform of the usury laws, 27 Feb., 8 Apr. 1824. He presented assorted Hertfordshire petitions against the coal duties, 18 Feb., and slavery, 15, 16 Mar.[16] He voted to refer the reports of the Scottish judicial commission to a committee of the whole House, 30 Mar. He spoke in support of the game laws amendment bill, 25 Mar., 12 Apr., and for the Hammersmith bridge bill, 13 Apr., because 'he detested monopolies of all kinds'. He did not join opposition in resisting the aliens bill, but he voted for inquiries into the Irish church establishment, 6 May, and the state of Ireland, 11 May, when he said that he 'objected entirely to trusting the inquiry to the management of the executive government'. He voted to end pluralities in the Irish church, 27 May. He supported the warehoused wheat bill, 17 May, and the beer duties bill, 24 May, approving of the latter in particular because it broke up the brewers' monopoly. He voted in condemnation of the trial of the Methodist missionary John Smith in Demerara, 11 June 1824. Although he supported the legislation to suppress the Catholic Association, Sebright told the House, 18 Feb. 1825, that the 'disgrace' of having to bring in such legislation would never have arisen 'but for our prejudice, injustice and cruelty towards the Catholics'; he voted that day to allow, as an act of justice, the Association's counsel to be heard against the bill. He presented a petition from Protestants of Carrick in favour of Catholic claims, 28 Feb.,[17] though he defaulted on the call of the House that day. He was excused, 1 Mar., when he voted for Catholic relief, 1 Mar., as he did again, 21 Apr., 10 May. On 6 May he observed that none of the arguments advanced against it 'required any answer'. He presented a Ware petition against the coal duties, 25 Feb.,[18] supported the game bill, 7 (when he was a teller for the favourable majority) and 24 Mar.,[19] backed Hume in his strong objections to the fees charged for admission to St. Paul's, 21 Mar., and approved the increase in police magistrates' salaries proposed by government, 21 Mar. He voted against the duke of Cumberland's grant, 30 May, 6 and 10 June, arguing that the duke's immorality furnished a good ground for objecting to anything more than adequate provision, and concluding with the observation that he 'appeared before them like an individual who requested the parish ... to enable him to maintain his own child. Oh fie!' He voted for action on chancery delays, 7 June, and was in the minority of 14 against the grant for the Irish Society for the Suppression of Vice, 13 June 1825.

He presented anti-slavery petitions, 15 Feb., 27 Feb., 7 Mar., 20 Apr., and divided against ministers on the Jamaican slave trials, 2 Mar. 1826.[20] On the government motion for a bill to consolidate the larceny laws, 9 Mar., he attributed most of the increase in rural crime to the game laws. He voted to regulate the Irish first fruits fund, 21 Mar., against the ministerial salary of the president of the board of trade, 13 Apr., for parliamentary reform, 27 Apr., and to curb electoral bribery, 26 May. He declared his opposition to the proposal to permit the emergency admission of foreign corn, 2 May, and two days later said that although he would like to see the ports open at a fixed duty, one of 12s. did not afford adequate protection. He upbraided ministers for panicking in response to 'the burning of a few looms'. On 5 May he again took them to task for resorting to 'this indirect mode' of altering the corn laws, claiming that his disappointment was the greater because he was 'more disposed to repose confidence ... [in them] than in any administration of which he had a recollection'. He duly voted against the admission of foreign corn, 8 May, and the second reading of the corn bill, 11 May 1826. Sebright, who in 1826 published *Observations upon Hawking*, in which he described his methods of training birds for falconry, stood again for the county at the general election that year. There was no threat of opposition, but he was assailed by a notorious local anti-Catholic for his support for emancipation. In reply, he conceded that Catholicism was

'dangerous to any state', but challenged his critic to 'produce a single instance where any religion was put down by persecution' and argued that the only way to neutralize the threat from Ireland was to 'throw open the portals of the constitution' to Catholics:

> He had never swerved from the right path during his parliamentary career; he had never been called a government man, who sat behind the treasury benches; and whatever support he gave to the present administration was founded on the conviction that take it all in all, it was the best the country ever had.[21]

Two months later his wife died.

Sebright opposed as 'extremely ill-timed' Western's amendment to the address on the subject of agricultural distress, 22 Nov. 1826, and he gave his 'hearty concurrence' to the corn bill, 1 Mar. 1827. He voted against the duke of Clarence's grant, 16 Feb., 2 Mar. 1827. He spoke against Hume's attempt to end corporal punishment in the army, 26 Feb., 12 Mar., being quite prepared to accept his share of 'public odium' for so doing. He spoke, 2 Mar.,[22] and voted, 6 Mar., in favour of Catholic relief. He presented a Dissenter's petition for general religious freedom, 26 Mar., and called again for reform of the game laws, 28 Mar., and a more open system of licensing public houses, 9 Apr.[23] He voted for inquiry into the Irish miscellaneous estimates and chancery delays, 7 Apr. On 11 May he declared his 'decided support' for Canning's ministry, despite his refusal hitherto to have anything to do with party: he attacked Peel and the other 'narrow-minded and prejudiced' former ministers, who would have been prepared to provoke rebellion in Ireland rather than concede Catholic relief, and asked whether it was better to rally to 'those who were disposed to pursue a liberal and enlightened policy, or go back again to the control of that miserable remnant which had been discarded'. Canning drew the king's attention to his speech.[24] Sebright did, however, vote for the disfranchisement of Penryn, 28 May. He presented a Hitchin petition for repeal of the Test Acts, 7 June, and supported a detail of the government bill to regulate arrests on mesne process, 15 June 1827.[25]

On 4 Feb. 1828 he urged the Wellington ministry to initiate 'a diligent inquiry into the finances of the country', and went on:

> I am far from intending to enter into the ranks of opposition to the new ministry; neither do I feel myself pledged to be their inveterate supporter on all occasions. Opposition has been, with one exception, my uniform course in public life; but not so from system. I have never ranged myself as a supporter of any government except that of Mr. Canning – there, indeed, I almost felt it a duty

to become a partisan, and to continue so, at least, until I had finally seen that great man firmly seated as minister.

He repeated his intention of judging 'measures not men', 11 Feb., when he said that he would not oppose the navy estimates if doing so would injure the public service, but counselled ministers to do their best to economize, on pain of being called to account. He presented Hitchin petitions for repeal of the Test Acts, 20 Feb., denying an assertion that most Dissenters were anti-Catholic, and he duly voted for repeal, 26 Feb. He again opposed curbs on army flogging, 10 Mar., saw no reason to restrict the activities of retail brewers, who 'tended to defeat the monopoly of the great breweries', 2 Apr., and approved Estcourt's alehouses licensing bill, 21 May. He voted for a pivot price of 60s. rather than 64s. in the corn duties scale, 22 Apr., and for inquiry into chancery delays, 24 Apr. He failed in his bid to secure permission for the bill for the erection of a new court house at St. Albans to be proceeded with despite an inadvertent failure to comply with standing orders, 29 Apr. He approved Robinson's bill to shorten the duration of borough polls, 6 May. He divided for Catholic relief, 12 May. The next day he was in the minority against the proposed provision for Canning's family, to the surprise and disappointment of Backhouse, Canning's former secretary, 'recollecting how handsomely he came over, very early, last spring'.[26] He condemned Calvert's proposal to throw the corrupt borough of East Retford into the neighbouring hundred as the worst possible solution, 2 June. He voted against government on the alleged waste of public money on Buckingham House, 23 June, but with them to maintain the salary of the lieutenant-general of the ordnance, which he thought the finance committee had been wrong to target, 4 July 1828.

When the Catholic question was aired at the annual dinner for the inauguration of the mayor of Hertford, 29 Sept. 1828, Sebright repeated his view that while Catholicism was 'founded on the darkest bigotry and the most degraded superstition', the state of Ireland demanded immediate remedial action and his belief that 'Catholic emancipation might be carried without the slightest danger to the Protestant establishment'.[27] He attested to the respectability of the signatories of an anti-Catholic petition from Hemel, 9 Feb. 1829, but deemed them to be misguided. He voted for emancipation, 6 Mar., endorsed a favourable petition from Hitchin, 11 Mar., paid tribute to Peel for his 'courage' and 'magnanimity', 27 Mar., when he entered a minor cavil over the inadequacy of the relief bill's restrictions on Jesuits, and voted for its third reading, 30

Mar. He voted for O'Connell to be allowed to take his seat unimpeded, 18 May, and saw nothing to object to in the case of two army officers who had been dismissed for refusing to attend a Catholic service while stationed abroad, 12 June. He voted for the transfer of East Retford's seats to Birmingham, 5 May, and for the issue of a new writ, which he preferred to the extension proposal, 2 June 1829, when he was also in the minority of 40 for Lord Blandford's parliamentary reform scheme.

Sebright was reported as saying that he would oppose Knatchbull's amendment to the address, 4 Feb., 'being satisfied that ministers ... would do everything in their power to alleviate the distresses of the country'; but he was listed in the minority who voted for it. He divided for the enfranchisement of Birmingham, Leeds and Manchester, 23 Feb., and the transfer of East Retford's seats to Birmingham, 5 Mar. At the Hertfordshire county meeting on distress, 13 Mar., he refused to commit himself to a specific plan of parliamentary reform, merely stating that he had always favoured 'that sort of reform which would afford to the people the greatest portion of liberty'. When he presented its petition, 16 Mar., he stated his conviction that 'there must be a reform of some kind in this House, and that the country will not be satisfied without it'. He voted for Russell's reform motion, 28 May. He took little part in the opposition campaign for tax reductions and retrenchment. He would not oppose the grant for maintaining the orphans of soldiers killed on active service, 8 Mar., but the following day he did vote to limit the funding of the volunteers. He divided 'against' the opposition motion on relations with Portugal, 10 Mar.[28] He also voted for inquiry into the management of crown lands, 30 Mar., after calling for the provision of a footpath from Waterloo Place to St. James's Park, which he thought was not much to ask in view of the money wasted on 'that ridiculous building at the end of the park'. He protested strongly against the cost of repairs and alterations at Windsor Castle, 3 May, declaring that he 'should be ashamed to look my constituents in the face' if he voted for the grant without prior inquiry; he then contrived to get shut out of the division. The chancellor of the exchequer believed that he had only spoken as he did because of the impending general election.[29] He voted for Jewish emancipation, 5 Apr., 17 May. He welcomed the government bill to regulate the beer trade, 8 Apr., though on 21 June he complained that it did not give due consideration to the vested property of publicans. He saw no merit in Knatchbull's proposal to prohibit sales for consumption on the premises, but voted for Maberly's amendment to outlaw them for two years, 1 July. He presented a number of petitions from Hertfordshire agriculturists for the imposition of a duty on rum commensurate with that proposed for corn spirits, 12, 17, 24 May, and he voted with government on the sugar duties, 21 June 1830.[30]

There was some talk in Tory circles of mounting an opposition to Sebright, who was supposed to have had a 'most unsuccessful canvass', at the 1830 general election, but it came to nothing.[31] Ministers numbered him among their 'foes', and he voted against them on the civil list, 15 Nov. 1830. He thought that Briscoe's scheme to provide the poor with small plots of ground was unlikely to work, 17 Dec. 1830, but he was willing to donate land of his own if the experiment was to be tried. He presented a Berkhampstead petition for the abolition of slavery the same day. Recurring to the subject of spending on Buckingham House and Windsor Castle, 15 Feb. 1831, he observed that this 'scandalous waste of public money' had 'done more to irritate the people, and even set their minds against a monarchical form of government, than any speech ever made in or out of this House'. He was upbraided by Goulburn, but defended by Lord John Russell against the charge of levelling personal accusations. Later that day he welcomed the Grey ministry's bill to deal with the game laws. On 26 Feb. he urged ministers, if the House rejected their forthcoming reform bill, to dissolve and appeal to the people. When Russell had finished detailing the measure, 1 Mar., Sebright broke the 'dead silence' which had fallen on a stunned House by seconding the motion for leave to introduce it and giving it his personal endorsement.[32] He voted for its second reading, 22 Mar. In a public letter of 26 Mar. he answered the question of a Watford freeholder by saying that conferring the vote on tenants with leases of under 21 year would put county elections at the mercy of large landowners and defeat the objects of the bill, but in general terms, he urged unanimity among reformers:

> This bill will be violently opposed, both directly or by the more dangerous mode of proposing amendments; and I think that those who are real friends to substantial reform should support the measure as proposed by the ministers. This ... is the line of conduct I shall adopt. Nothing will be more fatal to the measure than for its friends to *split* upon its minor points.[33]

His remark in the House, 30 Mar., that in the nature of things the Members for doomed boroughs could not be expected to cast disinterested votes on the details of the measure, was interpreted by some Tories as a suggestion that they should be debarred from voting in committee. He voted against Gascoyne's wrecking amendment, 19 Apr. 1831.

At the ensuing general election, when Sebright congratulated his constituents resident at Hertford on the defeat of the Hatfield House interest in the borough by two reformers, his contemptuous dismissal of the opposition threatened by Lord Verulam's son, just ousted at St. Albans, was vindicated when the latter backed down in face of the overwhelming current of opinion in favour of reform.[34] He voted for the second reading of the reintroduced reform bill, 6 July, and was a steady supporter of its details in committee at least until the end of the third week in August. He denied an allegation that the people of Hertfordshire were 'cooling down' on reform, 20 July, accused the opposition of wilfully obstructing the bill's progress, 29 July, and declared himself to be 'for the bill, the whole bill, and nothing but the bill', 5 Aug. On the presentation of the Hertford electors' petition complaining of evictions by Lord Salisbury in reprisal for their having opposed his nominee at the last election, 21 Sept., Sebright expressed his hope that reform would extirpate the 'improper influence of landlords', but voiced his concern over the likely effects of the Chandos clause enfranchising £50 tenants-at-will, who would 'have no more freedom of voting than the negro slave in the West Indies'; he had been criticized in the local press for his opposition to this proposal.[35] He voted for the passage of the reform bill later that day, and for the second reading of the Scottish bill, 23 Sept., after observing that O'Connell's complaint that the Irish measure was being neglected was another symptom of Irish paranoia. He made clear the alarm felt in Hertfordshire at plans to allow the use of molasses in brewing, 20 July, and presented a Bishop's Stortford maltsters' petition to this effect, 18 Aug. He divided with government on the Dublin election controversy, 23 Aug. He professed not to understand Gordon's assertion that the House was turning a blind eye to blasphemy by accepting certain petitions, 5 Sept. He argued that reform of abuses in the Irish church was imperative, 14 Sept., and criticized the Irish tithes system, 6 Oct. He promised full support for Campbell's general register bill, 20 Sept. 1831.

At the county reform meeting, 30 Sept. 1831, Sebright explained that he

> had considered it most advisable to support ministers throughout the discussions, because he thought that it would be most unfortunate for the reformers to split among themselves with respect to particular portions of the great measure. He had voted in every division except two or three, from which he was absent in consequence of indisposition.[36]

He voted for the motion of confidence in the ministry, 10 Oct. On the presentation of an anti-reform petition from Worcestershire, where he had an inherited estate, 16 Dec. 1831, he denied that it was representative of opinion there. The following day he voted silently for the second reading of the revised reform bill. Denis Le Marchant[†] wrote that afterwards at the Athenaeum Sebright, a 'sagacious, hardheaded man', whose 'opinion is generally esteemed of much weight', pronounced that the changes incorporated in it meant that there would be 'no difficulty with the Lords'. His view, which proved to be erroneous, was supposed to derive added credibility from his 'alliance and friendship with the Harewoods and other great Tories' (his sister Harriet had married Henry Lascelles, 2nd earl of Harewood, in 1794).[37] Sebright, who at last joined Brooks's, sponsored by Lords Dacre and Western, 4 Feb. 1832, again gave steady support to the details of the reform bill, and voted for its third reading, 22 Mar. He divided with government on the Russian-Dutch loan, 26 Jan., 12, 16, 20 July, and relations with Portugal, 9 Feb. He voted against interference with corporal punishment in the army, 16 Feb., and next day opposed Hume's call for military reductions, observing that if ministers deserved criticism, it was for not having increased the army in view of the disturbed condition of Ireland. He also maintained that the political corruption which had influenced promotion in his day was a thing of the past. As the owner of Norfolk property, he thought the assizes should be permanently removed from Thetford to Norwich, 3 Apr. He voted against the recommittal of the Irish registry of deeds bill, 9 Apr., and applauded Warburton's anatomy bill as a boon to the poor, 11 Apr. He voted for the address calling on the king to appoint only ministers who would carry the reform bill unimpaired, 10 May, and for the second reading of the Irish bill, 25 May, and against a Conservative amendment to the Scottish measure, 1 June 1832.

Later that month Sebright, together with Calvert, announced that he had decided to retire into private life when Parliament was dissolved. However, in response to a request from the county reformers, anxious to meet a Conservative threat as effectively as possible, they agreed to stand. Sebright topped the poll at the 1832 general election (his first contest, after 25 years as a Member), but he stood down at the next dissolution.[38] In 1836 he published *Observations upon the Instincts of Animals*. An improving landlord, and a generous benefactor of the poor in the vicinity of Beechwood, he died at Turnham Green in April 1846.[39] By his will, dated 14 Jan. 1846, he provided for his three surviving daughters, all unmarried (Emily,

who had married Frederick Franks in March 1822, had died seven months later).[40] He was succeeded in the baronetcy and the settled estates by his only son, Thomas Gage Saunders Sebright (1802-64).

[1] W. Blake, *Irish Beauty*, 20; E. Inglis-Jones, *Peacocks in Paradise*, 179; *Life of Wilberforce*, iii. 496; *Oxford DNB*. [2] *Edgeworth Letters*, 320-6, 332. [3] *County Chron.* 29 Feb.; *County Herald*, 18 Mar. 1820. [4] *The Times*, 18 May 1820. [5] *Lonsdale mss*, Beckett to Lowther, 19 Dec. 1820. [6] *The Times*, 24 Feb. 1821. [7] Ibid. 2 May 1821. [8] *Colchester Diary*, iii. 240. [9] *The Times*, 2 Feb. 1822. [10] Ibid. 22 Feb. 1822. [11] *Edgeworth Letters*, 370. [12] *The Times*, 1 May, 5 June 1822. [13] Ibid. 10 Feb. 1823. [14] Ibid. 28 June 1823. [15] Ibid. 3 May, 11 July 1823. [16] Ibid. 19 Feb., 16., 17 Mar. 1824. [17] Ibid. 1 Mar. 1825. [18] Ibid. 26 Feb. 1825. [19] Ibid. 25 Mar. 1825. [20] Ibid. 16, 28 Feb., 8 Mar., 21 Apr. 1826. [21] *Herts Mercury*, 3, 10, 17 June 1826. [22] *The Times*, 3 Mar. 1827. [23] Ibid. 27 Mar., 10 Apr. 1827. [24] *Geo. IV Letters*, iii. 1328. [25] *The Times*, 8, 16 June 1827. [26] *Harewood mss*, Backhouse to Lady Canning, 15 May 1828. [27] *Herts Mercury*, 4 Oct. 1828. [28] *Grey mss*, Howick jnl. 10 Mar. [29] *Add.* 40333, f. 101. [30] *Howick jnl.* 21 June. [31] *Hatfield House mss* 2M/Gen., Price to Salisbury, 29 July, reply [July]; *Herts Mercury*, 10 July, 14 Aug. 1830. [32] *Three Diaries*, 13. [33] *County Herald*, 9 Apr. 1831. [34] *Hatfield House mss* 2M, Sebright to Nicholson, 22 Apr.; *County Herald*, 7, 14 May 1831. [35] *County Press*, 23, 30 Aug., 6 Sept. 1831. [36] Ibid. 4 Oct. 1831. [37] *Three Diaries*, 168; *NLS mss* 24762, f. 49. [38] *Herts Mercury*, 23, 30 June, 7 July 1832. [39] *VCH Herts.* ii. 196, 200; *Gent. Mag.* (1846), ii. 93. [40] *PROB* 11/2039/541; *IR26/1753/483*; *Gent. Mag.* (1822), i.369; ii. 478. *Burke PB* wrongly attributes the marriage to Frederica Anne Sebright and the death to Franks.

D.R.F.

SEFTON, earl of [I] *see* **MOLYNEUX, William Philip**

SEVERN (formerly **CHEESMENT**), **John** (1781–1875), of Penybont Hall, Rad.

WOOTTON BASSETT	1807–25 Jan. 1808
FOWEY	1830–1832

b. 27 Oct. 1781, o.s. of Capt. John Cheesment, master mariner, of Mile End, Mdx. and 2nd w. Sarah, da. of Thomas Grace of Graceville, Castledermot, co. Kildare. *educ.* Eton 1796; Christ Church, Oxf. 1800; L. Inn 1801, called 1807. *m.* 30 Dec. 1811, Mary Ann, da. and h. of John Price, banker, of Penybont Hall and Devannor Park, Rad., 1s. 3da. *suc.* fa. 1783; took name of Severn in 'memory of William Severn late of Pall Mall esq. deceased' by royal lic. 1 Aug. 1807.[1] *d.* 17 Dec. 1875. Sheriff, Rad. 1811-12.

Severn, a socially ambitious barrister who had sat briefly for Wootton Bassett in 1807-8, 'began buying land in at least two parts of Radnorshire' in 1808 and consolidated his position in that county three years later through marriage to the 18-year-old heiress to the Penybont estate. He devoted part of his energies in the next few years to the rebuilding of Penybont Hall.[2]

He was returned unopposed for Fowey in 1830 on the interest of George Lucy*, presumably as a paying guest.[3]

The duke of Wellington's ministry regarded him as one of their 'friends', and he duly voted with them in the crucial civil list division, 15 Nov. 1830. He presented anti-slavery petitions from the Baptists of Llanbister and the inhabitants of Mynyddyslwyn, 25 Nov., but bowed to pressure not to have them printed, to save expense. He introduced a Stagecoach Regulation Act amendment bill, to improve passenger safety, 10 Dec. 1830, but it made no further progress. He presented a Fowey petition for repeal of the coastwise coal duty, 16 Feb. 1831. He divided against the second reading of the Grey ministry's reform bill, which proposed to disfranchise Fowey, 22 Mar., and for Gascoyne's wrecking amendment, 19 Apr. 1831. About this time Joseph Austen, the joint patron of Fowey, wrote that 'my friends connected with the mining interest ... feel very much obliged ... for your exertions in getting the [truck] bill so altered as not to affect our mining system'.[4] He was returned unopposed at the general election later that month.[5] He presented a Fowey petition for repeal of the duty on marine insurance policies, 29 June 1831. He voted against the second reading of the reintroduced reform bill, 6 July, and for an adjournment motion, 12 July, use of the 1831 census to determine the disfranchisement schedules, 19 July, and postponement of the consideration of Chippenham's inclusion in B, 27 July. On 21 July he recited statistics from a Fowey memorial to the home secretary against the borough's disfranchisement, to show that ministers 'do not practice what they preach, respecting the consideration of increasing commercial prospects, in their plan of disfranchising boroughs'; but he had no hope that they would reconsider their decision. He divided against the bill's passage, 21 Sept., and the second reading of the Scottish bill, 23 Sept. He paired against the second reading of the revised reform bill, 17 Dec. 1831, and voted against the enfranchisement of Tower Hamlets, 28 Feb., and the third reading, 22 Mar. 1832. In June he broached with Lucy and Austen the idea of vacating his seat immediately in favour of a friend, but was dissuaded because of the inconvenience involved. Lucy suspected that

> if he had found Parliament beneficial, as it might have been, if the reform measure had not spoilt it, I should never have heard a wish about his resigning. He wanted a seat for some particular object, which finding he cannot attain is disappointed, and backs out, or wishes to do so, with as little loss as he can'.[6]

Severn was absent from the divisions on the Russian-Dutch loan in July 1832, having paired off for the

session with Sir Thomas Winnington.[7] His parliamentary career ended with the disfranchisement of Fowey.

In October 1833 Sir John Benn Walsh*, on a visit to Penybont, noted in his diary that Severn was 'not a very popular man in this part of the world. He is supposed to be rather near, with a good deal of ostentation, and I believe there may be some truth in the charge. Yet he is an obliging man, with rather gentlemanlike manners'.[8] He died in December 1875 and was succeeded by his eldest son John Percy Cheesment Severn (1814-1900), a barrister.[9]

[1] R.C.B. Oliver, *Squires of Penybont Hall*, 29. The circumstances remain unclear, as no will of William Severn has been found. [2] Ibid. 22-23, 30, 35-37, 43-44. [3] *West Briton*, 30 July 1830. [4] Cornw. RO AD 275/3. [5] *West Briton*, 6 May 1831. [6] Treffry mss (History of Parliament Aspinall transcripts), Lucy to Austen, 14, 24 June, 23 July 1832. [7] *The Times*, 24 July 1832. [8] Oliver, 49. [9] Ibid. 59-63 for details of the will.

T.A.J.

SEYMOUR, Edward Adolphus, Lord Seymour (1804–1885), of 18 Spring Gardens, Mdx.[1]

OKEHAMPTON	1830–1831
TOTNES	17 Feb. 1834–15 Aug. 1855

b. 20 Dec. 1804, 1st s. of Edward Adolphus, 11th duke of Somerset, and 1st w. Lady Charlotte Hamilton, da. of Archibald Hamilton[†], 9th duke of Hamilton [S]. *educ.* Eton 1817-21; Christ Church, Oxf. 1823; European tour. *m.* 10 June 1830, Jane Georgiana, da. of Thomas Sheridan, paymaster at Cape of Good Hope, 2s. *d.v.p.* 3da. *suc.* fa. as 12th duke of Somerset 15 Aug. 1855; KG 21 May 1862; *cr.* Earl Saint Maur 19 June 1863. *d.* 28 Nov. 1885.

Ld. of treasury Apr. 1835-Nov. 1839; sec. to bd. of control Sept. 1839-June 1841; under-sec. of state for home affairs June-Sept. 1841; first commr. of woods Apr. 1850-Oct. 1851, of works and public buildings Oct. 1851-Mar. 1852; PC 23 Oct. 1851; first ld. of admiralty June 1859-July 1866.

Commr. of lunacy 1836-52; gov. R. Naval Coll. Portsmouth 1859-66; ld. lt. Devon 1861-*d.*

Seymour's father was a lifelong devotee of science and mathematics, a knowledgeable antiquarian and historian, and a member and patron of learned societies. Credited with 'great amiability of temper and gentleness of manners', he was reputedly henpecked by his Scottish wife, who carried domestic pennypinching to 'a very extraordinary length'. His politics were Whig, though his heart was not much in them. He made an unsuccessful bid for household office in 1796 and hankered after a blue ribbon, which he eventually obtained from Lord Melbourne's ministry in 1837.[2] Seymour's education was carefully attended to, and he inherited his father's intellectual curiosity, particularly for things mechanical. He was a bright but indolent boy, as his mother noted in 1815:

> He has a great deal of curiosity upon every subject and delights in receiving information, but can't bear the trouble of acquiring it from books ... He is very quick, extremely idle, and can't bear the least trouble, but his mind is activity itself. You would be surprised at the questions he asks, and the subjects upon which he reasons, the more so as his manner is particularly childish ... His character is very downright and open, and *I* think too much destitute of pride and ambition. I should like a little of the former and a great deal of the latter.

Three years later Somerset expressed concern about his son's character, observing that 'his levity and facility are not suited to this country. An Eton education seems the most likely to make him manly ... [but] if it does not, I do not know what else to do for him'. The regime at Eton apparently did the trick. Shortly before going to Oxford in 1823 Seymour had the idea of accompanying his father's friend Charles Babbage, the mathematical inventor, on his tour of the manufacturing districts, to examine the 'engines and machinery' which fascinated him, but practical difficulties put paid to the plan.[3] After leaving Oxford he travelled extensively in Europe, including Russia and Germany. Henry Fox*, who met him in Rome, found him to be a 'simple, unaffected, sensible young man; I was rather prepossessed by his manners. He seems to have a desire of improving his knowledge'.[4] His amorous exploits and marital prospects created gossip. Early in 1828 Lady Holland, rejoicing that he had 'escaped the toils' of the dowager countess of Sandwich and the 'brazen, hoydenish, old, rouged coquette' Mlle. D'Este, illegitimate daughter of the duke of Sussex, wrote that 'he is a person to be very happy with, and might with good connections become something remarkable; but it will depend upon the characters of the persons he is allied with'. In April 1830 Eleanor Fazakerley reported that he was 'paying prodigious attention' to one of the daughters of Cuthbert Ellison, the wealthy Member for Newcastle, but added that 'he is such a systematic flirt, that till he proposes to some girl I shall never believe he means anything'.[5] Soon afterwards he married 'the most lovely woman in England', Georgy Sheridan, one of the three attractive granddaughters of the dramatist (one of the others became Caroline Norton, who achieved notoriety as Melbourne's mistress). She was 'exquisitely beautiful', with 'clusters of the darkest hair and the most brilliant complexion [and] a contour of face perfectly ideal'. In 1839 she

presided as 'Queen of Beauty' at the Eglinton Castle tournament.[6]

Seymour had joined Brooks's Club, 28 Feb. 1827. He attended the Devon county meeting called to petition Parliament against Catholic emancipation, 16 Jan. 1829, when he seconded a pro-Catholic amendment and made what Lady Holland described as 'a good speech' on 'the liberal side', although he was eventually shouted down. He told a subsequent dinner meeting that no one was 'more zealous' than he in support of the principle of emancipation.[7] At the general election of 1830 he was returned for Okehampton on the Savile interest, which had been arranged for some time. Lady Seymour noted that he was 'very anxious to get into Parliament' and that 'his whole soul is in politics'; though he was 'very shy, he does not mind, but rather likes, speaking'.[8] The duke of Wellington's ministry listed him as one of their 'foes', and he duly voted against them in the crucial civil list division, 15 Nov. 1830. However, he was a conspicuous absentee from the Devon meetings on parliamentary reform in November 1830 and March 1831.[9] On 4 Mar. he caused a stir by speaking 'fantastically against' the Grey ministry's reform bill, which he condemned as the product of 'the law of popularity'. He announced that he had 'left the side of the House on which I have usually sat, and taken my place among those who, looking to the preservation of the constitution, the security of the throne, and the permanent good of the people, reject rash and revolutionary measures'. While Greville thought his 'defection' was 'unexpected', the duke of Bedford was not surprised by it.[10] Seymour divided against the bill's second reading, 22 Mar., and presented an Okehampton petition against disfranchisement, 13 Apr., but he voted with the government against Gascoyne's wrecking amendment, 19 Apr. 1831. He did not stand at the ensuing general election, when two firm anti-reformers came in for Okehampton.[11]

His father supported the reform bills in the Lords, and in the summer of 1832 Lord Grey considered Lord Ebrington's* suggestion that Seymour might be a suitable candidate for elevation to that House, acknowledging that 'the duke of Somerset is entitled to every consideration from us, and it must also be my wish, as it is my interest, to conciliate Lord Seymour'.[12] Nothing came of this, and in 1834 he was returned for Totnes, which lay near his father's Berry Pomeroy estate. He was soon a junior minister and subsequently held cabinet office in the Liberal administrations of Russell and Palmerston. He succeeded to his father's dukedom in 1855. Benjamin

Disraeli[†] credited him with 'great talent, which develops itself in a domestic circle', though he was 'otherwise shy' and had 'bad manners'. His friend John Cam Hobhouse* considered him to be 'a much more clever man than his look and manners would induce anyone to believe', and Lady Holland maintained that 'there cannot be a more estimable and agreeable man'.[13] He died in November 1885 and was succeeded in turn by his brothers Archibald Henry Algernon (1810-91), and Algernon Percy Banks (1813-94).

[1] See *Letters, Remains and Mems. of 12th duke of Somerset* ed. W.H. Mallock and Lady G. Ramsden, which prints correspondence now in Bucks. RO, Bulstrode mss D/RA/A. [2] Based on *Gent. Mag.* (1855), ii. 425-6; H. St. Maur, *Annals of Seymours*, 338-40; *Farington Diary*, x. 3572; xiv. 4911; *Faraday Corresp.* ed. F. James, i. 327, 347, 473; *Later Corresp. Geo. III*, ii. 1470; iv. 2837; v. 3966; *Prince of Wales Corresp.* iv. 1469; Add. 37183-6, *passim*. [3] *Somerset Letters*, 6-10; St. Maur, 342; *Two Brothers*, 207, 210, 220, 261; Add. 37183, ff. 66, 68. [4] Broughton, *Recollections*, iii. 260; *Fox Jnl.* 244. [5] *Lady Holland to Son*, 128; Add. 52011, Mrs. Fazakerley to Fox, 14 Apr. 1830. [6] Broughton, *Recollections*, iv. 27; v. 82; *Von Neumann Diary*, i. 211; *Disraeli Letters*, i. 234; iii. 992; *Howard Sisters*, 160-2, 173. [7] *Western Times*, 17 Jan. 1829; *Lady Holland to Son*, 94. [8] *Western Times*, 7 Aug. 1830; *Somerset Letters*, 24, 28. [9] *Western Times*, 27 Nov. 1830, 19 Mar. 1831. [10] *Greville Mems.* ii. 127; Add. 51576, Fazakerley to Holland [4 Mar.]; 51670, Bedford to Lady Holland [6 Mar. 1831]. [11] *Western Times*, 7 May 1831. [12] Devon RO, Earl Fortescue mss 1262M/FC88, Grey to Ebrington, 19 Aug. 1832. [13] *Disraeli Letters*, i. 283; Broughton, *Recollections*, v. 238; *Lady Holland to Son*, 201.

D.R.F./T.A.J.

SEYMOUR, Henry (1776–1849), of Knoyle House, Hindon, Wilts.; Northbrook Lodge, Devon, and 39 Upper Grosvenor Street, Mdx.

TAUNTON   1826–1830

b. 10 Nov. 1776, o.s. of Henry Seymour of Redland Court, Glos.[1] and Northbrook Lodge and 2nd w. Louise de la Martelliere, countess of Panthou. m. 12 Jan. 1817, Jane, da. of Benjamin Hopkinson of Blagdon Court, Som., 2s. 3da. suc. fa. 1805. d. 27 Nov. 1849. Sheriff, Wilts. 1835-6.

Seymour, a second cousin of the 11th duke of Somerset and the son of a groom of the bedchamber to George III, was detained in France, 1803-14, when he was 'one of the very few Englishmen exempted from close confinement', having obtained 'permission to remain at large ... from the Emperor Napoleon'. He returned to take up his inheritance, 'without having lost English sympathies by a long forced residence abroad'.[2] The owner of scattered properties in Somerset,[3] he offered for Taunton in 1820 in succession to Henry Powell Collins, the brother-in-law of Sir Thomas Lethbridge*, who had territorial influence in the borough. He declared himself to be 'a firm friend of the glorious constitution of this happy country' and 'a determined enemy to the innovating spirit of modern demagogues', who would give independent support to Lord Liverpool's ministry. At the end of polling he trailed the second-placed Whig candidate, John Ashley Warre, by five votes, but demanded a scrutiny on the ground that Warre and the other Whig, Alexander Baring, had secretly coalesced to prevent a free and fair election; the result was to widen Seymour's deficit to nine, and he withdrew his case.[4] He reappeared in the borough in the autumn of 1825, when feeling was running high against the Whig Members owing to their support for Catholic relief, and a canvass suggested that he was certain of success.[5] At the general election the following summer he was described as a local man from a venerable family, 'independent in property [and] beyond the remotest reach or suspicion of temptation', who would 'not espouse the side of Whig or Tory' but pursue an independent course. In his own words, he was 'a constitutional man' and a supporter of 'civil and religious liberty', but above all he was 'a Protestant and ... shall never deviate from this persuasion'. He advocated an unspecified revision of the corn laws, pointing to the interdependence of trade and agriculture. He was returned at the head of the poll after a lengthy contest.[6]

He divided against Catholic relief, 6 Mar. 1827. Affirming his hostility to Catholic claims, which 'it would be found impossible to ram ... down the throats of the people of England', he nevertheless announced his intention of supporting Canning's coalition ministry 'until that question came to be discussed', 2 May. He may have been the H. Seymour who voted with government against the Penryn election bill, 7 June. He presented petitions for repeal of the Test Acts from Taunton, 20 June 1827, and Fulwood, Somerset, 19 Feb., which suggests that it was possibly not he who voted against that measure, 26 Feb. 1828. He divided against Catholic claims, 12 May. He supported an individual's petition for compensation for property lost during the French Revolution, 23 June, observing that 'my father was robbed of his property in 1790' and 'I shall always consider that government owes me £3,000'. He presented a Taunton anti-slavery petition, 30 June. He may have voted for the corporate funds bill, 10 July 1828. The volte face performed by Seymour's patron Lethbridge on Catholic emancipation placed him in an awkward position. In February 1829 Planta, the Wellington ministry's patronage secretary, originally listed Seymour among those 'opposed to the principle', but his name was later scored through and added to the list of Members who would side 'with government'. His name did not appear in the published division lists of 6, 30 Mar., but a local newspaper was authorized to state that he had voted for emancipation on the first occasion.[7] He presented and concurred in a favourable petition from Taunton, 13 Mar., arguing that the measure would do nothing to harm Protestant establishments. When his colleague William Peachey presented a more numerously signed hostile petition from Taunton, 16 Mar., Seymour regretted its 'violent' wording and claimed that while the inhabitants were 'formerly unanimous against concession ... they have now improved much in liberality'. He presented a Taunton silk weavers' petition against the importation of foreign silk and drew the House's attention to the 'utmost distress and destitution' into which they had sunk, 13 Apr. It was probably he who voted against the silk bill, 1 May, and he presented a petition from two Somerset silk throwsters requesting compensation for the depreciation of their capital as a result of government measures, 5 May 1829. It may have been he who voted against the proposal to enfranchise Birmingham, Leeds and Manchester, 23 Feb. 1830. He reportedly voted with the majority to abolish the Bathurst and Dundas pensions, 26 Mar., and with the minority for inquiry into the management of crown land revenues, 30 Mar.[8] He presented a Taunton petition against renewal of the East India Company's charter, 6 Apr. He voted for restrictions to the sale of beer bill, 1 July 1830. In early June he announced that he had decided 'many months' before not to stand again at Taunton, but declared his attachment to Wellington's 'enlightened government' and its 'liberal and wise policy'. No evidence has been found to corroborate the claim made in local Whig circles that he had wished to offer but Lethbridge had refused to support him.[9] He did not contest another seat at that general election, but may have been the Seymour mentioned as a possible Tory candidate for Coventry in 1831.[10]

Seymour devoted the later years of his life to consolidating his estate in Wiltshire, where he laboured to 'fulfil the duties of an English gentleman and a Christian'.[11] He died in November 1849 and left his estates to his eldest son, Henry Danby Seymour (1820-77), Liberal Member for Poole, 1850-68.[12]

[1] Sold in 1811 for £13,000 (N. Kingsley, *Country Houses of Glos*, 203). [2] *Gent. Mag.* (1850), i. 212. His father's will was sworn under £17,500 (PROB 11/1462/440; IR26/123/338). [3] *VCH Som.* iii. 74; vi. 260; W. Phelps, *Som.* (1836), 332. [4] *Taunton Courier*, 9, 16 Feb., 15, 29 Mar., 12 Apr. 1820. [5] Ibid. 28 Sept.; *Bristol Mirror*, 8 Oct. 1825. [6] *Taunton Courier*, 21 June 1826. [7] Ibid. 18 Mar. 1829. [8] *The Times*, 1 Apr. 1830. [9] *Taunton Courier*, 9 June, 25 Aug. 1830. [10] Add. 36466, f. 410. [11] *VCH Wilts*. xi. 86-89, 91-92; *Gent. Mag.* (1850), i. 212. [12] PROB 11/2110/241; IR26/1881/203.

T.A.J.

SEYMOUR, Horace Beauchamp (1791–1851), of 23 Bruton Street, Mdx.[1]

LISBURN	22 Feb. 1819–1826
BODMIN	1826–1832
MIDHURST	1841–12 Dec. 1845
CO. ANTRIM	22 Dec. 1845–1847
LISBURN	1847–21 Nov. 1851

b. 22 Nov. 1791, 3rd s. of Hon. Hugh Seymour Conway[†] (afterwards Seymour) (*d.* 1801) of Hambledon, Hants and Lady Anna Horatia Waldegrave, da. and coh. of James, 2nd Earl Waldegrave; bro. of Hugh Henry John Seymour*. *educ.* Harrow 1803. *m.* (1) 15 May 1818, Elizabeth Malet (*d.* 18 Jan. 1827), da. of Sir Lawrence Palk[†], 2nd bt., of Haldon House, Devon, 2s. 1da.; (2) 9 July 1835,[2] Frances Selina Isabella, da. of William Stephen Poyntz*, wid. of Robert Cotton St. John Trefusis, 18th Bar. Clinton, *s.p.* KCH 1836. *d.* 21 Nov. 1851.

Lt. RN 1809; cornet 10 Drag. 1811, lt. 1812; lt. 18 Drag. 1814; capt. 60 Ft. 1815; capt. 23 Drag. 1815; capt. 1 Life Gds. 1815; brevet lt.-col. 1815; half-pay 1819, sold out 1835.

Gentleman usher to prince regent 1818-20, to George IV 1820-30, to William IV 1830-1; equerry to William IV 1832-7, to Queen Victoria June-July 1837; extra equerry to Queen Adelaide Mar. 1838.

Seymour's father, an army officer and long-serving Member, was a younger son of the 1st marquess of Hertford, and Seymour owed his advancement in life to his aristocratic connections. After a false start in the navy, he entered the army, and was described by Harriette Wilson (erroneously as to his parentage) as 'a gay, dashing son of Lord Somebody Seymour, of the 10th Hussars, whom everybody knows and few care much about'. Reputedly one of the strongest officers in the forces, he was said to have slain more men than anyone else at Waterloo. He received several promotions in 1815, including apparently one to the rank of lieutenant-colonel, as he was always thereafter known as 'Colonel' Seymour.[3] According to Lady Williams Wynn, in May 1818 his wedding took place

in St. George's [Hanover Square] at half past seven by owl light, the bridegroom having had half an hour to pass with the verger waiting for the rest of the company who likewise were waiting for the principal performer, the bishop of Gloucester, he being locked in the House of Lords for a division.[4]

That month, no doubt through his uncle, the 2nd marquess of Hertford, the lord chamberlain, and his wife, the regent's mistress, Seymour was appointed a gentleman usher of the privy chamber. He joined the half-pay list the following year.

Brought in by Hertford for his pocket borough of Lisburn in February 1819, Seymour was an inactive supporter of the Liverpool administration, like his brother Hugh, who represented county Antrim on the Hertford interest from 1818 until his death in 1821.[5] At the general election of 1820 he was returned for both Lisburn and Orford, one of Hertford's English boroughs, but chose to continue to sit for the former. His only known vote that session, unless it was his brother's, was against making economies in revenue collection, 4 July 1820. He divided in defence of ministers' conduct towards Queen Caroline, 6 Feb. 1821. Either he or Hugh paired against repeal of the additional malt duty, 3 Apr., and voted with government against economies, 28 May, 18 June 1821. He divided against reduction of the salt duties, 28 Feb., and abolition of one of the joint-postmasterships, 13 Mar. 1822. The 3rd marquess of Hertford, who had succeeded to his father's title that summer, pleaded with Peel, the home secretary, for 'something for Horace' as well as the Garter, as the price of his political support. It is not known if any position was offered to Seymour, but he thanked Hertford for his liberality, 2 Oct. 1822.[6] He was appointed to the corporations of Hertford's Suffolk boroughs, Aldeburgh and Orford, during that year.[7]

Seymour voted against abolition of the house tax, 10 Mar., repeal of the Foreign Enlistment Act, 16 Apr., reform of the Scottish representative system, 2 June, and inquiry into chancery administration, 5 June 1823. He divided against alteration of the representation of Edinburgh, 26 Feb., and inquiry into the trial of the Methodist missionary John Smith in Demerara, 11 June 1824. He voted for the Irish unlawful societies bill, 15, 25 Feb., and against the Irish franchise bill, 26 Apr. 1825. As he had, 28 Feb. 1821 and (pairing) 30 Apr. 1822, he divided against Catholic relief, 1 Mar., 21 Apr.; enticed away by Hertford's hospitality, he paired (probably with Croker) in this sense, 10 May 1825.[8] He was in the minority against the second reading of the spring guns bill, 21 June. In September 1825 Hertford commented that 'dissolution or no dissolution if I can job out something for Horace I shall be glad, if not I suppose I may well let him sell for his own advantage'. But the following March Hertford lamented that Seymour had again been passed over for military promotion.[9] Croker's arrangements for the return of himself and another Protestant Member for Aldeburgh were made conditional on some reward being granted to Seymour, but this linkage evidently came to nothing.[10] At the general election of 1826 he left Lisburn, which Hertford wanted for another of his cousins, and, again having no need to fall back on Orford, came in for Bodmin, where his patron was cultivating an interest.[11]

Following the death of his wife in January, Seymour was given leave from the House for two weeks, 12 Feb., and for a further month, 10 Apr. 1827. In February Hertford applied to the duke of Wellington, the commander-in-chief, for a posting for Seymour, but nothing came of a plan whereby Hertford would pay off his debts in order to allow him to purchase a full-pay commission.[12] He paired against Catholic relief, 6 Mar. Unless it was Henry Seymour, Member for Taunton, he voted against the Penryn election bill, 7 June. In November 1827, Sir Henry Hardinge* reported to Mrs. Arbuthnot that 'one of Lord Hertford's Members' had been 'desired to vote in any way the duke wishes – but Seymour, I am told, has been desired to do the same, *unless the duke of Wellington accepts* the office of *commander-in-chief*'.[13] When Wellington succeeded Lord Goderich as prime minister in January 1828, Hertford remarked that

as to myself, if I can muster strength to obtain two or three favours, not more than one Member of Parliament commonly gets, I shall not grumble, but I shall preserve my independence, which I will not barter for a favour to Horace S.C. (for whom *I* want none now) – nor does *he*; for the family doubt whether I have influence enough over him to get him down to the House of Commons and I have no fancy for a Bodmin re-election.[14]

He was probably the 'H. Seymour' who voted against repeal of the Test Acts, 26 Feb., and he again divided against Catholic relief, 12 May 1828.

In February 1829 Seymour confided to Hertford that he had hopes of marrying one of the Misses FitzClarence, but having bluntly told her father, the duke of Clarence, that his prospects were 'none', he needed a life interest of £1,000 a year; whether or not this was forthcoming, no marriage took place.[15] That month he was listed by Planta, the patronage secretary, as likely to be 'with government' on Catholic emancipation, and Hertford urged him, insofar as it was compatible with his wishes, to support administration.[16] Yet Seymour, who was a defaulter from the call of the House, 5 Mar., cast no votes on the subject. This was much to Hertford's embarrassment, as it put him in the wrong not only with ministers but with Davies Gilbert, the co-proprietor of (and other Member for) Bodmin. On 9 Mar. Seymour, who had misunderstood his instructions, wrote an anxious letter to his patron in Italy explaining that he had abstained because Hertford's opinions conflicted with those of his constituents, and concluding that 'I wish for my own sake you had been in Piccadilly, I could not then have done wrong which I am now much in doubt about'.[17] Unless it was his namesake Henry, he voted against the committal of the silk trade bill, 1 May 1829, and the enfranchisement of Birmingham, Leeds and Manchester, 23 Feb. 1830. He divided against transferring East Retford's seats to Birmingham, 11 Feb., reducing the admiralty grant, 22 Mar., Jewish emancipation, 17 May, and abolition of the death penalty for forgery, 7 June. Having been returned for Bodmin at the general election that year, he was listed by ministers among their 'friends', and he divided in their minority on the civil list, 15 Nov. 1830.

Seymour voted against the second reading of the Grey ministry's reform bill, 22 Mar. 1831, after which he was dismissed from his household position.[18] He divided with opposition in favour of Gascoyne's wrecking amendment, 19 Apr., which precipitated a dissolution. At the ensuing general election he was again returned for Bodmin, although he may have been the Seymour who was mentioned as a possible Tory candidate at Coventry, where Hertford also had an interest.[19] He voted against the second reading of the reintroduced reform bill, 6 July, to postpone consideration of the partial disfranchisement of Chippenham, 27 July, to censure the Irish government over the Dublin election, 23 Aug., and against the passage of the reform bill, 21 Sept. He divided against the second reading of the revised bill, 17 Dec. 1831, for Hunt's motion for giving the vote to all taxpaying householders, 2 Feb., and against the enfranchisement of Tower Hamlets, 28 Feb. 1832. He voted against the third reading, 22 Mar., and paired (with Sir Charles Paget) against the second reading of the Irish bill, 25 May. His only other known votes were with opposition against the Russian-Dutch loan, 26 Jan., 12 July. Partly through Hertford's influence, he was in September reinstated as an equerry, and Thomas Raikes noted that 'this nomination of an ultra-Tory to the household must prove to Lord Grey the real bias of the king'. Hertford, who called him a 'royal Hanoverian and no longer a Tory', observed that Seymour 'wished to retire from Bodmin rather than from the household'. He declined an opening in county Antrim at the general election in December 1832, when he found himself without a seat.[20]

According to Lady Bedingfeld, who had it directly from him, Seymour

> was left early an orphan, the sister and brothers were taken by different relations; his uncle, Lord Hertford, took him, and he was put in the army, and went young to India; he served all the war, he is now a widower with three children, a fine figure and handsome but a rather coarse, muddled complexion.[21]

Seymour, who returned to the Commons as a Conservative in 1841, died intestate at Brighton in November 1851.[22] His elder son Charles Francis (1819-54) was killed at the battle of Inkerman. The younger, Admiral Frederick Beauchamp Paget (1821-95), became in 1882 the first and only Baron Alcester.

[1] His surname is sometimes, e.g. in the *Returns*, given as Seymour-Seymour. [2] IGI. [3] A.M. Annand, 'Col. Sir Horace Seymour', *Jnl. for Soc. of Army Hist. Research*, xlvii (1969), 86-88; *Harriette Wilson Mems.* (1929), 410. [4] *Williams Wynn Corresp.* 208. [5] *HP Commons, 1790-1820*, v. 122-3. [6] Add. 40350, f. 28; Eg. 3261, f. 100. [7] *PP* (1835), xxvi. 2086, 2510. [8] Add. 60287, ff. 84, 87. [9] Ibid. ff. 114, 184. [10] Add. 38301, f. 208. [11] Add. 60287, f. 198. [12] Wellington mss WP1/883/6, 9; 884/15. [13] *Arbuthnot Corresp.* 92. [14] Add. 60288, f. 13. [15] Eg. 3261, f. 240. [16] Add. 60288, f. 107. [17] Ibid. ff. 122, 139, 163. [18] *Creevey Pprs.* ii. 225. [19] Add. 36466, f. 410. [20] Add. 60289, ff. 45, 70; *Raikes Jnl.* i. 79. [21] *Jerningham Letters*, ii. 395. [22] *The Times*, 25 Nov.; *Suss. Advertiser*, 2 Dec. 1851. Most sources wrongly give 23 Nov. 1851 as his death date, including *Gent. Mag.* (1852), i. 91-92.

S.M.F.

SEYMOUR, Hugh Henry John (1790–1821), of 244 Piccadilly, Mdx.

CO. ANTRIM	1818–2 Dec. 1821

b. 25 Sept. 1790, 2nd s. of Hon. Hugh Seymour Conway† (afterwards Seymour) (*d.* 1801) of Hambledon, Hants and Lady Anna Horatia Waldegrave, da. and coh. of James, 2nd Earl Waldegrave; bro. of Horace Beauchamp Seymour*. *educ.* Harrow 1803. *m.* 18 May 1818, Lady Charlotte Georgiana Cholmondeley, da. of George James, 1st mq. of Cholmondeley, 1s. *d.* 2 Dec. 1821.
Ensign 3 Ft. Gds. 1805, lt. and capt. 1811, capt. and lt.-col. 1815; equerry in ordinary 1818-*d.*; lt.-col. (half-pay) 71 Ft. 1820-*d.*

On Seymour's wedding day in May 1818, Lady Williams Wynn reported that he was to marry Lady Charlotte Cholmondeley

> *en grande cérémonie* at ten o'clock, under the auspices of [the] p[rince] r[egent], who is to give her away. I should not like to see my son receive a bride from such an unlucky hand, nor should I think my daughter's virgin purity unpolluted in approaching the altar through so gross an atmosphere.[1]

His father-in-law, a notorious lecher, was lord steward of the household and his uncle the 2nd marquess of Hertford, on whose interest he was twice returned for Antrim, was lord chamberlain, as well as the regent's cuckold. Seymour, who was not in the end challenged at the general election of 1820, continued to support the Liverpool government silently.[2] He voted against economies in revenue collection, 4 July 1820 (unless this was Horace), and in defence of their conduct towards Queen Caroline, 6 Feb. 1821. He divided against Catholic relief, 28 Feb. Either he or his brother paired against repeal of the additional malt duty, 3 Apr., and voted against economies, 28 May, 18 June. Reputed never to have wholly recovered from Walcheren fever, he obtained a month's sick leave, 9 May. He died, intestate and 'in the prime of life', in December 1821, less than three months after the birth of his son.[3] On 26 Jan. 1822 administration of his estate, including personalty sworn under £8,000, was granted to his widow.[4] A year later she was reported to be 'still in weeds and suffering the greatest anxiety about her baby, who is very weakly'.[5] She died in 1828, but Hugh Horatio Seymour survived until 1892.

[1] *Williams Wynn Corresp.* 207-8. [2] *Belfast News Letter*, 3, 24 Mar. 1820; *HP Commons, 1790-1820*, v. 123. [3] *Belfast News Letter*, 11 Dec. 1821; *Gent. Mag.* (1821), ii. 573. [4] PROB 6/198. [5] *Arbuthnot Jnl.* i. 197.

D.R.F.

SEYMOUR CONWAY, **Francis Charles**, earl of Yarmouth (1777–1842).

ORFORD	31 July 1797–1802
LISBURN	1802–1812
CO. ANTRIM	1812–1818
CAMELFORD	1820–17 June 1822

b. 11 Mar. 1777, o.s. of Francis Seymour Conway[†], 2nd mq. of Hertford, and 2nd w. Hon. Isabella Anne Ingram Shepheard, da. and coh. of Charles Ingram[†], 9th Visct. Irvine [S]. *educ.* Christ Church, Oxf. 1794; St. Mary Hall, Oxf. 1796. *m.* 18 May 1798, Maria Emily, legal[1] da. of John Baptist, Mq. Fagnani, 2s. 1da. *d.v.p. styled* Visct. Beauchamp 1793-4, earl of Yarmouth 1794-1822; GCH 1819; *suc.* fa. as 3rd mq. of Hertford 17 June 1822; KG 22 Nov. 1822. *d.* 1 Mar. 1842.

Minister plenip. to France June 1806; vice-chamberlain Mar.-July 1812; PC 20 Mar. 1812; warden of the stannaries Aug. 1812-d.; Garter mission to emperor of Russia 1827.

Custos rot. co. Antrim 1822-d.; vice-adm. Suff. 1822-d.; town clerk, Bodmin 1822; recorder, Coventry 1825.

Capt. Lisburn cav. 1796, Warws. militia 1803; col. commdt. R. Cornw. and Devon Miners 1814.

Yarmouth, who had joined Brooks's in 1795 and from 1797 had sat for three constituencies on the family interest, followed his father Lord Hertford in his support for Pitt's and subsequent Tory administrations. His principal allegiance was to the prince of Wales, who took his mother as a mistress in about 1807, appointed his father lord chamberlain when he became regent in 1812 and showered him and other relations with lucrative sinecures. However, by the mid-1810s Yarmouth's once considerable ascendancy over the prince had waned and, having already separated from his wife, he increasingly indulged his appetites for gambling, women and residence abroad.[2]

He retired from the representation of county Antrim at the dissolution in 1818, pleading ill health and personal reasons, which apparently had to do with his father's reluctance to see him continue in Parliament as 'his own master'.[3] He had already been evincing electoral ambitions in various Cornish boroughs, notably Camelford, of which he commented in June 1819 that 'I shall much prefer sitting for a place I find, and for myself, than for a family nomination'.[4] At the general election of 1820, when he wrested a seat from Lord Darlington's interest at Camelford, he commented to John Croker*, his factotum, that 'I don't care a D for the elections except [his friend Lord] Lowther's*, now I am got back to Seymour Place', his London house.[5] He evidently attended to some of his father's borough interests: for example, he oversaw Edmond MacNaghten's return for Orford at a by-election in May.[6] One of the silent supporters of Lord Liverpool's government who were angry at ministerial disarray, he 'stayed away altogether' from the division on the appointment of an additional Scottish baron of exchequer, 15 May.[7] The following month he complained of 'a cold and something like gout', and he was granted a week's leave on account of illness, 27 June 1820.[8] He cast no known votes that session.

In November 1820 Yarmouth, who expected the bill against Queen Caroline to be defeated in the Lords, wrote to Croker that

> I am sorry but do not wonder at your anxiety to see whatever sport there may be. To me there could be none, those with whom I would cheerfully have gone into opposition *totis viribus* have treated me unkindly and refused me the little favour I asked; and on the other hand the pleasure I might personally feel at their removal would be damped and destroyed by seeing you and Lord Lowther* and [John] Beckett* and some other friends dislodged from what amuses and is agreeable to you. *So* I am as well in a turnip field as anywhere.[9]

Despite being lukewarm towards ministers, he voted against censuring their treatment of the queen, 6 Feb. 1821. He paired against Catholic relief, 28 Feb. He divided against repeal of the additional malt duty, 21 Mar., 3 Apr., disqualifying civil officers of the ordnance from voting in parliamentary elections, 12 Apr., and the forgery punishment mitigation bill, 23 May. He voted against reduction of the barracks grant, 28,

31 May, and for the arrears payment to the duke of Clarence, 8, 18 June 1821.

In July 1821 he received the Knight Grand Cross of St. Anne of Russia. That month his father was forced into resigning from the household, where Lady Conyngham had succeeded Lady Hertford, the 'Sultana', as *maîtresse-en-titre*. Resentful of his fall from grace, Hertford renewed his application for a dukedom, which was refused by George IV, and insult was added to injury when early the following year the marquess of Buckingham was made a duke on coalescing with government with the remnant of the Grenvillite faction. As Yarmouth remarked in December 1821, 'so the Pitt party begin their *first honour* by breaking Pitt's promise to promote Lord Hertford if ever he promoted Lord Buckingham, but the latter has been an enemy, the former a firm friend'.[10] Suspecting that his father, who was apparently more or less 'out of his mind' by this time, might create legal difficulties over the succession, Yarmouth was obliged to follow his mother's interpretation of Hertford's desires concerning the by-election in county Antrim in January 1822. She told him that 'in short, you are the person who must manage all this', and he had to insist that his reluctant elder son, Lord Beauchamp, should go to Ireland to get himself elected.[11] He voted against more extensive tax reductions to relieve distress, 21 Feb., reduction of the salt duties, 28 Feb., and abolition of one of the joint-postmasterships, 13 Mar. He paired against the Catholic peers bill, 30 Apr. 1822, but, aware that Lowther, a junior minister, had 'found fault with *all* the Seymours for pairing', promised to attend in person on some unspecified occasion the following month.[12]

According to Countess Lieven, Yarmouth was 'waiting with indecent impatience the death of his father, but it should be said in his defence that the poor old man has become quite childish'.[13] When he succeeded as the 3rd marquess in June 1822 he inherited the bulk of personal wealth sworn under £300,000, estates in Ireland (valued at £57,000 a year), Warwickshire (£15,000), Suffolk (£10,000) and Scotland (£3,000), and the family's London residence in Manchester Square.[14] He took over his father's office of custos rotulorum of Antrim, being recommended by Henry Goulburn*, the Irish secretary, 'his weight being ... very great and his assistance while a Member of the House of Commons having been given very regularly and powerfully'.[15] Darlington won back the electoral patronage at Camelford, but Hertford, who was already building an interest at Bodmin, immediately sought seats elsewhere.[16] Lord

Yarmouth, as Beauchamp was now styled, exclaimed to his mother on 18 June that Hertford 'has already bought a borough in Parliament [Aldeburgh] and has given the Walkers 50,000 guineas for it – what do you think of that, and he is going to buy *two more* – what do you think of that!'[17] On the death of his cousin Lord Londonderry* in August 1822 he offered his seat at Orford to government and pressed them for some signal piece of patronage, such as a dukedom, as the price of his support.[18] Writing to Croker that month he told him that

> whenever you see Liverpool or Peel, if either talk to you, I think mystery always bad among intimates and therefore you had better say we talked it over last night and that I said I could fear no personal objection on His Majesty's part possessing as I do the king's letters since 1784 to 1819 ... Since the last date the king may have ceased to like frequenting Manchester House or our society but my poor father never failed a day on the queen's trial when he could be carried down and I after being out of Parliament got a seat to vote on her question as the king knows. I say nothing of this king's more peculiarly associating with Lord Hertford, but in your researches look whether any old household servants ever retired, without a change of sovereign or ministers, from long service without some step of rank or splendid mark of favour bestowed on him or his.[19]

Londonderry's garter was soon presented to him, and Creevey commented that Hertford owed it 'to his having purchased *four* seats in Parliament since his father's death, and to his avowed intention of dealing still more largely in the same commodity'.[20] Lady Williams Wynn, who recorded that Hertford complained of having '£60,000 *per annum* more than he can find what to do with', calculated that he controlled ten Members at the general election at 1826.[21] According to Lord Kenyon's diary, this figure had risen even higher by the dissolution in 1830, although many of his English borough interests were casualties of the Reform Act of 1832.

By his intimates, who included Croker and the strait-laced Peel, Hertford was well respected, and George Agar Ellis* commented on 29 Nov. 1822 that 'his faults make chiefly against himself – his qualities are many, though the world with its usual good nature dwells always upon the former and drops the latter'.[22] He played no further prominent part in politics; for instance, he declined William IV's offer of the lord chamberlainship in 1830 on the plea of poor health.[23] Instead he lapsed into a life of eccentricity and depravity, much of it spent in a secret love nest just off Park Lane. As Harriette Wilson described it:

He directed our attention to the convenience of opening the door, himself, to any fine lady who would honour him with a visit incognita, after his servants should have prepared a most delicious supper and retired to rest. He told us many curious anecdotes of the advantage he derived from his character for discretion: 'I never tell of any woman. No power on earth should induce me to name a single female, worthy to be called a woman, by whom I have been favoured. In the first place, because I am not tired of variety, and wish to succeed again: in the second, I think it dishonourable'.[24]

He died, having enjoyed a final debauch despite feeling unwell, in March 1842, when he was said to be worth over £2,000,000. By his extraordinary will, dated 25 Feb. 1823 with 29 codicils, he made (and unmade) numerous bequests, including one of over £20,000 and his wine cellar to Croker, and left several annuities to his lady friends, including a 'Mrs. Spencer'. A fraud case brought against Nicholas Suisse, a former servant and legatee, soon brought Hertford's private life into public notoriety. The bulk of the estates descended to his elder son, Richard Seymour Conway, 4th marquess of Hertford.[25] Greville's harsh verdict on the 3rd marquess was that

> no man ever lived more despised nor died less regretted. His life and his death were equally disgusting and revolting to every good and moral feeling. As Lord Yarmouth he was known as a sharp, cunning, luxurious, avaricious man of the world, with some talent ... He was a *bon vivant*, and when young and gay his parties were agreeable, and he contributed his share to their hilarity. But after he became Lord Hertford and the possessor of an enormous property he was puffed up with a vulgar pride, very unlike the real scion of a noble race ... After a great deal of coarse and vulgar gallantry, generally purchased at a high rate, he formed a connection with Lady Strachan [wife of Admiral Sir Richard Strachan], which thenceforward determined all the habits of his life ... There has been, as far as I know, no example of undisguised debauchery exhibited to the world like that of Lord Hertford, and his age and infirmities rendered it at once the more remarkable and the more shocking. Between 60 and 70 years old, broken with infirmities and almost unintelligible from a paralysis of the tongue, he has been in the habit of travelling about with a company of prostitutes, who formed his principal society.[26]

As well as other literary depictions, he appeared as Lord Monmouth in Benjamin Disraeli's[†] *Coningsby* (1844) and as the marquess of Steyne in William Thackeray's *Vanity Fair* (1847-8).[27]

[3] *Belfast News Letter*, 16 June 1818; *Croker Pprs*. i. 128. [4] Add. 60286, f. 162. [5] Ibid. f. 191; *R. Cornw. Gazette*, 11 Mar. 1820. [6] Add. 60286, f. 201. [7] Add. 30123, f. 157. [8] Add. 60286, f. 205. [9] Ibid. ff. 209, 210, 215. [10] Ibid. f. 232; Eg. 3261, f. 69. [11] *Palmerston-Sulivan Letters*, 151; Eg. 3261, f. 65; 3263, f. 130. [12] Add. 60286, f. 249. [13] B. Falk, '*Old Q's Daughter*', 117. [14] Add. 52471, f. 40; PROB 11/1659/372; IR26/911/705; *The Times*, 23 July, 16 Sept. 1822; *Gent. Mag.* (1822), 561; *Croker Pprs*. i. 239-40. [15] Add. 37299, ff. 228, 271. [16] *R. Cornw. Gazette*, 22, 29 June 1822; Add. 60286, ff. 238, 247, 250, 253, 256. [17] Eg. 3263, f. 142. [18] Add. 40350, f. 28. [19] Add. 60286, f. 261. [20] Eg. 3261, f. 90; Add. 38195, f. 116; 40304, f. 77; *Creevey Pprs*. ii. 56. [21] *Williams Wynn Corresp*. 308, 347. [22] *HP Commons, 1790-1820*, v. 127; Northants. RO, Agar Ellis diary. [23] *Arbuthnot Jnl*. ii. 367-9. [24] *Harriette Wilson Mems*. (1929), 275-6. [25] *The Times*, 3, 12, 14, 26, 29 Mar., 10 Aug. 1842; *Gent. Mag.* (1842), ii. 545-7; PROB 11/1964/405; *Croker Pprs*. ii. 415-22; Falk, 179-87. [26] *Greville Mems*. v. 19-20. [27] Falk, 175, 187-91; *DNB*; *Oxford DNB*.

S.M.F.

SEYMOUR CONWAY, Richard, Visct. Beauchamp (1800–1870).[1]

Co. ANTRIM	12 Jan. 1822–1826

b. 22 Feb. 1800, 1st s. of Francis Charles Seymour Conway*, earl of Yarmouth (later 3rd mq. of Hertford), and Maria Emily, legal da. of John Baptist, Mq. Fagnani. *educ.* private tutors; Exeter Coll. Oxf. 1818. *unm.* 1s. illegit. *styled* Visct. Beauchamp 1800-22, earl of Yarmouth 1822-42; *suc.* fa. as 4th mq. of Hertford 1 Mar. 1842; KG 19 Jan. 1846. *d.* 25 Aug. 1870.

Ensign 1 W.I. Regt. 1820; cornet 10 Drag. 1820, lt. 1821; capt. Cape corps cav. 1823; capt. 22 Drag. (half-pay) 1823-d.

Beauchamp, the elder son of Lord Yarmouth, the noted society playboy and friend of the prince regent, was probably, in fact, his only child, as a younger brother and a sister were apparently fathered by someone else. Brought up in Paris by his Italian mother, 'Mie-Mie', who had separated from Yarmouth, he was a bright but wayward boy, who received little formal education. Yarmouth's intention had been to take him to England to attend public school, but his wife's doubts about his health persuaded him to place Beauchamp with a tutor. He did not flourish, however, being incorrigibly idle and irked by English society; he wrote to his mother in 1816, asking her to pity him, 'for I do bore myself cruelly'.[2] That year he was duped by two army officers into losing an enormous sum of money at cards, a scandal which dogged him and his father for several years.[3] Early in 1817 Beauchamp reported to his mother the publication of Eaton Stannard Barrett's *Six Weeks at Long's* which

> gives an account of my business, and says I affect to speak bad English, that I wore false *favoris* and moustaches in Paris, etc., etc., etc. My name in the book is Don Exoticus

[1] Her paternity was in dispute between the 4th duke of Queensberry and George Augustus Selwyn[†]. [2] Add. 40296, ff. 29-30; *Peep at the Commons* (1820), 13; *HP Commons, 1790-1820*, v. 125-7.

Wistcoranzov. Exoticus on account of my having lived abroad all my life, and the other name on account of my *favoris* (my beard).[4]

For part of that year, and again during the Oxford vacation in 1819, he was apparently an attaché at the British embassy in Paris. He began a liaison with a woman 11 years his senior, Agnes Jackson, whose origins are obscure, although she was ostensibly the daughter of the self-styled baronet, Sir Thomas Wallace of Craigie Castle, Ayrshire, and the temporarily estranged wife of a City financier, Samuel Bickley. On 21 June 1818 she gave birth to Beauchamp's son, who was christened Richard Jackson. He was taken to France at the age of six and subsequently brought up by Lady Yarmouth, who was popularly supposed to be his mother.[5]

At Dover in October 1818, Lord Glenbervie[†] recorded meeting Beauchamp, 'just landed, looking so pale, so yellow and so jaded!', who 'unasked, told me he had just lost all his money at Paris'.[6] He purchased an ensigncy in the 1st West India regiment in February 1820 and the following month transferred to the Prince of Wales's Own light dragoons.[7] After the Liverpool government's decision to withdraw the bill of pains and penalties against Queen Caroline, which Beauchamp described as 'much the best thing that can happen, so there is an end of this disagreeable business', he took part in military action to defend the premises of the ministerialist *Courier* newspaper against the mob on the night of 11 Nov. 1820.[8] His father thought that his service did him good, as 'when he is steadily in town for a fortnight he grows languid but the morning air of his quarters soon restores him'.[9] Late the following year he bought a lieutenancy and joined the half-pay list, hoping, despite George IV's wish to have him reinstated, to be able to visit his ever indulgent mother in France.[10] However, to his inexpressible disgust, his father commanded him to offer himself on the current vacancy for county Antrim, in order to preserve the family interest, and engineered his return to a full-pay posting. 'So', as he complained to his mother, 'I shall not have a moment to myself in the whole year. But I told Lord Yarmouth that if he forced me to be in Parliament against my inclination I would give up the army'. Much against his wishes he set out for Ireland, and from Dublin reported that 'dirt, etc., is all that is to be found ... How I hate being here nobody knows and shall be delighted to find myself once more in Paris'.[11] A threatened opposition came to nothing, and in January 1822 he was duly returned for Antrim, where his grandfather, the 2nd marquess of Hertford, had his principal Irish estates.[12]

Beauchamp informed his mother of his success, adding that he was

> with great truth very sorry for it. I will *show* you how near I have been to quarrelling with Lord Yarmouth about it by his letters to me, etc. But I can assure you *nothing* will prevent me living a great deal more than I have abroad with you ... But you have too much good sense to perceive that I must live a great deal in this country *especially while Lord Hertford lives*, as much depends upon him with regard to me.

He chose to stay in the army that session, when parliamentary attendance would excuse him from his regiment, and to look for a way of leaving it in the autumn.[13] He paired against the Catholic peers bill, 30 Apr., apparently on an arrangement made by Yarmouth, who commented that 'I daresay Beauchamp will prefer Princess Esterhazy's ball'.[14] No other evidence of activity has been traced, though in May he reported to his mother that 'I have been attending to my parliamentary duties, answering the constituental [*sic*] letters and all that sort of thing, and hardly going out into the world at all'. But he also wrote: 'What a dreadful thing it is being quite *blasé* at my age, which I am very sorry to say is the case. Nothing amuses me, I don't know what is the matter with me and only hope it will not last'.[15] After Hertford died in June 1822, Lord Yarmouth (as he was now styled) complained of being left nothing directly, and commented of the extended entail that 'all I know is that I lose 1,000 a year by Lord Hertford's death, but now that *everything* is settled upon me without the possibility of selling it, I can do whatever I please with perfect impunity'.[16] John Croker[*], his father's man of business, expressed the hope that the 3rd marquess, 'who felt the inconvenience of a narrow and jealous system himself, will act handsomely' by Yarmouth.[17]

In early 1823, Hertford noted of his son, who left the army at this time, that he seemed in better health in England: 'I believe this dull country exhausts him much less than Paris for he soon picks up here'.[18] Yarmouth was credited with dividing in the majority for inquiry into the legal proceedings against the Dublin Orange rioters, 22 Apr. 1823, his only known vote in Parliament. He made no reported speeches and was said to have attended seldom and to have sided with ministers when he did so.[19] By the autumn of 1825 he had informed his father that he had no intention of continuing in the Commons, and he retired at the dissolution the following year.[20] Although he was again briefly an attaché in 1829, at Constantinople, he took no further part in politics, and his father wrote to him at the time of the dissolution in December 1834 that 'if you don't like Parliament, I don't wonder; I know [Lord Lonsdale's son, Lord] Lowther* and others would not sit but to please their papas'.[21] His was a life of unfilled potential. Countess Granville described him in 1832 as

> the greatest pity that ever was. Such powers of being delightful and captivating, *grandes manières*, talents of all kinds, *finesse d'esprit*, all spent in small base coin. He walks amongst us like a fallen angel, higher and lower than all of us put together.[22]

From the mid-1830s he resided in Paris, living reclusively at the Bagatelle villa in the Bois de Boulogne, and purchasing a vast collection of especially eighteenth-century art. In March 1842 he succeeded to the titles and estates of his father, by then a decrepit old roué.[23] According to Captain Gronow, the duke of Wellington remembered him as 'a man of extraordinary talents. He deserves to be classed among those men who possess transcendent abilities', and his father's old friend Sir Robert Peel* thought him

> a man of great comprehension; not only versed in the sciences, but able to animate his mass of knowledge by a bright and active imagination. In a word, if he had lived in London, instead of frittering away his time in Paris, he would no doubt have been prime minister of England.[24]

An epicurean figure at the decadent court of Napoleon III and one of the last of the absentee English 'milords', Hertford died in Paris in August 1870, shortly before the fall of the Second Empire at the battle of Sedan, and was buried in Père Lachaise cemetery.[25] He was succeeded as 5th marquess of Hertford by his second cousin, Francis George Hugh (1812-84), a household official, who inherited the entailed estates. But by his will, dated 1838 with several codicils dating from 1850 (which was proved in London with personalty under £500,000, 26 June, and in Dublin valued at £85,000 in Ireland, 12 Aug. 1871), he left his Irish and other estates to his illegitimate son, Richard (1818-90). He, who had changed his name from Jackson to Wallace in 1842, was given a baronetcy in 1871 and was Conservative Member for Lisburn, 1873-85. After the death of his widow in 1897 his father's superb artistic possessions passed to the nation and were subsequently opened to the public at the family's former residence in Manchester Square as the Wallace Collection.[26]

---

[1] Based on D. Mallett, *Greatest Collector: Hertford and Founding of Wallace Collection* (1979). [2] Eg. 3263, ff. 25, 29, 77; Mallett, 15, 17-20. [3] B. Falk, '*Old Q's Daughter*', 104-7. [4] Eg. 3263, f. 89. [5] Mallett, 28-30. [6] *Glenbervie Diaries*, ii. 331. [7] *London Gazette*, 4 Mar., 4 Apr. 1820. [8] Eg. 3263, ff. 97, 99. [9] Ibid. f. 39. [10] Ibid. ff. 108,

114, 126. [11] Ibid. ff. 130, 132, 134. [12] *Belfast News Letter*, 1, 8, 15 Jan. 1822. [13] Eg. 3263, f. 136. [14] Add. 60286, f. 249. [15] Eg. 3263, f. 138. [16] Ibid. f. 142. [17] *Croker Pprs*. i. 240. [18] Eg. 3263, f. 44. [19] *Session of Parl. 1825*, p. 492. [20] Add. 60287, ff. 117, 119. [21] Eg. 3263, f. 50. [22] *Countess Granville Letters*, ii. 121. [23] Mallett, 39, 42, 48-50; Falk, 204-93; 'Hertford and Eighteenth Century', *Burlington Mag*. xcii (1950), 153-4. [24] *Gronow Reminiscences*, ii. 323-4. [25] *The Times*, 27 Aug. 1870; Mallett, 110-12; Falk, 293-300; *Hertford-Mawson Letters* ed. J. Ingamells, 9-11. [26] Mallett, 112-13, 115; Falk, 301-3, 343; *Oxford DNB sub* Wallace.

S.M.F.

SHADWELL, Lancelot (1779–1850), of 36 Harley Street and 2 New Square, Lincoln's Inn, Mdx.

RIPON   1826–Nov. 1827

b. 3 May 1779, 1st s. of Lancelot Shadwell of Lincoln's Inn and 9 Upper Gower Street, Mdx. and 1st w. Elizabeth Sophia, da. of Charles Whitmore of Southampton, Hants. *educ*. Eton 1793; St. John's, Camb. 1796, BA 1800, fellow 1801-5, MA 1803; L. Inn 1797, called 1803. *m*. (1) 8 Jan. 1805, Harriet, da. of Anthony Richardson, merchant, of Powis Place, Great Ormond Street, Mdx., 6s. (4 *d.v.p.*); (2) 4 Jan. 1816, Frances, da. of Capt. Locke, 6s. (2 *d.v.p.*) 5da. (1 *d.v.p.*). *suc*. fa. 1815; kntd. 16 Nov. 1827. *d*. 10 Aug. 1850.

KC 6 Dec. 1821; bencher, L. Inn 1822, treas. 1833; v.-chan. Nov. 1827-*d*.; PC 16 Nov. 1827; member, judicial cttee. of privy council 1833; commr. of great seal Apr.1835-Jan. 1836, June-July 1850.

Shadwell was descended from a Staffordshire family who had acquired property at Beamish in Shropshire during the eighteenth century. His grandfather Lancelot Shadwell (1704-55) was in business as a chemist in Leadenhall Street, London. His father, the only surviving son, was born in 1750 and called to the bar in 1777. He specialized as a conveyancer, enjoying a high reputation and a lucrative practice. After the death of his first wife he married in 1797 Isabella, daughter of Sir Thomas Cayley of Brompton, Yorkshire, who was only a few years older than his eldest son Lancelot. Shadwell senior died in 1815, leaving to Lancelot real estate which had come to him by his first marriage.[1] His widow survived until 1854.

At Cambridge Shadwell became a friend of Thomas Denman*, with whom he made a punishing walking tour of Wales in 1797.[2] He was bred to the bar and practised successfully for 18 years as a junior in chancery. Like his father, he was an expert in real estate law. After taking silk in 1821 he sacrificed considerable income by declining to follow the fashion of taking briefs in more than one equity court, confining himself to chancery practice. When the Liverpool ministry reshuffled the legal hierarchy at the end of

1823 he was a serious contender for the post of solic-itor-general, but lord chancellor Eldon preferred his senior Charles Wetherell*.[3] Shadwell had become the 'man of business' of Elizabeth Sophia Lawrence, the parliamentary patron of Ripon, and she returned him for the borough with Frederick Robinson, the chan-cellor of the exchequer, at the 1826 general election. He continued to manage her affairs, including Ripon elections, until her death in 1845, when he received £15,000 and a life interest in £10,000 by her will.[4] Charles Williams Wynn* had described him as a 'Papist' in 1823, but three years later Sir John Copley* was reported as saying that he 'has had some new lights on the Catholic question, and thinks there might be great danger in granting further concessions to the Catholics' and that 'he is to be the next solicitor-gen-eral'.[5] Whether this change of mind had any connec-tion with Miss Lawrence's deep Anglican piety is not clear, but Shadwell duly voted against Catholic relief, 6 Mar. 1827. Yet when Peel was under attack for his apostasy on emancipation in 1829 Shadwell, acting on the Johnsonian dictum that 'in situations of distress the kind opinion of any one human being is always of some value', sent him a letter of encouragement and support.[6]

In his maiden speech, 29 Nov. 1826, he declared his wish to eradicate the 'evils' of high fees and long delays from conveyancing procedure.[7] On 14 Feb. 1827 he sought leave to introduce a bill to limit to 30 years the period within which the legal title to land might be disputed by writs of right and to sim-plify the law of dower. Some radicals dismissed it as a 'patch', but Shadwell, appealing to 'the spirit of reform in all useful matters [which] was now culti-vated by all classes of persons', argued that those who wanted revision of real estate law 'ought not to reject the remedy of one grievance because they could not obtain their wishes with respect to all'. Leave was given and Shadwell introduced the measure on 26 Feb. and steered it through the House by 10 Apr., despite continued criticism of its crudity. It was given a first reading in the Lords, 11 Apr., but no more was heard of it.[8] Shadwell presented Ripon petitions in favour of agricultural protection, 27 Feb.[9] On 13 Mar. 1827 he defended Peel's decision not to apply his criminal laws consolidation bills to Ireland.

On the formation of Canning's ministry the follow-ing month he was spoken of as a possible lord chancel-lor of Ireland. Williams Wynn was 'sorry for this as I think him a weak man though said to be a good lawyer and more of a gentleman than most in the court of chancery'.[10] Nothing came of the speculation. When

Robinson (now Lord Goderich) became premier in September 1827, Shadwell was confidently tipped by many observers to become solicitor-general in the revamped coalition with the Lansdowne Whigs. Mrs. Arbuthnot, noting that he was 'no politician', was not alone in wondering how the ambitious Whig Henry Brougham*, who was suspected of coveting the office, would 'swallow that'.[11] The Whig James Abercromby* warned Huskisson, the leader of the Commons, that Shadwell

> can never be of any use to the government. He has no principles, no opinions and no ... stability of mind. He will be a reformer of the law or an enemy to reform as his interest directs, but he will perform neither part with prudence or wisdom. It would be a very unpopular appointment with the bar. It will be set down as the act of Lord Goderich, who will be supposed ... to have an inter-est in promoting Shadwell on account of his influence with Miss Lawrence, who has great wealth to distribute.[12]

In the event Shadwell was not appointed, but at the end of October Goderich and lord chancellor Lyndhurst, in a manoeuvre blatantly designed to exclude Brougham, selected him as vice-chancellor in the room of Sir Anthony Hart, who unexpectedly became Irish chancellor. Goderich disingenuously informed Lansdowne, 24 Oct.:

> We cannot find a better man than Shadwell ... He has many excellent qualities, as I can testify from a long and rather intimate acquaintance; and from what I know of his general political sentiments (although that is of less importance, perhaps, as the vice-chancellor cannot be in Parliament) I should say that he is not gov-erned by antiquated prejudices, but sincerely approves of the principles and construction of the present administration.[13]

Shadwell, who was noted for his judicial courtesy and the rapidity with which he disposed of routine busi-ness, presided competently in the vice-chancellor's court for almost 23 years. Yet in 1833 lord chancellor Brougham's secretary Denis Le Marchant† wrote dis-paragingly of him:

> The vice-chancellor is a very good natured, careless person, of not very strong principles, a feeble judge and an inconsistent politician. He is a lively though not an interesting talker, and there is nothing about him agree-able besides the good-natured expression of his counte-nance and the buoyant gaiety of his manner.[14]

He declined Peel and Lyndhurst's request that he take the Irish great seal in December 1834 'on account of his numerous family of children', and the subsequent offer of a peerage did not change his mind.[15] In 1827 he had bought the manor of Northolt, Middlesex from Lord Jersey, and in the early 1830s he acquired a property at Barn Elms, Barnes, on the southern bank of the Thames, where he indulged his passion for outdoor bathing in the winter.[16] On 9 Dec. 1849 his second surviving son Louis Henry, a barrister, was found drowned in a ditch in the grounds of Barn Elms; he 'had for many years shown a degree of eccentricity, and always slept in the entrance lodge instead of the house'. It was assumed that he had 'accidentally fallen, in consequence of the fogginess of the evening, when on his way to his night's rest'.[17] Shadwell took it very badly. On 19 June 1850 he became for the second time one of the commissioners of the great seal, but five days later he was seized with 'a sudden and dangerous illness', which prevented him from sitting again during the continuance of the commission. He was still 'seriously unwell' when it ended on 15 July and he lingered at Barn Elms until 10 Aug. 1850. Denman was convinced that he had been 'killed by his son's lamentable death, co-operating with every derangement of the system, and ensuring the victory to bronchitis in its contest with life'.[18] In his will, dated 31 July 1850, he left £7,000 to his now second surviving son Charles Frederick Alexander, a naval officer, and the residue of his estate to his wife, the sole executrix. His personalty was sworn under £60,000 in the province of Canterbury and under £16,000 in that of York. He had already settled on his children the money bequeathed to him by Miss Lawrence.[19]

[1] PROB 11/1565/109. [2] Arnould, Denman, i. 16-18, 25. [3] Add. 40304, ff. 189, 191; 40329, f. 229; 51574, Abercromby to Holland [?30 Dec.]; 51586, Tierney to Lady Holland, 11 Dec.; 51659, Whishaw to same, 13 Nov.; 3 Dec. 1823; Hobhouse Diary, 108-9. [4] Lady Holland to Son, 229; Gent. Mag (1845), ii. 423; Add. 40489, ff. 127, 129, 274-9; 40490. ff. 229, 231; 40491, ff. 62-66; 40523, ff. 401, 403; 40526, ff. 16, 19; 40569, f. 90. [5] Buckingham, Mems. Geo IV, ii. 16; Life of Campbell, i. 437. [6] Add. 40398, ff. 255, 257. [7] The Times, 30 Nov. 1826. [8] Ibid. 27 Feb. 1827; CJ, lxxxii. 169, 405; LJ, lix. 250. [9] The Times, 28 Feb. 1827. [10] Canning's Ministry, 213; NLW, Coedymaen mss 195. [11] Arbuthnot Corresp. 90; Arbuthnot Jnl. ii. 143; Add. 38750, f. 95; Lansdowne mss, Abercromby to Lansdowne [?25 Aug.]; (3) 34, Holland to same, 3 Sept.; (3) 37, Rice to same, 4 Sept.; NLS, Ellice mss, Grey to Ellice, 8 Sept. 1827. [12] Add. 38751, f. 9. [13] HMC Bathurst, 646; Hobhouse Diary, 142; Lansdowne mss. [14] Foss, Judges of Eng. ix. 263-4; Oxford DNB; Three Diaries, 374. [15] Add. 40316, ff. 95, 97, 106. [16] VCH Mdx. iv. 114; VCH Surr. iv. 3; J.L. Roget, Hist. 'Old Water Colour Club', ii. 210-11. [17] Gent. Mag. (1850), i. 106. [18] Ibid. (1850), ii. 545-6; T.D. Hardy, Mem. Lord Langdale, ii. 258-9, 265, 267; Arnould, ii. 313. [19] PROB 11/2118/640; IR26/1883/677.

D.R.F.

SHARP, Richard (1759–1835), of Fredley Farm, Mickleham, Surr. and 23 Park Lane, Mdx.[1]

CASTLE RISING	1806–1812
PORTARLINGTON	1 Mar. 1816–3 Feb. 1819
ILCHESTER	1826–22 Feb. 1827

b. 1759 at St. John's, Newfoundland, 1st s. of Richard Sharp (d. 1765), an English officer of the garrison and Elizabeth Adams of St. John's. educ. by Rev. John Fell, dissenting minister, of Thaxted, Essex. unm. d. 30 Mar. 1835.
Dir. Hand in Hand Fire Office 1813

'Conversation' Sharp, who was said to talk 'better than any man in England', cast a wide spell of charm over his contemporaries. Once a wholesale hatter, whose 'very dark complexion' made it look 'as if the dye of his old trade ... had got engrained in his face' ('darkness that may be felt!' as one wag put it), he became a partner in a prosperous West India firm in London with Samuel Boddington[†], George Philips[*] and his brother-in-law Davis. It was as the host, companion, critic and travel guide of the literati that he made his name: Byron, Coleridge, Sir James Mackintosh[*], Moore, Rogers and Wordsworth were among his many friends and admirers. Miss Berry might dismiss him on a fleeting acquaintance as 'clever, but ... of little real depth of intellect', but those who knew him better did not doubt his mental powers. Byron thought him 'a very clever man'; Wordsworth rated him highly; and Francis Horner[†], who was captivated by him and stood in awe of his 'strong and purified understanding', described him as

> a very extraordinary man ... His great subject is criticism, upon which he always appears to me original and profound; what I have not frequently observed in combination, he is both subtle and feeling. Next to literature the powers of his understanding, at once ingenious and plain, show themselves in the judgement of characters ... He has paid much attention to metaphysics also.[2]

He had taken 'a very active part in the background' of Whig politics during his first period in the House, when he was one of the few nonconformist Members, but he never achieved the eminence to which he had originally aspired. Philips believed that 'he had not moral courage for Parliament', recalling that 'he was so awed there that his habitual fluency and correctness forsook him, and he could not speak without long and laborious preparation'. According to this account, Canning discovered Sharp's secret and on one occasion 'attacked him on that ground and exposed him to ridicule ... in such a manner as I think stopped his mouth forever afterwards'.[3] In 1820 he stood unsuccessfully for the third time at Milborne Port, and offered for the venal borough of Maidstone, where he maintained in his address that he had 'ever resisted, with equal earnestness, all attempts to disturb the peace of the community, or to innovate on our admirable constitution, by laws at once violent and ineffectual'. He condemned the 'waste of public money' and would not consent to any additional taxation 'before a considerate, but unsparing retrenchment has reduced the public expenditure to the public income'. He said he had witnessed 'with disgust, the endeavours of the unprincipled to vilify religion', and declared that his 'zeal for the support of the Protestant interest has been unfeigned'. He retired after the first day of polling, and a petition against the result was subsequently abandoned. George Tierney, the Whig leader in the Commons, thought Sharp had one of 'the strongest claims upon anything which party can do', and hoped he might come in for the surplus seat at Appleby, but the patron Lord Thanet disposed of it elsewhere.[4]

Mackintosh noted in July 1820 that Sharp seemed 'very old', later adding that he 'grows more and more into the rigidity of age ... characterized by a repetition of the same thoughts and phrases'. Others, including Maria Edgeworth and Thomas Creevey*, recorded similar impressions of him and found his company trying.[5] He inherited property at Norwood, Surrey, from his brother and business partner William in 1821, and took over responsibility for their ward Maria Kinnaird, an accomplished singer.[6] For the sake of her health he spent some of the next few years in foreign travel. At the general election of 1826 he was returned for Ilchester on Lord Darlington's interest.[7] The only known trace of his parliamentary activity before he and his colleague, the barrister John Williams, were unseated on petition is a silent vote against the Clarence grant, 16 Feb. 1827. Of Lord Goderich's coalition ministry he observed to Lady Holland that until her husband was in the cabinet, 'I cannot possibly feel ministerially disposed. I should go to the left hand of the Speaker as usual'. He left Paris for London in October 1828 intent on urging at Brooks's Club the importance of 'all men of Kent making a point' of attending the county meeting got up by the Brunswickers to oppose Catholic relief.[8] In his 'capacity of dry-nurse to rising men of talents', he held a dinner in honour of Thomas Macaulay* in 1830 and the two became fast friends, with Sharp giving the younger man valuable criticism and advice on his parliamentary oratory. On one occasion Macaulay fell in with him at the Athenaeum and they

had a long talk ... about everything and everybody, metaphysics, poetry, politics, scenery and painting. One thing I have observed in Sharp, which is quite peculiar to him among town-wits and diners-out. He never talks scandal. If he can say nothing good of a man he holds his tongue. I do not of course mean that in confidential communication about politics he does not speak freely of public men. But about the foibles of private individuals I do not believe that, much as I have talked with him, I ever heard him utter one word.[9]

Sharp published nine *Epistles in Verse* in 1828, followed by *Letters and Essays in Prose and Verse* in 1834, which enjoyed some success and went quickly to three editions.[10] He died in March 1835 and left all his real estate, which included freehold property in Fenchurch Street and his 80-acre retreat at Fredley, to Maria Kinnaird, the residuary legatee. He put his nephew Richard Davis, now Boddington's active partner, in possession of legacies due to himself as his brother-in-law's residuary legatee, and made him a joint executor, with power limited to that part of his estate which consisted of his father's share in the effects of his partnership with Boddington. His personalty was sworn under £140,000, and the value of his entire estate put at 'upwards of £250,000'.[11]

[1] See J. Wilson, *Biog. Index* (1808); P.W. Clayden, *Early Life of Samuel Rogers*, 122, 277-80, 303, 329, 332-3; C.K.P[aul], *Maria Drummond*, 11-16, 29-32, 46. [2] *Edgeworth Letters*, 66; S.J. Reid, *Sydney Smith*, 314; *Smith Letters*, i. 172; *Scott Jnl.* 191, 216-17, 222; A.W. Merivale, *Fam. Mems.* 210-11; *Berry Jnls.* ii. 344; *Shelley Diary*, i. 214; *Byron Letters* ed. R.E. Protheroe, ii. 341-2; v. 161; *Wordsworth Letters* ed. A.G. Hill, v. 68; *Horner Mems.* i. 240, 283. [3] Clayden, *Rogers and his Contemporaries*, i. 118; Wars. RO MI 247, Philips Mems. i. 350. [4] *Western Flying Post*, 6 Mar.; *Kentish Chron.* 7, 10 Mar.; Add. 51586, Tierney to Lady Holland, 12 Apr. 1820. [5] Add. 52444, f. 196; 52445, f. 53; *Edgeworth Letters*, 439; *Creevey Pprs.* ii. 275. [6] The will was sworn under £12,000 (PROB 8/214; 11/1645/361). [7] *Western Flying Post*, 12 June 1826. [8] Add. 51593, Sharp to Lady Holland, 5 Sept. 1827; 51572, Darnley to Holland, 6 Oct. 1828. [9] Ward, *Letters to 'Ivy'*, 347; *Macaulay Letters*, i. 272-3; ii. 18, 313 (quoted), 368, 376; vi. 275, 277. [10] Brougham mss, Sharp to Brougham, 30 Aug. 1834. [11] PROB 9/35 (24 Apr. 1835); 11/1846/263; IR26/1400/378; *Gent. Mag.* (1835), ii. 96-97.

D.R.F./T.A.J.

SHAW, Frederick (1799–1876), of 1 Lower Mount Street, Dublin and Kimmage Lodge, co. Dublin.

DUBLIN	1830–1831
DUBLIN	18 Aug. 1831–1832
DUBLIN UNIVERSITY	1832–9 Feb. 1848

b. 11 Dec. 1799, 3rd but 2nd surv. s. of Robert Shaw* (*d.* 1849), banker, of 31 Merrion Square and Foster Place, Dublin and 1st w. Maria, da. of Abraham Wilkinson of

Bushy Park, co. Dublin.[1] *educ.* Trinity, Dublin 1814, BA and MA 1832, LLB and LLD 1841; Brasenose, Oxf. 1816, BA 1819; King's Inns 1815; L. Inn 1817, called [I] 1822. *m.* 16 Mar. 1819, Thomasine Emily, da. of Hon. George Jocelyn, MP [I], of Newport, co. Tipperary, 5s. (1 *d.v.p.*) 3da. *d.v.p. suc.* bro. Robert as 3rd bt. 19 Feb. 1869. *d.* 30 June 1876.

Recorder, Dundalk 1826-8, Dublin 1828-76; sec. to master of rolls [I] 1827; bencher, King's Inns 1829; PC [I] 15 Jan. 1835.

Shaw, whose father was Member for Dublin, 1804-26, was mostly educated in England and practised at the Irish bar from 1822. Through his wife's cousin the 3rd earl of Roden, he gained legal office in Dundalk (his father-in-law's former parliamentary seat) in 1826, and the following year he was briefly secretary to his uncle Sir William MacMahon, the Irish master of the rolls, whose right to appoint to this office was disputed by the lord chancellor.[2] He came to prominence in March 1828, when, despite his youth and inexperience, he defeated a wide field of candidates to fill the vacant recordership of Dublin, with a salary of £2,000, of which £1,600 was paid by government.[3] This victory was mainly owing to the influence of Roden, who secured the backing of the Irish administration, and his staunchly Protestant allies, who carried weight with the corporation, on which Shaw's father was a (pro-Catholic) alderman. As Shaw boasted to Lord Ferrard:

I have indeed had a great triumph, with 12 opponents, George Moore [the sitting Tory Member] among them, and all having for a full week the circumstance to work upon of my being certain to come down first from the board of aldermen; with all their united efforts, the cry of party to aid them, they were only able to procure in the Commons 36 votes against me out of 120; in addition a great jealousy was excited there by the support of government.[4]

Although criticisms were still levelled against him and it was rumoured in 1829 that a bill would be introduced to redefine his status within the corporation, he quickly proved himself efficient in the execution of his judicial duties and dignified in his more ceremonial ones. According to Richard Sheil*, who thought him 'a most discreet and emphatic orator', he cut an imposing figure with 'his solemnity of aspect; his full, large black and brilliant eye; his handsome countenance, overspread with an air of Evangelical as well as judicial solemnity; his grave judicial walk and his recorder emphasis on every word'.[5]

On the eve of the general election of 1830 Lord Francis Leveson Gower, the Irish secretary, was wary of being seen to endorse his candidacy for Dublin, although he of course preferred him to the sitting Whig Henry Grattan. The Wellington administration considered his being in Parliament incompatible with his tenure of the recordership and thought that the law might have to be altered to prevent his receiving an official salary. At the same time, some of his speeches were considered hostile to ministers and Leveson Gower privately contradicted his public claim that he had had no hand in a recent unpopular attempt to reform the corporation.[6] In tandem with Moore, Shaw had the influence of the corporation and the leading guilds, but even among his natural supporters he had repeatedly to explain how he intended to arrange his judicial sittings around his periodic attendance in Parliament, a proposition which the liberal press found hard to accept.[7] On the hustings, 4 Aug. 1830, when he emphasized his sympathies for the church and the constitution but called for lower taxation and the abolition of slavery, he insisted that he was eligible to sit in the Commons and that his legal duties would, if necessary, be given priority over his parliamentary activities. He was returned in second place, behind Moore, after a violent, week-long contest against Grattan, who failed to pursue a petition against him.[8] According to one newspaper, this election cost him £10,000, as apparently did the two subsequent contests.[9]

As Lord Ellenborough recorded, Shaw made a speech before reading the Dublin corporation's loyal address to William IV, 27 Oct. 1830, 'a thing quite unprecedented and which might be inconvenient'.[10] He was listed by Planta, the patronage secretary, among ministers' 'friends', although a query was marked against his name. He presented Dublin anti-slavery petitions, 4, 5 Nov., and denied that most inhabitants of the city favoured repeal of the Union, 9 Nov. But he was absent from the division on the civil list, 15 Nov., and from the debates on 20 and 23 Dec. 1830, when the O'Gorman Mahon and Hume raised complaints about his inability to fulfil either his judicial or his parliamentary duties. In an extensive rejoinder, 10 Feb. 1831, he showed that the record of his constant sittings since 1828, which he moved to be produced, was owing to the backlog of cases which had needed clearing, and argued that new ones could be dealt with at intensive sittings held at monthly intervals.[11] He again attacked the O'Gorman Mahon, who had come off badly on the 10th, in relation to Dublin juries, 14 Feb., and the corporation, 17 Feb., when he accused his antagonist of deliberately attempting to provoke a row and disavowed the use of 'this sort of Irish political pugilism'. He was obliged to return to Dublin later that month by the illness of his mother, who died on 28 Mar., but was again active in bringing up constituency petitions and making minor contributions to debate in the Commons by the middle of March.[12] Stating that he would have voted for Catholic emancipation as accompanied by the franchise bill had he been in the House in 1829, he said that he favoured such moderate alterations as the enfranchisement of large towns, 22 Mar. 1831, when he condemned the Grey's ministry's reform bill for leading to the spoliation of the corporations and possible repeal of the Union, which he claimed that Daniel O'Connell*, acting with the 'characteristic disingenuousness of our countrymen', clearly intended. He voted against the second reading of the bill that night and presented the petition of the Dublin merchants' guild against it the following day.

Shaw, who, as he made clear in his address, had been travelling back to London when he learnt of the sudden dissolution, offered as an anti-reformer at the general election of 1831. His having missed the crucial division on Gascoyne's wrecking amendment (on 19 Apr.) was useful ammunition for those who opposed his sitting while serving as recorder, on which subject he was again forced on to the defensive, not least because those who had originally secured him the post, Lord Anglesey and William Lamb* (Lord Melbourne), were now key members of the Grey ministry.[13] Like Moore, for whom he plumped, he blamed his defeat at the hands of two reformers, after a bitter ten-day poll, on the creation of bogus freeholders and the direct interference of the Irish government.[14] He declined to contribute to the cost of the ensuing election committee, but on its unseating the Members in August, he immediately offered again at the subsequent by-election.[15] Nothing came of the bill, introduced by James Grattan, Member for Wicklow, 8 Aug., to prevent Irish recorders sitting in Parliament, or of Hume and O'Connell's objections to the grant for the Dublin recorder's salary, 31 Aug. Having persuaded the like-minded Lord Ingestre* to enter with him, Shaw gained widespread support among the high Tories and Protestants. By condemning the ministerial corruption prevalent at the general election, he managed to present himself in a moderate and independent light at the start of another severe contest, 18 Aug. 1831, from which he emerged a week later at the head of the poll.[16]

On 5 Sept. 1831, when an ultimately unsuccessful petition was entered against his return, Shaw took his seat and voted in the majority for John Benett's amendment to the motion to issue the Liverpool writ alleging gross bribery at the previous election there.

He brought up the first of a large number of Galway petitions relating to its franchise, 7 Sept., when he stated his opposition to reform and the disarming of the Irish yeomanry. He clashed with Henry Grattan, now Member for Meath, that day and again on the 9th, when he intervened against the ministerial plan for national education in Ireland. He divided for inquiry into how far the Sugar Refinery Act could be renewed with due regard to the interests of the West Indies and against going into committee on the truck bill, 12 Sept. He conceded the case for disfranchising government officials who held their posts during pleasure, 14 Sept., when he was brought up short by the Speaker on trying to justify his friends' conduct at the Dublin by-election, but he reiterated that police magistrates were independent of the Castle, which provoked another quarrel with Grattan, 21 Sept. He described his own involvement with the Irish master of the rolls in his dispute with the Irish chancellor over judicial patronage, which became the subject of parliamentary investigation, 16 Sept. He voted against the third reading, 19 Sept., and passage of the reintroduced reform bill, 21 Sept. 1831.

Shaw spoke in defence of the Protestant establishment on the address, 6 Dec., and, blaming the Irish government for yielding to the prevailing clamour over tithes as over much else, 15 Dec. 1831, he forecast that Ireland was 'fast approaching some calamitous convulsion'. He objected to the loss of the freeman franchise, including in Dublin, 12 Dec., and voted against the second, 17 Dec. 1831, and third readings of the revised reform bill, 22 Mar. 1832. He was in the minorities for Hunt's amendment to exempt Preston from the £10 householder qualification, 3 Feb., and Waldo Sibthorp's relative to Lincoln freeholders, 23 Mar. In addition to numerous short contributions to debate and continuous activity on Dublin affairs, from early February he spoke frequently to attack the intimidation used to prevent the collection of Irish tithes, voting against government on the arrears bill on 9 Apr., and repeated *ad nauseam* his criticism of the national education plan, against which he presented innumerable petitions. He urged the inclusion of the reference to Providence in the preamble to the cholera bill, 15 Feb., and called for the adjournment of the House, 20 Mar., so as not to continue proceedings into the national fast day on the 21st. He supported the bill to give the Irish master of the rolls the power to appoint his own secretary, 22 Feb., and introduced the Irish court of chancery bill, 13 Apr., but both measures were put off that session. He was a minority teller against the Catholic marriages bill, 2 Apr., and the recommittal of the Irish registry of deeds bill, 9 Apr. Having praised Wellington's attempt to form an administration, 18 May, he voiced fears about potential unrest in Ireland that day and on the 23rd. He spoke and voted against the second reading of the Irish reform bill, 25 May, when his prediction that revived Catholic fortunes under the reformed system would swiftly lead to the end of the Irish church and the Union plainly revealed him as an alarmist. (That he was not an extreme authoritarian was demonstrated by his support for restricting the use of the death penalty, 30 May, and showing leniency in a newspaper libel case, 31 May.) He clashed with the Grattans over the level of reform sentiment in Dublin, 1, 5 June, and brought up the corporation's hostile petition, 25 June, when he opposed the idea of doubling the city's representation since it would only give O'Connell the nomination of two more Members. He voted for Alexander Baring's bill to exclude insolvent debtors from Parliament, 27 June. His attempt to make rent the basis of the £10 qualification was much criticized, 29 June, and his defence of the rights of Irish freemen brought him close to endorsing calls for repeal of the Union, 2 July, when he was teller for his own unsuccessful motion to preserve the rights of Irish freemen admitted since 30 Mar. the previous year (defeated 128-39). He intervened several more times on the details of the Irish bill, 2, 6 July, and again defended the existing freeman franchise, 3 Aug. 1832.

Denying that he was himself an Orangeman, he damned the Irish party processions bill as a flagrant injustice since it outlawed Protestant but not Catholic ceremonials, 14, 25 June 1832. He warned that he would oppose it clause by clause, 27, 28 June, and on the 29th Smith Stanley, the Irish secretary, postponed it, conceding that it could not be passed in time for the Protestant marches in July. Shaw ruled out the introduction of poor laws as a means of dealing with distress in Ireland, 3 July. He was granted three weeks' leave on urgent business, 9 July, and so was presumably absent during the debates on Hume's failed bid to disqualify the recorder of Dublin from sitting in Parliament, 18, 24, 31 July. He spoke and voted against Sir John Burke's amendment to the Irish tithes bill, 1 Aug., and for Thomas Lefroy's against the retrospective character of the ecclesiastical courts bill, 3 Aug., and divided against going into committee on the Greek loan, 6 Aug. Furious to find the party processions bill revived when he was almost the only Irish Member still attending that session, he forced divisions against all its clauses, 8 Aug., when his constant apologies for having to abide by his self-imposed promise to obstruct its passage at every opportunity kept the chamber in fits of laughter. According to the

junior minister Tom Macaulay*, who described Shaw as 'an honest man enough, but a great fool and a bitter Protestant fanatic':

> We were all heartily pleased with these events. For the truth was that these 17 divisions occupied less time than a real hard debate on the bill would have occupied and were infinitely more amusing. The oddest part of the business is that Shaw's frank good natured way of proceeding, absurd as it was, has made him popular. He was never so great a favourite with the House as after harassing it for two or three hours with the most frivolous and vexatious opposition. This is a curious trait of the character of the House of Commons.[17]

Justifying his conduct as a response to ministers' apparent breach of faith about the bill, he announced he would give government no further trouble over it, 9 Aug. 1832.

Shaw was fully expected to stand for Dublin as a Conservative at the following general election, but he feared the popularity of the repealers; had he been able to pledge himself to vote against the Union, O'Connell would have been delighted to bring him in with a radical.[18] To the regret of the corporation, who voted him an address of thanks for his parliamentary services, he therefore transferred his pretensions to Dublin University, where he was admitted to a degree (on the basis of his Oxford one) to qualify for the elective franchise. Thwarting the hopes of the more extreme and eccentric Evangelical James Edward Gordon*, with whom he had an angry exchange of letters, he was returned with Lefroy after a contest against two Liberals in December 1832.[19] According to James Grant, who believed that he never fulfilled the expectations that his friends had held on his entering Parliament, Shaw was 'a voluble speaker, cold and monotonous on ordinary topics, but violent, both in matter and manner, in the highest degree, when the clergy, the church or the Orangemen are attacked'.[20] He was very influential during Lord Haddington's brief period as lord lieutenant, 1834-5, which became known as the Shaw viceroyalty, and was the acknowledged leader of the Irish Conservatives in the Commons in the 1830s. He retired from the representation of the College in 1848 and from the recordership of Dublin a few weeks before his death in June 1876. His father's baronetcy, which he had inherited from his elder brother in 1869, passed to his eldest son Robert (1821-95), who was a third cousin of the playwright George Bernard Shaw.[21]

[1] *Hist. Irish Parl.* vi. 263. [2] R.L. Sheil, *Sketches of Irish Bar* (1854), ii. 358-60. [3] *Dublin Evening Post*, 11, 22 Mar. 1828; *Cal. Ancient Recs. Dublin*, xviii. 255; *PP* (1835), xxvii. 112-113. [4] Add. 40397, f. 423; PRO NI, Anglesey mss D619/31F, pp. 15-23, 27-30;

PRO NI, Foster mss T2519/4/2167. ⁵ *Dublin Evening Post*, 1 Apr. 1828, 5 May 1829; Sheil, ii. 360-1; *New Monthly Mag.* (1831), ii. 2. ⁶ NAI, Leveson Gower letter bks. Leveson Gower to Gregory, 28 June, to Singleton, 11, 15, 30 July 1830. ⁷ *Dublin Evening Post*, 1, 6, 13, 20, 27 July; *Dublin Morning Post*, 21, 23 July 1830. ⁸ *Dublin Evening Post*, 5, 14 Aug. 1830. ⁹ *Freeman's Jnl.* 7 May 1831; *Oxford DNB*. ¹⁰ *Ellenborough Diary*, ii. 403. ¹¹ *PP* (1830-1), viii. 66-67. ¹² *Dublin Evening Mail*, 25 Feb. 1831. ¹³ Ibid. 29 Apr., 4 May; *Dublin Evening Post*, 3 May 1831. ¹⁴ *Dublin Evening Post*, 7, 19, 21 May 1831. ¹⁵ Ibid. 12 Aug.; Wellington mss, Holmes to Arbuthnot, 9 Aug.; NLI, Farnham mss 18611 (2), Lefroy to Farnham, 9 Aug. 1831. ¹⁶ *Dublin Evening Mail*, 15, 17, 19 Aug.; *Dublin Evening Post*, 20, 25, 27 Aug. 1831. ¹⁷ *Macaulay Letters*, ii. 173-4. ¹⁸ *Dublin Evening Post*, 18, 21 Aug., 1 Sept.; *Warder*, 6 Oct. 1832; *O'Connell Corresp.* iv. 1921, 1929. ¹⁹ *Cal. Ancient Recs. Dublin*, xix. 78-79; *Dublin Evening Post*, 15 Nov. 13, 20 Dec.; *Warder*, 1 Dec. 1832; J. Wolffe, *Protestant Crusade in Great Britain*, 75-76. ²⁰ [J. Grant], *Random Recollections of Commons* (1837), 151-2. ²¹ *The Times*, 1, 3 July; *Warder*, 1, 8 July 1876; *DNB*; *Oxford DNB*.

S.M.F.

SHAW, Robert (1774–1849), of Bushy Park, co. Dublin and 31 Merrion Square and Foster Place, Dublin.

DUBLIN   31 Mar. 1804–1826

b. 29 Jan. 1774, 1st s. of Robert Shaw, merchant, of Dublin and 1st w. Mary, da. of William Higgins of Higginsbrook, co. Meath. *educ.* Mr. Kerr's sch.; Trinity, Dublin 1788. *m.* (1) 7 Jan. 1796, Maria (*d.* 28 Mar. 1831), da. and h. of Abraham Wilkinson of Bushy Park, 6s. (3 *d.v.p.*) 3da. (1 *d.v.p.*);¹ (2) 2 July 1834, Amelia, da. of Benjamin Spencer, MD, of Bristol, Glos., *s.p. suc.* fa. 1796; *cr.* bt. 17 Aug. 1821. *d.* 10 Mar. 1849.

MP [I] 1799-1800.

Sheriffs' peer, Dublin 1797-1808; sheriff, co. Dublin 1806-7; alderman, Dublin 1808-41; ld. mayor 1815-16.

Cornet Rathfarnham cav. 1796, capt. 1803; capt.-commdt. S. Circular Road inf. 1805; col. R. Dublin city militia 1821.

Shaw, whose Scottish family had moved from Hampshire to county Kilkenny in the late seventeenth century, was the son of a prosperous Dublin merchant and minor government official. He followed his father into commerce and was elected a member of the common council of Dublin, but he declined the office of sheriff in 1797, paying a fine of 300 guineas, and served as a sheriffs' peer until chosen an alderman in 1808.² In 1797 he became a partner in the bank headed by Sir Thomas Lighton, former Member for Tuam and Carlingford, based in Foster Place, off College Green. From 1807 he was the senior partner in this firm, now known as Robert Shaw, Thomas Needham and Ponsonby Shaw (Ponsonby being his brother and a fellow corporator).³ He had opposed the Union in his brief career in the Irish Parliament, but from 1804 was an inactive and usually ministerialist Member for

Dublin. After winning the contest in 1806 (presumably the election which he later admitted had cost him £12,000), he was thereafter returned unopposed on the corporation interest, despite becoming a supporter of Catholic claims in about 1812.⁴

Shaw was criticized for being too indolent on constituency business and too close to the Liverpool administration, which in 1820 appointed his son and namesake to the position of accomptant-general of the Irish post office, in which his late father had served as comptroller. Yet he was not in the end challenged at the general election that spring, when he promised to press for lower (especially local) taxation and was again returned with his ailing colleague, Henry Grattan.⁵ One of several aldermen to be proposed for the office of lord mayor, 10 May, his defeat (by 88-23) was owing not so much to disrespect towards him as to the common council's determination to impose its own candidate.⁶ He defended the interests of Dublin in objecting to abolition of the Irish lord lieutenancy, 17 May, and supporting the continuance of the Union duties, 14 June, when he was a majority teller against inquiry into them. He brought in a bill to light Dublin with gas, 25 May; it passed that session despite his receiving a request from the corporation to withdraw it.⁷ He apparently remained neutral (and did not vote) in the divisive Dublin by-election which followed Grattan's death in June, although in the House he opposed the proposed exclusion of the winning corporation candidate Thomas Ellis as an Irish master in chancery, 30 June. He spoke up for Irish distillers on the sale of spirits bill, 12 July 1820. His loyalty to the government was rewarded with the colonelcy of the city militia and a baronetcy the following year.

He voted against censuring ministers' conduct towards Queen Caroline, 6 Feb., and stated that the sheriff of county Dublin had been 'indiscreet, but not corrupt' in forcibly closing the county meeting on this issue, 22 Feb. 1821. He voted against repealing the additional malt duty, 3 Apr., reducing the grant for the adjutant-general's office, 11 Apr., disqualifying civil officers of the ordnance from voting in parliamentary elections, 12 Apr. 1821, and abolition of one of the joint-postmasterships, 13 Mar. 1822. He unsuccessfully moved to repeal the Irish window tax, 16 May 1821, and gave notice that he would repeat the attempt, 28 Feb. 1822, when, as on several other occasions, he brought up a hostile Dublin petition; on 24 May he expressed his pleasure at government's decision to abolish it.⁸ He was appointed to the select committee on Dublin taxation, 20 Mar., and chaired its proceedings, 25, 30 Apr., 13 May.⁹ Like his colleague, he was thanked by the corporation for his exertions on both these subjects, 19 Apr., 19 July 1822.[10] He expressed the hope that much would be done for Ireland in the ensuing session at a Dublin sheriff's dinner in January 1823.[11] He voted for the grant for Irish church and glebe houses, 11 Apr., and against repeal of the Foreign Enlistment Act, 16 Apr., and reform of the Scottish representative system, 2 June. He several times chaired the reappointed committee on Dublin taxation, to which he gave evidence, 8 May. Having divided in the majority for the inquiry into the legal proceedings against the Dublin Orange rioters, 22 Apr., he made minor interventions, 6, 14 May, and was briefly examined by it, 23 May 1823.[12]

He was again named to the select committees on Dublin taxation, 8 Apr. 1824, 23 Feb. 1825. He continued to bring up numerous petitions from his constituents, such as one from the chamber of commerce against Ellis's Dublin coal trade bill, 5 Apr., although he acquiesced in the second reading of this measure, 13 Apr. 1824. Showing how he could occasionally busy himself with mercantile legislation, he was a majority teller against amendments to the Irish Equitable Loan Society bill, 1, 9 June, and secured its third reading, 10 June.[13] He divided against inquiry into the trial of the Methodist missionary John Smith in Demerara, 11 June. He pointedly failed to endorse the ascendancy interest at another shrieval dinner in October 1824.[14] He voted for the Irish unlawful societies bill, 15, 25 Feb., and (as he had on 28 Feb. 1821) for Catholic relief, 1 Mar., 21 Apr., 10 May 1825. He commented that nothing would so conciliate Irish opinion in favour of emancipation as the Commons agreeing to the securities of raising the elective franchise and paying Catholic priests, 28 Mar. 1825, adding that time should be given to Irish bankers to absorb the new financial regulations affecting them.[15] He declined the invitation to attend the O'Connellite dinner for the friends of civil and religious liberty in Dublin, 2 Feb. 1826.[16] As he had sometimes been obliged to do in the past, he presented the corporation's petitions for suppression of the Catholic Association, 27 Feb., and against Catholic claims, 27 Apr.[17] His only other known parliamentary votes were against the emergency admission of foreign corn, 8, 11 May 1826.

Shaw, who had long been criticized for being inefficient and insufficiently Protestant, declared his determination to stand at the following general election, despite the likelihood of his being opposed by a man of greater commercial expertise.[18] He duly offered on the basis of his past conduct and persisted as far as the nomination on the hustings, 10 June, when he insisted on his attachment to the interests of the city and explained his pro-Catholic votes as evidence of his independence. However, he withdrew at the end of that day, before polling could begin, ostensibly to prevent a violent partisan contest. Although it was said that he could have won if he had persevered, his retirement was attributed to a loss of confidence in him on the part of the Protestant corporation, who brought in the anti-Catholic George Moore at the cost of allowing Henry Grattan junior to secure the other seat.[19] He was mentioned as a possible candidate during electoral speculation in May 1827 and was again so considered by the Irish administration at the general election of 1830, when it was in fact his son Frederick who defeated Grattan.[20] In December 1830 he justified his pension, which he claimed to have inherited from his father, against Daniel O'Connell's* aspersions.[21] He voted for Frederick and Moore at the Dublin election of 1831 and for Frederick and Thomas Lefroy* in the University contest at the general election of 1832, when he proposed George Alexander Hamilton[†] for the county, and voted for the defeated Conservative candidates in the city of Dublin.[22] At the following general election, when he was again involved in the county contest, he was facetiously mentioned as a potential starter for the borough and may have had to give evidence to the subsequent election committee; he voted for the Conservatives Hamilton and John Beatty West[†] then and in 1837.[23] Proposing another Conservative, Thomas Edward Taylor[†], for county Dublin at the general election of 1841 (as he also did in 1847), he stated that 'when he, 15 years ago, withdrew from Parliament, the doctrines of the Whigs were different to what they put forward now. He was never for violent principles and therefore he was for a firm, strong, but moderate government'.[24] Shaw, whose bank of Sir Robert Shaw and Company was incorporated as the Royal Bank of Ireland in 1836, died, a highly respected country gentleman, in March 1849. He was succeeded in his title and estates in turn by his sons Robert (1796-1869) and Frederick, who sat for Dublin University until 1848.[25]

[1] *Hist. Irish Parl.* vi. 263. [2] *Cal. Ancient Recs. Dublin*, xv. 11-12, 20; xvi. 118. [3] Shaw mss (NRA 31216). [4] TCD, Donoughmore mss F/13/28; *HP Commons, 1790-1820*, v. 134-5. [5] Add. 40296, ff. 55-56; 40298, f. 16; *Dublin Evening Post*, 3, 5 Feb.; *Dublin Jnl.* 23 Feb., 10, 17 Mar. 1820. [6] *Dublin Evening Post*, 11 May 1820. [7] *The Times*, 26 May 1820; *Cal. Ancient Recs. Dublin*, xvii. 315-17. [8] *The Times*, 17 May 1821, 1 Mar., 18, 23 Apr., 9 May 1822. [9] *PP* (1822), vii. 175-7, 183. [10] *Cal. Ancient Recs. Dublin*, xvii. 453, 463, 471-3. [11] *Dublin Evening Post*, 16 Jan. 1823. [12] *PP* (1823), vi. 77-79, 750-5; *The Times*, 15, 24 May 1823. [13] *The Times*, 6 Apr., 11 June 1824. [14] *Dublin Evening Post*, 7 Oct. 1824. [15] *The Times*, 29 Mar. 1825. [16] *O'Connell Corresp.* iii. 1278. [17] *The Times*, 28 Feb., 28 Apr. 1826. [18] *Dublin Evening Post*, 10 Aug. 1824, 8 Aug., 27 Sept., 13 Dec. 1825, 9 Mar. 1826. [19] Ibid. 6,

10, 13, 15 June; *The Times*, 15 June; NLI, Farnham mss 18602 (19), Robinson to Maxwell, 12 June 1826. [20] *Dublin Evening Post*, 26 May 1827; NAI, Leveson Gower letter bks. Leveson Gower to Gregory, 28 June 1830. [21] *Dublin Evening Post*, 23 Dec. 1830; *Extraordinary Black Bk.* (1831), 481. [22] *Dublin Evening Post*, 19 May 1831, 18 Dec. 1832; *Dublin Univ. Pollbook* (1832), 27; *Dublin Pollbook* (1837), 167. [23] *Dublin Evening Post*, 3, 10, 13 Jan. 1835; *Dublin Pollbook* (1835), 15, 41-42, 134; *O'Connell Corresp.* v. 2299; *Dublin Pollbook* (1837), 167. [24] *Dublin Evening Post*, 10 July 1841; *The Times*, 11 Aug. 1847. [25] *Dublin Evening Mail*, 12 Mar.; *The Times*, 13 Mar. 1849; *Gent. Mag.* (1849), i. 541.

S.M.F.

SHAW LEFEVRE, **Charles** (1794–1888), of Heckfield Place, nr. Odiham, Hants.[1]

DOWNTON	1830–1831
HAMPSHIRE	1831–1832
HAMPSHIRE NORTH	1832–1857

b. 22 Feb. 1794, 1st s. of Charles Shaw Lefevre[†] of Heckfield and Helena, da. of John Lefevre of Heckfield. *educ.* Winchester 1806; Trinity Coll. Camb. 1811; L. Inn 1815, called 1819. *m.* 24 June 1817, Emma Laura, da of Samuel Whitbread[†] of Southill, Beds., 3s. *d.v.p.* 2da. (1 *d.v.p.*). *suc.* fa. 1823; *cr.* Visct. Eversley 11 Apr. 1857. *d.* 28 Dec. 1888.

Speaker of House of Commons 27 May 1839-11 Apr. 1857; PC 3 June 1839; bencher, L. Inn 1839; church estates commr. 1858-9; ecclesiastical commr. 1859-*d*.

Recorder, Basingstoke 1823-35;[2] chairman, Hants q.s. 1850-79; gov. I.o.W. 1857-*d*.

Lt. N. Hants yeoman cav. 1821, lt.-col. commdt. 1823-7, 1831; a.d.c. to Queen Victoria 1859.

Dir. Sun Fire Office 1815-41.[3]

Shaw Lefevre's paternal ancestors were from Yorkshire. His father, who was born Charles Shaw (1759-1823), sat for Newtown, Isle of Wight, 1796-1802, and Reading, 1802-20. He acquired his additional surname by his marriage to the heiress of John Lefevre (1722-90), who was of Huguenot descent and had made a fortune from banking and distilling. In about 1775 he had purchased Heckfield, an estate subsequently augmented and consolidated by the Shaw Lefevres, and described in 1859 as 'a large and handsome mansion, in an extensive and well-wooded park, near the confluence of ... two rivulets'.[4] From his own recollections, Shaw Lefevre's initiation into politics came early. As an infant he was dandled by George III, who used Heckfield as a staging post on his way to Weymouth, and as a boy he was taken to a Commons debate, where, upon witnessing an oration from Charles Fox, he was reputed to have asked his father 'why that gentleman was in such a passion?'[5] His Winchester headmaster William Goddard deplored

his continued adherence to the Whigs 'in spite of all I can say', but nonetheless believed him be of 'very high stamp' and, somewhat improbably, was alleged to have predicted his eventual ascent to the Speaker's chair.[6] At Cambridge, from his own account, his sphere of excellence was tennis, and his enthusiasm for field sports, which he retained into his dotage, led his mother to despair that he was 'only fit to be a gamekeeper'.[7] An obituary asserted that he 'grew to be one of the tallest and handsomest men of his generation', but a somewhat less flattering profile of 1838 described him as being of 'about the middle height, with a slight inclination to the athletic form ... a good-looking man, with a very intellectual expression of countenance'.[8] It was with a hint of fraternal jealousy that John George Shaw Lefevre (1797-1879), Member for Petersfield, 1832-3, and afterwards the holder of a succession of public offices, warned his future wife of his brother's vanity in 1824. This did not prevent her sister, Nevil Webb Edge, from finding Charles 'charming [and] very handsome', or from admiring his 'very fine figure, and the most good tempered amiable countenance I ever saw'.[9]

Like his father, a quondam Addingtonian who had gravitated towards opposition, Shaw Lefevre never joined Brooks's, though he strengthened his Whig associations by marrying Emma, the daughter of Samuel Whitbread and the niece of the 2nd Earl Grey, the future premier. Their families were already close. Shaw Lefevre had made a walking tour of the Scottish Highlands in 1814 with his future brothers-in-law, William Henry Whitbread* and Samuel Charles Whitbread*. The marriage settlement furnished the couple with an annuity of about £1,250, which Shaw Lefevre supplemented with his modest legal practice, and they settled initially at Burley, near Ringwood, Hampshire, a minor family estate which was sold in 1852.[10] Maria Edgeworth, who encountered them in March 1819, found them 'very agreeable, good and happy' with 'little to live on now, but [they] will have a little trifle of fourteen thousand a year when old Shaw Lefevre dies'.[11] If correct, this provision must have been by settlement, as his father left all his disposable property at his death in April 1823 to his widow, who survived until 1834 and made Shaw Lefevre her residuary legatee.[12] He succeeded directly to Heckfield, and to his father's local offices of recorder of Basingstoke and commandant of the yeomanry. Soon after assuming the latter responsibility, he complained to the duke of Wellington, the lord lieutenant, of the difficulties of underfunding and of enforcing attendance, and these frustrations led him to concur in the disbandment of the corps in 1828. After its reconstitution in the wake of the 'Swing' agricultural labourers' riots, he still found that his own dedication was not universally shared, for 'many persons who promised to join in the hour of danger ... proved faithless'.[13] His comparatively small stake of 2,400 acres proved no bar to his taking a leading role on the Hampshire bench, nor, as was demonstrably the case with other individuals, did his opposition politics.[14] He enjoyed cordial relationships with Sir William Heathcote, the Ultra Tory county Member, and Wellington, with whom he negotiated a property exchange along their mutual estate boundary in 1831, and who described him the following year as 'the best of neighbours and friends'.[15]

At the 1820 general election Shaw Lefevre apprised the electors of Reading of his ailing father's intended retirement as their Member (having initially assured them of his fitness to continue) and was active on behalf of his brother-in-law William Whitbread in Middlesex. According to an obituary, he 'canvassed electors, organised local committees, and addressed popular meetings from the hustings at Brentford, and other strongholds of the liberal cause'.[16] Other opposition contacts included Edward Ellice* and John Cam Hobhouse*, whom he vainly encouraged to come forward for Middlesex at the general election of 1830.[17] There was some advance expectation that Shaw Lefevre would stand on this occasion for Reading, where the family interest had been kept up, but in the event he found a seat for Downton on the interest of the radical 3rd earl of Radnor, whose brother Philip Pleydell Bouverie* had until recently been a banking partner of Shaw Lefevre's younger brother Henry.[18] Radnor made the offer, as he informed him, 11 June, because he understood him to be indifferent to place, 'ultra liberal' and inclined 'to do all you can to destroy the patronage of your patron'. With a degree of caution, Shaw Lefevre replied that his opinions were 'decidedly liberal' and allied to a general disposition 'to watch with great jealousy the proceedings of those in power whether Whigs or Tories'. He committed himself to support an extension of the franchise 'to every person ... who is capable of using it independently', election by ballot and 'the extinction of all parliamentary patronage', a line with which Radnor, a supporter of annual parliaments and universal suffrage, was evidently content.[19] He was returned unopposed, free of expense and without a visit to the constituency.[20] (Radnor had quashed a scheme to seat him instead for Cockermouth on the Lonsdale interest, as part of an arrangement involving Pleydell Bouverie, Henry Brougham* and the latter's brother James Brougham*.) In thanking his patron, Shaw Lefevre obsequiously concurred in Radnor's

wish 'that I should not ever *nominally* represent the borough of any other person'.[21]

Shaw Lefevre was reckoned a gain for opposition by Brougham, and, having been listed by the Wellington ministry among their 'foes', he voted against them in the crucial division on the civil list, 15 Nov. 1830. He presented a Basingstoke petition for parliamentary reform, 28 Feb., and at a Hampshire county meeting, 17 Mar. 1831, declared that he 'had always been a steady friend' to this cause 'and had given it his utmost support from a decided conviction of the public benefit which would ensue'.[22] He duly voted for the second reading of the Grey ministry's reform bill, 22 Mar., and against Gascoyne's wrecking amendment, 19 Apr. 1831. Before the ensuing general election he was invited by supporters of the bill to stand for Hampshire with Sir James Macdonald*. Their joint address of 21 Apr. presaged their entry to Winchester, 27 Apr. 1831, when Shaw Lefevre declared himself to be 'a most uncompromising supporter of parliamentary reform' and denounced the naked self-interest of its borough owning opponents, 'that band of pensioners ... who swallow up all the loaves and fishes themselves'.[23] He was proposed by the former county Member George Purefoy Jervoise at the nomination, when he produced figures to rebut claims that the bill would damage the parliamentary strength of the agricultural interest. He had no need of the seat held open for him at Downton, as he was returned unopposed after the withdrawal of the sitting Members.[24]

Before the opening of Parliament, Shaw Lefevre led yeomanry exercises at Basingstoke, 11 May, and Odiham, 29 May 1831.[25] He voted for the second reading of the reintroduced reform bill, 6 July, and against two motions for its adjournment, 12 July, and gave generally steady support to its details, though he was in the minorities for the complete disfranchisement of Saltash, over which government offered no clear lead, 26 July, and Aldborough, 14 Sept., and divided for Lord Chandos's amendment to enfranchise £50 tenants-at-will, 18 Aug. On 16 Aug. he disputed Hunt's assertions that the bill's allocation of five Members to Hampshire was excessive and that the county had hitherto been 'under the immediate influence of government'. He voted for the bill's passage, 21 Sept., and the second reading of the Scottish measure, 23 Sept. On 23 Aug. he was in two ministerial majorities on the Dublin election controversy. The Whitbread connection surely lay behind his presentation of a petition from Biggleswade, Bedfordshire against the use of molasses in brewing and distilling, 25 Aug. On 27 Sept. he seconded the unsuccessful motion for inquiry into the affair of Thomas and Caroline Deacle, the Hampshire farmers allegedly manhandled by William Bingham Baring* in the course of their arrest in the aftermath of the 'Swing' disturbances. His motive was to enable Baring to vindicate himself, though he objected to the implication of the court judgement that the use of handcuffs should depend on the social status of the detainee. He divided for Lord Ebrington's motion of confidence in the ministry, 10 Oct. 1831, when he was commended for his steady conduct at a Romsey reform meeting.[26]

Shaw Lefevre voted for the second reading of the revised reform bill, 17 Dec. 1831, steadily supported its details, and divided for its third reading, 22 Mar. 1832. He spoke warmly of proposals for a London to Southampton railway at a meeting of interested parties, 23 Jan., and was in the minority in favour of the Vestry Act amendment bill the same day.[27] He presented an Alton petition for abolition of the death penalty for offences against property, 18 Apr., and one from Hampshire coroners for an increase in their allowances, 22 June. He voted with government on the Russian-Dutch loan, 26 Jan., 12, 16, 20 July, relations with Portugal, 9 Feb., and military punishments, 16 Feb. He divided for the address calling on the king to appoint only ministers who would carry the reform bill unimpaired, 10 May, the second reading of the Irish bill, 25 May, and against a Conservative amendment for increased county representation for Scotland, 1 June. On other issues he showed some independence. He was in minorities for a select committee on colonial slavery, 24 May, and for a reduction in the barracks grant, 2 July. He voted against Baring's bill to exclude insolvent debtors from Parliament, 6 June 1832.

At the general election of 1832 Shaw Lefevre stood for the Northern division of Hampshire and topped the poll in a four-sided contest.[28] All his subsequent elections for North Hampshire were unopposed. He was selected to move the address at the opening of the 1834 session, and, according to Denis Le Marchant[†], produced 'an excellent speech'.[29] He chaired the 1835 committee on agricultural distress and directed his *Remarks on the Present State of Agriculture* (1836) to his constituents as an apologia for its inconclusive findings. In 1834 he was appointed to the royal commission on county rates. He chaired a similar body on rural policing, 1836-9, as he did the Commons select committee on procedure in 1838, when he was sketched as 'a man of great urbanity of manner [and] ... of extensive information on most of the topics which occupy the attention of the legislature'.[30] In 1837 he proposed the re-election of the Speaker, James Abercromby*, and he

was nominated by the Melbourne ministry to succeed him two years later. His victory, by 317-299, at the expense of the more experienced Henry Goulburn*, was seen as an important test of party strength, but his popularity and the absence of a viable alternative persuaded Peel to retain him after his accession as premier in 1841.[31] His tenure of the chair was marked by an improvement of discipline in the Commons, reform of its more arcane procedures and the almost unconscious elevation of the Speakership above the party conflict. According to a 1911 biographical profile, his steady stewardship owed much to his 'manly bearing ... handsome features and frank and open countenance [which] commanded the ready confidence of men of his own class'. His air of effortless authority apparently defied all contradiction, in spite of his occasional indulgence in creative extemporization on precedent rulings, a volume of which, edited by Robert Bourke, was published in 1857. Its preface quoted the view of the Tory Sir Robert Inglis* that he 'compressed into the period of his services more labour, more attention, and more successful energy than any one of his predecessors'; while Lord John Russell hailed him as 'the best Speaker I ever knew'. As befitted one for whom appearances were so important, he was an enthusiast for the ritual trappings which invested the Speakership with much of its latter day constitutional mystique, such as elaborate, formal dinners, and the custom of using dray horses to draw the state coach, which he originated. On his retirement in 1857, having served longer than any previous holder of the post except Arthur Onslow, he took the title of Viscount Eversley, a pension of £4,000 and the unsalaried position of governor of the Isle of Wight.[32] He declined the governorgeneralship of Canada in 1861 and was considered for the Irish lord lieutenancy in 1864, when Delane, editor of *The Times*, made the waspish remark that he would 'look the part well enough, and as looks are most part of the duties there would be no occasion to complain'.[33] Benjamin Disraeli[†] appointed him to chair the boundary commission of 1867. It was a mark of his increasing conservatism that he privately disapproved of the associated measure of parliamentary reform. He chaired the Hampshire quarter sessions from 1850 until 1879.[34]

Shaw Lefevre died at Heckfield in December 1888, one obituarist attributing his longevity to 'field sports and gardening'.[35] Latterly he had derived a handsome income from his partnership in the Whitbread brewery, but his personal life was blighted by misfortune.[36] The only one of his three sons to survive infancy died of measles in 1837, and his relationship with his wife, who had at first seemed an ideal match, deteriorated to the point where a formal separation was forestalled only by her death in 1857.[37] His younger daughters Helena and Elizabeth both married into the neighbouring family of St. John Mildmay of Dogmersfield. The eldest, Emma, remained at home, and according to a chronicler of her eccentricities, was 'very stout and moved with a sort of waddle ... and generally fell asleep at dinner, waking up at dessert in time to say 'Crown Derby', when the guests would all turn their plates upside down and examine the mark.'[38] By the terms of Shaw Lefevre's will, she inherited Heckfield and his London house in Eaton Square, while the Hackney and Bow estates of the Shaw family were earmarked for sale.[39] The same fate befell Heckfield in 1895, but the Eversley peerage was reconferred in 1906 on Shaw Lefevre's nephew George John Shaw Lefevre (1831-1928).[40]

[1] This biography draws on F.M.G. Willson, *A Strong Supporting Cast: the Shaw Lefevres, 1789-1936* (1993). [2] F. Baigent and J. Millard, *Hist. Basingstoke*, 474-5. [3] Willson, 50. [4] Ibid. 5, 21-31; *White's Hants Dir.* (1859), 523; *VCH Hants*, iv. 46-47. [5] V. Martineau, *John Martineau* (1921), 121-2. [6] H.C. Adams, *Wykehamica*, 164-5. [7] Willson, 49, 363; *The Times*, 29 Dec. 1888. [8] [J. Grant], *Random Recollections of Lords and Commons* (1838), ii. 181. [9] Willson, 63. [10] Ibid. 49-50, 59; *VCH Hants*, iv. 611. [11] *Edgeworth Letters*, 182. [12] PROB 11/1670/299; 1836/521; IR26/964/523; 1361/431. [13] Willson, 58; Wellington mss WP1/771/11; 934/34; WP4/3/2/1. [14] R. Foster, *Politics of County Power*, 12, 30-31, 44, 47. [15] F. Awdry, *A Country Gentleman of 19th Cent.* (1906), 91; Wellington mss WP4/3/4/12, 13; 4/1/15. [16] *Reading Mercury*, 21, 28 Feb. 1820; *The Times*, 29 Dec. 1888. [17] Add. 36464, f. 474; 36466, f. 161. [18] Bodl. MS. Eng. lett. c. 159, f. 47; Willson, 67-68, 72-73. [19] Wilts. RO, Radnor mss 490/1374, Radnor to Shaw Lefevre, 11 June; reply [11 June 1830], cited in Willson, 73-4 and R. K. Huch, *The Radical Lord Radnor*, 112-13. [20] Martineau, 122. [21] Radnor mss 490/1374, memo. of Radnor, 9 July, Shaw Lefevre to Radnor, 6 Aug. 1830. [22] *Hants Chron.* 21 Mar. 1831. [23] Wellington mss WP4/3/4/3/17; *Hants Chron.* 2 May 1831. [24] *Hants Chron.* 9 May 1831; Willson, 77-8; Radnor mss 490/1375, Boucher to Radnor, 24 Apr. 1831. [25] Wellington mss WP4/4/2/21, 22, 26; 5/2/12, 16. [26] *Hants Chron.* 17 Oct. 1831. [27] Ibid. 30 Jan. 1832. [28] Ibid. 17 Dec. 1832. [29] *Three Diaries*, 378. [30] Willson, 90-96; Grant, ii. 180. [31] Willson, 96-102; A.I. Dasent, *Speakers of the House of Commons*, 320-1. [32] Willson, 115-128, 152; Dasent, 321-5; J.A. Manning, *Lives of the Speakers*, 494-6; P. Laundy, *Office of Speaker*, 9, 24, 32, 294. [33] Willson 120, 233; Dasent, *John Delane*, ii. 123. [34] Willson 220-1, 230-36; Foster, 164; *The Times*, 29 Dec. 1888. [35] Hants RO 38M49/7/125/1. [36] Willson, 151-2; *The Times*, 6 May 1889. [37] Willson, 50, 59, 148-151. [38] Ibid. 164-5; Martineau, 122-5. [39] *The Times*, 6 May 1889. [40] *VCH Hants*, iv. 46-47.

H.J.S./P.J.S.

SHAW STEWART, **Sir Michael**, 6th bt. (1788–1836), of Ardgowan and Blackhall, Renfrew and 14 Carlton Terrace, Mdx.

LANARKSHIRE	16 Oct. 1827–1830
RENFREWSHIRE	1830–19 Dec. 1836

b. 4 Oct. 1788,[1] 1st s. of Sir Michael Shaw Stewart (formerly Stewart Nicolson), 5th bt., of Carnock, Stirling and his cos. Catherine, da. of Sir William Maxwell, 3rd bt., of Springkell, Dumfries; bro. of Patrick Maxwell Stewart*. *educ.* Christ Church, Oxf. 1807; L. Inn 1810; grand tour 1814-15. *m.* 16 Sept. 1819, Eliza Mary, da. of Robert Farquhar of Newark, Renfrew., 3s. 3da. (1 *d.v.p.*). *suc.* fa. as 6th bt. 3 Aug. 1825. *d.* 19 Dec. 1836.

Shaw Stewart, whose father had succeeded his uncle to the baronetcy and estates of the old Renfrewshire family of Shaw Stewart in 1812, was probably the 'Mr. Stewart Nicholson' who joined Brooks's Club on 11 July that year. He unsuccessfully contested Stirlingshire on the Whig interest in 1818. Yet his 'early friend' at Oxford was Robert Peel*, to whom he wrote in 1822 that, 'being free from all public political connection', he regarded him as 'the first public man of your day'.[2] He inherited extensive estates in Renfrewshire, including property in the port of Greenock, along with plantations in Trinidad and Tobago, from his father in 1825. Shortly afterwards it was suggested to Lord Melville, the Liverpool ministry's Scottish manager, that he might be a suitable candidate for Renfrewshire, if he would 'give us something like a pledge that he would not *systematically* oppose the government'.[3] In the event, he was returned for Lanarkshire at a by-election in October 1827 on the interest of the Whig 10th duke of Hamilton. His brother John, who represented him in his absence in Florence, stated that his 'general principles' were 'similar' to those of the deceased Whig Member, Lord Archibald Hamilton, and that he would accordingly support 'the present liberal and constitutional policy' of Lord Goderich's coalition ministry. In a subsequent address confirming his 'cordial support' for the government 'as ... at present constituted', he added that 'I deplore Mr. Canning's death every day'.[4]

He attended meetings of the West India planters and merchants,[5] and was presumably the 'Sir Matthew Stewart' who argued that if the duties on East and West Indian produce were equalized, an 'extensive' market for British manufactures 'would be thrown open', 16 June 1828. He voted against the duke of Wellington's ministry to reduce the grant for the Royal Cork Institution, 20 June, condemn the misapplication of public money for building work at Buckingham House, 23 June, and reduce the salary of the lieutenant-general of the ordnance, 4 July. He similarly divided against the East Retford disfranchisement bill, 27 June, and the additional churches bill, 30 June 1828. He presented petitions from Glasgow, Greenock and elsewhere in favour of Catholic emancipation, 4, 25 Mar., 7 Apr., and voted for the government's bill, 6, 30 Mar. 1829. He denied that a hostile petition from Greenock reflected the 'undivided opinion of the more respectable and intelligent part of the community', 16 Mar., and deplored the efforts by Church of Scotland ministers to 'excite a strong and prejudicial feeling throughout their congregations' by 'addressing them on this as a purely religious subject, both in and out of their pulpits'. He admitted that a 'great proportion' of the 'less well-informed' inhabitants in the West of Scotland were 'undoubtedly hostile to concession', 19 Mar., but observed that the 'lower orders' were 'ever ready to do anything ... [to] depress and keep back the Irish Catholics', who 'pour in upon them almost with every tide ... to compete with them in all their occupations ... materially lowering the rate of wages throughout the district'. He thanked ministers for their 'truly sanative, beneficent and just' decision to act, on which depended 'the tranquillity of the empire'. He objected to the Member for Perth Burghs being appointed to the committee on the Perth waterworks bill, 23 Mar., as this would be in 'violation' of the 'excellent rule' made by the House in the previous session. He successfully moved the second reading of the Lanarkshire roads bill, 16 Apr., and brought up the report of the committee on the Garturk and Garion railway bill, 4 May. He presented petitions from Hamilton cotton weavers and Glasgow out-pensioners for assistance to emigrate, 7 May, 1 June 1829, when he asked the government to state their intentions. He divided with them against Knatchbull's amendment to the address on distress, 4 Feb. 1830. However, he voted with the revived Whig opposition for tax reductions, 15 Feb., to get rid of the Bathurst and Dundas pensions, 26 Mar., and for returns of privy councillors' emoluments, 14 May, but was against Hume's amendment to reduce judges' salaries, 7 July. He presented more Glasgow petitions for assistance with emigration, 10 Mar., 14 May. When presenting a Glasgow weavers' petition for relief from distress, 18 Mar., he observed that 'thousands' were 'suffering the severest privation from the extremely low rate of wages', but doubted whether it was 'in the power of the House' to help, 'unless it be by opening the vast markets of India and China to the enterprise of their employers'. He presented petitions from Greenock, Port Glasgow and elsewhere against renewal of the East India Company's charter, 25 May, 11 June. He thought the Greenock petition for reduction of the duty on molasses 'well deserving' of government attention, 1 July, lamented that 'on many occasions the West India interest has been greatly overlooked' and hoped that 'Members ... connected with it will assert its claims more strongly in future'. He divided for Lord Blandford's reform bill, 18 Feb., and to enfranchise Birmingham, Leeds and Manchester, 23 Feb. He declared that the 'direct proof

of corruption' at East Retford 'calls for complete correction', 26 Feb., and voted to transfer its seats to Birmingham, 5 Mar. He divided for Jewish emancipation, 5 Apr. He expressed 'much satisfaction' with the Scottish judicature bill, 1 Apr., and attributed the 'liberal ... improvements and curtailments in the system of expenditure' to the 'enlightened mind' of Peel. He made several suggestions for the reduction of fees and the extension of trial by jury. He said he had received many contradictory communications on this bill, 18 June, but offered it his 'decided support' as a 'preliminary measure'. He presented Greenock petitions against the Port Glasgow harbour bill and the Clyde navigation bill, 3 May. He voted for inquiry into the state of Newfoundland, 11 May, and Labouchere's motion regarding the civil government of Canada, 25 May. He presented but dissented from the Glasgow petition for abolition of the death penalty for forgery, given 'the vast and ever undulating paper circulation of this country', 24 May, and argued that ministers had gone 'as far as ... prudent'; he paired against abolition, 7 June 1830. At the general election that summer he offered for Renfrewshire, in accordance with an agreement with John Maxwell, the retiring Member, and was returned unopposed. As a man of 'independent circumstances', he promised to pursue an 'independent' course and claimed to have 'supported ministers nine times out of ten'. He expressed the 'highest admiration' for Wellington and Peel, whose 'places could [not] be supplied', and hoped the 'free and spontaneous support of Parliament' would be given to them and that they would be 'strengthened by a union of their friends'. He pledged support for economy and retrenchment, 'as far as it could safely be done'.[6]

The ministry regarded him as one of the 'good doubtfuls', who was a friend 'where not pledged'. However, he voted against them in the crucial civil list division, 15 Nov. 1830. He was reportedly 'rather censured for not voting with ... Peel', who had apparently given 'something [of] late' to his brother Patrick.[7] He welcomed the Grey ministry's 'highly beneficial' plan to remove the expense of Scottish enfeoffments, 2 Dec. 1830. He joined a deputation of Scottish Members to the chancellor of the exchequer, Lord Althorp, regarding the proposed tax on steam vessels, 5 Mar., which he described to the House, 29 Mar. 1831, as 'gravely detrimental' to a trade that was 'in its infancy'.[8] He presented a petition from the West India planters and merchants of Glasgow, Greenock, Port Glasgow and Johnstone for compensation to slave owners, 28 Mar. He presented petitions for parliamentary reform from Greenock, Paisley, Eastwood and Stirling, 11 Feb. He supported the 'principle' of the government's English reform bill, which gave the 'franchise to wealth and population', 19 Mar., although he might 'perhaps disapprove of some of the details'; he divided for the second reading, 22 Mar. He claimed that there was a 'most decided and unanimous feeling in the West of Scotland' in favour of reform, 25 Mar., and considered its 'general policy' to be 'expedient and likely to produce the most beneficial effects to Scotland'. He voted against Gascoyne's wrecking amendment, 19 Apr. 1831. At the ensuing general election he was again returned unopposed for Renfrewshire, as an 'independent Scotsman' and a 'friend of the great measure of reform'. He explained that he had supported Wellington's ministry in expectation of 'a reform of some kind', but had 'heard with astonishment and dismay' the duke's anti-reform declaration. He described the Grey ministry's budget as 'an ill-digested measure', which had thankfully been 'thrown aside', and he favoured opening the East Indian trade, which was 'manifestly due to this part of the country'.[9]

Shaw Stewart criticized the sheriff of Lanarkshire for resorting to military force at the recent election, 29 June 1831. He presented a Greenock petition that day against renewal of the East India Company's charter, and ones from Greenock and Plymouth for repeal of the duty on marine insurance policies, 30 July. He divided for the second reading of the reintroduced reform bill, 6 July, steadily for its details and for its third reading, 19 Sept., and passage, 21 Sept. He presented, without comment, a petition from the Renfrewshire political union for modifications to the Scottish bill, 20 Sept., and divided for the second reading, 23 Sept. He expressed support for the bill, while reserving his opinion on details, 3 Oct., and described it as 'an act of common justice to Scotland', which had grown in wealth and population since the Union and whose 'present system of popular representation' was 'utterly inadequate'. However, he hoped it would be 'a final measure ... for our generation' and that ministers would 'take their constitutional stand' on it. He divided for Lord Ebrington's confidence motion, 10 Oct. He attended the Lanarkshire county meeting, 7 Nov., when he argued that Ebrington's motion had 'preserved the peace of the country' and expressed confidence that, 'backed by the irresistible power of the people', the reform bills would 'shortly become ... law'.[10] He voted with ministers to punish only those guilty of bribery at the Dublin election, 23 Aug. He divided for the second reading of the revised English reform bill, 17 Dec. 1831, its details in committee, the third reading, 22 Mar., and the motion for an address asking the king to appoint

only ministers committed to carrying an unimpaired measure, 10 May 1832. He informed *The Times* that he had paired for the second reading of the Irish bill, 25 May.[11] He divided against a Conservative amendment for increased Scottish county representation, 1 June, but advised ministers to postpone the registration clause to take account of various objections, 5 June. He opposed Cutlar Fergusson's motion to unite Port Glasgow with Greenock, 15 June, on the grounds that Greenock was 'the first seaport in Scotland' and 'fully entitled to ... one Member to itself', and that its interests were 'in constant conflict' with those of Port Glasgow. He moved that day, as a matter of 'common sense and common justice', to transfer Kilmarnock from the Renfrew to the Ayr Burghs, as the present arrangement effectively gave 'three Members to Ayrshire'; he was defeated, 67-35, acting as a minority teller. He divided with ministers on relations with Portugal, 9 Feb., and the Russian-Dutch loan, 12, 16, 20 July, but voted in the minorities to reduce the sugar duties, 7 Mar., and against the malt drawback bill, 2 Apr. He urged the postponement of Morton's patent ship bill, 28 Mar., warning that if the patent was renewed it would give an unfair advantage to foreign shipbuilders. He presented two Greenock petitions for protection to the West Indian colonies, 25 May 1832.

He offered again for Lanarkshire at the general election of 1832 on the 'same liberal and salutary principles which have hitherto guided me'. He advocated abolition of trading monopolies, retrenchment, a 'more equitable' distribution of the tax burden, municipal reform, a revised system of punishments, 'not only to take away their anomalous severity, but likewise to render them more effective, both for repressing crime and for reclaiming the criminal' and 'some wise and efficient scheme' to liberate the slaves. He was returned ahead of a Radical.[12] He sat until his death in December 1836, from 'an inflammation of the spine' apparently caused by 'a fall from his horse about a twelvemonth ago ... to which, at the time, he paid no attention'. He was succeeded by his eldest son Michael Shaw Stewart (1826-1903), Liberal-Conservative Member for Renfrewshire, 1855-65.[13]

[1] J. and S. Mitchell, *M.I. in Renfrewshire*, 137-40. [2] Add. 40353, f. 223. [3] NAS GD51/5/140. [4] *Glasgow Herald*, 3 Sept., 19, 26 Oct.; Lansdowne mss, Goderich to Lansdowne, 6 Sept. 1827. [5] Inst. of Commonwealth Stud. M915/4. [6] Glasgow City Archives, Maxwell mss T-PM 117/3/1; *Glasgow Herald*, 2 July, 13 Aug. 1830. [7] Hopetoun mss 167, f. 202. [8] *Glasgow Herald*, 11, 28 Mar. 1831. [9] Ibid. 13 May 1831. [10] Ibid. 11 Nov. 1831. [11] *The Times*, 29 May 1832. [12] *Glasgow Herald*, 30 July, 24, 28 Dec. 1832. [13] *Gent. Mag.* (1837), i. 317; PROB 11/1886/800; IR26/1468/1032.

T.A.J.

SHEIL, Richard Lalor (1791–1851), of Long Orchard, co. Tipperary.[1]

MILBORNE PORT	4 Mar. 1831–1831
CO. LOUTH	1831–1832
CO. TIPPERARY	1832–1841
DUNGARVAN	1841–Feb. 1851

b. 17 Aug. 1791, 1st s. of Edward Sheil of Bellevue, co. Waterford and Catherine, da. of John McCarthy of Spring House, co. Tipperary. *educ.* privately; Kensington House sch., Surr. 1802-4; Stonyhurst 1804; Trinity, Dublin 1807; King's Inns 1809; L. Inn 1811, called [I] 1814. *m.* (1) 1816, Miss O'Halloran (*d.* Jan. 1822), niece of Sir William McMahon, master of the rolls [I], 1s. *d.v.p.*; (2) 20 July 1830, Anastasia, da. and coh. of John Lalor of Cranagh and Long Orchard, wid. of Edmund Power of Gurteen, Clonmel, co. Tipperary, *s.p.* Took name of Lalor before Sheil 1830. *d.* 25 May 1851.

KC [I] 1830; commr. Greenwich Hosp. 1838-9; vice-pres. bd. of trade Aug. 1839-June 1841; PC 29 Aug. 1839; judge adv.-gen. June-Sept 1841; master of mint July 1846-Nov. 1850; minister plenip. to Tuscany 1850-*d.*

Dubbed 'the little spiteful, snarling Sheil' by Thomas Creevey*, but widely regarded as one of the 'most effective' and 'brilliant' parliamentary speakers of his age, Sheil was credited with 'an inborn gift of oratory', which he cultivated with 'great care and nicety', although his 'horrible' high-pitched voice, likened by William Gladstone[†] to 'a tin kettle battered about from place to place', and his 'detestable' Irish brogue, meant that he was 'not pleasant to listen to', and his speeches were 'better on paper than in the House'.[2] His father had been a successful merchant in Spain, and on returning to Ireland had purchased an estate in county Waterford and married into a family connected to Count MacCarthy of Toulouse and the earls of Clancarty. Educated by a refugee French priest, the Abbé de Grimeau, Sheil later attended the Jesuit schools at Kensington and Stonyhurst, where he recalled that there was a 'strong rivalry' between the English and Irish boys and the 'Jesuits themselves were all Englishmen' and 'occasionally exhibited that contempt for Ireland, which is exceedingly observable among the English Catholics'. In 1807 he entered Trinity, Dublin with 'a competent knowledge of the classics, some acquaintance with Italian and Spanish, and the power of reading and writing French as if it were his mother tongue'.[3] He was a member of its historical society, where a witness to his debut speech recounted how he 'jumped into the middle of the floor' and 'stamping violently, squealed forth the most inflated rhetoric that had ever been heard,

in the most discordant voice that could possibly be imagined'.[4] Following the bankruptcy of his father in 1808, relatives assisted with the cost of his studies in Dublin, where he had started to speak at meetings of the Catholic Board, and at Lincoln's Inn, where he joined the Eccentrics debating club. On returning to Ireland in late 1813 he delayed his call to the Irish bar in order to write *Adelaide* (1814), the first of a series of tragic dramas by which he attempted to make his fortune over the next decade. They enjoyed considerable success on the stage, aided by the performances of a celebrated Irish actress Eliza O'Neill, and in total netted him 'about £2,000'.[5] In 1816 his fortunes were further boosted by his marriage to a wealthy niece of Sir William MacMahon, the Irish master of the rolls, but his activities in support of emancipation were disapproved of and he derived no professional benefit from the connection, later remarking that the only thing he ever got from McMahon was breakfast.[6] His legal career was slow to develop, and in the lulls between briefs he wrote many of the popular 'Sketches of the Irish Bar' and other articles for the *New Monthly Magazine* that were posthumously reprinted as *Sketches, Legal and Political* (1855).

In January 1821 Sheil, who had steadily supported the vetoists on the Catholic Board in arguing that a crown veto over episcopal appointments would facilitate emancipation, launched a scathing attack on Daniel O'Connell*, the leader of the anti-vetoists, and his plan to set aside emancipation in favour of a campaign for parliamentary reform. 'I regret to see that his vetoistical folly is unchanged', observed John Barclay Sheil to O'Connell, 17 Jan., but 'if he knew how little is thought of such qualifying measures ... he would, I think, become an apostate from his present political creed and be forgiven'.[7] In a savage retort, O'Connell ridiculed the 'tragic wrath and noble ire of this Iambic rhapsodist', and it was only with difficulty that Sheil was dissuaded from challenging him to a duel.[8] Soon afterwards O'Connell was advised that Sheil had prepared an address for the next aggregate meeting 'full of the worst politics ... a kind of ode in prose in favour of the Pitt system', and that he should 'bring as many honest men as possible to the meeting to enable us to control any political rascality'.[9] In February 1821 Sheil welcomed William Plunket's relief bill, to which O'Connell was opposed, but the subsequent lack of progress reunited the Catholic factions.[10] On 8 Feb. 1823 he was formally reconciled with O'Connell at a dinner party at which it was decided to launch a new campaign for emancipation through the Catholic Association, of which he was a founding member.[11] Early the following year O'Connell's wife observed 'how much better' Sheil was 'getting on since he gave up his useless and foolish opposition'.[12] He spoke regularly at Catholic meetings, including those in honour of O'Connell in Dublin and Waterford, 4, 12 Aug. 1824, and the following month he and O'Connell invaded a bible meeting of the Munster Hibernian Society in Cork, at which the Protestant proselytiser James Edward Gordon* and the Baptist Wriothesley Noel were speaking, and over two days of 'orderly' argument 'routed them completely'. O'Connell later disclaimed any 'jealousy' at the dinner held to honour Sheil there, saying, 'it is the greatest compliment to me that he is thus treated', for 'whilst he differed with me he was totally disregarded'.[13]

In February 1825 Sheil was one of the deputation that went to Westminster to urge the case for emancipation, although O'Connell had privately decided against allowing him to give evidence, fearing that his 'voice, person and poetry would not answer for an exhibition at the bar' of the Commons.[14] During the debate on the Association's petition, 18 Feb., the backbencher Hudson Gurney observed O'Connell, the O'Gorman Mahon*, Sheil and two others 'under the gallery, a line of the most blackguard looking birds one shall see'.[15] In the event they were denied a hearing by the Liverpool ministry, following which O'Connell and Sheil, who were said to be 'very angry', waited on leading members of the Whig opposition.[16] George Tierney* believed that ministers had acted 'very foolishly, for the chances are ten to one that O'Connell and Sheil would furnish some new handle against themselves', but 'as it is they go back with a fresh grievance which every man will be able to understand'.[17] At the Catholic meeting at Freemason's Hall, 23 Feb., Sheil argued vehemently against the suppression of the Association, but the subsequent account implausibly attributed to him in *New Monthly Magazine* described his speech as 'a failure', in which he 'lost command over his throat' and 'wearied them with a laborious detail of uninteresting facts'.[18] Giving evidence to a Commons committee on Irish justice, 3 Mar., he declared that emancipation would end 'all religious faction in Ireland' and that he would 'take no further part in political concerns' thereafter, but he was vilified for his unfounded 'rhetorical artifice' that pensions were conferred by the Castle purely on sectarian grounds. O'Connell considered it a 'most comical examination'.[19] Following the rejection of the relief bill that summer, Sheil was named as the source in an article by William Cobbett† ascribing O'Connell's acceptance of the Protestant 'wings' to his desire for a patent of precedence, but Sheil assured O'Connell that he had 'never insinuated anything of the kind'

and hoped that the citation of his name had 'left no disagreeable impression'. Rumours of a breach persisted, however, and on 4 Dec. 1825 O'Connell's wife observed that Sheil was 'wheeling around again'.[20]

At the 1826 general election Sheil assisted in the return of the pro-Catholic Alexander Dawson for county Louth, speaking with the 'greatest success'.[21] At one meeting outside Dundalk chapel he 'astonished all parties' by likening the claim of Irish landlords to direct their tenants' votes to their feudal right 'upon the marriage of the daughter of any of his tenants, to conduct her to his own bed'. 'I tell you that your landlords have no more right to ask you to vote against your religion and your conscience, than they have to ask you for the virginity of your children', he declared, warning the Catholic freeholders that they had 'a choice between the cross and the distress warrant'.[22] Thereafter he adopted a far more militant line in the relaunched Association, which he predicted would soon be the 'master of the representation of Ireland', and initiated the Catholic census, which became a powerful tool of propaganda.[23] Describing one of his speeches at Bellinasloe, Durvergier de Hauranne recalled:

Five feet, eyes quick and piercing, complexion pale ... When you behold that little gacon figure in repose, it is impossible to suspect to what changes passion is capable of converting it ... His satire is shrewd and biting, his poetry dazzles, his enthusiasm carries you away ... His voice is meagre, harsh and shrill, but a profound emotion seems to regulate its vibrations ... Sheil possesses, in an eminent degree, the surprising faculty of exerting himself to the very verge of delirium, without once losing his complete self-possession.[24]

Speaking 'under the influence of some wine' in response to a royal toast in Mullingar, 14 Sept. 1826, he ridiculed the 'protestations about conscience' which had been urged against the relief bill in the Lords by the duke of York, 'an avowed and ostentatious adulterer ... hot and reeking from the results of a foul and most disgraceful concubinage'. 'That he should dedicate himself with an invocation to heaven to the everlasting oppression of my country!', he protested, is what 'sets me, and every Irish Catholic, on fire!'[25] Anticipating trouble, he left for Paris, where he contributed a number of anonymous articles on the condition of Ireland to *L'Étoile*.[26] The king, who took a 'personal interest' in his remarks, and Goulburn, the Irish secretary, regarded his speech as 'libellous', but after consulting the attorney-general the cabinet advised against prosecution, citing the effect it might have on the duke's health.[27] The 'general indignation and disgust' aroused by the speech, the home secretary Peel informed Lord Wellesley, the viceroy, 14 Nov. 1826, had 'inflicted upon the aggressor a severer punishment than could be awarded by a court of law'.[28] Speaking at the Association, 19 Jan. 1827, Sheil urged the Catholics to draw lessons about French military assistance from the recently published memoirs of the Irish insurgent Wolfe Tone, which Peel and Wellesley considered 'undoubtedly a seditious libel'.[29] Only Canning, the foreign secretary, doubted that there were sufficient grounds to prosecute, and on 29 Jan. Liverpool, the premier, resolved not to 'pass over unnoticed, a libel of so treasonable a character'.[30] The following month Sheil and Michael Staunton, the proprietor of the *Morning Register* which had printed his speech, were formally indicted, as *The Times* put it, for throwing out hints 'conducive to the success of the next invasion by the French'.[31] Shortly after the formation of Canning's ministry later that year, however, the case was dropped.[32]

Following Canning's death and the accession of the Goderich administration in August 1827, Sheil outlined plans for the formation of a central committee to correspond with all the parishes of Ireland where 'there is a priest and a curate', who, he contended, 'constitute a sort of intellectual aristocracy' and 'supply the place' of 'rank and wealth in which we are deficient'. Urging the necessity of such measures to O'Connell, 30 Sept. 1827, he wrote:

> We should not hide from ourselves, the public mind is beginning to cool. The reason is, I think, this: when Peel and Dawson and our decided antagonists were in office, the Catholics were exposed to perpetual affronts which kept their indignation alive ... But now that Lord Lansdowne is in, we say to each other, 'What a pity that our good friends in the cabinet cannot do us any service!' and, convinced that they cannot, we 'take the will for the deed'. In this view it would be almost better for us to have our open enemies than either our lukewarm and impotent advocates in power ... It behoves us therefore to make double exertions and I shall not, you may rely on it, be deficient in my efforts ... Our great object should be to bring the priests into efficient and *systematic* action. This is my plan and I shall do all in my power to rouse them.[33]

Sheil initially opposed O'Connell's plans to challenge the re-election of ministers appointed to the Wellington administration of 1828 as 'premature', but on 21 June he urged the Association to unseat Vesey Fitzgerald, president of the board of trade, in county Clare, on the grounds that 'they must show an increase of vigour' and 'make men exclaim, this question must be settled'.[34] Finding no suitable Protestant, Sheil urged O'Connell to stand and took a leading part in

his campaign. In a speech described by one observer as 'quite in the style of the French demagogues at the commencement of the revolution', 4 July 1828, he told the electors that 'Catholic emancipation is not the question, but it is the triumph of the people over the aristocracy, and the only way to effect it, is to make them fear you'.[35] Following O'Connell's return he boasted that 'we are the masters of the passions of the people' and warned the Protestants to 'awake to a sense of your condition ... Annihilate us by concession, if you do not, tremble for the result'.[36]

Rumours that month that Sheil would come forward for an expected vacancy at Galway prompted the retiring Member to write to Peel, again home secretary, with an offer to 'hold over for some time'.[37] To the alarm of ministers, however, Lord Anglesey, the new viceroy, advised Lord Francis Leveson Gower, the Irish secretary, that he saw 'no possible means' of 'depriving the demagogues of the power of directing the people', other than 'taking 'O'Connell and Sheil and the rest of them from the Association and placing them in the House'.[38] On learning of Sheil's candidacy he remarked, 'What harm will he do? None I verily believe', adding, 'he is to my mind a much more formidable character than O'Connell' and pointing out to Peel that he 'is the least likely of all the agitators to be caught', being 'in the habit of writing and well weighing what he means to say'.[39] The vacancy did not occur. That August Sheil, by now an occasional dinner guest at the Castle, privately agreed to use his influence in the Association to halt the growing number of processions of the peasantry which were threatening the peace of the country, including a grand Tipperary meeting in support of emancipation, which was called off.[40] On 18 Sept. 1828, in a widely circulated speech intended as an appeal for calm, he warned of the imminent danger of a civil war between the 'semi-Protestant north', where the Orangeman took up his 'blade clotted with the rusty blood of 1798', and the 'utterly Catholic south', in which 'a holocaust of Popish victims' would 'be offered up to the Moloch of orthodoxy'.[41] Reporting to Wellington a few days later, Maurice Fitzgerald* stated that he had 'announced explicitly, that if an affray should take place between the Orangemen and the Catholics of the north of Ireland ... it would be followed by a massacre of every Protestant man, woman and child in the south', and recommended immediate military preparations. Subsequent consideration of using the speech to expedite a prosecution of the Association came to nothing.[42] On 25 Sept. Sheil, notwithstanding complaints that he was an 'alarmist', successfully proposed resolutions halting the processions.[43] Commenting on the subsequent arrest of John Lawless, who had failed to heed the Association's recall, Sir Joseph Laffan observed to Anglesey, 16 Oct., 'I am sorry the lot had not fallen to Sheil instead of Lawless', as he has 'exasperated the Protestants' and 'lost the Catholics their cause', and 'matters would have been much more easily adjusted if he had been out of the way'.[44] Three days later, however, Anglesey assured Lord Holland that he was 'certain' that O'Connell and Sheil could be 'depended upon' and were 'sick of the present state of the country', although they had been 'provokingly foolish in not stopping after the Clare election'.[45]

On 24 Oct. 1828, in a move which Leveson Gower considered would 'do more to hurt his own cause by offending the English Protestants', Sheil attempted to speak at a Brunswick meeting at Penenden Heath in Kent, where he had recently acquired a freehold.[46] Denied a proper hearing by a hostile crowd, he retorted, 'You are afraid to hear me! You Brunswickers are afraid even of my voice, feeble as it is ... Is the argument on my side so strong that you will be deaf to it? They say justice is blind, but you make her deaf also'. Denying charges of personal ambition, he said that the object of emancipation was 'not for a few individuals to get into Parliament, nor to put a silk gown on my back, but to give tranquillity to Ireland and to restore the religious peace'.[47] Lord Darnley, who noted the 'disadvantage' to the other pro-Catholic speakers of his presence, wondered 'what could have provoked ... [him] to attend? I tried to stop him by remonstrance with a friend at whose house he was, but in vain. His reception must have mortified him much'.[48] Another commentator noted that 'Sheil, whom they would not hear, has the voice of a ventriloquist and the ways of a mountebank'.[49] The following day, however, Sheil insisted to O'Connell that 'although the Brunswickers had a majority in Kent, yet we had the preponderance of rank and wealth and also an immense body of the people'.[50] A copy of his intended speech appeared in the press that day and later as a pamphlet, much to the amusement of Mrs. Arbuthnot, who observed that he had written it 'the day before ... and sent it to be printed ... interlarding it with "(applause), (cheers), (immense cheering)", whereas he was hooted, and his brutality about the duke of York so exclaimed at, that not one word was heard. This has caused great ridicule against him'.[51] Jeremy Bentham, however, commented that 'so masterly an union of logic and rhetoric as Mr. Sheil's speech, scarcely have I ever beheld'.[52] Writing to Holland about the Catholic leaders, 28 Oct., Anglesey complained that they 'really are too indiscreet and put it almost out of the power of anyone to help them', but he hoped to take O'Connell 'in

hand' as 'well as Sheil', who 'is more to be depended upon'.[53] The following month Sir James Mackintosh* reported a rumour that Sheil, a widower for six years, had come to London 'to marry a great Popish fortune, a Miss Byrne', but no wedding took place.[54] He was back in Dublin by 18 Nov., when a German visitor recorded that 'as a speaker he is too affected, too artificial, and all he said too much *got up*', and that he was 'evidently jealous of his colleague O'Connell'.[55] Soon afterwards Greville heard that 'O'Connell and Sheil detest each other, though Sheil does not oppose him'.[56] In December 1828 Curtis, the Catholic primate, privately showed Sheil a letter indicating Wellington's willingness to settle the Catholic question.[57] Declaring that 'nothing can so well become us as mild behaviour and humility, when the least intimations of national pacification are held out', Sheil called for an immediate cessation of the Association's agitation, 3 Feb. 1829, but was asked to wait by O'Connell, who feared that a 'precipitate dissolution' would destroy his bargaining position in London with respect to the Irish 40s. freeholders.[58] Contrasting their attitudes, 8 Feb., Matthew Forde* noted that O'Connell 'is very wrong in using the violent language he still does' and that 'Sheil and Lawless seem to have a much better feeling'.[59] Four days later, to the fury of O'Connell, Sheil secured a resolution suspending the Association's activities with the aid of the 'Orange Papists', with whom the O'Connells alleged he had been 'conspiring'.[60] As he later explained to Pierce Mahony†, a former parliamentary agent of the Association who had the ear of government, 'it is ... much wiser to let the bill pass as it stands, and afterwards endeavour to modify it', as 'even the individuals who are most zealous in the cause of the forty shillingers ... admit that their franchises ought not to be weighed against the liberty and consequent tranquillity of the country'. On 29 Mar. he assured Mahony that where 'we were formerly interested in awakening, we are now equally interested and bound to allay the popular ferment', and predicted that 'in a few months time Ireland will be a new country', adding, 'what a relief it is to me to be liberated from the necessity of attending aggregate meetings'. Describing the advantages of emancipation to his friend William Curran, 28 Mar., he boasted of having recently received 'five briefs from an Orange attorney', and recalled how

> formerly, when I was about to leave Clonmel, a deputation of greasy liberals used to wait on me to beg that I would ... hold forth at a Catholic meeting ... I was then dragged to the Great Chapel, where some 5,000 peasants with a few Clonmel shopkeepers at their head were gathered in one dense and steaming mass of agitation. Placed

by a couple of brawny priests upon the steps of the altar, I held forth ... and was of necessity obliged to adapt myself to my audience. This was a dreadful need. I am now emancipated from it ... the perpetual reiteration of the same matter and of the same phrases was as wearisome to the repeater, as to the public.[61]

The previous month he had successfully defended Michael Staunton, who had been indicted by the Protestant archbishop of Tuam for a libel on himself and the church, and made what was described as a 'splendid' speech impugning the prosecution's motives.[62] On 7 Apr. 1829 he apprised Mahony that 'it would be of very great importance to me, especially after my recent success upon circuit, to get a silk gown', but that as it would probably 'not be given ... it behoves me to take a bold step'.[63]

In June 1829 he announced his intention of standing for a vacancy for Louth against a local Catholic proprietor, but offered to withdraw if a member of Anglesey's family came forward.[64] Later that month an anonymous informant advised Wellington that Sheil was 'disposed to be conciliatory' towards government, and suggested making him a king's counsel 'to ensure his loyalty'.[65] Wellington dismissed the notion and Sheil's apparent opposition to O'Connell's new anti-Union agitation, observing to Peel that 'they quarrel and reconcile their differences as frequently as children', and 'in the meantime they may separate the two countries'.[66] On 24 Oct. he added:

> I don't think that any promise or even appointment would give the government the support of Mr. Sheil, nor do I think it would be desirable to seek it ... It might be practicable to neutralize him and to separate him from any active co-operation with O'Connell by the promise or grant of a silk gown. But neither could be done without the consent of the king [and] the language of Sheil about the duke of York not yet three years old, his appearance last year in Kent, and his pretensions to the representation of ... Louth, founded on the radical Roman Catholic interest, are all topics of which we should never hear the end if we were to get into discussion ... I don't believe that in this country it has ever been the practice to appoint demagogues to be king's counsel.[67]

On 9 Nov., however, Greville reported that Leveson Gower was to meet Sheil with the approval of Peel, who was 'rather inclined ... to do anything to win him', despite the 'king's horror of the man'.[68] The previous month Mahony had urged Anglesey to support him in Louth in the event of his son declining, explaining that he 'is *at heart* a liberal Tory, one of your lordship's party', and that his 'character as a public man will not be *safe* until he is *seated* as a free representative

in the House of Commons', where 'I am convinced he would be as *useful* as he is *talented*' and 'would be as much your lordship's nominee, as any member of your noble house'.[69] On 19 Oct. 1829 Lord Cloncurry wrote in similar terms, saying that Sheil had 'good principles and great talent' and had 'never affected more of retirement or disinterestedness than he really felt: when an agitator he said he would not think as an Irishman but only as a Papist, he now says he must think only as a lawyer learning his trade'.[70]

It was in the 'pursuit of the regular path' of his profession that Sheil that month agreed to act as counsel for the Tory Lord George Thomas Beresford* in the forthcoming county Waterford by-election, prompting O'Connell to launch a 'ferocious attack' on him.[71] In a 'vindicatory letter' to the *Dublin Evening Post*, 8 Dec., Sheil insisted that by acting for the Protestant Beresfords he was helping to bury sectarian divisions made obsolete by emancipation. 'What is Sheil about?', asked one of O'Connell's supporters, observing that if he

> comes here for the Beresfords, I trust in God that our election will take place before that of Louth, and then I think you will see an address from the priests of Waterford to the priests of Louth to reject the claims of a man who roused the 40s. freeholders against the landlords, and who when emancipation is gained by their insurrection, joins those Beresfords whilst visiting the dupes of his fallacious promises with their direst vengeance. I warrant you I have something in store for Master Richard.[72]

His canvass at the end of the year was described as 'particularly successful' by Mahony, who informed Anglesey that 'Sheil now leads the aristocracy, the gentry, and the intelligent Catholics', 9 Dec. 1829.[73] Shortly thereafter Leveson Gower intimated to Arbuthnot that the duke of Northumberland, Anglesey's successor as viceroy, thought

> it would be an advantage to the government to have Sheil in Parliament as a supporter of its measures, and would be ready to furnish the money to buy a seat for the session if he could get one. This is entirely his own idea, but although he wishes to keep the whole transaction to himself, he would not consider himself justified in it unless he knew that it would not be disagreeable to the duke of Wellington ... If you think it too romantic to submit to the duke, put my letter in the fire.[74]

Writing to Peel, 23 Jan. 1830, Northumberland suggested that Sheil, 'having gained a dangerous, and as he now feels a detrimental notoriety in politics, is I suspect inclined to look for, and earn in due season the legitimate honour of his profession', and that 'he is viewed with great jealousy by O'Connell, and is an excellent counterbalance to him'.[75] Commenting on his work for the Beresfords at Waterford the following month, James Dwyer observed, 'Were I in his place I would not want to be seen much in public ... as the people will say that the hero of '26 is for the "unchanged" Beresford in '30'.[76] Beresford told Wellington that he was 'indebted to Sheil' following his return.[77] He was 'nearly murdered at Thomastown', reported Dywer, but 'his fortune is made'.[78] In April Leveson Gower was informed that Northumberland was keen to promote Sheil to be king's counsel.[79] Peel agreed that he 'ought not to be passed over', but advised Northumberland that the king had 'on several occasions expressed great and natural indignation at the gross insults' he had 'offered to the duke of York'. In reply, Northumberland assured Peel of Sheil's sincere 'penitence for his unjustifiable speech' and contended that his promotion would not only 'gratify the people of Ireland', but also put his 'comparatively quiet conduct' in a 'very beneficial contrast with the renewed agitation of O'Connell'.[80] The king's approval was secured and he took silk, 13 July 1830.[81] Later that month he married his second wife, a widow of 'considerable fortune'.[82]

At the 1830 general election Sheil came forward for Louth with the personal backing of Anglesey, but the claims of another candidate deprived him of the ministerial support he sought.[83] In a controversial four-day contest, he unsuccessfully fought the brother of a resident Catholic proprietor and a Protestant for second place, enabling the latter to slip in by splitting the Catholic vote.[84] 'I am not at all sorry for his defeat', a correspondent informed Thomas Wyse, the newly elected Member for county Tipperary, 'regarding it simply as the disappointment of his personal ambition and feeling no confidence whatever in his principles as a politician'.[85] The poet Thomas Moore reported 'great anxiety among his friends ... to get him into Parliament', but rumours of a petition against the return and plans to seat him for New Woodstock for the 'requisite' sum came to nothing.[86] In September Sir Henry Hardinge, the new Irish secretary, obtained assurances that he would 'support the government' in opposing repeal and considered seating him, 'not so much for his own individual value, as the advantage of separating him from O'Connell'.[87] Peel, however, cautioned:

We dread a parliamentary connection with Sheil, that is, we dread being instrumental in effecting his return, and thereby assuming the responsibility of whatever vagaries he may hereafter commit. We have no confidence in the discretion of Irish orators and (between ourselves) the communication made to you by Sheil does not encourage much confidence in his political honesty. He makes a

reservation on the score of reform, which he calls moderate reform, but this very question of reform may be the all-important, vital question.[88]

Following the fall of the Wellington ministry, Anglesey, the reappointed viceroy, warned the new Grey administration that having Sheil against them 'and even lukewarm upon the question of repeal would leave us quite helpless', and suggested that they enlist him, as he 'would be an immense card for us'.[89] Grey felt that government assistance might 'not be quite safe in this instance', as

there are sufficient grounds for a reasonable distrust of all these gentlemen. Sheil I hope is, and I believe him to be, from all I hear of him, a man of honour, but Melbourne has a letter from him today, which has rather the appearance of a threat, and we cannot be too careful.[90]

Sheil's letter concerned the approach made to him by Hardinge, but Anglesey assured Grey, 29 Jan. 1831, that it should not

be considered as a threat. What he tells me is that Hardinge was very anxious to have him in Parliament, that he promised him a seat *gratis* upon the express terms that he was to be at liberty to sit with the opposition, and to vote freely, except upon the repeal question, which he undertook to oppose with all his power, as also O'Connell in all his mischievous projects. I continue to think Sheil's being in Parliament of almost vital importance, and it is hardly possible that any question could arise with the present ministers that he would not warmly support. Upon the subject of reform, I should only fear that he would not go far enough ... Universal suffrage, vote by ballot, annual parliaments, he deprecates, and he is much averse to getting rid of the close boroughs of Ireland and thinks that if the right of voting were much more increased, none but Repealers would be returned ... Depend upon it, he will be worth his hire. It would be better for all parties that Sheil be enlisted by your government than by me.[91]

On 2 Feb. Anglesey was told that Grey disliked 'putting it in Sheil's power to say that government *money* had been applied, from secret funds, to bring him in', but that 'if matters could not be otherwise arranged', this should not stand in the way.[92] Plans were accordingly made to seat him for Cashel, where the son of the proprietor was ready to vacate, but with Sheil only able to provide £1,000 of the market price of £1,500, Anglesey insisted that Grey 'must meet any further demand', adding that if there were objections he would make his nominee George Stevens Byng 'give up Milborne Port and take Cashel instead'. Assuring Grey that Sheil would 'never take advantage of being assisted by government money', he added that his first explicit declaration in Parliament will have a powerful effect here, and particularly with the Catholic bar. At present he is paralysed. He was to be seated by the late government, and he has lost much at the bar by ... separating himself from O'Connell, whose followers amongst the attorneys no longer give briefs to Sheil.[93]

A lengthy negotiation ensued, during which Grey insisted that Anglesey 'must not tell Sheil' that 'anything is to be paid by government'.[94] Anglesey considered returning Sheil for his own nomination borough to be the 'worst possible arrangement', but on 12 Feb. Smith Stanley, the Irish secretary, advised him that there was probably no alternative.[95] Two days later Anglesey informed Holland, 'I am sending over Sheil and [Philip] Crampton*. I think you will like them both. I shall be most anxious about their debut'.[96] 'We shall have an agitator against an agitator', commented Creevey, adding, 'I shall be very curious to see how our one answers, he is a most powerful chap in private'.[97] A last minute attempt to find a berth for him at Saltash proved abortive, the 'Saltashites' making 'some difficulty about returning a Papist', and on 26 Feb. Smith Stanley reported to Anglesey that Sheil had 'set off without loss of time for Milborne Port', though he wished 'it could be otherwise'.[98] He was returned unopposed. 'Ministers have brought Sheil in to oppose O'Connell', remarked John Wilson Croker*.[99] On 7 Mar. Smith Stanley informed Anglesey that Sheil 'seemed highly pleased', but owned that he had 'some misgivings about him'.[100] He took his seat the following day, to the irritation of O'Connell, who reported to his wife, 10 Mar.:

> Sheil sat again last night perfectly silent. He does not speak to me. Indeed I believe, that is, I merely conjecture, that he was sent into the House for the very purpose of abusing me ... What other business could Lord Anglesey have of sending him here? But of course I do not care. If he attacks me I promise you he shall have his answer. I will not spare him of all men, as a renegade is the worst species of traitor.[101]

On 21 Mar. Sheil delivered his maiden speech in support of the second reading of the Grey ministry's reform bill. Speaking, according to the Whig Mackintosh, 'very cleverly and with a harsh voice and with much of our applause', he denied that the bill would destroy the influence of the aristocracy and, reminding the opposition of the 'evil' results of the 'years of agitation' and 'madness of delay' in Ireland, warned, 'let us beware how we put England through a similar process ... Concede, and that we may concede in safety, concede in time'.[102] Denis Le Marchant[†] later

recalled that 'after a few sentences, he nearly broke down, but ... by a great effort, he recovered the attention of the House, and from that time might be considered as one of its most eloquent Members'.[103] Thomas Macaulay*, with whom Sheil was on 'very civil terms' and had talked 'largely concerning Demosthenes and Burke', thought it 'an excellent speech, too florid and queer, but decidedly successful'.[104] The whip Lord Duncannon* considered it a 'most extraordinary speech, some of whose sentences were the most wonderful display I ever heard', but the minister Thomas Spring Rice* observed that although he had 'succeeded', it was 'more from physical than rational motives', and likened it to 'a bravura movement in a Jew's harp'.[105] 'It showed great readiness and imagination with some quick turns of pointed wit', noted the Tory Henry Bankes*, 'but his manner and attitudes were pantomimical, and his voice shrill and most unpleasing in its tone'.[106] The following day Smith Stanley informed Anglesey:

> Sheil did very well last night, brilliant in language, *almost too* brilliant ... I *think* he is landed as a debater, as an orator there is no doubt of him. Most people, however, are warmer in his praise than I am, and Plunket, who heard him, is quite delighted.[107]

He voted for the bill's second reading, 22 Mar., and against Gascoyne's wrecking amendment, 19 Apr. He denied that reform would destroy Protestant influence in Ireland, 29 Mar., and predicted that it would diminish support for repeal, 20 Apr. 1831.

At the ensuing general election he was first returned unopposed for Milborne Port and then for Louth, where the independent club invited him to stand and the Catholics reunited.[108] Afterwards Charles Thackeray complained to the primate that Sheil 'could not think his triumph perfect without an attack upon the church and its pastors', whom he denounced as 'pampered and bloated'.[109] He chose to sit for Louth, where, at his celebration dinner, 19 May, he promised not to offer again, except for Dundalk.[110] On 21 June he warned ministers of the growing support for repeal and urged them to 'pacify and conciliate' Ireland and 'tax the absentee'. He protested that the Irish freeholder franchise was 'far smaller' than in England, where the 40s. county franchise was to be preserved, 30 June. On 3 July he joined Brooks's, sponsored by Duncannon and Lord Sefton*. He voted for the second reading of the revised reform bill, 6 July, spoke and divided at least twice against adjournment, 12 July, and gave steady support to its details, though he voted against the division of counties, 11 Aug. Following the Newtownbarry massacre he demanded 'immediate action' against the yeomanry, 1 July, and he spoke and voted for printing the Waterford petition to disarm them, 11 Aug. He divided against the grant for the Society for the Propagation of the Gospels in the colonies, 25 July. He voted against disqualification of the Dublin election committee, 29 July, and with ministers on the controversy, 23 Aug. He demanded repeal of the Irish Subletting Act, 5 Aug. He clashed repeatedly with James Gordon, Member for Dundalk, over his 'offensive remarks' against Catholic priests and defence of the Newtownbarry yeomanry and Carlow grand jury, and called for Smith Stanley to 'always be present in the House when the affairs of Ireland are discussed', 9 Aug. He contended that the government had an 'obligation' to the 'phalanx of 40 popular Irish Members' who supported them, 10 Aug., and urged them to address the 'great grievances' of Ireland 'instead of rebuking us', 15 Aug. That month he was one of the deputation of Irish Members which threatened Grey with 'opposing the government' if 'their views of the policy fit to be pursued' in Ireland were not adopted.[111] Answering their critics in the House, he denied having tried to 'awe him into concession' with 'menacing language, menacing gesture, and menacing look', insisting that they merely wanted 'to tell the truth in a tone equally respectful and firm', 26 Aug. He wanted more Catholics to be appointed to Irish juries, 16 Aug. He argued against the grants to the Kildare Place Society, 23 Aug., and the Dublin Society, 29 Aug., but welcomed the new plan of Irish education, 9 Sept. In a speech which he boasted to Curran had been delivered 'in my old Association style, without fear', scoring 'a decided hit in the House', 29 Aug., he denounced the 'long and vitiated misrule' of Ireland and argued that 'something must be done to alleviate the dreadful sufferings' of a 'nation that stretches forth her hands for food'.[112] Calling for reform of the 'present system of pride and pomp' in the Irish church, 31 Aug., he asked, 'Shall the Whigs of parliamentary be the Tories of ecclesiastical reform? Shall there be no schedule A for my lords the bishops?' He divided for inquiry into the conduct of the Hampshire magistrates during the arrest of the Deacles, 27 Sept. He argued that improvements in the administration of English justice should also be applied to Ireland, 29 Sept. That month Anglesey observed to Holland that the Irish Members 'do not like Stanley' and that 'I suspect Sheil's course, which is not what he promised, proceeds from some slight in that quarter'.[113] Sheil doubted that there was any peaceful method of enforcing Irish tithes, 6 Oct., and was a minority teller against the ecclesiastical courts bill, 14 Oct. He voted for the third reading of the reform bill, 19 Sept., and

its passage, 21 Sept. On 27 Sept. he denied that its progress was being needlessly delayed by 'Irish local affairs', explaining that Irish Members had given ministers a 'persevering, undivided, unflinching sustainment' and were 'entitled to reciprocal fairness'. On 10 Oct., in what Greville termed a 'violent' speech, he supported Lord Ebrington's confidence motion, refuting 'insinuations' that Grey had 'resorted to reform in order to sustain the weakness and decrepitude of his government' and citing his bill of 1797 as evidence that it was not a 'new scheme'.[114] He believed that the Irish people 'unanimously' supported reform, but complained that 'justice had not been done to their country', which was 'entitled to 150 representatives', 17 Oct. 1831.

In a speech described by Le Marchant as 'not very forcible', 12 Dec., he questioned preserving the rights of Irish freemen created by birth and servitude and called for similar consideration for the 40s. freeholders who qualified in towns.[115] He voted for the second reading of the revised reform bill, 17 Dec. 1831, and gave general support to its details, but repeatedly pressed for more English nomination boroughs to be disfranchised and additional Members to be given to Ireland. His frequent recourse to statistics to support his case prompted O'Connell to hope that he would 'not keep us till August or September in summing up vulgar fractions', 23 Jan. He criticized the examination of voters at the poll with 'no formulae', 27 Jan., and urged Lord John Russell to adopt the Irish affidavit system rather than 'leave this matter to the bias, ignorance, or, perhaps, corruption, of the returning officer', 11 Feb. He voted against the enfranchisement of £50 tenants-at-will in the English counties, 1 Feb., when he observed that the enfranchisement of trustees 'in actual possession or receipt' of rents and profits related to their 'own profit' only and suggested that the word 'trustee' be struck out. On 21 Feb., in order to expedite the progress of the bill, he reluctantly agreed to withdraw his amendment to transfer Petersfield from schedule B to A, which he had hoped would establish a precedent for doing the same to Eye, Midhurst, New Woodstock and Wareham, much to the disappointment of the opposition.[116] He opposed similar proposals by other Members, saying the 'time has gone by for the discussion of this question', 2 Mar. He voted for the bill's third reading, 22 Mar., and for the address calling on the king to appoint only ministers who would carry it unimpaired, 10 May. He wanted the Irish bill to be made 'as far as possible the same' as the English, 25 May, but voted for its second reading that day. He asked why the Scottish universities were not to have 'even one Member' and divided for a Conservative amendment to increase Scottish county representation, 1 June. He campaigned steadily for the assimilation of the English, Irish and Scottish bills and the restoration of the 40s. freeholder franchise to Irish counties, for which he was a minority teller with O'Connell, 13 June. Attacking government plans that day to give one of the 'miserable five' additional Irish seats to Dublin University, where Catholics were 'excluded from fellowships and scholarships', he exclaimed, 'Whigs! Why do you do this? Is it because Ireland has deserved so ill, and Dublin ... so well at your hands that you are determined on offering a palpable affront to the one by conferring this baneful favour on the other?' He presented a petition for extending the franchise to all Dublin graduates, 13 July. He complained that 'no reason' had been given for setting the Irish leasehold qualification at £20 rather than the English level of £10 and was in the minority for O'Connell's motion to extend the Irish county franchise to £5 freeholders, 18 June. He protested at the 'constant evasion' of the property qualification for Members and called for its abolition, 27 June. On 29 June he argued that English and Irish £10 householders should qualify on the same basis and was a minority teller for his own amendment against the liability of Irish electors to pay municipal taxes before they could vote, which was defeated by 59-21. He pressed for the 40s. freehold voters in towns with a county status to be allowed to 'retain their right' as a 'counterbalance' to the Irish freemen, most of whom were Protestant and 'in favour of one political party', 2 July. He welcomed O'Connell's suggestions for improvements to the Irish leaseholder clauses and questioned the policy of making electors state the 'name of the street' where they lived at the time of registration, citing the '20 or 30 persons' who had been 'disfranchised' at the last Clare election 'because they lived in no street at all', 9 July. That day he urged that Newry be given the same boundary treatment as Dungarvan. He objected to Catholics swearing an oath of allegiance to the crown at registration, as it would perpetuate an 'unfortunate feeling of religious distinction', 18 July. In a speech criticised in the House by Hudson Gurney for being 'as full of *non sequiturs* as any speech can be', he asserted that the bribery clause was inoperable and 'a complete nullity', 30 July 1832.

In what was described by Holland as 'not only a good but a friendly and useful speech on the tithe question', he argued that it was 'folly to think of pacifying Ireland without an utter change in the ecclesiastical system', 15 Dec. 1831.[117] He objected to the Irish Subletting Act amendment bill, 20 Jan., and the 'impropriety' of holding its second reading at half-past-one in the

morning, 17 Feb. 1832. He campaigned relentlessly for abolition of the Irish tithes system, condemning the Protestant composition of the committee, 24 Jan., and their 'ignorance of tithe matters', 8 Feb., and warned that any attempt to enforce payment would be 'unjust in principle, preposterous in policy, and impossible of application', 14 Feb. He was a minority teller against their report, 8 Mar., when he contrasted the eagerness of ministers to press ahead with the reform bill, even at the expense of ignoring many of its defects, with their refusal to consider tithes, and urged them to 'awake, for God's sake, to a sense of the condition of Ireland', otherwise 'come the general election ... reform will have thrown the close boroughs open, the democracy will have become gigantic' and 'then will the people have their revenge'. Le Marchant afterwards overheard Lord Althorp saying that 'Sheil's speech has done us more harm than the division good' and congratulated Sheil for the 'valuable' support he had given the Tories:

> 'What would you have us do?', he replied. 'We shall get nothing by the reform. The Catholics and liberals return all the Members they can. The people insist on the abolition of tithe and unless we speak to that effect we shall have very little chance of being here the next Parliament. Besides the government have no claim upon us, we are quite different from Lord Killeen*, Sir Pat[rick] Bellew*, and others who have received favours'. This is the key to Sheil's conduct. He is, I fear, a mercenary man.[118]

On 13 Mar. he upbraided Smith Stanley for his 'infelicitous' language when he 'spoke of putting turbulence down and giving Ireland a lesson', and urged him to 'avoid all precipitate legislation'. He voted steadily against the tithes composition bill, condemning the 'haste' with which it had been 'concocted' and asking, 'Why, if you complain of boroughs without constituencies, may not we complain of churches without congregations?', 6 Apr. He was a minority teller against it, 16 Apr., 24 July, 2 Aug., but one of the Members 'usually opposing ministers' who supported Crampton's amendment regarding the payment of arrears, 9 Apr.[119] In a speech denounced by Smith Stanley for its 'hollow subterfuge' veiled in 'flowery eloquence', 16 Apr., he denied that his opposition to tithes betrayed his oath not to subvert the Protestant church. He condemned the tithes bill as a 'mockery of reform' which would 'East Retfordize the church', 5 July, presented numerous hostile petitions, 13 July, 2 Aug., and observed that the Protestant inhabitants of Lower Canada were exempt from supporting the established Catholic church, 23 July. He defended the legality of Irish anti-tithes meetings and insisted that Smith Stanley would need additional powers to suppress them, 20 July. On 24 July he called for the 'opulence' of the church to be 'cut down', arguing that the 'cry' from Ireland on this issue was as strong as that which had produced the 'concession on parliamentary reform'. That day he was a teller for his own amendment for the application of surplus church revenues to 'education and charity', which was defeated by 76-18. He criticized the false economy of sustaining the 'crozier by the bayonet' and paying 'an army of 30,000 men to protect the church', 26 July, but withdrew his motion to appropriate surplus revenues, 2 Aug. 1832, saying it was a 'subject that ought to be reserved for the new Parliament'. That day he spoke and was a majority teller for the reception of a petition urging the Irish people 'to resort to force' if troops were used to enforce tithe payments.

He voted with ministers on the Russian-Dutch loan, 26 Jan., 12, 16, 20 July, and relations with Portugal, 9 Feb. 1832. He was appointed to the select committee on the East India Company, 27 Jan. He defended the legality of charging fees to newly commissioned Irish magistrates, 7 Feb., and conjectured that a 'permanent committee' on Irish affairs would 'save much time', 15 Feb. He divided for information on military punishments the following day. He welcomed the anatomy bill, 27 Feb., but demanded its extension to Ireland in order to prevent the 'export of dead bodies' to England, 11 Apr. He condemned the unwarranted expense of the Irish registry of deeds bill, 3 Apr., was a minority teller against it that day and 9 Apr., and called for a reduction of the registrar's salary, 18 July. He was a minority teller against the establishment of a *nisi prius* court at Dublin, 3 Apr. He defended the Maynooth grant, 16 Apr., and refuted claims that the college fostered an 'anti-national and revolutionary spirit', 27 July. He welcomed the Irish party processions bill, 14 June, when he was a minority teller for giving king's bench the power to adjudicate student admissions to the inns of court. He spoke and voted for a tax on absentee landlords to provide permanent provision for the Irish poor, 19 June. He divided to make inquests public the following day. He spoke against Alexander Baring's bill to exclude insolvent debtors from Parliament, which was 'calculated to excite alarm' among the 'new class of constituents', 27 June, and presented petitions against it, 13 July. He voted for a system of representation for New South Wales, 28 June. He spoke and was in a minority of 12 against the retrospective effects of the ecclesiastical courts contempts bill, 3 Aug. 1832.

On 21 Oct. O'Connell was informed that 'the *great little patriot* Sheil' had been 'burned in effigy' at

Dundalk, following his last minute decision to withdraw and offer instead for county Tipperary at the 1832 general election. Four days later O'Connell declared that unless he gave 'the most explicit and unequivocal pledge to the repeal', which 'could not be explained away', he 'would not support him'.[120] A pledge was forthcoming and he was returned unopposed, Lord Rosslyn remarking to Wellington, 22 Dec. 1832, that Sheil

had proposed to Duncannon not many weeks or months ago to recommend to government to pass an Act to make it high treason to moot the repeal of the Union, and when the election came on he pledged himself to vote for the repeal in the strongest manner possible. When reproached ... he said only you may have other ways of getting into Parliament, but I have none and there I will be upon any terms.[121]

Sheil, who distanced himself from O'Connell's repeal agitation after 1835, sat for Tipperary until 1841, when he came in unopposed as a Liberal for Dungarvan. His 'career faded away into second class ministerial office' under the Liberal administrations of Melbourne and Russell, by whom he was appointed British plenipotentiary to the court of Tuscany in 1850.[122] He died in Florence 'of gout in the stomach' in May 1851, an obituarist recalling the 'expressions of delight with which he escaped from Downing Street to enjoy the fine vintages and bright sunshine of the south'. His remains were returned to Ireland for interment aboard a navy vessel, 24 Feb. 1852.[123]

[1] W. Torrens MacCullagh, *Mems. of Sheil* (1855). [2] *Creevey Pprs.* ii. 183; Lord Lytton, *Life of Lytton*, i. 426; J.R. O'Flanagan, *Irish Bar*, 272; *The Times*, 4 June 1851; J. McCarthy, *Hist. of Our Own Times*, i. 46; Glos. RO, Hyett mss D6/F32/13, Berkeley to Hyett, 25 June 1831. [3] MacCullagh, i. 5-6; *Sketches, Legal and Political* ed. M. Savage, ii. 305-6. [4] O'Flanagan, 266. [5] *Gent. Mag.* (1851), ii. 86. [6] MacCullagh, i. 91. [7] *O'Connell Corresp.* ii. 887. [8] MacCullagh, i. 150. [9] Torrens, *Melbourne*, i. 197-8; *O'Connell Corresp.* ii. 909. [10] W.E. Vaughan, *Hist. Ireland*, 67. [11] *O'Connell Corresp.* ii. 784, 1013; Torrens, i. 198. [12] *O'Connell Corresp.* iii. 1076. [13] Ibid. iii. 1105, 1112-13, 1125-6, 1132. [14] Ibid. iii. 1165, 1168. [15] Gurney diary. [16] PRO NI, Foster mss D207/73/120/243; *O'Connell Corresp.* iii. 1172, 1178; *Sketches*, ii. 19-54. [17] Grey mss, Tierney to Grey, 17 Feb. 1825. [18] *O'Connell Corresp.* iii. 1174; MacCullagh, i. 233; *Sketches*, ii. 49. [19] *PP* (1825), viii. 98, 101, 107; MacCullagh, i. 235; *O'Connell Corresp.* iii. 1180. [20] *O'Connell Corresp.* iii. 1248, 1268. [21] Brougham mss, Abercromby to Brougham, 12 July 1826. [22] Foster mss D562/14691; F. O'Ferrall, *Catholic Emancipation*, 138; *O'Connell Corresp.* iii. 1316. [23] *Dublin Evening Post*, 6 July 1826; *O'Connell Corresp.* iii. 1344. [24] *Lettres sur les Élections ... et sur la situation de L'Ireland* (Paris, 1827), 158-9. [25] MacCullagh, i. 306; *Speeches of Sheil* ed. T. MacNevin, 400. [26] Add. 37304, f. 219; *Oxford DNB*. [27] Add. 37304, ff. 215, 222, 224; *Geo. IV Letters*, iii. 1259, 1407. [28] Add. 37304, f. 241. [29] Add. 37305, ff. 15, 23; *O'Connell Corresp.* iii. 1436. [30] Add. 37305, ff. 22, 29. [31] MacCullagh, i. 333, 340; *The Times*, 6 Feb. 1827. [32] *O'Connell Corresp.* iii. 1436. [33] Ibid. iii. 1414. [34] MacCullagh, ii. 3, 13-14. [35] PRO NI, Anglesey mss D619/32A/2/82. [36] *Sketches*, ii. 149-56.

[37] Add. 40397, f. 113. [38] Wellington mss WP1/941/7. [39] Add. 51567, Anglesey to Holland, 1 July; 51558, Anglesey to Lamb [July 1827]; Anglesey mss 26/C/75-8. [40] J.A. Reynolds, *Catholic Emancipation Crisis*, 152; MacCullagh, ii. 24; Anglesey mss 32A/2/1/124; T. Wyse, *Hist. Catholic Assoc.* ii. p. clxxvi. [41] *Dublin Morning Register*, 19 Sept. 1828; PRO NI, Perceval Maxwell mss D3244/G/1/56. [42] Wellington mss WP1/955/16; 964/9. [43] MacCullagh, ii. 27. [44] Anglesey mss 32A/2/143. [45] Add. 51567. [46] Wellington mss WP1/961/12. [47] *Report of the speeches ... at Penenden Heath, 24 Oct. 1828*, pp. 19-24; *Sketches*, ii. 211. [48] Add. 51572, Darnley to Holland, 24 Oct. 1828. [49] Keele Univ. Lib. Sneyd mss SC17/40. [50] *O'Connell Corresp.* iii. 1497. [51] *Speech of Mr. Sheil as it was intended to have been delivered* (1828); *Arbuthnot Jnl.* ii. 218-19. [52] MacCullagh, ii. 41. [53] Add. 51567. [54] Add. 51655, Mackintosh to Holland, 6 Nov. 1828. [55] Prince Pückler-Muskau, *Tour by a German Prince* (1832), ii. 118. [56] *Greville Mems.* i. 224. [57] Reynolds, 123. [58] *O'Connell Corresp.* iv. 1516; O'Ferrall, 244. [59] PRO NI, Downshire mss D671/C/12/381. [60] *O'Connell Corresp.* iv. 1516. [61] Add. 40399, ff. 98, 108, 104. [62] *O'Connell Corresp.* iv. 1524. [63] MacCullagh, ii. 73. [64] *The Times*, 8 June 1829; Anglesey mss 32/A/3/1/212. [65] Wellington mss WP1/1066/18. [66] NLW, Coedymaen mss 211; Wellington mss WP1/1035/21. [67] Wellington mss WP1/1054/64. [68] *Greville Mems.* i. 327. [69] Anglesey mss 32/A/3/1/219. [70] Ibid. 3/1/223. [71] Ibid. 32/C/6; 32/A/3/1/267; PRO NI, Pack-Beresford mss D664/A/93. [72] *O'Connell Corresp.* iv. 1623, 1629. [73] *The Times*, 29 Oct. 1829; Anglesey mss 32/A/3/1/254. [74] *Arbuthnot Corresp.* 130. [75] *Greville Mems.* i. 327; Add. 40327, f. 97. [76] NLI, Wyse mss 15024 (10), Dwyer to Wyse, 21 Feb. 1830. [77] Wellington mss WP1/1099/7. [78] Wyse mss 15024 (10), Dwyer to Wyse, 4 Mar. 1830. [79] Add. 40338, f. 121. [80] Add. 40327, ff. 145, 161. [81] Wellington mss WP1/1122/66; 1123/44; NAI, Leveson Gower letterbks. Leveson Gower to Sheil, 3 July, to Singleton, 6 July 1830. [82] *Dod's Parl. Companion* (1833), 158-9; *O'Connell Corresp.* iv. 1786. [83] Anglesey mss 32C/4-5; Leveson Gower letterbks. Gower to Sheil, 17 May 1830; Wellington mss WP1/1117/44. [84] *Dublin Evening Post*, 17 July, 12 Aug. 1830. [85] Wyse mss 15024 (7), O'Hanlon to Wyse, 2 Sept. 1830. [86] *The Times*, 9 Oct. 1830; Add. 62081, f. 152. [87] Add. 40313, ff. 67-71, 136-7; A. Macintyre, *The Liberator*, 17. [88] Parker, *Peel*, ii. 161. [89] Anglesey mss 29B/4-7; 28C/19-21. [90] Ibid. 28A-B/37. [91] Ibid. 28C/53-7. [92] Ibid. 31D/13. [93] Ibid. 28C/66-7. [94] Ibid. 28A-B/40; 31D/14. [95] Ibid. 28C/69-71; 31D/17. [96] Add. 51568. [97] Creevey mss, Creevey to Miss Ord, 18 Feb. 1831. [98] Anglesey mss 31D/23-25. [99] *Croker Pprs.* ii. 109. [100] Anglesey mss 31D/30. [101] *O'Connell Corresp.* iv. 1784. [102] Add. 51655, Mackintosh to Lady Holland, 21 Mar. 1831. [103] Le Marchant, *Althorp*, 480. [104] *Macaulay Letters*, ii. 11. [105] Add. 51724, Duncannon to Lady Holland, 21 Mar.; 51573, Spring Rice to same, 21 Mar. 1831. [106] Dorset RO D/BKL, Bankes jnl. 173. [107] Anglesey mss 31D/35. [108] *Sherborne Jnl.* 5 May; *Drogheda Jnl.* 21 May 1831. [109] Pack-Beresford mss D664/A/245. [110] *Drogheda Jnl.* 24 May 1831. [111] Anglesey mss 28A-B/71. [112] MacCullagh, ii. 114. [113] Anglesey mss 27B/52. [114] *Greville Mems.* ii. 207. [115] NLS mss 24762, f. 49. [116] Le Marchant, 397. [117] Anglesey mss 27A/143. [118] Le Marchant, 399; *Three Diaries*, 211. [119] *The Times*, 10 Apr. 1832. [120] *O'Connell Corresp.* iv. 1928-9. [121] Wellington mss WP1/1239/38. [122] MacCarthy, i. 47. [123] *Gent. Mag.* (1851), ii. 88; *The Times*, 4 June, 26 July 1851.

P.J.S.

SHELDON, Ralph (1741–1822), of Donnington, nr. Newbury, Berks. and King Street, Mdx.

WILTON	24 May 1804–22 Nov. 1822

b. 14 Sept. 1741,[1] 1st s. of William Sheldon of Weston, Warws. and Margaret Frances Disney, da. of James Rooke of Bigsweir House, Mon. *educ.* St. Gregory's, Douai 1755. *m.* (1) 1780, Jane (*d.* 21 Mar. 1812),[2] da. of Adm. Francis Holburne† of Menstrie, Clackmannan and Lymington, Hants, 1s. 3da. (1 *d.v.p.*); (2) 17 June 1818, ?Sarah Broom of Great Titchfield Street, Mdx.,[3] *s.p. suc.* fa. 1780. *d.* 22 Nov. 1822.

Col. Oxford loyal vols. 1803; lt.-col. 3 Warws. militia 1808.

Mayor, Wilton 1808-9.

Ralph Sheldon, who was descended from the seventeenth-century antiquary of the same name, abandoned his family's traditional Catholic allegiance and was returned for Wilton, on the interest of the 11th earl of Pembroke, from 24 May 1804. That day he was also sworn in as a member of the corporation of Wilton, to which he had been elected in 1789, and in 1816 he signed the entry in the minute book for the return of Lord FitzHarris* at a by-election.[4] Following the death of his first wife, whose brother James Rooke was Member for Monmouthshire, 1785-1805, he remarried in 1818, aged 76. At the Wilton election that year his 'urbanity of manner and long acquaintance with the inhabitants' were commented on.[5] In 1819 he sold his ancestral home, Weston, Warwickshire, to the Manchester cotton manufacturer George Philips*, then Member for Steyning, though the property was rented for some years by Lord Clonmell, former Member for New Romney, before being rebuilt and occupied by its new owner.[6] In the Commons, Sheldon, who was again returned unopposed for Wilton at the general election of 1820, continued to be an inactive supporter of the Liverpool ministry. He voted in defence of their conduct towards Queen Caroline, 6 Feb., and against Maberly's resolution on the state of the revenue, 6 Mar., and repeal of the additional malt duty, 3 Apr. 1821. He paired against the forgery punishment mitigation bill, 23 May 1821. He voted against more extensive tax reductions to relieve distress, 11, 21 Feb., and abolition of one of the joint-postmasterships, 13 Mar. 1822, his last known vote. He had previously voted for Catholic relief, but was not listed in the majority in favour of this, 28 Feb. 1821. He made no reported speeches in this period.

Pembroke commented to Lord Normanton, 19 Nov. 1822, that 'from what I have heard I am led to fear that Sheldon is in such an alarming state of illness as to preclude much hopes of his recovery'.[7] He died, 'universally esteemed and respected', on the 22nd.[8] By his will, dated 6 Nov. 1822, he, 'mindful of my mortality', left his entire estate, which included personal wealth sworn under £1,000, to his wife, whom he named as 'Rebecca'.[9] A Rebecca Sheldon, supposedly his widow, died at her London home in Fludyer Street,

23 Feb. 1823.[10] As stipulated, Sheldon was buried in the family vault at St. Leonard's Church, Beoley, Worcestershire.[11] He was succeeded by his only son, Edward Ralph Charles (1782-1836), of Brailes, Warwickshire, Liberal Member for Warwickshire South, 1835-6, and his son, Henry James (1823-1901), the last of the line.[12]

[1] E.A.B. Barnard, *The Sheldons*, 74. [2] *Gent. Mag.* (1812), i. 395. [3] Ibid. (1818), ii. 81. [4] Wilts. RO, Wilton borough recs. G25/1/22, ff. 216, 252, 289. [5] *Salisbury Jnl.* 22 June 1818. [6] Barnard, 74; *VCH Warws.* v. 55. [7] Wilton House mss. [8] *Gent. Mag.* (1822), ii. 645. [9] PROB 11/1671/320; IR26/976/440. [10] *Gent. Mag.* (1823), i. 284; PROB 6/199. [11] Barnard, 88. [12] *Gent. Mag.* (1836), ii. 431; Barnard, 77-78.

S.M.F.

SHELLEY, Sir John, 6th bt. (1772–1852), of Maresfield Park, Suss.

HELSTON	21 Apr. 1806–1806
LEWES	13 Mar. 1816–1831

b. 3 Mar. 1772, o.s. of Sir John Shelley, 5th bt., of Michelgrove, Suss. and Wilhelmina, da. of John Newnham of Maresfield. *educ.* Westminster; Eton 1786-9; Clare, Camb. 1789; grand tour 1789. *m.* 4 June 1807, Frances, da. and h. of Thomas Winckley of Brockholes, Lancs., 4s. 2da. *suc.* fa. as 6th bt. 11 Sept. 1783; mat. uncle in Maresfield estate 1814. *d.* 28 Mar. 1852.
      Ensign 2 Ft. Gds 1790, lt. and capt. 1793; a.d.c. to duke of Sussex.
      Lt. Petworth yeomanry 1797.

By 1820 marriage and advancing years had reformed Shelley's rakish tendencies and curbed his gambling, though his passion for horse racing remained fervent. His abrasive sense of humour was also undimmed, as he demonstrated at the duke of Devonshire's in 1823, when he told his unamused host, resplendent in an elaborate gold waistcoat, that he looked 'like a mackerel just caught'.[1] Confounding hopes that he would offer for Sussex in 1820 against the errant Sir Godfrey Webster[†], he again came in for his local borough of Lewes, on this occasion unopposed.[2]

He continued to vote with the Whig opposition to Lord Liverpool's ministry on certain issues, particularly for economy and retrenchment, but in other respects he was becoming increasingly unreliable. He divided against Scottish parliamentary reform, 2 June 1823. He also continued to vote against Catholic relief, 28 Feb. 1821, 30 Apr. 1822, 1 Mar., 21 Apr. (paired), 10 May 1825. He spoke in favour of transferring Sussex elections to Lewes, 23 June 1820.[3] Four

days later, suffering from gout, he was excused from an election committee. Like his colleague Sir George Shiffner, he declined to be associated with the Lewes address to Queen Caroline in July 1820.[4] He divided for the motion condemning the omission of the queen's name from the liturgy, 23 Jan., and reportedly would have done so again, 26 Jan. 1821, but absented himself because of Lord Archibald Hamilton's attack on Canning's conduct in leaving the country.[5] To ministerial threats of resignation, 3 Apr., he retorted that 'he only wished them to resign a few of their oppressive taxes' and thus alleviate the distress which he observed in his locality. He was a majority teller against the appointment of a select committee on the game laws, 5 Apr. He was granted ten days' leave for urgent business, 7 May 1821. He vigorously defended the grant to his 'friend and patron' the duke of York, under whom he had served in Flanders, 15 Mar. 1822. He spoke against the leather tax, 1 May 1822, and declared that he had 'all his life been an enemy to the sinking fund, and would go on voting for the repeal of taxes until he got every shilling out of it'.[6] He joined in criticism of the agricultural distress committee's recommendation that farmers be subsidized to warehouse their surplus wheat, 6 May, and three days later supported an 18*s.* export bounty, which would be 'at all events better than the existing state of the corn laws'. He urged that the burden of taxation and poor rates on the landed interest must be eased, 10, 16 May,[7] and acted as a minority teller for Scarlett's bill to reform the poor laws, 31 May 1822. He advocated £2 million of further tax reductions, 6 Mar. 1823, when he was a minority teller against the sinking fund. However, he derided Hume's proposal next day that the yeomanry should pay for their equipment as an economy measure.[8] He blamed the distressed condition of the rural lower classes for widespread transgressions of the game laws, 11 Mar. He proclaimed field sports to be 'one of the political institutions of the country', 2 June, and expressed doubt that legalizing the sale of game would defeat poachers; he was a minority teller against this proposal next day. He paired against inquiry into arrears in chancery, 5 June 1823. In January 1824 he was reportedly 'very ill' and confined to his room with 'what they call rheumatic fever – spasms in the chest, gout in his hands'.[9] He recovered to pursue his chief preoccupation, the game laws, and provoked laughter with his dire warning that their relaxation would spell the end for country sports, 17 Feb. He suggested that the middle classes' demand for game should be met by their becoming possessed of landed estates, 11 Mar., and proceeded to enthuse upon the advantages of a resident gentry. He objected to details of the game law amendment bill, 25 Mar., 12 Apr., and was a majority teller against it, 31 May. He denied that the Foot Guards, in which he had served, were any costlier than other army corps, 17 Mar. He divided against Brougham's motion condemning the prosecution of the Methodist missionary John Smith in Demerara, 11 June 1824. Earlier that month a horse from his stable won the Derby, netting him £500, a triumph which 'made the last week one of the happiest of his life'.[10] He was granted a week's leave for urgent private business, 14 Apr. 1825. He pointed to the fall in the number of people gaoled under the game laws as an argument against the bill to amend them, 21 Apr., and was a minority teller against its third reading, 29 Apr. He was a majority teller against the spring guns bill, 30 June 1825. It was said of him at this time that he 'attended frequently, and voted with the opposition'.[11] He presented a Brighton petition in favour of the debtor and creditor bill, 7 Apr. 1826, his only recorded activity that session.[12] At the general election that summer his radical opponent at Lewes drew unfavourable comparisons between his attendance in the Commons and that at Newmarket, but he was narrowly returned in second place.[13]

At the duke of York's funeral, 20 Jan. 1827, Shelley was said to be 'lame and hobbling', and two days later he suffered a severe attack of gout.[14] He recovered in time to divide against Catholic relief, 6 Mar. He presented petitions against alteration of the corn laws, 8, 15 Mar. He defended spring guns as a deterrent to poachers, 23 Mar., and explained that 'he never set them up himself but ... put up a board to say he had done so'; he was a minority teller against the bill to ban them. He was a minority teller against the sale of game bill, 8 June. He was granted a week's leave for urgent private business, having served on an election committee, 1 May. As an 'advocate for a gradual and limited reform in parliament', 10 May, he once more supported the Sussex election bill, to move the venue for elections to Lewes. On 28 May 1827 he voted against Canning's ministry for the disfranchisement of Penryn and for Lord Althorp's election expenses bill. In January 1828 he wrote to Robert Peel, the leader of the Commons in the duke of Wellington's ministry, promising his 'strenuous though humble support'. Lady Shelley, in penning congratulations to the duke, to whom they had long been close, noted that 'Shelley for the future intends to be guided entirely by you', adding that 'this confidence we could neither of us have felt if Peel had become premier ... in spite ... of our high opinion of [his] talents ... [and] our liking for him personally'. However, Wellington declined to recommend Shelley for a peerage 'on the score of your being a friend of mine', observing that 'your claims of family are excellent, but those of fortune would fail you, at all events'.[15] He voted against repeal of the Test Acts, which he feared would pave the way for Catholic emancipation, 26 Feb., and divided against relief, 12 May. He announced that he would not oppose Stuart Worley's game laws amendment bill, 13 June, but he criticized its details, 19, 26 June, and wanted to limit the trial period to two years, 10 July. He voted with government on the ordnance estimates, 4 July 1828. In February 1829 Planta, the patronage secretary, listed him as one who was 'opposed to the principle' of Catholic emancipation. Mrs. Arbuthnot was sure that it would 'vex him very much to oppose the duke', but he presented a hostile petition from Lewes and spoke on the subject, while reporters were absent from the House, 5 Mar., and voted against emancipation the next day.[16] He presented petitions against the employment of children as chimney sweeps, 11 Mar., and for protection of the wool trade, 27 May 1829. He divided against Jewish emancipation, 5 Apr. 1830. He voted to abolish the death penalty for forgery, 24 May, 7 June, and spoke warmly of the new metropolitan police, 15 June. He voted for an amendment to the beer bill to prohibit consumption on the premises, 21 June 1830. The previous month, at a meeting in Lewes, he had blamed his lapses in parliamentary attendance on the gout, and claimed that 'when I am able to move, I go to the House at five and stay until three'. He maintained that while he belonged to no party, he gave general support to ministers, but 'when I think they are not quite right, I oppose them'. At the general election that summer he was returned in second place, ahead of a radical, and explained that his opposition to the beer bill was motivated by a desire to 'protect public morals'. He subsequently declared that he would 'never go to the length of my nose ... to support radical reform', but would 'use my utmost endeavours to promote a moderate reform'.[17]

The ministry regarded him as one of their 'friends', and he voted with them in the crucial civil list division, 15 Nov. 1830. He spoke in support of the Sussex juries bill, which proposed to divide the county for assize purposes, 9 Nov. He approved of the labourers' wages bill, 19 Nov., arguing that low wages were the cause of the 'Swing' riots. He admitted that the 'mass of crime which has prevailed in the country for years past' was 'in some measure to be attributed to the existing game laws', 15 Feb. 1831, and he offered no further resistance to their reform, though he warned against exaggerated expectations of what this could achieve. Next day he spoke in favour of landowners giving allotments to the poor, observing that 'feelings of amity and goodwill towards the higher classes' prevailed where this had already been done. It was around this time that Shelley provoked amazement with an audacious request for the barony of Sudeley to be revived for his benefit, to which the prime minister Lord Grey bluntly responded that he had no claim.[18] It is not clear whether this rebuff had any bearing on his announcement, 15 Mar., that he would oppose the government's reform bill. He explained on 22 Mar. that he favoured granting representation to large towns, but that he could not accept the sweeping borough disfranchisements being proposed or the exclusion of poor voters. He foresaw a weakening of the landed interest and a transfer of power to the Commons, and boldly predicted that no government could last for six months in such circumstances. He acknowledged that his stance would cost him his seat at Lewes, but congratulated himself on his political consistency. He divided against the bill's second reading that day, and for Gascoyne's wrecking amendment, 19 Apr. 1831. At the ensuing dissolution hopes of a backlash against reform led him to canvass Lewes on a platform of defending the rights of poor voters, but he made little headway and retired before the poll.[19]

By October 1831 Shelley's wife was noting that his 'personal comfort' had been greatly increased by his absence from Parliament and that he had 'entirely lost his wish to stand any more contests'. In a subsequent eulogy on his political career, she observed with satisfaction that the rise in poaching following reform of the game laws had been predicted by him.[20] He died in March 1852 after an attack of gout induced, his wife supposed, by a session of port drinking; an obituarist described him as a 'fine specimen of an English gentleman'. He was succeeded by his eldest son, John Villiers Shelley*.[21]

[1] Shelley Diary, i. 31-36; Bagot, Canning and Friends, ii. 171. [2] Petworth House mss, bdle. 76, Ashburnham to Egremont, 22 Feb.; Suss. Advertiser, 13 Mar. 1820. [3] The Times, 24 June 1820. [4] Town Bk. of Lewes, 1702-1837 ed. V. Smith (Suss. Rec. Soc. lxix, 1972-3), 230. [5] Castle Howard mss, G. Howard to Lady Morpeth, 28 Jan. 1821. [6] The Times, 2 May 1822. [7] Ibid. 11, 17 May 1822. [8] Ibid. 8 Mar. 1823. [9] Lonsdale mss, Beckett to Lowther, 27 Jan. 1824. [10] TNA 30/29/6/7/54. [11] Session of Parl. 1825, p. 484. [12] The Times, 8 Apr. 1826. [13] Brighton Herald, 20 May; Brighton Gazette, 15 June 1826. [14] Shelley Diary, ii. 150; Peel Letters, 95. [15] Add. 40395, f. 55; Wellington mss WP1/915/64; Shelley Diary, ii. 172. [16] Shelley Diary, ii. 192; Brighton Guardian, 26 May 1830. [17] Brighton Guardian, 26 May, 4 Aug.; Brighton Gazette, 17 Aug. 1830. [18] Wellington mss WP1/1175/2; Creevey Pprs. ii. 222. [19] Brighton Guardian, 13, 27 Apr. 1831. [20] Shelley Diary, ii. 211, 217. [21] Ibid. ii. 299-300; Gent. Mag. (1852), i. 516.

H.J.S.

SHELLEY, John Villiers (1808–1867), of Maresfield, Suss.

GATTON	1830–1831
GREAT GRIMSBY	1831–2 Aug. 1831
WESTMINSTER	1852–1865

b. 18 Mar. 1808, 1st s. of Sir John Shelley, 6th bt.*, and Frances, da. and h. of Thomas Winckley of Brockholes, Lancs. educ. Charterhouse 1819-23. m. 13 Aug. 1832, Louisa, da. of Rev. Samuel Johnes Knight of Henley Hall, Salop, 1da. suc. fa. as 7th bt. 28 Mar. 1852. d. 20 Jan. 1867.
  Ensign R. Horse Gds. 1825, lt. 1828; lt. 20 Ft. 1830; lt. (half-pay) 60 Ft. 1831; ret. 1832; lt.-col. 46 Mdx. Rifle Vols. 1861-d.

Shelley, who was the fourth successive generation of the line of Sussex baronets to sit in the Commons, appears to have inherited his father's lack of scholarly inclination. He chose an ornamental army career in preference to university, and was described by the duke of Bedford in 1828, à propos of a rumoured marriage, as 'no great catch, not a bit wiser than his father'. Harriet Arbuthnot was more complimentary on the occasion of his coming of age the following year, considering him to be 'a very fine young man, very good looking and gentlemanlike'.[1] At the general election of 1830 he was returned for Gatton, his distant cousin Lord Monson's pocket borough.

The duke of Wellington's ministry regarded him (like his father) as one of their 'friends', and he voted with them in the crucial civil list division, 15 Nov. 1830. He was added to the select committee on the renewal of the East India Company's charter, 15 Feb. 1831 (and reappointed, 28 June 1831). Delivering his maiden speech against the Grey ministry's reform bill, 2 Mar., he echoed his father's warnings that the measure would form a prelude to more radical change and that it would make government impossible. He provoked uproar with his remarkable defence of the close boroughs, whose representatives he characterized as 'the only really truly independent Members', as they had no constituents to answer to. He added a bizarre request for a separate Member to be assigned to the Westminster parish of St. George's, explaining that since 'the borough which I represent was held up as the first that ought to be disfranchised it would only have been fair if the parish in which I live should have a representative'. A radical commentator ridiculed this 'singularly absurd speech', which was 'even considered as such in the House'.[2] He divided against the bill's second reading, 22 Mar., and according to Thomas Creevey*, describing the scene at Crockford's

Club after the division, he did not swallow defeat with the dignity of most of his associates.[3] His was the sole voice raised against the 'great clamour' for reform at a Sussex meeting on the issue, 7 Apr., when he objected to the abolition of close boroughs and the disfranchisement of poorer voters and alleged that the measure was being pushed by ministers as a convenient distraction from the 'mass of blunders' in their budget. Wellington heard 'from the very best authority' that the speech was 'capital and ... gave great satisfaction to all but his opponents'; and even the radical *Brighton Guardian* could not but 'admire his cool intrepidity and the talent ... he displayed', adding prophetically that 'he is yet young, and we hope to see him reclaimed from the ranks of corruption'.[4] On the presentation of the resulting petition to the Commons, 18 Apr. 1831, he argued that Sussex contained many silent objectors and repeated his criticism of Whig fiscal policy. He voted for Gascoyne's wrecking amendment the next day. At the ensuing dissolution he was obliged to vacate his Gatton seat, which Monson required for another, and despite his youth he canvassed Sussex, only to abandon it for Grimsby, which was scheduled for partial disfranchisement and therefore likely to be receptive to his view of the reform bill as 'a crude and ill digested experiment'; he was narrowly returned in second place.[5] He divided against the second reading of the reintroduced reform bill, 6 July, and to use the 1831 census for the purpose of determining the disfranchisement schedules, 19 July 1831. He intervened in the discussion on Grimsby's partial disfranchisement, 25 July, to state that far from being a nomination or decayed borough, it was 'in a highly thriving and prosperous condition'. However, his tenure as the borough's representative proved to be short-lived, as his election was declared void on the ground of treating, 2 Aug. 1831, a judgement which he considered 'harsh in the extreme' when he spoke on behalf of the new Tory candidates.[6]

In October 1832 Shelley's mother reported that he was in Sussex 'reading hard and performing his duties as a magistrate', and a letter at this time from Charles Arbuthnot* suggests that he had to be dissuaded from offering for the eastern division of the county at the impending general election. When he finally stood a contest there in 1841, it was as a Whig, and he was soundly beaten.[7] He had been estranged from his parents for some years and in 1842 his father reported to Sir Robert Peel*:

It is painful to me to mention the cruel conduct of my eldest son, particularly to his devoted mother, but though we have been silent, I fear it is too well known that from the day we signed the marriage settlement by which we

made him an absolute gift of Maresfield, he has tried to fasten a quarrel upon us, with the object of avoiding the understood engagement that his home was to be our country house and home ... His determination remains unchanged never to let us enter his doors and the hope which induced us to make him independent is at last completely extinct.[8]

He was returned for Westminster in 1852, shortly after succeeding to his father's title, and his second political incarnation was as a Liberal and champion of further parliamentary reform. He became involved in the ill-fated Bank of London and, according to an obituarist, was 'never ... the same man' after its failure in 1866. He died of gout, 'the old enemy', in January 1867, whereupon his brother Frederic (1809-69) succeeded to the baronetcy, while the Maresfield estate passed to his only child Blanche.[9]

[1] *Shelley Diary*, ii. 128; *Arbuthnot Jnl.* ii. 255; Add. 51669, Bedford to Lady Holland, 30 June 1828. [2] *The Times*, 3 Mar. 1831; [W.D. Carpenter], *People's Bk.* 365. [3] *Creevey Pprs.* ii. 255. [4] *Brighton Guardian*, 13 Apr. 1831; *Shelley Diary*, ii. 207. [5] *Brighton Gazette*, 14, 21, 28 Apr. 1831; *Grimsby Pollbook* (1831), 5-6. [6] *Hist. Grimsby Election* (1831), 13. [7] *Shelley Diary*, ii. 217; Add. 40617, f. 2; *The Times*, 7 July 1841. [8] Add. 40504, f. 363. [9] *Gent. Mag.* (1867), i. 383; *Sporting Rev.* (1867), lvii. 159-60.

T.A.J.

SHIFFNER, Sir George, 1st bt. (1762–1842), of Coombe Place, nr. Lewes, Suss.

LEWES   13 Jan. 1812–1826

b. 17 Nov. 1762, 3rd but 1st surv. s. of Henry Shiffner† of Pontrylas, Herefs. and Mary, da. and coh. of John Jackson of Pontrylas, second in council, Bengal. *educ.* Bosma's acad. Amsterdam 1777-8; Pastor L'Honore's, The Hague 1778-80. *m.* 31 Oct. 1787, Mary, da. and h. of Sir John Bridger of Coombe Place and Coln St. Aldwyn, Glos., 4s. (1 *d.v.p.*) 4da. *suc.* fa. 1795; fa.-in-law 1816; *cr.* bt. 16 Dec. 1818. *d.* 3 Feb. 1842.

Cornet 11 Drag. 1782-8.

Capt. Suss. militia 1794-5, Lewes yeomanry 1795-1827, S. Lewes vol. batt. 1803.

Shiffner, the son of a failed Russia merchant, married well and in 1816 inherited Coombe Place at Offham, north of Lewes, where he had established an electoral interest. He was awarded a baronetcy by Lord Liverpool's ministry in 1818 and was returned for Lewes for the fourth time in 1820.[1] He was a fairly regular attender who continued to give loyal support to the government, though he seldom intervened in debate. Details of his attendance and voting record are supplemented by his personal diary, which also indicates his clear preference for local society over metropolitan, and the assiduity with which he performed his duties as a magistrate, militia commander and turnpike trustee.[2] Following his re-election in 1820 he feared he would not live to take his seat, as 'intermitting in my pulse' caused him to reflect on mortality and his Christian beliefs, 21 Mar. By the end of the month he had recovered and was 'thanking electors' in Lewes. He attended the opening of Parliament, 21 Apr., and took the oaths four days later. He recorded that he had received and presented two petitions regarding agricultural distress, 26 May, and that he attended the debate on this subject, 30 May, without staying for the division; next day he apparently voted for the inclusion of corn averages in the remit of the agricultural committee. In June he sat through the debates on the Queen Caroline affair. He spoke in favour of the Sussex election bill, which proposed to fix future contests at Lewes, 23 June.[3] He divided against economies in revenue collection, 4 July 1820. Later that month the local antiquarian Gideon Mantell condemned his 'arbitrary conduct' as a magistrate in preventing a travelling menagerie from stopping in Lewes. It is possible that he feared the exhibition would provide an excuse for a popular demonstration of support for the queen. Shortly afterwards he and his colleague Sir John Shelley refused to accompany the constables presenting an address to her from the borough, because they 'did not consider it consistent with their duty' as Members to 'take any steps which might appear like prejudging the case'.[4] He voted in defence of ministers' conduct towards the queen, 6 Feb. 1821. He divided against Catholic relief, 28 Feb. He presented a petition from Sussex landowners complaining of distress, 6 Mar.,[5] but privately noted that the widely favoured remedial measure of malt duty repeal would constitute 'too much loss to the government'. He divided against the disfranchisement of ordnance officials, 12 Apr. He was granted three weeks' leave owing to illness in his family, 2 May. Early that summer he toured the west of England, returning to London in time for the coronation on 19 July. On his wedding anniversary, 31 Oct. 1821, he reflected that he was 'quite happy in every respect, excepting the want of money owing to the pressure of the times on agriculture'. Nevertheless, he believed his locality would have been 'better without' the meeting on distress in January 1822, at which William Cobbett[†] spoke. He divided against more extensive tax reductions, 11, 21 Feb., abolition of one of the joint-postmasterships, 13 Mar., and reductions in diplomatic expenditure, 15 May. In his only known gesture of independence in this Parliament, 8 May, he voted with the minority for a fixed 40s. duty on imported corn. However, he recorded that he was in the majority next day against Ricardo's proposed sliding scale, and that he also paired against permitting the grinding and export of bonded corn, 10 June. He divided against inquiry into the resumption of cash payments, 12 June, and wrote approvingly that 'ministers have remitted four million taxes and reduced the expenditure by two million, making an aggregate saving of six million in twelve months'. He voted against the bill to relieve Catholic peers of their disabilities, 30 Apr. He divided against inquiry into the administration of the Ionian Islands, 14 May, and for the aliens bill, 5 June 1822.

He arrived in London for the new session of Parliament on 27 Feb. and voted against more extensive tax reductions, 3 Mar. 1823, before returning to Sussex to attend to local duties. He ensured that he was present to divide against Catholic relief, 17 Apr., and voted for the Irish insurrection bill, 12 May. He divided for the military and naval pensions bill, 18 Apr. He attended a Pitt Club dinner at the Merchant Taylors Hall, 28 May. He voted against inquiry into delays in chancery, 4 June 1823. He hastened to London 'in defence of Robinson's budget', 2 Mar. 1824, returning to Brighton the following day. He was back in attendance at the end of April, but grew tired of waiting for the warehoused wheat bill to be considered and went home on 15 May. He was present for the debate on the prosecution of the Methodist missionary John Smith in Demerara, 31 May, and voted against inquiry, 11 June. He again divided for the Irish insurrection bill, 14 June. His journey back to Coombe, 17 June 1824, took 'six hours exactly'. Of the debate on the address, 3 Feb. 1825, he recorded tersely, 'full House, much speechifying, no amendment'. He voted for the Irish unlawful societies bill, 15 Feb., recovered from illness to divide against Catholic relief, 1 Mar., 21 Apr., and voted against the Irish franchise bill, 26 Apr. He defended lord chancellor Eldon from Brougham's attack, 18 May, after the Lords had rejected the relief bill.[6] He was shut out of the division on the grant to the duke of Cumberland, 2 June, but voted for it, 6, 10 June 1825. He travelled to attend Parliament on 2 Feb. 1826, and was present for the division on the withdrawal of small banknotes, 13 Feb., which he evidently supported. He voted against reform of Edinburgh's representation, 13 Apr., and Russell's reform motion, 27 Apr. 1826. Next day he divided against the spring guns bill.[7]

In September 1825 Shiffner had informed his agent of his determination not to contest Lewes again. His Sussex neighbour John Smith* reckoned him to be a casualty of the uncertainty over the date of the general election, at which he seemed bound to face a contest. In his parting address he declared that the government had 'carried us triumphantly through times of difficulty and danger', with such success that 'individual exertion is not so much called for'.[8] Privately, he admitted that his decision stemmed from 'the great and constant expense and trouble' of maintaining his interest at Lewes, adding that 'my chief wish now [is] to make all matters in point of money as comfortable for my family as possible'. He was magnanimous enough to dine with the man who effectively displaced him, the Whig Thomas Read Kemp, 31 May 1826. Thereafter he made few diary references to politics, though it is clear that his conservative opinions never altered. In April 1831 he was a signatory to the Sussex antireform declaration.[9] He interpreted an attendance of 300 at the county meeting on reform, 4 Nov. 1831, as a 'complete failure to show confidence' in Lord Grey's ministry, and alleged that Lord Chichester had 'moved resolutions which he did not approve of'. The existing electoral system, he noted by way of approval, 5 May 1832, had been 'in practice for nearly three centuries'. He died in February 1842 and was succeeded in turn by his eldest surviving sons, Henry Shiffner (1789-1859) and George Shiffner (1791-1863).[10]

[1] Suss. Advertiser, 6 Mar. 1820. [2] E. Suss. RO SHR 827-9, Shiffner's diaries, 1820-32, for what follows. [3] The Times, 24 June 1820. [4] Jnl. of Gideon Mantell ed. C. Curwen, 23; Town Bk. of Lewes, 1702-1837 ed. V. Smith (Suss. Rec. Soc. lxix. 1972-3), 228-31. [5] The Times, 7 Mar. 1821. [6] Ibid. 19 May 1824. [7] Norf. RO, Gunton mss 1/21. [8] Brougham mss, Smith to Brougham, 3 Oct. 1825; E. Suss. RO SHR 305/7. [9] Suss. Advertiser, 25 Apr. 1831. [10] Gent. Mag. (1842), i. 552; PROB 8/235; 11/1968/638.

R.M.H./H.J.S.

SHIRLEY, **Evelyn John** (1788–1856), of Ettington, Warws.; Coolderry and Lough Fea, co. Monaghan, and 11 North Audley Street, Mdx.

Co. Monaghan	1826–1831
Warwickshire South	1 July 1836–May 1849

b. 26 Apr. 1788, 1st s. of Evelyn Shirley of Ettington and Phillis Byam, da. of Charlton Wollaston, MD, of Pall Mall, Mdx. educ. Rugby 1798; Bampton, Oxon. (Rev. George Richards); St. John's, Camb. 1807. m. 16 Aug. 1810, Eliza, da. of Arthur Stanhope of 1 Tilney Street, Mdx., 5s. (2 d.v.p.) 2da. suc. fa. 1810. d. 31 Dec. 1856. Sheriff, Warws. 1813-14, co. Monaghan 1824-5.

Shirley's father, a grandson of the 1st Earl Ferrers (1650-1717), married on 3 July 1781 the daughter of a London physician, whose grandfather was the scholar

and clergyman William Wollaston (1659-1724). In 1793 he was appointed sheriff of Warwickshire, where he had substantial property in Lower and Upper Ettington (otherwise Eatington). Evelyn, the third of 14 children, was baptized in Lower Ettington on 12 June 1788.[1] He was educated at a public school (of which he became a trustee in 1827) and by a private tutor (later vicar of St. Martin-in-the-Fields), before going up to Cambridge, where he kept one of several juvenile memoranda and notebooks.[2] In May 1810 he succeeded to the estates of his father, whose personalty was sworn under £70,000, and a few months later he married a second cousin of the 6th earl of Chesterfield, whose father was comptroller of the foreign letter department at the time of his death in 1836.[3] A Warwickshire county gentleman, he served as sheriff, 1813-14, and master of the fox hounds, 1822-5.[4]

Like his father before him, Shirley employed an agent to manage his large estate in the western half of the barony of Farney in Monaghan. Although it was reported as early as 1822 that he 'positively intends setting up for the county', it was not until he was obliged to fill the office of sheriff there in 1824 that he decided to bolster his interest and have his many Catholic tenants registered. Having rented a house at Coolderry, he set about constructing a new family mansion at Lough Fea, and thereafter usually resided in Ireland during the summer.[5] He was expected to win a seat in September 1825, when he noted in his pocket diary that he 'began canvassing with great success', but no dissolution occurred.[6] He was active at the general election of 1826, including at a dinner given by his tenants on 31 May, and although he failed to disclose his opinions on the Catholic question, he was thought certain to prevail.[7] His reticence was no doubt intended to mislead his Catholic tenants, who believed him to be a supporter of their cause, for, after accepting the backing of the leading patron Lord Cremorne, whose interest mostly went to Henry Westenra (the privately sympathetic son of the pro-Catholic Lord Rossmore), he had since the previous year been in alliance with Charles Leslie, the Orange Member.[8] 'Thank God I escaped the attack of the mob upon Col. Leslie and myself entering the town', was how he described the start of the poll, 24 June 1826, when he was introduced as a benevolent and independent landlord. After a fierce contest, he was returned with a substantial lead over Westenra, but the refusal of many of his tenants to give their second votes as he had instructed led to Leslie's ignominious defeat.[9] The eviction notices subsequently served on them earned him the long-lasting disgust of the local population.[10]

According to his diary, Shirley took his seat on 21 Nov. 1826 and voted for the first time, 19 Feb. 1827, in favour of the duke of Clarence's grant and the army estimates. Although he was present to hear the 'Catholic question discussed', 5 Mar., he apparently missed the division the following day.[11] He was granted one month's leave on account of ill health, 26 Mar. 1827. He presented, but declined to support, several local pro-Catholic petitions, 21, 29 Feb., 30 May, and brought up numerous hostile ones, 15, 17, 21, 28 Apr. 1828.[12] Having divided against repeal of the Test Acts, 26 Feb., he voted against Catholic relief, 12 May. At the Monaghan meeting on 10 Oct. 1828 he moved the resolution for establishing a county Brunswick Club.[13] In early 1829 his name appeared on the list of possible movers and seconders of the address compiled by Planta, the Wellington ministry's patronage secretary, who nevertheless had him down as 'opposed to the principle' of Catholic emancipation.[14] He privately recorded his surprise at the announcement of the measure in the king's speech, 5 Feb., and presented petitions against it from his county, 9 Feb., and various places in Monaghan, 16, 23 Feb., 2, 4, 24 Mar. During March 1829 he attended the debates on and divided steadily against emancipation.[15]

Shirley began his diary for 1830 with the pious comment, typical of his Evangelical outlook, that 'another year is commenced. God in his mercy grant that I may spend it better than the last'. However, as in other years, many of the dates which headed the daily entries were circled by him, and typical of his elliptical notes, which hint at some private and enduring cause of shame, was one which read: 'Without any efforts to resist, gave way as usual; made no trial of strength. Let me determine to resist and at all events do not give up without some resistance and I hope of *determined resistance*'.[16] He voted in the minority for restricting the army estimates to six months, 19 Feb., but against the enfranchisement of Birmingham, Leeds and Manchester, 23 Feb., and Jewish emancipation, 17 May. Criticized for being an absentee and intimidatory landlord, irregular in his attendance in Parliament and 'completely the reverse of liberal' in his principles, he was thought to be popular only with the extreme Protestants. However, he secured an alliance with another Tory, Lord Blayney's son Cadwallader Blayney, and was returned in second place behind him at the general election that summer, after another unruly contest with the now openly pro-Catholic Westenra.[17] He voted with Daniel O'Connell for repeal of the Irish Subletting Act, 11 Nov., and, despite having been listed by ministers among the 'moderate Ultras', divided in their minority on the

civil list, 15 Nov. 1830.[18] He voted against the second reading of the Grey ministry's reform bill, 22 Mar., and in the majorities for Gascoyne's wrecking amendment, 19 Apr., and to adjourn the House, 21 Apr. 1831.[19]

Apparently described by Daniel O'Connell* as 'a mongrel – half English, half Irish, and whenever he gives a vote as giving a slavish one', Shirley initially offered again at the ensuing general election, when he condemned reform as a 'violation of vested rights and chartered privileges' in his Monaghan address; he also signed the Warwickshire anti-reform declaration. Yet he soon withdrew in the face of a coalition between Westenra and Blayney, who were returned unopposed, ostensibly in order to preserve the peace of the county.[20] Rossmore boasted to the Irish secretary Smith Stanley, 13 July 1832, that he had 'beaten Mr. Shirley completely out of Monaghan', but deemed him 'a violent opponent, uncompromising'.[21] As a friend to the agricultural interest and a defender of the church, he was expected to succeed in Warwickshire South at the general election of 1832, but according to Sir George Philips*, who pushed him into third place, he stupidly 'abused all those who differed from him, in the most violent and unmeasured terms, and raised such a spirit of hostility against himself, as could not be repressed'.[22] However, he was elected there as a Conservative in July 1836 and sat until May 1849, remembered as 'an ultra Tory, opposed to every species of radical innovation and change, a thorough church and state man'.[23] He died at Lough Fea in December 1856 and was buried in the family vault in Lower Ettington the following month. He was succeeded by his eldest son, the distinguished antiquarian Evelyn Philip Shirley (1812-82), Conservative Member for Monaghan, 1841-7, and Warwickshire South, 1853-65.[24] His only son, Sewallis Evelyn (1844-1904), was Conservative Member for Monaghan, 1868-80.

[1] E.P. Shirley, *Hist. Co. Monaghan*, 278-9, 282; E.P. Shirley, *Stemmata Shirleiana* (1873), 224; *VCH Warws*. v. 79. [2] Rev. R. Morris, *Funeral Sermon preached ... on death of Evelyn John Shirley* (1858), 10; Warws. RO, Shirley mss CR 464/22-29. [3] PROB 11/1512/341; IR26/160/225; *Gent. Mag.* (1836), ii. 442. [4] *VCH Warws*. ii. 376. [5] *Co. Monaghan Sources*, 143-4, 152; PRO NI, Rossmore mss T2929/3/21, 49-51, 54; Morris, 10-15. [6] *Impartial Reporter*, 15 Sept.; Warws. RO, Shirley mss CR 229/174, Shirley diary, 26, 28 Sept. 1825. [7] *Belfast Commercial Chron.* 10 June; *Enniskillen Chron.* 15 June 1826; Add. 40387, f. 212. [8] *Dublin Evening Post*, 8, 24, 29 June 1826; PRO NI, Leslie mss MIC606/3/J/7/14/11-12, 31-32, 37-39, 111-12, 117-19, 120-1. [9] Warws. RO, Shirley mss CR 229/174, Shirley diary; *Newry Commercial Telegraph*, 30 June, 4 July; *The Times*, 1 July 1826. [10] See Co. MONAGHAN. [11] Warws. RO, Shirley mss CR 229/174, Shirley diary. [12] Ibid.; *Impartial Reporter*, 31 Jan. 1828. [13] *Belfast Guardian*, 17 Oct. 1828. [14] Add. 40398, f. 86. [15] Warws. RO, Shirley mss CR

229/174, Shirley diary, 5, 6, 17, 18 Mar. 1829. [16] Ibid. 1 Jan., 12 June 1830; Morris, 40-45. [17] Rossmore mss 10B/8, 21A; Leslie mss 3/J/7/17/15-18, 20-21, 35-36, 52-53; PRO NI, Barrett Lennard mss 170/3, Westenra to Barrett Lennard, 9 July; *Louth Free Press*, 7, 14, 21 Aug. 1830. [18] Warws. RO, Shirley mss CR 229/174, Shirley diary, 11 Nov. 1830. [19] PRO NI, Shirley mss D3531/J/2/3, Shirley diary, 21 Apr. 1831. [20] [W. Carpenter], *People's Bk.* (1831), 365; *Newry Commercial Telegraph*, 29 Apr., 10, 17 May; *Warwick and Warws. General Advertiser*, 14 May 1831. [21] Derby mss 920 Der (14) 122/2. [22] *Warwick and Warws. Advertiser*, 7 July, 15, 22 Dec. 1832; Warws. RO, MI 247, Philips Mems. i. 310; ii. 125-7. [23] Morris, 15-16. [24] *Gent. Mag.* (1857), i. 253; Morris, 20; Warws. RO, Shirley mss CR 229/8/2; 18/2; *Co. Monaghan Sources*, 146; *Oxford DNB sub* Evelyn Philip Shirley.

S.M.F.

SIBTHORP *see* WALDO SIBTHORP

SIDNEY, Philip Charles (1800–1851), of Penshurst Place, nr. Tonbridge, Kent and 25 Bolton Street, Piccadilly, Mdx.

EYE   19 Oct. 1829–Mar. 1831

b. 11 Mar. 1800, o.s. of Sir John Shelley Sidney (formerly Shelley), 1st bt., of Penshurst Place and Henrietta, da. of Sir Henry Hunloke, 4th bt., of Wingerworth Hall, Derbys. *educ.* Eton 1817; Christ Church, Oxf. 1820. *m.* 13 Aug. 1825, Sophia FitzClarence, illegit. da. of William, duke of Clarence, and Dorothy, illegit. da. of Francis Bland ('Mrs. Jordan'), 2s. (1 *d.v.p.*) 4da. (1 *d.v.p.*). KCH 1830; GCH 4 Mar. 1831; *cr.* Bar. De L'Isle and Dudley 13 Jan. 1835; *suc.* fa. as 2nd bt. 14 Mar. 1849. *d.* 4 Mar. 1851.
   Cornet and sub.-lt. 1 Life Gds. 1821, lt. 1823, capt. (half-pay) 1826.
   Equerry to William IV 1830-5; surveyor-gen. of duchy of Cornw. 1833-49; ld. of bedchamber Jan.-Apr. 1835.

Sidney was heir to Penshurst Place, which had been in the family since the reign of Edward VI. Through his father, the second son of Sir Bysshe Shelley of Castle Goring, Sussex (his first with his second wife Elizabeth Perry), he had a claim to the ancient barony of Lisle, formerly vested in the Sidneys and Dudleys, and he was coheir to the baronetcies of Berkeley and Tyes.[1] He was tutored privately in Kent and Brighton, and in 1818-19 toured the continent, where he acquired a reputation as 'a fine young man', who was 'very handsome, his manners very pleasing'.[2] Family letters record that early in 1821 he narrowly escaped involvement in a duel in Kent, where his father as sheriff had offended many by refusing to call a county meeting requisitioned to protest at the treatment of Queen Caroline.[3] He joined the Life Guards that year with a career as a soldier and courtier in mind and promoted the petition claiming the Lisle barony lodged by his father, who in 1824 employed

the services of the genealogist Sir Harris Nicolas; but after several adjournments, the committee of privileges of the House of Lords ruled against advising the king to allow the claim, 25 May 1826.[4] The previous August, with her father the duke of Clarence's 'full consent', Sidney had married the king's illegitimate niece Sophia, under a settlement designed to ensure that she did not forfeit her £500 a year from the crown.[5] Continued offers of assistance and support from the Clarences failed to secure Sidney the salaried post he coveted;[6] but, as courtiers and go-betweens, he and his wife, 'a very clever, agreeable woman' (Mrs. Arbuthnot), universally acknowledged as her father's favourite, socialized regularly with the duke of Wellington and other leading politicians to whom they addressed their claims.[7] Sidney is not known to have sought election to Parliament before 1829, when, shortly after the birth of his second son, his fellow soldier and courtier Sir Edward Kerrison* returned him for his borough of Eye, where the death of Sir Miles Nightingall had created a vacancy coveted by members of the Henniker family. No evidence has been found that he bought his seat, but Kerrison's name appeared on military promotion lists soon afterwards.[8]

Sidney, who is not known to have spoken in debate, voted against the Jewish emancipation bill, 17 May 1830. Clarence, on becoming William IV, appointed him one of his equerries with his other sons-in-law, and he retained his seat for Eye at the ensuing general election.[9] Wellington, replying to a letter of 12 Aug. 1830 from Sophia, pressing Sidney's case for elevation to the Lords as 'the sole representative of *eighteen peerages*' (a favour which she maintained George IV had personally asked her father to confer when he became king) reminded the couple, of whose negotiations with Lord Chandos* he was aware, that 'every addition that he [William IV] makes to the House of Lords will increase the difficulties of this government', and urged them 'to be patient and to use your influence with others to be likewise'.[10] The Wellington ministry counted Sidney among their 'friends' and he divided with them on the civil list when they were brought down, 15 Nov. 1830. Sir John Shelley in Kent and Kerrison at Eye, which it threatened with disfranchisement, strenuously opposed the Grey ministry's reform bill, so drawing attention to Sidney's conduct in the House and the embarrassing prospect of the king's son-in-law voting against his ministers. On 4 Mar. the cabinet resolved to use the forthcoming debates on the civil list and the report of the committee on salaries as a means of persuading the king to exert pressure on his retainers in Parliament to vote for the bill or lose their posts. General Wheatley, keeper of the privy purse, explained the situation to Sidney, who on the 5th wrote to inform William IV that he was resigning his seat. His private secretary Sir Herbert Taylor* replied, 6 Mar., that the king

> expressed himself most pleased with the handsome manner in which you met and acted upon the communication ... and approves of your accepting the Chiltern Hundreds. He gives you credit for the sacrifices you are making and full credit also for the correct and honourable principles which has produced that sacrifice as he is the last man who would wish or expect anyone to give a vote he could not reconcile to his conscience.[11]

By 8 Mar. Sidney was out of the House. It was common knowledge that 'his sentiments were not in favour of the reform bill', but 'he found it impossible to vote against the measure'.[12] Granville Dudley Ryder* thought the king had acted 'very improperly'.[13] A correspondent to the pro-reform *Suffolk Chronicle*, 12 Mar., and *The Times*, 16 Mar. 1831, however, maintained that Sidney had wished to vote for reform to please the king, but had been made to vacate by Kerrison.

Sidney, who with Kerrison was awarded the Grand Cross of the Guelphic Order of Hanover, 24 Mar., did not stand for Parliament again, but he appears to have assisted William Robert Keith Douglas* and other anti-reformers at the 1831 general election.[14] His wife hoped that the coronation in September 1831 'would have afforded the king an opportunity of complying with our wishes, without any reference whatever to *political sentiments or opinions*', and wrote requesting Taylor and Lord Brougham to raise the question of a peerage with him and Lord Grey, 25 July. The king, however, knew of the pressure on Brougham and current rumours that the Sidneys and Sophia's brother the earl of Munster were passing confidential information to the Tory opposition.[15] On 27 July he directed Taylor to inform Sophia, to whom with her sisters he now accorded the rank of marquess's daughter, that he was prepared to raise the question of Sidney's peerage with Grey but 'could not do so, unless he could add that Sir Philip Sidney would in the event of obtaining a peerage, support his government on all questions'.[16] The Sidneys replied that the 'sacrifice of principle and opinion ... [was] too high a price to pay', 31 July.[17] Sidney wrote to Thomas Lowndes, 13 Sept.:

> If ever I have the good fortune to go into the House of Lords, I must enter it with the *same feelings* that actuate me here ... It is indeed a time when we must be true to ourselves and repel firmly the base and scandalous attacks that are daily levelled by the public prints at the aristoc-

racy ... who have, I think, therefore proved themselves *worthy* of the land they live in.[18]

As the constitutional crisis over the reform bill deepened early in 1832, he argued against packing the Lords; and, in a bid to prevent it, he tried, with Sophia and Lord Strangford, to persuade Wellington to issue 'a declaration or resolution for moderate reform', and reassured him that the 'king was wavering and anxious to embrace a modified measure'.[19] Denis Le Marchant[†] recorded that he acted similarly in the Court and Conservative interests when the Grey ministry was almost brought down on the slavery question in June 1833.[20] Three months previously he had been appointed to the sinecure office of surveyor-general of the duchy of Cornwall, worth £1,500-2,000 a year.[21] When, in January 1835, he was created Lord De L'Isle and Dudley, Thomas Raikes made much of the peerage having been awarded under the auspices of a Whig ministry, and *The Times* printed a jibe at the numerous titles considered for Sidney; but the Conservative Sir Henry Hardinge* commented that 'friends and foes all admit that you have shown great judgement and the most scrupulous delicacy throughout this proceeding and we your personal political friends are quite proud of the result'.[22] He resigned from the royal household when Sir Robert Peel left office in April 1835, and complained bitterly against the Whigs in later life for refusing to pay his children £500 a year each, as promised in their grandfather's reign.[23] Sophia died in April 1837, a month after the birth of their youngest daughter, and the Conservatives subsequently rejected his patronage requests.[24] When asked by Lord Carlisle, as chief commissioner of woods and forests in 1849, to relinquish his surveyorship of the duchy, his complaint to Queen Victoria that his patrimony would be 'a very small one for a peer of the realm ... connected too with his late Majesty' was heeded, and he received an annual compensatory pension of £1,000.[25] He disentailed the 3,913-acre Kent estate to provide for his family after succeeding his father that year and died at Penshurst in March 1851, mourned by 'several of the family of his late Majesty'. He was succeeded as 2nd baron and third baronet by his only surviving son Philip (1828-98), who had married the daughter and heiress of Sir William Foulis of Ingelby Manor, Yorkshire.[26] By his will, dated 7 Dec. 1850, his effects at Penshurst and Warwickshire properties passed to Philip as life-tenant; and his personalty, town house and Kentish revenues provided legacies for his daughters, niece, grandson and servants. In 1853 his solicitor and trustee John Gregson* alleged irregularities in the administration of the will and estate by Adelaide

Augusta Wilhelmina Sidney (1827-1904), his eldest daughter and sole executrix.[27]

[1] *Burke PB* (1969-70), 756-8; LMA, Du Cane mss E/DCA/242-4; H.N. Nicolas, *Report on Claim to Barony of De L'Isle in House of Lords* (1829); *Ann. Reg.* (1849), Chron. p. 227. [2] Cent. Kent. Stud. De L'Isle mss U1500/C269/5, 6; C270/5, 6, 12-14; C271/1, 2; C284/2. [3] Ibid. C270/16-18; *The Times*, 19 Jan. 1821. [4] De L'Isle mss C212/1-5; L6/4, 27; V213/4; *Minutes of Evidence ... and Case of Sir John Shelley Sidney*. [5] De L'Isle mss C212/1-3; C213/4; C284/2. [6] Ibid. C212/1-4; C213/1. [7] *Arbuthnot Jnl.* ii. 313-15; *Von Neumann Diary*, i. 186. [8] De L'Isle mss C212/5; Suff. RO (Ipswich), Henniker mss S1/2/8/1.1; *Gloucester Jnl.* 19 Sept.; *Suff. Chron.* 15, 24 Oct. 1829; *Arbuthnot Jnl.* ii. 318. [9] De L'Isle mss C257/1; Wellington mss WP1/1125/40 *Suff. Chron.* 31 July; *Ipswich Jnl.* 7 Aug. 1830. [10] Wellington mss WP1/1134/8; 1137/42; de L'Isle mss C257/1. [11] *William IV-Grey Corresp.* i. 89, 136-50, 195; de L'Isle mss C240/1. [12] *Bury and Norwich Post*, 9 Mar.; *Ipswich Jnl.* 19 Mar. 1831. [13] Harrowby mss, Ryder to Harrowby, 8 Mar. 1831. [14] NAS GD224/507/3/19, 20. [15] M. Hopkirk, *Queen Adelaide*, 120; *Holland House Diaries*, 15; De L'Isle mss C235/3-5. [16] De L'Isle mss C240/2; L6/5; O15/2. [17] Ibid. C255/2; *Taylor Pprs.* i. 334-5. [18] Add. 37069, f. 296. [19] *Three Diaries*, 174-5; Wellington mss WP1/1213/14; NLW, Ormathwaite mss FG1/6, p. 30. [20] *Three Diaries*, 333-4. [21] De L'Isle mss O15/4. [22] *Raikes Jnl.* iii. 159; *The Times*, 6 Jan. 1835; De L'Isle mss C238/1. [23] Add. 40487, ff. 217-21; De L'Isle mss C236/10-12; C246/6, 7. [24] Add. 40426, f. 235; 40485, f. 344; 40486, f. 123. [25] *Ann. Reg.* (1837), Chron. pp. 139, 187; De L'Isle mss C236/1-8; O15/9. [26] *Maidstone Gazette*, 18 Mar.; *Ann. Reg.* (1851), Chron. p. 269. [27] PROB 11/2134/462; IR26/1874/397.

M.M.E.

SINCLAIR, George (1790–1868), of Ulbster and Thurso Castle, Caithness.

CAITHNESS	26 Aug. 1811–1812
CAITHNESS	1818–1820
CAITHNESS	1831–1841

b. 28 Aug. 1790, 1st s. of Sir John Sinclair[†], 1st bt., of Ulbster and 2nd w. Hon. Diana Jane Elizabeth Macdonald, da. of Alexander, 1st Bar. Macdonald [I]. *educ.* Harrow 1802; Göttingen Univ. 1806. *m.* 1 May 1816, Catherine Camilla, da. of Sir William Manners[†], 1st bt., of Buckminster Park, Leics., 3s. (2 *d.v.p.*) 3da. (1 *d.v.p.*). *suc.* fa. as 2nd bt. 21 Dec. 1835. *d.* 9 Oct. 1868.

When Sinclair asked Sir Walter Scott to sit on the committee of inquiry into Dr. John Knox's dealings with the Edinburgh body-snatchers in January 1829, the novelist wrote:

Sir John Sinclair is provided with a substitute to continue the trade of *boring*. When he is called to be a bore like some old classic amongst the heavenly constellations *haud deficiat alter*. I saw with a sick and sorry heart his eldest son, tall and ungainly like the knight himself with cheek as sleek as oil and a wit as thick as mustard. Young hopeful's business with me was to invite me to ... lend a hand to whitewash this much to be suspected individual. But he shall ride off on no back of mine ... The rest of

the committee are to be doctors and surgeons ... and I suppose the doughty Sir John at the head of them all and this young boar pig to swell the cry.[1]

Scott was unfair in tarring Sinclair with the same brush as his egregious father, whom he had never forgiven for his insensitive attempt to provide him with a second wife in 1826. Although Sinclair certainly took himself seriously, he was not given to inflicting his advice indiscriminately on all and sundry, and had more than his share of self-doubt, a weakness unfamiliar to his father, whose ineffable self-importance must have often embarrassed him.[2] One of the more preposterous attempts at self-aggrandizement by Sir John Sinclair, whose claims for a peerage in the 1820s were ignored, was his offer of 2 Apr. 1824 (five weeks short of his 70th birthday) to take on the Irish secretaryship (which was not vacant) in order to apply his economic expertise to the salvation of Ireland: if he went to Dublin, he told George's old schoolfellow Peel, the home secretary, 'I would take my son with me, to whose abilities you are no stranger, and it might be the means of introducing him into the line of public business for which he is so well qualified'.[3] Sir John also bombarded the king and his ministers with copies of George's *Narrative*, published in 1826, of his interrogation by Buonaparte 20 years previously, after being detained near Jena on suspicion of espionage.[4] For his own part, George Sinclair had become soon after his marriage a convert to Pentecostal Evangelicalism, which was thereafter the mainspring of his life.[5] To his wife, for instance, he wrote from Boulogne, 4 June 1822:

I am never more contented than in the bosom of my family; and I hope that my mind is in some degree weaned from an attachment to certain illusions, which education, example, habit, and practice, had for some time fostered and encouraged. I am, undoubtedly, conscious that my triumph is very imperfect ... but I should indeed be ungrateful to my heavenly Father, if I did not feel that some improvement has been wrought; that I am more humble, more contrite, more satisfied than I once was ... If I had no duties and obligations, incompatible with such an arrangement, I should like to retire with my children and you to the country; to give up London, with all its temptations and disappointments, and devote my time entirely to domestic quiet and enjoyment.[6]

Sinclair's marked independence during the 1818 Parliament, his support for parliamentary reform and his friendships with Sir Francis Burdett* and Joseph Hume* made him suspect in the eyes of the Liverpool ministry, while his radical leanings were unpopular with some of the Caithness lairds. His involvement in the county meeting of 1 Oct. 1823 which passed resolutions endorsing the Whig Lord Archibald Hamilton's recent Commons motion for reform of the Scottish county representation prompted the lord lieutenant, Lord Caithness, to put forward his brother James Sinclair* for the next general election. He sought and secured the support of Lord Melville, the minister responsible for Scotland.[7] The outraged Sir John Sinclair tried in vain to thwart this challenge, appealing to Melville and his Edinburgh underlings and furnishing a letter from George in which he asserted that his espousal of *'moderate'* parliamentary reform *'is now my only point of difference with ministers'*. At the same time he acknowledged that it was 'highly reasonable' that the consequence of his 'occasional votes against them' should be 'a complete exclusion from any personal emolument or advancement'.[8] In 1824 Sir John, begging Peel to intervene with Melville, insisted that George was 'well inclined to support the present government', but Peel declined to act.[9] Sinclair, encouraged by the Whig Dissenter William Smith*, stood his ground as the two factions struggled for supremacy, but at the rowdy and litigious 1826 general election he lost to James Sinclair by five votes in a poll of 41 freeholders.[10] Immediately afterwards his father asked Lord Radnor, an earlier recipient of a copy of the *Narrative*, to bring him in for Downton in the room of the poet Southey, whom he had returned without his knowledge or consent:

He was twice elected to represent ... Caithness ... and ... displayed talents that proved him capable of making a figure in the line of politics ... He had directed particular attention to the corn and currency questions which are to be decided in the course of the next or the ensuing session, *and on the decision regarding which the fate of the nation depends* ... I wish much that my son could be brought in for a couple of sessions ... that he may have an opportunity of stating his sentiments on ... [these] two most important subjects.

Radnor replied:

You cannot expect me to be actuated with the warmth of a parent. I consider myself as sufficiently excused by saying that I am sorry to be contributing to your disappointment, but so it must be.[11]

In November 1827 Sir James Mackintosh* recorded Lord Lansdowne's story that during the recent ministerial stalemate over the appointment of John Herries* as chancellor of the exchequer in the Goderich ministry, Sir John Sinclair had put himself forward for the post and added that 'he should still further provide for the public service by educating his son to supply his place when the fatal moment of decline should

arrive'.[12] Caithness did not return a Member in 1830, but at the general election of 1831 Sinclair, who since his defeat had continued his academic and theological studies, came forward as 'a moderate reformer'. There was widespread local support for the Grey ministry's reform scheme, and he encountered no opposition. On the hustings he spoke of

the necessity of setting the question at rest, by a final and satisfactory adjustment, an end which can only be attained by the adoption of a measure so comprehensive in its extent, so popular in its principles, so matured in its details, and so salutary in its operation, as to leave the visionary without influence, and the disaffected without excuse.

Portraying himself as 'a martyr to the cause' for 20 years, he argued that the proposed extension of the franchise would 'raise in the scale of political importance the middling classes of society, which are the boast and the bulwark of the land'. As ever, he emphasized his hostility to universal suffrage and annual parliaments; but he trusted that those not presently possessed of the requisite 'property' and 'intelligence' to be entrusted with the vote would be encouraged to 'look forward to its ultimate attainment, as an additional and powerful stimulus to economy and perseverance in industrious exertion'.[13]

The assertion of Sinclair's biographer, that 'whenever it was known that he was to make one of his great speeches, the House was sure to be filled with Members anxious to hear him', can be dismissed as fantasy.[14] He did, however, carry out his parliamentary duties with characteristic earnestness, and his periodic interventions in debate were clear and forthright, if nothing else. He presented a petition from the Highland Society of London for a bill to amend the Acts for its incorporation, 27 June. On 5 July he introduced the measure, which became law on 23 Aug. He voted for the second reading of the reintroduced English reform bill, 6 July, and against the adjournment, 12 July. He was a steady supporter of the details of the bill, and may have assisted Thomas Kennedy* in compiling for the government whips 'correct lists' of the votes of Scottish Members.[15] He voted for its third reading and passage, 19, 21 Sept. He divided with the minority for adjournment of the debate on the issue of the Dublin writ, 8 Aug., but voted with ministers in the first division of 23 Aug. on their alleged improper interference in the election there. He presented Caithness petitions for the abolition of slavery, 12 Aug., and against the use of molasses in brewing and distilling, 26 Aug. On 12 Sept. he suggested to the indignant Tory Colonel Sibthorp that his own 'vehemence of manner and gesticulation' had been largely responsible for an unflattering report in *The Times* of his speech of 6 Sept. Later that day he spoke and voted against government for inquiry into the effects of renewal of the Sugar Refinery Act on the West Indian colonies, each one of which contained 'a volcano of discontent, of which a very slight shock may be sufficient to cause the explosion'. On 26 Sept. he voted, as an elder of the Church of Scotland, to discontinue the Maynooth grant: he did so, he said, not out of personal hostility to Catholics, whose emancipation he had always supported, but because he was not prepared to subsidize the training of 'men who, from duty as well as inclination, must labour to subvert our Protestant establishments, and supplant our national faith'. He voted for the motion of confidence in the ministry, 10 Oct. 1831.

Sinclair voted for the second reading of the revised reform bill, 17 Dec. 1831. A month later he attracted public attention by refusing an invitation from William IV, his close friend of many years, to dine with him on a Sunday. Privately, he chided the king for his well-known hostility to the 'Saints', for it was 'by *them* that the spirit of true religion is kept alive':

I myself once despised those whom I am now most desirous to resemble. I myself once shunned that society which I now find most edifying and congenial. I myself was once 'a blasphemer, a persecutor, and injurious', walking according to the course of this world, and having my affections engrossed by 'seen and temporal objects'.[16]

To the consternation of some Edinburgh Whigs, who feared it reflected the king's views, he voted against government on the Russian-Dutch loan, 26 Jan. 1832.[17] He argued that they had failed to make out their case, and said that while he opposed them with 'great reluctance', he felt bound, on this as on all issues, 'to follow the dictates of my own judgement, without reference to parties or persons'. The following day, however, he warmly praised ministers for their 'courage' and 'honesty' in promoting reform which, amongst its many benefits, would rescue 'the people of Scotland from that state of political thraldom and degradation which had subsisted during so many centuries'. He supported the details of the English bill, though he opposed the enfranchisement of Merthyr Tydvil by the expedient of depriving Monmouthshire of a third Member, 14 Mar., when he asserted that 'my anxiety to support government is controlled by a sense of duty'. He voted for the third reading, 22 Mar. He sided with government on relations with Portugal, 9 Feb., but opposed the 'hasty and impolitic' malt drawback bill, 30 Mar., 2 Apr. He voted for the address asking the king to appoint only ministers who would

carry undiluted reform, 10 May, and two days later, at a moment of 'imminent and almost unprecedented peril', wrote to William begging him not to appoint the duke of Wellington prime minister, for to do so

would do more to lower the character of public men, more to endanger the royal authority, more to encourage political profligacy and abandonment of principles, than it is possible to exaggerate or to conceive. In his hands concession is deprived of all its grace, and of all its efficacy. The people ... would rather take *less* from Lord Grey than obtain *more* through the party which has undermined and supplanted him ... Not one of Lord Grey's supporters will be base enough to abandon him ... I myself, who never so much as exchanged with him a sentence of common civility, I, who have been often frowned at for occasional votes against the administration, and who had no personal favours, either to expect or to be grateful for, must honestly avow, that I consider myself bound ... to adhere to him in this emergency ... Should Parliament be dissolved, I myself shall retire to private life.[18]

With Grey reinstated, he voted for the second reading of the Irish reform bill, 25 May, and against a Conservative amendment to the Scottish measure, 1 June, when he said that 'our support has been given, not to reform for the sake of ministers, but to ministers for the sake of reform'. He was in the majority for a detail of the Scottish bill, 15 June. He spoke and voted for Sadler's proposal for a property tax on Irish absentee landlords, 'who grind the faces of the poor, and dissipate the income extorted from a famishing tenantry, in foreign luxuries or at English watering-places', 19 June. He belatedly presented petitions for the supplies to be withheld until the reform bills had become law, 20 June, along with petitions against the government's Irish education scheme. He supported the principle of Baring's bill to exclude insolvent debtors from Parliament, 27 June. He presented a Westminster petition for enforcing better observance of the Sabbath, 3 July. He rallied to government on the Russian-Dutch loan, 20 July, but on 30 July he cavilled at the proposed increase in the lord chancellor's pension, called for an increase in Scottish judicial salaries and placed on record his belief that the Irish viceroyalty, a source of 'intrigue and discord', should be abolished. He moved a wrecking amendment against Hume's bill to exclude the recorder of Dublin from the Commons, 31 July 1832, but the House was counted out.

Notwithstanding the 'nervous state of health' which had always handicapped him, Sinclair came in again for Caithness in 1832. Three years later he adhered to Peel's Conservative party with Sir James Graham* and Edward Smith Stanley*. He had lost control of his county seat by 1841, when he was beaten by two Liberals at Halifax.[19] A prominent participant in the Scottish non-intrusion controversy, he eventually joined the Free Church and became a prolific pamphleteer on religious questions.[20] The deaths of his first son Dudley (the youngest, Granville, had died in 1833), his mother and his sister Helen within a short period in 1844-5 cast a pall over him; and in 1847 he was taken to task by his friend John Croker* for turning his back on the world:

> You need no advice ... as to the true source of consolation; but I think there are minor helps which you seem to neglect too much. You should join your family in Edinburgh, and mix with the morning and evening thoughts of the world to come, the daily duties, avocations, and even amusements of the world in which we live ... Leave ... the hyperborean gloom of your castle near the pole, and ... [go] to Edinburgh, where old and new friends will convince you that, as long as heaven is pleased to leave us in this world, it provides us with the *pabulum vitae* – something worth living for.

Sinclair was still finding cause to regret 'the years misspent in faithless courts and fawning senates, neither doing nor deriving any good', in 1855, when he lamented the prevalent 'fatal mediocrity' in every sphere of life.[21] An attack of bronchitis in May 1867 drove him to Cannes for the winter, but he returned little improved and died in Edinburgh in October 1868.[22]

[1] *Scott Jnl.* 579-80. [2] R. Mitchison, *Agricultural Sir John*, 35, 228, 250-1. [3] Ibid. 255; Add. 40363, f. 235; 40382, f. 98. [4] *Geo. IV Letters*, iii. 1226; Add. 40385, f. 112. [5] B. Hilton, *Age of Atonement*, 92-95; J. Grant, *Sir George Sinclair*, 150-71, 258-61; NAS GD136/519/14, 17. [6] Grant, 55-56. [7] NLS mss 2, f. 68; 1054, f. 187; NAS GD51/1/198/6/16, 17; Mitchison, 258-9. [8] NAS GD51/1/198/6/17, 20. [9] Add. 40317, ff. 27, 30. [10] Sinclair mss, Smith to G. Sinclair, 3 Jan. 1824; Mitchison, 259-61; *Inverness Courier*, 12 July 1826. See CAITHNESS. [11] Sinclair mss, Sir J. Sinclair to Radnor, 11 July, reply, 18 July 1826. [12] Add. 52447, f. 119. [13] NAS GD136/519/21; *Inverness Courier*, 20 Apr., 4, 11, 18 May; *The Times*, 24 May 1831. [14] Grant, 121. [15] *Cockburn Letters*, 339-40. [16] Mitchison, 228; Grant, 254-61. [17] *Cockburn Letters*, 389. [18] Grant, 261-7. [19] Add. 40414, f. 29. [20] Grant, 267-99; Parker, *Peel*, iii. 73-79, 87-89. [21] *Disraeli Letters*, iv. 1475; *Croker Pprs.* iii. 182. [22] Grant, 472-4; *Oxford DNB*.

D.R.F.

SINCLAIR, Hon. James (1797–1856), of Braelangwell, Ross.

CAITHNESS 1826–1830

b. 24 Oct. 1797, 3rd but 2nd surv. s. of Sir James Sinclair, 7th bt., of Mey, Caithness, 12th earl of Caithness [S] (*d.* 1823), and Jane, da. of Gen. Alexander Campbell of Barcaldine, Argyll. *m.* 16 Mar. 1819,[1] Elizabeth, da. of George Tritton of West Hill, Wandsworth, Surr., *s.p. d.* 18 Jan. 1856.

2nd lt. 21 Ft. 1814; lt. 1st garrison batt. 1815; lt. army (half-pay) 1817; lt. 92 Ft. 1818; lt. (half-pay) 95 Ft. 1820; maj. army 1827, half-pay 1829, ret. 1841.

Lt.-col. Ross, Caithness, Sutherland and Cromarty militia.

Sinclair's father succeeded his own father as the 7th baronet of Mey in 1774, at the age of eight. In 1789 he succeeded his cousin John Sinclair, a suicide, as 12th earl of Caithness, but he did not assume the title until 4 May 1793, when his right was confirmed by the Lords. He was appointed lord lieutenant of Caithness, where his substantial estates centred on Barrogill Castle, near John O'Groats, in 1794, and postmaster-general of Scotland by the Perceval ministry in 1811. He was a Scottish representative peer, 1807-18. With his wife, a niece of Sir John Sinclair of Ulbster, Member for Caithness, 1790-6, 1802-6, 1807-11, he had six sons, of whom the eldest, John, died young in 1802, leaving the second, Alexander Campbell, heir to the earldom as Lord Berriedale. His next brother James Sinclair followed him into the army in 1814, but his career was desultory. When the 12th earl died impoverished in 1823 his successor applied successfully to the Liverpool ministry for the lord lieutenancy of Caithness, but failed to secure their support for his pretensions to a vacancy in the representative peerage, which had already been promised to Lord Errol. His wife Frances complained directly to her cousin Canning, the foreign secretary, and insinuated that Lord Caithness might turn against government, but she received a flea in her ear.[2] Soon afterwards Lord Caithness took advantage of local hostility to George Sinclair*, Ulbster's son and heir, who had represented the county, 1811-12, 1818-20, and now seemed to be espousing the cause of parliamentary reform, to put up his brother James as a candidate for the next general election. They secured the approval of Lord Melville, the ministry's Scottish manager, much to Ulbster's anger.[3] Sinclair, who had no property in the county, was provided with a parchment freehold. An attempt to effect a compromise failed, and at the general election of 1826 Sinclair defeated Ulbster's son by five votes in a poll of 41.[4]

He made no mark in the House, from which he was given six weeks' leave to attend to urgent business, 11 Apr. 1827. He voted with the duke of Wellington's ministry against repeal of the Test Acts, 26 Feb., and paired for Catholic relief, 12 May 1828. In January 1829, complaining that he and his wife were virtually destitute as a result of the bankruptcy of his father-in-law and that he had spent heavily to secure his election, he solicited a small pension for his wife, but to no avail.[5] As expected, he voted with the ministry for Catholic emancipation, 6, 30 Mar. 1829. He presented but made light of a hostile Caithness parish petition, 25 Mar., and brought up a favourable one from Helensburgh, 30 Mar. 1829. His only other known vote was in the minority for an amendment to the sale of beer bill, 21 June 1830. At the ensuing general election the return reverted to Buteshire, and at that of 1831 Sinclair waived his pretensions in favour of George Sinclair and endorsed him as a supporter of the Grey ministry's reform scheme.[6] In September 1832 he applied to the colonial secretary Lord Goderich for a post abroad, 'however small the emolument', bemoaning the fact that he had 'no means of subsistence' beyond his major's half-pay and claiming to have entered Parliament 'at great expense in order to support' Canning's administration, conveniently forgetting that it had not been formed until nine months after his return. Nothing could be done for him.[7] He died at Morton Cottage, Portobello, Edinburgh in January 1856.[8]

[1] *Gent. Mag.* (1819), i. 363. [2] Add. 40357, ff. 286, 287; Harewood mss, Lady Caithness to Canning, 25 Aug., reply, 31 Aug. 1823. [3] NLS mss 2, ff. 61, 68; NAS GD51/1/198/6/16, 17, 20-22; GD136/441/29. [4] *Inverness Courier*, 7 June, 5, 12 July 1826; NAS GD51/1/198/6/26, 27; GD136/729. [5] Wellington mss WP1/987/22. [6] *Inverness Courier*, 11 May 1831. [7] Add. 40880, f. 322. [8] *Gent. Mag.* (1856), i. 322.

D.R.F.

SKEFFINGTON (formerly **FOSTER**), **Hon. Thomas Henry** (?1772–1843), of Collon, co. Louth.

DROGHEDA	1807–1812
CO. LOUTH	27 Sept. 1821–20 Jan. 1824

b. ?1772, 5th but o. surv. s. of John Foster* and Margaretta, da. of Thomas Burgh, MP [I], of Bert, co. Kildare. *educ.* Eton 1784-9; Trinity Coll. Camb. 15 Apr. 1790, aged 18; L. Inn 1790. *m.* 20 Nov. 1810, Lady Harriet Skeffington, da. and h. of Chichester, 4th earl of Massereene [I] (whom she suc. 25 Feb. 1816 as *s.j.* Viscountess Massereene), 5s. 3da. Took name of Skeffington 8 Jan. 1817; *suc.* mother as 2nd Visct. Ferrard [I] 20 Jan. 1824; fa. as 2nd Bar. Oriel [UK] 16 Aug. 1828. *d.* 18 Jan. 1843.
　MP [I] 1792-1800.
　Commr. of revenue [I] 1798-99, of treasury [I] 1807-13; PC [I] 17 Oct. 1809.
　Trustee, linen board [I] 1808.
　Jt. gov. co. Louth 1805-28, gov. 1828-31; sheriff, co. Louth 1811-12, co. Antrim 1818-19.
　Col. co. Louth militia 1793-*d.*; 2nd capt. Collon inf. 1796.

Skeffington, son and heir of the last Irish Speaker John Foster, had given up the family seat at Drogheda in 1812, and although he was willing to serve there as mayor in 1816, he was disinclined to return to Westminster, feeling that his family had been neglected by government and that 'no man in the kingdom' had been 'so ill treated' as his father in his attempts to secure a United Kingdom peerage. 'I shall never look to Parliament', he stated, 11 June 1820, adding that he should prefer to see his first cousin John Leslie Foster* succeed his father as the family's representative for Louth.[1] On his father's elevation to a United Kingdom peerage the following year, however, Skeffington came forward for the vacancy. Rumours of an opposition came to nothing and he was returned unopposed.[2] His cousin Sir Ulysses Burgh* expressed a hope that 'Thomas will come over and be a regular attender', and when present, he supported the Liverpool ministry.[3]

He voted with them against more extensive tax reductions, 11, 21 Feb. 1822. On 25 Mar. Burgh advised his father that the 'sooner Thomas returns the better, as we shall have a good deal of business after the Easter holidays'.[4] He paired against the bill to relieve Catholic peers of their disabilities, 30 Apr., explaining that although he believed the 'peace and tranquillity of Ireland would never be restored' until the penal laws against Catholics were 'totally repealed', the present measure evaded 'the question of securities' and had taken the country 'by surprise', 10 May. He denounced the Irish grand jury presentments bill (on which he had been appointed a committee member, 3 May) as 'most destructive to the landlord, most injurious to the tenant, and fatal to the improvement of land in Ireland', 21 May, and presented two individuals' petitions against it, 4 July.[5] On 31 May he presented one from the landowners of Dundalk against the duties on imported butter and cheese.[6] He apprehended that the effects of the Irish tithes leasing bill 'would be rather to excite than to tranquillize Ireland', 13 June, voted against inquiry, 19 June 1822, and spoke against the Irish tithes commutation bill, but 'in so low a tone of voice' as to be inaudible, 18 Feb. 1823.[7] He divided against parliamentary reform, 20 Feb., tax reductions, 3 Mar., and repeal of the Foreign Enlistment Act, 16 Apr., but was in the majority for inquiry into the prosecution of the Dublin Orange rioters, 22 Apr. In his last known speech he opposed the Irish militia reduction bill and moved unsuccessfully for its postponement, 25 Apr. 1823.[8]

On the death of his mother in January 1824 Skeffington succeeded to her Irish viscountcy of

Ferrard, by which he was disqualified from sitting for an Irish constituency. 'Between ourselves', the Irish secretary Goulburn wrote to the home secretary Peel, his 'advancement ... will be a great gain as in addition to giving us Leslie Foster's support, it will rid me of Colonel Skeffington's conversation and advice'.[9] He was credited with 'making very material additions' to the former residence of his father, whom he succeeded in 1828, when he became sole governor of Louth.[10] His attempts to borrow against the family estates and settle his debts, to which were added the costs of his second son Chichester Thomas's unsuccessful candidature for Louth as a Conservative in 1835, led to a sordid lawsuit with his first son and heir John, 10th Viscount Massereene (1812-63).[11] He died in January 1843.

[1] J. D'Alton, *Hist. Drogheda* (1844), i. 257; PRO NI, Chilham (Foster) mss T.2519/4/1719. [2] *Dublin Evening Post*, 1 Sept. 1821; A. Malcomson, *John Foster*, 140; PRO NI, Redhall mss MIC582/1/69. [3] PRO NI, Foster Massereene mss D207/73/277; *Black Bk.* (1823), 192. [4] Foster Massereene mss 73/280. [5] *The Times*, 22 May, 5 July 1822. [6] Ibid. 1 June 1822. [7] Ibid. 19 Feb. 1823. [8] Ibid. 26 Apr. 1823. [9] *Drogheda Jnl.* 25 Feb. 1824; Add. 40330, f. 11. [10] J.C. Curwen, *Observations on the State of Ireland* (1818), 294. [11] Malcomson, 260, 333.

P.J.S.

SKIPWITH, Sir Gray, 8th bt. (1771–1852), of Alveston Villa, nr. Stratford-upon-Avon, Warws. and 6 Pall Mall East, Mdx.[1]

| WARWICKSHIRE | 1831–1832 |
| WARWICKSHIRE SOUTH | 1832–1834 |

b. 17 Sept. 1771, in Virginia, 1st s. of Sir Peyton Skipwith, 7th bt., of Prestwould, Mecklenburg, Virginia and 1st w. Anne, da. of Hugh Miller of Green Crofts, Blandford, Virginia. *educ.* Eton 1787-90; Trinity Coll. Cambridge 1790. *m.* 22 Apr. 1801, Harriett, da. of Gore Townsend of Honington Hall, Warws., 12s. (2 d.v.p.) 8da. *suc.* Sir Thomas George Skipwith†, 4th bt., to entailed estates 1790 and to Newbold Pacey Hall, Warws. 1832; fa. as 8th bt. 9 Oct. 1805. *d.* 13 May 1852.
Recorder, Stratford-upon-Avon 1823-35.[2]

Skipwith, a descendant through his mother (*d.* 1779), of the American Indian Princess Pocahontas, was born and raised in Virginia, where Sir Grey Skipwith, the 3rd baronet of Prestwould, Leicestershire, had settled after selling his English property to a follower of Cromwell in 1652. His father, a loyalist during the American War of Independence, bequeathed his Virginia estates to his younger sons, for Skipwith, his successor in the baronetcy, was already provided for as heir apparent to their childless kinsman Sir Thomas Skipwith (*d.* 1790), the 4th and last baronet of Newbold Pacey Hall, south of Warwick (the 1769-80 county Member), who had financed his English education.[3] Skipwith's influence in Warwickshire was also enhanced by his marriage to the 4th earl of Plymouth's granddaughter Harriett Townsend, which was noted for its fecundity.[4] Sir Thomas's widow (*d.* 1832) retained Newbold Pacey Hall for life, but she granted Skipwith £600 a year from the estate's £4,000 and adopted his daughter Selina (*b.* 1804).[5] He and his family meanwhile occupied the small Archer estate of Alveston, near Stratford-upon-Avon, where he acquired a reputation as an excellent quarter sessions chairman and able huntsman and became a trustee of Rugby School. Nimrod described him as 'a very pretty rider, always well mounted, generally in a good place and an excellent observer of hounds'.[6] A popular public figure on the hustings, he initially aligned with the Tories and was deemed suitable for the vacant county seat in October 1820, but his large family and small income forbade it.[7] He proposed and acted for the Whig moderate Sir Francis Lawley* in 1820 and 1826.[8] His wife's death, 7 July, precluded his participation in 1830 election.[9] In March 1831 he signed Sir Francis Burdett's* alternative requisition for a county reform meeting, 4 Apr., at which he declared unequivocally for the Grey ministry's bill. He was adopted as the compromise or unity candidate at a stormy nomination meeting, 4 May.[10] On the hustings that day, he confirmed his support for the proposed disfranchisements, £10 householder and copy and leaseholder franchises, but refused to pledge indiscriminately for 'all economies'. He added:

I have never until lately exhibited myself as a reformer, because, I confess, I could formerly see no hopes of success. I, however, embraced the first opportunity of expressing my sentiments, when I considered their expression might prove effectual ... My only fear is, that in attending to business connected with the great town of Birmingham, my abilities will not be equal to my zeal.[11]

He was returned unopposed.[12] Fêted at Stratford, 13 May 1831, he conceded that 'many excellent men he knew admitted the need for some reform, but thought that the bill went too far' by making the 'Commons too democratic' and increasing the risk of a revolution. He added: 'I have no fear of that kind. I have too high an opinion of the strong sense of Englishmen'.[13]

Acting with Lawley, Skipwith, who joined Brooks's, 16 July, voted for the reintroduced reform bill at its second reading, 6 July, and generally for its details, but against the total disfranchisement of Downton, 21 July 1831. His vote for Lord Chandos's clause for enfranchising £50 tenants-at-will, 18 Aug., reflected local opinion. He divided for the bill at its third reading, 19 Sept., and passage, 21 Sept., for the second reading of the Scottish measure, 23 Sept., and for Lord Ebrington's confidence motion, 10 Oct. He had written publicly to the leader of the Birmingham Political Union, Thomas Attwood†, following the bill's Lords' defeat, urging moderation and continued support for the Grey ministry, and the ensuing county meeting commended him for doing so, 8 Nov.[14] He divided for the revised bill at its second reading, 17 Dec. 1831, generally for its details and for the third reading, 22 Mar. 1832. He was absent 'in the country' when the House divided on the address calling on the king to appoint only ministers who would carry it unimpaired, 10 May. He voted for the second reading of the Irish reform bill, 25 May. He divided with government on the Dublin election controversy, 23 Aug. 1831, the Russian-Dutch loan, 26 Jan., 12, 16, 20 July, and relations with Portugal, 9 Feb. 1832. On slavery, an important local issue at the 1832 election, he was in Fowell Buxton's minority for the immediate appointment of a select committee to consider abolition, 24 May 1832.

Attending to constituency business, he presented and endorsed a petition criticizing the laws affecting debtors, 12 Oct. 1831, and brought up others on behalf of the distressed ribbon weavers, 28 Feb., and in favour of the Maynooth grant, 21 May, and the factory bill, 17 July 1832. His main concern was the fate of the beleaguered London-Birmingham railway bill. He brought up favourable petitions, 28 Feb., 13 Apr., and his speeches on 28 Feb., when he and Lawley thwarted attempts to kill the bill and carried its second reading by 125-40, reflected his knowledge of the statutory procedures for local bills and of their implementation in this instance. Addressing the railway's wealthy promoters at the *Thatched House Tavern*, 13 July, he extolled the scheme's merits and denounced the Tory peers who opposed it. When the Lords returned the bill amended, 17 July 1832, he recommended accepting it in a persuasive speech, which drew heavily on the engineer Telford's evidence to the select committee, and helped to secure its passage.

A Liberal and staunch churchman, but 'no radical', Skipwith moved to Newbold Pacey Hall in the summer of 1832 and topped the poll for Warwickshire South at the general election in December.[15] He resigned to avoid a contest in 1835 and was defeated in Warwickshire South in 1836 and Warwickshire North in 1837. He died at Hampton Lucy in May 1852, survived by at least 15 of his 20 children. He was suc-

ceeded in the baronetcy and estates by his eldest son Thomas George Skipwith (1803-63), the defeated Liberal candidate for Warwickshire North in 1852.[16]

[1] His first name is generally spelt 'Grey', but Gray in wills and his marriage settlement (PROB 11/1776/575; 2159/727; Warws. RO CR829/114; 2942/2). [2] *Aris's Birmingham Gazette*, 16 June 1823; *PP* (1835), xxiii. 253-8. [3] *Burke PB* (1999); PROB 11/1195/400; Warws. RO, unpubl. 'Jnls. of Selina, Lady Skipwith' ed. E.J. Shirley, TD64/41; *HP Commons, 1754-90*, iii. 442-3. [4] *Ann. Reg.* (1852), Hist. Chron. p. 281; *Warwick Advertiser*, 22 May 1852. [5] Warws. RO CR829/114; PROB 11/1799/255. [6] *Gent. Mag.* (1852), ii. 90-91; *The Times*, 6 Dec. 1827; *VCH Warws.* ii. 381. [7] Essex RO, Gunnis mss D/DGu/C6/1/6; Norf. RO, Kimberley mss KIM 6/37, Walton to J. Wodehouse, 7 Nov. 1820. [8] *Warwick Advertiser*, 28 Oct., 4 Nov. 1820, 10, 17 June 1826; *The Times*, 17 June 1826. [9] *Warwick Advertiser*, 17 July, 7 Aug. 1830. [10] Ibid. 26 Mar., 9, 23, 30 Apr., 7 May; Brougham mss, G. Philips to Brougham, 5 May 1831; Warws. RO (MI 247), Philips Mems. ii. 124-5. [11] *Coventry Mercury*, 8 May 1831. [12] *Warwick Advertiser*, 14 May 1831. [13] Ibid. 21 May 1831. [14] *The Times*, 12 Oct., 10 Nov.; *Warwick Advertiser* 5, 12 Nov. 1831. [15] Warws. RO CR829/77; *Warwick Advertiser*, 8, 15 Dec. 1832. [16] *The Times*, 17 Dec. 1834, 24 June 1836; *Warwick Advertiser*, 22 May 1852; *VCH Warws.* iii. 180, 214, v. 32, 89.

M.M.E.

SLANEY, Robert Aglionby (1791–1862), of Walford, Salop and 16 Tavistock Square, Mdx.

SHREWSBURY	1826–1834
SHREWSBURY	1837–1841
SHREWSBURY	1847–1852
SHREWSBURY	1857–19 May 1862

b. 9 June 1791, 1st s. of Robert Slaney of Hatton Grange, Salop and Mary, da. of Thomas Mason of Shrewsbury. *educ.* Trinity Coll. Camb. 1809; I. Temple 1810, called 1817. *m.* (1) 7 Feb. 1812, his cos. Elizabeth (*d.* 20 July 1847), da. of Dr. William Hawkins Muckleston, 3da.; (2) 4 Apr. 1854, Catherine Anne, da. of Rev. George Buckston of Bradborn Hall, rect. of Shirland, Derbys., wid. of Graves Archer of Mount John, co. Wicklow, *s.p. suc.* fa. to Hatton Grange 1834. *d.* 19 May 1862.
  Commr. health of towns 1843-8.
  Sheriff, Salop 1854-5.

The Slaneys of Hatton Grange, near Shifnal, were reputed to have come over from Bohemia in the twelfth century 'in the train of the Empress Maud'. By the sixteenth century they were established in Shropshire, where, as lords of the manor of Dawley, they supplemented the income from their 3,000-acre estate and the Kemberton and Lizard forges by leasing the mineral rights of Horsehay to the Darbys of Coalbrookdale and other entrepreneurs.[1] Slaney, the eldest of three sons and two daughters, was named after his father and the Warwickshire family of Aglionby with whom his forbears had intermarried. He and his next brother Thomas (d. 1819) shared a private tutor and went up to Cambridge together, but Slaney, who was also entered for the bar, left after two terms for an extended tour of Europe. He returned in 1811 and shortly afterwards married his cousin Eliza, on whom the Mucklestons' Walford estate, a London town house in Tavistock Square and £10,000 were settled.[2] On 18 Apr. 1815 he began to keep a journal, of which some 13 volumes survive.[3] His intention was 'not to chronicle events insignificant in themselves; but to spur me to exertion. I am of sanguine mind, but indolent indisposition, though from lassitude or want of reflection I have frequently wasted time'.[4] His sporting skills, a great asset in a Shropshire politician, already commanded attention, for he was a fine shot, excelled at cricket, which he played for the Marylebone and Shropshire teams, rode his own horses at Shrewsbury races, hunted regularly and supported the Baschurch coursing meetings.[5] He advocated the cause of the distressed colliers in 1816 and qualified as a barrister the following year, taking chambers in Hare Court, Inner Temple and practising on the Oxford circuit, where he sought briefs at Shrewsbury and Stafford. Drawing on local knowledge, his reading of Malthus and the strong sense of Whig philanthropy instilled in him by his father, in 1819 he published his first pamphlet, *An Essay on the Employment of the Poor*. It detailed living and labour costs and attributed the current level of unemployment to the national debt, the late wars and maladministration of the poor laws, his *bête noire*. He surmised that peacetime employment could be increased by 'profitable direction of national capital', but considered most job creation schemes to be 'fallacious' and argued that the employment prospects of 'the peasantry' had been reduced by 'several impolitic checks for investment of capital in agriculture'. Of his own prospects as the year closed, he noted:

> If London agrees with me I intend to visit it towards the end of January and remain there till summer, thus dividing our time: to attend sessions, Westminster Hall, etc., and keep up my law acquaintance; and, if not employed in gaining addition to fortune, I hope to be usefully occupied in laying up store for future use and in turning my attention with greater steadiness to political economy, not neglecting sessions law, agriculture, and perhaps a knowledge of mechanics [which] will fill up vacant time, and the education of my dear little girls will be an additional source of amusement to me. On every account, I shall try to keep up Italian and French.[6]

His first major public speech, a call for 'uniformity' and declaration for the moderate loyal address adopted at the Shropshire county meeting, 10 Jan.

1821, was well received.[7] Adhering to his plan, and with a parliamentary career in mind, he became a frequent observer of debates and election committee proceedings, fraternizing regularly in Shropshire and in London, notwithstanding their political differences, with Panton Corbett* and William Lacon Childe*, who made ministerial pamphlets and select committee reports available to him. The works of Godwin, Malthus, David Ricardo*, Smith, Robert Torrens* and Whately reinforced his confidence in political economy, capital investment and free trade, and his belief that Parliament and the poor laws should be reformed; and in 1821 he revised and republished his essay on employment as a pamphlet supporting James Scarlett's ill-fated poor bill, so securing introductions to the Whigs Henry Brougham*, John Calcraft*, and Sir James Mackintosh*. He canvassed Shropshire voters for Scarlett at the November 1822 Cambridge University by-election, attributed the Shropshire freeholders' rejection of the 'excellent individual' Childe that month to his pro-government votes on taxation and was relieved to see the coalition of grandees who supported him frustrated.[8] In July 1824, after many delays and revisions, he published his *Essay on the Beneficial Direction of Rural Expenditure*. A 'major defence' of 'an expanding industrial capitalism based on free trade', it advocated educating the poor and demonstrated the 'near impossibility' at current wage levels of agricultural labourers setting money aside to offset sickness or unemployment.[9] It met with his father's 'entire' approval, so serving as a means of restoring Slaney to his confidence after a difficult seven-year period; he remarked that 'if so, it has repaid me the time it cost a thousand times'.[10] He welcomed what he perceived as the conversion of Corbett and Childe 'to the liberal side' on the Catholic question in 1825;[11] and at the November hunt commenced his canvass for Shrewsbury, where he hoped to replace the disgraced radical Whig Grey Bennet at the next election.[12] Announcing his candidature in April 1826, he claimed that he stood 'upon independent or moderate principles, unfettered by party engagements', and stressed his 12 years of devotion 'to the study of those subjects connected with the extension and improvement of trade and manufactures and with the welfare and happiness of the middle and poorer classes'.[13] His hopes of an unopposed return were dashed by the late candidature of the Ultra, Thomas Boycott of Rudge, on whose retirement after a four-day poll he came in with Corbett.[14] On the hustings he criticized his adversaries for misrepresenting him as indifferent to the Protestant religion, blamed the Catholic church for refusing 'to let the people read the scriptures for themselves', alluded to his work for the Society for the Propagation of the Gospels and spoke of the 'Bible as the best guide in this life and the only foundation of our hope in the life to come'. His pamphlets were ridiculed, but he confirmed his commitment to the poor and insisted that his principles were moderate and that he 'would support good measures' from both sides of the House.[15]

In his first Parliament Slaney gave the Whigs 'uniform independent support', broadened his acquaintance, lobbied hard, often with scant success, on matters affecting the poor and the maltsters and divided sporadically with the Whig opposition. His maiden speech, 22 Nov. 1826, reiterated and endorsed the agriculturists' complaints against the duties on malt and beer, but failed in its objective of securing returns on account of a prior request by the Breconshire Member, Thomas Wood. Slaney resumed his campaign to little apparent purpose, 28 Nov. 1826, but was pleased to hear 'from authority I cannot doubt' that his speech 'attracted Mr. Canning's attention, who noticed me in consequence'.[16] He apparently abstained on Catholic relief, 6 Mar., and having served on the Coventry election committee, he was granted a month's leave, 19 Mar. 1827.[17] He seconded the political economist Wolryche Whitmore's abortive motion for inquiry into the India trade, 15 May. Learning that the Canning ministry had no plans to implement 'suggestions' in the 1817 and 1819 reports on the employment of the aged poor, he announced, 25 May, and introduced his own measures, 12 June, drawing heavily on the 1817, 1819 and 1825 committee reports and stressing the need to stem the recent rise in poor rates and pauperism, which was 'destructive to the independence and character of agricultural labourers and eventually to the whole capital and interests of agriculture'. He praised the Scottish relief system and vented his spleen against the prevailing practice in southern and south-western counties of topping up wages from rate revenues. The bill passed its first reading, 18 June, but, after being hastily considered and amended, it was ordered to be printed and was timed out, 22 June.[18] He presented petitions from Shrewsbury and its hinterland against corn law revision, 27 Feb., and for repeal of the Test Acts, 6, 7 June. He voted to disfranchise Penryn and for Lord Althorp's election expenses bill, 28 May, and for the Canadian waterways grant, 12 June 1827.

Slaney left his family in Shropshire for the 1828 session 'with natural regret'. He considered Brougham's six-hour speech advocating law reform, 29 Feb. 1828, 'most eloquent and laborious', and its conclusion

a noble specimen of stern and manly English eloquence worthy of the enlightened and independent man who (in spite of his failings, for he is but a man) has done more to clear away bigotry, to support rational freedom and to spread the cause of education and intelligence than any other person living.[19]

According to his journal, he attended the House 'pretty assiduously', devoting his time 'chiefly to two subjects', poor law reform and repeal and improvement of the laws affecting malt. He postponed his labourers' wages bill, 8, 27 Feb., 14 Mar., while he gathered 'information by abstracts, returns, etc.', and attended the select committee on parochial settlement, to which he was appointed, 21 Feb. He pointed to the close correlation between emigration, low agricultural wages, crime and poor law abuse when Irish migrant labour was considered, 19 Feb., and legislation on emigration proposed, 4 Mar., and obtained leave to bring in his bill based on the 1817 and 1819 reports, 17 Apr., when, though 'dismayed by poor attendance', he spoke for two hours as his speech 'could hardly be compressed from the facts and returns quoted'. He declared that he had no intention of 'meddling' with those parts of the law governing rating, settlement or relief to 'the lame, the impotent and the blind', advocated inquiry into fluctuating demands for labour, and suggested treating corn law and poor law reform conjointly, raising agricultural wages and ending systematic doles to able-bodied 'artisans, mechanics and agricultural labourers', who were suffering because of the misapplication of legislation originally intended for vagrants. He spoke of the increased burden that relief costs, which doubled every 20 years and associated litigation expenses, which did so in 12, placed on landed wealth, praised the Scottish system and voiced his customary criticism of poor law administration in the 16 counties south of a line from Gloucester to Stamford. He commended the Buckinghamshire petition, suggested a credit system linking parish employment to savings accounts and called for the appointment of a select committee. The bill was read a second time, 29 Apr., and its recommendations incorporated in the widely circulated report Slaney drafted as chairman of the 1828 select committee on the poor laws, which he hoped would 'lead to a practical measure next session for which I shall prepare!'[20] He publicized his study of brewing practices and the maltsters' plight when endorsing Shrewsbury's petition against the malt duties, 27 Feb. Bringing up similar petitions from Newport and Shifnal later that day, he riled the president of the board of trade Charles Grant by complaining that the system 'shackled the progress of that free and fair trade which, in other instances [he, Grant, had] advocated'. He repeated his call for concessions and an *ad valorem* duty on presenting the Sheffield maltsters' petition, 23 May, drawing criticism from the chancellor of the exchequer Goulburn, whom he had recently lobbied as spokesman for the Shropshire maltsters' delegation. He opposed the alehouse licensing bill, 21 May, 25 June 1828, when, as subsequently, he voiced support for Sunday opening.

He presented petitions, 25 Feb., and voted for repeal of the Test Acts, 26 Feb, but abstained on Catholic relief, 12 May, for which he presented Shrewsbury's petition, 6 May 1828. He thought East Retford deserved disfranchisement, 25 Feb., and explained before voting against recommitting the disqualification bill, 27 June, that although he usually supported the landed interest, in this case he thought the franchise should be transferred 'to a great town' like Birmingham. He also criticized the agriculturists for seeking high corn prices when commerce was depressed, and infuriated Nicolson Calvert by offering to support any plan that left East Retford disfranchised. He also divided against the ministry to lower the corn pivot price from 64s. to 60s., 22 Apr., and on the small notes bill, 5 June, the Buckingham House expenditure, 23 June, and the ordnance estimates, 4 July. He presented a petition against the friendly societies bill, 6 May, briefly endorsed the Shrewsbury anti-slavery petition, 19 June, and, alluding to its unpopularity in Shropshire, suggested withdrawing the additional churches bill for redrafting, 3 July. He voiced local concerns over the security of the Chester mail, 6 July 1828. Assessing his progress that session, he observed: 'I have become acquainted with more Members ... and have been kindly noticed by Lord Althorp and others of real weight, but feel greatly the want of an introduction-perseverance'.[21]

Reacting to the establishment of a Brunswick Club in Shropshire, Slaney knowingly placed his political future at risk by informing his constituents in an open letter that he was 'in favour of concessions to the Catholics under securities, i.e. denying them any vote in Parliament on questions connected with religion', 24 Nov. 1828. He stressed the difference between petitioning meetings, of which he approved, and clubs, which tended to perpetuate political divisions, and wrote to George Dawson*, the secretary to the treasury 'offering to support government in any conciliatory proposition'.[22] In his journal he expressed concern at the possible loss of his seat, fears (generated by Joseph Muckleston's illness) lest he mismanage Eliza's likely inheritance, and pride that Lord John Russell*, William Ward* and Althorp*, who with

Lord Tavistock* proposed his admission to Brooks's, 21 Feb. 1829, had approved his conduct.[23] Slaney felt exonerated by the 1829 king's speech, interpreting it as 'a death blow to the power of the Ultras in England' and 'likely to remove a great obstacle to my return at Shrewsbury'.[24] He attended the Commons and Lords debates, and, as the patronage secretary Planta anticipated, divided with government for emancipation, 6, 30 Mar.[25] 'Being well acquainted with the neighbourhood', he testified briefly to the 'respectability' of the clergy and other signatories to the Wolverhampton anti-Catholic petition, 11 Mar., and presented a favourable one from Cheswardine, 20 Mar. He predicted that Shrewsbury's fury at its Members' pro-emancipation votes 'will pass away, but at all events, if necessary I can resign the seat with content, well satisfied to have aided in passing two such liberal and excellent measures as the Catholic bill and the repeal of the Corporation and Test Laws'. He 'received no incivility on account of my vote' when he visited Shrewsbury in May 1829.[26]

Slaney aired his views on poverty whenever the topic was broached, and hearing from Peel that he, as committee chairman, should introduce changes based on his 1828 report, he did so, 24 Feb. 1829, with a warning that Beaufroy's 1740 prediction, that by 1840 poor rate expenditure would exceed £9,000,000 and one person in seven would be a pauper, had almost been realised. His detailed criticism of the administration of the 1603 Act apportioned particular blame to decisions made in 1795 and the way in which the word 'impotent' had been misconstrued to include children, so facilitating the introduction of rent and wage subsidies, bread scales and a minimum wage and contributing to depressed wages, population increases and a rise in crime. He asserted that the merit of his bill lay in its being a 'gradual remedy' calculated to end abuse of the Elizabethan poor law, not to supersede it, and claimed that it could not 'be considered impracticable, because it is the universal practice in the north of England, where ... the labourers are the most independent, happy and moral'. He aimed to reduce relief dependency by abolishing money payments to the able-bodied in employment, so drawing 'a line between the industrious and the idle, between the working man of good and the working man of bad character'. Allowances would continue during 'temporary illness', to widows and deserted wives unable to 'wholly maintain' their families, to those incapable of maintaining themselves through old age or infirmity and as a temporary expedient 'in case of urgent distress from fire or flood'. The first reading was carried, 26 Feb., but, after consultation with Althorp and Wellington, the second reading was deferred until 4 May. Favourable petitions were received from Gloucestershire, Somerset and Bristol, 25 Mar., and Westhoe, 21 May, but Leeds and Birmingham petitioned against it, 4 May, and the Tories Sturges Bourne and Sadler and the radical Hume condemned it as unworkable. On 22 May, after it had been thrice recommitted and reprinted, Slaney abandoned it, having carried the clause prohibiting overseers from paying wage supplements to labourers by 39-11, 15 May.[27] He wrote that McCulloch, whom he met for the first time, 25 Mar., 'greatly approved of my bill, but thinks eventually no able-bodied man ought to be relieved except by labour *in* a workhouse, his family being out. However, this appears to me impracticable at present'.[28] Defending it when the extension of the poor laws to Ireland was proposed, 7 May, he claimed that he had been misunderstood:

> It is supposed that I mean to take away by that bill all relief from every able-bodied man in this country who would not be able to procure employment. I mean no such thing. All that the bill states is, that relief shall be afforded to such persons in the form of work, and not in the form of money.

He brought in an abortive bill to regulate poor rate assessment in certain Scottish parishes, 1 June. Heeding Lord Milton's* advice, and with government clearly against him, he withdrew his proposed malt bill, which he claimed was 'no party question' and vital to the poor and the prosperity of the landed interest, 12 May 1829. His 'speech on the supply of malt liquor to the middle and poorer classes' discussed regional variations in malting practices by soil type and the prevalence of the tied houses he abhorred, and was 'printed voluntarily by Mr. Howell of Shrewsbury'.[29] In June he visited Brighton, Rotterdam and the principal towns of Holland, and joined the Society for the Dissemination of Useful Knowledge, anticipating that they would publish his *Considerations on the Wages of Labour and Welfare of the Working Classes*, with a view to educating them to be 'more provident and less clamorous', and *An Introductory View of the British Song Birds*, intended for the use of ladies and young persons. Both were issued in 1832.[30] He spent August 1829 at Barmouth on the Merionethshire coast with his family, and, returning to Shropshire, he dealt with complaints concerning the contentious route of the Holyhead road and prepared to 'persevere in the amendment of the poor laws, and laws affecting malt liquor', and to study

> the causes which depress and degrade the artisans and manufacturers, and endeavour to devise a remedy and call the public attention to it. The alternations and fluctu-

ations of wages demand the serious investigation of those who desire well to their fellows. [31]

Unsure how to react to the prospect of 'moderate liberals' among Canning's former supporters joining the Wellington ministry in January 1830, he consulted Althorp, whose reply, 'as we were end last session', seems to have done little to reassure him.[32] Returning to London he observed that

> parties are oddly divided, ministers about 120, Whigs about 90, Ultra Tories inveterate against government *now* 30. Huskisson and C. Grant, clever free trade men, also *now strong* in opposition, about 15, and the plot thickens as others come to town. I am rather desolate by myself and very inconveniently placed, but am, I trust, usefully occupied.[33]

He did not divide on the address, from which distress was omitted, 4 Feb., but he presented and endorsed petitions incorporating requests for government action to alleviate it, 16 Mar. He voted to transfer East Retford's seats to Birmingham, 11 Feb., and paired for this when out of town for his uncle Richard Slaney's funeral, 5 Mar.[34] He voted for Lord Blandford's reform proposals, 18 Feb., to enfranchise Birmingham, Leeds and Manchester, 23 Feb., for inquiry into the duke of Newcastle's abuse of his electoral influence, 1 Mar., and for parliamentary reform, 28 May. From 12 Mar. until 7 June he divided steadily with the revived opposition, whom he described as 'a body of independent Members who occasionally assemble at ... [Althorp's] rooms to consider public measures – Lord Milton, Lord Euston, Lord Nugent, Mr. Stanley, and about 35 of the best Whigs'.[35] He did not apparently vote on Jewish emancipation, but he informed Isaac Goldsmid, who sent him a copy of his pamphlet, that he 'was convinced before I received it of the necessity of giving fair equality of political privileges to those professing the Jewish religion, believing that the *more* support you have to your building the firmer it will stand'.[36] He voted to abolish the death penalty for forgery, 24 May, 7 June 1830.

As announced, 11 Feb., Slaney's poor law bill, a revision of his 1829 measure incorporating legislation on rating low rental tenements, was read for the first time, 22 Feb. 1830.[37] Supported by Althorp, he secured its second reading, 15 Mar.; but he failed to draft a labour rate clause acceptable to the country gentlemen, and the measure was strongly opposed in committee, where its provisions for separating pauper children from their parents were severely criticized from all sides of the House.[38] Before the clause authorizing parishes to maintain them was rejected (by 91-9),

26 Apr., he tried to explain that what he intended was little different to apprenticeship, and added:

> If I succeed this year in inclining Parliament to sanction the principle of the bill, it will give me great pleasure; but I shall not be disappointed if it be rejected, nor shall it prevent me again and again from urging it on the attention of Parliament, for so convinced am I of the importance of having some change in the present system of our poor laws, that as long as I have a seat in this House I shall not cease to press the matter on public attention.

The measure was recommitted, 3, 4 May, when it was split into two: a bill to prevent poor law abuse and one making landlords liable for payments on properties rated under £10.[39] He 'attended night after night till two o'clock' to promote it, 'the pressure of business always defeating me'.[40] He quipped when it was deferred from 24 to 27 May that 'the gentlemen who attend the Derby are not likely to care much about the matter', and demanded on the 27th that 'government should positively turn its attention to making some arrangement by which important bills like this may be properly debated'. Goulburn replied that Slaney 'makes his appeal to me nightly, but I cannot *make* another day'. Deferrals, hostile exchanges and petitions, notably from Merthyr Tydfil and Newcastle-under-Lyme, thwarted the progress of both bills, and directly George IV's death was announced he declared that he would hold them over until the next Parliament, 29, 30,[41] when, as agreed by the Whigs in April, he would also seek inquiry into the provision of open spaces in large towns.[42] He endorsed schemes to provide employment by capital investment in Ireland and declared against introducing the poor laws there, 9, 11 Mar., 3 June, and approved 'in principle' the bill for removing Irish and Scottish paupers, 26 May. He presented petitions against the truck system from Oldbury, 11 Mar., and Shifnal, 18 May, and despite reservations, 18 Mar., after sitting on the select committee on the labourers' wages bill, he gave it his support, 23 June. On 13 May 1830 he secured the appointment of a committee on employment fluctuations in manufacturing districts, which approved his scheme for 'combining savings banks and benefit societies in one club ... from which each member should have a right to draw during want of work in proportion to the amount of his contribution and the sum of his deposits'.[43]

He said that he intended seeking a select committee on the malt duties, 12 Feb., and presented petitions criticizing their effects on the poor, 22, 26 Feb., 1, 3, 4 Mar., but deferred to the successful ministerial measure, for which he voiced 'general support', 26 Apr 1830. He thought that 'the malt and beer question ... has aided me in the opinion of the House and at Brooks's' and that he 'ranked third' on the select committee on the sale of beer bill, which he considered to be 'one of the most important measures as regards the poorer classes that has been introduced to the attention of the legislature for some time past', 21 May. He praised it as a deregulatory measure, 21 May, 3, 6 June, but acknowledged that additional restrictions on on-consumption were desirable, 3, 4 May, and voted accordingly, 1 July. Voicing local concerns, he expressed support for the Birmingham Junction canal bill, criticized the attack on its solicitor Thomas Eyre Lee, 20 May, and promised to oppose any plan which omitted Shrewsbury from the route of the Holyhead road, 3 June 1830. By starting earlier, superior organization and his father's financial backing he defeated Corbett to come in for Shrewsbury with the local Tory nabob Richard Jenkins at the general election in August 1830. On the hustings, he gave a resumé of his parliamentary career to date and warned that, as in France, unrest might lead to revolution.[44] Reports circulated that he 'spent £8,000, and there is to be a petition against him for bribery'.[45] None was forthcoming, but he was so disgusted by the voters' venality that he contemplated retiring 'at the next election'.[46]

The Wellington ministry counted him among their 'foes', but although present to propose his own bills, to urge ministers to legislate for the poor and to criticize them for dissuading the king from attending the City dinner, 3, 8, 9, 11, 12 Nov., he was absent from the division on the civil list which brought them down, 15 Nov. 1830, having been summoned to Shropshire following the death of Muckleston on the 11th.[47] He was depressed by the incendiarism he found there, and busy as sole executor of Muckleston's will, which confirmed his life interest in the Shropshire, Staffordshire, Leicestershire and Derbyshire estates and London properties devised to his wife and daughters, and was proved under £180,000, 18 Dec. 1830.[48] In the House, 13 Dec., he declared that 'while the new government act in accordance with their professed principles of peace, retrenchment and reform, they shall have my most cordial support'. He welcomed the postponement during the unrest of the bill for the employment of the labouring poor, 17 Dec., and when a Sussex petition complaining of high taxes and tithes was presented that day, he annoyed the county Member Curteis by emphasizing the prevalence there of poor law abuse and low wages. He was convinced that 'despite some inflammatory publications', Ireland would remain quiet provided 'gentlemen would go down each to his own estate, and exert themselves in such a manner as the condition of the peasantry requires', 20 Dec. 1830. Backed by the wealthy merchant and political economist James Morrison, he expounded the merits of free trade when the barilla duties were considered, 7 Feb., disputed allegations made by Hunt that day that four-fifths of Staffordshire magistrates had a vested interest in the truck system, and presented petitions from Manchester for repeal of the duty on printed calicoes, and Shrewsbury protesting at the parish ballot, 10 Feb. 1831. He called for extracts to be read from the report of the select committee on the vestries' bill, criticized in the St. Martin-in-the-Fields's petition, 17 Feb. On Canada and the emigration bill, 18, 22 Feb. 1831, he repeated his call for capital investment and higher wages, attributed the current distress to poor law abuse and an excess of labour, and voiced support for subsidised passages, solely as a means of offering opportunity to the poor.

His much-deferred liability of landlords bill was committed, amended and reprinted, 23 Feb. 1831. Manchester petitioned in its favour, 28 Feb.; Newcastle, 7 Mar., and Merthyr Tydfil, 28 Mar., against it; and with his proposals to end poor law abuse and his motion for a select committee on open spaces it became a casualty of the dissolution.[49] Copies of his proposed bills and abstract returns were appended to his testimony to the Lords committee, 18 Feb., and therefore printed;[50] but when he sought to interest the S.D.U.K. in publishing them, he was peeved to find little enthusiasm for the project even after it had been endorsed by lord chancellor Brougham.[51] He was named as a defaulter, 16, 17 Mar., when he went to Shrewsbury for the reform meeting, and he presented and endorsed their petition for the ministerial measure with another from Ellesmere on the 21st.[52] Before doing so he protested at the tactics deployed to delay it and praised it on demographic grounds and as a response to the 'grand demand of the people', restoring them 'to the rights which their improved habits, their peaceable demeanour, and their increased intelligence prove that they deserve'. Refusing to be shouted down, he insisted that a vote against the second reading was 'against reform altogether' and divided for it, 22 Mar., and against Gascoyne's wrecking amendment, 19 Apr. 1831. At the general election that month 'white apronned flax dressers' rallied his supporters in Shrewsbury, and he defended his measures for the working classes, his votes for retrenchment and reform and the principles of the bill, adding that he was ready to 'go further' should ministers advocate it, and that those who now called for 'moderate reform' had always opposed it. He came in again with the anti-reformer Jenkins after Boycott and the Manchester reformer

Richard Potter[†] retired early during the poll.[53] He deliberately distanced himself from the contest for the county, where the sitting anti-reformers were re-elected; and, though present, he rarely spoke at reform dinners.[54]

He voted for the second reading of the reintroduced reform bill, 6 July, against using the 1831 census to determine English borough representation, 19 July 1831, and steadily for its details. When the enfranchisement of Manchester was considered, 2 Aug., he testified to the growth of the coalfields and manufacturing districts, and contrasted the annual average of £100 paid in assessed taxes by 38 schedule A boroughs with the £26,000 paid by 38 new boroughs. The reactionary Shropshire Member John Cressett Pelham commented caustically that 'to hear him one would imagine that manufactures are the road to population and wealth, and that agriculture is only the road to ruin'. He divided for the bill's third reading, 19 Sept., passage, 21 Sept., and Lord Ebrington's confidence motion, 10 Oct., and informed the Shrewsbury reformers that he lamented its loss in the Lords.[55] Writing from Walford to the Grey ministry's postmaster-general the 5th duke of Richmond, 15 Oct., as a self-appointed spokesman for steady supporters of the bill, he said that they hoped the next one would be 'somewhat less sweeping than the last':

It appears to me ... that some curtailment and alteration might take place which would render it safer and more palatable to a very large and respectable minority who would be glad (now they see reform *must* be carried) to meet us (as they ought) much more than half way! I know several Members ... who voted against the bill, who are desirous to support it, and settle the question, if some modification could be introduced. The same must be felt by many peers anxious to settle the question *safely*; I do not presume to say what alterations should be made, but think that if it were practicable to leave out great part of schedule B, to alter the uniformity of franchise, to make the £10 qualification (if such remain) *bona fide*, by introducing quarterly letting reservations of rent instead of mere weekly payments it would be a great improvement. Ten pounds reserved weekly and stopped out of wages on Saturday is not ten pounds per annum, but really the credit and class indicated hereby is not more than renters of six pounds per annum in quantity rent. I ... earnestly wish some approximation could take place in settling this great question, between honest and conscientious men belonging to the two great parties, as there are those who watch their contentions, and would rejoice to destroy them both when exhausted by the contest. The opinion of most persons in [Shropshire] ... is that the measure would be safe, if less extensive, and they are anxious for a *quiet* settlement.[56]

Before voting for the second reading of the revised bill, 17 Dec. 1831, he expressed regret 'that anything like a spirit of party should have manifested itself in the course of these debates' and called for calmness, moderation, and concessions on both sides 'without damaging the principle or the efficiency of the measure'. He contrasted the population, wealth and intelligence of rural and urban areas, rejected the notion that the latter enjoyed 'virtual representation' through such places as Gatton, and thanked Lord Clive for his conciliatory speech. Referring to the Whitchurch incendiaries, he concluded with a warning that 'to delay reform will make property insecure'. He voted against enfranchising all £10 poor rate payers, 3 Feb., called for 'prejudices be laid aside', as 'by this bill the representation of the country will be placed in the hands of the most intelligent and most deeply interested classes of the community', 19 Mar., and added:

> I do not think that the new constituent body will return a gentleman to this House, solely in consequence of his abilities as an orator, or in consequence of his usefulness to his party as a Whig or a Tory. These have too long been the qualifications to a seat in this House, while the most important one – namely a man's habits of business, and his capability to attend to the interests of his constituents – have been neglected. I think that, in a reformed Parliament, the political parties which now exist will have little weight, and men will not be sent here because they are gifted with great eloquence which they may occasionally be called upon to exert on grand occasions for the interest of their party. Those persons will be sent here who will sedulously devote their time and attention to the important business of the House, and who will anxiously watch over the interests of their constituents. You will not have men who only occasionally attend in their places, but those who are constant in their attendance, and who will be desirous to promote the well-being of the great communities who send them here.

He divided for the bill's third reading, 22 Mar., paired for the address requesting the king to appoint only ministers who would carry it unimpaired, 10 May, and voted against a Conservative amendment to the Scottish measure, 1 June. He questioned the decision to make Church Stretton rather than Much Wenlock the principal polling town for Shropshire South, 7 June. Nothing came of a suggestion that he should stand for the Northern Division following its passage.[57] He mistrusted and consequently opposed the anti-reformer Burge's advocacy of legislative colonial assemblies, 28 June, and engaged in several brief altercations with Hunt and Hume. He introduced the Irish boundaries bill, 5 June. He endorsed ministers' decision to postpone corn law reform, 1 June, and divided with them on the Russian-Dutch loan, 12, 16 July 1832.

Initially Slaney proceeded with his liability of landlords bill, 28 June, 8 July, and proposals for 'parks in populous towns', 22 June 1831, and he persisted in publicizing his views on poor law reform whenever the issue was raised. However, he conceded that reform 'must come from government', that 'individual good intentions ... will not do to correct an evil which has its roots in a general and most mischievous system', 28 June 1831. Blaming poor law abuse, rather than the laws themselves, he refuted Sadler's criticism of the political economists, and although, like Althorp, he offered 'general support' for the labourers' employment bill, 11 Oct., he criticized its sponsor Sadler's failure to appreciate the lack of uniformity and pockets of deprivation within the north-south divide, and by 1 June 1832 he was openly hostile to the measure. He also opposed Sadler's proposals for extending the poor laws to Ireland, 19 June, and pointed to possible abuses of the bill to remove Irish and Scottish vagrants, 28 June 1832. Writing to Brougham that day, after consulting Nassau Senior, he suggested that the new poor law commission should have no more than six members in London, who in turn would report on the findings of 'a like number of persons (or rather more) ... appointed as perambulatory or country commissioners'. He offered to serve in London with Senior, the Benthamite Walter Coulson, Bishop Blomfield of London and 'possibly [Lord] Sandon*, Sir Thomas Fremantle* and Thomas Grimston Estcourt*', and recommended two clergymen, John Thomas Becher and Charles David Brereton, the retired barrister Ward and Sir John Wrottesley* as country commissioners.[58] Although excluded from the commission, he submitted his opinions as the respondent to the 'rural queries' for the parish of Walford.

Slaney studied the 1832 cholera epidemic closely, and despite being much lampooned for this and his plans to educate the poor, he polled in second place at Shrewsbury, which returned him as a Liberal at the general election in December.[59] He maintained a high profile in the county and at municipal elections, and remained the Shrewsbury Conservatives' 'most dangerous foe, not only because of his readiness to spend, but also because of his ability to garner non-Whig votes'. Except for interruptions occasioned by defeat in 1835, his retirement for a single Parliament when Benjamin Disraeli[†] became a candidate in 1841, and when the local party favoured the Liberal-Tory George Tomline[†] in 1852, he kept his seat for life.[60] His overriding commitment was to improving conditions for the lower classes, especially in the industrial towns;[61] but he also found time for travel and to write poetry and other works.[62] On the recommendation of the prime minister Peel, to whom he offered his services 'independent of party', he became an unpaid commissioner on the health of towns, 1843-8.[63] *The Times* criticized Slaney in 1850 as 'a political hypochondriac', watching for the symptoms of disease instead of observing the general health, but his philanthropic exertions were universally commended, and his death at his London home in Bolton Row, Piccadilly, in May 1862, from complications following a minor fall at the opening of the International Exhibition, was widely mourned.[64] His will, proved 5 Sept. 1862, confirmed a number of family settlements and provided for his second wife Catherine (*d.* 10 Apr. 1883), to whom he entrusted his portrait by Pickersgill and journals drafted since 1854. His lands in Baschurch passed to his daughter Elizabeth Frances Eyton of Ryton, Shropshire; Hatton Grange, in which his brother William (*d.* 26 Dec. 1862) had a life interest, to his daughter Frances Catherine, wife of William Kenyon[†] of Walford, who took the name of Slaney, and his Leicestershire and Derbyshire estates and her mother's effects to his daughter Mary, wife of William Edward Wynne of Peniarth.[65]

[1] *VCH Salop*, i. 463; B. Trinder, *Industrial Revolution in Salop* (1981), 11, 15-16, 21-22; P. Richards, 'R.A. Slaney, the industrial town and early Victorian social policy', *Social Hist.* iv (1979), 88. [2] H.T. Weyman, 'MPs for Shrewsbury', *Trans. Salop Arch. Soc.* (ser. 4), xii (1929-30), 251; IR26/5110/342-56. [3] Birmingham Univ. Lib. Slaney mss 1-4, of which 1-3 are a record of his views and activities, Apr. 1815-Nov. 1817, Apr. 1825-Jan. 1826, and 4 is an undated travel jnl.; Salop Archives, Morris-Eyton mss 6003/1-9 cover 1818-Mar. 1825 and Feb. 1828-1849. [4] Slaney mss 1, 18 Apr. 1815. [5] *VCH Salop*, ii. 182, 184, 194; iii. 325; Salop Archives 6003/4, 28 May 1824. [6] Salop Archives 6003/1, 30 Dec. 1819. [7] *Shrewsbury Chron.* 12 Jan.; *Salopian Jnl.* 17 Jan. 1821. [8] Salop Archives 6003/1-4, *passim*; Birmingham Univ. Lib. Eyton mss 179-84; *Shrewsbury Chron.* 8, 15, 29 Mar. 1822. [9] Salop Archives 6003/1, 16 June, 15 Sept. 1820; 6003/2, 5 June, 29 July, 7, 15 Oct., 12-18 Nov., 22 Dec. 1821, 21 Mar. 1822; 6003/4, July 1824; Richards, *passim*. [10] Salop Archives 6003/2, 29-30 Sept. 1821, 13 Feb., 9, 25 Mar., 14 Apr. 1822; 6004/4, Oct. 1824. [11] Slaney mss 3, 12 May 1825. [12] NLW, Coedymaen mss 954; *Salopian Jnl.* 9, 16 Nov. 1825, 8 Mar. 1826. See J.A. Phillips and C. Wetherell, 'Great Reform Bill of 1832 and Rise of Partisanship', *JMH*, lxiii (1991), 633-4, 636. [13] *Shrewsbury Chron.* 21 Apr.; *The Globe*, 22 Apr.; *Salopian Jnl.* 26 Apr., 3 May; *The Times*, 1 May; Salop Archives 1066/136, diary of Katherine Plymley, 4 May 1826. [14] Eyton mss 185-6; *Salopian Jnl.* 3, 10, 17, 31 May, 7, 14, 21, 28 June; *The Times*, 12 June; Plymley diary, 12 June 1826; E. Edwards, *Parl. Elections of Shrewsbury*, 23-24. [15] Salop Archives 6001/3056, pp. 14, 18-22; Edwards, 24. [16] *The Times*, 23, 29 Nov. 1826; Salop Archives 6001/5, memo. Aug. 1828. [17] *CJ*, lxxxii. 199. [18] *The Times*, 19, 20, 23 June 1827; *CJ*, lxxxii. 575, 596. [19] Salop Archives 6003/5, 1-6 Feb. 1828. [20] *PP* (1828), iv. 137-99; *Quarterly Rev.* xliii (1830), 251; Salop Archives 6003/5, memo. Aug. 1828. [21] Salop Archives 6003/5, memo. Aug. 1828. [22] Ibid. Nov.-8 Dec.; *Shrewsbury Chron.* 14, 21, 28 Nov., 5 Dec. 1828. [23] Salop Archives 6003/5, 3 Dec. 1828-26 Jan. 1829. [24] Ibid. 6 Feb. 1829. [25] Ibid. 23 Feb. 1829. [26] Ibid. 25 Mar. [May] 1829. [27] Ibid. 30 Mar. 1829; *CJ*, lxxxiv. 82, 86, 100, 110, 117, 171, 243, 277, 307, 330, 350. [28] Salop Archives

6003/5, 25 Mar. 1829. [29] *CJ*, lxxxiv. 289; Salop Archives 6003/5, May, 14 July 1829. [30] Salop Archives 6003/5, June 1829; UCL, SDUK mss, Slaney 26-29. [31] Salop Archives 6003/5, June-Sept.; 6003/6, 30 Oct., 31 Dec. 1829. [32] Ibid. 6003/6, 23 Jan. 1830. [33] Ibid. 6 Feb. 1830. [34] Ibid. 6 Mar. 1830. [35] Salop Archives 6003/6, 15 Apr. 1830. [36] UCL, Goldsmid mss, letterbk. i. f. 211. [37] Salop Archives 6003/6, 20 Feb. 1830; *CJ*, lxxxv. 70, 90. [38] Salop Archives 6003/6, Mar. 1830. [39] *CJ*, lxxxv. 361, 375. [40] Ibid. lxxxv. 333; Salop Archives 6003/6, May-June 1830. [41] *CJ*, lxxxv. 399, 380, 385, 395, 399, 401, 403, 411, 416, 434, 436, 444, 459, 469, 490, 516, 524, 544, 548, 566, 574, 582. [42] Salop Archives 6003/6, 15 Apr. 1830. [43] Ibid. 15 June 1830. [44] Ibid. 30 June-2 Aug.; Salop Archives 840/159/441-3; *Shrewsbury Chron.* 6 Aug. 1830; Edwards, 25-26. [45] *Life of Campbell*, i. 475. [46] Salop Archives 6003/6, 25 July 1830. [47] Ibid. 5, 11 Nov.; *Shrewsbury Chron.* 12 Nov. 1830. [48] PROB 11/1779/715; IR26/1234/695. [49] *CJ*, lxxxv. 58, 18, 131, 134, 138, 142, 150, 155, 158, 171, 185, 198, 203, 235, 270, 326, 348, 451. [50] *LJ*, lxiii. 578-85. [51] SDUK mss, Slaney 27-29. [52] *Shrewsbury Chron.* 18 Mar. 1831. [53] *Wolverhampton Chron.* 4, 11 May; *Shrewsbury Chron.* 6, 13 May 1831; Edwards, 27; Trinder, 235; Phillips and Wetherell, 634-5. [54] NLW, Aston Hall mss C.235; *Shrewsbury Chron.* 27 May, 3 June 1831. [55] *Shrewsbury Chron.* 14 Oct. 1831. [56] W. Suss. RO, Goodwood mss 636, f. 84. [57] Aston Hall mss C.1018. [58] Salop Archives 6003/6, 16 July 1831-July 1832; Brougham mss, Slaney to Brougham, 28 June 1832. [59] *Shrewsbury Chron.* 28 Sept., 2 Nov., 14 Dec. 1832. [60] *VCH Salop*, iii. 323-8; Phillips and Wetherell, 636-9; Edwards, 41-43. [61] Richards, 85. [62] Slaney, *A Few Verses from Shropshire* (1846); *A Few More Verses from Shropshire* (1855); *Our Sources of Happiness* (1857); *Short Jnl. of a Visit to Canada and the States of America in 1860* (1861). [63] *Oxford DNB*; Slaney, *Reports ... on the Education and Health of the Poorer Classes in Large Towns* (1841); *Report on the State of Birmingham and Other Large Towns* (1845); Add. 40310, f. 287; 40580, ff. 350-4. [64] *The Times*, 7 Mar. 1850; Slaney, *A Plea to Power and Parliament for the Working Classes* (1847); *Gent. Mag.* (1862), i. 794; *Men of the Time* (1862), 705; *Shrewsbury Chron.* 23 May 1862. [65] PROB 11/1829/176; 2062/743; IR26/1367/127; 1787/883; 2307/1007; 5110/342-56.

M.M.E.

SLOANE STANLEY (formerly SLOANE), William

(?1780–1860), of Paultons, Romney, Hants and 21 Curzon Street, Mdx.

ORFORD	27 July 1807–1812
STOCKBRIDGE	1830–1831

b. ?1780,[1] 1st and o. surv. s. of Hans Sloane[†] of South Stoneham, Hants and his cos. Sarah, da. and coh. of Stephen Fuller, merchant and agent for Jamaica, of Clement's Lane, Lombard Street, London. *educ.* Eton 1791; St. Andrews Univ. 1798-9; Belvedere Coll. Weimar (M. Mounier) 1799-1800. *m.* 23 June 1806, Lady Gertrude Howard, da. of Frederick, 5th earl of Carlisle, 2s. 3da. *suc.* fa. 1824, having taken additional name of Stanley with him 28 Dec. 1821. *d.* 11 Apr. 1860.

Cornet 10 Drag. 1800, lt. 1801, ret. 1802.

Sheriff, Hants 1828-9.

Capt. St. James's, Westminster vols. 1803, S. Hants yeomanry 1803, Romsey yeoman cav. 1831.

Sloane Stanley's relationship with his father went from bad to worse during his early manhood. Money was at the bottom of their squabbles, which were exacerbated by the gulf in years and temperament between them. There were hints of trouble to come during Sloane Stanley's education in Scotland and Germany, when he ran up debts and was accused of gambling. His father envisaged a career in the diplomatic service for him, but he was set on joining the army. Hans Sloane, who had bought a 1,500-acre estate with his future in mind, and assured him that 'there will be few things you will not have a right to command', gave way and, after an initial setback, secured him a commission in the Prince of Wales's Hussars. Yet in little more than a year Sloane Stanley, complaining both of the expense and of 'the caprices of a most whimsical commanding officer, whose whole endeavour seems [to be] to run me into debt and to make me miserable', was begging to be released. Though slightly mollified by promotion to lieutenant as the prince's gift, he continued to moan, and incurred his father's displeasure by revealing new debts. The conclusion of peace gave him the chance to extricate himself from the army.[2]

He subsequently rebelled against the regime of academic study and foreign travel which his father sought to impose on him, preferring the field sports to which he was addicted. His outburst of resentment at being treated like 'a common gamekeeper' and his mounting debts so enraged his father that his uncle William Dickinson had to intervene as a peacemaker in November 1802. He was ordered to London for a showdown and advised to go abroad, in which case his father was prepared to increase his allowance from £700 to £1,000. There was another major row in the spring of 1805, when Sloane Stanley tried to get his hands on some of the substantial trust funds which his maternal grandfather had left between himself and his younger brother Stephen. (The latter, a clergyman, had also tested their father's patience by marrying an unstable widow at the age of 18.) Hans Sloane, who had been given the final say in the distribution of this money, which was subject to good behaviour, would not hear of it, though he accepted William's later apology and offered to settle his debts if he made a clean breast of them. At the end of that year Sloane Stanley entreated his father to resume negotiations with Lord Carlisle, who had refused his earlier offer of marriage to his daughter, and to overcome Carlisle's objections by making a partial entail of his estates on any son of such a union. Hans Sloane, sceptical of William's 'easily discarding the parade of expense and bustle of large societies', for all his promises to mend his ways, refused to go cap in hand to Carlisle, and threatened to impose the strictest entail on his son's inheritance if he continued to misbehave. In the

end, however, he relented, and sanctioned a settlement guaranteeing his daughter-in-law a widow's jointure of £1,200 a year, to be charged on certain estates which were entailed on the eldest son of the marriage.[3] These included property in county Down, where the Sloanes had come to prominence in the seventeenth century, and the Isle of Wight, as well as the potentially lucrative estate of Chelsea Park, Middlesex, bought by Hans Sloane's grandfather William Sloane (1651-1728) in 1717. (This should not be confused with the moiety of the nearby and even more valuable manor of Chelsea left by Hans Sloane's great-uncle Sir Hans Sloane (1660-1753) to his daughter Sarah, who married George Stanley of Paultons. Their son Hans Stanley (1720-80) left Paultons, subject to his two sisters' life interest, to Hans Sloane. He devised the reversion of the moiety of Chelsea manor not, as stated in some sources, to Sloane, but to the Cadogan family, who already owned the other moiety through the marriage of Sir Hans Sloane's other daughter.)[4]

Thereafter relations between father and son seem to have improved. Sloane Stanley, who made no mark as a Member of the 1807 Parliament, continued to devote most of his time to hunting and the turf. His brother, whose sinecure living of Gidney was the price extracted by his father for surrendering his seat in Parliament to suit the Grenville ministry, died in 1812. In his declining years Hans Sloane revelled in 'a scrambling life' divided between Paultons and his London house in Upper Harley Street, which was noted for its vile food and slovenly servants.[5] He died, aged 84, in the summer of 1824.[6] By his will, dated 9 Feb. 1824, he gave Lady Gertrude Sloane Stanley £500, provided generously for his domestic staff, and made William the residuary legatee of his personal estate, which was worth about £90,000.[7] In September 1827 Sloane Stanley visited northern Italy with his two sons, leaving his wife in Switzerland. He saw many 'fine things', but deemed the Milanese 'nasty' and 'horridly filthy', and was revolted by their water closets, which were 'like the French, abominable'.[8]

At the 1830 general election he was put up for Stockbridge by the 2nd Earl Grosvenor. His sister Maria's waggish husband Joseph Jekyll[†] noted that he 'canvassed and kissed the voters' wives with a bottle of wine in his pocket, which, being poured plentifully into the female stomach, had a great effect in winning the female heart'.[9] He was returned after a contest and, according to his Hampshire neighbour and friend Lord Palmerston*, afterwards entertained at Paultons with 'all the grandeur of an MP.'[10] His Whig brother-in-law, the 6th earl of Carlisle, reported that he was 'disposed to support government', who duly listed him among their 'friends', and he was in their minority on the civil list, 15 Nov. 1830.[11] In opposition to the Grey ministry, he divided against the second reading of their reform bill, 22 Mar., and for Gascoyne's wrecking amendment, 19 Apr. 1831. In his only known contribution to debate, 28 Mar. 1831, he spoke, as 'a large proprietor of British timber', on the comparative merits of oak and teak as shipbuilding material, and asked whether ministers intended to supply the dockyards with British or African timber. He retired from Stockbridge at the 1831 dissolution, when Grosvenor abandoned control of the borough.[12]

Although he was never again in Parliament Sloane Stanley, a personal friend of Sir Robert Peel*, was an active and zealous supporter of the Conservative interest in the southern division of Hampshire. Palmerston, smarting after his defeat there in 1835, found it hard to forgive his 'particular friend' for 'his offensive attack upon my personal character as a public man on the day of nomination'. He turned down Sloane Stanley's subsequent offer of a written public explanation, 'begged him to leave bad alone', and reflected that 'the only thing that can be said in his excuse is that he is a regular ass'.[13] Sloane Stanley capitalized on his Chelsea estate by turning parts of it over to urban development. The area of Camera Square was built up in the 1830s, and Paultons Terrace was erected in 1843. He died a reputed though probably not an actual millionaire in April 1860, 'aged 79', from 'an attack in the nature of apoplexy'. By his will, dated 20 May 1853, he left Lady Gertrude £10,000, plus an annuity of £400 to supplement her entitlement under their marriage settlement. He bequeathed £10,000 to make additional provision for his younger son George and two unmarried daughters, and devised Paultons to his elder son William Hans Sloane Stanley (1809-79), the residuary legatee. By a codicil of 13 Dec. 1855 he left George a freehold property with coal and mineral rights at Cadoxton-juxta-Neath, Glamorgan. He was credited by an obituarist with 'affability ... candour, and earnestness'.[14]

[1] *Burke LG* gives 1781, but his father commented that he had reached 'the mature age of 25' by 4 May 1805 (Hants RO, Paultons mss 28M57/67/26). [2] Ibid. 65/1-15; 66/1-65; 67/1-19. [3] Ibid. 66/63, 64; 67/20-32; 48M48/477; PROB 11/1063/160; 1330/653; *Palmerston-Sulivan Letters*, 116. [4] E. St. John Brooke, *Sir Hans Sloane*, 13, 35-36, 215-16; T. Faulkner, *Hist. Chelsea* (1829), i. 148, 150, 153-4, 373; *Survey of London*, iv. 48; A. Beaver, *Mems. Old Chelsea*, 117-18; PROB 11/1651/651. [5] Add. 40605, f. 464; *Gent. Mag.* (1812), i. 491; Paultons mss 46M48/100; *Jekyll Corresp.* ed. A. Bourke, 69, 83-84. [6] This corrects *HP Commons, 1790-1820*, v. 189, which reproduces the erroneous date of 1827 given in *Burke LG*. [7] PROB 11/1689/488; IR26/1020/939. [8] Paultons

mss 10MSS/326-9; 28M57/67/33-37; 46M48/101-4. [9] *The Times*, 27 July 1830; *Jekyll Corresp.* 245-6. [10] R.M.T. Hill, 'Stockbridge Elections', *Pprs. and Procs. of Hants Field Club*, xxiii (1968), 126-7; *Hants Chron.* 2, 9 Aug. 1830; *Palmerston-Sulivan Letters*, 241. [11] Add. 51578, Carlisle to Holland, 10 July [1830]. [12] *Hants Chron.* 2, 9 May; *Portsmouth Herald*, 8 May 1831. [13] Add. 40424, f. 21; 40513, ff. 361, 363; 40517, f. 67; Paultons mss 28M57/44, 45; *Jekyll Corresp.* 310; *The Times*, 14 Jan. 1835; K. Bourne, *Palmerston*, 537-8, 541; *Palmerston-Sulivan Letters*, 262. [14] Beaver, 118, 146-7; J. Summerson, *Georgian London* (1988), 281; *Gent. Mag.* (1860), i. 533.

D.R.F.

SMITH, Abel (1788-1859), of 15 Portland Place, Mdx.

MALMESBURY	30 Jan. 1810-1812
WENDOVER	1812-1818
MIDHURST	1820-1830
WENDOVER	1830-1832
HERTFORDSHIRE	1835-1847

b. 17 July 1788, 1st s. of Samuel Smith* and Elizabeth Frances, da. of Edmund Turnor of Stoke Rochford, Lincs. *educ.* Harrow 1800-5; Trinity Coll. Camb. 1805. *m.* (1) 28 Aug. 1822, Lady Marianne Leslie Melville (*d.* 22 Mar. 1823), da. of Alexander, 9th earl of Leven and Melville [S], *s.p.*; (2) 12 July 1826, Frances Anne, da. of Sir Harry Calvert, 1st bt., of Claydon, Bucks., 4s. 6da. *suc.* fa. 1834. *d.* 23 Feb. 1859.

Smith, who rose to greater eminence in business than any other of his generation of the family banking dynasty,[1] resumed his parliamentary career in 1820 when he was returned for the family borough of Midhurst. Maria Edgeworth judged him to be an 'agreeable young man', but his funeral oration, with its reference to an unnamed 'deep affliction' from which he suffered all his adult life, provides a possible clue as to why he was never a very active or vocal Member.[2] As in earlier Parliaments, he voted with the Whig opposition to Lord Liverpool's ministry on certain issues, but his political course was decidedly moderate. He gave no recorded votes on the question of parliamentary reform and, contrary to his previous line, he divided against Catholic relief, 30 Apr. 1822, 1 Mar., 21 Apr., 10 May 1825. He generally voted for economy and retrenchment during the sessions of 1820, 1821 and 1822, but, having divided for Brougham's motion for more extensive tax reductions, 11 Feb., he was against Lord Althorp's motion on the same issue, 21 Feb. 1822. He voted to restore Queen Caroline's name to the liturgy, 26 Jan., 13 Feb., and to condemn ministers' conduct towards her, 6 Feb. 1821. He divided for the motions accusing lord chancellor Eldon of a breach of privilege, 1 Mar., and condemning the prosecution of the Methodist missionary John Smith in Demerara, 11 June, but voted for the Irish insurrection bill, 14 June 1824. He voted for repeal of the usury laws, 17 Feb., and against the duke of Cumberland's grant, 30 May, 2 June 1825. It was said of him at this time that he 'attended frequently and voted with the opposition'.[3] He divided for inquiry into the silk trade, 24 Feb., and against any relaxation of the corn laws, 8, 11 May 1826. He was returned unopposed for Midhurst at the general election that summer.

He divided against Catholic relief, 6 Mar. 1827, but for repeal of the Test Acts, 26 Feb. 1828. He voted with the minority against the duke of Wellington's ministry to restrict the circulation of small bank notes in Scotland and Ireland, 5 June 1828. In February 1829 Planta, the patronage secretary, predicted that he would side 'with government' for Catholic emancipation, but in fact he continued to vote against it, 6, 30 Mar. He divided against the silk trade bill, 1 May 1829. He voted for Knatchbull's amendment to the address on distress, 4 Feb., but was presumably the 'J.A. Smith' who divided against reduction of the grant for South American missions, and the 'J. Abel Smith' who was against abolition of the death penalty for forgery, 7 June. In April 1830 Wellington had noted that Smith was ready to 'support the government without asking for anything', as was his uncle Lord Carrington, who returned him for his pocket borough of Wendover at the general election that summer.[4]

The ministry reckoned Smith to be one of the 'good doubtfuls', and in the event he voted with them in the crucial civil list division, 15 Nov. 1830. Reflecting a family concern, he presented an anti-slavery petition from a group of female Methodists, 10 Dec. 1830, and his religious devotion is hinted at in his presentation of petitions calling for a general fast, 10 Feb. 1831. The Smith family was divided over the Grey ministry's reform bill but, in accordance with his uncle and father's views, he divided against the second reading, 22 Mar. This stance led to his being offered the Tory interest in Hertfordshire (where his father owned property) at the anticipated dissolution, but he declined, telling Lord Salisbury that 'I neither find myself qualified for the situation, nor do I think I have any pretensions to it'. He also explained that he had earlier resolved to turn down 'an application of the same nature ... made by the opposite party, which I had reason to expect in the event of a dissolution ... previously to the agitation of the reform question'.[5] He confirmed his estrangement from the Whigs by voting for Gascoyne's wrecking amendment to the reform bill, 19 Apr. 1831. He was returned again for

Wendover at the ensuing general election. He divided against the second reading of the reintroduced bill, 6 July, for use of the 1831 census to determine the disfranchisement schedules, 19 July, and against the bill's passage, 21 Sept. He voted against the second reading of the revised bill, 17 Dec. 1831. In a letter to Salisbury the following month he indicated his support for a Hertfordshire anti-reform petition and observed that 'I shall not believe that new peers are to be created until it appears in the *Gazette*, although from the experience we have had of the present government, there is nothing too bad for them to do'.[6] In his only recorded speech in this period, 1 Feb. 1832, he attested to the independence of the £50 tenants-at-will who were to be enfranchised by the Chandos clause. He voted against the bill's third reading, 22 Mar. He divided against ministers on the Russian-Dutch loan, 26 Jan., 12 July 1832.

Smith rejected Salisbury's suggestion that he should stand for Hertfordshire at the impending general election, as he believed that 'under the excitement which still prevails on the subject of reform, more than one Tory Member would not be tolerated', and in any case he had 'neither time, nor inclination nor courage for such an undertaking'.[7] In 1834 he inherited the Woodhall Park estate in Hertfordshire from his father, and was the residuary legatee of personalty sworn under £500,000.[8] The following year he was returned for the county without difficulty and sat until his retirement in 1847. He remained a steady Conservative, but apparently declined a peerage from Sir Robert Peel* in order to devote his time to 'the pursuits of a country gentleman and resident landlord', notably the establishment and restoration of numerous churches.[9] He died in February 1859 and left Woodhall to his eldest son, Abel Smith (1829-98), Conservative Member for Hertfordshire, 1854-7, 1859-65, 1866-85, and East Hertfordshire, 1885-98.

[1] *Gent. Mag.* (1859), i. 542; H.T. Easton, *Hist. of a Banking House,* 51-52; J. Leighton-Boyce, *Smiths the Bankers,* 271-2. [2] *Edgeworth Letters,* 252; L.J. Barrington, *The Gain of Death,* 24. [3] *Session of Parl. 1825,* p. 485. [4] Add. 40309, f. 31. [5] Hatfield House mss 2M/Gen., Smith to Salisbury, 4 Apr. 1831. [6] Ibid. Smith to Salisbury, Jan. 1832. [7] Ibid. Salisbury to Smith, 23 June, replies, 26 June, 20 Oct. 1832. [8] PROB 11/1830/239; IR26/1367/153. [9] *Gent. Mag.* (1859), i. 542-4.

H.J.S.

SMITH, Christopher (?1749–1835), of 7 Adam Street, Adelphi, Mdx. and Starborough Castle, Lingfield, Surr.

ST. ALBANS	1812–1818
ST. ALBANS	1820–1830

b. ?1749, s. of a farmer at Harwell, nr. Abingdon, Berks. m. (1) 6 Sept. 1785,[1] Catherine (d. 10 Feb. 1802)[2], da. of James Church of Norwich,[3] 2s. 1da.[4]; (2) 22 Oct. 1807, Eleanor Wilkington.[5] d. 20 Jan. 1835.
Common councilman, London 1800-7, alderman 1807-d., sheriff 1807-8, ld. mayor 1817-18.
Pres. St. Thomas's hosp. 1818-d.
Dir. Atlas Assurance Co. 1812.

Smith had risen from humble and obscure rural origins to become a prosperous London wine merchant, with premises at 20 and 21 Queen Street, Cheapside. He took in his sons as partners on their coming of age, and in about 1820 added Edward Woodhouse, who married his only daughter Catherine Ann, with £12,000, in 1828. His own active involvement in the business had ceased by early 1825.[6] An alderman of London for almost 28 years, he had purchased the estate of Starborough Castle in eastern Surrey from Sir Thomas Turton, Member for Southwark, in 1812.[7] At the general election of 1820, when he was about 70 years of age, he stood again for the open and venal borough of St. Albans, where he had been turned out after one Parliament in 1818.[8] He comfortably topped the poll in a contest with two rivals.

As in the 1812 Parliament, Smith, who had a distant radical past, gave general support to the Liverpool ministry, though he occasionally took an independent line on specific issues. In the words of an obituary, 'he was no orator', and lacked 'the art of speechifying'; but he was by no means a silent Member. He voted against economies in revenue collection, 4 July, and voiced his support for the aliens bill, 12 July 1820. He 'deprecated the language of the answers' which Queen Caroline had returned to addresses of support for her, 31 Jan., voted in defence of ministers' conduct towards her, 6 Feb., and on 12 Feb. 1821 objected to the proposed grant of £50,000 to her, which he thought her unscrupulous advisers would use 'to increase that ferment, and perpetuate those disturbances, which had so long injured the public interests'. He also reproved the government for offering so large a sum at a time of economic distress, and complained of the 'immense annuity' enjoyed by the prince of Saxe Coburg. In a discussion on agricultural distress, 20 Feb., he took Sir Isaac Coffin to task for facetiously advising farmers to stop aping gentlemen: they were

already in 'a state of sufficient difficulty'.[9] He divided, as previously, against Catholic claims, 28 Feb. He suggested his notion of a fair price for bread in current circumstances, 15 Mar. He voted against parliamentary reform, 9 May, and paired against mitigation of the punishment for forgery, 23 May. He approved the principle of Martin's bill to prevent cruelty to horses, 1 June, and successfully proposed that asses be brought within its scope; but he failed in his attempts to amend Smith's bankruptcy bill, 4 June, and the metropolis gas light bill, 6 June 1821.[10] He supported Alderman Curtis's motion for inquiry into the orphans' fund coal duties, 20 Feb. 1822.[11] Although he voted with government against the opposition call for further tax reductions, 21 Feb., he said on 28 Feb. that the country was 'disappointed' that they had offered no remedy for agricultural distress other than a small diminution of the malt duty. That day he divided in the minority for inquiry into the assault on Alderman Waithman* at the queen's funeral. He spoke and voted against abolition of one of the joint-postmasterships, arguing that concession on this point would invite attacks on all offices held under the crown, 13 Mar. He voted against Canning's bill to relieve Catholic peers, 30 Apr. On 24 May he presented a petition from the guardians of Charlton against the poor removal bill and two London parish petitions in favour of the cruelty to animals bill. Later that day he objected to the principle of Bennet's public house licensing bill,[12] which he again opposed on its third reading, 27 June, when he said that it 'pressed too heavily on the publicans'. He divided with government on the lord advocate's dealings with the Scottish press, 25 June, and spoke against reduction of the salt duties, 28 June;[13] but he voted in the minority for inquiry into the Calcutta bankers' grievances, 4 July, and expressed his anxiety that nothing beyond the 'just debts' of the late queen should become a burden on the public, 31 July 1822.[14]

On the beer duties bill, 24 Mar. 1823, Smith said that it was desirable to get public houses out of the hands of the brewers. He spoke and voted against the measure at later stages, 12 May, 13 (when he admitted that he was 'not in the habit of opposing' the chancellor of the exchequer), and 17 June.[15] He presented the petition of St. Albans archdeaconry against Catholic relief, 26 Mar.[16] He joined in calls for repeal of the coastwise coal duties, 27 Mar., opposed Bennet's proposal to abolish punishment by whipping, which he considered a 'salutary infliction', 30 Apr., and applauded ministers' willingness to relax the Acts restricting the silk trade, 9 May.[17] He voted with them against repeal of the Foreign Enlistment Act, 16 Apr., and Scottish parliamentary reform, 2 June. He was one of the minority of

16 who opposed the clause of the London Bridge bill which gave the treasury control over the appointment of the engineer, 20 June 1823. He presented a London petition against the coastwise coal duties, 12 Feb., but expressed his dissent from the City petition against the aliens bill, 2 Apr. 1824.[18] He brought up a St. Albans petition for the abolition of slavery, 12 Mar.[19] He opposed inquiry into the method of collecting the beer and malt duties, 15 Mar. He presented a constituency petition in favour of the county courts bill, 5 Apr., and opposed the Westminster and London oil-gas bill, 12 Apr.[20] On the request of London fishmongers for a ban on the sale of mackerel on Sundays, 14 Apr., he observed that the 'conscientious feelings' which inspired them 'could not by any possibility operate upon the Jews'. He opposed Alderman Wood's Thames navigation debt bill as 'a mere job', 14 May, 9 June.[21] On 2 June he spoke against the orphans' fund bill, and was a teller for the minority. Later that day, when the appearance of Graham's balloon caused an exodus of curious Members, Smith, who, according to Thomas Creevey*, was 'a furious enemy of the Saints', had the House counted out after the division on the City bonds interest reduction bill, which he opposed, had revealed it to be inquorate: he thereby prevented the resumption of the debate on Brougham's motion for inquiry into the prosecution of the Methodist missionary John Smith for inciting insurrection by slaves in Demerara.[22] He said that repeal of the Combination Acts would do more harm than good to trade, 3 June 1824.[23] He presented a petition from the Cordwainers' Company (his own) for a repeal of assessed taxes, 18 Feb., and opposed the London Waterworks bill, 1 Mar. 1825.[24] He voted for the Irish unlawful societies bill, 25 Feb., and against Catholic relief, 1 Mar.; he only paired against the relief bill, 21 Apr., 10 May. He spoke and voted for repeal of the beer duties, 5 May, when he declared his hostility to 'any measure that had the effect of causing the poor to pay more than the rich'. When supporting the provision for the duke of Cumberland's family, 30 May, he deplored the 'malevolence' which had driven him abroad through 'innuendos and misrepresentations'; he voted again for the grant, 10 June 1825. The only trace of his parliamentary activity which has been found for 1826 is his vote with government against reform of Edinburgh's representation, 13 Apr. 1826.

He was subsequently returned again for St. Albans after a rare uncontested election, although it had been momentarily supposed there in the previous autumn that he intended to retire. Attacks on him as 'the complete tool of the ministers' and a bigot on Catholic relief proved ineffectual. On the hustings, he dealt only in the customary platitudes.[25] He duly voted against

Catholic relief, 6 Mar. 1827. He gave his 'warmest support' to the duke of Clarence's grant, 16 Mar. He favoured taking the corn averages over a period of six weeks to prevent fraud, 26 Mar, and he was in the minority against the corn bill, 2 Apr. 1827. He voted against repeal of the Test Acts, 26 Feb. 1828. He approved of the Wellington ministry's plan to amend the Stamp Acts as they affected fire insurances, 3 Mar., and he urged them to make a significant reduction in the duty, 25 Mar. He was in the minority of 15 against the motion that William Leadbetter had lied to the inquiry into electoral delinquency at East Retford, 7 Mar. He joined his colleague Easthope and the county Members in pleading in vain for the bill for the construction of a new court house at St. Albans to be sanctioned despite an inadvertent failure to comply with standing orders, 29 Apr. He voted against Catholic claims, 12 May. He supported a petition complaining of monopoly in the system of licensing hackney coach operators, 22 May, but dismissed that of some London bankers and merchants for the relocation of Smithfield meat market, 5 June. He divided against reduction of the salary of the lieutenant-general of the ordnance, 4 July 1828. Planta, the patronage secretary, listed him in February 1829 among those Members who would go 'with government' for Catholic emancipation; but he is not known to have voted either way in the divisions on the issue. He welcomed the Smithfield market improvement bill as likely to be 'productive of much practical advantage', 6 May, and spoke against reception of a petition against the London bridge bill, which he said was groundless, 8 May 1829.

Smith voted against the transfer of East Retford's seats to Birmingham, 11 Feb., and paired against the enfranchisement of Birmingham, Leeds and Manchester, 23 Feb. 1830. The previous day, in what turned out to be his last known contribution to debate, he had exceeded his customary brevity in a speech in support of the army estimates:

That distress prevails in every part of the country no one can doubt; and I admit that economy and retrenchment can alone relieve the people from their present miserable condition. Yet, by reason of the distressed state of the country, it appears to me the more necessary that a proper military force should be kept up, in order to quell any riot or disturbance, which is more likely to occur when the labouring class is out of employment and badly fed. Although ... I readily give my vote in favour of the army estimates, yet I feel equally disposed to support any motion for such retrenchment and economy as can be effected with propriety and justice. There are many sources from which considerable sums can be drawn, without material inconvenience, if ministers are disposed to avail themselves of them.

The only economy to which he could point was abolition of the additional allowances recently awarded to commissioners of excise; and his only recorded attempt in that session to practise what he preached was his vote against the Bathurst and Dundas pensions, 26 Mar. He voted for the grant for South American missions, 7 June 1830, and may have paired against abolition of the death penalty for forgery the same day.

Smith retired from Parliament at the dissolution of 1830. He died, 'aged 85', at his house in the Adelphi in January 1835, and was buried in the family vault in St. Antholin's church. It was said that despite his great age, 'an air of juvenility' had 'been always cast over his countenance by means of a curly wig to which he was for many years attached'.[26] By his will, dated 10 Feb. 1825, he left £100 and his copyhold orchard and two cottages at Harwell, Berkshire to his brother John Smith, who was then occupying them. (By a codicil of 2 Apr. 1834 he devised this property to John's daughters Charlotte Shorter, widow, and Rachael Smith, for whom he had made generous provision in his original will.) He created a trust fund to provide his wife with a life annuity of £1,000, and his nephew Abel Smith, the son of his late brother James, one of £35. (He was dead by 20 Feb. 1828, when Smith made the first codicil to his will.) He divided the residue of his personal estate between his sons and daughter, after whose marriage he made an appropriate adjustment to her share to take account of her dowry. He left the business premises in Queen Street to his elder son, and directed that all the rest of his real estate (apart from that at Harwell) should be sold: this included not only Starborough and the Adelphi house, but freehold property at Edmonton, Middlesex and premises at 19 and 22 Queen Street. His personalty was sworn under £90,000.[27] His widow died at Brompton, 'aged 86', 31 Jan. 1845. Her brief will, dated 17 Feb. 1843, consisted largely of bequests, totalling £1,300, to various London hospitals; by a codicil of 13 Dec. 1843 she left £300 to a charity school at Harwell. Her effects were sworn under £5,000.[28] Smith's wine business was carried on by his son Sebastian and survived into the 1860s.

[1] *Gent. Mag.* (1785), ii. 747. [2] Ibid. (1802), i. 275. [3] IGI (Norf.). [4] In *HP Commons, 1790-1820,* v. 191, Smith's sons are wrongly given as the issue of his second marriage. Newman Smith and Sebastian Smith were bap. at St. Antholin, Budge Row, London on 27 Mar. 1788 and 3 Dec. 1796 respectively (IGI). [5] The marriage took place at St. Michael, Cornhill, London (IGI). [6] IGI (London); PROB 11/1843/125. [7] *VCH Surr.* iv. 306. [8] Add. 76033, J. Harrison to Spencer, 25 Feb. 1820. [9] *The Times,* 21 Feb. 1821. [10] Ibid. 5, 7 June 1821. [11] Ibid. 21 Feb. 1822. [12] Ibid. 25 May 1822. [13] Ibid. 29 June 1822. [14] Ibid. 1 Aug. 1822. [15] Ibid. 18 June 1823. [16] Ibid. 27 Mar. 1823. [17] Ibid. 10 May 1823. [18] Ibid. 13 Feb., 3 Apr. 1824. [19] Ibid. 13 Mar. 1824. [20] Ibid. 6, 13 Apr. 1824. [21] Ibid. 15 May, 10 June 1824. [22] Ibid. 3 June 1824; *Creevey Pprs.* ii. 76. [23] *The Times,* 4 June 1824. [24] Ibid. 19 Feb., 2 Mar. 1825. [25] *Herts. Mercury,* 5, 12 Nov., 17 Dec. 1825, 10, 17 June 1826. [26] *The Times,* 22, 28, 31 Jan., 23 Feb. 1835; *Gent. Mag.* (1835), ii. 669. [27] PROB 11/1843/125; IR26/1399/57. [28] *Gent. Mag.* (1845), i. 327; PROB 11/2014/240; IR26/1720/108.

D.R.F.

SMITH, Sir Culling Eardley, 3rd bt. (1805–1863), of Bedwell Park, Herts. and Hadley, Mdx.

PONTEFRACT   1830–1831

b. 21 Apr. 1805, o.s. of Sir Culling Smith, 2nd bt. (*d.* 1829), of Bedwell Park and Hadley and Hon. Charlotte Elizabeth Eardley, da. and coh. of Sampson Eardley†, 1st Bar. Eardley [I], of Belvedere, Kent and Spalding, Lincs. *educ.* Eton 1820; Oriel, Oxf. 1823. *m.* 9 Feb. 1832, Isabella, da. of Thomas William Carr of Eshott, Northumb., 1s. 2da. *suc.* fa. as 3rd bt. 30 June 1829; took name of Eardley by royal lic. 14 May 1847. *d.* 21 May 1863.

Smith's maternal great-grandfather was Sampson Gideon, a wealthy Sephardi Jew and London stockbroker. In an early indication of the strength of his own Protestant convictions, although he obtained a second class degree in classics at Oxford he never graduated because he objected to 'some portions of the oaths' involved.[1] In 1829 he succeeded to his father's baronetcy, the Bedwell and other landed estates and the residue of personalty which was sworn under £30,000.[2] The following spring he expressed an interest in contesting Hertford at the next general election, but Lord Salisbury 'decidedly' objected to this, remarking that 'he is a man of considerable fortune, young, and does not appear to have any wish to attach himself to my party or to come in under my auspices'.[3] At the dissolution that summer his cousin reported that 'our new conservator' was canvassing the open borough of Pontefract, where he appears to have been the popular candidate. On the hustings he declared that in view of 'the influence which the government of this country exercised abroad', the 'extensive colonies which submitted to an English king' and 'the numerous interests, commercial, agricultural and manufacturing, which the unbiased statesman had equally to uphold and protect', he was resolved to 'be guided by what should seem to him to tend most to the welfare of the nation'; it was 'not for him to enter into the details of these subjects'. He adverted to the precarious state of France, where he hoped Britain would 'abstain from all interference', and delivered a eulogy on the prime minister the duke of Wellington, a distant relative (his great-uncle had married the duke's sister), describing him as 'fearless in war' but 'not alarmed in peace'. He was returned at the head of the poll.[4]

The ministry regarded him as one of their 'friends', and he voted with them in the crucial division on the civil list, 15 Nov. 1830. He presented an anti-slavery petition from Pontefract Wesleyans, 5 Nov. 1830, and one from the inhabitants for the declaration of a day of general fasting, 15 Feb. 1831. When Lord John Russell introduced the Grey ministry's reform bill, 1 Mar., Smith, in his only known speech, was the second Member to respond, professing his anxiety to 'support the true interests of his country'. After much consideration he had concluded that, given the changing circumstances of the country, there now existed 'a necessity for some reform'. He was convinced that 'the influence of the aristocracy is entirely too great in the House' and that 'in curtailing it to a considerable extent we deprive them of no right'. He approved 'in principle' of the proposed measure, but had reservations about 'some of the details', believing that 'the plan proceeds too much on the principle of population and too little on that of property'; ministers would have 'done better' to 'base it more on the wealth of many towns and districts'. There was also 'one striking deficiency' in that the bill made 'no provision for the more effectual prevention of bribery and corruption'. Having served on an election committee he was granted a month's leave to attend to private business, 7 Mar., and was therefore absent from the division on the second reading of the reform bill, 22 Mar. However, he voted for Gascoyne's wrecking amendment, 19 Apr. He quietly retired at the ensuing dissolution. He attended the Hertfordshire county meeting on reform, 5 May 1831, when he reportedly made a 'milk and water speech'.[5]

Smith subsequently emerged as a prominent Evangelical campaigner and religious philanthropist. He offered again for Pontefract in 1837 as a Liberal, standing on 'purity' principles, but was defeated. He unsuccessfully contested Edinburgh in 1846 as an anti-Maynooth candidate, and again failed to win a seat when he stood for the West Riding of Yorkshire in 1848. He founded the Evangelical Alliance in 1846 and was involved in the work of the London Missionary Society; he was particularly interested in improving the condition of the Jews abroad. He harboured a wish to see the Church of England disestablished and its liturgy reformed along more strictly Protestant lines, and expounded his views in several published letters. In 1847, following the death of his cousin, the 9th Lord Saye and Sele, he succeeded to the Belvedere estate of his maternal grandfather Lord Eardley, to which he had

been nominated as heir in 1812.[6] As the last representative of the Eardley family he assumed that name in lieu of Smith. He died in May 1863 after a three-week illness caused by a revaccination against smallpox.[7] His title and the Belvedere estate passed to his only son Eardley Gideon Culling Eardley (1838-75). He left Bedwell Park and the Kettlethorpe estate in Lincolnshire to his daughters Frances and Isabella respectively, and the Heugh estate in Northumberland to his nephew Hugh Culling Eardley Childers, a future Liberal cabinet minister. His gift to the nation was *Flight into Egypt* by the Spanish artist Bartolomé Esteban Murillo.

[1] *Gent. Mag.* (1863), ii. 110. [2] PROB 11/1759/452; IR26/1209/295. [3] Hatfield House mss 2M/Nicholson, Nicholson to Salisbury, 25 Apr., reply, 28 Apr. 1830. [4] Wentworth Woodhouse mun. J. W. Childers to Milton, 18 July; *Leeds Mercury*, 24 July; *Leeds Intelligencer*, 5 Aug. 1830. [5] Hatfield House mss 2M/Gen. Sutton to Salisbury, 6 May 1831. [6] PROB 11/1695/65; 1759/452. [7] *The Times*, 22 May 1863.

M.P.J.C.

SMITH, George (1765–1836), of Selsdon Park, Croydon, Surr. and 1 Upper Harley Street, Mdx.

LOSTWITHIEL	28 Mar. 1791–1796
MIDHURST	27 Dec. 1800–1806
WENDOVER	1806–1830
MIDHURST	1830–1831

b. 30 Apr. 1765, 5th s. of Abel Smith[†] (*d.* 1788), banker, of Nottingham and London and Mary, da. of Thomas Bird of Barton, Warws.; bro. of John Smith*, Robert Smith[†] and Samuel Smith*. *m.* 12 May 1792, Frances Mary, da. of Sir John Parker Mosley, 1st bt., of Ancoats, Lancs. and Rolleston, Staffs., 9s. 6da. (1 *d.v.p.*). *d.* 26 Dec. 1836.

Dir. Westminster Fire Office 1786-8; dir. E.I. Co. 1795-1833, dep. chairman 1805-6.

Maj. E.I. Co. vols. 1798.

Smith, a partner in the family's London and Hull banks until his retirement from business in 1829, and a director of the East India Company for 38 years, was again returned unopposed for his eldest brother Lord Carrington's nomination borough of Wendover at the 1820 general election. He continued to act with the conservative wing of the Whig opposition, but he was not a reliable thick and thin attender. He divided against the Liverpool ministry on the civil list, 5, 8 May 1820, and their prosecution of Queen Caroline, 23, 26 Jan., 6, 13 Feb. 1821. Unlike his elder brother and colleague Samuel, he voted for Catholic relief, 28 Feb. 1821. He was in minorities for army reductions, 14 Mar., ordnance economies, 21 May, and to omit arrears from the duke of Clarence's grant, 18 June; but he divided with ministers (and with Samuel) against repeal of the additional malt duty, 3 Apr. 1821. It is not clear whether it was he or Samuel who voted for more extensive tax remissions, 11 Feb. 1822. He divided for reduction of the salt duties, 28 Feb., and abolition of one of the joint-postmasterships, 13 Mar., 2 May. He was in Ricardo's minority of 25 for a maximum 20s. duty on wheat imports, 9 May. On 3 June he voted for reception of the Greenhoe petition for parliamentary reform, but he divided for none of the substantive reform motions of this period. He voted for criminal law reform, 4 June, inquiry into the lord advocate's dealings with the Scottish press, 25 June, and to abolish the lottery tax, 1 July. On the budget that day he 'said a few words in a low tone regarding the claim of the East India Company, and on the sinking fund'.[1] He voted for investigation of the Calcutta bankers' claims on the Company, 4 July 1822, having confirmed by request that their agent Prendergast, Member for Galway, had a 'clearly established' grievance.[2] Smith voted for ordnance economies, 19 Feb., but with government against Hume's motion for £2,000,000 tax reductions, 3 Mar. 1823. His only other known votes that session were for inquiry into the Irish church establishment, 4 Mar., and for proper use of the Bardados defence fund, 17 Mar. He voted to accuse lord chancellor Eldon of a breach of privilege, 1 Mar., for inquiries into the state of Ireland, 11 May, and Irish church pluralities, 27 May, to condemn the prosecution of the Methodist missionary John Smith in Demerara, 11 June, and, in a minority of 22, against the additional churches bill, 14 June 1824. He presented a Monk Wearmouth petition for the abolition of slavery, 4 May 1824.[3] He divided against the Irish unlawful societies bill, 15, 21, 25 Feb. 1825. A defaulter on a call of the House, 28 Feb., he attended and was excused next day, when he voted for Catholic relief, as he did on 21 Apr., 10 May. He divided against the duke of Cumberland's annuity, 2, 10 June 1825. No votes have been found for 1826, when he came in again unopposed for Wendover; 'indisposition' kept him away from the formalities and his eldest son stood proxy for him.[4]

Smith paired for Catholic relief, 6 Mar. 1827, and was present to vote for it, 12 May 1828. He divided for repeal of the Test Acts, 26 Feb. 1828. He put a question to a witness in the East Retford bribery inquiry, 7 Mar. 1828. He divided for Catholic emancipation, 6, 30 Mar. 1829. On the presentation of a petition from London East India merchants for a reduction in the duties on the importation of Indian silk goods, 13 Apr., 1829, he said there was no strong feeling on the issue in India. He voted for Jewish emancipation, 5

Apr., and paired for it, 17 May 1830. In early April 1830 Carrington informed the duke of Wellington that he, George and Samuel intended to support his ministry 'without asking for anything'.[5] He duly voted with them for the grant for South American missions and against abolition of the death penalty for forgery, 7 June 1830. At the general election that summer Smith transferred to Carrington's borough of Midhurst. Listed by ministers among the 'good doubtfuls', but reckoned to be in essence a 'friend', he was absent from the crucial division on the civil list, 15 Nov. 1830. Illness kept him away from that on the second reading of the Grey ministry's reform bill, 22 Mar. 1831, but he made it known that, unlike Samuel, and contrary to Carrington's wishes, he would have voted for it if present.[6] He paired against Gascoyne's wrecking amendment to the measure, 19 Apr. 1831, and retired from Parliament at the ensuing dissolution.

Smith, who left the East India Company direction in 1833, died at his Surrey residence at Selsdon in December 1836.[7] By his will, dated 23 Apr. 1834 and proved under £200,000, he provided handsomely for his many children, directed his sons and executors George Robert, Oswald and John Henry to sell his Midhurst property, divided residue of £79,178 between them and devised Seldson to George Robert.[8]

[1] *The Times*, 2 July 1822. [2] Ibid. 5 July 1822. [3] Ibid. 5 May 1824. [4] *Bucks. Chron.* 10 June 1826. [5] Add. 40309, f. 31. [6] *The Times*, 26 Mar. 1831. [7] *Gent. Mag.* (1837), i. 319. [8] PROB 11/1871/41; IR26/1465/15.

D.R.F.

SMITH, George Robert (1793–1869), of Woodside Cottage, Croydon, Surr.

| MIDHURST | 1831–1832 |
| CHIPPING WYCOMBE | 23 Oct. 1838–1841 |

b. 2 May 1793, 1st s. of George Smith* and Frances Mary, da. of Sir John Parker Mosley, 1st bt., of Ancoats, Lancs. and Rolleston, Staffs. *educ.* Eton c.1808. *m.* 4 May 1818, Jane, da. of John Maberly*, 2s. *suc.* fa. 1836. *d.* 23 Feb. 1869.

Sheriff, Surr. 1852-3
Treas. E. and W. India Dock Co. 1842-65.

Smith was one of six members of his family returned at the general election of 1831, when he succeeded to his father's seat for the pocket borough of Midhurst. Like most of his relatives he supported Lord Grey's ministry, though he did not join Brooks's Club until 1840. He divided for the second reading of the reintroduced reform bill, 6 July, and steadily for its details, its passage, 21 Sept., the second reading of the Scottish bill, 23 Sept., and Lord Ebrington's confidence motion, 10 Oct. 1831. He voted for the second reading of the revised reform bill, 17 Dec. 1831, and for its details. Most sources agree that it was he who rose with 'considerable diffidence', 23 Feb. 1832, to defend the transfer of Midhurst from schedule A to B. He accepted that the existence of nomination boroughs was 'against the letter and the spirit of the constitution', but maintained that the extended franchise would 'completely and irrevocably destroy' his family's interest at Midhurst and make it 'as independent as any borough in the country'. He divided for the bill's third reading, 22 Mar., Ebrington's motion for an address asking the king to appoint only ministers committed to carrying an unimpaired measure, 10 May, and the second reading of the Irish bill, 25 May. He voted with government on the Russian-Dutch loan, 26 Jan., 12 July, relations with Portugal, 9 Feb., and the navy civil departments bill, 6 Apr. 1832.

The sacrifice of most of his family's borough interests to the cause of reform left Smith without a seat at the general election of 1832. He inherited the Selsdon Park estate in Surrey from his father in 1836.[1] The following year he unsuccessfully contested Buckinghamshire, declaring that he was 'still strongly and sincerely attached' to 'liberal' principles. In 1838 the succession to the peerage of his cousin, Robert John Smith*, created a vacancy for him at Chipping Wycombe, but his second stint in the Commons ended in 1841, apparently owing to political differences with his increasingly conservative cousin.[2] He was a director of his family's banking concern at Derby for six years from 1837, and was admitted to the board of their London firm in 1850. He died in February 1869, when a fellow banker and lifelong friend, Samuel Jones Loyd*, Lord Overstone, paid tribute to his 'gentle and amiable character'.[3]

[1] PROB 11/1871/41; IR26/1465/15. [2] H.T. Easton, *Hist. of a Banking House*, 25; R.W. Davis, *Political Change and Continuity*, 138, 151. [3] NatWest Archives, Smith/2/1987; *Overstone Corresp.* iii. 1172.

H.J.S.

SMITH, John (1767–1842), of Blendon Hall, Kent and Dale Park, Suss.

WENDOVER	1802–1806
NOTTINGHAM	1806–1818
MIDHURST	1818–1830
CHICHESTER	1830–1831
BUCKINGHAMSHIRE	1831–1834

b. 6 Sept. 1767, 6th s. of Abel Smith† (*d.* 1788), banker, of Nottingham and London and Mary, da. of Thomas Bird of Barton, Warws.; bro. of George Smith*, Robert Smith† and Samuel Smith*. *m.* (1) 1 Dec. 1793, Sarah (*d.* 23 Sept. 1794), da. of Thomas Boone, commr. of customs, *s.p.*; (2) 6 Jan. 1800, Mary (*d.* 9 Apr. 1809), da. of Lt.-Col. Martin Tucker, 2s.; (3) 1 May 1811, Emma, da. of Egerton Leigh of West Hall, High Leigh, Cheshire, 2da. *d.* 20 Jan. 1842.

Vol. London and Westminster light horse 1798.

Dir. W.I. Dock Co. 1804-11, 1817-24, 1828-30, 1832-4, 1837-8, dep.-chairman 1812-13, chairman 1814; treas. bd. of agriculture 1807-16; dir. Imperial Insurance Co. 1813-31, Imperial Fire Insurance Co. 1831-4, 1836-40; commr. of exch. bill loans 1818-40.

Smith, 'one of the City's most eminent bankers', was with his brother George in effective control of the London bank of Smith, Payne and Smith from 1799, and he belonged to the boards of the family concerns in Derby, Hull and Nottingham.[1] With George he also shared the patronage of Midhurst, for which he again returned himself in 1820. He was an assiduous attender and frequent speaker, who continued to vote on most issues with the Whig opposition to Lord Liverpool's ministry, including parliamentary reform, 9 May 1821, 25 Apr. 1822, 24 Apr., 2 June 1823, 26 Feb. 1824, 13 Apr. 1826. He divided for Catholic relief, 28 Feb. 1821, 1 Mar., 21 Apr., 10 May 1825. On fiscal matters, in which his expertise was widely acknowledged, and in which the influence of David Ricardo* and other political economists is apparent,[2] he steered his own course. He called for 'the establishment of a permanent system of finance' to enhance confidence in the economy, 12 May 1820. While advocating repeal of the wool tax, 26 May, he cautioned that 'any measure tending to lessen the means of supporting the public credit should be viewed with some degree of alarm'. He queried an issue of exchequer bills to reduce the unfunded debt, 31 May. Responding to the budget, 19 June, he observed that 'the real state of our finances was very little known in the House' and called for their careful scrutiny, while he chided the chancellor of the exchequer, Vansittart, for his overoptimistic forecasts for debt reduction.[3] He spoke and voted for greater efficiency in revenue collection, 4 July 1820.

Encouraged by George Tierney*, Smith convened a meeting of London merchants, bankers and traders, 24 Jan. 1821, when he proposed resolutions in support of Queen Caroline.[4] Presenting the resulting petition, 2 Feb., he complained of the organized disruption of the meeting by opponents, and gave notice of a motion for the restoration of the queen's name to the liturgy. Thomas Creevey* noted that 'coming from him this motion may be considered as made from that City meeting, and must consequently produce a great impression'. The resulting speech was 'listened to with the deepest attention', 13 Feb., when Smith claimed that his only motive for acting was to end the 'disturbance and distraction which prevailed in the country on this subject'. While he might welcome the appointment of a Whig ministry, he neither sought nor expected to benefit personally from such a development. He also took the opportunity to attack the government's foreign policy and its inaction on domestic distress, though he was 'not among those who thought that agriculture was in a state of ruin'. His motion was lost by 298-178, and this was the last throw of the opposition campaign.[5] He supported repeal of the house and window taxes, 6 Mar., but his preference was for lifting the duty on salt. He opposed repeal of the additional malt duty, 3 Apr., suggesting that relief from agricultural distress might be more effectually achieved by reform of the poor laws and adherence to 'a rigid system of economy'. He denied that the agricultural interest had been damaged by the resumption of cash payments, 9 Apr. He supported a reduction in the army estimates, 30 Mar., declaring that 'no person should be employed by the state whose services were not absolutely necessary'. However, he only voted to reduce the ordnance office grant after Hume agreed to omit a number of proposed salary reductions from his amendment, 14 May. He spoke against the grant for Millbank penitentiary, 29 May.[6] He favoured mitigation of the punishment for forgery, 26 Mar., 13, 25 May, 4 June, explaining that its severity deterred many bankers from prosecuting.[7] In supporting the steam engines bill, 7 May, he expressed concern for the health of the poor. He approved of legislation against cruelty to horses, 1 June.[8] His bill to liberalize the bankruptcy laws gained a third reading, 4 June 1821, but made no further progress.

He advocated reduction of the 'odious' tax on salt, 28 Feb. 1822. He was critical of the privileges of the Bank of England and opposed the extension of its charter, 2 May. He blamed agricultural distress on the 'superabundant harvest', 13 May, when he expressed regret that illness had prevented him from opposing Wyvill's proposed tax reductions five days earlier. He warned that any attempt to reduce stockholders' interest would lead to disinvestment, and so to 'infamy and ruin'. In response to the budget, 1 July, he observed that the ruin of many small farmers would inevitably drive up prices and so relieve agricultural distress. Speaking as a member of the *London Tavern* relief committee, he informed the House of the gravity of the famine in Ireland, 17 June. He advocated Catholic relief, tithe reform and inquiry into the state of the

country rather than renewal of the Irish Insurrection Act, 9 July 1822, as the failure of repressive measures had been demonstrated. He was added to the select committee on foreign trade, 25 Feb. 1823 (and reappointed, 4 Mar. 1824). He defended the government's policy on the sinking fund, 3, 6, 11 Mar. He supported reform of the law regarding insolvent debtors, 11, 18 Mar., and on the former date backed the small debts recovery bill.[9] He derided the usury laws for their practical uselessness, 17 June, and was a tireless advocate of their repeal in the next three sessions, although this ran contrary to the majority view of the committee of bankers, of which he was chairman. His bill for the better protection of merchants' goods abroad gained royal assent, 25 July (4 Geo. IV c. 83). Surprisingly, *The Times* listed him as having voted with ministers against repeal of the Foreign Enlistment Act, 16 Apr.[10] He spoke in favour of the abolition of punishment by whipping, 30 Apr. He approved of the suppression of cruel animal sports, 21 May, but saw education as the best solution. He highlighted the success of non-denominational Sunday schools as a civilizing influence in Ireland, 12 May. In the debate on the prosecution of the Dublin Orange rioters, 26 May, he expressed disappointment that Canning's return to office had not signalled the adoption of a more liberal policy. He advocated government grants to promote employment in and encourage migration from Ireland, 23 June 1823.[11] Next day he complained of widespread abuses in that country's administrative machinery.

He approved of William Courtenay's bill to amend the bankruptcy laws, 18 Feb. 1824. He attacked puritanical attitudes towards debt, 23 Feb., arguing that 'credit was the basis of our prosperity and the foundation of all property in the country'. His speech that day against the tax on legal proceedings won a concession from ministers. He congratulated them for rescinding the duty on silk, 5 Mar. However, he was critical of grants for building work at Windsor Castle and for new churches, 9 Apr., and cited the education of the poor as a more deserving object of expenditure. He called for further measures to minimize the risk to traders operating abroad, 17 May, 1 June,[12] and was a teller for the marine insurance bill, 15 June. He advocated an end to flogging in the army, 11 Mar. He supported reform of the game laws, but not the use of hard labour as a punishment, 31 May.[13] In the context of the vagrants bill, 3 June, he argued for the effectiveness of solitary confinement in gaols. He demanded an inquiry into the cost of the Irish government, 12 Mar., and larded his subsequent speeches with examples of rough justice and maladministration. He defended the miscellaneous estimates grant with an assertion that 'much of

[England's] present splendour and prosperity derived from the humiliation of Ireland', 19 Mar. He regarded 'moral improvement' as an imperative for the Irish people and supported a select committee on education, 25 Mar. He queried the religious bias of voluntary subscription schools, 29 Mar. He backed Maberly's proposal for low interest loans to stimulate Irish manufacturing, 4 May, citing his experience as a commissioner of road and bridge building grants to illustrate the effectiveness of this kind of interventionist policy. Having no personal interest at stake he declined to be added to the select committee on the state of Ireland, 25 May, to the disappointment of Thomas Spring Rice, who praised his exertions on this subject.[14] He opposed the renewal of the Irish Insurrection Act, 14 June 1824. At the end of the year he attended the *London Tavern* meeting to raise a subscription on behalf of Spanish and Italian refugees.[15] He contrasted the government's readiness to suppress the Catholic Association with its failure to act against Orange Lodges, 10 Feb., and accordingly felt 'deep grief' at the unlawful societies bill, 23 Feb. 1825.[16] He spoke in favour of Catholic relief, which he saw as a matter of civil rights, 19, 21, 26 Apr., and praised the conduct and integrity of English Catholics. He favoured a reduction in the sugar duties, 28 Feb., and the transfer of the duty on beer to malt, 15 Mar. In opposing the quarantine laws as an unnecessary restraint on trade, 10, 30 Mar., 13, 19 May, he propounded the anti-contagionist theories then coming into vogue. He spoke in favour of restricting the hours worked by children in cotton mills, 6, 16, 31 May. He opposed the reduction proposed in the London tithes bill, 7 May 1825. That summer, after a fraud case involving his own bank had highlighted the inefficiency of the London police, he sought advice from Henry Brougham*, as he thought the committee of bankers might ask him to raise the matter. He complained that the home secretary Peel 'has often swaggered about in the ... Commons, but [he] is incapable of forming a national plan which might be adopted without any infringement of the liberty of the subject'.[17]

As crisis in the financial world loomed, Smith sought to allay fears about the depletion of the country bankers' gold reserves, 22 June, and the parallel over-circulation of paper currency, 27 June 1825. He told Brougham, 2 Sept., that the stock exchange panic of the previous month had been 'entirely attributable to the measures pursued by the Bank of England of diminishing their circulation', and warned that the directors' 'imprudence' had excited 'so strong a feeling ... among the leaders of the monied interest that I anticipate important consequences'. Six days later he

was more optimistic, reporting that 'the exchanges and the funds are rising so that I hope the commercial world will in time, though I fear not immediately, recover its former tranquillity'. In December 1825 he came to the aid of the stricken banking house of Pole, Thornton and Company, liaising with Bank of England directors, but he could not avert its eventual collapse.[18] At the opening of the parliamentary session, 2 Feb. 1826, he urged the chancellor of the exchequer Robinson to clarify his stated intention of allowing the Bank to open branches. He joined in the call for a return of bankrupt country bankers, 9 Feb., though he deplored the scapegoating of this group for the panic. He missed Robinson's speech the next day, owing to a 'severe indisposition', but, noting the particular sufferings of poorer holders of worthless paper currency, he supported the chancellor's proposal to limit the circulation of small notes, 13 Feb., as he believed that public disquiet made some form of action imperative. Nonetheless, he indicated support for a bimetallic currency standard, the favoured scheme of Alexander Baring, who moved the hostile amendment on this occasion. After the debate he told John Cam Hobhouse* that there was 'the greatest confusion and panic in the City'.[19] He approved the exemption of the Bank from the promissory notes bill, 20 Feb., and defended the conduct of its directors during the December panic. In keeping with his belief that 'the conduct of government, on this and other occasions, should be regulated by public utility', he urged ministers to make an exchequer bill issue to assist economic recovery. He expressed concern that the restrictions on the note issues from country banks were being imposed with undue haste, 28 Feb., 7 Mar. He condemned as 'absurd and ill-digested' an attempt to remodel the Bank's charter along the lines of the Bank of Ireland, 9 Mar., and showed himself to be more enamoured of the Scottish banking system, 14 Mar. About this time he wrote to a colleague that

> ministers have bungled the currency question most unpardonably. They have created a new panic, which I trust is subsiding, but which has occasioned great mischief. They treated my proposition of a committee with contempt, though they have displayed a complete ignorance of banking, and an entire distrust of those who knew something about it, and whose integrity they had no reason to suspect. This is Lord Liverpool's doing and not Huskisson's, who in his heart must be ashamed of the whole proceeding.[20]

He expressed understanding with Catholic antipathy to the Protestant charter schools in Ireland, 20 Mar., 14 Apr., 9 June. He called for inquiry into the condition of the Irish poor, 25 Apr., and the introduction of a poor law into that country, 27 Apr. He quizzed ministers over allegations of torture in New South Wales gaols, 14 Apr. He favoured a ban on spring guns, 27 Apr. His support for the government's plan to admit foreign corn, 1, 8 May, stemmed from his concern over urban distress, on which he privately consulted leading ministers, 24 July 1826, and was reassured.[21] At the general election that summer he again returned himself for Midhurst.

Outside Parliament, Smith's philanthropic efforts in the field of education were conspicuous during the mid-1820s, when he was deeply involved in the foundation of University College, London. A member of the first council, he corresponded with Brougham on the site of the new institution and the recruitment of subscribers, and was himself a generous benefactor of land and money. His commitment to the ethos of the project was evident in the 'great difficulties' he found over his relative William Wilberforce's* insistence on the inclusion of a Christian element in the curriculum as the price for his support.[22] At the same time, he reported on the success of an experiment in elementary education which he had initiated, involving the instruction of ten poor boys in French and Latin. In a letter of 1829 he proudly referred Francis Place to his 'little school', apparently located near the Sussex residence he had purchased in 1827, which had been honoured by a visit from James Mill. Later he collaborated with Place on similar projects in London.[23]

Smith supported an inquiry into Members' interest in joint-stock companies, 5 Dec. 1826, and denied that any of those in which he was involved, such as the Australian Company, were speculative ventures. His son subsequently noted that he was 'endeavouring to remove from his mind feelings of anger and animosity' towards newspaper editors who had impugned his motives for adopting this stance.[24] He called for bankruptcy cases to be removed from the jurisdiction of chancery and for a reduction in the number of commissioners, 27 Feb. 1827. He divided for Catholic relief, 6 Mar. He advocated non-denominational education in Ireland, 19 Mar., spoke against taxing Catholics to build Protestant churches, 3 Apr., and voted for inquiry into the Irish miscellaneous estimates, 5 Apr. He questioned the efficiency and honesty of customs officers, 13 Mar., and voted for information regarding the mutiny at Barrackpoor, 22 Mar. In presenting a Bolton petition for a minimum wage, 28 Mar., he argued that mechanisation, far from causing distress, was an engine of wealth creation.[25] He backed inquiry into London's gaols, 3 Apr. He presented petitions for repeal of the Test Acts, 30 May, 6 June 1827.[26] With

Lord John Russell, he was anxious to introduce the necessary legislation that session, but it was eventually deemed expedient to wait until the next. On 4 Feb. 1828 he apprized the House of the United Committee of Protestant Dissenters' resolution not to link their claims with those of the Catholics, and he presented numerous petitions that month. In seconding Russell's motion for repeal, 16 Feb., he observed that while the Test Acts were seldom enforced, their presence on the statute book was an insult to Dissenters, who were 'as intelligent ... loyal ... industrious and prosperous a clan of people as any within His Majesty's dominions'. The prejudice enshrined in these laws had no place in Smith's world view, in which progressive forces could not be 'gainsayed, or resisted'. He later cited his role in the repeal campaign as being among the proudest achievements of his parliamentary career. A numerously signed address from Liverpool Dissenters, 26 May, paid tribute to the 'active and distinguished part you have taken in bringing about this happy event', and praised his 'generous zeal in favour of the principles of religious liberty'. Ill health prevented his attendance at a commemorative dinner, 18 June, when his eldest son represented him.[27] He was not unfriendly towards Wilmot Horton's proposals for the encouragement of emigration, 4, 27 Mar., but was more enthusiastic about an allotments scheme which he had promoted to relieve unemployed labourers in one Sussex village. He recognized the need to halt migration from Ireland there, 18 Apr. He spoke against flogging in the army, 10 Mar. He voted against the duke of Wellington's ministry to extend East Retford's franchise to Bassetlaw freeholders, 21 Mar. He paired for Catholic relief, 12 May 1828, and continued to present numerous petitions in its favour. Ill health was surely the explanation for his non-attendance to support the government's emancipation bill in 1829, when there is no record of any parliamentary activity. In a letter to the editor of the *Edinburgh Review*, 13 Oct. 1829, he mentioned plans to visit Bath to cure a stomach complaint, and the recuperative effects of a sojourn in Perthshire earlier that year.[28]

He reappeared in the Commons to speak in favour of providing allotments for the poor, 9 Mar. 1830, citing the success of a scheme which he had originated in Essex and warning that 'unless something is done to assist the labouring classes, violence, murder and destruction of property will ensue'. He voted with the revived Whig opposition to omit the salary of the lieutenant-general of the ordnance, 29 Mar., and reduce the grant for Prince Edward Island, 14 June. He divided for Jewish emancipation, 5 Apr.,

17 May, and parliamentary reform, 28 May. In April, Wellington noted the conversion to ministerial politics of certain members of the Smith family, including Lord Carrington, who 'thinks he can neutralise his brother John Smith'. However, this proved to be a forlorn hope: Smith's personal attitude to Wellington can be guessed at from a nursery rhyme in his archive, written in his own hand, which characterized the duke as a baby-eater.[29] He presented a petition from several eminent bankers against the death penalty for forgery, 14 May, and voted accordingly, 7 June. He presented a petition against taxes on paper and newspapers from a self-improvement society of which he was a patron, 19 May, and one for the substitution of a solemn affirmation for oaths, 24 June. He called for information on Irish loans, 6 July 1830. At the general election that summer he accepted an invitation to stand for Chichester. His campaign emphasized his commitment to parliamentary reform, civil and religious liberty, and retrenchment and tax reductions, and he praised the government's efforts in the last area. He condemned the 'harsh application' of the game laws and pointed to his efforts to promote education. His religious affiliation came under scrutiny on the hustings and, though he denied being a Unitarian, he admitted to reading unorthodox pamphlets. He was comfortably returned in second place, ahead of a radical.[30]

The ministry of course listed him among their 'foes', and he duly voted against them in the crucial civil list division, 15 Nov. 1830. He presented anti-slavery petitions from Dissenting congregations, 4, 17 Nov., and one from Catholic freeholders in Galway for an extension of the elective franchise there, 16 Dec. 1830. He felt that magistrates had dealt too leniently with rioters in the agricultural districts, 8 Feb. 1831, and maintained that the distress in his Sussex locality was not of a magnitude to excuse such behaviour. However, he admitted the extent of the problem in western counties, and suggested emigration as a partial remedy. He supported another attempt to promote allotment schemes, 16 Feb., and the following month he chaired the inaugural meeting of the Sussex Association for Improving the Condition of the Labouring Classes.[31] His attempts to interest the House in the renewed problem of distress in Ireland received a muted response, 28 Feb., 18, 22 Mar. While professing reluctance to embarrass Lord Grey's ministry, he nevertheless savaged the budget proposal to tax the transfer of stock, 11 Feb. He asserted that had such an 'ill advised and dangerous' measure been in operation before, it would have been impossible to fund the French wars and the consequences of the financial crisis of

1825-6 would have been disastrous. He recommended an income tax on the wealthy as an alternative. His intervention may have helped to influence the government's decision to abandon its plan, for as Denis Le Marchant[†] noted, his was 'the speech that vexed us most ... as we knew him to be a friend'.[32] He spoke in favour of reforming the bankruptcy laws, 21 Feb. Commenting on the London merchants' reform petition, 26 Feb., he emphasized the number of signatories who were recent converts to the cause because they saw it as a necessary means of social containment. He made similar remarks on the petition from Chichester corporation, 4 Mar., when he observed that his anomalous position as a borough owning reformer had 'enabled me to do what I confess has given me delight, return one or two Whig Members to this House'. He admitted that the extent of the government's bill had 'taken away my breath, so surprised and delighted was I to find the ministers so much in earnest', though he foresaw 'difficulties in the execution of parts of the scheme'. One observer described his speech as being 'strongly in favour of the bill'.[33] He spoke in support of several Sussex reform petitions, 9 Mar., and divided for the bill's second reading, 22 Mar. In presenting a friendly petition from London merchants, 18 Apr. 1831, he argued that this refuted the charge that the measure was revolutionary, as 'the petitioners would be the first victims of revolution'. He voted against Gascoyne's wrecking amendment the next day. At the ensuing dissolution he declined an invitation to stand for London, owing to the arduous duties involved, but answered the call of the Buckinghamshire reformers to offer in place of his nephew Robert John Smith[*]. Possessed of no property in the county, he commended himself to the freeholders on the strength of his 'well known and ancient attachment to the cause of liberty in general, and above all, to reform in Parliament'. Among the benefits he anticipated from the government's measure were a fairer judicial system and an end to 'unnecessary wars', such as those against revolutionary France. He was returned after a contest, in which he was notably successful in attracting the votes of Dissenters.[34]

On hearing Thomas Macaulay's speech in support of the reintroduced reform bill, 5 July 1831, Smith paid him an emotional private tribute;[35] he divided for the second reading next day, and steadily for its details. He defended the inclusion of Midhurst in schedule A, 22 July, though he argued somewhat disingenuously for the incorruptibility of the burgage holders. When ministers failed to provide a lead in the case of Saltash, 26 July, he voted for its complete disfranchisement. That day he warned opposition leaders that their delaying tactics could provoke public unrest if the bill's passage was imperilled, and he suggested an earlier starting time for debates. He denied that support for the bill in the country was confined to the middle classes, though he would 'rather take [this] for a test than any other'. He was well disposed, as a former resident, to grant Tower Hamlets two Members, 4 Aug., seeing this as a 'safety valve opening a safe and constitutional channel for the expression of public opinion'. He divided for the third reading, 19 Sept., the second reading of the Scottish bill, 23 Sept., and Lord Ebrington's confidence motion, 10 Oct. He voted to punish only those guilty of bribery at the Dublin election, 23 Aug. He spoke in support of the general registry bill, 20 Sept., and revived his interest in reform of the bankruptcy laws, which he said was long overdue, 5, 12 Oct. He divided for the second reading of the revised reform bill, 17 Dec. 1831, and for its details. On 21 Feb. 1832 he faced opposition accusations that he had engineered the partial reprieve of Midhurst, which was now scheduled to retain one Member, and answered truthfully that under the new franchise his influence would be totally destroyed. In supporting the enfranchisement of Tower Hamlets, 28 Feb., he again referred to the threat of insurrection. He voted for the third reading, 22 Mar., Ebrington's motion for an address asking the king to appoint only ministers committed to carrying an unimpaired measure, 10 May, and against the Conservative amendment to increase Scotland's county representation, 1 June. He was named to the committee of secrecy on the renewal of the Bank of England's charter, 23 May. In supporting Sadler's proposal to impose a tax on absentee Irish landlords, 19 June, he expressed personal concern for the condition of the poor in Ireland and criticized the indifference of landlords to their plight. He was a majority teller against a call of the House, 12 July, before voting with ministers on the Russian-Dutch loan, as he did again, 20 July 1832.

Smith was again returned for Buckinghamshire at the general election of 1832 and sat until his retirement in 1834. He died in January 1842 as a result of draining a bottle of laudanum in mistake for cough medicine. He divided his real estate between his sons John Abel Smith* and Martin Tucker Smith*, and left personalty sworn under £250,000.[36]

[1] J. Leighton-Boyce, Smiths the Bankers, 127, 270; NatWest Archives, Smith/2/1987. [2] Brougham mss, Smith to Brougham, 19 Sept. 1825. [3] The Times, 20 June 1820. [4] Grey mss, Tierney to Grey, 13 Jan.; The Times, 25 Jan. 1821. [5] Creevey's Life and Times, 138. [6] The Times, 30 May 1821. [7] Ibid. 27 Mar., 5 June 1821. [8] Ibid. 2 June 1821. [9] Ibid. 12, 19 Mar. 1823. [10] Ibid. 22 Apr. 1823. [11] Ibid. 24 June 1823. [12] Ibid. 2 June 1824. [13] Ibid. 1 June 1824. [14] Ibid. 26

May 1824. [15] Northants. RO, Agar Ellis diary, 17 Dec. 1824. [16] The Times, 24 Feb., 8 Mar. 1825. [17] Brougham mss, Smith to Brougham, 14 Aug. 1825. [18] Ibid. Smith to Brougham, 2, 8 Sept. 1825; Leighton-Boyce, 126. [19] Add. 56550, f. 49. [20] Cockburn Letters, 138. [21] Brougham mss, Smith to Brougham, 25 July 1826. [22] Ibid. Smith to Brougham, 15 July, 14, 24 Aug., 2, 8, 16 Sept. 1825, 25 July 1826; C. New, Henry Brougham, 361, 365, 371. [23] Add. 34613, f. 278; 35149, ff. 203-4; 37950, f. 52; D. Miles, Francis Place, 220; A. Dale, Fashionable Brighton, 54. [24] W. Suss. RO Add. 22339. [25] The Times, 29 Mar. 1827. [26] Ibid. 31 May, 7 June 1827. [27] R.G. Cowherd, Politics of Dissent, 68; R. W. Davis, Dissent in Politics, 240, 244; W. Suss. RO Add. 22258, 22263, 22466. [28] Add. 34613, f. 278. [29] Add. 40309, f. 31; W. Suss. RO Add. 22249. [30] Chichester Election Procs. (1830), pp. 22, 64, 135-6, 146, 158. [31] BL C.T. 17. [32] Three Diaries, 9, 50. [33] Add. 51576, Fazakerley to Holland, 4 Mar. 1831. [34] Bucks. Gazette, 30 Apr., 7, 14, 21 May 1831; R.W. Davis, Political Change and Continuity, 94-95. [35] Macaulay Letters, ii. 63. [36] W. Suss. RO Add. 22514; PROB 11/1960/208; IR26/1623/148.

H.J.S.

SMITH, John Abel (1802–1871), of 1 Upper Harley Street, Mdx.

MIDHURST	1830–1831
CHICHESTER	1831–1859
CHICHESTER	21 Feb. 1863–1868

b. 2 June 1802, 1st s. of John Smith* and 2nd w. Mary, da. of Lt.-Col. Martin Tucker; bro. of Martin Tucker Smith*. educ. Eton c. 1814-18; Christ's, Camb. 1819. m. 26 Dec. 1827, Anne, da. of Sir Samuel Clarke Jervoise, 1st bt., of Idsworth, Hants, wid. of Ralph William Grey of Backworth, Northumb. 3s. suc. fa. 1842. d. 7 Jan. 1871. Capt. Suss. yeoman cav. 1831[1]

Treas. W. India Dock Co. 1838, E. and W. India Dock Co. 1839-40; dir. E. and W. I. Dock Co. 1842-9, New Zealand Co. 1844-58, Edinburgh Life Assurance by 1842-67.

As the son of a widely respected Whig banker and parliamentarian, Smith carried a weight of expectations that perhaps affected him as a young man. Although he matriculated in 1819 he had apparently not gone up to Cambridge by 1822, when he began to keep an intermittent private journal. This reads like a catalogue of self-reproach for his ill-natured and socially inept behaviour: on 29 Aug. he admitted to being 'most sadly hasty and passionate, which must lead in time to settled bad temper', and on 9 Nov. he recounted his 'struggle to overcome the dreadful vanity and pride which I feel on all occasions flying up and becoming the main spring of everything'. In the same entry he chided himself for his habitual mockery of his pious uncle and cousin, Samuel Smith* and Abel Smith*. On resuming his journal in 1826, having graduated the previous year, his state of mind had marginally improved, and he believed that travel in France and Switzerland had mellowed his temper.

When Lord Dudley Coutts Stuart* met him in Paris that March, he noted that 'he is an Englishman all over and full of our English good morality, ideas and views', although this did not prevent him from 'having very good, noble and generous sentiment'. The following year the brooding introspection of his journal gave way in part to comments on public affairs, initially occasioned by the formation of Canning's ministry, the staying power of which he doubted, fearing that 'the result of it all will be a high Tory administration'.[2] His marriage in December 1827 to the 'particularly fascinating' Anne Grey, a salon hostess, brought him two stepchildren.[3] He had joined Brooks's Club, 26 Nov. 1826. In April 1828 he contested the venal borough of Sudbury, as an advocate of 'that liberal policy' which had brought about 'important improvements in our civil and commercial regulations', and which he believed would 'consolidate and strengthen the constitution of the country'. However, the 'No Popery' cry was raised against him and he was narrowly defeated.[4] Two months later he spoke on his father's behalf at a dinner to mark the repeal of the Test Acts, which he regarded as 'a stimulus to further exertions' and 'a pledge of better things to come'.[5] At the dissolution in 1830 his name was mentioned in connection with Sudbury, Arundel and Chichester, but in the event he was returned unopposed for the family borough of Midhurst.[6]

The duke of Wellington's ministry naturally regarded him as one of their 'foes', and he duly voted against them in the crucial civil list division, 15 Nov. 1830. He divided for the second reading of the Grey ministry's reform bill, 22 Mar., and against Gascoyne's wrecking amendment, 19 Apr. 1831. At the ensuing dissolution his father's candidacy for Buckinghamshire created a vacancy at Chichester, for which he was returned after seeing off a radical challenge.[7] He voted for the second reading of the reintroduced reform bill, 6 July, and steadily for its details, though he was in the minority for the total disfranchisement of Aldborough, 14 Sept. He divided for the third reading, 19 Sept., the bill's passage, 21 Sept., the second reading of the Scottish bill, 23 Sept., and Lord Ebrington's confidence motion, 10 Oct. He voted to punish only those guilty of bribery at the Dublin election and against the motion censuring the conduct of the Irish administration, 23 Aug. He divided for the second reading of the revised reform bill, 17 Dec. 1831, and for its details. He was cheered by his own side for a neat riposte to Sir Richard Vyvyan's allegation of errors in the returns of the number of houses in Tavistock, 23 Jan. 1832. He voted for the bill's third reading, 22 Mar., and Ebrington's motion for

an address asking the king to appoint only ministers committed to carrying an unimpaired measure, 10 May, and was against the Conservative amendment for increased Scottish county representation, 1 June. He divided with ministers on the Russian-Dutch loan, 26 Jan., 12, 16, 20 July, relations with Portugal, 9 Feb., and the navy civil departments bill, 6 Apr. On 18 July he introduced a bill to regulate the payment of bills of exchange at places other than the drawee's residence: this non-controversial legislation gained royal assent, 8 Aug. 1832 (2 & 3 Gul. IV, c. 98).

Smith was again returned for Chichester at the general election of 1832 and sat, with one brief interruption, until his defeat in 1868. In 1842 he inherited Dale Park and other properties in Sussex from his father and was the joint residuary legatee of the estate, which was sworn under £250,000.[8] His public career emerged from the shadow of his father's and, like him, he won renown as a friend of religious toleration, leading the successful campaign to allow Jews to sit in Parliament in 1858. Though himself a 'low churchman', he was a friend of Pope Pius IX, and his early journal raises the curious possibility that he may have worshipped in a recusant chapel.[9] He became senior partner in his family's London banking firm, 1835-45, and sat on the boards of the associated banks in Derby, Hull and Nottingham. Railways and colonial development were chief among his other business interests.[10] In later life he evidently overcame the gaucherie of his youth, and the family historian describes him as being 'personable and affable'.[11] He died in January 1871.

[1] W. Suss. RO Add. 22507. [2] Ibid. 22339; BL Add. 52015, Stuart to Fox, 21 Mar. 1826. [3] H.T. Easton, *Hist. of a Banking House*, 30; W. Suss. RO Add. 22373. [4] W. Suss. RO Add. 22465; *Suff. Chron.* 12 Apr. 1828. [5] *Procs. of Dinner to commemorate Abolition of Sacramental Test* (1828) [BL 4135. bb. 44.]. [6] W.D. Cooper, *Parl. Hist. Suss.* 9; *Chichester Election Procs. (1830)*, pp. 16, 22, 108-9; NLW, Ormathwaite mss FG1/5, Walsh diary, 4, 6 July 1830. [7] *Chichester Election Placards* [BL 1856. b. 13.], f. 223. [8] PROB 11/1960/208; IR26/1623/148. [9] Easton, 26-28, 30; W. Suss. RO Add. 22339. [10] NatWest Archives, Smith/2/1987; Easton, 29. [11] J. Compton Reade, *Smith Fam.* 82.

H.J.S.

SMITH, Martin Tucker (1803–1880), of 43 Charles Street, Berkeley Square, Mdx.

MIDHURST	1831–1832
CHIPPING WYCOMBE	1847–1865

b. 6 July 1803, 2nd s. of John Smith* (*d.* 1842) and 2nd w. Mary, da. of Lt.-Col. Martin Tucker; bro. of John Abel Smith*. *educ.* Eton 1814-17. *m.* 8 July 1831, Louisa, da.

of Sir Matthew White Ridley, 3rd bt.*, 6s. (2 *d.v.p.*) 3da.
(1 *d.v.p.*). *d.* 10 Oct. 1880.

Dir. Canada Co. 1826-49, E.I. Co. 1838-58.

Smith, a member of the prominent Whig banking
dynasty, was returned for the family borough of
Midhurst in 1831, thus joining his father and brother
in the Commons. He divided for the second reading of
the Grey ministry's reintroduced reform bill, 6 July,
and steadily for its details, though he was in the minority for the total disfranchisement of Aldborough, 14
Sept. 1831. He voted for the bill's passage, 21 Sept.,
the second reading of the Scottish bill, 23 Sept., and
Lord Ebrington's confidence motion, 10 Oct. He voted
to punish only those guilty of bribery at the Dublin
election and against the motion censuring the conduct
of the Irish administration, 23 Aug. He divided for
the second reading of the revised reform bill, 17 Dec.
1831, and for its details. Although *The Times* credited
'Mr. M. Smith' with a speech in defence of the transfer
of Midhurst from schedule A to B, 23 Feb., this was
probably delivered by his cousin and colleague George
Robert Smith.[1] He voted for the bill's third reading,
22 Mar., and Ebrington's motion for an address asking
the king to appoint only ministers committed to carrying an unimpaired measure, 10 May. He divided with
government on the Russian-Dutch loan, 26 Jan., 12,
16, 20 July. He joined Brooks's Club, 5 Feb. 1832.

With the demise of his father's interest at Midhurst,
Smith had to wait 15 years before being returned for
Chipping Wycombe with the support of his cousin,
the 2nd Baron Carrington, as a free trader opposed to
the ballot. As a politician, he was always overshadowed
by his brother.[2] In 1842 he had inherited properties
from his father in Kent, Middlesex and Sussex, and
he was the joint residuary legatee of the estate, which
was sworn under £250,000.[3] He subsequently joined
the boards of the Smith banking houses in London,
Derby, Hull and Nottingham, eventually becoming
the senior partner of each. As a director of the East
India Company during its final year he 'devoted a considerable amount of time to the management of its
affairs'.[4] He died in October 1880.

---

[1] *The Times*, 24 Feb. 1832. [2] R.W. Davis, *Political Change and
Continuity*, 168, 216. [3] PROB 11/1960/208; IR26/1623/148.
[4] NatWest Archives, Smith/2/1987; H.T. Easton, *Hist. of a Banking
House*, 30.

H.J.S.

SMITH, Hon. Robert John (1796–1868).

WENDOVER	1818–1820
BUCKINGHAMSHIRE	1820–1831
CHIPPING WYCOMBE	1831–18 Sept. 1838

b. 16 Jan. 1796, o.s. of Robert Smith†, 1st Bar. Carrington,
and 1st w. Anne, da. of Lewyns Boldero Barnard of South
Cave, Yorks. *educ.* Eton 1805-11; Christ's, Camb. 1811.
m. (1) 17 June 1822, Hon. Elizabeth Katherine Weld
Forester (*d.* 22 July 1832), da. of Cecil Weld Forester†,
1st Bar. Forester, 1da.; (2) 10 Aug. 1840, Hon. Charlotte
Augusta Annabella Drummond Willoughby, da. of Peter
Robert Drummond Willoughby (formerly Drummond
Burrell†), 22nd Bar. Willoughby of Eresby, 3s. 2da. *suc.*
fa. as 2nd Bar. Carrington 18 Sept. 1838; took name of
Carrington by royal lic. 26 Aug. 1839. *d.* 17 Mar. 1868.
Ld. lt. Bucks. 1839-*d*; col. Bucks. militia 1839.

At the general election of 1820 Smith got his father
Lord Carrington's 'reluctant assent' to his offering
for Buckinghamshire, where their estate at Wycombe
Abbey gave them an interest, in the room of the retiring sitting Member. He stressed his 'independent
and disinterested conduct' as Member for the family
borough in the 1818 Parliament (where he had in
fact voted regularly with the Whig opposition to the
Liverpool ministry) and came in unopposed with the
sitting Tory Lord Temple, the son of the 2nd marquess of Buckingham. He subsequently established
himself as the representative of Buckinghamshire
Dissent.[1] Smith, who did not share his father's political conservatism, continued to vote with the mainstream Whigs on most major issues, but from the
1823 session his attendance fell away dramatically. It
is not clear whether it was he or Robert Percy Smith
who spoke in favour of the Grampound disfranchisement bill, 5 June; but he voted silently for parliamentary reform, 9 May 1821, 25 Apr. 1822, 24 Apr.,
2 June 1823, 27 Apr. 1826. His only recorded vote
for Catholic relief in this Parliament was on 21 Apr.
1825. Before his attendance lapsed he voted spasmodi-
cally for economy, retrenchment and reduced taxation. He divided for abolition of the death penalty for
forgery offences, 21 May 1823. He presented an anti-
slavery petition, 6 Apr., and divided to condemn the
prosecution in Demerara of the Methodist missionary John Smith, 11 June 1824. That autumn he took
up the cause of two Baptist preachers who had been
summarily goaled for vagrancy by an Anglican cleric
magistrate of Buckinghamshire.[2] He presented petitions from Newport Pagnell for enhanced protection
for domestic corn growers, 16 May 1820, and from
Chipping Norton complaining of agricultural distress,

15 Feb. 1822.[3] He voted in the protectionist minority against the corn bill, 11 May 1826. He secured the production of documents pertaining to the outstanding Austrian loan of 1795, 1 Feb., 14 Mar., but was persuaded to drop another similar motion on 22 June 1821. On 22 Feb. 1822 Smith, who four months earlier had seemed to his acquaintance Maria Edgeworth prematurely aged and 'much *worn* out', threatened to move resolutions deploring ministers' failure to call in the loan, but he did not do so.[4]

He was in the minority of magistrates who opposed Buckingham's veto of placing official advertisements in the oppositionist *Buckinghamshire Chronicle* at the October 1821 sessions. A year later he promoted a campaign for inquiry into county expenditure.[5] He was returned unopposed at the 1826 general election when, defying orchestrated 'No Popery' chants, he asserted his devotion to the cause of civil and religious liberty.[6] He voted for Catholic relief, 6 Mar. 1827, 12 May 1828, and presented a favourable petition, 8 May 1828. He presented and endorsed a petition from Buckinghamshire lace manufacturers for a reduction of the duty, 15 Mar., and voted against the corn bill, 2 Apr. 1827.[7] He brought up numerous Buckinghamshire petitions for repeal of the Test Acts, 7, 8, 15, 22 June 1827, 21 Feb., and divided to that effect, 26 Feb. 1828.[8] He voted against the Wellington ministry on the ordnance estimates, 4 July 1828. He divided for Catholic emancipation, 6 and (as pair) 30 Mar., presented favourable petitions, 17, 20 Mar., and voted to allow Daniel O'Connell to take his seat unhampered, 18 May 1829. He was in the minorities on the address, 4 Feb., and the estimates, 19, 22 Feb., 22, 29 Mar., and voted for the enfranchisement of Birmingham, Leeds and Manchester, 23 Feb., and the transfer of East Retford's seats to Birmingham, 5 Mar. 1830. A month later his father declared his own unconditional support for the government and told Wellington that he hoped to 'neutralize' his son.[9] He was not entirely unsuccessful, for Smith's only known votes in the remainder of the session were for Jewish emancipation, 17 May, against the grants for South American missions (as a pair), 7 June, and consular services, 11 June, and for abolition of the death penalty for forgery, 11 June; he had presented a Chesham petition on this subject, 24 May 1830.

At the general election that summer he was returned unopposed for the county, promising to act on 'independent principles' and expressing his 'detestation of slavery'. He was physically threatened by a mob assembled by his anti-Catholic Tory colleague.[10] Ministers listed him as one of their 'foes', but he was absent from the division on the civil list which brought them down, 15 Nov. 1830. He presented petitions in favour of the Grey ministry's reform bill, 19 Mar., and divided for its second reading, 22 Mar., and against Gascoyne's wrecking amendment, 19 Apr. 1831. He brought up an anti-slavery petition, 28 Mar. 1831. At the ensuing general election he gave up his county seat to enjoy a quiet return for Chipping Wycombe on the family interest; an uncle came in for Buckinghamshire after a contest.[11] He voted for the second reading of the reintroduced reform bill, 6 July, but was sparing in his active support of its details and cast wayward votes against the partial disfranchisement of Chippenham, 27 July, and Guildford, 29 July 1831. He voted for its third reading, 19 Sept., and passage, 21 Sept., but was a defaulter on a call of the House, 10 Oct., when he failed to divide for the motion of confidence in the government. He voted for the second reading of the revised reform bill, 17 Dec. 1831, consistently if not regularly for its details, and, despite being too ill to attend the Dorset election committee, 5 Mar., for its third reading, 22 Mar. 1832.[12] During the crisis of May he expressed to his uncle his 'indignant feeling at the conduct of the Tories' and told him that though 'still unwell ... I would, were I in bed, go to ... the House of Commons if the government want support there or any address proposed to His Majesty'; he duly attended to vote for the address calling on the king to appoint only ministers who would carry reform unimpaired, 10 May.[13] He divided with administration on the Russian-Dutch loan, 26 Jan., 20 July. He was 'disconsolable' at the sudden death from cholera of his 'young [28], beautiful' wife on 22 July 1832, twenty four hours after appearing at the opera 'in health and spirits'.[14]

Smith continued to sit for Chipping Wycombe until he succeeded his father to the peerage in 1838. He was one of the Liberal peers who opposed repeal of the corn laws in 1846. Five years later his county neighbour Benjamin Disraeli† (whom he had beaten at Wycombe in 1832 and 1835) described him as looking 'bored to death [and] absolutely disgusted by the necessity of living on his lands'.[15] He died in March 1868. He was succeeded by his eldest son Charles Robert (1843-1928), Liberal Member for Chipping Wycombe, 1865-8, who was created marquess of Lincolnshire in 1912.

Feb. 1822; *Edgeworth Letters*, 255. [5] Bucks. RO, Fremantle mss D/FR/46/9/9; 46/10/38; Davis, 62. [6] *Bucks. Chron.* 3, 10, 17, 24 June 1826. [7] *The Times*, 16 Mar. 1827. [8] Ibid. 8, 9, 16, 23 June 1827. [9] Add. 40309, f. 31. [10] *Bucks Gazette*, 7 Aug.; Stanhope mss C228, Carrington to Lady Stanhope, 10 Aug. 1830. [11] Add. 51663, Bedford to Holland [25 Apr. 1831]. [12] Southampton Univ. Lib. Broadlands mss SHA/PC/128; *CJ*, lxxxvii. 162. [13] NatWest Archives, Smith/2/2658. [14] *Raikes Jnl.* i. 65-66. [15] *Disraeli Letters*, v. 2043.

D.R.F.

SMITH, Robert Percy (1770–1845), of 20 Savile Row, Mdx. and Cheam, Surr.

GRANTHAM	1812–1818
LINCOLN	1820–1826

b. 7 May 1770, 1st s. of Robert Smith (*d.* 1827) of Bishop's Lydiard, Som. and Maria, da. of Isaac Olier of Bloomsbury, Mdx., late of Montauban. *educ.* King Edward's sch. Southampton; Eton 1779-88; King's, Camb. 1789, fellow 1792-7; France 1792; L. Inn 1793, called 1797. *m.* 9 Dec. 1797, Caroline Maria, da. and coh. of Richard Vernon[†] of Hilton Park, Staffs., 2s. (1 *d.v.p.*) 2da. *d.v.p. d.* 10 Mar. 1845.

Adv.-gen. Bengal 1803-11.

'Bobus' Smith's famously witty brother, the Rev. Sydney Smith, once said to him: 'Brother, you and I are exceptions to the laws of nature. You have risen by your gravity, and I have sunk by my levity'.[1] In fact Smith, blighted in spirit by the humiliating failure of his parliamentary début in 1812, and still more by the deaths of his daughters in 1814 and 1816, never fulfilled in public life the high expectations which were held of him. Yet, as Edward Littleton* noted in 1818, 'his friends did not on that account change their opinion of his talents':

I know no man whose mind is more luminous. The strength and soundness of his judgement can scarcely be surpassed. His perception is very rapid, and his power of reasoning surprising. Added to all this, his integrity is inviolable.[2]

Samuel Rogers ranked him with Sir James Mackintosh* and Thomas Malthus as 'the three acutest men with whom I was ever acquainted'; and Lord Holland, with whom he was a special favourite (though he was less popular with Holland's wife), reckoned him 'a library in himself'.[3] John William Ward* commended him in 1821 for

the vigour of his understanding, and the variety and extent of his knowledge. Besides, he is an excellent person, upright and kind-hearted. It is very provoking that his success in Parliament should have been so entirely disproportionate to his talents. It has made a less

happy and less useful man ... He shuns society which is so much benefited by his presence.[4]

Sydney Smith, perturbed by his brother's increasing fondness for 'solitude', supposed in March 1818 that

he will not go into Parliament again; then of course the evil will become worse. Whatever faults Bobus has, he has them in fee, his tenure is freehold, they are not to be touched or changed. This is true also of his virtues, which God be praised are many.[5]

As it happened, he gave up his purchased seat for Grantham and at the general election stood for Lincoln on the Monson interest. He was beaten into third place, at a personal cost of £3,000. Sydney, who could not get no word out of him on the subject, jocularly blamed his defeat on 'a trick played upon him' by the Lincoln Imp, who 'saw that he had not his clerical brother with him, and so watched his opportunity to do him a mischief'.[6] Later that year Caroline Fox reported to Holland from Littlehampton, where she was staying with the Smiths:

Bobus and his two sons are quite delightful. I have not seen him since his return from India so cheerful and conversible, full of everything animating and agreeable. Mrs. Smith says it is because he has books enough to read here, but not a whole library to absorb him and withdraw him from society. Be the cause what it may, the effect is delightful, and it does my head and heart good to see him so full of enjoyment himself, and imparting it to others.

He doted on his sons, in whom he sought compensation 'for what he has lost, losses which he has felt and still feels so deeply'.[7] In the winter of 1819 he was temporarily incapacitated by an attack of gout, to which he was always a martyr.[8] At the general election of 1820 he was returned *in absentia* (still gout-ridden) and free of expense for Lincoln, where a group of independent residents, disgusted by the efforts of the London freemen to barter the borough on the open market, subscribed to a fund to bring him in. In an address of thanks Smith, who had followed his own line in the House after Canning had disbanded his group in 1813, declared that 'unconnected with party, the only rule by which I have guided myself in Parliament is that of diligently attending to the questions as they arise, and voting upon them to the best of my judgement'.[9] Lord Morpeth[†] was glad to hear of his return to Parliament, 'for it is a great resource to him, and he has great ambition'.[10]

George Tierney, the Whig leader in the Commons, could not count Smith, who never joined Brooks's, as a partisan adherent, but supposed 'he will vote for us nine times in ten';[11] and so, by and large, he did. He divided with them on the civil list, 5, 8 May, the additional Scottish baron of exchequer, 15 May, the aliens bill, 1 June, 12 July, and the barrack bill, 17 July 1820. It is not clear whether it was he or Robert John Smith who, 'from a solicitude to establish parliamentary reform', but disavowing 'those wild theories which were advocated by would-be patriots', supported the Grampound disfranchisement bill, 5 June. It was surely 'Bobus' who condemned as 'a compilation of falsehood and nonsense' a Birmingham petition denouncing boroughmongers, 25 July. He favoured the exclusion of Thomas Ellis from the House as an Irish master in chancery, 30 June. In December 1820 he presented to Queen Caroline a congratulatory address from Lincoln, in which he fully concurred, on the abandonment of the bill of pains and penalties.[12] He did not vote in the division on the opposition censure motion, 6 Feb. 1821; but on the 13th he endorsed a Lincoln petition for the restoration of the queen's name to the liturgy, though he could not subscribe to its associated call for parliamentary reform, to which he 'looked with more apprehension of evil than hope of good'. He paired in favour of the restoration later that day. He voted for Catholic relief, 28 Feb. He divided for army reductions, 14, 15 Mar., and for at least eight other proposals for retrenchment during the rest of the session; but he sided with the Liverpool ministry against repeal of the additional malt duty, 3 Apr., and for the duke of Clarence's grant, 18 June. He supported Tennyson's amendment to the preamble of the Grampound disfranchisement bill, 19 Mar. He was in the minorities on placemen in Parliament, 31 May, and Sicily, 21 June. He voted for abolition of the death penalty for forgery, 23 May, 4 June. As a member of the select committee on the receivers-general of the land tax, he begged its critics not to obstruct implementation of its recommendations, 8 June 1821.[13] At the close of the session his wife reported that 'the House of Commons has not given Mr. Smith the gout'.[14]

Smith voted for the amendment to the address, 5 Feb., but divided with government against more extensive tax reductions, 11, 21 Feb. 1822. He voted for gradual reduction of the salt duties, 28 Feb., and admiralty economies, 1 Mar. He spoke and voted against a detail of the navy five per cents bill, 8 Mar.[15] He voted for abolition of one of the joint-postmasterships, 13 Mar., 2 May, and was in small minorities for army economies, 15, 18 Mar. That day he threatened to propose the extinction of the office of clerk of the rope yard at Woolwich but, on Croker's statement that he would thereby 'impede the progress of economy', he withdrew his motion with an ironical flourish, which raised a laugh.[16] On 22 Mar. he declined to support

Hume's motion to reduce the grant for garrisons, but a week later he backed his successful attack on the barracks estimates. He voted in the opposition minorities on the government of the Ionian Isles, 14 May, the embassy to the Swiss cantons, 16 May, the aliens bill, 5 June, 19 July, the Irish constables bill, 7 June, and chancery delays, 26 June. He presented a Lincoln petition against the poor removal bill, 31 May, and on 9 July he accused ministers of 'clandestinely' departing from the recommendation of the select committee to restrict the salaries of receivers-general to £600.[17] At about this time wide circulation was given to his 'caricature of a private conference between Joseph Hume* and Nicholas Vansittart* as a dialogue of penny-wise and pound-foolish'.[18] Soon afterwards Croker named him as one of the Members whom Canning would be able to 'command' should he go into opposition, but would not bring over with him if he joined the ministry.[19]

Smith presented and endorsed a Lincoln tradesman's position for repeal of the Insolvent Debtors Act, 10 Feb. 1823.[20] He voted in opposition minorities on the grant to the Royal Military College, 10 Mar., the merchant vessels apprenticeship bill, 24 Mar., and the military and naval pensions bill, 11, 18 Apr.; but he divided with government against repeal of the assessed taxes, 10, 18 Mar. He also sided with them against inquiry into the prosecution of the Dublin Orange rioters, 24 Mar., 22 Apr., and he took a part in questioning witnesses before the House, 7, 8, 9, 23 May. He opposed the grant for Irish glebe houses, 11 Apr., 1 July.[21] On the presentation of a Lincolnshire petition for parliamentary reform, 22 Apr., he declared that 'a more complete farce had never been played off' than at the meeting (which he had not attended) at which it had been voted; yet he voted for reform of the Scottish representative system, 2 June. He was in the minority of 37 for the abolition of punishment by whipping, 30 Apr. On the case of O'Grady, the Irish chief baron, 16 May, he suggested a precedent which might provide a basis for his removal, though he conceded that there were no grounds for impeachment.[22] He again called for some notice being taken of the issue, 17 June, and opposed dropping proceedings altogether, 9 July. He voted to equalize the East and West Indian sugar duties, 22 May, and to recommit the silk bill, 9 June, but divided with ministers against inquiry into the currency, 12 June. He almost certainly voted for investigation of chancery delays, 5 June. He voted for the Scottish juries bill, 20 June, and to include provision for jury trial in the New South Wales bill, 7 July. On 11 July 1823, as expected, he 'violently' opposed the clause in the East India mutiny bill permitting courts martial to try capital offences, but he was beaten by 40-13.[23] Smith voted to reduce the barrack grant, 27 Feb., in support of the complaint of breach of privilege against lord chancellor Eldon, 1 Mar., and against the aliens bill, 23 Mar., 2, 12 Apr. 1824. He favoured reform of the usury laws, 27 Feb., 8 Apr. On the game laws amendment bill, 25 Mar. he 'objected that any other penalty should be annexed to the violation of it than attached to ordinary trespassers'. He voted against the Welsh judicature bill, 11 Mar., but for Scottish judicial reform, 30 Mar. He spoke in favour of compensating court officials whose emoluments would be reduced by the county courts bill, 26 Mar., and on 24 May argued that it would be preferable to give the patronage of the places created by it 'to government at once, in its responsible capacity, than to leave them to be got at by jobbing'. He voted to end flogging in the army, 15 Mar., and successfully moved to relieve certain classes of vagrants from punishment by whipping, 3 June. He deemed the horses slaughtering bill 'unnecessary', 4 June 1824.

In April 1824 Smith was named as one of the 14 unsalaried commissioners appointed to investigate chancery administration, having been mentioned by the home secretary Peel as a person 'independent of the government' who 'would not lend himself to promote the hostile views of anyone, though he would act firmly on his own sense of what is right'.[24] He took his duties seriously (Lord Redesdale later called him the 'most troublesome' member of the commission),[25] but ill health, on account of which he was granted two weeks' leave, 21 Feb. 1825, restricted his attendance both there and in the House. He paired for Catholic relief, 1 Mar., 21 Apr., 10 May, and presented a Lincoln millers' petition against any change in the corn laws, 28 Apr. 1825.[26] In September he was 'confined in a horizontal position to my couch', but by November he had resumed attendance at the chancery commission. Caroline Fox was relieved that he did 'not seem the worse for it', though she feared, as ever, 'his overdoing exercise of mind and body, when once he is equal to any exercise of either'.[27] In March 1826 he was reported to be 'flourishing', having had 'less gout than usual', and to be 'pleased upon the whole with his chancery report'.[28] He defended it in the House against charges of prolixity, 18 Apr., and blandness, 18 May. He presented a Lincoln petition for the abolition of slavery, 3 Mar.[29] He spoke, 6 Apr., and voted, 7, 10 Apr., against the proposal to confer an official salary on the president of the board of trade. He presented a petition from some Lincoln landlords complaining that by a recent alteration of local jurisdiction they had been deprived of the vote, 18 Apr.[30] He had a hand in

Sykes's county elections bill, intended to deal with this problem, and made constructive comments on it, 26 Apr., 2 May 1826.

Ward commented that although Smith was 'no speaker, his known abilities and entire freedom from party views and party objects, give him no inconsiderable weight' in the House.[31] Morpeth wrote after his death that he rendered 'really eminent services as a most diligent and painstaking member of committees, which might have put many an idle mediocrity to the blush'. This is borne out by the frequency with which his name appears as a member of select committees.[32] On 10 Apr. 1826 Tierney told Holland:

> I walked home from the House with Bobus and am glad to find there is no truth in the report I had heard that he thought of quitting Parliament. I know no person who appears to me to enjoy a seat more than he does.[33]

He was mistaken, for three weeks later Smith announced his intention to retire from Parliament at the impending dissolution.[34] The harmful effects of attendance on his health may have decided him to step down: Sydney noted in May 1826 that he was not 'quite so well' as earlier, having been 'a good deal at the House of Commons, which never does him any good'; and two months later Lady Holland found him relishing 'extremely' his rural retreat at Cheam because 'his life has been improved by the complete restoration of his health'.[35]

Smith reacted stoically to the quite unexpected death of his younger son Leveson in April 1827, though it was another savage blow to one of his 'strong and ungoverned feelings'.[36] Less hard to bear was the loss a few weeks later of his eccentric father, who had repeatedly taken unfair advantage of his financial generosity and whose will bore all the signs of mental derangement. Smith, who had made a substantial fortune in India, was excluded from it at his own request, but he persuaded the old man to increase Sydney's legacy from £6,000 to £10,000.[37] He deemed Canning's death soon afterwards 'a great public misfortune'. Buoyed by much improved health, he mocked the hysteria with which the Ultra Tories reacted to Catholic emancipation in 1829: 'the Pope is expected at St. Paul's by ... [then], but many people think he will not come'.[38]

In December 1833 Tom Macaulay*, who was about to go out to India, met Smith at dinner:

> Bobus was very amusing. He is a great authority on Indian matters ... I asked him about the climate. Nothing, he said, could be pleasanter except in August and September. He never ate or drank so much in his life. Indeed his looks do credit to Bengal; for a healthier

man of his age I never saw ... We talked of the insects and snakes: and he said a thing which reminded me of his brother Sydney. 'Always, Sir, manage to have at your table some flashy, blooming, young writer or cadet, just come out, that the mosquitoes may stick to him, and leave the rest of the company alone'.[39]

On the other hand, in May 1834 Thomas Creevey* was made 'sick of learning' by the incessant witty prattle of Smith and Richard Sharp* at Rogers's table.[40] Smith, who lost his wife in 1833, increasingly kept himself to himself in 'his Elysium at Cheam', though he retained his sense of humour. Sending the Hollands a likeness of 'my very morose countenance', he wrote:

I have I believe outlived a great deal of ill temper since I was painted, but I can hardly think I ever looked so grim as the painter has made me. Sure I am that in more than 50 years I never met you with such a face, nor ever shall.[41]

His brother noted that he 'loves paradoxes', as he demonstrated in an exposition of his mature political views in 1841:

I am not sorry the Whigs are out. The country was tired of them, I think, and always will be after a short time. There is too much botheration in their politics for our people, who, though they have reformed more than all the nations of Europe put together, do not like scheming and planning reforms when the work is not in hand, and called for by some pressing occasion; they have something else to do, and talking about reform disturbs them. I do myself think the state of things best suited to our condition is a Tory government, checked by a strong opposition, and under the awe of a tolerably liberal public opinion.[42]

Smith, who inherited about £33,000 on the death of his brother Courtenay in 1843, was afflicted in his last years with progressive blindness, which he bore 'heroically'.[43] He died, resigned and composed, in March 1845, within three weeks of Sydney, whose son-in-law Dr. Henry Holland wrote that he had 'scarcely met with one who might compare in power and fullness of intellect with him'.[44] In his will, dated 8 June 1843, he provided for female relatives of his mother and two of his grandchildren.[45] He was commemorated by his only surviving son in an edition of his *Early Writings* (1850), which consisted chiefly of Latin verses composed between 1787 and 1792. Greville wrote that he was

perhaps more agreeable and more cultivated than Sydney, though without his exuberant wit and drollery: still he had great *finesse d'esprit*, and was very amusing, but in a quieter and less ambitious style.[46]

Holland had this to say of him in 1826:

If he seldom displayed his pleasantry and imagination, enough escaped him to satisfy even a superficial observer that he had in store, though he perhaps disdained to use it, as much of both those commodities as glittered in the conversation of his brother ... Perhaps the strict discipline to which Robert Smith had inured his mind even at Eton perverted rather than directed, encumbered rather than enriched it. Notions not very friendly to our species and crudely adopted from books while a boy, though quite foreign from his natural character, which was sanguine and gay as well as ambitious, checked him in the career of his profession, aggravated many little unavoidable but not insuperable disappointments, dimmed the brilliancy of his spirits, and though they could not extinguish the native warmth of his heart, confined its influence to too small a circle, and gave up, not to party, but to the parlour and the fireside, what was meant and admirably formed for mankind.[47]

Lady Holland, who had mellowed towards him with the passage of time, felt his death as 'a cruel blow', for 'he was so staunch a friend, and such a delightful companion'.[48]

[1] Sir F. Hill, *Georgian Lincoln*, 225. [2] Hatherton diary, 6 Feb. [1818]. [3] *Recollections of Table-Talk of Samuel Rogers* (1856), 194-5; Lord Ilchester, *Chrons. Holland House*, 86, 153-4. [4] Ward, *Llandaff Letters*, 292-3. [5] *Smith Letters*, i. 288. [6] *HP Commons, 1790-1820*, ii. 255; *Smith Letters*, i. 294-5. [7] Add. 51741, Caroline Fox to Holland [15, 17 Sept. 1819]. [8] *Smith Letters*, i. 327; Add. 51801, Caroline Smith to Holland, 15 Jan. 1820. [9] Hill, 225-8; *Lincoln, Rutland and Stamford Mercury*, 10, 17 Mar. 1820. [10] Castle Howard mss to Lady Morpeth [13 Mar. 1820]. [11] Grey mss, Tierney to Grey, 5 Apr. 1820. [12] *Drakard's Stamford News*, 24 Nov., i, 8, 15 Dec. 1820; *Fox Jnl.* 52. [13] *The Times*, 9 June 1821. [14] Add. 51801, Caroline Smith to Lady Holland, 8 July [1821]. [15] *The Times*, 9 Mar. 1822. [16] Ibid. 19 Mar. 1822. [17] Ibid. 1 June, 10 July 1822. [18] Buckingham, *Mems. Geo. IV*, i. 355; Bagot, *Canning and Friends*, ii. 134. [19] Add. 40319, f. 57. [20] *The Times*, 11 Feb. 1823. [21] Ibid. 12 Apr. 1823. [22] Ibid. 17 May 1823. [23] Ibid. 12 July 1823; Buckingham, i. 477. [24] Add. 40315, f. 135; 51801, Smith to Holland, 6 Aug. [1824]. [25] *Colchester Diary*, iii. 417. [26] *The Times*, 29 Apr. 1825 [27] BL OIOC Mss. Eur. C247/3, Smith to Rev. C.R. Smith, 2 Sept.; Add. 51746, Caroline Fox to Lady Holland, 6 Nov. [1825]. [28] Add. 51580, Carlisle to Lady Holland, 28 Mar. 1826. [29] *The Times*, 4 Mar. 1826. [30] Ibid. 19 Apr. 1826. [31] Ward, 293. [32] *Early Writings of R.P. Smith* ed. R.V. Smith, p. vi. [33] Add. 51584. [34] *Lincoln, Rutland and Stamford Mercury*, 5 May 1826. [35] *Smith Letters*, i. 448; *Lady Holland to Son*, 43. [36] *Gent. Mag.* (1827), i. 448; *Lady Holland to Son*, 43. [37] A. Bell, *Sydney Smith*, 2, 59, 64, 141; OIOC Mss. Eur. C. 247/3, Smith to fa. 19, 25, 30 Dec. 1817, 12, 14, 16, 21, 31 Jan., 26, 27 Sept. 1824, replies, 13, 18 Jan. 1818, 12 Mar., 28 Apr., 17 May 1824; PROB 11/1732/613. [38] OIOC Mss. Eur. C 247/3, Smith to Rev. C.R. Smith, 10 Aug. [14 Feb. 1829]. [39] *Macaulay Letters*, ii. 365. [40] *Creevey Pprs.* ii. 275. [41] *Smith Letters*, ii. 645; Add. 51801, Smith to Holland, 20 Sept. 1839. [42] *Smith Letters*, ii. 624, 734. [43] Ibid. ii. 778-9, 784, 807, 816, 820, 822. [44] *Gent. Mag.* (1845), i. 440-1; P.W. Clayden, *Rogers and his Contemporaries*, ii. 269. [45] PROB 8/238 (22 Apr. 1845); 11/2016/344; *Gent. Mag.* (1845), i. 667-8. [46] *Greville Mems.* v. 208. [47] Holland, *Further Mems.* 315-16. [48] *Lady Holland to Son*, 224.

D.R.F.

SMITH, Robert Vernon (1800–1873), of Savile Row, Mdx. and Farming Woods, nr. Thrapston, Northants.

TRALEE	9 June 1829–1831
NORTHAMPTON	1831–28 June 1859

b. 23 Feb. 1800, 1st and o. surv. s. of Robert Percy Smith* and Caroline Maria, da. and coh. of Richard Vernon† of Hilton Park, Staffs. *educ.* Eton 1814; Christ Church, Oxf. 1819; I. Temple 1822. *m.* 15 July 1823, Emma Mary Wilson, illegit. da. and coh. of John Fitzpatrick†, 2nd earl of Upper Ossory [I], 4s. (1 *d.v.p.*) 1da. *d.v.p. suc.* fa. 1845; *cr.* Bar. Lyveden 28 June 1859; took name of Vernon by royal lic. 14 July 1859; GCB 13 July 1872. *d.* 10 Nov. 1873.

Ld. of treasury Nov. 1830-Nov. 1834; jt.-sec. to bd. of control Apr. 1835-Sept. 1839; under-sec. of state for war and colonies Sept. 1839-Sept. 1841; PC 21 Aug. 1841; sec. at war 6-28 Feb. 1852; pres. bd. of control Mar. 1855-Mar. 1858,

Commr. of lunacy 1830-61.

On Smith's birth his witty uncle, the Rev. Sydney Smith, quipped that 'the immense fortune of the Smiths is free from the danger of being lost from want of heirs'. His father did subsequently make a substantial amount of money in India, but Smith's health, like that of his siblings, was so poor during his boyhood and youth that at times it seemed unlikely that he would live to inherit.[1] In 1816 he was thought to have 'turned the corner' and looked 'stout, healthy and well', but two years later he was again 'very alarmingly ill'. His father 'Bobus', whose life was blighted by the deaths of his daughters in 1814 and 1816, doted on him and his younger brother Leveson, and took considerable pains with their education at home. Caroline Fox wrote that 'too much cannot be said of the excellence of their heads, hearts, tempers and dispositions'. Illness continued to plague him at Oxford, where he was 'very kind and attentive' to Lord Holland's wayward son, Henry Edward Fox*, but he seems thereafter to have enjoyed better health.[2] Smith was generally 'agreeable' in society, but had not the same measure of charm as his father and uncle.[3] In a moment of peevishness in 1822 Fox, while acknowledging his debt to Smith 'for his kindness to me when I most needed it', commented that his 'unauthorized and unbounded conceit' was 'quite insufferable'.[4] Yet they remained friends. Like his father, Smith was of a generally liberal disposition in politics, and in March 1823 he suffered in silence at a dinner given by his Tory friend Lawrence Peel*, when the aged duchess of Richmond lambasted 'all our friends the opposition ... on the trite subject of the Catholic question'. As he told Fox:

Being alone, my politeness prevented my attacking them all in their own house, as I should have thought it the height of incivility in Daniel to have remonstrated with the lions on their naughty practice of eating gentlemen in their den.

Soon afterwards Smith, who liked his women's breasts to be '*hard*' and *springy*' (Fox preferred 'the voluptuousness of *soft* breasts'), became engaged to Holland's ward Mary Wilson, the illegitimate child of his mother's half-brother Lord Ossory.[5] His father, putting Holland 'in possession of what little I have to say on the subject', commented:

If I could have shaped events just as I wished I should have been glad if this matter had been brought to bear when they were a few years older, but in the absence of other objections I do not feel this from age to be of sufficient weight to induce me to say no. It is in some measure removed by a steadiness in Vernon's character which is beyond his age, and as a further corrective I have proposed, and I believe they both receive the proposal with pleasure, that if they marry they shall live with us at first ... I am bound to add that Vernon has never given us an hour's uneasiness, and that I think him as likely to make a good husband as any young man I have ever known.

He settled £20,000 on the couple, to supplement Mary's fortune of £12,000. They could also look forward to the reversion, on the deaths of Ossory's two legitimate spinster daughters, of his Northamptonshire estate at Farming Woods, near Daventry. Although 'Bobus' Smith attached 'a great deal of consequence' to Vernon's pursuing the law as a profession, and was 'perfectly satisfied with the way in which he takes to it', nothing seems to have come of this scheme.[6] Vernon 'hurt his knee and chin so much' in a fall from his horse that the wedding had to be postponed for three weeks: he was 'pale and in pain' during the ceremony.[7] The 'completely uncalculated' death of his brother, aged 26, in April 1827, brought him low, as he told Fox:

It not only turns all my pleasing recollections into painful regrets but makes me shudder for the future. It unhinges all my attachments to life, as it makes me tremble for their doubtful duration ... My nature always did and my situation and age now prevent my forming very close intimacies. Fate has deprived me of the most perfect unreserve I ever enjoyed ... When I recall the merry days of our boyhood, I cannot help the reflection ... that I am now left alone of the flourishing family to which I belonged when first you knew me.[8]

He remained 'nervous and unwell' for several weeks, but was 'much better' by the end of July.[9]

Two years later Smith purchased an Irish seat from Sir Edward Denny*. He was sworn in, 22 June 1829. In the tradition of his father, a quondam Canningite, he attached himself, though somewhat loosely, to William Huskisson* and Lord Palmerston*. He voted for the transfer of East Retford's seats to Birmingham, 11 Feb., 5, 15 Mar., the enfranchisement of Birmingham, Leeds and Manchester, 18 Feb., and inquiry into the duke of Newcastle's electoral domination of Newark, 1 Mar., but was in the majority against Lord Blandford's parliamentary reform scheme, 18 Feb. 1830. He divided against the grant for volunteers, 9 Mar. On 12 Mar. he was 'diverted', as he put it, from voting to censure ministers for appointing a salaried treasurer of the navy by the home secretary Peel's challenge 'not to judge him for an individual act, but to arraign him for his whole economical administration'. But on 22 Mar., after voting for admiralty reductions, he moved to reduce the grant for the navy pay office by £1,200:

> If I cannot administer to the wants of a suffering people, I will at least defer to their wishes. I shall vote against the committee [of inquiry into distress proposed by Davenport, 16 Mar.], because I think legislative enactments no cure for popular distress; but I do not think that the inattention of the legislature need provoke the prejudice of the people. For this reason, though £12,000,000 might not cure their grievances, I will not allow £1,200 to be added to their burdens.

He withdrew the amendment when Peel pledged government to effect a reduction, but was in the minority in the division forced by Hume that day. Thereafter he divided steadily with the revived opposition for economy and reduced taxation, and was in their minorities on the Terceira incident, 28 Apr., and the civil government of Canada, 25 May. He voted for Jewish emancipation, 5 Apr., 17 May, but against abolition of the death penalty for forgery, 7 June. On 18 May he presented a petition from Tralee against assimilation of the English and Irish stamp duties. He was in the minority for halving the grant for the Society for the Propagation of the Gospels, 14 June. He voted against an increase in the amount of security required of newspaper publishers under the libel law amendment bill, 6, 9 July, but opposed Hume's attempt to reduce judicial salaries, 7 July 1830.

At the 1830 general election he renewed his purchase of Tralee. On the motion of 11 Nov. 1830 for reappointment of the select committee on the Irish poor, to which he had been named, 11 Mar. 1830, Smith defended it against charges of dilatoriness, while admitting that his original 'prejudice in favour

of poor laws in Ireland' had been weakened by the evidence so far brought before it. He was a member of the new committee. The following day he was one of the minority of 39 who voted to reduce the duty on wheat imported into the West Indies. He had been listed by ministers as one of the 'Huskisson party', and he divided against them on the civil list, 15 Nov. On the accession of the Grey administration he accepted a place at the treasury worth £1,200 a year, his kinsman Lord Lansdowne having assured Grey that if Denny made difficulties about his re-election, he would be 'perfectly willing to be clerk of the ordnance' instead.[10] (He was re-elected without trouble.) Criticizing the new appointments, Denis Le Marchant[†] remarked, 'Lords Lansdowne and Holland have to answer for Vernon Smith, who, small deer as he is, has more enemies than many an experienced statesman'.[11] He presented a Tralee petition for the abolition of slavery, 11 Dec. 1830, and voted with his colleagues for the second reading of the ministerial reform bill, 22 Mar. 1831. On 13 Apr. he attended the Northamptonshire county meeting convened to support the measure. After considerable turmoil inside Northampton town hall the reformers, ignoring the protests of their opponents, adjourned to the open air (and heavy rain), where Smith, addressing a large assembly for the first time in his life, pronounced himself

> for the whole bill, for cutting off all the rotten boroughs root and branch. He trusted that the people would admit of no departure from the principle of the measure. There would be plenty of chaffering in the committee, plenty of attempts to destroy the efficacy of the bill. He wished, therefore, to impress on the meeting the necessity of demanding the bill unmutilated ... The country was bent upon reform, and reform must be had, and before long.

His admission that the electors of Tralee, where 'not a soul in the whole borough knew him', had 'no confidence in him', and the explicit recommendation of him by Robert Otway Cave* indicate that Smith had an eye on the county or borough representation. When the events at Northampton were discussed in the House, 19 Apr. 1831, he denied having mocked the Tory county Member Cartwright and defended the decision to abandon the hall on the grounds of public safety. He voted against Gascoyne's wrecking amendment that day.

At the ensuing general election he offered for Northampton as a reformer, denying allegations that he was a Catholic and defending the ministry's record on retrenchment, arguing that they had accomplished all that could be done in an unreformed Parliament. At the close of polling, 6 May, he was in second place, but he had to endure a scrutiny called for by Sir Robert Gunning*, the defeated anti-reform candidate, which did not terminate until 31 May. Returning thanks for his success, Smith declared that 'the middle and lower classes were worthy of the utmost extension of their privileges proposed by the bill'.[12] When Lord Chandos presented a petition from some Northampton electors complaining of the use made of neighbouring barracks to receive, treat and accommodate the supporters of Smith and his colleague Robinson at the election, 11 July, Smith retorted that he had ordered all the voters so housed to be ejected as soon as he learnt what was going on. He also pointed out that it had been customary for the supporters of the ministerial candidate to be so housed, in the interests of tranquillity, and that Gunning's voters had occupied the barracks in 1826. He asserted that the issue was being raised to prejudice the pending hearing of Gunning's petition, but in the event this was abandoned. Smith voted for the second reading of the reintroduced reform bill, 6 July, at least twice against adjournment, 12 July, and assiduously supported its details. He made a brief comment on borough population returns, 14 July. He divided with ministers on the Dublin election controversy, 23 Aug. On 19 Sept. he protested against premature discussion of the Deacles' case. He voted for the reform bill's passage, 21 Sept., for the second reading of the Scottish measure, 23 Sept., and for Lord Ebrington's confidence motion, 10 Oct. He was appointed to the select committees on West Indian commerce, 6 Oct., 15 Dec. 1831. He voted for the second reading of the revised reform bill, 17 Dec. 1831, and again supported its details, acting as a majority teller for the proposed restrictions on the freeman franchise, 7 Feb., and division of counties, 7 June 1832. He divided for the bill's third reading, 22 Mar. He voted against Hobhouse's vestry bill, 23 Jan. He was in the ministerial majorities on the Russian-Dutch loan, 26 Jan., 12, 16, 20 July, and relations with Portugal, 9 Feb. On 12 Feb. he belatedly joined Brooks's. He voted for the navy civil departments bill, 6 Apr. He replied to Hume's criticisms of the expense of parliamentary printing, 13 Apr., and the pension granted to Justice Stephens, 18 Apr. He presented petitions from Northampton in favour of Lord Nugent's bill for the registration of births, 18 Apr., 9 May, and gave it his backing, 18 May, 20 June, when he declared his intention of proposing that persons already alive could be registered retrospectively within a year, which would constitute 'a very material benefit' to 'a large class of the Dissenters of this country'. He voted for the address calling on the king to appoint only ministers who would carry the reform bill unimpaired, 10 May, for the second reading

of the Irish bill, 25 May, and against a Conservative amendment to increase the Scottish county representation, 1 June. He was appointed to the select committee on the renewal of the Bank of England's charter, 22 May. On 6 July he defended the grant of £1,000 for a survey of the possibility of establishing an efficient metropolitan water supply. He was a majority teller against adjourning the Irish tithes bill next day, and against the reception of a petition for their abolition, 2 Aug. Responding to the opposition attack on ministers over the Russian-Dutch loan, 16 July 1832, he declared:

> There can be but two objects in supporting this motion ... to turn out the present administration; and ... to make a splash upon the hustings ... Let Honourable gentlemen opposite ... raise at the hustings their promised cry of mock-economy, and we will meet them with our old battle cries, with no promises, but with boasts of performance ... of peace preserved, of retrenchment advanced, and of reform carried.

He was a majority teller on the issue that day.

At the 1832 general election Smith was re-elected in first place for Northampton as a Liberal. He successfully contested the borough at the next seven elections and held office in successive Liberal ministries until 1858. His tenure of the board of control in Palmerston's first administration, however, was a failure and he was removed to the Lords on the formation of his second in 1859.[13] He published editions of Horace Walpole's *Letters to the Countess of Ossory* (1848) and his father's *Early Writings* (1850). When the historian Sir Archibald Alison met him in 1861 he wrote:

> I had not been prepossessed in his favour, from his parliamentary appearances as secretary for India, but I was agreeably surprised by finding him not only polished and agreeable, but quick and intelligent in conversation. I did not see him long enough to be able to determine whether this was the result of native talent, or, as is often the case, of the advantage of having lived in superior and intellectual society.[14]

Smith died at his Northamptonshire country seat in November 1873. His property and the barony passed to his eldest son Fitzpatrick Henry Vernon (1824-1900).[15]

to Fox, 24 May 1827. ⁹ BL OIOC MSS Eur. C.247/3, R. P. to Rev. C.R. Smith, 29 July 1827. ¹⁰ Grey mss, Lansdowne to Grey [21 Nov. 1830]. ¹¹ *Three Diaries*, 6. ¹² . *Northampton Mercury*, 16, 23, 30 Apr., 7, 21, 28 May, 4 June 1831. ¹³ *Macaulay Letters*, vi. 220; *Greville Mems.* vii. 251. ¹⁴ A. Alison, *Autbiog.* ii. 325. ¹⁵ *The Times*, 13 Nov. 1873.

D.R.F./P.J.S.

SMITH, Samuel (1754–1834), of Woodhall Park, Herts. and 39 Berkeley Square, Mdx.

St. Germans	3 Sept. 1788–1790
Leicester	1790–1818
Midhurst	1818–1820
Wendover	1820–1832

b. 14 Apr. 1754, 4th s. of Abel Smith† (d. 1788), banker, of Nottingham and London and Mary, da. of Thomas Bird of Barton, Warws.; bro. of George Smith*, John Smith* and Robert Smith†. m. 2 Dec. 1783, Elizabeth Frances, da. of Edmund Turnor of Panton, Lincs., 3s. 7da. (2 d.v.p.). d. 12 Mar. 1834.
Lt.-col. commdt. Nottingham vols. 1799.

Smith was senior partner in the family's original Nottingham bank and had a substantial share in its branches in London, Derby and, until 1825, Hull.[1] At the general election of 1820 his eldest brother Lord Carrington transferred him from Midhurst to his other nomination borough of Wendover, where he came in with his younger brother George. He continued to act generally with the conservative wing of the Whig opposition to Lord Liverpool's administration, but he was not a dedicated attender. He was in the opposition minorities on the civil list, 5, 8 May, the additional Scottish baron of exchequer, 15 May, military expenditure, 16 May, the barracks establishment, 16 June, and economies in revenue collection, 4 July 1820. He divided against government on the Queen Caroline affair, 23, 26 Jan., 6, 13 Feb. 1821. He was at odds with George and their brother John in voting against Catholic relief (which he had once supported), 28 Feb. 1821, 30 Apr. 1822 (as a pair), 1 Mar., 21 Apr., 10 May 1825. He divided with opposition on the revenue, 6 Mar., and for army reductions, 14 Mar., but, like George, was in the ministerial majority against repeal of the additional malt duty, 3 Apr. 1821. He paired for the forgery punishment mitigation bill, 23 May. He voted against the payment of arrears in the duke of Clarence's grant, 18 June 1821.

Smith voted for the amendment to the address, 5 Feb. 1822. He may have divided for more extensive tax remissions, 11 Feb., but he was in the majority against a similar motion, 21 Feb. He voted to condemn Sir Robert Wilson's* dismissal from the army, 13 Feb., and interference with Members' letters, 25 Feb. He divided for admiralty economies, 1 Mar., abolition of one of the joint-postmasterships, 13 Mar., inquiry into diplomatic expenditure, 15 May, use of the sinking fund to pay the deadweight pensions, 3 June, and repeal of the salt duties, 3, 28 June. He voted for criminal law reform, 4 June. He was in the minorities for inquiries into Irish tithes, 19 June, and the lord advocate's dealings with the Scottish press, 25 June, and to curb the influence of the crown in the House, 24 June 1822. His only recorded votes in the next two sessions were for proper use of the Leeward Islands defence fund and inquiry into the coronations costs, 9 June 1823, to accuse lord chancellor Eldon of a breach of privilege, 1 Mar., and to condemn the prosecution of the Methodist missionary John Smith in Demerara, 11 June 1824. He divided against the Irish franchise bill as an adjunct of Catholic relief, 26 Apr., and against the duke of Cumberland's grant, 30 May, 2, 6 June 1825. He voted against proceeding with the ministerial proposals to deal with the recent banking crisis, 13 Feb. 1826. He divided for inquiry into distress in the silk trade, 24 Feb., was a teller for Hume's minority of 22 for reduction of the grant for the Royal Military College, 6 Mar., and voted against the emergency admission of warehoused corn, 8 May 1826. He came in again for Wendover at the general election a month later and, chairing the celebration dinner, promised to continue to act on 'independent principles' in Parliament.[2]

Smith voted against Catholic claims, 6 Mar. 1827, and paired with the hostile minority, 12 May 1828. He voted against the Wellington ministry for inquiry into the proposed restriction of small bank notes, 5 June 1828. Planta, the patronage secretary, thought he would side 'with government' for Catholic emancipation in 1829; but he divided against it, 6, 18, 27 and (as a pair) 30 Mar. He voted for the amendment to the address deploring official indifference to distress, 4 Feb. 1830. Two months later Carrington told the premier that Smith, like himself and George, would 'support the government'.[3] He voted against abolition of the death penalty for forgery, 7 June 1830. At the general election next month he was returned for Wendover with his eldest son Abel after a vexatious contest.[4] Ministers listed him as one of the 'good doubtfuls' who was in fact a 'friend', and he was in their minority in the crucial division on the civil list, 30 Nov. 1830. He was credited with an unlikely intervention, 18 Feb. 1831, urging the Grey ministry to introduce poor laws to Ireland, 'since nothing can be so dreadful as the accounts we are constantly receiving, that our fellow-citizens ... are dying of famine'. He was a spectator in the Lords for lord chancellor Brougham's speech on chancery reform, 22 Feb.[5] With Abel, and in accordance with Carrington's wishes, he voted against the second reading of the ministry's reform bill, 22 Mar., and for Gascoyne's wrecking amendment, 19 Apr. 1831. Returned unopposed for Wendover at the ensuing general election, he divided against the second reading of the reintroduced reform bill, 6 July, for use of the 1831 census to determine borough disfranchisement, 18 July, and against the partial disfranchisement of Chippenham, 27 July. From mid-August he paired with the convalescent Tom Macaulay.[6] He voted against the passage of the reform bill, 21 Sept., and the second reading of the revised measure, 17 Dec. 1831. In January 1832 he signed the Hertfordshire address to the king which professed support for moderate reform but called for suppression of the political unions and praised William's resistance to a mass creation of peers.[7] He voted against the third reading of the reform bill, 22 Mar. His only other known votes before his retirement from Parliament after Wendover's disfranchisement, having sat for 44 consecutive years without distinguishing himself, were against government on the Russian-Dutch loan, 26 Jan., 12 July, and in the majority against the production of information on military punishments, 16 Feb. 1832.

Smith died at his palatial Hertfordshire mansion of Woodhall in March 1834.[8] By his will, dated 30 Dec. 1830 and proved under £500,000, he made generous provision for his wife and seven surviving children. He devised the Hertfordshire manor of Beeches, Brent Pelham, to his second son Samuel George, for whom he had already bought the Goldings estate, and his Nottinghamshire properties to his third son Henry. Abel, his residuary legatee, succeeded him in the Woodhall estate.[9]

[1] J.A.S. Leighton Boyce, *Smiths the Bankers*, 194, 243, 270. [2] *Bucks. Chron.* 10 June 1826. [3] Add. 40309, f. 31. [4] *Bucks Gazette*, 31 July 1830. [5] *Three Diaries*, 10. [6] *Macaulay Letters*, ii. 87. [7] Hatfield House mss 2M/Gen. Smith to Salisbury, 7 Jan. 1832. [8] *Gent. Mag.* (1834), ii. 317. [9] PROB 11/1830/239; IR26/1367/153.

D.R.F.

SMITH, William (1756–1835), of Parndon, Essex and 6 Park Street, Mdx.[1]

SUDBURY	1784–1790
CAMELFORD	8 Jan. 1791–1796
SUDBURY	1796–1802
NORWICH	1802–1806
NORWICH	1807–1830

b. 22 Sept. 1756, o.s. of Samuel Smith, wholesale grocer, of Cannon Street, London and Clapham Common, Surr. and Martha, da. of William Adams of London, coh. of her cos. Anne, Viscountess Cobham. *educ.* French's sch., Ware, Herts. 1764-9; Daventry acad. Northants. 1769-72. *m.* 12 Jan. 1781, Frances, da. of John Coape of Oxton, Notts., 5s. 5da. (1 *d.v.p.*). *suc.* uncle James Adams 1779; fa. 1798; uncle Benjamin Smith 1803. *d.* 31 May 1835.

Dir. London Assurance 1803, Albion Insurance Co. 1811, British Herring Fishing Co. 1812; dep. gov. Soc. for British Fisheries 1817.

Commr. Highland roads and bridges 1803-18.

Chairman of Dissenting deputies 1805-32.

In 1820, when Smith, the Dissenters' parliamentary spokesman, secured his fifth but first unopposed return for Norwich, he was 63, his mercantile fortune was spent and his wholesale grocery firm bankrupt. Sales of his library, paintings, and Parndon and Park Street residences failed to prevent his financial decline and consequent dependence on his family; namely his sons-in-law W.E. Nightingale, George Nicholson and John Carter* and his eldest son Benjamin Smith[†], who, before the firm was wound up in 1823, made a fortune managing Cooke's distillery at Millbank.[2] To his friends, the Liverpool banker William Roscoe[†], who faced similar financial ruin, and William Wilberforce*, Smith intimated that his 'Necessarian' outlook and Unitarian beliefs sustained him in adversity, as they had done through the long campaigns for religious equality and the abolition of slavery in which, as chairman of the Dissenting Deputies of the Three Denominations (Baptists, Independents and Presbyterians) and a founder member of the London Society for the Abolition of Slavery, he remained a major figure. He was the only individual who belonged to the United Committee for repeal of the Test Acts in both 1786-90 and 1827-8.[3] A former supporter of Pitt, then Fox, he had been against going to war with revolutionary France and abhorred all violence. A 'consistent Whig', he shared their commitment to retrenchment, relieving distress and checking corruption, and backed Tierney for the Commons leadership in 1818. He did not support the radicals' demands for universal suffrage and short parliaments, but, as a committed reformer (he was a founder member in 1792 of the Society of the Friends of the People), he acknowledged their 'honest intentions' and was prepared to act with them on moral issues.[4] A stout, robust man, convinced of the educative merits of debate, he indefatigably spoke, presented petitions and requested official papers on the Dissenters' concerns and other issues, his prowess as a clear and erudite public speaker marred only by predictability and repetition.[5] Frequently acting as a teller, he supported measures for the better treatment of animals, children and felons, repeal of the usury laws, chancery reform and the abolition of military flogging throughout this period and divided steadily against the aliens bill.

On 5 May 1820 Smith criticized the Liverpool ministry for failing to keep their 1816 promise to inquire into the civil list and, as subsequently, ordered accounts of extents-in-aid to scrutinize for signs of revenue abuse. Becoming convinced that their deployment encouraged Irish unrest, he vainly attempted to introduce corrective legislation, 24 Apr. 1822.[6] He compared reductions in the standing army to parliamentary reform as 'one of those points, the advantage of which was always admitted, though the time for adopting it never arrived', 14 June 1820.[7] He condoned government spending on the British Museum, 26 May, the astronomer Herschel's pension, 5 July, and Westminster Abbey, 11 July, but opposed lavish expenditure on the household and the grants to the royal dukes, 3 July. As a minority teller with Hume the next day for economies in revenue collection, he criticized the way in which country bankers had become receivers of land tax, prompting a sharp response from the chancellor of the exchequer Vansittart.[8] (He voted for annual parliamentary scrutiny of revenue collection costs, 12 Mar. 1822.) Drawing on his experience as a Cornish Member, he spoke in favour of transferring the franchise of corrupt Grampound to Leeds, 19 May 1820, advocated a scot and lot franchise there, 2 Mar. 1821, and endorsed resolutions pronouncing Grantham guilty of electoral corruption, 12 July 1820.[9] He voted to disfranchise civil officers of the ordnance, 12 Apr., for parliamentary reform, 18 Apr., 9, 10 May 1821, 25 Apr. 1822, 20 Feb., 24 Apr., 2 June 1823, 13, 27 Apr. 1826, and Scottish burgh reform, 20 Feb. 1822, and was a minority teller for information on Inverness burgh elections, 26 Mar. 1823. He complained when endorsing the City corporation's reform petition, 17 May 1824, that he was 'denied a London vote' despite his 'considerable freehold', and spoke, 14 Mar., and voted to denounce electoral bribery, 26 May 1826.[10]

Smith backed the London merchants' distress petition suggesting lower taxes and a dual currency as remedial measures, 8 May 1820. He supported inquiry into agricultural distress, although he expected 'nothing' from it, 31 May, and criticized Holme Sumner's attempts to vet membership of the select committee, 1 June. He doubted the efficacy of Littleton's labourers' wages bill, 1 June. To prevent the newly established Unitarian Association and their

spokesman Matthew Wood* from usurping his role as the denomination's legislator and pressing prematurely for Test Act repeal, Smith pre-empted them by announcing a Unitarian marriage bill, 6 June, backed by petitions from London and the provinces, 6, 13 June; but he postponed it, 7 July.[11] He informed Lord Holland that the Dissenting Deputies' petition for repeal of the Test Acts which he presented, 13 July 1820, was the 'harbinger of the motion which ... I suppose I shall be desired to make next year'.[12] His kinsmen had waived their compensation entitlement for Savannah property captured in the American War, but Smith continued to represent the loyalists, supported their claims, 19 June 1820, 21 Mar., and was a majority teller when these were conceded, 6 June 1821. He also protested when difficulties in payment arose, 28 Mar. 1822.[13] On behalf of the London distillers, he resolutely opposed the admission of Irish spirits under the excess of spirits bill, 6, 10, 12 July 1820 (and again, 7 May 1821).[14] He voiced the concerns of the Protestant British and Foreign Schools Society, of which he was vice-president, over the minutiae of the Whig lawyer Henry Brougham's education bill, which, by applying the Test Acts, made employment as schoolmasters exclusive to practising Anglicans, 11 July, but otherwise he considered the scheme, which he also discussed in correspondence with Brougham, well suited to rural areas.[15] Alarmed at the investigation into Queen Caroline's conduct, he saw no inconsistency in voting for compromise, 22 June, and to kill inquiry by adjournment, 26 June 1820. He supported the parliamentary campaign on the 1821 queen's behalf and presented and endorsed the radical Norwich petition, 26 Jan.[16] Now based in London, he had moved his family 'back into trade' in Philpot Lane in December 1820; and another move, to rented property in Seymour Street, Portman Square, followed in 1823.[17]

Smith opposed the proposed redundancy payments for Scottish admiralty court officials, 15 Feb. 1821. He voted to repeal the additional malt duty, 21 Mar., 3 Apr., and against appointing a select committee to consider it in Scotland, to which he was nevertheless appointed, 12 Apr. He voted to restore official salaries to their 1797 levels, 30 Mar., and divided steadily against the army estimates, irritating ministers and delighting opposition with his sharp criticism of the £922 award for the 'superfluous' deputy quartermaster-general in Scotland, 11 Apr.[18] He voted to reduce the admiralty office grant, 4 May, but approved expenditure on Millbank penitentiary, 31 May, prisons, 4 June, criminal lunatics, the Bow Street police and St. Paul's Cathedral, 28 June. He opposed the lottery, 1 June, and the £3,000 salary for the governor of the slave colony of Sierra Leone, 28 June, on moral grounds. Excepting the Clarences' arrears, he now condoned the grants for the royal dukes, 8, 18, 29 June, but hoped to see the ostentatious coronation 'dispensed with', 29 June. He voted for the radical Whig Grey Bennet's abortive placemen bill, 30 May, and in protest against the appointment of Thomas Frankland Lewis* as an Irish revenue commissioner, 15 June, which he criticized as an abuse of crown patronage, 18 June.[19] He objected to 'purchasing from the colonies articles inferior to those which might be had nearer home', preferred the Norwegian to the Canadian or Russian trade, and voted to amend the timber duties accordingly, 16 Apr. He presented mercantile petitions from Norwich for repeal of the tax on foreign wool, 16 May, and against the proposed increases in tobacco duties, 18, 22 June 1821, and represented their interests throughout this period.[20]

Smith confined to procedural points his support for the campaigns on behalf of the radicals Thomas Davison, arbitrarily fined by Justice William Best† for contempt of court, 23 Feb., and Nathan Broadhurst, 7 Mar., and deliberately distanced himself from Henry Hunt's* friends before voting to receive the report on his conditions of detention at Ilchester, 21 June 1821.[21] Alluding to the case of the radical bookseller William Hone (whom he had defended in 1818), he maintained that *John Bull*'s libel against Grey Bennet, in which the foreign secretary Lord Castlereagh* was implicated, was 'personal rather than political', 9 May, and moved to have the printer, Weaver, taken into custody and reprimanded, 11 May, but this was superseded by an amendment consigning him to Newgate, 11 May. He presented the Protestant Dissenters of London and Westminster's petition for a reduction in the number capital offences and voted accordingly, 23 May 1821 (and again 4 June 1822, 21 May, 25 June 1823).[22] He urged reform of the courts of law in England, 9 May, and Newfoundland, 28 May, and was a minority teller for inquiring into the administration of justice in Tobago, 6 June 1821. Presenting the Unitarian Association's petition for amendment of the marriage laws, 8 June, he attributed the delay to his bill to 'pressure of public business' and assured Joseph Phillimore, whose clandestine marriage bill also languished, that the Unitarians would 'accept relief in whatever way the legislature will concede it'.[23] He steered the 1821 Westminster Improvement Act successfully through the Commons and presented the Fishmongers' Company's petition for repeal of the Elizabethan statutes prohibiting the development of the north bank of the Thames, 1 May 1821.[24]

Smith voted to amend the address, 5 Feb., against the government's coercive measures for Ireland, 7, 8 Feb., the dismissal of Sir Robert Wilson* from the army, 13 Feb., and for inquiry into the assault on Robert Waithman* for attempting to force the queen's funeral procession through the City, 28 Feb. 1822. He divided for more extensive tax reductions, 21 Feb., and was a minority teller with Hume, whose political leadership he praised, against the ordnance estimates, 27 Feb. He was granted further discussion of the government's navigation bill, 25 Feb., and, dissatisfied with its details, he explained when endorsing a hostile petition from London's silk merchants, 23 May, that he was 'favourable to the principle of free trade' but considered the current tax burden on shipping too great to make it competitive. He suggested retaining the barilla duty, on which the Scottish trade depended, on humanitarian grounds, although 'the first principles of political economy were at stake', 29 July.[25] He complained at the inconvenience to Members of prisoners such as Hunt using up their franks, 1 Mar.,[26] but voted for remission of his sentence on account of ill-treatment, 24 Apr. He voted to repeal the salt duties, 28 Feb., 28 June, and warned that their retention would ruin the fisheries, 11, 17 June.[27] He did not oppose the introduction of the naval and military pensions bill, 11 Mar., but he divided against it, 3 May, 3, 26 June, having urged that pensions be financed 'from the sinking fund without disguise' or 'any increase of establishments', 1, 24 May.[28] He sanctioned spending on civil and commercial improvements in Canada as a means of fostering its development 13 Mar., but divided against the Canada bill, 18 July. He queried the alterations made in the commercial credit bill, 17 Apr. He condemned the colonial trade bill as ill-conceived and criticized its details, but conceded (to taunts from the planters in the House) that something similar would have to be carried before further progress towards the abolition of slavery was possible, 1 Apr., 17 May.[29] He voted against the excise bill, 27 June, and seconded Edmond Wodehouse's unsuccessful amendment to have part of it repealed, 2 July. He divided against the royal burghs accounts bill, 19 July, although he had wanted to see its powers for acting against corrupt magistrates and the attendant £500 penalty extended to England and Wales, 17 June. He opposed the lotteries bill as previously, 1, 24 July, but condoned public expenditure on the arts, 17 July 1822.[30]

Smith, who had supported a similar motion, 9 Feb. 1821, was a minority teller for inquiry into the duties of the India board under the presidency of the Grenvillite Charles Williams Wynn*, 14 Mar. 1822.

He divided for inquiries into the government of the Ionian Isles, 14 May, and the dealings of the lord advocate with the Scottish press, 25 June (and again, 3 June 1823). He voted against the Irish constables bill, 7 June, to condemn the growing influence of the crown, 24 June, and for the production of papers on Colombian independence, 23 July 1822. He advocated government intervention to create employment for the Irish poor, 17 May, and testified to the success of similar initiatives by the London Companies of Drapers and Grocers as absentee landlords. He supported the Irish insurrection bill as 'a measure of mercy' and part of a long-term plan to remove 'the vestiges of centuries of Irish misgovernment', but foresaw little hope of tranquillity 'until he saw corn used, not as food for the still, but as food for man', 15 July. He presented several petitions backing his Unitarian marriage bill, 3 Apr., 21 May, and claimed that its sole objective was to grant English Unitarians equal privileges with Jews, Quakers and Scottish and Irish Dissenters, 17 Apr.[31] Government and the established church opposed it and, heeding the advice of Stephen Lushington* and his friends, he pre-empted its defeat by withdrawing it, 10 June, and securing leave for a new bill, which he brought in and had printed, 10 July.[32] Supporting Wilberforce, he ordered returns, 10 June, and seconded his successful motion for an address regretting the European powers' failure to implement their 1815 agreement prohibiting the trade in slaves, 27 June.[33] He described abolition as 'a sign of a Christian state', denounced the concept of the slave as property and condemned the trade at the Cape, 25 July, and in Trinidad, 5 Aug. 1822.[34]

Smith voted for large tax reductions, 28 Feb., 17, 18 Mar., and spoke against the national debt reduction bill, 6, 17 Mar. 1823. He quibbled over the estimates, pressed for reform of the pension system, 17 Mar., and divided against the military and naval pensions bill, 14, 18 Apr. He raised 'no immediate objection' to the passage of the merchant vessels apprenticeship bill, despite his long-standing opposition to impressment, 18 Apr.[35] He expressed support for equalization of the duties on East and West Indian sugars, which Huskisson as president of the board of trade was not prepared to concede, 3 Mar., and presented a favourable petition from Norfolk and divided for inquiry, 22 May.[36] He voted in a minority of eight against considering the warehousing bill, 21 Mar. He also suggested postponing the silk manufacture bill, which threatened the London and Norwich trades, to permit further inquiry, 21 Mar., and voted to recommit it, 9 June, although he conceded that certain clauses were beneficial, 9, 11 June. Convinced that state subsidies

and tithe abuse contributed to the unpopularity of the established church in Ireland, Smith voted for inquiry, 4 Mar., 21 Apr., and was a minority teller against the award for churches and glebe houses, 11 Apr., 1 July. He voted for inquiry into the prosecution of the Dublin Orange rioters, 22 Apr., and against renewing the Irish Insurrection Act, 12 May, 24 June, when he also complained that government measures 'were calculated solely to throw dust in the eyes of the public' and that tranquillity was impossible while 'six million people were denied the rights of the constitution, while one million ate up all the patronage, the honours and power of the country'. He voted for the Scottish juries bill, 20 June, and to amend the East India mutiny bill by transferring the trial of capital offences to the civil courts, 11 July. Despite his private disgust at the radical bookseller Richard Carlile's publications, he maintained that the blasphemous petition from 'ministers of the Christian religion for free discussion' should be received, as it was 'impossible to 'establish a safe test of opinion for the penal guidance of society', 1 July.[37] He ordered detailed returns of duties and drawbacks on the soft soap used in the Norwich worsted industry, 20 Feb.,[38] and presented his constituents' petitions for repeal of the Insolvent Debtors Act, 15 May, and the combination laws, 30 June. He failed in his attempt to have a clause added to the Scottish distilleries bill, freeing distillers from their obligation to give 12 months' notice before trading in England, 8 July. He was at Zachary Macaulay's house on 13 Jan. 1823, when the anti-slavery lobby agreed their tactics for the session, and was instrumental in establishing the London Society for the Abolition of Slavery.[39] He presented and endorsed abolitionist petitions, 27 Mar., 5 May, 30 June, 11 July,[40] expressed dissatisfaction with the vague time scale and inadequate enforcement strategy proposed in Canning's resolutions, 15 May, and joined Thomas Fowell Buxton* and Wilberforce in their negotiations with him.[41] On the slave trade consolidation bill, 5 July, he approved Lushington's abortive clause restricting slave transfers between the colonies and called for action against slave maltreatment in Demerara and Trinidad. He backed Wilberforce's motion for a select committee to examine the condition of the Honduras slaves, 11 July 1823, and, when it failed, ordered information on the slave populations of all British colonies.[42]

On the address, 4 Feb. 1824, Smith sought Canning's assurance that the country 'would not be a party to any arrangement which did not protect the Greeks'. Before voting to repeal the window tax, 2 Mar, and the assessed taxes, 10 May, he again criticized tax gathering costs and complained that the 'sinking fund had become a nickname for a thing that had gone into general disrepute' and would be better used for funding tax reductions. He voted, 15 Mar., and presented a petition from Norwich against the beer duties, 21 May.[43] He endorsed spending on the British Museum as previously, 1, 29 Mar., but voted against the grants for Windsor Castle, 5 Apr., and new churches, 9, 12 Apr., 14 June. He said that his opposition to the latter derived from his experience of the growth of urban Dissent and, citing the case of Norwich, whose redundant churches did not signify 'insufficiency, nor want of activity in the clergymen', he cautioned against assuming that buildings alone would boost church attendance, 9 Apr. He supported investigation of the disrepair of Londonderry Cathedral, 10 May. He voted for inquiry into the Irish church, 6 May, and against the Irish insurrection bill, 14, 18 June. He recommended granting diplomatic recognition to the 'independent' South American states 'sooner rather than later' on commercial and humanitarian grounds, 21 June. As in subsequent years, he presented and endorsed Norwich petitions for repeal of the duty on coastwise coal, 20 Feb., 29 Mar.[44] He approved the removal of protective tariffs on wool and silk, 5, 18 Mar., but endorsed the Norwich trade's petitions for concessions on stock-in-hand 19, 26 Mar. He presented a petition from Portsea for repeal of the combination laws, 19 Mar.[45] He introduced the successful Thames Tunnel bill as chairman of the attendant company, 22 Mar.,[46] opposed the St. Katharine's Docks bill, 2 Apr., and was a majority teller with Wood for the coal exchange debt bill, 9 June. Smith shared Buxton's disappointment with Canning's anti-slavery resolutions and assisted in the parliamentary campaign designed to expose the government's vacillation on the matter, 15, 16 Mar., and discredit the planters' claims that the Anti-Slavery Society sought the precipitate emancipation of all slaves, 15 June 1824.[47] He warned that the West India Company bill, against which he was a minority teller, 10 May, would worsen the slaves' plight, as the profitability of the Company would be paramount, and presented petitions, 1 June, and voted in condemnation of the indictment in Demerara of the Methodist missionary John Smith, 11 June.[48] Defending Hume, who as the presenter of a petition for the freedom of discussion was charged with cant and religious hypocrisy, Smith reiterated his opinion that 'religion must stand upon truth', which 'could only be discovered by discussion', and his tenet that 'prosecutions for religion's sake were ineffectual', 3 June. He interpreted the Carlile case as a question of 'whether an individual was to be subjected to excessive imprisonment for non-payment

of a fine, when his incapacity to pay it was evident', 11 June 1824, and again, 2 June 1825.[49] He was prepared to tolerate the whipping of vagrants, 3 June, but not impressment, 10 June 1824. As requested, on 24 June 1824 he reluctantly presented and endorsed the petitions which launched the Dissenters' premature campaign for repeal of the Test Acts, from which the Protestant Association held aloof.[50] During the recess he came to realize that the campaign could not succeed without the Association's support, and he also lobbied on behalf of the persecuted Swiss Protestants.[51]

Smith had divided for Catholic relief, 28 Feb. 1821, and expressed support for the English Catholics qualification bill provided Protestant Dissenters were not disadvantaged thereby, 28 May, 30 June 1823.[52] He divided against the Irish unlawful societies bill, 15, 18, 21, 25 Feb., and for Catholic relief, 1 Mar., 10 May, pairing for it, 21 Apr. 1825. Unnerved by Brougham's references to the Dissenters' differences on the issue, 18 Apr., he tried to demonstrate that with the exception of the Methodists', their petitions were predominantly pro-Catholic, 18, 19 Apr., and presented and endorsed favourable ones from Unitarian congregations, 9 May. He saw 'no inconsistency' in voting for the Irish franchise bill that day.[53] Briefed by Brougham, he warned the Dissenting deputies at their general meeting, 27 May, that their parliamentary friends were against 'touching' the Dissenters' question at present.[54] Having secured the backing of Lushington and the bishops, Smith saw his Dissenters' marriage bill, announced, 11 Feb., through the Commons, 23 Feb., 25 Mar., 6 May. However, his confidence that 'the legislature need attend only to the civil part of the business', as 'amply sufficient guards' were provided for 'accurate registration' and against clandestine marriages, proved to be misplaced; and, as predicted on 25 Mar. by Peel, the home secretary, to whom he had sent a book and printed sermon for guidance, he failed to prevent the bill being overloaded with amendments by Dissenters and high churchmen, and it was killed off in the Lords, 3 June.[55] He expressed reservations lest the Unitarians' petition against oath-taking should inadvertently jeopardize his plans, 21 June, and attributed it to their exclusion from the provisions of the Toleration Act. He defended government spending on the rehabilitation of slaves and the commission for suppression of the trade, 11 Mar., and wanted the Canadian wastelands bill be 'framed so as not to injure or prejudice the native Indians', 15 Mar. He repeatedly criticized Members for 'lauding and condemning architecture as if they knew all its rules' and joined in the clamour for a select committee on public buildings, 21, 28 Mar.[56] He inveighed to the last against the 'monopolistic' West India Company bill, which the abolitionists tried to wreck, condemning it as a private measure whose sole object was 'to bolster up a losing concern' and delay the abolition of slavery, 29 Mar., 16 May. By contrast, he praised the Mauritius trade bill as an experiment in self-sufficiency, 3 June. He advocated government intervention to put a stop to the 'abominable idolatry' of suttee, 6 June.[57] Convinced of the evils of spirit drinking among the poor and of its association with crime, he castigated ministers for lowering the retail duties on spirits, 22 Apr. 1825. He voted for revision of the corn laws, 28 Apr., which Norwich had petitioned for, 26 Apr., and to repeal the beer duties, 5 May.[58] On the 20th he divided against the Leith docks bill and voted to make puisne judges immovable. He acknowledged the administrative failings of the 1819 Factory Act and, backing Hobhouse's bill to amend it, he compared the Manchester children's plight unfavourably with that of West Indian slaves, 6, 16, 31 May.[59] On tithe reform, he admitted the shortcomings of the London bill, 17 May, and supported that for St. Olave's, 6 June.[60] He divided against subsidizing Irish emigration to Canada, 13 June, and for inquiry into the Irish church, 14 June. He criticized the distillery bill as unfair to Irish, Scottish and English distillers, claimed they would lose £100,000 by it and wished to see rum excluded from its provisions, 13 June. Clauses which he proposed exempting millers and other occasional distillers from its remit were withdrawn, 20 June.[61] He advocated paying compensation to Lecesne and Escoffery, 16 June. He protested strongly at the expulsion of the Wesleyan missionary Shrewsbury from Barbados and denounced the legislature there for failing to protect church property, 23 June. He endorsed Whitmore's proposals for establishing an independent stipendiary magistracy and jury trial under the combination of workmen bill, 27, 29 June 1825.[62]

Smith disputed Alexander Baring's argument that government had a duty to relieve individual merchants in the aftermath of the 1825-6 banking crisis, and called instead for 'substantial and immediate' measures to combat widespread distress, 14 Feb. 1826. He praised the Bank of England's initiatives to assist the country banks, 8 Mar.[63] He gave his customary speech as a minority teller for the abolition of bear-baiting, dog-fighting and cruel sports, 21 Feb., and was directed that day to assist with the cattle ill-treatment bill; but he opposed legislation against the improper treatment of dogs, to whom the law of misdemeanours already applied, 21 Apr. Endorsing the 72,000-signature London anti-slavery petition, 1 Mar., he singled out the recalcitrant legislature of Jamaica for

censure, 1 Mar., spoke and voted in condemnation of the Jamaican slave trials, 2 Mar., and presented anti-slavery petitions, 6, 7, 18, 21 Mar., when, goaded by the planters, he again denied that abolitionists sought the immediate emancipation of all slaves.[64] He spoke similarly, 20 Apr., when, clashing with Baring and the colonial under-secretary Wilmot Horton, he read out a list of charges of cruelty to slaves in Demerara and Berbice. He obtained returns of the government's slave holdings in Mauritius, 23 Mar., and was named to the select committee on the trade there, 9 May.[65] He voted for inquiry into the petition of James Silk Buckingham[†] concerning the liberty of the press in India, 9 May. He set out the grievances outlined in the Protestant Dissenters of London and Westminster's petition against the Test Acts, 18 May, and explained that legislation had been shelved that session, in favour of memorials and petitions.[66] Smith voted for reductions in the army estimates, 3 Mar., and called for free access to the Angerstein sculptures in Westminster Abbey, 16 Mar. He was in a minority of six against the grant for Irish charities, 23 Mar., and voted against approving Huskisson's official salary, 7 Apr. Maintaining that the 'state ought to suffer every class of persons to educate their children as they thought proper', he sympathized with Irish Catholics' demands for state funding for their schools, 14 Apr. He was a minority teller against the Irish church rates bill, 21 Apr. Norwich, where his unstinting support for the proposed assize transfer from Thetford and the recently defeated Norwich and Lowestoft navigation bill pleased both parties, returned him unopposed at the general election in June with the home secretary's brother Jonathan Peel, an ardent anti-Catholic. His son Benjamin paid Smith's £1,500 bill.[67] Writing to the Quaker leader Joseph John Gurney, 8 July 1826, Wilberforce rejoiced in Smith's re-election, but he was

> quite grieved ... to hear that he was to come into Norfolk this very week to take the chair in what is termed an Unitarian meeting. Indeed he mentioned it to me ... I had indulged a hope that he was rather retiring from his Unitarian opinions and this proof to the contrary has given me real pain.[68]

Smith succeeded in reviving the committee on standing orders, 24 Nov., expressed qualified support for the resolutions on private bills, 28 Nov. 1826, and was instrumental in securing the enactment of the Norwich and Lowestoft navigation port bill early in the new Parliament.[69] His defence of the Deist preacher Robert Taylor, a member of the Norwich Unitarian dynasty, for 'fairly' stating 'that he denied the truth of the Gospels, but ... firmly acknowledged the existence of God', 29 Nov., turned the London Evangelicals against him, weakening his influence within the Anti-Slavery Society and spawning an unsuccessful campaign to remove him as chairman of the Dissenting Deputies.[70] He advocated printing a rabid anti-Catholic petition from a Leicester parish, 2 Mar., but divided as hitherto for relief, 6 Mar. 1827.[71] When pressed by John Bowring of the Unitarian Association and others, he spoke out against the annual indemnity bill as a 'stalking horse ... for absurd oaths', without which the Test Acts would long ago have been abolished, 23 Mar. He spoke against the duke of Clarence's annuity bill, 16 Feb., 16 Mar., the army estimates, 20 Feb., and military flogging, 26 Feb. He supported inquiries into the allegations against Leicester corporation and county polls, 15 Mar.[72] After securing returns of exports and imports to and from the East and West Indies and Mauritius, 16 Mar., he criticized the 'unreasonable' protection which the annual duties bill gave to the East Indian sugar industry, 23 Mar., and later speculated that it was connected to the clandestine slave trade at Mauritius, 15 May.[73] He voted on humanitarian grounds for the spring guns bill, 23 Mar., and information on the magistrates' treatment of the Lisburn Orange marchers, 29 Mar. He voted to postpone the committee of supply until the ministerial uncertainty caused by Lord Liverpool's stroke was resolved, 30 Mar., and to inquire into the Irish miscellaneous estimates, 5 Apr. During Canning's ministry, he divided for the disfranchisement of Penryn, 28 May, for Lord Althorp's bill limiting election expenses, and also the Canadian waterways grant, 12 June. He presented contentious petitions for wage regulation, which he described as the 'worst remedy possible', though he conceded its palliative merits, from the distressed weavers and manufacturers of Norwich, 30 May.[74] He recommended awarding coloured freemen in the West Indies the legal rights and privileges of British subjects, 12 June.[75] The Dissenters' petitioning campaign for repeal of the Test Acts was already under way when Brougham warned them that Canning would put Catholics first, 3 May; but Smith, as chairman, persuaded the newly formed United Committee of the 24 Dissenting Deputies and their allies to delay legislating for it until 1828. Leaving Russell to gloss over disagreements over tactics among their ranks, 7 June, he emphasized the Dissenters' forbearance, on bringing up their petitions, 7, 13, 22, 29 June,[76] and used their moderation to good effect in the negotiations which secured ministerial backing for his Dissenters' marriages bill, which the Commons passed, 19 June 1827; it foundered in the Lords.[77]

After Canning's death in August, Smith wanted to postpone the repeal bill until a Whig administration favourable to it was appointed, but the Dissenting Deputies overruled his suggestion and, by arrangement with Russell, petitioning was set in motion directly the United Committee and the Protestant Society launched their joint campaign, 16 Jan. 1828.[78] Lobbied in turn by the Catholic Association, Smith used the opportunity afforded by presenting a pro-Catholic petition from Kilmainham to deny newspaper reports of collusion between the Catholics and the Dissenters, 6 Feb., adding that while the Dissenters acknowledged their disunity on the Catholic question, they agreed that 'civil and religious rights ought to be the same' and that 'no man should be deprived of the former by reason of the latter'. He closed with a personal plea for the swift passage of Catholic emancipation and repeal of the Test Acts. He sought and presented petitions for the latter, 15, 21, 22, 25, 26 Feb., and was a majority teller that day when their motion for considering it was carried, despite the Wellington ministry's opposition. He drafted the resolutions on which the repeal bill was based, and presented and endorsed favourable petitions, 14, 17, 18 Mar., when, knowing that the United Society objected to the 'Christian' declaration that he had negotiated as a security with Sir Thomas Acland*, Lord Lansdowne, the home secretary Peel and Russell, he explained that he had agreed to it solely to ease the bill's passage through the Lords.[79] He consulted Lansdowne and Wellington during its progress there, and stifled the Norwich Quaker banker Hudson Gurney's objections to their amendments, 2 May, accusing him of 'wasting his ingenuity'. At the celebration dinner at London's *Freemasons' Tavern*, 18 June 1828, the duke of Sussex hailed him as 'one of those friends I would trust in the dark', the United Society paid tribute to his political realism and Smith expressed relief that he was 'not in office' and therefore 'not in the situation of wanting a political keeper of my conscience'.[80] He informed Lord Holland that the Dissenters would press for Jewish emancipation to atone for the 'Christian' declaration, identified church rates, 'not tithes ... nonsense', as their only real remaining grievance and called for an end to

> fastidiously dwelling on the comparative trifles of difference that yet remain – treating the remaining prejudices of the clergy with moderation, as what must speedily yield to more familiar intercourse – not ostentatiously complaining of our want of a complete parochial registry, but leaving that to be settled, as I believe it will be, in a new arrangement for the whole kingdom upon the subject, which I know to be in exceedingly good hands

(the legal commission) and likely to be brought forward ere long. On the Unitarian marriages I have had several conversations with both the duke of Wellington and the bishop of London, and am thoroughly convinced of the good dispositions of both ... There are two or three other inconsiderable matters, paying turnpikes when going to meeting, assessment of chapels to parochial rates, which should be adverted to when occasion offers, but in fact are not purely Dissenters' objects, applying for the most part to all chapels not parochial.[81]

Repeating that there was 'no union between Catholics and Dissenters', he presented petitions, 25, 29 Apr., and voted for Catholic relief, 12 May. He reminded the House of the Quakers and Moravians' objections to oath-taking, 5 May, divided for inquiry into the Irish church, 24 June, and presented and endorsed petitions against the additional churches bill, 26 June, 8 July 1828, when he again called for toleration for Taylor.

Smith had discussed parliamentary tactics on slavery with Buxton, Lushington and Macaulay in October 1827, and he joined Buxton in criticizing the colonial under-secretary Wilmot Horton, 5 Mar. 1828.[82] He presented and endorsed anti-slavery petitions, 23 May, 3, 9 June, 17, 25 July, and supported the former colonial secretary Huskisson's request for a copy of his letter of 22 Sept. 1827 to the governor of Jamaica, disclosing much of its content, 1 July. Advocating reform, he peppered his speeches for Davies's abortive borough polls bill with references to Norwich, whose eight-man booths and one-day polls he praised, 21 Feb., 31 Mar., 15 May, and he supported the voters' registration bill, 19 June, and the corporate funds bill, 10 July. His examination of an East Retford witness was criticized as 'unduly harsh', 7 Mar. He divided against sluicing the franchise there, 21 Mar. He voted for more efficient collection of customs penalties, 1 May, and information on civil list pensions, 20 May. He presented Norwich petitions against the friendly societies bill, 30 Apr., and for the appointment of a committee to regulate wages, which, in view of the weavers' extreme distress, he moved for despite his personal reservations, knowing it would not be granted, 1 May. He presented various Norwich mercantile petitions, 20 May. He welcomed Peel's initiative on lunatic asylums, 19 Feb., and called for harsher penalties for cruelty to children under the offences against the person bill, 5 May, but withdrew his proposed amendment making the maltreatment of children and apprentices punishable by a four-year prison term, 6 June. He voted the same day to postpone the grant to the Society for the Propagation of the Gospel in the colonies. Before voting for army reductions, 13 June, he explained that he did so purely on account

of the state of the country and not 'to cast a censure upon, or to take a part in any systematic opposition' to the ministry, whose strength he praised. He cast critical votes on the cost of the Buckingham House refurbishment, 23 June, and ordnance expenditure, 4, 7 July 1828.

When Peel and Wellington conceded Catholic emancipation in 1829 Smith delegated the task of opposing the massive Norwich anti-Catholic petition to Hudson Gurney and excused the absence of a similar pro-emancipation petition as 'unnecessary', 19 Feb. Most Unitarian pro-Catholic petitions were forwarded to him for presentation, and he also presented that of the Dissenting Deputies, 6 Mar., when, controversially, he justified their decision to sign on behalf of their congregations by stating that the 'lower class of people cannot judge properly of this question'. As in 1825 and 1827, he exaggerated the Dissenters' pro-Catholic sympathies and tried to mask their differences by glossing over differences between the provinces and the metropolis and attributing anti-Catholic petitions to Calvinist and Wesleyan influences, 17 Mar.[83] He divided for emancipation, 30 Mar. He attributed his decision not to oppose the army estimates that year to recent improvements in management, 13 Mar. He voted to transfer East Retford's seats to Birmingham, 5 May, and for Lord Blandford's reform proposals, 2 June. He gave steady support to the labourers' wages bill, 25 Mar., 4, 12 May, and the anatomy bill, 8, 19 May, when he also endorsed proposals to amend the 1819 Factory Act. Dismissing a similar motion brought on by John Stuart Wortley as 'ill-conceived', he ordered returns to show the high mortality and administrative costs in Sierra Leone, 2 June, and he refused to sanction Otway Cave's resolution for freeing the children of all slaves born after 1830, 4 June. He requested a breakdown by colony of the entire slave population, 5 June 1829, and commented on the ecclesiastical courts bill that day. His financial affairs remained in disarray, partly on account of his attempt to recoup earlier losses by assuming the chairmanship of the ill-fated Thames Tunnel Company, whose operations were suspended amid charges of gross mismanagement after the tunnel collapsed for the second time, 12 Jan. 1828. Acrimonious exchanges followed between Smith and the engineer Brunel, whom he dismissed, and, after failing to secure adequate additional funding for the scheme from government and private sources, he relinquished his directorship in 1830.[84]

Smith dismissed Knatchbull's amendment condemning the omission of distress from the 1830 address as a ploy by the disaffected Ultras and divided with government against it, 4 Feb. He cautioned against forcing a division on reform, 5 Feb. He voted to transfer East Retford's seats to Birmingham, 11 Feb., 5 Mar., and registered his 'disgust' with the disfranchisement bill by voting to introduce the ballot there, 15 Mar. He voted for Blandford's reform scheme, 18 Feb., to enfranchise Birmingham, Leeds and Manchester, 23 Feb., to consider Newark's petition criticizing the electoral interference of the duke of Newcastle, 1 Mar., and for Russell's general reform proposals, 28 May. He suggested restricting the estimates, 19 Feb., and called for various economies, 9, 29 Mar., 14 June, including a £22,000 reduction in the public buildings grant, 3 May. He called for thorough investigation of the West India trade, 23 Feb. He divided for information on British involvement in Portugal, 10 Mar., and with the revived Whig opposition on the management of crown lands, 30 Mar., and for abolition of the Irish lord lieutenancy, 11 May. Dissenting from the motion for inquiry into privy councillors' emoluments, 14 May, he embarrassed its mover, Sir James Graham, by explaining that he would continue to vote with government whenever, as now, a question calculated to threaten their existence was raised, and against them on issues tending to increase public expenditure. He presented petitions, 25 Mar., 13 May, and voted for Jewish emancipation, 5 Apr., 17 May: 'a question of political expediency' which the Church of England was strong enough to survive. As he had intimated during the Ellenborough, 6 Apr., and Muskett proceedings, 28 Apr., he voted to reform the divorce laws, 3 June. He presented petitions, 6 Apr., 11 June, and voted for the forgery punishment mitigation bill, 7 June, and was a minority teller against accepting the Lords' amendments, 13 July. Backed by a Norwich petition, he called for inquiry into the employment of climbing boys, 11 June. He warned that intervention was needed if the evils of the truck system (the subject of his altercation on 16 Mar. with Hume) were to be checked, 23 June, and objected to considering it as a question of political economy rather than as a moral issue, 1 July. He supported the London distillers' campaign against altering the spirit duties, 10 Mar., 7 Apr., and endorsed Scottish petitions for continuing the fishery bounties, 27 Apr., but recommended that they be reduced by 75 per cent, 28 May. He presented the Norwich publicans' petition against the sale of beer bill, 11 May, opposed it on their behalf, 3 June, and voted to restrict on-consumption, 21 June, 1 July. He explained that day that he had initially favoured the measure but now dreaded the 'evil' and demoralizing consequences of 'deluging the country with small public houses'. Even so, he

conceded that he might ultimately vote for the bill to safeguard a £3,000,000 reduction in taxes. He voted against increasing recognizances under the libel laws, 9 July. According to his daughter Julia, Smith's prime concern had become the abolition of slavery, for which he pressed, 14, 15 June, 1, 13 July, when, 'not knowing what opportunity I might have of further expressing my opinions upon this subject', he spoke at length and was a minority teller for Brougham's inquiry motion.[85] He again defended the abolitionists' objectives when petitions were presented, 16, 20 July 1830. The repeal of the Test Acts in 1828 after a 40-year campaign and the near success in 1827 of his Dissenters' (Unitarian) marriage bill formed a fitting climax to Smith's parliamentary career. Speculation that he would stand again at Norwich at the 1830 general election proved false and he retired, heartened by the growing support for parliamentary reform and the emancipation of slaves.[86]

Out of Parliament, Smith welcomed Althorp's appointment as the Grey ministry's chancellor of the exchequer and leader of the House in November 1830, remained active in the anti-slavery movement and campaigned for a suitable memorial to Wilberforce (d. 1833) when abolition was achieved.[87] As in 1792, he organized support for the Poles, following the 1830 Russian invasion, and chaired their London committee. He resigned as chairman of the Dissenting Deputies in 1832.[88] He travelled in France with his wife and unmarried daughters in 1834 and died in May 1835 at Benjamin's house in Blandford Square, their home since 1830. Obituarists noted Smith's connections with the Clapham sect, his quarrels with Sir Walter Scott and the poet Robert Southey* and the political foresight and high moral principles he had shown as a tireless spokesman for the Dissenters and the Anti-Slavery Society.[89] By his will, dated 14 May 1833 and proved under £5,000 (the sum for which his life was insured), he bequeathed everything to his wife. Paintings auctioned after his death realized £276.[90] Benjamin Smith (1783-1860) became Liberal Member for Sudbury, 1835-7, and Norwich, 1838-47.

[1] Smith's life is reviewed in the unpublished recollections of his daughter Julia Smith (1799-1883) in CUL, William Smith mss Add. 7621/15. See also R.W. Davis, *Dissent in Politics, 1780-1830* (1971). [2] Hants RO, Calthorpe mss 26M62/F/C219; William Smith mss Add. 7621/29, 36, 37; Davis, 189-90; *HP Commons, 1754-90*, iii. 452-3; *HP Commons, 1790-1820*, v. 206. [3] William Smith mss Add. 7621/601; Brougham mss, Smith to Brougham [1830]; Davis, 96-97; *Committee for Repeal of Test and Corporation Acts* ed. T.W. Davis (London Rec. Soc. xiv), p. xix. [4] William Smith mss Add. 7621/31, 149; *Norf. Chron.* 11 Mar. 1820; *HP Commons, 1790-1820*, v. 206-14. [5] William Smith mss Add. 7621/149; Davis, 195; J. Stephen, *Essays in Ecclesiastical Biog.* (1849), ii. 297, 323. [6] *The Times*, 6 May

1820, 23 June, 4 July 1821, 9, 22 Feb., 25 Apr., 22 June 1822, 12 Feb. 1823. [7] Ibid. 15 June 1820. [8] Ibid. 5, 6 July 1820. [9] Ibid. 13 July 1820. [10] Ibid. 15 Mar. 1826. [11] Ibid. 7, 14 June, 8 July 1820; R.W. Davis, 'The Strategy of Dissent in the Repeal Campaign, 1820-1828', *JMH*, xxxviii (1966), 379. [12] Davis, *Dissent in Politics*, 216; *The Times*, 14 July; Add. 51573, Smith to Holland, 14, 16 July 1820. [13] *The Times*, 22 Mar. 1821, 29 Mar. 1822. [14] Ibid. 7, 11, 13 July 1820. [15] Ibid. 12 July 1820; Brougham mss, Brougham to Smith, 31 July 1820; Northants. RO, Gotch mss GK 1206. [16] *Norf. Chron.* 13, 20 Jan. 1821. [17] William Smith mss Add. 7621/15. [18] *The Times*, 6 Mar., 12 Apr. 1821. [19] Ibid. 16, 19 June 1821. [20] Ibid. 8, 17 May, 19 June 1821. [21] Ibid. 24 Feb., 22 June 1821. [22] Ibid. 24 May 1821. [23] Ibid. 9 June 1821; *CJ*, lxxvi. 166. [24] *The Times*, 18 Apr., 2 May 1821; *CJ*, lxxvi. 274, 281, 320, 425. [25] *The Times*, 26 Feb., 24 May, 30 July 1822. [26] Ibid. 2 Mar. 1822. [27] Ibid. 12, 18 June 1822. [28] Ibid. 12 Mar., 2 May 1822. [29] Ibid. 18 May 1822. [30] Ibid. 2, 18 July 1822. [31] Ibid. 4, 18 Apr. 1822. [32] Ibid. 22 May, 11 June, 11 July 1822; *CJ*, lxxvii. 179, 196, 332, 412. [33] *The Times*, 11, 28 June 1822. [34] Ibid. 26 July, 6 Aug. 1822. [35] Ibid. 18 Mar., 19 Apr. 1823. [36] Ibid. 4 Mar., 23 May 1823. [37] Ibid. 1, 2 July 1823. [38] Ibid. 21 Feb. 1823. [39] Davis, 252. [40] *The Times*, 28 Mar., 6 May, 1, 12 July 1823. [41] *Buxton Mems*. 133. [42] *The Times*, 12 July 1823. [43] Ibid. 22 May 1824. [44] Ibid. 21 Feb., 30 Mar. 1824. [45] Ibid. 6, 19, 20 Mar. 1824. [46] Ibid. 16, 23 Mar. 1824. [47] *Buxton Mems*. 145; *The Times*, 5, 11, 16, 31 Mar. 1824. [48] *The Times*, 2 June 1824. [49] Ibid. 3 June 1825. [50] Ibid. 18 June 1824; Davis, 220. [51] Add. 40370, f. 35; William Smith mss Add. 7621/142. [52] *The Times*, 1 July 1823. [53] Davis, *Dissent in Politics*, 220, *The Times*, 10 May 1825. [54] Brougham mss, Brougham to Smith, 26 May 1825; Davis, *Dissent in Politics*, 235. [55] *CJ*, lxxx. 105, 119, 266, 381; *LJ*, lvii. 979; *The Times*, 12, 24 Feb., 26 Mar. 1825; Add. 40375, f. 152. [56] *The Times*, 12, 22, 29 Mar. 1825. [57] Ibid. 17 May, 4, 6 June 1825. [58] Ibid. 27 Apr. 1825. [59] Ibid. 1 June 1825. [60] Ibid. 7 June 1825. [61] Ibid. 14, 21 June 1825. [62] Ibid. 28, 30 June 1825. [63] Ibid. 9 Mar. 1826. [64] Ibid. 2, 3, 7, 8, 19, 22, 24 Mar. 1826. [65] Ibid. 10 May 1826. [66] Ibid. 19 May 1826. [67] William Smith mss Add. 7621/143; Add. 40386, f. 269; 40387, ff. 17, 54, 56, 78, 248; Lansdowne mss, Empson to Lansdowne [9 Aug. 1830]. [68] Soc. of Friends Lib. Gurney mss Temp 434/1/423. [69] *The Times*, 25 Nov. 1826. [70] Ibid. 30 Nov. 1826; Davis, 208. [71] *The Times*, 3 Mar. 1827. [72] Ibid. 16 Mar. 1827. [73] Ibid. 17, 24 Mar. 1827. [74] Ibid. 31 May 1827. [75] Ibid. 13 June 1827. [76] Davis, *Dissent in Politics*, 237-40; *The Times*, 24 Mar., 8, 14, 23, 30 June; Brougham mss, Brougham to Smith, 3 May 1827. [77] *The Times*, 9, 11, 31 May, 20, 22 June 1827; Wellington mss WP1/917/1; *CJ*, lxxxvii. 442, 447, 552, 583; *LJ*, 427, 439, 450, 455, 466. [78] Davis, *Dissent in Politics*, 241-3; Wellington mss WP1/917/1. [79] *Committee for Repeal of Test ... Acts*, pp. xxii-iv, 202, 217, 220-1, 228, 230-48. [80] William Smith mss Add. 7621/31; Davis, *Dissent in Politics*, 246-7; *Report of Speeches and Proceedings at a Dinner to Celebrate the Passage of the Repeal of the Test Acts* (1828). [81] Add. 51573, Smith to Holland [1828]. [82] Brougham mss, Buxton to Brougham, 3 Oct. 1827; *Buxton Mems*. 203. [83] Davis, *JMH*, xxxviii. 391-3. [84] *The Times*, 3 Mar. 1825, 22 Aug., 22 Nov., 22 Dec. 1827, 14, 30 Jan., 18 Feb., 4 July 1828, 1 July 1829; Wellington mss WP1/1026/15, 18; 1107/14, 20; William Smith mss Add. 7621/505; L.T.C. Rolt, *Isambard Kingdom Brunel* (1970), 42-43, 47, 50-58, 62-65. [85] William Smith mss Add. 7621/15. [86] *Norwich Mercury*, 10, 17 July; *Norf. Chron.* 17 July 1830. [87] Add. 40880, f. 284; William Smith mss Add. 7621/141, 144; *Buxton Mems*. 329; Brougham mss, Smith to Brougham, 31 July, 13 Aug. 1834. [88] Davis, *Dissent in Politics*, 250-1. [89] *Gent. Mag.* (1835), ii. 204-5; William Smith mss Add. 7621/148. [90] PROB 11/1848/389; IR26/1400/341; William Smith mss Add. 7621/32.

M.M.E.

SMITH O'BRIEN, William (1803–1864).[1]

ENNIS	23 Apr. 1828–1831
CO. LIMERICK	1835–18 May 1849

b. 17 Oct. 1803, 2nd s. of Sir Edward O'Brien*, 3rd bt. (d. 1837), and Charlotte, da. and coh. of William Smith of Cahermoyle, co. Limerick; bro. of Lucius O'Brien*. *educ.* Welling, Kent ?1809; Harrow 1813; by Rev. Percy Scott, Harborough Magna, Warws. ?1818; Trinity Coll. Camb. 1821; L. Inn 1825. *m.* 19 Sept. 1832, Lucy Caroline, da. of Joseph Gabbett of High Park, co. Limerick, 5s. 2da.; 1s. 1da. illegit. Took name of Smith before O'Brien 1809. *d.* 18 June 1864.

With soaring aspirations, engendered by his elevated sense of family station, and only middling aptitudes, fitfully developed and not always steadily applied, the young Smith O'Brien rather smarted than flourished under his parents' kindly meant but misguided upbringing. Later, when he had ample to time to reflect on his self-inflicted misfortunes, he observed in his Tasmanian journal that

> it was supposed that a boy who suffered hardships, vexations and tyranny in his youth was better qualified than one brought up amidst kindly associations to contend with the difficulties and disappointments which never fail to surround if not overwhelm us in later years.

His character as an able and bold child was defined early on by his father, Member for Clare, who commented in 1808 that he was 'as quick and intelligent as any boy I ever saw of his age', and in 1813 described him, in comparison with his mild tempered elder brother Lucius, as 'a little more of a prickle'.[2] His destiny must also have been swiftly instilled in him, for not only was he conscious of his royal ancestor, but even as a younger son he was aware that he would have a sizeable inheritance. His maternal grandfather William Smith, at whose death in 1809 his surname was added to his own, had made his wealth as a lawyer; subject only to his mother and her sister's life interests, and notwithstanding the bogus claims of Smith's illegitimate children, the estate of Cahermoyle, county Limerick, and a fortune of £120,000 were eventually to come to him.[3]

Smith O'Brien was educated at a prep school in Kent and then spent three years at Harrow with Lucius before being sent to a crammer in Warwickshire. Originally studying science in order to equip him for his chosen career in the navy, he quickly changed to a concentration on more palatable arts subjects with a view to training as a lawyer. He explained his change of heart in two letters in March 1819 to his mother, whose Evangelical sensibilities he was at pains to mimic: in

September he informed her he had abandoned fishing and hunting as sinful occupations and in June 1820 he confessed his spiritual shortcomings to her.[4] Some time that year he addressed his father, who found him 'much improved, only anxious to leave Mr. Scott's', with a priggish affirmation of his intentions, writing that 'while other young men look to the honours of an university or to the laurels of military glory, my ambition is to serve and do good to my country'.[5] In 1821 he joined Lucius at Trinity College, where he belonged to the Apostles (though he is unlikely to have ever served as president of the Union) and it seems that he lost his excessive piety at this time.[6] By 1825, when he lodged with his father in London and accompanied him on a brief visit to Paris, he was reported to be reading widely but craving more entertaining pastimes; Sir Edward, who persuaded him to begin attending his dinners at Lincoln's Inn (and apparently also at the King's Inns in Dublin) to qualify him for future professional advancement, noted that he was 'an amiable man with good principles, but a little indolent and inclined to look to a higher class of society than I fear he will be able to keep'.[7] Yet, most likely referring to Smith O'Brien's failure to take his BA with honours, his father wrote to Lady O'Brien, 2 May 1826, that 'his unfortunate Cambridge affair will drive all idea of his going to the bar out of his head, if he ever was suited to so laborious a profession, which I much doubt'.[8]

It was expected that Smith O'Brien would be brought in on his father's interest for Ennis, where he had become popular locally as a member of the Mechanics' Institute, at the general election of 1826, but a paying guest was returned instead. He was nevertheless present for the proceedings there and for the election of his brother Lucius for Clare, 23 June, when he noted in his rough diary that he was 'toxicated'.[9] In his lengthy 'birthday reflections' of 17 Oct. 1826 he gave an honest appraisal of his limited abilities, including as an 'indifferent speaker' and a 'slow writer', but naively recorded that 'judgement predominates over imagination. Wit and invention I have none. Discrimination is the faculty in which I most excel'. Despite the self-exhortatory nature of such an exercise, over the following two years he largely neglected his legal studies and spent much of his time in riding and walking in the countryside, so developing a close identification with the Irish people.[10] In 1828 he drew up a list of 'grievances affecting the English Empire', which began with the exclusion of Catholics from Parliament (and continued with slavery, naval impressment and the like), and in 1848 he recorded:

From my boyhood I have entertained a passionate affection for Ireland. A child of its most ancient race, I have never read the history of their past wrongs, I have never witnessed the miseries and indignities which its people still suffer without a deep sentiment of indignation. Though myself a Protestant I have felt as acutely as any Roman Catholic – more acutely than many – the injustice to which the Roman Catholics of this country have been habitually subjected. Under the influence of these impressions I became a member of the Catholic Association before I entered public life and have never ceased to vindicate their claims to be placed in all respects upon a perfect equality with Protestants in regard of political advantages and civil privileges.[11]

Smith O'Brien, whose £5 subscription was handed in by Daniel O'Connell* at the Catholic Association, 24 Feb., was returned unopposed, on his father's nomination and at no little financial sacrifice, for the vacant seat at Ennis in April 1828.[12]

Relating to his wife that their son was intent on resuming his (in fact, never completed) legal studies, Sir Edward delighted in his prospects, noting that 'to William it is of great importance to have an object to give his mind full occupation and if he does not succeed in exerting himself, he will have nobody to blame but himself'.[13] He took his seat, 5 May, presented the Ennis pro-Catholic petition, 7 May, and, having been present during the several nights of debate on the question, voted for relief, 12 May 1828.[14] In his maiden speech he opposed the suppression of small Irish and Scottish bank notes, 3 June, and on the 4th his father recounted to his wife that evidently 'William does not intend to be a silent Member of the House and I have great satisfaction in hearing that he acquitted himself reasonably well. He is very attentive to the business of the House'.[15] He divided against the introduction of a bill to restrain the circulation of such notes, 5 June, when he supported Brownlow's Irish bogs bill, and its committal, 16 June. On the 12th, when he voted for the Irish assessment of lessors bill, he argued for the repeal of the Irish coal duties, which won him praise in his constituency's newspaper and, when the prime minister, the duke of Wellington, announced the abandonment of the tax, he wrote to his sister Anne some time that month that 'it is very satisfactory to be successful on these occasions, and though perhaps my speech had no great influence … yet my name stands the first who mentioned the subject'.[16] He later recalled that during this session, 'I gave no regular support to the Tory ministry', but he sided with it against reducing the salary of the lieutenant-general of the ordnance, 4 July 1828.[17]

On 19 June 1828 he was invited by Tom Steele, one of the Catholic Association's leaders, to oppose William

Vesey Fitzgerald, the newly appointed president of the board of trade, on his re-election for county Clare. But he declined to challenge his father's ally, not least because he was encouraged by the accession of another pro-Catholic to the cabinet and horrified by the threatened disruption of the customary connection between landlords and their tenants.[18] Although he had been praised by O'Connell in the Catholic Association, 5 June, and was so again by him from the hustings, 30 June, Smith O'Brien disapproved of his candidacy and the agitation which went with it.[19] Deploring the chaotic state of Ireland, he appealed for the immediate emancipation of the Catholics in the House, 3 July, and he unsuccessfully attempted to bring up a Clare petition against O'Connell's return, 16 July 1828. Like Lucius he signed the Irish Protestants' pro-Catholic declaration that autumn, when he took charge of the Ennis memorial complaining about the way in which the Clare Brunswick Club had been established.[20]

Smith O'Brien, who was listed by Planta, the patronage secretary, as likely to be 'with government' on the issue, was present to hear the announcement of the granting of Catholic emancipation in the king's speech, 5 Feb. 1829. It was because of this step that thereafter, in his more or less constant attendance over the next two years, he became an adherent of Wellington's administration, although he once stated that he had voted against it 'upon some questions which involved great constitutional principles'.[21] He sent in his resignation to the Catholic Association, 6 Feb., and in the Commons agreed to its suppression, it having now fulfilled its purpose, 10 Feb.[22] In the course of a ecstatic letter to Anne, 21 Feb., in which he gloried in the triumph of the Catholic cause and eulogized his father as one of its supporters, he declared that he felt 'like a slave who has shaken off his chains'.[23] He duly voted for emancipation, 6, 30 Mar. He spoke strongly for the related Irish franchise bill, 19 Mar., emphasizing that it would remove the influence of the priesthood from politics and improve proprietors' management of their estates. Such sentiments and the fact that he, as well as Lucius, left the House before the division on whether O'Connell should be allowed to take his seat unimpeded, 18 May, threatened to lead to a breach between them.[24] On O'Connell being required to have himself re-elected for Clare, Smith O'Brien issued a hostile address to the electors, 19 June 1829, in which he damned the Liberator for acting entirely from motives of self-interest. O'Connell forbore to reply to what he termed a 'very foolish and somewhat ferocious' production, but Steele, as a minor Clare landowner, resented his assertion that that it was 'not surprising' O'Connell 'should

not be an acceptable candidate to the gentry ... who see in him one who, in opposition to their *unanimous* wish, enticed the people, by false pretences, to displace the man of their choice'. A duel took place between him and Steele at Kilburn, 30 June, after which he almost had to fight Steele's second, the O'Gorman Mahon*, but he then stated that he had only meant 'unanimous' in the common sense of 'overwhelming' and the affair ended.[25] His father, who was forgiving about it, nevertheless pointed out that 'unanimous has been rather an unfortunate word for you and one which as a Member of Parliament you ought not to have used', and instructed him to 'in future weigh well and reconsider your paragraphs before you go to press'.[26] The sensation created by his intervention led to airy suggestions that he should himself stand for the county, which, at least in an undated letter to Anne, he was almost willing to countenance. But nothing came of this and by the time O'Connell, who threatened to attack his father's interest in the borough, was re-elected for Clare, 30 July 1829, he had already embarked on a short tour of the Low Countries and Germany.[27] By that summer, and possibly much earlier, he had begun an unfortunate liaison with Mary Anne Wilton, the sister of one of Lucius O'Brien's servants or agents; their first child, William O'Brien (1830-74), was born the following April, when, on condition of absolute secrecy being maintained, Lucius settled an annuity of £50 on the her, while another, Mary Wilton O'Brien (1831-1922), later married a Frenchman and had a family of her own.[28]

In January 1830 Smith O'Brien published a pamphlet entitled *Considerations relative to the renewal of the East India Company's Charter*, which advocated retaining the present system of governing India's peoples but called for relaxation of the China monopoly. It was welcomed by Peel, the home secretary, who thanked him for his 'approbation, confidence and support', and it secured him his appointment to the select committee on the Company's affairs, 8 Feb. (and again, 4 Feb. 1831).[29] He put in an almost constant attendance at it and, according to his proud father, he found his interest in politics rekindled and was 'delighted at coming almost daily in collision with men of superior mind'.[30] He divided against transferring East Retford's seats to Birmingham, 11 Feb., and parliamentary reform, 18 Feb., and was highly critical of O'Connell's radical reform proposals, 28 May. He voted for Jewish emancipation, 17 May. He divided against reducing the grant for South American missions and abolition of the death penalty for forgery, 7 June. Despite missing meetings of the Irish Members opposed to the increased Irish stamp and spirit duties, he insisted, in public letters dated 27 Apr. and 13 May, that he would resist ministers over this. He clashed with O'Connell about it, 30 June, and cast aspersions on his intentions, warning him to beware lest, 'in endeavouring to assume the character of a patriot, he does not overturn the existing institutions of the country'.[31] Unless it was his brother, he presented the county Clare petition against these tax rises, 2 July 1830, when he also brought up its one for alteration of the grand jury laws. Having canvassed and made hustings speeches in Lucius's unsuccessful campaign to retain his Clare seat, he was again returned for Ennis at the general election, but only after the O'Gorman Mahon had challenged his right to be brought forward.[32]

Smith O'Brien devoted much of that autumn to researching and consulting about another pamphlet, his *Plan for the relief of the poor of Ireland*, which on its appearance in November 1830 was admired for its recommendation of a voluntary system of local provision, although one rival commentator considered it futile and based on insufficient evidence.[33] He dismissed as worthless the previous session's select committee report on the Irish poor, 11 Nov., when he spoke and voted for O'Connell's motion for repeal of the Irish Subletting Act. Having been listed by ministers among their 'friends', he divided in their minority on the civil list, 15 Nov., and on the 20th, evidently in reply to a letter of commiseration, the out-going home secretary generously entreated him to ensure 'that no consideration of personal confidence in me may prevent you from taking any part in political affairs or forming any political connection which may best suit your views of the public interest'.[34] He gave notice for a bill founded on his ideas about Irish poor relief, 18 Nov., returning to this matter on 6, 9 Dec., and gave a cautious welcome to the Grey administration in relation to its intentions for Ireland, 23 Nov. 1830, when he ruled out appropriation of the revenues of the established church. Although he initially maintained contact with Peel, in January 1831 he began a supportive correspondence with the new Irish secretary Edward Smith Stanley about poor relief and other matters.[35] He obtained leave for his Irish poor bill, 8 Feb., when he congratulated the Irish government on its suppression of the O'Connellite repeal agitation, and secured its first reading, 15 Feb., but it was lost at the dissolution. He gave evidence against the validity of the return of the O'Gorman Mahon to the Clare election committee, 28 Feb., and on 14 Mar., having objected to the grant to the Kildare Place Society, he took a fortnight's leave in order to travel to Clare for the ensuing by-election. Supporting the unsuccess-

ful candidacy of his father, a reluctant reformer, his quarrel on the hustings with the O'Gorman Mahon's brother William Richard Mahon resulted in him fighting another, ultimately inconsequential, duel.[36] Perhaps fortuitously, given his family's ambivalent position, he missed the division on the second reading of the ministerial reform bill, 22 Mar., but he was in his place on the 30th to give a guarded endorsement to the programme of public works in Ireland.[37] He initiated a debate on the state of lawlessness in county Clare, 13 Apr., blaming the disturbances not on the indifference of local landlords but on the underlying poverty of the populace and calling for swift legislative intervention; however, on 10 May he privately admitted to Smith Stanley that he had unwittingly exaggerated his case.[38] He divided against Gascoyne's wrecking amendment to the reform bill, 19 Apr., but, as he had done on the 12th, on 20 Apr. 1831 he regretted that more additional seats had not been allotted to Ireland, if only because it strengthened the repeal cause, and denied that such an increase would give a greater than proportionate influence to the Catholic electorate.

Smith O'Brien had become a member of the Ennis Independent Club in March 1831 and was thought more than likely to continue as the borough's Member because of his considerable personal standing and liberal credentials, despite the eclipse of his father's electoral interests. However, he was forced to stand aside at the dissolution in April, perhaps owing to Sir Edward's disapproval of his recent parliamentary conduct, although by June, when he canvassed again, he was almost certain that his popularity would secure his re-election once the reform bill had been passed.[39] He provided most of the drive and initiative behind the abortive project to improve the navigation of the Fergus as far as Ennis, where he continued to maintain a high profile.[40] He kept up his increasingly liberal-minded correspondence with Smith Stanley, expressing his approval of the ministerial plan for national education in Ireland in September, and he wrote him a public letter in favour of alteration of the grand jury laws in December 1831.[41] The following month he issued a public address to O'Connell, condemning him as a mob orator and specifically criticizing him for failing to insist on a larger Irish representation at Westminster (he thought 125 Members a minimum) and for attacking rather than endeavouring to improve Irish legislation.[42]

Having raised suggestions about how to manage grand jury and other county assessments in August, on 9 Sept. 1832 Smith O'Brien announced that unforeseen personal circumstances had induced him to withdraw from Ennis. He claimed to have the support of five-sixths of the electorate and certainly incurred the displeasure of many of his political friends, but he may also have made enemies by his refusal to oppose the Union or to spend money.[43] This about-turn was caused by his rapid courtship of and marriage to the daughter of a Limerick alderman and country gentleman, which, combined with his parents' grudging decision to pass on part of the income from his grandfather's estate, naturally drew him more into the society and politics of the neighbouring county, although he did not take up residence at Cahermoyle until 1834.[44] There was at least one suggestion that he might try his hand in Clare and he was also invited to make a speculative attempt in county Limerick, but he did not stand for Parliament at the general election of 1832.[45] However, he was elected for county Limerick in 1835 and in the chamber, where he was respected as an unassuming politician and a clear speaker, he adopted the active Liberal principles of the former Limerick borough Member Thomas Spring Rice*, whom he had once described as 'my model'.[46] Denying that he ever had any pretensions as a party man, he later recalled that 'at each successive stage of my public career I enjoyed at least as much consideration in the House of Commons as my experience and abilities entitled me to expect', and that he had declined office because 'content with the moderate income which I possessed, I preferred independence to aggrandizement and held myself aloof alike from the obligations and from the rewards of party connection'.[47]

In this role he incurred the disdain of O'Connell, who believed him to be 'an exceedingly weak man, proud and self-conceited and, like all weak men, utterly impenetrable to advice'. Yet when he joined the Repeal Association in 1843 O'Connell welcomed him effusively, writing the following year that

I really think your accession quite providential – nothing less. You are by your 'antecedents' and your popular talents and your rank and religion just the 'beau ideal' of the person wanted to make the cause of repeal keep its course against the stream of persecution on the one hand and of otherwise inevitable desertion on the other.[48]

Yet, a year after O'Connell's death in mid-1847, Smith O'Brien was one of the Young Ireland leaders of the farcical 'cabbage patch' rebellion in Ballingarry, county Tipperary. He was convicted of high treason, 21 Sept. 1848, a judgment confirmed on appeal the following year, after which he was expelled from the Commons, 18 May 1849.[49] The original sentence of execution was commuted to one of transportation and he was held in Van Diemen's Land until 1854, when he was allowed

to return to Europe; he was granted a full pardon in 1856 and quietly lived out his days as a political writer. He died in June 1864, when Cahermoyle, which like his other estates had been in trust since before his trial, was inherited by his eldest son Edward William (1837-1909).[50] His statue by Thomas Farrell (1870), which stands very much overshadowed by O'Connell's on O'Connell Street, Dublin, gives his death date as 16 (not 18) June, an error which may have accidentally misled James Joyce in his choice of 'Bloomsday'. The struggles which Smith O'Brien endured, followed by his exile and homecoming, may bear superficial comparison with those of a latter-day Ulysses, but his life as a paradigm of lost opportunity was nonetheless a tragic metaphor for the shattered delusions of Ireland's mid-nineteenth century nationalists.[51]

[1] Based on R. Davis, *Revolutionary Imperialist: William Smith O'Brien, 1803-1864* (1998); R. Sloan, *William Smith O'Brien and Young Ireland Rebellion of 1848* (2000), and C. Heaney, *William Smith O'Brien, 1803-1864* (2004). [2] Davis, 11-13; Sloan, 12; *Rebel in his Fam.: Selected Pprs. of William Smith O'Brien* ed. R. and M. Davis, 4. [3] Davis, 10; Sloan, 12; I. O'Brien, *O'Brien of Thomond*, 196. [4] NLI, Smith O'Brien mss 426/1; 8655 (3), Smith O'Brien to mother, 10, 18 Mar., Sept. 1819, 5 June 1820; *Rebel in his Fam.* 4-6, 19-25. [5] Smith O'Brien mss 8655 (3), Smith O'Brien to fa. Sat. 18 [no month]; NLI, Inchiquin mss T23/2972, O'Brien to wife, 6 May 1820. [6] Sloan, 14-15, 29. [7] Inchiquin mss T24/3625, O'Brien to wife, 25 Feb.; 2979, same to same, 11, 30 Mar.; 3626, same to same, 18 Mar., 19 Apr. 1825; Davis, 18-19. [8] Inchiquin mss T24/3627; *Rebel in his Fam.* 25-26. [9] *Freeman's Jnl.* 27 May, 7 June 1826; Smith O'Brien mss 32717; Sloan, 16-17. [10] Smith O'Brien mss 32717; Sloan, 15-16; Davis, 20-22. [11] Smith O'Brien mss 464, draft address, pp. 15, 17; 32717. [12] Ibid. 449/3399; *Ennis Chron.* 1 Mar., 26 Apr. 1828; Davis, 23-24. [13] Inchiquin mss T24/2983, O'Brien to wife, 28 Apr., 1, 2 May 1828. [14] Smith O'Brien mss 32717. [15] Inchiquin mss T24/2983. [16] *Ennis Chron.* 21 June 1828; Smith O'Brien mss 18310 (1). [17] Smith O'Brien mss 10515 (4), Smith O'Brien to unknown, 25 Sept. 1844. [18] Ibid. 426/9-11; Davis, 28-30. [19] *Dublin Evening Post*, 7 June, 3 July; *Clare Jnl.* 7 July 1828. [20] *Dublin Evening Mail*, 8 Oct.; *Dublin Evening Post*, 15 Nov. 1828. [21] Smith O'Brien mss 10515 (4), Smith O'Brien to unknown, 25 Sept. 1844; 32717. [22] *Clare Jnl.* 12 Feb. 1829. [23] Smith O'Brien mss 18310 (1); Sloan, 19. [24] NLI, Stacpoole Kenny mss 18889 (13), W. to J. Macnamara, 24 May 1829; Sloan, 19. [25] *Clare Jnl.* 22 June, 6, 9, 13 July; *Dublin Evening Post*, 30 June, 4, 9 July 1829; Smith O'Brien mss 426/12-39; D. Gwynn, *O'Gorman Mahon*, 85-94. [26] Smith O'Brien mss 426/29. [27] Ibid. 18310 (1); Davis, 35, 40-41. [28] *Rebel in his Fam.* 6-7, 26-27, 82-83; H.W.L. Weir, 'William Smith O'Brien's Secret Pam.', *Other Clare*, xx (1996), 55-56. [29] Smith O'Brien mss 426/41. [30] Ibid. 32717; Inchiquin mss T26/3031, O'Brien to wife, 22, 25, 27 Feb. 1830. [31] *Clare Jnl.* 17, 20 May; *Dublin Evening Post*, 25 May 1830. [32] Smith O'Brien mss 32717; *Clare Jnl.* 22 July, 5, 12 Aug. 1830. [33] W.J. Fitzpatrick, *Life of Dr. Doyle*, ii. 232-4; *The Times*, 15 Nov. 1830; J. Connery, *The Reformer* (1831), 6-7, 22-30. [34] Smith O'Brien mss 426/45. [35] Ibid. 426/59, 62; Derby mss 920 Der (14) 122/5, Smith O'Brien to Smith Stanley, 2 Jan. 1831. [36] Smith O'Brien mss 32717; *Clare Jnl.* 14, 21, 24 Mar. 1831. [37] Sloan, 27. [38] Derby mss 122/5. [39] Ibid. Smith O'Brien to Smith Stanley, 15 June; *Clare Jnl.* 11 June 1831; Smith O'Brien mss 426/99, 100, 111, 112; 449/3398; 32717. [40] Smith O'Brien mss 427/140-74; *Clare Jnl.* 14 July, 3, 17, 20 Oct. 1831, 30 Jan., 2 Feb., 28 May, 23 July 1832. [41] Derby mss 122/5, Smith O'Brien to Smith Stanley, 18 Sept., 16 Dec.; *Dublin Evening Post*, 8 Dec. 1831; Sloan, 29-30. [42] *Clare Jnl.* 26 Jan. 1832. [43] Ibid.

30 Aug., 13 Sept. 1832; Smith O'Brien mss 427/170, 175, 181, 184; 449/3426-7; Sloan, 31-33; Davis, 61-62. [44] Sloan, 33-35; Davis, 62-65. [45] Smith O'Brien mss 426/135; 427/185. [46] Ibid. 18310 (1), Smith O'Brien to Anne O'Brien, n.d. [endorsed 1828]; [J. Grant], *Random Recollections of Lords and Commons* (1838), ii. 286-8. [47] Smith O'Brien mss 464, p. 13; 10515 (4), Smith O'Brien to unknown, 25 Sept. 1844. [48] *O'Connell Corresp.* vi. 2623; vii. 3061. [49] *CJ*, civ. 308-19. [50] *Limerick Chron.* 18 June; *The Times*, 20 June 1864. [51] *Gent. Mag.* (1864), ii. 252; *Weekly News*, 31 Dec. 1870; Sloan, 303; J. Joyce, *Ulysses*, ch. 6; Davis, p. vii; *Oxford DNB*.

S.M.F.

SMITH STANLEY, Edward, Lord Stanley (1775–1851), of Upper Grovsenor Street, Mdx.

PRESTON	1796–1812
LANCASHIRE	1812–1832

b. 21 Apr. 1775, 1st s. of Edward Smith Stanley[†], 12th earl of Derby, and 1st w. Lady Elizabeth Hamilton, da. of James, 6th duke of Hamilton [S]. *educ.* Eton 1789-92; Trinity Coll. Camb. 1792. *m.* 30 June 1798, his cos. Charlotte Margaret, da. of Rev. Geoffrey Hornby, rect. of Winwick, Lancs. 3s. 4da. (2 d.v.p.). *cr.* Bar. Stanley 22 Dec. 1832; *suc.* fa. as 13th earl of Derby 21 Oct. 1834; KG 2 Apr. 1839. *d.* 30 June 1851.
  Ld. lt. Lancs. 1834-d.
  Col. 2 R. Lancs. militia 1797; brevet col. 1797-1802.

Stanley, a staunch but inconspicuous Whig, was better known as a natural historian and collector than as a politician. In this he was hampered by his increasing deafness, poor looks and long period as heir apparent. His father, whose electoral interests he oversaw, was the head of the most powerful family in Lancashire, where he was lord lieutenant, influenced elections at Lancaster and Liverpool and returned one Preston and one county Member. Referred to affably by colleagues as 'Tongs' on account of his extreme thinness, large head and long limbs (a nick-name deliberately misconstrued when publicized by Henry Hunt*), Stanley was a shrewd, fairly consci-entious Member, who shared Derby's pro-Catholic sympathies and reservations on reform and took pride in select committee work and dealing with family and constituency business in Parliament. After the Peterloo massacre, radicals and Tories alike criticized his measured defence of the Manchester magistrates, the Lancashire grand jury (of which he was foreman at the summer assizes) and the Lancaster gaoler Higgins; and he also courted controversy by refusing to condemn outright the Liverpool ministry's repressive 'Six Acts'.[1] With Peterloo prosecutions, including that of Hunt, pending, and his eldest son, the future prime minister Edward George Geoffrey Smith Stanley*, too young to contest Preston as intended, the 1820

general election came at a difficult time for Stanley. He did not intervene at Lancaster or Liverpool, secured his third return for Lancashire with the eccentric Tory John Blackburne after a token poll, and assisted his brother-in-law Edmund Hornby* at Preston, where their interest prevailed in a severe contest involving Hunt.[2]

Stanley adhered to the main Whig opposition in the 1820 Parliament. A regular speaker on Lancashire issues, he occasionally challenged ministers in debate, but he was not a good orator and was eclipsed in this period by Edward. They were frequently confused in reports of parliamentary proceedings following the latter's return for Stockbridge on the Grosvenor inter-est in 1822. Stanley's support for the 1820 and 1821 parliamentary campaigns on behalf of Queen Caroline was unstinting although, like his father, who kept him informed of developments in the Lords, he privately admitted the 'impropriety of the queen's conduct'.[3] He pressed for the restoration of her name to the liturgy, 26 Jan., and effectively quizzed the leader of the House, Lord Castlereagh, over her £50,000 civil list award, 31 Jan. 1821. He divided for Catholic relief, 28 Feb. 1821, 1 Mar., 21 Apr., 10 May 1825. Bringing up a 10,000-signature Manchester pro-Catholic peti-tion, 10 May 1825, he contradicted the claim made by the home secretary Peel, on presenting a rival petition, that Lancashire was predominantly anti-Catholic. He voted to make Leeds a scot and lot borough under the Grampound disfranchisement bill, 2 Mar. 1821, knowing that the cotton towns of Manchester and Salford, who also coveted Grampound's seats, would accept a franchise more agreeable to the Lords.[4] He divided for Lord John Russell's reform proposal, 9 May 1821 (but not Lambton's, 18 Apr.), and again for reform, 25 Apr. 1822, 24 Apr., 2 June 1823, 26 Feb. 1824, 27 Apr. 1826. He attached 'great importance' to candidates' presence at elections and hated the notion of polling counties by districts, 20 Apr. 1826.[5] He voted in condemnation of electoral bribery, 26 May 1826.

Stanley was a principal speaker and majority teller for taking the printer Robert Thomas Weaver into custody after inquiry confirmed the involvement of Lord Londonderry (Castlereagh) in *John Bull*'s libel on Henry Grey Bennet, 11 May. 1821. Following his service on the 1817 and 1818 select committees, he had developed a keen interest in the poor laws and associ-ated issues, and he presented and endorsed petitions from Lancashire and elsewhere against the 1821 and 1822 poor bills, 4, 6 June 1821, 13, 20, 31 May 1822, when, as in 1824 and subsequently, he was a member of the select committee and planned legislation on vagrancy.[6] Canning scotched his attempt to embarrass government over apparent omissions and inconsistencies in diplomatic correspondence presented to the House, 24 Apr. He denied suggestions that the 30,000-signature Manchester petition for the abolition of colonial slavery (one of many he brought up in 1824 and 1826) was a forgery, 31 Mar. 1824.[7] He avoided declaring his views on abolition that day, but endorsed similar petitions, 24, 27 May, 1 June, and paired in condemnation of the indictment in Demerara of the Methodist missionary John Smith, 11 June 1824.[8]

Stanley undertook by far the greater share of constituency business and presented over 120 Lancashire petitions in the 1820 Parliament.[9] The revival in 1820 of the parliamentary campaign on behalf of the Peterloo radicals brought renewed criticism of Derby's county administration and his own conduct, but he easily refuted the radical George Dewhurst's allegations of ill-treatment at Lancaster gaol, 31 May 1820. He was unable to prevent the gaoler's failure to deliver letters to the convict Nathaniel Broadhurst that summer under the frank of William James from spawning breach of privilege motions, which, although defeated (by 86-33), 7 Mar. 1821, and (by 167-60), 25 Feb. 1822, tested him severely. He conceded on both occasions that there 'might be a breach of moral justice involved, but not one of law'. The Tory *Preston Sentinel* praised his 1822 speech.[10] Petitions brought up on behalf of the Peterloo veterans, 15 May 1821, also challenged his competence and, certain it would be defeated, he voted to concede inquiry to 'draw a line under the issue', 16 May. He reiterated his defence of the grand jury when a Liverpool petition cited its selection and oligarchic composition as factors in the 'failure to bring the Manchester yeomanry to justice', 12 June 1823. Accepting the sheriff Thomas Greene's* invitation to preside at the summer assizes, he wrote afterwards:

> I hardly know how to answer you, as I cannot suppose that you will be so hardy, when you recollect the anathemas that have lately been thrown out against the grand jury monopoly for this county, to persist in sanctioning so *wicked* a plan, by taking for your foreman one who must be of the fatal number of 38 monopolists. If, however, your courage carries you so far, I think I have already come in for so large a share of the censure, that it will make little difference whether I add another year to the score.[11]

He thwarted Liverpool's bids (1822-34) to replace Lancaster as Lancashire's assize town and con-

solidated his success in 1822-3 by carrying the 1824 Judges' Lodging Act, which ensured that facilities at Lancaster remained adequate.[12] Yet he remained a hostage to criticism by political rivals and aggrieved promoters of local bills that he opposed or otherwise failed to carry. When a partisan petition entrusted to Sir James Mackintosh from the Manchester attorney William Walker charged him with incompetence as chairman of the select committee on the Manchester gas light bill, it took the ingenuity of Edward, in his maiden speech, to spare him the embarrassment of seeing it accepted, 30 Mar. 1824. He fared better when Edward Curteis, who he pointed out had rarely attended the committee, renewed the attempt, 8 Apr. 1824.[13] He also had difficulty handling the Salford hundred court bill, which Bootle Wilbraham opposed for government, 13 May 1822; the Manchester and Salford loan company bill, which the president of the board of trade Huskisson condemned, 10 May 1824, and the Rochdale roads bill, 1 Mar. 1825. The Lowthers made him the scapegoat for the failure of the 1825 Liverpool-Manchester railway bill, which Derby opposed in the Lords, and he had to endure severe criticism in the press for failing to promote it when it was enacted in 1826.[14] He also had trouble in proving that his speech supporting the Lancashire grand jury's petition for revision of the game laws, 20 Apr., in which he allegedly criticized the authorities by stating that Lancashire was becoming increasingly lawless, had been misreported, even though he raised the matter in the House, where Bootle Wilbraham rallied to his assistance, 9 May 1826.[15]

Stanley's 'liberal' statements on trade were generally attuned to constituency interests and frequently endorsed by Huskisson, following his election for Liverpool in 1823. He echoed the Manchester Chamber of Commerce's pleas for easing commercial restrictions, 19 May 1820, 1 Mar. 1821, 20 May 1822; likewise their objections to increasing the duty on East Indian sugars, which, ignoring the chancellor of the exchequer Vansittart's denials, he insisted was a ploy to assist West Indian interests, 4 May 1821. He ordered papers to prove this, 7 May 1821, supported similar petitions, 3 May 1822, 9 May, and voted for inquiry, 22 May 1823.[16] He could be depended on to support the calico printers' campaign for lower duties, 29 June 1820,[17] and to oppose the truck system, which he equated with serfdom, 17 June 1822; but he would not endorse the prayer of the Manchester cotton workers' petition attributing their distress to new machinery, 25 Apr. He made it clear that he did not consider repealing the combination laws a suitable subject for a private Member's bill, 27 May 1823, called for 'caution' on bringing up petitions urging it, 15 Mar., 14 Apr. 1824, and warned Joseph Hume, who carried the 1824 repeal bill, of the 'personal risks to manufacturers testifying on combinations and the danger to which they would be exposed by the repeal of the existing laws'. He declined to approve petitions against their partial re-enactment, 25 Apr. 1825.[18] Dissatisfied with the government's policy, he presented petitions for repeal or revision of the corn laws, 22 Apr. 1825, 23, 27 Feb., 7 Apr., and voted for inquiry, 18 Apr. 1826. Endorsing a favourable petition from Bury, 5 May, he said he saw no point in releasing bonded corn untaxed, as dealers would be the sole beneficiaries, and suggested levying the duty in full and drawing on the revenue so generated to finance the work of the Committee for the Relief of the Distressed Manufacturers.[19] Canvassing and its cost preoccupied him at the general election of 1826, when lay-offs in manufacturing, corn law reform and Catholic relief were the main issues. He narrowly avoided a serious contest promoted by the Lowthers in the county, and Edward topped a 15-day poll at Preston, where their coalition with the corporation Tories had collapsed.[20]

Between January and April 1827 Stanley, who divided as hitherto for Catholic relief, 6 Mar. 1827 (and again, 12 May 1828), corresponded regularly with his constituents and colleagues on assistance for the depressed areas, corn, the East India Company's trading monopoly, local legislation, patronage and the projected transfer of Penryn's seats to Manchester. He attributed his infrequent attendance at this time to his father's gout and family problems.[21] His remarks on presenting petitions for corn law revision, 19, 26 Feb., 6 Mar. 1827, went unreported.[22] He voted against increased protection for barley, 12 Mar., and to delay supplies pending resolution of the succession to Lord Liverpool as premier, 30 Mar., and went over to government with his family after Canning took office, 1 May.[23] Anticipating concessions on Penryn, he pressed Manchester's case for enfranchisement, 8 May, when he candidly acknowledged local differences on the preferred voter qualification threshold, urged the prosecution of those guilty of bribery at Penryn and expressed unease at the prospect of sluicing the franchise there. Writing on 27 Apr. to the Manchester barrister George William Wood, he suggested a house-holder qualification of

£15 or £20. *I* certainly feel that if higher than the last mentioned rate, there would be great risk of making the election too much like a close borough, and on the other hand, possibly, lower than £15 (though *elsewhere* than in Manchester I should incline to £10) might let in *too* large a proportion of the *lower* orders. I certainly hope with

you that *some precautions* will be taken against excesses, but can you suggest any? For I fear it would be *impossible* to close all the public houses, as you have suggested. I should think it very probable that some endeavour may be made to limit the duration of any poll that might arise. Could you furnish me with any statement of the numbers of probable electors at *each* of the rates suggested either within the town of Manchester *alone*, or within the united towns of Manchester and Salford? For I think it would be hardly possible to separate *them*, though I do not think this idea should be admitted (which has been started) of including any of the adjoining townships, for it would be wholly impossible to draw any line, so as to include one, and exclude another.[24]

He presented and endorsed Manchester's petition for enfranchising 'populous towns' before voting to disfranchise Penryn, 28 May, and liaised with the Manchester delegation subsequently.[25] He brought up and endorsed further petitions for concessions in the India trade, 15 May, equal tariffs on East and West Indian produce, 21 May, and repeal of the Test Acts, 28, 30, 31 May, 6 June,[26] and introduced others for wage regulation, 18 May, and assisted emigration, 21 May 1827.[27] Representing the Lancashire colliery owners, he called for amendment of the Weights and Measures Act and suggested that government should sponsor legislation to relieve the county of the high cost of the Irish poor, 22 June 1827.[28] The prospect of Edward joining the junior ranks of Canning's administration and his own elevation to the Lords were broached in July but they held little attraction for Stanley. To his father, who saw it similarly, he explained:

As a Member for the county of Lancaster ... my present situation gives me a sufficiently respectable political character, *with employment*, which, if called up ... I must necessarily relinquish without obtaining any equivalent. I mean in the occupation of my time, and particularly with the possibility of Edward (who would, I conclude, probably succeed me for the county) having his time pretty well taken up in other ways, the business of the county would be thrown entirely upon the shoulders of the other Member ... Added to which is to be considered the pecuniary inconvenience of a simultaneous election both for the county and for Preston ... which might *possibly* occasion a failure there, and thus rather cause a loss than a gain to the very administration for the support of which the proposed measure is intended.

He refused to authorize Canning to move the Preston writ before the recess and dissuaded Edward from rushing to accept a seat on the treasury board.[29] Following Canning's death and after consulting Lord Lansdowne, he sanctioned Edward's appointment as under-secretary to Huskisson at the colonial office in Lord Goderich's coalition ministry.[30] Toeing the family line, he did not adhere to the incoming Wellington ministry in January 1828; but he delayed going into outright opposition until Penryn's fate had been decided, which coincided with the Huskissonite secession.[31]

He presented favourable petitions, 15, 22, 25 Feb., and voted to repeal the Test Acts, 26 Feb. 1828. He brought up petitions for Catholic relief 22 Apr., 9 May 1828. He was directed to bring in the abortive Penryn disfranchisement bill with Lord John Russell and the Manchester cotton manufacturer Sir George Philips, 31 Jan., and vainly opposed the attendant indemnity bill, 2, 3 Apr. He voted against sluicing the franchise at East Retford, 21 Mar., and recommitting the disfranchisement bill, 27 June. He brought up petitions for repeal of the Malt Act, 31 Mar., against the friendly societies bill, 18 Apr., 9 May, for permitting anatomical dissection, 22 Apr., 13 May, and urging the abolition of colonial slavery, 20 May. He delegated the contentious Manchester police bill, by which a £20 local franchise was established, to the Preston Member John Wood, who carried it, but handled the Manchester and Salford improvement bills himself.[32] He suggested minor changes to John Stuart Wortley's game bill, but conceded it was 'the best ... yet ... on the subject', 24, 26, 28 June. He divided against the archbishop of Canterbury's registrar bill, 12 June, and the proposed Buckingham House expenditure, 23 June, and voted for inquiry into the Irish church, 24 June. He made its late introduction and the government's refusal to hold it over his excuse for opposing the new churches bill, 30 June. He divided against them for ordnance reductions, 4 July. After reporting on the 7th from the committee on 'laws relating to Irish vagrants' (conceded to him, 12 Mar. 1828), he informed Edward:

> I think the committee generally understood and agreed with me, that till the Catholic question was over it was best not to stir in our question and, as our committee is pretty sure to take some time in discussion, for several have discordant propositions that they would wish to tack to the simple measure, I felt there was no chance of getting through this session.[33]

He also expressed misgivings lest his bill should be pre-empted by one proposing to introduce the English poor laws to Ireland.[34]

His soldier son Henry's gambling debts (which Derby agreed to assist with) and his stepmother's terminal illness preoccupied Stanley in 1829.[35] He divided for Catholic emancipation, 6, 30 Mar., and applauded its concession when presenting favourable petitions, 9, 16 Mar. Disparaging remarks he made on the 10th on the means by which anti-Catholic petitions had been procured, especially one from the Lonsdale hundred 'hawked about from house to house' and 'sent to the slate quarries to obtain the signatures of the miners', provoked damaging quarrels with its instigator Thomas Braddyll† of Conishead Priory, and presenter Greene, which Stanley rightly perceived presaged a bid by the Ultras to unseat him at the next election.[36] He criticized the proposed disbanding of his old militia regiment, 16 Mar., brought up petitions against 'huckshops' and for tax reductions that day, and several against altering the route of the Liverpool-Manchester railway, 23, 27 Mar. Illness prevented him from returning after the Easter recess, and he abandoned his Irish and Scottish poor bill for that session.[37] In August Edward made it known in Liverpool that he had a county seat in mind.[38] By December 1829 Stanley was fit for a long day's shooting and wrote waggishly to Edward of a family visit with his daughters and their families to Eaton Hall, where the Grosvenors' guests included 'Sir Foster Cunliffe* and Lady Cunliffe with two portentous misses, the younger the most horrible animal of the *manly* womankind that I ever had the misfortune to meet'.[39]

Stanley's minority votes for restricting the estimates to six months, 19 Feb., and the enfranchisement of Birmingham, Leeds and Manchester, 23 Feb., allayed but failed to silence speculation that the Derbys (and Grosvenors) would go over to government in 1830.[40] Making pressure of business their excuse, he and Edward boycotted the Whig meeting on 3 Mar., which invited Lord Althorp to become Commons leader.[41] Breaking his silence on distress when presenting a 13,000-signature petition from Manchester, 22 Mar., he acknowledged the severity of the economic downturn, but disputed the petitioners' claims that it was caused by 'currency change, military and naval expenditure and high public salaries', and said that although he welcomed Wellington's recent concessions, they did not go far enough. He added that he would vote for neither the radical Whig Edward Davenport's state of the nation motion nor the Ultra Curteis's amendment to it, 'because I do not think that their adoption is calculated to remove the evils complained of; but that on the contrary they will give rise to erroneous impressions and to unfounded hopes and expectations'. He divided against the navy estimates that day and sparingly with the revived Whig opposition (for tax revision, 25 Mar., against the Bathurst and Dundas pensions, 26 Mar., on Terceira, 28 Apr., the assistant treasury secretary's salary, 10 May, privy councillors' emoluments, 14 May, and Canada, 25

May). He endorsed the petitions he presented against the East India Company's trading monopoly, 22 Feb., 10, 15, 16, 22, 29 Mar., 12 May, and supported Littleton's truck bill, 3 17 May. He divided for Jewish emancipation that day and voted to abolish the death penalty for forgery, 7 June, for which he had paired, 24 May, and brought up favourable petitions 22 Mar., 26 Apr., 10, 17 May. He endorsed petitions against the sale of beer bill, 23, 29 Mar., 29 Apr., 4, 12, 17 May, criticized it as counter-productive, 29 Apr., 3 May, and voted to restrict its provisions for on-consumption, 21 June. He deemed petitions for temperance and Sunday closing 'laudable' in their general objective but not viable, 4 June. He praised the motives of the Cheshire, Derbyshire, Lancashire and Yorkshire calico printers in seeking to regulate their trade by limiting apprentice numbers and taxing machinery, 24 May. He cautioned against rushing through the 'half-pay apprentices' bill that Parliament, 11 June. Introducing his Irish and Scottish vagrants bill, 11 June, he portrayed it as a 'gradual' measure, calculated to relieve parishes through which the vagrants passed, 24 May, and conceded on the 26th that he had no prospect of carrying it that session. On 4 June he acknowledged that although he had anticipated hostility in London, he had been taken aback by Lancashire's opposition, for it had never been his intention, as his opponents maintained, to make removals compulsory. Blackburne's forthcoming retirement and the candidature of the Ultra John Wilson Patten had been announced in November 1829, and with other contenders manoeuvring Stanley attended closely to county business before the 1830 dissolution. He took charge of the Wigan-Newton, Warrington-Newton, St. Helens-Runcorn Gap and Stockport junction railway bills (succeeding with the first two). He also assisted with the Sankey Navigation and Liverpool Docks bills, and carried improvement bills for Bolton, Manchester and Salford in the teeth of strong opposition. He intended making way for Edward in the county in the event of a contest, but none ensued, so he came in with Wilson Patten, leaving Edward to defeat Hunt at Preston. On the hustings he praised Wellington for conceding emancipation, hoped he would promote reform and declared against the ballot and the East India Company's monopoly.[42] Discussing the election results with Henry Brougham* before the opening of the Liverpool-Manchester railway in September 1830, he wrote: 'I fear Wellington trembles, but what is to be the result if he fall? I see no one fit to seize the staff and to wield it properly'.[43]

Ministers naturally listed Stanley among their 'foes' and he voted to bring them down on the civil list, 15

Nov. 1830. He estimated that he presented over 120 Lancashire anti-slavery petitions that month. He and Derby corresponded closely on the November 1830 Liverpool by-election, unrest in the manufacturing districts, on which government sought their advice, Edward's appointment as the Grey ministry's Irish secretary and his subsequent defeat by Hunt at Preston.[44] Edward's office made Stanley an easy target for criticism by the Tory opposition. He presented petitions and lobbied against the truck system, 11 Dec., and the calico duties with Wilson Patten, 8, 9, 28 Feb. Differing from him, he endorsed the drawback on calicoes that the government proposed, 28 Feb. He presented favourable petitions but opposed the Preston-Manchester railway bill on behalf of the promoters of the rival Preston-Wigan scheme, 9, 25 Feb., 18, 21, 24 Mar. Opposition denounced the amendment he carried at its third that day reading as a 'job'. He handled the Leeds-Liverpool and Leeds-Manchester railway bills, 25 Feb., 18, 28 Mar., and reported from the committee on the bill to provide additional funding for the Liverpool-Manchester railway, 28 Mar.[45] Contradicting Hunt, he testified to the increasing groundswell for reform in Lancashire and denounced the ballot as a ploy to 'open the door to deceit and hypocrisy, occasioning the smiling to faces and the stabbing behind backs', 26 Feb. He declined to endorse a request for it in the Liverpool petition he presented that day and refused to comment on the recent bribery there or discuss the petitioners' demand for the enfranchisement of 'substantial' householders. He expressed full confidence in the ministerial reform bill, including its provisions for Lancashire, 9 Mar., brought up favourable petitions, 17, 18, 19, 22 Mar., and divided for its second reading, 22 Mar. He countered the anti-reformers' criticism of its 'generous provision' for county Durham and Lancashire, 25 Mar. He introduced favourable petitions from Broughton and Denton and elsewhere, 14 Apr. Unable to pre-empt or interrupt Hunt's tirade against the bill, 18 Apr., he retaliated by condemning the conduct of the radicals at recent mass meetings which Hunt had addressed, and criticized him severely for neglecting Lancashire business in the House, especially select committees. He voted against Gascoyne's wrecking amendment, 19 Apr. 1831. At the ensuing general election he dissuaded Edward from attempting Preston, supported his nephew Patrick Maxwell Stewart* at Lancaster and proposed a coalition between John Evelyn Denison* and William Ewart* at Liverpool. Wilson Patten's late decision to stand down dismayed him, but he acquiesced in the return of the Unitarian banker and reformer Benjamin Heywood as his colleague for the county.[46] An editorial in the Tory *Manchester Herald* quipped:

> Whatever may be said of the other candidates, Lord Stanley has had an easy time of it. His readiness to lop off thirty or forty English Members has saved him a world of trouble. If he has canvassed at all, it was within a very limited or a very *select* circle.[47]

Privately, he considered the bill's passage vital to allay unrest, but hoped for alterations in its details. Writing to Lord Holland from Liverpool, 8 June, he confided his misgivings:

> The rate of qualification which as it now stands will entail upon our large towns such as this and Manchester so enormous a host of voters. What think you of the agitation of a contest in either, with from 18,000 to 25,000, and some say, from 20 to 40,000 voters? And consider the class of voter! I hope the division of counties is not to be, as it at present appears ... I am *very* anxious it [Lancashire] should *not* be divided, and I *think* such is the general feeling. I fear that the result will be to throw the county representation too much out of the landed scale.[48]

Before returning to suffer 'the process of boiling in that human cauldron, London', he attended a calico printers' dinner in Manchester with Wilson Patten, 17 June 1831, and promoted the candidature of Lord Sandon* as Denison's Liverpool replacement.[49]

Stanley used Lancashire evidence to counter the former chancellor of the exchequer Goulburn's claims that the 1830 Sale of Beer Act had only caused problems in agricultural districts, and called on government to introduce remedial legislation, 30 June 1831. He divided for the reintroduced reform bill at its second reading, 6 July, and generally for its details. However, he cast wayward votes for the total disfranchisement of Saltash, which ministers no longer pressed, 26 July, and to award Stoke-on-Trent a second Member (for which he also spoke), 4 Aug., and voted 'without apology' against the proposed division of counties, 11 Aug.[50] He ably contradicted Hunt's assertions that Heywood was pledged to support universal suffrage, 8 July, and he upheld the right of English Members to comment on the bill's proposals for Scottish and Irish constituencies and *vice versa*, 4 Aug. He countered Wason's case for the separate enfranchisement of Toxteth Park by presenting another for a third Liverpool seat, which he neither pursued nor forced to a division, 6 Aug. He defended the bill's provisions for Lancashire, but acknowledged that the county sought additional representation, 10 Aug. He divided for the bill's passage, 21 Sept., and the second reading of the Scottish bill, 23 Sept. He was absent from the division on Lord Ebrington's confidence motion, 10 Oct. He

voted for the second reading of the revised reform bill, 17 Dec. 1831, against introducing a £10 poor rate franchise, 3 Feb., and for its provisions for Tower Hamlets, 28 Feb., and Gateshead, 5 Mar. 1832. He divided for its third reading, 22 Mar., and the address calling on the king to appoint only ministers who would carry it unimpaired, 10 May. He declined next day to present a hurriedly adopted Manchester petition requesting that supplies be withheld pending its passage.[51] According to the *Mirror of Parliament*, 11 May, he explained (after John Wood introduced the petition) that he considered this action too extreme, although he regretted the bill's mutilation in the Lords, and regarded its loss as a 'national calamity'. Appealing for calm and firmness, he added that should a ministry headed by Wellington 'bring forward a measure of equal extent and efficiency ... I should not be able to place confidence in them, nor do I believe that they would be able to give satisfaction out of doors'. Other reporters noted that he confirmed that the sentiments of the petition were those 'of the great majority of the people of Lancashire and the northern counties'.[52] He divided for the Irish reform bill at its second reading, 25 May, and against a Conservative amendment to the Scottish measure, 1 June. Justifying an amendment to the boundary bill substituting Newton for Wigan as the election venue for Lancashire South, he pointed out that 'all the railways go through Newton before getting to Wigan', 7 June 1832.

He voted in the minority for appointing 11 of its original members to the reconstituted Dublin election committee, 29 July, but divided with government on the election controversy, 23 Aug. 1831, against the Irish union of parishes bill, 19 Aug., on the Russian-Dutch loan, 26 Jan., 12, 16 July (paired), Portugal, 9 Feb., and the navy civil departments bill, 6 Apr. 1832. Bringing up a petition for a new Liverpool writ, 29 Aug. 1831, he criticized Benett's franchise bill as unfair to Liverpool freemen like himself who had not voted in November 1830 and those subsequently admitted, and warned that 'conjointly with the ... reform bill' it would throw 'the representation into the hands of the winning parties'. As usual, he brought up petitions on many local bills and issues, including flour imports, combinations and savings banks, 14 July 1831, and the unpopular general register bill, 13 Feb. 1832. His conduct as chairman of the committee on the Manchester-Leeds railway bill was severely criticized on the floor of the House, when a committee of appeal was conceded, 18 July, and again, 28 July 1831. He was also called on to justify his handling of legislation for the Warrington-Newton railway, 4, 9 Aug. He quizzed its instigator Hobhouse, 30 July 1831, and presented petitions in favour of the factory regulation bill, 13 Feb., 13, 14 Mar. 1832. He presented hostile petitions, 9, 10 Apr., and reported from the committee on the Manchester-Bolton-Bury railway bill, 11 May, and brought up petitions for the Birmingham-Leeds scheme, 22 May. He defended his conduct as a member of the committee on the Manchester improvement bill and as grand jury foreman, when they were criticized on 23, 26 Feb., 27 Mar. 1832 by Hunt, who used the October 1831 Preston riots to revive the campaign against the Peterloo magistrates and the grand jury.

Pleading increasing deafness, Stanley announced in July 1832 that he was standing down at the dissolution. The *Manchester Guardian* praised his 'constant accessibility' and 'devotion of time and talents to his constituents'.[53] As agreed in April 1831, he was raised to the peerage after the general election in December, when Edward came in for Lancashire North and Henry for Preston, where the Whig-Tory coalition was restored.[54] He succeeded as 13th earl in October 1834 and became a knight of the garter in 1839, but was denied (1837, 1839) the dukedom he coveted. He recovered from a stroke which cost him 'the use of the left side leg and arm', and died at Knowsley following another in June 1851. He was buried alongside his wife in the old family vault at Ormskirk. He was recalled as a president of the Linnaean Society (1828-34) and London Zoological Society (1834-d.) and as the founder at Knowsley of a museum and private zoo of 1,293 birds and 345 mammals, whose upkeep (£15,000 a year) severely encumbered his estates.[55] Although his will was proved under £12,000 in the province of York and £12,000 in Canterbury, 22 Oct. 1851, he was deemed insolvent. Edward, as 14th earl, executed his instructions for the disposal of his collections (by gift to the queen and to London Zoo and by sale), raising £7,000.[56]

¹ Lancs. RO HS3, grand jury minutes, 1800-33. ² J. Belchem, 'Orator' Hunt, 114-8; Cowdroy's Manchester Gazette, 19 Feb.; Lancaster Gazette, 18 Mar.; Manchester Mercury, 21 Mar. 1820. ³ Derby mss 920 Der (13) 1/161/19, 20. ⁴ Lancs. RO, Hulton mss DDHu/53/62. ⁵ The Times, 21 Apr. 1826. ⁶ Ibid. 5, 7 June 1821, 14, 21 May, 1 June 1822. ⁷ Ibid. 13, 23, 26 Mar. 1824, 28 Feb., 17 Mar., 20 May 1826. ⁸ Ibid. 25, 28 May, 2 June 1824. ⁹ Ibid. 17 May 1820, 27 Jan., 2, 29 Mar., 5, 7 June 1821, 16 Feb., 9 Mar., 1, 4, 11, 21, 31 May, 1, 4 June 1822, 26 Mar., 23 Apr., 10 May 1823, 6, 13, 16, 23, 26 Mar., 1, 6 Apr., 8, 12, 14, 22, 25, 28 May, 2 June 1824, 16, 22, 23, 30 Apr., 21 May, 1 June 1825, 24, 28 Feb. 17 Mar., 8, 13, 29 Apr., 6, 13, 20 May 1826. ¹⁰ Hulton mss 53/59; The Times, 8 Mar. 1821; Preston Sentinel, 2 Mar. 1822. ¹¹ HLRO, Greene mss GRE4/6, 7. ¹² Ibid. GRE4/1-5. The Times, 3 Mar., 1, 3 Apr. 1824. ¹³ The Times, 9 Apr. 1824. ¹⁴ Ibid. 14 May 1822; Blackburn Mail, 12 Apr. 1826. ¹⁵ Blackburn Mail, 3 May 1826. ¹⁶ The Times, 2 Mar., 8 May 1821, 4, 21 May 1822, 10 May 1823. ¹⁷ The Times, 22, 30 June 1820. ¹⁸ Ibid. 16 Mar. 1824. ¹⁹ Ibid. 23 Apr. 1825, 24, 28 Feb., 8 Apr. 1826. ²⁰ Ibid. 2, 10, 19 June; Manchester Mercury, 20 June

1826; Lancs. RO, Derby [of Knowsley] mss DDK 1740/3. ²¹ Derby mss (13) 2, Stanley's letterbks. vols. i and iii, passim. ²² The Times, 20, 27 Feb., 7 Mar. 1827. ²³ Stanley's letterbk. i, f. 39. ²⁴ Ibid. f. 36. ²⁵ Ibid. iii, ff. 97 et seq.; The Times, 29 May 1827; M.J. Turner, 'Manchester Reformers and the Penryn Seats', Northern Hist. xxx (1994), 152-4. ²⁶ Stanley's letterbk. i, f. 42; 3, ff. 93-97; The Times, 16, 19, 22, 29, 31 May, 1, 7 June 1827. ²⁷ The Times, 19, 22 May 1827. ²⁸ Ibid. 23 June 1827. ²⁹ Derby mss (12), Stanley to Derby [n.d. July]; Add. 51566, Derby to Holland, 14 July, Stanley to same, 14 July 1827. ³⁰ Add. 38750, f. 22. ³¹ A. Mitchell, Whigs in Opposition, 209. ³² LSE Lib. Archives Division, Coll. Misc. 0146, Potter mss, letterbk. xii, Brotherton to R. Potter, 23 Apr., Baxter to W. Harvey, 2 May 1828. ³³ Derby mss (14), Stanley to Smith Stanley [n.d.] ³⁴ Ibid. Stanley to Smith Stanley, [n.d.]. ³⁵ Ibid. (13) 1/161/23. ³⁶ Greene mss 4/16; Derby mss (13) 1/161/24. ³⁷ Derby mss (14) 63, Derby to Smith Stanley, 23, 27 May 1829. ³⁸ Albion, 31 Aug. 1829. ³⁹ Derby mss (14) 63, Stanley to Smith Stanley, 30 Dec. 1829. ⁴⁰ Mitchell, 236. ⁴¹ Castle Howard mss, Graham to Morpeth [3 Mar.] 1830; Mitchell, 227. ⁴² Manchester Guardian, 7 Aug. 1830. ⁴³ Brougham mss. ⁴⁴ Derby mss (13) 1/161/25-28; Add. 51835, Arbuthnot to Holland, 7 Dec. 1830. ⁴⁵ St. Deiniol's Lib. Glynne-Gladstone mss 197, T. to J. Gladstone, 18 Mar. 1831. ⁴⁶ Derby mss (14) 116/6, Winstanley to Smith Stanley, 25 Apr.; Brougham mss, Shepherd to Brougham [n.d.]; Lancaster Herald, 30 Apr., 7, 14 May 1831. ⁴⁷ Manchester Herald, 11 May 1831. ⁴⁸ Add. 51836. ⁴⁹ Ibid.; Manchester Guardian, 18 June 1831. ⁵⁰ Lancaster Gazette, 20 Aug. 1831. ⁵¹ Manchester Guardian, 12 May; Manchester Herald, 14 May 1832. ⁵² Parl. Deb. (ser. 3), xii. 893; The Times, 12 May 1832. ⁵³ Manchester Guardian, 7 July; Manchester Herald, 11 July 1832. ⁵⁴ PRO NI, Anglesey mss D619/27A/114; Devon RO, Earl Fortescue mss 1261M/FC88, Grey to Ebrington, 19 Aug. 1832. ⁵⁵ Manchester Guardian, 25 Oct. 1834, 2 July 1851; Derby [of Knowsley] mss DDK 33/8; Brougham mss, Smith Stanley to Brougham, 9 Sept. 1838. ⁵⁶ PROB 11/2140/780; IR26/1895/724; Lancs. RO, Lancs. Evening Post deposit DDPr 138/76; P.E. Stanley, House of Stanley, 284-6, 289; Oxford DNB.

M.M.E.

SMITH STANLEY, Edward George Geoffrey (1799-1869).[1]

STOCKBRIDGE	30 July 1822–1826
PRESTON	1826–Nov. 1830
NEW WINDSOR	10 Feb. 1831–1832
LANCASHIRE NORTH	1832–5 Sept. 1844

b. 29 Mar. 1799, 1st s. of Edward Smith Stanley, Lord Stanley* (later 13th earl of Derby), and Charlotte Margaret, da. of Rev. Geoffrey Hornby, rect. of Winwick, Lancs. *educ.* Eton 1811; Christ Church, Oxf. 1817, DCL 1852; American tour 1824-5. *m.* 31 May 1825, Emma Caroline, da. of Edward Bootle Wilbraham*, 4s. (2 *d.v.p.*) 2da. (1 *d.v.p.*). *styled* Lord Stanley 1834-44; *summ.* to Lords in his fa.'s barony as Lord Stanley of Bickerstaffe 4 Nov. 1844; *suc.* fa. as 14th earl of Derby 30 June 1851; KG 28 June 1859; GCMG 25 Mar. 1869. *d.* 23 Oct. 1869.

Under-sec. of state for war and colonies Sept. 1827-Jan. 1828; PC 22 Nov. 1830, PC [I] 10 Jan. 1831; chief sec. to ld. lt. [I] Nov. 1830-Mar. 1833, with seat in cabinet June 1831; sec. of state for war and colonies Apr. 1833-May 1834, Sept. 1841-Dec. 1845; first ld. of treasury 27

Feb.-28 Dec. 1852, 26 Feb. 1858-18 June 1859, 6 July 1866-29 Feb. 1868.

Ld. rect. Glasgow Univ. 1834-6; Sloane trustee, Brit. Mus. 1835-66; chan. Oxf. Univ. 1852-*d*.; elder bro. Trinity House 1852-*d*.

'Young Stanley', of whom it was reported in an apt but inaccurate overstatement that he was 'the only brilliant eldest son produced by the British peerage for a hundred years', proved himself one of the most gifted parliamentary debutants of his generation and a cabinet minister of considerable promise and distinction in this period.[2] Brought up at the family seat of Knowsley, near Liverpool, to cherish the vigorous Foxite Whiggery of his grandfather, the 12th earl of Derby, whose actress wife Elizabeth Farren apparently taught him how to make the most of his tenor voice, Smith Stanley escaped the dogged mediocrity of his father, Member for Preston and Lancashire, and the cloying piety of his mother (though his children's edition of the Parables attested to a youthful Evangelical streak) to become an accomplished classicist and a devoted sportsman.[3] Dashing, boyish and witty when seeking to charm, his many detractors would, however, invariably find fault with his overbearing superciliousness – Sydney Smith wrote of him, when fresh from Oxford, that 'a more unmannerly, ungracious person I never saw' – and not a few commentators, his grandfather apparently among them, were later to doubt whether he could scale the heights of statesmanship that seemed to await him.[4]

Smith Stanley, who joined Brooks's in 1819, was still just under age at the general election early the following year, when he was in Preston to assist in the return of his uncle Edmund Hornby, who thus continued to hold the family seat there as his locum.[5] Delighted by his travels in the early 1820s in Italy, where he was briefly incarcerated, he was equally pleased to be brought in quietly by Lord Grosvenor for his newly acquired borough of Stockbridge in the summer of 1822, although he insisted that he would not necessarily feel bound to vote as his Whig patron would wish on reform or any other issue.[6] He spoke with great effect on the hustings, but, perhaps at the behest of Derby, who hoped he would not be in a hurry to perform, he at first remained silent in the Commons.[7] Instead, ambitious of making a profession for himself in public life, he, for the second time, turned that autumn to Lord Lansdowne for a guide to the best historical and legal literature; thanking him for the daunting reading list which he received in reply, he expressed his relief at escaping the albeit alluring prospect of contesting Liverpool, where his grandfather's county influ-

ence might have led to him being put up in place of Canning, the new foreign secretary.[8] It was from the sober and moderate Lansdowne that he absorbed the political philosophy of broadminded Whiggism which he would retain throughout his career: a conception of the primacy of parliamentary politics as governed by the privileged position of aristocratic leadership and mediated through the workings of party connection.[9]

His first known votes were given against the military and naval pensions bill, 14 Apr., and for repeal of the Foreign Enlistment Act, 16 Apr. 1823. Like his father, who presumably took him under his wing, he was in the majorities for inquiry into the legal proceedings against the Dublin Orange rioters, 22 Apr., and against another into the currency, 12 June. He divided for parliamentary reform, 24 Apr. 1823, and alteration of the representation of Edinburgh, 26 Feb. 1824, 13 Apr. 1826. He voted for inquiry prior to the introduction of the Irish insurrection bill, 12 May, and to condemn the conduct of the lord advocate in the Borthwick case, 3 June 1823, and the lord chancellor over a breach of privilege, 1 Mar. 1824. He may sometimes have been confused in the parliamentary reports with Lord Stanley, who was more assiduous on local business, but on 25 Mar. he brought up several Lancashire anti-slavery petitions and one from Preston against the combination laws; having reverted to the latter the following day, he accepted the congratulations offered afterwards by Canning, who wrote to his wife on the 28th that 'they tell me he is by no means violently hostile'.[10] He made an admirable maiden speech, defending his father's handling of the Manchester gas light bill, 30 Mar., when Sir James Mackintosh publicly praised him and Hudson Gurney* privately recorded that he was 'the most promising *practical* beginner I have heard'.[11] To his grandfather's distress, he spoke and voted against Hume's motion attacking the Irish church establishment, 6 May, after which Charles Williams Wynn*, president of the India board, commented that it was 'the fashion of the opposition to bemoan the hard fate of poor Lord Derby in seeing his grandson act for himself and profess so much attachment to the church; his speech was really first rate'.[12] He slightly qualified his remarks, 11 May, when he was named to the select committee on the state of Ireland, and that month it was stated that George Tierney*, the former Whig leader, 'raves of his cleverness and promise'.[13] He voted with opposition to condemn the trial of the Methodist missionary John Smith in Demerara, 11 June 1824.

In what was politely considered a wild scheme, Smith Stanley and the other young 'fashionables'

John Evelyn Denison*, Henry Labouchere* and John Stuart Wortley* left England in June 1824 for an extensive and reflective tour of the United States and Canada.[14] He returned early the following year with a marked aversion to slavery and a sense of regret that, unlike the potential solution available of establishing a Catholic church in Canada, no such arrangement could be made in Ireland without endangering the Protestant religion there.[15] Anxious to be back before any possible dissolution, he was present to vote for Catholic relief, 21 Apr., 10 May 1825. According to his notebook of parliamentary proceedings, he divided to raise the elective franchise in Ireland, of which he wrote that he 'would have voted for it independently of the Catholic question', 26 Apr., and for paying Catholic priests, the other proposed 'wing', 29 Apr.[16] He was in the minority against the grant for the duke of Cumberland, 27 May 1825. Derby having waived any objections to his taking the daughter of a Tory neighbour in wedlock, he married on the 31st and for a time resided on the family estate at Ballykisteen, county Tipperary, where he rebuilt the mansion house. Although living in isolation there, he further developed his interests in Irish affairs, especially about the parlous state of the poor and the iniquities of tithe-holders and non-resident landlords, which he hoped could be partially alleviated through schemes of assisted emigration. Intending to remain at his father-in-law's till after the start of the new session, he doubted there would be much to dispute in Parliament.[17] Apart from moving the unsuccessful wrecking amendment against the Liverpool and Manchester railway bill, 6 Apr., his only significant speech that year was on 8 May, in support of the ministerial plan for the emergency admission of foreign corn, to which he briefly urged a minor amendment, 11, 12 May 1826.

Offering in lieu of Hornby for Preston as a supporter of Catholic claims and moderate reform at the general election of 1826, he made the best of a severe contest and was returned in first place with the advanced radical Whig John Wood, against the Tory Robert Barrie, whom (in line with the collapse of Derby's coalition with the corporation) he was obliged to disavow, and the radical William Cobbett†, who made him the butt of numerous offensive epithets (such as 'the honourable spitting box').[18] He seconded the motion for leave for the bill to authorize the sale of Canadian clergy reserves, arguing that this would help agricultural improvement without jeopardizing the stability of the Protestant church, 20 Feb. 1827. Noting the bitterness generated by the debate, he gave a silent vote for Catholic relief, 6 Mar. He was in opposition minorities for inquiry into the allegations against the corporation of Leicester, 15 Mar., information on the Orange procession and Lisburn magistrates, 29 Mar., and for referring the Irish miscellaneous estimates to a select committee, 5 Apr. He divided for Newport's unsuccessful amendment for a higher duty on flour, 19 Mar., but against Hume's for gradually lowering the duty on wheat to 10s., 27 Mar., and for the second reading of the ministerial corn bill, 2 Apr. He voted for Tierney's motion to postpone the committee of supply, 30 Mar., and against the newly installed Canning administration in favour of disfranchising Penryn, 28 May, 6 June.[19] Observing that there was no one who could obviously succeed as prime minister in the event of Canning's death, 19 May, Edward Littleton, Member for Staffordshire, added his regret that 'Mr. Stanley, a young man, competent to any post, is not brought into office'.[20] However, Smith Stanley divided with government for the Coventry magistracy bill, 11, 18 June, when he replied to the former home secretary Peel, the grant for water communications in Canada, 12 June, and the temporary corn bill, 18 June.[21] Under Lansdowne's aegis, he received an offer of a place at the treasury that month, but, although the family gave in its adherence to ministers, this was declined, partly because he required assurances that he would rise higher and partly, as with the suggestion of a peerage for his father, because of Derby's reluctance to sanction by-elections in Preston and Lancashire, where it was understood that he would eventually inherit a seat.[22] Following the death of Canning in early August 1827, it was suspected that he might be given an under-secretaryship at the foreign office, but, as a key element in the demands made by the Lansdowne Whigs in negotiating with the new premier Lord Goderich, he was offered one at the colonial department under Canning's political heir William Huskisson* the following month, apparently with the reversion of the office of Irish secretary whenever it was vacated by William Lamb*. He took up the work immediately and, despite his inexperience, was expected to shine as a man of business; Robert Wilmot Horton*, whom he refused to oblige by transferring to the board of trade, did not immediately resign the salary which came with the post and his appointment was not in fact gazetted.[23]

Tipped to be chancellor of the exchequer if the ailing Goderich administration gave way to a Whig one, in January 1828 Smith Stanley was witnessed by Countess Gower displaying 'negligence and apathy' towards the grave ministerial prospects. Lord Palmerston*, the secretary at war, reported to Lady Cowper on the 14th that 'Stanley, they say, considers himself now as attached to Huskisson and will at all events remain', but, Smith Stanley wrote to Lord Sandon* on the 17th that 'I hope, but hardly expect such a mixed government as I imagine you and I would both wish to see' and 'am quite ready to go out or stay in as things may turn out'.[24] On the duke of Wellington's appointment as premier later that month he seceded with the other Lansdowne Whigs, though Huskisson, who stayed at the colonial office, offered to retain him; his supporter Lady Holland, who considered him 'very ambitious' but 'far from popular with his young colleagues', observed that he 'was pleased with the business of the office and liked Mr. Huskisson personally very much' but had 'properly given in his resignation'.[25] Considered by Wellington as likely to be hostile on the finance committee, to which he was named on 15 Feb., he spoke in vindication of his conduct, 18 Feb. 1828, when he expressed his displeasure at Huskisson's abandonment of Canning's principles and his conviction that, nevertheless, 'the old and stubborn streak of Toryism is at last yielding to the increasing liberality of the age'.[26] His speech, which astonished Charles Baring Wall* was described by Charles Percy* as being *'offensive in so young a man, of no great talent and with more than fitting personality to Huskisson, considering that he held his late appointment by his kindness only'*.[27]

Smith Stanley voted for repeal of the Test Acts, 26 Feb., and Catholic relief, 12 May 1828. In early March he and Wood gave up their Preston poll bill, first introduced the previous year, which was opposed by the corporation.[28] Maintaining his interest in colonial affairs, he supported the passengers regulation bill several times that month and opposed the production of information on the Canada Company, 27 Mar. He divided against extending East Retford into the hundred of Bassetlaw, 21 Mar., and for transferring Penryn's seats to Manchester, 24 Feb. He argued that Huskisson's corn bill betrayed the principles of Canning's resolutions of the previous year, 22 Apr., when he acted as teller for John Calcraft's unsuccessful amendment for a lower pivot price, and voted against Henry Bankes and Edward Portman's unsuccessful amendments, 25 Apr., and again, 20 May, when he divided for information on civil list pensions. He welcomed Huskisson's appointment of a select committee on Canada, of which he became a member, 2 May, and, speaking 'very well and handsomely' according to Lord Seaford, vindicated Canning's memory in the debate on making provision for his family, 13 May.[29] He spoke, including in answer to Peel, now reinstated as home secretary, and voted for giving East Retford's seats to Birmingham, 19 May, when he declared that 'I am no theoretic reformer, but whenever a case

occurs when reform is necessary and practicable I will adopt it'. Following the subsequent dismissal of the Huskissonites, there was some thought that the bait of the Irish secretaryship might secure him to government, but nothing came of this and, as he carried all before him in the Commons, the cabinet minister Lord Ellenborough feared that 'now Stanley will lead the opposition and terrify Peel'; however, his attempt to organize a concerted assault on ministers was quashed by the Whig leadership.[30] Again speaking and voting against sluicing East Retford, 2 June, he noted in his journal that there was a 'great muster by government and threats of a dissolution, which is prevented by their satisfactory majority'. He presented and endorsed a Liverpool petition for its franchise to be confined to respectable householders only, 9 June. He intervened and divided (sometimes as a teller) for economies in relation to the archbishop of Canterbury's bill, 16 June, Buckingham House, 23 June, the salary of the lieutenant-general of the ordnance, 4 July, and the ordnance survey and North American fortifications, 7 July. He, at this stage at least, backed Nicolson Calvert's bill to disfranchise certain Retford electors, 24 June, when he was a minority teller for inquiry into abuses in the Irish church, and on again forlornly supporting the borough's disfranchisement, 27 June 1828, he attacked Peel and said that there had been 'a diminution of the small hope I had, that liberal and constitutional measures would proceed from this administration'.[31]

In July 1828 the Whig stalwart Sir James Graham* of Netherby, with whom his name was so often to be linked in the coming years, wrote to Smith Stanley, who now aspired to Canning's mantle, to urge him to hazard the leadership of a broad-based opposition, independently of Grey, Lansdowne and Henry Brougham*:

> I hope you will take the field in force and I think you will find a strong and respectful body willing to act under you. Much of course must depend on the events which may occur before Parliament reassembles, but the aspect of affairs is so clouded by difficulties that the chances are some capital blunder may be committed and there will arrive the golden opportunity of forming a party in the House of Commons in some broad and intelligible principle ... You are the person on whom I raise my hopes. You contain all the great requisites. You may reunite a scattered tribe which it is the interest of the country to see consolidated.[32]

According to Lady Jersey, he was 'very desirous of leading in the House of Commons' and that autumn he agreed with Lord John Russell* 'in the advantage of making the Catholic question a much more leading point of party than it has been made yet, and also of obtaining any points of union by which to consolidate a party of steady opposition'.[33] His rank and talents were recognized, but his frivolity and inexperience, compared for instance to Brougham or Lord Althorp*, told against him and he was distrusted. James Abercromby*, alluding to his endeavours earlier that year to gather his like-minded friends in support of the liberal part of the ministry, ruled him out, writing to Lord Holland:

I never find Stanley's name associated with the formation of a young party in the House of Commons without recollecting his move of last spring ... It is not agreeable to go into details in a matter that is so personal, but my impression is *now* strong that Stanley would not be a safe leader ... It may be that he has seen his error and is now inclined to a better issue, but I always recollect a golden rule that I learned from you – a man will commit a fault a second time, which he has committed once, *because* it is in his character. At any rate even the most charitable will agree that he should have a season of probation.[34]

Encouraged by Lansdowne, he intended to participate in what he hoped would be a concerted and decisive onslaught on ministers at the start of the 1829 session, over the disintegrating state of Ireland and the consequent necessity of granting Catholic emancipation, though he doubted whether the attempted exploitation of other topics would yield any advantage.[35]

In a detailed correspondence on this at the turn of the year with his Canningite friend Denison, to whom he lamented that 'you and I have happened hitherto to find ourselves in two different parties, between which, upon my conscience, I cannot, if put to the question, find any conceivable practical difference', he concurred that if Wellington was 'disposed to carry this question, even to a moderate extent, even requiring unnecessary securities against imaginary dangers ... I for one say with you that he ought to be cordially supported', but otherwise that their combined friends should unite in the middle ground, 'supporting no government which would *not* carry it and supporting any government *in* carrying it'.[36] The revelation of the ministerial concession of emancipation rendered an opposition assault pointless; welcoming it on expressing his approval of the suppression of the Catholic Association, 10 Feb. 1829, he however poisoned the atmosphere by condemning the Brunswickers with unnecessary asperity.[37] Thereafter he apparently left London for the rest of the month.[38] He voted for the emancipation bill, 6, 30 Mar., presented Preston and Lancashire petitions in its favour, 10, 18 Mar., and intervened on its details, 23, 24, 26 Mar. He went away

on 19 Mar. before the unanticipated division on the related Irish franchise bill, about which he now had qualms and only approved of on the 'ground of expediency and compromise'.[39] He divided for transferring East Retford's seats to Birmingham, 5 May, and urged alteration of the civil government of Canada, 14 May, 5 June. Nothing came of speculation in June that he would accept the offer of a place, but, as the best of the rising men in the House, Smith Stanley, who on a visit to Liverpool in August announced his future candidacy for Lancashire, continued to be thought a great catch.[40] In October the Ultra leader Sir Richard Vyvyan* described him as 'a man that should be obtained' for any potential administration, not least as 'a good decoy for the Whigs'; Palmerston privately thought him likely to 'jump at any offer that put him in into the cabinet with a seemly mixture of liberals'.[41] In November 1829 Thomas Creevey* recounted how he was at Knowsley when a letter arrived reporting that Huskisson had spoken of 'his return to office as a thing quite certain, and of Edward Stanley doing so too. Indeed he spoke of the latter as quite the Hope of the Nation!'; Creevey added that as 'the Hope of the Nation was present when this was read, it would not have been decent to laugh, but the little earl gave me a look which was quite enough'.[42]

Declaring himself to be 'very idle and very indifferent', on 13 Jan. 1830 Smith Stanley asked Brougham if he might be allowed to stay away from the opening of the session, but he was present to vote in the minority for Knatchbull's amendment to the address on agricultural distress, 4 Feb.[43] He was appointed to the select committee on the affairs of the East India Company, 9 Feb. As he had in the two preceding sessions, he obtained leave for his Irish ecclesiastical leases bill, 16 Feb., but he again failed to secure its passage. He spoke briefly for the principle of parliamentary reform, 18 Feb., but divided that day in the ministerial majority against Lord Blandford's proposals, and he voted for enfranchising Birmingham, Leeds and Manchester, 23 Feb., transferring East Retford's seats to Birmingham, 5, 15 Mar., and Russell's reform motion, 28 May. He gave government credit for the economies it had made, 19 Feb., and opposed Edward Davenport's motion for inquiry into the state of the nation as unnecessary and impracticable, 23 Mar., but he generally joined in the opposition's revived campaign for retrenchment and lower taxation that year. In early March he, like his father, pleaded pressure of business to excuse himself from the Whig meeting which chose Althorp as the new Commons leader.[44] On 6 Apr. Grey's heir Lord Howick*, noting that Smith Stanley had left without securing a pair on Daniel Whittle Harvey's motion about the management of crown land revenues, 30 Mar., recorded in his diary that 'I am afraid he is not quite what I would wish'; when talking about a possible Whig government, 13 May, Howick described his father as objecting to Althorp's suggestion of giving him a seat in the cabinet from the outset.[45] He divided for Jewish emancipation, 5 Apr., 17 May, and to abolish capital punishment for forgery, 24 May, 7 June. He was in minorities for Daniel O'Connell's bill to alter Irish vestry laws, 27 Apr., the abolition of the Irish lord lieutenancy, 11 May, and repeal of the Irish coal duties, 13 May. He spoke and voted to condemn ministers over Terceira, 28 Apr., and divided with opposition on Canada, 25 May. By late June and early July 1830, when ministers, Peel among them, were again contemplating an overture to him, he was closely involved with Whig operations, including a plan to disrupt the estimates, which was dished by Hume.[46]

Smith Stanley, whose father would have made way for him in Lancashire if he had been forced to a poll there, was again returned with Wood for Preston at the general election of 1830, when, having vindicated his parliamentary votes on the hustings and spent heavily on drink, he defeated the popular candidate Henry Hunt* in another violent contest.[47] In September Huskisson's fatal accident created a vacancy at Liverpool, for which he was briefly considered, partly to counter the potential candidacy of Peel; however, Derby's death, which would have removed him to the county seat, was thought to be imminent and, in any case, he was considered to be 'too decidedly anti-slavery'.[48] The loss of the leader of the former Canningites increased Smith Stanley's value to ministers: for example, Ellenborough that month urged his introduction, with Palmerston, 'to prevent the junction of the Whig aristocracy with the Radicals'.[49] On 1 Nov. Arbuthnot informed Peel of Wellington's negotiations with Palmerston and the Huskissonites, whom it was thought could be purchased at the cost of a commitment to limited reform, along with Graham and Smith Stanley. He added:

> I observed to Stanley that they would be exposed to all Brougham's attacks, but for this he did not care at all. He felt that by joining with Palmerston and the Grants he should be sufficiently covered, and Sir J. Graham had the same feeling. He did not know that Stanley wanted high office, or office at all at present, but he should say it would be wise to put him in office, as he would be most useful to Peel as an every-day man.[50]

Yet Wellington's declaration against reform, 2 Nov., killed the negotiation, and Smith Stanley, who early the previous month had been advocating a stronger

Whig union under Grey, at once became involved in the opposition preparations for Brougham's reform motion (on the 16th), which was expected to decide the duke's fate.[51] He raised the expense of the Rideau Canal, 5 Nov., and the salary of the clerk of the council, 15 Nov. 1830, when, having been listed earlier by ministers among their 'foes', he divided in the majority on the civil list, which precipitated their resignation.

Smith Stanley, of whom Abercromby snidely remarked to Holland that he 'is really a poor thing, that is with reference to the higher and nobler qualities of a man', 19 Nov. 1830, was named chief secretary to the lord lieutenant of Ireland, Lord Anglesey, on the formation of the Grey coalition ministry that month.[52] His predecessor Sir Henry Hardinge* welcomed his appointment 'as a man of ability and business', and Brougham, now lord chancellor, flattered him on his oratory and declared that 'you are the person I above all others look to as the powerful, eloquent and judicious champion of the good causes' in the Commons.[53] He initially expected an easy run at Preston, where he was obliged to offer himself for re-election, but the delay of the writ and Hunt's organized campaign led to his defeat, to the dismay of his ministerial colleagues, in December 1830.[54] He blamed his downfall on 'the stupidity or ill-will of the returning officer' who, by opening the poll to all comers, turned a sharp contest into a triumph for what he called 'mob law'; but his refusal to spend or to pledge for the ballot and alteration of the corn laws rendered him even more unpopular, while one observer commented that the radicals would never have tried their hand again but for his 'imprudent and offensive hauteur'.[55] Abandoning both the scrutiny he had promised and a petition, evidently because of the insurmountable legal difficulties of justifying his rightful election, he gratefully accepted the king's offer of a seat at Windsor, which would become available once the incumbent Sir Richard Hussey Vivian had been provided for.[56] This was considered a mark of royal favour towards ministers and Smith Stanley, who was duly returned unopposed at the by-election early the following year, used his speech there to hint at William IV's confidence in the government's moderate reform credentials.[57]

He was already embroiled in the affairs of Ireland, where mounting economic distress and growing calls for repeal of the Union, whipped up by O'Connell, had produced almost a state of insurrection. Writing to Holland from Dublin Castle, 2 Jan. 1831, he confided his hope that 'with cool heads and steady hands we may be too much for him at last', and at a shrieval dinner in the city on the 11th, when he portrayed himself as a resident Irish landlord, he expressed his ambitions for assisting in the development of the country.[58] Yet, as one observer wrote later that year:

> It was with some surprise that the people of Dublin saw in their new chief secretary an exceedingly juvenile and boyish looking functionary, with a demeanour which his shrewdness rescued from puerility, but in which a more than ordinary carelessness and a sort of harsh levity, not quite consistent with good breeding and alien from the nature of his duties, was observed.[59]

Certainly O'Connell, who, nicknamed him (as he did other inexperienced chief secretaries) a 'shave beggar' and was at some point to provoke him into an (unanswered) challenge, found him unacceptable and, particularly after his arrest on 19 Jan. for breaching the proclamation against the holding of seditious meetings, their mutual antagonism, which was frequently evident in their bad-tempered parliamentary encounters, influenced every aspect of Smith Stanley's tenure as Irish secretary.[60] Engrossed with numerous schemes of improvement, he took his seat, 11 Feb., when, as he was often to do, he dead-batted a query about Irish distress and unrest as being unfortunate but lying outside government's immediate remit; the following day he informed Anglesey that 'the temper of the House of Commons is *excellent* upon Irish matters and we shall be able to carry our affairs there with a high hand'. He indignantly denied that government had held out any secret political compromise in exchange for O'Connell pleading guilty to the charges against him, 14, 16 Feb., and, privately boasting that he had 'got the stock of him with the House', he attacked O'Connell for acting as a demagogue outside Parliament, 21 Feb., and kept the upper hand by insisting that it was he, not ministers, who had sued for terms over his trial, 28 Feb. 1831.[61]

Already deemed, in Holland's words, 'one of the main props of the government' in the Commons that month, he was anxious about the poor performance of his colleagues and confided to Anglesey, in relation to the as yet undisclosed parliamentary reform plan, that '*entre nous, I much* doubt its success'.[62] Althorp, the chancellor of the exchequer, showed him the extensive proposals just before Russell made his introductory statement, 1 Mar. 1831, so that he would be prepared to speak on it: he 'was so surprised that he burst into an incredulous laugh, but recovered himself by degrees and agreed to do as he was bid'.[63] Quietly optimistic about the bill's chances, he duly performed brilliantly in replying to Peel, 4 Mar., when his speech, which Sir Henry Bunbury, Member for Suffolk, described as 'statesmanlike, clear, pointed and effective', induced Grey to comment to Anglesey, who concurred, that

he 'is evidently to be, in due time, the leader of the House of Commons, and I am anxious to have him in the cabinet now'.[64] Aware of the absurdity of the Irish secretary being in the cabinet while his chief, the lord lieutenant, remained necessarily outside it, Smith Stanley, who declined to move to a different department and to incur a further £1,500 of expenses at Windsor, suggested that his duties should instead be transferred to the new office of a fourth secretary of state in charge of Ireland, but nothing came of this.[65] Among minor contributions on other government business, he derailed Sir John Newport's motion on Irish first fruits revenues, 14 Mar., explained the provisions of the Irish reform bill, 24 Mar., and defended his measures for relieving Irish distress, 30 Mar. Fearful of the Castle being left without immediate recourse to greater legislative powers, he strenuously opposed the option of a dissolution and even let it be known that he would resign rather than remain responsible for maintaining the peace in Ireland in such circumstances.[66] To the admiration of the Ultra duke of Newcastle, who thought him uniquely promising, he made another excellent speech, cautioning Members that the fate of the bill hung on the outcome, against Gascoyne's wrecking amendment, 19 Apr., though Thomas Gladstone* commented that he 'lost his temper sadly and spoke something like a desperate man'.[67] Having rebuffed approaches from Dublin, Preston and (slightly later) Liverpool at the ensuing general election, he made a major speech at Windsor in justification of the ministerial policies of peace, retrenchment and reform (in answer to which Wellington prepared a lengthy memorandum) and was returned unopposed.[68] On 14 May 1831 he reported to Grey from Dublin that the Irish elections, in which he was closely involved, were 'going on very well', and a week later he concluded that they would end 'about 66 to 34, or perhaps one more in our favour'.[69]

Reportedly furious that the Irish law officers had ruled that the prosecution of O'Connell should lapse with the life of the Parliament, Smith Stanley was forced to bow to Grey's decision that this was probably for the best, although bound to lead to unpleasant proceedings in the House.[70] Having been brought into the cabinet, somewhat against Anglesey's better judgement, to give him what Grey termed 'greater authority and efficiency in the House of Commons', he duly denied any compromise with O'Connell in the debate on the address, 21 June 1831, when he declared his belief that the state of Ireland was gradually improving, but hinted at the introduction of a system of poor laws to deal with the desperate levels of distress.[71] As he was often forced to do, he defended the yeomanry in relation to the Castle Pollard affair, 27 June, and repeated that justice was impartially administered despite occasional outrages like the one at Newtownbarry, 30 June; he made an 'inimitable' speech against Goulburn about official salaries that day, when he also presented statements on the reintroduced Irish reform bill and the issuing of £500,000 of exchequer bills to fund public works.[72] However, he blundered badly on introducing the Irish arms bill, 1 July, for his proposal to make the possession of unregistered arms in a proclaimed district an offence punishable by transportation, which had not been put before the cabinet, was pounced on by O'Connell; Althorp, who listened in astonishment and privately described it as 'one of the most tyrannical measures I ever heard proposed', informed his father Lord Spencer that 'we must stand by Stanley, but we must soften down his measure; it is at any rate a great scrape, for O'Connell will have the credit for forcing upon us any modification'.[73] He duly backtracked on the matter, 8 July, and although he was still considered a master in debate and a possible replacement as leader if Spencer's death removed Althorp to the Lords, O'Connell, whose juries bill was seconded by him on the 19th as an earnest of government intentions, noted that 'Stanley is much less self-conceited since I knocked up his arms bill'.[74] Now more confident about the viability of ministerial business, Smith Stanley, who the previous month had put off the tithes issue because it would 'afford the Tories the cry of revolution in the church following up revolution in the state', briefly objected to the repeated motions for adjourning proceedings on the reintroduced reform bill, 12 July, and opposed postponing the disfranchisement clauses, 13 July.[75] Thereafter, he made frequent interventions, some of them substantial, on its details in the committee, where, although not as active as Althorp or Russell, he seems to have had a quasi-superintending role. On the 28th he wrote to Anglesey that

at the present moment we can hear nothing but reform day and night. If this hot weather lasts we must die off fast – from 5 o'clock every night till 2 or 3 in the morning without interval, added to all the [Irish] office and government business in the day is more than flesh and blood can stand through August and September, and I see no hope of being through before Christmas. Our friends however are very staunch, and only very much annoyed when we give way on the fullest case being made out. Saltash was an instance the night before last, and they were some of them very sulky yesterday, but were reconciled by our defending strenuously a very bad case [on the partial disfranchisement of Chippenham] last night in which I believe we have done gross injustice, which was sanctioned by a large majority.[76]

He defended schedule B and denied that the representation of agricultural areas would suffer by it, 2 Aug. 1831.

Having, on 9 Aug. met, with petulance, criticisms that he was neglecting Irish business in the Commons, Smith Stanley also came under fire from a frustrated Anglesey, who protested to Grey on the 14th:

I have urged Stanley, over and over again, to press forward all his measures for the advantage of Ireland – that, at least, he would give notice of motions and thus take the initiative away from O'Connell, and from any of the factious Irish Members, the credit of originating measures. Unhappily, little, if any, of this has been done: and, by a strange fatality, every thing that has yet been announced has had the character of coercion, or of restriction or of taxation.[77]

Holland, who as a cabinet minister was privy to the lack of progress in formulating Irish policy, recorded in his diary that there was something 'in the complaints of Mr. Stanley's manner and the want of concert and consultation' with the Irish Members. Ironically, when Smith Stanley and Althorp met those favourable to administration, 18 Aug., Anglesey's plan for making the yeomanry a permanent establishment were totally rejected and the lord lieutenant was afterwards informed by his secretary, who conceded that the idea would have to be dropped, that 'their object is not to turn us out (which they will however do) but to force us into their measures, which I cannot allow them to do'.[78] At least Anglesey, who wrote to him from Dublin on the 20th that 'the *on dit* here is that you are *dismissed* for having opposed O'Connell about the yeomanry and that [the former viceroy Lord] Talbot is to relieve me from my labours', was delighted by his 'most brilliant display' in triumphantly defeating Robert Gordon's motion censuring the Irish government for exerting undue interference in the Dublin election, 23 Aug.[79] Although he concurred in opposing Sadler's motion on Irish poverty, in the hope of being able to bring in better proposals the following year, 29 Aug., he entered into a flurry of remedial legislation that autumn.[80] He obtained leave for a successful bill to improve the control of magistrates by establishing lord lieutenants in Irish counties, 15 Aug.; explained his plan for educating Protestants and Catholics together, in all subjects except religious instruction, at national schools that would be funded by an initial grant of £30,000, 9 Sept.; and published a (later abandoned) measure to alter Irish grand jury laws in order to end widespread financial abuses, 29 Sept. On 3 Sept. 1831 Anglesey, who understood Smith Stanley would transfer to the exchequer, deemed him 'too high and rough' for the Irish Members, but on the 23rd the latter, who feared the Irish reform bill would cause problems in debate, reported that they 'are at present in very good humour [and] I hope I may be able to keep them so'.[81]

Early that month, when his resignation was spoken of, he aligned himself with the duke of Richmond and the moderate reformers in the cabinet against asking the king for a creation of peers in order to ensure the reform bill's passage in the Lords.[82] Yet, he continued to give the measure his full support in the Commons, where on 20 Sept. 1831 he answered Croker by arguing that its defeat in the Upper House would increase not diminish the chances of revolution. He condemned as an outrageous slur Sir Charles Wetherell's suggestion that ministers had connived at the wave of public unrest which greeted the loss of the bill in the Lords, 12 Oct. He was warned against allowing the public appetite for reform to escalate out of control in a letter that day from Sandon, whose father Lord Harrowby, a leading 'Waverer', he visited early the following month, with Grey's approval, to confer about possible alterations to the bill.[83] Sympathetic to the sensitivities of the leading moderate Palmerston, who counted him among those of his colleagues who would be 'for modifications', his position lay somewhere between the advanced reformers, who favoured an even stronger bill, and Palmerston, to whom he wrote on 28 Oct.:

> The whole subject is fairly before us for reconsideration, and ... all we are pledged to as a government is to bring forward no measure which shall not go the full length of removing the grievances complained of, as effectually as the late bill did. I do not despair of our being able to agree on a measure ... which the peers may acquiesce in, and may satisfy our reasonable friends. But, I own, I think it would be more consistent of us to bring forward a measure even something larger than might go through both Houses, and which the peers might modify, than to run the risk of an imputation of insincerity, by so far reducing our proposals, as to leave it doubtful whether more might not have been obtained.[84]

After another row that month over the suggested appointment of O'Connell as an Irish law officer, which prompted Brougham and Holland to ruminate about moving him to a safer ministerial berth, he threw himself back into the affairs of Ireland, where, damned by Lord Donoughmore as an ignorant and dangerous 'puppy', he continued to be extremely unpopular.[85] He was reported by the patronage secretary Edward Ellice* to have said that 'the Irish hated him as much as he hated the Irish', while O'Connell condemned him as 'the snappish, impertinent, overbearing high church Mr. Stanley', who 'has rendered himself personally odious to every Irish Member' and 'is the sup-

porter of all existing abuses in Ireland', adding that he and his friends would support government if only their protagonist was '*promoted* off'.[86]

Smith Stanley was infuriated by the decisions, made at the cabinet meeting which he missed on 19 Nov. 1831, to adopt a broadly similar reform bill and to recall Parliament before Christmas, not least because he would be hard pressed to have his legislative proposals ready for the beginning of the session.[87] However, he got his tithes plan approved, despite some resistance, at other meetings and Holland subsequently commented to Anglesey that 'I like Stanley's views and measures much, infinitely better than his language and tone'.[88] He responded to Croker at the start of the debate on the address, 6 Dec., by arguing that altering tithes would fortify the Irish church just as reform would strengthen Parliament. Announcing the appointment of a select committee on Irish tithes, of which he became chairman, 15 Dec., he explained that changes had become essential because of the massive campaign of non-payment since the previous summer and indicated a two-fold strategy: first, in line with his strongly stated commitment to the established church, in enforcing payments; and second, as a concomitant concession, in removing the Catholics' genuine grievances. Charles Baring Wall reported that he 'gave great satisfaction' by his speech, though O'Connell predictably damned it by remarking that it had united all the Irish – both Protestants, who feared for the well being of their establishment, and Catholics, who wished him to go further – 'in unanimous execration of his plan'.[89] Speaking for once from a carefully prepared text, which his friends feared might make him less effective, he vindicated government's conduct on reform and its proposals in the revised bill, 17 Dec. 1831, when, primed by John Cam Hobhouse*, who was pleased with 'the genuine English spirit which breathed through all he said', he eloquently demolished Croker, whose comparison of the early 1830s with the disastrous 1640s was exposed as a tangle of historical inaccuracies. He was loudly cheered throughout, and Denis Le Marchant[†] recorded that many of the older Members thought that 'if not the best, it was one of the most effective speeches they had ever heard'. According to Greville, 'Grey said it placed him at the very top of the H. of C., without a rival' (though he added that, in his own view, this was perhaps 'jumping to rather too hasty a conclusion'). Sir John Benn Walsh* exclaimed in his journal of the author of this 'brilliant' speech: 'How much he is advancing, and how his powers of oratory and debate are expanding'.[90]

Optimistic about the prospects for reform, Smith Stanley, who was considered by Greville to hold the balance of power in the cabinet on the issue, sided with the moderates against asking the king for the immediate creation of 15 peers, 2 Jan. 1832.[91] Rightly believed that month to be at loggerheads with a resentful Anglesey and to be willing to resign rather than to allow the spoliation of the Irish church, Ellenborough speculated that he might join a 'Waverer' administration and that 'if he would lead the House of Commons, they would make a very strong government and put Peel aside'.[92] However, he again advocated reform on reintroducing the Irish bill, 19 Jan., when he explained the reasons for the additional five seats and the use of the 'beneficial interest' test, among other alterations, and insisted that the Protestant interest would not be overwhelmed by the increased Catholic electorate.[93] Exercising a strict control over the proceedings in the committee on tithes, the subject which earned him the sobriquet 'scorpion Stanley' that year, he defended the decision to exclude Catholic Members from it against O'Connell's objections, 24 Jan.[94] He dealt with complaints about the fees levied on Irish magistrates for renewing their commissions that day and again on 7 Feb., when Holland recorded that he showed his usual 'acuteness, self-possession, judgement and authority'.[95] According to Littleton's account of the debate on Portugal, 9 Feb.

> Stanley, who had been writing his report on Irish tithes on his knee, as he sat, all the evening, put by his paper when Peel began, and followed him in a very clever speech, full of high tone and animation – and considerable power. Peel winced under it.[96]

He emphasized that his tithes policy would embrace both enforcement and redress of grievances, 14 Feb., and, amid a welter of minor Irish business, he carried his Subletting Act amendment bill through the committee, 20 Feb., and repeated the principles behind the ministerial plan of national education, 6 Mar. In March he apparently declined leaving Ireland to become chancellor and leader of the Commons, as part of the potential rearrangement whereby Althorp would have been allowed to move to the Lords to supervise the reform bill there; in any case, Ellice doubted whether even he could make a success of it, such was his unpopularity among his fellow Whigs.[97] Again answering Peel, he closed the debate on the third reading of the reform bill, 22 Mar. 1832, with what Greville described as a 'good and dexterous speech', praised by all.[98] Holland's son Charles Fox*, who called his eloquence 'quite thrilling and splendid', was afterwards moved to exclaim, 'Stanley is a great man'.[99]

Smith Stanley, who had brought up his first report from the tithes committee on 17 Feb. 1832, was prevented from introducing his resolutions on it, 8 Mar., when Charles Brownlow, Member for county Armagh, sidetracked the debate with his unsuccessful amendment (defeated by 314-31) to postpone the discussion until the completion of the committee's deliberations. On the 13th he argued that the distress suffered by many clergymen necessitated swift action, but despite his pledge to counterbalance the initial coercive elements of his policy with future concessions, he again had to listen to the apprehensions of Irish radicals that he meant to subjugate their country. When proceedings were resumed, 27 Mar., he defeated Edward Ruthven's amendment for appropriation of the revenues of the Irish church (by 123-27) and secured his first three resolutions: to recognize the extent of resistance to payment; to advance £60,000 to distressed clergy; and to pay such advances in proportion to the value of each living. The next day he again encountered fierce opposition, so it was not until the 30th, when Henry Lambert's hostile amendment was rejected (by 130-25), that the final two resolutions were agreed: for enforcing the collection of the arrears (in order to repay government advances) and for the 'extinction' of tithes by commutation. These propositions formed the basis of his Irish tithes (arrears) bill, which he introduced, 2 Apr. He secured its second reading (by 119-21), 6 Apr., ensured its passage against further challenges in committee, 9 Apr., and had it agreed at third reading (by 52-10), 16 Apr., when, replying to a blistering attack by Richard Sheil, he reprobated the constant harassment he met with in endeavouring to ameliorate the condition of Ireland. It was enacted on 1 June. Having on 25 May complained that a draft of his second report had been printed in the *Dublin Evening Mail*, he on the 30th and 31st pursued the editor Thomas Sheehan, who was admonished by the Speaker, 1 June. He presented this final report, 4 June, and on its being read, 5 July, he clarified his use of the word 'extinction', which had raised unrealistic expectations in Ireland, by stating that he really meant compulsory and permanent commutation; in other words, that 'the object I have in view ... is to impose the burden, not upon the miserable occupying tenant of the soil, but upon the solvent and responsible landlord'. He defeated an O'Connellite amendment to abolish tithes (by 149-25) that day, and obtained leave for the subsequent Irish tithes (composition) bill (by 124-32) on the 13th. Having secured its second reading, 18 July, he spoke at length in favour of the dual principles of enforcement and concession in order to ensure its committal,

24 July, when a radical motion to add inquiry into other aspects of the church to the committee's brief was defeated (by 77-16), and made frequent interventions during its committee stage, 31 July-2 Aug. The third reading was uneventful, 6 Aug., and it was given royal assent, 16 Aug. 1832.[100]

Smith Stanley, who reported to Anglesey, 10 May 1832, that 'the king was much affected, and was in tears repeatedly' on ministers' resignation over the reform crisis early that month, signalled that he would also quickly relinquish his seat at Windsor.[101] At a party meeting at Brooks's, 13 May, he, according to Le Marchant, 'jumped on the table, and in a most stirring and eloquent speech attacked the new ministers and the Tory aristocracy most unsparingly', but, despite his violence, he in the end supported Althorp's successful resolution to back any reform measure that Wellington might propose. By the 16th, when he was quoted as saying that 'it was all settled and they had not been too hard upon the king', he and his colleagues had been reinstated.[102] Yet the following day a former Tory minister noted that 'Stanley says they are riding the king too hard in the matter of this creation of peers', and on 20 May he wrote to Sir Thomas Acland*:

> My chief satisfaction, while you seem to think that all is so smooth before us, is that the House of Lords will never forgive us the [illegible] violence which they have compelled us to use, and will take the earliest opportunity of turning us out as soon as the reform bill shall have passed and shall have brought in, as it will, an *aristocratic, agricultural* House of Commons.[103]

Whatever his personal reservations, he spoke twice for the second reading of the Irish reform bill, 25 May, and defended the use of the royal prerogative of creating peers, 5 June. Immersed in the details of the Irish measure, he repelled O'Connell's attempts to restore the county qualification to 40s. or at least lower it to £5 freeholders, 13, 18 June, and clashed with him over the leaseholder and freeman franchises, 25 June, 2 July. He provoked Protestant Tory opposition to his Irish party processions bill, 14, 25 June, but after announcing its postponement, 29 June, managed to carry it against last ditch resistance in the committee, 8 Aug. He expressed his sympathy for Sadler's motion to make provision for the Irish poor by a tax on absentees, but carried the previous question against it, 19 June. He attacked Peel for introducing party political considerations into the debate on the Ascot attack on the king, 20 June. O'Connell having threatened to have him impeached in the reformed Parliament, he made a lengthy rejoinder on his conduct towards Ireland

during his speech vindicating government over the Russian-Dutch loan, 20 July, and reacted angrily to the Preston anti-tithes petition, got up by Hunt and presented by Sheil, which called for his removal from office, 3 Aug. 1832.

Smith Stanley, who in June announced that he would leave Windsor to offer in place of his father, while his brother Henry came in for Preston, was returned unopposed for Lancashire North at the general election in December 1832, when he stated that the Reform Act was intended to be a final measure but advocated other liberal changes.[104] Reckoned by then to be second only to Peel as a parliamentary performer, James Grant recollected that 'all was anxiety and attention whenever he rose'. He dominated despite his faults, notably the 'spirit of mockery' in which he listened, the rancour which he displayed in speaking and the unashamed glee with which he exulted over his opponents; and he did so largely because, as the duke of Argyll wrote, 'the voice was beautiful, the sentences perfect in construction, the delivery easy and graceful. There was fire and fun and raillery, whilst occasionally Stanley rose to passages of great dignity and power'.[105] Tom Macaulay* was surprised to overhear him once say that 'my throat and lips ... when I am going to speak are as dry as those of a man who is going to be hanged', for he felt that 'nothing can be more composed and cool than Stanley's manner ... [he] speaks like a man who never knew what fear or even modesty was'.[106] Another colleague, Russell, later observed that during the reform debates it was he, rather than Althorp and other speakers, who

> by his animated appeals to the liberal majority, by his readiness in answering the sophisms of his opponents, by the precision and boldness of his language, by his display of all the great qualities of a parliamentary orator and an able statesman, successfully vindicated the authority of the government and satisfied their supporters in the House of Commons.[107]

Indeed, it was for his supreme brilliance in this respect that he later became well known as the 'Rupert of Debate', in the phrase from Sir Edward Lytton Bulwer's* 'The New Timon' (1845). Yet Russell was also aware of how, even on his first appointment as Irish secretary, 'his declarations in favour of the established church of Ireland, and his temper, little tolerant of opposition, gave warning of storms'.[108] These were frequent in his first two years in office, during which he not only often seemed to be flippant and arrogant in his relations with Irish Members and usually displayed a temperamental bias towards authoritarian policies, but was also at times hardly on speaking terms with Anglesey about official business, so that in Holland's words he became 'almost an obstacle to our government in Ireland'.[109] As the 'great authority' for Grey on Irish affairs, his position was not seriously challenged until the autumn of 1832, when disputes arose about his overly conservative proposals for reform of the Irish church, notably with Russell and Durham. However, at Grey's request, powerfully reinforced by Graham, he agreed not to insist on a pledge of unequivocal cabinet backing which risked endangering the administration, and, as the result of a promise made before the dissolution, in early 1833 he was finally transferred to another cabinet position.[110] As colonial secretary he carried the emancipation of slaves in British colonies, but his objections to Russell's opinions in favour of lay appropriation of Irish church revenues provoked his resignation the following year and by the end of the decade he had joined his old rival Peel in opposition.[111]

In October 1832 the young William Gladstone[†] wrote, with what turned out to be a double irony, that 'when I heard Stanley in the House of Commons, I thought him the cleverest man I had ever seen – he seemed quicker than thought itself – he is too good for them: I wish he were with us'. This sentiment was later echoed by Brougham in commenting that 'when Stanley came out in public life, and at the age of 30, he was by far the cleverest young man of the day: and at 60 he would be the same, still by far the cleverest young man of the day'.[112] Of course, by then, pained by gout and entering the last decade of his life, he had, as the 14th earl of Derby, been transmogrified into the long-serving leader of the Conservative party. Nonetheless, he was in some respects governed by the instincts that he had imbibed during his political apprenticeship, notably in his ultimately limited attitude to alteration of the corn laws; his paradoxically daring way of advancing the cause of parliamentary reform; and his obstinate, but neither unthinking nor uncharitable opposition to lay appropriation, the subject of one of his last, as it had been of one of his first, parliamentary speeches. Remembered as the prime minister who led three short-lived minority Conservative governments and presided over the passage of the second Reform Act in 1867, it could be argued that it was well before he inherited his peerage that he obtained the achievements recorded in the celebrated phrase formulated by Benjamin Disraeli[†], who has long overshadowed him in the historiography of their party, that 'he abolished slavery, he educated Ireland, he reformed Parliament'.[113] According to Sir Herbert Taylor[*], Derby

was greatly admired by a large party in the country – perhaps by the country generally – throughout a long life; and it was customary to call him 'chivalrous'. I think he was not chivalrous. He was a very able and capable man; he had force, energy and vivacity, and he was an effective speaker, always clear and strong, sometimes commonplace, but not seldom brilliant. He was not a man of genius; nor could it be said that he had a great intellect. He had the gifts of a party politician, such as eminent party politicians were in the generations immediately preceding his own rather than *in* his own – subsisting throughout his life, so far as literature is concerned, mainly upon the scholarship and academical accomplishments with which he began it and playing the game of politics with more of party than of public spirit, and without much perhaps of personal friendliness.[114]

On his death in October 1869 he was succeeded in his title and estates by his eldest son Edward Henry (1826-93), who served under him and Disraeli as foreign secretary, but joined the Liberals in 1879 before ending his days a Unionist.

[1] Apart from short lives by T. E. Kebbel (1890) and G. Saintsbury (1892), for many years the only study was W.D. Jones, *Lord Derby and Victorian Conservatism* (1956). However, there is now *The Forgotten Prime Minister: The 14th Earl of Derby*, 2 vols. (2007-8) by Angus Hawkins, in addition to his article on 'Lord Derby' in *Lords of Parl.* ed. R.W. Davis, 134-62, and his entry on Derby in *Oxford DNB*. [2] *The Times*, 25 Oct. 1869. [3] Hawkins, *Forgotten Prime Minister*, i. 5-18, 46-48; *Disraeli, Derby and Conservative Party* ed. J. Vincent, 184; *Conversations on Parables of New Testament* (1828); B. Hilton, *Age of Atonement*, 237-8. [4] Add. 51645, Smith to Lady Holland, 21 Oct. [1832]; *Ellenborough Diary*, ii. 71; *Greville Mems.* iii. 53. [5] *Manchester Mercury*, 29 Feb. 1820; Lancs. RO, Whittaker of Simonstone mss DDWh/4/99; W. Dobson, *Hist. Parl. Rep. Preston* (1868), 70. [6] Nottingham Univ. Lib. Ossington mss OsC 10; Bucks. RO, Fremantle mss D/FR/46/10/46; Derby mss 920 Der (13) 1/161/21; Grosvenor mss 9/13/20-25; Hawkins, *Forgotten Prime Minister*, i. 28-31. [7] *Salisbury and Winchester Jnl.* 5 Aug. 1822; *Creevey Pprs.* ii. 40. [8] Lansdowne mss, Smith Stanley to Lansdowne, 29 Aug., 20 Sept.; Derby mss (14) 115/1, Lansdowne to Smith Stanley, 12 Sept. 1822. [9] A. Hawkins, 'Lord Derby and Victorian Conservatism: A Reappraisal', *PH*, vi (1987), 281-5; 'Lord Derby', 136-40, and *Forgotten Prime Minister*, i. 33-43. [10] *The Times*, 26, 27 Mar. 1824; Harewood mss WYL 250/8/27. [11] Gurney diary. [12] *Creevey Pprs.* ii. 76; Buckingham, *Mems. Geo. IV*, ii. 73-74. [13] *Countess Granville Letters*, i. 294. [14] 'Pope' of Holland House ed. Lady Seymour, 250-1. [15] E. Stanley, *Jnl. of Tour in America* (1930); Jones, 8-10; Hawkins, 'Lord Derby', 141, and *Forgotten Prime Minister*, i. 33-43. [16] Lansdowne mss, Smith Stanley to Lansdowne, 11 Dec. 1824, 10 Feb. 1825; Derby mss (14) 2/3. [17] Ossington mss OsC 19, 25; Derby mss (14) 115/4, Smith Stanley to Forster, 14 Nov. 1825. [18] *The Times*, 3 May, 8, 13, 17, 24, 28 June; Lancs. RO, Disputed elections QDE/12, bdle. 1, Horrocks to Derby, 19 June, reply, 23 June, Smith Stanley to Horrocks, 21 June 1826; *Preston Election 1826*, pp. 3, 47, 121-3; T. Aspden, *Hist. Sketches of House of Stanley*, 49-57. [19] Derby mss (14) 2/3. [20] A. Aspinall, *Lord Brougham and Whig Party*, 280. [21] Derby mss (14) 2/3. [22] Ibid. (12), Stanley to Derby [June, July]; (14) Canning to Smith Stanley, 26, 27 June; Add. 51566, Derby to Holland, 14 July 1827; *Canning's Ministry*, 337; Hawkins, *Forgotten Prime Minister*, i. 55-56. [23] NLW, Coedymaen mss 202, 715; Chatsworth mss 6DD/GP1/1577; Add. 38750, ff. 22, 180, 231, 270; 38751, f. 325; 51687, Lansdowne to

Holland, 2, 5 Sept.; 52011, Stuart Wortley to Fox, 17 Nov.; Lansdowne mss, Abercromby to Lansdowne [Sept.], Goderich to same, 3, 13 Sept., Macdonald to same, 21 Oct. 1827. [24] *HMC Bathurst*, 651; *Howard Sisters*, 98; Southampton Univ. Lib. Broadlands mss BR23AA/5/1; Harrowby mss. [25] Add. 38754, f. 221; *Lady Holland to Son*, 67, 75, 149. [26] Add. 40307, f. 50. [27] Keele Univ. Lib. Sneyd mss SC12/86; 17/178. [28] Derby mss (14) 62, Palmer to Smith Stanley, 22 Feb., 8 Mar.; Lancs. RO DDPr 130/13, reply, 2 Mar. 1828. [29] Derby mss (14) 2/3; TNA 30/29/9/5/67. [30] *Ellenborough Diary*, i. 113, 128, 139; *Lady Holland to Son*, 86. [31] Derby mss (14) 2/3. [32] Hawkins, *Forgotten Prime Minister*, i. 58-61; Sir James Graham mss (IHR microfilm XR 80), 1, bdle. 2, Graham to Smith Stanley, 15 July 1828; Parker, *Graham*, i. 71. [33] *Ellenborough Diary*, i. 230; *Russell Early Corresp.* i. 282. [34] NLS mss 24770, f. 29; Add. 51834, Davenport to Holland, 18 Nov.; 51574, Abercromby to same, 19, 26 Nov. 1828; A. Mitchell, *Whigs in Opposition*, 211-12. [35] Brougham mss, Russell to Brougham, 15 Dec., Lansdowne to same, 26 Dec.; Lansdowne mss, Smith Stanley to Lansdowne, 31 Dec. 1828; Add. 51687, Lansdowne to Holland, 4 Jan. [1829;] Hawkins, *Forgotten Prime Minister*, i. 62-63. [36] Ossington mss OsC 63, 79. [37] Grey mss, Howick jnl.; *Arbuthnot Jnl.* ii. 240. [38] Derby mss (14) 63, Denison to Smith Stanley [Feb.], Lord Stanley to same [?20 Feb. 1829]. [39] Ibid. Derby to Smith Stanley, 8 Mar.; Brougham mss, latter to Brougham, 20 Mar. 1829. [40] *Ellenborough Diary*, ii. 60; NLW mss 10804 D/3, Williams Wynn to Bentinck, 16 June; *Albion*, 24 Aug. 1829; *Countess Granville Letters*, ii. 56. [41] *Palmerston-Sulivan Letters*, 234-5; Broadlands mss BR23AA/5/6. [42] *Creevey Pprs.* ii. 203. [43] Brougham mss. [44] Castle Howard mss, Graham to Morpeth [3 Mar. 1830]. [45] Howick jnl. [46] Ibid. 11 July; Derby mss (14) 117/3, Althorp to Smith Stanley, 5 July 1830; *Ellenborough Diary*, ii. 290, 297, 299, 301-2, 316; Mitchell, 229-30. [47] *The Times*, 2, 3, 9 Aug. 1830; Aspden, 63-64. [48] Derby mss (14) 116/1, Brougham to Smith Stanley [Sept.]; St. Deiniol's Lib. Glynne-Gladstone mss 196, T. to J. Gladstone, 17 Sept.; 243, Grant to same, 17 Sept. 1830. [49] *Ellenborough Diary*, ii. 347, 362-3. [50] Parker, *Peel*, ii. 163-6; J. R. M. Butler, *Passing of the Great Reform Bill*, 96. [51] Brougham mss, Smith Stanley to Brougham, 2 Oct.; Grey mss, Durham to Grey, 4 Oct.; Howick jnl. 7 Nov.; Add. 51564, Brougham to Holland [8 Nov.] 1830; 56555, ff. 42, 46; Hants RO, Carnarvon mss 75M91/E4/82; Mitchell, 244. [52] Add. 51575. [53] Derby mss (14) 116/8, Hardinge to Smith Stanley, 22 Nov.; 116/1, Brougham to same [Nov., Dec.] 1830. [54] Ibid. 116/6, Winstanley to Smith Stanley, 18, 22, 28 Nov.; 117/5, Grey to same, 10, 14 Dec.; *The Times*, 11, 13, 16, 18 Dec. 1830; *CJ*, lxxxvi. 119, 134-5. [55] *Greville Mems.* ii. 94; Broughton, *Recollections*, iv. 77; PRO NI, Anglesey mss D619/31D/6; Brougham mss, Shepherd to Brougham, 8 Feb. 1831. [56] *The Times*, 21, 27, 28 Dec. 1830; Aspden, 66-67; *William IV-Grey Corresp.* i. 20-21, 32-33, 45-46. [57] *Windsor and Eton Express*, 12 Feb. 1831. [58] Add. 51566; Anglesey mss 29B, pp. 37-38; *Dublin Evening Post*, 13 Jan. 1831. [59] *New Monthly Mag.* xxxii (1831), 112. [60] T.M. Torrens, *Life and Times of Sir James Graham*, i. 321-2; *Disraeli, Derby and Conservative Party*, 223-4; Jones, 19-21; Hawkins, *Forgotten Prime Minister*, i. 77-79, 90-91. [61] Anglesey mss 31D/13-23, 27. [62] Ibid. 27A/104; 31D/23-25; *Creevey Pprs.* ii. 219; *Three Diaries*, 56, 60. [63] Broughton, iv. 93. [64] Anglesey mss 28A-B/47; 28C, pp. 81-82; 31D/28-30; *Bunbury Mem.* 160; *Three Diaries*, 63, 65-66; *Greville Mems.* ii. 125; Hawkins, *Forgotten Prime Minister*, i. 81-82. [65] Brougham mss, Smith Stanley to Brougham, 5 Mar.; Grey mss, to Grey [10 Mar.] 1831; Hawkins, *Forgotten Prime Minister*, i. 82. [66] Anglesey mss 31D/35-37; *Three Diaries*, 80; Hawkins, *Forgotten Prime Minister*, i. 85-86. [67] *Unrepentant Tory* ed. R.A. Gaunt, pp. xxi, 38, 139, 148; Add. 51573, Rice to Holland [19 Apr.]; Glynne-Gladstone mss 198, T. to J. Gladstone, 20 Apr. 1831. [68] Derby mss (14) 121/2, Gosset to Smith Stanley, 25 Apr.; 116/9, Hodgson to same, 9 May; *Preston Chron.* 30 Apr.; *Windsor and Eton Express*, 30 Apr. 1831; *New Windsor Election 1831*, pp. 4-5, 9-10, 16-28; Wellington mss WP1/1207/1. [69] Grey mss; Hawkins, *Forgotten Prime Minister*, i. 86-87. [70] Derby mss (14) 117/5, Grey to Smith Stanley, 27 May 1831; *Arbuthnot Jnl.* ii. 425; Hawkins, *Forgotten*

Prime Minister, i. 86, 88. [71] Anglesey mss 28A-B/62, 63; 31D/42, 43; Hawkins, *Forgotten Prime Minister*, i. 88. [72] Hatherton diary. [73] Le Marchant, *Althorp*, 326. [74] Anglesey mss 27A/120, 122; TNA, Granville mss, Holland to Granville, 19 July [1831]; *O'Connell Corresp.* iv. 1825. [75] Anglesey mss 31D/42, 46. [76] Ibid. 31D/50. [77] Ibid. 28C, pp. 159-63; Add. 56555, f. 176. [78] Anglesey mss 31D/55; *Holland House Diaries*, 14, 26-27, 29, 33; Hawkins, *Forgotten Prime Minister*, i. 92-93. [79] Derby mss (14) 119/1/2, Anglesey to Smith Stanley, 20, 26 Aug. 1831; Anglesey mss 31D/57. [80] Anglesey mss 31D/59; Hawkins, *Forgotten Prime Minister*, i. 93-95. [81] Anglesey mss 27B, pp. 47-53; 31D/68. [82] Coedymaen mss 218; *Holland House Diaries*, 44-46; M. Brock, *Great Reform Act*, 236; Hawkins, *Forgotten Prime Minister*, i. 96. [83] Derby mss (14) 127/3; Brock, 246-7; Hawkins, *Forgotten Prime Minister*, i. 97-98. [84] Sir James Graham mss 1, bdle. 7, Smith Stanley to Graham, 27 Oct. 1831; Broadlands mss PP/GC/DE/61; RI/11. [85] *Holland House Diaries*, 68; Brougham mss, Holland to Brougham, 27 Oct.; Grey mss, Smith Stanley to Grey, 23 Oct. 1831; TCD, Donoughmore mss. [86] Broughton, iv. 151; *O'Connell Corresp.* iv. 1853-4. [87] *Holland House Diaries*, 81-82; Grey mss, Smith Stanley to Grey, 22 Nov. 1831; Hawkins, *Forgotten Prime Minister*, i. 98. [88] *Holland House Diaries*, 88, 90-91, 95; Anglesey mss 27A/139; Hawkins, *Forgotten Prime Minister*, i. 99-101. [89] *Howard Sisters*, 228; *O'Connell Corresp.* iv. 1861. [90] *Three Diaries*, 169-72; *Greville Mems.* ii. 230-1; Broughton, iv. 156; *Life of Campbell*, i. 526; ii. 3; *Holland House Diaries*, 97, 99; Le Marchant, 383; *Baring Jnls.* i. 91; NLW, Ormathwaite mss FG1/5, p. 242; M. D. George, *Cat. of Pol. and Personal Satires*, xi. 16834. [91] Anglesey mss 31D/77; Parker, *Graham*, i. 134-5; *Greville Mems.* ii. 234, 240. [92] *Arbuthnot Jnl.* ii. 440; *Personal Recollections of Lord Cloncurry*, 438; *Three Diaries*, 178, 186; Hawkins, *Forgotten Prime Minister*, i. 105-6, 109. [93] K.T. Hoppen, 'Politics, the law, and nature of Irish electorate', *EHR*, xcii (1977), 746, 757-8, 761, 772. [94] W.J. Fitzpatrick, *Life, Times and Corresp. of Dr. Doyle*, ii. 394, 404-5; A.D. Kriegel, 'Irish Policy of Lord Grey's Government', *EHR*, lxxxvi (1971), 29-30. [95] *Holland House Diaries*, 126. [96] Hatherton diary. [97] Add. 75941, Althorp to Spencer, 17 Mar. 1832; *Three Diaries*, 211; *Baring Jnls.* i. 93. [98] *Greville Mems.* ii. 272; *Three Diaries*, 215. [99] Add. 52058, C.R. to H.E. Fox, 11 Mar., n.d. [Mar.] 1832. [100] *CJ*, lxxxvii. 122, 175, 185, 227, 232, 237, 242-4, 254, 260, 279, 352, 360, 362, 363, 374, 462-3, 488, 491, 502, 519, 541, 544, 552, 560, 591; *PP* (1831-2), xxi. 1-540; Kriegel, 30-31; Hawkins, *Forgotten Prime Minister*, i. 106-8, 113-14. [101] P. Ziegler, *King William IV*, 197; Derby mss (14) 100/2/1, p. 113. [102] Le Marchant, 429; *Raikes Jnl.* i. 31; *Three Diaries*, 251, 261; *Disraeli, Derby and Conservative Party*, 4-5. [103] *Arbuthnot Corresp.* 166; Devon RO, Acland mss 1148M/21 (iv) 25. [104] *The Times*, 3, 20 Dec. 1832. [105] *Greville Mems.* ii. 374; [J. Grant], *Random Recollections of Commons* (1837), 158-63; *New Monthly Mag.* xxxii (1831), 113-14; *Argyll Mems.* i. 153. [106] *Macaulay Letters*, ii. 90. [107] Russell, *Recollections*, 91, 92. [108] Ibid. 68. [109] *Holland House Diaries*, 198, 200, 202; *Greville Mems.* ii. 310; *Creevey Pprs.* ii. 265; Mq. of Anglesey, *One-Leg*, 259-70, 277; Kriegel, 31-33; Hawkins, 'Lord Derby', 139-40, 143-5, and *Forgotten Prime Minister*, i. 75-76, 91-92, 104-6, 114-16. [110] Le Marchant, 452; Parker, *Graham*, i. 174-81; *Greville Mems.* ii. 366; Kriegel, 33-40; E.A. Smith, *Lord Grey*, 294-302; Hawkins, *Forgotten Prime Minister*, i. 114-27. [111] R. Stewart, *Foundation of Conservative Party*, 111-17, 223. [112] *Gladstone Autobiog. Memoranda* ed. J. Brooke and M. Sorenson, 25, 102. [113] *The Times*, 25 Oct. 1869; *Ann. Reg.* (1869), Chron. pp. 158-61; *DNB*; *Oxford DNB*; J.J. Bagley, *Earls of Derby*, 164-91. [114] *Taylor Autobiog.* i. 131.

S.M.F.

SMYTH, Sir George Henry, 6th bt. (1784–1852), of
Berechurch Hall, nr. Colchester, Essex.

COLCHESTER	1826–13 Apr. 1829
COLCHESTER	1835–Jan. 1850

b. 30 Jan. 1784, o.s. of Sir Robert Smyth, 5th bt.†, of
Berechurch and Charlotte Sophia Delaval Blake, spinster
(who was naturalized by Private Act, 21 Geo. III, c. 8,
12 Mar. 1781). *educ.* Paris; Trinity Hall, Camb. 1802. *m.*
28 July 1815, Eva, da. of George Elmore of Penton, nr.
Andover, Hants; 1 illegit. da. *d.v.p. suc.* fa. as 6th bt. 12
Apr. 1802. *d.* 11 July 1852.
Sheriff, Essex 1822-3.

Smyth was descended from a family of London
drapers and silk merchants. Robert Smyth (c. 1594-
1669), who was knighted in 1660 and created a baronet
in 1665, bought the Upton estate at West Ham. The 4th
baronet, Sir Trafford Smyth (c. 1720-66), inherited
from his uncle James Smyth (*d.* 1741) the Berechurch
property near Colchester.[1] He was succeeded by
Robert Smyth, the father of this Member, a strange
man who had a chequered political career. After a spell
as Member for Cardigan, 1774-5, he was returned for
Colchester in 1780 as an opponent of Lord North. One
of the St. Alban's Tavern group in January 1784, his
unsuccessful candidature for Colchester at the general
election in April was financed from Pitt's secret service
fund. He was seated on petition, sided with opposition
on the regency, 1788-9, became an enthusiast for the
French Revolution, retired from Parliament in 1790
and settled in Paris as a banker. He was a member of
the British revolutionary club and a close friend of
Tom Paine, and at the notorious dinner in Paris, 18
Nov. 1792, renounced his title, though this resolution was short-lived. On a visit to London two months
earlier he had been described to the foreign secretary
as 'extremely violent' and likely to 'do all the mischief
in his power'.[2] He died in Paris, leaving personal estate
sworn under £15,000, 12 Apr. 1802, six weeks before
his only son and residuary legatee, who had received
some of his early education there, matriculated at
Cambridge.[3]

George Smyth, who came into full possession
of the Berechurch estate in 1805, took a quite different approach to life and politics. He settled at
Berechurch, extended the estate and rebuilt the house,
made himself respected and popular in Colchester
and established himself as one of the leading figures
in the anti-Catholic Tory Blue party, which dominated municipal politics through the corporation.[4]
He chaired the meeting which led to the formation
of the Loyal Colchester Association to 'counteract

the diffusion of disloyal and seditious principles',
28 Feb. 1821.[5] He was active in the Colchester True
Blue or Pitt Club: at its anniversary dinner, 17 Nov.
1821, for example, he 'congratulated' its members on
'the increased ascendancy which True Blue principles
were gaining every day'.[6] At the general election of
1826 he was put up by the corporation to replace the
retiring ministerialist and was returned unopposed in
a compromise with the radical candidate. At the nomination he declared that he was 'an enthusiastic admirer
of the king; a firm supporter of the church and state;
and that to the utmost of his ability, he would walk in
the footsteps of the immortal Mr. Pitt'.[7]

Smyth presented petitions against Catholic relief
from the archdeaconry and inhabitants of Colchester,
2 Mar., and the corporation, 5 Mar. 1827.[8] He voted
accordingly, 6 Mar. He was in the ministerial majority
for the Clarences' annuity bill, 17 Mar., but in the protectionist minority hostile to the corn bill, 2 Apr. At
the True Blue Club dinner, 6 Nov. 1827, he said that
in the present unsettled political situation 'there might
be some difficulty as to the course which he should
pursue, but ... he would not take a seat with the Whigs,
nor with those who had come round to the True Blues
for the sake of place'. Dismissing the notion of 'security' to make Catholic emancipation acceptable to
Protestants, he called for resistance to the claims of
'men who deem us heretics, and would destroy us and
the Protestant establishment altogether, if they had it
in their power'.[9] He had presented a Colchester petition for repeal of the Test Acts, 14 June 1827,[10] but he
may have voted against that measure, 26 Feb. 1828. He
presented and endorsed Colchester corporation's petition praying the House, if it passed repeal, to 'guard
the country from the danger to which it was exposed
from the machinations of men who were avowedly
hostile to the church establishment', 17 Mar. At the
Colchester meeting to consider the formation of an
agricultural protection association, 9 Feb., he concurred in the decision to postpone the business until
the Wellington ministry had revealed its hand; he was
not directly involved in the establishment of the association in May.[11] He presented the archdeaconry's anti-
Catholic petition, 29 Apr., and voted against relief,
12 May. On 13 June 1828 he presented a Colchester
inhabitants' petition for the abolition of slavery.

At the Pitt Club meeting in November 1828 Smyth
urged the formation of a local Brunswick Club; he
duly became its first president, 8 Dec. At the mayoral
election, 30 Nov. 1828, he 'avowed himself a staunch
supporter of the Protestant cause', suggested that
ministers looked 'favourably' on the Brunswickers

and 'attributed the present quiet attitude of the Irish agitators to the soldiers that had been sent to Ireland by the duke of Wellington'.[12] He was astonished and outraged when the duke and Peel disclosed their decision to concede Catholic emancipation in February 1829: at the Colchester Loyal Association meeting on the 10th he declared that 'their unaccountable conversion from their former views ... had created a feeling of terror and alarm throughout this Protestant country'.[13] In the House he was one of the diehard opponents of emancipation, dividing doggedly against it throughout March and presenting many hostile petitions from his county. When bringing up those from the corporation, archdeaconry and inhabitants of Colchester, 6 Mar., he accused Peel of 'political apostasy', deception and betrayal, condemned Catholics as 'an intolerant and bigotted set ... not to be trusted' and said that if the measure was carried it would become 'a matter of indifference to me how short a time I continue to sit in this House'. He had the speech elaborately printed in gold letters on navy blue paper.[14] On 10 Mar, he complained of the 'indecent haste' with which the relief bill was being pressed, 'in direct opposition to the declared opinions of the great majority of the people of this country', and described the so-called 'securities' as worthless. On 17 Mar. he asserted that Parliament's disregard of popular opinion proved the need for its reform; and on the 23rd that emancipation would open the House to 'a crowd of demagogues, bold enough to go any lengths for the advancement of their religion'. He voted against the third reading of the bill, 30 Mar., and the following day informed Colchester corporation of his decision to resign his seat in protest at ministers' 'most extraordinary change of policy'. He could not be talked out of it and took the Chiltern Hundreds in mid-April. At the Colchester dinner to mark the return of his True Blue replacement, 17 July 1829, he said that he was 'disgusted with the House of Commons' and had 'done everything he could to oppose' emancipation, which would be 'the ruin of Old England'.[15]

Smyth remained prominent in Colchester politics. At a meeting called to petition for repeal of the beer and malt taxes, 19 Dec. 1829, he admitted to being 'wholly ignorant' on the currency question, hoped that the ministry would alleviate the tax burden and discounted the radical nostrum of a property tax. He did this again at the Essex county meeting, 11 Feb. 1830, when he demanded economy and retrenchment.[16] At the Essex by-election of March 1830, when he professed himself to be a 'Tory of the old school', he was instrumental in raising an opposition to the ministerialist Thomas Bramston*. He was one of the six candidates nominated for Colchester at the general election in July, but he withdrew before the poll.[17] At the True Blue Club dinner, 27 Nov. 1830, he attacked 'those demagogues who would overturn the constitution' and opposed all reform.[18] He nominated the corporation's absentee candidate against a reformer at the March 1831 by-election; and at the general election the following month was a prominent supporter of the unsuccessful Blue candidate.[19] He stood for Colchester at the general election of 1835 and was returned with another Conservative.[20] He held the seat, as an opponent of the Maynooth grant and repeal of the corn laws, until his retirement on account of 'age and infirmities' in early 1850.[21] He died without surviving issue at Berechurch in July 1852, commemorated as 'a fine specimen of the old English gentleman', notable for his 'warm-hearted, generous and hospitable disposition'.[22] The baronetcy became extinct, but Berechurch and his other real estate passed to the children of his illegitimate daughter Charlotte (1813-45), the late wife of Thomas White of Wetherfield, Essex.[23]

[1] VCH Essex, ix. 412. [2] Ibid. ix. 156, 168; HP Commons, 1754-1790, iii. 456-7; N and Q (ser. 9), i. 252; HMC Fortescue, iii. 472. [3] PROB 11/1377/500; IR26/64/159. [4] VCH Essex, ix. 413-14; A.F.J. Brown, Colchester, 84. [5] Colchester Gazette, 3 Mar. 1821; M.E. Speight, 'Politics in Colchester' (London Univ. Ph.D thesis, 1969), 183-4. [6] Colchester Gazette, 24 Nov. 1821. [7] Ibid. 3, 10 June, 22 July 1826; Bodl. MS. Eng. lett. c 159, ff. 38, 42; Speight, 103; Brown, 38. [8] The Times, 3, 6 Mar. 1827. [9] Colchester Gazette, 10 Nov. 1827; Speight, 169. [10] The Times, 15 June 1827. [11] Colchester Gazette, 16 Feb. 17 May 1828. [12] Ibid. 22 Nov., 6, 13 Dec. 1828. [13] Ibid. 14 Feb. 1829. [14] BL 650. c. 19. (1.). [15] Colchester Gazette, 28 Mar., 18 Apr., 18 July 1829. [16] Ibid. 26 Dec. 1829, 13 Feb. 1830. [17] Ibid. 13 Mar., 31 July 1830. [18] Ibid. 4 Dec. 1830. [19] Ibid. 2 Apr., 7 May 1831. [20] Brown, 84-85; VCH Essex, ix. 211, 225-6; The Times, 5, 8-10 Jan. 1835. [21] The Times, 2 Feb. 1850. [22] Gent. Mag. (1852), ii. 199-200. [23] Ibid. (1845), ii. 546; PROB 11/2158/668; IR26/1947/687.

D.R.F.

SMYTH, John Henry (1780–1822), of Heath Hall, nr. Wakefield, Yorks.

CAMBRIDGE UNIVERSITY	9 June 1812–20 Oct. 1822

b. 20 Mar. 1780, 1st s. of John Smyth[†] of Heath Hall and Lady Georgiana Fitzroy, da. of Augustus Henry Fitzroy[†], 3rd duke of Grafton. educ. Eton 1793-8; Trinity Coll. Camb. 1798; M. Temple 1801; European tour 1802. m. (1) 25 July 1810, Sarah Caroline (d. 29 May 1811), da. of Henry Ibbetson of St. Anthony's, Northumb., s.p.; (2) 16 Apr. 1814, his cos. Lady Elizabeth Anne Fitzroy, da. of George Henry Fitzroy[†], 4th duke of Grafton, 2s. 4da. suc. fa. 1811. d. 20 Oct. 1822.

Under-sec. of state for home affairs July 1804-Feb. 1806.

Capt. S.W. Yorks. yeomanry 1803.

Although the well-connected Smyth, a classical scholar of some distinction, had held office under Pitt, he was by inclination a liberal Whig, who had joined Brooks's on 3 May 1811 and voted steadily with opposition in the House. He was again returned unopposed for Cambridge University in 1820 but is not known to have voted or spoken in the first session of the new Parliament. Illness may have been responsible for this inactivity, for on 30 May 1820 he was given six weeks' leave on account of ill health. In 1821 he voted irregularly with opposition. He took no part in their attacks on the conduct of the Liverpool ministry towards Queen Caroline, but he voted in condemnation of the Allies' revocation of the new constitution in Naples, 21 Feb. He divided for army reductions, 14, 15 Mar., repeal of the additional malt duty, 21 Mar., 3 Apr., when he contended that this tax, which was costly to collect, could be abolished if savings were made in military establishments and that the best preparation for war was to 'husband our resources in peace'. In the same vein he declared, when supporting Hume's motion to reduce the grant to the Royal Military College, 30 Apr., that it was not 'of sufficient advantage to the community to be maintained in its present state during the existence of so much distress in the country'. He voted for repeal of the Blasphemous and Seditious Libels Act, 8 May, and in protest against delays in the inquiry into the courts of justice, 9 May. He was in the opposition minorities in favour of parliamentary reform, 18 Apr., 9 May, and reform of the Scottish county representation, 10 May. Yet his views on reform seem to have been essentially moderate: when Lambton presented a petition from some disfranchised freeholders of Lyme Regis, 12 Apr., Smyth contended that Lord Westmorland's legitimate electoral influence there should not be condemned as 'corrupt and improper'. He voted for inquiry into Peterloo, 16 May, and cuts in the ordnance estimates, 31 May. He divided for Catholic relief, 28 Feb., and on 16 Mar. challenged the hostile petition from the University, which Lord Palmerston, his ministerialist colleague there, had claimed to be a 'unanimous' representation of the scholars' opinions on the issue.[1] A dedicated opponent of slavery, he urged the government to put pressure on France and Portugal to ensure that the agreements they had signed prohibiting the slave trade were not flouted, 13 June.[2] On 27 June 1821 he voted for Hume's motion for economy and retrenchment.

For the whole of the 1822 session there is no record of activity. Illness presumably prevented his attendance, for, prior to his early death at Hastings in October 1822, he had 'been some months resident' there 'for the recovery of his health'.[3] His 'old and attached friend' Lord Lansdowne was pained by his loss.[4] His will was proved at York, under £5,000, 4 Mar. 1823.[5]

[1] The Times, 17 Mar. 1821. [2] Ibid. 14 June 1821. [3] Gent. Mag. (1822), ii. 472. [4] Add. 51690, Lansdowne to Lady Holland, 27 Nov. 1822. [5] IR26/977/758.

R.M.H.

SMYTH, Robert (b.1777), of Drumcree House, co. Westmeath.

Co. WESTMEATH   5 Mar. 1824–1826

b. Jan. 1777, 1st s. of William Smyth†, MP [I], of Drumcree and 1st w. Maria, da. of Mark Synnot of Drumcondragh, co. Armagh. educ. Trinity, Dublin 1793. m. 26 Jan. 1835, Elizabeth, wid. of Maj. Snodgrass, 2da. suc. fa. 1827.

Descended from seventeenth century Yorkshire settlers, the Smyths of Drumcree were part of a Westmeath dynasty with branches at Ballynegall, Gaybrook, Glananea and Barba Villa House, the ancestral home of William Meade Smythe, Member for Drogheda, 1822-6.[1] Smyth's father had sat for county Westmeath in the Irish Commons from 1783 and the Westminster Parliament from the Union on the declining interest of the 7th earl of Westmeath, but in 1808 had made way for the 2nd earl of Longford's brother.[2] In 1824 Smyth came forward for a vacancy in the county, allegedly as the 'locum tenens' of Sir Thomas Chapman of Killua, whose son was not yet of age. Citing 'political opinions ... nearly similar' to those of his father, he claimed to be 'truly independent' and 'not bound by any pledges, either of a public or private nature'. He was returned unopposed.[3] On 2 Apr. 1824 the Irish secretary Goulburn informed the under-secretary Gregory that he had received a letter 'from the new Member for Westmeath' in 'favour of five gentlemen' for the 'appointment of chief constable', which 'considering that he has not yet taken his seat ... promises well; at least it shows a very perfect idea of that part of his duty which consists in obtaining offices for his constituents'. Goulburn told Smyth that he would submit his request to the viceroy, Lord Wellesley, but that 'appointments of this nature' were 'extremely limited'.[4] Smyth, who is not known to have spoken in debate, voted with opposition to condemn the trial in Demerara of the Methodist missionary John Smith, 11 June 1824. He divided to suppress the Catholic Association, 15, 25 Feb., against Catholic claims, 1 Mar., 21 Apr., 10 May, and against the accompanying bill to disfranchise 40s. freeholders, 26 Apr. 1825.

At the 1826 general election he offered again with the support of Longford and the 'High Protestant interest', but denied allegations that he was a 'person of violent political opinions'. After a turbulent contest against a pro-Catholic candidate he was narrowly defeated.[5] The Catholic *Dublin Evening Press*, which had ridiculed him as an 'idiot' and 'the most stupid and silly man in the county', alleged that

on his first journey to London he put up from the stage-coach at a famous inn called *The Bull and Mouth*, in the city. He liked the accommodation, though it is three or four miles ... from St. Stephen's chapel, and accordingly [there] he remained while attending his parliamentary duties. Whether in reference to the inn, or to his mental or gastronomic or physical qualities ... to distinguish him from the nine or ten Smiths in the House, he was known by the prenomen of 'Bull and Mouth' Smyth. His voting was regulated by a most impartial and original rule. On any question that presented itself he voted as the first Smith he happened to follow voted ... Where it was his good luck to follow Mr. Smith of Norwich, he voted against the Marriage Act and in favour of the Unitarians. If he happened to light on John Smith of London, he voted with him against the slave trade and for emancipation. If another Smith, he voted for the West Indian planters and for the Orangemen of Ireland. In short Westmeath Smyth was all things to all men.[6]

Referring to 'how embarrassed he was in France owing to his ignorance of the language', the *Dublin Evening Post* quipped that he should 'make good use of his retirement' and 'get a master, and in seven years he may acquire some knowledge of French'.[7] His attempt to secure the seat by petition ended in failure in April 1828. Following his succession to the family's Drumcree estates in 1827 he began a lengthy lawsuit to recover other lands in county Westmeath which they had formerly held.[8] At the 1830 general election he started, but declined in favour of Chapman's son.[9] He came forward again in 1831, but was persuaded to retire at the nomination.[10]

The date of Smyth's death has not been ascertained. He was still acting as a magistrate in 1851, but on 16 Nov. 1866 his son-in-law Major Leicester Curzon (1829-91), who had married his elder daughter Alicia Maria Eliza, heiress to his 4,431-acre estate in February that year, assumed by royal licence the surname of Smyth.

[1] *Analecta Hibernica*, (1958), xx (1958), 279. [2] *HP Commons, 1790-1820*, v. 220. [3] *Westmeath Jnl.* 12, 26 Feb., 11 Mar. 1824. [4] *Mr. Gregory's Letter Box* ed. Lady Gregory, 275-6. [5] *Westmeath Jnl.* 8, 29 June, 6 July 1826. [6] *Dublin Evening Post*, 17 June 1826. [7] Ibid. 1 July 1826. [8] *Gent. Mag.* (1827), ii. 93; *Analecta Hibernica*, xx. 300. [9] NLI, Farnham mss 18602 (40), Hodson to Maxwell, 9 Aug. 1830.

[10] *Dublin Evening Post*, 12 May; *Roscommon and Leitrim Gazette*, 14 May 1831.

P.J.S.

SMYTHE, William Meade (1786–1866), of Westgate, Drogheda, co. Louth and Deer Park, nr. Honiton, Devon.

DROGHEDA 9 Mar. 1822–1826

b. 16 May 1786, 2nd s. of William Smythe (d. 1812) of BarbaVilla House, co. Westmeath and Catherine, da. and h. of William Meade Ogle, MP [I], of Drogheda. *educ.* by Mr. Foligny; Sidney Sussex, Camb. 1811. *m.* Aug. 1815, Lady Isabella Howard, da. of William, 3rd earl of Wicklow [I], 3da. (2 *d.v.p.*). *d.* 9 July 1866.

Smythe's father had married into the Meade Ogle dynasty of wealthy merchants who dominated the representation of Drogheda. His maternal uncle Henry Meade Ogle had sat there, 1806-7, 1812-20, with the backing of the corporation, of which his elder brother Ralph (1784-1814) was a leading alderman and its mayor in 1812.[1] On the death of the sitting Member in 1822, Smythe came forward citing his support for Catholic emancipation and his hope of regaining the 'honour which you have so often conferred on different members of my family'. With backing from the independent gentlemen and freemen, whom the Countess de Salis accused of 'rallying round' him, 'though an unpopular person, to save their town from the disgrace of being a second time bought by an attorney', he was returned at the head of the poll.[2] A radical commentary of 1823 stated that Smythe, who is not known to have spoken in debate, had shown 'no trace of attendance in the last three sessions', but two years later he was noted to have 'attended frequently, and voted with ministers'.[3] He presented a Drogheda petition for repeal of the Irish window tax, 1 May 1822.[4] On 6 June 1822 he applied to the Irish secretary Goulburn for the 'living of Collan in the county of Louth' on behalf of his younger brother John, explaining that

our family have been long soliciting this favour and have received many promises from government but never have obtained anything ... In a late interview I had with Lord Liverpool, he promised to speak to you on the subject; the living in question is a very small one, not £500 a year I believe, but from its situation it is particularly desirable for our family.[5]

He voted with the Liverpool ministry against inquiry into the parliamentary franchise, 20 Feb., and tax reductions, 13, 18 Mar. 1823. He divided against the production of papers on the Orange plot to murder the lord lieutenant of Ireland, 24 Mar. He voted for the grant for Irish churches and glebe houses, 11 Apr. He divided against repeal of the Foreign Enlistment Act, 16 Apr., and inquiry into chancery delays, 5 June 1823. He presented Drogheda petitions against repeal of the Irish fishing bounties, 3 May 1824, and against the county assessment, 3 June 1824.[6] He was granted a fortnight's leave on account of ill health, 15 Feb. 1825, but was present to vote for suppression of the Catholic Association, 25 Feb. He divided for Catholic claims, 1 Mar., 10 May 1825. He voted against condemnation of the Jamaican slave trials, 2 Mar. 1826.

At that year's general election Smythe offered again, denouncing the rival candidature of Drogheda's recorder Peter Van Homrigh*, whom he accused of breaking a promise not to intervene. A bitter struggle ensued, but following the appearance on the fourth day of another pro-Catholic candidate Smythe withdrew, claiming to have been 'deserted by the Roman Catholic interest of the town'.[7] He died at Scarborough, Yorkshire, in July 1866.[8]

[1] J. D'Alton, Hist. Drogheda, i. 257. [2] Dublin Evening Post, 2, 5 Mar. 1822; PP (1829), xxii. 9; Drogheda Jnl. 14 Aug. 1830; PRO NI, Foster mss D562/357, Salis to J.L. Foster, 1 Mar. 1822. [3] Black Bk. (1823), 194; Session of Parl. 1825, p. 485. [4] The Times, 2 May 1822. [5] Add. 37299, f. 202. [6] The Times, 4 May, 4 June 1824. [7] Drogheda Jnl. 7, 10, 14, 17, 21 June; Dublin Evening Post, 10, 17, 22 June 1826. [8] Gent. Mag. (1866), ii. 279.

P.J.S.

SNEYD, Nathaniel (c.1767–1833), of Ballyconnell, co. Cavan and 42 Upper Sackville Street, Dublin.

Co. CAVAN   1801–1826

b. c.1767, s. of Edward Sneyd, MP [I], wine merchant, of Dublin and Hannah Honora, da. of James King of Gola, co. Louth. m. (1) 29 Jan. 1791,[1] Alicia (d. 1793), da. of George Montgomery (formerly Leslie), MP [I], of Ballyconnell, s.p.; (2) 9 Aug. 1806,[2] Anne, da. of Thomas Burgh, MP [I], revenue commr., of Bert House, co. Kildare, s.p. suc. fa. 1781. d. 31 July 1833.
  MP [I] 1794-1800.
  Dir. Bank of Ireland 1802, dep. gov. 1816-18, gov. 1818-20.
  Sheriff, co. Cavan 1795-6, custos rot. 1801.
  Trustee, linen board [I] 1815.
  Capt. commdt. Ballyconnell vol. cav. 1798, 1803.

Sneyd had succeeded his father as a vintner specializing in clarets, and in 1829 Robert Peel, the home secretary, wrote that 'his house in the wine trade was the first in Dublin when I was in Ireland [in the 1810s] and ... I continued to have my wine from Mr. Sneyd after I left'.[3] Having, through the estate and influence inher-

ited by his first wife, secured a seat on the independent interest for Cavan on the eve of the Union, he became a ministerialist and, notwithstanding that his second wife had a pension of £400 on the Irish list, constantly sought patronage from the Liverpool government.[4] Professing constitutional principles at the same time as receiving liberal backing, he was returned for the last time for Cavan at the general election of 1820 without, in the end, having to stand a contest.[5] No evidence of parliamentary activity has been traced for that session, but he voted for the anti-Catholic Thomas Ellis* in the Dublin by-election in June 1820.[6]

Sneyd divided against censuring ministers' conduct towards Queen Caroline, 6 Feb., and with them against repeal of the additional malt duty, 3 Apr., disqualifying civil officers of the ordnance from voting in parliamentary elections, 12 Apr., and Russell's reform motion, 9 May 1821. He voted against inquiries into Irish tithes, 19 June, and the lord advocate's treatment of the press in Scotland, 25 June 1822, but for one into the legal proceedings against the Dublin Orange rioters, 22 Apr. 1823. He was listed in the ministerial majority against repeal of the Foreign Enlistment Act, 16 Apr. 1823, but was an absentee the following year. In June 1824 he admitted to Peel that 'I have been a truant this session, and have not laid eyes on St. Stephen's', to which he received the uncharacteristically warm reply: 'I shall be most happy to see you again, and quite as much from the satisfaction it will give me to shake by the hand an old friend, as from the additional vote which your presence will ensure'.[7] He divided for the Irish unlawful societies bill, 25 Feb., and, in his only reported intervention in debate, vindicated the conduct of the Bank of Ireland during the depression of 1817, 15 Mar. 1825. As previously, he voted against Catholic relief, 28 Feb. 1821, 30 Apr. 1822, 21 Apr., 10 May, and the related franchise measure, 26 Apr. 1825. In his only other known vote before the dissolution the following year, he divided for the grant to the duke of Cumberland, 30 May 1825.

By May 1824 it had become known that Sneyd's unopposed return in 1820 had been on the understanding that he would make way for, and give his support to, an advanced Whig at the following election. This angered the Orangeman Lord Farnham, whose nephew Henry Maxwell occupied the other seat, as it threatened to open the county to an emancipationist.[8] Yet, although it was thought that he would travel to Cavan in June 1826 and might stand at the general election, Sneyd withdrew before the start of the fierce contest that year.[9] He remained opposed to Catholic relief, since he chaired the Cavan meeting which established a Brunswick Club in the county, 13 Oct. 1828, and became president of the Swanlinbar branch.[10] He maintained his links with the county, of which he was custos, for example by signing the address of the sheriff and grand jury against agitation for repeal of the Union early in 1831, and he may again have been briefly considered as a possible candidate at the general election that year.[11] As well as signing the requisition for the Protestant county meeting in Cavan in January, he was active in Dublin, where, for instance, he presided at the meeting of the Protestant Conservative Society in April 1832.[12]

The senior partner in the firm of Sneyd, French and Barton, he was returning from the Bank of Ireland to his premises in Upper Sackville Street on 29 July 1833, when he was knocked to the ground by the force of a gunshot, which grazed his temple. His assailant, one John Mason, was described as having 'gazed on his victim for a few seconds and then, placing the pistol, which was four-barrelled, close to his forehead, he discharged the contents of one of the barrels into the head of Mr. Sneyd'. He apparently shouted 'Oh! I have done for you', as he ran off. Sneyd died speechless, after two days of excruciating agony, on the 31st. Mason, who was found to be deranged, could give no account of his actions save to insist that he had an unspecified grudge against the three partners, the death of any of whom would have pleased him equally well. Sneyd's estate was presumably divided among his relations, who attended his funeral on 5 Aug. 1833 in St. Mary's, Dublin, where it was intended to raise a monument in his memory.[13]

[1] IGI (Dublin). [2] Ibid. [3] Add. 40327, f. 9. [4] *Hist. Irish Parl.* vi. 302; *HP Commons, 1790-1820*, v. 220-1; Add. 40296, ff. 57-58; *Extraordinary Red Bk.* (1821), 219; *Black Bk.* (1823), 194; *Session of Parl. 1825*, p. 485. [5] *Dublin Evening Post*, 19 Feb., 9, 25 Mar.; *Enniskillen Chron.* 6 Apr. 1820. [6] *Correct Report of Speeches at Election* (Dublin, 1820), 76. [7] Add. 40366, f. 196. [8] PRO NI, Hist. Irish Parl. transcripts ENV5/HP/4/1, Coote to Clements, 12 May; Sneyd to Clements, 15 May; NLI, Farnham mss 18613 (1), Fox to Maxwell, 13 May 1824; Add. 40330, f. 108. [9] *Dublin Evening Post*, 27 May; Farnham mss 18602 (21), Thompson to Maxwell, 13 June; (26), Sneyd to same, 23 June 1826. [10] *Enniskillen Chron.* 23 Oct., 11 Dec. 1828. [11] *Dublin Evening Post*, 9 Apr. 1831; PRO NI, Orr mss D2934/14/29. [12] *Ballyshannon Herald*, 20 Jan., 27 Apr. 1832. [13] *The Times*, 2, 3 Aug. 1833; *Gent. Mag.* (1833), ii. 183-4, 560.

S.M.F.

SOMERSET, Lord Fitzroy James Henry (1788–1855), of Cefntilla Court, Usk, Mon. and 85 Pall Mall, Mdx.

TRURO	1818–1820
TRURO	1826–24 Feb. 1829

b. 30 Sept. 1788, 8th s. of Henry, 5th duke of Beaufort (d. 1803), and Elizabeth, da. of Hon. Edward Boscawen[†]; bro. of Lord Arthur John Henry Somerset[†], Lord Charles Henry Somerset[†], Henry Charles Somerset, mq. of Worcester[†], and Lord Robert Edward Henry Somerset*. *educ.* Westminster 1803. *m.* 6 Aug. 1814, Emily Harriet, da. of Hon. William Wellesley Pole*, 2s. (1 *d.v.p.*) 2da. KCB 2 Jan. 1815; GCB 24 Sept. 1847; *cr.* Bar. Raglan 11 Oct. 1852. *d.* 28 June 1855.

Cornet 4 Drag. 1804, lt. 1805; mission to Constantinople with Sir Arthur Paget[†] 1807; lt. 6 Garrison Batt. 1808, 43 Ft. 1808; a.d.c. to Sir Arthur Wellesley[†] in Portugal 1808; military sec. to Lord Wellington 1811-14; maj. 1811; lt.-col. 1812; capt. and lt.-col. 1 Ft. Gds. 1814; col. and a.d.c. to prince regent 1815-22; maj.-gen. 1825; col. 53 Ft. 1830; lt.-gen. 1838; gen. 1854; f.m. Nov. 1854; col. R. Horse Gds. 1854-5; c.-in-c. Crimea Feb. 1854-d.

Sec. embassy Paris 1814-15, 1815-18; sec. of ordnance 1818-27; military sec. war office 1827-52; master-gen. of ordnance 1852-5; PC 16 Oct. 1852.

Somerset received an annuity of £600 on his father's death in 1803, in addition to unspecified provision already made.[1] A professional soldier who lost an arm at the battle of Waterloo, he served for decades in various secretarial capacities to the duke of Wellington, his uncle by marriage. He had been returned for Truro in 1818 on the interest of the Tory patron, his cousin Lord Falmouth, despite strong opposition from a rival party within the corporation. However, in 1820 he was involved in a double return for the second seat and was defeated at the resulting by-election.[2] He accompanied Wellington to the congress of Verona in 1822 and in January 1823 was sent on a mission to Spain to convey the duke's suggestions for strengthening the government, in an unsuccessful attempt to avert French military intervention.[3] The following year the prime minister, Lord Liverpool, considered him as a possible candidate for the governorship of Madras.[4] On meeting him at dinner about this time, the Whig Thomas Creevey* declared, 'I never was more pleased with anyone than I was with him during our conversation'.[5] At the general election of 1826 he was returned unopposed for Truro, where Falmouth had regained control of the corporation.[6]

His appointment as military secretary at the horse guards, when Wellington became commander-in-chief in January 1827, helps to explain Somerset's sporadic attendance in the Commons. He divided against Catholic claims, 6 Mar. 1827, 12 May 1828. He voted with Wellington's government against repeal of the Test Acts, 26 Feb., presented a Truro petition against the small notes bill, 1 May, and voted against terminating the salary of the lieutenant-general of the ordnance, 4 July 1828. In February 1829 Planta, the patronage secretary, listed him as being 'with government' on Catholic emancipation, and he chose to vacate his seat that month rather than join with Falmouth in the Ultra opposition to Wellington.[7] Thereafter he concentrated on his military career. Following the Bristol reform riots in November 1831 he assisted with preparations for the defence of London against any revolutionary outbreak.[8] He was raised to the peerage as Lord Raglan in 1852 and two years later took command of the British expeditionary force to the Crimea, but he endured intense personal criticism for the campaign's military and logistical shortcomings before succumbing to dysentery in June 1855. As a former parliamentary colleague observed on learning of his death:

Poor fellow! I have not a doubt that it was welcome to him. The awful responsibility of his post, the apparent hopelessness of the struggle ... and above all the adverse comments of the press must have been almost sufficient without disease to weigh him down to the grave ... No man living had ever had such an opportunity of acquiring information about the military and diplomatic affairs of the world ... His personal appearance was highly in his favour, tall, well made, fair, with a remarkable bland and agreeable countenance and address, his whole air giving the appearance of a gentleman, you were won by him the moment you approached him ... In all his intercourse with others there was a conspicuous probity, a clearness and candour, a discretion and yet a kindness, which won your admiration and regard. Thus he had a swarm of friends in the army and never an enemy ... Few soldiers have ever enjoyed a more unquestionable character for intrepidity. All who had seen him in battle spoke of him as being apparently unconscious of danger, so calm and collected was he in the most critical moment ... That he possessed that vastness of comprehension, that power of mind that could embrace every object, reach every detail ... provide for every exigency, compel ready assistance by removing the tardy or unthoughtful and promoting the energetic, counselling and directing the government ... I doubt.[9]

He was succeeded by his only surviving son, Richard Henry Fitzroy Somerset (1817-84), but left all his real and personal estate to his wife. Parliament granted annuities of £1,000 to his wife and £2,000 to his son and his male heir.[10]

[1] PROB 11/1401/946; IR26/82/9. [2] *West Briton*, 10, 17 Mar., 9 June 1820. [3] *Wellington Despatches*, ii contains many letters regarding the Spanish mission. [4] *Arbuthnot Jnl.* i. 297. [5] *Creevey Pprs.* ii. 74. [6] *R. Cornw. Gazette*, 10, 17 June 1826. [7] *West Briton*, 6 Mar. 1829. [8] E.A. Smith, *Reform or Revolution*, 101-5. [9] C. Hibbert, *The Destruction of Lord Raglan*, passim; Hatherton diary, 4 July 1855. [10] PROB 11/2226/59; IR26/2074/18; *CP*, x. 724-5.

T.A.J.

SOMERSET, Lord Granville Charles Henry (1792–1848), of Troy, Mon. and 8 Clarges Street, Mdx.

MONMOUTHSHIRE 20 May 1816–23 Feb. 1848

b. 27 Dec. 1792, 2nd s. of Henry Charles Somerset[†], 6th duke of Beaufort (d. 1835), and Lady Charlotte Sophia Leveson Gower, da. of Granville Leveson Gower[†], 1st mq. of Stafford; bro. of Henry Somerset, mq. of Worcester*. educ. Christ Church, Oxf. 1811. m. 27 July 1822, Hon. Emily Smith, da. of Robert Smith[†], 1st Bar. Carrington, 3s. 2da. d. 23 Feb. 1848.
    Ld. of treasury Mar. 1819-Apr. 1827, Jan. 1828-Nov. 1830; PC 20 Dec. 1834; commr. of woods, forests and land revenues Dec. 1834-May 1835; chan. of duchy of Lancaster Sept. 1841-July 1846.
    Metropolitan lunacy commr. 1827-d.

Somerset, an anti-Catholic Tory, had represented Monmouthshire on his father the 6th duke of Beaufort's interest since 1816. A riding accident in infancy left him hunchbacked in appearance, and although the deformity did not impair his prowess as a sportsman and hunter after hounds, he was easily caricatured, which, with his brusque manner, impeded his promotion to high office.[1] Appointed a junior treasury lord in March 1819, he quickly demonstrated greater acumen and attention to departmental business than his elder brother Lord Worcester, Member for Monmouth Boroughs, unlike whom he assisted Beaufort in the management of their difficult constituency interests in Bristol and the counties and boroughs of Brecon, Glamorgan, Gloucester and Monmouth.[2] At the 1820 general election he monitored progress and negotiated support for their candidates in contests at Bristol, Cardiff and Monmouth Boroughs.[3] Despite rumblings of discontent from Whigs and protectionists, his own election for Monmouthshire with the head of the Tredegar family, Sir Charles Morgan, was not seriously challenged and was celebrated at Monmouth's *Beaufort Arms*.[4]

Somerset of course divided steadily with his colleagues in Lord Liverpool's government, and also against Catholic relief, 28 Feb. 1821, 30 Apr. 1822, 21 Apr., 10 May, and the attendant Irish franchise bill, 26 Apr. 1825. He divided against disqualifying civil officers of the ordnance from voting in parliamentary elections, 12 Apr. 1821, confirmed his hostility to reform in the divisions on 9 May 1821, 20 Feb., 2 June 1823, 26 Feb. 1824, 13 Apr. 1826, and voted against Lord John Russell's resolutions condemning electoral bribery, 26 May 1826. He voted against mitigation of the death penalty for forgery, 23 May 1821, and, notwithstanding his mother's Methodism, against condemning the indictment in Demerara of their missionary John Smith, 11 June 1824, and the Jamaican slave trials, 2 Mar. 1826.[5] When reports that he had missed the debate and division on Wilberforce's compromise motion on the Queen Caroline affair, 26 June 1820, were used to fuel constituency opposition to Beaufort in 1820-1, Somerset paraded with his father and another '200 persons of rank' at Monmouth races in October, and signed and endorsed the Breconshire loyal address, 21 Jan. 1821.[6] Although asked by the county meeting to do so, he chose not to present or endorse Monmouthshire's petition for abolition of sinecures and protection for agriculture, 6 June 1820,[7] but he presented others from Monmouthshire and Gloucestershire for action to alleviate agricultural distress, 26 Feb., 1 Mar., 23 May 1821. He campaigned for the unsuccessful candidate Sir John Nicholl* at the 1821 Oxford University by-election.[8] He dissociated himself from the radical demands in his constituents' distress petitions, 25 Mar., and disputed a claim by Joseph Hume that Monmouth's petition for parliamentary reform was signed by the majority of the burgesses, 28 Mar. 1822. They retaliated on the 30th by adopting remonstrances criticizing Somerset.[9] On 15 May 1822 he and Morgan confirmed that the distress complained of in Monmouthshire petitions (adopted during the 'Scotch cattle' riots) was genuine, but refused to sanction the abolition of 'unnecessary' pensions and places and tax reductions that they proposed as remedies.[10] Somerset brought up a Gloucestershire petition against the beer retail bill, 17 July 1822. When he married Lord Carrington's daughter on the 27th, Beaufort gave him £10,000 as part of his settlement and £30,000 was settled on his wife.[11]

Treasury meetings on the Hastings affair took up much of Somerset's time early in 1823.[12] He defended government policy on the barilla duties, insisting that the merchants who petitioned for their repeal had greatly exaggerated their distress, 5 June. He presented and endorsed Monmouthshire petitions against the Insolvent Debtors Act, 10 Mar., 12 May, and the truck system, 28 May, and one from the deanery of Stowe against concessions to Catholics, 15 Apr. 1823.[13] In 1824 he brought up petitions against West Indian slavery, 27 Feb., the proposed new theatre in Cheltenham, 6 Apr., and the beer duties, 7 May.[14] That month he conducted negotiations with Wyndham Lewis*, who, having forfeited the 2nd marquess of Bute's support, was keen to secure the Beaufort interest in Cardiff Boroughs at the next election.[15] On 18 Feb. 1825 he received a week's leave because of ill health, and he did not apparently speak in debate or present petitions that session. He voted in the minor-

ity for the Leith docks bill, 20 May, and on 13 July 1825 he was a majority teller for delaying the Western ship canal bill, in which his father had a vested interest, and voted against adding a clause restricting the rights of the corporation to the Bristol town dues bill. After Nicholl declined to stand at the February 1826 Oxford University by-election, Beaufort gave his interest to Thomas Bucknall Estcourt* for whom, perceiving his weakness, Somerset directed the Beaufort agents to secure every possible vote.[16] The Monmouthshire coroners entrusted their petition for increased allowances to him for presentation, 17 Apr. 1826.[17] At the dissolution in June it was erroneously reported that Somerset would contest Bristol, but he personally assisted Beaufort's candidates in difficult canvasses in the Monmouth and Cardiff Boroughs and came in unopposed for Monmouthshire.[18]

He divided against Catholic relief, 6 Mar. 1827, and was one of the 'underlings' whose resignations pleased the 'Protestant party' when the pro-Catholic Canning succeeded Liverpool as premier.[19] He divided with the Canning ministry against the disfranchisement of Penryn, 28 May, and presented a petition from Newport for repeal of the Test Acts, 1 June. He attributed his lifelong commitment to the cause of the insane to his appointment to the investigative committee on provision for pauper lunatics in Middlesex, 13 June 1827.[20] Somerset was in poor health when the duke of Wellington as premier appointed him a lord of the treasury in January 1828, and it was agreed that could remain in the country for a further two or three months and attend Parliament only 'if major principles are under discussion'.[21] He took his seat after re-election, 21 Feb., and voted against repeal of the Test Acts, 26 Feb. He divided against Catholic relief, 12 May, having presented and endorsed hostile petitions, 29 Apr. 8, 16 May, and against ordnance reductions, 4 July. He presented Monmouthshire petitions against the friendly societies bill, 18, 25 Apr. 1828. In August he was pleased to be consulted by the home secretary Peel over appointments to the metropolitan lunacy commission on which he was to serve, and attendant legislation.[22] Wellington's decision to concede Catholic emancipation in 1829 had Beaufort's approval, and Somerset chaired Peel's London committee for the Oxford University by-election and offered cautious advice on its progress.[23] He voted for the relief bill, 6, 30 Mar. 1829, but presented hostile petitions, 3, 13 Mar. Taking charge of the lunatic regulations amendment bill, 13 Feb., 16 Mar., 3, 6, 10, 14 Apr., and the madhouse regulation bill, 3, 13 Apr., he defended the application of public funds that they proposed, and the work of the 1828 select committee. The Monmouth county hall bill was also now entrusted to him.[24] In October 1829, estimating support for a coalition ministry, the Ultra leader Sir Richard Vyvyan* counted the Somersets among the government's most reliable supporters. Somerset voted with his colleagues against transferring East Retford's seats to Birmingham, 11 Feb., Lord Blandford's reform scheme, 18 Feb., and enfranchising Birmingham, Leeds and Manchester, 23 Feb. 1830. He divided against Jewish emancipation, 5 Apr., 17 May, and reducing the grant for South American missions, 7 June. He presented Monmouthshire petitions for tithe reform, 12 Mar., a £25 license fee for hawkers, 23 Mar., and abolition of the death penalty for forgery, 30 Apr., and against renewing the East India Company's charter, 18 May. He did 'nothing to oppose' the Merthyr police bill sponsored by Bute, and despite the threat it posed to the prosperity of the other Bristol Channel ports, he deliberately refrained from opposing the 1830 Bute (Cardiff) canal bill at its second reading, 15 Mar., reserving his objections until its committee stage, when he presented hostile petitions from the industrialist Richard Blakemore and rival canal companies, 26, 27 Apr., which delayed its passage.[25] He ordered detailed 'summary abstracts' of returns on pauper lunatics, 2 Mar., and tabled the metropolitan commissioners' July 1829 report, 25 May. Intervening with increasing confidence and frequency in debate, he was one of the principal speakers for the sale of beer bill, 4 May, when he endorsed the competition it sanctioned and the need to reduce gin drinking and adulteration of liquor. Forwarding the select committee's papers on the bill to Wellington afterwards, he conceded that they had relied too much on the testimony of brewers and publicans.[26] His return for Monmouthshire at the general election in August 1830 was 'perfectly safe' and was celebrated with great pomp. He attended to the other Beaufort constituencies and now brokered seats for the treasury.[27]

Somerset was of course in the government minority on the civil list, 15 Nov. 1830, and resigned with them. He proposed Peel as opposition leader in the Commons, 17 Nov., and became 'one of the small group of men who worked to keep the party together during the difficult years of the reform crisis'. He was also involved from the outset in the establishment and management of the Carlton Club.[28] He was visiting his father at his manor of Heythorp, Oxfordshire, in late November 1830 when they were threatened by rioters, and a deputation from Monmouthshire arrived to urge the duke, as lord lieutenant, to take firm action against the 'Scotch cattle'.[29] On 8 Dec. he presented several anti-slavery petitions and strongly defended

the exemption from coal duties enjoyed by Bristol Channel ports east of Cardiff. He attended a party dinner hosted by Wellington at Apsley House, 15 Dec. 1830.[30] Responding in his capacity as chairman of the metropolitan lunacy commission to criticism of their work by lord chancellor Brougham, 14 Jan., Somerset agreed that changes were necessary, but he hesitated to endorse those sanctioned by the Grey government and strongly opposed their Lunatic Act amendment bill, 23 Feb. 1831.[31] He presented a petition for repeal of the malt duties from Northleach, 8 Feb. He was appointed to the select committee on public accounts, 17 Feb., and was at the heart of discussions on opposition policy and tactics against the ministerial reform bill. He regarded its introduction, 1 Mar., as the 'first day of the revolution' and was dismayed at the futility of their opposition to it.[32] However, Greville and others subsequently blamed him (unfairly) for dissuading Peel from trying to kill the bill immediately, in order to safeguard, in the short term, Beaufort's constituency interests.[33] The Speaker refused to hear his observations on the coal duties, 23 Feb., and he failed, when introducing a petition from Newport, 7 Mar., and again, 14 Mar., to make Lord Althorp as chancellor disclose details of his proposals for equalizing them. Instead ministers ensured that Somerset's conduct at the treasury, where it emerged that one of Wellington's bills in the Burnell case had deliberately been left unpaid, came under scrutiny.[34] Undeterred, he criticized the government's proposals for taxing steam vessels, 16 Mar., and embarrassed them with pertinent questions on the coastal blockade when the navy estimates were presented, 25 Mar. Constituency opposition to Beaufort and the great landowners had increased, but (unlike Morgan and his son) it did not deter Somerset from voting against the reform bill at its second reading, 22 Mar., and he announced (before speaking on the truck bill), 12 Apr., that if it was committed he would move for the enfranchisement of Lincolnshire's large towns, to try to ensure that the principle of property and population-based representation which it purported to enshrine was equitably applied. He divided for Gascoyne's wrecking amendment, 19 Apr., but claimed at the ensuing general election that he would have preferred to see 'the bill continue in committee and passed in a modified form than for Gascoyne's amendment to be taken as a test issue'. Monmouthshire and Gloucestershire were 'in a ferment' and Somerset, who canvassed personally at considerable risk, saw Worcester defeated in Monmouth and their uncle Lord Edward Somerset stand down to avoid defeat in Gloucestershire.[35] Monmouthshire was certain to return the reformer

William Addams Williams, a lifelong Whig and Somerset's seconder in 1820 and 1830, and Somerset avoided a contest there only through Morgan's timely retirement.[36] Pressed on the hustings to justify his refusal to attend county reform meetings and present pro-reform petitions, he acknowledged that 'very much of the intelligence and respectability of the county' favoured reform and claimed that his votes against it were ones of conscience, as he considered the ministerial bill 'one of spoliation'. He insisted that being a Member was 'a sacred trust', not a 'mere feather in my cap', and refuted 'libellous' allegations that his family received £48,000 a year from public funds.[37] He recommended trying a test case under a quo warranto warrant before petitioning against Benjamin Hall's return for Monmouth and, although this was not done, he presented Worcester's petition, 22 June, and rejoiced in its success, 18 July 1831. He still doubted the legality of the Monmouth franchise, which the Commons committee had neglected to consider.[38]

Charles Arbuthnot* sought Somerset's assistance to ensure a good opposition attendance when Parliament met, and his contributions at pre-session briefings were praised.[39] He contrived to delay the reform bill's reintroduction with questions on nuisances in Waterloo Bridge New Street and the boundaries of the Forest of Dean, 23 June, and, anxious 'to maintain the war', he employed questions on steam navigation and exchequer accounts, 8 July, Sierra Leone and Fernandez Po, 25 July, and custom house agents, 9 Sept. 1831, to similar effect.[40] He voted against the reintroduced reform bill at its second reading, 6 July, to make the 1831 census the criterion for English borough disfranchisements, 19 July, and to postpone consideration of the partial disfranchisement of Chippenham, 27 July. He ordered returns of properties and tax assessments for Welsh towns, 4 Aug., and welcomed the decision to give Frome a Member, 5 Aug. Opposing the enfranchisement of Gateshead that day, he accused ministers of squandering the franchise wantonly on insignificant places while large and populous districts like Merthyr Tydfil remained inadequately represented. He endorsed the decision to give Glamorgan two county Members, 13 Aug., but joined Charles Williams Wynn in condemning the bill's provisions for voter registration, 20 Aug. On 7 Sept. he vainly proposed dividing the Monmouth Boroughs constituency by adding Chepstow to Monmouth and Usk, and Abergavenny and Pontypool to Newport. To justify the change he compared the needs of the South Wales coalfield, of which Monmouthshire formed a part, with those of 'over represented' Cumberland,

Durham and Northumberland. Rejecting the proposal, Russell accused him of failing to state 'whether he founds the claim of Monmouthshire on a comparison with the Welsh or English representation'. Somerset replied that counties represented by cabinet members had been given an unfair advantage and cited ratios of Members to population to substantiate his allegation. His subsequent proposal that Abergavenny, Chepstow and Pontypool be added to the Monmouth group also failed. On the 12th he informed Peel, who was out of town, that he and

> our friends think the sooner we get to the third reading the better, for delay no longer is of our service. There are notices of several amendments, but I do not think any of them likely to be strenuously supported excepting the revising the decision of the House so as to attempt to remove Guildford and the county towns out of B ... Althorp says he has not any amendments to propose with the exception of those of which he has given notice. He is to start them on taking the report into consideration tomorrow and I presume they will embrace some more Members for some of the Welsh counties.[41]

He corrected Althorp's claim that Pembrokeshire's second borough seat was new, 14 Sept. He voted against the bill's passage, 21 Sept., and the second reading of the Scottish measure, 23 Sept., and Beaufort voted to defeat the English bill in the Lords, 8 Oct. 1831.[42]

Somerset endorsed the Dublin election petition alleging undue interference by government, 20 Aug., and voted to censure them, 23 Aug. 1831. He was against issuing the Liverpool writ, in order to consider the bribery there, 5 Sept., and as chairman of the committee which found against the 1830 Tregony election petitions, he protested at being called repeatedly to the House to consider Richard Gurney's* petition against their decision and then finding the matter postponed, 5, 12, 14 Sept.[43] He assisted opposition candidates at the Dorset and Cambridgeshire by-elections, and was with his father in Bristol during the riots, of which he sent Wellington a detailed report, 3 Nov.[44] He realized immediately that the late decision to award Monmouthshire an additional county Member under the revised reform bill would be difficult to defend without sacrificing Merthyr, and deliberately refrained from voting at its second reading, 17 Dec. 1831.[45] He paired against it, 7 Feb., criticized its provisions for voter registration, 11 Feb., and polling, 15 Feb., and, having failed to delay schedules B and C, 23 Feb., voted against the proposed enfranchisement of Tower Hamlets, 28 Feb. 1832. Cheltenham, which he did not 'much care ... for having a vote at all, for I do not think it one of those places that stand in need of the franchise', had been awarded a Member, and though Somerset's suggestion that it qualified for two on population size was dismissed, 2 Mar., his arguments for including Pittville in the constituency were heeded and the clause postponed, 5 Mar. Complaining that ministers had treated Wales unfairly, he recommended enfranchising Merthyr instead of Gateshead, 5 Mar., or Walsall, 9 Mar., and spoke of the inadequacy of the bill's provision for the entire Bristol Channel area, compared to South Shields, 7 Mar. When Russell announced it on the 14th, he deplored the government's 'monstrous' decision to deprive Monmouthshire of a third Member in order to give Merthyr separate representation; but though he was supported by leading Conservatives and Welsh Members, he failed by 191-146 to defeat it and make ministers find Merthyr's seat elsewhere. He found less support when he complained again on the 19th. He divided against the bill's third reading, 22 Mar. He secured changes to the boundary bill favourable to the Beaufort interest in East and West Gloucestershire and Stroud, but not Tewkesbury, 7, 8, 22 June, and endorsed Portman's claim that Wareham should have been entirely disfranchised, 22 June. He supported a late attempt to have the writ for Aylesbury moved, 24, 25 July 1832.

As a member of the select committee that had recommended a gradual reduction in funding before closure of the Dublin Foundling Hospital, he criticized the large award made to them, 22 Aug. 1831. He co-operated with Addams Williams over the Monmouthshire roads bill and was glad to see the highways bill postponed and eventually timed out, 18 July 1832. He voted against Littleton's truck bill, which Monmouthshire's small ironmasters opposed, 12 Sept., but failed to have it amended, 12 Sept., or deferred, 5 Oct. 1831. Opposition divided with the West India Members against renewing the Sugar Refinery Act, 12 Sept. 1831, and Somerset spoke briefly for Burge's motion to reduce the levy on West Indian sugars, 9 Mar. 1832. He also voted against the Vestry Act amendment bill, 23 Jan., and the malt drawback bill, 2 Apr., and for inquiry into smuggling in the glove trade, 3 Apr. He threatened to press for an investigation into the operation of the 1830 Sale of Beer Act, 3 Feb., and enquired about appointments to the poor law commission, 13 Feb., 4 Apr. He divided against amending the Irish tithes bill, 9 Apr, and when drawn by George Lamb that day to comment on treasury minutes relating to the Irish registry of deeds, covering his period in office, he could only confirm the need for an investigative committee. He queried several items in the estimates, 13 Apr., 7 June, the

assessed taxes, 2 July, and civil list expenditure, 13 July. Attending to family business, he chaired the committee and helped to steer the Bridgwater and Taunton canal bill through the Commons, 27 Feb., 22 Mar., was a teller with Estcourt against the Purton Pill railway bill, 22 Mar., and expressed alarm at the manner in which the select committee's recommendations were thrown out at the third reading of the Exeter improvement bill, 13 June 1832. Somerset was named with Lamb and Robert Gordon to bring in a bill to regulate the care and treatment of the insane, 24 June, served on the select committee, and strongly opposed the Lords' amendments to it, 26 Sept. 1831. He was concerned that appointments were to be made by the home secretary and expenditure vetted by the Commons, and objected strongly to the right the Lords had given the lord chancellor to appoint commissioners, which the Commons rejected by 66-55, and helped to frame their objections for discussion at the ensuing Lords' conference.[46] He informed Beaufort:

> We turned over Lord Brougham and his amendments to the lunatic bill last night, which was good fun enough, more especially as I hear he is in a *fury* about it. He is the most grasping man after patronage that was ever known.[47]

He threatened to oppose the revised bill, introduced, 3 Feb., if ministers retained the 'objectionable clauses', was appointed to the select committee on the measure, 6 Feb., obtained returns of confined lunatics, asylums and licensed houses, 5 June, and when it was again delayed, urged Lamb to make his brother the home secretary give it the government's full backing, 15 June 1832. Declaring the Lords' amendments 'untenable', 3 Aug., he joined Charles Ross and Williams Wynn in calling again on Lamb to make government act decisively; the bill received royal assent, 11 Aug. 1832.[48]

Asked by Peel during the general election campaign in November 1832 whether he thought the party should back Goulburn or Williams Wynn against Littleton, should Manners Sutton resign as Speaker, he replied:

> Whether it be Wynn or whether it be Goulburn we shall not be enough to carry a Speaker against the ministers. I certainly hope we shall have even a stronger party than we had in this Parliament and I have no doubt ministers will have much less pliant majorities, nor do I think many of their professed friends will long adhere to them; but on the very first occasion that they should be so weak as to fail in their object of Speaker I cannot anticipate, and therefore we should rather argue on the supposition of defeat than success.

Setting personal preference aside, he chose Williams Wynn for being 'less intimately connected with our party' and the 'better to be vanquished'.[49] His time was now commanded by voter registration, the establishment of local committees, and the quest for funding and suitable Conservative candidates. Despite setbacks, which included defeats in Gloucestershire and Monmouth and compromise in Glamorgan, many durable networks of agents, attorneys, barristers and 'Conservative' landowners were formed, and notwithstanding his failure to introduce formal registration societies until 1841, he acquired a reputation as an outstanding party manager.[50] His return for Monmouthshire, where he was widely respected and had a strong committee, was not in doubt.[51] He retained his seat for life, contesting it only in 1847, when Worcester, as 7th duke, sought to oust him for supporting Peel's decision to repeal the corn laws.[52] His health did not recover after the ordeal and he died in February 1848.[53] He had held office again as commissioner of woods and forests and chancellor of the duchy of Lancaster and was admitted to the cabinet in 1843, but was denied the Irish secretaryship he coveted because of fears that he would be cruelly ridiculed in the Irish press.[54] Gladstone noted:

> Lord G. Somerset affords I think a remarkable instance of a very good tempered and good humoured man with reconciliatory modes of proceeding in business, and I confess also that he seems to me scarcely a statesman; but he has abundant talents for administration, and a mind quick in finding objections and consequently of great use in the department of intercepting what is crude and *rash*.[55]

He left everything as trustees to his widow and Lord Sandon*, having directed them to ensure that each of his five children received certain possessions to remember him by.[56]

[1] *Oxford DNB.* [2] H. Durant, *The Somerset Sequence*, 175; *HP Commons, 1790-1820*, v. 224. [3] E.M. Havill, 'Parl. Rep. Mon. and Monmouth Bor. 1536-1832' (Univ. of Wales M.A. thesis, 1949), 120-3; Merthyr Mawr mss CO/153/1-20; NLW, Vivian mss A124, 130; *Bristol Mercury*, 6, 13, 20 Mar. 1820. [4] *Cambrian*, 23, 30 Oct. 1819, 25 Mar.; *Keene's Bath Jnl.* 14 Feb.; *Bristol Mercury*, 21, 28 Feb. 1820; NLW, Baker-Gabb mss 683; NLW, Tredegar mss 45/1478, 135/778. [5] *Oxford DNB.* [6] *The Times*, 29 Sept.; *Bristol Mercury*, 20 Oct., 6, 20 Nov.; *Cambrian*, 21 Oct. 1820, 20 Jan.; *Seren Gomer*, iv (1821), 61-62. [7] *Bristol Mercury*, 27 Mar., 10 Apr.; *Cambrian*, 15 Apr.; Tredegar mss 45/1516; 135/795; *Seren Gomer*, iii (1820), 218-19. [8] Merthyr Mawr mss F/2/4, 20-24 Aug. 1821. [9] *The Times*, 9 Apr.; *Bristol Mercury*, 22 Apr. 1822; I.W.R. David, 'Pol. and Electioneering Activity in S.E. Wales, 1820-52' (Univ. of Wales M.A. thesis, 1959), 68. [10] *The Times*, 24 Apr., 1, 7, 15, 16, 22, 28 May; *Bristol Mercury*, 27 Apr., 4, 11, 25 May, 1, 22 June 1822; N. Gash, *Secretary Peel*, 346. [11] PROB 11/1858/138; 2075/434; *Gent. Mag.* (1822), ii. 178. [12] Wellington mss WP1/758/14. [13] *The Times,*

[14] Ibid. 28 Feb., 7 Apr., 8 May 1824. [15] Bodl. Hughenden dep. D/1/D/53. [16] Merthyr Mawr mss F/2/9, 30 Jan., 2 Feb. 1826; L/206/32; Add. 40385, f. 173; NLW, Maybery mss 6559-60. [17] *The Times*, 18 Apr. 1826. [18] Glam. RO D/DA12/94 i and ii, 100, 104; Hughenden dep. D/1/D/70, 73-76; *Cambrian*, 23 Dec. 1825, 27 May, 17 June; *Morning Chron.* 10 June; *The Times*, 10 June 1826. [19] Nottingham Univ. Lib. Denison diary, 14 Apr. 1827; *Croker Pprs.* i. 373. [20] T.G. Davies, 'Welsh Contribution to Mental Health Legislation in 19th Cent.', *WHR*, xviii (1996), 42-62, esp. 45-51. [21] Wellington mss WP1/914/21; 915/46. [22] Add. 40397, ff. 110-13, 219. [23] Add. 40398, f. 313; Gash, *Secretary Peel*, 62-63. [24] NLW, Beaufort mss II/9877-8, 10718; *CJ*, lxxxiv. 55, 119, 131, 145, 181, 186, 214, 220. [25] NLW, Bute mss L72/28. [26] Wellington mss WP1/1123/37. [27] *Mon. Merlin*, 10, 17 July, 7 Aug.; NLW ms 18541B, Jnl. of Iltyd Nicholl, 5 Aug. 1830; Cent. Kent. Stud. Stanhope mss U1590/C130/9, Mahon to Stanhope, 19, 23, 24, 26 May; C138/2, Strangford to same, 21 May, C318/2, Mahon to Lady Stanhope [1830]; NLW, Aberpergwm mss 11. [28] NLW, Ormathwaite mss FG1/6, 17 and *passim.*; *Three Diaries*, 243, 257, 306-8, 315, 340, 349; *Ellenborough Diary*, ii. 441; Gash, 'Organization of Conservative Party, 1832-46', *PH*, i (1982), 138; *Secretary Peel*, 668-9. [29] *Greville Mems.* ii. 74; Gash, *Secretary Peel*, 618; NLW ms 18541B, 6-12 Dec. 1830. [30] *Three Diaries*, 35. [31] Brougham mss, Somerset to Brougham, 14 Jan. 1831; Davies, 48. [32] *Three Diaries*, 52, 54, 57; *Croker Pprs.* ii. 108, 110; Bodl. Ms. Eng. lett. d. 153, f. 68; Stanhope mss C190/2, Somerset to Stanhope, 23 Mar. 1831. [33] *Greville Mems.* ii. 229-30, 408; Gash, *Sir Robert Peel*, 9. [34] Wellington mss WP1/1178/7. [35] D. Williams, *John Frost* (1939), 58-66; Cardiff Pub. Lib. Bute estate letterbks. ii. 274-5; *Three Diaries*, 91; Harrowby mss, Ryder to Harrowby, 6 May; *Mon. Merlin*, 19, 26 Mar., 2, 9, 16, 23, 30 Apr., 7, 14 May 1831. [36] W.T. Morgan, 'Co. Elections Mon. 1705-1847', *NLWJ*, x (1957-8), 176-7; NLW, Llangibby Castle mss A161; NLW, Bute mss L74/34; *Three Diaries*, 91; *Cambrian*, 30 Apr. 1831. [37] Gwent RO, Evans and Evill mss D.25.1401; *Spectator*, 30 Apr. 1831. [38] NLW, Sir Leonard Twiston Davies mss (Twiston Davies mss) 5927, 5936-7, 5954, 5963. [39] Add. 57370, f. 73; *Three Diaries*, 93. [40] Hatherton diary, 28 July 1831. [41] Add. 40402, f. 102. [42] Badminton mun. Fm M4/1/19, 22. [43] *CJ*, lxxxv. 358, 377; lxxxvi. 795-6, 825, 827, 835. [44] Wellington mss WP1/1199/13; 1201/6. [45] Llangibby Castle mss A162. [46] Badminton mun. Fm M4/1/19; *CJ* lxxxvi. 558, 577, 642, 748, 829, 867-8, 874-5. [47] Badminton mun. Fm M4/1/2. [48] *CJ*, lxxxvii. 67, 70, 75, 172, 528,573-4, 578, 584; Davies, 48-49. [49] Add. 40403, f. 105. [50] Bute mss L75/122, 133-46, 149, 149; Bute estate letterbks. ii. 276, 333-6, 346-7; iii. 1-13, 19, 36, 71; Add. 40303, f. 105; Gash, *PH*, i. 137-9; M. Cragoe, *Culture, Politics, and National Identity in Wales, 1832-1886*, pp. 85-86. [51] Bute mss L75/122, 133-146, 149; Twiston Davies mss 4304-7, 4324, 4355, 6005; *Mon. Merlin*, 23 June, 15, 22 Dec. 1832. [52] Morgan, 178-84; *The Times*, 11 May 1846, 31 July, 9 Aug. 16 Sept.; *Mon. Merlin*, 17, 24, 31 July, 7, 14, 21 Aug. 1847. [53] *The Times*, 24 Feb.; *Mon. Merlin*, 26 Feb., 3 Mar. 1848; *Von Neumann Diary*, ii. 278. [54] Gash, *PH* i. 138-9; *Sir Robert Peel*, 278; *Oxford DNB.* [55] Add. 44777, f. 184. [56] PROB 11/2075/434; IR26/1818/398.

M.M.E.

SOMERSET, Henry, mq. of Worcester (1792–1853).[1]

MONMOUTH	30 Dec. 1813–1831
MONMOUTH	18 July 1831–1832
GLOUCESTERSHIRE WEST	1835–23 Nov. 1835

b. 5 Feb. 1792, 1st s. of Henry Charles Somerset†, 6th duke of Beaufort, and Lady Charlotte Sophia Leveson Gower, da. of Granville Leveson Gower†, 1st mq.

of Stafford; bro. of Lord Granville Charles Henry Somerset*. *educ.* by Rev. Walter Fletcher at Dalston, Cumb.; Westminster until 1805; by Edward Vernon, abp. of York; Christ Church, Oxf. 1809. *m.* (1) 25 July 1814, Georgiana Frederica (*d.* 11 May 1821), da. of Hon. Henry Fitzroy, 2da. (1 *d.v.p.*); (2) 29 June 1822, at St. George, Hanover Square, and 21 Oct. 1823, at the Reform Church, Constance, Baden-Württemberg,[2] Emily Frances, half-sister of his 1st w., da. of Charles Culling Smith, 1s. 6da. *suc.* fa. as 7th duke of Beaufort 23 Nov. 1835; KG 11 Apr. 1842. *d.* 17 Nov. 1853.

Cornet 10 Drag. 1811, lt. 1811; a.d.c. to duke of Wellington 1812-14; lt. 7 Drag. 1815, 93 Ft. 1819; capt. 37 Ft. 1819, maj. 1819, half-pay 1821, ret. 1832.

Ld. of admiralty May 1815-Mar. 1819.

Lt.-col. commdt. Glos. Hussars 1834

High steward, Bristol 1836-*d.*

The 6th duke of Beaufort's heir Lord Worcester, noted for his dandified dress and accomplishments and escapades as a soldier, sportsman and courtier, successfully saw off a challenge from the Gloucestershire Whig John Hodder Moggridge in 1820, to secure his fourth return for Beaufort's borough of Monmouth and its contributories, Newport and Usk.[3] He had recently served without distinction on the admiralty board and attended little to the business of the House, voting only when obliged to as a placeman, to preserve Newport's exemption from the coal duties, and against Catholic relief, which, like all his family, he opposed.[4] He attributed his recent problems in reviving his military career to a lack of understanding and co-operation between his uncle by marriage, the duke of Wellington, and General Sir Henry Torrens.[5] As befitted 'one of the fancy' and a founder of the 'Four in Hand Club', Worcester devoted much time after the election to driving the 'Reading coach down to that town and back every day'.[6] A fall from his horse, 23 Aug. 1820, which it was initially feared might prove fatal, left him 'stunned and severely bruised, but not dangerously hurt'.[7] He divided with the Liverpool administration on the Queen Caroline case, 6 Feb., and the additional malt duty, 21 Mar., and paired, 28 Feb., and presented a petition from Clifton against Catholic relief, 2 Apr. 1821. Following their eviction for debt in March from their Upper Brook Street house, his wife had sought refuge at Apsley House, where she died, 11 May 1821, 'after a week's illness, of inflammation brought on by going into a cold bath after dancing at the ball at Carlton House'.[8] According to Mrs. Arbuthnot, her only regret was 'at leaving her children (two daughters) to the care of a father so inconsiderate and light minded'.[9] To Charles Greville it was 'the severest blow I ever had in my life' for 'I loved her like a sister'; and Henry Edward Fox* commented:

Such beauty, such youth and such a situation, poor woman! She never had a happy life. For *him* it is the worst thing that could happen. He will marry again, and some horrid thing or other like Miss Calcraft.[10]

Worcester had proved attentive during her illness, and, according to Wellington, who accompanied him to the funeral, he 'suffered severely', even if, as was widely predicted, he did 'not feel it long'.[11] Almost immediately he became engaged to the marquess of Anglesey's daughter, Lady Jane Paget, and in the spring of 1822 he was portrayed in satirical prints with her and a pregnant Miss Calcraft, daughter of the Member for Wareham. He was also lampooned with the duke of Cumberland, as rival suitors of the banker Thomas Coutts's widow, who had the means to pay off their debts.[12] To his parents' dismay, Worcester broke off his engagement, and caused a sensation in June by marrying his late wife's pretty twenty-one-year-old half-sister, over whom he had almost fought a duel with the duke of Gloucester. The couple left immediately for Paris.[13] Writing to her compatriot Metternich, Princess Lieven observed: 'the young woman's beauty consists in large black eyebrows and a great deal of hair on her face and arms – Englishmen cannot resist hairy arms. Isn't that an odd taste?'[14] Over the next two years Worcester and his father-in-law Culling Smith repeatedly sought counsel's opinion on the marriage, which, though not illegal, was voidable under the consanguinity laws, placing the legitimacy of any issue at risk. Culling Smith, whom Wellington rightly blamed for not having tried harder to prevent it, lobbied hard to have such marriages referred to a Lords select committee, and a validating clause appended to the 1823 Marriage Act. When this approach failed, he, Worcester, and the latter's friend Lord Avonmore explored the possibility of validating it under the Act as a foreign marriage. They found similar consanguinity prohibitions in force throughout Europe, but a dispensation was secured in Stuttgart, and the Worcesters were remarried in the reformed church at Constance, 21 Oct. 1823. To Worcester's dismay, for Emily was now pregnant, this marriage, though fully documented, was not admitted under the Act, because the couple had neither been resident in Württemberg nor married according to rites recognized by the Church of England. The 1822 wedding was confirmed retrospectively in February 1836, under the terms of the 1835 Act.[15]

Worcester had taken legal advice on his first marriage settlement (worth £2,000 a year, of which at least half was allocated to repaying debts) soon after his arrival in France, and he drafted a settlement and will in favour of Emily, whom he appointed guardian of his children, 15 Aug. 1822. Early fears that his mother would prevent his daughters joining him in Paris and keep them exposed to '*the pernicious influence*' and '*unfortunate increase of Methodism*' at Badminton proved unfounded.[16] He was concerned that when his uncle Lord Granville arrived in Paris as the new British ambassador, Lady Granville should 'receive' Emily, and threatened to bring libel actions against caricaturists who portrayed her as a pregnant bride watched over by her late sister. Wellington called on the Worcesters in Paris in October 1822, but the couple, who relied increasingly on loans procured through Culling Smith and his provision for Emily, were not reconciled with Beaufort until after the birth in February 1824 of an heir, to whom he agreed to be godfather. They returned to England after negotiations between Lord Fitzroy Somerset[†], acting for Beaufort, and Culling Smith had secured a £10,000 marriage settlement for Emily in August 1824.[17] That Michaelmas Worcester went to Swansea with his father to promote their interest in the Cardiff Boroughs constituency.[18] Publication of his erstwhile mistress Harriette Wilson's *Memoirs* early in 1825 put Worcester in the popular prints, which, as in 1817, depicted him as a dandy walking a clipped poodle.[19] He voted, 1 Mar., 21 Apr., and paired against Catholic relief, 10 May, and divided against disfranchising Irish 40s. freeholders under the attendant franchise bill, 26 Apr. 1825. He voted for the duke of Cumberland's annuity, 6, 10 June 1825. Opposition to the Beaufort interest in Monmouth and Usk persisted, but Worcester narrowly avoided a contest there in 1826 after a difficult canvass.[20]

He divided against Catholic relief, 6 Mar. 1827, 12 May 1828, and repeal of the Test Acts, 26 Feb. 1828, and presented a petition for repeal of the 1827 Malt Act from the maltsters of Monmouth, 29 Feb. 1828. Not surprisingly, he was one of the Members criticized by the Wellington ministry's patronage secretary Planta in March for failing to give them regular support despite the sums of public money awarded to their families.[21] In April Peel and Wellington turned down his requests for a civil knighthood for his friend Colonel Vaillant and church preferment for his former university tutor, Kenneth Mackenzie Reid Tarpley.[22] He divided with government against ordnance reductions, 4 July 1828. He and his wife were guests at Stoke in August, when the Catholic question and Peel and Wellington's treatment of Lord Anglesey as Irish lord lieutenant were much discussed.[23] As Planta had predicted in February, Worcester voted 'with government' for Catholic emancipation, 6 Mar. 1829.

He did not divide again on the issue and was refused government patronage that year for 'Beau' Brummell, Herbert Cornewall and Tarpley.[24] A vote against the enfranchisement of Birmingham, Leeds and Manchester, 23 Mar. 1830, is the only one recorded for him that session. At the proclamation of William IV in July and the general election in August, his constituents expressed satisfaction with him as a Member and returned him unopposed.[25] According to Greville, he was now the go-between in a liaison between Lady Fitzroy Somerset and the chancellor of the exchequer Goulburn.[26]

The ministry naturally counted Worcester among their 'friends' and he left Apsley House, where he was dining with Wellington, to vote with them on the civil list, 15 Nov. 1830, when they were brought down. Greville recalled that on returning he

> only said that they had had a bad division, 29. Everybody thought he meant a majority for government, and the duke, who already knew what had happened, made a sign to him to say nothing. He knew nothing himself, had arrived after the division; they told him the numbers, and he came away fancying they were for government.[27]

Worcester attended a grand dinner at the Prussian Embassy, 21 Nov., presented Monmouth's petition for repeal of the taxes on houses and windows, 23 Nov., and by 1 Dec. 1830 had joined his father and brother Granville at Heythorp, Oxfordshire, where they helped to eject and disperse a riotous mob.[28] Amid further outbreaks of 'jacquerie' in the winter of 1830-31, he refused to support his constituents' reform petitions, and a public meeting at Newport, 3 Feb. 1831, passed a resolution calling for representation by a reformer.[29] Undeterred, Worcester divided against the Grey ministry's reform bill at its second reading, 22 Mar., and for Gascoyne's wrecking amendment, 19 Apr. His declared opponent, the pro-reform squire and industrialist Benjamin Hall, had commenced canvassing, and Worcester was lucky to escape with his life after being cornered by the Newport mob, 28 Apr. On the hustings, he defended his decision to withhold his support from the Newport reform petitions, criticized the ministry's record on retrenchment and reform, and tried to capitalize on their decision to equalize the coal duties (so depriving Newport of its advantage over Cardiff). He also charged his 1830 supporters with inconstancy, and Hall with authorship of a handbill (later acknowledged to be the work of the Newport printer John Partridge), claiming (falsely) that Beaufort and his family received £48,000 annually from public funds.[30] Though now outpolled, Worcester was seated on petition, 18 July 1831, and new local committees were established to promote the Beaufort interest throughout Monmouthshire.[31]

He divided against the reintroduced reform bill at its third reading, 19 Sept., and passage, 21 Sept. 1831. The following day, briefing his father, who was about to set out to vote against it in the Lords, he claimed that Scarlett's failure to speak as intended had made little difference to the outcome of the division on the 19th and expressed great admiration for Peel and Wetherell's speeches on 21st. On the 27th, after visiting Stoke, he informed Beaufort that Lords Wharncliffe and Harrowby would continue to oppose the bill and praised his brother Granville's speech on the lunacy bill, 26 Sept., on which the government had suffered a setback.[32] He voted against the revised reform bill at its second and third readings 17 Dec. 1831, 22 Mar. 1832. He became a founder member of the Carlton Club with his father, and paired against government on the Russian-Dutch loan, 12 July 1832. He was then at Brighton with his family, seeking a cure for a rheumatic complaint, which left him almost unable to walk: 'being half an hour on my feet immediately brings on a return of the pain'.[33] It was to prompt his retirement from the army and prevented him canvassing early at the 1832 general election, when he was defeated by Hall.[34]

Worcester remained out of Parliament until 1835, when he was returned for Gloucestershire West.[35] His financial difficulties persisted after he succeeded as 7th duke in November that year, but reports of his ruin proved premature. He requested a diplomatic post in Vienna in September 1841, turned down that offered to him at St. Petersburg, and was delighted to be made a knight of the garter the following year. He further drained his resources by spending an estimated £20,000 trying to prevent Granville's election for Monmouthshire in 1847, when their differences over free trade were irreconcilable.[36] He died at Badminton in November 1853, recalled as one of the 'most popular sportsmen in England', and his figure dominates portraits of the Badminton and Windsor Hunts.[37] He left everything except jewellery and certain personal effects to his only son Henry Charles Fitzroy (1824-99), who from February 1846 until his succession as 8th duke was Conservative Member for Gloucestershire East.[38]

[1] Draws on the Badminton Muniments, seen by permission of His Grace the duke of Beaufort. (Fm O 1/9/2). [2] Badminton mun. [3] Cambrian, 10, 17 Mar.; Bristol Mercury, 13 Mar. 1820; K. Kissack, Monmouth, 73-76. [4] HP Commons, 1790-1820, v. 224-5. [5] Wellington mss WP1/629/22; 632/9; 633/5; 762/14; 763/10. [6] Keele Univ. Lib. Sneyd mss SC8/44. [7] Countess Granville Letters, i. 162-4. [8] Wellington mss WP1/644/10; 670/3; Nottingham Univ. Lib.

Portland mss PwH 84; Northants. RO, Agar Ellis diary, 6-11 May; Add. 51679, Lord J. Russell to Lady Holland [Mar.]; 51831, Lord Granville Somerset to Holland, 25 May 1821; Von Neumann Diary, i. 61. [9] Arbuthnot Jnl. i. 93-94. [10] Greville Mems. i. 119; Castle Howard mss, Fox to G. Howard, 21 May 1821. [11] Arbuthnot Jnl. i. 95-96; Add. 51667, Bedford to Lady Holland, 13 May; 51579, Morpeth to same, 15 May 1821; H. Durant, The Somerset Sequence, 182-3. [12] Arbuthnot Jnl. i. 123; M.D. George, Cat. of Pol. and Personal Satires, x. 14424-6. [13] Agar Ellis diary, 18 Mar., 4, 8, 9 July, 27 Sept. 1822; Arbuthnot Jnl. i. 141-2, 153, 171-2; Von Neumann Diary, i. 95; George, x. 14427. [14] Lieven Letters, 184-5. [15] Badminton mun. Fm O 1/9/2, bdles. marked 'Secret'; Wellington mss WP1/762/14; 763/10. [16] Badminton mun. Fm O 1/9/2. [17] Ibid.; George, x. 14427; Arbuthnot Jnl. i. 193; Add. 51668, Bedford to Lady Holland, 7 Mar.; Agar Ellis diary, 29 May 1824. [18] Cambrian, 2 Oct. 1824. [19] Harriette Wilson's Mems. ed. J Laver (1929), 127-8, 130, 142, 152, 163, 190, 195, 203-5, 234, 247; George, x. 14828, 14831, 14844, 14848-9, 14932, 15085. [20] Kissack, 56-101; NLW, Tredegar mss 57/45; Bristol Mercury, 8 May; Morning Chron. 10 June; The Times, 10, 15 June; Courier, 15 June 1826. [21] Arbuthnot Jnl. ii. 176. [22] Add. 40396, f. 189; Wellington mss WP1/968/27; 1023/19. [23] Greville Mems. i. 217. [24] Wellington mss WP1/1059/3; 1065/11; 1091/21; Greville Mems. i. 341. [25] Mon. Merlin, 7 Aug. 1830; D. Williams, John Frost (1939), 58. [26] Greville Mems. ii. 60. [27] Ibid. ii. 74. [29] Williams, 60-65; Mon. Merlin. 25 Dec. 1830, 5, 12 Feb., 19 Mar., 9, 23 Apr. 1831; Bristol Mercury, 28 Dec. 1830; The Times, 11 Feb.; Cambrian, 16 Apr. 1831. [30] Cambrian, 30 Apr.; Mon. Merlin, 30 Apr., 7 May, 31 Dec. 1831; M. Fraser, 'Benjamin Hall and Monmouth Boroughs, 1831-7', Presenting Mon. xii (1961), 10-11; Williams, 67. [31] Creevey mss, Creevey to Miss Ord, 6 May 1831; Greville Mems. ii. 143-4; Mon. Merlin, 14 May, 16, 23 July; Cambrian, 14 May, 23 July; The Times, 19 July 1831; NLW, Sir Leonard Twiston Davies mss (Twiston Davies mss) 4223-46, 4304-7, 5934-54; CJ, lxxxvi. 537, 643, 645, 665. [32] Badminton mun. Fm M 4/1/9. [33] Twiston Davies mss 6007; Lonsdale mss, Beckett to Lowther [June/July 1832]. [34] Twiston Davies mss 6008-9, 6053, 6071-7; Mon. Merlin, 7 July, 1, 15 Dec. 1832. [35] Illustrated London News (1853), ii. 448. [36] Add. 40488, ff. 292-7; Disraeli Letters, iv. 318-21; Von Neumann Diary, ii. 266; Greville Mems. vi. 141; The Times, 11 May 1846, 31 July, 9 Aug. 16 Sept. 1847. [37] Gent. Mag. (1854), i. 80-81; J. Evans, Funeral Sermon, 27 Nov. 1853. [38] PROB 8/248/315; 11/2187/182.

M.M.E.

SOMERSET, Lord Robert Edward Henry (1776–1842), of 5 Grosvenor Square, Mdx.

MONMOUTH	27 Mar. 1799–1802
GLOUCESTERSHIRE	14 Nov. 1803–1831
CIRENCESTER	6 Aug. 1834–1837

b. 19 Dec. 1776, 4th s. of Henry, 5th duke of Beaufort (d. 1803), and Elizabeth, da. of Hon. Edward Boscawen[†]; bro. of Lord Arthur John Henry Somerset[†], Lord Charles Henry Somerset[†], Lord Fitzroy James Henry Somerset*, and Henry Charles Somerset, mq. of Worcester[†]. educ. Westminster 1789. m. 17 Oct. 1805, Hon. Louisa Augusta Courtenay, da. of William, 2nd Visct. Courtenay, 3s. (1 d.v.p.) 5da. KCB 2 Jan. 1815; GCB 17 Oct. 1834. d. 1 Sept. 1842.

Jt. dep. paymaster-gen. 1807-13; lt.-gen. of ordnance June 1829-Nov. 1830, surveyor-gen. Dec. 1834-Apr. 1835.

Cornet 10 Drag. 1793, lt. 1793, capt. 1794; a.d.c. to duke of York in Holland 1799; maj. 12 Drag. 1799, 28 Drag. 1800; lt.-col. 5 Ft. 1800, 4 Drag. 1801; col. 4 Drag. in Portugal 1809; a.d.c. to king with rank of col. 1810; maj.-gen. i/c Hussar brig. 1813, i/c heavy cav. brig. in Netherlands 1815, i/c 1 brig. cav. France 1815-18; col. 21 Drag. 1818; inspecting gen. cav. 1818-25; col. 17 Lancers 1822, Royals 1829, 4 Drag. 1836; lt.-gen. 1825; gen. 1841.

Somerset, who received an annuity of £600 from his father's estate in 1803, in addition to other unspecified provision,[1] was a highly decorated hero of the Peninsular campaign and Waterloo. He was returned unopposed for Gloucestershire on his brother the 6th duke of Beaufort's interest for the sixth time in 1820, in conjunction with the Whig Sir Berkeley William Guise, after defending the Six Acts as 'indispensably necessary ... for the maintenance of our constitution, our religion and our property'.[2] He was a fairly regular attender, who continued to support Lord Liverpool's ministry but seldom spoke. He presented a Gloucestershire woollen trade petition against restrictions on imported wool, 16 May, and two from the agriculturists for higher protective duties, 26 May 1820.[3] He voted in defence of ministers' conduct towards Queen Caroline, 6 Feb. 1821. He divided against a reduction in the ordnance estimates, 16 Feb., repeal of the additional malt duty, 21 Mar., and Hume's motion on economy and retrenchment, 27 June. He presented petitions from Gloucestershire agriculturists for relief from distress, 20 Feb., and woollen manufacturers against the wool duties, 19 Mar.[4] He divided against Catholic claims, 28 Feb., and parliamentary reform, 9 May 1821. He voted against more extensive tax reductions, 11 Feb., and abolition of one of the joint-postmasterships, 13 Mar. 1822. He presented petitions from Gloucestershire agriculturists for greater protection, 26 Apr., 16 May.[5] He divided against removing Catholic peers' disabilities, 30 Apr. 1822. He presented anti-slavery petitions, 16 Mar.,[6] but voted against the motion condemning the trial of the Methodist missionary John Smith in Demerara, 11 June 1824. He was a majority teller for the second reading of the Cheltenham waterworks bill, 25 Mar. 1824. He divided for the Irish unlawful societies bill, 25 Feb., against Catholic claims, 1 Mar., 21 Apr., 10 May, presenting several hostile petitions,[7] and against the Irish franchise bill, 26 Apr. 1825. He presented a Gloucestershire woollen manufacturers' petition for revision of the corn laws, 22 Apr.,[8] and was a minority teller for the second reading of the Stroud and Severn railway bill, 28 Apr. He voted for the financial provision for the duke of Cumberland, 30 May, 6, 10 June. On 22 June 1825 he urged the Commons

to suspend judgement on his brother Lord Charles Somerset, governor of the Cape of Good Hope, until the commissioners investigating allegations of maladministration had reported. He divided against the motion condemning the Jamaican slave trials, 2 Mar., and reform of Edinburgh's representation, 13 Apr. 1826. He denied that his brother was evading his accusers, 8 May, and stated that Lord Charles was anxious to meet the 'gross and unfounded calumnies' levelled against him before the parliamentary recess, 19 May 1826.[9] At the general election that summer he was again returned unopposed for Gloucestershire after expressing confidence that the recent 'calamitous depression' was a temporary problem, which he attributed to the 'extensive but unfortunate spirit of enterprise and speculation which has prevailed to so great a degree amongst many classes of the community'.[10]

He presented several anti-Catholic petitions, 2, 5 Mar., and voted in this sense, 6 Mar. 1827. He presented petitions for repeal of the Test Acts, 15 June.[11] He voted for the Clarence annuity bill, 16 Mar., and was granted ten days' leave to attend the assizes, 2 Apr. He welcomed the decision to lay papers before the House regarding his brother's case, 17 May, and secured a statement from the minister Wilmot Horton, 29 June 1827, that the accusations of corruption and tyranny had not been substantiated. He claimed that 'the proceedings which had been adopted ... were the acts of individuals who had conspired together to effect their own private objects'. He divided against repeal of the Test Acts, 26 Feb., and presented a hostile petition from the archdeacon and clergy of Gloucester, 18 Mar. 1828. He presented numerous anti-Catholic petitions that session and voted accordingly, 12 May. He divided with the duke of Wellington's ministry against the motion condemning delays in chancery, 24 Apr., and reduction in the salary of the lieutenant-general of the ordnance, 4 July. He presented a Gloucestershire woollen manufacturers' petition against further regulation of their industry, 29 Apr., three petitions in favour of the circulation of small bank notes, 30 May, 7 July, and two against a lower duty on foreign silks, 12 June 1828. He presented anti-Catholic petitions, 9, 20 Feb., but, as the patronage secretary Planta had correctly predicted, he voted for Catholic emancipation, 6 Mar., and paired for it, 30 Mar. 1829. He explained that 'my sentiments on the subject remain in principle unchanged' but 'necessity ... controls me by presenting ... only a choice of evils', 9 Mar. He had been swayed by the state of 'discord' in Ireland, the promise of a raised Irish county franchise and confidence in Wellington. He presented a Cheltenham petition for repeal of the house and window duties, 20 Feb., and 'had an interview with the chancellor of the exchequer [Goulburn], who assured him that the circumstances complained of should be considered'.[12] He presented a Gloucestershire woollen manufacturers' petition against renewal of the East India Company's charter, 1 May. His appointment as lieutenant-general of the ordnance in June 1829 was regarded as a 'very Tory' one, helping to balance Whig appointments; George IV was reportedly 'well pleased' by it.[13] He divided with his ministerial colleagues against the transfer of East Retford's seats to Birmingham, 11 Feb., Lord Blandford's reform motion, 18 Feb., the enfranchisement of Birmingham, Leeds and Manchester, 23 Feb., and Jewish emancipation, 5 Apr., 17 May 1830. He refuted Lord Althorp's assertion that the duties of the master and lieutenant-general of the ordnance were identical, 29 Mar., and made several interventions to defend the ordnance estimates from radical attack, 30 Apr. He voted against the reduction of judges' salaries, 7 July. On 10 May 1830 he presented several petitions against the sale of beer bill and on-consumption in beerhouses, and presented and endorsed two from Gloucestershire against the truck system. He was again returned unopposed at the general election that summer.[14]

He of course voted with Wellington's ministry in the crucial civil list division, 15 Nov. 1830, and went out with them. He presented a 'numerously signed' petition from Gloucestershire woollen manufacturers and workmen against the truck system, 19 Nov., and promised to support Littleton's bill on the subject. He presented petitions from Stroud and Northleach against slavery, Cheltenham for repeal of the house and window duties and Stow-on-the-Wold for repeal of the malt duty, 23 Dec. 1830. He divided against the second reading of the Grey ministry's reform bill, 22 Mar., presented a favourable petition from Gloucester, with which he regretfully differed, 24 Mar., and voted for Gascoyne's wrecking amendment, 19 Apr. 1831. He again offered for Gloucestershire at the ensuing general election but was confronted by a formidable opposition from local reformers; his prospects were judged to be poor, 'shaken as he already is, in the house of his friends, by his vote on the ... Catholic bill'.[15] In his address, he explained that he had considered it his duty to oppose a reform bill 'pregnant with danger to the long established institutions of the country, unjust and delusive in its effects, and producing a much more sudden and extensive alteration in the constitution ... than was either necessary or expedient'. However, he professed willingness to support a measure that protected 'all those rights that deserve protection' and was 'consistent with the acknowledged principles of the constitution'. He withdrew the day before the poll.[16]

At the general election of 1832 Somerset accepted a requisition to stand for West Gloucestershire but was narrowly beaten into third place by two Liberals.[17] He was returned for Cirencester at a by-election in 1834 and held office in Peel's first ministry, before retiring from Parliament in 1837. In January 1842 he wrote to Peel from Rome to solicit support for his appointment as governor of Gibraltar or Malta whenever a vacancy arose, adding that 'I should infinitely prefer ... Malta ... as being likely to prove in many respects a more agreeable situation for myself and my family'; the premier's reply was non-committal.[18] He died in September 1842 and left the residue of his estate to be divided equally amongst his two sons and three unmarried daughters.[19]

[1] The will was proved under £70,000 (PROB 11/1401/946; IR26/82/9). [2] Gloucester Jnl. 20 Mar. 1820. [3] The Times, 17, 27 May 1820. [4] Ibid. 21 Feb., 20 Mar. 1821. [5] Ibid. 27 Apr., 17 May 1822. [6] Ibid. 17 Mar. 1824. [7] Ibid. 19 Apr., 4 May 1825. [8] Ibid. 23 Apr. 1825. [9] Ibid. 20 May 1826. [10] Gloucester Jnl. 5, 19 June 1826. [11] The Times, 3, 6 Mar., 16 June 1827. [12] Gloucester Jnl. 28 Feb. 1829. [13] Arbuthnot Jnl. ii. 277; Ellenborough Diary, ii. 43. [14] Gloucester Jnl. 7 Aug. 1830. [15] Harrowby mss, G.D. Ryder to Harrowby, 6 May 1831. [16] Gloucester Jnl. 9, 30 Apr., 7 May 1831. [17] Ibid. 7 July, 22 Dec. 1832. [18] Add. 40500, ff. 36-38. [19] PROB 8/235; 11/1968/639.

T.A.J.

SOMERVILLE, Sir Marcus, 4th bt. (?1772–1831), of Somerville, co. Meath.

Co. MEATH   1801–11 July 1831

b. ?1772, 1st s. of Sir James Quaile Somerville, 3rd bt., of Somerville and Catherine, da. of Sir Marcus Lowther Crofton, 1st bt., MP [I], of the Mote, co. Roscommon. educ. by Mr. Berington, Devon; Trinity, Dublin 1 Aug. 1791, aged 19. m. (1) 1 Oct. 1801, Marianne, da. and h. of Sir Richard Gorges Meredyth, 1st bt., MP [I], of Catherine's Grove, co. Dublin, 2s.; (2) 7 Apr. 1825, his cos. Elizabeth, da. of Piers Geale of Clonsilla, co. Dublin, s.p. suc. fa. as 4th bt. 1800. d. 11 July 1831.
    MP [I] 1800.
    Gov. co. Meath 1831-d.

Somerville, a 'constant resident' of county Meath, where he had originally been returned on the independent Catholic interest, had 'first joined the ranks of the government' in 1815, since when had obtained a crown solicitorship, a fishery inspectorate and a clerkship for his nominees. Following his unopposed return at the 1820 general election he was listed by the Liverpool ministry as seeking 'office for his brother' as his 'first object', silk for his lawyer kinsman Sir Henry Meredyth, and a 'small pension' for Lady F. Phillpot.[1]

A lax attender, he was granted leave on account of ill health for three weeks, 26 May, and a fortnight, 30 June 1820.[2] He was present to vote in defence of ministers' conduct towards Queen Caroline, 6 Feb., and against repeal of the additional malt duty, 3 Apr. 1821. He divided for Catholic claims, 28 Feb. 1821, 1 Mar., 21 Apr., 10 May 1825. His claims on government were sufficient for Goulburn, the Irish secretary, to advise the lord lieutenant to turn down Lord Bective's* request to succeed his father as colonel of the Meath militia in 1823, as it might be viewed as creating 'a monopoly ... in favour of one family to his future prejudice', and because Somerville's earlier 'application to be made a governor' had been unsuccessful owing to the viceroy's determination not to increase their number.[3] (Bective, however, was soon in place.) Somerville voted against the production of papers on Catholic office-holders, 19 Feb. 1824. In November that year he was considered by Liverpool and the duke of Wellington for an Irish peerage following a promise 'made by the king', which they were 'anxious to carry out', but it came to nothing.[4] He voted in the minority for hearing evidence on behalf of the Catholic Association, 18 Feb., presented Meath petitions against its suppression that day and 23 Feb., and divided thus, 21, 25 Feb. 1825.[5] On 25 Aug. 1825 he spoke at a county meeting to promote Catholic claims, which he promised to support 'till his last day'.[6] He attended the Association dinner for the 'friends of civil and religious liberty', 2 Feb. 1826.[7]

At the 1826 general election he offered again as a 'friend of liberty of conscience', citing his support for Catholic claims, a 'measure essential to the dearest interests of Ireland'. He was returned unopposed.[8] He voted for relief, 6 Mar. 1827, 12 May 1828, and presented favourable constituency petitions, 12 Mar. 1828. He voted with the Wellington ministry against ordnance reductions, 4 July. On 30 Sept. 1828 he left his 'sick bed, after a confinement of three days' to speak at a county meeting of the Catholic freeholders, who he declared could not fail if they acted 'prudently'.[9] He attended a Dublin meeting for the 'friends of civil and religious liberty', 20 Jan., and a county meeting in support of Lord Anglesey following his recall as Irish lord lieutenant, 26 Jan. 1829.[10] He presented multiple petitions for repeal of the Irish Vestries Act, 23 Feb. 1829, 25 May 1830. He presented petitions for Catholic emancipation, 23 Feb., and divided accordingly, 6, 30 Mar. 1829. He voted for Daniel O'Connell to be permitted to take his seat unhindered, 18 May 1829. He divided for Jewish emancipation, 5 Apr., 17 May 1830. He voted for repeal of the Irish coal duties, 13 May. He was appointed to the select committee

on Irish tolls, 25 May. He presented and endorsed a Meath petition against increases in Irish spirit and stamp duties, warning that the agricultural interest would 'greatly suffer' and that the additional duty on stamps would be a 'great embarrassment on all commercial dealings and cause the ruin of the press', 21 June. On 6 July Leveson Gower, the Irish secretary, asked Archdeacon Singleton:

> What can I say to Sir M. Somerville who presses to be made governor of his county? He states that he has supported government for *30* years and I really think that the appointment of Lord Clifton*, a political opponent, gives him some claim, particularly at the present moment, if it can serve him, however slightly, in his election interests.

A month later he wrote in similar terms, adding that Peel, the home secretary, 'also thinks, that it would be but fair to indulge Sir M. Somerville in his wish to become a governor after so many years of support' if 'the lord lieutenant should think proper'. He was in place by the following year.[11]

At the 1830 general election Somerville offered again with the backing of government, from whom he claimed that he had 'never received anything for himself or any of his family'. A threatened opposition by the Meath Independent Club prompted him to pledge support for economy and retrenchment, repeal of the Vestry Act, cessation of the Kildare Place Society grant, and 'a rational reform in the state of the representation', following which their candidate withdrew and he was returned unopposed.[12] He was listed by ministers as one of their 'friends', but was absent from the crucial division on the civil list, 15 Nov. 1830, when he was named to the select committee on Irish tolls. He voted for the second reading of the Grey ministry's reform bill, 22 Mar., and against Gascoyne's wrecking amendment, 19 Apr. 1831. At the ensuing general election he stood again, citing his support for reform and insisting that he was 'pledged to no party'. After a five-man contest he was returned in second place.[13] He was absent from the division on the second reading of the reintroduced reform bill, 6 July, and died five days later.[14] He was succeeded by his eldest son William Meredyth, Liberal Member for Drogheda, 1837-52, and Canterbury, 1854-65, who was Irish secretary in the Russell administration, 1847-52, and was raised to the Irish peerage as Baron Athlumney in 1863.

[1] *Dublin Evening Post*, 11, 18 Mar. 1820. [2] *Black Bk.* (1823), 194; *Session of Parl. 1825*, p. 485. [3] Add. 37300, f. 259. [4] Wellington mss WP1/805/9; 806/24, 25. [5] *The Times*, 19, 24 Feb. 1825. [6] *Dublin Evening Post*, 1 Sept. 1825. [7] *O'Connell Corresp.* ii. 762. [8] *Dublin Evening Post*, 8, 29 June 1826. [9] Ibid. 4 Oct. 1828. [10] Ibid. 8, 24, 27

Jan. 1829. [11] NAI, Leveson Gower letterbks. 7. B3. 33., Leveson Gower to Singleton, 6 July, 6 Aug. 1830; *R. Kal.* (1831), 389. [12] Wellington mss WP1/806/25; *Dublin Evening Post*, 3, 17, 19, 21 Aug.; *Westmeath Jnl.* 19, 26 Aug. 1830. [13] *Dublin Evening Post*, 3, 12, 14, 17 May; *Carlow Morning Post*, 16 May 1831. [14] *Dublin Evening Post*, 14 July 1831; *Gent. Mag.* (1831), ii. 177.

P.J.S.

SOTHERON (sometime **FRANK**), **Frank** (1765–1839), of Kirklington, Notts.

NOTTINGHAMSHIRE   11 Apr. 1814–1831

bap. 24 May 1765,[1] 3rd s. of William Sotheron (*d.* 1789) of Darrington Hall, Yorks. and Sarah, da. and h. of Samuel Savile and Elizabeth, da. and coh. of Robert Frank[†] of Pontefract; bro. of William Sotheron[†]. *m.* (1) 6 Oct. 1808, Caroline Matilda (*d.* 29 May 1812), da. and coh. of Thomas Barker of Potters Newton, Yorks., 1da.; (2) 13 Nov. 1813, Jane, da. of Wilson (Gale) Braddyll[†] of Conishead Priory, Lancs., *s.p. suc.* bro. William 1806 and took name of Frank until 1818 when he resumed name of Sotheron. *d.* 7 Feb. 1839.

Midshipman RN 1776, lt. 1783, cdr. 1792, capt. 1793, r.-adm. 1811, v.-adm. 1819, adm. 1830.

Sotheron, a Yorkshireman and naval officer, had apparently joined Brooks's Club in 1808, but represented Nottinghamshire on the duke of Newcastle's interest, as an inactive supporter of Lord Liverpool's administration, from 1814.[2] He offered again at the general election of 1820 and, regardless of expense, was determined to meet John Lumley's* challenge 'by polling the freeholders to the last vote'. After Lumley withdrew, Sotheron was again returned unopposed, although (as in 1818) he evidently incurred £1,000 of costs. He assured the electors of his political integrity, stating that 'his friends did not know what his political opinions were, and he himself scarcely knew what politics he had', but he was said to be 'diffuse and appeared overpowered' on declaring that he 'had only one little girl and wished to leave a good name behind him'.[3] He remained a country gentleman by inclination, attending occasionally to oppose Catholic relief and side with ministers.[4] He approved exempting the Aire and Calder navigation from the poor rates, 13 June, and was granted three weeks' sick leave, 27 June 1820.[5]

He voted in defence of ministers' conduct towards Queen Caroline, 6 Feb. 1821. He divided against barring civil officers of the ordnance from voting in parliamentary elections, 12 Apr., and parliamentary reform, 9 May. He voted against the forgery punishment mitigation bill, 23 May, and Hume's proposal for economy and retrenchment, 27 June 1821. He divided

against more extensive tax reductions to relieve distress, 11, 21 Feb., and spoke against reducing the number of junior lords of the admiralty, 1 Mar., but sided with opposition to abolish one of the joint-postmasterships, 2 May. He opposed dividing the constituency of Yorkshire, 7 June, and voted against inquiry into Irish tithes, 19 June, and repeal of the salt tax, 28 June 1822. He presented petitions from Nottingham and Southwell churchmen against the Marriage Act, 10, 14 Feb., and an anti-Catholic one from Mansfield, 15 Apr. 1823.[6] He divided for the grant for Irish churches and glebe houses, 11 Apr., and against repeal of the Foreign Enlistment Act, 16 Apr. He was in the majority for inquiry into the legal proceedings against the Dublin Orange rioters, 22 Apr., but sided with government against investigation of chancery administration, 5 June, and the currency, 12 June 1823. Sotheron divided against reform of Edinburgh's representation, 26 Feb. 1824, 13 Apr. 1826. He sided with ministers against inquiry into the trial of the Methodist missionary John Smith in Demerara, 11 June, and for the Irish insurrection bill, 14 June 1824. He voted against the Catholic peers bill, 30 Apr. 1822, and Catholic relief, 1 Mar., 21 Apr., 10 May, and the Irish franchise bill, 26 Apr., 9 May 1825. He brought up petitions from several Nottinghamshire towns against revision of the corn laws, 28 Apr., and voted for the duke of Cumberland's grant, 2, 6, 10 June 1825.[7] In May 1826 he conferred with his colleague Lord William Cavendish Bentinck about the malt trade concerns of their constituents.[8] He had previously been advised by Newcastle to announce that he would stand down if any challenger emerged in the county.[9] None appeared, and he was returned unopposed at the general election that summer, when, in a speech full of nautical allusions, he repeated his boast of independence and promised to co-operate with Lumley, the other Member.[10] John Evelyn Denison*, who privately upbraided him for allowing his seconder to characterize him as a reformer, wrote in his diary that Sotheron 'was annoyed, but made no answer. He is the greatest ass I ever talked to'.[11] Newcastle, who congratulated him on upstaging his new colleague, 17 June, signed a bond to him for £5,000 that month and paid a lachrymose visit to Kirklington, the childhood home of his former wife, in October 1826.[12]

During the following February and March he presented numerous Nottinghamshire petitions calling for agricultural protection, and he duly voted against the corn bill, 2 Apr. 1827.[13] He divided against Catholic relief, 6 Mar., and presented the hostile Nottingham petition, 6 Apr. He voted against the disfranchisement of Penryn, 28 May, and brought up East Retford's petition against the loss of its own seats, 18 June 1827.[14] He divided against repeal of the Test Acts, 26 Feb., and Catholic relief, 12 May 1828. He voted with the Wellington ministry against reduction of the salary of the lieutenant-general of the ordnance, 4 July. Believing that an anti-Catholic county meeting would be counter-productive, he refused Newcastle's request to initiate one in Nottinghamshire in December 1828, arguing that 'it would not accord with the professions repeatedly made at my election of being always ready to receive the instructions of my constituents but not to anticipate them'.[15] Listed by Planta, the patronage secretary, as 'opposed to the principle' of emancipation, he was indefatigable in presenting Nottinghamshire anti-Catholic petitions early the following session, angrily vindicating the validity of their signatures, 9, 20 Mar. 1829; he voted steadily against emancipation that month. Later that year the Ultra leader, Sir Richard Vyvyan*, included him among the 'Tories strongly opposed to the present government'. He voted against transferring East Retford's seats to Birmingham, 11 Feb., and the enfranchisement of Birmingham, Leeds and Manchester, 23 Feb. 1830. He presented his county's petition complaining of agricultural distress, 23 Mar. He divided against Jewish emancipation, 5 Apr., 17 May. He voted for the South American consular services' grant and against abolishing the death penalty for forgery, 7 June 1830.

Sotheron, who became a full admiral that year, was again returned unopposed at the general election of 1830, after Denison was persuaded, at the prompting of him and others, to avoid provoking a bitter contest.[16] On the hustings, he insisted that he remained independent and undertook, in relation to parliamentary reform, that 'if he was convinced more than he was at present, he would freely own his conviction'.[17] His Southwell agent, the Rev. John Thomas Becher, who had already urged him to retire in the face of growing discontent with him, warned him of his constituents' increasing support for reform that winter.[18] Although ministers listed him among their 'friends', Robert Peel, the home secretary, believed that he would side with opposition on its proposed reform motion in November 1830. He duly voted against government on the 15th, in the prior division on the civil list, which led to its resignation.[19] In March 1831 it was surmised that he would vote for the Grey ministry's reform bill out of fear, not affection for the new government.[20] Following the Nottinghamshire reform meeting that month, he told Newcastle that he would indeed do so, but would then resign his seat. The duke, a rabid anti-reformer, condemned this as inconsist-

ent and recorded that 'it is miserable to see so much want of character and firmness, and such a total blindness to future consequences'.[21] However, speaking in the debate on the second reading, 22 Mar., Sotheron explained that he had fully intended to follow his constituents in giving it his support, but that, alluding to Sir Edward Sugden's speech, 'after hearing the debate, I cannot in my conscience do it'. He acknowledged that this would anger the electors, but declared that 'I cannot vote for this bill', and, having made 'an extraordinary impression upon the House', duly divided in the minority against it. The minister Thomas Spring Rice* regretted that 'Sotheron has struck his reform flag', while the Tory Charles Arbuthnot* counted him among those who 'have expressed themselves as breast high with us'.[22] His defection, which Lord Grey had feared, 'gave token of desertion' by other country gentlemen.[23] He was praised for his conscientious vote by a moderate Nottinghamshire reformer, to whom he replied that 'I thought it more honourable for a man in my situation to vote against the second reading than to fritter away the bill in the committee; it must be almost remodelled even if the ministers carry it'.[24] He apparently did not vote in the division on Gascoyne's wrecking amendment, 19 Apr. 1831.

Sotheron, who had been warned that he would face a challenge in his county and had succumbed to a bout of illness, insisted on retiring at the ensuing dissolution, issuing a farewell address, 22 Apr. 1831. Becher, who was himself a reformer, blamed his sudden unpopularity on the manner and timing of his change of opinions on reform, but would have undertaken to obtain his re-election, if only after a damagingly expensive contest. It was alleged that he had tipped off his replacement, Denison, about the vacant seat before his withdrawal was announced, but Becher vindicated his entire political conduct at the county election, when he was generally praised for his long service.[25] He was, however, burnt in effigy as an anti-reform bogeyman at Radford, near Nottingham.[26] Among other private statements of regret at his departure that Sotheron received was one from Lord Manvers, 24 Apr., who assured him that 'if all those who are now called upon to *book up* with their constituents, could produce as fair *a ledger* as yourself, there would be far less difficulty in balancing their accounts'. In providing Sotheron with a statement of his recent services, 6 May 1831, the long-suffering Becher wondered whether 'by listening more to the counsel of your friend, and less to the arguments of Ultra Tories, you might not have smothered the reproaches of your adversaries', so preserving his good standing; but, he added, 'my consolation is that you are now released from your only care'.[27] In private life, Sotheron devoted himself to the management of his estates, though he did not relinquish his interest in local politics. Described as a 'correct specimen of the old English gentleman', he died in February 1839, and was buried, with befitting pomp, in a coffin reputed to weigh nearly half a ton.[28] By his will, dated 27 Aug. 1830, he devised his estates, and personalty proved under £50,000 in the province of Canterbury and under £14,000 in the province of York, to his only child, Lucy Sarah, and her husband, Thomas Henry Sutton Bucknall Estcourt*, who assumed the name of Sotheron (later Sotheron Estcourt).[29]

[1] IGI (Yorks.). [2] Burke Commoners, iii. 520-1; HP Commons, 1790-1820, iii. 828-9. [3] Nottingham Jnl. 11 Mar.; Nottingham Rev. 21 Mar.; Nottingham Univ. Lib. Ossington mss, J. to J.E. Denison, 17 Mar. 1820; Glos. RO, Sotheron Estcourt mss D1571 F732, 733. [4] Black Bk. (1823), 194; Session of Parl. 1825, p. 485. [5] The Times, 14 June 1820. [6] Ibid. 11, 15 Feb., 16 Apr. 1823. [7] Ibid. 29 Apr. 1825. [8] Notts. Archives, Tallents mss, Sotheron to Tallents, 13, 15 May 1826. [9] Unhappy Reactionary ed. R.A. Gaunt (Thoroton Soc. rec. ser. xliii), 44. [10] Nottingham Rev. 16 June 1826. [11] Nottingham Univ. Lib. Acc. 636, Denison diary, 28 July 1826. [12] Sotheron Estcourt mss F789; Unhappy Reactionary, 13, 52, 184. [13] The Times, 20, 22, 27, 28 Feb., 24 Mar. 1827. [14] Ibid. 19 June 1827. [15] Sotheron Estcourt mss F792, Newcastle to Sotheron, 11 Dec., reply, 13 Dec. 1828. [16] Ibid. F793, Denison to Sotheron, 6 July; Denison diary, 26 June 1830. [17] Nottingham and Newark Mercury, 7 Aug. 1830. [18] Sotheron Estcourt mss F793, Becher to Sotheron, 6 May 1831. [19] Ellenborough Diary, ii. 432. [20] Borthwick, Halifax archive, C. to F.L. Wood, 12 Mar. 1831. [21] Unhappy Reactionary, 77. [22] Ibid.; Add. 51573, Rice to Lady Holland [22 Mar. 1831]; BL, Herries mss, Arbuthnot to Herries, n.d. [23] M. Brock, Great Reform Act, 175-6; Baring Jnls. i. 84; Three Diaries, 71. [24] Sotheron Estcourt mss F793, Wright to Sotheron, 26 Mar., reply, 28 Mar. 1831. [25] Ibid. Wilkins to Sotheron, 31 Mar., address, 22 Apr.; Becher to same, 23, 26 Apr., 1, 4-6, 9 May 1831. [26] Lincoln, Rutland and Stamford Mercury, 6 May 1831. [27] Sotheron Estcourt mss F793. [28] Nottingham Rev. 15, 22 Feb., 1 Mar. 1839; Gent. Mag. (1839), i. 655-6. [29] PROB 11/1910/252; IR26/1529/162.

S.R.H./S.M.F.

SOUTHEY, Robert (1774–1843), of Greta Hall, Keswick, Cumb.[1]

DOWNTON   1826–8 Dec. 1826

b. 12 Aug. 1774, 2nd but 1st surv. s. of Robert Southey (d. 1792), linen draper, of Bristol, Glos. and Margaret, da. of Edward Hill, attorney, of Long Ashton, Som. educ. Westminster 1788; Balliol, Oxf. 1792; G. Inn 1797. m. (1) 14 Nov. 1795, Edith (d. 16 Nov. 1837), da. of Stephen Fricker, manufacturer, of Westbury, Wilts., 2s. (1 d.v.p.) 5da. (3 d.v.p.); (2) 4 June 1839, Caroline Anne, da. of Capt. Charles Bowles of E.I. Co., of Buckland Cottage, Lymington, Hants, s.p. d. 21 Mar. 1843.
    Poet laureate 1813-d.

Southey was descended from an old Somerset family of modest social origins.[2] He attended schools in Bristol and Corston, was expelled from Westminster for writing an article in the Flagellant against caning, and having been refused entry to Christ Church because of this, instead took up a place at Balliol, which he left without a degree. Imbued with the spirit of republicanism and Unitarianism, he, with his friend and brother-in-law Samuel Taylor Coleridge, planned to emigrate to America to establish a community embodying the principles of pantisocracy ('the equal government of all'), and aspheterism ('the generalization of individual property'), but nothing came of it.[3] He travelled in Portugal, 1800-1, the first of several visits abroad. He gave up potential careers in the church, medicine and the law, and, after an unhappy spell as private secretary to Isaac Corry[†], the Irish chancellor of the exchequer, 1801-2, he abandoned his ambitions for government service, though he retained hopes of a consular sinecure in southern Europe. In fact, he declined most later offers of employment because they would have drawn him away from Greta Hall, where he settled, with the Coleridges, in 1803. Reserved and temperamental by nature, it was only occasionally that his kind-heartedness showed through, as it did to Greville, who once described him as 'remarkably pleasing in his manner and appearance, unaffected, unassuming and agreeable'.[4]

Southey's prodigious output was largely the result of the regularity of his working day, which he described as

> three pages of history after breakfast ... then to transcribe and copy for the press, or to make my selections and biographies, or what else suits my humour, till dinner time; from dinner till tea I read, write letters, see the newspaper and very often indulge in a siesta ... Well, after tea I go to poetry, and correct and re-write and copy till I am tired, and then turn to anything else till supper; and this is my life, which, if it be not a very merry one, is yet as happy as heart could wish.[5]

The modest fees that he earned from his writing were supplemented by a pension of £160 a year from his friend Charles Williams Wynn*, which in 1807 was replaced by one of £200 a year from the Grenville ministry. With Coleridge and William Wordsworth he established the Lakes school of poetry and, thanks to Walter Scott's stepping aside, he was appointed poet laureate in 1813, with a salary of £100 a year.[6] He published many works as a historian, biographer, travel writer, translator, editor, pamphleteer, essayist, reviewer, social critic and story teller, and was involved in several periodicals, notably the Quarterly Review, to which he contributed nearly 100 articles.[7] He was awarded an honorary doctorate by Oxford in

June 1820, when the Whig Sir James Mackintosh* described him as 'a good deal oldened' though 'his mild manner, in spite of a touch of affectation, is very pleasant'.[8] Yet his contemporary reputation was generally low, Lord Holland judging that

> his vanity was inoffensive and diverting, and his enthusiasm, real or affected, about his literary pursuits pleasant and amiable ... yet, in spite of research and ardour, a sprightly imagination and great raciness and accuracy in his English, he was not only a credulous and almost silly historian, but a weak reasoner and tiresome poet, and neither in prose nor in verse captivated or warmed his reader, though he might occasionally surprise and divert him.[9]

Posterity has been scarcely less unkind.

Ever since the turn of the century, Southey's political opinions had been moving steadily to the right, so that by the mid-1810s he was, as Henry Crabb Robinson put it, 'an alarmist, though what he fears is a reasonable cause of alarm, *viz.* a *bellum servile*'.[10] Ten years later he was labelled by Charles Wood* as '*intolerantium intolerantissimus*'.[11] This was how he was widely perceived, and Whigs and radicals made great play of his apostasy from their cause. On the mischievous publication of his early jacobinical play *Wat Tyler* in 1817, the Unitarian William Smith* denounced him in the Commons, 14 Mar., when he was defended by Williams Wynn and supported by most of the House.[12] William Hazlitt scathingly summarized the argument of his ensuing *Letter to William Smith* (1817) as 'once admit that Mr. Southey is always in the right, and every one else is in the wrong, and all the rest follows'.[13] At the Westmorland election, 30 June 1818, Henry Brougham* accused him of having been bribed by place into changing his political outlook, a charge which he later retracted.[14] Southey took little part in electoral or county affairs, but in late 1819 he was the anonymous author of the Tory address against the calling of a Cumberland meeting on Peterloo.[15] In the preface to his *Vision of Judgment* (1822), a cruel satire on Southey's poem of the same name, Lord Byron declared of him that 'the gross flattery, the dull impudence, the renegado intolerance and impious cant of the poem ... are something so stupendous as to form the sublime of himself, containing the quintessence of his own attributes'.

Southey was robust in his own defence, arguing that his views had inevitably matured with age: 'I am no more ashamed of having been a republican, than I am of having been a boy'.[16] His son excused his conduct by arguing that he had naturally sided with radicals in the 1790s, when the main threat was perceived to come from a tyrannical government, and joined the conservatives in later life, when the danger of anarchy became uppermost in his mind and he had lost his belief in the perfectibility of human nature.[17] Yet he was never quite as extreme as he appeared, and although he argued in favour of a more powerful executive, he also advocated a great many social, economic, legal and humanitarian reforms, such as schemes for assisted emigration and national education, in order to ameliorate the effects of industrialization.[18] Not only in his overtly polemical writings, but also, for instance, in his *Life of Nelson* (1813), widely regarded as his most successful book, he assisted in the Tory appropriation of older opposition notions of patriotism and their transformation into a new idea of English nationalism. In this sense he was an essential link between the Toryism of Edmund Burke[†] and the Conservatism of Benjamin Disraeli[†].[19]

Integral to Southey's conception of the state was the centrality of the established church as the embodiment of the nation's spiritual achievement and the guarantor of its civilisation and freedom.[20] The publication of his *Book of the Church* in 1824 led to his 'parliamentary adventure' at the general election two years later, when, without his prior knowledge, the convinced Tory 2nd earl of Radnor, an admirer of this work, had him returned for his pocket borough of Downton as an opponent of Catholic claims. He was only nominally a Member: he declined to take his seat and refused even to use his privilege of franking letters, much to the irritation of his neighbours. The reasons he gave for his refusal were that he lacked a large enough estate, had a pension 'during pleasure', preferred his lakeland domesticity to the long hours of the House, which his health could in any case not have stood, and intended to devote his time to writing, rather than to speaking, in defence of the church. He might have avoided the problem over his pension by having it altered to one 'for life' or transferred to his wife, and he could have accepted the property which Sir Robert Inglis* and others offered to buy for him, but he was determined not to sit. He duly informed the Speaker that he was not qualified, and, as he wished, a new writ was issued, 8 Dec. 1826; otherwise he would have resigned his seat.[21] He declared that 'for me to change my scheme of life and go into Parliament, would be to commit a moral and intellectual suicide'; and his friend John Rickman, a Commons clerk, noted that 'prudential reasons would forbid his appearing in London' as a Member.[22] Another friend, his neighbour William Peachy, who had just been elected for Taunton, was given a triumphal greeting on his return home, but Southey was spared this as it was thought that he 'would not like it'.[23]

He was, of course, a steadfast opponent of the Wellington administration's decision to emancipate the Catholics in 1829. Later that year he published his *Colloquies on the Progress and Prospects of Society*, which provoked a famous and savagely destructive attack from Thomas Macaulay* in the *Edinburgh Review* early the following year. In January 1830 it was reported by Brougham that Southey would 'move or second the resolution that the [agricultural] distress is within the power of the legislature' to curtail, at the proposed Cumberland county meeting.[24] Encouraged by Rickman, he planned to write a pamphlet against parliamentary reform, and to this end he attended the Commons for the first time, 2 Nov. 1830, but nothing came of it.[25] Though prepared to accept some measures of reform, he was firmly opposed to the Grey ministry's bill, commenting that 'Lord John [Russell]'s budget', 1 Mar. 1831, 'is as much a masterpiece in its way as [the chancellor] Lord Althorp's. It really seems as if the aristocracy of this country are to be destroyed, so marvellously are they demented'. He believed that ministers had thrown in their lot with the radicals in order to survive in office, and he continued to hope that the mood of the country would turn against them.[26] Even after the bill's enactment he remained an alarmist, writing in March 1833 that

> this year will not pass away without greater changes than the last. It is already apparent that the reformed Parliament will not work. Government by authority has long been defunct. Government by influence was put to death by the reform bill and nothing is left but government by public opinion.[27]

In 1835 he declined the offer of a baronetcy from the premier, Sir Robert Peel, but accepted a pension of £300 per year.[28]

John Stuart Mill, who visited him in 1831, wrote this analysis of his character and career:

> Southey is altogether out of place in the existing order of society. His attachment to old institutions and his condemnation of the practices of those who administer them, cut him off from sympathy and communion with both halves of mankind. Had he lived before radicalism and infidelity became prevalent, he would have been the steady advocate of the moral and physical improvement of the poorer classes and denouncer of the selfishness and supineness of those who ought to have considered the welfare of those classes as confided to their care. Possibly the essential one-sidedness of his mind might then have rendered him a democrat; but now the evils which he expects from increase of the power wielded by the democratic spirit such as it now is, have rendered him an aristocrat in principle without inducing him to make the slightest compromise with aristocratic vices and weak-

nesses. Consequently he is not liked by the Tories, while the Whigs and radicals abhor him.[29]

Shortly after the death of his first wife he married his long-time correspondent, the poetess Caroline Bowles. She was his nursemaid, for he lapsed into imbecility a few months later. He died in March 1843, dividing his estate between his widow and surviving children.[30] His son Charles Cuthbert (1819-88), vicar of Askham, Westmorland, edited his *Life and Correspondence*.

[1] Based on *Life and Corresp. of Southey* ed. C.C. Southey (1849-50) and J. Simmons, *Southey* (1945). Southey's voluminous correspondence has been extensively published, notably in *Selections from Letters of Southey* ed. J.W. Warter, 4 vols. (1856); *Corresp. of Southey with Caroline Bowles* ed. E. Dowden (1881); and *New Letters of Southey* ed. K. Curry (1965). Good biographies include G. Carnall, *Southey and his Age* (1964) and K. Curry, *Southey* (1975). Recent experiments in rehabilitation are M. Storey, *Robert Southey: A Life* (1997) and W.A. Speck, *Robert Southey: Entire Man of Letters* (2006). [2] *Life and Corresp.* i. 2-3; *N and Q* (ser. 8), v. 141-2, 202-3, 241-3. [3] *Life and Corresp.* i. 221. [4] Ibid. vi. 1-14; *Barclay Fox's Jnl.* ed. R.L. Brett, 113; *Greville Mems.* ii. 58. [5] *Life and Corresp.* iii. 2-3. [6] Ibid. iii. 72-73; vi. 14-15. [7] For Southey's works, see *Allibone's Dict. of Eng. Literature* (1870), ii. 2182-7; Curry, *Southey*; E. Bernhardt-Kabisch, *Southey*. [8] Add. 52444, f. 162. [9] Holland, *Further Mems.* 385. [10] *Crabb Robinson Diary*, i. 282. [11] Glos. RO, Sotheron Estcourt mss D1571 F365, Wood to Bucknall Estcourt, 27 June 1826. [12] *Life and Letters of Rickman* ed. O. Williams, 187-9. [13] *Complete Works of Hazlitt* ed. P.P. Howe, vii. 187. [14] *Life and Corresp.* iv. 309; *The Times*, 4 July 1818. [15] *Letters of Southey*, iii. 148-54. [16] *Wilson's Noctes Ambrosianae* ed. R.S. Mackenzie, ii. 365. [17] *Life and Corresp.* iii. 5-7; v. 1-7. [18] Ibid. iv. 198-233; A. Cobban, *Burke and Revolt against 18th Cent.* 215-18; Carnall, 193-214. [19] D. Eastwood, 'Southey and Intellectual Origins of Romantic Conservatism', *EHR*, civ (1989), 308-31; 'Patriotism Personified: Southey's "Life of Nelson" Reconsidered', *Mariner's Mirror*, lxxvii (1991), 143-9; 'Southey and Meanings of Patriotism', *JBS*, xxxi (1992), 265-87; J. Mendilow, *Romantic Tradition in British Political Thought*, 47-82; P. Harling, 'Southey and Language of Social Discipline', *Albion*, xxx (1998), 630-55. [20] *Life and Corresp.* v. 308-9; S. Gilley, 'Nationality and Liberty, Protestant and Catholic: Southey's "Book of the Church"', in *Religion and National Identity* ed. S. Mews, 409-32. [21] *Life and Corresp.* v. 261-4, 271, 273-9; Add. 56368, f. 93; *The Times*, 4, 5 July 1826; *Letters of Sara Hutchinson* ed. K. Coburn, 326; *CJ*, lxxxii. 29, 109; Storey, 310. [22] *Letters of Southey*, iv. 7; *Colchester Diary*, iii. 444. [23] *Life and Corresp.* v. 265. [24] *Creevey Pprs.* ii. 147. [25] *Life and Letters of Rickman*, 259-60, 268; *Corresp. of Southey and Bowles*, 207. [26] *Life and Corresp.* vi. 90-91; *Corresp. of Southey and Bowles*, 219; Berks. RO, Pusey mss D/EBp C1/44. [27] *HMC 14th Rep.* iv. 568-9; *Life and Corresp.* vi. 199. [28] *Life and Corresp.* vi. 253-65. [29] *Mill Works*, xii. 83. [30] *The Times*, 1 Apr. 1843; *Gent. Mag.* (1843), i. 662-3; *DNB*; *Oxford DNB*.

S.M.F.

SPENCE, George (1787-1850), of 35 Pall Mall and 2 Stone Buildings, Lincoln's Inn, Mdx.

READING	1826-26 Mar. 1827
RIPON	2 Mar. 1829-1832

b. 1787, 2nd *s.* of Thomas Richard Spence (*d.* 1818) of Hanover Square and Cranford, Mdx. and *w.* Frances.[1]

educ. privately by Rev. Robert Delafosse at Richmond, Surr.; Glasgow Univ. 1802; I. Temple 1806, called 1811. *m.* 1819, Anne, da. of James Kelsall, solicitor, of Chester, 2s. *d.* 12 Dec. 1850.

KC 27 Dec. 1834; bencher, I. Temple 1835, reader 1845, treas. 1846-7.

Spence's father was a successful London dentist, who patented and marketed a brand of tooth powder and bought property at Cranford. His elder brother Thomas Richard Spence took holy orders and died at Rome in 1827; and his younger brother Henry Francis Spence (?1789-1856) entered the navy in 1803, saw action in various theatres and was paid off in 1814.[2] George Spence was recalled by one of his school contemporaries as 'an industrious and talented youth, who, by his gentleness and kindness of disposition, won the affection of his schoolfellows'. He was articled to a London solicitor, but eventually opted to train for the bar. A friend remembered that when he was making his way there he was

> very eccentric in his dress and appearance. His father was strict with him in money matters, which materially influenced him in his studies, to gratify his ambition, which was then very great, to get on in his profession, and to become independent.[3]

On his father's death in 1818 he inherited the Cranford property, subject to his mother's life interest, and £10,000 in consols.[4] He did well as an equity draftsman and was reputed to have had 'at one time, the largest business ever known to have been enjoyed at the chancery bar with a stuff gown'.[5]

In 1826 Spence published a treatise, dedicated to lord chancellor Eldon, on the *Origin of the Laws and Political Institutions of Modern Europe*, which he traced to those of Imperial Rome. At the general election that year he stood on the Tory True Blue interest for Reading, with which he had no connection, against the Whig sitting Members, in conjunction with the philanthropist Edward Wakefield. In a series of verbose and bombastic written addresses, he pledged support for the Liverpool ministry while they continued to promote 'the reduction of taxation, the improvement of our judicial institutions (a subject I have much at heart), the amelioration of the condition of all ranks of society, and the extension and establishment of liberty at home and abroad'. At the same time he laid claim to 'the most uncompromising independence'. On the hustings he denied having raised a 'No Popery' cry, but justified his avowed hostility to Catholic relief on the ground that he was 'averse to granting political power to a sect which had always abused it'. He advocated a 'diffusion of education and of the lights of

the gospel' as the likeliest remedies for the 'wretched condition' of Ireland. He was at odds with the sitting Members, he said, 'because he thought their opposition to ministers was systematic, and carried to a culpable extreme'. After an eight-day contest, which was reckoned to have cost him 'many thousand pounds', he edged one of them into third place by four votes.[6]

Spence soon showed his interest in judicial reform by speaking on Harvey's motion for returns of business in the exchequer court, 1 Dec. 1826, when he asserted that its judges wished it to be made 'efficient', with 'an active and extensive jurisdiction'. He thought the motion did not go far enough, and on 6 Dec. he moved for information on business transacted in the exchequer, rolls and vice-chancellor's courts, with the object of demonstrating that the underutilized equity jurisdiction of the exchequer could be employed to help clear the massive arrears in chancery. In the absence of the government law officers the home secretary Peel complained that the motions exceeded the terms of their notice, and Spence reluctantly agreed to their withdrawal.[7] Eldon, thanking Peel for his 'kind interposition', observed that Spence, 'a very good and respectable man', doubtless 'means well, but it is strong measure to propose alterations in the distribution of the business in the exchequer and chancery without mention to those who preside in them, or at least to him, who presides in one of them'.[8] Spence got into a procedural tangle when presenting a petition touching the disputed Denbigh election, 8 Feb. 1827. He presented a petition against Catholic relief, 19 Feb., and voted against the proposal, 6 Mar.[9] On 22 Mar. 1827 he was unseated on his opponent's petition, the inquiry having established that his majority was based on a number of illegal votes. Soon afterwards he sought an interview with Peel, leader of the Protestant interest in the Commons, 'on the subject of the future representation' of Reading, observing that 'the politics of the party by whom I ... [was] returned are I believe strictly in unison with your own'.[10]

Spence was returned on a vacancy for Ripon in March 1829 on the interest of Miss Sophia Lawrence, whose election manager Sir Lancelot Shadwell*, vice-chancellor of England, was his personal friend. He came in explicitly as an opponent of Catholic emancipation, against which he duly voted, 6, 27, 30 Mar. 1829. He presented petitions complaining of distress in the silk manufacturing industry, 28 Apr. He denounced the grant to the Catholic seminary at Maynooth, which 'fostered principles of the grossest idolatry', and voted in the minority of 14 against it, 22 May. He divided in favour of the issue of a new writ for East Retford, 2

June 1829. He voted against Lord Blandford's parliamentary reform scheme, 18 Feb., but was in the anti-government majority against the Bathurst and Dundas pensions, 26 Mar. 1830. He voted for Jewish emancipation, 5 Apr., 17 May and the abolition of capital punishment for forgery, 7 June. On 5 Apr. he moved for returns of the salaries and fees of chancery clerks and registrars, with a view to proposing ways of reducing the notorious delays and expenses of procedure in that court. Soon afterwards he published *Reform of the Court of Chancery*, in which he made detailed suggestions for improvements designed to save at least £35,000 a year. In the House, 17 June, he criticized the government's suits in equity bill, which proposed the appointment of an additional chancery judge, and its two related pending measures for reform of the registrars' and masters' offices: 'I cannot conceive that the appointment of a new judge, to send an additional number of causes to offices already encumbered, and so defective in their constitution, will prove of any advantage'. He declared that unless ministers proposed effective reform of equity jurisdiction he would take the initiative himself. The Whig lawyer Henry Brougham* thought his speech was 'excellent'.[11] Spence voted against Hume's attempt to reduce the level of judges' salaries as proposed in the administration of justice bill, 7 July. Thomas Frankland Lewis* later credited Spence with preparing amendments to this measure which saved Radnorshire from the loss of its assizes.[12] On 22 July 1830 he acquiesced in the law officers' temporary acceptance of an objectionable Lords' amendment, on the understanding that they would expunge it through a separate measure next session.

After the 1830 general election, when he came in again for Ripon, ministers listed Spence among their 'friends', but he was absent from the division on the civil list which brought them down, 15 Nov. 1830. He voted for the second reading of the Grey ministry's reform bill, 22 Mar., when he spoke briefly for it, and against Gascoyne's wrecking amendment, 19 Apr. 1831. According to an obituary notice the bill

> troubled the conscience of Mr. Spence. He had been returned as a Tory and sat for a close borough. He became convinced that it was his duty to vote for the bill, and he informed Miss Lawrence of his intention, resolving that if she objected he would resign his seat. She informed him that he might do as he pleased, and he voted throughout for the measure, having been again returned at the election of 1831.[13]

In fact, Spence was absent from the division on the second reading of the reintroduced bill, 6 July 1831, but he was present to vote for some of its details, 19,

27 July, 3, 9 Aug. Ill health, for which he took periods of leave, 12 Sept. and 7 Oct., accounted for his absence from the divisions on the passage of the bill, 21 Sept.,[14] and Lord Ebrington's confidence motion, 10 Oct. 1831. He voted for the second reading of the revised bill, 17 Dec. 1831, and occasionally for its details, though he was in the minority in favour of excluding borough freeholders from the county franchise, 1 Feb. 1832. He voted for the third reading, 22 Mar., and the address asking the king to appoint only ministers who would carry it unimpaired 10 May 1832. He did not vote in any of the divisions on other party issues for which full lists have been found; and his only other known vote after 1830 was with the minority for the vestries reform bill, 23 Jan. 1832.

Spence had continued to concern himself principally with his campaign for reform of equity jurisdiction. On 9 Nov. 1830 he gave notice that after Christmas he would move a series of resolutions on the simplification and improvement of chancery practice, but on 7 Dec. he postponed them until after Easter to give the new ministers the chance to take the matter into their own hands. He renewed his motion for returns of chancery fees, which had not yet been produced, 22 Nov., and on 9 Dec. was praised by the attorney-general Denman for his 'able statement' in explanation of his call for further documentary evidence. On 13 Dec. 1830 he drew attention to the scandal of the three civil offices, all part of the judicial bureaucracy, from which the Rev. Thomas Thurlow derived an annual income of £9,713. In the debate on Sugden's motion for information on chancery practice, 20 Dec. 1830, he dismissed John Williams's notion of transferring the bulk of equity business to the common law courts. Arguing that 'the House of Commons alone can reform the court of chancery', which successive governments had failed to touch, he detailed the abuses of delay and expense which originated in the inefficient and hidebound registrars' and masters' offices. He advocated payment of the chancellor by a fixed salary rather than by fees, abolition of the six clerks office, and the creation of a new, streamlined system of record keeping, which would 'get rid of three-fourths of the abuses'. He vowed to bring forward his own plan if ministers did not act:

> I am sure ... government will not consider that it is [in] the slightest spirit of hostility to them that I had formed this resolution, but I have been grievously disappointed by trusting to other governments, and feel it necessary, therefore, to narrowly watch this government.

He sent copies of the published versions of this speech and that of 17 June 1830, together with one of his 1830 pamphlet, to Jeremy Bentham.[15] He welcomed Campbell's plan to establish a general register of deeds in England and Wales, 30 June 1831, but advised postponement of its introduction until some groundless objections to it, especially in Yorkshire, had been overcome. He supported Campbell's fines and recoveries bill, 9 Dec. 1831, which would help to destroy 'the mystification of the law which relates to all transactions connected with real property'. He dismissed the objections of small landowners to a general register as unfounded, 20 Jan., 2 Feb. 1832; but when he presented a Ripon petition against it, 8 Feb. 1832, he wondered if a compromise could be affected by introducing 'a bill embracing a system of general registration, but allowing it to be conducted in counties or districts'. He was named to the select committee appointed to investigate the problem, 22 Feb. 1832. The same day he opposed Knight's Irish master of the rolls bill.

During 1831 Spence was invited by lord chancellor Brougham to assist in carrying out his scheme of chancery reform. He was entrusted with the preparation of a bill to regulate the masters' office, which was originally intended to be presented before Christmas, but Brougham subsequently decided that it would be preferable to embody in one bill proposals to reform all the offices connected with chancery. Thus on 15 Dec. Spence announced in the House that he was 'authorized to state' that measures were in train 'for the effectual reform of the most crying of the abuses'. Yet on 6 June 1832 he had to explain the long delay, and it was not until 10 July that he moved, successfully, for leave to introduce a bill to improve equity jurisdiction in connection with the administration of testators' estates. It was, he said, part of a general scheme of reform, and Brougham was about to introduce to the Lords an 'extensive' measure which would 'so construct the court of chancery as that a system will no longer exist for the benefit of the officers and practitioners of that court, but solely for the benefit of the public'. Spence's bill was presented and read a first time on 31 July 1832, but made no further progress before Parliament was dissolved. On 26 July he intervened in the squabble over the appointment of the chancellor's brother James Brougham* to two chancery sinecures, assuring the House that it was purely a temporary measure and that these offices would be abolished by pending legislation. In a discussion on judges' salaries, 30 July 1832, he replied to opposition criticism of the government's tardiness in introducing its chancery reforms. He provoked mocking laughter with his confession that the general reform bill had not yet been presented to the Lords because he had been

unable to complete the complex work of drafting an additional clause, requested by Brougham, to establish an appellate court within chancery. He concluded:

> I believe I shall not have another opportunity of addressing this or any other House of Commons ... From the moment I entered this House, I have laboured most assiduously to bring about a reform in the court of chancery. I have frequently ... seen a prospect of an effectual reform being introduced, and have been in some instances most grievously disappointed ... I hope and trust, however, that there is now a prospect of an effectual reform being completed.

Spence knew that his days as Member for Ripon were numbered. In July 1832 Benjamin Disraeli[†], who earlier in the year had described Mrs. Spence as being 'very silly, trying to apologize for her husband's ratting', reported that Miss Lawrence had 'turned violent Tory and *chassed*' Spence and his colleague Petit, another convert to reform, from the borough.[16] Brougham evidently asked the Russells if they could accommodate Spence for the next Parliament, but Lord John could only suggest an attempt on Huntingdon.[17] Nothing came of this, and Spence explained to Brougham, 31 Oct. 1832, after a holiday which furnished him with 'renovated health and renewed ardour to assist in perfecting your intended reforms':

> After much consideration I cannot but think that I shall be able to render much more effectual assistance out of Parliament than in. The distraction and consumption of time occasioned by having to attend the House together with the labour of chancery drawing leaves too small a portion of time to be devoted to so important a subject as chancery reform, especially for completing the most essential part, namely the orders and minor details.[18]

He accepted Brougham's offer of the first vacancy in the chancery masterships, which would enable him to use his 'utmost personal exertions' to make the reforms effective. Yet in July 1833 he declined Brougham's offer of remuneration for his 'time and trouble' in preparing chancery reform bills since leaving Parliament and, on being informed that a reduction in the number of masters was now in contemplation, waived his own pretensions if they would cause any 'embarrassment'. He continued to co-operate with Brougham in the slow work of chancery reform.[19] He took silk in December 1834 and hoped to try his fortune in the exchequer court if it was made an efficient part of equity jurisdiction. It was not, and as a king's counsel Spence never commanded the volume of work which he had enjoyed as a junior.[20]

In 1839 he published two *Addresses* on chancery abuses, in which he commended Lord Lyndhurst's scheme for the appointment of additional vice-chancellors as the only practical solution with any chance of immediate adoption. In 1842 he produced a *Summary of Documents* relating to the masters' office. His later years were largely devoted to the composition of his *magnum opus* on *The Equitable Jurisdiction of the Court of Chancery*. The first volume of this pioneering work, which is still regarded as the standard authority on the subject, appeared in 1846 and the second in 1849.[21] Spence began work on a third volume, but the labour involved had taken a heavy toll of his health and spirits. He also suffered a disappointment in 1847 when he failed in his bid to secure a vacant mastership in chancery, for which he asked Brougham to promote his claims with the lord chancellor.[22] In the last months of 1850 he 'slept worse and worse' and was 'constantly low spirited', having 'long been labouring under the delusion that he had a disease of the urethra or bladder', which had killed his father. In the small hours of 10 Dec. at his then residence at 42 Hyde Park Square he inflicted severe wounds to his neck, wrists and thigh. He lingered 'in a state of extreme depression' for two days and died 'from exhaustion and loss of blood', 'aged 63'. The inquest jury decided that he had tried to kill himself 'in a fit of insanity.[23] 'Alas!', wrote one of his friends, 'who would have thought that that life would have *thus* terminated, and he a man so single-minded and amiable, who knew no ill, and thought no ill?' Spence was credited with 'the art, or natural gift, of speaking upon abstruse and learned topics without using either abstruse or learned words'.[24] He left all his property to his wife for her life, thereafter to be equally divided between his two sons.[25] Both these, Henry Donald Maurice Spence (1836-1917) and Lancelot Molyneux Dalrymple Spence (1837-65), became clerks at the board of trade in 1855. Lancelot remained there until his early death, but Henry, who took the additional surname of Jones in 1904, subsequently entered the church and died as a long-serving dean of Gloucester and a prolific author of works of history and biblical commentary.

[1] PROB 11/1607/390. She was perhaps Frances, da. of Richard Rock of St. Martin, Ludgate, London. See *Reg. St. George Hanover Square*, i. 256. [2] *Gent. Mag.* (1827), ii. 473; (1856), i. 666. [3] *Law Rev.* xiii (1851), 431. [4] *Gent. Mag.* (1818), ii. 377; PROB 11/1607/390. [5] *Gent. Mag.* (1851), i. 435; *Oxford DNB.* [6] *Berks. Chron.* 15, 22, 29 Apr., 6, 13, 20 May, 3, 10, 17, 24 June 1826. [7] *The Times*, 2, 5, 7 Dec. 1826. [8] Add. 40315, f. 270. [9] *The Times*, 9, 20 Feb. 1827. [10] Add. 40393, ff. 163, 178. [11] NLS mss 24748, f. 96. [12] *Hereford Jnl.* 18 Aug. 1830. [13] *Gent. Mag.* (1851), i. 435. [14] *The Times*, 23 Sept. 1831. [15] See BL, C.T. 70. [16] *Disraeli Letters*, i. 140, 205. [17] Brougham mss, Russell to Brougham, 29 June [1832]. [18] Brougham mss. [19] Ibid. Spence to Brougham, 21 July, [Nov.] 1833, 14 Jan. 1835, 2 Aug. 1840. [20] *Law Rev.* xiii. 432. [21] *Oxford DNB.* [22] Brougham mss, Spence to Brougham, 29 Mar. 1847. [23] *Gent. Mag.* (1851), i. 435-6; *The Times*, 17 Dec. 1850. [24] *Law Mag.* xlv (1851), 131. [25] PROB 11/2128/156.

D.R.F.

SPENCER, Hon. Frederick (1798–1857), of Althorp Park, Northants. and 27 St. James's Place, Mdx.

WORCESTERSHIRE	1831–1832
MIDHURST	1832–1834
MIDHURST	12 Dec. 1837–1841

b. 14 Apr. 1798, 3rd but 2nd surv. s. of George John Spencer[†], 2nd Earl Spencer, and Lady Lavinia Bingham, da. of Charles Bingham[†], 1st earl of Lucan [I]; bro. of John Charles Spencer, Visct. Althorp.* *educ.* Eton 1808-11. *m.* (1) 23 Feb. 1830, Elizabeth Georgina (*d.* 7 Apr. 1851), da. and coh. of William Stephen Poyntz*, 1s. 2da. (1 *d.v.p.*); (2) 9 Aug. 1854, Adelaide Horatia, da. of Horace Beauchamp Seymour*, 1s. 1da. CB 13 Nov. 1827; *suc.* bro. as 4th Earl Spencer 1 Oct. 1845; KG 23 Mar. 1849. *d.* 27 Dec. 1857.
Midshipman RN 1811, lt. 1818, cdr. 1821, capt. 1822, r.-adm. 1852, v.-adm. 1857.
Equerry to duchess of Kent 1836-46; ld. chamberlain July 1846-Sept. 1848; PC 8 July 1846; chan. of duchy of Lancaster 1847; ld. steward of household Jan. 1854-Nov. 1857.

Born at the admiralty where his father, a Portland Whig, was first lord under Pitt, 1794-1800, Spencer followed his elder brother Robert into the navy in 1811 and saw active service off the Spanish coast, most notably at the siege of Tarragon and the evacuation of St. Phillippe Fort. He was made captain of the *Creole*, 26 Aug. 1822, when his younger brother George commented that 'having the command of a frigate ... at your age is a seasoning which must be of great service for your future prospects'.[1] In October 1827, as captain of the *Talbot* in the fleet sent to safeguard Greek independence, he 'fought with distinction' at the battle of Navarino, for which he was mentioned in dispatches and later decorated. He retired from active service the following year.[2] In 1830 he married his second cousin Elizabeth Poyntz who, according to his sister, was a 'most charming creature ... neither very young nor pretty, but he is most deeply in love with her'.[3]

Spencer, who considered 'a residence in London' to be 'contrary to my habits of life', declined to serve as private secretary to his brother Lord Althorp on his appointment as chancellor of the exchequer in the Grey ministry in November 1830.[4] At the 1831 general election, however, he was persuaded to come forward for Worcestershire, where the 'reform party' were 'zealously exerting themselves' and, as he informed his father, 27 Apr., had given him 'assurances of no expense'.[5] 'You must take care that it is clearly understood that you are to be carried free of all payment', Althorp warned, 29 Apr., adding, 'Father will come down with a thousand or two if necessary but unless they can carry you without expense the case ... is hopeless'.[6] Stating his political principles to be 'those of my brother', Spencer offered 'for this Parliament only, under the unequivocal pledge of voting for that most indispensable measure of reform'. He denied being a 'treasury candidate with the exchequer at my back' and Tory allegations that his family were Catholic, got up on account of the recent conversion of George, on which he was 'extremely sensitive'.[7] Althorp reminded him that 'reform is the main point but slavery is another on which you must be prepared', and 'on the hustings you may safely [pledge] yourself up to the ears against slavery, only saying that caution is necessary for the sake of the slaves themselves'.[8] After a week's 'tremendous struggle' the Tory candidate conceded defeat and Spencer was returned in second place.[9]

On 6 July 1831 his election was attacked by Wetherell, Tory Member for Boroughbridge, who, in a speech against the use of pledges, accused him of having impugned the 'honour and dignity' of the House by campaigning under the slogan 'Spencer and no corn laws'. Spencer, however, denied 'ever having been party to it', claiming that he had not 'on any public occasion alluded to the subject'; he was supported by his colleague Foley. He voted for the second reading of the reintroduced reform bill that day, at least twice against adjourning the debates, 12 July, and gave steady support to its details. On 6 Sept. he suggested that in order to 'avoid the continual expense of erecting temporary booths', permanent structures 'should be erected for taking the poll', but his advice went unheeded. He voted for the bill's passage, 21 Sept., and Lord Ebrington's confidence motion, 10 Oct. He presented a petition from the procurators of Berwickshire for repeal of the duty on attorneys' certificates, 5 Aug. At the 1831 Cambridgeshire by-election he served on the reformer Townley's London committee.[10] He divided for the second reading of the revised reform bill, 17 Dec. 1831, again supported its details, and voted for the third reading, 22 Mar. 1832. He divided with ministers on the Russian-Dutch loan, 26 Jan., 12 July, and the navy civil departments bill, 6 Apr., but was in minorities for inquiry into the glove trade, 31 Jan., 3 Apr., and colonial slavery, 24 May, and against restoration of the Irish registrar's salary, 9 Apr. He voted for the address calling on the king to appoint only ministers who would carry the reform

bill unimpaired, 10 May, and the second reading of the Irish bill, 25 May. He joined Brooks's, sponsored by Althorp and Sir Ronald Ferguson*, 23 May 1832.

At the 1832 general election Spencer redeemed his pledge to retire from Worcestershire and accepted an invitation from the electors of Midhurst, where he was returned unopposed on the interest of his father-in-law. He retired at the dissolution of 1834, explaining that an 'attendance in Parliament' was 'so irksome', that he 'could not be (as I fear I have not been) constantly in my place in the House, as I think your representatives ought'; but following the incapacity of his father-in-law, who replaced him, he came in again at the 1837 by-election. He was appointed equerry to the duchess of Kent in 1836, but on the advice of Althorp, who had succeeded as 3rd Earl Spencer in 1834, declined Lord Melbourne's offer of an additional household office on the accession of Queen Victoria. Since the death of Robert off Alexandria, 4 Nov. 1830, Spencer had been next in line to the peerage, and on Althorp's death without issue, 1 Oct. 1845, he succeeded to the family estates as 4th earl. He held senior household offices in the Russell, Aberdeen and Palmerston ministries, and was awarded an honorary doctorate by Cambridge University in 1847.[11]

Spencer died at Althorp in December 1857. By his will, dated 17 May 1854, he disinherited the convert George in the event of his succession to the peerage by directing that the family estates be entrusted to his nephew Lord Lyttelton for the use of his daughter Lady Sarah Isabella Spencer and her heirs. By a third codicil, dated 9 Aug. 1854 and revoking all others, special provision was made for any children from his second marriage. His estates passed to his elder son and successor in the peerage, John Poyntz (1835-1910), who at the general election in April 1857 had been returned as a Liberal for Northamptonshire South.

[1]BL, Althorp mss, G. to F. Spencer, 28 July 1823. [2]W.R. O'Byrne, Naval Biog. iii. 1103; Gent. Mag. (1858), i. 329; The Times, 14, 22 Oct., 15, 31 Nov. 1827. [3]Lady Lyttelton Corresp. 256. [4]E.A. Wasson, Whig Renaissance, 194; Althorp mss, address to electors, Dec. 1834. [5]Worcester Herald, 30 Apr. 1831; Althorp mss. [6]Althorp mss. [7]Worcs. RO BA 3762 b.899:31, Foley scrapbk. vol. 4, pp. 172-8; Worcester Herald, 7 May 1831. [8]Althorp mss, Althorp to Spencer, 28 Apr. 1831. [9]Worcester Herald, 21, 28 May, 4 June 1831. [10]Beds. RO, Russell mss R766. [11]Althorp mss, address to electors, Dec. 1834; Melbourne Pprs. 366; Wasson, 339.

P.J.S.

SPENCER, John Charles, Visct. Althorp (1782–1845), of Wiseton Hall, nr. East Retford, Notts.[1]

OKEHAMPTON	27 Apr. 1804–1806
NORTHAMPTONSHIRE	1806–1832
NORTHAMPTONSHIRE SOUTH	1832–10 Nov. 1834

b. 30 May 1782, 1st s. of George John Spencer†, 2nd Earl Spencer, and Lady Lavinia Bingham, da. of Charles Bingham†, 1st earl of Lucan [I]; bro. of Hon. Frederick Spencer*. *educ.* Harrow 1790-8; Trinity Coll. Camb. 1800-2; grand tour 1802-3. *m.* 13 Apr. 1814, Esther, da. and h. of Richard Acklom of Wiseton, *s.p. suc.* fa. as 3rd Earl Spencer 10 Nov. 1834. *d.* 1 Oct. 1845.
Ld. of treasury Feb. 1806-Mar. 1807; PC 22 Nov. 1830; chan. of exch. and leader of House of Commons Nov. 1830-Dec. 1834.
Cornet, Northants. yeoman cav. 1802, capt.-lt. 1805.

In a fragment of autobiography begun on his retirement from politics at the end of 1834, Althorp, the most personally attractive of the half dozen men who dominated the Commons in this period, wrote:

> There is only one object ... worthy of the ambition of a man of sense, and that is, to obtain the favour of God. Political pursuits and political rivalships are not the means to conduce to this end ... The occupations and the compliances which necessarily belong to a political man must ... have a tendency to diminish religious feelings.[2]

In March 1818 he told his friend Lord Milton* that 'my vanity was very near overpowering my reason' when he was asked by some Whig activists to undertake the leadership of the Whig party in the Commons: although he was aware of his 'total incapacity for the office' and 'decidedly refused', he recognized that he had strong credentials for it, in that his good relations with the mainstream Whigs George Tierney* and Henry Brougham* and the reformers Sir Francis Burdett* and John Lambton*, and his intimacy with Lord Folkestone* and Henry Grey Bennet* of the 'Mountain', with whom he had acted sporadically in the 1807 Parliament, made 'my personal influence in the ... Commons perhaps more general than that of any of our party'. His close friendship with Lord Lansdowne, a potential leader in the Lords, was another asset.[3] The death of his wife in childbed three months later devastated him and drove him for a time to a reclusive life at their home at Wiseton, where he took consolation in his simple religious faith, which was strengthened by his grief. Thereafter he surrendered himself to God's will and, unable to withdraw from politics because they were both a duty and a compulsion, perceived his political conduct in terms

of his relationship with God and his ultimate salvation. In effect if not in name an Evangelical, he sought atonement through public service. He gave up fox hunting (but not shooting) and intensified his interest in farming and the breeding of stock, which was his consolation in dark moments. He coupled his religious reading with a study of the tenets of political economy: both strands of thought influenced his subsequent career as one of the 'Young Whigs' who, despairing of the laziness and cynicism of the older Foxite leadership, sought to prevent the radicals from seizing the initiative in the promotion of a liberal agenda, which included parliamentary reform.[4] In person Althorp was 'short and corpulent', but robustly built. After his wife's death he invariably wore predominantly black clothes. His habit of keeping his double-breasted cashmere waistcoat 'buttoned up close to his chin', even in the hottest weather, doubtless enhanced the 'florid' hue of his face, which one observer wrote in 1837 generally bore a 'soft and stupid' expression: 'His appearance altogether is exactly that of a farmer, and his manners are remarkable for their unaffected simplicity'.[5]

Althorp's determined parliamentary opposition to the Liverpool ministry's repressive legislation after Peterloo and his appearance on the platform at the Westminster protest meeting, 8 Dec. 1819 (which annoyed his sour natured mother, from whom he was more or less alienated) prompted some of the Northamptonshire Tories to consider opposing him at the 1820 general election, but the notion ended in smoke and he came in unopposed again with the Tory Cartwright, in accordance with the tacit compromise which had operated since their return together in 1806.[6] Had he been faced with a contest, he would, as he had confided to his father, have retired from Parliament, both to save Lord Spencer and himself wasted expenditure and because 'attendance ... is a diminution instead of an increase of my happiness, and I have not the satisfaction of feeling that I do any good by the sacrifice I am making'. He anticipated a heavy defeat for the opposition and the early retirement through ill health of Tierney, the Commons leader since 1818, which would leave the Whigs 'worse off than ever', as Brougham, the only serious alternative, was not 'fit' to be a leader. Ironically, Tierney himself, telling Sir James Mackintosh* that he could not go on much longer, saw Brougham as the only choice and 'regretted that Lord Althorp, whom he most wished, was not acceptable to many'.[7] A half-expected bid to oust him as chairman of the county quarter sessions came to nothing. At the dinner, he toasted the royal family 'without the naming ... Queen

[Caroline] particularly, which is the Tory mode of doing it at present', but he 'thought it would be foolish to do anything which may produce anger, as everyone seemed to be in very good humour'. Stricken by 'a fit of gout', he went in mid-April 1820 to Leamington in order to 'get me into good trim to stand the House ... which will give me probably some pretty hard work'. After benefiting from the waters, he told his father, 23 Apr. 1820:

> I do not apprehend that the ... session will be a very busy one ... If the ministers are contented with the same civil list that the late king had, I should not think it would be adviseable for us to endeavour to reduce it ... By taking a conciliatory line with the people the country might be very well governed without the additional 11,000 ... [troops] raised in the autumn, but it would be a very disadvantageous question for us if we were to press for ... reduction ... at the very time when the disturbances in Yorkshire and Scotland have compelled the military to be called upon actual service ... There does not remain much to do, except any question relative to the queen should arise ... I shall have my hands quite full, for I must instantly begin upon the insolvent debtors.[8]

Althorp reintroduced his bill to amend the Insolvent Debtors Act, which had passed both Houses in the previous Parliament but had been overtaken by the dissolution, on 17 May 1820. It empowered three commissioners to investigate the affairs of debtors and gave creditors the right to compel them to surrender their effects after nine months' imprisonment. With the backing of the government law officers he saw the measure to a third reading, 16 June.[9] It was amended in the Lords and received royal assent on 26 July 1820. On 21 Feb. 1821 he secured leave to introduce a bill to improve further the system of recovering small debts by establishing new county courts, presided over by reputable barristers, to administer it. The measure was condemned by the attorney-general, 15 Mar., and Althorp abandoned it for the session on 11 May.[10] He tried again in 1823, when he had a select committee appointed, 18 Feb., and brought in a bill based on its report, which he did not press that session.[11] He reintroduced his measure in 1824 and 1825, when he unsuccessfully resisted ministerial attempts to include compensation for Westminster Hall lawyers for loss of income. In the latter session, when he secured the appointment of another select committee (15 Feb.) and accepted an element of compensation, the bill foundered in the Upper House on the intractability of lord chancellor Eldon, and Althorp gave it up as a hopeless cause as long as he remained in office. In the House, 27 Mar. 1826, he urged Peel, the home secretary, to take over the measure, as its only chance of

success. Peel's response was guarded, but Althorp left the business in his hands for the future.[12]

He attended a party meeting at Burlington House, 'the first which I ever attended that I thought likely to be useful', 4 May 1820, when it was decided that Brougham should attack the droits of admiralty as part of the civil list next day. He voted in the opposition minority, and again on the general civil list, 8 May, and told his father on the 12th that they had had 'two very good divisions' and that ministers seemed 'considerably alarmed at the state of things'.[13] He continued to divide regularly but mostly silently with opposition in this short session. He voted for referring agricultural distress petitions to a select committee, 30 May, though he expected nothing to be 'gained', especially when the inquiry's remit was restricted by ministers, and he observed to his father that by taking out repeated loans the chancellor of the exchequer Vansittart was 'going directly forward to ruin'; Tierney would 'not stir' on this issue, which Althorp and others wished to raise.[14] On 14 June he spoke and was a minority teller with his friend and mentor on economic issues Sir Henry Parnell for inquiry into the Irish Union duties. He had already predicted 'a terrible combustion in the party' over Queen Caroline, whose 'very indiscreet' championing by Brougham worried him;[15] but he was a teller for the minority against Wilberforce's compromise resolution, 22 June, and divided against the appointment of the green bag committee, 26 June. Condemning the barrack agreement bill, 10 July 1820, he 'protested vehemently' at the argument of the war secretary Lord Palmerston that troops were best kept isolated from the public.[16] After the session he moved from Spencer House into his 'old quarters' in the Albany, where he planned to set up a chemistry laboratory to investigate the application of science to farming, in which he was 'pretty sure I am more likely to be of use to my fellow creatures ... than in politics, for they are more hopeless than ever'.[17] His doing so 'without ever having dropped the slightest hint ... to me' angered his mother, who roundly condemned him:

> He is certainly the most unamiable and unsocial being ... reserved, suspicious, and repelling to a degree seldom seen ... I am sure he needed not to have feared any persuasion from me to alter his determination, since his society affords me very little else than regret at his unhappy disposition and strange lack of all affectionate feeling and openness of heart ... This additional instance of his poverty of mind and contraction of heart is ... only a confirmation of what I have had too long reason to know.[18]

Althorp, who believed the queen to be 'guilty, though I do not think it has been anything like proved', was against Milton's notion of calling a county meeting on the issue, while admitting that he approved of its 'objects' of demanding the dismissal of ministers and a prorogation of Parliament. At Althorp in October he found both parents 'stout anti-queenites', but at the Whig gathering at Holkham subsequently he discovered that she was there 'considered as nothing else than spotless innocence personified'. His private hope that the bill of pains and penalties would not come before the Commons was gratified by ministers' abandonment of it in mid-November.[19] He remained adverse to holding county meetings, both because he thought that thereby the Whigs would 'undo all the good' which ministers' 'extreme folly has done during the last few months', for the comparatively unimportant object of trying to secure the queen's rights, and because in the case of a Northamptonshire meeting, which he would be obliged to attend, it would be 'rather awkward to be obliged to differ ... with our friends as to the propriety of calling it'.[20]

Yet he was delighted with the Whig 'victory' at the Derbyshire meeting in January 1821, when he told Milton that he was 'rather inclined to think that notwithstanding all that has passed the ministers will be too strong for us this session'.[21] He was absent from the division on the omission of the queen's name from the liturgy, 23 Jan., but voted for its restoration and presented a Wellingborough petition for inquiry into the prosecution and for parliamentary reform, 26 Jan.[22] He attended but did not speak at the Surrey county meeting called to air the same issues, 2 Feb., and testified to its 'respectability' in the House, 8 Feb., having duly voted for the opposition censure motion on the 6th.[23] On 12 Feb. he wrote to his constituent John Gotch deploring 'the recent conduct of the House of Commons':

No man can now ... assert that they express the feelings of the country. If the people choose to submit, well and good, and they must be satisfied to be told by Lord Londonderry that they have been under a delusion; but if there is a grain of English spirit left, petitions for reform of Parliament will come from every parish ... I do not mean that they should be for universal suffrage or anything of that kind, but generally for such a reform as will give the people a greater influence on the decisions of the ... Commons.[24]

He spoke and voted for Milton's proposal to make Leeds a scot and lot borough if it got Grampound's seats, 2 Mar., wanted inquiry into the Lyme Regis petitioners' allegations of Lord Westmorland's electoral interference, 12 Apr., and divided for Lord John Russell's parliamentary reform motion, 9 May. He

voted for Catholic relief, 28 Feb. He divided only sporadically in support of the Mountaineers' campaign for economy and retrenchment. On 29 Mar. he said the ministerial proposals for the timber duties were 'quite at variance with true commercial principles'; but on 5 Apr. he opposed Parnell's attempt to reduce them on the ground that as long as the colonial system was maintained, reasonable protection was justified. He presented and endorsed petitions against the additional malt duty, 3 Apr., and urged Tory country gentlemen to disregard the empty government threat to resign if the repeal bill was carried against them;[25] he was in the minority for it, 12 Apr., when he supported (as ever) a proposal to repeal the usury laws. He was named to the select committee on agricultural distress, 7 Mar. He evidently gave up attendance for the session in the second week of May, partly on account of a severe attack of bilious gout, which took several weeks to shake off.[26] At a Holkham sheep-shearing dinner, 2 July, he described himself as 'but a young agriculturist' who had 'never expected any good' from the distress committee, which had largely ignored what he considered to be the root of the problem, excessive taxation.[27] In early October 1821 his brother George told their sibling Frederick that Althorp was

more eager than ever after his present hobby of cows, sheep and pigs ... It is ... the best employment for anybody who lives so much alone as he does ... and ... I never knew a person who knew as well how to get on by himself, without being more or less unfitted for society. I wish he would marry ... but I am convinced he is as much determined against that as ever. He says he lives alone more comfortably as he grows older, but I do not think he will find his account in it when he really grows positively old.[28]

At the turn of the year his brother-in-law William Henry Lyttelton[†] reported that he was

in much better health than he has had for many years, owing to prescriptions and rules of a Dr. Scudamore's, who put him upon a sensible, plain but nourishing diet, which he has kept now for five months ... He has had no cold nor any ailment at all for a long time, and can ride 45 miles *on end* without fatigue. He says he thinks he is as strong as ever again. He looks uncommonly well, and quite sufficiently fat ... and yet within these three months he has lost sixteen pounds.[29]

In January 1822 Russell, surveying the Commons scene after the ministerial reshuffle and absorption of the Grenvillites, judged the Whigs to be 'the strongest party in the House' and thought that Althorp 'might be leader of the band', with Brougham as 'first fiddle'.[30] This did not happen, but Althorp was much more

active in the Commons than in the previous year, even
though he missed the early divisions on the address
and against the repressive legislation for Ireland. He
voted for Brougham's motion for extensive tax cuts
to relieve distress, 11 Feb., and on the 15th, presenting a petition for abolition of the leather tax, pressed
ministers to act decisively on this issue.[31] On 21 Feb.
he proposed a resolution that their planned cuts were
'not sufficient to satisfy the just expectations of the
people', arguing that the £5,000,000 surplus could
be used to reduce taxes. He got 126 votes to 234.[32] He
voted fairly steadily for economy and retrenchment
until mid-March: he spoke for admiralty reductions, 1
Mar., and for taking 10,000 men from the army, 4 Mar.
A week later he wrote to Milton:

> I do not know whether I agree with you in wishing to see
> our friends in administration. I like some of them very
> much and I had much rather the ship should go ashore, as
> she indubitably will, when my adversaries are at the helm
> ... I do not see a possibility of our getting through our
> difficulties ... We shall go on in an alternation of agricul-
> tural and manufacturing distress. This must be the case
> with any country taxed out of proportion beyond the rest
> of the world ... Capital must leave us and we shall go from
> bad to worse, till our ruin is complete. I fear it is not in the
> power of man to prevent this and I therefore do not wish
> to see any of my friends in a situation where disgrace will
> accompany failure though there is no chance of success.[33]

Resuming attendance after Easter, he voted for
Russell's reform motion, 25 Apr. He threw 'a great
deal of cold water', as his mother reported, on an
unsuccessful Northamptonshire farmers' attempt to
secure a county meeting to petition for tax cuts and
reform; but when he presented the petition, 12 June,
he said that in refusing the requisition the sheriff had
'not exercised a sound discretion'.[34] He denounced the
leather tax, on behalf of his constituents, 30 Apr., but
defended ministerial relaxation of the navigation laws,
6 May.[35] Later that month he was mentioned again as
the 'best man' to lead the Whigs in the Commons, but
he was supposed to have approved Lord Tavistock's*
fanciful notion of installing Burdett at the helm.[36] He
divided with his friends on most major issues for the
rest of the session, including for criminal law reform,
4 June, but he appears to have absconded after 1 July.
He spoke and was a teller for the minority against the
'most arbitrary' Irish constables bill, 7 June, and was a
teller for the minority against the aliens bill, 14 June.
Although he agreed with it in principle, he declined to
vote for Wyvill's amendment for large tax reductions,
moved to oppose considering the agricultural distress
report, 8 May, because he considered the existing corn
laws to be 'so bad, that any of the proposed resolutions

would be much better'. In the committee, he contended that farmers wanted the 'steady price' which
a duty of 60-70s. per quarter would ensure. Next day
he moved for a duty of 20s. on wheat imports and an
enhanced bounty of 18s. on exports. Ricardo opposed
this proposal, which was beaten by 201-24. Althorp
then voted in the minority of 25 for Ricardo's plan for
a 20s. fixed duty. He complained that it was 'highly
unfair that it should be insinuated that all persons who
voted for a reduction of taxes contemplated a national
bankruptcy', 13 May. On 10 July 1822 he reluctantly
agreed to act on 'the Christian principle' by complying
with the urgent plea of James Abercromby* for him
to accompany him to Scotland as his second in a possible duel with the advocate William Menzies. They
reached Ferrybridge next day, but turned back on dis-
covering that the Commons had intervened to prevent
further action.[37]

Althorp agreed with Milton that it was 'foolish' to
move an amendment to the address in 1823, as some
intended, and decided to stay away. He confessed that
French aggression against Spain had put him in 'such
a fury that I have not proper possession of my faculties' and argued that ministers 'should have proposed
an offensive and defensive alliance with Spain on
condition of her acknowledging the independence of
South America': war was preferable to passivity while
'every vestige of liberty is destroyed on the continent
and everything is to be dependent on an oligarchy of
barbarian tyrants'.[38] He voted against the appointment of a lieutenant-general of the ordnance in peacetime, 19 Feb., and for inquiry into the parliamentary
franchise, 20 Feb. He was absent until 6 Mar., when
he voted against the national debt reduction bill. He
joined the Political Economy Club at this time. He
divided for a repeal of assessed taxes, 18 Mar. He told
Brougham, 17 Mar., that he thought the scheme of 'a
republican form of government for the opposition'
concocted by Lambton and Lord Duncannon* was
'rather a bad plan', but that he would not object to it if
Brougham endorsed it.[39] On 16 Apr. he got 110 votes
(to 216) for repeal of the Foreign Enlistment Act. He
voted for inquiry into the prosecution of the Dublin
Orange rioters, 22 Apr., for Russell's reform motion,
24 Apr., and reform of the Scottish representative
system, 2 June. He led the opposition to renewal of the
Irish Insurrection Act, 12 May, and advocated prior
inquiry into the state of the country; he was defeated
by 162-82. On 15 May he declared against the precipitate abolition of slavery and endorsed the government's amelioration resolutions as a step in the right
direction. He differed from Ricardo and John Maberly
in their wish to see malt rather than beer taxed, 28

May 1823. He divided for information on Catholic burials, 6 Feb., secured detailed returns relating to the state of Ireland, 19 Feb.,[40] and was a minority teller for an account of Irish Catholic office-holders, which would expose the prevailing 'exclusive system', 19 Feb. 1824. He divided for reform of Edinburgh's representation, 26 Feb., and in small minorities against items of the ordnance estimates next day. He presented petitions for repeal of the leather tax, 1 Mar.[41] He spoke and voted for Hobhouse's motion for repeal of the window tax, 2 Mar., but in so doing expressed approval of the government's plans for the silk and wool duties, though not for those on coal; he condemned the sinking fund system. He presented constituency petitions for improvement of the conditions of West Indian slaves, 2 Mar., and for the abolition of slavery, 22 Mar.;[42] but he did not vote to censure the prosecution of the Methodist missionary John Smith in Demerara, 11 June. (He had been 'unavoidably absent' the previous day.)[43] He moved unsuccessfully for information on the Irish government's dealings with ribbon men, arguing that the time was ripe for conciliation, 11 Mar. That day he was in a minority of 14 against the Welsh judicature bill and brought in a measure to restrict Irish landlords' right to distrain their tenants' growing crops. He abandoned this on 17 May, pending a select committee's report.[44] He acquiesced in the grant for the Society for the Propagation of the Gospels in the colonies, 13 Mar. On the 15th, when he voted to end army flogging, he objected to Maberly's proposal for the separate collection of the malt and beer duties. He offered to support the grant for Irish Protestant charter schools if ministers would concede an inquiry into Irish education, 15 Mar., but when this was refused he divided in the hostile minority of 33. He was in that of 27 against the grant for publishing Irish proclamations, 19 Mar. He spoke and voted against the aliens bill, though he wished Hobhouse had not called it a blot on the statute book, 23 Mar., and was a teller for the minority against the second reading, 2 Apr. He welcomed Canning's assurance that it would be allowed to lapse next year, 3 Apr. He voted for defence by counsel in felony trials, 6 Apr., and against the subsidy for new church building, 9, 12 Apr. He supported a motion for an advance of capital to Ireland, which he likened to a 'very rich' but 'out of condition' farm. He did not vote for Hume's motion for inquiry into the Irish church establishment, 6 May, but on the 11th he proposed investigation by select committee of the whole state of Ireland, recommending tax cuts, reform of the 'jobbing' culture and of grand jury presentments, a modest redistribution of church revenues and the abolition of all secret societies. He had a respectable minority of 136 to 184. He divided to end Irish pluralism, 27 May. He voted for repeal of the assessed taxes, 10 May, and of the leather tax, 18 May, and said that the warehoused wheat bill was a matter of 'perfect indifference' to the agricultural interest, 17 May 1824.

Althorp agreed with Brougham that opposition must make Ireland and Catholic relief, which had been 'opposed only by prejudice, folly and bigotry', their priority in the 1825 session, regardless of the potential threat to his electoral interests. He approved of the Irish Catholic leader Daniel O'Connell's* 'wise line'.[45] He spoke and voted against the bill to suppress the Catholic Association as 'an infringement of the liberties of the people', 15 Feb., and opposed it steadily thereafter. He was a teller for the minority in favour of allowing the Association to put its case at the bar of the House, 18 Feb. He was named to the select committee on the state of Ireland, 17 Feb., and on it shared in the examination of O'Connell, whom he had met socially beforehand.[46] He voted silently for Catholic relief, 1 Mar., 21 Apr., 10 May, and on 22 Apr. said that as a reformer he would support the attendant bill to disfranchise the 40s. freeholders because it would only 'deprive ... those who had no independent votes'. Supporting the first of Maberly's resolutions for repeal of the assessed taxes, 3 Mar., he commended ministers for the progress they had made towards 'bringing back our revenue to a sound and wholesome system', but urged them not to maintain these taxes 'against the wishes of the country'. He divided for repeal of the window tax, 17 May. He supported Whitmore's motion for revision of the corn laws, 28 Apr., but next day presented petitions against any alterations.[47] He supported the ministerial bill to rectify defects in Hume's Combination Act of 1824, 3 May, in order to 'secure from the effects of threats those workmen who were willing to labour'. He spoke and voted for Brougham's motion to make puisne judges immovable, 20 May 1825. No further parliamentary activity has been found for that session: he evidently did not join in the opposition to the duke of Cumberland's annuity bill. He had grave doubts about whether to subscribe to Brougham's scheme for a London University, fearing that it would be godless, even though he recognized that it would be 'a great benefit to the country to put scientific instruction within the reach of so many more people'. John Smith*, to whom Brougham showed his letter, commented that 'his motives are creditable ... but it confirms the opinion I always entertained of his capacity. He certainly has not the art of expressing himself clearly, which everyone with distinct ideas is sure to attain sooner or later'.[48]

Althorp saw no merit in calling a county meeting to petition for the abolition of slavery, as he told Milton, 11 Feb. 1826. Apart from not wishing to agitate his constituents so close to an election, when 'No Popery or corn' might be raised against him, he reckoned that such meetings were 'not so much intended and certainly not so much calculated to procure the emancipation of the slaves as to increase the power of the Methodists'. He hoped the government would be able to carry their bills to deal with the banking crisis, but was not convinced, as 'they appeared very weak in the House last night'.[49] One of the few leading Whigs who did not think that the Catholic question should be set aside until after the elections, he pressed Goulburn, the Irish secretary, to disclose ministerial plans for Ireland, 16 Feb. He subsequently let the issue alone.[50] He voted in the minority of 24 on the promissory notes bill, 20 Feb., and supported Maberly's call for the monthly publication of the amount of notes in circulation, 24 Feb. On the 28th he questioned the terms of the proposed exchequer bills loan. He voted with Hume for monthly bank returns, 7 Mar., and was named to the select committee on bank notes, 16 Mar. He presented anti-slavery petitions, 1 Mar., and next day, when he voted to condemn the Jamaican slave trials, told Gotch, who had sent the petitions to him, that 'we have gained a step, for I should think the colonial legislature will hardly venture to refuse to pass the measure proposed to them by government'.[51] He voted for army reductions, 3, 6, 7 Mar., and in the minority of 38 to exclude non-resident electors from Irish boroughs, 9 Mar. He divided against the salary arrangements for the president of the board of trade, 10 Apr., and for reform of Edinburgh's representation, 13 Apr., and seconded Russell's reform motion, which aimed to restore their lost 'power' to the people, 27 Apr. He had decided early in the session not to vote for Whitmore's motion for revision of the corn laws (18 Apr.), because 'nothing like a reasonable settlement can be expected just previous to a general election' and the measures to restrict the circulation of small notes required 'an importation of the precious metals' to stabilize the currency.[52] On 4 May, when he voted for Hume's state of the nation motion, he demanded a final settlement of the corn question; and he opposed the emergency admission of bonded corn as mere tinkering, 5, 8 May. On 19 Apr. he said that Littleton's proposals for the conduct of private bill committees 'did not go precisely ... to any ... of the causes of complaint' and 'must inevitably throw a great deal of additional labour on ... Members'. He spoke and voted for defence by counsel to aid uneducated prisoners, 25 Apr. He was in the minority of 13 against the Irish prison laws

bill, 5 May. His return for Northamptonshire at the general election in June 1826 was largely uneventful, but Cartwright's exposition of his views obliged him to follow suit, as he told Spencer:

> I spoke upon reform ... slavery, the Catholic question and the corn laws ... Some observations that were made upon the corn laws enabled me to explain again, and in more detail, to the farmers the principles that ought to be looked to ... and it appeared to satisfy them.

Afterwards he went to assist Tavistock in Bedfordshire, where he was standing on 'free election' principles.[53]

Russell, defeated in Huntingdonshire, publicly entrusted his planned measure to curb electoral bribery to Althorp in November 1826.[54] On the 2nd he secured the renewal of Russell's successful resolution of May 1826, which proposed that bribery cases should be referred to a select committee. He conceded that a bill embodying this would have no chance of passing the Lords, but bowed to the sense of the House and withdrew the proposition. He resumed the subject on 26 Feb. 1827, but his resolution was negatived. On 15 Mar. he obtained the appointment of a select committee (which he chaired) to consider means of reducing the cost of county elections, suggesting county-wide polling places and a more rational system of registration. He brought up the report, 16 May, and on 1 June introduced a bill for the registration of freeholders, which he had committed and left over to next session. On 8 May he brought in a bill to curb corruption and excessive expenditure in borough elections by banning the specious employment of electors as agents, musicians and runners. He carried the third reading by 26-10, 28 May, and got the House to accept the Lords' amendment excluding Scotland from its provisions, 18 June. It became law on 21 June 1827.

Althorp voiced his 'considerable regret' that ministers would not deal with the corn question before Christmas, 22 Nov. 1826. On the 28th he now concurred in Littleton's resolutions on private bill committees as 'a great improvement' worth a fair trial. He signed a requisition for and attended a 'thin' and non-political county meeting to vote condolences on the death of the duke of York, 1 Feb. 1827.[55] He saw great merit in Brougham's scheme for a Society for the Diffusion of Useful Knowledge, but hesitated to subscribe until he was satisfied that its potentially 'mischievous' publications would be effectively vetted.[56] He walked to the House on 6 Feb. with Hobhouse, and agreed with him that the grant for the duke of Clarence should not be opposed unless it was 'too large'. Yet it seemed to him to be so, and he denounced it as inappropriate at a time when 'distress and ruin [were] running through every part of the kingdom'. Grey's son Lord Howick* thought this a 'very good' speech, and the duke of Bedford deemed it 'plain, sensible and honest'. He was the teller for Hume's minority of 65 in favour of postponement. But Lord Holland was furious with him and the other Whig 'opposers', calling them 'a set of impracticable persons who never would come into place'.[57] Althorp urged Lord Rancliffe not to divide the House against the second reading of the bill, 22 Mar., arguing that while it was objectionable, it was 'not so important as to require a hostility so persevering'. He thought the allegations of improper electoral interference by Northampton corporation warranted investigation, 21 Feb., and he divided for inquiry into the activities of Leicester corporation, 15 Mar. He welcomed the ministry's proposals to relax the corn laws, 1 Mar. He reported that farmers at Northampton market had generally liked them, 8 Mar., but after some adverse constituency reaction had to admit on the 23rd that they had become hostile.[58] He would not support Whitmore's amendment to lower the duties on barley, 12 Mar.[59] He wanted the averages to be taken over six weeks rather than one and said that agriculturists did not want corn to be 'at a price oppressive to the manufacturers', 26 Mar.[60] Supporting the corn bill, 6 Apr., he argued that 'the principle of prohibition ... always gave rise to the most mischievous speculations'. He was in the minority for Catholic relief, 6 Mar. He divided for information on the Barrackpoor mutiny, 22 Mar., and the Lisburn Orange procession, 29 Mar. He spoke and was a majority teller for the spring guns bill, 23 Mar. 1827.

As the ministerial uncertainty which followed Lord Liverpool's stroke dragged on, Althorp predicted to Brougham, 26 Mar. 1827, that it was 'intended to patch up a divided administration with Lord Bathurst or some other King Log at the head of it'. While he thought that the Whigs would probably be able to 'support most of their measures of foreign and commercial policy', he felt that they would thereby be sanctioning 'an administration which acts upon a system quite contrary to every constitutional principle and highly detrimental to the real permanent interests of the country'.[61] He voted for Tierney's motion to withhold supplies until the crisis was resolved, 30 Mar., and for inquiries into the Irish estimates and chancery delays, 5 Apr. Speculation that he was to become secretary at war in the new Canning ministry was wide of the mark.[62] He disliked the Lansdowne Whigs' coalition with Canning, whom he had never trusted. 'Most of all', he feared that it might destroy the Whig party, which he was anxious to keep united. With Milton and Tavistock, he decided that they could not endorse a

junction with 'a divided and do-nothing government' which would not take up Catholic relief; but, viewing Canning's separation from Peel and the reactionary Tories as 'a great point gained', they resolved to 'take time and watch the government', supporting it whenever possible as the lesser of two evils. As he told Gotch, 1 June, 'I am not very sanguine as to any good being done, but there is a chance; if the old ministers came back into power, there would be no chance at all'. He and his close associates accordingly retained their seats on the opposition benches.[63] In the House, 7 May, he frankly explained his attitude to the ministry as an alternative to 'Toryism in its most odious forms', but stressed his differences from Canning on reform and repeal of the Test Acts. The son of Tierney, who had joined the government, reported that Althorp's speech and Milton's had 'worked miracles'; but Althorp told Thomas Creevey* that he was 'gratified ... at finding the line which I have taken approved of by all those with whom I first began my political life'.[64] He approved the government's small debts bill, but was not sure that £20 was the correct benchmark, 23 May. As a member of the Penryn election committee, he said on the 28th that 20 years' systematic corruption was indisputable and that the borough must be disfranchised; he voted in Russell's majority for this. On 30 May he announced that Dissenters' leaders had decided not to press for repeal of the Test Acts that session. He presented petitions for it, 15 June.[65] He considered Canning's budget 'too sanguine', 1 June, but would not follow Hume into the consideration of 'multifarious abstract questions'. He approved the intention to appoint a finance committee in 1828, but warned that 'if great economy were not introduced into all the estimates next year, he should feel himself obliged to withdraw his support from the government'. In late July 1827 he decided, after much agonizing, that his naval officer and favourite brother Robert could reasonably accept the offer of becoming private secretary to Clarence as lord high admiral. (He held the post until September 1828.) But it 'amused Lansdowne, a member of both coalition ministries, to see the Spencers 'brought into contact with royalty'.[66]

Althorp believed that Canning's death would cause 'a loss to our foreign politics ... beyond calculation', while domestically the king's decision to perpetuate the coalition was 'absolute annihilation to the Tories', and therefore 'some consolation'. He saw no 'reason to take a different course from the one we ... had taken already', as the Goderich ministry remained 'a less evil than a pure Tory one'. At the same time he expressed to Holland his hope that 'our friends will not hold office the moment after they are not able to forward'

Catholic relief.[67] Tavistock, believing that the Whigs had been humiliated by the rumoured appointment of the anti-Catholic John Herries* as chancellor of the exchequer at the king's behest, suggested to Russell, Holland and Spencer that Althorp should become their active Commons leader.[68] Althorp thought Tavistock was 'quite mad' to consider the notion, as he told Russell, 25 Aug., returning a letter from Holland to Russell detailing objections to Althorp, to which he himself could 'add many better arguments'. He went on:

> There is no chance whatever that it will be offered to you or to any man of decided character to take a place in this administration. They must have men of a more pliant disposition who will give up all the great principles on which we have acted for the sake of doing what I admit to be a good, viz., the [keeping] the Tories out ... I should certainly advise you or any other friend not to take upon yourself the responsibility of a cabinet office ... unless the Catholic question is to be made a government measure. There are many other questions which ought to be stipulated for, but this appears to me to be quite a *sine qua non* ... There is no change in the principles of the administration and therefore this ought to have our conditional but very jealous support.[69]

From the ministerial perspective, Alexander Baring* damned Althorp with faint praise by observing that 'if we are to have a second rate performer' as leader in the Commons, assuming Huskisson's health would not stand it, 'I always thought Althorp would please the House and satisfy the country better than anybody'.[70] The confirmation of Herries's appointment proved to Althorp, as he confessed to his father, that 'I was wrong in hoping that any good would come from ... Goderich's administration. I am afraid no good can be looked for in the present reign'.[71] The Tory whip Billy Holmes* believed that Althorp, Milton and Tavistock were 'quite furious and will go into decided opposition';[72] but Tierney had no reason to believe this of Althorp, while Abercromby, a supporter of the administration, told Lansdowne that he and Huskisson believed that Althorp

> thought that he could turn his character and talents to the best account by watching measures, supporting what he liked, urging what he thought useful, and opposing what he disapproved ... I was enabled from personal knowledge ... to confirm this view to the fullest extent. We understood, therefore, that though he was not to be reckoned an adherent ... he would on many occasions be a useful ally, and never a mischievous opponent.[73]

From Leamington, 9 Sept., Althorp gave his opinion of the situation to Holland, who had informed him of 'circumstances which ... must undoubtedly be consid-

ered to palliate the appointment of Herries'. Althorp conceded this, but criticized the Whig ministers for failing to attend the cabinet at which it was effected, which made it clear to 'the whole country that they are holding office without possessing any influence whatever':

> I can ... see no course for myself but to withhold my confidence from a government in which those ministers of whose principles ... I approve are without the power of doing any good. I must be ... quite independent and look only to measures ... Looking forward ... with horror to finding myself in this situation next session, still I think it is the only thing I can honestly do. If these ministers act upon the principles they have hitherto most of them professed, I shall almost always find myself supporting them. If they do otherwise, I ought to oppose them.

To his father the same day he confirmed that 'nothing ... shall at present shake me from the resolution ... of being in an armed neutrality'.[74] After consulting Grey, Althorp, Tavistock and Milton, Russell sent Tierney a list of 'six propositions' as conditions for their continued neutrality. Russell assured Tierney that Althorp was 'far ... removed from anything like a hostile or captious spirit', but was unwilling 'in his place [to] say that he had full and perfect confidence in the government', though he would support the propositions 'as beneficial to the country; in short, his only doubt is whether the ministry is strong enough at *Court* to carry such points'. Tierney was unable to secure the sanction of his cabinet colleagues for the bargain.[75] Althorp's neutral stance did not please the whip Duncannon, who thought it would hand 'absolute power to the crown; but Lyttelton considered his position, though uncomfortable, to be 'a very honourable one'.[76] Abercromby believed that Althorp had turned 'hostile' in mid-October, and a fortnight later Tierney heard that he was 'determined to *force* on the Catholic question as soon as Parliament meets': 'It is thought ... that we are endeavouring by some compromise to prevent its being moved ... and so the watchmen are to spring their rattles'.[77] In fact, Althorp was sticking to his line of 'favourable neutrality', as he assured Tierney, 2 Nov., when apprising him of an impending vacancy in the post of receiver-general of Northamptonshire, to which the appointment of the Whig aspirant would bolster the party in Northampton borough.[78] To Edward Davies Davenport* he wrote on 11 Nov. 1827:

> The most useful thing ... which public men can do in the present circumstances is to hang together and to compel the ministers to do that which they themselves think right, so that while the power of the king acts upon them in one direction to induce them to do that which is wrong,

a good strong party in the ... Commons may act upon them in the opposite direction ... If I can effect this I shall accomplish the highest object of my political ambition, for I have only one personal object, only one point on which I am aware that my personal feelings may lead me to act corruptly, and that is to keep myself in such a position that I may not be compelled to take office. Nothing shall ever persuade me to do so, but I should be sorry to be placed in such a situation as to avow this selfish feeling publicly, though I think it right that all those who wish to act with me should be aware of my decision.[79]

In the last week of November 1827 Tierney, having obtained the blessing of Goderich and Huskisson, but not Herries, asked Althorp whether he would take the chairmanship of the finance committee if it was offered. Althorp was inclined to accept it, as affording him a small means of doing some practical good, but he did not expect the offer to be made, having, as he told his father, been 'given to understand' when he had been sounded about office on the formation of the ministry, that 'the king would have objected to my being in the cabinet, had I not put a stop at once to any discussion on the subject'. He consulted and got the approval of Tavistock and Milton, and on 29 Nov. wrote to Tierney to 'accept the chair ... on the clear understanding that I am to support or oppose the views of government in that committee as I may think right'.[80] He had no direct part in the ministerial machinations, ostensibly over his chairmanship, which brought the ministry down, but he had talks with Tierney in mid-December 1827, when he expressed concern about being given a restricted remit and insisted that the annual estimates must be referred to the committee if ministers wished to be seen to be sincere in their professions of support for economy and retrenchment. His mother reported that he 'says unless they give some strong test of their acting up to the principles which they professed ... he will vote for turning them out'.[81] On Christmas Day Abercromby found him 'in point of feeling well disposed', but unhappy with 'what has been done as to church patronage', heavily in favour of Protestants, which 'destroys the argument that sacrifices must be made to keep out the Tories, for what they would do worse'.[82] Althorp, 'the most silent of very cheerful and sensible men', as Mackintosh referred to him,[83] regarded the final collapse of the government as 'an unmixed good', and turned his mind towards the task of reuniting the fractured Whig party, setting aside all recriminations with the coalitionists. He called off a planned meeting of the 'watchmen' and argued to Russell that if the expected Tory government was formed 'all persons who pretend to be Whigs will be in opposition' and that they and their associates should

'allow ourselves to be absorbed into the general Whig party'. Tavistock assured Hobhouse that Althorp 'has no wish to form a party or to put himself at the head of any set of men' and was 'quite free from all selfish or ambitious views ... and looks to no object upon earth than the public good'.[84] On better terms now with Lord Grey, after some years of coolness, Althorp had emerged as a figure of great stature in the party.[85]

He told an unknown spokesman for the Catholics, 25 Jan. 1828, that the new Wellington ministry, for all its professions of 'neutrality', was in reality 'decidedly hostile to your claims', for which the Catholics should agitate as before.[86] On the address, 29 Jan., he objected to criticism of Admiral Codrington for his action at Navarino, but questioned the policy and justice of the Treaty of London, approved the sending of British troops to Portugal and, still more, their subsequent withdrawal, and said he had 'no confidence whatever' in the ministry. Peel and Herries felt that they could hardly avoid naming him to the finance committee, 15 Feb., but he assured Peel in private that he was no party to rumoured plans of some members of the late government to propose him rather than Parnell as chairman, which had alarmed Wellington.[87] On 18 Feb. he stated the 'little' he knew of the events which had destroyed the Goderich administration, stressing the reluctance with which he had accepted the chairmanship of the committee. In reply to Herries's attack, he admitted that 'for the greater part of my life I have been a party man', but insisted that the events of the previous year had 'entirely separated me from party'. He presented several petitions for repeal of the Test Acts, 20, 21, 26 Feb., when he spoke and voted in the majority for that measure. He said on the 28th, when he presented the enabling bill, that the declaration which Peel proposed to substitute for the oath was unacceptable, but that he was willing to swallow 'securities compatible with Dissenters' consciences'. He would not vote for Waithman's motion to reduce the army to 80,000 men, 25 Feb., because the estimates were to be considered by the finance committee. On 6 Mar. he was given leave to bring in a new freeholders registration bill. He carried the second reading by 32-17, 25 Mar., but had to abandon it at the report stage, 13 June. He welcomed the government's plan to repeal the 1808 Life Annuities Act, as recommended by the finance committee, 12, 24 Mar. He spoke and voted for the transfer of East Retford's seats to Birmingham, 21 Mar. On the corn bill, 22 Apr., he expressed his preference for the measure of 1827 and voted for a pivot price of 60s. He saw much to commend in Macqueen's settlement by hiring bill, 29 Apr., but found fault with most of Peel's offences against the person bill, 5 May. He voted for Catholic relief, 12 May, having presented a Northampton Catholics' petition, 28 Apr. He was a teller for the majority for the second reading of Davies's borough polls bill, 13 May, when the House was counted out. That day he led the opposition to the provision for Canning's widow and family; when Stratford Canning asserted that he had a year ago promised to support Canning's ministry, he retorted that he had only said it was preferable to a Tory one. The Canningite Lord Seaford described it as a 'poor and miserable performance', while Abercromby reflected that Althorp 'must be rather ashamed of his company' in the minority.[88] On 16 May he confirmed that the finance committee, which was overwhelmed with work, was agreeable to the House's dealing with the military estimates before it reported. In passing, he said that naval impressment, though unpleasant, was 'necessary and unavoidable'. He later endorsed Parnell's amendment to get rid of the coastal blockade. He supported repeal of the usury laws and spoke and voted for Hume's motion for a return of civil list pensions, 20 May. A week later he was reported by Lord Rosslyn to be willing to support the ministry if Grey was brought into the cabinet; but Russell knew that in reality he remained 'just where he was'.[89] In the House, 12 June, he welcomed 'the more moderate tone' in which ministers, including Wellington, had discussed the Catholic question; but he deplored its being left open in cabinet when it was 'unanimously agreed that the state of Ireland is one of great danger'. He was in the minority of 21 for the Irish assessment of lessors bill that day, and voted against the archbishop of Canterbury's bill, 16 June, and the grant for Buckingham House refurbishment, 23 June. In the finance committee he was probably in the majority which rejected Goulburn's proposal to allocate a fixed annual sum to reduction of the national debt; he persuaded the committee to recommend the application of any surplus to the conversion of annuities.[90] When Peel abandoned his small debts bill for the session, 23 June, Althorp protested at the 'monstrous principle' of compensating the holders of patent offices for loss of fees, but admitted that the measure was an improvement on his own. On 2 July 1828 he wrote to Sir James Robert George Graham* from Althorp:

> I ... expected ... that the ministers would follow the advice of the financial committee as to reducing the salaries of the clerks in public offices, and perhaps the daily pay of the labourers in the dock yards; but that they would reject our advice whenever we recommended any reduction in political offices ... I had made up my mind as to the course ... to ... pursue ... on as fair and impar-

tial a consideration of the circumstances as a man very anxious to cull his ewes could be expected to give them. By being out of the way I have it in my power next session to say that I concluded that the recommendations of the finance committee would be attended to, but that, finding they were not, I for one decline being a party to such a delusion again. My main object being to see the Catholic question carried, I am inclined to sacrifice everything to this. But if there does not appear a prospect of this being done ... we must declare open war upon the government; and there cannot be a more hostile measure, or one more likely to be effective, than blowing up the finance committee upon the grounds which they are now about to give us ... I look forward with sanguine hopes of being relieved from my attendance ... next year and being at liberty to apply myself to other things of minor importance in which I am calculated to do much more good than by labouring at a subject above my abilities, and in a committee where consequently I have and ought to have no influence.[91]

In late August 1828 Althorp observed to his father that 'the Catholic question looks uncommonly well, thanks to O'Connell and the freeholders of Clare'. By the end of September he was almost sure that the government intended to 'do something for the Catholics'; but, still considering Wellington to be 'a man of a little mind', he feared, as he told Brougham, that he would

> propose some half measure ... This ... will be a great evil. It will be a fresh ground for our opponents to say nothing will ever satisfy ... [the Catholics]; and although it is not in the power of man to prevent the carrying of Catholic emancipation ... very soon, now that the Catholics are acting like rational beings, yet it will be a difficulty in the way of us who support them ... Whatever may be the degree of concession which they propose, we ought to accept it, unless it should be something which would amount to persecution ... I mean any measure calling upon all Catholics ... to subscribe something contrary to their religion ... If it is not the whole, we must enter our protest that it will ... and ought not to satisfy the Catholics. With respect to foreign politics, I find many of those with whom we have acted ... inclined to open war with the ministry ... Though the figure we are cutting ... is far from satisfactory, my political mind is so entirely absorbed by Ireland that I cannot bring myself to any very violent feelings on any other subject. If nothing is proposed for Ireland I am for open war, and will then gladly make use of any other topics of attack.[92]

Abercromby heard from Althorp in mid-October that a visit on farming business from his county neighbour Charles Arbuthnot*, the duke's confidant, had convinced him that nothing would be done and that he was now 'prepared to act decisively if he can get support'. Abercromby felt that if Althorp 'is stout, as I believe he will be', Grey, who wanted to hold off until ministers declared their hand, could have little influence on Whig Members.[93] Althorp poured cold water on the proposal of Holland and Russell to form a pro-Catholic club to counter the Brunswickers: 'We must beat them if we can whenever they come out of their holes and corners, and expose them to the ridicule and execration of all men of liberal minds, and then their ... exertions will have but little effect in a country as well educated as England is'.[94] Davenport, proposing to Holland the idea of a dining club of about 50 Members to co-ordinate hitherto chaotic opposition activity in the Commons, ruled out Althorp as a leader because he had 'kicked as if a bribe had been tendered' when Davenport had suggested such a plan in early 1828, and was now *'incomprehensible'* and not 'liberal' enough on foreign policy.[95] But John Fazakerley* thought that should Althorp be persuaded to press relentlessly for action on the Catholic question and promise 'firm opposition' if it was not conceded, 'everyone will rally round him' and even the prickly Edward Smith Stanley* would acquiesce in 'such an arrangement as should leave the ostensible lead of the party to Althorp', whose 'great experience, and courage, and weight in the House deserve it'.[96]

Althorp, who was 'lame' again in December 1828, favoured 'a good attendance on the first day' of speakers, but not of 'the foxhunters', for 'if the ministers intend to settle Ireland in a satisfactory manner they will want support [and] if they do not I hope they will be met by decisive opposition':

> I think Ireland of such critical importance now that if ministers will do their duty on that subject I would not annoy them on any other ... If ... not ... I would annoy them ... [and] ... attack them on every subject I could lay hold of and ... make every effort in my power to turn them out.

As for the growing notion that he should take a formal lead in the Commons, he wrote to Graham, 17 Dec. 1828:

> No man ever underrates himself; and I do not believe that any individual, except the person himself, is able to make any estimate of the abilities of a man who is discreet enough not to make attempts to which he is unequal. I agree with you that a great many of our party fancy that I should make a good leader ... but I know I should not. I should not have been two months before I should have fallen into the greatest possible contempt. At present I am overrated, then I should be underrated ... Ask Littleton, or some other person not particularly connected with me, what he thinks of my abilities as a member of the finance committee. If he will tell you the truth, you will be satisfied as to my capacity for a leader ... When anyone on whose judgement I can depend shall be equally well

informed with myself as to the qualities of my mind, and the amount of information which I possess, I shall admit him to be competent to controvert what I say when I assert that I am not equal to the post of the leader of a party.[97]

He interpreted Wellington's letter to Dr. Curtis as a sign that he would 'do nothing for the Catholics if he can help it', but admitted that Russell and others did not see it in that light. On the question of O'Connell's right to take his seat as Member for Clare, he gave Brougham his view that 'we ought to vote and speak against' as 'he has clearly no legal right to sit' and 'we shall damage ourselves and diminish our means of giving effectual support to the Catholic question' if they supported him.[98] He consulted Russell, who drew up two resolutions throwing on 'ministers the responsibility of not settling the question'. Althorp was not satisfied with them, but could offer nothing better.[99] Holland tried to persuade him to attack the government's foreign policy, but he would still have none of it, being unable to 'feel any interest in what happens in Portugal or Turkey or Russia or anywhere else, with a religious war impending ... at home'.[100] When it became clear that Wellington did intend to propose a measure of Catholic relief, Althorp argued that if it proved satisfactory and conceded the essential point of the right to sit in Parliament, 'I cannot be in opposition to such a government. There is plenty of fault to be found with their foreign politics, but ... conciliation and economy at home will cover a multitude of sins abroad'.[101] On the address, 6 Feb., he expressed 'great satisfaction' at the confirmation of the concession and praised the duke, but said he would prefer to see if emancipation gave a natural quietus to the Catholic Association than to have it suppressed by legislation. On 10 Feb. he sent through Arbuthnot a message to Peel to the effect that 'he and many of his friends cared very little' what the minister might say against the Association, but that as 'there were many fiery and violent spirits among them' it was 'very desirable' that he should not be provocative.[102] In the House that evening he acquiesced 'with a great reluctance' in the suppression bill. When he found that Mackintosh had given notice of a motion for papers on relations with Portugal, which 'must be considered as a motion of censure', he told Brougham that although he thought government had 'misbehaved grossly about the whole Portuguese business', he considered that it was 'of the highest importance that the ministers should feel confidence in our entire and cordial support and that they should not fancy that we have the slightest wish to take advantage of their unpopularity with their usual supporters to trip up their heels'. He would be obliged to vote against the motion, which was not 'likely to have a very good effect politically'. Mackintosh was persuaded to desist.[103] Althorp divided silently for the ministerial proposal to consider emancipation, 6 Mar. With Duncannon and Thomas Spring Rice*, he consulted Arbuthnot on the planned disfranchisement of Irish 40s. freeholders, with which he and many Whigs were unhappy. After being referred to Peel, who refused to give ground on it, Althorp convinced the majority at a party meeting that it must be swallowed in order to secure the greater object. He spoke in these terms, 18, 20 Mar., admitting his difference of opinion with Duncannon; but he had told Brougham a week before that he felt he ought to have spoken out sooner, and added that his failure of nerve 'proves to everybody what I have known myself long, that I am quite useless in any public situation'.[104] He presented petitions for emancipation, 12 Mar., and said that clergymen should not introduce politics to the pulpit, 19 Mar. He remained privately 'nervous' about the measure's chances of passing the Lords, but concluded that Wellington 'must know what he is about'. He pressed Arbuthnot to encourage the duke to turn out the junior ministers who were voting against the government, but accepted the argument that this might further enrage the king, who was threatening to change his mind and dismiss his ministers.[105] He voted silently for the third reading of the relief bill, 30 Mar., having argued to Brougham (who was on the circuit) that provoking a debate, as he wished, would only enable 'the Brunswickers' to delay the measure: a continuation of 'our quiet course' was the best option.[106] He was perplexed by an invitation from the lord mayor of London to attend the dinner on the day when Peel was to be given the freedom, as he told Brougham 1 Apr.:

> Going may appear as if I wished much more than I do to support or join with the government. I do not and cannot act quite as a solitary being; doing anything of this kind may commit others ... This ... applies to refusing to go as much as to accepting ... For myself ... the matter is one nearly of indifference, not being a man who would, under any circumstances, at least any conceivable one, submit myself to the trammels of office ... But ... I cannot act without involving others. What I have done is to accept ... in the first instance, and in case before the day arrives I should see reason for not going, I shall have business to do which shall force me to leave town.

He appears not to have attended the event, 8 Apr. A week later he was 'laid up' at Wiseton 'with a regular fit of the gout after having had it flying about me for six to seven months'.[107]

On 20 Feb. 1829 he said that even if ministers did not reappoint the finance committee, the House and country would expect them to 'make the greatest possible reductions', as they now had 'the materials to do so'. He acquiesced in the navy estimates, 27 Feb., and on 12 Mar. obtained information concerning the role of the Bank in management of the national debt. When he questioned Peel on his intentions for reform of small debt recovery, 8 May, the minister insisted that compensation was essential. Althorp urged Western to leave repeal of the tax on agricultural horses to ministers, 13 May, and approved the principle of the bill to prevent the payment of labourers' wages from the poor rates and of the anatomy bill, 15 May, when he did not get to bed until four next morning. He encouraged O'Connell privately and voted to allow him to take his seat unhindered, 18 May.[108] He opposed Hume's motion for a fixed duty on corn imports, 19 May, arguing that the 1828 sliding scale deserved a fair trial. He spoke and voted against the 'most wasteful' Buckingham House expenditure, 25 May. When Rosslyn took office as lord privy seal that month, Althorp remarked to his father that while he had 'no objection to any Whig joining the present ministry, if he can do so in such company as will enable him to have some degree of influence in the cabinet', he thought Rosslyn 'unwise'. He also expressed his disapproval of James Scarlett's* becoming attorney-general.[109] On a visit to the Arbuthnots at Woodford in mid-June, he had 'some political conversation' with Charles, whose wife recorded:

> He is a very honest, good kind of man but a weak liberal in politics, and certainly not a man whose support I would ever seek. He is, however, the sort of head of a party in the ... Commons who pretend to stand aloof and see what the ministers will do, and act accordingly and talk of the government strengthening themselves; that is to say, taking some of them in ... I heard him say ... the government was too weak in the ... Commons to go on as it was, and I remarked to him that, if everybody was to go on his principle of standing aloof, it was no wonder the government was weak ... To [Arbuthnot] he said that in the ... Lords the government would do perfectly, that the duke managed it excessively well and was very strong, but that in the Commons they had no party or power at all ... that his party considered the taking of Lord Rosslyn as a demonstration of cordiality towards them, but that they thought nothing of Scarlett ... He pretended that his party did not require offices (this is true as regards himself individually), though they would all have joined in a body if Lord Grey had come in; but he let out that the way to have them was to put one of their body in the ... Commons into the cabinet and to make Brougham *master of the rolls*![110]

News of this encounter apparently worried the king, who became 'alarmed at the idea of having more

Whigs forced upon him'; but Wellington knew better. Lord Camden thought that if the ministry could not conciliate the Ultras, they 'must get a few Whigs', including 'the Althorp people'.[111] To Brougham, 17 June 1829, Althorp gave his view on 'the state of the ministry', encouraging Brougham to say something about it in the House before the end of the session:

> They are so weak that they are unfit to govern ... I am doubtful whether it might not be expedient to say that, with every wish not to oppose them ... unless something is done to strengthen their hands before the next session, we shall feel it our duty not to allow the country to remain in such inefficient hands, if we can prevent it ... A great deal depends on the real wishes of the duke ... If he wishes to form a junction with us, and is only prevented by the bad humour of the king, it is perhaps the most prudent thing to say nothing. If ... he is absurd enough to think he can govern without the ... Commons, a gentle notice of this kind might tend to bring him to his senses ... I am rather, on the whole, inclined to think that they are favourably disposed.[112]

Althorp was outraged by Scarlett's instigation of *ex-officio* prosecutions of newspapers for libels of Wellington at the end of 1829.[113] In January 1830, when the Whig organizer Edward Ellice* identified 'the *Watchers* under Althorp' as one of four parties in the Commons (the others being 'government', 'Canningites' and 'Ultras'), he argued in favour of raising these prosecutions and some foreign policy issues on the first day, while avoiding specific motions on them which might 'involve ourselves in confederacy with the Ultra Tories and turn out the ministry, which, weak and inefficient as it undoubtedly is, is probably the best that under present circumstances we can hope for'. At the same time, he could not 'see how they can stand through the session'. Towards the end of the month he told Russell that he would support the government if Grey was a member of it, but Russell deemed this unlikely.[114] According to George Fortescue*, a notion of 'us Whigs ... organizing ourselves under the joint leadership of Althorp and Brougham' had been abandoned 'for the present'.[115] Althorp took a risk by dividing for the Ultra Knatchbull's amendment to the address, because it failed to stress the extent and severity of distress, 4 Feb. 1830, but he was careful to praise the ministry for carrying emancipation and to dissociate himself from the Ultras' agenda. A number of leading Whigs voted with government.[116] He voted for the transfer of East Retford's seats to Birmingham, 11 Feb., and again, 5 Mar., when he declared his support for the ballot to diminish 'the illegitimate influence of fear', but rebuked O'Connell for his condemnation of the aristocracy. He was in O'Connell's minority of 21 for incorporating the ballot in the East Retford bill, 15 Mar. Howick had found him 'very much inclined to oppose the government', but utterly 'hostile' to the Huskissonites, 14 Feb.[117] Next day he spoke and voted for Hume's motion for a large reduction in taxes, though he endorsed ministers' refusal to tinker with the currency. He called for repeal of the beer duty, 16 Feb., and reduction of the malt duty, 2 Mar. He could not go the whole way with Hume in army economies, 19 Feb., and welcomed those proposed by ministers, as far as they went; but he divided in small minorities that day and on 22 Feb. for less severe cuts than in Hume's original plan. His amendment to Lord Blandford's reform scheme, which stated the desirability of change, was negatived, 18 Feb., but he voted in the minority when Blandford divided the House. He voted silently for the enfranchisement of Birmingham, Leeds and Manchester, 23 Feb., and to receive the Newark petition complaining of the duke of Newcastle's improper electoral interference, 1 Mar. Next day he damned the press prosecutions as 'imprudent', but conceded that Scarlett had not exceeded his brief. Althorp, who thought the Commons was 'in a strange state', told Grey, 19 Feb., that 'if the ministers have strength enough to carry their measures I am very well satisfied to let them stay where they are'; but he felt that 'a ministry doing nothing' was 'nearly as bad' as one 'doing what is wrong'. Yet he gave them credit for genuinely believing that they had gone as far as was safe in military retrenchment.[118] He and Brougham intervened to prevent Graham from bringing on a motion criticizing the appointment of a treasurer of the navy, wanting Wellington to 'feel his weakness on reform' but 'not to carry a vote against him which might have the effect of overturning his administration, without any security as to what would succeed'; Grey washed his hands of this. But a few days later Grey's brother-in-law Lord Durham (Lambton) told Althorp, who included himself among the 'many in the ... Commons' who 'would not be supporters of any government' excluding Grey, that Grey 'reposed more confidence in him personally and those who acted with him, than in any other party'; Althorp seemed 'greatly pleased' to hear this.[119] At noon on 3 Mar. 1830, at the instigation of the influential backbenchers Edward Berkeley Portman II and Francis Lawley, there was a meeting at Althorp's Albany rooms of 27 Members, who included five county Members, Russell, Fazakerley, Howick and Henry Warburton of the 'Mountain'. They sought to 'form a party under the guidance of Lord Althorp with a view to take off some of the most oppressive taxes'. The Huskissonite Littleton commented cynically that

Althorp and Brougham between them had 'paralyzed the Whig party' and that the promoters of the meeting wanted to 'bind Althorp down to a certain line of conduct':

> But this object is only to be compassed in a manner flattering to Althorp, who is a vain man. He is a person of great respectability and purity of character, public and private, and withal rich in connection. Otherwise he has no qualifications ... except his industry.

'Very little was done', as Howick noted, because most of those present would not swallow a property tax, which Althorp favoured. However, he agreed to become leader for the purpose of promoting tax cuts if at least 45 Members turned up to a similar meeting planned for the 6th. He also wished to consult Brougham, Graham and Russell, whose blessing he obtained.[120] Over 60 Members attended on the 6th, when, according to Howick, there was again much disagreement, but it was resolved 'not to attempt any union with any other party and to endeavour as far as possible to promote every measure of economy'.[121] Althorp reported to Grey:

> The principle of the junction is that it is to extend only to measures of retrenchment and reduction of taxes. On all other points we are to continue as much disunited as ever. We have determined not on any pretence to hold any intercourse with the Tory or Canning party previous to measures being brought forward, but to support anything brought forward by either ... with perfect cordiality, if it comes within the principle of our union. I am to take occasion to state this determination ... before Goulburn brings forward his budget, in the hope – a vain one I fear – that it may have some influence ... There was so much variety of opinion in our meeting on ... [the 3rd], that I almost expected that the result of today would be to dissolve it; but today there was less difference of opinion, and I now hope that some good may be effected.[122]

In the House, 8 Mar., Althorp indicated that 'a union had been formed' to promote 'economy and reduction of taxes', but stressed that this party had no wish to turn ministers out.[123] Grey told Howick that he thought the 'object ... very laudable', but that he doubted 'the policy of avowing such a combination formally in the House and would have preferred to 'let it be seen and felt'. He went on:

> I quite approve of your connecting yourself with Althorp, of whose good sense and honour and integrity I have a high opinion. But I should doubt his having all the requisites for management of such a concern, above all readiness to take his part on the spur of the occasion and firmness to assert it by a direct, simple and open line of conduct.

Grey argued that ultimately the only feasible and creditable basis for a party was its projection as an alternative government to one which it opposed as inadequate; but he ruled himself out as too tired and old (66) to take office.[124] On 9 Mar. Althorp spoke and voted for reduction of the volunteers grant and, while dismissing Wilmot Horton's motion to consider the poor laws in committee of the whole House, admitted that they needed attention: those who married unwisely and procreated intemperately should be rendered worse off than the prudent. On 11 Mar. 1830 he left London to attend the Nothamptonshire county meeting called to petition for relief from distress and reform, having told Brougham the previous day:

> We hear that from two to two and a half millions of taxes will be the reduction proposed. I think they might safely take from four to five without substituting any tax, assuming that they can reduce the four per cents ... It is impossible to expect a comprehensive view of our finances, which alone will do any good, from our present financial ministers ... Huskisson undertook last night to move upon pensions ... I should have preferred this motion being in the hands of one of our own men, because I have no great confidence in Huskisson's spirit of economy; but still it is good to have him committed to the cause.[125]

Lady Spencer was 'happy' to hear Althorp say that 'since he has been in Parliament, he has never felt so much interest, never been so satisfactorily employed, never so conscious of having been so useful, nor ever been so capable, as to health, of his work sitting light upon him, as he feels himself at present'.[126]

On Goulburn's budget statement, 15 Mar. 1830, Althorp concurred in his assertion that the sinking fund was not a breach of faith with creditors and approved his selection of taxes for repeal, but thought he could have gone further. He supported Slaney's poor law amendment bill. When Cartwright presented the Northamptonshire distress petition, as that of the sheriff, 16 Mar., Althorp claimed that a more radical one for reform had had a majority. There had been another meeting at his rooms that morning, 'more numerously attended and less divided in opinion than the former ones'. More took place as the session progressed.[127] Althorp refused to support Davenport's motion on the state of the nation, 18 Mar., because it hinged on revision of the currency and was 'a direct censure' of ministers, whom he praised for declining to court popularity by interfering with the sugar duties. Howick thought he 'spoke ... well', while Lord Ellenborough, a member of the cabinet, heard that his tone was 'very friendly'.[128] He presented a Wellingborough petition for mitigation of the criminal code, 19 Mar. Next day he was in a deputation of nine who had an interview with Wellington and Goulburn on the banking system; and a week later he talked privately to Goulburn about the leather tax.[129] In the House, 22 Mar., he urged Goulburn to couple repeal of the malt and beer duties and spoke and voted for cuts in items of the navy estimates. On the 24th he told Thomas Francis Kennedy*:

> We are in a strange state; acting together pretty well and likely to do so better; but without any party views at all. I never saw people more inclined to be honest, and it is the first time I believe that a party could be brought to act together on an avowed principle of neutrality without any prospect of individual ambition.[130]

Supporting his protégé Poulett Thomson's motion for a revision of taxation, for which he was a minority teller, 25 Mar., he declared his preference for a property tax; but this, in Howick's view, 'frightened away' a 'great many of our own people' and reduced the minority to 78.[131] He approved the principle of Goulburn's plan to convert the four per cents, but spoke and voted against the Bathurst and Dundas pensions, 26 Mar. He acquiesced in the grant for a new naval hospital at Malta, 29 Mar., but supported Graham's bid to abolish the office of lieutenant-general of the ordnance. He divided for inquiry into crown lands revenues, 30 Mar. 1830.

After Easter he presented a Kettering petition for abolition of the death penalty for forgery, 26 Apr.; he voted to that effect, 24 May 1830. He divided with O'Connell for reform of Irish vestries, 27 Apr., and with the now resurgent opposition for inquiry into the Terceira affair, 28 Apr. Next day he explained his current views on the debtors laws, which turned on his wish to treat 'the unavoidably unfortunate' less harshly while bringing to book the 'fraudulent or willfully extravagant'. He gave his 'warmest support' that day to Brougham's scheme to establish cheap local courts. He spoke and voted for cuts in the ordnance estimates, 30 Apr., and the public buildings grant, 3 May. He was a majority teller for repeal of the usury laws, 6 May. 'Nearly satisfied' that the Irish lord lieutenancy should be abolished, he divided with Hume to consider this, 11 May. He did not think there were sufficient grounds for censuring the Irish solicitor-general John Doherty* over the Cork conspiracy trials and voted accordingly, 12 May,[132] but next day he supported repeal of the Irish coal duties. He endorsed and was a minority teller for Graham's motion for a return of privy councillors' emoluments, 14 May, and was a minority teller for one to reform Irish first fruits revenues, 18 May. He divided for Jewish emancipation, 17 May. He was willing to accept a salary of £5,000

for Welsh judges, but hoped it might be reduced to £4,000, 18 May. He spoke and voted for giving Canada an independent legislature, 25 May, and for inquiry into the revenue and expenditure of Ceylon, 27 May. Next day he refused to support O'Connell's radical reform motion because universal suffrage would ensure that 'one class alone will return the representatives', though he was content with triennial parliaments and the ballot. He divided silently for Russell's more moderate plan. He voted to reduce the grant for consular services, 11 June, and supported various cuts in colonial establishments, 14 June. On William IV's accession message, 30 June, he objected to hasty acquiescence in its contingent regency proposals and moved an adjournment, but was beaten by 185-139. His amendment that the House should complete the ordinary business of the session before the dissolution was rejected by 193-146; he was cross with Brougham for his 'violent' attack on Peel, which, he told Spencer, had 'split us into every sort of bad temper, quarrel and jealousy'.[133] He protested again at the precipitate dissolution, 2 July. He supported Robert Grant's motion on the regency, 6 July 1830, but he had not wanted a division on it and was not surprised when it was 'well beaten' (247-93). He told Spencer, 'I am happy to say that I shall not put my foot in the ... Commons any more this Parliament'.[134]

Althorp had drawn closer to Grey, who had shaken off his selfish indolence, during the second half of the session. In mid-May 1830 they talked of the possibility of an approach from Wellington, or even the formation of a new ministry, when the new reign began. According to Howick, Althorp 'said he should prefer not being in office, but if my father made it a *condition* he would consent'.[135] Mrs. Arbuthnot did not think Wellington would 'ever consent to try Lord Grey', but reckoned that Althorp 'would be the most powerful man for us to gain in the ... Commons'; and the minister Sir Henry Hardinge* thought he might be put at the board of trade, with Hobhouse at the exchequer, if Goulburn became Speaker.[136] Arbuthnot heard from Althorp's maternal uncle Lord Lucan that his (and Grey and Brougham's) aim at the beginning of July was 'not to break down the government' but to compel Wellington and Peel to turn to them 'for strength'. He reported that as late as 2 July Althorp had 'told Lucan that he feared the junction was now impossible, but that he was staying in London, not to excite further enmity, but to try to prevent it'.[137] In fact, on 4 July about 60 Members, including Brougham, Hobhouse, Graham and Hume, met at Althorp's and resolved to form after the elections a 'systematic' and 'vigorous opposition' with a view to turning out the government if they had not strengthened themselves by the time Parliament met. They ruled out coalition with the Huskissonites 'at present'.[138] The size of the ministerial majority on the regency question had convinced Althorp that the duke had no intention of recruiting from the opposition groups, and he reflected that 'I shall not be put to any difficulty about refusing office'.[139] Abercromby was 'very much pleased with what I hear of the union of the Whigs', adding that Althorp 'has his faults, but there is no more honest man, and it is always a cause of regret to me when ... he does not get all the help he might have'.[140] Richard Monckton Milnes[†] quoted to his sister the opinion of 'a very acute' observer that Althorp was 'certainly the most rising man in the House, and to whose party a young man ought to attach himself if he meant to stick by any party'.[141] Althorp busied himself with some electoral activities, which included chairing Hume's Middlesex committee and appearing (to no avail) at St. Albans, where his family had an interest, in support of Henry Gally Knight*. His own election, with Cartwright, was uneventful.[142]

Soon afterwards Poulett Thomson, wondering who might take up reform vigorously in the Commons in the wake of events in France, discounted Brougham and Graham and could 'see but Althorp, who from station ... character and ... honesty can do it', though 'his modesty and diffidence prevent his using all the power which he possesses'.[143] Althorp himself told Lord Ebrington*, 29 Aug. 1830, that he had agreed to 'continue' next session 'the arrangement which existed last' for meetings and concert, but did not

> conceal from myself that the difficulty of my situation will be very much increased. If I could back out I would, but I cannot ... I was ... just a little surprised at seeing you had said [in Devon] you were not opposed to the ministers, for I thought everyone must agree that they are so weak that they cannot carry on the government ... I shall on this ground declare open war when Parliament meets. I fear Brougham is likely to be more violent than in prudence he ought ... Perhaps both he and myself are more disgusted with the administration than others, from having been witness to the shabbiness ... of their conduct to ... Grey. My private opinion is that they are quite incapable from ability, as well as through weakness in numbers, to carry on ... the ... duke is as incapable as executing his office as any of the rest, while ... it is impossible to put any confidence in his integrity. How much of this it will be prudent to disclose is another thing.[144]

Althorp was reported by Brougham in late September, after Huskisson's death, to be keen on a junction with his followers; but two of these, Lords Palmerston* and Melbourne, told Holland that they 'did not feel any great confidence in the discretion' of either man.[145] On 5 Oct. Althorp informed Brougham that he would be in London on the 26th to discuss tactics:

> I am inclined to ground our opposition to the government *mainly, if not entirely*, on their total inefficiency. I think the thing most to be avoided, is the giving people an opportunity of saying that we were very moderate and mealy-mouthed as long as there was a chance of the duke ... taking us in, but that now we despair of this we are become violent ... We ought to be cautious how we urge anything against the ministers which might have been equally well brought forward last session. I should also be for giving them more credit for the quickness with which they acceded to the wishes of the people in acknowledging Louis Philippe.[146]

Privately, he still feared that Brougham would not 'confine his attack ... to such topics as will be intelligible to the country'. He also lamented the 'great scrape' into which his kinsman Lord Exeter had got himself by turning out hostile Stamford electors, which might oblige Althorp to 'vote against him on some violent resolution': 'it really appears as if grandees never could learn anything by looking at what was going on'.[147] Althorp, who was described by James Macdonald*, 22 Oct., as 'frightened and shrinking from his own position, but quite as hostile' to government as Brougham and Graham, organized on 31 Oct. an Albany meeting of Whigs 'to concert measures'. Howick recorded:

> It was not very numerously attended, but there was much less difference of opinion than at any of those last year. Althorp began by saying that at the beginning of the last session he had been unwilling to do anything which might have the effect of driving out the government, but that in consequence of its inefficiency and the apparent determination of the duke not to strengthen it he had no longer any such feeling ... It was agreed that retrenchment and parliamentary reform were to be our great objects ... Althorp ... gave notice that John Russell meant ... to give notice of the renewal of his motion for giving representatives to the three great towns, but the feeling of all present was so strongly expressed that such a motion as not going far enough ought not to be made that he engaged to write to John Russell to induce him to give it up.[148]

Althorp gave his own view of the meeting to Milton, 2 Nov.:

> We agreed for war against the ministry, but ... to be conducted in a reasonable manner. I am therefore to say today that I have no confidence in the government, but that if they propose good measures they may depend upon our support ... If ... any vote is proposed to which we feel favourable but which if carried would have the effect of removing the administration, this last circumstance will by no means prevent us from giving it our

support. Brougham is in a much more controllable state than he was.[149]

He duly spoke in these terms on the address later that day, approving the promise of economies and advocating 'extensive' parliamentary reform. Howick considered the speech 'injudicious', in that Althorp ought to have moved an amendment on the foreign policy element, but he accepted that he probably felt 'bound by [what] was agreed the other day'. John Campbell II, a new Member, told his brother that 'there is a better speaker than Lord Althorp in every vestry in England'.[150] On 7 Nov. Althorp discussed 'reform and the present situation of affairs' with Grey and Howick, and at dinner at Brougham's that evening with Smith Stanley, Denman, Hobhouse, Macdonald, Graham and Howick settled that the first major division would be on Brougham's reform motion on the 16th.[151] After presenting Dissenters' anti-slavery petitions, 8 Nov., he asked Peel to explain 'one of the most alarming events that I have ever known', the cancellation of the king's visit to the City. Next day he 'walked about some time' with Hobhouse, who described him as 'an excellent person, too good for a party man. He told me he should retire from public life the moment he got into the "Hospital for Incurables"'.[152] After a 'small party meeting' which 'went through lists of the House of Commons with reference to the reform motion', 12 Nov.,[153] he condemned Goulburn's 'confused arrangement for the civil list', voted in the minority of 39 to reduce the duty on West Indian wheat imports and supported the Irish Subletting Act amendment bill. On 13 Nov. he hosted a 'very unanimous' meeting of 'above 90 Members', which settled the terms of Brougham's motion. Next day he told Milton that he expected to 'divide 200 on it', but knew 'we shall be beaten pretty hollow'. Yet

> I never saw such a change in opinion on any question ... I used to think it never could be carried, but now I think that an administration favourable to it may effect it. I cannot at present foresee what will happen to the ministry. I hardly think we shall be able to carry any question which will have the immediate effect of turning them out, but still I do not think it possible they can carry on the business of the ... Commons ... I do not ... think there is any real danger [of insurrection], but people generally are much alarmed ... I can only write a political letter for I have nothing else in my head.[154]

He spoke and was a minority teller for Parnell's motion for inquiry into the 'monstrous' civil list, which brought the ministry down, 15 Nov. He was named to the select committee. He condemned the 'Swing' rioters, 18 Nov. 1830.

Grey, charged with forming a government, offered Althorp the premiership, which he flatly rejected. Grey browbeat him into becoming chancellor of the exchequer and leader of the Commons (on which Palmerston, the foreign secretary, deferred to him), by saying that otherwise he would give up the commission. Althorp consented with 'great reluctance' and on condition that he should not be asked to succeed Grey as prime minister and that Brougham must be persuaded to take the lord chancellorship rather than the mastership of the rolls, which would have made him a dangerous loose cannon in the Commons. He persuaded Brougham to swallow this and was also credited with securing the appointment of Poulett Thomson as Lord Auckland's efficient deputy at the board of trade.[155] Greville wrote on 1 Dec. 1830 that 'nobody expects much' from Althorp as a finance minister 'from anything that is already known about him'; and he certainly struggled in that role.[156] Croker thought that as leader of the House, where he was one of the worst speakers among those who regularly addressed it, he would be Palmerston's 'puppet'. Although he genuinely 'detested office' (he later told Russell that 'every morning when he woke, while he was in office, he wished himself dead') he confounded his critics and came to command through his unaffected 'sincerity' and capacity to inspire trust, plus his remarkably equable temperament, great influence and respect in the House.[157]

A week after the fall of the Wellington ministry Althorp wrote to Milton:

> The accounts from the country are very bad and certainly we come into office in as difficult a time as men ever had to engage with ... Attention to politics is a dangerous duty, and to no one ... more ... than to myself. I have a weakish head and a great inclination to please people, and I am therefore as likely as any man that ever came into office to do great jobs. I hope ... and ... feel sure that allowance must be made for the temptations in which we are placed. I am only placed in it because I thought that it was an imperative duty upon me to take office. And had I not thought so I should at the present moment be a happier man. I must however now buckle to and forget what I was and what my pursuits were ... I have hoisted the standard of reform in my advertisement to the freeholders of Northamptonshire.[158]

He was triumphantly re-elected on 6 Dec. 1830,[159] and in the House next day assured Parnell and Peel that ministers intended to look closely at the civil list and supported the principle of Lord Chandos's game bill. On 9 Dec. he said that the 'great evil' afflicting Ireland was 'the want of capital', but he thought O'Connell's remedial plan was too cumbersome. He secured the appointment of a select committee (which he chaired) on salary reductions, evincing the new ministry's determination to enforce 'the most rigid economy'. He defended the composition of the committee, 10 Dec., and, explaining the government's decision not to stop the trades' procession to St. James's Palace, caused a stir by extolling the tricolour as the symbol of the 'glorious' French revolution of July 1830.[160] He obtained a vote of credit of £100,000 to tide over the civil list till next session. He refuted charges that the government had already demonstrated its indifference to the problems of Ireland and asked for time, 11 Dec. On the 13th he declared that slavery should be abolished as soon as possible, but with due regard to the education and improvement of the slaves, and that ministers had no intention of fiddling with the currency. He defended the appointment of a chancellor of the duchy of Lancaster (Holland) and lord privy seal (Durham). He clashed with O'Connell over Irish pensions and judicial appointments and, while assuring Hume that he wished to 'relieve the country as much as possible from the ... dead weight' pension fund, disagreed with his contention that all military promotion should cease. Moving for a supply of £1,850,000 for the deficiency of 1830, he promised to try to keep down the 1831 estimates, but 'warned that inflated public expectations on this score were almost certain to be disappointed'. He had to tell Hume that ministers had been obliged to increase the army by 7,000 men, not because they wanted 'to govern by military, but in consequence of the disorders in the country'. On 14 Dec. he opposed Hume's motion for a select committee on truck payments as 'dangerous' in the circumstances of the manufacturing districts, and endorsed in principle Littleton's bill to abolish them. He confirmed that Bishop Phillpotts of Exeter would not be allowed to hold the living of Stanhope *in commendam* and said his reverence for the Church of England only intensified his 'regret' at the `abuses' which undermined it, 15 Dec. He persuaded the O'Gorman Mahon to drop his 'insidious' motion to name Irish magistrates who had been bankrupts. He did not oppose the withholding of the Evesham writ, as the Tories wished, even though he thought Peel's cited precedents were unconvincing, 16 Dec. The following day he received a devastating blow when he was called out of a cabinet meeting to be told that news had arrived of the death of his brother Robert from 'inflammation of the bowels' on board ship off Egypt on 4 Nov. This put him in 'a terrible state' and robbed him of all appetite for the House for a week; Palmerston deputized for him.[161] On 23 Dec., when he was 'tolerably well', he moved the adjournment of the House until 3 Feb. 1831 and fielded ques-

tions on a variety of subjects, but failed this time to prevent the O'Gorman Mahon from carrying his motion on bankrupt Irish magistrates.[162] On 28 Dec. he told Milton that his parents had 'borne their severe loss uncommonly well' and that

> the constant stretch in which my mind is kept very soon overcame the first terrible shock ... The necessity for the exertion very soon enabled me to make it. Our task is a very difficult one. At present we are very popular, but I suppose when it is seen how little we can do our popularity will be at an end. With respect to the corn laws, nothing can be done with them in an unreformed ... Commons. If we carry reform, as I feel pretty confident we can ... then will be the time for us to do good; till then we can only nibble at the various abuses of the present system. I have been a pretty strenuous advocate for reform a good while, but I never knew half the importance [of] and necessity for it till I became a minister.[163]

Robert Price* had told Milton, 15 Dec.:

> Althorp bears ... [the Commons] well, and puts down opposition by a conduct as plain and straightforward as that we used to see him display when sitting on the other side ... but still he is evidently annoyed by a want of confidence too early shown, and I believe, if he could have his choice would soon again be an independent Member and out of office.[164]

Next day Creevey informed Miss Ord, 'You have no conception how our *Clunch* is distinguishing himself in his *speaking* as well as honesty'.[165] Rumours persisted that he was unhappy in office and would soon go out, but the general Whig view was that he was 'doing excellently well'.[166] On Christmas Day 1830 Holland reported to Lord George William Russell* that Althorp had 'really done wonderfully ... and has gained character as a speaker as well as answered fully to the expectation formed of him as a man and a minister'; but Ellice, a born pessimist, thought Althorp and Grey were too complacent.[167]

Althorp had set his treasury team to work on tax collection and superannuations at the beginning of December 1830.[168] His well-intentioned attempts to prune the civil list quickly ran into trouble on the problem of life pensions granted by George IV, which had technically lapsed on his death. Althorp considered them to be debts of honour, which had to be continued, as William IV insisted. He also found the king reluctant to accept too radical an overhaul of the list, though he approved the removal of diplomatic salaries to the consolidated fund.[169] When he outlined his proposals to the House, 4 Feb. 1831, in what was generally thought to be a poor and garbled speech (he apologized, 17 Feb., for having 'mystified' the subject), he was attacked by Hume, and there was 'great disappointment' on the government back benches at the 'meagre' savings. Brougham urged him to make significant cuts in the list, in defiance of the king, but Althorp would not give way and threatened to resign.[170] Holland, however, thought that 'the unpopularity of the measure does not seem to shake the confidence and respect felt for ... [Althorp] both in and out of doors'.[171] On 7 Feb. he defended reduction of the barilla duty, an 'error' inherited from the Wellington ministry. (George Traill*, who had seen him privately on this subject, had found him 'a very fair and candid person, and quite unassuming and frank in his deportment'.)[172] Althorp had reported in mid-January that 'the state of Ireland is getting as bad as possible', that the government might be 'forced to adopt some very violent measures' and that O'Connell 'must be put down'. Yet a week later he expressed 'doubts of the legality of O'Connell's arrest' and surmised that if it proved to be illegal, ministers would be obliged to 'strike our colours, which to me at least, will be a most agreeable result': 'if I am once turned out', he told Spencer, 'they will have some difficulty in catching me again'.[173] In the House, 8 Feb., he answered the O'Gorman Mahon's furious rant against the Irish proclamation and O'Connell's arrest, stood by his view that O'Connell had been inciting violence and stated the government's determination to uphold the law and maintain the Union while pursuing measures of conciliation. On 10 Feb. he said that 'the whole system of colonial expenditure is vicious, and requires a strict investigation'. He now declared his dissent from Chandos's game bill, which obliged him to bring in an alternative. His first budget, presented as 'a bold experiment', 11 Feb., when he admitted that he was 'wholly unaccustomed to the statement of long financial details', was a humiliating botch. He proposed to repeal or reduce taxes on coals, slates, newspapers, candles, tobacco, glass and printed calicoes, which would yield a net saving of about £3,000,000. To balance the accounts, he planned to end colonial preference in the timber and wine duties, tax imports of raw cotton, coal exports and steamboat journeys, and, controversially, to impose a half per cent tax on transfers of real and funded property.[174] The House's initial reaction was favourable, but Goulburn attacked the whole plan (details of which had clearly been leaked) and made a strong case against the transfer tax as a 'breach of national faith'.[175] The City was soon in an uproar about it, and it became obvious that it could not be carried through the Commons. Althorp convened a meeting of over 200 Members and City men, 13 Feb., and reported to Grey afterwards:

I think we must give way. Now as to going out, I have considered it maturely, and though personally I should not be disinclined to do it, yet upon the very same principles which induced me to come in, I think we are bound to stay, if we can, till we have tried the question of reform. I think our going out just now would be producing the greatest possible danger, therefore we cannot be justified in doing so. I think the right way to retreat is to say that my opinion remains unchanged, but that I find I cannot carry it and therefore must give it up.

He offered his own resignation, but Grey refused to accept it.[176] On 14 Feb. Althorp had what Grey admitted to the king was the 'mortifying' task of announcing the abandonment of the transfer tax, which he said would oblige him to make other adjustments to the budget scheme.[177] Greville wrote:

A more miserable figure was never cut than his; but how should it be otherwise? A respectable country gentlemen, well versed in rural administration, in farming and sporting, with all the integrity of £15,000 a year in possession and £50,000 in reversion, is all of a sudden made leader in the ... Commons without being able to speak, and chancellor of the exchequer without any knowledge, theoretical or practical, of finance. By way of being discreet, and that his plan may be a secret, he consults nobody: and then he closets himself with his familiar Poulett Thomson, who puts this notable scheme into his head, and out he blurts it in the House ... without an idea of how it will be received, without making either preparations for defending it or for an alternative in case of its rejection ... The opposition cannot contain themselves.[178]

The Tory Thomas Gladstone* felt that Althorp had blundered 'in introducing what he was not determined to stand up to' and by failing to 'consult any of the authorities usually and naturally consulted on such occasions'.[179] Arbuthnot was delighted to see 'that Jacobin Lord Althorp ... in so great a scrape'.[180] But Holland told Lord Granville on 15 Feb. that while 'poor Althorp' had been 'discomfited', the 'retreat ... has been admirably conducted' and 'we have as firm a seat and as willing and powerful a horse as before'.[181] Althorp's humiliation was not over, however, for he was besieged by disgruntled cotton manufacturers, who persuaded him to reduce the tax on raw cotton imports. He also had to surrender the reduction of duties on tobacco and glass to make up for the loss of the transfer tax, and he made concessions on Cape wines and the steamboat tax. He defended himself in the House, 17 Feb., when he acquiesced in Parnell's motion for a public accounts select committee; but in private he was evidently still despondent and lamenting his own inadequacy. Brougham, who was never prone to self-doubt, urged him to stop his 'absurd' self-pity, to 'give up *abusing* yourself' and to 'borrow a little of Peel's' self-delight and approbation'.[182] The civil list and budget fiascoes damaged the government and Althorp's reputation.[183] The political economist McCulloch reckoned that 'everybody is now satisfied that Althorp is utterly unfit for his situation', for 'with the best intentions in the world, and incorruptible honesty, he has no knowledge and no power of speaking'.[184] Greville claimed that 'even' the Whig Lord Sefton* 'now confesses that Althorp is wretched ... *leading* the ... Commons without the slightest acquaintance with the various subjects that come under discussion, and hardly able to speak at all'.[185] Bedford observed that Althorp was 'no great *financier*, though an excellent and well-meaning man'; and Tavistock conceded that the budget had 'damaged him as a financier' and would 'shake his influence', though not permanently.[186] When Hobhouse visited him with a deputation of calico tradesmen in late February, he thought he 'did not seem to know much about the matter'.[187] James Hope Vere* heard on 28 Feb. 'a very strange thing. Someone wanting to please the Countess Spencer remarked that he thought Lord Althorp had done very well. The reply was, "I should like to know how you would define what is meant by *very bad*"'.[188] Althorp opposed Chandos's motion for inquiry into West Indian distress and refused to budge on the sugar duties, 21 Feb., when he defended the 'judicious' increase in the army. Next day he endorsed the ministerial emigration scheme. He replied to Hume's criticisms of details of the navy estimates, 25 Feb. 1831, and on the 28th insisted that O'Connell's speeches in Ireland were 'calculated to excite sedition'. That day Creevey, noting favourable articles in *The Times* and the *Morning Herald*, judged that 'we are recovering by gentle degrees from Althorp. He has very nearly killed us, poor fellow, honest as he is, but it must be admitted that he has been damned conceited'.[189]

Althorp was not one of the committee of four (Russell, Durham, Graham and Duncannon) to whom the task of drafting the English reform bill was entrusted in late November 1830, but he and Grey had a close supervisory role. In the first instance, he drew up a set of minimum proposals, which included the disfranchisement of 100 'seats', of which 42 would go to unrepresented manufacturing towns, and a £10 householder franchise in the boroughs. He also wanted the ballot, and got Duncannon to advocate this in the committee's deliberations.[190] (Lord John Townshend could not fathom how 'such an able and judicious man' could support such a 'crotchet'.)[191] Although the ballot was abandoned in the final scheme, Althorp, who was reported in early January to be 'coaxing the ultra radi-

cals' by dining 'Maberly, Hume and others of that stamp, in small select parties', was broadly satisfied with it: he 'should not be afraid of going further', but thought 'it will do'. He was not sure that it had not 'given too much power to the land', but reflected that 'the great principle of the measure is that henceforward there will be no privileged class and, the power of the country being placed in the hands of the intelligence of the country, we may be satisfied that any improvements which may hereafter be required may be easily made, for there will be nobody interested to oppose them as the proprietors of boroughs now are'.[192] Littleton found the eve of session dinner at Althorp's, 3 Feb., 'amusing':

> I sat next to Althorp, whom I like more and more daily. He has more simplicity and honesty about him than any man I ever knew. He laughed at the badgerings he has had in Parliament and said he cared less about them than he could have imagined, talked about his farms and his calves ... and his not having a minute night or day to himself ... He spoke most satisfactorily on the cordiality and union of the cabinet. Reform is to be brought on by Lord John Russell ... The government have thought it due to him not to take the question out of his hands, Althorp said he had always considered himself a pretty good radical before, but that he was ten times more so now, since he had been in office and had a peep behind the curtain.[193]

Greville thought giving the introduction of the bill to Russell was a 'pretence' of a compliment to him, but was really an expedient to take the burden off Althorp, who was 'wholly unequal to it'; but Brougham believed that he was entirely qualified to handle the measure if necessary.[194] Presenting a large number of reform petitions, 26 Feb., Althorp said he had only taken office to effect reform, without which 'there is no security for good government'. He 'spoke out manfully' for the English reform bill, 1 Mar., as Hobhouse recalled: he said that it aimed to 'remove all cause for discontent', to 'satisfy the people, and so avert all danger of a revolution' and to 'place the election of Members in the hands of the middle classes'.[195] Thomas Gladstone thought he 'bungled through' his speech, 'but was better than usual'; and Arbuthnot was told that Althorp, who believed that Peel had blundered by not opposing the introduction of the bill, had informed 'a near relative' that 'he could now breathe again, that he had had a weight upon his mind not to be imagined, but that the introduction of their reform bill had now relieved him'.[196] The king was still making difficulties over the civil list, which Althorp had had referred to a committee upstairs.[197] On 7 Mar. he said he could hold out no expectation of further tax cuts and denied

Chandos's allegation that ministers were 'encouraging' Members to 'inflame the public mind', with reference to George De Lacy Evans's diatribe at the *Crown and Anchor*, which he deplored as 'violent and foolish'. Ellenborough was well wide of the mark in commenting, 10 Mar., that Althorp 'is alarmed now and has more reform than he wants'. That day he was unable in the 'circumstances' to support Warburton's bill to ban tobacco growing in Ireland, but said this must be terminated as soon as possible. He saw off Chandos's motion to reduce the sugar duties by 147-49, 11 Mar., but said on the 14th that he hoped to be able to assist West India proprietors by other means. He defended reduction of the barilla duties against the complaints of Scottish Members and explained the transfer of the steamboat tax from passengers to tonnage of vessels, 16 Mar. Next day he saw Traill on the contentious subject of the use of sugar in distilleries.[198] On 18 Mar. he reported that while ministers could not apply money to relieve Irish distress locally, they were considering the general problem. He presented his modified proposals for the timber duties, of which he was privately 'very proud', but he was accused by Herries of deception, and a factious combination of opponents defeated them by 236-190.[199] He carried the previous question against Inglis's motion accusing *The Times* of breach of privilege in libeling anti-reform Members, 21 Mar. He voted silently for the second reading of the reform bill next day. In an angry debate arising out of the Cambridge University petition against the measure, 24 Mar., he maintained that it was 'not revolutionary'. He would not compromise on the disfranchisement of 'rotten boroughs', but indicated that ministers were willing to reconsider individual cases if errors had occurred in the 1821 population returns. On 25 Mar. he proposed a civil list of £11,530 more than that recommended by the finance committee and carried it against Hume's half-hearted opposition.[200] He dismissed Vyvyan's taunt of inconsistency on the issue of indifference to popular opinion, 30 Mar., when he secured an advance of money for local and temporary Irish relief. His humiliation over the budget was still haunting him, and even Brougham was critical of him behind his back.[201] By arrangement with Ellice, he wrote 'a circular, which will have more effect than a common treasury note', to muster attendance for the committee stage of the reform bill, 7 Apr.[202] On that and the following day he discussed and settled with Graham, Duncannon and Durham 'all the alterations' to be made to the measure.[203] On 12 Apr. he accepted Goulburn's suggestion that the £10,000 proposed for civil list 'emergencies' should be doubled, and carried it by 44-10. He now emphatically

declared his support for Littleton's truck bill. Next day he explained that schedule A boroughs which had been found to have populations over 2,000 would be transferred to B, but that the changes entailed would be 'very small'; and that the plan to reduce the membership of the House to 596 would be maintained unless it proved to be impractical, though it was not 'essential'. Before securing the third reading of the civil list bill by 72-17 and defeating amendments proposed by Hume and Davies, 14 Apr., he clashed with Goulburn over the merits of their respective schemes. He obtained a grant of £100,000 for the queen's widowhood, 15 Apr., when he opposed Buxton's motion for the immediate abolition of slavery, preferring an amendment condemning the failure of the colonial assemblies to act on the 1823 amelioration resolution and threatening commercial reprisals. On the 18th he led for the government in opposing Gascoyne's wrecking amendment to the reform bill, that the number of English and Welsh Members should not be diminished, arguing that 'we can no longer go on with a system of representation which is defensible only by prescription'. Grey thought his speech was 'quite excellent' and had taken 'the right tone and stated truly that, on the decision on this question ... the fate of the bill really depended'; but Mackintosh, who remarked on 'some unwonted spirit in Althorp's speech', heard that he 'left it somewhat doubtful' whether the outcome was to be so considered.[204] Ellenborough was told that 'while in the lobby Althorp, thinking they had a majority, begged people to stay, that they might go into committee at once'; but in the event the government was defeated by 299-291.[205] On 21 Apr. 1831 Althorp refused to answer Vyvyan's question as to whether ministers had secured a dissolution because the House had refused to reduce the number of English Members and failed by 142-164 to block William Bankes's motion for an adjournment. Next day, according to Hobhouse, he 'stood silent and quite unmoved' amid the sound and fury (chiefly of Peel) which was terminated by the arrival of Black Rod; he later commented, 'well, I think I beat Peel in temper'.[206] Through no fault of his own, he was dragged into a 'hazardous', protracted and expensive contest for Northamptonshire, where Milton allowed himself to be nominated by the local reformers, which prompted the Tories to put up another man with Cartwright. Condemned unfairly for a breach of trust, Althorp answered vigorously on the hustings and in print; but his indignation with Milton was intensified by his friend's refusal to appear in person or to bear his share of the costs. He headed the poll, and brought Milton in with him.[207]

During this distraction Poulett Thomson had kept Althorp *au fait* with exchange rates and the state of the bullion market.[208] He approved Grey's firm resistance at the end of May 1831 to the king's pressure for modifications to be made to the reform bill in order to conciliate the Lords and, convinced that the new voting qualifications must be preserved intact, was relieved when it appeared that 'we shall keep the franchise as it is'.[209] The death of his mother on 8 June obliged him to observe the decencies, but did not much upset him.[210] As he had hoped, there was no division on the address, 21 June, when he replied 'with spirit' to Peel's condemnation of the dissolution.[211] Next day he told Hume that he intended to persevere with the duty on raw cotton and the adjustment of the wine duties, and O'Connell that government would only introduce poor laws to Ireland as a last resort. He defended the Irish yeomanry and got leave for his bill to end tobacco cultivation, 27 June. He gave his view that 'any attempt to remedy the evils of the poor laws, upon correct principles, must be attended by severe pressure on the poor', 28 June. On the 30th he conceded that the 1830 Sale of Beer Act had created difficulties, but stood by its principle. He also forced the withdrawal of Alderman Wood's 'censure' motion for a revision of salaries to 1797 levels; this pleased him, as it 'showed that our men were very steady'.[212] He endorsed the appointment of a select committee on the use of molasses in brewing and distilling and justified the establishment of an Irish public works board. He had confided to his father, 25 June, that Milton had been 'imprudent' in 'talking about the corn laws without any conversation with me'. He feared that Milton's notice of a repeal motion would be 'injurious to me in the ... Lords', where he was already anticipating defeat by over 20 votes for the reform bill, even leaving the bishops out of the calculation. He admitted to Spencer on the 30th that a 'blunder' in the bill, by which claimants to the vote were required to pay their rents at least half-yearly, would have to be 'rectified instantly'. He was happy with the state of the revenue, but afraid that it would be lowered by cholera quarantine. He expected a Commons 'majority of about 150 on the reform bill', but bitterly regretted having gone the previous evening to hear Paganini, who 'made every noise that could be made with a fiddle, and a great many more than I ever heard before, but ... [with] no pretence of a tune'.[213] He got his customs duties through 'very easily', 1 July, when he refuted as 'absurd' Hunt's attack on Grey's blatant nepotism. He was horrified, however, by the Irish arms bill, which Smith Stanley, the Irish secretary, had surreptitiously changed into 'one of the most tyrannical measures I

ever heard proposed'. He told his father, 'We must stand by Stanley, but we must tone down his measure'.[214] On 4 July, when he was becoming increasingly worried by the prospect of conflict between Belgium and Holland, he admitted the government's mistake over rent payment, but denied that the draftsman Gregson was responsible for it. He was anxious to get the reform bill as quickly as possible to the Lords, even though he was sure they would reject it. He anticipated (wrongly) defeat there on the proposal to appoint lord lieutenants of Irish counties, but reasoned that this, unlike the reform bill, was not a resignation issue, though he would 'throw no obstacle in the way of resigning' if his colleagues wished to do so: 'I hate my situation more and more every day, and really go down to the House ... as if I was going to execution'. (Littleton noted that 'when once in the *melee* of the House, he recovered his spirits'.)[215] He spoke for the second reading of the reintroduced reform bill, 5 July. He admitted that it was proving difficult to root out 'abuse' in the system of exchequer accounts, 8 July. On the 11th he carried his modified wine duties, which favoured Cape produce, and, replying to Wetherell's jibe that he had filled his speech with figures, said that if he would 'show me how to state sums, and subtract one from another without the introduction of figures, I shall be very much obliged to him'. He got through the grant for civil services, which included £75,000 for pensions, 18 July, opposed a motion for information on Brazilian captures of British ships, 19 July, and refused to acceded to De Lacy Evans's demand for the official papers relating to the Deacles' allegations against William Bingham Baring*, 21 July, thinking privately that this would 'increase my power in the House' and 'soften' Alexander Baring's opposition to reform.[216] He answered questions on the Belgian situation, defended the grant for the Society for the Propagation of the Gospels in the colonies as a temporary expedient and the increased subsidy for the militia, and proposed an issue of exchequer bills to promote public works, 25 July. He produced the king's message concerning provision for the duchess of Kent and Princess Victoria, and crushed Hunt's amendment to halve it by 223-0, 3 Aug. Next day he forced an alteration to the terms of Attwood's motion for a copy of the authority by which the additional duty on wines had been levied; he called it 'a kind of impeachment against me'. Worried by the 'critical state' of foreign affairs, he appealed unsuccessfully to Vyvyan to drop his intended motion, which would jeopardize national interests, 6 Aug.; but he subsequently got Vyvyan to oblige.[217] He rejected Peel's suggestion of an inquiry into the administration of justice in Ireland, 10 Aug., and reluctantly opposed printing the Waterford petition for disarming the yeomanry, to avoid intensifying the 'violent party feelings' which blighted that country. He defended the Irish lord lieutenants bill and public works loan, 15 Aug. He and Smith Stanley had a hostile reception when they met 50 Irish Members 'professedly friendly to our government' to explain their plan to store the arms of and regulate the yeomanry, 18 Aug.; and he subsequently recommended abandonment of the scheme.[218] On 22 Aug. he pushed through the Irish estimates and justified the reduction of duty on French wines. The following day he put the ministerial case on the Dublin election controversy. Behind the scenes he thwarted the lord steward Lord Wellesley's attempt to apply some of the money voted for the coronation to the civil list.[219] He announced the good news that French troops had been ordered to leave Belgium, 25 Aug. He carried by 64-52 the previous question against Sadler's proposal for legislation for the Irish poor, arguing that it would be 'insane' to adopt such a vague resolution. He made a concession on the wine duties, 1 Sept., and repudiated Hume's accusation that he had violated an agreement, 7 Sept.; but he gave way again, 12 Sept. He secured the third reading of the game bill, 2 Sept. On the 6th he told Hume that ministers were considering a fairer distribution of Irish church revenues and opposed Alderman Wood's motion to repeal the quarantine duties and Hunt's for an Act of Grace for crown debtors on the occasion of the coronation. He failed by 73-77 to stop a motion for inquiry into the effects on the West India interest of renewing the Sugar Refinery Act, 12 Sept., but refused to suspend business in view of the smallness of the majority. He forced on the bill by 125-113, 28 Sept. When Hunt proposed consideration of the corn laws, 15 Sept., Althorp endorsed Hume's moving of the previous question. That day he admitted to Herries that 'the greatest portion' of his February budget had now been 'given up', but claimed credit for the reduction of duties on coals, candles and calicoes. He opposed De Lacy Evans's motion for inquiry into the Deacles' case, 22 Sept., and on the 27th denied the truth of O'Connell's allegation that 'the affairs of Ireland have not been attended to by this House'. He explained the make-up of the £163,670 still required to complete the work on Windsor Castle and Buckingham House, 28 Sept. Next day he upheld the recommendation of the public salaries committee to reduce the pay of the president of the board of control to £3,500. He carried by 67-37 an amendment to Hobhouse's vestries bill, which raised the required majority to two-thirds, 30 Sept. His ways and means statement, 3 Oct., forecast a surplus revenue of £493,000. He reiterated his faith in tax cuts as the way forward. He secured the appointment of a select committee on the condition of the West Indian colonies, 6 Oct., and uneasily defended the bill to abolish the Scottish exchequer court and award the chief baron, Abercromby, a compensatory pension, 7 Oct. 1831.

Althorp's part in guiding the reform bill through the hot, stinking, fractious and sometimes riotous Commons, 12 July-14 Sept. 1831, restored his battered reputation as a parliamentarian and did him great credit. On 11 July he held 'an immense meeting of reformers' at the foreign office to urge them to hang together, 'never quit the House' and 'support the government by our votes rather than speeches'. He was cheered to the echo, but 'stupid' and ungrateful Milton declared his intention of moving various amendments.[220] On the 12th he opposed the first of a succession of factious adjournment motions: he told Spencer next day that 'the enemy have injured themselves very much', would 'certainly quarrel with one another' and would offer 'vexatious, but unskillful and inefficient' resistance.[221] He and Russell, backed by their large working majority, got the House into committee on schedule A on 13 July, when Althorp defended in passing the £10 householder franchise and three Member counties proposals. The following day he justified the population benchmark of under 2,000 for total disfranchisement of boroughs which could not be rescued from 'corrupt influence', and on 15 July he got rid of Agnew's attempt to group these boroughs on the Scottish model. Consideration of individual boroughs began that day, and on the 19th Althorp opposed Mackinnon's amendment to base the disfranchisement schedules on the recent 1831 census, arguing that using the 1821 returns would 'remove all suspicion of partiality'. There was sudden alarm in the cabinet at this time at reports that Spencer was in 'very precarious health'. Grey and others could see no adequate replacement for Althorp as leader, but the crisis passed as his father recovered.[222] On 21 July Althorp provoked a furore by proposing that the House should bind itself to give precedence to the reform bill on all order days. Peel and Williams Wynn protested strongly and Althorp backed down, conceding that there should be an understanding, not 'a standing order'. Hobhouse thought he had taken his characteristic 'patience' too far and that 'our treasury bench is over-meek'; but Ellenborough, who heard that Althorp had been 'frightened out of his monstrous proposition ... by mere looks of firmness', acknowledged that in general 'he puts his points shortly and clearly ... When his points are good, he adheres firmly to them. When they are bad, he gives them up at once'.[223] But

Campbell, who was still inclined to denigrate Althorp, wrote that his 'reasoning' in discussions of detail 'consisted of saying "I think" and "I am of opinion" that so and so is the case, and he attempted nothing else'.[224] Althorp 'approved ... individually' of Littleton's suggestion that a select committee should be appointed to consider the boundaries of constituencies, but failed to convince the cabinet.[225] On 26 July, he committed what he admitted in private was 'a blunder' on the case of Saltash, which was proposed for total disfranchisement. He admitted that the case for this was 'one of the weakest' and, not expecting a division, seemed to concede the justice of transferring the borough to schedule B, but in a 'very indistinct' fashion. Hunt forced a division, and the transfer was carried by 231-150, with Althorp himself in the majority, but at least three ministers in the minority of uncompromising reformers. The patronage secretary Ellice, according to Littleton, 'went home in a rage', and Althorp confessed to his father that 'our friends were very angry'. He sought to appease them by making a stout stand for the partial disfranchisement of Chippenham next day, when opposition mustered strongly, and he carried this by 251-181. He told Spencer, 28 July:

> I stand my work very well. The hot weather does better for the House ... than the cold because we have the windows all open and have therefore fresh air. The progress ... is terribly slow and the people are becoming terribly impatient. Their fury will be directed against the opposition, but they are also beginning to blame me for not doing what is impossible ... It is not quite agreeable to be found fault with by one's friends, but there is this advantage in the impatience of the people, that it will prove to the ... Lords that the feeling in favour of the bill is not diminished.[226]

On 29 July he asked Hobhouse, whom he was seeing about his factories regulation bill, 'how the devil shall we get on with the [reform] bill?' Hobhouse facetiously replied that 'one way was not to let the attorney-general [Denman] make bad speeches'.[227] In a bid to 'expedite' the bill later that day, he proposed that as the House would not sit on Monday, 1 Aug., on account of the king's City dinner, it should convene on Saturday, 30 July. There were protests, but he eventually got his way, at the cost of losing even more time. Duncannon complained to Hobhouse that 'it was as much as he could do to keep Althorp and Graham ... to the sticking point', as they were 'wishing to give up'.[228] Schedule B was completed (with a couple of cases left over for further consideration) on 2 Aug., when Althorp defended the schedule C enfranchisements, especially those of the metropolitan districts. On 4 Aug. he was obliged to oppose and defeat by 230-102

Milton's attempt to give the schedule D boroughs two Members each instead of one. Next day he explained that the boundary commissioners would be empowered to extend boroughs to create viable constituencies and, stressing ministers' desire to avoid differences of opinion with their supporters, said, 'We are anxious, as far as it is in our power, to make this measure final'. Russell's fragile health had given way, and on about 10 Aug., when the committee had reached schedule F (the Welsh boroughs), Althorp assumed sole overall management of the bill's progress. Macaulay told his sister that of the ministers in the Commons, only Althorp was 'not either useless or worse than useless'. On 13 Aug. Holland found him 'better pleased at the attendance of our friends and prospects of the bill than I expected, though he was nettled by attacks in *The Times* on his successful defence of the division counties (carried by 241-132) on the 11th.[229] The only committee defeat which he suffered occurred on 18 Aug., when Chandos's amendment to enfranchise £50 tenants-at-will in the counties was carried against him by 232-148. He advised Grey that it would be unwise to try to overturn or materially alter this decision, and on the 19th had the relevant clause temporarily withdrawn for adjustments to be made. In any case, the whole complicated issue of urban voters in the counties had been exercising the cabinet for weeks, as the initial draft clauses turned out to have many defects; and at one point Althorp was driven to talk of resignation if he had to convey yet another change of mind to the government's supporters. On 20 Aug. he secured the adoption of the revised borough freeholders clause, which was partly intended to counteract the impact of the Chandos amendment.[230] He crushed by 123-1 Hunt's bid to impose a general borough householder franchise, which he considered tantamount to universal suffrage, and defeated by 225-136 Davies's amendment to confine urban freeholder electors to the boroughs, 24 Aug. He accepted some minor adjustments to the £10 franchise, but on 26 Aug. said that he was 'satisfied that we have not gone in it a step too far', as 'it was absolutely necessary for us to adopt some systematic plan of voting ... founded on so extensive a basis as to satisfy the wishes ... of the great body of the people'. Campbell had observed to his brother that Althorp, 'like Bottom the weaver, will play all the parts himself'; but after 'several consultations' with him he admitted that 'he appears to more advantage than in the House' and seemed 'to know more law than some of his legal advisers'.[231] Littleton wrote, 26 Aug.:

> The temper, good nature, the firmness, the thorough understanding of all the points of legal difficulty in the clauses, exhibited by Althorp are admirable. In

great debate he is nothing. As he said to me yesterday, 'My memory then fails me – I forget my topics, but a committee is my forte'.[232]

Another observer praised the 'calm, unpretending good sense, excellent temper and gentlemanlike feelings' on which his authority over the House rested.[233] But on 25 Aug. Althorp revealed to Brougham the personal unhappiness concealed by his calm and businesslike demeanour:

My being in office is nothing more or less than misery to me ... I have nothing to compensate me. I take no interest in any of my work. I see all of you interested in what you are doing, looking forward to success ... and therefore recompensed for present vexations and fatigues by the hope of future satisfaction. I have no such feelings of hope ... the only thing I can look forward to ... is the time when, consistently with my duty, I can be relieved from a situation to the duties of which I know I am unequal. This ... gives me ... some advantages, because it prevents me from being so much irritated as other people are by disappointments and attacks; for instance, being told I am incapable and unfit for my place has no effect upon me at all. I only rather wish that everybody would be convinced of it, for then I should at once be relieved.[234]

Next day he wrote to his father:

Since I have taken the management of the reform bill into my own hands, I have been so overwhelmed with work that I have not had a moment to spare. We are going on slowly, but well, in the ... Commons. I fear we have but little chance in the ... Lords, making allowance even for any number of coronation peers which is consistent with decency. The danger from the rejection of the bill, and consequent dissolution of the ministry, is great; but the relief to me will be so enormous, that my patriotism is not sufficient to induce me to look forward to it with any other feeling but that of hope. I do not consider the danger to be so great as some people do. It will undoubtedly be very difficult to govern; but the people are so accustomed to obedience to the law, that I do not apprehend any actual tumult. I keep quite well. I was knocked up a good deal last night, for I had to speak so very often ... I fall asleep the instant I am in bed, and do not wake till I am called.[235]

Macaulay dined with him on the 27th and found him

extremely pleasant ... We congratulated Althorp on his good health and spirits. He told us that he never took exercise now, that from his getting up till four o'clock he was engaged in the business of his office; that at four he dined, went down to the House at five, and never stirred till the House rose, which is always after midnight; that he then went home, took a basin of arrow root with a glass of sherry in it, and went to bed, where he always dropped asleep in three minutes. 'During the week', said he, 'which followed my taking office, I did not close my

eyes for anxiety. Since that time I have never been awake a quarter an hour after taking off my clothes' ... We talked about timidity in speaking. Althorp said that he had only just got over his apprehensions. 'I was as much afraid', he said, 'last year as when I first came into Parliament. But now I am forced to speak so often that I am quite hardened. Last Thursday I was up forty times'. I was not much surprised at this in Althorp, as he is certainly one of the most modest men in existence ... [and] simplicity itself ... My opinion of Althorp is extremely high ... His character is the only stay of the ministry. I doubt whether any person has ever lived in England who, with no eloquence, no brilliant talents, no profound information, with nothing in short but plain good sense and an excellent heart, possessed as much influence both in and out of Parliament. His temper is an absolute miracle. He has been worse used than any minister ever was in debate; and he has never said one thing inconsistent, I do not say with gentlemanlike courtesy, but with real benevolence. His candour is absolutely a vice in debate. He is perpetually showing excuses and ways of escape to his adversaries which they would never find themselves ... Althorp has the temper of Lord North[†] with the principles of [Sir Samuel] Romilly[†]. If he had the oratorical powers of either, he might do anything. But his understanding, though just, is slow; and his elocution painfully defective. It is however only justice to say to him that he has done more service to the reform bill even as a debater than all the other ministers together, Stanley excepted.[236]

A brief illness kept him from the House on 30 and 31 Aug., but he was back there on 1 Sept., when he explained and defended the plans for the boundary commission, which was 'rather too hard work for a convalescent to begin with', though he was 'not the worse for it' next day. 'Surprised' not yet to have had 'a great fall', he supposed 'I shall hold my popularity till we are all turned out together, and that is all ... that I can wish'.[237] In cabinet, 5 Sept., he 'questioned the propriety or rather condemned the expediency of making peers' to force the bill through the Lords, believing that the constitution surely must 'provide some means of correcting the consequence of a disagreement ... [amounting] to an obstacle to the conduct of public affairs'.[238] The bill left the committee stage on 14 Sept., and the report was quickly gone through. On the motion for its passage, 21 Sept. 1831, Althorp dissociated government from the Irish solicitor-general Crampton's statement that its rejection by the Lords would precipitate a dissolution and the withholding of writs from the schedule A boroughs. He contended that the measure created 'a representative system which, while it gives the power and influence which are due to the great manufacturing communities ... will also give a proper weight to the landed classes in this House'.

Althorp endorsed the Scottish reform bill, 23 Sept. 1831. (He had had discussions on it with Henry Cockburn, the Scottish solicitor-general, who wrote that 'everyone admits and admires [his] ... candour, plainness, sense and honesty ... but I am much struck with his talent'.)[239] He was also involved in talks with Russell, Smith Stanley, O'Connell and others on the Irish reform bill.[240] He had persuaded the cabinet to give both countries three additional Members, which he believed would 'greatly accelerate ... the progress of both bills'; but he kept 'mysterious silence' about this at a meeting with Scottish Members.[241] In the House, 4 Oct., he defended the Scottish bill's provisions and successfully resisted Tory attempts to increase the county representation. Privately, he admitted to Traill that he had made out a strong case for allocating Orkney and Shetland a Member each, but 'did not give me room to expect any change in the plans of government'.[242] Althorp now agreed with Brougham that if the Lords threw out the bill, 'we ought ... to endeavour to make *peers enough to carry it*'; but he told Campbell at about this time that if the bill was rejected he would 'not sleep the worse': 'he is a fellow of the most miraculous equanimity'.[243] However, when the second reading in the Lords was defeated by 41 votes, 7 Oct., which did not surprise him, he told his father next day:

A majority of 41 is not to be coped with ... The reasonable part of the country would not support us in making 50 peers. I am sure neither Grey nor myself can stay in unless we have a reasonable prospect of carrying a measure as large as the one we lost; and I do not see how we can say that we have a reasonable prospect of doing this ... According to ... [the] ordinary rule, we ought to resign. I am inclined to think ... that this is the only mode of carrying reform [which] will never pass the ... Lords unless it is brought forward by its enemies, as the Catholic question was. There is a great meeting of reforming Members ... today ... and much may depend upon it. I am sure our cabinet will break to pieces; but if I saw my own course clearly, which at present I do not, I should ... take my own line and form a government, if the means were placed at my disposal, whichever of my colleagues resigned; or, if the means were not placed at my disposal, state that this was the reason why I did not do so.[244]

The cabinet agreed that on Ebrington's confidence motion, 10 Oct., Althorp should, as the only minister to speak, declare that the government would resign unless they were able to bring in a new reform bill at least 'as efficient' as the last one. (Grey was to say the same in the Lords.) Palmerston, a reluctant reformer, unhappy with this, protested to Grey and argued that the only realistic way to secure reform was to modify the bill significantly. Althorp assured the premier that

he 'never had an idea of pledging Palmerston to anything', but had been aware of his unease and would not say a word by which he would be 'individually compromised'.[245] Before going to the House on the 10th he reported to his father news of the Derby riots and a consensus that 'our quitting office will be the signal for general confusion':

The Tories are now very much frightened by what they have done; and the leaders of the political unions are equally frightened, as they find they have set a machine in motion which they cannot control ... The speech I have to make tonight is terrific; one word in its wrong place may produce the most disastrous consequences. If we can weather the next fortnight without a convulsion, everything will do. But just now the crisis is rather awful.[246]

His speech, in which he asserted that 'by temperance, steadiness and perseverance, the cause of parliamentary reform must ultimately triumph', was a great success.[247] On 11 Oct. he confirmed that riots had occurred at Derby and that measures had been taken to suppress them. He allowed Sadler to bring in his bill to improve the condition of the labouring poor. Next day he defended against Vyvyan his public acknowledgement of a vote of thanks from the Birmingham Political Union: it was 'as innocent a letter as ever was written'. In it, he had beseeched Thomas Attwood[†] to prevent violence and defiance of the law.[248] He refused De Lacy Evans's request for papers on Poland because negotiations were in progress, 13 Oct., when he repudiated Wetherell's charge that government had not exerted themselves to prevent the destruction of the duke of Newcastle's Nottingham property because he was an anti-reformer. On the 18th he declined to answer a question about the dismissal of Lord Howe as lord chamberlain and said that a petition presented by Hunt for the exclusion of bishops from the Lords was unacceptable. He very reluctantly submitted to pressure from Brougham to try to press through his bankruptcy court reform bill before the prorogation: he did not think there was time, but it became law on the last day of the session. On the question of whether to offer office to O'Connell, which was discussed in cabinet on 13 Oct., Althorp favoured 'a more explicit communication with him without delay', but 'a half measure' was adopted.[249] Two days later his sister Lady Lyttelton called on him in Downing Street and found him

at his dinner, and so hurried and uneasy a meal I never saw ... He looked fagged and ill, just out of a long cabinet sitting, and before he had eaten one cutlet, arrived the governor of the Bank ... I felt quite oppressed with the air of Downing Street, and envying for Althorp every dandy and lounger I met afterwards with no responsibility on his mind.[250]

In the House, 19 Oct. 1831 Althorp (who was reported to General Dyott to have had 'the strongest propensity to republicanism' since his boyhood) said that the Birmingham Political Union's petition for a creation of peers, though a marginal case, should be received, and, moving the prorogation, reiterated ministers' determination to introduce a new reform bill at least as extensive as the one rejected by the Lords.

His period of rural respite was brief, for with Bristol in flames and unrest rife throughout the country, he was obliged to be back in London by 31 Oct. 1831. He organized precautions, which included bringing up guns from Woolwich and supplying the Bank with hand grenades, in case the White Conduit meeting on 7 Nov. went ahead. He was pleased that the new National Political Union, of which Burdett somewhat reluctantly became the president, did not seem to be flourishing, believing that such 'associations are really revolutionary', for 'revolutions do not originate in riots like those at Bristol'.[251] When the Birmingham Union later in the month called a meeting to promote non-payment of taxes, at which the members were urged to turn up armed, Althorp, to avoid using the government's contentious proclamation against illegal gatherings, got the Birmingham solicitor Joseph Parkes to transmit to Attwood his personal appeal for the meeting to be cancelled; Attwood complied.[252] From 11 to 26 Nov. Althorp was involved in a correspondence, which was later made public, with William Hulton of Hulton Park, chairman of the Lancashire bench at the time of Peterloo, who now resigned in response to Althorp's remarks supposedly denigrating the magistrates' conduct on that occasion during an earlier debate on the Deacles' affair.[253] On the question of when to recall Parliament, Althorp was initially in favour of 9 Jan. 1832, but, pressed by Brougham to consider an earlier date in order to avoid giving the impression that major changes to the reform bill were in contemplation, he came round to this view, and in cabinet, 19 Nov., was one of the majority of eight (to three) who decided on 6 Dec. 1831 as 'necessary and wise', though he was still not sure that the revised bill and its attendant documents would be ready in time.[254] On 18 Nov. Althorp gave Littleton

an amusing account of the manner in which the late bill was drawn and prepared. He seemed to speak of Mr. Gregson's draft of the bill in terms of very qualified praise – 'It was drawn decently enough … and yet when we came to get the great lawyers to look at it, they pulled every clause to pieces. I was obliged to make them all meet at my house, and to work with them, and so little would they pull together, when I was not with them, that … [when] I returned from a cabinet … I always found

them disputing about the very point which was under discussion when I left. The consequence was we were ill prepared, and obliged to make daily changes in the bill, as we advanced, and it frequently happened that at the hour at which the House met the amended clause was not drawn …'. All this he said with much merriment … [and] the same glee that he would have formerly talked of direful scrapes with his fox hounds after they were well got over.[255]

During November he worked with Russell in a bid to improve the bill and make it more palatable to the 'Waverer' peers. He successfully resisted Russell's wish to transfer urban freeholders from the counties to the boroughs, but made some other concessions. Their attempt to eliminate the single Member constituencies (schedules B and D) came to nothing.[256] In mid-November the governor of the Bank, John Horsley Palmer, who had been in consultation with the 'Waverer' leader Lord Wharncliffe, indicated to Althorp the modifications which would swing respectable, moneyed opinion behind the bill. Althorp did not commit the government, but acknowledged the usefulness of the information. Yet he told Smith Stanley that while some such provisions might be adopted with advantage, 'we must … look more to keeping the support of our friends than to conciliating our enemies. The first is possible, the second is not, and the bill at last must be carried by force and fear, not from conviction or affection'.[257] In Grey's absence, Althorp read to the cabinet on 25 Nov. Wharncliffe's detailed demands for modifications, but most of them were rejected as unreasonable. Althorp, who 'rather' hoped 'to be a country gentleman again before long', felt that 'entering into anything like a negotiation with him for the purpose of making … mutual concessions would be very unwise.[258] The problem of peerage creations had been raised by Graham, who wanted the cabinet immediately to secure the king's consent 'to make the requisite number' and to resign if he refused. Althorp, who still did not think a large creation was acceptable, persuaded Graham to talk to Grey on the 24th. To the premier, he laid out his own 'views at present', but admitted that they were 'not very steady or fixed':

I feel what I believe to be an insurmountable objection to overwhelming the … Lords by a large creation … but … if it was clearly proved to me that a revolution would be the consequence of not taking this step, and that not only the … Lords, but every other thing of value … would be overturned, it would be a very strong thing to say that it ought not to be taken. I should prefer making use of the privileges of the Commons for the purpose of forcing the … Lords, to using this prerogative of the crown ... Both, however, are desperate expedients ... If ... [Graham] perseveres in bringing the matter forward, and with the intention of resigning in case of failure, our days are numbered ... We are supposed by the reformers to have the full support of the king to the utmost extent of his prerogative ... I do not feel so much objection to requiring of the king that he should put this power in our hands – the possession of it would render the use of it unnecessary. If the king refused to give it to us, and we resigned now, our measure is carried; for no other ministry could be formed, and we should come back with such an overwhelming strength that the ... Lords must give way at once.[259]

Receipt of a letter from his father which advocated 'making a great many peers' surprised him, but he did not immediately change his mind. Yet he argued to Grey that if Graham went out 'the people will desert us because we have not followed his advice and the peers, knowing we have not secured the power ... will be totally unmanageable'. In that case, with no 'reasonable chance of carrying the bill', he and Grey were 'pledged to resign'.[260] There was no respite for him, and on 1 Dec. 1831 Littleton was told by Smith Stanley and Graham how he

> was instructing himself and his legal supporters ... how to defend his bill. He gave a dinner to ten lawyers, friends of the bill, among whom ... [was] Gregson ... After dinner Althorp and Gregson challenged the party to attack the bill. They went through it clause by clause, Campbell being the its acutest attacker; but Althorp always, except in two clauses, which were altered, being voted victor.[261]

On the address, 6 Dec. 1831, he defended the early recall of Parliament, said that renewal of the Bank and East India Company charters would be attended to in due course, declared that the revised reform bill would 'satisfy the just expectations of the great majority of the people of England' and accepted an amendment to the paragraph dealing with the treaty with Belgium. On 11 Dec. he was present at the inconclusive interview between Wharncliffe, Harrowby and Chandos, and Grey and Brougham: Chandos reported that he 'sat saying nothing, with his hands in his pockets, and then, after an hour, went away to Fishmongers' Hall', where he and Russell were sworn in as members of the Company.[262] Next day he told his father that while he thought 'on the whole the prospect of carrying the second reading ... in the ... Lords is improved' and 'the tone of the enemy is moderated', he was 'very low at the prospect before me' and 'bitterly' repented 'ever having had anything to do with politics'.[263] In the House later that day he followed Peel's 'angry' speech on the introduction of the bill with one of 'great vigour', and was thought by his friends to have put Peel in his place; but he was reckoned to have let Croker off lightly on the 16th, when he endorsed the second reading, as his 'good nature' prevailed.[264] At a cabinet dinner, 14 Dec., he read a letter from Ebrington which argued that Ireland was entitled to more Members than planned, but he and Smith Stanley stood firm against any increase. In his private reply to Ebrington, he contended that Scotland deserved more Members, as 'the population of Ireland is not sufficiently advanced in civilization to make it desirable that they should have any great preponderance in the legislative assembly of a highly civilized state'. However, he assured Ebrington that if he brought on a motion for an increase and 'the effect ... should be ... to oust us, I shall be under obligations greater to you than I shall ever be able to express'.[265] When Peel raised the controversial issue of the Russian-Dutch loan (which had already been paid), 26 Dec., Althorp confirmed that the law officers believed that the government was bound to honour it, but he had to force Denman to defend this opinion.[266] He did not oppose Herries's motion for information, 17 Dec., but he refused to discuss the subject further. On the question of peerage creations, he still agreed with Grey that they could not ask for more than 20 without bringing the ministry down: 'to make 40, 50 or 60 would be to effect a certain revolution with the view to preventing a contingent one'.[267] At the turn of the year the junior treasury minister Francis Thornhill Baring* noted that Althorp was 'low' in spirits.[268]

On issues relating to his department, he told Grey that conceding 'anything like prohibition' to distressed Coventry silk weavers 'would be ruinous to all our hopes of friendly commercial intercourse with France' and would 'injure the manufacturers of every other place'; and that the pensions of the widows of officers of the German Legion were probably indefensible, as 'pensions are the greatest grievance that presses upon the finances of the country'.[269] On 15 Jan. 1832 he confessed to Grey that he had discovered that he had been

> out on both sides of my account both in receipts and expenditure ... Instead of my having a surplus of £493,479 as I stated in October, I have a deficiency of £698,858. This is much too large, but we must endeavour to meet it by reduction of estimates. I must admit that my financial operations have not been brilliant, and you would have done just right ... if you had thrown me overboard as I recommended the day after my budget. You cannot do so now, at least until we have got the reform bill through, and you will therefore suffer for my rashness.[270]

He was 'full of sorrow and alarm' about the finances and this latest blunder, of which opposition soon got wind.[271] He was duly pilloried by Goulburn in the House, 6 Feb., when he admitted his mistake and, as Spring Rice reported, 'calmly and rationally explained how he intended to engineer a surplus of £164,000. Littleton thought that 'considering how bad his case was ... he defended himself with spirit, and spoke rather better than usual'.[272] His detestation of office led him to preside casually and indifferently over a near disaster for the ministry on the Russian-Dutch loan, 26 Jan., when they seemed certain to be defeated, as he resisted the opposition censure motion feebly and disregarded urgent messages from Grey and Brougham to 'get rid of the question by an adjournment or by some other side wind', which he considered would be 'disgraceful'. His intimation that he would resign if the motion was carried and an adroit rallying cry by Palmerston secured the government a majority of 24. Althorp confessed to Spencer next day that he now considered the case for payment of the loan a bad one and that he had at one point felt 'pretty sure that I should today be clear of all my annoyance'. Hobhouse reckoned that he 'never saw him look so lively as he did just before the division ... when he expected to be beaten, but his face fell when the majority was declared'.[273] Althorp refused Francis Baring's entreaties 'not to put the whole of the deadweight [pensions] in one estimate', having 'pledged himself to the king to support the political pensions'.[274] He declined to impose a duty on chicory, as a deputation of West Indians wanted him to do.[275] On 29 Feb. he agreed to postpone consideration of the sugar duties and moved for £100,000 in relief for West Indian colonies devastated by hurricanes. He made progress with the sugar duties bill, 23 Mar.[276] He conspired with Hobhouse, the new war secretary, to 'insinuate ... gradually' with Grey his plan to reduce the colonial forces.[277] On the army estimates, 17 Feb., he urged Members to ignore wild stories of the economies which could be made; and on 25 Feb. he privately rebuked Hobhouse for going 'too far' in telling the commander-in-chief Lord Hill that the colonial reductions were a *fait accompli*, which had prompted the colonial secretary Goderich to complain to Grey.[278] On 28 Mar. he confirmed that no significant cuts would be made in the domestic army. He defended the government's malt drawback proposals, 17 Feb., 1 Mar., 3 Apr., opposed a motion for modification of the soap duties, 28 Feb., and endorsed Poulett Thomson's acquiescence in the appointment of a select committee on the silk trade, 1 Mar. He resisted Hunt's motion for information on military punishments, 16 Feb., told Peel that ministers were considering the establishment of provincial police forces, 7 Mar., and disregarded Hunt's ironi-

cal invitation to second his motion for inquiry into Peterloo, 15 Mar. He thought Sadler's factories regulation bill could be improved in committee, 16 Mar., but felt that the intrinsically 'unwholesome' nature of labour in cotton factories was 'an evil which does not admit of remedy'. On 27 Mar. he allowed Ewart to prepare a bill to abolish the death penalty for certain offences, but resisted Trench's call for information on the costs of the Buckingham House refurbishment. He opposed Hunt's attempt to end corporal punishment in the army, 2 Apr. He defended the Scottish exchequer court bill, 10 Apr., approved Warburton's anatomy bill, 11 Apr., and boasted that there was at present 'no prospect' of war in Europe, 13 Apr. He supported repeal of the usury laws, 8 May 1832.

Althorp had been worried about the state of Ireland and O'Connell's intransigence since mid-December 1831, but he was eager to avoid coercion if at all possible.[279] In the House, 23 Jan. 1832, he dismissed Hume's charge that ministers intended to enforce the payment of Irish tithes. Next day he explained and defended the composition of the tithes select committee. On 14 Feb. he was obliged to clarify Grey's speech in the Lords in which he seemed to have threatened to 'deluge Ireland with blood' for the purpose of collecting tithes: he confirmed the government's determination to uphold the law, but stressed their wish to bring in a conciliatory measure also. Grey witnessed and approved of this speech.[280] Althorp differed with Grey in that he knew their supporters in the Commons would never accept the large increase in the army in Ireland which the premier favoured.[281] On 8 Mar. he held a meeting at the foreign office of almost 200 'English Members supporting government' (he had addressed the Irish Members the day before) to 'beg support for the government plan ... [for] the gradual extinction of tithes'. Littleton recorded the scene:

> Althorp opened the business. Surely never was there such a figure for an orator – especially to my eye – who had seen there on similar occasions Castlereagh, with his elegant and well-dressed figure and high-bred carriage, and Canning, with his air of quickness and intelligence greater than ever distinguished man. There stood Althorp at the top of the room, with his stout, honest face, and farmer-like figure, habited in ill-made black clothes, his trousers rucked up in a heap round his legs, one coat flap turned around, and exposing his posterior, and the pocket of the other crammed full of papers – his hat held awkwardly in one hand and his large snuff box in the other, with which he kept playing the devil's tattoo on his thigh – while he briefly and bluntly told his plain, unsophisticated tale with his usual correct feeling and stout sense, and was warmly responded to by the whole party.[282]

In the House that evening he supported Smith Stanley's motion to consider and reform Irish tithes, which was carried by 314-31; but he feared the consequences of Sheil's 'covert attack' on the Irish reform bill.[283] He defended the proposals, 13 Mar., and on 6 Apr. 1832 assured the House that the remedial measure had only been postponed because it was more complicated than the enforcement bill.

Althorp, who frankly and disarmingly admitted in private to the 'strongest prejudices of the old Tory school' which he had cast off at Cambridge, got the Commons into committee on the English reform bill on 20 Jan. 1832. A week later he told his father that having just obtained Hansard for the period 18 July-13 Aug. 1831, he was 'amused at seeing my name in the index with such a string of numbers to it' as indicated that he had 'spoken 292 times'.[284] He now repeated the process, steering the measure through over a seven-week stint of unremitting hard work, skilful advocacy and even-tempered defence of the details and technicalities. On 12 Feb. the lord advocate Francis Jeffrey*, who had been immediately captivated by Althorp's 'calm, clumsy, courageous, immutable probity and well-meaning', reported to Cockburn his 'pretended confession of faith and a sort of creed of his political morality' at a small dinner party:

[He] avowed that, though it was a very shocking doctrine to promulgate, he must say that he had never sacrificed his own inclinations to a sense of duty without repenting it, and always found himself more substantially unhappy for having exerted himself for the public good! We all combated this atrocious heresy the best way we could; but he maintained it with an air of sincerity, and a half earnest, half humorous face, and a dexterity of statement, that was quite striking. I wish you could have seen his beaming eye and benevolent lips kindling as he answered us, and dealt out his natural familiar repartee with the fearlessness as if of perfect sincerity, and the artlessness of one who sought no applause, and despised all risk of misconstruction, and the thought that this was the leader of the English House of Commons, – no speculator, or discourser, or adventurer, – but a man of sense and business, of the highest rank, and the largest experience both of affairs and society.[285]

Althorp carried by 215-89 the proposal to divide a number of counties, 27 Jan.; successfully resisted amendments to the £10 franchise (now based on rates rather than rent), 3 Feb.; saw off Hunt's attempt to lay the cost of booths and hustings on local authorities, 15 Feb., and secured the disfranchisement of Appleby (by 256-143), 21 Feb., and the partial disfranchisement of Helston (by 256-179), 23 Feb. He opposed and defeated (by 316-236) a Conservative amendment to

get rid of the metropolitan districts, 28 Feb. On 2 Mar. he denied having stated that the bill was 'not to be considered as a final measure'. On the 10th he presented the report and then went for a ride. There was serious talk in cabinet of his taking a peerage to conduct the bill through the Lords, as neither Grey nor Brougham felt equal to the task. The idea held strong appeal for him, not least because it would free him from the trammels of the 'odious' exchequer, but it foundered on the lack of a suitable man to replace him as leader of the Commons.[286] He spoke for the third reading of the reform bill, 19 Mar., and on the 26th carried it to the Lords with Russell, 'looking more triumphant than they felt'.[287]

From the beginning of the year Althorp had been tormented by the problem of whether to seek a creation of peers to get the measure through the Lords, which divided the cabinet and put him at odds with Grey, whom he had come almost to venerate and was reluctant to oppose. The king's acquiescence in mid-January in the cabinet's request that he pledge himself to create as many peers as proved necessary provided a temporary respite; but by the middle of February, when Althorp was determined to resign if the government were unable to send the bill to the Upper House without 'a moral certainty' of carrying it, and Grey, hoping that the 'Waverers' would secure the second reading, was now quite averse to pressing mass creations on the king, they seemed to be on a collision course. Althorp, who had removed his pistols from his bedroom to avoid the temptation to shoot himself in despair, and still spoke to Hobhouse of suicide as a way out of his torment, perceived that his own resignation would wreck the government, but that the likely outcome of that would be his succession as premier of a reform ministry kept in power by popular pressure, a prospect which appalled him. But he decided that he had no choice but conscientiously to try to convince Grey of the imperative need to insist on a creation and to resign, whatever the consequences, if this was refused. The cabinet was still divided and the issue unresolved when the bill passed the Commons, but Althorp was initially persuaded by Grey's plea for caution and threat to resign to try the Lords without the promise of a creation.[288] On 27 Mar., however, the cabinet 'unanimously' resolved to confront the king with 'the alternatives of resignation and creation' and to recommend 'the necessary creation of peers in the case of the bill being rejected on the second reading'. The king agreed, and on 28 Mar. Hobhouse found Althorp in a more optimistic mood, inclined to agree that they 'were on velvet'.[289] But a week later, to Althorp's annoyance, the king made difficulties about creating the requisite number of peers. Althorp told his father, 5 Apr.:

I am not sure that we shall be justified in going on till Monday [9th, when the second reading in the Lords was due to start] unless His Majesty gives way, for we must have the power of acting instantly, or we shall be ruined in our characters, in case we are beaten. I think by resigning now we might save a rag of character, but it is very doubtful whether we ought to give up our chance of success, considering that our resignation will be almost as bad as the defeat itself for the peace of the country. I think I must secure a passage in some packet for New York and have four horses to my carriage ready for the division in the ... Lords.

He anticipated a 'small majority' for the second reading, but an early defeat in committee, whereupon 'they would propose 60 peers, the king would refuse, they would resign', and Peel would 'come in and ... propose a moderate reform bill, which they would support'.[290] He was sure by the 9th that the second reading was safe, but assured Francis Baring that if he and his colleagues failed to secure reform, his own 'case' was 'very easy. At one blow I shall expiate the great fault of my life, having ever entered into politics'.[291] The majority of nine for the second reading, 13 Apr., exceeded his expectations and 'justified' ministers, as he saw it, 'so far in not having made peers', to which many of 'our staunchest men' in the Commons were averse. He even allowed himself to be 'sanguine enough to think that we shall get pretty well through the committee', as he left London to spend part of the recess at Wiseton, part at Leamington, hoping that 'some very awkward twinges in my foot' did not presage 'a fit of the gout'.[292] On 26 Apr. he and Grey were granted the freedom of the City by common council.[293] Anticipating defeat on Lord Lyndhurst's amendment to postpone consideration of schedules A and B, 7 May, when he went to the Lords to advise and support Grey, Althorp told Spencer that he was clear that they must then ask the king to create sufficient peers and to go out if he refused, but that Grey favoured immediate resignation.[294] The amendment was carried by 151-116, which Althorp considered to be 'as total a defeat first of the principle of the reform bill and secondly of the ministry as could well be imagined'. The leading members of the cabinet decided to send Grey and Brougham to Windsor to ask for a creation. The king refused and they resigned on 9 May, when Althorp told Spencer from Downing Street, 'I am quite clear of this horrid place. I recollect 1807 and how it is not easy for a Whig administration to get back even if they wish it and I certainly shall take all fair means to avoid coming back myself'.[295] Jeffrey

reported 'a characteristic scene' with the 'frank, true and stout-hearted' Althorp that day, when he called on him to discuss arrangements for the Scottish reform bill:

I was led up to his dressing-room, where I found him sitting on a stool in a dark duffle dressing-gown, with his arms (very rough and hairy) bare above the elbows, and his beard half-shaved and half staring through the lather, with a desperate razor in one hand and a great soap-brush in the other. He gave me the loose finger of his brush hand, and with the twinkle of his bright eye and radiant smile, he said, 'You need not be anxious about your Scotch bill for tonight, for I have the pleasure to tell you, *we are no longer His Majesty's ministers*'.

Jeffrey later recounted that on the following day Althorp bought plants for his garden at Althorp and wrote detailed 'plans for their arrangement'.[296] When he entered the House on 9 May to announce that ministers had resigned because the king had rejected their 'advice', he was greeted with the 'most deafening cheers'. He confessed to his father that 'it quite upset me and I spoke with a lump in my throat and as near crying as possible'.[297] He disapproved of Ebrington's notice of a motion for an address asking the king to appoint only ministers who would carry undiluted reform, as he explained to Spencer:

If it fails it will facilitate the formation of a new government, and if it succeeds will ensure the dissolution of Parliament and lose the great advantage we have gained in keeping the reform bill in existence so that it may be passed by the Lords, mutilated perhaps, but still must come back to us in a form to give to popular rights a great advantage. I am naturally in a state of considerable excitement, but it does not disturb my sleep, and I am quite well.

He failed to stop Ebrington from making his motion, 10 May, but made clear his disapproval of its timing when he spoke for it. He also said, 'in the most impassive manner, plainly and resolutely', as Hobhouse described it, that the 'advice' which had been spurned had been for the creation of enough peers to carry the bill: 'here the most tremendous cheers burst out from all quarters of the House'.[298] The motion was carried by 288-208, but Croker reported that 'the ministers looked ... *abattus*', and Althorp 'quite pale with agitation'.[299] In the House next day he urged reformers in the country to abide by the law. At a 'great Whig meeting at Brooks's', 13 May, called to consider a resolution declaring that no ministry formed by Wellington could enjoy the confidence of the country, Althorp, fearing that the rank and file 'were inclined to run very wild', as he told his father got upon the table to speak ... [and was received] with shouts and huzzas that must have been heard down to St. James's Palace. I took a decided line against the proposal ... and succeeded ... in bringing them to my opinion. This is very satisfactory, as it shows that my influence is complete and that it will depend upon me what line our party will take ... Wellington's having accepted office, pledged as I believe he is to carry through our reform bill with very few alterations, is ... the most disgraceful act of political profligacy ... ever ... recorded. But we must not let our anger get the better of our honesty and we must support the bill in whosoever hands it is.[300]

He stressed this in the House, 14 May, speaking 'with more warmth than usual'.[301] Next day Hobhouse was with him when the duke of Richmond came in 'and said: "Well, I have bad news for you; no shooting this year. Pack up your guns again ... Wellington has ... given up"'.[302] During the next three days, as the king cast about for a non-existent alternative government, Althorp, who was adamant that before resuming office he must have a guarantee of the bill's passage, either by a creation or the withdrawal of opposition in the Lords, kept his father abreast of developments.[303] Informing the House that negotiations were still in progress, 17 May, he 'dwelt on his pledge that no *essential* changes would be conceded'.[304] On 18 May 1832 he announced that ministers now had 'full security' for the passage of the bill, having been briefed at the last minute by Smith Stanley, who had been called out of the House by Grey.[305]

On 31 May 1832 he deplored press libels on public figures, but said government would not prosecute the publishers. He had to convince the king that it would be foolish to proceed against his libelers.[306] On 22 May he secured the appointment of a select committee on renewal of the Bank's charter and the system on which banks of issue were conducted. Ellice, who was sore at Althorp for paying no heed to his earlier pleas to be relieved of his post as patronage secretary, had warned Grey to make sure that the committee's remit was restricted, as Althorp would be no match for Peel, Goulburn and Herries in a wide-ranging investigation, and 'you will have a repetition of your budget of last year'.[307] Althorp, who believed that the time was not 'at present' ripe for emancipating the slaves, as they were not 'fit for the advantages of liberty', tried to persuade Fowell Buxton to drop or soften his motion for inquiry into the possibility of early abolition, but without success. On 24 May he moved and carried by 163-90 an amendment, in words supplied by Grey, binding the committee to inquire into abolition in terms consistent with the 1823 amelioration resolution.[308] His support of a bill brought from the Lords,

30 May, to abolish capital punishment for certain offences nettled the king, and Grey had to explain, more clearly than Althorp had done, that it was not a government measure and he had been speaking as an individual.[309] He opposed an attempt to amend the Sale of Beer Act, 31 May. On 4 June he gave an assurance that political considerations had been excluded from the boundaries bill. He supported the Lords' amendments to the English reform bill, 5 June, when he denied that the radical Colonel Jones was in communication with the government and affirmed his faith in 'the good sense of the people of England'. He backed Jeffrey on details of the Scottish reform bill, 4, 5, 6, 15 June, and said on the last day that the measure aimed to 'represent population combined with wealth'. His 'strange acquiescence' in Sir George Clerk's suggestion led to the introduction of a property qualification for Scottish burgh Members, which 'spread dismay' in Scotland and which he had to discard on the third reading, 27 June.[310] When Jeffrey subsequently abandoned the qualification for county Members, Althorp denied a Conservative charge that he had 'washed my hands' of the bill and 'given way to the representations of the political unions'. He opposed Baring's bill to exclude insolvent debtors from the Commons, 6, 27 June. On the 7th he refuted Sadler's allegation that 'our manufacturers conduct their factories in a manner which makes the loss of health and life inevitable'. On the boundaries bill that day, he laughed off Wetherell's allusion to the French Revolution and defended the division of Surrey. He denied any 'compromise' with the Lowthers over Whitehaven, but accepted the addition of Corfe Castle to Wareham as its Member George Bankes suggested, 22 June. He told De Lacy Evans that the Commons had no right to inquire into the management of the duchy of Cornwall, 8 June, and on the 13th said that ministers had never promised financial aid for the West Indian colonies. He proposed a loan for hurricane relief, 29 June. On the Irish reform bill, 13 June, he opposed O'Connell's attempt to restore the 40s. freeholder county franchise and defended the allocation of an additional Member to Dublin University. On the 18th he resisted a motion to enfranchise £30 tenants. Holland reckoned that Althorp and Smith Stanley were willing to concede some extension of the county franchise in order to 'smooth the passage of the bill';[311] and on 25 June he explained the decision to extend the £10 franchise to leaseholders as well as to freeholders. He opposed an amendment to the registration procedure because he thought it would encourage fraudulent voting, 6 July, and justified the enfranchisement of Dublin University Masters of Arts, 9 July. On 14

June he admitted to O'Connell that he had once spoken of the 'extinction' of Irish tithes, but insisted that this 'must be consistent with the rights of tithe-holders'. He defeated by 143-25 O'Connell's bid to adjourn the debate on the tithes composition bill, 5 July, and on the 10th declared that he could not 'empower the people of Ireland to set the law at utter defiance'. He carried the previous question against Bulwer's motion for repeal of the 'taxes on knowledge', a desirable object in principle, but damaging to the revenue. As an individual, he spoke and voted to open coroners' inquests, 20 June. On the 28th he and Milton were honoured at a Northamptonshire reform dinner, where he warned that while the Reform Act would have 'the most beneficial results ... it could not be expected that it would immediately produce miracles'. He declared his candidature for the county's southern division at the next general election.[312] In the House, 2 July, he confirmed that Durham and Richmond had decided to take up their official salaries, having originally resolved to forego them. Next day he opposed Waithman's resolutions on exports and imports, said Torrens had talked nonsense about bullion and expressed his dwindling hope that the Bank committee would be able to complete its work before the dissolution. Anticipating possible defeat in a renewed attack on the Russian-Dutch loan, 12 July, when he moved to go into committee on it, he told Spencer that in that case resignation would be the only option and that there could be 'no great objection to doing so' now that reform was secured. He took the same attitude ahead of the division of 16 July. According to Hobhouse, the government's 46 majority on the 12th 'did not satisfy' Althorp, who 'said ... that "the government was like a hard-pushed fox running fast, but which might be run in upon at any moment"'.[313] He and Grey formally received the freedom of the City at Guildhall on 11 July.[314] He declined to intervene to give defaulting ratepayers of Marylebone and elsewhere more time to pay and so qualify for electoral registration, 13 July, but on 7 Aug. offered to legislate to make the intention to pay sufficient. 'Strong opposition' forced him to abandon the idea, which 'disgusted some of his supporters, according to Greville.[315] He opposed abolition of the governorships of Londonderry and Culmore, 18 July, endorsed the grant for a National Gallery, 23 July, did not resist Hume's being given leave to introduce a bill to exclude the recorder of Dublin from the Commons but urged him to exempt the present incumbent, and justified the recent prosecution of unstamped publications, 24 July. Next day he defeated West Indians' attempt to reduce the duties on coffee and rum. On the

26th he opposed De Lacy Evans's call for a substantial reduction in the military establishment, admitting that he had been 'mistaken' in his belief that Catholic emancipation would enable the bulk of the troops to be withdrawn from Ireland. He seemed to dissociate himself from the controversy sparked by Brougham's appointment of one of his brothers to a chancery sinecure and his subsequent personal abuse of his critic Sugden, 26, 27 July.[316] In his budget statement, 27 July, he could not offer 'any sanguine views of the future, or congratulatory recapitulation of the past': he forecast a deficit of £464,000 for 1832 and 1833. On 30 July he detailed civil list charges and explained that pensions were to go on the consolidated fund. On 1 Aug., when Le Marchant noted that he remained 'most anxious to withdraw from office ... for he has a most impracticable team to drive in the Commons' and the Irish Members were 'perfect swindlers', he proposed the £4,000 pension for Speaker Manners Sutton on his anticipated retirement.[317] Next day he obtained leave for a bill to pay the lord chancellor and vice-chancellor fixed salaries instead of the traditional fees, refuted Hunt's allegation that the government had broken its promises on economy and pointed out that they had cut out places to the tune of £30,000 a year. He defended the level (£14,000) of the lord chancellor's salary, 8 Aug., and carried his pension of £5,000 against Hume's protest by 60-2, 9 Aug. On 2 Aug. he secured compensation for losses sustained by revocation of his patent as Irish king's printer for Sir Abraham King, who privately praised to O'Connell his 'candid and straightforward act'.[318] He explained details of the crown colonies relief bill and had it committed by 51-20, 3 Aug. He spoke in favour of honouring the Greek loan, 6 Aug. On 10 Aug. he blamed the fatal Clitheroe canvassing affray on outsiders. He insisted that De Lacy Evans's statement of the small number of electors who had registered in the Lancashire towns was a gross underestimate, 15 Aug. On 16 Aug. 1832 he rejected a strongly worded Irish petition for the abolition of tithes. When Parliament was prorogued later that day, he, Russell and Hobhouse were 'the only occupants of the treasury bench who attended the Speaker and some 80 Members to the House of Lords'.[319]

On 5 Oct. 1832 Althorp replied to Milton's argument that it was his 'duty to live at Althorp' during the election campaign:

> It is the endeavour to perform my duty which has placed me in the situation I now hold ... which makes me so miserable that my wish for death is only mitigated by the sanguine hope that I shall not remain long in this situation, and the intention whenever I can get out of it without

producing mischief to others of returning to private life. This you will say I ought to have thought of before I took office. I did so. I expected that I should sacrifice my happiness, but I certainly did not expect to acquire so much positive misery ... No one who has not tried what it is for a man accustomed to the habits of a country life to tie himself up in laborious office has a right to be the judge.[320]

At the general election of 1832 he was returned unopposed for Northamptonshire South, having considered an invitation from the reformers of Tower Hamlets when an expensive county contest briefly threatened.[321] He remained in harness for two more turbulent years until the death of his father in November 1834 removed him from the Commons and the exchequer and gave William IV, alarmed by Whig designs on Irish church revenues, a pretext to dismiss Lord Melbourne, who had replaced Grey as prime minister in July. Althorp largely retired from public life and, residing at Wiseton, devoted himself to farming and the struggle to eradicate the £500,000 encumbrance which his father's extravagance had placed on his inheritance.[322] He died, as his sister reported, 'as he had lived, in earnest piety and simplicity, and with more than resignation', wearing a locket containing a cutting from his wife's hair, in October 1845, three months after Grey.[323] He was succeeded in the peerage and entailed estates by his brother Frederick (1798-1857). Among the legacies assigned by his will was an annuity of £1,200 to the mysterious and unhinged Mrs. Wallace, who claimed to be his illegitimate daughter.

Greville, who did not know him well, but had 'a great respect and esteem for him', wrote:

> No man ever died with a fairer character, or more generally regretted. In his county he was exceedingly beloved and respected ... He had neither the brilliant or even plausible exterior which interests and captivates vulgar imaginations, but he had sterling qualities of mind and character which made him one of the most useful and valuable, as well as one of the best and most amiable men of his day. He was the very model and type of an English gentleman ... Modest without diffidence, confident without vanity, ardently desiring the good of his country, without the slightest personal ambition, he took that part in public affairs which his station and his opinions prompted, and he marched through the maze of politics with that straightforward bravery, which was the result of sincerity, singleness of purpose, the absence of all selfishness, and a true, genuine, but unpretending patriotism ... The greatest homage that ever was rendered to character and public virtue was exhibited in his popularity and authority during the four eventful years when he led the Whig government and party in the ... Commons. Without

one showy accomplishment, without wit to amuse or eloquence to persuade, with a voice unmelodious and a manner ungraceful, and barely able to speak plain sense in still plainer language, he exercised in the House ... an influence and even a dominion greater than any leader either after or before him ... His friends followed the plain and simple man with enthusiastic devotion, and he possessed the faculty of disarming his political antagonists of all bitterness and animosity towards him; he was regarded in the House ... with sentiments akin to those of personal affection, with a boundless confidence and a universal esteem.[324]

In an article written soon after his death, Russell observed:

> His diligence was indefatigable, his sagacity quick, his judgement seldom at fault ... If he ever fell into a mistake, it was from ... a trusting, believing, hoping nature ... His views were large and comprehensive ... Above all, his opinions upon questions both speculative and practical, were guided by a humble reliance on the goodness of God; and a conviction that he was bound in whatever he might think or do ... to follow the law of Christ ... The simplicity of his character ... made him understood, beloved and trusted beyond any man in [the Commons]... This was the more remarkable, as his tongue was far from eloquent; and, although his arguments were sound and comprehensive, he was so often wanting in words as to be obscure ... But the confidence of his friends, his party, and the country, supplied all deficiencies, and gave to his few and simple expressions, as much influence over his audience as had ever been obtained by the most admired eloquence of our greatest orators.[325]

Brougham paid tribute to him in his autobiography:

> Nobody ever hated office as he did ... He often said, when he got up in the morning, he wished he might be dead before night, but he always went through his duty manfully. There never was a man of real merit who had an opinion of himself so unaffectedly modest. Without a particle of cant, he was most deeply imbued with religion, and this, perhaps as well as any other part of his nature, indisposed him to exert himself to attain the usual objects of earthly ambition. Always undervaluing himself, he never could comprehend why he had attained so high a position in public life, and frequently expressed his astonishment at the great power he was conscious of exercising over men of all kinds and natures ... which proceeded from the complete conviction which all men felt in his thorough honesty and simple love of truth ... His powers were great. His ability was never so remarkably shown as in the reform bill ... He had a knowledge of all its details, and of all the numberless matters connected with it, that was almost supernatural.[326]

His career, Greville wrote, personified 'the simple and unostentatious practice of public and private virtue'.[327]

[1] The best modern biography is E.A. Wasson, *Whig Renaissance: Lord Althorp and the Whig Party, 1782-1845* (1987), on which this article draws. *Mem. of Visct. Althorp* (1876), by Sir Denis Le Marchant, a close personal acquaintance, is of value and contains original correspondence. [2] Le Marchant, pp. xv-xvi. [3] Fitzwilliam mss 92, Althorp to Milton, 21 Mar. 1818. [4] Le Marchant, 168-9, 536; B. Hilton, *Age of Atonement*, 238-9, 241; R. Brent, *Liberal Anglican Politics*, 28, 38, 123-8; Wasson, 96-104. [5] [J. Grant], *Random Recollections of Commons (1837)*, 180-1. [6] *The Times*, 9 Dec. 1819; *Lady Lyttelton Corresp.* 222; *Althorp Letters*, 100, 102; *Northampton Mercury*, 18 Mar. 1820. [7] *Althorp Letters*, 101; Add. 52444, f. 93. [8] *Althorp Letters*, 103-4. [9] *The Times*, 18 May, 17 June 1820. [10] Ibid. 22, 28 Feb., 12 May 1821. [11] Ibid. 28, 29 May, 4 June 1823. [12] Ibid. 27 Mar., 20 May 1824, 9, 15 Feb., 3-5, 17, 20 May 1825; Le Marchant, 182-6; Wasson, 110-12; *Althorp Letters*, 125. [13] *Althorp Letters*, 106, 107. [14] Ibid. 109-10. [15] Ibid. 108-9. [16] *The Times*, 11 July 1820. [17] *Althorp Letters*, 106-7. [18] Add. 75937, Lady to Lord Spencer, 15 Jan. 1821. [19] *Althorp Letters*, 110-11; Fitzwilliam mss 102/12. [20] Fitzwilliam mss 102/10; *Althorp Letters*, 112-13. [21] Fitzwilliam mss 104/3. [22] *The Times*, 27 Jan. 1821. [23] Ibid. 3, 9 Feb. 1821; HLRO, Hist. Coll. 379, Grey Bennet diary, 10. [24] Northants. RO, Gotch mss GK 1206. [25] *The Times*, 4 Apr. 1821. [26] *Althorp Letters*, 114. [27] *The Times*, 10 July 1821; B. Hilton, *Corn, Cash, Commerce*, 127, 143. [28] *Lady Lyttelton Corresp.* 239. [29] Ibid. 240. [30] Add. 51679, Russell to Lady Holland [Jan. 1822]. [31] *The Times*, 16 Feb. 1822. [32] Ibid. 22 Feb. 1822. [33] Fitzwilliam mss. [34] Add. 75937, Lady to Lord Spencer, 13 May; *The Times*, 13 June 1822. [35] *The Times*, 1, 7 May 1822. [36] Add. 56544, f. 6. [37] *Althorp Letters*, 118; Add. 75940, Althorp to Lady Spencer, 14 July 1822. [38] Fitzwilliam mss, Althorp to Milton, 3 Feb. 1823. [39] Add. 76369. [40] *The Times*, 11 Feb. 1824. [41] Ibid. 2 Mar. 1824. [42] Ibid. 2, 23 Mar. 1824. [43] Ibid. 11 June 1824. [44] Ibid. 18 May 1824. [45] Add. 76369, Althorp to Brougham, 14 Dec. 1824. [46] *O'Connell Corresp.* iii. 1172, 1176. [47] *The Times*, 30 Apr. 1825. [48] *Althorp Letters*, 125-6; Brougham mss, Smith to Brougham, 6 Sept. 1825. [49] Fitzwilliam mss 124/8. [50] Wasson, 146. [51] Gotch mss GK 1209. [52] Fitzwilliam mss 124/8. [53] *Northampton Mercury*, 3, 17 June 1826; *Althorp Letters*, 129-31. [54] *The Times*, 20 Nov. 1826; Wasson, 148. [55] *Althorp Letters*. [56] Add. 76369, Althorp to Brougham, 25 June 1827. [57] Broughton, *Recollections*, iii. 169; Add. 51663, Bedford to Holland [18 Feb.]; 51784, Holland to C.R. Fox, 17 Feb.; Grey mss, Howick to Grey, 17 Feb. 1827. [58] *Northampton Mercury*, 17, 24 Mar. 1827. [59] Broughton, iii. 177. [60] *The Times*, 27 Mar. 1827. [61] Add. 76369. [62] NLW, Coedymaen mss 194. [63] Le Marchant, 214-15, 222; *Canning's Ministry*, 272; Broughton, iii. 150-1, 188; Brougham, *Life and Times*, ii. 482; Add. 36463, f. 378; 76369, Althorp to Brougham, 18 Apr. 1827; Gotch mss GK 1210. [64] Bagot, *Canning and Friends*, ii. 398; *Creevey Pprs.* ii. 117. [65] *The Times*, 31 May, 16 June 1827; Gotch mss GK 1211. [66] *Althorp Letters*, 137; Add. 51687, Lansdowne to Holland, 31 Aug. [1827]. [67] *Cockburn Letters*, 178-9; Le Marchant, 225; Add. 51724, Althorp to Holland, 21 Aug. 1827. [68] Add. 51677, Russell to Holland, 16 Aug.; 76135, Holland to Spencer [c. 18 Aug. 1827]. [69] *Russell Early Corresp.* i. 258-9. [70] Lansdowne mss, Baring to Lansdowne, 1 Sept. 1827. [71] Ibid. Holland to Lansdowne, 22 Aug.; Add. 76380, Holland to Althorp, 28 Aug. 1827; Le Marchant, 225. [72] *Arbuthnot Corresp.* 89; *Arbuthnot Jnl.* ii. 142. [73] Lansdowne mss, Tierney to Lansdowne, 5 Sept., Abercromby to same [4 Sept. 1827]. [74] Castle Howard mss, Abercromby to Carlisle [Sept. 1827]; Le Marchant, 225-6; *Russell Letters*, ii. 104. [75] Hants RO, Tierney mss 61 (a) (b) (d); Wasson, 152. [76] Add. 51724, Duncannon to Holland, 29 Sept., Tuesday [Oct.], 10 Oct; Fitzwilliam mss, Lyttelton to Milton, 22 Nov. 1827; *Russell Letters*, i. 82, 84. [77] Castle Howard mss, Abercromby to Carlisle, 14 Oct.; Add. 51586, Tierney to Lady Holland, 1 Nov. 1827. [78] Tierney mss 4 (a). [79] JRL, Bromley Davenport mss. [80] Le Marchant, 226-7; *Althorp Letters*, 139; Tierney mss 66; Fitzwilliam mss, Althorp to Milton, 25 Nov., R. Price to same, 8 Dec. 1827; Add. 38752, ff. 104, 164; Wasson, 152-4. [81] Tierney mss 49 (c); Add. 75938, Lady to Lord Spencer, 13 Dec. 1827. [82] Castle Howard mss, Abercromby to

Carlisle, 25 Dec., Lady Carlisle to Morpeth, 29 Dec. [1827]. [83] Add. 52447, f. 136. [84] *Russell Early Corresp.* i. 271-2; Broughton, iii. 236; Add. 36464, ff. 166, 171; 51675, Althorp to Holland 10 Jan. 1828. [85] Wasson, 154-7. [86] Add. 76380. [87] Add. 40307, f. 50; 40395, ff. 219, 221, 241, 243. [88] TNA 30/29/9/5/67; Castle Howard mss, Abercromby to Carlisle, 17 May 1828. [89] *Ellenborough Diary*, i. 126; *Russell Letters*, ii. 87. [90] Hilton, *Corn, Cash, Commerce*, 253-4. [91] Parker, *Graham*, i. 72; Sir James Graham mss (IHR microfilm XR 80). [92] Add. 76369, Althorp to Brougham, 30 Sept. 1828. [93] NLS mss 24770, f. 23; Castle Howard mss, Abercromby to Carlisle [16 Oct.]; Duke Univ. Lib. Fazakerley mss, same to Fazakerley, 16 Oct. [1828]. [94] *Russell Early Corresp.* i. 283-4. [95] Add. 51834, Davenport to Holland [Nov.], 18 Nov. [1828]. [96] NLS mss 24770, f. 29. [97] *Cockburn Letters*, 204; *Althorp Letters*, 141; Fitzwilliam mss, Althorp to Milton, 5 Dec.; Brougham mss, Lansdowne to Brougham, 26 Dec. [1828]; Parker, *Graham*, i. 73-74. [98] Add. 51574, Abercromby to Holland, 28 Dec.; 76369, Althorp to Brougham, 28 Dec. 1828. [99] Add. 76369, Althorp to Brougham, 2 Jan.; Fitzwilliam mss, same to Milton, 24 Jan. 1829. [100] Add. 76380, Holland to Althorp, 6 Jan.; 51724, reply, 8 Jan. 1829. [101] *Cockburn Letters*, 205-6. [102] Parker, *Peel*, ii. 103. [103] Add. 76369, Althorp to Brougham, 14 Feb. 1829. [104] *Arbuthnot Jnl.* ii. 242, 250; Add. 76369, Althorp to Brougham [9], 11 Mar. 1829. [105] Add. 76369, Althorp to Brougham, 10, 18, 19 Mar., Thursday [Mar.] 1829; 76369, same to same, 27 Mar. 1829. [106] Add. 76369; *The Times*, 9 Apr.; Bromley Davenport mss, Althorp to Davenport, 15 Apr. 1829. [107] Add. 76369; *The Times*, 9 Apr.; Bromley Davenport mss, Althorp to Davenport, 15 Apr. 1829. [108] *Althorp Letters*, 143; *O'Connell Corresp.* iv. 1566. [109] *Althorp Letters*, 143; Wasson, 159. [110] *Arbuthnot Jnl.* ii. 285-6. [111] Ibid. ii. 290; *Ellenborough Diary*, ii. 60. [112] Add. 76369, Althorp to Brougham, 17 June 1829. [113] Ibid. same to same, 30 Dec. 1829; Add. 51680, Russell to Lady Holland [Jan.]; Fitzwilliam mss, Althorp to Milton, 20 Jan. 1830. [114] Grey mss, Ellice to Grey [18 Jan.]; Fitzwilliam mss, Althorp to Milton, 20 Jan.; Brougham mss, Russell to Brougham, 30 Jan. 1830. [115] Keele Univ. Lib. Sneyd mss SC10/91. [116] Add. 47223, f. 38; Wasson, 164-5. [117] Grey mss, Ellice to Grey 18 Jan. 1830. [118] Grey mss; Fitzwilliam mss, Althorp to Milton, 25 Feb. 1830. [119] Sneyd mss, Littleton to Sneyd, 24 Feb.; *Lieven-Grey Corresp.* 457, 459; Grey mss, Durham to Grey, 26 Feb. 1830. [120] Le Marchant, 243-6; Howick jnl. 3 Mar.; Castle Howard mss, Graham to Morpeth [3 Mar.]; Sneyd mss, Littleton to Sneyd, 3 Mar.; Grey mss, Ellice to Grey [5 Mar. 1830]. [121] Howick jnl. 6 Mar. [1830]. [122] Le Marchant, 267; Wasson, 168-9. [123] Add. 76369, Althorp to Brougham, 6 Mar.; Grey mss, Ellice to Grey [11 Mar. 1830]. [124] Grey mss GRE/B25/1C/85, 87. [125] Add. 76369. [126] Add. 75938, Lady to Lord Spencer, 11 Mar. 1830. [127] Howick jnl. 16 Mar.; *Russell Letters*, ii. 234; Salop RO 6003/1, Slaney diary, 15 Apr. 1830. [128] Howick jnl. 18 Mar. [1830]; *Ellenborough Diary*, ii. 215. [129] Add. 38758, f. 138; Gotch mss GK 1215. [130] *Cockburn Letters*, 226. [131] Howick jnl. 28 Mar. [1830]. [132] Add. 56553, f. 99. [133] Broughton, iv. 34; *Althorp Letters*, 151; Howick jnl. 11 July [1830]; Add. 40340, f. 223. [134] *Althorp Letters*, 151-2. [135] Howick jnl. 13 May [1830]. [136] *Arbuthnot Jnl.* ii. 366; *Ellenborough Diary*, ii. 290. [137] Add. 40340, f. 223. [138] Broughton, iv. 36-37; *Arbuthnot Jnl.* ii. 369; *Althorp Letters*, 150-1; Agar Ellis diary, 4 July; Derby mss 920 Der (14) 117/3, Althorp to Smith Stanley, 5 July; Fitzwilliam mss, Tavistock to Milton, 5 July; Howick jnl. 11 July [1830]; Add. 40340, f. 226. [139] *Althorp Letters*, 152. [140] Castle Howard mss, Abercromby to Lady Carlisle, 10 July 1830. [141] Reid, *Monckton Milnes*, i. 100. [142] Add. 36466, ff. 163, 219; *Althorp Letters*, 151-4; Wentworth Woodhouse mss G2/11, 27; *Northampton Mercury*, 10 July 1830. [143] Add. 61937, f. 116. [144] Devon RO, Earl Fortescue mss 1262M/FC 86. [145] Chatsworth mss, Brougham to Devonshire [21 Sept.]; Agar Ellis diary, 23 Sept.; Howick jnl. 27 Sept. [146] Le Marchant, 252-3. [147] Add. 252-3; Add. 75940, Althorp to Lady Spencer, 12 Oct. 1830. [148] Lansdowne mss, Macdonald to Lansdowne, 22 Oct.; Agar Ellis diary, 26 Oct.; Howick jnl. 31 Oct. [1830]; *Lieven Letters*, 260. [149] Fitzwilliam mss. [150] Agar Ellis diary, 2 Nov.; Broughton, iv. 56; Howick jnl. 2 Nov. [1830]; *Life of Campbell*, i. 483. [151] Howick jnl. 7 Nov.; Add. 51564, Brougham to Lady Holland [8 Nov. 1830]; 56555,

f. 42 ¹⁵²Broughton, iv. 64. ¹⁵³Agar Ellis diary, 12 Nov. [1830]. ¹⁵⁴Fitzwilliam mss. ¹⁵⁵Le Marchant, 259-60; *Three Diaries*, 5-6; Walpole, *Russell*, i. 159; Russell, *Recollections*, 67-68; Hatherton mss, Palmerston to Littleton, 17 Nov., Littleton to R. Wellesley, 19 Nov.; *Palmerston-Sulivan Letters*, 248; *Croker Pprs*. ii. 77; Brougham, *Life and Times*, iii. 78; *Ellenborough Diary*, ii. 440; Chatsworth mss, Brougham to Devonshire [18 Nov. 1830]. ¹⁵⁶*Greville Mems*. i. 298. ¹⁵⁷*Croker Pprs*. ii. 80; Russell, 129-30, 262. ¹⁵⁸Fitzwilliam mss, Althorp to Milton, 22 Nov. 1830. ¹⁵⁹*Northampton Mercury*, 11 Dec. 1830. ¹⁶⁰*Three Diaries*, 33. ¹⁶¹Agar Ellis diary, 17, 18 Dec.; *The Times*, 20 Dec.; *Howard Sisters*, 176; *Three Diaries*, 36; Add. 51578, Carlisle to Holland, 18 Dec.; 51569, Ord to Lady Holland, 21 Dec. [1830]; Wasson, 179. ¹⁶²Add. 51569, Ord to Lady Holland, 23 Dec. 1831. ¹⁶³Fitzwilliam mss. ¹⁶⁴Ibid. ¹⁶⁵Creevey mss. ¹⁶⁶Add. 57370, f. 66; Castle Howard mss, Abercromby to Carlisle, 30 Dec. [1830]. ¹⁶⁷*Russell Letters*, ii. 308; Broughton, iv. 78. ¹⁶⁸*Baring Jnls*. i. 80. ¹⁶⁹Add. 37310, f. 359; 57370, f. 69; 76373, Althorp to Grey [12 Dec. 1830]; Wasson, 195-7; Le Marchant, 270-1; *Arbuthnot Corresp*. 197, 198; *Grey-William IV Corresp*. i. 70, 91-94; Brougham, iii. 93-94. ¹⁷⁰*Three Diaries*, 8, 46; *Baring Jnls*. i. 80; *Greville Mems*. ii. 112-13; *Russell Letters*, ii. 320; *Grey-William IV Corresp*. i. 118-19; Le Marchant, 272; 157; PRO NI, Anglesey mss D619/27A/101. ¹⁷¹TNA 30/29, Holland to Granville, 11 Feb. [1831]. ¹⁷²Orkney Archives, Balfour mss D218/9, Traill to W. Balfour, 5 Feb. 1831. ¹⁷³Le Marchant, 288; Add. 76373, Althorp to Grey [?19 Dec. 1830]. ¹⁷⁴Le Marchant, 275-80. ¹⁷⁵*Baring Jnls*. i. 81; Add. 51569, Ord to Holland [11 Feb. 1831]; Anglesey mss 27A/100. ¹⁷⁶*Three Diaries*, 51; *Creevey Pprs*. ii. 218; Broughton, iv. 84; *Von Neumann Diary*, ii. 241-2; Anglesey mss 31D/17, 18; Add. 76373. ¹⁷⁷*Grey-William IV Corresp*. i. 127-9; Broughton, iv. 84; *Croker Pprs*. ii. 107. ¹⁷⁸*Greville Mems*. ii. 116-19. ¹⁷⁹St. Deiniol's Lib. Glynne-Gladstone mss 197, T. to J. Gladstone, 16 Feb. 1831. ¹⁸⁰*Arbuthnot Corresp*. 142. ¹⁸¹TNA 30/29. ¹⁸²*Three Diaries*, 52; *Croker Pprs*. ii. 107; Glynne-Gladstone mss 197, T. to J. Gladstone 18 Feb.; Lonsdale mss, Lowther to Lonsdale, 19 Feb.; Add. 76371, Brougham to Althorp [18 Feb. 1831]. ¹⁸³*The Times*, 23 Feb. 1831. ¹⁸⁴Add. 34614, f. 119. ¹⁸⁵*Greville Mems*. ii. 119 ¹⁸⁶*Russell Letters*, i. 167. ¹⁸⁷Add. 56555, f. 97. ¹⁸⁸Hopetoun mss 167, f. 222. ¹⁸⁹*Creevey Pprs*. ii. 220-1. ¹⁹⁰Wasson, 204-6; M. Brock, *Great Reform Act*, 142, 150-1; Broughton, iv. 75; *Life of Campbell*, i. 500; *Arbuthnot Jnl*. ii. 411; *Three Diaries*, 38-39; *Croker Pprs*. ii. 103; Le Marchant, 291, 294-5; Brougham mss, Russell to Brougham, 15 Nov. 1837; Hatherton mss, Althorp to Littleton, 1 Jan. 1831. ¹⁹¹Add. 51570, Townshend to Holland, 17 Dec. 1830. ¹⁹²Aberdeen Univ.Lib. Arbuthnot mss, Herries to Mrs. Arbuthnot, 3 Jan.; Lambton mss, Althorp to Russell [1831]; Earl Fortescue mss FC 87, same to Ebrington, 23 Jan.; Fitzwilliam mss, same to Milton, 6 mar. 1831; Wasson, 207-8. ¹⁹³Hatherton mss, Littleton to wife, 3 Feb. 1831. ¹⁹⁴*Greville Mems*. ii. 112; Brougham, *Life and Times*, iii. 103-4. ¹⁹⁵Broughton, iv. 88. ¹⁹⁶Glynne-Gladstone mss 197, T. to J. Gladstone, 2 Mar. 1831; Broughton, iv. 93; Parker, *Peel*, ii. 176. ¹⁹⁷*Grey-William IV Corresp*. i. 134-6, 148-50. ¹⁹⁸Balfour mss D2/8/9, Traill to W. Balfour, 16 Mar. 1831. ¹⁹⁹Add. 76373, Althorp to Grey [17 Mar. 1831]; *Three Diaries*, 68-69; Broughton, iv. 93; *Greville Mems*. ii. 131-2; *Arbuthnot Jnl*. ii. 414. ²⁰⁰Broughton, iv. 98. ²⁰¹*Arbuthnot Jnl*. ii. 417; Agar Ellis diary, 25 Mar. [1831]. ²⁰²Grey mss, Ellice to Grey [6 Apr.]; *Cockburn Letters*, 312-13; Glynne-Gladstone mss 454, Althorp to T. Gladstone, 7 Apr.; Add. 36466, f. 311; Hatherton mss, Althorp to Littleton, 7 Apr. 1831. ²⁰³Grey mss, Durham to Grey, 8 Apr. 1831. ²⁰⁴*Lieven-Grey Corresp*. i. 212; Add. 51655, Mackintosh to Lady Holland [19 Apr. 1831]. ²⁰⁵*Three Diaries*, 82-83. ²⁰⁶Broughton, iv. 105, 107. ²⁰⁷Le Marchant, 313-19; *Greville Mems*. ii. 144, 147; *Life of Campbell*, i. 514; Broughton, iv. 112. See NORTHAMPTONSHIRE. ²⁰⁸Add. 76373, Althorp to Grey, 6 May; 76382, Poulett Thomson to Althorp, 18, 21 May 1831. ²⁰⁹Grey mss, Althorp to Durham [29 May]; Add. 76373, same to Grey, 31 May 1831. ²¹⁰*Macaulay Letters*, ii. 46. ²¹¹Le Marchant mss, Althorp to Spencer, 21 June 1831; *Baring Jnls*. i. 88. ²¹²Le Marchant, 325. ²¹³Ibid. 323-5. ²¹⁴Ibid. 326. ²¹⁵Ibid. 326-7.

²¹⁶Le Marchant mss, Althorp to Spencer, 22 July 1831. ²¹⁷Le Marchant, 337. ²¹⁸*Holland House Diaries*, 33; *Arbuthnot Corresp*. 148; *Three Diaries*, 120; Add. 76377, Althorp to Grey [21 Aug. 1831]. ²¹⁹Add. 37311, f. 38. ²²⁰Le Marchant, 328-9; *O'Connell Corresp*. iv. 1826; *Three Diaries*, 103; Lonsdale mss, Croker to Lowther, 11 July [1831]; *Greville Mems*. ii. 164. ²²¹*Macaulay Letters*, ii. 70; Le Marchant, 333-4. ²²²*Holland House Diaries*, 5-6, 7; *Three Diaries*, 110; *Grey-William IV Corresp*. i. 310, 312; Fremantle mss 139/20/29. ²²³Broughton, iv. 123; *Three Diaries*, 109, 110. ²²⁴*Life of Campbell*, i. 526. ²²⁵Hatherton diary, 24 July [1831]. ²²⁶Ibid. 26 July; Add. 75941, Althorp to Spencer, 28 July 1831. ²²⁷Add. 56555, f. 169. ²²⁸Broughton, iv. 124; *Three Diaries*, 113; *Greville Mems*. ii. 175. ²²⁹Le Marchant, 335; *Macaulay Letters*, ii. 88; *Holland House Diaries*, 29. ²³⁰Brock, 222-9; Wasson, 221-5; *Holland House Diaries*, 29-30; *Three Diaries*, 116; Add. 76373, Althorp to Grey, Sat. night, 21 Aug. [1831]. ²³¹*Life of Campbell*, i. 518, 519. ²³²*Three Diaries*, 123. ²³³Le Marchant, 343. ²³⁴Add. 76369. ²³⁵Le Marchant, 335. ²³⁶*Macaulay Letters*, ii. 89-91. ²³⁷Gurney diary, 31 Aug. [1831]; *Lady Holland to Son*, 114; Le Marchant, 344. ²³⁸*Holland House Diaries*, 46-47. ²³⁹*Cockburn Jnl*. i. 23. ²⁴⁰*O'Connell Corresp*. iv. 1836. ²⁴¹*Holland House Diaries*, 521; *Life of Campbell*, i. 521. ²⁴²Balfour mss D2/3/14, Traill to J. Balfour, 1 Oct.; 8/13, to W. Balfour, 8 Oct. [1831]. ²⁴³Brougham, iii. 128-9; *Life of Campbell*, i. 522. ²⁴⁴Le Marchant, 354; *Baring Jnls*. i. 89-90; *Lady Lyttelton Corresp*. 263. ²⁴⁵*Holland House Diaries*, 66; *Grey-William IV Corresp*. i. 375-8; Southampton Univ. Lib. Broadlands mss PP/GC/GR/2355; Add. 76373, Althorp to Grey, 9 Oct. 1831. ²⁴⁶Le Marchant, 355. ²⁴⁷*Holland House Diaries*, 66, 69; Le Marchant, 356; Cornw. RO, Hawkins mss 16/2172; Broughton, iv. 141; *Howard Sisters*, 215. ²⁴⁸Le Marchant, 361-2; *Russell Early Corresp*. ii. 25. ²⁴⁹*Holland House Diaries*, 67-68. ²⁵⁰*Lady Lyttelton Corresp*. 264. ²⁵¹Le Marchant, 366; Add. 76373, Althorp to Grey [4 Nov. 1831]. ²⁵²Le Marchant, 367-8; Add. 76373, Althorp to Grey [18, 20 Nov. 1831]. ²⁵³*The Times*, 20, 23, 27 Dec. 1831. ²⁵⁴Earl Fortescue mss FC 87, Ellice to Ebrington, 26 Oct., Althorp to same, 3 Nov.; Add. 76373, Althorp to Grey [13 Nov.]; Hatherton mss, Althorp to Littleton, 22 Nov.; Derby mss Der (14) 117/3, Althorp to Smith Stanley, 24 Nov.; Hatherton diary, 18 Nov. 1831; *Holland House Diaries*, 79, 82; *Cockburn Letters*, 353. ²⁵⁵Hatherton diary. ²⁵⁶Add. 76373, Althorp to Grey, 20 Oct., Tuesday, Thursday night [Nov.]; Earl Fortescue mss FC 87, Althorp to Ebrington, 3 Nov.; Broadlands mss PP/GC/RI/11; Hatherton diary, 16 Nov. [1831]; Wasson, 230-1; Brock, 263-4. ²⁵⁷*Holland House Diaries*, 81; Sheffield Archives, Wharncliffe mss, Harrowby to Wharncliffe, 15 Nov.; Derby mss 117/3, Althorp to Smith Stanley, 15 Nov. 1831. ²⁵⁸Derby mss 117/3, Althorp to Smith Stanley, 24 Nov; Add. 76373, same to Grey [25 Nov. 1831]. ²⁵⁹Le Marchant, 370-2. ²⁶⁰Add. 76373, Althorp to Grey, 25 Nov. 1831. ²⁶¹Hatherton diary. ²⁶²*Three Diaries*, 162-3; *The Times*, 12 Dec. 1831; *Holland House Diaries*, 92. ²⁶³Add. 75941. ²⁶⁴Broughton, iv. 155; *Greville Mems*. ii. 228; *Lady Holland to Son*, 124; *Lieven-Grey Corresp*. ii. 305; Add. 51573, Spring Rice to Lady Holland [12 Dec.]; NLS mss 24762, f. 49; Wilts. RO, Hobhouse mss 145/2/b, Hobhouse to wife, 13 Dec. 1831; Anglesey mss 31D/78. ²⁶⁵*Holland House Diaries*, 93-94; Earl Fortescue mss FC 87, Althorp to Ebrington, 14 Dec. 1831. ²⁶⁶Add. 76373, Althorp to Grey, Tuesday [Dec.]; Hatherton diary, 17 Dec. ²⁶⁷Le Marchant, 374-5. ²⁶⁸*Baring Jnls*. i. 92. ²⁶⁹Add. 76373, Althorp to Grey, 8, 31 Dec. 1831. ²⁷⁰Add. 76373. ²⁷¹Hatherton diary, 19 Jan. [1832]; *Arbuthnot Corresp*. 161. ²⁷²*Three Diaries*, 189-90; Add. 51573, Spring Rice to Lady Holland, 6 Feb. [1832]. ²⁷³Add. 75941, Althorp to Spencer, 26, 27 Jan. 1832; *Three Diaries*, 184-5, 196-7; *Baring Jnls*. i. 92; *Holland House Diaries*, 119; Le Marchant, 389-92; *Russell Letters*, 111; Broughton, iv. 165-6, 169. ²⁷⁴*Baring Jnls*. i. 92. ²⁷⁵Glynne-Gladstone mss 199, T. to J. Gladstone, 9 Feb. 1832. ²⁷⁶*Holland House Diaries*, 138, 158; Grey mss GRE/B121/7/4; Glynne-Gladstone mss 199, T. to J. Gladstone, 27 Feb. 1832. ²⁷⁷Broughton, iv. 183. ²⁷⁸Ibid. iv. 185-6; Add. 47222, f. 146. ²⁷⁹*Holland House Diaries*, 99; Add. 51724, Althorp to Holland, 6 Jan. 1832. ²⁸⁰*Three Diaries*, 191, 195, 199; *Raikes Jnl*. i. 12; *Grey-William*

IV Corresp. ii. 226; Aberdeen Univ. Lib. Arbuthnot mss 3029/1/2/41. [281] *Holland House Diaries*, 129; Add. 75941, Althorp to Spencer, 20 Feb. 1832. [282] *Three Diaries*, 205-6. [283] Ibid. 211. [284] Ibid. 175; Add. 75941, Althorp to Spencer, 26 Jan. 1832. [285] Cockburn, *Jeffrey*, i. 322; ii. 243-4. [286] *Three Diaries*, 209, 211; *Baring Jnls*. i. 92; Le Marchant, 400-1; *Holland House Diaries*, 163; *Lady Holland to Son*, 131; Add. 75941, Althorp to Spencer, 10, 17 Mar. 1832. [287] *Three Diaries*, 215. [288] *Holland House Diaries*, 109, 134, 138, 144, 147, 149, 151, 158; Parker, *Graham*, i. 135; Add. 76369, Althorp to Brougham, 3, 7 Jan.; 76373, same to Grey [10 Jan.]; 75941, same to Spencer, 11, 13, 31 Jan., 20 Feb., 10 Mar. 1832; *Russell Early Corresp.* ii. 29-30; Le Marchant, 385-6, 40-6, 407-14; Broughton, iv. 178-81. 188-92, 194-6, 207-8; *Grey-William IV Corresp.* ii. 257-8, 262; *Three Diaries*, 214; Wasson, 232, 236-9. [289] *Russell Early Corresp,* ii. 30; Broughton, iv. 209. [290] Broughton, iv. 209; Add. 75941, Althorp to Spencer, 5 Apr. 1832. [291] Le Marchant, 415-17; *Baring Jnls*. i. 94. [292] Broughton, iv. 212, 213, 216; Add. 75941, Althorp to Spencer [14], 16 Apr. 1832. [293] *The Times*, 27 Apr., 4 May 1832. [294] Le Marchant, 419; Add. 75941, Althorp to Spencer, 7 May 1832. [295] Add. 75941, Althorp to Spencer, 7, 8, 9 May 1832. [296] Cockburn, *Jeffrey*, i. 330-2. [297] *Three Diaries*, 245, 247; Le Marchant, 423-4; Add. 75941, Althorp to Spencer [10 May 1832]. [298] Add. 75941, Althorp to Spencer [10 May 1832]; Broughton, 221-2; *Three Diaries*, 248; *Grey-William IV Corresp.* ii. 400-2; *Baring Jnls*. i. 97. [299] *Croker Pprs.* ii. 157. [300] *Life of Campbell*, ii. 10; *Three Diaries*, 251; Le Marchant, 429; Add. 75941, Althorp to Spencer, 14 May 1832. [301] *Croker Pprs.* ii. 165; *Three Diaries*, 254-5, 258. [302] Broughton, iv. 226; Cockburn, *Jeffrey*, i. 332; *Creevey's Life and Times*, 356-7. [303] Add. 75941, Althorp to Spencer [16], 17, 18 May 1832; *Three Diaries*, 263; *Holland House Diaries*, 183. [304] *Croker Pprs.* ii. 169. [305] Add. 75941, Althorp to Spencer, 18, 19 May 1832; Wasson, 240-4. [306] Le Marchant, 438-9. [307] Grey mss, Ellice to Grey [May 1832]. [308] *Buxton Mems.* 287; Grey mss, Howick to Althorp, 23 May, reply, 24 May; Bodl. (Rhodes House), Buxton mss Brit. Emp. s. 444, vol. 3, p. 29, Buxton to Althorp, 24 May 1832. [309] *Grey-William IV Corresp.* ii. 457-8. [310] *Holland House Diaries*, 196. [311] Ibid. 194. [312] *The Times*, 30 June 1832. [313] *Althorp Letters*, 157-8; Broughton, iv. 248. [314] Broughton, iv. 247 [315] *Greville Mems.* ii. 317. [316] Ibid. ii. 313, 315. [317] *Three Diaries*, 279. [318] *O'Connell Corresp.* iv. 1907. [319] Broughton, iv. 250. [320] Wentworth Woodhouse mss G17/2. [321] *Althorp Letters*, 159-60; Le Marchant, 442-3. [322] Wasson, 256-349; *Oxford DNB*. [323] *Lady Lyttelton Corresp.* 355; Le Marchant, 562-3. [324] *Greville Mems.* v. 230-2. [325] *Edinburgh Rev.* lxxxiii (1846), 251. [326] Brougham, iii. 253-4. [327] *Greville Mems.* v. 232.

D.R.F.

SPENCER CHURCHILL, Lord Charles (1794–1840), of Blenheim, Oxon. and 26 Grosvenor Street, Mdx.

ST. ALBANS	1818–1820
NEW WOODSTOCK	1830–1832
NEW WOODSTOCK	1835–1837

b. 3 Dec. 1794, 2nd s. of George Spencer† (afterwards Spencer Churchill), 5th duke of Marlborough, and Lady Susan Stewart, da. of John Stewart†, 7th earl of Galloway [S]; bro. of George Spencer Churchill, mq. of Blandford*. *educ.* Eton 1805-8. *m.* 24 Aug. 1827, Ethelred Catherine, da. of John Benett*, 2s. 3da. *d.* 29 Apr. 1840.[1] Ensign 68 Ft. 1811; 2nd lt. 95 Ft. and a.d.c. to Maj.-Gen. Hon. William Stewart† 1812; lt. 52 Ft. 1813; 1st lt. 95 Ft. 1813; capt. 60 Ft. 1815; capt. 85 Ft. 1815; half-pay 1823; capt. 75 Ft. 1824, maj. 1825; lt.-col. (half-pay) 1827, ret. 1832.

Spencer Churchill, whose profligate and impoverished father had succeeded as 5th duke of Marlborough in 1817 (when Spencer Churchill masqueraded as a clergyman to officiate at the mock marriage of his elder brother Lord Blandford to a young ingenue), was always short of money.[2] Two contested elections in the space of four months in 1818 for St. Albans, where his father had property, saddled him with considerable debts; and his still unpaid bills deterred him from showing his face in the borough at the general election of 1820.[3] In the 1818 Parliament he had acted, on the rare occasions when he was present, with the Whig opposition (he had joined Brooks's on 13 May 1818); but, like Marlborough, he now looked to the Liverpool ministry for a way out of his financial difficulties.[4] After the 1820 election, when an Oxfordshire Whig intervened successfully against his interest at Woodstock, Marlborough expressed the private view that as a one of their supporters had apparently '*opened the door of my dwelling*' by alerting him to the opportunity, ministers 'ought to assist my son Charles with a seat', for 'unless ... [he] gets in somewhere, he will be *arrested*'.[5] In 1821 Spencer Churchill sought a brevet promotion to major, approaching in the first instance the duke of Wellington, master-general of the ordnance, who passed on his memorial to horse guards. Nothing came of this, and he renewed his application in January 1823, shortly after returning from Malta. He was again unsuccessful, being told, as before, that without a specific recommendation, which Wellington felt unable to give, he had no chance of what amounted to preferential treatment.[6] His plight was worsened when he was placed on half-pay later in the year.

While he was in Paris in 1819 he had attracted the attention of the snobbish Mrs. Trelawny Brereton (soon to be widowed), who saw him as a socially desirable catch for her daughter Charlotte. Despite his pleas of poverty and his languid courtship during the next few years, she continued to construct fantasies:

> Every person gives him the character of being amiable and very good tempered, steady and prudent in his expenditure. I have never heard of his gaming, and am pretty certain he is a very sober man. As a soldier his character stands well. His being near thirty I believe ... [Charlotte] likes.[7]

Reality intruded when Spencer Churchill was hauled before the insolvent debtors court in the autumn of 1823. He was granted two extensions of time to file his schedule. At the final hearing, 9 Apr. 1824, it was revealed that he had paid off £3,000 of his St. Albans debts by borrowing from one Simpson, had contracted several other debts in London and had as his only income his captain's half-pay of 7s. a day and a discretionary allowance of £400 a year under the will of his late grandfather, the 4th duke, which had been occasionally withheld and latterly 'suspended' by the trustees. Counsel for his creditors complained that with such a modest income he had 'speculated with the property of others' to obtain a seat in Parliament, and called for a significant portion of his half-pay to be assigned for their benefit. On his behalf it was submitted that while his debts were large, their having been inflated by the notorious rapacity of St. Albans electors entitled him to lenient treatment. He was discharged without penalty.[8] Negotiations between the Marlborough and Trelawny Brereton lawyers soon afterwards produced a proposal that if Spencer Churchill married Charlotte, his debts would be paid and he would receive £10,000, while she would have £400 a year and £7,000 on her mother's death. He did not consider this acceptable, and the affair came to an end. Over the next few years his mother persuaded the Marlborough trustees to pay off his most pressing debts.[9] Shortly before the final bankruptcy hearing his parents appealed to Wellington, who granted him an interview, to endorse his bid for promotion. The duke was still unable to do more than offer a general recommendation, but in October 1824 Spencer Churchill obtained a captaincy in the 75th Foot, and he received a regular promotion in December 1825.[10] At the contested Woodstock election of 1826, when Blandford stood with a kinsman to reassert the supremacy of the Blenheim interest, Spencer Churchill, fighting 'without his shirt', joined him in a street brawl with supporters of their opponents.[11] Immediately after his marriage to the daughter of one of the Members for Wiltshire in August 1827, he unsuccessfully applied for the vacant post of inspecting field officer of militia in the Ionian Islands.[12] Four months later he was placed on a lieutenant-colonel's half-pay. He sought to step into the shoes of Lord Graves*, a suicide, as a commissioner of excise in February 1830, but Wellington, now premier, told him that no new appointment was to be made.[13]

At the general election of 1830 he stood for Woodstock with Blandford, who, outraged by the concession of Catholic emancipation, had espoused parliamentary reform and gone into opposition. In his own address, Spencer Churchill promised to 'maintain ... inviolate' the 'British constitution in church and state'. They were unopposed.[14] Ministers, tarring him with the same brush as his brother, listed him among

their 'foes', while Henry Brougham* claimed him as a gain for opposition. He duly voted with his brother against government on the civil list, 15 Nov. 1830. Unlike Blandford, however, he could not swallow the Grey ministry's reform bill, and he voted against its second reading, 22 Mar., and for Gascoyne's wrecking amendment, 19 Apr. 1831, after presenting an anti-reform petition from his constituency. At the ensuing general election, when Blandford stood down, Spencer Churchill was returned for Woodstock with another opponent of the bill after a token contest forced by a reformer who tried to establish the validity of a householder franchise.[15] He voted against the second reading of the reintroduced reform bill, 6 July, and at least twice for an adjournment, 12 July 1831. On the proposal to disfranchise Woodstock (which was eventually reprieved as a single Member borough), 26 July, he told an apparently indifferent House that it was 'one of the most independent constituencies in the kingdom' and that 'no influence whatever would induce the voters ... to swerve for one moment from the straightforward course':

> Honesty and independence have ever been their motto. I have been, from the earliest period of my life, a reformer; but I cannot bring myself to think there is any necessity of going to such lengths as ... [Russell] has proposed to go in his plan. I should be very willing to give the large manufacturing towns representatives, but not at the expense of those boroughs, which derive their right of franchise from ancient charters. I am not ... one of those who would rob Peter to pay Paul.

He voted to postpone considering the partial disfranchisement of Chippenham, 27 July, and to preserve the voting rights of non-resident freemen, 30 Aug. He divided against the passage of the bill, 21 Sept. Next day he was given a week's leave on account of illness in his family. At about this time opposition leaders persuaded his father to take his seat in the Lords and leave his proxy for use against the reform bill.[16] Spencer Churchill was absent from the division on the second reading of the revised bill, 17 Dec. 1831; and his only recorded votes in the last session of the unreformed Parliament were against its third reading, 22 Mar., and with opposition on the Russian-Dutch loan, 12 July 1832. He sold out of the army that year.

At the dissolution of 1832 he made way at Woodstock for Blandford. On the formation of Peel's first ministry two years later he pledged his support, in concert with his father and brother, but was an unsuccessful applicant for gainful employment.[17] He was returned unopposed for Woodstock at the general election of 1835, but was narrowly defeated there in

1837. Spencer Churchill, who was widowed in 1839, died, aged 45, in April 1840.[18] By his brief will, dated 8 Apr. 1840, he left all his property in trust to his five children, who were still minors, and by a codicil of the same date he gave £100 to a Miss Clarissa Parry 'as a testimony of my regards for her attention to myself and to my children'. His personalty, which yielded a taxable residue of £1,692, was sworn under £4,000, but his financial affairs appear still to have been in some disarray.[19]

[1] *HP Commons, 1790-1820*, v. 244, following *Burke PB*, gives 28 Apr.; but the 29th is confirmed by IR26/1543/476. [2] M. Soames, *The Profligate Duke*, 153. [3] *Althorp Letters*, 102. [4] Add. 38285, ff. 20, 67, 222; 38288, f. 112; 38289, ff. 19, 122, 177; 38290, ff. 315, 317, 323. [5] St. Deiniol's Lib. Glynne-Gladstone mss 290, Marlborough to J. Gladstone, 13 Mar. 1820. [6] Wellington mss WP1/669/18, 20; 754/14, 21. [7] A. Hill, *Trelawny's Strange Relations*, 17. [8] *The Times*, 24 Sept., 22 Nov. 1823, 10 Apr. 1824; *Arbuthnot Jnl.* i. 305. [9] Soames, 206-7; Hill, 17-18. [10] Wellington mss WP1/788/16; 789/13, 14. [11] *VCH Oxon.* xii. 404; Bodl. Ms. Top. Oxon. c. 351, f. 169. [12] Wellington mss WP1/895/49. [13] Ibid. WP1/1094/3. [14] *Jackson's Oxford Jnl.* 10 July; *Oxford University and City Herald*, 7 Aug. 1830. [15] *Jackson's Oxford Jnl.* 30 Apr., 7 May 1831; *VCH Oxon.* xii. 405. [16] Wellington mss WP1/1184/1; 1196/23; *Arbuthnot Corresp.* 150. [17] Add. 40405, ff. 76, 80; 40407, f. 28; 40409, ff. 183, 185. [18] *The Times*, 1 May 1840; *Gent. Mag.* (1840), ii. 205. [19] PROB 11/1932/560; IR26/1543/476.

D.R.F.

SPENCER CHURCHILL, **George**, mq. of Blandford (1793–1857).

CHIPPENHAM	1818–1820
NEW WOODSTOCK	1826–1831
NEW WOODSTOCK	1832–1834
NEW WOODSTOCK	11 May 1838–5 Mar. 1840

b. 27 Dec. 1793, 1st s. of George Spencer[†] (afterwards Spencer Churchill), 5th duke of Marlborough, and Lady Susan Stewart, da. of John Stewart[†], 7th earl of Galloway [S]; bro. of Lord Charles Spencer Churchill*. *educ.* Eton 1805-11.[1] *m.* 11 Jan. 1819, his cos. Lady Jane Stewart (*d.* 12 Oct. 1844), da. of George Stewart[†], 8th earl of Galloway [S], 3s. 1da.; (2) 10 June 1846, Hon. Charlotte Augusta Flower (*d.* 20 Apr. 1850), da. of Henry Jeffery, 4th Visct. Ashbrook [I], 1s. *d.v.p.* 1da.; (3) 18 Oct. 1851, his cos. Jane Frances Clinton, da. of Hon. Edward Richard Stewart[†], 1s. *styled* earl of Sunderland 1793-1817, mq. of Blandford 1817-40; *suc.* fa. as 6th duke of Marlborough 5 Mar. 1840. *d.* 1 July 1857.
Ld. lt. Oxon. 1842-d.
Capt. 3 R. Berks. militia 1812; capt. 1 Oxon. yeoman cav. 1817, lt.-col. commdt. 1845.

In 1811 John William Ward* described the 17-year-old Blandford as 'a very fine lad', who 'seems to have

good parts, and a good disposition'.[2] He did not improve with age, and four years later George Agar Ellis* referred to his 'drunkenness, obstinacy, indolence, shocking temper, duplicity and bad manners', which had contributed significantly to ruining his chances of securing the vacant seat for Oxfordshire.[3] Like his father, who succeeded as 5th duke of Marlborough in 1817 but barely had two pennies to rub together, he had the morals of a goat. In 1816 he had an affair with Lady Elizabeth Conyngham, which petered out. On 16 Mar. 1817 he went through a ceremony of mock marriage, performed by his soldier brother Lord Charles, posing as a clergyman, to Susannah Adelaide Law of Bayswater, who was not yet 17. They lived for a time in London as Captain and Mrs. Lawson, and he settled £400 a year on her. When she discovered the deception, Blandford, under pressure from her indignant parents, admitted the invalidity of the marriage but promised to take her to Scotland, where it could be regarded as legal by being publicly recognized. This he did in August 1818, five months after she had given birth to a daughter. Following Blandford's marriage to his aristocratic cousin in 1819, his association with Susannah ceased, but his mother continued to pay her the annuity, though it was subsequently reduced to £200 and she was forced to return some incriminating letters.[4] Blandford had also enjoyed the favours (widely bestowed) of his disreputable cousin Harriet Spencer, who in 1818 had his child, named Susan Harriet Elizabeth Churchill. She was taken in by Lady Bessborough, after whose death in 1821 she was raised at Brocket by Lady Caroline Lamb and her husband William Lamb*.[5]

In the family tradition, Blandford was at odds with his father, who in 1819 separated from the duchess and lived openly at Blenheim with his young mistress Maria Glover; she bore him half-a-dozen bastards.[6] As Member for Chippenham in the 1818 Parliament Blandford, who had joined Brooks's, 17 Feb. 1817, seems to have acted, when present, with the Whig opposition, though he rallied to the Liverpool ministry in support of the repressive legislation which followed Peterloo. He did not seek re-election for Chippenham in 1820. (It was reported ten years later that he 'still owed a large sum' there.)[7] He was expected to come in for Woodstock, where the Blenheim interest was dominant, but his father offered one seat to Lord Liverpool, who recommended John Gladstone*, a wealthy merchant, while James Langston*, a rich Oxfordshire Whig squire, made an opportunist bid for the second seat. In a curiously worded address Blandford, who admitted that his canvass had been unpromising, and seems to have been aiming at his father with his reference to a threat to the electors' 'independence', withdrew, on the pretext that he was not prepared to unite with another candidate.[8] The impecunious Marlborough, saddled with large estate debts, bombarded Liverpool with vain requests for employment and a remission of the tax on his post office pension during the 1820 Parliament.[9] In September 1825 Blandford declared his candidature for Woodstock at the next election, in tandem with his cousin Lord Ashley.[10] At the general election the following June, when he stressed that he was 'decidedly hostile' to Catholic claims, they were returned after a contest against Langston and a stranger, in the course of which Blandford was reported to have brawled in the street.[11]

He voted against Catholic relief, 6 Mar. 1827. On the 12th he was excused attendance on the Berwick election committee (which unseated Gladstone) on account of illness.[12] In his maiden speech, 23 Mar., he opposed the spring guns bill, arguing that the devices provided a 'salutary terror' and that objections to them stemmed from 'a kind of morbid sensitivity'. He secured a return of information on the number of persons killed by the guns in the last five years, 28 Mar.,[13] and was a teller for the minority against the third reading of the bill, 30 Mar. His father, who was denounced by one observer as 'a very shambling animal', switched his allegiance to Canning as prime minister, but Blandford was in the minority against the second reading of the government's corn bill, 2 Apr. 1827.[14] Like his father, he initially supported the duke of Wellington's administration.[15] He voted against Catholic relief, 12 May 1828. Planta, the patronage secretary, was 'doubtful' as to how Blandford would react to the ministry's concession of Catholic emancipation. In fact, he was enraged. In his fury he turned against the government, and he briefly occupied a position of quixotic prominence on the political stage. On 6 Mar. 1829 he accused Wellington and Peel of betraying the Protestant constitution, complained that the Commons was out of step with majority popular opinion and said that ministers had 'so conducted the affairs of the country, as to have involved us in the fearful alternative of rebellion and civil war, or instant and unconditional surrender to the insulting menaces and demands of Jesuits and Jacobins'. He voted against emancipation twice that day, and again on 18, 23, 27, 30 Mar. He presented a hostile petition, 17 Mar., and on the 27th called for the issue to be put before 'the tribunal of public opinion', and declaimed:

> We live in days of political experiment, and we daily witness established principles and acknowledged facts,

giving way to some gratis dictum about 'public expediency'; and a restless spirit of innovation, a spirit of gambling in codes and constitutions, seems to obtain, and is one of the strongly marked signs of portentous events hurrying fast on to the fullness of their completion.

He concluded with the observation that every 'sober' friend of the established church must now be convinced that 'the hour is now come, in which it is not only expedient, but highly necessary, that we should, without delay, honestly and effectually enter upon the consideration of the question of parliamentary reform'. He expanded on this theme, 5 May, when, speaking on the East Retford question, he raised the spectre of a Commons and state dominated by 'Roman Catholic wealth':

> By some method of parliamentary reform, care must be taken to prevent the increase of Popish influence within these walls, through the means of corrupt boroughs, which ... we had better at once erase from the political map of the country, than leave for the grasp of Papal ambition.

On the question at issue he abstained, approving neither of the proposal to transfer East Retford's seats to Birmingham, nor of sluicing the borough, not least because the latter plan was recommended by 'a government from whom recent events have compelled me to withdraw every degree of confidence'. On 2 June 1829, after warning of the potential 'influx and increase of the Roman Catholic party' and the threat posed to agriculture by the 'odious principle of free trade', and proposing the abolition of 'close and decayed boroughs' and the transfer of their seats to unspecified populous places, he moved two resolutions condemning corrupt boroughs, bribery and the buying of seats as 'disgraceful to the character of this House, destructive of the confidence of the people, and prejudicial to the best interests of the country'. He received support from O'Neill, Benett, Hume, Hobhouse and William Smith, but his first resolution was rejected by 114-40.[16] He gave notice the following day that he would raise the issue again next session. A few weeks later Sir Richard Vyvyan, the leader of the Ultras in the Commons, commented to associates that Blandford (who in one ludicrous newspaper plan of a new administration was named as home secretary and leader of the House) had 'done incalculable mischief' with his espousal of reform, and was to be approached with caution. He recalled that

> once or twice before the prorogation, a few words passed between us on that delicate subject; as I was not intimate with him, I could not of course enlarge upon the impolicy of his proceeding, but I touched upon it and found

him perfectly headstrong and resolved to make it a cause of his own.[17]

He duly listed Blandford among Tories 'strongly opposed to the present government' in October 1829.

On 4 Feb. 1830, after giving notice for the 18th of a motion for leave to introduce 'a bill for the better prevention of abuses in the election of Members', Blandford seconded the Ultra Knatchbull's amendment to the address, calling for action to deal with the current 'all-pervading and intolerable distress', specifically a large reduction of the tax burden:

It has been with too great justice remarked of this House, that its Members say a great deal, but that they do a very little ...These ... are not times for men to waste hours in lengthy orations, or be striving to outdo in effusions of frothy eloquence when they should be found acting. Neither are these times suited for the apprehensive sensibilities of the timid, or for the silky lispings of the mealy-mouthed.

He was a teller for the minority. On the report of the address the following day he appealed for and secured O'Connell's support for an amendment denouncing close and decayed boroughs and advocating reform. He 'rather foolishly', as Knatchbull's son saw it, disregarded Burdett's plea not to divide the House when so few reformers were present, and secured a derisory minority of 11 against 96.[18] He also stubbornly divided the House, which was promptly counted out, on his amendment demanding attention to distress before voting supplies, 9 Feb.; and in the same sense, he moved the adjournment of the committee of supply, 11 Feb., when he mustered ten supporters, including O'Connell, against 105. His similar motion of 15 Feb., brought on after voting for Hume's call for a reduction of taxes, was defeated by 189-9. Next day Mrs. Arbuthnot, Wellington's confidante, reflected that 'our opponents are just such as we might have chosen for ourselves', among them Blandford, 'who is said to have lost £26,000 at Doncaster races and not to have paid the debt'. (It seems that the loss had been incurred in 1827, when it was put at £15,000.)[19] Knatchbull confirmed Blandford's isolation and singularity with his comment to his wife, 15 Feb., that he was 'very perverse and obstinate, and has no weight in the House'.[20] He now voted for the transfer of East Retford's seats to Birmingham, 11 Feb. On 18 Feb. he unveiled his reform scheme, which proposed the establishment of a standing committee of 21 Members to scrutinise and report on delinquent boroughs and identify populous places with which to replace them, adopting a householder franchise. His plan also embraced the payment of Members; the disfranchise-

ment of non-resident voters, while allowing taxed householders to vote in their nearest borough; extension of the county franchise to copy and leaseholders and the abolition of Scottish parchment votes; reductions in the cost of the mechanics of polling; repeal of the Septennial Act and abolition of the property qualification for Members; the exclusion of all office-holders from the Commons, and the admission of clergymen. Hume seconded the motion. When Brougham urged him to accept a general resolution for reform, which would attract greater support, Blandford agreed and, with the support of Lord Althorp, a motion to the effect that reform was 'expedient' was put. It was negatived, and 'by some unaccountable confusion', as John Hobhouse remembered, several Whig reformers, including himself, Althorp, Brougham and Lord John Russell, voted for Blandford's motion for leave to introduce a bill, which was defeated by 160-57.[21] Some Whigs were unimpressed: Lord Howick, though he voted with Blandford, considered his speech 'a mere schoolboy's declamation with a few good sentences in it', and the scheme 'such a tissue of nonsense as never was seen'; the duke of Bedford and his son Lord Tavistock* thought Blandford was harming the cause, and Agar Ellis deemed his 'heads for his reform bill ... ridiculously absurd'.[22] Encouraged by the formation of the Birmingham Political Union in January 1830, Blandford had immediately communicated details of his plan to Thomas Attwood†, who was able to deliver the Union's public endorsement of it on 16 Mar.; and while it had little practical value, Blandford's initiative helped to stimulate the reviving interest in reform and to stir the Whigs into action.[23] He voted for Russell's proposal for the enfranchisement of Birmingham, Leeds and Manchester, 23 Feb., and O'Connell's amendment to incorporate the secret ballot in the East Retford bill, 15 Mar., and presented and endorsed a reform petition from a Norfolk parish, 18 Mar. 1830.

He divided for reductions in the army estimates, 19, 22 Feb., when, denying that his opposition to government proceeded 'solely from factious motives and the actuations of anti-Catholic spleen', he exclaimed that 'on the behalf of an abused and insulted people ... crying to this House for relief loudly, but in vain, I do protest against ... ministers being permitted to lay their sacrilegious hands upon the nation's money'. He presented petitions complaining of the practice of letting out the unemployed poor, 23 Feb., and against any alteration of the currency, 26 Feb. When he complained, 22 Mar., that the returns which he had ordered last session of the number of voters in every borough had not yet been produced, Peel told him that he was asking for the impossible. He voted for reductions in the army estimates that day. On 18 Mar. he was a teller for the minority of nine for O'Connell's attempt to adjourn the debate on Davenport's motion for inquiry into the state of the nation. Supporting the motion, 23 Mar., he called for tax remissions of over £10,000,000, the abolition of sinecures and the lowering of public salaries, and urged the people to address the king 'in the language of truth', as 'there is no longer sympathy between the people and the legislature'. He voted for a revision of taxation, 26 Mar., abolition of the Bathurst and Dundas pensions, 26 Mar., when he presented a petition for repeal of the beer and malt duties, and for economies in the ordnance department, 29 Mar. He presented a petition from Jews of Rochester and Chatham for emancipation, 2 Apr., and voted in that sense, 5 Apr., 17 May. He took great exception to Lord Ellenborough's divorce bill, 6 Apr., observing, in an astonishing display of hypocrisy, that Lady Ellenborough, 'young, giddy, thoughtless and inexperienced as she has been described to be, was neglected, abandoned and sacrificed'; he was a teller for the minority of 16 against the third reading. Later that day he presented a Shoreditch petition for a remission of taxation. He voted with O'Connell for the reform of Irish vestries, 27 Apr., and the production of information on the trial of the Doneraile conspirators, 12 May, and divided for abolition of the Irish lord lieutenancy, 11 May, repeal of the Irish coal duties, 13 May, and inquiry into Irish first fruits revenues, 18 May. He voted against government on the Terceira incident, 28 Apr., the treasury grant, 10 May, privy councillors' emoluments, 14 May, and the civil government of Canada, 25 May. On 17 May he secured 18 votes for his attempt to adjourn the debate on the third reading of Portman's parish watch bill. He voted for abolition of the death penalty for forgery, 24 May. He divided for O'Connell's radical reform bill, 28 May, and Russell's more moderate plan, 28 May, and presented an agriculturists' petition for reform, 17 June 1830.

At the general election that summer he recommended to the independents of Marlborough his friend Robert Torrens*, the political economist, who proved to be too radical for them, and whose persistence created considerable confusion.[24] He himself was returned unopposed for Woodstock with his brother Charles. In a long address, he denounced the betrayal represented by Catholic emancipation, which had failed to tranquillize Ireland, rehearsed his arguments for reform and dismissed as inadequate the government's measures of economy.[25] Ministers listed him among their 'foes'. It was expected in opposition circles that he would move an 'ultra-radical' amendment to the address 'about reform, universal suffrage,

etc.'; and he told Althorp that what he had in mind was 'so violent that he does not expect 10 people to vote with him and expects to be laughed at'.[26] He moved his amendment, 2 Nov. 1830, claiming to be doing so chiefly for the edification of the new king; it was seconded by O'Connell, but negatived without a division. Howick noted that the amendment was 'almost as long as a pamphlet and still more absurd than what he had said'; Agar Ellis considered it 'foolish', and James Hope Vere reported that the 'yard-long amendment' had 'excited much laughter'.[27] Blandford presented a Woodstock petition for the abolition of slavery, 5 Nov. He voted against government on the civil list, 15 Nov., and the following day presented and supported the prayer of a petition from Horsham for the ballot and shorter parliaments. The ever-needy Marlborough vainly sought a place from Lord Grey, the new premier, with an offer of his own and his sons' support.[28] Blandford was given three weeks' leave on account of the disturbed state of his neighbourhood, 6 Dec., but does not seem to have taken much advantage of it. On the 9th, recalling Grey's enthusiasm for reform in 1793, he expressed disappointment at his recent cautious statement, observed that the proceedings of the Calne and Knaresborough election committees gave him little confidence in the Whig reformers, and demanded, as essential immediate measures, an 'extensive' and 'radical' reform and a reduction of salaries to the standard of 1792. He presented a Diss petition for relief from distress, 10 Dec. On 18 Dec. 1830 he said that if the Liverpool petitioners against the bribery there did not persevere, he would raise the matter himself. A month later John Croker recalled:

> The last day I was in the House I had some serious talk with Blandford in the vote office, and I took leave of him with a 'good-bye, *Citizen Churchill*'. How men of rank and fortune, and above all, those who have nothing but rank and fortune, can lend themselves to a faction that seek to annihilate them, passes my comprehension. To do Citizen Churchill justice, however, he seemed to me to be alarmed and inclined to train off.[29]

He presented an Irish petition praying for the Catholics of Galway to be placed on the same footing as Protestants in the matter of the franchise, 9 Feb. 1831. Alarmed or not, Blandford, who was given a week's sick leave, 15 Mar., was present to vote silently for the second reading of the ministerial reform bill, 22 Mar., and against Gascoyne's wrecking amendment, 19 Apr. 1831. At the ensuing general election, being at odds with his father and brother on reform, he did not stand for Woodstock, which returned Lord

Charles and another anti-reformer.[30] Two months later, in anticipation of a rumoured vacancy which did not occur, he declared his hand for Oxfordshire, promising to 'support those measures which I shall deem best calculated for restoring that which time has impaired, for cleansing that which corruption has polluted, for rectifying that which craft has twisted aside from its proper use and real design'.[31]

Blandford, who in November 1831 secured a king's bench ruling for a criminal information against one Henry Jardis over an offensive letter concerning non-payment of a Doncaster gambling debt, was expected to be called to the Lords by the ministry if it proved necessary to create enough peers to carry the reform bill; but he later claimed that he had declined the proposal.[32] He was returned unopposed for Woodstock (now a single Member borough) at the general election of 1832, and drifted back towards the Conservatives. On the formation of Peel's first administration he pledged 'strenuous and constant support', but failed in his request for elevation to the Lords.[33] He made way for his brother at Woodstock at the next general election, but came in again in May 1838, when he narrowly defeated his Liberal youngest brother Lord John at a by-election. In November that year he was forced to go to law to establish the legitimacy of his first son and heir, following allegations in the *Satirist* that his marriage to Susannah Law was valid. He won the case, but the sordid evidence which was paraded reflected badly on his morals and earned him the censure of the judge.[34] He succeeded as 6th duke of Marlborough in 1840 and secured the lord lieutenancy of Oxfordshire from Peel two years later.[35] In 1853 his third wife, who was many years his junior, applied to the courts for custody of their son, accusing him of kidnap and of adultery with his housekeeper, Sarah Licence. He was forced to grant her free access to the child, but retained the services of Licence.[36] He spent his last years in a wheel chair, crippled by gout. He died, aged 63, in July 1851, so much forgotten that his obituarist dwelt at length on the life and exploits of his illustrious ancestor.[37] In his will, dated 27 June 1854, he tried to provide for his children from meagre resources, ignored his wife and left Licence £50 and £3 a week for life, together with items of furniture.[38] He was succeeded in the dukedom by his thoroughly respectable eldest son John Winston Spencer Churchill (1822-83), who served as viceroy of Ireland, 1876-80.

[1] *HP Commons, 1790-1820*, v. 244, following *Gent. Mag.* (1857), ii. 214, states that he matriculated at Christ Church, Oxford in 1811; but he is not listed as having done so in *Al. Ox.* There was talk in 1811 of his being sent to Scotland to continue his education

after leaving Eton (Ward, *Letters to 'Ivy'*, 129). [2] Ward, *Letters to 'Ivy'*, 129. [3] M. Soames, *The Profligate Duke*, 143. [4] Ibid. 152-3; A.L. Rowse, *The Later Churchills*, 203. [5] Soames, 177-8. She was educated in Switzerland, married a Swiss and died in 1882. See D. Howell-Thomas, *Lord Melbourne's Susan*. [6] Soames, 133. [7] St. Deiniol's Lib. Glynne-Gladstone mss 195, T. to J. Gladstone, 26 June 1830. [8] *Jackson's Oxford Jnl*. 19 Feb., 4, 11 Mar. 1820; *VCH Oxon*. xii. 404; Harewood mss HAR/GC/83, Gladstone to Backhouse, 28 Nov. [?1824]. [9] Add. 38285, ff. 20, 67, 222, 235; 38288, f. 112; 38289, ff. 19, 20, 122, 177; 38290, ff. 315, 317, 323; 38299, ff. 208, 209; 38371, f. 9. [10] *Oxford University and City Herald*, 3 Sept.; *Jackson's Oxford Jnl*. 8 Oct. 1825. [11] *The Times*, 6, 13 June; *Jackson's Oxford Jnl*. 10, 17 June 1826; Bodl. MS. Top. Oxon. c. 351, f. 169; *VCH Oxon*. xii. 404. [12] Glynne-Gladstone mss 194, T. to J. Gladstone, 12 Mar. 1827. [13] *The Times*, 29 Mar. 1827. [14] Add. 36463, f. 415. [15] Wellington mss WP1/939/7. [16] Broughton, *Recollections*, iii. 322. [17] Cornw. RO, Vyvyan mss, Vyvyan to Newcastle, 20 July, 25 Aug., to Sadler, 22 Aug. 1829. [18] Cent. Kent. Stud. Knatchbull mss U951 C38/8, C.H. to N. Knatchbull, 5 Feb. 1830. [19] *Arbuthnot Jnl*. ii. 334; Soames, 222. [20] Knatchbull mss C127/42. [21] Broughton, iv. 9. [22] J. Cannon, *Parl. Reform*, 193-5; Add. 36466, f. 23; Grey mss, Howick jnl. 18 Feb.; 51670, Bedford to Lady Holland, 20 Feb.; Northants. RO, Agar Ellis diary, 18 Feb. [1830]. [23] C. Flick, *Birmingham Political Union*, 39; Cannon, 194-5; M. Brock, *Great Reform Act*, 62; *Bill for Parl. Reform, as proposed by mq. of Blandford ... with Declaration of Birmingham Pol. Union thereon* (1831). [24] Wilts. RO, Marlborough (Burke) mss 124/4/2-6, 12, 13, 25. See MARLBOROUGH. [25] *Jackson's Oxford Jnl*. 10 July 1830. [26] *Life of Campbell*, i. 482; Fitzwilliam mss, Althorp to Milton, 2 Nov. 1830. [27] Howick jnl. 2 Nov.; Agar Ellis diary, 2 Nov. [1830]; Hopetoun mss 167, f. 177. [28] *VCH Oxon*. xii. 405. [29] *Croker Pprs*. ii. 100. [30] Add. 51604, Granville to Holland, 25 Apr.; *Jackson's Oxford Jnl*. 30 Apr. 1831. [31] *Jackson's Oxford Jnl*. 28 May 1831. [32] *The Times*, 19 Nov. 1831; *Greville Mems*. ii. 283; Add. 40405, f. 76. [33] Add. 40309, f. 289; 40405, ff. 76, 80; 40407, ff. 28, 47; 40408, f. 189. [34] *The Times*, 10, 19, 23 Nov. 1838; Soames, 153-6; J. Watney, *The Churchills*, 69. [35] Add. 40486, ff. 212, 214; 40506, ff. 110, 112. [36] Rowse, 212-13; K. Fleming, *The Churchills*, 107-8. [37] *Gent. Mag.* (1857), ii. 214-15. [38] PROB 11/2257/696; IR26/2105/764; Rowse, 213-15.

D.R.F.

SPOONER, Richard (1783–1864), of Glindon House, Warws.

BOROUGHBRIDGE	1820–7 June 1820
BIRMINGHAM	15 July 1844–1847
WARWICKSHIRE NORTH	1847–24 Nov. 1864

b. 28 July 1783, 5th s. of Isaac Spooner (*d.* 1816), nail manufacturer and banker, of Elmdon Hall and Barbara, da. of Sir Henry Gough†, 1st bt., of Edgbaston Hall. *educ.* Rugby 1796. *m.* 20 Dec. 1804, Charlotte, da. of Very Rev. Nathan Wetherell, DD, master of University Coll. Oxf. and dean of Hereford, 2s. *d.* 24 Nov. 1864.

Spooner's family had been established in the West Midlands since the fifteenth century. His grandfather Abraham bought a share in a Birmingham slitting mill in 1746 and built his own three years later. His father succeeded to this business and in 1791, with another manufacturer Matthias Attwood, opened what was only the fourth bank in Birmingham, Attwoods, Spooner and Company. The firm prospered and opened a London branch in Fish Street Hill in 1801.[1] Spooner's mother was the sister of the 1st Lord Calthorpe and his eldest sister was married to William Wilberforce*. In 1807 he wrote to Arthur Young, the agriculturist, describing himself as 'a young farmer' and seeking advice on crops; he remained a keen amateur farmer throughout this period.[2] He joined the bank 'at an early age' and was also involved in the family nail business. He received £4,000 as his share of his father's estate in 1816.[3] He first came to public notice in 1812, when he addressed the series of meetings held in Birmingham to protest against the orders in council. With Thomas Attwood[†], the son of his father's partner, who also worked in the bank, he was chosen to represent the views of Birmingham to the government. They gave evidence to a parliamentary committee and the subsequent revocation of the orders brought them great popularity in Birmingham. Spooner was elected high bailiff in 1813, in succession to Attwood, and immediately organized a mass meeting to denounce the East India Company's monopoly. The same year he orchestrated moves to establish a chamber of commerce in the town, of which he became the first president. Together Spooner and Attwood developed their currency theories, which Attwood in particular popularized some years later: their proposals for a paper currency which was not tied to gold, and the encouragement of 'productive expenditure', became known as the doctrines of the 'Birmingham School'.[4] He became a member of the Political Economy Club in 1821.

Spooner's first known involvement in a parliamentary election was at Boroughbridge in March 1819, when Marmaduke Lawson* was returned. It was reported that summer that he intended to 'offer himself if a vacancy happened', either at Boroughbridge or neighbouring Aldborough, and early in 1820 he was with Lawson in London apparently trying to secure candidates for the two boroughs. At the subsequent general election they contested Boroughbridge themselves, against the Tory nominees of the duke of Newcastle. There was a double return and the sheriff declared Spooner and Lawson elected, although the other candidates petitioned against the result.[5] During his brief sojourn in the Commons he spoke of the distress in Birmingham, 12 May 1820. On 19 May he postponed his notice of a motion on distress at the request of Lord Castlereagh, the leader of the Commons, but Attwood confidently told his wife that 'when R.S. speaks upon this subject it will have a great effect', adding that 'I shall advise R.S. respecting his speech and conduct'.[6] This did not come off, though he did speak on agricultural dis-

tress, 31 May, when he criticized the composition of the select committee on it, complaining that 'not one Member from the great manufacturing counties of Warwickshire, Staffordshire or Lancashire had been included'. His only recorded vote was against Lord Liverpool's ministry on the appointment of an additional Scottish baron of exchequer, 15 May. In the first week of June an election committee sat to decide on the Boroughbridge petition. Newcastle was informed that Spooner 'appears determined to try every point', but Lawson's mother reported that 'Spooner wrote ... in doleful plight' and observed that 'his eagerness for success makes him soon cast down if there is the least appearance of other ways'. The committee's verdict, 7 June 1820, was to unseat Spooner and Lawson. Newcastle heard that Spooner was 'mortified beyond description' and 'threatens to appeal', and that 'amongst other things' he 'talks of starting for Newark [another of the duke's boroughs] at the next general election'.[7] He petitioned against the committee's decision, 5 Feb. 1821, but this was rejected.

In the autumn of 1820 a vacancy occurred for Warwickshire and Spooner was immediately requisitioned as the champion of unrepresented Birmingham against the aristocratic interest. In his published address, he maintained his 'independence' and promised to uphold the town's interest in agriculture, trade and manufacturing. His supporters included the high bailiff of Birmingham, Joshua Scholefield, who later came to prominence with the Political Union, and the Tory industrialist Sir Robert Peel[†]. The near unanimous support he received from freeholders in Birmingham was insufficient to carry the county, however, and after his attempt to poll the freeholders of Coventry was thwarted, he was heavily defeated.[8] His petition to validate the Coventry votes, 9 May 1821, was rejected. In the interim he had suffered another disappointment, as an anticipated vacancy at Boston, where he had conducted a canvass, did not arise. Lawson's sister commented, 'he is so unlucky that I begin to despair of his ever getting into the House'.[9] For the next five years he concentrated on his business interests, helping to bring the railway to Birmingham, and he was instrumental in the foundation of the Birmingham Mechanics' Institute, becoming its first president, with Attwood as treasurer.[10] At the general election of 1826 he offered again for Boroughbridge, but Newcastle was now firmly in control and he was beaten. On his way home, he stopped at Knaresborough where he was invited to stand against the nominees of the Whig duke of Devonshire, but he declined.[11] Later that year he offered for the vacancy at Stafford, where he told the electors that in his opinion there was only 'one topic of importance', namely, 'the principle of free trade as connected with manufactures and the same principle considered with relation to the food we have to eat', and declared that 'he was upon both these grounds the advocate of free trade'. Although he reputedly spent £6-7,000 on the contest, the deeper pocket of his Whig opponent proved too much for him.[12] In June 1827, when Charles Tennyson proposed in the House that East Retford's seats be transferred to Birmingham, Spooner enthusiastically took up the cause and, with Attwood, organized a meeting in the town to promote the idea. Early the following year he was a member of the Birmingham delegation to the new prime minister, the duke of Wellington, to press Birmingham's case.[13] At a meeting in Worcester to establish a Brunswick Club, November 1828, Spooner spoke against the scheme and in favour of Catholic relief. The following year he helped organize a pro-emancipation meeting in Birmingham.[14] On 25 Apr. 1829 a large meeting was held in the town to protest at the distressed state of the country. Spooner and Attwood appeared and resolutions were adopted which reflected their currency doctrines. This meeting was the catalyst for the formation of the Birmingham Political Union, and was the last at which Spooner and Attwood spoke and acted in concert: from that point their politics diverged, and when Attwood formed the Union Spooner refused to join on account of his magisterial duties. They remained friends and business partners and continued to develop their currency theories. In July 1830 Spooner attended the public dinner given in honour of Sir Francis Burdett* and to celebrate the first anniversary of the Union, explaining that he was present merely to show his respect for Burdett's conduct as a reformer.[15] At the subsequent general election he spoke on behalf of the Whig Edward Ellice* at Coventry and briefly entered the contest as the third man, in the expectation of obtaining 'the second vote from each party'. He soon found that he had been deceived and abandoned the fight.[16]

Between 1830 and the general election of 1835 the transformation of Spooner's politics was completed. In December 1834 he was instrumental in the formation of the Birmingham Loyal and Constitutional Association, which later became the Conservative Association. He was appointed chairman and came forward in 1835 to contest a seat for Birmingham in opposition to Attwood, who thought he had been 'seduced by a knot of Tories', but still called him 'my own partner and intimate friend'.[17] He failed on this occasion and again in 1841, but he succeeded at a by-election in 1844 and became the first Conservative to represent Birmingham. He was returned for North Warwickshire in 1847 and was a prominent backbench Protectionist and Protestant, leading the campaign against the Maynooth grant. He died in November 1864 and divided all his real and personal estate equally between his two sons. One obituarist recorded that 'his sharp, harsh and somewhat singular features made him one of the most noticeable Members', and concluded that 'it will be impossible to find another more honest and conscientious'. A local newspaper recalled that he was 'always the same: frank, outspoken, courageous, manly and invariably good-humoured'.[18]

[1] VCH Warws. vii. 249, 265; C.M. Wakefield, Thomas Attwood, 2; F.G. Hilton Price, London Bankers, 156. [2] Add. 35129, ff. 458, 480; L.S. Pressnell, Country Banking, 348. [3] Gent. Mag. (1865), i. 240; PROB 11/1585/543; IR26/691/1919. [4] PP (1812), iii. 52; R.K. Dent, Old and New Birmingham, 349, 372; Wakefield, 27; D.J. Moss, Thomas Attwood, passim; S.G. Checkland, 'The Birmingham Economists, 1815-50', EcHR (ser. 2), i (1948), 4. [5] Leeds Mercury, 3 Apr. 1819; Nottingham Univ. Lib. Newcastle mss NeC 6624; T. Lawson-Tancred, Recs. of a Yorks. Manor, 336. [6] Wakefield, 75. [7] Newcastle mss NeC 6637, 6640; Lawson Tancred, 345. [8] Birmingham and Lichfield Chron. 12, 19, 26 Oct., 2, 9 Nov. 1820. [9] Lawson-Tancred, 347. [10] Wakefield, 94, 107. [11] Leeds Mercury, 15 June; Yorks. Gazette, 17 June 1826. [12] Staffs. Advertiser, 12 Aug., 16 Dec. 1826. [13] C. Gill, Hist. Birmingham, i. 203; Hatherton diary, 22 Feb. 1828. [14] G.I.T. Machin, Catholic Question in English Politics, 138. [15] Wakefield, 122-4, 146. [16] Coventry Mercury, 1 Aug. 1830. [17] Wakefield, 283. [18] Birmingham Post, 30 Nov. 1864; Gent. Mag. (1865), i. 240-2.

M.P.J.C.

SPOTTISWOODE, Andrew (1787–1866), of 9 Bedford Square, Mdx. and Broome Hall, Dorking, Surr.

SALTASH	1826–1830
COLCHESTER	1830–21 Mar. 1831

b. 19 Feb. 1787,[1] 4th but 3rd surv. s. of John Spottiswoode (d. 1805) of Spottiswoode, Berwick and Margaret Penelope, da. of ·William Strahan†, king's printer, of Little New Street, London. educ. Edinburgh h.s. m. 16 Mar. 1819,[2] Mary, da. of Thomas Norton Longman, printer, of 39 Paternoster Row, London, 2s. 3da (1 d.v.p.). d. 20 Feb. 1866.

King's printer, 1830-55.
Sheriff, London and Mdx. 1827-8.

Spottiswoode was descended from an old Berwickshire family, who in John Spottiswoode (1565-1639) could boast an archbishop of St. Andrews and lord chancellor of Scotland. His second son Sir Robert Spottiswoode (1596-1646) was executed by the Covenanters. Sir Robert's grandson John Spottiswoode (1666-1728), an eminent advocate and legal author, recovered the forfeited lands and barony of Spottiswoode in Berwickshire.[3] With his wife Mary Thompson of Fife he had two sons, John, the father of this Member, who succeeded to the family estate, and Robert, who became an attorney in London. In 1779 John Spottiswoode married the daughter of William Strahan, a master printer in London, who since 1770 had held a third share in the patent of king's printer, in which he was succeeded on his death in 1785 by his son Andrew Strahan, Member for various constituencies, 1796-1820. He operated as king's printer with Charles Eyre at 8 East Harding Street, Shoe Lane, off Fleet Street, and ran separately his private printing business in nearby Little New Street and New Street Square.[4]

John Spottiswoode, who evidently became a partner in his brother-in-law's private business in 1784, had six sons: of these, William, the second, died, aged 17, in 1800, and Henry, the youngest, died, aged 13, in 1806.[5] The previous year John, the eldest (1780-1866), succeeded his father, whose personalty was sworn under £12,500, to the Scottish estate and property in Tobago.[6] By his will, William Strahan had provided £5,000 for the benefit of the existing and future children of his daughter Margaret, who died in 1794. This was used to set up a fund, under the management of his trustees Andrew Strahan and Thomas Cadell, of £6,802 in the three per cents. From this Andrew Spottiswoode, John's third surviving son, obtained £2,871 when he came of age in 1808.[7] After schooling in Edinburgh, he began work in his uncle's private printing house, and eventually went into partnership with him. In 1819 he and his youngest surviving brother Robert, born in 1791, took over from Strahan the active management of the concern, which became known as A. and R. Spottiswoode. They installed steam printing and acquired and rebuilt additional premises in the area of New Street Square and Shoe Lane.[8]

At the general election of 1826 Andrew Spottiswoode was returned unopposed for Saltash on the Russell interest.[9] He presented an Edinburgh petition for repeal of the corn laws, 20 Feb. 1827.[10] He voted against Catholic relief, 6 Mar. He was in the Tory minorities against the disfranchisement of Penryn, 28 May, and the Coventry magistracy bill, 11, 18 June. He voted for the grant for Canadian water communications, 12 June 1827. He voted against repeal of the Test Acts, 26 Feb., and Catholic claims, 12 May, and presented a Saltash petition against the latter, 6 June 1828. He voted with the Wellington ministry on chancery delays, 24 Apr., the ordnance estimates, 4 July, and the customs bill, 14 July. On 5 June he commented that the London bankers and merchants who complained about the practice of driving cattle to slaugh-

ter through the streets of the City should be prepared to pay for an abattoir system out of their own pockets. He presented a Saltash petition for the abolition of slavery, 23 June 1828. Planta, the patronage secretary, predicted in February 1829 that Spottiswoode would vote 'with government' for Catholic emancipation, but he seems to have abstained, though he presented a hostile petition, 17 Mar. He was on holiday at Tunbridge Wells in September 1829.[11]

On 21 Jan. 1830, following the death of John Reeves the previous August, Spottiswoode received a 30-year patent as king's printer. He voted against the transfer of East Retford's seats to Birmingham, 11 Feb., Lord Blandford's reform scheme, 18 Feb., and the enfranchisement of Birmingham, Leeds and Manchester, 23 Feb. 1830. He divided against Jewish emancipation, 5 Apr., 17 May. He was in the Protestant minority against the Galway franchise bill, 25 May. On 13 May, presenting a petition complaining of the practice of interment in the churches and churchyards of London from an individual peddling a plan for a cemetery outside the city, he recounted from personal experience some of the vile nuisances which resulted. He called for the establishment of a permanent commission to regulate the whole metropolis, but did not move, as the petitioner wished, for the appointment of a select committee: 'I think that committees are more remarkable for finding out abuses than remedying them, and my object is not to blame but to remedy'. The following day he apologized for having unintentionally offended the vicar and parishioners of St. Giles's by his remarks on the state of their churchyard. He voted against abolition of the death penalty for forgery, 7 June. He thought it 'highly desirable' that reform of the magnitude proposed in Poulett Thomson's usury laws amendment bill should be 'thoroughly considered', 15 June. He had no confidence in Acland's much altered coach proprietors bill, which seemed to him to 'hold out encouragement to carelessness', 9 July 1830. At the general election of 1830 he was a late candidate for the open and expensive borough of Colchester, standing on the Blue interest with the backing of the corporation and declaring, among the customary cant, his 'firm attachment to the constitution in church and state'. He finished second in the poll to the radical sitting Member Harvey, well ahead of William Mayhew*, a reformer.[12] Ministers of course listed him as one of their 'friends'. Chairing the Colchester Blues' celebration dinner, 28 Oct. 1830, he claimed to have been returned unfettered and independent and promised to support and promote the agricultural interest, though he declined to commit himself to specific measures.[13]

On 5 Nov. 1830 Harvey's radical associate Hume raised in the House the question of Spottiswoode's patent as king's printer, complaining that in renewing it government had ignored the recommendation of the select committee of 1810, suggesting that it enabled its holder to profit greatly at the expense of the public, and alleging that it was an unwritten part of the contract that 'one of the king's printers is always to be in Parliament and vote for ministers'.[14] O'Connell seconded his motion for the production of the relevant papers. In his indignant reply Spottiswoode said that the costs to the public had been greatly exaggerated, and repudiated Hume's allegation that

> I have made a compact, by which I am to sit in this House and vote for ministers. I deny and cast back that aspersion in his teeth. No man here, or set of men shall have the control or command of my vote. Does it follow, because I differ from ... [Hume] in opinion, that I am corrupt? It is too much the practice now to use that kind of language, but I utterly deny its applicability to myself.

In a later exchange with Hume, he insisted that 'they are my own opinions, and none other, that govern my vote'. He was in the ministerial minority on the civil list, 15 Nov. The following day Mayhew petitioned against his return, alleging malpractice by the returning officer and bribery by Spottiswoode, but crucially arguing that his patent as king's printer disqualified him, as a government contractor.[15] At the anniversary dinner of the Essex and Colchester True Blue Club, 23 Nov. 1830, Spottiswoode observed sarcastically:

> The [Grey] ministry are pledged to bring forward measures of reform, which are to satisfy everybody, and restore the nation to its pristine brilliance and prosperity. If they do this, we have nothing more to say.

He deplored the disturbed state of neighbouring countries, where 'the spirit of turbulence and revolution, accompanied with diabolical practices', was rampant. He attributed the relative tranquillity of Essex to the benevolence and wisdom of its landlords, who knew that 'it is a false notion, by reducing the wages of the labourer a shilling, that the farmer relieves his own burdens'. Yet he wanted condign punishment for miscreants.[16] He gave somewhat evasive and unhelpful evidence to the select committee on the king's printers, 2 Mar. 1831.[17] On the 21st (the day before the second reading of the reform bill, which he would certainly have opposed) the Colchester election committee, deeming him to be disqualified by his patent, unseated him. Mayhew boasted in Colchester that he had 'thrown [Spottiswoode] back (never to emerge) into the press room of the king's printer,

and ... saved the country ... thousands per annum'.[18] Spottiswoode, who does not appear to have tried to re-enter Parliament, was again called before the select committee, 30 Mar. 1831.[19]

Andrew Strahan, a bachelor, died the following August 1831. By his will, dated 19 Mar. 1830, he left his property in Kent and Surrey to his great-nephew William Snow, who took the name of Strahan. He gave Andrew Spottiswoode a legacy of £15,000, and bequeathed to Robert his patent as king's printer and share in the stock and materials of that business. To both Spottiswoode nephews he left his house in Little New Street, two adjoining houses, the lease of the printing office in New Street Square and his share in copyright. They were entitled to an eighth share each in the £181,224 residue of a personal estate which was sworn under £800,000.[20] After the sudden death of Robert, aged 40, at Carlisle in September 1832, Andrew Spottiswoode (to whom his brother left £5,000) remained in sole charge of the private firm of Spottiswoode and Company for the next 16 years, as well as continuing to operate as king's printer with Eyre and Spottiswoode.[21] In 1837 he achieved some notoriety by organizing a nationwide subscription to help finance petitions against the return of Irish Catholic Members at the recent general election: he and his associates became known as 'The Spottiswoode Gang'.[22] In January 1845 he failed to convince Sir Robert Peel of the worth of a pamphlet by one Taylor advocating a return to 'a government paper currency to represent taxation, prices and a liberal minimum of wages for labour on public works'.[23] In 1848 he took in as partners in Spottiswoode and Company his second son George Andrew and Thomas Clark Shaw. He retired from the business in 1855, having already handed over his patent to his elder son William (1825-83), who achieved great distinction as a mathematician and was buried in Westminster Abbey. Thus the personal link between Spottiswoodes and Eyre and Spottiswoode, which were respectively continued by the two branches of the family, was ended.[24] Spottiswoode died in February 1866 at his London home at 12 James Street, Buckingham Gate. By his will, dated 7 Aug. 1860, he left his wife his shares in the Stationers' Company, together with his books, furniture and household goods. To William he devised his freehold property, to George a silver inkstand and to his daughters Rosa and Augusta equal shares in the proceeds of four life assurance policies and 13 shares each in the London Gas Light Company.

---

[1] Add. 48837, f. 11. [2] Gent. Mag. (1819), i. 274. Burke LG gives 5 Mar. [3] Oxford DNB. [4] HP Commons, 1754-1790, iii. 489-91;

HP Commons, 1790-1820, v. 301-2. R.A. Austen-Leigh, *Story of a Printing House* (1912), 10-11; W.B. Todd, *Dir. of Printers*, 186. [5] Add. 48837, ff. 11, 31. [6] *Gent. Mag.* (1805), i. 189; PROB 11/1424/302; IR26/98/208. [7] Add. 48837, ff. 32, 46. [8] Austen-Leigh, 36-38; P.A.H. Brown, *London Publishers and Printers*, 185; Todd, 182; Add. 48904, f. 309. [9] Lincs. AO, Tennyson d'Eyncourt mss H98/2d/30. [10] *The Times*, 21 Feb. 1827. [11] Add. 48905, ff. 65, 70, 73, 75, 80, 82. [12] *Colchester Gazette*, 31 July, 7 Aug. 1830. [13] Ibid. 30 Oct. 1830. [14] See also *Extraordinary Black Bk.* (1832), 572-3. [15] *CJ*, lxxxvi. 100. [16] *Colchester Gazette*, 4 Dec. 1830. [17] *PP* (1831-2), xviii. 23-29. [18] *CJ*, lxxxvi. 411; *Colchester Gazette*, 26 Mar. 1831. [19] *PP* (1831-2), xviii. 82-84. [20] *Gent. Mag.* (1831), ii. 274-5; C.H. Timperley, *Dict. of Printers*, 918; PROB 11/1790/542; IR26/1273/457. [21] *Gent. Mag.* (1832), ii. 386; PROB 11/1808/726; IR26/1306/705; Austen-Leigh, 38. [22] *O'Connell Corresp.* vi. 2472, 2515, 2520, 2531; *Holland House Diaries*, 376; *Greville Mems.* iii. 403-4. [23] Add. 40558, ff. 109, 111. [24] Austen-Leigh, 41, 51, 56.

D.R.F.

SPURRIER, Christopher (1783–1876), of Upton House, Poole, Dorset.

BRIDPORT   1820–20 June 1820

b. 16 Aug. 1783,[1] 2nd but 1st surv. s. of William Spurrier, merchant, of Poole and 2nd w. Ann, da. of Peter Jolliffe, surveyor of customs, of Poole. *m.* 22 Sept. 1814,[2] Amy, da. of George Garland†, merchant, of Poole, 2da. (1 *d.v.p.*). *suc.* fa. 1809. *d.* 13 Nov. 1876.
Sheriff, Dorset 1825-6.

The Spurriers, who became one of Poole's leading Newfoundland merchant families, appear to have come from the town of Wareham in the seventeenth century. Walter Spurrier, who was living in Fish Street in 1690, began as a sailor in the Newfoundland fishing fleets and became a merchant. His sons followed him into the business, opening up the previously unexploited fishing grounds off St. Mary's Bay, Newfoundland. One of them, Timothy (1672-1756), the chief architect of the family's rise to power and fortune, served as mayor of Poole three times between 1722 and 1731. In 1747 one of the six Spurriers in the corporation was William, who was mayor on four occasions between 1784 and 1802. He took over the Poole firm of Waldren and Young and by 1785 had become head of one of the largest and most prosperous Newfoundland trading companies.[3]

William's son and namesake with his first wife Mary (*d.* 27 July 1781), who had been a partner in the firm since at least 1791, died on 18 Apr. 1800, aged 37.[4] His younger half-brother Christopher, whose mother belonged to another of the principal mercantile families of Poole, replaced him as partner, and in 1804 became a member of the corporation.[5] He was encouraged by his ambitious father to stand for Poole, on the retirement of the wealthy merchant George Garland

at the general election of 1807, when he offered, in an address of 20 Apr., as a 'free and independent character', who made 'no professions of attachment to any men whether in administration or opposition'. However, confronted with a coalition, he backed down on 2 May and in the ensuing contest voted for his substitute, George's brother Joseph Garland. It was later revealed that William Spurrier had obtained the writ and delayed delivering it to the sheriff (his brother-in-law) to buy time for Christopher's nomination. For this transgression he received a severe reprimand from the Speaker in July 1808.[6] On the death of his father, 20 Mar. 1809, Christopher Spurrier succeeded to control of the family business, which included a bank in Poole. He took as partners his maternal uncle Peter Jolliffe and his nephew William Jubber Spurrier.[7] It is conceivable that he was the Christopher Spurrier who matriculated at St. Mary Hall, Oxford in December 1810, 'aged 26'; but it seems far more likely that this was one of his late brother's sons. He was listed among the stewards for a London meeting of the friends of Constitutional Reform in 1811.[8]

In 1809 Spurrier helped to return George Garland's son Benjamin Lester Lester* for Poole on the understanding that he would be supported by Garland, who spent several thousand pounds cultivating an interest for him, at a future election. Before his marriage to Garland's daughter (which took place the day after the marriage settlement had been signed on 21 Sept. 1814), Spurrier, whose wayward private conduct had already caused the Garlands alarm, threatened to break it off unless Lester made way for him at Poole. He was offered £2,000 by Garland towards a seat elsewhere and agreed not to stand, but he went back on his word in 1817, claiming that Garland had promised him support, and persisted in standing at the general election of 1818, when he finished bottom of the poll.[9] A gambler and a spendthrift, with little interest in supervising the family business, Spurrier built Upton House in 1818 'at great expense', diverting the turnpike road in order to enlarge the surrounding parkland.[10]

At the general election of 1820 Spurrier, who raised a £12,000 mortgage on his mansion and sold the Compton Abbas estate for £16,500 to finance the campaign, ducked another challenge at Poole and stood for the open and venal borough of Bridport, where he was helped by the retiring Member Henry Charles Sturt. After a severe contest, he was returned in second place as one of the 'popular' candidates.[11] He voted with opposition on the civil list, 5, 8 May, against the appointment of an additional baron of exchequer in Scotland, 15 May, for inquiry into military expenditure, 16 May, and against the aliens bill, 1 June. He was unseated on his opponent's petition alleging bribery, 20 June 1820. Although still bitterly aggrieved, Garland later that year attempted a reconciliation with the Spurriers, who resided in France in the early 1820s, but their quarrel was not patched up until 1824.[12] Spurrier was spoken of as a possible candidate at Poole during the speculation over the likelihood of a dissolution in September 1825, when he successfully tendered his vote in the mayoral election. He proposed William Ponsonby* at the general election in 1826, when he split for him and his Whig colleague Lester against Sturt.[13] He is not known to have taken any further part in politics.

There was no curb to Spurrier's profligacy and in 1825 he was forced to put Upton House up for auction; it was eventually sold in 1828 to Edward Doughty, formerly Tichborne. Paintings and plate went to pay off his mounting gambling debts and it is said that he wagered and lost his last silver teapot on a maggot race. In July 1830 the firm of Spurrier, Jolliffe and Spurrier, which had failed to diversify to compensate for the general decline of the Newfoundland trade, collapsed owing £26,077. There followed a sale of the company's Poole and Newfoundland properties, including a fleet of 11 ships and business premises in Placentia Bay, Oderin, Barren Island and the Isle of Allan. After the creditors had been paid, Amy Spurrier (d. 28 July 1841), who had lived largely apart from her husband after the crash, managed to recover £5,000 from his estate.[14] Their only surviving child, Amy, married Ernst, Baron de Linden of Württemberg, who probably had to support his father-in-law in old age. Spurrier, who apparently travelled abroad after 1830, died in Chelmsford in November 1876.[15]

[1] Ex. inf. I.K.D. Andrews, former Poole Borough Archivist, who kindly supplied other details upon which this biography is based. [2] Dorset RO, Lester-Garland mss D/LEG F23, f. 56. [3] D. Beamish, J. Hillier and H.F.V. Johnstone, *Mansions and Merchants of Poole and Dorset*, i. 13-16; C.N. Cullingford, *Hist. Poole*, 124, 137-8. [4] *Gent. Mag.* (1800), ii. 697; MI, St. James's, Poole; J. Hutchins, *Dorset*, i. (1861), 49. [5] Dorset RO, Poole borough recs. DC/PL CLA43. [6] Poole Mus. Service, addresses, printed poll list (1807); Beamish, i. 18; *HP Commons, 1790-1820*, ii. 137. [7] *Gent. Mag.* (1809), i. 286; PROB 11/1495/234; Beamish, i. 18. [8] Beds. RO, Whitbread mss W1/4455. [9] Lester-Garland mss F21, ff. 171, 173; F23, ff. 20, 48, 55, 60; F24; F62; *Late Elections* (1818), 257; Beamish, i. 18-19; *HP Commons, 1790-1820*, ii. 138. [10] Hutchins, *Dorset*, iii (1868), 308. [11] *Salisbury Jnl.* 13, 20 Mar.; *Star*, 14 Mar. 1820; Beamish, i. 19. [12] Lester-Garland mss F23; Beamish, i. 19. [13] *Dorset Co. Chron.* 22 Sept. 1825, 15 June 1826; Poole borough recs. S1660. [14] Beamish, i. 19-23; M. J. Bright, *Growth and Development of Commerce and Industry in Poole*, app. 2; *Gent. Mag.* (1841), ii. 331. [15] Beamish, i. 23-24; *Chelmsford Chron.* 23 Nov. 1876.

R.M.H./S.M.F.

STAFFORD JERNINGHAM, Hon. Henry Valentine (1802–1884), of Costessey, Norf.; Stafford Castle, Staffs., and 16 George Street, Mdx.

PONTEFRACT 1830–1834

b. 2 Jan. 1802, 1st s. of Sir George William Jerningham (afterwards Stafford Jerningham), 7th bt., 2nd Bar. Stafford, of Costessey and 1st w. Frances Henrietta, da. and coh. of Edward Sulyarde of Haughley Park, Suff. *educ.* Oscott Coll.; Magdalene, Camb. 1821. *m.* (1) 12 Feb. 1829, Julia Barbara (*d.* 19 Nov. 1856), da. of John Edward Charles Howard, *s.p.*; (2) 13 Sept. 1859, Emma Eliza, da. of Frederick Sewallis Gerard of Aspull House, nr. Wigan, Lancs., *s.p.* *suc.* fa. as 8th bt. and 3rd Bar. Stafford 4 Oct. 1851. *d.* 30 Nov. 1884.

Stafford Jerningham could trace his ancestry back to Hubert Gernegan, who held the knight's fee of the Suffolk honour of Eye in 1183. The Costessey branch of the family was founded in the sixteenth century by Sir Henry Jerningham, captain of Queen Mary's guard on the death of Edward VI, who received several grants of manors from her, including Costessey, which he made his principal residence. He and his descendants remained loyal to their Catholic faith. In June 1824 Stafford Jerningham's father finally secured the reversal of the attainder on the barony of Stafford, which had been in place since 1680, and successfully claimed the title, 6 July 1825; he became the 2nd baron and assumed the name of Stafford before Jerningham, 5 Oct. 1826. Stafford Jerningham, who his mother remarked in 1821 'represents to the life the truth of Lord Normanby's* speech for the Catholics', and who seemed '*desoeuvre* and humble, though with talent and judgement', undertook a tour in the summer of 1827 which included Belgrade, Budapest and Vienna.[1] He married a niece of the country's most eminent Catholic, the 12th duke of Norfolk, who sponsored his membership of Brooks's Club, 16 May 1829. His wife's cousin, Lord Surrey, became the first Catholic Member of the Commons after emancipation. At the general election of 1830 he offered for the open borough of Pontefract, with the encouragement of his brother-in-law Edward Petre*, and it was reported that his 'unassuming but fascinating manners' made him 'an universal favourite' there. He pledged support for 'the total abolition of slavery, reserving to himself ... a discretion as to the right of property, but always impressing upon the legislature that measures of a too gentle kind will never entirely destroy that curse which has been all but destroyed'. He promised to be 'a strict supporter of all means of retrenchment', but said he would not indulge in 'factious opposition to any government'. He was a friend of religious liberty, but 'at the same time a decided supporter of the rights and privileges of the established church'. On being returned in second place behind a Tory, he assured his constituents that he 'did not intend to make a coffee house of the House of Commons, but to devote much time to their interests in Parliament'. He left the next day for York, where his carriage adorned with blue ribbons (his colour at Pontefract, but that of the Tories in York) was attacked by a violent mob.[2] A petition against his return from the defeated radical candidate, alleging bribery, was dismissed by the election committee, 16 Mar. 1831.

The duke of Wellington's ministry listed him among the 'doubtful doubtfuls', and he voted against them in the crucial division on the civil list, 15 Nov. 1830. He presented anti-slavery petitions from Pontefract, 17 Nov., and Costessey, 16 Dec. 1830. He divided for the second reading of the Grey ministry's reform bill, 22 Mar., and against Gascoyne's wrecking amendment, 19 Apr. 1831. He stood again for Pontefract at the ensuing general election, when he explained that while he felt 'deeply indebted' to Wellington for 'that civil and religious liberty' which had enabled him to enter Parliament, he had come in as 'an independent man' and had not hesitated to vote against the duke's government on the civil list after the latter's 'famous declaration against all reform'. He was convinced that 'the general cry for reform upon the recurrence of distress, and upon the occurrence of disturbances of a revolutionary character in other countries', was 'decided proof that the system here had something in it that ought to be cured'. He therefore welcomed the 'wise, salutary and comprehensive' reform bill, and stated that it would be his duty to 'attend on every occasion on which that bill was brought forward, and to give it his most hearty and cordial support'. He reaffirmed his commitment to a general reduction of taxation, and praised ministers for showing that they 'had the interests of the poor at heart'. He was returned unopposed with an anti-reformer.[3] He divided for the second reading of the reintroduced reform bill, 6 July, steadily for its details, for its passage, 21 Sept., and for Lord Ebrington's confidence motion, 10 Oct. 1831. He voted to prosecute only those guilty of bribery at the Dublin election and against the motion censuring the conduct of the Irish administration, 23 Aug. He divided for the second reading of the revised reform bill, 17 Dec. 1831, its details, the third reading, 22 Mar., and the motion for an address asking the king to appoint only ministers committed to carrying an undiluted measure, 10 May 1832. He voted for the second reading of the Irish bill, 25 May, and against the Conservative amendment for increased Scottish

county representation, 1 June. In his maiden speech, 18 June, he replied to Daniel O'Connell's attack on English Catholic Members who had voted against enfranchising Irish 40s. freeholders, denying that he was 'indebted to those voters alone' for securing his emancipation and declaring that 'I cannot, even when a vote on their behalf is in question, surrender my right as a British representative of voting in that manner which, in my judgement, a comprehensive aspect of the interests of the whole empire demands'. He divided with ministers on relations with Portugal, 9 Feb., the navy civil departments bill, 6 Apr., and the Russian-Dutch loan, 12, 16, 20 July. However, he was in the minority against the government's temporizing amendment to Fowell Buxton's anti-slavery motion, 24 May. He voted in committee against the Sunderland Wet Docks bill, 2 Apr. 1832.

Stafford Jerningham was returned for Pontefract at the general election of 1832 and sat as a Liberal until his retirement in 1834. He was one of the prominent Catholics who took the pledge of temperance in September 1843 during the campaign of the Rev. Theobald Matthew, and he signed the address written by Dr. Wiseman in April 1848 calling for the restoration of diplomatic relations between Britain and the Vatican.[4] He died childless in November 1884 and was succeeded by his nephew Augustus Frederick Fitzherbert Stafford (1830-92).

[1] Jerningham Letters, ii. 210; Staffs. RO, Stafford Jerningham mss D641/3/P/13/50a. [2] Leeds Intelligencer, 29 July, 5 Aug.; Leeds Mercury, 7 Aug. 1830. [3] Leeds Intelligencer, 5 May; Leeds Mercury, 7 May 1831. [4] B. Ward, Sequel to Emancipation, ii. 64, 201.

M.P.J.C.

STANHOPE, Hon. James Hamilton (1788–1825), of 72 South Audley Street, Mdx.

BUCKINGHAM	23 June 1817–1818
FOWEY	1818–5 Mar. 1819
DARTMOUTH	8 Apr. 1822–5 Mar. 1825

b. 7 Sept. 1788, 3rd s. of Charles Stanhope[†], 3rd Earl Stanhope (d. 1816), and 2nd w. Louisa, da. and h. of Hon. Henry Grenville[†], gov. Barbados. educ. privately by Rev. Jeremiah Joyce, his fa.'s sec.; after 1802 by Rev. John Stonard. m. 9 July 1820, Lady Frederica Louisa Murray, da. of David William, 3rd earl of Mansfield, 1s. surv. d. 5 Mar. 1825.

Ensign 1 Ft. Gds. 1803; a.d.c. to ld. lt. [I] 1807-9; lt. and capt. 1 Ft. Gds. 1808; a.d.c. to Sir John Moore 1809; lt. and Gen. Thomas Graham[†] 1810-14; dep. asst. q.m.g. 1812, asst. 1813; brevet-maj. 1813, lt.-col. 1814; capt. and lt.-

col. 1 Ft. Gds. 1814-22; asst. adj. to duke of Wellington 1815; a.d.c. to duke of York 1815-*d*.; half-pay Portuguese service 1822-*d*.

Commr. of alienations 1806-*d*.

Stanhope, who had been damaged physically by the musket ball which lodged against his spine at the siege of Saint Sebastian in 1813, and emotionally by his unorthodox upbringing at the hands of his eccentric father, failed to find a seat in 1820. Later that year he married Lady Frederica Murray, 'of mathematical celebrity', whose family provided him with the affection which he had missed in his childhood.[1] In January 1822 his regiment was stationed in Ireland, from where he reported to his brother, the 4th Earl Stanhope, that 'the alarm has been most absurd and uncalled for'; in his opinion there was 'nothing religious or political in the riots'. On the problem of distress in England, he did 'not ... consider things in so desponding a view as you ... I believe landlords now not to be worse off than they were during the war, though the nominal amount of their incomes is much and must remain diminished'. He favoured repealing 'some of the taxes on the necessary articles of life, salt particularly', and imposing 'a proportionate income tax which should touch the fundholders', but thought this was 'as much as public faith will admit of'.[2] Three months later he was brought in for Dartmouth on the Holdsworth interest, as a supporter of Lord Liverpool's ministry. Ironically, he now found his second cousin the duke of Buckingham, to whose 'third party' line he had been unable to adhere when returned under his aegis in 1817, in alliance with the government.[3]

He divided against the removal of Catholic peers' disabilities, 30 Apr. 1822. He was in the protectionist minority of 24 in favour of a fixed duty of 40s. on imported corn, 8 May, but voted with government against repeal of the salt duties, 28 June. He divided for the aliens bill, 19 July 1822, arguing that 'no person would object to it, who had not done something wrong in his own country'; he thought his '20 minutes oration ... went off pretty well'.[4] He was devastated by his wife's death in childbirth, 14 Jan. 1823, and made no effort to hide his grief, commissioning Chantrey's celebrated memorial to her at Chevening. No trace of parliamentary activity by him has been found for that session, when he gave up his London house and moved in with the Mansfields at Kenwood, Hampstead.[5] He was present to vote against the motion condemning the trial of the Methodist missionary John Smith in Demerara, 11 June 1824. Later that year his behaviour gave cause for alarm: tortured by increasing pain from his wound, he lapsed into long bouts of depression and abstraction. He attended Parliament on the first day of the 1825 session and 'about seven o'clock left it and roamed about the whole night towards Battersea'. He was placed for a while under close surveillance, but this was relaxed when he showed signs of improvement. On the afternoon of 5 Mar. 1825 he created a 'sensation ... in the public mind' by hanging himself with his own braces in an outhouse at Kenwood. Lord George William Russell*, with whom he had served in the Peninsula, observed to Lord Lynedoch:

> What a sad and unexpected ending to our former gay companion. It is to be regretted he did not end his days in the trenches of San Sebastian, for he met with nothing but disappointments and misfortunes afterwards. He was cut by many on account of his *supposed* change in politics, he lost his wife, the fashionable world that thought him so agreeable in a capricious humour suddenly voted him a bore, and at last he finished his days by a desperate act of insanity.

The Whig George Agar Ellis* noted that Stanhope was 'a good and clever though not agreeable person'.[6] He was heir to the Revesby Abbey estate in Lincolnshire of his kinsman Sir Joseph Banks (1743-1820), the eminent botanist, subject to the life interest of Lady Banks. On her death in 1828 Revesby passed to Stanhope's only child, James Banks Stanhope (1821-1904), Conservative Member for North Lincolnshire, 1852-68. In his will, Stanhope charged other property in Lincolnshire, which likewise went to his son, with an annuity of £1,500 for his elder half-sister Hester, then living reclusively in Syria, whose affection had mitigated the harshness of his childhood. He also directed that in the event of his death before remarrying £10,000 should be paid 'as a mark of affectionate esteem' to Lady Mansfield's niece Elizabeth Barnett, to whom he was thought to be on the verge of marriage at the time of his suicide.[7]

[1] A. Newman, *Stanhopes of Chevening*, 195-8; Keele Univ. Lib. Sneyd mss SC8/41. [2] Cent. Kent. Stud. Stanhope mss U1590/C190/1. [3] Buckingham, *Mems. Geo. IV*, i. 304. [4] Stanhope mss U1590/C368/1. [5] Newman, 199. [6] Ibid.; Buckingham, ii. 224-5; *Gent. Mag.* (1825), i. 465; Northants. RO, Agar Ellis diary, 6 Mar.; Lonsdale mss, Lowther to Lonsdale, 7 Mar. 1825. [7] PROB 11/1698/228; Newman, 200.

D.R.F./T.A.J.

STANHOPE, Philip Henry, Visct. Mahon (1805–1875).

WOOTTON BASSETT	1830–1832
HERTFORD	1832–2 Apr. 1833
HERTFORD	1835–1852

b. 30 Jan. 1805, 1st s. of Philip Henry Stanhope†, 4th Earl Stanhope, and Hon. Catherine Lucy Smith, da. of Robert Smith†, 1st Bar. Carrington. *educ.* private tutors; Christ Church, Oxf. 1823. *m.* 10 July 1834, Emily Harriet, da. of Sir Edward Kerrison*, 1st bt., 4s. 1da. *suc.* fa. as 5th Earl Stanhope 2 Mar. 1855. *d.* 24 Dec. 1875.

Under-sec. of state for foreign affairs Dec. 1834-Apr. 1835; sec. to bd. of control Aug. 1845-July 1846.

Grandson of the radical 3rd Earl Stanhope, nephew of the famous Levantine traveller Lady Hester Stanhope and eldest son of a scholarly Whig turned Ultra Tory, who succeeded to the earldom in 1816, Mahon came from a family whose members were renowned for their diverse talents and eccentricities. He displayed a precocious ability at languages and composition, and excelled in the course of literary and practical education prescribed for him by his father.[1] He was taken on his first continental tour as a boy in 1812 and after studying at Oxford, where he was active in the Union, he spent several years abroad, visiting Belgium, Germany and Italy, March-April 1825, Belgium, France, Italy, Switzerland and Germany, July 1825-January 1826, and France, Spain, Gibraltar and Tangier, September 1827-May 1828. The Peninsula made a particularly strong impression on him, and he found the Spanish 'individually one of the finest races of men in the world although an oppressive government has rendered them nationally nothing'.[2] He made his reputation as a historian with his first work, *The Life of Belisarius*, the sixth-century Roman general, which was published in 1829.[3]

Mahon's father refused to countenance his desire to enter the army, having parliamentary ambitions for him instead. As he thought that there was no possibility of acquiring an 'independent seat', he wrote to advise Mahon to side with the 'government party', led by the prime minister, Lord Liverpool, as the lesser of two evils, 23 Apr. 1825. His son replied from Rome, 19 Feb. 1826, that it

> seems to me that the present unanimity of most people tends very much to diminish the importance of party, but I concur with you in thinking that from the present prosperous situation of the country, one would be most inclined to enlist with those to whom we are indebted for it, that is the present administration.[4]

Returned to England, he attended debates in the Commons: for example, he later commented there (22 Mar. 1831) that he had been present to hear Canning's speech on the silk trade, 13 Apr. 1826. No opening occurred at the general election later that year, and nothing came of soundings made by Stanhope in 1827 about vacancies in Ireland, which had been thought a possibility because Mahon, unlike his father, was strongly in favour of Catholic emancipation.[5] In May 1828 he hoped that, despite the 'singular and almost unparalleled' state of parties, the penal laws against Dissenters and Catholics would be lifted, though he opposed the idea of Jewish emancipation. Commenting on an approaching county meeting in Kent, where his father's principal estates lay, he wrote that he did 'not think that any moderate Catholics will have any chance at Maidstone on the 24th [Oct. 1828]; the contest will be between the Brunswickers and the blackguards Hunt and Cobbett'.[6]

On 18 June 1829 his close friend Philip Pusey*, whose writings on finance and politics he greatly admired, raised the possibility of one or other of them standing for two unnamed constituencies, which were almost certainly Rye and Seaford. Mahon replied that

> my father's wish as to my seat is not to give a round sum at once but to fix an annual payment and he has authorized me to offer as much as £1,000 a year. If the thing could be settled even at this 'eleventh hour' of the session I could make a payment immediately, but I fear that he would decidedly object to incurring the risk of a speedy dissolution by paying £3,000 down.

Their joint expenses at Seaford amounted to about £100, but while Pusey was successful at Rye in March 1830, Mahon was left empty-handed. On 5 Aug. 1829 he had his first interview with the diplomat Viscount Strangford, who also set about trying to find him a seat. Troubled by bouts of ill health throughout that year, he remained essentially optimistic about the march of events:

> For when I consider what numerous and terrible gales the vessel of the state has weathered and overcome during the last forty years, I can hardly imagine the possibility of any impending shipwreck, though not without apprehensions of tossing from a tempest. Increase of population beyond all reasonable means of maintenance – this is the circumstance which in my mind most darkens the horizon.[7]

Mahon's search for a constituency began in earnest in May 1830, when the king's death seemed imminent. Stanhope now put up £3,500 to buy him a seat, but none was initially available at that price. He considered Canterbury, where with his local connections he might have been able to replace the ministerialist Member, Stephen Rumbold Lushington, who was resident in India. Stanhope, however, strongly opposed the idea of Mahon engaging in what would probably prove to be an expensive contest there, though his friends advised him to keep the plan in reserve. On 21 May Strangford wrote that

between ourselves, I strongly suspect that Mahon has had some sort of intimation from Lord G[ranville] S[omerset]* that government, satisfied with the sort of general support which M[ahon] is disposed to give them, will not set up a candidate in opposition to him. This is merely my conjecture, but I think there must be something in it, from the change in Mahon's tone, within the last 48 hours, when speaking of the manifold inconveniences and vexations of a contest – of which he now, comparatively, makes light, and above all, from the more decided manner in which he talks of supporting government.

Mahon, however, pledged himself to take an independent stance and said that he 'would not as my mother advises accept of a treasury seat on any account', but he urged his father to agree, 24 May:

I fully admit the objections in my circumstances to a contest, and I only wish for one in case a purchase should be *impossible* at the price which we propose. You must not therefore look upon the alternative as a purchase but as not being in Parliament at all. Now many things are comparatively good which are not positively good. If I don't come into Parliament now, there is an end of my political prospects for *life*, since at the next election I should be too old to enter upon them with any prospect of success and should have fixed upon another (probably a literary) turn.

He nevertheless abandoned the idea of Canterbury when a ministerialist candidate started. Meanwhile, his maternal grandfather Lord Carrington had failed to bring him in for Hedon, where he would also have had to face a contest, or at any of his other boroughs, and he was just beaten to the purchase of a vacancy at Lymington.[8] By early July, however, he had secured a seat on Lord Clarendon's interest at Wootton Bassett, for which, under an undated electoral agreement, he was to pay £1,500 a year. But he could not escape the necessity of conducting a canvass, including a speech made 'from my horse like a Roman general to his troops', which he found extremely exhausting; Lord Porchester*, with whom he soon became friends, described him as 'a noble fellow'.[9] It was probably at this time that Pusey informed a deputation 'from a borough on the coast of Sussex' that Mahon, to whom they gave the erroneous title of colonel, had been 'summoned in another direction and was therefore obliged to decline the honour they intended him'.[10]

He was listed by the Wellington ministry among the 'doubtful doubtfuls', probably because he had left England, 11 Aug. 1830, to restore his health on the continent.[11] In a letter to Pusey, 18 Aug., he condemned the change of government in France on the grounds that the people would now

expect to find a revolution in future a sort of easy transfer from a bad government to a good one, without any infringement of vested property or legal rights, as a sort of storm, which is to last but a few days or hours, and end like other storms only in the clearing and purifying of the air.

On 2 Oct. he observed that 'of all forms of government none perhaps is so bad as progressive government which does not rest on institutions or look back to former periods of its national history but hurries forwards in pursuit of theories'.[12] Although sensitive to possible charges of indolence, he asked his father, 9 Oct., whether 'on public grounds should I not better consult my duty, by postponing my attendance till the second meeting in February than by entering upon it with a strength unequal to the duties it imposes?'[13] By 8 Nov., when he informed Lord Holland that he was 'poring over antiquities at Rome' rather than attending the 'very important session in London', he had decided to delay his return until the new year.[14] Porchester wondered whether he would continue to act with the 'Wellington party', but in a letter to Stanhope from Naples, 6 Dec., Mahon stated that

had I been in England my vote would have been with the minority the other night [15 Nov.], both on that question itself – for I think that retrenchment in the civil list is already carried to the utmost verge of national prudence or national dignity – and also with reference to the probably effect of a defeat in dissolving the ministry. I looked upon the talent and decision of the duke of Wellington as our safeguard for tranquillity at home, upon his renown in Europe as our best security for peace abroad and I much lamented that the country should be deprived of the services of the greatest hero she has ever, though fertile in heroes, produced.[15]

In a similar letter to Pusey, he added that

to curtail, I mean to any extent, our public salaries sounds popular, and is readily swallowed by the mob, and yet it is in fact a most aristocratical and exclusive system since it tends to prevent any man from entering the public service without a good patrimonial fortune of his own.[16]

With the occasional exception, such as over his allowance, Mahon and Stanhope rarely differed personally, but they did do so, albeit usually amicably, over politics. Mahon, for instance, could not follow the Ultra line in favour of parliamentary reform, and in a letter to Mrs. Arbuthnot, 19 Dec. 1830, he condemned the

> Protestant gentry and Protestant clergy, who if you get the soundest of them sometimes in private by their firesides, will tell you, very many of them, that the House of Commons does not properly represent the people or *that measure* [Catholic emancipation] could not have been *so* carried.[17]

Mahon arrived back in England, 26 Jan., and took his seat, 3 Feb. 1831.[18] In a lengthy maiden speech, 2 Mar., he pointed out inconsistencies in the ministry's reform proposals and between the aims of its various supporters. He said that he supported the enfranchisement of large towns, as had been proposed in the previous session, as 'legal and constitutional, founded on expediency and upheld by precedent', but he condemned the bill: 'we are told we must vote for this measure if we wish to avoid a revolution. Why, Sir, this measure itself is a revolution'. Denying that he had any electoral, party or personal interest to defend, he promised to oppose the bill, being 'convinced that our whole constitution would speedily sink under such a rash course of empirical experiment'. According to his own note, 'dates in my life', he said 'a few words more', 7 Mar.[19] He intended to introduce a bill on the subject of dramatic authorship, but none was forthcoming in this period.[20] On 22 Mar. he informed his father that

> I am now quite full of a speech I am to make tonight. Not finding a good opportunity, or not able to catch the Speaker's eye last night, I moved an adjournment at three this morning which was carried and which will give me 'possession of the House' as it is called at five this afternoon. Damned awful this prospect! I am in a great funk and much afraid of failure.[21]

Strangford related that he

> chose a bad moment for getting up, and much of the beginning of his speech was lost, owing to the confusion and shuffling of feet in taking places, etc. But when he was heard, he was heard with much attention, and had evidently a perfect command of the *good will* of the House.[22]

He started by rebutting several of the reformers' standard arguments, notably by denying that either Pitt or Canning, whose principles he claimed to follow, would have approved of the bill. His main point was that it would improve the House in talent, but that this would not be 'honesty', 'not practical information, not liberal knowledge, not statesmanlike views, but a low, selfish pettifogging sort of talent – I ought rather to have called it cunning'. Similarly, independent country gentlemen of the type of Sir James Graham would be replaced by 'some attorney's clerk – some

fellow without a virtue or a shilling', or men 'without any fixed principles of action – without any stake in the country', who were 'the delegates of local interests or particular prejudices'. He also declared that he had an 'eager and an anxious wish to satisfy the people', but only by 'changes that do not go the fearful length of establishing a new constitution', and he duly voted against the bill's second reading. Somerset reported to Stanhope the next day that 'I heard but one opinion of his performance. The House constantly cheered him'. His speech, which (like that of 2 Mar.) he corrected and published, was indeed widely praised, not least by Wellington, with whom he soon established a close friendship.[23] Fully aware of his father's fear that a declaration against reform would make him a 'marked man' in any popular contest, Mahon nevertheless decided to attend the Kent county meeting, 24 Mar.

> because I thought it right and becoming to show that I was not afraid of meeting the people the very next day after the vote I had given, and because I felt convinced that the great unpopularity which must at present necessarily attend that vote, would be not aggravated but diminished by my stepping forward firmly and boldly in vindication of it.[24]

His plea for more moderate reform was given an impatient and hostile hearing, and he was forced to write to the press to deny an allegation made by another speaker that he derived £1,000 a year from borough influence.[25] He was, however, congratulated for his stand against the reformers, and Wellington wrote to Lady Stanhope, 31 Mar., that he 'admired his spirit in coming forward to oppose them, and the temper with which he bore their taunts'. As he informed his father, 12 Apr., the former lord chancellor Lord Eldon called on him after his success and, like other Tories, evidently hoped to use his influence to win over Stanhope to their side in the Lords.[26] On 12 Apr. he asked Lord John Russell whether ministers considered that an alteration of the proportion of seats allotted to England, Ireland and Scotland would amount to a violation of the principle of the bill, but received no reply. He attended the first day's debate on Gascoyne's wrecking amendment to this effect, 18 Apr., which he summarized as 'much bad oratory and no result'. The following day he voted in the majority for the motion and, although he believed ministers might still persist, he acknowledged in private that talk of their resignation was prevalent.[27] His short satirical piece, *A Leaf from the Future History of England*, dated 19 Apr., described the beginnings of the 'English revolution' of 1831.[28] Partly because of his defence of the rights of the Maidstone freemen at the Kent meeting, he was solicited to offer at the subsequent general election, but he refused to consider standing there or for Kent. Instead, he successfully negotiated his return on the same terms for Wootton Bassett, where he and Porchester endured more arduous canvassing. He had feared widespread violence during the nationwide election and was dismayed at the Tory defeats, especially in the counties, which he felt deprived the opposition not only of physical but also of moral strength.[29] At the Pitt Club dinner, 28 May 1831, he spoke in praise of his kinsman, attacked the administration, advocated moderate reform and disclaimed any anti-Catholic sentiments.[30] It must have been at about this time that he became intimate with the leaders of the Tory party and attended meetings at Charles Street (for which he entered a subscription of £10, 25 Feb. 1832).[31] The following month he requested the attendance of Lord Carnarvon, Porchester's father, at a Conservative dinner, insisting that reform was 'not a party, but a national question'.[32]

He criticized ministers for advising a dissolution and complained that they had concealed the significant principles of the bill, 21 June 1831. He also condemned the recent elections, 'which did not proceed from the calm judgement of the country, but rather from its inflamed and misguided passion', and argued that the bill was only supported by those who thought it preferable to no reform at all, or those who saw it as a first step towards the overthrow of monarchical institutions. In default of a more senior alternative, Sidney Herbert† forwarded to Mahon the anti-reform petition of the resident bachelors and undergraduates of Oxford University, which he presented and endorsed, 1 July.[33] He voted against the second reading of the reintroduced bill, 6 July, but at least once with ministers against adjourning debate on it, 12 July. On 14 July he told Tom Macaulay*, who considered him a 'violent Tory, but a very agreeable man and a very good scholar', that 'friendships of long standing were everywhere giving way and that the schism between the reformers and anti-reformers was spreading from the House of Commons into every private circle'.[34] He divided for using the 1831 census to determine the boroughs in schedules A and B, 19 July, and to postpone consideration of the partial disfranchisement of Chippenham, 27 July. He raised a few points in what he admitted was a vain defence of Wootton Bassett, 26 July, when he had to apologize for calling Daniel O'Connell's allegations of corruption there 'indecent personalities'. He chaired a political dinner for Sir Edward Knatchbull, the former Member for Kent, at Sittingbourne, 3 Aug., when he spoke in praise of his conduct in the House.[35] Although one of those who

'voted generally against the bill', he sided with ministers for the division of counties, 11 Aug. He argued that Members should attend the coronation in court dress, 1 Sept., and divided for a select committee on the renewal of the Sugar Refinery Act, 12 Sept. He voted against the passage of the reform bill, 21 Sept. Mahon requested George Robert Gleig, perpetual curate of Ash, near Sandwich, to accept the editorship of a proposed Tory newspaper, 14 Sept., as 'I am convinced that in the present danger which threatens all our ecclesiastical as well as all our political establishments, there cannot be a higher moral duty than that of endeavouring to rescue both'.[36] Gleig wrote to Wellington, 21 Sept., to urge him to help stir Mahon, who was 'most zealous, most intelligent and most able', into taking a leading part in Kent against the bill.[37] He did write a *Letter to the Lords by a Member of the House of Commons*, dated 22 Sept., in which he advocated a period of delay so that the real anti-reform opinion of the people could become apparent, and he attended, but probably did not speak at, the Kent reform meeting, 30 Sept.[38] He continued to be involved with plans for establishing a newspaper, but his scheme to raise £10,000 by means of a subscription of £50 from each of 200 opposition Members was immediately dismissed by Wellington as impractical.[39] On 14 Oct. he informed his father that he had recovered from his inflammatory tendency, and had become 'particular friends' with Lord and Lady Salisbury. Four days later he reported to Pusey his belief that the king was firmly opposed to creating enough peers to ensure the bill's success and that this issue might split the cabinet, while Henry Labouchere* agreed with Mahon's view, 27 Oct. 1831, that opinion in the south of England was turning decisively against reform.[40]

Nevertheless, he wrote to his mother, 1 Dec. 1831, that 'in politics things look blacker than ever and it daily becomes more evident that the question is not one of privileges or of parties but of property'; and, on 7 Dec., that he had gone to London and had 'plunged at once into politics in which, sink or swim, I must continue immersed for many months'.[41] He objected to the uniform £10 borough qualification, 16 Dec., and argued that the revised bill excluded the higher and lower classes, which meant that 'under the present system all places are not represented, but all classes are; and that, in the new system, every place would be represented, but only one class'. He condemned ministers for not basing their measure on prescription, because

if you had but looked to practical grievance, rather than theoretical anomaly – if you had first enfranchised the large towns, and then, to make way for this increase, struck off an exactly equal number of small boroughs

– why you might have expected to frame, not only a moderate, but a final reform.

He boasted that his speech 'has been successful beyond my wildest expectations' and was considered superior to that of his colleague, which was a 'very high and certainly a very undeserved comment'. Others were critical, however, and thought it was chiefly notable for having provoked what Mahon himself, admiring 'merit in an adversary', called a 'great speech' by Macaulay.[42] He duly voted against the bill's second reading the following day. He supported the promotion of addresses to the king against the creation of a large number of peers, and he urged Pusey to speak and to take a leading part in opposing the bill's details.[43] He divided against going into committee on it, 20 Jan., and the enfranchisement of Tower Hamlets, 28 Feb. 1832. In moving the wrecking amendment against the bill's third reading, 19 Mar., he extolled the certain benefits of gradual and moderate reform in preference to the unforeseeable consequences that extensive alterations might have for the public funds, the distribution of property and the due influence of the landed and commercial interests. He argued that all but two of the 14 literary men and most of the eldest sons of peers in the House would be unseated by the implementation of the bill, and that it would not prevent future wars or high government expenditure. He ended by appealing to those who had voted for its second reading, but against its details, to listen to the changing voice of public opinion and to join him in defeating the bill. He, of course, voted for his amendment, 22 Mar., which was lost by 355-239. He may well have been absent for much of the session through poor health, and was, for example, overtaken by illness as he attempted to obey the call of the House for Lord Ebrington's motion for an address calling on the king to appoint only ministers who would carry the bill unimpaired, 10 May. He regretted missing a division 'in which not only the interest of one's party but the fate of one's country are so essentially involved'. He was praised for his speech at the Pitt Club dinner, 30 May, but he subsequently went out of town again several times.[44] He divided against the Russian-Dutch loan, 26 Jan., 12 July 1832, after which he wrote to Gleig that

this comes to you from a man half dead with sitting up in the House of Commons till five this morning at a temperature something like the famous Black Hole at Calcutta. I had however the satisfaction of seeing the ministers completely put down in argument and to observe how many of their friends had 'sudden business in the country' or 'severe indispositions' and stayed away from the division.[45]

While aware of the dangers of the 'vigorous opposition' inheriting the blunders of an 'imbecile administration', he continued to hope that the latter might be replaced, and, as he wrote to Pusey, 9 June, he thought that Wellington's attempt to form a government should have been

supported at all risks, because then we had a chance, nay a certainty, of greatly modifying the reform bill and of supporting the independent privileges of the House of Lords. Our feelings of delicacy have lost us this last opportunity of rescue. The bill has passed unmodified and the authority of the peers as an independent body has received a deep and perhaps deadly wound.

He regretted Peel's 'fatal hesitation' which had brought this about, but recognized, 5 Aug., that the

majority of our staunch friends were not yet convinced, as all discerning men nearer headquarters have been for many months, of the necessity, after what had passed, of granting a considerable measure. We have all become moderate reformers in London, though we never declared ourselves so as a party, but the country is still full of anti-reformers, and I think that had we pursued a different course collectively, we should have disgusted them without conciliating the enemy.[46]

Although he could make an impressive set speech, Mahon was not an able debater, and Lord Ellenborough thought he would never be very effective as a speaker. He was, however, active in the House, and apparently attended committee sittings regularly (at least on the reintroduced reform bill), as he once reported to his father that

we continue *billing* (but certainly not cooing, for we are very fierce and angry) on Wednesdays and sometimes on Saturdays, and you will therefore easily believe that all this especially on the dog days is very trying to the health and spirits.[47]

Facing the loss of his seat at Wootton Bassett, he was anxious to find an opening elsewhere. An initial sign that he might be supported at Sandwich came to nothing, and he also ruled out a contest for (probably the Eastern division of) Kent. He had hopes of Aylesbury, but lost the chance of what he considered would have been a seat for life when, in July 1832, Lord Nugent's expected appointment as commissioner of the Ionian Islands threatened a by-election (which did not, in fact, take place) and, as Mahon felt that he could not vacate and enter the lists so soon before a dissolution, his friends were obliged to switch their support to another candidate.[48] Instead, Salisbury put him up at Hertford, where, after succeeding in a violent contest, he was accused of bribery and unseated on petition.

However, he was returned there at the general election of 1835 and served out the rest of his Commons career as its Member.[49] To favourable reviews, he published his *History of the War of the Succession in Spain* in 1832, with a dedication to Wellington.[50] His subsequent stature as a historian rests mainly on his seven-volume *History of England* (1836-54) and his four-volume *Life of the Right Honourable William Pitt* (1861-2), but he pursued many other cultural interests and twice served briefly in minor office under Peel. He died in December 1875, being succeeded as 6th Earl Stanhope by his eldest son, Arthur Philip (1838-1905), Conservative Member for Leominster, 1868, and Suffolk East, 1870-5.[51]

[1] Cent. Kent. Stud. Stanhope mss U1590 C130/1, 2; C131/1, 3; A. Newman, *Stanhopes of Chevening*, 241-3. [2] Stanhope mss C130/3, 4; C296/1; C318/1; Berks. RO, Pusey mss D/EBp C1/7, 30; Newman, 226, 243, 298-300. [3] Newman, 280-1. [4] Stanhope mss C130/3; C316/1. [5] Ibid. C191/1, Stanhope to Cramer, 4 Apr.; C255, Mahon to Griselda Teckell, 18 May 1827; Newman, 251-2. [6] Stanhope mss C130/4, Mahon to Stanhope, 14 Oct. 1828; Pusey mss C1/21, 35. [7] Stanhope mss C296/1; Pusey mss C1/1, 4, 13, 26, 31, 36, 43. [8] Stanhope mss A122/1; C130/9, Mahon to Stanhope, 19, 22, 24, 26 May, Wed., Sun. [June]; C138/2, Strangford to same, 21, 26 May; C318/2, Mahon to Lady Stanhope, Wed. [n.d.] 1830. [9] Ibid. C138/2, Strangford to Stanhope, 6 July; C318/2, Mahon to Lady Stanhope, 5, 29, 30 July; C381/1; A122/1; Hants RO, Carnarvon mss 75M91/L12/2; *Devizes Gazette*, 1, 8 July 1830. [10] Stanhope mss C353, Pusey to Mahon [n.d.]. [11] Ibid. C296/1. [12] Pusey mss C1/32, 43. [13] Stanhope mss C130/9. [14] Add. 51835. [15] Carnarvon mss J3/17; Stanhope mss C130/11. [16] Pusey mss C1/41. [17] Stanhope mss C130/9, Mahon to Stanhope, 31 May 1830; Newman, 228-30, 252-3, 301-2; Aberdeen Univ. Lib. Arbuthnot mss. [18] Stanhope mss C296/1. [19] Ibid. [20] Ibid. C130/11, Mahon to Stanhope, 18 Mar. 1831; C381/1, Cromwell to Mahon, 25 Feb. 1832. [21] Ibid. C130/11. [22] Ibid. C138/2, Strangford to Stanhope, 26 Mar. 1831. [23] Ibid. C130/11; C190/2; C385/1; Pusey mss C1/8; Newman, 253; Earl Stanhope, *Conversations with Wellington*, p. v. [24] Stanhope mss C316/2, Stanhope to Mahon, 19, 25 Mar.; C130/11, Mahon to Stanhope, 26 Mar. 1831. [25] *The Times*, 25, 28 Mar. 1831. [26] Stanhope mss C130/11. [27] Ibid. C130/11, Mahon to Stanhope, 19, 20 Apr. 1831. [28] Ibid. C385/1. [29] Ibid. C130/11, Mahon to Stanhope, 22 Apr.; C381/1, Caney to Mahon, 1, 26 Apr., electoral agreement [n.d.]; A122/1; *Maidstone Gazette*, 19 Apr.; Pusey mss C1/44; Carnarvon mss L12/6; Keele Univ. Lib. Sneyd mss, Mahon to Sneyd, 5 May 1831. [30] Stanhope mss C130/11, Mahon to Stanhope, 30 May; *Standard*, 30 May 1831. [31] Pusey mss C1/9, 45; Stanhope mss A122/1. [32] Carnarvon mss B24/80. [33] Wilts. RO, Pembroke mss 2057/F5/15. [34] *Macaulay Letters*, ii. 21, 70. [35] *Maidstone Jnl*. 9 Aug. 1831. [36] NLS mss 3870, f. 19. [37] Wellington mss. [38] *Maidstone Jnl*; *Maidstone Jnl*. 2 Oct. 1831. [39] Wellington mss WP1/1195/22; 1196/14; 1199/10, 15; 1200/6, 7; A. Aspinall, *Politics and the Press*, 468-9, 471-3; NLS mss 3870, ff. 29, 33. [40] Stanhope mss C130/11; C381/1; Pusey mss C1/24. [41] Stanhope mss C318/2. [42] Ibid. C318/2, Mahon to Lady Stanhope [17], 19 Dec.; Add. 51569, Ord to Lady Holland [16 Dec.]; 51573, Rice to same [16 Dec. 1831]; NLS mss 3870, f. 70. [43] NLS mss 3870, f. 66; Pusey mss C1/1. [44] Stanhope mss C130/8, Mahon to Stanhope, Sun. [n.d.], Fri. [May]; C296/1; C316, Stanhope to Mahon, 1 June; *Standard*, 31 May 1832. [45] NLS mss 3870, f. 73. [46] Pusey mss C1/22, 32. [47] Stanhope mss C130/11, Mahon to Stanhope, Sun. [n.d.]; C255, same to Griselda Teckell, 4 July 1831; *Three Diaries*, 310; Newman, 253, 272, 276, 309-10. [48] Stanhope mss C130/8, Mahon to Stanhope, 19 June, 12, 21 July 1832; C381/1; NLS mss 3870, ff.

73-75; Pusey mss C1/23, 27, 31; Newman, 254. [49] Stanhope mss C130/8, 10; C318/2; C382; NLS mss 3870, ff. 75-81; Pusey mss C1/18, 22, 23, 40; V. Rowe, 'Hertford Borough Bill of 1834', *PH*, xi (1992), 103; Newman, 254-7. [50] Wellington mss WP1/1185/29; Newman, 285-7. [51] *The Times*, 25 Dec. 1875; *DNB*; *Oxford DNB*; Newman, 263-4, 272-5, 277-98.

S.M.F.

STANHOPE, Robert Henry (1802–1839), of 21 Chester Street, Grosvenor Place, Mdx.

DOVER   1831–1832

b. 21 Apr. 1802, 3rd but o. surv. s. of Hon. Henry Fitzroy Stanhope† and Elizabeth, da. of Capt. Robert Faulknor, RN. *m.* 29 Mar. 1830, Elizabeth Rosamund, da. of James Ward of Willey Place, Surr., *s.p. suc.* fa. 1828. *d.* 2 Mar. 1839.

Lt. RN 1824, cdr. 1828.

Gent. usher daily waiter to Queen Adelaide 1830-6.

Sub-inspector of constabulary, co. Leitrim 1836.

In August 1830 Thomas Creevey* witnessed a ludicrous episode at a fashionable gathering at Ascot races:

> Captain Stanhope of the navy ... is one of our visitors here, so Lord Sefton* said to him, 'You must go into the royal stand, Bob, as you know him'; an honour Bob would have willingly declined, but was made to do so, and nothing could be kinder than the king, who said, 'I have you always in my eye, Bob, and you shall have the first ship I can find for you'. As they sat down to luncheon immediately after this, the king said out aloud, 'Although Bob and I are very near relations, I don't think there is any family likeness', and after some pause he said to Lady Jersey, 'Do you think there is, Madam?'. So upon Sally's observing she did not exactly know what His Majesty alluded to, 'Why, Ma'am', said he equally publicly, 'my great aunt, the Princess Amelia, had a natural daughter who married Admiral Faulkner, and Mrs. Stanhope (Bob's mother) was their granddaughter'; and so you see it was true enough.[1]

It was almost true. Stanhope's maternal grandmother was the celebrated courtesan Elizabeth Ashe, known as 'little Ashe or the pollard Ashe', who was reputedly the bastard child of George II's daughter Amelia. (The later attribution of her paternity to the 1st Lord Rodney can be disregarded.) She was the companion in debauchery of Caroline Fitzroy and her libertine husband William Stanhope, 2nd earl of Harrington, Robert Stanhope's paternal grandfather. In 1751 Miss Ashe went through a form of bigamous marriage with the degenerate Edward Wortley Montagu†, who left her almost immediately afterwards.[2] Ten years later she attained respectability by marrying Captain Robert Faulknor, the naval hero of the hour. Poor health forced him to leave the service and he died at Dijon in 1769. His pregnant widow returned to England with their four children and, through the intercession of Amelia's brother, the duke of Cumberland, secured a pension. Her eldest son Robert Faulknor entered the navy in 1777, distinguished himself in the West Indies in 1794, but was killed in action, aged 31, 5 Jan. 1795. A monument to his memory was erected in St. Paul's.[3] His sister Elizabeth, a 'very pretty' woman much admired by the decrepit Horace Walpole, married in about 1786 Henry Fitzroy Stanhope, Harrington's second son.[4] He, a soldier in the family tradition, was Member for Bramber, 1782-4, when he became one of 'Fox's Martyrs'. He was a groom of the bedchamber in the prince of Wales's household, 1787-95, and in March 1812, with his cousin Charles Stanhope, an eccentric leader of fashion who succeeded as 4th earl of Harrington in 1829, he was appointed to a place in his household as regent. His daughter Harriet married the 3rd Lord Southampton in 1826 and he settled £10,000 on her. On his death, worth about £30,000, in 1828, the residue of his estate passed to his only surviving son, this Member.[5]

He took a post in the new queen's household in July 1830. At the general election of 1831 he stood for Dover at the invitation of a group of electors who wished to turn out one of the sitting Members, Sir John Reid, on account of his opposition to the Grey ministry's reform bill. Stanhope 'avowed his principles as a thorough reformer' and promised to support the measure 'as the first and surest blow against that corrupt influence which has so long stood between the people and the people's rights'. According to a hostile reporter, he spoke 'with more force than eloquence', but the strength of support for reform gave him and Poulett Thomson, a member of the government, a walkover.[6] At a dinner in his honour, 28 May 1831, Stanhope argued that the reform bill would 'ensure strict accountability and dependence of ministers towards the Parliament, and of the House of Commons towards the country'. At the same time, he warned against the raising of 'too sanguine anticipations of immediate benefits' from reform, in the shape of reduced taxation; rather, he forecast 'a more equal distribution of the public burthens'. He favoured a 'graduated income tax' and a cautious implementation of free trade.[7]

Stanhope, who joined Brooks's Club on 29 June 1831, sponsored by his kinsmen Sefton and Lord Tavistock*, made no mark in the House, where he is not known to have uttered a word in debate. He voted for the second reading of the reintroduced reform bill,

6 July, and at least twice against adjournment, 12 July. He voted steadily for its details, though he was in the minority for the disfranchisement of Aldborough, 14 Sept. He divided with government on the Dublin election controversy, 23 Aug. He voted for the passage of the reform bill, 21 Sept., the second reading of the Scottish bill, 23 Sept., and the motion of confidence in the ministry, 10 Oct. He divided for the second reading of the revised reform bill, 17 Dec. 1831. His name appears on the ministerial side in four of the 11 divisions in committee on the measure for which full lists have been found. He also voted for the disfranchisement of Amersham, 21 Feb. 1832. He voted for the third reading, 22 Mar., and for the address asking the king to appoint only ministers who would carry undiluted reform, 10 May. He was credited with a vote against government on the Russian-Dutch loan, 26 Jan., but he sided with them in the divisions of 12 and 20 July on the issue. He was in their majority on relations with Portugal, 9 Feb. 1832.

He stood for Dover at the general election of 1832, but finished in fourth place behind Poulett Thomson, Reid and John Halcomb[†], whose intervention as a Tory reformer helped to dish him.[8] Almost immediately he and Halcomb began vying to replace Poulett Thomson, who chose to sit for Manchester. Stanhope, who was backed by government and denounced his opponent as a 'political changeling', was confident of success; but Halcomb, supported by the duke of Wellington as lord warden of the Cinque Ports, the corporation and the friends of Reid, proved just too strong for him. Beaten by 69 in a poll of 1,399 (254 did not vote), he was reported to have flounced from the hustings in a huff, vowing never to return to Dover. An electors' petition challenging the validity of Halcomb's qualification was unsuccessful.[9]

Stanhope subsequently went to live in Ireland at Drumsna, county Leitrim, where he became a sub-inspector of police. On 17 July 1838, 'being sick and weak in body', he made a short will, by which he left everything to his wife.[10] He died 'after a long illness' in March 1839 at 81 Eaton Square, the London home of the widow Selina Marx.[11] His personalty was sworn under a derisory £450.[12]

[1] Creevey mss, Creevey to Miss Ord, 25 Aug. 1830. [2] Wraxall Mems. ed. H.B. Wheatley, i. 224-5; Horace Walpole Corresp. (Yale edn.), ix. 106-7, 129; xx. 289; xxxv. 195, 222-3; xxxvii. 433; HP Commons, 1715-54, ii. 556-7. [3] J. Ralfe, Naval Biog. iii. 308-9; Oxford DNB. [4] Walpole Corresp. xii. 33, 83, 136; M. D. George, Cat. of Pol. and Personal Satires, vi. 7746. [5] HP Commons, 1754-90, iii. 463; Williams Wynn Corresp. 342; Gent Mag. (1828), ii. 283; PROB 8/221 (27 Aug. 1828); 11/1745/505. [6] The Times, 25, 28, 29 Apr.; Kent Herald, 26 Apr., 5 May 1831. [7] Hastings Iris, 28 May 1831. [8] Kentish Chron. 27

Nov., 11, 18, 25 Dec. 1832. [9]*Kentish Gazette*, 4, 8, 18, 22 Jan., 26 Feb., 1, 8, 12 Mar. 1833; *Wellington Pol. Corresp.* i. 13, 16; *CJ*, lxxxviii. 190, 422-3. [10] PROB 11/1908/189. [11] *Gent. Mag.* (1839), i. 665. [12]PROB 8/232 (16 Mar. 1839).

D.R.F.

STANLEY, Edward John (1802–1869), of 38 Lower Brook Street, Mdx.

HINDON	1831–1832
CHESHIRE NORTH	1832–1841
CHESHIRE NORTH	1847–12 May 1848

b. 13 Nov. 1802, 1st s. of Sir John Thomas Stanley[†], 7th bt., of Alderley Park, Cheshire and Penrhos, Anglesey and Hon. Maria Josepha Holroyd, da. of John Baker Holroyd[†], 1st earl of Sheffield [I]. *educ.* Eton 1816; Christ Church, Oxf. 1822. *m.* 7 Oct. 1826, at Florence (and again, 26 June 1833, at Alderley), Hon. Henrietta Maria Dillon Lee, da. of Henry Augustus Dillon Lee[†], 13th Visct. Dillon [I], 4s. 8da. (3 *d.v.p.*). *cr.* Bar. Eddisbury 12 May 1848; *suc.* fa. as 2nd Bar. Stanley of Alderley 23 Oct. 1850. *d.* 16 June 1869.

Under-sec. of state for home affairs July-Nov. 1834; sec. to treasury Apr. 1835-June 1841; paymaster-gen. July-Sept. 1841, Feb. 1852, Jan. 1853-Mar. 1855; PC 11 Aug. 1841; under-sec. of state for foreign affairs July 1846-Dec. 1851; vice-pres. bd. of trade Feb. 1852, Jan. 1853-Mar. 1855, pres. Mar. 1855-Feb. 1858; postmaster-gen. Aug. 1860-July 1866.

'Ben' Stanley was how this Member was familiarly known, after his Oxford nickname 'Sir Benjamin Backbite', a character in Sheridan's *School for Scandal*, which he earned for his cutting satirical powers.[1] It also usefully distinguished him from his contemporary and distant relation Edward Smith Stanley*, who later sat in the Lords as Lord Stanley of Bickerstaffe and 14th earl of Derby.[2] Another Edward Stanley, Edward John's uncle, was bishop of Norwich, and had a son, Arthur Penrhyn Stanley, who became dean of Westminster. John Thomas Stanley, who was a Pittite Member for Wootton Bassett in the 1790 Parliament, retired from politics in 1796, but was wooed by the Whigs, and, having succeeded to his father's baronetcy in 1807, he became one of their leading supporters in Cheshire, where he had his principal estates.[3] From at least 1813 Edward John, the elder of his twin sons, was educated at 'Egglesfield House', probably a school in Eaglesfield, near Cockermouth, from where he recounted his early visits to the Lakes.[4] In 1816 his maternal grandfather, now earl of Sheffield, who thought him 'a stout, square, squat little fellow, just like his grandpapa', related an incident in which he was believed to have been drowned in the Thames at

Eton, but had actually just abandoned his clothes on the riverbank, and gone to dine in a borrowed outfit. By 1820 Sheffield had decided that Stanley should have a career in diplomacy, 'in which his talents will not be thrown away, in which he may pass his time most agreeably, and fit himself for the first offices in the state'.[5]

Stanley's tutor, the Rev. Charles Girdlestone, described him as 'giddy' on his first introduction to university life, and as not overly attentive to his studies. His coming of age was celebrated on his father's Anglesey estate in 1823, and the following year he may have spoken at a dinner on the construction of the Menai Straits Bridge and served on the Anglesey grand jury.[6] Later in 1824 he badly damaged, and may even have lost part of, a finger during a shooting accident at Kedleston Hall, Derbyshire.[7] Having taken his degree in 1825, he travelled via Brussels, Frankfurt and Geneva to Florence. From there he wrote to his mother, 15 Dec. 1825, that 'I feel it perfectly impossible to live the life of a quiet country gentleman; for from my present views and intimacies I could not bear the rough vulgarity of honest goodfellows'; and he explained his intention of residing in Italy for at least three years, perhaps as an attaché, in order to prepare for his career.[8] It was there, in the autumn of the following year, that he married a young woman of pronounced radical opinions, the daughter of the flamboyant but penurious Irish peer Lord Dillon, who was one of the leaders of Florence's émigré circle. He was elected to Brooks's, 24 Feb. 1828, sponsored by Lords Normanby* and Duncannon*. He attended the Cheshire Whig Club dinner in October that year, and the county meeting on reform, 17 Mar. 1831, at which his father took a prominent part.[9] It was possibly at about this time that he became, for a short period, private secretary to Lord Durham, the lord privy seal.[10] At the general election that year his father's Whig neighbour and political associate Lord Grosvenor put him up for his vacant seat at Hindon, and he was elected in second place, ahead of an anti-reformer.[11] At a meeting in Macclesfield, 4 May, he advocated moderate reform, and 'speaking of boroughmongers, said that they were in distress and hung out a sham banner of reform, with which they hoped to mislead and delude the people'. He seconded the nomination of the reformer George Wilbraham* at the Cheshire election, 13 May 1831.[12]

Stanley voted for the second reading of the Grey ministry's reintroduced reform bill, 6 July, at least once against adjourning proceedings on it, 12 July 1831, and thereafter with great regularity for its details. He made his maiden speech (as 'Mr. John Stanley'), 28 July, when, supporting the partial disfranchisement of Dorchester, he pointed out that the schedule B boroughs had been so chosen because they were too small to deserve two seats and that 'if I were of opinion that they were all mere nomination boroughs, I should come forward at once and move that they be transferred to schedule A'. He spoke against enfranchising Stoke, 4 Aug., arguing that, compared to a more populous county like Lancashire, Staffordshire was already sufficiently represented. He moved an amendment to, and made a suggestion on, the game bill, 8 Aug., and intervened in defence of Thomas Duncombe, 9 Aug. He opposed the idea of giving Merthyr Tydfil a separate seat, since Glamorgan was proportionately well represented, 10 Aug., and that day he defended ministers' treatment of Wales in the reform bill. He may have voted for, or abstained on, Lord Chandos's amendment, 18 Aug., because, as he later told the Cheshire electors:

> When the clause was introduced into the reform bill which gave the right of voting to £50 tenants-at-will, he felt upon principle that he could not oppose this extension of the franchise to a class he thought entitled to a voice in the choice of representative: but he had great fears of the result, in consequence of their necessary dependence; and he was sorry to say that his fears had been justified.[13]

He sided with ministers on the Dublin election controversy, 23 Aug. He voted for the third reading of the reform bill, 19 Sept., its passage, 21 Sept., the second reading of the Scottish bill, 23 Sept., and Lord Ebrington's confidence motion, 10 Oct. At the Cheshire county meeting, 25 Oct. 1831, he moved the address to the king, and, in a long reform speech, he opposed the tactic of withholding supplies, but insisted that there was no popular reaction against the bill and that delaying concessions to public opinion would be dangerous.[14]

He voted for the second reading of the revised bill, 17 Dec. 1831, the disfranchisement clauses, 20, 23 Jan. 1832, and again for its details. He praised the division of counties as a means of reducing costs, 27 Jan., on the grounds that 'the expenses of elections ... deters many independent men of moderate fortunes from engaging in a contest', and, making specific reference to Cheshire, that 'the arrangement will tend to increase the influence of the landed [over the manufacturing] interest'. He was added to the select committee on the East India Company's affairs, 1 Feb. He voted with government against the production of information on Portugal, 9 Feb. He moved for accounts of the

silk trade, 16 Feb., and on 1 Mar. he pointed out that distress in this industry extended beyond Manchester to Congleton and Macclesfield. He opposed uniting Gateshead with Durham and transferring its intended seat to Merthyr, 5 Mar. He told the House that the two principal arguments against reform, its inexpediency and unpopularity, had been overturned, 22 Mar., when he gave a lengthy recital of the Whig arguments in favour of restoring the constitution to its original purity. He ridiculed opposition for its pettiness in pointing out minor inconsistencies and declared that the solution to the prevailing evils was 'to destroy irresponsible power, which is tyranny, and to make it responsible, which is good government', and 'to restore sympathy between the governors and the governed'. He also denied the allegation of the Cheshire anti-reform petition that public opinion had turned against the bill, and of course divided with ministers in favour of the third reading that day. He voted against the recommittal of the Irish registry of deeds bill, 9 Apr. He voted in favour of Ebrington's motion for an address calling on the king to appoint only ministers who would carry the reform bill unimpaired, 10 May, and the third reading of the Irish bill, 25 May. He paired against increasing the county representation of Scotland, 1 June. His only other known votes in this Parliament were with ministers for the Russian-Dutch loan, 26 Jan., 12 and (pairing) 16 July 1832.

His seat at Hindon was abolished by the Reform Act, but having spoken in praise of reform, against pledges and reluctantly in favour of the ballot, he was elected as a Liberal for Cheshire North at the general election in December 1832.[15] He continued to represent his county, except during the 1841 Parliament, while his twin, William Owen Stanley, entered the House as Liberal Member for Anglesey in 1837, and subsequently sat for Chester and Beaumaris District. Stanley acted as Whig whip during Lord Melbourne's second ministry and was one of the founders of the Reform Club in 1836. He was given a peerage in 1848, and in 1850 he succeeded his father, who had been created Baron Stanley of Alderley in 1839. He held several ministerial offices and, as postmaster-general, sat in Lord Palmerston and Lord John Russell's cabinets. In 1834 the duchesse de Dino described him as 'une espèce de *faux dandy* parfaitement radical et de la plus mauvaise et vulgaire sorte'; and although Lord Malmesbury thought him 'a very amusing man, and clever', he was known to be a 'rough diamond'.[16] The family biographer Nancy Mitford wrote that 'he was a very disagreeable man indeed. I have heard it said, and I hope it is true, that on his death bed he apologized to his wife and children for his great nastiness to them at all times'.[17] He died in June 1869, in noticing which even *The Times* was drawn to comment that he was 'a man of ready and somewhat incisive wit', which 'has been accused of having in it the spice of ill-nature'. He was survived by his charming and intelligent wife, who was a fervent Liberal and one of the earliest champions of women's education. The bulk of his estate passed in trust to his eldest son, Henry Edward John (1827-1903), an eccentric diplomat and Muslim, who succeeded him as 3rd Baron Stanley.[18] His second son, John Constantine (1837-78), was colonel of the Coldstream Guards, and his fourth, Algernon Charles (1843-1928), was bishop of Emmaus, while his third, Edward Lyulph (1839-1925), who was Liberal Member for Oldham, 1880-5, succeeded as 4th Baron Stanley in 1903 and as 4th earl of Sheffield in 1909.

[1] *Greville Mems.* iii. 62-63; *Malmesbury Mems.* i. 285. [2] P. Draper, *House of Stanley*, 335; J.P. Earwaker, *E. Cheshire*, ii. 602-5. [3] *Girlhood of Maria Josepha Holroyd* ed. J.H. Adeane, 388-9; Cheshire RO, Stanley of Alderley mss DSA 12c, Wilbraham to Stanley, n.d. [4] Stanley mss 45; 136. [5] *Early Married Life of Lady Stanley* ed. J.H. Adeane, 368-9, 391, 414-15. [6] Stanley mss 4c, Mouton to J. T. Stanley, 28 Jan.; 45; 136, E.J. to Louisa Stanley, 18 Aug. 1824. [7] Ibid. 69. [8] Ibid. 45; P. Mandler, *Aristocratic Government in Age of Reform*, 68-69. [9] *The Times*, 11 Oct. 1828; *Chester Courant*, 22 Mar. 1831. [10] *Oxford DNB.* [11] *Devizes Gazette*, 5 May 1831. [12] *Chester Courant*, 10, 17 May 1831. [13] Ibid. 1 Jan. 1833. [14] Ibid. 1 Nov. 1831. [15] *The Times*, 21 Dec. 1832. [16] *Chronique de 1831 à 1862* ed. Princess Radziwill, i. 191; *Malmesbury Mems.* i. 285; *Letters of Lady Augusta Stanley* ed. A.P. Stanley, 230. [17] N. Mitford, *Ladies of Alderley*, p. xxii; *Stanleys of Alderley* ed. N. Mitford, p. xi. [18] *The Times*, 17 June, 28 Aug. 1869, 11 Dec. 1903; *Illustrated London News*, 26 June 1869; *Ann. Reg.* (1895), Chron. pp. 147-8; Lady St. Helier, *Mems. of Fifty Years*, 149-50; *DNB*; *Oxford DNB*.

S.M.F.

STANLEY, Lord *see* **SMITH STANLEY**, **Edward**

STANLEY *see also* **SLOANE STANLEY** *and* **SMITH STANLEY**

STANTON, **Robert** (1793–1833), of Highbury Place, Islington, Mdx.

PENRYN   10 May 1824–1826

b. 4 Jan. 1793, 1st s. of Robert Stanton, looking glass manufacturer, of 58 Lombard Street, London and Islington Green and Eleanor, da. of John Mason of Spilsby, Lincs.[1] *m.* 21 Mar. 1816,[2] Louisa, da. of Thomas Darby of St. Michael's Cornhill, London, 2s. (1 *d.v.p.*) 4da. (1 *d.v.p*) *suc.* fa. 1818. *d.* 3 May 1833.

The historical painter Benjamin Robert Haydon summed up Stanton's life in the following curiously constructed sentence: 'Staunton [sic] died in a mad house. He became after spending £80,000 a clerk to Charles Pearson, saved money became mad and died'.[3] While it has not proved possible to corroborate any of these statements, some hard facts have emerged about this obscure Member. He had a Nonconformist background. The Robert Stanton of George Yard, Lombard Street, who was interred in the Dissenters' burial ground at Bunhill Fields, City Road, London, on 19 Mar. 1784, may have been his grandfather. Certainly his grandmother Mary Stanton was buried there, aged 68, on 28 Oct. 1802.[4] By 1794 his father Robert Stanton was in business with Arthur Wilcoxon (?1758-1842) as a looking glass manufacturer at 58 Lombard Street. The firm was styled Stanton and Wilcoxon until about 1815, when it became Wilcoxon, Stanton and Company. With his wife Eleanor Mason, who died, aged 50, in July 1809, Robert Stanton had two sons, Robert and Charles, and seven daughters, Marianne, Sarah, Eleanor, Frances, Sophia, Harriet and Eliza. In his will, dated 28 Aug. 1809, he left his daughters £4,000 each on attaining their majorities, which he increased to £5,000 by a codicil of 4 May 1811. To Robert, the subject of this biography, he bequeathed his business and his house at Islington Green, plus £1,000 when he became 21. He devised the same sum to Charles, who was to take an equal share with Robert in the residue of the estate on their turning 30. As it happened Charles died, aged ten, on 27 Nov. 1811. Robert Stanton senior died at Plymouth, aged 61, on 7 Sept. 1818 and was buried on the 17th in the family grave which he had purchased in Bunhill Fields. His personalty was sworn under £80,000.[5]

His son Robert seems to have participated in the business for some years before coming into what must have been a handsome inheritance: he was described as a merchant in the baptismal record of his first child Louisa (6 Feb. 1817), when he was living at Dalby Terrace, City Road. In his evidence before the House of Lords committee on the Penryn disfranchisement bill, 8 May 1828, he said that he had been involved in looking glass manufacture for 'about five years'. The indications are that he withdrew from active participation, possibly by selling out, soon after succeeding his father. The firm's style had changed to Wilcoxon, Harding and Owen by 1820 and to Wilcoxon and Harding, who had added cabinet making to their repertoire, by 1825. The Harding involved was probably Stanton's brother-in-law and executor William Harding, the husband of his sister Frances. At the baptisms of his daughters Eleanor Darby (4 Jan. 1822) and Sophia Frances (21 Mar. 1823) Stanton, who was then a resident of Highbury Place, described himself as a 'gentleman'. He had at least one other daughter,

Marianne Maria, who died, aged three, in April 1833. His first son Robert lived for only two weeks and was buried in Bunhill Fields on 3 Dec. 1817; but he subsequently had another son, also named Robert, who was alive when he made his will on 21 Oct. 1822.[6] By this document, which made no mention of any business interests, he devised £500 to his wife, £50 to her cousin Maria Jane Ashmole and £50 to his nephew Robert Stanton Wise, the son of his sister Marianne. He left freehold premises in Fenchurch Street to his son, who was to be maintained from their rents during his minority, and directed that three insurance policies of £1,000 each on his own life should be cashed and the proceeds invested for the benefit of his surviving daughters. He left the residue of his estate to his wife for her life and thereafter to his surviving children as tenants-in-common. He appointed as his trustees and executors Harding, Thomas Clarke and Henry Smith.[7]

According to his own and Sir Christopher Hawkins's* evidence to the Lords committee, Stanton was introduced to Hawkins by a Mr. Simpson in about 1822 as a man who had 'come into a large fortune' and was 'very anxious to get into Parliament'. Hawkins could not help him then, but in April 1824 advised him to try his luck on a vacancy for the venal borough of Penryn, where he had a stake. The contemporary description of Stanton in the Cornish press as a London banker was evidently correct for, according to his own testimony, he had embarked on such a venture a few months before he went to Penryn. On 9 May 1828 Joseph Sowell, a Penryn maltster and enemy of the corporation, who acted as Stanton's leash-holder, gave the following enigmatic answer when asked by the Lords if he knew on what terms Stanton had gone there:

'No; I believe there could be no terms at all; for I believe if I had not come into the bank [at Falmouth] a person would have shot him in the bank; he had two loaded pistols with him'.
'Who would have shot him?'
'The gentleman that recommended him to go down'.

He was not required to elaborate. Stanton became involved in a bitter contest with a corporation candidate and won by six votes after a three-day poll of 300 electors.[8] His parliamentary career is soon dealt with, for his silent votes against Catholic relief, 1 Mar., 21 Apr., 10 May 1825, are the only traces of his activity which have been found. He evidently considered taking the Chiltern Hundreds in 1826, but in the event left Parliament at the dissolution in June that year.[9]

By then he was in serious financial trouble. His banking enterprise had failed 'about two months' after his election, which had cost between £2,000 and £3,000; he had paid back none of this by 1826.[10] His affairs were placed in the hands of trustees, who arranged the payment of 10s. in the pound on his 'considerable' debts. On 6 Feb. 1827 he was arrested on the suit of Cairne and Lake, bankers of Falmouth, who had advanced him £900 on his arrival at Penryn. He was committed to king's bench prison four days later but released on 20 Feb. 1827, having compromised the debt, which he repaid at 14s. in the pound. He was again confined to king's bench on 22 June 1827 at the suit of one Edward Jones for a debt of £75, and he remained there until 27 Aug.[11] It was during this second period of incarceration that he crossed the path of Haydon, who witnessed the celebrated mock election which took place within the prison, 12-16 July 1827. Stanton, who took the part of one of the 'Members', was reported to have 'particularly distinguished himself in the frolic, and appeared on each of the days dressed up in the most grotesque manner imaginable'. On 16 July the marshal of the prison sent in troops to prevent the planned chairing, and Stanton and the other ringleaders were put into 'close confinement'. Haydon commemorated these events in his paintings 'The Mock Election' and 'Chairing the Member': in the former he depicted Stanton, 'who, by his experience in the finesse of elections, was the moving spring of all the proceedings of this', as 'attired in the quilt of his bed, and in a yellow turban' and 'pointing, without looking at his opponent, with a sneer'.[12] He is not known to have been committed to king's bench subsequently.

The last trace of Stanton which has been found prior to his death is his appearance before the Lords committee on the Penryn disfranchisement bill, when he sorely tested the patience of his questioners with the evasiveness of his replies, particularly on the subject of his relationship with Hawkins. He denied Hawkins's allegation that he had advanced him £1,000 for the payment of his public house bills and insisted that Hawkins had made no claim on his estate thereafter. He also firmly but unconvincingly denied having authorized direct bribery at his election and attributed almost the whole of his expenses to the cost of food and drink.[13] Stanton, who evidently took up residence in Trinity Square, Southwark, died in May 1833. He was buried with his family in Bunhill Fields on the 9th. His 13-year-old daughter Eleanor joined him there on 27 Apr. 1835, but nothing has been discovered of the fate of his widow, son and other surviving daughters.[14] On 31 Aug. 1836 administration of his effects was granted to his widow, his surviving executors, Harding and Smith, having renounced probate.[15]

[1] IGI (London and Lincs.). Eleanor Mason was *bap.* 5 Oct. 1758. [2] *The Times*, 23 Mar. 1816. [3] *Haydon Diary* ed. W.B. Pope, iii. 215. [4] GL, Bunhill Fields M.I. recs. (897/4/14/144) and interment order bks. (1092/6, 9); TNA RG4/3989/96. [5] *Gent. Mag.* (1818), ii. 470; (1842), ii. 440; RG4/3991/106; 3992/83; 3994/105; PROB 11/1610/533; IR26/763/1128. [6] GLRO, Reg. St. Mary, Upper Street, Islington (P83/MRY1/1171, 1172, 1198); *LJ*, lx. 388; GL 1092/9, 14; RG4/3994/71; 3999/19. [7] PROB 11/1866/515. [8] *LJ*, lx. 385-6, 388-9, 391-2, 413; *R. Cornw. Gazette*, 1, 8, 15 May; *The Times*, 4, 15 May 1824. [9] *The Times*, 27 May 1826. [10] Cornw. RO, Johnstone mss AD 207/2, Edwards to Roberts, 7 Sept.; *West Briton*, 18 June, 2 July 1824; *LJ*, lx. 185-6, 205, 285, 388-92. [11] TNA Pris. 4/38/226; 39/55. [12] *The Times*, 17, 18 July 1827; *Haydon Diary*, iii. 209, 215; *Explanation of Picture of Mock Election* (1828), 3-6; *Haydon Autobiog.* ed. M. Elwin, 415, 446. [13] *LJ*, lx. 384-92. [14] GL 897/4/14/144; 1092/14, 15; RG4/3999/22, 63. [15] PROB 11/1866/515.

D.R.F.

STARKIE, Le Gendre Nicholas (1799–1865), of Huntroyde, nr. Padiham, Lancs.

PONTEFRACT	1826–1830

b. 1 Dec. 1799, 3rd s. of Le Gendre Pierce Nicholas Starkie (*d.* 1807) of Huntroyde and Charlotte, da. of Rev. Benjamin Preedy, DD, rect. of Great Brington, Northants. *educ.* by Dr. Charles Burney at Greenwich; Brasenose, Oxf. 1817. *m.* 23 Feb. 1827, Anne, da. of Abraham Chamberlain of Rylstone in Craven, Yorks., 3s. 1da. *suc.* bro. Le Gendre Starkie to Huntroyde 1822. *d.* 15 May 1865.
Lt. Craven yeomanry 1823, capt. 1827

Starkie came from the Lancashire branch of an ancient family, originating in Cheshire, who had acquired the Huntroyde estate through marriage in the fifteenth century. He had contemplated a career in the church, but the early deaths of his two elder brothers meant that in 1822 he inherited Huntroyde, other settled estates in Lancashire and the residue of personalty which was sworn under £40,000.[1] At the general election of 1826 he offered as the 'third man' for the open borough of Pontefract, making a populist declaration of his 'attachment to the constitution in church and state', and was returned at the head of the poll after an expensive contest.[2] A petition was presented against his return, alleging that he lacked the requisite property qualification, but this was dismissed, 14 Mar. 1827.

He made no mark in the House: his only recorded vote was against Catholic relief, 6 Mar. 1827, and he is not known to have spoken in debate. In February 1829 Planta, the Wellington ministry's patronage secretary, noted that he would be 'absent' from the divisions on

Catholic emancipation. He was granted three weeks' leave to attend to private business, 10 Mar. 1830, and quietly retired at the dissolution that summer.[3] He devoted the remainder of his life to 'the duties of a country gentleman' and took steps to develop his neglected estate, obtaining a private Act of Parliament in 1835 to enable him to exploit its coal deposits.[4] He was Provincial Grand Master of the West Lancashire freemasons for more than 25 years. He died in May 1865 and left Huntroyde to his eldest son, Le Gendre Nicholas Starkie (1828-99), Liberal Member for Clitheroe, 1853-57, and Ashton Hall, near Lancaster, which he had purchased late in life, to his second son John Pierce Chamberlain Starkie (1830-1925), Conservative Member for Lancashire North East, 1868-80. His funeral, held in Padiham, was conducted with 'full masonic honours'.[5]

[1] PROB 11/1660/404; IR26/929/841. [2] *Leeds Mercury*, 11 Mar., 29 Apr., 17 June 1826. [3] Ibid. 10 July 1830. [4] WYA (Leeds), Starkie/Armytage mss, Starkie to Charlotte Armytage, 24 Feb. 1835. [5] *Burnley Advertiser*, 27 May 1865.

M.P.J.C.

STAUNTON, Sir George Thomas, 2nd bt. (1781–1859), of Leigh Park, Hants and 17 Devonshire Street, Portland Place, Mdx.[1]

MITCHELL	1818–1826
HEYTESBURY	1830–1832
HAMPSHIRE SOUTH	1832–1834
PORTSMOUTH	26 Feb. 1838–1852

b. 26 May 1781, 2nd but 1st surv. s. of Sir George Leonard Staunton, 1st bt., diplomat, of Cargin, co. Galway and Jane, da. of Benjamin Collins of Milford House, nr. Salisbury, Wilts. *educ.* privately; M. Temple 1796; Trinity Coll. Camb. 1797. *unm. suc.* fa. as 2nd bt. 14 Jan. 1801. *d.* 10 Aug. 1859.
Writer, E.I. Co. (Canton) 1798, supercargo 1804; interpreter 1808; chief of factory 1816; jt. commr. of embassy to Peking 1816; res. 1819.

Staunton, a descendant of the Galway branch of the Staunton family of Nottinghamshire, was the son and protégé of the diplomat and colonial administrator George Leonard Staunton, who was awarded an Irish baronetcy in 1785. George Thomas, who, according to the dedication in Charles Butler's *Reminiscences*, had the same 'great and good qualities' as his father, was page to Lord Macartney during his embassy to China in 1791, and subsequently visited that country several times while in the service of the East India Company.[2]

On his retirement to England in 1817, he largely abandoned his study of the Chinese language, in which he was proficient, but he nevertheless produced a series of works, including a translation of Too Le-Shin's *Narrative of the Chinese Embassy to the Khan of the Tourgouth Tartars* (1821), and *Notes of Proceedings and Occurrences during the British Embassy to Pekin* (1824).[3] In 1823 he helped to found the Royal Asiatic Society, of which he became a vice-president, and to which he gave 3,000 Chinese books and manuscripts.[4] He was disappointed in his ambition of achieving some mark of recognition or employment from government, especially for his having been an unsalaried commissioner of embassy to Peking in 1816. For example, in 1823 his request to Lord Liverpool, the prime minister, for membership of the privy council was refused; and in 1831 his offer to work as an unpaid member of the India board was politely declined by the Grey ministry.[5] Instead, choosing not to reside at his ancestral home in Galway, he pursued the life of a country gentleman on his Hampshire estate, purchased in 1819, where he created a pleasure garden incorporating many Chinese elements.[6] In 1820 he was recommended for appointment as a local magistrate, but he did not qualify for at least ten years because of various periods of absence.[7] He evidently affected a Chinese manner in his conversation, as Henry Crabb Robinson, who met him at a Linnean Society dinner in 1829, commented that

> he amused me much … He has a jiffle and a jerk in his bows and salutations which give him a ludicrous air; but he is perfectly gentlemanly, and I believe in every way respectable. He is a great traveller, a bachelor and a man of letters.[8]

Late the following year, Maria Edgeworth described him as

> grown very old and lean and chou-chouing in quick time in the oddest manner. I never saw anything as droll as his bows and I thought they would never cease at every fresh word I said on meeting him – chou! chou! – as if he had been pulled by a string and brought up again by a spring to perpendicular then churning head and whole body up and down as you might push up and down a figure of old on spiral springs jumping up on opening a snuff box. Sir G. however is very good natured.[9]

'No opportunity of free election being as yet open to me', as Staunton later recalled, he was returned unopposed for Mitchell at the 1818 and 1820 general elections by the 4th Viscount Falmouth, as 'an affair of money', but 'on terms of perfect independence'.[10] Not the most assiduous of attenders, his voting behaviour was slightly wayward, though he generally sided with

ministers.[11] He voted against them on the appointment of an additional baron of exchequer in Scotland, 15 May, but with them against economies in revenue collection, 4 July 1820. Before the Commons and Lords select committees on foreign trade, 10 May, 8 July 1820, he was examined 'at considerable length' on the extent of American commerce with China, and he argued against the proposal to break the East India Company's monopoly by allowing private British merchants to trade there.[12] He divided in defence of ministers' conduct towards Queen Caroline, 6 Feb. 1821. He voted for repeal of the salt duties, 28 June 1822, against the military and naval pensions bill, 14 Apr., and for inquiry into the legal proceedings against the Dublin Orange rioters, 22 Apr. 1823. He visited Paris in early June 1823.[13] He voted for the production of information on Catholic burials, 6 Feb., to complain against the lord chancellor over an alleged breach of privilege, 1 Mar., and in condemnation of the trial of the Methodist missionary John Smith in Demerara, 11 June 1824. He divided for the Irish unlawful societies bill, 25 Feb., and (as he had done on 28 Feb. 1821) for Catholic relief, 1 Mar., 21 Apr., 10 May 1825. He voted for the duke of Cumberland's annuity bill, 10 June 1825, and spent the summer of that year in France.[14] He voted for a bill to disfranchise non-resident voters in Irish boroughs, 9 Mar., but with ministers to receive the report on the salary of the president of the board of trade, 10 Apr. 1826. He commented that the 'difference of opinion which existed between me and the patron of the borough' over Catholic emancipation led to his losing his seat at the general election later that year.[15]

In his *Memoirs*, Staunton related how the

> attendance and associations of a parliamentary life were, in the first instance and, I may say, for some years, highly gratifying to me, even under the disadvantage of sitting for a close borough. To hear matters of the highest and most momentous interest discussed night after night by the most splendid orators of the age, and especially the illustrious Canning, in the meridian of his glory, was an intellectual feast, not likely soon to pall upon the appetite. The opportunity also which my attendance in Parliament gave me to extend my acquaintance with public men, and generally with men eminent for their merits and talents, in all the higher walks of life, was extremely interesting and pleasant, and I readily concurred in opinion with those who pronounced the House of Commons to be (though rather an expensive one) the best club in London! Gradually, however, I became less contented with my position. I began to say to myself, with the Roman poet, '*semper auditor tantum, numquamne reponam?*' Still, never having had any practice in public speaking, I had not self-confidence sufficient to enable

me to break the ice without the stimulus of necessity, and *this* stimulus was never presented to a Member for a close borough. I had no constituents for whom it might have been both my *right* and my *duty* to plead, and I, therefore, naturally shrank from the ordeal of a first address to so awful an assembly, when I had no other plea than that of my own powers to amuse or instruct, for occupying its attention. I had literally *nothing to do*, and, therefore, I hope it will not be a very serious charge against me, that I *did nothing!*

He insisted, however, that he had given 'like many others, many a silent and, I trust, honest and conscientious vote'.[16] He admitted that his views had altered in response to changing circumstances, and wished merely 'to show that my political course has not been an *insulated* or *capricious* one; but adopted in general unison with a large political party', the liberal Tories and, later, the reformers.[17] He explained how his own concerns about the working of the electoral system had gradually increased:

There is another defect in the position of a Member for a close borough, of which I soon became deeply sensible, and which it appears to me impossible to any ingenuous mind to contemplate without some degree of humiliation and pain, and which consequently appears to me very much to strengthen the argument for the abolition of those boroughs. I felt that I entered the House under *false colours!* I felt that I was *not* what I professed to be, really the representative of the borough for which I was nominally returned. I came into Parliament by means which, under the circumstances of the case I conceived to be perfectly justifiable, but which, being *illegal*, I could not rise up publicly in my place and avow. It may have been useful and right that a certain number of seats in Parliament should be attainable by *purchase*, or through the *influence of certain wealthy commoners or peers*; but I consider the false position in which Members for close boroughs were placed in the House, under the old system, wholly indefensible.[18]

Staunton, who visited the continent from September 1826 to May 1827, and in January 1829, set off on another tour in May 1830, but travelled back on hearing of the death of George IV, 'with a view to a seat in the new Parliament'. Yet, although his return to the House at the subsequent general election, which he found 'most agreeable', was on 'the same terms of perfect independence' as before, it was for another rotten borough, Heytesbury, on Lord Heytesbury's interest.[19] He was listed by the Wellington ministry among the 'good doubtfuls' and as 'a friend, where not pledged', but he voted against them on the civil list, 15 Nov. 1830, principally because of the duke of Wellington's declaration against reform. He recorded, however, that

so reluctant, indeed, was I to give a vote against the party with which I had hitherto acted, that I hesitated to the last moment; and did not, in point of fact, go out into the lobby until I saw Sir Thomas Acland do so, of whose honesty and independence I had conceived the very highest opinion.[20]

He made his first reported speeches, 16 Dec. 1830, when he spoke briefly in favour of a Galway petition for extending the elective franchise to local Catholics, and, having served on the election committee, called for Evesham's disfranchisement. He argued that the newly installed Grey ministry had pledged itself

to bring forward some measure of safe, temperate and constitutional reform; I hope, therefore, that they will take the first step towards redeeming that pledge this night. I fear that our professions of a disposition in favour of reform generally, will be little valued if, when a practical case occurs, we flinch from our duty and decline to deal with it. I believe that most persons regret the half-measures which were pursued respecting East Retford in the last Parliament, and I trust we shall now set a better example. I hope that the representation of Evesham will be conferred on one of those great commercial cities whose non-representation is certainly the greatest blot in our elective system. All reformers, I conceive, of every shade and degree, must concur in that opinion. Even many of those who are against reform as a general measure, do not object to punish specific cases of delinquency.

He was appointed to the select committee on the East India Company, 4 Feb. 1831.

Staunton encapsulated his views on reform in a detailed private memorandum, dated 25 Feb. 1831, the first of a series that provides an unusual insight into the views of an ordinary backbencher during the reform crisis.[21] In advocating a 'moderate and rational' redistribution of seats from rotten boroughs to large manufacturing towns, he acknowledged the difficulties involved in such alterations, but stated his belief that

upon the balance of conflicting arguments and considerations the result promises on the whole to be beneficial. This is all which, with our limited capacities and in our uncertain state here on earth, can be predicated of any prospective measure whatsoever.

Indeed, while the aristocracy would retain its 'full and fair share of influence in the state', by 'giving the representation to the householders or middle classes the principle appears to me to be strictly conservative', and he doubted that it would lead to further popular reform measures, such as the ballot, which he abhorred. However, since he thought it 'safe and well to diminish the direct influence of the aristocracy by twenty or thirty votes, and yet very dangerous to do so to the extent of one hundred or more', he was shocked by the scale of Lord John Russell's reform proposals, 1 Mar. In notes dated 3 and 10 Mar. he expressed his admiration for much of the bill, particularly the provisions for counties, non-resident voters and unenfranchised towns, although he would have preferred a £20 borough qualification. His main objections, however, were to the 'violent and sweeping' nature of the disfranchisement, which he thought 'so great a change that no man who reasons calmly and impartially will venture to predict the result'; the lack of finality in its scope, as 'not only universal suffrage, but the ballot, *short parliaments* and the *exclusion of placemen* and pensioners from the House are now openly avowed as objects for further discussion'; and the replacement of the balance of monarchical, aristocratic and popular interests in the Commons by a republic, which 'is not nor never was the constitution of England'. Nevertheless, he continued to steer a middle course. He presented and endorsed a reform petition from neighbouring Havant, 19 Mar., when he expressed 'my regret that I cannot give my unqualified support to the bill as it stands at present'. He added, however, that 'I shall vote for the second reading, with a hope that the part which I object to may be amended in the committee'. Having duly divided in its favour, 22 Mar., he reiterated, 25 Mar., that the recent division 'appeared to me to be on the question of reform or no reform; and looking to the state of public feeling, and in deference to that, I agreed to the second reading. I trust that in the committee the measure will assume the character of a moderate reform'. He voted for Gascoyne's wrecking amendment to preserve the relative size of the English representation, 19 Apr. 1831, 'this being one of the modifications I required'.[22]

Staunton regretted that the government's defeat meant that the discussion on reform would be curtailed, and a dissolution made inevitable. He condemned the 'furious and unprincipled demagogues' who dominated the ensuing general election, and found it

> impossible not to fear that the Parliament now electing under the influence of the prevailing excitement will prove a revolutionary Parliament, a Parliament which will not allow the ministers to retrace their steps although anxious and willing to do so – which will fanatically persist in that which the people in their recovered senses will no longer desire.

By an address, dated 24 Apr. 1831, he declined to accept a requisition to stand for Hampshire, until the

bill had passed, and he defended his last vote against a clause which was a

> direct violation of the terms of those solemn compacts by which the legislative union of the three kingdoms had been effected, which, moreover left all our great colonies and vast possessions in the East and West Indies, as well as our various important commercial and funded interests, without the protection of either a *virtual* or a *direct* representation in Parliament.[23]

He was again returned unopposed for Heytesbury.

In a memorandum, 24 July 1831, he described Russell's speech reintroducing the reform bill that day as 'able and argumentative and historical', but he was irritated by it, and detailed instances 'of plausible and as he appears to think triumphant argument, which appeared to be decidedly false'. Although hostile to the bill, he still believed that a

> beneficial reform is very conceivable in theory – but it cannot be reduced to practice because its principles, though good, would not be popular – and that which is now popular, is decidedly not good. In this case, how much to risk with the view of saving the rest, is a difficult question.

He was convinced 'that the advocates of the measure hope and believe it would produce no effect at all', and that its opponents feared 'that it will not only do no good but a great deal of harm'. He was again appointed to the select committee on the East India Company, 28 June, when he spoke in defence of its monopoly of trade with China, for which he undoubtedly continued to press during its sittings.[24] He abstained from the division on the second reading of the reform bill, 6 July, 'meaning still to express approval of [the] principle of reform without sanctioning a bill which I now know from experience it is not intended to modify'. He voted in the minority in favour of hearing counsel on the Appleby petition, 12 July, 'because *admitting* the principle and rule of reform, we were bound to ascertain whether it *applied to this case*', but apparently against adjourning proceedings on the bill that evening.[25] He voted to postpone schedule A, 13 July, because the 'enfranchising of large towns' was the '*primary* object of the bill'. He was 'locked in and compelled to vote' for Sir Robert Peel's technical amendment, 14 July, the meaning of which he was unsure of, to ensure that the condemned boroughs were dealt with one by one. He divided in favour of an amendment to group the schedule A boroughs into single Member constituencies, 15 July, 'because admitting the principle [of disfranchisement], the object was allowed by less violent means'. The following day he noted his approval of the forebodings expressed by Peel, whom he now called 'the first statesman of the present age':

> The old road he admitted might be rough and even dirty, but the new he asserted was at the edge of a dangerous precipice – and although you might adopt it in defiance of his warning and escape for a time, his warning was not the less justifiable.

He was accidentally shut out, 19 July, and therefore unable to vote, as he had intended, for using the 1831 census to determine the boroughs in schedules A and B, 'conceiving that admitting population to be the measure of disfranchisement it ought to be the *actual* population'. He did, however, vote against the disfranchisement of Appleby that day, considering that if the borough was extended into neighbouring parishes, its population would have warranted the retention of one seat. He divided against the disfranchisement of Downton, 21 July, 'because it came under this rule, and the rule however good or bad, was better than no rule at all'. He voted against the disfranchisement of St. Germans, 26 July, for the same reason, and against the partial disfranchisement of Dorchester, 28 July, 'because although the *borough* is within the line, the *town* is above it'. However, he voted to remove one of the seats from Cockermouth, 28 July, 'because I do not object to take *one* Member from the small towns and because it diminishes the preponderance given by the bill to northern counties', and from Guildford, 29 July, as the town had 'no peculiar claims, having supported and petitioned for the bill'.[26] He left the House early, 3 Aug., 'but would have voted against the enfranchisement of the metropolitan districts, conceiving that the character of their representation would not be beneficial to the House and is not required by their peculiar interests'. He divided in favour of giving a second Member to Stoke, 4 Aug., 'not because it has any very strong claim in my opinion to have representation at all, but because the double representation is on many accounts preferable'. He voted against the enfranchisement of Gateshead, 5 Aug., since 'as a mere suburb of Newcastle it had no claim'. He sided with ministers over uniting Rochester with Chatham and Strood, 9 Aug., 'because of their contiguity and the influence of Chatham being beneficial rather than otherwise', and voted for Merthyr Tydfil to be grouped with Cardiff, 10 Aug., despite noting that it was large enough to justify having its own seat. He spoke in favour of the amendment to provide colonial representation, 16 Aug., the lack of which he considered a defect which was, 'if not the only, at least one of the principal of the obstacles which have deprived

me of the satisfaction of giving the bill in general my unqualified support'. He denied that there were insurmountable practical problems and, for the sake of consistency in promoting direct representation, he advocated the granting of two seats each to Jamaica and Calcutta. He voted for Lord Chandos's amendment to enfranchise £50 tenants-at-will, 18 Aug. He was absent from the division on the passage of the bill, 21 Sept., and two days later he was granted five weeks' leave on account of severe illness, so that he also missed the vote on Lord Ebrington's confidence motion, 10 Oct. 1831.[27]

Staunton's opinions changed back towards a grudging support for reform in the autumn of 1831 because of the popular unrest which followed the defeat of the bill in the Lords. 'Unfortunately the question now is', he wrote on 17 Nov., 'not how shall we improve the system of our representation, but how shall we prevent a revolution'. On 10 Dec. he commented that

> although I always have and always shall disapprove of the entire reform bill, thinking that it will on the whole do more harm than good, introduce or aggravate more abuses, than it will either remove or alleviate, I am by no means confident that I shall continue to resist it.

Acknowledging that there had been a major and permanent shift in public opinion and that changes were unavoidable, he judged that

> if the Whigs are the immediate, the Tories are the remote cause of our present difficulties. Their pertinacity in resisting the most moderate reforms, and their dissensions on the Catholic question, has thrown the country into the hands of their enemies; and since we cannot no [*sic*] longer hope to prevent mischief, let us do as little as possible ... In consequence of having so long refused to do anything, we are now driven to do too much.

By 24 Dec. 1831 he was reassured that the bill would bring some advantages, for example that there would be 'fewer very young men and mere loungers' in the House, and he now believed that there would be little further pressure to remove the still sufficiently powerful nomination interests. He voted for going into committee on the revised bill, 20 Jan. 1832, but the following day, in another private paper, he revealed his growing frustration with its progress:

> I have never entered very warmly into the merits of the details of the reform bill, especially those of the disqualification clause. Not only does the overwhelming importance of the measure put every other question connected with it in the shade; but I do not think that this question whether Malton or Calne is or is not within the line, has much to do with private justice.

He divided against the enfranchisement of Tower Hamlets, 28 Feb., when he was listed among those 'who generally vote for reform'. On 8 Mar., while pointing out that no significant changes had been made since the first bill, he observed on paper that 'the evils and dangers if not removed are considerably mitigated'. He listed the 'scale of houses and taxes' instead of population, the approximate restoration of the 'proportion between the three kingdoms', the Chandos amendment by which 'the legitimate influence of land is materially increased', a hope that the Lords would reverse the enfranchisement of the metropolitan boroughs, the proviso that £10 householders 'must also be ratepayers for a twelvemonth preceding', and the fact that schedule B was much reduced. According to his own account, however, he absented himself from the division on the third reading, 22 Mar., and left the House before the vote on Ebrington's motion for an address calling on the king to appoint only ministers who would carry the bill unimpaired, 10 May.[28] He had apparently intended to vote against the latter, 'because I consider the retirement of His Majesty's ministers a subject of great anxiety, but *not* of deep regret', yet he also for the first time genuinely feared an overthrow of the constitution on the model of the French Revolution: 'Lord Grey need not have brought in such a *sweeping* bill – the king needed not to have sanctioned it – but having once done this, it was at once become impossible for either party to stop in their career without more or less damage'. His only other known vote in this Parliament was against the production of information on Portugal, 9 Feb. 1832.

By the summer Staunton was publicly expressing himself reconciled to the provisions of the Reform Act, by which his seat at Heytesbury was abolished. Having declined to enter for Hampshire at the by-election in June, he accepted an invitation to stand for the Southern division later that year, and in his addresses he advocated reforms of the church, the corn laws, slavery, the Bank of England, the East India Company and the public finances, as well as a pacific foreign policy. Despite his poor record of voting in favour of reform, and John Croker's* opinion that he was 'as little cut out for a popular knight of a shire as any man I know', he 'went bowing unopposed through the country like a Chinese mandarin'.[29] By a 'happy accident', he was returned after a contest in December 1832, when he declared that

> he had never blindly followed the ministers of the day, but had voted for or against them as his judgement led him to approve or disapprove of their measures. Neither he nor his family has ever received one farthing of the public money, and private interest could not, therefore,

bias his votes, which he had ever given on all subjects that came before him, without personal consideration or partiality.[30]

He sat as a Liberal for Hampshire South for two years, and subsequently represented Portsmouth. Later in life he reviewed his political career:

> From the first day that I took my seat in the House of Commons, in January 1819, down to the present hour (January 1852), I have sided with that section of our great political parties which, previous to 1830, were usually denominated the 'Liberal Tories', who acknowledged Mr. Canning as their leader; and who, soon after his death, seceded from the Tories of Lord Liverpool's school, and became amalgamated with the Whigs. *With them*, I gave a general and independent *support* to Lord Liverpool's administration. *With them*, I invariably *opposed* Lord Liverpool and the Ultra Tories upon the Catholic question. *With them*, I finally and entirely separated from that party, on the occasion of the duke of Wellington's celebrated declaration of unqualified opposition to all parliamentary reform. *With them*, lastly, I have ever since given to the Liberal party a free and independent support.[31]

He retired at the dissolution in 1852 because of ill health.[32] He died in August 1859, when his baronetcy became extinct, and left his Irish and English estates to be divided between the heirs of his first cousin Victoire Cormick, the wife of Mark Lynch (*d.* 1822) of Duras, county Galway.[33]

---

[1] Based on his *Mems. of Chief Incidents of Public Life of Sir G.T. Staunton* (1856). [2] Ibid. 2-74; Sir G.T. Staunton, *Mem. of Life and Fam. of Late Sir G.L. Staunton*, 1-60, 145; *Oxford DNB*. [3] *Mems.* 1-2, 44-45, 76, 101-8. [4] Ibid. 173-6; *Trans. R. Asiatic Soc.* i (1827), 600-8. [5] *Mems.* 74-76, 176-84; Add. 38292, ff. 76, 139, 154. [6] *Mems.* 53, 169-73; J. King, *Poem on Leigh Park* (1829); D. Gladwyn, *Leigh Park*, 29-62, 119-28. [7] Hants RO, Malmesbury mss 9M73/ G2342, FitzHarris to Sturges Bourne, 11 Oct. 1820; Wellington mss WP1/657/7/1, 4; WP4/2/1/25. [8] *Crabb Robinson Diary*, ii. 60. [9] *Edgeworth Letters*, 450. [10] *Mems.* 76, 110, 192. [11] *Black Bk.* (1823), 194; *Session of Parl. 1825*, p. 486; *New Biog. Dict.* (1825), iii. 447. [12] *Mems.* 77; *PP* (1821), vi. 343-9; vii. 130-5; Sir G.T. Staunton, *Misc. Notes relating to China*, 317-84. [13] *Mems.* 153-4. [14] Ibid. 154-6. [15] Ibid. 116. [16] Ibid. 117-19. [17] Ibid. 110-11, 114. [18] Ibid. 119-20. [19] Ibid. 116, 156-60, 190. [20] Ibid. 110-11, 115. [21] These memoranda are in Duke Univ. Lib. Staunton mss, and are extensively quoted in M. O'Neill and G. Martin, 'A Backbencher on Parl. Reform', *HJ*, xxiii (1980), 539-63, from which unattributed quotations in the following paragraphs are taken. [22] A memorandum in the Staunton mss, dated 18 July 1831, lists 19 of Staunton's votes, Mar.-Aug. 1831, and gives his reasons for each of them. [23] *Hants Chron.* 2 May 1831; Wellington mss WP4/4/3/28. [24] *Mems.* 59-60, 77-78. [25] *The Times*, 1 Aug. 1831. [26] Ibid. [27] *Mems.* 123. [28] Ibid. [29] *Salisbury Jnl.* 11 June; *Hants Chron.* 6 Aug., 8 Oct. 1832; Add. 58772, f. 38; Keele Univ. Lib. Sneyd mss SC17/182. [30] *Mems.* 121-8, 192; *Hants Advertiser*, 15 Dec. 1832. [31] *Mems.* 110-11. [32] Ibid. 220-6. [33] *Gent. Mag.* (1859), ii. 318; *Burke Irish LG* (1904), 354-5, 564; *DNB*; *Oxford DNB*.

S.M.F.

STEPHENS *see* **LYNE STEPHENS**

STEPHENSON, Henry Frederick (1790–1858), of 5 Arlington Street, Mdx.

WESTBURY	15 July 1831–1832

b. 18 Sept. 1790, illegit. s. of Charles Howard[†], 11th duke of Norfolk (*d.* 1815), and Elizabeth, da. of Isaac Stephenson of Whitehaven, Cumb.[1] *educ.* Sedbergh; Trinity Hall, Camb. 1808; M. Temple 1811, called 1814. *m.* 27 Feb. 1826, Lady Mary Keppel, da. of William Charles, 4th earl of Albemarle, 6s. 9da. *d.* 30 July 1858.

Commr. of excise 1838-49, of stamps and taxes 1849, of inland revenue 1849-*d.*

Dir. Economic Life Assurance Co. 1829, chairman 1857-*d.*

Stephenson was the acknowledged son of the colourful and eccentric 'Jockey' of Norfolk, whose second wife was confined to a lunatic asylum shortly after their marriage in 1771, and Elizabeth, the daughter of Isaac Stephenson and his wife Mary, née Hodgson.[2] His illegitimacy did not unduly hinder his career, and Denis Le Marchant[†] recalled that he was 'as proud of his lineage as if his mother had been a duchess'.[3] According to an entry in Stephenson's diary, 28 Sept. 1812, he 'had some negotiation about standing for the borough of Plympton [Erle] but thought the event too uncertain and the expense very great'.[4] He was living with Norfolk at that time, and a few years later Lady Jerningham noted that he appeared 'strikingly' like his father.[5] He certainly took after him in his delight in high living, and in 1813 he joined the Sublime Society of Beefsteaks, of which he became treasurer and secretary.[6] Like Norfolk, he was a Protestant and an advanced Whig, and he also moved easily in the upper echelons of the Whig party.[7] He joined Brooks's, 24 Jan. 1819, sponsored by Lords Thanet and Bessborough, and was for many years a member of the Fox Club. However, reminding Lord Brougham, 23 Feb. 1831, that 'previous to the death of my father, the late duke of Norfolk, an intimacy commenced between you and me', he confessed that his demise, in 1815, had 'produced an unexpected, undeserved and serious wound upon my happiness and prosperity'. Surprisingly, Norfolk made no provision for Stephenson in his will, and initial attempts by Henry Brougham* (as he then was) to find him a place were unavailing.[8] In 1817 he applied to the 12th duke, claiming that he was not 'activated by any feelings of unkindness on account of the distribution of my father's property', but asking for a continuance of his former allowance of £400 a year.[9]

Stephenson fell back on his legal education, and from 1817 he was listed as an equity draftsman at 1 Garden Court, Temple, and, from 1835, at 3 Plowden Buildings. If Le Marchant is to be believed, he did not establish much of a reputation, being 'one of the most incompetent practitioners in chancery, as the little business he has ever done there abundantly testifies'.[10] He was employed by the duke of Sussex as an auditor, and from at least 1817 acted as his equerry and personal assistant.[11] Lady Jerningham described how Stephenson, when Sussex 'moves off to bed, generally serves him for a walking stick; being about 5 foot 5, and the duke 6 foot 4 and *large* in proportion, he winds his arm round the secretary's neck in a very affectionate way, and so they walk off'.[12] In 1824 Sussex presented him with a silver cigar case, inscribed with the names of some of his fellow Whigs, in gratitude for his services.[13] In May 1825 Lord Darlington offered to bring him into Parliament, but he declined.[14] This was presumably in relation to Petersfield, over which he issued a newspaper denial, although his candidacy was again rumoured prior to the general election the following year.[15] Of the duke of York's funeral in 1827, Thomas Creevey* related that the king's brothers were

> kept waiting in the cold chapel an hour and a half before everything was ready, during which period various peers made the most marked homage to *Billy* [the duke of Clarence, now heir presumptive], and as Stephenson was the duke of Sussex's train-bearer, he was privy to all that passed.[16]

Stephenson married into the Keppel family in 1826, but while his wife's father was apparently content with the match, her brother-in-law, Thomas William Coke, Member for Norfolk, was 'furious'.[17] That year also saw Stephenson take up the office of auditor to John George Lambton*, who was created Baron Durham two years later. As he had with Sussex, he set about a minute examination of Lambton's financial situation in order to advise him how to retrench. He also surveyed his estate and mining concerns, handled his legal affairs in London and acted as a parliamentary agent. Although he lived on terms of social equality with Lambton, relations were not always cordial, as was shown in August 1827, when Lambton 'directed *my auditor* to wait upon Lord Lansdowne, and to make that claim which I though I had a perfect right to, of being made a peer, but Stephenson refused to execute this commission'.[18]

In 1828 it was rumoured that he would be Lord Fitzwilliam's candidate at East Retford, and in early 1830 he, as Lord Holland put it, 'in a most manly, disinterested, but gentlemanlike and conciliatory manner', declined the offer from the marquess of Cleveland (as Darlington had become) of a seat for Winchelsea. This was because of his 'pledge to Ld. Fitz.' and his 'inability to support ministers', but nothing came of it. He was one of the counsel for the petitioners against the East Retford disfranchisement bill before the Lords between April and July.[19] He was pleased when the new cabinet was settled in November 1830, and wrote that it must

> steer its course by the three great principles on which it is avowedly formed – economy, reform and peace. The triumph to the Whigs and to their principles is great, and also to Lord Grey; for during the last ten years many of their principles have been reluctantly, but of necessity, adopted and carried by their political opponents, and Lord Grey is now by the voice of the country and the vote of Parliament forced into power ... I begin to feel a great interest in events and affairs as they are passing before me. The times are exciting; I am proud of my party and cannot help feeling elated that no dirty job, no intrigues of faction, has brought them into power; and that the regeneration and restoration of the country are thus committed to the judgement and abilities of those whom I have looked up to all my life.[20]

Having failed to gain an appointment when Canning had been premier, he doubly resented Brougham's failure to find him a legal office, especially as he had promised him a mastership in chancery if he were appointed lord chancellor. By February 1831 Stephenson interpreted this failure as a disparaging judgement on his abilities, and he wrote a highly charged letter to Brougham, which ended: 'you have thus for a long time sported with, and now wounded so many of my feelings so acutely, as to render it impossible for us to meet in future, except as the most perfect strangers. Farewell'. In another letter he haughtily refused the derisory offer of a commissionership of bankruptcy.[21]

In the last week of February 1831 Stephenson and William George Adam, a king's counsel, were asked to correct the reform bill, probably on the advice of Durham, who chaired the committee charged with its preparation, and it is unlikely that he played any larger role than this in its composition.[22] In July Sir Ralph Lopes, patron of and Member for Westbury, turned out his colleague, Henry Hanmer, because of his opposition to the bill, and replaced him with Stephenson. He voted against using the 1831 census to determine the boroughs in schedules A and B, 19 July, and thereafter divided steadily for the details of the reintroduced reform bill. Claiming 'some local knowledge of Gateshead' in his maiden speech, 5

Aug., he denied that it was to be enfranchised in order to increase the influence of a minister, presumably Durham, who lived nearby. He made the same point, 9, 10 Aug., when he stressed that the decision was in line with 'one of the great principles of the bill; namely, that of equalizing the representation'. It was probably Stephenson, rather than Lopes, who (as 'Hanmer') was the Member for Westbury forced to justify having cheered Lord Althorp in a 'marked manner', 10 Aug. He voted with ministers on the Dublin election controversy, 23 Aug., the passage of the reform bill, 21 Sept., the second reading of the Scottish bill, 23 Sept., and Lord Ebrington's confidence motion, 10 Oct. He divided for the second reading of the revised reform bill, 17 Dec. 1831, and its committal, 20 Jan. 1832, when he rebutted Croker's suggestions that he had entered the House as a dependant or had anything to do with the concoction of the bill:

> I have, however, always been the steady friend of parliamentary reform, and I have come into the House at my own request to support the present measure considering that the happiness, the welfare and the comfort of the country depend on the destruction of that detestable oligarchical power which has too long existed.

He again divided regularly in favour of its details. On 20 Feb. he indicated that he would move for the first ten boroughs to be disfranchised together, 'for it is impossible that there can be any discussion upon them', but dropped the idea when Lord John Russell expressed his disapproval. He also spoke in defence of the formula used to draw up the list of condemned boroughs, and the following day he reiterated that

> the vulgar rules of arithmetic are quite sufficient for the purposes required: and, indeed, are so accurately applied, as to place each borough as nearly as possible in its proper relative position, by adding the two sums of taxes and houses together, and dividing by a common divisor, say 100.

He voted for the third reading of the bill, 22 Mar., and Ebrington's motion for an address calling on the king to appoint only ministers who would carry it unimpaired, 10 May. He divided in the minority of ten against the second reading of the Liverpool disfranchisement bill, 23 May. He voted for the second reading of the Irish bill, 25 May, and against increasing the county representation of Scotland, 1 June. Although wanting it to be amended, he spoke in favour of the bill to exclude insolvent debtors from the Commons, 6 June, arguing that parliamentary privileges were 'never intended to enable a man to defraud his creditors'. He rebutted criticisms of the general register and anatomy bills, 2, 6 Feb., and denied that he had stigmatized opposition to such measures as 'ignorant clamour', 8 Feb. He voted against the production of information on Portugal, 9 Feb., and military punishments, 16 Feb. He divided against an amendment to the navy civil departments bill, 6 Apr., defended Sussex's ranger-ship of Hampton Court Park, 13 Apr., voted in the minority of 11 for requiring coroners to have medical qualifications, 20 June, and expressed his hope that the punishment of death bill would not be lost, 6 July. His only other known votes were with ministers for the Russian-Dutch loan, 26 Jan., 20 July 1832. By the Reform Act Westbury was deprived of one seat, which Lopes continued to occupy. Stephenson therefore left the House at the dissolution of 1832 and never sat again.

In his *Letter to Lord Henley* (1833), Stephenson argued in favour of church reform, stating that the

> voice of the nation is demanding in every public functionary a higher degree of zeal and purity, and public virtue; that abuses are no longer deemed sacred because they are venerable, nor improvements rejected as rash because they are extensive.

In *A Letter to James Abercromby* (1833) he advocated extensive reforms of municipal corporations. According to Sir Robert Heron*, after Durham had resigned from the government in 1833, Stephenson

> said, in a large company at dinner, 'That Lord Durham would return to the cabinet before the end of June, in a place of greater importance, though of inferior precedence'. This could not be said without design. It has not been realized.[23]

As an 'active member of the party at the bar', Stephenson seems to have retained his status in Whig circles for some years. However, either because his strictures against reckless expenditure proved too much, or because Sussex felt him in some way to blame for his failure to receive a larger grant from Lord Melbourne's administration, Stephenson left the duke's service in 1838.[24] In December 1838 he failed in his attempt to effect a reconciliation between ministers and Durham over the latter's report on Canada.[25] He continued to be employed as agent for the Lambton estates after Durham's death in 1840, but retired in 1853. He undertook similar work for other employers, such as Lord Bute, Fitzwilliam and Cleveland.[26] He nevertheless had to accept the offer of a commissionership of excise, in addition to one he already held for arbitration over compensation paid after the emancipation of the slaves. This plurality was noticed, for instance by Charles Greville, who wrote, 29 Feb. 1840, that there was

another job (or rather *jobbing*) coming forward, that of Stephenson, which though small in amount is very discreditable, and shows the laxity and system of favour which prevails with reference to individuals and party hangers-on.

Lord Granville Somerset* raised the matter in the House, 5 Mar. 1840.[27] Stephenson also held the offices of deputy ranger of Hyde Park and falcon herald extraordinary.[28] 'Booty', as he was sometimes known, died suddenly, of an aneurysm of the heart, in July 1858. His contemporaries

> wherever the remnants of the old Whig society still met, long missed the well known and well loved figure in the old-fashioned Hessian boots of the man who had been the friend and secretary of the royal duke of Sussex, the brother-in-law of Coke of Norfolk and the life and soul of all their gatherings.[29]

He was survived by his wife, who in 1868 married Samuel Charles Whitbread of Southill, Bedfordshire, Member for Middlesex, 1820-30, who had loved her since his youth.[30] Stephenson's eldest son, Augustus Frederick William Keppel (1827-1904), one of ten surviving children, became solicitor to the treasury and was awarded the KCB in 1885.

[1] Stephenson mss, *ex. inf.* M.G. Stephenson of Edgecliff, New South Wales, Australia, whose assistance is gratefully acknowledged. [2] Ibid. [3] *Three Diaries*, 14. [4] Stephenson mss. [5] Holland, *Further Mems.* 146; *Jerningham Letters*, ii. 284. [6] Boase, *Modern Eng. Biog.* iii. 734. [7] H.F. Stephenson, *Letter to Lord Henley* (1833), 11; Le Marchant, *Althorp*, 296. [8] Brougham mss; Stephenson mss, Symonds to Stephenson, 10 Nov. 1817; PROB 11/1577/93. [9] Arundel Castle mss C314. [10] *Three Diaries*, 14. [11] *Ann. Reg.* (1817), Chron. p. 113; Brougham mss, Stephenson to Brougham, 1 May 1820, 1 Jan. 1823, 29 Dec. 1836; *Creevey Pprs.* ii. 6, 47, 155, 329; Wellington mss WP1/1100/5; 1149/8. [12] *Jerningham Letters*, ii. 145. [13] Sir H. Keppel, *Sailor's Life under Four Sovereigns*, 97. [14] Stephenson mss. [15] *Hants Telegraph*, 4 Apr. 1825; Grosvenor mss 9/9/26. [16] *Creevey's Life and Times*, 234. [17] *Creevey Pprs.* ii. 97. [18] Ibid. ii. 126; D. Spring, 'Agents to Earls of Durham in 19th Cent.', *Durham Univ. Jnl.* liv. 3 (1962), 104-6. [19] Fitzwilliam mss, Crompton to Milton, 21 May; Stephenson mss, Dundas to Stephenson, 6 June 1828; Add. 51785, Holland to Fox, 7 Feb.; Grey mss, Durham to Grey [8 Feb. 1830]; *Lords Sess. Pprs.* cclxxx. 3. [20] Stirling, *Coke of Norf.* 543-4. [21] Brougham mss, Stephenson to Brougham, 23 Feb., to unknown [n.d.] 1831. [22] *Three Diaries*, 14; Le Marchant, 296. [23] Heron, *Notes*, 207. [24] Stirling, 407; M. Gillen, *Royal Duke*, 215-16. [25] *Melbourne Pprs.*, 443; C.L. New, *Lord Durham*, 486-7. [26] Spring, 106; *Lady Charlotte Guest* ed. Lord Bessborough, 135, 145, 149-50, 152-3; Stephenson mss. [27] *Greville Mems.* iv. 251. [28] *The Times*, 4 Aug. 1858; *Burke's Fam. Recs.* (1897), 552. [29] *A Royal Corresp.* ed. J. Stephenson, 9; *Spencer Stanhope Letter-Bag*, ii. 126; Keppel, i. 96; ii. 219; iii. 27; *Gent. Mag.* (1858), ii. 316. [30] *Spencer Stanhope Letter-Bag*, ii. 151.

S.M.F.

STEPHENSON, Rowland (1782–1856), of Marshalls, nr. Romford, Essex.[1]

LEOMINSTER   19 Feb. 1827–4 Feb. 1830

b. 19 May 1782, 3rd surv. s. of John Stephenson, banker (d. 1822), of Great Ormond Street, Mdx. and Mary, da. of James Broadley of Mersham, Kent. educ. Eton 1796–9. m. 23 Apr. 1807, his cos. Mary Eliza, da. of Edward Stephenson, banker, of Farley Hill, Berks., 8 ch. d. 2 July 1856.
Treas. St. Bartholomew's Hosp. 1824–9.

Stephenson's father, a member of the Cumbrian (Alston) branch of the family, had married a niece of the naval commander Thomas Broadley in 1771, and embarked on a career as a merchant and victualling agent in Florida, where he became (by 1776) a member of the king's council at Pensacola. His business collapsed when Spain captured the colony during the American War of Independence, and Stephenson was born at sea during the family's return passage to London, where his father became a partner in his uncle Rowland Stephenson's[†] Lombard Street bank, Stephenson, Remington and Company. Stephenson himself joined them from Eton College, and succeeded his father as a partner in 1822.[2] Like his great-uncle Rowland and his uncle and father-in-law Edward Stephenson (1759-1833), an authority on the composer Johann Sebastian Bach and collector of Cremona violins, 'the dapper little banker' and his wife Mary who, like him, was small and delicate, delighted in patronising the arts. They also entertained their London friends at Sunday parties and musical soirees at Marshalls, the 'pretty villa' with 300 acres near Romford, Essex, which Stephenson purchased in 1816, adding to it the manor lordship of Cockermouth, the How Hatch estate at Braintree and other local properties.[3]

Stephenson was also ambitious, with his brother-in-law John Norman Macleod*, to be elected to Parliament. Thwarted at Carlisle in 1816 and possibly elsewhere from lack of funds, he intensified his efforts after his wife died in October 1821.[4] His contacts and partnership at Remingtons enabled him to mount bold and costly by-election challenges to the Irish secretary Goulburn at West Looe in February 1822 (followed up with a petition), and to the Welsh judge Jonathan Raine in March 1823 at Newport; and, having desisted at Carlisle in 1825, he was again expected to oppose the duke of Northumberland's nominees in the Cornish boroughs at the 1826 election.[5] In the event he availed himself of the late retirement at Leominster of his fellow banker Sir John Lubbock, who had represented

the borough, 1812-20. Lord Hotham topped the poll and Thomas Bish[†] came second, but a double return was made after Stephenson's counsel protested that Bish, who ran the lottery, was disqualified, as a government contractor, from standing.[6] Hotham's election was confirmed directly Parliament met, 21 Nov. 1826, and Stephenson's on petition, 19 Feb. 1827.[7] Bish protested that he had 'found his way into Parliament *not* by the suffrages of the people ... but by the ingenuity of his legal advocates'.[8] He also facilitated through London brokers the election of Macleod for Sudbury in April 1828, but refused to canvass with him.[9] He voted against Catholic relief, 12 May, and with the Wellington ministry against ordnance reductions, 4 July 1828, but no speeches or contributions by him to the business of the House were recorded, and his parliamentary career was distinguished solely by his manner of leaving it.

When unsecured advances authorized by his assistant John Henry Lloyd came to light late in December 1828, Remingtons suspended payment and Stephenson immediately left St. Bartholomew's Hospital, where, as treasurer, he had an apartment. Taking passages aboard fishing smacks from Bristol and Clovelly, he and Lloyd reached Angle Bay, near Milford Haven, and boarded the *Providence*, bound for Savannah, Georgia. The lord mayor of London, believing that they had absconded with £200,000 in exchequer bills, had issued a writ for their arrest, rewards of £1,000 and £300 were offered for their detention, and reports of alleged sightings and further misdeeds proliferated long after their departure, coverage of which dominated the newspapers and delighted the gossips.[10] Remingtons' bankruptcy, which affected many provincial banks, was gazetted, 4 Jan. 1829, and an indictment charging Stephenson with embezzlement was issued at the Old Bailey, 16 Jan., as a prelude to outlawry proceedings in king's bench. Despite rumours to the contrary, the largest single debt proved against his estate was for £6,700.[11] His assets, the Essex estates, a mansion and its contents in Dover, a box at Drury Lane theatre, paintings, antiques, and the contents of David Garrick's villa at Hampton, Middlesex, which he had purchased in 1823, were auctioned by Shuttleworth's, 29 Jan.-3 June 1829. He forfeited his parliamentary seat when he was formally bankrupted under the twelve-month rule, 19 Jan. 1830.[12]

Stephenson's treatment on his arrival in the United States, 27 Feb. 1829, aroused as much interest as his flight from England. His assumed name of Smith (Lloyd's was Larkin) proved no disguise, and he was arrested and detained in a debtors' prison in New York, where extradition proceedings failed as he was not a convict. He was released, 26 Mar.[13] In a declaration drafted on 21 Jan. 1829 and sent to Stephenson's family, Lloyd accepted full responsibility for the losses at the bank and Stephenson's plight, but the effect of Stephenson's recent heavy investment in Thomas Horton's Regent's Park Colosseum, which opened in January 1829, remains unexplained.[14] His relations supported Stephenson financially in exile and cared for his children. His eldest son Rowland Macdonald Stephenson (1808-95) visited him in the summer of 1829 and afterwards paid 15,000 dollars for Dr. William Shippen's 170-acre estate, Farley, on the Delaware River, in Bensalem township, near Bristol, Pennsylvania, where Stephenson settled in October 1829.[15] He died there in July 1856 and was buried in the churchyard of St. James's Episcopal Church. An obituary in the *Bucks. County Intelligencer* described him as 'formerly a banker in England', long since settled in Bristol, where 'he was universally esteemed for his benevolence and kindness to the poor and distressed'. His will was proved at Doylestown, Pennsylvania, 16 July 1856, and, as he had directed, his goods were sold, debts paid and the residue sent to Rowland with family memorabilia. Rowland was knighted in October 1856 for his services as a civil engineer and managing director of the East India Railway Company.[16]

---

[1] Information from Rowland Stephenson, 12 Denmark Road, Exeter, concerning Stephenson's birth at sea, flight to Pennsylvania and his will, is gratefully acknowledged. [2] *N and Q* (ser. 12), x. 421, 491; xi. 88-89; *Gent. Mag.* (1814), i. 518; ii. 188-9; (1822), i. 478, 565-6; GL ms 6667; PROB 11/1664/613. [3] *New Grove Dict. of Music and Musicians* (Edward Stephenson); *Gent. Mag.* (1807), i. 375; Lord W.P. Lennox, *Fifty Years Biog. Reminiscences*, ii. 48-52; *VCH Essex*, vii. 71. [4] *HP Commons, 1790-1820*, ii. 91-94; *The Times*, 24 Oct. 1821. [5] *R. Cornw. Gazette*, 22, 29 Mar.; *West Briton*, 4 Apr. 1823; Brougham mss, Stephenson to J. Brougham, 29 Mar., 1 Apr. 1825; *N and Q* (ser. 12), x. 421, 491; xi. 88-89. [6] *Globe*, 8, 12, 15 June; Macleod of Macleod mss 1061/2, 5, 7; Hull Univ. Lib. Hotham mss DD HO/8/4, J. Hall to Hotham, 18 June; *Worcester Herald*, 24 June 1826. [7] Keele Univ. Lib. Sneyd mss SC12/78, B. Percy to Sneyd [Feb. 1827]. See LEOMINSTER. [8] *Hereford Jnl.* 21 Feb. 1827. [9] Macleod of Macleod mss 1062/7, 13. [10] *Hereford Jnl.* 31 Dec. 1828; *The Times*, 2, 3, 5, 6, 8 Jan., 14 Feb.; Grey mss, Ellice to Grey [Jan. 1829]. [11] *Gent. Mag.* (1829), i. 78. [12] *The Times*, 3-5 Feb., 15 May, 3 June 1829; *Sale Catalogues of Libraries of Eminent Persons* ed. A.N.L. Munby, 12; *Sale Catalogues of Libraries of Eminent Persons* ed. J.F. Arnott, 1-175 (Garrick); *CJ*, lxxxv. 3-4; *Globe*, 11 Feb. 1830. [13] *Gent. Mag.* (1829), i. 361; *The Times*, 10, 11, 14, 22, 27, 29 Apr. 1829. [14] Letters *ex inf.* Rowland Stephenson; R. Hyde, *Regent's Park Colosseum*. [15] Letters *ex inf.* Rowland Stephenson; *Globe*, 11 Feb. 1830; D. Green, *Hist. Bristol* (1911), 143. [16] Bucks. will book 14, p. 95 (*ex inf.* Rowland Stephenson); *Oxford DNB*.

M.M.E.

STEUART, Robert (1806-1843), of Alderston, Haddington and 10 Upper Belgrave Street, Mdx.[1]

HADDINGTON BURGHS	1831–10 Aug. 1831
HADDINGTON BURGHS	1832–1841

bap. 9 July 1806,[2] 1st s. of Robert Steuart of Alderston and Louisa Clementina, da. of John Drummond, of Logie Almond, Perth. *educ.* Braesnose, Oxf. 1824. *m.* 7 July 1827, Maria, da. of Col. Samuel Dalrymple of Nunraw and North Berwick, Haddington, 1s. 2da. *suc.* fa. 1827. *d.* 15 July 1843.

Ld. of treasury Apr. 1835-May 1840; chargé d'affaires and consul general to Colombia 1842-*d.*

Steuart's father, who maintained in his will that he was one of the Grantully branch of that family (they relinquished trusteeship of his estate at probate) had business interests in Calcutta, administered for him in later life by his brother-in-law William Hastie (*d.* 1818) and the latter's sons. He purchased a 315-acre estate and several holdings in Alderston and nearby Haddington and in 1805 married a granddaughter (*d.* 1823) of the 3rd earl of Dunmore, on whom property in Nicolson Street, Edinburgh, had been settled. Her brother William Drummond (*d.* 1828), a writer and diplomat, represented St. Mawes, 1795-6, and Lostwithiel, 1796-1802, on the treasury interest. Robert Steuart died 1 Feb. 1827, worth an estimated £18,000 at probate (including two original shares in East India Company stock), having willed his estates and the bulk of his fortune to Steuart, the eldest of his four children, then an Oxford undergraduate. With the consent of his trustees, his brother-in-law Norman Pringle and the minister of the episcopal chapel in Haddington, James Craill, in July 1827 at North Berwick he married Maria Dalrymple, the daughter of an East Indian army colonel who had died in Madras in 1821.[3]

Steuart became a commissioner of supply for Haddingtonshire, where he rallied support for the reformers and the Grey ministry at mass meetings and dinners in the winter of 1830-1. After successfully canvassing the councils of Jedburgh and Haddington (who appointed him their delegate), he declared for Haddington Burghs at the general election precipitated by the reform bill's defeat and was returned by three votes to two after a riotous contest dominated by the kidnapping of the Lauder baillie.[4] The ministry's election managers perceived that this 'abstraction' was 'a sad scrape for Alderston, for it involves him in a committee and may void the election', and he did not contest the petition against his return.[5] He voted for the second reading of the reintroduced English reform bill, 6 July, signed a declaration next day under the 1829

Controverted Election Act that he would not seek re-election for Haddington Burghs that Parliament and ceased attending directly it was presented, 8 July 1831. He had been granted leave that day to introduce a bill to regulate the appointment of solicitors as chief magistrates in the royal burghs. The Haddington return was amended in favour of the defeated candidate Sir Augustus John Dalrymple, 10 Aug. 1831.[6]

Advocating the ballot, civil registration and church reform, Steuart regularly addressed reform meetings in 1831-2, canvassed continuously and was returned unopposed for Haddington Burghs as a Liberal at the general election of 1832.[7] A tall, dark, commanding figure, with 'an abundant crop of hair' and 'partial to large whiskers', by 1838 he was a well known politician 'much respected by all parties'.[8] He proved to be an effective parliamentarian and junior treasury minister under Lord Melbourne, but his tenure at Haddington became increasingly dependent on government support, and he was defeated there in 1841, seven months after resigning from office on being passed over for the Irish secretaryship.[9] In August 1841 he accepted a diplomatic posting to Colombia, where he died of a fever in July 1843.[10] His widow (d. 1886) later married William Henry Rainsford Hannay (d. 1856) of Kirkdale, Kirkudbright. His only son Robert Dalrymple Steuart (1836-64) took the additional names of Grossett and Muirhead by royal licence following his marriage in 1863 to the daughter and co-heiress of the late Henry Du Vernet Grossett Muirhead of Bredisholm, Lanarkshire.[11]

[1] Draws on *E.I. Reg.* 1800-57, and Steuart's obituaries in *Kelso Chron.* 29 Sept. and *The Times*, 17 Oct. 1843 [2] IGI (E. Lothian), which also gives 9 Aug. 1806. [3] Ibid.; MI in Haddington church; PROB 11/1652/13; 1726/325; IR26/897/82; 1144/315; *Gent. Mag.* (1821), ii. 474; *Caledonian Mercury*, 20 Nov. 1823, 17 Feb.; *Edinburgh Weekly Jnl.* 18 July 1827; *HP Commons, 1790-1820*, iii. 623-5. [4] *Berwick Advertiser*, 12, 26 Feb., 12, 19 Mar.; *Edinburgh Evening Courant*, 28 Mar., 4, 9, 25, 30 Apr.; *Caledonian Mercury*, 28 May; *Scotsman*, 28 May 1831. [5] *Cockburn Letters*, 320; *CJ*, lxxxvi. 551. [6] *CJ*, lxxxvi. 741; *The Times*, 9 July, 11 Aug. 1831. [7] *Berwick Advertiser*, 10 Sept., 19, 26 Nov. 1831, 19 May, 16 June, 22 Dec. 1832. [8] [J. Grant] *Random Recollections of Lords and Commons* (1838), ii. 318-20. [9] *The Times*, 9 Aug. 1836, 13, 14 May 1840; *Scottish Electoral Politics*, 221, 227, 242, 266-7. [10] *Gent. Mag.* (1843), ii. 546. [11] *The Times*, 10 Aug. 1863, 11 May 1886.

M.M.E.

STEWART, Alexander Robert (1795–1850), of Ards, Letterkenny, co. Donegal.

CO. LONDONDERRY	1818–1830

b. 12 Feb. 1795, 1st s. of Alexander Stewart[†] of Ards and Lady Mary Moore, da. of Charles Moore[†], 1st mq. of

Drogheda [I]. *educ.* Woodnesborough, Kent (Rev. John Smith); St. John's, Camb. 1815; continental tour. *m.* 28 July 1825, Lady Caroline Anne Pratt, da. of John Jeffreys Pratt[†], 1st Mq. Camden, 1s. *suc.* fa. 1831. *d.* 24 Mar. 1850. Sheriff, co. Donegal 1831-2.[1]
Maj. co. Londonderry militia ?1819, lt.-col. 1823-*d.*

'Alick' Stewart was elected for county Londonderry in 1818, in place of his father, on the interest which the latter held in combination with his elder brother, the 1st marquess of Londonderry. Stewart, a silent and inactive Member (though an occasional committeeman), who had spent some of the intervening two years on the continent, nevertheless offered on the basis of his past conduct at the general election of 1820, when he was again returned unopposed.[2] He continued to follow the lead given by his first cousin Lord Castlereagh, foreign secretary in the Liverpool administration, through whom he had some influence over Irish patronage.[3] He voted against economies in revenue collection, 4 July 1820, and in defence of ministers' conduct towards Queen Caroline, 6 Feb. 1821. Like Castlereagh, he divided for Catholic relief, 28 Feb. He voted against repeal of the additional malt duty, 3 Apr., omitting the arrears from the grant to the duke of Clarence, 18 June, and Hume's motion for economy and retrenchment, 27 June 1821. He was in ministerial majorities against more extensive tax reductions to relieve distress, 21 Feb., and abolition of one of the joint-postmasterships, 13 Mar. 1822. He voted against inquiry into the conduct of the lord advocate relative to the press in Scotland, 25 June, and repeal of the salt duties, 28 June 1822, and the assessed taxes, 18 Mar. 1823.

The family claimed that Londonderry (as Castlereagh had become) had intended to transfer the colonelcy of the Londonderry militia to Stewart, who was described by the other county Member, George Dawson, as 'a very good colleague', but after his suicide in August 1822 it was given to the city Member, Sir George Hill, one of the rival Beresford set.[4] Stewart's relations, notably the 3rd marquess of Londonderry and the 1st Marquess Camden, bombarded ministers with complaints. However, their cause was not helped by his father, who, in Stewart's absence abroad with his sick brother, accepted the offer of the lieutenant-colonelcy on his behalf.[5] Londonderry's efforts peaked in July 1823, when various compromises were explored, including a notion that Stewart's father would become the colonel, with Stewart running the regiment as his lieutenant.[6] In fact, despite repeated assurances of Hill's amicable attitude, it was not until the end of the year that Stewart finally accepted the promotion, telling the lord lieutenant, among other quibbles, that 'I never could look upon the commission he then offered me as a satisfaction of the claim that the family had to the command of the regiment'. Peel, the home secretary, sarcastically described Stewart's grudging letter of acceptance as 'the happiest specimen of the unreasonable'.[7]

It was believed that Stewart would remain loyal to his cousin Londonderry, who, although highly dissatisfied by his treatment at the hands of ministers, considered it right for the family to give them general support.[8] In early 1824 he thought, like his father, that the offer of a rapprochement from the Beresfords was a sign that they would co-operate with the Stewarts for the present, with a view to taking advantage of their reduced influence at a future date, but he was dubious about retaining a long-term interest in the county unless Londonderry challenged them at the next election.[9] He divided against condemning the trial of the Methodist missionary John Smith in Demerara, 11 June 1824. He voted for Catholic relief, 1 Mar., 21 Apr., 10 May 1825. In July that year he married one of Camden's daughters, whose aunt was the widow of the 1st marquess of Londonderry, but only after the 3rd marquess had intervened to extract a proper settlement from Camden.[10] Declining to attend the Dublin dinner of Irish Catholics, 29 Jan. 1826, he informed Daniel O'Connell* that he had always voted for relief 'from no party considerations, but from an honest and sincere conviction that, until that long and often discussed measure is satisfactorily arranged ... no permanent tranquillity can be secured for Ireland'; yet he deplored 'angry threats or impassioned language' as counterproductive.[11]

Stewart absented himself from Londonderry during the general election of 1826 on the ground that his wife was nearing her confinement (although there was no surviving issue of this pregnancy). He was returned unopposed with Dawson, but his brother John was defeated in county Down, where he had been nominated in case Londonderry's son, Lord Castlereagh*, was petitioned against as being under age.[12] He was granted six weeks' leave because of illness in his family, 21 Feb. 1827. Although his father signed the anti-Catholic petition from the noblemen and gentlemen of Ireland early that year, he declined to support the hostile county Londonderry petition. He missed its presentation by Dawson in the Commons, 2 Mar., when Brownlow indicated that Stewart would soon forward a pro-Catholic petition from the county, and the division on the question, 6 Mar.[13] Having given birth to their only surviving child (5 July), his wife

died on 7 Oct. 1827. Stewart, who may have been the Member of that name listed in the minority against finding Leadbeater guilty of lying in evidence on the East Retford disfranchisement bill, 7 Mar., was again absent from the division on Catholic relief, 12 May 1828. He was reckoned by Planta, the Wellington ministry's patronage secretary, as likely to be 'with government' on emancipation in February 1829. He was named as a defaulter on the call, 5 Mar., but brought up a petition from Kilrea in favour of the measure, 13 Mar., and, in his only reported speech, 16 Mar., declared that he would give the bill his 'most anxious support'. His last known vote was for the third reading, 30 Mar. 1829. He was granted three weeks' leave to attend the assizes, 11 Mar. 1830. Later that month, on the announcement that Hill would become governor of St. Vincent, Camden requested Wellington to appoint him to the colonelcy of the Londonderry militia, but the post went to Lord Garvagh.[14]

Since at least 1826 relations had cooled between Stewart, who had chosen a 'neutral and independent position' in politics, and Londonderry, who resented his cousin's indifference and considered him 'totally impracticable'. Deterred by the prospect of an expensive contest, Stewart gave no clear indication of whether he would stand again and refused to co-operate with Londonderry's financial offer to try to secure the family interest.[15] Despite being given some credit for his consistency, compared to the turncoat Dawson, by mid-1829 he was considered to have no chance of re-election by his Beresford opponents.[16] Amid an anti-Catholic backlash in the county, he probably reckoned his prospects poor and, in any case, his father's death would terminate the lease of the Mercers' Company estates, which was the basis of the Stewart interest, so he retired at the dissolution in 1830.[17] His brother-in-law Lord Brecknock* wrote to him that 'I wish Dunfanaghy [in co. Donegal] was a nice rotten borough with half a dozen electors. I should be sorry not to have you a *Parliament man*, but I think you could not do otherwise than you have done'. In August 1830 a reconciliation was achieved between Londonderry and Stewart's father.[18] He and his father both signed the Down requisition against agitating the issue of the Union in March 1831, when, as a self-confessed 'old Tory', he privately condemned the Grey ministry's reform proposals as 'well calculated to hurry on a crisis'.[19] On the death of his father in late 1831, he inherited the bulk of his personal and real estate, including the residence at Ards, which was rebuilt at about this time.[20] He was said to be 'disliked by his own tenantry and the county at large' in Donegal, where, as sheriff, he caused controversy by prematurely closing the county reform meeting in January 1832.[21] He never sat in the Commons again and, for instance, he scorned the idea of offering for his former county in November 1839, when Londonderry urged:

> Believe me, Alick, you would be more looked up to by all the connection if, with your large fortune, you would do as your dear father did before you – make some effort to uphold and aid the family and house of Stewart which you belong to, I mean *politically*, in these strange, reforming times.[22]

Stewart died in March 1850, being succeeded by his only son Alexander John Robert (1827-1904).[23]

[1] Not 1830-1 as erroneously stated in *HP Commons, 1790-1820*, v. 270. [2] PRO NI, Stewart-Bam mss D4137/B/1/8-21 (NRA 40263); *Belfast News Letter*, 10 Mar. 1820. [3] Add. 40296, ff. 11, 58-59; *Black Bk.* (1823), 195; *Session of Parl. 1825*, p. 486. [4] Add. 38291, f. 152; PRO NI, Hill mss D642/202. [5] Add. 40328, f. 217; 40352, f. 164; Stewart-Bam mss B/2/5; Cent. Kent. Stud. Camden mss U840 C504/2, 5. [6] Add. 38295, ff. 160, 172; Stewart-Bam mss A/6/18, 19; Wellington mss WP1/767/11; 769/13. [7] Add. 40329, ff. 214, 243, 249. [8] Norf. RO, Blickling Hall mss, Londonderry to Lady Londonderry, 14, 29 Dec. 1822, 20 Feb., 2 July 1823. [9] PRO NI, Castlereagh mss D3030/N/135, 136. [10] Ibid. T2, p. 94; Q1, Londonderry to Lady Londonderry n.d. [?1828]; Stewart-Bam mss A/7/2. [11] Stewart-Bam mss B/11/1; *O'Connell Corresp.* iii. 1286. [12] *Belfast County Chron.* 12, 24 June 1826; Castlereagh mss N/157, 158. [13] Add. 40392, f. 5; Stewart-Bam mss B/11/2. [14] Wellington mss WP1/1104/3. [15] Ibid. WP1/1124/13; Stewart-Bam mss A/6/21; Castlereagh mss T2, p. 99; Q1, Londonderry to Lady Londonderry, n.d. [?1828]. [16] PRO NI, Pack-Beresford mss D664/A/89; PRO NI, Primate Beresford mss D3279/A/4/12, 13. [17] Add. 40304, f. 86; Castlereagh mss N/135; *Belfast Guardian*, 9, 16 July 1830. [18] Stewart-Bam mss B/6/12; 2/30. [19] PRO NI, Dufferin mss D1071/B/C/20/1/94a, 602. [20] *Gent. Mag.* (1831), ii. 476; PRO NI D1825/C/1/2; M. Bence-Jones, *Guide to Irish Country Houses*, 11. [21] PRO NI, Anglesey mss D619/33B/3; *Ballyshannon Herald*, 13, 20 Jan. 1832. [22] Stewart-Bam mss B/2/37; 11/7, 8. [23] *Londonderry Sentinel*, 29 Mar. 1850.

S.M.F.

STEWART, Charles (1801–1891), of 28 Oriental Place, Brighton, Suss.

PENRYN   1831–1832

b. 30 Sept. 1801, 3rd but 2nd surv. s. of Capt. Philip Stewart (*d.* 1837) of Lisburn, co. Antrim and his cos. Anne, da. of Capt. William Smyth. *educ.* L. Inn 1835; M. Temple 1836, called 1838. *m.* in Paris, 21 July 1861, Emily Constantia, da. of John Parland of St. Petersburgh, 1s. *d.* 30 June 1891.

Stewart belonged to a branch of an old Perthshire family which had migrated to Ulster in the early eighteenth century and had a strong tradition of military service. His father was born at Kinsale in 1765, entered the army in 1782, attained the rank of major in 1805, and was captain successively of the 5th (1805),

9th (1807) and 2nd (1819) Royal Veteran Battalions until his retirement on full pay in 1820 (he eventually settled at Brighton). His mother was a great-granddaughter of John Vesey, archbishop of Tuam, 1668-1716.[1] He stood for the venal borough of Penryn on the anti-corporation interest at the 1830 general election, purporting to be 'perfectly independent of party', but gave up after three days' polling left him a poor third.[2] He thought better of his threat to petition, continued to cultivate the borough and offered again at the general election of 1831, when he 'declared some reform to be necessary, but not that set forth in the [Grey ministry's] bill', which proposed the partial disfranchisement of Penryn; he was narrowly returned in second place.[3]

He divided against the second reading of the reintroduced reform bill, 6 July, at least four times for adjournment motions, 12 July, and for use of the 1831 census to determine the borough disfranchisement schedules, 19 July 1831. He voted for the total disfranchisement of St. Germans but against that of Saltash, 26 July, and he was in the minority next day to postpone consideration of the fate of Chippenham. He was presumably the 'Sir Charles Stuart' who recommended the inclusion of 'the important parish' of Hove in the new borough of Brighton, 5 Aug. He acquiesced in the proposed amalgamation of Penryn with Falmouth to form a two Member constituency, 9 Aug., but protested on behalf of Penryn's ratepayers, who he claimed were 'as pure and incorrupt as the voters in any other open town', at their inevitable subjugation to the £10 householders of Falmouth. He called for the borough qualification in the West of England generally to be significantly lowered, arguing that 'the influence of property will operate more on the lower classes of voters than on £10 householders'. He also expressed his hope that 'the first fruit of the union' of Penryn and Falmouth would be his own re-election. Around this time he made private representations to ministers about local anxieties regarding the boundaries of the Penryn portion of the new borough.[4] He divided against the bill's passage, 21 Sept. He was in the small minority for the Irish union of parishes bill, 19 Aug., voted to censure the Irish administration for undue interference in the Dublin election, 23 Aug., and divided against the Maynooth grant, 26 Sept. 1831.

Stewart voted against the second reading of the revised reform bill, 17 Dec. 1831, the motion to go into committee, 20 Jan., and the enfranchisement of Tower Hamlets, 28 Feb. 1832. He secured the adoption of an amendment prohibiting acting borough returning officers from serving as churchwardens or overseers of the poor, 14 Mar. Before dividing against the bill's third reading, 22 Mar., he warned that its 'dangers' far outweighed its dubious benefits:

It unsettles completely the relative weight of the different interests represented in this House; it takes from the land that power which it has so long and so properly possessed, and gives the preponderance to the commercial and manufacturing interests ... At the first election for a reformed Parliament, the vote by ballot and universal suffrage will be clamoured for by those classes whom you are now about to call into political power. I believe they will demand the abolition of the corn laws, an equitable adjustment of the national debt, and the destruction of church property; but ... the excited appetite of the people will not be restrained here, and the abolition of the hereditary peerage and the downfall of the monarchy will sooner or later follow the adoption of this ill-fated measure.

He appealed to the Lords to reject the bill. He was in the small minority for an attempt to preserve freemen's voting rights under the Irish bill, 2 July. He voted against ministers on the Russian-Dutch loan, 26 Jan., 12 July, and paired against them for the division on the affairs of Portugal, 9 Feb.[5] He was credited with a vote in Hunt's minority of 28 for information on army punishments, 16 Feb., and divided against the government's temporizing amendment to Fowell Buxton's motion for inquiry into the abolition of slavery, 24 May 1832.

He duly stood for Penryn and Falmouth at the general election in December 1832, promising to 'act in accordance with ... [the] spirit' of the Reform Act and to support 'a speedy abolition of colonial slavery ... a just commutation of tithes and ... reform of the abuses which may exist in our institutions'. He was humiliated, finishing bottom of a four-man poll with only 88 votes, 340 behind the successful Conservative Lord Tullamore*, whom he publicly accused of blatant bribery.[6] However, he did not carry out his threat to petition and his parliamentary career was over at the age of 31. He subsequently trained for the bar and after his call in 1838 was listed for many years as a special pleader on the northern circuit, but he probably never practised. His father died intestate at Brighton in 1837, leaving effects valued at under £800.[7] By the 1850s he and his brother William were living in Paris, where in 1861 he married a goddaughter of the tsar of Russia.[8] Towards the end of his life he returned to England, where he died in June 1891. He left all his property in England and France to his only child, Charles Edward Stewart (1862-1933), a non-practising barrister educated at Eton, Oxford and the Inner Temple.[9]

[1] Hist. Mems. Stewarts of Fothergill ed. C.P. Stewart, 47-56. [2] R. Cornw. Gazette, 10-31 July, 7 Aug. 1830. [3] Ibid. 14 Aug. 1830, 30 Apr., 7 May 1831. [4] Ibid. 13 Aug. 1831. [5] The Times, 9 Feb. 1832. [6] R. Cornw. Gazette, 30 June, 10, 24 Nov., 1-29 Dec. 1832. [7] Gent. Mag. (1837), ii. 101; PROB 6/213 (27 May 1837). [8] Gent. Mag. (1857), i. 498; Hist. Mems. Stewarts, 54. [9] The Times, 6 July 1891.

D.R.F.

STEWART, Edward (1808–1875).

WIGTOWN BURGHS   1831–1834

b. 9 Oct. 1808, 1st s. of Hon. Edward Richard Stewart[†] (d.1851) of 7 York Place, Portman Square, Mdx. and Lady Katharine Charteris, da. of Francis Charteris[†], Lord Elcho, of Amisfield, Haddington. educ. Eton 1823; Oriel, Oxf. 1826; L. Inn, called 1834. m. 27 Feb. 1838, Louisa Anne, da. of Charles John Herbert of Muckruss, co. Kerry, 2s. 5da. d. 21 Mar. 1875.
   Priv. sec. to first ld. of admiralty Dec. 1830-May 1831.
   Vic. of Sparsholt, Hants 1842-d.; rect. of Lainston, Hants 1850-d.

Stewart's father, a younger son of the 7th earl of Galloway, had a brief military career and sat for Wigtown Burghs on the family interest from 1806 until January 1809, when he was made a commissioner of the navy victualling board by the Portland ministry. He was subsequently, under the auspices of the Liverpool administration, paymaster of marines (1812-13), and a commissioner of the navy board (1813-19), of customs (1819-21) and of audit (1821-7). His marriage in 1805 connected him to the Charteris family, claimants to the attainted earldom of Wemyss. His brother-in-law Francis Charteris was created Baron Wemyss in 1821 and on the reversal of the attainder in 1826 became 6th earl of Wemyss.[1] Edward, the eldest of Stewart's three sons, was conventionally educated in England. He entered Lincoln's Inn in March 1830 and in December was made private secretary to his father's Whig nephew, Sir James Graham*, first lord of the admiralty in the new Grey administration. At the general election of 1831 his cousin Lord Garlies*, eldest son of the 8th earl of Galloway, returned him for Wigtown Burghs as a supporter of the ministerial reform scheme. He resigned his place at the admiralty and duly voted for the second reading of the reintroduced English reform bill, 6 July, and against the adjournment, 12 July 1831. He gave fairly steady support to its details, pairing on at least two occasions (5, 9 Aug.), but he was absent from the division on its passage, 21 Sept., and was given three weeks' leave on account of ill health two days later. He attended to vote for the motion of confidence in the ministry, 10 Oct. It was probably not he who divided for the Irish union of parishes bill, 19 Aug. He was in the government majorities on the Dublin election controversy, 23 Aug. He presented Lowland farmers' petitions against the use of molasses in brewing and distilling, 9 Aug. He voted for the second reading of the revised English reform bill, 17 Dec. 1831, steadily for its details and for the third reading, 22 Mar. 1832. He was in the ministerial majorities on the Russian-Dutch loan, 26 Jan., and relations with Portugal, 9 Feb., but he divided in the minorities of 41 against the malt drawback bill, 2 Apr., and of 26 for inquiry into the glove trade, 3 Apr. He was added to the select committee on the East India Company, 23 Feb., and named to that on the silk trade, 5 Mar. On 8 May he presented a petition in favour of the Edinburgh and Glasgow railway bill. He voted for the address calling on the king to appoint only ministers who would carry reform unimpaired, 10 May, and the second reading of the Irish reform bill, 25 May, after presenting petitions for supplies to be withheld until reform was secured. He was given a fortnight's leave on account of ill health, 9 July 1832.

Stewart was returned for Wigtown Burghs as a Liberal after a contest at the general election of 1832 and retired from Parliament at the dissolution in 1834. He was called to the bar that year but never practised, and made a change of direction by entering the church. He was ordained deacon in 1841, became vicar of Sparsholt, Hampshire in 1842 and in 1850 obtained the living of Lainton. On the death of his father in 1851 he received a legacy of £2,000 and a quarter share in residue of personal estate calculated for duty at £27,989.[2] He died in his sister Jane's house at 14 New Steine, Brighton, 21 Mar. 1875.[3] His elder son Herbert Stewart, aide-de-camp to Queen Victoria, had a distinguished military career, which was terminated by death from wounds sustained in Egypt in 1885.

[1] HP Commons, 1790-1820, v. 271. [2] PROB 11/2140/755; IR26/1915/666. [3] The Times, 27 Mar. 1875.

D.R.F.

STEWART, **Frederick William Robert**, Visct. Castlereagh (1805–1872).

Co. Down   1826–1852

b. 7 July 1805, o.s. of Charles William Stewart[†], 3rd mq. of Londonderry [I] and 1st Bar. Stewart [UK], and 1st w. Lady Catherine Bligh, da. of John Bligh[†], 3rd earl of Darnley [I]. educ. Eton 1814; Christ Church, Oxf. 1823. m. 2 May 1846, Hon. Elizabeth Frances Charlotte Jocelyn, da. of Robert Jocelyn*, 3rd earl of Roden [I], wid. of Richard Wingfield[†], 6th Visct. Powerscourt [I],

s.p. styled Visct. Castlereagh 1822-54; suc. fa. as 4th mq. of Londonderry [I] and 2nd Bar. Stewart [UK] 6 Mar. 1854; KP 28 Aug. 1856. d. 25 Nov. 1872.

Ld. of admiralty July 1829-Nov. 1830; vice-chamberlain Dec. 1834-Apr. 1835; PC 23 Feb. 1835.

Col. N. Down militia 1837; ld. lt. co. Down 1845-64.

'Cas' or 'Young Rapid', as the rakish Frederick Stewart was known,[1] was a grandson of the 1st marquess of Londonderry and the eldest son of the army officer and diplomat Charles Stewart, who sat for county Londonderry until he was created Baron Stewart in 1814. After the death of his mother in 1812, and in the absence of his father as ambassador in Vienna, he was cared for in vacations from Eton by his uncle Lord Castlereagh*, the foreign secretary, at North Cray Farm, Kent. On a visit to him there in 1821, his stepmother described him, evidently after a spell of illness, as 'quite recovered and as strong as ever, intelligent and beautiful'.[2] When Castlereagh was excluded from his Down seat on Londonderry's death that year, the family interest was given to a local stopgap, Mathew Forde, on the understanding that it would eventually revert to Frederick, of whom Castlereagh wrote that he 'seems to inherit the family propensity for election and enjoyed much his county prospects'.[3] After Londonderry's suicide in August 1822, Frederick, who now took the courtesy title of Lord Castlereagh, recorded that he 'certainly thought my poor uncle unlike himself for a long time; so much was he altered in his way of speaking and doing anything'.[4] He, of whom Lord John Russell* observed that 'he talks, but does not seem mad', bore himself well as chief mourner at his uncle's funeral,[5] and soon afterwards travelled to Vienna to be with his father, the new marquess, with whom he had an emotional reunion.[6] Londonderry complained of neglect by ministers, for instance that the Londonderry militia colonelcy was not safeguarded for Castlereagh's future enjoyment, but extracted from them a United Kingdom earldom (Vane) with special remainder to his sons with his second wife.[7] Through her he had come into extensive estates in county Durham and he informed his father-in-law Lord Camden, 9 Oct. 1822, that he considered 'England and Wynyard as my most natural home', but added that 'I am aware however that I have a duty towards Ireland to perform for Frederick and for the family name, and that I am fully determined to do'.[8]

Castlereagh returned to England for a period of intensive study under his tutor John Matthias Turner, before going up to Christ Church in January 1823.[9] However, in May he participated in a series of noisy night-time disturbances and was one of a number of students subsequently sent down. His family were said to be 'greatly afflicted', not least because it precluded him from taking up a promised commission in the army. But once the dean had removed his name from the register his expulsion could not be reversed, and Dr. Charles Lloyd, the regius professor of divinity, recorded that 'everybody speaks of him as of a young man who, if he had not fallen on unhappy times, might have gone through the university not only without disgrace, but with credit and distinction'.[10] Thereafter he seems to have travelled intermittently on the continent, including in 1824 to Scandinavia, where he contracted venereal disease.[11] That year Londonderry petulantly rebuffed Lord Liverpool's offer of a junior diplomatic posting for Castlereagh, asking instead that

> Mr. Robinson* [at the board of trade] or your lordship might employ him (out of remembrance to the name he bears) in any of the offices at home in a confidential and private manner, to give him a better habit of office detail, before he came into Parliament.[12]

Ministers agreed to provide something, in part to keep on friendly terms with the wayward Londonderry, but were still trying to accommodate him two years later.[13]

As early as July 1824 Castlereagh was taking soundings about standing for Down, and his father reported from their residence, Mount Stewart, that month that 'Frederick has been very handsomely admitted into the Down Hunt, and I think his conduct since his arrival here has given satisfaction'.[14] One of the family's supporters, the Rev. Mark Cassidy, commented the following year that, although it would depend on undertaking a detailed personal canvass, his success was certain.[15] He returned from the continent in time to offer at the dissolution in 1826, when Forde, alleging betrayal, was forced to withdraw.[16] Ignoring what he called the 'morally impossible' ideas of his father, who remarked that 'I hope, as a young and ardent mind, he is not too sanguine', the underage Castlereagh arranged for a cousin to stand against him and Lord Arthur Hill, the brother of Lord Downshire, with whom Londonderry was in cahoots. Despite the disgust shown by the independent interest, the poll was thereby kept open for nearly two weeks, and Castlereagh was elected with Hill on the day after his 21st birthday.[17] Cassidy sent him a long letter of encouragement and advice, warning him against servility to ministers and inattention to local concerns.[18] In fact, Castlereagh, who was expected to support the Liverpool government, was active in the affairs of both counties Down and Durham, where his father also had electoral interests.

Castlereagh presented Down petitions for Catholic relief, 27 Feb., 2 Mar., and voted in this sense, 6 Mar. 1827.[19] Sir James Mackintosh* noted on the 4th that 'Young Castlereagh has they say made a very becoming short speech'; thereafter he spoke rarely, but wittily and well.[20] He asked about government's intentions towards the Irish constabulary, 23 Mar., when he was granted a month's leave to attend the assizes.[21] Following the line set out by his father, who retained the family's hostility to Canning, Castlereagh declared his opposition to the new premier, 4 May, in what Hudson Gurney* described as 'a speech of great violence'.[22] On 25 May he repeated that he saw no prospect of the administration being able to deliver emancipation. Sir Henry Hardinge* reported to Londonderry, 11 Dec. 1827, that he had 'seen Castlereagh and ventured to suggest a fling off on the Greek and Turkish question, which he seems inclined to adopt'; nothing apparently came of it in the House.[23] Castlereagh again voted for Catholic relief, 12 May 1828. Londonderry, who continued to bear grudges against ministers, was angry that the duke of Wellington, the prime minister, passed over Castlereagh for office in January and June that year.[24] Mrs. Arbuthnot, who thought it a pity that Wellington should give him up just because the home secretary, Peel, 'does not like him', recorded that Londonderry 'says everybody is preferred to office rather than his son, who has talent, is excessively well disposed, but who, he insinuated, would go into opposition in consequence of being overlooked'.[25] According to General Dyott, writing in October 1828, Castlereagh was 'a lively pleasant young man, but [had] none of the satire of his celebrated uncle'.[26]

He declined Wellington's offer of the colonelcy of the South Down militia in February 1829.[27] That month Planta, the patronage secretary, listed him as likely to be 'with government' on Catholic emancipation and considered him a possible mover or seconder of the address.[28] Castlereagh welcomed the new policy as a means of calming Ireland, 9 Feb., objected to the inflammatory tactics of the Ultras, 9 Mar., and, as 'the representative of the most Protestant county of Protestant Ulster', called for continued prosperity and good government under the Union, 17 Mar. He brought up more favourable petitions, 3, 13, 27 Mar., and voted for emancipation, 6, 30 Mar. He divided for Daniel O'Connell being allowed to take his seat unimpeded, 18 May. The following month Mrs. Arbuthnot again pleaded his cause with Wellington, recounting the story that Liverpool had more or less promised him a reversion to office at Londonderry's funeral in 1822 and arguing that, 'though his father was behaving so ill, still ... the young man had done nothing and that he had claims, that he was clever and that it was hard to set him down as an idler merely because, having nothing to do, he did nothing'. Castlereagh having accepted the proffered vacancy at the admiralty, she observed that 'if he has any good sense and application it will make a man of business of him ... He is very clever but so flighty, I doubt his doing much'.[29] Her husband noted that it was 'a popular appointment in every quarter except that in which it ought to be the most so'; and Lord Ellenborough commented that Londonderry, who was disappointed at not obtaining a position himself, was 'much annoyed at Castlereagh's taking office. He neither likes the expense of an election for Downshire, nor losing a vote he thought he could dispose of'.[30] Expecting a challenge, Castlereagh left immediately for Ireland, but with the tacit support of the Downshire interest he was re-elected unopposed in July 1829.[31]

Both he and his father were said to be 'sulky with the duke' in early 1830, when Castlereagh commented privately that the Commons 'is in a strange state' and that 'we shall be either out of office next week, or stronger than we ever were'.[32] He nevertheless divided with his ministerial colleagues that session. He spoke against abolition of the Irish lord lieutenancy, 11 May. He stated his reluctant support for the continued duties on seaborne coals, 13 May, but warned the chancellor that he would have to heed the outcry against the higher Irish stamp and spirit taxes. Having been addressed on this subject in the *Northern Whig*, he offered his resignation rather than jeopardize his seat, but Wellington refused it and, in any case, the tax changes were soon reversed.[33] He sent a message of approval to the county Down meeting on this subject, 9 May, and supported the ensuing petition in the House, 14 June 1830. The following month he received, but evidently ignored, a request from the dismissed lord lieutenant of Ireland, Lord Anglesey, to join opposition.[34] His parliamentary stance on the taxes, together with active canvassing and government influence, enabled him to see off a serious challenge from Forde and the independent interest at the general election that summer, when he headed the poll.[35]

At Londonderry's request, on 7 Oct. 1830 Castlereagh reported his grievances to Wellington, who replied that 'I can quite understand and enter into your uncomfortable position with your father, in being separate in politics. But this is no fault of mine, and he should have thought of this himself'.[36] Having of course been listed by ministers among their 'friends', he divided in their minority on the civil list, 15 Nov. He left office with them a few days later and, with his

income falling from £3,000 to £200, was obliged to make economies, as he wryly reported to Cassidy.[37] The new prime minister, Lord Grey, attempted to entice Londonderry and his son into supporting parliamentary reform by holding out offers of the lord lieutenancy of Down to the former and the colonelcy of the county militia to the latter, but nothing came of it.[38] Castlereagh refused to present the favourable Down petition and condemned government's extensive measure both privately and in the Commons, 22, 25 Mar. 1831.[39] He voted against the second reading, 22 Mar., and for Gascoyne's wrecking amendment, which precipitated a dissolution, 19 Apr. 1831. Aware that he faced a strong opponent in the reformer William Sharman Crawford[†] and the Independent Club, he despaired of carrying Down once the Hills threw in their lot with them, but his father, an arch anti-reformer, inspired him to persevere.[40] On the hustings he spoke for limited reform, but criticized the abolition of so many English seats, the loss of the Irish corporation boroughs and the ballot. After a six-day poll he was returned behind Hill, to whom he still owed considerable covert support.[41]

He divided against the second reading of the reintroduced reform bill, 6 July, for postponing consideration of the partial disfranchisement of Chippenham, 27 July, and with Hunt to make proven payment of rent a qualification for voting in boroughs, 25 Aug. 1831. He brought up petitions for the grant to the Kildare Place Society, 15 July, 8 Aug., 27 Sept., when he claimed that its discontinuation was unpopular with northern Irish Protestants. He voted against the passage of the reform bill, 21 Sept.; Londonderry's hostile vote in the Lords the following month led to him being physically attacked by a street mob.[42] He divided against the second reading of the revised bill in the Commons, 17 Dec. 1831, the enfranchisement of Tower Hamlets, 28 Feb., and the third reading, 22 Mar. 1832. He supported the *regium donum*, 5 Mar., and brought up Ulster petitions against the ministerial plan for national education in Ireland, 14, 30 Mar., 18 Apr. On 30 Apr. he suffered a severe accident when his horse took fright and he was thrown out of his cabriolet.[43] Claiming that government had bought the support of Irish Members by selling out the establishment to the Catholics, he seconded the wrecking amendment to, and voted against, the second reading of the Irish reform bill, 25 May. Early the following month he was expected to join the Protestant Conservative Society of Ireland.[44] He divided against the Irish party processions bill, 25 June, and for preserving the voting rights of Irish freemen, 2 July. His only other recorded vote was against government on the Russian-Dutch loan, 12 July 1832.

O'Connell observed in October that it was 'shocking that an Irish county should return a man who bears the odious title of the assassin of his country – Castlereagh'; but, a founder member of the Carlton Club that year, he was again returned as a Conservative for Down at the general election of 1832.[45] Early the following year Lady Holland maliciously reported that the actress 'Madame Vestris, for the first time in her life, is with child. Lord Castlereagh, for the honour of Ireland, is enchanted at his feat'.[46] This was just one of the amorous escapades enjoyed by Castlereagh, who in later years travelled a good deal, including to the Near East. He retired from the Commons in 1852 and two years later succeeded to his father's Irish titles and estates.[47] Following a decade of mental illness he died, apparently intestate, at an asylum in Hastings in November 1872. The English and Irish halves of the family were then reunited, for he was succeeded as 5th marquess of Londonderry by his half-brother, the former North Durham Member, George Stewart, 2nd Earl Vane (1821-84).[48] His son Charles, Viscount Castlereagh (1852-1915), was Conservative Member for Down from 1878 until he inherited the marquessate in 1884.

[1] H.M. Hyde, *The Londonderrys*, pp. xv, 44. [2] Lady Londonderry, *Life and Times of Frances Anne, Marchioness of Londonderry*, 66. [3] PRO NI, Castlereagh mss D3030/Q2/2, pp. 256, 261-2. [4] W. Hinde, *Castlereagh*, 277. [5] Add. 51679, Russell to Lady Holland [Oct. 1822]; I. Leigh, *Castlereagh*, 365-6. [6] Castlereagh mss Q2/2, pp. 306, 308; Lady Londonderry, 85. [7] Cent. Kent. Stud. Camden mss U840 C504/5; Add. 38291, f. 321; 38293, f. 76; Lady Londonderry, 119-20. [8] Castlereagh mss Q1. [9] Add. 38291, f. 80. [10] Add. 40342, ff. 117, 119, 121; *The Times*, 19 July 1823. [11] Castlereagh mss T2, Bloomfield to Londonderry, 5 June 1824. [12] Add. 38298, ff. 190, 192. [13] Camden mss C257, Robinson to Camden, 10 Aug. 1826. [14] Castlereagh mss N/147; T2, p. 96. [15] PRO NI, Cassidy mss D1088/45. [16] *The Times*, 31 May; *Belfast Commercial Chron.* 10, 21 June 1826. [17] Castlereagh mss N/157, 158; PRO NI, Londonderry mss D654/B4/2, Londonderry to Castlereagh, 6, 15, 20, 26, 29 June, to Downshire, 15 June; *Belfast Commercial Chron.* 19, 28 June, 12 July 1826. [18] Cassidy mss 39. [19] *The Times*, 28 Feb., 3 Mar. 1827. [20] Add. 52447, f. 48; Hyde, 44. [21] *The Times*, 24 Mar. 1827. [22] TCD, Donoughmore mss G/7/7; PRO NI, Fitzgerald mss MIC639/12/6/49, 52; Gurney diary. [23] Durham CRO, Londonderry mss D/LO/C/83/10. [24] Castlereagh mss Q1, Londonderry to Dowager Lady Londonderry [?1828]; Wellington mss WP1/934/24; 979/13; Lady Londonderry, 149-50. [25] *Arbuthnot Jnl.* ii. 192-3. [26] *Dyott's Diary*, ii. 39. [27] Wellington mss WP1/993/56; 1000/18. [28] Add. 40398, f. 86; 40399, f. 1. [29] *Arbuthnot Jnl.* ii. 282-5; Wellington mss WP1/1029/22. [30] *Arbuthnot Corresp.* 120; *Ellenborough Diary*, ii. 55; Lady Londonderry, 159-62. [31] PRO NI, Nugent mss D552/A/6/6/21; Wellington mss WP1/1025/20; *Belfast News Letter*, 3, 17 July 1829. [32] Grey mss, Durham to Grey, 5 Feb.; Hatherton mss, Castlereagh to Littleton, 8 Feb. 1830. [33] PRO NI, Pilson diary D353/1, 10 May 1830; Wellington mss WP1/1113/18. [34] PRO NI, Anglesey mss D619/32C/9. [35] Castlereagh mss N/211, 231, 252; Wellington mss WP1/1126/24; 1131/18; *Newry Commercial Telegraph*, 2 July, 3, 17, 20, 24 Aug. 1830. [36] Lady Londonderry, 164-6. [37] Cassidy mss 92. [38] Anglesey mss 28A-B/48, 49. [39] Cassidy mss 80. [40] Wellington mss WP1/1184/15, 20; Add. 40402, f. 52; PRO NI, Downshire mss D671/C/2/451; M. Brock, *Great Reform Act*, 192. [41] PRO NI, Meade mss MIC259/2, Brush to Meade, 8 May; *Newry Commercial Telegraph*, 13, 17, 20, 27 May 1831. [42] Lady Londonderry, 171-2. [43] *The Times*, 2 May 1832. [44] NLI, Farnham mss 18611 (3), Lefroy to Farnham, 4 June 1832. [45] *O'Connell Corresp.* iv. 1929; *Newry Commercial Telegraph*, 11, 21 Dec. 1832. [46] *Lady Holland to Son*, 140. [47] *CP*, viii. 115; Hyde, 44-49; Lady Londonderry, 259. [48] Hyde, 50-51; *Downpatrick Recorder*, 30 Nov., 7 Dec. 1872; *Ann. Reg.* (1872), Chron. pp. 170-1.

S.M.F.

STEWART, Sir Hugh, 2nd bt. (1792–1854), of Ballygawley Park, co. Tyrone.

CO. TYRONE 1830–1834

b. 14 May 1792, 1st s. of Sir John Stewart*, 1st bt., of Ballygawley and Mary, da. of Mervyn Archdall[†] of Castle Archdall, Enniskillen, co. Fermanagh. *educ.* Trinity, Dublin 1810; L. Inn 1815; King's Inns 1817. *m.* (1) 19 Jan. 1826, Julia (*d.* 29 Nov. 1830),[1] da. of Marcus McClausland Gage of Bellarena, co. Londonderry, 1s. 1da.; (2) 28 Feb. 1837, Elizabeth, da. of Rev. Henry Lucas St. George, rect. of Dromore, co. Tyrone, 2s. 3da. *suc.* fa. as 2nd bt. 22 June 1825. *d.* 19 Nov. 1854.

Jt.-ld. treasurer's remembrancer, exch. [I] 1825-35.
Sheriff, co. Tyrone 1827-8.

The Stewarts of Ballygawley (or Athenry) were descended from the seventeenth-century Scot Captain Andrew Stewart of Gortigal, county Tyrone, whose elder brother James was the forbear of the neighbouring Stewarts of Killymoon. Like his father, who brought this branch of the family to prominence, Hugh received a legal education, but he apparently never practised. He inherited his father's baronetcy in June 1825, when he set about remodelling Ballygawley as a classical residence.[2] That August, on the death of Lord Donoughmore, he and his brother Mervyn received the sinecure office of lord treasurer's or second remembrancer in the Irish court of exchequer, the reversion to which had been negotiated by their father 22 years earlier on his retirement as Irish attorney-general.[3] Stewart, who had signed the requisition for the anti-Catholic county meeting in February 1825, was thought that summer to have 'hereditary pretensions' to fill the parliamentary vacancy created by the death of Sir John, who had represented Tyrone for a total of 17 years. However, evidently deterred by the entry of the younger son of the leading magnate Lord Belmore, he issued an address stating that his father's Tory 'views and principles are mine' and promised to offer on another occasion.[4] To the regret of his supporters among the minor independent interests, he also declined at the dissolution the following year. An active participant in Protestant county meetings, he moved the resolutions against Catholic relief, 1 Dec. 1826, for the formation of the Tyrone Brunswick Club, 26 Sept., and against emancipation, 2 Dec. 1828.[5] In January 1830 he was solicited to stand in place of the valetudinarian William Stewart of Killymoon and, having begun negotiating for the support of the Belmore and minority Abercorn interests, he issued a preparatory address in April.[6] On the retirement of his distant cousin at the general election that summer, when he sought to head off a ministerial challenger by assuring the premier, the duke of Wellington, that he would not join opposition, he was introduced as a worthy successor to his father and was elected unopposed.[7]

Stewart was listed by ministers among their 'friends', with 'q[uer]y' written beside his name, but he missed the division on the civil list which led to their resignation, 15 Nov. 1830. This was perhaps owing to the condition of his wife, who was shortly to bear him a son; following her death he was given leave of the House for three weeks, 11 Feb. 1831. He voted against the second reading of the Grey ministry's reform bill, 22 Mar., and for Gascoyne's wrecking amendment, 19 Apr. A silent but 'decided anti-reformer', he was returned without opposition at the ensuing general election.[8] He was absent from the division on the second reading of the reintroduced reform bill, 6 July, but his name appeared in the ministerial majority against using the 1831 census to determine the disfranchisement schedules, 19 July. His only other recorded votes that session were against the passage of the bill, 21 Sept., the second reading of the Scottish reform bill, 23 Sept., and the Maynooth grant, 26 Sept. He paired against the second reading, 17 Dec. 1831, and third reading of the revised reform bill, 22 Mar., and divided against the enfranchisement of Tower Hamlets, 28 Feb., and the second reading of the Irish bill, 25 May 1832. He sided with opposition against the Russian-Dutch loan, 26 Jan., but having been granted three weeks' leave on urgent business, 9 July 1832, he was absent from the divisions on this later that month. He retained his seat as a Conservative at the general election of 1832 and sat for another two years. In 1835 he was deprived of his sinecure in a legal reorganization which saw him superseded by a practising barrister.[9] He died of cholera in St. Helier, Jersey, in November 1854, and was buried the following month in the family vault in Termon, county Tyrone. He was succeeded by his eldest son John Marcus (1830-1905), who, like his two half-brothers and the subsequent holders of the baronetcy, was a professional army officer.[10]

[1] Ten days after the birth of their son on the 19th (*Belfast News Letter*, 14 Dec. 1830). [2] M. Bence Jones, *Guide to Irish Country Houses* (1988), 22. [3] *HP Commons, 1790-1820*, v. 275. [4] *Strabane Morning Post*, 8 Feb., 21 June 1825; PRO NI, Belmore mss D3007/H/7/9. [5] *Belfast Commercial Chron.* 10 June, 9 Dec. 1826; *Belfast News Letter*, 3 Oct., 5 Dec. 1828. [6] PRO NI, Stewart of Killymoon mss D3167/2/310; Add. 43234, f. 191; *Strabane Morning Post*, 13 Apr. 1830. [7] PRO NI, Richardson mss D2002/C/26/16; Wellington mss WP1/1124/21; *Enniskillen Chron.* 15, 22 July, 12, 26 Aug. 1830. [8] [W. Carpenter], *People's Bk.* (1831), 371; *Enniskillen Chron.* 5, 26 May 1831. [9] R.B. McDowell, *Irish Administration*, 128. [10] *Tyrone Constitution*, 1 Dec. 1854.

S.M.F.

STEWART, Hon. James Henry Keith (1783–1836).

WIGTOWN BURGHS   1812–16 Feb. 1821

b. 22 Oct.1783, 6th surv. s. of John Stewart[†], 7th earl of Galloway [S] (*d.* 1806), and 2nd w. Anne, da. of Sir James Dashwood, 2nd bt.[†], of Kirklington Park, Oxon.; bro. of Hon. Edward Richard Stewart[†], George Stewart, Visct. Garlies[†], Hon. Montgomery Granville John Stewart[†] and Hon. William Stewart[†]. *educ.* Charterhouse 1796-1801; Trinity Coll. Camb. 1801; M. Temple 1802. *m.* 10 Aug. 1819, Henrietta Anne, da. of Rev. Spencer Madan, DD, rect. of Ibstock, Leics., 3s. 1da. CB 1815. *d.* 18 July 1836.

2nd lt. 95 Ft. 1803, 1st lt. 1804, capt. 1805; brigade maj. to bro. William in Egypt 1807, afterwards to Maj.-Gen. Edward Paget[†] in Sweden and Portugal; brevet maj. 1812; maj. 7 W.I. regt. 1813; brevet lt.-col. 1813; lt.-col. 3 Ft. Gds. 1814, ret. 1820.

Commr. of customs [GB] 1821-3 and [I] Feb.-Sept. 1823; comptroller of army accts. 1823-6; chairman, commn. of stamp duties 1826-8; asst. sec. to treasury 1828-Jan. 1836.

Stewart, one of five brothers with parliamentary experience, was again returned for the family's district of burghs at the general election of 1820. He continued to support Lord Liverpool's ministry, dividing with them against economies in revenue collection, 4 July 1820. He presented a Wigtown petition for restoration of Queen Caroline's name to the liturgy, 5 Feb. 1821,[1] but next day he voted in defence of ministers' prosecution of her. Ten days later he vacated his seat to accommodate a junior minister who had been defeated at the general election. He was rewarded with a customs place and was subsequently promoted to comptroller of army accounts, chairman of the stamp duties commission and finally assistant treasury secretary.[2] He held this post for over seven years, but retired from it six months before his death in July 1836.

[1] *The Times*, 6 Feb. 1821. [2] Add. 38296, f. 54; 38302, f. 45.

D.R.F.

STEWART, **John** (1784–1873), of Belladrum, Inverness.

BEVERLEY   1826–1830

b. 29 May 1784, s. of Thomas Stewart of Keithmore, Aberdeen and Ann, da. and h. of Francis Gordon of Mill and Kincardine, Aberdeen. m. 15 Dec. 1814, Jamesina, da. of Capt. Simon Fraser of Fanellon, Inverness, wid. of Lt.-Col. William Campbell of 78 Ft., 2s. d.v.p. 2da. d. 5 Mar. 1873.

Stewart was descended from the Stewarts of Drumin, Banffshire, through whom he was related to the prominent East India merchant Charles Forbes*, Member for Beverley in the 1812 Parliament. He was in the same line of business. He told parliamentary select committees in 1830 that between 1800 and 1817 he had visited China seven times and had been to most parts of India as 'mate and commander of a ship, and agent for the transaction of business connected with the ships I commanded'. He added that he had 'had other ships, with their cargoes, consigned to me in China' and that he had for a time traded on his own account to a limited extent.[1] Whether he had any connection with John Stewart and Company, East India merchants and agents, of 23 Threadneedle Street, who were listed in the London directories between 1828 and 1831, is not clear. At the general election of 1826 he offered for Beverley, where money was the key to success, with the endorsement of Forbes, Member for Malmesbury since 1818. He also received the active backing of the local landowner Henry Burton Peters*, who waived his own pretensions to a seat. Stewart declared his support for the abolition of slavery, but otherwise confined himself to the customary cant of professing 'perfectly independent principles'. He spent heavily and topped the poll by a considerable margin.[2]

Stewart voted in the opposition minority against the grant to the Clarences, 16 Feb. 1827. His vote for Catholic relief, 6 Mar., prompted Burton Peters to accuse him of breaching an understanding that he would oppose relief and to withdraw the future support of 'the party' which had returned him. Stewart, who presented but dissented from Beverley corporation's petition against Catholic claims, 22 Mar., defended himself in a letter to Burton Peters. Their correspondence was made public. On 20 Apr. he issued an address to the freemen of Beverley in which he claimed that he had been influenced in his vote by the 'able speech' of Plunket, the Irish attorney-general, and had 'since seen no cause to regret' it.[3] He voted in Hume's minority of 44 for information on the Barrackpoor mutiny,

22 Mar., but with the Canning ministry against the Coventry magistracy bill, 18 June. On 8 June 1827 he presented a Beverley petition for repeal of the Test Acts, but he did not vote for that measure, 26 Feb. 1828. He was in a minority of 15 for reduction of the navy estimates, 11 Feb. He opposed the disfranchisement of East Retford and the transfer of its seats to Birmingham, 25 Feb., and spoke against the Penryn disfranchisement bill, 14, 28 Mar. On 27 June he seconded Tennyson's motion to defer the East Retford bill till next session, explaining that while he considered the evidence of corruption too insufficient to justify disfranchisement, he did not want the borough to be sluiced by throwing it into the hundred of Bassetlaw, which 'would be merely transferring it into the hands of the aristocracy'. He divided for Catholic relief, 12 May. He urged the Wellington ministry not to abandon the building of ships of the line at Bombay, 19 May. Supporting Mackintosh's motion for information on debtors imprisoned in India, 22 May, he stated that four or five years earlier he had been one of a deputation sent to examine the debtors' gaol in Calcutta, where 'the scene of misery we beheld surpasses every power of description'. Later that day he warmly supported the pensions for Canning's widow and son. His attempt to insert in the stamp allowances bill a clause to halve the required commission was unsuccessful, 23 May. He argued for equalizing the duties on East Indian sugar and cotton with those on West Indian produce, 9 June. He divided against the compensation clause of the archbishop of Canterbury's bill, 16 June, and spoke and voted to reduce the salary of the governor of Dartmouth, 20 June. He drew attention to the 'enormous' duties imposed by the United States on British goods, 4 July, but on 18 July welcomed the home secretary Peel's speech in favour of the relaxation of trade restrictions. On 8 July he raised the issue of Governor Darling's harsh and fatal treatment of two soldiers accused of theft in New South Wales. He secured a return of information on the revenues and trade of Ceylon, 14 July 1828.

As expected by Planta, the patronage secretary, Stewart supported the concession of Catholic emancipation in 1829. He voted for the principle, 6 Mar., gave the relief bill his 'most zealous and unqualified approbation', 16 Mar., and paired for the third reading, 30 Mar. He cast doubt on the credibility of many witnesses in the East Retford inquiry, 10 Apr., and voted for the issue of a new writ, 2 June. He was in the minority for reduction of the hemp duties, 1 June. On 4 June he obtained an account of the civil and military establishment of Ceylon during its administration by the East India Company, 1796-8. He declared his support for allowing native Indians to sit on juries, 5 June. He joined in the successful opposition to the bill to enclose Hampstead Heath, 12, 19 June 1829. He again opposed interference with East Retford, 11 Feb., but his attempt to secure the insertion in the bill of a clause requiring any man returned for the borough in future to swear that bribery had played no part in his success came to nothing, 2, 8 Mar. 1830. He voted against the enfranchisement of Birmingham, Leeds and Manchester, 23 Feb., but was in the minority of 26 to ban Members from voting in committee on bills in which they had a personal interest, 26 Feb. He was named to the select committee on the East India Company, 9 Feb., after speaking knowledgeably on the affairs of India. He presented a Farsley clothiers' petition against renewal of the Company's charter, 29 Mar. On 4 Mar. he moved for inquiry into the dispute between the Company and the Bombay judicature. The motion was defeated by 106-15 on the 8th, when he was a teller for the minority. He pressed for a ministerial statement of intent on the Darling affair, 5 Mar., 13 May. He was in the minority of 16 against the third reading of Lord Ellenborough's divorce bill, 6 Apr. He endorsed petitions for equalization of the Scottish and English stamp duties, 8 Apr., and reduction of the duties on shipping, 6 May. He voted to reduce the salary of the assistant secretary to the treasury, 10 May, and for reform of the civil government of Canada, 25 May. On 14 May he secured a return of information on the Scottish house tax. He divided for Jewish emancipation, 17 May. His motion for inquiry into the commerce, revenue and administration of Ceylon, which was supported by Forbes, 27 May, was defeated by 82-48. He paired for abolition of the death penalty for forgery offences, 7 June, and on 20 July urged rejection of the measure after its mutilation by the Lords; his amendment was rejected by 74-10. He supported government against a proposal to reduce the consular services grant, observing that they had 'already effected great reductions in the expenditure of the country', 11 June; but he objected to the money laid out for propagating the gospels in the colonies being exclusively devoted to the Church of England, arguing that the many Presbyterian inhabitants of Canada were entitled to a fair share. He voted with Hume for inquiry into the conduct of the commissioners of St. Luke's church, 17 June, when he withdrew his motion for an address on the Darling case after being assured that all the relevant documents would be produced. He called for reduction of the sugar duties to aid the suffering East India interest, 21 June. On 8 July 1830 he defended the report of the East India select committee and urged its reappointment in the next Parliament,

with Members not connected with the Company or with shipping and manufacturing interests, but with first hand knowledge of India.

Stewart retired from Parliament at the dissolution later that month. Nothing is known of his long later life. He died at his elder daughter's London house in Queen Anne Street, Cavendish Square in March 1873.[4]

---

[1] *PP* (1830), v. 322; vi. 393. [2] Hull Univ. Lib. Hotham mss DDHO/8/4, Hall to Hotham, 4, 10, 24 June; *Hull Advertiser*, 2, 9, 16 June 1826. [3] Humberside RO DDBC/11/81; 21/58. [4] *The Times*, 6 Mar. 1873.

M.P.J.C.

STEWART, Sir John, 1st bt. (1758–1825), of Ballygawley Park, co. Tyrone.

Co. Tyrone	1 Mar. 1802–1806
Co. Tyrone	1812–1 June 1825

b. ?1758, 1st s. of Rev. Hugh Stewart, rect. of Termon, co. Tyrone, and Sarah, da. of Ven. Andrew Hamilton, DD, adn. of Raphoe. *educ.* by Rev. R. Norris, Drogheda; Trinity, Dublin 1 Nov. 1774, aged 16; L. Inn 1779; King's Inns 1781, called [I] 1781. *m.* 4 June 1789,[1] Mary, da. of Mervyn Archdall[†] of Castle Archdall, Enniskillen, co. Fermanagh, 2s. 1da. *d.v.p. suc.* fa. 1800; *cr.* bt. 21 June 1803. *d.* 1 June 1825.
   MP [I] 1794-1800.
   KC [I] 1795; counsel to commrs. of revenue [I] 1797; bencher, King's Inns 1798; solicitor-gen. [I] June 1798-Dec. 1800, att.-gen. [I] Dec. 1800-Oct. 1803; PC [I] 23 Dec. 1800.
   Sheriff, co. Tyrone 1809-10.
   Trustee, linen board [I] 1802.
   Commdt. Omagh vols.; capt. Omagh inf. 1796.

Stewart, who owed much to the 1st marquess of Abercorn, no doubt a distant cousin of his mother, retired as an Irish law officer in 1803 in exchange for a baronetcy and a pension. Returned for his native county on the Abercorn interest, 1802-6, and again, with the assistance of Lord Belmore, from 1812, he usually supported the Liverpool administration and, as an Orangeman, opposed Catholic relief.[2] In March 1820, when he signed requisitions for county meetings on George IV's accession and on illicit distillation, he was again returned unopposed with his kinsman William Stewart of Killymoon.[3] He spoke against investigation of the Drogheda election, 25 May, and for his abortive Irish still fines bill, 7 June. Displaying his occasionally independent streak, he on 14 June divided for inquiry into Anglo-Irish trade, his only recorded vote that session. He was granted a month's leave on urgent private business, 23 June 1820. He moved the resolution for a loyal address to the king at the Tyrone meeting, 24 Jan., but missed the division on ministers' conduct towards Queen Caroline, 6 Feb. 1821.[4] He voted against Catholic claims, 28 Feb. 1821, 30 Apr. 1822. He sided with ministers against Maberly's resolution on the state of the revenue, 6 Mar., and repeal of the additional malt duty, 3 Apr., but was credited with a vote complaining of delays in the inquiry into the courts of justice, 9 May 1821. He voted against more extensive tax reductions to relieve distress, 11 Feb., but cast a wayward vote to permit the grinding and export as flour of bonded corn, 10 June 1822.

Remarking that 'many of the most loyal inhabitants of that country felt sore' regarding the legal proceedings in Ireland against the Orange rioters, Stewart hinted that he would raise the matter again, 18 Feb. 1823.[5] According to Thomas Creevey*, who called him 'a damned fool withal as I ever beheld', he was to have introduced a definitive motion on the 24th, when, however, he merely repeated his opposition to the actions of William Plunket, the Irish attorney-general.[6] He apparently missed the division on this issue, 22 Apr., although he was involved in the questioning of witnesses, 5-7 May. He voted against repealing £2,000,000 of taxes, 3 Mar., and for the grant for Irish churches and glebe houses, 11 Apr. He presented anti-Catholic petitions from Killyman, 16 Apr., and Tyrone, 17 Apr., and intervened on the Irish tithes bill, 16 May, 16 (when he divided against its committal), 18 June.[7] He voted against reform of the Scottish representative system, 2 June, but to condemn the conduct of the lord advocate in the Borthwick case, 3 June 1823. No trace of parliamentary activity has been found during the 1824 session. He voted for the Irish unlawful societies bill, 15 Feb., and, having brought up petitions for suppression of the Catholic Association from Ardstraw and Tyrone, 17, 23 Feb., he divided for the last time against Catholic relief, 1 Mar. 1825.[8] Later that year, 'being enfeebled by long and severe indisposition', he lost control of his carriage when the horses bolted and he died of his injuries four days after the accident. He was succeeded in his title and estates by his elder son Hugh Stewart*.[9]

[1] IGI (Co. Dublin). [2] Add. 40298, f. 40; *Extraordinary Red Bk.* (1821), 222; PRO NI, Leslie mss MIC606/3/J/7/21/4; *Hist. Irish Parl.* vi. 343-4; *HP Commons, 1790-1820*, v. 275-6. [3] *Belfast News Letter*, 17, 28 Mar. 1820. [4] Ibid. 2 Feb. 1821. [5] *The Times*, 19 Feb. 1823. [6] Creevey mss, Creevey to Miss Ord, 21 Feb. 1823. [7] *The Times*, 17, 18 Apr., 19 June 1823. [8] Ibid. 18, 24 Feb. 1825. [9] *Belfast News Letter*, 7 June 1825; *Gent. Mag.* (1825), ii. 466.

S.M.F.

STEWART, Patrick Maxwell (1795–1846), of Ardgowan, Renfrew and 11 Upper Brook Street, Mdx.

LANCASTER	14 Mar. 1831–1837
RENFREWSHIRE	1841–30 Oct. 1846

b. 28 Feb. 1795,[1] 5th but 4th surv. s. of Michael Stewart (formerly Stewart Nicolson) (*d.* 1825) of Carnock, Stirling and his cos. Catherine, da. of Sir William Maxwell, 3rd bt., of Springkell, Dumfries; bro. of Sir Michael Shaw Stewart, 6th bt.* *unm. d.* 30 Oct. 1846.
   Agent, Tobago 1826-*d.*
   Chairman, London and Westminster Bank 1834-*d.*, West India Colonial Bank 1837-*d.*

Unlike his older brothers, Sir Michael, Admiral Sir Houston Stewart (1791-1875) and the advocate John Shaw Stewart (1793-1840), little can be said with certainty about Stewart's early life. He joined the London firm of P. Stewart trading at Winchester House, Great Winchester Street before October 1812, when, writing as a merchant, he advised his father, who had recently succeeded to the baronetcy and estates of Sir John Shaw Stewart of Blackhall and Ardgowan, so becoming the largest landowner in the Clydeside port of Greenock, to switch from the Baltic to the West India trade and develop the family's Houston and Roxborough plantations in Tobago.[2] He probably toured the continent with Michael in 1814 and 1815 and was certainly in Paris in 1819 to see Louis XVIII crowned.[3] By July 1830, when he first canvassed Lancaster on the Whig interest of the 10th duke of Hamilton,[4] he was trading independently in Great Winchester Street and Upper Brook Street, and was one of the founders and a director of Shaw's Water Company, Greenock, and of the Inverkip Gas Company, both of them joint-stock ventures established after Michael succeeded their father in 1825. He had also (as the nominee and successor of William Robert Keith Douglas*) been a member since 8 Apr. 1829 of the standing committee of West India planters and merchants and an agent (since 1826) for Tobago.[5] Though authorized, his agency was not fully ratified while the Tobago legislature and successive governors remained in dispute.[6]

A bold public speaker and persuasive negotiator, with a reputation for conviviality and wit, he was instrumental in securing support for Sir Michael when he successfully contested Lanarkshire at the 1827 by-election, and helped to effect his switch to Renfrewshire at the general election of 1830, when they failed in their attempt to bring in their kinsman John Maxwell* for Lanarkshire.[7] Explaining that his candidature was 'merely postponed', Stewart declined a contest at Lancaster in 1830, when the outcome was uncertain and the sitting Tory Cawthorne in poor health; but he declared directly Cawthorne's death was announced, 1 Mar. 1831, and came in unopposed on the 14th as a 'decided reformer and ardent free trader', committed to ending the monopolies of the East India Company and Bank of England. On the hustings and at the Lancaster reform meeting next day he praised Lord Grey's administration and commended their reform bill as a means of restoring property based representation.[8] The diplomat John Macpherson Grant of Ballindalloch, who met him in London afterwards, told his father that he expected Stewart to promote their campaign to raise the voting qualification in Scottish counties to £50 and commended him as 'a very clever intelligent fellow ... likely to be of use on Scotch matters'.[9]

Brought in to strengthen the West India lobby, promote reform, and attend to Scottish and commercial issues affecting his relations and their political allies, Stewart was admitted to Brooks's on Lord Lansdowne's nomination, 27 Mar., and attended West India committee strategy meetings on 28 Mar. and 13 Apr. 1831.[10] Generally, but not slavishly, he divided with his brother, becoming an imposing figure in the House in his own right. He testified to the overwhelming support for the reform bill on presenting the Lancaster petition, 19 Mar., and voted for its second reading, 22 Mar., and against Gascoyne's wrecking amendment, 19 Apr. Opposing the appointment of a committee on slavery, 15 Apr., he criticized the colonial under-secretary Lord Howick for making the colonial legislatures the scapegoats for ineffective policy and, warning of the dangers of precipitate abolition, he pointed to the short-sightedness of the Dissenters who petitioned for it and demanded a 'searching, uncompromising inquiry' to establish a means of ending slavery 'compatible with the well being of the slaves themselves, with the safety of the colonies and with a fair and equitable consideration of the interests of private property'. The Liverpool West India merchant Thomas Gladstone* remarked that he 'spoke well and modestly, evidently prepared', but many of his supporters in Lancaster, where the *Herald* printed his speech, were abolitionists and angry at being duped.[11] Stewart made light of the issue and paid only a brief visit to Lancaster at the general election in May, when he and his colleague Thomas Greene came in unopposed as reformers.[12] He assisted in Renfrewshire and Lanarkshire, where he was caught up in the tumult following Maxwell's defeat.[13] In the House, 29 June 1831, he endorsed his brother's statement that the dis-

turbance could have been quelled without troops, and attributed the blame to the sheriff's decision to mount his horse, giving himself an 'unruly horse as well as an unruly mob' to manage.

He voted for the second reading of the reintroduced reform bill, 6 July 1831, and gave it steady support in committee, taking care to inform the press if his name was omitted from the division lists.[14] He divided for its third reading, 19 Sept., and passage, 21 Sept., and the second reading of the Scottish bill, 23 Sept. Speaking on the latter, 3 Oct., as 'one of the Scotchmen billeted on England', he ridiculed the anti-reformers' assertions that the tenantry of Scotland were 'averse to their own enfranchisement' and its people 'indifferent' to the bill's fate. Citing current population totals, voting statistics and rateable values, he commended the measure as a means of establishing the franchise where it 'scarcely now exists' and curtailing the electoral power of the parchment voters and burgh councils. He voted for Lord Ebrington's confidence motion, 10 Oct., and annoyed the corporation of Lancaster, where his speech on the Scottish bill had been circulated, by turning the civic feast on the 22nd into a celebration of reform.[15] He divided for the revised English reform bill at its second reading, 17 Dec. 1831, steadily for its details and for its third reading, 22 Mar. 1832. He voted for the address calling on the king to appoint only ministers who would carry it unimpaired, 10 May, and for the second reading of the Irish reform bill, 25 May. Opposing a Conservative amendment to increase the Scottish county representation, which he dismissed as 'a little bit of a gasconade', 1 June, he spoke again of the likely benefits of the measure and pointed out that Scots like himself could still come in for English seats. Undeterred by ministers' hostility, he joined Michael in promoting their local interests, 15 June, when they opposed Cutlar Fergusson's amendment (defeated 73-47) to join Port Glasgow to the new Greenock constituency, and failed by 35-67 to have Kilmarnock transferred from the Renfrew to the Ayr district, and Inverary and Campbeltown moved from Ayr to Renfrew. He voted against the amendment to prevent the dismemberment of Perthshire that day, and on the 27th supported an unsuccessful motion to join Peeblesshire and Selkirkshire, in order to give Orkney and Shetland separate representation. On the Dublin election controversy, he voted in the minority for postponing the new writ, 8 Aug., but with government against censuring the Irish administration, 23 Aug. 1831. He also divided with them on the Russian-Dutch loan, 26 Jan., 12, 16, 20 July, and relations with Portugal, 9 Feb. 1832.

Stewart was added to the planters and merchants' subcommittee 'for managing the question of the admission of molasses to use in breweries and distilleries', 30 June,[16] and presented the Liverpool merchants' petition against renewing the Sugar Refinery Act, on which government faced possible defeat, 5 Sept., and divided against them, 12 Sept. 1831. He argued that day that the measure contravened the principles of free trade and was likely to boost sugar production where slavery was permitted, so impoverishing British West Indian planters and doing nothing to assist the slaves. He reaffirmed his opposition to the bill's principle, 13 Oct. 1831, but refrained from further criticism, encouraging speculation by Robert Gordon and others of 'a job'. Supporting Lord Chandos's amendment for lowering the sugar duties, 7 Mar. 1832, he quoted extracts from Huskisson's speech of 21 June 1830 (which he had heard) to try to boost the merchants' case and demonstrate the anti-colonial temper of the House. He naturally pressed for concessions for the West Indies under the customs duties bill, 25 July 1832. An Act of 21 July 1831 passed by the Tobago legislature naming their former speaker Christopher Irvine as agent had compromised Stewart's status and business as the colony's banker, and between 10 July and 27 Nov. 1832, when matters were finally resolved in his favour, he engaged in acrimonious written exchanges with Howick and his principal Lord Goderich, during which he applied independently to the colonists for support, rallied the merchants and planters and threatened to raise the matter in the House.[17]

Stewart was returned unopposed for Lancaster as a Liberal in 1832 and 1835, despite mounting concern over his stance on slavery and joint-stock enterprises. Defeated there in 1837, at the 1841 general election he recaptured the Renfrewshire seat lost to the Conservatives following his brother's death in 1836.[18] A leading opponent of the Bank's London monopoly and financier of utility and transport companies, he died unmarried at Carnock House, in October 1846, a fortnight after contracting a cholera-like illness.[19] By his will, dated 14 Oct. 1840 and proved under £30,000 in the province of Canterbury, 16 Nov. 1846, he ordered the sale of Charlottesville, his Tobago estate, bequeathing the proceeds to his brother Houston, to whom, with his brother-in-law John Osborne and partner George Smith Cundell, he left his heritable property in Scotland and English assets, less £8,000 placed in trust for the children of his late brother John.[20]

[1] J.F. Mitchell, 'Renfrew M.I.' [BL J/X705/84]. [2] Glasgow Central Lib. Shaw Stewart of Ardgowan mss (NRA 14672), T-ARD1/6354; T-ARD9/3, 4; Ardgowan estate mss (NRA 14672), bdle. 98, Stewart to fa. Oct. 1812; H.I. Woodcock, *Hist. Tobago* (1867), app. [3] Ardgowan estate mss, bdle. 69, Stewart to fa. 25 Apr. 1819; bdle. 98, same to same, Feb. 1814; bdle. 100/9/1 (Sir Michael Shaw Stewart's journal of his continental tour, 1814-15). [4] *Lancaster Gazette*, 24 July 1830. [5] R. Thom, *Shaw's Water Scheme* (1829) [BL C.T. 226.]; Inst. of Commonwealth Stud. M915/4/3, 20, 26, 43, 49, 72, 77, 82, 90, 92, 95. [6] TNA CO285/30/104; 31/140; 32/106, 249, 319, 358; H. Craig, *Legislative Council of Trinidad and Tobago*, 18. [7] Derby mss 920 Der (14) box 62, Huskisson to Smith Stanley, 12 Sept., Stewart to J. Maxwell, 21 Sept. 1827; *Greenock Advertiser*, 13, 17 Aug. 1830. [8] *Lancaster Gazette*, 7 Aug. 1830; *Lancaster Herald*, 5, 12, 19, 26 Mar. 1831. [9] Macpherson Grant mss 361, J.M. to G. Macpherson Grant, 2-4 Apr. 1831. [10] Inst. of Commonwealth Stud. M915/4/167, 169. [11] St. Deiniol's Lib. Glynne-Gladstone mss 198, T. to J. Gladstone, 16 Apr.; *Lancaster Herald*, 23 Apr. 1831. [12] *Lancaster Herald*, 30 Apr., 7 May 1831. [13] *Glasgow Herald*, 9, 16 May 1831. [14] *The Times*, 18 July, 10 Aug. 1831. [15] *Lancaster Herald*, 15 Oct., 5 Nov.; *Lancaster Gazette*, 22 Oct. 1831. [16] Inst. of Commonwealth Stud. M915/4/181, 191. [17] TNA CO285/38/82-88; 39/356-9; 286/7/72-78; Add. 40880, f. 337. [18] *Lancaster Herald*, 15 Dec. 1832; N. Gash, *Politics in Age of Peel*, 363; *Scottish Electoral Politics*, 256, 266. [19] L. Ragatz, *Fall of Planter Class in British Caribbean*, 95; *Renfrewshire Advertiser*, 7 Nov. 1846; *Gent. Mag.* (1847), i. 85-86. [20] PROB 11/2045/840; IR26/1755/848; *The Times*, 27 Nov. 1846.

M.M.E.

STEWART, Randolph, Visct. Garlies (1800–1873).

COCKERMOUTH   1826–1831

b. 16 Sept. 1800, 1st s. of George Stewart[†], 8th earl of Galloway [S], and Lady Jane Paget, da. of Henry, 1st earl of Uxbridge. *educ.* Harrow 1814-17; Christ Church, Oxf. 1819. *m.* 9 Aug. 1833, Lady Harriet Blanche Somerset, da. of Henry Charles Somerset[†], 6th duke of Beaufort, 6s. (1 *d.v.p.*) 7da. (1 *d.v.p.*). *styled* Visct. Garlies 1806-34. *suc.* fa. as 9th earl of Galloway [S] 27 Mar. 1834. *d.* 2 Jan. 1873.

Ld.lt. Kirkcudbright 1828-45, Wigtown 1828-51.

This Member's father, a distinguished naval officer and political follower of the younger Pitt, had (as Lord Garlies) represented Saltash, 1790-95, Cockermouth, 1805-6, and Haselmere, 1806, before succeeding as 8th earl of Galloway in November 1806.[1] His mother, a sister of the 1st marquess of Anglesey, preferred living in London to Galloway House, their family seat on Wigtownshire's Machars peninsula, and most of Garlies's childhood was spent in England. He travelled on the continent after leaving Oxford, returning in January 1826 to take over the management of the 79,000-acre family estates in Kirkcudbright and Wigtownshire from his ailing father, who wished to spend less time there.[2] Garlies was disqualified, as the eldest son of a Scottish peer, from representing the Wigtown Burghs on his family's interest, but his

return was assured through an exchange of seats negotiated in May 1825 with the 1st earl of Lonsdale, who
20 years earlier had obliged his father similarly.[3] He
was accordingly returned *in absentia* for the Lowther
borough of Cockermouth at the general election of
1826, and afterwards took a town house in Hanover
Street for the parliamentary session.[4]

Of a retiring disposition, Garlies was lax in his parliamentary attendance and made no reported speeches
in the House. At his father's request, in the winter of
1826-7 he and their London attorney William Vizard
sought to adjust provisions made for his sisters and
others, that overencumbered their entailed estates
(he was appointed to the investigative committee on
Scottish entails, 27 Feb. 1829).[5] He was free to vote
independently of the Lowther 'ninepins', and did so
for Catholic relief, 6 Mar. 1827, and again for Catholic,
6, 30 Mar. 1829, and Jewish emancipation, 5 Apr., 17
May 1830. When arrangements were made for him to
take over the lord lieutenancies of Kirkcudbright and
Wigtownshire from his father in November 1828, he
dealt adroitly with his rivals for the post, Sir Andrew
Agnew* and Sir William Maxwell*.[6] He presented
Wigtown's petition against the Scottish gaols bill, 14
May 1829. That October, at his parents' behest and
against his better judgement, he sought patronage for
his former tutor John Perkins, for whom he had little
respect.[7] He brought up a Wigtown petition against
the proposed additional tariff on spirits, 14 May, and
voted against the Galway franchise bill, 25 May, and
abolishing the death penalty for forgery, 7 June 1830.
Although peeved by his tardy application, the Lowthers
again returned him for Cockermouth at the general
election that summer.[8] He now spent much time at
Titness Lodge, near Sunninghill, Berkshire, with Lady
Caroline Stewart and at the Travellers' Club.[9]

The Wellington ministry listed him among their
'friends', but he was absent when they were brought
down on the civil list, 15 Nov. 1830. He presented a
reform petition from Wigtown, 3 Feb., and voted for
the Grey ministry's English reform bill at its second
reading, 22 Mar. 1831. He presented an anti-slavery
petition from New Woodstock, 29 Mar. The arrangement with the Lowthers lapsed at the dissolution
precipitated by the reform bill's defeat, 19 Apr. In
December 1831 and January 1832, he declined offers
of a peerage conditional on his support for the government's reform bills in the Lords.[10] Though subsequently expected to contest Wigtownshire, Garlies did
not stand for Parliament again.[11]

His courtship of the duke of Beaufort's daughter
Blanche, whom he married in 1833, had his family's

approval but was initially forbidden by the duchess
of Beaufort, because he was a strict Episcopalian and
refused to espouse Evangelicalism.[12] After succeeding
his father as 9th earl of Galloway in 1834, he consistently supported the Conservatives in the Lords, where
he sat by virtue of his British barony of Stewart. 'In
feeble health', he relinquished both his county lord
lieutenancies by 1851 and died at Galloway House in
January 1873, survived by his widow (*d.* 1885) and
11 of their 13 children. His will was confirmed at
Wigtown with personalty sworn under £40,000, 17
Sept. 1873.[13] He was succeeded in the peerage and
estates by his eldest son Alan Plantaganet Stewart
(1835-1901), Conservative Member for Wigtown
1868-73, on whose death without issue they passed to
his second son Randolph (1837-1920).

[1] *HP Commons, 1790-1820*, v. 271-2. [2] NLS, Galloway mss Acc.
6604/1, Galloway to Young, 2 Feb., to Garlies, 24 Nov., 3, 5 Dec.,
Vizard to Garlies, 27 Feb., Garlies to Galloway, 30 Nov. 1826, Young
to Vizard, 20 Mar. 1827. [3] Lonsdale mss, A. Stewart to Lonsdale,
23 May 1825. [4] Lonsdale mss, Garlies to Lowther, 11 June; *Cumb.
Pacquet*, 13 June; Galloway mss Acc. 6604/1, Galloway to Garlies, 3
Dec. 1826. [5] Galloway mss Acc. 6604/1, Galloway to Garlies, 5 Dec.
1826, 20 Mar. 1827. [6] Wellington mss WP1/930/13; 944/7, 8; 947/15;
1050/23; Galloway mss Acc. 6604/1, Agnew to Garlies, 7 Nov.,
Garlies to Maxwell, 11, 16, 17 Nov. 1828. [7] Galloway mss 6604/1,
Lord and Lady Galloway to Garlies, 28, 29 May 1830; Wellington
mss WP1/1050/23. [8] Lonsdale mss, Lowther to Lonsdale, 18,
20, 24 July, Lonsdale to Lowther, 18, 20, 24 July 1830. [9] NLW,
Ormathwaite mss FG1/5, pp. 122, 124, 131-2. [10] Galloway mss Acc.
6604/1, J. Stewart to Garlies, 20 Dec. 1831, 3 Jan. 1832. [11] *Westmld.
Advertiser*, 2 Apr., 7 May 1831; I.G.C. Hutchinson, *Pol. Hist.
Scotland*, 8. [12] Galloway mss Acc. 6604/1, Lady Galloway to Garlies,
3, 4 Sept., 17 Nov. 1832, 2 Jan. 1833, duchess of Beaufort to same,
3 Oct. 1832, 10 Jan. 1833, Beaufort to same, 20 Dec. 1832. [13] *The
Times*, 3, 4 Jan., 10 Oct.; *Galloway Advertiser*, 9 Jan. 1873.

M.M.E.

STEWART, Robert, Visct. Castlereagh (1769–1822),
of Mount Stewart, co. Down; North Cray Farm, nr.
Bexley, Kent, and 9 St. James's Square, Mdx.[1]

TREGONY	12 May 1794–1796
ORFORD	1796–19 July 1797
CO. DOWN	1801–July 1805
BOROUGHBRIDGE	18 Jan. 1806–1806
PLYMPTON ERLE	1806–1812
CO. DOWN	1812–6 Apr. 1821
ORFORD	28 Apr. 1821–12 Aug. 1822

b. 18 June 1769,[2] 2nd but 1st surv. s. of Robert Stewart,
MP [I], 1st mq. of Londonderry [I], of Mount Stewart
and 1st w. Lady Sarah Frances Seymour Conway, da.
of Francis, 1st mq. of Hertford. *educ.* R. Sch. Armagh
1777; by Rev. William Sturrock, Portaferry 1781; St.

John's, Camb. 1786; continental tour 1791-2. *m.* 9 June 1794, Lady Amelia Anne Hobart, da. and coh. of John Hobart†, 2nd earl of Buckinghamshire, *s.p. styled* Visct. Castlereagh 8 Aug. 1796-6 Apr. 1821; KG 9 June 1814; GCH 1816; *suc.* fa. as 2nd mq. of Londonderry [I] 6 Apr. 1821. *d.* 12 Aug. 1822.

MP [I] 1790-1800.

Kpr. of privy seal [I] 1797-1801; ld. of treasury [I] 1797-1804; chief sec. to ld. lt. [I] Mar.-Nov. 1798 (ad. int.), 1798-1801; PC [I] 20 Oct. 1797, [GB] 19 Dec. 1798; pres. bd. of control July 1802-Feb. 1806; sec. of state for war and colonies July 1805-Feb. 1806, Mar. 1807-Nov. 1809; sec. of state for foreign affairs Feb. 1812-*d.*; plenip. at Chatillon 1813, Paris 1814, 1815, Vienna 1814-15, Aix-la-Chapelle 1818.

Lt.-col. co. Londonderry militia 1793, col. 1798-*d.*; gov. co. Londonderry 1805, custos rot. 1821.

For the last ten years of his life Castlereagh, Pitt's leading disciple, was the most influential politician in Britain. He was the principal architect of the European post-war settlement, which he sought to safeguard with a flexible, pragmatic foreign policy of circumspect involvement and co-operation with the leading continental powers, executed partly through the network of personal contacts which he had built up. The rise of new issues in Europe, on which British interests were at odds with those of the Holy Alliance, made this line increasingly difficult to hold. Domestically, he was the most powerful member of the cabinet, close at times to being *de facto* prime minister, as Lord Liverpool's relationship with George IV deteriorated. Despite his glaring defects as an orator, he had become a combative and generally effective government leader in the Commons. Yet the Whig James Macdonald* wrote just after his tragic death:

His character will not be very easily defined in the page of history in which it must stand so conspicuously from the great events with which it has been connected. No man certainly ever traded so largely on so small a capital, but presence of mind, some sagacity, a good temper and good manners supplied the place of knowledge and eloquence.[3]

Over 20 years later Sir George Philips*, another political opponent, recalled that

[Sir James] Mackintosh* used to say of Castlereagh that he had all the inferior qualities of a leader in an extraordinary degree. Though his language was often ungrammatical, his metaphors and figures so strangely perplexed and confused as to set the House a laughing, yet I have heard him speak in such a powerful, impressive and eloquent style as would have done honour to any man. The more he was pressed ... the better he spoke, both in matter and manner. He was a handsome, fine looking man, good natured, high bred, and his courage was so

undoubted that he could allow people to take liberties with him, or disregard them, as unworthy of his notice, which other men might have lost reputation by not resenting.[4]

William Wilberforce* wrote that when Castlereagh

was in his ordinary mood, he was very tiresome, so slow and heavy, his sentences only half formed, his matter so confined, like what is said of the French army in the Moscow retreat, when horse, foot and carriages of all sorts were huddled together, helter-skelter; yet, when he was thoroughly warmed and excited, he was often very fine, very statesmanlike ... and seemed to rise quite into another man.[5]

In a mature assessment, Lord John Russell* observed:

Castlereagh, who had been often pointed out as the successor of Pitt, wanted the large views of that great man ... [He] was an obscure orator, garnishing his speeches with confused metaphors ... He had no classical quotations, no happy illustration, no historical examples ... Yet his influence with his party was very great, and he was, till near the close of his life, a successful leader of the House of Commons. For this end he possessed ... very considerable advantages. He was, as a man of business, clear, diligent, and decided. His temper was admirable – bold and calm, good humoured and dispassionate. He was a thorough gentlemen; courteous, jealous of his own honour, but full of regard for the feelings of others. No one doubted his personal integrity, however much they might dislike his policy.[6]

His greatest asset and most attractive feature was his 'cool and determined courage', which, as Greville noted, 'commanded universal respect and ... gave an appearance of resolution and confidence to all his actions, inspired his friends with admiration and excessive devotion to him, and caused him to be respected by his most violent opponents'.[7] He had plenty of these, and indeed by the end of 1819, following Peterloo and the passage of the Six Acts, was probably without rival in popular and radical demonology. To the savage attacks of Robert Southey*, Tom Moore, Lord Byron, William Cobbett† and many others he remained, outwardly at least, coolly indifferent. As Edward Littleton* perceived, however, his 'smooth, polished exterior' and 'phlegmatic manner' concealed 'an anxious temperament', which eventually gave way under the pressure of an unforgiving and excessive workload in testing times.[8]

In mid-January 1820 Castlereagh, on his way to a shooting party in Norfolk for 'a fortnight's relaxation, which, after our short but active session, I in some measure *require*', informed Prince Hardenberg:

As far as we can judge, our measures have operated very favourably on the internal state of the country. Radical stock is very low indeed at the present moment, and the loyal have resumed their superiority and confidence. The provisions of the laws which have been enacted will, no doubt, do a great deal to repress the mischief; but ... whatever our reformers may choose to say, the voice of Parliament is in itself still all-powerful in this country, when clearly pronounced.[9]

Three weeks into the new reign he told his half-brother Lord Stewart, ambassador to Austria, that in view of 'the magic trance into which the country has been thrown by the late bills', the government had decided on an early dissolution, so as 'not to give our opponents time to agitate anew the public mind'.[10] He was presumably oblivious to the discussions with Lord Liverpool initiated at this time by his cabinet colleague and rival George Canning*, in which it was rather idly speculated that he might be persuaded to go to the Lords in his father's lifetime in order to enable Canning to take the Commons lead which he deemed essential if he was to remain in high office at home rather than go out to govern India.[11] Yet Princess Lieven surmised that George IV's replacement of Lord and Lady Hertford, Castlereagh's relatives, as royal favourites by the Conynghams would reduce his previously powerful influence, and reported to Metternich that he was 'sulking' at the prospect.[12] Be that as it may, it was Castlereagh, who, having initially started to clear his desk at the foreign office in the expectation of the ministry's dismissal, took the leading role in persuading the king not to insist on having a divorce from Queen Caroline and thereby 'hazard the scandal of a public inquiry'.[13] The Cato Street conspirators were reported to have wrangled over claiming the honour of cutting his throat. He felt that he and his colleagues had managed the whole affair 'without a fault' and as 'tolerably cool troops'; and he took delight in flourishing at the dinner table, 28 Feb. 1820 (to the alarm of Princess Lieven), the two loaded pistols which he carried everywhere.[14] A week later he went to Ireland for his quiet election for County Down and to visit his ailing father.[15]

Although he had privately welcomed the Carlsbad decrees of December 1819, by which Metternich sought to tighten his control over German liberalism, he was obliged to take another line in public, maintaining and emphasizing the cardinal tenet of British non-interference in the internal affairs of other states unless European peace or national interests were seriously threatened. He set out this position in his state paper of 5 May 1820, which deprecated the Russian plan for the mutual guarantee by the Powers of their respective governments. It was approved by his colleagues and sent to the Allies; and he instructed his brother to urge these views at the subsequent Congresses of Troppau and Laibach.[16] At the start of the new Parliament, which an attack of gout forced him to miss, he confided to Metternich that 'although we have made an immense progress against radicalism, the monster still lives, and shows himself in new shapes; but we do not despair of crushing him by time and perseverance'. He correctly anticipated a 'troublesome' session.[17] He opposed Hamilton's motion condemning the appointment of an additional baron of exchequer in Scotland, 15 May 1820, when he deplored 'sweeping assertions' that 'the only object of ministers was the patronage of office'. The Tory backbencher Henry Bankes thought he 'made as good a stand as the nature of the case admitted of'.[18] His motion for the previous question was carried by only 12 votes, and while the division was in progress he rallied ministerialist Members in the lobby. He defended various aspects of the civil list, 17, 18 May. The following day he did not stand in the way of the second reading of the Grampound disfranchisement bill, indicating that he saw it not as a question of parliamentary reform but one of hitting on the best practical solution for a specific problem: he preferred following the precedent of sluicing the borough with freehold voters to transferring its seats to Leeds. The duke of Wellington, master-general of the ordnance, complained to Mrs. Arbuthnot, 20 May, that ministers had come 'badly' out of the discussion: 'We have too many nice and curious feelings upon every subject which Lord Castlereagh has not the power of explaining to the world'.[19] He had no objection to the production of the latest Scottish electoral rolls requested by Lord Archibald Hamilton, 25 May, but he refused to be seduced into a discussion of reform. He was surprised and irritated, blaming himself for laxity, when Holme Sumner's motion for an inquiry into agricultural distress was carried against him by 150-101, 30 May; but he reasserted his authority the following day, when he 'came down with all his forces' to secure the passage, by 251-108, of an instruction confining the committee's remit to an investigation of frauds in taking the corn averages.[20] On 1 June he restricted the scope of the inquiry into the Welsh judicature secured by John Frederick Campbell, and got leave, by 149-63, to continue the Aliens Act for two years. He opposed Mackintosh's proposed additional clause to the aliens bill, which would have given the right of appeal to the privy council, complaining of 'the foul calumny which it tended to throw upon ministers'. He explained that gradual reduction of the Irish linen duties was a necessary prelude to the total repeal which ministers contemplated, 2 June, when he replied to attacks by Hume and Grey Bennet on the sinecure exchequer tellerships. He said that inquiry, sought by Parnell, into the Irish Union duties would 'produce a great deal of commercial jealousy' at a time of economic uncertainty, 14 June. On 16 June he endorsed the government plan to bale out the Bank of Ireland and defended the secret service grant. He paid lip service to the principle of Brougham's bill for the education of the poor, 28 June, but urged him not to press it that session; and later that day he said that there was no need to introduce an insurrection bill for Ireland, as Foster demanded. He agreed that in future Irish masters in chancery should not be allowed to sit in the Commons, 30 June, but argued that in fairness to Henry Ellis the proposed legislation should not have a retrospective operation. He dismissed Hume's motion concerning the private property of the late king and got rid of Hamilton's for the continuance and revival of the Scottish judicial commission, 4 July.[21] He had no quibble with Parnell's proposal to bring in an Irish tithes bill, provided it was understood that it did not trench on the general question of commutation, 5 July. He supported the plan to repeal the ban on the import of raw Irish spirits, 6, 12, 24 July.[22] On 11 July 1820 he said that it was not for Parliament to interfere in the matter of Sir Manasseh Masseh Lopes's* gaol sentence and objected to the production of information on negotiations between France and Argentina for the establishment of a Bourbon dynasty in South America, asserting that 'the honour of every individual power who was a party to ... [the] Holy Alliance ... was untainted'.

At the beginning of the session he had written to Metternich:

Much will depend on the course Her Majesty shall think fit to pursue. If she is wise enough to accept the *pont d'or* which we have tendered her, the calamities and scandal of a public investigation will be avoided. If she is mad enough or so ill-advised as to put her foot upon English ground, I shall, from that moment, regard Pandora's box as opened.[23]

As it turned out, it fell to him to bear almost single handed the burden of handling the business in the Commons, as a result of which even more popular opprobrium was heaped on him. On 6 June he laid the king's message concerning Caroline and the 'green bag' documents on the table, 'prudently', as Bankes thought, ignoring provocative remarks from Brougham. The following day, after Brougham had formally notified the House of the queen's intention to return and fight her corner, Castlereagh moved, in what John Croker* heard was a 'long and vague'

speech, for the appointment of a secret committee to inquire into her conduct, concluding with a hit at Brougham and her other advisers who would 'tempt her into crooked, and thorny, and dangerous paths'. Princess Lieven perceived his 'obvious aversion' to the whole business, and Bankes too saw that 'the embarrassment and reluctance which he felt were not counterfeited'. He was 'obliged to consent' when opinion in the House, prompted by Wilberforce, showed itself to be strongly in favour of adjournment.[24] He and Wellington represented the king in the subsequent abortive negotiations with Caroline's lawyers, on which he reported to the House, 19 June. Privately, he reflected that

upon the whole, I do not think matters, up to the present point, could have worked more favourably ... His Majesty has had all the forbearance without conceding anything; and the mind of Parliament has been gradually brought to settle to the calamity of a public trial of the queen as an inevitable evil, from which no prudential effort could relieve them'.[25]

On Wilberforce's compromise resolution, 22 June, when his admirer Mrs. Arbuthnot thought he 'spoke remarkably well', but Littleton felt that he 'talked in his usual vague manner', he 'stoutly upheld the king's right to regulate the liturgy' and angrily accused opposition of trying to 'prevent all accommodation'. Like Liverpool and lord chancellor Eldon, he did not wish the bill of pains and penalties, by which ministers decided to proceed in the Lords, to go as far as divorce.[26] On 3 July he moved seven grants for members of the royal family, excluding the queen, and, when Hamilton complained on that score, said that it would be 'time enough' for him to do so 'when he found ministers disbursing the public money without any legal authority'. He insisted that the coronation would cost far less than Creevey anticipated. He saw off a motion for inquiry into the Milan commission, 6 July, when, securing yet another postponement of Commons proceedings on the queen, he claimed that George IV 'had never betrayed the slightest symptom of a vindictive spirit'. In a lighter moment, 16 July, he showed Princess Lieven 'the changes he has made in his country house' at North Cray Farm. She told her lover Metternich:

It has been much enlarged; but what taste in furnishing! The story of Don Quixote carpets his study, and Sancho is being tossed in a blanket just in front of his desk. He says that gives him a pleasant sensation, and he thinks its position is excellent. Join me in laughing![27]

He was reckoned to have given Dr. Lushington 'a most handsome and proper dressing' when quashing his motion for papers concerning the queen's plate, 17 July.[28] He said that if Wetherell persisted in his call for action to be taken against the *Western Luminary* for a libel on the queen, 25 July, he would press for a like response to attacks on the king. A week later Princess Lieven had the uncomfortable experience of waltzing with him at a fete at North Cray: 'heavens, what hard work to keep the minister in revolution'. When Caroline provocatively took a house next to his in St. James's Square, he initially reacted with his usual 'intrepid coolness', deciding to stay put; but in the end wiser councils prevailed, and he 'had his bed installed in the foreign office, in the room where he gives audience to ambassadors'.[29] He moved the adjournment of the Commons for four weeks, 21 Aug. 1820, when he observed that Osborne's motion for an address to the king for a prorogation was designed to 'keep the country in constant fever and agitation, open to every daring spirit, fit for the purposes of every base conspirator and political adventurer'.

Castlereagh, whom Creevey encountered at the Lords trial of the queen in mid-August 'smiling as usual, though I think awkwardly', was additionally exercised by continental developments, particularly the military rising in Portugal and the Austrian moves to crush the liberal regime in Naples. Others were concerned at the prospect of his having to fight the queen's battle in the Commons, if the bill of pains and penalties reached there, virtually unaided; and Wellington asked Mrs. Arbuthnot to consider what would happen 'if he should be taken ill'.[30] He had no difficulty in securing further adjournments of the House, pending the outcome of proceedings in the Lords, 18 Sept., 17 Oct., when he put Hume in his place over his 'romance' concerning an alleged ministerial conspiracy in the Franklin case.[31] He displayed his customary sang-froid when Mrs. Arbuthnot tackled him on the reports of the king's 'dissatisfaction' with and 'abuse' of his ministers:

> He lamented very much the king's indiscretion in talking of those who he still retained as his ministers in so indecorous a manner, and said that such conduct and feelings entirely destroyed any pleasure there might be in serving him. He did not, however, seem to believe that the king had any fixed plan for getting rid of us, but only thought he was uneasy about the progress of the bill and vented his ill humour in abuse of his ministers.

When he attributed much of this spleen to the intrigues of the king's mistress Lady Conyngham, 'who was indignant because the ministers' wives had not invited her to their houses', Mrs. Arbuthnot told

him that his own wife was the 'chief offender'; but he sprang fiercely to her defence.[32] At the end of October he told his brother that as 'the fate of the bill still hangs in suspense, and ... fresh food for inquiries seem to present future resources for opposition', 'our *danger* is diminished, but not our *difficulties*'. He doubted whether the bill could be carried, but was hopeful of establishing the queen's guilt beyond doubt. Although he was 'roughly handled' by her supporters at the theatre, 8 Nov., and continued to be on the sharp end of the king's tongue, he was pleased with the eventual outcome of the affair, being mightily relieved at the abandonment of the bill, which he had dreaded having to handle in the Commons, and was reported in late November to have 'declared that nothing shall remove him but an earthquake'.[33] He began recruiting for an attendance for the next session in early December 1820.[34] The failure of the attempt to bring in Robert Peel* after Canning's resignation was partly attributable to Castlereagh's unwillingness to 'give him the leadership of the House of Commons'; and Wellington continued to fret that 'if ... [he] should have the gout we shall be undone'. The poor health of Lord Londonderry was another source of worry. Apart from the fact that Castlereagh was, according to Princess Lieven, 'very wretched at not being allowed to see him', his father's death would necessitate his vacation of his Irish seat and his being returned elsewhere, which, it was feared, would create delay and uncertainty. However, the princess understood that the disruption would be minimal, for contingency plans had been laid; and in the event Londonderry temporarily rallied.[35]

Meanwhile, Castlereagh had been grappling with problems of foreign affairs, notably the developments in Portugal and Naples. He pressed the Portuguese king to return to settle with the liberals, and eventually succeeded. Regarding Naples, he considered Austria entitled to intervene against the new regime, the tenor of which alarmed him; but he was keen to prevent a joint operation by the Allies, and particularly anxious to keep Russia out of it. He sent Stewart to the October conference at Troppau as an observer, while letting it be known through his usual channels that he would only remain there if the tsar stopped making declarations which were repugnant to British public opinion. He deplored the Allied protocol affirming their determination to intervene against unacceptable governments. Although it was abandoned, it was replaced with an almost equally objectionable paper which tried to involve Britain and France in the collective decisions of Troppau. In January 1821 Castlereagh issued a riposte, endorsed by his colleagues, which nettled

Metternich and earned its author much credit, but did not prevent the decisive Austrian invasion of Naples.[36]

Castlereagh and Liverpool found the king amenable enough on an eve of session visit to Brighton to discuss the speech from the throne.[37] On 23 Jan. 1821 Castlereagh, in what the 'Mountaineer' Grey Bennet dismissed as 'a bad, spluttering, halting, wretched speech', protested against Wetherell's motion for papers on the liturgy question and secured its defeat, before, on the address, reviewing government policy.[38] The following day he kept 'very cool' in refusing to be drawn into discussion of the issues raised by the hundreds of petitions being presented in support of the queen; but Edward Bootle Wilbraham* remained afraid that he would 'not be equal to the fatigue of the campaign, which he has to manage singly'.[39] His fighting speech against Hamilton's motion deploring the omission of the queen's name from the liturgy, 26 Jan., delivered at four in the morning, was considered 'able and manly' by his friend Sir Henry Hardinge, who reported that it was received 'with loud and continued cheers on our side, and silent, deep attention on the other'. The young Whig George Howard*, watching from the gallery, thought it 'bad in everything that constitutes an orator, but very dextrous for his purpose'. According to Grey Bennet, he 'came to the bar and with great agitation of manner kept watching those who had gone forth' into the opposition lobby, but government had a majority of 101.[40] He was, as Creevey noted, thrown into a 'rage' by Brougham's communication of the queen's defiant message, 31 Jan.; but, as ever, anger made him more effective. He said that Caroline, badly advised, was 'erecting herself into a great power in the state' and accused opposition of seeking nothing more than office for themselves.[41] The following day he urged caution in asserting the privilege of Parliament against the press and deplored the unconstitutional language put into the queen's mouth in her answers to addresses. He had a personal triumph on 6 Feb., when, speaking against the opposition censure motion, he defended the conduct of ministers, lashed opposition for trying to 'get themselves into power at any desperate hazard to the crown and state', and exposed Brougham's 'trickery'. Yet Von Neumann later recited

a couple of phrases which created much laughter. Wishing to justify the government in having given instructions to the embassies abroad that they should arrange for the queen not to be received by foreign courts, he said that had they acted otherwise she would have returned to this country with a weapon in her hand which would have served as a pretext for being treated in the same way here. In speaking of Mr. Brougham, despatched to St. Omer

to negotiate with the queen, he said that he should have kept himself open, and the queen open, to consider other propositions.

For his own part, Castlereagh considered that the crushing defeat of the motion 'seems to leave the issue no longer doubtful, and will, I trust, in conjunction with the display of loyalty which has shown itself both in addresses and upon His Majesty's late visit to the theatre, restore confidence and abate the popular fermentation'. However, it was thought that his public remonstrance with Lady Conyngham's son Lord Mount Charles* for threatening to vote to reduce the queen's allowance would only continue his and his wife's 'open war' with the royal favourites.[42] He had an angry exchange with Denman on the liturgy question, 8 Feb.[43] Replying to Hobhouse's jibe, 13 Feb., that in 1790 he had advocated reform of the Irish House of Commons, he admitted the fact, but said that he had ceased to do so from 1793; and he professed supreme indifference to Newport's attack on him for his part in effecting the Union. He dealt easily enough with the last flings of opposition on the queen's case in the following few days, although Grey Bennet condemned his speech of 15 Feb. 1821 as 'one of his vapouring displays, very insolent and presumptuous, assuming everything and proving and reasoning nothing'.[44]

Questioned by Gooch, 5 Feb. 1821, as to what ministers intended to do about agricultural distress, Castlereagh said that nothing 'specific' was in contemplation, as distress was created by 'causes beyond the control of the legislature'; but he expressed willingness to sanction another inquiry if required. (It was appointed on 7 Mar.) On 12 Mar. he opposed Hume's motion for a return to the 1792 military establishment and defended the army estimates:

He would not be understood as opposing retrenchment ... but he did protest against the language of exaggeration and inflammation. He did not see that the distress of the country could be removed or alleviated by painting that distress in glaring and unwarrantable colours; and, that any such reduction could be effected in the military expenditure as would sensibly lighten the burdens of the people, was an assertion which no honest man who saw his way to the end of the proposition could be justified in making.

As proceedings dragged on until four in the morning, with the House in a 'disorderly' state, he 'kept his temper all the time, spoke not, and seemed to sleep with the greatest complacency'.[45] At the end of the debate on repeal of the additional malt duty, which was carried against ministers, 21 Mar., he warned that it would destroy public credit; and he spoke in the same sense when the government forced a reversal of the vote, 3 Apr. He opposed reduction of the revenue collecting service, 22 Mar., when he made fun of Mackintosh, and repeal of the tax on agricultural horses, 5 Apr. The following day, insisting that ministers had been justified in taking a stand on the malt duty, he described Creevey as the 'protester-general against the measures of government, and libeller-general of Parliament'. (Lady Holland told her son that 'the wags say Lord Castlereagh likes all taxes, but *syntax*.)[46] On 21 Feb., replying at length and with 'force' to the opposition attack on British policy towards Naples, he defended the Austrian intervention and reiterated the sacred principle of British non-interference: 'it was now strange to him to find ... ministers censured for not having committed this government to a war with the greatest military powers in Europe'.[47] He had more to say on the subject, again justifying the Austrian action, 20 Mar. He conceded, as arranged, Hume's request for information on the government of the Ionian Islands under Sir Thomas Maitland[†], 23 Feb., but deprecated his premature criticisms. He assured the House that no British agent had been involved in the execution of Murat or the Naples affair, 23 Feb. He sought to correct some misapprehensions regarding the unpaid Austrian loan, 14 Mar. He spoke and voted in favour of Catholic relief, 28 Feb., and on the relief bill, 23 Mar., urged 'the adoption of that wiser as well as more liberal plan, which, instead of separating a large class of the community from the rest of their fellow-subjects in political sentiment and situation, would give the Catholics an interest in the state, and the state a confidence in the Catholics'. Charles Williams Wynn, who was pleased to see that Castlereagh '*now* seems quite in earnest' for relief, thought he 'spoke better than I ever heard him'; and Grey Bennet privately acknowledged that his 'conduct has been excellent during the whole of this question'.[48] He discountenanced Davison's complaints against William Best[†] the judge, 23 Feb. and 7 Mar. He would have preferred giving Grampound's seats to the East Riding of Yorkshire rather than to Leeds, and was not prepared to accept a scot and lot franchise there, 2 Mar. He was initially averse to referring the Carlisle petition complaining of the interference of the military in an election to the committee of privileges, 15 Mar. 1821, but changed his mind as the debate revealed uncertainties in the case.

While he could be pleased with his performance and the strength of the ministry in the first two months of the session, he still conspicuously lacked able support on the front bench, and told his brother, 21 Mar., that his parliamentary labours were 'difficult

to endure'. Yet when he was offered assistance he rejected it, putting up unexpected opposition to the proposal to replace Nicholas Vansittart as chancellor of the exchequer with Peel. As he explained to Charles Arbuthnot*, who passed it on to his wife, he

> objected to this, stating that in his position as leader of the House of Commons it was certainly not desirable that there should be a chancellor of the exchequer who, from the nature of his office, *ought* in time of peace to be the most powerful member of the government and who, if he were ambitious, might make a party against him in the House of Commons; that it would be very unfair upon Mr. Vansittart, and that Mr. Peel had never done anything to entitle him to so high a place.

None of this was very convincing, or fair to Peel: it is not clear whether Castlereagh genuinely feared an enhancement of the anti-Catholic party, lacked confidence in his own ability to keep Peel in his place, or was betraying early symptoms of the paranoia which eventually destroyed his reason. At this time he frankly asked Liverpool whether he intended to retire, and the premier told him that although he was anxious to do so on personal grounds, he would remain while he had the support of his colleagues and their party, but that in the event of his going, he looked to Castlereagh as his successor, perhaps with Canning at the foreign office. (The previous month Wellington had posited such an arrangement to Mrs. Arbuthnot, with the additional proviso that Liverpool should become president of the council to lead the Lords, which would help to neutralize the drawbacks of Castlereagh's unpopularity and support for Catholic relief.)[49] The death of his father in early April 1821, which 'greatly afflicted' him, obliged him to vacate Down and come in for his uncle Lord Hertford's borough of Orford, where he had briefly sat 25 years earlier. Londonderry, as he now was, rallied behind Liverpool in his successful resistance to George IV's preposterous attempt to install a creature of the Conynghams as a canon of Windsor. In early May 1821, in conversations with the premier and Wellington, he stood by his objections to Peel's appointment to the exchequer and thereby put an end to the project.[50]

In the House, he opposed efforts to reduce the army estimates, 30 Apr., 2 May, and on the ordnance estimates, 18, 21 May, objected to Members making 'bold and exaggerated assertions' which bore no relationship to the facts and accused opposition of trying to fan 'the dead embers' of the Queen Caroline affair by carping about the approaching coronation. He upheld the principle of British non-interference in the internal affairs of European states, 4 May; said that the Russian army currently marching south would not pass beyond her boundaries and defended Russia and Austria against charges of tyranny, 7 May; declined to prejudice on-going negotiations over the Austrian loan, 31 May and 22 June;[51] opposed inquiry into Maitland's regime in the Ionian Islands, 7 June; saw off Hely Hutchinson's motion condemning Allied suppression of European liberalism, 20 June, when he claimed to be 'as sincere a friend to rational liberty as ... any other man', and the next day, with 'a daring speech in his confident tone' (Grey Bennet) defeated a motion criticizing British acquiescence in the crushing of liberalism in Sicily and insisted that British policy was founded 'as a rock' on the principles set out in the declaration of January.[52] In the agricultural distress committee, Londonderry, to the disquiet of its protectionist members, sug-gested the adoption of a report recommending no alteration of the corn laws and the rescinding of the 1820 committee's proposal to include Irish corn in the returns. He had clearly lost faith, as had other leading ministers, in the ability of a highly protected domes-tic agriculture to supply the country's needs; but he saddled Huskisson, a non-cabinet minister, with the opprobrious task of defending the policy of inactiv-ity.[53] However, he conceded repeal of the husbandry horses tax in deference to 'the extreme depreciation of the agricultural interest', 18 June, though he warned that it might have to be replaced with another.[54] He failed to prevent those responsible for libelling Bennet in *John Bull* being committed to Newgate for breach of privilege, 11 May. Opposing inquiry into Peterloo in 'an animated and forcible speech' (Bankes), 16 May, he declared that 'the danger of treason had dis-appeared before the thunder of Parliament'. Grey Bennet thought it was 'one of his most audacious and insolent speeches', which went largely unanswered.[55] He was against abolition of the death penalty for forgery, 23 May, and successfully divided the House against the measure, in what Grey Bennet consid-ered a low 'trick', 4 June.[56] He encouraged Scarlett to persevere with his poor bill, 24 May. He recom-mended acquiescence in the Lords' amendments to the Grampound disfranchisement bill and approved the activities of the Constitutional Association against 'disloyalty and sedition', 30 May. He saw nothing to be gained from Grant's slaves removal bill, 1 June, but accepted as 'a moral appeal' Wilberforce's address calling for action against the foreign slave trade, even though he found much of it offensive as 'a diplomatic instrument'. Opposing a commission of inquiry into the Owenite settlement at New Lanark, 26 June, he objected to 'Parliament being made the tribunal for investigating every abstruse principle and every

scheme for remodelling the existing order of society'; Grey Bennet deemed this a 'rational' line.[57] That month he carried, in the face of persistent opposition, the duke of Clarence's annuity, and dealt with attacks on the decision to exclude Caroline from the corona-tion.[58] Replying for government to Hume's motion for economy and retrenchment, in what Grey Bennet deplored as 'one of his most insulting and triumph-ing speeches', 27 June, he claimed that much had been achieved since the war and, while refusing to 'satisfy any excited feelings of the country, by deluding the people with a show of impractical retrenchment', he promised that during the recess ministers would produce a 'safe' and 'practical' scheme.[59] He defeated Wilson's attack on the grant for the aliens office, 29 June. Winding up the session, 3 July, he facetiously

> rejoiced to observe the good humour which now pre-vailed on the other side of the House, but to which the gentlemen opposite appeared, at times, to be entirely strangers ... They appeared to have receded in a consider-able degree from that political and constitutional Utopia which they had originally set up.

He reported that since January, the Commons had sat for an average of over eight and a half hours on each working day.[60] On the last, 10 July 1821, he refused to answer Lord Tavistock's question as to whether the army of occupation in France was to be reduced following Buonaparte's death. Arbuthnot, reviewing a 'stormy' and 'laborious' session, told his son that Londonderry 'has done wonders, and his reputation stands very high indeed'; and Grey Bennet wrote that he had been the only 'defender' of the beleaguered ministry 'whom the House would listen to', though he thought that the opposition front bench had failed to test his 'problematical character'.[61]

At the end of May 1821 Londonderry, 'suspi-cious' of Liverpool's motives in inviting Peel to join the ministry without specifying an office, had been 'excessively discontented' on learning of the business, but, according to Arbuthnot, was 'pacified' by assur-ances that 'nothing would induce Lord Liverpool to admit Mr. Peel into the treasury, and that he would consult Lord Castlereagh's wishes and feelings in preference to any one else'.[62] In the subsequent dis-cussions about bringing Canning into the cabinet, he, with Wellington, Lord Bathurst and Lord Sidmouth, succeeded in curbing what they saw as the premier's overeagerness, and putting the affair on hold until Liverpool had got over his wife's recent death. In mid-June Londonderry, who had no firm objection to Canning's admission, provided he was not forced on the king, told Mrs. Arbuthnot that 'he wished he could slip his neck out of the collar and have done with the whole thing'. In July the Grenvillite leader Lord Buckingham, whose group was also in the running for office, reported that he had found Londonderry

> very *boutonné*, very low and very cold. He referred everything to the [king's] return from Ireland, and told me that until that took place the government was *paralysed* in all its parts, and nothing of any sort could be done till then. He said he did not apprehend any *fatal* result, as the king did not seem at all inclined to change his system as to foreign powers or domestic economy.[63]

At the coronation he was, in the words of Lady Lyttelton, 'stately and conscious of it' in his garter regalia.[64] He accompanied the king to Ireland, and it fell to him on board ship at Holyhead to give him the news of Caroline's death, which, he told Eldon, 'cannot be regarded in any other light than as the greatest of all possible deliverances, both to His Majesty and to the country'. To the surprise of Londonderry, who told his wife that 'never did Providence preside over any barren transaction more auspiciously than over this visit', and the fury of opposition, his own reception in Ireland was little short of ecstatic.[65] The king returned more angry than ever with Liverpool, who, in addition to pressing for Canning's recruitment, was resisting his attempt to appoint Lord Conyngham as lord chamberlain. Londonderry, in contrast, was reported to be 'in the highest possible favour'; and he told Mrs. Arbuthnot that the king, who 'says he cannot and will not go on with Lord Liverpool any longer', had pressed him to 'agree to be the premier', which he had refused to do. He thought that 'the king's dissatisfaction [was] entirely personal to Lord Liverpool' and that it 'might be got over' after his return from Hanover, where he went as minister in attendance towards the end of September 1821.[66]

In addition to these domestic vexations, he had on his mind the Greek revolt against Turkey and the threat of Russian intervention on behalf of the former, which would threaten European stabilty and British interests. He had already made a personal appeal to the tsar not to take unilateral action, while affirming his confidence in the value and importance of the Alliance. He was anxious to concert measure with Metternich, who shared his alarm, and arranged to meet him in Hanover for private talks. They agreed on a course of action designed to effect a diplomatic solution to the problem.[67] According to Metternich, the king again proposed to Londonderry, whom he excepted from the abuse which he levelled at his ministers, that he should step into Liverpool's shoes. Londonderry did not rule this out entirely, but insisted that Liverpool should

retire voluntarily rather than be forced out. Eventually George, indicating that he was willing to compromise on the household appointment and to accept Canning provided he had no personal contact with him and that he was got rid of to India as soon as possible, charged Londonderry with the task of trying to effect a reconciliation with the premier. He returned in advance of the main party to do so, complaining to his wife that he was 'very much out of sorts', troubled with 'the blue devils' and disenchanted with 'the sad trade' which he plied.[68] He saw Liverpool as soon as he arrived, reporting to him the king's improved temper and disposition, and took on himself much of the credit for bringing about a restoration of something resembling harmony. He told Princess Lieven, to whom he was growing ever closer:

> 'The result of my negotiation is good in fact; and it will be good as experience; for the king will learn that it is not so easy to dismiss a minister, and the prime minister will learn that it must be remembered that the king is master'. In short, he seems absolutely convinced that the government is now immovable. He gives you [Metternich] a great deal of credit for the reconciliation, because you mollified the king.[69]

He and Liverpool had a cordial reception from the king when they saw him at Brighton to explain their plans for the reconstruction of the ministry, which involved putting Peel in the home office, sending Lord Wellesley and Henry Goulburn* to Ireland and taking in the Grenvillites, with Canning being excluded and earmarked for India. Londonderry conducted direct negotiations with the Grenvillites: he had little time or respect for them, but thought it important to secure their adhesion in order to 'destroy the intrigue of a third party in the House of Commons', and sought to soften the asperities which courting them created in some quarters. He told his brother that with himself, Peel and Williams Wynn on the front bench, 'I think we could carry on the government in the Commons with efficiency'.[70] There was unrest in Ireland, but he was insistent that ministers should not panic and, by resorting to a military solution, limit their ability to deliver their promised reductions and economies. He wrote to Sidmouth, 19 Dec. 1821:

> Our parliamentary campaign, perhaps our moral influence to carry the country through its difficulties, depends on having good ground to stand on in our military reductions. It can afford any temporary effort, which internal safety and tranquillity may require, if you take it on grounds of temporary policy and upon a case made out ... Were we upon the present Irish alarm ... to rescind our decision of July ... we should shake all confidence and be supposed to have been looking out for an excuse to

mobilize a feeling which is already imputed to the Horse Guards, of wishing to keep up cavalry beyond the wants of the country, at least beyond its means.[71]

The following day Croker told a friend:

> Londonderry goes on as usual, and ... like Mont Blanc continues to gather all the sunshine upon his icy head. He is *better* than ever; that is, colder, steadier, more *pococurante*, and withal more amiable and respected. It is a splendid summit of bright and polished frost which, like the travellers in Switerland, we all admire; but no one can hope, and few would wish to reach.[72]

Londonderry, who was pleased with Wellesley's initial proceedings in Ireland, pressed for an attend-ance of Members from there for the opening of the 1822 session, when he expected opposition to 'try our strength as early as possible upon some question which will give them the chance of shaking our landed support'.[73] On the address, 5 Feb., he outlined the gov-ernment's intentions to deal with agricultural distress and to retrench, and condemned and defeated Hume's 'most extraordinary' amendment 'in a very civil speech and subdued tone', according to Hobhouse.[74] Mrs. Arbuthnot found him unruffled by the 'unpleas-ant temper' of the House and the restiveness of the Tory country gentlemen: 'he is so calm minded that he never is alarmed by anything. He assured me, though, that nothing should induce him to remain in office if our financial system was broke in upon'.[75] He intro-duced and defended the Irish insurrection and habeas corpus suspension bills, 7, 8 Feb. Lady Holland reported that in doing so he 'showed a glorious jumble of ideas, or rather complete ignorance of language', by referring to his 'general *hydrophobia* for martial law'.[76] On 11 Feb. he brushed aside Grey Bennet's motion for inquiry into the disturbances at the queen's funeral before replying to Brougham's motion for extensive tax reductions to relieve distress, deploring the 'cloaked and mysterious terms' in which he had 'hinted at the measures to which the landed interests were to look for protection'. His motion for the previ-ous question was carried by 211-108. Goulburn told Wellesley that his speech was 'most triumphant', and Mrs. Arbuthnot, a spectator, thought he spoke 'very well'; but to Creevey it was 'an impudent, empty answer, clearly showing the monstrous embarrass-ments the ministers are under, as to managing their pecuniary resources and their House of Commons'.[77] Hudson Gurney* thought he made a 'bad' defence of the dismissal of Wilson from the army, 13 Feb.[78] Although Von Neumann and Mrs. Arbuthnot consid-ered that his exposition that day of the government's relief package, which consisted of a reduction in the

malt duty and the application of surplus revenue to reduction of the national debt by converting the five per cents to four, gave general 'satisfaction' to the House and the Tory backbenchers; but Creevey was astounded by his ineptitude:

> Such *hash* was never delivered by man. The folly of him – his speech as a composition in its *attempt* at style and ornament and figures, and in its real vulgarity, bombast and folly, was such as, coming from a man of his order, with 30 years parliamentary experience and with an audi-ence quite at his devotion, amounted to a perfect miracle ... Brougham ... played the devil with him.

The duke of Bedford commented that Londonderry had been 'more than usually ridiculous, but the Tory country gentlemen will nevertheless carry him through thick and thin to his journey's end at the close of the session'. Mackintosh was told that he had 'outdone himself in his peculiar eloquence ... when he said that the repeal of taxes would be to *contradict the causes of nature*'.[79] He secured the appointment of a select committee on agricultural distress, 18 Feb., when he advised Hamilton to leave his proposed bill for aboltion of the inferior Scottish consistory courts to the lord advocate.[80] He did not oppose Creevey's motion for information on civil list pensions, 27 Feb., but mocked his 'crane-necked research' and 'severity of manner which was at all times so alarming'. He said that reduction of the salt duties would destroy public credit by a side wind, 28 Feb., and the following day defended the ministerial relief scheme against accusa-tions of breach of faith, but was defeated on the grant for the navy pay office. Mrs. Arbuthnot wanted him to issue an ultimatum of resignation to recalcitrant and fractious country gentlemen, but feared that he was

> so good natured that I dare say he will not ... He says they only give these votes occasionally to make a figure in the columns of the opposition papers and please their con-stituents and they trust to our good luck that their votes will only lessen not overturn our majority.[81]

He quashed the rumour that government intended to reduce the army half-pay and condemned the distur-bances at the queen's funeral as an 'atrocious' attempt to disturb the peace and obstruct the law, 6 Mar.[82] He was dismissive of agriculturists' calls for parlia-mentary reform and tax reductions, 7 Mar., when his joke that Thomas Coke I's* recent marriage ought to have put him 'in a better temper' was taken amiss by Macdonald, who said that Coke 'held a place in the esteem and love of the people' which Londonderry never would. He made detailed comments on the five per cents reduction bill, 8 and 10 Mar.,[83] and endorsed the superannuation scheme outlined by Vansittart,

11 Mar. He and Liverpool had a 'most satisfactory' audience of the king, when they persuaded him to make a 'voluntary' sacrifice of ten per cent on his privy purse payments.[84] Opposing abolition of one of the joint-postmasterships, 13 Mar., he told the country gentlemen that 'if they truckled to the spirit and the clamour which was now abroad, they would betray their own situation, and what was worse, they would betray the people themselves'. He scouted Russell's bid to have Arbuthnot's letter summoning Members to attend to resist opposition attacks declared a breach of privilege, 15 Mar. He opposed Creevey's attack on the Barbados pensions fund, 25 Mar., and defended ministerial plans to increase the number of gaol deliveries, 27 Mar. 1822. The following day Princess Lieven, who believed that 'he loves me with all his heart', though she assured Metternich that their relationship was entirely platonic, wrote that

> when he meets me he fastens on to me; we spend whole evenings sitting together and he never leaves me ... He knows very few people in society ... It is strange how timid he is in society, as if he were just beginning ... I find him thoroughly entertaining ... His phrases are always unexpected.[85]

Londonderry was instrumental in persuading Plunket not to bring on the general Catholic question that session,[86] and spoke in that sense when approving Canning's Catholic peers bill, 10 May 1822. He defended the secret service grant, 1 Apr., and angrily accused Grey Bennet of trying to seduce the public into a 'most flagrant deviation from sound policy as well as common honesty' by advocating a change in the currency system, 3 Apr., when he invoked Ricardo's views to bolster his familiar argument that tax reductions would afford no significant relief to agriculture. He was too hoarse to speak against parliamentary reform, 25 Apr.[87] Denis Le Marchant[†] was told by a member of the agricultural distress committee that its proceedings were 'conducted with much warmth and bad temper', and that it required all Londonderry's 'tact and decision' to maintain order, though he was said to have taken little part in its deliberations.[88] On the committee's report, 29 Apr., he outlined the ministerial proposals to advance capital to parishes; to lend £1,000,000 for the purchase and warehousing of British corn, and the same sum to create employment in Ireland, both to be funded by the Bank via the reduced five per cents; to extend the Currency Act to 1833, protect country bankers over the issue of small notes and facilitate the formation of joint-stock banks; to lighten the dead weight of the army and navy half-pay by converting it into a long annuity, which

would provide an operating surplus of £1,800,000 to be applied to as yet unspecified tax reductions, and to introduce a modified sliding scale to regulate corn imports when prices were between 70s. and 80s. Unfortunately, as even Mrs. Arbuthnot admitted, he was at his worst on this occasion, 'so confused and involved in his language that the House did not in the least understand' the scheme.[89] He supported Vansittart in his explanation of the naval and military pensions plan, 1 May, expressing sarcastic surprise at opposition's sudden tenderness for the sinking fund. That day he declined to say whether the government had or would formally recognize the new independent republics of South America.[90] On 2 May ministers were defeated by 216-201 on the abolition of one of the postmasterships. In committee on the agricultural distress report, 6 May, Londonderry proposed the scheme for the advance of £1,000,000 for warehoused corn, but testily withdrew it when the agriculturists, whose spokesmen had recommended it against his personal wishes, 'tamely' allowed opposition to ridicule it. Mrs. Arbuthnot blamed the country gentlemen for the fiasco, but Buckingham thought there was 'no excuse' for Londonderry's weakness and vacillation.[91] In continued debates on the subject, 7, 8, 9, 13 May, he carried his corn law resolutions against a variety of alternative proposals. His explicit threat of the goverment's resignation if they were defeated on the issue of diplomatic expenditure, 15 May, and Williams Wynn's brother's embassy to Switzerland the following day, into which he was apparently goaded by Peel after a row in cabinet, had the desired effect, though it infuriated opposition.[92] He assured the House that every effort was being made in Ireland to raise subscriptions for the relief of distress, 17 May, and upbraided Hume for making unwarranted statements on the Irish civil list which were 'calculated to produce false and painful impressions', 21 May. He supported the Marriage Act amendment bill, 20 May, again endorsed the military pensions scheme, 24 May, and expressed strong reservations over certain crucial provisions of Scarlett's poor bill, 31 May 1822.

At this time he was again infuriated by the meddlesome Lady Conyngham, who, unknown to him, sought to exclude Lady Londonderry from the dinner in honour of the prince and princess of Denmark. At the king's instigation, Princess Lieven successfully intervened with Lady Conyngham and, as she flattered herself, ended the 'quarrel of two years standing'. However, she was astonished by Londonderry's reaction when she told him what had occurred, for he 'suddenly flew into a positive rage' and talked wildly of resigning if matters did not improve. He also said that he would wash his hands of the proposed journey to the autumn conference of the Allies in Vienna, on which the king was insisting on going himself, with his mistress in tow. His brother, whom he sent to the Princess to tell her that his mind was made up, said that he was 'disgusted with everything', that 'this women's quarrel' was the last straw, that he was suspicious of Peel and believed that all his colleagues, including Wellington, were conspiring against him: 'He told me that Lord Londonderry was broken-hearted, and that he had never seen a man in such a state'. Certainly he was under a terrible strain and showing symptoms of mental and physical exhaustion, for at this time he buttonholed the Whig Lord Tavistock*, with whom he had only a slight acquaintance, in Hyde Park, and

> lost no time in unbosoming himself upon the state of public affairs. He described the *torment* of carrying on the government under the general circumstances of the country as beyond endurance, and said if he could once get out of it, no power on earth should induce him into it again.

On 10 June 1822 Princess Lieven, who wondered if his brother was feeding his paranoia about Wellington, noted that he 'looks ghastly. He has aged five years in the last week; one can see that he is a broken man'. A week later, however, she found him 'radiant', having received assurances from the king concerning the visit to the Allied Congress.[93]

In the House, 3 June 1822, he opposed reception of the Greenhoe reform petition because it was couched in the language of 'insult'. That day he said that the new corn bill was not intended to create a perfect law and that 'if Parliament waits until the agriculturists were agreed upon a remedy, they might wait till doomsday, and to no purpose, for ... they did not always understand their own interests'.[94] He defeated Canning's proposed clause to permit the grinding of foreign corn, 10 June. He supported the aliens bill, 5 June, when he denied that ministers had promised a formal inquiry into the state of Ireland, for whose problems they were trying to find practical solutions.[95] He backed the constables bill (7 June) and the tithes leasing bill (13 June) as examples of this policy. He opposed the resumption of cash payments, 12 June, and on the 14th clashed with Russell over his statement that 'overwhelming necessity' might justify reduction of the interest on the national debt. He said that in alleging that the influence of the crown was increasing, 24 June, Brougham 'wished to sap the foundation of the character of Parliament'. He opposed inquiry into the conduct of the lord advocate towards the Scottish press, 25 June. Next day he had a 'terrible battle' with

Creevey, Grey Bennet and Brougham over Sidmouth's pension.[96] As in the previous year, he swallowed Wilberforce's remonstrance on the foreign slave trade, but pointed out that if France and America refused to co-operate, it was almost impossible to make much progress. He opposed repeal of the salt duties, 28 June. He held out the prospect of 'a moderate compromise only' on the matter of the Austrian loan, 1 July. He failed to persuade Spring Rice to defer his planned motion impugning chief baron O'Grady until the next session, 4 July. He welcomed Nolan's poor law amendment bill because its object was to 'bring back the system to what it was' and told Stuart Wortley that he was optimistic of getting Portugal to rescind her additional duty on imported wool, 10 July.[97] On 12 July he again spoke in favour of the Marriage Act amendment bill; according to Henry Fox*, he said that 'the nullity feature was buried in the womb of futurity'.[98] He caused a stir among those accustomed to his normally infallible memory, 5 July, by professing utter ignorance of the taking of a British merchant ship by the Spanish.[99] He made his apologies, 15 July, when he also refused to commit the government to active intervention on behalf of the Greek insurgents, who he deemed to be as steeped in blood as the Turks. He called for tempers to be cooled in discussion of the Borthwick case, 17 July, preferring 'indirect censure' to anything of greater severity. He wished to proceed with the Canada bill despite the lateness of the session, 18 July, but was forced to bow to demands for its postponement, 23 July. Defending the Superannuation Act amendment bill against Canning's criticisms, 26 July, he observed that in seeking to reduce public salaries as near as possible to the standard of 1792 ministers were merely carrying out the recommendations of the select committee. In his last reported speech in the House, 30 July 1822, he exonerated the government from any 'supineness' in protecting British shipping in the South Sea.

Londonderry and Metternich had succeeded in averting Russian intervention in support of the Greeks, and persuaded the tsar to submit the Eastern question to the Vienna conference. However, the Russian scheme for an Allied invasion of Spain to rescue King Ferdinand from the liberals posed another threat to peace, and Metternich was anxious that Londonderry, who was also exercised by the problem of the Spanish South American republics, should attend the Vienna meeting, if not that scheduled for later in Verona to discuss Italian affairs. Given all his difficulties with the king, who eventually opted to visit Scotland, and Lady Conyngham, it was not until late July 1822 that Londonderry could be sure of going to Vienna. He planned to leave England with his wife in mid-August and to arrive three weeks later for preliminary talks with Metternich.[100] On 31 July, after the close of the session, Princess Lieven found him in 'good spirits' and 'delighted' at the prospect of seeing Metternich; but the following day Joseph Planta*, under-secretary at the foreign office, noted that after the most 'wearying, troublesome and disagreeable session' he could remember, his chief, who delegated little of his official business, was 'more tired in *mind* than I have seen him'.[101] At the cabinet meeting to approve his plans for the conference, 7 Aug., he was, as Wellington recalled, 'very low, out of spirits and unwell'.[102] The following day, at Cray, he told one of his staff that he was 'quite worn out' in the mind and dreading the conference, 'a fresh load of responsibilty [which] is more than I can bear'.[103] He had already told Mrs. Arbuthnot that he was being blackmailed for an alleged homosexual offence; and when he took his leave of the king on 9 Aug. he was raving in the same strain, accusing himself of that and all manner of other crimes. The king urged him to seek medical advice and subsequently alerted Liverpool, who did not take him seriously. Later that day Londonderry produced a similar performance for Wellington, who was about to set out for the Netherlands. The duke told him that he was not in his right mind and advised him to see his doctor, Charles Bankhead, whom he personally alerted, along with the Arbuthnots. (There is no concrete evidence that Londonderry had committed a homosexual act, but it seems that a few years earlier he had been enticed into a brothel by a man disguised as a woman, and that he was being blackmailed on that score. The case of the bishop of Clogher, which was currently the talk of the town, probably impinged on his disturbed mind.)[104] Bankhead had him cupped, sent him to Cray for the weekend and followed him there. He remained in a fretful state, ranting wildly about conspiracies and threats to his life, but no special watch was kept on him, though his pistols and razors were removed. At about 7.30 on the morning of 12 Aug. 1822 he sent for Bankhead, who found him in a dressing room seconds after he had severed his carotid artery with chilling surgical precision, using a small knife which had been overlooked. He died almost instantly, but not before he had exclaimed, 'My dear Bankhead, let me fall upon you; it is all over'.[105] The inquest held at Cray the following day decided that he had destroyed himself while in 'a state of mental delusion'. While overwork and mental stress clearly played a part in his loss of reason, it seems likely that he was the victim of a psychotic depressive illness.[106] News of his death, which was at first ascribed to natural causes, created a sen-sation, though Greville, on his return to London on 13 Aug., met

> several people who had all assumed an air of melancholy, a *visage de circumstance*, which provoked me inexpressibly, because it was certain that they did not care; indeed, if they felt at all, it was probably rather satisfaction at an event happening than sorrow at the death of the person.

The king, his cabinet colleagues, especially Wellington, Mrs. Arbuthnot, Princess Lieven and others close to him were devastated; but, naturally, working politicians of all persuasions were not slow in beginning to calculate the immense consequences of his death for domestic and foreign affairs.[107] His half-brother blamed his suicide on 'that royal conduct which wounded him in the tenderest and most acute quarter', more specifically 'the intrigues that were carried on by the women surrounding the king', which 'gave additional friction to all his other torments'.[108] George Agar Ellis* reflected on this 'proof of the nothingness of human grandeurs: here is a man who has raised himself to the highest point of them, and then finds that they have not charms enough to induce him merely to live to enjoy them'. He considered it 'a still greater proof ... of the sad effects which disappointment and chagrin may have on a mind in which religion is not uppermost, for I have no doubt that the sad and apparently irretrievable state of affairs in England was the real cause of ... [his] unfortunate state of mind'.[109] At the insistence of Lady Londonderry, he was buried on 20 Aug. in Westminster Abbey, next to Pitt. While the crowds which lined the funeral route were generally respectful and decorous, there was cheering when the coffin was taken out of the hearse at the Abbey door.[110] By his will, dated 14 Aug. 1818, the settled estates in County Down passed to his half-brother, who succeeded him as 3rd marquess of Londonderry. He left other Ulster property, his London house and North Cray to his wife. His personalty within the province of Canterbury was sworn under £35,000.[111]

Creevey defied

> any human being to discover a single feature of his character that can stand a moment's criticism. By experience, good manners and great courage, he managed a corrupt House of Commons pretty well, with some address. This is the whole of his intellectual merit. He had a limited understanding and no knowledge, and his whole life was spent in an avowed, cold-blooded contempt of every honest public principle. A worse, or if he had had talent and ambition for it, a more dangerous public man never existed.[112]

Sir Robert Wilson, another political opponent, believed that there had never been 'a greater enemy to civil liberty or a baser slave'.[113] Brougham was slightly more generous, acknowledging his abiding courage, and reflecting that 'his capacity was greatly underrated from the poverty of his discourse' and that he was 'far above the bulk of his colleagues in abilities', though his natural gifts were 'of the most commonplace' kind.[114] Mrs. Arbuthnot, who grieved long and bitterly for him (there circulated a 'ridiculous story' that he had 'killed himself for love' of her) wrote:

In discussing matters of business I used to remark that he was slow at finding words and had an involved way of explaining a subject, but it was always plain that the idea was right and clear in his mind, and nothing could exceed his strong good sense ... He had a natural slowness of constitution of which he was himself quite aware ... Nothing ... could exceed his tact and judgement in dwelling on the strong points of his own arguments or the weak ones of his antagonists; and his management was so good, and he was himself so gentlemanlike and so high minded, that he was one of the most popular leaders the government ever had.[115]

Croker observed that 'absence of all vanity and perfect simplicity of mind always characterized him'.[116] Many years after his death Lord Aberdeen, one of his successors as foreign secetary, told Bishop Wilberforce that Londonderry was 'a very bold man – not very scrupulous – I do not mean a positively dishonest man in anything – but, having great purposes, would not stick at the means of carrying them out'.[117] Hobhouse of the home office, who thought his loss 'irreparable', praised his abilities as a manager of the Commons, notwithstanding his 'disposition to compromise' and his deficiencies as a speaker:

Amid these defects, he rose by dint of a noble person, an heroic mind, an undaunted soul, strong power of argument, personal courage, and the manners and demeanour of a most polished gentlemen, which never deserted him in the hottest and bitterest debate. It has been often remarked that he always spoke best when most severely attacked. He has been likened to a top, which spins best when it is most whipped.[118]

Lord John Russell summed him up as 'a man of business, endowed with common sense and discretion, but bound by traditional Toryism'.[119] Agar Ellis, who 'had known him for some years', paid tribute to his 'many redeeming virtues and good qualities':

He was a man of a strong and cool head and a resolute judgement, considerable abilities and much application. His speaking in Parliament was for the most part confused and bad ... [but] he sometimes spoke well ... In temper he was unmatched as a leader of the ... Commons ... In private life he was most amiable ... His conversation was

occasionally agreeable, rarely though – it was generally too drawling in manner, and with an air too little interested in what was going on. A steady friend, and a forgiving enemy. I doubt whether he cared much for the constitution; he had been too long in the mire of politics for that.[120]

Unfailing courage and, until it betrayed him at the end, a clear head raised Londonderry above many men of greater natural gifts. He was a political giant, at the centre of momentous events; and his reputation has been rescued by the perspective of posterity and by cool appraisal from the infamy visited on him by his contemporary critics.

[1] See the biographies by Ione Leigh (1951), C.J. Bartlett (1966) and Wendy Hinde (1981), and the survey by J.W. Derry (1976). For Castlereagh as foreign secretary and diplomat in the post-war period see Sir Charles Webster, *The Foreign Policy of Castlereagh, 1815-1822* (1947). [2] He was baptized a Presbyterian at Strand Street, Dublin, 5 July 1769. [3] Lansdowne mss, Macdonald to Lansdowne, 18 Aug. [1822]. [4] Warws. RO, MI 247, Philips mems. i. 377. [5] *Life of Wilberforce*, v. 259. [6] Russell, *Recollections*, 26-27. [7] *Greville Mems*. i. 127. [8] Hatherton diary, 13 Dec. [1831]; M.D. George, *Cat. of Pol. and Personal Satires*, x. 13504, 13515-20, 13531, 13534. [9] *Castlereagh Letters*, xii. 174 [10] PRO NI, Londonderry mss D3030/Q2/2, Castlereagh to Stewart, 19 Feb. 1820. [11] Harewood mss HAR/GC/26, Canning to wife, 28 Jan., 20 Feb. 1820. [12] *Lieven Letters*, 7. [13] *Castlereagh Letters*, xii. 210-14; *Arbuthnot Jnl*. i. 2-3; *Hobhouse Diary*, 9; Buckingham, *Mems. Geo. IV*, i. 72; *Croker Pprs*. i. 161; Londonderry mss Q2/2, Castlereagh to Stewart, 19 Feb. 1820. [14] *Lieven Letters*, 16, 17; *Von Neumann Diary*, i. 18-19; Hatherton diary, 8 Mar. [1820]. [15] *Arbuthnot Jnl*. i. 8; *Geo. IV Letters*, ii. 795. [16] *Oxford DNB*; Hinde, 257-8; Webster, ii. 192; Derry, 204-8. [17] *Castlereagh Letters*, xii. 258-9; *Althorp Letters*, 106. [18] Dorset RO D/BKL, Bankes jnl. 117. [19] Wellington mss. [20] *Althorp Letters*, 109; *Lieven Letters*, 37; Brougham mss, Brougham to Grey [1 June 1820]; Add. 52444, f. 122. [21] *The Times*, 5 July 1820. [22] Ibid. 25 July 1820. [23] *Castlereagh Letters*, xii. 259. [24] *Croker Pprs*. i. 174; *Lieven Letters*, 40; *Greville Mems*. i. 95; Bankes jnl. 118 (6, 7 June 1820). [25] *Arbuthnot Jnl*. i. 23; *Hobhouse Diary*, 25; J.E. Cookson, *Lord Liverpool's Administration*, 242. [26] *Arbuthnot Jnl*. i. 24; Hatherton diary, 22 June 1820; *Hobhouse Diary*, 29-30. [27] *Lieven Letters*, 53. [28] Buckingham, i. 51-52. [29] *Lieven Letters*, 57, 59, 62; *Arbuthnot Jnl*. i. 31-32; *Hobhouse Diary*, 36. [30] *Creevey Pprs*. i. 306; *Arbuthnot Jnl*. i. 37; *Colchester Diary*, iii. 163. [31] *Von Neumann Diary*, i. 41. [32] *Arbuthnot Jnl*. i. 42-43. [33] *Londonderry mss Q2*, Castlereagh to Stewart, 29 Oct. [1820]; *Arbuthnot Corresp*. 15; *Hobhouse Diary*, 36-38, 44; *Countess Granville Letters*, i. 189; *Creevey Pprs*. i. 338; Buckingham, i. 78, 82; *Life of Campbell*, i. 389; Cookson, 263, 267. [34] Londonderry mss, Castlereagh's circular letter, 5 Dec. 1820; Cookson, 282; *Arbuthnot Corresp*. 18. [35] *Hobhouse Diary*, 46; *Lieven Letters*, 101, 105; Cent. Kent. Stud. Camden mss U840 C530/6; Wellington mss, Wellington to Mrs. Arbuthnot, 21 Dec. 1820; Lonsdale mss, Beckett to Lowther, 17 Jan. 1821. [36] Hinde, 261-4; Derry, 204-10; *Arbuthnot Jnl*. i. 65; *Castlereagh Letters*, xii. 364. [37] *Arbuthnot Jnl*. i. 63-64. [38] HLRO, Hist. Coll 379, Grey Bennet diary, 2. [39] Buckingham, i. 113; *Colchester Diary*, iii. 201. [40] Camden mss C530/7; Castle Howard mss, Howard to Lady Morpeth, 28 [Jan. 1821]; Grey Bennet diary, 7. [41] *Creevey's Life and Times*, 137; Add. 43212, f. 180. [42] N. Gash, *Secretary Peel*, 287; *Lieven Letters*, 113-14; *Von Neumann Diary*, i. 50; *Castlereagh Letters*, xii. 364. [43] *The Times*, 9 Feb. 1821. [44] Grey Bennet diary, 21-22, 26. [45] Ibid. 35. [46] *Lady Holland to Son*, 5. [47] *Von Neumann Diary*, i. 52. [48] Buckingham, i. 142-3, 146; Grey Bennet diary, 46. [49] Hinde, 266-7; Londonderry mss Q2/2; *Arbuthnot Jnl*. i. 76, 82-83; Cookson, 309-11; Gash, 290-1. [50] *Geo. IV Letters*, ii. 914;

Hobhouse Diary, 52-53; *Arbuthnot Jnl.* i. 89, 90, 92. [51] *The Times*, 1 June 1821. [52] Grey Bennet diary, 103. [53] B. Hilton, *Corn, Cash, Commerce*, 105-6, 108-10. [54] Grey Bennet diary, 85, 101. [55] Bankes jnl. 128; Grey Bennet diary, 82-83. [56] Grey Bennet diary, 96. [57] Ibid. 105. [58] *Geo. IV Letters*, ii. 933, 934, 966. [59] Grey Bennet diary, 106-7, 111. [60] *Geo. IV Letters*, ii. 938. [61] *Arbuthnot Corresp.* 20; Grey Bennet diary, 118, 121. [62] *Arbuthnot Jnl.* i. 97. [63] *Hobhouse Diary*, 61, 62, 64, 66; Buckingham, i. 164-5, 169; *Arbuthnot Corresp.* 19; *Arbuthnot Jnl.* i. 102; *Croker Pprs.* i. 198-9; Add. 38370, ff. 25, 57; Bucks. RO, Fremantle mss D/FR/46/11/52; 51/5/15. [64] *Lady Lyttelton Corresp.* 237. [65] Twiss, *Eldon*, ii. 432; *Arbuthnot Corresp.* 22; *Croker Pprs.* i. 201-2; Lady Londonderry, *Castlereagh*, 61-62; *Creevey Pprs.* ii. 30; *Arbuthnot Jnl.* i. 115-16. [66] Buckingham, i. 195-6, 202, 209-10; *Arbuthnot Jnl.* i. 116, 117, 121. [67] Hinde, 269-71; Derry, 211-15. [68] *Geo. IV Letters*, ii. 957-9; Add. 38566, f. 71; *Arbuthnot Corresp.* 25; Hinde, 271-2; Webster, 369. [69] *Geo. IV Letters*, ii. 966; *Arbuthnot Jnl.* i. 124-5; *Hobhouse Diary*, 77; Buckingham, i. 227; *Lieven Letters*, 142-3. [70] Add. 51600, Lady Cowper to Lady Holland [28 Nov.]; *Geo. IV Letters*, ii. 973; *Arbuthnot Corresp.* 26; *Arbuthnot Jnl.* i. 133; BL, Fortescue mss, Buckingham to Grenville, 2 Dec., Wynn to same [5 Dec.]; Londonderry mss Q2, Londonderry to Stewart [9 Dec.]; Aberdeen Univ. Lib. Arbuthnot mss, Londonderry to Wellington [9 Dec.]; Harrowby mss, Bathurst to Harrowby, 12 Dec. 1821. [71] Cookson, 342-3. [72] *Croker Pprs.* i. 219. [73] *Arbuthnot Corresp.* 26. [74] Add. 56544, f. 60. [75] *Arbuthnot Jnl.* i. 140. [76] *Lady Holland to Son*, 9. [77] Add. 37298, f. 158; *Arbuthnot Jnl.* i. 142; *Creevey Pprs.* ii. 33. [78] Gurney diary, 13 Feb. [1822]. [79] *Von Neumann Diary*, i. 91; *Arbuthnot Jnl.* i. 144; *Creevey Pprs.* ii. 34; *Russell Letters*, ii. 6; Add. 52445, f. 49. [80] *The Times*, 19 Feb. 1822. [81] *Arbuthnot Jnl.* i. 146-7. [82] *The Times*, 7 Mar. 1822. [83] Ibid. 9, 12 Mar. 1822. [84] *Arbuthnot Corresp.* 26; *Wellington and Friends*, 20. [85] *Lieven Letters*, 157, 166. [86] Buckingham, i. 307, 309-10. [87] Ibid. i. 318. [88] Le Marchant, *Althorp*, 203-4; Hilton, 156. [89] *Arbuthnot Jnl.* i. 156, 160. [90] *The Times*, 2 May 1822. [91] *Arbuthnot Jnl.* i. 161; Fremantle mss 46/12/2. [92] *Arbuthnot Jnl.* i. 163; Add. 75937, Lady to Lord Spencer, 13 May 1822. [93] *Lieven Letters*, 157, 159, 167, 170, 171-5, 177-81; *Arbuthnot Jnl.* i. 163-4; *Creevey Pprs.* ii. 38; Broughton, *Recollections*, ii. 187; Leigh, 347-53. [94] *The Times*, 4 June 1822. [95] Ibid. 6 June 1822. [96] *Arbuthnot Jnl.* i. 171. [97] *The Times*, 11 July 1822. [98] *Fox Jnl.* 136. [99] *The Times*, 6 July 1822; H. Montgomery Hyde, *The Strange Death of Lord Castlereagh*, 171-2. [100] Hinde, 274-7; Webster, 469-82, 537-49; Leigh, 354; Buckingham, i. 355. [101] *Lieven Letters*, 187; Bagot mss (History of Parliament Aspinall transcripts), Planta to Bagot, 1 Aug. 1822. [102] Wellington mss WP1/720/9; *Wellington Despatches*, i. 255. [103] Sir A. Alison, *Lives of Lord Castlereagh and Lord Stewart*, iii. 180-1. [104] *Arbuthnot Jnl.* i. 177-9; *Wellington Despatches*, i. 251-4, 255-8; *Lieven Letters*, 189-90, 194; J. Richardson, *Recollections*, i. 285-8; *Hobhouse Diary*, 92-93; Montgomery Hyde, 149-90. [105] *Wellington Despatches*, i. 255-8; *Croker Pprs.* i. 224-5; Glos. RO, Bledisloe mss D 421/X 17; Montgomery Hyde, 36-70. [106] *The Times*, 14, 15 Aug. 1822; Hinde, 280-1; Montgomery Hyde, 1-25. [107] *Greville Mems.* i. 126; *Croker Pprs.* i. 224; *Life of Wilberforce*, v. 134-5; *Lady Palmerston Letters*, 107-8; *Fox Jnl.* 141; Add. 36459, ff. 297, 299; *Arbuthnot Jnl.* i. 238; *Lieven Letters*, 189, 192; *Hobhouse Diary*, 126; Buckingham, i. 364; *Von Neumann Diary*, i. 102; J. Bagot, *Canning and Friends*, ii. 133; Bessborough mss, Tierney to Duncannon, 14 Aug.; Add. 51564, Mackintosh to Lady Holland, 15 Aug. 1822. [108] Norf. RO, Blickling Hall mss, Londonderry to Emily Londonderry, 25 Aug. 1822. [109] Northants. RO, Agar Ellis diary, 16 Aug. [1822]. [110] *The Times*, 21 Aug. 1822; Twiss, iii. 465; *Hobhouse Diary*, 90-91; *Croker Pprs.* i. 226. [111] PROB 11/1670/296; IR26/964/449. [112] *Creevey Pprs.* ii. 42. [113] Lambton mss (History of Parliament Aspinall transcripts), Wilson to Lambton, 26 Aug. 1822. [114] *Hist. Sketches* (ser. 2), 121-31. [115] Agar Ellis diary, 21 Sept. [1822]; *Arbuthnot Jnl.* i. 181-2. [116] *Croker Pprs.* iii. 192. [117] R. Wilberforce, *Samuel Wilberforce*, 236. [118] *Hobhouse Diary*, 91-92. [119] Russell, 47. [120] Agar Ellis diary, 16 Aug. [1822].

D.R.F.

STEWART, William (1781–1850), of Killymoon, co. Tyrone.

CO. TYRONE   1818–1830

b. ?1781, 1st surv. s. of James Stewart[†], MP [I], of Killymoon and Hon. Elizabeth Molesworth, da. and event. coh. of Richard, 3rd Visct. Molesworth [I]. *educ.* Christ Church, Oxf. 26 Oct. 1797, aged 16. *unm.*; 3da. illegit. *suc.* fa. 1821. *d.* 2 Oct. 1850.

Capt. Cookstown inf. 1803; lt.-col. co. Tyrone militia 1805-*d.*; capt. Newmills inf. 1822.

Stewart's Whig father James, whose family had long held one of the principal electoral interests in Tyrone, represented his county at Dublin and Westminster from 1768 to 1812. William regained the seat at the general election of 1818 with the support of local magnates and Lord Liverpool's administration, but sided with opposition in the Commons, except (following his father's example) on Catholic relief.[1] He was again returned unopposed in March 1820, when he signed requisitions for county meetings on George IV's accession and on illicit distillation.[2] He voted against the appointment of an additional baron of exchequer in Scotland, 15 May, and Wilberforce's compromise motion on the Queen Caroline affair, 22 June, and for economies in revenue collection, 4 July 1820. Having inherited his father's estate on 18 Jan. 1821, he took six weeks' compassionate leave, 12 Feb., so it was probably not he, but William Stuart, Member for Armagh, who divided against Catholic claims on the 28th.[3] He apparently suggested the temporary postponement of the Irish tithes leasing bill, 15 Mar.[4] He voted for repeal of the additional malt duty, 3 Apr., and to disqualify civil officers of the ordnance from voting in parliamentary elections, 12 Apr. 1821. Although by no means a thick and thin attender, during the following three sessions he divided fairly steadily with the Whig opposition on most issues, including for parliamentary reform, 25 Apr. 1822, 20 Feb., 24 Apr., 2 June 1823. He voted against the Catholic peers bill, 30 Apr. 1822. He divided for inquiries into Irish tithes, 19 June, Irish distress, 8 July 1822, the Irish church establishment, 4 Mar. 1823, 6 May 1824, the legal proceedings against the Dublin Orange rioters, 22 Apr. 1823, and the state of Ireland, 11 May 1824. He voted for securing the proper use of Irish first fruits revenues, 25 May, and against Irish clerical pluralities, 27 May, and the Irish insurrection bill, 18 June 1824. He was granted six weeks' sick leave, 10 Feb. 1825, and apparently missed the rest of the session. The inhabitants of Cookstown congratulated him on his recovery that autumn and early the next year he was reported to be ready to resume his parliamentary duties.[5] However, the sole piece of evidence for attendance which has been traced that year was his probable vote against flogging in the army, 10 Mar. 1826.

He confidently asserted in his address that he would be well enough to attend Parliament, nothing came of a rumoured challenge and he was returned unopposed at the general election of 1826.[6] He signed the requisition for, but apparently was not present at, the Tyrone Protestant meeting at the end of that year.[7] Having also signed the anti-Catholic petition from the landed proprietors of Ireland, he presented his county's hostile one, 5 Mar. 1827.[8] Yet he was listed as an 'absentee' from the division the following day and was granted another six weeks' sick leave on 2 Apr. No evidence of parliamentary activity has been traced for the 1828 session and Planta, the Wellington ministry's patronage secretary, noted that he was 'Protestant' but 'absent' at the start of the following year. He missed the Tyrone meeting on 2 Mar., but was credited with a vote (his last) in favour of Catholic emancipation, 6 Mar., and he may have been the Stewart who spoke in its favour, 16 Mar. 1829.[9] Late that year it was expected that he would vacate, and his hand was forced by the resolutions passed at a meeting of freeholders in January 1830, when approaches were made to his distant kinsman Sir Hugh Stewart* to replace him. Recognizing that he was 'incapable of that attendance which the fulfilment of my duties as their representative requires', he promised them he would resign at the dissolution, and in an address issued from Paris, 8 July 1830, he confirmed his retirement.[10] At the general election of 1831, when he claimed to have always been a reformer, he wrote to his mother that 'were I less poor or stronger I would try my luck once more for Tyrone', but nothing ever again came of such an ambition.[11]

In his youth Stewart had lived for some years with Ellen, daughter of Edmund Power of Curragheen, county Waterford, with whom he had had three daughters. She afterwards married John Home Purves, a younger son of Sir Alexander Purves of Purves Hall, Berwickshire, who passed off the children as his own, although, as Greville noted, 'nothing could be more notorious than the original connection and the real paternity'. Later still she married the Commons Speaker Charles Manners Sutton, so ending her days (in 1845) as Viscountess Canterbury.[12] Stewart died at the soon to be sold Killymoon in early October 1850. By his will he left the rest of his Tyrone estates to his unmarried sister Mary Eleanor and thereafter to the family of his other sister Louisa, wife of Henry John Clements† of Ashfield Lodge, county Cavan.[13]

[1] Hist. Irish Parl. vi. 339-42, 354; HP Commons, 1790-1820, v. 273-4, 296. [2] Belfast News Letter, 17, 28 Mar. 1820. [3] In what follows, Whig votes are attributed to this Member regardless of the spelling of his surname in the division lists. [4] The Times, 16 Mar. 1821. [5] Belfast News Letter, 25 Sept. 1825; Impartial Reporter, 23 Feb. 1826. [6] PRO NI, Leslie mss MIC606/3/J/14/73,4; Belfast Commercial Chron. 12, 24 June 1826. [7] Impartial Reporter, 30 Nov., 7 Dec. 1826. [8] Add. 40392, f. 5; The Times, 6 Mar. 1827. [9] Impartial Reporter, 5 Mar. 1829. [10] Add. 43234, ff. 80, 82; PRO NI, Stewart of Killymoon mss D3167/2/310, 311; PRO NI, Richardson mss D2002/C/26/16; Belfast News Letter, 9 Apr., 23 July 1830. [11] Stewart of Killymoon mss 2/335. [12] Greville Mems. iii. 178. [13] Tyrone Constitution, 11 Oct. 1850; Gent. Mag. (1850), ii. 565; PRO NI D21/1.

S.M.F.

STEWART see also **SHAW STEWART**

STEWART MACKENZIE, James Alexander (1784–1843), of Brahan Castle, nr. Dingwall, Ross.

Ross-shire	1831–1832
Ross and Cromarty	1832–Mar. 1837

b. 23 Sept. 1784, 2nd but 1st surv. s. of Hon. Keith Stewart† (d. 1795) of Glasserton, Wigtown and Georgiana Isabella, da. of Simha D'Aguilar. educ. Charterhouse 1795-1802; Trinity Coll. Camb. 1802. m. 21 May 1817, Hon. Mary Elizabeth Frederica Mackenzie, da. and h. of Francis Humberston Mackenzie†, 1st Lord Seaforth, wid. of V.-Adm. Sir Samuel Hood†, 1st bt., 3s. (1 d.v.p.) 3da. Took additional name of Mackenzie on marriage; suc. bro. Keith Stewart to Glasserton 1795. d. 24 Sept. 1843.

Commr. bd. of control Dec. 1832-Dec. 1834, jt.-sec. Apr.-Dec. 1834; PC 5 Apr. 1837; gov. Ceylon 1837-40; ld. high commr. Ionian Islands 1840-3.

Provost, Dingwall.

Stewart Mackenzie's father, a naval officer, had received the Wigtownshire estate of Glasserton from his father, the 6th earl of Galloway, in 1763, and was Member for the county from 1768 to 1784, when, as a staunch Pittite, he received the sinecure place of receiver-general of the land tax in Scotland. He died in March 1795 and was followed to the grave three months later by his eldest son Keith Stewart, a midshipman on the Queen Charlotte, who 'fell into the sea and was drowned' while watching the ship's carpenter repairing damage sustained in the action off Port L'Orient.[1] Thus Stewart Mackenzie (whose mother, a naturalized Sephardic Jewess, married in 1797 Richard Fitzgerald of the Life Guards, who was killed at Waterloo) became the owner of Glasserton at the age of ten. He was evidently taken under the care of his cantankerous uncle, the 7th earl of Galloway, with whose youngest son James Henry Keith Stewart* he was educated in England. He espoused Whig politics and was elected to Brooks's on 3 June 1816. A year later he married Lady Hood, the widowed daughter and heiress of the 1st Lord Seaforth, chief of the Mackenzie clan (*d.* 1815). She, who had gypsy looks and 'an almost lawless spirit of adventure', and beguiled Sir Walter Scott with her 'warm heart and lively fancy', brought him an additional name and the extensive Seaforth estates in Ross-shire, centred around Brahan Castle, near Dingwall, but including also the Isle of Lewis in the Outer Hebrides.[2] Stewart Mackenzie sold Glasserton in about 1819, but retained the eastern Ayrshire property of Muirkirk, which contained lucrative coal and mineral deposits, exploited on lease by the Muirkirk Iron Company.[3] At the general election of 1818 he and his wife supported the unsuccessful candidature for Ross-shire of Alexander Fraser of Inchcoulter, one of a group of West India merchants with estates in the county, and they subsequently sought to enhance their interest.[4] When the county's leading lairds held a meeting to adopt a loyal address to the regent in the wake of the Peterloo incident, 12 Nov. 1819, Stewart Mackenzie, who declared himself to be 'neither an alarmist nor a radical reformer', sent the convener an open letter denouncing it as inexpedient, calling for inquiry into the massacre and asserting that the existing laws were adequate to curb and punish seditious 'blasphemies', which he deplored.[5] At the general election four months later he again backed Fraser, but the Liverpool ministry, previously neutral, now backed the sitting Member, Thomas Mackenzie of Applecross, despite Stewart Mackenzie's direct appeal to their Scottish political manager, the 2nd Lord Melville. Fraser was obliged to withdraw.[6]

At a county meeting, 1 May 1820, Stewart Mackenzie moved resolutions for an extension of the bounties granted to Scottish fisheries.[7] He witnessed the trial of Queen Caroline in the Lords in August 1820 and took no part in the Ross-shire meeting to express loyalty to the king, 4 Jan. 1821.[8] A man who hated the 'cant' of Methodism, he visited Lewis in September 1822 and found the house at Seaforth Lodge, near Stornaway, in a decrepit state. He expressed regret for the sale of Glasserton and experienced a passing temptation to get rid of the bankrupt Seaforth estates, but concluded that he was bound to meet his obligations towards the tenantry and bring 'the word of God' into their lives. He implemented a programme of retrenchment at Brahan and kept Lewis, where in August 1825 he hosted a Stornoway celebration of the third anniversary of George IV's visit to Scotland. But his purchase for £16,000 of the

far western property of Torriden earned him a rebuke from his wife.[9] By June 1824 he had decided to stand at the next opportunity for Ross-shire, where Sir James Wemyss Mackenzie of Scatwell had replaced the dead Applecross in 1822; but he was on good personal terms with Scatwell, and made no move against him at the general election of 1826.[10] Nor did he in 1830, when he issued an address explaining that he had planned to stand if Scatwell retired, but declining to disturb the peace.[11] In December 1830, with the Whigs in power under Lord Grey, he sought the advice of his friends Lord Lansdowne and James Abercromby* as to whether he should declare himself as a candidate for the next vacancy. His pretensions were considered by Lord Grey, Sir James Graham*, the first lord of the admiralty, and the patronage secretary Edward Ellice*, who assured him of 'any disposition you can desire in ... [London] to promote your views', but suggested that open endorsement by the treasury might not go down well with the freeholders of Ross-shire. Stewart Mackenzie accordingly kept quiet for the time being.[12] At the county meeting at Dingwall, 24 Dec. 1830, he moved a resolution for reform of the Scottish representative system and was named as chairman of the committee set up to promote the cause. In March 1831 he convened a Dingwall meeting to express support for the ministry's reform scheme and wrote open letters indicating his personal approval of it. At an Edinburgh meeting, 9 Mar., he seconded the motion for an address to the king in support of reform and, claiming always to have been a reformer, praised William IV and lord chancellor Brougham. He argued that the plan was not 'revolutionary' but was rather 'a restitution' of the constitution, and disputed Peel's recent assertion that it involved 'confiscation', which the aristocratic Whigs would never sanction. He did not attend the Ross-shire meeting at Tain, 24 Mar., but sent a letter asking for its adjournment until 5 Apr., when a meeting organized by the Dingwall reform committee was to be held. This was rejected by the anti-reformers, who attacked the committee and carried a resolution condemning the reform scheme as 'too sweeping'. On 25 Mar. Stewart Mackenzie made known his intention of standing for the county at the next election, which prompted Scatwell to announce his retirement and Colin Mackenzie of Kilcoy to offer as a moderate reformer. At the meeting on 5 Apr. Stewart Mackenzie's resolution that the reform plan was 'wise and practicable', though open to amendment, was rejected in favour of one condemning it.[13] At the general election precipitated by the defeat of the English reform bill, Stewart Mackenzie and Kilcoy were joined in the field by another reformer, Sir

Francis Alexander Mackenzie of Gairloch. Stewart Mackenzie's chances were not at first rated very highly, but he rejected an attempt to entice him to contest the venal Anstruther Burghs.[14] He was distracted by an appeal for support from Sir Andrew Agnew, the sitting Member for Wigtownshire, who had voted for the second reading of the English reform bill but expressed strong reservations about borough disfranchisement. After corresponding with him and the lord advocate, Francis Jeffrey*, Stewart Mackenzie decided to give him the benefit of the doubt and, despite fatigue and raging toothache, he interrupted his own campaign to go to Wigtown, chair the election meeting and secure Agnew's return with his casting vote.[15] At his own election nine days later some collusion with the friends of Gairloch, who withdrew, enabled him to beat Kilcoy by seven votes. Returning thanks, he insisted that 'a timely and effectual reform' was essential, but admitted the force of some of the detailed objections levelled against the Scottish measure by Hugh Rose Ross of Cromarty and, acknowledging that he was at odds with a number of his constituents on the issue, promised to try to improve the bill without endangering its principle. In a written reply to a congratulatory address from Dingwall, where he was fêted, he repeated this declaration, agreed to support economy and tax cuts, while stressing the need to uphold public credit, and said he would 'endeavour to diffuse universally that first of blessings, a religious education, and knowledge among all ranks of the people'.[16] Ellice asked him to attend Parliament no later than 21 June 1831, while Sir James Miller Riddell of Ardnamurchan, Argyllshire, wrote to his wife:

> Stewart's parliamentary career begins at a very momentous period ... Bid him to beware! Tell him to steer clear of faction. I admonish him as a sincere friend thoroughly to sift that portentous bill ... and not to be led into an approbation of all its parts by the clamours of the mob.[17]

Repudiating Gairloch's subsequent reproach that he had not acted quite honestly, Stewart Mackenzie insisted that his supposed 'information as to my being opposed to reform at any time is quite erroneous. It is true I object to universal suffrage and ballot, but a reformer I have ever been'.[18]

He voted for the second reading of the reintroduced English reform bill, 6 July, and was a general but silent supporter of its details, though he was in the minority for the disfranchisement of Saltash, 26 July 1831, when ministers did not press the issue. He voted for the third reading, 19 Sept., and passage of the measure, 21 Sept. He divided against censuring the Irish administration for interfering in the Dublin election, 23 Aug. On 1 Sept. he secured production of a copy of the report on public charities. Next day he wrote to his wife that he hoped to improve the condition of their Lewis tenantry 'and not squander the produce of their industry on the expensive luxuries and debaucheries of a distant capital'.[19] He was named to the select committee on malt drawback, 5 Sept. He voted for the second reading of the Scottish reform bill, 23 Sept., and on the 28th dissented from the prayer of a Ross-shire petition objecting to its proposed merger with Cromartyshire, which he considered to be eminently sensible, and argued that the bill would 'confer the most essential benefits upon Scotland'. He was in the ministerial majority on the motion of confidence, 10 Oct. He was shocked by the reform riots in Derby and Nottingham, but thought the country was on the whole tranquil. He chaired a Ross-shire meeting to consider precautions against the cholera, which worried him greatly, 15 Nov. 1831.[20]

Stewart Mackenzie relished Macaulay's bravura speech of 16 Dec. 1831 in support of the second reading of the revised English reform bill, for which he duly voted the following day. In a desperate bid to solve his worsening dental problems, he evidently had some of his teeth extracted and false ones made; it did little good, and he was still being tortured over a year later.[21] He spent Christmas at Hastings with his two young sons Keith and George, who were at school at Cheam. He left his name at Brighton Pavilion on 6 Jan. 1832, when he dismissed stories that the king was willing to create 60 peers to carry reform. Before Parliament reconvened he was vexed by 11-year-old Keith's nail-biting habit (he had at least stopped bed-wetting) and trouble with his ears, one of which yielded up a coffee bean to medical examination. He pined for his wife, but was cheered on the eve of the session by her affectionate letters.[22] He voted to go into committee on the reform bill, 20 Jan., was again a steady supporter of its details, and divided for the third reading, 22 Mar. He was absent from the division on the Russian-Dutch loan, 26 Jan., but voted with ministers on it in July. He was in their majorities on relations with Portugal, 9 Feb., and against the production of information on military punishments, 16 Feb. He was named to the select committee on the East India Company, 27 Jan., and chaired some of its sittings.[23] He argued that the malt drawback bill would encourage illicit distillation in Scotland and diminish the revenue, 17 Feb., 31 Mar.; he was a teller for an unsuccessful wrecking amendment, 2 Apr. He was appointed to the select committee on the silk trade, 5 Mar., and on 7 Apr., defending its decision not to issue a report that session, claimed to have sat 'patiently and pretty assiduously' on it for almost four months: he doubted the effectiveness of legislative interference to relieve distress. He presented and endorsed petitions from Glasgow flax-spinners and Kirkcaldy linen manufacturers against the 'ill judged' bill to restrict children's factory hours, 7 Mar., and on the 16th contended that it would handicap British industry. That day he reluctantly paired on the ministerial side for continuance of the existing sugar duties, informing his wife that 'I never gave a vote with more pain'.[24] He divided for the address asking the king to appoint only ministers who would carry reform unimpaired, 10 May. On 23 May he presented a Ross-shire petition commending the appointment of a Lords select committee on West Indian slavery and hoping for a fair settlement of the problem. He voted for the second reading of the Irish reform bill, 25 May. On the Scottish measure, he voted against Conservative amendments to increase the county representation, 1 June, and rescind the dismemberment of Perthshire, 15 June, when he again defended the annexation of Cromartyshire to Ross-shire. He voted against Baring's bill to exclude insolvent debtors from Parliament, 6 June, and to make coroners' inquests open, 20 June 1832.

At the general election in December 1832, when he replaced Macaulay at the board of control, Stewart Mackenzie easily defeated a Conservative for the Ross and Cromarty seat. He won a narrower victory in 1835, after privately trying to convince a young kinsman who believed he was '*not desirous* to preserve the great institutions of this country', that to 'reform, repair and amend what is amiss and with caution to remove defects when glaring ... is the duty of every well wisher to ... [their] continuance'.[25] He left the Commons in March 1837 to become governor of Ceylon. He transferred in December 1840 to the Ionian Islands, where he served for two years. He died at Southampton in September 1843. By his will, dated 18 May 1843, he left all his property to his wife.[26] He was succeeded by his elder son Keith William (1819-81), whose son and heir James Alexander Francis Humberstone Mackenzie (1847-1923) was created Baron Seaforth in 1921 but died without issue.

[1] *HP Commons, 1754-1790*, iii. 483; *Gent. Mag* (1795), ii. 615. [2] *Macaulay Letters*, ii. 338; *Scott Jnl.* 561; *Ordnance Gazetteer of Scotland* (1895), iv. 508; Lord Teignmouth, *Reminiscences*, i. 341. [3] NAS GD46/1/24; 2/8, 23. [4] *HP Commons, 1790-1820*, ii. 574-5; NAS GD46/4/122. [5] *Inverness Courier*, 18 Nov. 1819. [6] NLS mss 1054, f. 174; NAS GD46/4/124/2, 5, 8-10, 12-15; GD51/5/749/1, p. 170; *Inverness Courier*, 16, 23 Mar. 1820. [7] *Inverness Courier*, 25 May 1820. [8] NAS GD46/15/23/8; *Inverness Courier*, 11 Jan. 1821. [9] NAS GD46/15/23/8; 15/25/7; 15/29/6, 13; 15/32/13, 17; *Inverness Courier*, 31 Aug. 1825. [10] Add. 39193, ff. 73, 86; NAS GD46/15/29/6, 13; *Inverness Courier*, 5 July 1826. [11] *Inverness Courier*, 28 July 1830. [12] NAS GD46/4/129/1-3. [13] *Inverness Courier*, 26 Dec. 1830, 16, 23, 30 Mar., 13 Apr. 1831. [14] Ibid. 4 May 1831; NAS GD46/4/132/18, 21-23. [15] NAS GD46/4/130/1, 2; 4/132/25, 26, 33; 4/135/3. [16] *Inverness Courier*, 25 May, 1 June 1831; NAS GD46/4/133/1, 4; 15/38/14. [17] NAS GD46/4/131/4; 4/133/6. [18] NAS GD46/4/133/8, 13. [19] NAS GD46/15/39/15. [20] NAS GD46/15/40/10, 15; *Inverness Courier*, 23 Nov. 1831. [21] NAS GD46/15/41/20, 25; 15/46/14; 15/52/1. [22] NAS GD46/15/42/2, 21, 40, 43, 50, 57. [23] *Macaulay Letters*, ii. 146. [24] NAS GD46/15/44/8. [25] Add. 39193, f. 114. [26] PROB 8/237; 11/1991/42.

D.R.F.

STOPFORD, James Thomas, Visct. Stopford (1794-1858).

CO. WEXFORD   1820-1830

b. 27 Mar. 1794, 3rd but 1st surv. s. of James George Stopford[†], 3rd earl of Courtown [I] and 2nd Bar. Saltersford [GB], and Lady Mary Montagu Scott, da. of Henry, 3rd duke of Buccleuch [S]. *educ.* privately; Christ Church, Oxf. 1812. *m.* (1) 4 July 1822, his cos. Lady Charlotte Albinia Montagu Scott (*d.* 29 Feb. 1828), da. of Charles, 4th duke of Buccleuch [S], 3s. (1 *d.v.p.*); (2) 29 Oct. 1850, Dora, da. of Edward Pennefather, 3s. *styled* Visct. Stopford 1810-35. *suc.* fa. as 4th earl of Courtown [I] and 3rd Bar. Saltersford [GB] 15 June 1835. *d.* 20 Nov. 1858.

Sheriff, co. Wexford 1833-4, custos rot. 1845-*d.*

Stopford, whose grandfather and father, a Pittite Member of Parliament, 1790-1802 and 1803-10, were courtiers, was educated by John Giffard Ward (dean of Lincoln, 1845-60), who 'came to be my tutor when I was eleven years old and remained with me in that capacity until I left Christ Church'.[1] In 1818, when his father was captain of the gentleman pensioners, he stood unsuccessfully for county Wexford on the combined interest of his family, who were 'powerful', but whose Protestant principles were 'detested', and that of Lord Mountnorris, who blamed him for the defeat of his pro-Catholic coalition partner Lord Valentia*. At the 1820 general election he rejected the terms of another coalition and offered again with the apparent backing of the Liverpool ministry, citing his hostility to leaving the representation in 'the hands of one or two individuals' and his residence in the county. At the last minute Valentia withdrew and he was returned unopposed.[2] A poor attender, who is not known to have spoken in debate, when present he generally supported government, who listed him as seeking a clerkship for a Mr. Devereaux and a position on the assessors list for a Mr. Bates.[3] He voted against economies in revenue collection, 4 July 1820, and in support of ministers on the Queen Caroline affair, 6 Feb., and the revenue, 6 Mar. 1821. He divided against Catholic relief, 28 Feb. 1821,

30 Apr. 1822, 1 Mar., 21 Apr., 10 May 1825. He voted against government for repeal of the additional malt duty, 21 Mar., but reversed the vote on 3 Apr. 1821. He divided against parliamentary reform, 9 May, for the forgery punishment mitigation bill, 23 May, 4 June, and against an opposition motion for economy and retrenchment, 27 June 1821. He voted against condemning the trial of the Methodist missionary John Smith for inciting slave riots in Demerara, 11 June 1824. On 27 Sept. 1824 a county Wexford informant warned him that his 'political opponents' were 'particularly active' and, noting a report in that month's *Patriot* that his Catholic tenantry would not support him at the next election, complained of his unnecessarily 'explicit' letter to an opponent which would serve as a 'knock-him-down argument in the hands of your enemies'. Stopford replied:

> You may rest assured that though I oppose the Roman Catholic claims in Parliament, it is from no enmity towards them. On the contrary, I never have or ever will make the smallest distinction between those of different persuasions in this country. With regard to what you say about a counter paragraph, I can have no objection to it, as I think such a testimony coming from a Roman Catholic friend would be of great service to me.[4]

That year he was listed as one of the 'committee of the Grand Orange Lodge'.[5] He divided for the Irish insurrection bill, 14 June 1824, and for suppression of the Catholic Association, 15, 25 Feb. 1825.

On 24 Feb. 1826 he declared his intention of offering again for Wexford on the 'independent interest alone'.[6] His canvass showed clear support from Protestants and opposition from Catholics, one of whom advised him that his stance on relief formed 'the only bar to what your known character as a landlord and resident ... entitles you'.[7] On the hustings he repeated that he was opposed to relief 'solely on principle' and had 'no enmity to Catholics'. His controversial alliance with the pro-Catholic sitting Member forced another pro-Catholic candidate to withdraw and he was returned unopposed.[8] He signed the petition of Irish landed proprietors against Catholic claims in February 1827 and voted thus, 6 Mar. 1827, 12 May 1828.[9] He was granted three weeks' leave on urgent private business, 13 Mar. 1827. On 3 Feb. 1828 his father, who had left the household the previous year on the formation of the Canning ministry, informed Peel, home secretary in the new Wellington ministry, that Stopford was in Rome and could not attend Parliament at present as his wife was too ill to travel; she died there later that month.[10] Stopford chaired the first meeting of the Newtownbarry Brunswick Club, 16 Nov. 1828, and

was secretary to the Gorey Brunswick Club presided over by his father, which drew up a declaration promising 'to resist all attempts to disorganize society ... should it be necessary at the expense of our lives', 5 Jan. 1829. The following month Planta, the patronage secretary, correctly predicted that he would be 'absent' from the divisions on Catholic emancipation. (On 24 Jan. his father, in an apparent volte face, had offered Wellington his proxy in the hope that some measure would be taken to grant emancipation.)[11] Stopford voted against allowing Daniel O'Connell to take his seat unhindered, 18 May 1829. He divided against the transfer of East Retford's seats to Birmingham, 11 Feb., and the enfranchisement of Birmingham, Leeds and Manchester, 23 Feb. 1830. He voted against Jewish emancipation, 5 Apr. He was granted a month's leave on account of ill health, 28 Apr., and divided against the Galway franchise bill, 25 May 1830.

At the 1830 dissolution Stopford retired without explanation. He was a 'staunch supporter' of the anti-reformer Valentia, his erstwhile opponent, at the 1831 general election, when he complained that the Grey ministry, which had come to power 'pledged to reduction of taxation, economy and reform', had

> augmented the army and ordnance estimates, thereby increasing the burdens of the people ... [and] brought forward a budget which was the laughing stock of the country ... Finding they were becoming unpopular in the country and abused by their own friends, they then brought forward this wild and revolutionary scheme of reform.

Contending that if the bill passed the 'lowest class' would be 'entirely excluded from the representation', he warned, 'Look at what has happened in France, look at the effect of a revolution brought about by the folly of an obstinate king and wicked ministers'.[12] In June 1834 he helped fund the abortive attempt of his brother Colonel Edward Stopford to come forward as a Conservative for the county.[13] Next year he succeeded to his father's peerage and estates.

During the Bedchamber crisis of 1839 Stopford informed Peel that 'it would not be unreasonable ... if I, who have always given my warm support in both Houses to the Conservative party, wish to follow the example of my father ... but the fact is that ... life about a Court ... would entail a longer residence in London than would suit my health', and recommended his brother.[14] On the formation of Peel's ministry in 1841 he declined an offer of a lordship-in-waiting, saying his income was 'too small'.[15] Thereafter he regularly solicited government patronage, especially on behalf of his brother-in-law, the Rev. Abel John Ram.[16] In

1842 he voiced his 'most decided objections' to Peel's plan of Irish education and recommended a subsidy to safeguard the 'schools of the *established church*'.[17] He died at his seat of Courtown House in November 1858 and was succeeded in the peerage by his elder son James George Stopford (1823-1914).[18]

[1] Add. 40426, f. 383; 40575, f. 384. [2] *Dublin Evening Post*, 11, 21 Mar. 1820; Add. 38283, f. 241; TCD, Courtown mss P/33/14/1. [3] *Black Bk.* (1823), 195; *Session of Parl. 1825*, p. 486. [4] Courtown mss 14/11, 12, 18. [5] PRO NI, Leslie mss MIC 606/3/J/21/4. [6] Courtown mss 14/79. [7] Ibid. 14/124. [8] *Wexford Evening Post*, 16, 20 June; *Dublin Evening Post*, 20 June 1826. [9] Add. 40392, f. 5. [10] Add. 40395, f. 203. [11] Wellington mss WP1/991/8. [12] Courtown mss 14/136. [13] Ibid. 14/136a. [14] Add. 40426, f. 383. [15] Add. 40487, ff. 394-5. [16] Add. 40489, f. 147; 40523, ff. 292-4; 40541, f. 281; 40549, ff. 94-97; 40558, f. 447; 40572, ff. 235, 238, 240; 40575, ff. 384-6. [17] Add. 40500, f. 249. [18] *Gent. Mag.* (1859), i. 101; *The Times*, 23 Nov.; *Dublin Evening Post*, 23 Nov. 1858.

P.J.S.

STORMONT, Visct. *see* **MURRAY**, **William David**

STRICKLAND, **George** (1782–1874), of Hildenley and Boynton, Yorks. and Parliament Street, Mdx.

YORKSHIRE	1831–1832
YORKSHIRE (WEST RIDING)	1832–1841
PRESTON	1841–1857

b. 26 Nov. 1782, 2nd but 1st surv. s. of Sir William Strickland, 6th bt., of Boynton and Henrietta, da. and coh. of Nathaniel Cholmley† of Whitby Abbey and Howsham. *educ.* L. Inn 1803, called 1810. *m.* (1) 1 Mar. 1818, Mary (*d.* 10 Jan. 1865), da. and h. of Rev. Charles Constable of Wassand, 3s. (1 *d.v.p.*) 1 da.; (2) 25 Mar. 1867, Jane, da. of Thomas Leavens of Norton, *s.p. suc.* fa. as 7th bt. 1834; to estates of maternal grandfa. and took name of Cholmley by royal lic. 17 Mar. 1865. *d.* 23 Dec. 1874.

Strickland, though a hypochondriac of a sickly disposition, believed he was destined to live a long life since he was 'obliged to be careful'. 'I am never a very strong person', he told his confidant James Brougham*, 'and never could learn to eat and drink like you and the duke of York'.[1] His family were supposedly a cadet branch of the Stricklands of Sizergh, Westmorland. William Strickland, Member for Scarborough, 1558-86, purchased Boynton after returning from voyages of discovery in the New World during his youth. His grandson, also William, was created a baronet in 1641, and represented Hedon and the East Riding, and all the successive baronets down to the fifth, Sir George, this Member's grandfather, sat in the House. Strickland's finances were tight during

his early adult life and led to frequent disputes with his father-in-law, the Rev. Charles Constable, over his marriage settlement, which were exacerbated by his wife's long term 'nervous' illness. Matters came to a head in 1828 when, as he explained to Brougham, his wife, who had been suffering 'strange nervous attacks since she was a girl', became delirious and plunged her hand into the fire, seriously burning herself. Strickland packed her off to Constable to convalesce and determined that she should never again be left alone with any of their children until she was cured, nor would he live with her until then. They were estranged for the next 37 years. Charged by Constable with 'unkindness', he told Brougham, 'as to old Constable, I care nothing about him, and thanks to my resolute plans of economy ... I feel very independent of his cursed money'.[2]

In public life Strickland was principled and an entertaining public speaker, but not without his critics. 'With all respect to so great a reformer and patriot', Robert Price* informed Lord Milton*, 15 Dec. 1830, 'I have always thought ... Strickland to be a disagreeable personage'.[3] His political activism had been initiated, he informed the House, 23 Feb. 1832, by Peterloo. He signed the requisition for the Yorkshire county meeting to discuss the incident, at which he spoke, 14 Oct. 1819, alleging that the local Tories were insincere in their support for inquiry.[4] At the 1820 general election he seconded the nomination of the Whig Milton.[5] Strickland's father entrusted him to communicate his opinion to Milton on the proposed transfer of Grampound's seats to Yorkshire, 31 May, while Earl Fitzwilliam, Milton's father, asked his son to canvass the opinion of 'trusted people', including Strickland, on the propriety of holding a county meeting in support of Queen Caroline, 9 Nov. 1820.[6] Seconding a proposal for a pro-reform petition at a county meeting, 22 Jan. 1823, Strickland argued that it was necessary to restore the confidence between the people and government and scoffed at the discussion about what reform ought to consist of:

> This great cause is not a new one, it has agitated men's minds for nearly a century, and we are now to be asked, what is meant by the term parliamentary reform? Its meaning is written in the distress of the country.[7]

That September he was appointed to a committee to investigate the requirements for an extension to York Castle gaol and wrote an open letter to Henry Brougham* outlining his opposition to the demolition of Clifford's Tower to enable an enlargement to take place. When the proposals were finally made they included no alteration to the tower, and the extension that was begun in March 1826 incorporated this into its plans.[8] On 7 Feb. 1825 Strickland wrote to James Brougham in support of his brother's speech on Catholic emancipation at the opening of the session, observing, somewhat resignedly, that he was leading 'an idle, farming, fishing, hunting, kind of life'.[9] During the rumours of dissolution that autumn, Milton received intelligence that Lord Morpeth*, the Whigs' preferred candidate for Yorkshire at the next general election, would not receive the financial backing of his relation, the 6th duke of Devonshire. On 18 Dec. Milton informed Lord Althorp* that 'if this is really to be the case, it will be far better to withdraw him and press forward Strickland'.[10] Milton joined Strickland and other leading Yorkshire Whigs at Wheatley, the home of Sir William Cooke, the following week to discuss the situation, where it was decided to press ahead with a requisition to Morpeth, which Strickland unsuccessfully urged him to accept, 25 Dec. 1825.[11] Thereafter Strickland was repeatedly spoken of as a candidate, but in the event did not come forward.[12] Instead he chaired the Whig committee at the 1826 general election and seconded Milton at the nomination, when he denounced the corn laws as 'injurious to the manufacturing part of the country' and the game laws as a 'remnant of feudal tyranny', and argued in favour of Catholic emancipation.[13] That December, when he was suffering from a 'violent inflammation upon the lungs', he predicted to James Brougham that the war in Portugal would result in Britain keeping troops there 'till France withdraws hers from Spain' and hoped that Henry Brougham, who had been 'long enough in opposition', would 'shake off old Hume and his Greek loan, and join the Canning part of administration'. At Brougham's request he took a £100 share in the new London University, but thought it money 'thrown away'.[14]

Anticipating the formation of a Canning ministry following Lord Liverpool's incapacity, Strickland expressed a desire to visit London in the spring of 1827 to 'see how the Whigs look', having 'never expected' to see them 'in office again'.[15] In December 1827 he published a *Discourse on the Poor Laws of England and Scotland, on the state of the Poor in Ireland and on Emigration*, addressed to Lord Landsdowne, home secretary in the short-lived Goderich ministry, in which he asserted that the poor laws encouraged population growth, increased the poor rates, and thereby augmented 'the burthens of the landowners', while 'the advance of manufactures, and the success of mercantile speculation, all tend to the same result; a predominating influence of the mercantile classes over the landed proprietors', which he feared would

lead to a collapse of the aristocracy. To prevent such social calamity he recommended repealing much of the existing poor laws, so that they 'expressly provided alone for the lame, impotent, old, blind, and such others, being poor and not able to work', and called for the establishment of a relief system and public education in Ireland. He reacted to reports that Henry Brougham was to be made master of the rolls by telling James that it had 'always appeared to me a very hard case that a man ... should be excluded from high judicial situations on account of party politics'. He continued:

> He ought to be chancellor, if that cannot be, then he ought not to refuse the rolls. He is the only person who could effect any reforms in the state of the law ... If he waits for a pure Whig administration, he must die labouring in an inferior situation ... The Tories who are to govern the country must be very unlike the old stamp of Tories. They must be reformers, and economists of public money, and very like Whigs, similar except in name.[16]

He advised Brougham that the establishment of Brunswick Clubs in Yorkshire had attained only 'partial success', 4 Nov. 1828.[17] As Constable refused to pay him the agreed amounts under his marriage settlement, and even failed sometimes to pay anything for short periods, Strickland's income by now was only £900 per annum.[18] He had little desire to re-establish his home life with his wife as he feared 'incessant interference' from his in-laws. He confided to Brougham, 7 Apr. 1829, that Constable's 'only chance of getting Mary and myself together is to act honourably, and that he will not do'. Brougham, one of the trustees of the settlement, did his best for his friend, but was able to bring him little satisfaction. Strickland's father, too, tried to mediate, but to no avail. When Strickland wished to send his children to school, he could not afford the fees. Constable had promised to pay, but only on condition that Strickland's second son lived at Wassand with him and his other children spent their holidays there. Strickland refused the conditions. Constable threatened to take the matter to the courts in March 1830 and Strickland sought the advice of Henry Brougham, Daniel Sykes, a lawyer and Whig Member for Hull, and Althorp. His wife's dementia had not improved and she had sent him a series of letters in which she conceded on the one hand that he had always treated her with 'kindness and compassion', but on the other likened him to 'the demonical possession described in the New Testament'. He sought a loan from his father in June 1830, but was refused, whereupon he contemplated emigrating.[19]

In the aftermath of the Wellington ministry's concession of Catholic emancipation Strickland told James Brougham, 4 July 1829, that 'if Wellington imitates Pitt and continues sole minister of England it will shorten his life'. However, he thought the Tories too powerful to allow any power or patronage to the Whigs, whose only chance was that the Tories 'render themselves so contemptible that measures of reform and retrenchment may be carried against them'. He concluded that Wellington was frustrated because 'whatever he may have done with Huskisson, he cannot have Henry [Brougham] or Hume cashiered, or tied up and flogged, whenever he likes'.[20] In November 1829 he asked James Brougham if anything could be done 'with [James] Abercromby* or through some other means' to assist Morpeth, whose relations had again refused to pledge financial support for his candidacy for Yorkshire at a future election.[21] Following the confirmation of Milton's retirement from Yorkshire in May 1830, Strickland participated in meetings to adopt Morpeth as the Whigs' first candidate, but was initially hostile to suggestions that Henry Brougham might start as their second, as 'not being a Yorkshire man would not do, and ... such an attempt would create jealousies'.[22] At a full meeting of the county's Whigs in York in July, however, he was instrumental in persuading the country gentlemen of the East and North Ridings to join the commercial men of the West Riding in supporting Brougham, in order to preserve unanimity.[23] He served on both of the ensuing election committees and accompanied Brougham on his early canvass of the West Riding, from where Brougham reported to Lord Holland, 31 July:

> I assure you the difficulty is to keep them from setting up Strickland with me. He was actually proposed two or three times on our progress, and not by mobs ... It was necessary to prevent this as it would have driven Morpeth to the wall.[24]

Following Brougham's acceptance of a peerage and the woolsack in the new Grey administration, Strickland backed Sykes for the vacancy, but reluctantly accepted the candidacy of Sir John Johnstone. At a meeting of the Whigs, 2 Dec., he regretted that 'the commercial interests of this country are not adequately represented; the Members whom we return being all closely connected with the highest branches of the aristocracy and church' and hoped that Johnstone would support a thorough reform bill, which gave no compensation to borough proprietors, and the secret ballot, without which it was 'quite impossible that anything like freedom of election can exist'.[25] When the sheriff asked if there were any other candidates at the nomination, 7 Dec. 1830, Strickland stepped forward, saying that he had read reports of Johnstone's speeches before the Leeds Cloth Halls which had 'rendered it impossible' for him to continue to support him, as he was not a thorough reformer and had not made up his mind on the ballot. He then proposed Sykes, prompting a bitter debate, but Sykes refused to stand, whereupon Strickland, responding to the clamour of the crowd, said he would be willing to do so if nominated. As none of the Whigs on the hustings would perform the task, two freeholders obliged. Strickland won the show of hands and Johnstone demanded a poll. Strickland then asked the crowd how the ballot could be considered 'unEnglish', as Johnstone had alleged, when it was used for the election of a registrar in the West Riding, but Edward Baines, editor of the *Leeds Mercury*, pointed out that this was not the case, as he often published the final list of voters and their votes. As no preparations for a poll had been made, the contest was adjourned until the following day. Strickland told Lord Brougham, 12 Dec., that 'Baines and the Leeds party and Dan Sykes, almost on their knees, begged me to retire'.[26] He did so after the poll had only been open for a few hours, with the votes at 361 to Johnstone against Strickland's 104. At the declaration Strickland said that he had received many promises of support, especially from the West Riding, and would have kept the poll open longer if he could have been sure of success. He emphasized to Brougham that he had not retired at the behest of the Leeds delegation, but because 'there was no time for anything'. Brougham had offered him £1,000 towards his expenses and Strickland hoped to be able to call on it again at a future election. Indeed, he thought his giving up had been a 'great mistake', despite the fact that his father had taken 'the part of the squires, in fury' and had had 'his doors ... shut against me'. In his parting address, 15 Dec., he denied that there had been any preconceived plan, claiming that he had acted purely in order to advance the cause of reform, and promised to come forward at the next opportunity.[27] Confiding to James Brougham that he felt 'ill used by some who ought to have been my friends', 22 Dec. 1830, he complained that he had done more than anyone to return Morpeth, who 'now despises my advice and is doing the greatest of follies, having gone along with Sir John Johnstone [on] a canvassing tour of the West Riding', adding, 'be assured this is working well for myself and Sykes'.[28] On 27 Mar. 1831 the newly formed Leeds Association successfully requisitioned Strickland to stand at the next opportunity. In his address he promised to support an effective reform, economy, the abolition of slavery, the extinction of all monopolies and Hobhouse's proposed factory reform bill.[29]

At the 1831 general election he duly came forward as a reformer, telling the crowds at the hustings that the 'best judges of public virtue and senatorial talent' were not 'an old wall at Aldborough, a summer house at Gatton, or a mound at Old Sarum'. He was returned unopposed with three other Whigs.[30] An assiduous attender and keen contributor to debate, Strickland hardly let a day go by without making some comment on proceedings. In his maiden speech, 27 June 1831, he sympathized with O'Connell's criticism of the Irish yeomanry, which was 'not a good species of force', promised to support any motion O'Connell cared to bring forward to disband them and urged the creation of a police force for Ireland. He presented a petition from Hedon and Holderness calling for the two to be united to return two Members, 4 July. On 6 July he welcomed the reintroduced ministerial reform bill's abolition of nomination boroughs and extension of the franchise, denied Wetherell's charge that those pledged to support it were not free agents, insisting that he was at least as unshackled as Wetherell, who represented only 'a few decayed cottages', but expressed a fear that the division of counties would increase the influence of landed proprietors and create 'nomination counties' and regretted that some anomalies would remain, wishing that 'the bill could have gone a little further'. He voted for the second reading that day, against the adjournment, 12 July, and gave general support to its details, though he campaigned steadily for more Members to be given to Yorkshire and even contemplated moving an amendment to give the East Riding four, only to abandon it out of 'respect' for the conduct of ministers, 22 July. He welcomed Milton's suggestion that the boroughs in Schedule D ought to return two Members each rather than one, as it afforded a means of increasing the representation of Yorkshire, and denied that such a course would destroy the balance between commerce and agriculture, 4 Aug. He spoke and voted with government on the Dublin election controversy, 23 Aug., and was in the minority against issuing a writ for the Liverpool by-election, 5 Sept. That day he agreed with Thomas Houldsworth that it would be impossible to poll the West Riding in two days, and although he approved the principle of limiting the duration of elections, he thought an exception ought to be made in this case. Presenting a Manchester petition for weekly tenants paying £10 annual rent to be given the vote, 7 Sept., he observed that the petitioners' willingness to forego their request, if it should impede progress, was proof of working class support for the bill. When Wetherell

renewed his criticism of Members pledged to the bill, 15 Sept., Strickland took it as a personal attack and again sought to justify his stance. He concluded by saying that he thought 'no good can arise from these kind of personal observations', but they engaged in a few more exchanges. He voted for the reform bill's passage, 21 Sept., and for the second reading of the Scottish measure, 23 Sept. He presented a Halifax petition for election by ballot, wondering whether 'the division of counties and the admission of tenants at will to the right of voting will not render the establishment of this most important system absolutely necessary for the protection of the freedom of election', 26 Sept. He spoke and divided for Lord Ebrington's confidence notion, 10 Oct. At a Yorkshire county meeting to address the king in support of ministers two days later, he boasted that he had attended every debate and division on the reform bill with only 'one or two exceptions' when he was 'delayed by illness'.[31] Endorsing the ensuing petition, he declared that the bill 'would have a considerable effect in restoring the prosperity and tranquillity of this country', 7 Dec. 1831.

Strickland welcomed proposals for the resettlement of the poor, 28 June 1831. He thought a gradual reform was best and hoped a limited system could be introduced to Ireland, but he declined to support Sadler's proposals for the provision of poor relief there, 29 Aug., believing that 'no form of poor law will ever act well which ... attempts to give employment to the able bodied labourer'. He presented a Dewsbury petition in favour of the Leeds and Manchester railway bill and was appointed to the committee on it, 29 June. He disapproved of those Members who had not attended one of its sittings before they turned up on the last day to vote, and supported Morpeth's motion to consider a petition of appeal against the committee's decision, 21 July. He unsuccessfully moved for a committee of appeal, 25 July, and presented a petition of complaint, 28 July, but was forced to withdraw it when it was ruled out of order. He criticized John Campbell's general register bill, which would 'give rise to many inconveniences', 30 June, and campaigned against it at every stage thereafter, advocating local registers, similar to the one that already existed in Yorkshire, as a cheaper and better alternative, 20 Sept., demanding that Yorkshire be exempted from the bill's provisions as initially indicated, 4 Oct., 7 Dec., and presenting numerous petitions against it. Before voting for civil list pensions, 18 July, he said that in future such proposals ought to go before a committee. He objected to a critical petition from the West Riding magistracy and clergy against the Sale of Beer Act, 3 Aug., observing that the vast increase in public houses would soon fall when many of the ventures failed. He voted against the Irish union of parishes bill, 19 Aug. On the game bill, 2 Sept., he objected to the summary power to be vested in a single magistrate and the prospect of accidental trespassers being brought before them, and threatened to divide the House, but relented after denouncing the existing laws as 'a perfect mess of injustice and feudal barbarity'. He did not approve of intervening between master and employee but promised to support the truck bill as the working classes felt aggrieved with things as they stood, 12 Sept. He believed that Buckingham House was 'useless and extravagant', 28 Sept., but agreed to a grant of £100,000 as it would cost more to put it to other uses, 28 Sept. That day he welcomed Hobhouse's cotton factories apprentices bill as 'absolutely called for', but regretted that it was limited to such factories. After he and Morpeth came under attack in some of the Yorkshire newspapers for their 'indifference' to the bill, Strickland wrote to the *Mercury*, 14 Nov., to deny the criticisms of Richard Oastler that he had been absent during crucial stages. He welcomed the labourers' house rent bill, which sought to clarify the law and prevent rents being paid out of poor law funds, 29 Sept., and said he would be glad of any improvement to the Vestry Act, especially the abolition of close vestries, 30 Sept. He was appointed to the select committees on the West Indian colonies, 6 Oct., 15 Dec. Perhaps surprisingly, he backed Morpeth's defence of the *Leeds Mercury* and Baines after Hunt had accused the paper of libel, 14 Dec. 1831.

Strickland voted for the second reading of the revised reform bill, 17 Dec. 1831, again supported its details, and divided for the third reading, 22 Mar. 1832. He approved making York the polling town for the North Riding, said that Wakefield would be suitable for the West, but thought Beverley inconvenient for the East, 24 Jan. He reiterated his misgivings that the proposed division of counties would make some of them nomination seats, but argued that it would 'not be worth while to the minister of the day to make a bargain with a person who can return one or two Members', 27 Jan. He presented a petition from the residents of Ripon praying that the borough be extended to encompass Boroughbridge and some other townships, to prevent it remaining a close borough of Miss Lawrence, 6 Feb. He supported Morpeth's call for Huddersfield to be extended to include the parish to prevent it coming under the control of Sir John Ramsden, who owned almost all the town, 5 Mar., 8 June. On 9 Mar. he asked why Doncaster had been omitted from the representation and again charged ministers with underrepresenting Yorkshire. He voted for the address calling on

the king to appoint only ministers who would carry the reform bill unimpaired, 10 May, and testified to the frustration of his constituents, whose petitions on the issue he had repeatedly deferred 'in conformity with the generally expressed wish' of the House, 18 May. 'At the United Services Club', Denis Le Marchant[†] recorded, 15 May, 'Strickland showed me a letter from some of his leading constituents at Saddleworth. They have told him that people were tired of signing petitions and addresses – they wished to fight it out at once, and the sooner, the better'.[32] He presented three Yorkshire petitions for supplies to be withheld until the bill passed, 23 May. He divided for the second reading of the Irish reform bill, 25 May, and expressed his hope that it would help 'ameliorate' the evils there, 14 June. He voted against a Conservative amendment to increase Scottish county representation, 1 June. He presented petitions from the townships of Halifax parish seeking inclusion in the borough, 5, 14 June, and spoke thus, 8 June. He was in the minority on Whitehaven's boundary, 22 June. He attempted to present a petition from the Leeds Political Union for a more extensive Irish reform bill, 27 June, but it was refused acceptance by the Speaker. During the debate on the Liverpool franchise bill, 4 July, he rhetorically asked why Liverpool had been selected for 'public execration', suspecting that the reason lay only in the size of the bribes involved and not the principle of bribery itself, and concluded that the bill was unnecessary as 'the reform bill will do much to put a stop to such a system'.

Strickland welcomed Sadler's factories regulation bill, 15 Dec. 1831, presented petitions in its favour from Halifax, 10 Feb., 23 May, and Morley 19 Mar., and was appointed to the committee on the bill, 16 Mar. 1832. He attended the county meeting in its support next month and endorsed the ensuing petition, 27 June. He was in the minority for the second reading of the Vestry Act amendment bill, 23 Jan. 1832. He resumed his opposition to the general register bill, 22 Feb., when he was appointed to the committee on it, and welcomed Lord Nugent's births registration bill, 18 May, believing that it would not interfere with other plans for a general register and would satisfy the wishes of the Dissenting community. He endorsed a Leeds petition for poor laws in Ireland, 23 Jan., and spoke and was in the minority for Sadler's motion for their introduction, 19 June. He welcomed another from Dewsbury calling for education reform there, 28 Mar., and one from the West Riding supporting nondenominational teaching, 9 Apr. He voted with ministers on the Russian-Dutch loan, 26 Jan., 12, 16 July, and relations with Portugal, 9 Feb. He believed that the only way to check the spread of cholera was to improve the conditions of the poor, 13 Feb. He moved the second reading of the South Shields and Monkwearmouth railway bill, 14 Feb., and urged Sir Hedworth Williamson to pursue his objections at the committee stage. When he declined and divided the House that day, Strickland was a teller for the majority. He presented a Sculcoates petition for inquiry into Peterloo, 23 Feb., and divided accordingly, 15 Mar. He presented a petition for relief from distress from Beeford and Skipsea, 29 Feb. On the presentation of a petition highlighting distress in the silk trade, 1 Mar., he said the whole subject ought to go before a committee of the House and demanded action to curtail smuggling. He seconded Ewart's motion to abolish the death penalty for horse, sheep and cattle stealing and for burglary where no person was endangered, 27 Mar., saying that it was 'high time' for reforms in the criminal law. He voted with ministers on the navy civil departments bill, 6 Apr., but was in the minority against confirming an increase in the Irish registrar's salary, 9 Apr. The following day he called for a reduction in the number of Scottish judges. When Inglis said that a petition calling for a separation of church and state was inadmissible, 8 May, Strickland insisted that 'the people have a right to petition on all great constitutional questions'; he was appointed to a select committee on the subject next day. He presented a Hemel Hempstead petition for the abolition of slavery, 23 May, and spoke and voted for Fowell Buxton's motion for a select committee to investigate the best means of effecting it, 24 May. He was a majority teller against amending the Sale of Beer Act, 31 May. He voted against Alexander Baring's bill to exclude insolvent debtors from Parliament, 6 June. On the 8th he opposed a clause in Campbell's dower bill, which he claimed would adversely affect widows with large families to support, and was a majority teller against it. He backed calls for financial recompense for coroners, voted for public inquests, but also suggested that they be given powers to hold private ones, 20 June. On 27 June he asked Kenyon to have his labourers' employment bill printed and held over to the next session, which he refused. He protested that it went 'totally against all the principles which ought to govern us with respect to poor laws' and was a minority teller against it, 9 July. When the report was brought up next day, he again objected to it, complained that he had not been given sufficient opportunity to voice his opposition, and said he would divide the House on it, but was prevented from doing so by the Speaker. He endorsed a petition presented by Johnstone for a nondenominational university at Durham, 29 June. He welcomed

the tithes prescription bill, believing it to be of importance to the clergy, acceptable to the landed gentry and an improvement on the 'most objectionable' existing law, 5 July 1832.

At the 1832 general election Strickland was returned unopposed as a Liberal for the West Riding, where he sat until 1841, when he successfully contested Preston. He retired at the dissolution of 1857. On 9 Jan. 1865 he wrote to Lord Brougham, 'I consider you to be the oldest friend I have left in the world. Life is a most uncertain profession, all my early companions, by living too well, killed themselves off'. He explained that he had just succeeded to the estates of the Cholmley family, worth 'about £10,000 a year', after the death of a descendant of his maternal grandfather, whom he had only seen two or three times. The terms of the will meant he had to change his name, but, he added, 'all this may be useful to me if I should retain my health, which never was strong'.[33] Following the death of his wife, 10 Jan. 1865, he informed Brougham, 15 Feb.:

> Lately she had an independent fortune of about four thousand a year. After a separation of 37 years she has left that quite as I could wish, to my only daughter ... What has surprised some people is that she has left a legacy to me of £500 ... 'as proof that I leave this world with no enmity to him'. The fact is that she was sensible that I had done all I could to be kind to her.[34]

Two years later he remarried. He died in December 1874, the last surviving Member for the former united county of Yorkshire. He had accumulated property in all three Ridings, but principally in the East, where he owned over 26,000 acres, worth £35,000 a year.[35] By his will, dated 16 Feb. 1870, most of his estates were divided between his two surviving sons, Charles William Strickland (1819-1909), his successor in the baronetcy, and Henry Strickland Constable. Boynton, the family seat, and £70,000 passed in trust to Walter William Strickland, his eldest grandson and later the 9th baronet. He left his second wife two estates, Thorpe Bassett and Norton, both near Malton, as well as his London house at 118 Piccadilly, and gave his brother Nathaniel £20,000 and his brother John a villa in Hampshire.

[1] Brougham mss, Strickland to J. Brougham, 10 Jan. 1827, 24 July 1828. [2] Ibid. 17 Oct., 18 Nov. 1828. [3] Fitzwilliam mss. [4] *Leeds Mercury*, 9, 16 Oct.; *Yorks. Gazette*, 16 Oct. 1819. [5] *Leeds Mercury*, 25 Mar. 1820. [6] Fitzwilliam mss 102/11. [7] *Leeds Mercury*, 25 Jan. 1823. [8] *Yorks. Gazette*, 25 Mar. 1826. [9] Brougham mss. [10] Add. 76379. [11] Castle Howard mss. [12] Ibid. Abercromby to Carlisle, 30 Dec. 1825. [13] E. Baines, *Yorks. Election 1826*, p. 74. [14] Brougham mss, Strickland to J. Brougham, 16 Dec. 1826. [15] Ibid. 10 Jan. 1827. [16] Ibid. 30 July 1828. [17] Ibid. 4 Nov. 1828. [18] Ibid. 18 Nov. 1828. [19] Ibid. 7 Apr.

1829, 24 Mar., 30 May, 4, 26 June 1830. [20] Ibid. 4 July 1829. [21] Ibid. 14 Nov. 1829. [22] Wentworth Woodhouse mun. G3/23, Strickland to Milton, 31 July 1830. [23] Ibid.; *Leeds Mercury*, 27 July 1830 [24] Add. 51562. [25] *The Times*, 26 Nov.; *Yorks. Gazette*, 4 Dec.; *Leeds Mercury*, 4 Dec. 1830. [26] Brougham mss, Strickland to Lord Brougham, 12 Dec. [1830]. [27] Ibid. 12, 15 Dec. 1830. [28] Ibid. 22 Dec. 1830. [29] *Leeds Mercury Extraordinary*, 27 Apr. 1831. [30] *Leeds Mercury*, 7 May 1831. [31] Ibid. 15 Oct. 1831. [32] *Three Diaries*, 258. [33] Brougham mss. [34] Ibid. [35] J.T. Ward, *East Yorks. Landed Estates*, 19.

M.P.J.C.

STRUTT, **Edward** (1801–1880), of St. Helen's House, Derby; Kingston Hall, Notts., and 17 Cork Street, Mdx.

DERBY	1830–22 Mar. 1848
ARUNDEL	16 July 1851–1852
NOTTINGHAM	1852–July 1856

b. 26 Oct. 1801, o.s. of William Strutt of St. Helen's House and Barbara, da. of Thomas Evans of Derby. *educ.* Manchester Coll. York 1817; Trinity Coll. Camb. 1819; L. Inn 1823; I. Temple 1825. *m.* 28 Mar. 1837, Amelia Harriet, da. of Rt. Rev. William Otter, bp. of Chichester, 4s. (2 *d.v.p.*) 4da. *suc.* fa. 1830; *cr.* Bar. Belper 29 Aug. 1856. *d.* 30 June 1880.
PC 30 Oct. 1846; chief commr. of railways 1846-8; chan. of duchy of Lancaster Dec. 1852-June 1854, member of council 1854; vice-pres. Univ. Coll. London 1862-71, pres. 1871-9.
Sheriff, Notts. 1850-1, chairman, q. sess. 1855, ld. lt. 1864-*d.*

Strutt's grandfather was the Unitarian cotton manufacturer Jedediah Strutt (1726-97), an inventive engineer and innovative businessman, whose partnership with the celebrated Richard Arkwright established the family fortunes. His three sons, who continued to trade as W., G. and J. Strutt, were equally gifted, in different ways: William was the technical expert, George Benson the manager of the mills and estates, and Joseph the head of the commercial side of the enterprise.[1] The Irish poet Tom Moore, who noted that the brothers had 'more than 40 thousand a year' and 'a million of money pretty equally divided between them', was delighted to recount in 1813 that their families were 'fond of literature, music and all those elegancies which their riches enable them so amply to indulge themselves with' and were 'to crown all, right true Jacobins after my own heart, so that I passed my time very agreeably amongst them'.[2] Together they were enormously influential in the development of Derby, not only as builders of fine houses and benefactors of educational establishments, but as leading members of the Dissenting community and advanced Whig stalwarts on the corporation.[3] William Strutt,

who was described by Samuel Taylor Coleridge as 'a man of stern aspect, but of strong, very strong, abilities', inherited much of his father's ingenuity, his inspired creations including a method of constructing fireproof buildings and a convection system for heating Derbyshire General Infirmary, which he designed himself. A friend of Erasmus Darwin, whom he succeeded as president of the Derby Philosophical Society in 1802, and of Richard Lovell Edgeworth, another member of the Birmingham Lunar Society, William's bent for scientific experimentation won him election to the Royal Society in 1817.[4]

His only son, this Member, who had much of the family's yearning for intellectual inquiry and Unitarian sobriety of aspect, was noticed while still a child by Edgeworth, who found him 'fond of mechanics'. His daughter Maria Edgeworth agreed that Strutt was 'a boy of great abilities, affectionate, and with a frank countenance and manner which win at once'.[5] Educated at Manchester College in York from 1817, the year that his uncle Joseph became its president, he seems to have imbibed his father's enthusiasm for learning and went up to university two years later.[6] Paternal confidence in his capacity to guard himself from being 'infected' by 'such a sink of vice and profligacy' seems to have been justified, since, despite his £5,000 allowance, it was later reported that 'he used to be noted at Cambridge for fearing an inroad of friends lest they might drink some of his wine'.[7] He was president of the Union in 1821 and became closely associated with the group of liberal-minded intellectuals, including Charles Buller II*, Thomas Babington Macaulay*, John Moultrie, Winthrop Mackworth Praed*, John Romilly and Thomas Hyde Villiers*.[8] He was introduced to John Stuart Mill and his circle through Charles Austin, the Cambridge exponent of the doctrines of Jeremy Bentham, and became reacquainted with Robert Owen in London in July 1821, when he observed that the peers 'who had been peculiarly hostile to the queen' were subjected to the 'hissing and the murderous cries' of the crowd at the coronation of George IV.[9]

After taking his degree in 1823, Strutt began to study at the inns of court, but was never called. On his return from the continent that summer, his father congratulated him on being invited to visit Bentham, which would be reckoned 'a feather in your cap', and James Abercromby*, which would 'of course lead to attentions from the duke of Devonshire'. He added:

These things are coming in some degree to your own merits, and some how or other derived from Cambridge

I suppose. I think I remember observing to you that the eye of the public would be upon you at a certain time; that time is arrived, you are beginning to be thought of for a public station.[10]

He at some point became a partner in the firm, though he did not take an active part in it, and participated in family initiatives in Derby, where he was a corporator, such as the establishment of a mechanics' institute in the mid-1820s.[11] During election speculation in August 1824 he was named as a possible future Member for the borough, and Abercromby, pointing out the significant local influence of his 'opulent, numerous and powerful family', recommended him to Devonshire, in preference to Samuel Crompton*, as more likely to consolidate his electoral interest.[12] However, Strutt stood aside in favour of Crompton, whose candidacy he seconded at the general election of 1826. With his first cousin William Evans*, he secured a petition for alteration of the corn laws at a meeting in Derby, 9 Nov. 1826.[13] In September 1827 Bentham wrote to Lafayette that Strutt, 'a young man of more than ordinary promise', who was searching for a parliamentary seat, 'agrees with us, I believe, entirely on the subject of government as well as that of religion'. According to Bentham, his literary reputation secured his association with the *Westminster Review*, but he did not publish.[14] He assisted John Ramsay McCulloch and William Eyton Tooke with clarifications about the development of Arkwright's inventions for articles they intended to write.[15] He was an enthusiastic supporter of the educational ideals of the new University of London, where he attended John Austin's lectures on jurisprudence.[16] In 1829 the Society for the Diffusion of Useful Knowledge declined to publish his 'Treatise on Wages'.[17]

John Romilly, with whom he proposed to travel in Scotland, wrote to him on 21 Aug. 1829, perhaps in relation to a possible parliamentary opening, that he regretted that Strutt's 'Wiltshire visit did not lead to an immediate *arrangement*'. Strutt informed his sister Fanny, 26 May 1830, of a plan to 'bring me into Parliament for Newcastle[-under-Lyme] ... for £1,200!'. Exactly a month later his uncle Joseph informed him of Crompton's sudden resignation and that the Devonshire interest had been placed at his disposal: 'the duke and Mr. Abercromby are written to, and you must come by the mail ... to settle the address'.[18] It was later reported, but whether or not this was to Crompton is unclear, that Strutt had 'previously agreed to lend £19,000 for 10 years upon a borough without interest'.[19] He requested his father to subscribe £25 to assist the canvass of the advanced

Whig John Wood* at Preston, 'as I know him very well and as I shall probably see a good deal of him in the House'.[20] Thanking the electors for his unopposed return, he declared that

> the friends to improvement in Parliament can do but little unless they are supported by the voice of the people out of doors. And I consider it to be one of the most encouraging signs of the present times that public opinion is daily acquiring greater influence over the deliberations of the legislature and measures of the government.

He advocated education as the best security for social order and good government, the abolition of colonial slavery provided the circumstances were right, the adoption of a system of rigid economy, the removal of unnecessary restrictions on trade, judicial changes and such radical reforms as shorter parliaments, an extended franchise and the ballot.[21]

Strutt, who was counted by the Wellington administration among their 'foes' and by Greville as a 'Radical',[22] took his seat among his friends on the opposition backbenches, 2 Nov. 1830. The following day he observed to Fanny that the king's speech was

> a bad one, containing nothing about reform or political improvement of any kind, little about economy, an attempt to excite alarm about Ireland and Kent and a very objectionable passage about Belgium, particularly in calling the king's government *enlightened*.

He accompanied his colleague Henry Cavendish to the levée and was elected to Brooks's that day. He voted to reduce the duty on wheat imported to the West Indies, 12 Nov. Having divided in the majority on the civil list that precipitated the government's fall, 15 Nov., he reported to Fanny on the 19th that the new ministry was to consist 'exclusively of the Whigs and the remains of the Huskisson party and to contain no Ultra Tories'.[23] He made his maiden speech on presenting and endorsing the Derby petition for reducing the stamp duties on newspapers, 8 Dec., and he brought up the first of many reform petitions, also from his constituency, 16 Dec. 1830. His father, who shared his favourable views about the revolutions in various European countries that year, died on the 29th, a loss to society, Owen remarked, 'of one of the most valuable men that the last century has produced'. Strutt inherited St. Helen's House, a valuable estate in Nottinghamshire and personalty sworn under £30,000.[24] In February 1831 Strutt, who expected to find 'some gross jobs' as a member of the select committee on the expenditure on Buckingham House, opined that 'the new ministers did not make a good figure' on Lord Althorp's budget and that 'they have, as I feared they would, done little to satisfy the public'. Elected to the council of the University of London, 23 Feb., he found the ensuing dinner a 'Whiggish and dullish' affair and a subsequent internal quarrel a great nuisance. On 28 Feb. he was appointed to the select committee to consider the reform petitions, one of several which occupied his time and bored him with 'stupid debate'. Following Lord John Russell's statement, 1 Mar., Strutt commented the next day that the Grey ministry had

> proposed a tolerably sweeping measure of reform, a much more extensive and better one than I think was expected by anybody. It has no doubt great defects, but if it is carried (as it must be *eventually*) all the rest must follow. It has of course *horrified* a great proportion of the House and I have no expectation that they can carry the measure in its present shape through the present Parliament; but I hope they will not permit it to be frittered away, and if they remain firm it must be carried at last.

A week later he believed that the 'prospect of the bill's passing the second reading improves', and a week after that he was pleased at '*how* the reform bill goes on prosperously'. After having been put on the second reading committee of the cotton factories apprenticeship bill, 14 Mar., he wrote in exasperation to his sister 'that you may suppose I am not idle; and to mend the matter I caught a very bad cold'. Reporting that he was 'still fast upon this abominable [Petersfield] election committee' and that there was no truth in the rumour of his impending resignation, 21 Mar., he added that if he had not been hoarse he 'might possibly have said a few words in the [reform bill] debate'.[25] He voted for the second reading of the bill the following day. Writing to Fanny, 18 Apr., he observed that

> reports are very industriously circulated (but whether on any authority no one can tell) that the king will not dissolve if ministers are in the minority. In that case they must of course go out, which would make a tremendous sensation throughout the country. There will of course be a very full attendance tonight. The House has been by no means *thin* of late, though the divisions may not have been large at particular times and on questions of no great interest.

He was in the minority against Gascoyne's wrecking amendment, 19 Apr. 1831, but, as he put it in other letters to his sister on the 21st and 23rd, he and his Whig friends were 'rather jubilant' and 'in great glee' at the news of the dissolution.[26]

Strutt offered again for Derby as a reformer at the ensuing general election, arguing that the country's welfare depended on the bill's success, without which the 'name of representation was an empty mockery

and delusion'; he was returned unopposed.[27] He voted for the second reading of the reintroduced reform bill, 6 July 1831, and steadily for its details. He sided with opposition against the grants for professors' salaries at Oxford and Cambridge, 8 July, and civil list services, 18 July. He was in minorities for swearing the original Dublin committee, 29 July, and to print the Waterford petition for disarming the Irish yeomanry, 11 Aug., but divided with ministers against charges of improper interference in the Dublin election, 23 Aug., and for issuing the Liverpool writ, 5 Sept. He cast wayward votes against the truck bill, 12 Sept., and for the total disfranchisement of Aldborough, 14 Sept. Having secured the adjournment, 19 Sept., he spoke the next day of his 'warm and zealous support' for the reform bill, which he claimed 'contains so much substantial good, and offers to the people so important an additional security for good government'. He repudiated all objections to the bill, but regretted the exclusion of 'more effectual measures' to extinguish the undue influence of property and believed the people 'fully competent to select their own representatives'. He voted for the passage of the bill, 21 Sept., the second reading of the Scottish reform bill, 23 Sept., and Lord Ebrington's confidence motion, 10 Oct. He attended the Derby meeting at the end of September, when he again hailed the importance of government's appeal to the strength of favourable public opinion, and the Derbyshire county reform meeting in early October 1831, when he seconded the resolution to petition the Lords for the bill.[28]

In December 1831 Strutt was described by his friend John Heywood Hawkins*, along with Joseph Hume, Robert Torrens and Henry Warburton, as being among the (radical) 'economists' in the Commons who were not always uniformly supporters of government.[29] He divided for the second reading of the revised reform bill, 17 Dec. 1831, and again mostly for its details. However, he was in the minority against retaining the Chandos clause for the enfranchisement of £50 tenants-at-will, 1 Feb. 1832. He divided for the Vestry Act amendment bill, 23 Jan., and was named to the select committee on the renewal of the East India Company's charter, 28 Jan. He was in government majorities for the Russian-Dutch loan, 26 Jan., and on relations with Portugal, 9 Feb., but voted for the production of information on military punishments, 16 Feb. He was among the Members invited to dine at the patronage secretary Edward Ellice's, 18 Feb. 'That, you see, is what one gets by a patient servility to his Majesty's ministers', he joked to his sister, adding that 'the prospect of the reform bill's passing is … generally thought to be improving'. He was at Westminster,

13 Mar., but preferred to remain in the library 'whilst some of the stupid practice freshmen were talking'. He had to 'walk down to the House every morning before breakfast for more than a week to put my name on the Speaker's paper', before being able to present and endorse the Macclesfield petition against the stamp duties, 2 Apr. He attended the debate on the second reading of the reform bill in the Lords, relishing the 'complete dusting' which Lord Grey gave the bishop of Exeter, 13 Apr. 1832.[30]

Going much further than Ebrington in attacking Wellington and the Tories as unfit to take charge of the reform bill, Strutt seconded the motion for an address calling on the king to appoint only ministers who would carry it unimpaired, 10 May 1832, when he declared:

> Let this House come forward and place itself in its proper station at the head of the people; let this House show itself true to its former professions; let it show the people that, as long as they are true to themselves, this House will not desert them; and that, instead of looking for leaders elsewhere, they have only to look to the ranks of the reformers in this House for their real and natural supporters.

He was a teller for the majority that day, his conduct being approved by his proud family and constituents.[31] He voted for the second reading of the Irish reform bill, 25 May, and against increasing the Scottish county representation, 1 June, when he said that it was absurd to attempt to settle the question of the corn laws on the 'very eve of parliamentary reform'. He supported the ministerial plan for Irish national education and objected to the stamp duties as taxes on knowledge, 14 June. He voted to reduce the barracks grant, 2 July, but again with ministers for the Russian-Dutch loan, 12, 16, 20 July. He attended the reform celebrations in Derby that summer and was returned as a Liberal after a contest at the general election of 1832.[32]

One of the mainstream, if conventional, philosophic radicals in the reformed Parliament, Strutt was thought likely to contribute, perhaps financially, to a new monthly review during the mid-1830s, but Mill later castigated him as an 'apostate radical' for his political moderation.[33] He increasingly saw himself as independent of his electors, but continued to sit for Derby until unseated in 1848, and retired from the Commons in 1856 to take a seat in the Lords, supposedly as the first mill owner to do so.[34] In the words of Henry Taylor, Strutt

> was a man of sound knowledge and solid understanding, simple and honest-minded. He had a large fortune, obtained a good position in the House of Commons,

became a member of the government, and was eventually raised to the peerage by the title of Lord Belper, which was probably all the success in life to which he aspired, if indeed he was troubled with any aspirations of that kind.[35]

He died in June 1880, being succeeded by his second son Henry (1840-1914), who was Liberal Member for Derbyshire East, 1868-74, and Berwick, 1880.[36]

[1] See R.S. Fitton and A.P. Wadsworth, *The Strutts and the Arkwrights, 1758-1830: A Study of the Early Factory System* and *Oxford DNB* sub Jedediah Strutt. [2] *Moore Jnl.* i. 342, 344-5; Fitton and Wadsworth, 178-9. [3] Fitton and Wadsworth, 184-91. [4] Ibid. 169-81; C.L. Hacker, 'William Strutt of Derby', *Derbys. Arch. Jnl.* lxxx (1960), 49-70. [5] Derby Local Stud. Lib. Strutt mss, W. to E. Strutt, 23 Jan. 1811, Edgeworth to same, 3 May 1812; Fitton and Wadsworth, 177. [6] Strutt mss, W. to E. Strutt, 1 Oct. 1817; Fitton and Wadsworth, 171-3. [7] Fitzwilliam Mus. Camb. mss 15-1948; W. Thomas, *Philosophic Radicals*, 189. [8] P. Cradock, *Recollections of Camb. Union*, 22-23; J. Hamburger, *Intellectuals in Politics*, 11. [9] Strutt mss, E. to W. Strutt, 21 July 1821; J.F.C. Harrison, *Robert Owen and the Owenites*, 156; Fitton and Wadsworth, 182-3. [10] Fitton and Wadsworth, 182. [11] Ibid. 186, 189; *PP* (1835), xxv. 443. [12] *The Times*, 28 Aug. 1824; Chatsworth mss 6DD 1017, 1020. [13] *Derby Mercury*, 14 June, 15 Nov. 1826. [14] *Bentham Corresp.* xii. 379-81; H. Grote, *Personal Life of George Grote*, 59. [15] Brougham mss, Strutt to Tooke, 24 Feb. 1828. [16] *Derby Mercury*, 6 Feb. 1828; H.H. Bellot, *University of London*, 187. [17] *Mill Works*, xiii. 742. [18] Strutt mss. [19] Derbys. RO, Gresley of Drakelow mss D77/38/5. [20] Strutt mss, E. to W. Strutt, 13 July 1830. [21] *Derby Mercury*, 30 June, 4 Aug. 1830. [22] *Greville Mems.* ii. 57. [23] Strutt mss. [24] Fitton and Wadsworth, 179, 184, 191; PROB 11/1782/115; IR26/1271/91. [25] Strutt mss, E. to F. Strutt, 11, 25 Feb., 2, 3, 9, 16, 21 Mar. 1831; J. Wigley, 'Derby and Derbys. during Great Reform Bill Crisis', *Derbys. Arch. Jnl.* ci (1981), 140-1. [26] Strutt mss. [27] *Derby Mercury*, 27 Apr., 4 May 1831. [28] Ibid. 28 Sept., 5 Oct.; *The Times*, 10 Oct. 1831. [29] Cornw. RO, Hawkins mss 10/2175. [30] Strutt mss, E to F. Strutt, 20 Feb., 14 Mar., 3, 14 Apr. 1832. [31] Ibid. J. to E. Strutt, 13 May 1832; Le Marchant, *Althorp*, 426. [32] Wigley, 146-7. [33] Thomas, 3, 189, 206; Hamburger, 115, 207; *Mill Works*, xii. 198, 202, 211, 246, 333. [34] Wigley, 149. [35] *Taylor Autobiog.* i. 81. [36] *The Times*, 1 July, 14 Aug. 1880; *DNB*; *Oxford DNB*.

S.R.H./S.M.F.

STRUTT, Joseph Holden (1758–1845), of Terling Place, Witham, Essex.

MALDON	1790–1826
OKEHAMPTON	1826–1830

b. 21 Nov. 1758, 2nd but 1st surv. s. of John Strutt[†] of Terling and Anne, da. of Rev. William Goodday, rect. of Strelley, Notts. *educ.* Felsted; Winchester 1768; Brasenose, Oxf. 1778. *m.* at Toulouse, 21 Feb. 1789, Lady Charlotte Mary Gertrude Fitzgerald, da. of James, 1st duke of Leinster [I] (she was cr. Baroness Rayleigh 18 July 1821), 2s. (1 *d.v.p.*) 2da. *suc.* fa. 1816. *d.* 11 Feb. 1845.

Lt.-col. western batt., Essex militia 1783-96; col. S. Essex militia 1798, 1803-5, 1809, W. Essex militia 1823-31; brevet col. during service 1798.

Strutt, a short man with piercing blue eyes, was the grandson of a prosperous miller. On the death of his overbearing father 'Black Jack' Strutt in 1816 he acquired 6,000 inherited and purchased acres in Essex, to which during his lifetime he added 2,330, at a cost of £103,000, drawn entirely from savings.[1] An undistinguished, mostly silent but conscientious parliamentarian, he had succeeded his father as Pittite Tory Member for Maldon in 1790 and, sustained by his friends in the corporation, had by 1820 extended their combined period of unbroken possession of the seat to almost 46 years. He was conceited and smug, under a cloak of false humility. He had married the daughter of an Irish duke at the age of 20 and since the turn of the century had vainly pestered successive Tory ministries for a British peerage for her, on the strength of his own and his father's electoral and militia services in Essex. In a fragment of autobiography, intended as a lesson in filial obedience and civic duty for his troublesome son John James (1796-1873), he boasted that he had 'obtained the approbation' of Pitt, Dundas, Addington, Perceval, Lord Liverpool and George IV, among others; but in reality they considered him tiresome and importunate.[2]

He was returned again unopposed for Maldon at the 1820 general election. Notwithstanding his later ludicrous claim that he had 'declined' the offer of a place, 'preferring penury which induced me and my daughters to breakfast on a penny worth of milk with water and dry bread, that I might be free in public life as an MP', he remained generally steady in his support of the Liverpool administration.[3] He was, however, credited with a vote in the minority against Wilberforce's compromise resolution on the Queen Caroline affair, 22 June 1820.[4] When the election for Colchester of the radical Whittle Harvey was declared void a week later, ministers encouraged Strutt to put up his son at the by-election; but his enquiries revealed divisions among the local Tories which made it a hopeless case.[5] On 14 Dec. 1820, hearing that Western, the 'violent' Whig county Member, planned to urge the lord lieutenant Lord Braybrooke to convene a meeting to condemn ministers' conduct towards the queen, Strutt dashed the 27 miles from Terling to Audley End in a successful bid to forestall him. Like Braybrooke, Strutt saw the dangers involved in 'assembling the county to address against the clamour of the day', which could end in embarrassing defeat; but he believed that 'the minds of the people are coming round to sound consideration' and that the issue could not 'long infatuate' them.[6] He duly voted against the opposition censure motion, 6 Feb. 1821. As before, he divided against Catholic claims, 28 Feb. 1821, 30 Apr. 1822, 1 Mar., 21

Apr., 10 May 1825. On 9 May he was in the minority against the bill to disfranchise the Irish 40s. freeholders as a security for relief. He was in the ministerial majorities against repeal of the additional malt duty, 3 Apr., military economies, 11 Apr., 28 May, retrenchment, 27 June, the disfranchisement of ordnance officials, 12 Apr., and parliamentary reform, 9 May 1821. That summer his claim for a British peerage for his wife was finally conceded as one of the coronation creations. Returning obsequious thanks to Liverpool, Strutt described the honour as 'requiting the long constitutional conduct in and out of Parliament of my ... father and of my humble constant exertions within the sphere of a country gentleman'; but he 'lived long enough to repent' of settling for this arrangement, which gave his son precedence of rank over him, and to wish that he had insisted on the peerage being granted 'in my own person'.[7]

Strutt voted against more extensive tax reductions, 11, 21 Feb., and abolition of one of the joint-postmasterships, 13 Mar., and for the Irish estimates, 22 July 1822. He divided with government against repeal of the assessed taxes, 18 Mar., and of the Foreign Enlistment Act, 16 Apr., for the grant for Irish glebe houses, 11 Apr., and against inquiry into chancery delays, 5 June 1823. That month he and his son attended and were toasted at the anniversary dinner of the Maldon Pitt Club.[8] His only known vote in the 1824 session was against the abolition of army flogging, 5 Mar. He voted for the Irish unlawful societies bill, 25 Feb., and the duke of Cumberland's grant, 2, 10 June 1825. In April he had told Liverpool that 'if no particular circumstance should arise to me or any of my family, prior to a dissolution of Parliament, I at present intend that my son and myself should be in the next, provided that your Lordship remains at the head of government'.[9] In September 1825, when a dissolution was expected, Strutt informed the electors of Maldon that he would follow his father's example and, with the country now 'in the plenitude of honour and glory with the world, and in rising prosperity', hand over the seat to John James. However the latter, who had recently been converted from a rake into an Evangelical religious maniac, had only reluctantly agreed to come in; and in March 1826, after a furious row with his father, he withdrew from the scheme, thereby ending the family's 52-year tenure of the seat.[10] Strutt presented Witham and Maldon anti-slavery petitions, 3 Feb., 11 May, but voted in defence of the Jamaican slave trials, 2 Mar. 1826.[11] He divided for the president of the board of trade's ministerial salary, 10 Apr., and against reform of Edinburgh's representation, 13 Apr. 1826.

At the general election in June he was returned *in absentia* for Okehampton on the Savile interest, presumably as a paying guest; he proclaimed his 'firm adherence to the principles of our glorious constitution'.[12] He was given eight days' leave of absence on account of ill health, 13 Feb., but was present to vote against Catholic relief, 6 Mar. 1827. He was granted a fortnight's sick leave, 30 Mar. On 18 June 1827 he was in the Tory minority against the Coventry magistracy bill. He divided against repeal of the Test Acts, 26 Feb. 1828. He got two weeks' leave on account of illness, 1 Mar., but was in the minority of 15 against punishing a prevaricating witness in the East Retford inquiry, 7 Mar. 1828. He voted against Catholic relief, 12 May, and the provision for Canning's family, 13 May, and with the Wellington ministry on the ordnance estimates, 4 July 1828. Planta, the patronage secretary, thought he would side 'with government' for Catholic emancipation, but he voted steadily against it in March 1829, presenting hostile petitions from Terling and Fairsted on the 17th. Although the Ultras did not count him as one of their own in October 1829, he divided against administration on the Terceira affair, 28 Apr., the army estimates, 30 Apr., and the grant for South American missions, 7 June 1830. He voted against Jewish emancipation, 17 May, and in minorities for amendments to the sale of beer bill, 21 June, 1 July 1830. Now aged 71, he left Parliament at the dissolution that month.

On his wife's death in 1836 Strutt had the mortification of seeing his son seated in the Lords, but they subsequently buried the hatchet.[13] In his declining years he was consoled and nursed by his unmarried daughter Emily Anne (1790-1865), for whose future comfort he bought in 1840 St. Catherine's Court, near Bath, where he mostly spent the last five years of his life.[14] In his egotistical memoir he claimed that

> whenever his consideration and judgement permitted him to exert himself (which was not so often as he wished) upon public business, success usually followed, affording credit to him, and advantage to those interested and the public. My dear children, would it not have been melancholy to know that your father had been despised of men? Is it not pleasing to cherish in recollection that he was approved by men, so as to receive consideration, esteem and honour [for] high incorruptible conduct?

In 1843 he moaned to his distinguished soldier brother William Goodday Strutt:

> What a miserable state the nation is in! Twenty years ago I said it was at its zenith, and Sir R. Peel has precipitated its downfall by free trade ... what a frightful state we are in – Radicals, Chartists, distressed manufactories,

an income declining, debt increasing, interest not paid or paying *though there is a property tax*, Ireland upon the verge of rebellion, the duke of Wellington old and Peel not of strength of *mind* to govern the nation.[15]

Strutt died at Bath in February 1845, four weeks after being forced by a fire in his bedroom to take to the street in his nightshirt.[16] In his interminable will, dated 25 Nov. 1844, he asked to be carried to his grave by Terling estate labourers. He left Emily an annuity of £1,075, in addition to a sum of £1,000 in three per cent consols given to her in 1844, and settled on her St. Catherine's and property at Marshfield, Gloucestershire. He gave his married daughter Margaret Drummond an annuity of £425 and £3,000 for the purchase of land, and left his brother £5,000 and Blunt's Hall, near Terling. His entailed real estate passed to his son.[17]

[1] C.R. Strutt, *Strutt Fam. of Terling, 1650-1873*, pp. 56, 60; Sir W. Gavin, *Ninety Years of Farming*, 1-7. [2] *HP Commons, 1754-1790*, iii. 493-5; *HP Commons, 1790-1820*, v. 303-5; Strutt, 30, 45-46. [3] *Suff. Chron.* 11 Mar. 1820; *Session of Parl. 1825*, p. 486; Strutt, 54. [4] *The Times*, 26 June 1820. [5] Add. 38458, f. 331. [6] Add. 38288, f. 303. [7] Add. 38575, ff. 8, 10; Strutt, 50-51; Lord Rayleigh, *Baron Rayleigh*, 5. [8] *Colchester Gazette*, 21 June 1823. [9] Add. 38576, f. 63. [10] Strutt, 69-74; *Colchester Gazette*, 24 Sept. 1825; *Kent and Essex Mercury*, 21 Mar. 1826. [11] *The Times*, 4 Feb., 12 May 1826. [12] *Alfred*, 13 June 1826. [13] Strutt, 75-75. [14] Ibid. 100-2; Gavin, 21. [15] Strutt, 35, 55. [16] Ibid. 60. [17] PROB 11/2016/337; IR26/1720/256.

D.R.F.

STUART, Lord Dudley Coutts (1803–1854), of 16 Wilton Crescent, Mdx.

ARUNDEL	1830–1837
MARYLEBONE	1847–17 Nov. 1854

b. 11 Jan. 1803, 8th s. of John Stuart†, 1st mq. of Bute (*d.* 1814), and 2nd w. Frances, da. of Thomas Coutts, London banker. *educ.* privately by Rev. Edmund Mortlock; Christ's, Camb. 1821. *m.* 1824, Christina Alexandrine Egypta, da. of Lucien Buonaparte, prince of Canino, 1s. *d.* 17 Nov. 1854.

Stuart was the grandson of Lord Bute, George III's prime minister, and his family boasted an impressive parliamentary pedigree: his father, three uncles and three half-brothers all sat in the House before 1820. The only son of a late second marriage, he was brought up by his mother in Naples after his father's death in 1814. It was to her firm character, according to an obituarist, that he owed his 'strong feelings of indignation against oppression and compassion for misfortune which were the ruling principles of his life'.[1] As a youth he inspired great admiration: his uncle Sir Francis

Burdett* had 'but one fault to find with him – he is too handsome'; Lady Holland heard that he was 'universally beloved at Cambridge', and Henry Edward Fox*, who befriended him when he was travelling with his mother in Italy after leaving university, described him as 'a most amiable, noble, fine-spirited character ... I quite love him'. Eleanor Fazakerley considered it a great merit that he had 'avoided singularities in his habits more than one would have thought easy in his family'.[2] Further tribute to the youthful Stuart and his emerging humanitarian qualities was paid in a Charles Dickens story entitled *The Italian Prisoner* (1860), an idealized account of how he secured the release of a political prisoner while in Italy. It was there that he formed a liaison with Napoleon's niece 'Christine' Buonaparte. She was five years his senior and had been abandoned by her husband, the Swedish count Aarvid de Posse; an annulment had apparently been sought but not granted. Notwithstanding this, Stuart secretly married her at a Catholic church near Rome in 1824, and a son was born the following year. On reports of de Posse's death they married again according to Anglican rites in Florence, 21 May 1826, and may have gone through another ceremony in England that autumn. Fox found her 'very clever' and noted that 'her conversation and conduct have captivated him completely'; but George Agar Ellis* expressed the society view of this 'deplorable business':

> She is old, ugly, humpbacked ... of a bad character, a foreigner, a widow ... A fortnight ago the husband died ... and Dudley took that opportunity of marrying her and bringing her to England. To make the matter worse Dudley had long been engaged to his cousin Lady Georgiana North, to whom he has behaved disgracefully ill, and Mr. Coutts was just going to make him a partner in the banking house, which is now at an end forever. Never did a young man by one false step so completely blast his prospects in every way.

Concerned for the status of his son, Stuart spent the summer of 1826 in consultation with lawyers to obtain the papal dispensation necessary for a mixed marriage, but this plan was scuppered by de Posse's reappearance early in 1827. An annulment was then sought on the ground that de Posse's marriage had never been consummated, and Stuart was obliged to pay him £5,000 to undergo a medical examination to establish his impotence. The dissolution was declared in Sweden, 3 Apr., and confirmed in Rome, 17 Sept. 1828, when a dispensation was finally granted. The couple's problems did not end there, however, as the Buonaparte family pushed for another marriage ceremony, apparently without success, and both families exerted pressure on the opposite party to change religion.[3]

Lady Bute, who seems to have warmed to her daughter-in-law, was ambitious for her 'dearest Pea' (her nickname for Stuart) to pursue an active parliamentary career, and in August 1829 she quoted the veteran Whig George Tierney* as having 'spoken of you almost with tears in his eyes. He said you must come down to the House of Commons amongst them'. Her hopes were realized in 1830 when he was returned unopposed for Arundel at the general election, ostensibly independently of the Whig patron, the duke of Norfolk. Lady Bute advised him to be 'collected and cautious, and not allow any private feeling or family feeling [to] ... carry him beyond himself'.[4] The duke of Wellington's ministry listed Stuart as one of the 'doubtful doubtfuls', and he voted against them in the crucial civil list division, 15 Nov. 1830. His former tutor Mortlock attended a dinner on his behalf at Arundel shortly afterwards and reported that 'everybody seems pleased with your vote'.[5] In his maiden speech, 7 Mar. 1831, he supported the Grey ministry's reform bill, denying that it would negate the 'just influence of property' and maintaining rather that it would oblige proprietors to 'live more in the country and attend more to the wants and wishes of the people, thus cementing together the different classes of society'. He approved the enfranchisement of the middle class, 'which in all communities is the most virtuous, but which in England is the pride and flower of the country', but thought the total exclusion of other classes 'rather hard'. Despite the possible loss of his seat at Arundel, which was to be partially disfranchised, he thanked ministers for bringing forward a measure which he did 'not consider to be revolutionary' and which he was 'convinced can perpetuate to us the blessings of the glorious revolution'. Lord Holland congratulated him on his 'good debut' and his mother praised his 'manly speech, so fine in content and imaginary usage, without flourish'.[6] He divided for the bill's second reading, 22 Mar., and against Gascoyne's wrecking amendment, 19 Apr. 1831. At the ensuing general election it was feared that the intervention of another reformer might cost Stuart his seat, but in the end he faced only a late, weak challenge, and though hampered by an attack of measles he was easily returned.[7]

He divided for the second reading of the reintroduced reform bill, 6 July 1831, and steadily for its details. He asserted that Arundel was 'perfectly free from nomination' and professed his independence of Norfolk, 26 July. Next day he said he felt bound to support the borough's partial disfranchisement, though 'nothing [could] be more painful' to him. On 19 Aug. he presented a petition from the mayor of Arundel in favour of the ballot (which he did not endorse) and complaining of Members with vested interests voting in private bill committees, which he refused to withdraw despite objections. He received an assurance that scot and lot voters temporarily unable to pay poor rates would not suffer permanent disfranchisement, 30 Aug. He divided for the bill's third reading, 19 Sept., its passage, 21 Sept., the second reading of the Scottish bill, 23 Sept., and Lord Ebrington's confidence motion, 10 Oct. He voted to punish only those guilty of bribery at the Dublin election, 23 Aug. He divided for the second reading of the revised reform bill, 17 Dec. 1831, and generally for its details, but he voted against the enfranchisement of Gateshead, 5 Mar. 1832. That day he announced his conversion to the view that Merthyr Tydvil and Cardiff should be granted a Member each, as they had no community of interest. Though a 'zealous reformer', he was prepared to oppose the government on this issue in order to further 'the great end and object of reform ... to take away all just ground of complaint from the people'. He voted for the third reading, 22 Mar., Ebrington's motion for an address asking the king to appoint only ministers committed to carrying an unimpaired measure, 10 May, the second reading of the Irish bill, 25 May, and against the Conservative amendment for increased Scottish county representation, 1 June. However, he vigorously opposed the boundary commissioners' proposal to unite Arundel with Littlehampton on the ground of their incompatibility and because it would deliver the borough into Norfolk's hands. He presented hostile petitions from the inhabitants, 4 June, and sought to demonstrate that Arundel satisfied the criteria for returning one Member alone. He dismissed opposition jibes that his support for the reform bill was wavering and continued to plead Arundel's case, 7, 8 June, winning praise from Edward Littleton* for his 'zeal and perseverance'; this was finally rewarded when the boundary was left unchanged. He voted for amendments to the boundary bill to lessen proprietorial influence in Whitehaven and Stamford, 22 June. He voted in the radical minorities for an amendment to the Vestry Act to relax the property qualification, 23 Jan., and for information on military punishments, 16 Feb. He divided with ministers on the Russian-Dutch loan, 26 Jan., 12, 16, 20 July, and relations with Portugal, 9 Feb. He voted against recommitting the Irish registry of deeds bill, 9 Apr., and to make coroners' inquests public, 20 June. While he agreed with the principle of the ecclesiastical courts contempt bill, to remove Members' immunity from their jurisdiction, he objected to a clause which appeared to make the provisions retrospective and voted for an amendment, 3 Aug. He presented peti-

tions from manufacturers criticizing the failure of the select committee on the silk trade (of which he was a member) to produce a report, 7 Aug., and described the distressed state of the industry in Spitalfields. He blamed cheap imports and attacked Joseph Hume, 'the great upholder of the free trade system', suggesting that he 'condescend to gain a little practical knowledge before he insists on our adopting his speculative theories'. He argued that another cause of distress was the increase in smuggling, which often involved 'respectable' people, and he thought 'the punishment in the case of a rich man offending in this manner should be much heavier than in the case of a poor man who may be considered as the rich man's servant'.

At the general election of 1832 Stuart was again returned for Arundel, and he sat as a Liberal until his defeat in 1837. After a ten-year absence from the House he was elected for Marylebone. It was said of him that while he 'never submitted entirely to the trammels of party his support of liberal measures was firm and undeviating'. The great political passion of his life, the independence of Poland, did not manifest itself until after 1832, although it was in December 1831 that he was 'deeply moved' on first hearing Prince Adam Czartoryski speak on the country's plight. His increasing devotion to the Polish cause impeded conventional political advancement and he reportedly refused several offices, 'declaring that the only appointment he should accept would be that of ambassador at the court of Warsaw'.[8] His controversial marriage failed and in January 1840 he stopped an allowance to his wife, then living in Italy.[9] He died in Sweden, where he had gone to win support for the Poles, in November 1854. The bulk of his estate passed to his son, Paul Amadee Francis Coutts Stuart, who had sustained brain damage in a riding accident, with remainder to the family of his niece Elizabeth Townshend, with whom he had lived latterly at Balls Park, Hertfordshire.[10]

[1] E.H. Coleridge, *Life of Thomas Coutts*, ii. 182; *Gent. Mag.* (1855), i. 79. [2] Bodl. Eng. Hist. c. 297, Burdett to Lady Guilford, 23 Mar. 1821; *Lady Holland to Son*, 33; *Fox Jnl.* 214; Add. 52011, Eleanor Fazakerley to Fox, 16 Sept., 8 Dec. 1825. [3] Harrowby mss vol. 24 (Latey précis); Northants. RO, Agar Ellis diary, 16 June, 3 July; Lambeth Palace Lib. ms 2877, ff. 86-146, Stuart's letters to Dr. John Lee, 1826-9; *Fox Jnl.* 325. [4] Harrowby mss vol. 22, ff. 110, 134, 172; W.D. Cooper, *Parl. Hist. Suss.* 9. [5] Harrowby mss vol. 23, f. 107. [6] Ibid. vol. 22, f. 204; 1057, f. 8. [7] Ibid. vol. 22, ff. 210-11, 216. [8] *Jewish Chron.* 24 Nov. 1854; *News of the World*, 26 Nov. 1854; *Gent. Mag.* (1855), i. 79; 'Letters of Adam Czartoryski to ... Lord Dudley Stuart', *Slavonic Rev.* xxix. (1950), 155. [9] Brougham mss, Lady Dudley Stuart to Brougham, 14 Aug. 1841. [10] PROB 11/2216/647; Harrowby mss vol. 1063, ff. 420, 475.

H.J.S.

STUART, James (1774–1833), of 63 Portland Place, Mdx.

HUNTINGDON   14 May 1824–1831

bap. 12 July 1774, illegit. s. of William Stuart, 9th Bar. Blantyre [S] (*d.* 1776), and Harriet Teasdale of Iver, Bucks. *educ.* by William Rutherford at Uxbridge Common. *m.* 23 Sept. 1822, Charlotte, wid. of Charles Chapman of E.I. Co. (Bengal), 2da. *d.* 6 Apr. 1833.
  Writer, E.I. Co. (Bengal) 1791; asst. in sec.'s office, revenue dept. 1791; commr. ct. of requests 1791; asst. registrar, Nizamut Adawlut, Calcutta 1793; dep. registrar, Sudder Dewanny and Nizamut Adawlut 1796-9, registrar 1801; sec. in revenue and judicial dept. 1801; judge and magistrate, Agra 1804, Benares 1805; 3rd judge, provincial ct. Benares 1807; 3rd judge, ct. of appeal, Benares 1808; puisne judge, Sudder Dewanny and Nizamut Adawlut 1809; member, supreme council and pres. of bd. of revenue 1817; res. 1822.
  Director, E.I. Co. 1826-*d.*

Stuart was one of the four illegitimate children fathered by the 9th Lord Blantyre in his liaison with Harriet Teasdale: Colonel John Stuart died of wounds received at the battle of Rolica in 1808, and Major Charles Stuart (?1777-1854) served in the Bengal army.[1] Their sister Ann Maria married Thomas Brooke of the Bengal civil service. According to Mrs. Littlehales, James and Charles had 'delicately fair complexions, like the inside of a bivalve shell'.[2] Blantyre died intestate in 1776, but appears to have made provision for his children. Harriet Teasdale subsequently became a favourite of the 5th earl of Sandwich, and bore him two bastards, of whom William Augustus Montagu, Member for Huntingdon, 1818-20, was one. James Stuart was educated at Uxbridge and earmarked for service with the East India Company. He arrived in India in June 1791, enjoyed rapid promotion and was one of the civil servants specifically commended by Sir John Shore on his resignation as governor in 1798. He took over the registrarship of the courts of Sudder Dewanny and Nizamut Adawlut at an annual salary of 5,000 rupees, but subsequently relinquished it on account of ill health. He convalesced at the Cape and in May 1799 was recommended for leave. He returned to Bengal in February 1801 and resumed his deputy registrarship. In March he was appointed secretary in the revenue and judicial departments, but shortly afterwards succeeded as registrar of the Sudder Dewanny and Nizamut Adawlut. He continued to hold a number of important judicial and administrative posts and by 1808 was third judge in the court of appeal at Benares. His report on the police and judicial arrangements of the province was subsequently published in the fifth report of the select committee on

the East India Company in 1812.[3] He was appointed puisne judge of the Sudder Dewanny and Nizamut Adawlut in 1809. He was again recommended for leave, to return with his rank, and was appointed second member of the council of the College of Fort William in 1811. His illegitimate son James Stuart was born in Bengal in April 1812 as a result of his copulation with Maria Fenelon. In 1814 he was compelled by illness to quit the presidency and recuperate at the Cape. His total annual income in 1816 was estimated at 55,000 rupees. He was given seniority over Lord Liverpool's nominee and appointed to the supreme council of Bengal in 1817. He became president of the board of revenue in December the same year and, according to an obituary, acquired a comprehensive knowledge of Indian affairs. He resigned from the Company's service on 23 Feb. 1822, returned to England and in September married the widow Charlotte Chapman.[4]

Stuart was brought forward for Huntingdon in May 1824 by the Dowager Lady Sandwich on Lord Ancram's succession to the peerage; he appears to have been a substitute for his half-brother Montagu, who was then preoccupied with his naval career.[5] He was attacked by the liberal *Huntingdon Gazette* as a placeman, and at the election was forced to swear an affidavit as to his property qualification. He presented himself as a ministerialist, but repudiated the charge that he had 'imbibed slavish principles' in India. In what the *Gazette* called a 'specious address', he boasted of his determination to protect national prosperity: no man was more attached to the 'free constitution'. He was elected ahead of the anti-corporation candidate after a contest forced in an effort to try the eligibility of the votes of the inhabitant householders.[6] John Drakard, editor of the *Stamford News*, predicted that he would not find his seat 'altogether so pleasant as he may have anticipated'.[7] A petition against his return was presented on 21 May 1824, but it was not finally rejected until 1 Mar. 1825. An appeal against this decision was rejected, 17 Apr. 1826.[8] The cost of defending his seat amounted to over £3,046. Lady Sandwich, astonished at the expense, contributed over £1,572, but Stuart remained indignant and considered that his colleague John Calvert ought to bear some share.[9]

Stuart voted with the Liverpool ministry in defence of the prosecution of the Methodist missionary John Smith in Demerara, 11 June 1824, and for the Irish unlawful societies bill, 25 Feb. 1825. He divided against Catholic relief, 21 Apr., but, much to Huntingdon corporation's dismay, voted for it, 10 May 1825. Lady Sandwich was reported to have demanded his compliance on the ground that the question did not relate to India.[10] An East India Company stockholder since 1824, he was defeated by Henry Alexander* in the ballot for the vacant directorship, 8 Mar. 1826. Undaunted, he stood as a candidate in the annual election to the court of directors the following month. The *Huntingdon Gazette* attributed his absence from the division on the ministerial salary of the president of the board of trade, 10 Apr., to his active canvass. Supported by the deputy chairman Hugh Lindsay* and all 16 directors, he was duly elected, 12 Apr., and immediately appointed to the Company's shipping and private trade committee.[11] The *Gazette* ironically attributed his absence from the division on the reform of Edinburgh's representation, 13 Apr., to his 'deserved contempt' for so 'limited a franchise'; and he was censured for missing the division on inquiry into economic distress, 4 May.[12] On 11 May 1826 he was added to the select committee to consider the appeal of James Silk Buckingham,† the proprietor of the *Calcutta Journal*, who had been expelled from India for his criticism of the Company.

Stuart was returned unopposed for Huntingdon in 1826 despite rumours that he would retire to provide William Henry Fellowes* with a safe seat. Challenged to explain his equivocation on Catholic relief, he denied that he had bowed to the 'petticoat government' of Lady Sandwich: he had opposed it in deference to public opinion, but had subsequently voted for it because it would improve the condition of Ireland. He refused to be drawn on the equity of an extended franchise at Huntingdon; but, currying favour with the freemen, he claimed that the failure of the householders' petition had confirmed their privileges against 'speculative and factious attacks'.[13] In the House, 11 June 1827, he secured information on Anglo-Indian shipping.[14] He was credited with a speech against the second reading of the East Retford disfranchisement bill, 22 June, though the reporter for *The Times* failed to catch his name: he was not prepared to see the House pledged to transfer its seats to Birmingham and proposed as an alternative one of the Scottish counties, 'where there was neither bribery nor corruption'.[15] On 11 Mar. 1828 he moved for further information on Anglo-Indian shipping, and had the papers printed, 21 Mar. He voted against the archbishop of Canterbury's estate bill, 16 June, and the modified East Retford disfranchisement bill, 27 June. He voted with the duke of Wellington's government against reduction of the salary of the lieutenant-general of the ordnance, 4 July 1828. He had sent his illegitimate son to Frome grammar school and, as a director of the Company, successfully endorsed his application for a writership on the Prince of Wales

Island establishment, 10 Dec. 1828.[16] Planta, the patronage secretary, predicted in February 1829 that he would vote 'with government' for the concession of Catholic emancipation. According to the *Gazette*, Lady Sandwich directed her Members to do so, but Stuart voted against consideration of the measure, 6 Mar. 1829.[17] He divided against the transfer of East Retford's seats to Birmingham, 11 Feb., and reduction of the South American consular grant, 7 June 1830. In a debate on the bill framed to authorize the Company to compensate those whose property had been lost as a consequence of the Madras registrar's malversation, 9 July 1830, he warned against attaching too much weight to it as a precedent, regretted that it had not undergone the discussion 'which its importance demands' and defended the court of directors.

Stuart stood again for Huntingdon in 1830, presenting himself as an independent, and was returned after a nominal contest. He declared that he would go to Parliament 'unfettered as to the tea monopoly', but that as ministers had his confidence on 'most points' he would generally defer to them.[18] They listed him among their 'friends', and he voted with them in the division on the civil list which brought them down, 15 Nov. 1830. He divided against the second reading of the Grey ministry's reform bill, 22 Mar., and for Gascoyne's wrecking amendment, 19 Apr. 1831. He did not seek re-election at Huntingdon at the ensuing general election.[19]

Stuart died in April 1833. In his will, dated 22 July 1830 and proved under £20,000, he made provision for his wife and confirmed her jointure of £800 for life. He left £10,000 to furnish marriage settlements for each of his two daughters. Among the residuary legatees were his son James (d. 31 Aug. 1833), Charlotte Chapman, a daughter of his wife's first marriage and his remarkable nephew, Sir James Brooke (1803-68), the first raja of Sarawak.[20]

[1] V.C.P. Hodson, *Officers of the Bengal Army*, 204. [2] G.L. Jacob, *Raja of Sarawak*, i. 2. [3] *PP* (1812), vii. 573-86. [4] *Gent. Mag.* (1833), i. 466-7. [5] Add. 38292, f. 52. [6] *Huntingdon, Bedford and Peterborough Gazette*, 1, 8, 15, 22, 29 May, 5 June 1824. [7] *Drakard's Stamford News*, 28 May 1824. [8] *CJ*, lxxix. 394; lxxx. 641; lxxxi. 246. [9] Hunts. RO, Sandwich mss Hinch/8/198-200; 8/214/1-2; *VCH Hunts*. ii. 51-52. [10] *Huntingdon, Bedford and Peterborough Gazette*, 3 Dec. 1825. [11] *The Times*, 9, 21 Mar., 14 Apr.; *Huntingdon, Bedford and Peterborough Gazette*, 15 Apr. 1826. [12] *Huntingdon, Bedford and Peterborough Gazette*, 22 Apr., 13 May 1826. [13] Ibid. 15 Apr., 6 May, 10 June 1826. [14] *The Times*, 12 June 1827. [15] Ibid. 23 June 1827. [16] BL OIOC J/1/45, ff. 329, 333. [17] *Huntingdon, Bedford and Peterborough Gazette*, 14 Feb., 7 Mar. 1829. [18] *Huntingdon, Bedford and Peterborough Gazette*, 31 July, 7 Aug. 1830. [19] Ibid. 30 Apr. 1831. [20] *Gent. Mag.* (1833), i. 466-7; ii. 285; PROB 11/1815/26; IR26/1336/35.

S.R.H.

STUART, **Hon. John** (1797–1867), of Cambus Wallace, Doune, Perth.

NEWPORT I.o.W.   18 Feb. 1825–1826

b. 25 Jan. 1797, 2nd s. of Francis, 10th earl of Moray [S] (*d.* 1848), and 1st w. Lucy, da. and coh. of Maj.-Gen. John Scott[†] of Balcomie, Fife. *educ.* Chobham. *unm. suc.* bro. Francis Stuart as 12th earl of Moray [S] 6 May 1859. *d.* 8 Nov. 1867.
    Cornet 3 Drag. 1815, lt. 1816, half-pay 1817; lt. 13 Drag. 1822; capt. (half-pay) 1825-*d.*

Stuart's grandfather Francis, 9th earl of Moray, was a Scottish representative peer from 1784 to 1796, when he was created Baron Stuart of Castle Stuart in the British peerage. His two eldest sons died young and it was the third, this Member's father, who succeeded him as 10th earl of Moray in 1810. He was lord lieutenant of Elginshire from then until his death in 1848. His first wife, the mother of his two eldest sons, died in 1798, aged 23. Two years later her sister Joan Scott married George Canning*, who as premier in 1827 successfully recommended Moray to George IV for a vacant green ribbon, even though he was 'of such retired habits, that he would never seek such a distinction'.[1]

John Stuart, Moray's second son, entered the army three weeks after Waterloo and, in what was a nominal career, rose no higher than half-pay captain. He was described in 1822 as 'six feet in stature, dark complexioned, and handsome'.[2] Three years later Lord Liverpool, the prime minister, named him for a vacant seat at Newport, which the Worsley Holmes trustees had placed at the government's disposal for the remainder of the Parliament. He was returned unopposed *in absentia*.[3] A lax attender, who is not known to have spoken in debate, his only recorded votes were for Catholic relief, 1 Mar., 21 Apr., 10 May 1825, and in government majorities on the duke of Cumberland's annuity bill, 6 June 1825, and the Jamaican slave trials, 2 Mar. 1826.[4] At the 1826 dissolution he retired. Later that year he was one of a committee of three deputed by the Celtic Society to present Sir Walter Scott with a 'most splendid broadsword'.[5] In 1859 he succeeded his elder brother, who had been incurably insane since their schooldays, to the peerage and the family's extensive estates in north-eastern Scotland. He died at Doune in November 1867, having 'for many years taken no part whatever in public affairs'. He was succeeded in turn by his half-brothers Archibald George Stuart (1810-72) and George Philip Stuart (1816-95).[6]

[1] *Gent. Mag.* (1848), i. 305; *Geo. IV Letters*, iii. 1361. [2] *CP*, ix. 191. [3] Berks. RO, Mount mss D/EMt F14, pp. 1-7, 21. [4] *Session of Parl. 1825*, p. 486. [5] *Scott Jnl.* 70-71. [6] *Gent. Mag.* (1867), ii. 815.

D.R.F./P.J.S.

STUART, **William** (1798–1874), of Tempsford, nr. Sandy, Beds.; Aldenham Abbey, nr. Watford, Herts, and Hill Street, Mdx.

ARMAGH   1820–1826

BEDFORDSHIRE   1830–1831

BEDFORDSHIRE   1832–1834

b. 31 Oct. 1798, 1st s. of Hon. and Rt. Rev. William Stuart, bp. of St. Davids and abp. of Armagh, and Sophia Margaret Juliana, da. of Thomas Penn of Stoke Poges, Bucks. *educ.* St. John's, Camb. 1815. *m* (1) 9 Aug. 1821,[1] Henrietta Maria Sarah, da. of Adm. Sir Charles Morice Pole[†], 1st bt., of Aldenham Abbey, 3s. 3da. (2 *d.v.p.*); (2) 31 Aug. 1854, Georgiana Adelaide Forester, da. of Gen. Frederick Nathaniel Walker of the Manor House, Bushey, Herts., *s.p. suc.* fa. 1822. *d.* 7 July 1874.
    Registrar, probate ct. [I] c. 1821-57.
    Recorder, Banbury 1828; capt. Beds. militia 1831; sheriff, Beds. 1846-7.

Stuart's father, who was born in 1755, was the fifth and youngest son of the 3rd earl of Bute, George III's early favourite and prime minister, 1762-3. After leaving Cambridge he entered the church, becoming vicar of Luton, where his father's Bedfordshire estate lay, in 1779, though he lived two miles away at Copt Hall, which Bute placed at his disposal. During an outbreak of smallpox he had almost 2,000 local people inoculated at his own expense. A shy man of commendably few words, he was introduced to Dr. Johnson, 10 Apr. 1783, by Boswell, who wrote that 'with all the advantages of high birth, learning, travel and elegant manners', he was 'an exemplary parish priest in every respect'.[2] As Bute's health collapsed in the years before his death in 1792, his wife took it on herself to press the king for preferment for Stuart. A bid for the bishopric of Exeter in August 1792 was unsuccessful, but the following year he was made a canon of Windsor and in 1794 he was promoted to the see of St. Davids. Six years later the king, taking his usual stand on appointing a non-Irish bishop to the primacy of Ireland, insisted on his becoming archbishop of Armagh, dismissing his qualms over the effect of the 'humid climate' on his 'infirm state of health' and the 'great expense of taking possession', which would 'utterly ruin my children'. As it turned out, he did very well financially out of his 22 years in the post.[3] His primacy was not without controversy. In its first weeks he had to be nudged by the king into vetoing the Irish government's plans to replace the anti-Catholic Member for Armagh with a supporter of relief.[4] Later in 1801 he blustered and threatened to resign over the promotion of an Irish bishop of whose lax morals he disapproved; he was ignored.[5] He was quick to take umbrage at perceived personal slights, and his relations with the Portland, Perceval and Liverpool administrations were sometimes strained. The bishop of Limerick, anxious to smooth Stuart's path with the prince regent, portrayed him behind his back in 1811 as a man who 'from his retired habits is but little known and very much misunderstood', but was 'a very sensible, clear-headed man of business', with 'very good understanding' as well as 'many oddities'. In 1813 Limerick described him to the regent's secretary as

a high, proud, independent man, but with honourable principles and excellent understanding. He is a constant resident in his see of Armagh, which he has much improved, and by his attention and example, the established church in Ireland has been highly benefitted and greatly extended. Within the last seven years the number of churches has been doubled, and the resident clergy in the same proportion.[6]

William Stuart, the elder by six years of the primate's two sons, spent much of his boyhood in Armagh. At the time of the general election of 1818 his father extracted from ministers, as the price of his co-operation in a desired electoral arrangement for Armagh, which he controlled as head of the church, an assurance that if after two years he wished to bring William into Parliament, a seat would be provided for him either for Armagh, by the retirement of the sitting Member, or elsewhere, at government expense. Peel, the Irish secretary, thought it 'more than probable that the primate will never claim for his son the fulfilment of the promise'; but at the general election of 1820, when Stuart was only five months into his majority, the archbishop returned him for Armagh.[7] Shortly before the new Parliament met the primate wrote to him in London:

If you represented any other borough it would be a matter of indifference, to me at least, with which party you voted; but representing Armagh you have no option, and must support the established government. Armagh does not belong to me but to the church, and, whatever may be my private opinion, I should act dishonourably were I not in this matter to consult the interest of that church, which is manifestly to support the minister for the time being. Besides, the questions which will come before the House of Commons during the session ... so personally concern the king – the revenue of the crown, the rights of the queen, etc., etc. – that a man who joins opposition must do so for the express purpose of degrading and insulting Majesty.

He gave Stuart permission to second any motion by Newport for having the Irish parochial reports printed, but no more, and promised to send him further coaching and instruction in the defence of the church. He advised Stuart, who was suffering from a swelling in his face, to decline any request from ministers that he should move the address.[8]

It was surely Stuart who voted in defence of their conduct of the Queen Caroline affair, 6 Feb.; but it is not clear whether it was he or William Stewart, Member for Tyrone, who divided against Catholic claims, 28 Feb. 1821. The 'few words' which he uttered on the relief bill, 2 Apr., were 'perfectly inaudible in the gallery'.[9] He voted with government against repeal of the additional malt duty, 3 Apr.,[10] and Hume's attempt to disfranchise ordnance officials, 12 Apr. He introduced, 9 Mar., and steered through a bill to regulate public notaries in Ireland, which became law on 28 May 1821 (1 & 2 Geo. IV, c. 36).[11] Two months later he married the daughter and heiress of Sir Charles Pole, former Member for Newark and Plymouth and groom of the bedchamber to the duke of Clarence, whose death in 1830 was to bring him his Hertfordshire property at Aldenham Abbey. His marriage settlement was a very generous one, which gave him an annual income of £1,000 and his wife a jointure of £2,000, together with a trust fund of £40,000.[12] Stuart divided against more extensive tax reductions to relieve distress, 21 Feb., but was credited with a vote in support of Hume's call for information on navy victualling, 22 Feb. 1822, which may have been the work of William Stewart. He voted against the bill to relieve Catholic peers of their disabilities, 30 Apr. Six days later his sickly father died tragically at his London house in Hill Street, where, as a result of blunders by a servant and his wife, who were probably flustered by his own impatience and bad temper, he took a fatal dose of embrocation, containing laudanum and camphorated spirit, in mistake for medicine just prescribed for him by his doctor. Mrs. Stuart was reported to have rushed into the street 'in a state of speechless distraction', while one of his daughters was said a week later to have 'never spoken since'.[13] By his father's will, dated 1 May 1822, Stuart, who was given a month's compassionate leave, 5 June, became entitled to an invested £20,000 on the death of his mother (though she lived for another 31 years). He received the Hill Street house and the residue of his father's real and personal property, which included an estate at Sutton Cheney, near Market Bosworth, Leicestershire. The primate's personalty was sworn under £250,000 in the province of Canterbury, and the residue calculated for duty at £141,078.[14]

Stuart voted with government against inquiry into the parliamentary franchise, 20 Feb., for the national debt reduction bill, 3, 13 Mar., and against repeal of the Foreign Enlistment Act, 16 Apr. 1823. On 4 Mar. he 'expressed his strong disapprobation' of Hume's motion for inquiry into the Irish church establishment and repudiated as 'totally unfounded' his attack on his late father on the issue of clerical non-residence. However, he seems to have supported Hume's attempt to halve the grant for the Irish yeomanry, which he thought would 'do good', 10 Mar.[15] He voted for inquiry into the prosecution of the Dublin Orange rioters, 22 Apr., and may have been in Hume's minority of 32 on naval promotions, 19 June 1823. He voted against reform of Edinburgh's representation, 26 Feb., the abolition of army flogging, 5 Mar., and inquiry into the trial of the Methodist missionary John Smith in Demerara, 11 June, and for the Irish unlawful societies bill, 14 June 1824; but he was listed in the minority of 33 for an advance of capital to Ireland, 4 May. In 1825, when he was reckoned to have 'attended occasionally, and voted with ministers',[16] he divided again for the Irish unlawful societies bill, 15, 25 Feb., and against Catholic relief, 1 Mar., 21 Apr., 10 May, and the Irish franchise bill, 26 Apr. He was improbably credited with a vote for the abolition of army flogging, 10 Mar. 1826. He presented an Armagh petition for the abolition of slavery, 9 May 1826.[17]

In 1825 Stuart bought for £64,000 the Payne estate at Tempsford, about seven miles from Bedford in the east of the county.[18] He apparently sought the support of his cousin, the 2nd marquess of Bute, for an attempt on the county at the next general election in January 1826, but Bute was unable to oblige him on this occasion, preferring to back the candidature of Sir Robert Inglis* (which came to nothing) as 'the best way of keeping my interest altogether'.[19] Bute, who had installed him as nominal recorder of Banbury, where he had inherited a dominant electoral interest, in 1828, did support Stuart when he offered for Bedfordshire at the 1830 general election, when he was seen as 'one of the new party, called Wellington Tories'. The disaffected Tory sitting Member gave up, and Stuart was returned unopposed with the Whig Lord Tavistock, son of the duke of Bedford. At the nomination he applauded the fact that 'the terms Whig and Tory, which have so long been the watchword of party feuds and political animosities, have become almost obsolete'. Expressing his admiration for the duke of Wellington, he said that 'the bias of my mind may incline me in general to the support of his administration, but I will bind myself to no party'. In his victory address, he wrote that

> although I cannot concur in the wild and visionary theories of those who, erroneously attributing the consequences of individual corruption to defects in the form and fabric of the state, would introduce dangerous and unnecessary innovations, I shall be ever ready to promote those moderate and rational improvements which the diffusion of knowledge, and the consequent advancement of human intellect, may render expedient.

He blamed the distress of agricultural labourers on defects in the poor laws, and that of the farmers on the 'erroneous principles and calculations' on which the corn laws were based, and declared his support for 'every prudent measure' to ameliorate the condition of slaves in the West Indian colonies and so lead eventually to abolition. According to Bedford, Bute 'left him in the lurch ... as to expense, and Mr. S. had to pay *the whole*, which he did not much like'.[20] Ministers listed him among their 'friends', but he voted against them on the civil list, 15 Nov. 1830, though his name was initially omitted from the hostile majority.[21] He voted against the second reading of the Grey ministry's reform bill, 22 Mar., and for Gascoyne's wrecking amendment, 19 Apr. 1831. He stood again for Bedfordshire at the ensuing general election, professing support for any 'moderate plan of reform', but condemning the bill as 'a rash experiment, introducing extensive *innovations in the state*'. On the hustings, he said that he was willing to give the vote to leaseholders and copyholders and to enfranchise large industrial towns, but admitted that he now repented of having helped to vote the Wellington ministry out of office, as their successors were 'endangering the constitution'. He was always up against it, with the tide of enthusiasm for reform running strongly against him, and he finished a poor third behind a second reformer. The election cost him about £4,000.[22]

He kept up his interest in the county and was considered a likely starter in October 1831 if Tavistock was called to the Lords.[23] From at least 1821, possibly earlier, Stuart seems to have been the joint holder with the Rev. Sir John Robinson, the nephew of a previous archbishop of Armagh, of the sinecure place of registrar of the Irish probate court, the duties of which were executed by deputies. On Robinson's death in May 1832 he evidently became the sole incumbent of the post, which was reckoned to be worth over £1,000 a year. He held it until the Irish probate system was rationalized by statute in 1857.[24] He stood again for

Bedfordshire as a Conservative at the general election of 1832, and was successful after a contest which relieved him of over £11,000.[25] Soon afterwards he mortgaged the Tempsford estate to Bute and others for £40,000.[26] He retired from Parliament at the dissolution in December 1834 because of ill health, but he saw his brother Henry sit for Bedford, 1837-8 and 1841-54, and his eldest son William Stuart (1825-93), a barrister and colonel of militia, do likewise, 1854-7 and 1859-68.[27] In 1857 Stuart, who lived mostly at Aldenham for the last 40 years of his life, having made over Tempsford to his eldest son, privately published 22 copies of *Stuartiana*, a collection of family and personal anecdotes, verses and correspondence.[28] He died in July 1874. By his brief will, dated 4 Sept. 1854 at St. Leonards, he left £5,000 to his second wife (who later married the 9th earl of Seafield) and all the rest of his property, apart from a few trifling legacies, to his eldest son.

[1] *Gent. Mag.* (1821), ii. 176. [2] *Oxford DNB*; *Admissions to St. John's, Camb.* iv. 499; *Prime Minister and his Son* ed. E. Stuart Wortley, 215; *Edgeworth Letters*, 87, 319; *Boswell's Life of Johnson* ed. G.B. Hill and L.F. Powell, iv. 199, 517. [3] *Geo. III Corresp.* i. 733, 775, 780; iii. 2091, 2098, 2191, 2194-7, 2267, 2271-2, 2275. [4] Ibid. iii. 2329, 2333, 2336, 2338; *Glenbervie Diaries*, i. 394-5. [5] M. MacDonagh, *Viceroy's Post-Bag*, 97-119; *Geo. III Corresp.* iv. 2592. [6] *Prince of Wales Corresp.* viii. 3093, 3273; *Geo. IV Letters*, i. 358. [7] Add. 41295, ff. 131, 136, 146, 149, 155. [8] Beds. RO, Wynne mss WY 997/1. [9] *The Times*, 3 Apr. 1821. [10] PRO NI, Rossmore mss T.2929/3/14. [11] Ibid. 16 Mar. 1821. [12] *VCH Herts.* ii. 427; Wynne mss 990/46; 997/2, 3, 67, 10, 1219, 24, 26. [13] *Oxford DNB*; *Gent. Mag.* (1822), i. 469-70; *Edgeworth Letters*, 399, 400; Wynne mss 997/33-34, 39. [14] PROB 11/1656/236; IR26/892/409; Wynne mss 937; 997/ 35, 36, 40. [15] *The Times*, 11 Mar. 1823. [16] *Session of Parl. 1825*, p. 486. [17] *The Times*, 10 May 1826. [18] Wynne mss 279, 300-1; 998/5, 6, 8, 9, 13, 14, 19, 23, 26-29, 33. [19] Ibid. 999/1. [20] Ibid. 1009/2; *Russell Letters*, i. 141; *Herts. Mercury*, 10, 17, 24, 31 July, 7, 14 Aug. 1830; Add. 51663, Bedford to Holland [25 Apr. 1831]. [21] *The Times*, 26 Nov.; *Herts. Mercury*, 27 Nov. 1830. [22] Hatfield House mss 2M/Gen., Bute to Salisbury, 3 Apr.; *Cambridge and Hertford Independent Press*, 30 Apr.; 7, 14 May; Fitzwilliam mss, C. Hill to Milton, 29 Apr. [1831]; Wynne mss 1009/4. [23] *Cambridge and Hertford Independent Press*, 1 Oct.; Wellington mss WP1/1199/19. [24] Wynne mss 997/11, 13; Wynne mss 16, 18, 20, 23; *Gent. Mag.* (1832), i. 462. [25] Wynne mss 999/19, 20, 22, 24, 25, 28, 29;1009/6, 7; *Russell Letters*, iii. 25. [26] Wynne mss 307-8. [27] Ibid. 1009/8; J. Davies, *Cardiff and marquess of Bute*, 107. [28] The copy in BL 9918. aa. 7. is inscribed by Stuart himself to his youngest son, Clarence Esme Stuart (1827-1903), who became a Plymouth Brother. His second son, Charles Pole Stuart (1826-96), was a lawyer.

D.R.F.

STUART, Lord *see* **CRICHTON STUART**, **Patrick James Herbert**

STUART *see also* **VILLIERS STUART**

STUART WORTLEY, Hon. Charles James (1802–1844), of Wortley Hall, Yorks.

BOSSINEY   1830–Feb. 1831

b. 3 June 1802, 2nd s. of James Archibald Stuart Wortley* (*d*. 1845) and Lady Elizabeth Caroline Mary Creighton, da. of John, 1st Earl Erne [I]; bro. of John Stuart Wortley*. *educ*. Harrow 1812. *m*. 17 Feb. 1831, Lady Emmeline Charlotte Elizabeth Manners, da. of John Henry, 5th duke of Rutland, 2s. 1da. *d*. 22 May 1844.
  Cornet 10 Drag. 1819, lt. 1822; half-pay 1825; capt. 4 Ft. 1826; half-pay 88 Ft. 1829.

Stuart Wortley, like his father, initially pursued a military career. In April 1830 it was reported that he was to marry the daughter of Admiral Frank Sotheron, Member for Nottinghamshire, but this did not come off.[1] At the general election that summer he was returned on the family interest for Bossiney, probably as a locum for his elder brother John, who had quit his seat there to contest Perth Burghs. The duke of Wellington's ministry listed him as one of their 'friends', and he voted with them in the crucial civil list division, 15 Nov. 1830, his only recorded action in the Commons. His brief parliamentary career ended in February 1831 when he vacated for his brother, who had been unseated on petition. At the general election that spring the Tory party managers in London sent him and James Lockhart, the editor of the *Quarterly Review*, to contest Milborne Port, but they found Lord Anglesey's interest to be impregnable and beat a hasty retreat.[2] In February 1831 he married Lady Emmeline Manners, who had once been courted by Prince Leopold of Coburg, and who subsequently became a well-known poet and author.[3] He apparently knew the prince and was reacquainted with him when he travelled to Belgium in December 1832 to observe the siege of Antwerp. Although he had no official standing, he carried letters from the foreign secretary Lord Palmerston* to Sir Robert Adair[†], the special envoy to Brussels, and to Colonel John Hobart Cradock*, the government's observer at Antwerp. He published a record of his experiences in his *Journal of an Excursion* (1833). He died, apparently intestate, at his brother's London house in May 1844.[4]

[1] Lonsdale mss, Beckett to Lowther, 9 Apr. 1830. [2] Cent. Kent. Stud. Stanhope mss U1590/C 346. [3] *Oxford DNB sub* Lady Emmeline Stuart Wortley. [4] *Gent. Mag.* (1844), i. 103.

M.P.J.C.

STUART WORTLEY, James Archibald (1776–1845), of Wortley Hall, Yorks.; 15 Curzon Street, Mayfair, Mdx., and Belmont, Perth.

BOSSINEY	1802–1818
YORKSHIRE	1818–1826

b. 6 Oct. 1776, 2nd s. and event. h. of Hon. James Archibald Stuart[†] and Margaret, da. of Sir David Cunynghame, 3rd bt., of Milncraig, Ayr. *educ.* Charterhouse 1789-90. *m.* 30 Mar. 1799, Lady Elizabeth Caroline Mary Creighton, da. of John, 1st Earl Erne [I], 3s. (1 *d.v.p.*) 2da. (1 *d.v.p.*). Took additional name of Wortley (with his fa.) 17 Jan. 1795; additional name of Mackenzie 17 June 1826; *suc.* fa. 1818; *cr.* Bar. Wharncliffe 12 July 1826. *d.* 19 Dec. 1845.

Ensign 48 Ft. 1790; lt. 7 Ft. 1791; capt. 98 Ft. 1794, maj. 1794, brevet lt.-col. 1796; lt.-col. 12 Ft. 1796; capt. and lt.-col. 1 Ft. Gds. 1797, ret. 1801; lt.-col. S.W. Yorks. yeomanry 1803, commdt. militia 1810.

PC 16 Dec. 1834; ld. privy seal Dec. 1834-Apr. 1835; ld. pres. of council Sept. 1841-*d.*

Ld. lt. Yorks. 1841-*d.*

According to Greville, Wortley, as he was usually known, occupied a 'place in the political scale' which 'was that of the most conspicuous and important of the country gentlemen'. A 'forcible' rather than 'eloquent' debater, whose speeches were 'more argumentative than ornamental', at the 1820 general election he offered again for Yorkshire, where he had been returned unopposed in 1818 as part of an unpopular compromise between the leading interests.[1] He had asked his uncle Sir William Cunynghame for a loan of £7,000 to enable him to stand again, which made his total debt to him £8,000.[2] Defending his record at the Leeds Cloth Halls, where he was received with much hissing, 4 Mar., he called for repeal of the recent wool tax, which 'every principle of political economy was against', justified his votes for the Six Acts, arguing that 'it was better to endure a temporary suspension' of liberty 'than to incur the evils of anarchy', and explained that although he was no reformer, he would listen carefully to the arguments on both sides for enfranchising Leeds.[3] He canvassed the West Riding extensively, describing to his wife, 13 Mar., 'such a hooting and hissing from an immense mob at Sheffield as never was heard ... the Barnsley radicals too made a delightful noise ... By the respectable people, everywhere, I am received with open arms'.[4] At the nomination, 20 Mar., Edward Baines, editor of the Whig *Leeds Mercury*, criticized his failure to support the county meeting over Peterloo and votes for the Six Acts, whereupon Wortley again defended his record, insisting that 'he had not forfeited one pledge which

he had given, and he left it to the freeholders to say, whether his conduct had not squared with his professions'. They had no chance to do so as he was returned unopposed. At his celebration dinner he warned that there were

but now two parties. One was those who loved the constitution and would support it; the other, those who talked about it, but united with the radicals. The time ... may not be far distant when we shall be called upon to support the principles we profess, for the present state of things cannot long exist. The party calling themselves Whigs must either entirely amalgamate with the radicals, or the radicals will pull them down.[5]

In the House Wortley resumed his line as an independent supporter of the Liverpool ministry, who paid close attention to matters of procedure. Despite what he had said during the election, he was suspected of being 'not very much in earnest' about repeal of the wool tax;[6] but in the early stages of the 1820 Parliament he devoted much time to it. He condemned it as a 'cruel measure' and urged its repeal, 3 May, brought up multiple petitions against it from the West Riding that month, and when his colleague Lord Milton introduced his repeal motion, 26 May, asserted that it was the 'universal opinion' of those involved in the woollen industry that the tax had been 'a deadly blow'. That day he presented a Forfar petition to extend the linen bounties, as enjoyed by Irish producers, to the manufacturers on the mainland. He reaffirmed his opposition to the wool tax, which 'had almost ruined the export trade in wools, and had been quite inefficient to protect the grower', 18 June 1821.[7] During discussion of the remit of the newly appointed committee on agricultural distress, 31 May 1820, he backed the ministerial proposal to limit its scope, noting that although the agriculturists were entitled to 'every protection which could be consistently extended to them', they of all classes 'were suffering the least' and their distress 'bore no proportion to that of the manufacturers'. When the government sought to appoint a secret committee to investigate the behaviour of Queen Caroline, 7 June, Wortley said that he had 'very little hope of any compromise' before judicial proceedings against her were instigated, but as many thought a delay would help, he urged the House 'to consider whether it ought not to make that small sacrifice'. Ministers failed in their own attempt to broker a deal a few days later, and on 22 June Wilberforce introduced his own compromise motion, which Wortley seconded, warning that if it was rejected there was no other option but to proceed with the inquiry and 'for months to come, the country would be plunged into a state of agitation'. The motion passed and Wortley, Wilberforce, Sir Thomas Acland and Henry Bankes were deputed to present the resolutions to the queen, 24 June. They were received 'in the most impertinent manner' and her reply, read to them by Henry Brougham*, was a flat refusal. On leaving they were forced to make a dash for their carriage under a barrage of bricks and abuse from a large crowd that had gathered outside.[8] Wortley reported on the failed mission to the House and later to Lord Liverpool.[9] The motion to proceed with the inquiry was reintroduced, 26 June, when Wortley contended that the ministerial proposals were the 'best adapted for the emergency of the case'. Over the next few months he vacillated in his opinion of the wisdom of introducing the bill of pains and penalties against the queen, and when her trial began became convinced that she would 'damn herself by her own witnesses', noting that her counsel, 'seeing that their case was ruined', were 'catching at straws'.[10] On 29 Oct. he advised his wife that 'the second reading of the bill in the Lords will be carried', which, he informed Liverpool, 'would be the worst and most dangerous thing for the country possible'. Yet he predicted to his wife that it could 'never go through the ... Commons, and will therefore probably be got rid of *some how* before it goes there'.[11] After its abandonment Liverpool sought Wortley's opinions, 30 Nov. In reply, 18 Dec., he expressed amazement that anyone with the evidence before them could have voted for her innocence, but ascribed the failure of the bill to the king's actions, adding that whatever course ministers decided upon, they should act 'in deference to the feelings of the better part of the community ... and by no means in deference to any personal feelings of the king's'. He agreed with Liverpool's determination to exclude the queen from the liturgy, she having forfeited 'all moral right', and urged him to put the question before Parliament as soon as possible. This, he contended, would 'do more to strengthen your government than any other step'. He had no firm opinion on her being given a palace, but said that if she was granted an annuity of £50,000, it should be unconditionally, though personally he had 'very great doubts' about giving the queen 'any such sum'. He concluded by declaring that it was unlikely that a Yorkshire county meeting to support her would take place because of disagreements between the Whigs and radicals.[12] Arbuthnot, the patronage secretary, thanked Liverpool for an account of the letter, which he believed was 'very important', while Seymour Bathurst* told Lady Wortley that it 'did my heart good ... it was worthy of a *Blue* and coming from a *Bottled Green*, it gave me, if possible, more satisfaction'.[13]

Wortley defended ministers on the issue, asserting that they had not yet 'lost the public confidence so much as to reconcile the country to having the gentlemen opposite as their successors', 31 Jan., and voted against their censure, 6 Feb., and a motion to restore the queen's name to the liturgy, 13 Feb. 1821. The dowager duchess of Devonshire told his wife, 7 Feb., that his 'firmness and manly expression of his opinions does him great credit everywhere'.[14] Following the presentation of a petition complaining of the conduct of the sheriff of Cheshire, 9 Feb., he condemned all the sheriffs who had lately refused to hold county meetings in defiance of properly signed requisitions. After the queen's death he asked ministers if pensions would be provided for all members of her household as was the custom, 13 July 1822. On being told that some would be excluded, he threatened to move an amendment to assert their rights, but never did so.[15] He presented and endorsed a West Riding petition for inquiry into the stamping of woollen cloth, 8 Feb., and moved for one, to which he was appointed, 28 Mar. 1821.[16] On 12 Feb. he spoke and was a majority teller against Nicolson Calvert's amendment to the Grampound disfranchisement bill transferring its seats to a divided county of Yorkshire (two Members for the West Riding, two for the East and North). Dismissing claims that giving Leeds the Members would make them the puppets of the clothiers, he argued that the House would benefit from the presence of representatives of manufacturing, that there was neither precedent nor machinery for dividing the county, and that the result of giving Members to counties rather than towns would be 'that the whole of the representation would fall into the hands of the aristocracy'. On 2 Mar. he welcomed the proposed enfranchisement of Leeds but spoke against adopting a £10 voting qualification, as it would produce too large an electorate, and moved as an amendment £20, which would 'include every person of the rank of tradesman ... and give a body of voters of between 2,000 and 3,000'. After Milton's proposal for a scot and lot franchise was rejected, Wortley's amendment was carried, which induced Lord John Russell, the bill's initiator, to abandon it. Taking it up himself Wortley moved the report, 5 Mar., and successfully pressed for the bill's recommittal on the ground that his amendment had been misunderstood, explaining that he had not intended to limit the franchise to the owners of houses with an annual rental value of £20, but to enfranchise all occupiers 'paying scot and lot on an annual rental of £20'. In moving the third reading, 19 Mar. 1821, he hoped ministers would refrain from using their influence in the Lords to defeat it.[17] Liverpool was apparently dismayed, but by a compromise suggested by Lord Castlereagh and moved in the Lords by Liverpool in May, it was proposed that the seats should go to the county of Yorkshire as a whole.[18] When the bill returned to the Commons, 30 May, Wortley protested that the Lords had 'placed them in a more cruel situation than they had ever before stood in': not only had they abrogated to themselves greater power, but their solution would satisfy nobody. He accordingly urged the rejection of the bill and a separate one to disfranchise Grampound, leaving the question of the disposal of the seats to be settled later, but the bill passed as amended. When Milton moved the Yorkshire election polls bill to alter the way the poll would be taken in consequence of the additional Members next day, Wortley observed that many gentlemen of all political persuasions and from all the ridings opposed the scheme.[19] He presented hostile Huddersfield and York petitions, 29 Apr., 14 May 1822, and was a majority teller against it, 7 June 1822.

Wortley was in the opposition minority for printing the Nottingham petition for the impeachment of ministers, 20 Feb. 1821. To Sir Robert Wilson's assertion that he could prove murder at Peterloo, 21 Feb., he retorted that the 'place for preferring such a charge was surely a court of law', and to those who complained that no inquiry had taken place he suggested, 'why not set the question at rest by prosecuting any of the parties for common assault?' He spoke in similar terms against Burdett's motion for inquiry, 16 May. Commenting on the meeting of the Allied monarchs over Naples, 21 Feb., he declared that 'if such a tribunal ... was suffered to exist', not only Europe but 'the British constitution was not safe'. He 'spoke on the matter in a manner becoming a great English gentleman', John William Ward* later informed the bishop of Llandaff.[20] After the Allied sovereigns had issued the Laibach declaration Wortley, moving for a copy to be laid before the House, 21 June, argued that Britain ought to point out that the 'doctrines advanced in that document were not consonant with those on which the government of this country acted', adding that while those sovereigns had the right to determine how to govern their own people, 'the moment they stepped out of their own territories ... to promulgate principles hostile to the existence of liberty, it became necessary for that House to express its opinion'. His motion was lost by 113-59. He voted for Catholic relief, 28 Feb., and dissented from a hostile petition from the clergy of York which he presented, 26 Mar.[21] On 9 Mar. he contended that the *Morning Chronicle* was guilty of a breach of privilege for a 'very foul libel' in its report of one of Castlereagh's speeches and moved that the printer and publisher attend at the bar, but was eventually prevailed upon to desist. He voted against repeal of the additional malt duty, 3 Apr. On Lambton's motion for parliamentary reform, 17 Apr., he said that although there was 'a strong and general' feeling for it in the country, he believed that 'even as constituted at present' the Commons 'was the only assembly for successfully carrying on the business of the nation'. He conceded that the constitution had evolved through innovations, but maintained that the effect of making elections too popular 'would be to do away with the House of Lords', and that if the 'wild visions' of some were realized, 'the limited monarchy of England would be converted into a republic, and an end would be made to our glorious constitution'. He was granted ten days' leave on private business, 7 May. He presented a Settle petition for revision of the criminal law, 17 May, and voted for abolition of the death penalty for forgery, 3 June. On 18 June he denied a charge of inconsistency in supporting both the estimates and repeal of the tax on husbandry horses, explaining that while he was in the general habit of voting with ministers, the repeal of a tax was 'a very different case ... where every man exercised his own judgement as to its necessity'. He divided against Hume's proposals for economy and retrenchment, 27 June. Writing to his wife, 20 July 1821, he observed that 'although I hesitated a long time about going to the coronation, I confess I am glad I did go, for certainly nobody can see a more magnificent spectacle', and predicted that owing to the queen's affair, the bitter wrangle over the promotions in the Irish peerage and the resignation of Lord Hertford as lord chamberlain, 'I fully expect that the government will not be in office long'.[22] During a stay at Wortley Hall, Edward Littleton* noted in his diary, 3 Nov. 1821, that he was

> rather disappointed in this visit, as far as the agrémens of place and establishment go, for I have seldom witnessed less show and splendour in the place of a gentleman of £5,000 a year. He got elected for the county during his father's lifetime, and having been obliged to observe economy and parsimony, he seems now to be unable to shake off the habit and expand his mode of life with his means.[23]

However, Wortley was still indebted to Cunynghame, and his accounts for 1822 show that his household expenditure alone came to over £10,000 that year.[24]

He accepted that 'it was the duty' of the House 'to enforce the severest retrenchment', but opposed the amendment to the address because ministers had pledged themselves to that course and it was only fair to wait to see how far they would redeem their promise, 5 Feb. 1822. He voted with them against Brougham's motion on the distressed state of the country, 11 Feb. On the motion for a select committee on agricultural distress, to which he was appointed, 18 Feb., he denied that the landed interest 'had arrived at their present condition principally through their own fault', cited the expenses that the recent wars had inflicted on the country, and endorsed the government's proposals for retrenchment rather than tax reductions, hoping that the money saved would be put into the sinking fund to reduce the national debt and thereby lower interest rates. He criticized the scheme to issue exchequer bills to help relieve parishes, however, and insisted that the great object must be to 'prevent that great influx of corn which was likely to pour in ... immediately after the price of grain reached the maximum now established by law'. He voted with ministers against further tax reductions, 21 Feb., and reducing the salt duties, 28 Feb., but was in the opposition majority for admiralty cuts, which the 'circumstances of the times made it imperative' to support, 1 Mar. Alarmed, the treasury circularized the country gentlemen to rally to government, and on Lord Normanby's motion for abolition of one of the joint-postmasterships, 13 Mar., Wortley announced that 'there was a point at which resistance must be made by those who wished to preserve the just influence of the crown' and divided in the government majority. When Normanby reintroduced his proposal, 2 May, and ministers intimated that they might be willing to concede an inquiry, an outraged Wortley, having given his previous vote with 'considerable hesitation', declared that he would now vote with Normanby and led '40 other country gentlemen who a month ago had voted against' into the opposition lobby to ensure the government's defeat.[25] He refused to back the superannuation amendment bill until more details were known, 11 Mar., supported the call for Henry Hunt* to be released from gaol, 14 Mar., and recommended equalization of the distillation laws of Ireland and the mainland to benefit barley growers, 27 Mar. He supported a similar adjustment of the Scottish distillery regulations, 29 Apr., and presented a Forfar petition for the export of whisky to England, 6 May.[26] Presenting a Linlithgow petition complaining of distress, 1 Apr., he agreed that the tax reductions had been inadequate and endorsed its suggestion that government intervene to purchase £1,000,000 of corn, observing that the Bank of England, 'by refusing to discount at a lower rate of interest, had contributed materially to the distress of the country'. He presented a Sculcoates petition to simplify the recovery of small debts, 18 Apr., and one from Burlington ship owners

against the West Indies and American trade bill, 29 Apr.[27] He presented West Riding petitions against the importation of foreign wool that day and 30 May, when he again complained that the wool tax had driven the British manufacturer out of the foreign market. On 10 July he sought assurances that ministers would try to reverse the Portuguese doubling of import duties on British wool.[28] He presented petitions against the poor removal bill, 17, 31 May, and for revision of the criminal code, 17 May, 4 June. He brought up a Howden tanners' petition against the leather tax, 17 May, and when presenting another from Sheffield, 20 May, suggested that relief would be best afforded by repeal of some of the assessed taxes, 20 May. He presented a Whitby petition against any alteration in the navigation laws that day,[29] a York petition against alterations to the corn laws, 3 June, and a West Riding petition for equalization of the East and West Indian sugar duties, 25 June. The previous day he spoke against Brougham's motion alleging an increase in influence of the crown, perceiving its real object to be a reform of Parliament. He voted for repeal of the salt duties, 28 June, although he believed it would be of little benefit to the country.[30] He contended that the begging of the Irish poor in London should be stopped by giving them proper relief, 8 July 1822.[31]

In August 1822 John Croker*, writing to Peel about the political prospects following Lord Londonderry's death, named Wortley as likely to be 'inclined' to join Canning if he did not go to India and went into opposition.[32] However, Canning's confidant Charles Ellis* warned Lord Granville, 20 Oct., 'Pray be on your guard in talking to Wortley. I suspect that he is by no means friendly'. Writing again, 28 Nov., he added:

> What you report of Wortley's language is exactly what I had expected. He feels certain that C[anning]'s management of the House of Commons will not suit his book. He wants a man who will consent to bring forward a parcel of foolish measures which he and the Boodle's cabinet may have the credit of throwing out. His pride is to take a rural gentleman to the minister, and to astonish his simplicity by the disagreeable things which he will say about government, and his mind misgives him that he cannot do this by Cannning.[33]

At the Yorkshire county reform meeting, 22 Jan. 1823, Wortley was the only speaker against the resolutions. Before a hostile crowd, he extolled the 'great and magnificent blessings' of the constitution, defended legitimate aristocratic influence and predicted 'anarchy and revolution' from wholesale reform. He and Richard Fountayne Wilson, later Ultra Member for the county, were the only dissentients from the petition. William

Blackwood, editor of the *Blackwood's Edinburgh Magazine*, later praised him for having 'bearded the lion in his den'.[34] Wortley reiterated his objections when Milton presented the petition, 22 Apr., and voted against reform of the Scottish electoral system, 2 June, as he had against inquiry into the parliamentary franchise, 20 Feb. 1823. After the Commons had reconvened Canning, now leader of the House and foreign secretary, informed Liverpool, 9 Feb. 1823, that he had asked Wortley to show restraint about the developing crisis in the Peninsula, and warned the premier that

> the mischief he may do if he opens the subject again, to limit and qualify and warn against war is incalculable. My apprehension is that he will *fancy* that HIS! expressions of disapprobation of the conduct of France will more than compensate for his pacific admonitions to the government, but it will do no such thing.[35]

When Canning informed the House, 14 Apr., that the French had declared war on Spain, he was strongly attacked, but he seemed to find solace in telling Peel that it had been 'very well worth it ... not the less so as I find that Wortley is at Newmarket, and not likely to be in town till late in the week'.[36] On 28 Apr. the Whig James Macdonald moved a vote of censure against ministers for their conduct in the affair, whereupon Wortley, declaring that 'the true question [was] whether they did or did not approve ... the course they had taken during recent negotiations', moved a pacific amendment, pouring scorn on Macdonald's 'totally visionary and unfounded' view and asking what more ministers could have done without endangering Britain's neutrality. The ensuing debate lasted three days, enabling Canning to deliver a robust defence, and resulted in a majority of 372-20 for Wortley's amendment. On 14 Feb. he presented a Bradford petition against the Insolvent Debtors Act, which he said had produced 'no good effect' and required 'some remedial measure', 13 Mar.[37] He thought that Whitmore's motion to reduce the import price of corn to 60s. did not go far enough, 26 Feb., as 'there was no safety for the agriculturalist unless the ports were kept constantly open, with a regulating duty', before voting for it. He divided against Hume's attempt to cap the sinking fund, 13 Mar., when he was appointed to the select committee on the game laws. When Lord Cranbourne proposed to revise them, 2 June, Wortley said that he was 'anxious' for some change, that the first step should be legalizing the sale of game, and that although the bill would not end poaching, it would help to diminish it and that therefore he would support it. He saw no necessity for the division of counties

bill, 17 Mar.[38] He was a minority teller against the wheat warehousing bill, 21 Mar. On 14 Apr. Charles Williams Wynn, president of the board of control, informed the duke of Buckingham that in a bid to limit the damage the pro-Catholic cause was likely to receive when Plunket introduced his motion to consider their claims, 'we are trying in secret' to persuade Wortley, amongst others, to 'rise immediately after Plunket' and 'propose an adjournment'. This, he added, Wortley would be willing to do 'to avoid offending ... Orange constituents and the government'.[39] In the event, however, the motion was abandoned. He voted against inquiry into the prosecution of the Dublin Orange rioters, 22 Apr. He presented a Whitby petition for repeal of the leather tax, 26 May, and a York one to make permanent the temporary Act for the use of sulphuric acid in bleaching, 28 May.[40] He welcomed proposals for altering the combination laws, 27 May. Next day he seconded Lord Nugent's motion to put British Catholics on a par with the Irish, by enabling them to vote and fill certain offices. On 3 June his son John was returned for the family's pocket borough of Bossiney, and thereafter there is some difficulty in distinguishing between them. When Milton presented a Leeds petition for repeal of the duty on foreign wool, 4 June, Wortley declared that 'little benefit' would be derived from free export as the foreign manufacturers would not resort to this country for wool that could be had on better terms elsewhere. He presented a Halifax petition against the workmens' wages regulation bill, 9 June, Leeds and Manchester ones against repeal of the linen stamping bill, 18 June, and several from Yorkshire, and one from Bury, against any alteration in the wool duties, 24, 25 June.[41] He presented a Whitby petition against the reciprocity of duties bill, 30 June, and spoke thus, arguing that 'the protecting duty on grain could not be long continued, but must be brought nearer to the standard of the European markets', 4 July 1823.

Wortley presented a Barnsley petition for repeal of the combination laws, 10 Feb., was appointed to the select committee to investigate them, 12 Feb. 1824, and, the same day, defended the legality of prisoners on remand being made to use the treadmill.[42] Seeking leave to bring in a game laws amendment bill, 17 Feb., he said that 'there could be no subject more important to the comfort, to the morals, and the well being of the people of this country' and dismissed the fears of landowners as 'unfounded', arguing that the bill would facilitate the preservation of game by legalizing its sale, establishing shooting rights and facilitating punishments for persistent poachers. It received its second reading after he had made some minor concessions, 11

Mar., but although he secured the bill's recommittal, 25 Mar., it was lost in committee, 31 May, whereupon Wortley gave notice that he would resurrect it next session. On 24 Feb. he condemned the government's decision to reduce the duty on foreign wool and allow its free export, claiming that the manufacturers faced an act of 'extreme injustice' and demanding that they be either invited to direct talks with the government or allowed to appear at the bar of the House. He present multiple petitions against the proposals, 2 Mar., when he warned that long wool, the 'exclusive growth of this country', was essential to our own manufacturers and ought not to be exported, and between 4 and 26 Mar.[43] He condemned the wool import and export bill, 21 May, arguing that it would be ruinous to both agriculturalists and manufacturers, that it was wrong to give up a natural advantage without any reciprocity, and that the measure had nothing to do with free trade. Despite his protests it passed the House, 24 May 1824. He was a majority teller against reform of Edinburgh's representation, 26 Feb., when he complained that such motions 'tended to cherish republican sentiments' and 'encouraged vituperation of the existing system'. He presented multiple petitions from the licensed victuallers of several Yorkshire towns against the duty on excise licenses, 25, 26 Feb., 1 Mar., 12 May.[44] He voted against ending flogging in the forces and brought up a York petition for continuing the bounty on low linens, 5 Mar. He presented petitions from Huddersfield and Halifax for repeal of the Union duties, 8 Mar., Yorkshire petitions for repeal of the house and window taxes, 12, 31 Mar, and a Northallerton petition against the county courts bill, 19 Mar.[45] He asked ministers to justify levying a tax of 6s. on seaborne coal, but only 1s. on that transported inland, 29 Mar., and insisted that northern coal owners sought no advantage, but only equal treatment, 1 Apr. During March and May he presented six petitions from the tanners of Yorkshire against the hides and skins bill (and one for repeal of the leather tax), and four from the county's butchers in its favour. He submitted West Riding petitions against the beer retail bill, 12, 21 May. When presenting petitions from civil service clerks against paying five per cent superannuation, 13, 21 May, he complained of the hardship they suffered under the Superannuation Act of 1822 and defended the bill to abolish their payments, 12, 21 June. He presented Bradford and Whitby petitions for inquiry into the trial of the Methodist missionary John Smith for inciting slave riots in Demerara, 25, 26 May, but voted against condemning it, 11 June. He criticized Members who voted in private bill committees after hearing none of the evidence, 27 May, and hoped that

'some better means would be devised for punishing those who harbour vagrants' during a debate on the vagrants bill, 5 June 1824.[46]

On 15 Feb. 1825 he complained to his wife that the House had already spent three days debating 'one question of the bill for putting down the Catholic Association', but observed, 'I don't however hold myself bound to listen to all the human voice that is so uselessly expended ... I get away to dinner always'.[47] He voted for the bill, 25 Feb. Speaking in favour of the 'just claims of the Catholics' three days later, he dismissed the 'chimerical apprehension' that the Catholic clergy wanted to overthrow the established church and warned that there would be no 'substantial peace in Ireland until the question was conceded. He divided accordingly, 1 Mar., when he boasted to his wife that he had been credited with assisting the motion 'by my eloquence', 21 Apr. (as a pair), 10 May.[48] He voted for repeal of the usury laws, 17 Feb., next day telling his wife that 'today is one of the busiest days of the year with me, being the last day for presenting petitions for private bills'.[49] On 17 Feb. he had reintroduced his game laws amendment bill, threatening to 'wash his hands' of it if any attempt was made to limit its scope to legalizing the sale of game, which was his secondary aim, his first being 'to give every occupier of land a right to the game ... and protection against the poacher and trespasser'. Despite his strenuous efforts the bill was again rejected. He presented petitions in favour of the county courts bill that day and 10 May, and one from Doncaster for repeal of the house and window taxes, 9 Mar.[50] He brought in a bill to regulate the cutlery trade, 24 Mar., but it appears to have proceeded no further. He was appointed to the select committee on the combination laws, 29 Mar., presented a petition from the manufacturers of Sheffield complaining of the consequences of their repeal, 27 May, and spoke on the combination of workmen bill, 30 June, emphasizing that he did not wish to come between master and employee, but to prevent 'any combination of journeymen from exercising a cruel tyranny over the honest industry and the labour of any other workman'.[51] He presented Yorkshire petitions against the change in linen duties, 25 Apr., and alteration of the corn laws, 25, 26, 28 Apr.[52] That day, before voting for Whitmore's critical motion, he 'entreated' ministers to pledge themselves to consider the laws at the beginning of the next session. He spoke and voted for the spring guns bill, 21 June 1825.

Anti-Catholic agitation in Yorkshire, led by the *Yorkshire Gazette*, had been steadily growing since the last general election, and the candidates for the next increasingly became the subject of speculation through 1825. Perhaps with his eye on this Wortley had hoped to use the annual Pitt dinner in Sheffield to explain his pro-Catholic stance, but on 20 Oct. Sir John Beckett* told Lowther that the gathering would be cancelled 'in order to prevent him'.[53] By early December it was clear that two anti-Catholic Tories, William Duncombe* and Fountayne Wilson, would offer for the county. Milton was expected to come forward again, and with Richard Bethell*, a pro-Catholic Tory, also in the field, a contest looked certain. On 4 Dec. Lord Althorp* reported to his father that he feared that 'Wortley and Bethell will fly'.[54] Wortley, however, stuck firmly to his principles, and wrote to the *Gazette* and *Leeds Mercury*, 29 Nov., to deny a suggestion in that week's *York Chronicle* that he would not in future support Catholic relief.[55] Taking up his pen again to reply to the vicar of Bradford over a similar rumour, 10 Dec., he declared:

> For nearly 25 years I have heard the question of Catholic emancipation argued and discussed, by men, perhaps, of the greatest reasoning powers that ever adorned this country. It is impossible that I should not have made my mind up on it ... The gentlemen who are now, for the first time, asking the confidence of the freeholders may be justified in taking steps at this period to bring their pretensions before them, while I cannot but feel that some of the duty which has been entrusted to me, is still to be performed, and that until the whole is concluded, I can have no right to ask for their renewed support ... Whenever the proper time comes, I shall again present myself to the county.[56]

The Whigs, calculating that Wortley would probably be defeated by Duncombe, Wilson and two Whigs, discussed the means of helping him and Bethell by splitting votes with them. However, as early as 22 Dec., James Abercromby* reported hearing that 'there are rumours of great promotion in the peerage, and unless they have determined not to add to the House of Lords, Wortley may be made a peer'.[57] Nevertheless, his friends pressed on with arrangements, holding a private meeting in Leeds at the end of December, when they declared that he was 'strong in *solid* votes'.[58] Wortley spent Christmas and the New Year in Paris, but returned to attend to electioneering, 4 Jan. 1826.[59] He met his committee in York, 12 Jan., and the following day declared himself a candidate, telling his wife:

> Bore as all this journey has been to me, I have at least the satisfaction of feeling that it has been useful to me, and it has certainly been most gratifying and flattering to me to find myself so kindly and cordially received by almost all my old friends, and by a very considerable number of

new ones. At the same time I cannot conceal from myself that nothing but a feeling that I have done my duty to the county, and a dependence upon my integrity and independence, could have carried me through against the feeling of the lower and middle classes, which is undoubtedly strong on the 'no Popery' subject.

With Lord Morpeth* refusing to come forward for the Whigs, he hoped he might succeed without a contest.[60] Before the opening of the 1826 session, Wortley told his wife that Sir Charles Stuart's conduct during the negotiations over the independence of Brazil were out of character and 'certainly not approved by Canning', but he suspected that he had 'a complete defence', as Stuart appeared 'quite satisfied'. On the commercial and financial crisis, he wrote that 'all confidence between mercantile men is entirely gone ... I do not think that the government are aware of the full extent of the difficulties'.[61] He presented Sheffield petitions for reduction of the tobacco duties, 23 Feb., and the abolition of slavery, 27 Feb., 7 Mar.[62] Perhaps with his thoughts on a contest for Yorkshire, he brought in a bill to increase the number of polling booths at the county's elections to facilitate more efficient polling, 20 Apr., but it went no further. That day he also expressed his determination to press on with his campaign for reform of the game laws. He voted for revision of the corn laws, 18 Apr., recommended postponing the freeholders in districts bill, 2 May, and divided against Russell's proposal to curb electoral bribery, 26 May 1826.

Shortly before the 1826 general election John Whishaw assured Lady Holland that Wortley was still expected to come in for Yorkshire.[63] On 27 May, however, when John Marshall*, a Leeds linen manufacturer, finally agreed to become the second Whig candidate, it had become known that Wortley would receive a barony. Although many suspected the motives behind his elevation, the duke of Bedford reported that it was the king's 'own gracious and spontaneous act', 30 May.[64] Wortley considered taking Stuart as his title, but eventually settled on Wharncliffe, the name of one of his Yorkshire estates. Lady Caroline told her mother, 10 June, 'the king was beyond measure kind and gracious to [him] at Ascot, and when he told him his latest decision, *approved*, but added, "My good fellow you will now be the Dragon of Wharncliffe all the rest of your life"'.[65] On 3 June Beckett advised Lowther that 'the Dragon' would 'show at the nomination and propose Bethell, but all his vapouring won't do'.[66] Wortley did appear, but only to thank the county for past support. However, he was prevented from doing so until after the protracted nominations, and when he did eventually step forward to speak he was frustrated by 'an incessant clamour' from the anti-Catholics. He tried again after the show of hands, but 'was often interrupted'.[67] Bethell withdrew from the contest that evening, and Beckett wrote gleefully to Peel, 20 June:

> Wortley's peerage was very ill-timed, and has been ill-received. He thought he could put Mr. Bethell into his shoes for the county. But he could not get a hearing even at York ... and was not allowed to speak till all was over and *he* left to himself, and some of *Lord Milton's friends*![68]

A public dinner to thank Wharncliffe for his services to the county was held in Sheffield, 14 Sept. 1826, when he denounced the escalating cost of elections, saying that 'if the freeholders wish to have independent Members, they must endeavour to prevent this enormous expense', otherwise 'the county might as well be put up for auction'. He insisted that he would have stood the contest, despite the cost, if he had not been made a peer, and defended his barony, claiming that he had never asked for it, and had only accepted it as a personal favour from the king.[69] In 1830 Wharncliffe tried to arrange a compromise with Milton to cut the cost of the Yorkshire election by agreeing that candidates would not pay for travelling expenses, but the plans were disturbed by the candidacy of Martin Stapylton on principles of purity.[70] The results of the 1830 general election convinced him of the need for a measure of reform and he played a pivotal role in the crisis after the reform bill was defeated in the Lords in October 1831. He became the chief broker between the government and those Tory peers who supported reform, but wanted a less radical measure. His negotiations on behalf of the 'Waverers' managed to deliver a majority for the second reading, 14 Apr. 1832. Desperate to repair his rift with the Conservative party, however, he voted for Lord Lyndhurst's motion to postpone the disfranchising clauses, 7 May, and so made himself 'odious to both parties'. He later served under Peel, in 1835 as lord privy seal, and in 1841 as lord president of the council, 'but he was disappointed in not having a more important office'. He lacked sufficient weight in cabinet to extend the educational reforms as far as he would have liked, and was 'one of the sturdiest opponents' of repealing the corn laws, although many expected that eventually he could have been won round.[71] His edited *Letters and Works of Lady Mary Wortley Montague*, his grandmother, was published in 1837.

Wharncliffe died intestate in December 1845 at his London house, following a short illness of suppressed gout and apoplexy induced, his son James claimed, by 'anxiety about public affairs'.[72] Administration of his estate was granted to his widow and his eldest son and successor John (1801-55).[73] Greville wrote:

> In public life [Wharncliffe played] a secondary, but an honourable and useful part, in private life he was irreproachable, amiable, and respected ... No man died with fewer enemies, with more general goodwill, and more sincerely regretted by everyone belonging to or intimate with him.[74]

[1] *Greville Mems.* v. 342; *Ann. Reg.* (1845), Chron. p. 320; *Yorks. Gazette*, 4 Mar. 1820. [2] Sheffield Archives, Wharncliffe mun. WhM/426, Cunynghame to Wortley, 22 Feb., 1 Mar. 1820. [3] *Yorks. Gazette*, 11 Mar. 1820. [4] Wharncliffe mun. T.687. [5] *Yorks. Gazette*, 25 Mar. 1820. [6] Wentworth Woodhouse mun. F48/171. [7] *The Times*, 19 June 1821. [8] *Arbuthnot Jnl.* i. 25. [9] Wharncliffe mun. 553b/1. [10] Ibid. 553a/14, 19, 20, 21. [11] Ibid. T.714; 553a/23. [12] C.D. Yonge, *Lord Liverpool*, iii. 114-19. [13] Add. 38574, f. 232; Wharncliffe mun. 574/4. [14] Wharncliffe mun. 575/11. [15] *The Times*, 13 July 1822. [16] Ibid. 9 Feb., 29 Mar. 1821. [17] Ibid. 20 Mar. 1821. [18] J.E. Cookson, *Lord Liverpool's Administration*, 306. [19] *The Times*, 1 June 1821. [20] Ward, *Llandaff Letters*, 278. [21] *The Times*, 27 Mar. 1821. [22] Wharncliffe mun. T.761. [23] Hatherton diary. [24] Wharncliffe mun. 618. [25] *Arbuthnot Jnl.* i. 161. [26] *The Times*, 15, 28 Mar., 30 Apr., 7 May 1822. [27] Ibid. 19 Apr. 1822. [28] Ibid. 31 May, 11 July 1822. [29] Ibid. 1, 18, 21, May, 1,5 June 1822. [30] Ibid. 4, 26 June 1822. [31] Ibid. 9 July 1822. [32] Add. 40319, f. 57. [33] TNA 30/29/9/5/18, 19. [34] *Sheffield Mercury*, 25 Jan. 1823; Wharncliffe mun. 449a. [35] Add. 38193, f. 179. [36] Add. 40311, f. 25. [37] *The Times*, 15 Feb., 14 Mar. 1823. [38] Ibid. 18 Mar. 1823. [39] Buckingham, *Mems. Geo. IV*, i. 449. [40] *The Times*, 27, 29 May 1823. [41] Ibid. 5, 10, 19, 25, 26 June 1823. [42] Ibid. 11 Feb. 1824. [43] Ibid. 5, 19 Mar. 1824. [44] Ibid. 26, 27 Feb., 2 Mar., 13 May 1824. [45] Ibid. 6, 9, 13, 20 Mar.; 1 Apr. 1824. [46] Ibid. 1 Apr., 13, 14, 18, 22, 25-27 May, 7, 14 June 1824. [47] Wharncliffe mun. T.824. [48] Ibid. 826. [49] Ibid. 825. [50] Ibid. 25 Feb., 10 Mar., 11 May 1825. [51] Ibid. 28 May, 1 July 1825. [52] Ibid. 26, 27, 29 Apr. 1825. [53] Lonsdale mss. [54] *Althorp Letters*, 127. [55] *York Chron.* 24 Nov.; *Yorks. Gazette*, 26 Nov. 1825. [56] *Leeds Mercury*, 10 Dec. 1825. [57] Fitzwilliam mss, Tottie to Milton, 12 Dec. 1825; Castle Howard mss. [58] Fitzwilliam mss, Sir F. Wood to Milton, 1 Jan. 1826. [59] Wharncliffe mun. T.839. [60] Ibid. T.840. [61] Ibid. T.835. [62] *The Times*, 24, 28 Feb., 8 Mar. 1826. [63] Add. 51659. [64] Add. 51668. [65] Wharncliffe mun. 553b/7. [66] Lonsdale mss. [67] E. Baines, *Yorks. Election 1826*, p. 110. [68] Add. 40387, f. 207. [69] *Sheffield Mercury*, 16 Sept. 1826. [70] M. Brock, *Great Reform Act*, 95. [71] Ibid. 275-7; *Greville Mems.* v. 343. [72] C.B.S. Wortley and C. Grosvenor, *Lady Wharncliffe*, ii. 353. [73] PROB 6/222/270. [74] *Greville Mems.* v. 344.

M.P.J.C./P.J.S.

STUART WORTLEY, John (1801-1855), of 15 Curzon Street, Mdx.

BOSSINEY	2 June 1823-1830
PERTH BURGHS	1830-11 Dec. 1830
BOSSINEY	16 Feb. 1831-1832
YORKSHIRE (WEST RIDING)	1841-19 Dec. 1845

b. 23 Apr. 1801, 1st s. of James Archibald Stuart Wortley* and Lady Elizabeth Caroline Mary Creighton, da. of John, 1st Earl Erne [I]; bro. of Hon. Charles James

Stuart Wortley*. *educ.* Harrow 1812-17; Christ Church, Oxf. 1818. *m.* 12 Dec. 1825, Lady Georgiana Elizabeth Ryder, da. of Dudley Ryder†, 1st earl of Harrowby, 3s. 2da. *suc.* fa. as 2nd Bar. Wharncliffe 19 Dec. 1845 and took additional name of Mackenzie. *d.* 22 Oct. 1855.

Sec. to bd. of control Feb.-Dec. 1830.

Maj. S.W. Yorks. yeomanry 1822, lt.-col. 1841; col. commdt. 1 W. Yorks. militia 1846.

Stuart Wortley, who as a small boy had the 'great treat' of becoming his mother's 'bedfellow' when his father was away, passed much of his childhood in Yorkshire, under the supervision of his maternal grandmother Lady Erne. When he was six his mother admitted that 'he is too like myself in many respects not to make me feel uncomfortable as to his future temper and feelings'.[1] As a Harrow schoolboy he went with his parents to Spa and Paris in the late summer of 1814; and from October 1817 until June 1818, three months after his father succeeded to the family's Yorkshire and Scottish estates, he was with them and his siblings visiting Paris, Rome, Naples, Venice and Innsbruck.[2] In February 1819, after a delay since matriculating, he went up to Christ Church, where he was industrious and happy, and became close friends with Henry Edward Fox*, William Henry Greville and George William Howard, Visct. Morpeth*, who came from Whig families, and Lawrence Peel*, whose political background, like his own, was Tory.[3] In a letter to Fox in June 1821 he deplored the disfranchisement of Grampound and transfer of its seats to Yorkshire, maintaining that 'the county is considerably against it and it seems to me to satisfy nobody at all, besides ... it certainly was not at all necessary'. The following month, after attending the coronation, he judged Queen Caroline's conduct there 'disgusting', but thought the king had 'behaved rather like a naughty child about it'.[4] At his examination in December 1821 he took a first in mathematics and a second in classics, with which he claimed to be 'perfectly satisfied'. He hunted for the rest of the winter, postponed a planned visit to Ireland until the next summer and contemplated without relish the prospect of his first London season.[5] In November 1822 he persuaded Fox to join him on a European jaunt at the end of the winter, though for a time it was threatened with delay by the possibility of an immediate vacancy on his father's interest at Bossiney. They left London for Paris, 22 Feb. 1823, and travelled into Italy and Switzerland. Their mutual friend Robert Vernon Smith* told Fox that he would find Stuart Wortley 'a very pleasant companion', adding that 'if he does not find you so, it can only be from his inveterate habit of disagreeing with the opinion of everybody

else'. He was still away in June when he was returned for Bossiney after a contest with an interloper; he survived a petition against the return.[6] That summer Fox, for whom Stuart Wortley was now a half-hearted rival for the hand of Theresa Villiers, daughter of the disgraced former paymaster of marines (though he had, or so he said, 'prejudices ... against early marriage'), assessed his friend:

> Wortley has plain good sense, a correct taste, but a total want of imagination. His desire of knowledge and his industry in procuring it is very great: but when he has got it it produces nothing, for he is so straightforward that what is not matter of fact appears to him falsehood. He has an excellent heart and a clear understanding, but has a brusquerie and coldness of manner that will make him unpopular.[7]

Like his father, he voted with Lord Liverpool's ministry against reform of Edinburgh's representation, 26 Feb., and the abolition of flogging, 5 Mar. 1824. Canning, the foreign secretary, to whom he was drawn politically, reckoned that his own speech in support of the aliens bill next day kept Stuart Wortley, who had 'half a mind' to 'go astray', in the government lobby.[8] A few days later he went for a month to The Hague as the guest of the ambassador, Lord Granville, whose wife at first thought him 'such a love', but just before his departure told Lady Harrowby that he was 'an odd fish':

> He sits for ages quite silent with his head upon his shoulder, looking comfortable, but like a bird at roost ... He is a selfish person, and for a young man wonderfully so. Yet I cannot make him quite out, for he is more ready to do anything, go anywhere than anybody. I think him to begin with uncommonly pleasing. He is so refined, has such an accomplished mind. There is such manliness and good sense, such a freedom from all the vanities and littleness of his kind. On the other hand, I never saw anyone make so little effort to surmount any little cloud of *humeur, chagrin* or *ennui* for the benefit of the society he is in, and he never puts his best leg foremost to promote the satisfaction or amusement of those he is with ... If he is not in the vein there is no feeling of civility, good fellowship, or what is called helping a lame dog over a stile that will induce him to move a finger.

He was in the Commons, 'fresh from the steam vessel', on 6 May.[9] He joined his father in the minority against repeal of the prohibition on the export of long wool, 21 May 1824. That summer he went with John Evelyn Denison* Edward Smith Stanley* and Henry Labouchere* on an extended tour of North America and Canada: they visited New York, Quebec, Boston, Washington ('a sort of straggling village ... magnificent in its plan, of great space, thinly and unequally inhabited'), Baltimore and Halifax, and met Lafayette and ex-President Adams ('one of the few remaining distinguished revolutionists', now in 'melancholy old age').[10] He arrived back in London in early June 1825 and shortly afterwards wrote to Fox, who was in Italy:

> I have been doing nothing but sit at home excepting a few dinners since I returned, and feel no sort of inclination to squeeze into the beau monde again. The House of Commons will be up in a fortnight and I am come in so late for the session and am so behindhand in everything that is going on that I have hardly been there.[11]

In August he assumed 'the solid and sturdy character of a *magistrate*' in Yorkshire. Two months later, in 'ecstasy', he informed Fox of his impending marriage to the Harrowbys' daughter Lady Georgiana Ryder (whom Fox had once described as 'sensible, hard-headed, severe, vain, and spoiled by the admiration of all the many that worship') after a courtship 'of three weeks', although it was 'an old attachment ... on his part'. While he was said to be 'desperately in love', it was generally believed that she was 'not a bit in love with him'. The wedding took place shortly before Christmas 1825 and the honeymoon was spent at Trentham, the Staffordshire home of the marquess of Stafford, Lady Georgiana's uncle.[12]

Stuart Wortley was chosen to move the address, 2 Feb. 1826, in his parliamentary debut. Briefly straying from the traditional formula, he suggested that the current commercial distress was 'temporary and ... the worst had passed over'. Denison thought he 'spoke sensibly and without embarrassment, but too low in tone, and with too colloquial an expression', while the Whig Lord Carlisle, Lady Georgiana's kinsman, heard that he was 'sensible, prudent and distinct'; the prime minister approved his performance.[13] He voted with government on the Jamaican slave trials, 2 Mar. The previous month Greville had reported to Fox that their friend seemed 'very happy, but looks just as dismal as if the most severe calamity had befallen him', and in March he himself confirmed his 'happiness', which he 'never knew ... really before', telling Fox that he would 'find me an old married man ... living quietly before my own fireside without much digression, and talking about currency and committees'. Yet he was reported to be looking 'more dead than alive' and in a 'melancholy state of health' at Brighton in late April.[14] He was again returned for Bossiney at the general election that summer.[15] In July 1826 his father's elevation to the peerage as Lord Wharncliffe was gazetted.

On 29 Nov. 1826 Stuart Wortley, who was described at this time as being 'very thin and amiable', and who had apparently had his courage screwed up by his wife,

earned praise in the House from the home secretary Peel for a speech on the 'dry and tedious subject' of controverted election precedents. Lord Holland told his wayward son Fox that his friend's effort had been 'very advantageous: a good speech, and what is better than a good speech much parliamentary knowledge, good parliamentary manner and a promise of taking a part and shining in debate'. The Whig lawyer James Abercromby* (who relished such topics) commented to Carlisle that 'young Wortley seems to be very zealous and industrious, and with these properties ... he will make a better name for himself than men of higher talents'.[16] In April 1827 his mother reported that he had

> been gaining immense credit in a committee by the clearness and soundness of his arguments in a very difficult case ... All I hear of him encourages me to think that he is in the way to distinguish himself in no common way ... I am so delighted at his having taken so much to his parliamentary duties.[17]

While he never scaled any great political heights, he did become a diligent and respected parliamentarian. He divided for Catholic relief, 6 Mar. 1827, and subsequently supported Canning's administration.[18] He called for reform of the game laws, 4 May,[19] and advised Smith Stanley to allow his planned bill to regulate Preston elections to be subsumed in Lord Althorp's general measure, 14 June. He defended the government's legislation on the corn trade, 21 June. In November 1827 he wrote to Fox that the members of Lord Goderich's crumbling administration

> appear to me to bear much resemblance to the ring of toadstools which often mark the spot where the great oak fell. I do not deny that they may be some of them very good *fungi*, but I am afraid they are as little united and as weak as worse ... I cannot help thinking that when a session comes, if they will stay in, it will be only because there is nobody to turn them out. Their condition in Parliament appears to me to be that in the Upper House they have leaders enough but lack votes, in the lower they have votes enough but lack leaders.

The feckless Fox, who had renounced Parliament, condescendingly noted that the letter was

> much better expressed and fuller of clever thoughts than his letters used to be. Perhaps his marriage, which I have always hitherto lamented, has served to nerve and excite him, for that is all he wants. He has very fair abilities, but great indolence and constitutional indifference.[20]

In January 1828 Edward Littleton* remarked to Peel, back in office under the duke of Wellington, that Stuart Wortley, his brother-in-law Lord Sandon and a few other 'young men' formed 'the most important party at this time in the House of Commons'; they 'hang much together and ... though having different party connections [are] all united against High Tory principles'.[21] As one of the small Huskissonite squad, Stuart Wortley initially supported Wellington's ministry, but Canning's nephew Lord George Cavendish Bentinck* could scarcely credit his assertion that 'he cannot see any political hostility to Mr. Canning's principles in anything the duke said or did last year'.[22] He gave his 'undivided support' to the steamboat passengers regulation bill, 18 Mar. He voted against sluicing East Retford with freeholders of the hundred of Bassetlaw, 21 Mar., and with government against inquiry into delays in chancery, 24 Apr. He was reassured by Huskisson's statement regarding the scope of the select committee on the civil government of Canada, 2 May. He questioned the fairness of the grant to the Society for the Propagation of the Gospels in Canada, where most of the inhabitants were Dissenters, 6 June, and laid 'a large portion of the blame' for Canadian disaffection on the colonial office, 14 July. He presented petitions for Catholic relief, 6 May, and voted in that sense, 12 May. Next day he supported the provision for Canning's family as an 'act of generosity and justice'; he found the acrimonious debate 'very painful'.[23] When Huskisson and the other leading Canningites resigned from the ministry that month, Stuart Wortley sympathized with them and was twice listed as one of their parliamentary group.[24] On 22 May he introduced a bill to curb poaching at night, which his father had carried through the Lords; it gained royal assent, 19 July (9 Geo. IV, c. 69). He also took up, 30 May, a bill to regulate the sale of game which had originated in the upper House with Lord Salisbury, but he abandoned it on 6 June and secured leave to introduce a new one, which was endorsed by Peel. He described it as 'an experimental measure' and a 'first step towards gradual reform of the whole system', 24 June, but it was later thrown out by the Lords. (A similar bill the following year met with the same fate.) He argued that the 'flourishing' colony of New South Wales should be 'freed from the disagreeable inconvenience of being made a receptacle for convicts', 30 May, and pointed to this as an obstacle to the introduction of jury trial there, 20 June. He voted for revision of the usury laws, 19 June. He supported the compensation claims of British merchants on Denmark and Sweden, 4 July, when he divided in the opposition minority for ordnance reductions.[25] He was in the majority for the bill to prevent the use of municipal funds for election purposes, 10 July 1828.

On 8 Feb. 1829 Stuart Wortley, informing Fox of the ministry's surprising decision to concede Catholic emancipation, commented:

> It has been amusing enough to witness the many incredible convulsions wrought in so short a space of time, and it is no small satisfaction to us to see that obstinate and haughty [Whig] party entrapped and exposed, though at the same time one must confess, somewhat provoking to find those very men getting credit for this great measure and using the language of conciliation and wisdom, who not two years ago killed poor Canning, and so embarrassed the king as almost to stop the course of government, with no other excuse than their pertinacious resistance to the very same arguments ... We are looking with anxiety to the papers from Ireland and news of the [Catholic] Association ... *All parties* are agreed upon their interest and duty, but there is no reckoning on Irishmen, and still less on Irish demagogues.[26]

In the House, 27 Feb., he argued that while 'popular clamour' was undoubtedly hostile to emancipation, 'public opinion', or 'the sense and intelligence of the country', was for it. He voted, 6, 30 Mar., and spoke again, 24 Mar., for the measure. He confessed his dislike for the accompanying bill to disfranchise Irish 40s. freeholders, 19 Mar., but with 'considerable difficulty' swallowed it as a matter of 'absolute necessity'. He voted to allow Daniel O'Connell to take his seat unhindered, 18 May. He welcomed ministerial assurances that the grant to the Society for the Propagation of the Gospels in the colonies would not be used to establish 'an exclusive church', 6 Apr., and denied Hume's assertion that the Canadians were innately hostile to Britain. He secured information on the management and economy of Sierra Leone which, he argued, could not be 'retained with advantage', 19 May, and returns of military mortality in the West Indies, 2 June. He supported Labouchere's call for information on communications between the colonial office and the Canadian governments and lamented the colonial secretary Murray's evasive response, 5 June. He voted for the transfer of East Retford's seats to Birmingham, 5 May. He supported Warburton's anatomy bill, 15, 18 May, when he was a majority teller for its third reading. He spoke contemptuously and voted against the grant for the sculpture of the marble arch, 25 May 1829. Shortly afterwards, according to Mrs. Arbuthnot, who despised him as one of the 'rank Canningites', Peel considered recruiting him for a place at the admiralty board, but nothing came of it.[27]

In January 1830, however, Wellington offered Stuart Wortley the vacant secretaryship to the board of control. In an interview with Peel, who found him 'in a very good temper of mind and very much flattered', he sought and received assurances that the government did not intend to renew the East India Company's charter without prior inquiry or to depart from their liberal commercial policy, and that as a minister he would be free to vote as previously on the East Retford question. He said 'not a word about Tories or junction with any party', clarified matters with Wellington and, having hastily consulted his family and a few accessible friends, took the office.[28] His father told Littleton (who six years later recalled sourly that his acceptance came only a week after a conversation at Sandon 'in which he expressed the strongest opinions against the ... government and discussed with me the various modes of attacking and demolishing it'):

> His communications with the duke ... and Peel were so satisfactory that I am quite sure there were no principles at stake to give him the least excuse for [refusing] ... and therefore, if he has made up his mind to official life, he could not do otherwise in my opinion than accept this, which at this moment is likely to be an office of considerable work and importance, and to open a door to anything for which he may be fitted by his abilities.

Yet Huskisson, who asked Denison, 'does this make the government less harlequin?', took rather a dim view, reflecting that Wellington was 'a very clever recruiting sergeant'.[29] Mrs. Arbuthnot decided that it was 'an excellent appointment as he is one of a knot of young men who are rather inclined to oppose the government'; Lord John Russell* considered it 'a very fair one, much better than the duke's usual nominations', but Greville doubted 'his being of much use' to a government to which he had previously been 'rather inimical'. Lady Granville reported a wag's comment that Stuart Wortley 'between Lords Ashley* [a commissioner of the board] and Ellenborough [its president] will be the tame elephant between the wild ones'.[30] He was duly named to the select committee on the East India Company, 9 Feb. 1830. He supported the prayer of a Sheffield petition for the franchise, as he had been 'particularly requested' to do, 23 Feb., but later that day voted with his colleagues against the enfranchisement of Birmingham, Leeds and Manchester. He was, however, in the minority for the transfer of East Retford's seats to Birmingham, 5 Mar. He spoke and was a majority teller against O'Connell's 'sweeping' reform scheme, which aimed 'to exclude the influence of property from the House of Commons', 28 May. He was in the ministerial minority against the Galway franchise bill, 25 May, and voted against abolition of the death penalty for forgery, 7 June. He maintained that the northern coal owners were anxious for full inquiry into the London

trade, 11 Mar. He regarded Labouchere's motion for reform of the Canadian administration, 25 May, as an 'unfair and unjust ... censure' of the government. As a minister, he now took the line that the grant to the Society for the Propagation of the Gospels in the colonies was not for the establishment of a 'dominant' church, 14 June, and next day he opposed withdrawal from Sierra Leone, suggesting that Britain was 'not paying so heavy a price for the colony as some appear to suppose'. He made only a handful of interventions on departmental business: Ellenborough thought he did 'very well', speaking 'very officially and properly', on the awkward question of Indian half-castes, 4 May, when he showed 'forbearance' in passing over the chance to make a flashy speech.[31] He was evidently not particularly happy as a government underling. He told John Cam Hobhouse* at the end of May that 'he expected the ministry would not last long' and 'confessed it was no very pleasant task acting under Peel' in the House: 'his manners were cold, and very little assistance was required by him from anybody'.[32] He felt unable to vote with government on the regency issue and abstained, 30 June, when Wharncliffe and Harrowby divided against ministers in the Lords. Next day, claiming to have acted quite independently of them, he offered his resignation, initially to Peel and Ellenborough, who expressed regret and referred him to Wellington. On 2 July 1830 Ellenborough recorded in his diary:

> I saw Wortley who ... was much distressed, and evidently regrets extremely that he tendered his resignation ... He was going to see Peel and afterwards the duke. He told me the government could not be conducted in the House of Commons unless some more ministers would speak – that there must be a change ... Spoke to the duke about Wortley. He said he had written a kind note to him, and told him he had been too hasty. He should have spoken to some of the ministers first. The duke evidently intends the thing to blow over. Spoke to Lord Wharncliffe ... He said he would neither have voted nor have spoken against government ... if he had had an idea of Wortley's resigning, because it gave the appearance of concert, and there really was none ... He said he thought Wortley altogether wrong. That a young man, having joined a government, had no right, for a difference on a single point, to resign ... He afterwards talked to the duke, and I have no doubt Wortley will remain.

So he did, withdrawing his resignation, and he reportedly had 'tears in his eyes' when talking to Ellenborough of Wellington's 'kindness of heart'.[33] At the general election that summer he made way at Bossiney for his brother Charles and stood for Perth Burghs, where his father's property in Forfarshire and

Perthshire gave him a stake. He was returned after a fractious contest with a representative of the Airlie interest, but faced a certain petition.[34]

Before the election Stuart Wortley had been authorized by his father to inform his ministerial colleague Charles Arbuthnot*, who passed it on to Wellington, that Lord Palmerston* and Charles Grant* were willing to join the cabinet and for their leader Huskisson to be excluded. Nothing came of this, but he made another approach in early September, when Peel and Arbuthnot agreed that he had been 'fishing' and seemed disposed 'to leave us if we are supposed to be not strong'. A Whig observer suspected that Wharncliffe was trying to promote a coalition in order to 'keep his son in place'.[35] On 6 Nov. 1830 Stuart Wortley confided to Ellenborough his belief that 'we cannot go on', as Wellington's 'declaration against reform had made it impossible for any to join them, and upon the question of reform it is doubtful if we should have numbers enough'. He considered the cancellation of the king's visit to the City soon afterwards 'a sad business, and fatal to the government'. Yet, on 11 Nov. he maintained that 'the spirits of our friends are improved, and those of our foes lowered, the last few days, as to reform'.[36] In the House, 15 Nov., he vainly tried to have consideration of the Perth Burghs petition deferred until after Christmas. Later that day he voted in the ministerial minority in the crucial civil list division. He resigned in due course with his colleagues, pleased at least that the defeat had not come on reform and that the Whigs and their allies now had 'the burden of bringing [it] forward ... as a government measure'.[37] He expressed qualified support for the principle of Lord Chandos's game bill, 18 Nov., and presented an anti-slavery petition, 25 Nov. On 11 Dec. 1830 he lost his seat when the Perth Burghs election was declared void, but early in the 1831 session his brother stepped aside for him at Bossiney.[38] Shortly before his return Ellenborough, who doubted whether he would be staunch in opposition, noted that while other Tories were laughing at the Grey ministry's budget embarrassments, Stuart Wortley 'seemed sorry for them'.[39] In the House, 17 Feb. 1831, he supported Chandos's proposal to disfranchise Evesham if electoral corruption, of which he had 'little doubt', was proved. He was added to the East Indian committee, 22 Feb. (and reappointed, 28 June 1831, 27 Jan. 1832). He thought repeal of the coastwise coal duty would be of little benefit to Londoners unless other restrictions on the trade were lifted, 23 Feb. He argued that 'the principles of political economy, in the strict sense' were inapplicable to 'human affairs in the complicated relations of a great nation', 11 Mar., and

gave a cautious welcome to the government's colonial trade bill. He approved, with some reservations, their plan for the timber duties, 15 Mar. He introduced a bill to regulate the fees and emoluments of officials of the Indian supreme court, 17 Mar., but it made no further progress that session. Nor did the measure which he presented on 21 Mar., in accordance with a committee's recommendation, to amend the municipal sett of Dundee, one of the constituent burghs of the Perth district. He complained that Scotland had been unfairly treated in the matter of the tax on steam navigation, 29 Mar. He voted silently against the second reading of the government's reform bill, 22 Mar., but in supporting a petition from Anstruther Easter Burghs against disfranchisement, 28 Mar., he indicated that he would support the principle of the Scottish bill. He endorsed an assertion that opinion in Yorkshire was not unanimous for reform. He voted for Gascoyne's wrecking amendment to the reform bill, 19 Apr. 1831. The 'Tory party in Leeds' invited him to stand for Yorkshire at the ensuing general election, but his father thought better of it; 'animated to a degree you never saw' by the crisis, as his mother reported, he was returned unopposed for Bossiney.[40]

Stuart Wortley presented a petition from the grain dealers of St. Andrews for better protection of buyers' rights, 22 June 1831. He pressed ministers to make the renewed East India committee smaller than the last one, 28 June, as there had been 'much more of desultory conversation than of regular examination'. He supported the case for St. Andrews to be united with five other Fife burghs to return a Member and called for separate representation for Perth, 30 June. He voted against the second reading of the reintroduced reform bill, 6 July, for use of the 1831 census for the purpose of scheduling boroughs, 19 July, and against the partial disfranchisement of Chippenham, 27 July. He persuaded ministers to add Wednesday to the two weekly order days as an 'experiment' to expedite business, 13 July. Two days later he endorsed Agnew's ludicrous amendment to have disfranchised schedule A boroughs combined into 'convenient' districts to return Members and insisted that the 'dangerous' bill, which could have 'lamentable consequences', was supported by 'mere popular clamour' rather than by 'real public opinion'. He offered no resistance to the proposed disfranchisement of Bossiney, 20 July, but insisted that it was 'an open corporation' where the only influence was legitimate. He argued for the inclusion of Dunster parish to save Minehead, 22 July, and harried ministers over the inconsistency with which they had treated this and other cases, 2 Aug. He also proposed to have Salford included in the new

Manchester constituency, but gave way after hearing an explanation of the reason for their separation. He criticized the enfranchisement of Wolverhampton, 4 Aug., Gateshead, 5 Aug., and Walsall, 6 Aug. He complained that giving the boundary commissioners the final word on constituency limits made 'a perfect mockery of legislation', 5 Aug., and suggested increasing the majority required to fix their decisions, 13 Sept. He approved the plan for Yorkshire to have six county Members, 10 Aug., but thought Buckinghamshire entitled to four and that giving two to Glamorgan strengthened the case for augmenting the Scottish county representation, 13 Aug. He failed in an attempt to have the amended county franchise clause set aside for further consideration, 19 Aug. He denied being 'irritated' when he attacked the £10 householder clause, 24 Aug., but asserted that through it ministers had 'destroyed the old constituency', 26 Aug. He lamented the 'great injustice' of the partial disfranchisement of the county towns of Dorchester, Guildford and Huntingdon, 15 Sept. He divided against the bill's third reading, 19 Sept., and its passage, 21 Sept. Two days later he spoke and voted for the second reading of the Scottish bill, though he warned that he did not anticipate being able to support its details as they stood. He opposed an amendment to the game bill, 8 Aug. He voted to censure the Irish administration for interfering in the Dublin election, 23 Aug. He secured a minor change to the wine duties bill, 7 Sept., and denied that the northern coal owners were monopolists, 15 Sept. He questioned ministers about the contingency plan for the administration of justice in Prince of Wales Island, 19 Sept. On 29 Sept. 1831 he finally brought on a motion condemning the proposed reduction of the salary of the president of the board of control; it was negatived.

In the crisis following the rejection of the reform bill by the Lords, Stuart Wortley was approached by his former associate Palmerston, the foreign secretary, who 'expressed a desire that some compromise should be effected between the government and the opposition leaders'. He contacted his father and Harrowby, and they and Sandon 'discussed the matter and came to a sort of general resolution as to the basis on which they could treat'. This led to negotiations with ministers for a modified bill which Wharncliffe, Harrowby and the other 'Waverer' peers could support.[41] In the House, 12 Dec. 1831, after the revised bill had been detailed, Stuart Wortley was one of those in opposition who tried to soothe the 'irritation' caused by Peel's 'very injudicious speech'. Yet he made it clear that despite certain 'improvements', he could not support the still 'objectionable' measure, and appealed

to ministers to play their part in resolving the crisis 'by mutual concession and ... statesmanlike views'; one observer reckoned that he was 'not attended to'.[42] He was said to have spoken 'very well' in the same sense before voting against the second reading, 17 Dec. 1831, when he applauded the Lords' rejection of the previous bill and indicated that he and those who felt like him would accept a limited degree of disfranchisement, the enfranchisement of large towns and a modest widening of the franchise. He told Denison that if those who really disliked the measure continued nevertheless to vote for it, it had 'no chance of being mended'.[43] After questioning ministers, he denounced the 'absurdity' of fixing in advance the number of boroughs to be included in schedule A, 20 Jan. 1832, but he did not vote in the opposition minority on the issue that day.[44] He argued that York was preferable to Beverley as a polling place for the East Riding, 24 Jan. He condemned the plan to give some counties three Members as 'absurd and inconsistent', 27 Jan., mocked the separate representation proposed for the Isle of Wight, 1 Feb., and, supporting an amendment to the £10 householder clause, 3 Feb., complained of the 'extreme scantiness of information furnished to the House'. He was unhappy with the registration clause, 7 Feb., and next day ridiculed the proposal to retain the freeholder franchise in the surviving sluiced boroughs. He voted against the enfranchisement of Tower Hamlets, 28 Feb., objected to the revised plans for Manchester and Salford, 5 Mar., said it was preposterous to give South Shields separate representation, 7 Mar., and voted silently against the bill's third reading, 22 Mar. He supported an unsuccessful bid to increase the Scottish county representation, 1 June, but secured an alteration allowing town clerks to act as returning officers, 27 June. He divided against ministers on the Russian-Dutch loan, 26 Jan., 12 July. He welcomed the proposed appointment of poor law commissioners, 15 Mar. He approved the principle of the Indian juries bill, 18 June, and voted for Baring's measure to exclude insolvent debtors from Parliament, 27 June 1832.

Nothing came of talk of Stuart Wortley's standing for the West Riding at the general election of 1832, and the disfranchisement of Bossiney left him without a seat.[45] But for his narrow defeat in Forfarshire in 1835 he would have become colonial under-secretary in Peel's first ministry. He was subsequently offered a place at the treasury, but declined because it would appear 'too much like a desire of holding office merely for the sake of its emoluments', when he had no parliamentary seat.[46] In 1841 he won a notable victory in the West Riding, but his father's death in December 1845 removed him from the Commons. An improving agriculturist, who published a short treatise on the currency in 1833, he later suffered much from 'sorrows and ill health'; he spent part of the winter of 1854-5 in Egypt, where he grew a beard.[47] He died of consumption in October 1855 and was succeeded by his eldest son, Edward Montague Stuart Wortley (1827-99), who was created earl of Wharncliffe in 1876.[48]

[1] C. Grosvenor, The First Lady Wharncliffe and her Fam. i. 65, 141, 145, 163. [2] Ibid. i. 198-211, 223-5, 233-52. [3] Ibid. i. 257-8; Add. 52011, Stuart Wortley to Fox, 31 Dec. 1820, 22, 31 Jan., 23 Aug.; 52059, Vernon Smith to same, 6 July [1821]. [4] Add. 52011, Stuart Wortley to Fox, 5 June, 25 July 1821. [5] Ibid. Stuart Wortley to Fox, 20 Dec. 1821, 13 Jan., 2 Feb., 11 July 1822; Fox Jnl. 62, 95, 130. [6] Add. 52011, Stuart Wortley to Fox, 3, 16 Nov., 29 Dec. 1822 [16, 30 Jan.]; 52059, Smith to same [3 Mar. 1823]; Fox Jnl. 157, 166; West Briton, 30 May, 6 June 1823. [7] Add. 52011, Stuart Wortley to Fox, 2 Oct. [1823]; Fox Jnl. 175, 182. [8] Harewood mss, Canning to wife, 4 Apr. 1824. [9] Countess Granville Letters, i. 279, 288-91; TNA 30/29/9/5/30. [10] Grosvenor, i. 316-19; Add. 52011, Stuart Wortley to Fox, 21 Oct. 1824, 11 Feb., 14 Mar. 1825. [11] Add. 52011, Stuart Wortley to Fox, 25 June 1825. [12] Ibid. Stuart Wortley to Fox, 24 Aug., 16 Oct.; 52012, Greville to same, 8 Nov.; 52017, Townshend to same, 12, 30 Oct., 20 Nov. 1825. [13] Grosvenor, ii. 2; Nottingham Univ. Lib. Denison diary, 2 Feb.; Add. 51580, Carlisle to Lady Holland, 5 Feb.; Sheffield Archives, Wharncliffe mun. WhM/T.842, Lady C. Stuart Wortley to Lady Erne, 6 Feb. [1826]. [14] Add. 52011, Stuart Wortley to Fox [6 Mar.]; 52012, Greville to same, 9 Feb.; 52017, Townshend to same [29], 30 Apr. 1826. [15] West Briton, 2, 16 June 1826. [16] Grosvenor, ii. 9, 10; Castle Howard mss, Morpeth to Lady Carlisle, 25 Nov., Abercromby to Carlisle [9 Dec.]; Add. 51749, Holland to Fox, 3 Dec. [1826]. [17] Grosvenor, ii. 12. [18] Ibid. ii. 15; Arbuthnot Corresp. 83. [19] The Times, 5 May 1827. [20] Add. 52011, Stuart Wortley to Fox, 17 Nov. 1827; Fox Jnl. 249. [21] Hatherton diary, 29 Jan. 1828. [22] Add. 38755, f. 158; Nottingham Univ. Lib. Portland mss PwH 145. [23] Broughton, Recollections, iii. 261-2. [24] Add. 38756, f. 222. [25] Denison diary, 4 July [1828]. [26] Add. 52011, Stuart Wortley to Fox, 8 Feb. 1829. [27] Arbuthnot Jnl. ii. 282. [28] Ellenborough Diary, ii. 158, 181; Lady Holland to Son, 107; Wellington mss WP1/1089/13. [29] Hatherton mss, Stuart Wortley to Littleton, 30 Jan., Huskisson to same, 30 Jan., Wharncliffe to same, 1 Feb. 1830; Nottingham Univ. Lib. Ossington mss OsC 72. [30] Arbuthnot Jnl. ii. 328; Greville Mems. i. 365; Countess Granville Letters, ii. 60. [31] Ellenborough Diary, ii. 329. [32] Broughton, Recollections, iv. 25. [33] Add. 40401, ff. 1, 3, 5, 18; Wellington mss WP1/1123/4, 20; Ellenborough Diary, ii. 295, 297-9, 302. [34] Edinburgh Evening Courant, 26, 28 Aug. 1830; Wellington mss WP1/1126/27. [35] N. Gash, Secretary Peel, 640; Add. 40340, ff. 226, 230, 232, 234; Brougham mss, Agar Ellis to Brougham, 4 Oct. 1830. [36] Ellenborough Diary, ii. 416, 423, 429. [37] Ibid. ii. 435. [38] West Briton, 11, 25 Feb. 1831. [39] Three Diaries, 47, 51. [40] Grosvenor, ii. 74-75, 76, 78; Creevey mss, Creevey to Miss Ord, 30 Apr.; West Briton, 29 Apr., 6 May 1831. [41] Greville Mems. ii. 214; Three Diaries, 158; M. Brock, Great Reform Act, 245. [42] Grosvenor, ii. 102; NLS mss 24762, f. 49. [43] Grosvenor, ii. 102, 104; Holland House Diaries, 97. [44] Croker Pprs. ii. 149. [45] Wharncliffe mss, Stuart Wortley to bro. James, 9 July 1832. [46] Add. 40405, f. 185; 40406, ff. 49, 255; 40407, f. 218; 40411, f. 297; Greville Mems. iii. 145; Grosvenor, ii. 220-3. [47] Add. 52011, Wharncliffe to Holland, 8 Sept., 18 Oct., 20, 22 Nov., 6 Dec. 1854, 19 Jan. 1855, Lady Wharncliffe to same, 8 July [1856]. [48] Gent. Mag (1855), ii. 643.

D.R.F.

STURGES BOURNE (formerly **STURGES**), **William** (1769–1845), of Testwood, nr. Southampton, Hants.; Acton Hall, nr. Droitwich, Worcs. and 15 South Audley Street, Mdx.

HASTINGS	3 July 1798–1802
CHRISTCHURCH	1802–1812
BANDON BRIDGE	24 Mar. 1815–1818
CHRISTCHURCH	1818–1826
ASHBURTON	1826–1830
MILBORNE PORT	1830–7 Mar. 1831

b. 7 Nov. 1769, o. s. of Rev. John Sturges, DD, preb. of Winchester, and Judith, da. of Richard Bourne of Acton Hall. educ. Winchester 1782; Christ Church, Oxf. 1786; L. Inn 1789, called 1793. m. 2 Feb. 1808, Anne, da. of Oldfield Bowles of North Aston, Oxon., 1 da. suc. uncle Francis Page[†] (formerly Bourne) to Acton Hall, and took additional name of Bourne by royal lic. 6 Dec. 1803; fa. 1807; uncle Richard Bourne Charlett (formerly Bourne) to Steeple Aston and Thrupp, Oxon. 1821. d. 1 Feb. 1845.

Sec. to treasury May 1804-Feb. 1806; ld. of treasury Mar. 1807-Dec. 1809; PC 10 Aug. 1814; commr. bd. of control Sept. 1814-June 1816 (unsalaried), June 1818-Feb. 1822 (salaried); sec. of state for home affairs Apr.-July 1827; commr. of woods, forests and land revenues July 1827-Feb. 1828; poor law commr. 1832-3; eccles. commr. 1832-5.

Vol. Bloomsbury corps; capt. New Forest vols. 1803-5; chairman, Hants q. sess. until 1822; warden, New Forest 1827.

Sturges Bourne's 'personal appearance ... was unprepossessing', and 'his manner in public neither dignified nor impressive'; but, as his obituarist noted, 'being thoroughly familiar with the affairs of government, and capable of producing, as occasion required, the varied information which long official experience usually imparts, he acquired slowly but surely the favourable opinion of the House of Commons'.[1] He was the close personal friend, long-standing political associate and occasional butt of George Canning*, who had saddled him with the nickname of 'Scroggs', and under whom he served at the board of control.[2] At the general election of 1820 he came in again unopposed for Christchurch on the Rose interest. He is not known to have made a single Commons speech on Indian affairs during the remaining two years of his tenure of his place. He was, however, a pundit on the poor laws and related problems, and had had some success in legislating on them in the two preceding Parliaments. On 6 June 1820 he expressed his willingness to assist Parnell in any attempt to eradicate abuses in the treatment of vagrants forcibly returned to Ireland, though he pointed out that his own poor law amendment bill of 1819 had stipulated that they should not suffer physical punishment. He accordingly supported Parnell's motion for leave to introduce a bill, 14 June, having 'no objection to make the poor laws more perfect than they are at present'. At the same time, he advised Parnell that Irish paupers could obtain settlements by service or renting property, although his own efforts to extend the scope of the settlement regulations had been rejected by the House. He divided with his ministerial colleagues against economies in revenue collection, 4 July. On 6 July 1820 he was a teller for the minority against Chetwynd's bill to end the public whipping of women. In the autumn, according to Mrs. Arbuthnot, he was the government emissary sent to Sir William Heathcote* to investigate his claims that Sir William Gell, Queen Caroline's chamberlain, had given perjured evidence at her trial.[3]

When Canning, feeling compromised by the queen's affair, resigned from the government in December 1820, he 'persuaded' Sturges Bourne to remain in place.[4] He only paired against the opposition censure motion, 6 Feb. 1821. On 9 Feb. he echoed his colleague Lord Binning's indignant repudiation of suggestions that Canning was still receiving his official salary. He paired in favour of Catholic relief, 28 Feb. He was named to the select committee on agricultural distress, 7 Mar. He voted against repeal of the additional malt duty, 21 Mar., 3 Apr., a revision of public salaries, 30 Mar., parliamentary reform, 9 May, and abolition of the death penalty for forgery, 23 May. He voted steadily thereafter in the ministerial majorities against the radical-inspired campaign for economy and retrenchment. As a former chairman of the poor laws committee, he concurred in the principle of Scarlett's proposed amendment bill, 8 May, and urged him to incorporate in it provision for the encouragement of select vestries, on which he had himself legislated in 1818. On 7 June, however, he joined in attacks on the inadequacies of the measure.[5] He belatedly expressed concern over the 'latitude of examination pursued in the House' in the *John Bull* breach of privilege case, 11 May. He was a teller for the minority against reducing the compensation for General Desfourneaux as low as £3,500, 28 June 1821. That month John Croker* dismissed as nonsense a story that Sturges Bourne was about to replace him as secretary to the admiralty.[6]

In July 1821 Sturges Bourne succeeded his uncle, Richard Bourne Charlett (the brother of his benefactor of 1803), to estates in Oxfordshire.[7] This addition to his personal wealth underpinned his voluntary retirement from office, with Binning, at the turn of

the year, as part of the reshuffle which brought in the Grenvillites. Binning told William Huskisson* that 'it is well known that Sturges retires because he *bona fide* wishes to withdraw finally from all official situation, and I do not know that it would break his heart if he were to be out of Parliament'. Sturges Bourne himself, like Binning, was adamant that Huskisson should remain in as commissioner of woods and forests, no matter how justifiably disgruntled he felt at not being promoted; and his surprise and disappointment at Canning's decision to take the government of India made him 'doubly glad that I took this opportunity of getting my release'. It was clearly understood, however, that he still had a 'strong wish to support the government', and that his 'retreat may be considered as unconnected with Canning's'.[8] His only known votes in the 1822 session were with government against more extensive tax reductions, 11, 21 Feb., relaxation of the salt duties, 28 Feb., and abolition of one of the joint-postmasterships, 13 Mar. He objected to the wording of Maberly's motion for returns of public accounts as implying that they were inaccurate, 4 Mar.;[9] he was named to the subsequent select committee, 18 Apr. He was also a member of the select committee on poor returns, 12 Mar. 1822. He divided with government against repeal of the assessed taxes, 18 Mar., and of the Foreign Enlistment Act, 16 Apr., and on the prosecution of the Dublin Orange rioters, 24 Mar., 22 Apr. 1823; he had a technical point to make on the latter inquiry, 23 May.[10] He 'objected decidedly' to Grey Bennet's bid to abolish punishment by whipping, 30 Apr. 1823, arguing that 'in the case of a hardened offender it was often attended with most beneficial effects'. He defended government policy on the war between France and Spain, 17 Feb. 1824, and moved a successful amendment, applauding their neutral stance, against Lord Nugent's call for further information. He voted against reform of Edinburgh's representation, 26 Feb., and was a teller for the majority against a clause proposed to be added to the county courts bill, 24 May. He objected to a petition complaining of the conduct of George Chetwynd, Member for Stafford, as a county magistrate, 27 Feb., and to the bill to raise funds for repairs to Londonderry Cathedral, 10 May, and recommended postponement of the mariners' apprentices settlement bill, 21 May. He favoured printing the evidence given before the South London Docks committee, 2 June 1824.[11] The following month an incredulous Robert Ward* reported a story that Canning had once offered the chief justiceship of Madras to Sturges Bourne, 'a privy councillor, a member of the control, a man of fortune, and his own most attached friend', and that he 'could hardly answer him with gravity'. Commenting on this unlikely tale, Charles Williams Wynn*, the president of the board of control, observed that

> in the difficulties which have attended the disposal of the governor[ship] of Madras, we should have been but too happy to put forward as respectable a candidate as Scroggs; but it never entered into my mind to offer it to a man with a very easy fortune, and only one daughter in miserable health, especially after he has quitted so easy an office as the India board from wishing to have more leisure.[12]

In the summer of 1824 Sturges Bourne went abroad for several months.[13]

He was appointed to the select committee on Ireland, 17 Feb., and voted for the Irish unlawful societies bill, 25 Feb. 1825. He divided for Catholic relief, 1 Mar., 21 Apr., 10 May 1825, though he was ready in private to admit 'the increased aversion of the people of England to any further concession'.[14] He supported the bill to disfranchise Irish 40s. freeholders as a means both of purifying the electorate and removing the incentive for the subdivision of land, 12 May. He was named to the select committees on the export of machinery, 24 Feb., and the combination laws, 29 Mar. On 22 Mar. he obtained leave to introduce a bill to clarify elements of the laws of settlement; it received royal assent as 6 Geo. IV, c. 57 on 22 June 1825. He divided for the duke of Cumberland's annuity, 6, 10 June. He seconded Littleton's motion for the appointment of a select committee on the constitution of committees on private bills, 7 June, and was duly made a member of it. He was at pains to ensure that William Kenrick, a former Member, was given the right of reply to the charges levelled against him, 14, 21 June; and doubted whether an election committee was best suited to investigate the rights of the electors of West Looe, 20 June 1825.[15] In January 1826 Peel, the home secretary, commented that had Sturges Bourne 'been a Protestant, he would have been a good man' for the current vacancy for Oxford University.[16] On 17 Feb. he declared in the House that the case against Kenrick amounted to virtually nothing, went 'only to investigate the moral character of an individual' and would establish a precedent 'full of danger'. He divided with ministers in defence of the Jamaican slave trials, 2 Mar., and against reform of Edinburgh's representation, 13 Apr. He was named to the select committees on emigration, 14 Mar., and promissory notes, 16 Mar. Although he wanted Wilson to restrict the scope of his motion for information on tavern expenses incurred by commissioners of bankrupts, 15 Mar. 1826, he thought that those who had abused the system should be brought to book.

At the end of April 1826 Henry Goulburn* reported that Sturges Bourne had been 'for some time laid up with a violent attack of gout. He is confined to his chair and still in great pain, but is I hope on the high road to be better. He is one of those who are in great uncertainty as to again coming into Parliament'.[17] At the general election in June he made way for a member of the Rose family at Christchurch, and came in for Ashburton on the Clinton interest, presumably as a paying guest. He formally proposed the re-election of Manners Sutton as Speaker, 14 Nov. 1826, but seemed 'embarrassed what to say', according to the Whig Member George Agar Ellis.[18] He was appointed to the select committee on Northampton corporation, 21 Feb. 1827. Still 'gouty and indolent', he talked incessantly at home of 'Ireland, Catholics, corn and ministry' at this time; and he voted for Catholic relief, 6 Mar. He was trapped for five hours a day on an election committee later that month.[19] During the negotiations for the formation of Canning's ministry in April he initially 'refused all office' and, though anxious that the approach to the Lansdowne Whigs should succeed, 'hugs himself at having nothing to do with it all', in his daughter's words.[20] On 26 Apr., however, when matters had reached a seeming impasse over Lansdowne's reluctance, as home secretary, to be responsible for the expected appointment of a Protestant executive in Ireland, Canning pressed Sturges Bourne to save the day by taking the home seals until the end of the session. He evidently asked for time to consider, but that evening tried to wriggle off the hook:

> I have endeavoured in vain since we parted to persuade myself that I might execute the duties of the home department without discredit to you as well as to myself. But I feel my first opinion to have been correct. And though I should certainly be anxious to relinquish the office almost as soon as I had learned my task, yet I cannot disguise from myself that such a speedy surrender of the post would look very like a proof of my insufficiency, when I know and feel that such an opinion would be well founded. Under these circumstances I think it may be convenient to you that I should relieve you from any suspense respecting me ... I am ... sure that any facility which my acceptance of office would give to your arrangements, would be more than counterbalanced by having such a situation inadequately filled. I sincerely hope that a better arrangement may present itself to you.

Canning would have none of it, telling Sturges Bourne that 'my administration *wholly* depends upon your helping me for two months as home secretary'; and under such pressure he had no choice but to submit. His daughter wrote that 'nobody ever lamented more what the greater part of the world would consider such a piece of good fortune'.[21] Huskisson, who became a member of the administration, described Sturges Bourne as 'a very efficient man, of excellent understanding, and much respected in the House', whose appointment would be 'generally approved'; while Peel wrote to the duke of Wellington that 'I know not what better arrangement could have been made and I wish it were to be a more permanent one'.[22] On the other hand, two opponents of the new ministry, of contrasting political complexions, were contemptuous: the anti-Catholic Tory Mrs. Arbuthnot dismissed Sturges Bourne as one of the 'little click of his own personal friends' whom Canning had put in as '*warming pans*'; and the duke of Bedford thought how 'ridiculous' it was to see a man, 'who I remember a briefless barrister, brought forward by Mr. Pitt, with scarce any pretension to a subordinate office', in such an exalted station.[23]

There was no difficulty about Sturges Bourne's re-election, but the brief interval during which he was out of the House enabled him to get to grips with his official business without distractions. As soon as he took his seat, 11 May, he was mischievously asked to confirm that his appointment was 'only provisional': his evasive answer did not please his questioner. Despite this, his daughter described him the following day as being 'very well and in good spirits'.[24] He had agreed that Peel should proceed with his legislation to reform the criminal code, and he welcomed his bills to abolish benefit of clergy and increase the punishment for second offences, 18 May, and to facilitate the recovery of small debts, 20 June. He did not object to the introduction of the Coventry magistracy bill, 22 May, though he did not wish to have evidence relating to it heard at the bar of the House; he presented a petition in its favour, 1 June. He announced that steps were being taken to revise the rules of confinement in the Fleet prison, 22 May; but on the 25th said that he had no measure in contemplation to provide for the employment of the aged poor.[25] Closing the debate on the Penryn election bill, 28 May, he argued that it was 'contrary to every principle of justice' to penalize the whole borough on account of the misconduct of half the voters, and he divided with Canning in the minority against Russell's amendment for disfranchisement. On 7 June, however, he supported the third reading of the bill in deference to the expressed will of the House. He presented an Ashburton petition for repeal of the Test Acts, 1 June, acquiesced in the appointment of a commission to investigate London's water supply, though he would have preferred a select committee, 11 June, and sanctioned Gordon's motion for a com-

mittee on the treatment of pauper lunatics, to which he was named, 13 June.[26] He stated that a measure was in preparation to deal with estreated recognizances, 14 June, suggested that the House was guilty of 'great extravagance in sanctioning the printing of so many petitions', 16 June, and explained why there was as yet no public access to parts of Regent's Park, 22 June 1827.[27] His handover of the home seals to Lansdowne in July was briefly put in doubt by a notion that the latter might become foreign secretary, but he resigned on the 16th, replacing Lord Carlisle as first commissioner of woods and forests and retaining his seat in the cabinet. As Binning put it, 'Sturgeon Burgeon falls soft, and gladly, from his present eminence into the rural lap of woods and forests'.[28] The Whig Sir James Mackintosh* saw it as a reward 'for the fatigues and ridicule of three months as nominal secretary of state'.[29]

On Canning's death, 8 Aug. 1827, Sturges Bourne and Lord Goderich were immediately summoned to Windsor, where the king invited Goderich to form an administration on Canning's principles and pressed Sturges Bourne to become chancellor of the exchequer and government leader in the Commons. He shied at the prospect, and on 11 Aug. formally declined the offer, as he did the king's subsequent suggestion that he might return to the home office. He was, however, willing to remain where he was, though his personal preference would have been for complete retirement.[30] On his refusal, the exchequer was offered to the anti-Catholic Tory John Herries*, whose appointment was unacceptable to many of the Whig supporters of Canning's administration. Goderich's difficulties were increased by the king's refusal to admit Lord Holland to the government. Sturges Bourne was 'sadly tired and worried' by all this aggravation, as his daughter reported, and pitied Goderich, who he thought had 'not nerves nor the strength to keep together very heterogeneous materials'. Once the king had explained to him the grounds of his objections to Holland, which had 'reference to the feelings of foreign sovereigns', he saw them as 'so much more reasonable and valid than any which I anticipated, that I almost regret that they could not be communicated' to Holland himself.[31] As Huskisson's arrival from Paris was awaited, Lord Palmerston* wondered whether, if he would not take on the exchequer, Sturges Bourne 'may be persuaded to devote himself for a session in order to save the government'; but on 29 Aug. he informed a friend that 'Bourne says that if the fate of the government depends on his taking the exchequer, the government must prepare for dissolution, for that on no consideration will he do any such thing'.[32] The following day, however, Huskisson thought at one point that he had prevailed on Sturges Bourne to take the exchequer, if only for a year, and was near to persuading Herries to settle for woods and forests and the chairmanship of the finance committee. Yet George Tierney*, the master of the mint, perceived in the early evening that Sturges Bourne was 'perfectly wretched at the prospect'; and four hours later he wrote to Huskisson:

> After I left you today, and was able to collect my thoughts, I felt that, though the case had not arisen, by Herries being satisfied, which made my decision necessary, yet that I had perhaps given more reason to expect that I would take the seal of the exchequer than I could upon a moment's reflection confirm. I therefore hastened back to the chancellor [Lord Lyndhurst] and Knighton [the king's secretary] to put them out of doubt upon the subject.

Lyndhurst, reporting his 'fixed determination', saw that it would be 'impossible to induce him to change his resolution'; and all efforts to do so duly failed.[33] Sturges Bourne, who tried unsuccessfully to persuade Huskisson to take the exchequer, explained and justified his conduct to Lansdowne, 31 Aug.:

> I had at no time yesterday acquiesced in the proposal, though when so painfully pressed as I was upon the subject, it is difficult in seeking information, in order to ascertain all that belongs to the question, not to depart in some degree from the language of peremptory refusal; and I necessarily allowed the case to be put to Mr. Herries as if I had acquiesced, in order to see whether his feelings could be satisfied, which I understood was a *sine qua non*. And I stated more than once to the chancellor that I considered the proposal to me as premature till that was ascertained. The first moment however that I was once more left to my own reflections, the vastness of such an undertaking occurred to me so forcibly, that I determined to put an end to all doubt on the subject. But I do not consider the preliminary point as gained ... If the case had arisen, I would again have made a sacrifice of my peace and comfort in life, if that had been all that was had been required of me. But I am called upon to undertake the most arduous office in the state ... having, as I had already assured the king, a certain and entire conviction of my own incompetence to discharge its duties without disgrace to myself and discredit to the government. That opinion is informed by all the reflection which I can give the subject, and I must so far regard myself as to decline sacrificing not only my peace, comfort and health, but my reputation, such as it is, also.

He was active in the successful efforts to persuade Lansdowne and the other Whigs to accept Herries's appointment and stay in office, though he did not expect Lansdowne, for one, to 'remain long with us'. While he was inclined to blame Goderich for all the trouble which had occurred, he thought that it would have been avoided had Huskisson been on the spot when Canning died.[34] His daughter was delighted that he had managed to 'persuade people that it was not necessary to sacrifice himself', and that he had returned to Testwood 'the same Herr Wald und Forts commissioner that he went and very well'; but others took a less charitable view of his conduct. Georgiana Agar Ellis thought him 'provoking'; Lady Granville complained that he was 'beyond my patience'; Lord Seaford considered his refusal of the exchequer to have been 'quite inexcusable', and even Huskisson had 'not forgiven him' for his 'desertion' three days later.[35]

Sturges Bourne had an 'uncomfortable' time of it in November and December 1827, when cabinets on the conflict with Turkey necessitated several journeys to and stays in London; but he was back in Hampshire before Christmas, and remained there throughout the crisis which put an end to Goderich's ministry. Williams Wynn kept him informed of developments, and he replied that 'as I could have been of no use I am well pleased to be absent'. He was uneasy at the prospect of war in the aftermath of Navarino.[36] He told Huskisson in January 1828 that even if he was not turned out by the duke Wellington, he wished to retire, partly because, having been party to the reconciliation of Lansdowne to Herries (both of whose conduct he considered to have been 'more than irreproachable') in September, he did not wish to make himself 'an accomplice ... *ex post facto*' to the anticipated removal of the former and retention of the latter. He also observed that the 'enmity and malevolence towards Canning' shown by some of Wellington and Peel's subordinates 'must make it painful to meet them on terms of daily and official familiarity'. He was duly replaced by Charles Arbuthnot*: his daughter construed it as 'a great relief', though she resented the failure of the ministers to give him 'any private account' of the new arrangement, which he gleaned from the newspapers, and the indecent haste with which the Arbuthnots took possession of the commissioner's house in Whitehall.[37] Williams Wynn believed that he had 'urged Huskisson as strongly as he could to decline the junction' with Wellington.[38] He was seen as a contender for the contentious chairmanship of the finance committee, and Charles Percy, a government backbencher, preferred 'Sturgy Burgy ... an independent and upright man', to all others. He was offered the position, but turned it down, claiming that the state of his wife's health, which might force them to go abroad, made it impossible for him to put himself in 'a situation of such long confinement to London', as well as observing that as a member of a government which had been broken up over the chairmanship, he did not wish to become involved in a possible renewed contest for it.[39] On the ministerial explanations in the House, 21 Feb., Sturges Bourne queried some of Herries's allegations and deplored his 'tone of contempt and sarcasm' towards Goderich. He presented petitions for repeal of the Test Acts, 20 Feb., and attended the debate on Russell's motion, 26 Feb., but did not vote in the division.[40] In the absence of Acland, Member for Devon, it fell to him on 18 Mar. to propose the insertion in the repeal bill of a declaration to be made by Dissenters appointed to office which was designed to satisfy both supporters and opponents, but it was rejected in favour of an alternative put forward by Peel. That day he extolled the beneficial effects of his Select Vestries Act, and expressed surprise that the report on London's water supply had been so long delayed. He thought that Macqueen's bill to deal with settlement by hiring had 'little bearing' on the poor laws and would merely redistribute paupers, 29 Apr. On the offences against the person bill, 5 May, he argued that attempted murder should remain a capital offence; and later that day he pressed for magistrates to be given a summary power of determining cases of assault. He voted for Catholic relief, 12 May. He defended the cost of the royal yachts and spoke of 'the economical spirit of the admiralty', 19 May. The same day he explained that, as last session, he had opposed the disfranchisement of Penryn, but that he was prepared to support that of East Retford and the transfer of its seats to Birmingham:

I have ever been, and ever will be, an enemy to parliamentary reform, but I think I shall be the best friend to the cause I espouse, by taking away a franchise when it is proved to be notoriously only a vehicle for corruption. The transfer ... will be of great service to ... [Birmingham] as well as take away one of the most popular arguments from those who advocate the general principle of reform.

After the resignation from the government of the former Canningites which was precipitated by Huskisson's disagreement with his cabinet colleagues on this question, Sturges Bourne was listed as one of their parliamentary group.[41]

When he arrived in London for the 1829 session, his head, as his daughter reported, was 'in a state of the greatest amusement and interest' over the rumoured concession of Catholic relief.[42] In the House, 19 Feb., he sarcastically commented that the promoters of the much vaunted Norwich anti-Catholic petition clearly 'had better means of appreciating the condition of Ireland – and were themselves wiser – than the king's cabinet'. He voted for emancipation, 6 Mar., and

presented and endorsed a favourable petition from Southampton, 9 Mar. In committee on the relief bill, he said that a Catholic would 'outwit himself as well as the House' by refusing to take the oath provided for him (23 Mar.), and that only a Protestant secretary of state could authorize the disposal of church property (24 Mar). He disputed Inglis's claim that Catholics had no cause to complain of interference with the 'free exercise of their religion', 26 Mar., and voted for the third reading of the bill, 30 Mar. On Hobhouse's motion for a committee on select vestries, to which he was appointed, 28 Apr., he said that those which had been regulated by his own Acts of 1818 and 1819 should not be tarred with the same brush as the London ones: 'nothing can be so improper as to lay down one general rule on this subject'. According to Hobhouse, in the committee, 15 May, Sturges Bourne 'gave me a sort of lecture, under which I was not very docile'.[43] He doubted whether Slaney's labourers' wages bill would achieve its object, 4 May, when he called for the removal of the limitation to 20 acres which had been imposed by the Lords on his own bill of 1819 facilitating parochial purchases of land for cultivation by the able bodied poor. He voted, with the other Huskissonites, for the extension of East Retford's seats to Birmingham, 5 May, and spoke against the issue of a new writ for the borough, 7 May. He presented an Ashburton petition for repeal of the coal duties, 19 May. On Peel's bill regulating the appointment of justices of the peace, 27 May, he opposed Hume's proposal to extend the qualification to all freeholders, but at the same time suggested that the bill as it stood would deter many worthy men from taking seats on the bench.

An improvement in his wife's health made it unnecessary for Sturges Bourne to go abroad in the winter of 1829, as he had at one point contemplated. Looking ahead to the next session, he commented to Huskisson that 'the government will have a large body of steady and zealous friends, and a yet smaller body of organized and combined opponents, and in that will consist its strength, if strength it can be called'. He thought that ministers had some awkward explaining to do on their foreign policy, especially in relation to Turkey and Portugal.[44] His own plans for parliamentary attendance in 1830 were disrupted by a severe attack of gout, which had him on crutches in February and, after a relapse, in bed the following month. By mid-April he was 'very well', and he arrived in London in time to vote with opposition for information on the Terciera incident, 28 Apr.[45] He divided against Jewish emancipation, 17 May, and the abolition of the death penalty for forgery, 7 June. He was named to the committee on the labourers' wages bill, 3 May, and the select committee on manufacturing employment, 13 May. He objected to a clause of the Scottish and Irish paupers removal bill, 26 May, and on 4 June dwelt on its inadequacies, arguing that it was desirable to give parishes entire discretion in the matter of relief, in order to deter the 'sturdy beggar'. He was unhappy that Hamerton's divorce bill had come to Parliament without the sanction of a verdict at law, 3 June. He again gave annoyance to Hobhouse, who described him as 'the most egregious coxcomb I ever met', in committee on his vestries reform bill, 14 June 1830.[46] Shortly after the king's death, his daughter warned her regular correspondent to prepare herself for a 'final cessation' of franks, as it seemed almost certain that he would not come in again: 'He has many things that make politics at present not very interesting or pleasant to him, and yet I think he will feel the difference'. In the event, the 1st marquess of Anglesey, believing it to be 'of consequence that Sturges Bourne should be in Parliament', as he told Huskisson, offered him a seat for Milborne Port:

> He very conscientiously told me that upon the subject of reform he did not go the length that many liberals did, and could not for instance go in hand with Lord John Russell. It is not very probable that S.B. and I should materially differ upon such matters, and if we do, it is very easy to separate.[47]

After his unopposed return ministers of course listed him as one of the 'Huskisson party'; and in early September 1830 Huskisson met and conferred with Palmerston at Testwood before setting off on his ill-fated journey to Liverpool. There was evidently some speculation about his standing there after Huskisson's death, but Lord Carlisle commented that he 'would not be active enough'. Later that month Sturges Bourne toured North Wales with his wife and daughter.[48] He did not vote in the division on the civil list which brought down the Wellington ministry, 15 Nov. 1830, and he was back in Hampshire a week later.[49] There he received a 'Swing' letter 'threatening my life'; and he joined in the steps taken under the aegis of the duke of Wellington to organize 'persons who have anything to lose' in order to combat disorder.[50] In early January 1831 Lord Grey, seeking to accommodate Sir Richard Vivian, who was proving reluctant to vacate his seat for Windsor in favour of the Irish secretary, Edward Smith Stanley, suggested to Anglesey, now lord lieutenant of Ireland, that Sturges Bourne, to whom 'I cannot think it can be an object of much importance to ... continue in Parliament', might be sounded 'as to his resignation' by Palmerston, the foreign secretary.

He evidently declined to retire, but a fortnight later Grey thought of his seat as a berth for one of the Irish lawyers, Philip Crampton* or Richard Sheil*, whom ministers were anxious to bring in. Anglesey was willing to make one Milborne Port seat available for this purpose, but the difficulty lay in deciding whether it should be Sturges Bourne's or that of his colleague, George Byng, Anglesey's son-in-law and a member of his vice regal household. Stanley told Anglesey at the beginning of February that

> upon this there has been much discussion, and the general opinion of the cabinet seems to be that it would not be desirable that Sturges Bourne should be urged to retire. His vote, and his weight with some of the country gentlemen, are thought of great importance upon the reform question, as well as any measure which may be brought forward connected with the English poor laws.

Anglesey acknowledged the force of this argument, and in the event, it was Byng who made way for Sheil.[51] On 16 Feb. 1831 Sturges Bourne warmly welcomed Briscoe's bill to extend the scope of his own Act of 1819 for parochial land purchases, which would 'do more to relieve parishes from the present enormous burden of the poor rates than any other measure that I can think of'. He had reservations about Lord Chandos's bill to disfranchise Evesham, 18 Feb., because no reliable evidence of the venality of the resident voters had been adduced. He presented a Milborne Port petition for the abolition of slavery, 2 Mar. 1831. In November 1830, Lord Sandon* had named Sturges Bourne as one of the 'sober and peaceable' men who were 'inclining' to parliamentary reform; but when the ministerial scheme was unveiled he found it too extreme, and surrendered his seat to Anglesey. Grey was peeved, feeling that it was 'now very much to be regretted that his seat was not vacated instead of Byng's'; but Anglesey was more sympathetic, as he told the premier:

> I am truly sorry ... that you will not have the support of Sturges Bourne. I regret it much, because he is a very influential man. I think he is mistaken about Canning. Had he lived in 1831, I feel confident that he would have supported the measure of reform. I have so written to Sturges Bourne, and have expressed a strong desire that he would retain his seat and support you, but I have also begged that if he cannot bring himself to do this, he will immediately resign, in favour of George Byng.

Stanley, too, was 'sorry' to lose Sturges Bourne, though he had been 'afraid it might be so, and that the reform plan would be too sweeping for him to venture upon'. Sturges Bourne's mind was made up, and he vacated his seat in the first week of March, thereby doing, as his daughter saw it the most honourable thing between his reluctance to oppose government in a measure on which their existence, and perhaps our safety, depend, and an equal reluctance to give up the opinions of his whole life, and incur the charge of great inconsistency ... I hope nobody will say that he shirks difficulties, and they need not think either that he entirely disapproves of the bill, in which there are many good things. He was always for transferring to large towns the franchises of corrupt boroughs and thinks that had more been done in this way, we might have been saved so sweeping a measure.[52]

Shortly before the general election of 1831, when he cast anti-reform votes for Southampton and Winchester, Sturges Bourne, in his daughter's words, was 'nearly as busy and excited as if he were in Parliament, always going about to hear the latest thing and his friends coming to talk it all over and pick his brains'.[53] According to Littleton, he refused in July 1831 to become a boundary commissioner, being 'frightened out of ... [his] wits at the reform bill'; and in December he was critical of the 'injudicious policy' of the Tory opposition 'during the whole of the reform debates'. In April 1833 Littleton found him still

sadly alarmed about the country's political state. He expresses his conviction that Lord Althorp is in heart a republican, and that it is now too late to stop that downward tendency which monarchical institutions have derived from his influence on public affairs. He lamented pathetically the want of sound understanding and good sense on the part of the king ... Sturges Bourne, however, is a great alarmist by nature.[54]

In 1832 he was appointed to the royal commissions on the poor laws and ecclesiastical revenues; and in the former capacity he corresponded with John Fazakerley* on the knotty problem of the bastardy laws, and the 'excess of population', which he thought was the 'besetting evil' and 'cause of all that are called the abuses of the poor laws'.[55] Greville reported that Lord George Cavendish Bentinck* invited him to stand for King's Lynn at the 1835 general election, 'but he would not hear of it'; and soon afterwards he wrote to Peel, who had sent him some correspondence about the career of Canning's only surviving son:

I rejoice to see *young* men of such character and talents attaching themselves to you, in order that your principles may long endure and actuate our councils. It was the object of Mr. Pitt ... to rally round him such persons in their early manhood. How much more important is such an object now, when those who, like myself, being past the maturity of life, feel themselves unequal to the conflict of the hustings and the more formidable labours of the House of Commons ... No person can be more anxious than I am for the success of your administration.[56]

Sturges Bourne, who, so Sydney Smith said in 1839, 'makes his wife and daughter leave off wine in order to do his own gout good',[57] died at Testwood in February 1845. By his will, dated 15 June 1836, he left all his property to his wife, who survived him by five years, with remainder to his daughter.[58] An anonymous obituarist wrote that he would enjoy no 'large amount of posthumous reputation, but his career will not utterly pass away from our minds as a man or a minister'.[59] Littleton commemorated him as

a very sensible, honest and excellent man ... It was difficult to say of him whether he was more a liberal Tory, or a moderate Whig. Till the period of Huskisson's death, all his sympathies seemed to be with ... the remnant of the Canning party, but when on Lord Grey's accession to the government, that party became parliamentary reformers, Bourne, who was a very cautious man, became alarmed, and though no longer in Parliament himself, was a very useful ally of Peel's more immediate party, in clubs and in society. Canning had a particular regard and respect for him. With much information, and a great delight in that kind of wit, which he found in the Canning circle in its best days ... he nevertheless was totally free from the vice of humour himself. Gravity and deliberation and solidity were the ornaments of a mind eminently judicial. He was consequently a respected, and a very useful friend ... The death of such a man is a great loss.[60]

[1] *Gent. Mag.* (1845), i. 434. [2] *Greville Mems.* i. 92. [3] *Arbuthnot Jnl.* i. 41. [4] Harewood mss, Binning to Liverpool, 20 Dec.; TNA, Dacres Adams mss, Courtenay to Adams, 21 Dec. 1820. [5] *The Times*, 8 June 1821. [6] *Croker Pprs.* i. 188. [7] *Gent. Mag.* (1821), ii. 93; *VCH Oxon.* xi. 63; xii. 192; PROB 11/1649/595. [8] Add. 38743, ff. 65, 83; Buckingham, *Mems. Geo. IV*, i. 273; *Hobhouse Diary*, 85; NLW, Coedymaen mss 615. [9] *The Times*, 5 Mar. 1822. [10] Ibid. 24 May 1823. [11] Ibid. 3 June 1824. [12] Buckingham, ii. 107, 112. [13] Add. 37061, f. 44. [14] *Colchester Diary*, iii. 369. [15] *The Times*, 21, 22 June 1825. [16] Add. 40342, f. 307. [17] Surr. Hist. Cent. Goulburn mss Acc 304/67A, Goulburn to wife, 30 Apr. 1826. [18] Northants. RO, Agar Ellis diary. [19] St. Deiniol's Lib. Glynne-Gladstone mss 276, Huskisson to J. Gladstone, 10 Dec. 1826; Hants RO, Sturges Bourne mss 9M55 F5/4, 7. [20] Sturges Bourne mss F5/8, 11, 13. [21] Ibid. F5/8; *Canning's Ministry*, 250-1, 261; *Hobhouse Diary*, 144-5. [22] *Huskisson Pprs.* 224; Wellington mss WP1/887/49. [23] *Arbuthnot Jnl.* ii. 109; *Canning's Ministry*, 290. [24] Sturges Bourne mss F5/14, 15. [25] *The Times*, 23, 25 May 1827. [26] Ibid. 2, 12 June 1827. [27] Ibid. 15, 18, 23 June 1827. [28] *Canning's Ministry*, 336, 340, 343; *HMC Bathurst*, 638, 643; Add. 37305, f. 133; *Hobhouse Diary*, 139; Sturges Bourne mss F5/25; Bagot, *Canning and Friends*, ii. 407. [29] Add. 52447, f. 108. [30] *Geo. IV Letters*, iii. 1377, 1381, 1386, 1400; *Croker Pprs.* i. 382; *Palmerston-Sulivan Letters*, 190; Bagot, ii. 420, 423; *Huskisson Pprs.* 226; Add. 38750, f. 39; TNA 30/29/9/5/51; Harrowby mss, Sturges Bourne to Harrowby, 11 Aug. 1827. [31] Sturges Bourne mss F/28; Harrowby mss, Sturges Bourne to Harrowby, 19 Aug. 1827. [32] *Palmerston-Sulivan Letters*, 197, 199. [33] Add. 38750, ff. 145-9, 152, 158, 162; 51586, Tierney to Lady Holland, 30, 31 Aug. [1827]; TNA 30/29/9/5/56; Southampton Univ. Lib. Broadlands mss PP/ GMC/17; Coedymaen mss 200, 202; *Palmerston-Sulivan Letters*, 200; *Greville Mems.* i. 187. [34] Lansdowne mss; Add. 38750, f. 216; Harrowby mss, Sturges Bourne to Harrowby, 7 Sept. 1827. [35] Sturges Bourne mss F5/29; *Howard Sisters*, 91; *Countess Granville*

Letters, i. 424; *Bagot*, i. 426-7; Add. 38750, f. 188. ³⁶Coedymaen mss 252-5. ³⁷Sturges Bourne mss F5/37, 39-41; F6/2-4; Add. 38754, ff. 159, 240; Wellington mss WP1/915/41. ³⁸Coedymaen mss 735. ³⁹Keele Univ. Lib. Sneyd mss SC12/85; SC17/36; Add. 40395, ff. 226, 244. ⁴⁰Sturges Bourne mss F6/8. ⁴¹Bulwer, *Palmerston*, i. 278-9; *Palmerston-Sulivan Letters*, 205; *Colchester Diary*, iii. 568; Nottingham Univ. Lib. Ossington mss OsC 67a. ⁴²Sturges Bourne mss F7/1. ⁴³Add. 56554, ff. 11-12. ⁴⁴Add. 38758, f. 50. ⁴⁵Sturges Bourne mss F8/7-9, 11, 13. ⁴⁶Add. 56554, f. 114. ⁴⁷Ibid. F8/18, 19; Add. 38758, f. 198. ⁴⁸*Palmerston-Sulivan Letters*, 241; Sturges Bourne mss F8/25; Add. 51580, Carlisle to Lady Holland, 2 Oct. 1830. ⁴⁹Sturges Bourne mss F8/30, 31. ⁵⁰Coedymaen mss 257-9. ⁵¹PRO NI, Anglesey mss D619/ 28a-B/32, 37; 31D/13. Derby mss 920 Der (14) 119/2, Anglesey to Smith Stanley, 4 Feb. 1831. ⁵²Harrowby mss, Sandon to Harrowby, 12 Nov. 1830; Anglesey mss 28A-B/46; 28C, pp. 79-80; 31D/30. ⁵³Sturges Bourne mss F9/6,7. ⁵⁴Hatherton diary, 22 July 1831; *Three Diaries*, 170, 319. ⁵⁵Duke Univ. Lib. Fazakerley mss, Sturges Bourne to Fazakerley, 4 Oct. 1832. ⁵⁶*Greville Mems*. iii. 118; Add. 40413, ff. 261, 297. ⁵⁷*Smith Letters*, ii. 689. ⁵⁸*Gent. Mag.* (1845), i. 661; PROB 11/2013/183; IR26/1696/262. ⁵⁹*Gent. Mag.* (1845), i. 434. ⁶⁰Hatherton diary, 4 Feb. 1845.

D.R.F.

STURT, Henry Charles (1795–1866), of Crichel House, Wimborne Minster, Dorset.

BRIDPORT	28 Mar. 1817–1820
DORCHESTER	10 Apr. 1830–1830
DORSET	1835–2 Feb. 1846

b. 9 Aug. 1795, o.s. of Charles Sturt† of Crichel and Brownsea Castle, Poole and Lady Mary Anne Ashley Cooper, da. of Anthony, 4th earl of Shaftesbury. *educ.* Harrow c.1806; Christ Church, Oxf. 1814. *m.* 15 Aug. 1820, Lady Charlotte Penelope Brudenell, da. of Robert Brudenell†, 6th earl of Cardigan, 3s. (1 *d.v.p.*) 4da. *suc.* fa. 1812. *d.* 14 Apr. 1866.
Sheriff, Dorset 1823-4.

Sturt's quixotic, Foxite father, who matched his wife in the adultery which wrecked their marriage and exposed them to public humiliation in 1801, encumbered his son's inheritance. After his death in 1812 his personalty was sworn under £10,000, and the following year his estate was in chancery. Fortunately for Sturt, who was granted letters of administration in 1832, his father's executors were able to rectify matters.¹ In 1817 he sold Brownsea Island in Poole harbour, where he had spent much of his boyhood, for £8,000; but he came to enjoy 'a splendid inheritance' of land in Dorset, together with the valuable Pitfield estate at Hoxton in east London, which had been brought into the family by his paternal grandmother. He lent £1,000 to his cousin Charles Sturt (1795-1869), the Australian explorer, who had saved him from drowning off Weymouth in 1813.²

Sturt, whose politics were indeterminate, made no mark in the House as Member for Bridport, where the family interest was evidently in decline. He 'relinquished his pretensions' there at the dissolution in 1820, when a contest loomed.³ Remaining neutral as sheriff, on 12 Feb. 1823 he told his friend Henry Bankes* that he was bound to win the vacant Dorset seat; however, at the by-election that month he declared the show of hands to be in favour of Bankes's opponent, Edward Portman.⁴ At the request of his uncle the 6th earl of Shaftesbury, Sturt seconded Bankes at the Dorset by-election in February 1826, repeating the courtesy at the two following elections.⁵ As had been rumoured during the previous two years, at the general election of 1826 he stood for Poole, competing for the second seat with the Whig William Ponsonby*, who was married to his first cousin Barbara, daughter of the 5th earl of Shaftesbury.⁶ On the hustings Sturt declined to

> enter into any detail upon politics because it is unnecessary ... I am generally inclined to ministerial measures because I imagine them to be the most correct, but I am not tied or pledged to any measure whatever. I am free and uncontrolled as the winds.

He was beaten into third place in the contest, which cost him at least £500, but did not carry out his threat to petition against Ponsonby's return.⁷

In April 1830, when he became a freeman of the borough for the purpose, Shaftesbury brought him in for Dorchester in the room of one of his sons.⁸ There was no opposition, but he was quizzed by one voter, who wished to know whether, if Shaftesbury subsequently required him to vacate his seat, 'he would come forward as a candidate for the free votes of the electors'. Sturt refused to answer and spoke mainly in conventional platitudes, though he was reported to have declared that

> wherever he saw a willingness to diminish undue patronage, wherever he saw a willingness to diminish the expenditure and burdens of the nation, and a desire to relieve it from its distress, he should deem it his duty to support such measures.⁹

There is no evidence that he acted up to these professions in the House, where he took his seat, 26 Apr. He divided with the Wellington administration against the Galway franchise bill, 25 May, and for the grant for South American missions, 7 June, when he voted against the abolition of the death penalty for forgery. He is not known to have spoken in debate and at the general election of 1830 he made way for Shaftesbury's heir, Lord Ashley.¹⁰ He voted for the sitting Members

Bankes and Portman, who were opposed by John Calcraft*, at the general election of 1831.[11] The Hollands heard him spoken of as a possible reform candidate for the vacancy created by Calcraft's suicide in September 1831, but it was Ponsonby who came forward.[12] He signed the requisition to Bankes, who declined, and voted for the eventual anti-reform candidate Ashley, whose brother had feared that he was 'inclined to Ponsonby'.[13] Sturt was also touted as a replacement for Ponsonby at Poole, but it was reported that while 'his friends appeared anxious to introduce him' there, 'unless he will pledge himself to the support of a full and complete reform, the electors will not think of him'.[14]

Sturt secured a county seat as a Conservative in 1835 and occupied it until 1846 when, with his cousin Ashley, he resigned it, being then a convert to free trade, but representing an overwhelmingly protectionist constituency. To the prime minister, Peel, who tried to make him sit tight, he administered a 'gentle' rebuke, by wondering whether repeal of the corn laws 'might not have been managed without stranding others and myself'.[15] Sturt, who was 'not generally prominent in the management of the county business', preferring to pursue his interests in science and archaeology, was described as 'a man of mark in his generation', and credited with a 'naturally acute and inquiring mind', a large store of knowledge, and an 'unusually genial temperament and great conversational powers'. He died in April 1866, being succeeded by his eldest son Henry Gerard (1825-1904), a noted sportsman, who was Conservative Member for Dorchester, 1847-56, and for Dorset from 1856 until 1876, when he was created Baron Alington.[16]

[1] M. Soames, *Profligate Duke*, 51-52, 94-112; *Gent. Mag.* (1812), i. 596; (1866), i. 912; PROB 11/1535/347; IR26/561/475.   [2] J. Hutchins, *Dorset* (1868), i. 648; Mrs. N.G. Sturt, *Charles Sturt*, 2, 14, 319-20; M. Langley, *Sturt of the Murray*, 30, 228, 237.   [3] *HP Commons, 1790-1820*, v. 319; *The Times*, 22 Feb. 1820. [4] Dorset RO, Bankes mss D/BKL; *Western Flying Post*, 24 Feb. 1823. [5] Bankes mss, Sturt to Bankes, 2 Dec. 1825; *Dorset Co. Chron.* 23 Feb., 22 June 1826, 12 Aug. 1830. [6] *Salisbury Jnl.* 18 July 1824, 26 Sept. 1825, 5 June 1830. [7] *Dorset Co. Chron.* 1, 8, 15 June; *The Times*, 5, 12, 14 June 1826; Dorset RO, photocopy 348 (from Crichel House mss). [8] *The Times*, 15 Apr. 1830; C. H. Mayo, *Municipal Recs. of Dorchester*, 434. [9] *Dorset Co. Chron.* 8, 15 Apr. 1830. [10] Ibid. 22, 29 July 1830. [11] *Dorset Pollbook* (1831), 63. [12] PRO NI, Anglesey mss D619/28A-B/80; *Lady Holland to Son*, 116. [13] Bankes mss, requisition, 15 Sept. 1831; *Dorset Pollbook* (Sept.-Oct. 1831), 92; Shaftesbury mss OF 50/32. [14] *The Times*, 23 Sept. 1831. [15] Add. 40583, ff. 280, 282; Parker, *Peel*, iii. 335, 337; N. Gash, *Sir Robert Peel*, 571, 613. [16] *Gent. Mag.* (1866), i. 912; Hutchins, iii. 127.

D.R.F./S.M.F.

SUGDEN, Edward Burtenshaw (1781–1875), of Tilgate Forest Lodge, Slaugham, Suss. and 71 Guildford Street, Mdx.[1]

WEYMOUTH & MELCOMBE REGIS	20 Feb. 1828–1831
ST. MAWES	1831–1832
RIPON	1837–Sept. 1841

b. 12 Feb. 1781, 2nd s. of Richard Sugden, hairdresser, of Duke Street, Westminster and w. Charlotte Burtenshaw of St. George, Hanover Square. *educ.* privately; L. Inn 1802, called 1807. *m.* 23 Dec. 1808, Winifred, da. of John Knapp, 7s. (3 *d.v.p.*) 7da. (1 *d.v.p.*). kntd. 10 June 1829; *cr.* Bar. St. Leonards 1 Mar. 1852. *d.* 29 Jan. 1875.

KC 6 Dec. 1821; bencher, L. Inn 1822, treas. 1836; solicitor-gen. June 1829-Nov. 1830; PC [UK] 16 Dec. 1834, [I] 15 Jan. 1835; ld. chan. [I] Dec. 1834-Apr. 1835, Oct. 1841-July 1846; ld. chan. Feb.-Dec. 1852; member, jud. cttee. of PC 1852.

High steward, Kingston-upon-Thames.

'There are few instances in modern times of a rise equal to that of Sir Edward Sugden', wrote Thomas Fowell Buxton* in 1836.[2] His father, a well-to-do London hairdresser, married Charlotte Burtenshaw in November 1778, and their first son, John Baynes Sugden, was baptized at St. Andrew, Holborn, the following August. Sugden himself was baptized at St. Clement Dane's.[3] Far from trying to disguise his humble origins, he gloried in his rise to eminence by virtue, as he was fond of boasting, of his own abilities and determination; his 'secret' was his resolution to make all the legal knowledge he acquired 'perfectly my own, and never to go to a second thing, till I had entirely accomplished the first'.[4] Soon after he attained the pinnacle of his profession in 1852 it was said that 'someone is supposed lately to have twitted him with being the son of a barber, whereupon he retorted, "Yes, but if you had been the son of a barber, you would have been a barber yourself"'.[5] He was employed as a clerk with a firm of London solicitors before being taken on by the conveyancer Lewis Duval, from whom he passed to William Groome. His father was dead by the time he was admitted to Lincoln's Inn in September 1802. That year he published *A Brief Conversation with a Gentleman of Landed Property about to Buy or Sell Lands*, in which he displayed his talent for the accurate condensation and clear exposition of complex subjects. He began independent practice as a certificated conveyancer in 1805, when he produced *A Practical Treatise of the Law of Vendors and Purchasers of Estates*, which had modest financial success (though the later of its many editions brought him as much as 4,000 guineas), but, more importantly, identified him as a pundit on property law and put abundant work his way. Having originally, according to his contemporary George Pryme, been 'not anxious for the honours of the profession' and more concerned to make a living, he decided to risk the bar, and for a few years after his call in 1807 he combined court work with his large chamber practice.[6] In 1808 he published *A Practical Treatise of Powers*, which became a standard text and ran to several editions.

Before he entered Lincoln's Inn Sugden had formed a liaison with Winifred (baptized, 2 Mar. 1783, as 'Winifruite') Knapp, his kitchen maid. They had at least four children, including Richard, the eldest son, who went to Oxford in 1820, before they married at St. Giles-in-the Fields in December 1808. They had their children Edward, Juliet and Laura baptized at St. Pancras Old Church on Christmas Day.[7] The following year Sugden wrote *A Series of Letters to a Man of Property, on the Sale, Purchase, Lease, Settlement, and Devise of Estates*, which he followed with an annotated edition of Gilbert on *Uses and Trusts* (1811) and slighter works on *Repealing the Annuity Act* (1812), *Attestation of Instruments* (1814) and *Redeemable Annuities* (1816). Although he had a growing family, which eventually numbered 14, he had gambled by resolving to confine himself to court work, having found the burden of combining it with chamber practice too much even for his iron constitution. His rise at the chancery bar was swift and decisive, and by 1817 he held the commanding position there, with an annual income of at least £15,000. With his great erudition and forensic skill he was a formidable advocate; but his supercilious manner, sharp temper and fondness for wounding sarcasm made him unpopular with his colleagues.[8] He acquired a Sussex property near Cuckfield, and at the general election of 1818 stood for the county, promising independent support for 'the general march of government'. One of the sitting Members, Sir Godfrey Webster, announced his retirement, and his aristocratic sponsors were at a loss for a suitable candidate willing to stand a contest. Sugden was within a whisker of being formally returned when some of Webster's more radical friends revived his candidature. Although he told Webster to his face that he was 'not a fit person to represent the county', he gave up when a few hours' polling left him 50 votes adrift in third place.[9]

Sugden, who produced a tract on *Surrender of Terms* in 1819, took silk two years later. In 1825 he responded to attacks in the Commons on chancery administration by John Williams with a published *Letter*: he professed support for rational reform of its glaring defects, but deplored its portrayal as 'an odious dungeon' and opposed sweeping changes. In June 1825, when the Whig sitting Member announced his intended retirement at the next general election, Sugden declared his candidature on 'constitutional principles' for New Shoreham, the extended boundaries of which included his own property. In an unsuccessful bid to win the support of the duke of Norfolk he claimed to be 'a decided friend of Catholic emancipation'; but in his address he asserted that 'I have pledged myself, at the desire of a numerous body of you, to oppose the introduction of Catholics into Parliament'.[10] On the eve of the election in 1826 his chances seemed excellent, and he reiterated his anti-Catholic pledge. To his embarrassment, however, his opponents exposed his duplicity, which was given wider publicity by *The Times*. He claimed that he had been persuaded to change his mind by the strength of hostility to Catholic relief among the electors of Shoreham and condemned disclosure of his approach to Norfolk as a breach of private confidence. He repeated these excuses on the hustings, where he advocated adjustment of the corn laws to secure 'steadiness of price', denounced slavery, but argued that immediate abolition was impractical, and bragged of his rise from obscurity through 'his own honest, unwearied industry'. He polled respectably, but gave up after four days.[11] Later that year he outlined his ideas on 'reform of the law of real property' in a *Letter to James Humphreys*. He continued to cultivate Shoreham, but early in 1828 stood on a vacancy for Weymouth, with which he had no previous connection.[12] He was apparently recommended by the duke of Wellington, recently appointed prime minister, who had turned down an invitation to put up his son. He was supported by a majority of the corporation but opposed by a candidate on the Johnstone interest, who was also a friend of the new ministry. After boasting of his 'unassisted' rise and 'undeviating integrity', he declared his unabated hostility to Catholic emancipation, though he kept his options open by indicating that when they were prepared to accept adequate 'securities' he would 'advise the people of England to open their arms to them'. After an expensive contest he had a majority of 120 in a poll of 524.[13]

He made his début by opposing as too unsettling Brougham's motion for inquiry into the state of the law, 29 Feb. 1828, when he approved the government's proposal to set up separate commissions on the common law and the law of real property and stated his willingness to rationalize chancery procedure. He opposed Kennedy's bill to alter the Scottish law of entail, 6 Mar., and Davies's borough polls bill, 31 Mar., 23 May. Defying interruptions, he opposed inquiry into chancery administration, 24 Apr., when he said he was prepared to accept 'cautious improvement' but would never agree to the separation of bankruptcy administration. Sugden, who presented a Horsham petition against Catholic relief, 29 Apr., and voted thus, 12 May, gave an earnest of his wish to get rid of blatant chancery 'anomalies' by securing leave, 6 May, for a bill to amend the laws for facilitating the payment of debts out of real estate. Introduced on 19 May, it passed the Commons, 9 June, but had only a formal first reading in the Lords. He also brought in for consideration measures to reform the laws concerning estates vested in trustees, the property of infants and lunatics and illusory appointments. When seeking leave for the first, 20 May, he again had difficulty in holding the attention of the House, where his self-satisfied demeanour, rapid and monotonous delivery and squeaky voice made him fair game for the bored and unruly. More dominant than ever in the chancery court during Lord Lyndhurst's early days as chancellor, he sustained a formidable workload there and in the Commons by virtue of his physical toughness and prodigious powers of apprehension and application.[14] Although he wanted to see the usury laws properly modified, he considered Poulett Thomson's amendment bill half-baked, 20 May; but he was at a loss for a satisfactory solution, 19 June. He supported Spring Rice's rights of executors bill, 21 May, and, differing from the lord advocate, pressed for its extension to Scotland, 4 June, when he also approved Fergusson's Indian real property bill. He urged the extension of East Retford's franchise to the hundred, 27 June, supported the additional churches bill and scorned Hume's talk of parochial elections of ministers, 30 June, and voted with government on the ordnance estimates, 4 July, and the silk duties, 14 July 1828.

On 12 Feb. 1829 Sugden announced in the House that he would support Catholic emancipation as a matter of expediency to avert 'a general convulsion' in Ireland, but exhorted ministers to crack down on political subscriptions and religious meetings and to promote the country's economic development and moral improvement. He voted for the measure, 6, 30 Mar., and opposed Inglis's amendment to the oath, 23 Mar. His insistence that Daniel O'Connell could not sit without taking the oath of supremacy led to a petulant clash with Brougham, 15 May; but three days later, while maintaining the same line, he complimented O'Connell on his 'talent and temper'. He reintroduced his four real property law amendment bills, 13, 15 Apr., and had them printed for further consideration, 1 May. They passed the Commons, 11 May, and were formally introduced to the Lords the following day. He

objected to Baring's plan to apply money belonging to chancery suitors to payment of the unfunded debt, 8 May. He offered constructive criticisms of Kennedy's tailzies reform bills, 11 May, and advocated the adoption of a more 'cautious' approach to the problem, 22 May 1829.

Sugden, whom Greville considered 'a great rogue', had been mentioned as the next solicitor-general in March 1829, and he duly succeeded Tindal on his promotion to the bench in June.[15] Less than a month later Lord Bathurst, lecturing Arbuthnot on the need to strengthen the ministry by a junction with the Whigs, suggested that Sugden might be made the new equity judge and be replaced by Brougham; but this was idle speculation.[16] When Alexander, editor of the Ultra *Morning Journal*, printed an allegation that Lyndhurst had procured Sugden's appointment in return for a loan or bribe of £30,000, he was successfully prosecuted for libel.[17] At his re-election for Weymouth, where he was accompanied by John Gordon, one of the other sitting Members, Sugden was manhandled and abused for his support of Catholic relief and failure to pay all his bills of 1828. Ignoring his 'ill state of health' and constant barracking, he insisted that he would pay no more than the £6,000 he had already laid out, for he had not authorized the 'ruinous expenses' which had been incurred in his name. His attempted explanation of his support for emancipation was shouted down. His opponents nominated a prisoner in king's bench but withdrew him after a token poll.[18] On 11 Dec. 1829 Sugden had a furious altercation in the chancery court with Sir Charles Wetherell*, who accused him of interrupting him. A duel seemed likely to ensue until they were hauled before a magistrate and bound over.[19] Sugden voted with his colleagues against the transfer of East Retford's seats to Birmingham, 11 Feb., and the enfranchisement of Birmingham, Leeds and Manchester, 23 Feb. 1830. Seeking leave to reintroduce his law amendment bills, 11 Feb., he outlined an additional measure to alleviate the hardships of prisoners confined for contempt of court, whose plight he had investigated at first hand. All these bills reached the statute book (11 Geo. IV & 1 Gul. IV, cc. 36, 46, 47, 60, 65). On 2 Mar. he gave guarded approval to Taylor's bill to reduce the costs of lunacy commissions in difficult cases. He answered O'Connell's criticisms of the administration of justice bill, 9 Mar., and opposed Harvey's call for inquiry into crown lands revenues, 30 Mar. He introduced a bill to amend the Insolvent Debtors Act, 1 Apr., and explained and defended it, 29 Apr.; it became law, 16 July 1830 (11 Gul. IV & I Gul. IV, c. 38). He expressed general support for the government's Scottish judicature bill, 1 Apr., but advised the lord advocate to try to reduce the number of Scottish appeals to the Lords. He said that Jewish emancipation would 'sever the church from the state', 5 Apr., was a teller for the hostile minority, and voted against it when it was rejected, 17 May. He unsuccessfully opposed Poulett Thomson's usury laws amendment bill, 26 Apr. He defended British intervention at Terceira, 28 Apr. The following day he poured cold water on Brougham's scheme for the establishment of local judicatures, indicating his preference for making existing institutions cheaper. He was suspicious of O'Connell's bills dealing with Catholic charitable bequests and marriages, 4 May, and opposed his motion for papers on the Cork trials of October 1829. On 14 May he defended separate bankruptcy and insolvency jurisdictions against the attacks of Hume, whose motion for information on the four-and-a-half per cent duties, he scorned as 'a bad precedent', 21 May. He justified the dismissal of Barrington from the Irish admiralty court and was a teller for the majority against his being allowed to address the House, 22 May. He objected to Smith Stanley's Irish and Scottish paupers bill, 26 May, and spoke and acted as a teller against inquiry into the divorce laws, 3 June. He had been sounded by Peel at the turn of the year on his bill to mitigate the penalties for forgery.[20] On its third reading, 7 June, he opposed Buxton's attempt to abolish capital punishment and was a teller for the minority in the division. When Wetherell questioned the need for the proposed new equity judge, 10 June, Sugden accused him of pre-empting the second reading of the bill. Having been consulted by the cabinet on provision for a regency, he opposed Grant's motion for an address to the crown, 6 July 1830. In the course of his speech he made a disparaging remark about Fox, which elicited a telling sarcasm from Brougham, who subsequently savaged Sugden and made him, Denis Le Marchant† wrote, 'appear so ridiculous, that the whole treasury bench seemed convulsed with laughter'.[21] His appearance on the hustings at Weymouth at the general election provoked some 'strong marks of disapprobation', but he was returned unopposed and proclaimed that 'if ever there was a government ... which wished to render the people happy and were desirous of reducing the expenditure, I believe it is the government you now have'.[22]

On 9 Nov. 1830 Sugden obtained leave to bring in a bill to amend the Statute of Frauds. Questioned by Hume and others, he declared his hostility to the idea of a 'pocket-volume' or 'code' of laws. He objected to O'Connell's plan to repeal the Irish Subletting Act, 11 Nov., accusing him of wishing to deny cheap law

to Irish landlords. He voted in the minority with his ministerial colleagues on the civil list, 15 Nov. Shortly before his removal from office he got leave, 19 Nov., to bring in a bill dealing with the attestation of instruments. He introduced it with his frauds bill, 14 Feb. 1831, but neither measure made any progress before the dissolution. He joined in attacks on the Grey ministry for dismissing Hart from the Irish chancellorship and creating pensions for him and chief baron Alexander, 9 Dec. 1830. On Hume's demands for the abolition of sinecures, 13 Dec., he commented that while many were indefensible, it was necessary to retain some 'as a remuneration for men who perform much useful business in the House'. As anticipated, he objected to Campbell's scheme for a general register of deeds, 16 Dec.[23] Later that day he expounded his mature ideas on chancery reform, which the late ministry's fall had prevented him from implementing. He reiterated his antipathy to any separation of bankruptcy administration from chancery, though he conceded that the former required revision. He advocated the abolition of all patent places and reversionary incomes; putting the rolls court on the same regular footing as that of the vice-chancellor, who would become entirely independent; having the chief baron of exchequer devote all his time to equity business; promoting one of the other exchequer judges to a position of superiority; creating an equity exchequer chamber to hear appeals; streamlining procedures through technical improvements, and reforming the six clerks, report, registrars and masters offices. His hatred and jealousy of Brougham, whose professional abilities he held in low esteem, had been intensified by his appointment as lord chancellor in the Grey ministry; and he now criticized him for appointing practising solicitors to certain lucrative chancery offices and was attacked in his turn by Denman, the attorney-general.[24] He retorted that Brougham was a fair target for criticism and boasted that no solicitor-general who had held office for so short a time as himself had 'done more'. He carried his vendetta with Brougham into court, where in January 1831 he theatrically drew attention to the chancellor's habitual inattention on the bench.[25]

Sugden condemned the proposed stock transfer tax, 'as deliberate a violation of public faith as revolutionary France ever did', 11 Feb. 1831. He opposed the emigration bill and failed to get leave to legislate to extend the law of mortmain to Ireland, 22 Feb. On 17 Mar. he supported Davies's motion for inquiry into secondary punishments and brushed aside Hunt's allegations of the maltreatment of reformers gaoled under the suspension of habeas corpus in 1817. According to Lord Ellenborough, he wanted to answer Jeffrey, the lord advocate, in the debate on the ministerial reform bill, 4 Mar.; 'but Peel having first told Croker, who was next to him, to speak, Sugden took offence and would say nothing'.[26] On 21 Mar. he asserted that its 'great object' was to keep in power ministers 'who have gained their places on the strength of popular ferment' and 'now seek, by looking to the voice of the people, to maintain that power'. He said that it must lead sooner or later to universal suffrage, the ballot and shorter parliaments. He denied the 'moral power' of the House to disfranchise boroughs and pointed out that the measure was riddled with 'absurdity' and inconsistencies, not least those consequent on the adoption of the 1821 census returns as the criterion for disfranchisement. He provoked uproar by accusing ministers of compromising the intended prosecution of O'Connell in return for his support for reform. Smith Stanley, the Irish secretary, privately considered it a 'most impudent attack'; but subsequent events vindicated Sugden. According to the duke of Newcastle, at least one vote was gained by his speech, 'the very best and fullest of matter [we] have heard'; while the minister Francis Thornhill Baring* deemed it a 'good performance'.[27] Sugden voted against the second reading, 22 Mar. A fortnight later he was accused in *The Times* of having before the last election made a secret bargain with Gordon whereby he was to enjoy a free seat for Weymouth on the strength of Gordon's position as a Johnstone trustee for as long as he wanted it, in return for allowing Gordon to sell two of the other seats and using his influence with Lords Goderich and Grantham to secure him a peerage. The case against Sugden, which had emerged in the course of a Scottish prosecution brought against Gordon by his former agent over alleged debts, seemed less than watertight; and in two letters to *The Times*, 7, 9 Apr., he firmly denied the substance of the charges.[28] In the House, 12 Apr., he ridiculed Lord John Russell's statement on the population figures used for framing the reform bill, but welcomed the government's provision in their Irish justice bill of relief for those suffering under convictions for contempt. The following day, when he argued that the proposed alterations in the reform bill would set the agricultural and manufacturing interests at odds, O'Connell taunted him with the Weymouth scandal. An angry altercation ensued, in which the Speaker had to intervene. Russell observed that Sugden's written denials had not entirely allayed the suspicion of his 'improper conduct' and encouraged O'Connell to instigate a full inquiry; but no more was heard of it in the House. In formally seconding Campbell's motion for bills to amend the laws of real

property, 14 Apr., Sugden, whose hostility Campbell attributed to 'jealousy' of his chairmanship of the commission, indicated his reservations and objections.[29] He gave a silent vote for Gascoyne's wrecking amendment to the reform bill, 19 Apr. 1831.

At the ensuing general election Sugden abandoned Weymouth and stood on the duke of Buckingham's interest for St. Mawes, having made terms with the duke on the basis of their common 'political sentiments ... usually called moderate Whig or liberal Tory', which recognized that 'some reform must be conceded in the present excited state of the country'.[30] He was returned after a token contest forced by a local reformer. He reintroduced his bills on frauds and attestation of instruments, 23 June 1831, but they got nowhere that session. He voted against the second reading of the reintroduced reform bill, 6 July, and on the 8th asserted that it was 'not understood by the people'. He deplored ministers' refusal to allow counsel to be heard on behalf of threatened boroughs, 12 July, when he voted for the first motion of adjournment before leaving the chamber. In what Ellenborough considered 'a very good speech' for postponing consideration of the disfranchisement schedules, 13 July, he contended that the new bill was 'in almost all respects, a complete departure from the principle' of the original.[31] Irritated by tomfoolery at the bar, he observed that 'I care little whether or not I ever enter this House again. My seat here is attended only with pain and anxiety'. With Croker and Wetherell he led the opposition attack on the details of the bill in committee. While his style tended to be tedious, he was acute and pertinacious and by no means a negligible opponent.[32] Frequently barracked and mocked from the government side, he easily lost his temper, though he generally responded with studious politeness to Althorp's habitual courtesy. He argued that for all Russell's much vaunted concessions the bill was still founded on 'arbitrary and capricious principles', 2 Aug., and that ministers well knew that it could not be a final measure. Opposing the enfranchisement of Tower Hamlets, 4 Aug., he said that the removal of freeholders with £10 houses in that and other metropolitan districts from the county would throw Middlesex into the hands of the 'very lowest class of freeholders'. On 12 Aug. he pointed out that as it stood the borough freeholder clause virtually disfranchised those substantial landlords whose property conferred a £10 borough vote on their tenants. On 17 Aug. Althorp announced that to meet this objection ministers had decided to modify the clause so that the urban freeholder should not lose his county vote unless he qualified for a borough vote by virtue of his own occupancy of his freehold. Sugden denounced this as 'a root and branch cutting up of the power of the aristocracy and of the influence of land on the return of county Members'.[33] He supported Lord Chandos's amendment to enfranchise £50 tenants, 18 Aug., and backed Davies's unsuccessful attempt to exclude all borough freeholders from the counties, 24 Aug. He drew attention to the very uneven effect of the £10 borough franchise, 25 Aug. While his objection to the appointment of boundary commissioners had been removed by the intention to submit their proposals to parliamentary scrutiny, he remained uneasy at the 'monstrous powers' delegated to them, 1 Sept. The following day he complained that the decision to place the four sluiced boroughs on the same footing as others by enfranchising £10 householders and excluding the freeholders of their hundreds would give Worthing a commanding influence over the representation of Shoreham. Without obvious irony, he observed that his own candidacy there in 1826 had been 'attended with a good result, for it compelled the Members to pay more attention to their constituents than they did before'. Later that day he attacked the registration provisions as 'an innovation' which would 'produce a most unpleasant state of confusion and inconvenience'. He voted in the majority for suspension of the Liverpool writ, 5 Sept., deplored reformers' attempts to intimidate the Lords, 7 Sept., and voted against the passage of the reform bill, 21 Sept. On the grants for Buckingham House and Windsor Castle, 28 Sept., he protested at the radicals' boast that 'as soon as the people alone are represented in this House, they will take to themselves the hereditary revenues of the crown'. He fell with relish on Brougham's bankruptcy court bill, 5 Oct., remarking that the chancellor's professional 'despatch', much lauded by Williams, might prove 'a very great evil' and advising him to spend less rather than more time in court. He alleged that by this measure Brougham would obtain for himself more money for less labour than his predecessors but establish 'an inferior jurisdiction in the place of one of high importance'. As a cheaper alternative he suggested a two-thirds reduction in the number of bankruptcy commissioners, who should be adequately paid and permanently in session. On 11 Oct. 1831 he opposed the general register bill, denied being a defender of abuses and called for the law commissioners' work to be terminated.

When seconding the killing amendment to the second reading of the revised reform bill, 16 Dec. 1831, Sugden said it had been framed to ensure 'the entire elevation of the democratic over the landed interest' and 'for the purpose of bestowing on the political

unions the masterdom of the country'. The reformers Ord and Spring Rice dismissed his speech as 'feeble' and 'a lawyer's *rechauffé* of many bygone arguments'.[34] Sugden presented a Gloucester solicitors' petition against the general register bill, 20 Jan.; pressed ministers to condemn and punish those in Ireland who blatantly evaded payment of tithes, 23 Jan.; said that there was no justification for increasing Scottish judicial salaries given the cost of implementing Brougham's bankruptcy reforms, 24 Jan.; spoke and voted against government on the Russian-Dutch loan, 26 Jan., and expressed support for restriction of children's factory hours, 1 Feb. 1832. He again took a leading share in the detailed criticism of the reform bill in committee: he was particularly harsh on the registration and rating provisions, which would create 'a regular annual election from one end of the kingdom to the other', 1 Feb., and would 'fall in so nicely with your political unions, that they will be able to carry everything with a high hand at the poll', 8 Feb. He accepted Russell's invitation to draw up an amendment to the clause dealing with voters' oaths, 11 Feb. He hinted at political chicanery in the treatment of some boroughs, but had to admit that he had no proof, 9 Mar. On the third reading of the bill, 22 Mar. 1832, he again predicted that it would lead to repeal of the corn laws, disestablishment of the church, universal suffrage and the ballot.

Sugden wanted the general register bill to be considered in committee of the whole House rather than by select committee, 22 Feb. 1832. He thought there were grounds for investigating Lord Plunket's alleged misdemeanours as Irish chancellor, 6 Mar. He deplored Irish Members' encouragement of resistance to tithes collection, 25 Mar., and objected to the presentation of an anti-tithes petition which Grattan admitted he had not read, 13 Apr. In the debate on the ministerial crisis, 14 May, he defended Wellington against Russell's attack, though he personally disclaimed 'any idea of accepting office', of which there was 'not the shadow of a shade of a probability'. Le Marchant thought he spoke 'in the style of a pettifogging attorney, and only plunged the cause deeper into the mire'.[35] He accused Hume and his like of seeking to 'inflame large multitudes' against the bishops and peers who had opposed the bill, 15 May. On the Lords' amendments, 5 June, he denounced the means by which it had been forced through and attacked Lord Milton* and the chancellor's brother William Brougham* for withholding payment of their taxes, trusted to 'the good sense, the moderation and the conservative principles of the great body of the people' to avert calamity and called for the unions to be suppressed. On 20 June he drew attention to the fact that Campbell's four 'most important' real property law bills had been passed almost unnoticed; he was one of the seven leading Commons lawyers who sent a written protest to Brougham.[36] He objected to the addition of Corfe Castle to Wareham and forced a division against it, 22 June. He voted against the second reading of the Irish reform bill, 25 May, and described as 'astonishing' O'Connell's complaints of its shortcomings, 2 July, observing that it gave Catholics 'a power which was never contemplated when the relief bill was passed'. He thought the decision to dispense with Members' property qualification under the Scottish bill was another sop to the unions, 27 June. When attacking the Russian-Dutch loan, 12 July, he provoked derision with his remark that as a Member for 'a nomination borough' he felt 'a greater responsibility than if I had the largest constituency, for I have felt myself not answerable to only a class of persons, but that I was responsible to the country at large'. He sought to establish that ministers were not pledged to the abolition of Irish tithes, 22 July, and divided the House unsuccessfully against Hume's motion for a bill to disqualify the recorder of Dublin from Parliament, 24 July. The following day he disingenuously mentioned the recent appointment of Brougham's brother James Brougham* to the chancery office of clerk of patents, vacated by the death of Lord Eldon's son. In court on 23 July he had notified Horne, the solicitor-general, that he planned to ask a question on the subject, but he claimed that a riding accident on his way to the House had prevented him from doing so that day. In the ensuing tetchy discussion Horne admitted that he had not had a chance to apprise Brougham of Sugden's intentions, while most speakers, including Althorp and Peel, suggested that the appointment was meant to be a temporary one until Brougham's bill to abolish chancery sinecures became law. Brougham was enraged, and in the Lords, 26 July, made what was generally reckoned to be an 'indecent' attack on Sugden, to whom he gave credit for being motivated by the thirst for knowledge which distinguished men 'not only from the insect that crawls and stings ... but from that more powerful, because more offensive creature, the bug, which, powerful and offensive as it is, is still but vermin'. Even Lord Eldon and Wellington rallied to Brougham's defence; and in the Commons Sugden, who became involved in a quarrel with William Brougham, complained that 'there is evidently an effort, on the part of certain persons, to run me down'. When he drew attention to Brougham's remarks, 27 July, Smith Stanley had him called to order; but he insisted that he had been 'personally insulted and abused in the grossest manner'. Greville thought that Brougham

came out worse from the episode, while on 2 Aug. Sugden gave notice of a motion, intended to expose Brougham's inadequacies, for inquiry into chancery administration next session and declared his intention of trying to have Brougham's Bankruptcy Act referred to a select committee. He and Brougham were eventually reconciled and became friends.[37] Sugden accepted the salary increase for Scottish judges and the proposed retirement pension of £5,000 for the chancellor, 30 July, but wanted full details of the latter's fees to be furnished before the salary of £14,000 was ratified. He was anxious that the dead fund should not be used to finance Brougham's chancery reforms and that impediments to suitors getting hold of small sums due should be removed. He bowed to the 'strong public feeling' in favour of the forgery punishment bill, 31 July, but lamented that 'we are travelling fast towards the abolition of all capital punishment'; he applauded the Lords' restoration of the death penalty for certain offences, 15 Aug. He questioned the necessity of the emergency bill to extend the time allowed for the payment of rates to qualify for a borough vote, 7 Aug., condemned the Clitheroe affray as 'premeditated', 10 Aug., and said that the difficulties over registration merely proved his case against the Reform Act's 'anomalies', 15 Aug. 1832.

St. Mawes was disfranchised by the Reform Act, and at the 1832 general election Sugden, having declined an invitation to stand for New Shoreham, unsuccessfully contested Cambridge. He failed again there in June 1834.[38] Peel made him Irish lord chancellor in his first ministry, but within weeks he resigned because his wife was refused reception at court in Dublin. He was talked out of it, but the government fell soon afterwards.[39] The 'flippant and conceited' Sugden, who acquired a property at Boyle Farm, on the Thames opposite Hampton Court, was returned for Ripon in 1837 and 1841, but vacated his seat to become Irish chancellor in Peel's second administration. He was lord chancellor in Lord Derby's first ministry, but turned down the office in 1858 on account of his age.[40] Roundell Palmer, who knew him only after he had left the bar, recalled him as

a very clever man, profound in conveyancing and case-law; waspish, overbearing, and impatient of contradiction. In Ireland, where everybody did homage to his superiority, he made a good judge; but in England, both as chancellor and in the House of Lords, the quality of his judgments suffered from his inability to endure a brother near the throne.[41]

While he resisted sweeping legal reforms, he instituted legislation to improve the lot of the indigent insane and penurious debtors.[42] He died at Boyle Farm in January 1875; 'for the full term allotted to man', wrote an obituarist, 'his name has been on men's lips'.[43]

[1] See *Oxford DNB* and J.B. Atlay, *Victorian Chancellors*, ii. 1-52. [2] *Buxton Mems.* 406. [3] *Reg. St. George Hanover Square*, i. 293; IGI (London). [4] *Buxton Mems.* 46. [5] *Life of Campbell*, ii. 305. [6] Pryme, *Autobiog. Recollections*, 67. [7] IGI (London); *Greville Mems.* iii. 177. [8] T.A. Nash, *Lord Westbury*, i. 55-56. [9] *Suss. Weekly Advertiser*, 22, 29 June 1818; *Late Elections* (1818), 342-3. [10] *Brighton Gazette*, 23, 30 June, 7, 14 July 1825, 8 June 1826. [11] Ibid. 6 Apr., 18, 25 May, 1, 8, 15, 22 June; *The Times*, 13 June 1826; W.D. Cooper, *Parl. Hist. Suss.* 32; G.I.T. Machin, *Catholic Question in English Politics*, 73. [12] *Brighton Gazette*, 6, 20 July 1826; *Brighton Herald*, 1 Sept. 1827; *Dorset Co. Chron.* 7 Feb. 1828. [13] *The Times*, 31 Jan. 4-6, 11, 12, 14-16, 18, 19, 21, 22, 26 Feb. 1828. [14] Atlay, ii. 9-10, 12. [15] *Greville Mems.* i. 280; Add. 40399, f. 336; *Ellenborough Diary*, ii. 49. [16] *Arbuthnot Jnl.* ii. 293. [17] *Ellenborough Diary*, ii. 53; Atlay, ii. 13-14; M. D. George, *Cat. of Pol. and Personal Satires*, xi. 15910, 16009. [18] *Dorset Co. Chron.* 11, 18 June 1829. [19] *The Times*, 12, 15 Dec. 1829; George, xi. 16020. [20] Add. 40399, f. 417. [21] *Ellenborough Diary*, ii. 232, 283; *Greville Mems.* ii. 407; Le Marchant, *Althorp*, 248. [22] *Dorset Co. Chron.* 5 Aug. 1830. [23] *Life of Campbell*, i. 478. [24] *Wellington Pol. Corresp.* i. 377; Arnould, *Denman*, i. 327-8. [25] *Greville Mems.* ii. 108. [26] *Three Diaries*, 63. [27] Surr. Hist. Cent. Goulburn mss Acc. 304/67B, Goulburn to wife [22 Mar.]; PRO NI, Anglesey mss, Smith Stanley to Anglesey, 22 Mar; Nottingham Univ. Lib. Newcastle mss. Ne2 F4/1/5; *Baring Jnls.* 84. [28] *The Times*, 5-9, 11-13 Apr. 1831. [29] *Life of Campbell*, i. 478. [30] Bucks. RO, Fremantle mss D/FR/139/20/14; *West Briton*, 6 May 1831. [31] *Three Diaries*, 105. [32] Le Marchant, 335, 339; M. Brock, *Great Reform Act*, 219. [33] See Brock, 226-9. [34] Add. 51569, Ord to Lady Holland; 51573, Rice to same [16 Dec. 1831]. [35] *Three Diaries*, 255; Le Marchant, 431-2. [36] Brougham mss, memo. [c. June 1832]. [37] Atlay, ii. 20-24; Arnould, 382-3; *Greville Mems.* ii. 312-16. [38] Add. 40617, f. 8; *Cambridge Chron.* 2, 30 Nov., 14 Dec. 1832; *The Times*, 9-14 June 1834. [39] *Greville Mems.* iii. 124, 177-8, 180; *Smith Letters*, ii. 610. [40] *Life of Campbell*, ii. 301, 305-6; *VCH Surr.* iii. 463. [41] Lord Selborne, *Mems.* pt. I, vol. ii, p. 333. [42] *Oxford DNB*. [43] *The Times*, 30 Jan. 1875.

D.R.F.

SUTTIE *see* **GRANT SUTTIE**

SUTTON *see* **MANNERS SUTTON**

SWANN, Henry (1763–1824), of Lower Green, Esher, Surr. and New Close Wood, Ufford, Northants.

YARMOUTH I.o.W.	1 Oct. 1803–20 Feb. 1804
PENRYN	1806–26 Feb. 1819
PENRYN	1820–24 Apr. 1824

bap. 15 Nov. 1763, 1st surv. s. of John Swann of Wansford, Northants. and w. Mary Adams of Stamford Baron St. Martin, Lincs.[1] *educ.* I. Temple 1787, called 1792. *m.* 21 Jan. 1785, Katherine, da. and h. of Robert Symes of Esher, 4s. (1 *d.v.p.*)[2] 2da. *suc.* fa. 1797.[3] *d.* 24 Apr. 1824.
Commr. for issuing exch. bills 1817-*d.*

Brought before king's bench for judgement, 17 Nov. 1819, after being found guilty of electoral bribery at Penryn, 'Lawyer' Swann made a rambling speech in which he admitted that proven corruption warranted 'exemplary' punishment, but claimed that 'in Parliament he had ever acted as a conscientious, independent man, unshackled by ministerial or other influence, and was therefore unlikely to be guilty of wilful or corrupt bribery'. He was sentenced to a year in the Marshalsea.[4] Three months later Sir Alexander Cray Grant* reported that on a visit to the prison he had seen 'that wretch' Swann dining with Henry Brougham* and Joseph Hume*:

> He avows himself to be compiling a history of all transactions involving jobbery or profligacy of any kind as connected with Parliaments as well as the conduct of the royal family in pecuniary matters, etc., which he means to publish or (we may conclude) to use as a means of extorting money. He says he is sure of his election for Penryn [at the forthcoming general election] without expending a shilling![5]

His renewed candidature for Penryn was promoted by his many friends in the borough, where he had built up a strong interest, partly through his success in securing a contract for the use of local granite in the construction of the new Waterloo Bridge.[6] At the end of the debate on the second reading of the bill to suspend the writs for Penryn, Barnstaple, Camelford and Grampound, 21 Feb. 1820, Lord John Russell answered Sir Joseph Yorke's complaint that Swann had been harshly treated 'in the language of the poet – "*Rara avis in terra nigroque similima cygno*"'. The bill's subsequent rejection by the Lords cleared the way for a contest at Penryn, where Swann was returned in second place after a three-day poll.[7] A petition was lodged against his return, 9 May, and on the motion of Charles Harvey, 1 June 1820, he was given permission to appear 'in custody' at the bar of the House on the 13th, if he wished to defend himself.[8] The election committee confirmed his return, 16 June. On Russell's motion for the early release of Swann's fellow scapegoat Sir Manasseh Masseh Lopes*, imprisoned for bribery at Grampound, 11 July, several Members called for mercy to be shown also to Swann, who was supposed to have 'two children at death's door'. However, the motion was withdrawn and Swann served his full term. His release, 16 Nov. 1820, was celebrated by his supporters at Penryn, who formally addressed him in acknowledgement of his services to the borough.[9]

He continued his practice of giving general support to the government of the day, while displaying his independence on certain occasions. He voted in defence of the Liverpool ministry's conduct towards Queen Caroline, 6 Feb., and paired against Catholic relief, 28 Feb. 1821. He divided for Russell's parliamentary reform motion, 9 May, and was in small minorities against including arrears in the grant to the duke of Clarence, 8, 29 June. He was a majority teller for adjourning the debate on the Newington select vestry bill, 16 May 1821. As the owner through marriage of the Oxford plantation in Jamaica, he attended general meetings of the West India interest in 1822 and 1823.[10] He paired against relieving Catholic peers of their disabilities, 30 Apr., and for the aliens bill, 5 June,[11] and voted against repeal of the salt duties, 28 June 1822. That autumn James Macdonald* facetiously remarked that if Canning succeeded in his rumoured plan to make the Speaker governor-general of India in order to remove Charles Williams Wynn from the board of control to the Speakership, opposition should put up Swann or Billy Holmes, the shady government whip, against him.[12] Swann divided with ministers against repeal of the Foreign Enlistment Act, 16 Apr., and inquiries into the prosecution of the Dublin Orange rioters, 22 Apr., and delays in chancery, 5 June 1823.

He died in April 1824, having previously signified his intention of vacating his seat.[13] He gave his wife a life annuity of £150, charged on the Oxford plantation, which he left in trust for his younger sons Frederick Dashwood, a half-pay captain in the Grenadier Guards, and Charles Henry, subject to the jointure of one Georgiana Elizabeth Malthus. On her death it was to be sold or mortgaged to raise £4,000 to be invested for the benefit of his eldest son John Thomas and his daughter Caroline Gibson. He distributed his property in the area between Stamford and Peterborough, which variously lay in Huntingdonshire, Lincolnshire, Northamptonshire and Rutland, among his children. His personalty was sworn under £800.[14]

[1] IGI (Northants.). [2] Gent. Mag. (1811), i. 275, 396. [3] Ibid. (1797), ii. 806. [4] The Times, 18 Nov. 1819. [5] NLI, Vesey Fitzgerald letterbks. 7858, pp. 169-70. [6] West Briton, 11 Feb., 24 Nov. 1820; Add. 58977, f. 171. [7] West Briton, 25 Feb., 3, 10, 17 Mar. 1820. [8] The Times, 2 June 1820. [9] R. Cornw. Gazette, 18 Nov.; West Briton, 24 Nov. 1820. [10] Inst. of Commonwealth Stud. M915/4/1, 80. [11] Add. 52445, f. 86. [12] Cockburn Letters, 69. [13] Gent. Mag. (1824), ii. 185; R. Cornw. Gazette, 1 May 1824. [14] PROB 11/1686/1320; IR26/1018/486.

D.R.F.

SYKES, Daniel (1766–1832), of Raywell and 16 Bowlalley Lane, Kingston-upon-Hull, Yorks.[1]

KINGSTON-UPON-HULL	1820–1830
BEVERLEY	1830–1831

b. 12 Nov. 1766, 5th s. of Joseph Sykes (d. 1803) of West Ella, Yorks. and Dorothy, da. of Nicholas Twiggs of Bakewell, Derbys. educ. Pocklington (privately by Rev. Miles Popple, DD); Trinity Coll. Camb. 1784, fellow 1790-5; M. Temple 1787, called 1793. m. Aug. 1795, Isabella, da. of Matthew Wright of Stamford Bridge, Lincs., s.p. d. 24 Jan. 1832.
Recorder, Kingston-upon-Hull.

Sykes's ancestors, originally from Cumberland, had settled in Leeds in the sixteenth century and become successful merchants. Richard Sykes had been its chief alderman at the town's first incorporation and one of its first mayors, and had purchased the title of lord of the manor of Leeds from the crown in 1625. It was his grandson, also Daniel, who moved to Hull in the mid-seventeenth century, becoming an eminent merchant there. Sykes's grandfather, another Richard, produced three sons, including Mark with his first wife, who established the Sykeses of Sledmere and became baronets, and Joseph with his second wife, this Member's father, who remained in Hull. Both branches were prominent in East Riding politics, but whereas the former were Pittites and Tories, those from Hull were Whigs and, later, Liberals. Sykes's father and elder brothers John and Nicholas served as mayors and sheriffs of Hull while his sister Mary Ann married Henry Thornton†.[2] His father, a staunch Whig and associate of Lord Rockingham, Sir George Savile† and the Rev. Christopher Wyvill, was said to be able to return one Member for Hull, but this exaggerated his influence. He had made his fortune as the exclusive importer of iron from the White Iron Mines in Sweden, whose produce was used by the cutlers of Sheffield, and was one of the few shareholders in the Hull Dock Corporation. It fell to him and his sons to sustain Rockingham's interest in Hull after his death, in which they were supported by Lord Fitzwilliam and his son Lord Milton*.[3] Daniel, who had always been a sickly child, suffered from repeated illness whilst at university, and after three years his father tried to lure him away from Cambridge, but the prospect of a fellowship, to which he was elected, kept him there. When the recordership of Hull became vacant a few years later, his father wanted to secure him the post but he again declined, preferring to persist with his law studies. He took up practice at the bar, only to be struck low by a near fatal illness. This persuaded him to become a provincial barrister and he moved back to his native town to take up practice and assist his father's business. It was during this period that he took on himself the task of educating the son of his brother Richard; he later founded the first primary school in Hull. In 1802 he took his first known part in elections, canvassing the Hull voters resident in York. By 1806 he was totally engrossed in the Whig cause in the East Riding, where he played a key role at York and Beverley, and in 1808 he helped to establish the Whig newspaper, *The Rockingham and Hull Weekly Advertiser*. In 1812 he unsuccessfully tried to secure the re-election of Lord Mahon for Hull. He was the principal speaker at a meeting in the town that October held to mark the retirement from the county of his friend and neighbour William Wilberforce*, whose victory in abolishing the slave trade he claimed was greater than any secured by Napoleon or Wellington. Despite Hull corporation being generally opposed to his politics, he was elected recorder in 1817, and the following year he and his eldest brother Richard secured the return of James Robert George Graham*. Around this time he withdrew from legal practice and became an East Riding magistrate.[4]

At the 1820 general election Sykes received an invitation to stand for Liverpool, which he declined, saying he had no desire to enter the Commons. Prospective candidates were spoken of at Hull, but when none materialized he was urged to offer by a section of the freemen, who offered him upwards of 1,000 votes. At the nomination he agreed to stand, observing that

had a fit and discreet person, in the words of the writ, offered himself, you would not have seen me in this situation ... A seat in Parliament has no charm for me. I do not desire to leave the comforts of private life for a burden I am not fit to bear, but I could not endure to see your state during the last two days.

He was returned unopposed but was obliged to pay a *parva consuetudo* for the promised votes. At the declaration he insisted that he would be his own man:

I am solely your representative. I will not be found truckling to public offices, bandied from board to board, or attending the levées of the minister or the bureau of the chancellor of the exchequer. I will not attend to private matters out of Parliament, only to private bills in Parliament; and there I will watch every act of the legislature that can effect the meanest subject. I will beg no favours. If you want them you must go elsewhere.

Following his election he sold his stake in the *Rockingham*.[5]

A regular attender, Sykes voted steadily with the Whig opposition to the Liverpool ministry on most

major issues, including economy, retrenchment and reduced taxation.[6] In his maiden speech, 5 June 1820, he called for the freeholders of the county corporate of Hull, who were unable to vote in county or borough elections, to be enfranchised in line with freeholders in other county towns, such as Bristol. (He introduced a bill to this effect in 1826, but abandoned it at its second reading, 2 May.) In early December 1820 he reported to Fitzwilliam that an attempt to organize a county petition in support of Queen Caroline, in which he had been involved, had failed, since many thought its aims too restrictive and would only act if reform was included. He urged Fitzwilliam to abandon plans for a county meeting and suggested that more localized petitions would be preferable. The Whig leader Lord Grey regarded this failure as a significant setback, but although Sykes regretted it, he believed 'the late unconstitutional proceedings about the queen to be but a small item in the catalogue of grievances for which ministers are answerable'.[7] He presented a Hull petition in her support, 24 Jan. 1821, when he denied that the petitioners were 'radicals'. On 19 Feb. he moved the second reading of the Hull sailors poor rates bill, which sought to make the shipping interest liable for a contribution to the local poor rates.[8] He voted for Catholic claims, 28 Feb. 1821, 1 Mar., 10 May 1825, and spoke against a hostile petition, 26 Mar. 1821. He divided for making Leeds a scot and lot borough if it received Grampound's seats, 2 Mar., for parliamentary reform, 18 Apr. 1821, when he spoke at length of the need for the Commons to represent 'the feelings and wishes of the people', 25 Apr. 1822, 24 Apr. 1823, 27 Apr. 1826, and for reform of the Scottish representative system, 2 June 1823. He argued for warehoused corn from abroad to be allowed into the domestic market, 30 Mar. 1821, 17 Feb., 13 May, 7 June 1825. He joined Brooks's, sponsored by Fitzwilliam and Graham, 10 May 1821. He urged government to extend the law granting bounties to the Greenland fishermen, 1 Feb. 1822.[9] He presented four petitions complaining of agricultural distress, 11 Feb., demanded action, 18 Feb., and argued that a reduction in taxation was 'the only remedy', 13 May. On 8 Mar. he gave notice of his intention to bring in a bill to repeal the tax on tallow candles. He secured returns of the duty paid, 11 Mar., spoke in support of Curwen's motion for their repeal, 20 Mar., and presented his own measure, 9 May 1822, but it went no further. He made another unsuccessful attempt, 11 Apr. 1823, brought up petitions in its support, 5, 23 Mar. 1824, 14 Mar. 1826, and returned again to the subject, 28 Apr. 1825.[10] He presented a petition from the merchants of Hull against the navigation bill, 6

May 1822, and spoke and voted against the merchant vessels apprenticeship bill, fearing that it would place new constraints upon commerce, 24 Mar. 1823.[11] He presented a petition against the liability of ship owners to penalties for smuggling by their employees, 3 June, and urged caution on the reciprocity of duties proposals while the shipping interest assessed their probable impact, 6 June 1823.[12]

Sykes voted to abolish flogging in the navy, 5 Mar. 1824, 10 Mar. 1826, condemned it as 'inhuman' and 'barbaric', 11 Mar. 1824, 11 Mar. 1825, and was a minority teller on the issue, 9 June 1825. He presented and endorsed petitions against naval impressment, 18 Mar., 26 May 1824, 13 June 1825.[13] He brought up others for the abolition of slavery, 13, 16, 26 Mar., and against the combination laws, 17, 19 Mar. 1824. He welcomed the county courts bill, 26 Mar., 24 May. He spoke and voted for an advance of capital to relieve distress in Ireland, 4 May, and for inquiry into the state of that country, 11 May 1824. On 21 Feb. 1825 he contended that the bill to suppress the Catholic Association 'would be wholly ineffectual' and urged the necessity of conceding Catholic claims. He spoke in similar terms, 23 Mar., 4 May. He called for a reduction in the hemp and iron duties, to relieve the shipping interest, 28 Feb., and in a speech against the sugar duties, 18 Mar., declared, 'I shall never cease to advocate the cause of free trade all over the world'. He predicted that a re-enactment of the combination laws would result in violence, 25 Apr., and brought up a petition against their renewal, 17 May. He presented another from Hull corporation for the Hull docks bill, 11 May, and from Hull merchants for a reduction of foreign timber duties, 16 June, and against the removal of tax on seed rape, 18 June 1825. During the rumours of a dissolution that September Sykes privately told his friend John Smith* that he was undecided about whether or not he would offer again for Hull, where 'I stand very well with the voters of all classes, but the polling money is a sad stumbling block'. Later that month Smith brought Sykes to the attention of Henry Brougham*, saying that he had 'a little coterie of liberal friends about him who would subscribe at his bidding' for shares in the proposed London University. Sykes purchased two shares himself, despite being sceptical of the university's success, and helped to found the Mechanics' Institute in Hull, of which he was president until his death.[14] On 1 Mar. 1826 Sykes, who was by now chairman of the Hull Anti-Slavery Society, urged ministers to hasten the introduction of measures for the total abolition of colonial slavery. He attacked the Scottish steam vessels bill, saying that more regulations were unnecessary, 9

Mar., and presented a ship owners' petition against the navigation laws, 26 May 1826.[15] He welcomed proposals to consolidate the criminal laws, 9 Mar., 17 Apr. 1826.

At the 1826 dissolution Sykes, after some hesitation, announced his retirement from Hull, citing his objection to having to pay in order to do fulfil a role that was deleterious to his 'health, strength and leisure'. A requisition signed by over 1,000 freemen urged him to reconsider, however, and on 10 June he accepted, stating that he would pay no polling money, but advising Milton that he would spend up to £3,000 for another seat if defeated. The *Hull Advertiser* criticized him for having supported Lord John Russell's motion to curb electoral bribery, but he was not listed as such, 26 May 1826, and the *Rockingham* defended him against all charges. Unpopular with the 'lower order of voters', he issued a defence of his past conduct, describing his support for tax reductions, Catholic relief, the abolition of slavery, a revision of the corn laws and 'the extension of your docks, the promotion of your commerce and the support of your shipping'. His hopes for an unopposed return were dashed at the last minute, but after a close contest he was returned in second place. A celebratory dinner was held in Hull in early July 1826, but he was unable to attend, again because of ill health. It would appear that he paid for the votes he received.[16] He called for measures to end impressment, 12 Feb., and for the abolition of corporal punishment, 12 Mar. 1827. He voted against the grant to the duke of Clarence, 16 Feb. He presented and endorsed Hull petitions for Catholic relief, 16, 27 Feb., and divided accordingly, 6 Mar. He was appointed to the select committee to investigate Northampton corporation, 21 Feb., and moved and was a minority teller for inquiry into Leicester corporation, which he claimed had illegally created freemen and used corporation funds for electoral purposes, 15 Mar. He was in the minority to lower the corn duties, 9 Mar. He welcomed proposed reforms of the navigation laws, 19 Mar. He voted for information on the Barrackpoor mutiny, 22 Mar., and for the spring guns bill next day. He was in the minority for information on the Lisburn Orange procession, 29 Mar. He divided for Tierney's amendment to withhold the supplies, 30 Mar. Following the accession of Canning as premier next month, Sykes informed a friend:

> Altogether I cannot make up my mind on the late changes. I believe that I must go with the rest of my friends; but still my old opposition feelings stick to me; and strongly disliking Canning, I cannot cordially support his administration. However, there are cases in which what is strictly right must give way to what is strongly expedient.

He presented a Hull petition against the Malt Act, 8 Feb. 1828. He brought up others from the Protestant Dissenters against the Test Acts, 14, 19, 22, 25 Feb., and voted for their repeal, 26 Feb. He called for army reductions, 25 Feb. He presented petitions for the Wakefield and Ferrybridge canal bill, 29 Feb., and spoke at length of its superiority over the Aire and Calder navigation bill and the likely benefits to Hull, 3 Mar. During the debates on the East Retford disfranchisement bill, he defended the banker Foljambe, saying he was sick and would give a satisfactory explanation of himself when well, 4 Mar., and his friend Henry Compton Cavendish* from the charges made by Daniel Whittle Harvey, 10 Mar. He presented a Hull petition against the stamp duties, 11 Mar. He resurrected the plight of Hull's disfranchised freeholders that day, and obtained leave to bring in a bill to enfranchise freeholders in corporate counties, 20 Mar., which was read a first time, 24 Mar., but was lost in committee. He secured returns on British shipping, 17 Mar., and drew attention to the economic difficulties facing that industry, 20 Mar. He divided against extending East Retford's franchise to Bassetlaw, 21 Mar. He was in the minority for a reduction of the corn duties, 29 Apr. He presented a petition from Hull corporation against Catholic claims that day, but of course voted in favour, 12 May. On 2 May he presented and endorsed a petition complaining of the conditions in Horsham gaol. He brought up others for the abolition of slavery and against the friendly societies bill, 12, 16 May, 2 June. He supported plans to introduce summary convictions for petty felonies, 13 May, and called for inquiry into the usury laws, 15 May. That day he welcomed a bill to shorten the duration of polls. Next day he called for a voluntary scheme to replace impressment. He presented and endorsed a petition for the repeal of restrictions on the circulation of county bank notes, 19 May. He was in the minority for information on the civil list, 20 May. He brought up Hull petitions for measures to cultivate the science of anatomy and against the alehouse licensing bill, 21 May, and for repeal of the assessed taxes, 4 June. He spoke against the corn importation bill, 23 May 1828.

Planta, the Wellington ministry's patronage secretary, predicted that Sykes would support their concession of Catholic emancipation, for which he brought up petitions, 16, 27 Feb., 10 Mar., and duly voted, 6 (as a pair), 30 Mar. 1829. He criticized the methods by which a hostile Hull petition presented by his colleague had been got up, 10 Mar., and endorsed Sir William Amcotts Ingilby's complaints of malpractice by anti-Catholic petitioners, 20 Mar. He called for a repeal of the game laws, 17 Feb. He brought up Hull petitions against the stamp and house duties, 23 Feb., and one from Kilkaranmore against the Irish Subletting Act, 10 Mar. He advocated removal of the silk import duties, 10 Apr. He welcomed elements of the juvenile offenders bill that would speed up convictions, 12 May, and proposals to exempt horses employed in husbandry from taxation next day. He presented and endorsed a constituency petition for the equalization of duties on East and West Indian produce, 19 May. On the 28th he rejected claims that free trade had caused distress. He brought up a petition for the speedier recovery of small debts, 1 June 1829, and spoke in the same sense, 17 Feb. 1830. He urged a reduction of the duties on imported hemp and timber that day, when he was in the minority to reduce the former, and gave notice that he would introduce a motion to lower the latter next session, 2 June 1829. That day he argued that 'the evidence is not sufficient to warrant the conclusion that East Retford should be deprived of its franchise' and was in the minority for the issue of a new writ. He divided for Lord Blandford's parliamentary reform resolutions, 2 June, when he objected to the proposed tax on merchant seamen for the support of Greenwich Hospital. He presented Hull petitions against the East India Company's monopoly, 2 June 1829, 3, 8 Mar. 1830. He was in the minorities for more extensive tax cuts, 15 Feb., and military reductions, 19 Feb. He voted for Blandford's parliamentary reform scheme, 18 Feb., for the enfranchisement of Birmingham, Manchester and Leeds, 23 Feb., and Russell's motion for reform, 28 May. He secured returns of Baltic timber imported by British ships, 24 Feb. He was in the minority for the transfer of East Retford's seats to Birmingham, 5, 15 Mar. Throughout March he supported the Leeds and Selby railway, promoting it as the essential link for the wool trade between Leeds and Hamburg via Hull. He voted steadily with the revived opposition for economy and reduced taxation from that month onwards. He presented a Hull petition against the poor law removal bill, 16 Mar. Next day he presented but dissented from a petition for the abolition of the death penalty in all cases except murder, stating his belief that 'many cases may happen where the security of society would require the infliction of death, even where murder has not been committed'. He brought up more petitions against the East India Company's monopoly, 19 Mar. He insisted that free trade would result in the greatest extension of imports and exports into and from every country in the world' and thereby benefit the shipping interest, 2 Apr. He voted for Jewish emancipation, 5 Apr. (as a pair), 17 May. He advocated repeal of the usury laws, which were 'equally absurd and impolitic', 6 May. He divided for abolition of the Irish viceroyalty, 11 May. That day he argued that the reduction of the duty on soap and tallow candles was 'absolutely essential to the comfort of the poor' and far more imperative than any reduction of the duty on beer. He presented petitions against the sale of beer bill and for the abolition of slavery next day. He paired for the abolition of the death penalty for forgery, 24 May, 7 June, and spoke against the practice, 3 June. He voted for a reform of the divorce laws that day. He was in the minority of 17 for repeal of the Irish Vestry Acts, 10 June 1830.

At the 1830 dissolution Sykes, who had incurred the displeasure of the ship owners for his advocacy of free trade, determined not to offer for Hull again, explaining that 'advancing years and declining strength render me less able to discharge the constant duties of a representative of a large commercial town'. There was an opportunity to represent the county and many wished him to seek the position, but in the event he agreed to withdraw his pretensions in favour of Brougham, for the sake of unanimity. He initially rejected a requisition from Beverley, but when it became clear that John Wharton* would definitely not stand there he agreed to come forward. Still in York, he proposed Lord Morpeth* for the representation of the county at a meeting of Whig freeholders and seconded Brougham. He was returned in second place for Beverley, but refused to pay the 210 guineas demanded for his freedom by the corporation. At Hull he assisted the return of William Battie Wrightson after abandoning Gilbert John Heathcote*. At his victory dinner he condemned the French government's conduct and looked forward to the reign of William IV with some optimism. A public dinner was held in Hull during September 1830 to commemorate his services as a representative.[17] He presented petitions for the abolition of slavery, 4, 9, 10, 11, 15, 16 Nov. 1830. He was, of course, listed by the Wellington ministry as one of their 'foes' and he voted against them in the crucial division on the civil list, 15 Nov. Anticipating the formation of a new ministry two days later, he declared, 'whom it may be composed of I know not, but ... I never shall give my support to any administration which refuses to grant freedom to the slave, real representation to the people, and a large reduction of taxation to the public'. He was solicited to stand for Yorkshire at the by-election caused by the elevation of Brougham to the woolsack, but again made way for another candidate, Sir John Johnstone*, for whom he actively campaigned.[18] Early in 1831 his health began to fail and he endured considerable pain, though he continued to be a regular

attender. He complained that much unrest in the countryside was caused by the operation of the game laws, 8 Feb. 1831. He concurred with petitions calling for repeal of the stamp duties and secured accounts of soap duties, 14 Feb. He welcomed the Grey ministry's reform proposals as likely to 'secure the people's rights' and 'produce peace and satisfaction throughout the country', 4 Mar. In the timber duties debate, 15 Mar., he defended his position on free trade and the shipping interest, arguing that although 'the shipping interest ought to receive every protection from the government ... the true way to benefit our shipping is to endeavour to extend our commerce in every direction, by removing all burdens upon it'. In line with this policy he sought leave to bring in a bill, in conjunction with Battie Wrightson and George Schonswar, to alter the method of settlement on apprentice seamen the following day. He paired for the second reading of the reform bill, 22 Mar., and divided against Gascoyne's wrecking amendment, 19 Apr. 1831.

At the ensuing dissolution Sykes retired from Beverley, explaining that poor health disabled him 'from the efficient performance of the duties of a Member'. He refused a requisition to stand for Yorkshire, but clearly envisaged returning to the House if his health improved, telling a supporter, 'if you will return me, in a reformed Parliament, for the East Riding, I may again buckle on my armour'. He actively supported the return of William Marshall* as his successor at Beverley and spoke in favour of the four reform candidates for the county at Hull, where he became embroiled in a bitter dispute with the corporation over the failure of his freeholders in districts bill, which he insisted they had forced him to abandon. He relinquished his recordership of Hull that summer and soon afterwards discovered he had cancer.[19] He declined over the winter and died in January 1832. By his will, proved 8 May 1832, his estate was divided between his wife and his brothers Richard and Henry and their families. The Mechanics' Institute raised a subscription of £300 to erect a seven-foot statue to his memory in Hull.[20]

[1] Unless otherwise indicated, this biography is based on G. Pryme, Mem. Daniel Sykes (1834). [2] Gent. Mag. (1832), i. 178-82; J. Foster, Peds. Yorks. Fams.; R.V. Taylor, Leeds Worthies, 337-41; J.J. Sheahan, Hist. Hull, 400. [3] Fitzwilliam mss, box 39, Rev. R. Sykes to Fitzwilliam, 23 Nov. 1783, 3 May 1784, 4 June, J. Sykes to same, 11 June 1790; Sheahan, 400; HP Commons, 1790-1820, ii. 447. [4] Hull Rockingham, 2 Jan. 1808; Sheahan, 664. [5] Hull Advertiser, 10 Mar. 1820. [6] Black Bk. (1823), 196; Session of Parl. 1825, p. 486. [7] Fitzwilliam mss 102/4, 6; A. Mitchell, Whigs in Opposition, 152. [8] The Times, 20 Feb. 1821. [9] Ibid. 2 Feb. 1822. [10] Ibid. 9, 12 Mar., 10 May 1822, 12 Apr. 1823. [11] Ibid. 7 May 1822. [12] Ibid. 4 June 1823. [13] Ibid. 27 May 1824, 14 June 1825. [14] Brougham mss, Sykes to

J. Smith, 12 Sept., Smith to Brougham, 16 Sept.; Fitzwilliam mss, Sykes to Milton, 25 Sept. 1825. [15] *The Times*, 27 May 1826. [16] Fitzwilliam mss, D. Sykes to Milton [1826]; *Hull Rockingham*, 3, 10 June; *Hull Advertiser*, 9, 13 June 1826; Add. 37236, f. 72. [17] *Hull Rockingham*, 24, 31 July, 7, 14 Aug. 1830; *Hull Advertiser*, 30 July, 6 Aug. 1830; Lincs. AO, Ancaster mss X111/B/5g. [18] *Hull Advertiser*, 3, 10 Dec. 1830; *Hull Rockingham*, 4 Dec. 1830. [19] *Hull Rockingham*, 30 Apr., 6, 14 May 1831; Sheahan, 645. [20] PROB 11/1800/324; Sheahan, 645.

M.P.J.C.

TALBOT, Christopher Rice Mansel (1803–1890), of Penrice Castle and Margam Park, Glam.[1]

GLAMORGAN   1830–1885

MID-GLAMORGAN   1885–17 Jan. 1890

b. 10 May 1803, o.s. of Thomas Mansel Talbot of Margam and Penrice Castle and Lady Maria Lucy Fox Strangways, da. of Henry Thomas Fox Strangways[†], 2nd earl of Ilchester. *educ.* Harrow 1814-17; Oriel, Oxf. 1819. *m.* 28 Dec. 1835, Lady Charlotte Butler, da. of Richard, 1st earl of Glengall [I], 1s. *d.v.p.* 3da. *suc.* fa. 1813. *d.* 17 Jan. 1890.

Ld. lt. Glam. 1848-*d.*

Talbot was descended from the earls of Shrewsbury through the Hensol Castle, Castle Talbot and Lacock branches of the family. His forefathers had purchased the Abbey and most of the 18,725-acre parish of Margam at the Dissolution, and intermarried with the Mansels of Oxwich and Penrice to become Glamorgan's largest resident landowners (34,000 acres). Margam's political hegemony had lapsed, but as manorial lords of Kenfig and proprietors in Aberavon, their interest remained decisive in the struggle between the 6th duke of Beaufort and the 2nd marquess of Bute for control of Cardiff Boroughs, while in Glamorgan Talbot's father had led the 'independent' party against the absentee aristocracy and rebuilt Penrice, where by 1820 the annual rent revenues reached £15,000.[2] He died in 1813, having entrusted his estates to his cousin Michael Hicks Beach[†] (*d.* 1830) of Williamstrip Park, Gloucestershire, Beach's namesake son, Member for Malmesbury, 1812-17, and the rector of Margam, the Rev. Dr. John Hunt. His widow, who in 1815 married Sir Christopher Cole*, had full control of her jointure and Penrice until Talbot married or attained the age of 25. Talbot received £1,000 annually from the age of 21, increasing to £2,000 if he was travelling abroad or a Member of Parliament.[3] Trust funds were also released for Cole to contest Glamorgan in 1817 and 1820, and on 30 Mar. 1825, the balance stood at £16,421 2*s.* 6*d.* in Talbot's favour.[4] His sister Jane Harriot had married John Nicholl[†] of Merthyr Mawr,

the son and heir of the Member for Great Bedwyn, and the family's influence in Glamorgan was further strengthened by the marriages of his sisters Isabella to Richard Franklen of Clemenston, and Charlotte to the Rev. John Montgomery Traherne of Coedarhydyglyn. In 1833 Emma married John Dillwyn Llewellyn of Penlle'rgaer, son of Lewis Weston Dillwyn[†].[5]

Talbot is reputed to have refused to sign the thirty-nine articles, but he gained a first in mathematics at Oxford in 1824, when, to his dismay, his coming of age was a great county occasion.[6] Congratulating him on his academic achievement, Sir John Nicholl* had observed that the 'young S_r of Margam might so distinguish himself as to possess that weight and influence in Glamorganshire which his ancestors heretofore held' and advised him

> to abstain very cautiously from committing yourself to any party or set of men, until you had a full opportunity by considerable experience of forming a deliberate judgement which set of measures generally pursued or recommended by contending parties were upon the whole most conducive to the real interests of the country, for if once you became a party man, you were no longer quite as independent, and perfect independence should in no degree be sacrificed but on most mature consideration guiding the judgement.

Replying, Talbot described 'knowledge gained' at university as 'rather curious than useful', and dismissed his examination success as an endeavour to please his tutor. He concurred that the distinction between the parties 'is so inconsiderable that it is no easy matter to make up the mind to either, however, I never shall approve of the maxim *medico tutisimus ibis*'.[7] He indulged his love of sailing and foreign travel while he familiarized himself with the management of his estates, their mineral deposits, and Glamorgan politics, where Bute observed that he found it difficult to escape the bonds of loyalty incurred by Cole and the trustees in and before 1820.[8] Talbot was indeed under pressure to provide financial support for the 'independent' interest in Glamorgan.[9] He favoured banking exclusively in London and, grieved by the losses incurred by his agents through the collapse in December 1825 of Gibbins and Eaton's Swansea bank, he consulted Nicolson Calvert* in London in May 1826 and took action afterwards to prevent his father's lessees, the English Copper Company, exploiting his land.[10] At the general election in June he declared late for and seconded Bute's brother Lord James Crichton Stuart* in Cardiff Boroughs, and attended Cole's election in Bridgend.[11] He spent most of the next eighteen months aboard his yacht *Guilia* in the Mediterranean, whence he assumed control of family finances, monitored the activities of the Porth Cawl Company and commissioned plans to develop his port of Aberavon, realized later through the establishment of Port Talbot. He informed his agent Griffith Llewellyn, 21 July 1827:

It has always been my grand object to restore Margam to what it ought to be, the park and residence of the owner of the property. If it depended only on myself, I should have little difficulty, but there appears to have been on the part of those who held the purse strings, an anxious wish to get rid of the cash by every possible means. I mention this, because it will now depend more *on you* than on me, whether I am ever enabled to put my project into effect. I can easily limit my expenditure to £2,000 per annum even with my large establishment here, and if you would also limit the expenditure of the estate to what is absolutely necessary, I should soon be enabled to begin operations. There is a wide difference between conducting the affairs of a trust and of an individual.[12]

In 1829, after an extended visit to his cousin, the pioneer photographer William Henry Fox Talbot†, at Lacock Abbey, Talbot returned to his family at Penrice. He stewarded the races at Cardiff, for which Bute lent Cole the Castle, planned his new mansion, and kept a close watch on transport schemes, for he saw 'grounds to dislike the introduction of an *Act of Parliament* on land which belongs *exclusively* to myself'.[13] When George IV lay dying he met his trustees to settle the accounts and informed his agent, 7 June 1830:

I have also had a conversation with the earl of Ilchester respecting the money spent in electioneering, and in consequence of his communications to me, I have not the least further delicacy with regard to coming forward as a candidate for the county. I have received a letter from Sir Christopher ... stating his intention to resign at the next dissolution ... and I mention these things in confidence to you in order that you may be prepared, as soon you see his advertisement of resignation, to retain the legal men for me as soon as possible afterwards. It is unlikely there will be any opposition, but I am prepared if there is to raise a sum of money on the purchased estates which will be conveyed to me by the trustees. At all events, who is there in the county who has both a claim to represent the county, and money to support that claim? I have paid Miss Talbot's fortune and Miss Emma's. There now only remains Mrs. Traherne's unpaid, and the trustees have agreed to take my personal bond for that, which will leave the purchased estates unencumbered.[14]

Cole announced his retirement and Talbot, frequently accompanied by Dillwyn, canvassed the gentry with his agents directly after the king's funeral.[15] Attempts to raise an opposition failed, and he was returned at Bridgend, 10 Aug. On the hustings he said that occasional conflicts of interest between the agricultural, manufacturing, shipping and commercial interests were inevitable, and described himself as 'a sincere friend to every measure calculated to promote the liberty of the subject', reduce public spending and taxation, improve the condition of the labouring poor and promote trade and commerce'. He praised the duke of Wellington's policies on religious toleration, hinted at future support for his ministry and expressly denied that Cole had been his *locum tenens*.[16] From Cowes, where he joined Cole and the rest of his family, he wrote to Fox Talbot, 18 Aug. 1830:

Nothing can be more satisfactory than the result of the English elections. We are not, however, as fortunate in Wales. Carmarthenshire and Pembrokeshire and Breconshire and Monmouthshire return all government men. Glamorgan is pre-eminent in returning two Whig Members. I marvel how Lord Lansdowne has managed about Calne. I see too Mr. Gye has left Chippenham.[17]

Thomas Bucknall Estcourt* hoped Talbot would 'not be disinclined to exert himself'.[18]

Talbot arrived in London after the October races, too late to present the Glamorgan address. He was confident the Wellington ministry would be defeated on reform and 'must go out',[19] but was absent from the division on the civil list, which brought them down, 15 Nov. 1830. From London, 18 Dec., he dismissed the incendiarism in Glamorgan as the work of aggrieved labourers, incited by travellers, and added:

As to *Swing*, that is all humbug and hoax, but I do confess I am quite astonished that those who do receive their letters should publish to the world that they have.[20]

He returned to Penrice, where county landowners and radicals solicited his support, 23 Dec. 1830, and on 25 Feb. 1831 presented petitions from the hundred of Cowbridge for tithe reform and from Bridgend for election by ballot.[21] He brought up further reform petitions, 15 Mar., and was surprised to find that Kenfig was not to be disfranchised under the Grey ministry's bill.[22] He divided for its second reading, 22 Mar., and afterwards left for Dover, where he was 'kept by contrary winds and might just as well have stayed in town to talk'. He considered the majority of one, 'small as it is ... as good as 100', and hoped Parliament would not be precipitately dissolved, so that the Glamorgan roads bill and concessions on the coastwise coal duties were not forfeited (both were enacted).[23] He presented the county's petitions for reform and additional representation, 28 Mar., 15 Apr. As requested by the Merthyr Tydfil meeting, 8 Apr., he accompanied a 'deputation to Lord Althorp*', 18 Apr., 'to try for a Merthyr Member, but in vain'.[24] He knew before he divided against Gascoyne's wrecking amendment, 19 Apr., that the industrialist William Crawshay of Cyfarthfa, the former county Member Sir John Edwards Vaughan*, and Alderman William Thompson*, a joint-proprietor of the Penydarren works, were scheming against him in Glamorgan.[25] Ignoring requests to declare against the bill at the ensuing election, he campaigned assiduously, assisted by the popular tide for reform. He had already privately agreed to back Dillwyn for the second county seat conceded to Glamorgan, 18 Apr. 1831, for which his brother-in-law Nicholl now canvassed as an anti-reformer.[26] At his election, Talbot explained that he supported reform because the population, wealth and education had increased and communities had outgrown their political institutions.[27]

He had declined a militia captaincy in 1829, and the June 1831 Merthyr rising confirmed his belief 'that a force acting together only eight days in the year must be wholly inefficient for any practical purposes'.[28] He gave up his hotel rooms and took a house in Chesterfield Street in July 1831 to make Commons attendance easier, and divided for the reintroduced reform bill at its second reading, 6 July, and steadily for its details, except where they conflicted with his personal and Glamorgan interests.[29] He thus cast a wayward vote against taking a Member from Chippenham (which Fox Talbot hoped to represent), 27 July. He declined to promote Merthyr Tydfil's cause in the Commons '*lest he should hamper* the bill', but he acknowledged that it had a good case for separate representation, voted against its inclusion in the Cardiff Boroughs, 10 Aug., and lobbied to ensure that it was not awarded the separate franchise granted to Swansea (with Aberavon, Kenfig, Loughor and Neath), whose petition he presented, 16 Aug.[30] He voted for Lord Chandos's amendment enfranchising £50 tenants-at-will, 18 Aug. He divided for the reform bill's passage, 21 Sept.,[31] and Lord Ebrington's confidence motion, 10 Oct. He was privately relieved that the home office heeded 'the awful power of the lower classes' at Merthyr Tydfil, which remained a contributory designate of Cardiff in the revised reform bill.[32] He returned to London to vote for its second reading, 17 Dec. 1831, and later maintained that pressure to attend the House during its committee stage delayed his recovery from influenza.[33] He divided for the schedule A disfranchisements, 20 Jan., but either failed to vote for or divided against schedule B, 23 Jan. (for which only a majority list survives), although he voted for the Vestry Act amendment bill that day. He

voted with other South Wales Members to substitute Merthyr Tydfil for Gateshead in Schedule D, 5 Mar., but deemed the government's decision, announced on 14 Mar., to award it the extra Member designated for Monmouthshire

> very unwise in them, because everyone knows that if the duke of Beaufort had not been supposed to have great influence, the thing would not have been done. It is a job, and will tend to throw great discredit on ministers.[34]

He divided for the bill's third reading, 22 Mar., but was 'absent in the country' when a ministry headed by Wellington was contemplated. He divided for the second reading of the Irish reform bill, 25 May, and against a Conservative amendment to the Scottish measure, 1 June 1832. He divided with government on the Dublin election controversy, 23 Aug. 1831, the Russian-Dutch loan, 26 Jan., 12 July, and relations with Portugal, 9 Feb. 1832.

Costly building work at Margam between 1830 and 1832 forced Talbot to find £5,000 that year, but he attributed rumours that he was heavily in debt, which greatly annoyed him, to 'my being arbitrator for Lord Portarlington in the case of a gambling bond transaction, wherein I hope I have benefited his lordship by my decision to an amount of £10,000, but certainly not at my own expense'.[35] The admissions of many Kenfig burgesses had been deliberately kept unstamped to cut costs, and he had these removed from the books before the reform bill was enacted.[36] Canvassing Glamorgan in June 1832, he declared that 'no single Member ... can represent agriculture, commerce, industry and the county'.[37] Anticipating opposition from 'the Merthyr men', Edwards Vaughan's son, and the Conservatives, he attended closely to voter registration before the general election in December, but Bute refrained from intervention in return for Dillwyn and Talbot's acquiescence in the return of John Nicholl for Cardiff Boroughs.[38] Asked by Bute to define his politics and attitude towards the Conservative party, Talbot had replied, 16 Sept. 1832:

> I think it very possible to be both 'conservative' and friendly to the present ministry, but until I know what are the objects of the Conservative party, and what those of the present ministry, I should feel it disingenuous in me to solicit support as the adherent of either. I regret extremely that any pains should be taken to perpetuate the existence of two parties whose ancient cause of dispute is now at an end. I know not on what grounds or pretences we should speak of reformers and anti-reformers, Whigs and Tories, now that the hopes of one party and the fears of the other have met with a common fate in the passing of the bill. When I first became a Member ... I placed entire confidence in the administra-

tion of the duke of Wellington. It is my firm belief that his grace possessed more power to benefit this country than any minister of modern times. He was looked up to by the ... Commons, and by the country, for his noble and unostentatious retrenchments and for his perfect disinterestedness. The ball was at his feet, he would kick it, it came to Lord Grey, and *he* gave it, I am willing to allow, an unreasonably hard kick. In my humble opinion, it was then too late to attempt even modification, and I, with many others, found myself compelled either to support the whole reform bill, or to have none at all: an alternative which I considered tantamount to revolution. In a word, I supported the ministry of Lord Grey because I thought it would eventually prove more strictly speaking a 'conservative' one than that of his opponents ... I am no admirer of the present ministry either in regard to their financial views, or their foreign policy: I believe more practical good to have been done by the exertions of Sir Robert Peel and ... Wellington than is likely to be effected by ... Grey and Lord Althorp, and I think that in any measures which may come before Parliament, Conservative, or from whatever source, predilection for neither one set of men nor for another would influence my line of conduct in favour of either.[39]

Notwithstanding his protectionist principles, Talbot represented Glamorgan as a Liberal until the boundary changes of 1885, and subsequently Mid-Glamorgan, where he encountered strong constituency opposition after opposing Irish Home Rule in 1886. He died a millionaire and 'father of the House' in January 1890, having declined Gladstone's offer of a peerage in 1869, as his only son Theodore, who predeceased him in 1876, refused to stand for Glamorgan.[40] He bequeathed his real estate, including an estimated £1,000,000 stake in the Great Western Railway Company, to his unmarried daughter Emily Charlotte (*d.* 1918), whom he charged with the care of her sister Emma, and left his shares in the London and South Western Railway Company to his married daughter Bertha Elizabeth, whose grandson John Theodore, the son of Andrew Mansel Talbot Fletcher (1880-1951) of Saltoun Hall, East Lothian, succeeded to the estates in trust on Emily's death.[41]

[1] For a review of Talbot's political career see T.M. Campbell, 'CRM Talbot (1803-90): A Welsh Landowner in Politics and Industry', *Morgannwg*, xliv (2000), 66-104. [2] H.M. Thomas, 'Margam Estate Management, 1765-1860', *Glam. Historian*, vi (1969), 16; P.D.G. Thomas, *Politics in 18th Cent. Wales*, 14-15, 51-53; P. Jenkins, 'From Edward Lhuyd to Iolo Morgannwg', *Morgannwg*, xxiii (1979), 41; I.G. Jones, 'Margam, Penrhudd and Brombil', ibid. xxxiv (1990), 7-9; Glam. RO D/D/Ma/E/1; NLW, Penrice and Margam mss 9222; *HP Commons, 1790-1820*, ii. 499-501. [3] PROB 8/206; 11/1546/389; Penrice and Margam mss 6556. [4] Penrice and Margam mss 9235, J.W. Smith to G. Llewellyn, 30 Mar., 30 June, 16 July 1825. [5] *Glam Co. Hist.* vi. 2-4; Penrice and Margam mss 6488; 9238, Talbot to G. Llywellyn, 15 Apr. 1830. [6] J.V. Hughes, *The*

Wealthiest Commoner, 11-14; *The Times*, 18 Jan. 1890; *Cambrian*, 15 May 1824; British Library, Talbot collection, Isabella Franklen to Fox Talbot. [7] Merthyr Mawr mss L/205/7. [8] Penrice and Margam mss L1324-5; 9235, Wyndham Lewis to T. Llewellyn, 23 Sept.; 9236, Talbot to G. Llewellyn, 8 Aug. 1825; Glam. RO D/DA11/17, 47; 12/116, 135-6; NLW, Bute mss L67/23. [9] Merthyr Mawr mss F/51/7. [10] Penrice and Margam mss 9235, W. to T. Llewellyn, 19 Dec.; 9236, Talbot to G. Llewellyn, 24 Dec. 1825, 14 May 1826. [11] Merthyr Mawr mss L/206/37; *Cambrian*, 17, 24 June 1826. [12] Penrice and Margam mss 9236, Talbot to G. Llewellyn, 21 July 1827 and *passim*. [13] Ibid. Talbot to G. Llewellyn, 15 Nov. 1828, *et seq.*; 9237, same to same, 29 Nov.; NLW, Penllergaer mss, diary of Lewis Weston Dillwyn, 12-14 Oct. 1829. [14] Penrice and Margam mss 9238, Talbot to G. Llewellyn, 7 June 1830. [15] Bute mss L73/78; Penrice and Margam mss 9238, Talbot to G. Llewellyn, 7, 18 July; Dillwyn diary, 6, 16-18, 26, 27, July, 5, 7 Aug.; Cardiff Pub. Lib. Bute estate letterbks. ii. 240; NLW, Vivian mss, Talbot to J.H. Vivian, 7 July; *Cambrian* 10, 17 July 1830. [16] Bute estate letterbks. ii. 228; Fox Talbot mss, Talbot to Fox Talbot, c. 14 July; *Cambrian*, 24, 31 July, 14 Aug. 1830. [17] Fox Talbot mss. [18] Ibid. Estcourt to Fox Talbot, 21 Oct. 1830. [19] Penrice and Margam mss 9238, Talbot to G. Llewellyn, 16 Aug., 8 Nov. 1830. [20] Penrice and Margam mss 9238, Talbot to G. Llewellyn, 10, 18 Dec.; *Cambrian*, 18 Dec.; *Bristol Mercury*, 28 Dec. 1830. [21] Bute estate letterbks. ii. 260; *Cambrian*, 28 Jan. 1831. [22] Penrice and Margam mss 9238, Talbot to G. Llewellyn 7, 15 Mar.; *Cambrian*, 12 Mar. 1831. [23] *Cambrian*, 27 Nov., 24 Dec. 1830, 26 Feb., 5 Mar. 1831; Fox Talbot mss, Talbot to Fox Talbot [24 Mar. 1831]; E. Ball, 'Glamorgan: A Study of the Co. and the Work of its Members in the Commons, 1825-1835' (Univ. of London Ph.D. thesis, 1965), 90-92. [24] Penrice and Margam mss 9238, Talbot to G. Llewellyn, 19 Apr.; *Cambrian*, 19, 26 Mar., 23 Apr. 1831. [25] Penrice and Margam mss 9238, Talbot to G. Llewellyn, 19, 20 Apr. 1831. [26] Bute mss L74/30, 32, 34; *Mon. Merlin*, 14 Apr.; Dillwyn diary, 20 Apr.; Penrice and Margam mss 9239, Talbot to G. Llewellyn, 27 Apr., 1 May; *Cambrian*, 30 Apr., 7 May 1831. [27] Dillwyn diary, 2, 6 May; *Cambrian*, 14 May; *Mon. Merlin*, 21 May 1831. [28] Bute mss L72/85; L74/124, 137; Penrice and Margam mss 9239, Talbot to G. Llewellyn, 18 June 1831. [29] Penrice and Margam mss 9238, Talbot to G. Llewellyn, 28 July 1831. [30] NLW, Maybery mss 6585; Ball, 171-8. [31] *The Times*, 23 Sept. 1831. [32] Penrice and Margam mss 9239, Talbot to G. Llewellyn, 4 Nov., 15 Dec. 1831. [33] Ibid. Talbot to G. Llewellyn, 13 Jan. 1832. [34] Ibid. same to same, 20 Mar. 1832. [35] Thomas, 28; Penrice and Margam mss 9239, Talbot to G. Llewellyn, 3 Apr. [2 June] 1832. [36] Penrice and Margam mss 9237, Talbot to G. Llewellyn, 27 Sept. 1829; Thomas, 26; I.W.R. David, 'Pol. and Electioneering Activity in S.E. Wales, 1820-1852' (Univ. of Wales M.A. thesis, 1959), 259. [37] *Cambrian*, 30 June 1832. [38] Dillwyn diary, 23, 24 June, 20-29 Sept., 5, 7, 16, 17 Oct.; Penrice and Margam mss 9239, Talbot to G. Llewellyn, 26 June, 29, 31 July, 1, 12 Aug., 7 Sept.; Bute mss L75/93, 101; Bute estate letterbks. ii. 346-7; iii. 36, 50; NLW, Mansel Franklen Coll. 6575 E, pp. 82-83; *Cambrian*, 18 Aug. 1832. [39] Bute mss L75/145. [40] *Glam. Co. Hist.* vi. 9-18; K.O. Morgan, *Wales in British Politics, 1868-1922*, pp. 72, 112; P. Jenkins, *Making of a Ruling Class*, 274-5; Add. 44423, ff. 140-1, 252, 318, 347; Hughes, 15-34; *The Times*, 18 Jan.; *Illustrated London News*, 25 Jan. 1890; W.B. Rubinstein, *Men of Property* (1981), 252. [41] *The Times*, 17 Apr. 1890; I.G. Jones, *Morgannwg*, xxxiv. 9-12.

M.M.E.

TALBOT, Richard Wogan (1766–1849), of Malahide Castle, co. Dublin.

Co. Dublin	1807–1830

b. 1766, 1st s. of Richard Talbot of Malahide Castle and Margaret, da. of James O'Reilly of Ballinlough, co. Westmeath (*cr.* Baroness Talbot of Malahide [I] 28 May 1831). *m.* (1) lic. 28 Nov. 1789, Catherine (*d.* c.1800), da. and h. of John Malpas of Chapel Izod and Rochestown, co. Dublin, 1s. 1da. both *d.v.p.*; (2) 15 Mar. 1806, Margaret, da. of Andrew Sayers, timber merchant, of Drogheda, co. Louth, *s.p.* suc. fa. 1788; mother as 2nd Bar. Talbot of Malahide [I] 27 Sept. 1834; *cr.* Bar. Furnival [UK] 8 May 1839. *d.* 29 Oct. 1849.

MP [I] 1790-1; PC [I] 28 Dec. 1836.[1]

Maj. Ward's Ft. 1794; lt.-col. 118 Ft. 1794, 23 Ft. 1800; capt. commdt. Malahide vols. 1803, col.

Talbot, whose father's family had held the castle and lordship of Malahide, on the coast north of Dublin, from the earliest period of English occupation under Henry II, was also illustriously descended through his mother, who came from the Milesian princely house of Breffney. Born a Catholic, he converted (as a child) with his father in 1779, and, after unsatisfactory army, cotton manufacturing and banking careers, in 1807 he won back the county Dublin seat which he had briefly held in his mid-twenties.[2] A relatively inactive Whig, he was narrowly returned again, with the backing of the independent interest, at the general election of 1820. On 11 May 1820 he attended the city dinner in honour of the Whig Alderman Thomas McKenny, but no trace of parliamentary activity has been found for that session.[3]

He was criticized for missing the meeting held at Kilmainham on 30 Dec. 1820, when the sheriff forcibly adjourned the proceedings rather than allow the county to pronounce in favour of Queen Caroline, but he chaired another which met to deplore this outrage, 11 Jan. 1821.[4] Having voted for her name to be reinstated in the liturgy, 23, 26 Jan., 13, 15 Feb., and to censure ministers' conduct towards her, 6 Feb., he spoke and voted in condemnation of the sheriff's actions, 22 Feb. He divided for Catholic relief, 28 Feb. 1821, 1 Mar., 21 Apr., 10 May 1825. As well as siding regularly with opposition in its campaign for economies and reduced taxes in 1821, he was in minorities for information on Naples, 21 Feb., and lowering the number of place-holders in the Commons, 9 Mar. He was granted six weeks' leave on urgent private business, 1 May. He voted for parliamentary reform, 18 Apr. 1821, 25 Apr. 1822, 24 Apr., 2 June 1823. He divided for abolition of one of the joint-postmasterships, 2 May, but, out of personal regard for his distant kinsman the duke of Buckingham, he abstained on the opposition attack on the costs of Henry Williams Wynn's[†] embassy to the Swiss Cantons, 16 May 1822.[5] Talbot, who missed the county Dublin meeting in January 1823 to address the lord lieutenant after the Orange theatre riot, was criticized not only for failing

to instruct his tenants to vote for the Whig Henry White*, but also for giving his own to the Tory candidate Sir Compton Domvile* at the by-election there the following month.[6] He voted for lower taxation and reductions in the national debt, 28 Feb., 3, 6, 17 Mar., and repeal of the Foreign Enlistment Act, 16 Apr. He was in the majority for inquiry into the legal proceedings against the Dublin Orange rioters, 22 Apr. He was listed in the opposition minority for an inquiry into chancery administration, 5 June, but in the government majority against one into the currency, 12 June 1823. He voted for an advance of capital to Ireland, 4 May, repeal of the assessed taxes, 10 May, and inquiry into the state of Ireland, 11 May 1824. His praises were sung at a meeting of the Catholic Association, 16 Oct. 1824, when his contribution to the Catholic rent was received.[7] He divided steadily against the Irish unlawful societies bill, which was designed to suppress the Association, in February 1825. He accepted the invitation to attend the O'Connellite dinner of the friends of civil and religious liberty in Dublin, 2 Feb., signing the ensuing pro-Catholic petition from the Protestants of Ireland; he brought up the city manufacturers' petition for reduction in the coal duties, 3 Mar. 1826.[8]

Talbot, who had already twice authorized statements that he had formed no union with any potential challenger, was forced to deny that he had joined the Tory candidate George Alexander Hamilton[†] at the general election of 1826, when he successfully relied on his past record and, with the support of the Catholics, was returned in second place, behind White, after a violent contest.[9] He attended the county Catholics' meeting in October 1826, but apparently missed the division on their claims in the Commons the following March. He presented the Swords and Malahide pro-Catholic petitions, 18 Mar., and voted in this sense, 12 Mar., while he also divided for economies, 23 June, 4, 7 July 1828. But he was a defaulter on emancipation, 5 Mar. 1829, and his only known vote that session was the pair he gave for the third reading of the relief bill, 30 Mar. The following month his wife unsuccessfully applied to the prime minister, the duke of Wellington, for a peerage and a pension, mentioning that their son's death the previous year had left them in financial difficulties.[10] He divided for Jewish emancipation, 5 Apr., 17 May 1830. He sided with Daniel O'Connell against the Irish vestry laws, 27 Apr., 10 June, and divided to repeal the unpopular Irish coal duties, 13 May, and to make Irish first fruits no longer nominal, 18 May. He attended the meeting of Irish Members in London to lobby against the increased spirit and stamp duties, 6 May, and probably brought up his county's petitions against them, 25, 28 May.[11] His only other known votes were for parliamentary reform, 28 May, alteration of the divorce laws, 3 June, and reducing the grant for South American missions, 7 June 1830, when he also apparently paired for abolition of the death penalty for forgery.

It was expected that Talbot, whose inactivity and government backing now told against him, despite his 24 years' experience, would be forced to withdraw at the general election of 1830. Although he persisted as far as the third day of the poll, this proved to be the case; Wellington commiserated with him, but no peerage was forthcoming.[12] He made no attempt to regain his seat at the following election, but in May 1831 he signed the requisition for a county Dublin meeting in favour of reform. That month his mother received a barony from the Grey ministry, this arrangement permitting the title to pass to her now childless eldest son, who was thus considered a potential lord lieutenant of the county, and then to his brothers. He chaired the monster reform meeting in Dublin, 14, 15 May 1832, and voted for O'Connell and Edward Southwell Ruthven* in the city contest at the general election.[13] Having inherited the Irish peerage in 1834, he spent much of that decade involved in legal cases over his claims to compensation for the loss of ancient rights to duties in the port of Malahide and to a seat in the Lords on the basis of his being heir to the receiver of an original writ of summons.[14] The latter question was resolved by the award of a United Kingdom barony in 1839. Talbot, who joined Brooks's, 3 Feb. 1841, died after a 'long life of uniform liberal policy' in October 1849.[15] His Irish title and estates passed to his next brother James (?1768-1850), and then to James's son and namesake (1805-83), Liberal Member for Athlone, 1832-4. Talbot's widow, who rose from humble origins to aspire to be 'a leading star in the world of fashion', died in November 1861.[16]

[1] Not the 25th, as erroneously given in *HP Commons, 1790-1820*, v. 331. [2] *Convert Rolls* ed. E. O'Byrne, 266; *Hist. Irish Parliament*, vi. 373-4. [3] *Dublin Evening Post*, 26, 29 Feb., 16, 21, 24, 30 Mar., 1, 8 Apr., 13 May 1820. [4] Ibid. 2, 4, 11, 13 Jan. 1821. [5] Buckingham, *Mems Geo. IV*, i. 322-3, 327-9. [6] *Dublin Evening Post*, 9, 11, 30 Jan., 6 Feb. 1823. [7] Ibid. 16, 19 Oct. 1824. [8] *O'Connell Corresp.* iii. 1278; *The Times*, 4 Mar.; *Dublin Evening Post*, 23 Mar. 1826. [9] *Dublin Evening Post*, 10 Sept. 1825, 2 Mar., 13 May, 6, 10, 13, 15, 24 June, 4, 6 July 1826. [10] Wellington mss WP1/1011/7; 1013/13. [11] *Dublin Evening Post*, 8 May 1830. [12] Ibid. 10, 17 July, 5, 10, 14, 24 Aug.; *Dublin Morning Post*, 28 July, 14 Aug.; NAI, Leveson Gower letter bks. Leveson Gower to Brabazon, 6 July 1830; Wellington mss WP1/1135/23; 1139/5. [13] *Dublin Evening Post*, 16 June, 25 Aug. 1831, 15, 17 May 1832; *Dublin Pollbook* (1837), 178. [14] Bodl. Talbot mss (NRA 29936); *Gen. Mem. of Fam. of Talbot of Malahide* (1829), 8; *CP*, vol. xii, pt. i. 626. [15] *Dublin Evening Post*, 1 Nov. 1849; *Gent. Mag.* (1850), i. 83-84. [16] *Gent. Mag.* (1862), i. 105.

S.M.F.

TAPPS, George William (1795–1842), of Hinton Admiral, Christchurch, Hants and 4 Stratford Place, Oxford Street, Mdx.

NEW ROMNEY	1826–1830
CHRISTCHURCH	1832–1837

b. 24 May 1795, o.s. of Sir George Ivison Tapps, 1st bt., of Hinton Admiral and Sarah, da. of Barrington Buggin, merchant, of 16 Harpur Street, Red Lion Square, Mdx. *educ.* Ealing (Mr. Goodenough); Trinity Coll. Camb. 1812; L. Inn 1815, called 1821. *m.* 26 Sept. 1825, Clara, da. of Augustus Eliott Fuller† of Rose Hill and Ashdown House, Suss., 3s. 1da. *suc.* fa. as 2nd bt. 15 Mar. 1835 and took additional name of Gervis by royal lic. 3 Dec. 1835. *d.* 26 Oct. 1842.

Tapps was a direct descendant of Richard Tapps, who married Catherine, the last surviving coheiress of George Gervis (1635-1718) of Islington. On the death without issue in 1751 of her eldest sister Lydia, the widow of Sir Peter Mews (?1672-1726), the latter's property at Hinton Admiral passed to the Tapps family. This Member's grandfather George Gervis Tapps bought property at Northchurch, Berkhampstead, from the Duncombes.[1] The implication of the phraseology of his will, made two months before his death in May 1774, was that the chief beneficiary George Ivison Tapps and his sister Jane Ivison Tapps were not his legitimate children, though they were living with and maintained by him. The will was left unadministered by its executors and on 4 July 1795 probate was granted to George Ivison Tapps, who had received a baronetcy in 1791 and served as sheriff of Hampshire, 1793-4.[2] He and his only son George William, who was bred to the bar but seems not to have practised, showed an interest in a seat for Christchurch on a vacancy in January 1818, but Lord Malmesbury dismissed their chances: 'They are not much liked. Sir George is a very narrow minded penurious fellow'.[3] Nothing came of it. At the general election of 1826 George William Tapps was returned for New Romney on the Dering interest. He made no mark in the House, where his only known votes were against Catholic relief, 12 May 1828, and emancipation, 6, 18, 30 Mar. 1829; this after being listed among the 'doubtful' on the issue by Planta, the Wellington ministry's patronage secretary. He is not known to have spoken in debate in this period and he gave up his seat at the 1830 dissolution.

Tapps came in unopposed as a Conservative for the greatly enlarged constituency of Christchurch in 1832 and 1835, when he succeeded to the baronetcy and, in accordance with his father's wish, took the additional name of Gervis.[4] He played a part in the urban development of eastern Bournemouth, and his marriage added property in Sussex to his holdings.[5] He died in October 1842, having directed in his will of 22 Jan. 1835 that 'one artery in each of my arms and legs shall be opened before my burial'. His personalty was sworn under £35,000.[6] On the death of his brother-in-law Owen John Augustus Fuller Meyrick in 1876 the Meyrick estates at Bodorgan, Anglesey, passed to Tapps's eldest son and successor Sir George Eliott Meyrick Tapps Gervis (1827-96), who took the further additional name of Meyrick.[7]

[1] *CB*, v. 278. [2] PROB 11/998/206. [3] Hants RO, Malmesbury mss, Malmesbury to Fitzharris, 17, 19 Jan. 1818. [4] R. Lavender, *From Pocket Borough to Parliamentary Democracy*, 14-15; PROB 11/1851/523. [5] *VCH Hants*, v. 81, 84, 134. [6] PROB 11/1970/747; IR26/1610/785. [7] E.H. Fellowes, *Descendants of Richard Garth*, 3.

D.R.F.

TAVISTOCK, mq. of *see* **RUSSELL**, **Francis**

TAYLOR, **Charles William** (1770–1857), of Burcott House, nr. Wells, Som. and Hollycombe, nr. Midhurst, Suss.

WELLS   1796–1830

b. 25 Apr. 1770, 2nd s. of Peter Taylor[†] of Burcott House and Purbrooke Park, nr. Portsmouth, Hants and w. Jane Holt. *educ.* Magdalen, Oxf. 1787. *m.* 25 Apr. 1808, Charlotte, da. of John Buncombe Poulett Thomson of Waverley Abbey, Roehampton, Surr., 1s. 1da. *suc.* bro. Robert Paris Taylor[†] 1792; *cr.* bt. 21 Jan. 1828. *d.* 10 Apr. 1857.
Lt. Som. militia 1789, capt. 1793, res. 1793.

Taylor, having succeeded to the family property on the death of his disreputable elder brother, whose last twelve years were spent in a debtors' prison, secured his position at Wells in 1796 through an alliance with Clement Tudway[†], whom he apparently obliged 'with an exchange of lands near his mansion'.[1] From 1815 Taylor, whose own moral reputation was dubious, shared the representation with Tudway's nephew John Paine Tudway, a Tory, and they were returned unopposed at the general election of 1820. He was an occasional attender who continued to act with the Whig opposition to Lord Liverpool's ministry, but is not known to have spoken in debate. He divided against the civil list, 5, 8 May, and the appointment of an additional baron of exchequer in Scotland, 15 May 1820. He was granted a month's leave for urgent private business, 9 June, and this was extended for

another month, 30 June 1820. He voted to restore Queen Caroline's name to the liturgy, 26 Jan., 13 Feb., but was absent from the division on the opposition censure motion, 6 Feb. 1821. He also missed the division on Catholic relief (which he had previously supported), 28 Feb 1821. He was allowed another month's leave, 18 May 1821. He voted for parliamentary reform, 25 Apr., and abolition of one of the joint-postmasterships, 2 May 1822. He divided against the naval and military pensions bill, 14 Apr., but was reportedly with ministers against repeal of the Foreign Enlistment Act, 16 Apr. 1823.[2] He voted to accuse lord chancellor Eldon of a breach of privilege, 1 Mar., repeal the window tax, 2 Mar., and reform the Scottish courts of justice, 30 Mar. 1824. He was absent from the call of the House relating to Burdett's Catholic relief motion, 28 Feb. 1825, and though he attended next day a newspaper later claimed that he had deliberately avoided voting.[3] He took no part in the other divisions on this issue, 21 Apr., 10 May 1825. His reticence on the Catholic question arose from the fact that his earlier support for emancipation was helping to fuel the growing opposition to him at Wells, as was his alleged failure properly to discharge his obligations as a Member. During the fiercely contested general election in 1826 his arch critic, the Tory county Member Sir Thomas Lethbridge, alleged that in 'the many and vital questions which had agitated [the] House [Taylor] had seldom if ever been found on one side or the other', although admittedly 'of late ... he had seen Mr. Taylor more frequently there'. Taylor's alliance with Tudway saved him, and a petition against their return was rejected.[4] He was almost entirely inactive in the 1826 Parliament. Unless he was the Taylor who made a brief intervention in defence of the Arigna Mining Company, 5 Dec. 1826, he did not speak in debate in this period. The Goderich ministry recommended him for a baronetcy in late 1827, and the award was confirmed by their successors.[5] In February 1829 Planta, the Wellington ministry's patronage secretary, listed him as likely to vote 'with government' for Catholic emancipation, and he divided accordingly, 6, 30 Mar. 1829. At the dissolution in 1830 it was reported that he would again stand for Wells, despite the opposition party having taken control of the corporation from Tudway, but no election address was issued and he quietly disappeared.[6]

Taylor spent the remainder of his long life playing the role of a hospitable and philanthropic country squire at his Hollycombe estate in Sussex, which he had acquired in about 1800 and where he had a house built from designs by Nash. It was said of him that in his habits Taylor was one of the last survivors of the

Regency age, 'when sporting adventure, witty society, and free indulgence in the luxuries of the dinner table, composed the daily and nightly routine of most men of wealth and fashion'. He had been a favourite companion of the prince of Wales and was regularly seen at Carlton House and Brighton. Fittingly, however, for one who lived into the more sober climate of the mid-Victorian years, Taylor's pious obituarist noted:

A consolation of a yet higher order than the reflection upon a mere amiable character or humane disposition is afforded ... by the knowledge that the advancing years and declining health of the venerable baronet had inspired him with solemn thoughts of a preparation for a future world ... A large portion of his time, of late years, was dedicated to religious meditation and reading.[7]

He died in April 1857 and was succeeded by his only son, Charles Taylor (1817-76); his personalty was sworn under £120,000.[8]

[1] *The Times*, 31 Aug. 1831. [2] Ibid. 22 Apr. 1823. [3] *Bristol Mirror*, 10 Sept. 1825. [4] Ibid. 8 July 1826. [5] Bucks. RO, Buckinghamshire mss, Goderich to George IV [Nov. 1827]. [6] *Bristol Mirror*, 17 July 1830. [7] *Gent. Mag.* (1857), i. 617-18. [8] PROB 11/2252/420; IR26/2112/401.

T.A.J.

TAYLOR, Sir Herbert (1775–1839), of Fan Court, Chertsey, Surr. and Little Camden House, Kensington, Mdx.[1]

NEW WINDSOR   1820–Feb. 1823

b. 29 Sept. 1775, 2nd s. of Rev. Edward Taylor (*d.* 1798) of Bifrons, nr. Canterbury, rect. of Patrixbourne, and Margaret, da. of Thomas Payler (formerly Turner) of Ileden, Kent. *educ.* privately on continent, 1780-92. *m.* 5 Oct. 1819, Charlotte Albinia, da. of Edward Disbrowe†, vice-chamberlain to Queen Charlotte, of Walton-upon-Trent, Derbys., 2s. *d.v.p.* 1da. KCH 1819; GCH 1825; GCB 16 Apr. 1834. *d.* 20 Mar. 1839.

Clerk, foreign office 1792-4; asst. mil. sec. and a.d.c to c.-in-c. 1795-8; mil. and priv. sec. and a.d.c. to ld. lt. [I] 1798-9; priv. sec. and a.d.c. to duke of York 1799-1805; priv. sec. to George III 1805-12, to Queen Charlotte 1812-18; mil. sec. to c.-in-c. 1820-7; first a.d.c. to George IV 1827-30; dep. sec. war office May-Aug. 1827; surveyor-gen. of ordnance 1828-9; adj.-gen. of forces 1828-30; priv. sec. and first a.d.c. to William IV 1830-7; first a.d.c. to Queen Victoria 1837-*d.*

Cornet 2 Drag. Gds. Mar. 1794, lt. July 1794, capt. 1795, maj. 1801; lt.-col. 9 W.I. Regt. 1801, half-pay 1803; capt. and lt.-col. 2 Ft. Gds. 1803; brevet col. 1810; maj.-gen. 1813; col. 85 Ft. 1823-*d.*; lt.-gen. 1825.

Master, St. Katharine's Hosp., London 1818-*d.*

Taylor was descended from a Shropshire family. His great-grandfather, John Taylor (1655-1729), bought Bifrons and other estates in Kent. His elder son, Brook Taylor (1685-1731), an eminent mathematician, left only a daughter and was succeeded at Bifrons by his brother Herbert (1698-1763), a clergyman. Herbert's first son and namesake died unmarried in 1767, when the estate passed to the second son, Edward Taylor, the father of this Member. He entered the church, becoming rector of the parish adjoining Bifrons, but was more interested in literature and agriculture than the ministry. In 1769 he married Margaret Payler, who, as well as three daughters, bore him five sons: Edward, who was Member for Canterbury, 1807-12; Herbert; the twins Brook and William, and Bridges. In 1780 the Rev. Taylor took his wife and children to Europe, where he wished his sons to be educated. Mrs. Taylor died, aged 36, at Brussels, in April that year. In 1782 the Taylors moved on to Heidelberg, and the following year to Carlsruhe, where they stayed until they returned briefly to England in 1788. From a succession of private tutors Herbert Taylor acquired a good knowledge of French and German and the rudiments of Italian, which he was able to improve when the family went to Italy in the summer of 1789, leaving behind Bridges, who was destined for the navy. The Rev. Taylor's house in Rome was a social centre for British residents and visitors, and it was there that Herbert, whose military ambitions were discouraged by his father, 'laid the foundations of friendships which became and continued very valuable at various stages of my subsequent career'. He made a particularly good impression on the 1st Lord Camelford, Pitt's cousin, who helped to obtain for him a clerkship in the foreign office, of which his kinsman (and later son-in-law) Lord Grenville was the head.[2]

Taylor was installed there in August 1792, after again wintering in Rome and travelling home through Switzerland and Germany. He was followed into the office by his brothers Brook, who later served as Grenville's private secretary and went on to carve out a distinguished career in diplomacy, and William, who was drowned in a boating accident on the Thames in 1797. Herbert Taylor was befriended and guided by the under-secretary, James Bland Burges†, and was occasionally given confidential employment by Grenville, who in December 1792 made him secretary to Sir James Murray† on his special mission to Prussian military headquarters at Frankfort. When Murray left to become adjutant-general to the duke of York's army based at Antwerp, Taylor took temporary charge in Frankfort. As he later recalled, 'my 17 years, my knowledge of languages and music, my official employment, with a moderate share of impudence, gave me access to almost every circle'. In April 1793 Murray secured Taylor's transfer to army headquarters as his secretary, remaining on the foreign office establishment at a salary of £300. Grenville and Bland Burges were at pains to obtain the Rev. Taylor's permission for this move, which had the object of 'bringing him forward in a manner which ... must infallibly advance his fortunes even beyond any expectation you may have formed', and to allay his fears for Herbert's physical safety. At Antwerp Taylor was presented to the duke of York. After a brief visit to London to equip himself, he returned to headquarters, now established at Bruges, and was present as a volunteer at the actions of May 1793 and the sieges of Valenciennes and Dunkirk. The awkwardness of his having nowhere officially to mess was solved by Murray's obtaining an open invitation from the duke of York to share his table. Taylor later wrote:

> Henceforth I was on velvet. But the few weeks' probation did me good. I had been brought forward early, and made much of at Frankfort; I was a great man in my own estimation. During several weeks after I joined at headquarters I found myself a sort of outcast from its circle. I was lowered a few pegs, and found my level. Still, I had brought with me too much of foreign manners and habits, and with these, a good share of assurance, not to say impudence, which led me to put myself forward in conversation with my seniors and betters, and to sport opinions very freely. Of this I was very soon corrected by remarks made in my presence ... The check was mortifying, but it was very salutary and useful ... I became more cautious and discreet ... Otherwise I was of a happy disposition, never lacking employment, or caring for difficulties, and I very soon received the kindest treatment on all hands; perfectly ready to work hard if necessary, but very fond of ... boy's play, amusement and every sort of fun ... and I enjoyed excellent health.

Taylor, whose linguistic skills made him particularly useful, remained with York as his assistant secretary when Murray returned to England in 1794. That year he obtained a commission in the 2nd Dragoon Guards, which terminated his connection with the foreign office, and he generally joined the regiment when it was in action. On York's departure in 1795 Taylor stayed on as assistant secretary to two successive commanders-in-chief of the British forces, Harcourt and Dundas.[3]

He went back to London in September 1795 to take up his duties as aide-de-camp and assistant military secretary to York as commander-in-chief of the army, working mainly in the office at Horse Guards. In July 1798 he went to Ireland as secretary to the lord lieu-

tenant, Lord Cornwallis, who came to rate him highly and, when York wished to recall him in November to become his own private secretary, asked for and obtained permission to retain his services until the end of January 1799: 'Captain Taylor, with great readiness and quickness of parts, is most indefatigable in business; and in honesty, fidelity and goodness of heart he has no superior'.[4] Taylor, whose father died while he was in Ireland, published anonymously in 1799 an *Impartial Relation* of the military operation against the French invasion of August 1798. He attended York as his aide-de-camp on the Helder expedition in September 1799, and saw action there. He continued as York's secretary, rising through the ranks of the army, until July 1805, when Pitt secured his appointment as private secretary to George III, whose sight was rapidly failing. The king placed every confidence in Taylor, who, as Lord Holland acknowledged, performed his delicate task with great 'discretion and judgement'.[5]

When the household was remodelled under the regency Taylor, who was made one of the statutory commissioners for managing the king's estate, became private secretary to Queen Charlotte on the Windsor establishment, but only after he had scotched the initial proposal to appoint him secretary to the groom of the stole in the king's household, which he considered a humiliation.[6] Had Sir Henry Bunbury* gone as governor to the Ionian Islands in December 1812, Taylor would have replaced him as under-secretary for war. As it was, a year later he got leave to go to Holland to liaise with the new provisional government and to make arrangements for the landing of British troops. In the subsequent campaign he commanded two brigades under General Thomas Graham†, who wrote to Bunbury, 15 Jan. 1814:

> He goes beyond all that I had heard of him. There is nobody I should wish more to keep. He will be a most serious loss to us ... He would make an excellent *chef d'etat major* to any army. His judgement and arrangement are so clear and good on all occasions, and he seems to like service as if he had always lived in a camp instead of a Court.

Taylor went to London in early March, and returned to the continent later that month on a special mission to Prince Bernadotte, commanding the Swedish army in Germany. On his arrival in London in April 1814 he learned that his youngest brother had been drowned on active service off Brindisi.[7] On the death of the queen in November 1818 Taylor, who was one of her executors, was without employment for sixteen months, though he enjoyed a civil list pension of £938.

He married a daughter of the late queen's chamberlain in 1819, was knighted that year and built a new mansion on a property which he had bought near Chertsey, but which he not long afterwards sold.[8]

It was 'very much against his inclination' that he submitted to the insistence of the new king that he come in for Windsor on the Court interest at the general election of 1820. He had agreed to do so when York pressed him to become military secretary at Horse Guards. Although he anticipated difficulties in combining the two roles and, according to his sister Mary, the wife of Edward Bootle Wilbraham*, 'would willingly have declined ... if he could have done so with propriety', he took up the post.[9] Charles Knight, editor of the *Windsor and Eton Express*, recalled Taylor at this period of his life:

> Sir Herbert was a man not versed in the common affairs of the outer world. He had been the depository of many a political secret which he could confide to no friend. Shy, painfully cautious, I have heard him break down in the most simple address to the electors when he first stood for Windsor; and yet a man of real ability.[10]

Taylor made no mark in the House, where he of course supported the Liverpool ministry, and is not known to have uttered a syllable in debate. He voted against economies in revenue collection, 4 July 1820. In June he had joined in the representations to Lord Liverpool for permanent provision to be made for certain of the late king's servants, who would otherwise be reduced to penury.[11] In September 1820 the duke of Wellington, master-general of the ordnance, who thought that the Horse Guards authorities were 'managing the affairs of the army exceedingly ill' by allowing soldiers to 'form combinations among each other' to air grievances, wrote to Taylor on the subject, 'pointing out to him how destructive such a system must be and strongly advising that severe measures should be taken to put a stop to it'. In reply Taylor, who was in the House for the debate of 18 Sept. on Queen Caroline's case, but was soon afterwards briefly troubled by a 'severe indisposition', assured Wellington that 'the necessity of extraordinary vigilance at this period is felt, and that this feeling is acted upon'. At the same time, he suggested that

> extreme caution must be used to avoid creating an impression that the fidelity of the troops is suspected, for this might produce the very evil which it is intended to avert. Nor do I believe that there is any cause to suspect their fidelity, or to apprehend that any serious effect has been or will be produced by the industrious attempts of the disaffected ... There is, however, one circumstance which has occurred to me ... that, whether from a sense

of his own increased importance which the soldier has acquired during the late war, or from being influenced to a certain extent by the latitude of opinion and observation upon public questions which has been assumed by the lower classes, grievances, whether real or supposed, are brought forward and urged in a more decided tone than heretofore, and the grievance of a few individuals is discussed and taken up by the large body, and brought forward as the common interest and object of the whole ... To what this may lead in time God knows; but if I am founded in this observation the natural inference is, that there never was any period when the utmost care and vigilance of the commanding officer was more required to guard even against the necessity of explanation.

He did not, however, think the problem serious enough to warrant the issuing of a general order, as Wellington proposed.[12]

Taylor voted in defence of ministers' conduct towards Caroline, 6 Feb. 1821. He voted against Catholic claims, 28 Feb. 1821, and the Catholic peers relief bill, 30 Apr. 1822. He was on the ministerial side in the divisions on repeal of the additional malt duty, 21 Mar., 3 Apr., the army estimates, 11 Apr., parliamentary reform, 9 May, miscellaneous services, 28 May, the duke of Clarence's grant, 18 June, economy and retrenchment, 27 June, and the alien office grant, 29 June 1821. That month he was instructed by York to let it be known that his decision not to accept the grand mastership of the Orange Lodges did not reflect any abatement of his hostility to Catholic relief.[13] Communications with Sir Robert Wilson*, dismissed from the army for inciting disorder at the queen's funeral, were made through Taylor, who privately thought he would condemn himself out of his own mouth when he protested his innocence in the House.[14] He voted against more extensive tax reductions, 11, 21 Feb., mitigation of the salt duties, 28 Feb., and abolition of one of the joint-postmasterships, 13 Mar. 1822. Finding the combined labour of his two positions impossible to sustain, he retired from Parliament at the start of the 1823 session, when he was replaced by his brother-in-law, Edward Disbrowe, and soon afterwards accepted the colonelcy of the 85th Foot.[15]

Taylor continued to 'drudge' at Horse Guards until the death in January 1827 of York, whose declining days he described that year in a chronicle of his *Last Illness*.[16] Having poured cold water on the king's scheme to take personal command of the army, with Taylor as adjutant-general, he remained in his post under Wellington, the new commander-in-chief.[17] When Wellington resigned on the formation of Canning's ministry, the king again made a bid for the command, with Taylor as the efficient secretary.

This plan was thwarted, and for the four months until Wellington was reinstated after Canning's death Taylor carried out the duties of his former post as deputy to Lord Palmerston,* the secretary at war and acting commander-in-chief. On stepping down from this 'situation of extreme anxiety and delicacy', as one observer characterized it, he was without employment for several months: he resisted pressure to take the military command in India, and waived his pretensions to the governorship of the Cape, which he would have preferred, in favour of Sir Lowry Cole*.[18] In March 1828 he was appointed surveyor-general of the ordnance in Wellington's ministry; and in September he was 'delighted' to become adjutant-general, at the pressing request of George IV, who was said to like him 'better than anybody' of those about him. (He had made Taylor his principal aide-de-camp, a new post, the previous year.) In 1828 he moved into the newly built lodge of St. Katharine's Hospital in Regent's Park, in the mastership of which he had succeeded his father-in-law in 1818.[19]

It was with 'great reluctance' that Taylor submitted to William IV's desire to appoint him as his private secretary on his accession. He turned down an offer of the privy purse, the £3,000 salary of which was divided equally between himself and Sir Henry Wheatley. As he told his brother:

> This is less by £500 than I had and I quit a situation more permanent, more satisfactory and less laborious; but this circumstance places me on high ground, and will assist me materially in maintaining the independent footing and tone which are most essential towards enabling me to overcome various difficulties that may occur.

Within a month he found 'the fatigue ... beyond any I ever experienced, although God knows my life has not been an idle one'.[20] Yet he served the king in this capacity, writing most of his letters in his own hand and being the channel for all his communications with his ministers, for the duration of his reign. He had a particularly tricky course to steer while the reform bills were before Parliament, but Lord Grey, according to his son, was entirely satisfied with the way in which Taylor 'acquitted himself of the very difficult and delicate duties of his situation' and felt that the influence which he undoubtedly exercised over the king was 'only used for the purpose of allaying the feelings of irritation created at times in his ... mind, and of smoothing any difficulties that arose between him and his ministers'. Taylor, who feared above all 'a schism and collision' between the two Houses of Parliament, and had come to believe by June 1831 that 'a revolutionary spirit' was threatening the country, saw that

reform had to be effected; and he played a significant role in persuading Tory peers to abandon their opposition on the reinstatement of the Grey ministry, with the king's promise of a creation to carry the bill, in May 1832. Denis Le Marchant[†] commented that this intervention was

> more to his honour, as he was a Tory of the old school, and had always kept up some connection with the party. He said to me at the time,'I should have opposed the bill in every stage had I remained in the House of Commons, but I see that it is for the king's interest that it should be carried, and I have done my best to assist the ministers accordingly'.

Lord Holland, whose suggestion of a peerage for Taylor in September 1831 was not taken up, thought him 'a laborious, distinct, discreet, and honourable man'.[21] Inevitably, there was criticism of Taylor at various points during the passage of the bills from both the opponents and supporters of reform; but he was generally reckoned to have conducted himself with tact, discretion and honesty, and to have kept the king to constitutional paths. Perhaps the most serious charge that could be levelled against him was that he was 'too fond of writing', and 'voluminously inclined' in his letters to ministers.[22]

On the death of William IV Taylor, whose health had been impaired by his secretarial labours, retired, though he was made principal aide-de-camp to Queen Victoria. After tidying up the king's affairs, he went with his wife and 12-year old daughter Charlotte Mary Louisa, known as 'Chaddy', to Cannes, where he had bought land on which a 'most elegant and convenient' villa was being built. (His sons, Edward Herbert and Frederick, born in 1823 and 1826 respectively, had not survived infancy; and there was no truth in the story that David Urquhart, a future Member for Stafford, was his illegitimate son.)[23] In the summer of 1838 he was at Lake Como, from where he wrote *Remarks on an Article in the Edinburgh Review*, repudiating personal attacks by Lord Brougham on George III, Queen Charlotte and George IV.[24] He wintered in Rome, but his health collapsed, and he died peacefully there, not long after saying 'Good night, Pussy' to his daughter, as usual, in March 1839. After temporary burial in the British cemetery, his remains were returned to England for interment in the chapel of St. Katharine's in June 1839.[25] By his brief will, a memorandum drawn up at Brighton, 30 Jan. 1834, Taylor left all his property, which consisted chiefly of insurance policies on his own life, to his wife, his sole executrix.[26] An obituary acknowledged his 'able and indefatigable administration' of army business, and paid tribute to his 'urbanity, kindness and attention' in that capacity.[27] Despite their differences, Brougham commended him as a royal secretary:

Sir Herbert Taylor's exercise of such a delicate office ... was throughout marked by the most unsullied honour towards all parties with whom he came into contact ... Upon all occasions his best advice was offered according to the dictates of a scrupulous conscience, and a judgement hardly to be surpassed in clearness and calmness, although certainly biased by what we should call some very erroneous opinions – the result of early prejudices not yet thrown off ... In the exercise of a most difficult and laborious duty he was one of the ablest, indeed the most masterly men of business who ever filled any public employment.[28]

[1] Based on *Taylor Pprs.* ed. E. Taylor (1913), which contains (pp. 1-45) Taylor's personal reminiscences of his early life. See also *Oxford DNB.* [2] *Taylor Pprs.* 1-16. [3] Ibid. 17-51. [4] Ibid. 50-57; *Cornwallis Coresp.* ii. 352-3, 430-1, 436, 446; iii. 40. [5] *Taylor Pprs.* 57-58; *Colchester Diary*, ii. 16; *Geo. III Corresp.* iv. 3123; Holland, *Further Mems.* 61. [6] *Taylor Pprs.* 70-76; *Prince of Wales Corresp.* viii. 3308, 3310, 3312. [7] *HMC Bathurst*, 222; *Taylor Pprs.* 86-165. [8] *Taylor Pprs.* 172-80; Add. 62954, f. 182; E.W. Brayley and E. Walford, *Hist. Surr.* ii. 18. [9] *Taylor Pprs.* 184-5; *Colchester Diary*, iii. 126; *The Times*, 24 Feb., 8 Mar. 1820. [10] C. Knight, *Passages of a Working Life*, i. 229-30. [11] Add. 38285, f. 174. [12] *Arbuthnot Jnl.* i. 38; *Wellington Despatches*, i. 144-8. [13] *Taylor Pprs.* 185-6. [14] *HMC Bathurst*, 511, 514; Add. 40344, f. 337. [15] *Taylor Pprs.* 186. [16] *Geo. IV Letters*, iii. 1085; *Taylor Pprs.* 189-94. [17] Parker, *Peel*, i. 434-4; *Hobhouse Diary*, 125; *Arbuthnot Jnl.* ii. 72; *HMC Bathurst*, 621. [18] *Taylor Pprs.* 194-5, 206-13; *Wellington Despatches*, iii. 645-6, 647-9; iv. 82-83, 100-1; *Colchester Diary*, iii. 485; *Canning's Ministry*, 210, 283, 296; *Geo. IV Letters*, iii. 1355; *Hobhouse Diary*, 139; *Arbuthnot Corresp.* 83; *Prince of Wales Corresp.* viii. 3463. [19] *Wellington Despatches*, iv. 302, 668, 670-2; *Geo. IV Letters*, iii. 1530, 1531; *Greville Mems.* i. 223-4; *Taylor Pprs.* 205, 218. [20] *Taylor Pprs.* 319; Add. 62953, ff. 167, 171, 178, 180, 185; *Arbuthnot Jnl.* ii. 357; *Croker Pprs.* ii. 67. [21] *Grey-William IV Corresp.* vol. i. pp. xiii-xiv; Add. 62953, ff. 188; 62954, ff. 70, 126; Le Marchant, *Althorp*, 434; Russell, *Recollections*, 107-8; *Arbuthnot Corresp.* 163; *Holland House Diaries*, 55, 181. [22] *Windsor and Eton Express*, 2, 9, 16 Apr.; *The Times*, 9, 18 Apr. 1831; Add. 62954, f. 48; *Three Diaries*, pp. xvi, 174, 260, 262; *Taylor Pprs.* 339-58; *Grey-William IV Corresp.* vol. i, p. xiv; *Greville Mems.* ii. 387. See M. Brock, *Great Reform Act*, 174-5, 272, 303, 304-5; E.A. Smith, *Lord Grey*, 264, 267, 272, 275-7. [23] *Taylor Pprs.* 393, 398, 411, 413-98; *Holland House Diaries*, 337, 382. [24] *Taylor Pprs.* 498-504; *Von Neumann Diary*, ii. 88; *Edinburgh Rev.* lxvii (1838), 1-80; lxviii (1838-9), 191-262. [25] *Taylor Pprs.* 505-12; Add. 62954, f. 183; *The Times*, 28, 30 Mar., 11 Apr. 1839. [26] PROB 11/1912/399; IR26/1530/385; *Gent. Mag.* (1830), ii. 670. [27] *Gent. Mag.* (1839), ii. 654. [28] *Edinburgh Rev.* lxviii. 192.

D.R.F.

TAYLOR, Michael Angelo (1757-1834), of Cantley Hall, nr. Doncaster, Yorks. and Whitehall Yard, Mdx.

POOLE	1784-1790
HEYTESBURY	22 Dec. 1790-Feb. 1791
POOLE	25 Feb. 1791-1796
ALDEBURGH	1796-7 Mar. 1800
DURHAM	17 Mar. 1800-1802
RYE	1806-1807
ILCHESTER	1807-1812
POOLE	1812-1818
DURHAM	1818-1831
SUDBURY	1832-16 July 1834

bap. 13 July 1757,[1] o.s. of Sir Robert Taylor, architect, of Spring Gardens, Mdx. and his w. Elizabeth (*d.* 27 Dec. 1803). *educ.* Westminster 1766; Corpus, Oxf. 21 Oct. 1774, aged 17; I. Temple 1769; L. Inn 1770, called 1774. *m.* 7 Aug. 1789, Frances Anne, da. and h. of Rev. Sir Henry Vane, 1st bt., of Long Newton, co. Dur., *s.p.* *suc.* fa. 1788. *d.* 16 July 1834.

Recorder, Poole 1784-*d.*; member of council, duchy of Cornw. 1808; PC 23 Feb. 1831.

Maj. commdt. Skirack vols. 1804.

A diminutive, pompous and well-meaning barrister committed to reforming the court of chancery, Taylor had abandoned Pittite Toryism shortly after entering Parliament in 1784 and thereafter he consistently advocated the removal of religious disabilities, the abolition of sinecures, parliamentary and criminal law reform and lower taxes. Recalled by John Hobhouse* as 'an incredible coxcomb, but good-natured and not altogether without capacity', his boast in 1827 that he had supported the Whigs, who made his Whitehall house their rendezvous, 'for eight and thirty years at an expense of above £30,000' was substantially correct. He also routinely marshalled snippets gleaned at his dinner table and elsewhere into informative letters to Lords Darlington and Grey and the Whig hierarchy.[2] They, according to the Tory Lord Lowther*, the target of misinformation circulated by Taylor at Doncaster races in 1825, used him as 'a sort of common crier or parrot that will repeat and blazon about anything that is told him'.[3]

Taylor's second return for Durham in 1818 on his wife's interest had not been contested, but a family dispute and futile appeal to chancery that year by Mrs. Taylor, who opposed the marriage of her niece and joint custodian of the Vane interest, Lady Frances Vane Tempest, to Lord Castlereagh's* half-brother and heir, Lord Charles William Stewart[†], prompted a challenge to him at the general election of 1820 by Stewart's friend and prospective brother-in-law Sir Henry Hardinge. The Tory Richard Wharton's[†] decision to contest the county restored Lambton-Tempest control in Durham without a contest and for the next decade Taylor represented the city with Hardinge as the nominee of the county Member, John Lambton, notwithstanding the residual Vane interest he commanded.[4] On the hustings at the 1820 city and county elections he defended Lambton and denounced the repressive legislation enforced by Lord Liverpool's administration after Peterloo, although his parliamentary speeches had condoned restrictions on public meetings.[5]

A steady but unaffiliated supporter of the Whig opposition led by Tierney in the 1818 Parliament, Taylor divided with them on most major issues in that of 1820, voting also occasionally with his friend and frequent guest Thomas Creevey and the 'Mountain' for economy, retrenchment and reduced taxation and consistently for criminal law reform, against military flogging and to end West Indian slavery. A radical publication of 1825 noted correctly that he 'attended frequently and voted with opposition; spoke often'.[6] However, except on matters affecting the courts and the London area, his views were rarely heeded. Drawing on his experience as a prison visitor and victim of a personal assault and robbery in July 1820, he supported the call for an improved police system, 17 Apr. 1821; but he voiced his reservations about the merits of the metropolitan force established by Peel, 15 June 1830.[7] He supported the 1820-1 parliamentary and extra-parliamentary campaigns on behalf of Queen Caroline, but did not speak on the subject after his questions on the Milan commission were ridiculed on both sides of the House, 24 June 1820.[8] Two days later he received ten days' leave on private business. He voted, 28 Feb. 1821, and paired, 1 Mar. 1825, for Catholic relief, but he stated in the House, 28 Mar., and to Darlington afterwards, that as an opponent of the attendant franchise bill, he could not give further support to the 1825 measure.[9] He stewarded at the *London Tavern*, 3 Apr. 1821, and divided for parliamentary reform, 9, 10 May 1821, 25 Apr. 1822 (as a pair), 2 June 1823, 27 Apr. 1826, having missed the division on Lambton's proposals through dining with him, 18 Apr. 1821.[10] He joined its presenter Thomas Coke I in denouncing William Cobbett's[†] radical Norfolk petition as the work of an anti-reformer, a 'mass of absurdities ... false statements ... [and] a farrago of inconclusive reasoning', 24 Apr. 1823.

Undeterred by the rejection of his annual schemes to reduce chancery delays, he resumed his campaign directly the queen's case was resolved by proposing a resolution of intent, committing the House to address the issue early in 1822, which ministers narrowly defeated (by 56-52), 30 May 1821. He reviewed his attempts since 1808 to reform chancery, highlighted

Sir Samuel Romilly's[†] role in securing inquiry in 1811 and discussed the shortcomings of the court without criticizing its personnel or lord chancellor Eldon.[11] His next attempt, which failed by 51-108, 26 June 1822, targeted the vice-chancellor's court and was backed by the chancery barrister John Williams, who, by making the attack a personal one on Eldon, caused ministers to initiate an inquiry in the Lords. Taylor supported Williams in a major speech, 28 Apr., was a minority teller for adjourning his motion, 4 June 1823, and divided for it the next day.[12] He denounced the terms of the 1824 commission (established in his absence and packed with government supporters), 31 May, and supported further inquiry, 7 June 1825. When the attorney-general Sir Charles Wetherell moved to effect the commission's recommendations, 18 May 1826, Taylor conceded that their report was not without merit, blamed Eldon for failing to recommend setting up a separate court for bankruptcy proceedings and refuted suggestions that chancery arrears were illusory. He also suggested appointing a deputy Speaker for the Lords to give the lord chancellor more time to attend to the business of his court, an idea subsequently taken up by Brougham and included in the 1830 Act. On other judicial matters, he recommended giving a criminal jurisdiction to the court of pleas, 3 July 1821,[13] and, harrying the lord advocate, he backed the Whig Thomas Kennedy's proposals for the Scottish court of session and the Scottish juries bill, 12, 14, 16 Feb. 1821, 26 Apr., 28 June 1822.[14] He objected to the compensation payments proposed for former Irish exchequer court officers, 21 Mar. 1821,[15] and backed Lord Cawdor's abortive scheme for abolishing the Welsh courts of great sessions and judicature, 23 May 1822. He called for a full investigation into the lord advocate's conduct in the Borthwick case, observing that it 'had little to do with Scottish law', 3 June, and urged prompt inquiry into allegations against the Irish chief baron O'Grady, 13 June 1823. He defended the principle of the 1824 county courts bill and had the county clerk of Durham, previously overlooked as a bishop's appointee, added to the list of court officers to be compensated, 26 Mar. 1824.

Taylor's examination of the printer Weaver helped to confirm the involvement of Lord Londonderry (as Castlereagh had become) in *John Bull*'s libel on Henry Grey Bennet*, 9 May, and he contributed to the clamour for printing the evidence, 10, 11 May 1821.[16] He was for investigating the Constitutional Association's libel action against the proprietor of the *Examiner*, 28 May 1823, but made it clear that he would have no truck with Hume and the radicals' defence of Deist publications, 3 June 1824. As the president of the India board Charles Williams Wynn had anticipated,[17] he voted in the opposition majority for inquiry into the prosecution of the Dublin Orange rioters, 22 Apr., and intervened repeatedly during it, 2, 23 May. 1823.[18] He opposed the Irish tithes composition bill and complained that the Irish church hierarchy were grossly overpaid, 30 May 1823. Taylor's large head and small limbs (which Gilray caricatured) were hard to disguise, and according to Creevey he was 'smoaked instantly ... and got most infernally hustled' when he 'went as a Jew peddler and knife seller' to the masquerade that July.[19]

Taylor's 1821 bill to control the nuisance of steam engine smoke, which he claimed affected his London home, was hatched in the investigative committees he secured in 1819 and 1820 and shaped to promote the chimney system patented by the Warwick manufacturer Parkes, which he viewed on 11 Apr. 1820, and described in the House, 2 May 1820, 18 Apr. 1821. He overcame opposition from the mining and iron districts of Cornwall, Staffordshire and South Wales, Londonderry's hostility and complaints by Fowell Buxton and other opponents of compulsion to carry the bill's committal by 83-29, 7 May, and third reading, 10 May. It received royal assent, 28 May 1821, after he had added a rider exempting mine engines (1 & 2 Geo. IV, c. 41).[20] The author of the 1817 London Paving and Lighting Act (57 Geo. III, c. 29), he spoke regularly on metropolitan matters, and his stage coaches bill received royal assent, 6 June 1820 (1 Geo. IV, c. 4). He presented the wharfingers' petitions on the dangerous state of London Bridge, 1 May 1820, and called for the construction of a new one, 29 Apr. 1822.[21] He brought up the report on the contentious Stoke Newington vestry bill, 27 Mar. 1821. He supported inquiry into the water supply, although he disputed its instigator William Fremantle's account of the water companies, 6 Feb. 1821. He later backed the corporation of London's petition criticizing the 'bubble' Metropolitan Waterworks Company, 11 Mar., and called for better regulation, 18 May 1825. He opposed the establishment of University College, London from a conviction that the discipline and education at Oxford were superior and that Brougham's liberal views were bound to fail, 3 June 1825.[22]

As recorder, Taylor retained a keen interest in matters affecting Poole, where his standing had plummeted following repeated failures to secure concessions for or inquiry into the Newfoundland trade. As his interventions of 5 June 1820 and 23 Feb. 1821 on the timber duties presaged, he opposed relaxa-

tion of the navigation laws because it would 'transfer the trade of England to the opposite shores', 7, 20 May 1822.[23] Alluding to the damage wrought by the American concessions on the Newfoundland trade and the need for help from all quarters, he backed both Wilmot Horton's abortive Newfoundland laws bill, 25 Mar., and Hume's proposal for inquiry into the fisheries, which Horton opposed, 14 May 1823. He presented and endorsed the South Shields petition against the reciprocity duties, 1 July 1823.[24] Attending to constituency business, he presented and endorsed petitions for changes in the laws affecting debtors, 20 May 1822, and against the bankruptcy, 11 June 1823, hides and skins, 29 Mar., and beer retail bills, 17 May 1824.[25] Deputizing for Lambton, he presented petitions from the coal owners of Sunderland against the new shipping regulations, 18 May 1824, and several against slavery, 24 Feb., 9, 20 Mar., 18 Apr. 1826.[26] On the hustings at Durham at the general election in June, when he was unopposed, he reviewed his 'sixty-nine years' and defined a Whig as a man who would not accept office 'unless by his intervention the people were allowed to have their due weight and influence' in the Commons. He also accounted for his stance on Catholic relief in 1825 and advocated reform of chancery and the civil courts and the abolition of slavery.[27] In October 1826 he joined the Whig and Durham hierarchy at Lambton races.[28]

Taylor added his voice to Horton's in defence of the Australian Mining Company, 5 Dec. 1826. Except on the chancery question, he kept a low profile in the House while the succession to Lord Liverpool as premier was determined. He divided for Catholic relief, 6 Mar., and a 50s. pivot price for corn imports, 9 Mar., was a minority teller on the Dublin election petition, 20 Mar., and voted for information on the Barrackpoor mutiny, 22 Mar. 1827. He stressed that the protectionist petitions he presented from Sunderland's ship owners, 21 Mar., and millers, 2 Apr., were motivated solely by distress.[29] With Williams out of Parliament, he drafted a motion to remove bankruptcy jurisdiction from chancery, but withdrew it pending the announcement of favourable ministerial proposals, 27 Feb. Dissatisfied with the reforms announced by the master of the rolls Copley, 'a tub to catch the whale', 23 Mar., he voted in Harvey's minority for inquiry, 5 Apr., and on 22 May revived his 27 Feb. motion, which now also served to test support for the new Canning administration and failed by 37-134. Ministerial backing for separation had evaporated and Brougham, who had endorsed similar proposals by Williams, but now supported ministers, declined to vote. The experience confirmed Taylor in his mistrust of Canning and his administration, which 'dissected both Whigs and Tories'.[30] On 14 June 1827 he withdrew his proposals to end the system of appointing nominees to election committees, in deference to Williams Wynn.[31]

Writing to Grey, 23 Jan. 1828, Taylor described the duke of Wellington's new administration as a 'liberal government founded upon the exclusion of the Ultra Tories' and a reputed expedient until George IV could be persuaded to make the home secretary Peel prime minister.[32] He had shared in the unease over Codrington's victory at Navarino and stated his opposition to the treaty behind the battle, 31 Jan. 1828.[33] After much 'whingeing to Eldon' about the ministers 'and vice versa',[34] he prefaced his motion of 12 Feb. for chancery reform with a statement directly criticizing the system, not past and present lord chancellors. Now projecting himself as an individual fighting vested interests, he protested at his deliberate exclusion from the 1825-7 chancery commission, spoke of the cost and delay to claimants and the absurdity of the lord chancellor's position as head of both chancery and its appellate court, the House of Lords. George Bankes and Brougham, believing that the remedy lay in distributing business to 'cheaper' local courts, would have none of it, and the motion was rejected. Taking a less dogmatic approach, he moved for inquiry into 'the actual state of chancery', 24 Apr., but Peel deemed his proposal too abstract and killed it, 91-42. He continued to press ministers, request returns and table motions while legislation was awaited from the Lords, 10 May 1828, 5, 6, 10 Feb., 25 May 1829, when he asked Peel to hold over the chancery bill to allow time for discussion. He presented several petitions (18 Feb.-29 Apr.) and voted for repeal of the Test Acts, 26 Feb., and divided for Catholic relief, 12 May. 1828. He was shut out of the division on civil list pensions, 20 May, voted against the archbishop of Canterbury's registrar bill, 16 June, and divided for ordnance reductions, 4 July. He supported Durham petitions for repeal of the stamp duty on receipts under £20, 25 Feb., and against the small debts bill, 23 June 1828. That day, making the department of woods and forests and their 'unauthorized' payments to the architect Nash for work on Buckingham House his particular targets, he proposed a critical resolution setting out the sums spent without parliamentary consent (£250,000, 10 Mar. 1826-30 June 1827), which was defeated by 181-102. He reiterated his complaints against Nash, 12 May 1829.

The prosecution at Marlborough Street on 9 Jan. 1829 of his former footman for disrupting one of Taylor's dinners and keeping his livery created a stir and was widely reported.[35] He divided for Catholic

emancipation, 6, 30 Mar., having presented and endorsed favourable petitions, 20 Feb., and he commended the government's decision to concede it and Peel's candidature for Oxford University when hostile petitions were presented from South Shields, 4 Mar., and Durham, 10 Mar. He seconded Alderman Wood's motion to have Lowther, whose office as commissioner of woods and forests was in abeyance pending the issue's resolution, added to the committee on private bills, 17 Mar., and presented petitions for referral to it that day on the Clarence railway bill. He also defended the conduct of the crew of the Sunderland collier brig *Rosanna*, who had been denied compensation after being sunk by a navy vessel, 22 May 1829. He voted to transfer East Retford's seats to Birmingham, 5 May 1829, 11 Feb., and paired 5 Mar. 1830.

As one of the '28 opposition Members' who voted against Knatchbull's amendment to include reference to distress in the address, 4 Feb., Taylor explained (12 Feb., 2 Mar. 1830) that the Whig party with whom he had long acted had 'dwindled away', and that he would remain a lifelong Whig, unconnected with ministers, but prepared to support them on retrenchment and to oppose currency reform.[36] He voted for Lord Blandford's reform scheme, 18 Feb., and paired for Lord John Russell's, 28 May, having voted for inquiry into Newark's allegations against the duke of Newcastle, 1 Mar., but not the enfranchisement of Birmingham, Leeds and Manchester, 23 Feb. He welcomed proposals to prevent Members voting on bills in which they had a pecuniary interest, 26 Feb. He voted, 5 Apr., and paired, 17 May, for Jewish emancipation, likewise the abolition of capital punishment for forgery, 7 June, which he had urged when presenting Durham petitions, 12 Mar., 29 Apr., and again, 13 May. He voted against the proposed expenditure on Woolwich, 30 Apr., public buildings, 3 May, and South American missions, 7 June. He advocated inquiry into the Irish church, 4 Mar., and voted in the minorities on Irish first fruit revenues, 18 May, and for inquiry into the conduct of the church commissioners, 17 June. He monitored the progress of the chancery bill closely in the Lords and made it known that he would not permit it to fail 'without generating some discussion', 18 May, and that he was prepared to compromise to avoid further time-wasting inquiry, 10 June. Highlighting the notorious case of Lord Portsmouth's lunacy, he proposed legislating to give the lord chancellor the right to refer similar cases to courts of record, 2 Mar., so prompting the disclosure on the 18th that such power already existed. On the administration of justice bill, he poured scorn on the arguments for preservation of the Welsh judicature, but expressed regret that its abolition facilitated the appointment of only one additional chancery judge, 17, 18 June 1830. He topped the poll in a three-cornered contest at Durham at the general election in August, when the Ultra Gresley, as Londonderry's nominee, defeated the Whig Chaytor to become Hardinge's replacement; but he had to spend £5,000-£7,000 and he was compromised by allegations of collusion, and severely criticized for failing to divide frequently with the revived Whig opposition.[37] In September 1830 he accompanied his wife and Creevey to North Wales, whence he attributed Huskisson's fatal railway accident to a partial paralysis caused by a prostate complaint.[38]

The Wellington ministry listed Taylor among their 'foes', and he divided against them on the civil list when they were brought down, 15 Nov. 1830. He presented and endorsed Durham petitions against debtors' prisons, 3 Nov., and West Indian slavery, 5, 11, 17, 23 Nov., ordered chancery returns as hitherto, 10 Nov., and moved the adjournment by which Sugden's inquiry motion, calculated to embarrass Brougham as the new Grey ministry's lord chancellor, was postponed, 16 Dec. He rallied for administration when it came on on the 20th. Responding to opposition criticism that day, he maintained that he had voted in 1823 to try O'Grady solely with a view to enabling him to clear his name, and no longer thought there were grounds for prosecution. Creevey, to whom Taylor confided his disappointment that Grey had omitted to reward his loyalty with a peerage, membership of the privy council or a secure Commons seat, claimed the credit for securing his admission to the council in February 1831 and duly ridiculed the event.[39] Promoting reform, Taylor sent a letter of support to the Durham meeting, 7 Jan., and presented and endorsed their petition, 3 Feb., when 'as a reformer of many years standing' he urged the House to back the forthcoming ministerial measure 'with one voice'.[40] He presented and endorsed further favourable petitions, but not the ballot, 8 Feb., 14 Mar., and voted for the second reading of the ministerial bill, 22 Mar., and against Gascoyne's wrecking amendment, 19 Apr. 1831. He stood down at the ensuing dissolution after belatedly canvassing Durham, where the dissatisfaction of the disfranchised freemen was directed against him and the reformers, resenting his refusal to spend or support Chaytor's son at the recent by-election, made him the scapegoat for their failure to return two Members.[41] Vexed at being deprived of the pleasure of seeing Taylor returned for Durham, his wife blamed the Lambtons for deserting him and the party for forgetting his sacrifices for Grey.[42]

Taylor applied in vain to Grey for a coronation peerage and church patronage for his nephew by marriage, the Rev. 'Jack' Vane, with whose assistance he brokered an introduction to the venal borough of Sudbury, which returned him as a Liberal at the general election of 1832.[43] He died without issue at his London house, 16 July 1834, recalled by Creevey as a 'gentleman of small stature and modest sagacity, but greatly assisted to some distinction by his clever and ambitious wife'.[44] By his will, dated 14 July 1831 and proved under £100,000, he bequeathed a life interest in his London property and Bank stocks to his wife, with reversion to Vane as his executor and residuary legatee. He provided generously for his servants, left his racing cups to his friends William Joseph Denison* and Sir Ronald Ferguson*, and gave £50,000 in Irish currency to Oxford University to endow the Taylor language scholarship in memory of his father.[45]

[1] IGI (Mdx.). [2] Broughton, *Recollections*, ii. 177; *Creevey Pprs.* i. 211; ii. 65, 89-91, 105, 116; Brougham mss, Darlington to Brougham, 29 Mar. 1821; Grey mss, Darlington to Grey, 8 Sept. 1825. [3] Lonsdale mss, Lowther to Lonsdale, 24 Sept. 1825. [4] Durham CRO, Londonderry mss D/Lo/C83/3(1), 13(1), 14, 16(1), 17; *Crabb Robinson Diary*, i. 312; Brougham mss, Taylor to J. Brougham, 5 Feb. and n.d.; NLI, Vesey Fitzgerald mss 7858, A.E. Grant to Vesey Fitzgerald, 9 Feb.; PRO NI, Londonderry (Castlereagh) mss D3030/Q2/2; *The Times*, 18 Feb.; *Newcastle Courant*, 19 Feb.; *Durham Chron.* 4, 25 Mar. 1820; A.J. Heesom, *Durham City and Its MPs*, 23-24. [5] *The Times*, 7, 13 Mar. 1820. [6] *Session of Parl. 1825*, p. 487. [7] *The Times*, 18 July 1820, 18 Apr. 1821. [8] Add. 52444, f. 172; Dorset RO, Bond mss D/BoH C15, Jekyll to Bond, 4 July; *Newcastle Courant*, 9, 16 Dec. 1820. [9] Grey mss, Darlington to Grey, 8 Apr. 1825. [10] *The Times*, 4, 5 Apr. 1821; Broughton, ii. 150. [11] *The Times*, 20 June 1820; HLRO, Hist Coll. 379, Grey Bennet diary, 90. [12] *The Times*, 27 June 1822, 29 Apr. 1823. [13] Ibid. 4 July 1821. [14] Ibid. 13 Feb. 1821, 27 Apr., 29 June 1822. [15] Ibid. 22 Mar. 1821. [16] Ibid. 10-12 May 1821. [17] Buckingham, *Mems. Geo. IV*, i. 446. [18] *The Times*, 3, 24 May 1823. [19] *Creevey's Life and Times*, 186. [20] Arnould, *Denman*, 131-2; *The Times*, 29 Apr. 1820, 20 Apr., 1, 8 May 1821; *CJ*, lxxvi. 329, 383. [21] *The Times*, 29 Apr., 2, 6, 17 May 1820, 30 Apr. 1822. [22] Ibid. 4 June 1825. [23] Ibid. 24 Feb. 1821, 8 May 1822. [24] Ibid. 2 July 1823. [25] Ibid. 21 May 1822, 12 June 1823, 30 Mar., 18 May 1824. [26] Ibid. 19 May, 1824, 25 Feb., 10, 21 Mar., 19 Apr. 1826. [27] Ibid. 30 May, 2, 6 June; *Durham Chron.* 17 June 1826. [28] *Creevey's Life and Times*, 223. [29] *The Times*, 10 Mar., 3 Apr. 1827. [30] Ibid. 5, 6 Dec. 1826, 10 Mar.; Grey mss, Taylor to Grey [Feb.]; *Creevey Pprs.* ii. 116; NLS, Ellice mss, Grey to Ellice, 31 May 1827. [31] *The Times*, 15 June 1827. [32] Grey mss, Taylor to Grey, 23 Jan. 1828. [33] Ibid. Taylor to Grey, 16 Nov. 1827. [34] *Creevey Pprs.* (1912 edn.) 494. [35] *The Times*, 10 Jan. 1829. [36] A. Mitchell, *Whigs in Opposition*, 218. [37] Derbys. RO, Gresley of Drakelow mss D77/38/5, Durham to Gresley, 2 July, W.E. Mousley to same, 29 July; Londonderry mss C86/13-15; Creevey mss, Creevey to Miss Ord, 25 Aug.; *Procs. at Durham City Election* (1830), 17-23. [38] *Creevey Pprs.* ii. 213; Add. 51594, Luttrell to Lady Holland, 23 Sept. 1830. [39] Creevey mss, Creevey to Miss Ord, 7 Jan 1831; *Creevey's Life and Times*, 334, 337. [40] *Newcastle Chron.* 15 Jan. 1831. [41] *Durham Co. Advertiser*, 29 Apr., 6 May; Londonderry mss C86/17; Creevey mss, Creevey to Miss Ord, 3 May; Wellington mss WP1/1184/3; Grey mss, Chaytor to Grey, 16 May 1831. [42] Creevey mss, Mrs. Taylor to Creevey [30 Apr. 1831]. [43] Grey mss, Taylor to Grey, 18 June, 22 Sept. and n.d., Grey to Sefton, 23 Sept.; Creevey

mss, Creevey to Miss Ord, 23 Sept. 1831; NLW, Ormathwaite mss FG 1/6, pp. 93, 157, 159, 161, 167-75, 187-9. [44] *Creevey Pprs.* ii. 284. [45] PROB 11/1848/352; IR26/1400/429.

M.M.E.

TAYLOR *see also* WATSON TAYLOR

TAYLOUR, Thomas, earl of Bective (1787–1870).

Co. Meath   1812–24 Oct. 1829

b. 4 May 1787, 1st. s. of Thomas Taylour, 1st mq. of Headfort [I], and Mary, da. and h. of George Quin of Quinsborough, co. Clare. *educ.* Harrow 1798-c.1803; Trinity Coll. Camb. 1811. *m.* (1) 29 Jan. 1822, Olivia (*d.* 21 July 1834), da. of Sir John Stevenson, D. Mus., of Dublin, wid. of Edward Tuite Dalton of Fennar, co. Meath, 3s. 3da.; (2) 5 Apr. 1853, Frances, da. of John Livingstone Martyn of co. Tyrone, wid. of Sir William Hay MacNaghten, 1st bt., and of Col. James C. McClintoch of the Bengal army, *s.p. styled* Visct. Headfort 1795-1800, earl of Bective 1800-29; *suc.* fa. as 2nd mq. of Headfort [I] 24 Oct. 1829; *cr.* Bar. Kenlis [UK] 10 Sept. 1831; KP 15 Apr. 1839. *d.* 6 Dec. 1870.
 Ld. of bedchamber June 1835-June 1837; ld. in waiting June 1837-Sept. 1841; PC [I] 30 May 1835.
 Ld. lt. co. Cavan 1831-*d.*
 Col. R. Meath militia 1823.

Bective had joined Brooks's, 19 Dec. 1810, sponsored by Lord Bessborough, but once seated for Meath on his family interest voted with government and in favour of Catholic claims.[1] On 29 June 1816 costs of £10,000 were awarded against him for the 'seduction' of the wife of Lord George Thomas Beresford*. It was probably in settlement of this that a note of sequestration was later served on his London house in Stanhope Street, Mayfair, while he was abroad.[2] At the 1820 general election he was returned unopposed for Meath and proposed Nathanial Sneyd* for county Cavan, where his family also had a 'leading' influence.[3] Listed by the Liverpool ministry as 'strongly recommending' silk for Sir Henry Meredyth, he voted in defence of their conduct towards Queen Caroline, 6 Feb. 1821, and against repeal of the additional malt duty, 3 Apr. He argued against inquiry into the conduct of the sheriff of Dublin, who he contended had 'conducted himself with great judgement and propriety', 23 Feb. He divided for Catholic relief, 28 Feb. 1821, 1 Mar., 21 Apr., 10 May 1825. He voted against more extensive tax reductions, 21 Feb. 1822. On 19 June 1822 Goulburn, the Irish secretary, wrote 'again' to Lord Wellesley, the Irish viceroy, concerning Bective's 'anxiety' for a church living for one Mr. Pepper.[4]

Following the birth of his first son, 1 Nov. 1822, Lady Spencer, whose daughter Georgiana had married Bective's younger brother George, informed her husband:

> It is your regret at Lord Bective's having a son. I have ever considered poor Gin's children as so absolutely barred from any future accession of fortune or rank, that it actually made no impression on me to hear of that profligate race being perpetuated through that infamous channel ... It is surely better that the disappointment should take place early than late and at Lord Bective's age it even might be looked to as probable ... As for poor Gin she must submit to it [and] exert herself to make the best of it ... These are the considerations which really make me read of the notice of Lord Bective's having an heir with the same indifference that I should any other blackguard having one.[5]

On 21 Feb. 1823 Goulburn cautioned Wellesley against the 'dangerous precedent' of allowing Bective to succeed his father as colonel of the Meath militia, as it might be viewed as creating 'a monopoly ... in favour of one family', and urged that he be offered the custos rotulorum instead; but Bective was appointed colonel later that year.[6] He divided against inquiry into the currency, 12 June 1823. No trace of parliamentary activity has been found for 1824. Apparently without warning, he voted against suppression of the Catholic Association, 15 Feb., whereupon Goulburn informed Wellesley that he was 'most surprised at Lord Bective's opposition', and again, 25 Feb. 1825.[7] He presented a Newcastle petition against the measure, 21 Feb., and one from county Cavan for Catholic claims, 19 Apr., which he claimed had been 'signed by 12,500 persons who possessed property to the amount of £60,000 per year', 26 Apr.[8] He endorsed a county meeting against alteration of the corn laws, 24 Apr., and attended one to promote Catholic claims, 30 Aug. 1825.[9] The following month, when there were rumours of a dissolution, Goulburn complained to the home secretary Peel that Bective had put his father's interest in county Cavan at the disposal of Robert Henry Southwell, 'a radical', apparently 'with a view to secure Roman Catholic support for himself' in Meath, and urged the adoption of 'any means to produce a change in Lord Headfort's decision'. This was apparently unsuccessful, for on 24 Sept. 1825 Lord Farnham reported to Peel that 'there would not have been any opposition' in Cavan 'had not Lord Bective given his support to Southwell, who stands on the Roman Catholic interest'.[10] Bective attended the Catholic Association dinner for the 'friends of civil and religious liberty', 2 Feb. 1826.[11]

At the 1826 general election he stood again for Meath, citing his 'decided conviction that the concession of Catholic claims was essential'. Rumours of an opposition came to nothing and he was returned unopposed.[12] In county Cavan he proposed Southwell.[13] He brought up Meath petitions for Catholic claims, 2, 5 Mar., and divided accordingly, 6 Mar. 1827, a visitor to Headfort House noting that Bective 'was obliged to leave us at night, on his way to attend Parliament, on the Roman Catholic question, of which he is a warm supporter'.[14] He brought up a constituency petition against alteration of the corn laws, 8 Mar. 1827.[15] He was granted leave for a month to attend the assizes, 14 Mar., and for a fortnight on account of family illness, 1 May 1827. He presented multiple petitions for Catholic relief, 29 Apr. 1828, when he warned that 'postponement' of the question would be 'received in Ireland with dismay', 1 May, and voted thus, 12 May. He attended county meetings to promote the cause and draw up favourable petitions, 30 Sept. 1828, 26 Jan. 1829, and helped chair one in the Rotunda, Dublin, 20 Jan. 1829, when he urged 'all the friends of civil and religious liberty in Ireland to unite in one determined body' and condemned the recall of Lord Anglesey, the Irish viceroy.[16] He presented 40 petitions for emancipation (13 from Meath) and argued that 'if the Catholic Association be dangerous, the Brunswick and Orange Clubs are doubly so' and 'also ought to be suppressed', 12 Feb. He presented dozens more petitions for emancipation and repeal of the Subletting and Vestry Acts throughout February and March, insisted that emancipation would 'extinguish all those religious and political differences which have long stood in the way of the improvement and prosperity of Ireland', 19 Feb., and voted accordingly, 6, 30 Mar. He had been listed by Planta, the Wellington ministry's patronage secretary, as 'opposed to securities', but on 19 Feb. he conceded that 'the one bill cannot be carried unless the other bill is carried also' and suggested that the disfranchisement of the 40s. freeholders would 'prove to be but as a light cloud, which for a while may diminish the brightness of the sun's rays'. On 26 Mar. he welcomed the raising of the minimum freehold qualification to £10 as 'the best remedy we can apply to the present abuses', but warned that increasing it to £20 'would deprive a large portion of the really respectable freeholders of their franchises'. He presented a petition from the Meath militia for compensation under the Militia Suspension Act, 19 Mar., and one in similar terms from the Westmeath militia, 24 Mar. He voted for Daniel O'Connell to be allowed to take his seat unhindered, 18 May. On 3 July 1829 Leveson Gower, the Irish secretary, informed him of the success of his request for the living of Newtown and assured him of his 'due appreciation of the

support received by government in Parliament from your lordship'.[17]

On the death of his father in October 1829 Bective succeeded to the Irish marquessate of Headfort. Reviewing the claims of the leading families in Meath to the vacant governorship, Wellington advised the Irish viceroy that 'Headfort is the most important, but by English rules cannot be appointed to succeed his father'.[18] In September 1831 the Grey ministry gave him a United Kingdom peerage as Baron Kenlis, George Agar Ellis* noting that 'like a true Irishman' he went to the Lords 'without his patent, so his introduction was obliged to be deferred till tomorrow'.[19] He was appointed the first lord lieutenant of county Cavan under the Irish Lord Lieutenants Act later that year. He held household posts under the second Melbourne administration. Greville observed that he became 'quite frightened' when Guizot committed a 'great gaucherie' and upset the queen's table sittings, 22 Sept. 1840.[20]

Bective died at Headfort House in December 1870 and was succeeded in the peerage by his eldest son Thomas (1822-94), Conservative Member for Westmorland since 1854.

[1] *Black Bk.* (1823), 139; *Session of Parl. 1825*, p. 450. [2] *The Times*, 1 July, 14 Dec. 1816. [3] *Dublin Evening Post*, 25, 30 Mar.; *Enniskillen Chron.* 6 Apr. 1820; Add. 40331, f. 147. [4] Add. 37399, f. 238. [5] Add. 75937, Lady to Lord Spencer, 9 Nov. 1822. [6] Add. 37300, f. 259. [7] Add. 37303, f. 196. [8] *The Times*, 22 Feb., 20, 27 Apr. 1825. [9] *Dublin Evening Post*, 21 Apr., 1 Sept.; *The Times*, 5 Sept. 1825. [10] Add. 40331, f. 147; 40381, f. 367. [11] *O'Connell Corresp.* iii. 1278. [12] *Dublin Evening Post*, 8, 22, 29 June 1826. [13] *Newry Commerical Telegraph*, 23 June 1826. [14] *The Times*, 3, 6 Mar. 1827; *Mems. Joseph Gurney* ed. J. Braithwaite, i. 329. [15] *The Times*, 9 Mar. 1827. [16] *Dublin Evening Post*, 4 Oct. 1828, 31 Jan. 1829; *O'Connell Corresp.* iv. 1507; *The Times*, 24 Jan. 1829. [17] NAI, Leveson Gower letterbks. M. 736. [18] Wellington mss WP1/1059/39. [19] Northants. RO, Agar Ellis diary, 13 Sept. 1831. [20] *Greville Mems.* iv. 289.

P.J.S.

TEMPLE, Henry John, 3rd Visct. Palmerston [I] (1784–1865), of Broadlands, nr. Romsey, Hants and 9 Great Stanhope Street, Mdx.[1]

NEWPORT I.o.W.	1807–24 Mar. 1811
CAMBRIDGE UNIVERSITY	27 Mar. 1811–1831
BLETCHINGLEY	18 July 1831–1832
HAMPSHIRE SOUTH	1832–1834
TIVERTON	1 June 1835–18 Oct. 1865

b. 20 Oct. 1784, 1st s. of Henry Temple, 2nd Visct. Palmerston [I][†], and 2nd w. Mary, da. of Benjamin Mee, merchant, of Bath, Som. *educ.* by Gaetano Ravizzotti, an Italian tutor; Harrow 1795; Edinburgh Univ. 1800; St.

John's, Camb. 1803. *m.* 16 Dec. 1839,[2] Hon. Emily Mary
Lamb, da. of Peniston Lamb, 1st Visct. Melbourne [I][†],
wid. of Peter Leopold Louis Francis Nassau, 5th Earl
Cowper, *s.p.* legit.; 2s. 2da. illegit. *suc.* fa. as 3rd Visct.
Palmerston [I] 16 Apr. 1802; GCB 6 June 1832; KG 12
July 1856. *d.* 18 Oct. 1865.

Ld. of admiralty Apr. 1807-Oct. 1809; sec. at war Oct.
1809-May 1828, with seat in cabinet Apr. 1827; PC 1
Nov. 1809; sec. of state for foreign affairs Nov. 1830-Nov.
1834, Apr. 1835-Sept. 1841, July 1846-Dec. 1851; sec.
of state for home affairs Dec. 1852-Feb. 1855; first ld. of
treasury 10 Feb. 1855-25 Feb. 1858, 18 June 1859-*d.*

Capt. Fawley vol. inf. 1803-4; lt.-col. commdt. S. W.
Hants militia 1809.

Ld. warden, Cinque Ports 1861-*d.*; master, Trinity
House 1862-*d.*; ld. rect. Glasgow Univ. 1862-*d.*

By 1820 Palmerston, who had inherited his dilettante father's indebted estates and Irish title in 1802
and had sat, despite his pro-Catholic sentiments,
for Cambridge University since 1811, was an odd
amalgam of the Regency buck, whose boyish good
looks had earned him the nickname 'Lord Cupid',
and the inconspicuous, as yet apparently unambi-
tious, bureaucrat.[3] As secretary at war, a post described
by the prime minister Lord Liverpool as that of 'the
finance minister of the army', with a salary of £2,480,
he was an unrelenting pen-pusher, although he was
responsible for the introduction of useful organiza-
tional and humanitarian alterations, and, as in the
major row over the army returns in March 1820, he
was never shy of asserting his competing jurisdic-
tional claims with those of the commander-in-chief,
the duke of York.[4] His contributions in Parliament,
which were adequate to the purpose – although, as in
his correspondence, the clarity of his expressions was
sometimes undermined by his vituperative tone – were
limited to the annual departmental business of carrying the army estimates and the militia bill; his senior
colleague George Canning* later lamented his inability to bring 'that three-decker Palmerston' into action
in debate.[5] Although lacking strong personal connections with any of the leading ministers, he was already
on the 'liberal' side of the government; of course he
invariably divided with them in the Commons, where
he was often a teller on military matters, and sat on
several select committees, including those on the
militia estimates.[6] Yet, at the same time, he devoted
himself to the dizzying social whirl of Almack's and
the race course, and was an unconscionable philanderer, keeping a record of his conquests in his pocket
book. He was noticed by the Irish poet Tom Moore in
May 1819, 'sitting faithfully close to his old flame Lady
Cowper – a vulgar man', of whom Canning reportedly
said, 'he looks like a footman who thinks his mistress

is in love with him, *and who is mistaken*'.[7] With her, his
equally wayward principal mistress, he had already
fathered two children: his eventual heir, William
Francis Cowper[†], later Baron Mount-Temple, and his
favourite 'Minny', mother of his future private secretary Evelyn Ashley[†]. Another child, 'Fanny', born on
9 Feb. 1820, was probably also his, although by then he
was involved with Eliza Blackburn, the wife of a school
and university contemporary. Despite his limited
financial means, he for many years had to provide for
a Mrs. Emma Murray (later Mills), whose son John
Henry Temple Murray was supposedly his bastard.
Nothing came of the perhaps not entirely serious
proposal he made to Lord Minto's sister Lady Anna
Maria Elliot in 1820, nor of his attempts in 1825 to
woo Lady Georgiana Fane, whose refusals were probably prompted by the meddling of her jealous sister,
Lady Jersey.[8] A year or so later he propositioned the
wife of Edward John Stanley* with a brusque, 'Ha ha,
I see it all – beautiful woman neglected by her husband
– allow me – etc.'[9]

The compromise with his Whig colleague still
holding, Palmerston was returned unopposed for his
university at the general election of 1820, when it
was briefly rumoured that he would accept a United
Kingdom peerage.[10] As well as intervening against
the radical John Cam Hobhouse* in Westminster, he
attempted to influence the choice of candidates for
Hampshire, where, though this was really the duke
of Wellington's bailiwick, he continued to play a
role in the Tory resistance to seditious activities and
helped to establish a patriotic Southampton newspaper early that decade.[11] He cited the necessity of the
armed forces in the preservation of internal peace and
freedom on resisting calls for a select committee on
military expenditure, 16 May, and for a reduction in the
size of the army, 14 June. He easily carried his limited
parliamentary business that session, during which
his only other intervention was against the exclusion
of Thomas Ellis, the Irish master in chancery, from
the House, 30 June. He had believed it unlikely that
George IV would persist with a prosecution of Queen
Caroline and in mid-October 1820 he commented on
the likely failure of the bill of pains and penalties in a
letter to his former guardian Lord Malmesbury, whose
death the following month aroused painful feelings in
him.[12]

Palmerston voted for Catholic relief, 28 Feb., and,
on presenting his constituents' hostile petition,
expressed his support for this and the intended securities, 16 Mar. 1821.[13] He introduced the army estimates,
claiming that economies had been made and that it

was delusory to hope for a return to the expenditure levels of 1792, 12 Mar. For the next two months he fought a successful rearguard action against the concerted opposition of radicals and advanced Whigs, who divided the House on at least a dozen occasions, including on the grant for volunteer corps, 16 Apr., when he stated that, although the war had ended in 1815, this had been only the first year of 'domestic peace'. Lady Cowper commented to her brother Frederick Lamb in early May that

> I am very glad to find Lord Palmerston has done himself such credit by the talent, discretion and temper he has displayed during all this time and if Hume has not managed to reduce the estimates, he has at least reduced the secretary at war, for he has grown as thin again as he was.[14]

Nevertheless, that summer he gave Liverpool proposals for large additional savings, noting that the ones relating to three household cavalry regiments 'are those which in all the discussions we have had in the House of Commons have excited the most attention and upon which we have had the least favourable divisions'.[15] In November 1821 he declined Liverpool's bid, as a means of providing for William Huskisson*, to demote him to the Lords and the department of woods and forests (while awaiting a vacancy at the post office), opining that such an arrangement 'would be liable to misconstruction'.[16] The following month Lord Binning*, referring to Palmerston's survival instincts, called him 'a very shy cock. An old pheasant is not more dexterous in eluding dogs, beaters and guns'.[17]

Having spoken briefly against Hume's amendment to the address, 5 Feb., Palmerston was, in Hudson Gurney's* word, 'wretched' in his sneering defence against Sir Robert Wilson's censure motion, 13 Feb. 1822; then, as on most occasions that the cases of aggrieved officers were brought before the House, he stood his ground wholly on the king's prerogative to dismiss him from the army.[18] Boasting that he had implemented the economies requested by opposition, 4 Mar., he saw his departmental accounts through the committee of supply that month with his now characteristic flippancy and informed his brother William Temple, a diplomat, on the 25th that

> I have not had half the trouble with estimates this year that I had last year: indeed, we had made such large reductions, that little was left for Hume to object to, and the body of the Whigs did not support him much in his objections even to that little.[19]

In August 1822, in the aftermath of Lord Londonderry's suicide, which he regretted – not

least because it was a toss-up whether the more brilliant Canning, who became foreign secretary, or the more reliable Robert Peel, the home secretary, should succeed as leader of the House – he was considered for promotion, but John Wilson Croker*, who admitted his 'readiness and nerve', wrote to Peel that

> Palmerston's deficiency is exactly that which we are now considering how to supply – that *flow* of ideas and language which can run on for a couple of hours without, on the one hand, committing the government or, on the other, lowering by commonplaces the station of a cabinet minister.[20]

He retained his office in the ensuing reshuffle, though he did himself no favours by exasperating Liverpool over another turf war with York early the following year.[21] Apart from skirmishes over the mutiny bill's provisions relating to the dismissal of officers, 6, 14 Mar. 1823, Palmerston secured his army estimates without difficulty that session. No doubt so as not to antagonize his constituents, whose increasing Protestantism had been demonstrated by the return of the arch anti-Catholic William Bankes at a by-election late the previous year, he made no comment on presenting their petition against Catholic relief, 16 Apr.; he brought up another from the university for the abolition of colonial slavery, 22 Apr.[22] He departed from his usual inactivity by making a major speech in defence of Canning's policy of not threatening force of arms against France over its invasion of Spain, 30 Apr., his first outing on foreign affairs since 1808.[23] On 7 May 1823 he was forced up to explain his part in the prosecution and execution of the poacher Charles Smith, who had shot at his gamekeeper, an affair which William Cobbett† elevated into a radical *cause célèbre*.[24]

Palmerston gave an account of his visit to Holland and Germany that autumn in a series of amusing letters to his sister Elizabeth. After an initial period of being 'at slack water' in the Commons, he recounted to her husband Laurence Sulivan, a subordinate at the war office, 26 Feb., that the 'estimates went off like smoke from a steam engine', but he was obliged to defend the practice of flogging in the army, 5, 11, 15 Mar. 1824.[25] He was named to the select committee on the Irish Insurrection Act, 11 May, and, having chaired most of its sittings, he brought up its first report, 31 May, and justified its proceedings, 24 June.[26] On 30 Dec. 1824 he concurred in Peel's decision to suppress the Catholic Association without prior recourse to parliamentary inquiry.[27] He again took charge of the committee on the state of Ireland, which was reappointed on 17 Feb. 1825, presenting three of its four reports that session.[28] Although on 15 Mar. he brought up the hostile petition of Cambridge University, he of course voted for Catholic relief, 1 Mar., 21 Apr., 10 May, and was privately optimistic about its chances.[29] He observed that granting it would do much to facilitate military reductions in Ireland, 4 Mar., when, as on the 7th, he denied that modest increases in the size of the army were related to matters of internal unrest or official patronage. In September 1825, and again a year later, he visited his county Sligo estates, where he busied himself with an ambitious programme of practical improvements.[30]

Although in January 1825 he had found 'things looking very prosperous' at Cambridge University, his future prospects were soon reckoned to be so doubtful that he was expected to retreat to the Lords.[31] He was grateful that no dissolution took place that autumn, but was shocked to have to embark on an extensive canvass there in December, when a rumour briefly arose that he was to be governor-general of India.[32] Not only was he challenged by Bankes, but, to his fury, both the staunch anti-Catholics John Singleton Copley, the attorney-general, and Henry Goulburn, the Irish secretary, also offered, with the backing of like-minded ministers. As the Whigs, such as the Rev. Adam Sedgwick, who had no candidate of their own, rallied to him as a long-standing pro-Catholic Member, he knew by January 1826 that his continued exertions gave him a fighting chance, but he made his displeasure at this deeply embarrassing situation abundantly clear to Liverpool that month in a strongly worded protest; in this he blamed the prime minister, whose reply was unsatisfactory, for failing to abide by the rule of cabinet neutrality on the Catholic question.[33] In February he had his hostile views on slavery relayed to his constituents, and he presented and endorsed their petition for its abolition on the 28th.[34] Amid further squabbles with York that spring, he vindicated the expense and size of the army, 3, 7 Mar., but was unconvincing, 13 Mar. 1826, in his rejection of Hume's motion to end flogging, a practice which he was quietly endeavouring to restrict.[35]

After a six months' 'nightmare' of strenuous canvassing, including agonizing about how far to share splits with his rivals, Palmerston was returned in second place behind Copley at the general election of 1826, at the cost of at least £750.[36] He had told Liverpool, who he thought 'acted, as he always does to a friend in personal questions, shabbily, timidly and ill', that he would have resigned if defeated, and, although he saw his triumph as securing his own seat and as a setback for the 'no popery' cause generally, he wrote in his short autobiographical memoir that 'this

was the first decided step towards a breach between me and the Tories, and they were the aggressors'. He confided to his brother:

> As to the commonplace balance between opposition and government, the election will have little effect upon it. The government are as strong as any government can wish to be, as far as regards those who sit facing them; but in truth the real opposition of the present day sit behind the treasury bench; and it is by the stupid old Tory party, who bawl out the memory and praises of Pitt while they are opposing all the measures and principles which he held most important, it is by these that the progress of the government in every improvement which they are attempting is thwarted and impeded. On the Catholic question, on the principles of commerce, on the corn laws, on the settlement of the currency, on the laws regulating the trade in money, on colonial slavery, on the game laws ... on all these questions, and everything like them, the government find support from the Whigs and resistance from their self-denominated friends. However, the young squires are more liberal than the old ones, and we must hope that heaven will protect us from our friends, as it has from our enemies.[37]

In July 1826 Canning suggested moving him to the post office with a peerage, and also raised the idea of his taking on Frederick John Robinson's departmental and Commons duties at the exchequer, although he admitted that Palmerston's 'only fault is a habit of non-attendance on ordinary occasions, a fault wholly inconsistent with the *existence* of a chancellor'. Liverpool scotched this, and it was possibly at this time that Palmerston declined two offers of postings in India.[38] Disturbed that autumn by the incipient civil war in Ireland, where he noted in a memoranda book that he would vote for any fair securities, 'not as safeguards against a danger I foresaw, but as the price to be paid to respectable prejudice for the purchase of substantial justice', he regretted the anti-Catholicism of his colleagues, observing to Temple that

> I can forgive old women like the chancellor [Eldon], spoonies like Liverpool, ignoramuses like Westmorland, old stumped-up Tories like Bathurst; but how such a man as Peel, liberal, enlightened and fresh minded, should find himself running in such a pack is hardly intelligible ... *But the day is fast approaching, as it seems to me, when the matter will be settled, as it must be.*

Such sentiments put him firmly on the reformist wing of the administration, although he hardly qualified as a Canningite.[39]

Palmerston was privately delighted by Canning's sterling pre-Christmas speech in favour of British intervention in Portugal.[40] He responded angrily to Hume's criticisms of the war office, 30 Nov., 8 Dec.

1826, 14 Feb. 1827, saw off opposition to his army estimates, 19, 20 Feb., and again defended flogging, 12 Mar. He presented the petition of the Catholics of county Sligo for their claims, 21 Feb., and voted accordingly, 6 Mar.[41] On 9 Apr. he distanced himself from any responsibility for the Cornwall and Devon Mining Company, one of the ill-fated entrepreneurial concerns with which he became embroiled in the mid-1820s and which seriously exacerbated his worrying financial problems.[42] On the accession of Canning as premier that month, when he was also considered for the home office, he accepted the invitation to become chancellor (a position he had declined in 1809) in order to support him both at the treasury and in the Commons. However, to avoid his re-election becoming mixed up with a contest which was already due to take place at Cambridge University, his appointment was postponed to the end of the session. Lady Cowper reported him to be 'very well pleased' with this arrangement, especially since he joined the cabinet with immediate effect.[43] As he had done briefly after York's death in January, he served as acting commander-in-chief following what he saw as the regrettable resignation of Wellington, and, having helped to stifle the king's plan to exercise this role personally, he drew up a memorandum on this, 11 June, and explained his role to the House, 21 June.[44] In his only other interventions that session, he gave lukewarm support to the Penryn disfranchisement bill, 7 June, and favoured the East Retford measure only in so far as the existence of such electoral abuses strengthened the hand of radical reformers, 11 June 1827.

Palmerston, who approved of Canning's intention 'to found his government upon public opinion rather than borough interests', welcomed the exclusion of the bigoted Tories and the inclusion of moderate Whigs in subordinate roles.[45] Mrs. Arbuthnot, who liked him despite his quarrelsome nature, was aghast at this about-turn, remarking in June 1827 that 'he *professes* now to be a Whig, having been for 15 years in office upon high Tory principles, and he makes this profession just at the moment when the Whigs get into power in order to keep his place'. So she was delighted to hear that he might suffer the indignity of being dropped.[46] Perhaps because of rumours of his alleged improprieties over share dealing, but more probably simply because the premier's vexed political arrangements required him to hold the chancellorship himself, Canning, at about this time, asked him to relinquish the promise of the exchequer. This Palmerston did with a good grace, putting the interests of the government ahead of his own, and perhaps only in retrospect was he to attribute such moves to

displace him to the underlying hostility of George IV. Subsequently, he later recorded, the prime minister offered him the governorship of Jamaica, at which 'I laughed so heartily that I observed Canning looked quite put out', and the governor-generalship of India, about which, as when Liverpool had made such a suggestion, he repeated that 'my ambition was satisfied with my position at home'.[47]

Although, as Lady Cowper put it, Palmerston was 'quite a late convert', he was described by her to have been as 'completely devoted' to Canning as her brother William Lamb*, the Irish secretary, and he was consequently devastated by his death in August 1827.[48] Canning's successor Lord Goderich (as Robinson had become) soon revived the offer of the chancellorship, but, on the king insisting on the appointment of John Charles Herries*, Palmerston, who had vainly urged William Sturges Bourne* to take it, retracted his acceptance 'in the handsomest manner'.[49] During the tortuous imbroglio that ensued, owing to the struggle to have this decision reversed, he acquitted the king of acting on motives of political partisanship, as the Whigs reckoned, but was aware that some element of personal animus lay behind it, since George IV had told Princess Lieven, the wife of the Russian ambassador, that '*il y a quelque chose en lui qui me déplait, il a toujours l'air si fière* [sic]'. Nevertheless, he was of the opinion that the king, at the instigation of his secretary Sir William Knighton, wished to insert his supposed creature Herries, whom Palmerston in fact judged to be a man of talent and integrity, at the exchequer, so as to pave the way on 'a hundred questions connected with the privy purse, the crown revenue and royal expenditure which are constantly arising'.[50] Thus, while Henry Brougham*, for instance, privately advanced Palmerston's merits, writing that 'I abhor Herries – I love Palmerston, an excellent, honourable, liberal man, and of good Whig stock, and I have remonstrated with *The Times* for him strongly, and against Herries', he and the studiously calm Palmerston agreed that the Whig leaders should do all they could to preserve the existing parliamentary majority of the ministry and particularly the 'preponderance of liberal views in the cabinet'.[51] To his brother Palmerston argued that otherwise either Goderich would have to take back some of the secessionist Tories, which would create a government 'just like Liverpool's, consisting of men differing on all great questions, and perpetually on the verge of a quarrel, the result of which is that nothing is done', or 'the Tories would come in bodily', which 'would be most unfortunate in every possible way'.[52]

By early September 1827, when he saw through the king's rather too obvious flattery of him during an explanatory interview, he was content to remain where he was.[53] It had been reported the previous month that 'the army is going to the devil under Palmerston' and that he was 'a good deal quizzed for having gone in uniform to the review of the Coldstream Regiment', so he was relieved to relinquish his additional duties to Wellington, the reappointed commander-in-chief, with whom, however, professional disagreements soon arose.[54] Rumours had emerged that he might have been president of the board of trade, but on the leadership of the Commons, for which Croker deemed him unsuited because he had 'not fluency nor industry, nor a general knowledge of business', he gladly deferred to Huskisson, the colonial secretary. Displaying his usual lack of ambition, he confided to Sulivan, of this position, that

> there are few things indeed in this world which I should so much dislike; even if I felt that I was fit for it. But in various ways I should be unequal to it. To go no further than one point, the person so placed must be in a perpetual state of canvass; and of all irksome slaveries there is none more difficult to me than that; besides the character of the government is, as it were, identified with the debating success of the individual.[55]

The following month he escaped for a few weeks to Ireland, and that winter he took a close interest in foreign affairs, noting that the battle of Navarino 'will smooth and not increase our difficulties'.[56] In December 1827 he was kept in the dark about a ministerial scare, for which he forgave the prime minister, but he was scathing about the collapse of the ministry the following month.[57] According to his later account, which Herries's son and biographer found to be inaccurate in this and other respects, Palmerston wrote that Huskisson, who now led the Canningites

> blamed me for not having stood out. He said if I had insisted upon the fulfilment of Goderich's promise [of the exchequer], that promise would not have been retracted, especially as it had been spontaneously made, and Herries would not have been thrown like a live shell into the cabinet to explode and blow us all up. At the appointed time he did explode. He picked a quarrel with Huskisson ... Goderich had not energy of mind enough to determine in favour of one or the other ... and gave the king to understand that he had no advice to give, and did not know what to do. But George knew very well what he had to do: he bid Goderich go home ... and he immediately sent for the duke of Wellington ... The king was the great plotter, and [William] Holmes* and [Joseph] Planta* worked upon Goderich, and persuaded him he could never overcome the difficulties he would have to encounter.[58]

However, he yet again survived in the cabinet, to the despair of Mrs. Arbuthnot, who exclaimed that Palmerston, 'the shabbiest of all', had 'told me himself that he was a Whig and would always remain so'.[59]

Yet Palmerston's course was governed less by love of place than by concern for public principles, for example the continuation of cabinet neutrality over Catholic relief, as guaranteed by the retention of a sufficient number of like-minded friends, or 'liberals', to counterbalance the extreme Tory 'pigtails'. Following negotiations in January 1828 it was agreed, among other concessions, that Huskisson's presence was essential, 'as a security for the maintenance of those liberal principles which we both profess'. At the same time, although he regretted the retreat of Lord Lansdowne's moderate Whigs (with whom he would not have sat in the Commons had he too left office), Palmerston judged Peel, the reinstated home secretary, to be 'QUITE as *liberal* on every point except the Catholic question as Huskisson or Canning', and considered that Lord Dudley's

> continuance in the foreign office ... would give a security that our foreign relations would be kept up in the same spirit as hitherto, while Huskisson's superintendence of our colonial system and [the president of the board of trade Charles] Grant's management of our commercial arrangements would preclude any departure from the much calumniated principles of free trade.[60]

Believing Wellington was '*not* a bigot' over emancipation, he was cautiously prepared to give him the benefit of the doubt and, having persuaded himself that the inclusion of Herries should not be made an insuperable objection, he, with the other members of the 'triumvirate', Dudley and Grant, nudged Huskisson into accepting the final ministerial arrangement. This he almost settled at a meeting on the 18th, when, however, he raised additional demands for the fair treatment of pro-Catholics over official or electoral patronage and the exclusion of rigid Protestants from the Irish administration, to which the new premier laughingly replied that 'the first was asking him whether he was an honest man, and the second whether he was a madman'. He later recorded that 'Dudley, Lamb, Binning [soon to become 9th earl of Haddington], Grant and myself met at Huskisson's house', and accepted Wellington's offer, 'not as individuals, but as a party representing the principles, and consisting of the friends, of Mr. Canning'. The ministry was settled by the 21st and Palmerston opined that 'I think it will *do*, and the government will be strong and liberal, at least if it is not the latter, it will soon cease to be the former'.[61]

Palmerston, ever ready to express his stoutly held opinions in cabinet, stated his reservations about Wellington remaining as commander-in-in-chief at its meeting, 24 Jan. 1828.[62] Anxious that no revelation of internal splits over religion should place power in the hand of the 'illiberals', he made careful preparations for his low-key speech on the address, 29 Jan., when, as the only minister present in the Commons, he reported its uneventful approval to the king.[63] He fended off embarrassing questions about the new government, 31 Jan., and during the ministerial explanations on 18 Feb. he insisted that it would remain Canningite in its foreign and commercial policies. He clashed with Hume on introducing the curtailed army estimates, 22 Feb., and his request for papers on the full and half-pay lists, 12 Mar.; he thought these matters much better left to the finance committee, to which he gave evidence in person, 10 Mar., and he continued to suggest economies, for instance over the militia.[64] He wound up the debate on the Test Acts, apologetically remarking that they had, in any case, been 'to all intents and purposes practically repealed', 26 Feb.; Mrs. Arbuthnot, who complained that he 'scarcely ever speaks' and 'sneaks about ashamed (as well he may) of showing his face', wryly observed that he 'argued for the repeal and voted against it!'[65] As he recorded in his journal, in March Palmerston was dissatisfied with the new corn bill, but agreed to it as a compromise, considering that 'the great object was to get established the principle of protection by duty, instead of prohibition'; on Grant threatening to resign over the duty being fixed at too high a rate, he eventually persuaded him to stay since otherwise both Huskisson and himself would then have been forced to depart over this issue.[66] The following month he sent Wellington a summary of his objections on foreign policy, especially over the proposals for Greek independence, which, on behalf of the diffident Dudley, he constantly raised in cabinet.[67] However, writing to Temple, 25 Apr., he remarked that, partly because of the finance committee, 'our session has hitherto been one of the most inactive I ever remember', and, detecting the decline of the agriculturists and the end of the 'reign of Toryism', he was even hopeful of the eventual concession of Catholic relief, for which he gave a silent vote, 12 May 1828.[68]

He spoke for the grant to Canning's family, 13 May 1828, much to the delight of the embittered widow of the late premier, and the following day, in response to an attack from Lord Chandos, he declared 'that as the principles which emanated from him are followed, just in that proportion will those who adopt them conduce to its interest and advantage, and obtain for their government the confidence and approbation of the people'.[69] This sensational 'mutiny', as the prime minister described it, apparently gave 'mortal offence' to Wellington, who, already at odds with Palmerston personally, especially at his 'always *pecking*' in cabinet over the endlessly postponed issue of relations with Russia, and regretting the accession of the Huskissonites altogether, meditated some kind of reprimand in the Lords.[70] Before an opportunity arose, however, both the hesitant Huskisson, who had pledged himself in cabinet to vote for transferring the seats of at least one corrupt borough to a large town, and the nonchalant Palmerston, who understood that its meeting on 19 May had agreed the matter was not to be considered a government question, divided that night, against Peel, for transferring East Retford's seats to Birmingham. Palmerston, who had told him to 'stay where you are' and later remarked that 'if Huskisson had had to move, instead of sitting still, he would have voted the other way', was certainly responsible for their votes, but he knew nothing of his colleague's blundering written apology, which Wellington, despite Palmerston's subsequent explanations, insisted on interpreting as a letter of resignation.[71] The lord privy seal, Lord Ellenborough, who reckoned that 'Palmerston's loss can be easily supplied', recorded that Wellington had said that 'Palmerston must follow Huskisson, and he did *not choose to fire great guns at sparrows*'; so, with the prime minister evidently prepared to eject them, Palmerston left office with Dudley and Grant in late May 1828. Dudley, who was the only one to waver, felt himself bound to follow the sterling example of Palmerston, who later noted that 'We joined as a party; as a party we retired'.[72] Wellington, who thought that 'Palmerston never liked me', later confided that 'I may be wrong, but I have always suspected him of having put Huskisson up to the move which led to the tender of his resignation. He imagined that without Huskisson and his friends ... I should not be able to get on'.[73]

Palmerston's justificatory Commons statement on this affair, 2 June 1828, was satisfactory to both his former colleagues and the Huskissonites, or 'ejected liberals', who sat below the treasury bench on the government side. He compiled a list, 'respectable both in its number and composition', of 'gentlemen in Parliament who may be supposed as agreeing pretty much in opinion and likely to find themselves voting the same way'; the three versions of it, each of which placed him second after Huskisson, comprised about 26 MPs and about 11 peers.[74] Commenting that 'it is so many years since I have been my own master that I feel it quite comical to have no tie', he relinquished the war office, whose clerks were ecstatic at his departure, but, having requested Sulivan to supply him with the relevant papers, he made interventions on the previously postponed army estimates, 13, 20 June.[75] He spoke and voted for the usury bill, 19 June. He urged the enfranchisement of disturbed manufacturing towns as a prophylactic against radical alterations, declaring himself in favour of the transfer of East Retford's seats, 'not because I am a friend to reform in principle, but because I am its decided enemy', 27 June. He divided with opposition that day, and again on Fyler's amendment to the silk duties, which was carried with government support, 14 July. He judged that the session 'went off languidly, and without any events of particular interest', but was smugly pleased that, except on the Catholic question, ministers appeared to be more liberal than before the exit of the Huskissonites, perhaps being 'disposed to do things, when they have the credit of doing them, which they refused to do when it would have been supposed that we were urging them to do them'. Thus, as he had predicted the previous August, the reshuffled government had become 'essentially Tory, with a garnish of liberals to keep up appearances'; but he thought that, unless overwhelmed by the growing pro-Catholic tide, 'the ship will sail well enough in fair weather, and the business of the crew must be to keep her out of storms'.[76] By the end of July 1828 he was astounded that Wellington had reverted to Canning's foreign policy, at least as far as Turkey was concerned, and informed Lady Cowper that

all points on which we had almost angry disputes at every cabinet from January to May, and upon which I thought it impossible we ever should agree, and out of which I daily expected a break up of the government to take place; *all* of these points have now been settled exactly in conformity with *our* opinions.[77]

By the following month, when, according to lists he sketched in his journal, he seems to have envisaged serving under Wellington as chancellor or under Lansdowne as colonial secretary, he was speculating that the ministry's apparent weakness would lead to another reorganization once Parliament was recalled, although he had determined 'to make the [settlement of the] Catholic question a *sine qua non* to my return to office'.[78]

He visited Ireland in the wake of what he saw as the epochal Clare election that autumn, conferring with the lord lieutenant, Lord Anglesey, on the desirability of Catholic relief, and in December 1828 he welcomed the revelation that Wellington, whose foreign policy he again found deficient, was, as had long been suspected,

preparing the ground for emancipation. His visit to Huskisson's Sussex estate at Eartham that month, in the company of Goderich and Lord Melbourne (as Lamb had become), gave rise to speculation that what Croker jokingly referred to as the 'party of the three viscounts' might be attempting to position itself to exploit the ministerial split that Palmerston imagined would arise if Peel refused to give up his entrenched anti-Catholicism.[79] He was in Paris for most of January 1829, enjoying its high society and political gossip, but, particularly concerned about the still uncertain future of Ireland, he returned before the meeting of Parliament, crossing from Calais with Hobhouse, who observed that 'he "talked" liberal just as well and as freely as if he had played that part all his life'.[80] On the announcement of emancipation, after which he privately considered himself 'as *landed* at Cambridge', he congratulated ministers in the House, although not without disapproving of the suppression of the Catholic Association, 10 Feb.[81] He of course voted for emancipation, 6 Mar., and on the 18th delivered a major speech in its support, which 'astonished everybody' by its unexpected oratorical brilliance, so much so that the former Whig leader George Tierney* said that it was 'an imitation of Canning, and not a bad one'.[82] Among the congratulations he received on circulating a printed version of it was one from Horace Twiss*, who asked him whether 'I am not justified in the opinion which I have more than once ventured to give you, that you were doing great injustice to yourself and to the country, by keeping your parliamentary talents so much in the shade?'[83] To his brother, he explained, of Wellington's achievement of emancipation, that 'neither Canning nor any other minister could, *this year*, have done the thing, because nothing has brought the king to agree to it but his being check-mated by having no other move left on the board', in the form of a viable anti-Catholic government; nevertheless, he judged the ministry to be weak in the Commons and wrote that 'we must have a turn out upon foreign politics before the session is over'.[84] He criticized the punitive disfranchisement of what he deemed to be independent 40s. freeholders in Ireland, 19 May, dividing in minorities against the bill that day and the next, when he suggested that the measure might be made temporary. According to his pocket diary, he continued to attend Parliament throughout that month, and he again voted for relief, 30 Mar. 1829.[85]

Palmerston contented himself with a silent vote for enfranchising Birmingham, 5 May 1829, commenting to Temple the following day that, with the Catholic question becoming forgotten, 'parties are returning to their ancient demarcations' and 'our division last night upon East Retford brought us nearly to the status ante'.[86] He objected to the introduction of poor laws to Ireland, preferring to advocate English capital investment, 7 May. He divided for allowing Daniel O'Connell to take his seat unimpeded, 18 May, and to reduce the hemp duties, 1 June. That night, rising at 1 am, he strongly condemned Britain's tacit neutrality towards the Portuguese tyrant Dom Miguel and urged the government, by diplomatic interference rather than military intervention, to assist the supporters of the rightful queen, Maria; he also denounced the reversal of Canning's policy in relation to Greece and complained that the reputation of Britain, as a country governed by public opinion rather than physical force, had been gravely damaged. He again wrote out this well-prepared and ably presented speech to be printed, and, in its resonance with the popular mood, which had been one of his aims, it confirmed his arrival as a significant national politician, especially coming after his recent triumph on emancipation.[87] In mid-June he privately expressed his frustration that 'the Whigs were too coquetting with the treasury bench' to reinforce his assault on ministers' vulnerability over foreign affairs, and, doubting that any of the Huskissonites would rejoin them, 'because we would then have no security against being obliged to concur in measures which we disapprove', he forlornly speculated that 'the best government would be one composed by a union of Huskisson and Lansdowne; in short, the government of Goderich, with a better head and some changes'.[88] Although that summer it was supposed by Lord Londonderry that Palmerston might take the Commons lead in the king's desired liberal Tory government, Sir Henry Hardinge* had heard the rumour that the Huskissonites and 'low Whigs' would unite under him; the latter commented that 'Palmerston must look sharp, for the university in a general election say they will not tolerate *two* Whigs', but he was apparently aware of this danger, since, for his electioneering foray there in July 1829, with the newly elected Whig William Cavendish, he drafted an (in the end unused) speech extolling his own independent conduct.[89]

Sir Edward Knatchbull* questioned whether Palmerston could be separated from the Huskissonites, but the Ultra chief Sir Richard Vyvyan* believed that, if handled with care, he might be caught.[90] He duly sounded Palmerston during a long conversation, 3 Oct. 1829, offering him flattering promotions, including the position of colonial secretary, in the Ultra ministry that he hoped to establish that autumn. Palmerston, who confided to Lady Cowper that he found the idea

of a government led by Lord Mansfield and his ilk faintly ludicrous, declined to commit himself to, but evidently led on, Vyvyan, who subsequently recorded that

> by detaching Lord P. from the Huskisson party, which may be done effectually, *provided a favourable change takes place*, we have dislocated the strength of that party and gained a most valuable auxiliary, a good speaker, a man of business and, if necessary, *a competent leader in the House of Commons*.[91]

In fact, he had no intention of abandoning Huskisson and, for instance, in November he attempted to encourage Melbourne to participate in his planned assaults, especially on foreign policy, in the following session.[92] In Paris, where he predicted a possible change of ministry and even of the French regime, he talked at length to Minto, who reported to Lansdowne, 16 Dec. 1829, that he was 'eager, very eager I think, to attack our great duke', including by concerted liberal efforts to oust him, and that 'I think he feels his own value and that you will see him next session take his own line as a leader'; on 6 Jan. 1830 he added that Palmerston, who did not labour under the disadvantages which beset the more talented Canning, 'goes home I think quite resolved to take up his own position as a rallying ground for liberal opinions'.[93] That month, Edward Ellice*, who relayed to Lord Grey a rumour that he was to replace Ellenborough, counted the 'direct and active opposition' led by Palmerston and Melbourne as one of four distinct parties in Parliament.[94]

Despite wanting to raise foreign affairs at the start of the session, Palmerston contented himself with voting for Knatchbull's amendment on distress, 4 Feb. 1830.[95] The following day he explained that he had been bound to do this, given the factual inaccuracy of the address, but saw the agricultural depression as a temporary effect of the beneficial return to a metallic currency; he also criticized ministers' conduct towards Portugal and on the 9th gave notice of a censure motion on this topic. He made what Hobhouse described as a 'furious speech' on the government's failure to guarantee the independence of Greece, 16 Feb., when, in response to an irate intervention by Peel asking who he stood for, he declared that 'I stand here ... as one of the representatives of the people of England ... I also stand here ... as one of that body which represents or which, at least, ought to be the maintainers of, the honour and interests of England'.[96] It was perhaps in relation to their 'brisk skirmish' that day, which marked a breach between them, that Lord Holland surmised that the session might end in the formation of 'two parties, of one of which Peel, of the other Palmerston, will be the leader'.[97] He voted for transferring East Retford's seats to Birmingham, 11 Feb., 5 Mar., and the enfranchisement of Birmingham, Leeds and Manchester, 23 Feb., but against the Ultra Lord Blandford's reform bill, 18 Feb. He stated that he would divide against restricting the grant for the army to six months, 19 Feb., but sided with opposition against filling the vacant treasurership of the navy, 12 Mar., and spoke and voted for inquiry into the revision of taxation, 25 Mar. As George Agar Ellis* put it, Palmerston 'spoke admirably and bitterly respecting the conduct of government', commending to ministers the maxim 'Be just and fear not', on introducing his unsuccessful motion for papers on relations with Portugal, 10 Mar., which was defeated by 150-73.[98] The speech, which he had published, led to a lively debate, during which he was again pitted against Peel, and provoked further contributions to the continuing pamphlet war on the subject.[99] Palmerston, who according to Joseph Jekyll†, 'looked pale and jaded, and five years older since last summer, from his parliamentary anxieties and displays', asked a question about a reported amnesty in Portugal, 6 Apr., and voted for Grant's resolutions on the affair at Terceira (which he had criticized on 10 Mar.), 28 Apr.[100] He divided for Jewish emancipation, 5 Apr., 17 May. He voted to repeal the Irish coal duties, 13 May, for a return of privy councillors' emoluments, 14 May, and to end capital punishment for forgery, 24 May, 7 June 1830.

What Palmerston considered that spring to be the 'very disjointed state' of parties, with a weak administration and an indifferent opposition, was heightened by the instability generated during the final illness of George IV, which may have been partly the reason why he received an abortive approach from Grey via Princess Lieven in April 1830.[101] Following the king's death, he criticized ministers for failing to consider regency proposals and for precipitating a dissolution because they were unable to carry their business through the Commons, 30 June, and, having made an anxious canvassing visit to Cambridge, he probably divided for settling the regency, 6 July.[102] He voted against colonial slavery, 13 July. He was mentioned by Wellington in the course of his overture to Melbourne that month as another potential adherent of government, but that putative arrangement collapsed because of Melbourne's demands for the inclusion of Huskisson and Grey. Palmerston, who told Huskisson that if they returned to the cabinet they would be in an even more powerless position than they had been in 1828 and would incur public odium as unprincipled place-hunters, privately noted that

my mind was quite made up that I, for one, would not accept the very best offer which it was possible for the duke to make us, supposing he was willing to treat us as a party ... without a general or larger reconstruction of his administration.[103]

He was nevertheless supposed to want to rejoin singly, possibly replacing Goulburn as chancellor (as Hardinge surmised), although Peel was reported to have said that Palmerston 'would be too discreditable and unsafe, that he would not come alone and would be paralysed in speaking by fear of attacks from those he quitted'.[104] As no Tory in the end stood, he was returned unopposed with Cavendish at the general election of 1830. This, he believed, brought no significant gains for Wellington, and, buoyed up by the simultaneous revolution in France, an event he hailed as 'decisive of the ascendancy of liberal principles throughout Europe', he predicted the slow demise of the ministry; government, he quipped, was a word which could 'only be rendered by the paraphrase of vacillation in public measures and jobbing in patronage'.[105]

Greville, who had heard conflicting reports of his joining either Grey or Wellington, wrote in his journal, 20 Aug. 1830, that 'it seems odd that Palmerston should abandon his party on the eve of a strong coalition [with the Whigs], which is not unlikely to turn out the present administration', but on the 29th he met Palmerston and could 'from the tenor of his language infer that he has no idea of joining government'.[106] Amid reports of suspected negotiations that summer, Palmerston was one of those participants reported by Anglesey to Edward John Littleton*, 1 Sept., to be 'ripe for mischief, full of fight', and he was certainly in touch with Huskisson, possibly with a view to concocting plans for the forthcoming session, before the latter's fatal accident in mid-September.[107] Thomas Creevey* conjectured that Huskisson's removal would smooth the way for the return of his supporters to office, and Hardinge reckoned that now was the time for Palmerston to do so.[108] Yet he continued to stand aloof, informing Littleton on 25 Sept. 1830 that the difficulties for the Huskissonites of uniting with Wellington 'are increased instead of being diminished' by the death of their leader, 'because they would enter his cabinet more completely destitute of means of influence to carry their opinions into action'; whereas, in relation to joining the Whigs, he averred that 'our maxim should be co-operation whenever practicable, but no incorporation'. In his letter to Grant of the same date, he similarly ruled out accepting any offer from the 'dictator', if indeed one was forthcoming, and, as well as lamenting the loss of Huskisson's extensive talents, guessed that the duke would retain power, just as he had over Catholic emancipation, by enfranchising a token number of manufacturing towns.[109] Brougham, who judged that he would 'return to insignificance with a ruined character' if he left the ranks of opposition, was soon rejoicing that Palmerston wished to 'take council together' with the equally delighted Hollands the following month.[110]

In late September 1830 Wellington contemplated inviting Palmerston to succeed Sir George Murray* as colonial secretary, and, at the suggestion of Mrs. Arbuthnot, who considered him 'the best of that party and certainly a good speaker', he decided to use as an intermediary Lord Clive*, who was an old friend of Palmerston and had involved him with his Ludlow constituency affairs.[111] Clive dutifully embarked on a series of letters and interviews, which resulted in stalemate since, according to Palmerston's later account, he insisted that 'in no case would I join the duke's government singly', and that

> the friends with whom I was politically acting were Melbourne and Grant; but that, to say the truth, I should be unwilling, and I believed they would be so too, to join the duke unless Lansdowne and Grey were to form part of his government.

Likening Wellington's offer to 'asking me whether I was disposed to jump off Westminster bridge', he determined to stick to his and Huskisson's former resolution, which still had Melbourne's support, to hold out for a general rearrangement, a proposal which the prime minister refused to contemplate.[112] To his brother, Palmerston wrote that Wellington 'is playing over again the game of January 1828: he wants us to help him go on, and if by-and-by, when he has got on by our aid, he should be able to stand alone, he would get rid of us again with as little ceremony as before'; so, to avoid further embarrassment, in mid-October he escaped briefly to Paris, where he enjoyed the thrill of the continuing political agitation.[113] Egged on by the Arbuthnots, partly because they had heard, via Littleton, that Palmerston would not insist upon the inclusion of such advanced Whigs as Brougham, the duke met Palmerston again on the 30th, only for their talks to collapse on Wellington's repeating his refusal to countenance a wholesale reconstruction.[114] The question of parliamentary reform seems to have been mentioned during these negotiations, and Wellington's declaration in the Lords against even moderate alterations, 2 Nov. 1830, confirmed Palmerston in the rectitude of his decision.[115] He later recorded, of another Tory approach, that

Croker called on me a few days afterwards to try to persuade me to reconsider the matter. After talking some time he said, 'Well, I will bring the matter to the point. Are you resolved, or are you not, to vote for parliamentary reform?' I said, 'I am'. 'Well, then', said he, 'there is no use in talking to you any more on this subject. You and I, I am grieved to see, shall never again sit on the same bench together'.

By that time, having been sounded out by the Whigs, he and some of the former Canningites, or what Lord Althorp* called the 'Palmerston party', had agreed to vote for Brougham's intended motion on reform, provided it was vaguely worded, and he also promised to ask the Ultras to support it.[116]

Palmerston, who (so Croker assured Peel) was, like Grant, easily answered, as they were 'really nothing but froth', raised a question about Portugal on the address, 3 Nov., and criticized the government's legislative programme and its civil list proposals, 12 Nov. 1830.[117] He divided for Parnell's amendments to reduce the duty on wheat imported to the West Indies, 12 Nov., and to refer the civil list to a select committee, to which he was appointed, 15 Nov., when ministers decided to resign prior to their expected defeat on reform the following day. Palmerston's truncated autobiography ended with the sentence, 'As soon as Lord Grey was commissioned by the king to form an administration he sent for me'; but this was not quite true, since Lord Tavistock*, who thought it 'not a very popular appointment', recorded that both Lansdowne and Holland had declined the foreign office before he accepted it (and the salary of £6,000, soon reduced to £5,000).[118] He had been considered a potential leader of the House, but nothing came of rumours that he had been so appointed. He did propose himself for it to Grey, but declared himself quite content on the new prime minister indicating that this position was to be filled by Althorp, the chancellor; the exchequer, like the home secretaryship (which went to Melbourne), was an office to which Palmerston might reasonably have expected to succeed.[119] He thus led the reduced rump of non-Tory Huskissonites, the 'small political party' which he believed had been the instrument for carrying him into his new position, back into office with the Whigs, with whom he was from then on to be associated.[120] Although, as in the form of Winthrop Mackworth Praed's* cruel parody ('I'm not a Tory now') he remained vulnerable to allegations of being a placeman, others, such as his Cambridge friend George Pryme†, gave him credit for having made a principled stand on emancipation and East Retford.[121] His re-election for the university was a formality, 30 Nov., and, as 'prompter to the puppet', as Croker had maliciously observed, he deputized for the absent Althorp over routine Commons business for much of December 1830.[122] He failed to make a good impression in this role, but as James Abercromby* opined at the end of the year, 'I think the danger is now that they may underrate Palmerston, for I strongly incline to believe in his being manly, firm and honourable in all things'.[123]

According to his official biographer William Henry Lytton Earle Bulwer*, a diplomat, in November 1830 Palmerston's appearance was that

> of a man in the full vigour of middle age, very well dressed, very good looking, with the large thick whiskers worn at the time. His air was more that of a man of the drawing room than of the senate; but he had a clear, short, decisive way of speaking on business which struck me at once.[124]

He was reported by Greville to 'have begun very well' in diplomatic circles, although on 22 Dec., a month after his arrival at the foreign office, Palmerston wrote that 'I have been ever since my appointment like a man who has plumped into a mill-race, scarcely able by all his kicking and plunging to keep his head above water'.[125] Assisted by his colleagues, the gossipy Holland and the sedate Lansdowne, but above all by Grey, whose constant supervision he soon found irksome, he usually overcame residual Whig suspicions of him in cabinet, not least because he circulated papers widely and encouraged discussion on them; for example, early the following year Sir James Graham*, the first lord of the admiralty, commented on 'his honesty and his stoutness', and Althorp told Littleton that 'he is doing his work as well as it is possible to do it; we are all in admiration of him'.[126] He was certainly required to employ immense reserves of application and self-confidence in the role, and he devoted long hours to the rapidly increasing volume of paperwork, which probably contributed to his haggard looks and irritable behaviour; in later years, his idiosyncrasies only worsened, most notably in the form of his appalling unpunctuality and brusque insensitivity. He drove his clerks unmercifully, famously insisting that they write a large and legible hand, and his unpopularity was increased by his endeavours to improve the efficiency of the office and, following parliamentary pressure, to make economies.[127] Princess Lieven, who claimed she had influenced her old lover Grey in favour of the appointment, which she thought 'perfect in every way', of Palmerston (himself probably one of her former paramours), wrote to Lady Cowper in January 1831 that he was 'adorable, *controlling* foreign affairs in every sense of the word'.[128] However, she was later

to change her opinion, not least because Palmerston, who was nobody's fool, soon demonstrated an indomitable spirit and an assured autonomy of action that was quite at odds with his former lowly ministerial subservience. Nothing effected this transformation more than the daunting task, which he inherited on taking over the foreign office, of chairing the newly appointed London conference on Belgium, which had recently won its independence from Holland. These time-consuming, complex and exhausting negotiations, which lasted throughout 1831 and beyond, gave him a fiery apprenticeship in what was an incredibly demanding, but also highly prestigious, cabinet post.[129]

Except in answering numerous questions and making minor interventions, Palmerston was not called on to make many speeches on foreign policy, although when he was, he always ensured that he had fully mastered his subject.[130] He defended the government's suppression of Irish repeal agitation, 8 Feb., and its slight expansion of the army, 18 Feb. 1831, but otherwise, as Greville noted, did almost nothing in the House that month.[131] Refusing Hume's request for the release of the conference's initial protocols on the independence, neutrality and future security of Belgium, he vindicated his principle of non-violent interference in the cause of preserving the general peace of Europe, 18 Feb.[132] But he was considered by Ellenborough to have been too lackadaisical in manner and by Francis Thornhill Baring* to have been unsatisfactory and incautious in content, while Holland informed Lord Granville, the reinstated ambassador in Paris, on the 24th that 'Palmerston does not hit [?suit] the temper of our friends and of the House, so well as I had hoped he would'.[133] Privately, he was pleased at the king's confidence in ministers and, despite his doubts about Lord Durham's radical tendencies, at the popularity of their reform proposals, which, he opined, 'whatever the Tories may say, will not be revolution, but the reverse'.[134] In the words of the Commons clerk John Rickman, he 'lashed himself up to an uphill speech', which was considered a failure, in favour of the reform bill, 3 Mar., when, as well as the more common reasons he adduced for reform, he commented that Canning's genius might have recognized the necessity of it and that the intention was to give the vote to the respectable middle classes.[135] Tavistock admitted on the 10th that Palmerston 'has cut but a sorry figure', and, after he had proved himself no match for Peel in a clash over the Irish reform bill, 24 Mar., Agar Ellis regretted that 'Palmerston, Graham and Grant have all failed lamentably in speaking and in courage'.[136] He was involved in a squabble over his future prospects at Cambridge on bringing up university petitions for and against the reform bill, 30 Mar. Representing Clive's views as an example of a Tory who would be willing to back a more moderate reform bill, Palmerston wrote at length to Grey, 8 April 1831, to urge him to consider such alterations as would ensure its parliamentary passage without incurring the dangerous risk of a dissolution or a dismissal of the government:

> Notwithstanding the applause which has been bestowed upon the bill, we must not disguise from ourselves, that there is a vast mass of intelligence, of property, of liberality and even of Whiggism by which its provisions are looked upon, with some uneasiness, as too sweeping and extensive, and to whom considerable modifications would be exceedingly acceptable; and the points to which the most frequent objections are directed are the extent of disfranchisement, the lowness of the £10 qualification and the reduction in the English representation.

On the last point, he correctly predicted (as Gascoyne's successful wrecking amendment demonstrated later that month) that 'my confident belief is, that we shall be beat, if we resist it'. Although his pleas were partly motivated by concern for his own standing in Cambridge, where he exclaimed that 'I have scarcely met six people who approve of our bill!', a pained Grey refused to alter the principles of it.[137] Palmerston's unequivocal public endorsement of and votes for the bill aroused massive opposition in the university and, despite extensive and expensive canvassing, he and Cavendish were defeated by two Tories in the only major contest to go against the government at the general election of 1831.[138] He expressed hopes of being able to regain the seat, but Lord John Russell*, the paymaster-general, felt he should have been compensated with a safe berth in a county and there was speculation he would make a suitable Member for Liverpool, should he choose to stand there.[139]

Enclosing a cutting from *The Times*, which argued in favour of the will of the people overriding the resistance of the peers, Palmerston complained to the prime minister in May 1831 that such sentiments 'inspire me with unpleasant misgivings that we are hurrying on too fast'. Grey, however, refused to rein back and his 'expressions were so strong that they silenced Palmerston' at the cabinet meeting, 29 May, when the latter was the only minister present who did not agree 'that a very probable consequence of attempting to conciliate the House of Lords by concession would be to lose the House of Commons'.[140] The cabinet split on reform continued in June, when he presented it with Littleton's list of Members hostile to the £10 rate of qualification.[141] Rumours abounded that month that Palmerston would resign over minor humiliations perpetrated by cabinet colleagues on foreign affairs, and Princess Lieven commented that, being dependent on the administration for a treasury seat, he was unfortunately 'forced to bend, to give way and to obey'.[142] The duke of Bedford described Palmerston as 'by no means of the first *calibre*' as foreign secretary, but Grant and Graham confirmed to Littleton that he was cordially respected in the cabinet for his diligent and skilful diplomacy.[143] He was brought in on the government interest for Bletchingley, at a cost of £800, 18 July, and the following year he was reluctantly obliged to pay a further £500.[144] He took his seat on the 19th, when, in a letter to Granville, Holland ruled him out as a possible replacement as leader for Althorp, whose ailing father's death would have removed him to the Lords, as he

> is not popular with the bulk of our House of Commons supporters, and has not, as [Edward Smith] Stanley *perhaps* has, that promptitude and talent in debate which by gratifying the eagerness of the moment overcomes any prejudice of partisans in their leader.[145]

He declined to oppose the disfranchisement of Bletchingley, 20 July 1831, and divided silently for the reform bill's details when present that summer, being, like Grant, as Tom Macaulay* suspected, 'idle and ... not very hearty' on the subject.[146]

It may also have been because Palmerston was distracted by foreign affairs, since, having produced papers on Belgium, 27 July, he was assailed by questions about the French retaliatory military action following the invasion by the disaffected Dutch of its former possessions, 3, 6, 8 Aug. 1831.[147] A petition from the Westminster Union of the Working Classes calling for his removal was presented by Henry Hunt on the 8th, when he ruled out any discussion of the Polish uprising. He persuaded Vyvyan to postpone his hostile motion on France's intentions, 9, 11 Aug., and, confiding that he reckoned that the Tories viewed the possibility of a European war as their last chance of killing the reform bill, he wrote frantically to Granville, instructing him to ascertain whether the French would reciprocate if the Dutch could be persuaded to withdraw.[148] On Croker introducing an unsuccessful motion for papers, with the intention of establishing that the foreign secretary had deceived the House, 12 Aug., Palmerston refused to enter into details and sneeringly dismissed his antagonist with the words, 'I, for one, do not write in the newspapers'; this put-down was, in fact, of doubtful accuracy, but Littleton privately noted that 'indifference and contempt were never expressed with more good humour, or in a more gentlemanly manner'.[149] Lord Valletort's question about French naval actions off Portugal 'fell very flat', 18 Aug., and, since it failed to elicit any information relating to the continuing negotiations, Vyvyan's motion, 20 Aug. 1831, 'led to nothing, Palmerston saying nothing at all' of any substance.[150] Thanking Granville for having obtained the requested reassurances from France, Palmerston commented that 'our opponents are now obliged to tender us their *doleful congratulations* upon our fortunate escape from what they looked forward to as a certain piece of luck'.[151] He stifled Thomas Peregrine Courtenay's repeated attempts to request information on Portugal towards the end of the session.

In the summer Palmerston had imagined that the creation of 'a few peers' would have secured the passage of the reform bill through the Lords, but by late August 1831 Holland was disappointed to notice that he and Lansdowne were 'disinclined to any measure vigorous enough to be effectual', and by the following month the foreign secretary was canvassing his cabinet colleagues on the lengths they were prepared to go in manipulating public opinion as a means of pressurizing the upper House.[152] In a letter to Lady Cowper, 8 Oct., he expressed his surprise at the size of the majority against the second reading of the reform bill in the Lords the previous night, but noted that 'at least it has one good effect, it puts out of the question any idea of making a batch of peers to carry the bill'. Although determined to stand by his fellow ministers, he differed from most of them in believing that the only way to secure its passage was by making enough concessions to obtain sufficient support, as a bill which did not give 'too great and sudden an increase of power to the democratical influence' would please 'the great bulk of the gentry of the country'; on each of the next three days he protested to Grey against Althorp committing him by a prospective pledge to a bill just as extensive in scope as the one which had been lost, since, for all that he approved of the general outline of the measure, he insisted that its more dubious details were still subject to discussion and alteration in cabinet.[153] At the urgent request of Melbourne and others not to risk a split in the ministry, he decided against stating this punctilio during the debate on Lord Ebrington's confidence motion, 10 Oct. 1831, perhaps because Althorp purposely avoided compromising him directly. On the 14th Grey resentfully denied that such statements of government intent precluded making such changes as were found to be necessary, while Holland privately recorded his qualms about Palmerston's 'strange scruples' and Durham, discerning 'the cloven foot in Palmerston's letter very plainly', called him a 'thorough anti-reformer'.[154]

Later that month Palmerston began to attempt to create a consensus for alterations in the reform bill among his more moderate colleagues, including Smith Stanley, who found him 'very dissatisfied' especially at the antics of the more extreme members of the government, whose friendly newspapers were 'identifying ourselves with the radicals and breaking down all our established institutions, etc.'[155] By mid-November 1831 he had also opened discussions with Lord Wharncliffe about possible Tory co-operation over certain parts of the bill, one of the first attempts to initiate negotiations with the 'Waverers' in the Lords.[156] He had thought that 'the natural disinclination which all ministers must have to so unnecessary a renewal of a laborious attendance' would prevent the 'violents' from carrying their attempt to have Parliament recalled before Christmas, but he was in the minority of three against this (with Grey and the duke of Richmond) in cabinet, 19 Nov.[157] He wrote furiously to Melbourne, one of four absentees, the following day that, had time been given to complete his talks

> we could not only have improved the measure, but have ensured a majority in the House of Lords for that and all other purposes *before* Parliament had met. How this is now to be done I hardly see. John Russell is tomorrow three weeks to expound what we call the principles, but what, as we well know from experience, will be all the *details*, of the bill. From that point all negotiation is over.[158]

In fact, Palmerston renewed his discussions with Wharncliffe and continued to urge modifications to the bill, though he was so worried by some of the suggested changes, including the proposals to omit the division of counties and to substitute scot and lot for the householder franchise, that he commented, in relation to the opponents to the bill, that 'we have caught at the letter of their arguments without regarding the spirit', thus serving only to increase their objections. Despite having his own complex ideas for changing schedules B and D, on which he had done some detailed work, he was willing to agree to Grey's compromise of the bare minimum of significant changes at a heated cabinet meeting, 30 Nov. 1831.[159]

Assisted by a rapprochement with France, Palmerston secured an international treaty on Belgium, 15 Nov. 1831, which he described as 'a great thing done', and two days later Littleton noted in his diary that 'his success, through a thousand difficulties and constantly impending war, and other machinations and lies and evil forebodings of party, is a signal triumph'.[160] Speaking on the address, he denied that the settlement had been forced on the people of

Belgium, 7 Dec. By then, as what Creevey described in a letter to Miss Ord on the 6th as 'the ringleader of the insurgents', he was pressing openly for co-operation with the 'Waverers', but, although he had assured them that only schedule A and the £10 franchise were regarded as unalterable principles, it transpired that no real concessions were on offer when, at Palmerston's behest, they met Althorp, Brougham and Grey on the 10th.[161] On Russell introducing the revised reform bill, 12 Dec. 1831, he apparently 'came in late and seemed to go to sleep'.[162] Still hankering after alterations, he strongly objected to the future creation of a large group of new peers, an issue on which it was imagined he might resign, at the cabinet's meeting on 2 Jan. 1832, and thereafter he supported the idea of calling up only the heirs to existing titles, as well as Scottish or Irish lords, and attempted to restart negotiations with Wharncliffe and his friends.[163] Greville recorded that month that he and Melbourne were 'now heartily ashamed of the part they have played about reform. They detest and abhor the whole thing ... and they do not know what to do, whether to stay in and fight this unequal battle or resign'.[164] However, for all that it was bad tempered and tardy, his intervention in vindication of the Russian-Dutch loan (in other words, of the payments which, the United Provinces not having quite yet been formally dissolved, Britain was still obliged to make), rescued the government, 26 Jan. 1832.[165] Althorp informed his father the following day that 'Palmerston made a capital speech at last and saved us, for we know that he converted solo enough to account for nearly the whole majority', which fell as low as 20 in one of the two divisions.[166]

Granville commented to Holland, 23 Jan. 1832, that 'I think with you that Palmerston's foreign politics are essentially good and liberal, but he is constantly apprehensive, not of being duped, but of being thought to be duped by Talleyrand and the French government'.[167] The French ambassador was said by Raikes to have 'got Palmerston in his *wily embrace*', and a strikingly lifelike double portrait of them in a cartoon entitled 'the lame [Talleyrand] leading the blind' aroused his intense resentment at this time.[168] His worries about the parliamentary treatment of his departmental responsibilities were illustrated by the way he anxiously briefed Littleton to assist him in answering Vyvyan's hostile questioning over the Belgian settlement, 3 Feb.; he again had to respond on this and about a convention with France on the slave trade, 6 Feb.[169] He had been restrained by the cabinet from becoming too involved, as the French navy had done, with the military activities of Dom Pedro, on behalf of his daughter Maria, but Courtenay's motion for information on Portugal, 9

Feb., forced him to defend his active diplomatic interference against the Miguelite regime, a concentrated and protracted policy of attempting to facilitate the return of the legitimate ruler which he nevertheless claimed did not abrogate his principle of non-intervention.[170] In response to bellicose questioning from Vyvyan about French military ambitions in Italy, 7, 13 Mar., he calmed fears of a European war; wishing to keep both France and Austria as much as possible out of the vacuum of collapsing Italian states, including the Papacy, he made determined efforts that year to encourage them to establish viable governmental institutions.[171] The airing of criticisms by Lord Eliot, who echoed the usual Tory objection that Palmerston was too close to the French, 26 Mar., led him into a lengthy vindication of his policies towards Belgium and Portugal, particularly as having been carried out in accordance with Britain's overall interests. He ridiculed Dixon's allegation that he had 'repeatedly shuffled away' from his inquiries about compensation due from Brazil to British merchants, 13 Apr., and did enough to prevent his pressing his motion for papers to a division, 16 Apr. 1832.

Since February 1832 Palmerston, still resolutely opposed to peerage creations, had been confident that the reform bill would be read a second time in the Lords and that, with Grey being more reasonable, no amendments 'which we shall not be prepared to agree to', would be forced on the government.[172] Ministerial differences persisted the following month, with Russell complaining that 'Palmerston especially had never "given his mind to it" or cared at all about it', although Durham, of whom Palmerston caustically observed that he 'would make 70 peers to secure one Member for Gateshead', was heartened by the fact that 'even Palmerston had declared he would stand by the franchise'.[173] According to Holland's diary, 3 Apr., he was 'as usual civil, courteous and fair' in stating his reservations about the cabinet's contingency plans in the event of the bill's defeat, hinting that he would personally, despite having the most to lose financially, prefer resignation to a dissolution or the manufacture of an artificial majority in the Upper House.[174] He was disappointed that the government only carried the second reading in the Lords by nine votes, 13 Apr., but, relieved that by its removing speculation about his personal vulnerability his diplomatic hand would be strengthened, he instructed Frederick Lamb, the ambassador at Vienna, to 'boldly present this division as the Waterloo of parties in England, and as deciding the continuance of the present ministry in office. I hope it may produce an effect upon Metternich'.[175] Concerned at the mustering of the Tories, he arranged and hosted another meeting between Grey and Wharncliffe, 28 Apr., when he understood the latter to have promised not to vote for putting off the disfranchisement clauses.[176] He therefore felt betrayed when the 'Waverers' divided in the majority for Lord Lyndhurst's wrecking amendment, 7 May, and surprisingly, at the emergency cabinet on the 8th, it was he who called for the immediate creation of up to 50 peers.[177] He informed Lamb that, unlike his fellow moderates, he

> felt strongly that as we had prevented the making of peers at a time when the king gave Grey the power to do so, if now in consequence of none being made we are defeated, we were to insist upon dissolving the government, we should be accused and with some show of plausibility, of a scheme to defeat the bill and to play false to our colleagues.

As well as considerations of public unrest in necessitating reform, he added:

> Had we been beat on a clause of the bill, the metropolitan districts, the rating of the ten pounders, the exclusion of the county freeholders living in represented towns or anything of that kind, I should not have agreed to make peers for that; but this proposal was either nothing but a mere preference of arrangement or it was an opinion against disfranchisement. If it was the former, the making it a pitched battle and a defeat of the government was intended for the purpose of compelling the government to resign; if the latter, it attacked a fundamental principle of the bill. In either case we have no longer any power over our own measures in the Lords and must either strengthen ourselves or retire.[178]

Refusing to apologize for any change in his own opinions in the Commons, 14 May, he justified ministers' conduct in resigning, the king having chosen this course over the cabinet's request for peerage creations. He was delighted by the decision made by the Whigs at Brooks's that night to oppose any reform bill emerging from the putative Wellington government, commenting to Lamb the following day that 'the debate of last night was the most remarkable expression of public opinion, upon the political conduct of public men, which I ever remember to have witnessed, and that has been the immediate cause of the duke's failure'.[179] Pleased to be back in office, he wrote on the 18th that, not least because of the irresponsibility of the Tories, it was

> impossible to disguise from oneself that the events of the last ten days have struck a harder blow at royal and aristocratical power in this country than any thing since the days of Charles I, saving the expulsion of James II, because a ministry and a measure odious to the peers and distasteful to the king have been forced upon both by the House of Commons as backed by the great mass of the nation.[180]

Thereafter, he grudgingly accepted the bill as the best an essentially conservative reformer could hope for in the way of limiting concessions to democratic demands, and, apart from declining O'Connell's invitation to back the re-enfranchisement of the Irish 40s. freeholders on 13 June 1832, he made no further speeches on it.[181]

That month Palmerston, who was given the grand cross of the order of the Bath as a personal mark of favour by William IV, was annoyed by what he considered quite improper press attacks, inspired he suspected by Durham and Ellice, on his employing Tories as diplomats; his approval of Durham to lead a special mission to Russia was partly designed to satisfy the violent Whigs in this respect.[182] He had long played down calls for intervention in aid of the Polish rebels and, aware that they had popular support, he agreed to Cutlar Fergusson's motion for papers and noticeably failed to condemn O'Connell's scurrilous attack on the tsar for perpetrating atrocities against them, 28 June 1832.[183] As he put it, the government 'beat the Tories handsomely about the Russian-Dutch loan, though they counted upon a victory', 12 July, but he again had to defend the payments to Russia, 16 July, and it was not until the 20th, when he spoke admirably in defence of his policy of stabilizing Belgium, that he could finally dispose of the question.[184] He saw off the disaffected Bulwer's motion for papers on the German Diet's Austrian inspired repression of personal and press freedoms, 2 Aug., when, in an important speech, he remarked that 'constitutional states I consider to be the natural allies of this country' and, rejecting 'non-intervention' as a French word, he reiterated his principal of 'non-interference by force of arms' combined with the occasional expedient of 'interfering by friendly counsel and advice'; to the king, who as elector of Hanover had approved the Diet's resolutions, Palmerston presented on the 5th what Holland called 'a long and spirited' remonstrance in favour of liberal institutions.[185] Although, in line with his initially philhellenic policies, he obtained his committee on a loan to guarantee the independence of Greece, 6 Aug., he had by this time realized the necessity of propping up the Ottoman Empire, particularly against Russian and Egyptian aggression.[186] He was obliged to remain in London for parliamentary and official business that month and, despite Lady Cowper's assertion that 'a person of less sanguine disposition than his would have been quite worn out long ago' by the still unsettled affairs of Belgium and Portugal, in late September 1832 he was desperate for a holiday, having not had a full week off in nearly two years.[187]

By the autumn of 1832 Palmerston, still flatteringly called 'the Romsey dandy' and also known as 'Protocol Palmerston', had earned the nickname 'Lord Pumicestone' for his abrasive foreign policy, which in a later age would became characterized as 'gunboat diplomacy' and 'brinkmanship'.[188] His former admirer Princess Lieven, who thought him a mule 'rushing headlong towards liberalism', denounced him as 'a poor, small-minded creature, wounded in his vanity, who wants a great warlike demonstration behind which he hopes to conceal his blunders'.[189] Yet her intrigue to engineer his replacement by Durham, her latest dupe, spectacularly misfired when he contrived to have her husband recalled two years later, a banishment for which she never forgave him.[190] By this time he was again occupied in releasing information to, and even drafting articles for, reliable newspapers; he had explained to Lady Cowper in 1831 that he could 'impel' the inclusion of favourable paragraphs but not 'control' the appearance of critical ones, but this did not prevent him from joining the fray by assisting the *Globe*, his preferred vehicle, as a counterweight to the hostility of *The Times*.[191] As Greville later wrote, in a unsympathetic assessment which could equally well refer to this period:

> Palmerston, the most enigmatical of ministers, who is detested by the *corps diplomatique*, abhorred in his own office, unpopular in the House of Commons, liked by nobody, abused by everybody, still reigns in his little kingdom of the foreign office, and is impervious to any sense of shame from the obloquy that has been cast upon him, and apparently not troubling himself about the affairs of the government generally, which he leaves it to others to defend and uphold as they best may.[192]

Nevertheless, he was a colossus of a foreign secretary, who, while sometimes content to work within the confines of the concert of Europe, but also bold enough to nurture the development of constitutional states, was ultimately, like his mentor Canning, governed by considerations of Realpolitik, as encapsulated in his later dictum that 'we have no eternal allies, and we have no perpetual enemies. Our interests are eternal and perpetual, and those interests it is our duty to follow'.[193]

Palmerston, who realized he had no chance of regaining his seat at Cambridge University and turned down offers from several other constituencies, was eventually satisfied that he had sufficient backing in Hampshire South and was returned as a Liberal for his native county after a contest at the general election of 1832.[194] He lost his seat there in 1834, but thereafter sat for Tiverton and held high office almost continuously for the rest of his life, twice serving as prime minister. Talleyrand judged him to be

> certainly one of, if not quite the ablest of statesmen I have ever met with in all my official career. He possesses all the aptitude and capacity which most contributes to form such a man in England – extensive and varied information, indefatigable activity, an iron constitution, inexhaustible mental resources and great facility of speech in Parliament. Without being what is called a great *debater*, his style of eloquence is biting and satirical, his talent lying more in his power of crushing an adversary under the weight of his irony and sarcasm, than of convincing his auditors; and furthermore, he has great social qualities and highly finished manners.[195]

In his oratory, which was not very evident in his early years at the foreign office, he was certainly more effective than eloquent.[196] But in this, as in other respects, his character was full of contradictions: although bred on an ideology of aristocratic paternalism, he was nothing if not a practical politician; although exploiting the growing assertiveness of public opinion, he was never more than a conservative reformer at home; although avowing liberal sentiments abroad, he was always and conspicuously a patriot; and above all, despite being a devilish old roué, even after his marriage to Lady Cowper in 1839, he was the supreme epitome of Victorian pride, respectability and self-assurance.[197] Of his death in harness, 18 Oct. 1865, just after the general election of that month and two days before his 81st birthday, Philip Guedalla, in a famous envoi, later wrote '... and the last candle of the eighteenth century was out'; and yet undoubtedly more accurate, since by then he was the acclaimed embodiment of the national character, was the *Daily Telegraph*'s obituary notice of him as 'the most English minister'.[198]

[1] Palmerston's pprs., some of which are accessible at www.archives.soton.ac.uk/palmerston, form part of the Broadlands mss at Southampton Univ. Lib. These were partly printed in Sir Henry Lytton Bulwer (Lord Dalling), *Life of Henry John Temple, Visct. Palmerston*, 5 vols. (1870-6) [hereafter cited as Bulwer]; following Dalling's death, the last three volumes of this work were edited and written by the Hon. Evelyn Ashley, who prepared a revised and enlarged edition, *Life and Corresp. of Henry John Temple, Visct. Palmerston*, 2 vols. (1879) [hereafter cited as Ashley]. P. Guedalla's influential but romanticized portrait, *Palmerston* (1926) and H.C.F. Bell's workmanlike *Lord Palmerston*, 2 vols. (1936), were echoed in a number of routine 20th century biographies, to which D. Southgate's study, *'The Most English Minister': The Politics and Policies of Palmerston* (1966), was a worthy companion. J. Ridley's generally reliable *Lord Palmerston* (1972 edn.) has been superseded by the most recent life, J. Chambers, *Palmerston: 'The People's*

Darling' (2004); while, as a basic introduction, M. Chamberlain, *Lord Palmerston* (1987) is preferable to P.R. Ziegler, *Palmerston* (2003). For the first half of his career, the authoritative account is K. Bourne, *Palmerston, The Early Years, 1784-1841* (1982), which is much relied on here; as, for his diplomacy, is Sir C. Webster, *Foreign Policy of Palmerston, 1830-1841: Britain, the Liberal Movement and the Eastern Question*, 2 vols. (1951). [2] Not the 11th, as erroneously stated in *HP Commons, 1790-1820*, v. 348. [3] Chambers, 51-52; Ridley, 93; Bourne, 80-82, 115, 181-2, 227. [4] Broadlands mss PP/GC/LI/184-5, 192-3; Bourne, 90-92, 96, 103-5, 110-11, 115-19, 122, 142-4, 146, 161, 170-2; M. Partridge, 'Palmerston and War Office', ch. 1 in *Palmerston Stud.* ed. D. Brown and M. Taylor, ii. 1-23. [5] Bulwer, i. 145-6; Ashley, i. 86-87, 102-3. [6] Bulwer, i. 150; Bourne, 234-5. [7] Guedalla, 100-2; *Moore Jnl.* i. 174; Hatherton diary, 17 Mar. 1836. For his future wife, see Countess of Airlie, *Lady Palmerston and her Times*, 2 vols. (1922) and F.E. Baily, *Love Story of Lady Palmerston* (1938). [8] Bourne, 182-224. [9] '... and Mr. Fortescue' ed. O.S. Hewett, 162. [10] *Cambridge and Hertford Independent Press*, 19, 26 Feb., 11 Mar. 1820; Bourne, 241. [11] Broadlands mss PP/GC/WE/55; SLT/22; BR195/12-17, 20-25; *Palmerston-Sulivan Letters*, 148; Bourne, 157-8, 232. [12] *Palmerston-Sulivan Letters*, 148-9; Hants RO, Malmesbury mss 9M73/404; *Malmesbury Letters*, ii. 537-8. [13] *The Times*, 17 Mar. 1821. [14] *Lady Palmerston Letters*, 79. [15] Add. 38194, ff. 78, 80. [16] Ibid. f. 83; Broadlands mss PP/GC/LI/190; TE/167. [17] Add. 38743, f. 75. [18] Gurney diary; Chambers, 88, 91-92. [19] Bourne, 135-6; Ashley, i. 88. [20] *Palmerston-Sulivan Letters*, 151-3; *Croker Pprs.* i. 230-1. [21] *Palmerston-Sulivan Letters*, 156-9; Bourne, 172-3, 238-9. [22] *Palmerston-Sulivan Letters*, 153-5; Bourne, 241-2; *The Times*, 17, 23 Apr. 1823. [23] Broadlands mss PP/SP/A/4. [24] Ridley, 105-11; *Cobbett's Rural Rides* ed. G.D.H. and M. Cole, 467-70, 483-4. [25] *Palmerston-Sulivan Letters*, 161-6, 170, 171. [26] *PP* (1825), vii. 1-458; *The Times*, 25 June 1824. [27] Parker, *Peel*, i. 357. [28] *PP* (1825), viii. 1-845. [29] Broadlands mss PP/GC/TE/171. [30] Bulwer, i. 158-9, 161, 174-9; *Palmerston-Sulivan Letters*, 174-5, 183-6; *Arbuthnot Corresp.* 78; D. Norton, 'On Lord Palmerston's Irish Estates in 1840s', *EHR*, cxix (2004), 1255-7. [31] *Palmerston-Sulivan Letters*, 172; Buckingham, *Mems. Geo. IV*, ii. 249. [32] Add. 40381, f. 437; 51659, Whishaw to Holland, 3 Dec.; *Cambridge Chron.* 9, 16, 30 Dec. 1825; Bulwer, i. 161, 164-6; *Palmerston-Sulivan Letters*, 176-7. [33] CUL Add. 8339/2, 14, 15, 23, 32, 33, 36, 39, 58, 64; *Palmerston-Sulivan Letters*, 177-81; J. W. Clark and T. McK. Hughes, *Life and Letters of Sedgwick*, i. 268-70, 275-7; *Eng. Hist. Docs.* xi. 105-8; Broadlands mss, Liverpool to Palmerston, 23 Jan. 1826; Bourne, 242-6. [34] CUL Add. 8339/90, 122. [35] Bourne, 139-41, 174-5. [36] CUL Add. 8339/152, 181, 184, 185; *The Times*, 14-17 June 1826; Bulwer, i. 166-70, 373; *Palmerston-Sulivan Letters*, 181-3. [37] Broadlands mss, Palmerston to Liverpool, 31 May 1826; Bulwer, i. 167, 169-72, 374. [38] Add. 38301, f. 261; 38568, f. 129; Bulwer, i. 372; Bourne, 139, 248, 250-1. [39] Broadlands mss PP/D/25; Bulwer, i. 178-81; Bourne, 249-50; A. Aspinall, 'Canningite Party', *TRHS* (ser. 4), xvii (1934), 215. [40] Bourne, 249. [41] *The Times*, 22 Feb. 1827. [42] Bourne, 253-64. [43] Bulwer, i. 188-9, 374-5; *Palmerston-Sulivan Letters*, 187; *Canning's Ministry*, 118, 240. [44] Bulwer, i. 186-7, 191; Bourne, 175-7; *Palmerston-Sulivan Letters*, 189; *The Times*, 22 June 1827. [45] Bulwer, i. 189-92. [46] *Arbuthnot Jnl.* i. 419; ii. 129, 135. [47] Bulwer, i. 375-7; Bourne, 252-3, 263-5. [48] *Lady Palmerston Letters*, 173; *Palmerston-Sulivan Letters*, 190. [49] Broadlands mss PP/GMC/17; Bulwer, i. 196-8, 377-8; *Geo. IV Letters*, iii. 1392; *Huskisson Pprs.* 227-9. [50] *Palmerston-Sulivan Letters*, 193-5, 198. [51] Ibid. 196-9; A. Aspinall, *Politics and the Press*, 132, 221; Brougham mss, Palmerston to Brougham, 22 Aug., 1 Sept. 1827; Bourne, 267-8. [52] Bulwer, i. 198. [53] Ibid. i. 378; *Palmerston-Sulivan Letters*, 200. [54] *Creevey Pprs.* ii. 123; Wellington mss WP1/895/22; *Palmerston-Sulivan Letters*, 197; Bourne, 177-9. [55] Wellington mss WP1/895/15; Lonsdale mss, Croker to Lowther, 11 Aug. [1827]; Bulwer, i. 193-6. [56] Bulwer, i. 200-5; *Melbourne's Pprs.* 108-9. [57] Add. 40862, f. 233; *Palmerston-Sulivan Letters*, 204. [58] Bulwer, i. 210, 378-9; E. Herries, *Mem. of Public Life of Herries*, i. 128-30, 162-3, 193-5, 234; ii. 77-86. [59] *Arbuthnot Jnl.* ii. 159, 162-3. [60] Broadlands mss PP/GMC/18;

BR23AA/5/1, 5; Powis mss, Palmerston to Clive, 15 Jan. 1828; Bulwer, i. 217-20, 379-80. [61] Broadlands mss PP/GMC/24-28; BR23AA/5/2; Add. 38754, ff. 132, 152, 157; Bulwer, i. 380. [62] Broadlands mss PP/CAB/1; Bourne, 179. [63] Broadlands mss PP/GMC/28; Add. 40395, f. 167; Bourne, 280. [64] Bulwer, i. 231; Wellington mss WP1/928/5. [65] *Arbuthnot Jnl.* ii. 166-7, 177. [66] Bulwer, i. 231-5, 239-46. [67] Ibid. i. 223-4, 230-1, 238, 246-50; Wellington mss WP1/926/9. [68] Ashley, i. 140-1. [69] A. Aspinall, 'Last of the Canningites', *EHR*, l (1935), 645. [70] Add. 38756, f. 247; *Arbuthnot Jnl.* ii. 187; *Ellenborough Diary*, i. 98, 103-4, 106-7, 109; *Greville Mems.* i. 208; Bulwer, i. 250; Broadlands mss PP/D/2, ff. 18-25; Ashley, i. 143-6. [71] Bulwer, i. 234-5, 253-68; Broughton, *Recollections*, v. 203-4; Wellington mss WP1/980/29. [72] *Ellenborough Diary*, i. 113, 116; Broughton, iii. 271; Bulwer, i. 272-6, 380-1; Wellington mss WP1/933/10; 935/45; Ward, *Letters to 'Ivy'*, 339. [73] G.R. Gleig, *Personal Reminiscences of Wellington*, 41-42. [74] Broadlands mss PP/GC/TE/200; Bulwer, i. 277-9; *Palmerston-Sulivan Letters*, 205-6; Aspinall, 'Canningite Party', 224-6; Bourne, 288, 290. [75] Ashley, i. 163; *Arbuthnot Jnl.* ii. 190; *Palmerston-Sulivan Letters*, 205; Bulwer, i. 268. [76] Bulwer, i. 282-7; *Palmerston-Sulivan Letters*, 206-7; Broadlands mss BR23AA/5/3; Ashley, i. 164-6. [77] Broadlands mss BR23AA/5/4; Bulwer, i. 287-95. [78] Broadlands mss PP/D/2, f. 73; *Palmerston-Sulivan Letters*, 212, 213. [79] Bulwer, i. 299-313; Broadlands mss PP/D/2, ff. 92-93; *Palmerston-Sulivan Letters*, 211-19; Bourne, 293-4. [80] Bulwer, i. 313-25; *Palmerston-Sulivan Letters*, 223-9; Broughton, iii. 300. [81] *Palmerston-Sulivan Letters*, 230. [82] *Greville Mems.* i. 274, 283; Bourne, 295-6. [83] Broadlands mss PP/SP/A/9, 11-17. [84] Bulwer, i. 327-33. [85] Broadlands mss PP/D/5. [86] Ibid. PP/GC/TE/204. [87] Ibid. PP/D/5; SP/A/18; Bulwer, i. 333-4, 340-6; *Greville Mems.* i. 296; Heron, *Notes*, 178; Guedalla, 139-40. [88] Bulwer, i. 334-7. [89] Durham CRO, Londonderry mss C83/25; *Arbuthnot Corresp.* 120; Broadlands mss SP/B/1. [90] Cornw. RO, Vyvyan mss, Knatchbull to Vyvyan, 26 Aug., replies, 31 Aug., 7 Sept. 1829. [91] Ibid. Vyvyan to Cumberland, 6, 22 Oct. 1829; Broadlands mss BR23AA/5/6; *Palmerston-Sulivan Letters*, 232-6; B.T. Bradfield, 'Sir Richard Vyvyan and Fall of Wellington's Government', *Univ. of Birmingham Hist. Jnl.* xi (1967-8), 148-9. [92] Broadlands mss BR23AA/5/8; Bourne, 304-6. [93] Bulwer, i. 347-59; Lansdowne mss. [94] Grey mss, Ellice to Grey, 18 Jan., [1 Feb.] 1830. [95] Nottingham Univ. Lib. Ossington mss OsC72. [96] Add. 56554, f. 65. [97] *Greville Mems.* i. 374; Add. 51786, Holland to Fox, 3 Mar. 1830; Bourne, 307, 309. [98] Northants. RO, Agar Ellis diary; Grey mss, Howick jnl.; *Howard Sisters*, 125. [99] *Letter to Friend in Paris by one of Minority on Lord Palmerston's Motion* (1830); W. Walton, *Letter addressed to Visct. Palmerston* (1830); Bourne, 307, 667. [100] *Jekyll Corresp.* ed. A. Bourke, 229. [101] Bourne, 310-11. [102] *Palmerston-Sulivan Letters*, 240. [103] Broadlands mss PP/GMC/33; Bulwer, i. 381; Bourne, 312-13; J. Milton-Smith, 'Earl Grey's Cabinet and Parliamentary Reform', *HJ*, xv (1972), 61. [104] *Ellenborough Diary*, ii. 306, 312, 316; *Arbuthnot Jnl.* ii. 373. [105] Sir James Graham mss (IHR microfilm XR 80), 1, bdle. 2, Palmerston to Graham, 28 July; *Cambridge Chron.* 30 July, 6 Aug. 1830; Harewood mss WYL 250/11/60; Airlie, i. 172-4; Milton-Smith, 62; Webster, i. 80. [106] *Greville Mems.* ii. 33, 39. [107] *Unrepentant Tory* ed. R.A. Gaunt, 121, 125; Hatherton mss; *Palmerston-Sulivan Letters*, 241. [108] *Creevey Pprs.* ii. 213; *Arbuthnot Corresp.* 139. [109] Hatherton mss; Broadlands mss PP/GMC/34, 35, 38. [110] Chatsworth mss, Brougham to Devonshire [21, 30 Sept.]; Agar Ellis diary, 25 Sept., 1 Oct. 1830. [111] *Arbuthnot Jnl.* ii. 389-90; *Palmerston-Sulivan Letters*, 14. [112] Bulwer, i. 381-2; Broadlands mss PP/GMC/36-40; Add. 51599A, Palmerston to Holland, 12 Oct.; Hatherton mss, same to Holland, 12 Oct. 1830; Bourne, 319-23. [113] Ashley, i. 212; *Palmerston-Sulivan Letters*, 242-7. [114] *Arbuthnot Jnl.* ii. 393; Parker, ii. 165; Bulwer, i. 382-3; Broadlands mss PP/GMC/42; Hatherton mss, Littleton to Wellesley, 20 Dec. 1830. [115] Powis mss, 'mem.' [Nov. 1830]; *Ellenborough Diary*, ii. 418; *Arbuthnot Jnl.* ii. 397-8. [116] Bulwer, i. 383; Broughton, iv. 60; Agar Ellis diary, 12, 13 Nov.; Fitzwilliam mss, Althorp to Milton, 15 Nov. 1830; Bourne, 324-7. [117] *Croker Pprs.* ii. 74. [118] Bulwer, i. 383; Walpole, *Russell*, i. 160; G.

M. Trevelyan, *Lord Grey of Reform Bill*, 379. [119] Grey mss, Durham to Grey, 4 Oct.; Powis mss, Holmes to Powis [c.17 Nov.]; Hatherton mss, Palmerston to Littleton, 17 Nov. 1830; Le Marchant, *Althorp*, 260; *Palmerston-Sulivan Letters*, 248; Bourne, 328-9. [120] P. Ziegler, *Melbourne*, 119; Webster, i. 19-22; Aspinall, 'Last of the Canningites', 659, 663, 668-9. [121] Ridley, 210-11; *Autobiographic Recollections of George Pryme* ed. A. Bayne, 177. [122] *Croker Pprs.* ii. 80. [123] Bucks. RO, Fremantle mss D/FR/139/14/73; *Three Diaries*, 2-3. [124] Bulwer, ii. 17. [125] *Greville Mems.* ii. 88-89; *Palmerston-Sulivan Letters*, 248. [126] E.A. Smith, *Lord Grey*, 262, 279-81; Webster, i. 31-35; Bourne, 499-501; Lambton mss (History of Parliament Aspinall transcripts), Graham to Durham, 31 Jan. 1831; *Three Diaries*, 91. [127] Bulwer, ii. 130; Webster, i. 58-60, 64, 72; Sir E. Hertslet, *Recollections of Old Foreign Office*, 24-25, 34-35; Sir J. Tilley and S. Gaselee, *Foreign Office*, 50-60, 63-69; Bourne, 415-26, 430-4, 438-9, 441, 445, 449. [128] *Lieven Letters*, 276; *Lieven-Palmerston Corresp.* 24; Bourne, 330-1. [129] Webster, i. 91-92, 104-18; Bourne, 332-4. [130] Webster, i. 42-43, 57; ii. 782-3. [131] *Greville Mems.* ii. 118. [132] Webster, i. 119-30. See also J.A. Betley, *Belgium and Poland in International Relations, 1830-1831*. [133] *Three Diaries*, 54; *Baring Jnls.* i. 81; TNA, Granville mss 30/29. [134] Bulwer, ii. 45, 48; Milton-Smith, 67. [135] O. Williams, *Life and Letters of Rickman*, 275; *Three Diaries*, 63; Broughton, iv. 90; N. Gash, *Politics in Age of Peel*, 13-14. [136] *Russell Letters*, ii. 327-8; St. Deiniol's Lib. Glynne-Gladstone mss 197, T. to J. Gladstone, 25 Mar.; Agar Ellis diary, 25 Mar. 1831. [137] Grey mss; Trevelyan, 301; Milton-Smith, 67; Bourne, 505-6. [138] Ashley, i. 258-9; *Palmerston-Sulivan Letters*, 248-9; *Cambridge Chron.* 29 Apr., 6, 13 May 1831; Bourne, 508-10. [139] Add. 51600, Palmerston to Lady Holland [8 May]; 51680, Russell to same [?3 May]; Glynne-Gladstone mss 198, T. to J. Gladstone, 7, 10 May 1831. [140] Grey mss, Palmerston to Grey, 14 May, reply [15 May], Althorp to Durham [29 May 1830]; Trevelyan, 301-2. [141] Milton-Smith, 67; *Three Diaries*, 98. [142] *Arbuthnot Corresp.* 146; *Arbuthnot Jnl.* ii. 425-6; *Creevey's Life and Times*, 345-6; *Lieven Letters*, 305. [143] *Russell Letters*, ii. 350; Hatherton diary, 30 June 1831. [144] Bourne, 509-10, 534-5. [145] Granville mss. [146] *Macaulay Letters*, i. 91. [147] Webster, i. 132, 137-9. [148] Ibid. i. 139; Bulwer, ii. 98, 102-3, 120. [149] Surr. Hist. Cent. Goulburn mss Acc. 304/67B, Goulburn to wife [12 Aug.]; Hatherton diary, 12 Aug. 1831; Bulwer, ii. 18-21; Bourne, 480. [150] *Greville Mems.* ii. 186; *Three Diaries*, 120. [151] Bulwer, ii. 120. [152] Hatherton diary, 18 July; Herts. Archives, Panshanger mss, Palmerston to Melbourne, 3 Sept. 1831; Milton-Smith, 68; *Holland House Diaries*, 43. [153] Broadlands mss BR23AA/5/9; PP/GC/GR/2355-7; Trevelyan, 313-14. [154] Ziegler, 147; *Holland House Diaries*, 66, 69; Add. 76373, Althorp to Grey, 9 Oct.; Grey mss, Durham to same [11 Oct.], Grey to Palmerston, 14 Oct. 1831. [155] Broadlands mss PP/GC/DE/61; RI/11; Sir James Graham mss 1, bdle. 7, Smith Stanley to Graham, 27 Oct. 1831. [156] Broadlands mss BR23AA/5/17; *Greville Mems.* ii. 214-5; Bourne, 514-15. [157] Broadlands mss BR23AA/5/10; Bourne, 515-16. [158] *Melbourne's Pprs.* 140-2. [159] Wellington mss WP1/1202/13; Broadlands mss PP/HA/D/5; BR23AA/5/20, 21; Milton-Smith, 71; Bourne, 516-17. [160] Webster, i. 145; Hatherton diary. [161] Creevey mss; *Holland House Diaries*, 98; Wellington mss WP1/1204/19, 21. [162] *Croker Pprs.* ii. 141. [163] *Holland House Diaries*, 108, 113; *Three Diaries*, 178; Trevelyan, 331; Bourne, 518-19. [164] *Greville Mems.* ii. 234. [165] *Holland House Diaries*, 119; *Three Diaries*, 185, 197; Hatherton diary. [166] Add. 75941. [167] Add. 51604. [168] *Raikes Jnl.* i. 9; M.D. George, *Cat. of Pol. and Personal Satires*, xi. 16937; *Talleyrand Mems.* ed. duc de Broglie (1891), iv. 191-2. [169] Hatherton diary, 2, 3 Feb. 1832. [170] Webster, i. 237-51; R. Bullen, 'Party Politics and Foreign Policy', *BIHR*, li (1978), 37-41. [171] Webster, i. 200-20; A. J. Reinerman, 'An Unnatural "Natural Alliance": Metternich, Palmerston and Reform of Papal States', *International Hist. Rev.* x (1988), 541-58. [172] Add. 60463, f. 20; *Three Diaries*, 202; *Greville Mems.* ii. 256-9. [173] *Three Diaries*, 205; Add. 60463, ff. 36, 44; Broughton, iv. 198. [174] *Holland House Diaries*, 167-8. [175] Add. 60463, f. 67; *Three Diaries*, 205; Bourne, 351-2, 520. [176] Add. 51599A, Palmerston to Holland, 20 Apr.; Sheffield Archives, Wharncliffe

mss, 'mem.' 28 Apr. 1832; *Holland House Diaries*, 172; Bourne, 520. [177] *Three Diaries*, 242; *Greville Mems.* ii. 293. [178] Add. 60463, f. 92; Milton-Smith, 72. [179] Parker, *Graham*, i. 143; Add. 60463, f. 105. [180] *Lady Palmerston Letters*, 190; Add. 60463, f. 107. [181] Bourne, 522. [182] Devon RO, Earl Fortescue mss 1262M/FC 88; *Lady Palmerston Letters*, 194; *Three Diaries*, 275, 277. [183] Add. 60463, f. 134; Webster, i. 181-91; Bourne, 352-7. [184] Add. 60463, f. 139; 51644, Jeffrey to Lady Holland [20 July 1832]. [185] Webster, i. 225-36; ii. 799-800; Bourne, 367-72; Castle Howard mss, Holland to Carlisle, 6 Aug. 1832. [186] Webster, i. 82, 87, 257-89; Bourne, 374-8; M. Vereté, 'Palmerston and Levant Crisis, 1832', *JMH*, xxiv (1952), 143-51. [187] Add. 60463, ff. 153, 192; *Lady Palmerston Letters*, 199, 200; Webster, i. 152-76, 248-53. [188] *Jekyll Corresp.* 302, 307; Chambers, 88, 137. [189] *Lieven-Palmerston Corresp.* 43; *Lieven Letters*, 332; Webster, i. 197. [190] Webster, i. 191-9, 320-32; Bourne, 359-65. [191] Add. 47355, f. 187; Webster, i. 45-52; Aspinall, *Politics and the Press*, 191-2, 238, 241; Bourne, 476-91. [192] *Greville Mems.* iv. 138. [193] Webster, i. 3, 55, 76, 81-82; ii. 780-1, 784-95; Bourne, 386-7, 404-6, 523-4, 621-2, 624-8, 631; *Oxford DNB*; S. M. Lee, 'Palmerston and Canning', ch. 1 in *Palmerston Stud.* i. 7-11. [194] Broadlands mss BR195/30-43, 55; *Palmerston-Sulivan Letters*, 252-4; *The Times*, 9, 15 Oct., 12 Nov., 20, 21 Dec. 1832; Bourne, 535-8; D. Brown, 'Palmerston, S. Hants and Electoral Politics', *Hants Pprs.* xxvi (2003), 6-17. [195] *Talleyrand Mems.* iii. 281. [196] [J. Grant], *Random Recollections of Commons* (1837), 226; Lord Teignmouth, *Reminiscences of Many Years*, ii. 214; Bourne, 502; J.S. Meisel, 'Palmerston as Public Speaker', ch. 3 in *Palmerston Stud.* i. 48-51. [197] *DNB*; Webster, i. 55-57; ii. 793; Chamberlain, 1-3; D. Brown, *Palmerston and Politics of Foreign Policy*, 4-13. [198] *The Times*, 19 Oct. 1865; Guedalla, 9, 93-94, 459; Southgate, pp. xxviii, 566.

S.M.F.

TEMPLE NUGENT BRYDGES CHANDOS GRENVILLE, Richard Plantagenet, Earl Temple (1797-1861).

BUCKINGHAMSHIRE   1818-17 Jan. 1839

b. 11 Feb. 1797, o.s. of Richard Temple Nugent Grenville†, 2nd mq. and 1st duke of Buckingham and Chandos, and Lady Anne Elizabeth Brydges, da. and h. of James Brydges†, 3rd duke of Chandos. *educ.* Eton 1808; Oriel, Oxf. 1815. *m.* 13 May 1819, Lady Mary Campbell (div. 19 Jan. 1850), da. of John, 4th earl of Breadalbane [S], 1s. 1da. *styled* Earl Temple 1813-22, mq. of Chandos 1822-39. GCH 1835; *suc.* fa. as 2nd duke of Buckingham and Chandos 17 Jan. 1839; KG 11 Apr. 1842. *d.* 29 July 1861.

Ld. privy seal Sept. 1841-Feb. 1842; PC 3 Sept. 1841.

High steward, Winchester.

Col. Bucks. yeomanry.

Temple, a spoiled only child, became a handsome young man, who combined beguiling charm with an egotism equal to that of his odious father. His uncle Charles Williams Wynn* observed in 1846 that 'neither of them ... [had] ever been subjected to moral control or education, both ... learning no other lesson but that the world was made for them and that everything and everybody was to give way to their will and caprice'. He had a taste for low company and a shrewd eye for popular issues, but in the first part of this period was more interested in his corps of yeomanry than politics. A philanderer by nature, before his ill-fated marriage in 1819 to a strait-laced, Evangelical Scottish aristocrat, he had had an affair with an unsuitable woman, who ended her days in Bedlam, and fathered an illegitimate daughter, Anna Eliza (d. 1887).[1]

In his first Parliament he had followed the Whig alarmist and neutral line adopted by his father, head of the Grenvillite rump, but through the influence of his mother, he was hostile to Catholic relief, of which the rest of his senior male relatives were conspicuous supporters. On his unopposed return for Buckinghamshire on the family interest in 1820, one observer reported that he was 'quite Tory, over and above, ultra royalist, anti-Catholic'.[2] He presented petitions from distressed Buckinghamshire agriculturists, 12, 16 May, and on 31 May 1820 (when he was given a fortnight's leave on urgent private business) acquiesced in the appointment of a select committee of inquiry, though he doubted its usefulness and said he would oppose any attempt to 'add to the price to be paid by the labouring classes for their corn or bread'.[3] Temple, who received £6,000 a year from his father, had moved into the family's second county home at Wotton, near Aylesbury, after his marriage, but in late October 1820 it was destroyed by fire. He wrote to his great-uncle Thomas Grenville[†]:

> In this world it is our duty to struggle against misfortunes and to bear our losses with firmness and composure; and if I have been able in the least to succeed in this enviable policy, I owe it entirely to the example of my dearest mother ... It is impossible for me ever to repay the kindness, the affection or the generosity of my parents, and though delightful it may be to see poor Wotton rise from its ashes, yet my residence in it would be embittered by the latest moment of my life if I thought that either their comfort or their income were in the least crippled or diminished. The expense ... will be heavy, but I hope that by diminishing my own establishment I shall be able to assist considerably with the savings of my own income.[4]

These were empty words, for he was already deep in debt. The house was rebuilt over three years and was partly furnished with articles from the house at Gosfield, Essex, which nominally belonged to Temple's uncle Lord Nugent, Whig Member for Aylesbury, and which Temple occupied in the interim.[5]

Lord Buckingham, angered by the foreign secretary Lord Castlereagh's* attack on his uncle Lord Grenville over his part in the 1806 Milan commission, was initially inclined to prevent Temple from attending to divide with the Liverpool ministry against the opposition censure motion on their conduct towards Queen Caroline, 6 Feb. 1821; but at Grenville's request he relented and allowed his son to cast a silent vote.[6] He was 'sorry' that Temple's 'feelings' on the Catholic question made him abstain from the division of 28 Feb., but told his confidant William Fremantle* that he had 'written to him to say what mine are, but that I leave him free. Nothing can be more considerate or affectionate than his letter. His opposition may prove embarrassing to me and will annoy Lord Grenville'. Temple voted against the second reading of the relief bill, 16 Mar.[7] He presented Buckinghamshire agricultural distress petitions, 28 Feb.[8] He divided with government against repeal of the additional malt duty, 3 Apr., and on the army estimates, 11 Apr. He got leave for three weeks on private business, 9 May 1821. His father was rewarded with a dukedom for delivering the formal support of his squad to the ministry in January 1822, and Temple took the courtesy title of marquess of Chandos.[9] He voted against more extensive tax reductions, 11, 21 Feb., his father having ordered Fremantle, now a member of the board of control, to 'stick close to him to keep him in the right way'; but on the 29th he angered Buckingham by dividing for gradual relaxation of the salt tax. The Whig Sir James Mackintosh* heard that the duke, who was additionally vexed because he had 'two or three days before on the first report of Lord Chandos wavering assured Lord Liverpool that he had spoken to his son and would answer for him', dealt with him 'so sorely ... that many such interviews it is supposed would make the young lord a Whig'. Buckingham let Liverpool know through Williams Wynn, his representative in the cabinet, that Chandos had given 'assurances that his support in future shall be *steady*'; and he went up to vote against abolition of one of the joint-postmasterships, 13 Mar.[10] He voted against Canning's bill to relieve Catholic peers, 30 Apr. By May Buckingham was complaining to Fremantle of the 'insults' offered to him by ministers, which he said Chandos also felt 'strongly'; and he sanctioned his son's vote in the minority of 24 for enhanced protection of domestic corn producers, 8 May. The day before he had presented a Buckinghamshire agriculturists' petition expressing alarm at the notion of releasing warehoused foreign corn.[11] He obeyed his father's order to vote for the aliens bill, 5 June, divided in defence of the lord advocate's treatment of the Scottish press, 25 June, and next day said that all grants of public money to his yeomanry had been legitimately spent.[12] In late July, conjuring with the notion of getting the king to visit Stowe on his way back from Scotland, he complained to Fremantle that ministers were 'not very anxious to assist us in ... county patronage'; and he recurred to this two weeks later when observing that Canning was 'the only person at all calculated to supply the deficiency' created by Lord Londonderry's suicide. Fremantle's nephew Sir Thomas Fremantle*, reporting that Chandos was unlikely to attend a county dinner, commented that 'if we were farmers and clowns instead of gentlemen we might have a chance of being favoured with his company'.[13]

He was 'not to be had' as a mover of the address in 1823, when he declined Canning's request, against the advice of his father, who observed that 'he hates the House of Commons'.[14] He did little there in that and the next session, when his only recorded vote was against inquiry into the parliamentary franchise, 20 Feb. 1823. In mid-April Buckingham told Fremantle that 'Chandos's conduct makes me very low and unhappy';[15] but on the 25th Chandos defended him in the House against an allegation of abuse of power as a Hampshire magistrate. At the end of the year Buckingham, though disgruntled with 'the general inattention and indisposition' of ministers, exhorted Fremantle to intervene with Lord Melville, first lord of the admiralty, on behalf of Captain Jervoise, whose dismissal from his ship for inflicting unduly harsh punishments had enraged his friend Chandos. The duke was anxious to avoid an embarrassing situation:

> Chandos ... is warm in his affections and inveterate in his enmities and stands by Jervoise ... with a warmth which one cannot blame however much one may feel the inconvenience of it. Chandos's determination is unless the admiralty gives Jervoise another ship, or in some way right him, to bring the subject before the House of Commons and this determination I *cannot shake*.

Chandos was apparently persuaded not to raise the matter in the House, but at the start of the 1824 session Buckingham reported that he

> complains of general inattention, of Canning's never having invited him even to his parliamentary dinners, or *speaking to* him. He is gone up to London most hostilely inclined, and I regret to say that government cannot count upon his support. I believe that he means to see Lord Liverpool to explain his situation ... Nothing will induce him to vote on any question with opposition, but he means to desire that notes may not be sent to him. Lord Melville might prevent this if he chose, but no one else can.

Chandos was credited with supporting the prayer of a Winchester petition for repeal of the assessed taxes, 22 Mar., but was otherwise inconspicuous.[16] Two months later he was being treated with 'marked and unusual

courtesy' by both Canning and the king's anti-Catholic brother the duke of York. Buckingham, who was glad of this, noted that Jervoise was 'no longer the immense object in Chandos's eye which he was'; but in May York invited him to discuss the case, which made Buckingham apprehensive of his receiving 'a long No Popery tirade'. Chandos subsequently raised the matter with the duke of Wellington, but to no avail.[17] His absence from the division on the opposition call for inquiry into Irish disturbances, 11 May, was 'accidental', for he 'went home at one, being tired'.[18] In June 1824 (when Thomas Creevey* saw the deranged victim of Chandos's youthful fling in Bedlam) there was a week-long 'junket' at Stowe to celebrate the christening of his first (and only) son. Lady Williams Wynn, a guest, commented sourly on 'the perfect frigidity' of Chandos and his wife, and on his obsession with his yeomanry, who were 'paraded about and made ... much too prominent throughout the whole gala'.[19]

Chandos divided silently against Catholic relief, 1 Mar., 21 Apr., 10 May, but vowed to oppose it to the bitter end when presenting a hostile petition from Buckingham, 18 Apr. 1825.[20] He voted against the Irish franchise bill, 26 Apr. In June his father wrote, without his knowledge, to ask Melville to try to procure him a place at the admiralty, being 'very anxious to bring ... [him] forward ... into public life', preferably just before the anticipated dissolution, to avoid two elections. Liverpool's response was encouraging, and Buckingham then informed Chandos of what he had done.[21] Before the close of the session he ordered Chandos to tell Canning of his preposterous desire to be made governor-general of India if Lord Amherst was recalled. In September Chandos was employed in the canvassing of directors of the East India Company. As the business dragged on Chandos, who Fremantle believed 'rules his father', matched the duke in the intensity of his 'unmeasured' anger with ministers, most especially Williams Wynn, for what they regarded as a breach of faith. Buckingham told Fremantle that as Williams Wynn had failed to promote his interests, he felt they would be 'safer' in the care of Chandos, who was now 'turning out what I did not expect he would, a man of business'.[22] He was mentioned as a possible candidate for the vacancy for Oxford University in January 1826, but Peel, the home secretary and sitting Member, discounted him as the eldest son of a peer.[23] In early February he was sent by Buckingham to order Fremantle to promise not to speak in the House on anything relating to the Indian fiasco. He was satisfied with Fremantle's reservation of his right to speak on departmental business, but asked him to warn Williams Wynn that if on the 23rd Hume mentioned the subject when moving for information on the Barrackpoor mutiny, he would 'explain ... the whole of the conduct which his father has pursued'. Fremantle, who saw that the duke and Chandos were absurdly aiming to 'drive out Wynn and to continue friends with government', told his nephew that he had 'cautioned ... [Chandos] against a reply from Canning, who has materials and will not fail to make use of them in exposing their conduct, to their serious injury'. As he expected, Chandos kept quiet.[24] He presented a petition for the abolition of slavery, 13 Apr.[25] He divided with ministers against reform of Edinburgh's representation, 13 Apr., but was in the protectionist minority against the corn bill, 11 May, having lamented to his father the lack of a 'leading agriculturist in the House who can contend with ministers, supported as they are by the manufacturing party'.[26] He was Buckingham's emissary to Fremantle in talks to decide whether the latter could continue to sit on the duke's interest after his appointment to a household place and to ascertain Buckingham's 'situation with government'. Fremantle convinced him that only a direct approach to the king or Liverpool would answer. Buckingham shied from this, but Chandos eventually convinced him that it would not be 'politic ... at the *present* moment to quarrel with the government' and that he should 'remain quiet' until either India or Ireland (which he also coveted) fell vacant, when he could '*demand* ... fulfilment of the promise'. At the same time he urged Fremantle, who was assured of his return for Buckingham, to try to extract 'one word' of 'kindness' from the king.[27]

At the general election in June 1826 Chandos, many of whose bills from 1820 remained unpaid, reached an agreement with the Whig sitting Member Robert John Smith which was designed to save money on dinners and canvassing; but it collapsed and he spent £2,500 on his unopposed return. His father would not hear of his suggestion of transferring to Buckingham and agreed to pay his current election debts. On the hustings he condemned the government's proposal to admit bonded corn, declared himself 'decidedly hostile' to slavery, but stressed the rights of the planters, denied being 'a ministerial man' and, echoing the 'No Popery' cries of an intimidating and regimented group of his supporters, 'gloried' in having opposed Catholic relief. He preached agricultural protection and resistance to Catholic claims at a series of celebration dinners, prompting Fremantle to wonder if his conduct arose from some '*malady*' which blinded him to the best long-term county interests of himself and his family; he also marvelled at Buckingham's 'submis-

sion to it'. In January 1827 he commented that if the fat duke '*stomachs*' Chandos's scarcely veiled threats to intervene against his nomination of pro-Catholics for Buckingham at the next election, 'he had better at once retire and make room for his son's succession'.[28]

In February 1827 Buckingham applied to Liverpool through Chandos for the Indian post and received a 'flat refusal'. Chandos now argued that his father must separate himself from the government, but Fremantle, who believed that Chandos was 'leading him to his political disgrace' by trying to 'get his father abroad and himself ... in possession and command of his influence and property', persuaded the duke to stay his hand until Chandos had seen Wellington to establish where he stood. Wellington sent 'general expressions of kindness' which temporarily mollified Buckingham.[29] Chandos presented petitions against further interference with the corn laws, 21, 23 Feb., when he also brought up one from distressed Buckingham lace-makers. Presenting and endorsing two parish petitions against Catholic relief, 2 Mar., he called for 'a decided negative' to kill the question; and he wrote what Buckingham, who believed he was deluding himself, called 'a note of *unfeeling joy*' to inform him of the majority against it, 6 Mar.[30] He demanded to know why the Catholic Association had been allowed to assume the 'character of a legislative body', 6 Apr. On the 2nd he presented more petitions against relaxation of the corn laws before voting against the corn bill.[31] He was involved in the early April exchanges between Buckingham and Wellington over the terms on which the Grenvillites had joined the ministry in 1822, and he continued to press his father's claim to India, which Canning, the new premier, summarily dismissed.[32] Later in the month the Fremantles blamed the duke's vacillation over fulfilment of his engagement to return Sir Thomas for Buckingham in place of the retiring William on Chandos's pernicious and dominating influence over his father and his wish to secure the seat for an anti-Catholic. William Fremantle thought he was 'outrageous at being disappointed in getting rid of his father' and would 'never forgive those who would not join with him in the attempt'. Chandos did not risk opposing the return of Sir Thomas, but he pointedly stayed away from the formalities; he was one of the borough burgesses required by the duke to resign their gowns.[33] Canning's coalition with the Lansdowne Whigs had convinced Chandos that the king had 'given way on the Catholic question and that the government are to support the measure'.[34] He said as much in the House, 2 May, when he presented an anti-Catholic petition, declared his hostility to the ministry and entreated the country to come forward 'in a manner so decisive as to drive the question ... for ever from the door of Parliament'. On 7 May he said that 'the character of an English Whig' had been 'disgraced and degraded' by the coalition. He presented a Chipping Wycombe petition for repeal of the Test Acts, 23 May.[35] Buckingham, who directed his other Members to remain neutral for the present 'and not to sit with Lord Chandos nor appear to belong to his party', complained to Fremantle that his son had aligned himself with Peel and the Tory opposition 'without communication with me', and noted in his diary that he had 'broke off political connection' with Chandos, who 'thinks himself the head of a Protestant party instead of his father's'. Nugent was horrified by his 'absurd violence' on the issue; but Chandos told his wife five years later that 'there was a time when I thought that political matters could not so materially affect me, but I was called forward by the Catholic question'.[36] Buckingham was preparing to leave England for a extended stay in Italy in a bid to save money; but he made light of Chandos's address to his yeomanry in mid-June, which Fremantle, who warned him of the 'alarming' danger of leaving his son to run riot in the county, considered to be 'of a political character highly objectionable'. In July 1827 Buckingham pledged to the king his own and his Members' support for the government as ministers of the crown; but Chandos immediately saw Wellington and Peel in what Fremantle construed as an attempt to undermine this. The news of Canning's death prompted Chandos to ask Fremantle whether the ensuing change 'might once more give ... [Buckingham] an opening for India', which Fremantle believed remained 'Chandos's only object'.[37] As he, his mother and Sir Edward East* began to look into the duke's financial affairs, he was shocked by the enormity of the debts and the discovery that Buckingham had violated the terms of his marriage settlement by diverting the Chandos estates to himself. (At the instigation of the duchess, this was subsequently rectified by a private Act.) He also found that his paternal inheritance had been tampered with; but he too was in debt, to the extent, as East ascertained, of over £130,000.[38] In December 1827 he entertained Wellington and Peel at Wotton and orchestrated a dinner in Buckingham to honour Wellington for his military services. The affair, which offended Chandos's great-uncles, was ostensibly non-political; but its anti-Catholic undertones were obvious.[39]

Chandos was offered a place at the admiralty by Wellington when he became prime minister in January 1828, but he declined it, claiming that acceptance would risk 'a diminution' of his county influence. At the same time, he pledged his 'best' support for the

ministry and sought employment for a constituent, one Wyndham, though initially without success.[40] He presented Dissenters' petitions for repeal of the Test Acts, 14, 26 Feb., when he voted against that measure, and brought up a dozen more hostile petitions, 17 Mar. He presented and endorsed petitions for reform of the poor laws, 5 Mar., 1 May, and more anti-Catholic petitions, 2, 6, 8 May; he voted against relief, 12 May. That day he brought up a Newport Pagnell agriculturists' petition against the revised corn duties. On the 14th he stated his 'decided objection' to the provision for Canning's family and condemned Canning's 'principles and policy'. Williams Wynn's brother reckoned that he had 'lowered himself very much by ... leaving the House lest anybody should answer him'.[41] He voted against repeal of the usury laws, 19 June, and ordnance reductions, 4 July, and presented an Olney petition for the abolition of slavery, 10 July 1828. Three weeks later he informed Wellington that he was ready to accept a West Indian governorship if a vacancy occurred. This arose from negotiations with his father over his financial situation. When Chandos threatened to resign his seat unless his allowance was raised to £8,000, Buckingham gave way and agreed to pay his debts.[42]

In the autumn of 1828 Chandos, who was described by Lady Holland as 'living with inferiors and always accompanied by a led captain, his *bully back*', promoted the formation of the Buckinghamshire Brunswick Club, though he took a moderate tone in his speech as chairman of its dinner, 21 Oct.[43] On the recall of the viceroy Lord Anglesey from Ireland in January 1829 he reminded Wellington of his father's 'great anxiety to obtain that appointment'; but Buckingham subsequently disclaimed all knowledge of this.[44] Wellington's decision to concede Catholic emancipation enraged Chandos, as he showed in the House, 5 Feb. He made his father's Pall Mall house a rendezvous for the parliamentary opponents of emancipation and was one of the principal promoters of protest meetings and petitions, which he presented and endorsed by the bushel in February and March; on 16 Feb. he clashed openly with Nugent in the Commons.[45] In defiance of his father he organized a meeting of the three hundreds of Buckingham, 21 Feb., when, after giving a public breakfast at Wotton, he went with his guests to Buckingham to declare that 'though I may not live to see the day ... if this law now passes England will know the period when blood must be shed in defence of her liberties'. His father was furious when he learned of this display, issued a public letter condemning it and told Sir Thomas Fremantle that he must persevere in 'ceasing to consider my son as speaking my political language or leading my political friends'.[46] Chandos divided steadily against emancipation, acting as a minority teller in divisions on 6, 18, 23, 30 Mar. On the 24th he complained that its opponents had not had a fair hearing and was defeated by 218-98 in his bid to prevent a Catholic becoming first lord of the treasury. Yet he was not permanently alienated from the ministry, and once the relief bill had passed the Commons he wrote to Wellington asking to be given 'official employment' as soon as possible. Wellington was sympathetic, as was Peel, on whom Chandos also pressed his claims, but nothing could readily be found for him and in May the cabinet 'rejected immediately' a suggestion that he be made lord privy seal, as he was 'not of sufficient calibre'. According to Mrs. Arbuthnot, he was 'very uneasy' at the recruitment of the Whigs Lord Rosslyn and James Scarlett* and 'intimated that he would oppose any further such appointments'. The value of his formal attachment to the government as a means of securing the good will of 'all the respectable part of the Tory party' was clear to several ministers; but he could not persuade Peel to make his constituent Wyndham receiver of the new metropolitan police.[47] He was at first disposed to decline an invitation from the committee of West India planters and merchants to become their chairman, but after consulting Wellington, who endorsed his view that he might be of service to the government in that capacity, he accepted it. He presided at the committee's dinner in honour of Wellington, 25 June, and a few days later led a deputation to the premier to explain the West Indians' concerns.[48] In late July, when it was falsely rumoured that he had 'refused offers or at least repelled advances' from Wellington, the Ultra leader Sir Richard Vyvyan* considered Chandos to be virtually lost to his faction; and when the king's Ultra brother the duke of Cumberland sounded him, Chandos 'told him there was not a word of truth in the report, but let him know ... that he was perfectly well inclined to accept office if offered to him'. In mid-October, however, Cumberland assured Lord Eldon that Chandos was '*all right*, sees things in the true point of view, is ... of opinion that it is impossible for the present government to go on as they are now constituted [and] says that many of the county Members have declared they will not serve under Peel as a leader'.[49] William Fremantle thought Chandos, whose 'great object' was to 'get rid of his father and to send him to die at Calcutta', was 'fully prepared to take office', but had 'assumed the ministry will not take him, unless he can bring unconditionally the whole parliamentary influence of his father with him'; Fremantle doubted that the duke would sanction this 'without some arrange-

ment for himself'. In late October, shortly before Buckingham returned to England, Chandos, who had recently raised £30,000 by a 'most ruinous' annuity, told Fremantle that he was determined to mount a challenge to Nugent at Aylesbury at the next election, that his father intended to 'claim an engagement from the duke of Wellington' that he should be made Irish viceroy on the next vacancy and that he himself was to go as governor to Jamaica:

> Chandos ... ended by begging me to speak well of him to the king ... he was in constant communication with the duke of Cumberland, which will do him no good. The more I ... know of him, the more I am confirmed in my conviction of his being the most profligate, unprincipled, abandoned public political character that at his age and in his station ever existed.

Fremantle remained sure that Chandos, whose 'best quality, and the one he most values, is that of hatred and revenge', would not allow his father to 'play a friendly game' between Nugent and himself.[50]

Wellington, who visited Chandos at Wotton at the turn of the year and received him in London at the head of a West Indian deputation, 16 Jan. 1830, offered him the mastership of the mint on the 26th. After three days' thought he turned it down, against the advice of his father (who had been urged by Wellington to persuade him to take it), pleading his 'unpleasant' situation in Buckinghamshire 'from the peculiar difficulties I now have to contend with'. It was thought that infuriated Ultras would have organized a challenge to his necessary re-election, though 'some people' surmised that he had turned down the offer because it did not include membership of the cabinet. He and Buckingham pledged support for the ministry.[51] Buckingham, who attributed 'the *refusal* ... [to] a feeling of anger and a wish not to be bound up with *me*', and was set on a line of 'steady downright support' of government, warned Sir Thomas Fremantle 'not to let any quirks or crotchets of *his*, either in consequence of his own feelings or the instigation of constituents, respecting currency, malt tax, etc., be considered as *mine*'.[52] Chandos did present and endorse a Stony Stratford petition for repeal of the malt and beer duties and currency reform, 17 Feb.; but when bringing up one for repeal of the malt duty, 19 Mar., he said that he had been 'much gratified' by ministers' tax reductions, especially repeal of the beer duty. He expressed to Peel 'a particular wish' to be placed on the select committee on the East India Company, and was duly obliged, 9 Feb.[53] He voted against the transfer of East Retford's seats to Birmingham, 11 Feb., and the enfranchisement of Birmingham, Leeds and Manchester, 23 Feb. On 22 Feb. he got leave to bring in a bill to amend the game laws, which, as he told Sir Thomas Fremantle, was intended to 'preserve property and protect the gentlemen'.[54] The measure met strong opposition and Chandos gave it up for the session on 5 July. He presented and endorsed petitions from West India merchants and planters for reduction of various duties, 23 Feb., 19 Mar., 30 Apr., 14, 21 June. On 18 May he failed to make Peel promise to relieve the West Indian colonies, and on 14 June he was beaten by 102-23 in an attempt to secure a cut in the duties on their produce. He complained that East Indian sugar planters had received preferential treatment and was defeated by 88-36 in a bid to redress the balance, 30 June.[55] A 'lucky' vacancy occurred in late April to enable ministers to find a job for Wyndham;[56] but this did not deter Chandos from voting against the sale of beer bill, 4 May, 21 June. He divided against Jewish emancipation, 17 May. On 9 July 1830 he presented the Glasgow West India body's petition for protection and compensation for losses inflicted by the recent order-in-council on slavery.

In May 1830 Chandos and Buckingham jointly raised a loan of £35,000 to meet the latter's needs, in return for which Chandos had the rise in his allowance confirmed and was given a £3,000 annuity from the estate, which he used to borrow £45,000, theoretically to pay off his crippling annuity loans. Yet he remained in deep trouble and, like his father, was now in marital difficulties, having been detected in adultery.[57] Buckingham vetoed any interference against Nugent at the 1830 general election, when Chandos, who tried unsuccessfully to upset the Carrington interest at Wendover (to the annoyance of his great-uncles), was returned unopposed but not cheaply for the county. At the nomination he claimed that he had 'never truckled to power nor struck my colours to any political party whatever' and denied being 'opposed to the freedom of slaves'. At subsequent celebration junkets he boasted of his resistance to Catholic emancipation, called for fair protection for the agricultural interest, again paid lip service to the amelioration of slavery and declared that 'church and king have always been the anxious objects of my support'.[58] Ministers listed Chandos, whose father had been made lord steward of the household on the accession of William IV, among their 'friends'; but his recommendation of his Whig father-in-law Lord Breadalbane for the lord lieutenancy of Perthshire was disregarded.[59]

He was an absentee from the division on the civil list which brought down the ministry, 15 Nov. 1830. That month he was active at the head of his yeomanry in dealing with 'Swing' rioters.[60] On 18 Nov. he repudiated Daniel O'Connell's allegation that some of Buckingham's Irish tenants had been driven to penury by the tyranny of his local agent and got leave to reintroduce his game bill, slightly modified, which was superseded by the Grey ministry's subsequent measure. He was named to the select committee on public salary reductions, 9 Dec. On the 13th he presented the West India body's petition for protection of legally acquired property and deplored 'unjust' abolitionist attacks on the planters. He presented an anti-slavery petition from Buckingham, 18 Dec. 1830, and on 14 Feb. 1831 secured information on Jamaican slave manumissions and the sugar trade. That day he demanded to know if it was true that ministers had compromised with O'Connell over his threatened prosecution; he was satisfied with the explanation, 16 Feb. He rallied the West India interest against aspects of the budget and on 21 Feb. was only persuaded by Peel's personal appeal to withdraw a resolution declaring their right to relief, which some thought would have been carried against ministers. His initial anger with Peel was soothed by the whip William Holmes's* discreet intervention to get the West India committee to write him a letter of thanks.[61] His amendment to reduce the sugar duties, 11 Mar., when he complained of the planters' great distress, was defeated by 147-49; and he failed to persuade ministers to allow sugar and molasses to be used in brewing and distilling, 22 Mar. In a bid to sidetrack the anticipated ministerial reform scheme, Chandos took up the case of Evesham, where 'flagrant' corruption had been exposed by inquiry into the last return. On 16 Dec. 1830 he carried a motion to have the writ suspended until the evidence had been printed. He got leave to introduce a bill to disfranchise the borough and transfer its seats to Birmingham, 18 Feb. 1831, but gave way to ministers' insistence on his postponing the date for the attendance of witnesses from 28 Feb., the day before the reform plan was to be unveiled, to 7 Mar.[62] The measure was rendered nugatory by the government's reform bill, against the introduction of which Chandos believed Peel should have divided the House.[63] On 7 Mar. he alleged that supporters of the ministry were 'going abroad amongst the people, trying to influence the minds of the lower classes' and to 'intimidate Members' hostile to the scheme. He could not convince Peel that a preferable alternative to opposing the second reading was the submission of an alternative plan which, while it 'satisfies the moderate reformer and protects the timid politician, will ensure the safety of the country and preserve its tranquillity'.[64] He was a teller for the minority when the second reading was carried by one vote, 22 Mar.; and on the 29th he declared his 'most decided opposition' to the bill, even though he professed to want 'a moderate, proper and constitutional reform' and to like 'one or two' features of the measure. He presented petitions for the English and against the Irish bills, 13 Apr., and divided for Gascoyne's wrecking amendment, 19 Apr. 1831. At the ensuing general election (during which his wife found more strong evidence of his philandering) he promoted an unsuccessful intervention against his uncle at Aylesbury and was himself easily but expensively returned for the county after a four-day contest forced by the disorganized local reformers. Under questioning on the hustings, he claimed again to be 'a friend to moderate and constitutional reform', in favour of 'extending the elective franchise, giving representatives to large and populous places and disfranchising every borough that should be proved to be corrupt', and professed to desire the abolition of slavery, being 'equally disposed to do his duty both by blacks and whites'. Ever the populist, he portrayed himself as 'a country gentleman, determined to support the agricultural and general interests of the country, without hope of profit or emolument from ... government'.[65]

By now Chandos occupied a prominent position in the opposition hierarchy: he was at the meeting which decided to adopt Joseph Planta's* Charles Street house as a headquarters, 16 June 1831, and hosted a gathering which set up a managing committee a month later.[66] He was a teller for the minority against the second reading of the reintroduced reform bill, 6 July, and divided for use of the 1831 census to determine the disfranchisement schedules, 19 July, and to postpone consideration of Chippenham's inclusion in B, 27 July. He objected to the allocation of three county Members to Buckinghamshire, 13 Aug. On the 18th he proposed and carried against government, by the impressive margin of 84 votes, the enfranchisement in the counties of £50 tenants-at-will, whom he described as 'independent', after exploiting a procedural blunder by Colonel Waldo Sibthorp, Member for Lincoln, who had tried to make an identical proposal. Ministers, having already resolved to extend the right of borough freeholders to vote in the counties, accepted this reverse, optimistically expecting the Lords to overturn it.[67] Chandos was one of the Tories 'dissatisfied' with Peel's decision to give up stubborn resistance to the details of the bill and 'prepared to go on interminably'.[68] He was a teller for the majority against issuing the Liverpool writ, 8 July, voted in the same sense, 5 Sept., divided for the transfer of Alborough to schedule A and failed to have Evesham treated likewise, 14 Sept., and voted against the passage of the reform bill,

21 Sept. He provoked a warm debate by demanding an explanation of why the prosecution of O'Connell had not gone ahead, 27 June, protested against the possible disarming of the Irish yeomanry, 18 Aug., and voted to censure the Irish administration for interfering in the Dublin election, 23 Aug. He presented the petition of Northampton electors complaining of the use of barracks to house out-voters in the ministerial interest at the last election, 11 July, but did not pursue the matter. On 22 July he said that 'some protecting duty' was necessary to safeguard domestic corn production. He badgered ministers for information on the situation in Belgium, 25 July, 6, 11, 17 Aug. He suggested significant alterations to their game bill, 8 Aug., and later briefed Wellington on how to amend it in the Lords.[69] On 30 July he presented the West India merchants and planters' petition against renewing the Sugar Refinery Act until the House had considered its implications for their interest and continuance of the foreign slave trade. He was reported to have told the abolitionist Thomas Fowell Buxton* that as chairman of the West India committee he would 'agree to a parliamentary measure for emancipation if a loan or an indemnity to the amount of five million were given to the planters'. Nothing came of this, but he was named to the select committees on the state of the West India interest, 6 Oct., 15 Dec. 1831.[70]

Chandos, who was included as chancellor of the duchy of Lancaster in Lord Ellenborough's sketch of a putative interim administration to carry moderate reform, sent Wellington information about potential opponents of the reform bill in the Lords ahead of its defeat there.[71] In the Commons, 17 Oct. 1831, he urged ministers to offer a reward for the capture of those responsible for burning Nottingham Castle. He was privy to the attempts of the Tory 'Waverer' peers to effect a compromise on reform with ministers (he seemed to be 'satisfied with the concessions of the government' in late November), and in early December, at an audience of the king ostensibly on the subject of the West Indies, he obtained 'a sort of authority' to renew the negotiations. He arranged a meeting between Lords Harrowby and Wharncliffe on the one side, and Grey, Althorp* and Brougham on the other, 10 Dec., but it ended in failure.[72] In the House, 12 Dec. 1831, he expressed a wish for conciliation and took a markedly more moderate line than Peel on the revised reform bill; but his assertion that it retained 'many' objectionable features convinced ministers that compromise was unattainable.[73] In early January 1832 Chandos, who was on the committee of six appointed to set up a club for the anti-reformers, tried unsuccessfully through the king to renew the negotiations in order to prevent a mass creation of peers.[74] He voted against going into committee on the reform bill, 20 Jan., and to condemn ministers over the Russian-Dutch loan, 26 Jan. (and again, 12 July). He welcomed their retention of his clause enfranchising tenant farmers, 1 Feb. Confident of success, he moved on 28 Feb. to get rid of the proposed new metropolitan electoral districts, but he was beaten by 316-236.[75] He voted against the third reading of the reform bill, 22 Mar. Presenting a West Indian colonists' petition for reduction of the sugar duties, 7 Mar., he said that some planters were in 'absolute poverty'; his motion for a reduction of 4s. was beaten by only 148-134. He wanted information on the slave insurrections in Jamaica and elsewhere, 9 Mar. During the crisis of May he was one of the leading Conservative backbenchers who vainly tried to persuade Peel to take office to carry a measure of reform.[76] On 24 May he presented and endorsed the West India body's petition for immediate relief and divided against the government's temporizing amendment on abolition; he was named to the select committee on this, 30 May. He voted against the second reading of the Irish reform bill, 25 May. He voted for Alexander Baring's bill to exclude insolvent debtors from the House, 27 June, and failed to get a response from ministers on British involvement in the Greek loan, 5, 13 July 1832.

Chandos topped the poll for Buckinghamshire in 1832, 1835 and 1837 and succeeded to the dukedom in 1839. As the self-styled 'Farmer's Friend', he was the leading Protectionist in the Commons in the 1830s. His status earned him a place, as lord privy seal, in Peel's 1841 cabinet, but he resigned after six months in protest at the premier's relaxation of the corn laws, and was compensated with the garter. This ended his political career.[77] The rest of his life was a sordid saga of personal extravagance, financial catastrophe and sexual scandal, marked by the enforced sale of the contents of Stowe in 1848 and divorce in 1850 after his proven adultery with the wife of a House of Lords clerk. He spent his last years as a pensioner, living in lodgings and hotels on money provided by his son and whatever he could scrounge, and editing and publishing selections from his family's political correspondence. He died, bankrupt, in the Great Western Hotel, Paddington, in July 1861, having succeeded with his father in squandering a vast fortune and wasting a glittering inheritance in a period of only 34 years. On the death in 1889 of his worthy son Richard, Protectionist Member for Buckingham, 1846-57, and a member of the Derby and Disraeli ministries, 1852 and 1866-7, who managed to stave off complete ruin during his lifetime, the dukedom became extinct. Adverse eco-nomic conditions subsequently ensured that the family's landed inheritance had been alienated by 1921, when Stowe was sold to become a public school.[78]

[1] J. Beckett, *Rise and Fall of the Grenvilles*, 106, 112-16; R.W. Davis, *Political Change and Continuity*, 72-73; *HP Commons, 1790-1820*, v. 350-1. [2] J.J. Sack, *The Grenvillites*, 201; *Fox Jnl.* 312; Essex RO, Gunnis mss D/Dgu Z1 C1/1/5; *Jackson's Oxford Jnl.* 26 Feb., 18 Mar. 1820. [3] *The Times*, 17 May 1820. [4] Add. 41859, f. 20. [5] Beckett, 111, 121-2, 137. [6] Bucks. RO, Fremantle mss D/FR/46/11/45; 46/12/36. [7] Ibid. 46/12/34; Add. 58967, f. 138. [8] *The Times*, 1 Mar. 1821. [9] Buckingham, *Mems. Geo. IV*, i. 256. [10] Fremantle mss 46/10/15, 17, 18; Add. 52445, f. 64. [11] Fremantle mss 46/10/32; 46/12/22; *The Times*, 8 May 1822. [12] Fremantle mss 46/12/77; *The Times*, 27 June 1822. [13] Fremantle mss 46/10/42, 52, 57. [14] *Arbuthnot Corresp.* 38; Fremantle mss 46/12/69. [15] Fremantle mss 46/1/80. [16] Ibid. 46/11/88, 91; *The Times*, 23 Mar. 1824. [17] Fremantle mss 46/11/99; 51/5/21; Wellington mss WP1/797/18; 807/21; 808/19. [18] Buckingham, ii. 74. [19] *Creevey's Life and Times*, 198; *Bucks. Chron.* 19 June 1824; *Williams Wynn Corresp.* 316-20; Beckett, 145. [20] NLW, Coedymaen mss bdle. 18, Fremantle to Williams Wynn [18 Apr. 1825]. [21] NLI, Melville mss, Buckingham to Melville, 19, 23 June, reply, 21 June 1825. [22] Fremantle mss 46/12/55, 64, 67; 138/12/2, 5, 8, 9; Christ Church, Oxf. Phillimore mss, Fremantle to Phillimore, 5 Oct. 1825; Coedymaen mss 950, 957; Add. 40331, f. 243; *Arbuthnot Jnl.* i. 434; Wellington mss WP1/834/13. [23] Add. 40342, f. 307. [24] Fremantle mss 51/8/1; 138/16/18. [25] *The Times*, 14 Apr. 1826. [26] D. Spring, 'Lord Chandos and the Farmers', *HLQ*, xxxiii (1969-70), 258. [27] Fremantle mss 46/11/133, 135; 46/12/90; 51/8/3; Fremantle to Buckingham, 3 May 1826. [28] Beckett, 111; Sack, 21; *Bucks. Chron.* 3, 10, 17, 24 June, 19, 26 Aug. 1826; Fremantle mss 138/16/1; 138/18/7; 138/21/1/5. [29] Fremantle mss 46/12/100, 101; 51/8/4; 138/21/1/7, 8; *Canning's Ministry*, 15; Wellington mss WP1/883/4. [30] *The Times*, 22, 24 Feb., 3 Mar. 1827; Fremantle mss 46/11/155; 138/21/1/10. [31] *The Times*, 3 Apr. 1827. [32] *Canning's Ministry*, 64, 69, 76; Wellington mss WP1/887/9; Fremantle mss 51/8/5. [33] Fremantle mss 46/10/47, 48; 49/1/8; 138/21/2/5, 7, 8, 10; 138/28/2. [34] Ibid. 49/1/17. [35] *The Times*, 24 May 1827. [36] Fremantle mss 46/12/113; 49/1/17; 138/28/3; Add. 52447, f. 76; Sack, 211-12; Spring, 258. [37] Fremantle mss 138/21/2/11-15; Fremantle to Buckingham, 19 June 1827; Add. 40394, f. 128. [38] Beckett, 148-53. [39] Fremantle mss 138/22/2-6, 8; 138/21/2/17, 21-24; *Bucks. Chron.* 15, 22, 29 Dec. 1827. [40] Wellington mss WP1/914/19; 915/50; 918/6; 920/43; 939/1; Add. 40395, ff. 109, 112, 265, 269, 271. [41] TNA 30/29/9/5/67; NLW ms 2796 D, Sir W. to H. Williams Wynn, 27 May 1828; *Arbuthnot Jnl.* ii. 187. [42] Wellington mss WP1/943/18; Beckett, 153; Sack, 22. [43] Wellington mss WP1/955/6; *Lady Holland to Son*, 88; Fremantle mss 139/2/2-4; *Bucks. Chron.* 20, 27 Sept., 25 Oct. 1828; Davis, 73; Sack, 212-13. [44] *Wellington Despatches*, v. 440; Wellington mss WP1/998/13; Fremantle mss 139/10/5, 7. [45] *Colchester Diary*, iii. 597, 601; Fremantle mss 139/10/14, 17; Lonsdale mss, Lowther to Lonsdale, 10 Feb.; Dorset RO D/BKL, Bankes jnl. 166 (5 Mar. 1829). [46] Fremantle mss 139/10/14, 36; *The Times*, 24 Feb. 1829. [47] Wellington mss WP1/1011/14; *Ellenborough Diary*, ii. 6, 19, 42, 55; Add. 40399, ff. 181, 183, 242, 243, 270, 278; *Arbuthnot Jnl.* ii. 287, 290. [48] Wellington mss WP1/1019/10; 1022/16; 1024/26, 32; 1025/26; 1027/19; 1030/35; *Windsor and Eton Express*, 27 June 1829. [49] Add. 51655, Mackintosh to Lady Holland, 31 July; *Arbuthnot Jnl.* ii. 298; Cornw. RO, Vyvyan mss, Vyvyan to Newcastle, 20 July, reply, 15 Aug.; Cumberland to Vyvyan, 17 Aug., Knatchbull to same, 26 Aug.; Eldon mss, Cumberland to Eldon, 16 Oct. 1829. [50] Fremantle mss 139/10/47, 49, 54, 55, 64. [51] *Arbuthnot Jnl.*, ii. 321, 324, 328; *Ellenborough Diary*, ii. 173, 180, 181, 185; Wellington mss WP1/1065/40; 1085/19; 1019/35, 38; *Wellington Despatches*, vi. 436-7, 441, 455; Fremantle mss 46/12/118; Lonsdale mss, Lowther to Lonsdale, 25, 28 Jan., reply, 26 Jan; Add. 51575, Abercromby to Holland, 3 Feb.; 51680, Russell to Lady Holland, 6 Jan.; NLS mss 24770, f. 39; Grey mss, Ellice to

Grey [27, 30 Jan., 1 Feb.]; Howick jnl. [1 Feb. 1830]. ⁵² Fremantle mss 139/14/9. ⁵³ Ibid. 139/14/11. ⁵⁴ Ibid. 139/14/3. ⁵⁵ Wellington mss WP1/1120/19. ⁵⁶ Ellenborough Diary, ii. 232; Wellington mss WP1/1110/13. ⁵⁷ Beckett, 116, 155. ⁵⁸ Davis, 26, 85; Cent. Kent. Stud. Stanhope mss U1590 C228, Carrington to Lady Stanhope, 10, 11 Aug.; Bucks Gazette, 7, 28 Aug. 1830. ⁵⁹ Wellington mss WP1/1144/17; 1148/25. ⁶⁰ Wellington mss WP4/2/2/6, 11; Wellington Despatches, vii. 368; Three Diaries, 25. ⁶¹ Arbuthnot Corresp. 143; Croker Pprs. 108; St. Deiniol's Lib. Glynne-Gladstone mss 197, T. to J. Gladstone, 22 Feb. 1831; Add. 34614, f. 119. ⁶² Glynne-Gladstone mss 197, T. to J. Gladstone, 19 Feb. 1831. ⁶³ Fremantle mss 139/20/9. ⁶⁴ Add. 40402, ff. 15, 17; 57420, f. 58. ⁶⁵ Fremantle mss 139/20/16, 20, 22; Wellington mss WP1/1182/21; 1186/1; Add. 37185, f. 538; Bucks Gazette, 30 Apr., 7, 14 May; The Times, 6, 7, 9, 10, 13 May 1831; Beckett, 116; Davis, 90-91; Sack, 21, 26; M. Brock, Great Reform Act, 196. ⁶⁶ Three Diaries, 93, 97, 108. ⁶⁷ Brock, 228; Holland House Diaries, p. xxxii; Three Diaries, 119-20. ⁶⁸ Peel Letters, 134; Add. 40320, f. 183. ⁶⁹ Wellington mss WP1/1198/9. ⁷⁰ Holland House Diaries, 55-56. ⁷¹ Three Diaries, 147, 151; Wellington mss WP1/1198/1. ⁷² Brock, 260; Grey-William IV Corresp. ii. 14-15, 21-24; Three Diaries, 160, 162-3; Holland House Diaries, 92; Arbuthnot Jnl. ii, 437-8; Croker Pprs. ii. 140; Wellington Despatches, vii. 124-5; Fremantle mss 46/12/20; 130/5/7, 8. ⁷³ Grey-William IV Corresp. ii. 25, 28; Croker Pprs. ii. 141; Holland House Diaries, 97; NLW ms 2797 D, Sir W. to H. Williams Wynn, 18 Dec. 1831. ⁷⁴ NLI, Farnham mss 18602; Russell Early Corresp. ii. 29-30; Three Diaries, 174; Grey-William IV Corresp. ii. 181; Wellington Despatches, viii. 147 ⁷⁵ Three Diaries, 178; Glynne-Gladstone mss 199, T. to J. Gladstone, 1 Feb. 1832. ⁷⁶ Three Diaries, 251, 256; Hants RO, Carnarvon ms 75M91/H5/4. ⁷⁷ Spring, 257-82; Beckett, 192-3. ⁷⁸ Beckett, 100, 192-267; D. and E. Spring, 'Fall of Grenvilles', HLQ, xxix (1955-6), 165-90.

D.R.F.

TENNANT, Charles (1796–1873), of 62 Russell Square and 2 Gray's Inn Square, Mdx.

ST. ALBANS   1830–1831

b. 1 July 1796, 2nd s. of George Tennant (d. 1832) of Southampton Row and Margaret Elizabeth, da. of Thomas Beetson of St. Andrew's, Holborn.¹ educ. Harrow 1806-7. m. 11 Sept. 1847, Gertrude Barbara Rich, da. of Adm. Henry Theodosius Browne Collier, 1s.3da. d. 10 Mar. 1873.

Tennant came from a north country family. Christopher Tennant (d. 1678) of Milbeck, Dent, Yorkshire, had a son Richard (1672-1719), whose younger son and namesake was born in 1705, lived at Poulton-le-Fylde, Lancashire, and died in 1760. His elder son John Tennant, born in 1733, was admitted as an attorney in 1755, had a practice in Wigan and lived at Standishgate there. He married Alice Latham of Wigan in 1759 and died in 1767. His only son George Tennant, the father of this Member, was baptized at Wigan, 21 Jan. 1766.² By 1792, when he married Margaret Beetson, he was settled in London; and by 1796 he was in practice as an attorney at 2 Gray's Inn Square in partnership with Thomas Green. In 1816, he bought the Glamorgan estate of Rhydings, just

north of Neath, and soon afterwards he acquired the adjoining property of Cadoxton. His scheme to revive and improve the defunct Glan-y-wern canal received no support from local landowners, but he went ahead on his own initiative in 1817, and by the autumn of 1818 had completed a four-mile navigation from Neath to the River Tawe, with a shorter branch to Glan-y-wern. In 1820, aiming to encourage the development of the collieries and iron works of the Neath Valley and give them improved communications with the sea at Swansea, he decided to extend his canal beyond Neath Abbey to join the Neath canal at Aberdulais. Tennant began the work, without an Act of Parliament, the following year; and, after overcoming considerable difficulties, he saw the canal (the longest private one in Britain, after the duke of Bridgwater's) opened at a lavish ceremony, 13 May 1824. At the Swansea end there was an outlet to the sea at Port Tennant, on the eastern side of the Tawe, though Tennant's plans for a floating dock came to nothing. The canal, initially styled the Neath and Swansea Junction, but soon familiarly known as Tennant's, cost at least £20,000, probably very much more; but it operated at a good profit, despite the restrictions imposed by the inability of Port Tennant to take vessels of over 80 tons. In 1826, Tennant, who had publicized the canal enterprise in his Narrative two years earlier, obtained an Act for the construction of a railway along the Dulais Valley, but it was never built.³

Tennant's elder son Henry, born in 1795, was educated at Oxford (he was a fellow of New College, 1813-21) and Gray's Inn, and called to the bar in 1820, though he did not practise. Charles was articled to his father in November 1812 and admitted as an attorney in partnership with him and Richard Harrison in 1821. In August that year he embarked on a tour of the Low Countries, Germany, Switzerland, Savoy and France, which, with characteristic immodesty, he described in two published volumes in 1824. In the pretentious preface he wrote (p. vi):

> I believe that if the superiority of the English nation, as a people, in respect of general information over other nations, be attributable more to one circumstance than to another, it is to that restless spirit of enquiry, the predominant trait in the English character, and which marks the Englishman in every portion of the globe.

On 5 Sept. 1829 he wrote to Peel, the home secretary, asking him to consider the plight of George John Thicknesse Touchet, 20th Baron Audley, who was in severe financial difficulties, and to whom he had gullibly given £10 of his own money. He was informed by the duke of Wellington, the prime minister, that the eccentric Audley had already received more than his fair share of government assistance.[4] In 1830, Tennant, who was attracted to the doctrines of Utilitarianism, published a *Letter to Sir George Murray*, in which he expounded his scheme for 'systematic colonization' as a challenge and alternative to the '*inadequacy* and the ruinous *expense*' of the plans advocated by Robert Wilmot Horton*.

At the general election later that year he came forward as the third man for the open and venal borough of St. Albans. Never inclined to use one word when he could resort to a dozen, he produced an introductory address of striking verbosity:

> My religious creed will be found in the Christian doctrines of our church, which teach universal benevolence and toleration. My political principles will lead me to support a government, which, as respects the governed, can combine the greatest portion of individual happiness with the least portion of human distress; which can unite protection with freedom; forbearance with power; and which can shield that labour to which every government must, at the last, owe its existence. The present administration appears to me to be directed by principles which have this tendency; and so far as these principles may hereafter be directed to the consummation of those most important objects, the present administration will receive my humble support.

On the hustings, he proclaimed himself 'a lover of civil and religious liberty' and 'a staunch and independent advocate of freedom'. He said that he was 'inclined to support the present government' while it acted in the national interests. He attributed Wellington's recent admission that the system of taxation required revision to pressure from 'the voice of the people'; and, to laughter, went on to say that 'I rejoice in this power in the people, and thus you see, my friends, I am a radical also'. He declared his support for the existing constitution, but denounced slavery and promised to oppose 'all monopoly', notably those of the brewers and the East India Company, and to promote the diffusion of knowledge:

> I ... will not cease till the oppressions which have bowed down the labouring classes of England have been relieved, until the mists of ignorance are dispelled, and the chains drop from the hands of the slave.

After his return in second place above a Whig he said that 'I have promised all my efforts and will use them; but I cannot pledge myself that their exercise will ensure the taking off taxation'.[5]

Tennant condemned Brougham's scheme for the establishment of local jurisdictions in England and Wales as expensive and inefficient, 10 Nov. 1830.

Ministers had listed him among their 'friends'; but after he was added to the published list of their minority on the civil list, 15 Nov., he made it known through a local newspaper that he had in fact not voted.[6] As 'a decided enemy' to the 'odious and barbarous' game laws, he called for their abolition in preference to the half-baked measure of reform proposed by Lord Chandos, which he admitted he had not studied, 7 Dec.; he was talked out of executing his threat to divide the House on his killing amendment. The following day he called on the Grey ministry to repeal the duties on seaborne coals, a particular grievance for those who, like his family, had 'expended our fortunes' in collieries in the Swansea and Neath area, and resented the statutory exemption enjoyed by Newport coals carried east of Flatholm. He opposed Littleton's bill to abolish truck payments, 13, 14 Dec., arguing that such interference in the relations between masters and workmen was 'based upon principles of unphilosophical legislation' and was an 'entire departure from the principle of political economy'; he preferred inquiry by select committee. On 20 Dec. he gave notice that at the earliest convenient moment next session he would move for a commission of inquiry into the colonization of waste lands in Canada, South Africa and Australia; his attempt to expatiate on the benefits of organized colonization was nipped in the bud by the Speaker. He tried again, 23 Dec. 1830, when presenting a St. Albans petition for repeal of the coal duties, but he was barracked into silence.

Tennant, who had quickly acquired a reputation in the House as a bore, welcomed government's plans for civil list economies and auditing, 4 Feb. 1831, when he spoke from the opposition benches. He seconded a motion to print a petition for the holding of a national synod, 11 Feb., and presented petitions from Chorley and Salford calico printers for repeal of the duty on cotton goods. The House would not allow him to deliver his views on the budget, 14 Feb. Two days later he pressed for the tax on coal exports to be removed rather than merely reduced, and was laughed at when he stated that even if the present consumption of coal increased tenfold, there was enough to last for a thousand years. Ministers had to wring out of him his 'entire approbation' of their proposal to repeal the duty on seaborne coals; and he persisted in calling for an end to the export tax, peevishly denying that he was being wilfully obstructive and ungrateful. When ministers unveiled their bill to encourage the unemployed poor to emigrate, 22 Feb., Tennant attacked and rejected it, along with the ideas of Wilmot Horton, on which it was based. He confessed that the latter had told him that no subject was more guaranteed to empty the House, and so forbore on this occasion to detail his own notions, which he said would require a speech of two or three hours. He set them out in a substantial pamphlet, entitled *Letters forming part of a correspondence with Nassau William Senior*. He advocated emigration on such a scale as would permanently raise wages in Britain, to be financed by the colonists by 'certain arrangements which would confer wealth on the colonies'. He proposed that all persons of the appropriate age should be given free passage, that only childless married couples and young single adults should be eligible and that there should be no forced settlement of wildernesses. He sprang a surprise, 9 Mar., when he applauded the ministerial plan of reform as a 'great and good service rendered to the country'. Despite the obvious restiveness of his audience, he sought to demonstrate by means of arithmetical principles that the bill would correct an imbalance which had distorted the constitution; and he voted for its second reading, 22 Mar. He opposed the Manchester and Leeds railway bill as a threat to a perfectly adequate canal, 11 Mar. He repeated his objections to legislation against truck payments, 12 Apr., hinting that emigration was the best means of eradicating distress and with it the need for payment in kind. He was probably in Hume's minority of 15 against the bill; and he secured one amendment to it in committee, but failed with another. He supported a motion to revive the committee on the Colne River Waterworks bill, 20 Apr., speaking as a member of the former committee who had dissented from every recommendation of his colleagues. He voted against Gascoyne's wrecking amendment to the reform bill, 19 Apr. 1831. He did not stand for St. Albans at the ensuing general election, ostensibly because he did 'not wish to involve himself in the expense of a contested election ... against two powerful and wealthy opponents'.[7] He was never again in the House, which was thus spared a full exposition of his views on systematic colonization.

Tennant's father died, worth £10,000 in personalty, 27 Feb. 1832. By his will, dated 30 Aug. 1831, he left all his property to his wife, after providing his two unmarried daughters with modest annuities; and to Tennant he devised all property vested in him by mortgage or trust.[8] Tennant, who continued to live in his father's house at 62 Russell Square, became head of the firm, in which Harrison remained a partner. In August 1832, recalling his 'not unserviceable' parliamentary labours on colonization, he asked the colonial secretary Lord Goderich for a place in the service for a young man of 'liberal education', the 'son of a gentleman who once possessed considerable property', but had died leaving

the individual in question a 'burden' on Tennant's family. No realistic hope could be held out to him; and in response to this rejection he informed Goderich's secretary that he

> had formed no expectation of success. I recollected the polite attention which I had received from Lord Goderich when I was in Parliament, and when I had the honour of an interview with his Lordship on a subject which was considered to be one of much public importance, and which cost me much labour, time and expense ... Certainly I never entertained the thought of the slightest personal advantage to myself ... The young man on whose behalf I was induced to make my application, is one of many dependants upon me, and I am now ill able to bear the weight. But though unsuccessful, I have no ground for disappointment.[9]

In 1834, the seemingly shameless Tennant inflicted on the world a truly execrable epic poem on *The State of Man*, in which he sought to 'exhibit, in a concise form, a view of the Divine purpose in the creation of Man'. (Conciseness is by no means its leading characteristic, as it runs to 4,026 turgid lines.) His letters of February 1838 to lord chancellor Brougham, in which he claimed to have 'intelligence of state importance' bearing on the Canada bill, in so far as it adversely affected the interests of an unnamed peer for whom he was acting, seem to have been ignored.[10] In 1846, he tried unsuccessfully on behalf of his mother to secure compensation for injury to the canal's prospects from the projected Vale of Neath railway. (This and other railways progressively eroded the canal's profitability, but it was not until about 1934 that it ceased to carry commercial traffic.)[11] After marrying at the age of 51, Tennant became even more prolific with his pen in the promotion of what he described to Brougham in 1858 as 'those higher laws which more immediately concern the government and welfare of human beings'.[12] His most substantial contribution to the cause of rational improvement was his treatise of 1857 on taxation, *The People's Blue Book*; but between 1856 and 1869 he published at least nine other works on the Bank of England and decimal coinage; national defences; the American and Irish questions; Utilitarianism; railways, and the franchise. Tennant, whose brother died, apparently in rather straitened circumstances, in 1865 (his effects were sworn under £100, 12 Dec. 1866), seems to have retired from his legal practice the following year. At some time after this he moved his London residence to 2 Richmond Terrace, and it was there that he died in March 1873. By his will, dated 1 Aug. 1853, he left all his property, other than that vested in him as a trustee, to his wife, his sole executrix. His only son, Charles Coombe Tennant (1852-1928), became the owner of Cadoxton.

[1] IGI (London). [2] Ibid. (Lancs.). [3] C. Hadfield, *Canals of S. Wales* (1967), 19, 77-88, 254-5; *Glam. Co. Hist.* v. 162, 286, 434, 441, 462, 470; *Glam. Historian*, ii (1965), 96; C. Baber, 'Canals and Economic Development of S. Wales', *Modern S. Wales* ed. Baber and L.J. Williams, 28, 35, 37. [4] Wellington mss WP1/1043/19. [5] *Herts Mercury*, 10, 17 July, 7, 14 Aug.; *The Times*, 17 July 1830. [6] *The Times*, 19 Nov.; *Herts Mercury*, 27 Nov. 1830. [7] *The Times*, 27 Apr. 1831. [8] PROB 11/1799/256; IR26/1303/157. [9] Add. 40880, ff. 388, 390. [10] Brougham mss, Tennant to Brougham, 2, 6 Feb. 1838. [11] Hadfield, 87-88. [12] Brougham mss, Tennant to Brougham, 24 Sept. 1858.

D.R.F.

TENNYSON, Charles (1784–1861), of 4 Park Street, Mdx. and Bayons Manor, Lincs.

GREAT GRIMSBY	1818–1826
BLETCHINGLEY	1826–1831
STAMFORD	1831–1832
LAMBETH	1832–1852

b. 20 July 1784, 2nd s. of George Tennyson† of Bayons Manor and Mary, da. and event. h. of John Turner of Caistor. *educ.* Louth g.s. 1798; St. John's, Camb. 1801-5; I. Temple 1801, called 1806. *m.* 1 Jan. 1808, Frances Mary, da. of Rev. John Hutton, rect. of Lea, 5s. 3da. *suc.* fa. (who had disinherited his e.s. George) and took additional name of D'Eyncourt 30 July 1835. *d.* 21 July 1861.
  Clerk of ordnance Dec. 1830-Feb. 1832; PC 6 Feb. 1832 (*honoris causa*).
  Capt. 1 regt. N. Lincs. vols. 1803.

Tennyson, a tenacious and independent liberal Tory before 1820, had been returned for the notoriously venal borough of Great Grimsby in 1818 with the aid of his father, who formerly headed the Red interest, and the money of his brother-in-law Matthew Russell*. He spent the interval before the next election attempting to consolidate his position. His agent engaged in buying up property, but delays in paying the freemen threatened to nullify any advantage that he had gained over the Whig Lord Yarborough, who had previously possessed the major influence. Rumours of a liaison with Yarborough during 1819 further damaged his cause, but his opposition to the Hull dock bill and the provision of 'Christmas boxes' raised his stock.[1] Anticipating the general election, he asked Russell, 31 Jan. 1820, what he wished him to do at Great Grimsby. Russell replied, 5 Feb., that he would pay the outstanding cost of the previous election and that henceforth Tennyson was 'unshackled' and could do what he pleased with the interest he had established.[2] (Tennyson continued to assist Russell in his electoral affairs at Bletchingley, county Durham and Saltash until his death in May 1822. Thereafter

he was largely given a free hand in running them by Russell's son and successor William Russell*, and unashamedly used the seats at his disposal to try to gain preferment for himself.) On 5 Feb. Tennyson's agent Joseph Daubney advised him that if he paid the election money, he 'would get two Members easily'. However, the death of the king with the freemen still unpaid 'raised people's wrath and disappointment almost to fury ... They will have the money or you need not come again'.[3] Assurances of payment followed, and at the dissolution Tennyson entreated the electors to reserve both their votes as he would introduce a second candidate. The freemen were duly paid, and in the expectation of further largesse, he and his colleague were returned with a large majority.[4] His wife's uncle William Hutton of Gate Burton, however, warned Tennyson that future elections would not pass so easily, as Yarborough was determined to regain his influence.[5]

Tennyson, who had displayed some independence in his votes and favoured a degree of electoral reform, was nominally a supporter of the Liverpool ministry, but on 22 Jan. 1820 the Tory Lord Lowther* advised Lord Lonsdale that he had gone over to opposition.[6] This assessment was somewhat premature and Tennyson received the government's request for his attendance at the opening of the new Parliament.[7] He acted as Sir William Manners's† nominee to the Grantham election committee when he petitioned against the return of James Hughes, 11 May. When Manners was confined to Newgate for failure to attend the committee, Tennyson presented his petition for release, 18 July. On 8 June he introduced a bill 'for enabling landlords more speedily to recover possession of farms unlawfully held over by tenants', explaining that his aim was to reduce litigation. The bill received royal assent, 25 July, when he gave notice that he would propose another measure in the next session to facilitate the recovery of illegally held small tenements. Although there is no record of his voting in this session, it appears that he initially supported ministers on the Queen Caroline affair, and he probably divided with them against Wilberforce's compromise motion, 22 June 1820. Thereafter, however, growing disquiet in Great Grimsby prompted him to reassess his position. In a pamphlet addressed to his constituents early in 1821, he admitted that he had begun to view events with a 'growing anxiety' and quoted extensively from canon and constitutional law in support of the queen. In his preface he added that George Canning's* conduct throughout the affair and his recent resignation had 'nobly vindicated his political character'.[8] Tennyson had spoken to Canning in Paris the previous

October and November, and had then determined that he would withhold his support from ministers should he leave the government.[9]

He voted accordingly in the 1821 session, joining the Whig campaign on the queen's behalf and presenting a constituency petition in her support, 24 Jan. On 13 Feb. he seconded and was a minority teller for a motion to restore her name to the liturgy, in which he drew on the arguments and evidence contained in his pamphlet, saying that ministers occupied a 'supercilious position' and that 'the country at large considered the omission ... an insult and an injury, proceeding from the dictates of disappointed vengeance'. Thereafter he divided steadily with the opposition to the ministry on most major issues, including economy, retrenchment and reduced taxation. Ignoring a warning given in 1819 that a pro-Catholic vote would be received with much disapproval in Great Grimsby, he voted for relief, 28 Feb. 1821, 1 Mar., 21 Apr., 10 May 1825. He divided to make Leeds a scot and lot borough if it received Grampound's seats, 2 Mar., and successfully moved to omit the words from the preamble declaring that when Grampound was disfranchised the number of burgesses serving in Parliament would become incomplete, arguing that no 'fixed or immutable' number had ever been set, 19 Mar. 1821. He voted for parliamentary reform, 9 May 1821, 25 Apr. 1822, 24 Apr. 1823, and for reform of the Scottish representative system, 10 May 1821, and of Edinburgh's representation, 26 Feb. 1824, 13 Apr. 1826. He gave notice of a gamekeeper bill, 19 Apr., and was a majority teller to bring it in, 15 May 1821, but it came to nothing.[10] He was a minority teller against the committal to Newgate for libel of the editor of *John Bull*, 11 May. He voted for abolition of the death penalty for forgery, 23 May, 4 June. In a speech 'inaudible in the gallery', he apparently opposed the sale of game bill, 2 June 1821.

Tennyson's elder brother George Clayton Tennyson (father of the poet Alfred) had been mentally unstable for a number of years, as a result, so he claimed, of his rejection by his parents in favour of Charles. Tennyson cared for him and in 1822 and 1823 spent periods with him at Cheltenham, where he was seeking a cure, to the detriment of his attendance in the House.[11] He continued to vote regularly when present, but he made no reported speech in these two sessions. On 15 Apr. 1822 he informed his father, 'I have reason to think that Canning has thought of offering me a situation with him in India', which he thought he would have to decline as he 'could not consent to leave those whom I might never again see'.[12] After Lord

Londonderry's* suicide that summer, John Croker*, assessing the potential support Canning would have in the House if he did not go to India but went into opposition, included Tennyson among those 'inclined to him'.[13] News of his likely return to government prompted Tennyson to write to him, 11 Sept. 1822, pledging to support ministers if he occupied a 'very prominent position', for although he had recently acted with opposition, he had managed not to identify himself with them, and Londonderry had been 'the chief promoter of those measures which rendered me inimical to the administration'. He thought it 'indispensable' that Canning should have the foreign office, adding that if he needed to bolster his claim by a demonstration of his numerical support, he could depend on the two seats for Great Grimsby and those controlled by William Russell.[14] On returning from France the following year, however, he informed Canning, 24 Apr. 1823, that although he was still attached to him personally, he had been alienated by what he perceived as his failure to direct foreign affairs and to have a wider influence on the general tenor of government policy, and could neither support ministers as he had intended, nor go over to opposition. His nephew Russell, he said, felt the same, and perceiving that there were others of a similar mind in the House, he thought they might form 'a body ... actuated by liberal but moderate political feelings' which would 'steer a middle course between the two parties'.[15] Tennyson duly drew up a set of rules for a 'third party', whose general principle should be to 'express the mixed and moderate tone of both [other parties] and thus more effectually represent the average public feeling of the country'. More specifically it would stand for

> a rational economy of the public money, Catholic emancipation, and parliamentary reform to be effected by a series of measures consistent with the ancient frame and existing spirit of the constitution ... It shall promote a foreign policy which shall tend to advance the cause of rational liberty, civil and religious, in other countries ... while it shall at the same time be consistent with the honour and interests of this country.[16]

This manifesto was in practice little more than a statement of Tennyson's own views. His party never materialized and although Russell was content to follow him, he was an infrequent attender. Tennyson voted to abolish the death penalty for larceny, 21 May, against the Irish tithes composition bill, 16 June, and for the usury laws repeal bill next day. On 1 July he informed his father that he had been asked to go to Paris to help 'settle some claims on the French government in conjunction with our ambassador', but in the event ill health had forced him to decline.[17] He divided against the use of flogging in prisons, 7 July 1823.

Tennyson voted for information on Catholic burials, 6 Feb. 1824. He belatedly joined Brooks's, sponsored by Lords Tankerville and Kensington†, 23 Feb. On 1 Mar. 1824 he 'animadverted in strong terms on the incongruous absurdities that were manifested in the modern additions of mongrel architecture evinced in the new entrance to the House of Lords'. During discussion of the game laws amendment bill, 17 Feb. 1825, he argued for more gradual reform but hoped that 'the illegality of traps to catch the unwary as well as the guilty would be put beyond all doubt'. He successfully moved an amendment to the bill repealing the indemnity of gamekeepers to kill trespassers, 28 Mar., and was a majority teller for its third reading, 29 Apr., when he stated that although he still entertained objections to several of its provisions (which he had failed to reverse in committee), he approved of its general character.[18] Moving the second reading of his own measure to outlaw the use of spring guns, 21 June, he claimed that they were so repugnant that 'the inhabitant of another planet would suppose men to be a species of destructive vermin'. He argued that in normal circumstances homicide could only be justified in order to prevent a crime which was punishable by a death sentence, or in self-defence. As trespass was not even a criminal offence, and spring guns could not be used in self-defence, he entreated the House to sanction his measure 'for putting an end to this anomalous barbarity'. He was a majority teller that day and for the third reading, 29 June, but spoke and voted against its passage that day after an amendment to allow the use of spring guns in gardens and orchards was approved, following which the bill was lost by 32-31. He was a minority teller for the cattle bill, 21 June, and divided against the clause in the combination bill which excluded factory masters from being chosen as justices, 27 June 1825. He again introduced a bill to outlaw spring guns, 14 Apr., and was a minority teller for its third reading, 27 Apr. 1826, when it was rejected by 25-24. He divided to allow defence by counsel for persons charged with a felony, 25 Apr. 1826.

At the 1826 general election Tennyson retired from Great Grimsby, where, despite spending £12,000 since 1818, his pro-Catholic votes had made him unpopular with the Reds and Yarborough's nominees had been canvassing since March. (To his alarm, these included his friend George Heneage*, prompting rumours of a coalition between his family and Yarmouth which he was keen to dispel.) Lord Grey promised to help him, but he did not wish to be 'under obligation to a party from which I am now at liberty if I please'.[19] Instead, he accepted William Russell's offer of a seat for Bletchingley, where he was returned unopposed, having passed up a requisition from Boston, 22 May.[20] He retained an influence at Great Grimsby for the rest of this period, although he did not directly intervene in any of the elections. He voted for Catholic relief, 6 Mar., and for inquiry into Leicester corporation, 15 Mar. 1827. He divided to go into committee on the duke of Cumberland's annuity bill, 16 Mar., explaining that it was the country's duty to establish some fixed scale of provision and that until it did he could not conscientiously vote against this grant. He voted for information on the Barrackpoor mutiny, 22 Mar. He reintroduced his spring guns bill, 8 Mar., and in moving to go into committee on it, 23 Mar., stated that since the last time he had brought the measure forward 'a multitude of dreadful incidents had occurred ... [all of which] had fallen to the lot of innocent individuals'. He was a majority teller on his motion that day, and for the third reading, 30 Mar. When the bill returned from the Lords, 17 May, Nicolson Calvert moved that spring guns be allowed in houses, gardens and hothouses, to which Tennyson replied that a number of 'commensurate' improvements had been made in the Lords, where a similar motion had been 'ineffectually proposed'. He was a majority teller to accept the Lords' amendments and reject Calvert's that day, and the bill received royal assent, 28 May.[21] On 18 May he brought in a game laws amendment bill which passed its third reading, 21 June, but was lost in the Lords, 26 June. He voted against the corn bill, 2 Apr., and for the election expenses bill, 28 May. During May he arranged with Canning, now prime minister, for William Lamb, the new Irish secretary, to come in for Bletchingley in the room of Russell, who had gone abroad.[22] He presented petitions for repeal of the Test Acts, 7 June, and voted with government for the grant to improve water communications in Canada, 12 June 1827.

Tennyson embarked on a personal crusade to enfranchise Birmingham, 11 June 1827, when he moved the special report of the election committee (of which he was a member) on East Retford. He detailed the evidence of corruption there and argued the case for disfranchising the borough and transferring its seats to a larger and more populous place, citing the apparent overrepresentation of Nottinghamshire in comparison to Warwickshire, and the lack of effectual representation for Birmingham. The resolution for the House to give the matter its attention was agreed and Tennyson immediately moved for leave to introduce a bill to disfranchise East Retford and transfer its seats to Birmingham, which was given its first reading that day. He was a majority teller for its second reading, which he sought 'as an assurance that the House would support him in the next session, and would not in the meantime issue the writ to Retford', and successfully moved that the House should not issue a new writ before the expiration of 14 days of the next session, 29 June 1827. When he heard that John Evelyn Denison* would be vacating his place in the lord high admiral's council that September, he applied to the new premier Lord Goderich for the appointment, reminding Goderich of his attachment to Canning and of having provided Lamb with a seat. He bolstered his request by pointing out that he had been trained for the bar and was 'accustomed to business'. Goderich acknowledged his support of Canning and his promises of backing for his administration, but turned down his request in general, and for that post in particular, because Denison had not vacated it. When the latter did so in December, Tennyson again sought the office, but without success.[23] On 14 Dec. 1827 he advised Lamb that Russell wished to resume his seat at Bletchingley, but when Russell eventually returned from the continent an opening for county Durham proved more attractive.[24] Grey told Edward Ellice* in early February 1828 that 'Tennyson is gone down to the north with £10,000 to see if he can bring his nephew in', while Tennyson assured John Cam Hobhouse*, 6 Feb. 1828, that 'all is going smoothly'. Russell was returned unopposed the following week.[25]

Tennyson visited Birmingham during January 1828, telling his father on the 14th: 'I was treated in the handsomest manner. They will have it I am to be [their] Member when they get the right, but I fear the change of ministry will extinguish our hopes'.[26] (The accession of the duke of Wellington as premier that month created difficulties for Tennyson, as the Canningite Lamb remained in office. On 27 Feb. he informed his father, 'Lamb still occupies William's seat at Bletchingley. We are somewhat delicately situated. We do not profess to oppose the administration and I am trying to settle matters satisfactory to all parties'.) He was given leave to reintroduce his disfranchisement bill, 31 Jan., and headed a deputation to Wellington and Peel, the home secretary, 22 Feb., but reported to his father that they had given 'no definite answer'.[27] In seeking the second reading of the disfranchisement bill, 25 Feb., Tennyson declared that his 'sole object' was to 'go into committee and hear evidence in support of the allegation of the bill'; it was committed that day. He concluded his questioning of witnesses, 4 Mar., but he was forced to defend the role of the Whig Lord Fitzwilliam at the last East Retford election, 10 Mar., when he made the amazing claim

that although Fitzwilliam had paid money towards the expenses, his conduct had 'no bearing on the case'. Ministers had decided that they would appease the reformers by supporting the transfer of Penryn's seats to Manchester, but that East Retford must be sluiced into the hundred of Bassetlaw. Therefore, after Tennyson had moved his bill's recommittal, 21 Mar., Calvert, who was aware of the cabinet's decision, moved an amendment that East Retford be thrown into its hundred. Tennyson reiterated the proofs of corruption, argued Birmingham's case and dismissed comparisons with other boroughs that had had their franchises extended into the hundred as a result of corruption. He concluded:

I trust, therefore, that the House will not, by acquiescing [in Calvert's motion], take a course at once useless, anomalous, and obsolete ... [and] leave me under the painful feeling that I have being doing worse than wasting my time, by deciding this question with reference to a bundle of precedents, faulty in principle, futile in practice, and totally inapplicable to the case of this borough ... I trust the House will not confer on the freeholders of the hundred any privilege which they do not seek for or desire to possess; while on the other hand, in so doing, the House will disappoint the flourishing and populous town named in the bill, and defeat its just hopes and expectations.

He was a minority teller against Calvert's amendment, after which he confessed that he was unsure how to proceed, adding that much would depend on what happened to the Penryn bill. Peel denied any ministerial collusion with Calvert, 24 Mar., but it was with their concurrence that he had carried his amendment. Tennyson was a majority teller on the Penryn bill, 28 Mar., and while that measure was in the Lords he secured a number of postponements of the East Retford bill to await the outcome. However, when the Penryn bill was withdrawn, he sought to revive his original bill, 19 May. Again Calvert successfully substituted the hundred for Birmingham, but despite continued government backing for Calvert's plan, the ministers Huskisson and Palmerston, partly through a misunderstanding, voted with Tennyson. This resulted in the Huskissonites' departure from office. During the committee stage, 2 June, Tennyson said he could not allow the substitution of Bassetlaw for Birmingham and proposed an adjournment, which was negatived by 221-24. That day, after a heated exchange with Peel, he urged the postponement of the bill and, when the report was brought up, flippantly suggested that it be thrown out, which earned him a rebuke from the Speaker. In obtaining a further postponement, 9 June, he said that if he failed to carry his point on enfranchising Birmingham next time he would hand his bill over to Calvert, but warned that he would 'wage all manner of war against a measure the character of which will be opposite to that which I originally introduced'. Calvert obtained permission to bring in a separate bill to disqualify certain freemen, 24 June. Seeking the disfranchisement bill's recommittal, Tennyson called on Peel to act on his previous assertion that 'if Penryn were opened to the hundred' then 'this forfeited franchise should be transferred to a great town', 27 June. In an attempt to force the issue he proposed a postponement until the next session, but his suggestion, for which he was a minority teller, failed by 55 votes. He then acted as a minority teller for Lord Howick's attempt to transfer the Members to Yorkshire and supported Russell's unsuccessful proposal for absolute disfranchisement. Calvert now had control of the bill and Tennyson delivered a scathing attack on the 'unfair, unjust, uncandid, impolitic, and grossly unconstitutional' actions of the government that day. He presented an East Retford petition against the freemen's disqualification bill, 30 June. He welcomed Calvert's decision to postpone his bills until the next session, 11 July, and gave notice of his own intention to bring in two measures, one for the absolute disfranchisement of East Retford and the other to enable Birmingham to return Members, 25 July 1828.

He voted for repeal of the Test Acts, 26 Feb., opposed the Llanelly railway bill, 26 Mar., and promised to bring forward proposals to deal with some outstanding problems associated with landlords and tenants if the solicitor-general failed to resolve the matter, 2 Apr. 1828. He divided for Catholic claims, 12 May. Three days later he was a majority teller for the recommittal of the borough polls bill. He voted for inquiry into pluralities in the Irish church, 24 June, and against the additional churches bill, 30 June. On 10 July he proposed an amendment to the game bill to mitigate the penalty for trespass where it was clear that it was accidental, but it was negatived without a division. Writing to Huskisson, 19 Dec., he explained that he was reluctant to raise the East Retford question 'precisely in the way in which it has now been repeatedly discussed', and, believing the borough 'irretrievably transferred *from the monied to the agricultural interest*', thought it 'expedient' to devise some other plan. He outlined a scheme which proposed to overcome one common objection to reform by maintaining the proportion of representation allotted to each country in the Union, via an absolute addition of 13 Members (two to Ireland, one to Scotland, the rest to England). To counter objections that giving the additional Members to commercial towns would

unbalance the constitution he planned to give seven to the great towns (two each to Birmingham, Leeds and Manchester, and one to Glasgow), four to English counties and one to an Irish county. Thus the manufacturing and commercial interest would gain seven, the agriculturists would obtain the same (he included the Bassetlaw seats in this calculation) and one would be neutral. Huskisson replied, 25 Dec. 1828, that 'however ingenious your scheme, I feel upon full consideration, great doubt respecting it, viewed either practically or theoretically'. He recommended the total disfranchisement of East Retford, but no redistribution of the seats until another borough had been similarly disfranchised for corruption, when two seats could be given to a large town, and two to the agricultural interest. In reply, Tennyson suggested giving one seat to a great town and one to the agriculturists immediately, with each to be given a second when another borough was convicted, 8 Jan. 1829.[28] He gave notice that he would bring forward his bills, 5 Feb. 1829, but repeatedly delayed their introduction in deference to the proceedings connected with the Wellington ministry's concession of Catholic emancipation. He questioned the legitimacy of a Bristol petition against relief, 26 Feb., and to the suggestion that the proposed concessions would infringe the constitution of 1688, referred the staunch Protestant Sir Robert Inglis to its text and challenged him to find 'any reference whatever to Catholics, except the provision that excludes them from the throne', 4 Mar. He voted for emancipation, 6, 30 Mar., when he brought up a favourable petition, and insisted that majority opinion in Lincolnshire favoured it, 20 Mar. He spoke against George Lamb's attempts to have a new writ issued for East Retford, 10 Apr., 5 May, when he introduced his bills to disfranchise the borough and transfer its seats to Birmingham. He was a minority teller for his proposals and against Calvert's successful motion for a bribery prevention bill. He joined forces with Calvert as a majority teller against the issuing of a new writ, 2 June, when it was agreed to postpone the matter until the next session. That October Tennyson declined attending the low bailiff's dinner in Birmingham on the advice of Joseph Parkes, one of the leading campaigners to enfranchise the town. This was simply to avoid too close an association with the town's Whigs, but a generous toast was drunk in his honour, and Parkes paid a handsome tribute to his efforts on Birmingham's behalf.[29] Tennyson was a strenuous opponent of the London Bridge approaches bill, by which the corporation of London proposed to continue the collection of the orphans' fund to pay its costs. It was, he said, 23 Mar. 1829, 'a monstrous imposition of tax on the poor', and he claimed that the fund would soon be paid off, thereby 'setting at liberty £30,000 or £40,000', which would help cover the expenses. He opposed the proposed charges for the carriage of coal, 8 Apr., and secured a select committee to investigate the orphans' fund, to which he was appointed, 7 May. On the report stage of the bridge bill next day he objected to the coal duties, which he claimed would raise £25,000 over the sum needed to pay off the loan. Herries, master of the mint, informed Colonel James Wood, 15 June, that Tennyson had recommended 'the expediency of continuing the wine duty ... with the concurrence of the City authorities', as a possible solution.[30] Tennyson supported the archbishop of Canterbury's estate bill, 10 Apr., and suggested deferring the second reading of the West India docks bill, 14 Apr. 1829.

He voted for Knatchbull's amendment to the address, 4 Feb. 1830, when he gave notice that he would reintroduce his proposal for East Retford. When Calvert brought on his bribery prevention bill, 11 Feb., Tennyson, admitting that he was 'pertinacious of my own view upon this question', stressed the economic distress of the country, especially in those places that were unrepresented, and claimed that the people 'ascribe that distress to the misconduct and corruption of Parliament, and these to the imperfect state of the representation'. The result, he said, was a rising demand for parliamentary reform which had 'already had the effect of reducing my proposal ... to comparative insignificance'. He was a minority teller for his amendment to transfer the seats to Birmingham, which was lost by 27 votes. He voted for Russell's motion to enfranchise Birmingham, Leeds and Manchester, 23 Feb., repeated his objections to Calvert's bill, 26 Feb., and failed by 33 votes to substitute Birmingham for Bassetlaw, 5 Mar. This marked the end of his campaign and he merely spoke to register his objection to the disfranchisement bill, 8, 15 Mar., when he divided against the third reading. He voted for parliamentary reform, 28 May 1830.

He asked ministers to divulge the amount of reductions they proposed to make, 15 Feb., and divided in favour of preventing Members from voting in committee on issues in which they had a personal stake, 26 Feb. 1830. He voted for information on the interference of British troops in the affairs of Portugal, 10 Mar., and for the critical motion on the intervention of British forces at Terceira, 28 Apr. He was a member of a delegation to Wellington to lobby for revision of the banking laws, 20 Mar., and paired to deduct the salary of the lieutenant-general from the ordnance estimates, 29 Mar.[31] He insisted that it was essential

that evidence be printed to allow the House to make a fair decision on Lord Ellenborough's divorce bill, 1 Apr. On the London Bridge and Fleet bill, 29 Apr., he welcomed Knatchbull's amendment to remit half the duty on coals for Gravesend, and asked Herries what the government intended to do about the surplus on the orphans' fund once it had been paid off. He reminded him that his committee had recommended its 'liberation, extinction or other appropriation', and said that he had a clause ready. Although government concurred in the report, Herries asked Tennyson to delay his motion until the next session, which he did, 13 July. He voted for abolition of the Irish viceroyalty, 11 May, and repeal of the Irish coal duties, 13 May. He paired for Jewish emancipation, 17 May. He voted to abolish the death penalty for forgery, 24 May, 7 June, when he also voted to reduce the grant for South American missions, and to reform the divorce laws, 3 June. Referring to the king's poor health, he informed his father, 7 June, 'The scene must shortly close. In the meantime all goes on as usual, but there are rumours of a strong league against the duke of Wellington. We keep aloof from all party at present'.[32] On 7 July he apprised Huskisson that he had had a conversation with the duke of Sussex, who had expressed his hope that Huskisson and Grey could be united in an administration.[33] On 8 July 1830 he presented and endorsed a Birmingham petition for compensation for losses suffered at Copenhagen in 1807.

Anticipating the general election, Tennyson began to make preparations in May 1830, telling his father on the 15th, 'I am to be again returned for Bletchingley or Saltash. There are some reasons why Saltash may be fixed on, but the other seats will be reserved for the present'. He added, 24 May, that the seat was gratuitous 'of course' and that 'I do not fear any extraordinary expenses at Saltash except the journey in case I should have to go down, which will probably not be deemed necessary'.[34] By 5 July it was decided that he should be returned for Bletchingley, but soon afterwards he received a requisition to stand for Lincoln.[35] However, as he explained to Gilbert John Heathcote*, 14 July:

> I have now made up my mind most reluctantly to give up all further thought of contesting Lincoln. It is most vexatious, since [I am] confident of success on every ground but the absurd prejudice which I told you yesterday has arisen against me on the part of several of the inferior class of voters, on account of my vote in favour of Lord Althorp's bill against staffmen and cockades in 1827.

He recommended Heathcote to the freemen, but retained thoughts of Lincoln should Heathcote decline, or one of the others give up.[36] On 19 July he told his father that while he was at Newark he had received a deputation from Stamford.[37] He presumably gave them a positive answer before proceeding to Durham, where he co-ordinated Russell's campaign.[38] He took the precaution of having himself returned for Bletchlingley and duly offered for Stamford, asserting that his sole object was to release the electors from their subjugation to the Tory marquess of Exeter, whose family had controlled the borough for nearly a century. His political opinions, he declared, were well known, and though his 'opinions on reform of Parliament and some other public matters by no means keep pace with those entertained by some of the warm supporters', he believed his 'general tone ... harmonizes tolerably well with the average political feeling now existing throughout the country'.[39] After a violent four-day contest, in which he repeatedly complained of intimidation by his opponents, he was defeated in third place. He donated 500 guineas to the newly established Purity of Election Society and all his voters received a small portrait of him.[40] On 3 Aug. he advised his father that the expenses were £600-£700, which Russell had promised to settle, but that 'the town propose to pay, them having *sent for* me'. He had decided not to petition because of the expense, but reported that 'the town make it their own cause, and I have already disclaimed it as mine'.[41] He left for Durham to complete work for Russell's campaign and returned to Stamford to host a dinner, 30 Aug. He gave a ball two days later, and on 2 Sept. 1830 a dinner was held in his honour, at which he was presented with a silver cup.[42]

On 7 Sept. Lord Durham, Grey's son-in-law, who believed that Tennyson 'inclines towards the Huskisson connection', told Henry Brougham* that he had pointed out the necessity of filling Russell's seats with 'efficient persons', but that Tennyson had been content to leave the stopgaps in place and wait to see how 'the cat jumps'.[43] Ministers, of course, listed Tennyson among their 'foes'. Criticizing the king's speech for not mentioning parliamentary reform, 3 Nov., he explained that although he sat for a rotten borough, he considered himself 'a representative of the whole people of England' and would not be 'base enough to contend for the continuation of that degraded and degrading system'. In a warning to Wellington, he added that 'public opinion has determined in favour of reform, and that opinion must ere long prevail'. He argued that the country was entitled to know what reductions ministers planned before supply was granted, 5 Nov., defended the presentation of petitions as one of the most important duties of a Member, 9 Nov., and urged an early decision on the

local jurisdiction bill, 10 Nov. He voted against government in the crucial division on the civil list, 15 Nov. Next day he notified his father:

> I intended to have spoken but had no opportunity ... What the result may be no one can tell. The duke may make a discreditable struggle, but he will sink at last. He might have made a minister 50 years ago but the age has moved past him. The folly of the cabinet is beyond anything which could have been conceived of schoolboys.[44]

Informing his father of the latest rumours on the composition of the incoming Grey ministry, 17 Nov., he commented, 'I see my name in the *Chronicle* as likely to have office, but I know not upon what foundation'.[45] When he was not offered a place he complained to Durham, the new privy seal, that he felt 'unkindly overlooked', 27 Nov. Had he been given something, he explained, he would have 'contributed to the cause by endeavouring to obtain the admission into the House of Commons of any gentleman equally pledged to our views whose presence the government might require'. It appears that he was offered the chairmanship of ways and means at an early stage in the new arrangements, but vacillated on the advice of Brougham, now lord chancellor, who tried to get the clerkship of the ordnance for him. On 20 Dec. 1830 he was offered it by Grey and accepted.[46] The seats that he controlled were quickly pressed into government service, with Palmerston, Thomas Hyde Villiers and Sir William Horne being accommodated.

Tennyson unsuccessfully sought extra time for the recognizances on the Stamford election petition, 30 Nov. 1830. According to Thomas Gladstone*, he had planned to introduce a bill, based on his proposed franchise for Birmingham, to enfranchise all those who had 'three years unremitted payment of rates' prior to an election. Gladstone feared that his idea would 'not give sufficient influence to property and too much to those who have nothing at stake', but conceded that 'he is a very agreeable man'.[47] Tennyson appears to have dropped his proposal after his appointment to office. He urged very careful consideration of the regency bill before it was agreed, 10 Dec., and viewed 'with some degree of suspicion' the request by Lord Chandos to delay the new writ for Evesham, 16 Dec. He challenged Warrender's assertion that there was no evidence that a majority favoured parliamentary reform, insisting that opinion for it was 'diffused throughout the mass of the population', 21 Dec. 1830. On 3 Jan. 1831 he informed Edward Littleton that it was his 'earnest and anxious desire' to see him elected as Speaker, but confessed that, since others had told him he would be a suitable candidate, he harboured thoughts of the post himself.[48] He returned himself for Bletchingley after his appointment to office, 10 Jan. 1831. When Waldo Sibthorp, Tory Member for Lincoln, expressed his surprise that Tennyson should support the ministerial reform bill, as it would disfranchise his constituents and deprive his relation of a valuable possession, 7 Mar., Tennyson declared that 'the vote which my seat has given me' had been 'uniformly exercised for the benefit of the people' and stated that Russell was happy to sacrifice his boroughs for the good of the country. He voted for the second reading of the bill, 22 Mar., telling his father, 'we should I think do better if we dissolved now' and that after reform he would be 'secure of either of Stamford or Birmingham free of cost', 28 Mar.[49] On 13 Apr., after presenting a petition against slavery, he introduced his ordnance estimates, explaining that they represented a saving of £270,627 over the previous year. Although he ascribed some of that to the previous ministry and some to the balance in hand, he claimed credit for a saving of over £100,000. He was a teller for the government majority on the civil list next day and divided against Gascoyne's wrecking amendment to the reform bill, 19 Apr. When the Ultra Vyvyan made a furious attack on the government for dissolving Parliament, 24 Apr. 1831, Tennyson interrupted by making points of order, and when the Speaker permitted Vyvyan to continue, 'Tennyson disputed his opinion, which enraged the Speaker'.[50]

At the ensuing general election he offered again for Stamford as a reformer, having rejected an invitation to start for Lincoln and abandoned thoughts of contesting the county on the advice of his land agent, who believed that the defeat of Exeter in Stamford would 'secure' the Kesteven division after reform. After a three-day contest he was returned in second place, the first Member elected in opposition to the Cecil family for nearly 100 years.[51] He immediately left to vote for Palmerston at Cambridge University, warning his father, 3 May, 'there will be a petition'.[52] He was chaired a second time on his return, 6 May, and then went to Lincoln to support Sir William Amcotts Ingilby* for the county. He provided dinner for the freemen, 17 May, and later hosted a ball. A reform dinner was given to him and Amcotts Ingilby, 24 May, and he attended one at Oakham, 30 May.[53] He had again taken the precaution of returning himself for Bletchingley, but, opting to sit for Stamford, placed the seat at government's disposal in July. On 3 June Tennyson had received a letter from his colleague Lord Thomas Cecil charging him with calling Exeter 'an execrable man' and 'a tyrant' on the hustings and demanding a public retraction.[54] In reply, Tennyson denied using the words 'execrable man', admitted that

he might have used the word 'tyrant', though only in relation to Exeter's electoral interference, but put it down to 'excited feelings' and said that he had meant nothing personally disrespectful. Cecil accepted this explanation, but was incensed three days later by a report of the Oakham election dinner, at which Tennyson accused his family of 'invading the rights of the people', and demanded another apology. Tennyson refused, saying the eviction of tenants on account of their votes was an invasion of their rights according to 'the declaration of the House of Commons'. Cecil therefore asked Tennyson to send a representative to see his friend Colonel Standen, 'who will arrange the only alternative left me'. Tennyson engaged William Maberly* and gave him full authority to act for him. Maberly maintained that Tennyson had 'a constitutional right' to use the words he did, and as he had made clear that he meant no personal offence, he refused to accede to a duel. Cecil denounced Tennyson and Maberly in a speech at Stamford, 14 June, and they both demanded an apology the following day. Cecil informed Maberly that he meant him no offence, but refused to give any assurance until their former dispute was settled. Tennyson therefore agreed to the duel, 18 June. Maberly declined to be Tennyson's second as he was implicated in the proceedings, and so Amcotts Ingilby accompanied him to Wormwood Scrubs that afternoon. He and Cecil exchanged shots, neither was injured and both professed themselves satisfied. They were all taken into custody, but 'as the parties were reconciled ... the matter was dismissed'.[55] Tennyson informed his father, 21 June 1831:

> The course I have pursued is unanimously approved and even the opposition party speak well of me and think Cecil was wrong ... It is said that this is only number one of a series of reform duels, and it is thought a very proper thing that the clerk of the ordnance should commence the shooting season ... Lord Durham acted in the most kindly manner and was on the point of acting as my second if he had not been advised that as a cabinet minister ... it would be improper'.[56]

On 27 June Tennyson brought forward 'almost precisely similar' ordnance estimates to those he had introduced before the dissolution. He of course voted for the second reading of the reintroduced reform bill, 6 July, was a steady supporter of its details, and acted as a teller for the government majority against using the 1831 census, 19 July. He divided with his colleagues on the Dublin election controversy, 23 Aug., for the passage of the reform bill, 21 Sept., the second reading of the Scottish measure, 23 Sept., and Lord Ebrington's motion of confidence in ministers, 10 Oct. He expressed his hope that the boundary commissioners would take local influences into account when determining the new limits, 1 Sept., and cited the example of St. Martin's parish adjacent to Stamford, which if it was included in an enlarged borough would restore Exeter's electoral control. He voted for the Irish union of parishes bill, 19 Aug., and the same day, when Sir George Clerk moved to bring the Great Grimsby returning officer before the House to explain his actions at the last election, said that he was 'at a loss to know how withholding the return for three or four days' could have helped Yarborough. He was a teller for the government majorities for the oaths before lord stewards bill, 20 July 1831.

Tennyson had suffered from poor health for some time and his ordnance office was never to his liking. He coveted a less demanding place, but thought it unlikely that he would get one. Government wanted his office for Thomas Kennedy*, but had no alternative to offer him. He had hoped for the post of secretary at war, but found that had been promised to Hobhouse, and therefore Grey offered to make him a member of the privy council if he left office. As part of the deal Tennyson was to allow government to continue using the Bletchingley seats. He accepted the terms, resigned, 2 Feb., and was sworn of the privy council, 6 Feb. 1832. On 1 Feb. he advised his father:

> The rank is that nearest to the peerage, and giving the title of 'Right Honourable', it is a distinction *for life* ... I might have toiled in here for three or four or five years as [Sir Henry] Hardinge* did without attaining any office which would give this rank as an appendage, and it is deemed more personally favourable when given to a man out of office which is in fact *very rare*.[57]

Writing that day to his wife, James Stewart Mackenzie* reported:

> Tennyson has resigned and what will much amuse you is that he did so because it was *infra dig* to be called a clerk of the ordnance ... His daughter had an excellent offer of marriage which depended on his not being called clerk, for the parents made it an objection to the match. Can you believe this? Yet 'tis true.[58]

He voted for the second reading of the revised reform bill, 17 Dec. 1831, and again supported its details. On 19 Mar., however, he presented and endorsed a petition for the franchise in scot and lot boroughs not in schedule A to be preserved, rather than limited to the existing holders, and, in response to questioning, indicated that he had pressed for this while he was in office.[59] He gave notice that he would move an amendment to this effect after the third reading, for which he voted, 22 Mar., but he withdrew it because of the late hour and short notice he had given. He voted for the second reading of the Irish reform bill, 25 May. He remained critical of the boundary bill, telling his father, 23 Feb., 'What folly to embarrass the reform bill by all this unnecessary matter. They have as I suspected let in Lord Exeter to sluice Stamford'.[60] He presented a Stamford petition against the bill, 19 Mar., when he said that his constituents would rather forego representation than again be subjugated to Exeter. He voted for the address calling on the king to appoint only ministers who would carry the reform bill unimpaired, 10 May, but concurred in the king's decision to seek alternatives before consenting to create peers, 15 May. Reporting that some Whigs were annoyed with him, 18 May, he explained to his father:

> I do not feel that it is necessary for me to join in a cry against the king because I am a reformer ... I trust ... we shall temper the measure of reform as attempted in the boundary bill, although it is now possible that the reform bill itself may pass without much or any change.[61]

On 22 May he denied rumours that he had used a recent audience with the king to influence him into inviting Wellington to form an administration, in which he had been promised a position, insisting that it had always been his opinion that only a ministry headed by Grey could carry a satisfactory measure of reform. His stance on the king's actions, however, upset his supporters in Birmingham, who told him in June that he would no longer be welcomed as a candidate.[62] The Blues in Stamford supported his efforts on the boundary bill, and suggested that if he could not expunge the addition of St. Martin's, he should try to secure the addition of The Deepings, the only locality where Exeter had no influence.[63] His amendment against the inclusion of St. Martin's, for which he was a teller, was defeated by 172-19, 22 June. That day he was in the minority against Whitehaven's proposed boundaries. He presented a petition from Stamford complaining of the partisanship of its corporation, 16 July, and one from chemists and drug dealers against the customs duty bill, 18 July. He divided with government on the Russian-Dutch loan, 26 Jan., 12, 16 July, and relations with Portugal, 9 Feb., and to postpone inquiry into the abolition of slavery, 24 May. He was one of only 15 who divided to end flogging in the army, 19 June 1832, and next day voted to make coroners' inquests public.

Disconsolate at the news that he would be unwelcome at Birmingham, he advised his father, 14 June, that although he expected that there would be a dissolution in November, he was undecided as to whether or not he would seek re-election.[64] Estimates by the Blues showed that he would still have a fair chance of success at Stamford, despite the addition of St. Martin's, although they expected that Exeter would soon be able to reassert his full control of the borough.[65] Towards the end of June he was invited to stand for the new metropolitan district of Lambeth.[66] On 30 June he reported:

> I know you hate the thought of Grimsby, and that you would perhaps prefer that I should go out of Parliament. Stamford after all is far from hopeless ... However, I have ... sent to Stamford my farewell address, and in the papers you will see my acceptance of the undeniable offer from Lambeth.[67]

He was returned there after a contest at the 1832 general election and continued to represent the constituency until he retired from the House at the 1852 dissolution. His views became increasingly progressive: he introduced motions to shorten the duration of parliaments in 1833, 1834 and 1837, and advocated household suffrage, election by ballot and religious liberty, although he was a supporter of the established church.[68]

His father, who tenuously claimed a descent from the Norman family of D'Eyncourt, had bought the original family lands in Lincolnshire in 1783, but despite Tennyson's best efforts he refused to revert to the ancient family name. Tennyson applied to use it in 1832, but Lord Melbourne, the home secretary, refused permission.[69] However, Tennyson managed to persuade his father to include the change of name as a condition in his will, which disinherited his insane elder brother, and on succeeding him in 1835, he added the name to his own.[70] He also undertook a grandiose rebuilding programme at Bayons Manor, turning the house into an extravagant Gothic castle based on his own design. The poet Tennyson mocked his uncle in 1836:

> See his geegaw castle shine
> New as his title, built last year.

Tennyson never attained the high office or peerage he coveted. Although he retained political credibility he became a figure of ridicule in Lincolnshire. After the death of his favourite son Eustace in 1851 he became morose, and composed an elegy in his memory. He later regretted the conversion of Bayons, exclaiming late in life, 'I must have been mad'.[71] He died in July 1861. By his will, dated 8 Dec. 1848, he left his wife £1,000 and an annuity of £600. He bequeathed his surviving sons and daughters varying amounts and small annuities. The residue and his real estates passed to his eldest son George Hildeyard Tennyson

D'Eyncourt (1809-71). Writing a year after his death, Granville Fletcher remarked that 'his efforts over East Retford gained for him the familiar soubriquet of the "modern father of reform"'.[72]

[1] S. Humberside AO (SHAO), Tennyson D'Eyncourt mss box 1, *passim*. [2] Durham CRO Brancepeth mss D/BR/F 294; Lincs. AO (LAO), Tennyson D'Eyncourt mss TdE H108/24. [3] SHAO, Tennyson D'Eyncourt mss, box 1. [4] *Grimsby Pollbook* (Squire, 1820); *Lincoln, Rutland and Stamford Mercury*, 3 Mar. 1820. [5] LAO, Tennyson D'Eyncourt mss 2Td'E H103/4. [6] Lonsdale mss. [7] LAO, Tennyson D'Eyncourt mss Td'E H33/11; *Black Bk.* (1823), 197; *Session of Parl. 1825*, p. 487. [8] C. Tennyson, *Observations on Proceedings against the Queen* (1821). [9] LAO, Tennyson D'Eyncourt mss Td'E H1/87. [10] *The Times*, 20 Apr. 1821. [11] A. Wheatcroft, *Tennyson Album*, 31. [12] LAO, Tennyson D'Eyncourt mss Td'E H88/18. [13] Add. 40319, f. 57. [14] LAO, Tennyson D'Eyncourt mss Td'E H1/87. [15] Ibid. 93-95. [16] Ibid. 91. [17] Ibid. H89/14. [18] *The Times*, 29 Mar. 1825. [19] LAO, Tennyson D'Eyncourt mss Td'E H98/6, 14. [20] Ibid. 2Td'E H17/30. [21] *CJ*, lxxxii. 494. [22] LAO, Tennyson D'Eyncourt mss Td'E H1/103-105. [23] Ibid. 108-111. [24] Add. 38753, ff. 3, 4. [25] NLS mss 15012, ff. 39-41; Add 36464, f. 213. [26] LAO, Tennyson D'Eyncourt mss 2Td'E H85/3. [27] Ibid. 9. [28] Add. 38757, ff. 147, 155, 184. [29] J. Buckley, *Joseph Parkes of Birmingham*, 40. [30] Wellington mss WP1/1025/27. [31] Add. 38758, f. 138. [32] LAO, Tennyson D'Eyncourt mss 2Td'E H85/28. [33] Add. 38758, f. 193. [34] LAO, Tennyson D'Eyncourt mss 2Td'E H88/18, 22. [35] Ibid. 35. [36] LAO, Ancaster mss xiii/B/5bb, 5ee. [37] LAO, Tennyson D'Eyncourt mss 2Td'E H88/44. [38] Ibid. 47. [39] *Drakard's Stamford News*, 16, 30 July 1830. [40] Ibid. 6 Aug. 1830. [41] LAO, Tennyson D'Eyncourt mss 2Td'E H89/2. [42] *Drakard's Stamford News*, 27 Aug., 10 Sept. 1830. [43] Brougham mss. [44] LAO, Tennyson D'Eyncourt mss 2Td'E H89/47. [45] Ibid. 50. [46] Ibid. Td'E H33/5; 2Td'E H89/53, 60, 67, 70. [47] St. Deiniol's Lib. Glynne-Gladstone mss 196, T. to J. Gladstone, 6, 8 Dec. 1830. [48] Hatherton mss. [49] LAO, Tennyson D'Eyncourt mss 2Td'E H91/53. [50] *Greville Mems.* ii. 137. [51] Ancaster mss xiii/B/6d, Tennyson to G.J. Heathcote, 28 Mar. 1831; LAO, Tennyson D'Eyncourt mss Td'E H27/11-15; H36/6, 13-16; *The Times*, 3, 4, 5 May 1830. [52] LAO, Tennyson D'Eyncourt mss 2Td'E H92/2. [53] *Drakard's Stamford News*, 13, 20, 27 May 1830. [54] Unless otherwise stated this section is based on LAO, Tennyson D'Eyncourt mss Td'E H22, the 'duel corresp.' [55] *Drakard's Stamford News*, 24 June 1831. [56] LAO, Tennyson D'Eyncourt mss 2Td'E H92/22. [57] Ibid. Td'E H111/3; K. Bourne, *Palmerston*, 534. [58] NAS GD46/13/42/1. [59] For more details see P. Salmon, *Electoral Reform at Work*, 187-8. [60] LAO, Tennyson D'Eyncourt mss Td'E H111/11. [61] Ibid. 36. [62] Ibid. 38. [63] Ibid. Td'E H36/36. [64] Ibid. Td'E H111/38. [65] Ibid. Td'E H36/41. [66] Ibid. Td'E H111/41, 42. [67] Ibid. 46. [68] *Dod's Parl. Companion* (1847), 155-6. [69] LAO, Tennyson D'Eyncourt mss Td'E H33/10. [70] Wheatcroft, 46. [71] Ibid. 16. [72] G. Fletcher, *Parl. Portraits*, iv. 214.

M.P.J.C./P.J.S.

THICKNESSE, Ralph (1768-1842), of Beech Hill, nr. Wigan, Lancs.

WIGAN   1831-1834

b. ?1768, o.s. of Ralph Thicknesse, MD, of The Oaks, Cheshire and Wigan and w. Anne Dorothy Bostock. *m.* 20 Dec. 1798,[1] Sarah, da. of John Woodcock of Newburgh House, nr. Ormskirk, Lancs., 1s. *suc.* fa. 1790. *d.* 1 Nov. 1842.

Thicknesse's ancestors were active in the Newcastle area of Staffordshire in the thirteenth century. They acquired a property at Balterley, about six miles away, and supplied Members for the borough in the late fourteenth century. Ralph Thicknesse of Balterley (b.?1663), a non-juror, married Elizabeth, daughter and heiress of Thomas Stockton of The Oaks, Cheshire. His son, successor and namesake, who was born in 1693, married Alethea, daughter of Richard Bostock (1690-1747), a physician of Shrewsbury. He apparently 'squandered idly away' his patrimony and left his children 'wholly unprovided for'. His eldest son, another Ralph Thicknesse, was educated at Brasenose College, Oxford. (He has sometimes been confused with his father's cousin, Ralph Thicknesse (1709-41), of Farthinghoe, Northamptonshire, who was educated at and became a fellow of King's College, Cambridge.) He qualified as a physician and, having disposed of Balterley, settled and practised in Wigan. His marriage to his kinswoman Anne Bostock was financially advantageous to him. In 1749 he published *A Treatise on Foreign Vegetables*. On his death, 12 Feb. 1790, he was variously described as 'a man of the nicest feeling, and of a compassionate disposition'; and as 'a victim ... to the blue demon of dismay', who 'as an acquaintance ... was capricious; as a master, a tyrant; and as a physician, trifling, unscientific, and generally unsuccessful'.[2]

By then his only son, imaginatively named Ralph, was established as a banker in Wigan. He was subsequently in partnership with Thomas Woodcock of Bank House, who presumably was his brother-in-law. He had a residence at Beech Hill, just to the north of the town centre, and became 'extensively engaged in the coal trade' at Birkett Bank and Ince; he was a co-proprietor of the lucrative Kirklees colliery.[3] His politics were liberal, and on 10 Mar. 1831 he chaired a Wigan meeting called to express support for the Grey ministry's reform bill. He said that while the measure might have disappointed the advocates of the ballot and universal suffrage, it 'exceeded' the expectations of most reformers, whom he called on to back the king and his ministers against the boroughmongers. A few days later he announced his intention of standing for Wigan when the bill had become law.[4] As it happened, he came forward as a reformer and the opponent of the Balcarres interest at the general election precipitated by the defeat of the measure. At the nomination he declared that 'a moderate reform, such as had been proposed by the enemies of the present bill, would never meet with the confidence of the nation'. He advocated free trade, and in particular abolition of the East India Company's monopoly:

The situation of the working classes of England was most deplorable; but he believed that if an opening was made in the Indian seas, our trade would be so much improved, that artisans of any description would get wages sufficient to keep them in happiness and comfort.

A serious outbreak of violence forced an adjournment of proceedings, but when order was restored the next day Thicknesse topped the poll.[5]

He never joined Brooks's, and in the House acted with the advanced wing of the government's supporters. He voted for the second reading of the reintroduced reform bill, 6 July, was a reliable voter for its details and divided for its third reading, 19, and passage, 21 Sept. 1831. He was in the minority of 27 against the grant for the Society for the Propagation of the Gospels in the colonies, 25 July. He voted with O'Connell to proceed with the Dublin election committee, 29 July, and was in the minority for disarming the Irish yeomanry, 11 Aug.; but he divided twice with ministers on the findings of the Dublin committee, 23 Aug. He was in minorities on the Liverpool writ, 5 Sept., and for inquiry into the Deacles' allegations against William Bingham Baring*, 27 Sept. He voted for the Scottish reform bill, 23 Sept., spoke at the Wigan reform meeting, 26 Sept.,[6] and divided for the motion of confidence in ministers, 10 Oct. Thicknesse voted for the second reading of the revised reform bill, 17 Dec. 1831. He generally supported its details, but he was one of the minority of 32 who opposed the enfranchisement of £50 tenants, 1 Feb. 1832. He divided for the third reading, 22 Mar. He voted for the vestries bill, 23 Jan., and the abolition of Irish tithes, 16 Feb., but sided with ministers on the Russian-Dutch loan, 26 Jan., 16, 20 July, and relations with Portugal, 9 Feb. He voted against Warburton's anatomy bill, 27 Feb., 11 May, when he was a teller for the minority of four. On 8 Mar. he presented and endorsed a petition against the factories regulation bill from the mill owners of Wigan who, he explained, were of opinion that reduced hours must entail lower wages. He divided with government on the navy civil departments bill, 6 Apr., but voted against the Irish registry of deeds bill, 9 Apr. He presented petitions for mitigation of the severity of the criminal code, 8 May, and voted for the Liverpool disfranchisement bill, 23 May, and against the government's temporizing amendment on the abolition of slavery, 24 May. He voted for the address calling on the king to appoint only ministers who would carry the reform bill unimpaired, 10 May, and presented a Wigan petition for supplies to be withheld until it had been passed, 18 May. He voted for the second reading of Irish reform bill, 25 May, and against a Conservative amendment to the Scottish measure, 1 June, but was in the minority for preservation of the voting rights of Irish freemen, 2 July. When ministers proposed an amendment to the boundaries bill to make Newton rather than Wigan the place of nomination for South Lancashire, 7 June, he argued strongly against it and, despite the county Member Lord Stanley's reasoned plea, insisted on dividing the House: he got five votes to 54. He was in the minorities on the boundaries of Whitehaven and Stamford, 22 June. He voted for a tax on Irish absentees and to suspend flogging in the army, 19 June, to make inquests public, 20 June, and to reduce the barracks grant, 2 July. He supported Alexander Baring's bill to exclude insolvent debtors from Parliament, 27 June, and presented a Wigan magistrates' petition against the vagrants removal bill, 16 July 1832.

Thicknesse topped the poll at Wigan at the general election of 1832, when he advocated repeal of the corn laws and the abolition of tithes and boasted of his 'non-attachment to any party'.[7] By the time he stood down at the dissolution of 1834, he had withdrawn from the Wigan bank, which was now styled Woodcock and Son. He died, 'aged 74', at Beech Hill, 1 Nov. 1842.[8] By his will, which was proved at Chester, 9 Jan., and in London, at £1,000, 16 Sept. 1843, he left all his property, including mines and collieries, to his only child, Ralph Anthony Thicknesse (1800-54), pro-ballot Liberal Member for Wigan from 1847 until his death.[9] As Ralph Anthony's only son predeceased him, Beech Hill passed to his daughter Anne, whose husband, Francis Henry Coldwell, later bishop of Leicester, took the name of Thicknesse in 1859.

[1] IGI (Lancs.). [2] Gent. Mag. (1790), i. 185, 273, 399-400, 521. [3] E. Baines, Hist. Lancs. (1825), ii. 617-19; Gent. Mag. (1843), i. 657. [4] Preston Chron. 12, 19 Mar. 1831. [5] Manchester Guardian, 30 Apr., 7 May; Liverpool Mercury, 13 May 1831. [6] Bolton Chron. 1 Oct. 1831. [7] The Times, 12 Dec. 1832. [8] Preston Pilot, 5 Nov. 1842; Gent. Mag. (1843), i. 657 incorrectly gives 10 Nov. [9] PROB 8/236; 11/1986/667; IR26/1656/6.

D.R.F.

THOMPSON, George Lowther (1786–1841), of Sheriff Hutton Park, Yorks.

HASLEMERE   15 Apr. 1823–1830

YARMOUTH I.o.W.   1830–1831

b. Dec. 1786, o.s. of George Wentworth Thompson of York and Sheriff Hutton and Jane Sarah, da. of John Dell of Dover, Kent. educ. Harrow 1798-1802; Trinity Coll. Camb. 1804. m. Mary Ann, da. of Rev. Edward Waldron, rect. of Hampton Lovett, Worcs., 3s. (2 d.v.p.) 1da. d.v.p. suc. fa. 1802. d. 25 Dec. 1841.

The Sheriff Hutton branch of the Thompson family was established by Edward Thompson (c.1639-1701), a York wine merchant, who represented that city in three Parliaments during the reign of William III. His son and grandson followed the same line of business, while his great-grandson, this Member's father, was a captain in the 4th Hussars, who had retired by 1794 and died in 1802.[1] Apart from the provision he made for his wife and daughter, he devised all his real and personal estate, proved under £10,000, to his only son. The remainder of Thompson's education was placed under the supervision of his father's cousin John Lowther* of Swillington.[2] It was on the interest of the latter's brother, the 1st earl of Lonsdale, that Thompson was returned for Haslemere in 1823. He had been promised the seat on the first intimation of the sitting Member's resignation some months prior to the actual return, which was apparently timed to suit his convenience.[3] A fairly regular attender, like the rest of Lonsdale's parliamentary squad he was a supporter of the Liverpool ministry, but he is not known to have spoken in debate.[4] Lonsdale's son Lord Lowther* surely had Thompson in mind, among others, when he bemoaned to his father the lack of oratorical talent among their connections, 11 Jan. 1830.[5] Thompson voted against repeal of the Foreign Enlistment Act, 16 Apr., and inquiries into the prosecution of the Dublin Orange theatre rioters, 22 Apr., chancery delays, 5 June, and the currency, 12 June 1823. He divided against Scottish parliamentary reform, 2 June 1823, and reform of Edinburgh's representation, 26 Feb. 1824. The government request for his presence to oppose a motion censuring their conduct over the war between France and Spain seems to have been met, 17 Feb. 1824, although no majority list survives. That day Lowther informed his father that he had 'begged' Thompson to stay for the debate on chancery delays which took place without a division, 24 Feb.[6] He voted against Brougham's motion condemning the trial of the Methodist missionary John Smith for inciting slave riots in Demerara, 11 June 1824, and repeal of the usury laws, 17 Feb. 1825. He divided for suppression of the Catholic Association, 25 Feb., and against Catholic relief, 1 Mar., 21 Apr., 10 May, and the Irish franchise bill, 6 Apr. He was in the majorities for the duke of Cumberland's annuity bill, 6, 10 June 1825. No trace of parliamentary activity has been found for 1826.

At the 1826 general election Thompson was again returned for Haslemere. He voted for the duke of Clarence's annuity bill, 16 Mar., and the grant for Canadian waterways, 12 June 1827. With other Lowther connections he divided against the bill to reform the Coventry magistracy, 18 June 1827. He voted against repeal of the Test Acts, 26 Feb. 1828. That April Lonsdale, concerned at the Wellington government's vulnerability on the East Retford question, asked his son, 'Is Thompson come up? If not there is perhaps time to send for him'.[7] No majority list survives for that session on that subject, but he was in his place to present a petition against changes to the corn law from Sheriff Hutton, 16 May, and to vote against ordnance reductions, 4 July 1828. He voted against Catholic relief, 6 Mar. 1827, 12 May 1828, and the ministry's concession of emancipation, 6, 18, 27, 30 Mar. 1829. He divided against the transfer of East Retford's seats to Birmingham, 11 Feb., Lord Blandford's parliamentary reform motion, 18 Feb., and the enfranchisement of Birmingham, Leeds and Manchester, 23 Feb. 1830. He voted against abolition of the death penalty for forgery and reduction of the grant for South American missions, 7 June, and against cuts to judges' salaries, 7 July 1830.

At the 1830 general election Thompson retired from Haslemere, where his seat had been earmarked for the government chief whip William Holmes. After weighing the alternatives, Lonsdale bought him a seat at Yarmouth on the Worsley Holmes interest for £3,000.[8] This was apparently facilitated by the financial saving effected by Lonsdale's compromise with his opponents in Westmorland.[9] Ministers listed Thompson among their 'friends', but he was absent from the crucial division on the civil list, 15 Nov. 1830. In February 1831 Lonsdale lamented that Thompson was suffering from an 'unfortunate' illness, given the imminent introduction of the Grey ministry's reform bill, and considered replacing him. Lowther hoped that 'if we do not find a useful successor, perhaps Thompson might be induced to come up for the second reading'.[10] He was granted two weeks' leave on account of ill health, 1 Mar., but attended to vote against the second reading of the reform bill, 22 Mar., and for Gascoyne's wrecking amendment, 19 Apr. 1831. At the ensuing dissolution he retired from Parliament and public life.

Thompson died at Leamington Spa in December 1841. By his will, dated 29 Oct. 1840 and proved under £104,000, Sheriff Hutton was settled on his son Leonard, while property in neighbouring Silling passed to his wife, along with an annuity of £1,500. He also provided for the widow and child of his cleric son Edward.[11]

[1] *Foster's Yorks. Fams.* ii. [no pagination]. [2] PROB 11/1381/723; IR26/67/120; Clwyd RO, Lowther mss 146. [3] Lonsdale mss, Beckett to Lowther, 30 Jan., R. Ward to Lonsdale, 17 Feb., 21, 24, 26 Mar.

1823. [4] *Session of Parl. 1825*, p. 487. [5] Lonsdale mss. [6] Ibid. Lowther to Lonsdale, 11, 17 Feb. 1824. [7] Lonsdale mss. [8] Ibid. Lowther to Lonsdale, 24 July, Beckett to Lowther, 27 July 1830. [9] J.R. McQuiston, 'Lonsdale Connection and its Defender', *Northern Hist.* xi (1975), 143-79. [10] 10 Lonsdale mss, Lowther to Lonsdale, 19, 21, 25 Feb. 1831. [11] *Gent. Mag.* (1842), i. 228; PROB 11/1957/59; IR26/1623/114.

H.J.S./P.J.S.

THOMPSON, Paul Beilby (1784–1852), of Escrick Park, Yorks. and 29 Berkeley Square, Mdx.

WENLOCK	1826–1832
YORKSHIRE (EAST RIDING)	1832–1837

b. 1 July 1784, 3rd s. of Sir Robert Lawley, 5th bt.[†] (*d.* 1793), of Canwell Priory, Staffs. and Jane, da. of Beilby Thompson of Escrick and sis. and h. of Beilby Thompson[†]; bro. of Francis Lawley* and Sir Robert Lawley[†], 6th bt.. *educ.* Rugby 1795; Christ Church, Oxf. 1803; fellow, All Souls 1806-17. *m.* 10 May 1817, Hon. Caroline Neville, da. of Richard Aldworth Griffin (formerly Neville)[†], 2nd Bar. Braybrooke, 4s. 1da. *suc.* uncle Richard Thompson to Escrick 12 Sept. and took name of Thompson by royal lic. 27 Sept. 1820; *cr.* Bar. Wenlock 13 May and took name of Lawley before Thompson by royal lic. 1 June 1839; *suc.* bro. Francis as 8th bt. and to Salop estates 30 Jan. 1851. *d.* 9 May 1852.
Ld. lt. Yorks. (E. Riding) 1840-7.

Lawley, as he was first known, was named after his maternal great-grandfather, Beilby Thompson (*d.* 1750), and great-uncle (1742-99), Member for Hedon and Thirsk, whose Yorkshire estates, worth almost £16,000 a year in 1813, he inherited in 1820 on the death of his uncle Richard Thompson, whose name he then took.[1] His father, who represented Warwickshire, 1780-93, 'under Whig auspices', died when he was eight and his eldest brother Robert, 16 years his senior, succeeded to the Lawley baronetcy and estates in Shropshire, Staffordshire and Warwickshire. As stipulated in their father's will, Lawley and his elder brother Francis remained in their mother's care and were provided for by Sir Robert, who, having failed to realize his political ambitions in Warwickshire and at Wenlock, where he had land and a claim to the barony, sat for Newcastle-under-Lyme as a Whig, 1802-1806, before leaving for Naples, where he devoted himself to art collecting.[2] Lawley remained at Oxford until he married, when Sir Robert made Bourton Cottage, near Much Wenlock, available to him. He improved the property, oversaw management of the estate and sponsored local charities.[3] At the general election of 1820, after securing the support of Edward Littleton*, Richard Thompson and his wife's cousin, the Grenvillite Sir Watkin Williams Wynn*, who possessed the second largest interest at Wenlock, Lawley belatedly announced his candidature for the borough, ostensibly to prevent Cecil Weld Forester of Willey Park returning two new Members, his brother Francis Forester and the anti-Catholic heir to Kinlet, William Lacon Childe.[4] He was defeated, and from Florence, 1 Apr., Sir Robert wrote:

> I have long from the papers been informed of your attempt upon Wenlock and of its result; and I am sorry to say that I cannot afford you my approbation upon that subject. You have no right to avail yourself of your accidental residence upon that estate to procure to yourself any personal advantage unless it is yours, or without the express approbation of myself and of Francis, whom it appears you have not consulted in the business.[5]

He nevertheless offered his future assistance, provided 'you determine to pursue patriotic and independent principles in Parliament'.[6] Over the next two years, and with Richard Thompson's wealth to draw on,[7] they foiled Weld Forester's attempt to take the title Baron Wenlock when he became a coronation peer;[8] and, by instigating civil actions, so threatened his purse and his supremacy at Wenlock, that he agreed to share the nomination with Williams Wynn. On 18 June 1822 Lord Forester, as he now was, shook hands with Thompson, as Lawley had become, as Member for Wenlock at the next election.[9] To precipitate it, Thompson offered his interest to Childe at the Shropshire by-election in December 1822, but nothing came of it,[10] or of his prospects the following year of securing the Whig nomination for Yorkshire, where he now resided.[11] He was returned for Wenlock at the general election of 1826, when, despite constituency pressure and his dissatisfaction with the Wynnstay agent, he steadfastly refused to promise to oppose Catholic relief.[12]

Thompson, a silent Member, who acted in opposition to the Weld Foresters, and apparently independently of the Williams Wynns, cast his few known votes with his brother Francis, who since coming in for Warwickshire in November 1820 had divided steadily with the Whig moderates.[13] He voted for Catholic relief, 6 Mar., but presented Wenlock's petition against it, 23 May 1827.[14] During the recess he travelled on the continent, where, according to Sir Brook Taylor, who met him in Munich, he said that he thought the coalition ministry had been strengthened by Canning's death.[15] He divided for Catholic relief, 12 May 1828. Thompson was one of 15 Members that the Wellington ministry's patronage secretary Planta predicted in February 1829 would 'probably support

the securities rather than endanger' Catholic emancipation and he divided for it 6, 30 Mar. 1829. He voted to transfer East Retford's seats to Birmingham, 5 May. He is unlikely to have been the 'P. Thompson' listed in a minority of 12 for imposing fixed duties on corn imports, 19 May 1829. He was granted a fortnight's leave 'on account of illness in his family', 2 Mar. 1830. He presented and endorsed his constituents' petition for criminal law reform and abolition of the death penalty for forgery, 29 Mar., and paired for the latter, 14 May. He seems to have lacked Francis's commitment to the revived Whig opposition, but divided with them on the ordnance salaries, 29 Mar., and the Terceira affair, 28 Apr., and for Jewish emancipation, 17 May 1830. He was included in the deputation from the select committee on the Holyhead roads bill which pressed the duke of Wellington to sanction changes in the route through Shropshire, 14 June.[16] Before the dissolution in July he hurried to Wenlock, where, assisted by Williams Wynn, he came in unopposed, after the local ironmasters decided against fielding a candidate. On the hustings he promised 'to vote for every proper measure of retrenchment and economy, to support our establishment in church and state, and to preserve my own independence'.[17]

Ministers counted Thompson among their 'foes', but he was absent from the division on the civil list which brought them down, 15 Nov. 1830. He was granted a fortnight's leave on urgent private business after sitting on an election committee, 14 Feb. 1831, and another week on account of ill health, 11 Mar. He divided for the Grey ministry's reform bill at its second reading, 22 Mar., and against Gascoyne's wrecking amendment, 19 Apr. 1831. His return at the general election that month was unopposed.[18] He divided for the reintroduced reform bill at its second reading, 6 July, against adjournment, 12 July, and using the 1831 census to determine borough representation, 19 July 1831, and sparingly for its details. He voted for the partial disfranchisement of Chippenham, 27 July, and Dorchester, 28 July, and paired against enfranchising town and city voters in counties corporate, 17 Aug., and for the enfranchisement of Greenwich, 3 Aug. Sir Robert Lawley became Baron Wenlock at the coronation, and the brothers attended a meeting of the bill's supporters at Lord Ebrington's house, 21 Sept.[19] Thompson voted for its passage that day, and for Ebrington's confidence motion, 10 Oct. 1831.

Despite their differences with the Williams Wynns on reform, the Thompsons remained regular guests at Wynnstay, and acted as political advisers to Caroline Thompson's nephews Henry and Sir Stephen Glynne when they came in for Flint Boroughs as reformers in 1831-2.[20] Thompson paired for the revised reform bill at its second reading, 17 Dec. 1831, and voted for its provisions for voter registration, 8 Feb., Appleby, 21 Feb., Helston, 23 Feb., and Gateshead, 5 Mar., having also paired for the enfranchisement of Tower Hamlets, 28 Feb. 1832. He divided for the bill's third reading, 22 Mar., the address requesting the king to appoint only ministers who would carry it unimpaired, 10 May, and the second reading of the Irish measure 25 May. He voted with government on relations with Portugal, 9 Feb., but is not known to have voted on the Russian-Dutch loan. He voted to make coroners' inquests public, 20 June. Later that month he funded reform celebrations at Lawley Bank[21] and in Yorkshire, where he stood as the 'Liberal Orange candidate' for the new East Riding constituency at the general election in December and was returned unopposed.[22] The Williams Wynns considered his conduct on his retirement at Wenlock, where he neglected to assist Charles Williams Wynn's son-in-law James Milnes Gaskell[†], 'very shabby', notwithstanding his willingness to support Charles Williams Wynn in preference to the Whig, Littleton, for the expected vacancy in the Speakership.[23]

Thompson was admitted to Brooks's, 26 July 1834, and remained a lifelong Liberal, although he opposed them over the appropriation of Irish church revenues in 1836. He lost his seat in 1837, and in 1839 was created Baron Wenlock, which title had been in abeyance since his brother's death without issue in 1834, and was of no interest to Francis (d. 1851), whose heir in the baronetcy he remained.[24] Appointed lord lieutenant of the East Riding in 1840, he resigned in 1847 because of failing health, and died in May 1852 at Escrick, which he had largely rebuilt, and where, as throughout his estates, he had endowed a village school, introduced cottage allotments and promoted agriculture. He was buried in the Thompson family vault at Escrick, whose church, consecrated in 1857, became his memorial.[25] He was succeed in his titles and entailed estates by his eldest son Beilby Richard Lawley (1818-80), Liberal Member for Pontefract, 1851-2, having settled the Yorkshire estates of Kelfield and Stillingfleet, which were to provide incomes for his four younger children, on his widow (d. 1868) for life.[26]

[1] J.T. Ward, 'E. Yorks. Landed Estates in 19th Cent.' *E. Yorks. Local Hist. Ser.* xxiii (1967), 21; *HP Commons, 1790-1820*, v. 366. [2] PROB 11/1230/159; *HP Commons, 1790-1820*, iv. 393-4. [3] Hull Univ. Lib. Forbes Adams mss DDFA/39/45/2-19. [4] Salop Archives, Weld Forester mss 1224, box 337, corresp. C.W. Forester and Sir. W. Williams Wynn, 25, 26, 28 Feb., B. Lawley to C.W. Forester, 1, 2 Mar.; Forbes Adams mss 39/45/20; J.D. Nichol,

'Wynnstay, Willey and Wenlock', *Trans. Salop Arch. Soc.* lviii (1965-8), 220-31. [5] Forbes Adams mss 39/45/21. [6] Ibid. [7] PROB 11/1634/453; Forbes Adams mss 39/46; *Salopian Jnl.* 18 Oct.; Salop Archives, Corbett of Longnor mss 1066/125, diary of Katherine Plymley, 2 Nov. 1820. [8] Forbes Adams mss 39/45/23-27; Add. 38369, f. 332. [9] Weld Forester mss, box 337, private mem. made in London; J. Pritchard jun. to sen. 18 June; NLW ms 2794 D, Lady Williams Wynn to H. Williams Wynn, 18 June 1822. [10] Buckingham, *Mems. Geo. IV*, i. 395; Staffs. RO, Weston Park mss D.1287/10/4a, Childe-Forester corresp. [Nov. 1822]. See CHILDE and SHROPSHIRE. [11] Fitzwilliam mss 114/2/1. [12] Salop RO, Blakemore mss 604, box 8, Lord Forester's letterbk. pp. 120-1; *Salopian Jnl.* 14 June 1826. [13] Norf. RO, Wodehouse of Kimberley mss KIM6/37, Walton to J. Wodehouse, 7 Nov. 1820. [14] *The Times*, 24 May 1827. [15] NLW ms 2796 D, Taylor to H. Williams Wynn, 18 Oct. 1827. [16] Wellington mss WP1/1119/11; 1159/53. [17] NLW ms 2797 D, Lady Williams Wynn to H. Williams Wynn, 13 July; *Wolverhampton Chron.* 14, 28 July, 4 Aug. 1830. [18] *Salopian Jnl.* 27 Apr.; *Shrewsbury Chron.* 29 Apr. 1831. [19] *Greville Mems.* ii. 283. [20] NLW, Glynne of Hawarden mss 32, 5204; UCNW, Mostyn of Mostyn mss 265, E.M.L. Mostyn to fa. 17 Mar. 1832. [21] *Shrewsbury Chron.* 29 June 1832. [22] *York Herald*, 22 Dec. 1832. [23] NLW ms 2797 D, Fanny to H. Williams Wynn, 7 Nov. 1832; NLW, Coedymaen mss 234. [24] *The Times*, 4 May 1839. [25] *VCH Yorks. E. Riding*, iii. 14, 19-21, 28, 164; *York Herald*, 15, 22 May; *Illustrated London News*, 22 May; *Gent. Mag.* (1852), i. 617-18; Ward, 21, 68, 72. [26] PROB 11/2158/676; *Illustrated London News*, 28 Aug. 1852; Ward, 20, 72.

M.M.E.

THOMPSON, William (1792–1854), of Dyer's Hall Wharf, Upper Thames Street, London and 12 Gloucester Place, Mdx.

CALLINGTON	12 June 1820–1826
LONDON	1826–1832
SUNDERLAND	4 Apr. 1833–8 Sept. 1841
WESTMORLAND	22 Sept. 1841–10 Mar. 1854

bap. 23 Jan. 1792, 2nd s. of James Thompson (*d.* 1841) of Grayrigg, Kendal, Westmld. and Agnes, da. of John Gibson of Orton, Westmld.[1] *educ.* Charterhouse. *m.* 1817, Amelia, da. of Samuel Homfray[†] of Penydarren Place, Merthyr Tydfil, Glam. and Coworth Park, Berks., 1 da. *d.* 10 Mar. 1854.

Alderman, London 1821-*d.* (father of the City 1851-*d.*), sheriff 1822-3, ld. mayor 1828-9; master, Ironmongers' Co. 1829, 1841.

Chairman, Lloyd's 1826-33; treas. Hon. Artillery Co. 1826-9, v.-pres. 1829-43, pres. 1843-*d.*; dir. Bank of England 1827-*d.*; treas. King's Coll. London 1828-*d.*; pres. Christ's Hosp. 1829-*d.*; trustee, Patriotic Fund 1833-*d.*; dep.-chairman, St. Katharine's Dock Co. 1848-51, chairman 1851-*d.*

Lt.-col. London militia 1835-51, col. 1851-*d.*

Thompson's ancestors had been settled at Kendal for four generations, but his great-uncle William Thompson was a London silk merchant at 8 Basinghall Street. His father, the first son of James Thompson and his wife Isabel Dent of Crosby Ravensworth,

Westmorland, was baptized at Kendal on 5 Aug. 1750, and apparently remained in the locality until his death in November 1841. He had two younger brothers, William and Robert, baptized respectively on 20 Jan. 1754 and 6 Feb. 1757.[2] Both became involved in the iron trade. William signed the London merchants' loyal declaration of 1795 as an iron merchant of Paul's Wharf, and before the turn of the century was head of the firm of Thompson, Forman and Homfray of Bankside, which by 1802 had settled in Upper Thames Street. His partners were actively concerned in the South Wales iron manufacturing industry. From 1786 Richard Forman had been a partner with the brothers Francis, Jeremiah and Samuel Homfray in the Penydarren works at Merthyr Tydvil. He died in 1794, and his successor William Forman was William Thompson's associate in the London business and also a partner in Penydarren. In 1790 Robert Thompson, having married the widowed sister of Richard Crawshay, became a partner in the iron merchants firm of Richard and William Crawshay and Company of George Yard, Upper Thames Street, which handled the products of the Crawshays' massive Cyfarthfa works at Merthyr. The Crawshays and the Homfrays later became connected by marriage. Robert Thompson, who was the manager of the Guest family's Dowlais iron works at Merthyr, acquired the Tintern works, near Chepstow, Monmouthshire, in 1798, and left the London business. He subsequently invested in iron works at Llanelli and Ebbw Vale, while William became a partner with Samuel Homfray and William Forman in the Tredegar and Aberdare works.[3]

Their nephew William Thompson, James's second son (his elder brother John was baptized at Grayrigg on 10 Apr. 1786), was sent to London, where he attended Charterhouse and then entered the counting house of his pious uncle William's firm in Upper Thames Street.[4] On 15 June 1807 the latter, a bachelor, made a will, by which he left to Thompson's father the estate of Lambert Ash at Grayrigg and provided for his children other than William, 'now under my care', whom he named as his residuary legatee. He put the management of his businesses during William's minority in the hands of his brother Robert, his sole executor, in whom he vested discretionary power to redistribute his property among James's other children should William 'not turn out to be a man of business, industrious and attentive'. Thompson made the grade and on his uncle William's death, 'after repeated attacks of apoplexy', at his home at Laurence Pountney Hill, 30 Apr. 1815, inherited £110,072 in residuary personal estate and became head of the Upper Thames Street firm of Thompson and Forman.[5] Two years later he married the daughter of Samuel Homfray of Penydarren, and he subsequently became a partner in the iron works. His sister Isabel, who was born in 1788, married in about 1815, as his second wife, William Crawshay (1788-1867), head of the Cyfarthfa works.

At the general election of 1820 Thompson and the banker Matthias Attwood stood for Callington on the 'independent interest' against the nominees of Lord Clinton. They were defeated at the poll but successfully petitioned and were seated in June.[6] Thompson gave general support to the Liverpool ministry, but was prepared to oppose them on specific issues. He divided with them against economies in revenue collection, 4 July 1820. In December that year Lord Lonsdale secured some 'favour' for Thompson and Attwood from Lord Liverpool.[7] Thompson did not, however, vote in defence of ministers' conduct towards Queen Caroline, 6 Feb. 1821. He divided against Catholic relief, 28 Feb. 1821, 30 Apr. 1822. He voted with government on the revenue, 6 Mar., and against repeal of the additional malt duty, 3 Apr., parliamentary reform, 9 May, and economy and retrenchment, 27 June; but he divided against them for inquiries into the currency (as one of a minority of 27), 9 Apr., and the administration of justice in Tobago, 6 June. He presented a petition in favour of the Thames wharves improvement bill, 10 May 1821.[8] In August he was elected unopposed as a London alderman for Cheap ward, declaring that 'he had ever been bred up in reverence of the king and for the established constitution'.[9] Thompson voted with ministers against more extensive tax remissions, 11, 21 Feb., but divided in the minorities for gradual reduction of the salt tax, 28 Feb., and admiralty economies, 1 Mar. 1822. He voted for the production of information on the alleged assault on Alderman Robert Waithman* in the aftermath of the queen's funeral, 28 Feb. On the presentation of the London livery's reform petition, 2 Apr., he said that while distress was 'severely felt by the trading and shipping interests', as well as by agriculture, he 'was not a friend to those sweeping propositions which were sometimes advanced from the other side of the House, although he would always be willing to remedy any clear case of corruption'.[10] He was in small minorities for a 20s. duty on imported wheat, 9 May, against the export of ground bonded corn, 10 June, and for inquiry into the currency, 12 June; but he voted with government in defence of the lord advocate's dealings with the Scottish press, 25 June. He voted for Grey Bennet's alehouses licensing bill, 27 June 1822.

He divided against inquiry into the parliamentary franchise, 20 Feb., and the £2,000,000 tax remissions proposed by Hume, 3 Mar., but for an amendment to the national debt reduction bill, 17 Mar. 1823. On 4 Mar. he expressed his hope that the dispute between the admiralty and Lloyd's over piracy in the West Indies could be amicably settled. He called for 'mature consideration' of the warehousing bill, 17 Mar.,[11] and approved the beer duties bill, 24 Mar., when he voted to reduce the grant for colonial agents and for information on the alleged plot to assassinate the Irish viceroy; he again voted against government on the latter issue, 22 Apr. He urged revision of the Insolvent Debtors Act, 26, 27 Mar. He voted with administration against repeal of the Foreign Enlistment Act, 16 Apr., Scottish parliamentary reform, 2 June, and investigation of chancery delays, 5 June. On 9 May he endorsed a London silk manufacturers' petition for repeal of the 'pernicious' Spitalfields Acts. In common council, 10, 23 June, he was one of the aldermen who opposed the grant of £1,000 in support of Spanish liberals.[12] He was in the very small minorities against a temporary increase in the barilla duties, 13 June, and treasury control over the appointment of engineers for the new London Bridge, 20 June, when he was a teller for the minority of four against the third reading of the bill. He spoke and voted in the minority of 19 in favour of ending capital punishment for stealing from shops attached to houses, 25 June.[13] He presented a London merchants' petition complaining of excessive duties on foreign seed, 2 July, and spoke and voted in the minority of 15 against the reciprocity bill, 4 July 1823.[14]

On 20 Feb. 1824 Thompson 'deprecated the impolicy of imposing high duties on low-priced commodities' such as wool and raw silk. He voted against reform of Edinburgh's representation, 26 Feb. He welcomed ministers' sanction of Hume's call for information on committals by magistrates in and around London, 2 Mar. He presented a London silk mercers' petition for drawback to be extended to cut goods, 19 Mar., and spoke to this effect on the silk bill, 22 Mar. On the 30th he presented a London merchants' petition in favour of the St. Katharine's Docks bill, but in common council next day he opposed petitioning against the aliens bill.[15] On 17 May Thompson, though not yet a subscriber to Lloyd's, acted as their spokesman against Fowell Buxton's 'uncalled for' marine insurance bill, which threatened their monopoly. His attempt to wreck the measure, 28 May, was defeated by 51-33; and his motion for the appointment of a select committee by 29-25, 3 June, when he also failed with an amendment to make every member of a joint-stock insurance company separately liable to the insured, and was thwarted by 30-7 on a clause to compel com-

panies to register their partners' names in chancery. He unsuccessfully opposed the third reading, 14 June.[16] He opposed and voted in the minority of 20 against lifting the ban on the export of long wool, 21 May. He divided with government in defence of the prosecution of the Methodist missionary John Smith in Demerara, 11 June, and for the Irish insurrection bill, 14 June 1824.

A member of the government dismissed Thompson's performance in seconding the address, 3 Feb. 1825, as 'wretched'.[17] He supported the St. Katharine's Docks bill, 22 Feb. He presented and endorsed a London petition for reduction of the tobacco duties, 24 Feb., and voiced disappointment when they and the brandy duties were ignored in the budget statement, 28 Feb., though he applauded proposed remissions on hemp and iron (being 'largely interested' in the latter trade) and, bragging that he was 'not afraid of foreign competition', proclaimed himself to be 'a warm advocate of liberal commercial principles'.[18] On 25 Mar. he gave his 'approbation' to all aspects of the ministerial proposals to relax the customs duties, which would 'afford the greatest relief to commerce and would eventually extend our trade', and denied that he had colluded with ministers over the iron duties. He voted against Catholic claims, 1 Mar., 21 Apr., when he presented a hostile petition from 3,000 'respectable' Londoners and disputed the claim of Wood, one of the City Members, that majority opinion there was favourable to relief. He voted against the Irish franchise bill, 26 Apr., presented a Cardiff anti-Catholic petition, 5 May, and divided against the relief bill, 10 May. He brought up petitions for the London water works bill, 3 Mar., and the Tees railway bill, 4 Mar., when he was a majority teller for its second reading. He presented a Tower ward petition for repeal of the assessed taxes, 17 Mar.[19] He gave qualified support to Martin's bill to increase the penalties for cruelty to animals, 24 Mar. He presented a petition from Thames fishermen against the Metropolitan Fish Company bill, 28 Mar., and next day supported the West India Company bill.[20] He presented a London corn merchants' petition for revision of the corn laws, 29 Mar., urged 'the necessity of an alteration' at the City meeting, 13 Apr., called on ministers to act, 25 Apr., and voted in the minority of 47 on the issue, 28 Apr.[21] On 2 May he tried unsuccessfully to reduce the duty on bonded corn to 5s. He presented a number of petitions calling for protection for employers against violent and lawless workmen, 30 June.[22] He divided with administration for the duke of Cumberland's annuity, 2 June, and voted for the St. Olave tithe bill, 6 June 1825.

In common council, 8 Feb. 1826, Thompson supported financial aid for distressed Spitalfields silk weavers and, in response to questioning, said that he had 'done all in his power to procure a change in the corn laws, which he considered a disgrace to a civilized country'.[23] In the House, 13 Feb., he criticized the timing of the ministerial plans to deal with the financial crisis, which he blamed on an excessive issue of paper and a general spirit of speculation, forecast that the planned restriction of small notes would 'create a convulsion' and denounced the proposed interference with the Bank of England as 'a mere delusion'; he was in the minorities of 39 and seven at the end of the debate. The Whig Member Agar Ellis found his speech 'unbearable'.[24] Thompson abandoned his resistance to the promissory notes bill, 24 Feb. He opposed ministers on the question of the president of the board of trade's salary, 7, 10 Apr.[25] He endorsed the London livery's petition for relaxation of the corn laws, 17 Apr., and voted in that sense next day. He presented petitions against Littleton's potteries regulation bill, 21 Apr. 1826. He had by then offered for London at the approaching general election, when he came forward as a spokesman for the shipping and commercial interests; his anti-Catholic views secured him strong Tory backing. He confirmed this stance at the nomination, claimed that he had 'always acted with a spirit of independence' and advocated repeal of the corn laws. He was impressively at the head of the poll.[26]

At the common hall meeting to petition for revision of the corn laws, 19 Oct. 1826, Thompson demanded abolition of the landowners' 'grievous monopoly'.[27] In the Commons, 30 Nov., he praised ministers' 'liberal' commercial policy and argued that it was pointless to inquire into trade, as Parnell wished, while the corn question remained unsettled. He presented and endorsed a petition for reduction of the duty on insurances and pressed for a thorough overhaul of stamp duties, 8 Dec. 1826.[28] He supported the prayer of the London livery's petition for free trade in corn, 19 Feb.,[29] and generally welcomed the government's proposals, 1 Mar., though he thought that the pivot price for imports was set too high. He was in the minorities for lower protection, 9, 12 Mar. He voted against Catholic relief, 6 Mar., and for the duke of Clarence's annuity, 16 Mar. On the London ship owners' petition complaining of distress, 19 Mar., he 'very much doubted' if legislation could help, and suggested that relaxation of the navigation laws had done less damage than was alleged. He was given a fortnight's leave on account of illness in his family, 2 Apr. At the common council meeting held to promote an address to the king on the change of ministry, 23 May, Thompson, while willing to concur in it as an expression of loyalty to the crown, expressed qualms about its

> two-fold character. It appeared to intimate support to the ... [Canning] administration, and to that he must certainly refuse to pledge himself. When he considered the persons with whom Mr. Canning was now associated, he could not give him his implicit confidence. He was ... anxious not to give a decided opinion upon ... [Canning's] government, and he wished the court to be equally anxious on that point.[30]

He presented Bishopsgate petitions for improvement of the process for recovering small debts, 8 June, endorsed one brought up by Hume for reduction of the duty on insurances, 15 June, and presented one to the same effect from London merchants and shipowners, 21 June. He was unhappy with some details of the customs duties bill, but failed in his attempt to modify it, 19 June 1827.[31]

In late January 1828 Lord Ashley* told Peel, home secretary in the duke of Wellington's new ministry, that Thompson, who was now a director of the Bank, 'liked everything' about it except the duke's combining the premiership with the command of the army.[32] Thompson promised to support the common council petition for repeal of the Test Acts, 24 Jan.[33] He duly did so, 11 Feb., and he presented similar London ward and parish petitions, 18, 22, 26 Feb., when he voted for repeal. He was named to the select committee on the police of the metropolis, 28 Feb. (and again, 15 Apr. 1829), having attributed rising crime to 'the low price of ardent spirits' and the practice of compromising felonies. He had been considered by ministers as a possible nominee to the finance committee, but was not selected.[34] As the representative of the 'first' body of ship owners in Europe, he gave his 'most strenuous support' to the passengers regulation bill, 20 Mar., though he wanted to amend it in committee. Next day he voted with the parliamentary reformers against throwing the delinquent borough of East Retford into the hundred of Bassetlaw. He urged greater magisterial authority to control retail wine outlets, 24, 31 Mar. He presented and supported a petition from 16 assurance companies for a reduction of stamp duties, 25 Mar. He brought up a Putney petition against the Battersea enclosure bill and was a teller for the majority against its second reading, 31 Mar. Next month he presented several petitions against the friendly societies bill. He saw no virtue in a fixed minimum wage, 21 Apr. The following day he voted in the minority of 58 to lower the pivot price for corn imports. On 28 Apr. he presented and endorsed a London merchants' petition against a clause of the London Docks bill and supported the prayer of one from wool merchants against the new duty on foreign goods. He brought up the Sion College petition against Catholic relief, 6 May, and voted in that sense on the 12th. He defended the corporation of London's policy on relocating Smithfield market, 5, 12, 13 June, when he expressed strong objections to the usury laws amendment bill. He voted against the measure to restrict Scottish and Irish small bank notes, 5 June, voiced fears of an undue contraction of the currency and tumbling prices and voted in Hume's minority of 24, 16 June, and divided in the hostile minority of 13, 27 June. He voted against the additional churches bill, 30 June, and the silk bill, on which he had made representations to ministers, 14 July.[35] On 15 July 1828 he pressed for the enforcement of British merchants' claims on Spain, opposed any increase in the barilla duties, but defended that of the duty on lead ore.

At Michaelmas 1828 Thompson was chosen lord mayor of London; he professed pleasure at being so honoured 'at a time when political distinctions were rather nominal than real'.[36] In February 1829 the diehard anti-Catholic Lord Lowther* reported that Thompson was 'undeviating in his hostility' to emancipation, but Planta, the patronage secretary, expected him to vote 'with government' for it. He decided to do so on pragmatic grounds, as he privately told Wellington and Peel and explained in the House, 2 Mar., when he presented Sion College's hostile petition. He voted to consider the proposal, 6 Mar.; supported the favourable London corporation petition and argued that emancipation would 'form a basis for sound legislation' for Ireland, 9 Mar.; 'stayed away' from the division on the second reading of the relief bill, 18 Mar., but attended to vote for its third, 30 Mar.[37] He presented petitions against the London Bridge bill, 16, 23 Mar., and the anatomy bill, 27 Mar. He made known the worries of brokers and auctioneers over the auction duties bill, 6 Apr., and applauded its abandonment by ministers, 1 May. On 8 May he defended their scheme to refund subscribers to the recent exchequer bills issue. In July 1829 Peel endorsed Thompson's claim to a baronetcy, which had been put to him by Lowther, on account of his 'manly support for emancipation'. Wellington was sympathetic, but felt that he could not then recommend it to the king, whose desire to make his dubious friend Nash the architect a baronet he was trying to resist.[38]

Thompson refused to support Knatchbull's amendment to the address, 4 Feb. 1830, wishing to give ministers 'time to develop their views ... as to the best means

of removing the distress which now overwhelms the country'. Yet he warned from personal observation that matters were very serious, particularly in the manufacturing districts, and urged government to 'exercise an unsparing economy' and to establish a sound paper currency. He was named to the select committees on the East India Company, 9 Feb., 4 Feb., 28 June 1831, 10 Feb. 1832. He carried the second reading of the St. Katharine's Docks bill, 1 Mar. He voted silently for the transfer of East Retford's seats to Birmingham, 11 Feb., and the enfranchisement of Birmingham, Leeds and Manchester, 23 Feb. On 1 Mar. he opposed naval economies, for the sake of British merchant shipping, but said he would approve 'all practicable reductions' in the civil establishment. He disclaimed, curiously, any special interest in the Merthyr petition complaining of distress in the iron trade which he presented on 9 Mar., and gave a personal view that the problems were 'temporary'. He presented and supported the prayer of a London licensed victuallers' petition against the sale of beer bill, 11 Mar.; he voted for unsuccessful amendments to the measure, 21 June, 1 July. On 11 Mar. he spoke for the London corporation sponsored motion for an inquiry into the coal trade, to which he was named. On the London merchants' petition for a reduction of taxation, 13 Mar., he observed that the City's retail business was 'very far from being in a prosperous condition'. After the budget statement, 15 Mar., he insisted that ministers could go further with remissions, advocated a property tax as the only 'effectual' solution and demanded reduction of the punitive levies on insurances. He opposed inquiry into the state of the nation, 23 Mar., contending that the 'universal' distress could not be blamed on ministerial policy; but he divided against government on the Bathurst and Dundas pensions, 26 Mar. He approved Peel's proposals to mitigate the punishment for forgery, 1 Apr. Next day he supported reductions in the ordnance establishment. At a common hall meeting on distress, 5 Apr., he again advocated a tax on the 'great and ... unproductive accumulations of capitalists' and acquiesced in the resolution calling for a reduction of public salaries.[39] When the petition was belatedly presented, 17 May, he said that while trade and manufacturing had improved, retailers were still in trouble, and promised to vote for a reduction of salaries and the enfranchisement of large towns. He divided for Jewish emancipation, 5 Apr., 17 May. He pressed for urgent inquiry into the Insolvent Debtors Act, which bore 'with peculiar severity upon the retail trader', 29 Apr. On 19 May he endorsed a petition for reduction of the newspaper stamp tax and got leave to introduce a charitable institutions bill to relieve the Bethlem and royal hospitals from a rate levy. It foundered in committee, 30 June.[40] He welcomed the ministerial promise to curb Cuban piracy, 20 May. He called for repeal of the 'ruinous' soap duty, 21 May, 7 June. He defended the Bank's arrangements for the transport of specie and the Ironmongers' Company against Harvey's allegations of 'abandoned practices', 4 June. On the 7th he agreed with Hume that magistrates should be empowered to have unmuzzled dogs destroyed and voted for the grant for South American missions. He disliked the 'degrading' clause of Littleton's truck bill which made manufacturers liable to prosecution on the word of informers, 5 July 1830.

Thompson was returned unopposed for London at the general election at the end of the month, when he advocated 'a change in ... [the] present system of taxation' and stood by his support for Catholic emancipation.[41] Ministers listed him as one of their 'friends'. He was among the City dignitaries summoned to the home office to be informed by Wellington of the decision to cancel the king's planned visit and, according to Lord Ellenborough, he approved of it and was 'almost in tears' at the thought of 'the apprehended danger to the duke'. In the House, 8 Nov. 1830, he defended ministers and the City magistrates, but disowned the alarmism of the new lord mayor, Key; he spoke in the same vein in common council, 15 Nov.[42] That day he got leave to reintroduce his charitable institutions bill (which he lost by 36-7 on its second reading, 7 Dec.), presented a petition for the abolition of slavery and voted in the ministerial minority on the civil list. On 14 Dec. he supported suspension of the Evesham writ as the traditional preliminary to dealing with corrupt boroughs and supported the London corporation petition for repeal of the coal duties, for which he presented ward petitions, 7, 11 Feb. 1831. He defended the Grey ministry's reduction of the barilla duties, 23 Dec. 1830, 7 Feb. 1831. He presented ward petitions for repeal of the assessed taxes, 3 and 14 Feb. On the budget, 11 Feb., he expressed his 'decided dissent' from the proposed tax on transfers of funded property and criticized plans to equalize the timber, wine and cotton duties, but welcomed reductions on coals, candles and calicos. He applauded the abandonment of the transfer tax, 14 Feb., but, by request of the shipping interest, remonstrated against the timber duties proposals and sought modification of the scheme for wine for the sake of the Cape trade. He conveyed his constituents' hostility to the planned tax on steamboat passengers, 17 Feb., complained of ministers' refusal to allow drawback on the export of printed calicos, 28 Feb., 8 Mar., and had more to say on the timber duties, 11, 15 Mar., having denounced them at a mercantile

dinner on the former day as 'a breach of faith with the colonies and ship owners'.[43] He presented London merchants' petitions for a reform of bankruptcy administration, 21, 22 Feb. He partially approved of Frankland Lewis's bill to regulate the London coal trade, 28 Mar., but argued that the fundamental cause of high prices was the 'monopoly' of the north-eastern coal owners. He presented a petition for the abolition of slavery, 29 Mar. 1831.

Thompson took a blatantly opportunist and insincere line on parliamentary reform. He presented and endorsed a London bankers and merchants' petition for moderate reform, 26 Feb. 1831, but he was taken aback by the scale of the ministerial bill. In common council, 4 Mar., he said that while he was 'convinced of the necessity of some change in the representation' and 'anxious to see the constitution repaired', he felt that 'although the bill would do a great deal of good, it would also do a great deal of evil'.[44] In the House later that day he indignantly repudiated Hunt's attack on the City corporation as 'a set of jobbers and scavengers, and managers of all the dirty work in London', and announced that he would not decide on his course on the reform bill until the livery met on the 7th. He indicated that if they decided to support the measure despite its ostensible threat to their franchises, he would 'feel released from the compact into which I entered with them, to support ... their rights'. Yet at the meeting, which, according to Denis Le Marchant[†], he later described as 'a decided failure', he declared that he would support the bill as the livery instructed.[45] He duly gave a silent vote for the second reading, 22 Mar. At a Mansion House meeting of merchants and bankers, 25 Mar., he promised to support 'in the most uncompromising manner' the detailed provisions of the bill, which 'would not only give strength and security to the monarchy, but satisfaction to the great body of the people'.[46] He presented a favourable ward petition, 29 Mar., and voted against Gascoyne's wrecking amendment, 19 Apr. 1831. At the ensuing general election he stood for London as 'an uncompromising advocate of retrenchment in the public expenditure' and supporter of the bill. He was returned with three other reformers, pledged to endorse the measure 'at every stage'. He repeated his commitment at the livery reform dinner, 9 May 1831.[47]

The precise extent of Thompson's stake in the Penydarren and associated iron works by this time is not entirely clear, though it was certainly considerable. After the death of William Forman he appears to have become chief partner in Penydarren, with Forman's son Thomas Seaton Forman, John and Samuel

Homfray and John Addenbrooke.[48] At the general election of 1831 in Glamorgan he spoke against the sitting Member Talbot and tried to rally the other ironmasters to thwart what he mistakenly perceived as collusion between Lord Bute and the radical Josiah Guest* of Dowlais to secure the latter's return for Merthyr if, as many hoped, it was eventually given separate representation.[49] Thompson seems to have become the owner of Penydarren House, in the centre of Merthyr, but he made only occasional visits. In the destructive and bloody workers' riots which occurred in the town in the first week of June 1831, the house was occupied by troops and became the seat of authority. Thompson, who went to see the state of affairs for himself on 7 June, conceded to Hunt in the House on the 27th that the rank and file of the Glamorgan yeomanry had behaved badly, but he defended the officers. His claim on government for compensation for the shambles to which the army had reduced the house dragged on for almost two years.[50]

Speaking in the Commons as 'a manufacturer', 24 June 1831, Thompson recommended a fixed duty on imported corn, contending that unrestricted free trade would be risky. On 1 July he advised Lord Althorp, the chancellor of the exchequer, not to transfer the duty from soap to tallow and deplored his postponement of the proposed repeal of the tax on candles. He voted for the second reading of the reintroduced reform bill, 6 July, but landed himself in hot water with the livery on the 12th by speaking, from local knowledge, and voting in the minority for Appleby's claim to be allowed to return one Member to be heard by counsel at the bar. Later that night he divided with ministers against the adjournment motions. Next day he stated that his Appleby vote did not vitiate his general and genuine support for the bill and applauded its abolition of 'nomination boroughs' and £10 householder franchise. He was called to account by a 'junta' of the livery on 14 July, when, according to a newspaper report, he attributed his vote to 'inadvertence', in that, being tired and not having heard 'a word' of the debate, he had assumed that the amendment had been merely to permit the evidence of an obvious clerical error in the 1821 census return, which had led to a significant underestimate of the borough's population, to be put fairly before the House:

As to the suspicion entertained against me ... because I have been a Tory, I ... have never been of any party ... I have ... acted hastily and inadvertently, but nothing of the kind shall occur again. I had undergone great fatigue at the time I committed the error ... I have pledged myself to support the government. I repeat that pledge.

A resolution was carried accepting his explanation and, in view of his renewed pledge, reaffirming confidence in him as Member. In a highly embroidered account of the episode written later in the year, he was depicted as a 'weeping, repentant and degraded alderman', reduced to a state of 'trembling servility'.[51] Wellington and Greville took a dim view of Thompson's submissive conduct, though the former reckoned that 'more than half the Members of the present Parliament' had been returned as 'delegates' for reform.[52] When Thompson had meekly voted with government for the disfranchisement of Appleby, 19 July, Lowther commented that he had '*finished* his political career in avowing himself a cowardly ninny' and had 'sunk into perfect contempt with friend and foe in the City'.[53] He was careful to divide steadily with government for the details of the bill during its passage through committee. On 3 Aug., taunted, not for the first time, by Wetherell over his subservience to his constituents, he defended his conduct and denied being 'a disgraced, or degraded, or shackled Member'. He briefly argued Merthyr's case for separate representation, 5 Aug. He addressed the common hall meeting called to petition the Lords in favour of the bill, 19 Sept.,[54] and voted for its passage, 21 Sept., and for the second reading of the Scottish bill, 23 Sept. He voted for the motion of confidence in the ministry, 10 Oct. On other issues, he called for a reduction of the duty on tiles, 21 July, and economies in the consular service, 25 July; objected to the wine duty proposals, 22 Aug., 7 Sept., and refuted Hunt's allegation that the new London Bridge was 'a City job', 6 Sept., when he divided the House for immediate repeal of the 'oppressive and unjust' quarantine duties, losing by 64-20. He spoke and voted for inquiry into the effects of the Sugar Refinery Act on the West Indian colonies, whose 'total ruin' he forecast, 12 Sept., when he voted also in the minority of 24 against Littleton's truck bill. He generally liked lord chancellor Brougham's bill to reform bankruptcy jurisdiction, 13 Oct. 1831, but made it clear that he had 'considerable objection' to some of its details, especially those concerning the appointment of official assignees.

In the disputed lord mayoral election of 1831, Thompson backed the livery's eventually successful attempt to re-elect the trusted reformer Key.[55] He voted for the second reading of the revised reform bill, 17 Dec. 1831, and divided steadily for its details. He welcomed the concession of separate representation to Merthyr, while disclaiming any personal interference, 14 Mar. 1832. He voted for the third reading of the bill, 22 Mar. He voted against government on the Russian-Dutch loan, 26 Jan., and may have done so again, 12 July; but he was in their majority on the navy civil departments bill, 6 Apr. On 21 Feb. he confirmed that there was 'overwhelming distress' among London silk weavers, but argued that 'prohibitory enactments' against foreign goods were not the answer. He persuaded Althorp to consider modifying the soap duties, 28 Feb., and presented and endorsed a London merchants' petition for relaxation of the hemp duties, 2 Apr. He presented petitions in favour of Sadler's factories regulation bill, 6 Mar. He denounced Dom Pedro and ministers' support for him in Portugal, 26 Mar., and joined in pressing them to act against Brazilian piracy, 16 Apr. He supported the London corporation petition for the supplies to be withheld until reform was carried 'whole and entire', 10 May, and voted for the address to the king on the issue later that day. But at the common hall meeting the following day, which was attended by a deputation from the Birmingham Political Union, he provoked disapprobation by refusing to commit himself to voting against granting the supplies. On the 14th he approved the studied language of common council's address to the king.[56] In the House later that day he supported the livery's petition, but confessed his qualms about obstructing the supplies, and denied Hunt's charge that the Bank could not cope with the demand for gold. He paired for the second reading of the Irish reform bill, 25 May, and voted with government against any increase in the Scottish representation, 1 June. He was named to the select committee on the Bank, 22 May. He thought the customs duties proposals on the whole 'most judicious', though he regretted some omissions, 15 June; and he was teller for the minority for an amendment concerning West Indian coffee, 25 July, when he demanded a reduction of the duty on currants. He was in the minority for an Irish absentee tax, 19 June. He voted for Alexander Baring's bill to exclude insolvent debtors from Parliament, 27 June. It was from the opposition benches that he questioned Althorp about the relief grant for some West Indian colonies, 29 June. He denied that the Bank had been negligent in the affair of the forger Fauntleroy, 10 July, and on 26 July 1832 he thanked ministers for resisting Easthope's 'ill-timed' motion for information on the Bank's management of the 1825-6 financial crash.

Thompson did not stand for London, where he probably would have had little chance, at the general election of 1832. He contested the new constituency of Sunderland and finished bottom of the poll, but was successful at a by-election four months later. Despite his steady drift to Conservatism, he was returned there at the next three general elections, but in September 1841 he transferred to his native county, where he

had acquired the estate of Underley, near Kirkby Lonsdale. He was by now an unabashed protectionist, and he opposed repeal of the corn laws in 1846. In 1833 Lady Charlotte Guest of Dowlais had described him as 'the *Alderman* in every sense', who 'has not the uprightness which I should have been inclined to give City merchants credit for'.[57] His Welsh and London iron businesses made him extremely wealthy, and he became a substantial investor in shipping, railways, lead mining, landed property and South American mining ventures.[58] He died at Bedwellty House, Monmouthshire, in consequence of a cold caught while visiting his iron works, in March 1854.[59] By his will, dated 2 Mar. 1853, he left his wife his London house in Park Street, Westminster, an annuity of £1,500 and his Westmorland estates, with reversion to his only child Amelia, who had married Lord Bective* (later 3rd Marquess of Headfort). He gave her an annuity of £1,000 in addition to her marriage settlement. He created a trust fund of £8,000 to provide for the children of his late brother James, and left the Penydarren and Tredegar works in trust to all James's sons except the eldest.[60] Penydarren works stopped production in 1858 and was bought the following year by Dowlais.[61]

[1] IGI (Westmld.); B.B. Orridge, *Citizens of London*, 185. [2] Orridge, 185; IGI (Westmld.); *Gent. Mag.* (1841), ii. 666. [3] A.H. John, *Industrial Development of S. Wales*, 25, 33-36; J.P. Addis, *Crawshay Dynasty*, 9-10, 153; *Iron in the Making* ed. M. Elias, 1, 18, 19, 33, 34, 75, 78, 81-84, 138-40, 149-51, 207-8, 213; *Glam. Co. Hist.* vi. 111. [4] *Gent. Mag.* (1854), i. 650; C. Wilkins, *S. Wales Coal Trade*, 396. [5] PROB 11/1569/283; *Gent. Mag.* (1815), i. 475; IR26/657/357. [6] *West Briton*, 11 Feb., 3, 10, 24 Mar., 16 June 1820; *CJ*, lxxv. 125-6, 305. [7] Add. 38288, f. 343; 38574, f. 232. [8] *The Times*, 11 May 1821. [9] Ibid. 3 Aug. 1821. [10] Ibid. 3 Apr. 1822. [11] Ibid. 18 Mar. 1823. [12] Ibid. 11, 24 June 1823. [13] Ibid. 26 June 1823. [14] Ibid. 3 July 1823. [15] Ibid. 31 Mar., 1 Apr. 1824. [16] C. Wright and C.E. Fayle, *Hist. Lloyd's*, 310-14; *The Times*, 1 June 1824. [17] Buckingham, *Mems. Geo. IV*, ii. 217. [18] *The Times*, 25 Feb. 1825. [19] Ibid. 4, 5, 18 Mar. 1825. [20] Ibid. 29 Mar. 1825. [21] Ibid. 30 Mar., 14 Apr. 1825. [22] Ibid. 1 July 1825. [23] Ibid. 9 Feb. 1826. [24] Keele Univ. Lib. Sneyd mss SC8/79. [25] *The Times*, 11 Apr. 1826. [26] Ibid. 10 Mar., 4 May, 10, 20 June 1826; A.B. Beaven, *Aldermen of London*, i. 293. [27] *The Times*, 20 Oct. 1826. [28] Ibid. 9 Dec. 1826. [29] Ibid. 20 Feb. 1827. [30] Ibid. 24 May 1827. [31] Ibid. 9, 16, 19, 20 June 1827. [32] Add. 40395, f. 132. [33] *The Times*, 25 Jan. 1828. [34] Add. 40395, f. 221. [35] Add. 40397, f. 144. [36] *The Times*, 30 Sept. 1828. His engagement diary, which contains nothing of interest, is GL ms 501. [37] Lonsdale mss, Lowther to Lonsdale, 10 Feb., 19 Mar. 1829; Wellington mss WP1/1001/4; Add. 40399, f. 19. [38] Wellington mss WP1/1033/19; 1036/3. [39] *The Times*, 6 Apr. 1830. [40] *CJ*, lxxxv. 447, 448, 468, 599. [41] *The Times*, 27, 31 July 1830. [42] *Ellenborough Diary*, ii. 421; Grey mss, Howick jnl. 8 Nov.; *The Times*, 16 Nov. 1830. [43] *The Times*, 14 Mar. 1831. [44] Ibid. 5 Mar. 1831. [45] Le Marchant, *Althorp*, 301-2; *The Times*, 8 Mar. 1831. [46] *The Times*, 26 Mar. 1831. [47] Ibid. 25-30 Apr., 10 May 1831; Add. 40309, f. 243. [48] PROB 11/1765/24; Glam. RO, Homfray mss D/D Pe 9 (NRA 8735). [49] See GLAMORGAN. G.A. Williams, *Merthyr Rising*, 97; NLW, Penrice and Margam mss 9238. [50] Williams, 151, 159, 161, 169, 210; C. Wilkins, *Hist. Merthyr*, 168. [51] *The Times*, 15 July 1831; *Ann. Reg.* (1831), Hist.

pp. 167-8. ⁵²Wellington mss WP1/1191/11; *Greville Mems.* ii. 168. ⁵³Lonsdale mss, Lowther to Lonsdale, 22 July 1831. ⁵⁴*The Times,* 20 Sept. 1831. ⁵⁵Ibid. 11, 15, 22, 25 Oct. 1831; Orridge, 162. ⁵⁶*The Times,* 12, 15 May 1832. ⁵⁷*Jnl. of Lady Charlotte Guest* ed. earl of Bessborough, 41. ⁵⁸*Oxford DNB*; C. Wilkins, *Hist. Iron, Steel, Tinplate and Other Trades of Wales,* 136, 140-1. ⁵⁹*Gent. Mag.* (1854), i. 650; Wilkins, *S. Wales Coal Trade,* 397. ⁶⁰PROB 11/2193/495; IR26/2012/521. ⁶¹*Glam. Co. Hist.* v. 120.

D.R.F.

THOMSON *see* **POULETT THOMSON**

THORNTON *see* **ASTELL**

THROCKMORTON, Robert George (1800–1862), of Buckland House, nr. Faringdon, Berks.

BERKSHIRE 1831–1834

b. 5 Dec. 1800, 1st s. of William Throckmorton (*d.* 1819) of 2 Old Square, L. Inn, Mdx. and Frances, da. of Thomas Giffard of Chillington, Staffs. *m.* 16 July 1829, Elizabeth, da. of Sir John Francis Edward Acton, 6th bt., of Aldenham Hall, Salop, 5s. (1 *d.v.p.*) 4da. (1 *d.v.p.*). *suc.* uncle Sir Charles Throckmorton, 7th bt., of Coughton Court, Alcester, Warws., Weston Underwood, Bucks. and Buckland as 8th bt. 3 Dec. 1840. *d.* 28 June 1862.
Sheriff, Berks. 1843-4.

Throckmorton came from a very old Catholic family, originating in Worcestershire, who had acquired the Warwickshire estate of Coughton by marriage in the first half of the fifteenth century. A later generation obtained the Olney property at Weston Underwood, Buckinghamshire by the same means.¹ The 1st baronet, so created in 1642, was Sir Robert Throckmorton (*d.*1650), whose estates were sequestered in the Civil War. His grandson, Sir Robert Throckmorton (1662-1721), the 3rd baronet, one of the Catholic non-jurors, married Mary Yate, who brought him an estate at Buckland, at the north-western extremity of Berkshire. His younger son, Robert Throckmorton (1702-91), succeeded him to the baronetcy. He in turn was succeeded as 5th baronet by his eldest grandson, John Courtenay Throckmorton, who had younger brothers George, Charles and William, the latter being the father of this Member. Sir John Courtenay Throckmorton, who was born in 1753, was a founder member of the Catholic Committee in 1782 and one of the leaders of the advanced or Cisalpine party of the Catholic laity, who sought to restrict papal interference in British church affairs. His coadjutors included his kinsmen the 9th Lord Petre and Sir Henry Englefield of Whiteknights, another Berkshire Catholic. In his two *Letters to the Catholic Clergy*

of 1790 and 1791 he denied the right of the pope to meddle in the appointment of English bishops. A headstrong, wilful man, he was a personal friend of Fox and a member of Brooks's and of the Association of the Friends of the People. In his pamphlet of 1806, *Considerations arising from the Debates in Parliament on the Petition of the Irish Catholics,* he explained why English Catholics had taken no part in the campaign in support of the Irish Catholic petition the previous year, and called for the adoption of 'an enlarged system of policy' to prepare the way for emancipation: 'the higher orders among the Catholics ... their bishops, and their clergy, should be invited to use their influence on the great mass of society'.² He was one of the principal speakers at the Berkshire parliamentary reform meeting of 11 Feb. 1817.³

On his death without issue in January 1819 he was succeeded as 6th baronet by his next brother George, who had been born in 1754 and had a childless marriage, as did the next in line for the baronetcy, his brother Charles, now aged 61. Their nephew, Robert George Throckmorton, eldest son of their youngest brother William, was therefore the heir presumptive. William Throckmorton, who was born in 1762, entered Lincoln's Inn in 1786 and appears to have practised as a certificated conveyancer. He was in Paris in the company of other English Catholics in November 1802. Like Sir John, he was a member of the Catholic Board, which replaced the Committee in 1808.⁴ He died at Brighton, aged 56, 31 Mar. 1819, less than two months after proving his eldest brother's will. A widower, he died intestate, leaving three sons and two daughters under age. Administration of his effects, which were sworn under a paltry £800, was granted to Sir John's widow (who was a sister of William's late wife) and Charles Courtenay, an uncle, the legal guardians of the children.⁵

It is not known where Robert George Throckmorton received his education, but the Rev. Joseph Berrington, chaplain at Buckland, may have had a hand in it. In the summer of 1821 he travelled from France to Italy, where he spent the following winter, staying first in Naples and then in Rome. His travelling companions included the widow and children of Sir John Francis Edward Acton, 6th baronet (1736-1811), formerly commander-in-chief and prime minister of Naples, who in 1800 had been given papal dispensation to marry his brother's teenage daughter, his junior by almost 50 years. Throckmorton spent the winter of 1823-4 in Italy.⁶ He was admitted to Brooks's on 18 Feb. 1826, was in London in the spring, and after the general election told Denis Le Marchant† that the successful intervention of the Catholic Association in counties Monaghan and Waterford had 'certainly frightened many moderate persons who favoured the party on account of its political insignificance'.[7] Soon afterwards his uncle Sir George died and was succeeded as 7th baronet by Charles. Throckmorton seems to have lived mostly at Buckland from about this time, though in the summer of 1828 he visited Scotland, returning reluctantly to Berkshire in September for the 'honour and bore' of acting as steward of some local races. In 1829 he married Acton's daughter Elizabeth.[8]

At the general election of 1830 Robert Smith, the Whig Member for Buckinghamshire, solicited his support in case he was threatened with a 'No Popery' opposition.[9] In Berkshire the aged and long-serving Whig Member Charles Dundas, who was possibly grooming Throckmorton as his successor, asked him to second his nomination. He complied, and delivered what was probably his first public speech, a brief eulogy of Dundas as 'the most uncompromising foe of corruption and bigotry'.[10] He attended the Berkshire county meeting of 16 Mar. 1831 to express approval of the Grey ministry's reform bill, but did not speak.[11] Throckmorton, whose first child, a boy, was born on 1 Apr., was regarded by the Berkshire reformers as a good potential candidate for the next general election. When John Berkeley Monck, the former Member for Reading, resisted pressure from Lord Radnor to come forward after the defeat of the reform bill, arguing that Throckmorton was a better bet, having 'everything to recommend him, family, property, a good name, and good principles', he agreed to stand.[12] He did so as a firm supporter of the 'salutary [and] constitutional' measure. His position was strengthened by county-wide meetings which pledged to support him with Dundas, and by the voluntary withdrawal of the veteran radical reformer William Hallett, who had contested the county on three previous occasions. The other sitting Member, Robert Palmer, a Tory, who had voted for the second reading of the bill but opposed it on Gascoyne's amendment, because he regarded it as too sweeping, submitted to the tide of opinion against him and retired on the eve of the election, leaving the way clear for the reformers. At the nomination Throckmorton, who was proposed by the radical hero Sir Francis Burdett* and seconded by Monck, both of whom made much of his relationship to the late Sir John, his youth and his independent wealth, proclaimed himself to be 'the uncompromising advocate' of the entire bill. He denounced the 'specious pretext of moderate reform' and deplored 'the perjury, the misery, and the vice under which the country had so long groaned, owing to the boroughmongering

monopoly'. He emphasized his devotion to the interests of agriculture and called for a speedy abolition of slavery, provided it was attended with 'proper regard to the property of the West Indian interests ... and to the sufferings of the miserable slaves'. In response to questions, he expressed his approval of Lord Althorp's bill to reform the game laws, but evaded the issue of renewal of the East India Company's charter, which he thought the next Parliament would not have time to consider. At the formal election proceedings, he asserted that the reform bill, though not 'revolutionary', would 'sweep away bribery and corruption, from whence had flowed by far the greatest part of those evils which had so long bowed this suffering country to the ground'.[13] His wife told her brother: 'If you could see the faces of the parsons – a popish radical – the poor dear church!'[14] From Charles Butler, one of Sir John Throckmorton's closest allies on the Catholic Committee, he received a letter of congratulation and advice:

> You cannot serve the cause of reform, or to speak more properly the great cause of liberty, better, than by watching your own friends and keeping them firm in the popular principles of their party ... In my long life I have seen the Whigs three times called into power, and at each time losing their character and their strength by too great sacrifices to aristocratic feelings. From reproach on this head the present ministry are not free. But it would be invidious to mention particulars. Their conduct, however, deserves your serious attention. The abolition of sinecures, and undeserved pensions, the exercise of office by deputy, the non-residents and pluralities of the clergy, the absence of the prebendaries from their stalls, and the neglect of the religious education of the poor loudly called for remedy. The public expects both a serious and speedy reform of all these particulars, and will take the measure into their own management, if the ministers delay it, or deal it with a sparing hand. I hope to see you at the head of those who promote these substantial and necessary reforms. I hear from Berkshire that your speeches were most favourably received. They certainly have been praised in London ... I hope it will not be long before you hear your own voice in Parliament. Every day's delay adds to the difficulty of a speaker for the first time. You may be assured that at present, public opinion is greatly in your favour.[15]

At a celebration dinner at Newbury, 25 May 1831, Throckmorton proclaimed 'the triumph of reform over a little knot of oligarchists, who had so long usurped their rights', portrayed himself as 'the avowed enemy of all jobs' and said that he would be found 'foremost in the ranks of the advocates of the comprehensive and enlightened policy' of the government.[16]

He made little mark in the House. He voted for the second reading of the reintroduced reform bill, 6 July, and twice against adjournment, 12 July 1831. He was a generally steady supporter of the details of the bill, but he voted against the proposed division of counties, 11 Aug., and for the enfranchisement of tenant farmers, 18 Aug. Explaining the former vote, 12 Aug., when he approved the proposal to create some three Member counties (of which Berkshire was one), he said that division would 'tend to nomination'. At the same time, he insisted that in his constituency the measure had 'in all its details given very great satisfaction'. He had presented a Newbury agriculturists' petition for all occupiers paying rates of a certain amount to be given the county vote, 20 July. He voted with ministers for the prosecution of those found guilty of giving bribes at the Dublin election, 23 Aug., but not against the opposition censure motion which followed it. On 19 Sept. he presented a petition from the Vale for reduction of the duty on fire insurance. He voted for the third reading of the reform bill later that day, and for its passage, 21 Sept. He voted for the second reading of the Scottish reform bill, 23 Sept. At the Berkshire meeting to petition the Lords to pass the English bill, 5 Oct., he professed to be 'convinced' that they would do so

as it appeared impossible that they could resist the power of public opinion so vehemently expressed ... It had been said that the question now was, reform and peace, or insurrection and bloodshed; but he denied that it was so, for he felt convinced that a little patience only was necessary, and that after one more session at the utmost, they would see their hopes fully accomplished, even if the cup was now dashed from their lips.[17]

After the rejection of the bill he told his Tory brother-in-law, Sir Ferdinand Richard Edward Acton, whose known desire for a peerage at that moment was something of an embarrassment to him, that London was 'perfectly quiet and no apprehension is entertained I believe except in Scotland, where the people are furious'. He voted for Lord Ebrington's confidence motion, 10 Oct. 1831, and spent the recess at Buckland, Coughton and the Acton residence in Shropshire.[18]

He went up to vote for the second reading of the revised reform bill, 17 Dec. 1831. He was absent from the divisions of 20 and 23 Jan. 1832 on the bill, though he was in London on the 24th, when he told his wife, to whom he wrote frequently, and in terms of great affection, but with whom he seems to have had a passing tiff:

I have just got your darling letter, angel. How sorry I am at what I said. I am so afraid sometimes you do not know how I adore you and I am always trying to do what will please you, so forgive me when I have a jealous fit, darling ... I wish I had never got into this beastly Parliament and that I could get out this year. I hate it. We were so happy and well with our child before.[19]

He was one of the reformers who voted against government on the Russian-Dutch loan, 26 Jan., and he divided for inquiry into distress in the glove trade, 31 Jan. He voted for the £10 householder clause of the reform bill, 3 Feb., after which he paired off, 'except on Belgium', with Lord Villiers until schedule A came under consideration. He was therefore absent from the division on relations with Portugal, 9 Feb.[20] He resumed attendance in the last week of February, and voted with government in the committee divisions on Appleby, 21 Feb., Helston, 23 Feb., Tower Hamlets, 28 Feb., and Gateshead, 5 Mar. To his great delight, his wife and child joined him in London at Thomas's Hotel in early March; and later in the month he took possession of a house at 71 Pall Mall on a two-year lease.[21] He went to the House for the debate on the third reading of the reform bill, 20 Mar., but, disappointed to learn that there was no chance of a division that night, told his wife, 'I am sorry I came, though it looks bad only just coming in for the division'. While he could scarcely credit a rumour that his uncle would be offered a peerage if creations proved necessary to get the bill through the Lords, he thought ministers would 'make a point of not passing over the Catholics'.[22] He duly voted for the third reading, 22 Mar. He divided in the minority against restoring the salary of the Irish registrar of deeds to its original level, 9 Apr., but he voted for the address asking the king to appoint only ministers who would carry the reform bill unimpaired, 10 May. He voted against the government's temporizing amendment to Fowell Buxton's motion for an inquiry into colonial slavery, 24 May, and on 18 June he presented a petition for abolition from Wantage Baptists. His attendance in Parliament to vote for the second reading of the Irish reform bill, 25 May, was his excuse for staying away from that day's county meeting to petition the Lords in favour of reform.[23] He voted against a Conservative amendment to the Scottish reform bill, 1 June, and to make coroners' inquests public, 20 June. He did not vote in the divisions on the Russian-Dutch loan, 12, 16, 20 July 1832.

Throckmorton stood again for Berkshire at the general election of 1832 and was returned in second place, but he retired from Parliament at the dissolution of 1834. He succeeded his uncle to the baronetcy and estates in five counties in 1840.[24] He died at his

London home at 14 Hereford Street, Park Lane in June 1862. As his eldest son, Robert Charles Courtenay Throckmorton, had died in 1853, he was succeeded in the baronetcy by his second son, Nicholas William George (1838-1919), who was in turn succeeded as 10th baronet by his brother Richard Charles Acton (1839-1927). Throckmorton's third daughter Emily survived until 1929.

[1] A.L. Rowse, *Ralegh and Throckmortons*, 1-2. [2] B. Ward, *Dawn of Catholic Revival*, i. 46-47, 90, 93, 111-12, 116-17, 121, 153, 332, 340; ii. 39-40, 46, 51-52; and *Eve of Catholic Emancipation*, i. 39 – 40, 66, 102, 112, 173; D. Mathew, *Catholicism in England* (1948), 158; M.D.R. Leys, *Catholics in England*, 137-8; M.D. Petre, *Lord Petre*, 121, 126 – 7, 157, 205; *Burke Corresp.* vii. 482-3; *HMC Fortescue*, ix. 194, 299. [3] *Jackson's Oxford Jnl.* 15 Feb. 1817. [4] *Berry Jnls.* ii. 201; Ward, *Eve of Catholic Emancipation*, i. 102. [5] *Gent. Mag.* (1819), i. 181, 380; PROB 6/195 (13 May 1819); 11/1613/96. [6] Warws. RO, Throckmorton mss CR 1998/Tribune/folder 4/7-8; folder 21/1. [7] Cambridge Univ. Lib. Acton mss, Add. 8121 (4)/185; *Baring Jnls.* 46. [8] Acton mss 354, 355; Throckmorton mss CR 1998/Tribune/folder 17/1-7. [9] Throckmorton mss folder 11/2. [10] Ibid. folder 11/3; *The Times*, 9 Aug. 1830. [11] Acton mss 316; *The Times*, 17 Mar. 1831. [12] Acton mss 359, 360; Throckmorton mss folder 10/1, 9. [13] Throckmorton mss folder 16/24-29, 31, 33, 34; box 61/folder 5, Throckmorton to Sir C. Throckmorton, 9 May; *Reading Mercury*, 25 Apr., 2, 9, 16 May 1831. [14] Acton mss 317. [15] Throckmorton mss 11/4; Petre, 280-3. [16] *Reading Mercury*, 30 May 1831. [17] Ibid. 10 Oct. 1831. [18] Acton mss 318-20, 365. [19] Throckmorton mss folder 16/52. [20] Ibid. folder 16/56, 57; Acton mss 323. [21] Acton mss 324-6; Throckmorton mss folder 16/49, 58, 59. [22] Throckmorton mss folder 16/49, 51, 60. [23] *The Times*, 26 May 1832. [24] PROB 11/1941/148; IR26/1589/72.

D.R.F.

THYNNE, Lord Edward (1807–1884), of 2 Richmond Terrace, Mdx.

WEOBLEY	1831–1832
FROME	1859–1865

b. 23 Jan. 1807, 6th s. of Thomas Thynne[†], 2nd mq. of Bath (*d.* 1837), and Hon. Isabella Elizabeth Byng, da. and coh. of George, 4th Visct. Torrington; bro. of Lord Henry Frederick Thynne*, Thomas Thynne II, Visct. Weymouth[†] and Lord William Thynne*. *educ.* Charterhouse 1820-1; Oriel, Oxf. 1825. *m.* (1) 8 July 1830, Elizabeth (*d.* 6 Mar. 1849), da. of William Mellish of Woodford, Essex, *s.p.*; (2) 4 July 1853, Cecilia Anne Mary, da. of Charles Arthur Gore, 1st Life Gds., 1da. *d.* 4 Feb. 1884.
2nd. lt. 60th rifle corps 1828, lt. 1829, ret. 1830; lt.-col. Som. yeoman cav. 1830; cornet Wilts. yeoman cav. 1855; lt. 13th Som. rifle vols. 1863.

The only one of the 2nd marquess of Bath's sons to be educated at Charterhouse, Thynne, an inveterate gambler who may have been intended for the church, took his degree at Oxford in 1828, before being bought a commission in the duke of York's rifle corps. He

resigned it less than two years later on his marriage to the heiress Elizabeth Mellish, whose father had made his fortune as a navy contractor.[1] Six months of negotiations had produced a settlement whereby Mellish granted his daughter £100,000 in three equal shares, and Thynne received £10,000 charged on his father's Irish estates.[2] His maternal uncle, the 6th duke of Bedford, observed: 'The saints always marry among themselves. They will become *degenerate* from what we farmers call *breeding in and in*'.[3] To cover his gaming losses, on 25 Oct. 1830 he granted the first of a series of annuities illegally charged to his marriage portion.[4] He had not been found out in 1831, when at the general election his father returned him with his brother Henry for the family borough of Weobley, which was to be disfranchised under the Grey ministry's reform bill. He is not known to have spoken in debate and rarely attended the House in 1831-2. He voted with Henry and their uncle Lord John Thynne against the reintroduced reform bill at its second reading, 6 July, against taking a Member from Chippenham, 27 July, and the bill's passage, 21 Sept. 1831. He neglected to attend a call of the House, 10 Oct., in order to travel to Bath for the mayor's inaugural dinner, where he responded to the toast to the Somerset yeoman cavalry, of which his father had made him a lieutenant-colonel.[5] He voted against the revised reform bill at its second reading, 17 Dec. 1831, and paired against the third reading, 22 Mar. 1832. He divided against government on the Russian-Dutch loan, 12 July 1832.

At the 1834 and January 1835 Finsbury elections, Thynne, whose financial and marital affairs were in disarray, canvassed against Thomas Slingsby Duncombe*, to whom he owed over £10,000, and who sued him and his wife repeatedly for debt. Being estranged from him, she claimed to be divorced when seeking credit, but sought a married woman's indemnity when brought to court for non-payment.[6] Lord Bath, who was prosecuted by another of his creditors, John Lyde, provided £60,000 in 1835 to write off his debts and guarantee him an allowance, 'because I am certain he would be arrested and it would be out of my power to relieve him'.[7] Denied family funds following his father's death, he was imprisoned for debt, charged with outlawry and obliged to file for bankruptcy in August 1837.[8] His wife failed to obtain a larger share of the Mellish fortune by securing a judgement against her sister and brother-in-law, the 2nd earl and countess of Glengall, in 1847; and her estate, in which Thynne retained a life interest, had dwindled to £3,000 at probate, 18 May 1849.[9] He married the only daughter of the popular novelist Mrs. Gore in 1853, and after failing there in 1856 and 1857, he was returned for

Frome in 1859 as an 'anti-ballot Conservative' for a single Parliament.[10] He died intestate at his Wiltshire home, The Hill, Laverstock, near Salisbury, in February 1884, and was buried with his second wife in nearby Fisherton Anger.[11] Capital from his first marriage settlement passed to the Chateris family, and a balance of £259 2s. 3d., from his life insurance was paid to his nephew John Alexander, 4th marquess of Bath (1831-96), who had stood surety for him, and claimed to be his sole 'legal, personal representative'.[12] His only daughter, Mary Isabella Emma Thynne (d. 1906), left less than £25 to be administered by her former husband, Stephen Ormston Eaton of Tolethorpe Hall, Rutland, from whom she was divorced.

[1] Add. 52011, Eleanor Fazakerley to H.E. Fox, 8 Jan.; *Russell Letters*, ii. 235; *Bath Chron.* 22 July 1830. [2] Longleat mun. Lord Edward Thynne 115, 01/01/1830, 08/07/1830; *The Times*, 28 Apr., 1 May 1847. [3] Add. 51670, Bedford to Lady Holland [Feb. 1830]. [4] Longleat mun. Lord Edward Thynne 150, 25/10/1830. [5] *Bath Herald*, 15 Oct. 1831. [6] Longleat mun. Lord Edward Thynne 150, 06/08/1833 (ix-xii); *The Times*, 3, 5, 6, 28 Jan. 1835, 22 Apr., 14 June 1847. [7] Longleat mun. Lord Edward Thynne 130, 15/11/1834; 150, 25/10/1830, 19/08/1831, 22/05/1833, 03/08/1836, 06/08/1833 (i-xx). [8] Ibid. Lord Edward Thynne 150, 06/08/1833 (xxi-xxii); *The Times*, 27 July, 19 Aug. 1837. [9] *The Times*, 28 Apr., 1 May, 23 Aug. 1847; Longleat mun. Lord Edward Thynne 115, 08/07/1830, 18/07/1865; PROB 6/225. [10] *The Times*, 8, 23 July 1856, 11, 28 Mar. 1857, 7, 11 Apr., 2 May; *Western Times*, 9, 16 Apr., 7 May; *Warminster Herald*, 7 May 1859; *Salisbury and Wilts. Jnl.* 7 June 1879. [11] *The Times*, 5 Feb.; *Salisbury and Winchester Jnl.* 9 Feb.; *Warminster and Westbury Jnl.* 16 Feb. 1884. [12] Longleat mun. Lord Edward Thynne 115, 20/09/1884; 150, 24/03/1858 (i-vii).

M.M.E.

THYNNE, Lord Henry Frederick (1797–1837), of 6 Grovesnor Square, Mdx.

WEOBLEY	4 Feb. 1824–1826
WEOBLEY	12 June 1828–1832

b. 24 May 1797, 2nd but 1st surv. s. of Thomas Thynne†, 2nd mq. of Bath, and Hon. Isabella Elizabeth Byng, da. and coh. of George, 4th Visct. Torrington; bro. of Lord Edward Thynne*, Thomas Thynne II, Visct. Weymouth†, and Lord William Thynne*. *educ.* Eton bef. 1811. *m.* 19 Apr. 1830, Harriet, da. of Alexander Baring*, 2s. 1da. *styled* Visct. Weymouth Jan.-Mar. 1837; *suc.* fa. as 3rd mq. of Bath 27 Mar. 1837. *d.* 24 June 1837.
    Entered RN 1810, lt. 1817, cdr. 1821, capt. 1822, transf. to signals 1828.

Thynne, the eventual heir of the 2nd marquess of Bath, was intended for the navy, and at the age of 13 he left Eton, which he attended with his brother John (1798-1881), the future dean and canon of Westminster, to go to sea as a supernumerary gentleman volunteer in the *Royal William*.[1] Over the next

six years he served as a volunteer and certificated midshipman in the *Fortune*, *Tigre*, *Royal George*, *Blake*, *Malta*, *Impregnable*, *Royal Sovereign* and *Tennant*. After passing as a lieutenant, 7 Aug. 1816, he joined the *Ganymede*, and was considered for the *Active*, *Cambrian* and *Glasgow* before being posted to the Mediterranean and the East Indies in the *Tagus* and the *Alacrity*, whose captain, Henry Stanhope, recommended him for promotion.[2] He was made commander of the sloop *Frolick*, 9 June 1821, and soon afterwards volunteered for the *Suspect*, on the South American station, but he was passed over and sent back in the *Superb* in May 1822 to solicit further employment. Appointed to captain the *Termagant*, 30 July, he embarked in the *Alligator*, 22 Sept. 1822, to join her at Cochin in the East Indies.[3] Hearing in Bombay that his ship had sailed for England, he took a passage home in the *Dauntless*, and was placed on half-pay on his arrival, 7 Sept. 1823. His service record, particularly his recent embarrassments, was singled out in the Commons by Joseph Hume when his father was made a knight of the garter in July 1823, as an example of 'needless promotion' by 'interest and family connections'; and Bath's placeman Member for Weobley Sir George Cockburn was called upon to justify Thynne's naval promotion 'over the heads of 3,588 lieutenants ... and 755 commanders' despite his apparent failings and inexperience.[4] He remained unplaced when he was brought in for the Weobley seat vacated by his cousin Lord Frederick Cavendish Bentinck in February 1824.[5]

Thynne was added to the select committee on foreign trade shortly after taking his seat, 22 Mar. 1824. No speeches by him were reported and he generally toed the political line set by his father and his uncle Lord John Thynne, with whom he was described in a radical publication of 1825 as a Member who 'attended occasionally and voted with ministers'.[6] He voted against condemning the indictment in Demerara of the Methodist missionary John Smith, 11 June 1824. He divided for the bill outlawing the Catholic Association, 25 Feb., but left the House before the division on Catholic relief, 1 Mar. 1825, declaring that 'he would not vote with government and would have voted with ... [the Whigs] but for his father'.[7] On 11 Mar. the admiralty authorized his appointment to captain the *Ranger*, a 28-gun frigate bound for South America, where she was deployed conveying diplomats and consular officials, on coastal patrols and in survey work. He joined her at Portsmouth, 2 Apr., and was on embarkation leave when he confirmed his differences with his family on the Catholic question by pairing for the relief bill, 10 May. He sailed, 10 July

1825, and was replaced at Weobley at the 1826 general election by his soldier brother William.[8]

Thynne and the *Ranger*, which had been deliberately ordered back from South America by the Wellington ministry in March, were off Spithead when Cockburn came in for Plymouth on the admiralty interest, 7 June 1828.[9] He docked at Portsmouth on the 11th after a 60-day journey from Rio de Janeiro with a cargo of 1,200,000 dollars, 21 chests of gold and £16,000 worth of diamonds from Dom Pedro, and was returned for Weobley the next day.[10] His personal log of the voyage contains no entries for 11 and 12 June.[11] He applied to the admiralty for leave and half-pay, 26, 30 June, and was probably the Lord G. Thynne listed in the government majority against ordnance reductions, 4 July 1828, the day he took his seat. He transferred to the signal corps, 6 July, and did not serve at sea again.[12] In October 1828 he attended the Bath corporation dinner with his family.[13] Thynne was a declared opponent of the Wiltshire anti-Catholic petition and voted for Catholic emancipation, 6, 30 Mar. 1829.[14] Estimating support in the Commons for a putative coalition in October, the Ultra leader Sir Richard Vyvyan* listed him with Members whose 'sentiments are unknown'. He is unlikely to have been the 'Lord Thynne' who divided against Jewish emancipation, 5 Apr. 1830.[15] His marriage that month to Harriet Baring, daughter of the financier and Member for Callington, pleased both families and brought him settlements worth £750 a year. According to Lady Holland, wags familiar with Thynne's drinking habits and her vanity dubbed their union 'bottle and glass'.[16] He was returned for Weobley with William at the general election in August, and they attended the Bath corporation dinner in October 1830.[17]

Ministers counted the Thynnes among their 'friends' in the new Parliament, but Bath failed to give Wellington his proxy and Thynne, who cut a 'magnificent' figure at the theatre, 14 Nov., was absent from the division on the civil list, 15 Nov. 1830, which brought them down.[18] He received two weeks' leave 'because of the disturbed state of his neighbourhood' during the 'Swing' riots, 2 Dec. 1830.[19] He was named as a defaulter, 16 Mar. 1831, soon after the birth of his heir, divided against the second reading of the Grey ministry's reform bill, by which Weobley was to be disfranchised, 22 Mar., but 'came into the House so dreadfully tipsy that they were obliged to carry him out' before he could vote for Gascoyne's wrecking amendment, 19 Apr. 1831.[20] He was returned for Weobley with another brother, Edward, at the ensuing general election. The Thynnes voted against the reintroduced reform bill at its second reading, 6 July, against taking

a Member from Chippenham, 27 July, and the bill's passage, 21 Sept. 1831. Bath deliberately stayed away from the Lords in October, but the Thynnes signed the Wiltshire anti-reform declaration,[21] and voted against the second reading of the revised reform bill, 17 Dec. 1831, the enfranchisement of Tower Hamlets, 28 Feb., and the third reading, 22 Mar. 1832. Henry Hepburne Scott*, Thynne's partisan and fellow guest at Charles Baring Wall's* Hampshire estate in January 1832, considered him 'nearly the best' shot in England.[22] He and his wife dined regularly in London with supporters of the Conservative opposition, and he divided with them on the Russian-Dutch loan, 26 Jan., 12 July 1832.[23]

Left without a seat in 1832, Thynne, whose clubs were Boodles and the Travellers, pursued the life of a country gentleman. His eldest brother Thomas had long been estranged from their father, and his sudden death without issue in January 1837 left Thynne, whom Bath now made his sole executor, heir to the marquessate and land in county Monaghan, Shropshire, Somerset and Wiltshire, to which he succeeded in March. He died suddenly at Longleat in June 1837, 'having only enjoyed his title a few months', and was buried at Longbridge Deverill.[24] As 3rd marquess of Bath, he had ordered the prompt payment of wages and annuities, but refused further assistance to his brother Edward, whose debts had already inconvenienced him as party to his marriage settlement.[25] His will, dated 2 May 1835, failed to take account of his succession, and was proved under £25,000, 26 July 1837, five days before that of his father. By it, he left all household effects to his widow, assigns and executors, making the latter (his late father and Lord Ashburton) trustees of his real estate and all personal estate clear of debt. It was to be used to support his widow until remarriage or death, and his children until they married or came of age.[26] Probate and division of the estate according to the 2nd marquess's will, which Ashburton was also appointed to execute, could not be completed until after the death of Thynne's widow, 2 Jan. 1892. Asked to account for the discrepancy between the 1837 valuation and the £59,175 on which legacy duty was now paid, his children, John Alexander, 4th marquess of Bath (1831-96), Henry Frederick Thynne (1832-1904), Conservative Member for Wiltshire South, 1859-85, and Lady Louisa Isabella Harriet Fielding, volunteered a further £315, and testified that his estate had 'consisted almost entirely of the residuary estate of Thomas, [2nd] marquess of Bath, on which £10,704 2s. was charged in annuities which have all fallen in'.[27]

[1] Longleat mun. 3rd mq. 120, 04/09/1810. [2] Ibid. 06/08/1811, 25/08/1811, 19/10/1811, 27/12/1811, 06/01/1812, 12/01/1813, 13/02/1815, 04/03/1815, 13/03/1815, 22/07/1816, 07/08/1816, 20/07/1817, 28/09/1817, 29/09/1817, 27/11/1817, 21/02/1821; TNA ADM 1/1284/A.32; 1286/A.369, A.407; 1288/A.772; ADM 12/197. [3] Longleat mun. 3rd mq. 120, 09/06/1821, 27/10/1821, 30/07/1822; ADM 1/2619/Cap.T.28 (1822); ADM 12/208. [4] ADM 1/2619/ Cap.T.37-38 (1823); ADM 12/214; ADM 51/3496; ADM 52/3690; Parl. Deb. (n.s.), ix. 1085-1101; Add. 38295, ff. 22-23. [5] ADM 1/2619/Cap.T.38 (1823); Cap.T.2 (1824); ADM 12/221. [6] Session of Parl. 1825, p. 487. [7] Add. 75938, Lady to Lord Spencer, 4 Mar. 1825. [8] ADM 1/2620/Cap.T.5, 11 (1825); Cap.T.18-19 (1826); Cap.T.2, 7, 22 (1827); ADM 3/207, 11 Mar. 1825; ADM 12/228, 236, 244; ADM 51/3402; Longleat mun. 3rd mq. 120, 15/03/1825; Von Neumann Diary, i. 152. [9] Lansdowne mss, Spring Rice to Lansdowne, 17 Sept. 1827; ADM 3/216, 13 Mar. 1828; ADM 12/252; ADM 51/3402; Longleat mun. 3rd mq. 120, 10/02/1828; Woolmer's Exeter and Plymouth Gazette, 31 May, 7, 14 June 1828. [10] Exeter Weekly Times, 21 June 1828. [11] Longleat mun. 3rd mq. 120, 10/02/1828. [12] ADM 12/252, 260, 268, 275, 283, 289, 297, 307, 319, 331. [13] Bath Herald, 11 Oct.; Bath Chron. 16 Oct. 1828. [14] Glos. RO, Sotherton Estcourt mss D/1571/X114, W. Long to Estcourt, 26 Jan. 1829. [15] The Times, 24 Feb., 1 Mar. 1830. [16] Howard Sisters, 127; Russell Letters, ii. 235-7; Bath Chron. 22 Apr. 1830; PROB 11/1881/521. [17] Bath Chron. 30 Sept., 14 Oct. 1830. [18] Howard Sisters, 165; Greville Mems. ii. 57. [19] Add. 41315, f. 149. [20] Wilts. RO, Pembroke mss 2057/F4/50. [21] Add. 63010, ff. 3, 9; Devizes and Wilts Gazette, 11 Aug. 1831. [22] NAS GD157/2411/21. [23] NLW, Ormathwaite mss FG1/6, p. 40. [24] Gent. Mag. (1837), i. 219, 537; ii. 204; Greville Mems. i. 294; PROB 11/1877/326; 11/1881/521; Longleat mun. 2nd mq. E7 box B1; 3rd mq. 195, 08/02/1868; Salisbury and Wilts. Herald, 24 June, 1 July; Salisbury and Winchester Jnl. 26 June 1837; Raikes Jnl. iii. 146, 220. [25] Longleat mun. 3rd mq. 115, 08/07/1830; 130, 15/11/1834; 150, 27/03/37 (xi & xii). [26] PROB 11/1881/519, 521; IR26/141/627. [27] Longleat mun. 3rd Mq. 195, 26/07/1837, 10/03/1838, 01/12/1839, 13/05/1848, 26/04/1858, 08/02/1868, 16/06/1887, 04/11/1892.

M.M.E.

THYNNE, Lord John (1772–1849), of 15 Hill Street, Berkeley Square, Mdx.

WEOBLEY	1796–23 Nov. 1796
BATH	8 Dec. 1796–1832

b. 28 Dec. 1772, 3rd s. of Thomas, 1st mq. of Bath (d. 1796), and Lady Elizabeth Bentinck, da. of William, 2nd duke of Portland.; bro. of Lord George Thynne† and Thomas Thynne I, Visct. Weymouth.† educ. St. John's, Camb. 1792. m. 18 June 1801, Mary Anne, da. of Thomas Master† of The Abbey, Cirencester, Glos., s.p. suc. bro. George as 3rd Bar. Carteret 19 Feb. 1838.[1] d. 10 Mar. 1849.

Vice-chamberlain 1804-12, (Windsor) 1812-20; PC 11 July 1804; member, bd. of trade May 1805; dep. groom of stole 1812-20.

Maj. Wilts. vol. cav. 1797; lt.-col. Hanover Square vol. inf. 1799-1804.

Thynne's appointment to the royal household, worth £1,200 a year, terminated on the death of George III, which left him, his wife and his brother George unplaced.[2] His recent mediation had failed to heal the rift between his brother the 2nd marquess of Bath, whom he had succeeded as Member for Bath in 1796, and the latter's eldest son Thomas Thynne II, Viscount Weymouth†.[3] Weymouth's Weobley seat was accordingly placed at the disposal of the treasury at the general election of 1820, with the suggestion that it be offered to Sir George William Gunning†, one of Thynne's key supporters on the corporation of Bath, where the recorder, the 2nd marquess of Camden, was intriguing on behalf of his heir Lord Brecknock*.[4] In the event, the return for Weobley of the lord of the admiralty Sir George Cockburn posed no threat to Thynne, a staunch and generally silent ministerialist opposed to Catholic relief, and he topped the token poll to come in with his former liberal colleague Charles Palmer.[5]

Never one to delight in public speaking, Thynne was joined in the Commons by his indolent nephews Lords Frederick Cavendish Bentinck and Edward, Henry and William Thynne. No longer committed as a placeman, his recorded votes in the 1820 Parliament were sparse, and his role as a member of select committees diminished. He remained staunchly anti-Catholic, and voted against concessions, 30 Apr. 1822, 1 Mar., 21 Apr., 10 May 1825 (but not on 28 Feb. 1821). A radical publication in 1825 noted that he 'attended occasionally and voted with ministers'.[6] He held aloof from the Queen Caroline affair, notwithstanding its popular appeal in Bath,[7] and demonstrated his support for Lord Liverpool's government in the divisions on the revenue, 4 July 1820, tax reductions, 11 Feb., retrenchment, 27 June 1821, the salt duties, 28 Feb. 1822, and the prosecution of the Dublin Orange rioters, 22 Apr. 1823. He voted against condemning the indictment in Demerara of the Methodist missionary John Smith, 11 June 1824. He divided for the duke of Cumberland's grant, including the award for Prince George's education, 30 May, 2, 10 June 1825. He regularly attended corporation dinners and functions in Bath, where, in the autumn of 1825, Camden prevailed on several of his supporters to give second votes to Brecknock, so enabling him to defeat Palmer at the general election of 1826, when Thynne, hailed again as a 'No Popery' candidate, topped the poll.[8]

He voted against Catholic relief, 6 Mar., received a fortnight's leave on urgent business after serving on the Wells election committee, 1 May, and presented a petition of complaint against the regulations of the Royal College of Surgeons from its members in Bath, 22 June 1827.[9] He voted against repealing the Test Acts, 26 Feb., and Catholic relief, 12 May, and divided with the duke of Wellington's ministry against ordnance reductions, 4 July 1828. In view of the turmoil generated by Palmer's recent by-election challenge to Lord Brecknock, Bath and his sons Henry and Edward accompanied Thynne to the mayor's dinner in Bath in October.[10] Notwithstanding his constituents' dismay and hostile petitions, Thynne, as predicted, divided 'with government' for Catholic emancipation, 6, 30 Mar. 1829.[11] His prospects of re-election were consequently 'doubtful', and he stayed away from Bath that Michaelmas.[12] He voted against Lord Blandford's reform scheme, 18 Feb., and the enfranchisement of Birmingham, Leeds and Manchester, 23 Feb., and was probably the 'Lord Thynne' who divided against Jewish emancipation, 5 Apr., 17 May 1830. At the general election that summer, he eventually prevailed at Bath at Brecknock's expense through a late surge of split sympathy votes from Palmer's supporters.[13] His nephews Edward and Henry supported him at the corporation dinner in October.[14]

Lord Bath, who had hoped for timely concessions on reform, caused comment by leaving town in November 1830 without giving Wellington his proxy; and Thynne, who had been listed among his ministry's 'friends', was absent from the division on the civil list when they were brought down, 15 Nov.[15] His support for the Somerset magistrates' anti-reform petition and votes against the Grey ministry's reform bill at its second reading, 22 Mar., and for Gascoyne's wrecking amendment, 19 Apr. 1831, made him unpopular with the populace of Bath, where, though taunted, hissed and pelted, he was returned unopposed with Palmer at the ensuing general election.[16] Whereas Lord Bath adopted an increasingly sanguine approach to the reform bill, Thynne, like their brother Lord Carteret, remained a committed anti-reformer, but confined his votes to key divisions.[17] He voted against the reintroduced reform bill at its second reading, 6 July, paired for adjournment, 12 July, and divided against the partial disfranchisement of Chippenham, 27 July, and the bill's third reading, 19 Sept., and passage, 22 Sept 1831.[18] He voted against government on the Dublin election controversy, 23 Aug. New appointments were made to the corporation of Bath before the October dinner, which coincided with the fervent pro-reform petitioning which followed the bill's defeat by the Lords and calls for Thynne's ejection.[19] He voted against the revised reform bill at its second reading, 17 Dec. 1831, and against enfranchising Tower Hamlets, 28 Feb., and the third reading, 22 Mar. 1832. He divided with opposition on the Russian Dutch loan, 26 Jan., 12 July 1832. With no prospect of success, he did not seek re-election, and at the October 1832 dinner he proposed the toasts to the mayor and

corporation of Bath and thanked them for electing him six times in 36 years.[20]

Thynne succeeded his brother to the Carteret barony and estates in Bedfordshire, north Cornwall and Somerset and a personal fortune of almost £46,000 in 1838. He died without issue at his seat, Hawnes Place, near Ampthill, Bedfordshire, in March 1849 after a short illness, whereupon the barony became extinct.[21] His will, dated 3 Dec. 1846, was administered by his nephew and residuary legatee, Lord John Thynne (1798-1881), dean and canon of Westminster, whose succession to the Carteret estates it confirmed.[22]

---

[1] Not 22 Feb. as stated in W.R. Williams, *Herefs. MPs*, 171. [2] *Black Book* (1820), 83; *The Times*, 16 Aug. 1831. [3] TNA C13/2630, Weymouth *v*. Bath. [4] Add. 38283, f. 127; 38458, f. 285; *HP Commons, 1790-1820*, ii. 343-4; iv. 119-20. See also WEOBLEY and BATH. [5] *HP Commons, 1790-1820*, v. 382-3; *HMC Fortescue*, x. 454; *Bath Chron*. 9, 16 Mar.; *Keenes' Bath Jnl*. 13, 27 Mar. 1820. [6] *Session of Parl*. 1825, p. 487. [7] *Keenes' Bath Jnl*. 13, 20 Nov. 1820. [8] Ibid. 16 Oct. 1820, 15 Oct. 1821, 14 Oct. 1822, 13 Oct. 1823, 15, 22 Oct. 1825; Cent. Kent Stud. Camden mss U840 C202/11/14; *Bath Herald*, 10 June, *Bath Chron*. 15 June 1826. [9] *The Times*, 23 June 1827. [10] *Bath Chron*. 12 June, 28 Sept., 16 Oct. 1828. [11] Ibid. 26 Feb., 12 Mar. 1829. [12] Camden mss C38/1; *Bath Chron*. 24 Sept., 1, 7, 15 Oct. 1829. [13] *Bath Chron*. 8, 22, 29 July, 5 Aug.; *Bath Herald*, 10, 17 July, 7 Aug. 1830. [14] *Bath Chron*. 30 Sept. 1830. [15] *Greville Mems*. ii. 57. [16] Glos. RO, Sotherton Estcourt mss D1572/E411, Salmon to Estcourt [Mar.]; Camden mss C202/4-5; *Keenes' Bath Jnl*. 18 Apr., 2 May; *Bath and Cheltenham Gazette*, 26 Apr., 3 May; *Bath Herald*, 30 Apr.; *Devizes and Wilts. Gazette*, 5 May 1831; S. Brooks 'Bath and Great Reform Bill', in *Bath in Age of Reform, 1830-41* ed. J. Wroughton, 21-31. [17] Add. 63010, ff. 3, 9. [18] *The Times*, 16 July 1831. [19] *Bath Chron*. 19 May, 14 July, 29 Sept.; *Bath Herald*, 1, 15 Oct. 1831. [20] *Bath Chron*. 12 July, 4, 11, 18 Oct.; *Bath Herald*, 13 Oct. 1832. [21] *Ann. Reg*. (1849), Chron. p. 225; *Gent. Mag*. (1849), i. 537-8; IR26/1477/241. [22] Longleat mun. Carteret 132, 21/07/1846; 29/03/1849; PROB 11/2089/178; IR26/1829/181.

M.M.E.

THYNNE, Lord William (1803–1890), of Longleat, Wilts.

WEOBLEY   1826–1831

b. 17 Oct. 1803, 4th s. of Thomas Thynne†, 2nd mq. of Bath (*d.* 1837), and Hon. Isabella Elizabeth Byng, da. and coh. of George, 4th Visct. Torrington; bro. of Lord Edward Thynne*, Lord Henry Frederick Thynne* and Thomas Thynne II, Viscount Weymouth†. *m.* 19 Dec. 1861, Belinda, da. of George Archer Brummell, attorney, of Morpeth, Northumb., *s.p.*[1] *d.* 30 Jan. 1890.

Ensign R. Fus. 1820, lt. 1822, capt. 1825, maj. 1830, lt.-col. (half-pay) 1838, ret. 1844.

A career soldier, Lord William Thynne was brought in for his father's borough of Weobley in 1826 in place of his brother Henry, then absent on naval service. No speeches by him were reported, and although he could be relied on to support the duke of Wellington's ministry his attendance was spasmodic. He received a week's leave after serving on the Dublin election committee, 3 May 1827. He voted against investigating chancery delays, 24 Apr., Catholic relief, 12 May, and ordnance reductions, 4 July 1828; and as their patronage secretary Planta predicted, he voted 'with government' for Catholic emancipation, 6, 30 Mar. 1829. He was given three weeks' leave on urgent private business, 8 Mar. 1830, but may have been the 'Lord Thynne' who divided against Jewish emancipation, 5 Apr., although it was probably his uncle Lord John Thynne. He was returned *in absentia* at the general election in August and promoted to major later that month. The ministry listed him among their 'friends' and, unlike his relations, he divided with them on the civil list, 15 Nov. 1830, when they were brought down. He did not vote on the Grey ministry's reform bill, which proposed Weobley's disfranchisement, and made way for his younger brother Edward at the dissolution in April 1831.

Thynne, who was based mainly in Gosport while on active service, tried hard to secure a reconciliation between Edward and his estranged first wife.[2] His own late marriage proved childless. He maintained a residence at 24 Mount Street, Grosvenor Square, following his wife's death in 1869, but spent his later days at Ditton Park, Slough, the home of his sister Charlotte Anne, dowager duchess of Buccleuch, where their brother Charles, a former dean and cannon of Canterbury and convert to the Roman Catholic church, was chaplain. Invalided by a stroke, Thynne died there in January 1890 and was buried in nearby Datchett churchyard.[3] His will, dated 19 Mar. 1884, was proved in London, 2 Feb. 1890, and administered by his nephews Francis John and Alfred Walter Thynne, sons of his brother Lord John Thynne (1798-1881), dean and canon of Westminster. Alfred and his three younger brothers were Thynne's joint residuary legatees, but the main beneficiary was his manservant Samuel MacLean, who received '£700 and his master's clothes'.[4]

[1] Information from Thynne's marriage certificate. Not therefore 1864, as stated in *Burke PB* and W.R. Williams, *Herefs. MPs*, 174. [2] Longleat mun. Lord Edward Thynne 150, 06/08/1833 (ix, x, xix). [3] *Warminster and Westbury Jnl.* 1 Feb.; *The Times*, 6 Feb.; *Slough, Eton and Windsor Observer*, 8 Feb. 1890. [4] Longleat mun. Lord William Thynne 195, 22/01/1890.

M.M.E.

TIERNEY, George (1761-1830), of 11 Savile Row, Mdx.[1]

COLCHESTER	6 Apr. 1789–1790
SOUTHWARK	21 Dec. 1796–1806
ATHLONE	1806–1807
BANDON BRIDGE	3 Aug. 1807–1812
APPLEBY	29 Dec. 1812–1818
KNARESBOROUGH	1818–25 Jan. 1830

b. 20 Mar. 1761, 3rd s. of Thomas Tierney of Limerick, prize agent at Gibraltar, and w. Sabina (*d.* 23 July 1806). *educ.* Boteler's, Warrington;[2] Eton 1776; Peterhouse, Camb. 1778; L. Inn 1780, called 1784. *m.* 9 July 1789, Anna Maria, da. of Michael Miller of Bristol, 1s. 3da. *d.* 25 Jan. 1830.

Treas. of navy June 1803-May 1804; PC 1 June 1803; pres. bd. of control Oct. 1806-Apr. 1807; master of mint May 1827-Feb. 1828.

Lt.-col. commdt. Loyal Southwark vols. 1803-4, Somerset Place vols. 1803-4.

At the start of this period Tierney sat uneasily in the unenviable position of leader of the Whig opposition in the Commons to which he had been nominated (not entirely *faute de mieux*, for he was a formidable parliamentarian) in 1818. Although he had received scant support from the selfish and idle Lord Grey, he had generally performed well in a difficult situation. Yet he was being undermined by indifferent health: after suffering a collapse in the House towards the close of the 1819 emergency session, he had told Grey and the whip Lord Duncannon* that if he was to continue as leader, he must be allowed to act 'upon a limited scale'.[3] It was not only unreliable health which led contemporaries habitually to refer to Tierney as 'old', even before he reached his sixtieth birthday in March 1821.[4] His innate pessimism, a nervous temperament (Lord Althorp* commented that he was 'so anxious that it tears him to pieces')[5] and a timidity in council which contrasted strikingly with his bold assertiveness in debate, of which he was a master, gave an impression of weakness and indecision, to the exasperation of the party's more adventurous spirits. Shortly before the dissolution which followed the death of George III, Tierney, by taking an avowedly neutral line in the House on the case of Queen Caroline, while trying to prevent ministers from fudging the issue, not only annoyed her more violent partisans, such as Henry Brougham* and Joseph Hume*, but upset some of the moderates. Backed as he subsequently was by Grey and Lord Holland, he stood by what he had said, remarking to the former that 'there can be no middle line between cashiering and giving her all her rights. If she is not fit to be acknowledged by the king, she is not entitled to be supported at the expense of the country'.[6]

Accepting the offer of the 6th duke of Devonshire to bring him in again for Knaresborough at the 1820 general election, Tierney (who was also returned for Appleby on the interest of the 9th earl of Thanet, as part of a contingency plan arising out of the Cumberland election), wrote from his Savile Row house, 16 Feb.:

> My room is a sort of office for electioneering and I do nothing but write and talk about contested counties, cities and boroughs ... Personally, it would be of little moment to me if I never again entered the House of Commons. I am growing old, and my health is not what it was, but I am willing to carry on the war, as well as I am able, so long as it is thought I can be of any service to the cause of my friends.[7]

In the course of his journey to Knaresborough with his colleague Sir James Mackintosh he said that 'he could no longer attend regularly or even frequently in the hot weather' and, ruling out Mackintosh and Lord Althorp for different reasons, envisaged Brougham as his successor as leader.[8] He calculated an overall gain of about six for opposition, but reported to Grey that 'government people are much discomposed at the result of the elections, and it is the fashion to call it the triumph of the radicals'.[9] In early April Lord Granville recorded that Tierney was 'evidently much disposed to make parliamentary reform a party question, and wishes the Whigs to head the reformists'; but the following day Tierney himself wrote gloomily to Grey:

> Anything like constant attendance in the House of Commons ... is quite out of the question. Of this I gave Duncannon and others fair notice before Christmas, so that no fault ought to be found with me. I am it is true at this moment in good health, but I know by experience what I have to expect from two or three long nights in a bad atmosphere, even if exposed to nothing more than my share of work. I am greatly mistaken, however, if in the next session there is not a demand upon me for stronger nerves, better spirits and more temper than I pretend to possess, and if, to execute the office of leader, it is not found necessary to have requisites which do not fall to my lot. As for authority, except with a certain number, I have it not, and in your absence, I do not see where it is to come from; and yet if I were to withdraw they tell me – and I am afraid with truth – I should disband the whole opposition. A pleasing prospect this.[10]

From Brighton, where he went for a short spell of recuperation, he told Lady Holland, 10 Apr. 1820,

that he 'never had less inclination for a parliamentary campaign than I have for that which is approaching'.[11] Grey, who, to Tierney's irritation, gave no 'hint at the possibility of his coming to town', observed to Duncannon that 'his health forbids us to hope that he will be able to bear hard work and constant attendance, and without this a leader must be in a great degree inefficient'.[12]

On his return to London he was reported to be of opinion that it would be 'infinitely better to make good use' of the Peterloo massacre 'collaterally in debates than to bring forward any substantive motion respecting it'.[13] His anodyne observation on the address, 27 Apr. 1820, that he was not disposed to disturb the 'prevailing unanimity' of the House at the start of a new reign, was privately condemned as 'very bad' and 'shabby' by Hobhouse, the advanced Whig Member for Westminster.[14] He harried Vansittart, the chancellor of the exchequer, on ministers' intentions regarding the civil list, 27, 28 Apr., 1, 2 May.[15] He spoke and voted for the opposition motions on the subject, 3, 5, 8 May, protesting against 'voting away the public money in the dark, during a season of great public pressure', and throwing out hints about provision for the queen.[16] Althorp informed his father a few days later that he

> has hitherto kept well, but we have not been later than twelve yet, and he has not been called upon to make a long speech. Whenever this happens I am afraid he will fail, and we have all agreed to insist upon his not hazarding his health in the least by coming down when he is not quite able to bear it, and we must fight under Brougham during his absence.

Sydney Smith told Grey that he was 'well, but very old, and unfit for anything but gentle work'.[17] He was hopeful of beating government on the question of the appointment of an additional baron of exchequer in Scotland, 15 May, when he accused them of clinging to power through 'patronage and influence'; but a poor opposition muster and a ministerial promise of inquiry saw the motion defeated by 189-177. He was blamed by some for the subsequent procedural bungling which 'wrecked the effect' of the debate; and Holland told Grey, still taking his ease in Northumberland, that he was 'timid and inactive'.[18] Tierney again attacked government on the civil list, 17 May. Supporting the transfer of Grampound's seats to Leeds as an indication to the 'middle classes' that the House was willing to implement reasonable improvements to the electoral system, he castigated Lord Castlereagh and his colleagues for their obscurantism. Yet to the disgust of Brougham, who complained that he had 'got

Castlereagh out of the worst scrape he ever was in', he supported the ministerial restriction of the scope of the inquiry into agricultural distress, 31 May.[19] The following day he supported the imposition of a duty on the import of foreign linen yarn and voted against the aliens bill; but Althorp reported that 'many' Whigs were irritated by his refusal to attack Vansittart over his policy of borrowing to finance the national debt.[20] He called for the creation of a contingency fund to provide for the sisters of deceased naval officers, 9 June. He spoke and voted for Hume's motion for economies in revenue collection, 4 July, when he said that 'at bottom, all the abuses on this subject were attributable to influence', and voted against the barrack agreement bill, 13 July 1820.

He had scarcely credited reports earlier in the year that the queen intended to come to England, and indeed had bet Brougham, of all people, a guinea that she would not appear within six months. In mid-May, sensing the possibility of a 'new era', which might benefit the Whigs, though basically inclined to the view that the affair would end in 'a compromise disgraceful to her, the king and the administration, and their renewal of their lease for another year for those who can neither possess the good opinion of the crown nor the confidence of the country', he implored Grey to come to London to direct operations:

> No man can estimate more highly than I do the comfort of being out of the reach of political warfare at such a moment as the present, for, though I put as good a face upon the matter as I can, I am most heartily sick of the House of Commons and its bustle, and should be happy if I could devise the means of passing my few remaining years in peace and quiet ... I know it is said by some that the business of the queen ought not to be made a party question. I do not see it exactly in that light, but, if it is to be so considered, you are the only person who can place it upon the right footing, and if anything should occur to render it expedient that we should all act together as a body, you ought to be here to take the lead.[21]

Grey did not go up for another four weeks. On the motion for the appointment a secret committee, 7 June, Tierney 'thanked God' that he had had nothing to do with the negotiations, but insisted that 'before any money was voted to the queen, some course ought to be taken which would establish either her innocence or her guilt'. He attacked ministers, who had 'acted with injustice to the queen, disrespect to Parliament, and above all with the most marked indifference to the feelings and dignity of their master', and, opposing the committee, argued that compromise was not possible under present circumstances. The Tory Member Henry Bankes noted that in doing so he indulged in

some 'levity and jocularity'.[22] To Grey he condemned the conduct of government, who had 'contrived to create a general interest in her favour', as 'disgustingly disgraceful'; and he told Lady Holland that he was 'satisfied that the line I took ... on this business was the right one'.[23] Soon afterwards Tierney, like Holland and Lord Lansdowne, was sounded by emissaries from the king (in his case Lord Hutchinson), who 'assured me that the ministers would be immediately dismissed if I would say that I advised him to press the king to do so'. He refused to give such advice, pointing out that 'the management of his present ministers had given such a turn to the opinion of the country, and made such an impression upon the House of Commons, that I was satisfied no administration could be formed capable of stemming the tide of popular feeling'. He observed to Grey, who now had no option but to go to London, that 'a sudden dismissal of the ministry in a moment of wrath would have been the worst possible thing for us'; but, while he did not trust George IV, he was not entirely dismissive of the chances of the Whigs being able to form and sustain a ministry:

> You know that I have always felt, or, as you would perhaps say, exaggerated, the difficulty of our forming an administration ... *Are we to confine ourselves to our own ranks, or are we to look for alliances?* This is the main embarrassment ... In other respects a variety of circumstances concur to render the present a favourable moment for a new administration to commence its labours. The distressed state to which this country has been brought in its finances, trade and agriculture is so universally admitted that it constitutes in itself a sort of claim upon public support in aid of those who, without having contributed to the mischief, are to be employed in endeavouring to avert or mitigate it. The question of the queen, too, having been disposed of, the civil list settled and the budget for the year arranged gives infinite advantage to those who might, ten days hence, be called to office, and who would have six months before them, uninterrupted by parliamentary duties, to form their plans and prepare for a future campaign. These apparently favourable circumstances must not, however, be allowed to mislead you, or make us overload the probable difficulties we should have to encounter in the next session. I always speak with reference to the House of Commons.[24]

When Grey did arrive in London, he complained to his wife, 21 June, that he had no idea what Tierney intended to do on Wilberforce's motion of the following day for a compromise settlement, which he thought should be opposed.[25] Tierney, who, according to Mackintosh thought ministers would soon be forced out office,[26] duly took this line in the House, and he spoke and voted for the opposition adjournment motion, 26 July, when he strongly attacked ministers and called for a change of government. He forced Castlereagh to concede that they had plans to provide financially for the queen, 3 July 1820. On the 6th, discountenancing Ferguson's earlier motion for the production of papers on the Milan commission, which drew ironical cheers from the ministerial benches, he declared that he would 'keep his mind clear and unbiased', so that when the queen's affair came regularly before the House, he could consider it 'without regarding popular clamour on the one hand or Court influence on the other'. He admitted in private at the end of the month that he was 'considerably alarmed' at the threat posed to public order, especially in London, by popular support for Caroline, whom he was later inclined to consider as 'mad'.[27]

On 21 Aug. 1820 he opposed Hobhouse's attempt to prorogue Parliament, prompting Lord Morpeth[†] to condemn 'the violence of the queen's friends and the irresolution of Tierney'.[28] A month later a backbencher complained that 'Tierney contrives to be out of town' on the occasion of Hobhouse's renewed attempt to force a prorogation.[29] A 'slight bilious attack' at about this time decided Tierney, whose sister's son William Robarts, Member for St. Albans, was causing him great anxiety as he lapsed into what soon proved to be a fatal illness, to stay away from the queen's trial in the Lords, as he told Holland, 1 Oct.: 'I do not ... think it would be a very wise action unnecessarily to expose myself to the heat of one House of Parliament when I shall so soon be obliged to encounter the other'.[30] He attended the Commons, 17 Oct., when his milk and water countering of the ministerial proposal for a five week adjournment with one for a fortnight and his failure to condemn the bill of pains and penalties led to a clash with a furious Creevey (who had come in in his room for Appleby). Creevey, who had dubbed Tierney 'Mrs. Cole', after the brothel keeper in a Foote farce much given to proclaiming her own virtues, reflected:

> Alas poor Cole! I had always a misgiving that she would get her death from me, and last night I fear the presentiment was nearly verified ... I had not pronounced two sentences before one and all of his troops deserted him. The roar that resounded from every part of the benches behind him (which were very full) was as extraordinary to me as it must have been agreeable to him.

Morpeth, however, took Tierney's side, and got the impression that he had 'had some influence with his irregular troops'. The Hollands, too, were outraged by Creevey's behaviour.[31] After the debate he 'had a word' with Hobhouse:

He said the bill would not pass the Lords, but what would the queen get? 'She will get her name in the liturgy', said I. 'Oh yes, for that, but all will be forgot and quiet in six months'. 'What', said I, 'won't you hang these ministers?' 'Ah', replied Tierney, 'I wish I had my life on so good a tenure as the ministers have their places'.[32]

On 23 Nov. 1820 Tierney joined in the rowdy opposition attempt to delay the prorogation by Black Rod so that Brougham could deliver a message from the queen. Lord John Russell*, in Paris, found it hard to 'fancy the cautious Tierney applauding a schoolboy riot'.[33] Yet Lord Buckingham heard a month later that he was 'very angry with his radical friends and they with him'.[34] He was approached by Lord Donoughmore at the behest of the king, who, furious with his ministers after the abandonment of the bill, wished to negotiate with Grey. In his absence Tierney was cautious and non-committal, and nothing came of the business. Indeed, they agreed in early December that no further overtures from third parties should be entertained.[35] Tierney and Holland took the lead in attempting to promote county and other meetings to petition in support of the queen. To an initially dubious Grey he argued that 'everything depends upon the public mind being kept thoroughly alive during the next two months': 'The nail to drive is the restoration of the queen to the liturgy ... All clamour for change of ministers I am quite against'. He was discouraged by setbacks in Yorkshire and Cumberland, but persevered into the new year, with ultimately encouraging results.[36] There was a ludicrous episode in December 1820 when Tierney, in a jocular answer to the question of Decaze, the French minister, as to what the Whigs would do with Buonaparte if they came to power, said that they would 'put him on the throne of France'. The remark, relayed to Metternich, caused 'a diplomatic frisson' at the Congress of Troppau, and in the ensuing fuss Tierney, who was described at this time by Henry Fox* as 'one of those wise-acres who always see into a mill-stone', was 'frightened out of her wits' at the possible consequences, as a delighted Creevey put it.[37]

At Cassiobury in the last days of 1820 Tierney, just recovered from 'a terrible cough and cold', told Sir Robert Wilson* that he was 'all for refusal of [the] queen's allowance, be the sum what it may ministers propose to offer, until her name is restored to the liturgy'.[38] 'Lively and witty' at Holland House, 3 Jan. 1821, he was heartened by the success of Devonshire, to whom he wrote a fawning letter of congratulations, in carrying a successful amendment to a Tory motion for a loyal address at a Derbyshire county meeting. He worked to ensure a good attendance, though he did not doubt that government would have a majority in any division on the queen, and urged Grey to come up for the start of the session to assert his authority, 'however limited'. Unlike Grey, he was not keen on an amendment to the address, but he met Brougham, James Scarlett* and James Abercromby* to consider the matter, 14 Jan. In the event, none was moved.[39] On 23 Jan. Tierney, supporting Wetherell's call for papers on the liturgy question, responded to Castlereagh's comment that he should use his influence to prevent such obstructive motions being made with the observation that while the minister tried to

> represent the opposition as an army invariably acting under the orders of a general ... [he] disavowed the power and command which ... [he] ascribed to him; if such a power were offered to him he would decline the responsibility attached to it.[40]

On the address, in a speech described by the Grenvillite Member William Fremantle as 'tame',[41] he demanded a more active line in the protection of European liberalism, welcomed the promise of retrenchment but noted the disastrous state of the economy and deplored recent attempts by sheriffs to suppress county meetings in support of the queen. He gave a silent vote for her restoration to the liturgy, 26 Jan., after being delayed in his appearance in the House by an 'indisposition'. He received his share of blame for the procedural disarray into which the opposition campaign on behalf of the queen had fallen.[42] On 31 Jan., in what even Creevey considered to be 'one of his very best speeches',[43] Tierney, having called Castlereagh to order for accusing opposition of stirring up agitation in the country in the hope of gaining office, retorted that he would 'rather die on a dung hill' than hold power on the same terms and by the same methods as Castlereagh. Admitting that he had been accused by some of his political associates of being 'too lukewarm' in the queen's business, he now roundly condemned the government's treatment of her, which had been 'marked by a little, petty, rancorous malevolence'. When supporting the opposition censure motion, the crushing defeat of which seemed to confirm ministers' security in office for the immediate future, 6 Feb., he argued that there would be no advantage in a change of government without 'a change of system', specifying Catholic emancipation, repeal of the Six Acts and an instalment of parliamentary reform, of which he had always been 'a warm friend', sufficient to 'make the House a real representative of the Commons of England'. He concluded with a denunciation of the corrupt system developed by Pitt and his successors, which

had given them such a root in the church, in the army, and in the navy, as proves, when a strong resistance is made against them, that the sense of the people is opposed to them, since a great number of the people are absolutely under their fangs.

Henry Labouchere*, a spectator at the debate, was disappointed with the 'eloquence and debating talent' displayed, but said that 'Tierney alone exceeded my expectations'. John Whishaw noted that he 'has spoken very well, but is declining in vigour. His health is quite unequal to these late nights'.[44] He spoke and voted for Mackintosh's motion deploring the Holy Alliance's suppression of the liberal regime in Naples, 21 Feb., when he alleged that Castlereagh 'approved in his heart of the conduct of Austria'. He voted silently for Catholic relief, 28 Feb., and protested against unwarranted delay in proceeding with the subsequent bill, 19 Mar.[45] On 2 Mar. he said that the Grampound disfranchisement bill would be rejected by the Lords if it sought to deprive the untainted electors of that borough of a vote for Cornwall.[46] He voted for Maberly's motion on the state of the revenue, 6 Mar., and Macdonald's attempt to reduce the army by 10,000 men, 14 Mar. 1821.

In mid-February 1821 Henry Grey Bennet, reflecting on the increasing enthusiasm of opposition for the 'Mountain's' campaign for economy and retrenchment, hoped 'the leaders will take an interest in the whole affair', but thought that 'if not it will be necessary to come to an understanding with Tierney, who is not to be allowed to take our exertions amiss if he absents himself on any plea except bad health from his daily attendance in the House'.[47] However, in the first week of March Tierney formally resigned the leadership.[48] Lady Cowper observed that 'the reason is ill health and bore and above all that nobody attends him'; while Lady Palmerston reported that he 'says nobody minds him, and he is sick of politics'; but she noted that

> many of our rational friends think it will be better and that when ... there is no leader, there will be less jealousy of him, and that his opinion will have more weight and that perhaps the whole party may hang better together or, if not this, that they will quite divide and the violent ones walk off together.[49]

In fact the party, which Tierney, ground down by indifferent health and left to sink or swim by Grey, felt unable any longer to control, was 'now completely disorganised', in the words of John Campbell II*.[50] Yet Tierney himself told Joseph Jekyll† that 'his health failed under the duties' and that 'one late night was not recruited by three days' quiet'. He added that 'absence on motions by opposition friends was misinterpreted into dissent by the public and unpleasantly felt by the party', but denied that 'there was any schism or mutiny in his troops', who 'manifested implicit deference to his opinions, except perhaps a few intractable ultras'.[51] Abercromby, reviewing the episode some years later, wrote that to the 'assigned' reasons of poor health and the bad impression created by selective attendance must be added 'the violent course pursued by ... Creevey and others acting with him, who not only did not yield that respect and obedience which the party principle requires, but on occasions manifested personal opposition towards the views and conduct of ... Tierney'.[52] 'With the exception of the cause', the duke of Bedford was 'not sorry that Tierney has abdicated the command', for 'he had no authority over his troops', and was 'too old, too wary and too cautious for the enterprising spirit of the present day'. At the end of what he regarded as 'a sorry campaign' for opposition, Bedford told Lady Holland that 'though I most sincerely wish that Tierney's health may be completely restored, I trust I shall never again see him come forward as our *leader*. He is not to blame, as he was forced into the situation, but the experiment has wholly failed'.[53] Grey Bennet, from the perspective of the 'Mountain', condemned Tierney's initial 'indecision in reference to the queen', which had 'damped the spirit of everyone' from the outset, and his 'indifference', shared with other occupants of 'Rotten Row' (the opposition front bench) to the economy campaign.[54]

Tierney agreed with Creevey, 6 Apr. 1821, that distress petitions had been disregarded, but he was not prepared to countenance the denunciation of the dismissal of Lord Fife* from his household post for voting for repeal of the additional malt duty which Creevey had incorporated in his amendment against going into committee of supply. Later that day, however, he voted to reduce the war office grant. He voted for further army economies, 11, 16 Apr. On 12 Apr. he supported Hume's motion for the disfranchisement of civil officers of the ordnance as a remedy for a specific grievance at Queenborough, but said he was not willing to conflate it with 'the grand question of parliamentary reform'. He gave silent votes for Lambton's, 18 Apr., and Russell's, 9 May, motions on that subject, and for reform of the Scottish county representation, 10 May. He divided for repeal of the Blasphemous and Seditious Libels Act, 8 May, and inquiry into Peterloo, 16 May. He voted to censure of delays in the proceedings of the commission of judicial inquiry, 9 May, and was named to the select committee on the Irish report, 26 June (and again, 19 Mar. 1823). He voted fairly regularly for economies during

May, and was in the minority for Hume's general motion for retrenchment, 27 June 1821. He voted for mitigation of the punishment for forgery, 23 May, 4 June. He divided for inquiry into the administration of justice in Tobago, 6 June, and in condemnation of the suppression of liberalism in Sicily, 21 June. He was, however, one of the few Whigs who supported the grant of £6,000 to the duke of Clarence, as he explained on 8 June 1821.[55]

Tierney and his wife spent the late summer at Sandgate, near Folkestone, and moved in mid-September to Dover. Though not 'much surprised' that Wilson's 'indiscretion' had got him into 'a scrape', he was 'sincerely sorry' for him after his dismissal from the army on account of his conduct at the queen's funeral, and advised him as to his best course of action when he called on his return from the continent. In early October, telling Grey that he was otherwise out of the way of political news, he wrote:

> My aversion to the present system does indeed daily increase, but, as I do not see how I can contribute to its overthrow, I may as well not set my bile afloat by worrying myself about it, at least during the recess. When Parliament meets ... I shall, if I continue as well as I am at present, have quite enough of storms and bitterness in the course of what will probably be the bustling and angry session which I shall witness.[56]

In December 1821 he convinced himself that the recruitment by the ministry of the Grenvillites and the Irish appointments of Lord Wellesley and William Plunket* indicated that 'the king is friendly to [Catholic] emancipation, and that it is nearer at hand than many imagine'. He maintained this view, notwithstanding Grey's cynicism, and refused to believe that he would 'find a good many flying off this year on the Catholic question'.[57]

On the eve of the 1822 session, when he was 'in good health and spirits', he could 'never remember town so empty when the meeting of Parliament was so close at hand' and admitted that he knew 'nothing of the intention of opposition'. He told Mackintosh that 'he thought none of us (barring unforeseen calls) should speak, but should leave the ministers and the country gentlemen to squabble', though he placed little faith in the reports that 'the country gentlemen are coming up in a rare humour, and are to frighten ministers out of their wits': 'I do not take the wrath of Messrs. Gooch and Co. to be quite so formidable'. He was critical of Russell for writing public letters on the corn laws to Huntingdonshire farmers.[58] Provoked by Londonderry's (Castlereagh) comments into speaking on the address, 5 Feb., when he voted for Hume's amendment (on which he did not want to divide), he nevertheless appealed to the disgruntled country gentlemen for support, and, showing some of 'his old spirit and vigour', called for sweeping retrenchment and abolition of the sinking fund (of which he had hitherto been a staunch supporter) to facilitate tax reductions.[59] He voted against the suspension of habeas corpus in Ireland, 7 Feb., and for Wilson's motion on his dismissal, 13 Feb., reporting to Grey that it had gone off 'very satisfactorily'.[60] He also voted for the motion in support of Alderman Robert Waithman*, 28 Feb. He would not support Brougham's motion for further tax reductions, 11 Feb., believing it to be too strong; but on the 21st he spoke and voted for Althorp's more moderate one, taking the opportunity to avow his change of opinion on the sinking fund, and arguing that to continue it, when the real surplus was only £5,000,000, was 'to throw dust in the eyes of the country'. On 22 Feb. he mocked Vansittart, who 'had for many years got so entirely out of his understanding, his accounts and speculations had become so indistinct, that for five years he [Tierney] had not troubled his mind with them'; but later that day he 'went out of the House to avoid voting' on Hume's motion for information on naval pay.[61] He voted for the production of detailed estimates, 27 Feb., gradual diminution of the salt duties, 28 Feb., and admiralty reductions, 1 Mar., when he denounced the government's 'manoeuvre' in remitting part of the malt duty, but he left the chamber before Hume's motion for army reductions, 4 Mar.[62] He claimed to have no objection to the principle of the navy five per cents bill, 8 Mar., but voted for an amendment to extend the time allowed for dissent. He voted for abolition of one of the joint-postmasterships, 13 Mar. The following day he supported Creevey's motion for inquiry into the India board, though he complained that he had not been given notice of it. He was shocked by Creevey's subsequent 'Billingsgate' attack on the Grenvillites, but felt he had committed himself to vote for the motion.[63] Fremantle, a member of the board, thought that 'nothing could be more absurd than Tierney's conduct, speaking entirely against Creevey, and by his vote identifying himself with the opposition'.[64] At this time Brougham, writing to Duncannon from the northern circuit of what he considered the folly of opposition in quarrelling amongst themselves, condemned Tierney: 'The mischief he does is quite incalculable ... He sows distrust and disheartens everyone except the enemy, who he cheers daily by his complaints *to them of us*'.[65] On 29 Mar. Tierney encouraged Plunket to bring on the Catholic question, but failed to draw him. He was present, 16 Apr., at a meeting with the Members

Plunket, Newport, Parnell, Canning, Charles Grant, Phillimore and Charles Williams Wynn to consider the best course to adopt on the question. He 'expressed a very strong opinion as to the detriment the general question had received from not having been taken up immediately upon the meeting of Parliament' (he told Lady Holland that 'the Catholic interests have been strangely and grievously mismanaged'), but he acquiesced in the decision to shelve it, though he carried his point that 'the postponement should be Plunket's own act, and not a measure advised by the friends of emancipation'.[66] He objected to reception of a petition from the synod of Glasgow against Canning's bill for the relief of Catholic peers, 17 Apr.[67] He voted for parliamentary reform, 25 Apr., 3 June, abolition of one of the joint-postmasterships, 2 May, and Hume's motion for the payment of military pensions from the sinking fund surplus, 3 May. He spoke and voted in the minority of 37 for Wyvill's call for a large remission of taxation to ease agricultural distress, 8 May. Supporting the motion for cuts in diplomatic expenditure, 15 May, he urged the Tory country gentlemen to call Londonderry's resignation bluff. Sir Watkin Williams Wynn* thought the speech 'ingenious and good'; but Tierney voted in censure of his brother Henry's appointment to the Swiss embassy the following day.[68] He voted for criminal law reform, 4 June. He divided against the aliens bill, 14 June, 10 July, in protest against the present influence of the crown, 24 June, and for inquiry into chancery delays, 26 June, and repeal of the salt duties, 28 June. He voted for inquiry into the conduct of the lord advocate towards the Scottish press, 25 June, and called for the miscreant Hope to be speedily punished for breach of privilege, 9, 17 July. He voted for inquiry into the Calcutta bankers' claims, 4 July, and was in Hume's minority of 20 on the burgh accounts bill, 19 July 1822.

Tierney was at Worthing in August, and moved on to Brighton towards the end of the month. He anticipated no major changes following Londonderry's suicide; wrongly predicted that Canning would still go to India; thought that there was not the remotest chance of an approach being made to the Whigs, who were 'as much out of the question as if they were out of the world', and supposed that the government, however reconstituted, would 'have a sore time of it' in Parliament' but, 'in the present state of their opponents' would 'contrive to keep their heads above water'.[69] Brougham, anxious that opposition should be prepared in the unlikely event of an overture, urged Grey to take the appropriate steps and suggested that as he could not give up his profession, Tierney might 'go on' as a 'nominal leader ... taking it just as easily as he chose' and relying on Brougham's 'constant support'. Grey replied that only Brougham could provide effective leadership. Brougham, who asked Duncannon, if he saw Tierney, to 'make him be quiet and not go telling Charles Long,* etc., every sort of twaddle that is against the party, which they immediately carry to Carlton House', also exhorted the Hollands not to indulge in premature cabinet-making. Having been sent 'a long quotation' from Brougham's letter by Lady Holland, Tierney commented:

> I quite agree that it is foolish for any of our friends to proclaim the impossibility of our having the means within ourselves to form a government, but I must be forgiven if I think that it would be a very difficult undertaking, and if I confess myself entirely in the dark as to the manner in which it might be managed ... To constitute anything which could deserve the name of an administration there must be a great deal more than a mere muster of noblemen and gentlemen ready to accept the principal places. This I should say under any circumstances, but more especially in the present state of public affairs.[70]

Tierney, who was worried by the illness of two of his children, welcomed Hume's reported disavowal of his connection with the Whigs, and was made 'sick' by the adulation of Canning on his promotion to the foreign office: 'Anyone would suppose he was some young man of great promise but untried talents, instead of being an old battered politician who has been spouting all over the country for the last 20 years'. He was reported as believing that the introduction of Canning had made the ministry 'stronger'; but at the close of 1822, writing from Russell Farm, near Watford, which his widowed sister rented, he observed that 'if our friends act with common prudence and will have but a little patience they may occupy a more advantageous position than six months ago they could have hoped for'.[71]

Bedford, deploring the opposition hierarchy's desertion of Hume when he attacked the recent appointment of a lieutenant-general of the ordnance, 12 Feb. 1823, commented that Canning had 'laid himself particularly open, and it would have been a fine opportunity for old Tierney in his better days, *mais ces beaux jours ... sont passés*'.[72] Tierney spoke and voted for Maberly's motion for tax remissions of £7,000,000, 23 Feb., though with slight reservations as to the amount. On 3 Mar. he criticized the budget statement and voted for Hume's call for £2,000,000 in reductions.[73] He joined in the attack on the national debt reduction bill, 6, 13, 17 Mar., producing forceful speeches on the last two occasions. He was in Creevey's minority on the Barbados defence fund, 17 Mar., but not

Maberly's for repeal of the assessed taxes the following day. Campbell now quoted him as saying that 'the game is up', and that 'the party may almost be considered as dissolved'.[74] He cast silent votes against the naval and military pensions bill, 11, 14, 18 Apr. On 17 Apr., speaking 'very well', as George Agar Ellis* thought, he reaffirmed his support for Catholic relief, but said it would never be carried unless a government was formed which would take it up fairly, and accused Canning of trifling with Catholic hopes and the Grenvillites of betraying the cause through their 'eagerness to get into power'.[75] He supported inquiry into the prosecution of the Dublin Orange rioters, 22 Apr. He voted for Russell's reform motion, 24 Apr., and Scottish reform, 2 June. He divided for abolition of the death penalty for forgery, 21 May. He voted in condemnation of the lord advocate's conduct in the Borthwick case, 3 June, and was pleased with the strong opposition muster.[76] He voted against government on chancery delays, 5 June, and the coronation expenses, 19 June. He said that chief baron O'Grady should be heard in his own defence at the bar of the House, 17 June. He was in the majority for the Scottish juries bill, 20 June. Two days later he breakfasted with Brougham at Holland House, and was described by Lord George William Russell* as 'sententious and sarcastic, but very agreeable'.[77] He voted for Brougham's motion for further consideration of the Catholic petition complaining of the administration of justice in Ireland, 26 June, and against the grant for Irish glebe houses and for the petition of complaint against James Crosbie*, 1 July 1823.

Tierney voted for information on Catholic burials, 6 Feb., and the criminal jurisdiction of the Isle of Man, 18 Feb. 1824. He divided for reform of Edinburgh's representation, 26 Feb. He voted for Hume's attempts to reduce the ordnance estimates, 27 Feb., when he also voted for repeal of the usury laws, as he did again, 8 Apr. He spoke and voted in support of Abercromby's charge of breach of privilege against lord chancellor Eldon, 1 Mar. The following day he voted for repeal of the window tax. Like Brougham, he thought inquiry preferable to Heron's proposed bill to end the necessity of a renewal of offices on a demise of the crown, 4 Mar. On 15 Mar. he was in the opposition minorities on the beer tax, flogging in the army, and the grant for Protestant charter schools; and he voted against the provision for the publication of Irish proclamations, 19 Mar. Although 'a fast friend to the principle of free trade', he applauded Alexander Baring's efforts to persuade government to hear the representations of the silk manufacturers before proceeding with the reduction of duties, 18 Mar. He opposed the aliens bill, 23

Mar., 2 Apr., when, following Canning, he stressed the importance of Britain's maintaining 'not a nominal but a real neutrality' in European affairs; Canning's friend Charles Ellis* thought he spoke 'very well'.[78] He voted to refer the reports of the Scottish commission of judicial inquiry to a committee of the whole House, 30 Mar. He voted against ministers on the grant for the refurbishment of Windsor Castle, 5 Apr., after joining in futile demands for assurances that no more money would be required. He voted against the grant for building new churches, 9 Apr. He divided for an advance of capital to Ireland, 4 May, and, when supporting inquiry into the state of Ireland, 11 May, gave Canning what was considered a 'deserved ... dressing': he accused him of indifference to the Catholic cause and of 'playing fast and loose' with opposition who, though 'anxious for the success of parliamentary reform', were not, as he alleged, pledged to introduce it if they came in. Fremantle reported that Tierney was 'cheered in thunders by an immense band of opposition, and [there was] no attempt to put it down by the government'.[79] Tierney, who was in the opposition minorities on Irish first fruits, 25 May, and pluralities, 27 May, presented a Knaresborough petition for inquiry into the prosecution of the Methodist missionary John Smith in Demerara, 1 June, but he did not vote for Brougham's motion on the subject, 11 June.[80] He was in Hume's minority of 38 for inquiry into naval impressment, 10 June. The following month Lady Holland reported that he 'keeps perfectly well' and 'defies even punch and turtle'; but he was unable to ascertain what lay behind the almost daily cabinet meetings, as he told Grey, 29 July 1824: 'All our politicians are quite in the dark, and the government secrets are well kept'.[81]

He did not write to Grey again until mid-January 1825, having just arrived in London, where he had not spent a fortnight since the summer. He could not guess how Canning would handle the Catholic question, but, hearing that many Whigs approved the conduct of the Catholic Association, was clear as to his own line:

> My vote will be given as it always has been, but I must be pardoned if I steer clear of anything that looks like making common cause with Messrs. [Daniel] O'Connell* and Co. Indeed, they have parted company with us, their oldest and most tried friends, and have thrown themselves upon Sir F. Burdett* and [William] Cobbett†. Let my opinion, however, of their proceedings be what it may, I am more and more convinced of the pressing necessity which exists of granting their just claims, and I lament that the intemperate speeches with which the Association commenced its sittings should have frightened away some of their former supporters.

Gratified that Grey and Holland agreed with him, he planned to remain silent, if possible, until the 'regular question of emancipation' came on. He approved of Canning's policy towards the independent South American states, but found it 'really amusing' to see him being 'cried up as the champion of liberal principles', though acknowledging that he was infinitely preferable to the Tory old guard.[82] He felt obliged to attack the bill to suppress the Association and to urge the 'pressing necessity' of conceding Catholic claims, 11 Feb., when he made a splash with an attack on Plunket and his ministerial colleagues in his best and inimitably sarcastic style. One backbencher reported that it was 'quite delightful and kept the House in a continued roar of laughter'; while according to Hobhouse, even his victims 'could not help joining in the laugh'. Yet Fremantle noted that 'although the House was amused', Tierney's raillery 'did not lessen one iota the impression made by Plunket'; and Mrs. Arbuthnot thought it was entirely 'irrelevant' and 'had nothing to do with the question'.[83] Tierney, who did not subscribe to the view of many Whigs that 'public opinion has undergone a material change in favour of emancipation', confided to Grey his regret that Brougham had by his speeches identified himself so closely with the Association.[84] But he voted for Brougham's motion to hear their case against the unlawful societies bill at the bar of the House, 18 Feb., and was generous in his praise of his speech. He welcomed of the decision of the Association leaders, reached in concert with Burdett and Brougham, to bring on the Catholic question by resolution on 1 Mar., though he was worried that the interval which must necessarily elapse before a bill was brought in would allow the anti-Catholics to rally. According to Canning, Tierney assured him privately in the House, 21 Feb., that there would be no more serious resistance to the progress of the unlawful societies bill, which he voted silently against that evening, and on the 25th. He went over the lists with Duncannon, and correctly predicted a majority for the consideration of relief.[85] He was named as a defaulter, 28 Mar., but attended and was excused, 1 Mar., when he duly voted for it. He divided for repeal of the assessed taxes, 3 Mar. On the Catholic relief bill, he urged Burdett to resist ministerial pressure to delay its second reading, 22 Mar., denied, as one of the committee who had drawn it up, that O'Connell was its author, 23 Mar., and reserved judgement on the proposals to pay the Catholic clergy and disfranchise Irish 40s. freeholders, 28 Mar. He voted for the second and third readings, 21 Apr., 10 May, but was suspected by the Grenvillites of intriguing with Grey to ensure that it did not become law.[86] He voted for revision of the corn laws, 28 Apr. He opposed the grant to the duke of Cumberland, an 'unwarrantable precedent', 30 May, 2, 6, 9, 10 June. He wanted William Kenrick's[†] conduct as a Surrey magistrate to be investigated, 21 June, and condemned, 28 June. He was in Hume's minority of 18 for his amendment to the combination bill concerning intimidation, 27 June 1825.

Tierney and his wife went to Brussels in the second week of September, but he was laid low with diarrhoea and a 'derangement' of his liver. To his surprise and amusement Cumberland, who was also there, was uncommonly civil to him, and they 'vowed everlasting friendship'. Expecting a 'confounded dissolution', which did not in the event take place, he returned to London earlier than planned. He took a pessimistic view of prospects for the Catholic question, and had 'no idea of again being in a majority [on it] when the present Parliament is no more', for 'the sense of the country is against us'. He had misgivings about Lord Tavistock's[*] address to Bedfordshire declaring that at the next election he would neither solicit votes nor spend money; but Bedford, Tavistock's father, dismissed them as an example of his 'usual way of croaking'.[87] Towards the close of the year he kept a concerned eye on the commercial crash and the 'gloom' and 'panic' in the City, not the least disturbing aspect of which, he thought, was the handle which it gave to 'Lord Eldon's tribe' to 'talk of the mischievous effects of liberal principles'. In mid-January 1826 he wrote to Lady Holland from London:

> With Grey I have not exchanged a line since he went out of town ... The meeting of Parliament is now near at hand and, though there are no longer any of the old party battles to be fought, I suspect there will be plenty of debating. Corn, currency and trade will it is most probable furnish many a long night, to say nothing of the state of slavery in the colonies ... and the Catholic question ... Of the state of the country as to money and trade there are many and contradictory reports, but, if I am rightly informed, the full effect of the late alarm has not yet been felt and great distress in the commercial world is to be looked for. Happily there seems to be no prospect of the peace being interrupted or the prospect would be very discouraging ... I have nothing to complain of but that I grow older every day and feel it.[88]

In the House, 9 Feb. 1826, Tierney got Robinson, the chancellor, to admit that the Bank had not made any formal proposal for the establishment of branches in the country. His initial impression of the measures proposed by government to deal with the banking crisis was favourable; but on 17 Feb., a few hours after Peel, the home secretary, had told the duke of Wellington that he seemed 'indifferent', he attacked

the promissory notes bill as an abrogation of their stated principle of 'a speedy return to a metallic currency'. He called for the issue of £5,000,000 in exchequer bills on 'proper security', which would facilitate a 'return to a wholesome state of things ... a large circulation of paper, founded on a solid, substantial metallic currency'. Greville thought this speech 'admirable'.[89] On 20 Feb. Tierney spoke and voted in the minority of 24 against the ministerial proposal to allow banks to issue small notes until October. He told Holland that while he did 'not see things in quite so gloomy a light as many of my neighbours', he thought that 'commercial credit is for the moment at an end'. He wanted ministers to act decisively, and even harboured a fear that 'all this may end in our falling back into a paper system', which 'the Ultra members of administration' would like to foist on Canning and the liberal group. He saw that he would be obliged to support Thomas Wilson's motion for an issue of exchequer bills, 28 Feb., though he was resolved 'if I say anything to take care distinctly to mark my opinion on the relative merits of the two contending parties so that my vote shall not be misunderstood'; in the event, the motion was withdrawn, as ministers revealed their own plans. That day Tierney criticized their scheme to indemnify the Bank for its advances to relieve distress, which was 'all soap and oil – no one could get hold of it'. He also attacked what he later described to the Hollands as their 'shabby', and 'miserable and mischievous ... subterfuge' of getting the Bank to issue exchequer bills. He reckoned that they owed him thanks for exposing it, for 'if I had made a formal motion with a few days notice, I should have run them very hard, and if nobody but Lord Liverpool had been concerned I would have done it'. Tierney, who voted against government on the Jamaican slave trials, 2 Mar., the army establishment, 3 Mar., Hume's amendment to the notes bill requiring country banks to make monthly returns, 7 Mar., and Newport's attempt to disfranchise non-resident Irish borough voters, 9 Mar., told Holland a few days later that economically, 'things are certainly a little better', though a return to prosperity was some way off. He anticipated an 'abundance of bitterness and animosities' on the corn laws, for there was 'plenty of suppressed wrath fermenting which only waits for a good opportunity to vent itself against Canning and Huskisson'. He applauded Peel's plans for reform of the criminal code: 'Opposition as a party is extinct, and my only object being now to support that branch of the administration whose opinions come the nearest to my own, I rejoice in whatever annoys and disgraces those with whom I think it is nearly impossible that I should ever agree'. He sympathized with the outcry in Scotland against the proposal to prevent the issue of promissory notes below the value of £5: 'if we had proposed to screw every Highlander into a pair of tight leather breeches we could not have created more alarm'. He was named to the select committee on the subject, 16 Mar., but did not expect a bill to result. On a personal note, he confessed to Holland that 'though on the score of health I have nothing to complain of, I feel every day more and more that which I do not accomplish soon I may never accomplish at all'. Irritated by the reluctance of the Hollands' son Henry Fox* to embark on the parliamentary career which had been earmarked for him, he commented that 'all the young ones appear to me to want that sort of energy and ambition which used to animate us old boys when in our youth'.[90] He presented a Knaresborough petition for the abolition of slavery, 20 Mar.,[91] when he voted to reduce the grant for Irish chartered schools. He was in the minority on Irish first fruits revenues the following day. A 'very troublesome cough ... which is tolerably quiet all day but plagues me sadly at night' drove him to Brighton, 'without reaping much if any benefit', in early April. On the 7th he spoke and voted against the proposal to give the president of the board of trade a separate ministerial salary, and he did so again on the 10th, when he made a hard-hitting, sarcastic speech at Canning's expense, and repeated the reference to 'His Majesty's Opposition' made earlier in the debate by Hobhouse; he was subsequently credited with coining the phrase. He was surprised, he told Holland, by the continued 'general stagnation of trade' and 'want of confidence'.[92] He voted for reform of Edinburgh's representation, 13 Apr., and Russell's reform motion, 27 Apr., when he was pleased with some of the opposition speeches but disappointed with 'a bad division' (247-123).[93] He voted for Whitmore's motion for revision of the corn laws, 18 Apr. He welcomed the unexpected ministerial proposal to give themselves the power to open the ports at their discretion for the importation of corn at a duty of 12s., 1 May, but found himself at odds with the Whig protectionists, as he informed Holland:

All the landed interest are in a terrible commotion ... I have had no private communication with anybody but G[rey] and I then saw enough to satisfy me that the less I meddled the better as I might subject myself to the imputation of beating up for recruits against those with whom I am most sorry to differ. Upon my own opinion I must vote, and, if it be necessary, speak. The conduct of government has been very unaccountable and is, I admit, liable to much animadversion, but having supported Whitmore's motion ... it is impossible for me not to give my countenance to a measure which provides some remedy for the evil which I deprecate ... I cannot say that I am in the sweetest possible temper.

He was 'vexed' to see Grey (to whom he seems not to have written after the summer of 1825), 'after professing to withdraw from all political activity', joining Lord Malmesbury and 'the most violent of the Tories' in attacking the government on this issue in the Lords, 1 May. From the other side of the protectionist fence, Bedford commented that 'old Tierney *the consumer*' had 'always been the enemy of the agricultural interest, without understanding a jot of the subject. All he cares about is *cheap bread*, and when he gets it, what a pretty state the country will be in!'[94] Tierney voted for inquiry into the state of the nation, 4 May 1826. Reported to be 'in great health and vigour' later in the month, on the 26th, as one of the 'dissentients' from the report of the small notes committee, he reviewed and criticized the ministry's financial policy that session, wishing to

clear himself from having given any assistance to, or having participated in, what he conceived to be a system of delusion ... He washed his hands of it ... He felt no hostility to Lord Liverpool. He wished him every possible good ... as a man whom he respected; and he also wished him a little more nerve and firmness as a minister.[95]

Later that day he was in the majority for Russell's resolution proscribing electoral bribery. He came in again for Knaresborough at the general election the following month.

Tierney stood by his support for the opening of the ports, even though it turned out that the legislation was 'so worded that it will not meet the case'.[96] When Peel's brother-in-law George Dawson* asked him in early October 1826

what kind of campaign the opposition intended to carry on, he said, 'There is no opposition now. I and others have long since given it up, the parties now are the government and the Canningites, and I and a great many others are of the latter class'.[97]

Three months later, when Hobhouse found him with Burdett, 'discussing in what form the Catholic question ought to be brought on', he 'lamented that there was no opposition, no man to whom the country looks up'.[98] In the House, 16 Feb. 1827, he voted with government for the grant to the duke of Clarence, to the disgust of Creevey and the surprise of Bedford, who asked: 'What became of old Tierney? Is he, who is always so stout and plain spoken on these subjects, looking to the future favours of William IV?'[99] He voted for Catholic relief, 6 Mar., and information on the Orange procession at Lisburn, 29 Mar. 1827. In the early stages of the period of uncertainty created by Liverpool's stroke, he told Peel that opposition 'meant very soon to ask a question as to the state of the government', and that 'for sixpence I would make a motion myself'. He did so on 30 Mar., when, with Brougham absent on the circuit, he took the initiative in moving to postpone going into committee of supply until 'a strong, an efficient, and a united administration' was in place. He at first seemed satisfied with Canning's assurance that the king intended to replace Liverpool, and a considerable number of Members left the House, thinking there would be no division. But Tierney subsequently demanded a promise that the new ministry would be announced before the Easter holidays, which Canning refused to give; and, 'at the instigation of some persons around him', he divided the House, which rejected his motion by 153-80.[100] He voted for inquiry into the Irish miscellaneous estimates and information on chancery delays, 5 Apr. On 12 Apr., when Williams Wynn moved the writ for Newport, Isle of Wight, where Canning was to come in after his appointment as first lord of the treasury, and an adjournment of the House to 1 May, Tierney 'faintly opposed' the latter, but did not force a division. He told Holland that he would have had a majority, 'but then it would have been a majority of Tories, so it was best avoided'. Ruminating on the mass resignation of the anti-Catholic ministers, he went on:

How the new minister is to carry on the war is beyond my comprehension, that is to say with any strength of his own. He cannot hazard a single division without an assurance of our full support. Indeed I do not see how he is to form his staff without our help and though I now begin to think he must ask for it, I own I do not understand how it is to be obtained. Without us I should say Canning's administration, unless he can whistle back the Tories, cannot last through the session ... I am afraid ... [Grey] is under evil influence.

Indeed Tierney, who was not particularly well, was upset by reports of Grey's 'ill considered invective' against Canning, though he claimed to be unwilling to '*pledge myself* either to support or oppose the new administration' without knowing what line Canning intended to take on the Catholic question. He observed to Holland in mid-April:

There never was a moment in which we were called upon for so much firmness, circumspection and temper, and what remains of our character will revive or be extinguished as we conduct ourselves. The state of the country requires a government bearing upon the face of it the appearance of stability ... God forbid that I should see ... [Eldon's] gang brought back again and above all that I should see it restored to power in such a way as to induce a belief that their services could not be dispensed

with. Now a short-lived ministry with Canning at its head would I am afraid have just such an effect.[101]

Soon afterwards he was quoted in Tory circles as saying that there was 'no chance' of the Whigs forming an alliance with Canning; and there was a curious report that he, like Grey, was actually 'adverse' to a junction.[102] This was not the case, though he continued to dither as negotiations commenced between Canning and Lord Lansdowne. He did not wish the latter to be 'pushed into administration' by the cabal at Brooks's led by Brougham; and he refused to take the blame for fouling the negotiations by 'stipulating for a Catholic government in Ireland', though he admitted that he had 'heartily concurred' in this demand, which was the very least that the Whigs were entitled to press. He told Holland that 'the more I think of it the less inclination I have to take office without Grey or you', and claimed that only concern for the future welfare of his son George, a junior diplomat with delicate health, prevented him from washing his hands of the business:

If I close my political life (and to withdraw at this moment would be to do so, as well as to give offence to a very great majority of my friends) I leave him as unprotected as I was myself when I began the world, and deprive him of the only advantage which can in any degree serve to counterbalance the follies of my own life, and the little use I have made of the talents which *you* at least I know will not accuse me of overrating from any vanity and self conceit ... People of all ranks and degrees seem to me to be gone mad about a junction with Canning. Some are actuated by a natural hatred of the Tory faction, some by being heartily sick of the thing called opposition, and not a few by a wish for office. All that can be said for them is that in giving their support to Canning they are not conscious of any dereliction of principle. The junction I am persuaded would in the first instance be popular, but how long such a temper as now prevails may last is another question. Unless the great mass of the Whig interest can cordially co-operate in giving and have some satisfactory security for receiving support by the projected union, the experiment is full of danger.[103]

Holland strongly urged him to take office, arguing that it would be 'folly' to refuse on account of scruples about offending Grey, and that no dereliction of principle would be involved. He also pressed Lansdowne to ensure that Tierney was given 'a post of honour and profit'. Tierney still hesitated, fearful that the Catholics would be sacrificed to the king's prejudices.[104] On 26 Apr., however, he agreed to enter Canning's cabinet, as master of the mint, with Lansdowne and Lord Carlisle, although their appointments were not to take place until Canning had managed to settle the Irish government to the satisfaction of the pro-Catholics. Lansdowne, communicating Tierney's acceptance to Canning, 'strongly' urged him not to require Tierney to undertake to oppose parliamentary reform.[105] The wags made play of his playful reference to Canning in his speech of 30 Mar. by imagining a 'circular letter' to the London press:

My speech on Canning's '*Master-mind*'
One great mistake contains, I find:
Please to correct the gross mis-print
Of 'Master-mind', for 'Master-Mint'.[106]

Bedford deplored the coalition, but told Holland that

what pleases me best in all these ridiculous transactions is to see *old Citizen Tierney* become a cabinet minister after 40 years' hard labour to attain that eminence. I am pleased at it, because I like him and admire him personally, very sincerely; because I think it will cheer his old age, and he will not be troubled with any 'compunctious visitings'.[107]

Tierney sat on the second bench on the government side of the House, 1 May, and on the treasury bench, 7, 16 May, when he moved the adjournment, in what was his sole reported contribution to debate during the life of the ministry. He told his son that their victory on 7 May, when, on Gascoyne's motion for inquiry into the shipping interest, 'the enemy were afraid to come up to the scratch and ran fairly away', was 'by far the most satisfactory thing that he has seen yet'.[108] Canning offered him the governor-generalship of India as an alternative to the mint, but he was not interested. It became necessary to expedite the Whigs' entry to the cabinet sooner than intended; and they meekly swallowed a stipulation that the Catholic question was to remain an 'open' one, as in Liverpool's ministry.[109] Tierney had an untroubled re-election for Knaresborough, 24 May. His absence from the Commons for the debate on the budget, 1 June, was taken as one of the signs of the ministry's weakness; and at the end of the month, when Lansdowne and Canning were supposed to be at loggerheads, he was reported as saying, 'We cannot go on; the coach must be all unpacked and repacked again'.[110] Mackintosh noted in early July 1827 that Tierney had recently 'suffered alarmingly from a singular complaint ... a hardening and swelling of a small and delicate but important organ which nature has unusually exposed to danger'. He was 'confined six weeks to the sofa and took 350 grams of blue pill at 15 grams a day without touching his gums. He cannot yet take much exercise, but is in good general health'.[111] According to John Denison*, on 7 Aug. Tierney assured the ailing

Canning that his strong constitution would pull him through: he was dead within hours.[112] Lady Cowper, speculating as to what might now happen, noted that 'Tierney would hate being leader, it is too much work for him; but I believe he would not decline it for the sake of keeping things together if he was sure of powerful support'.[113] The Tory Lord Lowther* predicted that although his health was not equal to 'every night's work', he was one of the cabinet ministers who would 'stick to the last, as they have little chance of again gaining six months salary or patronage'.[114] Brougham, expecting the worst of Tierney, urged Holland

by main force [to] keep ... [him] from his wonted course of twaddle. I see him shaking his head and looking wise and saying we can't carry on the government in the House of Commons now Canning is dead. Let him speak for himself. I say we can. I say he himself is more than a match for all Peel can bring against him. But I say whether he is or not, I am, and I say it without the least vanity, but because there are always some Tierneys ... who, distressing themselves, choose also to be so kind as to distress all their friends and to be fainthearted for others.

Holland, however, assured him that 'Tierney's head was never more *fixed*, nor his heart less appalled than upon this occasion'; Brougham was glad to hear it.[115] Tierney agreed initially to stay on with Lansdowne under Lord Goderich, but objected 'strenuously', with 'hasty and coarse expressions', to the proposed appointment of the anti-Catholic John Herries* as chancellor of the exchequer, on which the king insisted. The resultant impasse seemed at one point almost certain to end in the resignation of the Whig ministers, though the Canningite Lord Palmerston* thought that Tierney only 'affects' to be outraged: 'Will any man living believe that he would willingly go out if he had a decent excuse for staying on?'[116] Holland, whom Tierney and Lansdowne were anxious to have admitted to the cabinet, whenever the king's objections could be overcome, strongly urged him, 22 Aug., to resist Herries's appointment to the death, even at the cost of resignation. Tierney agreed 'entirely', but could not

feel as confident as you do that our friends and the public will support us if the result is to be our retiring ... I am afraid that some of our adherents and a large portion of the country will ... strongly express their disapprobation of the part we act. We do not live in times when anything that savours of resistance to power is likely to meet with encouragement or even countenance ... As things stand at the moment [25 Aug.] all I can say to you is that ... if the Canningites are steady and act with us, as I am sure we wish to act with them, the king, so far as relates to

Herries, cannot do otherwise than give way. If there is to be temporizing, timidity and concession, our days are numbered.[117]

He hoped for salvation from the offer of the exchequer to William Sturges Bourne*, but on his refusal was thrown back into agonies of indecision, as he told Lady Holland, 31 Aug.:

> We have a most delicate and difficult game to play, and I do not doubt we shall be severely censured whatever we do. If we stay in with Herries we shall be said to disgrace ourselves. If we resign we shall be charged with breaking up the government and letting in the Tories. Would that some creditable middle course could be devised, but I hardly see how it can be looked for.[118]

He was by now, however, convinced that the nomination of Herries had originated not with the king but with Goderich and, while claiming that this did not 'alter my opinion as to the unfitness of the appointment, which I still think a most improper one', he did not feel that he could advise Lansdowne to refuse the entreaty which the king was expected to make to him to withdraw his tendered resignation, for the sake of the public service, 1 Sept. 1827. He wrote to this effect to Lansdowne before he went to Windsor that day, 'after a sleepless night', and confessing that 'I never had a harder battle than between my feelings and my discretion'. He entirely endorsed Lansdowne's submission to the king's request: 'I heartily rejoice that you tendered your resignation, but I think, there being no sacrifice or even compromise of any principle in question, you would not have been justified if you had continued to press it after the earnest manner in which His Majesty was pleased to appeal to you'.[119] The Tories were contemptuous of the Whig ministers' capitulation: the Arbuthnots wondered how Tierney, in particular, could stay in after 'saying that he would rather starve than sit in the cabinet with Herries'.[120] Bedford, however, was inclined to blame Lansdowne and acquit 'the old Citizen', who had been 'stout and held out to the last', but, quite rightly, 'would not desert him' at the crunch.[121]

Russell found Tierney, who got into a panic over the impending Lanarkshire by-election, fearing 'an end to all cordial co-operation with the friends of liberal principles in Scotland' if the lord advocate was allowed to continue supporting the Tory candidate against a Whig, 'much out of humour' when he met him at the Hollands' Bedfordshire home at Ampthill just after the crisis had been resolved. Yet Lady Holland reported that he was 'more at ease since the last breeze ... and has become quite fond of Lord Lansdowne and praises and extols him to the skies for his com-

pliance'.[122] He did his best to recruit support for the government, especially from Althorp and the young Whigs. He conducted negotiations with Russell, who submitted six propositions, endorsed by Grey, Althorp, Milton and Lord Tavistock, which amounted to stipulations of what was required to ensure their neutrality. Tierney, who insisted that there must be 'nothing like a bargain', preferred to regard them as 'hints'; in any case, he was unable to persuade his cabinet colleagues to agree to them.[123] Mrs. Arbuthnot heard in late October that he and Lansdowne were 'very uncomfortable in their seats'; but Bedford had a 'good account' of him from Lady Holland, which dispelled his own worries about his well-being:

> What I wrote to you some time ago was simply from my own observation. I passed two days with him, and three or four hours *tête à tête*, and thought he had lost much of that lively fancy, cheerfulness and *gaieté de coeur*, which used to delight us all; but I did not mean that he was going to hang himself, *au pied de la lettre!*[124]

Tierney, whom Holland found infuriatingly and unusually '*boutonné*' at Brighton in early November 1827, assured Lady Holland that the story that ministers were 'endeavouring by some compromise' to prevent the Catholic question from being brought on next session was no more than malicious gossip.[125] Tierney was worried about the popular and possible parliamentary reaction to the destruction of the Turkish fleet at Navarino, though he hoped that 'satisfactory explanations will be given and ... all will end well'; but it was said in ministerial circles that his 'want of power to conceal his apprehensions is complained of as hurtful'.[126] Grey, regretting the lapse of their friendship, blamed him, along with Brougham, for spreading 'injurious' tales attributing his hostility to the coalition ministries to personal pique and snobbish distaste for Canning.[127]

In mid-November 1827 Tierney suggested to Goderich that Althorp should be appointed to the chairmanship of the finance committee. Herries, who later denounced Tierney as 'an old rogue, the very focus of intrigue, descending to all kinds of tricks', appeared at first to acquiesce, but subsequently raised strong objections and threatened to resign. Certainly Tierney, disregarding an understanding with Huskisson, carried on covert negotiations with Althorp. The deadlock created by Herries's intransigence led to the collapse of the government, as the feeble Goderich threw in the towel in early January 1828.[128] Tierney was dismissed by the duke of Wellington when he formed his ministry, though he promised to do what he could for his son, who aspired to be secretary of embassy at The Hague, where he was currently second secretary; had he wanted it, he could have applied for a commissionership of customs or excise.[129] Tierney was said by a Tory to be 'inexpressibly sad at losing a salary which he hugged', while Palmerston, who joined the ministry with the other former Canningites, noted that Herries's appointment as master of the mint would make him 'doubly furious'.[130] To his son he wrote, 21 Jan. 1828, of his

> disgust ... that the friends of Canning, in return for the cordial and efficient support they received from the Whigs, should so readily avail themselves of an opportunity to exclude us from the cabinet, and to form a junction with those who have been his and their most inveterate enemies ... The compromise between Herries and Huskisson is most curious ... Herries appears to Huskisson a harmless cabinet minister when changed into the master of the mint. But all this is too contemptible to be talked of ... How all this will go down in the House of Commons remains to be seen, but I confess that I rather expect it will succeed, at least in the outset. I do not see how we are to embark at once on a systematic and furious opposition without exposing ourselves to the same censures which we heaped upon our opponents last year. At any rate so far as I am concerned I have no stomach for attacking anything but such measures as may seem fairly to provoke a battle. A great deal will depend upon the manner in which the recent change shall be received in Ireland.

Advising his son of Wellington's friendly disposition, he wrote: 'Do not trouble your head about my politics except to remember that they are very near their end, and that there is very little probability of my ever being again in office'.[131] Anxious to set the record straight, both on his own and the Lansdowne Whigs' account, he gave his version of events in the House, 18 Feb. 1828, after Huskisson and Herries, whose statements he described as 'not altogether accurate'. He ironically expressed the hope that Wellington 'may be enabled to control the jarring and discordant elements over which he has been called upon to preside', criticized the former Canningites for their treatment of the Whigs, and insisted, unconvincingly, that Canning's policy as prime minister on the Catholic question had been quite distinct from that of his predecessor. He was generally thought to have 'shattered ... [Herries's] statement to atoms', though Abercromby wished he had been 'less abusive of the Canningites', and a Tory observer thought that while he was 'very entertaining', he had 'impugned little of Herries's statement'.[132]

This marked the effective end of Tierney's political career. He was 'very far from well' in the spring of 1828, but recovered by slow degrees at Brighton, from

where he wrote at the end of April that Wellington had 'a very difficult game to play' on the Catholic question, and that the Whigs 'ought to be very well satisfied with what he has done'. He was 'not sorry to have been away' from the reportedly fractious proceedings of the finance committee, to which he had been named, 15 Feb. He was agreeably surprised by the majority to consider Catholic relief, 12 May, when he took a pair. It was rumoured in late August that he was 'breaking up' and close to death; but he was in fact tolerably well, and he improved still more when he returned to Brighton in the autumn.[133] His son, meanwhile, had applied to Wellington and the foreign secretary Lord Aberdeen for promotion, and he was rewarded at the end of the year with a posting to Munich as secretary of legation.[134] In early January 1829 Tierney had 'a bad cold', but he was optimistic of decisive ministerial action on the Catholic question. In the event he told Holland that if, as was reported, Catholics were to be admitted to Parliament, he 'should be disposed to accept it almost on any terms', no matter how unpalatable the 'securities' might be.[135] He voted silently for emancipation, 6, 30 Mar. (Curiously, Planta, the patronage secretary, had included him the previous month among those whose attitude was 'doubtful', though this may have had more to do with his stance on securities than with his views on the main question.) When Greville told him that there had been 'great disappointment that he had not answered Sadler' on the 17th, he 'said that he could not speak for coughing', and 'talked of the duke's management of this business with great admiration'.[136] He voted for the transfer of East Retford's seats to Birmingham, 5 May. In his last reported speech in the House, 15 May, he argued that O'Connell should be allowed to state at the table his reasons for objecting to swearing the oath of allegiance before taking his seat, having debated the merits of this issue, 'bill in hand', with Grey at Lady Jersey's that morning.[137] In his last known vote, he supported O'Connell's right to take his seat without hindrance, 18 May 1829. Three weeks later he told Greville that unless Wellington was careful, and avoided such blunders as the current ministerial support for the anti-Catholic George Bankes* against a Whig in the Cambridge University by-election, he would 'offend more people than he would conciliate': 'the way he went on was neither fish nor flesh'. Later in June, observing the ministry's crying want of additional strength and paucity of debating skill, he 'said it was very lamentable that there should be such a deficiency of talent in the rising generation, and remarkable how few clever young men there are now in the House of Commons'.[138]

Tierney was 'quite well, and in good spirits' in August 1829, and, having lost another Robarts nephew in October, he went to London from Russell Farm in early January 1830.[139] There was a report that he planned to attend on the opening day and, as Huskisson later put it, make 'a grand exposé with all the solemnity of a farewell speech, and to have concluded by the earnest prayer of a dying man to the House to support the duke of Wellington, as the only hope of salvation'.[140] The Commons were spared this exhibition, for in the afternoon of 25 Jan. 1830 Tierney was found dead in his chair at his Savile Row home by his servant, who had 'returned only five minutes after having taken a parcel off the table, to announce some visitor'; he had suddenly succumbed, 'without a struggle and apparently without a groan', to 'organic disease of the heart'.[141] He was 'a great loss to all his friends', commented Greville, though 'his political life was already closed'.[142] He died intestate, and administration of his estate, which was sworn under £2,000, was granted to his widow, 10 Mar. 1830. It was reckoned that he had 'left scarcely £1,000 a year for his family, having rather encroached on his wife's fortune', though he had 'never placed himself under a pecuniary obligation ... to ... any of his family'. Holland saw this as 'very painful proof of the little advantage he has derived from his long services in public life'[143] There was considerable shock and sadness at his death. Lord Ellenborough, a political opponent, was 'very sorry'.[144] Grey was 'quite overwhelmed', as he told Princess Lieven:

He was one of my oldest friends, and almost the only one remaining of those with whom I was connected on my setting out in public life. There never has been any interruption of our mutual regard, though some divergence in our political feelings and conduct on one or two occasions ... But I can think of nothing now but his many amiable and valuable qualities, which render his loss irreparable.[145]

The Hollands were deeply upset. Lord Holland lamented the loss of 'one of my best and oldest friends, and the pleasantest one that public life ever procured me. Indeed, so agreeable a man I do not think is left behind him'. Bedford wrote of him as 'a valued and excellent friend ... and a constantly cheerful and kind hearted companion'; while Russell said he would miss his 'kind, friendly, agreeable conversation'. Holland's son Charles Fox* observed that 'he was of all the older set of Holland House the one I loved and liked the most'.[146] Abercromby wrote that he was 'in some respects a man by himself', who would always 'be remembered with pleasure by those who have known him'; Lord Carlisle regarded his death as 'a great

blow', and Lord Essex observed that 'we have indeed lost a *most valuable friend* and one not to be *easily replaced*'.[147] On a less effusive note, Milton commented that 'Tierney would have made a great gap some years ago', but 'now one has only to lament the loss of an acquaintance'; while the king's creature Sir William Knighton, a man not fit to lace Tierney's shoes, noted in his diary, 4 Feb., that like all 'contemptible' politicians, he would 'not be remembered a week hence, and ought not'.[148] Tierney's widow was 'deeply hurt to find that the writ for Knaresborough is to be moved without any tribute of respect' to him; but Holland, after consulting several leading Whigs, advised her that the practice of pronouncing posthumous panegyrics in the House had been abandoned, 'by a sort of understanding or consent among leading public men', after one or two unhappy recent examples.[149] However, on 12 Feb. 1830 Lord Morpeth, as Lord Lansdowne related, introduced into his speech 'quite naturally as arising out of the subject of finance and economy, some observations on Tierney's public services that were admirable both in taste and feeling'.[150] The Wellington ministry subsequently granted Mrs. Tierney a civil list pension of £400 a year; but her son made no immediate headway in his bid for a move back to The Hague.[151]

Tierney was a man of great personal charm and a genuine master of debate, although, as he told Tom Macaulay*, 'he never rose in the House without feeling his knees tremble under him'.[152] Sir George Philips* later described him as

one of the cleverest debaters in a clear, simple, condensed, unpretending style, appropriate, as to its language, to the matter that I ever knew. He never affected eloquence and imagery, and no man had the same talent for putting down and ridiculing all his opponents who attempted flights of eloquence.[153]

He would almost certainly have made a fortune had he opted for a career at the bar. As a politician he was often weak, pessimistic and indecisive, and perhaps too much given to intrigue. Hobhouse wrote three days after his death:

The panegyrics in the newspapers seem to me to be true as to his parliamentary capacity, but false as to his integrity. My father, who knew him well, told me he was as great an intriguer as ever lived. I also think that no statesman ever took such false views of coming events ... His conjectures, so far as I ever heard of them, were never happy.[154]

Holland, who thought he was 'much more disinterested than his sometimes grovelling way of talking of public virtue led superficial men to imagine', commented:

It was hardly in his nature to take any step without some previous hesitation or some subsequent misgivings ... His oratory, though of no elevated, commanding or even brilliant kind, was perhaps the most popular and the most agreeable, and certainly by far the most original, then left in Parliament ... In truth his irresolution was fed, if not engendered, by that very sense of humour which enabled him to discern so keenly and to expose so admirably whatever was ridiculous in other public men. His pleasantry and easy manners shed a charm over all intercourse with him, even on the driest matters of business and detail ... Though not destitute of spirit, and though his physical courage was redundant rather than deficient, he had perhaps less pride and certainly far less vanity than any man of equal talents and acquirements whom I ever had an opportunity of observing ... In his capacity as leader of a party he was sometimes too readily offended at insignificant deviations, and disproportionately alarmed at the indiscretion of individuals. He was ... always striving to be more circumspect in conducting other men than is compatible with preserving any authority over them at all; and yet by a contradiction not uncommon in the caution which has its source in timidity, he was occasionally so enamoured of some crotchet or refinement of his own that he was hurried into courses hazardous and rash.[155]

Brougham, who detested his 'doctrine of self-distrust and stultification', later wrote:

He possessed sufficient industry to master any subject, and, until his health failed, to undergo any labour. His understanding was of that plain and solid description which wears well ... To any extraordinary quickness of apprehension he laid no claim; but he saw with perfect clearness, and if he did not take a very wide range, yet, within his appointed scope his ideas were strongly formed, and ... luminously expressed ... Everything refined he habitually rejected; partly as above his comprehension, partly as beneath his regard; and he was wont to regard the efforts of fancy still lower than the feats of subtlety ... A man undeniably of cool personal courage; a debater of as unquestioned boldness and vigour, he was timid in council; always saw the gloomy side of things; could scarcely ever be induced to look at any other aspect; and tormented both himself and others with endless doubts and difficulties ... It is probable, however, that this defect in his character as a politician had greatly increased as he grew older ... He was one of the surest ... speakers ... and his style ... seemed so easy and so natural to the man as to be always completely at his command ... He was wanting in decision and vigour ... until he rose, when a new man seemed to stand before you.[156]

Tierney's son wrote to Holland, 4 Nov. 1831:

His shrewdness and penetration were employed not in refining upon that which was plain in itself, but in stripping from truth, or rather from the *simplicity* of truth, all the colouring with which he found it disguised. Of all the men I ever knew he was perhaps the easiest to be amused, the most tolerant of a bore, and the best natured apologist for dullness and mediocrity in others ... [He was marked by] a total absence of all vanity and pretension.[157]

Mackintosh recalled him as 'so shrewd and droll – the words seemed made for him'.[158]

[1] The only biography to date is the inadequate one by H.K. Olphin (1934). [2] According to E. Baines, *Lancs.* (1824-5), ii. 585. [3] NLS mss 5319, f. 195; Grey mss, Tierney to Grey [28 Dec.]; Bessborough mss, same to Duncannon, 28 Dec. 1819. [4] See, e.g., *Life of Campbell*, i. 396; *Smith Letters*, i. 355; Add. 51667, Bedford to Lady Holland [16 Mar. 1821]. Mrs. Arbuthnot thought he was 'above 70' in August 1827 (*Arbuthnot Jnl.* ii. 135). [5] *Althorp Letters*, 101. [6] Grey mss, Tierney to Grey, 22 [23], 27 Feb. 1820. [7] Hants RO, Tierney mss 21c; Chatsworth mss; Add. 51571, Thanet to Holland [18 Mar. 1820]. [8] Add. 52444, f. 93. [9] Grey mss, Tierney to Grey, 17, 22 Mar., 5 Apr. 1820; *Arbuthnot Corresp.* 14. [10] BL, Morley mss, Granville to Morley, 4 Apr.; Grey mss, Tierney to Grey, 5 Apr. 1820. [11] Add. 51586. [12] Ibid. Tierney to Lady Holland [12], 19 Apr.; Bessborough mss, Grey to Duncannon, 9 Apr. 1820. [13] JRL, Bromley Davenport mss, Macdonald to Davenport, 24 Apr. [1820]. [14] Broughton, *Recollections*, ii. 126. [15] *The Times*, 28, 29 Apr., 2 May 1820. [16] Grey mss, Tierney to Grey, 18 May 1820. [17] *Althorp Letters*, 107; *Smith Letters*, i. 355. [18] Dorset RO D/BKL, Bankes jnl. 117 (15 May); Grey mss, Tierney to Grey, 18 May, Grey to Lady Grey, 20 May 1820; Add. 30123, f. 157. [19] Brougham mss, Brougham to Grey [1 June 1820]; Add. 52444, f. 122. [20] *Althorp Letters*, 109-10. [21] Grey mss, Tierney to Grey [29 Feb.], 5 Apr., 18 May 1820. [22] Bankes jnl. 118. [23] Grey mss, Tierney to Grey, 8, 10 June; Add. 51586, Tierney to Lady Holland [9 June 1820]. [24] Grey mss, Tierney to Grey, 12 June 1820 (two letters). [25] Ibid. [26] Add. 52444, ff. 192, 196. [27] Buckingham, *Mems. Geo. IV*, i. 53; *Countess Granville Letters*, i. 175-6. [28] Add. 51578, Morpeth to Holland, 25 Aug. [1820]. [29] Essex RO, Barrett Lennard mss D/DL C60, T.B to Sir T.B Lennard, 19 Sept. 1820. [30] Add. 51586. [31] *Creevey Pprs.* i. 327-8, 329, 330, 336; Add. 51579, Morpeth to Lady Holland, 19, 22 Oct. 1820; 56541, f. 84. [32] Add. 56541, f. 85. [33] *Hobhouse Diary*, 42; Add. 51679, Russell to Lady Holland [3 Dec. 1820]. [34] Bucks. RO, Fremantle mss D/FR/46/11/38. [35] *Geo. IV Letters*, ii. 878, 881; Grey mss, Tierney to Grey, 21, 24, 25 Nov., 7 Dec. 1820. [36] Grey mss, Tierney to Grey, 24 Nov., 7, 9, 13 Dec. 1820, 13 Jan. 1821. [37] *Fox Jnl.* 51, 54; *Creevey Pprs.* ii. 5. [38] Add. 30123, f. 233; 51586, Tierney to Lady Holland [28 Dec.]; Lonsdale mss, Ward to Lonsdale, 27 Dec. 1820. [39] *Fox Jnl.* 60; *Cockburn Letters*, 14-15; Chatsworth mss 6DD/GPI/486; Grey mss, Tierney to Grey, 10, 13 Jan. 1821. [40] HLRO, Hist. Coll. 379, Grey Bennet diary, 2. [41] Buckingham, i. 112. [42] *Colchester Diary*, iii. 201; *Creevey Pprs.* ii. 5; *Arbuthnot Jnl.* i. 66; Add. 38742, f. 171. [43] *Creevey's Life and Times*, 137. [44] *Smith Letters*, i. 374; Add. 43212, f. 180; Harrowby mss, Labouchere to Sandon, 12 Feb. 1821; *Pope of Holland House* ed. Lady Seymour, 234-5. [45] *The Times*, 20 Mar. 1821. [46] Ibid. 3 Mar. 1821. [47] Grey Bennet diary, 23. [48] Harrowby mss, Castlereagh to Harrowby, 8 Mar. 1821. [49] Lady Airlie, *Lady Palmerston and her Times*, i. 86; *Lady Palmerston Letters*, 74. [50] *Life of Campbell*, i. 396; *Colchester Diary*, iii. 212; *Von Neumann Diary*, i. 54; Hants RO, Carnarvon mss 75M91/E4/27. [51] Dorset RO, Bond mss D/BoH C16, Jekyyll to Bond, 20 Mar. 1821. [52] NLS acc. 10655, Abercromby's pol. memorandum. [53] Add. 51667, Bedford to Lady Holland, Friday [16 Mar.], Tuesday [June 1821]. [54] Grey Bennet diary, 120-1. [55] Ibid. 113. [56] Add. 51586, Tierney to Lady Holland,

11, 21 Sept., 7, 11, 13 Oct.; Grey mss, same to Grey, 3, 10, 31 Oct. 1821. [57] Grey mss, Tierney to Grey, 3 Oct., 11, 30 Dec. 1821, 23 Jan. 1823. [58] Add. 52445, f. 31; Buckingham, i. 282; *Cockburn Letters*, 41; Grey mss, Tierney to Grey, 23 Jan. 1822. [59] Add. 52445, f. 35; 56544, f. 61. [60] Grey mss, Tierney to Grey, 14 Feb. 1822. [61] *The Times*, 23 Feb. 1822; NLW, Coedymaen mss 621. [62] Bankes jnl. 134 [63] Add. 52445, ff. 66-67. [64] Buckingham, i. 294; Fremantle mss 46/10/20. [65] Bessborough mss, Brougham to Duncannon [15 Mar. 1822]. [66] Buckingham, i. 314; Coedymaen mss 633; Add. 51586, Tierney to Lady Holland 16 Apr. 1822. [67] *The Times*, 18 Apr. 1822. [68] *Arbuthnot Jnl.* i. 163; NLW ms 2794 D, Sir W. to H. Williams Wynn [15 Mar. 1822.] [69] Bessborough mss, Tierney to Duncannon, 14 Aug.; Add. 51586, same to Lady Holland, 23, 26 [30] Aug. [4], 22 Sept. 1822. [70] *Brougham and Early Friends*, iii. 46; Bessborough mss, Brougham to Duncannon [4 Sept. 1822]. [71] Add. 51584, Tierney to Holland, 21 Oct; 51586, same to Lady Holland, 6, 28 Oct., 31 Dec. 1822; Buckingham, i. 392. [72] Add. 51667, Bedford to Lady Holland [23 Feb. 1823]. [73] *The Times*, 4 Mar. 1823. [74] *Life of Campbell*, i. 416. [75] Northants. RO, Agar Ellis diary, 17 Apr. [1823]. [76] Add. 51586, Tierney to Lady Holland, 6 June 1823. [77] Blakiston, *Lord William Russell*, 101. [78] TNA 30/29/9/5/25. [79] Buckingham, ii. 75; *Arbuthnot Jnl.* i. 310-11. [80] *The Times*, 2 June 1824. [81] *Lady Holland to Son*, 27; Grey mss. [82] Grey mss, Tierney to Grey, 19, 31 Jan. 1825. [83] Cumbria RO, Howard mss D/HW8/48/6; Broughton, iii. 86; Agar Ellis diary, 11 Feb.; Bankes jnl. 153; Buckingham, ii. 211; *Arbuthnot Jnl.* i. 376. [84] Grey mss, Tierney to Grey, 17 Feb. 1825. [85] *Ibid.* same to same, 21 Feb. 1825; Buckingham, ii. 216. [86] Lonsdale mss, Long to Lonsdale, 23 Mar.; Buckingham, ii. 232, 239, 241; Fremantle mss 46/11/116. [87] Add. 51584, Tierney to Holland, 24 Sept., 13, 14 Oct.; 51586, same to Lady Holland, 24 Oct.; 51663, Bedford to Holland, 28 Oct. 1825; Carnarvon mss 824/8. [88] Add. 51586, Tierney to Lady Holland, 25 Nov. 2, 19 Dec. 1825, 16 Jan. 1826. [89] Fitzwilliam mss 124/8/1; Wellington mss WP1/850/9; *Greville Mems.* i. 158. [90] Add. 51584, Tierney to Holland, 23 Feb., 12, 24 Mar.; 51586, same to Lady Holland, 3 Mar. 1826; Wellington mss WP1/852/11. [91] *The Times*, 21 Mar. 1826. [92] Add. 51584, Tierney to Holland, 10 Apr. 1826; Broughton, iii. 129-31, 191. [93] Add. 51586, Tierney to Lady Holland, 28 Apr. 1826. [94] Add. 51584, Tierney to Holland, 4 May; 51663, Bedford to same, 9 May [1826]; *Russell Letters*, i. 52. [95] Add. 51668, Bedford to Lady Holland, 23 May; Nottingham Univ. Lib. Denison diary, 19 May [1826]. [96] Add. 51586, Tierney to Lady Holland, 2 Sept. 1826. [97] Add. 40389, f. 123. [98] Broughton, ii. 161. [99] Add. 51784, Holland to C.R. Fox, 17 Feb.; *Creevey Pprs.* iii. 106; Add. 51663, Bedford to Holland [18 Feb. 1827]. [100] Wellington mss WP1/885/6; *Geo. IV Letters*, iii. 1299; *Canning's Ministry*, 66; *Colchester Diaries*, iii. 475. [101] *Canning's Ministry*, 124; Add. 51584, Tierney to Holland, 12 [?13] Apr. [1827]. [102] *Canning's Ministry*, 150, 233; Wellington mss WP1/887/28; Bagot, *Canning and Friends*, ii. 395; Lonsdale mss, Lowther to Lonsdale, 24 Apr. 1827. [103] Add. 51584, Tierney to Holland [22 Apr. 1827]. [104] *Canning's Ministry*, 222, 234, 247; Add. 51586, Tierney to Holland, 24 Apr. [1827]. [105] *Canning's Ministry*, 254, 255, 259; Chatsworth mss 1469, 1477, 1478. [106] Cent. Kent. Stud. Stanhope mss U1590 C138/1, Strangford to Stanhope, 28 Apr. 1827. [107] Add. 51663, Bedford to Holland, 5 May [1827]. [108] Gurney diary, 1, 7, 16 May 1827; Bagot, ii. 397. [109] *Canning's Ministry*, 272, 297, 299, 305, 307-9; Tierney mss 15a, 15c, 43c; *Greville Mems.* i. 174-5; *Arbuthnot Jnl.* ii. 120. [110] *Creevey Pprs.* ii. 120; *Colchester Diary*, ii. 520. [111] Add. 52447, f. 87. [112] Denison diary, 7 Aug. [1827]. [113] Lady Airlie, i. 140. [114] *Croker Pprs.* i. 393. [115] Add. 51562, Brougham to Holland Aug.; Brougham mss, reply [13 Aug. 1827]. [116] *Palmerston-Sulivan Letters*, 194, 199; Ward, *Letters to 'Ivy'*, 328-9; *Croker Pprs.* i. 391-2; Add. 38750, f. 39; Lonsdale mss, Lowther to Lonsdale, 28 Aug. 1827. [117] Tierney mss 37c; Add. 51584, Tierney to Holland [28 Aug.]; 51586, same to Lady Holland, 22 Aug. 1827. [118] Add. 51586. [119] Add. 51584, Tierney to Holland, 1 [2] Sept.; 51586, to Lady Holland, 3 Sept.; Lansdowne mss, to Lansdowne, [1], 5 Sept.; Tierney mss 43b, 43d, 43f; *Greville Mems.* i. 187. [120] Add. 40340, f. 200; *Arbuthnot Jnl.* ii. 141; *Arbuthnot Corresp.* 89. [121] *Russell Letters*, i. 74. [122] Fitzwilliam

mss, Russell to Milton, 6 Sept. 1827; Add. 38750, ff. 280, 283, 286; *Russell Letters*, i. 76. [123] *Russell Letters*, ii. 104; Add. 51586, Tierney to Lady Holland [19 Sept. 1827]; Tierney mss 61a-e; E.A. Wasson, *Whig Renaissance*, 152. [124] *Arbuthnot Jnl.* ii. 146; Add. 51669, Bedford to Lady Holland, 26 Oct. [1827]. [125] Lansdowne mss, Holland to Lansdowne, 4 Nov.; Add 51586, Tierney to Lady Holland, 1, 8 Nov. [1827]. [126] Add. 51586, Tierney to Lady Holland, 15 Nov.; 51655, Mackintosh to same [19 Nov. 1827]. [127] NLS, Ellice mss, Grey to Ellice, 15, 16, 23, 27 Dec. 1827. [128] Tierney mss 4c, 66, 85b; Add. 38752, ff. 104, 164; 51663, Bedford to Lady Holland [21 Dec. 1827], 15 Jan. [1828]. [129] Wellington mss WP1/913/8; *Creevey Pprs.* ii. 141; *Croker Pprs.* i. 406; *Greville Mems.* i. 197; Wasson, 154. [129] Wellington mss WP1/914/22; 915/25; Southampton Univ. Lib. Broadlands mss BR 23AA/5/1; Tierney mss 85a. [130] Devon RO, Sidmouth mss, H. Addington to Sidmouth, 23 Jan.; Broadlands mss PP/GMC/26. [131] Tierney mss 85a. [132] Tierney mss 43g; Hatherton diary, 18 [Feb.]; *Greville Mems.* i. 206; Castle Howard mss, Abercromby to Carlisle [19 Feb. 1828]; Keele Univ. Lib. Sneyd mss SC12/86. [133] *Lady Holland to Son*, 79; Add. 51586, Tierney to Lady Holland, 30 Apr., 11, 16 May, 22 Aug. 5 Oct. [1828]; Hatherton mss, Warrender to Littleton, 31 Aug. 1828. [134] Wellington mss WP1/936/15; 939/13969/15, 36; 971/32; Tierney mss 2. [135] Duke Univ. Lib. Fazakerley mss, Ord to Fazakerley [Jan.]; Add. 51584, Tierney to Holland [3 Feb.]; 51586, same to Lady Holland [31 Jan. 1828]. [136] *Greville Mems.* i. 274. [137] Ibid. i. 292. [138] Ibid. i. 95, 298-9. [139] Add. 51669, Bedford to Lady Holland, 11 Aug.; 51584, Tierney to Holland, 27 Aug.; 51586, same to Lady Holland, 5, 8 Jan. [1829]. [140] Nottingham Univ. Lib. Ossington mss OsC 72. [141] Grey mss, Ellice to Grey [27 Jan.]; Add. 51785, Holland to C.R. Fox, 7 Feb.; *The Times*, 28, 29 Jan. 1830; *Gent Mag.* (1830), i. 270. [142] *Greville Mems.* i. 363. [143] PROB 6/206; Grey mss, Ellice to Grey [3 Feb.]; Add. 51785, Holland to C.R. Fox, 7 Feb. 1830. [144] *Ellenborough Diary*, ii. 177. [145] *Lieven-Grey Corresp.* i. 422-3. [146] *Countess Granville Letters*, ii. 57; Add. 51670, Bedford to Lady Holland [Jan.]; 51674, duchess of Bedford to Holland [4 Feb.]; 51680, Russell to Lady Holland, 26 Jan.; 51785, Holland to C.R. Fox, 7 Feb.; 52058, C.R. to H.E. Fox, 1 May 1830. [147] Add. 51575, Abercromby to Holland [28 Jan.]; 51578, Carlisle to same, 27 Jan.; 51596, Essex to same, 26 Jan. 1830. [148] Add. 51836, Milton to Althorp, 30 Jan. 1830; *Geo. IV Letters*, iii. 1575. [149] Add. 51584, Mrs. Tierney to Holland [Feb.]; 51574, Abercromby to same [Feb. 1830]; Tierney mss 75b. [150] Add. 51687, Lansdowne to Holland [12 Feb.]; 51670, Bedford to Lady Holland, 14 Feb. [1830]. [151] Wellington mss WP1/1121/38; 1122/65, 71; 1127/8; 1141/2; 1143/27, 37. [152] *Macaulay Letters*, ii. 12, 44, 90. [153] Warws. RO MI 247, Philips mems. i. 363. [154] Broughton, iv. 6. [155] Add. 51785, Holland to C.R. Fox, 7 Feb. 1830.; Holland, *Further Mems.* 265-7. [156] Add. 30115, f. 100; *Hist. Sketches* (1839), ii. 144-6, 152, 155. [157] Add. 51836. [158] *Mackintosh Mems.* ii. 475.

D.R.F.

TINDAL, Nicholas Conyngham (1776–1846), of 43 Bedford Square, Mdx.

WIGTOWN BURGHS	4 Mar. 1824–1826
HARWICH	1826–7 May 1827
CAMBRIDGE UNIVERSITY	11 May 1827–June 1829

b. 12 Dec. 1776, 1st s. of Robert Tindal, attorney, of Coval Hall, nr. Chelmsford, Essex and 1st w. Sarah, da. of John Pocock of Greenwich, Kent. *educ.* Chelmsford g.s.; Trinity Coll. Camb. 1795, BA 1799, fellow 1801-9, MA 1802; L. Inn 1795, called 1809. *m.* 2 Sept. 1809,

Merelina, da. of Capt. Thomas Symonds, RN, of Bury St. Edmunds, Suff., 3s. (1 *d.v.p.*) 1da. kntd. 27 Nov. 1826; *suc.* fa. 1833. *d.* 6 July 1846.

Auditor, Camb. Univ. 1811-25, counsel 1825-9; solicitor-gen. co. palatine of Durham 1823-6; solicitor-gen. Sept. 1826-June 1829; bencher, L. Inn 1826; l.c.j.c.p. 1829-*d.*; PC 10 June 1829; sjt.-at-law 1829; member, jud. cttee. of PC 1833.

Tindal was descended from the Rev. John Tindal (*d.* 1674), a native of Kent, who became rector of Beerferris, Devon. His eldest son was Matthew Tindal (1657-1733), the eminent deist and author of *Christianity as Old as the Creation* (1730). Matthew's nephew, the Rev. Nicholas Tindal (1687-1774), sometime vicar of Waltham, Essex, translated and continued Rapin's *History of England* and died as chaplain of Greenwich Hospital.[1] Of his three sons John, the eldest, was rector of Chelmsford, 1739-74; while James, the youngest, had an army career and was the father of the antiquary, the Rev. William Tindal (1756-1804), who committed suicide in the Tower of London, of which he was chaplain.[2] Nicholas's second son George Tindal (*d.* 1777) reached the rank of captain in the navy and acquired the property of Coval Hall, near Chelmsford. His eldest son Robert Tindal (*b.* ?1750), the father of this Member, practised for many years as an attorney in Chelmsford. His wife died in 1818, and two years later, aged about 70, he married Elizabeth Robinson of Chelmsford. He subsequently moved to Taunton[3] Three of his six sons, John Pocock, George and Charles, entered the navy: the two former died young on active service abroad in 1797 and 1805 respectively.[4] Robert, the youngest, became a military surgeon and died unmarried in Mexico in 1834; and Thomas (*d.* 1850), the last survivor, was a successful Aylesbury attorney.

According to some of his Chelmsford schoolfellows, Nicholas Conyngham Tindal gave early indications of 'those quick parts and that solid talent which afterwards marked his career'.[5] He was articled to his father before going to Cambridge, where he was academically successful and was elected a fellow of Trinity. He became a pupil of Sir John Richardson, and by 1805 was in practice as a special pleader below the bar at 3 King's Bench Walk, Inner Temple. He did well, being known as 'thoroughly learned', and briefly had Henry Brougham* among his pupils. In 1809 he married and decided to take his chance at the bar.[6] He went the northern circuit, where he was Brougham's friendly rival, and though he found 'very little fame as an advocate', he acquired extensive and lucrative business on the strength of 'his learning, his industry, and his high reasoning faculties'. His great erudition extended

to many legal by-ways. In 1818, for example, he successfully demonstrated that trial by battle, for which a client opted, was still a valid process; an Act (59 Geo. III, c. 46) was subsequently passed to abolish it.[7] In February 1818 his wife died, leaving him with four young children; and sometime afterwards his spinster sister-in-law Juliana Symonds became 'the lady who presides in my house', as he put it in 1827.[8] He was chosen by Brougham as one of the supporting counsel for Queen Caroline in 1820. (Had he not been so engaged, he would have been retained for the crown.) He gave, in Brougham's words, 'able and useful assistance'; but he was overshadowed by Brougham, John Copley* and Thomas Denman*, and did not enhance his reputation.[9]

At the end of 1823 Tindal, though neither a king's counsel nor a Member of Parliament, was one of a number of men considered by Lord Liverpool's ministry for the vacant office of solicitor-general. While his friend Goulburn, the Irish secretary, whom he had taught at Cambridge, thought him 'a man of talent and judgement', well suited to the position, he admitted to the home secretary Peel that Charles Wetherell*, the eventual choice, had a superior claim. Tindal was in any case handicapped by being, like Copley, the new attorney-general, a common lawyer, for lord chancellor Eldon was 'always very desirous' of having one of the law officers in his own court. In the more extensive reshuffle which would have occurred had Sir Thomas Plumer† been willing to retire as master of the rolls, Tindal would probably have become solicitor, with Wetherell as attorney.[10] As it was, ministers clearly wanted him in the House; and early in March 1824, when his London home was at 9 Brunswick Square, he was brought in for Wigtown Burghs on the interest of the 8th earl of Galloway, replacing a junior member of the government who had been given an audit office place. He did not prove to be a great asset as an orator. An obituarist noted:

We can say but little for his qualifications as a public speaker. His manner was cold, dry, and unimpressive; his political and historical knowledge displayed itself to small advantage; it bore upon few questions, and not even upon those with much power. One would have expected that his talents and learning as a lawyer must have often enabled him to enlighten the House on legal difficulties, yet he had not a popular mode of discussing even questions of law.[11]

Tindal voted for the usury laws repeal bill, 8 Apr. 1824. His maiden speech, in opposition to Brougham's condemnation of the trial and conviction of the Methodist missionary John Smith in Demerara, 11 June, was applauded with 'considerable cheering'. He divided for the Irish insurrection bill, 14 June 1824, and the Irish unlawful societies bill, 25 Feb. 1825. A defaulter, 28 Feb., he appeared and was excused the following day, when he voted against Catholic relief. He did so again, 21 Apr., 10 May, and voted against the Irish franchise bill, 26 Apr. He was in the ministerial majorities for the duke of Cumberland's grant, 30 May, 2, 6, 10 June. He credited the commissioners of inquiry into chancery administration with 'an honest, faithful and careful' investigation, 7 June 1825. He kept a low profile in the House in 1826, when he opposed George Lamb's bid to introduce a bill to allow defence counsel for persons charged with felonies to address the jury, 25 Apr: 'it would effect such an alteration in the tone, the temper, and the character of a criminal accusation, as could not fail to be mischievous to the prisoner'. He was a teller for the hostile majority. On 18 May 1826 he again defended the chancery commissioners, whose recommended reforms, to be taken up by government, 'would produce the most beneficial effects'.

At the general election of 1826 Tindal came in for the treasury borough of Harwich. On the circuit a month later he was the guest, with Tom Macaulay* and James Parke, of the Rev. Sydney Smith at Foston.[12] When Copley became master of the rolls in September and was succeeded as attorney-general by Wetherell, he assured Lord Liverpool that Tindal was 'the fittest person at the bar, to be made solicitor-general': not only was 'no man ... so universally respected in the profession' but he was expected to have 'considerable influence' over the mercurial Wetherell.[13] Tindal voted against Catholic relief, 6 Mar., and for the spring guns bill, 23 Mar. 1827. Named as a defaulter, 28 Mar., he failed to attend the following day and, to 'a great deal of merriment', was ordered to be taken into custody.[14] He announced his intention of proposing an additional clause to safeguard the interests of children and married women under the writ of right bill, 30 Mar., and defended the revenue commissioners' adverse report on the County Fire Office, 10 Apr. 1827, even though it 'contained a great deal of bran amongst the flour'. Wetherell refused to remain in office under Canning but Tindal, despite his hostility to Catholic relief, decided to stay. It was at first assumed that he would be promoted to attorney-general; but Canning was keen to have the Whig James Scarlett* and Tindal, 'with admirable humour and good taste', as the premier put it, consented to be passed over.[15] Copley's elevation to the woolsack as Lord Lyndhurst created a vacancy for Cambridge University. Tindal started for it, along with Goulburn,

who had resigned with the former ministers, and William Bankes, Member for the University from 1822 until his defeat in 1826. All were Trinity men and opposed to Catholic relief. When Goulburn withdrew shortly before the election Tindal, who had been criticized for giving only silent votes against Catholic claims, sought to counter the effects of Bankes's more rabid anti-Catholicism by issuing a circular declaring his 'decided and firm support' for 'the ascendancy of the Protestant church'. He secured a majority of 101 in a poll of 857 over the largely discredited Bankes, whose support came mostly from the rural clergy; he won Trinity by 191 votes to 78. He was left in no doubt, however, that he was expected in future 'zealously [to] oppose the dangerous experiment of granting political power to the Papists' with his voice as well as his vote.[16] He got leave to introduce a bill to prevent arrests for debt on mesne process for sums under £20, 23 Mar. 1827, when he declined to pledge support for George Bankes's proposed measure to exempt Catholics from a double land tax assessment. He voted with his ministerial colleagues against the disfranchisement of Penryn, 28 May. On 1 June he killed off Hume's frivolous arrests bill, which he said 'contained too sweeping a remedy, and was calculated to introduce an entirely new machinery into the system of law'. He carried his own bill through the House, grafting additional clauses onto it, 15, 22 June.[17] It became law, 2 July 1827 (7 & 8 Geo. IV, c. 71).

In late July 1827 Peel told the duke of Wellington that 'I rather think that the solicitor-general has no great desire to remain'.[18] He was in fact sounded about elevation to the bench as chief baron of the exchequer in the room of Sir William Alexander, who was in line for the Irish chancellorship. Brougham, whom Canning wished to bind to his ministry without having him as a dangerous rival in the Commons, had already turned it down. Tindal did likewise, indicating to Lyndhurst that 'he wishes, as the ultimate object of his ambition, the common pleas'. Canning, seeking a handy solution, commented to Lyndhurst:

> Tindal's note rather puzzles me. You are the best judge ... whether the stipulation which he asks, of succession hereafter to the common pleas, be a reasonable one. If it be so, and if Tindal takes the place of chief baron only *in transitu*, it is obvious that Brougham, by waiting that turn, will be ... only where he would be now: with both chief justiceships filled up against him. Is it not possible that this consideration might alter Brougham's views as to present acceptance? I presume Tindal would be satisfied to wait where he is for the common pleas. Indeed, from the tone of his note, I should think he would prefer doing so ... Is it not at least worthwhile to bring this

new state of the case under Brougham's contemplation? Could not Tindal be made useful in doing so?

While Lyndhurst was 'persuaded' that Tindal would 'do whatever we wish', he advised Canning, if he really wished Tindal to decline the office of chief baron, not to risk his accepting it by coupling it with 'the contingent promise of the common pleas'. Canning explained that he wished Brougham to be invited to reconsider 'on Tindal's refusal to take the exchequer without a promise of the common pleas hereafter, giving Tindal the promise of common pleas, if he chooses to wait for it as solicitor-general'. Brougham was not to be tempted, however, and Canning's death soon afterwards put an end to the business.[19] Tindal remained in office under Lord Goderich. There was continued speculation that he was to become chief baron; but in the event Alexander was passed over for the Irish seals in favour of Sir Anthony Hart, the vice-chancellor, whom Tindal was not professionally qualified to succeed, in order to avoid creating a vacancy in the solicitor-generalship which it would have been impossible to deny to Brougham.[20] During the ministerial crisis which brought down Goderich it was thought that Tindal would 'certainly' go out if Herries resigned from the exchequer.[21] On the formation of Wellington's ministry he acquiesced in Wetherell being reinstated as attorney-general over his head.[22]

Tindal did not resist Taylor's motion for information on chancery administration, 12 Feb., but he gave a silent vote against inquiry into delays, 24 Apr. 1828. He voted against repeal of the Test Acts, 26 Feb. Replying for government to Brougham's motion for a commission of inquiry into the common law, 29 Feb., he announced their intention to appoint separate commissions on that and the law of real property and repudiated many of Brougham's arguments. While he professed willingness to 'use the pruning knife' with 'unrelenting severity' on 'superfluous and unnecessary' excrescences, he declared his hostility to root and branch reform and warned that law could never be cheap. His ministerial colleague Croker was unimpressed with his speech, which he considered 'clear but feeble'.[23] He urged Graham to withdraw his customary tenure bill pending the law commissioners' investigations, 11 Mar.; he eventually had his way, 3 June. He made what he considered 'a fair offer' of concessions on the Catholic land tax to Bankes, who agreed to drop his bill, 18 Apr. He presented a petition against Catholic relief from the archdeacon and clergy of Ely, 30 Apr., and, mindful of the university's wishes, spoke against Burdett's motion, 8 May, before voting in the hostile minority, 12 May. He opposed amendments to

the offences against the person bill, 23 May, 6 June, endorsed the prayer of the Cambridge University petition calling for implementation of the 1823 resolutions for the amelioration of slavery, 3 June, and defended the archbishop of Canterbury's bill against Hume's attack, 16 June. He was a teller for the ministerial majorities in the subsequent divisions, as he was in that for the third reading of the Scottish and Irish banknotes bill, 27 June, after explaining its objects. He was in the government majority on the ordnance estimates, 4 July. He carried a bill to enable the holders of lay and clerical benefices to provide for their families, which became law, 28 July 1828 (9 Geo. IV, c. 94).

In late October 1828 Wellington, raising the possibility of persuading or even forcing Wetherell to become a puisne baron of exchequer and replacing him with Scarlett, whom the king wanted as attorney-general, wondered whether Tindal could fairly be passed over again. He was inclined to think not, even though Lyndhurst, anxious for the change, thought that Tindal would 'have no feeling upon the subject'. Lord Bathurst, lord president of the council, also felt that in the unlikely event of Wetherell's agreeing to move, Tindal must have first refusal on succeeding him, if only because of 'the strong Protestant feeling which exists at present'. Wellington accepted this view and informed Lyndhurst accordingly; but in the event no change occurred.[24] Peel thought Tindal might resign over the government's decision to implement Catholic emancipation, but Lord Ellenborough, president of the board of control, did not doubt his loyalty.[25] He announced his pragmatic change of mind to the House, 6 Feb. 1829, when he presented a petition against relief from the dean and chapter of Chester:

> With these sentiments my own fully concur; and if I saw any probability of success in resisting these claims, I should still hold myself bound to oppose them. But as the tranquillity of Ireland, and in my judgement, the security of the whole empire call upon the legislature to receive with deliberate attention the claims made upon it, I do think I shall better discharge ... [my] duty ... by bestowing whatever time and labour I can on the framing, devising and perfecting of such full and sufficient securities as shall establish permanently and inviolably the Protestant ascendancy in this country, than by devoting myself to a single and fruitless opposition to all concession.

He presented an Ely petition for suppression of the Catholic Association and against emancipation, 13 Feb. Later that day and on 16 Feb. he explained and carried amendments to the suppression bill, which he had helped to draft under Peel's supervision, along with the relief and franchise bills.[26] He attended cabinet meetings to discuss the details of the legislation, and on one occasion, according to Ellenborough, mistook 'Regulars of the church of Rome' for 'Regulars of the army': 'and so *solvuntur risu tabulae*'. Ellenborough did 'not think much' of Tindal, whom he judged on the strength of these performances to be 'evidently not fit to be made attorney'. He also recorded a 'curious scene' which occurred when Tindal, leaving the House in the early hours of 5 Mar., panicked on learning that there was 'a hitch' with the king: 'He was quite astonished and shocked, and cried out, "O Lord, I am committed, I am pledged. We shall all fall together!"'[27] He voted for relief, 6 Mar.; explained and defended clauses of the bill, 23 and 24 Mar.; joined in attempts to persuade Wetherell that his fears that Catholics would be able to interfere in the running of Protestant charter schools were groundless, 27 Mar., and before voting for the third reading of the relief bill, 30 Mar., argued that unless it was implemented, 'the Protestant church in Ireland will fall, and the Protestant church in England will be in danger'. His bill to introduce fixed dates for law terms, 13 May, got no further than its second reading. He replied to O'Connell's appeal to be allowed to take his seat for Clare unimpeded, 18 May, contending that he was not entitled to do so without swearing the oath of supremacy; he was a government teller in the division. He had more to say on the subject, 19, 21 May 1829, when he explained the government's insistence that O'Connell must seek re-election. There had been speculation in Cambridge that Tindal would replace Wetherell, who was dismissed for his violent opposition to emancipation.[28] In fact, Wellington was now determined to 'get rid of Tindal' and make Scarlett attorney-general; and the only question was that of how he was to be paid off. An attempt to open the rolls for him by persuading Sir John Leach† to retire was unsuccessful; but in late May 1829 Wellington, with the aid of the king, got Sir William Best† to vacate the chief justiceship of the common pleas for him.[29]

It was as lord chief justice that Tindal, who presented a marked contrast to his irascible and frequently partial predecessor, did full justice to his talents. He was, in the words of William Ballantine, 'a most painstaking judge':

He was certainly not a man of startling characteristics, but upon the bench presented a singularly calm and equable appearance. I never saw him yield to irritability, or exhibit impatience ... He was made for the position that he filled, and sound law and substantial justice were sure, as far as human power could prevail, to be administered under his presidency.[30]

Serjeant Robinson reckoned that 'there never was a more considerate, humane, and intelligent judge', and that 'while few judges bore a higher reputation for a thorough knowledge of the law, no one could show greater kindness, courtesy and benignity than he invariably displayed'.[31] His professional decorum concealed 'a vein of grave, sly humour'.[32] Tindal's father died at Bath, 'in his 83rd year', 8 Jan. 1833. By his will, dated 13 Mar. 1824, he authorized the sale of his real estate in Essex, Huntingdonshire and Oxfordshire, which included a six-acre pasture at Chelmsford, for the benefit of Tindal, in accordance with the terms of an indenture of 1816. Tindal also became entitled to whatever remained of an £8,000 trust fund created by the sale of property at Great Haddow, Essex. As it was, the personal estate was sworn under a paltry £450.[33] Tindal added a residence on Hampstead Heath to his town house in Bedford Square.[34] In 1842, he lost his eldest son Nicholas, vicar of Sandhurst, Gloucestershire, at the age of 32. He himself died in harness in July 1846 at Folkestone, where he had gone on medical advice after recently being 'seized with paralysis of the left leg'. By his will, dated 2 Sept. 1842 (just after the death of his son), he left freeholds at Chelmsford to his elder surviving son, Louis Symonds Tindal, a naval officer. He devised a freehold windmill and cottage at Chelmsford and a close at Aylesbury to his other son, Charles John Tindal, a barrister, who was to die, aged about 37, in New South Wales in 1853. He gave his daughter Merelina £2,000, having 'already amply provided for her' on her marriage to James Whatman Bosanquet, a London banker. His remaining property was to be converted into money to provide an annuity of £200 for his sister-in-law, who was still living under his roof, and to create a trust fund of £8,000 for the benefit of his late son's widow and her two infant daughters. The residue of his estate was equally divided between his sons.[35]

[1] *Oxford DNB*. [2] Ibid. [3] *Gent. Mag.* (1818), i. 641; (1820), ii. 634; PROB 11/1813/191. [4] *Gent. Mag.* (1805), ii. 877. [5] Ibid. (1846), ii. 199. [6] *Oxford DNB*; *Gent. Mag.* (1846), ii. 199; E. Foss, *Judges of Eng.* ix. 283. [7] Brougham mss, Tindal to Brougham, 24 Sept. 1812; *Creevey's Life and Times*, 69-70; *Gent. Mag.* (1846), ii. 199; Foss, ix. 283; C. New, *Brougham*, 248. [8] *Gent. Mag.* (1818), i. 468; Add. 42584, f. 177; PROB 11/2039/546. [9] Brougham, *Life and Times*, ii. 380-1; *Geo. IV Letters*, ii. 833; *Creevey Pprs.* i. 328; *Gent. Mag.* (1846), ii. 199; Foss, ix. 284. [10] Add. 40329, ff. 229, 247; 40359, f. 147; *Hobhouse Diary*, 108. [11] *Gent. Mag.* (1846), ii. 199-200. [12] *Macaulay Letters*, i. 215. [13] Add. 40305, f. 217; *Geo. IV Letters*, iii. 1250. [14] *The Times*, 30 Mar. 1827. [15] *Canning's Ministry*, 133, 150, 200, 204; Arnould, *Denman*, i. 206; Lansdowne mss, Twiss to Lansdowne, 3 Aug. 1844. [16] *Cambridge Chron.* 20, 27 Apr., 4, 11, 18, 25 May 1827. [17] *The Times*, 16, 19, 23 June 1827. [18] *Wellington Despatches*, iv. 65. [19] *Canning's Ministry*, 358, 361, 362, 364. [20] *Arbuthnot Jnl.* ii. 143; Devon RO, Sidmouth mss, Stowell to Sidmouth, 24 Oct. 1827; *Hobhouse Diary*, 142-3; NLW, Coedymaen mss 204; Durham CRO,

Londonderry mss D/Lo/C83 (10) (1). [21] *Croker Pprs.* i. 400; Grey mss, Ellice to Grey [Jan. 1828]. [22] Add. 40307. f. 23; Arnould, i. 206. [23] *Croker Pprs.* i. 407-8. [24] *Wellington Despatches*, v. 179-80, 189-90, 203-5, 217-18. [25] *Ellenborough Diary*, i. 321. [26] *Peel Mems.* i. 351. [27] *Ellenborough Diary*, i. 370, 374, 376, 378. [28] *Cambridge Chron.* 13 Mar., 15 May 1829. [29] *Colchester Diary*, iii. 613; *Ellenborough Diary*, ii. 29; *Arbuthnot Jnl.* ii. 269, 276, 277. [30] W. Ballantine, *Some Experiences of a Barrister's Life*, i. 143, 244-5. [31] B.C. Robinson, *Bench and Bar* (1891), 130. [32] Ibid. 132; Arnould, ii. 27. [33] *Gent. Mag.* (1833), i. 93; PROB 11/1813/191; IR26/1335/88. [34] Add. 34589, f. 231. [35] *Gent. Mag.* (1846), ii. 200, 660; PROB 11/2039/546; IR26/1753/530.

D.R.F.

TOLLEMACHE, Felix Thomas (1796–1843), of 1 Hyde Park Place, Mdx.

ILCHESTER	22 Feb. 1827–1830

b. 16 Feb. 1796, 2nd s. of Sir William Manners[†] (afterwards Talmash or Tollemache), 1st bt. (*d.* 1833), of Buckminster Park, Leics. and Catherine Rebecca, da. of Francis Grey of Lehena, co. Cork; bro. of Frederick James Tollemache* and Lionel William John Tollemache*. *educ.* Harrow 1805-10. *m.* (1) 1 Oct. 1825, Sarah (*d.* 1831), da. of James Gray of Ballincar, King's Co., 1s. 1da.; (2) 27 Apr. 1833, Frances Julia, da. of Henry Peters of Betchworth Castle, Surr., *s.p. d.* 5 Oct. 1843. Ensign and lt. 1 Ft. Gds. 1815, half-pay, 1819, ret. 1835.

Tollemache, who was described as 'one of the handsomest young men in the kingdom',[1] stood unsuccessfully in 1818 and 1820 at Grantham, where a hostile coalition had been established against his father's interest. On the latter occasion his brother Hugh acted for him in his absence, which allegedly arose from his elopement to France with an 'artful, profligate, infamous married woman'.[2] In 1826 he and his elder brother Lionel were defeated at Ilchester, where their father also had influence, but they were subsequently seated on petition.[3]

He is not known to have spoken in debate, and there is some difficulty in differentiating his votes from those of his brothers, particularly Frederick, Member for Grantham. He may have been the 'H. Talmash' listed as voting to go into committee on the Clarence annuity bill, 16 Mar., and it was possibly he rather than Frederick who voted to do so on the spring guns bill, 23 Mar., and against the corn bill, 2 Apr. 1827. It was most probably he who presented a Hampstead petition complaining of the burden imposed by the maintenance of itinerant Irish paupers, 29 June 1827.[4] He may have voted against repeal of the Test Acts, 26 Feb. 1828, although it seems more likely that this was Frederick. One of them divided with the Wellington ministry against inquiry into delays in chancery, 24 Apr. He was

probably the 'F. Talmash' in the favourable majority rather than the minority list on Catholic claims, 12 May, as Frederick's hostility at this time is known from later evidence. He may have voted for the usury laws amendment bill, 19 June, while one of the brothers voted against reducing the salary of the lieutenant-general of the ordnance, 4 July, and for the corporate funds bill, 10 July, and the customs bill, 14 July 1828. In February 1829 Planta, the patronage secretary, expected him to vote 'with government' for Catholic emancipation. He was named as a defaulter, 5 Mar., but may have attended to vote for emancipation, 6 Mar., and certainly divided for the relief bill, 30 Mar. He may have voted to issue a new writ for East Retford, 2 June 1829, and against transferring its seats to Birmingham, 11 Feb. 1830. He may have divided for Jewish emancipation, 5 Apr., 17 May, and to abolish the death penalty for forgery, 24 May; he definitely did so on the latter, 7 June 1830.

At the general election of 1830 he offered again at Ilchester with his younger brother Algernon, but they were defeated by the candidates standing on Lord Cleveland's interest. On being nominated, he had repudiated the accusation circulating in the town that 'his vote on the Catholic question had not been given on principle', maintaining that 'he had voted on that question independently and contrary to the wishes of his family'.[5] A petition against the result was rejected. It appears that at the 1831 general election he and Frederick canvassed at Ilchester, hoping to capitalize on discontent with the borough's imminent disfranchisement under the Grey ministry's reform bill, but they withdrew before polling.[6] Instead, he and Algernon offered at Grantham, but they were unsuccessful and he came bottom of the poll.[7] On his father's death in 1833 he received a quarter-share of the proceeds of the sale of real property in Surrey and Suffolk, but a separate bequest of £10,000 had already 'been raised' in his father's lifetime.[8] He inherited only a gold snuffbox from his grandmother, Countess Dysart, in 1840.[9] Experiencing financial difficulties, he turned to his eldest brother, now earl of Dysart, for a loan of £10,000, which would be of great assistance to 'a small fish like myself'.[10] When he died in Oct. 1843 his mother hoped that he would be 'rejoicing in the change. No longer languishing under pain and sickness; no longer molested by the harsh and overbearing temper of his unfeeling wife'.[11] He left his real and personal property in trust for the benefit of his children, William and Caroline, and an annuity of £150 to his wife, in addition to the provisions made under their marriage settlement; she was also given the option of purchasing his property at Tongs Wood, Kent, for £12,000.[12]

[1] *Lincoln, Rutland and Stamford Mercury*, 12 June 1818. [2] *The Times*, 15 Feb.; *Drakard's Stamford News*, 3, 24 Mar. 1820. [3] *Western Flying Post*, 12 June 1826; *The Times*, 23 Feb. 1827. [4] *The Times*, 30 June 1827. A note by his fa.'s agent, 9 July 1829, gives an address for him at Westend, near Hampstead (Tollemache (Dysart) mss 71). [5] *Sherborne Jnl.* 5 Aug. 1830. [6] Tollemache mss 72. [7] *Lincoln, Rutland and Stamford Mercury*, 29 Apr. 1831. [8] PROB 11/1815/257. [9] PROB 11/1940/94. [10] Tollemache mss 3587. [11] Ibid. 3592. [12] PROB 8/236; 11/1990/889.

T.A.J.

TOLLEMACHE, Frederick James (1804–1888), of Ham House, Surr. and 1 Hyde Park Place, Mdx.

GRANTHAM	1826–1830
GRANTHAM	1837–1852
GRANTHAM	1857–1865
GRANTHAM	1868–1874

b. 16 Apr. 1804, 5th s. of Sir William Manners[†] (afterwards Talmash), 1st bt., Lord Huntingtower (*d.* 1833), of Buckminster Park, Leics. and Catherine Rebecca, da. of Francis Grey of Lehena, co. Cork; bro. of Felix Thomas Tollemache* and Lionel William John Tollemache*. *educ.* Harrow 1811. *m.* (1) 26 Aug. 1831, Sarah (*d.* 3 Jan. 1835), da. of Robert Bomford of Rahinstown, co. Meath, 1 da. *d.v.p.*; (2) 4 Sept. 1847, Isabella, da. of George Gordon Forbes of Ham, 1 da. *d.* 2 July 1888.

One of Lord Huntingtower's four sons who sought a seat at Grantham in this period, Tollemache, 'a very tall and uncommonly handsome young man', was the only one to succeed.[1] His father, who also had influence at Ilchester, headed the Blue party at Grantham, but had been unable to secure a seat there since 1812, as a result of the predominance of the Red party, headed by Lord Brownlow, and the determined opposition of some independent freemen. Shortly before the 1826 general election, one of the sitting Members, Sir Montague Cholmeley, announced his retirement, creating an unexpected opening, for which Tollemache came forward with good prospects of success, 5 June, it being noted by the press that the feeling of the freemen towards his family was now 'so different ... to that which some time ago existed in the town'. At the nomination Tollemache described himself as 'an enemy to Catholic emancipation' and 'hoped that no further pledge of political conduct would be required'. After a severe four-day contest against two other Tories he was returned in first place.[2]

He presented a Lincolnshire petition for agricultural relief, 20 Feb. 1827.[3] Thereafter, his parliamentary record is difficult to distinguish from that of his brothers (especially Felix), who were seated for Ilchester on petition, 22 Feb. He may have voted for the spring

guns bill, 23 Mar. Either he or Felix divided against the corn bill, 2 Apr. He voted against the disfranchisement of Penryn, 28 May, and was probably the Tollemache who divided for the election expenses bill that day, and the grant to improve Canadian water communications, 12 June 1827, against repeal of the Test Acts, 26 Feb., and inquiry into chancery delays, 24 Apr. 1828. He voted against Catholic claims, 12 May. Either he or Felix voted for the usury laws amendment bill, 19 June, and one of the brothers voted with ministers against ordnance reductions, 4 July, amendments to the corporate funds bill, 10 July, and for the customs bill, 14 July 1828. In early February 1829 Planta, the Wellington ministry's patronage secretary, predicted that he would vote 'with government' for their concession of Catholic emancipation, and he was probably the 'F. Tollemache' who divided thus, 6, 30 Mar. On 26 Mar. he presented a Newton petition against Catholic claims, but noted that when it was signed the government's proposals were not known. 'If they had been', he declared

> they would have petitioned not against them, but in their favour. For my own part I have twice voted against Catholic claims, but I have since felt it right to come to a different conclusion, and shall accordingly now give a different vote on the question, as I consider that the fullest securities are given for the Protestant establishment by the disfranchisement of the 40s. freeholders ... By that wholesome measure, the priests and the Catholic Association are deprived of that tremendous power which for some time past they have exercised over the population of Ireland.

Either he or Felix divided for the issue of a new writ for East Retford, 2 June 1829, and against the transfer of its seats to Birmingham, 11 Feb. 1830. One of them voted against Jewish emancipation, 5 Apr., 17 May, and for abolition of the death penalty for forgery, 24 May, 7 June 1830.

At the 1830 general election Tollemache belatedly offered again for Grantham, amid reports that none of Lord Huntingtower's sons was 'desirous of being in Parliament', and having told an enquiring London meeting of Grantham electors that he 'did not know who his father should choose to put up'. Attacked by *Drakard's Stamford News* for his failure to support reform, retrenchment and reduced taxation, on the hustings he defended his parliamentary record and promised to perform his duties 'satisfactorily' if re-elected. After a four-day contest he was defeated in third place, owing, it was alleged, not to 'any personal feelings' towards him but to his father's 'neglect' and 'oppressive habits'.[4] A petition against the return failed and an attempt by his brothers to recapture the borough in 1831 was unsuccessful, but in 1832 his brother Algernon headed the poll as a Conservative. On the latter's retirement in 1837 Tollemache came in, after a contest, as a 'moderate Conservative'. He lost the seat in 1852, by when he had moved into the ranks of the Liberals, but was returned again in 1857, defeated in 1865, re-elected in 1868 and retired in 1874.[5] He died at Ham House, which he shared with Algernon, in July 1888.[6] The bulk of his estate was divided equally between Algernon and his son-in-law Charles Douglas Richard Hanbury Tracy, 4th Baron Sudeley.

[1] *Drakard's Stamford News*, 16 June 1826. [2] Ibid.; *Grantham Pollbook* (Storr, 1826), *passim*.; [3] *The Times*, 21 Feb. 1827. [4] Lincs. AO, Ancaster mss xiii/B/5x, 5y; *Drakard's Stamford News*, 2 July; *Lincoln, Rutland and Stamford Mercury*, 16 July 1830; *Grantham Pollbook* (Storr, 1830), *passim*. [5] *Dod's Parl. Companion* (1847), 247; (1852), 290; (1869), 307. [6] E.D.H. Tollemache, *Tollemaches of Helmingham and Ham*, 127.

M.P.J.C./P.J.S.

TOLLEMACHE, Lionel William John (1794–1878), of 1 Hyde Park Place, Mdx.

ILCHESTER 22 Feb. 1827–1830

b. 18 Nov. 1794, 1st s. of Sir William Manners[†] (afterwards Talmash or Tollemache), 1st bt., and Catherine Rebecca, da. of Francis Grey of Lehena, co. Cork; bro. of Felix Thomas Tollemache* and Frederick James Tollemache*. *educ.* Harrow 1805-10. *m.* 23 Sept. 1819, his cos. Maria Elizabeth, da. of Sweeney Toone of Keston Lodge, Kent, 1s. *d.v.p. styled* Lord Huntingtower 1833-40. *suc.* fa. as 2nd bt. 11 Mar. 1833; grandmo. Louisa Tollemache as 8th earl of Dysart [S] 22 Sept. 1840. *d.* 23 Sept. 1878.

Tollemache, who was 'strikingly handsome as a young man',[1] stood unsuccessfully in 1818 and 1820 at Ilchester, where his father's control had been broken by the Whig Lord Darlington. He was similarly unfortunate in contesting the by-election at Grantham, 21 July 1820, which arose from a petition after the general election when his brother Felix had been the defeated candidate.[2] In 1826 he and Felix were defeated at Ilchester but they were subsequently seated on petition.[3]

He was a very inactive Member, who is not known to have spoken in debate, and few votes can definitely be attributed to him rather than his brothers. The 'J. Talmash' whose name appeared in several division lists was more likely to have been Frederick James. He was presumably the 'B.L. Talmash' who voted to go into committee on the Clarence annuity bill, 16 Mar. 1827. He voted with the duke of Wellington's ministry against inquiry into delays in chancery, 24 Apr. 1828. He divided against Catholic claims, 12 May. One of the brothers voted against reducing the salary of the lieutenant-general of the ordnance, 4 July, and for the corporate funds bill, 10 July, and the customs bill, 14 July 1828. In February 1829 Planta, the patronage secretary, predicted that he would side 'with government' on Catholic emancipation, and he apparently voted for the third reading of the relief bill, 30 Mar., although according to the *Mirror of Parliament* he paired against the second reading, 18 Mar. 1829, and for the third. He may have divided against Jewish emancipation, 5 Apr., and to abolish the death penalty for forgery, 24 May, but he definitely voted against the Galway franchise bill, 25 May 1830.

He retired from Parliament at the 1830 dissolution. In 1833 he succeeded to his father's baronetcy and landed estates in Lincolnshire, Leicestershire and Somerset.[4] On his grandmother's death in 1840 he succeeded to the earldom of Dysart and inherited her estate in Surrey.[5] He had declined the duke of Rutland's offer in 1836 to put his name forward as a justice of the peace for Leicestershire, explaining that 'I lead so retired a life' that 'I fear I should on no occasions be induced to devote any of my time to magisterial duties – indeed nothing short of civil commotion would induce me to take a different course'.[6] In his later years he gained a reputation as a miser and a hermit, and finally 'he would see no one', confining himself to one room of his London residence, where 'his meals were handed to him through a trapdoor'.[7] He died in September 1878 and was succeeded by his grandson, William Tollemache (1859-1935).

[1] E. Tollemache, *Tollemaches of Helmingham and Ham*, 128. [2] *Western Flying Post*, 13 Mar.; *Drakard's Stamford News*, 21 July 1820. [3] *Western Flying Post*, 12 June 1826; *The Times*, 23 Feb. 1827. [4] The will was sworn under £40,000 (PROB 11/1815/257; IR26/1323/173). [5] The will was sworn under £140,000, but the residuary legatee was his younger bro. Algernon (PROB 8/234/; 11/1940/94). [6] Tollemache (Dysart) mss 3571. [7] Tollemache, 128.

T.A.J.

TOMES, John (1760–1844), of Jury Street, Warwick, Warws.

WARWICK 11 Feb. 1826–1832

bap. 28 Mar. 1760, 1st s. of John Tomes, innholder of Southam, and w. Jane. *m.* bef. 1785, Ann, 2s. *d.v.p.* 3da. (2 *d.v.p.*). *d.* 31 Jan. 1844.

Tomes, who frequently testified to his humble origins when addressing his constituents, was born in the small Warwickshire town of Southam (six miles south-east of Leamington), where the family had settled by the sixteenth century and engaged in the victualling and agricultural trades.[1] Little is known of his early life. His father, the lessee in 1761 of the *Lord Craven Arms* and 195 acres, was also a local mortgagor and had made substantial additions to his holdings before Tomes, who was also a lifelong dealer and speculator in property, took a house in Warwick in 1783.[2] He had by then qualified as an attorney and he soon established himself among the leaders of the Warwick reform or independent party. He supported the London banker Robert Ladbroke[†] at the 1784 election, extended his legal practice and became a partner in 1791 in the Whig banking firm of Dawes, Tomes and Russell of New Street (afterwards Tomes, Russell and Tomes), drawing on Ladbroke and Company. He was also in 1805 the joint-proprietor of a navigation mill at Emscote.[3] He was the agent in 1792 for Robert Knight*, the challenger to Lord Warwick's Castle interest, addressed borough and county meetings in 1797, 1815, and 1816 to protest against high wartime taxation and successfully promoted the return for Warwick from 1802 of the East India Company director Charles Mills.[4] Already well known as a sponsor of the races, improvement bills and the committee for the poor, he had turned down a requisition to contest Warwick in 1818, when Mills's support for Lord Liverpool's administration was resented, and presided at the 1820 election dinner in Mills's absence.[5] He was a spokesman for the Whig Sir Francis Lawley* at the 1820 Warwickshire by-election and a requisitionist and speaker at meetings in support of Queen Caroline.[6] Anticipating a dissolution, and with no 'moderate' forthcoming, he canvassed and declared his candidature as Mills's replacement in September 1825 and easily defeated his ministerialist opponent George Winn* when Mill's death necessitated a by-election in February 1826. The 'No Popery' cry was raised against him, and on the hustings he was forced to defend his low birth and membership in 1819-20 of the Warwick Union for Civil and Religious Liberty.[7]

Like his acquaintance Thomas Attwood subsequently, Tomes found his strong Midland accent a handicap in the House, where he made little mark. He is not known to have spoken in debate, presented petitions or served on major committees, but his voting record and the testimony of his partisans, the Unitarian William Field and the reforming cleric Arthur Savage Wade, who monitored his parliamentary conduct, indicates that he attended the House

regularly.[8] He voted for inquiry into the silk trade, 24 Feb., in condemnation of the Jamaican slave trials, 2 Mar., for reductions in military expenditure 6, 7 Mar., and for parliamentary reform, 27 Apr. 1826. An attempt to substitute Chandos Leigh of Stoneleigh for Tomes foundered and he and Greville were unopposed at the general election in June.[9] Returning to Westminster in February 1827,[10] Tomes voted for Catholic relief, 6 Mar., and in the minorities for inquiry into Leicester corporation, 15 Mar., and the Lisburn Orange magistrates, 29 Mar. He was for postponing the supply debates during the ministerial uncertainty following Lord Liverpool's stroke, 30 Mar., and inquiry into the Irish miscellaneous estimates, 5 Apr. The Warwick independents celebrated obtaining a mandamus against the corporation with a dinner in his honour, 1 May, at which he praised the king for appointing the pro-Catholic Canning as premier, expressed regret at ministers' failure to introduce measures of genuine retrenchment, and promised to 'continue to oppose the lavish expenditure of public money'.[11] His stewardship of the September races was interrupted by the death of his wife, who was eulogized in an obituary in the *Warwick Advertiser*, 8 Sept. 1827. Tomes voted to repeal the Test Acts, 26 Feb., against sluicing the franchise at East Retford, 21 Mar., and for Catholic relief, 12 May 1828. As expected, he divided for Catholic emancipation, 6, 30 Mar. 1829. He voted to transfer East Retford's seats to Birmingham, 5 Mar., and for inquiry into taxation, 29 Mar., and divided fairly steadily with the revived Whig opposition until 7 June 1830. He was in Daniel O'Connell's minority of 12 for information on the Doneraile conspiracy, 12 May. He held aloof from the activities of the Birmingham Political Union that preoccupied his son-in-law William Collins in July 1830, and his return at the general election, when he and his sponsors made retrenchment and reform the main issues, was unopposed.[12]

The Wellington administration naturally listed Tomes among their 'foes' and he divided against them on the civil list when they were brought down, 15 Nov. 1830. He encouraged the adoption of reform petitions in Warwick and the county and voted for the Grey ministry's reform bill at its second reading, 22 Mar. 1831. Prompted by the campaign to bring in Knight's son-in-law Edward Bolton King for Warwick as a reformer, he canvassed personally during the Easter recess and issued addresses emphasizing his consistent conduct and the support for the king and his ministers for reform. He divided against Gascoyne's wrecking amendment, 19 Apr.[13] He topped the Warwick poll after a bitter and violent contest at the ensuing general election, when King, with whom he denied coalescing, was in second place. He paid tribute on the hustings to those who had defied the Castle by electing him and called again for reform.[14] Tomes voted for the reintroduced reform bill at its second reading, 6 July 1831, and gave it generally steady support in committee. His wayward votes against the Saltash disfranchisement that ministers no longer pressed, 26 July, and the division of counties, 11 Aug., and for the enfranchisement of £50 tenants-at-will, 18 Aug., were identical to King's, and the last two were attuned to local interests. He voted to disfranchise Aldborough, 14 Sept.[15] He returned briefly to Warwick for the coronation celebrations, and divided for the reform bill's third reading, 19 Sept., and passage, 21 Sept., the second reading of the Scottish bill, 23 Sept., and Lord Ebrington's confidence motion, 10 Oct. 1831. On 22 Oct. he wrote to thank his constituents for expressing confidence in his conduct and petitioning in protest at the bill's Lords' defeat, and he was fêted by them at the mayor's feast, 1 Nov.[16] He voted for the revised reform bill at its second reading, 17 Dec. 1831, steadily for its details, and for its third reading, 22 Mar. 1832. Summoned by Lord Althorp, he left Warwick by chaise, 8 May, and voted for the address calling on the king to appoint only ministers who would carry the bill unimpaired, 10 May.[17] He divided for the second reading of the Irish reform bill, 21 May, and against a Conservative amendment to the Scottish bill, 1 June, but was in the minorities for extending the Irish freeholder franchise, 18 June, and against making all Irish borough voters liable to pay municipal taxes, 29 June. He voted to change the boundary bill's provisions for Stamford, 22 June. He did not vote when party loyalties were tested on the Russian-Dutch loan in January and July, but he divided with government on Portugal, 9 Feb., and the navy civil departments bill, 6 Apr. 1832. He voted with the radicals for inquiry into the Deacles' case, 27 Sept. 1831, and Peterloo, 15 Mar. 1832, and for reductions in civil service expenditure, 18 July 1831, and the Irish registrar's salary, 9 Apr. 1832. As requested by Leamington Political Society, he voted for a select committee on slavery, 24 May, and provision for the Irish poor, 19 June.[18] A coroner for over 30 years, he voted to make inquests public, 20 June 1832.

Making his long residence and support for retrenchment, reform and the abolition of slavery the cornerstones of his campaign, Tomes commenced canvassing at the Warwick reform dinner of 30 June 1832 and was dismayed to be defeated at the general election through the chicanery of the earl of Warwick.[19] He did not stand for Parliament again. He transferred his banking assets to Henry Jephson and Collins as trustees of the Warwick and Leamington Bank in 1834, but he remained a co-partner of the attorney and dealer Charles Handley, and retained investments in local businesses and utilities. He died at his house in Jury Street in January 1844, predeceased by his brother Edward (1771-1837), a prosperous Southam farmer, and his son Richard (1790-1838), with whom he held many properties in common.[20] His obituarist noted Tomes's continued popularity despite a recent downturn in his commercial interests and recalled the opinion of Samuel Parr twenty years previously, who in 'Mr. Tomes of Warwick always admired the vigorous understanding and useful activity by which he is distinguished in private life' and 'applauded the consistency and integrity of his public conduct'.[21] On 26 June 1849 the court of probate in London granted his principal creditor Felix Ladbroke the right to seize and administer Tomes's entire estate (sworn on personalty under £4,000). The intended beneficiaries of his will, dated 21 Dec. 1838, were his trustees, Collins and Edward Tomes's son-in-law Henry Thomas Chamberlayne of Stoney Thorpe. His daughter Jane Collins and his grandchildren had relinquished their rights.[22] A subscription paid for the passages to New South Wales that year of his orphaned granddaughters (Richard's children).[23]

[1] IGI (Warws.); H. Smith, *Hist. Southam.* [2] Warws. RO, Craven [of Coombe Abbey] mss CR 8/134; Stockton, Sons and Fortescue [of Banbury] mss CR 580/516/5-10, 14, 15; P. Styles, 'Corporation of Warwick', *Trans. Birmingham Arch. Soc.* lix (1935), 96. [3] Styles, 96-97, 104; *VCH Warws.* viii. 508. [4] T.H. Lloyd, 'Dr. Wade and the Working Class', *Midland Hist.* ii (1974), 64; Styles, 102; T. Kemp and A.B. Beavan, *Warws. MPs*, 24-29. [5] Warws. RO, Greville [of Warwick Castle] mss CR 1886, box 613/11; *Warwick Advertiser*, 11 Mar. 1820. [6] *Warwick Advertiser*, 11, 18 Nov., 23, 30 Dec. 1820, 13 Jan.; *The Times*, 2 Jan. 1821. [7] *Warwick Advertiser*, 20 Nov., 4 Dec. 1819, 14 July 1820, 21 Sept., 1 Oct. 1825, 4, 11, 18 Feb. 1826; Keele Univ. Lib. Sneyd mss SC12/67; *The Times*, 8, 14 Feb. 1826. [8] Lloyd, 68; Greville mss CR 1886, box 613/11; *Warwick Advertiser*, 5 May 1827. [9] Warws. RO, Heath and Blenkinsop mss CR 611/32-38; *Warwick Advertiser*, 3, 10, 17 June; *Times*, 10 June 1826. [10] *Warwick Advertiser*, 24 Feb. 1827. [11] J. Parkes, *Report of inquiry into ... Warwick Corporation*; W. Collins, *King and Burgesses of Warwick v. Mayor and Eight Aldermen of Warwick* (1827); *The Times*, 24 Nov. 1826; *Warwick Advertiser*, 5 May 1827. [12] *Warwick Advertiser*, 24, 31 July, 7 Aug. 1830. [13] Ibid. 12, 19, 26 Mar., 9, 16 Apr.; *The Times*, 11 Apr. 1831; Greville mss CR 1886, box 613/11. [14] *Warwick Advertiser*, 30 Apr., 7 May 1831; [15] See COVENTRY. [16] *Warwick Advertiser*, 17, 24 Sept., 29 Oct., 5 Nov. 1831. [17] Ibid. 12 May 1832. [18] Ibid. 19 May, 9 June 1832. [19] Ibid. 14 July, 8, 15, 1832; *VCH Warws.* viii. 503. [20] Heath and Blenkisop mss CR 611/479, 482, 484, 506, 564/32-35, 571/19; 1453/18, pp. 108, 147; *Warwick Advertiser*, 15 Apr. 1837, 6, 20 Oct. 1838, 3 Feb. 1844; *VCH Warws.* viii. 445, 508. [21] *Warwick Advertiser*, 10 Feb. 1844. [22] PROB 8/242; 11/2095/478-9; IR26/1850/497. [23] *Gent. Mag.* (1845), ii. 325; Shakespeare Birthplace Trust RO, Stoneleigh and Adlestrop mss DR 671/328.

M.M.E.

TOMLINE, William Edward (1787–1836), of Riby Grove, nr. Great Grimsby, Lincs.

CHRISTCHURCH	1812–1818
TRURO	1818–1820
TRURO	1826–24 Feb. 1829
MINEHEAD	1830–1831

b. 27 Feb. 1787, 1st s. of Rt. Rev. George Tomline (formerly Pretyman), bp. of Lincoln and later of Winchester, and Elizabeth, da. and coh. of Thomas Maltby of Germans, Bucks. *educ.* privately; Trinity Coll. Camb. 1804. *m.* 18 Apr. 1811, Frances, da. and h. of John Amler of Ford Hall, Salop, 3s. 2da. *suc.* fa. 1827 (but not to the baronetcy of Pretyman to which his claim was established in 1823). *d.* 25 Mar. 1836.
Sheriff, Lincs. 1824-5.
1st maj. Lindsey regt. Lincs. militia 1809, lt.-col. 1814; col. R. North Lincs. militia 1831, col. 1835-*d.*

Tomline, the son of Pitt's confidant and biographer, was returned for Truro on Lord Falmouth's interest in 1818, but he and his colleague Lord Fitzroy Somerset were again opposed in 1820 by two candidates representing a section of the corporation hostile to the patron. A local newspaper reported that, 'finding he had no chance of success', Tomline '*cut and run*, without taking leave', and that he made an approach to his former constituency of Christchurch. In the event, no opening was available there and he came bottom of the poll at Truro.[1] By 1826, however, Falmouth had re-established control over the borough and Tomline and Somerset were returned unopposed.[2]

His attendance was very poor, and he is not known to have spoken in debate. He divided against Catholic relief, 6 Mar. 1827. Early in 1828 he wrote to the new prime minister, the duke of Wellington, claiming that he was entitled to a baronetcy (he had been unable to succeed to the Pretyman title when his father died the previous year), but consideration of his application was postponed.[3] He presented petitions from Lincolnshire sheep farmers for a protective duty against imported wool, 5 Mar., and from Stamford against the Malt Act, 20 Mar. He voted against repeal of the Test Acts, 26 Feb., and Catholic relief, 12 May 1828. His failure to vote on the Penryn disfranchisement bill that session angered Falmouth, and prompted Tomline to clarify his understanding of their political connection. He maintained that he had been 'brought ... into Parliament as a sincere Tory and an opposer both of parliamentary reform and the Catholic claims', while on other issues he was 'free and unfettered'. Although he disliked the Penryn bill and would not vote for it, he also thought it 'possible that by occasionally yielding to popular feeling in particular cases like the present, an additional power may be gained in the means of resisting all general questions of reform'. He declared himself to be 'Tory enough to dislike opposing a measure of a government conducted by the duke ... whom I still regard with the same unbounded confidence I ever did', and who required cordial and steady support in order to resist 'many measures proposed by persons whose politics you and I equally dislike'.[4] In February 1829 he resigned his seat, having changed his mind on the question of Catholic emancipation, to which his patron remained opposed. He explained that 'when I see Ireland ... without any government at all except the Catholic Association, and see only one man superlatively fit to be at the head of the government in England', it was clearly impossible for the present arrangements in Ireland to continue and essential that ministers be supported in their 'exertions to remedy evils which experience proves them no longer able to control'. The only alternative, he argued, was to allow the Whigs to take office, and any emancipation measure of theirs would be 'carried probably in a manner less conciliatory to the feelings and less consistent with the principles of every zealous Protestant'. In regretfully accepting Tomline's decision, Falmouth cautioned him against seeking or accepting a peerage, which 'I think I have heard you say might be desirable to you', but which would destroy his reputation for integrity.[5] There is no indication that any such offer was made.

Tomline briefly reappeared in the Commons as Member for Minehead, where he was returned unopposed at the general election of 1830 with the borough's patron, John Fownes Luttrell. The Wellington ministry reckoned him as one of their 'friends', and he duly voted with them in the crucial civil list division, 15 Nov. 1830. He divided against the second reading of the Grey ministry's reform bill, 22 Mar., and for Gascoyne's wrecking amendment, 19 Apr. 1831. The ensuing dissolution marked the end of his parliamentary career. Tomline's father had accumulated a fortune during his career in the church, leaving on his death in 1827 a personal estate which was sworn under £200,000.[6] According to Thomas Raikes, Tomline took 'great care' of his inheritance and after his death in May 1836 his personalty was sworn under £400,000. He distributed large sums of money amongst his children and left the residue to his eldest son, George Tomline (1812-89), Conservative Member for Sudbury, 1840-1, and Shrewsbury, 1841-7, and Liberal Member for Shrewsbury, 1852-68, and Great Grimsby, 1868-74.[7]

[1] *West Briton*, 10, 17 Mar. 1820. [2] Ibid. 9 June 1826. [3] Wellington mss WP1/920/22. [4] Suff. RO (Ipswich), Tomline mss HA 119/562/726, Tomline to Falmouth, 27 Mar. 1828. [5] Ibid. Tomline to Falmouth [n.d.], reply, 13 Feb. 1829. [6] IR26/1151/792; *Black Bk.* (1820), 83-84; (1823), 225, 301. [7] *Raikes Jnl.* ii. 371; PROB 11/1865/456; IR26/1432/409.

T.A.J.

TORRENS, Robert (1780–1864), of Stonehouse, Devon and 12 Fludyer Street, Mdx.

IPSWICH	1826–26 Feb. 1827
ASHBURTON	1831–1832
BOLTON	1832–1834

b. 1780,[1] 1st s. of Robert Torrens of Herveyhill, co. Londonderry and Elizabeth, da. of Skeffington Bristow, preb. of Rasharkin, co. Londonderry. *educ.* ?Derry diocesan sch. *m.* (1) 8 Nov. 1801, Charity (div. by 1818),[2] da. of Richard Chute of Roxburgh, co. Kerry, 1s. 1da.[3] (2) 12 Dec. 1820, Esther Jane, da. of Ambrose Serle, solicitor to bd. of trade, ?1da.[4] *d.* 27 May 1864.
Lt. R. Marines 1797, capt. 1806; maj. army 1811, lt.-col. 1819, half-pay 1823; maj. R. Marines 1831, ret. 1834.
Chairman, crown commrs. for colonization of S. Australia 1835-9.

Torrens, whose grandfathers were both Irish clergymen and who was a cousin of Sir Henry Torrens, adjutant-general of the armed forces, combined for some years a military career with literary and philosophical pursuits. In March 1811 he was the commander of a 380-strong garrison on the island of Anhalt, which repulsed a Danish force of 4,000. Although it was 'a minor action' the 'sweeping victory caught the public imagination' and Torrens, who was seriously wounded, earned both celebrity and promotion.[5] His numerous publications included two novels, but he achieved greater distinction through his contributions to the development of political economy, becoming an active figure in Whig-radical intellectual circles and helping to found the Political Economy Club in 1821. He was one of the first theorists to emphasize the role of land, labour and capital as the three instruments of production and to expound the law of diminishing returns. In 1808 he attacked the views of Thomas Spence regarding the primacy of agriculture as the foundation of national wealth, and by 1815 he advocated free trade in corn, which he saw as necessary to generate overseas demand for British manufactures. However, he was 'outside the mainstream of Ricardian monetary and fiscal policies' in that he favoured an income tax as a means of 'diverting resources from the drones to the socially useful', and because he opposed the resumption of cash payments on the ground that

currency depreciation would likewise redistribute wealth from landlords and other *rentiers* to the productive classes. He also retained certain 'mercantilist proclivities' and regarded foreign trade as an instrument for acquiring colonies and augmenting national power.[6] Early in his career he lacked financial independence, and in 1818 he lamented that he had been about to marry a 'lady whose sudden death has ... deprived me of all that love and ambition could desire, an intellect of the first order and a fortune more than sufficient for my wants'.[7] During the 1820s, perhaps thanks to his second marriage, he acquired an impressive stable of newspapers and periodicals, including the *Nation*, *True Briton* and *Athenaeum*. He tried unsuccessfully in 1821 to gain control of the *Morning Chronicle*, in the hope of establishing himself 'in the confidence of the Whig party'. In 1823 he amalgamated two London evening papers, the *Globe* and the *Traveller*, which provided a 'forum for the political economists' and which he edited for a time in the late 1820s, maintaining close connections with Henry Brougham*. After 1830 the *Globe and Traveller* was the 'avowed ministerial organ' of the Whigs and by the middle of that decade it sold 3,000 copies nightly and yielded annual dividends of £5-6,000. Torrens continued to write many of its leading articles and was 'still the chief, although ... nearly dormant proprietor' in 1860.[8]

He stood for Rochester in 1818 as an opponent of Lord Liverpool's ministry but came bottom of the poll; he did not contest the seat again in 1820.[9] In 1826 he apparently sought government support for his candidature at Ipswich, by expressing to the minister Robert Wilmot Horton* his 'uncompromising allegiance to the government generally, and specially to the foreign policy of Canning, the free trade of Huskisson and the criminal law reform of Peel'. In the event, he was opposed by two ministerialists but was returned with a Whig banker after a 'desperate struggle' which cost him £5,000.[10] It was suspected that his 'ambition is to supply [David] Ricardo's* place in the ... Commons', and he immediately planned to 'publish a declaration against the corn laws', but on arriving at Westminster he was reportedly 'somewhat puzzled with the annoyance of his pretended Whig friends', who advised him 'not to do anything this session ... [or he] will lose himself'.[11] He presented numerous anti-corn law petitions between November 1826 and February 1827.[12] However, he also adopted a more friendly tone towards the landed interest, which may have reflected his changing perspective on the dangers of inflationary growth and the desirability of saving, in the light of the recent financial crisis, or may have resulted from a desire to improve his chances of obtaining official employment.[13] He emphasized the interdependence of agriculture and industry and declared that he 'considered the value of land as the true barometer of national opulence', 24 Nov. 1826, but he warned that agriculturists risked their own ruin by seeking artificially high prices. He argued that manufacturers had no need for protection and only required repeal of the corn laws to make their products more competitive, 30 Nov. He predicted that agricultural shortages in the spring would show the 'evil' of the present system of protection, 1 Dec. Though 'generally speaking a friend to free trade', he was prepared to make an exception for the export of machinery, 6 Dec. 1826, as he believed in 'the policy of each country reserving to itself the sole benefit of those exclusive advantages which, either from nature or by acquisition, it might enjoy'. He regarded emigration as the 'only efficient remedy' for the nation's economic ills, 15 Feb. 1827, maintaining that it was 'merely the application of the redundant capital and population of the United Kingdom to the redundant land of the colonies' and that it would save England from 'the alarming and destructive increase of her poor rates'. On 5 Dec. 1826 he announced his intention of introducing a bill for the pacification of Ireland, and he argued next day that if Catholics were given political power they would seek to retain it by acting responsibly.[14] Nothing came of this, as he did not contest the petition against his return for Ipswich, which alleged that the count had been inaccurate; he was unseated, 26 Feb. 1827.

Shortly afterwards Torrens accepted an invitation to stand as a supporter of Canning's ministry at Canterbury, where an early vacancy was expected, but this did not materialize and he eventually withdrew his name.[15] In August 1827 he proposed himself for the vice-presidency of the board of trade in Lord Goderich's ministry, claiming that his appointment would be 'acceptable to the great manufacturing and commercial interests', but the post had already been filled.[16] At the dissolution in July 1830 the Ultra Lord Blandford* recommended him as a suitable candidate for Marlborough, describing him as 'a person of ... sound constitutional independent politics'. However, the local Tories suspected that he was really 'a radical' and doubted whether he could 'show a qualification, or that his money is forthcoming', and they threw him over.[17] He offered instead for Pontefract as the champion of independence and opponent of slavery, but came bottom of the poll. He afterwards complained to the premier the duke of Wellington that he had stood in the expectation of receiving government support, which had not been forthcoming, and he requested

that another seat be found for him; the duke pleaded ignorance of the matter and Torrens's petition was rejected.[18] In March 1831, having returned to active military service, he applied to Lord Grey's ministry for the office of adjutant-general of the marines, but was considered too junior.[19] When Parliament was dissolved the following month he received financial assistance from the government to contest Ashburton as a supporter of their reform bill, and he was returned in second place, ousting an anti-reformer.[20]

He argued that peace and security must be restored to Ireland before measures were taken to alleviate distress, 22 June 1831, but suggested that an 'equitable' reform of Irish church revenues might provide some relief. He believed that 'rash' currency reforms were largely to blame for Ireland's depressed state and favoured public works projects such as 'the draining of ... bogs and morasses' to provide 'employment for [the] poor', 25 July. He rejected calls to promote manufacturing in Ireland, 10 Aug., arguing that its agriculture must be improved through investment and the consolidation of farms, with the surplus population migrating to the colonies. He objected to a legal and permanent provision of poor relief in Ireland, 29 Aug., as this would 'aggravate and perpetuate the misery of that country' by undermining wealth creation and further increasing the population. He considered it 'most unfair' to tax Irish Catholics for the support of an education system which was 'directed against themselves', and he favoured allowing the various denominations to educate their young according to their own tenets, 14 July. He deplored Anglican petitions against the Maynooth grant, 2 Sept. He voted to print the Waterford petition for disarming the Irish yeomanry, 11 Aug., and for the Irish union of parishes bill, 19 Aug. He warned that 'no permanent union could be kept up' between Britain and Ireland if the latter had its own Parliament, 16 Aug., and he wanted the inhabitants of the two countries to be 'rendered one people, by being governed by one system of laws ... equally and ... impartially administered', 31 Aug. He voted to swear in the 11 Members chosen for the Dublin election committee, 29 July, and to postpone issuing the writ, 8 Aug. He objected to the reference in the Dublin election committee's resolutions to unconstitutional practices, when similar abuses had occurred in other constituencies such as Ashburton, 23 Aug., and he voted to punish only those guilty of bribery and against the censure motion on the Irish administration. He dismissed criticisms of the anomalies in the reintroduced reform bill, 5 July, declaring that the precise rules for voting and redistribution were a matter of 'comparative indifference', since the measure was founded on the crucial principle that 'the constituent body should be so extensive as to have an identity of interest with the community at large'; he was confident that 'honest and able men will be returned to Parliament'. He also rejected claims that popular excitement on the subject was a temporary phenomenon, observing that public opinion had been growing for 50 years and that 'when thus formed [it] becomes omnipotent and the voice of the people is the voice of God'. He divided for the second reading, 6 July, and steadily for its details. He put the case for removing Ashburton, 'the principal seat of a large manufacturing district', from schedule B, 27 July, and called for Bolton to be given two Members as it was the second most important manufacturing town in Lancashire, 5 Aug. On 21 Sept., when he voted for the bill's passage, he appeared at the Westminster reform meeting where he moved, in provocative terms, to petition the Lords in its favour, suggesting that if they continued to resist the will of the people they might be added to schedule A. Two days later he explained in the House that this expression had been 'used hypothetically', but the outraged king demanded his dismissal from the marines for having 'shown the cloven foot'. He was only saved by ministers' fear that they would fatally undermine their own position if they were seen to be bowing to royal pressure at that moment.[21] He divided for Lord Ebrington's confidence motion, 10 Oct. He voted to condemn the bribery committed during the Liverpool election, 5 Sept. He maintained that it was 'only owing to the grossest mismanagement' that New South Wales and Van Diemen's Land were costing Britain money, and that with the 'sale of colonial lands' they would be financially self-sufficient, 18 July. He regretted that the island of Fernando Po was not to be retained, 25 July, as it might have become a valuable 'commercial depot' in West Africa and given Britain greater influence in putting down the slave trade. He thought the only relief that could be given to the West Indian planters was to reduce their costs by revising the navigation laws and working to abolish slavery worldwide, 12 Sept. He favoured a measure for enforcing better observation of the Sabbath, which would benefit working men, 2 Sept., but was wary of interfering with their recreations. He observed on 12 Sept. that 'while our corn laws remain, and our oppressive taxes continue', abolition of the truck system could 'do little for the people', as profits were too low for employers to be able to pay better wages. However, he was willing to support abolition as a temporary experiment. He voted to postpone the grant for Windsor Castle and Buckingham House, 28 Sept. He gave notice of a bill for the next session to repeal all taxes paid for out of

wages and profits and substitute for them a modified property tax, 12 Oct. 1831.

He announced his intention of moving for the repeal of all prohibitions on foreign imports, 6 Dec. 1831, but did not do so. He warned that prohibiting glove imports would damage other manufacturers, 15 Dec. 1831, and maintained that the real cause of industrial distress was that 'England is oppressed by taxation and a high price of food', 31 Jan. 1832. He blamed the corn laws and high taxes for manufacturers' low profits and the long hours worked by factory children, 1 Feb., but was prepared to support the factory bill as 'it is impossible to argue that the principles of political economy are opposed to those of humanity', 7 Feb. He supported the vagrants removal bill on the ground that English labourers needed to be 'protected in some way ... from the competition of the Irish', 28 June 1832. He advocated repeal of the taxes on newspapers, 7 Dec. 1831, as 'the salvation of this country depends upon the general promulgation of sound political knowledge ... by allowing well informed and upright men to set the people right'. He divided for the second reading of the revised reform bill, 17 Dec. 1831, steadily for its details and for the third reading, 22 Mar. 1832. He rejected fears that reform would lead to democracy, 20 Mar., arguing that this confused cause and effect since the bill had been 'produced by that democratic change which the progress of society has already completed'. It was 'impossible any longer to govern this country by means of a nomination Parliament', as 'the aggregate of the wealth and knowledge of the middle class now exceeds ... [that] of the upper orders', but if the aristocracy recognized this fact 'their superior wealth and their leisure for acquiring superior knowledge will still secure to them important advantages, and they will continue to be the natural leaders of the country'. He voted for Ebrington's motion for an address asking the king to appoint only ministers committed to carrying an unimpaired measure, 10 May. In presenting a Bolton petition for withholding supplies until reform was secure, 17 May, he warned that continued resistance by the Lords would encourage demands for universal suffrage. He voted for the second reading of the Irish bill, 25 May, and welcomed reform as 'the means to a magnificent end ... of securing good government, cheap government and the universal prosperity of the people', 5 June. From his own experience of Bolton and Manchester, he said it was untrue that the new registration system was inefficient, 15 Aug. He divided with ministers on the Russian-Dutch loan, 26 Jan., 12, 16 July, and relations with Portugal, 9 Feb. He was named to the select committee on the East India Company, 27 Jan. He protested 'in the name of the people' against Britain incurring any expense for the civil establishments in the colonies, 17 Feb., and voted for a representative system for New South Wales, 28 June. He divided for reform of Irish tithes, 27 Mar., insisted there should be no coercion bill until a tithes measure was ready for simultaneous passage, 6 Apr., and voted to postpone the subject until the next Parliament, 13 July. He advocated a redistribution of Irish church property so that 'a sufficient Catholic clergy may be paid out of it to meet the wants of the majority of the people', 6 Apr., and maintained that since Irish Catholics paid taxes they were entitled to a fair share of their appropriation for such purposes as education, 11 Apr. He divided for the government's navy civil departments bill, 6 Apr., but was in the minority for reduction of the barracks grant, 2 July. He voted for inquiry into the inns of court, 17 July 1832.

In November 1832 Torrens informed Lord Brougham that while he had been offered two Irish borough seats and had 'secured Bolton', he was 'not very desirous of remaining in Parliament'. He thought his opinions were likely to place him 'in opposition to government on commercial questions' and resented the 'treatment I have received from Lord Althorp', the leader of the Commons, who he claimed had reneged on a promise made the previous year to appoint him to an unspecified Irish commission in return for agreeing to contest Ashburton: 'I never recovered from this staggering blow ... [and] never afterwards went straight or entered the House except under feelings of disappointment and mortification'. He requested Brougham's help in securing the governorship of Van Diemen's Land 'or an appointment at home equivalent to the promised Irish commission', but nothing could be done. The following year he again expressed a wish to be 'permanently employed on a government board'.[22] At the general election of 1832 he was returned at the head of the poll for Bolton and sat, as an advocate of 'Whig principles, inclining in some particulars to radicalism', who favoured 'the ballot and the immediate abolition of slavery', until his defeat in 1835. A parliamentary journalist described him as having a 'gentlemanly and prepossessing' appearance and judged that he had achieved 'some status in the House': he possessed 'considerable talents and often made very effective speeches', but his delivery was marred by 'something hard and unmusical about his voice' and there was 'a good deal of affectation and pomposity in his manner'.[23] In 1835 he was appointed chairman of the commission for promoting the colonization of South Australia. Meantime, his involvement with the South Australia Land Company made him a 'disciple' of Edward Gibbon Wakefield and he became

convinced that systematic colonization was the only way of avoiding a glut of capital at home. His later writings on political economy developed his vision of a 'vast colonial empire populated by persons of British stock', and he was increasingly drawn to the idea of an 'imperial zollverein' and believed free trade should only be adopted on a reciprocal basis.[24] Though 'not in the first rank' of political economists, 'among men of the next grade his standing was not negligible', and his views on banking reform influenced Peel's legislation of 1844. He was 'firm in his grasp of general principles but lacking perhaps the intensity of vision to push through to the elaboration of a complete system'.[25] He died in May 1864 and left property in South Australia and New Zealand to his only son, Sir Robert Torrens (1814-84), Liberal Member for Cambridge, 1868-74.

[1] IGI (Dublin). [2] In Oct. 1818 he said that he had 'long been separated and for some time divorced' (Add. 37949, f. 79). [3] His will mentions a da. named Charity. [4] His 2nd da. was named Jane. [5] F. Fetter, 'Robert Torrens: Colonel of Marines and Political Economist', *Economica*, n.s. xxix (1962), 152-65. [6] S. Meenai, 'Robert Torrens, 1780-1864', ibid. xxiii (1956), 49-61; L. Robbins, *Robert Torrens and the Evolution of Classical Economics*, *passim*; B. Semmel, *Rise of Free Trade Imperialism*, 60-64, 78-79; B. Hilton, *Corn, Cash, Commerce*, 63, 263-4. [7] Add. 37949, f. 79. [8] J. Grant, *Newspaper Press*, 69-73; A. Aspinall, *Politics and the Press*, 243-4; A. Mitchell, *Whigs in Opposition*, 51-52; S. Koss, *Rise and Fall of Political Press*, i. 45; NLS mss 24748, f. 30; Brougham mss, Torrens to Brougham, 3 July 1860. [9] *Kentish Gazette*, 25 Feb., 3 Mar. 1820. [10] TNA 30/29/9/6/43; *Suff. Chron.* 29 Apr., 13, 20 May, 10, 17 June 1826. [11] TNA 30/29/9/6/43; G. Wallas, *Francis Place*, 178-9. [12] *The Times*, 25, 29, 30 Nov., 5, 14 Dec. 1826, 9, 17, 23 Feb. 1827. [13] Hilton, 228-9. [14] *The Times*, 6 Dec. 1826. [15] *Kentish Chron.* 6, 10 Apr. 1827, 7 Oct. 1828. [16] Hatherton mss, Torrens to Littleton, 13, 18 Aug. 1827. [17] Wilts. RO, Marlborough (Burke) mss 124/4/6,7,9, 14, 15, 20, 22. [18] *Leeds Mercury*, 7 Aug. 1830; Wellington mss WP1/1149/24. [19] Brougham mss, Graham to Brougham, 7 Mar. 1831. [20] *Trewman's Exeter Flying Post*, 5, 12 May; Brougham mss, Ellice to Brougham, 17 May 1831. [21] *Morning Chron.* 22 Sept. 1831; Parker, *Graham*, i. 125-7. [22] Brougham mss, Torrens to Brougham, 26 Nov. 1832, 26 Aug. 1833. [23] *Dod's Parl. Companion* (1833), 167; [J. Grant], *Random Recollections of Commons* (1836), 188-91. [24] Robbins, 4-8, 77-231; Semmel, 186-98; Hilton, 263-4. [25] Robbins, 6, 257-8.

T.A.J.

TOTTENHAM, Charles (1807–1886), of Ballycurry, co. Wicklow and New Ross, co. Wexford.

NEW ROSS	1831–9 July 1831
NEW ROSS	18 Mar. 1856–May 1863

b. 14 Nov. 1807, 1st s. of Charles Tottenham[†] of Ballycurry and Catherine, da. of Sir Robert Wigram[†], 1st bt., of Walthamstow House, Essex. *educ.* by Mr. Bird of Burghfield, Berks.; Trinity Coll. Camb. 1825. *m.* 14 Jan. 1833, Isabella Catherine, da. of Lt.-Gen. Sir George Airey, 3s. 2da. *suc.* fa. 1843. *d.* 1 June 1886.

Sheriff, co. Wicklow 1845-6, co. Wexford 1846-7.

Tottenham came from a leading family of New Ross property owners and corporators (nominally headed by their kinsmen the marquesses of Ely), who since the Union had taken turns with the Leighs of Rosegarland to nominate the borough's Member. His father had sat there from 1802 until July 1805, when he retired in favour of his uncle Ponsonby Tottenham. At the 1830 general election Tottenham appears to have broken ranks with his family and subscribed £100 towards the return of Henry Lambert as a reformer for county Wexford.[1] At the 1831 general election he came forward for New Ross, where it was his father's turn to nominate, with the support of Lambert and was returned unopposed. The local press assumed that he had been sent 'into Parliament for the avowed purpose of supporting' the Grey ministry's reform bill, for which he voted at its second reading, 6 July, but on the 9th he took the Chiltern Hundreds, apparently because his father wanted a 'thorough-going Tory'.[2] He offered again in 1835 as a Conservative, but was beaten by a Liberal, and sat from 1856 to 1863, when he retired in favour of his son Charles George Tottenham (1835-1918). Tottenham died at Ballycurry in June 1886.[3]

[1] *Wexford Herald*, 7, 18 Aug. 1830. [2] *Wexford Independent*, 13 May; *Dublin Evening Post*, 26 May; *Wexford Herald*, 17 Aug. 1831. [3] *The Times*, 4 June 1886.

P.J.S.

TOWNLEY, Richard Greaves (1786–1855), of Fulbourn, Cambs. and Beaupré Hall, Norf.

CAMBRIDGESHIRE   1 Nov. 1831–1841

CAMBRIDGESHIRE   1847–1852

b. 20 July 1786[1], 1st s. of Richard Greaves Townley of Belfield Hall, Rochdale, Lancs. and Margaret, da. of John Sale of Whitehaven, Cumb. *educ.* Eton 1799; Trinity Coll. Camb. 1802; L. Inn 1807. *m.* 23 Aug. 1821, Cecil, da. of Sir Charles Watson, 1st bt., of Wratting Park, Cambs., 5s. (1 *d.v.p.*) 1da. *suc.* fa. 1823. *d.* 5 May 1855.

Townley belonged to a cadet branch of the old Lancashire family of Towneley. His great-grand-father Richard Townley (1689-1762), the son of Abraham Townley of Dutton, near Blackburn, settled in Rochdale as a mercer in 1717. He became steward to Alexander Butterworth, formerly sheriff of Lancashire, who left him the Belfield Hall estate on his death in 1728. Richard Townley married Jane, the daughter of William Greaves of Gartside Hall, Rochdale, and sister of William Greaves of

Fulbourn, about five miles south-east of Cambridge, which he had bought in 1742.[2] William Greaves, who was commissary of Cambridge University, 1726-79, married the daughter and heiress of Beaupré Bell of Beaupré Hall, on the Norfolk-Cambridge border near Wisbech, and took the additional names of Beaupré Bell. Richard Townley's only surviving son and name-sake was educated at Cambridge, served as sheriff of Lancashire, 1752-3, and in 1791 published at Whitehaven a rather tedious *Journal kept in the Isle of Man*. He died at Ambleside in 1802. With his first wife Ann, daughter of Thomas Western of Abington Hall, Cambridgeshire, he had an only son, Richard Greaves Townley, the father of this Member.

He, who was born in 1751, was educated at Rochdale, Eton, Manchester Grammar School, Trinity College, Cambridge and the Middle Temple. He was in the 15th Hussars, 1778-84, and married the following year. On the death of his great-uncle William Greaves Beaupré Bell in 1787 he inherited all his real estate, including Fulbourn, Beaupré Hall and property in Lancashire and Yorkshire.[3] Townley made Fulbourn his principal residence and was sheriff of Cambridgeshire, 1792-3. He took command of the county's provisional cavalry with the rank of lieutenant-colonel in 1797 and, as a deputy lieutenant, was one of those who stood in for Lord Hardwicke, the lord lieutenant, during his absences as Irish viceroy.[4] He died, worth £10,000 in personalty, at the Cork Street Hotel in London, 5 Feb. 1823. A local admirer wrote of him:

> In his political life he was a Whig of the old school, and such was his nice sense of the high degree of liberty the *people* ought to enjoy that, although possessed of extensive property, he would never *even ask* a tenant or a tradesman with whom he dealt, for a vote in support of that interest to which he himself was attached.[5]

His eldest son Richard Greaves Townley, whose younger brothers William Gale and Charles entered the church, inherited all his real estate, which was variously charged with provision for his mother and two youngest siblings. (William Gale Townley, as incumbent of the 'valuable' living of Upwell cum Welney, was deemed thereby to be 'very amply pro-vided for'.)[6] Townley also succeeded his father as a conservator of the corporation of Bedford Level, which enabled him to make a mark in county affairs.[7] He shared his father's Whig politics, but, like him, never joined Brooks's. At the 1820 general election he nominated the sitting Whig county member, Lord Francis Godolphin Osborne, a personal friend, whose residence at Gogmagog Hills lay close to Fulbourn. He deplored the current 'outcry of danger' fomented by the Liverpool ministry, who might try 'through their influence in Parliament to stifle the liberties of the people', but could not prevent the return of popular and independent Members such as Osborne.[8] Townley attended the county meetings in support of Queen Caroline, 16 Jan., and parliamentary reform, 13 Mar. 1821, but on each occasion confined his oratorical contribution to moving and seconding votes of thanks. He was a silent attender at the meeting on agricultural distress, 28 Feb. 1822.[9] In October 1824 it was reported that he had returned to Fulbourn with his wife and two baby sons 'after a long absence, during which the building had undergone considerable repairs and improvements'.[10] A year later there was a story that at the next general election he would be nominated by the independents to challenge the Tory county Member, Lord Charles Manners, the duke of Rutland's brother; but nothing came of this, and in 1826 he nominated Osborne.[11]

At the county meeting called to petition for repeal of the malt and beer taxes, 22 Jan. 1830, Townley seconded a resolution requesting the county Members to support it, which was defeated by the radicals in favour of an amendment instructing them to do so.[12] He seconded Osborne's nomination at the 1830 general election, when Manners was beaten by Henry Adeane, standing on the independent interest. Townley, who gave his second vote to Adeane, declared after the close that 'the county had coalesced for the purpose of turning out Manners'.[13] At the meeting to consider convening the county to petition for parliamentary reform, 27 Nov. 1830, he voiced the majority view that the new Grey ministry should first be given the chance to show its hand:

> He had been brought up in the principles which advocated reform ... It was with satisfaction that he heard that ... ministers had come into office pledged to that measure, and he could not help thinking that something was to be hoped from them.[14]

His was the second signature on the requisition for a county meeting to endorse their reform bill, 18 Mar. 1831, when he proposed the loyal address but did not speak on the main question.[15] He was chairman of Osborne's committee at the 1831 general election and seconded him at the nomination, but he took the opportunity to make a public apology to Manners for an unguarded expression which had caused offence the previous year.[16]

When Osborne retired on health grounds in early October 1831 Townley, who was plausibly reported to have been tipped off well in advance, offered in his room, in response to a formal requisition from the

leading county independents and reformers.[17] He was opposed by Charles Yorke, Hardwicke's nephew, who had the backing of Rutland and portrayed himself as a moderate reformer and champion of the agricultural interest.[18] Townley, who was warmly supported by the duke of Bedford, members of his family and other leading Whigs, claimed to be 'no tool of faction, nor delegate for party purposes', and stressed his vested interest in safeguarding agriculture, to which the reform bill was not a threat. On the hustings, he conspicuously refused to give any 'pledge respecting the bill' and denied his opponents' charge that he was committed to support all its details: 'he had nothing to do with the details of the bill', but would support 'a full and efficient measure of reform'. He comfortably defeated Yorke by 536 votes in a four-day poll of just over 3,400; his expenses were paid by subscription.[19] Townley, who took his seat, 7 Dec. 1831, did nothing to draw attention to himself in his first session. He voted for the second reading of the revised reform bill, 17 Dec., and was a steady supporter of its details in committee, with the exception of his vote against the enfranchisement of Gateshead, 5 Mar. 1832. He divided for the third reading, 22 Mar. 1832. He voted with government on the Russian-Dutch loan, 26 Jan., 12, 20 July, and relations with Portugal, 9 Feb. His only other known votes were against a Conservative amendment to the Scottish reform bill, 1 June, and to make coroners' inquests public, 20 June. He is not known to have spoken in debate in this period. He presented petitions from Chatteris in favour of the factories regulation bill, 2 Mar.; from Royston and Wisbech for the abolition of slavery, 18 May, and from the hemp and flax growers of Upwell for compensation for losses anticipated from the customs duties bill, 13 July 1832.

Townley successfully contested the county in 1832 and 1835, was unopposed in 1837, but went out in 1841, when three Conservatives came in. It was as a Protectionist that he was returned for the last time in 1847. He died at Fulbourn in May 1855. He was commemorated as 'a man of sterling worth and great benevolence', whose 'amiable qualities much endeared him to his friends', and 'to no one more than to those who dissented from his political opinions'.[20] By his will, dated only a week before his death, he confirmed the provision made in his marriage settlement for his wife and younger sons, allowed his brother William to continue as tenant of Beaupré Hall; and left all his Cambridgeshire and Norfolk estates to his eldest surviving son, Charles Watson Townley. (The first born, Richard Greaves Townley, had died in India in 1847.) By a private Act of 26 June 1846, Townley had had the rectory of Upwell divided into three; and he directed that after his brother's incumbency his younger sons should be presented to these livings if they so wished.[21] Charles Watson Townley (1823-93) was lord lieutenant of Cambridgeshire 1874-93; the second son, Thomas Manners Townley (1825-95), was a Cambridge University cricket Blue, served with the cavalry in the Crimea and found fame as a steeplechase jockey; and the other sons, William (1827-69) and Francis Mitford Townley (d. 1874) duly entered the church.

[1] Ex. inf. Stephen Lees. [2] R. Gardner, Hist. Cambs. 214-15. [3] Gent. Mag. (1787), i. 277; PROB 11/1151/108; VCH Cambs. iv. 209. [4] Add. 35664, f. 262; 35666, f. 141; 35667, f. 345; 35668, ff. 46, 61, 92, 93; 35671, f. 257; 35750, f. 308. [5] IR26/976/417; Cambridge and Hertford Independent Press, 1, 8 Feb. 1823; Gent. Mag. (1823), i. 186. [6] PROB 11/1671/327. [7] Gent. Mag. (1855), ii. 437. [8] Cambridge Chron. 24 Mar. 1820. [9] Cambridge and Hertford Independent Press, 20 Jan., 17 Mar. 1821, 2 Mar. 1822. [10] Ibid. 23 Oct. 1824. [11] Ibid. 24 Sept. 1825, 24 June 1826. [12] Ibid. 23 Jan. 1830. [13] Ibid. 14, 21 Aug. 1830. [14] Ibid. 4 Dec. 1830. [15] Ibid. 12, 19 Mar. 1831. [16] Ibid. 14 May 1831. [17] Three Diaries, 151; Cambridge and Hertford Independent Press, 1, 8, Oct. 1831. [18] Cambridge Chron. 7, 14 Oct. 1831. [19] Cambridge and Hertford Independent Press, 8, 15, 22, 29 Oct.; Cambridge Chron. 4 Nov. 1831; Three Diaries, 154. [20] Gent. Mag. (1855), ii. 436-7. [21] PROB 11/2217/652; IR26/2047/753.

D.R.F.

TOWNSEND FARQUHAR, Sir Robert Townsend,
1st bt. (1776–1830), of 13 Bruton Street and 2 Richmond Terrace, Whitehall, Mdx.

NEWTON	11 Feb. 1825–1826
HYTHE	1826–16 Mar. 1830

b. 14 Oct. 1776, 2nd s. of Sir Walter Farquhar, 1st bt. (d. 1819), apothecary and physician, of Great Marlborough Street, Mdx. and Ann, da. of Thomas Stevenson of Barbados, wid. of John Harvie, physician, of Wardour Street. educ. Westminster 1787. m. 10 Jan. 1809, Maria Frances Geslip, da. and coh. of Francois Joseph Louis de Lautour of Madras and Devonshire Place, 1s.; 1 illegit. s. cr. bt. 21 Aug. 1821. Took name of Townsend bef. Farquhar 19 July 1824. d. 16 Mar. 1830.

Writer E.I. Co. (Madras) 1795; asst. under accountant to board of revenue 1796; asst. under resident at Amboyna 1797, dep. commercial resident 1798, commercial resident 1798-1802; commr. for adjusting British claims in Moluccas 1802; lt.-gov. Prince of Wales Island (Penang) 1804-5; gov. Mauritius 1811-23.

Dir. E.I. Co. 1826-8.

Townsend Farquhar came from a cadet branch of the Farquhars of Gilminscroft, Ayrshire, who migrated to Aberdeenshire in the seventeenth century. His grandfather, the Rev. Robert Farquhar (1699-1787), was minister of Garioch. Robert's fourth son

Walter, who was born in 1738, studied medicine at Aberdeen, Edinburgh and Glasgow, but did not graduate. He entered the army medical service and took part in the expedition to Belle Isle in 1761. On leave of absence he pursued his studies in France for 18 months, before quitting the army on account of poor health. He settled in London, set up and flourished as an apothecary and was transmogrified into a physician. He built up a fashionable practice, and in 1788 Edward Gibbon (whose last illness he was to treat unsuccessfully five years later) recommended him as 'lequel sans être de la faculté les a supplanté les Medicins dans les premières maisons de Londres'. In 1796 he obtained the degree of MD from Aberdeen, was admitted a fellow of the Edinburgh College of Physicians and a licentiate of the London College and created a baronet (1 Mar.) Four years later he was appointed personal physician to the prince of Wales, with whom he remained a firm favourite. He attended Pitt in his fatal illness in January 1806 and became one of his many posthumous creditors, to the tune of 1,000 guineas.[1] It was said that his 'professional forte' lay in his 'acute' recommendation of 'suitable medicine'; but John William Ward* blamed him in 1811 for the early death of the duke of Devonshire, 'another [added] to the list of Farquhar's victims'. By 1809 it was reckoned that his star was on the wane:

> Sir Walter Farquhar had a run for some time, being supported by the duchess of Gordon, Mr. Pitt, etc., but he is now only in the third or fourth line. He never had the opinion of the other physicians with him, and it has been observed that unless a physician is supported in his reputation by the acknowledgement of his claim by the corps of physicians his reputation will only be temporary.[2]

Farquhar largely retired from practice in 1813 and died on 30 Mar. 1819; his personalty was sworn under £40,000.[3]

He had provided in his lifetime for his three sons, on whom he doted.[4] The eldest, Thomas Harvie Farquhar (1775-1836), became a partner in the London bank of Herries, Farquhar and Company. The two younger, Robert Townsend and Walter, entered the service of the East India Company, the former after being instructed in book-keeping by James Pierson of Castle Street.[5] He went out to Amboyna, one of the Indonesian islands recently captured from the Dutch. He became commercial resident there in 1798, but in 1801 was severely censured by the Madras government for exceeding his brief in organizing a successful attack on the neighbouring Dutch settlement of Ternate. He was superseded by a soldier and declined the option of continuing as resident with restricted powers. Even though he was 'deprived of all emolument, of all command, and [was] indisputably in a state of degradation', and had 'already suffered much from the climate, by repeated attacks of the epidemical Banda fever', he martyred himself by voluntarily remaining until May 1802 to assist his successor.[6] On reaching Calcutta in October he beseeched the governor-general, Lord Wellesley, to whom he submitted an elaborate defence of his conduct, to intercede to clear his name. Wellesley, who had taken a benevolent interest in Townsend Farquhar's career from the start, was sympathetic, and secured his appointment as commissioner to supervise the restoration of the former Dutch settlements in the Moluccas.[7] He then made him lieutenant-governor of Penang, in the Malayan peninsula, and commended him to Lord William Henry Cavendish Bentinck*, the new governor of Madras:

> Your Lordship must be fully apprised of his meritorious character and services, and ... his zeal, integrity, and attainments ... Mr. Farquhar's conduct in both these situations has been highly meritorious and exemplary, and merits my entire approbation. In addition to these public considerations, I feel a great personal regard for Mr. Farquhar, and I take a most cordial interest in his welfare and success.[8]

Whether Townsend Farquhar obtained from the East India Company the compensation which he sought for serving in the Moluccas on a reduced salary is not clear. What he did get early in 1805 was a blow in the form of news that he was to be superseded in the government of Penang, where new arrangements were to be introduced. Wellesley, alerted by Sir Walter Farquhar, who invoked his aid 'for the revival of my son's hopes and the amelioration of his prospects', was extremely supportive. He offered Townsend Farquhar an equivalent position in India or, if he wished to return to England, passage there in his own suite on his impending departure from Bengal. Townsend Farquhar, who bemoaned 'the triumph of interest over every consideration of justice and propriety' (though as 'Leadenhall Street never was the meridian of either' he had half expected this setback), was keen to return home, if only 'to prove to the directors, or at all events to an impartial public, that their new arrangements respecting this Island have neither been planned with common prudence and circumspection, nor exercised with common zeal for the public interests'. He commended to Wellesley's protection his brother Walter, collector of revenue at Penang, who stood to lose 40,000 rupees a year. (Walter was subsequently provided for in India, but died at St. Helena in 1813.) As

it happened Townsend Farquhar was unable to leave for England until early 1806. He did so furnished with a complimentary letter of introduction from Bentinck to his father, the 3rd duke of Portland.[9]

It was with the encouragement of Wellesley and Portland's fledgling ministry that Townsend Farquhar stood for Canterbury in conjunction with Stephen Rumbold Lushington* at the general election of 1807. Lushington would have compromised with their opponents for one seat, but Townsend Farquhar, who was not quite open with him, would have none of it. On the hustings he endorsed Lushington's attack on the late Grenville government's attempt to force the king's conscience on Catholic relief, paid lip service to 'independence', promised residence if he was elected and declared his support for the plan to link the city to the sea by canal. He and Lushington were comfortably beaten after a heavy poll, at a personal cost of about £5,000 each.[10] The same year Townsend Farquhar published *Suggestions* for supplying the West Indian colonies with labourers from China after the abolition of the slave trade and made another unsuccessful bid to secure the governorship of Penang.[11] In 1810 he joined the expedition sent against the French islands of Bourbon and Mauritius by Lord Minto, the governor-general of India, who on 30 Mar. earmarked him to assume the interim administration of both in the event of success. Townsend Farquhar, who wrote in anticipation to Wellesley, now foreign secretary, asking him to secure his confirmation in these posts, took control at Bourbon on 8 July and at Mauritius on 6 Dec. 1810.[12] To his father, who had already pestered ministers on the subject, he wrote:

> As this is to be a *king's* government, the *bugbear* will be that I am a Company's servant. As I have no *mark in the hand* which stamps me a Company's servant, or disqualifies me from serving the king, I can only say that I offer my resignation and hereby again authorize you to give it in, if that be an obstacle. *I expect that Lord Wellesley and all the ministers will support me.* You must take an immediate opportunity of urging my claims and bringing to their recollection that I exerted myself when in England to support their cause at a heavy and ... very inconvenient expense to myself, for which hitherto I have not received the compensation which all others similarly situated have already obtained. I sacrificed my views in Leadenhall Street and every prospect in the world to Lord Wellesley. He and his colleagues have it now in their power to realize their promises and make me compensation for my services ... I can hardly anticipate so unjust a measure as my supercession, yet until I receive my confirmation from home, I cannot but feel anxious about the success of a question, involving all my future prospects in life.[13]

It was rumoured that he was to be replaced by Lord Robert Somerset*, but he was confirmed in the government, worth £10,000 a year, in March 1811. He was briefly in England soon afterwards, and returned to Mauritius in the late summer.[14]

Just before receiving his confirmation Townsend Farquhar wrote to Wellesley:

> The improvement of my circumstances, occasioned by a very happy marriage, and the recovery of some property at Madras, have already placed me in a very independent state, and I trust that three or four years more on this side of the Cape will enable me to return to my family and friends with sufficient means, not only to live, but to do good to them, and to enable me to gratify the honourable ambition ... of ranging myself under your Lordship's banners, in political life.[15]

As things turned out, he found himself in a very difficult situation in Mauritius, where the transition to British rule was painful: charges of impropriety in his administration of its affairs were to haunt his later years and dog him to the grave. In an early dispatch, 15 Feb. 1811, he reported that the 'laws, customs and usages' of Mauritius, which he had been instructed to safeguard, included a flourishing slave trade, essential to the island's economic survival, and argued, mistakenly, that the British Abolition Act of 1807 did not apply to colonies subsequently acquired. He insisted that he was 'not by any means disposed to be a supporter of slavery', but feared that 'any sudden alteration' in policy on the trade would agitate the colony's 60,000 slaves, who seemed to expect immediate emancipation. The colonial secretary, Lord Liverpool, emphatically corrected his 'extraordinary misapprehensions' regarding the legality of the slave trade and instructed him to take every step to suppress it. Although the trade was formally abolished in Mauritius in 1813 and vice-admiralty courts were established to deal with offenders, it is clear that for the next few years the illicit traffic in slaves continued on a significant scale. Townsend Farquhar, anxious to conciliate the French settlers, and inadequately furnished with means of law enforcement, adopted a lenient attitude, which to his critics seemed tantamount to connivance. On 23 Oct. 1817, however, he concluded a treaty with King Radama of Madagascar, which promised effectually to check the trade.[16]

Townsend Farquhar had been painfully unwell in 1812 (when his spirits were temporarily lifted by a false report that Wellesley had become prime minister) and a recurrence of illness forced him to take leave of absence in November 1817. On his arrival in London he found his father terminally ill and himself suffered a relapse, but he lost no time in paying court to Liverpool, now premier.[17] His deputy in Mauritius, General John Gage Hall, was soon complaining to the British government that the slave trade had 'attained to a daring pitch' there, but Townsend Farquhar countered that he was confusing the trade with slavery. He failed, as he had all along, to interest ministers in his ideas for the establishment of a strong British influence in Madagascar, which he had had charted for the first time.[18] He had discussions with William Wilberforce* and other abolitionists on the best means of suppressing the slave trade off east Africa. At one such gathering in March 1819 Maria Edgeworth recorded that 'I never heard one word he said nor do I believe he said any one worth hearing'.[19] By the end of that year Townsend Farquhar's health was improved and he was ordered to resume his post, but he did not depart without seconding Lushington's successful nomination for Canterbury at the 1820 general election and soliciting 'some public mark of the approbation and confidence of my government', particularly one which, given the dangers posed by a tropical climate to his ravaged constitution, could be passed on to his son: he received a baronetcy in 1821.[20] By then Townsend Farquhar, who claimed that Hall and Ralph Darling, acting governor, 1819-20, had stirred up trouble among the slaves, had renewed the treaty with Radama, which Hall had broken. A treaty with the Imaum of Muscat followed and when Townsend Farquhar finally left Mauritius in May 1823 he assured Lord Bathurst, the colonial secretary, that 'it is a source of great satisfaction to me to leave this island freed from the stigma of the slave traffic'.[21] He lost no time in fawning on Liverpool on his arrival in London in September 1823.[22] George IV's request that Bathurst should 'take care' of 'that good man, Sir Robert Farquhar' related to a forthcoming treasury report in the financial administration at Mauritius of Theodore Hook, the accountant-general, who had been held responsible for a deficiency of £12,000 and sent home a prisoner in 1818. The report implicated other officials but not Townsend Farquhar who, as Bathurst replied to the king, would 'stand clear of any charge except what may arise from the facility with which his amiable disposition allowed others to practise upon him'.[23] In mid-November 1823 he declared his candidacy for the next vacancy in the East India Company's direction, but he did not secure election until March 1826.[24] In February 1824 local difficulties dished an attempt by the duke of Wellington to have him adopted as ministerial candidate for Berwick-upon-Tweed at the next general election; but in April 1824 he indicated that he would stand for Canterbury if there was a vacancy.[25] In February 1825 he secured his return as a supporter of government on a vacancy for Newton on the Legh interest.

Townsend Farquhar divided in the minority for repeal of the usury laws, 17 Feb. 1825. He voted for Catholic relief, 1 Mar., 21 Apr., and the duke of Cumberland's annuity, 6, 10 June. In the debate of 17 May on the customs consolidation bill, by which the produce of Mauritius was placed on the same footing as that of the West Indian colonies, he responded to Bernal's insinuation that the slave trade still prevailed there with the assertion that 'there had been no slave trade in the island for the last five years at least'. The issue was discussed at greater length on 3 June when Townsend Farquhar, who was supported by Huskisson, president of the board of trade, insisted that although there had been some smuggling of slaves by French privateers before 1820, the traffic had since been eradicated at Mauritius and was confined to Bourbon (returned to France at the peace). He supported the customs bill, both then and on 6 June 1825, as an act of justice to Mauritius, whose commerce, 'sacrificed to European policy', had been allowed to stagnate.[26] He voted in the minority of 39 against the government's proposed bank restriction, 13 Feb., but divided with them in defence of the Jamaican slave trials, 2 Mar., and the salary of the president of the board of trade, 10 Apr., and against parliamentary reform, 13 Apr. 1826. The exchanges of 1825 on the slave trade had presaged the attack which the abolitionist Thomas Fowell Buxton, primed by Hall and Edward Byam, former commissary-general of police at Mauritius, launched the following session. The government directed commissioners to visit the colony to investigate. In the House, 9 May 1826, Buxton moved for the appointment of a select committee to inquire into whether and to what extent the trade had prevailed at Mauritius. He alleged that there had been 'a regular, systematic and unceasing importation of slaves' from 1810 'almost to the present moment' and implicated Townsend Farquhar, along with his private secretary Telfair and the colony's administrative hierarchy, in connivance in the traffic. In reply, Townsend Farquhar complained that Buxton had 'artfully spread his facts over a space of 16 years, taking very good care to direct the attention of the House to the earlier period, keeping altogether clear of the last six years', when only a single incident of smuggling had occurred. He denied the charges against Telfair and, while admitting that up to 1820 there had been 'several extensive debarkations of slaves', stated that they had been 'to a comparatively trifling extent'. He tried to explain away defects in the slave register and the demographic evidence adduced by Buxton, made light

of his dispatch of 1811, disclaimed any responsibility for slave trading in the distant Seychelles, detailed the treaties with Madagascar and Muscat and, courting 'the fullest inquiry', observed:

> Every measure of his government ... had for its object to put an end to that trade. But he had not thought it expedient to tell those who had been employed in the trade that they were felons, his wish being to avoid irritating the people. His object had been to produce a just moral feeling on the subject in the minds of the people ... From the anomalous state of the law, he did not think it prudent to proceed with the utmost severity ... He had done all he could, with the tools he had ... A moral feeling, a disgust towards slavery, had taken place in the Mauritius. By this means, and the measures he simultaneously took, he had been enabled to state last year, that the slave trade had ceased there.

He was defended by Wilmot Horton, the colonial under-secretary, who accused Buxton of pursuing a personal vendetta; but Canning, government leader in the Commons, sanctioned the inquiry 'upon the ground of its being a question of national honour'.[27] Townsend Farquhar was named to the committee which, in the event, sat for only six days in May, being handicapped by Hall's illness and overtaken by the dissolution. Its brief report and minutes of evidence were inconclusive, but the former welcomed the government's continued commitment to sifting the business to the bottom.[28]

At the general election of 1826 Townsend Farquhar declined an invitation to stand for Canterbury and was returned unopposed for Hythe, where money and Company patronage were telling factors.[29] Buxton, aided by Dr. Stephen Lushington*, continued to collect evidence on the Mauritian slave trade, in particular from soldiers who had served there. Bathurst was inclined to obstruct the proceedings of this 'self-elected court', but Horton pointed out that ministers were 'in a certain degree' pledged to support them. He agreed with Bathurst that the evidence so far published was 'anything but conclusive', yet thought it had to be assumed that Buxton, whose credit and that of his associates was 'very deeply implicated in this business', had a substantial case:

> My opinion of the weakness of their case would be extremely increased, were it not for the *easiness* of Farquhar's character ... I acquit him *in toto* of knowledge, much more of participation, but I think it possible that he may have been systematically juggled and deceived, and consequently I do not share the absolute conviction which he appears to entertain that the whole is a farce from beginning to end, and that Buxton has not a shadow of case behind, although he has made so poor a figure (which I admit) in the committee.[30]

On 21 Feb. 1827 Buxton tried to secure a renewal of the inquiry but, failing to get ministerial support, he postponed his motion until 26 May. Townsend Farquhar voted for Catholic relief, 6 Mar. He again declined to stand for Canterbury that month.[31] When William Smith alleged, 15 May, that a clandestine slave trade continued at Mauritius, Townsend Farquhar stood by his declarations of the previous two years. He complained that the case against him, which in his opinion had virtually collapsed, rested on evidence procured in the 'most scandalous and foul manner, from the lowest and most profligate persons', and angrily challenged Buxton to prove his allegations. Buxton retorted that he would show that the trade 'had been carried on to a most enormous extent' under Townsend Farquhar's administration, but four days later he suffered a nervous collapse, from which he did not recover until the day designated for his motion had passed. His health remained precarious and in March 1828 he offered to hand over his evidence to the Wellington ministry if they would take up the case. Huskisson, now colonial secretary, declined to do so, assuring Buxton that the trade had long since ceased and exhorting him to await the outcome of the commission of inquiry.[32]

Townsend Farquhar had personally promised his support to Wellington on his appointment as prime minister in January 1828: '"A Wellesley ... in the cabinet and a Wellesley in the field" is the surest pledge for the maintenance of the national honour and fame abroad, and the general prosperity of all classes at home'. He asked Wellington to obtain a junior diplomatic posting for his legitimate son Walter when he left Oxford, and the duke secured his attachment to the Vienna embassy, though he observed privately to the foreign secretary Lord Aberdeen that 'I am very unfortunate in having a very numerous acquaintance of gentlemen in Parliament who have served in their different lines and whom I cannot convince that although the minister of the country I can do nothing to forward their views or those of their friends and relations'.[33] Townsend Farquhar voted for Catholic relief, 12 May, and in the ministerial majority on the silk duties, 14 July 1828. At the end of the year he was accused in the *Anti-Slavery Reporter* of having done nothing during his government of Mauritius to ameliorate the appalling conditions in which the slave population existed. Invited to comment by the new colonial secretary Sir George Murray*, he replied that the allegations were 'a tissue of atrocious calumnies' invented by the abolitionists to advance their 'visionary experiments'. He boasted that he had 'effectually done at least as much ... to abolish the slave trade,

foreign as well as English, as the whole [abolitionist] party put together'.[34] He had been suffering from 'severe indisposition', but was present to vote, as expected, for Catholic emancipation, 6, 30 Mar. 1829. In August 1829 he sent Wellington extensive material on his pet scheme for the introduction of 'mint notes' to replace metal coins. The duke gave it short shrift: 'We cannot make ourselves inhabitants of the moon'.[35]

Townsend Farquhar secured a number of returns bearing on the Mauritian slave trade, including his reply to the *Reporter*, 6 Apr., and presented and endorsed the petition of Jean Roudeaux of Mauritius for liquidation of his claims on the French government, 4 May 1829. On 25 May he was goaded by the West Indian Bright to repeat his previous assertions regarding the trade, which prompted Buxton to explain why he had not pressed the issue for over two years. Townsend Farquhar then complained that it was 'extremely hard that a public servant should have a charge hanging over his head for three years, when it might be so easily brought forward and investigated'. When Buxton moved for papers concerning the treatment of slaves in Mauritius, 3 June, Townsend Farquhar challenged him either to renew the inquiry or apologize in his place. Buxton pledged himself to reopen his case next session and, while he conceded that Townsend Farquhar's 'courting inquiry' seemed to tell in favour of his innocence, warned him that he would expose a sordid tale of cruelty, deception and greed. Tempers flared out of control as the exchanges continued, and Townsend Farquhar rounded on ministers:

In this long and almost unprecedented persecution of me, I have not received, neither have I craved, the assistance, support or countenance of any of the officers of government ... Whether from intimidation, or from the principle of government, daily gaining ground, of conciliating the enemy, or from the love of ease ... I cannot say; but ... those from whose department I might naturally have expected support have rather, if anything, lent themselves to the opposite party; and, instead of throwing their shield over one of their own servants, whose conduct and services had been approved by his king and country, they have kept aloof, and afforded the means to my enemies of protracted delay ... All I ask for is fair play, and the termination of the inquiry, involving my character, which has been now suspended for upwards of three years.

A week later Townsend Farquhar, in a letter to Murray, dismissed the commissioners' report, which he had been invited to peruse, as 'the most inconclusive, vague, incoherent and frivolous rhapsody that was ever produced in the shape of a public document'.

He protested, too, that preceding ministries had gone behind his back in altering the commissioners' terms of reference with 'special instructions', and insisted that if Buxton failed to proceed with the case, ministers should publicly repudiate him. The report, in which the commissioners blamed a conspiracy of silence in Mauritius for their failure to get properly to the bottom of allegations that civil servants had connived at or participated in the trade, indicated that the illicit traffic had continued for several years after the British takeover. Yet it acknowledged the importance of Townsend Farquhar's treaties with Madagascar and Muscat and stated that there had been no direct import of a whole cargo of negroes since March 1821.[36] Buxton was bent on prosecuting the case in the next session, but Townsend Farquhar's sudden death in March 1830 put him out of reach. The following month, according to Buxton, Murray privately admitted that 'slave trading to a *vast extent* had prevailed at the Mauritius, and that *all our statements had been well founded*'.[37] To the delight of the abolitionists, Murray said almost as much in the House, 13 May, when he attributed the great increase in the Mauritian sugar output to the illegal import of 'a great number of slaves'; but on 17 May 1830 he tried to correct this 'erroneous impression' by explaining that those imports had occurred between 1814 and 1821.

In his will, dated 21 Mar. 1820, Townsend Farquhar provided his wife with £3,000 a year, gave legacies of £1,000 each to his four sisters and left £2,000 to his bastard son Walter Farquhar Fullerton and £500 to one George Harrison, 'whom I have taken under my protection and educated'. His personalty was sworn under £20,000, 22 Mar. 1830, and resworn under £16,000, 19 May 1832. His estate was left unadministered by his brother, and on 3 July 1841, after his widow and brother-in-law, the two other surviving executors, had renounced probate, administration was granted to William Morgan, one of his creditors.[38] His only legitimate son, Sir Walter Minto Townsend Farquhar, 2nd bt. (1809-66), represented Hertford as a Conservative, 1857-9, 1865-6, and was succeeded in turn to the baronetcy, which became extinct in 1924, by the first four of his six sons with the illegitimate daughter of the 7th Lord Reay. His fifth son, Horace Brand Townsend Farquhar (1844-1923), was Liberal Unionist Member for West Marylebone, 1895-8, and died childless as 1st Earl Farquhar.

[1] *Oxford DNB*; *Gibbon Letters* ed. J.E. Norton, iii. 700, 867, 874, 875; *Prince of Wales Corresp.* iv. 1440, 1562, 1564, 1821; vi. 2292; Add. 34456, ff. 315, 336; 42772, ff. 286-93; *HMC Bathurst*, 51; *Farington Diary*, vii. 2673, 2708; viii. 2869. [2] *Farington Diary*, viii. 2809; x. 3536; Ward, *Letters to 'Ivy'*, 144. [3] PROB 8/212 (30 June 1819). [4] PROB 11/1617/271. [5] BL OIOC J/1/15, ff. 216-17. [6] *Gent.Mag.*(1802), i. 69; Add.13869, ff. 15, 16, 19, 24, 29 and *passim*. [7] Add. 13869, f. 1; 13870, ff. 1, 3. [8] Add. 13712, f. 184. [9] Add. 13712, f. 203; 13870, ff. 115, 156, 162, 163; 13874, ff. 164, 166; 37283, f. 280. [10] Add. 38281, f. 11; Cent. Kent. Stud. Harris mss C67/37/1; *Kentish Chron.* 1, 5, 8, 12, 15 May 1807. [11] Wellington mss WP1/177/107. [12] Add. 37292, ff. 17, 137, 173. [13] Add. 37292, ff. 103, 171, 278, 282; 38323, f. 109. [14] *HMC Fortescue*, x. 123; *PP* (1816), xiii. 322. [15] Add. 37292, f. 264. [16] *Imperial Reconstruction* ed. F. Maddon and D. Fieldhouse, 780-2; *PP* (1826), xxvii. 136-8; H.T. Manning, *British Colonial Government*, 466-73; *Camb. Hist. British Empire*, ii. 110, 473; A. Toussaint, *Hist. Mauritius*, 58-61, 66-67, 77; J. Addison and K. Hazareesing, *New Hist. Mauritius*, 45; C. Lloyd, *Navy and Slave Trade*, 197-9; D. Napal, *British Mauritius*, 1-6, 33. [17] Add. 37293, ff. 165, 240, 242; 38270, f. 246. [18] *PP* (1821),xxiii. 353; (1825), xxv. 814; (1826), xxvii. 279, 344-5; Toussaint, 77; L. Geoffroy, *Chart of Madagascar* (1819); Add. 38276, f. 314. [19] *Edgeworth Letters*, 185. [20] Add. 38276, f. 314; 38281, ff. 11, 13, 15; *Kentish Chron.* 10 Mar. 1820. [21] Loudon mss, Townsend Farquhar to Hastings, 11 Dec. 1820 (NRA 15459, p. 509); Add. 41265, ff. 1, 25, 28, 53, 64; *HMC Bathurst*, 522; Lloyd, 199; Wellington mss WP1/767/13. [22] Add. 38296, f. 273; 38298, f. 4. [23] *HMC Bathurst*, 544; *Geo. IV Letters*, iii. 1088. [24] *The Times*, 6 Jan. 1824. [25] Wellington mss WP1/784/11; *Kentish Chron.* 23 Apr. 1824. [26] *The Times*, 7 June 1826. [27] Bodl. (Rhodes House), Buxton mss Brit. Emp. s. 444, vol. 2, p. 239, Hannah to E. and H. Buxton, 10 May 1826; *Buxton Mems.* 182-6. [28] Lloyd, 200; *PP* (1826), iii. 87; (1826-7), iv. 287. [29] *Kentish Chron.* 14 Mar. 1826. [30] *Buxton Mems.* 189-95; *HMC Bathurst*, 607-12. [31] *Kentish Chron.* 27 Mar. 1827. [32] *Buxton Mems.* 201, 206; R.H. Mottram, *Buxton the Liberator*, 78-79, 86. [33] Wellington mss WP1/913/30; 951/62; 1032/4; 1036/1; 1085/8; *Wellington Despatches*, vi. 42-43. [34] *Anti-Slavery Monthly Reporter*, ii. 332-40, 374-5; iii. 13-14, 19-24, 45-49; *PP* (1829), xxv. 95-101. [35] Wellington mss WP1/1039/8; 1044/1; 1048/17; *Wellington Despatches*, vi. 146-8. [36] *PP* (1829), xxv. 49-93, 135-9; *Buxton Mems.* 224-8. [37] *Buxton Mems.* 228-30. [38] PROB 8/223 (22 Mar. 1830); 11/1768/166.

D.R.F.

TOWNSHEND, Lord Charles Vere Ferrers Compton (1785–1853), of 20 Cavendish Square, Mdx. and Rainham Hall, nr. Fakenham, Norf.

TAMWORTH	1812–1818
TAMWORTH	1820–1834

b. 16 Sept. 1785, 2nd. s. of George, 2nd Mq. Townshend (*d.* 1811), and Charlotte, da. and coh. of Eaton Mainwaring Ellerker of Risby Park, Yorks. *educ.* Harrow 1797-9. *m.* 24 Mar. 1812, his cos. Charlotte, da. of Gen. William Loftus† of Stiffkey, Norf., *s.p. d.* 5 Nov. 1853. Maj. Norf. rangers 1808; capt. Norf. yeoman cav. 1831.

Townshend's family had held one of Tamworth's seats from 1765 until 1818, when Townshend fought desperately but unsuccessfully to retain it, having been disadvantaged by the enforced sale of the Tamworth Castle estate by the Townshend trustees which had followed the death of his father in 1811. His elder brother George, who had succeeded to the peerage, and with whom the public were 'well acquainted' owing to his alleged homosexuality and failure to consummate his marriage, had been partially disinherited and lived abroad. By their father's will Townshend, who had married his cousin, a 'pretty young modest looking person', eventually came into possession of the entailed estates at Rainham, with their 'very large income' of about £15,000 a year, in 1832, but in the meantime was embroiled in a series of bitter legal disputes over his father's entrusted properties. In 1820 Lady Jerningham observed that he lived 'in a *very* small house' and 'at present he has not £2,000', and his case was described as 'one of singular hardship' in a letter sent to Sir Francis Burdett* in 1831, shortly before he obtained 'unrestricted possession' of Rainham Hall.[1]

At the 1820 general election Townshend offered again for Tamworth in opposition to the Peel interest and their assumption of both seats. Rather than face another stiff contest, Sir Robert Peel stepped down, leaving his son William and Townshend to come in unopposed.[2] A regular attender, Townshend gave generally steady support to the Whig opposition to the Liverpool ministry on most major issues, including economy, retrenchment and reduced taxation.[3] He voted against Catholic claims, 28 Feb. 1821, 1 Mar. 1825. He divided for parliamentary reform, 9 May 1821, 25 Apr. 1822, 24 Apr., 2 June 1823, 13, 27 Apr. 1826; but in his only known intervention in debate, 24 Apr. 1823, he 'censured the revolutionary principles contained in the Norfolk petition' presented that day in favour of reform. At the 1826 general election Townshend, whose uncle Lord John Townshend† had been assured by Robert Peel, the home secretary, that his father had 'no thoughts of proposing at the ensuing election more than one of his sons', was again returned unopposed for Tamworth.[4] He voted for the disfranchisement of Penryn, 28 May 1827, against extending East Retford's franchise to the hundred of Bassetlaw, 21 Mar. 1828, and for transfer of its seats to Birmingham, 5 May 1829, 5 Mar. 1830. He voted to condemn delays in chancery, 24 Apr. 1828. He voted for repeal of the Test Acts, 26 Feb. 1828, but was absent from the division on Catholic claims, 12 May. The following day he voted against the provision for Canning's family. He divided for inquiry into the Irish church, 24 June, and to adjourn the additional churches bill, 30 June 1828. In February 1829 Planta, the Wellington ministry's patronage secretary, predicted that he would be 'opposed' to securities to counterbalance Catholic emancipation. His name appears in none of the divisions of the following month except a minority of 17 against the Irish franchise bill, 19 Mar. 1829. He voted for the enfran-

chisement of Birmingham, Leeds, and Manchester, 23 Feb., and parliamentary reform, 28 May, and divided steadily with the revived opposition from March 1830. He voted for leave to introduce a bill for Jewish emancipation, 5 Apr., but against the second reading, 17 May 1830.

At the 1830 general election Townshend stood again for Tamworth where, following the candidature of Robert Peel, 'the borough was in a state of great excitement' and preparations were under way for a 'strenuous contest' if Peel's brother William did not step down. Townshend, who hoped that the electors 'would never suffer the borough to be closed by any family compact', considered it 'unnecessary' to 'declare his political principles', other than to observe that he had 'always voted for all necessary reductions in public expenditure' and had 'never been connected with any ministerial jobs'. After the withdrawal of William Peel he was returned unopposed.[5] He was listed by the Wellington ministry as one of their 'foes', and divided against them in the crucial division on the civil list, 15 Nov. 1830. He was absent from the division on the second reading of the Grey ministry's reform bill, 22 Mar., but present to vote against Gascoyne's wrecking amendment, 19 Apr. 1831. At the ensuing general election he offered again for Tamworth, urging the 'propriety and necessity of parliamentary reform', which would be 'of essential benefit to the community, and by no means dangerous to the constitution'. He had 'expected that a recent vote he had conscientiously given would probably have separated him from some of his chief friends, but the reception he met with convinced him that Tamworth ... was favourable to the disfranchisement of such places as Gatton, Old Sarum and Castle Rising'. Rumours of a third candidate came to nothing and he was again returned unopposed.[6] He voted for the second reading of the reintroduced reform bill, 6 July, at least twice against the adjournment, 12 July 1831, and gave generally steady support to its details, although he divided against the proposed division of counties, 11 Aug., and for Lord Chandos's clause to enfranchise £50 tenants-at-will, 18 Aug. He voted for the bill's passage, 21 Sept., and Lord Ebrington's confidence motion, 10 Oct. He divided with ministers on the Dublin election controversy, 23 Aug. 1831.

Following the reform bill's rejection in the Lords, Townshend was considered for possible inclusion in a list of 'heirs apparent or presumptive to the peerage, whose immediate elevation to the House would have no tendency towards the permanent augmentation of the numbers of that assembly'. In a report sent to Peel by William Holmes*, 6 Jan. 1832, he was rumoured to be one of 20 creations about to be 'immediately ordered' by the king, but nothing came of this.[7] He voted for the second reading of the revised reform bill, 17 Dec. 1831, and again generally supported its details, although he was in the minority against the inclusion of Helston in schedule B, 23 Feb. 1832. He divided with government on the Russian-Dutch loan, 26 Jan., 12, 20 July, and relations with Portugal, 9 Feb. 1832. He divided for the reform bill's third reading, 22 Mar., but was absent from the division on the address calling on the king to appoint only ministers who would carry it unimpaired, 10 May. He voted for the second reading of the Irish bill, 25 May 1832.

At the 1832 general election Townshend was re-elected unopposed for Tamworth, where he sat as a Liberal until the dissolution of 1834, when he retired.[8] Following the death in 1833 of John Robins, who had bought the family's Tamworth estate in 1814, Townshend, in collaboration with the family trustees, repurchased the Castle and some of the adjoining land.[9] He also aspired to succeed to the peerage, but his claims were uncertain. The Marchioness Townshend, who had never divorced his brother, had in 1809 taken at Gretna Green a second husband, John Margetts, with whom she had a son John (1811-1903), styled Lord John Townshend, 1823-8, and then earl of Leicester, under which name he was returned as a Conservative for Bodmin in 1841. His claims, as one commentator put it, threatened to 'cast the honour of this distinguished family upon an alien brood', and in 1843 Townshend obtained a private Act of Parliament declaring that the children of the Marchioness 'are not, nor were, nor shall they or any of them be taken to be, or be deemed, the lawful issue of the said George Ferrars, Marquess Townshend'. The self-styled earl changed his name to John Dunn Gardner shortly thereafter.[10]

Townshend died at St. Leonard's-on-Sea in November 1853. By his will, dated 12 Aug. 1853, he left all his personal estate to his wife. The family estates at Rainham, of which he was 'tenant for life', and Tamworth Castle passed to the next male heir, his cousin Captain John Townshend (1798-1863), who sat for Tamworth as a Liberal, 1847-53, and succeeded Townshend's elder brother as the 4th Marquess Townshend in 1855, when the earldom of Leicester became extinct.[11]

[1]*Gent. Mag.* (1811), ii. 93, 664; *Jerningham Letters*, ii. 185; *The Times*, 14 June 1819; Sheffield Archives, Arundel Castle mss MD 2613. [2] N. Gash, *Secretary Peel*, 296; *Staffs. Advertiser*, 4 Mar. 1820. [3]*Session of Parl. 1825*, p. 487. [4]Add. 40385, f. 321; *Staffs. Advertiser*, 10 June 1826.

[5] *Lichfield Mercury*, 16, 23, 30 July, 6, 13 Aug.; *Staffs. Advertiser*, 24, 31 July, 7 Aug. 1830. [6] *Lichfield Mercury*, 29 Apr., 6 May; *Staffs. Advertiser*, 30 Apr., 7 May 1831. [7]Arundel Castle mss MD 2613; Add. 40402, f. 175. [8] *Dyott's Diary*, ii. 187-8. [9] *White's Staffs. Dir.* (1834), 383; (1851), 620; C. Palmer, *Hist. Tamworth*, 499. [10] Arundel Castle mss MD 2613; *Gent. Mag.* (1853), ii. 631; *CP*, xii. 812-13. [11] *Gent. Mag.* (1853), ii. 631; H. Wood, *Borough By Prescription* (1958), 69; PROB 11/2188/247; IR26/2011/176.

P.J.S.

TOWNSHEND, Hon. Horatio George Powys (1780–1843), of 2 Chapel Street, Mdx.

WHITCHURCH	13 Aug. 1816–1826
WHITCHURCH	25 Feb. 1831–1832

b. 6 Feb. 1780, 3rd s. of Thomas Townshend†, 1st Visct. Sydney (*d.* 1800), and Elizabeth, da. and coh. of Richard Powys† of Hintlesham, Suff. *educ.* Eton 1787-91. *unm.* kntd. (and KCH) 25 Sept. 1835. *d.* 25 May 1843.
   Ensign 1 Ft. Gds. 1795, lt. and capt. 1799, capt. and lt.-col. 1809; brevet col. 1819; lt.-col. commdt. 1 Ft. Gds. 1821; half-pay 1830.
   Dep. ranger, St. James's and Hyde Parks 1823-31; lt.-gov. Windsor Castle at *d.*

Townshend, a veteran of Waterloo, was again returned by his eldest brother Lord Sydney for the family borough at the 1820 general election.[1] A regular attender, he continued to give mostly silent support to the Liverpool ministry.[2] He voted with them on the Queen Caroline affair, 6 Feb., repeal of the additional malt duty, 3 Apr., the army estimates, 11 Apr., and the disfranchisement of ordnance officials, 12 Apr. 1821. He divided against parliamentary reform, 9 May 1821, and reform of the Scottish county representation, 2 June 1823, and Edinburgh's electoral system, 13 Apr. 1826. He voted against Catholic relief, 28 Feb. 1821, 30 Apr. 1822, 1 Mar., 21 Apr., 10 May 1825. He divided against more extensive tax reductions, 11, 21 Feb., abolition of one of the joint-postmasterships, 13 Mar., and censure of the lord advocate's dealings with the Scottish press, 25 June, and for the aliens bill, 19 July 1822. He sided with ministers against repeal of the house tax, 10 Mar., and the Foreign Enlistment Act, 16 Apr., and inquiries into the legal proceedings against the Dublin theatre rioters, 22 Apr., and currency reform, 12 June 1823. Townshend, who was commanding officer of the Grenadier Guards from 1821 until his retirement in 1830, voted against the abolition of flogging in the army, 5 Mar., and refuted allegations that it was routinely inflicted in his regiment, 11 Mar. 1824. He paired with ministers against inquiry into the prosecution of the Methodist missionary John Smith for inciting slave riots in Demerara, 11

June 1824. He divided for suppression of the Catholic Association, 25 Feb., and the duke of Cumberland's annuity bill, 30 May, 2, 6 June 1825. He was in the minority against the second reading of the spring guns bill, 21 June 1825. Replying to opposition complaints against the housing of soldiers in barracks on the doorstep of Parliament at Charing Cross, 6 Mar. 1826, he declared that 'the army would soon run to confusion and disorder if the barrack system were abolished'. On 10 Mar. he insisted that 'gentlemen were much mistaken who thought that the discipline of the army could be maintained without corporal punishment'. He divided against Russell's resolutions on electoral bribery, 26 May 1826.

At the 1826 general election Townshend made way for his nephew, but on the latter's succession to the peerage early in 1831 he resumed the family seat. He voted against the second reading of the Grey ministry's reform bill, by which Whitchurch stood to be completely disfranchised, 22 Mar., and for Gascoyne's wrecking amendment, 19 Apr. At the ensuing general election he offered again as an opponent of the bill, which he described as an 'infernal nuisance', and was returned unopposed.[3] He voted against the second reading of the reintroduced reform bill, 6 July 1831. On 26 July he abandoned as futile his intention of pleading for a reprieve for Whitchurch 'on the grounds of its being a burgage tenure', but insisted that his motives for resisting reform were 'honourable':

> If I for a moment thought that the ... [bill] was likely to be attended with advantage to my country, I would be among the foremost ranks in its support. But as, on the contrary, I conceive it to be fraught with danger and mischief to our constitution, I shall ever, with heart and hand, give my assistance in preventing it being made one of the laws of the land.

He divided against some of its details, 27 July, 2 Sept., and its passage, 21 Sept. He paired with the minority of diehards opposed to the Maynooth grant, 26 Sept. He voted against the second reading of the revised reform bill, 17 Dec. 1831, and was in the minorities against going into committee on it, 20 Jan., the enfranchisement of Tower Hamlets, 28 Feb., and the third reading, 22 Mar. 1832. He voted against the second reading of the Irish measure, 25 May. He divided against ministers on the Russian-Dutch loan, 26 Jan., but was in their majority against inquiry into military punishments, 16 Feb. He was in the minority of 17 against the malt drawback bill, 29 Feb. 1832. His parliamentary career ended with the disfranchisement of Whitchurch.

Townshend died unmarried at his home in Bolton Street, Piccadilly, in May 1843. By his will, dated 3 Apr. 1843, he left bequests of about £22,000, including £5,000 to his sister Lady Dynevor, £5,000 to each of his godchildren Lady Harriet Janet Sarah Moore and the Rev. Edward Moore, and £5,000 to his niece, Harriet Lucy Rice. His personal estate was sworn under £60,000. The residue passed to his nephew and executor Lord Sydney. At his request his burial pall was dressed in the ceremonial colours of the Grenadiers and his coffin carried to the family vault at Chislehurst by regimental survivors of Waterloo.[4]

[1] *Salisbury Jnl.* 13 Mar. 1820. [2] *Black Bk.* (1823), 198; *Session of Parl. 1825*, p. 487. [3] *Portsmouth Herald*, 8 May 1831. [4] *Gent. Mag.* (1843), ii. 202; PROB 11/1981/442; IR26/1657/489.

D.R.F./P.J.S.

TOWNSHEND, Lord James Nugent Boyle Bernardo (1785–1842), of Yarrow House, Bintree, Norf.

HELSTON   1818–1832

HELSTON   1835–1837

b. 11 Sept. 1785, 6th s. of George Townshend[†], 1st Mq. Townshend, and 2nd w. Anne, da. and coh. of Sir William Montgomery, 1st bt., MP [I], of Magbie Hill, Peebles; half-bro. of Lord Charles Patrick Thomas Townshend[†] and Lord John Townshend[†]. *educ.* Eton 1796; Harrow 1797–9. *m.* 8 May 1813, Elizabeth Martha, da. of P. Wallis, government cooper, of Halifax, N.S., *s.p.* KCH 1835. *d.* 28 June 1842.

Entered RN as midshipman, lt. 1806, cdr. 1806, capt. 1809, ret. 1840.

Maj. commdt. Norf. Rangers 1822; capt. Norf. yeoman cav. 1831.

Townshend, a naval officer, was returned for Helston for the second time in 1820 on his brother-in-law the 6th duke of Leeds's interest, after a contest forced by an 'independent' party among the freemen.[1] He was an almost silent Member who continued to give general support to Lord Liverpool's ministry, but he was a poor attender. He presented a Helston petition for a small debts recovery bill, 11 May 1820.[2] He was granted a fortnight's leave on account of ill health, 5 July 1820, and another month for the same reason, 15 Mar. 1821. He voted against the removal of Catholic peers' disabilities, 30 Apr., and presented a Helston corporation petition for repeal of the salt duty, 24 May 1822.[3] He divided against inquiry into the borough franchise, 20 Feb., and the prosecution of the Dublin Orange rioters, 22 Apr. 1823. He voted for the Irish unlawful societies bill, 25 Feb., and against Catholic relief, 1 Mar. 1825. According to *The Times*, it was he who voted against the financial provision for the duke of Cumberland, 27 May 1825.[4] He was returned unopposed for Helston at the general election of 1826.[5]

He divided against Catholic relief, 6 Mar. 1827, 12 May 1828. He was granted a week's leave to attend the assizes, 23 Mar. 1827. He acknowledged the request from Peel, the leader of the Commons in the duke of Wellington's ministry, to attend at the opening of the 1828 session, but explained that his arrival was likely to be delayed by a 'severe fit of gout'.[6] He presented a Helston anti-slavery petition, 12 June. He stated from personal experience that the fortifications at Dartmouth were 'in good order' and had 'done good service', 20 June. However, he voted against ministers to condemn the misapplication of public money for building work at Buckingham House, 25 June 1828. In February 1829 Planta, the patronage secretary, listed him as being likely to vote 'with government' for Catholic emancipation, which accorded with the wishes of Leeds, a member of the royal household; he paired for the measure, 18, 23, 27 Mar. 1829. He was granted a month's sick leave, 1 Mar. 1830. At the general election that summer he was returned unopposed for Helston.[7] The ministry regarded him as one of the 'good doubtfuls', who was one of their 'friends ... where not pledged', but he was absent from the crucial division on the civil list, 15 Nov. He was granted three weeks' leave on account of the disturbed state of his neighbourhood, 2 Dec. 1830. He divided against the second reading of the Grey ministry's reform bill, 22 Mar., and for Gascoyne's wrecking amendment, 19 Apr. 1831. At the ensuing general election he was returned unopposed for Helston, which was scheduled to lose one of its Members.[8] Shortly afterwards he was given command of the frigate *Dublin* on the South American station, and Leeds expected him to vacate, but in the event he retained his seat despite his absence from the House.[9] He retired at the dissolution in 1832 but sat again for Helston as a Conservative from 1835 to 1837; contrary to the statement in an obituary, he never 'voted with the Whig party'.[10] He died childless in June 1842 and left all his property, including land in St. John's, Newfoundland, to his wife; his personalty was sworn under £25,000.[11]

[1] *R. Cornw. Gazette*, 11 Mar. 1820. [2] *The Times*, 12 May 1820. [3] Ibid. 25 May 1822. [4] Ibid. 30 May 1825. [5] *West Briton*, 9, 16 June 1826. [6] Add. 40395, f. 158. [7] *West Briton*, 7 Aug. 1830. [8] Ibid. 6 May 1831. [9] Wellington mss WP1/1184/27. [10] M. Stenton, *Who's Who of British MPs, 1832-1885*, p. 382; *Gent. Mag.* (1842), ii. 423-4. [11] PROB 8/235; IR26/1625/554.

T.A.J.

TOWNSHEND, Hon. John Robert (1805–1890), of 3 New Burlington Street, Mdx.

WHITCHURCH   1826–20 Jan. 1831

b. 9 Aug. 1805, 2nd but o. surv. s. of John Thomas Townshend†, 2nd Visct. Sydney, and 2nd w. Lady Caroline Elizabeth Letitia Clements, da. of Robert, 1st earl of Leitrim [I]. *educ.* Eton 1817-20; St. John's, Camb. 1822. *m.* 4 Aug. 1832, Lady Emily Caroline Paget, da. of Henry William Paget†, 1st mq. of Anglesey, *s.p. suc.* fa. as 3rd Visct. Sydney 20 Jan. 1831; GCB 10 Mar. 1863; *cr.* Earl Sydney 27 Feb. 1874. *d.* 14 Feb. 1890.

Groom of bedchamber Sept. 1828-Nov. 1830; ld. of bedchamber Jan.-Apr. 1835; ld. in waiting Sept. 1841-July 1846; capt. of yeomen of the guard Dec. 1852-Mar. 1858; PC 4 Jan. 1853; ld. chamberlain of household June 1859-July 1866, Dec. 1868-Mar. 1874; first plenip. on spec. mission to king of Belgians 1866; ld. steward of household May 1880-June 1885, Feb.-Aug. 1886.

Ld. lt. Kent 1856-d.; capt. Deal Castle 1879-d.

Capt. W. Kent militia 1827, W. Kent yeomanry 1830; col. Kent artillery militia 1853.

Townshend's father had held junior office in Pitt's first ministry from 1784 until his succession to the peerage in 1800, when he became a courtier. He was a lord of the bedchamber until 1810 and ranger of Hyde and St. James's Parks, with £1,732 a year, from 1807. His son with his first wife, the daughter of Lord De Clifford, who died in childbirth in 1795, did not survive infancy, and his second wife died in the act of giving birth to this Member in 1805. After a conventional education Townshend spent the winter of 1824-5 in Italy, where he became friendly with Lord Holland's son Henry Edward Fox*, whose initial impression of him was that of a 'good-natured youth, not likely to inflame either Thames or Tiber'.[1] They went together from Rome to Naples in January 1825 when Fox, whose only reservation about him was that he lacked 'depth of feeling', reported:

> Townshend is happy in the good cuisine ... and revels among truffles and green peas ... I delight in ... [him]. His character and disposition are thoroughly amiable and his understanding, if more cultivated, which I dare say it will be, will be very adequate to all the purposes he can wish to turn it.[2]

Townshend returned to Rome in April 1825 and travelled via Florence, Venice, Verona and the Tyrol to Paris, intending to witness the coronation of Charles X at Rheims. He became a favourite with Lady Granville, the wife of the British ambassador who, as he informed Fox receives in her garden every Tuesday at two. Eating, dancing and petit jeu go on ... in the latter amusement ladies run about the garden to be caught by men. They call it le coup. George Howard must perform this feat with the fat Lady Helena Robinson who, sad to say, made a great exposure, her ladyship falling with George on her, and showing what my decency forbids to write. The French women were all delighted.

He went with the suite of the duke of Northumberland, the British ambassador extraordinary, to the coronation, which was 'well worth seeing, though very inferior to our own'.[3] On returning to England in June 1825, he spent an enjoyable five weeks in London society, where he fell in love with Lord Harrowby's daughter Lady Georgiana Ryder. Recuperating during August at the family home at Frognal in Kent, he informed Fox, 'I ... am now rather enjoying the dullness of a country life, after the hustle of a year's voyage. I am getting up my history and my health by a regular and early life'. He visited the Ryders at Sandon at the end of the month, but six weeks later was chagrined to learn of Lady Georgiana's engagement, after 'an affair of three weeks', to John Stuart Wortley*. He was also 'very much annoyed' at his favourite half-sister Mary's marriage, at the age of 31, to George James Cholmondeley of Boxley who, at 73, was '13 years older than her father'.[4] (This match, which provoked much gossip, the more so as Mary Townshend stood to inherit £45,000 on the death of her maternal uncle Lord De Clifford, produced a daughter ten months later.)[5]

Townshend went to Paris in November 1825 and, determined not 'to marry this 8 or 10 years', contented himself with 'making love to married women'.[6] Fox's parents, who were also there, took to him. Lady Holland thought him 'an excellent tempered and well conditioned young man in all respects', with 'a very plain understanding', and her husband found him 'agreeable in looks and manners and, if not brilliant, not the least deficient in conversation'.[7] Mrs. Fazakerley, however, complained that 'without meaning to be ill natured or to do harm', he was too much the scandal-monger for his own good.[8] At the end of April Townshend, who had been troubled by the recurrence of a venereal complaint which he had contracted at Naples, returned to London to go as one of the duke of Devonshire's attachés on his special mission to the coronation of Tsar Nicholas of Russia.[9] From St. Petersburg he wrote to Fox that 'the Russian women provoke me to the highest degree. They are all very pretty, very coquettish, very civil in their own houses, and most reserved in other society'. After the ceremony, which was delayed until 3 Sept. 1826, he returned to London via Germany and France with his

friend Lord Morpeth* 'to attend our respective duties in Parliament', having been returned in absentia, and two months under age, for the family borough at the general election that June.[10]

Townshend attended the opening of Parliament, where he sided with the Liverpool ministry, and later told Fox, 'I take very kindly to Parliament, and I think it will amuse me very much', though 'it interferes sadly with one's dinner'.[11] In March 1827 his father expressed to the home secretary Peel his hope that 'my son Mr. Townshend is a good attender in the House of Commons', which he appears to have been.[12] He privately welcomed the government's proposals for adjustment of the corn laws, noting that as 'the ultras of each party disapprove' he was disposed to believe 'there is something really good in the medium'.[13] He voted against Catholic relief, 6 Mar. 1827, 12 May 1828. Lord Sydney was reputedly of a mind to resign his rangership in protest at Canning's accession to the premiership in April 1827, but he did not do so.[14] Townshend was in the minority of 31 against the disfranchisement of Penryn, 7 June 1827. At the end of that year, when the Goderich ministry was tottering, he wrote to Fox of 'the weakness of the government' and 'the melancholy state of the country, four millions deficiency of revenue and the probability of a war, in which if we succeed, our own interests in the Mediterranean must be destroyed'.[15] On the formation of Wellington's ministry Sydney wrote to Peel to

again beg to recommend my son ... be employed in public business. I have written to the duke of Wellington soliciting, and most earnestly, an employment at one of the public boards ... You know my political principles and those of Mr. Townshend are the same. I have looked to you as the minister of the crown, to whom I wished to attach myself in politics, and probably you have long given me credit for what I now declare.

Peel replied cordially but was unable to oblige.[16] Townshend voted against repeal of the Test Acts, 26 Feb. 1828. He was in the government majority on the ordnance estimates, 4 July 1828. Two months later he was appointed a groom of the bedchamber. In Febuary 1829, when he was considered as a possible mover or seconder of the address, he was expected by Planta, the patronage secretary, to forego his previous hostility to Catholic relief and support the ministerial concession of emancipation. He voted accordingly, 6, 30 Mar. 1829, when, in his only known speech, he explained that he did so

on the ground of expediency, because I think that it is much better to run the risk of incurring a minor mischief, rather than to encounter the ... certainty of a greater ... In taking this course, I do not admit the abstract right of the Roman Catholics to those privileges which the legislature is about to confer on them ... but, I contend, that things cannot remain as they are ... I cannot blind myself to the distracted state of society in Ireland, to the utter depression of trade and commerce in that country, and to the cessation of social intercourse between man and man.

He divided against parliamentary reform, 11, 18, 23 Feb., Jewish emancipation, 17 May, and abolition of the death penalty for forgery, 7 June 1830.

At the 1830 general election he was again returned unopposed. He was one of the 'friends' of government who voted in their minority on the civil list, 15 Nov. 1830. He went out of place on the change of ministry and was removed from the Commons by his father's death in January 1831.[17] As a peer he opposed the Grey ministry's reform bill. He held household office in both Peel's administrations and, after initial misgivings, supported repeal of the corn laws in 1846. He subsequently gravitated with other Peelites to the Liberals and held senior household posts in all their governments between 1859 and 1886, being on particularly close terms with William Gladstone[†].[18] On his death without issue in February 1890, Queen Victoria observed:

He is a great loss, and was ever such a loyal devoted servant of the crown, much devoted to me personally, a man full of knowledge and experience to whom one could turn at all times.[19]

Lord Lansdowne, the viceroy of India, recalled him as a man with 'much knowledge of the world', together with 'excellent business abilities' and 'sound judgment'.[20] By his will his estates at Frognal and Matson, Gloucestershire passed on the death of his widow in 1893 to his nephew Robert Marsham (1834-1914), the only son of his half-sister Mary and her second husband, the 2nd earl of Romney.

[1] *Fox Jnl.* 201. [2] Ibid. 224; Add. 61937, Fox to Mrs. Fazakerley, 25 Jan. 1825. [3] Add. 52017, Townsend to Fox, 4, 25 Apr., 11, 18 May: 61937, Fox to Mrs. Fazakerley, 15 Feb. 1825. [4] Add. 52017, Townsend to Fox, 2, 21 June, 5 July, 1, 6, 30 Aug., 13, 30 Oct.; 52011, Mrs. Fazakerley to Fox, 29 Aug., 25 Oct. 1825. [5] *Arbuthnot Jnl.* i. 423; *Williams Wynn Corresp.* 324, 338-9; *Gent. Mag.* (1830), ii. 567. [6] Add. 52017, Townshend to Fox, 20, 29 Nov. 1825. [7] Add. 51766, Lady Holland to Fox, 5 Jan. 1826; 51749, Holland to Fox, 8 Jan. 1826. [8] Add. 52011, Mrs. Fazakerley to Fox, 21 Mar. 1826. [9] Add. 52017, Townshend to Fox, 17 Jan. , , 30 Apr., 6 June 1826. [10] Ibid. 24 June, 21 July, 10 Sept., 9 Nov. 1826. [11] Add. 52017, Townshend to Fox, 22 Dec. 1826. [12] Add. 40393, f. 104. [13] Add. 52017, Townsend to Fox, 5 Mar., 29 July 1827. [14] *Canning's Ministry*, 142, 312. [15] Add. 52017, Townsend to Fox, 27 Dec. 1827. [16] Add. 40395, ff. 61-62. [17] Add. 40398, f. 87; PROB 11/1782/114. [18] Add. 40409, ff. 122, 321; 40583, ff. 286, 288; 40593, ff. 384, 388; 44318, ff. 355-511; *The Times*, 15, 21 Feb. 1890. [19] *Victoria Letters* (ser. 3), i. 568. [20] Ibid. 572.

D.R.F./P.J.S.

TRACY *see* **HANBURY TRACY**

TRAILL, George (1787–1871), of Castlehill, nr. Thurso, Caithness and Hobister, Orkney.

ORKNEY AND SHETLAND	1830–1834
CAITHNESS	1841–Aug. 1869

b. 5 Nov. 1787,[1] 1st s. of James Traill, adv., of Hobister and Rattar Dunnet, Caithness and Lady Janet Sinclair, da. of William, 10th earl of Caithness [S]. *educ.* Westminster 1801-5; Edinburgh Univ.; adv. 1811. *unm. suc.* fa. 1843. *d.* 29 Sept. 1871.

Traill's father, the son of Dr. George Traill (*d.* 1785) of Hobister, minister of the north Caithness parish of Dunnet, 1751-84, was born in 1758, admitted an advocate in 1779 and became sheriff of Sutherland and Caithness. He was served as heir general to his father in the Orkney estate of Hobister, near Kirkwall, in 1787, but resided mainly in Caithness. He was not on the freeholders' roll there, but was in Orkney, where his estate was described in 1788 as a 'good' one.[2] His son George Traill was educated for the Scottish bar, to which he was admitted in 1811, by when he too was on the Orkney roll as George Traill junior of Hobister; but he lived chiefly in Caithness, at Castlehill.[3] He and his father had been parties to the Orkney electoral pact of 1818, whereby they and a group of independent proprietors had agreed with Thomas Dundas, 1st Baron Dundas, to an alternating system of nomination for, in the first instance, the next two general elections, in order to overturn the currently dominant interest of Sir William Honyman, Lord Armadale (SCJ). At the general election of 1820, when it was the turn of the lairds to put up the Member, Traill and his father were active in promoting the candidature of the latter's old friend, 69-year-old John Balfour of Trenabie, who had represented the county in the 1790 Parliament and now lived in and near London. Traill overcame 'the desponding view' of John Balfour's nephew and Orkney man of affairs, Captain William Balfour, and the election resulted in Balfour's defeat of Armadale's son.[4] In 1823 James Traill tried to obtain from the Liverpool ministry an exchange of his shrievalty for a commissionership of bankrupts for his younger son and namesake, but apparently did not succeed; James Traill junior later became a metropolitan police magistrate.[5] The electoral pact had been renewed for the next two elections soon after the election of 1820, and in 1825 Captain George Heneage Dundas*, brother of the 2nd Baron Dundas (the 1st Baron having died in June 1820) and Member in the 1818 Parliament, announced his candidature for the anticipated general election. However, one of the signatories to the pact, the Whig Samuel Laing[†], declared his intention of standing against him. According to Captain Balfour, writing to John in late September 1825, 'a hint' had been given to Traill soon after the 1820 election that 'if it should prove inconvenient for any of the Dundas family to come forward' next time, 'their turn should be given up to him'; and he thought that Traill and 'his friends had spoken a little unguardedly' about this. At the same time, he felt that he himself was in honour bound to support Dundas if he persevered, and reported that Traill and his father had also promised Dundas their support.[6] George Traill confirmed this to Captain Balfour, and explained 'the views I have entertained with respect to myself' regarding the county at the election after the next:

> I have always said that if you would consent to become a candidate ... you should have my most zealous support ... but as you have heretofore declined it in so decided a manner, and having been myself encouraged by the wishes expressed in my favour by several friends connected with Orkney, I trust it will not be thought presumptuous in me to say that for some time I have looked to this situation as a desirable object, the attainment of which would probably afford me, for the active part of my life, an ample employment suited to my inclination and turn of mind ... But neither for the attainment of this nor of any personal gratification to myself will I be the cause of disunion ... still less of risking the dissolution of that intimate connection of friendship which has for so long subsisted between our families. Therefore if, when it comes to our turn to elect, you shall be disposed to bring forward another candidate ... I will at once withdraw my pretensions ... With respect to party, it being admitted that a regular opposition is essential to the existence of our system of government, it follows that provided the candidate is otherwise a proper person, his belonging to that party can be no sufficient objection to him ... but if you should object to me on this score, I shall ... give way. All I would ask in that case is that before determining against me, you would give me an opportunity of stating my sentiments at the time; because although I am a Whig in principle and cannot anticipate any change in that respect, yet it does not necessarily follow that I must always be an oppositionist, whatever may be the character and conduct of the existing administration.[7]

Captain Balfour replied that he would be guided by his uncle, while he lived, and by Traill's father thereafter, and declined to commit himself so far in advance, but said that it was 'very improbable I shall not support you' and 'impossible I should oppose you'.[8] In early January 1826 Captain Balfour, commenting to his uncle that Traill's recent interest in plans for facilitating the transport to market of 'the productions of his estate' was out of character, observed:

He spends two or three weeks there once in the year it is true, but he is (when well) employed from morning to night rather for preparing for his expected seat in Parliament by reading Adam Smith, Ricardo* and McCulloch on political economy than in planning the improving of his estate.[9]

On 21 Feb. Traill informed Captain Balfour from Southampton that he had heard that the Honyman and Henderson families had coalesced with Laing, which seemed to make Dundas's success unlikely and thus threatened their own long term prospects. He suggested trying to persuade John Balfour to stand for re-election, with the concurrence of the Dundases, which he was prepared to seek in person, on the understanding that the Dundas interest would have the nomination at the election after next. If John Balfour declined and the chance was offered to him, he would 'try it', though he acknowledged that his 'chance of success at the election is nothing like so certain' as Balfour's and that the Dundases would be less 'likely to put me forward, because they would not have the subsequent return'.[10] To John Balfour the captain wrote, 25 Feb., that Traill's notion of brokering such a deal with the Dundases on his behalf was 'a mere compliment', for, as Traill knew full well, the arithmetic of the votes was all against their beating Laing.[11] Nothing came of this. On 29 Apr. Traill wrote at length to Captain Balfour, again from Southampton, confirming that he and his brother had consulted John Balfour and discovered that he had no intention of standing at the next election. He had then broached to Captain Dundas the suggestion of his family's 'offering us the first nomination', but found him unreceptive and confident of his own chances. Traill was willing to assist him as best he could, in point of honour and as the best means of securing their own interests in the long run. As to his own views:

> It is of course decided that when our turn comes Mr. [John] Balfour resumes his place, if he can be induced to accept. If not ... so far from considering you as under the slightest pledge to me ... I shall certainly not come forward unless it meets with your entire approbation *at the time* ... If it should so happen that ... you shall wish to support any other person ... I shall not stand in your way.[12]

Captain Balfour was satisfied with this, though he thought that some of Traill's speculations of votes to be gained for the old coalition were optimistic and perceived that, like himself, he rather wanted Dundas to give it up, though 'for a different reason'.[13] A month before the election Captain Balfour discovered that Traill and his father had tied off with two Hendersons, so that they need not attend the election, and expressed his strong disapproval. After a flurry of correspondence it proved possible to secure their release from this arrangement.[14] In the event Laing withdrew at a late hour, leaving Captain Dundas to walk over. A month after the election Traill was testing the waters for the next one.[15] In May 1827, when he was trying to open a new market for kelp in America, he alerted Captain Balfour to the forthcoming sale of the Honyman estate and attached superiorities and offered to take an equal share with the Balfours in their purchase. He also suggested making 'a general and formal offer' of support to John Balfour at the next election. This was done, and, as Traill had presumably anticipated, Balfour signified his determination not to enter Parliament again, which left the way clear for Traill at the next election.[16] In November 1827 he asked Captain Balfour for advice on how to respond to an overture from Lord Dundas, who accepted that Traill was to be the candidate at the next election, but suggested an agreement that in return for support then it was to be understood that a Dundas nominee would be put up at the election after that. Traill concurred in Balfour's view that any such engagement should be avoided at that distance from the event, and he subsequently had a satisfactory talk with Dundas's agent on this matter.[17] He was in London in mid-June 1830, when he anticipated the king's death and informed Captain Balfour of reports that the struggling Wellington ministry was to be 'very materially changed by an infusion of new strength from the liberals'; in this event, he wanted to see Charles Grant, Member for Inverness-shire, made chancellor of the exchequer, which would aid his efforts to secure legislation to alleviate the problems of the kelp trade. He had already discussed the problem and possible solutions, which included a scheme for 'commutation of the window duty' to boost the production of glass, with Grant and James Loch*, a candidate for Tain Burghs, and they had not entirely negative talks with Goulburn, the incumbent chancellor.[18] On the dissolution in July he announced his candidature for Orkney, and he was returned unopposed, 1 Sept. 1830. Returning thanks, he promised to act 'in the most independent and conscientious manner' and to continue his co-operation with Loch to 'revive the kelp trade'.[19]

Ministers listed Traill as one of their 'friends', but after consulting John Balfour, to whom he turned constantly for advice and guidance, he went to the Commons on 15 Nov. 1830 intending to vote against them on the civil list, only to discover that 'the lobby was shut a few minutes before my arrival'.[20] He presented petitions for the abolition of slavery from Orkney and Caithness, 16 Nov., 6, 18 Dec. 1830. He gleaned from Thomas Kennedy*, whose draft Scottish reform proposals had been taken up by the Grey ministry, that their scheme would enfranchise at least 100 £10 owners and occupiers in Orkney, exclusive of Shetland. He approved of this, and in January 1831 gave Captain Balfour the impression that his uncle's 'ideas on reform go rather further than his'. This surprised the captain, who was suspicious of Traill's motives in creating the impression that he consulted John Balfour 'most unreservedly on every point connected with our public affairs'. He thought there could be strong opposition in Orkney to a Member who was 'inclined to carry ... [reform] so far as George Traill is supposed to do', and foresaw trouble at the next election if the Dundases asserted their right to fill the seat, as he was sure that Traill had no intention of stepping quietly aside.[21] On 5 Feb. Traill wrote at length to Captain Balfour from Edinburgh of his efforts to improve the kelp trade, which he thought had 'favourable' prospects of success, though he had felt unable to support Loch's new scheme to secure a repeal of the glass duties to compensate for the reduction of those on barilla without consulting his constituents, having been mandated by them to co-operate with the glass makers for a commutation of the window tax. He also doubted the practicality of the West Highland proprietors' proposals for a small increase in the duties on salt and barilla. He explained his controversial attempt to improve the postal service to Orkney. In his frequent communications with the treasury on these matters he had found Spring Rice, the financial secretary, and Lord Althorp, the chancellor of the exchequer, 'very satisfactory' to deal with. On the issue of parliamentary reform, he wrote:

> That this measure will and must be carried is now admitted *almost universally*, but whether before or after a dissolution ... is not so certain, from there being about 30 Members representing treasury boroughs and put in by the late ministers, and from the pertinacity and blindness of some of the borough proprietors, who notwithstanding the signs of the times seem determined to cling to their patronage. If a dissolution is resorted to, there can be no question ... as to the result, but from the present state of the public mind there is no saying what disturbances this might give rise to or how they might terminate. Had it not been for the duke of Wellington's opportune resignation, I do not think the peace of the country could have been maintained, and if the present ministry were obliged to go out on this question, the result would be still more certain. But of this I conceive there is no chance, and as it appears the ministers are quite agreed as to the measure which they are to propose, I confidently hope it will be such as to satisfy the influential and middling

classes of the community and, if so, the labouring class, notwithstanding the efforts of demagogues, will very soon be reconciled.

He had been advised by John Balfour not to raise directly with Lord Grey the possibility of separating Orkney and Shetland for electoral purposes, though he calculated that reform might create barely a dozen electors in the latter. Anticipating a dissolution in May whatever happened, he sought a renewal of Captain Balfour's support.[22] In the House, 26 Feb., he presented reform petitions from Stromness and Wick, and later in the discussion said that 'if public meetings in Scotland to petition for reform have not been numerous, it is not because the people are opposed to the question, but because they did not wish to agitate it before it had been taken up by government ... Nearly all the wealth, respectability and talent of the country are prepared to support ... ministers on this point'. On 12 Mar. he informed Captain Balfour that he had high hopes of ministers' agreeing to abolish the glass duties, but opined that a property tax, which he favoured, could not be achieved in an unreformed Parliament. He claimed that John Balfour entirely agreed with him that the government's English reform bill

neither should nor could be counteracted. The system of rotten boroughs in particular, by which both the government and the people are kept in subjugation, has of late been so completely exposed that no force could maintain it for two ... months. The legitimate power which the aristocracy obtain by the addition to the county Members will be a much more effectual support to their interests than the invidious possession of close boroughs, while the qualification of £10 will secure a much better class of voters than those who have lately exercised that right at Liverpool and Preston. My opinion of this plan is that it is so reasonable that it will permanently satisfy the people ... The determination to reform Scotland is so universal that even if the question was lost with respect to England it would be applied to Scotland.[23]

A report that ministers were going to permit the use of sugar instead of barley grain in distilling sent him scurrying in protest to the treasury, where he found Spring Rice willing to allow the argument against this to be fully aired.[24] On 21 Mar. Traill presented 50 Scottish petitions in support of the ministerial reform scheme, drawing attention to one from merchants, bankers, manufacturers, traders and other inhabitants of Glasgow with 24,000 signatures and another from Glasgow town council. Next day he divided for the second reading of the English reform bill. He took up the case for giving Orkney and Shetland a Member each, the more urgently when he discovered that the Scottish reform bill would enfranchise around 110

Shetlanders; he had an interview with Lord John Russell, who promised to lay the case before Grey.[25] Laing now told him that if Parliament was dissolved before reform was carried, he would not oppose his re-election, but that he would definitely stand as an enthusiastic reformer at the first election under reformed conditions. Captain Balfour's view, vouchsafed to his uncle, was that in the latter case Laing would be unbeatable and it might be advisable to make terms with him to ensure a share in the future representation, or, less appealingly, to strike an alliance with the Shetlanders; James Baikie was of the same opinion.[26] Nevertheless, they began a canvass for Traill. When Balfour, who was privately at a loss to understand why the 'ambitious' Traill 'took it into his head to be a reformer', when Laing's credentials as such were far more convincing, explained their views to him, Traill replied on 8 Apr. that he had decided not to seek re-election, even in the event of a dissolution before reform was secured (which he did not expect), for in that case he would be a lame duck Member, and recommended George Dundas as the man to put up against Laing. On a more positive note, he had established from Spring Rice that the proposal to allow distilling from sugar was 'at a stand' for the moment.[27] He authorized some of his friends in Caithness, where he had earned popularity through his attention to local interests and some reformers were keen to see him returned, to start a preliminary canvass and put him up for that county.[28] Captain Balfour had many objections to Dundas's candidature, as he told his uncle, 21 Apr., and he wrote to Traill in an attempt to persuade him not to retire and continued the canvass for him.[29] He was unaware of the ministerial defeat on Gascoyne's wrecking amendment to the reform bill, 19 Apr. (when Traill was in their minority), which precipitated a dissolution four days later. On 21 Apr., anticipating this, Traill informed Captain Balfour and Baikie that he had extricated himself from Caithness and, having discovered that George Dundas had no wish to come in at present, had decided to offer again for Orkney, though he professed willingness to step aside if they strongly preferred another man.[30] Captain Balfour decided to support him as the least objectionable candidate in the circumstances, though his dalliance with Caithness, which had done better from the reform scheme than had Orkney, laid him open to local resentment. He reasoned also that the slim chance of obtaining separate representation for Orkney and Shetland might be enhanced by returning 'a thick and thin supporter' of the reform scheme.[31] Traill broke his 'unpleasant journey [north], arising from the extreme cold of the weather, and the state of my health not being well adapted for travelling', with a discussion in Newcastle with his kelp agent, who told him that the glass manufacturers wanted a repeal or significant reduction of the window duties, which Traill knew ministers would not concede. In Edinburgh he tackled the lord advocate Francis Jeffrey* for the third time on the Orkney case against the junction with Shetland, but was told that there was not 'the slightest hope' of succeeding in it; he felt that 'our only remaining chance is by bringing our case directly under the cognisance of Lord Grey, which ... may be accomplished through the medium of Lord Dundas'.[32] He was returned unopposed, but Laing wanted the freeholders to instruct him to oppose the Scottish reform bill 'in every stage' unless the separation of Orkney and Shetland was conceded. He was persuaded by Baikie to substitute a request that Traill should use his best endeavours to secure this.[33]

Traill voted for the second reading of the reintroduced English reform bill, 6 July, steadily for its details and for its passage, 21 Sept. 1831. Before voting for the second reading of the Scottish bill, 23 Sept., he presented the petition of Shetland proprietors for separate representation. He also brought up a Caithness malt distillers' petition against the use of molasses in distilling, having been named to the select committee on that subject, 30 June. He voted in defence of the conduct of the Irish administration during the Dublin election, 23 Aug. On 1 Oct. he told John Balfour that, pursuing his so far fruitless attempt to 'preserve our political independence' by persuading ministers to separate Orkney and Shetland, he was to have that day another interview with Althorp. He had given notice of an appropriate amendment to the Scottish bill, but expected the English one to be thrown out by the Lords, which 'will give us some breathing space'. A week later he asked Captain Balfour to send him 'without delay' Orkney petitions to both Houses for separate representation and reported that his earlier interview with Grey had been inconclusive, but that the one with Althorp (when he had been supported by Sir Francis Burdett*) had been slightly more encouraging, in that Althorp had conceded that he had made out a strong case, though he held out no hope of a concession. He claimed to have the support of Joseph Hume*, Daniel O'Connell*, Lord Dundas and others, as well as Burdett, and affirmed: 'If I had been striving for my life I could not have done more and Lord Althorp volunteered to give me a certificate that I had left no means untried. I know it is unnecessary to say this to you, but I wish it to be known by others'. He divided for Lord Ebrington's motion of confidence in the Grey ministry, 10 Oct. 1831, having attended the meeting of their supporters two days earlier, when this course was decided on as 'the only means by which the country can be saved from a tremendous convulsion'.[34] He subsequently enlisted the active support of Lord Dundas, to whom in mid-November he sent a digest of statistical and other information on Orkney and Shetland designed to show their divergent interests, which Dundas transmitted to Althorp for consideration by the cabinet.[35] Laing, however, remained dissatisfied with his efforts and urged Captain Balfour to call a county meeting to instruct Traill 'not to vote away the political existence of his constituents':

It is a delicate situation in which Mr. Traill stands. He is bound to support the measure of reform by principle and in acting with a party he must support all the details even to the extent of voting away the political existence of his constituents, unless his constituents ... by the most decided instruction put it in his power to show his party that he is not free to vote away the political existence of ... Orkney.[36]

Detained in Scotland by his concern for his poorly father, Traill got permission from the whips to pair off with James Balfour until Christmas, and he was thus in Edinburgh at the time of the division of the second reading of the revised English reform bill, 17 Dec. 1831.[37] He was present to vote for schedule A, 20 Jan. 1832. On the 25th he was elected a member of Brooks's Club, sponsored by Burdett and Sir Ronald Ferguson*. He was in the ministerial majorities on clause 27 of the reform bill, 3 Feb., the disfranchisement of Appleby, 21 Feb., the enfranchisement of Tower Hamlets, 28 Feb., and Gateshead, 5 Mar., and the third reading, 22 Mar. He divided with government on the Russian-Dutch loan, 26 Jan., and relations with Portugal, 9 Feb., but was one of the Scottish Members who voted against the third reading of the malt drawback bill, 2 Apr. He presented petitions against the Edinburgh police bill, 16 Apr. His last recorded vote in this period was for the address calling on the king to appoint only ministers who would carry reform unimpaired, 10 May. Four days later he informed Captain Balfour that the duke of Wellington's attempt to form a Conservative reform ministry was on the verge of collapse.[38] On 6 June, to register his protest against the junction of Orkney and Shetland, he argued the case for separating them, but acknowledged that there was no hope of persuading ministers to concede this. (As he later told Captain Balfour, 'everyone knows that I might as well expect to add a cubit to my height as to add a Member' to the Commons.) He thought that should be the end of the matter for the time being, but was pressured by others to move a technically dubious amendment to the third reading, 27 June, the effect of which would be to give Orkney and Shetland a Member each by the expedient of disfranchising one of the burgh districts. Ministers of course would not have it, and he withdrew, satisfied that he had made out a case 'consistent with the claims of justice'. He told Captain Balfour that the question was now 'placed in a better position for being taken up in the next Parliament' and that he was 'so satisfied that I have done my utmost that I am not afraid of any strictures on that head'.[39] He was given a month's leave to attend to urgent business, 29 June 1832.

John Balfour thought that Traill, who was unwell in the autumn, might have done more to protect the interests of Orkney as against those of Shetland and Caithness, and Laing publicly condemned him as a charlatan and party hack; but there was no opposition to his return for the county as a Liberal at the 1832 general election.[40] He was defeated by Captain Balfour's son in 1835, unsuccessfully contested Caithness in 1837, was returned unopposed there as a Liberal in 1841 and sat for 27 years.[41] He died in September 1871.

[1] W. Traill, *Traills of Orkney*, 66. [2] Ibid. pp. xi-xii, 65; *Pol. State of Scotland 1788*, p. 247. [3] *Pol. State of Scotland 1811*, pp. 112-13. [4] Orkney Archives D14/1, Traill to J.T. Urquhart, 19 Jan., 16 Feb.; *Inverness Courier*, 20 Apr. 1820. [5] Orkney Archives, Balfour mss D2/25/4, W. to J. Balfour, 6 Feb. [1823]; Traill, 66. [6] Balfour mss D2/24/1, W. to J. Balfour, 23 Sept. 1830. [7] Ibid. D2/8/13, Traill to W. Balfour, 3 Oct. 1825. [8] Ibid. D2/28/11, W. Balfour to Traill, 10 Oct. 1825. [9] Ibid. D2/3/10. [10] Ibid. D2/28/11. [11] Ibid. D2/3/10. [12] Ibid. D2/8/13. [13] Ibid. D2/3/10, W. to J. Balfour [May]; D2/8/11, to Traill, 23 May 1826. [14] Ibid. D2/28/11, W. Balfour to Traill, 9 June; D2/23/11, J. Ker to A. Dallas, 12 June, to Traill, 21 June 1826. [15] Ibid. D2/3/10, W. to J. Balfour, 29 Aug. 1826. [16] Ibid. D2/8/13, Traill to W. Balfour, 19 May 1827. [17] Ibid. D2/8/24, Traill to W. Balfour, 2, 10 Nov. 1827, 18 Mar. 1828. [18] Ibid. D2/8/9, Traill to W. Balfour, 11 June 1830. [19] Ibid. D2/8/9, Traill's address, 1 July, Traill to W. Balfour, 16 July; *Inverness Courier*, 8 Sept. 1830. [20] Balfour mss D2/8/9, Traill to W. Balfour, 16 Nov. 1830. [21] Ibid. D2/3/14, W. to J. Balfour, 13 Dec. 1830, 3, 31 Jan., 11 Feb. 1831. [22] Ibid. D2/8/9. [23] Ibid. [24] Ibid. Traill to W. Balfour, 16 Mar. 1831. [25] Ibid. Traill to W. Balfour, 28 Mar. 1831. [26] Ibid. D2/3/14, W. to J. Balfour, 30 Mar.; Baikie to same, 1 Apr.; *Scotsman*, 30 Apr. 1831. [27] Ibid. D2/31/26, Traill to W. Balfour, 8 Apr. 1831. [28] Ibid. D2/23/11, Traill to Baikie, 21 Apr. 1831; NAS GD136/536/8. [29] Ibid. D2/3/14, W. to J. Balfour, 21 Apr. 1831. [30] Ibid. D2/23/11. [31] Ibid. D2/3/14, W. to J. Balfour, 11 May 1831. [32] Ibid. Traill to Balfour, 13 May 1831. [33] *Caledonian Mercury*, 30 Apr., 11 June; Wellington mss WP1/1185/35; Balfour mss D2/3/14, W. to J. Balfour, 1 June 1831. [34] Balfour mss D2/3/14, Traill to J. Balfour, 1 Oct.; D2/8/13, to W. Balfour, 8 Oct. [1831]. [35] Ibid. D2/3/14, Traill to Dundas, 19 Nov., reply, 23 Nov. 1831. [36] Ibid. D2/35/19, Laing to W. Balfour, 19 Nov. 1831. [37] Ibid. D2/3/14, Traill to J. Balfour, 8 Dec. 1831; *Cockburn Letters*, 359, 363. [38] Balfour mss D2/8/9. [39] Ibid. D2/37/6. [40] Ibid. D2/20/11, J. to W. Balfour, 20 July, 1 Oct.; D2/28/11, Laing's address to the electors, 22 Dec. 1832. [41] *Dod's Parl. Companion* (1861), 297.

D.R.F.

TRANT, **William Henry** (1781–1859), of 31 Portland Place, Mdx.; Farrincantillon, co. Kerry and Drumonby, co. Limerick.

OKEHAMPTON	2 June 1824–1826
DOVER	11 Feb. 1828–1830
OKEHAMPTON	1831–8 July 1831

b. Feb. 1781,[1] 2nd s. of Dominick Trant, MP [I] (*d.* 1790), of Dunkettle, co. Cork and 2nd w. Eleanor, da. of John Fitzgibbon, MP [I], of Mount Shannon, co. Limerick. *educ.* Eton 1789-95. *m.* (1) 25 Nov. 1812 at Calcutta, Charlotte Anne, da. of John Lumsden, jun. merchant in E.I. Co. (Bengal), 1s. 1da.;[2] (2) 11 May 1842, Eleanor, da. of John Richards of Datchet, Bucks., *s.p.*[3] *d.* 1 Oct. 1859. Writer, E.I. Co. (Bengal) 1798; asst. in gov.-gen.'s office 1803; 2nd asst. to resident at Hyderabad Mar. 1806; asst. to coll. of 24 Pergunnahs Aug. 1806; asst. to sec. to govt. (mil. dept.) Mar. 1807; asst. to sec. to board of commrs. in ceded and conquered provinces Sept. 1807; accountant to board 1808, jun. member 1817; registrar to Bareilly court Oct. 1807; coll. of Bareilly 1810; judge of Dewanny Adawlut of 24 Pergunnahs June 1811; sec. to board of revenue 1811, coll. of 24 Pergunnahs 1815; to Europe Dec. 1819; out of service by 1823.

Trant's family was of Danish extraction and had long been prominent in the Dingle promontory. He was a collateral descendant of Sir Patrick Trant, who followed James II to France and was attainted in 1691. His grandfather Dominick Trant, a prosperous merchant, acquired extensive estates in Kerry and Tipperary. By his first marriage, to his kinswoman Catherine Trant, he had two sons, James and Dominick. In his will, dated 31 Oct. 1755 and proved in 1759, he left most of his property to the latter, supposedly passing over James, whom he provided with a life annuity of £30, because he had entered some foreign service. Dominick Trant became a successful Irish barrister, who did good business on behalf of the smuggling gentry of the south-west. His main residence was at Dunkettle, which Arthur Young described as 'one of the most beautiful places I have ever seen in Ireland'.[4] He was a man of cultivated tastes, with an interest in geology and fine art, who travelled widely in Europe. He sat in the Irish Parliament for St. Canice, 1781-3. Early in 1787 he published *Considerations on the Present Disturbances in Munster*, in which he defended tithes and called for punitive action against the insurgents, but also advocated prison reform and the promotion of education. Some passages in it angered Sir John Conway Colthurst of Ardrum, who fought a duel with Trant near Bray on 14 Feb. 1787. Colthurst was hit and died of his wounds five days later. An inquest returned a verdict of manslaughter in self-defence, but Trant was said to have 'had no peace' after the incident.[5] His first wife, whose third husband he was, was dead by the spring of 1775.[6] His second wife's brother John Fitzgibbon became Irish chancellor and Lord Fitzgibbon in 1789 and earl of Clare in 1795; and her sister Elizabeth was married to William Beresford, archbishop of Tuam (1794) and 1st Baron Decies (1812). With her he had a daughter Maria, who in 1802 married Henry Sadleir Prittie, 2nd Baron Dunalley*, and two sons, John Frederick and William Henry. In December 1789 Dominick Trant was appointed advocate of the Irish admiralty court, but he died six months later, when his sons were beginning their Eton careers.[7] John Frederick Trant (?1777-1838) went to Oxford, was entered at Lincoln's Inn and became a captain of dragoons. He sold most of the family property near Dingle to Lord Ventry in 1809. He also disposed of Dunkettle, and settled at Dovea, near Thurles, Tipperary, where he was succeeded by his son and namesake.

William Henry Trant was placed with the East India Company and arrived in Bengal in September 1799. He returned to Britain two years later, but was back in India by the end of 1803. He served in a variety of administrative posts until ill health forced him to come home 16 years later.[8] His father-in-law John Lumsden, a director of the East India Company from 1817 until his death in December 1818, left him £6,000, and he became a proprietor of Company stock.[9] A member of the committee set up to administer the Irish relief fund in 1822, he seems initially to have divided his time between Ireland, where he bought estates in Kerry and Limerick, and London, where his mother lived. By 1823 he was an Irish absentee landlord and was living in Grove End Road, St. John's Wood. In June 1824, when he was resident in Portland Place, he came in on the Savile interest for Okehampton, where his sister's widower Dunalley made way for him.[10]

Trant, a conscientious attender and forthright debater, gave general support to the Liverpool ministry, but had a pronounced independent streak.[11] He divided with government in defence of the prosecution of the Methodist missionary John Smith in Demerara, 11 June 1824. Next day, in his first known speech, he supported the superannuation fund bill.[12] He welcomed the Irish insurrection bill, without which Ireland would 'relapse into a state of anarchy and confusion', 14 June, and approved the treaty with Netherlands ceding Indian settlements to Britain, 17 June 1824. On the address, 4 Feb. 1825, he argued that suppression of the Catholic Association would encourage the investment of capital in Ireland, and he

duly voted for the unlawful societies bill, 25 Feb. He voted against Catholic relief, 1 Mar., 21 Apr., when his speech was shouted down,[13] and 10 May. He divided against the disfranchisement of Irish 40s. freeholders, 26 Apr., 9 May. He approved the government's 'cautious course' on the reduction of import duties, 10 Mar.; and on 18 Mar., when he agreed with Hume that the Irish linen board was 'utterly incompetent', he once more advocated caution, even though he claimed to be of the same mind as 'those who were for removing all restrictions upon trade'. He supported the Mauritius trade bill, 3 June.[14] He favoured the establishment of provincial banks in Ireland, 15 Mar., and, on the strength of a government promise to investigate the whole subject, concurred in the grant to facilitate Irish emigration to Canada, 15 Apr. He supported Newport's proposal to limit Irish church pluralities, 14 Apr., acknowledging the 'disordered state of the church establishment'; but he could not swallow Hume's motion for a redistribution of church revenues, 14 June, when he said that Hume, who 'meddled with all sorts of things, and who did not know much of Ireland', had 'done the question of Catholic emancipation more harm by his resolution than he had ever done it good'. He opposed Hume's call for information on the Indian army, 24 Mar., warned that it would be 'highly dangerous' to intervene too precipitately against Hindu religious rites, 6 June, and threatened to move next session for inquiry into the administration of justice in India, 13 June.[15] He welcomed inquiry into the Combination Acts, 29 Mar., and was friendly to the principle of Hobhouse's cotton mills regulation bill, 31 May.[16] He voted against the Leith docks bill, 20 May, joined in criticism of the current regulations governing private bill committees, 2 June, and voted for the spring guns bill, 21 June. He voted with government for the duke of Cumberland's grant, 30 May, 2, 6, 10 June, but was in the minority of 26 for Hume's motion on the clerk to the committee of stationery in Bengal, 7 June 1825. Trant divided with ministers on the Jamaican slave trials, 2 Mar., the salary of the president of the board of trade, 10 Apr., and reform of Edinburgh's representation, 13 Apr. 1826. He went against them by supporting inquiry into the grievances of James Silk Buckingham[†] about curbs on press freedom in India, 9 May. He was named to the select committee, and two days later denied the home secretary Peel's 'imputation' that he had gone into the investigation with his mind already made up.[17] He was a critic of the East India Company's training college at Haileybury, 16 Mar., 28 Apr. On 16 Mar. he also moved a successful wrecking amendment against Martin's cruelty to cattle bill. He objected to the 'latitudinarian principle' of Spring Rice's attempt to empower Irish Protestant vestries to assess parishes for the building and repairing of Catholic and Presbyterian places of worship, 21 Apr. He was in the protectionist minority against the corn bill, 11 May, and voted for an amendment to the alehouses licensing bill the next day. He voted against Russell's bid to curb electoral bribery, 26 May 1826.

Trant found no seat at the general election that year. In January 1828 he came forward on a vacancy for Dover, where anti-Catholicism flourished. He was regarded as the candidate favoured by the Wellington ministry and the representatives of Lord Liverpool, the dying lord warden of the Cinque Ports, though he does not seem to have been explicitly recommended by them. Of his previous period as a Member, he claimed that he 'was never away a day, and gave his vote without influence, according to the dictates of his conscience'. He had 'supported the administration of Lord Liverpool with conscientious views, and never asked a favour of government'. He was supported by a coalition of the lord warden's and independent parties and comfortably beat a rival of broadly similar political opinions. Returning thanks before hastening to London because 'a near and dear relative' was 'dangerously ill', 11 Feb., he proclaimed himself to be 'highly favourable to the existing government', but 'unfettered'.[18] He survived his opponent's petition. Trant was sworn in on 20 Feb. and voted against repeal of the Test Acts, 26 Feb. 1828. He welcomed a government amendment to the repeal bill, 2 May, which seemed to show their desire to safeguard the Irish church. He presented petitions against Catholic relief, 24 Apr., 9 May, and voted accordingly, 12 May. He applauded a backbencher's proposal to clarify the Indian laws of real property and called for an annual detailed review of Indian affairs, 25 Mar. He favoured inquiry into the claims of sufferers by the defalcation of the late registrar of Madras, 18 Apr., 22 May, when he also approved the idea of native Indians being allowed to serve on grand juries, but opposed Hume's attempt to reduce Indian legal fees. He was unwilling to remove at a stroke the advantages enjoyed by West over East Indian sugar producers and advocated a 'more equitable system' of trading arrangements with India, 9 June. He saw no reason to countenance the grievances of privileged Calcutta merchants against the stamp duties, 11 June, but he criticized a detail of the Indian justice bill, 7 July, and complained of high imposts on barilla and silk, 15 July. He voted with ministers against inquiry into chancery delays, 24 Apr. He attacked Davies's borough polls bill, 28 Apr., 6 May, when, speaking 'disinterestedly' as 'an absentee', he also called for the introduction of a modified system of poor laws to Ireland, which might 'rescue millions from ... starvation'. He voted against the archbishop of Canterbury's bill, 16 June, but sided with government on the ordnance estimates, 4 July. He voted for reform of the usury laws, 19 June, and presented a petition for the abolition of slavery, 24 June. He objected to Otway Cave's bill to prevent corporations using their funds for electoral purposes, 1, 8 July, when he commented that it was unfair that such organizations as the Catholic Association should be allowed to do so; he was in the minority of ten against its third reading, 10 July. He voted in the minority on the silk duties and attacked the superannuation allowances bill, 14 July. On 18 July 1828 he praised Peel for his attack on America's protectionist tariff and encouraged ministers to continue their good work of exploiting the 'extensive and various resources of India' and 'cultivating a more just and liberal intercourse of commerce with her'.

Trant, anticipating the ministry's volte face on Catholic relief, joined English and Irish Brunswick Clubs in the autumn of 1828. When Parliament met in the new year he took a seat on the opposition benches and became one of the most active and vociferous opponents of emancipation. On the address, 5 Feb., he condemned the 'sophistry' used by ministers to justify the concession, which was nothing more than a surrender to the Catholic Association's intimidation. The 'extraordinary change' in Peel's views, he said on 9 Feb., could 'only be compared to a species of Hoenlhoe miracle', though he subsequently acknowledged that Peel's motives were 'most conscientious', 5 Mar. He called on Protestants to deluge the House with petitions, 9 Feb., and he went on to present his own share, including one from Dover, 3 Mar., when the Whig Lord Howick* thought his speech was 'very violent and very tiresome'.[19] On 15 Feb. his kinswoman Clarissa Trant wrote:

> After church walked with my father to call on Mr. Trant, whose head is so full of the resistance which he has made and still purposes making in the House to ... Catholic emancipation that he can neither talk or think of anything else. C'est une *vraie manie*! ... My father entreated him to be more guarded in his expressions, but he said he certainly should go on as he had begun.[20]

So he did, with constant tirades against the admission to Parliament of men whose 'ulterior objects' were to 'tear down the Protestant church of Ireland in the first instance, and when that ruin is accomplished, to tear down the Protestant church of England':

> I think a little leaven would leaven the whole lump. I am what is called a good sitter in this House. I come early and

remain late, and I know well what may be done by a few Members bent upon a common object.

Trant, who voted to the last ditch against the measure during March, made set speeches against its introduction, 5 Mar., second reading, 18 Mar., and third reading, 30 Mar., when he described it as 'part of a perpetual Popish plot against the Protestant establishments of the country'.[21] Planta, the patronage secretary, was wrong in his prediction that once the principle of emancipation had been carried Trant would 'support the securities'. He denounced them as 'mere delusions', 5 Mar., spoke, without being listened to, against the second reading of the Irish franchise bill, 19 Mar., and was a teller for the hostile minority of 17. Next day, when he argued that it would 'create a most fertile source of discontent among the Catholic population of Ireland', he was one of the 20 who voted for the amendment to prevent fraudulent registration. According to Clarissa Trant, he was 'quite low-spirited at the defeat of his party', and she heard that 'he is christened the duke of "Oh Trant Oh"'.[22] He was at pains to ensure that no Catholic lord of the admiralty could interfere with the disposal of church patronage under the Greenwich Hospital bill, 14, 16 Apr. Curiously, he was credited with voting in the minority in favour of O'Connell being allowed to take his seat unimpeded, 18 May. John Hobhouse* thought Trant 'looked silly' when he asked him if he intended to join the procession to Windsor with an anti-Catholic address organized by John Halcomb† (his Dover opponent of 1828).[23] He seized on the need to renew the Irish Arms Act, 2 June 1829, as a vindication of his forecast that emancipation would not pacify Ireland, whose people would continue to exercise 'their peculiar forte', a 'propensity to disturbance'.

Trant spoke against any further reduction of the volunteer force, 20 Feb., but supported Hume's bid to end military flogging, 10 Mar. 1829. He defended the subsidy for the Society for the Propagation of the Gospels against Hume's attack, 6 Apr. He was horrified by the notion of a system of non-scriptural Irish education, 9 Apr., 22 May, when he declared that its adoption would 'destroy in me any little confidence which I now have left remaining in the good intentions of the present government'. He again called for the introduction of 'some measure for the permanent relief' of Irish poverty, 7 May. He complained of Hume's 'vexatious and unreasonable' opposition to the ecclesiastical courts bill, 21 May, 3 June, arguing that 'any reform of those courts' must be 'beneficial'; but he thought Hume was entitled to seek information on the excessive fees charged in Doctors'

Commons, 5, 12 June. He demanded a reduction in the advantage given to Caribbean sugar producers as an act of 'substantial justice to the East Indies', 25 May, and looked askance at free trade theories, 22 June 1829.

The Ultra leaders listed Trant among 'Tories, strongly opposed to the present government' in October 1829, and he resumed his place on the opposition benches in the 1830 session. He voted for the amendment to the address, 4 Feb., when, according to Clarissa, he gave Daniel O'Connell 'a friendly hint' to remove his hat as he rose to deliver his maiden speech.[24] The following day he insisted that agricultural distress was widespread and called for 'a revision of our recent measures of free trade' and currency reform; but he told Hume that country gentlemen would not be seduced into attacking tithes by his blandishments, 8 Feb. He supported Harvey's bid to prevent Members from voting in committees on private bills in which they had a personal interest, 26 Feb. He was one of the disaffected Tories who voted regularly against government in favour of economical reform: he supported a reduction of the navy pay office grant, 22 Mar., for example, to prove to them that 'we are determined on retrenchment'. On 23 Mar., in fulfilment of his pledge to a meeting of the Committee for the Relief of Distressed Manufacturers, he demanded inquiry into the country's 'great and overwhelming distress'. Yet he was not such a stickler for economy that he would countenance reductions in the Irish yeomanry, 22 Feb., the dockyard labour force, 26 Mar., or the Irish ordnance grant, 6 Apr. He also voted against his Dover colleague Poulett Thomson's motion for a revision of taxation, 25 Mar., as he later admitted to a group of his constituents. His explanation that he had done so according to his honest judgement was accepted, and his supporters voted him thanks for his 'unwearied attention to his duties', with special reference to his resistance to Catholic emancipation.[25] Trant deplored ministers' concession of a commission of inquiry into the Irish church, which was of a piece with their 'absurd, and miserable, and shuffling system of policy', 4 Mar. 1830. He warned against casual acceptance of petitions for repeal of the Union, 22 Mar., and described O'Connell's Irish vestries regulation bill as part of his plan 'to overthrow the Protestant church', 27 Apr. After the appointment of a select committee on Irish poverty, 11 Mar., he moved as an instruction that it should consider how far the statute of 1601 was applicable there, but the Speaker deemed this unnecessary. Hume tried to have Trant added to the committee, but the Irish secretary would not wear it. Trant supported the idea of introducing a system of poor laws to Ireland, 3 June, but could not concur in an absentee tax, 7 June. He voted against the Galway franchise bill, a violation of corporate rights which gave 'an overwhelming influence' to Catholics, 24, 25 May. He complained that the Irish arms bill was not stringent enough, 27 May, and on 24 June accused O'Connell and Sheil of deliberately fomenting agitation. He was a resolute opponent of Jewish emancipation, which went 'to the abandonment of Christianity', 17 May. Trant, who spoke and voted against Lord Ellenborough's divorce bill, 6 Apr., was concerned that Protestant soldiers should not be compelled to attend Catholic church services, 30 Apr., 16, 17 June. He joined in calls for mitigation of the penal code, 18 Mar., expressed his disappointment that 'total abolition' of the death penalty was not included in Peel's forgery punishment bill, 1 Apr., 19, 24 May, and voted for the abolition, 7 June. He took exception on constitutional grounds to the central control proposed for the Irish constabulary, 30 Mar., and the metropolitan police, 15 June, preferring parochial accountability. He supported inquiry into the finances of Ceylon, 27 May, and Mackintosh's bill to force the East India Company to compensate claimants against the registrar of Madras, 19 June. He dismissed Hume's allegations of corruption against the commissioners for the building of new churches, 8 June, though he thought the exorbitant cost of St. Pancras church should be investigated, 17 June; and he was sure that if Protestant churches were built in Ireland, there would be no shortage of worshippers to fill them, 15 June. He was in the minority for an amendment to the sale of beer bill, 21 June 1830.

On the message from the new king, 30 June 1830, Trant, who had voted for Hume's motion of 3 May to ensure continuity of constitutional government on the demise of the crown, seconded the amendment against an immediate dissolution: 'I have not acted in factious opposition to the government, but neither will I pretend to say, that I have that confidence in it which I formerly had'. He trusted that 'something like justice' would soon be done to East Indian sugar producers and argued that 'the consequences must be dreadful' if Ireland did not receive aid from public funds, 1 July. On 7 July he called for adequate salaries to be paid to Commons officials, to replace the corrupt fees system, spoke and voted for Hume's bid to reduce judicial salaries and supported the Madras registrar compensation bill. Next day he expressed a hope that the next Parliament, in which he did not expect to sit, would investigate a 'flagrant breach of faith' perpetrated against the natives of the western provinces of India over land revenues. He was in the

minority against increased recognizances under the libel law amendment bill, 9 July. On 13 July 1830 he called for improved regulation of the administration of the estates of persons dying intestate in India and begged again for financial aid to be given to Ireland, accusing ministers, 'in their adherence to political economy', of preventing the House 'from saving the people of Ireland from starvation'. He recommended those who would deal next year with the renewal of the East India Company's charter to safeguard the 'happiness and welfare' of the natives and warned against a too hasty introduction of western 'improvements'. Later that day he spoke and voted against the Lords' amendments restoring the death penalty to the forgery punishment bill.

Trant did not stand for Dover at the 1830 general election: he was reported to be 'tired of all the business', besides having 'reasons which would prevent him from supporting the measures of the duke of Wellington'.[26] He did not find an opening elsewhere, but at the 1831 general election he came in again for Okehampton, supposedly as a friend to 'moderate reform' who could not accept the 'sweeping measure' proposed by the Grey ministry.[27] On the address, 21 June 1831, when he sat with the Tory opposition, he accused ministers of making 'a most imprudent, unconstitutional, and mischievous use of the king's name' and of recklessly encouraging 'excitement and agitation', which placed Parliament 'under the constant dread of violence from the people'. In particular, he attacked Graham, first lord of the admiralty, and the double turncoat John Calcraft, who 'by the most extraordinary tergiversation ever witnessed, has been manufactured into a county Member'. (It was taunts such as this which drove Calcraft to suicide three months later.) On 22 June Trant presented an anti-reform petition from Durham out-voters, said that one presented by Hume for abolition of the Irish church establishment showed what could be expected if the reform bill passed and, to a chorus of 'derision', backed Inglis's complaint that at a time when the country was 'threatened with war, pestilence, and famine', no reference had been made in the king's speech to 'Providence'. He provoked more ridicule, 24 June, by asking free traders what would become of the manufacturing population if trade with the Baltic was stopped by cholera: it was 'no laughing matter', he retorted, for he had had the disease himself. He objected to Evans's corporate funds bill, 27 June, and the following day, in a discussion on the salary of the president of the board of control, appealed to Hume and other radicals:

We ought not, especially in these times, to give countenance in this House to an idea too prevalent out of doors, that men came here to perform no labour, but to fill their pockets and to live upon the public. I have spent many anxious weary hours in this House, and have never obtained or looked for a farthing from it. The country cannot prosper, if insinuations go forth to the public, that we are merely a set of rogues who come here for our own profit, for the country will place no confidence in us.

He could not go the whole way with Hume in his criticism of the cost of royal palaces, 1 July, but thought the House should look closely at 'those expenses which may not be immediately necessary'. Soon after voting against the second reading of the reintroduced reform bill, 6 July 1831, he vacated his seat to accommodate the Ultra leader Vyvyan, who had been beaten in Cornwall at the general election.

Trant gave evidence before the Commons select committee on the revenue of the East India Company, 10, 12 Apr. 1832.[28] In December 1834, writing from Taplow, Buckinghamshire, he lectured Peel on the folly of rising to the bait of the Whig Dr. Stephen Lushington's* public reference to him and Wellington as 'convicted swindlers':

> I speak feelingly indeed on this subject. It was my father's hard fate to accept a challenge arising out of political circumstances, and to kill his challenger ... I thank God that before I was well a man I was enabled to make a resolution that under no possible circumstances would I either give or accept a challenge ... How much evil has been done by the example of public men in this respect ... In these days of rebuke and blasphemy, can it be expected that the people will 'honour the king' if their rulers do not show that they 'fear God', who has said, 'Thou shalt do no murder', 'vengeance is mine I will repay, saith the Lord'.[29]

The remainder of Trant's life is obscure. He was a resident of New Windsor in 1842, but spent his last years at Torquay, where he died in October 1859.[30] By his will, dated 31 Dec. 1854 (five days after the death of his second wife), he left a life annuity of £200, charged on his Irish estates, to Henry John Trant, his son by his first wife, who 'from the state of his health' was 'incapable of managing his own affairs'. He instructed his trustees to save and invest as much as possible each year from this sum, his object being to 'ensure an adequate personal provision' for Henry, while leaving him under the control of the trustees. He devised all his English and Irish real estate and his personal estate to his daughter Madalina Elinor, who had married in 1840 Neil Benjamin Edmonstone. By a codicil of 18 Dec. 1856 he increased his son's annuity to £300.

[1] BL OIOC 3/1/17, ff. 278-9. [2] Ibid. N/1/9, ff. 47, 113; *Gent. Mag.* (1818), ii. 643; PROB 11/1611/570. [3] Marriage certificate (Eton district registry). [4] S.T. McCarthy, *Trant Fam.* 4-7, 13-16, 42-44; *Jnl. of Clarissa Trant* ed. C.G. Luard, 66-67. [5] McCarthy, 16-18; R.B. McDowell, *Irish Public Opinion*, 125. [6] Eg. 1969, ff. 22, 28, 39. [7] *Hist. Irish Parl.* vi. 433-4; *Gent. Mag.* (1790), ii. 669. [8] W. Prinsep, *Madras Civilians*, 390; *PP* (1831-2), xi (i), 166; B.B. Mishra, *Central Administration of E. I. Co.* 143; *Corresp. of Lord W. Bentick* ed. C.H. Philips, 405-6. [9] PROB 11/1611/570. [10] *Jnl. of Clarissa Trant*, 138. [11] *Session of Parl. 1825*, p. 488. [12] *The Times*, 14 June 1824. [13] Ibid. 22 Apr. 1825. [14] Ibid. 4 June 1825. [15] Ibid. 14 June 1825. [16] Ibid. 1 June 1825. [17] NLW ms 10804 D, C. Williams Wynn to Amherst, 29 May 1826. [18] *Kentish Gazette*, 29 Jan., 1, 5, 8, 12 Feb. 1828; Bodl. MS. Eng. lett. c. 159, ff. 171, 173. [19] Grey mss, Howick jnl. 3 Mar. 1829. [20] *Jnl. of Clarissa Trant*, 254-5. [21] Brougham mss, Smith Stanley to Brougham, 20 Mar. 1829. [22] *Jnl. of Clarissa Trant*, 259. [23] Add. 56554, f. 5. [24] *Jnl. of Clarissa Trant*, 282. [25] *Kentish Gazette*, 14 May 1830. [26] Ibid. 2 July 1830. [27] *N. Devon Jnl.* 5 May, 21 July; *Western Times*, 7 May 1831. [28] *PP* (1831-2), xi (i), 166-74, 192-3. [29] Add. 40405, ff. 92-97, 150, 220. [30] *Gent. Mag.* (1859), ii. 544.

D.R.F.

TREMAYNE, John Hearle (1780–1851), of Heligan, nr. St. Austell, Cornw. and 8 New Street, Spring Gardens, Mdx.

CORNWALL   1806–1826

b. 17 Mar. 1780, o.s. of Rev. Henry Hawkins Tremayne of Heligan (who *suc.* his kinsman Arthur Tremayne of Sydenham, Devon 1808) and Harriet, da. and coh. of John Hearle of Penryn, vice-warden of the stannaries. *educ.* Eton 1793-6; Christ Church, Oxf. 1798. *m.* 11 Jan. 1813, Caroline Matilda, da. of Sir William Lemon, 1st bt.*, 3s. 3da. (1 *d.v.p.*). *suc.* fa. 1829. *d.* 27 Aug. 1851.

Lt. St. Austell vols. 1798; maj. R. Stannary artillery 1803, lt.-col. 1808, lt.-col. commdt. 1812.

Sheriff, Cornw. 1831-2.

Tremayne, who was returned unopposed for the county for the fifth time in 1820, with his Whig father-in-law Sir William Lemon, had numerous family connections across the Cornish political spectrum, including the Tory 1st Baron De Dunstanville and the prominent reformer John Colman Rashleigh. He declared that he adhered to the same 'independent' principles on which he had first been elected, and in the past he had often voted with the Whig opposition to Lord Liverpool's ministry, before associating himself briefly with the Grenvillites. A remark to his father in 1818, that he 'abhorred' Catholic emancipation and parliamentary reform, betrayed definite Tory leanings, and he had supported the government's repressive legislation in late 1819.[1]

He continued to attend regularly and speak occasionally, while serving on many select committees; Thomas Grenville† described him as being 'in the highest class of honourable, independent and effective

Members'.[2] He divided with the minorities to consider the droits of the crown and the admiralty as sources of revenue for the civil list, 5 May, against the appointment of an additional baron of exchequer in Scotland, 15 May, and for economies in tax collection, 4 July 1820. He presented Cornish petitions for relief from agricultural distress, 11, 18 May 1820.[3] Following the debate on the restoration of Queen Caroline's name to the liturgy he reported to his father, 29 Jan. 1821, that the government was 'very triumphant' and the queen 'in the way of being forgotten', noting that 'there was no mob about the ... Commons nor any excitement of the people'.[4] He voted to defend the conduct of ministers, 6 Feb. He urged them to 'turn their attention to the civil establishments of the navy, which ... were capable of great reduction', 2 Feb., and divided for military retrenchment, 16 Feb. (when, as a member of the finance committee, he reportedly 'protested against the expense of the ordnance department'),[5] 14, 15 Mar., 11 Apr., 9, 11, 12 May. He complained to his father, 17 Feb., that the Commons was 'very flat and tiresome' and apparently disinclined to 'make any [effort] in saving public money'. Although he was 'quite sure' the country could be saved from 'ruin' by 'proper reductions and attention to the collection of revenue ... nobody will attend to that', whereas 'if there is a proposition to take a tax off, they will come down in shoals and vote for it, thus endeavouring to lessen the ways and means without reducing the expenditure'.[6] He accordingly voted against repeal of the additional malt duty, 3 Apr., and Hume's economy and retrenchment motion, 27 June. He divided against the payment of arrears in the duke of Clarence's annuity bill, 29 June. When the chancellor of the exchequer, Vansittart, offered to appoint a committee to inquire into the receivers general of taxes and stamp distributors, 22 Mar., Tremayne was, in the eyes of a Whig Member, the 'only person of character' proposed for it among the 'sham country gentlemen'.[7] He wrote that he had 'swallowed the vote in ... favour' of the conduct of the sheriff of Cheshire, which 'went hard with me', 20 Feb., for although the sheriff had been 'partial' in his handling of the county meeting, there had to be 'a very strong case to warrant a committee'.[8] In March he told the organizers of the petition arising from the meeting in Cornwall that he sympathized with their grievances about agricultural distress and believed 'few were inclined to go further than myself' in the direction of economy and retrenchment, but that he saw little hope of any 'immediate remission of taxation'. Moreover, he 'totally differed' from the petitioners with respect to Queen Caroline and had 'seen nothing to make me alter the opinion I had formerly expressed by my

vote'. He also adhered to his belief that in any 'great and general' reform of the representation 'our risk of loss was greater than our chance of gain', although he did not 'preclude myself from reforming any particular abuse that might occur even by disfranchisement, holding as I do that the elective franchise was a political trust granted for the benefit of the state and which the legislature might without injustice resume whenever the welfare of the state required it'.[9] He voted against Russell's reform resolutions, 9 May. On being named to the select committee on agricultural distress, 7 Mar., he said he was 'convinced that agriculture was the sure and stable anchor of the health and prosperity of the country', but emphasized that any measures of relief must be extended to 'all branches of the community', as they were 'inseparably connected'. In letters to his father while the committee was examining witnesses, he observed that the land agents 'give a rather more favourable account of the general state of things than the practical farmers', with the former reporting that rents had fallen by 20 to 33 per cent since 1812-13, while the latter implied that 'land is absolutely worth nothing'. One 'bold theorist' who gave evidence maintained that 'the goodness or badness of the harvest had no effect on the price of corn', but as Tremayne noted, 'everyone is more or less mad on some topic, and he is so on the question of a depreciated currency'. It was his impression that while some committee members 'make a very good thing of it ... others make very little', and he had 'no idea to what result we shall come'.[10] When the committee began to consider its report in May, he was 'quite clear we can do nothing to relieve the present distress', and his own inclination was to 'hold fast [to] the protection we have by a prohibition up to 80s. [rather] than such a high fixed duty, which in a time of scarcity would be clamoured against and speedily repealed'. Towards the end of the month he wrote that 'we have got so far as to determine that a report shall be drawn, which we may pull to pieces and alter', but he suspected that 'if we change at all hereafter it will be rather towards a free trade in corn than the other way'. In his final surviving letter on the subject, 7 June, he groaned that 'we are debating the report inch by inch, and I am afraid I shall have to come up again tomorrow if not also on Saturday, so that my Whitsuntide holidays will be greatly interfered with'. He vowed that 'never again will I undertake such a mass of committees as I have this year', as 'it has so completely occupied my time that I am sure no salaried officer of government has had fewer leisure hours or less time for exercise'.[11] In fact, he served on eight committees that session. He divided against Catholic relief, 28 Feb., but after the bill was rejected by the Lords he remarked to his father that it was 'the very worst state of things that can be to have the two Houses at variance on such a subject', and 'considering the perfect certainty of its passing within a few years ... I cannot say I wish it longer withheld'.[12] He declared himself 'favourable to the general principle' of the steam engines bill, but doubted whether it could be applied 'in the mining districts', 18 Apr. He voted against the forgery punishment mitigation bill, 23 May 1821.

He was granted ten days' leave on account of family illness, 22 Apr., but returned to present a Cornish petition for relief from agricultural distress, 29 Apr. 1822.[13] He divided against the removal of Catholic peers' disabilities, 30 Apr., and the Irish constables bill, 7 June. He voted to abolish one of the joint-postmasterships, 2 May, when he explained that 'a pledge had been given, on the passing of the pension bill, to reduce all sinecures ... which he should never consider redeemed while the two [offices] remained'. He wrote to his father, 20 May, that he had 'made a bad hit in coming up' in the hope of attending a debate on the corn bill, as 'it is the week of Epsom races and people are full of that and nothing else'. On 6 June he thought it was 'a pretty thing to come 200 miles to see a House adjourned for want of Members at 4 o'clock', because 'all the world are gone to ... Ascot races'.[14] In late May he 'asked Vansittart across the House whether he meant to allow any drawback on salt used on fish exported', in the proposed revision of the salt duties, and was informed that this would be a 'matter for consideration'. Fearing that 'the small curers will be certainly annihilated' by the plan to remove their exemption from the duty, he 'sat up a great part of Friday night writing letters to different parts of the county, which I left for Sir William's [Lemon's] signature and which will go down by his post'. Since there was 'no bill yet in the House and the holidays will last some days', he hoped the fishermen would 'move actively on the subject', although it involved the 'necessity of my being more in London than I wish or can well stomach this year'. He reported on 8 June that he had received a petition from the fishing adventurers to present to the Commons, and intended to 'have an interview also with Vansittart, who ... is a shuffling little fellow'; he had 'no hopes of doing any good with him but by frightening him'. He 'implored' Vansittart in vain 'not to listen to the revenue board on this subject', 11 June.[15] He mentioned that 'we had a long tedious night' on Western's motion for inquiry into the currency, 10 July, and 'no division after all'.[16] He attended a county meeting to condemn the proposed removal of Falmouth's packet service,

25 Oct. 1822, when he emphasized the need to ensure that 'the interests of the country might not be whispered away'.[17]

He divided against repeal of the Foreign Enlistment Act, 16 Apr., reform in Scotland, 2 June, and inquiry into delays in chancery, 5 June 1823. He voted with the minority to introduce trial by jury in New South Wales, 7 July 1823. He described the prorogation of Parliament that month as 'the flattest ... I ever witnessed'.[18] A radical publication referred to him at this time as 'a *sincere* alarmist, a supporter of ministers from real dread of the people'.[19] He presented petitions against the coastwise coal duty, 13, 18 Feb.,[20] and expressed support for its gradual repeal, 1 Apr. 1824. He voted with the minority for the motion accusing lord chancellor Eldon of a breach of privilege, 1 Mar. He similarly divided against the grants for Irish charter schools, 15 Mar., and repairs to Windsor Castle, 5 Apr. He presented anti-slavery petitions, 1, 16, 18 Mar.[21] He thought it would be a 'great improvement' to punish smugglers 'by hard labour' rather than by imprisonment, 6 Apr. 1824.[22] He served on nine committees that session. He voted for the Irish unlawful societies bill, 25 Feb., and against Catholic relief, 1 Mar., presenting hostile petitions from Cornish clergymen, 28 Mar., 18 Apr. 1825.[23] Yet, according to Charles Williams Wynn*, he privately 'declared his determination to vote' for Catholic relief, 'at the hazard, indeed the extreme probability, of an opposition in Cornwall at the next election'; in fact he was absent from the divisions on 21 Apr. and 10 May.[24] Early in March he was 'alarmed' to find that 'the government has declared war against the protecting duties on metals', and he and other interested Members met the president of the board of trade, Huskisson, to ascertain his intentions.[25] He maintained that he had 'no wish ... to oppose the principles of free trade', 11 Mar., but pointed out that large sums had been invested in Cornish copper mines 'on the faith of a continuance of the existing system' and warned of 'the most mischievous effects' if they were exposed to South American competition. He complained that the House was 'losing sight' of the principles laid down by the finance committee, 7 Mar., and felt that no case had been made for the increased army estimates. He 'cordially concurred' in the motion to reduce judges' salaries, 16 May, and voted against the financial provision for the duke of Cumberland, 30 May, 6, 9, 10 June. He divided against the spring guns bill, 21 June 1825. Surprisingly, it was said of him at this time that he 'attended occasionally and voted with ministers'.[26] He presented several anti-slavery petitions, 14, 27, 28 Feb., 1, 2, 17 Mar.,[27] and voted to condemn the Jamaican slave trials, 2 Mar. 1826. He divided for reduction of the navy estimates, 21 Feb., the army estimates, 3 Mar., and abolition of the treasurership of the navy, 7 Apr. He thought that 'estimates previous to expenditure' on public buildings would be 'more useful than accounts afterwards', 13 Mar.[28] He divided against a proposal to reform Edinburgh's representation, 13 Apr., but for Russell's resolutions to curb electoral bribery, 20 May. He voted against the corn importation bill, 11 May 1826, as there was 'nothing in the state of the country' to justify altering the existing system. At the general election that summer he offered again for Cornwall on the same 'independent' principles, but was caught up in the struggle between other Whig and Tory candidates. He observed that 'a strict adherence to party might be right in those who had in view the attaining office', but 'a Member for a great county should watch all parties without being entangled with any'. One of his sponsors maintained that 'during the 20 years he had sat in Parliament he had never asked or received a favour from ... ministers'. Tremayne emphasized that he had 'supported every measure of economy' recommended by the finance committee. However, he admitted to 'feelings of difficulty and doubt' on the Catholic question, and while he could not 'make up his mind to grant the ... claims', he saw that continued resistance might lead to 'the separation of Ireland and the consequent dismemberment of the empire'. He thought emancipation would be 'less objectionable' if the Irish franchise qualification was raised. His hope that he might be spared the expense of a contested election, on account of his long service to the county, was disappointed, and he withdrew before the poll.[29]

In September 1827, after the formation of Lord Goderich's coalition ministry, Tremayne wrote to a friend that 'the Whigs have opened themselves most terribly, and they catch it most roundly in every quarter', although their only mistake in his opinion was to make their objection to the appointment of John Herries* as chancellor of the exchequer 'so public a point'. He found it 'quite ridiculous to witness the feeling that exists that the Protestant church is considerably more secure' because of Herries's presence.[30] On his father's death in 1829 he inherited his landed property in Cornwall and Devon and was the residuary legatee of the personal estate, which was sworn under £35,000.[31] As sheriff of Cornwall he convened county meetings on the Grey ministry's reform bill, 23 Mar., 26 Oct. 1831, and after the latter he expressed the hope that the issue might 'be so settled as to secure the permanence of the constitution and the happiness of the country'.[32] He declined an invitation from

leading Conservatives to stand for East Cornwall at the general election of 1832.[33] He 'dropped down suddenly and expired at the railway station at Dawlish' in August 1851, leaving his estates to his eldest son, John Tremayne (1825-1901), Conservative Member for East Cornwall, 1874-80 and South Devon, 1884-5.[34]

[1] E. Jaggard, *Cornw. Politics in Age of Reform*, 46; *West Briton*, 25 Feb., 24 Mar. 1820; Cornw. RO, Tremayne mss DD/T/2514. [2] Buckingham, *Mems. Geo. IV*, ii. 282-3. [3] *The Times*, 12, 19 May 1820. [4] Tremayne mss 2563. [5] HLRO, Hist. Coll. 379, Grey Bennet diary, 22. [6] Tremayne mss 2571. [7] Grey Bennet diary, 42. [8] Tremayne mss 2573. [9] Ibid. 1922. [10] Ibid. 2575-7. [11] Ibid. 2588, 2591, 2599, 2602. [12] Ibid. 2548. [13] *The Times*, 30 Apr. 1822. [14] Tremayne mss 2654, 2662. [15] Ibid. 2657, 2662, 2663; *The Times*, 12 June 1822. [16] Tremayne mss 2669. [17] *West Briton*, 1 Nov. 1822. [18] Christ Church, Oxf. Phillimore mss, Tremayne to Phillimore, 22 July 1823. [19] *Black Bk.* (1823), 198. [20] *The Times*, 14, 19 Feb. 1824. [21] Ibid. 2, 17, 19 Mar. 1824. [22] Ibid. 7 Apr. 1824. [23] Ibid. 29 Mar., 19 Apr. 1824. [24] Buckingham, ii. 242-3. [25] Tremayne mss 2735. [26] *Session of Parl. 1825*, p. 488. [27] *The Times*, 15, 28 Feb., 1, 2, 3, 18 Mar. 1826. [28] Ibid. 14 Mar. 1826. [29] *West Briton*, 9, 16 June 1826. [30] Phillimore mss, Tremayne to Phillimore, 10 Sept. 1827. [31] PROB 11/1755/251; IR26/1208/136. [32] *West Briton*, 25 Mar., 28 Oct. 1831. [33] Carew Pole mss CC/N/65, circular letter, 30 Aug., Buller to Pole Carew, 1 Sept. 1832. [34] *Gent. Mag.* (1851), ii. 653; PROB 11/2146/78; IR26/1945/17.

T.A.J.

TRENCH, Frederick William (?1777–1859), of 7 Bolton Street, Piccadilly, Mdx.

MITCHELL	1806–15 Dec. 1806
DUNDALK	21 Feb. 1812–1812
CAMBRIDGE	3 Dec. 1819–1832
SCARBOROUGH	1835–1847

b.?1777, 1st s. of Michael Frederick Trench of Heywood, Queen's Co. and Anne Helena, da. and h. of Patrick Stewart of Killymoon, co. Tyrone. *educ.* Trinity, Dublin 1793; Trinity Coll. Camb. 6 Apr. 1797, aged 19; L. Inn 1797. *unm. suc.* fa. 1836; kntd. 22 Feb. 1832; KCH 1832. *d.* 6 Dec. 1859.

Ensign and lt. 1 Ft. Gds. 1803, lt. and capt. 1807; q.m.g.'s staff, Sicily 1807, Walcheren 1809, Cadiz 1811; maj. and asst. q.m.g. Kent 1811; lt.-col. and dep. q.m.g. Holland 1813; half-pay 1813; col. and a.d.c. to the king 1825; maj.-gen. 1837; lt.-gen. 1846; gen. 1854.

Storekeeper of ordnance June 1829-Dec. 1830; sec. to master-gen. of ordnance Dec. 1834-Apr. 1835, Sept. 1841-July 1846.

Trench, a verbose and egregious Irishman, whose father held his property in Queen's County as a tenant of the Earls Stanhope, was the 'great confidant and friend' of the 5th duke of Rutland.[1] He had been returned for Cambridge as a supporter of the Liverpool administration (his flirtation with opposition in 1812 publicly admitted but repented of) on Rutland's controlling interest at a by-election in December 1819. He took a prominent part in the borough's ceremonial celebrations of the accession of George IV, which required him to fund a distribution of bread to the poor and a dinner for the inmates of the gaol. These gestures did nothing to lessen his unpopularity with the unfranchised residents of Cambridge, who loathed him as a foreigner and Rutland's puppet. When he stood again at the 1820 general election, only three months after his first return, amid rowdy scenes, he boasted of his efforts to rescue the poorer classes from 'harpies of the law' by promoting a scheme to facilitate the recovery of small debts, but had to admit that 'my plans are yet in their infancy'. He applauded the recent coercive legislation against 'atheism and rebellion', deplored the Cato Street conspiracy and asserted that 'there cannot be found in the whole world a constitution so beneficial, so full of moderation and freedom' as the British. He laid claim to principles as 'independent' as the 'ample fortune' provided for him by his father. He and Rutland's other nominee comfortably won a contest forced by the independent party opposed to the duke's hegemony.[2] In his first known speech in the House, 2 June 1820, Trench fancifully defended the system of military education at Sandhurst. He voted with government against economies in revenue collection, 4 July 1820. On 6 Feb. 1821 he dismissed as an expression of minority opinion the Cambridge bankers and merchants' petition for the restoration of Queen Caroline's name to the liturgy, carried at a meeting which the authorities had refused to sanction;[3] and later that day he voted in defence of ministers' conduct towards her. He was given ten days' leave to deal with urgent private business, 14 Feb., and did not vote in the division of 28 Feb. on Catholic relief, which he had supported in 1812, but to which Rutland and most of his constituents were implacably opposed. He was in the government majorities on the additional malt duty, 3 Apr., the army estimates, 11 Apr., parliamentary reform, 9 May, and the duke of Clarence's grant, 18 June 1821. His brief speeches against reduction of the quartermaster's establishment, 11 Apr. 1821, were denounced by his Cambridge enemies as attempts to preserve his own salary.[4] He divided against more extensive tax reductions, 11 Feb., and abolition of one of the joint-postmasterships, 13 Mar. 1822. He lost his temper when rebutting Hume's 'foul' insinuation that army officers were slaves of the crown, 12 Mar., and was forced to apologize to the House. He defended a detail of the army estimates, 15 Mar.[5] He voted against the emancipation of Catholic peers, 30 Apr. He called for measures to relieve 'the

great distress' prevalent in Ireland, where crop failures had caused 'absolute starvation', 7 May. On the question of Irish tithes, he told his father, he was

> so completely imbued with the subject and so sincerely anxious about it that I shall not require any preparation and had much rather avail myself of it to try my own bottom than make any attempt at a regular speech. Regular speeches are always long, smell of the lawyer and are not tolerated except from Canning or some great gun. But a ready and evidently unprepared attack in reply is much more useful to the speaker and more agreeable to the hearer. I wish I had something to defend.[6]

He expressed disappointment that ministers were not prepared to propose 'such a commutation of [Irish] tithes as would sustain the just rights of the church, and effect the general tranquillity of the country', 15 May; but he divided with them against Newport's call for a comprehensive commutation, 19 June. He presented Irish petitions for protection against imported butter, 20 May.[7] Supporting the Irish insurrection bill, 15 July 1822, he urged the gentry to 'raise the peasantry of Ireland from their degraded condition', condemned the 'absentee system' as 'a very great evil' and advocated relaxation of the 'oppressive' excise laws.

On the eve of the 1823 session Arbuthnot, the patronage secretary, mentioned Trench to Huskisson, president of the board of trade, as one of a number of possible movers and seconders of the address: 'when I was at Belvoir a little while ago the duke of Rutland begged me to bring him forward. He is *not* very presentable, but *faute de mieux* he might do'.[8] He was not chosen. He voted with government on the franchise, 20 Feb., the assessed taxes, 10 Mar., and the sinking fund, 13 Mar. He supported the prayer of a petition from the grand jury of Queen's County for a commutation of tithes, 10 Feb., welcomed the government's temporary measure as 'a great improvement', 6 Mar., and vouched for the efficiency of the Irish yeomanry, 7 Mar.[9] At this time Rutland pressed on Lord Liverpool Trench's claims for present or future employment: 'he is desirous of becoming a sedulous man of business, and to devote his whole time to that object'. Liverpool, who pleaded a demand for places in excess of the supply, could not oblige.[10] Trench opposed ministers by seconding and voting for Barry's motion for information on the alleged Orange plot against the Irish viceroy, 24 Mar.,[11] and was in the majority for inquiry into the legal proceedings against the miscreants, 22 Apr. He repeated his hope that good would come of the tithes composition bill, 21 Apr., 16 May; claimed that Catholic priests had improperly interfered in the last Dublin election, 22 Apr.,[12] and applauded the principle of Browne's bill to discourage joint tenure in Ireland, the source of electoral bribery and disorder, 27 May. He voted with ministers against inquiries into chancery delays, 5 June, and the currency, 12 June. He supported the Irish insurrection bill, 30 June,[13] and the distilleries bill, which had put this question on 'a proper and fair footing', 8 July 1823. Trench, who had some skill as a draftsman and drawer, had by now ingratiated himself with George IV and his mistress Lady Conyngham; his sketches of her husband's Irish residence at Slane Castle were much admired by the Court circle.[14]

He voted with government against the production of papers on Catholic office-holders, 19 Feb., and reform of Edinburgh's representation, 26 Feb. 1824. He paired for the aliens bill, 2 Apr.[15] On Irish matters, he praised the ministerial bill to encourage the permanent residence of the clergy, 16 Feb., and rejected the opposition amendment, which would 'create a revolution in the whole church property of both countries'. He found fault with ministers for repealing the linen bounties, which would damage the growing trade of south-west Ireland, 26 Feb., 18 Mar., 3 May. He was one of a deputation of 11 Members and peers who vainly laid before Huskisson and Robinson, the chancellor, the case for continuing the bounties, 8 Apr.[16] He took a personal interest in the proposed Irish ordnance survey, which he welcomed, 27 Feb., 10 Mar., when he was appointed to the select committee on it.[17] He supported Maberly's motion for the advance of £1,000,000 capital to Ireland, where the irresponsibility of the gentry had been 'productive of the most mischievous effect', 4 May,[18] and endorsed the government measure to remove restrictions on the establishment of banks in Ireland, 17 May, but he argued that Owen's 'visionary plan' for the promotion of Irish education and employment would 'destroy the very roots of society' 26 May. He attacked the Catholic Association, Daniel O'Connell* and the nationalist leaders, 'a set of artful, cunning, unprincipled demagogues', for fomenting unrest over tithes, 31 May, though he thought the Catholic clergy ought to be better provided for.[19] He supported the insurrection bill, 14, 18 June, presented an Upper Ossory petition for an absentee tax and parish relief for the poor, 21 June, and had the House counted out before it could divide on Hely Hutchinson's motion for production of the evidence taken before the inquiry into Irish disturbances, 24 June.[20] He presented a Cambridge petition for the abolition of slavery, 4 Mar., petitions from Wisbech, 8 Mar., and Cambridge, 11 Mar., in support of Lord Althorp's county courts bill, and one from Cambridge against the coal duties, 11 Mar.[21] He supported Bankes's motion for inquiry into the expense of the new Westminster law courts and was named to the select committee, 23 Mar. On 4 May he presented the petition of George White, town clerk of Cambridge (who later fled abroad to evade trial for forgery), for compensation for losses sustained under the county courts bill; his amendment to include such provision in the measure was rejected by 112-31, 24 May.[22] During the 1824 session he came under pressure from the corporation of Cambridge, who were 'very jealous of attention' and became 'angry' with him, to secure government intervention to enable them to finance the erection of a new gaol. Partly with an eye on the next election, he raised the problem several times with Peel, the home secretary, who was unwilling to amend the pending gaol bill, but held out the prospect of future enabling legislation for town gaols.[23] He voted with government in defence of the prosecution of the Methodist missionary John Smith in Demerara, 11 June 1824.

Trench rated himself highly as an urban improver and designer of fine buildings, and had hatched a grandiose scheme for the embankment of the Thames from Charing Cross to Blackfriars. He had the support not only of Rutland and his wife, but of the king's brother, the duke of York, who took the chair at an inaugural meeting on the lord mayor's barge, 17 July 1824, when Trench explained his scheme, which he also set out in a published *Prospectus*, to an audience of the great and the good. He estimated that it would cost less than £500,000 and would yield a return of five per cent. A committee of management was formed and a subscription opened.[24] Trench lobbied assiduously, secured 'honeyed words' of praise from the king and won over Liverpool who, he claimed, was 'absolutely *enamoured* with my project':

> I have now little doubt of its success, and even if it had failed I flatter myself the part I have taken and the luck I have had in overcoming difficulties would have been *eminently* useful to me as a public man.

George Agar Ellis* conceded that the project 'seems [to be] getting on in public opinion', but doubted 'the possibility of its execution'. By January 1825, when he was hobnobbing with Wellington, York and Lords Anglesey and Hertford at Belvoir, Trench believed it would be 'carried into effect not exactly as quickly as I could wish and as my project would effect it, but as effectually, and at all events it will be done *honestly* and *impartially* and skilfully'.[25] When he presented the petition for a bill to implement the Thames Quay scheme, as it was known, 18 Feb., Sir Joseph Yorke warned the House that the pillars, arches and promenades envisaged in it would create 'a receptacle for ...

the offensive filth which this great city was constantly pouring into the river, and which, so accumulated, would, in all probability, occasion a pestilence'. There was opposition from several Members, including Peel, when Trench, who pointed out that the main object of the project was to improve river navigation, moved for leave to introduce the bill, 15 Mar.; but he was supported by Lord Palmerston, the secretary at war, and carried his motion by 85-45. The bill had a first reading the next day, but the opposition of landlords, notably the duke of Norfolk, and wharf owners was so fierce that Trench had to abandon it, 15 Apr., when he nevertheless spoke confidently of being able to dispel the 'ignorance' which had frustrated him before the next session.[26] In December 1825 he inflicted on a dismayed Palmerston a 'long note' about 'his cursed quay';[27] but he never reintroduced the plan to Parliament, though he tried to revive it in 1827 with the publication of *A Collection of Papers relating to the Thames Quay*. He presented a petition from the deacon and clergy of Ely against Catholic claims and the Catholic Association, 18 Feb. 1825.[28] When supporting the Irish unlawful societies bill, 21 Feb., he argued that 'the seeds of happiness, peace and tranquillity' sown by recent enlightened legislation were at risk from the association; Sir John Nicholl* thought the speech was 'plain and sensible' and contained 'some useful facts'.[29] Trench voted for the bill, 25 Feb. He divided against Catholic relief, 1 Mar., 21 Apr., 10 May, and on 6 May contended that emancipation could not be conceded as long as an 'ignorant and degraded' populace were in thrall to the priests, who aimed at 'supreme power'. He supported the proposed disfranchisement of Irish 40s. freeholders on its own merits, 9 May, and deplored its defeat, 12 May. He did not carry out his threat to try to prevent attorneys practising in county courts under the terms of Althorp's revised bill, 19 May. He voted for the duke of Cumberland's grant, 30 May, 6 June 1825. His first attempt to secure appointment as an extra aide-de-camp to the king as a 'special mark' of royal favour was unsuccessful, despite Rutland's intervention with York, the commander-in-chief; his promotion to colonel, it was thought, would mean that 'a very considerable number of officers highly distinguished by their services in the field would be passed over.[30] On 27 May 1825, however, he was one of 21 men named as aides-de-camp in a general promotion. Five weeks later a scandalized Mrs. Arbuthnot recorded a curious episode at Rutland's in which, after dinner, the duke asked Lady Caroline Powlett if she was '*ready to be smothered*' and, on her answering in the affirmative, disappeared with her and Trench behind the closed door of an adjoining room.[31]

Mrs. Arbuthnot had cause to notice Trench again before the year was out for, describing a visit with her husband, now commissioner of woods and forests, to Wellington's home at Stratfield Saye in October, she wrote:

> We had Col. Trench to show us some plans he has for new buildings. He wants to have a palace in ... [Hyde] Park on ... [Bugden Hill], and the execution of his plan would cause half Hyde Park to be occupied by building, courts and gardens. It is the worst plan of a house I ever saw, and quite colossal, for he proposes a statue gallery 500 feet long, a drawing room 190, and other rooms in proportion. It is the most ridiculous plan I ever saw for, added to it, is the idea of a street *200 feet wide* extending from the end of Hyde Park opposite the new palace to St. Paul's!! The king and the duke of York are madly eager for this plan; but the former says he supposes his d____d ministers won't allow it. Mr. Arbuthnot was very angry with Col. Trench, for he said it was too bad anybody should go and get the king's ear and set him against everything that is being done for him. Col. Trench has persuaded him that Buckingham House will always be a damp hole unfit for him to live in; and the ministers, in consequence of the king's determination to have no other palace, during the last session obtained money from Parliament, obtained the king's approval of the plan and immediately set to work to build there for him.

Arbuthnot, who referred slightingly to Trench in front of the others as 'a gentleman who fancies himself a man of taste', told him that he had informed Liverpool of his disruptive interference. In a bid to clear his name 'from an imputation of thrusting myself forward', Trench immediately sent the premier a long, tedious, self-exculpatory letter, explaining how he had come to lay the project before the king. He enclosed with it the plans, but Liverpool returned them unseen. This rebuke did not prevent Trench from publicizing his scheme for an alternative palace in the press at the end of the year.[32]

On the Irish Catholic petition for an education grant, 14 Apr. 1826, he denounced the idea as 'injudicious' and advocated the creation of 'a sort of neutral ground, in which both Catholics and Protestants might meet in harmony'. He saw little merit in the proposal temporarily to open the ports to foreign corn, 5 May, but did not oppose it, though he suggested that Ireland might become a reliable source of grain if its people could be taught 'habits of industry'. He did not think much of his leading constituents (he referred in private to 'our blessed Cambridge corporation'), who had pestered him in 1825 on the subject of the university police bill, and into whose factional squabbles he was always liable to be dragged. He had been making himself known at Scarborough, where Rutland controlled one seat, currently occupied by Speaker Manners Sutton: 'I think much of my future political comfort and ease will depend on my success there, and I have a substitute ready for Cam[bridge]', he told his father.[33] Yet it was for Cambridge that he stood again at the 1826 general election, when he declared his pride in being Irish, hypocritically complained of 'not having enough to do' in the matter of safeguarding local interests, emphasized his unflinching hostility to Catholic claims and quibbled at the extent of recent moves towards free trade. He was confronted with allegations that he had spoken contemptuously of his constituents, possessed a dossier of information on every elector and was involved in a plot to revise the bye-laws to hamstring the corporation's opponents. He denied the first and third charges, but admitted and made light of the second. He and the other Rutland nominee were returned after a token contest.[34]

In January 1827 Rutland, writing to congratulate Wellington on his appointment as commander-in-chief, strongly recommended Trench, who was 'filled with ambition to be put forward in public life', for employment: 'with his disposition to business, and his indefatigable attention to whatever concern may be entrusted to him, I think you are acquainted'.[35] The following month Trench submitted to Wellington proposals to reduce the electoral power of the Irish 40s. freeholders and reform the Irish Catholic church. The advanced Whig Thomas Creevey* liked the plan (of which Trench had given notice in the Commons), but the duke saw insuperable practical difficulties.[36] Trench voted against Catholic relief, 6 Mar. 1827. He said that subsidized emigration was anything but the solution to Ireland's economic problems, 9 Mar., and deplored 'any system of proselytism' as a 'great impediment' to the promotion of Irish education, 19 Mar. He opposed the abolition of army flogging, 12 Mar., and the spring guns bill, which was inspired by 'a feeling of morbid sensibility' characteristic of 'the new system of philosophy and political economy', 23 Mar. During the ministerial crisis which followed Liverpool's stroke, he was a conduit for the opinions of Rutland and like-minded 'old Tory' peers who sought in vain to prevent Canning's accession to power. He tried to impress on Wellington, apparently irritating him in the process, Rutland's wish that he should stand forward 'as the champion of the Protestant and Tory party'.[37] He caused a splash, 6 Apr. 1827, when, with no question before the House, he launched an attack on Plunket, the Irish attorney-general, for his 'inflammatory' speech in favour of Catholic relief a month earlier and his failure to act decisively against the Catholic Association. Ignoring attempts to silence

him, he propounded from a prepared paper, which had 'cost him much labour', his own scheme for a settlement of the Irish problem: suppression of the Association; subsidized temporary employment of the poor; promotion of education; agricultural improvement; generous payment of the Catholic clergy; franchise reform, and the appointment of county governors. Eventually the 'long drawling cry of "Oh! Oh!"' which had been 'regularly set up' on the opposition benches overwhelmed him. Peel and Plunket defended themselves, but Trench insisted that he had been right to speak his mind 'as an Irishman and an honest man', and said that first hand experience of 'the evils which arose from the system pursued by the Irish Catholics' had brought him to see the folly of the support he had naively given to their claims in 1812.

He voted against repeal of the Test Acts, 26 Feb. 1828. He repeated his view that agricultural improvement, the creation of a market for articles of 'comfort', and an end to the 'infinite subdivision of land', rather than emigration or the introduction of poor laws, would bring prosperity to Ireland, 31 Mar., 1 Apr. He voted against Catholic relief, 12 May, and with Wellington's government on the ordnance estimates, 4 July. Rejecting criticism of Gordon's plan to remove Smithfield livestock market from the City, 12 June (he had, of course, drawn up a scheme of his own at his own expense), he said that he would be 'glad to see Millbank penitentiary converted into a giant abattoir'. The following day he brandished figures to prove his assertion that, thanks largely to the late duke of York, the cost of 'the bravest and most economical army in the world' was relatively less than in 1792. On 24 June 1828 he called for action to relieve the shipping industry from distress, and accused Huskisson of disregarding the complaints of the ship owners of Scarborough in a speech delivered 14 months ago; Huskisson gave him short shrift. Later that day he opposed Wilmot Horton's Irish emigration scheme and again peddled his own nostrum of agricultural improvement, through which Ireland would 'become the Sicily of this part of the world; and, instead of having two millions of half-naked wretches, we should have so many comfortable, happy peasantry, contributing to the support of the manufactures of England.'

He presented a petition for the abolition of slavery, 30 June 1828. A month later Rutland told Wellington that Trench, to whom he gave the original credit for the suggestion that Wellington's son Lord Douro* might enter the Commons on Rutland's interest, feared that he had 'displeased' the duke by urging on him his 'wishes for civil employment'. Trench was relieved to be assured by Wellington in November that he had caused no offence; but the premier informed Rutland, who had hinted that Trench might be made surveyor-general of the ordnance, that it was 'impossible at present' to find a niche for him.[38] The decision to concede Catholic relief created difficulties for Trench, who was expected by Planta, the patronage secretary, to side 'with government' for it. Rutland, who agreed to Wellington's request that he should not pledge himself either way in advance, told Mrs. Arbuthnot, 25 Feb. 1829:

> Trench writes me today in the following terms: 'I have had letters from Ireland today and I confess that every moment increases my doubts of resisting what cannot fail (if resistance be successful) to throw us into the power of the ultra Whigs, and of absolute unconditional surrender without the shadow of a security'.[39]

Two days later Trench presented a petition from Cheveley, where Rutland's Cambridgeshire house was sited, against emancipation, but stressed that it acknowledged the 'wisdom' of ministers' recommendation that the question be settled. Having resolved to support emancipation, combined as it was with adequate securities, he voted for the second reading of the relief bill, 18 Mar.; and the next day he wrote at length to one of Rutland's leading supporters at Cambridge, where there was considerable anger at his change of mind, explaining and justifying it on the grounds that

> our case is almost that of children contemplating amputation to save the life of a beloved parent, a choice between *partial* and *total* revolution ... We cannot sink Ireland into the ocean; and we must either conciliate or coerce.[40]

On the Irish franchise bill, 26 Mar., he opposed Moore's amendment to extend its operation to the boroughs, and welcomed it as 'a great national security to Protestant interests, and to the Protestant church'. He spoke and voted in the minority for Moore's subsequent attempt to raise the voting qualification to £20. He again explained his conduct in a speech delivered for Rutland's benefit, 27 Mar., and voted for the third reading of the relief bill, 30 Mar., though he made an unsuccessful bid to add a clause making it a misdemeanour for any Christian minister to prohibit reading of the Scriptures. Lord Londonderry encouraged Rutland, 1 Apr., to turn Trench out; but the duke, who compromised on emancipation by voting for the second reading of the relief bill and sending a proxy vote against the third, and made it clear that his basic confidence in the ministry was undiminished, evidently had no fault to find with him.[41] Trench was offered the post of storekeeper of the ordnance by

Wellington in late May 1829. After a reconnaissance at Cambridge, which convinced him that standing for re-election there would 'do *good* rather than *harm*' to Rutland's interest, he accepted. The king was 'well pleased' with the appointment, a 'very Tory one', seen as a counterpoise to the simultaneous recruitment of Lord Rosslyn and James Scarlett*.[42] At his re-election Trench attributed his support for emancipation, which was resented by many of his constituents, to his 'honest and conscientious conviction' of its necessity. He was assailed by Samuel Wells, the eccentric Huntingdon radical, who had been rewarded for his apostasy; but there was no threat to his return, and he subsequently boasted that by confronting Rutland's 'false friends' he had rendered the interest impregnable.[43] He voted with his colleagues against parliamentary reform, 11, 18, 23 Feb., and the Galway franchise bill, 25 May, and for the grant for South American missions, 7 June 1830. He paired against abolition of the death penalty for forgery, 7 June. As an official man, he curbed his tongue in debate. He supported a Scarborough ship owners' petition for relief, 15 Mar.; briefly defended aspects of his departmental estimates, 2, 30 Apr.; presented a Cambridge petition against prohibition of arrest for debts of under £100, 10 May, and expressed 'strong objections' to Smith Stanley's Irish ecclesiastical leases bill, 16 June. In a ludicrous episode, 9 July 1830, he proposed an addition to Acland's stage coach bill, but left the House immediately; it was negatived in his absence. There was no opposition to him and the other sitting Member at the 1830 general election, but incessant barracking prevented him from obtaining a hearing.[44]

Trench was in the ministerial minority on the civil list, 15 Nov. 1830, and went out of office on the change of administration. He presented Irish petitions against any further grant to the Kildare Place Society, 13 Dec. 1830. Opposition loosened his tongue. On 15 Feb. 1831 he got leave to introduce a bill, which he presented the next day, to amend the Acts governing Irish elections: it sought to give the vote to the owner of two or more freeholds with a combined value of £10 and to oblige candidates to warn every would-be voter against voting unless properly qualified. Trench, who supported the prayer of another Scarborough ship owners' petition for protection against foreign competition, 1 Mar., was one of the opposition understrappers who seemed to Lord Ellenborough to be made 'low' when the scope of the Grey ministry's reform bill was revealed.[45] He complained of attempts to intimidate Members by an appeal to mass agitation, 9 Mar. On 22 Mar. he asserted that the Irish people would inevitably prefer the more radical reform advocated by O'Connell, of whose 'flirtation' with the authorities he was very suspicious. Later that day he divided against the second reading of the English reform bill. Although ministers incorporated his proposals to validate votes from combined freeholds in the Irish bill, Trench insisted, 24 Mar., on pressing on with his own measure so that it would be law in time for the dissolution which he anticipated when the English bill was defeated. It had a second reading, 28 Mar., but Trench's attempt to add to it provisions to secure the vote for freeholders on tenure for three lives, 14 Apr., was thwarted, and the measure was overtaken by the dissolution. On the government proposal to make a loan of public money for Irish relief, 30 Mar., Trench called for the advance of a smaller sum without securities to provide immediate help. He criticized both the resident gentry and 'political agitators', but largely blamed the latter for the disturbances in Clare, 13 Apr., when he clashed with O'Connell. He voted for Gascoyne's wrecking amendment to the reform bill, 19 Apr. 1831, and the next day demanded that the Wellington ministry be given due credit for the economies which they had effected in the ordnance department. In his address to Cambridge, where the great enthusiasm for reform had no electoral impact, Trench likened the dissolution to Pride's Purge, argued that the Irish bill would hand that country over to the nationalist agitators and forecast the speedy annihilation of church, aristocracy and monarchy if the ministerial plan became law. He paid the usual lip service to his willingness to support a 'judicious and temperate measure of reform' of indefensible abuses: he was 'not an anti-reformist but an anti-revolutionist'. He and his colleague were re-elected without opposition amid a barrage of abuse from the unfranchised populace. They were burnt in effigy after their hasty departure from Cambridge.[46]

In the House, 5 July 1831, Trench declared that the consequences of passing the reintroduced reform bill would be

> the invasion of public property, and, at no very distant period, the ruin of the public creditor. I ... think this measure rash, improvident, ill-considered, ineffective for its own professed object, and revolutionary in its tendency.

Replying to opposition descriptions of Cambridge as a rotten borough, he said that Rutland's influence was 'legitimate and honourable and unpurchasable', and that 'the realm of England does not possess any body of constituents more pure, more upright, and more independent'. He paired against the second reading of the bill next day, but voted to the bitter end

for the adjournment, 12 July. He was in the opposition minorities on the 1831 census, 19 July, the partial disfranchisement of Chippenham, 27 July, and the voting rights of non-resident freeholders in sluiced boroughs, 2 Sept., and voted against the third reading and passage of the bill, 19, 21 Sept. He voted for legal provision for the Irish poor, 29 Aug., but insisted that there was 'a combination to resist the payment of tithes' in Ireland, 6 Oct. He thought the Deacles' allegations against William Bingham Baring* had their origin in 'a conspiracy', 27 Sept. On 11 Oct. he praised the police for their handling of the crowd converging on Parliament the previous night, and the following day had an angry exchange with Hume, which required the Speaker's intervention, over his supposed failure to prevent the attack on Wellington's house: 'the time, perhaps, is not very far distant, when a Jacobin club may overawe the proceedings of this House'. The defeat of the reform bill in the Lords and the Tory victory in the Dorset by-election encouraged Trench to predict a national reaction against reform, 17, 20 Oct. 1831.

He rode his royal palace hobby horse (in which he failed to interest Wellington)[47] into Parliament, 18 July 1831, when he moved an instruction to the committee on the works at Buckingham House to consider an alternative use for it. Arguing that it was not fit even for a private residence, let alone the site of the Court, he recommended using it partly for a national picture and statue gallery and partly to accommodate King's College, London, whose new buildings on the east side of Somerset House he would employ as government offices. He claimed that this arrangement would effect a saving of £1,749,081, which could be applied to the erection of a new and superior palace at no public cost. The motion, which was seconded by Hume, was agreed to. On the grant for works at Windsor Castle and Buckingham House, 28 Sept., he went over all this ground again, and complained that the chairman of the committee had spurned his offer to give evidence; he was disregarded. On 8 Aug. he secured the appointment of a select committee, which he chaired, to investigate the possibility of improving the accommodation and conditions of the House. On a pretext, 12 Aug., he outlined his own preferred scheme for the extension of the chamber into the lobby and the provision of better ventilation and access to the benches. He admitted that his original estimate of £2,000 had been £1,000 short. Trench was thanked by some Members, but he had the embarrassment, 6 Oct., of presenting a report which concluded that although the existing House was inadequate, there was no prospect of improving it satisfactorily, and that the only alternative was to build a new one, a proposal deemed to be beyond the committee's remit.[48] It emerged, 11 Oct. 1831, that in his advocacy of Benjamin Wyatt's extension scheme, the cost of which he now put at £10,000, Trench had been in a minority of one on the committee; and he was mercilessly mocked by Croker, one of its members, who dismissed the plan as ludicrous.

Trench voted against the second reading of the revised reform bill, 17 Dec. 1831, and was in the opposition minorities against going into committee, 20 Jan., the enfranchisement of Tower Hamlets, 28 Feb., and the third reading, 22 Mar. 1832. He voted against government on the Russian-Dutch loan, 26 Jan., 12 July, and condemned their interference in the Portuguese civil war, 26 Mar. He endorsed the popular view that the general register bill was a 'job', 8 Feb.; complained of potentially dangerous economies in the Holyhead packet service, 13 Feb.; said that proposals for army reductions, which had been taken to their limit by the Wellington ministry, went too far, 17 Feb., and argued that Warburton's anatomy bill would encourage rather than curb burking, 27 Feb. He was knighted that month. His motion to revive the select committee on the Commons buildings, 14 Feb., when he blamed Hume for the deadlocked fiasco of the last one, was coldly received, and he dropped it. He again attacked the expense of Buckingham House, 29 Feb., failed in his bid to obtain papers after once more rehearsing his own alternative scheme, 27 Mar., and on 13 Apr. defiantly predicted that the building would 'never be occupied by the monarch'. He joined in the attack on Plunket, now Irish chancellor, for nepotism, 6 Mar., said he would be glad to see the Irish Catholic priests paid by the state if they would forsake their 'narrow system' of seminary education, 11 Apr., and asserted that the clergy were entitled to tithes as long as most Irish property belonged to Protestants, 13 Apr. He paired against the second reading of the Irish reform bill, 25 May. On 31 May he attributed the disturbances in the hitherto peaceful Queen's County, where his relatives were at the mercy of 'self-elected lawgivers', to a deliberate 'reign of terror', which he called on government to crush. Although he approved the Irish party processions bill, 29 June, he belatedly attacked ministers for sanctioning, as almost their first act on coming into office in 1830, the trades' procession to address the king. He criticized the mooted extension to the Commons library as 'plain and ugly', 25 July, when he also expressed his belief that Lord Brougham's appointment of his brother to a chancery sinecure had been intended to be permanent; he defended Sugden's part in exposing this job the next day. He sought to justify police intervention against a

meeting at Blarney and protested at the removal of the naval base from Cove, 2 Aug. The following day, when he voted against the crown colonies relief scheme, he stated that a major objection to single women being allowed to serve as jurors was the fact that juries were often 'locked up all night together in a room'. He also accused ministers of having encouraged the agitation against Irish tithes which they were now trying to disown and suppress. He thought that army officers with ten years' service who took holy orders should remain entitled to their half-pay, 8 Aug. 1832.

The Reform Act freed Cambridge from Rutland's control. At the 1832 general election Trench contested Scarborough on the duke's interest, but was beaten by two Liberals. He fought successful contests there at the next three elections and retired in 1847. Peel employed him in both his ministries, though whether on his own merits or as a sop to Rutland is not clear.[49] On the death of his father, aged 90, in 1836, Trench inherited all the freehold and leasehold property held under Stanhope, the contents of Heywood, £1,000 in three per cent consols and an equal share with his spinster sister Mary in the residue of the estate.[50] He was centrally involved in what Greville, expressing the views of many, described as the 'gross job' of commissioning the sculptor Matthew Cotes Wyatt, Benjamin's brother, to produce the giant and much derided equestrian statue of Wellington which was sited on the arch at Hyde Park Corner.[51] He tried to resuscitate his embankment scheme, which now included an overhead railway and an extension to London Bridge, in a public *Letter* in 1841; but the embanking of the Thames was not begun until four years after his death in Brighton in December 1859. By his will, dated 8 Nov. 1859, he left most of his disposable real estate, including his leasehold London house at 47 Lower Grosvenor Street and property in Queen's County inherited from his brother, the Rev. Segar Stewart Trench (?1782-1853), to Mary Trench. Property at Moyvannon Castle, Roscommon, had already been settled on another sister's children. He left Mary a snuff box given to him by George IV as a token of friendship and in memory of the duke of York, and, ludicrous to the end, bequeathed to Rutland's successor 'a picture of myself in a dressing gown hard at work about the Thames Quay in which his father took so much interest'.

[1] PROB 11/1862/326; *Arbuthnot Jnl.* ii. 94. [2] *Cambridge Election* (1819), 17; *Cambridge Chron.* 11, 25 Feb., 3, 10 Mar.1820. [3] *The Times*, 7 Feb. 1821. [4] Ibid. 12 Apr.; *Cambridge and Hertford Independent Press*, 14 Apr. 1821. [5] *The Times*, 16 Mar. 1822. [6] Add 53816, f. 24. [7] *The Times*, 21 May 1822. [8] Add. 38744, f. 49. [9] *The Times*, 7, 8 Mar. 1823. [10] Add. 38292, f. 346; 38393, f. 21. [11] *The*

Times, 25 Mar. 1823. [12] Ibid. 23 Apr.1823. [13] Ibid. 1 July 1823.
[14] Add. 53816, ff. 12, 16, 30. [15] Northants. RO, Agar Ellis diary, 2 Apr..
[16] Ibid. 8 Apr. [1824]. [17] Add. 38298, f. 61. [18] The Times, 5 May 1824.
[19] TCD, Donoughmore mss D/43/62, C. Hely Hutchinson to
Donoughmore, 2 June 1824. [20] The Times, 19, 22, 25 June 1824.
[21] Ibid. 5, 9, 12 Mar. 1824. [22] Ibid. 5, 25 May 1824. [23] Add. 40361,
f. 109; 40364, ff. 85-90; 40365, ff. 119, 121. [24] Oxford DNB; Agar
Ellis diary, 17 July; The Times, 20 July 1824. [25] Add. 53816, ff. 20,
21, 23, 28, 34, 36; Agar Ellis diary, 20 Dec. [1824]. [26] Agar Ellis
diary, 1, 2, 14, 15 Mar.; The Times, 17 Mar. 1825. [27] Palmerston-
Sulivan Letters, 177. [28] The Times, 19 Feb. 1825. [29] Merthyr
Mawr mss F/2/8, Nicholl diary, 21 Feb. 1825. [30] Add. 58316,
f. 26. [31] Arbuthnot Jnl. i. 407. [32] Ibid. i. 420; Add. 38300, f. 51;
38380, f. 171;Wellington mss WP1/829/17; Trench, Coll. of Pprs.
150. [33] Add. 40379, f. 322; 53816, f. 36. [34] Cambridge Chron. 1, 16
June 1826. [35] Wellington mss WP1/880/16. [36] Ibid. WP1/884/4,
21; Creevey mss, Creevey to Miss Ord, 10 Dec. 1826. [37] Arbuthnot
Jnl. ii. 94; Rutland mss (History of Parliament Aspinall transcripts), Londonderry to Rutland, 23 Mar. [1827]; Wellington mss
WP1/885/1; 887/27. [38] Wellington Despatches, v. 314; Wellington
mss WP1/943/217; 966/18. [39] Wellington Despatches, v. 489-94;
Wellington mss WP1/995/3; Arbuthnot Corresp. 119. [40] Wellington
mss WP1/1069/33. [41] Rutland mss; Wellington Despatches, v.
583; Wellington mss WP1/1003/3; 1014/17. [42] Wellington mss
WP1/1023/10, 13; Arbuthnot Jnl. ii. 269, 277-8; Ellenborough
Diary, ii. 42-43; Greville Mems. i. 295. [43] Cambridge Chron. 5, 12
June 1829; Wellington mss WP1/1023/10. [44] Cambridge Chron.
16, 30 July, 6 Aug. 1830. [45] Three Diaries, 57, 63. [46] Cambridge and
Hertford Independent Press, 30 Apr., 7 May 1831. [47] Wellington
mss WP1/1191/8. [48] PP (1831), iv. 657. [49] York Herald, 22
Dec. 1832; N. Gash, Politics in Age of Peel, 209-10; Add. 40405,
ff. 104, 107; 40406, f. 110; 40407, f. 34. [50] PROB 11/1862/326;
IR26/1432/265. [51] Croker Pprs. i. 328; Greville Mems. iv. 70.

D.R.F.

TREVOR see HILL TREVOR

TROUBRIDGE, Sir Edward Thomas, 2nd bt. (?1790–1852), of Rockville, North Berwick, Haddington.

SANDWICH   1831–1847

b. ?1790,[1] o.s. of R.-Adm. Sir Thomas Troubridge, 1st
bt., and Frances, da. of Capt. John Northall, wid. of
'Governor' Henry Richardson of Marylebone, Mdx.
educ. Dr. Charles Burney at Greenwich.[2] m. 18 Oct.
1810, Anna Maria, da. of V.-Adm. Hon. Sir Alexander
Forrester Inglis Cochrane[†] of Lamancha, Peebles, 4s. (3
d.v.p.) 3da. (1 d.v.p.). suc. fa. as 2nd bt. 1 Feb. 1807; CB 19
July 1838. d. 7 Oct. 1852.
   Entered RN 1797, midshipman 1801, lt. 1806, cdr.
1806, capt. 1807; c.-in-c. Cork 1831-2; r.-adm. 1841.
   Naval a.d.c. to William IV and Victoria 1831-41; ld. of
admiralty Apr. 1835-Sept. 1841.

Troubridge followed his mercurial father, who
received a baronetcy in 1799, into the navy. He saw
action at the battle of Copenhagen and served in the
Victory under Nelson, his father's friend, 1803-4. In
February 1806 he was promoted to lieutenant in the
Blenheim, his father's flagship as commander-in-chief

in India. Soon afterwards he was given command of
the Harrier, in which he destroyed a Dutch brig, 4
July, and participated in the capture of a frigate and
two Indiamen, 26 July. His father wrote from Penang
to John Markham[†], a lord of the admiralty in the
Grenville ministry, 23 Aug.:

> How fortunate my cruises have been. It was a bold dash
> and I have great pleasure in saying Elphinstone says Tom
> in the Harrier behaved like a brave, good fellow; had he
> done otherwise I would with great composure put a pistol
> ball through his nob ... I have made him post into the
> Dutch frigate ... May I request your influence with the
> first lord to confirm him ... I know you will make allow-
> ances for my pressing request, and attribute it to the
> anxiety of a parent to see his son as high in the service as
> it will admit.

Troubridge's promotion to commander was subsequently confirmed, and it was reported that his share
of the prize money for the capture was £26,000.[3] His
father, enraged at being relegated to the command at
the Cape, ignored advice that the Blenheim was not
seaworthy and left Madras in pique early in 1807.
The Blenheim was last seen in severe distress in a
cyclone off Madagascar, 1 Feb. Troubridge was sent
to look for her, and his fruitless search inspired James
Montgomery to write a poem beginning:

> He sought his sire from shore to shore,
> But sought his sire in vain.

Troubridge was invalided home in January 1808.[4]
When his father's will was proved the following
August he inherited £10,000 in three per cents and
£29,297 as his share of the residue of the estate. (His
sister Charlotte received £23,746.)[5]

   In September 1809 Anna Maria Cochrane assured
her father that there was no truth in reports that she
was engaged to Troubridge:

> I think him an amiable, pleasant young man, but that is
> not to say that 'he loo's me, or I loo' him' ... At present
> the baronet is flirting and dancing away with the ladies in
> Edinburgh, so that does not look as if he were desperate
> and as for me, I am as lively, and more so I think, than
> when he was here.[6]

They married a year later, when Troubridge made a
brief will (26 Oct. 1810), by which he confirmed the
terms of their settlement and transferred his holding
of £33,333 6s.4d. in three per cent consols to a trust
fund for the benefit of himself, his wife and their
children.[7] He commanded the Armide in American
waters, 1813-15, and led a naval brigade at the battle
of New Orleans. Troubridge, one of whose sons was

born in Florence in 1817, bought 'a gentlemanlike residence without a large estate' near North Berwick, where his brother-in-law Charles Stuart Cochrane had property, but he and his wife spent most of their time on the continent in the 1820s.[8] In the spring of 1828 they settled at Tours, with the ailing Sir Alexander Cochrane, and they moved with him to Paris for the winter. Troubridge, who had to make arrangements for the education not only of his own sons, but those of his wife's brother Sir Thomas Cochrane[†], governor of Newfoundland, periodically visited London. When there, he did what he could to try to resurrect the military career of his wife's disreputable uncle Andrew Cochrane Johnstone[†], but was careful not to become involved in his tangled financial affairs.[9] On one such visit in February 1829 he was pleasantly surprised by the duke of Wellington and Peel's conversion to Catholic emancipation, proof that 'miracles will certainly never cease':

Whether it will tranquillize Ireland to the extent expected I much doubt, but it will conciliate the English Catholics and the moderate Irish; and if not received by O'Connell and the rabble it will at least give the government a better case to act on than they would have had without making this attempt.[10]

He moved his family to Boulogne in the summer of 1829, when he spent a few days at the Cowes regatta. He was at North Berwick with his dying sister-in-law Jane Bruce at the end of the year.[11]

Troubridge's hopes of sending his first son, Thomas, to university and obtaining an East India Company writership for his second, Edward, were frustrated. (Thomas entered the army in 1834 and Edward continued the family's naval tradition.) Rockville had become 'a great loss' to him, costing about £1,000 a year; and at the end of July 1830 he went to Britain in an unsuccessful attempt to find a buyer.[12] Before going to Scotland to pack up books, minerals and other effects, he made his 'bow to the *Blue Jacket* king', William IV. He hankered after appointment as a naval aide-de-camp, which would be 'very flattering to the memory of my father and may tend to bring me forward upon some future occasion'; but he was disappointed.[13] Back in Boulogne by October, he told his brother-in-law that 'this confounded revolution in Belgium has quite deranged our plans, as we intended to have wintered at Brussels'. He considered moving to Dover, or buying a house in Brighton, but in the event decided to keep his wife and younger children in France. On recent political developments he wrote:

think the march of intellect, as everything is now called, together with the example of revolution shown by so large a portion of the continent, will oblige us to reform at home. Brougham as MP for Yorkshire, supported by Lords Morpeth* and Milton*, is coming forward very strong, and the boroughmongers are not a little frightened. They are making good use of the present time, £1,000 to £1,500 being the price of a seat to be independent on all questions but borough reform, which you are expected to vote against on all occasions.[14]

He returned to England in December, when, chagrined at being passed over as a Companion of the Bath in a recent creation, he submitted to the admiralty a statement of his past services in support of his pretensions. Although he got no satisfaction on this he was 'gratified' by the attention he received from the new premier Lord Grey and Graham, first lord of the admiralty, at a royal reception at Brighton, 27 Dec. 1830.[15] In March 1831 his offer of a renewal of his professional services was accepted and he was appointed to the command at Cork, due to fall vacant at the end of May, with a broad pennant in the *Stag*, which he joined on 15 Apr. He obliged Grey by taking on his nephew as a midshipman and planned to move his family to Cove once the official house there had been refurbished.[16] These plans were disrupted by the snap general election of 1831, when Troubridge was sent to stand for Sandwich on the government interest as a reformer. He was returned in second place after a three-day contest, his expenses apparently being borne by government. To his wife he wrote: 'I feel I have embarked in a good cause and I both hope and believe it will prove so ... I never felt better in my life, and the late activity has done wonders for me'.[17] At a Deal celebration dinner, 11 May, he promised to support 'the great measure of reform, retrenchment and an extensive reduction of taxation'. He told his wife that 'Wellington or even Napoleon could not have been better received' than he was on his triumphal entry to the town. Yet he dreaded the inevitable shoal of patronage requests, 'for every man that voted for me thinks he has a right to ask for something'.[18]

Troubridge, who spent some time with his ship at Plymouth before attending the opening of Parliament, 21 June 1831, now successfully applied for a vacant post as naval aide-de-camp. He took to the treasury a petition from Deal to have it and Walmer united to Sandwich, which had been scheduled to lose one Member by the first reform bill, to form a new two Member constituency. This scheme was incorporated in the new bill, to the considerable benefit of Troubridge's standing with his constituents.[19] He briefly defended his role in this affair in the House, 26 July. He voted for the second reading of the bill, 6 July, and steadily for its details until early August when, having joined Brooks's on the 6th, he went to the *Stag* at Spithead.[20] He was present to vote for clause 22 of the bill, 30 Aug., and was given formal confirmation of a week's leave of absence from his ship, 2 Sept.[21] He was in the minority for the total disfranchisement of Aldborough, 14 Sept., but voted for the third reading, 19, and passage of the bill, 21 Sept. He got permission to leave the *Stag*, which he had sailed from the Downs to Portsmouth, in early October, but evidently arrived too late to vote for the motion of confidence in the ministry, 10 Oct. 1831. He was 'astonished' at the size of the Lords majority against the bill, which had 'brought the bishops into disrepute and in my opinion completely upsets the Tory party for ever'. Troubridge, who 'made a point' of attending the funeral of one of his crew killed in a fall from the masthead, and tried to get a pension for his widow, expected to leave at last for Ireland after going by sea to Leith to collect some household effects from Rockville.[22]

As it happened, he went no further than the Channel. He got leave to attend the new session of Parliament and was present to vote for the second reading of the revised reform bill, 17 Dec. 1831, and its borough disfranchisement schedules, 20, 23 Jan., and with government on the Russian-Dutch loan, 26 Jan. 1832.[23] Soon afterwards the *Stag* went to Ireland under the temporary captaincy of Commander Herringham, but she was back at Plymouth by late March.[24] Troubridge, whose wife wintered in Paris, continued to attend and vote for the reform bill in committee, and was in the ministerial majority on relations with Portugal, 9 Feb. He tried to make himself 'master' of Graham's proposal to unite the admiralty and navy boards 'in case an opportunity opens to say anything in the House';[25] it did, 14 Feb., when, after appealing for an abandonment of 'party spirit' on the question, he praised the bill and its authors in extravagant and partisan terms. His last known vote in this Parliament was for the third reading of the reform bill, 22 Mar. 1832.

Next day he was summoned to the admiralty and ordered to take the *Stag* to Madeira and to keep a neutral watching brief on naval developments in the Portuguese civil war. He remained there for at least two months and became 'sorely disappointed at being kept there so long', as he complained to his wife. News of the reform bill's rejection by the Lords and Grey's resignation, which he received on 23 May, appalled him:

I dread to think of the consequences not only for poor England but for all the world. It is the death blow to Pedro's success, and also to the present French ministry. The king of Holland will also take advantage to keep

the Belgic question open. In short, I see nothing but war and mischief ... If the House of Commons remain of the same opinion as when I left, then I cannot understand how the Tory party can possibly carry on the government ... I ... still hope to hear the king has made some arrangements to get the bill passed.[26]

By July 1832 Troubridge, who dined with Dom Pedro on the ship of Admiral Sartorius and then showed him over the *Stag*, was cruising off the Portuguese coast, still fretting to be allowed home:

I am really glad the reform bill is done with, and the more I reflect the more certain I am that no power could have avoided revolution; and revolution in England is quite another thing to revolution in France. Lord Grey in my opinion stands as high as a man can stand ... I am almost sick of a sea life. However, I am happy to say I have given satisfaction in all I have done both with the admiralty and Admiral Parker and I am glad to have had an opportunity of showing myself not a *blockhead*.[27]

Later in the year he was offered a transfer to the *Malabar*, with the 'chance of foreign service'; but he demurred on account of his constituents' insistence during his canvass for the 1832 general election that he should not go abroad. He wished instead to retain the *Stag*, and the Irish command, but no effort was made to accommodate him; and, privately furious with the admiralty, he found himself 'a gentleman at large once more'.[28] He successfully contested Sandwich, survived a vindictive attempt to unseat him on the ground that he had been promoted captain when two years under the prescribed minimum age, came in there at the next three general elections and held office in Lord Melbourne's second ministry. Troubridge, whose son Edward died on naval service in the Far East in 1850, died in October 1852 at his house in Eaton Place, Belgrave Square.[29] Administration of his effects was granted to his only surviving son Sir Thomas St. Vincent Hope Cochrane Troubridge (1815-67), who lost his right leg and left foot at Inkerman in 1854.[30]

[1] PROB 11/2166/65. [2] NLS mss 2272, f. 68. [3] *Markham Corresp.* (Navy Recs. Soc. xxviii), 245-6, 370. [4] *Oxford DNB*; *Gent. Mag.* (1853), i. 197-8; L. Troubridge, *Memories and Reflections*, 159-60 and *Life among the Troubridges* ed. J. Hope Nicholson, 183-4. [5] PROB 11/2166/697; IR26/138/277. [6] Troubridge, *Life*, 184-6. [7] PROB 11/2166/65. [8] NMM, Troubridge mss (Ms 84/070) 3/14, Troubridge to wife, 17 Oct. 1831. [9] NLS mss 2270, ff. 151, 159, 163, 165, 201, 213, 267. [10] NLS mss 2271, f. 20. [11] NLS mss 2272, ff. 10, 25, 27. [12] NLS mss 2272, ff. 67, 97. [13] Troubridge mss 3/13, Troubridge to wife, 20 [Aug.], 12 Sept. [1830]. [14] NLS mss 2272, ff. 134, 165. [15] Troubridge mss 3/213, Troubridge to admiralty, 22 Dec., to T.H. Troubridge, 28 Dec. 1830. [16] Ibid. 3/14, Grey to Troubridge, 9, 25 Mar., reply [13 Mar.], C. Wood to Troubridge, 18 Mar., E.N. Troubridge to Lady Troubridge, 10 Apr. 1831. [17] *The Times*, 26 Apr.; *Kentish Chron.* 3, 10 May; Troubridge mss 3/14, Troubridge to wife, 9 May 1831. [18] *Kentish*

Chron. 17 May; Troubridge mss 3/14, Troubridge to wife, 13 May 1831. [19] Troubridge mss 3/14, E. N. Troubridge to Lady Troubridge, 20 June, Troubridge to same, 25, 30 June; *Kent Herald*, 2 June; *Kentish Chron.* 19 July 1831. [20] Troubridge mss 3/14, E. N. Troubridge to Lady Troubridge, 22 Aug. 1831. [21] Ibid. Foley to Troubridge, 1 Sept. 1831. [22] Ibid. Hardy to Troubridge, 8 Oct., Troubridge to wife, 17 Oct. 1831. [23] Ibid. Foley to Troubridge, 25 Oct.; Warren to same, 27 Oct., Hardy to same, 5 Dec. 1831. [24] Ibid. 3/15, Hardy to Troubridge, 27 Jan. 1832. [25] Ibid. Troubridge to wife, 7 Feb. 1832. [26] Ibid. Hardy to Troubridge, 23 Mar., Troubridge to wife, 24 Apr.; 3/16, same to same, 18, 28 May 1832. [27] Ibid. 3/16, Troubridge to wife, 2 July [1832]. [28] NLS mss 2270, f. 230. [29] Troubridge, *Memories*, 161; *Gent.Mag.* (1853), i. 197-8. [30] PROB 11/2166/65; IR26/1978/14; Malmesbury, *Mems. of an Ex-Minister*, ii. 214.

D.R.F.

TUDOR, George (1792–1857), of 28 Park Crescent, Marylebone, Mdx.

BARNSTAPLE	1830–1831

b. 1 Aug. 1792, 2nd s. of Henry Tudor (*d.* 1803), manufacturer, of Sheffield and 2nd w. Elizabeth, da. of John Rimington of Carlton, nr. Barnsley, Yorks. *educ.* M. Temple 1817, called 1822. *m.* bef. 1838, Elizabeth Mary, da. of John Jones of London, *s.p. d.* 24 Dec. 1857.

Tudor was descended from a Montgomeryshire family, prominent in the affairs of Welshpool, where his father Henry was born in 1738. He was apprenticed in London as a silversmith, but moved to Sheffield, where in 1758 he married Elizabeth Dodworth, the sister-in-law of Thomas Bolsover, the inventor of the silverplating process. Soon afterwards, in partnership with Thomas Leader, he established a silversmith's business, which became the first to exploit the commercial possibilities of silverplating. He lived in a fine Adam house close to his factory and received a grant of arms in 1775. His first wife died childless in 1781 and two years later he married Elizabeth Rimington, with whom he had two sons, Henry (1788-1864) and George, and four daughters. His second wife died in 1800 and he died, a wealthy man, in 1803.[1] Neither of his sons, who were still well short of their majorities, seems to have taken any part in the business, which was broken up in about 1812. Henry Tudor was called to the bar in 1822 but did not practise. He published a *Narrative of a Tour in North America* (1834), a eulogy of American people and institutions; and *Domestic Memoirs of a Christian Family* (1848), an extended homily dedicated to the Church Missionary Society, of which he was a prominent member.

George Tudor was also bred to the bar, but did not persevere in that line. At the general election of 1830 he came forward for the venal borough of Barnstaple as the 'popular candidate' of the resident freemen, who were at odds with the corporation. In his address he claimed to be 'entirely free from the spirit and engagement of party', but he said he would 'cordially support the government in such measures as may tend to ameliorate the burthens of the people'. Yet at the nomination he was reported to have 'avowed his principles to be "decidedly ministerial"'. He was returned in second place, at a reputed cost of £8,000.[2] The Wellington ministry numbered him among their 'friends', but he voted against them in the crucial division on the civil list, 15 Nov. 1830. He presented Barnstaple petitions in favour of parliamentary reform, 26 Feb., 19 Mar., but he voted against the second reading of the Grey ministry's reform bill, 22 Mar., and for Gascoyne's wrecking amendment, 19 Apr. 1831. At the ensuing general election when, so he said, he declined an invitation to stand for 'a considerable borough' in Norfolk, he offered again for Barnstaple, but found himself in difficulties as a result of his prevarication on reform. Lamely claiming that his vote against the Wellington ministry 'proved him to be a reformer' and that he had been a constant attender, he tried to justify his opposition to the 'highly dangerous' and 'revolutionary' bill, which he felt posed a threat to the monarchy, the church and the Union. His efforts were unavailing, and his defeat at the poll ended his brief, undistinguished and expensive parliamentary career.[3]

Tudor subsequently moved from Park Crescent to 41 Portman Square and acquired a freehold house and hotel on the Avenue de Matignon in Paris. In 1854 he bought East Cowes Castle on the Isle of Wight, the residence built in 1798 by the architect John Nash for his own use.[4] He died at Folkestone in December 1857. By his will, dated 1 May 1838, he left all his property to his wife.[5] She, who lived until 1880, became in 1861 the second wife of the 3rd Viscount Gort.

[1] *Misc. Gen. et Her.* (ser. 3), i. 21-22; *Mont. Colls.* xxiv. 327-8; J. Hunter, *Hallamshire* (1869 edn.), 156, 168; J.D. Leader, *Recs. Burgery of Sheffield*, 393-7, 443, 485; *Torrington Diaries* ed. C. Bruyn Andrews, ii. 25, 133-4. [2] *The Times*, 23 July; *Western Times*, 24, 31 July, 7 Aug. 1830; *Trans. Devon Assoc.* lxxiii (1941), 190. [3] *N. Devon Jnl.* 28 Apr., 5 May; *The Times*, 3, 6 May 1831. [4] *VCH Hants*, v. 198. [5] *Gent. Mag.* (1858), i. 227.

D.R.F.

TUDWAY, John Paine (1775–1835), of New Street, Wells, Som.

WELLS   19 July 1815–1830

b. 21 Apr. 1775, 1st s. of Robert Tudway of Wells and Mary, da. of Rev. Thomas Paine, canon of Wells; *educ.* St. Mary Hall, Oxf. 1793. *m.* 1806, Frances Gould, da. of Lucas Pulsford of Wells, 2s. 7da. *suc.* fa. 1800; uncle Clement Tudway[†] 1815. *d.* 28 June 1835.
    Lt. Wells yeoman cav. 1800, capt. 1818.

Tudway, the third generation of his family to represent Wells, in an unbroken succession dating back to 1754, had effectively inherited the seat in 1815 from his uncle Clement, along with properties in Somerset and the 1,096-acre Parham Hill plantation in Antigua.[1] He was the residuary legatee of his father's property in Wells, where the family's political influence derived from control of the corporation and generous support for local causes.[2] He was again returned unopposed at the general election of 1820, in alliance with Charles William Taylor, a Whig.

He was a very poor attender and is not known to have spoken in debate. He divided with Lord Liverpool's ministry against more extensive tax reductions, 11 Feb. 1822. A radical publication of 1823 exaggerated only slightly when it claimed that there was 'no trace of this man's attendance' during the previous three sessions.[3] He voted against Scottish parliamentary reform, 2 June 1823, and inquiry into the prosecution of the Methodist missionary John Smith in Demerara, 11 June 1824. He divided against Catholic relief, 1 Mar., 10 May 1825. It was said of him at this time that he 'attended very seldom and voted with ministers'.[4] His neglect of his parliamentary duties was an ostensible reason for the opposition that emerged to him at Wells in the mid-1820s. One inhabitant dismissed him as 'a sort of amphibious, ambiguous, nondescript and indescribable character, of whom it is difficult to say to what party he belongs'. Sir Thomas Lethbridge, the county Member and a prominent supporter of the opposition party, accepted that poor health might have prevented Tudway from fulfilling his responsibilities, but argued that he should retire. Tudway's connection with the pro-Catholic Taylor was a more serious liability, but their alliance remained firm during the bitter general election contest of 1826 and the subsequent unsuccessful attempt to unseat them on petition.[5] He divided against Catholic relief, 6 Mar. 1827. In February 1829 Planta, the Wellington ministry's patronage secretary, listed him as likely to be 'with government' for Catholic emancipation, but in fact he voted against it, 6, 18, 23 Mar. Having lost control of Wells corporation

in 1828, he retired at the dissolution in 1830, expressing regret that the city had become 'inflamed by party zeal and embittered by political animosities'.[6]

He died in June 1835, 'a martyr to that excruciating tormentor, the gout'.[7] His properties in Somerset and Antigua had been placed in trust for his eldest son Robert, and the proceeds from the sale of his remaining real estate were invested for the benefit of his nine-year-old son, Henry; his personalty was sworn under £14,000.[8] Robert Tudway (1808-55) renewed his family's connection with the representation of Wells as a Protectionist, 1852-5.

[1] The personalty was sworn under £70,000 (PROB 11/1572/480; IR26/658/744); V.L. Oliver, *Antigua*, iii. 152-3. [2] PROB 11/1354/139; *Bristol Mercury*, 11 July 1835. [3] *Black Bk.* (1823), 199. [4] *Session of Parl. 1825*, p. 488. [5] *Bristol Mirror*, 1 Apr., 8 July 1826. [6] Ibid. 10 July 1830. [7] *Bristol Mercury*, 4 July 1835. [8] PROB 11/1854/678; IR26/1402/800; Oliver, iii. 151-2.

T.A.J.

TUFTON, Hon. Henry (1775–1849).

ROCHESTER   1796–1802

APPLEBY   1826–20 Apr. 1832

b. 2 Jan. 1775, 4th s. of Sackville, 8th earl of Thanet (*d.* 1786), and Mary, da. of Lord John Philip Sackville[†]; bro. of Hon John Tufton[†]. *educ.* Westminster 1786; Angers mil. acad. *unm.* 1s. 1da.[1] *d.v.p. suc.* bro. Charles as 11th earl of Thanet 20 Apr. 1832. *d.* 12 June 1849.
    Ensign 26 Ft. 1790; capt. ind. co. Ft. 1793, half-pay 1793-1826.
    Hered. sheriff, Westmld. 1832-*d.*; ld. lt. Kent 1841-6.

Tufton, a French-trained soldier, espoused the Whiggism and pro-Catholic sympathies of his father and brothers, the 8th, 9th and 10th earls of Thanet, on whose interest he had successfully contested Rochester in 1796. 'A fierce Buonapartist and Jacobin', he returned to France soon after the Peace of Amiens in 1802, and he remained there as one of Buonaparte's *detenus* until 1813, and afterwards by choice.[2] He inherited part of the Kent estate of Hothfield Place on the death of his eldest brother Sackville in January 1825; but his brother Charles, as 10th earl, refused him an annuity on account of their parlous finances and would not hear of his standing for Westmorland, preferring to return him for Appleby, which he controlled jointly with the Tory Lord Lonsdale, at the general election of 1826.[3]

Tufton, who is not known to have spoken in debate, voted against the award to the duke of Clarence, 16 Feb., to separate bankruptcy jurisdiction from chancery, 11 May, and for the disfranchisement of Penryn, 28 May 1827. He divided for Catholic relief, 6 Mar. 1827, 12 May 1828. He divided for Catholic emancipation 6, 30 Mar., and to permit Daniel O'Connell to sit without swearing the oath of supremacy, 18 May 1829. He voted to transfer East Retford's seats to Birmingham, 5 May, and to lower the hemp duties, 1 June 1829. Returning late for the 1830 session, he divided steadily with the revived Whig opposition, 3 May-14 June, including for Jewish emancipation, 17 May, parliamentary reform, 28 May, revision of the divorce laws, 3 June, and abolition of the death penalty for forgery, 7 June. Under the 'Westmorland Treaty' agreed in July between his brother, James Brougham* and Lonsdale, he was initially expected to come in for Cockermouth at the general election of 1830, but a compromise with Lord Radnor made Appleby again available to him.[4]

The Wellington ministry naturally listed Tufton among their 'foes' and he divided against them on the civil list when they were brought down, 15 Nov. 1830. He voted for the Grey ministry's reform bill, which proposed Appleby's disfranchisement, at its second reading, 22 Mar., and paired against Gascoyne's wrecking amendment, 19 Apr. 1831. At the ensuing general election he came in for Appleby as previously.[5] He divided for the reintroduced reform bill at its second reading, 6 July, against adjournment, 12 July, and generally voted or paired for its details. He is not known to have voted on the disfranchisement of Appleby, 19 July, for which the division lists are incomplete, but according to Lonsdale's heir Lord Lowther* 'he took an active part' against it.[6] He was absent from the division on the bill's passage, 21 Sept. He divided for the revised reform bill at its second reading, 17 Dec. 1831, and voted for its committal, 20 Jan., the schedule B disfranchisements, 23 Jan., the enfranchisement of Tower Hamlets, 28 Feb., and the third reading, 22 Mar. 1832. He divided with government on the Russian-Dutch loan, 26 Jan. 1832. Elevated to the Lords and made hereditary sheriff of Westmorland by the death of his brother, 20 Apr., he was portrayed to Lord Holland by Lord Brougham as a 'very stout politician' who would 'be as he has been in the Commons, a most regular attender'.[7] He returned his nephew Charles Barham as his replacement and sought advice on the likely impact of Appleby's disfranchisement on the county constituency before directing his agents to support Barham's elder brother John in Westmorland at the 1832 general election.[8]

Thanet, who sustained his own household in Paris, was well placed to scotch reports circulating in 1832

that his brother Sackville had fathered an illegitimate daughter there.[9] He acknowledged his own children with Julie Durieux and died after a long illness in June 1849. By his will, dated 21 Dec. 1848, he devised the shrievalty of Westmorland and some 40,000 of the 60,000-acre family estates in Kent, Westmorland and Yorkshire, which he had freed from encumbrances, to his French-born son Richard Tufton (1813-71), the residuary legatee. Charles Barham, Durieux and his London housekeeper Sarah Fuller were the other main beneficiaries.[10] The Thanet peerage lapsed and Tufton, whose naturalization was effected by an Act of 1 Aug. 1849, was created a baronet, 16 Jan. 1851. His son Henry James (1844-1926) was raised to the peerage as Baron Hothfield, 11 Oct. 1881. The hereditary shrievalty, which Barham also coveted, was abolished by the 1849 and 1850 Acts.[11]

[1] Brougham mss, Miss Elizabeth Tufton to Brougham, 11 Aug. [1838], records his sudden departure for Paris 'on account of the illness of a daughter not expected to be alive on his arrival'. [2] *Letters of William and Dorothy Wordsworth* ed. A.G. Hill (1979), v (pt. i), 369-70. [3] Lonsdale mss, Lowther to Lonsdale, 27 Jan., 31 Mar., 12 July, 14 Sept., [W.D.] to same, 7 Feb., Lonsdale to Lowther, 16, 24 Sept.; Brougham mss, Lonsdale to Brougham, 10 July 1825, J. Brougham to Atkinson, Aug. 1826; Heron, *Notes*, 252; *The Times*, 15 June; *Westmld. Advertiser*, 17 June 1826. [4] Lonsdale mss, bdle. on 1830 election; Wilts. RO, Radnor mss 490/1374; *Westmld. Gazette*, 7 Aug. 1830. [5] *Westmld. Advertiser*, 7 May 1831. [6] Lonsdale mss, Lowther to Lonsdale, 22 July 1831. [7] Add. 51564, Brougham to Holland [26 Apr.]; 51590, Dover to Lady Holland, 26 Apr. 1832. [8] *Westmld. Advertiser*, 28 Apr., 19 May, 16 June; Brougham mss, J. Heelis the elder to J. Brougham, 28, 29 May, 4 Aug. 1832. [9] Add. 51837, Stuart de Rothesay to Holland, 16 Aug., Thanet to same, 10 Dec. 1832. [10] PROB 11/2102/805; IR26/1853/837; *The Times*, 10, 11 July 1849. [11] *Ann. Reg.* (1849), Chron. p. 73.; *LJ*, lxxxi. 371, 439, 602.; *Kendal Mercury*, 15, 30 June, 21 July; Brougham mss, R. Tufton to Brougham, 22 Aug., 12 Sept. 1849, 12 Aug., 19 Sept. 1850.

M.M.E.

TUITE, Hugh Morgan (1795–1868), of Sonna, co. Westmeath.

| Co. WESTMEATH | 1826–1830 |
| Co. WESTMEATH | 1841–1847 |

b. 1795, 2nd but 1st surv. s. of Capt. Hugh Tuite of Sonna and Sarah Elizabeth, da. of Lt.-Col. Daniel Chenevix of Ballycommon, King's Co. *educ.* Christ Church, Oxf. 1814. *m.* (1) 6 Feb. 1826, Mary (*d.* 14 Mar. 1863), da. of Maurice O'Connor of Mount Pleasant, King's Co., 1s. 1da.; (2) 8 Oct. 1863, Hester Maria, da. of John Hogan of Auburn, co. Westmeath, *s.p. suc.* fa. 1843. *d.* 15 Aug. 1868.
Sheriff, co. Westmeath 1822-3, co. Longford 1837-8.

Tuite, 'the son of a gentleman of about £5,000 per annum', was a permanent resident of Westmeath, where the local press commended his family for giving 'perpetual employment to a number of our poor' and spending 'a splendid fortune'.[1] Following the death of one of the county's sitting Members in 1824 he made a 'limited canvass' as a supporter of Catholic claims, but on finding 'the strong interests combined' against him quit the field, hinting that he intended to stand at the next general election.[2] In 1826 he duly offered as a pro-Catholic in opposition to the dominant Protestant interests, stressing his independence from 'any particular line of politics', his belief that emancipation would restore 'peace and good order' and his wish to deliver the county 'from the degradation of being considered a sort of family property, or hereditary borough'. He was actively assisted by the Catholic Association and after a 'severe struggle' returned in second place, amidst accusations of widespread electoral misconduct by his supporters.[3]

He informed the Commons, 14 Feb., that he would not defend his return against his beaten rival's petition, but his associates successfully petitioned to be admitted as parties for his defence, 8 Mar. 1827. He was absent from the division on Catholic claims, 6 Mar., as he 'could not vote, not having defended his election'.[4] A commission of inquiry into his return was established, 3 May 1827, but it disintegrated the following year, whereupon a committee was appointed, 18 Apr., and decided in his favour, 28 Apr. 1828.[5] In his first reported action in the House Tuite, who is not known to have spoken in debate in this period, voted for Catholic relief, 12 May 1828. He divided against restricting the circulation of Irish and Scottish small notes, 5 June 1828. He was a convenor for the meeting of the 'friends of civil and religious liberty' at the Rotunda, Dublin, 20 Jan., and of course voted for the Wellington ministry's concession of emancipation, 6 Mar. 1829.[6] He was granted three weeks' leave on account of ill health, 12 Mar. 1830. He was in the minorities for O'Connell's Irish vestries bill, 27 Apr., and repeal of the Irish coal duties, 13 May. He paired for the second reading of the Jewish emancipation bill, 17 May. He voted to reduce the grants for consular services, 11 June, and Nova Scotia, 14 June, and was in the minority of 30 against the administration of justice bill, 18 June 1830.

At the 1830 general election Tuite offered again, citing his avoidance of 'all coalitions' and opposition to 'every measure tending to increased taxation'. Faced with alliance between his former opponents, and abused for not pledging his unqualified support to Daniel O'Connell*, he 'apologized for voting for the emancipation bill, clogged as it was with the disfran-

chisement of the 40s. freeholders', and explained that he had withdrawn his support from the vestries bill in order to please both Catholics and Protestants. After a warm contest, in which he was 'rather remiss' in his canvassing, he was defeated; the *Westmeath Journal* observed that he had 'sailed into the emancipation bog [and] run on vestry sands'.[7] At the 1831 general election he started as a supporter of the Grey ministry's reform bill but withdrew after a brief canvass.[8] It was erroneously reported in *The Times*, 4 July 1838, that he had been created a baronet. He sat for Westmeath as a Liberal, 1841-7.[9] He died at Sonna in August 1868 and was succeeded by his only son Joseph (1828-1910).[10]

[1] Brougham mss, Abercromby to Brougham, 12 July; *Westmeath Jnl.* 8 June 1826. [2] *Westmeath Jnl.* 26 Feb. 1824. [3] *Dublin Evening Post*, 8, 15, 20, 24, 29 June, 1 July 1826; *Westmeath Jnl.* 15 June; Add. 40334, f. 171. [4] *The Times*, 10 Mar. 1827. [5] *CJ*, lxxxii. 16, 168, 293, 429; lxxxiii. 244, 277. [6] *Dublin Evening Post*, 8 Jan. 1829. [7] *Westmeath Jnl.* 8, 15 July, 5, 12, 19, 26 Aug.; *Dublin Evening Post*, 29 July, 1 Aug. 1830. [8] *Dublin Evening Post*, 3 May 1831. [9] *Dod's Parl. Companion* (1846), 241. [10] *The Times*, 19 Aug. 1868.

P.J.S.

TULK, Charles Augustus (1786–1849), of 19 Duke Street, Mdx.

| SUDBURY | 1820–1826 |
| POOLE | 1835–1837 |

b. 2 June 1786, 1st s. of John Augustus Tulk (*d.* 1845) and 1st w. Elizabeth Carey. *educ.* Westminster 1801-5; Trinity Coll. Camb. 1805; L. Inn 1807. *m.* 8 Sept. 1807, Susanna, da. of Marmaduke Hart, merchant, of Hampstead, Mdx. 12ch. (4 *d.v.p.*). *d.* 16 Jan. 1849.

Tulk, a close correspondent of the poet Coleridge and the phrenologist Spurzheim, was a member of the London branch of a Dorset family who had prospered as wine merchants (Tulk and Lovelace) and married well. In 1795 his father, an original member of Robert Hindmarsh's Theosophical Society devoted to the Christian teachings of the Swedish philosopher Emanuel Swedenborg, succeeded his brother James Stuart Tulk (*d.* 1791) to the Middlesex estates of Leicester Fields (Leicester Square) and Honiton previously owned by the latter's brother-in-law Sir George Yonge†.[1] Tulk was sent up to Cambridge and entered for the bar, but, 'partly from disenchantment' and 'partly because his father's fortune rendered it unnecessary', he never practised.[2] Of 'middle height ... benevolent smile ... [and] remarkable gentleness and courtesy', he married a merchant's daughter and close connection of the sculptor John Flaxman, whose religious orientation they shared, and relocated his family regularly to scenic locations in Britain and France to broaden their horizons. Tulk invariably devoted several hours daily to reading and writing religious tracts and the affairs of the Swedenborgian Society, of which he was a founder and committee member, 1810-43, and chairman in 1814 and 1843.[3] Encouraged by Coleridge, whom he first met in 1817, he contributed anonymously to the newspaper campaign for factory legislation and, like Swedenborg, entered politics as a means of addressing social issues.[4] At the general election of 1820 he was considered for Maidstone before successfully contesting the venal borough of Sudbury as the candidate of the Dissenters and the 'low party'. He insisted that he would eschew party affiliation and act solely according to his conscience.[5]

Tulk made a few short speeches and attended regularly in his first Parliament. He sat with the radical opposition and forged a close personal friendship with Joseph Hume, with whom 'his general opinions closely coincided'. However, as his biographer, Hume's daughter Mary Catherine, noted, 'the character of their minds was totally different', and Hume could not depend upon his vote.[6] Nevertheless, a radical publication in 1825 described him as a Member who 'attended regularly and voted with the opposition'.[7] He voted with the Whig opposition to restore Queen Caroline's name to the liturgy, 26 Jan., but against their censure motion criticizing the Liverpool ministry's handling of the affair, 6 Feb. 1821. Tulk, who worshipped at home, saw no need for a separate sectarian church and never officially left the Anglican communion,[8] was steadfastly opposed to Catholic relief: he voted against it, 28 Feb. 1821, 30 Apr. 1822, 1 Mar. 1825, and declared his objections to concessions when presenting hostile petitions from Sudbury, 23 Mar. 1821.[9] He supported the parliamentary campaign on behalf of the 'mistreated' radical prisoner Nathan Broadhurst in the division on 7 Mar., and was a majority teller against the contentious Newington select vestry bill, 16 May 1821. He abhorred violence and voted against capital and corporal punishment, 23 May 1821, 4 June 1822, 30 Apr. 1823, and for the spring guns bill, 21 June 1825.[10] He voted for parliamentary reform, 2 June 1823, 26 May 1826. On slavery, he voted in condemnation of the indictment in Demerara of the Methodist missionary John Smith, 11 June 1824, and of the Jamaican slave trials, 2 Mar. 1826.

Tulk accepted Swedenborg's arguments in favour of a metallic currency, reductions in taxation and repeal of the usury laws, and voted for the last, 8 Feb.

1825.[11] He became inclined to withhold support for economies whose prime purpose he perceived to be to embarrass government; and although he voted against the appointment of an additional Scottish baron of exchequer, 15 May 1820, he rarely divided in Hume's small minorities on the estimates after May 1821, and he voted with government on the revenue, 6 Mar., the grant to the duke of Clarence, 18 June, and taxation, 27 June 1821. He voted against Brougham's vague proposals to relieve distress, 11 Feb. 1822, but for Lord Althorp's, 21 Feb., and for admiralty reductions, 4 Mar., and abolition one of the joint-postmasterships, 13 Mar., 2 May 1822. He voted to reduce taxation on salt, 28 Feb., and malt, 2 July, and for the third reading of Grey Bennet's alehouses licensing bill, 27 June 1822. He voted against raiding the sinking fund to finance massive tax cuts, 5, 13, 18 Mar., and against reopening the currency question, 12 June 1823. He was in the minority of eight against the committal of the warehousing bill, 21 Mar. 1823, and presented Sudbury's petition against the coal duties that day.[12] He voted for information on the prosecution of the Dublin Orange rioters, 24 Mar., but was in the government minority, when defeat made them concede inquiry, 22 Apr. 1823. True to his family and Dorset interests, he strenuously supported the Newfoundland bill and testified to the 'absolute need' to improve justice and administration to safeguard the fisheries and save the island from 'absolute ruin', 25 Mar. He voted against the silk manufacture bill, 9 June, and the beer duties bill, 13 June 1823.

In February 1824 Tulk consulted the home secretary Peel preparatory to ordering papers on the state of the Lancashire and Cheshire cotton factories that session, but in great distress throughout his wife's final illness, he moved with his family to Worthing, where she died, 17 Oct.[13] Testifying to the 'atrocious cruelty' of the current factory system, he spoke, 16 May, and presented petitions in favour of Hobhouse's cotton factories regulation bill, 31 May 1825, when he moved an amendment to restore its provision for an eleven and a half hour day, which he reluctantly withdrew after Huskisson warned that it placed the entire measure in jeopardy. He voted to defeat the controversial Leith Docks bill, 20 May, against increasing the duke of Cumberland's grant, 27 May, and with Hume for information on the Indian army, 24 Mar., and the Rev. Bryce's appointment as clerk to the committee of stationery in Bengal, 1 June 1825.[14] He voted against the president of the board of trade's proposed salary, 7, 10 Apr., and to consider corn law reform, 18 Apr. 1826. He voted for and was named to the select committee appointed to inquire into James Silk

Buckingham's[†] allegations concerning press censorship in India, 9 May 1826.

Tulk had dined with the corporation and stated his intention of seeking re-election for Sudbury when a dissolution was anticipated in the autumn of 1825, but criticism of his idiosyncratic cross-party stance augured against his success and he withdrew after John Wilks II*, Benjamin Rotch and Bethell Walrond* entered the fray at the general election of 1826.[15] By then Tulk was engulfed in a religious controversy prompted by John Clowes's pronouncement that his editing of Swedenborg's writings proclaimed 'idealistic and gnostic notions denying the reality of the Lord's incarnation' tantamount to heresy.[16] He defended himself, under the pseudonmyn 'Mr. Collins', in *The Intellectual Repository*, a religious periodical which he and his father had financed since 1812, but he was soon exposed and became estranged from his father on account of their doctrinal differences. He launched and funded the *New Jerusalem Magazine* (1826-9) to publicize his views, but Clowes retaliated at the Swedenborgians' 1828 meeting at Warwick by carrying a series of doctrinal resolutions that he knew Tulk could not accept.[17] Assisted by his son-in-law John Gordon, Tulk (who faced further charges of heresy in 1842), published his *Record of Family Instruction* in 1832 and *The Science of Correspondency*, a digest of his numerous religious articles, in 1846.[18] He was defeated at Poole, where Dissent and the Newfoundland lobby were well represented but the reformers were divided, at the October 1831 by-election and the general election of 1832, but was returned there as a Liberal in 1835.[19] After retiring from Parliament in 1837, he remained an active Middlesex magistrate and chairman of the management committee of Hanwell lunatic asylum, 1839-47.[20] He did not remarry, remained close to his five surviving sons and three daughters and died in January 1849, having bequeathed his valuable property in Leicester Square, which was the subject of protracted litigation, equally between them, excluding only his 'beloved eldest son Marmaduke' Hart (*d.* 1853), for whom his maternal grandfather had already provided.[21]

[1] IGI (Dorset, London, Mdx., Surr.); PROB 11/837/131; 1213/345; 1813/200; 2011/165; *Gent. Mag.* (1791), 789, 868; *Public Characters* (1799-1800), 418; Swedenborgian Soc. (London) archives K 59, 'Annals of the New Church', i. 483. [2] M.C. Hume (afterwards Rothery), *Brief Sketch of the Life, Character and Religious Opinions of Tulk* ed. C. Pooley (1890), 7-8. [3] Ibid. 9-13, 24; Add. 39781, ff. 152, 480; Swedenborgian Soc. (London) archives A9. [4] Hume 14, 16, 18; 'Annals of the New Church', i. 260. [5] *Bury and Norwich Post*, 8, 15 Mar. 1820. [6] Hume, 14, 16. [7] *Session of Parl. 1825*, p. 488. [8] Hume, 13-14; *Dorset Co. Chron. and Som. Gazette*, 6 Dec. 1832. [9] *The Times*, 24 Mar. 1821. [10] Hume, 16. [11] C. Hasler and

J. Kaczmayck, *Emanuel Swedenborg*, 27. [12] *The Times*, 22 Mar. 1823. [13] Add. 40361, f. 44; 40363, f. 233; Swedenborgian Soc. (London) archives K4, 42, 74; *The Times*, 19 Oct. 1824. [14] *The Times*, 25 Mar. 1825. [15] *Ipswich Jnl.* 15 Oct. 1825; *The Times*, 6 June 1826. [16] 'Annals of the New Church', i. 275, 306, 332. [17] Ibid. i. 335, 343, 351, 258-62; *Oxford DNB*. [18] Swedenborgian Soc. (London) archives K4; 'Annals of the New Church', i. 559; *New Church Mag.* (1890), 102. [19] *The Times*, 11 June, 22 Sept. 1832, 17 Dec. 1834; *Dorset Co. Chron. and Som. Gazette*, 29 Nov., 6, 13 Dec. 1832, 8 Jan. 1835. [20] *The Times*, 6 July 1837, 30 Mar. 1838, 4 Dec. 1839, 3 Sept. 1844; Hume, 15. [21] *The Times*, 7, 22 Dec. 1848, 12 Feb. 1849; *Oxford DNB*; PROB 11/2088/148.

M.M.E.

TUNNO, Edward Rose (1794–1863), of Llangennech, nr. Llanelli, Carm.; Boverton Castle, Llantwit Major, Glam., and 19 Upper Brook Street, Mdx.

BOSSINEY   1826–1832

bap. 26 Nov. 1794, o. surv. s. of John Tunno, merchant, of 6 Old Jewry, London and w. Margaret (née Rose?).[1] *educ.* Harrow 1806-13; Trinity Coll. Camb. 1813; L. Inn 1816, called 1823. *m.* 8 Oct. 1825, Caroline, da. of Job M. Raikes of Portland Place, Mdx., *s.p.*[2] *suc.* fa. 1819. *d.* 8 Mar. 1863.
   Sheriff, Carm. 1835-6.

Tunno's origins are obscure. His father, who may have been a Scot, was in business in London as a merchant and underwriter by the late 1780s, and from about 1810 seems to have had premises in New Broad Street Court; he had acquired a town house at 18 Devonshire Place by 1803. Two of his father's brothers, Adam and William, were in partnership in a business based at Charleston, South Carolina, and another, Robert, was 'for many years a respectable member of the Stock Exchange'.[3] Tunno received a conventional gentleman's education and on his father's death in 1819 was the residuary legatee of his estate, which was sworn under £500,000. It is not clear whether this included the Boverton Castle estate in Glamorgan, or whether Tunno himself bought it. He certainly purchased the Llangennech estate, near Llanelli, which contained coal deposits.[4] He stood as the 'independent' champion of the resident freeholders at a by-election at Bossiney in June 1823, but his attempt to open the borough was thwarted by the returning officer and his petition against the result was eventually rejected.[5] However, he subsequently established himself as joint-patron of Bossiney, and by the time of the general election in 1826 was strong enough to ensure his return after a token contest. He retained the seat unopposed until Bossiney was disfranchised by the Reform Act of 1832.[6]

He was a poor attender, who is not known to have spoken in debate or to have presented a single petition. He divided for Catholic relief, 6 Mar. 1827. He voted against repeal of the Test Acts, 26 Feb., but was absent from the division on the Catholic question, 12 May 1828. He voted with the duke of Wellington's ministry against reduction of the ordnance estimates, 4 July 1828. He divided for Catholic emancipation, 6, 30 Mar., and in favour of Daniel O'Connell being allowed to take his seat unimpeded, 18 May 1829. He was named as a defaulter, 1 Mar. 1830, and, after failing to attend an election committee ballot the following day, was taken into custody. He voted for the grant for South American missions and against abolition of the death penalty for forgery, 7 June 1830. After the general election that summer ministers reckoned him as one of the 'doubtful doubtfuls', but this assessment was subsequently annotated with the comment that he was 'a friend'. He was at first listed as an absentee from the crucial division on the civil list, 15 Nov. 1830, but a week later he 'authorized' a newspaper to state that he had in fact voted in the ministerial minority.[7] He was granted three weeks' leave to attend to urgent private business, 9 Feb. 1831. He divided against the second reading of the Grey ministry's reform bill, 22 Mar., and for Gascoyne's wrecking amendment, 19 Apr. In the new Parliament he divided against the second reading of the reintroduced reform bill, 6 July, to postpone consideration of the partial disfranchisement of Chippenham, 27 July, and against the bill's passage, 23 Sept. He voted to censure the Irish administration's conduct during the Dublin election, 23 Aug. He was absent from the division on the second reading of the revised reform bill, 17 Dec. 1831, but was present to vote against going into committee, 20 Jan., the enfranchisement of Tower Hamlets, 28 Feb., and the third reading, 22 Mar. 1832. His only other recorded vote was against government on the Russian-Dutch loan, 12 July 1832.

Soon after retiring from Parliament Tunno bought the Hampshire estate of Warnford Park. At the general election of 1835 he offered for Andover (where he also had a residence at Red Rice House) as the 'advocate of that great cause in which was concentrated liberty without licentiousness, and freedom in its only perfect sense'; he finished a distant fourth in the poll.[8] He made no further attempt to re-enter the House. He died in March 1863 and left the bulk of his real estate, including Warnford and Llangennech, to his nephew Edward John Sartoris (1814-88), Liberal Member for Carmarthenshire, 1868-74, the son of his sister Matilda with Urban Sartoris of Paris.[9]

[1] At St. Botolph without Aldgate (IGI). [2] Gent. Mag. (1825), ii. 368. [3] Ibid. (1803), ii. 1084; (1840), i. 216; The Times, 28 Dec. 1803, 3 Aug. 1811, 2 Nov. 1814; Add. 38255, f. 21; PROB 11/1616/247; 1922/64. [4] PROB 11/1616/247; IR26/800/549; Gent. Mag. (1819), i. 493; H.M. Thomas, Glam. Estate Maps, 39. [5] West Briton, 30 May, 6 June 1823. [6] Ibid. 2, 16 June 1826, 30 July, 6 Aug. 1830, 30 Apr., 7 May 1831. [7] The Times, 19, 22 Nov. 1830. [8] VCH Hants, iii. 270-1; Hants Chron. 12 Jan. 1835. [9] In the Sartoris pedigrees in Burke LG, Matilda is incorrectly identified as Edward Rose Tunno's da.

D.R.F.

TWISS, Horace (1787–1849), of 15 Serle Street, Lincoln's Inn Fields, Mdx.

WOOTTON BASSETT	1820–1830
NEWPORT I.o.W.	1830–1831
BRIDPORT	1835–1837

b. 28 Feb. 1787,[1] 1st s. of Francis Twiss of Bath and Frances, da. of Roger Kemble, actor and theatrical manager. educ. I. Temple 1806, called 1811. m. (1) 2 Aug. 1817, Anne Lawrence Serle (d. 24 Mar. 1828), 1da.;[2] (2) 3 Apr. 1830, Ann Louisa Andrewanna, da. of Rev. Alexander Sterky, Swiss minister and reader to Princess Charlotte, wid. of Charles Greenwood, Russia merchant, of 6 Rood Lane, London, 1s. suc. fa. 1827. d. 4 May 1849. Commr. of bankrupts 1819-27; counsel to admiralty and judge adv. of fleet Feb. 1824-June 1828; KC 12 June 1827; bencher, I. Temple 1827, reader 1837, treas. 1838; under-sec. of state for war and colonies May 1828-Nov. 1830; vice-chan. of duchy of Lancaster Nov. 1844-d.

Twiss's father was born in 1759, the younger son of an English merchant then residing in Holland, who subsequently settled in Norfolk. He was descended from a junior branch of the Twiss family of Killintierna, county Kerry. His elder brother Richard (1747-1821) made a faintly ludicrous name for himself as a traveller and miscellaneous writer and ended his days in penury after squandering a handsome inheritance in futile attempts to perfect the manufacture of paper from straw.[3] Francis Twiss, who was educated at Cambridge, reputedly nourished a hopeless passion for Sarah Kemble (later the celebrated Mrs. Siddons) before settling for marriage in 1786 to her less talented but equally beautiful sister Fanny, who promptly abandoned her undistinguished stage career. She later opened a fashionable girls' school at 24 Camden Place, Bath, in the running of which she was assisted by her husband and their three daughters. Her niece Frances Anne Kemble recalled her 'great sweetness of voice and countenance' and 'graceful, refined, feminine manner'. She remembered Francis Twiss as a 'grim-visaged, gaunt-figured, kind-hearted gentleman and profound scholar'.[4] The author and Welsh judge George Hardinge described Mrs. Twiss in her mature years as being 'big as a house, in very good looks. Her manner is affected; her voice and expressions measured; but she is very good-natured, and by no means deficient in materials for society or chat'. Of her husband he wrote:

> [He is] very thin, and stoops. His face is ghastly in the paleness of it. He takes absolute clouds of snuff; and his eyes have an ill-natured acuteness in them. He is a kind of thin Dr. Johnson without his hard words (though he is often quaint in his phrase); very dogmatical, and spoilt as an *original*.

His scholastic bent led him to compile a *Complete Verbal Index to the Plays of Shakespeare*, a work of great labour but little practical use; mercifully, 542 of its 750 copies were consumed by fire in 1807.[5]

Horace Twiss, whose younger brother John joined the Royal Engineers in 1816, was markedly influenced by this bohemian background. He was bred to the bar, went the Oxford circuit and subsequently practised successfully in the equity courts; but he inherited his mother's family's love of the theatre and had literary aspirations and pretensions as a wit and raconteur. It was reckoned that he was retarded in his profession by his vulgar, raffish image and apparent lack of gravitas. He shone as a member of various debating societies, and one of his dinner party pieces was a series of imitations of great parliamentary orators, past and present. He composed the farewell address which his aunt delivered on her retirement from the stage in 1812, and in 1814 published some clever *Posthumous Parodies* of famous poets and the words to *A Selection of Scotch Melodies*.[6] On 13 May 1819 his tragedy *The Carib Chief* was performed at Drury Lane, with Kean in the title role. It was 'received with great applause', but later sank into well-merited obscurity.[7] It was at about this time that Tom Moore attended 'an odd dinner' given by Twiss in Chancery Lane, 'in a borrowed room, with champagne, pewter spoons, and old Lady Cork'.[8] On a weightier note, he contributed to the *Edinburgh Review* in 1810 (xvi. 1-30) a piece on the anonymous *Letter on the French Government*; and in 1812 he published *Influence or Prerogative*, in which he argued that the admitted increase in the influence of the crown since 1688 was merely a necessary and largely benign compensation for the corresponding diminution of the royal prerogative.[9]

Twiss had parliamentary ambitions. In 1816 and 1818 he contested Wootton Bassett on the interest of the 2nd earl of Clarendon, but on both occasions he was narrowly beaten and failed with a petition.[10] He was successful at the general election of 1820 and in turn survived a petition. He aligned himself with the Liverpool ministry, voting against economies in revenue collection, 4 July 1820. In his maiden speech, against the motion of censure on ministers for their treatment of Queen Caroline, 5 Feb. 1821, he carried the attack to the Whig opposition, who frequently barracked him. Thomas Creevey* sneered that 'the daring, dramatic Horace Twiss made his first, and probably his last appearance on the stage'; but he was not to be so easily silenced.[11] He voted for Catholic claims, 28 Feb., and scored a considerable success with his speech in support of the relief bill, 23 Mar. The 'Mountaineer' Henry Grey Bennet thought it 'remarkably good', the Whig George Agar Ellis* noted that he spoke 'well' and the independent Tory Henry Bankes* recorded that the speech was 'much and deservedly commended'.[12] However, Twiss failed to scale these heights again, so that Cyrus Redding could observe that he 'should have been called single-speech'. Redding claimed to have spied on him with a friend through the keyhole of the door to his Inner Temple chambers as he rehearsed a speech intended for the Commons:

> We ... saw him address the tongs, placed upright against the bars [of the fireplace] as 'Mr. Speaker' ... [He] preserved wondrous gravity, and the tongs falling, said to himself, 'Aye, now the Speaker has left the chair'.[13]

Nothing came of his promised initiative to improve bankruptcy administration, 16 Feb., 1 Mar.[14] He spoke against the disfranchisement of ordnance officials, 12 Apr. On 17 Apr. he opposed Lambton's parliamentary reform scheme, arguing that 'it was better, in most cases, for the House to be a little behind public opinion, than a little before it' and that 'the inconvenience of our present system – for some there were – we willingly bore as the price of our freedom'. He voted against Lord John Russell's reform motion, 9 May, and dismissed Burdett's demand for inquiry into the Peterloo massacre, 16 May, in a speech which Grey Bennet reckoned was 'rather ingenious', but 'only showed the base nature of thieving lawyers and the length they will go to secure the favour of the crown'.[15] He divided with ministers for the duke of Clarence's grant, 18 June, and against economies, 27 June 1821.

Twiss voted against more extensive tax cuts, 11, 21 Feb., and abolition of one of the joint-postmasterships, 13 Mar 1822. He opposed Wilson's attempt to bring the circumstances of his dismissal from the army before the House, 13 Feb. On 25 Apr. he spoke at length against Russell's reform scheme, which he said would lead to the 'total subversion of the monarchy', but the Speaker, according to Mrs. Arbuthnot, allowed him to be 'coughed down'.[16] He defended the aliens bill, 5 June, and voted with government against the attack on the lord advocate, 25 June, and for the Irish estimates, 22 July. He supported the Scottish juries bill, 20 June, because a prisoner in Scotland currently had the odds stacked against him, but he objected to the proposal to ballot for jurors. When opposing abolition of the vice-chancellor's court, 26 June, he deplored 'this restless activity of change, so much the rage of the day' and forecast that lord chancellor Eldon's judgments would come to be 'looked up to as monuments of legal excellence'. He denied that judges ever imposed harsh sentences out of personal spite, 1 July.[17] He introduced a bill to regulate the appointment of assessors at parliamentary elections, 8 July 1822, but it made no significant progress then, or when he reintroduced it in 1823 and 1825.[18] He voted against reform, 20 Feb., the remission of £2,000,000 in taxes, 3 Mar., repeal of the Foreign Enlistment Act, 16 Apr., and inquiry into the legal proceedings against the Dublin Orange rioters, 22 Apr. 1823. He defended British neutrality in the Franco-Spanish conflict, 30 Apr., but the 'growing impatience' of the House cut him short. He was a teller for the majority in favour of introducing a bill to regulate the issue of writs of *capias utlagatum* in Ireland, 28 May. He spoke and voted against Scottish electoral reform, 2 June, praising the existing constitution for its 'faculty of self-adaptation to the circumstances of all times'. He was a teller for the majority against inquiry into Middlesex county court, 19 June, and now divided with government against the Scottish juries bill, 20 June. In reply to Hume's assault on the blasphemy laws, 1 July 1823, he vindicated the role of the state as 'a sort of moral police, as well as a civil one'.

In his quest for professional advancement, which began as soon as he entered the House, Twiss, as a pro-Catholic, attached himself to the foreign secretary Lord Londonderry, through whom he applied to Eldon for a mastership in chancery. Eldon refused him this, but held out the prospect of a Welsh judgeship whenever a vacancy occurred. After Londonderry's suicide in August 1822 Twiss lost no time in sending Canning, his successor as leader of the Commons, an 'exposition of his pretensions and expectations'. Canning, aware that the Welsh judicature and the propriety of its members being allowed to sit in the Commons were under critical parliamentary scrutiny, suggested to Lord Liverpool that a mastership 'of the first, second, or third vacancy' would be the best way to cater for Twiss, whose elevation to the Welsh bench 'would infallibly bring that question forward under most unpropitious circumstances'. When a vacancy occurred in March 1823 Liverpool, who had a low estimate of Twiss's abilities, had no compunction in preferring the more senior and respectable Jonathan Raine*. Yet the promise made by Londonderry and Eldon remained, and when the puisne judgeship of Chester fell vacant in September 1823 Twiss duly applied for it through Canning, who told Liverpool:

> I really do not see how this application is to be refused, unless we determine never to make a Welsh judge again in the House of Commons (and that determination would come awkwardly after Raine) or never to make a *friend* (and that would be hardly stateable *to* friends) ... [Twiss] has unquestionably the best claim of any man on our side. I feel all the inconvenience of the run that may be made against him. But I think it would be injustice in the government to pass him over, and it would certainly be very hard upon *me*, after Lord Londonderry's promises. If it is thought expedient to make his going out of the House ... a condition, I have no objection. It would be one thing to say that we will not risk the question of his seat in Parliament, but it is quite another to say that parliamentary services shall be the *reverse* of a qualification for preferment.

On the other hand, the Welshman Charles Williams Wynn*, president of the board of control, urged the need for 'care in the selection', especially as the chief justice of Chester, Charles Warren*, had come to be unusually reliant on his associate judge, because of his own defective knowledge:

> Under these circumstances the puisne judgeship requires a person of more knowledge and ability than might be necessary with a different chief justice ... You will probably be applied to by Mr. Twiss, but though he is a good speaker and might be appointed a puisne judge on one of the other Welsh circuits where there is an able chief, I fear that his professional reputation is not such as would render his nomination to this office, which is superior in emolument to any of the other appointments but the chief justiceship of Chester, creditable to the government or useful to the public.

An attempt to fob Twiss off with the chief justiceship of Bombay foundered on the objections of the East India Company directors. In the end Liverpool, feeling obliged to provide for him, but convinced that his elevation to the bench would entail 'the annihilation of the Welsh judicature', gave the puisne judgeship to Thomas Jervis, whose post of counsel to the admiralty was conferred on Twiss.[19]

He was not much in evidence in the House in 1824, when he objected to Hume's attempt to name committing magistrates, 27 May, opposed the game bill, which would 'considerably increase crime among the lower orders', 31 May, and appealed to the Catholic Association to dissolve itself before government intervened, 10 June. He voted with ministers on the case of the Methodist missionary John Smith, 11 June, and for the Irish insurrection bill, 14 June 1824. He divided for the Irish unlawful societies bill, 25 Feb., was a defaulter, 28 Feb., but appeared and was excused, 1 Mar., when he voted for Catholic claims. He divided for the relief bill, 21 Apr., and spoke at length for its third reading, 10 May, when he sat down to 'loud and repeated cheering from all sides of the House'. He defended the level of Eldon's income from fees, 27 May, and voted for the duke of Cumberland's annuity, 2, 10 June, and for the spring guns bill, 21 June 1825. He opposed parliamentary reform proposals, 13 Apr., 26 May 1826. On the criminal justice bill, 17 Apr., he made a suggestion concerning depositions which ministers would not accept; and he again diverged from the home secretary Peel and the attorney-general by supporting George Lamb's bill to allow persons on trial for felony offences to conduct their defence through counsel, 25 Apr. He paired (with Agar Ellis) against the immediate abolition of colonial slavery, 19 May 1826.[20] That year he published *An Enquiry into the Means of Consolidating and Digesting the Laws of England*, in which he put the case for a classification of municipal law by experts in its various branches, under the direction of 'a small superintending body'. At the general election he stood again for Wootton Bassett under the aegis of the 3rd earl of Clarendon, in harness with the Whig George Philips, whose sponsor Lord Bolingbroke had hoped that Clarendon would 'find a better man' than Twiss, 'a great talker' who 'cannot pay'. They were returned after a contest and survived a petition, but it was not the ideal seat for a man with an eye to any political promotion which required re-election.[21] Twiss's father died on 28 Apr. 1827, having neglected to alter his will of 1814, in which he had left everything to his wife, who had died in 1822. Horace, who received a gold watch by it, was granted probate of the estate, which was sworn under a paltry £2,000.[22]

In the House, he suggested improvements to Shadwell's writ of rights bill, 30 Mar., and Lord Althorp's elections regulation bill, 8 May 1827; in the later case, by establishing a means of determining the validity of dubious votes on the spot. He claimed 17 years later that had Nicholas Tindal* been made attorney-general in Canning's administration, as was at first expected, he would have replaced him as solicitor-general. When this fell through, Canning gave him the option of taking silk or becoming under-secretary at the home office, and he opted for the former.[23] At the swearing-in there was, according to John Campbell II*

a general laugh when, on reading poor Twiss's patent, it turned out that he was expressly told by the king that he was to have *no wages*, whereas our royal master allows the rest of us £40 a year. This exception in Twiss's patent is to preserve his acceptance of the office from vacating his seat in Parliament.[24]

To add to his difficulties he was obliged, 'at no small sacrifice of revenue for higher considerations', as he later complained, to give up not only his assize and sessions business, but his commissionership of bankrupts.[25] Supporting Canning in power, he voted against the disfranchisement of Penryn, 28 May, and answered a question from Hume on the ministry's attitude towards Portugal, 8 June. After Canning's death he attached himself to Huskisson and Lord Palmerston* as members of Lord Goderich's administration. When the chief justiceship of the Brecon circuit fell vacant in December 1827 he applied for it, informing Huskisson that although he still coveted a mastership in chancery, this place would in the interim, when combined with 'the now reduced receipt of the admiralty', provide him with an official income of £1,500. His injunction to secrecy, lest news of his application encouraged a 'heavily expensive' and 'anxiously vexatious' opposition to his re-election for Wootton Bassett, proved unnecessary, for he was passed over for Nathaniel Clarke.[26] He voted against repeal of the Test Acts, 26 Feb. 1828. He made comments during the investigation of electoral corruption at East Retford, 4, 7 Mar., when he voted in the minority to exonerate a witness from the charge of perjury. On 24 Apr. he spoke and voted for inquiry into chancery delays: his own solution to the problem was to transfer the equity business of exchequer to chancery, to appoint a additional chief baron and to have the master of the rolls sit daily. He voted for Catholic relief, 12 May. He seconded Sugden's motion for a bill to amend the Act of 1826 concerning the real estate of infants and lunatics, 20 May, and on 23 May 1828 successfully proposed the addition to Eden's bankruptcy bill of a clause allowing the chancellor discretion to dispense, in certain cases, with the service of a personal notice of a composition on creditors.

In the reorganization necessitated by the resignation of the Huskissonites from his government in May 1828 the duke of Wellington, at Peel's prompting, offered Twiss the under-secretaryship at the colonial office 'with an assurance', as Twiss told Huskisson, 'that I am to be perfectly free upon the Catholic question':

The only members of the late government to whom I am at all bound are yourself and Lord Palmerston. And

I sincerely say to you, as I have said to him, that if Mr. Canning's friends ... are of opinion that my services can in any way be useful to him as a party disconnected from the government, or that my connections with them, on account of my obligations to Mr. Canning, are such as would make my acceptance of office at present a breach of faith to them, or in any respect a disparagement to my own honour, I shall be most truly obliged by your telling me so, in the frankest manner; I shall then at once decline the offer. If, on the other hand, you concur with Lord Palmerston in the feeling (by which I mean of course a cordial and unqualified feeling) that there is no reason why I should not accept the offer, I shall do myself the pleasure to accept it accordingly.

No objection was raised and Twiss took the office, which did not require re-election.[27] His elevation earned the disapproval of Wellington's confidante Mrs. Arbuthnot, who thought he had 'no merit but being a good parliamentary speaker. He has a very indifferent character among the lawyers and is not a gentleman, either in habits or principles'.[28] According to Peel, Wellington 'said to Twiss, "You will have to give up your profession". Twiss replied, "That does not signify so much when a government is sure to be permanent"'.[29] Yet within six months he got cold feet over his enforced abandonment of the admiralty counsellorship 'without retaining any resource in the event of a political change', for he had not held it long enough to qualify for a pension. He asked Peel to appoint him to the vacant post of gazette writer in the state paper office, worth about £450 a year, as 'some little refuge against a total reverse'. He appears not to have got this, for one William Gregson was appointed, though in 1841 Twiss was in receipt of compensation 'in respect of an abolished office'.[30] Henry Taylor, senior clerk in the colonial office, described Twiss as 'the fleshliest incubus' of 'all the under-secretaries who had ever laid the weight of their authority' on its business and recalled that he was

> obstructive through timidity and indecisiveness ... for ever occupied with detail and incapable of coming to a conclusion – routing and grunting and tearing up the soil to get at a grain of the subject.[31]

Many of his interventions in debate after his appointment were on routine colonial matters, but he opposed investigation of Baron de Bode's compensation claim, 1 July 1828. He handled some legal business, too, such as the fraudulent devises bill, 5 June, the bankruptcy bill, 9 June, and the lunatics' estates bill, 12 July 1828. He spoke in favour of Catholic emancipation as 'the boldest and the safest [measure] that was ever propounded for the settlement of an empire', 18 Mar. 1829. He was a teller for the government

majorities on the ecclesiastical courts bill, 21 May, 5 June 1829. Early in 1830 Wellington considered him for the secretaryship to the board of control. Lord Ellenborough, the president, judged him to be 'a clever man, but rather vulgar', who, as 'a lawyer and a very good speaker', would 'do very well'; but nothing came of this.[32] Twiss reiterated his hostility to reform when opposing Lord Blandford's scheme, 18 Feb., and Russell's proposal to enfranchise Birmingham, Leeds and Manchester, 23 Feb. The Whig Lord Howick* did not think much of these efforts, but two months later he was 'not a little astonished' to hear lord chancellor Lyndhurst talk openly of 'Twiss's failure' in the House.[33] On 28 Apr. Twiss outlined the facts on which the government rested its case on the Terceira incident. Accused by Russell of reading a prepared speech, he claimed merely to be using copious notes, and received an apology. He voted against Jewish emancipation, 17 May, and was a ministerial teller in the division against reform, 28 May. He defended the appointment of an additional equity judge, 17 June, and was a teller for the government majorities for the suits in equity bill, 24 June, and the increase in judicial salaries, 7 July. He acted likewise for the division against the immediate abolition of slavery, 13 July. On 16 July 1830 he pressed Otway Cave to retract his assertion that if emancipation did not occur soon, the slaves would be morally justified in resorting to violence: he disapproved of slavery, but it was a form of property enshrined in law.

At the general election of 1830 Twiss transferred to Newport, Isle of Wight, on the Holmes interest. According to Palmerston, who was being vainly courted by Wellington, Twiss called on him on 7 Oct. 1830 'to say that Peel wished to promote him in course of changes now in contemplation, and he hoped that if I came in, I would help him on instead of opposing any obstacle to his promotion'.[34] Within seven weeks of this bid to smooth his future path Twiss, who was surprisingly absent from the division on the civil list which brought down the ministry, 15 Nov. 1830, found himself out of office, with no regular source of income. His friend Frederick Pollock* did not at first think he would go out with his colleagues on account of his friendship with Palmerston, who was expected to come into office; but the evening after the vote he

> walked home with Twiss ... [who] considers he is out and has lost £2,000 a year. He is about to let his house furnished, put down his carriage, go into lodgings and in the manly way I was sure he would do meet the emergency, live within his income and wait for better times.[35]

Twiss supported the Grey ministry's proposal for an inquiry into the possibility of reducing official salaries, 9 Dec. 1830, but only because it was 'exceedingly desirable to disabuse the public mind, and to expose the monstrous exaggerations and enormous errors which prevail'. He wished them joy of their clamorous radical allies, 13 Dec. On 21 Dec. he endorsed Inglis's assertion that the desire in the country for reform was 'not so great as some suppose it to be' and doubted whether the government could produce a scheme which would satisfy all reformers. He defended Darling, the governor of New South Wales, against Hume's attack, 23 Dec. 1830. In January 1831 he stayed with Peel at Drayton, from where his fellow guest Sir John Beckett* reported that he was

> very *Swiss*, and would fight under any banners ... I wish heartily that he could get any decent permanency from the present people that would take him out of Parliament (for he could not with any decency stay in the House if he joined them). He will be of no use to us, for his *heart* is *not* Tory, and his interests will soon be *Whig*. Liking him personally and wishing him well, I wish he was out of Parliament and poverty.[36]

In the House, 8, 10 Feb. 1831, he was inclined to excuse alleged improprieties in the management of Fisherton gaol. He opposed calls for the abandonment of the colonies, 10 Feb., and criticized the Canada bill, 18 Feb. After Russell had expounded the government's reform proposals, 1 Mar., Twiss, who, according to Thomas Gladstone*, 'gained an apparent hold on the attention and even feeling of the House that I was not prepared for',[37] outlined his instinctive 'strong objections' and declared that

> until a few short months ago, the most radical reformer was not sanguine enough to dream of beholding a day when the ministers of the British crown – of a mixed monarchy – would bring down to Parliament a bill, sweeping away at once all the proportions of the representation, all the fixed landmarks between the ancient estates of the kingdom.

The disfranchisement of boroughs, he argued, was 'a violation' of the constitutional settlement of 1688; and, far from the Commons being unrepresentative, 'the will of the people already but too often overpowers the calmer and better judgement' of its Members. The real security required by the House was 'against the passions and follies of the people themselves, against the efforts of a blind, but a gigantic strength, to pull down the pillars of a constitution, whose fall must be our common ruin'. He claimed to have voted for the transfer of the representation of Grampound (1821) and East Retford (1828) to large towns and still to favour this piecemeal

approach as delinquent boroughs were identified. He spoke of the £10 householders whom ministers planned to enfranchise as 'persons of whom a large proportion must be men of narrow habits, scanty information and strong prejudices, little shopkeepers and small attornies', who were 'not men fitted to exercise a discretion in political affairs'. This outburst, from which Peel quickly dissociated himself, provoked accusations, both inside and outside the House, that Twiss had ridiculed and belittled 'the middle classes'.[38] He denied this, 17 Mar., claiming that he had in mind 'a totally different order of persons', well below the middle class in 'property and intelligence', and that he had been seeking to expose the 'absurdity' of placing the entire machinery of government at the mercy of 'the uninformed, however respectable, householders of the manufacturing towns'. His fury and dismay at the scope of the bill made him fair game for the cartoonists; and Tom Macaulay*, describing the scene in the House when the second reading was carried by one vote, 22 Mar., wrote that when the result was called 'the face of Twiss was as the face of a damned soul'.[39] On 30 Mar. he sarcastically suggested that reform should be handed over to 'the mob, from whom it would be very easy to raise any number of petitions'. He opposed the immediate abolition of slavery, 15 Apr., and voted for Gascoyne's wrecking amendment to the reform bill, 19 Apr. 1831.

Twiss's connection with Newport was known to be of '*a very precarious nature*', and at the 1831 general election Lord Yarborough, the most influential of the Holmes trustees, returned ministerialists. Twiss stood unsuccessfully for Hindon and Wootton Bassett. At this time Sir John Benn Walsh* wrote of him:

> He was not particularly well received by the House ... He has the advantage of a very elegant *distingué* appearance, and particularly gentlemanlike manners ... [and] a certain easy assurance which seems to stand his friend in all societies ... He has a delicate, consumptive constitution and a great want of natural flow of animal spirits; though his conversation is occasionally enlivened with anecdote, yet the serious is his style. He is thoroughly ambitious, aspiring and actively pushing, and ... extravagantly vain.[40]

Soon afterwards Sydney Smith, mocking the fallen Tory ex-ministers, called him 'Beelzebub Twiss'.[41] Tory talk of his being accommodated at Dundalk or St. Ives came to nothing.[42] Later in the year Edward Littleton* was

> much amused to hear Twiss's opinion of the late government ... He had been taken from his practice at the bar, and made under-secretary ... No man had in public or private fought more stoutly for his party. But he is now thrown back into the ranks of his profession, and without

a shilling has to commence anew. He had failed in getting a pension for his wife, while [William] Holmes*, their whipper-in, had one, and Sir W[illiam] Rae* also one for his wife. His abuse was worth hearing.[43]

In April 1832 Twiss published *Conservative Reform*, outlining a counterplan to the reform bill which might be brought forward by the opposition in the Lords. He conceded an unspecified degree of disfranchisement of rotten boroughs, to be replaced by large towns, but suggested that all the adult male inhabitants should choose an electoral college of 100-200, to form 'an intermediate, permanent and highly-qualified body of electors, to guard against the danger of sudden caprices, fluctuations and tumults, on the part of the multitude'. If, in the event of the Grey ministry's fall, Wellington and Peel still refused to carry a moderate reform scheme, he envisaged 'a temporary administration of other less distinguished statesmen' to settle the question 'on a conservative, rather than on a radical principle'.

He did not stand at the 1832 general election, but in 1835 he secured an expensive return for Bridport after unsuccessfully asking Peel for a place in his new ministry (as judge advocate or admiralty secretary) to tide him over until the chancery mastership which he had been encouraged to expect fell vacant.[44] He was beaten at Nottingham in 1837 and at Bury St. Edmunds in 1841, when he made his will, which largely catered for the settlement of debts in excess of £14,000, 'in case any accident should deprive me of my life in the excitement of the now pending election, much pains having been taken to excite the populace by false representations'.[45] Desperately short of cash and yearning for a mastership or some equivalent office, he supplemented his professional income though journalism, which included sitting behind the Commons clock as a condensing reporter for *The Times*.[46] He also secured a contract to write a *Life of Lord Eldon*. When this appeared in 1844 its quality surprised many observers, and its success helped Twiss to obtain the post of vice-chancellor of the duchy of Lancaster, worth £600 plus fees. The chancellor, Lord Granville Somerset*, had observed to Peel:

> The person ... who struck me as having a claim on *us as a party*, and on the whole not unfit for the situation, is Twiss ... [whose] publication ... which has been so generally lauded, has placed him in a better position before the public than he had before, and would, I think, compensate for any of his previous absurdities.

Peel, who had a soft spot for Twiss, replied:

> I think very favourably of Horace Twiss. In all my intercourse with him he has acted like a man of honour and

independent spirit, and I really believe him to be in point of knowledge and ability much higher than his reputation. He has had the misfortune to make himself a sort of bye-word by little foolish peculiarities which ought not, however, to detract from his real merits.[47]

Twiss had time to experience one more electoral defeat, at Bury St. Edmunds in 1847, before he dropped dead while addressing a meeting of the Rock Assurance Society at Radley's Hotel, Blackfriars in May 1849. His personal estate went to his widow for her life and thereafter to his son Quintin William Francis Twiss (1835-1900), and he left a piece of land in Carlton Gardens, on which he had built a house at a loss, to his daughter Fanny, who successively married two editors of *The Times*, Bacon and Delane.[48] John Stuart Mill dismissed Twiss as one of 'the hack official jobbing adventurer Tories', and Macaulay too considered him to be 'a mere political adventurer'.[49] Campbell reckoned him to have been

> the impersonation of a debating society rhetorician. I have often heard his case cited against debating societies. When he got into the House of Commons, though inexhaustibly fluent, his manner certainly was very flippant, factitious, and unbusinesslike; but, without being in a debating society, I doubt whether he would have gained any eminence whatever.[50]

His sworn enemy John Cam Hobhouse*, noting his death, commented, 'Just the sort of man whom the newspapers lament, but I who knew him ...'.[51] Redding recalled his 'grave countenance' and 'solemnity sometimes passing for extra wisdom', but gave him credit as 'an honest, upright man'.[52] Although he was in many ways preposterous and vulgar (his gluttony was legendary), Twiss, as Peel perceived, was not without ability and redeeming features.[53] Many found him a delightful and entertaining companion; and to his cousin Fanny Kemble he was 'one of the readiest and most amusing talkers in the world', always 'clever, amiable, and good-tempered'.[54]

[1] IGI. [2] *Reg. Temple Church Burials*, 83. She was described in *Gent. Mag.* (1849), i. 652 as o. da. of Col. Serle of Montague Place, but it has not proved possible to verify this. *Oxford DNB* erroneously gives her death date as 20 Feb. 1827. [3] *Oxford DNB*; *Farington Diary*, vi. 2221; P. Fitzgerald, *The Kembles*, i. 227-32. [4] *Glenbervie Diaries*, ii. 59; F.A. Kemble, *Rec. of a Girlhood*, i. 20-24. [5] J. Nichols, *Illustrations of Literary Hist.* iii. 37-38. [6] *Life of Campbell*, i. 143; *Crabb Robinson Diary*, i. 152, 173; *Farington Diary*, xi. 4151; *Berry Jnls.* ii. 501. [7] J. Genest, *English Stage*, viii. 690-1; *Gent. Mag.* (1819), i. 478; Add. 38523, f. 46. [8] *Moore Mems.* ii. 320. [9] *Oxford DNB*. [10] *The Times*, 11 July 1816, 26 June 1818. [11] *Creevey Pprs.* ii. 12. [12] HLRO, Hist. Coll 379, Grey Bennet diary, 43; Northants. RO, Agar Ellis diary, 23 Mar.; Dorset RO D/BKL, Bankes jnl. 126 (23 Mar. 1821). [13] Redding, *Fifty Years' Recollections*, iii. 223. [14] *The Times*, 17 Feb., 2 Mar. 1821. [15] Grey Bennet diary, 82. [16] *Arbuthnot*

Jnl. i. 160. [17] *The Times*, 2 July 1822. [18] Ibid. 14, 15 Mar. 1823, 17 Mar. 1825. [19] Add. 38193, ff. 166, 190, 192; 38195, f. 153; 38296, f. 356; 40311, f. 15; 40359, ff. 274, 307. [20] Agar Ellis diary. [21] *The Times*, 21 June; Brougham mss, Bolingbroke to Holland, 11 Sept. 1826; Add. 40391, f. 301. [22] *Gent. Mag.* (1827), i. 476; PROB 8/220; 11/1726/333. [23] Lansdowne mss, Twiss to Lansdowne, 3 Aug. 1844. [24] *Life of Campbell*, i. 446. [25] *Huskisson Pprs.* 275. [26] Ibid. 274-5. [27] Add. 38756, f. 206. [28] *Arbuthnot Jnl.* ii. 192. [29] *HMC Bathurst*, 654. [30] Add. 40397, ff. 333, 334, 336; 40486, f. 353. [31] *Taylor Autobiog.* i. 117-18. [32] *Ellenborough Diary*, ii. 158. [33] Grey mss, Howick jnl. 18, 23 Feb., 6 May [1830]. [34] Southampton Univ. Lib. Broadlands mss, memo. 30 Oct. [1830]. [35] CUL, Pollock mss Add. 7564 A/4, Pollock to Alexander , 17 Nov.; Hatherton diary, 24 Nov. [1831]. [36] *Dyott's Diary*, ii. 102; Lonsdale mss, Beckett to Lowther, 13 Jan.; Pollock mss 7564 C/1, Pollock to Alexander, 24 Jan. [37] St. Deiniol's Lib. Glynne-Gladstone mss 197, T. to J. Gladstone, 2 Mar. 1831. [38] Le Marchant, *Althorp*, 300. [39] M.D. George, *Cat. of Pol. and Personal Satires*, xi. 16602, 16626, 16636-8, 16673, 16691, 17136; *Macaulay Letters*, ii. 10. [40] *Kentish Gazette*, 15 Mar.; *The Times*, 30 Apr., 3 May 1831; NLW, Ormathwaite mss FG 1/6, p. 179. [41] *Macaulay Letters*, ii. 33. [42] NLI, Farnham mss 18606 (1), Arbuthnot to Farnham, 4 May 1831; Wellington mss WP1/1186/9. [43] Hatherton diary, 24 Nov. 1831. [44] Add. 40309, f. 362; 40408, f. 207; *Wellington Pol. Corresp.* ii. 781. [45] *The Times*, 23, 30 July 1841; PROB 11/2029/637. [46] Add. 40423, f. 87; 40486, ff. 353-6; 40497, ff. 292, 365; 40543, ff. 249, 251. [47] Add. 40552, ff. 24, 26, 40, 47, 49, 51; *Macaulay Letters*, iv. 202, 205; *Smith Letters*, ii. 844; *Gent. Mag.* (1849), i. 649-55. [48] PROB 8/242 (19 Aug. 1849); IR26/1851/685. [49] *Mill Works*, xii. 345; *Macaulay Letters*, iii. 267. [50] *Life of Campbell*, i. 143. [51] Broughton, *Recollections*, vi. 237. [52] Redding, iii. 223-4. [53] *Greville Mems.* iii. 203-4; *Gronow Reminiscences*, ii. 84; *Disraeli Letters*, iv. 1226. [54] Kemble, i. 142.

D.R.F.

TYNTE *see* KEMEYS TYNTE

TYRELL, Charles (1776–1872), of Polstead, Plashwood and Gipping, Suff.

SUFFOLK	1830–1832
SUFFOLK WEST	1832–1834

b. 1776, o.s. of Rev. Charles Tyrell, vic. of Thurston and rect. of Thornham Magna and Thornham Parva, and Elizabeth Baker of Stow Upland. *educ.* Emmanuel, Camb. 1793. *m.* (1) 8 June 1801, Elizabeth (*d.* 22 Aug. 1826), da. and h. of Richard Ray of Plashwood, 2s. 3da. (1 *d.v.p.*); (2) 9 Sept. 1828,[1] Mary Anne, da. of John Matthews of Wargrave, Berks., wid. of Thomas William Cooke of Polstead. *suc.* fa. 1811. *d.* 2 Jan. 1872. Sheriff, Suff. 1815-16.

The Tyrell family, major landowners in Essex and Suffolk since Domesday, had owned the Gipping estates, which were frequently bedevilled by mortgage problems, since the sixteenth century. Tyrell's father, one of the Stowmarket branch of the family, benefited from Lord Henniker's patronage and inherited Gipping from his cousin Edmund Tyrell in 1799.[2] Two years later Charles, who had been 'brought up to be a well educated country gentleman', married

Elizabeth Ray, which strengthened family ties with the Oakes family of Nowton Court, bankers at Bury St. Edmunds, and gave him control of the Plashwood estate near Haughley, where he settled.[3] He took pride in family paintings by Sir Peter Lely and Vandyke and built up a collection of early books. In 1811 he inherited Gipping (which was then let to Sir John Shelley*) and the major part of his father's personal estate, valued at under £10,000.[4] After serving as sheriff, 1815-6, he remained active in county politics as a supporter with his friend the wealthy Felixstowe merchant Samuel Sacker Quilter, of the Member Thomas Gooch and the Tory interest.[5] He attended the 1821 and 1822 county meetings which petitioned for relief from distress, and afterwards signed declarations dissenting from their adopted resolutions of no confidence in government and in favour of parliamentary reform.[6] He was a founder member in 1821 of the Suffolk Pitt Club, and in 1825 organized a meeting of owners and occupiers of land in West Suffolk to petition Parliament in support of Gooch's case against changing the corn laws.[7] His wife died in 1826, and after he remarried in 1828 he moved to Polstead Hall near Hadleigh, which his bride had inherited, with personal estate worth almost £20,000, from her first husband in 1825. Tyrell's marriage settlement, to which three Suffolk Whigs, Sir Robert Shafto Adair†, the Rev. John Staverton Matthews and Sir William Rowley*, were parties, gave him a life interest in the Cooke estates.[8] He signed the requisition for and attended the county meeting that petitioned for relief from agricultural distress, 6 Feb. 1830, but although he spoke briefly he shied away from proposing explanations or remedies for current grievances.[9] There is no indication that Tyrell sought to represent the county before July 1830. On the 11th he was approached by a group of Tories led by Quilter, who failed to persuade him to stand. Nevertheless, on the 19th he turned down a request to second Gooch's nomination and, apparently still keeping Gooch abreast of developments, on the 24th, following discussions with the attorney Richard Dalton, he agreed to contest the seat as a liberal Tory.[10] He canvassed as an advocate of religious freedom and the abolition of slavery, committed to agriculture and 'practical constitutional reform', but strongly opposed to annual parliaments and universal suffrage, and easily defeated Gooch.[11] Allegations of collusion with the Whig Sir Henry Bunbury, with whom he shared 988 of the 1,725 votes polled, were rife; but the Wellington ministry's patronage secretary Joseph Planta*, Lord Lowther* and the Whig Henry Brougham* were all convinced that Suffolk had replaced Gooch with another 'government man'.[12]

Tyrell's contributions to debate were few and brief, but he voted conscientiously and attended to constituency and committee business. He presented numerous Suffolk anti-slavery petitions, 11, 15, 18 Nov. 1830. Although listed among the Wellington ministry's 'friends', he divided against them when they were brought down on the civil list, 15 Nov. 1830. He presented and endorsed petitions for repeal of the newspaper stamp duty, 8 Feb., and the malt duties, 11 Feb.;[13] for reductions in taxes and tithes, 16 Mar., and for parliamentary reform, 16, 18 Mar. 1831. He declared his support for the Grey ministry's reform bill that day and divided for its second reading, 22 Mar., and against Gascoyne's wrecking amendment, 19 Apr. He also endorsed Sudbury's petition against the bill's proposal to deprive it of its second seat, 15 Apr. He was returned unopposed at the general election in May 1831 amid accusations that he, like Bunbury, had sacrificed agricultural to commercial interests in the wake of the popularity of reform. On the hustings, he announced that he would not vote slavishly for the bill's details, but would press Sudbury's case to retain two Members and seek amendments to safeguard and extend the rural vote.[14]

He voted for the second reading of the reintroduced reform bill, 6 July, and against adjournment, 12 July, and using the 1831 census to determine borough disfranchisements, 19 July 1831. Taking each clause on its merits, and under close scrutiny from the local press, he voted against the disfranchisement of Downton, 21 July, but for that of St. Germans, 26 July; and to make Chippenham, 27 July, Dorchester, 28 July, and Guildford, 29 July, single Member constituencies, but not Sudbury, which he argued was 'the only manufacturing town in Suffolk, contains a numerous population and is in a flourishing condition', 2 Aug. He voted for the enfranchisement of Greenwich, 3 Aug., and Gateshead, 5 Aug., and to unite Rochester with Chatham and Strood, 9 Aug., but against the proposed division of counties, 11 Aug. He divided for Lord Chandos's amendment to enfranchise £50 tenants-at-will, 18 Aug., and against granting county votes to freeholders in cities corporate, 17 Aug., or to borough copyholders and leaseholders, 20 Aug.[15] He voted against preserving the voting rights of all freemen, 30 Aug., and an amendment calculated to deny the freeholders of Aylesbury, Cricklade, East Retford, and Shoreham special status, 2 Sept. He divided for the bill's passage, 21 Sept., the second reading of the Scottish measure, 23 Sept., and Lord Ebrington's confidence motion, 10 Oct. He signed the requisition for and attended the Suffolk reform meeting which requested the king to back the bill and his ministers, 11

Nov. 1831, but stipulated that despite his support for the 'whole bill', he reserved the right to oppose certain clauses.[16]

He voted for the revised bill, which spared Sudbury its second seat, at its second reading, 17 Dec. 1831, and to proceed with it in committee, 20 Jan. 1832, where apart from wayward votes to prevent borough freeholders voting at county elections, 1 Feb., and for the enfranchisement of £10 poor rate payers, 3 Feb., he gave it steady but silent support. He voted for its third reading, 22 Mar., and the address calling on the king to appoint only ministers who would carry it unimpaired, 10 May. He divided with government in both divisions on the Dublin election controversy, 23 Aug. 1831, the Russian-Dutch loan, 26 Jan., 12, 16, 20 July, and relations with Portugal, 9 Feb. 1832. He voted to tax absentee landowners to provide for the Irish poor, 19 June, and to make coroners' inquests public, 20 June 1832. Tyrell was appointed to the select committee on the use of molasses in breweries and distilleries, 1 July, and presented a series of petitions, which he had encouraged Suffolk corn growers to adopt, complaining of the practice, 20, 21, 30 July, 2 Sept. 1831.[17] He presented and endorsed others for amending the Sale of Beer Act, 6 Feb., against the friendly societies bill and the hemp duties, 13 Apr., and for the labourers' employment bill, 5 July 1832. He wrote to lord chancellor Brougham, 15 Sept. 1831, 13 Mar. 1832, apparently without success, requesting that copies of the report of the 1800 committee on public records be sent to the corporations of Bury St. Edmunds and Ipswich for 'research' and 'reference'.[18]

Tyrell was named as a candidate for Suffolk West in June 1832, announced it in October, when he was assured of Bunbury's personal support, and topped the poll at the general election in December as a 'reform' and 'anti-slavery' candidate committed to agricultural causes.[19] The hitherto supportive but Tory *Bury and Suffolk Herald* now criticized

> his subservience to Sir H. Bunbury in St. Stephen's and to ... [his] faction in Suffolk, notwithstanding that he had opposed the one and the other all his life before ... [which] betokened a mind ready to break faith with an old friend the moment it was found a more beneficial collusion could be made with an old enemy.[20]

He retired at the dissolution in 1834, but continued to support Liberals in West Suffolk.[21] Following his wife's death in 1849 he moved back to Plashwood, where he died in January 1872, 'shortly before his 96th birthday'. He was buried with his first wife in the Ray family vault at Haughley. Obituaries highlighted his contribution towards passing the first reform bill and roles as a magistrate, deputy lieutenant and militia commander.[22] He was succeeded in his estates and manors by his elder son Charles Tyrell (1805-87) to whom, by a deed of gift dated 8 May 1871, he had previously bequeathed his personal estate. His will provided for other family members, including his 'poor daughter Eleanor', then aged 68, whose care he entrusted to a servant, Mrs. Hannah Sawyer, in return for a cottage and a cow. A painting of Tyrell and his family in 1805 by Henry Walton was sold for £48,000 in 1981.[23]

[1] Gent. Mag. (1828), ii. 270. [2] Tyrrell Fam. Hist. Soc. iv (2), 23; Suff. RO (Ipswich), Tyrell mss S1/5/1; W. Copinger, Suff. Manors, vi. 181, 191. [3] G.M.G. Cullum, Ped. of Ray of Denston (1903), 20; White, Suff. Dir. (1844), 269, 564. [4] PROB 8/205; 11/1530/99. [5] Bury and Norwich Post, 9 Jan. 1872. [6] Ipswich Jnl. 17, 31 Mar. 1821, 19 Jan., 2 Feb. 1822; The Times, 21 Mar. 1821, 31 Jan. 1822; Suff. RO (Bury St. Edmunds) HA/521/14, Oakes diaries, 29 Jan. 1822, 7 Apr. 1823; Ipswich Jnl. 9 Feb., Bury and Norwich Post, 24 Apr., 1 May 1822. [7] Bury and Norwich Post, 25 Apr. 1821, 20 Apr. 1825. [8] PROB 11/1704/516; 2110/243; IR26/1038/1059; 1881/153. [9] Bury and Norwich Post, 27 Jan., 3, 10 Feb. 1830. [10] Ibid. 16, 30 June, 14, 28 July; The Times, 17 June; Ipswich Jnl. 10 July; Lincs. AO, Ancaster mss, J. May and C.C. Western to G.J. Heathcote [July 1830]. [11] Bury and Norwich Post, 28 July, 11 Aug.; Ipswich Jnl. 7 Aug.; The Times, 12 Aug. 1830. [12] Globe, 20 July, 12 Aug.; Bury and Norwich Post, 4, 18 Aug.; The Times, 12 Aug.; Lonsdale mss, Lowther to Lonsdale, 12 Aug. 1830; Add. 40401, f. 125; Wellington mss WP1/1134/6. [13] The Times, 12 Feb. 1831. [14] Bunbury Mem. 161; Bury and Norwich Post, 27 Apr., 4, 11 May 1831. [15] Bury and Norwich Post, 27 July, 10, 24, 31 Aug. 1831. [16] Ibid. 9, 16 Nov.; The Times, 12 Nov. 1831. [17] Bury and Norwich Post, 27 July 1831. [18] Brougham mss. [19] Suff. Chron. 30 May, 6, 20 June, 17 Oct.; Bury and Suff. Press. 17 Oct.; Bury and Norwich Post, 14 Nov., 19, 26 Dec. 1832. [20] Bury and Suff. Herald, 26 Dec. 1832. [21] Suff. Chron. 27 Sept., 13 Dec. 1834; Suff. RO (Bury St. Edmunds) Acc. 296/54. [22] PROB 11/2110/234; IR26/1881/153; Bury and Norwich Post, 9, 16 Jan.; Illustrated London News, ix (1872), 51. [23] IR26/2757/647; Tyrell Fam. Hist. Soc. iv (2), 23.

M.M.E.

TYRELL, **John Tyssen** (1795–1877), of Boreham House, nr. Chelmsford, Essex.

ESSEX	1830–1831
ESSEX NORTH	1832–1857

b. 21 Dec. 1795, 1st s. of Sir John Tyrell, 1st bt., of Boreham and Sarah, da. and h. of William Tyssen of Cheshunt, Herts. educ. Felsted; Winchester; Trinity Coll. Camb. 1813; Jesus, Camb. 1814. m. 19 May 1819, Elizabeth Anne, da. of Sir Thomas Pilkington, 7th bt., of Chevet, Wakefield, Yorks., 2s. d.v.p. 3da. suc. fa. as 2nd bt. 3 Aug. 1832. d. 19 Sept. 1877.

Capt. W. Essex militia 1815, lt.-col. by 1820, col. 1831-52.

Tyrell belonged to a junior branch of an old Essex family, whose members included Walter Tirel (fl.

1100), the reputed accidental killer of William Rufus, and Sir Thomas Tyrell (d. 1502), the supposed murderer of the princes in the Tower. The baronetcy conferred on John Tyrell (?1637-73) of East Horndon in 1666 became extinct on the death in 1766 of his great-grandson Sir John, the 5th baronet. This Member was descended from Thomas Tyrell of Buttsbury, a younger brother of the father of the first baronet, John Tyrell (1597-1676) of East Horndon, who was knighted in 1628 and sat for Maldon, 1661-76. Thomas's great-grandson John Tyrell (?1714-86), of Hatfield Peverill and Wakering, was sheriff of Essex, 1770-1. He had acquired the Boreham estate through his first and childless marriage to Sarah, the daughter and heiress of John Higham. With his second wife Anne Master of East Haddingfield he had a son John, the father of this Member.[1] John Tyrell was a stalwart of the Essex Blue or Tory party, received a baronetcy from the Portland ministry in 1809 and served as sheriff, 1827-8. His elder son John Tyssen Tyrell, whose brother Charles (1803-58) entered the church and took the additional name of Jenner in 1828, chaired the anniversary dinner of the Maldon Pitt Club, 18 June 1821.[2] After his marriage in 1819 to a nineteen-year-old Yorkshire woman, a ward in chancery, who brought him £45,00, he lived at Pitt's Place, near Coggeshall; but on the death of his mother in 1825 he and his family of females moved in with his father at Boreham. On 19 Nov. 1827 his wife Elizabeth eloped with the Rev. Humphrey St. Aubyn, one of the many bastards of the Whig dilettante Sir John St. Aubyn, whom she had met during a visit to her mother that summer. While he was reconnoitring the Chelmsford area to plan the elopement, St. Aubyn disguised himself as a Jewish pedlar. The couple were run to ground in London at Jannay's Hotel, Leicester Fields, masquerading as Mr. and Mrs. Johnson, but they later fled to France. On 22 Feb. 1828 Tyrell's crim. con. action in common pleas ended in an award of £1,500 damages, which St. Aubyn, who had to resign his Cornish living, could not pay. Tyrell obtained a definitive sentence of divorce in the London consistory court and had it ratified in 1829 by an unopposed parliamentary bill, which received royal assent on 14 May.[3] Two weeks later his father observed to a county friend that Tyrell was well out of the marriage 'without any attempt to impugn his character' and 'must be very unlucky indeed if ever he meets with such another woman'.[4]

Tyrell started belatedly for Essex at the general election of 1830, seeking to replace the retiring Blue Member. At the nomination he declared his support for the existing constitution in church and state; said that free trade theories could not safely be applied to agriculture; described himself as 'the advocate of economy and retrenchment', who would support repeal of at least half the malt tax; claimed to be 'totally unconnected with any party', and endorsed the 'gradual' abolition of slavery. During a prolonged and bitter contest forced by the independent William Long Wellesley*, who was attacking the Whig-Tory compromise which had divided the county for two generations, Tyrell professed his support for the disfranchisement of corrupt boroughs and the introduction of poor laws to Ireland. He was returned at the head of the poll, with the Whig sitting Member Western in second place.[5] His inclusion by the Wellington ministry in a list of their 'friends' was subsequently queried; and for the Whig opposition Henry Brougham* reckoned that he was unlikely 'to vote with government'. Tyrell presented and endorsed an anti-slavery petition from Langham, 5 Nov., and brought up several more from the county in the following five weeks. He was in the majority which brought down the administration on the civil list, 15 Nov. On 23 Dec. 1830 he was in the minority of four for the motion of Quintin Dick, Member for Maldon, for the printing of a petition for repeal of the oath of abjuration. On the Grey ministry's budget, 11 Feb. 1831, he criticized their failure to reduce the malt duty and said that the proposed tax on stock transfers would be 'a very great clog to the monied interest' and 'a blow ... at the national faith'. He rebuked Hume and Whittle Harvey, Member for Colchester and Long Wellesley's principal supporter, for making remarks hostile to the Church of England, 16 Feb., when he tried unsuccessfully to persuade the chancellor of the exchequer to implement reduction of the candle duty immediately rather than in October. On 7 Mar. he opposed the Grey ministry's reform bill as 'sweeping, oppressive, tyrannical and ... revolutionary', argued that 'what the majority of my constituents mean by a parliamentary reform is a reform of ... taxation' and attacked Harvey for advocating 'republican' government at a recent Essex meeting. When charged by Barrett Lennard, Whig Member for Maldon, with having paid lip service to reform during his election campaign, 9 Mar., he replied that it was 'a question of degree'. He pleaded by letter his duties as a member of the Petersfield election committee as the reason for his absence from the county reform meeting, 19 Mar., when he was denounced as a turncoat by Long Wellesley, who claimed to have

> met him in the coffee room of the House ... the evening before last, deep in a rump steak, and a bottle of port deep in him, and he pressed him to attend this meeting, and [said] that if he should be taken into custody for absence

from his committee, he would pay his fees, but ... [Tyrell] declined, alleging that he could not leave the committee.[6]

After deploring the 'precipitancy' with which the reform bill was being pressed through, 22 Mar., he voted against its second reading. He welcomed the advance of £50,000 for Irish relief, 30 Mar., but urged ministers to introduce a modified poor law, which would 'at once strike at the root of the evil'. He contended that the Essex reform petition did not represent respectable majority opinion and upbraided Harvey for attacking the church, 13 Apr. They clashed angrily on this, 15 Apr. Tyrell voted for Gascoyne's wrecking amendment to the reform bill, 19 Apr. 1831, and next day presented four Essex petitions for the abolition of slavery. He stood again for the county, with Western and Long Wellesley, at the ensuing general election, claiming to favour the enfranchisement of 'great commercial places', the extinction of corrupt boroughs and a modest extension of the franchise, but insisting that the reform bill would unbalance the constitution and damage the agricultural interest. At the nomination he accused ministers of preferring 'a paltry political triumph to the passing of a measure which would have satisfied all the various interests of this county' and boasted that he had 'proved himself a more sincere friend to retrenchment and economy than the Whigs who, when they came into office, adopted a Tory civil list'. During the contest he was credited with the observation that

> he was no advocate for the boroughmongers, but if there was in future to be no other channel for getting into the ... Commons than by the popular voice, he thought that a certain number of boroughs should be reserved to be sold publicly by auction – the money to be applied to the exigencies of the state – so as to afford a number of independent Members the means of getting into Parliament, where they might express their unbiased opinions free from the trammels of mobs and democrats.

Tyrell, who apparently received assistance from the Tory opposition's election fund, was soundly beaten into third place by Long Wellesley.[7]

He succeeded his aged father, whose personalty was sworn under £16,000, in August 1832.[8] At the general election four months later he topped the poll for the Northern division of Essex, where he sat as a Conservative and Protectionist for 25 years. His leader Sir Robert Peel privately regarded him as a 'blockhead', and the whip Fremantle considered him 'insignificant and stupid'; but he had the last laugh by helping to vote Peel out of office after corn law repeal in 1846.[9] He died at the Royal York Hotel, Brighton in September 1877. The baronetcy died with him, while

Boreham passed to his grandson, John Lionel Tufnell, the son of his eldest daughter Eliza Isabella.

[1] P.G. Laurie, *Tyrells of Heron*, 1-11; F. Chancellor, *Ancient Sepulchral Mons. of Essex*, 175; *HP Commons, 1660-90*, iii. 618. [2] *Colchester Gazette*, 23 June 1821. [3] *The Times*, 25 Dec. 1827, 23 Feb. 1828; *LJ*, lxi. 79, 112, 231-2, 271-6, 378, 396, 397, 399, 441, 454; *CJ*, lxxxiv. 234-5, 242, 249, 267, 273. [4] Essex RO, Rayleigh mss D/DRa F69, Tyrell to Strutt, 28 May 1829. [5] *Essex Election, Aug. 1830*, pp. 18, 49; *Essex Co. Election* (1830), 5-6, 160. [6] *The Times*, 21 Mar. 1831. [7] Ibid. 25, 28 Apr., 6, 10, 12 May; Essex RO D/DRh F25/13, Round diary, 26, 29 Apr., 7 May 1831; *Arbuthnot Jnl*. ii. 421; PRO NI, Wellington mss T2627/3/2/296, Arbuthnot to Wellington, 17 Aug. 1831. [8] PROB 11/1804/545; IR26/1305/503. [9] *Arbuthnot Corresp*. 226; D.R. Fisher, 'The Opposition to Sir Robert Peel in the Conservative Party' (Camb. Univ. Ph.D. thesis, 1970), 56; Add. 40476, f. 20; 40485, f. 295; 40486, f. 30; N. Gash, *Sir Robert Peel*, 267, 602.

D.R.F.

TYRWHITT DRAKE, Thomas (1783–1852), of Shardeloes, nr. Amersham, Bucks. and St. Donat's Castle, Glam.

AMERSHAM	31 Jan. 1805–1832

b. 16 Mar. 1783, 1st s.of Thomas Drake Tyrwhitt[†] (afterwards Tyrwhitt Drake) of Shardeloes and Anne, da. and coh. of Rev. William Wickham of Garsington, Oxon.; bro. of William Tyrwhitt Drake*. *educ.* Westminster; Brasenose, Oxf. 1801. *m.* 15 Oct. 1814, Barbara Caroline, da. of Arthur Annesley[†] of Bletchington Park, Oxon., 4s. 8da. *suc.* fa. 1810. *d.* 23 Mar. 1852.
  Sheriff, Bucks. 1836-7.
  Capt. S. Bucks. yeomanry 1803.

Tyrwhitt Drake, one of the wealthiest commoners of his day, with inherited landed estates in half a dozen counties, continued to sit for the family pocket borough until it was disfranchised.[1] It was later said that during his time in Parliament the 'minister of the day' described him and his brother as

two of the best Members of Parliament – neither of them refused a vote, when required by duty to give it, or ever made a useless speech, or ever asked a favour for themselves or their families.[2]

In reality he was a lax attender, whose posthumous reputation for proud independence was grossly inflated.[3]

He only paired in defence of the Liverpool ministry's conduct towards Queen Caroline, 6 Feb. 1821. He voted against Catholic relief, 28 Feb., took a month's leave, 1 May, and attended to vote with government against retrenchment, 27 June 1821, as he did again, 11 Feb., 13 Mar. 1822. He divided against Canning's bill to relieve Catholic peers of their disabilities, 30

Apr. 1822, and parliamentary reform, 20 Feb., 2 June 1823. He presented an Amersham petition for the abolition of colonial slavery, 18 Mar. 1824.[4] He voted against Catholic relief 1 Mar., 21 Apr., 10 May, and the Irish franchise bill, 26 Apr. 1825. His only known deviation from his support for the ministry in the 1820 Parliament was his opposition to the duke of Cumberland's annuity, 30 May, 2, 6, 9, 10 June 1825.

Returning thanks for his election in 1826 Tyrwhitt Drake declared that he was 'determined to support our glorious constitution in church and state' and to 'vote for the abolition of what were really unnecessary sinecures and pensions'. He considered the government's recent regulation to permit the release of bonded corn to be 'of little consequence', but trusted that there would be no further tampering with the corn laws, because 'everything emanated from the land, and unless agriculture flourished none of our manufacturers would'.[5] He voted against Catholic relief, 6 Mar. 1827. He divided for a separate bankruptcy jurisdiction, 22 May, and against the disfranchisement of Penryn, 28 May, 7 June 1827. He voted against repeal of the Test Acts, 26 Feb., and paired against Catholic relief, 12 May 1828. He was in the minority against the provision for Canning's family, 13 May, but divided with the duke of Wellington's government against ordnance reductions, 4 July 1828. He stayed aloof from the Buckinghamshire Brunswick Club promoted by Lord Chandos*, but presented a petition against Catholic emancipation, 6 Feb. 1829, and, as expected, was one of its diehard opponents in the lobbies the following month.[6] He voted against the sale of beer bill, 4 May, 21 June, 1 July, for repeal of the Irish coal duties, 13 May, and against Jewish emancipation, 17 May. He divided with the Whig opposition in the first division on the regency question, 30 June 1830, but was 'driven away' from the second by Brougham's intemperate speech.[7]

Tyrwhitt Drake, whom ministers listed among the 'moderate Ultras' after the 1830 general election, presented an anti-slavery petition, 15 Nov., but absented himself from the civil list division which brought down the government later that day. He voted against the second reading of the Grey ministry's first reform bill, 22 Mar., and for Gascoyne's wrecking amendment, 19 Apr. 1831. He divided steadily against the reintroduced bill in July, and voted against its passage, 21 Sept. He voted against the revised bill, by which Amersham was transferred from schedule B to A, at its second reading, 17 Dec. 1831, and on the motion to go into committee, 20 Jan. 1832. He presented the Amersham inhabitants' petition against total disfranchisement, 24 Jan.

He was in the majority against an attempt to restrict polling in the smaller boroughs to one day, 15 Feb. On 21 Feb. 1832, when Amersham's fate was confirmed, he protested against the way in which its boundary had been drawn, leaving a 'large portion' of the town 'unjustly excluded'. He voted against the third reading of the bill, 22 Mar. He was in the majority against Hunt's attack on military punishments, 16 Feb., but divided with the Conservative opposition against the second reading of the Irish reform bill, 25 May, and the Russian-Dutch loan, 12 July 1832.

After 1832 Tyrwhitt Drake 'scarcely ever took any active part in national or county politics, further than to support generally the principles he approved'.[8] Peel's abandonment of protection in the 1840s disgusted him. He was 'an excellent sportsman' and esteemed master of hounds, remembered by John Fowler of Aylesbury as 'a stern, determined man, and a scrupulously good landlord'.[9] He died in March 1852, leaving his widow £1,000 and a life annuity of £1,500, payable from the trust fund which he directed to be set up to provide for his 11 younger children.[10] The settled estates passed to his eldest son, 'Squire' Thomas Tyrwhitt Drake (1817-88), who was a more colourful character than his father. Fowler recalled trying with a friend to persuade him to stand for the county on a vacancy in 1863:

> After listening to all we had to say, he replied, 'You two fellows have known me all your lives, haven't you?'. 'Yes', we answered. 'Well, you know I have always associated with gentlemen?' 'Certainly'. 'Then why the deuce do you want to send me to the House of Commons?' He then spurred his horse, galloped down one of the rides of Tittershall Wood, and viewed the fox away, and that was the last attempt made to nominate him for Parliament.[11]

His first cousin once removed, Sir Garrard Tyrwhitt Drake, told this story of him:

> He was one day travelling by train from London to Brighton and a lady in the same carriage tried hard to get into conversation with him without much success. As a last effort she said: 'I suppose you will bathe in the sea when you get to Brighton, Mr. Tyrwhitt Drake?'. The Squire's reply was: 'No, Mam, I have been sick in it far too often to want to wash in it'.[12]

[1] *Gent. Mag.* (1852), i. 521. [2] J.K. Fowler, *Recollections of Old Country Life*, 6. [3] *Black Bk.* (1823), 199; *Session of Parl. 1825*, p. 461. [4] *The Times*, 19 Mar. 1824. [5] *Bucks. Chron.* 10 June 1826. [6] R.W. Davis, *Political Change and Continuity*, 77. [7] Grey mss, Howick jnl. 11 July [1830]. [8] *Gent. Mag.* (1852), i. 521. [9] Fowler, 1-2. [10] PROB 11/2152/392. [11] Fowler, 3. [12] Sir G. Tyrwhitt Drake, *My Life with Animals*, 5-7.

D.R.F.

TYRWHITT DRAKE, William (1785-1848), of Shardeloes, nr. Amersham, Bucks.

AMERSHAM   21 Nov. 1810-1832

b. 21 Oct. 1785, 2nd s. of Thomas Drake Tyrwhitt† (afterwards Tyrwhitt Drake) (*d.* 1810) of Shardeloes and Anne, da. and coh. of Rev. William Wickham of Garsington, Oxon.; bro. of Thomas Tyrwhitt Drake*. *educ.* Westminster 1801; Christ Church, Oxf. 1803. *m.* 22 Aug. 1832, Emma, da. of Joseph Thompson Halsey of Gaddesden Park, Hemel Hempstead, Herts., 2s. 1da. *d.* 21 Dec. 1848.
Cornet R. Horse Gds. 1805, lt. 1807, capt. 1811; brevet maj. 1815; maj. R. Horse Gds. 1820; brevet lt.-col. 1820; ret. 1825.

Colonel Tyrwhitt Drake, who had fought at Waterloo, continued to sit for the family borough. He was an even worse attender than his elder brother Thomas, but was marginally more inclined to oppose the Liverpool ministry on specific issues.[1] He voted in defence of their conduct towards Queen Caroline, 6 Feb. He divided against Catholic relief, 28 Feb. 1821, 30 Apr. 1822, 1 Mar., 21 Apr., 10 May 1825. He divided with government against parliamentary reform, 20 Feb. 1823, but against them on grants to the royal dukes, 18 June 1821, 6, 9, 10 June 1825, the beer duties bill, 24 May 1824, and the admission of bonded corn, which his brother accepted, 8 May 1826. He voted against Catholic relief, 6 Mar. 1827, 12 May 1828. He was in the Wellington ministry's majority on ordnance salaries, 4 July 1828, but, as expected, was a diehard opponent of their concession of Catholic emancipation in 1829. In the 1830 session he voted against the sale of beer bill, 4 May, 21 June, 1 July, for repeal of the Irish coal duties, 13 May, and against Jewish emancipation, 17 May. Like his brother, he was listed among the 'moderate Ultras' by ministers after the 1830 general election, and he too abstained from the civil list division of 15 Nov. 1830 which brought them down. He was a steadfast opponent of the Grey ministry's reform bills, on which his voting record was almost identical to that of Thomas. He voted against the government on the Russian-Dutch loan, 26 Jan., 12 July, but with them against Hunt's motion for information on military punishments, 16 Feb. 1832. He is not known to have uttered a syllable in debate and his parliamentary career was ended by the disfranchisement of Amersham.

Soon afterwards Tyrwhitt Drake married, two months short of his 48th birthday. He lived for a short time at Paulswalden, near Hitchin, Hertfordshire. He died 'suddenly of diseased heart ... in Piccadilly' in December 1848, 'having just met his son, who was on his way home for the Christmas holidays'.[2] He had made provision for the establishment of a trust fund to support his wife and children.[3]

[1] *Black Bk.* (1823), 199; *Session of Parl. 1825*, p. 461. [2] *Gent. Mag.* (1849), i. 319. [3] PROB 11/2086/20.

D.R.F.

UPTON, Hon. Arthur Percy (1777–1855), of The Albany, Piccadilly, Mdx.

BURY ST. EDMUNDS   1818–1826

b. 13 June 1777, 3rd s. of Clotworthy, 1st Bar. Templetown [I] (*d.* 1785), and Elizabeth, da. of Shuckburgh Boughton of Poston Court, Herefs.; bro. of John Henry Upton[†], 2nd Bar. Templetown [I], and Hon. Fulke Greville Howard*. *educ.* Palgrave, Suff.; Westminster 1786; Berlin mil. acad. *unm.* CB 4 June 1815. *d.* 22 Jan. 1855.
Ensign 2 Ft. Gds. 1793, lt. and capt. 1795; a.d.c. to Sir R. Abercromby 1799; maj. 13 Ft. 1807; lt-col. 7 W.I. regt. 1807, capt. and lt.-col. 1 Ft. Gds. 1814; a.d.c. to duke of York 1815; maj.-gen. 1821; lt.-gen. 1837; gen. 1851.
Equerry to the queen 1810; to the duchess of Kent 1835.[1]

Upton, the subject in 1817 of Richard Deighton's six portraits of the man 'Up-Town', was a distinguished career soldier, courtier, cricketer and amateur violinist, who enjoyed the patronage of the duke of York, and had received the order of Maximillian Joseph in 1815 in recognition of his service as correspondent with the Bavarian army.[2] Following the death of Queen Charlotte, to whom he was an equerry, he moved regularly between Oatlands, London and Paris, where his sister and brother-in-law, the Grenvillite 5th earl of Bristol, resided from 1817 to 1822.[3] Like his brother Templtown previously, from 1818 he had occupied Bristol's seat at Bury St. Edmunds as locum for his nephew Lord Frederick William Hervey*, a minor, who nevertheless deputized for him there at the general election of 1820.[4] Inactive in his first Parliament, in his second, Upton, a sporadic attender for whom no speeches are known, lent occasional support to the ministry of Bristol's brother-in-law Lord Liverpool. He voted consistently for Catholic relief, 28 Feb. 1821, 1 Mar., 21 Apr., 10 May 1825, and against parliamentary reform, 20 Feb., 2 June 1823, and divided with government on the Queen Caroline affair, 6 Feb. 1821, tax relief, 21 Feb. 1822, and the window tax, 10 Mar. 1823. He was in their minority against inquiry into the prosecution of the Dublin Orange rioters, 22 Apr. 1823. He voted against condemning the Jamaican

slave trials, 2 Mar. 1826. In 1825 Thomas Maclean and others caricatured him as a client of the courtesan Harriette Wilson, whose published memoirs described his gallantry and her discovery of him *deshabillé* after a dalliance with her sister Amy.[5]

Upton would have made way for Hervey at Bury St. Edmunds directly he came of age in 1821, had he then been offered the command of a crack regiment, and did so at the dissolution of 1826, having also canvassed for him at the 1822 Cambridge University by-election.[6] He did not stand for Parliament again. A popular dinner guest, correspondent and sportsman, he travelled widely on the continent and his anecdotes of court and army life enlivened the memoirs of his friends Captain Gronow, Herbert Taylor* and Thomas Raikes.[7] He achieved the rank of a full army general in 1851 and died unmarried and without issue at Brighton in January 1855. He was buried in Kensal Green cemetery, London.[8]

[1] *The Times*, 8 May 1835. [2] *Prince of Wales Corresp.* ii. 792; vii. 2961; *Gent. Mag.* (1855), ii. 306; *Arbuthnot Jnl.* i. 374. [3] *Gronow Reminiscences*, i. 91. [4] *HP Commons, 1790-1820*, v. 427; *Oakes Diaries* ed. J. Fiske (Suff. Recs. Soc. xxxiii), ii. 250-1. [5] M.D. George, *Cat. of Personal and Pol. Satires*, x. 14817, 14828; *Harriette Wilson's Mems.* ed. J. Laver, 141-2. [6] Suff. RO (Bury St. Edmunds), Hervey mss 941/56/71, Upton to Bristol, 6, 13 July 1821; *Arbuthnot Jnl.* i. 196; *Oakes Diaries* ii. 310-11. [7] *Arbuthnot Jnl.* i. 390, 424; *Gronow Reminiscences*, ii. 293; *Raikes Jnl.* i. 146, ii. 114; *Taylor Pprs.* 479, 506. [8] *The Times*, 25 Jan.; *Gent. Mag.* (1855), ii. 306; PROB 11/2211/8; IR26/2050/300; W.H. Upton, *Upton Family Recs.* 112.

M.M.E.

URE, Masterton (1777–1863), of 8 Lower Grosvenor Street and 16 Lower Brook Street, Mdx.

WEYMOUTH & MELCOMBE REGIS   9 June 1813–1832

b. 3 Apr. 1777,[1] 4th s. of Rev. Robert Ure (*d.* 1803), DD, minister of Airth, Stirling, and Anne, da. of James Laurie of Burngrange. *educ.* Glasgow Univ. 1790. *unm. d.* 10 Mar. 1863.
Writer to signet 1799.

Ure, an obscure Scottish attorney, was a younger son of a Stirlingshire minister, whose wife (*d.* 8 Aug. 1817, in Edinburgh) was the niece of James Masterton, ministerialist Member for Stirling Burghs, 1768-74.[2] As the leading trustee of the estate of the late Sir John Lowther Johnstone[†] of Westerhall, Dumfriesshire, and guardian of his son George Frederic Johnstone[†], Ure managed the turbulent borough of Weymouth, where he returned himself from 1813. At the general election of 1818 he came to terms with his principal opponents, allowing the 'town' interest to return two

Members, while he was elected with Thomas Wallace, vice-president of the board of trade, on behalf of the 'trustees'.[3] This 'union' compromise was repeated at the general election two years later, when he issued an address professing his strong attachment to the constitution 'in church and state' and was returned unopposed.[4] That year he again expressed his confidence in the prime minister, Lord Liverpool, who replied that he entertained 'a just sense of your friendly support to government', but declined to provide him with a sinecure compatible with a seat in Parliament or to promote his brother James, comptroller of customs at Leith.[5]

Ure, who was active in the political affairs of Weymouth, was entrusted with the corporation's loyal addresses to George IV in early 1820 and oversaw the passage of the Weymouth bridge bill that year.[6] Yet his influence was by no means secure, and his wayward handling of property acquisitions and local patronage increasingly lost him the confidence of Lady Johnstone, the young heir's mother, and her friends.[7] It may even have been at her behest that he was denied a clerkship in the court of session, to which her brother John Gordon*, who coveted his seat, had heard that Ure was to be appointed.[8] An attempt was also made to select a collector of rents at Weymouth who would be independent of the Johnstone trustees, as it was said that this would 'abridge Ure's power' and that 'he will have no ground whatever of making a charge of remuneration for his trouble, so that the £1,000 a year he has been charging will be done away'.[9] In July 1820 he rebutted Wallace's accusation that he had begun to usurp the interest for his own ends, writing that

> I will not here recapitulate all that passed at the last election. But I will assert without the hazard of contradiction that my conduct towards yourself, was as *friendly and as honourable as that of any man on earth could be*. It has ever been my anxious wish to do all in my power to promote Lady Johnstone's wishes in the management of the affairs. And I opposed these in the cases I have mentioned because I felt it my duty to the family to do so.[10]

Whatever the extent of his influence, it was gradually eclipsed over the following decade, as the young baronet approached his majority, and Gordon and Lady Johnstone's second husband Richard Weyland* played an increasingly assertive part in electoral matters.

Ure, who usually divided silently with ministers when present, voted against Lord John Russell's parliamentary reform resolutions, 9 May, and reform of the Scottish representative system, 10 May 1821. He obtained leave to introduce the Irish and colonial secu-

rities bill, 28 Mar., and presented it, 2 Apr.; it became law on 24 June 1822.[11] He voted against repeal of the Foreign Enlistment Act, 16 Apr., and inquiries into the legal proceedings against the Dublin Orange rioters, 22 Apr., and chancery administration, 5 June 1823. He accompanied Wallace on his visit to Weymouth in November 1823, and presumably oversaw his unopposed return at a by-election early the following year.[12] No evidence of parliamentary activity has been found for the 1824 session, although in the following one he was reported to have 'attended occasionally, and voted with ministers'.[13] He divided for the Irish unlawful societies bill, 25 Feb., and (as he had on 28 Feb. 1821 and 30 Apr. 1822) against Catholic relief, 1 Mar., 21 Apr., 10 May 1825. He secured leave to introduce the Weymouth harbour bill, 17 Mar., and sponsored its passage through the Commons.[14] Commenting on the West India Company bill, he deprecated attacks on slavery, 29 Mar. He attended the mayoral dinner in Weymouth, 21 Sept. 1825, when he praised the national economic recovery and various local improvements.[15] He voted against condemning the Jamaican slave trials, 2 Mar., and against altering the representation of Edinburgh, 13 Apr. On 19 Apr. 1826 he told James Brougham*, whom he consulted on his affairs, that illness had forced him to leave the Commons the previous night.[16]

At the general election that summer Ure was so strongly attacked that he was afterwards forced to publish his accounts in order to vindicate his financial rectitude as a trustee of the Johnstone interest.[17] Not only was he accused of mismanagement, but one anonymous handbill condemned him for having 'always been a mere aye and noe automaton in the House, innocently and immaculately nodding this way and that, just as the minister of the day directs'. He defended his conduct at a meeting in Weymouth, 22 May, issued explanatory addresses on 7 and 28 June 1826 and praised his supporters for rallying to him. But he was opposed first by Weyland and then by Gordon, who jointly threatened him with legal action on behalf of the family. Although he was returned in fourth place, with Wallace, his other nominee was defeated by Gordon after a bitter contest.[18] On receiving a peerage in early 1828, Wallace recorded that he had tried to consult Ure, 'but he is not come from Brighton; I wonder at this because it was so probable that if there was a change of government my seat would be in one way or other affected'.[19] He presumably gave his support to Edward Sugden*, the ministerialist candidate, at the subsequent by-election, when Sugden's opponent Weyland was assisted by Gordon, who soon became a trustee for the Johnstone family and considerably undermined Ure's position.[20] Ure divided against Catholic relief, 6 Mar. 1827, 12 May 1828, and repeal of the Test Acts, 26 Feb. He voted with the Wellington ministry against inquiry into chancery administration, 24 Apr., and reduction of the salary of the lieutenant-general of the ordnance, 4 July 1828. In February 1829 he was listed by Planta, the patronage secretary, as likely to vote 'with government' for Catholic emancipation, but in fact he cast no known votes that session. In June 1829 he applied to Wellington for assistance in securing Sugden's return at a by-election, but seems to have played little part in it.[21] He voted against transferring East Retford's seats to Birmingham, 11 Feb., and the enfranchisement of Birmingham, Leeds and Manchester, 23 Feb. 1830. He divided against Jewish emancipation, 5 Apr., 17 May. He was returned unopposed for Weymouth at the general election in August 1830, when he declared that although he had opposed emancipation he believed that it had done no harm, and he expressed his approval of other ministerial measures.[22]

Ure's name was omitted from ministers' survey of the new Commons (unless he was the 'M. Vere' listed among their 'friends'), but he divided in their minority on the civil list, 15 Nov. 1830. He presented the Weymouth anti-reform petition, 21 Mar., and voted against the second reading of the Grey ministry's reform bill, 22 Mar., and for Gascoyne's wrecking amendment, 19 Apr. 1831. At the ensuing general election he was returned after a token contest, during which he said that he favoured disfranchising out-voters and enfranchising large towns, but opposed expanding the Irish Catholic representation and reducing the number of Weymouth seats from four to two.[23] He was involved in the brief abortive attempt to return Michael George Prendergast* against Gordon's candidate at the by-election which occurred later that summer, when he otherwise acquiesced in the return of Charles Baring Wall.[24] He divided against the second reading of the reintroduced reform bill, 6 July, and for postponing consideration of the partial disfranchisement of Chippenham, 27 July. He stated that he objected to the bill 'so far as it affects towns, where no decay has taken place in the population' according to the 1831 census, 6 Aug., when he urged that Weymouth and Melcombe Regis be allowed to retain three Members. He voted against the passage of the bill, 21 Sept., and the second reading of the Scottish reform bill, 23 Sept. He divided against the second reading of the revised reform bill, 17 Dec. 1831, paired against going into committee on it, 20 Jan., and voted against the enfranchisement of Tower Hamlets, 28 Feb., and the third reading, 22 Mar. 1832. His only other known votes were against

the third reading of the malt drawback bill, 2 Apr., and with opposition against the Russian-Dutch loan, 26 Jan., 12 July 1832. As Johnstone had come of age in January that year, Ure's powers as trustee and guardian no doubt lapsed, and he exercised no further influence at Weymouth. It was announced in October that the 'extremely precarious' state of his health would deprive his constituents of his assiduous services at the dissolution, and there was no question of Johnstone inviting him to stand at the general election in December 1832.[25] He is not known ever to have sought a seat elsewhere. He died in March 1863, at his then residence, 45 Park Street, Middlesex.[26]

[1] Soc. of Writers to Signet (1936), 351. [2] Burke LG (1846), ii. 1126; Gent. Mag. (1817), ii. 189. [3] HP Commons, 1790-1820, ii. 143-7; v. 428. [4] Western Flying Post, 28 Feb., 13 Mar. 1820. [5] Add. 38282, f. 329; 38283, ff. 95, 121; 38288, ff. 278, 280. [6] Western Flying Post, 27 Mar., 22 May 1820; Weymouth and Melcombe Regis borough recs. 110.MB1, p. 293; CJ, lxxv. 128, 177, 290, 336, 353. [7] Northumb. RO, Middleton mss ZMI/S76/34/1; 40/3, 5-7, 9, 11, 13, 23. [8] Ibid. S76/40/8. [9] Ibid. S76/40/25. [10] Ibid. S76/30/23; 34/1-7. [11] The Times, 29 Mar. 1822. [12] Salisbury Jnl. 1 Dec. 1823. [13] Session of Parl. 1825, p. 488. [14] CJ, lxxx. 217, 225, 242, 460, 479. [15] Dorset Co. Chron. 29 Sept. 1825. [16] Brougham mss. [17] Dorset RO D705 L2, Extracts from the Accounts of Masterton Ure, Esq. Sworn by him on the 10th of May 1825. [18] Dorset Co. Chron. 6 Apr., 25 May, 1, 8, 15, 22, 29 June, 6, 20 July; The Times, 22, 24, 30 June 1826. [19] Middleton mss S76/49/25. [20] The Times, 5 Feb. 1828; [W. Carpenter], People's Bk. (1831), 374. [21] Wellington mss WP1/1025/31. [22] Dorset Co. Chron. 5 Aug. 1830. [23] Ibid. 5 May 1831. [24] Brougham mss, Prendergast to Brougham, 8 June 1831. [25] Dorset Co. Chron. 18 Oct. 1832. [26] Gent. Mag. (1863), i. 532.

S.M.F.

VALENTIA, Visct. *see* **ANNESLEY**, George Arthur

VANDEN BEMPDE JOHNSTONE, Sir John, 2nd bt. (1799–1869), of Hackness Hall, nr. Scarborough, Yorks. and 60 Grovsenor Street, Mdx.

YORKSHIRE	7 Dec. 1830–1832
SCARBOROUGH	1832–1837
SCARBOROUGH	1841–24 Feb. 1869

b. 28 Aug. 1799, 1st s. of Sir Richard Vanden Bempde Johnstone, 1st bt., of Hackness Hall and 2nd w. Margaret, da. of John Scott of Charterhouse Square, London. *educ.* Rugby 1810; Trinity Coll. Camb. 1818; L. Inn 1820. *m.* 14 June 1825, Louisa Augusta, da. of Rt. Rev. Edward Venables Vernon (afterwards Harcourt), abp. of York, 2s. 4da. (1 *d.v.p.*). *suc.* fa. as 2nd bt. 14 July 1807. *d.* 24 Feb. 1869.

Cornet Yorks. Hussars yeomanry 1821, capt. 1824; maj. W. Riding yeoman cav. 1843, lt.-col. 1859-*d*.

Sheriff, Yorks. 1824-5.

This Member's ancestor, William Johnston, 2nd earl of Annandale, plotted both for and against James II, but was elevated to a marquessate in 1701 after making terms with William III. In 1718, he took Charlotte Van Lore as his second wife, without the permission of her wealthy father John Vanden Bempde, a London merchant who had purchased Hackness Hall in about 1707. Annandale died in 1721, leaving one son by each of his wives, of whom the elder, James, succeeded him but died unmarried in 1730, bequeathing the title and estates to the second, George, who took the name of Vanden Bempde. In 1792 he also died unmarried, leaving Hackness to his uterine brother, Richard Johnstone, this Member's father, who assumed the surname of Vanden Bempde by Act of Parliament in 1793 and obtained permission by sign manual to take the name of Johnstone in addition, 9 June 1795. A few weeks later he was created a baronet. He died in 1807, when his title and estates passed to John, his elder son, then six years old. On coming of age Johnstone took a post in the county militia, but by the terms of his father's will he did not succeed to his estates until his 23rd birthday.[1]

In 1824 he became sheriff and took as his chaplain for his year of office the Whig wit, the Rev. Sydney Smith, the first indication of his politics.[2] That September uncertainty arose over one of the seats for East Retford when the sitting Member Samuel Crompton announced his intention of stepping down at the dissolution. The banker Henry Foljambe, agent to Earl Fitzwilliam, whose nominee Crompton was, suggested that Johnstone, 'a very worthy young man and a good politician', might be 'a proper person, in case he wishes to have a seat', 30 Sept. On 18 Oct. Foljambe informed Fitzwilliam that he had 'had a letter from Johnstone, by which he seems disposed to offer himself ... though he does not speak decidedly, but leaves the matter till he has had an opportunity of conversing with me'.[3] While Johnstone hesitated, Fitzwilliam introduced his nephew. In January 1826 the Whig hierarchy in Yorkshire decided to requisition Viscount Morpeth*, son of the earl of Carlisle, to contest a seat for the county at the next general election. Johnstone, accompanied by Smith, presented this request, 14 Jan., but Morpeth declined the invitation and Johnstone appears to have taken no further part in the Whig campaign.[4] At a similar meeting prior to the 1830 general election Johnstone again proposed Morpeth, who this time accepted, but his attempts to prevent the candidature of Henry Brougham*, who he feared 'would cause a division in the religious interest of the country' and never be accepted by the country gentlemen, proved unsuccessful. Johnstone headed Morpeth's committee, nomi-

nated him on the hustings and chaired the Whig victory dinner, 6 Aug 1830.[5] That November Brougham accepted a peerage and the post of lord chancellor in the Grey administration, creating a vacancy for Yorkshire. The manufacturers of the West Riding were keen to replace him with a like-minded man, but the gentry of the other Ridings were determined not to be usurped again, and Johnstone emerged as their favourite. On 22 Nov. he issued an address promising to pursue 'a liberal and enlightened policy, which by the removal of all injurious monopolies, will open new channels to the commerce and manufacturers of Great Britain'. Next day he visited Leeds to 'wait upon several of the most influential supporters of Lord Brougham with a view to conciliate them in his favour'. The *Yorkshire Gazette* doubted 'that the commercial gentlemen in the West Riding will acquiesce in Sir John's election', and on 26 Nov. the 'liberal men' of Leeds, led by John Marshall junior, son of the former county Member, opted for Daniel Sykes, Whig Member for Beverley and a commercial man.[6] Sykes, however, declined their invitation and the disappointed West Riding Whigs reconvened and reluctantly endorsed Johnstone. Addressing the Leeds Cloth Halls, 30 Nov., he declared that 'freedom in trade should be the rule, restriction the exception', advocated a revision of the corn laws, blaming 'fluctuations in the price of grain' for the 'greater part of the misery of this country', condemned the East India Company's monopoly and called for the abolition of slavery, economy and retrenchment. He expressed his support for reform but refused to be pledged on the secret ballot, explaining:

> I shall lend a patient hearing to all the arguments, *pro* and *con*, upon the subject, and, should I learn from them that there cannot be a reform without it, I shall not hold up my opinion against that of the House; but I do consider the vote by ballot an un-English practice.[7]

After the retirement of another candidate it was expected that he would be returned unopposed, but at the nomination, 7 Dec. 1830, George Strickland* of Boynton, a leading Yorkshire Whig, said that as a result of Johnstone's refusal to sanction the ballot, he could no longer support him and stood against him. After a brief token poll Strickland resigned and Johnstone, whose victory speech was 'received with much disapprobation', was returned.[8]

He presented a Hackness petition for repeal of the coal duty, 7 Feb., and endorsed a Leeds petition in favour of parliamentary reform presented by Morpeth, 26 Feb. 1831. In his maiden speech, 7 Mar., he welcomed the Grey ministry's reform bill as a 'restorative' and 'purifying' measure, which would give the middle classes 'a stake in the country' and 'result in a considerable improvement in the habits and feelings of the people'. 'Under the operation of it', he declared, 'we may expect to see within these walls, as the representatives of the people, the wisest of her sons'. It was a 'good and sensible' speech, William Ord* informed Lady Holland, 7 Mar.[9] On 16 Mar. he added his backing to the numerous Yorkshire petitions in support of the bill presented by Morpeth. He was appointed to the select committee on cotton factories, 18 Mar. Presenting a Scarborough petition in favour of reform next day, he denied the claims of Edmund Phipps, the borough's Member, that it did not represent the views of the majority of the inhabitants or corporation. He voted for the second reading of the reform bill, 22 Mar., defended another favourable petition from Yorkshire against the criticism of William Duncombe, the sitting Tory, 28 Mar., and divided against Gascoyne's wrecking amendment, 19 Apr. 1831. At the ensuing general election Johnstone offered again, promising to 'never swerve' from the principles he professed. Alluding to a speech in the Commons, of which no trace has been found, the Tory press accused him of having 'misrepresented' the workers of Huddersfield who were 'engaged in the fancy trade', by denying that the West Riding was in a depressed state. He 'met with a boisterous reception' in the town, but his published explanation was said to have removed 'every unpleasant feeling from the minds of the fancy operatives in the neighbourhood'. Rumours of an opposition came to nothing and he was returned unopposed with three other reformers.[10]

Seconding the address at the opening of the new Parliament, 21 June 1831, Johnstone claimed that during his recent canvass there had been 'one feeling' and 'one common sentiment', in both 'the agricultural as well as the manufacturing districts', in favour of 'an extensive plan of reform'. He voted for the second reading of the reintroduced reform bill, 6 July, and gave generally steady support to its details, although he divided for the enfranchisement of £50 tenants-at-will, 18 Aug. He presented a Wakefield petition for reform, 8 July. On the 13th he accused the bill's opponents of 'insulting the people of England with impunity' and caused a stir by likening the actions of the Wellington administration to those of Catiline. He spoke against Wrangham's motion to give Yorkshire ten county Members, 10 Aug., believing that by allotting four to the West Riding, in addition to enfranchising the manufacturing towns, the balance between them and the agricultural interest would be upset. He objected to Thomas Duncombe's motion for the total disfranchisement of Aldborough, 14 Sept.,

arguing that an exception should not be made in order to punish it, and criticized Wetherell's defence of the duke of Newcastle, whose nomination borough it was. He voted for the third reading, 19 Sept., and passage of the bill, 21 Sept. On 10 Oct. he spoke and voted for Lord Ebrington's motion of confidence in the government, describing the defeat of the bill in the Lords as 'a national calamity' and warning that 'upon these resolutions depends the tranquillity of the north of England'. He presented a petition against the North Shields road bill, 19 July. He criticized members of the Manchester and Leeds railway bill committee, of which he was a member, for voting 'without having heard one word of the evidence', 21 July. He said that if the aim of the cotton factories apprentices bill was to prevent the overworking of children, there was no reason to exempt Scotland from its provisions, and insisted that even the 'upright manufacturers of Yorkshire' required the measure as it was necessary to protect the interests of good employers from the unfair competition of unscrupulous ones, 27 July. On 22 Aug. 1831 he presented and endorsed a Wakefield petition against the settlement of the poor bill, which would 'relieve the agricultural districts at the expense of the manufacturing districts', and recommended a settlement based on the parishes in which the poor had 'spent their early and best years'.

Johnstone voted for the second reading of the revised reform bill, 17 Dec. 1831, again supported its details, and divided for the third reading, 22 Mar. 1832. He voted for Ebrington's motion for an address calling on the king to appoint only ministers who would carry the measure unimpaired, 10 May. When Morpeth presented a number of Yorkshire petitions for withholding supplies until the bill passed, 22 May, Johnstone suggested that circumstances were now so changed as to render such extreme measures unnecessary. He divided for the second reading of the Irish reform bill, 25 May, and against a Conservative amendment to increase the Scottish county representation, 1 June. He declined to give his wholehearted backing to a Leeds petition against the levying of tithes in Ireland before the poor had been clothed and fed, as he had been requested to do, 23 Jan. He voted with ministers on the Russian-Dutch loan, 26 Jan., 12, 16, 20 July. On 2 Feb. he welcomed the general register bill, though he acknowledged its unpopularity in Yorkshire, where there was already a local register system of which he approved. He spoke and was a minority teller against a motion for a select committee on the expediency of establishing a general register of deeds, to which he was appointed, 22 Feb. On 9 Apr. he defended a Yorkshire petition supporting the government's proposed education reforms in Ireland, denying that the petitioners were unqualified to form a judgement and contending that 'the opening of the schools to the Protestant, as well as to the Catholic, will eventually lead to the welfare of both'. He welcomed another for the factories regulation bill, 27 June, when he praised conditions in the mills of the West Riding that he had visited, noting that the majority of the children working in them could read and write and regularly attended Sunday school, but warned that if the petitioners' intention was to restrict working to ten hours regardless of the report of the select committee, he could not go along with them. He presented a Scarborough petition for students of all denominations to be admitted to the proposed Durham University, 29 June 1832.

At the 1832 general election Johnstone, who never joined Brooks's, retired from Yorkshire and successfully contested Scarborough as a Liberal. Some confusion surrounds his subsequent political affiliations, with different sources listing him as a Liberal and a Conservative at the 1835 general election, when he was returned again for Scarborough, and in 1837, when he was defeated, and 1841, when he was re-elected.[11] (His colours, however, were orange, traditionally that of the Liberals in Scarborough.) He was for many years a member of the council of the Royal Agricultural Society.[12] In February 1869 he fell from his horse while hunting in Northamptonshire, and as well as breaking his collar bone, sustained a punctured lung. He returned to his London house in Belgrave Square, and 'great hopes were entertained ... for his recovery', but a few days later 'an unfavourable change ensued, and he expired without a struggle'.[13] By his will, dated 26 July 1856, he left his wife the freehold on his London house, a £3,000 legacy and an annuity of £400. In addition he granted her free use of Grange House on his Hackness estate and devised to her income derived from £15,000 invested in stocks and interest on another £5,000. The remainder of his estate passed to his eldest son and successor in the baronetcy, Harcourt Vanden Bempde Johnstone (1829-1916), who succeeded him in the representation at Scarborough and sat as a Liberal until he was created Baron Derwent in 1881.

[1] PROB 11/1468/819. [2] Smith Letters, i. 407. [3] Fitzwilliam mss 118/6, 7, 11. [4] Leeds Mercury, 21 Jan. 1826. [5] Yorks. Gazette, 7, 14 Aug. 1830. [6] Ibid. 27 Nov. 1830. [7] Ibid. 4 Dec. 1830. [8] Ibid. 11 Dec. 1830. [9] Add. 51589. [10] Yorks. Gazette, 30 Apr.; Leeds Mercury, 30 Apr., 7 May 1831. [11] Dod's Electoral Facts ed. H.J. Hanham, 277; McCalmont's Parl. Pollbook ed. J. Vincent and M. Stenton, 258; Dod's Parl. Companion (1847), 191; (1857), 223. [12] W.W. Bean, Parl. Rep. Six Northern Counties, 1059. [13] The Times, 26 Feb. 1869.

M.P.J.C.

VANE, Henry, Visct. Barnard (1788–1864), of Selby, Welford, Northants.

DURHAM CO.	1812–July 1815
WINCHELSEA	12 Feb. 1816–1818
TREGONY	1818–1826
TOTNES	1826–1830
SALTASH	1830–1831
SHROPSHIRE SOUTH	1832–29 Jan. 1842

b. 6 Aug. 1788, 1st s. of William Harry Vane[†], 3rd earl of Darlington, and 1st w. Lady Catherine Margaret Powlett, da. and coh. of Harry Powlett[†], 6th duke of Bolton; bro. of Hon. William John Frederick Powlett* and Hon. Harry George Vane[†]. educ. Christ Church, Oxf. 1806. m. 18 Nov. 1809, Lady Sophia Poulett, da. of John, 4th Earl Poulett, s.p. styled Visct. Barnard 1792-1827, earl of Darlington 1827-42; suc. fa. as 2nd duke of Cleveland 29 Jan. 1842; KG 11 Apr. 1842. d. 18 Jan. 1864.

Cornet 7 Drag. 1815; lt. 2 Life Gds. 1817, capt. 1818; maj. (half-pay) 2 Ceylon Regt. 1823; maj. 75 Ft. 1823, lt.-col. 1824; half-pay 1826-d.; brevet col. 1838; maj-gen. 1851; lt.-gen. 1857; gen. 1863.

Col. co. Dur. militia 1842-d.

Barnard's father, Lord Darlington, who was worth over £1,000,000 and owned almost 100,000 acres when (as marquess of Cleveland) he died in January 1842, returned Members in this period for Camelford, Ilchester, Totnes, Tregony and Winchelsea. He also had decisive interests in Milborne Port (until 1825), Shrewsbury, Shropshire and county Durham, where he was colonel of the militia and lord lieutenant.[1] Returned for that county in 1812, Barnard was ineffective and relinquished the seat in 1815 to pursue what proved to be a high ranking but essentially nominal military career, which left him free to sit for his father's boroughs and indulge his love of hunting. With his brother and successor as Member for county Durham William Powlett, he generally followed the Whig, pro-Catholic line adhered to by Darlington, whose reservations on parliamentary reform they shared, but after being checked in 1818 from veering too closely to Lord Liverpool's administration, Barnard had spent the next session abroad.[2] His return for Tregony at the general election of 1820, when he also defended Darlington's electoral interests in Camelford, county Durham, Ilchester and Milborne Port, was contested and petitioned against. The House ruled in his favour, 15 Feb. 1821.[3]

Barnard's votes were subject to confusion with those of the Irish Members Lord Bernard and Thomas Bernard. He seems to have divided with the main

Whig opposition with Darlington's Members on most major issues in the 1820 Parliament. According to a radical publication of 1825, he 'attended frequently and voted in opposition to government', but his attendance was no more than episodic, and he made no reported speeches and served on no major committees.[4] He supported the parliamentary campaign on behalf of Queen Caroline in 1821, when the death on 8 Jan. of his sister Louisa kept him away at the start of the session.[5] He divided for Catholic relief, 28 Feb. 1821, 1 Mar., 10 May 1825, for parliamentary reform, 9 May 1821, 25 Apr. 1822, 24 Apr., 2 June 1823, 13 Apr. 1826, and in condemnation of electoral bribery, 26 May 1826. It was almost certainly he who voted to abolish the death penalty for forgery, 23 May, 4 June 1821, and for a fixed 20s. duty on wheat, 9 May 1822. He attended successfully to Darlington's interests at by-elections for Camelford and Shropshire in 1822. From then until the general election of 1826 he was party to protracted and duplicitous negotiations and litigation concerning the vote houses and corporation of Tregony and his own candidature for Totnes, where, having been requisitioned, he was furious to be taken to a poll and at finishing in second place. He stated on the hustings that he was 'no merchant adventurer' and was committed to defending local interests.[6] Camelford, Ilchester and Tregony were also hotly contested in 1826, and he was a member of the committee that confirmed the return of Darlington's Tregony nominees, 23 Mar. 1827.

Now on half-pay, he retained a low profile in the House until 1830, when his father went over to the duke of Wellington's administration. He voted for Catholic relief, 6 Mar., and inquiry into the allegations against Leicester corporation, 15 Mar. 1827. He was in France with his youngest brother Harry when Canning succeeded Lord Liverpool as premier, so his allegiance to his administration and to its successor led by Lord Goderich, to whom Darlington owed his promotion to the marquessate of Cleveland, was not tested.[7] Now styled Lord Darlington, he took a house in Brook Street and joined his father and brother in refusing to sign the requisition for a Durham county meeting to address Wellington during his tour of the North East that month.[8] They refrained from deliberate hostility to the duke's ministry in 1828, when Barnard's only reported votes were for Catholic relief, 12 May, and against ordnance reductions, 4 July, and according to the secretary at war Sir Henry Hardinge*, he 'gave in a general adhesion' to the government at the close of the session.[9] Cleveland secured a diplomatic posting to St. Petersburg for Harry during the recess, and as directed and the patronage secretary Planta predicted,

Darlington divided 'with government' for Catholic emancipation, 6, 30 Mar. 1829.[10]

Ministers had passed over him as mover of the 1829 address, and his selection in 1830 was interpreted by the Whig James Abercromby as a deliberate ploy to allay the opposition of Henry Brougham, who despite Cleveland's entreaties, had exchanged his Winchelsea seat for the Whig duke of Devonshire's borough of Knaresborough.[11] On 4 Feb., making his maiden speech after 17 years in Parliament, he made a virtue of his previous silence and loose political alignment, praised Wellington and maintained that Whig measures, especially retrenchment, which he had advocated consistently, were now promoted by Tory ministers. As an 'independent' Member, he was free to support them. The Ultra Knatchbull contrasted and exploited references in the speech to recent increases in exports and a decline in home consumption, claiming they were symptoms of the distress the address had ignored.[12] Ill-equipped to counter Huskisson's criticism, Darlington eventually did so briefly, before voting against transferring East Retford's seats to Birmingham, 11 Feb. He divided against Lord Blandford's reform scheme, 18 Feb., and the enfranchisement of Birmingham, Leeds and Manchester, 23 Feb., when his brother voted for it. Opposing the Jewish emancipation bill (for which Powlett voted), 17 May, he argued that the admission to Parliament of all non-Christians was 'too great a reform in the institutions of the country'. His vote against the forgery mitigation bill cancelled Powlett's for it, 7 June, but both voted for the grant for South American missions that day. Darlington presented and endorsed petitions from Stockton against foreign flour imports, 28 May, and for the release of grain from bonded warehouses (for grinding), 15 June. He resisted attempts by the opposition to revive the regency question following William IV's accession, 6 July 1830. He held his colleague and co-patron, the vice-president of the board of trade Thomas Courtenay, directly responsible for his defeat at Totnes at the general election that summer, when Cleveland's candidates were also opposed at Ilchester and Tregony. Afterwards he was hastily returned for Saltash on the interest of the Whig William Russell, whose election, with Powlett, for county Durham Cleveland supported.[13] In September Darlington asked the home secretary Peel to help him to broker a mutual pact for Totnes at the next election with Courtenay.[14]

Ministers listed Darlington among their 'friends', and he divided with them on the civil list when they were brought down, 15 Nov. 1830. In December,

Cleveland, who had applied to Wellington in vain for promotion in the peerage, the Order of the Bath, or the Garter, declared for Grey's reform ministry and expected his sons to do the same.[15] Undeterred and notwithstanding his avowed intention to support his Whig 'friends' in office 'whenever possible', on 2 Mar. 1831 Darlington, who hitherto had 'only sipped but never dived into political discussions',[16] created a stir by differing openly from his father and making a major speech against the ministerial reform bill, by which Camelford, Ilchester, Tregony and Winchelsea were to be disfranchised and Totnes deprived of a Member. *The Times*, then pro-reform, reported that he was barely attended to and 'transiently heard in the gallery'.[17] He conceded the case for granting the middle classes a 'voice in government' and that many boroughs were 'too small' or 'rotten', suggested levying a rate on the newly enfranchised towns to compensate the disfranchised boroughs and their proprietors and cautioned that the ballot, universal suffrage and any extension of the franchise to the lower classes were harbingers of revolution. He divided against the bill at its second reading, 22 Mar., when Powlett, who had also criticized its details, divided for it. He proposed a 20 per cent reduction in the civil list salaries of the royal household, 28 Mar. He delayed presenting Saltash's petition and case for continued representation until 18 Apr. 1831, and voted (with Powlett) in the majority for Gascoyne's wrecking amendment next day. Cleveland denied them his interest at the ensuing general election.[18] Darlington hurried in vain to Saltash in search of a seat and afterwards tried his luck at Totnes, where he came third. His canvassing address evaded the 'great question of reform' and concentrated on local issues, but on the hustings he said that the bill would have had his support had it not proposed an overall reduction in representation. He said he supported the principle of transferring Members from rotten boroughs to large towns.[19]

Out of Parliament, Darlington, like Powlett, moved to Norfolk, settling at the Vane estate of Snettisham Hall, near King's Lynn. At the general election of 1832 his father's former Shropshire Member Cressett Pelham made way for him in the Conservative stronghold of Shropshire South, which he represented until Cleveland's death in January 1842.[20] He applied in vain to Peel in 1841 to be called to the Lords in his father's lifetime and was passed over as his successor in the lord lieutenancy of Durham.[21] He died without issue at Raby Castle in January 1864, predeceased in 1859 by his wife and recalled as an ardent Conservative and sportsman, who had been instrumental in making owners liable for rates under the 1834 poor law.[22] His

will was proved in London by his nephew and executor Mark Milbank, 3 Mar. 1864. As agreed with Powlett, his successor as 3rd duke, who was also childless, the unentailed estates passed directly to their heirs, their brother Harry (1803-91), Liberal Member for Durham South, 1841-59, and Hastings, 1859-64, and nephew Sir Morgan Vane (1809-86).[23]

[1] *The Times*, 31 Jan., 7 May 1842; PROB 11/1960/243; IR26/1603/321. [2] *HP Commons, 1790-1820*, ii. 151; v. 430. [3] Lincs. AO, Tennyson d'Eyncourt mss 2Td'E H108/32, Russell to Tennyson, 21 Feb.; Grey mss, Tierney to Grey [29 Feb.], Darlington to same [Mar.]; *West Briton*, 3, 10, 17 Mar. 1820; Add. 30115, f. 165. [4] *Session of Parl. 1825*, p. 450. [5] Grey mss, Darlington to Grey, 16 Jan. 1821. [6] NLW, Aston Hall mss C. 1087; Add. 43507, ff. 34-51; *West Briton*, 23 Sept., 7 Oct. 1825; 2, 16, 20 June; *The Times*, 19 Feb., 3 June 1826. [7] Add. 43597, ff. 55-57; Brougham mss, Darlington to Brougham, 18 Apr. 1827. [8] Aberdeen Univ. Lib. Arbuthnot mss, Hardinge to Mrs. Arbuthnot, 6 Oct. 1827. [9] Durham CRO, Londonderry mss D/LO/C83 (24). [10] Wellington mss WP1/971/16; 974/29; 990/12; 995/22; 1004/34; Brougham mss, Cleveland to Brougham, 10 Feb. 1829. [11] Wellington mss WP1/1092/14; 1098/7; Add. 40395, f. 85; 40400, f. 40; 51517 5, Abercromby to Holland [30 Jan.]; Brougham mss, same to Brougham [Jan.]; Grey mss, Durham to Grey, 20 Jan. 1830. [12] *Durham Chron.* 6, 13 Feb.; *Western Times*, 13 Feb. 1830. [13] Add. 40501, 238; *Western Times*, 31 July; *Exeter Flying Post*, 12 Aug. 1830. [14] Add. 40401, f. 155. [15] Wellington mss WP1/1126/4; 1152/6; 1154/45; Lonsdale mss, Lowther to Lonsdale, 12 Dec. 1830; Brougham mss, Cleveland to Brougham, 24 Jan. 1831. [16] Rutland mss (History of Parliament Aspinall transcripts), Douglas to Rutland, 23 Apr. 1831. [17] *The Times*, 3 Mar.; *Durham Chron.* 11 Mar.; *Durham Co. Advertiser*, 11 Mar.; *Plymouth Herald*, 19 Mar. 1831. [18] St. Deiniol's Lib. Glynne-Gladstone mss 198, T. to J. Gladstone, 20 Apr.; Stair mss (History of Parliament Aspinall transcripts), Murray to Dalrymple, 24 Apr.; *Durham Co. Advertiser*, 29 Apr. 1831. [19] *R. Devonport Telegraph*, 30 Apr., 7 May; *Western Times*, 7 May 1831; W.P. Courtney, *Parl. Rep. Cornw.* (1889), 160, 162; Devon RO D1579 A/12/20. [20] NLW, Coedymaen mss 230; *Salopian Jnl.* 14 Nov.-26 Dec. 1832; *VCH Salop*, iii. 315. [21] Add. 40501, ff. 228-44. [22] *The Times*, 7 Oct. 1842, 3 Mar. 1846, 3 Oct. 1854, 3, 6 June 1857, 13 Apr. 1861, 19 Jan.; *Durham Co. Advertiser*, 22 Jan. 1864. [23] *The Times*, 8 Feb., 14 Mar. 1864.

M.M.E.

VAN HOMRIGH, Peter (1768–1831), of Listoke, co. Louth.

DROGHEDA   1826–1830

b. 1768, 3rd s. of John Van Homrigh of Drogheda and w. Alicia Marshall. *educ.* Drogheda sch. by Dr. Richard Norris; Trinity, Dublin 1784-9; King's Inns 1790; M. Temple 1790, called [I] 1792. *unm. d.* 5 Mar. 1831.
Recorder, Drogheda 1796-*d.*, mayor 1811-12.

Van Homrigh, a 'Dutch Irishman', was probably descended from Bartholomew Van Homrigh, Member of the Irish Parliament for Londonderry, 1692-3, 1695-9, whose name was taken by his eldest brother.[1] It was either Bartholomew or Beaver Van Homrigh, another older brother and attorney, who in

1797 acquired a highly favourable lease on 'ground at Legavoran' from the corporation of Drogheda, where Van Homrigh had been elected recorder the previous year and later served as mayor.[2] Shortly thereafter both brothers died, Beaver's will being proved on 31 May 1804, by which time Van Homrigh's mother had remarried, and Batholomew's on 17 Nov. 1809, with the direction that he be interred in 'the burial place of my family' at St. Peter's, Drogheda.[3] Van Homrigh, who in both cases seems to have been the principal legatee, was supposedly 'distinguished as a classical scholar, but a disposition unsuited to the dry and severe study of the law diverted him from a close application to his profession, and he retired early from practice'.[4]

Following the 1818 Drogheda election, when the corporation-backed candidate secured a narrow victory, the independent challenger Thomas Wallace II* fought a duel with Van Homrigh in which, 'after discharging each a case of pistols, they quitted the ground attended by their seconds'.[5] The victor over Wallace at the 1820 general election was listed by the Liverpool ministry as seeking public office for Van Homrigh, but this appears to have come to nothing. At the 1826 general election Van Homrigh came forward himself at the request of 'a large body of freeholders', professing principles which were 'known to have been liberal from the earliest period of his life' and support for Catholic emancipation, and armed with a long purse. (In a financial arrangement of 29 Apr. 1825, the corporation had discontinued his salary of £100 per annum and 'in lieu thereof' issued him with 'nine debentures of £100 each', bearing 'interest at the rate of five per cent per annum', with the 'remaining £55 ... applied to effecting an insurance on his life, to create a fund for the payment of such debentures'.)[6] After a bitter struggle with the sitting Member, who accused him of saying that 'if the representation was offered to him, from his time of life, he would decline it', and with Wallace, who entered the field on the fourth day alleging that both his opponents were 'incapacitated' by their purchase of votes, Van Homrigh was returned at the head of the poll.[7] Rumours of a petition came to nothing and Van Homrigh insisted in the House, 28 May 1827, that he 'owed his election to the unbought, unsolicited suffrages of the town'.

In his maiden speech, 2 Mar. 1827, he defended the Catholic bishop Dr. Curtis against 'the charge of improperly interfering in matters of state'. He voted for Catholic relief, 6 Mar., and told an inattentive House that 'if I were a Catholic ... I would never be satisfied until I had completely succeeded in vindi-

cating my claims to equal rights with the rest of my fellow-subjects', 23 Mar. He considered it 'deplorable' that 'there were more than five thousand paupers in Drogheda and its vicinity', 9 Mar., and presented a petition for employment of the 'distressed poor' there, 14 Mar.[8] He argued that the unpopularity of the Irish viceroy Lord Wellesley with Protestants and Catholics had arisen because when he 'administered justice in such a way as was pleasing to one party, he was attacked in the *Evening Mail*, and when his conduct pleased the other party, he was attacked in the *Morning Register*', 16 Mar. That day he divided for the duke of Clarence's annuity bill. He voted for the spring guns bill, 23 Mar. He presented a Drogheda petition against the Irish coal duties, 27 Mar.[9] He divided with Canning's ministry against the disfranchisement of Penryn the following day, asserting that 'there was no proof of corruption against its two representatives', and again, 7 June, when he complained that if the bill passed it would be 'the first instance in the annals of Parliament that a select committee should declare the ... Members ... duly elected' and subsequently 'disfranchise the same borough on account of acts connected with that very election'. He was appointed to the select committee on Irish grand jury presentments, 6 June 1827, against which he presented a Drogheda petition, 27 June 1828. He voted for the grant to improve Canadian water communications, 12 June 1827. He denounced the Coventry magistracy bill as 'novel, capricious, and calculated to do no credit to the House' and voted against it, 18 June 1827. He presented a Drogheda petition for 'unqualified and unconditional' Catholic relief, 5 May, and voted thus, 12 May 1828. He cautioned against the practice of immediate execution for convicted murderers, 5 May. He voted with the Wellington ministry against ordnance reductions, 4 July, and for their silk duties, 14 July. On 20 Sept. 1828 the Irish secretary Lord Francis Leveson Gower informed Peel, the home secretary, that Van Homrigh had

called on me this morning with an urgent request for the office in the commission of judicial inquiry ... His application was pressing, and he described the state of his personal circumstances as very distressing. I should be glad if you would inform me of the degree of interest which you would be inclined to take in him. I am told he is among the most constant and sleepless supporters of government in the House of Commons and I think a claim of that nature is not to be neglected.[10]

A few days earlier Van Homrigh had written what was described as a 'very peremptory' letter to Lord Ellenborough, Lord Melville's successor at the board of control, 'demanding that a promise of a cadetship made by Lord Melville to his son should be performed'.[11] Both applications seem to have come to nothing.

Van Homrigh presented two Drogheda petitions for the Wellington ministry's concession of Catholic emancipation, 11 Mar., warned that 'there never will be peace in Ireland, or permanent security for life, so long as this great question remains unsettled', 16 Mar., and voted accordingly, 30 Mar. 1829. He considered the accompanying Irish freeholders bill a 'gain' for Catholics, as although it 'may curtail their present privileges, the other measure will present them with more than counterbalancing advantages', 26 Mar. He defended the conduct of Irish proprietors towards the poor, declaring that 'a body of landlords more generous, indulgent, or liberal, than those of Ireland, does not exist', 7 May. He divided for Daniel O'Connell to be allowed to take his seat unhindered, 18 May 1829. He voted against the transfer of East Retford's seats to Birmingham, 11 Feb., Lord Blandford's parliamentary reform scheme, 18 Feb., and the enfranchisement of Birmingham, Manchester and Leeds, 23 Feb. 1830. He dismissed as 'totally unfounded' allegations by O'Connell that Drogheda corporation had misappropriated 'upwards of £20,000 with which they were entrusted for purposes of education', 22 Mar. He divided against the abolition of the death penalty for forgery, 7 June. He voted against reductions of the grants for South American missions that day, and for Prince Edward Island, 14 June 1830.

At the 1830 dissolution Van Homrigh retired from politics, evidently on account of financial difficulties. That December, following the accession to power of the Grey ministry, he wrote to the new home secretary Lord Melbourne, whom he had considered 'a friend of mine' when he was in Ireland (1827-8), to ask for assistance towards the 'expenses of my election to the late Parliament', explaining:

My attendance there involved me in debts which I am unable to pay and I am in deplorable distress. Lord Killeen*, Sir M[arcus] Somerville*, Mr. J[ames] Grattan*, Mr. A[lexander] Dawson* and other of my friends have contributed to my temporary relief, but I am in hopes that you and His Majesty's ministers will give me that substantial relief which will prevent me from dying in the jail of this town of which I have been recorder 33 years. I am in hopes that you and they will do something handsome to avert such a calamity from a Member of the late Parliament.

Melbourne, however, was 'totally unable to give any assistance'.[12]

Van Homrigh died 'suddenly' in March 1831, after falling off his chair whilst 'reading in the public news room' at Drogheda.[13] By his death Drogheda corporation's 'insurance was effected', and with the money they received the 'debentures were thereupon paid off'.[14]

[1] Ellenborough Diary, i. 221; M. MacDonagh, The Viceroy's Post-Bag, 295. [2] PP (1835), xxviii. 420; Drogheda Jnl. 8 Mar. 1831; J. D'Alton, Hist. Drogheda, i. 257, ii. 375. [3] Irish Genealogist, ii (Oct. 1943), 28. [4] Drogheda Jnl. 8 Mar. 1831. [5] The Times, 13 July 1818. [6] PP (1835), xxviii. 435. [7] Dublin Evening Post, 6, 8, 17, 22 June; Drogheda Jnl. 14, 17, 21 June 1826. [8] The Times, 15 Mar. 1827. [9] Ibid. 28 Mar. 1827. [10] Add. 40335, f. 120. [11] Ellenborough Diary, i. 221. [12] Herts. Archives, Panshanger mss, Van Homrigh to Melbourne, 3 Dec. 1830, with endorsement by Melbourne. [13] Drogheda Jnl. 8 Mar.; Belfast News Letter, 11 Mar. 1831. [14] PP (1835), xxviii. 435.

P.J.S.

VANSITTART, **Nicholas** (1766–1851), of 10 Downing Street, Whitehall, Mdx.

HASTINGS	1796–1802
OLD SARUM	1802–May 1812
EAST GRINSTEAD	8 June 1812–1812
HARWICH	1812–4 Feb. 1823

b. 29 Apr. 1766, 5th s. of Henry Vansittart (d.?1770) of Foxley, Berks., gov. Bengal, and Emilia, da. of Nicholas Morse, gov. Madras. educ. Gilpin's sch. Cheam; Christ Church, Oxf. 1784; I. Temple 1786; L. Inn 1788, called 1791. m. 22 July 1806, Hon. Catharine Isabella Eden, da. of William Eden†, 1st Bar. Auckland, s.p. cr. Bar. Bexley 1 Mar. 1823. d. 8 Feb. 1851.

Envoy to Denmark Feb.-Mar. 1801; sec. to treasury Apr. 1801-May 1804, Feb. 1806-Apr. 1807; chief sec. to ld. lt. [I] Jan.-Sept. 1805; PC 14 Jan. 1805; chan. of exch. May 1812-Jan. 1823; chan. of duchy of Lancaster Feb. 1823-Jan. 1828.

Lt. Westminster vols. 1795-8, (dismounted) capt. 1798; lt.-col. St. Margaret's and St. John's vols. 1803.

Bencher, L. Inn 1812; commr. for building new churches 1818.

High steward, Harwich.

George Canning* likened the 'pious and demure looking' Vansittart to 'the honest attorney who brings in the real will at the end of the play'; and John Mallet described him as 'indefatigable at his pen' and 'made to be an actuary to an insurance office'.[1] His mumbling delivery rendered him largely useless in Commons debate, where he was propped up by Lord Castlereagh. (When the witty 'Bobus' Smith* saw a letter from Vansittart asking Edward Littleton to postpone a question on the circulation until he could 'speak *distinctly* and positively' on the subject, he remarked, 'Why, damn him, we may wait to all eternity, if we are to wait till then!')[2] By the death of his mother in August 1819 Vansittart, as her residuary legatee, inherited something in the region of £100,000;[3] and it was this windfall which made his cabinet colleague William Wellesley Pole* wonder in January 1820 whether he 'might probably not be anxious to remain' in harness. When Robert Ward* observed that 'Vansittart's heart and pleasure seemed to be in office', Wellesley Pole replied that 'he was afraid he was doing ill, and was not much approved by the moneyed interest'.[4] Indeed, Vansittart seemed a fixture at the exchequer, notwithstanding the derision with which his post-war financial expedients, propounded with a benign complacency maddening to his critics, were regarded by many pundits. He was nothing if not diligent and, above all, still enjoyed the confidence of Lord Liverpool. Yet by 1820 his position had been weakened by his defeat over the resumption of cash payments and the related success of the Canningite William Huskisson* in persuading the premier that there must be an efficient sinking fund, based on real surplus revenue.[5]

After coming in again for the treasury borough of Harwich, Vansittart answered opposition questions on the civil list, 27, 28 Apr., when he told Lord Archibald Hamilton that to encourage the Scottish poor to emigrate to America would be to 'transport them to poverty on a foreign shore'.[6] He refused to amend the Scottish malt duty, 1 May, and parried criticism of the civil list, as he did again, 2, 3 May. Opposing inquiry into the droits of the crown, 5 May, he boasted of a saving of over £238,000 since 1816. In reply to Maberly's call for exchequer bill accounts, 11 May, he declined to divulge his financial plans, but defended his policy in general terms. He was willing to receive the Oldham petition complaining of military outrages, 12 May; but when Hamilton attacked the Scottish representative system, 25 May, he warned the gullible against concluding that it 'must necessarily be defective, because it differed from that of England'. He opposed repeal of the tax on foreign wool, 26 May, and explained the contract for the funding of £7,000,000 of exchequer bills, 31 May. On 1 June he endorsed the government amendment to the proposed inquiry into the Welsh judicature. Later that day he climbed down from his resistance to consideration of the linen bounties when Frederick Robinson, president of the board of trade, explained that he had promised the mover, Maberly, that he would not be opposed. He replied tartly to Creevey's attack on the pensions charged on the Barbados defence fund, 2 June. It fell to him to move the adjournment when news arrived of Queen Caroline's arrival in England, 5 June 1820.[7]

Vansittart moved resolutions to continue the Irish Union duties for a limited period, 8 June, and defeated a motion for their immediate repeal, 14 June. After stating the terms of the loan contracted for raising £5,000,000 by annuities, 9 June, he replied to Ricardo's general criticism of his system of public borrowing. He said government could not intervene to alleviate the distress caused by Irish bank failures, 14 June, but two days later announced a loan of £500,000 by way of relief. He also defended the increase in barrack expenditure, which had been forced on government by the 'agitated state of the country'. Vansittart made his budget statement to a House still restless after Castlereagh's presentation of papers concerning the queen, 19 June. To meet the requirements of expenditure he proposed to borrow £12,000,000 from the sinking fund, in addition to the £12,000,000 already raised in loans. He predicted a surplus of £3,500,000, short of the £5,000,000 deemed requisite the previous year, and the result of a sluggish economy.[8] He defended the modest expense of the coronation, which would stimulate employment, 3 July, and accused Dr. Lushington of encouraging the people to indulge in 'extremities and outrage'. He opposed Hume's call for economies in revenue collection and persuaded him to drop his motion for information on the value of the late king's private property, 4 July. When Hamilton moved for restoration of the differential Scottish malt duty, 5 July, Vansittart offered a partial concession, but it failed to appease Hamilton, whose motion was defeated by 53-43. He explained modifications to the lottery bill, 6 July, disclaimed responsibility for the finance committee's alleged suppression of its findings on the audit office, 7 July, but reluctantly acquiesced in the production of papers, 12 July, and defended the barrack agreement, 10, 11, 13, 17 July.[9] He sought to justify the clause of the spirits bill which would allow the import of Irish raw spirits under certain conditions, 12 July, but abandoned it when even Castlereagh denounced it as 'nugatory'. He outlined plans for the future regulation of Irish distillation, 14 July, and blocked inquiry into the subject, 18 July.[10] Vansittart, who featured prominently in the collective discomfort of the government front bench as the furore over the queen unfolded, denied that ministers had left her short of legal aid, 18 Sept., and, speaking for the longer adjournment, 17 Oct., defended lord chancellor Eldon against Whig attacks. He privately thought the bill of pains and penalties 'wisely given up' and welcomed the prorogation, which would allow 'spirits to cool'. Ministers, he told Ward, 'were bound in honour, at whatever expense of struggle and courage, to stand by the king as long as he was firm to *them*'.[11] On Canning's resignation from the India board in November 1820 Vansittart 'very handsomely offered' to move there if the exchequer was required to accommodate Robert Peel.[12]

Vansittart spoke briefly against restoration of the queen's name to the liturgy, 23 Jan. 1821. Creevey claimed that when he condemned the duke of Wellington's recent reference to the 'farce' of public meetings in her support, 26 Jan., 'Mouldy', as he called Vansittart, tried 'to punish me, but was instantly smothered in universal derision'.[13] He refused to commit government to repeal of the agricultural horse tax and said it was not possible to appropriate civil list money to provide for the queen, 13 Jan. He did not oppose Maberly's motion for an account of the deficiency on the consolidated fund, 1 Feb., but boasted that the country 'had arrived at a period, when it might bid adieu either to loans or new taxes'. He argued that trade was improving, repudiated Grenfell's attack on the 'dilapidated' sinking fund, and hoped for an increase of revenue. He defended the navy estimates, 2, 6 Feb., and, in the face of Creevey's calls for economies to relieve distress, 9 Feb., promised a reduction of at least £1,000,000 in the year's estimates. In the absence of Castlereagh, he denied knowledge of British and Allied intervention in Naples, 9, 12 Feb.[14] He again resisted repeal of the Union duties, 16 Feb., agreed to streamline the procedure for presenting the annual estimates, 19 Feb.,[15] and opposed receipt of Davison's petition against Justice William Best[†], 23 Feb. Vansittart, who voted as usual against Catholic relief, 28 Feb., spoke against Curwen's attempts to repeal the agricultural horse tax and to impose a duty on stock transfers, 5 Mar.: the latter would 'bring down destruction upon public faith'. Replying to Maberly's motion for repeal of the house and window taxes, 6 Mar., he argued that the promotion of capital circulation and the maintenance of public credit would do more to mitigate distress than the fanciful nostrums peddled by 'political charlatans'. He outlined the bill to advance the resumption of cash payments, 19 Mar. His denial of Wilson's suggestion that he had two years earlier encouraged the manufacture of coffee substitute from wheat, 12 Mar., led to angry words, private explanations and a public apology from Vansittart, 14 Mar.[16] After speaking against the financial claims of American loyalists, he vainly opposed repeal of the additional malt duty, 21 Mar. As an amendment to Hume's motion for abolition of revenue offices, 22 Mar., he offered and carried a select committee of inquiry.[17] He spoke against Hume's motions for a revision of public salaries, 30 Mar. and 6 Apr., when he insisted that the government had made

'reductions to a considerable extent', with more in the offing. He repented his hostility to repeal of the husbandry horse tax, 5 Apr.,[18] and opposed inquiry into the possibility of establishing a dual currency standard, 9 Apr. He carried by 56-17 his proposal to refer petitions against the Scottish malt duty to a select committee, 12 Apr., and accepted an amendment to the cash payments bill, 13 Apr. On 17 Apr. Lambton, opening his speech in support of parliamentary reform, mocked the emptiness of the treasury bench, where there sat only Vansittart and Charles Bathurst, chancellor of the duchy of Lancaster, 'those right honourable twins, so lovingly united in affection, in principle, and in representation of the oyster-dredgers of Harwich'. Vansittart, opposing the motion, denied that majority opinion in the country was for reform and extolled the 'degree of practical liberty' enjoyed under the existing constitution. He deflected Parnell's motion for inquiry into trade with Ireland, 19 Apr. At about this time the Canningite John William Ward*, who considered 'Van's anti-arithmetical propositions' of finance 'a disgrace to Parliament', marvelled at his 'cool intrepidity' in the face of economic adversity, though he reflected that 'Van's courage may be the result of short-sightedness and phlegm'.[19] The ministry's continued weakness in Commons debate, now exacerbated by the loss of Canning, had already tempted Liverpool to consider taking advantage of Vansittart's offer of the previous December in order to bring in Peel, but the scheme foundered, largely on Castlereagh's fear of Peel as a dangerous rival in the potentially powerful office of chancellor. Lord Melville, who was to have replaced Lord Sidmouth at the home office, thus vacating the admiralty for Canning, endorsed Liverpool's reconsidered view that he

> knew from experience that he could go on perfectly well with Van as his chancellor, but that at best it would be an experiment with Mr. Peel and, if it failed, his position would be an extremely unpleasant one; and, as there was no fault to be found with Van in his financial capacity, that it would be a pity to run such a risk.

By early May 1821 there was no immediate threat to Vansittart's place.[20]

In reply to Hume's carping on the army estimates, 2 May 1821, he said that it was 'well known' that his own post 'was not overpaid'. (It was worth about £5,300 a year plus, in Vansittart's case, the Downing Street house.) He vindicated the preference given to West over East Indian sugar, 4 May, defended the bill authorizing a loan of £500,000 from the Bank of Ireland in return for allowing it to extend its capital, 9,

10 May, and opposed repeal of the Irish window tax, 16 May, and a call for stringent economy, 18 May.[21] He announced that there would be no need for an additional vote of money for the coronation, 21 May, defended the extraordinary civil list grant, 28 May, and defeated by 64-31 Maberly's motion for equalization of the interest to be paid on Irish treasury and exchequer bills, 30 May. In his financial statement, 1 June, he claimed a reduction in expenditure from 1820 of £1,771,888, promised continued efforts to economize, admitted that a clear sinking fund surplus of £5,000,000 had not yet been attained, but said that £4,000,000 was within reach. Boasting of the large reduction in the unfunded debt in the last three years, he painted a rosy picture of the country's 'immense inherent resources' and 'solid means'.[22] He again refused further compensation for American loyalists, 6 June, denied an assertion that the country was deeper in debt than at the end of the war, 8 June, and opposed as unnecessary Newport's bid to spell out the right of Catholics to become Irish Bank directors, 13 June. The following day he had the humiliation of seeing Curwen's motion for repeal of the agricultural horse tax carried against his defence of the government record on economy by 141-113.[23] His implied threat to overturn the verdict when the bill came in provoked an outcry; and on 18 June he backed down, in deference to 'the sense of the country'. He professed to be shocked by a Whig's reference to the coronation as an 'absurd and expensive ... pageant', 21 June, when his 'very angry' retort that no one else in the country shared that view provoked 'a loud laugh and shout' from the opposition benches.[24] Next day, in another climb-down, he announced the provision of £60,000 for loyalists. He would not be drawn on Hume's allegation of partiality in government patronage of Irish newspapers, 28 June, and opposed repeal of a vexatious clause of the Beer Duties Act, 29 June.[25] He had to admit that there were after all additional, though small coronation expenses, 30 June, and promised to do what he could to relieve Scottish brewers of genuine hardship, 10 July 1821.[26] He was in the minority of six who opposed a reduction in the compensation to General Desfourneaux.[27]

In that month the Grenvillite William Fremantle* claimed that Wellington agreed with him that Vansittart and Bathurst were 'perfect cyphers' in the Commons. In their negotiations with Liverpool during the recess the Grenvillites made a dead set at Vansittart: Charles Williams Wynn*, for example, wrote in early October that his 'retirement from the exchequer is indispensable'.[28] In a discussion with Liverpool, 30 Nov., Lord Buckingham, though generally happy with the terms offered, tried to have Vansittart replaced by the pro-Catholic Huskisson:

> I stated ... that the real ground of the weakness of the government was Mr. Vansittart's inadequacy to his task in the House of Commons ... that Lord Liverpool must know ... that his own friends and the country gentlemen in particular were loud in disapprobation of the manner in which the chancellor ... conducted his business in the House ... that the proposition of a junction would come much stronger recommended if we could see any prospect of a change in that department, without injury to Mr. Vansittart's fair claims.

Liverpool retorted that

> the first lord of the treasury in the House of Lords could not carry on the government without his chancellor of the exchequer being wholly, exclusively and entirely in his confidence, that it would not do to have a chancellor ... in any way independent of the first lord ... or belonging to another party in the government ... That he knew Lord Londonderry's [Castlereagh] wish was not to have anyone else in that situation ... That he was quite aware of Vansittart's faults, that he was no orator, that he had an ungracious and undecided way of doing business, but that the consideration he had stated more than counterbalanced those inconveniences.

Buckingham, who stood to gain a dukedom, was ready to acquiesce in Vansittart's retention, but his uncle Lord Grenville, nominal head of the group, still thought he deserved no mercy. Londonderry intervened to impress on Buckingham, among other considerations, the folly of insisting on Vansittart's removal as a *sine qua non*. He pointed out that if Peel or another 'man of considerable talent' and Protestant views was at the exchequer, which in normal circumstances carried with it the lead in the Commons, his own supremacy and the success of the Catholic question would be endangered. He added that

> no one could act with Lord Liverpool at all times, and under all circumstances, like Van; that Lord Liverpool was accustomed to his odd ways and Vansittart's to Lord Liverpool's; that at all moments of sulk, indisposition or worry Vansittart could get Lord Liverpool to do business when no one else could.

Moreover he, like Wellington, hinted that Vansittart might soon depart voluntarily, having 'come to a certain time of life ... wound up his revenue ... tided through all the difficulties attending the return from war to peace ... [and] concluded his retrenchments'. The Grenvillites duly joined the ministry with Vansittart still in place.[29] He was said to be predicting, more accurately than perhaps he realized, 'constant botheration on economy' in the forthcoming session.[30]

In cabinet Vansittart advocated the provision of cheaper credit as the most effective remedy for agricultural distress. He wished to convert the five per cents into four, in order to reduce the charge on the debt, leave scope for tax remissions and encourage interest rates to fall. He planned to borrow £3,000,000 from the Bank for the year's supply and advance £4,000,000 to the landed interest in exchequer bills; but the latter plan ran into difficulties when the banks refused to lend because farmers could not offer adequate security. It was therefore decided to make a loan of £4,000,000 at three per cent to parishes, on the security of their rates.[31] When Hume moved an amendment to the address calling for extensive tax reductions, 5 Feb. 1822, he handed Vansittart a copy of his detailed statement of the national finances. Vansittart, as one unimpressed backbencher saw it, 'stammered a short answer', in which he said the best remedy for distress was 'an extension of the currency', promised modest tax reductions, paid lip service to the value of the alliance with the Grenvillites, and argued that Hume's scheme would destroy the sinking fund and public credit. The Whig Member Sir James Mackintosh thought that Vansittart 'spoke very intemperately and injudiciously'.[32] It was Londonderry who detailed the government's proposals for the relief of distress, 15 Feb.; and at the close of the debate on Lord Althorp's critical resolution, 21 Feb., Vansittart again insisted that the sinking fund must be 'religiously guarded and properly applied to redeem the debt'. He pointed to the 'improving' condition of trade and manufacturing and declared that a large reduction of taxes, which 'did not appear a matter of indispensable necessity', would be 'dearly purchased by any interference with the delicate subject of public credit'. The following day he was given an uncomfortable time over apparent discrepancies in the public accounts, on which subject he agreed under pressure to appoint a select committee. He also announced that he would not repeal the Irish window tax, but that he would extend to Ireland remission of the malt duty, though he subsequently admitted, 28 Mar., that it would do little good.[33] On 25 Feb. he laid before the House his plan to convert the five per cents, which would effect an annual saving of £1,230,000. Londonderry told the king that its terms had been 'very generally approved' and, less convincingly, that Vansittart had given 'very clear and satisfactory answers' to the various queries which were raised. This, Vansittart's most successful financial stroke, eventually realized a saving of £1,140,000 at the cost of an addition of £7,000,000 to the capital debt.[34] He directly opposed gradual reduction of the salt duties, 28 Feb., when Maria Edgeworth, a spectator in the ventilator,

noted that of all the speakers, he used 'the best language and most correct English, though there is little in what he says'. (The Speaker, she was told, once said that Vansittart 'never makes a mistake in grammar'.)[35] He repeated his promise to instigate inquiry into the means of simplifying the public accounts, 1 Mar.,[36] but when he made the proposal, 18 Apr., he refused to enlarge its scope as Maberly and others wished. He defended the payment of a fee to the Bank for managing the stock conversion, 4 Mar. He opposed reduction of the Scottish house tax, 28 Mar.[37] He tried to justify the size of John Herries's* salary as Irish commissary, 29 Mar., announced that he would mitigate the tax on mortgage transfers to help agriculture, 1 Apr., promised 'considerable reductions' in the allowances of stamp distributors, 17 Apr., and denied that the leather tax was oppressive and expressed reluctance to interfere with extents in aid, 24 Apr.[38] He voted against Canning's bill to relieve Catholic peers, 30 Apr. 1822.

On 11 Mar. 1822 Vansittart outlined his measure to lessen the expense of public salaries by making deductions to create a general superannuation fund. Fremantle commented that the bill (which became law as 3 Geo. IV, c. 113) would 'create a great deal of discussion', which Vansittart 'will not mend by his explanations'.[39] On 1 May he explained the associated scheme to relieve the immediate burden of naval and military pensions by granting contractors a fixed annuity of 45 years. Although Ricardo and others exposed it as a blatant 'invasion' of the sinking fund, the House accepted Vansittart's resolutions. The plan was soon in trouble, however, for no contractors were willing to take the risk. Buckingham thought that

nobody but such a blockhead as Van would have thought of submitting his plan to the City just at the moment when the government was loudly proclaiming everywhere, that its existence was to depend upon the next division, and when the opposition was boasting and betting you would [be] beat [on the joint-postmastership, 2 May]. The eve of failure is not the day when a man borrows money to the greatest advantage.[40]

Accordingly Vansittart announced, 24 May, a modification of the scheme, whereby trustees were to manage a fund raised by exchequer bills on the sale of annuities. He claimed that this new debt would not trench on the sinking fund, and proposed compensatory remissions of the taxes on leather and salt, and repeal of the Irish window tax and the tonnage duty.[41] His plea that the post office was under investigation by a commission failed to prevent the success of Lord Normanby's motion for abolition of one of the postmasterships, 2 May. The same day he denied allegations that he had not given due notice of negotiations for renewal of the Bank's charter. He dismissed Wyvill's 'revolutionary' proposal for the repeal of £20,000,000 in taxes, 8 May, and opposed as impractical the notion of a tax on absentees, 16 May. To much jeering from the opposition benches, he signified his acquiescence in Grenfell's suggestion that the national debt commissioners be allowed to apply their funds to the purchase of the naval and military pension annuities, 3 June. Later that day he opposed total repeal of the salt tax. He did so again, 5, 11 June, but on 14 June he announced a modification of his original proposals.[42] He expressed sympathy with the grievances of Irish tanners against the leather tax, 19 June,[43] but threatened to abandon its proposed reduction if the House voted to repeal the salt tax, 28 June. In his budget statement, 1 July, he predicted a surplus of £5,000,000 for the sinking fund and claimed that the success of the stock conversion demonstrated the 'solid foundation of British credit'. The following day he opposed repeal of the house and window taxes, while indicating that the latter would be reviewed in future, and boasted that 'in no other country of Europe had so large a remission of taxation been made' since 1815. He successfully resisted an attempt to repeal the 1821 Beer Duties Act, 9 July, and insisted that ministers had been more than fair in their financial dealings with the late queen, 24 July.[44] He easily got rid of Hume's alternative budget, 25 July. When Canning attacked the superannuation bill, 26 July, Vansittart was assisted in his defence of it by Londonderry. On its third reading, 29 July, he carried amendments which his opponents deemed unintelligible. He reiterated the government's refusal to settle the queen's debts, 31 July 1822.[45] Vansittart's political credibility had been irreparably damaged by the ineptitude and evasiveness of his performance in the 1822 session. Yet when Huskisson described him, just after Londonderry's suicide, which increased his vulnerability, as 'the real *blot* and *sin* of the government', John Croker*, secretary to the admiralty, replied that 'Van, though not a very creditable chancellor ... was a very useful one', if only, to take a cynical view, because his willingness to eat his words had helped to keep the ministry in office. Croker subsequently reflected that however much Huskisson might covet his place, Vansittart was at least 'as safe and as work-withable a chancellor', and that 'the general opinion seems to leave Van in the quiet possession of his dead weight and his small remnant of sinking fund'; but Canning's acceptance of the foreign secretaryship with the lead in the Commons prompted renewed speculation about Vansittart's future at the exchequer, where his days seemed to be numbered.[46]

Canning, frustrated by Buckingham in his initial bid to remove Williams Wynn from the India board and replace him with Huskisson, turned his attention to Vansittart in early October 1822 when, to his 'infinite surprise', he drew from Liverpool an admission that he was 'not immovable'. Liverpool, who conceded that Vansittart was 'absurd, ridiculed and deserted by everybody', said he would 'get him out' if a satisfactory arrangement could be reached. He was quite sure that Vansittart would never voluntarily surrender the exchequer to Huskisson, as Canning's man, and felt the India board would be 'the surest lure' to him. Canning was aware that 'all chance of success with Van depends upon ... [Liverpool] not appearing to make his approaches at anyone's instigation, or as a matter of compact'. ('It was of the utmost importance' he later wrote, 'that my cloven foot should not appear in the scheme'.) He persuaded Huskisson to settle for the board of trade in succession to Robinson for whom, as Londonderry's favourite, Vansittart would have no qualms about vacating the exchequer to go to the India board.[47] It proved impossible, however, to shift Williams Wynn and, to create a suitable niche for Vansittart, Canning next aimed to secure the retirement of Bathurst from the duchy of Lancaster. By early December Bathurst, after negotiations conducted through his brother-in-law Lord Sidmouth, now a cabinet minister without office, had agreed to stand down from both place and Parliament.[48] On 14 Dec. 1822 Liverpool informed Vansittart of this development and, reminding him of his offer of two years earlier to move aside for Peel, offered him the duchy, which was

> a situation ... highly honourable in itself, and which may save you from some of those eventual embarrassments which nearly always grow out of so great a change in the government as has unavoidably arisen in consequence of the death of ... Londonderry.

He informed Vansittart of the plans for Robinson and Huskisson, and invited him to consult Sidmouth, still his closest political associate. (There is no truth in the spiteful story recorded by Lord Colchester that Liverpool's letter was 'not even written in his own hand'.)[49] Vansittart, who had recently bought a Kent estate at Foot's Cray, near Bromley, where he was having a house built for his eventual retirement (when not in Downing Street he lived with his spinster sister Sophia in the Blackheath house which she had inherited from their mother) asked for time to consider. He approved the idea of Robinson as his successor, but hinted at reluctance to take the duchy with a seat in the Commons:

I have long felt myself growing unequal to the labour of the House of Commons; and ... I think nothing could reconcile me to enter upon another Parliament. My inclination therefore would rather lean to a total retreat, if it could be managed without the appearance either of public or private difference: but this it might not be so easy to avoid.[50]

After consulting Sidmouth he told Liverpool, 16 Dec., that having pondered whether 'this is a time when I can voluntarily relinquish active employment with credit', and whether 'the mode proposed to me [is] an honourable one', he had concluded that 'the opportunity, though not peculiarly eligible, is at least not discreditable', and that the arrangement was 'not less honourable than a simple retirement, though less agreeable to myself'. Anxious, in the first instance, to ensure that no one but Robinson succeeded him, he urged Liverpool to put the offer to him.[51] When Liverpool told him of Robinson's acceptance, 21 Dec., Vansittart, who was to meet the premier on the 26th to discuss his own destination, indicated that 'I have by no means made up my mind to accept the duchy', as there were 'several considerations on both sides'. The following day he explained his 'considerable objections' to Sidmouth, who was keen for him to accept. Its only merit from a personal standpoint was its being 'a disguised pension', though inferior, 'from its precariousness', to what he was entitled to under the Act of 1817, which he would have claimed in preference had financial provision been 'decidedly essential to my future conduct'. As against this, acceptance would 'keep continually hanging over my head a second resignation and final retirement'. Above all, he jibbed at the prospect of remaining in the Commons as a superannuated minister with little to do and shorn of 'all consideration and importance', which must be the consequence if he was to 'obtain any material relief' from the drudgery and strain of constant attendance:

> Any minister in the House of Commons who would not be utterly insignificant, is in a situation very unfavourable to health and comfort, especially as in addition to the evening labour, I should always be obliged to pass the mornings in committees, of which the burden and vexation has been continually increasing of late.[52]

Nor could he believe that Liverpool attached 'any real importance' to his remaining in the cabinet. Before leaving London he unburdened himself obliquely but clearly enough, to Arbuthnot, secretary to the treasury, who, doubtless as Vansittart intended, immediately notified Liverpool of what it was he really wanted:

> He more than once said that had he been a peer he could have had no hesitation in accepting the duchy ... He is

anxious to quit the House of Commons altogether, and it would ... delight him if you were to propose to him a peerage with the duchy of Lancaster for immediate possession, and to have the warrant for his pension signed so that he might as a thing of course come into the receipt of it whenever he shall be deprived of the duchy.

Liverpool, aware of the king's aversion to multiplying peerages and dubious of Vansittart's fitness in status and wealth to sustain one, hoped Sidmouth would be able to talk him out of it, but Vansittart dug in his heels. At their meeting on 26 Dec. 1822 Liverpool 'not very willingly' agreed to recommend the peerage to the king, though he absolutely refused to attach to it 'any collateral remainders', consoling himself with the reflection that it would almost certainly expire with the childless Vansittart, a widower for 12 years and now approaching 57 years of age. Vansittart who, Arbuthnot commented, 'rates his financial merits very high', was slightly miffed, but settled readily enough for what, in all the circumstances, was an excellent personal bargain. The king sanctioned the whole arrangement, which had been kept largely secret, on 2 Jan. 1823.[53]

Canning was delighted with himself for having engineered 'poor V's euthanasia'.[54] Lord Bathurst, the colonial secretary, welcomed the settlement, which had spared his old friend the humiliation of being forced out of the exchequer: nor was it any more than Vansittart deserved, for 'the public do not do justice to the real energy of his character and the fertility of his resources'. Lord Harrowby thought that 'Van's retreat is most handsomely covered', though he did 'not expect much assistance from his eloquence in our House'.[55] Sir Watkin Williams Wynn* observed that it would be 'a great relief to the House of Commons not to have poor Van's croaking any more'.[56] According to Canning, who had great difficulty in reconciling Huskisson to his exclusion from the cabinet, Vansittart talked to him 'with perfect good humour' of what had passed, but made it plain that to have stood aside for Huskisson would have been 'a disgrace to which he could never have submitted'.[57] Once the news was out, many a joke was made on the subject of Vansittart's title. Charles Williams Wynn, who believed 'he trusts still to his own loins to perpetuate the peerage', though 'Old Nick ought to be Viscount Van, for alliteration sake'.[58] Henry Fox* recorded that the Whig wags

> talk of Ld. Caravan, Ld. Woold and Coold, which is the way he pronounces would and could, and which is meant to be a parody on Saye and Sele. The best, however, is that he cannot take the name of his birthplace, Maidenhead.[59]

Canning put it about that 'Van is to be Ld. Cockermouth'.[60] Sidmouth noted that he received the congratulations of his friends with his customary 'great complacency', but a farewell cabinet dinner, planned for 28 Jan., had to be cancelled because he was 'very unwell and confined to his bed'.[61] As soon as Parliament met he and Charles Bathurst vacated their Harwich seats for Canning, who was tired of sitting for Liverpool, and Herries, the new financial secretary to the treasury. According to Hobhouse of the home office, Vansittart scotched Canning's bid to secure 10 Downing Street for his own use and relegate Robinson to a smaller house.[62] His peerage, with the prosaic title of Bexley, was conferred on 1 Mar. 1823. Two weeks later Sidmouth reported that he 'still bears the marks of his illness' and could surely 'not have stood the service of another session in the House of Commons'.[63] Vansittart moved back into his London house at 31 Great George Street (let since 1812) and set himself up at Foot's Cray Place when rebuilding was completed in 1824.[64] Peel made fun of him, 24 Aug. 1823, when he told his wife of a social call from him: 'You may judge what a desert London must be when a visit from Van is thus recorded'.[65]

He took an occasional but not important part in Lords debates. On the collapse of the Liverpool ministry in 1827 he enhanced his reputation as 'a twaddle' by first agreeing to continue in office under Canning, then tendering his resignation, and finally being 'silly enough' to agree, under pressure from Canning and the king, to stay on. He remained in office under Lord Goderich, would have resigned had Lord Holland been admitted to the cabinet, and was ditched by Wellington in January 1828, when the blow was softened by the grant of his 'first class' pension of £3,000 a year.[66] He continued his active promotion of Evangelical Christianity and related good works, and became president of the British and Foreign Bible Mission.[67] An unrepentant opponent of Catholic relief, he attended the Kent county meeting, 24 Oct. 1828, but did not try to make his feeble voice heard. Instead, he published an Address to the Freeholders, which put the case against concessions and created a minor stir.[68] He spoke and voted against emancipation in 1829. He opposed the Grey ministry's reform bills, and was one of the 22 diehards who voted against the third reading of the final English bill, 4 June 1832.

Vansittart, whose sister died intestate and worth £60,000 in 1836,[69] died at Foot's Cray in February 1851, when his peerage became extinct. By his will, dated 26 July 1848, he devised his London house to his nieces Emilia and Selina Parry, who also received an annuity of £1,000 for their joint lives. He left his Kent estate and property at Upton St. Leonards,

Gloucestershire, to his cousin Arthur Vansittart (1807-59) of Shottesbrook, Berkshire, who was succeeded by his son Coleraine Robert Vansittart (1833-86). The residue of his personal estate was divided equally between his Parry nieces and their sister Eliza, wife of John Thornton of Clapham.[70] A sour obituary acknowledged his 'perpetual good-nature' and 'the primitive simplicity of his manner', which had 'obtained for him many friends', but marvelled that he should have risen so high in politics 'with no very conspicuous exercise of talents, knowledge or energy'. As for his oratorical abilities, 'not one man in a hundred understood him'.[71]

[1] B. Hilton, *Corn, Cash, Currency*, 165. [2] Hatherton mss, Vansittart to Littleton, 1 Apr. 1822; Hatherton diary, 17 Mar. 1836. [3] PROB 11/1619/401; IR26/807/693. [4] Phipps, *Plumer Ward Mems.* ii. 47. [5] Hilton, 33-35, 39-40, 42, 46, 48, 65, 87. [6] *The Times*, 28 Apr., 1 May 1820. [7] *Williams Wynn Corresp.* 247. [8] Gurney diary, 19 June [1820]; J.E. Cookson, *Lord Liverpool's Administration*, 228. [9] *The Times*, 8, 12, 13 July 1820. [10] Ibid. 19 July 1820. [11] Phipps, ii. 96, 97, 101. [12] *Hobhouse Diary*, 45; NLW, Coedymaen mss 595. [13] *Creevey Pprs.* ii. 9. [14] *The Times*, 7, 10, 13 Feb. 1821. [15] Ibid. 20 Feb. 1821. [16] Ibid. 13, 15 Mar. 1820; Add. 30115, ff. 20, 22. [17] HLRO, Hist. Coll. 379, Grey Bennet diary, 42. [18] *The Times*, 6 Apr. 1821. [19] Ward, *Llandaff Letters*, 281, 284. [20] *Arbuthnot Jnl.* i. 82, 94; Buckingham, *Mems. Geo. IV*, i. 142, 163; *Hobhouse Diary*, 62; Cookson, 308-9, 311-12. [21] *The Times*, 10, 17 May 1821. [22] Grey Bennet diary, 94. [23] *The Times*, 9, 14, 15 June 1821; Grey Bennet diary, 100. [24] *The Times*, 22 June 1821; Grey Bennet diary, 104. [25] *The Times*, 23, 29, 30 June 1821. [26] Ibid. 2, 11 July 1821. [27] Coedymaen mss 609; Grey Bennet diary, 111. [28] Buckingham, i. 173, 210, 229; Cookson, 335; *Arbuthnot Jnl.* i. 133; Coedymaen mss 946. [29] BL, Fortescue mss, Buckingham to Grenville, 30 Nov., 3 Dec., memo. 30 Nov.; Grey mss, Tierney to Grey, 11 Dec. 1821. [30] Bagot, *Canning and Friends*, ii. 123. [31] Cookson, 346-50; Hilton, 157. [32] Gurney diary, 5 Feb. [1822]; Add. 52445, f. 35. [33] *The Times*, 23, 29 Mar. 1822. [34] *Geo. IV Letters*, ii. 1004. [35] *Edgeworth Letters*, 370. [36] *The Times*, 2 Mar. 1822. [37] Ibid. 29 Mar. 1822. [38] Ibid. 2, 18, 25 Apr. 1822. [39] Buckingham, i. 297. [40] Bucks. RO, Fremantle mss, Buckingham to Fremantle, 19 May 1822. [41] *Oxford DNB.* [42] *The Times*, 6, 12, 15 June 1822. [43] Ibid. 20 June 1822. [44] Ibid. 10, 25 July 1822. [45] Ibid. 30 July, 1 Aug. 1822. [46] *Croker Pprs.* i. 228-9, 230, 232; *Colchester Diary*, iii. 259; Buckingham, i. 372-3, 374, 375; *Wellington Despatches*, i. 261-2, 263-4; *Hobhouse Diary*, 95; Cookson, 365-6; Northants. RO, Agar Ellis diary, 12 Jan. [1832]. [47] Cookson, 378-81; Add. 37843, ff. 217, 224, 227. [48] Cookson, 382-4; *Arbuthnot Corresp.* 32; *Arbuthnot Jnl.* i. 194, 198-200. [49] C.D. Yonge, *Life and Administration of Lord Liverpool*, 111, 208; Add. 31232, f. 294; *Colchester Diary*, i. 272. [50] Add. 31232, f. 290; 38291, f. 205. [51] Add. 31232, f. 297; 38193, f. 171; 38291, ff. 211, 218. [52] Add. 31232, f.303; Sidmouth mss, Vansittart to Sidmouth, 22, 23 Dec. 1822. [53] Add. 31232, f. 299; 38291, ff. 237, 264, 272, 293; 40862, f. 83; *Arbuthnot Corresp.* 32. [54] Bagot, ii. 154-6, 159. [55] HMC Bathurst, 537-8. [56] *Williams Wynn Corresp.* 299. [57] Add. 38193, f. 171. [58] Buckingham, i. 410. [59] *Fox Jnl.* 154. [60] Bagot, ii. 159. [61] Sidmouth mss, Sidmouth to C. Bathurst, 22, 28 Feb. 1823. [62] *Hobhouse Diary*, 102-3. [63] Sidmouth mss, Sidmouth to Bathurst, 18 Mar. 1823. [64] Add. 38298, f. 257. [65] *Peel Letters*, 49. [66] *Canning's Ministry*, 84, 85, 88, 89, 95, 98, 104, 124, 130; *Hobhouse Diary*, 130; Bagot, ii. 387, 392; *Palmerston-Sulivan Letters*, 187, 247; Hilton, 244; HMC Bathurst, 650; *Wellington Despatches*, iv. 202-3; *Geo. IV Letters*, iii. 1463; *Von Neumann Diary*, i. 18; *Colchester Diary*, iii. 482. [67] *Oxford DNB.* [68] *The Times*, 25 Oct., 1 Nov. 1828. [69] PROB 6/212. [70] PROB 11/2126/96; IR26/1889/93. [71] *The Times*, 12 Feb. 1851.

D.R.F.

VAUGHAN, Sir Robert Williames, 2nd bt. (1768–1843), of Nannau Hall, nr. Dolgellau, Merion.

b. 29 Mar. 1768, 1st. s. of Sir Robert Howell Vaughan, 1st bt., of Hengwrt, Merion. and Anne, da. and h. of Edward Williames of Ystumcolwyn, Mont. and Meillionydd, Caern. *educ.* Jesus, Oxf. 1787. *m.* 23 Sept. 1802, Anna Maria, da. of Sir Roger Mostyn[†], 5th bt., of Mostyn, Flints. and Gloddaeth, Caern. *suc.* fa. as 2nd bt. 13 Oct. 1792. *d.* 22 Apr. 1843.
  Sheriff, Merion. 1837-8.
  Commdt. Dolgellau vol. inf. 1798; maj. commdt. Cader Idris vols. 1803, lt.-col. commdt. 1804.
  Member, bd. of agriculture 1802, vice-pres. 1816.

Vaughan's surgeon father, who had been awarded a baronetcy in 1791 on the recommendation of the Grenvillite Lord Bulkeley, had acquired control of the locally prestigious estate of Rûg through his second son Edward (*d.* 1807) in 1780, and inherited Hengwrt and Nannau on the death of his elder brother three years later. However, it was left to his eldest son Vaughan, a well-built and at times uncouth country-man over six feet tall, to realize their shared ambi-tion to succeed their kinsman Evan Lloyd Vaughan of Corsygedol in the representation of Merioneth. Vaughan, who made no reported parliamentary speeches before 1820, consistently opposed parlia-mentary reform and Catholic relief and professed allegiance to 'church and king'; but he was never more than a sporadic attender, who enjoyed living among his constituents and the prestige of represent-ing them. He associated as readily with Tories as with his Whig in-laws, who shared his love of the chase, were bilingual and sponsored bards.[1] He announced George III's death by calling for a county meeting to adopt the customary addresses of condolence and congratulation, 28 Feb. 1820, when he extolled the blessings of the last reign, and made it known that he would seek re-election.[2] There was little prospect of opposition, for his 12,000-acre Nannau estate in the parish of Llanfachreth was renowned as the seat of power in Merioneth, where his younger brother Griffith ap Howell Vaughan, the constable of Harlech Castle, had inherited Hengwrt and Rûg, making them the county's premier resident landowners. The Tory *North Wales Gazette* commended Vaughan as a county Member and following his election at Harlech, 14 Mar., he reaffirmed his independence and commit-ment to 'church and state politics'.[3] Later that year he had a bilingual tribute to the late George III inscribed on a new extension to Llanfachreth church.[4] Vaughan was the last surviving trustee under the will of Lady

Essex Ker, and prosecuted as such by rival claimants to the 1st and 3rd dukes of Roxburghe's estates in the courts of session and the House of Lords, 1823-32 (as previously, 1805-12). His attendance in the Commons often coincided with litigation concerning the case in the Lords, Mar.-June 1823, Mar.-May 1825, and Dec. 1830-Apr. 1831.[5]

He welcomed the development of Porthmadog, and amid fears that the coastwise coal duties would stunt the growth of the North Wales slate industry by increasing the cost of steam power, on 18 May 1820 his brother chaired the Merioneth meeting which petitioned against them. Vaughan presented the peti-tion, 12 June.[6] Soon afterwards he suffered an illness, for which he received six weeks' leave, 23 June, having paired for ministers on Wilberforce's compromise resolution on the Queen Caroline affair, 22 June 1820. He divided against parliamentary reform, 9 May 1821, but cast a wayward vote for inquiry into the prosecu-tion of the Dublin Orange rioters, 22 Apr. 1823. Lord Bulkeley had informed the duke of Buckingham when Vaughan voted against enfranchising Catholic peers, 20 Apr. 1822, that he was one of North Wales's 'ultra anti-Catholics', who were generally ready to support 'government under your standard ... but upon the Catholic question they are raving mad'.[7] He pre-sented a petition from the clergy of Bangor archdea-conry against changing the law on Catholic marriages, 3 May 1824,[8] and several from Caernarvonshire and Merioneth against Catholic relief, 15, 19 Apr.,[9] and divided against the measure, 21 Apr. 1825. He voted against the attendant bill to disfranchise Irish 40s. freeholders, 26 Apr. 1825. According to a radical publication of that year, he 'appeared to attend very seldom and to vote with opposition'.[10] Vaughan's large stature and reputation for capitalizing on enclo-sure and promoting new turnpikes had earned him the nickname 'Colossus of Roads', but he played no part in the passage of the 1824 Radnor, Hereford and Merioneth roads bill through the House.[11] The coming of age of his eldest son Robert Williames Vaughan junior ('Y Fychan'), 25 June 1824, was cel-ebrated in verse and with subscriptions, dinners and illuminations throughout Merioneth and on the family estates in Conway and Meillionydd, Caernarvonshire, and Llanfyllin and Llansantffraid, Montgomeryshire, while 200 guests were entertained in a specially erected pavilion at Nannau, where Sir Robert spoke at length but 'Y Fychan' was too overwhelmed to utter a word.[12] Thomas Clarkson recorded in his diary, 17 Aug. 1824, how difficult it was to muster support for the Anti-Slavery Society 'in the teeth of Sir Robert Vaughan', but he presented and endorsed petitions for the abolition of colonial slavery from 'some towns in Caernarvonshire', 9 Mar., and Barmouth, Corwen, Dolgellau and Towyn, 16 Mar. 1826.[13] He faced no opposition at the general election.

Vaughan had mellowed towards the Methodists, whom he steadfastly denied permission to build chapels on his estates, and he neither presented petitions nor divided on repeal of the Test Acts in 1828.[14] He voted against Catholic relief, 6 Mar. 1827, 12 May, having presented hostile petitions, 8 Apr., 2 May 1828.[15] In December he became vice-president of the Brunswick Club that William Ormsby Gore* established at Criccieth.[16] The Wellington ministry's patronage secretary Planta listed him as 'opposed to the principle' of Catholic relief in February 1829, but he neither brought up petitions nor voted on the measure. Instead, he co-operated in the preparation of hostile petitions from Merioneth and elsewhere and entrusted them to Ormsby Gore or Lord Eldon.[17] In view of recent malicious gossip concerning his parliamentary conduct, on 20 Apr. he asked the anti-Catholic *North Wales Chronicle* to explain 'that had he not been confined to his room with a severe attack of gout, a longer time than was taken to carry the Catholic relief bill through the Commons, he would have attended in his place and opposed the measure in every stage'.[18] He advocated protection as a means of alleviating agricultural distress, divided against revision of the corn laws, 2 Apr. 1827, and presented petitions from the maltsters of Caernarvonshire for repeal of the 1827 Malt Act, 26 Mar., and from his constituents for tariffs on foreign wool, 1, 15 May 1828. He was also instrumental that session in securing the passage of the Dyffryn-Nantlle railway and Llanfrothen enclosure bills. During the summer recess he was involved in a dispute with Sir Watkin Williams Wynn*, the lord lieutenant of Merioneth, over access rights to an unenclosed sheepwalk in the parish of Llanuwchllyn, and negotiated a £12,700 loan (finalized in March 1829) to Aethelstan Corbet of Ynysmaengwyn.[19]

He signed the Merioneth gentry's memorial asking the justice commission to investigate the expediency of assimilating the Welsh courts of great sessions and judicature into the English assize court system, with his brother and their political associates, 7 Nov. 1828, and delegated the task of giving the commissioners his views to the chairman of the magistrates, R.W. Price of Rhiwlas.[20] The commissioners' 1829 report designated Dolgellau as the assize town for Merioneth, north Cardiganshire and west Montgomeryshire, when the great sessions were abolished; but the partitioning of counties this entailed was widely resented

and Vaughan was one of several Welsh Members to oppose the 1830 administration of justice bill that encapsulated the proposals, on this count.[21] Making his only reported parliamentary speech at the bill's committee stage, 27 May 1830, he argued that the attorney-general should have treated the two issues (abolition and assimilation) separately and added:

> As the representative of a county, which feels strongly on this subject and the majority of whose constituents are strongly opposed to this measure, I feel bound to give it my opposition; and I oppose it on the ground of its abolishing the ancient jurisdiction of the country, and one to which the people are with justice attached. The charges which [the home secretary Peel] has brought against the opponents of this measure shall not prevent me from pursuing this course; and, aware of the ultimate object of this bill, I should betray my duty to those who sent me here did I not endeavour, by every means in my power, to prevent its passing into law.

Despite his strong words, he failed to divide with the 'Cambrian Warriors' against the bill's recommittal, 18 June, when, having received a month's leave on account of ill health, 5 Apr. 1830, he had remained in London on business.[22] He had divided with the revived Whig opposition on the Bathurst and Dundas pensions, 26 Mar., supply, 3 May, the Irish coal duties, 13 May, and privy councillors' emoluments, 14 May; but he paired against Jewish emancipation, 17 May 1830. He gave Ormsby Gore his interest against the marquess of Anglesey's brother Sir Charles Paget* in Caernarvon Boroughs at the general election that summer, when his own return was naturally unopposed.[23]

Ministers listed Vaughan as one of the 'moderate Ultras' and endorsed the entry to 'friend', but he was absent when they were brought down on the civil list, 15 Nov. 1830. He received a month's leave on account of ill health, 30 Nov. 1830, and Merioneth's anti-slavery petitions were now entrusted to others. Urgent private business, for which he was granted a month's leave, 9 Feb. 1831, kept him away from the House when it considered the Ffestiniog railway bill, over which opinion in Merioneth was divided, and which failed on a technicality.[24] He voted against the Grey ministry's reform bill at its second reading, 22 Mar., and for Gascoyne's wrecking amendment, 19 Apr. 1831. His canvassing address at the ensuing general election made no statement of policy and he was not denied his eleventh unopposed return.[25] He chaired the county meeting at Dolgellau, 17 June 1831, which petitioned requesting that Merioneth be granted borough representation, and was praised for his impartiality. Griffith ap Howell was the petition's principal opponent, and Vaughan tactfully persuaded its advocates that their views would carry greater weight if presented by Lord John Russell rather than himself.[26] He divided against the reintroduced reform bill at its second reading, 6 July, and to make the 1831 census the basis for borough disfranchisement, 19 July, and paired against the bill's passage, 21 Sept. 1831. *The Times* had recently written of him: 'In this gentleman there remains the finest specimen of the old country Tory school. The race is nearly extinguished'. [27] He offered the Rhuddlan votes of certain tenants at Rûg to the Glynnes at the Flint Boroughs by-election in September,[28] and received three weeks' leave on urgent business on the 29th. Though still regarded as staunch anti-reformer, he is not known to have voted on the revised reform bill, which made no additional provision for Merioneth, and was absent when party affiliation was tested on the Russian-Dutch loan, 26 Jan., 12, 16 July 1832.

Vaughan's offer of hospitality to the duchess of Kent and Princess Victoria during their visit to North Wales in the summer of 1832 was not taken up.[29] The appearance of his name as an early requisitionist of the Conservative Ultra Lloyd Kenyon* in Denbighshire prompted an opponent to remind readers of the *Chester Courant* that Vaughan's stake in that county was 'very small', and to urge the voters of Merioneth to reject him and the 'parasites who daily glut themselves at the cost and pamper the pride of the uninformed but well-intentioned host of Nannau'. The writer acknowledged that Vaughan was 'a very meritous country gentleman', but claimed that he was 'not fitted for the great duties of a Member', and made much of his erratic attendance and tendency to 'divide' and 'pair' rather than to 'discuss or listen to the discussion'.[30] Undeterred, the Vaughans supported Ultras in Denbighshire and Caernarvon Boroughs at the general election in December, when *The Times* found the squires conspicuously absent from his election at Harlech.[31] He kept his seat until ill health forced him to retire in 1836, when he was succeeded by his chosen nominee, Richard Richards of Caerynwch, whose father had facilitated his own return in 1792. Vaughan had chaired annual meetings in Wales of gentlemen educated at Jesus College since at least 1819, and the county commemorated his long service with a subscription which funded the Vaughan exhibition for Merioneth scholars at Oxford.[32] His son's marriage in June 1835 was celebrated with the customary ostentation and family settlements, revised to take account of his brother's debts.[33] These stood at almost £250,000, and required further action in 1842

and January 1843.[34] Vaughan died in April that year and was commemorated in a long eulogy in the Welsh language by Meurig Idris. Among many stipulations about his funeral at Llanfachreth he had requested that the woollen cloth used for mourning hat-bands for his tenants and workers should be of sufficient size and thickness to make each a waistcoat later.[35] His will, dated 19 May 1835, was proved, 7 Sept. 1843, after his failure to appoint an executor had been dealt with. He left his 'entire estate' to his son, the last quadruple possessor of Nannau, Hengwrt, Meillionydd and Ystumcolwyn, who died without issue in 1859, whereupon the baronetcy lapsed and the estates were scattered. He also allowed his wife £500 in addition to her settlement, and made many small bequests to servants and friends.[36]

[1] *HP Commons, 1790-1820*, v. 445-6. [2] *N. Wales Gazette*. 2, 9 Mar. 1820. [3] Add. 40266, f. 141; *N. Wales Gazette*. 9, 23 Mar. 1820. [4] UCNW, Nannau mss 712-14. [5] *LJ*, lv. 806; lvii. 108, 132; lxii. 148, 213; lxii. 191, 406 [6] *N. Wales Gazette*, 18 May; *Cambrian*, 27 May; *The Times*, 26 June 1820; NLW, Porthmadog mss 279; *CJ*, lxxv. 302. [7] Buckingham, *Mems. Geo. IV*, i. 334. [8] *The Times*, 4 May 1824. [9] *CJ*, lxxx. 309, 321; *Cambrian*, 30 Apr. 1825. [10] *Session of Parl. 1825*, p. 488. [11] C. Thomas, 'Merion. Estates, 1790-1850', *Merion. Hist. and Rec. Soc.* v (1965-6), 222, 234-5. [12] Nannau mss 719-48; *N. Wales Gazette*, 21 June, 1 July 1824. [13] NLW ms 14984 A, p. 3; *The Times*, 10, 17 Mar. 1826. [14] J. Hughes, *Methodistiaeth Cymru*, i. 604-11. [15] *The Times*, 3 Mar. 1827; *CJ*, lxxxii. 256; lxxxiii. 277, 305. [16] *N. Wales Chron.* 1 Jan. 1829. [17] Ibid. 19 Mar. 1829; UCNW, Mostyn of Mostyn mss 7450. [18] *N. Wales Chron.*, 16, 23 Apr. 1829. [19] Nannau mss 755, 756, 3783. [20] *N. Wales Chron.* 8, 15 Jan. 1829; *PP* (1829), ix. 382, 413. His name was entered as 'W.H.M.E. Vaughan' in the commissioners' report, an error not made in the *N. Wales Chron.* [21] *PP* (1829), ix. 42-44. [22] UCNW, Plas Newydd mss i. 759. [23] Ibid. ii. 218; G.I.T. Machin, 'Catholic Emancipation', *Trans. Hon. Soc. Cymmrodorion* (1962), 81-92. [24] NLW, Maybery mss 2316; *Caernarvon Herald*, 30 Apr. 1831; 'Mems. of Samuel Holland, 1803-92', *Merion. Hist. and Rec. Soc.* extra publications ser. i, no. 1, pp. 18-19. [25] *Chester Courant*, 3, 17 May 1831. [26] *Salopian Jnl.* 22 June; *Shrewsbury Chron.* 24 June; *The Times*, 25 June 1831; *CJ*, lxxxvi. 611. [27] *The Times*, 16 Aug. 1831. [28] NLW, Glynne of Hawarden mss 5399. [29] Nannau mss 760. [30] *Chester Chron.* 3, 17 Aug.; *Chester Courant*, 7 Aug. 1832. [31] *N. Wales Chron.* 11 Dec.; *The Times*, 25 Dec.; *Caernarvon Herald*, 29 Dec. 1832. [32] *Cambrian*, 13 Nov. 1819; *Caernarvon Herald*, 23 July 1836; Nannau mss 3787A. [33] Nannau mss 767-82, 3784, 3785. [34] Ibid. 793, 794. [35] Ibid. 783, 795; *Caernarvon Herald*, 29 Apr. 1843. [36] PROB 8/236; 11/1986/668; Nannau mss 3769-71; *DWB*.

M.M.E.

VAUGHAN *see also* **EDWARDS VAUGHAN**

VENABLES, William (1785–1840), of 17 Queenhithe, London.

LONDON   1831–1832

bap. 8 May 1785, 1st s. of William Venables (*d.* 1818), paper maker, of Cookham, Berks. and w. Mary Green.[1] *m.* 15 Sept. 1814, Ann Ruth, da. of Peter Fromow of Newport, I.o.W.,[2] 5s. 3da. *d.* 30 July 1840.
    Alderman, London 1821-*d.*, sheriff 1821-2, ld. mayor 1825-6.
    Master, Stationers' Co. 1824-5.

Little is known of Venables's antecedents. His father, William Venables, was 'a paper maker on a small scale' at Cookham, Berkshire, where he married Mary Green in 1782. Venables, the eldest of four surviving sons, went to London in about 1806 and entered business as a wholesale stationer (presumably supplied by his father) with two partners in Brewer Street, Golden Square. After the death of one partner he dissolved his connection with the other and operated alone, before moving in about 1816 to 17 Queenhithe, where his premises remained for the rest of his life. By 1826 he was in partnership with one Wilson, who was joined in about 1831 by William Tyler.[3] Venables's father was buried at Cookham on 2 Jan. 1819, aged 57. By his will, dated 27 Dec. 1818, he left equal shares in the residue of his estate, which included personalty sworn under £5,000, to Venables and his younger brothers Charles, of Hampton Grey House, Woodstock, Oxfordshire, and George, of Cookham, who were paper manufacturers with mills at Wooburn and Taplow, Buckinghamshire, south-east of Wycombe near the Berkshire border.[4]

Venables, whose wife was of Huguenot descent and who had his first three sons baptized at the Independent Chapel in Carey Street, Lincoln's Inn Fields, 1815-19,[5] stood for an aldermanic vacancy for Queenhithe ward in May 1821. His opponent was John Capel*, a wealthy stockbroker and outsider, whom the Queenhithe common councillors sought to impose on the ward. As the residents' candidate, with the watchwords of 'honesty and integrity', Venables declared his support for sensible reform:

> The best things are liable to abuse. I wish ... that abuse may be corrected when discovered; but I do not wish to see rash and intemperate nostrums tried upon the constitution, which might endanger that which we are all desirous of supporting. If our house needs repair, we repair and not demolish it.

He was elected by 50-31.[6] In July 1821 he was chosen as one of the City's sheriffs, though he was nominated

against his personal inclination and refused to canvass for votes.[7] In common council, he supported their reform petition, 29 Jan. 1823. He was appointed to the committee to manage their grant to the Spaniards resisting French aggression, 10 June 1823, defended the principle of the grant, 18 Mar., and on 31 Mar. 1824 said that the argument that the Aliens Act had not been abused by government 'would go to support the existence of a Star Chamber'.[8] His mayoralty, 1825-6, was marked by the publication by his Evangelical chaplain, Robert Dillon, of a laughably overblown and bombastic account of his visit by water to Oxford in his official capacity as conservator of the Thames; it made Venables and his entourage look ridiculous and was mercilessly sent up by Theodore Hook in *John Bull*.[9] While in office Venables came forward for London at the general election of 1826, having confirmed his intention at a Mansion House dinner in early March, when, declaring that he was not 'a rash, daring, "thick and thin" politician', he observed:

> Although neither his education nor habits had led him to consider himself fitted to take a lead in politics, he yet had long since made up his mind on the chief questions ... Power must reside somewhere, and its tendency was always to increase and perpetuate itself; but it was the great excellence of our constitution, that ... if there occurred at any time an error or excess in any one branch, it was intended to be corrected or controlled by the others ... He was most anxious that the House of Commons should be a free, fair, and full representation of the people ... He was a friend of liberty.

At the nomination, he described 'constitutional liberty' as the best foundation for economic prosperity and applauded the Liverpool ministry's 'enlightened views' on commercial policy; but he urged 'the greatest caution' in the application of free trade theories, though he favoured revision of the corn laws. He promised to be 'guided by the opinions of his constituents' on the Catholic question, declared his 'unequivocal support' for the abolition of slavery, reiterated his desire for sensible reform and advocated education of the poor and the dissemination of religious knowledge. He was fourth in the poll after the first day, but slipped to fifth on the second and remained there throughout. He blamed his failure on the mischievous intervention of a candidate who had no chance.[10] In common council, 23 May 1827, he expressed guarded approval of Canning's ministry, and on 26 Feb. 1829 'spoke strongly in favour' of the City corporation petition for Catholic emancipation; he later claimed that his pro-Catholic views had cost him a certain return for London in 1830.[11] On 25 Mar. 1831 he proposed one of the London merchants' resolutions in favour of the Grey ministry's reform bill, which was 'eminently calculated to promote the welfare of the country'; and in common council, 31 Mar., he moved the vote of thanks to Lord John Russell*.[12] At the general election of 1831 he stood as a 'decided' supporter of the bill, 'a just, a wise and a salutary measure', and was returned unopposed with three other reformers. He told the livery reform dinner, 9 May 1831, that 'those who opposed them wished to carry on an irresponsible government, not for the good of the many, but for the benefit of the few'.[13]

Venables, who never joined Brooks's, duly voted for the second reading of the reintroduced reform bill, 6 July 1831. On the 15th he claimed that the measure, 'if not absolutely perfect', had given 'general satisfaction' and 'won the affections of the people of England'; and on 22 July he denied a Tory allegation that the London Members were 'restrained' by pledges to support it blindly. He voted steadily for its details in committee, though on 18 Aug. he was in the majority for the enfranchisement of £50 tenants-at-will, on the principle that it extended the franchise. This vote earned him a reprimand from the livery's reform committee, 25 Aug., when he defended himself and denied having 'made a promise of implicit adherence to every clause' of the bill; but a newspaper report claimed that his critics were so forceful that he gave 'an assurance that there should be no further cause of complaint'.[14] In the House, 26 Aug., he supported his colleague Wood's plan to disfranchise the owners of finance house premises who did not pay rates and taxes, 26 Aug. In common council, 6 Sept., he denied having promised undeviatingly to toe the reform line and argued that he 'had done everything to promote the bill and its ultimate success'.[15] He divided for the passage of the measure, 21 Sept. He assured the House that the City corporation had no vested interest in Frankland Lewis's London coal bill, 1 July, and welcomed ministers' intention to regulate the capital's hackney and cabriolet trade, 8 July. An explanation by Lord Althorp, the chancellor of the exchequer, persuaded Venables to vote with him on civil list pensions, 18 July, but he did not wish it to be thought that he approved of their continuance. He welcomed the grant of £1,000,000 for public works to provide employment for the poor, 26 July. On the 29th he was in Daniel O'Connell's minority on the proceedings of the Dublin election committee. He secured a return of information on the malt duty, 2 Aug., and objected to the proposed levy on Cape wines, 8 Aug., 7 Sept. He was in the reformers' majority against the issue of a new writ for Liverpool, 5 Sept., but divided in the minority of 20 on the quarantine duties the follow-

ing day. On 7 Sept. he joined in the condemnation by London Members of the petition presented by Hunt calling for inquiry into alleged structural defects in London Bridge. That day he was added to the select committee on steam navigation, and on 20 Sept. he applauded the government's decision to regulate the operation of steamboats to protect the public from 'the thoughtlessness or the avarice of individuals'. He was named to the select committees on the commercial state of the West Indian colonies, 6 Oct., 15 Dec. 1831). He thought the arrangements for the appointment of assignees in lord chancellor Brougham's bankruptcy bill would 'work well', 15 Oct. After the reform bill's defeat in the Lords he voted for the motion of confidence in the ministry, 10 Oct., and attended the London merchants' meeting to address the king in their support, 13 Oct. 1831.[16]

Venables voted for the second reading of the revised reform bill, 17 Dec. 1831, was again a reliable supporter of its details and divided for its third reading, 22 Mar. 1832. On 9 Dec. 1831 he raised the case of the recent compromise at £20,000 of the prosecution of Leaf and Company, a London silk firm, for smuggling; and on the 15th, when successfully moving for the relevant papers, he argued that the compromise system was 'most injurious', though he gave ministers 'full credit for endeavouring to protect the trade to the utmost of their power'. Hunt, his seconder, was less charitable towards them. On 20 Jan. 1832 he approved their apparent willingness to impose prison sentences on convicted silk smugglers: 'I am not friendly to prohibition, but ... the manufacturers of this country are entitled to the full enjoyment of ... protection against foreign competition'. He spoke in the same sense, 21 Feb., when, presenting a London silk manufacturers' petition for enhanced protection, he stated that 'the present situation of the weavers in Spitalfields is far worse than ever it was'. He handed over the question to Lord Grosvenor, Member for Cheshire, but on 1 Mar. he secured returns of silk exports and duties, and he was named to the select committee on the trade, 5 Mar. He presented a petition from distressed Woodstock glovers, 31 Jan. He was added to the select committee on the East India Company, 10 Feb. Suspicious of the provisions of the fines and recoveries bill touching compensation to officers, 20 Jan., he observed that 'the House should be very cautious in its expenditure of the public money'. On 17 Feb. he denied that cholera had broken out in Hoxton, as Hunt alleged. He voted with government for the navy civil departments bill, 6 Apr., but was in the minority for reduction of the Irish registrar of deeds's salary, 9 Apr. He supported the Gravesend pier bill, 10 Apr., and, as instructed, endorsed London corporation's petition in favour of the new Irish education scheme, 16 Apr. On 10 May he supported their petition for supplies to be withheld until the reform bill was passed and voted for the address calling on the king to appoint only ministers who would carry it unimpaired. At a meeting of the London livery, 11 May, he said:

> The refusal of the supplies was an extraordinary measure, but was the means ... which the constitution lodged in the House of Commons, as the guardian of the people's rights and purses, to restrain the other branches of the legislature from arbitrary measures ... The bill must pass, if not by Lord Grey, by some other minister.[17]

In the House later that day, however, he said that a Tory ministry, even if it carried reform, would 'not give satisfaction to the country'; and on 14 May he called for the reinstatement of the Grey administration:

> If ... the reform bill should not be carried ... the country will be torn to pieces ... If the duke of Wellington and a Tory government should, after so long opposing the bill, at length, on getting into office, carry it, their doing so would be such a dereliction of all public principle as to be productive of as much evil as the reform bill may be expected to produce good.

He supported London reform petitions, 24 May, paired for the second reading of the Irish bill next day,[18] and on 4 July supported the London corporation petition calling for it to be made more radical. He voted against opposition amendments to the Scottish bill, 1, 15 June. He defended the City's policing organization, 4 June, and on the 20th deplored the attack there on Wellington, which had been 'confined to the very lowest classes'. He was in small minorities for an Irish absentee tax, 19 June, and to reduce the barracks grant, 2 July, but he divided with government on the Russian-Dutch loan, 12, 16, 20 July. He voted to open coroners' inquests to the public, 20 June, and supported an attempt to divert some of the Irish Society's funds to the cost of the Foyle bridge at Londonderry, 18 July. On 25 July he criticized the appointment of Brougham's brother to a chancery sinecure, said that arrangements were in hand for the burial of London cholera victims outside the city, called for severe penalties for smuggling to be incorporated in the customs duties bill and supported attempts to reduce the levies on coffee and currants. He supported a petition complaining of evidence given to the silk trade committee, which the Speaker would not accept, 3 Aug., and on the 7th presented a London manufacturers' petition to the same effect, recommended removal of the duty on the raw material and urged ministers to show 'the

greatest tenderness' towards the distressed weavers. He backed George Evans's warnings of possible large-scale disfranchisement in the new metropolitan districts if practical problems involved in the payment of rates were not addressed, 9 Aug. 1832.

Venables initially offered for London at the general election of 1832 as 'a decided friend of efficient reform in every department of the state': he stressed the need for church reform, including the appropriation of ecclesiastical revenues; advocated a property tax and relaxation of the corn laws; declared his support for triennial parliaments and (as a recent convert) the ballot, and called for the speedy abolition of slavery, revision of the Bank's charter and opening of the trade with India. With four other reformers in the field, he was prevailed on to withdraw a fortnight before the election for the sake of unity in the face of a Conservative challenge.[19] On the death of the veteran reformer Waithman two months later Venables started in his room, but he was comfortably beaten by the unsuccessful Conservative candidate at the general election. He blamed his defeat on broken promises and the spiteful behaviour of the extreme radicals – 'political renegades' – who had impugned his sincerity as a reformer.[20]

Venables, who had acquired a West End house at 4 Arlington Street, died at Cowes, Isle of Wight, in July 1840.[21] By his will, drawn up in haste, 29 July, he left his property at Clapton, Buckinghamshire to his wife, together with an annuity which, with Clapton rents, would bring her £800 a year. He devised his four cottages at Cookham and £300 to his sister Elizabeth and a token 20 guineas to one Charlotte Bayley, 'now residing in my family'. He made donations to the Church Missionary Society, the Society for the Propagation of the Gospels and the London Missionary Society. He created a trust fund to give a life annuity of £250 to his eldest son William, who also received a £4,000 share of the residue of his personal estate. He distributed the rest among his seven other children and provided for his brother Stephen, as required by the terms of his father's will. His personalty was sworn under £90,000.[22] His eldest son, born in 1815, was educated at Charterhouse, Oxford and the Inner Temple and practised medicine, but died on his passage to Madeira in 1845.[23] His third son, Edmund Venables (1819-95), was educated at Merchant Taylors' and Oxford, entered the church and published books on local history. Venables's fourth son, George Henry Venables, born in 1824, eventually became the owner of the Clapton and Princes paper mills. The Queenhithe stationery business of Venables, Wilson and Tyler, later Venables, Tyler and Son, was still in existence in 1902.

[1] IGI (Berks.). [2] *The Times*, 16 Sept. 1814. [3] *VCH Berks.* i. 382; *Gent. Mag.* (1840), ii. 435. [4] Berks. RO, Cookham par. reg.; PROB 11/1617/299; IR26/807/546; *VCH Berks.* i. 382; D.C. Coleman, *British Paper Industry*, 197, 241; *PP* (1840), v. 122; A. Dykes Spicer, *Paper Trade*, 192. [5] IGI (London). [6] A.B. Beaven, *Aldermen of London*, i. 195; *The Times*, 23-25 May 1821; *Gent. Mag.* (1821), i. 555. [7] *The Times*, 26-30 June, 2, 3 July 1821. [8] Ibid. 31 Jan., 11 June 1823, 19 Mar., 1 Apr. 1824. [9] Ibid. 30 Sept. 1825; Add. 40382, ff. 217, 219; 40385, f. 42; Beaven, ii. 204; R.C. Dillon, *Lord Mayor's Visit to Oxford* (1826); *Oxford DNB sub* Dillon. [10] *The Times*, 10, 18 Mar., 10, 12, 17 June 1826. [11] Ibid. 24 May 1827, 27 Feb. 1829, 12 Feb. 1833. [12] Ibid. 26 Mar., 1 Apr. 1831. [13] Ibid. 25, 30 Apr., 10 May 1831. [14] Ibid. 26 Aug. 1831. [15] Ibid. 7 Sept. 1831. [16] Ibid. 14 Oct. 1831. [17] Ibid. 12 May 1832. [18] Ibid. 30 May 1832. [19] Ibid. 16, 27 Oct., 24, 27 Nov. 1832. [20] Ibid. 7, 9, 12, 18, 26, 27 Feb., 1, 2 Mar. 1833; GL, Noble Coll. C.78 T. 1833. [21] *Gent. Mag.* (1840), ii. 435. [22] PROB 8/233 (6 Oct. 1840); 11/1935/732. [23] *Gent. Mag.* (1845), ii. 326.

D.R.F.

VENABLES VERNON, Hon. **George John** (1803–1866), of Sudbury Hall, Derbys. and 25 Wilton Crescent, Mdx.

DERBYSHIRE	1831–1832
DERBYSHIRE NORTH	1832–1835

b. 22 June 1803, o.s. of George Charles Venables Vernon (formerly Sedley), 4th Bar. Vernon, and Frances Maria, da. and h. of Adm. Sir John Borlase Warren†, 1st bt., of Stapleford, Notts. *educ.* Eton 1814; Christ Church, Oxf. 1822. *m.* (1) 30 Oct. 1824, Isabella Caroline (*d.* 14 Oct. 1853), da. and coh. of Cuthbert Ellison*, 3s. (1 *d.v.p.*) 3da.; (2) 14 Dec. 1859, his cos. Frances Maria Emma, da. and h. of Rev. Brooke Boothby, preb. of Southwell, *s.p. suc.* fa. as 5th Bar. Vernon 18 Nov. 1835; mother to Stapleford 1837 and took name of Warren instead of Venables Vernon by royal lic. 14 Oct. 1837. *d.* 31 May 1866.

Capt. Burton yeomanry 1831; capt. commdt. Sudbury vols. 1859; maj. 2 batt. Derbys. rifle vols. 1861, hon. col. 1864; constable, Tutbury Castle.[1]

Venables Vernon's grandfather, the 3rd Baron Vernon, a younger son of the 1st Baron with his third wife, was the older brother of Edward Venables Vernon, archbishop of York. This Member's father, a former soldier and an enthusiast for naval architecture, married the heiress to Stapleford, where their only child was born in 1803. As a youth, Venables Vernon seconded the nomination of Francis Mundy* at the Derbyshire by-election in November 1822, and, a Whig like his father, he was admitted to Brooks's in 1826, sponsored by Lord Althorp* and George Lamb*. He married one of the daughters of the

Tory Member for Newcastle-upon-Tyne in 1824 and apparently lived for a time in Italy (where his first son was born in February 1829), so acquiring an interest in Italian literature. His father succeeded to the barony in March 1829. Venables Vernon, whose suitability had been drawn to the attention of the duke of Devonshire, was invited at short notice to stand as a second Whig candidate for Derbyshire at the general election of 1831 by Lord Waterpark*, in loose alliance with the Cavendish Member. Although he had no funds and suspected that this request was an attempt to make him subservient, he accepted and his canvassing apparently involved him (then or soon afterwards) in making speeches even in small towns and villages.[2] His popularity was such that one supporter reported to Lord Vernon that, at a meeting of freeholders, the 'natural, honest and unaffected manner in which he answered their questions and addressed them pleased them infinitely more than the most splendid oratory would have done'.[3] Despite his youth and inexperience, he declared himself an 'old reformer', who believed in giving the people 'as much civil and religious liberty as they could possibly enjoy consistently with the safety and security of the state'. Having averred that he was for abolishing colonial slavery, a 'firm friend' to retrenchment and economy, a 'staunch advocate' of free trade and an 'enemy of war', he was returned unopposed.[4] Worried about his election expenses and that he was to be made a dupe of the Tories, he insisted that he would speak on the side of the people and should decline the situation of groom of the bedchamber as 'I'd not be independent enough, and even though I were so in reality, my constituents might fancy the contrary'.[5] In the House he joined his father's cousins George Granville Venables Vernon and Granville Harcourt Vernon (as well as William Venables, who was no relation).

Venables Vernon presented the Chesterfield petition for its own enfranchisement, 25 June, and pressed for legislation to ameliorate the condition of slaves in the West Indies, 27 June 1831. He voted for the second reading of the Grey ministry's reintroduced reform bill, 6 July, and generally for its details. Admitting that he could not speak and had in fact 'made a sad mess of speaking at my election', he informed his father, 19 Aug., about his effort on the 11th that

> from not sufficiently raising my voice, I was not much heard by the other side of the House. I thought all the time that I was speaking in a stertorian tone, but still my own side kept crying 'speak out, speak out'. At one time I lost myself completely from sheer fright but the House crying 'hear, hear', I was enabled to resume.

He argued in favour of splitting counties into smaller, more accessible and less expensive divisions, and wrote to Lord Vernon on the 23rd that he had voted for this because he was pledged to support the whole bill, adding, however, that 'since Lord Chandos's amendment [to enfranchise £50 tenants-at-will], which I consider to have violated the principle of the bill, has been carried, I consider myself at liberty to vote against it (if I wish) on bringing up the report'.[6] He divided for printing the Waterford petition calling for the disarming of the Irish yeomanry, 11 Aug., but with ministers against charges of improper interference by the Irish government in the Dublin election, 23 Aug., although he was in the minority for Benett's amendment that there had been gross bribery at the Liverpool election, 5 Sept. He voted for the passage of the reform bill, 21 Sept., the second reading of the Scottish bill, 23 Sept., and Lord Ebrington's confidence motion, 10 Oct. He voted for the second reading of the revised reform bill, 17 Dec., and again for its details and the third reading, 22 Mar. 1832. He was one of the 'old friends' attending John Cam Hobhouse's re-election for Westminster in February.[7] He spoke for the factories regulation bill to prevent children falling 'victims of avarice', 20 Feb., and supported its referral to a select committee because he had received 'so many complaints from the master manufacturers of Derbyshire'. He voted for Ebrington's motion for an address calling on the king to appoint only ministers who would carry the reform bill unimpaired, 10 May, and brought up Derbyshire petitions for withholding supplies, 22 May. He paired for the second reading of the Irish reform bill, 25 May, and voted against increasing the Scottish county representation, 1 June. He divided for making coroners' inquests public, 20 June, and backed the Derby coroner's petition complaining of inadequate remuneration, 6 July. He was added to the select committee on the renewal of the East India Company's charter, 28 June. He sided with ministers for the Russian-Dutch loan, 26 Jan., 12, 16, 20 July 1832.

Late the previous year Venables Vernon had come under pressure from Devonshire to state that he would stand with the sitting Cavendish Member for the Northern division of the county, but, since his father's estates were in south Derbyshire, he chose to offer for that division. This arrangement meant that he did not risk his friend Thomas Gisborne's* candidacy for Derbyshire North; it might have jeopardized Waterpark's, but they were both returned for Derbyshire South after a contest at the general election of 1832. He sat as a Liberal until his defeat two years later.[8] He inherited his father's title and estates in 1835

and changed his surname to Warren on coming into his mother's property in 1837. From 1839 he resided in Italy, claiming that life in England reminded him of the four ubiquitous 'T's: 'turnips, trustees, turnpike-gates and top-boots'. Not only did he become a Dante scholar of considerable repute, publishing a luxury edition of the poet's works (in three volumes, 1858-65), but in later life he developed a monomaniacal interest in rifle shooting, as recollected by his younger son William John Borlase Warren Venables Vernon (1834-1919). He died in May 1866, being succeeded as 6th Baron Vernon by his elder son Augustus Henry Venables Vernon (1829-83).[9]

[1] *Derby Mercury*, 6 June 1866. [2] Vernon of Sudbury mss, Waterpark to Vernon, n.d., Venables Vernon to same, 24 Apr., 10 May, Devonshire to same, 28 Apr. 1831; G.E. Hogarth, 'Derbys. Parl. Elections of 1832', *Derbys. Arch. Jnl.* lxxxix (1969), 72-73, 76; Chatsworth mss 2330, 2334. [3] Vernon of Sudbury mss, Lockett to Vernon, 28 Apr. 1831. [4] *Derby Mercury*, 27 Apr., 11 May 1831; Derby Local Stud. Lib. BA 324, election ballads. [5] Vernon of Sudbury mss, Venables Vernon to Vernon, 10, 12 May 1831. [6] Ibid. [7] Add. 56556, f. 59. [8] Hogarth, 75-82. [9] W.W. Vernon, *Recollections of 72 Years*, 13, 14, 18, 24, 205, 207, 254, 258, 354; H.C. Barlow, *On the Vernon Dante*, 1-4, 33-34; J. Forster, *Life of Dickens* (1846), 416-17; *Gent. Mag.* (1866), ii. 108-9; *DNB*; *Oxford DNB*.

S.R.H./S.M.F.

VERE *see* **HOPE VERE**

VEREKER, Hon. John Prendergast (1790–1865).

LIMERICK 25 July 1817–3 July 1820

b. 1 July 1790, 1st s. of Charles Vereker[†], 2nd Visct. Gort [I], and 1st w. Jane, da. of Ralph Westropp of Attyflyn, wid. of William Stamer of Carnelly, co. Clare. *educ.* Harrow 1803. *m.* (1) 15 Dec. 1814, Maria O'Grady (*d.* 4 Apr. 1854), da. of Standish, 1st Visct. Guillamore [I], c.b. exch. [I], 6s. (3 *d.v.p.*) 5da. (2 *d.v.p.*); (2) 10 June 1861, Elizabeth Mary, da. and h. of John Jones of London, wid. of George Tudor*, *s.p. suc.* fa. as 3rd Visct. Gort [I] 11 Nov. 1842. *d.* 20 Oct. 1865.[1]
  Mayor, Limerick 1831-3.[1]
  Capt. Limerick city militia 1804, maj. 1811; col. Limerick city artillery 1842-*d.*
  Rep. peer [I] June 1865-*d.*

Vereker's father Lord Gort, like several of his recent Prendergast and Smyth ancestors, had previously sat on the family interest for Limerick. He inherited his uncle's title and estates of Roxborough in county Limerick and Loughcutra Castle in county Galway, where he was a governor, in 1817. Vereker, who had been Byron's fag at Harrow, replaced his father as Member for Limerick that year and, while being but a pale shadow of him, replicated his Tory and Orange politics.[2] At the general election of 1820, when his brother-in-law Standish O'Grady came in for the county, he was, for the third time in less than three years, attacked by Lord Limerick, in alliance with the mainly Catholic 'friends to the independence of Limerick'. Having defended his support for the Liverpool ministry's repressive legislation, he defeated Limerick's son-in-law Thomas Spring Rice at the borough poll, but was unseated on petition three months later.[3] He never found a way back into the House, but remained on the corporation of Limerick. Serving a double term as mayor, he refused permission for a meeting to petition in favour of the English reform bill in November 1831, and presided at the return of two Repealers at the general election in December 1832, when his cousin John Vereker junior was the defeated Conservative candidate.[4]

Vereker's egotistical father, a representative peer from 1823, had done spectacularly well out of the spoils system, but his bid for ornamental office under the duke of Wellington in 1834 was rejected, as were his claims for improved compensation for the abolition of his Irish sinecure in 1842, a few months before his death.[5] Vereker's inheritance was encumbered with debts of £50,000, and his attempts to extricate himself from these financial difficulties were blighted by the famine of 1847. He was forced to sell almost all his Irish estates to pay his creditors and was reduced to a state of penury. In 1853 he begged the Aberdeen ministry to save him and his 'large and helpless family' from 'actual starvation' by giving him domestic and diplomatic employment. Better still, he wished to be 'provided for, upon the civil list, with apartments at Hampton Court and thus be enabled to support myself and family without entering into a line of life for which I was neither born nor educated'.[6] Nothing seems to have been done for him either then or the following year when, after his first wife's death, his renewed plea to be rescued from 'a deplorable state of actual destitution' was supported by over 60 peers with a stake in Ireland.[7] He obtained some relief in 1861 by marrying, at the age of 70, a widow of similar years, who provided him with a residence on the Isle of Wight. 'Ever a warm supporter of the Conservative party', he died there, four months after his election as a representative peer, in October 1865.[8] His second son Standish (1819-1900), succeeded to the Irish viscountcy.

[1] M. Lenihan, *Limerick, its Hist. and Antiquities*, 707. [2] *Hist. Irish Parl.* ii. 274-5; vi. 115-16, 293-4, 298-9, 465-7; *HP Commons, 1790-1820*, v. 447-9; PRO NI, Leslie mss MIC606/3/J/7/21/4. [3] *The Times*, 17 Feb.; *General Advertiser and Limerick Gazette*, 29 Feb., 24

Mar., 11, 14 Apr., 7 July 1820. [4] *Limerick Evening Post*, 8 Nov. 1831; *Limerick Herald*, 17, 24 Dec. 1832. [5] Add. 40298, f. 27; 40405, f. 127; 40408, f. 19; 40508, ff. 83-86. [6] Add. 43250, ff. 169-73; *CP*, vi. 29. [7] Add. 43256, ff. 93-98. [8] *The Times*, 23 Oct. 1865; *Gent. Mag.* (1865), ii. 797.

D.R.F./S.M.F.

VERNON (afterwards **HARCOURT**), **George Granville Venables** (1785–1861), of 19 Hanover Square and Stable Yard, Mdx.

LICHFIELD	1806–1831
OXFORDSHIRE	1831–19 Dec. 1861

b. 6 Aug. 1785, 1st s. of Hon. and Rev. Edward Venables Vernon (afterwards Harcourt), vic. of Sudbury, Derbys., and Lady Anne Leveson Gower, da. of Granville Leveson Gower[†], 1st mq. of Stafford; bro. of Granville Venables Harcourt* (formerly Vernon). *educ.* Westminster 1798; Christ Church, Oxf. 1803; continental tour. *m.* (1) 27 Mar. 1815, Lady Elizabeth Bingham (*d.* 9 Sept. 1838), da. of Richard Bingham[†], 2nd earl of Lucan [I], 1 da.; (2) 30 Sept. 1847, Frances Elizabeth, da. of John Braham of London, wid. of John James Henry Waldegrave of Navestock, Essex and of George Edward, 7th Earl Waldegrave, *s.p.* Took name of Harcourt (his fa. having *suc.* to Oxon. estates of William Harcourt[†], 3rd Earl Harcourt) 15 Jan. 1831. *suc.* fa. 1847. *d.* 19 Dec. 1861.

Vernon, scholarly and 'naturally fond of reading', whose father was bishop of Carlisle, 1797-1807, and archbishop of York from 1807 until his death 40 years later, had sat since 1806 for Lichfield on the Trentham interest of his uncle, the 2nd marquess of Stafford, with whom he had deserted opposition in 1815, having previously been a moderate Whig. At his unopposed return at the 1820 general election he expressed relief that Lichfield had not succumbed to 'the calamitous tumults of sedition' and urged the necessity of upholding 'that harmony and subordination in all classes, without which commerce would not flourish nor industry be secure'.[1] A poor attender, he was credited with having 'voted with ministers' by a radical commentary of 1825, but this was not always the case.[2] He voted with the Liverpool ministry over the omission of Queen Caroline's name from the liturgy, 23 Jan., but was in the opposition minority for Hamilton's motion on the issue, 26 Jan. 1821, when, according to the ministerialist Lord Ancram*, he was one of 'our friends' who 'voted against us merely because their father or brothers disapproved of the bill [of pains and penalties] in the other House'.[3] A letter from his aunt conveyed the approval of Lord Stafford, whose 'sentiments and yours perfectly coincide', and of his father, whose own speech had been 'very well expressed and delivered' and who was 'the individual peer who had the most cause for satisfaction'.[4] 'He was much relieved by the conversation he had with you in the House which removed any doubt from his mind on Hamilton's motion', his aunt later informed George Macpherson Grant*, adding that she hoped 'no other' questions would 'arise on which any further scruple can be felt in going with' ministers.[5] On 29 Jan. he dissented from a petition presented by Anson, his Whig colleague at Lichfield, in support of the queen, claiming that it did not express 'the unanimous sense of the inhabitants' and that a protest against it 'had been signed by about 300 persons'. He added that in voting for Hamilton's motion 'he had not been influenced by any view of overturning the present administration', but had merely been motivated by the 'original omission of the queen's name', and called for an address to the king to authorize Parliament to 'prescribe such a form of prayer' as would 'prevent the recurrence of similar controversies'.[6] He divided against the opposition censure motion, 6 Feb. He voted for Catholic relief, 28 Feb. 1821, 1 Mar., 21 Apr., 10 May 1825. He divided against parliamentary reform, 12 May, but for the forgery punishment mitigation bill, 23 May 1821. On 16 Aug. 1822, after Lord Londonderry's* suicide, he wrote a letter of strong support to Canning, arguing that his 'resolution to accept the government of India' was 'most deeply to be regretted' and that it was 'most essentially important to the House of Commons and the public interest, that you should remain here to fill that station which naturally belongs to you'. He added that he had 'not taken the least interest in party politics nor formed any connection with any member of the government which I have been generally supporting' since 1812, when he had attempted 'to bring the leading members of the opposition, with which I was then connected, into co-operation with you', and considered himself 'therefore perfectly at liberty ... to support any line of conduct in relation to the present administration' and Canning's putative leadership of the House of Commons. Writing again, 25 Oct. 1822, he denied having aspired to the vacant under-secretaryship at the foreign office, which he thought had already been filled:

If you had been enabled to offer the under-secretaryship to me, of which your letter shows me very unexpectedly the kind intention ... I should have felt myself under some difficulty, because having never since 1812 contemplated office as a good even without the sacrifice of a seat in Parliament, I was by no means prepared to ... relinquish this, even for ... the only official situation of which ... the duties and circumstances would be pleasant to me ... I have taken so little interest in the business

of Parliament for some years, and have derived so little amusement from its debates, that I should probably have consulted better for my own happiness and enjoyment of life by preferring your office.[7]

He divided for abolition of the death penalty for larceny, 21 May 1823, repeal of the usury laws, 8 Apr. 1824, and the Irish unlawful societies bill, 25 Feb. 1825.

At the 1826 general election he offered again for Lichfield where the Trentham interest, following his uncle's decision to sever all connection with Staffordshire politics, had been sold to his Whig kinsman Lord Anson, whose support he now received. A 'most severe contest' ensued, during which his headquarters were 'violently assailed' and stones were thrown at him, but after seven days the independent candidate conceded defeat, accusing Vernon and Anson of achieving their victory through 'the violation of all law'.[8] Vernon voted for Catholic relief, 6 Mar. 1827. On 18 Apr. he informed the moderate Whig leader Lord Lansdowne of his father's 'authentic account' of 'the interview between the king and his prelates of Canterbury and London' and the 'immense importance of enabling Canning to succeed if possible in giving Ireland a fit government'. 'If he fails', he warned, 'the Tories will resume their influence, and if they choose to appeal to the people on the Catholic question, I fear they may be much strengthened'. In offering his support, he again disclaimed all personal interest in office, having 'supported government for twelve years without it', and believing that 'under present circumstances it could scarcely be worth my while to risk another contest at Lichfield'. He regretted that his connection and coincidence of political opinions with Lord Stafford in 1815 had prevented him from taking 'the course of personal connection with you, which was always most suited to my inclination'.[9] He was in the ministerial minority against the disfranchisement of Penryn, 28 May 1827. He voted for Catholic relief, 12 May 1828, and the Wellington ministry's concession of emancipation, 30 Mar. 1829. His only known votes in the rest of this Parliament were against Lord Blandford's parliamentary reform scheme, 18 Feb., and the enfranchisement of Manchester, Birmingham and Leeds, 23 Feb., and for Jewish emancipation, 17 May 1830.

At the 1830 general election Vernon offered again, claiming to have given 'fair and steady support to the government'. Faced with stiff opposition from the independent candidate Sir Edward Dolman Scott*, on the third day of polling a deal was struck whereby Vernon would 'be returned this time', but 'whenever the period of another general election should arrive, he would not offer' again.[10] He was listed by the Wellington ministry as one of their 'friends' and divided in their minority on the civil list, 15 Nov. 1830. Unpredictably, he voted for the second reading of the Grey ministry's reform bill, 22 Mar., and against Gascoyne's wrecking amendment, 19 Apr. 1831. At the ensuing general election he duly retired from Lichfield, highlighting his 'recent support of the reform bill', and offered instead for Oxfordshire where, following the death of the 3rd Earl Harcourt in June 1830, his father had succeeded to the estates of Stanton Harcourt and Nuneham Courteney, which they refurbished at a total cost of £70,000.[11] In his published addresses Harcourt, as he was now styled, claimed to have discharged 'the duty of an independent Member ... neither joining in a factious opposition to any existing administration, nor giving to any unqualified support', and to have been 'the advocate of reform at time when reform was unfashionable', coming as he did from 'a most respectable reforming family'. His opponents, however, accused him of advocating 'measures which he has hitherto invariably opposed' and alleged that his 'pockets and those of other members of his family, are filled with money drawn from the public purse'. Granville Ryder* considered him 'a bad canvasser' who 'would otherwise be pretty sure of Oxfordshire', and noted that he had 'made a poor job of it, in Oxford market place, coquetting with the farmers'. After a three-day poll he was returned when the Tory candidate Lord Norreys* (who later became his son-in-law) withdrew.[12]

Vernon spoke briefly on a technicality during a debate on the truck bill, 25 June 1831. He voted for the second reading of the reintroduced reform bill, 6 July, when it was observed by John Hobhouse that during Peel's speech 'some of our converts, Harcourt Vernon for instance, winced under his whipping', and gave general support to its details.[13] He voted for Lord Chandos's amendment to enfranchise £50 tenants-at-will, 18 Aug. He divided for the bill's passage, 21 Sept., the second reading of the Scottish bill, 23 Sept., and Lord Ebrington's confidence motion, 10 Oct. He voted with ministers on the Dublin election controversy, 23 Aug. 1831. He divided for the second reading of the revised reform bill, 17 Dec. 1831, and again gave general support to its details, although he was in the minority for his brother's amendment to enfranchise all ratepayers above £10 annual value, 3 Feb. 1832. He voted for the bill's third reading, 22 Mar., and the address calling on the king to appoint only ministers who would carry it unimpaired, 10 May. He divided with ministers on the Russian-Dutch loan, 26 Jan., relations with

Portugal, 9 Feb., and the navy civil departments bill, 6 Apr. 1832.

He was returned again as a reformer at the 1832 general election and sat for Oxfordshire for the rest of his life, but, as his nephew later observed, 'he had not sufficient energy to make much mark in Parliament, although his abilities were considered above average'.[14] He died Father of the House in December 1861 at Strawberry Hill, Middlesex, the property of his second wife, the Dowager Countess Waldegrave, following 'a fall, on landing from France, on the Dover pier'. By his will the Harcourt estates passed to his eldest surviving brother, the Rev. William Vernon Harcourt (1789-1871), canon of York.[15]

[1] E.W. Harcourt, *Harcourt Pprs.* xiii. 1; *Lichfield Mercury*, 10 Mar. 1820. [2] *Black Bk.* (1823), 200; *Session of Parl. 1825*, p. 488. [3] NLW, Coedymaen mss 604; Add. 43212, f. 180 [4] *Harcourt Pprs.* xiii. 34-35. [5] Macpherson Grant mss, Lady Stafford to Macpherson Grant, 1 Feb. 1821. [6] *The Times*, 1 Feb. 1821. [7] W. Yorks. AS Leeds, Stapleton mss 887/7/2. [8] E. Richards, 'Influence of Trentham Interest', *Midlands Hist.* (1975), iii. 141; *Aris's Birmingham Gazette*, 19, 26 June; *The Times*, 15 June; *Staffs. Advertiser*, 17, 24 June 1826. [9] *Canning's Ministry*, 163. [10] Bodl. GA Staffs. b. 6, election posters; *Lichfield Mercury*, 30 July, 6 Aug.; *Staffs. Mercury*, 7 Aug. 1830. [11] *Harcourt Pprs.* xii. 219-20; *The Times*, 3 Aug. 1830. [12] Bodl. GA Oxon b. 195, election posters; Harrowby mss, G.D. Ryder to Harrowby, 6 May 1831. [13] Broughton, *Recollections*, iv. 120. [14] *Harcourt Pprs.* xiii. 36. [15] Ibid. 42-47; *Gent. Mag.* (1862), i. 230-1.

P.J.S.

VERNON *see also* **VENABLES VERNON**

VESEY FITZGERALD (formerly **FITZGERALD**), **William** (?1782-1843), of Inchicronan, co. Clare.

ENNIS	25 Feb. 1808-1812
ENNIS	4 Jan. 1813-1818
CO. CLARE	1818-June 1828
NEWPORT	20 Mar. 1829-1830
LOSTWITHIEL	1830-13 Dec. 1830
ENNIS	1831-3 Jan. 1832

b. ?1782, 2nd but 1st surv. s. of James Fitzgerald[†] of Inchicronan and Catherine (*cr.* Baroness Fitzgerald and Vesey [I] 31 July 1826), da. of Rev. Henry Vesey, warden of Galway. *educ.* Christ Church, Oxf. 23 Oct. 1799, aged 17; L. Inn 1799. *unm.* 1s. 1da. illegit. Took name of Vesey before Fitzgerald 13 Feb. 1815; *suc.* mother as 2nd Bar. Fitzgerald [I] 3 Jan. 1832; fa. 1835; *cr.* Bar. Fitzgerald [UK] 10 Jan. 1835. *d.* 11 May 1843.

Commr. of treasury [I] Dec. 1809-Aug. 1812; PC [I] 10 Feb. 1810, [UK] 13 Aug. 1812; chan. of exch. [I] Aug. 1812-July 1817; ld. of treasury [UK] Oct. 1812-Jan. 1817; envoy extraordinary to Sweden 1820-3; paymaster-gen. July 1826-July 1828; treas. of navy Feb. 1828-Dec. 1830; pres. bd. of trade June 1828-Feb. 1830; pres. bd. of control Oct. 1841-*d*.

Trustee, linen board [I] 1815.

Gov. co. Clare 1815, ld. lt. 1831-*d*.

Maj. co. Clare militia 1805, col. 1832-*d*.; capt. Ennis inf. 1817.

Vesey Fitzgerald, an ambitious, talented, likeable but unsteady Irishman, with a relaxed moral code, was undermined in politics by unreliable health and lack of nerve. He owed such eminence as he achieved in his chequered political career after 1820 almost entirely to his personal friendship with Robert Peel*, which was cemented during the latter's period as Irish secretary, 1812-18. He had ceased to be chancellor of the Irish exchequer and a lord of the treasury when the two establishments were amalgamated in 1817, having refused the Irish vice-treasurership as beneath him, thereby confirming the premier Lord Liverpool's low estimate of his judgement and temper. Beset by financial problems and keen to obtain an Irish peerage for his aged father (which had been refused him in 1815), he was bitterly disappointed at being passed over as Peel's successor, and remained disgruntled and dissatisfied during the 1818 Parliament, though he continued his general support for the ministry.[1] In October 1819 he was offered the embassy to Sweden, and after hesitating 'for a short time' he decided to accept it, though he was not expected to go out for some months.[2] In January 1820 he thanked Charles Arbuthnot*, the patronage secretary, for his 'anxious and active friendship', but went on:

> What may be my feelings as to the treatment I have met with from the government is I am quite aware of little moment to them. I have not deserved it, but I shall never condescend to remonstrate or to complain of it and they probably in the plenitude of their power would be very careless if I did. But I have satisfaction in knowing the interest which my friends have felt and their solicitude for me.[3]

At the general election two months later he was returned again unopposed for county Clare, where his family had a leading interest.[4] He apparently still had doubts as to whether he would actually go to Stockholm; but in late May 1820, appeasing a disgruntled supporter concerned that he was taking his seat for granted, he explained that having agreed to serve

> for a short time, it is not my intention to relinquish Parliament, but on the contrary to give up the mission ... if I find it expected that I should continue there ... I certainly do not contemplate being absent longer than for one session.[5]

He attended the first session of the new Parliament. As an Irish Member, he supported Holme Sumner's motion for inquiry into agricultural distress, 30 May 1820, and he was placed on the resultant select committee next day. He claimed to be 'averse to protecting duties', 2 June, but sought reassurance from the chancellor, Vansittart, that the Irish linen duties were not under threat. He said that precipitate repeal of the Union duties would cause 'serious inconvenience and injury' in Ireland, 8 June, and on the 14th he spoke and was a teller for the majority against Parnell's attack on them. That day he regretted government's initial refusal to relieve the distress produced by Irish bank failures (he applauded their decision to advance £500,000 on the 16th); paid a personal tribute to the dead Henry Grattan I*, though the Whig Member Sir Mackintosh thought he did it 'ill',[6] and opposed army reductions, warning that 'unless some precaution was taken before the next session the force now in Ireland would be insufficient' to maintain order in the west. On 28 June he stated that 'the moral amelioration of its poorer inhabitants' was 'peculiarly necessary' there. He approved the government's proposal to regulate the importation of Irish spirits, 12 July. His appointment to Stockholm was officially ratified on 7 Aug. and he arrived on 19 Sept. 1820.

The principal object of the mission, which brought him £4,900 a year, was to persuade Bernadotte to repay the large sums lent by Britain during the French wars. In this Vesey Fitzgerald was unsuccessful. Still smarting over his treatment by ministers (he observed to one correspondent, 14 Sept. 1821, that 'the long services and claims of my father, my family and myself' were 'so much waste paper'), he told Peel, when congratulating him on his appointment as home secretary, 24 Dec. 1821, that he had been 'long in low spirits from many causes', but in terms of health was 'much better than I was a month ago'.[7] He had not expected to have to endure a second Scandinavian winter and had applied for leave of absence in the autumn of 1821, but it was refused. Aggrieved and tempted to resign altogether, he reluctantly accepted his fate, but in the spring of 1822 made the most of Peel's enhanced influence in government to obtain a furlough, ostensibly to attend Parliament, 'particularly on the Irish questions', and to look after his interest in Clare, 'which would otherwise be materially prejudiced'. Yet, typically, he now complicated matters by telling Peel at the end of March that recurrent 'fever' and a debilitating 'rheumatic attack' had made him unable to undertake a long journey for several weeks. He was in any case anxious to be rid of the mission, 'which I now see leads to nothing, and which is to me as ungrateful as

any pursuit that I have followed, or any other sacrifice which I may have made'. In the event he returned
to England in mid-May 1822 and never went back to
Stockholm.[8]

Vesey Fitzgerald supported the principle of the
Irish constables bill, 7 June 1822. On 17 June he
pressed Goulburn, the Irish secretary, to relieve distress, for 'the awful situation' in Ireland 'no longer
admitted of delay'. He made a few minor contributions to debates on Irish matters in the following three
weeks.[9] His mission was terminated in a 'style' which
irked him (though he was not formally replaced until
April 1823) and he was 'harassed to death' during a
visit to his constituency.[10] Liverpool's aversion to him
was undiminished, and when William Huskisson*
pressed for promotion from woods and forests in
August the premier told him that if he vacated the
office Vesey Fitzgerald would want it: if he was given
it he 'might make himself a very inconvenient personage ... by getting into relations with the king'; but if he
was passed over he 'would be furious and in opposition
might become very troublesome'.[11] Vesey Fitzgerald's
name cropped up in the speculations which followed
Lord Londonderry's* suicide; but the Speaker was
under the impression that he 'would prefer foreign
employment to any office within reach at home'.[12]
Likewise, John Croker* told Peel, 25 Aug. 1822, that
a false report that Vesey Fitzgerald had now accepted
the Irish vice-treasurership had driven him to 'blazing
indignation' and 'fury':

> I am on the whole glad to find, from his own conversa-
> tion, that his views are still directed to diplomacy ... [and]
> that he does not appear to look for something at home,
> because I am sure he will never, in Lord Liverpool's time
> at least, get anything that he would think it right to take ...
> Vesey looks high as to foreign employment.[13]

When Huskisson was moved to the board of trade
in December 1822 Peel pressed Liverpool at least to
offer woods and forests to Vesey Fitzgerald, but the
premier would not hear of it.[14] However, prompted
by Canning, who felt that Vesey Fitzgerald '*must* be
soothed, if not satisfied', he offered him the vice-presidency of the board of trade when Thomas Wallace I*
resigned it in January 1823; to Liverpool's annoyance,
he rejected it.[15]

In the Commons, 10 Feb. 1823, Vesey Fitzgerald
joined in calls for a revision of Irish tithes. He welcomed the government's composition bill as 'calculated to redeem all the promises which had been
made', 6 Mar. Yet he wanted it to go to a committee
upstairs, 21 Apr., when he deplored Hume's inflammatory encouragement of Irish Catholics to take up

arms; and on 16 May he denounced the measure,
which he now felt 'would not relieve the distresses of
the people, but would ... augment the revenues of the
clergy'. He repeated this criticism, 30 May, 6 June, and
voted in the hostile minority, 16 June. He defended
the Irish yeomanry against Hume's 'most unfair and
illiberal' attack and supported the ministerial proposal to place them under military control, 11 Feb.
He divided with government against inquiries into the
parliamentary franchise, 20 Feb., and the prosecution
of the Dublin Orange rioters, 22 Apr., and repeal of
the house tax, 10 Mar. He supported renewal of the
Irish Insurrection Act, 12 May, contending that 'the
misfortunes of Ireland were to be attributed, not to
the conduct of those by whom she had been governed,
but to moral causes, which no government could effectively control'. Despite his pro-Catholic sympathies,
he deprecated the 'calumnies ... against the magistracy
and the people' contained in their petition for a more
equitable administration of justice in Ireland, 26 June.
He was named to the select committee on employment of the Irish poor, 20 June 1823. Soon afterwards
he broached his wish for a senior diplomatic posting
to Liverpool, ruling out the 'odious' embassy to the
United States, which he claimed to have turned down
in 1819. He made little impression, and when Peel,
whom he had asked to put in a good word for him,
reported that Liverpool had mentioned Portugal as
spoken for but had 'pointed at America', he became
indignant:

> I see that from Lord Liverpool I am to expect nothing
> and I must make up my mind to my future. I must not
> blame Mr. Canning, on whom I have neither political or
> personal claim, if Lord Liverpool does not think that I
> am entitled even to his intervention ... I do not think my
> conduct towards the present government ought to have
> led to ... an offer which was to produce my retiring from
> Parliament for such a mission ... I have spoken with Lord
> Liverpool and Mr. Canning for the last time on these
> points ... They shall not again insult me ... I ought not
> perhaps to express what I feel towards your colleagues ...
> But it is hard to suppress one's feelings for ever. When I
> look back on the two past years and call to mind what I
> have experienced, I cannot think that even you will blame
> me.[16]

At Cheltenham in August 1823 he sang the praises
of the duke of Wellington's political acumen, which
he had recently discovered, to Mrs. Arbuthnot, but
damned his brother Lord Wellesley's 'absurd pomp
and assumption of all the attributes of royalty' as Irish
viceroy.[17]

In February 1824, through Peel, he renewed his
application for an Irish peerage, this time for himself,

letting it be known that it might reconcile him to the American embassy and would give him 'an honourable exit from my representation of Clare', which he was finding increasingly tiresome. Peel put his 'strong claim on the justice of the government' for acquiescing in the abolition of his office in 1817, adding that 'considering the prominent part which Ireland is likely to bear in our discussions, it would be politic to connect with the government one who, from ability and local information, has the power of rendering so much service'. Liverpool would not have it, pointing out that a peerage would not advance his diplomatic pretensions, which were in an case inflated, and suggesting that he would 'be as anxious for office and employment after he gets the peerage as he was before. It will not satisfy him, but rather in his opinion give additional weight to his claims'. Vesey Fitzgerald whined to Peel that 'my prospects are as bad as possible, and hopeless as I thought them, I never looked at them with more painful feelings'.[18] He was reported at this time to be 'not in favour' with the king, who was 'displeased with him about ... a lease of a house in Pall Mall'.[19]

In the House, 10 Feb. 1824, he opposed Hume's motion for information on non-resident Irish clergy as 'casting a most undeserved stigma on the bishops of Ireland'. He defended the Kildare Place Association's educational work and stated that in parts of southwest Ireland there had been 'no partiality' towards Protestants in the establishment of schools 9 Mar. He was named to the select committees on Irish land valuations, 10 Mar., and Irish disturbances, 11 May (and again, 17 Feb. 1825). He argued strongly against the government's proposal to get rid of the Irish linen bounties, 18, 19, 22 Mar., and was one of a deputation of Irish Members who urged their temporary continuance on the chancellor, 8 Apr.[20] He saw little merit in the bill to remove restrictions on the formation of Irish local banks, 18 May. He voted with ministers on the case of the Methodist missionary John Smith, 11 June. He spoke and voted for renewal of the Irish Insurrection Act as a necessary evil, 14 June 1824, arguing that magistrates had enforced it 'with the least possible oppression'. His name was still being linked with the American mission, and it was formally offered to him, but he continued to agonize in the late summer of 1824, initially telling Peel that 'it would be madness in me to think of it without a peerage', for if he did so he would have to surrender his seat and would then

come home at the end of three years, a general election having taken place in my absence, after a wretched abode in Washington, perhaps with ruined health, to look again to the honourable feeling of a ministry who have shown me that they think no more of me than a sucked orange,

to lay a claim to promotion or employment after I have in fact abandoned political life at home and in retiring from Parliament sealed that abandonment.

Having secured an assurance that his peerage claim would be favourably considered in due course, he still hesitated, fearing that going to America would not, given his past shabby treatment by Liverpool, open the door to more congenial senior European postings. On the advice of Peel, to whom he unburdened himself at great length in tortured letters, he more or less committed himself at the end of September to accepting the appointment. Yet he continued to play for time and confessed to Peel that he would 'prefer the peerage, if I can obtain it through you, to any other object':

I should feel that I had not been passed by in *every* line and for everybody. I should while in the full enjoyment of an ascendancy in my county and while every motive of retirement must be suspected get rid possibly of a representation that tires me and which ... obliges me to an hundred acquiescences, to civilities which are burdensome, applications which are odious and the approaches of Popish lawyers and others whom in the end I am sure I shall offend ... If you can accomplish it for me I would rather finish now with this object than remain perhaps seven years more, with embittered and resentful feelings ... With this object I should not object to go to America or anywhere else or to remain at home without looking for anything. In a couple of years I might go abroad to occupy myself better than I can do here in my present mortifying position.[21]

After a visit to Paris, where he bought paintings on Peel's behalf, in November, he found Liverpool, who had been approached on the matter by Peel, very receptive to his wish to have the Irish peerage conferred on his mother, with remainder to himself. To get himself out of the American mission he had seized on the alarming state of Ireland, where the Catholic Association was threatening to create chaos. Liverpool did not attach much 'importance' to this, but Canning, to whom Vesey Fitzgerald appealed in December 1824, was more indulgent and released him from his engagement and agreed to let it be known that far from prevaricating, he had 'relinquished a most important mission from a sense of duty' and had not prejudiced his future claims. Feeling 'quite light hearted', Vesey Fitzgerald acknowledged the handsomeness of Canning's conduct, and Peel congratulated him on such an 'advantageous' outcome.[22]

On the eve of leaving Ireland for the 1825 session Vesey Fitzgerald concluded a long report to Peel on the state of that country with the observation that 'everything which I have seen ... confirms me in the impression ... that there is no *immediate* danger of insurrection or movement among the people'.[23] Supporting the unlawful societies bill, 15 Feb., he argued that the Catholic Association were 'justified in much that they had said and done' and had been 'instrumental to a great degree in restoring peace to Ireland', but had thrown 'the Protestant mind ... into a state of panic which it would be difficult to describe'. He voted again for the bill, 25 Feb., but presented a hostile petition from Clare Catholics, 1 Mar.,[24] before dividing for Catholic relief. He voted for the relief bill, 21 Apr., 10 May, when he endorsed a favourable petition from Galway Protestants; he spoke briefly on a detail of the measure, 6 May. As a member of the select committee on Ireland, he quizzed Daniel O'Connell*, among other witnesses.[25] He presented petitions from Sligo, 9 Mar., and Galway, 15 Mar., for the establishment of provincial banks.[26] On 22 Mar. he opposed Grattan's plan to introduce poor laws to Ireland, which would 'perpetuate its poverty and degrade its population for ever'. He welcomed the appointment of a select committee on the linen trade, to which he was named, 14 Apr., when he concurred in Newport's motion for leave to introduce a bill to regulate Irish pluralities and episcopal unions, though he put in a word for Wellesley's efforts to remedy these abuses. He supported items in the Irish miscellaneous estimates, 15 Apr. On 26 Apr. he spoke for the bill to disfranchise Irish 40s. freeholders, irrespective of its connection with Catholic relief, though he would have preferred the qualification to be raised even higher; he was a teller for the majority that day. On 9 May he backed Foster's attempt to widen its scope as 'a measure of general reform of the system of voting in Ireland'. He shared Peel's reservations about Newport's proposal to prosecute the perpetrators of abuses in Irish charter schools, 9 June, but 'should be ashamed not to give it his support' if it was pressed to a division (which it was not). He divided with ministers for the duke of Cumberland's grant, 30 May, 10 June 1825.

In mid-September Wellesley wrote to Liverpool enthusiastically endorsing Vesey Fitzgerald's wish to have the Irish peerage conferred on his mother. Nothing was done in December, as Wellesey recommended, and in January 1826 Vesey Fitzgerald, who felt that the viceroy had perhaps overdone things, fretted that Liverpool, 'the last [man] that ought to forget my family or me', might cast him aside again. Peel persuaded him to be patient.[27] He regretted Peel's brother-in-law George Dawson's* attack on O'Connell and Richard Sheil*, as 'we have hitherto had the gentleman's advantage over the Catholic Association that the personality was exclusively theirs'.[28] He was not

much in evidence in the House that session. He presented a petition from the Hibernian Bank Company for a bill to amend their Act, 16 Feb.[29] He opposed Grattan's amendment to the Irish church rates bill to empower vestries to assess parishes for poor relief, 27 Apr. He voted against reform of Edinburgh's representation, 13 Apr., and Lord John Russell's resolution condemning electoral bribery, 26 May 1826, when he presented a Clare petition against alteration of the currency.[30] He gleefully accepted Liverpool's offer of the 'high' and 'gentlemanlike' office of paymaster-general in the minor reshuffle at the dissolution, and was additionally delighted by the conferring of the Irish peerage on his mother. A few technical hitches caused him anxiety, but he came in unopposed for his county and all was settled by the end of July 1826.[31]

Vesey Fitzgerald justified the size of the estimates, 19 Feb. 1827. He was a teller for the ministerial majority on the Clarences' annuity bill, 8 Mar. He voted for Catholic relief, 6 Mar., and presented favourable Clare parish petitions, 16 Mar.[32] On 15 Mar. he replied to Burdett's attack on Peel's jocular allusions to Peregrine Pickle and Roderick Random in the debate on Leicester corporation, whose critics, he suggested, had like Smollett 'shown more of the novel writer and the political pamphleteer, than of the liberal and impartial narrator of events'. He presented a Clare millers' petition for restrictions on the importation of foreign flour, 19 Mar.[33] In the ministerial crisis which followed Liverpool's stroke O'Connell tried to force Vesey Fitzgerald to side with Canning and the pro-Catholics by threatening to make a run at him in Clare if he went with Peel. After consulting his friend and pondering for a while, he accepted Canning's offer to retain him in his office in his new coalition ministry, though it was reported in June that Canning was already keen to ditch him.[34] He supported the grant for the new harbour at Dun Laoghaire, 11 May, and presented a Clare landowners' petition for reform of the system of grand jury presentments, 23 May;[35] he was named to the select committee on this, 6 June. He divided with his colleagues against the disfranchisement of Penryn, 28 May, and for the grant for Canadian canals, 12 June. On the Preston election bill, 14 June, he observed that the example of countries where the secret ballot was used showed that it was 'not free from influence and by no means favourable to liberty'. After returning from Canning's funeral, 16 Aug. 1827, Vesey Fitzgerald reflected that he had 'died fortunately for his own fame', before insuperable difficulties had overwhelmed him.[36] He remained in office under Lord Goderich, whose situation he did 'not envy'; and on the ignominious collapse of his administration he lamented the 'melancholy' state in which he had left national affairs:

> God knows in these times neither office or power are much the objects of ambition. In the difficulties of the country, it would be ... to be wished perhaps that the Whigs had been tried for a couple of months. The task of their successors would be more easy.[37]

He stayed in under Wellington, pleased to be reunited in office with Peel, on whom he unsuccessfully urged his brother Henry the dean of Kilmore's claims to preferment.[38]

On the address, 31 Jan. 1828, Vesey Fitzgerald praised Admiral Codrington for his victory at Navarino and, on Ireland, defended the new ministry's leaving the Catholic question as an open one within the cabinet. 'As a Protestant and proprietor of landed property', he presented and endorsed several Irish pro-Catholic petitions, 4, 5, 7, 25 Feb., 7 May, and voted silently for relief, 12 May. He divided against repeal of the Test Acts, 26 Feb., and two days later came to Peel's defence over his premature exit from the debate. He was appointed to the finance committee, 15 Feb., and to the select committee on Irish education, 11 Mar. He acquiesced in the granting of leave for Grattan's Irish assessment of lessors bill, 20 Mar., though he thought it would need alteration. On the East Retford issue next day he favoured sluicing the borough with the freeholders of Bassetlaw. He supported the life annuities repeal bill, 25 Mar. He spoke in favour of the Hibernian Company bill, 22, 24 Apr., when he was in the government majority against inquiry into chancery delays. On 28 Apr. he denied a radical allegation that he and other Irish Members had persuaded ministers to have the corn averages calculated at Irish ports. He deplored the 'warmth of feeling' which entered the debate on provision for Canning's family, 14 May, when he praised Canning's 'talents ... zeal and ... earnestness'; he spoke in the same sense, 22 May. On the 16th he vindicated the finance committee in reply to Hume's strictures. He presented and supported a petition from resident Irish aristocrats and gentry for a grant of money to employ the starving poor. He defended details of the Irish estimates, 10 June 1828.

In mid-May Lord Ellenborough, anticipating the resignation of Huskisson and his associates from the ministry, noted a view that of their possible replacements Vesey Fitzgerald was 'the cleverest and is useful, but he is unpopular, and would rather discredit a government'.[39] He was on a flying visit to Ireland to comfort his ailing father when Peel notified him, 28 May, that Wellington (who had decided against his original plan to offer him the secretaryship at war) wished him to replace the formidable Huskisson as president of the board of trade, with a seat in the cabinet. He came over and, though fearful that he would, as he told Peel, 'disappoint you and others in such an office', considering his 'own little competency' for it, decided to accept and to 'do my best'.[40] According to Lord Colchester, 'everybody' disapproved of the appointment, which was generally thought to be Peel's doing.[41] The Huskissonite Lord Palmerston* commented that Vesey Fitzgerald was 'unpopular in the House of Commons and though a clever man and able speaker doers not hit the House, as Burke said, between wind and water'.[42] He had to seek re-election for Clare, where O'Connell was persuaded to stand against him and, in a sensational and significant contest, easily defeated him, with the backing of the Catholic Association, the priests and a mass subscription.[43] Advised by Peel not to rise to the bait of his traducers, he delivered an even tempered but occasionally tearful valedictory speech; but he told Peel that 'no one can contemplate without alarm what is to follow in this wretched country'. In cabinet, 15 July, he 'gave an awful account of the state of Ireland' and argued unsuccessfully for O'Connell to be unseated for refusing to take the oaths and for legislation to declare Catholics to be ineligible to sit in Parliament.[44]

He was apparently offered a seat for Aldeburgh by his friend Lord Hertford; but in mid-August he found that Wellington had arranged his return for Tralee, whose sitting Member had recently died.[45] However, this arrangement fell through, and he was without a seat for nine months. He was already panicking about his ability to cope with his office and asked Peel to try to secure his removal to the board of control, the business of which he would be able to do 'respectably':

> The subjects [of trade] are so new to me, the details so difficult and complicated, the responsibility so great and my own sense of inferiority so painful when I have to communicate with the persons who represent different interests, and my consciousness, my conviction that I shall *not* acquit myself to my own satisfaction, to yours, or the duke's when I come to treat these points in public, are so intense that if ... I might be transferred ... I should feel not only gratified and obliged but I should be relieved from what is at times almost an agony of mind.

After consulting Wellington, who thought it essential that the head of the board of trade should be in the Commons, Peel told him that 'he ought to remain where he is [and] that having held the office of chancellor of the exchequer in Ireland he must be conversant with the business generally of the board of trade'.[46]

Vesey Fitzgerald, who considered Dawson's pro-Catholic speech at Londonderry, 12 Aug. 1828, 'very bold and imprudent', but likely to have a good 'moral effect', was closely involved in the cabinet's deliberations on how to deal with the crisis in Ireland and corresponded at length with Peel on the problem. Yet according to Von Neumann, he complained in November that it was 'particularly embarrassing for the government in view of the divergence of opinion which it had produced in the cabinet', who had already 'allowed matters to go too far'.[47] Ellenborough observed on 24 Dec. 1828 that in cabinet he 'expresses himself well ... takes a good deal of part, and does everything in a very gentlemanlike and unassuming manner'; but a week later Mrs. Arbuthnot wrote that Wellington

can't bear Mr. Fitzgerald who, he says, is an ill tempered, ill conditioned blackguard with whom it is quite disagreeable to him to be in society with. I think, if the consideration of the Catholic question is put off, it will be a great consolation to the duke if it frees him of Mr. Fitzgerald, who is always dissatisfied, always wanting to change his office and always talking of going. He says now he must go if the Catholics are not satisfied this session; but, when the time comes, he won't go, I'll answer for it.[48]

After Lord Anglesey's recall as viceroy, which he blamed on his own 'vanity', Vesey Fitzgerald entreated Peel to urge caution on Wellington, whom he considered to be surrounded by incompetent advisers. Ellenborough found him 'rather Irish' in cabinet, 21 Jan. 1829, when, because he 'hates the 40s. freeholders who ousted him', he argued for 'giving a pecuniary provision for the clergy'. He was one of the committee of four charged with the task of drafting a measure to control the freeholders to complement the concession of Catholic emancipation, and he did not shy away from their 'open disfranchisement'.[49] In the small hours of 7 Mar. he wrote to congratulate Peel on his speech detailing the government's plans, which he was sure had thereby been 'absolutely accomplished'.[50] His hopes of a seat for Sandwich were dashed, but in early March Wellington persuaded the duke of Northumberland, the new Irish lord lieutenant, to bring him in for his Cornish borough of Newport for the remainder of the session.[51] He was returned on the 20th, was sworn in on the 23rd and the following day, after hinting at his proposals to deal with the distressed silk trade, spoke on a detail of the Catholic relief bill. He opposed passionately and at length a Protestant attempt to try to extend the franchise bill to the Irish boroughs, deploring such vindictiveness as a threat to the stability of the settlement and disclaiming any personal resentment of his ejection from Clare, though

he admitted that he had felt it 'deeply'. Towards the close of the debate on the third reading of the relief bill, 30 Mar., he replied vigorously and effectively, witnesses thought, to the Ultra Sadler's 'lucubrations on the state of Ireland'.[52] On 6 Apr. he presented but dissented from a petition from distressed Coventry ribbon manufacturers against any reduction in the silk duties; and on the 13th, opposing Fyler's motion for inquiry into the trade, set out his plan to lower them. The matter had caused him anxiety in the preparation, but the Whig Member Agar Ellis thought his speech showed 'considerable ability'.[53] He pressed the measure through to its third reading, 8 May. On the 11th he dismissed the notion of re-imposing a protecting duty on foreign wool imports. He opposed reception of a petition from the inhabitants of Upper Canada against the pending administrative legislation, 14 May, when he gave an assurance that ministers contemplated no further interference with the corn laws, replied sharply to Hume's attack over the East Indian trade monopoly and, explaining his proposals for the customs duties, lost his temper with 'Bum' Gordon, whom he accused of 'pointing out to me my duty, of which I am able to judge sufficiently well myself'. He was also irritable when denying ministerial indifference to the problems of the shipping interest, 19 May. He resisted Hume's motion for a fixed duty on corn that day, and on 2 June 1829 deplored Fyler's apparent linking of the recent Spitalfields weavers' riots with the rejection of his motion for inquiry. He also refused to countenance the continuance of fishery bounties beyond the current financial year. Soon afterwards the Whig Lord Althorp*, commenting on ministerial weakness in Commons debate, observed that Vesey Fitzgerald, 'though sharp and clever, offended everybody by his ill-temper, his violence and vulgarity'.[54] His generous speeches of March had encouraged O'Connell to seek a compromise whereby if he was allowed to take his seat for Clare unimpeded he would not oppose him next time; but the House's rejection of his claim to sit, which forced him to stand again, hardened his heart, and he made it clear that it would be 'folly' in Vesey Fitzgerald to contest the issue.[55] It was thought in mid-May 1829 that he could be found another seat, but in the event he remained Member for Newport, with Northumberland's blessing.[56]

At the close of the session Greville, noting that the 'great want' of the administration was 'that of men of sufficient information and capacity to direct the complicated machinery of our trade and finances and adjust our colonial differences', observed that Vesey Fitzgerald 'knows nothing of the business of his office, still less of the principles of trade; he is idle but quick'.[57] Curiously, the Ultra leader Sir Richard Vyvyan considered him as a potential member of a coalition ministry, but his ally Sir Edward Knatchbull scoffed at the idea, arguing that he would '*stick* to the duke'.[58] So too thought Palmerston, who had 'a very indifferent opinion of his morale, although he certainly is a clever man'.[59] In early October Vesey Fitzgerald gave the cabinet 'bad' accounts of Ireland and the state of 'trade generally', and later in the month at Sudbourne talked 'a great deal of politics' with Mrs. Arbuthnot, apparently complaining as 'usual' of Peel's 'coldness and bad management' of the Commons and 'thinking of nothing but getting the Huskisson party back'; for this she deemed him 'a most miserable coward'.[60] He was by now nearing the end of his tether, and in late November, when he was ill, he begged Peel to secure if possible his 'release from a position in which I shall disappoint and embarrass you all, as well as disparage myself', though he expressed willingness to soldier on if necessary. Peel tried to calm him down, but in December Vesey Fitzgerald, who complained to Greville of the king's reckless extravagance and his own wretched health, which made it almost impossible to carry on the business of an office whose remit had been increased by Huskisson, confessed that 'I feel every day more terrified at the responsibility'. Peel advised him to attend to his diet and take regular exercise; but a week later he threw himself on Peel's mercy:

I feel my health seriously impaired, my sight is very much affected, and ... my spirits are depressed to a degree that I am unwilling to confess ... I fall almost daily into a state of nervousness which not only incapacitates me for doing my daily duties, but which is made more distressing by the anxiety which my office imposes, and the tremendous responsibility which hangs upon me ... I am ... deeply sensible of what will be my situation when Parliament meets, and when the pressure on my brain will break me down.[61]

In January 1830, when he apparently suffered an 'apoplectic seizure', he resigned his office, despite Wellington's attempt to make him reconsider, and, on doctor's orders, decided to stay away from Parliament for the whole of the approaching session.[62] Croker, who half suspected him of malingering, until Peel disabused him, thought that his nervous collapse had been produced by 'a sensitive delicacy about being *pitted* against O'Connell' in debate.[63] The Whigs recognized his departure from the scene as a blow to the government's debating prowess in the Commons and 'a great loss to Peel' in particular. Thomas Spring Rice* was generous: 'his conduct at the board of trade was in all respects admirable, and his zeal for the interests of Ireland was equalled by a knowledge of the actual condition of that country not possessed by any other member of the cabinet'.[64]

The Irish secretary Lord Francis Leveson Gower reported from London, 5 Feb. 1830, that Vesey Fitzgerald's 'unfortunate dejection at this moment is irreparable'.[65] He was in better shape by early April, when he thought ministers should take 'a very high tone' against Jewish emancipation.[66] Next month he went to Paris (where Ellenborough thought he hankered to be British ambassador) and he was kept abreast of political developments at home by Croker.[67] After the death of George IV he told Peel:

If an election takes place I suppose I ought to go over instantly, for I shall have an arrangement to make of some kind if I am not willing perhaps to be excluded from the House of Commons. At all events perhaps I ought to be over, and to pay my duty to the king. I have no ambition but I do not like being altogether on the shelf.[68]

Soon afterwards Ellenborough, who wished 'he was well and could come into office again', heard from Sir Henry Hardinge* that he 'seems eager about politics'. He went to London in late July, when Greville found him 'aware of the difficulties' of the ministry 'and the necessity of [their] acquiring more strength'.[69] At the general election he found a berth for Lostwithiel on Lord Mount Edgcumbe's interest. There was pressure on him to 'return to office', but his health and nerve were not up to it and he went back to France at the end of August 1830.[70] He was unwell in Paris in early September when Wellington formally invited him to rejoin the cabinet, but he declined, even though he knew that he was damaging his future prospects.[71] He vacated Lostwithiel at the end of 1830. A report that he would be nominated for county Clare at the by-election in late March 1831 came to nothing.[72] At the general election a month later he returned himself for Ennis. He was in the House to oppose the printing of a Glasgow Protestants' petition against the Maynooth grant, 19 July, and to present one from Galway Catholics for equal treatment with Protestants in the exercise of the local franchise, 18 Aug. He paired against the passage of the Grey ministry's English reform bill, 21 Sept. 1831. He became the first lord lieutenant of county Clare that autumn, having 'behaved very well about it', as the Irish secretary Edward Smith Stanley thought.[73] He was named to the select committee on Irish tithes, 15 Dec. 1831, but observed to Peel from Clare a week later that 'the course which the government are taking makes the matter hopeless'.[74] His mother's death in January 1832 made him an Irish peer and so ineligible to continue sitting for Ennis. He did not come in elsewhere, though he was one of the Conservatives' Irish election management committee.[75]

The following year, still in 'miserable health', Vesey Fitzgerald sought Wellington's support for his pretensions to an Irish representative peerage, 'now the only door which is likely to be opened for my entering either House'. The duke, who rebuked him for his almost indecipherable handwriting, eventually persuaded the leading Irish Conservatives to support him on the second vacancy, after Lord Bandon.[76] He was noted by Wellington as a candidate for diplomatic office when Peel formed his ministry in December 1834. He was disappointed to be passed over ('without any good cause', as Peel thought, having actually turned down an offer), but was appeased with a United Kingdom peerage, two weeks before the death of his father.[77] He was not initially included in Peel's 1841 cabinet, but when Ellenborough vacated the board of control to go to India in October he was brought in. The outgoing Whig prime minister Lord Melbourne described him to Queen Victoria as

a very able public man ... if not the most able they have; but [I am] told by others, who know ... [him] better, that ... [I overrate] him. He is a very good speaker, he has not naturally much industry, and his health is bad, which will probably disable him from a very close and assiduous attention to business.[78]

He was poorly in the spring of 1842, recovered briefly, but fell mortally ill with 'a liver complaint' on 5 May 1843. He lingered in severe distress until his death at his house in Belgrave Square in the early hours of the 11th.[79] His private secretary recorded his last conversation with him 'upon public matters' on the 10th: 'I have no reason to be ashamed of my character, or conduct as a public man. After Lord Castlereagh I was the first Irishman who succeeded in obtaining a seat in the cabinet'.[80] Greville, who noted that 'he never ought to have taken office, for his constitution was unequal to its anxieties and fatigues, and he was too nervous, excitable, and susceptible for the wear and tear of political life', was flattering in his assessment:

He is a great loss in all ways, and few men could be more generally regretted. He was clever, well-informed, and agreeable, fond of society, living on good terms with people of all parties, and universally popular. He was liberal in his opinions, honourable, fair, and conciliatory ... His death is a public misfortune.[81]

An anonymous writer took a more sober view:

[He was] considered a good man of business and was greatly esteemed in private life, but it never could be said that his talents or qualifications as a statesmen were of the

highest order; still ... they were of that efficient and useful character which makes his loss as a minister, though not irreparable, much to be regretted.[82]

Another described him as 'a man of accomplished understanding, graceful in manners, and intelligent in office', and 'a very interesting speaker upon occasions, less forcible than finished, and less declamatory than pointed'.[83] His British peerage became extinct and he was succeeded in the Irish barony by his brother Henry, on whose death in 1860 it lapsed. By his will of 23 Aug. 1838 he left his estates in Clare to Henry and directed that the rents of his property in Galway should accumulate for the benefit of Henry's eldest son. (Henry died without male issue and the ultimate beneficiaries were the families of their married sisters Lady Mahon and Letitia Foster.) He gave one Mary Ann Pineau a life annuity of £150 in addition to one of £50 which she received from his father. He left his recently purchased Croagh estate in Limerick to his bastard son William Robert Seymour Vesey Fitzgerald (1816-85), Conservative Member for Horsham, 1848, 1852-65, 1874-5, and governor of Bombay, 1866-72.[84] His personalty, which William Robert shared with his illegitimate sister, was sworn under £30,000 in England and under £120,000 in Ireland.[85]

[1] *HP Commons, 1790-1820*, iii. 756-7; NLI mss 7857, p. 82, Vesey Fitzgerald to Vandeleur, 19 Mar. 1819. [2] NLI mss 7857, p. 267, Vesey Fitzgerald to Castlereagh, 30 Oct. 1819; 7858, pp. 120, 134, Strangford to Vesey Fitzgerald, 6 Jan., Vesey Fitzgerald to Massey, 24 May 1820. [3] NLI mss 7858, p. 42. [4] Ibid. pp. 13, 58, 68, Vesey Fitzgerald to Massey, 15 Feb., to Egremont [Mar.], Hickman to Vesey Fitzgerald, 19 Feb. 1820. [5] Ibid. p. 120, Vesey Fitzgerald to Massey, 24 May 1820. [6] Add. 52444, f. 151. [7] NLI mss 7859, p. 158; Add. 40322, f. 1. [8] NLI mss 7859, pp. 109, 216, Vesey Fitzgerald to Wade, 25 May 1821, 28 Mar. 1822; Add. 40322, f. 8; 40345, ff. 187, 188. [9] *The Times*, 20, 21, 28 June, 2, 3, 6 July 1822. [10] Add. 40322, f. 16. [11] Add. 38743, f. 192. [12] Add. 40350, f. 248. [13] Add. 40319, f. 57. [14] Add. 40304, ff. 98, 100. [15] Add. 38744, f. 21; 40304, f. 223; Buckingham, *Mems. Geo. IV*, i. 417. [16] Add. 40322, ff. 35, 37. [17] *Arbuthnot Jnl*. i. 250, 252. [18] Add. 40304, ff. 218, 223; 40322; ff. 42, 60; *Arbuthnot Jnl*. i. 295. [19] PRO NI, Wellington mss T2627/3/2/296, Wellington to Mrs. Arbuthnot, 25 Mar. 1824. [20] Northants. RO, Agar Ellis diary, 8 Apr. [1824]. [21] Buckingham, ii. 113; Add. 40322, ff. 46, 56, 64, 80, 86. [22] Add. 40322, ff. 88, 98, 103, 111. [23] Add. 40322, f. 113. [24] *The Times*, 2 Mar. 1825. [25] *O'Connell Corresp*. iii. 1176. [26] *The Times*, 10, 16 Mar. 1825. [27] Add. 37303, f. 239; 40322, ff. 133, 139. [28] Add. 40322. f. 140. [29] *The Times*, 17 Feb. 1826. [30] Ibid. 27 May 1826. [31] Add. 37304, ff. 137, 141; 40322, ff. 146, 148, 152, 158, 160, 163; *Colchester Diary*, iii. 436. [32] *The Times*, 17 Mar. 1827. [33] Ibid. 20 Mar. 1827. [34] *O'Connell Corresp*. iii. 1364; Lansdowne mss, O'Connell to Knight of Kerry, 24 Apr. 1827; Add. 40322, ff. 169, 171; *Arbuthnot Jnl*. ii. 128. [35] *The Times*, 12, 24 May 1827. [36] Add. 40322, f. 181. [37] Add. 40322, ff. 173, 188, 194, 197, 215, 227. [38] Add. 40322, ff. 233, 235, 241. [39] *Ellenborough Diary*, i. 107. [40] Wellington mss WP1/980/30; Add. 40322, ff. 247, 249, 252; *Ellenborough Diary*, i. 125, 144. [41] *Colchester Diary*, iii. 569; *Creevey Pprs*. ii. 160; TNA 30/29/9/5/71. [42] Southampton Univ. Lib. Broadlands mss PP/GC/TE/201. [43] Add. 40322, ff. 263, 265, 270; *Ellenborough Diary*, i.

153, 157; *O'Connell Corresp.* iii. 1463, 1466; *Colchester Diary*, iii. 577; *Arbuthnot Jnl.* ii. 196-7; *The Times*, 7, 9, 10 July 1828. See COUNTY CLARE. [44] Add. 40322, ff. 268, 270; *Clare Jnl.* 7 July 1828; Wellington mss WP1/941/12; *Ellenborough Diary*, i. 162-3. [45] Add. 40322, f. 278. [46] Add. 40322, f. 278; Wellington mss WP1/948/3. [47] *Greville Mems.* i. 219-20, 283-5; *Ellenborough Diary*, i. 200, 203, 230; Grey mss, Ellice to Grey [1828]; Add. 40322, ff. 303, 310, 320, 328, 329, 331, 337, 341, 378; *Von Neumann Diary*, i. 193-4. [48] *Ellenborough Diary*, i. 283; *Arbuthnot Jnl.* ii. 229-30. [49] Add. 40323, ff. 7, 12, 15, 31; *Greville Mems.* i. 231-2; *Ellenborough Diary*, i. 307, 347-8, 349-50, 358. [50] Add. 40323, f. 38. [51] *Arbuthnot Corresp.* 116; Wellington mss WP1/1002/18, 20; 1007/11, 12. [52] *Croker Pprs.* ii. 12; Brougham mss, Abercromby to Brougham [31 Mar. 1829]; Dorset RO D/BKL, Bankes jnl. 166. [53] Add. 40323, f. 42; Agar Ellis diary, 13 Apr. [1829]. [54] *Arbuthnot Jnl.* ii. 285. [55] *Greville Mems.* i. 287; *O'Connell Corresp.* iii. 1474; iv. 1552, 1555a, 1569, 1577, 1584, 1586. [56] Wellington mss WP1/1018/22; 1022/10. [57] *Greville Mems.* i. 225, 228. [58] Cornw. RO, Vyvyan mss, Knatchbull to Vyvyan, 26 Aug., reply, 31 Aug. 1829. [59] Broadlands mss BR23AA/5/6. [60] *Ellenborough Diary*, ii. 102, 108; *Arbuthnot Jnl.* ii. 311-12, 316. [61] Add. 40323, ff. 50, 56, 58, 81, 84; *Greville Mems.* i. 345-6. [62] *O'Connell Corresp.* iv. 1628a; *Creevey Pprs.* ii. 147; *Greville Mems.* i. 350, 352-3; Wellington mss WP1/988/16; 1083/13, 15; 1084/20; 1087/24; 1091/12; *Ellenborough Diary*, ii. 158, 169; *Arbuthnot Jnl.* ii. 323-4, 328; Grey mss, Ellice to Grey [18 Jan. 1830]. [63] *Croker Pprs.* ii. 55; Add. 40320, ff. 143, 145. [64] Add. 51534, T. Grenville to Holland, 14 Jan.; 51580, Carlisle to same, 7 Jan.; 51586, Tierney to Lady Holland, 5, 8 Jan. 1830; NLS mss 24770, f. 39; Torrens, *Melbourne*, i. 327-8. [65] NAI, Leveson Gower letterbks. 23. G. 39/4. [66] Add. 40323, f. 106. [67] *Croker Pprs.* ii. 57-69; Add. 40323, ff. 115, 124, 134, 144, 153; *Ellenborough Diary*, ii. 259. [68] Add. 40322, f. 157. [69] *Ellenborough Diary*, ii. 306; *Greville Mems.* ii. 11. [70] *Greville Mems.* ii. 25; *Arbuthnot Jnl.* ii. 377-8, 381. [71] Wellington mss WP1/1140/20; 1143/10. [72] Derby mss 920 Der (14) 121/1/2, Gosset to Smith Stanley, 16 Mar. 1831. [73] PRO NI, Anglesey mss D619/31D/59. [74] Add. 40323, f. 169. [75] *Three Diaries*, 266. [76] *Wellington Pol. Corresp.* i. 190-2, 201-2, 213-14, 637, 644, 650-1, 702. [77] Ibid. ii. 227, 449; Add. 40323, ff. 193, 194, 196, 198; *Gent. Mag.* (1833), i. 318. [78] Parker, *Peel*, ii. 578; *Victoria Letters* (ser. 1), i. 435. [79] *The Times*, 11, 12 May 1843; *Raikes Jnl.* iv. 258. [80] Add. 40463, f. 280. [81] *Greville Mems.* v. 91-92. [82] *The Times*, 12 May 1843. [83] *Gent. Mag.* (1843), ii. 92. [84] *Oxford DNB*. [85] PROB 11/1980/399; IR26/1641/293; *The Times*, 1 June 1843.

D.R.F.

VILLIERS, Frederick (1801–1872), of 11 Paper Buildings, Lincoln's Inn, Mdx.

SALTASH	1831–1832
CANTERBURY	1835–27 Mar. 1835
SUDBURY	1841–14 Apr. 1842

b. 24 Mar. 1801,[1] ?4th (?2nd illegit.) *s.* of Charles Meynell (*d.* 1815) of The Grove, Ashbourne, Derbys. *educ.* Eton 1814; Trinity Coll. Camb. 1823; L. Inn 1825, called 1831. *m.* Anna. *d.* 27 May 1872.

Villiers was born in Derbyshire and descended from the Meynell family, who had been established in that county since the twelfth century. His father was the youngest son of Hugo Meynell of Bradley, Member for Lichfield and other boroughs, 1762-80. According to Charles Meynell's will, he left at his death in 1815 two sons, Charles and Francis Meynell, and two other 'natural sons', Charles and Frederick Villiers, who were 'now receiving their education at ... Eton'. Frederick inherited £1,500 and a half-share of certain 'trust money', payable on the death of his father's second wife.[2] He qualified as a barrister in January 1831 and at the general election that spring was returned unopposed for Saltash as a supporter of the Grey ministry's reform bill, on the interest of his friend William Russell*.[3]

He informed *The Times* that he had not been absent from the division on the second reading of the reintroduced reform bill, 6 July 1831, but had voted for it.[4] He voted steadily for the bill's details, although he supported the transfer of Saltash from schedule A to B, 26 July, on the ground that the borough and the parish of St. Stephen's were 'completely identified'; he praised the government's fairness in allowing the House to decide the matter. He divided for the third reading, 19 Sept., but stated next day that while his objections to certain clauses had been removed, others still remained. He particularly regretted the inclusion in the preamble of 'highly derogatory' expressions regarding 'the composition of this and preceding Parliaments', which, by implying that they had been 'illegally constituted', seemed 'calculated to diminish the respect due to its authority' and were likely to encourage some to 'call in question the legality of many contracts founded on the decision of this House'. These 'inflammatory discourses' had 'furnished the enemies of existing institutions and vested rights with a fresh weapon' and exacerbated the violence of popular feeling. He would have preferred to see the case for reform explained in terms of the need to 'keep pace with the improved intellect of the people'. He also feared that the proposed division of counties was 'pregnant with mischief' for the aristocratic interest, as many of the constituencies thus created would be dominated by the manufacturing towns within them, and the representatives of divided counties would carry less weight in the House. He maintained that 'no representative legislature can ever be permanent and secure, unless it contains ... a large portion of those who form the natural aristocracy of the country'. He ended by expressing his 'total disapprobation' of the clamour raised in the country against the Lords, in an attempt to inhibit 'the exercise of its proper jurisdiction'. Benjamin Disraeli[†] later recalled how his 'old acquaintance' had 'distinguished himself by voting for the bill in all its stages and then delivering a violent philippic against it', as a result of which 'a certain coolness ... ensued between himself and his old ally, Edward Lytton [Bulwer*]'.[5] He voted for the bill's passage, 21 Sept., and Lord Ebrington's confidence motion, 10 Oct. He divided for the second reading of the revised bill, 17 Dec. 1831, its details, including the enfranchisement of Tower Hamlets, 28 Feb.,[6] the third reading, 22 Mar., and Ebrington's motion for an address asking the king to appoint only ministers committed to carrying an unimpaired measure, 10 May 1832. His only other known votes were with ministers on the Russian-Dutch loan, 26 Jan., 12 July. He was named to the select committee on the renewal of the East India Company's charter, 27 Jan. 1832.

Villiers wrote to lord chancellor Brougham in January 1832 requesting that if he should 'ever wish for any man willing to work and anxious to earn his hire, to fill any place which may be at your disposal', he might 'take my case into consideration'. He explained that

> owing to my constant attendance in the House last year, for the purpose of giving my support to the reform bill, I was prevented applying to my profession so closely as I was wont to do. I was compelled to absent myself both from the sessions and from the circuit. It even happened that the week the circuit was at Exeter ... was the exact week in which the debate upon Saltash ... came on. As my colleague does not support ministers thoroughly, I was entreated to remain in town. Your Lordship is aware how prejudicial it is to a man working his way at the bar to absent himself from his sessions or circuit. I fear that I may be called upon again this year to make the same sacrifice, for my constituents are very much discontented at finding Saltash in schedule A.[7]

No offer was apparently forthcoming, but Villiers was relieved of his constituency obligations by the Reform Act. His subsequent choice of seats to contest was singularly unfortunate. He was returned for Canterbury in 1835 as 'a decided advocate of triennial parliaments and vote by ballot, a staunch friend to civil and religious liberty, a resolute economist, and a determined abolisher of unearned pensions', only to be unseated on petition. In 1841 he was elected at Sudbury, but this was later declared void and the constituency disfranchised for gross venality.[8] He evidently did not persevere at the bar, and was reportedly living at Genoa in the 1860s. By the time of his death in 1872 he had become Frederick Villiers Meynell; his widow Anna resided in London and Nice.

[1] *Al. Cant.* [2] PROB 11/1567/198. [3] Brougham mss, Ellice to Brougham, 2 May; *Western Times*, 7 May 1831. [4] *The Times*, 12 July 1831. [5] *Disraeli Letters*, i. 146. [6] *The Times*, 1 Mar. 1832. [7] Brougham mss, Villiers to Brougham, [Jan. 1832]. [8] *The Times*, 7, 9, 10 Jan., 27 Mar. 1835, 15 Apr. 1842.

T.A.J.

VILLIERS, Hon. John Charles (1757–1838).

OLD SARUM	6 Jan. 1784–1790
DARTMOUTH	1790–1802
TAIN BURGHS	1802–24 May 1805
QUEENBOROUGH	1807–1812
QUEENBOROUGH	1820–7 Mar. 1824

b. 14 Nov. 1757, 2nd s. of Thomas Villiers[†], 1st earl of Clarendon (*d.* 1786), and Lady Charlotte Capel, da. (and coh. of her mother) of William, 3rd earl of Essex, and 1st w. Jane, da. of Henry Hyde[†], 4th and last earl of Clarendon. *educ.* Eton 1766; St. John's, Camb. 1774; L. Inn 1774, called 1779. *m.* 5 Jan. 1791, his cos. Maria Eleanor, da. and coh. of Adm. Hon. John Forbes, MP [I], 1da. *d.v.p. suc.* bro. Thomas Villiers[†] as 3rd earl of Clarendon 7 Mar. 1824. *d.* 22 Dec. 1838.

KC duchy of Lancaster 1782-6; surveyor of woods in northern parts of duchy 1786-1825; comptroller of household Feb. 1787-Feb. 1790; PC 19 Feb. 1787; member, bd. of trade 1790; c.j. in eyre north of Trent 1790-*d.*; prothonotary of common pleas, co. of Lancaster 1804-*d.*; minister plenip. to Portugal Nov. 1808-Feb. 1810; clerk of the peace, Lancs. 1825-*d.*

Col. 1 fencible cav. 1794-1800, Mdx. yeomanry 1803.

Recorder, New Windsor 1789-1806; town clerk, Wootton Bassett 1794-*d.*

At the general election of 1820, Villiers, whose brother held the revived earldom of Clarendon and had an estate at The Grove, Watford, Hertfordshire, resumed a parliamentary career which had begun in the first weeks of Pitt's minority administration by securing (after a break of eight years) his second return for the government borough of Queenborough. Armed with two sinecures worth almost £5,000 a year, he was 'one of the treasury phalanx'.[1] He paired against economies in revenue collection, 4 July 1820. He voted in defence of ministers' conduct towards Queen Caroline, 6 Feb., against a revision of official salaries, 30 Mar., and repeal of the additional malt duty, 3 Apr., and for the alien office grant and the payment of arrears on the duke of Clarence's annuity, 29 June 1821. He was on the government side in the divisions on tax reductions, 11, 21, 28 Feb., the joint-postmastership, 13 Mar., Irish tithes, 19 June, the lord advocate's dealings with the Scottish press, 25 June, the Canada bill, 18 July, and the aliens bill, 19 July 1822. In his only known speech in this period, 5 July, he welcomed 'the liberal contributions now making for the sufferers in Ireland, and for which every post showed the inevitable necessity'; and he was named to the select committee on employment of the poor there the following year.[2] Charles Rose Ellis* wrote to Lord

Granville, 6 Sept. 1822, that the offer of the exchequer with the lead of the Commons to George Canning
was 'little short of an insult (and I am very glad to find
John Villiers entertains the same feeling, for I know
no one whose bias is usually so strongly in favour of
Canning's accepting office on almost any terms)'.[3] He
voted against repeal of the Foreign Enlistment Act, 16
Apr., and inquiries into the legal proceedings against
the Dublin Orange rioters, 22 Apr., and chancery
administration, 5 June 1823. He evidently remained
neutral on Catholic relief.

After succeeding his brother as earl of Clarendon in
early 1824 he took little active part in politics, though
he continued to exercise control over the corporation
and one parliamentary seat at Wootton Bassett. He
supported the Whigs in power from 1830, but in 1835
urged Sir Robert Peel* to defy the odds against his
ministry in the Commons, as Pitt had done in 1784.[4]
When corresponding with Dr. Butler of Shrewsbury
on endowed schools in 1820 he stressed the importance
of 'implanting and cultivating a due disposition of
piety in the useful [sic] breast'; and he largely devoted
his later years to the promotion of religious and charitable causes, which were deemed to have suffered 'a
very serious loss' by his death in December 1838.[5]
He was succeeded in his titles and estates, but apparently not in his fortune (which went to his wife and
her family), by his nephew George William Frederick
Villiers (1800-70), the defeated candidate at Newport,
Isle of Wight, in 1831, who capped his ministerial
career as lord lieutenant of Ireland, 1847-52.[6] The
4th earl's brothers were Thomas Hyde Villiers* and
Charles Pelham Villiers, who had been unsuccessful at
Hull in 1826, but sat as a Liberal for Wolverhampton
from 1835 till his death in 1898.

[1] *Black Bk.* (1823), 200. [2] *The Times*, 6 July 1822. [3] Harewood
mss WYL 250/8. [4] *Holland House Diaries*, 244-5; Add. 40418, f.
263. [5] Add. 34585, ff. 40-42, 51, 61; *The Times*, 28 Dec. 1838; *Gent.
Mag.* (1839), i. 207-8; *DNB*; *Oxford DNB*. [6] *CP*, iii. 271.

D.R.F.

VILLIERS, Thomas Hyde (1801–1832), of 8
Suffolk Street, Haymarket and 6 Cleveland Court,
Westminster, Mdx.

HEDON	1826–1830
WOOTTON BASSETT	1830–1831
BLETCHINGLEY	18 July 1831–3 Dec. 1832

b. 27 Jan. 1801, 2nd s. of Hon. George Villiers† (*d.* 1827)
and Hon. Theresa Parker, da. of John Parker†, 1st Bar.
Boringdon. *educ.* at home and by Thomas Wright Hill at
Kensington, Mdx.; St. John's, Camb. 1817; L. Inn 1831.
unm. d. 3 Dec. 1832.

Jun. clerk, colonial office 1822-4, sen. clerk 1824-5; sec.
to bd. of control May 1831-*d.*

Agent, Berbice and Newfoundland ?1825.

Villiers's courtier father, known to his family as
'The Governor', was appointed paymaster of marines
in 1792. It emerged in 1810 that his official accounts
were in chaos and that, as a result of incompetence
rather than criminality, he was in default to the tune
of over £200,000. He duly resigned but, as a royal
favourite, suffered no worse consequences than public
humiliation.[1] For the last 17 years of his life he was
precariously sustained by an allowance from his eldest
brother Thomas, 2nd earl of Clarendon, and the proceeds of two colonial sinecures. From 1812 he and
his family shared Kent House, Knightsbridge, with
the family of his wife's brother the 1st earl of Morley,
Canning's close friend. The distractions of Villiers's
financial problems and poor health limited his authority over his children, who were influenced more significantly by their forceful and intelligent mother, the
'Queen Bee'.[2] In 1819 she told Morley that her second
son Hyde, who had been too delicate to follow his elder
brother George to Christ's Hospital, 'would have
been fit for nothing if he had gone to *any* school'.[3] At
Cambridge, where he became friendly with Thomas
Macaulay* and other serious-minded young men,
'Comely Villiers with his flaxen hair', who was constantly encouraged and hectored by his mother, sought
to repair the defects of his early education.[4]

On leaving university Villiers, whose elder brother
was set up in the diplomatic service in 1820, idled for
a while before entering the colonial office as a junior
clerk, earning £150 a year, in October 1822. George
IV, who had a soft spot for his father, was keen for provision to be made for his younger brothers Charles
and Edward; and when, through Canning's influence,
a commissionership of customs was in the offing for
George in 1823, his mother speculated that if she could
'get anything better for Hyde' she 'should not despair
of getting Edward into Hyde's shoes'. Nothing came
of this and Villiers, who was promoted to senior clerk
with £600 a year in January 1824, stayed at the colonial office.[5] In August 1824 he was in Corfu, whence he
wrote to Canning's secretary Stapleton of his fear that
the naval force at the disposal of the Ionian authorities
would not be sufficient to cow the belligerent Greeks.[6]
He became friendly with his junior colleague Henry
Taylor, who in old age recalled him as follows:

Hyde's face was that of a fair and distinguished looking
child grown to the stature of manhood (he was very tall),

with as little alteration as might be of its delicate features. He had a large forehead, large eyes, and a sensitive mouth beautifully chiselled. He was slenderly made, with a feminine roundness of the muscular fabric. His manners ... were invariably highbred, and under all ordinary circumstances expressively courteous. He was calm, self-governed, ambitious, but with a far-sighted ambition, caring little for present, unless in so far as they might conduce to ultimate results; cool and not vain, patient and resolute, enduring bodily pain with unshaken fortitude, and encountering danger and difficulty with an undisturbed mind.[7]

His family's recent political tradition was Tory, but his mother was more liberal and, like her, he sympathized with Queen Caroline in 1820.[8] He and his brother Charles mixed in London with Macaulay, Austin, Romilly, Strutt and other young men of progressive views, who associated with James and John Stuart Mill and subscribed to Benthamite ideas. He was a member of the debating society promoted by the younger Mill and in March 1825, according to Taylor, made a splash there with a speech on colonization, which was 'able, orderly, and distinct; with no grace of language other than harmony and simplicity'. Yet soon afterwards Villiers reproved Taylor, with whom he shared a house in Suffolk Street, for imputing to him 'further community' with the 'Utilitarians' than he was prepared to avow.[9] Certainly he was no doctrinaire, and his political opinions remained somewhat indeterminate. He left the colonial office on account of poor health in July 1825, having secured the agencies of Berbice and Newfoundland to keep his head above water.[10]

At the general election of 1826 he stood for the venal borough of Hedon as a supporter of the Liverpool ministry. Whether he denounced Catholicism, as was alleged, is not clear; but his brother Charles, who unsuccessfully contested neighbouring Hull at the same time, was equivocal in his pronouncements on the subject. Villiers was returned in second place and survived a petition alleging bribery.[11] According to his elder brother's biographer, Villiers had, before standing, accepted an offer to defray all his expenses by a loan of money from 'a certain wealthy young peer', an unsuccessful suitor of his sister Maria Theresa, 'the pleasantest girl in London'. Evidently this benefactor, contrary to what he had led Villiers to expect, renewed his courtship of Theresa after the election. In 1827 unpleasant rumours began to circulate concerning the nature of the bargain and George Villiers, head of the family after their father's death in March, was obliged to intervene. He demanded from the peer immediate settlement of the unpaid expenses to 'secure Hyde from a recurrence of those distressing difficulties which have been as detrimental to his credit as the

reports circulated against him have been to his honour' and gave a personal pledge for full repayment of the debt as soon as circumstances permitted, 'to relieve Hyde from an obligation, the contracting of which I fear he will long have cause to regret'.[12]

Villiers, who seems to have been somewhat loosely associated with Canning, did not immediately draw attention to himself in the House. One observer had noted that as he had his agencies, 'if he fails as a speaker he is only where he was'.[13] He was probably the 'very clever and agreeable' Mr. Villiers encountered by Mrs. Arbuthnot at a gathering of ministerialists at Hatfield House in January 1827.[14] He voted for Catholic relief, 6 Mar. 1827. He spoke in favour of the sale of game bill, 7 June, and voted in the minority against the Coventry magistracy bill, 18 June 1827.[15] Immediately after Canning's death, when it was falsely rumoured that Wilmot Horton was to resign as under-secretary for war and colonies, Stapleton observed to Huskisson that Villiers had acquired 'a great reputation for understanding the business of that office'.[16] Early in 1828 he travelled in Ireland with George, who was engaged there on the work of unifying the two excise boards, concluded that 'Catholic emancipation *must* be granted, or a convulsion ensue' and marvelled that the Wellington ministry 'stands still, looking on, and doing nothing'.[17] He spoke and voted for relief, 8, 12 May 1828. His attempts to amend Gordon's pauper lunatics bill, 27 Mar., and the government's offences against the person bill, 23 May, were unsuccessful; in the latter case, ministers thought his proposal to transport offenders found guilty of wounding in cases where, had death ensued, the charge would have been manslaughter, was too dangerous an extension of the present law. He divided with government against inquiry into chancery delays, 24 Apr., and ordnance reductions, 4 July; but he voted for Otway Cave's corporate funds bill, 10 July, and was in the minority on the silk duties, 14 July. He voted for the usury laws amendment bill, 19 June 1828. Lord Colchester listed him among 'the *rump of the Canning party*', but Lord Palmerston did not include him in his own similar list.

A letter of early 1829 from Villiers to George in Ireland, which indicated the government's sentiments on Catholic relief, came to the attention of Richard Sheil*, who used it to hasten the voluntary dissolution of the Catholic Association.[18] Villiers voted for emancipation, 6, 30 Mar. 1829, when he declared that 'there never was a period when the country had more reason to be satisfied with its House of Commons'. He voted against the continued exclusion of O'Connell, 18 May. On 12 Mar., as a member of the select committee which had recommended a bill to regulate the supply of corpses for anatomical research, he advocated such a measure. After it had been dropped he was named to the revived committee, 7 Apr., and helped to steer the new bill through the House. On the Newfoundland fisheries bill, 7 Apr. 1829, he deplored ministers' failure to promise an inquiry into 'the whole condition of the colony'. The following year he protested to the colonial office against the French assumption of sovereign fishing rights along the Newfoundland coast, but could not persuade the government to intervene.[19] He voted against Lord Blandford's parliamentary reform scheme, 18 Feb., but for the enfranchisement of Birmingham, Leeds and Manchester, 23 Feb. 1830. He was in the opposition minority for a revision of taxation, 25 Mar., and voted to end capital punishment for forgery, 24 May. In June 1830 he sent to the home secretary Peel, at the request of the author, a copy of the second edition of his friend Professor John McCulloch's *Principles of Political Economy*.[20] On the 15th he moved for information on the state of Britain's commercial relations with Portugal, having been twice frustrated earlier in the session and so prevented from now calling for an inquiry, as he had originally intended. He condemned the Methuen treaty of 1703, which gave Portuguese wines an unfair advantage over superior French products, and stressed 'the immense importance to this country of our continuing to extend our markets' and 'unlocking the trade with France'. The speech made a considerable impact, as Monckton Milnes noted: 'They are talking much of a Mr. Hyde Villiers, who seems to have made a great impression on the House. He has been four years in Parliament, and never had an opportunity of making himself heard'.[21]

At the general election of 1830 Villiers abandoned Hedon and came in for Wootton Bassett, where his uncle John, 3rd earl of Clarendon since 1824, had a strong interest.[22] In his calculation of gains and losses Brougham reckoned Villiers as a ministerialist, but government listed him as one of the 'doubtful doubtfuls'. He was absent from the division on the civil list which brought them down, 15 Nov. 1830. On 14 Dec. 1830, speaking from the Grey ministry's benches, he expressed reservations about Littleton's proposed bill to increase the penalties on employers who paid wages in truck. He voted for the second reading of the ministerial reform bill, 22 Mar., and against Gascoyne's wrecking amendment, 19 Apr. 1831. At the ensuing general election Clarendon denied him backing at Wootton Bassett for supporting reform. He went to the poll, but was defeated..[23] His hopes of a seat for St. Ives came to nothing and an offer of one for Saltash, subsidized by government, was rejected by his brother for reasons 'connected with family feelings and arrangements'.[24]

Immediately after the elections he was chosen by Lord Grey 'on the grounds of his parliamentary reputation' to become secretary to the board of control in the room of Lord Sandon*, who resigned because he could not support reform. Lord Holland noted that he was 'reported as clever, and entitled to reward from the reformers, having lost his seat in support of that cause'; while Greville wrote:

> Hyde Villiers has been appointed to succeed Sandon ... as a Whig and a reformer. He was in a hundred minds what line he should take, and had written a pamphlet to prove the necessity of giving ministers seats in both Houses as in France, which he has probably put in the fire. I am very glad he has got the place; and though his opinions were not very decided before, he has always been anti-Tory, and has done nothing discreditable to get it, and it was offered to him in a very flattering manner.[25]

There was talk of his being put up for Liverpool, where a seat was surplus to requirements, but there were, as Grey noted, 'great objections on account of his situation at the India board'. In the event government secured and financed his return for Bletchingley on the Russell interest.[26]

On 25 July 1831 Villiers was attacked in the House by George Richard Robinson as a sinecurist who, as agent for Newfoundland, had 'not been of the slightest service' to the colony. The under-secretary Lord Howick repeated a previous statement that since his appointment to the board of control Villiers, whose services to Newfoundland he praised, had ceased to draw his £300 salary as agent; the agency for Berbice, it seems, had been abolished earlier. Villiers then spoke in his own defence and the matter was dropped. Next day he was added to the select committee on the East India Company. On 22 Aug. he appealed for support for the government's bill to equalize, in accordance with his own suggestion of the previous year, the duties on French and Portuguese wines. He voted steadily with his colleagues for the reform bills throughout the sessions of 1831 and 1832 and was present for all the other divisions on party issues for which full lists have been found. He voted in favour of public inquests, 20 June, and opening the inns of court to merit, 17 July 1832.

Villiers was one of only two Members to whom Mill thought 'there would be the least use' in Gustave D'Eichthal sending a copy of the Saint-Simonian journal *Le Globe*.[27] Although he spoke only occasionally on Indian matters in 1832, he was immensely busy. Possibly prompted by his friend Nassau Senior, in January 1832 he suggested the appointment of a royal commission on the poor laws, which the government put in place two months later.[28] In addition to the demands of parliamentary attendance and the dispatch of routine official business, his time was consumed by the organization and supervision of the work of the East India committee, renewed on 28 Jan. 1832.[29] His chief, Charles Grant*, was notoriously feckless and Villiers, as Taylor wrote, had the 'perpetual toil' of forcing him to make decisions, 'a waste of time and spirits which those only can estimate who have known what it is to act under the inactive and decide for the indecisive'. Taylor continued:

> These burthens he bore with a steady and invariably tranquil outward demeanour, never complaining of them as oppressive, partly perhaps from a feeling that it was injurious to a man's reputation to have it supposed that he felt his business to be too much for him. But in point of fact, whilst there was an excess of energy in his mind, there was too little elasticity. He became more and more deeply involved in intellectual labours, from which he could not or did not withdraw himself for intervals of relaxation.[30]

He had problems with Robert Gordon*, a new commissioner of the board, who, according to Macaulay, was trying to reduce him to the status of 'a mere copying clerk'.[31] He also had the vexation of securing a seat in the first reformed Parliament. He declined an invitation to stand for Perth because he had hopes of Lymington, but these were dashed.[32] He was unwell with 'a stomach complaint' at the end of July and 'very ill' two months later, when Macaulay was 'seriously alarmed about him'. Despite suffering agonies from an abscess in his head he travelled to Cornwall in mid-November to canvass Penryn. He seemed to have every chance of success but, broken down by his exertions, he fell into a coma and died, unmarried and intestate, at Carclew, the seat of Sir Charles Lemon*, 3 Dec. 1832.[33] His effects were sworn under a meagre £800, 6 May 1833.[34] Villiers, who was reckoned to have 'fallen a victim to his zealous and indefatigable discharge of his public duties', was considered 'a great loss, not only to his friends, but to the public service'.[35] Raikes described him as 'a young man of very superior talents' and Denis Le Marchant[†] as one 'of great promise', whose 'industry and clear understanding, set off, as they were, by a most pleasing address and considerable powers of speaking, had already marked him for political eminence'.[36] Mill wrote to Carlyle:

> One of the most likely *doers* among the young men, the only one among the official young men, has departed from us ... He was an earnest workman, who would have plied his trade of politics honestly, and if not with first rate talents, yet with such as well used had been sufficient to do much. Take him for all in all we shall not soon find his equal among that class of men.[37]

[1] *HP Commons, 1790-1820*, v. 452-4. [2] Maxwell, *Clarendon*, i. 8-30; G. Villiers, *A Vanished Victorian*, 28-30, 35-38. [3] Add. 48232, f. 236. [4] *Oxford DNB*; Maxwell, i. 17-21; *Three Diaries*, 283. [5] *Prince of Wales Corresp.* viii. 3425; Maxwell, i. 46. [6] *Canning Official Corresp.* i. 222-4. [7] *Taylor Autobiog.* i. 74-75. [8] Maxwell, i. 12; Villiers, 46. [9] *Taylor Autobiog.* i. 75-77, 86; J.S. Mill, *Autobiog.* (1924), 54-56, 88; *Taylor Corresp.* 4-5. [10] *Gent. Mag.* (1833), i. 84. [11] *Hull Advertiser*, 9, 16, 23 June 1826; M.T. Craven, *New Hist. Hedon*, 136, 141, 146-8. [12] Maxwell, i. 57-59; *Fox Jnl.* 112. [13] Northumb. RO, Middleton mss ZMI/5/76/52/8. [14] *Arbuthnot Jnl.* ii. 73. [15] *The Times*, 8 June 1827. [16] Add. 38750, f. 36. [17] Villiers, 63. [18] W. T. McCullagh, *Mems. Sheil*, ii. 57. [19] A.H. McLintock, *Establishment of Constitutional Government in Newfoundland*, 118-19. [20] Add. 40400, ff. 196, 198. [21] Reid, *Monckton Milnes*, i. 100. [22] Cent. Kent. Stud. Stanhope mss U1590 C318/2, Mahon to Lady Stanhope, 5 July [1830]. [23] *Devizes and Wilts. Gazette*, 28 Apr. 1831. [24] *R. Cornw. Gazette*, 30 Apr.; Aberdeen Univ. Lib. Arbuthnot mss 3029/3/1/1; Brougham mss, Ellice to Brougham [2 May 1831]. [25] *Gent. Mag.* (1833), i. 84; TNA, Granville mss, Holland to Granville [?13 May 1831]; *Greville Mems.* ii. 147-8. Greville's reference to Villiers's pamphlet may be the basis for the statement in M. Brock, *Great Reform Act*, 181 that Villiers 'saw the defects of the bill, and indeed wrote a pamphlet about them'. Brock, who mistakenly describes Lord Clarendon as Villiers's father, suggests that as 'an aspirant for office' his support for reform 'may not have been wholly disinterested'. [26] Grey mss, Stanley to Grey, 22 May, reply, 27 May, Ellice to Grey [7 Nov.]; St. Deiniol's Lib. Glynne-Gladstone mss 198, T. to J. Gladstone, 29 May; Brougham mss, Ellice to Brougham [17 May 1831]; *Macaulay Letters*, ii. 31. [27] *Mill Works*, xii. 90. [28] P. Mandler, *Aristocratic Government in Age of Reform*, 135; Grey mss, Villiers to Howick, 19 Jan. 1832. [29] NLW, Harpton Court mss C/571, Villiers to Lewis, 21 Dec. 1831; Grey mss, same to Howick, 4 Feb. 1832. [30] *Taylor Autobiog.* i. 147-50. [31] *Macaulay Letters*, ii. 139-40. [32] *Corresp. of Southey with Caroline Bowles* ed. E. Dowden, 243-4, 248; *The Times*, 15 Dec. 1832. [33] *Macaulay Letters*, ii. 157, 158, 179, 196, 208-9; *The Times*, 24 Nov., 4, 6 Dec. 1832. [34] PROB 6/209/294. [35] *The Times*, 8 Dec. 1832. [36] *Raikes Jnl.* i. 117; Le Marchant, *Althorp*, 467; *Three Diaries*, 282-3. [37] *Mill Works*, xii. 134.

D.R.F.

VILLIERS, Visct. *see* **CHILD VILLIERS, George Augustus Frederick**

VILLIERS STUART, **Henry** (1803–1874), of Dromana, co. Waterford and Bramfield, Herts.

CO. WATERFORD	1826–25 June 1829
BANBURY	1830–19 Apr. 1831

b. 8 June 1803, 1st s. of Lord Henry Stuart and Gertrude Emilia, da. and h. of George Mason Villiers, 2nd Earl Grandison [I]. *educ.* Eton c.1816-19; Christ Church, Oxf. 15 Dec. 1820. *m.* [illegit.] 12 Jan. 1826,[1] Theresia Pauline Ott of Vienna, 1s. 1da. *suc.* fa. 1809. Took name of Villiers before Stuart by royal lic. 17 Nov. 1822; *cr.* Bar. Stuart De Decies [I] 10 May 1839. *d.* 23 Jan. 1874.
Ld. lt. co. Waterford 1831-*d.*, Waterford city 1832-*d.*; col. Waterford militia.
PC [I] 1837.

Villiers Stuart was orphaned in 1809 by the death of his father and shortly afterwards his mother, from whom he inherited the Dromana estates of his grand-father Earl Grandison. On coming of age in 1824 he made Dromana his main residence, began lavishly entertaining, and instructed his agents to issue new leases and attend to the neglected registration of his tenants, over 600 of whom were soon on the county Waterford rolls. By August he had been appointed to the grand jury and at the end of the year he joined the Catholic Association.[2] During the rumours of a dissolution in the autumn of 1825, he started campaigning against the anti-Catholic sitting Member Lord George Beresford with the assistance of a committee of local Catholic activists led by Thomas Wyse*, who described him as 'young', 'untried', and 'inferior indeed, in the ... possession of government patronage, in high title, and in extensive pecuniary resources, to his adversary'.[3] His public proposal not to oppose Beresford if he abandoned his opposition to Catholic claims was rejected as 'insidious and offensive', whereupon he formed a junction with the other pro-Catholic sitting Member, Richard Power.[4] On 28 Dec. 1825 he advised one of his supporters that he had yet to 'receive a invitation to the Catholic dinner', adding, 'It is what I would willingly avoid attending but for the proverb "needs must", etc.'[5] At the 1826 general election he came forward as a liberal Protestant supporter of Catholic emancipation, appealing to the freeholders not to be intimidated by the 'unconstitutional' appointment of a stipendiary magistrate and an 'army of troops' at the behest of the Beresfords. After an 'astonishing' nine-day contest, noted for its humiliation of the Beresfords and desertion of the Catholic tenantry from their Protestant landlords, he was returned in second place with the assistance of Daniel O'Connell* and other leaders of the Association, in what became celebrated as the *Bliain an Stuaird* (year of Stuart). At the declaration he promised to support tax reductions and 'to oppose any administration that did not make emancipation the *sine qua non* of its policy'.[6] A petition against his return complaining of bribery and interference by the priests came to nothing. The settlement of his election expenses, somewhat improbably estimated at £30,000 in 1829, plagued him for years. On a visit to Waterford in April 1828 he was 'besieged' in the 'most violent manner' by a mob of furious creditors, from whom he had to be 'rescued' by a special constable before fleeing to Dromana. That year he sold his Hertfordshire property.[7]

In his maiden speech, 12 Feb. 1827, he urged the necessity of emancipation, disputing claims that Catholic doctrines were 'totally incompatible with the British constitution' and contrasting the enlightened rule of India and Canada with the 'persecution and oppression' of Ireland. He was in the opposition minority against the grant to the duke of Clarence, 16 Feb. He asserted that there was no surer way to abolish the Association than to remove Catholic disabilities, 2 Mar. In what George Agar Ellis* considered an 'admirable' speech, 5 Mar., he defended the conduct of the Catholic priests in the Irish elections against the 'groundless aspersion and unmerited obloquy' of defeated anti-Catholic candidates, asking, 'Could it be expected that in England any candidate would be elected whose interests ... were directly opposed to those of his constituents? Why should it then be expected in Ireland?'.[8] He 'manfully defend[ed] his allies the priests without offending the House, who hate them', commented Sir James Mackintosh* that day. 'Villiers Stuart, quite a boy in appearance ... made a very good speech', remarked John Hobhouse*, adding, 'Brougham said it was the best maiden speech that had been made for twenty years'. 'The latter part ... was good', but 'he has the most affronting impudence', John Robert Townshend* informed Henry Fox*.[9] On 16 Mar. he presented and endorsed a constituency petition against the appointment of a stipendiary magistrate and 'additional military' during his campaign, condemning the Irish government's actions as 'unconstitutional', 'uncalled for' and 'one of the boldest attacks on the pure administration of justice', and successfully moved for related papers. (The previous October he had signed a requisition for a county meeting on the issue.)[10] Reporting his remarks to Lord Wellesley, the Irish viceroy, 19 Mar., Goulburn, the Irish secretary, complained:

> He was unnecessarily violent in his expressions, both as regarded you ... and myself, but the fact is that Mr. Stuart is a vain young man who will when he grows older receive a severe rebuff if he pursues a similar line of conduct. I thought it better to treat what he said as the speech of a young man and rather to express surprise at the tone of his expression after the kindness which he had received from you ... than to express any indignation ... If it had been possible to divide the number who voted with him would have been extremely limited.[11]

On the 25th he joined Brooks's, sponsored by Lords Jersey and Duncannon*. He divided for information on the Lisburn Orange procession, 29 Mar., against the supplies, 30 Mar., and for inquiry into chancery delays, 5 Apr. He welcomed the formation of the Canning ministry, which had the 'general approbation' of the Irish population, and presented a constituency petition for Catholic claims, 8 May.[12] He divided for the disfranchisement of Penryn, 28 May 1827.

Following the accession of the Wellington ministry, 5 Feb. 1828, he explained that although he had changed seats 'twice' he had 'never changed sides':

> When I entered the House, I found the government of Lord Liverpool ... decidedly against ... Catholic claims. I was therefore opposed to it. In the governments of Mr. Canning and Lord Goderich ... there was ... a preponderance in favour of ... Catholic claims, and I felt it my duty to support them ... It is my fixed resolution to oppose the present government as being composed of as anti-liberal materials as ... could possibly have been got together.

He presented constituency petitions for relief that day and 1 May, and voted accordingly, 12 May. He presented but dissented from a petition for repeal of the Irish Subletting Act, which he believed was 'better calculated' than any other measure to 'benefit and strengthen the impoverished population', 19 Feb. He recommended a 'well organized scheme of emigration' to 'alleviate' the surplus population of Ireland that day, and denied claims that the passenger regulation bill would impede voluntary emigration, 18 Mar. He voted for repeal of the Test Acts, 26 Feb. Commenting on the arrival in London of Madame Wyse, the estranged wife of Wyse, 29 Feb., Lady Holland informed her son that 'the *on dit*, though don't say it I beg, is that she is under the protection of Villiers Stuart'.[13] He presented and endorsed a constituency petition for repeal of the 'cruelly oppressive' Irish Vestry Act, 20 Mar. He voted to disfranchise East Retford in favour of a large unrepresented town, 21 Mar., 27 June. He was in the minorities against chancery delays, 24 Apr., and for the more efficient recovery of customs penalties, 1 May. On 9 May he argued that the Union had failed to produce benefits for Ireland, warned of growing agitation for its repeal and demanded that England and Ireland be placed on an equal constitutional footing. 'Young Villiers Stuart was fluent and showed some talent', noted John Croker*.[14] He voted to censure public expenditure on Buckingham House, 23 June, and for inquiry into Irish church pluralities, 24 June. He presented a petition against slavery, 3 July. He divided for ordnance reductions, 4, 7 July, but defended the grant for the survey of Ireland, asserting that 'more litigation arises ... from a want of good a survey than from any other cause', 7 July. He demanded a 'quick' implementation of the Irish butter trade bill that day and 10 July. Following the establishment of the County Waterford Brunswick Club that October, he published a letter in the press to Dr. Kelly, the Catholic bishop of Waterford, condemning the 'formation of illiberal and bigoted clubs', renewing his £20 subscription to the Catholic Association and asserting his 'determina-

tion to oppose every ministry, however formed, which continued to withhold ... the rights and privileges of a free state' from the Catholics, 3 Nov. 1828.[15] He signed the Protestant declaration in support of emancipation at the end of that year.[16]

Villiers Stuart welcomed the Wellington ministry's 'enlightened' concession of emancipation and declared his willingness to accede to the accompanying securities, including the suppression of the Association to which he belonged, 10 Feb. 1829. He presented favourable petitions, 20 Feb., 19 Mar., 2 Apr., and voted accordingly, 6 Mar., when he praised 'ministers, who regardless of personal considerations, have had the magnanimity to sacrifice their bonds to party to secure the internal prosperity of the nation', and 30 Mar. He dismissed a hostile constituency petition as 'unrepresentative', 9 Mar. In what Edward Smith Stanley* deemed 'an admirable speech in the point of boldness and effect', he regretted that the concession was accompanied by 'so unpalatable a measure' as the disqualification of the 40s. freeholders, which in other circumstances he would have opposed, but urged its acceptance, 19 Mar.[17] On 7 May he presented a petition and argued for the introduction of a system of Irish poor laws, which would promote an 'increased circulation of money' and industry, but on finding little support withdrew his motion for inquiry. In his last known vote of this Parliament, he divided to allow O'Connell to take his seat unhindered, 18 May 1829.

On 6 May, in what O'Connell considered 'a dereliction of duty' and the *Waterford Mail* ridiculed as 'a suicidal act of patriotic heroism', Villiers Stuart had unexpectedly announced in the press his intention to resign, citing the 'pain' of having to acquiesce in the disfranchisement of the 40s. freeholders, by whom he had been 'so proudly returned', and his inability to continue as their representative. Declining to offer again, he explained that he could no longer 'make an effectual registry'. 'The opinion gains ground that Stuart will not vacate until the next meeting of Parliament', noted a Beresford agent, 16 June, adding that 'his friends' had 'asked him not to vacate until then'. To O'Connell's 'great annoyance', however, on 25 June he took the Chiltern Hundreds, amidst reports that he had been 'bought out' by ministers in return for elevation to his grandfather's dormant peerage or a safe borough seat, and had received 'hard cash' from the Beresfords to alleviate his financial difficulties. (His creditors had met earlier that month to appoint representatives.) In response, he vigorously denied having had any 'communication ... with any party or parties whatsoever', but refused to comment further.

His retirement has 'occasioned some perplexity' and 'rewards his friends by leaving them in the lurch at the mercy of the common enemy', observed *The Times*, adding that if he had 'made a secret bargain ... it would indeed be a paltry job'.[18] 'I do not think my friend Villiers Stuart's resolution an unwise one', Thomas Spring Rice* later remarked, noting his own disaffection with life in the Commons, but after visiting Ireland that October he returned 'in the same ignorance ... of the motives which induced [him] to give up his county'.[19] On 6 Oct. Lord Beresford reported hearing that Villiers Stuart had 'again taken it into his head to start as a candidate for the county', and thought 'there is some appearance of it from his returning there, and giving notice for the registry ... though it is uncertain what he is about'.[20] Speculation that he would offer again, however, came to nothing and he 'considered it unadvisable' to attend a meeting later that month about the ensuing 1830 by-election, in which he kept a low profile.[21] It was feared by the Beresfords that he would be 'a powerful antagonist' against them at that year's general election, but in the event he remained neutral.[22]

At the general election he was returned unopposed for Banbury as the nominee of his first cousin, the 2nd marquess of Bute.[23] He presented constituency petitions against slavery, 4, 10 Nov. 1830. Next day, when he was appointed to the select committee on the Irish poor, he defended the Irish Subletting Act as the 'poor man's best and only security ... against injustice and extortion' by landlords, and urged its amendment rather than repeal. He had been listed by Henry Brougham* as one of the incoming Members likely to oppose ministers but by the Wellington ministry one of the 'good doubtfuls', and he voted in their minority in the crucial division on the civil list, 15 Nov. He was granted a month's leave on account of ill health, 22 Nov. 1830. On 10 Feb. 1831 he presented a Carrickfergus petition complaining of forged names on a petition against the return of Lord George Augusta Hill. He pressed O'Connell about whether it was his intention to bring forward the repeal question, 4 Mar. In his last known speech, 21 Mar., he explained that in order to defend his 'constituents' on the corporation of Banbury, he would vote against the second reading of the Grey ministry's reform bill, but that he 'would be worse than a hypocrite ... to deny' that he personally approved of the measure and would relinquish his seat as soon as practical. He divided accordingly next day. That month Wyse suggested that he come forward for county Waterford as a 'champion of the popular cause' against Beresford at the next election, but he declined, 3 Apr., explaining that a

'constant attendance in the House' was 'altogether incompatible with the preservation of my health, suffering as it still does ... from the ... cramp by which I was attacked last year in Paris'.[24] On 19 Apr. 1831, three days before the dissolution, he took the Chiltern Hundreds.

He was appointed the first lord lieutenant of county Waterford, 17 Oct. 1831, and Waterford city, 2 May 1832.[25] Defending his selection on non-partisan grounds in the House, 6 Oct. 1831, Sir John Newport explained that he had 'only been a temporary Member ... in consequence of the expense he had incurred in a contested election' and that he was the 'proprietor of a very large and valuable estate' in the county, where he would now 'take up ... permanent residence'. In July 1832 he successfully quashed mass anti-tithes rallies in the county, urging the necessity of 'less intimidating meetings'.[26] Responding to applications from his uncle Lord James Stuart and Lord Lansdowne for him to be given a peerage that year, Lord Grey explained that nothing would him 'greater pleasure' than to assist 'a person so strongly recommended', but he was 'beset with applications' and could only add his name to the list.[27] At a Dublin dinner held in his honour in 1836 he spoke with 'extreme violence of language' against Lord Lyndhurst and the Conservative dominated Lords for pursuing a 'campaign of hatred' against Ireland.[28] Two years later a well-wisher informed him of a private dinner at which O'Connell had spoken 'most warmly as to the generous and noble part you had acted in emancipating your country', observing that 'when the history of the struggles' came to be recorded, it would 'not be forgotten that you, in taking your stand against the oppressors ... had to cast away the prepossessions and prejudices of *"your order"*, upon whom you waged war'.[29]

Villiers Stuart, whose younger brother William sat as a Liberal for county Waterford, 1835-47, was given an Irish barony by the Melbourne administration in 1839.[30] On his death in January 1874 his estates passed to his eldest son Henry Windsor Villiers Stuart (1827-95), Liberal Member for county Waterford, 1873-4, 1880-5, who, finding no proof of his parents' marriage, was unable to succeed to the barony, which became extinct.[31]

---

[1] No records survive of the marriages that allegedly took place at the Roman Catholic chapel of St. James's, Spanish Place, and in Scotland under Scottish law (*CP*, xii, pt. 1, pp. 408-9). [2] NLI, Villiers Stuart mss 24682, 24685, 24686, 24691; F. O'Ferrall, *Catholic Emancipation*, 121. [3] T. Wyse, *Hist. Catholic Association*, i. 267. [4] Add. 40381, f. 208; Villiers Stuart mss 24682, Facthlegg House agreement, 25 Aug. 1825. [5] Villiers Stuart mss 24682, Stuart to Sir William Homan. [6] *Dublin Evening Post*, 15, 22 June, 1 July;

Waterford Chron. 29 June, 1 July 1826; M. Kiely and W. Nolan, 'Politics, land and rural conflict in county Waterford, c.1830-1845', in *Waterford Hist. and Society* ed. W. Nolan and T. Power, 460. [7] *Waterford Chron.* 28 Nov. 1826; *The Times*, 12 Apr. 1828, 20 July 1829. [8] Northants. RO, Agar Ellis diary, 5 Mar. 1827; *The Times*, 3, 6 Mar. 1827. [9] Add. 52447, f. 51; 52017, Townshend to Fox, 5 Mar. 1827; Broughton, *Recollections*, iii. 173. [10] Villiers Stuart mss 24690, requisition to Henry Bush, 28 Oct. 1826. [11] Add. 37305, f. 53. [12] *The Times*, 9 May 1827. [13] *Lady Holland to Son*, 77. [14] *Croker Pprs.* i. 418. [15] *Dublin Evening Post*, 8 Nov. 1828. [16] Wyse, ii. p. ccxxvi. [17] Brougham mss, Smith Stanley to Brougham, 20 Mar. 1829. [18] *Waterford Mail*, 13, 24, 27 June, 1 Aug. 1829; NLI, Wyse mss 15028 (4), Power to Wyse, 19 June 1829; *O'Connell Corresp.* iv. 1583; *The Times*, 16 June 1829. [19] NLI, Spring Rice mss Ms. 549; Derby mss 920 Der (14) 63. [20] PRO NI, Pack-Beresford mss D664/A/100. [21] *The Times*, 17 Oct. 1829. [22] Pack-Beresford mss A/154, 158. [23] *Jackson's Oxford Jnl.* 7 Aug. 1830. [24] Wyse mss 15024 (13), Villiers Stuart to Wyse, 3 Apr. 1831. [25] Villiers Stuart mss T. 3131/I/2/1, 2. [26] Kiely and Nolan, 468. [27] Lansdowne mss, Grey to Lansdowne, 16 Jan. 1832. [28] *The Times*, 29 Sept. 1836. [29] Villiers Stuart mss T.3131/I/1/6. [30] *The Times*, 4 May 1839. [31] *Oxford DNB* sub Henry Windsor Villiers Stuart.

P.J.S.

VINCENT, **Sir Francis**, 10th bt. (1803–1880), of Debden Hall, nr. Saffron Walden, Essex.

ST. ALBANS   1831–1834

b. 3 Mar. 1803, 1st s. of Sir Francis Vincent, 9th bt., of Stoke d'Abernon, Surr. and Debden Hall and Jane, da. of Hon. Edward Bouverie[†] of Delapre Abbey, nr. Northampton. *educ.* Eton 1817. *m.* 10 May 1824, Augusta Elizabeth, da. of Hon. Charles Herbert[†], capt. RN, 1da. *suc.* fa. as 10th bt. 17 Jan. 1809; grandmo. Mary Vincent (née Chiswell) to property at Debden 1826.[1] *d.* 6 July 1880.
Cornet 9 Drag. 1818, ret. 1821.

Vincent belonged to a very old family, which had possessed land in Leicestershire in the early fourteenth century, migrated to Northamptonshire and settled in Surrey, where the estate of Stoke d'Abernon, near Leatherhead, came into their hands by marriage into the Lyfield family. The baronetcy was conferred on Francis Vincent, later Member for Surrey, in 1620. His direct descendants, the 5th, 6th and 7th baronets, made financially advantageous marriages into London mercantile families; and the 3rd, 5th, 6th and 7th baronets were Members of Parliament. The last, Sir Francis Vincent (*d.* 1775), this Member's great-grandfather, sat for Surrey from 1761 until his death. His son and successor, Sir Francis Vincent, who was born in 1747, married in 1779 Mary, the daughter and heiress of Richard Muilman Trench Chiswell, Member for Aldborough, 1790-7, whose Essex estate at Debden thus came to the Vincents.[2] Sir Francis, who was supposed to have kept as a mistress a Mrs. Harris, one of the women debauched by James Hare[†]

during his Cambridge days, was appointed resident consul at Venice in February 1791, but died there only 18 months later.[3] Like his two predecessors, he died intestate. His son Sir Francis Vincent, 9th baronet, was born in 1780, educated at Cambridge and called to the bar from Lincoln's Inn in 1804. His wife of only two years died the following year. He was a Whig in politics, and on the formation of the Grenville ministry in February 1806 he gave up the law to accept an appointment as under-secretary at the foreign office under Fox. He remained there under Fox's successor Lord Howick (subsequently 2nd Earl Grey). Nothing came of a plan to find him a seat at the 1806 general election, and he went out of office on the fall of the government in March 1807.[4] He was admitted to Brooks's, sponsored by Lord Fitzwilliam, three months later. He died, aged 28, 17 Jan. 1809, 'after four days illness, brought on by a cold, with which he had been some time affected'. He too had not made a will, and administration of his estate, which was sworn under £7,000, was granted to his mother, Dame Mary Vincent, the guardian of his infant boys Francis and Edward William.[5] She survived until 1826.

After Eton, Francis Vincent had a perfunctory career in the cavalry. The Stoke d'Abernon estate had been disposed of by the time of his marriage into another Whig family, soon after coming of age, in 1824.[6] He had joined Brooks's the previous year. At the general election of 1831 he stood as 'a staunch reformer' for the open and venal borough of St. Albans, where he was returned with a barrister of the same politics after a contest with the Tory sitting Member.[7] He lost no time in making his parliamentary debut, speaking in support of the second reading of the Grey ministry's reintroduced reform bill, 5 July, when he gave it his 'cordial support'

> not because the system of representation has grown materially worse of late years, but ... [because] the eyes of the people are opened to its defects, and ... it is no longer possible to persuade them that the system works well for the nation, however it may for the governors, which has crippled and paralyzed its resources, and brought upon it an overwhelming burden of debt.

An effective reform, he contended, would ensure that the people would 'no longer give a willing ear to those wild theories which have been propounded to them for the last 15 or 20 years by various political quacks'. He voted for the bill next day, and went on to give general support to its details, though he cast wayward votes for the disfranchisement of Saltash, 26 July, against the division of counties, 11 Aug., against giving borough freeholders a county vote, 17 Aug., for the enfranchisement of £50 tenants-at-will, 18 Aug., and for the disfranchisement of Aldborough, 14 Sept. On 29 July he argued that the partial disfranchisement of Maldon would not adversely affect the agricultural interest in Essex, being more than compensated for by the addition of two county Members and the opening of Harwich. He voted for the passage of the bill, 21 Sept., and the motion of confidence in the government, 10 Oct. He divided against ministers in favour of a reduction in the grant for civil list pensions, 18 July. He made much of this vote at a constituency dinner for his supporters, 30 July, and also paid tribute to the power of the press as 'an overwhelming and irresistible instrument when employed to effect *good*'.[8] On Hume's presentation of a petition complaining of prosecutions for the sale of unstamped pamphlets, 5 Sept., Vincent observed that

> the more restraints are put upon the diffusion of knowledge by means of the press, the more ingenious and the more numerous will be the devices resorted to for the purpose of evading the laws imposing those restrictions.

He was in the minority for printing the Waterford petition for disarming the Irish yeomanry, 11 Aug., but sided with government on the Dublin election controversy, 23 Aug. He was chosen to second the address, 5 Dec., when he declared that the recent Cambridgeshire by-election proved that there was 'no symptom of that reaction [against reform], which some would fain pretend to have taken place'. He voted for the second reading of the revised reform bill, 17 Dec. 1831, gave it steady support in committee and divided for its third reading, 22 Mar. 1832. He was named to the select committee on the East India Company, 27 Jan. He spoke and voted in defence of ministers on the Russian-Dutch loan, 26 Jan., and divided with them on relations with Portugal, 9 Feb. He presented a St. Albans petition in favour of the factories regulation bill, 28 Feb., and one from interested landowners against the London and Birmingham railway bill, 4 Apr. He voted in Hunt's minority of 31 for inquiry into Peterloo, 15 Mar., but was in the ministerial majority on the navy civil departments bill, 6 Apr. On 18 Apr. he declared his 'deep interest' in 'the fate of unfortunate Poland', and contended that it was time to 'make a stand' against Russian aggression. He took the same line when supporting George Evans's motion on the subject, 7 Aug: 'there are some persons in this House who do not think that truckling to a powerful and ambitious nation is the best mode of preserving peace'. He voted for the address calling on the king to appoint only ministers who would carry the reform bill unimpaired, 10 May, and spoke at the

St. Albans meeting on the subject, 16 May.[9] He voted for the second reading of the Irish bill, 25 May, but was one of O'Connell's minority for the enfranchisement of £5 freeholders, 18 June. He secured returns of information on the New South Wales veteran companies, 22 May, and voted to make coroners' inquests public, 20 June. He voted against ministers in favour of a speedy abolition of slavery, 24 May, the suspension of flogging in the army, 19 June, and to reduce the barracks grant, 2 July; but he paired with them on the Russian-Dutch loan, 12 July, and voted with them in person, 16, 20 July. To confirm his alignment with the radical wing of their supporters, he spoke and voted against the Greek loan, 6 Aug. 1832.

At the St. Albans reform festival, 28 June 1832, Vincent declared his intention of standing for the borough at the forthcoming general election:

> He had been sent to Parliament a pledged man, but had not been obliged to profess doctrines and opinions which he had formerly condemned. His political principles were the same as they had ever been – they were the principles of a Chatham, a Fox, a Grey, a Brougham.[10]

He topped the poll, but stood down in 1834. He subsequently became the author of triple-decker, silver fork novels, producing *Arundel, a Tale of the French Revolution* in 1840, and four others, equally execrable, in a late burst of creativity between 1867 and 1872. He seems to have spent much time in the fashionable watering-holes of Europe: Greville encountered him at Baden-Baden in 1843, and the opening scene of his last novel, *The Fitful Fever of a Life*, was set in one of the gambling halls there. Indeed, according to Captain Gronow, Vincent was one of the many victims of the 'French hell' of the Salon des Etrangers in Paris: he 'contrived to get rid of his magnificent property and then disappeared from society'.[11] Gronow's assertion is given credence by the fact that Vincent seems to have died intestate, in the family tradition, in July 1880. Debden Hall passed to his only child Blanche, the wife of John Raymond Trevilian. The baronetcy was assumed by his cousin, the Rev. Frederick Vincent (1798-1883).

[1] PROB 11/1709/121. [2] T. Wright, *Essex*, ii. 141. [3] *Glenbervie Diaries*, i. 1. [4] *HMC Fortescue*, ix. 42, 421. [5] *Gent. Mag.* (1809), i. 94; PROB 6/185/705. [6] *VCH Surr.* iii. 458; Nottingham Univ. Lib. Portland mss PwL 253-6. [7] *The Times*, 25, 29 Apr.; *County Herald*, 30 Apr., 7 May 1831. [8] *County Press*, 2 Aug. 1831. [9] *County Herald*, 1 May 1832. [10] *County Press*, 3 July 1832. [11] *Greville Mems*. v. 111; *Gronow Reminiscences*, i. 122. *CB*, i. 159 assumes Vincent's father to be the subject of Gronow's allegation; but chronology and the context of the story point to Vincent himself.

D.R.F.

VIVIAN, Sir Richard Hussey (1775–1842), of Beechwood House, nr. Lyndhurst, Hants.[1]

TRURO	1820–1826
NEW WINDSOR	1826–3 Feb. 1831
TRURO	1832–1834
CORNWALL EAST	1837–1841

b. 28 July 1775, 1st s. of John Vivian of Truro, vice-warden of the Stannaries, and Betsy, da. of Rev. Richard Cranch, vic. of St. Clement's, nr. Truro, Cornw. *educ.* Truro g.s. 1783; Lostwithiel g.s. 1784-7; Harrow 1789; Exeter Coll. Oxf. 1790. *m.* (1) 14 Sept. 1804, Eliza (*d.* 15 June 1831), da. of Philip Champion De Crespigny† of Aldeburgh, Suff., 2s. 3da. (1 *d.v.p.*); (2) 10 Oct. 1833, Letitia, da. of Rev. James Agnew Webster of Ashfield, co. Longford, 1da. KCB 2 Jan. 1815; KCH 1816; *suc.* fa. 1826; *cr.* bt. 19 Jan. 1828; GCH 1831; *cr.* Bar. Vivian 19 Aug. 1841. *d.* 20 Aug. 1842.

Ensign 20 Ft. 1793; lt. Independent Ft. July 1793, 54 Ft. Oct. 1793; capt. 28 Ft. 1794; capt. 7 Drag. 1798, maj. 1803; lt.-col. 25 Drag. 1804; lt.-col. 7 Drag. 1804-15; a.d.c. to prince regent 1811; col. army 1812; maj.-gen. 1814; col. 12 Lancers 1827; lt.-gen. 1830; col. 1 Drag. 1837-*d.*

Equerry to prince regent 1812-20, to George IV 1820-30; inspector gen. of cavalry 1825-30; groom of bed-chamber 1830-7; c.-in-c. [I] 1831-6; PC [I] 23 July 1831; master-gen. of ordnance May 1835-Sept. 1841; PC [GB] 27 May 1835.

Vivian belonged to the Trewen branch of a very old and extensive Cornish family. His great-grand-father was Thomas Vivian (1685-1759), of Kenwyn, Truro, whose only son and namesake was vicar of Cornwood, Devon, from 1747 until his death in 1793. His eldest son, John Vivian, this Member's father, was born in 1750. He became an adventurer in Cornish copper mines in 1771 and acquired a personal stake in about eight. In 1785 he co-operated with Matthew Boulton of Birmingham and Thomas Williams† of Anglesey to form the Cornish Metal Company, which had offices in Truro and was intended to divide the national copper market between the producers of Cornwall and Anglesey. Five smelting companies agreed to process its ores at fixed prices. Various problems arose, and in 1790 Vivian and Williams engineered a new arrangement, which effectively put an end to the Metal Company. Vivian, who was an agent for Williams's Parys Mine Company and a partner in the Truro Miners' Bank of Willyams and Company, gave some controversial evidence before the Commons select committee on the copper mining industry in 1799. The following year he transferred his interest in the Hayle smelting works to that run by the Cheadle Copper Company at Penclawwd, near Swansea.[2]

Richard Hussey Vivian, his eldest son, made an educational visit to France in 1791. He was initially destined for the law, in the footsteps of his great-uncle, Richard Hussey, Member for three Cornish boroughs, 1755-70, and attorney-general to the queen, 1761-70, after whom he had been named, and in 1793 he was articled to a Devonport solicitor as a preliminary to entering the Middle Temple. He preferred, however, a military career, on which he embarked in July that year. He saw much action in Flanders in 1794, was stationed at Gibraltar, 1796-8, and went on the Helder expedition in 1799. During a period at home, 1799-1808, he made a runaway marriage and cemented his friendship with Lord Paget† (later marquess of Anglesey), his colonel in the 7th Dragoons. In the autumn of 1808 Vivian commanded the regiment in Spain, where he performed with distinction in covering the retreat to Corunna. Back in England, he was Paget's second in his duel with Captain Cadogan, 30 May 1809.[3] Vivian's father had made him a partner in the Penclawwd smelting business, and that year he became one, with his younger brother John Henry (1785-1855), in the family's new and larger scale enterprise at nearby Hafod.[4] He served in Ireland, 1800-13, and was made an aide-de-camp (1811) and equerry (1812) to the prince regent. He went to Spain in August 1813 and took command of cavalry brigades. A bad wound received during the advance on Toulouse, 8 Apr. 1814, forced him to return home, where he was knighted and put in charge of the Sussex military district. In April 1815 he joined Wellington's army in Belgium as a commander of a brigade under Paget. He missed the action at Quatre Bras, but played a significant role at Waterloo, for which he was voted thanks by both Houses of Parliament. He was with the army of occupation until 1818.

At the general election that year he stood for his native town of Truro, a corporation borough, where his father was the focus of local opposition to the controlling interest of Lord Falmouth, under the patronage and encouragement of the regent's crony Lord Yarmouth*, warden of the Stannaries. Vivian and his colleague were beaten by one vote, and the petition lodged on their behalf was rejected.[5] In 1819, he was given a command in the north, where he dealt with disturbances in and around Newcastle and Glasgow, whence he issued his initial address when offering again for Truro at the 1820 general election. On his arrival, he stressed his local connections and deplored the Cato Street conspiracy and the prevalence of blasphemy and sedition, though he refused to pledge himself as to his future conduct. He was returned at the head of the poll.[6] General Grant, who 'knows Sir Hussey Vivian well', told Mrs. Henry Bankes that he 'believes him to be opposition in grain when he dares to follow his own inclination. Should this turn out so, Lord Yarmouth will have made a bad exchange for his master'.[7] As it was, Vivian proved to be a reliable supporter of Lord Liverpool's ministry, if not the most assiduous of attenders. He was a teller for the government majority against inquiry into military expenditure, 16 May, and on 14 June 1820 spoke against opposition proposals for army reductions, arguing that it was 'the duty of government to protect the well-affected' and asserting that many of the inhabitants of the Glasgow area had 'forgotten their duty to their magistrates, to their ministers, and even to their God'. His frequent letters to his brother, who managed the smelting business and extended it to Liverpool, Birmingham and London and greatly increased its profitability, contained copious advice on matters appertaining to it, and Vivian himself sometimes dealt in London with various problems as they arose, including negotiations with other copper manufacturers.[8]

A spectator at the trial of Queen Caroline in the Lords,[9] he voted in defence of ministers' conduct towards her, 6 Feb. 1821. He voted against the principle of Catholic relief, 28 Feb., but according to Charles Williams Wynn*, he indicated his 'intention of not voting in the committee' on the relief bill.[10] He presented a Truro petition for relief from agricultural distress, 1 Mar.[11] Opposing army reductions, 12 Mar., he criticized the 'inconsistency' of opposition Members who, while they urged ministers to intervene on behalf of the liberals of Naples, 'would refuse that amount of military force which was essential to enable government to prosecute such a war with effect'. At the same time, as he later explained to his brother, he suggested that 'the events now passing in Italy were such as ought to be viewed with a most jealous eye and might very probably before long demand an interference, however ministers might at present be disposed to avoid it'. This observation, he admitted, 'very much annoyed' Lord Castlereagh, the foreign secretary, though a week later he flattered himself that the minister must now be 'satisfied I was not far wrong'.[12] When opposing a further call for army reductions, 14 Mar., Vivian, goaded by Hume, declared that he was 'a sincere supporter' of the government. He raised a laugh with his mockery of the notion that to save money, cavalry going on foreign service should take no horses with them: 'they were to learn to ride in this country, and when they went abroad they were to take

their saddles on their backs till they met with horses to their liking'.[13] He voted against repeal of the additional malt duty, 3 Apr., and on 1 May drew attention to the 'great hardship' suffered by major-generals on half-pay. He was given six weeks' leave, 4 May, on account of the illness of his youngest brother Thomas, whose death in Truro in September 1821 he witnessed.[14]

He voted against more extensive tax reductions, 21 Feb., and relaxation of the salt duties, 28 Feb. 1822. He said that army economies had been 'carried as far as they possibly could', 4 Mar., and thanked ministers for having adopted his suggestion that half-pay major-generals should receive their full regimental allowance. He 'hoped that the advantages of a good and general system of equitation for the cavalry would never be given up', 15 Mar.[15] He paired against Canning's bill to relieve Catholic peers of their disabilities, 30 Apr. He denied that agricultural distress was caused by excessive taxation, scorned Wyvill's scheme for large remissions and supported the government's modest adjustment of the corn laws, 9 May. He presented a Truro petition for repeal of the salt duties, 20 May 1822.[16] He was given a week's leave to attend to urgent private business, 17 Feb. 1823. He divided with government against repeal of the assessed taxes, 18 Mar., and of the Foreign Enlistment Act, 16 Apr., inquiry into the prosecution of the Dublin Orange rioters, 22 Apr., and Scottish parliamentary reform, 2 June 1823. He led the resistance to Hume's proposal to ban corporal punishment in the army, 15 Mar. 1824, and was a teller for the majority. Later that day he successfully opposed Hume's bid to end the 'farce' of commission purchase certificates. He voted to go into committee on the usury laws repeal bill, 8 Apr., but was listed in the majority against the second reading of the reintroduced measure, 17 Feb. 1825. With a growing family, his finances were in some disarray (his father had long felt that he and John Henry were 'spending much more than we ought') and in August 1824 he staked his claim with the king for the governorship of the Royal Military College, or a suitable alternative command:

> The state of my finances make it absolutely necessary that I should take some steps in order to relieve myself from difficulties which will otherwise oppress and inconvenience me ... Unless a man makes known his wishes ... he is constantly passed over under the impression that he desires to remain unemployed.[17]

The College was spoken for, but Vivian was made inspector-general of cavalry towards the end of the following year.

He voted for the Irish unlawful societies bill, 25 Feb., and against Catholic relief, 1 Mar., 21 Apr., and the Irish franchise bill, 26 Apr., 9 May 1825. He presented a constituency petition against Catholic claims, 2 May.[18] On 28 Feb. he asked ministers not to reduce the import duty on foreign copper below a level which would afford fair protection for Cornish producers. With the county Members and Pascoe Grenfell, Member for Penryn and a commercial rival, he saw Huskisson, the president of the board of trade, on the subject, 4 Mar., when he learnt that the duty was to be halved. He told his brother that this, by opening the way for large quantities of South American produce, would 'make a strange revolution in the copper trade', of which it was 'hardly possible to say what will be the consequence'. Although he personally had 'no great fear' of the results, he was seriously alarmed at the prospect of any further diminution; and it was with the intention of forestalling such a development that he spoke at some length on its effects on the Cornish industry, 25 Mar., though he expressed approval of the ministry's 'general policy' of relaxing restrictions on commerce. Vivian, who had strongly advised his brother against becoming involved in speculation in South American mining ventures – 'be content to go on with the copper trade, where we well know what we are about' – complained particularly of the threat posed by the South American Mining Company.[19] He brought up Cornish petitions against any alteration of the corn laws, 28 Apr.,[20] and the following day unsuccessfully opposed the third reading of Stuart Wortley's game laws amendment bill. He voted for the duke of Cumberland's grant, 30 May, 2 June 1825.

When a dissolution was expected in the autumn Vivian, on military duty in Newcastle, and already assured of a return for Windsor on the Court interest, announced that he would not stand again for Truro, where his position had been undermined by Lord Falmouth. He asserted that 'on all great questions' he had supported 'an administration under whose guidance the country had risen to a state of prosperity its most sanguine friends had not anticipated' and reiterated his hostility to Catholic claims.[21] Soon afterwards Mrs. Arbuthnot (whose stepson was later to marry Vivian's eldest daughter) visited him at his New Forest residence at Beechwood, but it was Lady Vivian who left the more abiding impression on her, as

a very pretty woman, a great coquette ... [who] practises her art with great success on my eldest brother ... I don't like her at all, for she is the most complete Mrs. Candour I have ever met with, and an amazing gossip. He is a good-natured, rough hussar.

(Vivian himself wrote that his wife was 'violent, jealous and touchy, but she has a good heart at bottom and is

open and honourable to an extreme'.)[22] The commercial crisis of December 1825, which for a time seemed to threaten the Truro bank, took him to London and prompted him to urge his father and brother, without success, to get 'well out' of banking and restrict their activities 'simply to the copper trade'. Indeed, as he told his brother, he could envisage their eventual withdrawal from direct involvement even in the latter, though he did not labour the point:

I am very delicately circumstanced. It is a profitable concern and a safe one and I know not how money could be better laid out ... but still I have invariably said that I have no right to expect you to work for me and my family, whilst on the other hand I have no right to press giving up that which is of more importance to you than to me.[23]

He said in the House that a story of the victimisation of a trooper in the 10th Hussars by his adjutant had been much exaggerated, 28 Feb., 6 Mar. 1826, when he also defended the grant for the Royal Military College. On 3 Mar. he acknowledged the general efficiency of yeoman cavalry but thought it desirable that they should be inspected by regular officers. He voted with ministers in defence of the Jamaican slave trials, 2 Mar., but presented a Truro petition for abolition, 20 Apr.[24] It was almost certainly Sir Richard Vyvyan, Member for Cornwall, rather than he who voted against the corn bill, 11 May. Vivian was nettled to be lectured by his brother, at the age of 51, on the dangers of gambling, to which he denied being in any way addicted. He conceded that John Henry was 'quite right as to my having a fine income on which I ought to live, and so I determine to do, but I have many demands on me'. He pleaded this excuse when, admitting that 'I am a careless fellow about money', and 'I have spent very much more than I ought to have done', he had to ask his brother to help him out of a scrape with his army agent's bills at the end of May 1826:

I could sell Beechwood and take a small house in town and live no doubt on £2,000 a year ... I could get a command and go either to the East or West [Indies] but this would be for ever separating myself from the man in the world I love best ... To accept it would be to bury my father as far as I am concerned whilst he yet lives. I could live at Beechwood on a somewhat reduced establishment, but it would be out of the question to live in the county and give up its amusements ... My present income is however more than equal to such an expenditure as I should require. The difficulty is to meet the incurred debt. I could give up Windsor [which would initially cost him about £1,000], but were I to do so I might offend the king, and moreover sacrifice that which may be of use to myself and my family, the interest and consequence that it necessarily gives me ... I hardly know what I had best do, and therefore beg of you to consider for me, and above all things *do not lecture me for that would only add to my misery without convincing me of my folly one jot more than I am already convinced of it, or make me more sensible than I am of the necessity of retrenchment.*[25]

He was duly returned for Windsor at the general election two weeks later, when he promised on the hustings to 'oppose Catholicism and to support the Protestant faith'.[26] Not long afterwards Vivian, who was pessimistic of his chances of managing on £2,000 a year, as his brother suggested, was again 'in a great stew' over the bank.[27] His anxiety on this score was ended by his father's death from the effects of an accident, 7 Dec. 1826, which terminated the Vivians' involvement in it. By his father's will, Vivian was entitled to an equal share with John Henry in his 'chattels'. He proved it, under £14,000, 12 Feb. 1827, but subsequently left the estate unadministered.[28]

He denied Hume's allegation of chicanery in the placing of soldiers on the retired list, 19 Feb. 1827.[29] He opposed a call for the abolition of army flogging, which was essential to 'maintain a proper degree of discipline', 26 Feb., and again, 12 Mar., when he said that pro-abolition speeches created disaffection in the ranks and thus necessitated the infliction of exemplary punishment. He only paired against Catholic relief, 6 Mar., at a time when he was 'very unwell',[30] but he voted in person for the duke of Clarence's annuity, 16 Mar. On 22 Mar. he defended and praised the conduct of Anglesey's brother, Sir Edward Paget†, commander-in-chief in India, in suppressing the mutiny at Barrackpoor. Next day he opposed the spring guns bill. He had egged on Anglesey to seek the master-generalship of the ordnance when it was vacated by Wellington's anticipated appointment as commander-in-chief on the death of the duke of York. Ministers initially frustrated Anglesey, but in the uncertain situation created by Liverpool's stroke Vivian urged him to attach himself personally to the king and to steer clear of the aristocratic Tory cabal, led by Rutland and Londonderry, which was working to prevent Canning from becoming premier:

I am no Canningite myself and I should be very glad to see a government formed the principles of which should in many respects differ from the present, but my fear is that the day is not yet arrived when it can be brought about.

He regretted Peel's resignation on personal grounds, and felt that he and the other anti-Catholic seceders would only drive Canning into the arms of the Whigs and thus 'actually go to force on the country the very measure that they deprecate and also force it on the

king'.[31] To the latter he made known Anglesey's wish to support Canning's administration. When Anglesey was duly appointed master-general it was widely assumed that Vivian would become clerk or secretary of the ordnance; but he told his brother that he had 'refused everything but the lieutenant-generalship', where no change was made.[32] It was probably Vyvyan who voted against the third reading of the Penryn election bill, 7 June. In October 1827 Mrs. Arbuthnot noted that Anglesey, backed by the king, was trying to have his 'dear friend and toady' Vivian made commander-in-chief in Ireland, but that Wellington was determined to prevent it. In any case, Vivian's lack of rank as a 'young major-general' was a decisive factor against him.[33] The following month he accepted the Goderich ministry's offer of a baronetcy, which had once been declined by his father.[34]

In January 1828 he wrongly predicted that Wellington would form a government

of Ultras ... He is a fool if he does not. The Whigs have cut such a poor miserable figure in many respects that they are very low in estimation, and a good regular Tory administration would have many supporters; besides which a thing of patchwork would never do. It must be one or other, Whig or Tory.

He told his brother that if the new ministry opted for a dissolution, he might well resign his seat, as 'I do not much fancy the Ultra Tories'.[35] The inclusion of the former Canningites, not to mention Anglesey's appointment as lord lieutenant of Ireland, presumably satisfied him. He thought that Admiral Codrington was 'thrown over' in the slighting reference to Navarino in the king's speech.[36] He spoke against army reductions, 22 Feb., arguing that the military shambles of 1793-4 showed the folly of ill conceived cutbacks, and opposed the abolition of flogging, 10 Mar. 1828. He voted against repeal of the Test Acts, 26 Feb., and Catholic relief, 12 May. It was probably Vyvyan who voted against the provision for Canning's family, 13 May. At the end of that month Anglesey was forced to accept Sir John Byng* rather than Vivian, his preference, as Irish commander-in-chief.[37] Vivian objected to Stuart Wortley's bill to legalize the sale of game, which he said would encourage poaching, 13, 24 June. Although he favoured inquiry into the nature of the Holdsworth family's long monopoly of the governorship of Dartmouth Castle, 20 June 1828, he deplored the abolition of such means of keeping deserving officers from penury. Later that day he defended the grant for Chelsea Hospital.

He spoke against further reductions in the cavalry, 20 Feb. 1829. The patronage secretary Planta predicted that he would side 'with government' for Catholic emancipation; and on the motion to consider it, 6 Mar., he rose after Anglesey's son, Lord Uxbridge, who opposed it, to speak at some length in its support on pragmatic grounds. At the same time, he made it clear that he swallowed it with 'great reluctance' and expressed strong reservations, based largely on his suspicion of the Irish Catholic agitators. The backbencher Hudson Gurney thought this 'proved it was against the grain at headquarters'. His vote for emancipation that day was the only one he cast. Three years later he bragged that in this speech, he had accurately 'foretold [Daniel] O'Connell's present course'.[38] Replying to his brother's compliments on his performance, he observed that

it contained my honest sentiments. What I used to say was that I hoped to be [a] Member of Parliament, a lieutenant-general and a GCB. As to the future, God knows. The duke of Wellington will never bring me into office. Was Lord Anglesey [recently recalled from Ireland] to come into power I might no doubt have a high office. He asked me two days since if I would under such circumstances take office. To that I replied, with him but not else. Strange things, depend on it, will take place before 12 months pass over. I expect in the first instance a ministry of Ultra Tories, and then if the duke of Clarence comes to the throne I expect Lord Anglesey will come in as a liberal.[39]

He voted in the minority for the issue of a new writ for East Retford, 2 June 1829. When his brother sent him an alarming account of a 'falling off in our trade' that month, Vivian told him that

come what may there is one mischief which I earnestly entreat you not to incur and that is loss of health by worrying ... Times must be bad indeed if between us, what with soldiering and coppering, we cannot raise the wind to maintain ourselves and our children out of a joint purse.

He advised against joining forces with the Grenfells, if the difficulty proved to be anything more than a temporary reflection of commercial depression, and suggested that their own agents, James Palmer Budd and Octavius Williams, should be made partners (which they were in 1831). In December 1829 the Vivians withdrew from the Association of Copper Companies.[40]

Vivian voted against the transfer of East Retford's seats to Birmingham, 11 Feb. 1830. He objected to opposition pressure for further army reductions, 19 Feb., when he said that ministers had done everything possible to economize and welcomed their new regulations for military pensions. Opposing inquiry

into the state of the nation, 18 Mar., he insisted that distress was not as intense or widespread as was alleged and that there was 'still an elasticity, a spring of health within the country'. He dismissed protection, retrenchment and currency reform as panaceas. He gave the House the benefit of his recent researches into distress in Hampshire and Cornwall, undertaken while suffering from an illness which had interfered with his attendance: overpopulation and high prices were largely to blame, but in Cornwall, where distress was negligible, intelligent enterprise and low prices had maintained high levels of employment. He later took credit to himself for having in this speech 'clearly anticipated the outrage' of the 'Swing' disturbances.[41] On 23 Mar. he denied O'Connell's charge that he was the advocate of wage reductions. On the problem of imports of South American ore, he privately thought that unless the Cornish producers were willing to 'make some concessions', such as accepting a lower duty on foreign copper in return for an increase in that on ore, the government would 'yield nothing'. Alarmed by the extravagance of his eldest legitimate son, Charles Crespigny Vivian[†] (1808-86), a cavalry captain of dragoons, who was threatening to 'make ducks and drakes' of his patrimony, Vivian took steps in April 1830 to tighten the reins.[42] He presented a petition from licensed victuallers of Windsor and Eton against aspects of the sale of beer bill, 11 May. He paired against abolition of the death penalty for forgery, 7 June. He defended the army's practice of paying respect to local religious observances when on foreign service, 17 June 1830. That month he was in consultation with ministers over a proposed restriction on smoke emissions from factories, which posed a threat to the Hafod works. A sudden deterioration in his wife's health forced him to leave the problem in the hands of Wynne Pendarves, Member for Cornwall.[43]

Just after the death of George IV Vivian, who was about to lose his inspectorship as a result of his promotion to lieutenant-general, sought to succeed Sir Herbert Taylor[*] as adjutant-general, though not, he stressed, over the head of Taylor's deputy Macdonald, who was duly appointed.[44] Since he was also deprived of his place as an equerry, worth £2,000 a year, he was inclined, as he told his brother, to give up his seat and public life unless he found that there was 'something in reserve' for him, a step which he would 'by no means regret', in view of his wife's parlous condition. He contemplated selling Beechwood and going abroad, but his appointment as a groom of the bedchamber evidently reconciled him to coming in again for Windsor at the 1830 general election, when he explained his reasons for supporting Catholic emancipation.[45] In the wake of the revolution in France he commented that

> it is not possible to look to the state of Europe without fear or exaltation: fear lest the dictation of the people may be carried too far; exaltation that those of France have had courage enough to put down the most outrageous attempt on their liberties ever conceived even in the most despotic times of Napoleon.

He remained intent on selling Beechwood, which was considered to be too damp for his wife's good, but he now thought of wintering in Brighton and Leamington.[46]

Ministers listed him among their 'friends', but, writing from Dover, 9 Nov. 1830, he thought that Wellington 'must go out after his most uncalled for, imprudent and unwise speech about reform'. He later observed that the duke had 'cut his own throat by his silly speech on reform', for 'had he met the wishes and the feelings of the people and come forward with some moderate measure of reform, he might have formed the strongest government possible'. He nevertheless went up to vote with ministers on the civil list, 15 Nov. Two days later he informed his brother:

> If Lord Anglesey takes office – and it has been offered him – he wishes me to come in with him, and although I believe I should be happier and in Eliza's state better perhaps out of office, still for the sake of my children and for other reasons I think I cannot decline. If Lord Anglesey does not take office then I shall resign my appointment as groom and place myself in a perfectly independent position in Parliament, for having paid every farthing of expense for my seat I shall not feel myself bound on all occasions to support Lord Grey.

Depending on which office Anglesey took, Vivian anticipated becoming military secretary at horse guards, lieutenant-general of the ordnance, Irish secretary, commander-in-chief in Ireland or secretary at war. As it was, Anglesey was made lord lieutenant of Ireland and Vivian agreed to take the command there when Byng retired in the spring of 1831.[47] He was at the head of cavalry on guard against disturbances in Hampshire in late November 1830, and on 2 Dec. was given a fortnight's leave on this account.[48] In the House, 13 Dec., he expressed astonishment at Hume's demand for army reductions of 20,000 men and regretted that ministers had not inquired into the causes of unrest:

> I admit that distress has been in some places the cause of the disturbances; but I cannot allow it to have been the only cause, or even the principal ... The truth is, the lower orders have been tampered with ... They have been taught to read, but have not been taught to profit by edu-

cation ... in every little pot-house ... you meet with some of those inflammatory publications that are so common ... The poison has been administered, but the antidote has nowhere been provided – the people have been taught that the distress has arisen from the taxes, and the government have been assailed as the cause, not only out of doors, but by Members of this House, but nowhere have they been taught to understand that if the government were overturned tomorrow their distress would be ten times greater than it has ever been.

He urged ministers and country gentlemen to set aside party rancour and co-operate to restore tranquillity, and recommended a programme of waste cultivation to provide employment. On 23 Dec. 1830 he joined in calls for an adjournment of only two weeks.

Vivian envisaged retaining his seat until he went to Ireland, and perhaps even keeping it then; but in late December 1830 ministers, with the approval of the king, claimed it immediately for Smith Stanley, the Irish secretary, who had been embarrassingly defeated when seeking re-election for Preston. Anglesey was too squeamish to press Byng to bring forward his retirement, even though Byng himself had offered to do so, and took it for granted that Vivian, guaranteed the succession in June, would make no difficulties about surrendering his seat.[49] In fact, he was extremely reluctant to comply, as he made clear first to Smith Stanley and then to Grey, who interviewed him on 9 Jan. 1831, when he moaned about

> the inconvenience of vacating his seat before he was appointed; his liking for the business of Parliament; the belief that he had at Windsor, in consequence of the declarations both of the late king and the present, a seat for life; a hope that he might have retained it, as was done by Sir George Murray; the difficulty that might occur at a new election if a fair and ostensible reason, such as his actual appointment might afford, were not apparent for his resigning it, etc., etc.

He left Grey under the impression that he was 'finally quite satisfied' with the proposal, put to him at Smith Stanley's suggestion, to appoint him to the Irish staff until he took over from Byng, with an additional assurance that if the ministry fell, Smith Stanley would hand the Windsor seat back to him. Yet within hours he wrote to Ellice, the patronage secretary, to rehearse the 'many and considerable' objections which now occurred to him:

> It would in the first place carry with it the appearance of a job ... and perhaps might even be noticed in the House of Commons. In Ireland it might be unpleasant to Byng having me as his successor under his command, and it might be unpleasant to me to be so situated. With a large

family I should have no home to go to on getting there; or if I lived on I should have all the misery of changing in a few months.

He suggested that it would be much simpler if Byng could be persuaded to resign at once, perhaps with the sweetener of the promise of a governorship:

I assure you I grieve most truly at going out of Parliament. It has always been a great object to me to have a seat, and it is by no means incompatible with the command in Ireland ... and moreover I had flattered myself [I] possibly might have been occasionally of some use to you in the House.

At the same time, he acknowledged that, sitting as he did on the Court interest, he had little choice but to acquiesce in the king's wishes; but he told Ellice that he 'must in return, at some future day, if I require it, help me back again into the ... House', possibly for a Cornish borough. Although Grey, in his reply to Ellice, expressed 'some dissatisfaction' at Vivian's conduct, he declined to interfere, and told Anglesey that he was inclined to 'look out for another seat for Smith Stanley and another commander-in-chief'.[50] Vivian evidently agreed to the Irish staff arrangement, for which the king's approval was obtained, 11 Jan., though some objections were raised to it by Lord Fitzroy Somerset*, military secretary at the war office. To Grey's intense annoyance, as he informed Anglesey, Vivian almost immediately afterwards wrote to Ellice from Dover

saying that Lady Vivian is so ill that he cannot leave her and therefore declining the appointment at present; but stating that he holds himself ready, at the meeting of Parliament, to vacate his seat for Windsor. Nobody can be more ready than I am to admit the validity of such an excuse, but coupling it with all that had previously passed, I do not think that we can rely with certainty on his eventually taking over the appointment of commander-in-chief. I have found out, in the course of these proceedings, that he would have preferred a civil to a military office, and that his real wish was to be appointed secretary at war. At all events it is necessary that we should know what we have to count upon.

For his own part, Vivian told his brother, 12 Jan., that he was to go to Ireland in June and that ministers could have his seat now, as 'in poor Eliza's dreadful state I can think of but one thing'. The following day, contemplating her inevitable early death, which would leave him with 'three motherless girls', he confided to John Henry:

I sometimes think I shall give up Ireland altogether and go abroad with my whole family for two or three years.

In short, I know not what to think or determine on. It is a grievous affliction to look forward to, but it must come ere long.

He duly vacated his seat when Parliament met, though he pleaded the desperate condition of his wife, who died five months later, for pulling out of an arrangement to hold Smith Stanley's hand at the by-election.[51]

Vivian took over the Irish command, which brought him £3,600 a year, in addition to £2,600 from his regimental colonelcy and wounds pension, on Byng's retirement, and held it for five years. John Croker*, for one, was 'glad to see a man of decision there'.[52] From Dublin in March 1832 he put something of a gloss on the circumstances surrounding his retirement from Parliament and his appointment to the command by asserting, for public consumption, that Lady Vivian's illness had 'prevented my attending my duty', and that 'immediately before I came to this country I was offered the appointment of secretary at war, but I preferred pursuing the line of my profession': no evidence has been found to substantiate this claim.[53] He was also economical with the truth when, standing for Truro as 'a friend to the great measure of reform' at the 1832 general election, he attributed his resignation from the Windsor seat to a belief that he could not honourably, as Member for that place, act in accordance with his conviction that in 1831 'the time for granting an efficient reform had arrived'. He claimed to have been 'friendly to reform ... throughout his life', to have turned down the offer of a seat in 1802 because it had entailed a commitment to oppose reform, and to have made and kept a promise never to vote against it after his first election for Truro.[54] He was returned after a contest, and his brother came in as a Liberal for the Swansea district, but his eldest son was beaten at Bodmin. Vivian was defeated at the polls in 1835, when his son was successful at Bodmin, was made master-general of the ordnance in Lord Melbourne's second ministry, and successfully contested East Cornwall in 1837. He was created a peer in 1841. John Hobhouse* referred to him the previous year as 'not a wise, though a good man'.[55] Vivian sold Beechwood and bought an estate at Glynn, near Bodmin. In December 1841 he complained to his brother of financial problems and, rather than take the drastic option of selling Glynn, he decided to go abroad for eighteen months in the following spring. He planned to go to Rome and Naples, which he had never seen, but he died at Baden-Baden in August 1842.[56] By his will, dated 24 Sept. 1841, he left his second wife £2,000 and an annuity of £1,500, and smaller annuities to his younger children. By a codicil of 14 May 1842 he devised his property at Newnham, Cornwall, to his second son, John Cranch Walker Vivian (1818-79), who sat as a Liberal for Penryn, 1841-7, Bodmin, 1857-59, and Truro, 1865-71. His share in the family business became part of his residual estate. He was succeeded in the peerage and the Glynn estate by his eldest son. He left £100 as a token of affection to his illegitimate son, Robert John Hussey Vivian (1802-87), who had been brought up as one of the family and, described by Benjamin Disraeli[†] as 'a baddish style of man with his glass always to his eye', found a place in the *Oxford Dictionary of National Biography* on the strength of his services with the Indian army.[57]

---

[1] His grandson Claud Vivian's *Memoir* (1897) covers his life to Waterloo, but deals with the following 26 years in three pages. Vivian's own autobiographical reminiscences, written on 9 Mar. 1832, were published in *Letters of Sir Walter Scott to Rev. R. Polwhele* (1832), 69-79. See also *Oxford DNB*. [2] J.R. Harris, *Copper King*, 43, 56-70, 85, 97-98, 125-6; D.B. Barton, *Hist. Copper Mining*, 24, 36, 56; H. Hamilton, *English Brass and Copper Industries* (1967), 170-1, 176, 183, 197-9, 209, 324; Add. 38421, f. 227; *House of Commons Sess. Pprs. of 18th Cent.* ed. S. Lambert, cxxii. 319-25, 327-8, 346-8, 351, 373, 375, 377-8, 396, 397; *Glam. Co. Hist.* v. 58. [3] *Farington Diary* ed. J. Grieg, v. 175; Mq. of Anglesey, *One-Leg*, 103. [4] *Glam. Co. Hist.* v. 58; Barton, 56. [5] *HP Commons, 1790-1820*, ii. 88; *Late Elections* (1818), 351; *CJ*, lxxiv. 95-96, 393-4, 399. [6] *West Briton*, 11, 18, 25 Feb., 3, 10, 17 Mar.; *The Times*, 4 Mar. 1820. [7] Dorset RO D/BKL, Bankes mss, diary of Mrs. Henry Bankes, 21 Mar. 1820. [8] See NLW, Vivian mss A 997-1261. [9] *Creevey Pprs.* i. 309. [10] Buckingham, *Mems. Geo. IV*, i. 135. [11] *The Times*, 2 Mar. 1821. [12] Vivian mss A 1006. [13] *The Times*, 15 Mar. 1821. [14] Vivian mss A 1008; *Gent. Mag.* (1821), ii. 379. [15] *The Times*, 16 Mar. 1822. [16] Ibid. 21 May 1822. [17] Vivian mss A 1003, 1009; *Geo. IV Letters*, iii. 1175. [18] *The Times*, 3 May 1825. [19] Vivian mss A 1017-23. [20] *The Times*, 29 Apr. 1825. [21] *West Briton*, 16, 23 Sept. 1825. [22] *Arbuthnot Jnl.* i. 417; Vivian mss A 1070. [23] Vivian mss A 1036-44. [24] *The Times*, 21 Apr. 1826. [25] Vivian mss A 1050-4. [26] *Berks. Chron.* 17 June 1826. [27] Vivian mss A 1055-8, 1061-5. [28] PROB 11/1722/121; IR26/1148/93. [29] *The Times*, 20 Feb. 1827. [30] Vivian mss A 1074. [31] Anglesey, 155, 167, 367; PRO NI, Anglesey mss, Vivian to Anglesey, 23 Mar., 12, 13 Apr. 1827. [32] *Geo. IV Letters*, iii. 1315; *Canning's Ministry*, 166; Bagot, *Canning and Friends*, ii. 391. [33] *Arbuthnot Jnl.* ii. 146; Add. 40325, f. 51. [34] Vivian mss A 1079; Durham CRO, Londonderry mss D/LO/C 83 (11). [35] Vivian mss A 1087, 1097. [36] Ibid. A 1092. [37] Add. 40325, ff. 49, 51. [38] *Scott Letters*, 78; Gurney diary, 6 Mar. [1829]. [39] Vivian mss A 1120. [40] Ibid. A 1122; UCNW mss 13069. [41] *Scott Letters*, 78. [42] Vivian mss A 1124. [43] Ibid. A 1126-30. [44] *Taylor Pprs.* 319-20. [45] Vivian mss A 1131, 1132; *Windsor and Eton Express*, 31 July 1830. [46] Vivian mss A 1133-5. [47] Ibid. A 1135b, 1137, 1138. [48] *Three Diaries*, 22. [49] Grey mss, Taylor to Grey, 6 Dec., *Grey-William IV Corresp.* i. 20-21, 32-33; Anglesey mss D619/28A-B/28; 28C, pp. 19-24. [50] NLS, Ellice mss, Vivian to Ellice, 9 Jan.; Anglesey mss 28A-B/32. [51] *Grey-William IV Corresp.* i. 44-46; Anglesey mss 28A-B/34, 36; Vivian mss A 1141, 1142; Derby mss 920 Der (14) 124/4, Vivian to Gosset, 25 Jan., to Smith Stanley, 1, 3, 6 Feb. 1831. [52] *Croker Pprs.* ii. 98. [53] *Scott Letters*, 77, 79. [54] *The Times*, 27 July, 8 Oct., 11 Dec.; *West Briton*, 12 Oct., 16 Nov., 7, 14, 21, 28 Dec. 1832. [55] Broughton, *Recollections*, v. 273. [56] Vivian mss A 1252; *Gent. Mag.* (1842), ii. 542-4. [57] PROB 8/236; 11/1975/141; *Disraeli Letters*, iii. 1089.

D.R.F.

VYVYAN, Sir Richard Rawlinson, 8th bt. (1800-1879), of Trelowarren, nr. Helston, Cornw. and 24 Great George Street, Mdx.

CORNWALL	27 Jan. 1825-1831
OKEHAMPTON	14 July 1831-1832
BRISTOL	1832-1837
HELSTON	1841-1857

b. 6 June 1800, 1st s. of Sir Vyell Vyvyan, 7th bt., of Trelowarren and Mary, da. of Thomas Hutton Rawlinson of Lancaster. *educ.* Harrow 1813-17; Christ Church, Oxf. 1818; grand tour. *unm. suc.* fa. 1820. *d.* 15 Aug. 1879.

Sheriff, Cornw. 1840-1.

Vyvyan was descended from a very old Cornish family who had resided at Trelowarren since the reign of Henry VII: the first baronet had been a Royalist during the Civil War and the third was imprisoned as a Jacobite in 1715. He inherited his father's title and all his freehold estates in January 1820, before he came of age.[1] John Hearle Tremayne, the Tory county Member, visited the 'young baronet' shortly afterwards and wrote that

> I have seldom seen a young man whom I liked better on a short acquaintance. His conversation is very animated and he seems alive on all subjects. I am much mistaken if he does not one day [aspire to] the representation of this county, and I really think it a great thing ... to have the prospect of a person so well able and willing to serve it.[2]

He left Oxford in the summer of 1820 and spent much of the next four years travelling on the continent.[3] In 1823 he was spurned by Lady Frances Stuart, daughter of the marquess of Bute, and wrote an embittered letter to her brother in which he declared that 'all my romantic visions are vanished and I must never more see that person for whom I thought myself born ... I am indifferent about what becomes of me'; he never married.[4] His decision to take up permanent residence at Trelowarren in the autumn of 1824 was propitious, as the death that December of the Whig county Member, Sir William Lemon, created an opening for him. He offered at the resulting by-election on 'principles completely independent ... influenced by no party feeling', although a Whig newspaper claimed that he was 'in the fullest sense of the term, an Ultra Tory, strenuously opposed to every amelioration of existing systems'. He maintained that he was 'attached to the constitution in church and state' which embodied 'the real Whig principles of our ancestors', although the 'party now assuming the name of Whigs had abandoned' them, and he accepted the right of 'Dissenters

... to the participation of civil rights, where they do not admit a foreign influence'. He questioned whether the present prosperity was due to the liberal commercial policy of Lord Liverpool's ministry and promised to oppose it if Cornwall's mining interests were threatened. He was returned unopposed after the Whig, Edward Wynne Pendarves*, declined to be nominated.[5]

He divided against Catholic relief, 1 Mar., 21 Apr., 10 May, and the Irish franchise bill, 26 Apr. 1825. He warned that the free importation of South American copper would 'have the effect of shutting up some of the principal mines of Cornwall', on which 'one fourth of the population' depended for employment, 25 Mar. He voted for the financial provision for the duke of Cumberland, 2, 6, 10 June, but against the judges' salaries bill, 17 June 1825. He divided with the minorities to condemn the Jamaican slave trials, 2 Mar., and against the corn bill, 11 May 1826. In the autumn of 1825 he had canvassed Helston, apparently in search of a safer seat, but he offered again for Cornwall at the general election of 1826. He defended his vote for the Cumberland grant, which was necessary to ensure that the possible future king was educated in England, and denied that he was a ministerial candidate, insisting that his support of the government 'depended on their line of policy'. In fact, 'he did not approve of the present conduct of ministers', who were 'the real authors of all the calamities that had befallen the country', and he condemned their devotion to the 'abstract principles of political economy', which threatened Britain's agricultural and mining interests. He repeated his opposition to Catholic relief, observing that 'they should not as Protestants hate the Catholics' but that 'he distrusted them because they hated Protestants'. He was returned unopposed with Wynne Pendarves after Tremayne retired from the contest.[6]

Vyvyan gradually became more active in his second Parliament and usually served on a couple of select committees each session. He mobilized his supporters to promote petitions from Cornish parishes in favour of agricultural protection, and he presented eight of them, 12, 21 Feb., 8 Mar. 1827.[7] He reported to a constituent that Canning's statement on the corn laws, proposing 'a range of duties like a thermometer', 1 Mar., had satisfied neither the free traders, who considered it 'too favourable to the landed interest', nor the landowners, who were 'inclined to treat the proffered boon with scorn'; the debate had nevertheless been 'carried on with the greatest moderation'. While the proposed sliding scale was 'vastly inferior to the

prohibitory system', he admitted that it did not seem 'altogether bad' if the pivot price was 'placed higher up, say at 65s. or 66s.'. To another correspondent, a week later, he wrote that Canning had 'thrown himself into the arms of the economists' and that 'the struggle will soon begin' as 'we are going to fight the *principle* of the old law and then for 64s. ... instead of 60s.'. He added that 'the country gentlemen are united to a certain degree' and 'we have had some meetings', but 'they all speak at once'; he feared that 'we are not strong in orators'. After the debate he expressed satisfaction that there had been 'no inconsiderable harmony of opinion' among the country gentlemen, which was 'so difficult to obtain in that august body'.[8] He divided against Catholic relief, 6 Mar. He presented petitions from Helston and Truro Dissenters for repeal of the Test Acts, 12 June, having assured one of the organizers that while he objected to Catholic claims on account of 'my conviction that Catholic ascendancy is hostile to civil and religious liberty', the 'same principles' made him 'anxious to witness the extension of liberty of conscience to every individual, and to remove any hindrance to the free exercise of his own form of worship', provided this did not endanger the established church or the constitution.[9] He voted for the spring guns bill, 23 Mar. Early in May he sent information to George Legh Keck, who was preparing the Penryn election bill, to show the effect of throwing open the borough's franchise to the Penwith and Kerrier freeholders, and hoped that 'you will put an end to the system of giving a power to landholders to make votes, by granting small tenements on life leases', as there was 'no system more prejudicial to the independence of a county than the sort of manufacturing of votes which goes on to a great extent where a contest is expected'.[10] He divided against the amended bill, 7 June. In late May he joined a deputation of Cornish and Devon Members to the president of the board of trade, Huskisson, and 'strenuously advocated' the continuation of export bounties on pilchards.[11] He voted with Canning's coalition ministry for the grant to improve water communications in Canada, 12 June 1827. He apparently contemplated a motion for information regarding 'the state of Turkey and the treaty said to be in existence between the courts of London and St. Petersburg relating to the dissensions in the Turkish dominions', but nothing came of it. This was presumably the occasion when Lord Palmerston*, the secretary at war, who had 'frequent communications' with Vyvyan on 'foreign and domestic' subjects, took him to the foreign office 'to read over a mass of papers', which 'so far succeeded in altering his opinions' that he refrained from making a motion.[12] He explained to a

Cornish clergyman hoping for a church living for a son that he would 'feel considerable embarrassment and difficulty' in asking lord chancellor Lyndhurst for any favours, and that 'independence of principle induces me to avoid being under any degree of obligation to a government which I have not supported'.[13] Later that year, in a revealing memorandum, Vyvyan wrote of his desire to 'take advantage of the situation ... in which I am placed ... to lead a quiet and philosophical life':

The happiness of such an inexhaustible fund of calm contentment as the pursuit of philosophy is alone experienced by those who have inclination and courage to adopt it. Those who have never done so, will ridicule the naturalist or scientific man. Could they but know the independence of his soul, how would they envy him! His delights are a foretaste of eternal bliss ... I feel I have had some experience of his pleasure, but in an evil hour the tempter came and offered me the gratification of my selfish passions. I knew the worthlessness of the distinction, the material inconsequence of the raving hunger of ambition ... I knew this and *fell* with my eyes open. Yet even then I made a resolution like a yielding sinner, to reform by and bye ... For five years I meant to run the wild career of selfishness, to jostle others and follow the fools called politicians, then if I found myself no greater than when I first commenced, it was my resolution to retire into private life. Three years are nearly passed: I have not altered my resolution. I am no greater than I was when I commenced; politics are like the labours of those ghosts of pagan evil, whose punishment was to draw a *sieve* from a well instead of a *bucket* ... I cannot labour heartily when I know the *end* of it, even if I succeed.[14]

He presented more Dissenters' petitions for repeal of the Test Acts, 25 Feb. 1828, but did not vote on this issue next day. He divided against Catholic relief, 12 May. He opposed the duke of Wellington's ministry by voting for information regarding civil list pensions, 20 May, and against the additional churches bill, 30 June. In May he circularized his supporters urging them to organize memorials to Cornish borough Members against the government's small notes bill, 'one of those momentous questions which extend their influence to every branch of society'. He was convinced that only a 'continuance of a £1 note circulation will save us from stagnation in our mines and agriculture, a depreciation of value in every article of produce, and a melancholy want of employment'.[15] He presented petitions from St. Columb and Breage in this sense, 3 June, and voted against the small notes (Scotland and Ireland) bill, 5, 16, 27 June. He presented anti-slavery petitions from Marazion and Falmouth, 23 June 1828.

In February 1829 Planta, the patronage secretary, listed Vyvyan as being 'opposed to the principle' of Catholic emancipation, and he emerged that session as

one of the leading figures in the 'revolt of the Ultras'. He presented 16 hostile petitions from Cornwall, which he claimed 'represented the feelings of a large portion of the wealth ... intelligence and ... respectability of the county', 24 Feb. He declared that Wellington and Peel's conduct had 'entirely destroyed my confidence in public men', as there were 'no reasonable grounds for their conversion', and he insisted that 'an administration might have been formed on the principle of adhering to the constitution of 1688 ... anti-Catholics might have been found capable of directing the affairs of the country'. He accepted that the consequences of resistance might be 'civil war' but was unwilling to 'surrender' the constitution. He asserted that a 'great conspiracy' was 'in progress throughout Europe' to destroy the 'civil and religious liberty of nations', inspired by 'absolute or would be absolute sovereigns and by the Papal power', whose principal agents, the Jesuits, had achieved 'immense' power in England. Catholic emancipation was therefore no 'mere provincial subject' but part of the 'warfare between religious liberty and religious despotism'. He believed that ministers should have proceeded 'more gradually' and 'tried at first to procure the admission of Catholic peers to the House of Lords', rather than 'taking the nation by surprise'. The Whig Lord Howick* thought that Vyvyan 'certainly showed a good deal of power of speaking, though what he said was very open to answer'.[16] He divided against the emancipation bill, 6, 18, 23, 27 (when he was a minority teller), 30 Mar., and presented more hostile petitions, 10, 24 Mar. He attended a meeting of Ultras at Lord Chandos's* house, 16 Mar., and talked of organizing a county meeting 'to address the king to dismiss his ministers and dissolve Parliament'; nothing came of this.[17] On 27 Mar. he moved an amendment to insert words into the new parliamentary oath requiring Catholics to renounce the murder of heretics and the Papal dispensing power, but this was negatived. He also moved that Jesuits in all of 'His Majesty's dominions' should be required to register, in order to prevent them 'subverting constitutions and erecting a new anti-national power in every state', but he withdrew after receiving assurances about registration in the colonies. Another amendment to prohibit Jesuits and other Catholic monks from acting as schoolmasters was eventually withdrawn. One Whig Member described Vyvyan's speeches that day as 'very absurd'.[18] He voted against the silk trade bill, 1 May. He expressed regret, 12 June, that for reasons including 'the Epsom races, a matter of great import to the senators of this country', no time had been found for his motion for inquiry into distress. He deemed it 'indecorous and dangerous' that Members were about to disperse without considering the subject, and took the opportunity to blame the withdrawal of small bank notes for 'creating the existing state of distress' and argue that there was 'no hope of improvement but by adopting some ameliorated system of paper currency'. He opposed the anatomy bill, 18 May, as Warburton would not agree to prohibit the dissection of murderers, and was a minority teller against the third reading. In June Sir James Mackintosh* wrote of the 'angry underlings' who resented the Whigs' support for Wellington, and noted that 'Vyvyan says ... he wishes an end to a state of things in which "the unplaced retainers of ministers occupy the opposition benches"'.[19] During the summer and autumn he was in communication with fellow Ultras, including George IV's brother, the duke of Cumberland, to whom he looked as the 'champion' of the 'Protestant party' and as a channel of communication between them and the king, who needed encouragement to change his ministers. He was anxious that Wellington should not be granted an early dissolution, as 'the influence of the treasury must always be paramount in a general election' and the result would be a Commons even more compliant to the duke's wishes. He told the duke of Newcastle that given the 'conduct of the Irish Catholics' since emancipation and the 'deplorable state of trade', Wellington was becoming 'more unpopular every day' and his ministry 'may not last six months'. It was therefore essential for the Ultras to act with 'firmness and unity of purpose'.[20] Vyvyan looked to the formation of a 'Tory government upon Tory principles', but while he was prepared to see certain members of the present government retained in office, he was adamant that Wellington, the 'arch deceiver', must not be included as this would 'ruin' the 'Tory party' and lead to the advent of a Whig administration. He was confident that the personnel for a new government, headed perhaps by Lord Mansfield, could be found, but he argued that Lord Blandford* had disqualified himself by his 'headstrong' pledge to raise the question of parliamentary reform, which 'in the present state of affairs ... would be nothing more or less than the commencement of a revolution ... more fearful even than that of France' in 1789.[21] In late September he showed Cumberland his analysis of the state of the Commons, which suggested that the projected government would have 278 'certain supporters', comprised of those Tory Members who had either opposed emancipation or not voted at all, while the sentiments of another 89 who had supported the third reading were 'unknown'. Shortly afterwards he had an interview with Palmerston, whom he hoped to

detach from the Huskissonites with the proposal that he should lead the Commons in a 'Mansfield, Eldon, Newcastle and Knatchbull administration', in which Vyvyan seems to have envisaged himself as foreign secretary. He advised Cumberland that if decisive action was taken at the opening of Parliament 'a government might be formed almost entirely of Tories, which would probably be as strong as any that has been in power for the last 20 years', but he feared the consequences if nothing was done and 'we form *part* of a discordant opposition' to Wellington:

> With some few exceptions, the Tory party in both Houses, however staunch and firm they may be, are not the men to act well together in *opposition*, many of them are persons in easy circumstances and liable to be discouraged by being in small minorities, nor have they sufficient energy or policy to combine in a systematic opposition and to keep together for some time.[22]

By the end of November 1829, he was dismayed to find that there seemed little prospect of the 'Protestants' striking 'an immediate blow' and he detected signs of 'gradual defections from their ranks'. He was increasingly suspicious that Wellington was acting as part of a 'new Holy Alliance', with Metternich, Polignac, the tsar of Russia and the 'apostolical party', to 'put down representative governments', and felt that his removal from office 'alone will save Europe'.[23]

Early in 1830 it was rumoured that Vyvyan would move an amendment to the address enunciating his 'high Tory and currency' opinions,[24] but in the event he divided for Sir Edward Knatchbull's amendment on distress, 4 Feb. He and Knatchbull were the leaders of a group of some 30 hard core Ultras who engaged in more or less outright opposition to ministers that session, and he reportedly told the Tory whips that 'his object was to reduce the government majorities as much as possible and to make the government as contemptible as possible'. He voted consistently with the revived Whig opposition on retrenchment issues.[25] On 16 Mar. he announced that he would not press his call of the House for that evening, as there was already a 'very full attendance' for Davenport's motion for inquiry into the state of the nation. Two days later he maintained that distress 'pervades all ranks except the monied interest and presses most heavily upon the productive classes'. The country was 'in a state of peril' and unless action was taken to alleviate the problem and 'calm the public sentiment of exasperation against the legislature', he feared that 'this House will not meet for three sessions more in its present form and the equilibrium of our government may be destroyed'. He doubted whether overpopulation was the cause of distress, as there were sufficient means to feed everyone, and some undoubted causes, such as 'improvements of machinery' which were 'appalling to the present generation' but 'ultimately ... productive of great benefits to civilized society', were beyond Parliament's control. However, the currency question was 'intimately connected with the subject', as the withdrawal of small notes from circulation had 'annihilated a great portion of that ... property ... founded upon credit which ... found its way into the remotest corners of the kingdom', with the result that the 'prosperity of the greater part of the agricultural population' had been undermined. Falling prices meant that the burden of the national debt, arising from the necessary wars against revolutionary France, had grown, and ministers were unable to make tax reductions because military establishments had to be maintained. He therefore predicted that the government must soon either 'have a paper currency or commit an ... overt act of national bankruptcy'. He denied that he and his friends considered ministers to be 'unworthy of the confidence of the nation', but they would not 'blindly place themselves at the disposal' of government and resented being accused of 'factious motives'. He declared that 'the landed interest have their all at stake' and 'may probably save themselves' by voting for inquiry; he was a minority teller, 23 Mar. He claimed on 8 June that 'we have gradually gained an accession of strength' on the currency question, which would 'continue to press upon the House like an incubus', and that the only opponents of inquiry were 'the holders of pensions [and] the well-paid officers of the crown ... now receiving 30s. for every £1 granted them by Parliament during the depreciation'. He was named to the select committee on the East India Company, 9 Feb. (and again, 4 Feb., 26 July 1831). He divided against Blandford's reform plan, 18 Feb., and Jewish emancipation, 5 Apr., 17 May. He was one of a handful of Ultras who voted for Palmerston's motion regarding British interference in the internal affairs of Portugal, 10 Mar.[26] He condemned the government's foreign policy, 2 July, declaring that 'never was England in a more disgraceful position', distrusted by other countries, and he gave the example of the unwise military intervention against Turkey. He openly expressed his 'fear, almost amounting to a conviction', that ministers were acting with 'the despotic governments of Europe' to 'depress the spirit of liberty in different countries', and he sought reassurance that there was no intention of intervening in France. He warned that the militia ballot suspension bill might lead to the 'extinction of the constitutional force' and leave nothing but a 'large standing army', 25

May. He moved for a return of the number of metropolitan police officers, 28 May, and expressed concern about 'the unconstitutional character of this establishment and the ultimate intentions of the government', 15 June. It was necessary to preserve the system of 'self-government' as a 'safeguard of our liberties', and he 'dreaded' the extension of the London model to other parts of the country, which would make the home secretary 'supreme' and create the potential for 'an efficient army'. He moved to adjourn the debate on the sale of beer bill owing to the late hour, 3 June, and said he regarded this measure as 'lowering the magistracy' by leaving beer houses 'entirely without regulation'. He thought consumption on the premises should be allowed, but wanted to see a 'distinction between tippling and drinking a glass in passing ... no tippling should be allowed'; he was a minority teller. However, he voted against on-consumption, 21 June, 1 July, when he complained that the bill was being 'forced on us as a pet measure' of ministers, regardless of the warnings of the 'unpaid magistracy', who were 'disliked by the executive power'. Referring also to the police and militia measures, he detected signs of the 'art of enslaving a free people'. He divided to abolish the Irish lord lieutenancy, 11 May, and against the Galway franchise bill, 25 May. He voted for abolition of the death penalty for forgery, 7 June, and against increased recognizances in the libel law amendment bill, 6, 9 July. He regretted that the export bounties on fish had not been made an 'exception to the doctrine' of free trade, 28 May, and gave notice of an amendment in committee on the labourers' wages bill to restrict its operation in the Devon and Cornwall stannaries, 3 July. He thought the decision to dissolve Parliament quickly, without making proper arrangements for supply, was 'unnecessary so far as the interests of the country are concerned', 2 July 1830, and saw it as proof that the government had lost the confidence of the Commons, although there had been 'no coalition between the three sections of opposition'. He felt obliged to express his 'total want of confidence' in ministers, 'whether I look at their home policy, their commercial or foreign policy'. At this time he wrote another memorandum describing his feelings about his decision to enter politics:

> Five years have passed and I am still in Parliament, but greater than I was – living with the first men of the party with which I am connected – in the confidence of princes – and powerful enough to direct the balancing party in the House of Commons against the minister – possibly to upset his government. Another five years of statesmanship, and unless I am in power I will cease to climb the giddy height.[27]

He stood again for Cornwall at the general election that summer and delivered a lengthy speech defending his conduct during the previous two sessions. He declared that he was 'so decidedly opposed' to the principles of Wellington's government that he 'must range himself in the ranks of a decided opposition' to it. He accused the premier of 'destroying party', by drawing support from the old Whig opposition, and likened his policies on the police and the militia to those of Polignac, from which he concluded that 'the great struggle between despotism and freedom was not now confined to one country'. He maintained that it would 'give him no pain to see the Whigs, as a body, in power', and though 'he should probably be amongst their opponents', this would be for the sake of 'keeping up the wholesome spirit of party' rather than 'from any personal objection'. Until this happened, he thought it 'behoved ... Whigs and Tories to oppose the present mixed government by forming a Conservative, or anti-Wellington party, or a country party, on the principle of resisting [Wellington's] attempt ... to concentrate all power in himself'. He insisted that 'Whigs and ... Ultra Tories ... might coalesce with honour', and he 'commented with severity' on the conduct of Lord Althorp's 'independent party', which had saved the government in the division on Knatchbull's amendment. He observed that 'the monied interest will muster powerfully' in the next Parliament and give 'zealous support' to ministers, and he lamented to see the power of the country gentlemen being 'crushed' as a result of the government's commercial and financial policies. After receiving promises of support from some prominent Whigs, who accepted him as a champion of 'liberty', he explained that he could give 'no pledge' to support parliamentary reform, as 'he apprehended danger from any [general] plan', and that he would not 'vote for such a change until he found that the present system, under proper direction, had ceased to work well'; the 'future conduct of the ... Commons would determine his views on that point'. He emphasized that he would never support military intervention to restore Charles X, who had 'so grossly outraged the constitution of his country', to the French throne, and argued that this proved he was not an Ultra, in the original meaning of the term. He was returned unopposed with Wynne Pendarves. One Tory peer commented on Vyvyan's speech that 'I have never before seen joined together, such power of expression and such weakness of judgement, such a strong charge for his musket, and so blind in taking aim'.[28]

The ministry of course listed him among the 'violent Ultras'. He presented 53 anti-slavery petitions from Cornwall, 12 Nov. 1830. Following a meeting of his and Knatchbull's Ultra friends, he and they voted against the government in the decisive civil list division, 15 Nov., playing a crucial part in its downfall.[29] It is not clear whether he was sounded as to the possibility of joining Lord Grey's ministry, but when the Ultra duke of Richmond accepted office he declined to follow him. During the next few months attempts to reunite the Tory opposition in the Commons under Peel's leadership came to nothing, and the state of political confusion was magnified by divisions of opinion amongst the Ultras themselves. Vyvyan and Knatchbull led one group, who were personally hostile to Peel and determined to take an independent line on the government's reform bill. Henry Goulburn* lamented that the 'most formidable' of the difficulties facing the opposition was 'the obstinacy of ... Vyvyan and others', who 'insist on moving a resolution in which we find it impossible to concur inasmuch as it would pledge us to an extent of reform little short of that which the bill proposes to effect'. The arguments of leading Tories had made 'some impression upon him', but 'with a man so uncertain and obstinate it is not possible to say what we may be ultimately able to effect'.[30] On the morning of 21 Mar. 1831 the Vyvyan-Knatchbull group met to discuss their tactics on the second reading of the ministerial reform bill, and it was agreed that Vyvyan should move its rejection that evening. He explained to the House that since taking his seat in 1825 he had 'abstained from voting upon parliamentary reform', except for his opposition the previous session to the ballot, and he admitted the 'necessity for occasional changes and improvements in all human ordinances'. However, he did not believe it was 'safe at any time to attempt an entire change in the constitution of a country', as this was 'most dangerous to the whole superstructure of society', yet ministers were proposing their 'fearful experiment' at a time of instability in Britain, Ireland and Europe. The bill was therefore 'full of danger to the throne and our existing institutions'. Whereas the constitutional settlement of 1688 had been 'a revolution of the aristocracy', ministers were proposing 'a revolution of the democracy', and he knew of no instance in history where this had been achieved 'without eventually throwing the supreme sovereignty of the state into the hands of an absolute king or a military despot'. He observed that 'two years of severe distress in the agricultural and manufacturing interests' had caused the people to demand relief, and claimed that it was the refusal to grant an inquiry that had made 'the legislature and the executive ... unpopular' and given rise to 'a renewed cry for parliamentary reform', which was seen as a 'panacea for the evils of the country'. He warned that reform would lead to attacks on tithes, rents and funded property, which included 'all the accumulations of the savings banks, amounting to 20 millions of the poor man's property'. He specifically objected to the bill because it gave 'an undue and anti-agricultural influence to towns', and because the abolition of small boroughs with varied franchises removed the means by which 'all the great interests of the country' obtained their 'due weight in the indirect but yet efficient representation'; he particularly feared that colonial interests would suffer as a result. He stated that if the bill was rejected he would move a 'declaratory resolution', to show the House's determination to 'strengthen and extend the representation' at a more appropriate time, and he indicated that 'any plan ... I might offer hereafter would go nearly to the extent of that which I believe it was the intention of ... ministers to propose before they came into office'. However, the second reading was carried by 302-301, 22 Mar. Mackintosh described Vyvyan's oration as 'shewy' and 'rambling', but one Whig minister noted that it was 'much cheered' on the opposition benches and had probably helped to sway the votes of a 'few' who had deserted the government. Lord Granville Somerset* thought the speech 'able', while Henry Bankes, a rival Ultra, agreed it was 'clever and argumentative' but regretted that, 'like many other county Members ... fear of his constituents and of a dissolution' had driven Vyvyan to 'declare himself friendly to some moderate reform'.[31] He acknowledged that his hostile vote had provoked opposition to him in Cornwall, 29 Mar., but declared that he would never 'basely yield to the ill-advised clamour ... now raised throughout the country'. He denied that he had acted from factious motives in opposing reform and the timber duties, 30 Mar. He voted for Gascoyne's wrecking amendment, 19 Apr, but insisted two days later that this was not 'for the purpose of throwing out the bill', as the Commons had merely sought to 'uphold the Protestant religion of this country' by opposing increased representation for Ireland. He condemned the resulting dissolution, 22 Apr. 1831, denounced ministers as 'the most incapable ... inconsistent ... least efficient body of men that ever attempted to govern a great country', and warned that they were 'about to incur a fearful responsibility' by raising unrealistic expectations amongst 'every class' as to the benefits of reform. As he continued to speak, the sound of cannon fire heralding the king's approach was heard in the chamber, and a Whig diarist noted how 'at each discharge of the guns the ministerialists cheered loudly, as if in derision of the orator's solemn sentences'. Finally, 'the roaring of the cannon, the laughter and our cheering ... beat the baronet, and

he suddenly sat down'. On the other hand, Greville judged that, 'excited as he was', Vyvyan's speech had been 'very well done'.[32] At the ensuing general election he offered for Cornwall with Lord Valletort*, but they faced strong opposition from Wynne Pendarves and another Whig. He insisted that he was a 'moderate reformer' and claimed that 'ministers did not wish their bill to pass and had made it violent, that it might be rejected'. He repeated his opposition to 'wild theories of free trade', favoured an 'adjustment' of tithes and declared his support for the 'gradual abolition' of slavery, with due regard to the rights of the planters, the welfare of the slaves and the 'general interests of the empire'. He and Valletort were defeated after a contest lasting five days. Lord Grey was afterwards informed that that 'ill-conditioned and most unpopular man' could 'never show his face in Cornwall again'.[33]

In July 1831 a vacancy was created for Vyvyan at Okehampton, where the Savile interest predominated, and after being returned at the by-election he sought to organize the depleted ranks of the Ultras.[34] He voted to use the 1831 census for the purpose of scheduling boroughs in the reintroduced reform bill, 19 July. He warned on 29 July that if ministers persisted in their plan to devote five days per week to the bill the opposition would be driven to the 'unpleasant alternative' of moving an adjournment the next day. While not taking an active part himself in the reform debates, he defended the right of Members to protect the interests of their constituents by engaging in detailed opposition, 4 Aug. He divided to preserve the voting rights of non-resident freemen for life, 30 Aug. He feared that government appointment of the boundary commissioners risked placing 'boroughs more under undue nomination than they are under this present system', 1 Sept. He supported Waldo Sibthorp's amendment to prevent Members from being appointed as boundary commissioners, 13 Sept., on the ground that ministers would otherwise be able to 'delegate to a body of their own friends and adherents a power so despotic'. He was convinced that 'this bill never can pass', once the revelation of such 'gross ... anomalies' awoke the nation from its 'delusion' that the measure was 'meant for ... great national objects'. He admitted that he was 'now a reformer to a greater extent than when the bill was first brought forward', but thought it would be 'dangerous to offer any plan of reform as a counter-project, whilst we are discussing this bill'. He believed the approaching crisis would 'try the firmness' of the peers, who had 'an opportunity for deciding how far they are free senators of a great empire'. One Whig Member wrote that the 'barrage of ... Vyvyan, who had been got up to be very effective ... was infinitely absurd'.[35] Though he could not 'go to the full extent' of Waldo Sibthorp's amendment to disfranchise persons holding civil offices during the pleasure of the crown, 14 Sept., he felt 'the substance of [it] ought to have been embodied in the bill', to prevent the government from 'interfering in election matters' by 'exercising a direct control' over public servants. He argued that 'without universal suffrage the ballot would be the most unfair system of election that could be possibly adopted', 21 Sept., as those excluded from the franchise had a right to know how those included had voted. He divided against the bill's passage, 21 Sept. He mentioned on 11 Oct. that he had voted against Lord Ebrington's confidence motion the previous day. In what Greville described as a 'furious attack', 12 Oct., he condemned the 'novel and dangerous ... practice' of ministers corresponding with the political unions, which had 'set themselves in array against the legislature'. He hoped the rejected bill would be amended to make it acceptable to the Lords, but suspected that ministers would prefer to exploit popular clamour.[36] He argued that Ireland had no case for increased representation because she 'does not contribute to the revenue to the extent which she ought in proportion to her population', 17 Oct. He objected to the language used in a Birmingham Political Union petition, 19 Oct., and exclaimed, 'God protect us from the government of clubs or unions!' He trusted that such bodies would never be allowed to 'dictate to this House what course it should pursue', and said he would prefer to see 'riots in some parts of the country than that the peace should be kept by means of these unions'. He maintained that the House had no right to withhold the Liverpool election writ for 'anything done before the present Parliament was in existence', 12 Oct., and considered it 'hard for such a place ... to be without two representatives'. He agreed to postpone his motion for papers regarding the Belgian crisis, while diplomatic negotiations were continuing, 6 Aug., but insisted that he was 'fully justified' in raising the matter as the government's conduct had been 'highly detrimental to this country' and 'may involve us in war'. After reluctantly agreeing to further postponements, 9, 11 Aug., he brought on his motion, 18 Aug., when he defended the right of the Dutch king, who had been 'abandoned and sacrificed' by the London conference of the Powers, to send troops into Belgium, and argued that the king had always been faithful to 'his professed principles of toleration and national feeling', in difficult circumstances. It would be detrimental to Britain's 'faith and honour' in the eyes of the 'minor powers', if the British fleet took action against the Dutch, and he hoped the 'mistake of

Navarino' would not be repeated. The Belgian revolt had been organized by an 'alliance of the ultramontanes and the liberals', the 'precise counterpart of what is now going on in Ireland', and a similar combination in France, a 'power behind the government and the throne', was bent on provoking war with Britain. He urged ministers 'for the safety of the country and for the peace of Europe', to 'offer a firm, bold, and determined resistance to the policy of that party wherever it may be found'. He explained that 'those who have been falsely called "Ultras" in this country are widely different ... from the persons who were originally so termed in France', because those in Britain were 'desirous to maintain order' and 'make as few alterations as possible to support the ancient institutions, authority and honour of the country', whereas the French Ultras 'wanted a government by edicts and ordinances ... destructive of the liberties of the people'. He withdrew his motion when the foreign secretary, Palmerston, declined to give any information. Sir Henry Hardinge* thought Vyvyan had been 'very poor in his motion and very indiscreet'. It may have been conceived as a diversionary attack on the government.[37] He congratulated ministers on the news that French troops had been withdrawn from Belgium, 27 Sept. He objected to the Commons receiving the North Western Union petition against the Queen's Dower Act, 19 Aug., as this would establish 'a most dangerous precedent'. He voted to censure the Irish administration for using undue influence in the Dublin election, 23 Aug. He complained the same day that the Beer Act had caused 'disorder and inconvenience', and warned that if beer houses were not 'placed more effectually' under magisterial control 'there must be an increased necessity for a larger police'. In the debate on the wine duties, 7 Sept., he criticized ministers for sacrificing the existing trade with Portugal in the 'delusive hope' of increased trade with France, and complained that they were 'trifling with the interests of our great colonial system' by proposing to expose Cape producers to French competition. He feared that 'our colonies will cease to regard the metropolitan part of the empire ... with respect and confidence'. He called that day for 'measures ... to render our currency less fluctuating', and questioned the restrictions on private banks and the need for a state bank, observing that 'the present system, both of currency and banking, is calculated to throw every impediment in the way of safe speculation'. He voted for inquiry into the effects on the West India interest of renewing the Sugar Refinery Act, 12 Sept. Next day he expressed doubts that the banning of threshing machines would create employment, as this would 'cause land now in cultivation to be thrown out of it'. He approved of the vestries bill, 30 Sept., having 'long entertained' the view that the 'whole of those who pay rates ought to be entitled to vote', but he hoped it would be amended to give extra weight to larger property owners, so that they were not 'borne down by numbers'. He urged ministers to take immediate steps to 'isolate places infected' with cholera, 18 Oct. 1831.

He elicited that the government did not intend to set up an inquiry into distress, 12 Dec. 1831. Three days later he observed that the 'inevitable consequence' of free trade policies was that such manufactures as gloves were being 'driven out of the market by ... foreigners', which must 'inevitably diminish the employment of our own workpeople, unless ... you increase the means of consumption'. He admitted that 'if we were about to establish an entirely new system of government, no doubt we ought to be in favour of free trade, for the abstract truths of its benefits cannot be denied', but thought it was 'impossible to make any alteration in existing trade without creating much misery'. He declared that 'the free trade system has had its trial and ... has completely failed', 31 Jan. 1832. He considered the Coventry ribbon makers' case 'a very hard one' which merited inquiry, 21 Feb., described the appointment of a committee on the silk trade as 'a great triumph', 1 Mar., and successfully moved that Alderman Waithman be added to it, as a 'practical man' was needed, 6 Mar. He argued that statistics proving the growth of trade did not show whether the labourers were 'in as comfortable a condition as formerly', 3 July, and he complained that Parliament had shown insufficient attention to their interests, having 'on every occasion rather regarded the interests of the capitalist'. He pointed out that he and other opponents of reform had supported inquiries into distress, although some had 'lost their seats ... in consequence of the excitement which prevailed on the subject of reform', and he thought it 'right that the country should know who are its true friends'. He dissented from Hume's claim that 'the property of the church is national property', 14 Dec. 1831, and he divided against the government amendment to the Irish tithes bill, 9 Apr. 1832. He asked what Hume would do about advowsons and lay improprietors, 10 Aug. 1832, 'because if we once admit the principle that property ... is to be taken away from the holders at pleasure, there is an end of all government and all justice'. He said he would again oppose the anatomy bill unless the clause giving over murderers' bodies for dissection was omitted, 15 Dec. 1831, observing that 'if ... you wish to further the ends of science, by allaying the prejudices that exist against dissection,

you must remove that feeling of degradation which is now associated with it in the public mind'. He believed that 'those who die in the poor house ... are as much entitled to the protection of the law as those who die in palaces'. He expressed regret the same day that ministers had not tried the 'experiment of isolation' to stop the spread of cholera, but he agreed that it was 'necessary to give all the powers that are requisite' and that 'all party considerations ought to be thrown aside', 14 Feb. 1832. He concluded that given the separation of Belgium from Holland, Britain was 'no longer liable' to pay the interest on the Russian-Dutch loan, 16 Dec. 1831, and he voted accordingly, 26 Jan. 1832. He hoped the forthcoming London conference of the Powers would show the Dutch king 'fair and even handed justice', 17 Dec. 1831, observing that 'Holland is sure to be a more serviceable ally to this country than Belgium, which must always be under the influence of France'. He agreed, apparently on Wellington's advice, to postpone his motion on the Dutch-Belgian treaty until it had been fully ratified, 6 Feb. 1832, and it was suspected on the ministerial side that he had also been influenced by the likelihood of cutting 'a bad figure in the division'; the motion never came on.[38] He again voted against the Russian-Dutch loan, 12 July, complained that the House was being asked to give a 'blind vote of confidence' when insufficient information had been provided, 16 July, and suggested that payment should be seen 'in the light of a bribe to Russia', 20 July. He sought information regarding the landing of French troops at Ancona, which he feared would 'again excite a civil war in Italy', 7 Mar. He emphasized that 'as an Englishman and an admirer of our constitution', he considered the government of the duke of Modena to be 'of a character which no man ... can approve of', while 'that ... of the Pope is such as no love of liberal proceedings can sanction'. He denounced the 'hostile invasion of the Papal territory' by France, which was claiming 'a right of uncontrolled discussion in the affairs of Europe', 13 Mar., and he urged the government to 'maintain the honour and interests of England'. Believing that 'we must take foreign governments as we find them', he argued that 'we are bound by treaties to preserve the peace and maintain the balance of power in Europe'. A Whig Member remarked that Vyvyan had 'become a good speaker', but was 'unfair and mischievous'.[39] In the general debate on foreign policy, 26 Mar., he accused Palmerston of securing peace by allowing France to 'gain all her points', in Algiers, Portugal, Italy and Belgium, 'without opposition', although he denied that he wished to 'plunge the country into war'. Following conversations with Palmerston and the Dutch ambassador in late July 1832, he reported to Peel that 'it may now be prudent to allow the session to terminate without saying anything more on foreign politics'.[40]

He divided against the second reading of the revised reform bill, 17 Dec. 1831. In January 1832 there was speculation that he might be included in a ministry formed by the Tory 'Waverers', Lords Harrowby and Wharncliffe, but there is no evidence of any direct communication with them; he remained hostile to Tory reunion under Peel.[41] He complained that ministers were apparently resolved to disfranchise a certain number of boroughs without allowing the House to consider the merits of individual cases, 20 Jan. 1832, when he was a minority teller against going into committee. However, he offered his 'cordial vote in support' of the clause to 'prevent the creation of fictitious freeholders', which had been 'introduced to overpower the real constituency of a county', 1 Feb. He also admitted the benefits of a 'well conducted registration', 8 Feb., since 'the idea of confining the representation of a county to the three or four families in it who may have the money requisite to undertake a contest' was 'in contradiction to the general freedom of elections and the principles of the constitution'; but he objected to revising barristers being given the power to decide who could register, as there was a danger of political bias entering into their decisions. Sources differ as to whether he voted for the registration clause that day or abstained. He thought the two-day interval between the nomination meeting and the election for counties should be increased to seven, to prevent surprise candidatures, 11 Feb., or else 'cunning and trick will constitute the chief weapons at an election'. He criticized the 'errors' committed by the boundary commissioners in the case of Helston, which was to lose one Member, 23 Feb., and urged that the case be adjourned. He voted against the enfranchisement of Tower Hamlets, 28 Feb., and argued that Gateshead, which 'may be considered as one town' with Newcastle, had no claim to separate representation, 5 Mar. He accepted that the reform question must be 'speedily settled', 20 Mar., but advised ministers to present a 'more moderate' plan in order to conciliate the peers and the country. He objected to the total disfranchisement of any borough, except where corruption had been proved, and deplored ministers' determination to 'assail the corporations' and 'infringe upon and destroy charters', which must 'endanger all property'. He suggested that through the 'partial disfranchisement of a sufficient number' of boroughs, using size of electorate as the criterion, it would be possible to provide for 'new constituencies in towns and counties', although increased representation for London was 'unnecessary' as it was 'virtually represented by nearly half the House'. He argued that the £10 borough franchise was 'arbitrary' and set a 'fearful precedent', as 'there is but one abstract right of voting which can be brought forward by pure theorists, and that is universal suffrage'. If the bill was passed he foresaw the introduction of a property tax, repeal of the corn laws and an attack on church revenues. He warned ministers that 'in their attempt to enjoy a long tenure of office', by means of the bill, 'they and the aristocracy of their own party are committing an act of suicide'. A sketch of an alternative reform plan in Vyvyan's hand, evidently from this time, proposed that there should be no change in the proportionate representation of England, Scotland and Ireland, and that 74 boroughs drawn by lot, from among those with under 100 voters or a population of under 5,000, should each lose one Member. Of the seats made available for redistribution, two each should be given to 27 counties and the other 20 to the towns listed in schedule C, except Merthyr Tydfil and one other. Those remaining boroughs with under 100 voters should be thrown open to the hundred, while in boroughs with large populations a variable household franchise of up to £20 should apply. All existing voting rights should remain except for the out-voters, who should have a vote for life where they resided.[42] He divided against the third reading, 22 Mar., and for Waldo Sibthorp's amendment regarding Lincoln freeholders, 23 Mar. In April he submitted to the marquess of Salisbury a proposed amendment to the bill's preamble, which he regretted not having moved in the Commons, embodying the principle that there should only be partial disfranchisement of an unspecified number of boroughs. He observed that if in the Lords committee, 'where proxies do not count (and that must be a benefit to your cause in the present state of the House), you could carry [this] proposition ... I should think you might succeed'. Thus, 'the principle of Lord Grey's bill will be overthrown and the entire measure ... emasculated'. Nothing came of this, and he afterwards expressed to another correspondent his hope that the Lords would reject the bill, as 'time is everything' and 'a better measure may be more acceptable in a few months'. He feared that if the bill passed and Parliament was dissolved, ministers 'must have a war-cry, and in these days I know of none which can be raised without advantage to the Jacobin party'.[43] On 10 May, following the resignation of Grey's ministry, he attended a meeting of opposition Members at Peel's house to discuss their response to Ebrington's motion that evening, for an address asking the king to appoint only ministers committed to carrying an unimpaired bill.[44] After the address was carried he objected to its being presented as the view of the Commons, when there had only been a majority of 80 in favour of it. This raised the important question of 'whether the other branch of the legislature is to be dictated to by the king's ministers for the time being', and he warned that if it was accepted that the government had the power to change the composition of the Lords, it would be 'utterly impossible for that body to act as a free assembly'. During the ensuing constitutional crisis, when Wellington attempted to form a government in order to carry a similar reform bill, Vyvyan was reportedly 'not amenable' to the explanations offered to justify this course.[45] However, on 18 May he defended Wellington's willingness to 'sacrifice ... himself and ... his personal opinions', arguing that 'his acceptance of office might have saved the independence' of the Lords. He also said that he understood Peel's refusal to serve, as he had 'made more decided and solemn protestations on ... the reform bill'. He described the Whig proposal to create new peers as 'so gross and outrageous to the spirit of the constitution' as to be 'akin to treason'. William IV had shown himself 'a greater friend to the liberties of the country' than the Whigs, and he was confident that if a general election were held 'the sober, reflecting and calmly judging people of England' would show their approval of the king's conduct. Early in June he wrote a desperate letter to Cumberland urging that the Lords should postpone the bill's third reading, for if it passed:

I do not believe that any earthly power can save this country from a social revolution. The present House of Commons will not venture to destroy the unions ... because each Member will look to his future election, and the ministry will feel that their existence depends upon the aid of these societies ... On the other hand, a Tory government might recommit the bill in the Lords, make such alterations as were necessary and (if the Commons rejected the bill) they might dissolve with such a bill before the country as the Lords might be induced to pass without incurring the charge of slavery. There may be danger on one side, but there is irresistible ruin on the other.

However, he was advised that nothing more could be done.[46] After the bill's passage he continued to talk of forming an 'old Tory party', separate from Wellington and Peel, but as Sir John Benn Walsh* noted, though a 'clever, subtle fellow with a good deal of ingenuity and penetration', Vyvyan was 'rather crotchety in his views and far fetched in his ideas'.[47] He favoured referring the boundaries bill to a select committee in order to 'proceed with greater rapidity', 4 June. He divided

for Alexander Baring's privileges of Parliament bill, 27 June, when he remarked that since political power had been placed 'in the hands of the bulk of the community', it was necessary to ensure that 'those without property' should not be allowed to 'vote away the public money'. He warned against the provision in the bribery at elections bill allowing Members to be petitioned against for two years after an election, 30 July 1832, as this would hold over them 'a scourge ... which might altogether destroy their independence'; he advised that the matter be left to the next Parliament, since so few Members remained in London.

At the general election of 1832 Vyvyan was returned at the head of the poll for Bristol, where he sat as a 'Conservative' until his retirement in 1837. By then most of the Ultras had been reconciled to Peel's leadership and Vyvyan had become an isolated figure. He was described about that time as 'a man of middle size ... slenderly and delicately made', with 'something of a pensive cast' about his countenance and a 'rather sallow' complexion, whose 'voice and manner' were nevertheless 'pleasant'.[48] In another personal memorandum, in 1837, he wrote:

Before the ten years were completed, I succeeded in overthrowing an administration. I was instrumental in placing men in office who have done great mischief ... I have been courted by all parties, and at last I was indirectly consulted by two British sovereigns, and in communication with the first foreign statesmen in the world. Still my resolution remained unbroken. The ten years have elapsed ... I am *not* in power, and I thank my good fortune for it. I am no longer in Parliament. My retirement has been optional. All Hail philosophy ... All Hail religious peace! I have fulfilled my vow. Vain pomp and glory of the world farewell.[49]

In fact, he was returned for Helston in 1841 and sat until his final retirement in 1857, but he was never again a major force in the House. He published several works on philosophical and scientific subjects, and on one occasion he mentioned an unpublished volume, 'so arranged as to pretend to something like a system', in which he attached particular importance to 'the chapters on the laws of matter and geology, and the last chapter in which I have attempted to prove the *subordinate* agency'.[50] He died in August 1879 and was succeeded by his nephew, the Rev. Sir Vyell Vyvyan (1826-1917).

[1] Five younger children shared all the property from a marriage settlement, £25,000 charged on the real estate and the residue. The personalty was sworn under £16,000 (PROB 11/1628/244; IR26/846/292). [2] Cornw. RO, Tremayne mss DD/T/2545. [3] *R. Cornw. Gazette*, 16 Oct. 1824. [4] Harrowby mss, Vyvyan to Lord Dudley

Stuart, 3 Mar. 1823. [5] *West Briton*, 17 Dec. 1824, 7, 28 Jan. 1825.
[6] Ibid. 11 Nov. 1825, 16, 23 June 1826. [7] Cornw. RO, Vyvyan mss
DD/V/BO/47, letters from Roberts, 1 Feb., Shepherd, 17 Feb., Pole
Carew, 17, 21 Feb.; *The Times*, 13, 22 Feb., 9 Mar. 1827. [8] Vyvyan
mss 47, Vyvyan to Avery, 2 Mar.; Carew Pole mss CC/N/60, Vyvyan
to Pole Carew, 8, 21 Mar. 1827. [9] Vyvyan mss 47, Vyvyan to Rev.
Moore, 26 May; *The Times*, 13 June 1827. [10] Vyvyan mss 44, Vyvyan
to Legh Keck, 6 May 1827. [11] *West Briton*, 1 June 1827. [12] Vyvyan
mss 47, Vyvyan to Lord John Russell, 12 June 1827; *Palmerston-
Sulivan Letters*, 231. [13] Vyvyan mss 47, Vyvyan to Rev. Polwhele,
25 June 1827. [14] Ibid. memo. 4 Dec. 1827. [15] Ibid. circular letter,
26 May 1828. [16] Grey mss, Howick jnl. 24 Feb. 1829. [17] *Colchester
Diary*, iii. 608. [18] Gurney diary, 27 Mar. 1829. [19] Add. 52655, f. 156.
[20] Vyvyan mss 48, Vyvyan to Cumberland, 13 July, 9 Aug., to
Newcastle, 20 July 1829. See generally, G. I. T. Machin, *Catholic
Question in English Politics*, 181-7; P. Jupp, *British Politics on Eve
of Reform*, 280-4; B.T. Bradfield, 'Sir Richard Vyvyan and the
fall of Wellington's Government', *Birmingham Univ. Hist. Jnl.* li
(1967-8), 141-56. [21] Vyvyan mss 48, Vyvyan to Cumberland, 22, 29
Aug., to Newcastle, 25 Aug., to Knatchbull, 31 Aug., 7 Sept. 1829.
[22] Eldon mss, Cumberland to Eldon, 25 Sept.; Vyvyan mss 48,
analysis of Commons, n.d., Vyvyan to Cumberland, 22 Oct.
1829; *Palmerston-Sulivan Letters*, 231. [23] Vyvyan mss 48, Vyvyan
to Eldon, 30 Nov. 1829, memo. n.d. [24] Nottingham Univ. Lib.
Ossington mss, Huskisson to Denison, 30 Jan.; Hatherton mss,
Wharncliffe to Littleton, 1 Feb. 1830. [25] *Ellenborough Diary*, ii. 186;
Arbuthnot Jnl. ii. 331-2. [26] Howick jnl. 10 Mar. 1830. [27] Vyvyan mss
BO/47, memo. June 1830. [28] *West Briton*, 13 Aug.; Cent. Kent. Stud.
Stanhope mss U1590/C130/9, Mahon to Stanhope, 15 Aug. 1830.
[29] M. Brock, *Great Reform Act*, 128-9. [30] Ibid. 135-6, 172-5;
Bradfield, 'Sir Richard Vyvyan and the Country Gentlemen, 1830-
1834', *EHR*, lxxxiii (1968), 731-3; Surr. Hist. Cent. Goulburn
mss Acc 304/67B, Goulburn to wife, 19 Mar. 1831. [31] Add 51655,
Mackintosh to Lady Holland, 21 Mar.; 51764, Duncannon to same,
21 Mar.; 51724, Duncannon to Holland, 22 Mar.; Dorset RO D/
BKL, Bankes jnl. 173, 21-22 Mar.; Stanhope mss C190/2, Somerset
to Stanhope, 23 Mar. 1831. [32] Broughton, *Recollections*, iv. 104-5;
Greville Mems. ii. 137. [33] *West Briton*, 29 Apr., 6, 13, 20 May;
Grey mss, Bedford to Grey, 19 May 1831. [34] Bradfield, 'Vyvyan
and Country Gentlemen', 733-4. [35] Add. 61937, f. 125. [36] *Greville
Mems.* ii. 209. [37] Aberdeen Univ. Lib. Arbuthnot mss, Hardinge to
Mrs. Arbuthnot, 19 Aug. 1831; Bradfield, 'Vyvyan and Country
Gentlemen', 735. [38] Hatherton diary, 6 Feb. 1832. [39] Gurney diary, 13
Mar. 1832. [40] Add. 40403, f. 57. [41] Bradfield, 'Vyvyan and Country
Gentlemen', 735-6. [42] Vyvyan mss 47, 'Reform plan of Sir Richard
Vyvyan, 1832'. [43] Ibid. Vyvyan to Salisbury, 18 Apr. 1832, with
enclosed sketch; Vyvyan to ?, n.d. [44] *Croker Pprs.* ii. 154. [45] *Three
Diaries*, 257. [46] Vyvyan mss 47, Vyvyan to Cumberland, 3 June 1832,
Lyndhurst to Vyvyan, n.d. [47] NLW, Ormathwaite mss FG1/6, p. 88.
[48] J. Phillips, *Reform Bill in Boroughs*, 73-83, 92-100; Bradfield, 'Vyvyan
and Country Gentlemen', 738-43; *Dod's Parl. Companion* (1833),
171; [J. Grant], *Random Recollections of Commons* (1837), 154-6.
[49] Vyvyan mss 47, memo. Aug. 1837. [50] Add. 60993, f. 98.

T.A.J.

WAITHMAN, Robert (1764–1833), of New Bridge
Street, Blackfriars, London; 7 Woburn Place, Mdx.,
and Reigate, Surr.[1]

LONDON 1818–1820

LONDON 1826–6 Feb. 1833

b. 1764, *s.* of John Waithman (*d.* 1764), turner, of
Bersham, nr. Wrexham, Denb. and w. Mary *née* Roberts.
educ. Mr. Moore's, ?Wrexham. *m.* 15 July 1787, his cos.

Mary Davis of Red Lion Street, Holborn, Mdx., 4s. (1
d.v.p.) 2da. *d.* 6 Feb. 1833.

Common councilman, London 1795-1818, alderman
1818-*d.*, sheriff 1820-1, ld. mayor 1823-4.

Master, Framework Knitters' Co. 1815-16.

Waithman, a Welshman and London retail linen
draper, with a shop at 103-4 Fleet Street, in which
he was partnered by his sons John and William from
about 1812, played a crucial role in the revival of
reforming politics in the City in the first two decades
of the nineteenth century. An energetic and combative man, he was proud, touchy, honest and brave, but
often self-righteous and tiresome: there can have been
few moments of repose in his life after his entry into
London politics as a relentless opponent of the French
wars, which he considered unnecessary and unjust
until the end of his days. While he regarded himself as
the champion and spokesman of his class, his reform-
ism was essentially moderate and conciliatory – too
much so for such extreme radicals as William Cobbett[†]
and Henry Hunt[*], who saw him as a Whig lick-spittle
and City jobber, and whose distaste he returned with
interest. In the eyes of Tories and some aristocratic
Whigs, he was a dangerous revolutionary.[2] His anger
over Peterloo landed him in hot water with the Tory
majority in the court of aldermen, who attempted to
prosecute him for obstructing the mayoral election
of Michaelmas 1819 by trying (in temporary alliance
with Hunt) to introduce resolutions condemning the
affair and the Liverpool ministry. The dispute dragged
on until king's bench discharged the rule against
Waithman and his coadjutors without costs, 8 June
1820. During it Waithman and his chief persecutor,
Sir William Curtis[*], who had lost his seat for London
in the opposition triumph in which Waithman had
shared in 1818, carried on a bitter personal vendetta.
At the end of 1819 Waithman hit back with an attack,
which he relentlessly pursued, on Curtis's practice as
collector of the orphans' fund coal duties of keeping
large balances in his own hands.[3] These controversies
were aired at the 1820 general election, when Curtis,
benefiting from a reaction to Peterloo and the Cato
Street conspiracy, had his revenge: Waithman, who
ranted interminably on the hustings and complained
of being made a scapegoat, was narrowly squeezed into
fifth place. His post-election dinner, 1 Apr. 1820, when
he called for future unanimity among 'the friends of
liberty', was attended by the opposition Members
Henry Grey Bennet, George Byng, Charles Calvert,
John Cam Hobhouse and Samuel Whitbread.[4] The
working class radical Samuel Bamford met Waithman
at this time and described him as 'a dissatisfied, bilious
looking man'.[5]

Waithman, who spoke 'at great length' for common council's parliamentary reform petition, 26 May 1820, took a prominent part in the City in support of Queen Caroline, though he played second fiddle to his radical rival Alderman Matthew Wood, one of the Members. He was pleased with the 'perfectly miraculous' and 'quite new' parish organizations which were set up to sustain the campaign and was present when Caroline attended St. Paul's to celebrate the abandonment of the bill of pains and penalties, 29 Nov. He was the leading promoter of common council's address calling on the king to dismiss his ministers, 1 Dec., when he perorated that 'it was impossible' that they 'could subjugate the people to the sword'; and in the court of aldermen, 5 Dec. 1820, he put up fierce but ultimately vain resistance to their loyal address. He spoke heatedly for common council's petition for restoration of Caroline's name to the liturgy, 11 Jan. 1821.[6] As sheriff of London, he was a conspicuous figure on horseback at the queen's funeral procession, 14 Aug. 1821; and when a section of the crowd attending the Hammersmith funeral of the two men shot dead by the Guards that day on the 26th clashed with troops outside Knightsbridge barracks, Waithman, who was apparently trying to keep the peace, was manhandled. He and his supporters in common council made an issue of the incident; but Wood's motion for inquiry into the 'outrage', 28 Feb. 1822, was opposed by ministers and crushed.[7] In early September 1821 *John Bull*, seeking to thwart Waithman's mayoral ambitions, published pieces implying that he had handled stolen goods. Waithman, who complained at the mayoral election that 'attacks upon his public character having failed, a systematic warfare was organized against him, to ruin ... his private fortunes', and, when endorsing common council's vote of thanks to Joseph Hume for his parliamentary services, 26 Oct. 1821, reflected that 'for a man to be constantly struggling against misrepresentation and calumny required patience, temper and talents of no ordinary description', sued for libel. He won £500 in damages, 20 Apr. 1822.[8] He took the lead in promoting common council's 'constitutional reform' petition, 29 Jan., supported tithe reform at a City meeting, 27 Feb., and backed votes of money for embattled Greek and Spanish liberals in June 1823.[9] The king never forgave him for his espousal of the queen's cause and was evidently tempted to veto his election as lord mayor at Michaelmas 1823, but wiser counsels prevailed.[10] George IV was furious with the cabinet ministers Canning and Charles Williams Wynn for attending Waithman's official dinner at Easter 1824, despite an earlier collective decision to boycott it.[11] After a Mansion House dinner for the

Greeks, when 'the Waithman family, both male and female, were in all their glory', Thomas Creevey* 'could not help thinking ... what they must think of the *shop*, poor things, when they return to it after all their finery'.[12] At about this time Waithman handed over active management of the shop to John and William. His youngest son Henry was by now in business as a silk broker in Old Bond Street, and for a few years either side of 1830 Robert, the eldest, ran a furniture printing and upholstery enterprise at 244 Regent Street. Waithman called for revision of the corn laws in common council, 7 Apr., and at a public meeting, 13 Apr. 1825; but in common council, 8 Feb. 1826, he attributed distress in the Spitalfields silk trade and other industries to 'nefarious speculations ... [and] a vicious paper system', and called for reduced taxation and judicious protection of domestic manufactures.[13] The following month he offered for London on his usual platform of 'freedom and purity of election', as the spokesman for the livery; and at the general election in June, when his torrent of words included the observation that 'men of honesty, who could speak common sense, and would not be afraid to speak it, were the men that the country wanted in Parliament', he was returned second in the poll.[14] Greeted in common hall with 'tumultuous approbation', 19 Oct. 1826, he expressed his 'warmest support' for repeal of the corn laws, but argued that a complete change of financial system was required to underpin it.[15]

On the address, 21 Nov. 1826, Waithman demanded 'immediate consideration' of the corn laws and curbs on the fraudulent speculations which had precipitated the 1825-6 commercial crisis, and challenged Brogden, the chairman of ways and means, to explain his involvement in the Arigna Mining Company. Yet he was one of the 'many of the opposition' who voted against Hume's amendment.[16] On 24 Nov., when he declined to join in praise for ministerial relaxation of the corn laws, he renewed his attack on Brogden after he had reluctantly given up the chairmanship. He pursued the Arigna issue, 28, 30 Nov., 1 Dec., and on 5 Dec. moved for the appointment of a select committee of inquiry into joint-stock companies, 1824-6, but acquiesced in the government amendment to restrict it in the first instance to the Arigna Company.[17] He called for a reduction in insurance duty, 8 Dec. 1826, and queried the cost of king's counsel, 12 Feb. 1827.[18] He voted against the Clarences' grant, 'one of the most ill-timed measures that was ever submitted to Parliament', 16 Feb., 2, 16 Mar. On 20 Feb. he spoke and voted in a minority of 15 for army reductions, and next day he supported inquiry into Northampton corporation's alleged interference in elections; he voted in the same sense on Leicester, 15 Mar. He divided silently for Catholic relief, 6 Mar. He defied the barracking of agricultural Members to demand a lower import price for corn, 9 Mar., and complained of their renewed 'clamour', 12 Mar., when he voted against increased protection for barley.[19] He presented but reserved judgement on a London ship owners' petition against erosion of the navigation laws, 22 Mar. He voted for the spring guns bill, 23 Mar. He was in the opposition minority for supplies to be withheld until the uncertainty following Lord Liverpool's stroke was resolved, 30 Mar. On 9 Apr. he presented a petition from aggrieved subscribers to the Devon and Cornwall Mining Company and personally attacked Wilks, Member for Sudbury, one of its directors; his comment that Wilks was 'the last man alive whom I would trust myself with for five minutes, except in the presence of a third person', earned him a rebuke from the Speaker. He withdrew a motion for inquiry under pressure from Brougham, 15 May. He indicated his 'wish to support' Canning's ministry if possible, 7 May, but in common council on the 23rd he explained that 'he had not changed his seat in the House of Commons because ... a man representing a large body of persons ought not to be dragged from one side ... to the other by any party'.[20] He called for Penryn's seats to be given to Manchester, 8 May, and spoke and voted in that sense, 28 May, arguing that it would be preferable to have 'the abuses of the representation left in their hideous deformity' than to adopt 'the delusive farce' of sluicing the borough. He supported the disfranchisement of East Retford, 11 June. Having spoken in common council for repeal of the Test Acts, 9 May, he presented favourable petitions, 18 June 1827, 18, 19 Feb., 3, 18 Mar., supported the one from London corporation, 11 Feb., and voted silently for repeal, 26 Feb. 1828.[21] On 19 June 1827, foreshadowing a familiar future refrain, he suggested that ministers had gone too far in their application of free trade principles, which 'could never be carried fully into effect, without a considerable reduction in taxation'.[22]

Waithman, who was widowed in September 1827, voted in Hume's minority of 15 against the Wellington ministry's navy estimates, 11 Feb. 1828. He was in one of eight on the same issue next day, when he deplored the automatic granting of supplies and the notion of unquestioning 'confidence in ministers'. He had plenty more to say on this theme, 22, 25 Feb., when his attempt to reduce the army by 10,000 men failed. He declared on the former day that he was 'sufficiently an aristocrat' to wish to see 'the sons of the great and wealthy families ... watching over and checking the extravagances of ministers, not making provi-

sions for themselves'. He urged repeal of the Small Receipt Stamp Duty Act, which relied on 'a system of informers' against tradesmen, 19 Feb. He argued that the object of the select committee on the policing of the metropolis proposed by Peel, the home secretary, should be the prevention rather than the punishment of crime, and voiced confidence in the 'perfect and complete' arrangements which operated in the City. He was keen for justice to be visited on prevaricating witnesses in the East Retford inquiry, 3, 4, 7 Mar. (when he made a fool of himself by supposing the borough to be in Yorkshire), and spoke and voted for transferring its seats to Birmingham, 21 Mar., but was admonished by Peel for suggesting that taxation without representation was an 'absolute tyranny' which justified physical resistance. He was indignant at ministers' opposition to this practical reform, 24 Mar., 19 May, 2, 27 June. He attacked the 'fallacious' Canada Company project, but withdrew his motion for papers after annoying the Speaker, 27 Mar., and opposed the Hibernian Company bill, 24 Apr. He favoured reform of select vestries, 31 Mar., 9 June. He supported the principle of Lord Althorp's borough polls bill, 31 Mar., 28 Apr., pointing to the example of London to demonstrate that by sensible organization large numbers could be polled in a short time; he was named to the committee on it, 2 Apr. He was dismissive of Wilmot Horton's plan to finance education by allowing parishes to mortgage their poor rates, 17 Apr. He presented petitions against the friendly societies bill, 21 Apr., when he denied assertions that the silk trade was recovering. He presented a Norwich weavers' petition complaining of distress on account of low wages, 1 May, but dissented from its call for wage fixing. He pressed for inquiry into chancery delays, 24 Apr., and was in the minority of 39 on excise prosecutions, 1 May. He divided for Catholic relief, 12 May, and against the provision for Canning's family next day. On the army estimates, 16 May, he criticized ministers' failure to reduce the 'enormous and needless expenditure' to combat distress. Supporting Hume, 30 May, he condemned details of the miscellaneous estimates. He was in Hume's minority of 28 against the grant for the Society for the Propagation of the Gospels, 6 June, and he voted in protest at the cost of refurbishing Buckingham House, 23 June, when he also questioned the 'extraordinary appropriation of public money' to pay reduced and retired army officers. He divided against the Irish and Scottish small notes bill, 5 June. On the 13th he defended the City authorities' policy on Smithfield meat market, having seen 'nothing' there that morning 'to frighten even old women and children', and opposed the inquiry, to which, however, he was subsequently named. He denounced the additional churches bill, which authorized churchwardens arbitrarily to tax parishioners, 23, 30 June. He contended that 'excessive taxation' and unrestricted foreign imports had wrecked the glove trade, 26 June, when he was in a minority of ten on cider excise licences. He presented and endorsed a London glove manufacturers' petition for protection, 8 July, arguing that free trade must be reciprocal. He was apparently not present for the division on the ordnance estimates, 4 July, but he spoke and voted against a detail of them, 7 July 1828. Next day, opposing more Canadian expenditure, he appealed to Members to 'act from their own unbiased conviction, and show some regard to the feelings and interests of their constituents'.

Waithman, who fell foul of Hunt during the latter's unsuccessful campaign for election to the common council in December 1828,[23] supported the Irish unlawful societies bill, 13 Feb. 1829, when he gave full credit to ministers for their 'honourable' conduct on Catholic emancipation and persuaded them to omit a couple of 'inquisitorial' clauses from the relief bill. He supported it in common council, 26 Feb., and alleged that many hostile petitions were fraudulently signed,[24] as he did relentlessly in the House, 27 Feb., 3, 11, 13, 16, 18, 19 Mar., when he squabbled petulantly with Inglis. He voted for emancipation, 6, 30 Mar., and lavishly praised Peel and Wellington when endorsing London corporation's petition, 9 Mar. He voted for Daniel O'Connell to be allowed to take his seat unimpeded, 18 May. 'With every disposition to confide in the ministry', he still carped at their practice of evading the issue of economy by passing the buck to the finance committee, 27 Feb. On their proposals for the silk trade, 14 Apr., he expounded at length the views on free trade which he consistently maintained thereafter, arguing that current circumstances required 'prohibition' and that a unilateral application of free trade dogma would ruin the industry:

> I do not understand the doctrine of free trade. I have read many pamphlets and books on this subject, and on political economy, but they only bewilder me; and I do not know, after reading them, whether I have any common sense or not. Things that once appeared certain, quite lack that property.

He accordingly opposed the silk bill, 28 Apr., 1 May, when he was in the minority of 22 for a wrecking amendment, 4, 7 May. On the budget statement, 8 May, he deplored but did not altogether condemn the recent silk weavers' riots, disputed official statements that distress was abating and demanded inquiry and tax remissions:

> I throw no fault on the present administration, who do pretty much like their predecessors, tread in the beaten path, though I much wish they would strike into a new and better one. I do not wish for any change of administration; for I frankly own I do not see how the country could be benefited by it.

He objected to the calico duties, 27 May, voted for reduction of those on hemp, 1 June, and the following day struggled against country gentlemen's mockery to advocate relaxation of the corn laws. The silk bill confirmed his belief that the 'great trading interests' should be represented in Parliament, and he accordingly voted for the transfer of East Retford's seats to Birmingham, 5 May, and for Lord Blandford's reform scheme, 2 June. He defended the London Bridge bill, 6 May, and saw no reason to extend the metropolitan police bill to the City, 25 May. On 4 June 1829 he put to the House the stark choice between protecting domestic trade and industry and the 'far more dangerous experiment' of returning to a paper currency.

In October 1829 Waithman wrote to *The Times* from the house which he had acquired at Reigate about the fatally dangerous state of the local turnpike, and in common council, 5 Nov. 1829, he called for measures to reduce London coal prices.[25] He seconded Protheroe's abortive amendment to the address, 4 Feb. 1830, and voted for Knatchbull's, having declared that he had 'nothing to hope or to expect from any party' and that, though he had 'been charged with being a Jacobin, a republican, and everything else that implies hatred to our government', he wanted 'reform ... to prevent the necessity of revolution'. He again supported the transfer of East Retford's seats to Birmingham, 11, 26 Feb., 5 Mar., when he accused ministers of 'wantonly playing at cudgels in a china shop' by resisting it; he was in O'Connell's minority of 21 for having elections there conducted by secret ballot, 15 Mar. He did not vote for Blandford's reform scheme, 18 Feb., but divided for the enfranchisement of Birmingham, Leeds and Manchester, 23 Feb. He was in the minority of 13 for O'Connell's radical reform bill, 28 May, and voted later that day for Lord John Russell's more moderate proposal. On 5 Feb. he insisted that the 'true value' of exports had significantly diminished since the war, a theme to which he returned on the 9th, when he secured a return of accounts to prove his point. Furious that ministers were glossing over the country's problems, he opposed going into committee of supply without better information, 11 Feb., but on Peel's explanation admitted that he 'may have misunderstood the matter'; he voted in Hume's minority of nine for an adjournment, and divided with him for tax reductions, 15 Feb., though he pointed out to him, 19 Feb., when he voted against the army estimates, that it was idle to expect ministers to make retrenchments. In common council, 25 Feb., he contended that no benefit would accrue from ending the East India Company's trading monopoly.[26] In the House that day he spoke and voted in a minority of 26 for Harvey's proposal to prevent Members from voting in private bill committees on measures in which they had an interest. In a discussion provoked by his presentation of a London merchants' and ship owners' petition complaining of excessive taxation, alteration of the currency and erosion of commercial reciprocity, 12 Mar., he disputed the doctrinaire views of Maberly and Hume and the political economists:

> I have some experience on these subjects, more, I believe, than any other person who now hears me, having been 40 years in trade ... I stand here ... on a better footing than ... three-fourths of the Members who hear me, having been returned to Parliament free of all expense ... by the votes of ten or twelve thousand individuals ... Things are not likely to mend till there is a reform; and if we do not take that business into our hands, it will be done out of the House, by a suffering, but intelligent community. It is impossible to go on with a representation suitable to a population of five millions and no debt, now that we have a population of twenty millions, and £8,000,000 of debt. The people are everywhere in distress ... and why ... to increase the foreign trade of the country; and although it has been increased three or four millions by forcing a trade ... we have not succeeded ... though we have ground down the labourer to the dust [and] ruined our substantial farmers and merchants.

He seconded Burdett's unsuccessful motion for inquiry into distress, 16 Mar., and spoke at length in the state of the nation debate, 19 Mar., rehearsing his usual arguments and answering his critics. He spoke and voted for a reduction in the navy estimates, 22 Mar., and divided for ordnance economies, 29 Mar, and inquiry into crown lands revenues, 30 Mar. On 2 Apr. he opposed the St. Giles vestry bill and supported the prayer of a Hull ship owners' petition on distress. At a thinly attended common hall on this subject, 5 Apr., he confessed that he 'saw no probability of ... reform being carried ... soon' and blamed distress on 'a pernicious meddling with trade'.[27] In the House that day he voted for Jewish emancipation, as he did again on 17 May. He was in the minorities against Lord Ellenborough's divorce bill, 6 Apr., and for reform of the law, 3 June. He presented petitions for abolition of the death penalty for forgery, 26, 27 Apr. He paired against the grant for public buildings, 3 May. He voted for abolition of the Irish lord lieu-

tenancy, 11 May, repeal of the Irish coal duties, 13 May (having been named to the select committee on the coal trade, 11 Mar.), information on privy councillors' emoluments, 14 May, and the four-and-a-half per cent duties, 21 May, inquiry into the government of Ceylon, 27 May, and against the grant for consular services, 11 June. He was appointed to the committee on Littleton's truck bill, 3 May, and warmly supported the measure, 4 May. He welcomed the sale of beer bill, 4 May, but recanted on 1 July, when he voted for an amendment to restrict on-sales. After presenting a London ship owners' distress petition, 6 May, he voiced his weariness with the 'dictatorial lectures' of the free trader Poulett Thomson. He saw no point in investigating the condition of the poor as Slaney proposed, 13 May. Next day he condemned the 'extraordinary expense' of bankruptcy administration and called for its reform. He pressed for repeal of the house and window taxes, 28 May. He spoke and voted for Hume's motion for inquiry into the church building commissioners' oppressive dealings with the parish of St. Luke, 17 June 1830. At the general election that summer he was returned unopposed for London, despite his refusal to canvass. At the nomination he admitted that tax reductions would be difficult to implement without a breach of faith towards the public creditor and pronounced that in Parliament 'a little less talk and a little more work ... would be more desirable'.[28] He was criticized for declining to attend a *London Tavern* meeting to subscribe for the French revolutionaries, 17 Aug. 1830, but in a public rejoinder explained that he was 'not in very good health or spirits' and doubted the efficacy of such displays.[29]

In the House, 3 Nov. 1830, he lamented the lack of any reference to distress in the king's speech and the government's refusal to countenance reform; and on the 5th he reiterated his view that it was now a question of 'a reform or a convulsion'. He attacked government for obscurantism on this and for believing the alarmist aldermen who had advised them to cancel the king's visit to the City: ministers had 'virtually and effectually signed their own death warrant'. In the court of aldermen, 9 Nov., and in common council, 15 Nov., he savaged Aldermen Key and Hunter for unilaterally recommending cancellation.[30] He thought Spring Rice's motion for a select committee on the Irish poor was futile, 11 Nov. He helped to vote the Wellington ministry out of office on the civil list, 15 Nov. On 6 Dec. he withdrew a motion for a reduction of public salaries in order to give the Grey ministry time to formulate their policies; but he promised to reveal after Christmas the results of his personal investigations into distress, which had brought him to recant his support of the resumption of cash payments. Later that day he questioned the sense of lavishing money on Canadian waterways and argued that 'however plausible in theory', free trade ideas had proved to be 'most mischievous in practice'. He presented petitions for the abolition of slavery, 8 Dec., and of the truck system, 14 Dec., when he endorsed the City petition for repeal of the coastwise coal duties. He criticized ministers for maintaining the salary of the ambassador to France at £10,000 and warned them that 'the country will expect performances as well as promises', though he praised the 'liberality and fairness' of the chancellor Althorp's subsequent observations on the estimates. On 17 Dec. he joined in calls for repeal of the duty on printed cottons and calicos and asserted that the reduction of taxes which bore on 'the middle classes' was essential for the restoration of full employment and general prosperity; he presented an Aldgate petition for repeal of the 'monstrous' assessed taxes, 22 Dec. 1830. Next day he attacked pensions which he mistakenly took to belong to members of Lord Bathurst's family, but he backed down gracefully when his blunder was pointed out.

Waithman, whose aspirations to the chamberlainship of London in January 1831 came to nothing,[31] presented a petition from his ward for an extension of the franchise and the ballot, which he now favoured, having seen at close quarters the effects of corporate influence in London, 4 Feb. He insisted that foreign imports had wrecked the silk industry, 7 Feb., and next day demanded reform of the bankruptcy laws for the benefit of creditors, as he did on the presentation of the City petition, 21 Feb. On the budget, 11 Feb., he approved the removal of the duty on printed cotton, but 'talked a good deal of nonsense', as one Whig saw it, about the proposals for wine and timber, and was 'rather hostile' to the notion of a tax on land and stock transfers.[32] In any case, he added, nothing effectual could be accomplished without 'reform and retrenchment'. He welcomed ministers' abandonment of the transfer tax, 15 Feb., before unleashing on a restless and bored House a string of 27 statistical resolutions (which he had leaked to the press a month earlier)[33] designed to prove his case that the real value of exports had fallen and that the root cause of economic distress was depreciation of the currency since the 1819 settlement. Ministers carried the previous question, but Waithman sided with them against Hume on the navy estimates, 25 Feb. He had no serious objections to the proposed transfer of duty from printed calicos to raw cotton, 28 Feb., but pressed government to extend the time allowed to claim drawback. He spoke

against equalization of the timber duties at a merchants' dinner, 11 Mar.[34] He approved of Frankland Lewis's bill to regulate the coal trade, 28 Mar. He presented London petitions for reform, 26 Feb., and cited Reigate as an example of a borough under domineering 'influence', 28 Feb. As 'an old reformer', he 'rejoiced' at the scope of the ministerial reform bill, which he endorsed in common council and the House, 4 Mar., when he repudiated Hunt's attack on London corporation as a set of jobbers, and at a tumultuous meeting of the livery, 7 Mar. He was one of the delegation which presented the City reform address to the king, 9 Mar.[35] On 9 Mar. he hailed the bill as 'a measure of necessity', called for 'by circumstances and ... recommended by the concurrent voice of the people'. He presented more favourable petitions, 16 Mar.; voted for the second reading, 19 Mar.; spoke at a London merchants' reform meeting, 25 Mar.;[36] stated on 14 Apr. that 'by this measure you satisfy the wise and the reasonable, and draw a line of distinction between them ... and dangerous or wild theorists'; contradicted Hunt's allegation that Spitalfields silk workers had reacted against the bill, 18 Apr. 1831, and voted against Gascoyne's wrecking amendment the following day. At the ensuing general election he was returned unopposed on a joint platform with three other reformers; he denounced the self-styled 'moderate reformers' and urged vigour and unanimity to thwart 'the proprietors of rotten boroughs' in the Lords.[37]

Waithman spoke at the livery reform dinner, 9 May 1831, and in common council three days later ranted against the West India Dock Company as 'one of the most disgraceful jobs ever perpetrated in the City'.[38] In the House, 22 June, he said that pro-reform feeling was 'nearly universal' in Wales and presented a Spitalfields silk workers' reform petition. Next day he had a rather childish clash with Hunt, whom he charged with verbal diarrhoea and egotistical use of 'I'; Hunt retorted that ten minutes of Waithman's ponderous oratory was an unbeatable opiate.[39] Waithman voted silently for the second reading of the reintroduced reform bill, 6 July, and on the 8th confirmed the strength of his constituents' support for it, despite the threat which it posed to the votes of many of them. He voted against the adjournment motions of 12 July, exhorting ministers not to submit to such 'vexatious and factious' obstruction. He was a steady supporter of the bill's details. He dismissed borough proprietors' demands for compensation for disfranchisement as 'the height of insolence and arrogance', 19 July. On 22 July he likened the captious Tory barrister Wetherell to 'lawyer *Endless* in the play', and 'demolished' the renegade Whig Scarlett, who had tried to exploit the livery's reprimand of his City colleague Thompson for a wayward vote. Littleton wrote that he had 'never heard more bold, coarse, blackguard, just or successful vituperation', which could only have been effectively delivered by someone with 'the Alderman's peculiar qualities of mind'. Creevey, who relished the 'licking', had 'never ... heard a more powerful execution of a culprit'.[40] Waithman complained of opposition time-wasting, 29 July, 3 Aug. He pressed for the whole of Wrexham parish to be included in the Denbigh district, 10 Aug. On 24 and 30 Aug. he denied that there had been any reaction against the bill in the City and exhorted its supposed friends to stop proposing hair-splitting amendments. He reckoned that two days were enough for borough polls, 6 Sept. In common council the following day he contended that 'the great principle of the bill had been preserved throughout, and any alterations ... were only introduced to strengthen it'.[41] He presented a Manchester petition for the ballot in county elections and a householder franchise in boroughs, 13 Sept. At a common hall to petition the Lords in favour of the bill, 19 Sept., he proclaimed that 'the king, the government and the people were firmly united for it' against a segment of the aristocracy, and added that while he 'did not think the bill went far enough', he was 'willing to take it as it was' to secure the vital extinction of rotten boroughs.[42] He divided for the passage of the bill, 21 Sept., and for the motion of confidence in ministers after its defeat in the Lords, 10 Oct. He attended but did not speak at the London merchants' meeting which resolved to address the king in support of the government and the bill, 13 Oct.[43] He supported the grant for the duchess of Kent and Princess Victoria, 3 Aug. He spoke and voted in support of ministers in the Dublin election controversy, 23 Aug., and called lord chancellor Brougham's bankruptcy reform bill 'a most excellent measure', 14 Oct. 1831.

Waithman quarrelled with some of the wilder reformers in the livery that month by dissociating himself from their reported wish to nominate him in the protracted lord mayoral election farce as they sought to force the re-election of Key on the court of aldermen. His refusal in common hall, 14 Oct., to be made the 'tool' of a faction provoked a commotion, and he subsequently defended himself in letters to the press.[44] In the House, 12 Dec. 1831, he asserted that his own inquiries had convinced him that the sensational story that the convicted burkers had confessed to dozens of murders was not true. He voted silently for the second reading of the final reform bill, 17 Dec. 1831, two days before the death of his son William.[45] Waithman, whose own health was now failing, voted

to go into committee on the bill, 20 Jan. 1832, when he repeated his axiom that unrestricted foreign competition was destroying the silk trade. He again gave steady support to the bill in its passage through committee. He said on 27 Jan. that he would swallow the division of counties because the benefits outweighed the dangers. In an angry exchange with Croker over Tory obstruction, 2 Feb., he addressed the Speaker as 'my lord mayor'. Later that day he made a personal attack on Wetherell over his flight from the Bristol riots, and claimed to have missed only one day's debate on the reform bill, as a result of illness on 30 Jan. He supported the clauses concerning parochial relief and registration, 8 Feb., and the cost of booths and clerks, 15 Feb., condemned the boroughs of Amersham, 21 Feb., and Great Grimsby, 23 Feb., and endorsed the provisions for additional metropolitan Members, 2 Mar. He voted for the third reading, 22 Mar. He divided with government on the Russian-Dutch loan, 26 Jan., and relations with Portugal, 9 Feb., and exonerated them from blame for 'a great waste of money' on some naval works begun by their predecessors, 13 Feb. He said that he would support the restriction of children's hours in factories but that it would be 'wrong to force grown-up men out of employ', 10 Feb. He welcomed Alexander Baring's bill to exclude insolvent debtors from the House and end Members' exemption from arrest, 14 Feb. On 1 Mar. he presented and endorsed weavers' petitions from Spitalfields, Coventry and Macclesfield for inquiry into distress, and later supported Grosvenor's successful motion for the appointment of a select committee and criticized Poulett Thomson's mealy-mouthed speech. Although Vyvyan had not consulted him before proposing that he be added to the committee, 6 Mar., he agreed to serve in order to counter its free trade bias. He obtained a return of silk imports but agreed to drop his demand that firms found guilty of illegal trading be named, 15 Mar. He spoke and voted for Davies's motion for inquiry into distress in the glove trade, 3 Apr. He welcomed the government's cautious and sensible approach to the abolition of slavery, 4 Apr. Despite feeling unwell, he spoke in support of common council's motion to petition for supplies to be withheld until the reform crisis was favourably resolved, 10 May, and secured the appointment of a committee to monitor events.[46] He backed the petition in the House later that day, admitting that poor health had recently interfered with his attendance, and voted for the address calling on the king to appoint only ministers who would carry the reform bill unimpaired. Next day he supported the livery's petition, remarking that the Lords 'might quote bits of Latin [but] there was not a boy of 14 who could not teach them practical sense'.[47] He spoke for the petition in the House, 14 May, when he mocked Wellington's 'futile' attempt to form a ministry and warned that if the Commons deserted the people there would be 'no answering for public tranquillity'. He approved common council's address to the king that day, but suggested that 'the best course was to uphold the House of Commons, and let the battle be fought there'.[48] When presenting a supplies petition from the churchwardens of St. Bride's, Fleet Street (where he was to be buried nine months later), he said that no parishioners had been involved in the recent disruption of a sermon by the bishop of Lichfield. He was delighted at the reinstatement of the Grey ministry, voted for the second reading of the Irish reform bill, 25 May, and on 4 July endorsed London corporation's petition calling for the principles of the English bill to be applied to it. On a motion for inquiry into the effects on trade of changes in the navigation laws, 22 May, he deployed his familiar arguments on free trade and depreciation. He presented a petition for the lifting of theatre censorship, 31 May. He was unhappy with the fining powers given to coroners by Warburton's bill, 20 June. On 3 July he submitted 32 resolutions, all of which were negatived, on the economy, supported them in a long and tedious speech and, replying to his many critics, expressed his contempt for the free trade 'philosophers and poets' who 'think they know better than practical men'. He presented and approved a petition from St. Andrew's, Holborn against the vagrants removal bill, 5 July. In his last known utterance in Commons debate, 7 Aug. 1832, he presented and vigorously supported a silk weavers' petition complaining of the way in which the select committee had taken evidence. He maintained that it had been packed to promote free trade dogma and attacked Poulett Thomson, whose smile when he inadvertently referred to him as 'Member for the board of trade' drove Waithman to redoubled ranting rage.

He was returned in third place for London at the general election of 1832, but was too ill to take his seat in the reformed Parliament before his death at his house in Woburn Place in February 1833.[49] By his will, dated 21 Apr. 1832, and proved under a modest £14,000 (later £12,000), he left his remaining interest in the Fleet Street shop to his son John, who carried it on for about ten years. Henry, who continued in business as a silk broker, received £500, and his sisters Maria and Mary Ann equal shares in a trust fund of £8,000. The residue, which included the properties at Reigate and Winchmore Hill, Middlesex, but yielded no money, went to John and his eldest brother Robert,

who evidently retired from the upholstery business.[50] In the summer of 1833 a St. Bride's parish committee erected an obelisk in memory of Waithman at Ludgate Circus, on the site of his first shop in Fleet Market, and facing the column commemorating Wilkes.[51] Noticing Waithman's death, *The Times* patronisingly commented that 'had his early education been better directed, or his early circumstances more favourable to his ambition, he might have become an important man in a wider and higher sphere' than City politics, his natural stamping ground, but conceded that 'his conduct up to the last was fearless and consistent'.[52]

[1] See J.R. Dinwiddy, *Radicalism and Reform* (1992), 63-86; *Biog. Dict. of Modern British Radicals* ed. J.O. Baylen and N.J. Grossman, i. 504-6; *Oxford DNB*; *DWB*. [2] J. Belchem, 'Orator' Hunt, 44, 69. [3] R.R. Sharpe, *London and the Kingdom*, iii. 311-12; Belchem, 120; *The Times*, 15, 18, 30 Sept., 9, 13, 22 Oct., 8, 15, 16, 20, 27 Nov., 7, 8, 17, 29 Dec. 1819, 20, 26, 29 Jan., 29 Apr., 12, 25 May, 9 June 1820. [4] *The Times*, 26, 28 Feb., 6, 8-11, 13-17 Mar., 13 Apr.; Add. 38568, f. 78; Lonsdale mss, Long to Lonsdale, 11 Mar. [1820]. [5] S. Bamford, *Passages in the Life of a Radical* ed. W.H. Chaloner, i. 232. [6] *The Times*, 27 May, 13 June, 14 July, 4 Aug., 23, 29 Sept., 20, 31 Oct., 2, 6, 11, 16 Dec. 1820, 12 Jan. 1821; *Creevey Pprs*. i. 341; *Geo. IV Letters*, ii. 884; Add. 37949, f. 87; 40120, f. 152; J.A. Hone, *For the Cause of Truth*, 351. [7] *Creevey Pprs*. ii. 18; *Geo. IV Letters*, ii. 953; *Ann. Reg.* (1821), Chron. pp. 127, 134-5; *Arbuthnot Jnl*. i. 115-16; *The Times*, 29, 31 Aug., 12 Sept., 27 Oct., 7 Dec. 1821, 1 Feb. 1822. [8] M.D. George, *Cat. of Pol. and Personal Satires*, x. 14244; *Colchester Diary*, iii. 235; *The Times*, 1, 27 Oct. 1821, 22 Apr. 1822; *Ann. Reg.* (1822), App. pp. 404-7. [9] *The Times*, 20 Dec. 1822, 30 Jan., 28 Feb., 11, 14, 24 June 1823. [10] Ibid. 30 Sept. 1823; *Geo. IV Letters*, iii. 1108. [11] Buckingham, *Mems. Geo. IV*, ii. 65-66; *Arbuthnot Jnl*. i. 306; *Wellington Despatches*, ii. 251; *Wellington and Friends*, 43; *Hobhouse Diary*, 110; *Geo. IV Letters*, iii. 1163; *Croker Pprs*. i. 266. [12] *Creevey's Life and Times*, 192. [13] *The Times*, 8, 14 Apr. 1825, 9 Feb. 1826. [14] Ibid. 18 Mar., 4 Apr., 12, 18 May, 3, 10, 12-17, 20 June 1826. [15] Ibid. 20 Oct. 1826. [16] *Baring Jnls*. i. 51. [17] *The Times*, 6 Dec. 1826; Add. 36463, f. 228. [18] *The Times*, 9 Dec. 1826, 13 Feb. 1827. [19] Ibid. 13 Mar. 1827. [20] Ibid. 24 May 1827. [21] Ibid. 10 May, 19 June 1827. [22] Ibid. 20 June 1827. [23] Belchem, 180. [24] *The Times*, 27 Feb. 1829. [25] GL MS 10409; *The Times*, 3, 6 Nov. 1829. [26] *The Times*, 26 Feb. 1830. [27] Ibid. 6 Apr. 1830. [28] Ibid. 28, 31 July 1830. [29] Ibid. 18, 21, 23 Aug. 1830. [30] Ibid. 12, 16 1830. [31] Add. 56555, ff. 86-87, [32] Add. 51569, Ord to Holland [11 Feb. 1831]. [33] *The Times*, 19 Jan. 1831. [34] Ibid. 14 Mar. 1831. [35] Ibid. 5, 8, 10 Mar. 1831. [36] Ibid. 26 Mar. 1831. [37] Ibid. 25-30 Apr. 1831. [38] Ibid. 10, 13 May 1831. [39] George, xi. 16722. [40] Hatherton diary, 22 [July]; Creevey mss, Creevey to Miss Ord, 23 July 1831. [41] *The Times*, 8 Sept. 1831. [42] Ibid. 20 Sept. 1831. [43] Ibid. 14 Oct. 1831. [44] Ibid. 13, 15, 18, 20, 21 Oct. 1831. [45] *Gent. Mag.* (1831), ii. 570. [46] *The Times*, 11 May 1832. [47] Ibid. 12 May 1832. [48] Ibid. 15 May 1832. [49] Ibid. 27 Oct., 13 Nov., 10-13 Dec. 1832, 31 Jan., 7 Feb. 1833. [50] PROB 11/1815/265; IR26/1340/249. [51] *The Times*, 20 Feb., 7, 26, 28 June 1833; *Gent. Mag.* (1833), i. 634. [52] *The Times*, 7 Feb. 1833; *Gent. Mag.* (1833), i. 179.

D.R.F.

WALDO SIBTHORP, Charles De Laet (1783–1855), of Canwick Hall, Lincs.[1]

| LINCOLN | 1826–1832 |
| LINCOLN | 1835–14 Dec. 1855 |

b. 14 Feb. 1783, 2nd s. of Humphrey Sibthorp[†] (afterwards Waldo Sibthorp) (*d.* 1815) of Canwick and Susannah, da. of Richard Ellison, banker, of Thorne, Yorks. and Sudbrooke Holme, Lincs.; bro. of Coningsby Waldo Waldo Sibthorp*. *educ.* Chiswick; Brasenose, Oxf. 1801. *m.* 21 Feb. 1812, Maria, da. and coh. of Ponsonby Tottenham[†] of Merrion Square, Dublin, 4s. *suc.* bro. 1822. *d.* 14 Dec. 1855.

Cornet 2 Drag. 1803, lt. 1806; capt. 4 Drag. Gds. 1811, ret. 1822.

Lt.-col. R. South Lincs. militia 1822, col. 1852-*d.*

Colonel Sibthorp (as he was always known) was a colourful and preposterous Member, an excessively hirsute man dressed in a regency frock coat, top hat and Wellington boots, who always carried a magnifying glass. Poorly educated (he did not graduate from Oxford), but possessing 'an acuteness surpassed by few', he expressed his unshakeable prejudices with an often comical and sometimes offensive bluntness. He became one of the House's great entertainers and his 'peculiarities' were generally indulged.[2] He served in the Penisula with the cavalry, but retired from the army four months after succeeding his elder brother to the old family property at Canwick, on the southern edge of Lincoln, in March 1822. His military bent found a new outlet with his appointment as lieutenant-colonel of a regiment of the county militia in September. He had declined an invitation to stand for Lincoln in his brother's room.[3] He claimed to be 'perfectly neuter' in the county by-election of late 1823.[4] The following year he fought a duel with the reformer Dr. Edward Charlesworth of the county hospital.[5] At the county meeting called to petition against the unhindered importation of foreign corn, 23 Dec. 1825, Sibthorp defended his conduct as chairman of a recent agricultural show dinner in intervening to prevent William Johnson, the radical Member for Boston, from introducing politics and, repudiating a charge that he had been afraid to have liberal views aired, boasted that 'he had never known fear in his life'. He admitted that 'his early pursuits had rendered him unfit to offer an opinion on agricultural subjects', but he advised the agriculturists to 'confide in the conduct of ministers, to whom the country owed both gratitude and confidence'.[6] At the general election of 1826 he accepted an invitation to stand for Lincoln on the Tory and corporation interest which had sustained his

father and brother. Professing 'an honest independence ... founded upon a firm attachment to our *glorious* constitution in church and state', he declared with 'emphatic emotion' his abhorrence of Catholic claims. He was returned in second place after a contest with two men of liberal opinions. At a Lincoln dinner, 11 Nov. 1826, he 'desired his constituents to observe his very movements in Parliament, for he was no party man, nor slave to any one'.[7]

Sibthorp presented four Lincolnshire petitions requesting continued protection for agriculture, 27 Feb., spoke briefly in that sense, 12 Mar., 9 Apr., and voted against the corn bill, 2 Apr. 1827. He divided against Catholic relief, 6 Mar. He called the revenue commissioners' report on the County Fire Office 'unfair ... assassination', 10 Apr. Soon afterwards he gave his constituents the 'earliest notification' of Canning's appointment as prime minister.[8] He brought up Lincolnshire agriculturists' petitions against the importation of foreign wool, 25 May, voted against the disfranchisement of Penryn, 28 May, 7 June, and the Coventry magistracy bill, 18 June, and opposed the game bill, 21 June 1827.[9] He presented two Lincolnshire petitions for repeal of the Test Acts, 31 May 1827,[10] but he divided against that measure, 26 Feb., and Catholic relief, 12 May 1828. Supporting inquiry into criminal commitments, 5 Mar., he called for close attention to be given to the theft of livestock. He endorsed the Lincoln city freeholders' petition for a county vote, 6 Mar., supported Sykes's motion for inquiry into the franchise in counties corporate such as Lincoln, despite being 'an enemy to abstract reform', 11 Mar., and welcomed the resultant bill, 20 Mar. In May and June he was a determined opponent of Davies's borough polls regulation bill, which he said would increase election expenses and curtail 'constitutional enjoyments'; he was a minority teller in the divisions of 13 and 27 May. He opposed Lord Nugent's voters' registration bill, 19 June, and the 'harsh, ungenerous and illiberal' corporate funds bill, 8, 10 July, when he was a teller for the hostile minority. He demanded 'considerable additional protection for domestic agriculture', 31 Mar., and criticized the Wellington ministry's proposed corn duties as 'most unfavourable to the farmer', 22 Apr. On 28 Apr, he moved resolutions for increased protection for barley, which were defeated by 104-47, and said that if the corn law revisionist William Jacob[†] 'had to farm some of the poor soils' of Lincolnshire 'he would be very glad to throw his book into the fire'. He alleged that there was 'a disposition, amongst a large body in this House, to destroy the very best interests of the farmer', 20 May, and he supported a vain attempt to keep out warehoused foreign grain, 23 May. He

presented and endorsed more wool producers' petitions, 8, 15 May. He was in the ministerial majorities
against inquiry into chancery delays, 24 Apr., and on
the Ordnance estimates, 4 July, and the customs bill,
14 July. He voted against the provision for Canning's
widow, 13 May, and when seconding Hume's wrecking amendment to it, 22 May, insisted that he was
'bound to no party'. He divided against the small
notes restriction bill, 5 June, and supported a hostile
Lincoln petition, 16 June. He opposed the game bill,
24 June, and unsuccessfully proposed the abolition of
legacy duty on small sums deposited in savings banks,
14 July 1828.

In December that year Sibthorp's dirty domestic linen was washed in public with his wife's uncontested suit for separation *a mensa et thoro* on account
of his adultery since 1826 with Sarah Ward, a woman
'of low character'. His net annual income from rents
was reckoned at £8,536 and he disclosed ready cash
of £10,000, though he claimed to have debts equal
to that. Alimony was set at £2,200, inclusive of
Maria Sibthorp's existing annuity of £300. Sibthorp
appealed against this as 'rather excessive', 7 Dec. 1829,
but the matter went no further as an amicable settlement was reached.[11] Sibthorp's notorious appetite for
rough sex was a key element in an amusing tale related
to Greville in April 1829:

> Mackintosh ... went one day to the House of Commons at
> eleven in the morning to take a place. They were all taken
> on the benches below the gangway, and on asking the
> doorkeeper how they happened to be all taken so early,
> he said, 'Oh, sir, there is no chance of getting a place,
> for Colonel Sibthorp sleeps at the bawdy house close by,
> and comes here every morning by eight o'clock and takes
> places for all the Saints'.[12]

Sibthorp was astonished and outraged by ministers' 'unaccountable and unexpected' concession of
Catholic emancipation, which he considered 'a violation of the constitution', in 1829, and was permanently
alienated from the government by it. He presented
numerous hostile petitions and ranted repeatedly
against the measure in February and March, voting
to the last ditch as one of its diehard opponents. On 6
Mar., when he denounced Peel's 'political apostacy',
he provoked laughter with his assertion that emancipation would 'sap the foundations of the constitution'. His attempts to prevent Catholics from voting
on the disposal of Protestant charitable funds, 24,
27 Mar., were unsuccessful; and on 30 Mar. he was
defeated by 233-17 when he pressed this to a division. He complained that Irish Catholic prelates had
unlawfully appropriated Episcopal titles, 7, 11 May,

ridiculed the notion that emancipation had tranquil-
lized Ireland, 21 May, and next day spoke and voted
against the Maynooth grant. Being 'averse to the prevailing cry of reform and retrenchment as unbecoming a great country', he opposed a reduction in militia
staff, 16, 23 Mar., 4 May; he was now sitting on the
opposition benches. He was in the minority of 22
against the silk bill, 1 May, and on the 11th said that
'unless ministers abandoned the horrible system of
free trade, the country will be totally unable to pay the
taxes charged upon it'. He voted for the issue of a new
writ for East Retford, 2 June. Supporting a Blackburn
petition for inquiry into distress, 12 June 1829, he
deplored the early prorogation and ministerial indifference to anything but their 'foolish, detestable and
atrocious' Catholic relief bill, and described Irish
Catholic priests as 'devils incarnate'. In October he
was counted by Sir Richard Vyvyan*, the Ultra leader,
as one of the two dozen 'Tories strongly opposed to
the present government'.

At the county meeting to petition for repeal of the
beer and malt taxes, 8 Jan. 1830, Sibthorp concurred
in this plan and also condemned the government's
'shameful encouragement' of the consumption of
French goods; he spoke to the same effect at a constituency dinner later that day. At a city meeting, 1 Feb.,
he called for a limited return to a paper currency and
attacked pensions and sinecures. The former Tory
minister Lord Wallace dismissed these ravings as of
'no importance', for Sibthorp did not carry 'much
weight', being 'hostile to government *generally* on
account of the Catholic bill' and under the delusion
that 'the actual state of the country arises ... from free
trade'.[13] Sibthorp was in Hume's minority of nine
to postpone going into committee of supply, 11 Feb.
Presenting and endorsing the Lincoln taxation petition next day, he vowed to 'divide the House to all
eternity, till some measures are effected to remove the
burdens of the people'. He voted with Hume for tax
remissions, 15 Feb., and against the army estimates,
19 Feb., attended the City distress meeting, 22 Feb.,
and the following day accused ministers of 'culpable
neglect of the concerns of the country' and asserted
that 'the absurd, the damned system of free trade' had
ruined domestic wool producers. On 26 Feb. he said
that he would like to see 'the statements with regard
to the condition of the country ... contained in ... petitions printed in letters of gold, and hung up in the
treasury chambers ... for the information of ministers'; but he could not go along with Hume in opposing that day's grant for the Royal Military College.
On 1 Mar. he tried to secure a return of passports
issued since 1826, with a view to checking landlord

absenteeism, but he was persuaded to desist. He voted for reductions in the navy estimates that day and on 22 Mar., and for ordnance economies, 29 Mar. He obtained returns of lay pluralists and the holders of reversionary places, 9 Mar. Next day he voted against government on British interference in the affairs of Portugal. On 16 Mar. he expressed disappointment at the 'small amount' of the tax reductions proposed by ministers. Supporting Davenport's state of the nation motion, 19 Mar., he said that 'I have ... upon former occasions, declared myself an enemy to reform, but the events which have lately occurred in the country have decidedly induced me to become, though not a radical, yet a moderate reformer'. He supported petitions for reduction of the newspaper stamp duty, 25 Mar., 2, 5 July. He spoke and voted for abolition of the Bathurst and Dundas pensions, 26 Mar. He opposed Jewish emancipation, 5 Apr., 17 May. He presented and endorsed Lincoln petitions against the sale of beer bill, 7 Apr., 10 May, opposed its second reading, 4 May, predicted on 3 June that it would 'make every house in the parish not only a common drinking house, but ... a common bawdy house' and supported unsuccessful attempts to emasculate it, 21 June, 1 July, when he facetiously proposed that it should be entitled 'a bill to increase drunkenness and immorality and facilitate the sale of smuggled spirits'. He voted to reduce the grants for the Royal Military Academy, 30 Apr., public buildings, 3 May, consular services, 11 June, when he condemned all 'extravagant expenditure', and Prince Edward Island, 14 June, and to cut the assistant treasury secretary's salary, 10 May. He was a vehement critic of the northern roads bill, 'a mere job', 20 May, 3 June. He opposed the militia ballot suspension bill, 25 May, when he was in the Protestant minority against the Galway franchise bill, and Littleton's truck payments bill, 11 June. He divided against the abolition of the death penalty for forgery offences, 7 June. After the king's death, 30 June, he cautioned ministers 'how they attempt to recommend a dissolution ... when the country has such just reasons to be dissatisfied with their apathy, their neglect and their maladministration', and rebuked Peel for 'the smile of complacency' with which he acknowledged the cheers of his sycophantic supporters. On 6 July 1830 Sibthorp predicted 'great pressure' if not 'ruin' from the wretched state of the economy, endorsed the opposition motion on a regency and spoke and voted for a successful bid to reduce newspaper recognizances in libel prosecutions. Next day, however, he opposed Hume's attempt to lower the new judicial salaries, even though he proclaimed himself 'the most zealous advocate for retrenchment and economy'.

He enjoyed an unopposed return for Lincoln at the 1830 general election, when he stressed his resistance to Catholic emancipation, was circumspect on the slavery question and promised to 'watch with a jealous eye the expenditure of the public money'. Nominated for the county without his consent, he demurred, claiming to be a county Member in all but name, as he dedicated himself to scrutinizing ministers' 'apathy and rapaciousness' from an independent stance.[14] He was listed by them as one of the 'violent Ultras'; and he strongly attacked them at a county meeting on taxation, 8 Oct. 1830.[15] In the House, 5 Nov., he explained that had he not been 'detained in the country by particular business' he would have voted for the amendment to the address on the 2nd, and demanded from ministers 'some cataplasm ... to relieve the agonies of mind of the impoverished people', though he censured all 'riotous conduct'. He complained that no minister was present to explain the cancellation of the king's visit to the City, 8 Nov. A week later he helped to vote them out of office on the civil list. He protested against 'the country being saddled with any portion of the expenses attending the support of the metropolitan police force', 18 Nov. From the opposition benches he badgered the new Grey ministry to make 'a considerable reduction' in public salaries and pensions, 2, 9, 13 Dec., when he dropped his intended 60-point interrogation on the assurance of the chancellor of the exchequer, Lord Althorp, that they meant to act. He presented but did 'not entirely concur' in a Lincoln anti-slavery petition, 8 Dec., and deplored the abolitionists' wilder allegations and insisted on the right of the planters to compensation, 13 Dec. Presenting a Lincoln petition for the extension of local jurisdiction, 10 Dec., he voiced pleasurable anticipation of lord chancellor Brougham's promised law reforms. He supported Lincolnshire petitions for repeal of the insurance tax and the coal duties, 15 Dec., and on the 17th said that the farmers 'must, shall, and will have protection' and opposed free trade in corn, though he favoured repeal of the taxes on malt, hops, soap and candles, to benefit the labouring classes. He was in the minority of four for printing a petition against abolition of the oath of abjuration, 3 Dec. 1830, when he carped at the length of the impending prorogation but welcomed the ministerial statement of intent on civil list pensions.

At the county reform meeting, 28 Jan. 1831, Sibthorp expressed 'great confidence in the present ministry', advocated repeal of the malt and assessed taxes, opposed shorter parliaments, universal suffrage, the ballot and the enfranchisement of large towns, but came out for 'a moderate, gradual, and sound reform', including the extinction of rotten boroughs, an enhanced county representation and a copyholder franchise.[16] When the petition was presented, 26 Feb., along with one from Lincoln which, given Sibthorp's hostility to radical reform, had been entrusted to the county Member Amcotts Ingilby, he reiterated his support for sensible reform to end 'the shameful abuse of public money' and 'of patronage'. He felt 'extreme disappointment' with the tax cuts proposed by Althorp, 11 Feb., though he welcomed those on tobacco, coals, candles and printed calicoes. He fixed the blame for the 'improper expenditure' on Windsor Castle and Buckingham House improvements on the Wellington administration, 15 Feb. He objected to augmenting the army with fresh recruits, 21 Feb., said that much Irish distress could have been alleviated by adoption of his cherished absentee tax, 23 Feb., and protested against the proposal to make the treasurer of the navy temporary paymaster of marines, 25 Feb. He urged repeal of the 'odious and unjust' assessed taxes, 7 Mar., when, appalled and enraged by the scope of the government's 'partial, unjust, and ... tyrannical' reform bill, he accused its framers of political bias in the selection of boroughs for disfranchisement and called for use of the pending 1831 census to frame the schedules. He wanted compensation for calico manufacturers affected by repeal of the duties, 9 Mar. On 11 Mar. he denounced the corporate funds bill (he was a minority teller against proceeding with it, 28 Mar.) and, complaining of misrepresentation by the government press of the basis of his hostility to the reform bill, denied being any man's nominee. He refused to join in Hume's opposition to the garrisons grant, which included pensions for deserving officers, 14 Mar., and on 16 Mar. moved an unsuccessful wrecking amendment to the rabies bill. Next day he asked Althorp to extend the period for presenting petitions as he was being unfairly abused in Lincoln for not having brought some up. On 19 Mar. he presented reform petitions from the inhabitants and the corporation, dismissed as 'absurd' the report that he was 'not a radical, but a root-and-branch reformer' and therefore an 'apostate' and said that the corporation's decision to support the bill had at least 'released' him from 'one difficulty'. He voted against the second reading, 22 Mar., and insisted next day that while he could not accept 'any measure which goes to invade the constitution', he was 'prepared to go beyond temporizing reform'. He supported grants for the Royal Military Asylum and Chelsea Hospital, 23 Mar., but criticized the civil list contingent fund and accused ministers of 'another abandonment of principle' on public salaries, 25 Mar. He spoke and voted, in a minority of 17, for

Hume's bid to reduce civil list pensions, but opposed his amendment to reduce the grant for the royal dukes, 14 Apr. On 30 Mar. he claimed that his demonstration that the reform bill would reduce the Lincoln electorate by two-thirds had prompted a reaction against it among his constituents. He conceded that the government's changes to the measure had made it 'less objectionable', 12 Apr., but said that far more substantial modifications were required before he, 'a great reformer', could support it. He voted for Gascoyne's wrecking amendment, 19 Apr. Next day he applauded the reinstatement of some freemen's voting rights, but he endorsed Hunt's assertion that 'the people of England are not content with this bill'. On 21 Apr. he voiced 'astonishment and disgust' at the activities of the Parliamentary Candidate Society and called for an extension of the franchise to 'honest farmers'. Although he was burnt in effigy at Lincoln for his opposition to the reform bill he defied his critics at the ensuing general election, delivered 'a flaming speech' and, thanks to the local reformers' failure to find a third man, came in unopposed. When the reform question was raised at a Lincoln dinner to mark the king's birthday, 28 May 1831, he and his cronies walked out.[17]

Sibthorp pronounced the speech from the throne 'a decided humbug', 22 June; said that heavy taxes on the agricultural interest made protection 'imperative', 24 June; criticized aspects of the military estimates, 27 June, and spoke and voted, in a minority of 13, for a reduction of public salaries to 1797 levels, 30 June 1831. He alleged that there had been a popular reaction against free trade, as well as reform, 1 July, when he reiterated his wish for an absentee tax and queried the cost of refurbishing Holyrood House. He supported the grant for Oxford and Cambridge professorships, but objected to that for Dissenting ministers, 8 July, and complained of delays in the distribution of the Deccan prize money, 11 July. He opposed the militia ballots suspension bill, 14 July, demanded a reduction in the 'enormous brigade of consuls', 18 July, and pressed for stringent regulation of the 'execrable' and 'desperate set' of London hackney coachmen, whose 'filthy' contraptions were likely to spread cholera, 19, 20 July. His eminently sensible suggestion that cabs should be required to carry a table of fares was dismissed, 1 Sept. He approved a government amendment to the game bill to increase fines for poaching, but failed to effect other changes, 8 Aug., and on 2 Sept. he damned the whole bill. Having lost two relatives in the *Rothesay Castle* steamboat disaster, he urged ministers to investigate and to introduce a bill for 'summarily punishing' negligent operators, 22 Aug. He continued to harp on this subject, 26 Aug., 5 Sept., and on 6 Sept.

he secured the appointment of a select committee of general inquiry, which he chaired. He promised legislation, 20 Sept., and endorsed an individual's handy method of improving safety, 28 Sept. He voted to censure the Irish government for interference in the Dublin election, 23 Aug., and attacked the increase in the grant for the Irish secretary's office, 29 Aug. 1831.

Sibthorp was a determined and sometimes splenetic opponent of the reintroduced reform bill. After presenting a Hitchin agriculturists' petition for the enfranchisement of yearly tenants, 6 July, he opposed the second reading of the 'most abominable' measure, a 'chaos of nonsense and absurdity', riddled with blunders, anomalies and inconsistencies, which could not be final, as O'Connell and the radicals were well aware:

> I contend that this project of reform is little better than a dream ... that it is concocted in ignorance, and that even according to its advocates it is at least but a cataplasm to allay public irritation and enable an incompetent ministry to retain their places.

He took exception to Lord William Lennox's subsequent remark that ministers had reduced the bill 'to the level of his understanding', but after hurried negotiations upstairs Lennox, who recalled that Sibthorp had 'looked as if he could eat me alive', furnished a satisfactory explanation.[18] He voted five times (once as a teller) for the adjournment, 12 July, denying 'factious motives' in doing so. He divided for use of the 1831 census to determine the disfranchisement schedules, 19 July, and next day claimed that in rural areas 'many persons ... who were formerly as hot as pepper for the reform bill, are now cooling down, and becoming convinced that it will prove dangerous, unless it be greatly modified'. This spurious notion of a popular reaction against reform became one of his constant themes. On 21 July he avowed that he would 'rather go out of this House with a few having justice on my side, than be one of the phalanx who obey the *sic volo sic jubeo* mandate of ministers'. His allegation next day that reports of debates and meetings on the bill were distorted by a biased and 'venal press, paid by ministers', provoked uproar. He claimed that there were at least 20 crucial errors in the 1821 census returns and voted against the partial disfranchisement of Chippenham, 27 July. He opposed that of Grimsby, 28 July, and Maldon, 29 July, when he professed indifference to 'the groans, the smiles, or the frowns' of ministerialists. He alleged that 'partiality' had ensured preferential treatment for county Durham at the expense of the agricultural interest elsewhere, 10 Aug., and said that the division of counties would increase 'bribery and corruption' and 'party feeling', 11 Aug., and that the proposed division of Lincolnshire would 'render it a direct nomination county' in at least one district, 12 Aug. He was opposed to giving the Isle of Wight two Members, 16 Aug. On 18 Aug., at some length, he proposed to a deliberately inattentive House an amendment to clause 16 to enfranchise £50 tenants-at-will. However, he blundered in his timing and the question could not be put at that time; and later in the debate he was beaten to it by Lord Chandos, who moved an almost identical amendment. Sibthorp was furious, complaining that Chandos had taken 'by force my adopted child'; but he stayed with a bad grace to vote in the majority of 232 (to 148) for the plan. When ministers acquiesced in the amendment next day Sibthorp admitted to 'great disappointment at not being the leader instead of the follower', but Chandos laughed in his face. Thus the celebrated 'Chandos clause' could easily have become known as the 'Sibthorp clause'; and Sibthorp bore his grudge about this to the grave.[19] He asked an incomprehensible question about the votes of freeholders of counties corporate, 20 Aug. Supporting an attempt to exclude borough freeholders from the counties, 24 Aug., he said that the 'odious tendency' of the bill was to harm the agricultural interest. When interrupted and heckled he protested that 'ministers ... do not wish me to be listened to, because I always thrust it home'. When the debate grew even rowdier he tried to secure an adjournment. Defending his conduct next day, he observed that the £10 householder franchise would give the vote to 'a set of people ... who will not have a shirt and a half among the whole company'. He spoke and voted in small minorities for the preservation of freemen's rights, 27, 30 Aug. He objected to the powers given to the boundary commissioners and the inclusion of the Members Littleton and Gilbert among them, 1 Sept., and to the lord chancellor's control over the appointment of revising barristers, 3 Sept., when he admitted that he wished to retard the bill in order to expose its 'gross inconsistencies'. On its last clause, 6 Sept., he bade 'farewell to all the existing institutions of the country' and, becoming heated, swore eternal opposition to the bill; he was ridiculed. On 12 Sept. he got seven votes to 73 for his motion to have the printer and publisher of *The Times* charged with breach of privilege in a report of these proceedings. He deemed the concession to allow freemen who resided within seven miles of their boroughs to vote 'a complete mockery', 13 Sept., when he moved but was prevailed on to withdraw a proposal to redistribute Lincoln freeholders in the county according to their location north or south of the River Witham. He voted against the third reading, 19 Sept., and passage of the reform bill, 21 Sept., although 'bodily indisposition' restricted him to hoping that 'the greatest blow ever aimed at the liberties of this country' would be deflected by the Lords. He divided against the second reading of the Scottish bill, 23 Sept. On 26 Sept. he spoke and vote against the Maynooth grant, lamenting 'the march of imbecility' away from the established church and towards repeal of the Union. Next day he disputed O'Connell's allegation of English indifference to the Irish reform bill: he claimed to have missed no more than 14 days' attendance since he became a Member. He spoke and voted, in a minority of 12, with Hume, 'that Cerebus of the revenue', to postpone the grant for Windsor Castle and Buckingham House repairs, 28 Sept. He presented a Lincoln petition against the general registry bill, which he felt would 'put the small landowners to great and increased expense', 4 Oct. Opposing the motion of confidence in the government, 'a trick of ... disappointed ministers', 10 Oct., he attacked Macaulay and rejoiced in the 'destruction' of the reform bill by the Lords. On 12 Oct. he said that he had been harangued in the lobby by a delegate from a political union who had mistaken him for a reformer: 'I have been hooted as I have gone along the streets, as an anti-reformer, but I have told the people ... that I am one, and will continue one'. He quoted letters from Stamford and Hull to illustrate his argument that popular opinion had turned against the bill, 17 Oct. 1831. *Drakard's Stamford News*, a thorn in his flesh, reported that 'Don Whiskerandos', conscious of his unpopularity in Lincoln, had let Canwick for the hunting season; but this was categorically denied by Sibthorp's nephew John Hawkins, reforming Member for Tavistock, who told his father:

He is heartily sick of his steam navigation committee, and very wrath with his fellow committee men ... He seems to have undertaken the job under the impression that the chairman of a parliamentary committee has nothing to do but sit in the chair and listen to the evidence. The committee say that when they met to arrange their proceedings he had not a single proposition to make, or a single idea to offer. I fear he now finds himself in the situation of a man who has no amusement but business, and [has] not application for that.[20]

Sibthorp was 'very lame from rheumatism' that winter;[21] and in the House, 12 Dec. 1831, when he again berated Chandos for stealing his 'plumes', he said that he had been 'for some weeks past tortured with excessive bodily pain'. He had to explain himself to Chandos on 14 Dec. He attacked the 'newly improved edition' of the reform bill at its second reading, 17 Dec., though he acknowledged that some improvements had been made, arguing that it still gave 'an unfair preponderance ... to a class of persons who are fit representatives neither of the property nor the intelligence of the community', would destroy the agricultural interest, 'reduce the country to the greatest distress' and 'be the cause of general confusion'. He expressed his 'continued detestation' of the measure, 24 Jan. 1832 when he spoke and divided the House (64-195) against the proposed division of Lincolnshire. Hawkins reported, 28 Jan., that 'the Colonel ... looks wretchedly' and 'complains' of "sciatica" in his hip': 'he is more quiet in conversation, but as vehement in his parliamentary declamation as ever'.[22] To prove this point, Sibthorp proclaimed on 27 Jan. that Lincolnshire had 'not only been anatomised and cut up, but actually burked' by the reform bill. He opposed Hume's bid to expunge the Chandos clause, observing that the 'healthy yeomanry' were more deserving of votes than 'that multitudinous assemblage which we see coming out of St. Giles's and out of those cholera morbus places', 1 Feb. He quarrelled with Amcotts Ingilby over the state of opinion in Lincolnshire, 2 Feb. On 8 Mar. they clashed again over the recent premature dismissal of the South Lincolnshire militia. Hawkins told his father that Amcotts Ingilby's comment that Sibthorp 'growls and grumbles like Mount Etna' but issued 'nothing but smoke and rubbish' had 'elicited the loudest and longest peals of laughter I ever heard in the Honourable Assembly'. Sibthorp retorted that Amcotts Ingilby could not tell a gun from a bayonet, was an expert only on smoking his filthy cigars and had been put up to this attack by *Drakard's*.[23] Laughter drowned his speech of 9 Mar. when he remarked that the absent Amcotts Ingilby was probably 'snugly smoking upstairs'. He voted against the enfranchisement of Tower Hamlets, 28 Feb. On 14 Mar. he unsuccessfully divided the House (162-16) to adjourn debate on the reform bill, but he found no seconder for his similar motion on the third reading, which he duly voted against, 22 Mar. 1832. Next day, on the pretext of proposing redistribution of the Lincoln city freeholders (rejected by 169-27), he ranted against the 'unintelligible and absurd' measure and castigated the 'imbecility' of ministers for ignoring 'the universal stagnation which prevails'; he was admonished by the Speaker for replying to speeches made on earlier occasions. During the whole of this performance the House resembled a bear garden, as Hawkins reported:

The moment the colonel rose, he was saluted with a volley of cheers, which were repeated at the conclusion of every sentence, the intervals between being filled up with every variety of laughter and schoolboy noise – the cry of an owl and the mewing of a cat being, ever and anon, heard from the gallery.[24]

Sibthorp voted silently against government on the Russian-Dutch loan, 26 Jan., 12 July 1832. He attacked the general register bill, 27 Jan., and criticized Hume's silence on matters of retrenchment since the advent of the reform bill, 13 Feb. On the grant for Chelsea and Kilmainham Hospitals, 17 Feb., he condemned 'the paltry and disgraceful deduction of one shilling in the pound from the pension of the poor soldier' by an Act of George II. He was a forceful critic of Warburton's anatomy bill, suggesting that horse thieves should be strung up on the spot and used for dissection, 27 Feb., when he was a teller for the minority of 13 against a particularly 'disgusting' clause of the bill. He spoke in the same sense when objecting to the cost of transporting convicts who could be more economically executed, 26 Mar., called the bill 'a measure ... to legalize the disposal, joint by joint, of the bodies of the lower orders of society', 11 Apr., and was a teller for the minority of five against it, 11 May. He defended the 'excellent conduct' of the yeomanry at Peterloo when opposing inquiry, 15 Mar., complained of the 'shameful manner' in which parliamentary proceedings were reported by 'a base and profligate press', 28 Mar., and repudiated some of Hume's allegations of the horrors of army flogging, 2 Apr. He divided against the government's resolution for a clergy relief fund as part of Irish tithe reform, 27 Mar. After the address calling on the king to appoint only ministers who would deliver reform unimpaired had been carried, 10 May, he observed that 'a hundred ought to be deducted from the majority as expecting to be made peers'. Boasting that 'I belong to no party', 14 May, he asserted that the reform bill did not have the king's blessing and claimed to be 'a constitutional reformer'. He deplored the Grey ministry's return to power, 18 May, heatedly ascribed to the Irish reform bill 'all the leading features of a revolution', 21 May, and voted against the second reading, 25 May. Dissenting from the Lincoln petition for supplies to be withheld until reform was secured, 24 May, he professed confidence of retaining his seat at the next general election and said that the economy was ruined: 'there is scarcely a sixpence in the treasury, and we are overwhelmed with debt'. That day he opposed the immediate abolition of slavery. He protested that the Lords had been 'bullied' into passing the 'illegal' reform bill, 5 June, and pointed to the 'inconsistency and absurdity' of the boundary bill, 7 June. He dismissed Alderman Wood's 'mongrel' steam vessels regulation bill, 6 June, moaning that advantage had been taken of his temporary absence; but Wood replied that the committee had been unwilling to entrust a measure to Sibthorp. He voted against the Irish party processions bill, 25 June, but sided with government against the 'vehement' opposition of some Irish Members to their tithes proposals, 10 July. He voted for Alexander Baring's bill to exclude insolvent debtors from the House, 27 June. He was frustrated in his attempts to get straight answers and accurate information from ministers about the prevalence of cholera, 17, 18, 26 July. He approved of the grant for a national gallery, but spoke and voted, in a minority of 17, against the government's Irish education scheme, 23 July. He was one of eight Members who divided against the Maynooth grant, 27 July. His splenetic diatribes against the electoral bribery bill, 30 July, 6 Aug., excited much merriment; but his wrecking amendment found no backers, 7 Aug. He accused the government of having achieved 'nothing at all' on economy and retrenchment despite their 'many professions', 2 Aug., and on the 8th he repudiated their counter claims and asked Hume, 'the president of a political union', if he would undertake to press for a general reduction of public expenditure in the next Parliament, to which he himself felt 'tolerably sure' of being returned. He was in minorities of 20 and 16 against the crown colonies relief bill, 3 Aug., and the Greek loan, 6 Aug., and was a teller for the minority against printing the Preston petition condemning the use of troops to enforce the payment of Irish tithes, 3 Aug. On 9 Aug. he exulted in ministers' embarrassment over the possible disfranchisement of large numbers of borough voters by late payment of rates; moved for information on the cost of the reform bill; said that £4,000 was a fair pension for the lord chancellor; condemned railways as 'a fanciful invention, which may be here today and gone tomorrow', and, having the previous day divided the House eight times against the Irish party processions bill, moved, though with no intention of pressing, a wrecking amendment to its third reading. Macaulay privately execrated 'that hairy, filthy, blackguard Sibthorp' for 'glorying in the unaccommodating temper which he showed and in the delay which he produced'.[25] On 10 Aug. 1832 Sibthorp pressed ministers to settle the Deccan prize money business, damned reckless cabriolet drivers and threatened in the next Parliament to propose measures to curb public disorder: 'I will not hesitate to avow that I am an anti-reformer'.

This stance cost him his seat at the 1832 general election, but he regained it in 1835 and topped the poll at the next four elections. He continued his rabid protests against the expansion of the Catholic church in England, goaded to greater fury by his clerical brother Richard's sensational conversion to Rome in 1841. He was instrumental in securing a £20,000 cut in the grant for Prince Albert in 1840, opposed repeal of the corn laws in 1846 and denounced the Great Exhibition of 1851.[26] Dickens poked fun at him in chapter 18 of *Sketches by Boz* as a

> ferocious looking gentleman, with a complexion almost as sallow as his linen, and whose huge black moustache would give him the appearance of a figure in a hairdresser's window, if his countenance possessed the thought that is communicated to those waxen caricatures ... He is ... the most amusing person in the House. Can anything be more exquisitely absurd than the burlesque grandeur of his air, as he strides up the lobby, his eyes rolling like those of a Turk's head in a cheap Dutch clock? ... He is generally harmless, though, and always amusing.

The 'embodiment of honest but unreasoning Tory prejudice', Sibthorp died at his London house in Eaton Square in December 1855.[27] By his will, dated 14 July 1855, he confirmed his former wife's annuity, left £10,000 in trust for his three younger sons, who were to share in the proceeds of the sale of property in Durham, Northumberland, Nottinghamshire and Yorkshire, after payment of his debts, and left £1,000 to Sarah Ward (now Bentham).[28] He was succeeded at Canwick and in the Lincoln seat by his eldest son Gervaise Tottenham Waldo Sibthorp (1815-61).

[1] For an inconsequential sketch see C. Sykes, 'Colonel Sibthorp', *History Today*, i (1951), 14-20. [2] *Gent. Mag.* (1856), i. 84-85. [3] *Lincoln, Rutland and Stamford Mercury*, 22 Mar. 1822; Sir F. Hill, *Georgian Lincoln*, 229, 231. [4] *Lincoln, Rutland and Stamford Mercury*, 5 Dec. 1823. [5] Hill, *Georgian Lincoln*, 278. [6] *Lincoln, Rutland and Stamford Mercury*, 30 Dec. 1825. [7] Hill, *Georgian Lincoln*, 231; *Lincoln, Rutland and Stamford Mercury*, 2, 9, 16 June, 17 Nov. 1826. [8] *Lincoln, Rutland and Stamford Mercury*, 20 Apr. 1827. [9] *The Times*, 26 May, 22 June 1827. [10] Ibid. 1 June 1827. [11] *The Times*, 5 Dec. 1828, 8 Dec. 1829; Sir F. Hill, *Victorian Lincoln*, 17. [12] *Greville Mems.* i. 287. [13] *Lincoln, Rutland and Stamford Mercury*, 15 Jan., 5 Feb. 1830; Northumb. RO, Middleton mss ZMI/S77/3/1. [14] *Lincoln, Rutland and Stamford Mercury*, 23 July, 6, 13 Aug. 1830. [15] Ibid. 15 Oct. 1830. [16] *Drakard's Stamford News*, 21 Jan., 4 Feb. 1831. [17] Ibid. 29 Apr., 6 May, 3 June 1831. [18] Lord W.P. Lennox, *My Recollections*, i. 239-40. [19] N. Gash, *Politics in Age of Peel*, 92. [20] *Drakard's Stamford News*, 21 Oct. 1831; Cornw. RO, Hawkins mss 10/2174. [21] Hawkins mss 10/2177. [22] Ibid. 10/2179. [23] Ibid. 10/2187; Lincs. AO, Tennyson D'Eyncourt mss H36/49; M.D. George, *Cat. of Pol. and Personal Satires*, x. 16974. [24] Hawkins mss 10/2190. [25] *Macaulay Letters*, ii. 174. [26] *Oxford DNB*; Hill, *Victorian Lincoln*, 30. [27] *The Times*, 17 Dec. 1855; *Gent. Mag.* (1856), i. 84-86. [28] PROB 11/2229/240; IR26/2078/16.

D.R.F.

WALDO SIBTHORP, Coningsby Waldo (?1782–1822), of Canwick Hall, Lincs.

LINCOLN   21 May 1814–9 Mar. 1822

b. ?1782, 1st s. of Humphrey Sibthorp[†] (afterwards Waldo Sibthorp) of Canwick and Susannah, da. of Richard Ellison, banker, of Thorne, Yorks. and Sudbrooke Holme, Lincs.; bro. of Charles De Laet Waldo Sibthorp*. *educ.* Louth g.s. 1791; Westminster 1797; Corpus, Oxf. Nov. 1800, aged 18. *unm. suc.* fa. 1815. *d.* 9 Mar. 1822.
  Capt. R. South Lincs. militia 1804, maj. 1808, lt.-col. 1813.

At the general election of 1820 Sibthorp stood again for Lincoln, where he had sat, like his father before him, since 1814, on the strength of his wealth, residence at Canwick Hall on the city's southern edge and connection with his uncle Richard Ellison, a local banker and former Member. Despite being 'too much indisposed to appear in the open air' (his clergyman brother Humphrey stood in for him), he topped the poll after a contest forced by a third man.[1] As previously, he was inconspicuous in the House, partly on account of his poor health. He refused to present the address of a public meeting in support of Queen Caroline in December 1820, on the pretext that he did 'not consider such a service as within the range of his parliamentary duties'. He promoted a meeting to get up a loyal address to the king, 14 Dec. 1820, when he deplored the 'enormous abuse' of the right of free speech in 'disgusting and disgraceful attempts ... to vilify and degrade' the monarch, and provoked anger with his assertion that Caroline's supporters had 'treason in their hearts'. His address was overwhelmingly rejected, but was subsequently made available for signatures.[2] He voted in defence of the Liverpool ministry's prosecution of the queen, 6 Feb., and on the 13th dissented from the prayer of the Lincoln petition in her support:

> He had never been able to bring himself to consider the proceedings against Her Majesty as unjust, illegal and inexpedient; and as to parliamentary reform, he ever should oppose every system which, under the pretence of reform, threatened to endanger the best principles of our constitution.

Ten days later he was 'severely and dangerously hurt', suffering 'paralysis in the lower part of the back', when a wheel flew off his carriage in Lincoln Minster Yard; sabotage was suspected but never proved.[3] Although he partially recovered, his parliamentary career was over: no further votes or speeches have been found and on 9 May 1821 he was given six weeks' sick leave. He was reported to be on the mend after 'a severe relapse', 15 Feb., but he died at Canwick, 'aged 40', in March 1822. According to a fulsome and scarcely credible obituary

> in his more immediate neighbourhood he left a void which will not easily be supplied ... His manners were those of a perfect gentleman, polite, courteous, and unassuming. There was an inexpressible suavity in his demeanour that endeared him to all ... His powers of conversation threw instruction and delight all around him ... His intellectual attainments were of a very superior quality.[4]

By his will, dated 6 Nov. 1821, he left a life annuity of £300 and a legacy of £1,000 to his mother and a life annuity of £100 to Margaret Browne, 'spinster, now residing at Canwick'. To Humphrey he devised a legacy of £8,000, plus £4,00 in shares and bonds, fee farm rents at Bristol worth £60 a year and a freehold house in Broadway, Blackfriars, London. He gave his brother Richard £8,000 and provided £3,000 to be invested for the benefit of the children of his sister Mary Hawkins. His real estate in Lincolnshire and Oxfordshire and the residue of personal estate sworn under £45,000 passed to his next brother Charles, who replaced him in the Lincoln seat.[5]

[1] *Lincoln, Rutland and Stamford Mercury*, 3, 10, 17 Mar. 1820; Sir F. Hill, *Georgian Lincoln*, 79, 227-8. [2] Hill, 228-9; *Drakard's Stamford News*, 8, 15, 22, 29 Dec. 1820. [3] *Lincoln, Rutland and Stamford Mercury*, 2, 9 Mar. 1821. [4] Ibid. 15 Feb., 15 Mar. 1822; *Gent. Mag.* (1822), i. 280-1. [5] PROB 11/1656/220; IR26/927/339.

D.R.F.

WALHOUSE *see* **LITTLETON**

WALKER, Charles Arthur (?1790–1873), of Belmont House, co. Wexford.

WEXFORD   1831–1841

b. ?1790, 1st s. of Thomas Walker of Tykillen, co. Wexford and Maria, da. of William Acton of West Aston, Kilmacurragh, co. Wicklow. *educ.* Trinity, Dublin 17 July 1806, aged 16; L. Inn 1812. *m.* 10 Feb. 1836, Eleanor, da. of Joseph Leigh of Tinnekelly House, co. Wicklow, 2s. 3da. *suc.* fa. 1837. *d.* 29 Oct. 1873.

Walker's family originated in Cheshire, whence they migrated to Ireland in the seventeenth century. His great-grandfather Peter Walker acquired the Wexford property by marriage. Peter's son Charles Walker, a barrister, was an Irish master in chancery from 1754 until his death in 1790, when he was succeeded in that post by his eldest son Thomas Walker, this Member's father, who held it until 1806. Charles Arthur Walker,

whose younger brother Thomas entered the army, was educated for the bar, but was not called. At the general election of 1831 he stood for the local borough of Wexford as a 'liberal' but not a 'revolutionary' reformer having, so he claimed, rejected earlier invitations to do so because he was 'of retired habits [and] attached to country pursuits'. The strength of feeling in favour of the Grey ministry's reform bills frightened off the sitting Member and Walker was returned unopposed, calling on his fellow Protestants to unite with Catholics in support of reform and the redress of Irish grievances.[1]

He followed Daniel O'Connell and Richard Sheil in criticizing the amended county franchise contained in the reintroduced Irish reform bill, 30 June 1831, arguing that it would deliver Wexford into 'the hands of the aristocracy'. He took no part in the debates on the reintroduced English bill, but voted for its second reading, 6 July, and steadily supported its details, with the exception of a vote against the division of counties, 11 Aug. He voted for the bill's passage, 21 Sept., and for the second reading of the Scottish bill, 23 Sept. He was much concerned with the repercussions of the recent massacre of civilians by yeomanry at Newtownbarry in Wexford, which he condemned, 23 June, and demanded inquiry into, contending that 'the employment of the yeomanry force in Ireland is one of the most fertile causes of discontent and disaffection in that country', 30 June. He spoke and voted for disarming the yeomanry, 11 Aug., and had more to say on the subject, 31 Aug., 9 Sept., 3, 12 Oct., when he presented petitions in similar terms. He divided against government to reduce the grants for civil list services, 18 July, and the Society for the Propagation of the Gospels in the colonies, 25 July. He was in O'Connell's minorities on the Dublin election controversy, 29 July, 8 Aug., but he sided with ministers in the first division of 23 Aug., though he did not stay on to vote on Gordon's censure motion. He voted to suspend the Liverpool writ, 5 Sept. He divided against the Irish union of parishes bill, 19 Aug., and for legal provision for the Irish poor, 29 Aug. He was in the small minorities for inquiry into the Deacles' allegations, 27 Sept., and against the grant for repairs to royal residences, 28 Sept. On 6 Oct. he denied that there was 'any illegal combination' against the payment of tithes in his diocese of Ferns, but admitted that 'a very strong and very natural disinclination to pay tithes, which are frequently extortions, exists to a great extent among both the Protestant and Catholic inhabitants'. His attack on the bishop of Ferns for pursuing a legal vendetta against a distressed farmer drew protests from supporters of the Protestant ascendancy, but he stood his ground, protesting that 'we see the land-lords of a county coming forward with premiums to encourage agriculture and industry in Ireland, and the church instantly endeavouring to crush the rising spirit of improvement by taxing it'. He voted for Lord Ebrington's confidence motion, 10 Oct. 1831.

Walker voted for the second reading of the revised reform bill, 17 Dec. 1831, again supported its details, and divided for its third reading, 22 Mar. 1832. He voted with ministers on the Russian-Dutch loan, 26 Jan., 16, 20 July, relations with Portugal, 9 Feb., and the navy civil departments bill, 6 Apr., but was in the minorities for vestry reform, 23 Jan., informa-tion on army flogging, 16 Feb, and inquiry into the Peterloo massacre, 15 Mar. He repeated his calls for tithe reform, 24 Jan., 14 Feb., when he deplored Lord Grey's threat to 'deluge Ireland once more with blood' to enforce their collection. He voted in the small, mainly Irish, minorities on the issue, 8, 27 Mar., and on 30 Mar. criticized the government's plan for a levy to recover arrears, urging them to combine coercion with remedial action and arguing in favour of a thor-ough reform of the Irish church establishment. He voted against the arrears of tithes bill, 6 Apr. He had reservations about the retrospective aspect of the Irish subletting bill, but considered it 'a great improvement' on the existing law, 20 Feb. He voted for the address calling on the king to appoint only ministers who would carry reform unimpaired, 10 May, the second reading of the Irish reform bill, 25 May, and against Conservative amendments to the Scottish measure, 1, 15 June. In committee on the Irish bill, he was in the minorities for the enfranchisement of £5 freeholders, 18 June, and against the payment of municipal taxes as a prerequisite of registration, 29 June; but he wel-comed its extinction of the voting rights of future Irish freemen, 2 July, though he wanted the clause requiring Catholics to take the qualification oath to be amended, 18 July. On 23 May he opposed Parnell's motion for inquiry into the efficiency of the Irish coer-cive laws, arguing that the disturbances in Queen's County had been provoked by 'acts of gross oppres-sion'. He divided for the immediate abolition of colo-nial slavery, 24 May, was a teller for the minority of four against Alexander Baring's bill to exclude insol-vent debtors from Parliament, 30 May, and divided for Hunt's bid to suspend military flogging and for a tax on Irish absentee landlords to provide for the poor, 19 June. He voted for coroners' inquests to be made public next day and for a system of representation for New South Wales, 28 June. He opposed the introduc-tion of the 'extremely partial' Irish tithes composition bill, 13 July, and brought up petitions for the abolition

of tithes, 17, 26 July. On 25 July he resisted Hume's attempt to reduce the salary of the Irish registrar of deeds. He was in the minority of 16 for Sheil's call for more radical tithe reform, 24 July, objected to pro-ceeding with the composition bill when there were only five Irish Members present, 31 July, and voted in two tiny minorities for amendments to the bill, 1 Aug., when he demanded 'legislation accompanied with justice instead of injustice'. Next day he asserted that most Irish landlords were hostile to the measure. He presented more petitions for the abolition of tithes, 11 Aug. 1832.

Walker, a pragmatic Repealer, was returned unop-posed for Wexford at the next three general elections. He died at Tykillen in October 1873.[2]

[1] *Wexford Independent*, 26, 29 Apr., 6, 10, 17 May 1831. [2] *O'Connell Corresp.* iv. 1934; *Wexford Independent*, 12, 15, 19 Dec. 1832; *Illustrated London News*, 8 Nov. 1873.

D.R.F.

WALKER, Joshua (1786–1862), of Hendon Place, Mdx. and 9 Mansion House Street, London.[1]

ALDEBURGH   1818–14 May 1829

b. 28 Sept. 1786, 2nd surv. s. of Joshua Walker (*d.* 1815) of Clifton House, nr. Rotherham, Yorks. and Susanna, da. of Samuel Need, textile manufacturer, of Arnold, Notts. *m.* 18 Dec. 1805, Anna Maria, da. and coh. of Allan Holford of Davenham, Cheshire, 6s. 2da. *d.* 22 Jan. 1862.

The Walkers of Rotherham were Nonconformists who owed their wealth to successful iron founding, lead manufacture and intermarriage with other indus-trial dynasties. Joshua, like his elder brother Henry, was trained for an administrative role in the family businesses, in which he inherited partnership shares on his father's death in 1815. His cousin and co-part-ner Samuel Walker[†] had returned himself and Joshua as Members after purchasing the de Crespigny inter-est in the borough of Aldeburgh for £39,000 in 1818, but the post-war decline in the iron trade that pre-cipitated a reduction in the capital value of their busi-ness from over £200,000 in 1821 to under £36,000 in 1832 made their political commitment unsustainable.[2] Samuel stood down in 1820, having returned Joshua, who was in London developing his banking and lead manufacturing concerns, with a promoter of the West India planters' interest, James Blair.[3]

A silent anti-Catholic Tory opposed to parliamen-tary reform, against which he voted, 2 June 1823, Walker attended regularly and divided steadily with

Lord Liverpool's ministry, except when he felt that their policies compromised his religious beliefs (he was a Methodist) or commercial interests in Walker and Company of Rotherham and Sheffield, and in Everett, Walker and Company of London.[4] He brought experience of pioneering workers' pension and benefit schemes to the select committee on the orphans' fund to which he was appointed to, 20 Feb. 1822, and of manufacturing James Watt's steam engines to that on the export of tools and machinery, 24 Feb. 1825.[5] He voted against Catholic relief, 28 Feb. 1821, 30 Apr. 1822, 1 Mar., 21 Apr., 10 May 1825, and against condemning the indictment in Demerara for inciting a slave riot of the Methodist missionary John Smith, 11 June 1824. On the currency, he voted in Alexander Baring's minority of 27 for inquiry, 9 Apr. 1821, but against Western's motion, 12 June 1823; and he also voted to repeal the usury laws, 8 Apr. 1824, and paired (in a minority of 39) against appointing a select committee on the Bank Charter Act, 13 Feb. 1826. Walkers, Eyre and Stanley's Rotherham and Sheffield banks survived the 1825-6 crisis, but Everett, Walker and Company was forced to suspend trading by January 1826, whereupon Walkers' London agency passed to Barclay, Tritton, Bevan and Company.[6] Walker, whose lead manufacturing partnership with Maltby was dissolved in 1824, was keen to remain in Parliament and made a futile canvass of East Retford after the sale of the Walker interest in Aldeburgh to the 2nd marquess of Hertford in 1822.[7] At the general election of 1826 he retained his seat for Aldeburgh as the nominee of the 3rd marquess of Hertford, whom he declined to pay £4,000 to vote freely.[8] Hertford later commented: 'A seat in Parliament was a feather in his cap, while the solid value of the borough was an agreeable weight in his pocket'.[9]

Walker cast his customary votes against Catholic relief, 6 May 1827, 12 May 1828, but voted to repeal the Test Acts, 26 Feb. 1828.[10] His refusal to be guided by his patron's view 'that a government formed on the principle of resistance to Catholic emancipation is *now* an impossibility' cost him his seat despite his vote to consider the issue, 6 Mar. 1829.[11] Resigning, he wrote 'openly and candidly' to Hertford, 17 Mar.:

It is with extreme pain and reluctance that I find myself compelled to make known to your Lordship that I can neither bring myself to concede to the Catholics that which this bill proposes to give them, nor to believe it will have the effect so confidently anticipated by the legislature with regard to Ireland ... I think I might without hesitation assert that such has been my confidence in His Majesty's present ministers, that there is no *other* question upon which I would not surrender my opinion to

theirs ... I therefore without hesitation voted in favour of a committee to consider the subject ... [but] my opinions and feeling remain unchanged.[12]

Hertford, who authorized his tenure 'in perfect freedom' until a suitable replacement was available in May,[13] confessed to John Croker* that

he gives me a little touch on his understanding how he was to sit, meaning as a perfect Protestant ... But you know if besides sitting for nothing he is to discuss with me and decide on all questions, even the right of discussing each Member would make a borough valueless. But he retires and unless he makes any remarks we had better let him go *over the best bridge* and thus an end of it.[14]

There is no evidence of Walker's continued attendance. Out of Parliament, he remained a partner and director of his family's banking and lead manufacturing companies and played a prominent role in the success of their Lambeth lead works. He sold his interest in the declining iron company in 1833, thus avoiding the bankruptcy that befell his cousin Samuel. In March 1843 Peel dismissed his request for a government post in Canada for his son Edward, then farming in the colony.[15] Following Walker's death in January 1862 his estate was divided equally between his seven surviving children and his lead company shares passed to the two sons he had already brought into the partnership.[16]

[1] Draws on A.H. John, *Minutes relating to Messrs. Samuel Walker & Co. Rotherham, iron founders and steel refiners, 1741-1929*; A.H. John, *Messrs. Walker, Parker and Co. lead manufacturers*; A.H. John, *The Walker Family – iron founders and lead manufacturers, 1741-1893*. [2] *Oxford DNB sub* Walker family; *HP Commons, 1790-1820*, ii. 369; v. 467. [3] BL, J. Glyde, 'Materials for a Hist. of Aldeburgh, Framlingham and Orford', 166; S. Pollard, 'Fixed capital in industrial revolution in Britain', *Jnl. Ec. Hist.* xxiv (1964), 310; *Ipswich Jnl.* 11 Mar.; *Suff. Chron.* 11 Mar.; *Morning Chron.* 13 Mar. 1820. [4] Nottingham Univ. Lib. Newcastle mss NeC F1/1, 241. [5] R.S. Fitton, *Strutts and Arkwrights* (1958), 38 and *passim*. [6] *The Times*, 17 Nov. 1825, 4, 5 Jan. 1826. [7] Newcastle mss NeC F1/1, 241; Add. 40370, ff. 201, 203; 60286, f. 376; Fitzwilliam mss 118/2-4; John, *Walker Family*, 36. [8] Add. 38301, f. 208; 60287, f. 215; 60288, f. 116. [9] Add. 60288, f. 147. [10] Ibid. f. 37. [11] Ibid. ff. 116, 144. [12] Ibid. ff. 150-1. [13] Ibid. f. 147. [14] Ibid. ff. 152-6. [15] Add. 50562, ff. 342, 344. [16] A.H. John, *Walker Family*, 36-38; Add. 60562, ff. 342, 344.

M.M.E.

WALL, Charles Baring (1795–1853), of Norman Court, East Tytherley, Hants.

GUILDFORD	10 Feb. 1819–1826
WAREHAM	1826–1830
GUILDFORD	1830–1831
WEYMOUTH & MELCOMBE REGIS	1 Aug. 1831–1832
GUILDFORD	1832–1847
SALISBURY	1847–14 Oct. 1853

bap. 1 May 1795, o.s. of Charles Wall, merchant, of St. Peter le Poor, London and Norman Court and Harriet, da. of Sir Francis Baring[†], 1st bt., of Stratton Park, Hants. *educ.* privately by Dr. Pearson, dean of Salisbury; Eton 1811; Christ Church, Oxf. 1813; European tour 1815.[1] *unm. suc.* fa. 1815. *d.* 14 Oct. 1853.

Wall's father amassed a considerable fortune from his partnership in the mercantile house of Baring and Company and left his only son, who apparently took no part in the business, his Hampshire estate and the bulk of his personal estate, which was sworn under £125,000.[2] Wall lived the life of a fashionable aesthete, using his inheritance to indulge his interest in fine art and pursue a political career. Emily Eden, the novelist, wrote enviously after a visit to Norman Court in 1827: 'Such luxuries! Such riches! It is too disgusting that little Wall should have it all'. Her host, she condescendingly noted

> makes one laugh, which is a merit, and he is a warm friend, and if he is a little ridiculous, it is no business of ours. Heaven help Mrs. Wall, if there ever should be one. But there never will.[3]

Wall probably owed his *entrée* to the representation of Guildford to his father's ownership of nearby Albury Park, although he did not inherit the estate, which was sold in 1819.[4] He was again returned unopposed in 1820, despite some criticism of his support for Catholic relief. He voiced qualified approval of Lord Liverpool's ministry and its recent emergency measures, but 'could not give his support to restraints on the press', and he spoke favourably of Lord John Russell's parliamentary reform plan. To his friend and political confidant Ralph Sneyd he expressed concern that the age and health of George IV and his brothers might produce a series of dissolutions: 'I fear many interferences of Providence in favour of the radicals to give us annual parliaments'.[5]

He was a fairly regular attender who followed an independent course, as promised. In his only known speech of the Parliament, 1 June 1820, he condemned the Aliens Act as an infringement of liberty and voted

accordingly. He divided with government against economies in revenue collection, 4 July 1820. He voted against the omission of Queen Caroline's name from the liturgy, 26 Jan., 13 Feb., but was absent from the division on the opposition motion condemning ministers' conduct towards her, 6 Feb. 1821. He divided for Catholic relief, 28 Feb. He subsequently remarked to Sneyd on the large number of absentees from this division, hinted at a liberal view of foreign policy and confided that 'I have a quiet fancy for a little speech on Lambton's [parliamentary reform] motion'; he is not recorded as having spoken or voted for it, 18 Apr.[6] He privately expressed satisfaction that 'the king supports the government', 24 Mar., but he opposed them by voting for repeal of the additional malt duty, 3 Apr. 1821.[7] Early in 1822 he was involved in discussions with George Agar Ellis* and others regarding the formation of a small 'independent' party, to uphold the national interest; nothing came of this.[8] He divided against the opposition motions for more extensive tax reductions, 11, 21 Feb. 1822. That autumn it was reported that he had been ill and 'near losing the sight from one of his eyes'.[9] No trace of parliamentary activity has been found for the 1823 session: in the summer he was in Milan and then Venice, buying paintings and complaining of police harassment.[10] He voted in the minorities for information regarding the government's stance towards the Franco-Spanish conflict, 17 Feb., inquiries into the Irish church, 6 May, and the state of Ireland, 11 May, and to condemn the prosecution of the Methodist missionary John Smith in Demerara, 11 June 1824. He divided for the Irish unlawful societies bill, 15, 21 Feb., and for Catholic relief, 1 Mar., 21 Apr., 10 May 1825. He voted for the financial provision for the duke of Cumberland, 6 June 1825, but was in the minority next day for inquiry into delays in chancery. In February 1826 he wrote in praise of Canning and Huskisson's speeches on banking and currency reform, which were 'so bitter, so true, so effective', but he worried about the attitude of the country bankers.[11] He voted in the minorities to condemn the Jamaican slave trials, 2 Mar., reform Edinburgh's representation, 13 Apr., and consider the state of the corn laws, 18 Apr. 1826. At the dissolution that summer, faced with a contest at Guildford, he found refuge at Wareham, where he was returned on the interest of his friend John Calcraft*.[12]

In January 1827 he told Sneyd, possibly in reference to the controversy over the vacant post of commander-in-chief, that 'we are all in great spirits about the extreme want of temper and conduct Peel has displayed ... when there was nothing to rattle him'. After Liverpool's stroke the following month he reported rumours about the composition and leadership of the ministry, without making clear his own views, though he presumably supported Canning; he voted for Tierney's motion calling for a speedy resolution of the situation, 30 Mar.[13] He divided for Catholic relief, 6 Mar., and a select committee on the Irish miscellaneous estimates, 5 Apr. By October 1827 he could not see how Lord Goderich's ministry, 'stripped of all patronage, can stand long', but his prognostications in February 1828 for the duke of Wellington's administration were less accurate:

> I can find no confidence in a government with a premier and a home secretary both against the Catholics, who I think have a worse chance now than they did ten years ago. The present men are supported by those who are against ... commercial and religious liberty.

He also complained that Huskisson had behaved 'in the basest manner' towards Lord Lansdowne.[14] He admired the contributions of Peel and John Cam Hobhouse to the debate on the battle of Navarino, 14 Feb., and was on the spot next day to report from that on the appointment of the finance committee.[15] He divided for repeal of the Test Acts, 26 Feb., having solved his dilemma of the previous year when he had been 'much puzzled' as to how to vote on this issue, given the king's reported antipathy.[16] He divided for Catholic relief, 12 May. His admission to Brooks's Club, 1 Mar., appeared to signal a move towards the Whigs, and in June he hoped that Lord Grey would shortly join the cabinet.[17] He voted to recommit the East Retford disfranchisement bill, 27 June, and for reduction of the salary of the lieutenant-general of the ordnance, 4 July. He attended the Kent meeting on Catholic emancipation in October 1828 and was impressed by the oratory of William Cobbett†, but by the end of the year he had 'lost all interest in politics, for I feel that whatever is done will be so soon reversed'.[18] In letters to Sneyd he shed no tears over the recall of Lord Anglesey from the lord lieutenancy of Ireland, 11 Jan. 1829, but, apparently reanimated by the prospect of Catholic emancipation, he predicted victory for Peel in the Oxford University by-election. He observed that 'the Lords are coming round by the dozen', 24 Feb., and was impressed by the resolve he detected in the Commons to carry a measure, 4 Mar.[19] He presented a pro-Catholic petition from Guildford, 2 Mar., and cast aspersions on the legitimacy of one of the opposite prayer, 9 Mar. He divided for the government's emancipation bill, 6, 30 Mar., although he privately jibbed at the clause against the Jesuits. He praised Peel's 'gracious' speech introducing the measure, but told Sneyd that 'it quite

settles my mind that he is no great man'.[20] He voted to transfer East Retford's seats to Birmingham, 5 May 1829. That summer he reported from Paris on the instability of the French government.[21] He divided for Knatchbull's amendment to the address on distress, 4 Feb. 1830. He voted for the transfer of East Retford's seats to Birmingham, 11 Feb., and the enfranchisement of Birmingham, Leeds and Manchester, 23 Feb., but against Lord Blandford's reform scheme, 18 Feb. He divided with the revived Whig opposition to condemn the appointment to the vacant treasurership of the navy, 12 Mar., and British interference in Portuguese affairs, 28 Apr., to obtain returns of privy councillors' emoluments, 14 May, and inquire into the civil government of Canada, 25 May; he paired for reduction of the grant for consular services, 11 June. He divided for Jewish emancipation, 5 Apr., 17 May, and abolition of the death penalty for forgery, 24 May, 7 June. He voted against increased recognizances in libel cases, 9 July 1830. At the general election that summer he was returned for Guildford at the head of the poll and celebrated, according to a local newspaper, with a dinner 'given in the style worthy of [his] well known liberality'.[22]

The ministry listed Wall as one of their 'foes', yet at the end of October 1830 Georgiana Ellis found him to be in 'a most anti-liberal state', though she believed persuasion would make him 'reasonable on all subjects' except Brougham's anticipated motion on parliamentary reform. On the other hand, his cousin Francis Thornhill Baring* reckoned he would 'certainly' support this motion.[23] He voted against ministers in the crucial civil list division, 15 Nov. On 1 Dec. 1830 Georgiana Ellis reported that the extent of disaffection revealed by the 'Swing' agricultural disturbances had left Wall 'in a most desponding state since his expedition into Hampshire', and that 'he talks as if it was all over with the landed property'. She again noted his antipathy to reform, about which he was 'very unhappy', in February 1831. When Lord John Russell introduced the Grey ministry's bill, 1 Mar., Wall turned to Hobhouse and twice exclaimed, 'They are mad!'[24] Speaking from the opposition benches the next day, he condemned the bill as too democratic and biased towards northern and commercial interests. He argued that the prevailing 'spirit of reform ... that pervades all our institutions [and] animates all our public men' made such a sweeping measure unnecessary and, dwelling on the alleged divisions among ministers, he expressed a wish to see Peel at the head of the government in the Commons. This speech was widely hailed as one of the best from the opposition side, though Georgiana Ellis wished 'for his own sake' that he had not joked that the proposed partial disfranchisement of Guildford would leave him 'but half a man'; Lord Auckland, the master of the mint, on hearing the quip, commented that 'he overstates it very much'.[25] He attended the Hampshire meeting on reform, 17 Mar., when, speaking against a great clamour, he decried the bill as an 'anomalous, unjust, unconstitutional and revolutionary measure'. In a pamphlet dated two days later he reminded his constituents that 'this bill talks not of inherent rights or principles' but was 'proposed to you as a mere question of expediency', and he advised them to 'be sure that your remedy is the right one for the grievances you complain of'. He warned of the increased influence the bill would give to country gentlemen, radical demagogues and 'Papal Ireland', and criticized the 'slovenly manner' of its framing, the peculiar distinction it drew between 'due' and 'undue' influence, and the proposal to deprive Guildford of a Member. Without being specific, he stood by his election pledge to support a measure of moderate reform, and excused his vote on the civil list thus:

I always entertained a firm conviction that the Whigs would be unable to form an administration upon purely Whig principles. I imagined (simple minded as I was) that the party to whom they naturally looked for support, and who afterwards did unite with them, would have insisted on some conditions with regard to the reform question.[26]

He voted against the bill's second reading, 22 Mar., and for Gascoyne's wrecking amendment, 19 Apr. 1831. At the ensuing general election he was soundly defeated at Guildford, and told Sneyd afterwards that from 'what I saw there I feel convinced ... there is no resisting the torrent'.[27]

By mid-May 1831 Wall had recovered enough optimism to predict a Huskissonite desertion of the government, who he reported had 'decided on a budget ten thousand times more absurd than the last'.[28] His anxiety to return to the Commons led him in August to Weymouth and Melcombe Regis where, aided by a decision on the local franchise in his favour, he defeated a reformer after an eight-day poll. Later that month he signed the Wiltshire declaration against the reintroduced reform bill.[29] In the House, 5 Aug., he argued that on the basis of their separate populations the conjoined boroughs which he represented were entitled to return three Members. Somewhat inconsistently, he then raised 'insuperable objections' to schedule B and single Member boroughs, suggesting instead the complete disfranchisement of all places with a population under 3,000. He moved for returns of towns and cities whose population exceeded 10,000 and which

remained unrepresented under the provisions of the bill, 30 Aug., and next day cast doubt on the impartiality of the boundary commissioner Bellenden Ker. On 5 Sept. he embarrassed ministers by drawing attention to letters sent to local officials requesting their cooperation with commissioners whose names had yet to be approved by the Commons; he told Sneyd that he was 'mad about this part of the bill'. He also reported to his friend on the coronation, claiming that

the king's figure was ludicrous, he could hardly grasp the orb ... What a king and government it is, I dare not say what I think of both ... We have a majority in the Lords, but I have a conviction that Lord Grey will pass the bill somehow, how is indifferent to him.[30]

In attacking the bill's inconsistencies, 20 Sept., he remarked that 'it would seem as if ministers were frightened at the results which their own [measure] will produce, for they will not push them to their legitimate result'. He predicted that the bill as it stood would not only entrench existing oligarchies and restrict social mobility, but spell an end to the monarchy. He voted against its passage the next day. Early in December he met Lord Wharncliffe, one of the leaders of the Tory 'Waverers', and hoped that the meagre concessions offered to them would convince them of 'the uncompromising and unreliable spirit of the government'.[31] He divided against the second reading of the revised bill, 17 Dec., when he went so far as to admit the justice of the schedule A disfranchisements but predicted 'disappointment and reaction' once the popular excitement over the bill had abated. Writing to Sneyd, 2 Feb. 1832, he confessed himself 'puzzled' as to the course the opposition should adopt, but doubted if the bill was susceptible to worthwhile amendment given that it was 'revolutionary in its principle'. He appeared to favour a line of unwilling acquiescence, assuming that ministers would create peers to pass it in any case, and 'if they do, the game is up ... [for] we are in that situation that no government can go on without an efficient and strong measure of reform being carried'. He attended a meeting at Peel's house to discuss tactics before he voted against the enfranchisement of Tower Hamlets, 28 Feb.[32] He divided against the third reading, 22 Mar., and the second reading of the Irish bill, 25 May. On 22 June he opposed the proposal to enlarge his former constituency of Wareham to include the whole of the Isle of Purbeck, protested at the division of Dorset and warned that 'many of the counties under the new system will be complete rotten boroughs'. He voted for his uncle Alexander Baring's bill to deprive Members of their immunity from prosecution for debt, 27 June. He divided against ministers on the Russian-Dutch loan, 26 Jan., 12 July, but with them on military punishments, 16 Feb. He voted for a system of representation for New South Wales, 28 June 1832. Towards the end of the session he admitted to Sneyd that 'I am very low about everything ... Let us go abroad together as soon as the Parliament is dissolved'.[33]

In the summer of 1832 Wall canvassed Guildford 'with a heavy heart', but he succeeded in displacing one of the sitting reformers at the general election later that year.[34] Soon afterwards his political and personal reputation was threatened by a charge that, in the early hours of 28 Feb. 1833, he had indecently assaulted a policeman in Harley Street. At the trial, 11 May 1833, the policeman, John Palmer, testified that Wall had initially engaged him in vulgar conversation in which he had railed against religion and the system of government. Palmer claimed that after the alleged offence had taken place, Wall first attempted to bribe him and then tried to escape arrest. Wall's counsel, Sir James Scarlett*, seized on minor inconsistencies in the story to suggest that it was an extortioner's fiction. After listening to 19 of Wall's friends, relatives and servants testify to the spotlessness of his character and his inability to utter blasphemy, the jury acquitted him. However, two earlier letters to Sneyd suggest that his interest in the uniformed forces of law and order was such as to render Palmer's tale at least plausible. In August 1828, after meeting 'two good looking soldiers', Wall remarked that 'I wish I lived in a disturbed district'; and in October 1829 he had written of the new metropolitan police force, 'I delight in them all'. Charles Greville, while anticipating Wall's acquittal, observed that 'nobody can be plunged into such mire without smelling of it more or less ever after'.[35] Nevertheless, his parliamentary career continued without interruption and he was eventually classed as a Liberal, having supported repeal of the corn laws. He also established a reputation as an authority on artistic matters. Evidently he was not socially ostracized, as he continued to entertain lavishly at 44 Berkeley Square, where he had resided since 1827 in what Benjamin Disraeli[†] described as 'a house the most beautiful I ever entered'. To the surprise of Hobhouse, the dinner guests in April 1841 included William Bankes*, another Member who had been dubiously acquitted of a homosexual offence and was about to repeat his transgression.[36] Wall died in October 1853 and left his entire property to his cousin Thomas Baring, Conservative Member for Huntingdonshire, 1844-73.[37]

[1] *The Times*, 13 May 1833. [2] PROB 11/1571/407; IR26/662/356. [3] *Miss Eden's Letters* ed. V. Dickinson, 128-9, 152. [4] *VCH Surr.*

iii. 74. [5] *Surr. Herald*, 11 Mar. 1820; Keele Univ. Lib. Sneyd mss SC17/15, 17. [6] Sneyd mss SC17/19. [7] Ibid. 20. [8] Northants. RO, Agar Ellis diary, 19, 21 Feb. 1822. [9] *Miss Eden's Letters*, 78. [10] Sneyd mss SC17/24, 25. [11] Ibid. 28. [12] Ibid. 21, 26; *Baldwin's London Weekly*, 6 June 1826. [13] Sneyd mss SC17/30, 31. [14] Ibid. 33, 34. [15] Ibid. 36. [16] Ibid. 30. [17] Ibid. 191. [18] Ibid. 40, 41. [19] Ibid. 43, 44, 183. [20] Ibid. 46. [21] Ibid. 51. [22] *County Chron.* 31 Aug. 1830. [23] *Howard Sisters*, 151; *Baring Jnls.* 70. [24] *Howard Sisters*, 171-2, 186; Broughton, *Recollections*, iv. 87. [25] *Howard Sisters*, 190-1; *Baring Jnls.* 84; Sneyd mss, Mahon to Sneyd, 5 May 1831. [26] *The Times*, 18 Mar.; C.B. Wall, *To the Electors of Guildford* (1831). [27] Sneyd mss SC17/57. [28] Ibid. 58. [29] *The Times*, 30 July, 4 Aug.; *Devizes Gazette*, 11 Aug. 1831. [30] Sneyd mss SC17/59. [31] Ibid. 64. [32] Ibid. 60, 65. [33] Ibid. 67. [34] Ibid. 182. [35] *The Times*, 13 May 1833; Sneyd mss SC17/39, 52; *Greville Mems.* ii. 364. [36] *Gent. Mag.* (1853), ii. 643-4; *Disraeli Letters*, ii. 514; Broughton, vi. 14, 97. [37] PROB 11/2181/844; IR26/1985/674.

H.J.S.

WALLACE, Thomas I (?1768–1844), of Carleton Hall, Cumb.; Featherstone Castle, Northumb., and 33 Portman Square, Mdx.

GRAMPOUND	1790–1796
PENRYN	1796–1802
HINDON	1802–1806
SHAFTESBURY	1807–1812
WEYMOUTH & MELCOMBE REGIS	1812–9 June 1813
COCKERMOUTH	27 Nov. 1813–1818
WEYMOUTH & MELCOMBE REGIS	1818–2 Feb. 1828

b. ?1768, o.s. of James Wallace[†] of Asholme, Northumb. and Elizabeth, da. and h. of Thomas Simpson of Carleton Hall. *educ.* Eton 1777; L. Inn 1785; Christ Church, Oxf. 10 June 1785, aged 17; continental tour 1788. *m.* 16 Feb. 1814, Lady Jane Hope, da. of John, 2nd earl of Hopetoun [S], wid. of Henry Dundas[†], 1st Visct. Melville, *s.p. suc.* fa. 1783; *cr.* Bar. Wallace 2 Feb. 1828. *d.* 23 Feb. 1844.

Ld. of admiralty July 1797-July 1800; commr. bd. of control July 1800-Feb. 1806, Apr. 1807-June 1816, Feb. 1828-Feb. 1830; PC 21 May 1801; vice-pres. bd. of trade Jan. 1818-Apr. 1823; master of mint[1] Oct. 1823-May 1827.

Maj. Edenside rangers 1802, Cumbrian rangers 1803, lt.-col. 1803; lt.-col. commdt. W. Northumb. militia 1824.

Wallace came from a Northumberland family, though it was in Brampton, Cumberland, where his grandfather and namesake was an attorney, that he was said to have been born, probably in 1768.[2] His father was Member for Horsham, 1770-83, and one of Lord North's[†] law officers, and when Wallace followed him into Parliament in 1790, he supported Pitt, and held junior ministerial office almost continuously from 1797. Having inherited properties in Cumberland and Northumberland, though he disposed of the former in the late 1820s, he had some electoral influence in the north, where he was well respected. As his Northumberland neighbour James Losh of the Grove, Jesmond, later commented, he was

> an honest man and very industrious, and has shown what may be done by these good qualities without any considerable talents. His connections enabled him to get into Parliament, and his political opinions (or rather those of his great friends Lord Melville, etc.) made him steady to that party.[3]

The prime minister Lord Liverpool, who like Canning was a friend from university, thought that Wallace, a petulant and unashamedly ambitious colleague, overrated his own abilities and, being a reluctant speaker, made little contribution to the standing of the government in the Commons. Despite being several times passed over for more senior positions, he was appointed vice-president of the board of trade, with a salary of £1,500, in 1818.[4]

At the general election that year he was returned after a contest for Weymouth, where he had sat briefly in the previous Parliament. This was on the Johnstone family interest, which, during the minority of the 7th baronet, was managed by the principal trustee, and Wallace's ministerial colleague there, Masterton Ure. On the eve of another dissolution, he wrote to his friend, Sir Charles Monck of Belsay, 10 Feb. 1820, deploring his decision to retire from Parliament and admitting that 'I believe I should not be sorry to follow your example'.[5] He was, however, returned unopposed for Weymouth at the general election that year, with Ure and two town Members under the 'union' compromise, and drank to 'union and independence' at his election dinner. On 29 Mar. his agent Joseph Horsford informed him that Lady Johnstone, the 6th baronet's widow, was convinced of his loyalty and that 'as long as you wished, that seat should be filled by you', but the following month Horsford suspected that she and Ure wanted him to be dislodged.[6] In July Wallace differed seriously with Ure over the handling of the borough and local patronage, which Wallace exercised as a Member in his own right, through government, and via his wife's son the 2nd Viscount Melville, the first lord of the admiralty.[7] In an undated letter to Ure he angrily asserted that he was 'bound to avail myself of nothing to be given in Weymouth but for the advantage of the Johnstone family' and, indicating that Ure was acting without the sanction of the family and the other trustees, stated that he had 'never abandoned my right of private judgement to *you* or anyone'.[8] Nevertheless, the quarrel was apparently smoothed over.

In the House, Wallace continued to divide, for the most part silently, with his ministerial colleagues. In May 1820 he was asked by Horsford to give advice on the Weymouth bridge bill.[9] He was appointed to the select committee on foreign trade, 5 June, and chaired its sittings. On presenting its report, 18 July, he outlined the existing state of distress and advocated for its relief the greatest practicable measure of free trade, recommending the relaxation of the navigation laws, the extension of the warehousing system and the simplification of the laws relating to commerce. He hailed the committee's findings, at the start of a series of ground-breaking reports, as 'the first and most material step of this country to a departure from the course of restrictive policy which its legislature had hitherto pursued, and to the establishment of a more enlarged and liberal policy towards foreign states than any which had yet prevailed'.

He was chairman of the foreign trade committee during the following four sessions, and much of his parliamentary work was concerned with sponsoring the ensuing legislation.[10] Wallace spent that autumn in Buxton, explaining to Charles Arbuthnot* that 'I have been so ill since I came to this place as to be hardly capable of doing anything'. The other treasury secretary, Stephen Rumbold Lushington, reassured him by letter, 18 Oct., that 'you were not at all wanted last night', when no division had occurred on the bill of pains and penalties against Queen Caroline.[11] During his stay he corresponded with his friend John Gladstone* about his commercial proposals and expressed his anxiety about the progress of the queen's trial.[12] According to Robert Ward*, he listened to the Lords debate, 4 Nov. 1820, and 'came out very sanguine for a large majority, which he said would have great weight with people out of doors, and bring them round'.[13] He commended government's decision to withdraw the bill against Caroline, hoped that the loyal addresses would help to calm the agitation of her supporters and doubted rumours of ministerial changes; but he noted that there would be a good deal of violent opposition in Parliament 'and if we are to form any conjecture from what passed at the time of the prorogation, there seems to be no extent of it for which we ought not to prepare ourselves'.[14]

He commented on an alleged breach of privilege, 9 Mar. 1821. He moved for the reappointment of the select committee on foreign trade, 6 Feb., when he indicated that government would take the inquiry in hand and bring forward measures for relief. Having answered questions about the future of the timber duties, 14, 16 Feb., 27 Mar., he moved resolutions to repeal them, 29 Mar., on the ground that it was more economic to import timber from northern Europe than to rely on uncompetitive colonial produce, and spoke in favour of the timber duties bill, 5, 12, 16, 19 Apr.[15] It was no doubt in recollection of one of these occasions that Hudson Gurney* later recorded in his diary that Wallace 'made a very long and heavy speech on the timber trade. On coming out of the House Lord Londonderry [Castlereagh], being stopped by a timber dray conveying an immense timber, called out, "There goes Wallace's speech to be printed".'[16] The chancellor of the exchequer announced his appointment as the head of the commission of inquiry into the Irish revenue, 15 June, when he answered Hume's objections by saying that he had waived any emolument because he was already in receipt of an official salary. Reiterating his customary arguments in favour of free trade, he moved resolutions for amending the Navigation Acts, 25 June, when Henry Grey Bennet* recorded that 'he made, as usual, a dull, though by no means a bad speech. His principles were good, but I have no doubt the merchants and their interests will prevail'.[17] It was probably of this debate that Gladstone wrote to him, 24 Sept., in praise of the 'liberal, enlarged, comprehensive and statesmanlike view which you have taken of the great commercial and mercantile interests of the country'.[18] Wallace related to John Herries*, one of his fellow commissioners, 8 Aug., that

> it is clear to me from what passed [in conversation with Liverpool] that a great deal is expected from us and if we fulfil the intentions and wishes of government we must be prepared to cut very deep, in fact that we are to be the instruments of changing completely the actual system of governing Ireland by *patronage*.[19]

He spent the autumn taking evidence in Dublin, from where he reported to Liverpool, 3 Dec., and to Gladstone, 5 Dec. 1821, that he and his colleagues were unanimous in their recommendations, which included abolition of the separate Irish customs and repeal of many of the duties on Irish trade.[20]

Wallace agreed with Gladstone, 7 Jan. 1822, that government had 'purchased' the Grenvillites 'at a price much beyond the value of any strength or credit they bring to our support', and although he approved of most of the ministerial changes that month, he added that 'I hope it will answer, but I cannot help having my fears'. Anticipating some busy months of legislative activity for himself, he admitted in another letter, 21 Jan., that ministers' 'great difficulty in the ensuing session will arise from the agriculturists, who I suspect will make a violent assault upon our taxation, with

what success it is in these times impossible to say'.[21] He secured the reappointment of the foreign trade committee, 25 Feb., and was a teller for the majority of three to one against James Drummond being added to it, 28 Feb., when the House was counted out. On 27 Feb. he presented his proposals on the Irish revenue, the first of the 22 reports which he oversaw (the last was ordered to be printed by the Commons, 9 July 1830).[22] Having put off the discussion on his navigation bill, 6 May, he spoke in its favour, 20 May, arguing that the changed circumstances of overseas trade made it necessary to remove the existing restrictions, which would not endanger the country's shipping and commercial interests, but would lead to more general economic prosperity. He repeated this opinion, 23 May, 4 June when he was a teller for the majority in favour of the third reading.[23] He postponed the warehousing bill to the following session, 21 June 1822, promising that an investigation would be made into the silk trade. He admitted privately that he 'had determined to make my escape some time before Parliament rose', and rested at Carleton Hall until he had to resume his Irish revenue work, although he did not in fact visit Ireland that autumn.[24]

In December 1822 Frederick Robinson, the president of the board of trade, accepted Liverpool's invitation to succeed Nicholas Vansittart as chancellor, but warned the prime minister that Wallace considered that his services entitled him to take over the department (which was to go to Huskisson), and 'may therefore require a little soothing, when it comes to the point'. Canning and Arbuthnot agreed, and suggested that Liverpool take the chance to express ministers' gratitude for his useful work before broaching the new arrangements. Liverpool finally informed Wallace of the changes by letter, 8 Jan. 1823, stressing that Huskisson was the only commoner he would consider placing over his head. As expected, Wallace, who was described as being 'most indignant', was extremely disappointed, and reacted (as he had in 1816) by resigning. He did offer to take the presidency without a salary, when that was raised as a sticking point, and urged Liverpool to consider

> my situation fairly, consider my time of life and that my political views are drawing very fast to a close. Am I never to have the gratification of anything but a subordinate office? Is nothing more due to me? If so it is time for me to retire.

Liverpool, who was acutely sensitive to his friend's distress, endeavoured to dissuade him, and even proposed that Wallace and Arbuthnot, who was to go to the department of woods and forests, should exchange places. This was much to the discomfiture of Arbuthnot, whose wife believed the problem to be that 'Lady Melville will not allow Mr. Wallace to remain where he is'. Other solutions were suggested, the most feasible being that Wallace should succeed Lord Maryborough as master of the mint, but in the end all that could be held out to him was the vague promise of a future office.[25] Of his resignation, Wallace confided to Gladstone, 6 Feb. 1823:

> I own to you I did it with great reluctance because it gave me advantages in prosecuting my views in opening and relieving the commerce of the country, but I really was placed by the new arrangement in a situation in which, consistently with my honour and character, I could not hesitate.[26]

Despite his low profile in government, his departure was regretted by his constituents, who voted him an address of thanks for his services, 8 Feb. 1823, and this was matched by others, notably from several hundred London merchants.[27] Ministers were quick to praise his achievements. Arbuthnot stressed his experience when he wrote to Liverpool that

> Wallace in this respect, had he consented to remain, would have had an advantage which I possess not. He had laboured so well and so zealously that Robinson had become the cypher; and so fair has been the fame that he has acquired, that not even Huskisson himself would eclipse him.[28]

When he moved for the reappointment of his committee and commented on the improved economic situation, 12 Feb., Wallace was complimented on his efforts by Ricardo, Hume and Canning; and Peel privately congratulated him 'on the just and most gratifying testimonies which you received'.[29] Robinson added to these encomiums when, in the course of his budget statement, 21 Feb., he said that nothing

> in the course of my political life has given me more satisfaction than to have found in him a colleague, imbued with the same principles upon all these subjects, as those which I have at all times advocated, and upon which I have endeavoured to act.

Wallace, who continued to give ministers largely silent support, voted against parliamentary reform, 20 Feb., and alteration of the Scottish representative system, 2 June. He divided against repeal of the assessed taxes, 18 Mar., and the production of information on the plot to murder the Irish lord lieutenant, 24 Mar. He spoke for the warehousing bill, 21 Mar. (when he was teller for the majority in its favour), 24 Mar., 21 Apr. He voted against repeal of the Foreign Enlistment Act, 16 Apr., and inquiry into the legal proceedings against the Dublin Orange rioters, 22 Apr. He defended the reduction of duties on Irish cloth, 2 May. He called the Spitalfields Acts 'a disgrace to the statute book', 9 May, and supported the silk bill, 21 May. He spoke in defence of the reciprocity of duties bill, 6 June, 4 July, and the distilleries bill, 30 June, 8 July 1823.[30]

The death of Lord Cornwallis later that year allowed a relieved Liverpool to make Maryborough master of the buckhounds and so 'reward the indefatigable labours of Mr. Wallace as chairman of the parliamentary commission, and repair in some degree the injury he thought he received'; however, the king was reportedly displeased 'that a place in his household should be made subservient to an accommodation for Wallace'. He welcomed his appointment to the undemanding office of master of the mint, and acquiesced in the decision to deny him a seat in the cabinet, although admitting privately that he still thought his claim was 'full as good a one as Huskisson's'.[31] He was congratulated by the corporation of Weymouth, 10 Oct., and was elected a capital burgess, 24 Nov. 1823, during a visit to the town, after which he complained of 'having been detained amongst my constituents subject to all the slavery of such a situation preparatory to an election'. He was returned unopposed at the by-election in February 1824, when he advocated free trade, commented on the increasing economic recovery and opposed involvement in any foreign wars.[32] With the exception of slavery, Ireland and the Catholic question, he observed to Gladstone, 5 Feb., that 'I do not see that the parliamentary prospect has anything in it of a disagreeable nature'.[33] He voted against the production of papers on Catholic office-holders, 19 Feb. He criticized the proposal to adopt a decimal coinage as impracticable, 25 Feb. He denied that a pledge had been given to repeal the hemp duties, 26 Feb., and, having for the last time been appointed chairman of the foreign trade committee, 4 Mar., he urged opening the silk trade to competition, 8, 22 Mar. He promised in the following session to introduce a measure to equalize the English and Irish currencies, 24 June 1824.[34]

Wallace supported the St. Katharine's Docks bill, 22 Feb. 1825. As he had on 28 Feb. 1821 and 30 Apr. 1822, he voted against Catholic relief, 1 Mar., 21 Apr., when he spoke at length on the issue, and 10 May, and presented an anti-Catholic petition from Weymouth, 18 Apr. 1825.[35] Among other select committee appointments, he chaired one on the combination laws, although Gladstone warned Huskisson that 'from having seen very much of your chairman in the foreign trade committee, I do not hesitate to say to *you* that I have not confidence in either his nerve or his judgement; I hold him unequal to the task'.[36] However, the radical Francis Place was of a different opinion of Wallace's performance in the chair, noting that

> he was a man singularly well qualified for his office, conversant with parliamentary business, not too wise for the purposes of his masters, but more than sufficiently conceited with his own wisdom and his own importance. In many ways he was perhaps the most unmanageable man that could have been pitched upon. He had a purpose to accomplish, and would attend to no suggestions from those who were opposed to him. The committee was informed that about half-a-dozen gentlemen would be examined, and then a bill would be submitted to the committee to remedy the evils complained of.[37]

Insisting that some level of protection against combinations should be retained, he spoke in favour of the committee's recommendations for a bill to abolish the Combination Acts, 16, 23, 27, 29 June, when he was a teller for the majority in its favour.[38] He argued the case for assimilating the Irish and English currencies, 12 May, and oversaw the bill to achieve this, which became law, 27 June 1825. The following year the lord lieutenant, Lord Wellesley, wrote that 'Ireland is as prosperous as any country can be, under the auspices of poverty, discord and disease, with the currency of Wallace in possession and with a famine price of potatoes in reversion'.[39]

In February 1826 Wallace was said 'to be dying',[40] and his only known votes that session were for receiving the report on the salary of the president of the board of trade, 10 Apr., and against reform of the representation of Edinburgh, 13 Apr. He agreed that the rates of postage in England and Ireland ought to be made equal, 21 Apr.[41] At the general election that summer he offered again for Weymouth, where he was returned with Ure on the interest of the trustees, despite the fact that their differences with the Johnstone family provoked a long contest. He was roundly condemned for helping to uphold the 'union' against the family's challenger John Gordon*, and for suggesting that the mayor summon the military to suppress the disturbances caused by his supporters. His expenses amounted to £1,216.[42] Senior ministers considered various changes during July 1826, and Canning proposed that Wallace be made either secretary at war or postmaster, having 'earned just that sort of reputation which would render the placing him at the head of a great department, in which there is much to set right, or to improve'. Nothing came of it.[43] He was still in very poor health at the beginning of the following year,[44] and his last known vote in the Commons was that given

against Catholic relief, 6 Mar. 1827. He requested the postponement of a motion relating to foreign trade, 23 Mar., and, after several changes of plan, was able to attend the Commons to defend the Irish revenue commission's findings, 10 Apr.[45] He was among the anti-Catholics whom Canning tried to recruit when forming his ministry that spring, but he declined a peerage and the home office. As the 3rd marquess of Londonderry noted, 'Wallace was offered *carte blanche*, but gallantly threw up'.[46] In August the king apparently wished to have him appointed president of the board of trade, but Canning's successor Lord Goderich (as Robinson now was) persuaded him that to appoint a 'Tory-Protestant-seceder' to the cabinet would alienate the Whigs.[47] In November 1827 he was listed by the new master of the mint George Tierney* among those intended for inclusion on the finance committee.[48]

Although disappointed at being again passed over for high office, he decided not to impede the formation of the government in January 1828, and so acquiesced in the duke of Wellington's offer of a peerage. He merely stipulated that it should be announced at the same time as the cabinet in order to 'produce the impression I am anxious should be generally received that although not holding an official situation I am identified with your grace's administration'.[49] This duly occurred, and he returned to office as a member of the board of control. Lord Ellenborough, the new lord privy seal, was one of those who regretted his exclusion as a result of the junction with Huskisson, believing that 'Wallace's name was as good for the commercial interest'.[50] Despite his protestations of support, Wallace was also concerned at the scope for dissension within the coalition ministry and differed with ministers over Catholic emancipation, which he voted against by proxy, 4, 10 Apr. 1829. He left the government in February 1830, blaming the long-standing 'mutual *repulsion*' between himself and Peel for his failure to win a cabinet place. He was strongly opposed to the Grey ministry's reform bills and for many years voted silently with the Conservatives in the Lords.[51] Wallace, one of the minor actors in the emergence of liberal Toryism in the early 1820s, died in February 1844, when his peerage became extinct. He left his papers to Monck, his executor, who failed to honour an apparent agreement whereby the survivor was to have written a biography of his late friend, but his estates passed to his wife's nephew Lieutenant-Colonel James Hope (1807-54), Conservative Member for Linlithgow, 1835-8, who took the additional name of Wallace.[52]

[1] Not master of the mint [I] as erroneously stated in *HP Commons, 1790-1820*, v. 468. [2] C. Rogers, *Bk. of Wallace*, i. 224-5; J. Hodgson, *Northumb.* pt. 2, vol. iii. p. 92; *Gent. Mag.* (1844), i. 426. [3] *Diaries and Corresp. of James Losh* ed. E. Hughes (Surtees Soc. clxxxiv), 34-35. [4] *HP Commons, 1790-1820*, v. 468-72; *Black Bk.* (1820), 443. [5] *Northumb.* RO, Middleton mss ZMI/B16/V. [6] Ibid. S76/40/5, 7, 8; *Western Flying Post*, 13, 20 Mar. 1820. [7] Middleton mss S76/29/9, 11, 18, 43; 30/70; 34/1-7; 40/23, 29. [8] Ibid. S76/30/23. [9] Ibid. S76/40/13, 14. [10] B. Hilton, *Corn, Cash, Commerce*, 179, 185, 195-7. [11] Middleton mss S76/30/81; 31/11. [12] Ibid. S76/31/6, 7; St. Deiniol's Lib. Glynne-Gladstone mss 319, Wallace to Gladstone, 22 Sept., 18, 26 Oct. 1820. [13] *Plumer Ward Mems.* ii. 76. [14] Glynne-Gladstone mss 319, Wallace to Gladstone, 11, 15, 29 Nov., 16 Dec. 1820. [15] *The Times*, 15, 17 Feb., 28 Mar., 6, 13, 20 Apr. 1821. [16] Gurney diary, 24 Mar. 1824. [17] HLRO, Hist. Coll. 379, Grey Bennet diary, 104. [18] Glynne-Gladstone mss 319. [19] Add. 57401. [20] Northumb. RO, Hope-Wallace mss ZHW/2/5; Add. 38290, f. 113; Glynne-Gladstone mss 319. [21] Glynne-Gladstone mss 319; Hilton, 128. [22] *The Times*, 26, 28 Feb. 1822. [23] Ibid. 7, 24 May, 5 June 1822. [24] Glynne-Gladstone mss 319, Wallace to Gladstone, 8 Aug. 1822; Add. 38291, ff. 185, 187. [25] Add. 38291, ff. 223, 233, 236, 335, 344, 347, 351, 398, 406; 38292, f. 160; 38744, ff. 17, 19, 26, 28; Buckingham, *Mems. Geo. IV*, i. 417; *Arbuthnot Corresp.* 35, 36, 42, 43; *Arbuthnot Jnl.* i. 201-2, 204-5, 208; Wellington mss, Wellington to Arbuthnot, 16 Jan. 1823; W. D. Jones, *'Prosperity' Robinson*, 66, 96-97. [26] Glynne-Gladstone mss 319. [27] *Salisbury Jnl.* 17 Feb. 1823; *Gent. Mag.* (1844), i. 426. [28] *Arbuthnot Corresp.* 36. [29] Add. 40354, f. 216. [30] *The Times*, 3 May, 1 July 1823. [31] Middleton mss S76/49/3-5; Add. 38296, f. 168; 38425, ff. 149, 151; 57401, Wallace to Herries, 28 Aug. 1823; *Geo. IV Letters*, iii. 1079; *HMC Bathurst*, 542. [32] Weymouth Mus. Weymouth and Melcombe Regis borough recs. 110.MB2, pp. 384, 391-2, 396-9; Middleton mss S76/49/7; *Salisbury Jnl.* 27 Oct., 1 Dec. 1823; *Dorset Co. Chron.* 12 Feb. 1824. [33] Glynne-Gladstone mss 319. [34] *The Times*, 25 June 1824. [35] Ibid. 19 Apr. 1825. [36] *PP* (1825), iv. 569-989; Middleton mss S76/49/12. [37] G. Wallas, *Life of Place*, 229. [38] *The Times*, 17, 24, 30 June 1825. [39] Wellington mss WP1/860/14. [40] Keele Univ. Lib. Sneyd mss SC8/79, Ellis to Sneyd, 13 Feb. 1826. [41] *The Times*, 22 Apr. 1826. [42] Ibid. 22, 27, 30 June; *Dorset Co. Chron.* 6 Apr., 15, 22, 29 June, 6 July 1826; Middleton mss S76/49/20; 52/2-4, 7, 8, 12. [43] Add. 38301, f. 261; 38568, f. 129. [44] Add. 62097, f. 188. [45] Add. 36463, ff. 311, 313, 329; *The Times*, 24 Mar. 1827. [46] Add. 36463, f. 378; *Canning's Ministry*, 150, 166, 182, 210. [47] Jones, 155. [48] Add. 38761, f. 269. [49] Wellington mss WP1/913/28, 41, 48; Hope-Wallace mss 2/7; Middleton mss S77/1/2. [50] *Ellenborough Diary*, i. 4, 31; Lonsdale mss, Beckett to Lowther, 15 Jan., Lonsdale to same, 23 Jan. 1828. [51] Middleton mss S77/1/2, 8; 3/1; 5/9; *Gent. Mag.* (1844), i. 429. [52] *Tyne Mercury*, 5 Mar.; *The Times*, 30 July 1844; PROB 11/2002/600; Middleton mss S77/20/1, 2; *Gent. Mag.* (1844), i. 429-30; (1854), i. 420-1; *DNB*; *Oxford DNB*.

S.M.F.

WALLACE, Thomas II (1765–1847), of Belfield, Donnybrook, co. Dublin.

YARMOUTH I.o.W.	21 Aug. 1827–1830
DROGHEDA	20 Oct. 1831–1832
CO. CARLOW	1832–1834

b. 13 Apr. 1765, o.s. of James Wallace, woollen manufacturer, of Meath Street, Dublin and w. Deborah Bedford. *educ.* Trinity, Dublin 1789; G. Inn 1795; King's Inns 1795, called [I] 1798. *m.* ?Katherine Chapman, 1s. *d.* 9 Jan. 1847.

KC [I] 1816.

According to a contemporary account of the Irish bar, Wallace was

in several respects a remarkable man. He has for many years held an eminent station in his profession, and is pre-eminently entitled to the self-gratulation of reflecting, that his success has been of that honourable kind in which neither accident nor patronage had any share.

The sketch, first published in July 1826, credited him with 'the composed and dogged ardour of a Scotchman', though this was apparently not a hint as to his origins.[1] According to King's Inns admission records, he was born in Bristol, and his parents, for whom no marriage date has been found, were dead by 1795. The James Wallace listed as his father has not been found in the Dublin directories, where a William Wallace appears as a woollen draper in Bridge Street from 1762 to 1791 and a merchant of the same name is recorded at 22 North Cumberland Street in 1792 and 1793. Both premises were occupied by Wallace himself during the early years of the next century, indicating a family link. His presumed marriage has been adduced from the King's Inns admission record of his only son Thomas, who was born on 31 Mar. 1817. Of his background, his 1826 biographer revealed only that he was without 'competence or connections' in his youth and had set upon 'a solitary plan of self-instruction' to qualify himself for Trinity.[2] From there he progressed to the Irish bar, where, according to a hustings panegyric from Walter Blackney*, his colleague in county Carlow in 1832, he 'rose by his great talents' to eminence, but, remaining faithful to his origins, was known as a 'zealous advocate of the poor'. Regarding his politics, Blackney asserted, somewhat misleadingly, that 'the company he kept in 1798 shows how his heart beat' and cited his defence of the United Irishman James Napper Tandy 'and many others like him'. He was not among the principal advocates named before the celebrated trials of 1800 and 1801.[3]

Wallace, who retained 'all the compactness and rotundity of early youth' with a figure 'a little above the middle size', was said to radiate 'masculine energy' in the courtroom. His reputation was established in jury trials, where his 'skill in dissecting a knavish affidavit' was displayed to the best advantage. But for 'his political sympathies with Mr. [Henry] Grattan I* and friends of Ireland', noted his bar profile, his promotion to king's counsel would have occurred much sooner.[4] In June 1827 he was suggested as a candidate for the post of serjeant-at-law by Lord Wellesley, the Irish viceroy, to Canning, the premier, who replied that he knew Wallace 'by reputation, and I rejoice in his promotion'.[5] Although the appointment was not made, the regard for his ability in official circles was further demonstrated by a backhanded compliment from William Lamb*, the Irish secretary, who referred to him in October as one of the '*ugly* customers' at the Irish bar, from whom a lord chancellor might expect trouble.[6] It was with a hint of bitterness that Daniel O'Connell* recorded next month that he was 'the first of my juniors who got a silk gown for his merits'. (O'Connell had earlier heard a rumour that Wallace was to be made Irish solicitor-general, an honour which, it was later claimed, he had at some unspecified point declined.)[7] The two men, who were virtual contemporaries, had fallen out in 1813, when Wallace had demanded that O'Connell take responsibility for his libellous defence speech at the trial of John Magee, the editor of the *Dublin Evening Post*.[8] Wallace had long harboured political and literary pretensions. His first venture into publication was prompted by sheer pique, after it had emerged that his *Variations in the Prose Style of the English Language* (1796) had been ignored in a Royal Irish Academy prize essay competition in favour of an entry from one of the judges.[9] In 1798 he produced *Manufactures of Ireland*, which, drawing on his family's experiences, advocated economic protection for the Irish woollen industry. He provoked several ripostes with his *Vindication of the Conduct of the Irish Catholics during the late Administration* (1807), which sought to rescue the Catholics from the charge of having caused the downfall of the 'Talents' ministry by their clamour for emancipation. Denouncing Lord Redesdale, the former Irish chancellor, as a 'loquacious and busy bigot', he put the blame on the ministry for its 'culpable inertness' in failing to deal with endemic anti-Catholicism in the state, especially among the magistracy. Under the same pseudonym of 'A Protestant', he published *The Orange System Exposed* (1823), in which he called for the disbandment of Orange societies and praised Wellesley for his 'equal and impartial administration'. His subsequent literary forays included *A Review of the Doctrine of Personal Identity* (1827), a fairly light treatment of the works of several philosophers, including John Locke, and his *Observations on the Discourse of Natural Theology by Lord Brougham* (1835), which took issue with the lord chancellor's materialist belief in the mortality of the soul, which, Wallace contended, took 'fear from the sinner and hope from the saint!'

He made his first known attempt to enter Parliament in 1818, when he offered for Drogheda on the independent interest. He added further colour to a fierce contest by fighting a duel with the town's recorder, 'in which two shots were fired on each side, but fortunately without injury to either party'. After a narrow defeat, he petitioned unsuccessfully against the return.[10] At a pro-Catholic meeting at the Dublin Rotunda the following February he made a name for himself by silencing a disruptive Orange element with 'stern, determined, almost terrific energy', after Grattan himself had been ineffective.[11] Although he declined to stand again for Drogheda at the 1820 general election, he was nominated 'without his consent' by his supporters. In his absence on the circuit, he was defeated after a five-day poll. A petition lodged by his partisans was not pursued. At the same election he gave a plumper for Richard Talbot, the sitting Member for county Dublin, and on the hustings said a few words against his wealthy challenger, Thomas White.[12] Press speculation before the 1826 general election suggested that Wallace had abandoned Drogheda to act as agent for Lord George Beresford* in county Waterford, but he confounded this report by making a grand entry to the borough 'in the company of the Grattans' (presumably Henry junior, shortly to become Member for Dublin, and his brother James, Member for county Wicklow). He retreated on finding another independent candidate in the field, but reappeared four days into the contest to renew his claims. After a declaration in favour of Catholic relief and a narrow escape from assault by a mob, he polled his travelling contingent of 24 out-voters and departed. If he contemplated a challenge to the return, it never materialized.[13]

His quest for a berth ended in August 1827, when he came in on a vacancy for Yarmouth, Isle of Wight, where the seats were at the disposal of the trustees of Sir Leonard Thomas Worsley Holmes*. His profile of the previous year had predicted that once in the House 'his career there will be neither "mute" nor "inglorious"', but in the event he did not live up to such expectations, though he was a willing speaker, primarily on Irish issues. On other matters, he tended to side with ministers. He spoke in favour of petitions for Catholic relief, noting that 'it is impossible for things to go on as they are in Ireland', 19 Feb., and presented two from county Meath, 20 Mar., and one from Drogheda, 5 May 1828. He voted accordingly, 12 May, when he made a prolix and ill-judged attempt to convince Peel, the home secretary, that denial of Catholic claims was a contravention of the Glorious Revolution settlement. Richard Sheil* cited the speech as a prime example of the 'accident and obstinacy' that caused Wallace to disappoint as a Commons performer:

> He rose at three in the morning, on the fourth night of the Catholic debate, and commenced with the Treaty of Limerick. He plunged, as I have heard it observed, at once into one of the old moats of that ancient city, and lost himself in the ooze, if I may so call it, with which his infelicitous topic was overspread.[14]

John Hely Hutchinson I* later recalled that the House, 'though tired to death, was anxious to hear him', until he 'wasted twenty minutes in endeavouring to show how the law officers of the crown in Ireland might have put down the Catholic Association. Nothing could have been more uncalled for or more injudicious'.[15] Wallace spoke against the Irish Subletting Act, which he believed would unfairly penalize the small landholder, 19 Feb. He presented a Drogheda petition for its repeal and expressed his particular concern at the possibility of its retrospective operation, 21 Mar. From personal experience, he called for Irish sheriffs to be subjected to a legal requirement of promptitude in compiling returns of jurors, 20 Mar. On 2 Mar. he was appointed to the select committee on the civil government of Canada. (The previous month, he had been sent a petition from French Canadians complaining of their treatment at the hands of their Scottish Presbyterian neighbours, though there is no record that he presented it.)[16] He welcomed Sugden's bill to facilitate the payment of debts out of real estate, 6 May 1828.

Wallace called for a more precise wording for proclamations to be inserted in the Irish unlawful societies bill in order to assist its enforcement, 13 Feb. 1829. He did not think that a measure to drain Irish bogs would 'produce any good effect', 26 Feb. On 9 Mar. he introduced a bill to extend the law against the abuse of charitable trusts to Ireland, which was given a second reading, 12 Mar., and passed the House, 23 Mar., but progressed no further. As Planta, the Wellington ministry's patronage secretary, had predicted, he voted for the concession of Catholic emancipation, 6 Mar. He asserted that many signatories to anti-Catholic petitions were influenced by 'undue means' and were therefore not competent to judge the question, 12 Mar. In private, however, he warned Peel that the bill's definition of a Catholic might be too loose to ensure their effective exclusion from church appointments.[17] Commenting on a petition against alleged abuses of the Irish office of sub-sheriff, he insisted that legal redress was already available, 14 Apr. 1829. That day he presented two petitions against the Irish Subletting Act, which he complained was being exploited by unscrupulous landlords. He welcomed the ensuing amendment bill, 16 Feb., 5 Mar. 1830. He voted against Lord Blandford's parliamentary reform scheme, 18 Feb., and the enfranchisement of Birmingham, Leeds and Manchester, 23 Feb. In March he was again mentioned as a candidate for the Irish serjeantcy, though Lord Francis Leveson Gower*, the Irish secretary, offered him little encouragement and privately considered that he had no political claims to the position.[18] On 10

May he presented petitions for the construction of a road leading north from Waterloo Bridge and from a Mayo clergyman against libels allegedly contained in petitions previously presented by O'Connell, whom he ritually exonerated. He voted against Jewish emancipation, 17 May 1830. Next day he presented a petition from Kilkenny printers for the equalization of Irish and English newspaper stamp duties.

At the 1830 dissolution Wallace retired from Yarmouth. It was widely expected that he would offer again for Drogheda, but on 'finding the field preoccupied' at the nomination he declined.[19] Following the accession of the Grey administration, Wallace professed 'sincere respect for Lord Anglesey', the reappointed Irish viceroy, 'and a wish to support his government', but deemed ministers' prosecution of O'Connell for unlawful assembly to be 'erroneous'. Despite their long-standing quarrel, he wrote to O'Connell to say so, 19 Jan. 1831, with the rider that 'no just inference can be made of any adoption on my part of your political principles'. The gesture signalled a reconciliation, despite O'Connell's subsequent unauthorized publication of the letter, much to the consternation of the Irish government.[20] Anglesey described Wallace's intervention as 'very indecorous' on the part of a king's counsel, while Hely Hutchinson ascribed it to frustrated ambitions for office and found in it confirmation of his view that 'whatever his character may be as a lawyer, he has no common sense'.[21] Later that year Wallace offered his opinion on two Irish judicial appointments to Lord Melbourne, the home secretary, 'perhaps too freely', as he later admitted.[22] In April 1831, however, Anglesey assured Grey that he had 'knocked under', and when he offered for Drogheda at the general election shortly afterwards he obtained the support of ministers.[23] His past record on the subject notwithstanding, he proclaimed himself 'unqualifiedly favourable to reform', whereupon a local newspaper retorted that he had previously been a 'thick and thin supporter of ministers to the extent of muzzling the press'. After an eight-day poll he was defeated, for which he blamed the freemen out-voters.[24] O'Connell, however, privately noted that 'Wallace, on whom I relied for Drogheda, is doing only mischief. There are some men born with heads that see all matters upside down and act accordingly'.[25] Nothing came of Wallace's threat to challenge the eligibility of his opponent, John Henry North, before the latter died in September. On offering for the vacancy, Wallace declared himself 'a thorough radical reformer', though he actively sought the support of his erstwhile enemies on the corporation, and the strictures he had so recently passed on his late adversary gave way to eulogies of 'his much lamented and estimable friend'. He was returned unopposed, according to Edward Smith Stanley*, the Irish secretary, 'by mere bragging', as 'he had not a shilling and would not have stood a poll'.[26]

Wallace voted for the second reading of the revised reform bill, 17 Dec. 1831, gave steady support to its details, and voted for the third reading, 22 Mar. 1832. He presented a petition from Drogheda landholders against grand jury assessments and tithes and for the extension of the vote to Irish £10 leaseholders, 26 Jan. He voted with ministers on relations with Portugal, 9 Feb. He objected to an amendment bill to the Irish Subletting Act on the premise that the law was intrinsically a bad one, and was a minority teller against a clause allowing absolute power to landlords to prevent subletting, 20 Feb. He presented a petition from the procurators-general of the Dublin court of prerogative and faculties against a precipitate response to the report of the Irish ecclesiastical commissioners, 5 Mar. On 15 Mar. he introduced a bill to delay implementation of the provisions of the Friendly Societies Act of 1830, which passed, 16 Apr. and gained royal assent, 23 May (2 Gul. IV, c. 37). He divided for an address asking the king to appoint only ministers who would carry the reform bill unimpaired, 10 May, and, citing the 'intense anxiety' that prevailed among his constituents, spoke against a call to adjourn the debate on withholding the supplies, 14 May. He voted for the second reading of the Irish reform bill, 25 May, but was in the minorities for O'Connell's motion to extend the franchise to £5 freeholders, 18 June, and for removing the liability of electors to pay municipal taxes before they could vote, 29 June. He made brief interventions on the wording of two clauses, 25 June, and proposed an amendment to prevent 'vexatious' objections to freeholder registrations, 6 July, which he withdrew after receiving ministerial assurances. He was in the minority of 29 against the bill to exclude insolvent debtors from Parliament, 6 June. On 4 July he endorsed the petition of a sacked Dublin post office employee. He voted with ministers on the Russian-Dutch loan, 12, 16 July. In the belief that 'every judicial officer should be placed in situation above all suspicion', he was a majority teller for disqualifying the recorder of Dublin from sitting in Parliament, 24 July 1832.

According to Blackney, at some late point in 1832 Wallace crossed the floor to sit 'at the back of Mr. O'Connell', a gesture prompted by his disenchantment with ministers over the issue of Irish tithes.[27] On 14 Feb. he welcomed their efforts to meet grievances, praising Smith Stanley's 'very able exposé', but

two days later he was in the minority for printing the Woollen Grange petition for the abolition of tithes. On 8 Mar. he denounced the 'hasty and injudicious' report of the select committee, notably its recommendations for the recovery of arrears, although he conceded that ministers' actions were 'generally characterized by frankness and candour'. He reiterated his objections, 13 Mar., was in the minority for a thorough overhaul of the tithe system, 27 Mar., when he warned that 'the peace of Ireland is at hazard', and voted against a levy for arrears, 30 Mar. He proposed a lengthy amendment to the report endeavouring to justify the 'passive opposition' offered to tithe payment, 2 Apr., and was appointed to the select committee on Irish unrest, 31 May. He was in a minority for postponing the tithe bill until the next Parliament, 13 July, being of the opinion that the proposed reforms were 'a mockery, if not an insult' and would do nothing to satisfy Irish opinion, 24 July. That day he was a teller for the minority of 16 for an amendment to appropriate Irish first fruits revenues. On 1 Aug. 1832 he proposed an amendment for the 'complete extinction' of tithes and a new land survey to set a fair replacement charge, which was lost by 60-8. He was in another minority on the bill that day, when his numerous interventions on minor details led Lord Althorp to charge him with resorting to delaying tactics.

At the 1832 general election Wallace abandoned Drogheda, where his failure to give an unequivocal pledge in support of repeal of the Union had provoked dissatisfaction. At O'Connell's behest, it was claimed, he stood for county Carlow, to which he possessed no obvious link. His proposer pledged 'honest Tom' to support the abolition of tithes and vote by ballot, but again he refused to be bound to support repeal of the Union. A hostile squib dismissed him as a political adventurer and condemned his hustings performance as 'unmeaning verbiage, pitiful special pleading, and nisi prius sophistry', but admitted that there was not 'a single blemish' on his private character. He was elected and survived a petition.[28] In the reformed Parliament he was classed as a Liberal and continued to speak on Irish matters. His initial address before the 1835 election was noted to have contained a typographical error, which, to the delight of his opponents, pledged him 'to stand by the country, and its deformed constitution'.[29] As O'Connell had anticipated, he declined another contest, according to the local press because of a lack of funds, and he made no further bid to re-enter Parliament.[30] In September 1834 he had written to Melbourne expressing his desire 'to promote the success and stability of your lordship's administration' and urging the appointment of Irish judges 'of sound and liberal principles', though he denied that it was himself that he had in mind.[31] His antipathy to O'Connell had returned by 1843, when he urged Peel, the Conservative premier, to adopt repressive measures.[32]

Wallace died in January 1847 at his Belfield residence just south of Dublin, 'after a very brief illness'.[33] His only son and heir was listed at this address as a practising barrister in 1853, having previously shared his father's chambers at 76 St. Stephen's Green. He had disappeared from the directories ten years later, but Belfield apparently remained in the family until the end of the century.

[1] W.H. Curran, *Sketches of the Irish Bar* (1855), 325, 327. [2] Ibid. 326. [3] *Carlow Sentinel*, 1 Dec. 1832; *The Times*, 12 May, 20 Nov. 1800. [4] Curran, 327-9, 334-6. [5] *Canning's Ministry*, 320, 326. [6] Brougham mss, Lamb to Brougham, 14 Oct. 1827. [7] *O'Connell Corresp.* iii. 1399; *Carlow Sentinel*, 1 Dec. 1832. [8] *O'Connell Corresp.* i. 475; iii. 1431. [9] Curran, 353-4. [10] *The Times*, 10 July 1818; *CJ*, lxxiv, 23, 83. [11] Curran, 350-2; *The Times*, 16 Feb. 1819. [12] *Dublin Evening Post*, 14, 18, 25, 28 Mar. 1820; *CJ*, lxxv. 162, 293. [13] *Drogheda Jnl.* 10, 14, 17, 21 June 1826. [14] R. Malcolmson, *Carlow Parl. Roll*, 43. [15] TCD, Donoughmore mss E/372, Hely Hutchinson to Donoughmore, 30 Jan. 1831. [16] Add. 38755, f. 36. [17] Add. 40399, f. 91. [18] NAI, Leveson Gower letterbks. 3, Leveson Gower to Wallace, 5 Mar., to Singleton, 13 Mar. 1830. [19] *Drogheda Jnl.* 27, 31 July 1830. [20] *O'Connell Corresp.* iv. 1751a-1754. [21] Add. 51568, Anglesey to Holland, 23 Jan. 1831; Donoughmore mss E/372, Hely Hutchinson to Donoughmore, 30 Jan. 1831. [22] Add. 37307, f. 168. [23] PRO NI, Anglesey mss, Anglesey to Grey, 30 Apr. 1831. [24] *Dublin Evening Post*, 5, 10, 14 May 1831. [25] *O'Connell Corresp.* iv. 1802. [26] *Drogheda Jnl.*, 2, 15, 22 Oct.; Grey mss, Smith Stanley to Grey, 23 Oct. 1831. [27] *Carlow Sentinel*, 1 Dec. 1832. [28] Ibid. 15 Sept., 1, 15, 22 Dec. 1832; *CJ*, lxxxviii. 115, 161, 241, 414. [29] *The Times*, 1 Jan. 1835. [30] *O'Connell Corresp.* iv. 2143, 2148; *Carlow Sentinel*, 29 Nov., 13 Dec. 1834. [31] Add. 37307, f. 168. [32] Add. 40525, f. 231. [33] *Dublin Evening Post*, 12 Jan. 1847.

H.J.S./P.J.S.

WALPOLE, Horatio, Lord Walpole (1783–1858), of Wolterton, Norf. and 11 Berkeley Square, Mdx.

KING'S LYNN	9 Mar. 1809–15 June 1822

b. 14 June 1783, 1st s. of Horatio Walpole[†], 2nd earl of Orford, and 1st. w. Sophia, da. and coh. of Col. Charles Churchill[†] of Chalfont, Bucks.; bro. of Hon. John Walpole*. *educ.* Eton 1797-1801; Trinity Coll. Camb. 1801. *m.* 23 July 1812, Mary, da. and coh. of William Augustus Fawkener, clerk of PC, of Brocton Hall, Salop, 3s. 2da. *suc.* fa. as 3rd earl of Orford and 4th and 6th Bars. Walpole (of Wolterton and Walpole) 15 June 1822. *d.* 29 Dec. 1858.

Attaché at St. Petersburg 1806, at Madrid 1808; ld. of admiralty June 1811-Oct. 1812; sec. of embassy and minister *ad. int.* St. Petersburg 1812-15; commr. bd. of control June 1818-Feb. 1822.

Constable, Castle Rising 1822-*d.*; high steward, King's Lynn 1822-*d.*, Great Yarmouth 1833-6.

Col. W. Norf. militia 1822-*d.*

The diminutive placeman and former diplomat Lord Walpole, who acquired a reputation as an inveterate gambler, anti-feminist and 'poseur', neglectful of his wife, was returned *in absentia* for King's Lynn on his father's interest in 1820, when family illness detained him at Dresden.[1] An anti-Catholic Tory for whom no Commons speeches are reported after 1820, he returned to the continent after taking his seat, spent the summer in Italy and informed his friend and fellow diplomat Edward Cromwell Disbrowe*, in Switzerland, that he was taking his family to Vienna for the winter, in order to 'hear what is going on' in England, and to shorten his journey to the Commons, when summoned.[2] Although 'Canning's secession' made him 'less inclined' to do so, he returned for what he envisaged as six weeks in late January 1821 to support Lord Liverpool's ministry on the Queen Caroline affair and other issues.[3] He divided with them as required until 13 Mar. 1822, when, probably as a reaction to losing his seat on the India board as a result of the Grenvillite accession, he created a stir by casting a wayward vote for the abolition of one of the joint-postmasterships.[4] He had voted against parliamentary reform, 9 May, and he brought up a petition from King's Lynn against the poor law amendment bill, 4 June 1821.[5] He voted against permitting Catholic peers to take their seats in the House of Lords, 30 Apr. 1822. He was elevated there by his father's death in June, and returned his brother John for King's Lynn, where at Michaelmas he became high steward.[6]

From 1825 financial difficulties induced Orford, who privately had little respect for the Liverpool and Goderich ministries and esteemed Canning (whose corn bill he paired against, 18 June 1827) only as foreign secretary, to seek diplomatic employment.[7] However, he turned down offers from Canning and the duke of Wellington of a mission to Mexico as unsuitable for his family and, with no alternative forthcoming, he sold his London home and went abroad pending further sales.[8] His applications on behalf of John also failed.[9] A lifelong Conservative and leader of the local party in Norfolk, 1846-58 (Conservative ministries never considered him trustworthy and 'sanguine' enough for office), he gave Wellington his proxy for Catholic emancipation in 1829, despite continued misgivings, opposed parliamentary reform with his Carlton Club colleagues and harried Lord Grey in the Lords on the French invasion of Belgium and other foreign policy issues, 1831-3, notwithstanding his brother's preferment during his ministry.[10] He died at Wolterton in December 1858, estranged from his wife (*d.* 4 Feb. 1859), and was succeeded in his titles and estates by his eldest son Horatio William Walpole

(1813-94), Conservative Member for Norfolk East, 1835-37, and a convert to Roman Catholicism. Orford had settled a sum on his putative daughter Wilhelmine in St. Petersburg at her marriage in 1833-4, and his will, dated 7 Apr. 1852, invoked other family settlements and provided generously for his younger sons Henry (1818-76) and Frederick Walpole (1822-76), Conservative Member for Norfolk North, 1868-76. By a codicil of 19 Mar. 1858, he left £2,000 and £1,500 respectively to Miss Charlotte Lait of Regent's Park and his housekeeper Caroline Anne Biddiscombe.[11]

[1] W. Rye, *Later Hist. of Fam. of Walpole of Norf.* 33-37; *HP Commons, 1790-1820*, v. 474-5; *Bury and Norwich Post*, 8, 15 Mar. 1820. [2] *Recs. of Stirring Times* ed. M. Montgomery-Campbell, 276-7. [3] Ibid. 277-9. [4] Gurney diary, 13 Mar. 1822. [5] *Recs. of Stirring Times*, 277-8; *The Times*, 5 June 1821. [6] *The Times*, 19 June; *Norf. Chron.* 22, 29 June 1822. [7] *Geo. IV Letters*, iii. 1362; Lord Walpole of Wolterton mss 14/48A; 17/4/84 [NRA 43212, pp. 163, 168]; Wellington mss WP1/937/17; 992/5. [8] All Souls, Oxf. Vaughan mss, Orford to Vaughan, 26 July 1827, 3 July 1829; Wellington mss WP1/984/11; 1054/82. [9] Wellington mss WP1/952/23; 957/21. [10] Ibid. WP1/998/16; 999/7; 1054/82; 1185/19; 1216/5; Vaughan mss, Orford to Vaughan, 16 Feb., 3 July 1829; *Three Diaries*, 94, 136, 341; *Holland House Diaries*, 31; Lord Walpole of Wolterton mss 16/10, 12, 13 [NRA 43212, p. 145], *The Times*, 19 Nov. 1836, 6 Aug. 1843. [11] *The Times*, 31 Dec. 1858; *Gent. Mag.* (1859), i. 219; Lord Walpole of Wolterton mss 14/4/55 [NRA 43212, pp. 164-5].

R.M.H./M.M.E.

WALPOLE, Hon. **John** (1787–1859), of 58 Jermyn Street, Mdx.

KING'S LYNN   29 June 1822–1831

b. 17 Nov. 1787, 4th but 2nd surv. s. of Horatio Walpole[†], 2nd earl of Orford (*d.* 1822), and 1st. w. Sophia, da. and coh. of Col. Charles Churchill[†] of Chalfont, Bucks.; bro. of Horatio Walpole, Lord Walpole*. *educ.* Eton 1802. *unm. d.* 10 Dec. 1859.

Lt. 1 Ft. Gds. 1808, capt. and lt.-col. 1814, ret. 1825.

Private sec. to sec. of state for foreign affairs (Lord Palmerston*) Nov. 1830–Apr. 1833; consul-gen. Chile 1833, plenip. 1837, chargé d'affaires 1841, ret. 1849.

Walpole, the 2nd earl of Orford's youngest son, initially pursued a military career, punctuated with sojourns attending his eldest brother Horace on diplomatic missions to St. Petersburg, Vienna and Dresden. Henry Williams Wynn[†], who first met him there in 1805, found him 'much more *comme il faut* than the rest [of English travellers], he also appears to more advantage as he talks French tolerably well, which few of my countrymen do'.[1] A veteran of the siege of Burgos, which cost him the use of his left arm, he was consigned to the home service following the death of his brother William in 1814, and it was anticipated that

he would replace Horace as the Walpole or corporation member for King's Lynn on their father's death. He experienced little opposition when he deputized for his absent brother at the general election of 1820; but in what proved to be the first of four violent contests which marked his tenure of the seat, his election on 29 June 1822, shortly after the 2nd earl's funeral, was bitterly opposed, as dissidents on the corporation and the anti-corporation party combined to back Sir William Henry Browne Ffolkes*, whose father had previously represented the borough.[2]

Walpole, who made no reported speeches and generally followed his brother the 3rd earl's political leadership, was condemned by his opponents as a placeman and recipient of an army pension of £700 a year.[3] He divided with Lord Liverpool's ministry on taxation, 3, 10, 13 Mar., and the prosecution of the Dublin Orange rioters, 22 Apr. 1823. He voted against Scottish parliamentary reform, 26 Feb., and against condemning the indictment in Demerara of the Methodist missionary John Smith, 11 June 1824. He took charge of the 1824, 1825 and 1826 Eau Brink bills on the corporation of King's Lynn's behalf.[4] His votes against Catholic relief, 1 Mar., 21 Apr., and the Irish franchise bill, 26 Apr. 1825, were the last attributed to him in that Parliament. He came in at great cost with Lord William Cavendish Bentinck at the 1826 general election.[5] He voted against Catholic relief, 6 Mar. 1827, and repeal of the Test Acts, 26 Feb. 1828. His brother's uncertain allegiance to the Canning, Goderich and Wellington ministries was tempered by vain hopes of diplomatic preferment to ease his financial difficulties.[6] Walpole's own finances fluctuated with those of the Potosi La Paz and Peruvian Mining Association, of which he was a director with the government whip William Holmes*, the former sheriff of London Sir Francis Desanges and Thomas Thistleton, and which in 1827 became the subject of a 'great scam'.[7] He applied unsuccessfully for preferment after a Potosi board meeting on 22 Aug. 1828 had called for a subscription of a pound a share, and Orford suggested him for the vacant post of surveyor-general of the ordnance, but he was informed by Wellington that only 'a gentlemen who has attended to business and who has the reputation of having attended to business more than your brother has' would do.[8] As the patronage secretary Planta had predicted, he voted 'with government' for Catholic emancipation, 30 Mar. 1829.[9] He voted against transferring East Retford's seats to Birmingham, 11 Feb., and enfranchising Birmingham, Leeds and Manchester, 23 Feb., and divided against Jewish emancipation, 17 May 1830. His opposition to reform was the reason given for forcing a poll at King's

Lynn at the general election in August when Browne Ffolkes came in for the county.[10]

The Wellington ministry counted Walpole among their 'friends' and he divided with them on the civil list, 15 Nov. 1830, when they were brought down.[11] His surprising appointment at £300 a year as private secretary to the foreign secretary Lord Palmerston in Lord Grey's administration was authorized on personal and compassionate grounds arising from his readiness to stand surety for a brother officer who had absconded for debt, and a king's bench ruling in a test case, Temple v. Walpole and others (4 Mar. 1830), that he was personally liable for the Potosi debts.[12] His votes for the government's reform bill at its second reading, 22 Mar., and against Gascoyne's wrecking amendment, 19 Apr. 1831, failed to satisfy his opponents in King's Lynn at the ensuing general election that he was a reformer, and he was obliged to retire before the poll to avoid a costly defeat.[13]

Walpole made several statements to the House on behalf of the foreign office, but he did not stand for Parliament again. After much prevarication, for he wanted a European posting, preferably St. Petersburg, he agreed to go to Chile as consul-general, and arrived there in December 1833.[14] His diplomatic career is detailed in official dispatches and his private correspondence with Palmerston. He negotiated and signed the slave trade treaty of 19 Jan. 1839 with Chile, was promoted to chargé d'affaires shortly before securing agreement on the Chilean Convention of 7 Aug. 1841 and remained there until independence was declared in 1847.[15] He subsequently received a pension of £365 a year. He never married and died intestate at Sydenham in December 1859. On 19 Jan. 1860 administration of his estate was granted at the principal registry to Maria, the wife of Martin John West of Leeds, the eldest of his four surviving sisters. His library and other effects from his house in Jermyn Street were sold at auction in 1860.[16]

[1] *Williams Wynn Coresp.* 87; *HP Commons, 1790-1820,* v. 474-5. [2] H. Hillen, *King's Lynn,* ii. 558-67; *Bury and Norwich Post,* 8, 15 Mar. 1820, 3, 10 July; *Norwich, Yarmouth and Lynn Courier and Norfolk Gen. Advertiser,* 29 June, 6, 13 July 1822. [3] *Norwich, Yarmouth and Lynn Courier and Norfolk Gen. Advertiser,* 6, 10 July 1822. [4] Nottingham Univ. Lib. Portland mss PWJe 77, 112. [5] *Bury and Norwich Post,* 7, 14 June 1826; J. Rosselli, *Lord William Bentinck,* 76; Portland mss PwJe 121, 1079. [6] All Souls, Oxf. Vaughan mss, Orford to Vaughan, 26 July 1827, 3 July 1829 [NRA 10564]; Wellington mss WP1/937/17; 952/23; 984/11; 992/5; Southampton Univ. Lib. Broadlands mss GC/OR/6; GC/GR/1935. [7] *Morning Herald,* 24, 30 Oct., 2, 3, 7-10, 12-14 Nov., 22 Dec.; *The Times,* 2, 8, 12, 14 Nov. 1827. [8] *London Gazette,* 30 Sept. 1828; Wellington mss WP1/952/23; 957/21. [9] Wellington mss WP1/992/5; 998/16; 999/7; 1007/34. [10] *Norfolk Mercury,* 10, 24, 31 July, 7 Aug. 1830. [11] Wellington mss WP1/1054/82. [12] *Morning Herald,* 5 Mar. 1830;

[13] *Norfolk Mercury,* 16, 30 Apr.; *Bury and Norwich Post,* 4, 11 May 1831; Lord W.P. Lennox, *50 Years Biog. Reminiscences,* ii. 158-9, 162-3. [14] *Raikes Jnl.* i. 46; TNA FO16/22, ff. 1-99; Broadlands mss GC/WA/39; Bourne, 428. [15] FO16/22-23, 25-28, 30-32, 34-35 *passim.* Broadlands mss GC/WA/40-74. [16] *Norwich Mercury,* 14 Dec. 1859; *Gent. Mag.* (1860), i. 195; Lord Walpole of Wolterton mss 24/48 [NRA 43212, p. 132].

M.M.E.

WALROND, Bethell (1801–1876), of Clifton Street, Bond Street, Mdx. and Dulford House, Montrath, Devon.

SUDBURY	1826–1831
SALTASH	1831–1832

b. 10 Aug. 1801, 2nd *s.* of Joseph Lyons Walrond (*d.* 1815) of Antigua and Montrath House, Broadhembury, Devon and Caroline, da. of Edward Codrington, merchant, of Broad Street Buildings, London. *m.* 10 Nov. 1829, Lady Janet St. Clair Erskine, da. of James St. Clair Erskine†, 2nd earl of Rosslyn, 5ch. (1s. 1 da. surv.). *suc.* bro. Lyons Walrond 1819. *d.* 28 May 1876.

Cornet 1 Life Gds. 1818, sub-lt. 1821, half-pay 1822.

Walrond, who proudly traced his ancestry to Edward I and held the titles of a Spanish grandee, was born and raised at his parents' London home in Grosvenor Place and named after his mother's late uncle and guardian, Sir Christopher Bethell.[1] The family's West Indian wealth derived from his father's service as manager of the Codrington estates in Antigua, where the Lyons and Walrond families were merchant planters, and from his trusteeship of the Davis, Gray, Jaffreson and Ronan estates.[2] His death precluded his family's return there after the war, and control of his English and Antiguan estates, valued at £75,000 at probate, passed to his widow, his brother Maine, cousin John Lyons and friend and attorney William Osgood. Bequests worth an estimated £52,000 to his two sons were conditional on their surviving to 1 Feb. 1823 and 1 Jan. 1825. By his elder brother Lyons's death in 1819, Walrond inherited both shares in 1825.[3] He neglected his army career to embark on the life of a west country squire and gentleman, and entered Parliament in 1826 as Member for the venal borough of Sudbury, where he started late, deposited £10,000 in the bank and, failing to satisfy the powerful 'No Popery' faction on the corporation that his opposition to Catholic relief was genuine, reputedly bought off one of the front runners, Benjamin Rotch, who retired before the poll.[4] A petition alleging this from the defeated candidate Charles Ogilvy was not proceeded with, but few believed Lord Belhaven's assertion that his return cost Walrond only £1,500.[5]

Tall, fair and handsome, Walrond was dogged by his reputation as a gambler and 'Lady Ashbrook's old flirt', and made no major speeches in the House, where, despite his voting inconsistencies and absenteeism, he was considered a 'thorough-going ministerialist'.[6] He voted, 6 Mar. 1827, and paired, 12 May 1828, against Catholic relief, but voted to repeal the Test Acts, 26 Feb. He divided with the duke of Wellington's ministry on the ordnance estimates, 4 July 1828. Their patronage secretary Planta predicted that he would vote 'with government' for Catholic emancipation in 1829, but he divided against it 6, 18, 30 Mar. He voted to transfer East Retford's seats to Birmingham, 5 May 1829. By his marriage that December he became the son-in-law of the 2nd earl of Rosslyn, a former Foxite, who in June 1829 had joined the ministry as lord privy seal. He voted against Lord Blandford's reform scheme, 18 Feb., and the enfranchisement of Birmingham, Leeds and Manchester, 23 Feb., but for Jewish emancipation, 5 Apr., 17 May 1830. From Sudbury, he presented petitions for abolition of the death penalty for forgery (which he voted against, 7 June), 24 Apr., and against the beer bill's provisions for on-consumption, 10 May 1830. His return there at the general election in July was unexpected and unopposed.[7] His new colleague, Sir John Benn Walsh, now deemed him a 'loose hare-brained thoughtless fellow, and very lax and tricky in his principles ... so slippery a fellow that I do not feel inclined to embark in [a coalition] ... with him'.[8]

The ministry counted Walrond among their 'friends', but he was absent from the division on the civil list by which they were brought down, 15 Nov. 1830. He was granted ten days' leave to attend the assizes, 16 Mar., and did not divide on the Grey ministry's reform bill at its second reading, 22 Mar., but he voted for Gascoyne's wrecking amendment, 19 Apr. 1831.[9] At the ensuing dissolution, he decided against canvassing Sudbury for 'several thousand cogent reasons in the shape of election bills incurred on the last occasion', and came in for Saltash (which was then designated for disfranchisement) as a reformer, on his own and the Buller interest.[10] According to his marriage settlement, he had Saltash burgage properties worth an estimated £12,000.[11] On the hustings, he 'pledged to support the bill' notwithstanding his vote with Gascoyne.[12] Walrond was absent from the division on the second reading of the reintroduced reform bill, 6 July 1831, and voted to adjourn its committal, 12 July. After the schedule A boroughs (from which Saltash was temporarily removed) had been dispatched, he voted for the bill's provisions for Chippenham, 27 July, Greenwich, 3 Aug., and

Gateshead, 5 Aug., and its third reading, 19 Sept., and passage, 21 Sept.[13] He voted for Lord Ebrington's confidence motion, 10 Oct. He divided for the revised reform bill (which confirmed Saltash's disfranchisement) at its second reading, 17 Dec. 1831, steadily for its details, and for the third reading, 22 Mar. 1832. He divided for the address calling on the king to appoint only ministers who would carry it unimpaired, 10 May. He paired for the second reading of the Irish reform bill, 25 May, and against a Conservative amendment for increasing the Scottish county representation, 1 June.[14] He divided with government on the Russian-Dutch loan, 26 Jan., 12, 16 July, and relations with Portugal, 9 Feb., but was in Hume's minority of ten to omit the reference to Divine Providence in the preamble to the Scottish cholera bill, 16 Feb.[15] He presented the corporation's petition against the Saltash floating bridge bill, 7 Feb. 1832.

Walrond did not stand for Parliament again. His claim to the ancient barony of Welles was acknowledged following his mother's horrific death after her clothes caught fire, 6 Nov. 1833, but he was not awarded the title.[16] His marriage had become volatile and unhappy, and his failure to make up his wife's marriage settlement in full by 1836 led to a breach with his brother-in-law James St. Clair Erskine*, who, after succeeding as 3rd earl of Rosslyn in 1837, pursued the matter in a series of acrimonious court cases involving several family members.[17] Walrond's counter-prosecutions failed, and he economized by taking his family to the continent, whence he returned to Devon in 1852 with his only surviving son Henry Walrond (1841-1915), leaving his wife (from whom he separated formally in 1850) and daughter Harriet in Frankfurt. Divorce proceedings were not initiated, but legal action ensued and in 1856 Walrond drafted a will prohibiting his wife and daughter from inheriting any part of his estate, which he devised solely to Henry.[18] His breach with the latter in 1862 prompted further litigation and a new will in 1868, in which Walrond disinherited his entire family in favour of his Devon friends. He anticipated but failed to prevent its being contested following his death in May 1876.[19] An out-of-court settlement of 13 June 1877 gave Henry possession of the Devonshire estates, valued at £14,000 at probate, 1 May 1877, 25 June 1878, encumbered with £19,000 in mortgages, outstanding bequests of over £26,000, and heavy litigation costs; but 'The Great Devonshire Will Case', with its ghoulish appeal, was revived and pursued at law until 1884. Evidence submitted during it portrayed Walrond as a devoted father, excellent administrator and able soldier, magistrate and county lieutenant, whose many 'eccentricities' included a belief in the immortality of dogs.[20]

[1] *The Times*, 16 June 1877. [2] *Gent. Mag.* (1801), ii. 763; V.L. Oliver, *Antigua*, i. 145, 170, 173, 194; ii. 35, 109; iii. 50, 119, 180-3; R. Lowe, *Codrington Corresp.* 3, 32. [3] *Gent. Mag.* (1815), i. 187; PROB 8/208; 11/1569/286; IR26/661/223. [4] NLW, Ormathwaite mss FG1/5, pp. 75-76; G37, f. 3; *The Times*, 6, 9, 14, 19 June; *Bury Gazette*, 21 June 1826. [5] *CJ*, lxxxii. 59-60, 92, 124, 307; Ormathwaite mss G36, f. 18. [6] Ormathwaite mss FG1/5, p. 69; G35, f. 98. [7] *The Times*, 9, 12, 19 July; *Colchester Gazette*, 7 Aug. 1830. [8] Ormathwaite mss FG1/5, pp. 86-87. [9] *The Times*, 24, 26 Mar., 21 Apr. 1831. [10] Ibid. 28 Apr.; *Plymouth Herald*, 30 Apr.; *Cornubian*, 6, 13 May; *Colchester Gazette*, 7, 14 May 1831. [11] Devon RO 1926/B/W/FS/19a; *The Times*, 27 July 1838. [12] Brougham mss, Ellice to Brougham, 6 Apr.; *Western Times*, 7 May 1831. [13] *The Times*, 2, 9 Aug. 1831. [14] Ibid. 28 May, 4 June 1832. [15] Ibid. 18 Feb. 1832. [16] Ibid. 13 Nov. 1833; TNA PCAP 1/18. [17] Brougham mss, Walrond to Brougham, 26 July; *The Times*, 27 July 1838. [18] TNA J46/1364. [19] *Exeter and Plymouth Gazette*, 1 June 1876. [20] TNA J15/1351/2464; J121/2853; 3043 (i), (ii); J165/35-39; *The Times*, 31 May, 2, 8, 9, 14, 19, 21 June 1877.

M.M.E.

WALSH, Sir John Benn, 2nd bt. (1798–1881), of Warfield Park, Berks. and 28 Berkeley Square, Mdx.

SUDBURY	1830–1834
SUDBURY	27 Mar. 1838–29 May 1840
RADNORSHIRE	10 June 1840–16 Apr. 1868

b. 9 Dec. 1798, 5th but 1st surv. s. of Sir John Benn Walsh[†], 1st bt., of Ormathwaite, Cumb. and Warfield Park and Margaret, da. of Joseph Fowke, E.I. Co. service, of Bexley, Kent, niece and h. of John Walsh[†] of Warfield Park. *educ.* Faithfull's sch. Warfield 1808-11; Eton 1811-13; priv. tutor 1814-17; Christ Church, Oxf. 1816. *m.* 8 Nov. 1825, Lady Jane Grey, da. of George Harry, 6th earl of Stamford and Warrington, 2s. (1 *d.v.p.*) 2da. (1 *d.v.p.*). *suc.* to estates of gt.-uncle John Walsh 1819; fa. as 2nd bt. and to Ormathwaite 7 June 1825; *cr.* Bar. Ormathwaite 16 Apr. 1868. *d.* 3 Feb. 1881.
Ld. lt. Rad. 1842-75.

Walsh, whose five brothers, including his twin William, died at or soon after birth, was born heir to and named after his maternal great-uncle, John Walsh (1725-95). The latter's East Indian fortune and estates in Berkshire, county Cork and county Kerry had been bequeathed to his mother in trust until her male heir came of age, provided her husband (his executor John Benn) assumed the name of Walsh. A protégé, through his guardian uncle Dr. William Brownrigge, of the North ministry's treasury secretary John Robinson[†], Benn Walsh represented Bletchingley as a supporter of Addington's ministry and was created a baronet in 1804. He had amassed an £80,000 fortune and met his wife, a goddaughter of Lady Clive, in India, where she had joined her father and brother, Joseph and Francis Fowke, in the late 1780s and pioneered the collection of Hindustani airs. Tall and imposing, she exerted a profound influence over her son Walsh, who commemorated her in an unpublished six-volume biography.[1] He also kept a journal record of his own life from his departure from Faithfull's school at Warfield for Eton in 1811 until his sight failed in 1871, when he delegated the task to his secretary.[2]

Walsh recalled his childhood at Warfield and his parents' London house in Harley Street among East Indian friends and relations as 'brilliant and happy'.[3] He was withdrawn early from Eton, where he was 'ill and unhappy', and tutored by a 'Mr. Wilson', whom he described as 'good', but with 'no means of control', and went up to Oxford, where he formed lasting friendships with Panton Corbett[*], William Stratford Dugdale[*], Sir Roger Gresley[*] and Edward Protheroe[*], 'deficient in knowledge of the classics'.[4] He sought to improve his 'connections' through European tours (he made his first in 1816), triennial visits to his Irish and Cumberland estates and introductions to London, Berkshire and Brighton society, and hoped to enter Parliament at the first opportunity.[5] His father, who in any case considered the attempt premature, suffered a paralytic stroke in March 1820 shortly after making overtures on his behalf for a treasury seat, and nothing came of his own negotiations with Evan Baillie[†] for Tralee and Thomas Spring Rice[*] for Limerick, in the course of which Walsh professed support for Lord Liverpool's ministry and for Catholic relief.[6] 'Ambitious and discontented', he afterwards criticized his great-uncle Walsh for spending on elections at Worcester and Pontefract, where he could acquire no proprietary interest, and for purchasing 'scattered ... tracts of land in remote parts of the kingdom, where there was neither a residence nor a possibility of living'. He dismissed Warfield Park as a 'mere villa in a county where it was impossible he could ever obtain any extent of ground, or create any considerable county interest ... a mere plaything for which I have no taste', but appreciated the £3,600 per annum it brought him.[7] Eager to 'join the oligarchies of birth and political influence', Walsh saw marriage and an independent parliamentary seat as the keys to progress and resolved to live by his father's mantra, 'Do as much as I have done John and you will be a peer'.[8] Lady Charlotte Charteris, whom he courted from 1823 to 1825, turned him down, but on 11 Sept. 1825, three months after succeeding his father as 2nd baronet and to an estimated £119,000, the Whig Lord Stamford's daughter Lady Jane Grey accepted his marriage proposal. His annual income was then £7,402.[9]

Walsh was abroad at the dissolution in 1826, 'irritated and disappointed at the unpleasant conduct' of his 'wife's family and the apparent failure' of his expectations from the connection.[10] By 1830 his confidence had been boosted by the birth of two sons, successful overtures to his Fowke cousins, whose Radnorshire properties he proposed adding to his own with a view to representing the county, and the éclat generated by musical entertainments at his £13,000 house in Berkeley Square and favourable reviews of his pamphlet on Irish poverty.[11] 'Composed without concert, or consultation with any human being, without even reference to books ... my style as well as my ideas was all my own', it was acclaimed by Edward Smith Stanley*, Sir Henry Parnell*, Malthus, McCulloch, and Lords Limerick and Maryborough, and caused Spring Rice to invite him to testify before the Commons select committee on the Irish poor. (Nothing now came of it, but he was appointed to the revived committee, 11 Nov. 1830).[12] His mother encouraged him to seek a seat directly the king's health deteriorated in April 1830, and he made overtures to Sir Edward Dering*, who invited offers over 5,000 guineas for New Romney and 'quite rejected any annual consideration'; to Sir Charles Forbes* and through him to the broker Vizard, who suggested openings on the Foster Barham* interest at Stockbridge, or as second man to William Henry Trant* in Dover; and to William Stephens, the attorney handling his Berkeley Square property and an influential figure in Taunton. That seat was under offer, but Stephens sent him to Walter Montriou, an acquaintance of the town clerk of Sudbury Edmund Steadman, who briefed him on the sitting Members and arranged for him to go down to meet the corporation on 28 June.[13] Setting aside his family and friends' concerns over Sudbury's venality, Walsh grasped the opportunity afforded by the proclamation of William IV during his visit to declare as a 'church and state' candidate, and eventually came in unopposed at an initial cost of £4,000 with the 2nd earl of Rosslyn's son-in-law Bethell Walrond.[14] He attributed the general shortage of seats at the election to the 'aristocracy buying them up, a few disfranchisements, and an oversupply' of candidates.[15] He surmised:

Had I entered Parliament at 21 in 1820, I should have come in a timid bashful unknown youth, I should have found the Tory ministry of Liverpool firm as a rock offering no probabilities of change, no opening for talent, little anxious to bring forward the young, or to recruit its ranks with fresh accessions of talent. In such an atmosphere and at such a time, I should certainly never have stepped forward actively. The title of MP might have assisted me in society, but the moment would have been

unfavourable for my acquiring a grain of political importance. I should have acquired a habit and the character of a cypher, and it is difficult indeed to divest oneself of a character once stamped. Had I entered in 1826 the time would have been more favourable. The brilliant genius of Canning had illuminated the dullness of the Tory cabinet, new views, new ideas, new measures were in agitation, the stagnant intellects of Eldon, Castlereagh and Sidmouth no longer weighed down all talent, men's minds were beginning to ferment and there was the hope that the active and clever might work their way to notice. But yet I see little cause to regret that I did not then come into the House. The sacrifice of money would have inconvenienced me and my nerves and health were not in a state to have fortified my exertions. Since that period we have been steadily and uniformly progressive and single and unaided as we have been, have done much towards rendering our names known and establishing both a solid and a showy position in the world.[16]

He presented Sudbury's loyal address to William IV, 4 Aug. 1830.[17]

The Wellington ministry counted Walsh among their 'friends' and he took the seat he recalled as his father's 'on the left hand on entering under the gallery ... understanding that this was the neutral ground for those Members who were independent, but inclined to ministers'.[18] Returning to Warfield, as he did regularly that autumn, he discussed with his mother, who mistrusted Wellington, how he should vote on the address if the king's speech mentioned interference in Belgium, which he thought 'most impolitic' and likely to 'light up a general war between governments and people throughout Europe'.[19] He considered the speech 'injudicious', 2 Nov., but his ambition was whetted by the evident shortage of good government speakers in the ensuing debate. Regrettably for Walsh, who quickly gained a reputation as an excellent attender, energetic politician and party hack, his halting delivery would preclude him from high office.[20] According to his journal, he was not as commonly stated absent from the division on the civil list by which the ministry were brought down, 15 Nov. 1830, but voted, 'rather against my opinion on the particular case', in their minority, having perceived that Parnell's amendment was a 'catching' one on which they would be 'run hard'.[21] He played a leading part in organizing local resistance to the 'Swing' riots in Berkshire that month, and found sitting on the Forfar election committee, 2-11 Dec., a tedious, but useful experience.[22] After much prevarication, he chose to make his maiden speech for Newport's resolutions on Irish grand juries, 9 Dec. 1830, his 32nd birthday. It was, he acknowledged, 'rather a lame effort ... not altogether a breakdown, though I fear it will not materially increase my reputation'.[23] Unwell with a heavy cold, he gave a dinner in Sudbury, where his civil list vote was criticized, 22 Dec. 1830, and was foreman of the Berkshire grand jury in Reading when the 'Swing' rioters were tried the following week. There, realizing that his publications were more likely to advance his political career than his speeches, he commenced *Popular Opinions on Parliamentary Reform Considered*, which, when he developed erysipelas in January 1831, was transcribed by a local schoolmaster to ensure its pre-session publication. It was widely acclaimed.[24]

Walsh resumed his seat on the 'neutral ministerial benches', 14 Feb. 1831, determined to oppose the Grey ministry's transfer tax, but to 'see what their reform plan would prove' before taking any decided line. He witnessed its introduction and the sensation it caused from a 'seat inside the bar on the opposition side' to which he had been opportunely summoned by Charles Ross, 1 Mar.[25] Next day, drawing on his pamphlet and its argument that 'an entire remodelling of the constitution' was intended, he spoke 'nervously' and ineffectively against the bill.[26] He informed his mother:

I am not quite easy about this reform question. It appears to me that it is making ground very rapidly, and the prevailing opinion is that it will be carried. I look at it with great hostility. The giving Members to counties has caught many, but altogether it seems to me a true Whig scheme, occupying all the avenues to political power and distinction by the high aristocracy on one side and by the radicals on the other and sacrificing all the intermediate classes of the gentry, and placing the nobility in so invidious a position with respect to the rest of the community, that they will speedily be overpowered.[27]

He voted against the bill at its second reading, 22 Mar., presented a hostile petition from Sudbury, from which it proposed taking a seat, 15 Apr., and divided for Gascoyne's wrecking amendment, 19 Apr.[28] As privately discussed with Wellington and others, 24 Mar., he countered his incompetence in debate with a new pamphlet, published in April 1831, *Observations on the Ministerial Plan of Reform*.[29] *The Times*, then pro-reform, dismissed it as useless, but the anti-reformer Lord Ellenborough thought it enough to secure Walsh 'a good efficient place' should the Tories return to office.[30] Walsh perceived that

newspapers all approached it with the same deference and respect and the Tories were more pleased with it, because, always rather distrusting the Whigs as statesmen, their late radical measures had inflamed me against them; and I infused into the tone of it a certain subdued bitterness and contempt, in place of the strictly impartial dispassionate and philosophical discussion of the first.[31]

His return for Sudbury at the general election that month was assured; and, denying the former Tory Member John Norman Macleod, whom he disliked, a coalition, he applied to their committee in Charles Street for a second man, so securing the defeat of the reformer Windham and bringing in Lord Aberdeen's former private secretary Digby Cayley Wrangham as his colleague.[32] Afterwards he assisted the anti-reformer Robert Palmer* in Berkshire.[33]

Partly through Wrangham, whose high connections and recourse to party funds to pay his way he resented, Walsh was privy to the manoeuvring, meetings and private dinners that accompanied opposition policy making and the eventual formation of the Carlton Club in 1831-2.[34] He thought the response to the address

very badly managed. None of the great points were dwelt upon: the state of Europe, the squadron at Spithead, the riots at the elections, the subsequent disturbances, the connection between them. Instead ... the whole ... was taken up with little petty frivolous personalities, which it was quite right to bring forward, but not to the exclusion of everything else. I attended a meeting of the Tories and Ultra Tories at Peel's ... It was there determined that no obstruction should be offered to the bringing in of the [reform] bill, and that the point of the Irish and Scottish bills being simultaneously before the House should be insisted upon. This was conceded. We are in a very critical situation. They seem to think that the peers will be firm, and that the bill can only be carried by a large creation of new ones. In the fashionable world I continue to make a rapid progress, though Jane's illness prevents its being quite a solid one.[35]

He accepted a late invitation from William Holmes* to open the debate on the reform bill's second reading, 4 July, and moved to kill it by adjournment in a 40-minute speech that capitalized upon the recent riots in Banbury, Merthyr, Rye and Wigan and condemned the measure as a threat to the constitution and social and class harmony.[36] It was easily trounced by the bill's architect Lord John Russell, who compounded Walsh's woes by claiming that his pamphlets showed him to be 'grossly ignorant of the history of England'. He realized soon afterwards that he was being deliberately excluded from the Charles Street subcommittee organizing opposition to the bill.[37] He considered their attempts to adjourn its committee stage 'injudicious. I divided the first time with the ministry and then left the House', 12 July.[38] He chose not to divide on the schedule A boroughs, but voted to postpone consideration of the partial inclusion of Chippenham in schedule B, 27 July. He also presented a hostile petition from the corporation and freemen of Sudbury that day, and set out their case for removing the borough from schedule B in speeches, 29, 30 July, 2 Aug., when he and Wrangham lost the division by 157-108.[39] It hinged on the inaccuracy of the 1821 census returns and the accuracy of archive evidence which he had discovered, and Russell refuted, proving that the suburb of Ballingdon (its inclusion made depriving Sudbury of a Member untenable on population grounds) was legally part of the parish and borough, and administratively distinct from the county of Essex in which it was geographically situated.[40] He travelled regularly over the next ten weeks between London and his family in Ryde.[41] He voted to retain existing voting rights, 27 Aug. Arriving in London, 13 Sept., he was vexed to find that Peel's decision to waive unnecessary opposition to the bill in the Commons had cost him a fortnight's sailing and would probably deprive him of an opportunity to propose an amendment creating university representation for Scotland. Ignoring Sir George Murray, who prepared a similar proposal, Walsh had liaised only with the mathematician Chalmers, a family friend.[42] He voted silently against the English bill's passage, 21 Sept., and the second reading of the Scottish bill, 23 Sept., and announced his clause for Scottish university representation after voting to end the Maynooth grant, 26 Sept. It called for two University Members for Edinburgh and St. Andrews, and two for Glasgow and Aberdeen, and became a casualty of the bill's adjournment, 4 Oct. 1831.[43]

Walsh found a place by the throne to hear the Lords debate the English bill, 7 Oct. 1831, and stayed there to witness its defeat.[44] In conversation afterwards with Philip Pusey*, he agreed that Peel 'retired too much into himself, and did not enough bring forward the young men of his party'.[45] He attended the Marylebone reform meeting and dined at the Travellers with George Johnson on his way to the House, 10 Oct., where Lord Porchester* informed him 'that the committee in Charles Street had determined ... to adopt the most conciliatory language, to avoid attack upon the ministers with a view of not increasing popular excitement out of doors'.[46] Walsh 'quite disapproved':

> Ebrington's resolution reasserted the principle of the reform bill, and expressed general confidence in the ministry. Now I would have wholly passed over the question of reform, but upon that of general confidence in the ministry, I would have arraigned their policy upon the various other assailable points. The ministry are not popular in the country, though the reform bill is. By attacking them upon different ground, we should have put them on the defensive, without at all increasing the excitement out of doors.[47]

With bad grace, he attended a Sudbury dinner (21 Oct.) to celebrate the bill's defeat with Wrangham, whose superiority to him as a speaker and 'overweening ambition and conceit' he resented.[48] After a week assisting the Tory Charles Philip Yorke's* London committee during the Cambridgeshire by-election, he returned to Berkshire, where he ultimately failed to procure an anti-reform address.[49] While there, he assisted Steadman with further inquiries concerning Sudbury, which, as he had hoped, retained two Members under the revised reform bill, announced, 12 Dec. 1831.[50]

Walsh had resolved to make a concerted effort to revive his political career through publications, 'little dinners and entertainments' when Parliament reassembled; and as his confidence grew he became increasingly aware of the infidelities and individual foibles and idiosyncrasies of his colleagues and recorded them in his journals: thus he noticed when opposition met at Peel's after the king's speech, 6 Dec. 1831, that John Croker seemed 'restive and likes to move *parsi parssu*'.[51] He regretted not responding in debate to the Irish secretary Smith Stanley, 15 Dec., but although his interest in Irish issues persisted (24 Feb., 8 Mar. 1832), his mind was full of his next pamphlet on parties and reform,[52] for which he gleaned ideas during the debate on the bill's second reading, 17 Dec. 1831. He described Smith Stanley's speech for government that day as 'brilliant' and the division 'a poor one for opposition'.[53] He attended the House assiduously, but divided sparingly, voting against the bill's committal, 20 Jan., the enfranchisement of Tower Hamlets, 28 Feb., when he was delighted to see the government's majority reduced to 20, and the third reading, 22 Mar. 1832.[54] He quibbled briefly over the proposed three Member counties (Berkshire was one) as being conducive to 'unfortunate struggles and great expense', 27 Jan., but 'felt embarrassed and did not acquit myself well'.[55] He compensated with his judiciously distributed pamphlet, the *Present Balance of Parties in the State* (published, 26 Jan. 1832), which was highly praised in Tory circles, and responded to by Montague Gore for the Whigs.[56] It made Walsh a popular dinner guest and committee member, and he took particular pride in his work at the Carlton Club, where he was instrumental in securing Jephson's appointment as secretary, and was an active member of the subcommittees on 'newspapers' and 'candidate selection'.[57] To Walsh, Parliament comprised ministerial Whigs, liberal Tories and radicals, the old Canning-Huskisson opposition, High Tories and independents. Each party's essence rested on 'political principles peculiar to itself'. The Whigs had been destroyed by the shock of the French revolution, the 'diminution of party spirit after the peace of 1815', and 'liberal policies and the threat of subversive reform', for the interests of aristocratic Whigs and popularists were incompatible. Lord Grey's administration could not be based on the three Whig principles of 'economy, non-interference with foreign affairs and reform'.[58] Denouncing his Conservatism and moderate reform, 'Philo-radical' wrote in *The Times*, 26 Mar. 1832:

> Walsh takes the lead and because he writes well and with facility, considers he writes wisely and constitutionally. He represents his own thousands, and though he condemns corruption by his pen, yet stoutly supports it by his vote. He certainly becomes the venal borough of Sudbury better than he would do any of the proposed enfranchised towns.[59]

Privately, meanwhile, Walsh assessed his situation thus:

> I have now a firm and a flattering position in society and I will own that I enjoy it. I have learned to value it, to understand it. I have acquired by my long experience a certain tact ... [and] become more at my ease.[60]

He believed that further Lords' defeats made peerage creations to carry the bill inevitable, and knew before the division on Ebrington's resolutions, 10 May, that Peel would refuse to serve in the quasi-reform ministry contemplated in the king's overture to Wellington.[61] With its outcome still uncertain, he divided his time between London and Berkshire, where, having secured the writ, he canvassed for Palmer, the successful candidate at the June by-election. He also now learnt that he risked disqualification for treating, should he attempt Sudbury again.[62] He voted against the Irish reform bill at its second reading, 25 May, and, withdrawing his amendment to the Scottish bill, 4 June, he said that university representation would have not have been enough to counter the measure's 'oppressive' evils and that he was no longer prepared to risk inciting strong feelings by pressing it. He divided against government on the Russian-Dutch loan, 26 Jan., 12 July, and although he agreed with Peel that it would be 'wrong to turn out the ministers on the issue', he was disappointed when Hume and the radicals deserted them before the latter division.[63] He had turned down an invitation from Sir Richard Vyvyan* in June 1832 to join an 'Old Tory' or 'sort of country party independent of the duke and ... the Whigs'.[64]

Walsh had repeatedly sought and grudgingly received confirmation from Wrangham of his superior claim to the corporation and Conservative vote in Sudbury, which returned him with the Whig veteran

Michael Angelo Taylor* at the general election in December 1832 after Wrangham retired during the poll.[65] He stood down there at the dissolution in 1834 when his prospects were poor, but following defeats in Radnorshire (1835) and Poole (1837) and unsuccessful forays in Abingdon (1836) and Birmingham (1837), he topped the Sudbury poll in dubious circumstances in 1838.[66] In 1840 he realized his ambition to sit for Radnorshire, which he retained for the Conservatives until his elevation to the Lords by Lord Derby in April 1868. He was made lord lieutenant of Radnorshire on Peel's recommendation in 1842 and was instrumental in quelling the 1843 Rebecca riots there. On his death at Warfield Park in February 1881 the barony and estates passed to his elder son Arthur (1827-1920), Conservative Member for Leominster, 1865-8.[67]

[1] *HP Commons, 1754-90*, iii. 602-3; *HP Commons, 1790-1820*, iii. 174-5; *Oxford DNB sub* Fowke and Walsh; NLW, Ormathwaite mss FE5/1-6; FG1/43, pp. 115, 123; G. Parry 'Intro. to Ormathwaite Pprs.' (NLW, 1990), pp. i-vi. [2] Ormathwaite mss FG1/1-43. [3] Ibid. FG1/1, pp. 5, 97, 193; 1/5, p. 25. [4] Ibid. FG1/1, pp. 103, 141; G35, f. 2. [5] Ibid. FG1/1, 97, 253; FG1/43, pp. 62-74, 76-79, 81; J.S. Donnelly, 'Jnls. of Sir John Benn Walsh relating to management of his Irish Estates, 1823-64', *Jnl. of Cork Hist. and Arch. Soc.* lxxix (1974), 86-123; lxxx (1975), 15-42. [6] Ormathwaite mss FG1/5, p. 61; G15, ff. 4, 5, 14-16, 22, 27-29, 36-39, 61-71, 83, 88. [7] Ibid. FG1/3, pp. 253-65. [8] Ibid. pp. 266-74; FG1/4, pp. 20-29, 40-80, 110-30. [9] G. Parry, intro. to Ormathwaite mss [NRA 33331], pp. i-viii; FG1/4, pp. 107-201. [10] Ormathwaite mss FG1/5, p 61. [11] Ibid. pp. 25, 30-40, 52-62; Walsh, *Poor Laws in Ireland Considered.* [12] Ormathwaite mss FG1/5, pp. 22-24, 30, 31, 33, 39. [13] Ibid. pp. 68-77; G35, ff. 78, 103-4; G37, ff. 3-4. [14] Ibid. FG1/5, pp. 78-92; G35, ff. 90-102, 107-21; G36, f. 18; G37, ff. 3-8; *The Times*, 12 July; *Bury and Norwich Post*, 4 Aug. 1830. [15] Ormathwaite mss FG1/5, pp. 67-68. [16] Ibid. pp. 64-65. [17] *The Times*, 5 Aug. 1830. [18] Ormathwaite mss FG1/5, pp. 117-22. [19] Ibid. pp. 123-4, 130-3. [20] Ibid. pp. 126-7. [21] Ibid. pp. 133-4; *Bury and Norwich Post*, 24 Nov. 1830. [22] Ormathwaite mss FG1/5, pp. 135-44. [23] Ibid. pp. 142-3. [24] Ibid. pp. 145-67. [25] Ibid. pp. 168-9. [26] Ibid. pp. 169-70; *The Times*, 3 Mar. 1831. [27] Ormathwaite mss G39, f. 43. [28] Ibid. FG1/5, p. 171. [29] Ibid. p. 172. [30] *The Times*, 11 Apr. 1831; *Three Diaries*, 77. [31] Ormathwaite mss FG1/5, p. 174. [32] Ibid. pp. 176-80; *Bury and Norwich Post*, 27 Apr., 4, 11 May 1831. [33] Ormathwaite mss G39, f. 54. [34] Ibid. FG/1/5, pp. 183-4, 192. [35] Ibid. G39, f. 59. [36] Ibid. FG1/5, p. 189; *The Times*, 9 July 1831. [37] Ormathwaite mss FG1/5, pp. 189-90. [38] Ibid. p. 191. [39] *The Times*, 3 Aug. 1831. [40] Ormathwaite mss FG1/5, pp. 193-5. [41] Ibid. pp. 195-9. [42] Ibid. pp. 199-202; G39, f. 74. [43] Ibid. FG1/5, p. 203; G39, f. 98. [44] Ibid. FG1/5, pp. 204-6. [45] Ibid. p. 207. [46] Ibid. p. 208. [47] Ibid. p. 211-3. [48] Ibid. pp. 214-30; G39, f. 112. [50] Ibid. pp. 229, 240. [51] Ibid. pp. 231-6. [52] Ibid. p. 241; FG1/6, p. 33; G42, f. 16. [53] Ibid. FG1/5 pp. 241-2; FG1/6, pp. 5-7, 12. [54] Ibid. FG1/6, p. 31. [55] Ibid. p. 13. [56] M. Gore, *Reply to Sir John Walsh's Pamphlet.* [57] Ormathwaite mss FG1/6, pp. 13-66. [58] Walsh, *Present Balance of Parties*, 36-38, 56-57, 99. [59] *The Times*, 26 Mar. 1832. [60] Ormathwaite mss FG1/6, p. 42. [61] Ibid. p. 77. [62] Ibid. pp. 77-87; *The Times*, 8, 18 June 1832. [63] Ormathwaite mss FG1/6, pp. 100-102, 109. [64] Ibid. pp. 88-90. [65] Ibid. pp. 97, 104, 153-4, 159, 163, 167, 170, 172; G42, ff. 108-22; *The Times*, 3, 14 Dec.; *Bury and Norwich Post*, 19 Dec. 1832. [66] Ormathwaite mss FG1/43, pp. 116-7. [67] *The Times*, 10 June 1840, 5 Feb. 1881; Ormathwaite mss FG1/13, pp. 38-121; FG1/43, pp. 137, 144.

M.M.E.

WARBURTON, Henry (1784–1858), of 45 Cadogan Place, Mdx.

BRIDPORT	1826–7 Sept. 1841
KENDAL	9 Nov. 1843–1847

b. 12 Nov. 1784, 1st s. of John Warburton, timber merchant, of Eltham, Kent and ?Anne, da. of Abel Aldridge of Uxbridge, Mdx. *educ.* Eton 1799; Trinity Coll. Camb. 1802. *unm. suc.* fa. 1808. *d.* 16 Sept. 1858.
  Fellow, R. Soc. 1809; member of council, London Univ. 1827, fellow 1836; pres. Geological Soc. 1843-4.

The Warburtons' Baltic timber business had been in existence since at least 1757, and Henry may have been the grandson or great-grandson of the Norway merchant John Warburton of Rotherhithe, Kent, who died, aged 91, in 1765. Although his grandparents have not been traced, it is known that Henry's father John married, on 23 Nov. 1780, the sister (*d.* 9 Feb. 1787) of John Clater Aldridge of New Lodge, St. Leonard's Forest, Sussex, Member for Queenborough, 1784-90, and New Shoreham, 1790-5.[1] One of their four surviving children, Frances, married in 1803 the army officer and later baronet John Elphinstone, whose mother Amelia was the daughter of the Somerset herald, another John Warburton (1682-1759), possibly a kinsman.[2] This Member's father, who signed the London merchants' declaration of loyalty in 1795, died 19 Jan. 1808, when his London home was at 2 Parliament Street, Westminster. By his will, dated 9 Dec. 1807, he left annuities for his children Charles, Frances and Harriet, and bequeathed his commercial and residential properties and the residue of his estate, which included personalty sworn under £50,000, to Henry.[3] As he later informed a Commons select committee, Henry then succeeded as a 'yard keeper' or wholesale dealer in foreign timber, which he sometimes imported on his own account. This was carried out at premises in Lambeth, variously listed as Cuper's Bridge, Waterloo Bridge and Commercial Road, until he finally retired from the concern in 1831.[4] He was active in defence of his business interests: for example in 1820 he forwarded to the prime minister, Lord Liverpool, the petition from the timber merchants of London against the timber duties, which was presented to the Lords by Lord Lansdowne on 16 Aug.[5] Once in the House he frequently pressed the case for the duties on Baltic timber to be equalized with the more favourable tariffs on colonial American woods, and he played a part in the eventual abolition of those duties.[6]

Warburton, who had been placed as 12th wrangler at Cambridge in 1806, was a 'scholar and man of science' and was elected a fellow of the Royal Society in 1809, but published nothing on mathematics until late in life.[7] Described by one admiring society lady as 'a good looking scientific youth', and by an eminent physician as 'the *all* powerful and omniscient Warburton', he initially devoted himself to intellectual pursuits.[8] John Whishaw, who in late 1815 thought that he 'seemed to fall considerably short of the proper degree of *indignation* against the conduct of the Allies', wrote of him that he was 'very severe' on provincial society and 'a stranger hearing him would have supposed that he was a great admirer of the political conversation of the metropolis, the only difference being that he extremely dislikes one society and entirely neglects the other'.[9] Maria Edgeworth made a similar comment in 1822, that he was

> a young man of fortune, benevolence, pleasing manners, agreeable conversation, excessive shyness and [had] something incomprehensible about him. He vanishes from time to time from London and country society and no one, not even his favourite sister Lady Elphinstone, can tell where he is or anything about him till it be his pleasure to reappear.[10]

Probably on those occasions he was undertaking geological surveys, of the kind that he reported on at length to Whishaw in 1814.[11] In the Commons, he sometimes intervened in favour of a new survey of Britain and Ireland, as well as on scientific subjects, such as longitude and cholera.

Schooled in politics by James Mill and befriended by David Ricardo*, Warburton, a member of the Political Economy Club from its foundation in 1821, was a Utilitarian, although less doctrinaire than some of the other philosophic radicals.[12] At the general election of 1826 he was introduced to Bridport by the retiring Whig Member James Scott and was returned unopposed, on the radical Dissenting interest, with a Tory, Sir Horace St. Paul.[13] As the Dorset newspaper later put it, Warburton was 'Mr. Hume's Echo' in the Commons, where he often seconded Joseph Hume's motions, supported him in debate and acted with him as a teller.[14] An extremely active member of the 'Mountain', he almost invariably spoke and voted for economies and reduced taxation, and was a consistent advocate of free trade and an opponent of monopolies. One of the most frequent speakers, as well as a regular committeeman, he made interventions on a wide variety of topics, including cases of personal injustice, local legislation and the organization of business in the House, and regularly moved for returns of papers and presented constituency petitions.[15] He voted for Hume's amendment to the address, 21 Nov., and made his maiden speech on the corn laws, 24 Nov. 1826, though the following day Lansdowne wrote to Lord Holland that 'Warburton I hear did not speak like a man of the sense and talent we know him to possess'.[16] He commented on postage to the West Indies, 28 Nov., advocated lowering coroners' fees, 30 Nov., and insurance duties, 8 Dec., and urged free trade in timber, 30 Nov., machinery, 6 Dec., and corn, 7 Dec. 1826.[17] He condemned naval impressment, 13 Feb., and the practice of flogging, 12 Mar. 1827. He voted for a lower import price for corn, 9 Mar., and against increased protection for barley, 12 Mar., attacked the method of calculating the averages, 23, 27 Mar., and spoke and acted as a teller for the minority for Hume's amendment to reduce the duty on corn to 10s. by 1833, 27 Mar. He presented the Manchester petition for repeal of the corn laws, 28 Mar., objected to Knatchbull's amendment for a fixed duty, 9 Apr., and declared that the corn bill 'would afford no substantial relief to the country', 12 Apr.[18] He voted for inquiry into the allegations against the corporation of Leicester, 15 Mar., and information on the mutiny at Barrackpoor, 22 Mar., and on the Orange procession and Lisburn magistrates, 29 Mar. He divided for reform of chancery administration, 5 Apr., and to consider separating bankruptcy jurisdiction from it, 22 May. As John Evelyn Denison* noted on 1 May, he, like Hume and others, 'kept their old seats' on the appointment of Canning as prime minister; and he sided with the minority of ten for repeal of the Blasphemous and Seditious Libels Act, 31 May, thus placing himself with those 'irreconcilables' opposed to the new ministry.[19] He criticized the notion of extending Penryn into the neighbouring hundreds, 26 May, and voted in this sense, 28 May; he suggested the introduction of the ballot, 14 June. He opposed the grant for water communication in Canada, 1 June, and was teller for the hostile minority, 12 June.[20] He was a teller for the majority for considering the third reading of the Coventry magistracy bill rather than the orders of the day, 18 June 1827.

Warburton insisted that the finance committee be allowed to examine its subject in depth, 12 Feb., and as originally constituted, 25 Feb. 1828. It was during that session that Edward Davies Davenport* named him among the handful of Members who 'appeared most willing' to join his parliamentary club of like-minded reformers.[21] He voted for repeal of the Test Acts, 26 Feb. He spoke against the passengers regulation bill, 4, 18, 20, 24, 25 Mar., and higher duties on insurance, 10, 25 Mar., 1 Apr. He voted against extending East Retford into the hundred of Bassetlaw, 21 Mar., and spoke against the bill treating Penryn in the same way

if not accompanied by the ballot, 28 Mar. He opposed Wilmot Horton's schemes for assisted emigration unless he could 'distinctly prove by a pounds, shillings and pence statement, that this country will be a gainer by our voting considerable sums', 17 Apr., and repeated this point, 24 June. He brought up a petition from surgeons complaining of the difficulties of obtaining bodies for dissection, 22 Apr., and obtained a select committee on the subject. He again voted for inquiry into chancery administration, 24 Apr. He seconded and acted as a teller for Hume's motion for the transition to a low fixed duty on corn, 29 Apr. He divided against making provision for Canning's family, 13 May, and for the usury bill, 19 June. On 24 June, when he denied that there was distress in shipbuilding, he rebutted Gascoyne's suggestion that he had a personal interest in the matter. He divided for disqualifying certain East Retford voters that day, when he also sided with opposition for inquiry into the Irish church, and he voted against recommitting the East Retford disfranchisement bill, 27 June. On 7 July he stated that although he was 'on the economical benches', he would not oppose the grant for the survey of Ireland, but he did object, as he had often done, to further expenditure in Canada, 'inasmuch as the colony is of no value, but a source of great expenditure and waste'. Having chaired the select committee on anatomy, he wrote its rigidly Benthamite report, which he presented to the House, 22 July 1828.[22]

As he had on 6 Mar. 1827 and 12 May 1828, Warburton divided for Catholic emancipation, 6, 30 Mar. 1829. He obtained leave to bring in his anatomy bill, 12 Mar., when he argued that, despite the public distaste for the use of pauper cadavers for dissection, there was no other way to advance the vitally important medical science of anatomy. Peel, the home secretary, gave him guarded support, but the bill attracted widespread popular hostility, particularly from Tories and some radicals, so that Warburton had to concede another select committee on it, 7 Apr., from which he reported, 1 May. He saw off several attempts to amend and wreck the bill, 15, 18 May, but it was defeated in the Lords, 5 June.[23] He voted to transfer East Retford's seats to Birmingham, 5 May, and for Lord Blandford's reform proposals, 2 June. He called for revision of the corn laws, 14 May, when he also attacked the India board as a 'mere nursery for statesmen', and he voted for Hume's motion on the corn duties, 19 May. He divided in favour of allowing Daniel O'Connell to take his seat without swearing the oath of supremacy, 18 May, and against the ecclesiastical courts bill, 21 May. He raised a question about a loophole in the Small Notes Act, 22 May, objected to protection of the shipping trade,

1 June, when he voted for reduction of the hemp duties, and expressed caution about natives being allowed to serve on grand juries in India, 5 June 1829.

He sided with Lord Howick in the ministerial majority against Knatchbull's amendment to the address, 4 Feb. 1830, but in early March attended, 'as the representative of the Mountain', the Whig meeting at which Lord Althorp* was chosen as leader.[24] He voted to transfer East Retford's seats to Birmingham, 11 Feb., 5 Mar., and condemned the influence of landlords, peers and government there, 5, 8, 15 Mar., when he divided against the disfranchisement bill and for O'Connell's amendment to include the ballot. He voted for parliamentary reform, 18 Feb., and the enfranchisement of Birmingham, Leeds and Manchester, 23 Feb. He commented on the state of distress and the need to reform the system of taxation, 23, 25 Mar., 8 June. He advocated mitigating the punishment for forgery, 8 Apr., 13 May, and divided for this, 24 May, 7 June. He voted for Jewish emancipation, 5 Apr., 17 May. He voted with opposition for alteration of the laws relating to Irish vestries, 27 Apr., 10 June, abolition of the lord lieutenancy, 11 May, and information on the conduct of the Irish attorney-general, 12 May. Having observed how important its trade was to his constituency, he divided for inquiry into the state of Newfoundland, 11 May. He was in the minority for consideration of the civil government of Canada, 25 May, and condemned the payment of its expenses, 14 June. He was active in the opposition to the labourers' wages bill, 23 June, 1, 3, 5, 9 July, and expressed his hostility to the libel bill, 6 July, when he voted in the majority against requiring additional securities to be given by printers. He divided to abolish slavery, 13 July. He was returned unopposed for Bridport at the general election that summer. He successfully insisted on Hume being allowed to stand for Middlesex and, as chairman of his committee, helped to oversee his return, though John Cam Hobhouse*, who noted that Warburton 'cannot write', had to draft the necessary addresses.[25] He presided at the meeting at the *London Tavern*, 17 Aug. 1830, when he spoke in support of resolutions congratulating the French on their recent revolution.[26]

In November 1830 he attended the Whigs' planning meeting for Henry Brougham's intended motion on parliamentary reform, recommending him 'to say as little as possible for fear of making it necessary for the radical reformers to qualify their vote'.[27] Listed, of course, by ministers among their 'foes', he divided against them on the civil list, 15 Nov. He presented Bridport petitions for reform and the ballot, 16 Nov., and against slavery, 25 Nov., and urged abolition of

the duty on coastwise coal as it adversely affected the fortunes of his borough, 8 Dec., when, as on other occasions, he commented on the causes of economic distress. Like Hume and others, he was displeased at the extremist turn of the Middlesex reform meeting which he attended on 15 Dec.; in related matters, he came to Hume's defence over his attitude to the beer bill, 16 Dec., and supported his call for the ballot, 21 Dec. 1830.[28] He stated that he would reintroduce his anatomy bill at some point, 9 Feb. 1831, when he acceded to Lord John Russell's request to postpone his motion on the ballot until after the general reform question had been raised. He welcomed the proposed alteration of the timber duties, 11 Feb., but criticized Althorp's budget that day. He pressed for the abolition of tobacco planting in Ireland, 21 Feb., 10, 25 Mar., objected to Howick's emigration plan, 22 Feb., and continued to urge the case for lower timber duties, 11, 15, 18 Mar. Richard Carlile's petition for the remission of the remainder of his sentence was forwarded to him on 22 Feb., but in the end it was John Wood who brought it up (on 3 Aug.).[29] He voted for the second reading of the Grey ministry's reform bill, 22 Mar., and against Gascoyne's wrecking amendment, 19 Apr. He was returned unopposed for Bridport at the ensuing general election, when he presumably again assisted Hume in Middlesex.[30] He informed Brougham, 7 May 1831, that he believed 'Whigs and reformers ought not now to be quarrelling', but stated that he would have felt obliged to support Leslie Grove Jones† if he had persisted in his candidacy for Southwark.[31]

Considered as one of the three main candidates for chairmanship of the National Political Union later that year, Warburton remained a respected radical Member, although Francis Place had written a few months earlier, 'I can hardly tell you how much I esteem him, and yet his old bachelor sort of prudence, spite of his enlarged views and accurate reasoning, makes a droll thing of him sometimes'. One of Althorp's 'most confidential friends', he helped to moderate radical attitudes towards the government and, while he continued very often to attack ministers and vote against them on financial and economic questions, he gave consistent support to the reform bills.[32] Thus, he divided for the second reading of the reintroduced English bill, 6 July, at least twice against adjourning proceedings on it, 12 July 1831, and steadily for its details. He spoke against St. Paul's amendment to remove Bridport from schedule B, 27 July, Littleton's attempt to enfranchise Stoke, 4 Aug., and saving both seats at Dorchester, 15 Sept. He voted for the minority for swearing the original Dublin election committee, 29 July, but with ministers against censuring the Irish government on this, 23 Aug., and against Benett's amendment against issuing the Liverpool writ, 5 Sept. Edward Littleton* noted on 11 Aug. that 'the Mountain (Hume, Warburton and others) were refractory and were disposed to oppose the government' on the division of counties.[33] He was listed in the minority for printing the Waterford petition for disarming the Irish yeomanry that day, but in the majority against the Irish union of parishes bill, 19 Aug. He declared that the Chandos amendment to enfranchise £50 tenants-at-will had 'completely overturned the balance between town and county representation', 20 Aug., when he was in a minority of one against giving urban copyholders and leaseholders the right of voting in counties. He voted for the third reading, 19 Sept., and passage of the reform bill, 21 Sept., the second reading of the Scottish bill, 23 Sept., when he opposed giving representation to Scottish universities, and Lord Ebrington's confidence motion, 10 Oct. While acknowledging the need for reform of the bankruptcy laws, he raised strong objections to Brougham's bankruptcy court bill, 12-15, 17, 18 Oct. 1831.

Warburton reintroduced his much simplified anatomy bill, 15 Dec., and secured its first reading, 17 Dec. 1831. He was accused of bringing the matter forward because of the fear of a renewed outbreak of 'Burking' and under cover of the continuing furore over reform, but he insisted in the House, 17 Jan. 1832, and in private, for instance to Holland on the 29th and to Brougham on the 30th, on the validity of his timing and purpose.[34] He faced strong attacks on the bill, notably by radicals such as Henry Hunt and Tories such as Sir Robert Inglis, at every stage. He presented petitions in its favour from the Royal College of Surgeons of Edinburgh, 6 Feb., the Medical Society of London, 24 Mar., and the National Political Union, 8 May, and had to defend the bill (and act as a teller against hostile amendments), 17, 24, 26 Jan., 6, 27 Feb., 15, 16 Mar., 11, 18 Apr., 8, 11 May.[35] At least he had the support of John Hawkins, Member for Tavistock, who reported to his father, 13 Apr., that the bill

is of great importance as a matter of principle, and Warburton deserves much credit and all the support which we can give him, in carrying through a measure which exposes its proposer to the daily risk of undergoing the death of St. Stephen.[36]

It was eventually given royal assent, 1 Aug. 1832.

Warburton voted for the second reading of the revised reform bill, 17 Dec. 1831, to go into committee on it, 20 Jan. 1832, and again generally for its details, though on the 17th and other occasions he criticized

the method of devising the schedule of condemned boroughs. He divided for Hobhouse's vestry bill, 23 Jan. He was appointed to the select committee on the East India Company, 27 Jan., and heard evidence on its financial affairs.[37] He admitted that he had taken notes on 26 Jan., when he voted with government on the Russian-Dutch loan, and so was implicated in the complaint of a breach of privilege on the publication of that day's debate, 31 Jan. Persuaded to do so by Place, he urged that the franchise should not be given to ratepayers because they were dependent on their landlords, 3 Feb., and he voted against giving the vote to all £10 ratepayers that day.[38] He voted against the production of papers on Portugal, 9 Feb., but to omit the reference to Providence in the preamble to the cholera bill, 16 Feb., and for Hunt's motion for inquiry into Peterloo, 15 Mar. He divided for the third reading of the reform bill, 22 Mar., and Ebrington's motion for an address calling on the king to appoint only ministers who would carry it unimpaired, 10 May. In a letter to Place that month he condemned the mobbing of the duke of Wellington, and he did much to deflate radical expectations in order that some measure of reform might be allowed to pass.[39] He stated that he had several Dorset petitions for withholding supplies, 17 May, and brought up one from Bridport, 25 May, when he divided for the second reading of the Irish reform bill. He was a teller for the minority against the second reading of the Liverpool franchise bill, 23 May, and for the majority for his own spontaneous motion requiring coroners' inquests to be held in public, 20 June. He spoke and voted for Buxton's motion for a select committee on the abolition of slavery, 24 May. He advocated extending the borough of Wareham to include Bere Regis and Corfe Castle, 22 June, when he voted to amend the boundaries of Whitehaven and Stamford. He divided for giving New South Wales a system of representation, 28 June. He again objected to the bankruptcy bill, 5, 9, 20, 26, 30 July, when he described the bribery at elections bill as worthless and cited his own conduct on reform as evidence that radicals need not be labelled as obstinate. He divided with ministers for the Russian-Dutch loan, 12, 16, 20 July. On 11 Aug. 1832 he suggested that the Reform Act might be amended in the reformed Parliament.

Warburton, who laid the foundation stone of the Working Men's Institute in his constituency on 2 July 1832, was returned with another reformer for Bridport after a contest at the general election in December 1832.[40] He continued to sit for that borough until revelations about the practice of making customary payments to the electors forced his resignation in 1841, and he was thereafter Member for Kendal. Although he was 'not among the first class of *political* wranglers' and was not active on the City platform, in 1840 it was observed of his career as a Radical that

> his speeches from the beginning were invariably short, but always to the point ... He has very rarely fallen below the point of promptitude and energy requisite in a practical reformer at such a period as the present, and he has never damaged his cause by over zeal, rashness of judgement or the impulses of personal vanity.[41]

His university friend, the political economist George Pryme[†], remembered

> Russell at a dinner at his house gently rallying Warburton on his having been called by the *Examiner*, 'the Nestor of the Radical camp', and he *was that*; for though he was far more radical than any of us Whigs, there was a kind of temper and judgment about him which moderated what otherwise might have been extravagant in his views.[42]

'Philosopher' Warburton, as he was known, 'a man of high character and integrity', died in September 1858, leaving his estate to his great-nephew Howard Warburton Elphinstone (1830-1917), only son of Sir Howard Elphinstone, who was Liberal Member for Hastings, 1835-7, and Lewes, 1841-7.[43]

[1] *PP* (1835), xix. 337; *Gent. Mag.* (1765), 247; (1780), 542; (1787), i. 186. [2] Warburton the herald (see *Oxford DNB*) had a son John, an antiquarian of Dublin, who was clearly not Henry Warburton's father; and therefore the suggestion in Elphinstone's obituary (*Gent. Mag.* (1846), ii. 93) that he married his 'cousin german' must be wrong. [3] *Gent. Mag.* (1808), i. 94; PROB 11/1473/80; IR26/131/276. [4] *PP* (1835), xix. 337. [5] Add. 38286, f. 169; *LJ*, liii. 369; *The Times*, 17 Aug. 1820. [6] D.M. Williams, 'Henry Warburton and Free Trade Movement', *Procs. Dorset Natural Hist. and Arch. Soc.* xc (1968), 287-9, 293. [7] *Oxford DNB*; *Procs. R. Soc.* ix (1859), 555-6. [8] *Countess Granville Letters*, i. 200; *Gentlemen of Science: Early Corresp.* ed. J. Morrell and A. Thackray (Cam. Soc. ser. 4, xxx), 31. [9] '*Pope' of Holland House* ed. Lady Seymour, 122. [10] *Edgeworth Letters*, 270, 390. [11] '*Pope' of Holland House*, 300-6. [12] *The Times*, 21 Sept. 1858; *Oxford DNB*; W. Thomas, *Philosophic Radicals*, 13. [13] Add. 51659, Whishaw to Lady Holland, 4 June; *Dorset Co. Chron.* 8, 15 June 1826. [14] *Dorset Co. Chron.* 13 Dec 1832. [15] P. Jupp, *British Politics on Eve of Reform*, 203, 231. [16] Add. 51687. [17] *The Times*, 29 Nov., 1, 9 Dec. 1826. [18] Ibid. 29 Mar., 10 Apr. 1827. [19] Nottingham Univ. Lib. acc. 636, Denison diary; W. Harris, *Radical Party in Parl.* 199. [20] *The Times*, 2 June 1827. [21] JRL, Bromley Davenport mss, 'mem.' 1828. [22] *PP* (1828), vii. 1-122; R. Richardson, *Death, Dissection and the Destitute*, 108-9, 113, 166-7, 332. [23] *CJ*, lxxxiv. 129, 209, 260, 263, 277, 290-1, 308, 323; M.D. George, *Cat. of Pol. and Personal Satires*, xi. 15777; Richardson, 151-2, 157-8. [24] Castle Howard mss, Graham to Morpeth [3 Mar. 1830]. [25] *Dorset Co. Chron.* 15 July, 5 Aug. 1830; Add. 56554, f. 134; Broughton, *Recollections*, iv. 29-30; D. Miles, *Francis Place*, 138. [26] Add. 56555, f. 13; *The Times*, 18 Aug. 1830. [27] Add. 56555, f. 52. [28] Ibid. f. 74. [29] Add. 35149, f. 22. [30] *Dorset Co. Chron.* 28 Apr., 5 May 1831. [31] Brougham mss. [32] G. Wallas, *Life of Place*, 278; Miles, 187, 212; *The Times*, 21 Sept. 1858. [33] Hatherton diary. [34] J. Belchem, '*Orator' Hunt*, 189; Add. 51836; Brougham mss; Richardson, 177-9, 183, 185-7, 191-2, 194, 197-205. [35] *CJ*, lxxxvi. 27, 32, 35, 49, 53-54, 147, 268-9, 287-8, 308. [36] Cornw. RO, Hawkins mss 10/2192. [37] *PP* (1831-2), x. pt. 1, p. 37. [38] Wallas, 325. [39] Add. 35154, f. 135;

The Times, 21 Sept. 1858. [40] *Sherborne Jnl.* 5 July, 13 Dec. 1832. [41] *Saunders' Portraits and Mems. of Eminent Living Pol. Reformers*, 119. [42] *Autobiog. Recollections of George Pryme* ed. A. Bayne, 231-2. [43] *The Times*, 21 Sept. 1858; *Gent. Mag.* (1858), ii. 531-2; *DNB*; *Oxford DNB*

S.M.F.

WARD, John (1779–1855), of Holwood House, Keston and Calverley, Tunbridge Wells, Kent.

LEOMINSTER   11 Feb. 1830–1830

b. 22 Dec. 1779, 2nd *s.* of William Ward (*d.* 1811) and Catherine, da. and h. of Thomas Nevill of Blackburn, Lancs. *m.* 27 Nov. 1806, Jane Frances, da. of Robert Lambert of Elland Hall, nr. Halifax, Yorks., 5s. (3 *d.v.p.*) 2da. *d.v.p. d.* 24 Feb. 1855.

Sheriff, Kent 1835-6.

Despite the existence in nineteenth century editions of *Burke's Landed Gentry* of pedigrees covering five generations of this Member's family, some obscurities remain concerning his immediate antecedents. His father William Ward (*b.*1743) was the youngest son of Samuel Ward (1707-47), described by Burke (although it cannot be verified) as a barrister, and his wife Elizabeth Dodgson of Leeds. After being widowed, she raised their sons in a house in the precincts of York Minster, inherited by her first husband. William Ward married a Lancashire heiress, probably the daughter of a Blackburn attorney, and was in business by 1795 as a merchant in London, trading variously as Ward and Company or William Ward and Son of 3 Basinghall Street. The Blackburn property and their father's trading fortune (his will was proved under £25,000, 19 Feb. 1813) devolved upon Ward, then of Grove House, Tooting and his brother Samuel Nevill Ward (1773-1850) of Balham House, Surrey.[1] Ward and Lambert, Irish linen and calico factors, Ward's partnership with his in-laws, shared the same trading address in the 1811 London directories (33 Cateaton Street) as William and John Ward, merchants and insurance agents. That firm became Samuel and John Ward and Company in 1812, had moved to 46½ Coleman Street by 1813, and from 1815, when their brother-in-law William Edwards (formerly of Tokenhouse Yard) joined their broking firm, Ward and Edwards, they traded at 3 Packers Court, Coleman Street. Ward and Lambert disappeared from trade directories by 1817. The Packers Court firms were listed until 1824.[2] Retiring from trade, the Ward brothers invested in land in the Bromley area of Kent, where Samuel acquired the estate of Baston, near Hayes, and John purchased Holwood, once the property of the younger William Pitt[†], and the adjoining duchy of Lancaster manor of Farnborough in 1823. He replaced Pitt's modest house with a Grecian mansion designed by the architect Decimus Burton and bought the Calverley estate in the Mount Pleasant area of the spa resort of Tunbridge Wells, where Burton was responsible, 1828-35, for a development of fashionable villas and terraces, with a park, shops and other amenities, inspired by Nash's Regent's Park scheme. Calverley House, where Princess Victoria stayed in 1827, was enlarged and opened as an hotel in 1840.[3]

In January 1830, having made overtures in London the previous year, Ward came forward on a vacancy for the open and venal borough of Leominster, where the incumbent Rowland Stephenson had been bankrupted under the twelve-month rule. Notices described him as a man of 'large property' and 'independent principles', with no party affiliation. Having 'tied up his election' before the writ was ordered, 4 Feb., he easily saw off his challengers.[4] He took his seat, 9 Mar. 1830, and, aligning with the revived Whig opposition, voted to halve the grant for volunteers that day. No parliamentary speeches by Ward were reported, but he divided against government on the East Retford disfranchisement bill, 15 Mar., and steadily with opposition until 9 July, including for Jewish emancipation, 5 Apr., 17 May, and parliamentary reform, 28 May. Confusion surrounds his votes on the abolition of capital punishment for forgery, 24 May, 7 June: on the first occasion he was twice listed in the majority in its favour but omitted from a 'corrected' list; on the second he was named on both sides in different lists.[5] Transferring his local interest to the young Yorkshire squire William Marshall*, he stood down at Leominster at the dissolution of 1830. Although mooted there subsequently as a 'rich stranger' and toasted by the Kent reformers in June 1831, he did not stand for Parliament again.[6] He stated in his resignation notice, 20 July 1830:

To my great regret that great object [remaining a healthy and active Member] has been disappointed by the want of method and arrangement in the conduct, or rather in the mismanagement, of the business of the ... Commons, where the time and health of its Members have been sacrificed without result, and where desultory conversations and equally frivolous discussions have absorbed nearly the whole of that attention which should have been occupied by useful business; so that during the late laborious session of six months, no more business has been effected than might well have been performed in a single month.[7]

Ward's investment in urban development was matched by his brother, who in 1845 owned 39 leasehold houses in Albany Street, Gloucester Terrace,

Park Square and St. Andrew's Place on the Regent's Park scheme. John Ward had properties in Clarence Terrace and York Terrace in the same area, and he seems to have sold Holwood to the railway contractor Thomas Brassey before he made his will, 13 Aug. 1852. He died in February 1855 at his London residence in Park Street, Grosvenor Square, having devised and divided the Calverley estate and his other property equally between his surviving sons Arthur Wellesley Ward (1813-1900) and Neville Ward (1814-72).[8]

[1] *Burke LG* (1846), ii. 1516; (1855), 1282; W.A. Abram, *Hist. Blackburn*, 401; PROB 11/1542/110; IR26/595/56. [2] *Kent's London Dir.* 1793-1815; *London Post Office Dir.* 1815-24. [3] *Arch. Cantiana*, xxiv (1900), 157-8; lix (1946), 12-13; C. Freeman, *Hist. Bromley*, 33; G. Clinch, *Antiquarian Jottings*, 140-1; W.H. Hewlett Cooper, *Old Keston*, 20-21; F.S. Gammon, *Story of Keston*, 27; J. Britton, *Descriptive Sketches of Tunbridge Wells*, 44, 53-56; J. Phippen, *New Guide for Tunbridge Wells*, 47-51; H.R. Knipe, *Tunbridge Wells*, 19, 22, 26-29. [4] *The Times*, 21 Dec. 1829; *CJ*, lxxxv. 3-4; *Hereford Jnl.* 6, 13 Jan., 17 Feb. 1830; Derbys. RO, Gresley of Drakelow mss D77/36/7. [5] *The Times*, 1 June 1830. [6] *Hereford Jnl.* 4, 18 Aug. 1830, 4 May, 28 Dec.; *The Times*, 8 June 1831. [7] *Hereford Jnl.* 28 July 1830. [8] PROB 8/248 (13 Mar. 1855); 11/2124/929; 2209/277; Hewlett Cooper, 20-21; *Gent. Mag.* (1855), i. 445.

D.R.F./M.M.E.

WARD, Hon. John William (1781–1833), of Himley Hall, Staffs.[1]

DOWNTON	1802–7 July 1803
WORCESTERSHIRE	18 July 1803–1806
PETERSFIELD	1806–1807
WAREHAM	1807–1812
ILCHESTER	1812–1818
BOSSINEY	8 Apr. 1819–25 Apr. 1823

b. 9 Aug. 1781, o.s. of William Ward[†], 3rd Visct. Dudley and Ward, and Julia, da. of Godfrey Bosvile of Gunthwaite, Yorks. *educ.* privately at Paddington; Edinburgh Univ. 1797-8; Oriel, Oxf. 1799 (BA, Corpus 1802). *unm. suc.* fa. as 4th Visct. Dudley and Ward 25 Apr. 1823; *cr.* earl of Dudley 5 Oct. 1827. *d.* 6 Mar. 1833.
Sec. of state for foreign affairs Apr. 1827-May 1828; PC 30 Apr. 1827.
Capt. Dudley vols. 1803, lt.-col. 1803

In 1838 Lord Melbourne read Ward's private journal (later destroyed by his executors because it contained pornographic descriptions of his remorseless but joyless sexual exploits with women 'both in high and low life'): it was 'full of nothing but discontent and dissatisfaction' with himself, for 'he was always doubting whether he made the most of his position and his fortune, and amused himself in the best way'.[2] Lord Hatherton (Edward John Littleton*), one of the executors, wrote of the journals, 23 Aug. 1838:

> There is really nothing worth preserving; and it is a remarkable circumstance that a man of ... [his] talents and observation should have kept a journal for so many years, without contriving to insert matter of more interest and importance. His object seems to have been merely to keep a mirror in which to contemplate himself ... What I have read has produced a melancholy and painful impression on me. They prove indisputably that rank, wealth, talents and reputation were largely possessed by one of the most unhappy of men.[3]

Ward was undermined by self-doubt and prone to bouts of abject depression which rendered him purposeless and made his entire existence appear a nullity. He gave his own explanation of this 'malady' to his friend Lord Aberdeen in 1822:

> I have little doubt that it derives its origin from the brutal neglect and unkindness with which I was treated in my early years. There is something in habitual terror, subjection and persecution of which one never gets the better. I was bred under a task-master [his father], and the sound of the lash is never quite out of my ears. This early misfortune added to a somewhat more than average quantity of mistakes on my part furnishes abundant matter for disagreeable reflections whenever I am disposed to indulge in them.[4]

Politically, Ward had come full circle by 1820: he had entered the House as a supporter of Pitt; joined the Whig opposition in 1804; abandoned them for Canning in 1812 only to be stranded by the disbandment of his party a year later, and generally supported the Liverpool ministry, *faute de mieux*, after Canning joined it in 1816. There was no truth in the rumour that he had 'gone over to the opposition' early in 1820.[5] He ignored a possibility of coming in for Worcestershire at the general election and retained his seat for Bossiney on the interest of James Stuart Wortley*. Before the new Parliament met he wrote to his friend Edward Copleston, later bishop of Llandaff:

> The government must not quarrel with the Tories. I wish with all my heart there were moderate Whigs enough to save the country, for nobody has a greater disgust to Tory prejudices than I have. But unhappily the Tories compose the main body of the army with which the Jacobins are to be opposed.

He voted against the aliens bill (as he had in 1816), 1 June, and denounced it as 'paltry' and 'unnecessary', 7 July 1820. The Whig Sir James Mackintosh* considered this

a most brilliant speech in which he showed how an old subject could be made new. It was perfectly prepared. He had even arranged beforehand all the mistakes and corrections and repetitions and hesitations which were to give it an unpremeditated air. He acted an extempore speech as well as possible.[6]

During the summer he was unwell: depressed by the poor weather, he craved the unattainable 'paradise' of 'English comforts, English society, English interests, and an Italian sun' and considered wintering in the Mediterranean. He was disgusted by most aspects of the Queen Caroline affair and would 'rather read about it by an Italian daylight, than vote upon it in an English fog'. In the event he stayed at home to witness Canning's resignation, which he believed would not harm his future prospects once the queen's business was laid to rest. According to Lord Holland's son Henry Fox*, Ward and Canning 'sneered at the queen, and contended that the popular feeling was deadened about her, and would be so still more before Parliament met'. When, on the contrary, there was an upsurge of support for her Ward, still 'full of his sneers about reform and the Whigs', predicted that the ministry would be 'outdebated' but not 'outvoted'.[7] He felt vindicated in this view by the outcome of the debate on the omission of her name from the liturgy, 26 Jan. 1821, when he left the House before the division, though it was said that he was one of the 'stragglers' who sympathized with the Whigs on the issue and 'would have voted with opposition if Canning had not been attacked' by Lord Archibald Hamilton. He was reported to have been 'writhing with vexation at the ill taste' of Charles Ellis's 'unsatisfactory' explanation of Canning's absence.[8] He did not vote in the division on the opposition censure motion, 6 Feb. 1821.

Ward still saw parliamentary reform as an evil threat to a constitution under which 'the people not only enjoy nearly as much happiness as it is in the nature of government to confer', but 'possess an ample share of power, to prevent them from ever being deprived of their present advantages by the arbitrary will of their rulers'. At the same time he acknowledged the growth of pro-reform sentiment among non-partisan men of 'understanding and education' and, aware that a 'discredited constitution' could not be defended on the score of '*practical benefit*', was prepared to remedy the more flagrant defects of the existing system as a defensive measure. It was in this spirit that he advocated the transfer of Grampound's seats to Leeds, 12 Feb. 1821, when Charles Williams Wynn* thought that opposition's success in carrying the proposal by two to one against ministers owed 'much' to Ward's speech. The radical Whig Henry Grey Bennet* interpreted it (wrongly) as 'pretty decisive that Canning is becoming more tempered on these topics'.[9] Ward made what George Agar Ellis* considered 'a good short speech' against Mackintosh's motion of 21 Feb. for information on the government's response to the Holy Alliance's suppression of the new constitution in Naples, which he saw as one of no confidence in ministers; but he strongly condemned these events as 'the most alarming circumstances that had occurred in Europe for a long period of time'.[10] He hoped, as he told Coplestone, that his own and other speeches would check the 'Barbarian Triumvirate' and compel ministers to 'observe an *honest* neutrality', to which he suspected 'they were not inclined to adhere'. On 20 Mar. 1821 he upheld the principle of British neutrality but criticized government for 'skulking in the rear of the allied powers' and denounced 'the monstrous principle of interference on the part of the despotic monarchs of Europe, to put down any principle of liberty'. His speech delighted Lady Holland, from whom he had been estranged for several years.[11]

Ward, who claimed no expertise on economic questions, but was attracted by the idea of making silver as well as gold legal tender, argued against repeal of the additional malt duty, 3 Apr. 1821, and urged those 'members of the Pitt Club' who had defeated government on it earlier to take a course 'more consistent with their own principles'. He voted against the disfranchisement of ordnance officials, 12 Apr., and parliamentary reform, 9 May, and on 11 May opposed the imprisonment of the author of a libel on Grey Bennet because the Whigs had declined to inflict so severe a punishment on the perpetrator of a far worse attack on Canning in 1819.[12] He voted for Catholic relief, 28 Feb., and criminal law reform, 23 May, 4 June. In his last known speech in the Commons, 22 June, he endorsed ministers' refusal to press Austria for the immediate repayment of Pitt's war loans, but delivered a scathing attack on every aspect of Austrian government and society. The ministerial view that his diatribe was inspired as much by 'the slights offered to him at Vienna' in 1818 as by his hatred of despotism was confirmed by Canning, who told Mackintosh, 'You know he hates the Austrians. The Austrian postilions are so slow. The society at Vienna is dull and sometimes inaccessible. The lodgings are bad and dear'. He voted with ministers against economy and retrenchment, 27 June 1821, but soon afterwards it was said that, anxious to see Canning restored to office, 'he talks of nothing but their weakness'.[13]

Ward spent the winter at Nice and did not return to London until 24 June 1822.[14] During his absence

he continued to lament the incapacity of ministers, though he could see no credible alternative to them, and feared that Canning would put a 'singular and unsatisfactory' end to his career by deciding to become governor-general of India. By June 1822 he had been encouraged to think that the events of the current parliamentary session had undermined the case for parliamentary reform and

> must have convinced all reasonable men, that though the present House of Commons is not the direct and complete representative of the people ... it is quite as far removed from being a servile tool in the hands of the government. Public opinion strongly expressed is sure to control its votes.

In April 1822 he had a bad fall from his horse on his way to Florence, where he was taken ill and attacked by his 'old enemy' melancholia. He attended the Commons to vote against the aliens bill, 1 July 1822, but was by now close to nervous collapse:

> Anxiety, regret for the past, apprehensive uneasiness as to my future life, have seized upon me ... I dread solitude, for society I am unfit, and every error of which I have been guilty in life stands constantly before my eyes.

Yet on 5 July he 'ventured into the sanctuary of Whiggism' at Brooks's and gave Mackintosh 'an hour of more pleasant conversation than I should have had with an orthodox Whig'.[15] Overall, however, he remained in a 'deplorable state' for several weeks, but in mid-August claimed a 'partial recovery', though he felt that

> a somewhat darker shade is to be spread over the remainder of my life. Up to a certain period hope triumphs over experience – after that, experience gradually extinguishes hope. One sees pretty clearly the best that can come of this life, and that this *best* is not very good.

He expected Canning to be restored to the cabinet after Lord Londonderry's* suicide, but discounted himself for office for the 'honest and sufficient reason' that he was temperamentally and physically unfit for it. In September he toured southern England with Lady Davy and contemplated returning to the continent.

On 21 Sept. 1822 Canning, now foreign secretary, asked Ward if he would take the post of under-secretary, which Lord Binning* had declined. In doing so Canning, as he confided to Lord Granville, was merely offering Ward a placebo: 'I wish him *not* to accept the offer but ... think the offer itself may be mentally and medicinally good for him'. Ward, tempted to accept but wracked with indecision, unwittingly called Canning's bluff by asking for time to consider and consult his friends. Canning, who now professed himself happy for Ward to take the job provided his health was equal to it and he genuinely wanted it, gave him 'all the latitude he asked'. Ward explained his first impressions to Copleston:

> The office is altogether subordinate, and it involves going out of Parliament. These seem objections; but then I prefer subordination to responsibility, and Parliament is no great object to me, as I am quite sure never to cut any figure in it. Then the under-secretaryship is an occupation, and that too of an agreeable and interesting sort. Yet, perhaps, any fatigue, particularly coming in the shape of a task, is what I ought not to venture upon, and I am not free from apprehension lest the acceptance of such a situation should be held as a degradation.

He said he was determined 'not to accept it if my father should declare himself positively against it'; but when Lord Dudley did precisely that, arguing that it would destroy his 'independence', he could not submit gracefully.[16] Ellis, who had initially ascribed Ward's hesitancy to his 'morbid inability to come to a decision', told Granville:

> He read to me a part of his reply, in which he pressed his father to revise his opinion, on the ground of the occupation which the business of the office would afford him, and the great discomfort which he now felt from the want of such distraction. This letter was written in the tone of a person, not undecided as I had supposed, but anxious for the situation; and if his father's objections are not very strong, they ought to yield to an anxiety so strongly expressed and so rational in itself.

Dudley reluctantly gave way, but Ward still hesitated. He obtained a further extension of time and moaned that 'Do what I may, my character must be lowered and my feelings wounded'. On 14 Oct. 1822 he declined the offer. Ellis thought it 'really quite lamentable to see such fine talents rendered useless by such weakness of character'; and Canning '*almost*' feared that 'he begins to repent'.[17] At first Ward, who nurtured vague hopes of 'diplomatic employment' at a future date, did not regret his decision, though he smarted at the thought that it would appear that he had made it because he considered the job beneath his dignity and talents. This was certainly the view of many casual observers; and Mackintosh commented that he would have been 'no more than a piece of ornamental furniture in Canning's office'.[18]

Within two months Ward concluded that he had made an irredeemable mistake and, having lapsed into 'what is now my natural state of depression', he considered going to Paris, 'not as I should formerly have done to amuse myself, but to hide myself'. To Aberdeen, who tried to rally him, he wrote:

> The source of my happiness and misery lie more exclusively than you appear to imagine within the circle of private life. I do not mean to cant about ambition, or to pretend that I should not have been better pleased to play a distinguished part. But ... I shall not be made unhappy by the want of fame and power. They have always been too far off.[19]

He stayed in England, but his sense of failure and remorse was undiminished when he wrote to Copleston, 4 Jan. 1823:

> I think the decision wrong to which I came after such long and anxious doubts ... As to Parliament I am only anxious to withdraw from it as quietly and as decently as I can ... It is a bad bargain to worry one's spirits and impair one's health for the sake of a little, third-rate, precarious, fictitious reputation, unattended by any solid self-satisfaction, or by any real influence on human affairs. I meditate a speedy retreat ... and I shall then try what literature and society will do for me during the remainder of my days.

He was considered for seconding the address, but Canning thought he 'would not have undertaken it in my absence from the House'.[20] He supported ministers silently and hopelessly, voting with them on parliamentary reform, 20 Feb., the Irish estimates, 11 Apr., the Foreign Enlistment Act, 16 Apr., and the legal proceedings against the Dublin Orange rioters, 22 Apr. 1823. According to Thomas Creevey,* he believed that the government was doomed, Peel being 'incompetent' and Canning having 'no one of any party with him': 'a pleasant statement this to be made by a man who calls Canning his master, or at least who has called him so'.[21] His father's sudden death that month removed him to the Lords, 'where he has long wished to be', as Agar Ellis, who found him 'nervous and rather low', believed.[22] He wrote gloomily to Lord Lansdowne of his change of circumstances and the inheritance of extensive Staffordshire and Worcestershire estates, which included coal and mineral deposits and brought him £120,000 a year, 6 May 1823:

> Whether I shall be happier for it depends something upon my prudence, and something upon my luck ... Such an accession of wealth is not received by me as it perhaps would have been twenty years ago. After a certain age and beyond a certain amount is valuable chiefly as power. As a purchaser of gratification it has lost a good deal of its power, especially to me who have not much natural taste for personal expense. Besides ... I am to a certain degree confounded and made nervous by so large a share of the goods of fortune devolving upon a person that has done so little to earn them ... I almost envy the self-complacency of twenty blockheads as rich and as undeserving

as myself who strut about the world as if all this were a matter of course, and who seem never once to suspect that their existence is one of the miracles of human society, and that it requires a tract of refined though just reasoning to show that they ought not to be condemned to work for their bread, and their estates given to be divided among wiser and stronger men. However, I shall endeavour to fulfil my duties towards society and towards the order to which I belong. My efforts ... will probably be of no long duration. At present I am well, but I am quite aware that mine is a frame calculated to last but a few years more.[23]

Four years later he belatedly attained the public eminence he craved by accepting Canning's invitation to become foreign secretary in his ministry. He was curious 'to have a peep at official life', but was little more than Canning's instrument. After Canning's death he stayed in office under Lord Goderich, on whose first resignation in December 1827 he was even spoken of as a possible premier: ludicrously, thought Mrs. Arbuthnot, for he 'is as mad as Bedlam, knows nothing of business and is proverbially idle'.[24] Princess Lieven called him 'an amateur minister' who 'combines much real ability with so exaggerated a diffidence that he is capable of asking his colleagues if he dare say "perhaps"'; while William Lamb* (Melbourne) remarked that 'without the experience of a clerk, he has the tone of one'.[25] He retained his office in the Wellington ministry but resigned (very reluctantly, it seems) with his fellow Canningites in May 1828.[26] His tenure of the office, though not disastrous, was largely undistinguished and memorable chiefly for his notorious affair with Lady Lyndhurst, wife of the lord chancellor, which spawned the joke that he was trying to 'put a Ward in chancery'. He may well have succeeded, for she later claimed that one of her daughters was his child.[27]

Dudley made his last speech in the Lords against the Grey ministry's reform bill, 5 Oct. 1831. His later years were marked by his increasing 'absences and oddities', particularly his 'inveterate trick of talking to himself': 'Dudley talking to Ward', as the wags said. In April 1832 he exhibited 'every mark of harmless derangement' and was placed under restraint at Norwood.[28] Thomas Raikes commented:

Here is a man with high rank, character, very cultivated talents, and a colossal fortune, courted in society, surrounded with every means of receiving and conferring happiness – the most enviable position perhaps in life that could be pictured – and what is the result? One single dispensation annihilates the whole![29]

The duke of Bedford remarked:

It is melancholy to see so fine an intellect and well cultivated a mind laid prostrate. With all his obliquities, he had some good points about him, and it is to be hoped that with proper care and skill he may recover his reason.[30]

He never did, but was at least oblivious to the unsavoury stories which circulated concerning his relationship with Lady Lyndhurst, who seems to have blackmailed him shortly before his confinement.[31] Littleton visited Norwood in June 1832 and

saw him, evidently much weakened by frequent depletions from fear of paralysis ... I afterwards saw proofs of increasing mental decay, in writings of his. His great amusement is billiards, at which his resident surgeon and attendants play with him, taking especial care to leave the victory on his side. His constant book is Tacitus. His whole life has been one constant enjoyment of the classics, and now his relish for them has survived every other enjoyment. He is driven out about 15 miles daily, and fancies he is journeying to London. If he were a sovereign, he could not be better attended, or his susceptibility of enjoyment improved.[32]

He died after suffering a stroke in March 1833.[33] His barony of Ward of Birmingham passed to his cousin William Humble Ward (1781-1835), 'a mad parson', on whom he settled £4,000 a year. Most of his vast fortune went to his heir's son William Ward (1817-85), who was created earl of Dudley in 1860. By a codicil to his will, which was proved under £350,000, he left annuities of £2,000 to Lady Lyndhurst ('the wages of prostitution', thought Agar Ellis) and £800 to Susan, wife of the poet William Spencer, and a legacy of £25,000 to one of her sons, 'whom he always tacitly acknowledged'.[34]

On reading Ward's journal Littleton was struck by the absence of

a single trace of anything like rural tastes or the slightest knowledge of rural affairs. Frequent expressions of envy when he sees persons enjoying the sports of the field, and lamentations of his father's neglect of a cultivation of a taste for those objects in his early years ... If his parents had given him in early life opportunities of imbibing the usual tastes of his class and enjoying the associations that belong to them, he would probably have been a more conspicuous man; at all events, his time would not have been engrossed with the idle pursuits of the town. Nothing would have destroyed his vigorous understanding or checked his pursuit of knowledge.[35]

Lord Holland wrote of him:

A man of highly cultivated mind and of exquisite and refined though somewhat elaborate wit. He was accused of wanting affections but I think that, although confined to a few and certainly not in proportion to his bitter hatreds and unwarrantable resentments, he was not entirely devoid of benevolence and even generosity.[36]

Henry Brougham* paid him a generous and perhaps inflated tribute as

one of the most remarkable men that have appeared in this country ... He possessed one of the most acute and vigorous understandings that any man ever was armed with ... His wit was of the brightest order ... His powers of reasoning ... were admirable ... Vast expectations were raised of his success. Nor can it be said with any truth that these were disappointed ... His capacity and his acquirements were fully developed, and bore him to high honours, to great fame, and to exalted station. But he had an over-sensitiveness, an exquisitely fastidious taste, a nervous temperament ... Unsteadiness of purpose, therefore, unwillingness to risk, and reluctance to exert, incapacity to make up his mind ... greatly chequered his existence as a public man during the latter years of his brilliant, but unhappy life.[37]

[1] Based on Ward's *Letters to bp. of Llandaff* (1841), 241-377, except where otherwise stated. See also *Oxford DNB*. [2] *Melbourne Pprs.* 379; *Greville Mems.* iv. 254; v. 438. [3] Add. 61937, f. 136. [4] Add. 43231, f. 36. [5] Lonsdale mss, Lowther to Lonsdale, 22 Jan. 1820. [6] Add. 52444, f. 192. [7] *Fox Jnl.* 50, 61; TNA 30/29/6/7/47. [8] Grey mss, Ellice to Grey, 15 Jan.; Castle Howard mss, G. Howard to Lady Morpeth, 28 [Jan.]; Add. 38742, f.173; Macpherson Grant mss 361, G. Macpherson Grant to Lady Stafford, 27 Jan. 1821. [9] Buckingham, *Mems. Geo IV*, i. 123; HLRO, Hist Coll. 379, Grey Bennet diary, 18. [10] Northants. RO, Agar Ellis diary, 21 Feb. 1821; Grey Bennet diary, 27. [11] *Lady Holland to Son*, 4. [12] Grey Bennet diary, 80. [13] Add. 51654, Mackintosh to Lady Holland, 15 July 1821. [14] Northumb. RO, Blackett Ord mss 324/A/33, Ward to Ord, 26 Oct. 1821. [15] Add. 52445, f. 94. [16] Harewood mss, Canning to Granville, 21, 25 Sept. 1822; TNA 30/29/8/6/293-5. [17] TNA 30/29/6/3/57; 8/6/297; 9/5/16-18. [18] Add. 51654, Mackintosh to Lady Holland, 3 Oct. 1822. [19] Add. 43231, f. 36. [20] Add. 38744, f. 49; *Arbuthnot Corresp.* 43. [21] *Creevey Pprs.* ii. 69. [22] Agar Ellis diary, 26, 28 Apr. [1823]. [23] Lansdowne mss. [24] Add. 43231, f. 228; *Arbuthnot Jnl.* ii. 152. [25] *Lieven Letters*, 107; Herts. Archives, Panshanger mss D/Elb F78, W. to F. Lamb, 3 Dec. 1827. [26] Agar Ellis diary, 26, 27 May 1828; *Arniston Mems.* 346. [27] *Fox Jnl.* 234-5; *Lady Holland to Son*, 70; *Creevey Pprs.* ii. 141; *Creevey's Life and Times*, 252-3, 255; *Williams Wynn Corresp.* 366; *Three Diaries*, 205-6; Hatherton diary, 8 May [1832]. [28] *Lady Holland to Son*, 93, 132; *Croker Pprs.* ii. 170-1; *Macaulay Letters*, ii. 43; *Greville Mems.* ii. 273-4; Hatherton diary, 18, 20, 23 Mar., 8 May; Agar Ellis diary, 2 Apr. [1832]. [29] *Raikes Jnl.* i. 19-20, 22. [30] Add. 51671, Bedford to Lady Holland, 5 Apr. [1832]. [31] *Lady Holland to Son*, 140; *Three Diaries*, 225-6; Aberdeen Univ. Lib. Arbuthnot mss 3029/1/2/53; Hatherton diary, 8 May [1832]. [32] Hatherton diary, 17 June [1832]. [33] *Gent. Mag.* (1833), ii. 367-9, 558; *Oxford DNB*. [34] Agar Ellis diary, 9 Mar. [1833]; *Greville Mems.* ii. 364; *Creevey's Life and Times*, 363; PROB 11/1821/566; IR26/1317/615/. [35] Hatherton diary, 8 Mar. 1840. [36] *Holland House Diaries*, 165. [37] *Edinburgh Rev.* lxvii (1838), 77-79.

D.R.F.

WARD, Robert (1765–1846), of Pall Mall, Mdx. and Hyde House, Chesham, Bucks.

COCKERMOUTH	1802–1806
HASLEMERE	10 Jan. 1807–Apr. 1823

b. 19 Mar. 1765, 6th s. of John Ward (*d.* 1791), merchant, of Gibraltar and London and Rebecca *née* Raphael of Spain. *educ.* Macfarlane's sch. Walthamstow, Essex; ?Westminster; Christ Church, Oxf. 1783; I. Temple 1781, called 1790; continental tour. *m.* (1) 2 Apr. 1796, Catherine Julia (*d.* 28 Dec. 1821), da. of Christopher Thompson Malling of West Herrington, co. Dur., 1s. 3da. *d.v.p.*; (2) 16 July 1828, Jane (*d.* 26 Mar. 1831), da. and coh. of Rev. the Hon. George Hamilton, canon of Windsor, wid. of William Plumer* and of Richard John Lewin, cdr. RN, *s.p.*; (3) 14 Feb. 1833, Mary Anne, da. of Sir George Anson*, wid. of Rev. Charles Gregory Okeover of Okeover, Staffs., *s.p.* Took name of Plumer bef. Ward 16 July 1828. *d.* 13 Aug. 1846.

Under-sec. of state for foreign affairs Jan. 1805-Feb. 1806; ld. of admiralty Apr. 1807-June 1811; clerk of ordnance May 1811-Apr. 1823; auditor of civil list 1823-31.

Dir. Commercial Dock Co. 1812.

Sheriff, Herts. 1832-3.

Maj. Bloomsbury vols. 1803; commdt. Gilston yeomanry.

Ward, a protégé of Pitt and brother-in-law of the cabinet minister the 1st earl of Mulgrave, had attached himself like a limpet to the 1st earl of Lonsdale, who returned him again for his borough of Haslemere at the general election of 1820.[1] As a junior minister he continued to be one of the dependable government phalanx in the House, where he acted as a teller on at least 15 occasions in this period. Once a supporter of Catholic relief, he paired against it, 28 Feb. 1821, 30 Apr. 1822, in deference to Lonsdale's hostility. The radical Whig Henry Grey Bennet* attributed the former 'very discreditable action' to the dictation of the duke of Wellington, Ward's chief at the ordnance since 1818.[2] He voted against parliamentary reform, 9 May 1821, 20 Feb. 1823. As previously, he rarely strayed beyond his departmental brief in debate; but his annual presentation of the ordnance estimates involved him in sharp exchanges with Hume and other sticklers for economy. On 2 June 1820, for example, Ward insisted that the military establishment was 'not greater than the circumstances of the country demanded'; and on 11 May 1821, under attack from Hume, he tried to 'prove the entire necessity of the present extensive arrangements'. On 14 May 1821 he hit out at his tormentor, who 'seemed to be always in a reverie about the ordnance'. He was able to detail an actual saving of £83,000, 25 Mar. 1822, though Hume

was still not satisfied. Ward led the ministerial resistance to his motion for the disfranchisement of civil
officers of the ordnance, 12 Apr. 1821, and replied to
his condemnation of the appointment of a lieutenant-
general of the ordnance in peacetime, 19 Feb. 1823.
On the last occasion, a Whig observer thought that he
had failed to answer Hume 'except by rant and declamation, bold assertions, coarse abuse, and jibes and
jeers'; but a friend congratulated him on 'the complete
drubbing which you so genteely gave him'.[3]

Extracts from Ward's political journal during the
period of Queen Caroline's trial, 14 Oct.-22 Nov. 1820,
were published by his biographer in 1850: they convey
a vivid impression of ministers' anxieties, as the affair
seemed to threaten their hold on power. For his own
part, Ward passed on to members of the cabinet on 15
Oct. a hint from an 'opposition man' that some of the
queen's 'violent friends' were so sure of her guilt that,
while they would not swallow the bill of pains and
penalties, they would settle for a lucrative divorce. In a
conversation with the Whig Commons leader Tierney
two days later Ward

> observed, the only remedy, the only possibility of things
> returning to their former state, was a rebellion, and the
> troops ... quelling it with a high hand. He replied, that
> was the disease. I said, neither he nor I should live to see
> society where it had been and ought to be; to which he
> assented. I have no doubt he is sincere; yet he and his
> party are the real authors of the spirit we deplore.

Conscious of the weakness of government, especially
in the Commons, where they 'seemed like victims',
and believing that it had come to a question of whether
the country 'would ... be governed by any administration', he encouraged Wellington to consider stepping in to form a stronger ministry. The duke looked
askance at the idea. Ward thought that ministers
were entitled to disregard the popular support for the
queen, as expressed through the 'ridiculous' medium
of petitions 'carried by force':

> The House would be much more formidable, indeed,
> after all, the only thing that was formidable, but with a
> verdict of guilty, which the second reading must amount
> to, I did not fear it. I thought the country gentlemen
> would stand by us ... The Radicals might mouth, and the
> Whigs might support them, but these latter never gained
> one inch of ground, and we should triumph as we had
> done before.

Once the second reading of the bill had been narrowly carried in the Lords, which constituted 'a complete justification of ministers', he hoped it would
never be sent to the Commons. He duly applauded
its abandonment, though he had some doubts about

Lord Liverpool's speech on the occasion, which he
felt amounted to 'a confession that radicalism had
triumphed by the threats and clamour out of doors'.
In a broader view, he deplored the Whigs' 'admirable
policy of questioning motives, and attributing everything in office, or friends to office, to corruption,
by which they have nearly destroyed the very roots
of society'. Sickened by 'the scoundrel spirit of the
times', he reflected:

> There was a time when I should have felt such things
> acutely; but with many feelings as warm, nay as roman-
> tic as ever, to political feeling I am almost dead, and the
> nil admirari is to me, not only the most just, but the only
> maxim by which I wish to govern myself. There is not a
> leader in the state capable of swaying parties with proper
> authority, nor do I think (such is the change on the side
> of personal vanity throughout all ranks) Mr. Pitt himself
> could lead as he did. Everyone is for himself – of course
> everyone differs. Authority is gone.[4]

Although Ward's wife was in poor health from late
1819, she rallied 'so often' that he 'blindly and pre-
sumptuously refused to believe in her danger' until her
death two years later. He was 'bent before the blow',
and was also afraid that the government reshuffle of
January 1822 might 'take me from the ordnance';
but Wellington shielded him for the moment. Seven
months later his 'sunk heart' seemed to have 'lost all
interest with the rest of the world': it was as though
'everything' had 'receded from me in one great loss'.
Yet he appears to have recovered some of his spirits
by September 1822, when he informed Lonsdale of
Canning's impending appointment as foreign secretary.[5] The death of his wife was more than an emotional blow, for since his resignation as under-secretary
in 1806 she had enjoyed a pension of £1,000 a year,
which was contingent on his not resuming office at a
salary of £2,000 or more. Although he secured a grant
of a pension of £1,000 for himself in respect of his
services as clerk of the ordnance, 14 May 1822, he was
still currently out of pocket, as his official remuneration had recently been reduced by government economies to about £700.[6] Faced with the 'ridiculousness'
of 'continuing to serve ... in an office of the labour and
responsibility of mine, for less than I can receive by
law, by going out of it', he set about trying to negotiate
a better deal for himself. By late January 1823 it was
thought probable, as Lonsdale's son Lord Lowther*
reported, that Ward was to become a commissioner of
taxes, which would vacate his seat. Lowther prompted
his father to select a replacement Member, but at the
same time advised discretion, as it was said that Ward
was 'not well pleased at quitting Parliament', which
he considered 'a great wound to his dignity': nothing

was yet settled, and careless talk would only give him an excuse to 'say, as he once before hinted, that we wanted to get rid of him'. On 29 Jan. 1823, according to Lowther, Ward wrote a long letter to Lushington, the new patronage secretary, 'of which we could not make out purport or meaning', beyond the fact that he was 'in great ill humour and much dissatisfied'.[7] Three weeks later Ward wrote to Lonsdale to complain of 'slight, abandonment and total injustice on the part of the government', who, for all their honeyed words, had made no real effort to treat him fairly:

I gave up £2,000 a year at the bar, on the invitation of Mr. Pitt, and the *promise* to be taken care of in proportion to what I gave up. Hence the late king's order recognizes the principle in terms, when it says that in order to compensate to me or *my family* the sacrifice I made, my wife should have £1,000 a year, so long as I had not two *under* the government. My place is reduced to less than one ... Yet though the defalcation of the peer gave them the fairest opening to raise the salary, though the committee of finance would have willingly raised it to £2,000, they neither have the courage to raise this miserably paid place, nor to renew the pension according to the intentions of the king; nor to make the least attempt at such a arrangement as to any other parliamentary office as might, by being tenable with my parliamentary pension, equalize my government income with what was promised and intended ... Thus ... I am fairly *forced* out of Parliament by the cowardice of those who say ... they want to keep me there.

He was further miffed at being pressed to retain his seat until he had dealt with the ordnance estimates, though he could hardly refuse. If he hoped that Lonsdale would intervene with ministers on his behalf he was disappointed, for his patron's reply 'pointed all to retirement'.[8]

This was far from the end of the affair. On 28 Feb. 1823 Lowther wrote that Ward had now opted to become auditor of the civil list by which, 'united to his pension', he would enjoy £2,000 a year 'with easy duty', though he would still have to vacate his seat. Within a fortnight he changed his mind again and reclaimed the tax office place, but it had been given to another man.[9] In the House, 17 Mar., Ward replied to Creevey's attack on the use of the Leeward Islands duties as a pension fund and handled the ordnance estimates. Next day Arbuthnot, Lushington's predecessor as patronage secretary and now commissioner of woods and forests, asked Lowther whether, 'as Ward was going out of Parliament', Lonsdale would be willing to replace him as Member for Haslemere with the Scottish solicitor-general Wedderburn on a short-term basis. Lowther, who naturally assumed

that Arbuthnot was speaking of behalf of government, told him that Lonsdale was already engaged to return his kinsman George Lowther Thompson.*[10] Unaware of this episode, Ward made a last, desperate bid to cling on to his seat. On 20 Mar. he called on Lowther, who related their conversation to his father:

He began by asking me if you had fixed upon anyone to succeed him at Haslemere; I told him you had ... [and] that I believed you had made the proposition and that it was accepted. He then told me that he was in negotiation with some member of one of the boards to exchange his auditorship for a place tenable with Parliament, and wished to know if he could retain his seat if this arrangement was made; that he had never announced his intention of accepting the tax office or the auditorship if he could have got a place to improve his income and at the same time sit in Parliament, and that all his negotiations were coupled with this reservation. I observed upon this that it was perfectly understood he was going; that he himself had consulted me which of the two offices that were offered he should accept; and that even the government were so impressed at his having accepted the auditorship that they had made an application to bring in a friend of theirs to succeed him at Haslemere. To this he had nothing to say, but shifted his tack to inquire if you were anxious to have his seat. I repeated again that as it was understood he was retiring from Parliament you had provided yourself with a person to supply the vacancy ... He will write you a letter today setting forth his hopes of making an arrangement with someone to change offices ... but I am sure that Lord Liverpool has not yet been consulted, and from what I have heard I do not think that he is likely to agree to such a proposition. Now it comes to the point I perceive Ward is catching at every straw to save himself from retiring from Parliament. He will very likely tell you that the government are very anxious that he should remain in the House of Commons; from what I heard today I should be inclined to draw quite another inference.[11]

Ward duly wrote to Lonsdale, claiming that it had all along been understood that his preferred option was an office tenable with a seat, advising him that he had a good chance of effecting an exchange and asking permission to pursue this negotiation with a view to continuing to sit for Haslemere. The exchange which he had in mind was with William Henry Fremantle*, secretary to the board of control, whose patron the duke of Buckingham and chief Charles Williams Wynn* approved the swap, though it had not yet been submitted to Liverpool. Ward also told Lonsdale that 'circumstances might arise to make me content to remain even at the ordnance itself', namely a 'difficulty' about finding a successor and the prospect of war. In his answer, which Lowther thought 'very proper and conclusive', Lonsdale evidently made it clear to Ward that there was to be no reneging on the arrangement with Thompson, mentioned the supposed approach from government as further proof of the understanding that he had decided to retire and rapped his knuckles for his shuffling conduct.[12] Ward, as Lowther reported, was mortified, and on 24 Mar., in the Speaker's room, he delivered

> a most intemperate oration of the ill usage he had experienced from the treasury in having informed you that he was about to accept the auditorship ... He added that it was now proved that he had enemies and that they wished to get rid of him and that no one had ever been so ill treated. He was in much too great a *tantrum* and so wrongheaded that he could not be reasoned with. I told him that the fact of his having accepted the auditorship was too notorious to be denied ... Ward keeps writing long letters to Lushington, which he puts in the fire and does not answer ... Ward has plagued the government so much about his concerns that if this place had not been given him he would have got nothing at all. It seems singular that he should appear in ill humour when he has got a permanent situation of £1,400 a year, added to which he can hold half his pension ... His great wrath is against the government [for] having proposed someone to succeed him; he does not know who it was that made the proposition and who the person was that they wished to come in, and upon this point he had better remain in ignorance ... Ward is searching ... with such watchfulness for a grievance that it is quite dangerous to talk to him without a witness. Lushington and Arbuthnot will have no further communication with him.[13]

Ward tried to explain himself to Lonsdale by letter later that day, but he evidently received a dusty answer. He may well have had some cause to complain of Arbuthnot's characteristically officious interference, which turned out to have been on his own initiative. He soon identified the culprit and on 26 Mar. wrote at length to Lonsdale, mixing sycophancy with defiance, to allege that Arbuthnot's 'manoeuvres' had cheated him out of his seat. As parting shots, he threw out his suspicion (which was unfounded) that the person on whose behalf Arbuthnot had approached the Lowthers was Lushington's son, and rather unconvincingly cited his own personal feelings as the true reason for his reluctance to surrender his seat: 'I, too, have a son, who when his father is forgotten is not likely to be remembered'.[14] Lonsdale's reply seems to have been a frosty one, and Ward had to retract his slur on Lushington, though he stuck by his complaint against Arbuthnot. He indignantly denied Lonsdale's assertions that he must all along have been aware that Wellington 'might wish to have a person of his own nomination in my place' and that Liverpool did not think much of his abilities.[15] The Lowthers indulged

Ward's wish to 'cling to the ship as long as possible' by deferring the vacating of his seat until after Easter, but they were anxious to wash their hands of him, especially as he continued to broadcast his grievances. Lowther commented, 1 Apr.:

> No person could possibly have been treated with more kindness, consideration and indulgence ... He had the offer of two offices; he made a selection, and now coming with an *afterthought* and saying it was always with an understanding that it was provided he could not get a place tenable with Parliament is quite idle and I think quibbling ... Even if his own statements or allusions were admitted I should think he was much to blame for not being more explicit ... about the plans that were working in his own mind ... Your delicacy and kindness to him ... seem to have produced these unreasonable demands ... Ward appears to me to be exerting his ingenuity ... to endeavour to catch at an expression or a word to found a grievance upon ... Taking all the circumstances into consideration, I think you are very lucky to have got rid of him.

'Any stranger to the transaction', Lowther observed next day, 'would imagine he was turned out without a sixpence'.[16] Eighteen months later Ward was asked to us his pen against those elements in the government who were hostile to Canning. To Buckingham, whose confidant he had now become, he reported:

> I found I was supposed to be neither more nor less than out of humour, and ill used both at the ordnance and the treasury, and not ill disposed to show my feelings upon it. I put the matter to rest in an instant by a very simple explanation; for I found to my amusement, though also to my vexation, that I was supposed to have quitted the ordnance in a *quarrel* with the duke [of Wellington], and had left Parliament in disgust. I felt bound therefore to set things right, and say that I had parted from the duke the best friends possible, and still admired him, as I still loved Lord Lonsdale ... That it was very true I felt I had been tricked out of the seat, and betrayed in my best interests, either from negligence or design, by others; but this would not make me quarrel with old friends, whom, though I felt little obligation to, I could not oppose with pleasure or credit in the way hinted at.[17]

In his retirement Ward became a successful novelist. His *Tremaine, or, the Man of Refinement*, published anonymously in 1825, received considerable acclaim, as did its successor *De Vere, or, the Man of Independence* (1827), one of whose principal characters was a composite of Bolingbroke, Canning and Pitt. Benjamin Disraeli[†] admired it, and Ward's friend Peter George Patmore put him on a par with Scott; but both works, together with *De Clifford, or, the Constant Man* (1841), have long been buried in deserved obscurity.[18] Reconciled to being on the fringe of affairs and delighted with his literary success, Ward wrote to a friend on Canning's accession to power in April 1827:

> You looked for mine or my son's name, you say, in the late changes; mine you will see no more. All my feelings forbid it. I have now lost every man to whom I looked up, or could ever follow, and I would not lead, even if I could. In short I am grown old, and am content to be so, knowing what I know, and feeling what I feel. The place I have is just the very best I could have with these feelings, keeping me just enough in the political world to say I am not out of it, and giving me, therefore, precisely the quantum of public interest to make me the more relish my dear private life. Hence nothing Mr. Canning could have given me could have equalled what I have. Had he doubled my public income (which he could not), I must have spent the difference, exchanged a certainty for an uncertainty, and quiet for turmoil, by no means compensated by returning to Parliament and being Right Honourable. This I fairly told a noble friend of mine, who came twice to me, observing, that he believed they wanted me in more active office ... But though I had lost all ambition as to myself, I had occasion to observe its workings in others, with no very raised opinions of its effects on human nature ... In short, it is no affectation to say, that I have realized what Tremaine only dreamed, and view the world at a distance.[19]

(No evidence has been found to suggest that Ward was even considered for office, let alone made an offer.)

Marriage to a widow in 1828 brought him an estate on the borders of Hertfordshire and Essex and an extra name; but a succession of calamities awaited him. In August 1830 the two eldest of his three daughters died on consecutive days. Soon afterwards, Charles Russell* met him in the street: 'He is quite a cripple from rheumatic gout, very deaf, and instead of his former animated manner, or of any appearance of melancholy, he spoke with a silly vacant simper'.[20] Seven months later, to Ward's 'infinite astonishment', his wife died. In 1832 rumours circulated about 'the secret history of Gilston', where a 'series of rows ... beyond conception' were supposed to have occurred. 'The Wards', reported Disraeli, 'say that Madame killed the girls, and the recrimination now is, that the young Wards killed her'.[21] It was later alleged that both Ward and his son, having been 'always over head and ears in debt', were 'quite ruined' and that Mrs. Plumer Ward's 'property turned out only £400 per annum'. Certainly, although she left Ward real estate in six counties, her personalty was sworn under a paltry £100.[22] Ward's finances were not improved by the loss of his office in 1831, when the Grey ministry incorporated it into the treasury and so deprived him of £900 a year. (He lost the salary of £1,400, but

became entitled to the other half of his pension.) Ward considered himself to be the victim of political spite, and he was outraged when Lord Althorp, the chancellor of the exchequer, described the auditorship in the House, 4 Feb. 1831, as 'a sinecure', the duties of which were mostly performed by deputy. He got Goulburn and General Phipps to clear his name, 28 Mar.: they forced Althorp to admit that he had 'performed all the duties required of him, himself'.[23] Another source of mortification to Ward, who condemned the authors of the reform bills as 'robbers', was his son's espousal of radical views.[24] (After a brief diplomatic career Henry George Ward (1797-1860), who was at dagger's drawn with his stepmother, sat for St. Albans, 1832-7, and Sheffield, 1837-49. He supported the ballot, triennial parliaments and household suffrage; and his motion of 1834 for the appropriation of Irish church revenues precipitated the collapse of the Grey ministry and became thereafter an annual parliamentary ritual.)

The illness of his surviving daughter in 1832 drove Ward to Brighton, where he met his third wife. She brought some domestic happiness to his last years, despite the death of his daughter in 1835. After a period of residence abroad he returned to England in 1837 and the following year, abandoning Gilston to his son, who was 'very welcome to all the cockneys and radicals of Herts', he went to live at his stepson's home in Staffordshire. In addition to his third novel, he published *Illustrations of Human Life* (1837), an *Historical Essay on the Revolution of 1688* (1838) and *Pictures of the World at Home and Abroad* (1839).[25] In 1841 he applied unsuccessfully to Peel for a baronetcy, both as a mark of his status as representative of the Plumer family, who had held one in the seventeenth century, and as compensation for his victimization by the Whigs.[26] The next year he struck Crabb Robinson as 'a very lively and pleasant man', notwithstanding his debilitating deafness.[27] Ward wrote from Hastings in January 1845:

> I am in the greatest danger of going off in a fit of indolence; for I have no other complaint. Lounging, in both body and mind, gets more and more hold of me, and this soft climate makes it worse ... My life ... passes in a happy, if indolent reverie, which I take to be the true paradise of fools; and while that is the case, I don't want to be among the wise.[28]

Later that year he suffered 'severe attacks of painful indigestion'. Early in 1846, riddled with 'perpetual and painful illness', he moved into his father-in-law's official residence at Chelsea hospital.[29] After a brief rally he died there in August 1846, a few weeks after his son's appointment as secretary to the admiralty in the Russell ministry.[30] Ward had settled his real estate, including Gilston, on Henry George in 1831. By his will, dated 23 Feb. 1844, he left his wife £1,000 in addition to her jointure. Among the possessions of which he disposed was a 'letter attempted to be written by Mr. Pitt when wandering in mind on his death bed'.[31] An obituarist credited him with 'fine intelligence and boundless information'; and Patmore, his uncritical admirer, wrote of 'that strong and clear good sense which was the marking and guiding feature of Mr. Plumer Ward's singularly varied intellect'.[32] Four years after his death Croker, reviewing his biography, recalled him as an 'amiable and clever man'.[33]

[1] Lonsdale mss, Ward to Lonsdale, 6 Mar. 1820. [2] HLRO, Hist. Coll. 379, Grey Bennet diary, 28-29. [3] Add. 51667, Bedford to Lady Holland [23 Feb. 1823]; Phipps, *Plumer Ward Mems.* ii. 104. [4] Phipps, ii. 58-101. [5] Lonsdale mss, Ward to Lonsdale, 6, 23 Mar. 1820, 22 Jan., 10 July, 10 Sept. 1822. [6] *Geo. III Corresp.* iv. 3173; *Black Bk.* (1820), 86; *Extraordinary Red Bk.* (1821), 237; *PP* (1821), xv. 309; (1822), xix. 91; (1823), xiii. 133; (1830-1), vi. 574. [7] Lonsdale mss, Lowther to Lonsdale, 24, 25, 29 Jan. 1823. [8] Ibid. Ward to Lonsdale, 17 Feb., 21 Mar. 1823. [9] Ibid. Lowther to Lonsdale, 28 Feb., 12 Mar 1823. [10] Ibid. Lowther to Lonsdale, 18, 19 Mar. 1823. [11] Ibid. Lowther to Lonsdale, 21 Mar. 1823. [12] Ibid. Ward to Lonsdale, 21 Mar., Lowther to same, 21 Mar. 1823. [13] Ibid. Lowther to Lonsdale, 24 Mar. 1823. [14] Ibid. Ward to Lonsdale, 24, 26 Mar., Lowther to same, 24, 25 Mar.; Bucks. RO, Fremantle mss, Buckingham to Fremantle, 27 Mar. 1823. [15] Lonsdale mss, Ward to Lonsdale, 1 Apr. 1823. [16] Ibid. Lowther to Lonsdale, 27 Mar., 1, 2 Apr., Long to same, 1 Apr. 1823. [17] Buckingham, *Mems. Geo. IV*, ii. 129. [18] Phipps, ii. 106-13; 133, 156; P. G. Patmore, *My Friends and Acquaintance*, i. 240, 262; *Disraeli Letters*, ii. 24, 62; *Oxford DNB*. [19] Phipps, ii. 171-2. [20] *Gent. Mag.* (1830), ii. 189; Bodl. MS. Eng. lett. c. 160, ff. 192-3. [21] Phipps, ii. 172-3; Patmore, i. 247; *Disraeli Letters*, ii. 146. [22] *Disraeli Letters*, iv. 260X; PROB 11/1784/248; IR26/1275/148. [23] Phipps, ii. 173-84. [24] Hatfield House mss 2M/Gen., Ward to Salisbury, 13 Jan. 1832; Add. 40494, ff. 177, 179, 181. [25] Phipps, ii. 186-222; Patmore, ii. 61, 72, 74, 96-97. [26] Add. 40494, ff. 177, 179, 181. [27] Crabb Robinson *Diary*, ii. 231. [28] Phipps, ii. 224. [29] Patmore, ii. 196, 200; Phipps, ii. 226-7. [30] *Gent. Mag.* (1846), ii. 650. [31] PROB 8/239 (23 Dec. 1846); 11/2047/940. [32] *Gent. Mag.* (1846), ii. 651; Patmore, i. 285. [33] *Quarterly Rev.* lxxxvii (1850), 275.

D.R.F.

WARD, William (1787–1849), of 34 New Broad Street, London and 40 Bloomsbury Square, Mdx.

LONDON   1826–1831

b. July 1787, 2nd s. of George Ward (*d.* 1829), merchant, of Broad Street and Northwood Park, Cowes, I.o.W. and Mary, da. of Henry Sampson Woodfall, printer, of Ivy Lane, Paternoster Row, London. *educ.* Winchester 1800-4. *m.* 26 Apr. 1811, Emily, da. of Harvey Christian Combe†, brewer, of Cross Street, London and Cobham Park, Surr., 4s. (1 *d.v.p.*) 4da. (2 *d.v.p.*). *d.* 30 June 1849.

Dir. Bank of England 1817-36; commr. of lunacy 1828-31; master, Musicians' Co. 1830-1.

Ward's father, who was born in 1751, was the eldest brother of the barrister and novelist Robert Ward, Pittite Member for Cockermouth, 1802-6, and Haslemere, 1807-23. Their father, John Ward (*d.* 1791), a merchant based in Gibraltar, where he was chief clerk of the ordnance, had married a Spaniard and settled in England in 1782. George Ward became a prosperous and respected London merchant, specializing in Spanish and Mediterranean produce, with premises in Broad Street. He invested heavily in land, acquiring estates in Hampshire and on the Isle of Wight around Cowes, where he built Northwood House. Farington, a guest at his 70th birthday dinner in 1821, was told by his neighbour John Nash, the architect, that he possessed 'great property, a landed estate of £8,000 per annum', was 'very rich in money' and that 'when he married he resolved to settle £2,000 on every child he might have'.[1]

William Ward, his second son, was born at his London home in Highbury Place, Islington. After leaving Winchester, where his elder brother George Henry was also educated, he spent some time in an Antwerp banking house, acquiring an expertise in the foreign exchanges. On his return he worked for his father, who in 1810 took him into partnership with George Henry and one Thompson, a clerk. This arrangement lasted until 1817, when Ward and his younger brother Henry took over the business, which was now based at 34 New Broad Street. From 1825 it was in Ward's hands alone, and in about 1828 he moved it to 50 Lothbury.[2] In April 1817, at the age of 29, Ward became a director of the Bank of England. He gave evidence to the Lords and Commons select committees on the resumption of cash payments in February 1819, describing himself as 'a cambist and Mediterranean merchant' and advising 'excessive caution' in the restriction of paper in order to ensure a smooth transition. He was an advocate of the Ricardian ingot plan and dissented from the general opinion of his senior colleagues at the Bank that currency regulation had no bearing on the foreign exchanges: subsequent developments vindicated Ward's view, of which he secured the adoption as Bank orthodoxy in 1827. He was one of the directors who signed the London merchants' free trade petition presented to the Commons on 8 May 1820.[3] Ward, a tall, powerfully built man, had another string to his bow, for he was one of the four outstandingly talented cricketers of the pre-Victorian era. In July 1820, in an innings begun on his 33rd birthday, he scored 278 for the Marylebone Cricket Club against Norfolk, which remained the highest individual score made at Lord's until it was surpassed by Holmes of Yorkshire 105 years later. Ward saved the ground from the builders in 1825 by buying the lease for £5,000 from Thomas Lord, who was on the verge of turning over a large part of it for the erection of houses.[4]

Ward was one of the leading supporters of Thomas Wilson*, spokesman for the City's commercial and shipping interests, at the general election of 1820, when, at Wilson's adoption meeting, he declared that there were 'two sorts of independence', namely 'independence from any administration' and, 'much more valuable, independence of popular clamour'.[5] At a merchants' meeting called to petition for relaxation of the corn laws, 13 Apr. 1825, he recommended steps to ensure 'a regular supply by a fixed duty'.[6] At the general election of 1826 Ward, who was described by Lord Lansdowne as 'a good sort of man but no Whig', offered for London in Wilson's room. When publicly asked whether he would take an alderman's gown he declined, citing Wilson's example. He repeated this at his adoption meeting, when he expressed very guarded support for piecemeal parliamentary reform:

There was a great difference between corruption proved and ... asserted. Reform, as Mr. Canning had ... [said] could only be effected by reverting back to the old system, or by the reconstruction of our political edifice ... [which] must ... be preceded by the demolition of our present edifice, to which he never would consent ... If parliamentary reform, of which universal suffrage was a part, were adopted, every ... trader's clerk, and everyone bearing the form of man, who presented himself, would be entitled to a vote, and the rights and privileges of the City would be proportionately affected.

He refused to give a pledge on the Catholic question, but was assumed to be hostile to relief; and his committee were accused of surreptitiously playing the 'No Popery' card. He was returned third in the poll.[7]

Ward was named to the select committee on the Arigna Mining Company, 5 Dec. 1826. In the House, 15 May 1827, he denied an allegation that he had attended it 'sometimes, but not regularly', claiming to have 'voluminous notes' to prove otherwise. He voted silently against Catholic claims, 6 Mar. 1827, but afterwards told John Hobhouse* that 'he should not have cared if the majority with which he voted had turned out to be the minority'.[8] He supported the London livery's petition for free trade in corn, 19 Feb. (as he had spoken in common hall, 19 Oct. 1826),[9] and argued in that sense when criticizing as inadequate the Liverpool ministry's modification of the corn laws and defending the 1819 currency settlement against disgruntled agriculturists, 8 Mar. He spoke and voted in the minority of 38, with his three London colleagues,

against the proposed increase in the protection for barley, 12 Mar.; but he voted with government for the duke of Clarence's annuity bill, 16 Mar. He was in the minority of 18 against the spring guns bill, 23 Mar. He approved Wrotteseley's bill to curb the powers of Coventry magistrates, 22 May. He objected to a clause in the customs bill, 15 June. He regretted that the corn laws had 'remained for a whole year unsettled', but 'disclaimed imputing any blame whatever' to the Canning ministry, 19 June; and on their corn bill, 21 June, he decried 'prohibitory' regulations, while defending the existing warehousing system, and encouraged ministers to 'proceed boldly in a measure of this general degree of usefulness, and leave the responsibility of defeating it at the doors of others'.[10] That summer he scored 42 and 20 for England against the round-arm bowling of Sussex and 'said he should have made more in the second innings had he not been thinking of a coming corn law debate'. He made an undefeated 96 for the Gentlemen against the Players.[11] In the autumn he informed James Macdonald*, a junior minister in the Goderich administration, of the 'high good humour' of the City with Lansdowne as home secretary.[12]

Ward was one of the Wellington ministry's supporters appointed to the finance committee, 15 Feb. 1828.[13] He voted for repeal of the Test Acts, 26 Feb., but against Catholic claims, 12 May. He defended the corn bonding system, 31 Mar., presented London corn merchants' petitions for permission to grind corn into flour for export, 18, 22 Apr., and on 25 Apr. acquiesced in the ministerial corn bill as a 'safe' measure, even though he felt it set the price for free imports 'much too high'. He again upbraided the currency cranks, 28 Apr., when he presented and strongly endorsed a London wool merchants' petition against the threatened duty on foreign produce. On the Scottish bank note restriction, which he described, unaccountably, as 'one of the most interesting subjects that can engage the attention of an English House of Commons', 5 June, he put the Bank's point of view, which largely coincided with the government's, and said that country bankers had 'done much to militate against a sound currency'. He voted with ministers on the ordnance estimates, 4 July, and supported their grant for canals as 'the most economical mode of defending Canada', 8 July. On the 11th he urged them not to abandon or infringe the sinking fund, as investors had 'as much right to have it maintained as the landholder has to the corn bill', and defended the Bank's relationship with government against Hume's criticisms. He assured the House, 15 July 1828, that remittances of bullion from India were 'not likely to produce any ruinous effects upon the trade with that country'. Towards the end of the year he spoke privately 'in very high terms' of Lord Ellenborough, president of the India board, who was flattered by this testimony from 'a great citizen'.[14]

Ward was considered by ministers as a possible seconder of the address at the opening of the 1829 session, when the decision to concede Catholic emancipation was to be disclosed.[15] He was not selected, but Planta, the patronage secretary, expected him to vote 'with government'. As it was, he paired against consideration of the measure, 6 Mar. On the presentation of the City corporation's favourable petition, 9 Mar., he announced his continued hostility to 'further concessions', but gave credit to Peel and the duke of Wellington for good intentions and promised not to oppose the relief bill after recording his objection to its principle; he did so with a speech and vote against the second reading, 18 Mar., when he sought to correct an impression that he had been guilty of 'lukewarmness or vacillation'. He presented hostile petitions, 10 Mar. He presented petitions against the London Bridge bill, 2, 3, 13 Apr. He was named to the select committee on vestries, 28 Apr. 1829, as he was again, 9 Feb. 1830. He defended the government's funding of exchequer bills and upheld the sinking fund, 11 May 1829, asserting that 'the resources of the country are abundant, if its affairs be administered in a plain and intelligible manner'. He spoke and was a minority teller for the Smithfield market bill, 15 May. On 2 June 1829 he presented the petition of a London silk manufacturer complaining of the lawless conduct of Spitalfields journeymen weavers, whose resort to 'combination and outrage', in order to extort higher wages, he condemned.

Ward was chosen to second the address, 4 Feb. 1830, when he said that repeal of the malt tax would afford only partial and currency reform no relief to distressed agriculturists. He clashed with Knatchbull, a spokesman for the latter, protesting that ministers had not put words in his mouth.[16] At the particular request of Wellington, who was godfather to his youngest son Arthur Robert, born the previous year, he became chairman of the select committee on the East India Company's affairs, 9 Feb. He reported part of its evidence and told Hume to keep his nose out, 4 Mar., and brought up its final summarizing report, 8 July, when he stated that it had sat for 22 weeks and put over 6,000 questions, and repudiated an accusation that it had acted partially. His involvement with the committee did not excuse him when his name was drawn in the ballot for the Wexford election committee, 2 Mar., but in the event he was not appointed to it. He endorsed a petition for Jewish emancipation, 22 Feb., and paired for that measure, 5 Apr., 17 May. He supported the St. Katharine's Docks bill, 1 Mar. Next day he opposed further inquiry into his father's friend Nash's conduct over crown leases. He also called for a speedy settlement of the vestry dispute in St. Giles parish; and he spoke and was several times a majority teller for the regulation bill, 1, 2 Apr. He voted against Lord Blandford's reform plan, 18 Feb., and the enfranchisement of Birmingham, Leeds and Manchester, 23 Feb.; but it is not clear whether he was the 'C. Ward' credited with a vote for inquiry into the Newark petition complaining of electoral interference by the duke of Newcastle, 1 Mar. On 12 Mar. he dissented from that part of a London merchants' relief petition

> which ascribes ... distress ... to the malconstruction of this House. I do not mean to say that a small number of commercial towns, under certain circumstances, ought not to have representatives; but, at present, I am decidedly opposed, on general principles, to the large question of parliamentary reform.

Opposing inquiry into the state of the nation, 16 Mar., he argued that agricultural rents were too high, that currency reform was a red herring and calls for a double standard foolish, and that distress was attributable to bad harvests, increased poor rates, the spread of machinery and the influx of unemployed Irish labourers. He denied Warburton's assertion that the Bank, the East India Company and 'other large bodies' exercised significant influence in City elections, 25 Mar. He excused himself from attending the common hall meeting which petitioned for 'radical' reform and a reduction in public salaries, 5 Apr., on the plea of his duties on the East India committee, but promised to assist in conveying its sentiments to the House.[17] He duly supported the petition when it was presented by his colleague Wood, 17 May, and now declared that the enfranchisement of such towns as Birmingham, Leeds and Manchester, 'so far from endangering the constitution ... would be a public benefit'. On 26 Apr. he presented petitions for abolition of the death penalty for forgery, for which measure he spoke and voted, 24 May, and for reduction of the duty on the domestic cultivation of tobacco. He presented a Bethnal Green petition against the sale of beer bill, 4 May, and was in the minority for an amendment to restrict sales for on-consumption, 1 July. He supported the grant for South American missions in the spirit of Canning and for the sake of British commerce, 7 June. He dismissed Attwood's currency nostrums and defended the Bank's handling of the 1825-6 panic, 8 June. He may have voted against the requirement for printers to give additional security under the terms of the libel law amendment bill, 6 July 1830.

Ward stood again for London at the general election at the end of that month and was returned unopposed with the other three sitting Members: he made no reported political pronouncements. Ministers listed him as one of their 'friends', but he was absent from the crucial division on the civil list, 15 Nov.; he was named to the ensuing select committee, and to that on a reduction of public salaries, 9 Dec. He endorsed a London householders' petition for mitigation of the penal code, 19 Nov., and one from the corporation for repeal of the duty on coastwise coals, 14 Dec. 1830. 'Extremely' surprised by the Grey ministry's budget proposal to tax transfers of funded stock, he declared his 'decided hostility', 11 Feb., and welcomed their capitulation over it, 14 Feb. 1831. Next day he refused to support his radical Whig colleague Waithman's motion for an inquiry into trade and, unhappy with the chancellor of the exchequer Lord Althorp's explanation of his statement that the governor of the Bank, John Horsley Palmer, favoured the transfer tax, read a statement which he had extracted from Palmer earlier that day, to clarify the matter. He attended a dinner of merchants at which the ministerial proposals to equalize the Canadian and Baltic timber duties were denounced, 11 Mar.[18] Ward could not stomach the reform bill. At a meeting of the livery, 7 Mar., he alone of the City Members refused to obey their instruction to support it in the House. He was subsequently pressed to resign his seat by a committee formed to find a replacement, and replied that he would do so if half the corporation signed a written request to that effect.[19] He promoted a City anti-reform petition, which he presented after speaking and voting against the second reading of the bill, 22 Mar., when he described it as 'a formidable experiment' introduced at a dangerous time, and defended close boroughs as havens for men of talent.[20] He presented a Guildford petition expressing qualified support for the measure, 30 Mar., and voted for Gascoyne's wrecking amendment, 19 Apr. He initially offered for the City at the ensuing general election. In his address, he rejected annual parliaments, universal suffrage and the ballot, and reform as a means of 'abolishing tithes, of repealing the corn laws entirely, and of remitting taxation to such an extent as will leave the public creditor unpaid', but professed support for limited change, noting that the bill as it stood would disfranchise many liverymen and increase Catholic representation. He was targeted by the Parliamentary Candidate Society and opposed by four reformers with a united committee; and on the day of nomination, 29 Apr. 1831, he announced that on the advice of his own committee he had decided to

withdraw in deference to the overwhelming 'sense of the livery'.[21] When Wellington questioned his reported observation at a public meeting in May that his and Peel's fall from power was the price they had paid for bargaining for the support of natural adversaries, as they had on Catholic emancipation, Ward explained that his meaning had been misrepresented:

> I neither said nor hinted that you had proposed the relief bill in any connection with the spirit of compromise. I feared that some of my Tory friends might think that I had retired under a compromise with reformers, who were to bring me in hereafter in consideration of my retiring now. I stated that caution was necessary even in accepting the support of adversaries and that yours had cheered you on while you were recommending a measure that was agreeable to them, but that they turned their backs when that measure had become law ... I have contended for the seat in the City under every possible disadvantage, because I believed it to be due to the principles I have advocated and the cause I have upheld ... I could have polled one third of the livery in my favour ... I have gulped my little disappointments, but I cannot conceal my uneasiness and concern at the present posture of public affairs ... and ... the current that has so strangely set in against every existing institution.[22]

During the crisis precipitated by the defeat of the reform bill in the Lords in October 1831, Ward and Palmer had a series of meetings with Lord Wharncliffe, one of the Tory 'Waverer' peers keen to effect a compromise: they impressed on him the general feeling for reform in the City and suggested modifications which would strengthen ministers' position. With the knowledge and approval of Lords Grey and Althorp, they sought to promote a City address in favour of a diluted bill.[23] Ward's evidence to the Commons select committee on the Bank's charter in June 1832 included another defence of its handling of the financial crisis of 1825-6.[24] He promoted a City loyal address to William IV after his dismissal of the Melbourne ministry in December 1834, when he offered as one of three coalesced Conservative candidates for London at the general election called by Peel in an attempt to sustain his fledgling administration. He condemned those who wished to disturb the supposedly 'final' settlement of 1832 and argued that while 'it was impossible they ever could have a government so strong as governments used to be', it was feasible to secure 'a government of administrative efficiency'. He privately hoped for 'an exhibition of strength' rather than victory, but he finished a distant sixth as the Conservatives were humiliated.[25]

By now Ward was on the verge of personal ruin, through no fault of his own. On the dissolution of their partnership in 1817 his father had executed a trust deed of £30,000 for the benefit of Ward's children, but had allowed the money to remain in Ward's hands in the business's capital. Ward's brother George Henry, the trustee, remained ignorant of the existence of the fund until it was revealed by their father's will, which was proved under £200,000, 24 Apr. 1829. When George Henry applied to William for recovery of the money, he was told that full repayment would inevitably and immediately bankrupt him. After a legal mediation he sought restitution by instalments. Only £8,000 had been paid by 1835, when George Henry called in the rest, forcing William to have his business, which had moved to Warnford Court, Throgmorton Street, declared bankrupt, 6 Feb. 1836. A meagre dividend of 1s. in the pound was declared on 23 Aug. 1836.[26] The previous summer Ward, who had foregone his turn as deputy-governor of the Bank in view of these difficulties, and his four daughters had sold the lease of Lord's to J.H. Dark for £2,000 and an annuity of £425 for the remaining 58 years of its term.[27] He resigned from the Bank direction in 1836 and left his town house in Bloomsbury Square for a more modest residence at 76 Connaught Terrace, Edgware Road. In 1842 his affairs were in chancery, where the following year lord chancellor Lyndhurst ruled that contrary to the claim made on behalf of Ward's children, their uncle George Henry had not been guilty of breach of trust in failing to press for recovery of the fund until 1832.[28] In December 1842 Ward, who explained that he had been 'maintained by others for some years past', was reduced to soliciting from Peel a place in the patent office which turned out not to exist.[29] He lost his eldest daughter in 1839, his third son Matthew, of the Bengal cavalry, to 'spasmodic cholera, seven days after his marriage', in 1843 and his third daughter in 1845.[30] In 1840 he published a pamphlet on *Monetary Derangements*, in which he advocated replacement of the permanent government debt to the Bank with a short annuity and revision of the discounting system in order to guarantee a sound, reliable metal-based currency. In 1847 he unleashed *Remarks on the Monetary Legislation of Great Britain*, in which he complained that successive governments had undermined mercantile confidence with their inept interference. Ward died at his then London house at 4 Wyndham Place, Bryanston Square in June 1849.[31] By his will, dated 15 June 1849, he transferred his entitlement to half his late son's share in the trust fund and one twentieth of his late eldest daughter's to his second daughter Alicia Frances and second son Henry; his late third daughter's portion had already been assigned to his two other younger children, Arthur and Georgina. Artefacts which he distributed among his family included two

marble cricketing figures, his 'only remaining cricket bat and ball' and an engraving of a Sussex against Kent match at Brighton. His personalty was sworn under a paltry £200 and the entry in the estate duty register was docketed 'insolvent'.[32] Three months later his bother George Henry died without issue, and the extensive and lucrative Northwood and other estates passed to Ward's eldest son William George (1812-82), who had already embarked on his controversial career as a leader of the Oxford Movement, having been received into the Catholic church in 1845.[33]

[1] *Gent. Mag.* (1849), ii. 206; W.P. Ward, *William George Ward and Oxford Movement* (1890), 1-2; *VCH Hants*, v. 250, 268-9; *Farington Diary*, xvi. 5746-7. [2] *Oxford DNB*; *Gent. Mag.* (1849), ii. 206; *The Times*, 14 Jan. 1842, 27 Apr. 1843. [3] *PP* (1819), iii. 75-86, 421-8; (1831-2), vi. 126-49; B. Hilton, *Corn, Cash, Commerce*, 42, 62, 89, 174; Sir J. Clapham, *Bank of England*, ii. 116-17. [4] Lord Harris and F.S. Ashley Cooper, *Lord's and the M.C.C.* 28, 39, 46, 49, 63, 73, 75; Sir P. Warner, *Lord's*, 19-20, 23-24; G.B. Buckley, *Fresh Light on Pre-Victorian Cricket*, 75, 79, 88, 93, 117, 133, 171, 206. [5] *The Times*, 18 Feb. 1820 [6] Ibid. 14 Apr. 1825. [7] Add. 51690, Lansdowne to Holland, 18 Apr.; *The Times*, 8, 13 May, 10, 16, 17, 20 June 1826. [8] Broughton, *Recollections*, iii. 176. [9] *The Times*, 20 Oct. 1826, 20 Feb. 1827. [10] Ibid. 16, 20, 22 June 1827. [11] Harris and Ashley Cooper, 46, 81. [12] Lansdowne mss, Macdonald to Lansdowne, 21 Oct. [1827]. [13] Add. 40395, f. 221; Hilton, 247. [14] *Ellenborough Diary*, i. 261. [15] Ibid. i. 312; Add. 40398, ff. 83, 85, 87; Grey mss, Ellice to Grey, 31 Jan. [1826]. [16] Cent. Kent. Stud. Knatchbull mss U951 C38/8. [17] *The Times*, 6 Apr. 1830. [18] Ibid. 14 Mar. 1831. [19] Ibid. 8, 15 Mar. 1831. [20] *Three Diaries*, 66; *The Times*, 21 Mar. 1831. [21] *The Times*, 25, 27-30 Apr. 1831. [22] Wellington mss WP1/1186/4, 9; Add. 40309, f. 243. [23] *Greville Mems.* ii. 216; Wellington mss WP1/1262/24; M. Brock, *Great Reform Act*, 247; *The Times*, 23-25 Nov. 1831. [24] *PP* (1831-2), vi. 126-49; Hilton, 203, 208. [25] *The Times*, 23, 24, 29, 30 Dec. 1834, 3, 5-8 Jan. 1835; *Greville Mems.* iii. 125, 132, 134, 136; Add. 40407, ff. 213, 215; 40409, f. 82. [26] *The Times*, 8, 16, 27 Apr., 22 July, 24 Aug. 1836, 14 Jan. 1842; PROB 11/1755/256; IR26/1212/83. [27] *The Times*, 30 Dec. 1834; Harris and Ashley Cooper, 49, 97, 266; Warner, 20. [28] *The Times*, 14, 15, 17, 18, 22 Jan. 1842, 27 Apr. 1843. [29] Add. 40520, ff. 142, 144. [30] *Gent. Mag.* (1839), i. 101; (1844), i. 110; (1845), ii. 543. [31] *Gent. Mag.* (1849), ii. 206-7. [32] PROB 11/2097/562; IR26/1854/389. [33] *Gent. Mag.* (1849), ii. 554; *Oxford DNB*.

D.R.F.

WARING MAXWELL, **John** (1788–1869), of Finnebrogue, co. Down.

| DOWNPATRICK | 1820–1830 |
| DOWNPATRICK | 1832–1834 |

b. 1788, 3rd but 1st surv. s. of John Charles Frederick Waring of Belvedere Place, Dublin and Dorothea, da. of Robert Maxwell of Finnebrogue. *m.* 26 Aug. 1817,[1] Madelina Martha, da. of David Ker of Portavo, co. Down, *s.p. suc.* fa. 1802; took additional name of Maxwell by royal lic. 9 Apr. 1803. *d.* 22 Dec. 1869.
   Sheriff, co. Down 1817-18.
   Capt. Inch yeomanry 1811.

Waring Maxwell's father John, lieutenant-colonel of the Down militia, belonged to the Waring family of Waringstown, county Down, one of whom, Samuel, had represented Hillsborough in the early eighteenth century Irish Commons. John was the son of Richard Waring and Sarah, daughter of the Ven. John Maxwell of Falkland, archdeacon of Clogher. In 1783 he married his first cousin, Dorothea, whose father (*d.* 1769), son of the Irish Member and privy counsellor Henry Maxwell of Finnebrogue, was head of a cadet branch of the Maxwells, Lords Farnham. She was heiress to her eldest brother Edward, in recognition of which Waring informally adopted the additional surname of Maxwell. He died 26 Oct. 1802, when, by his will (proved in 1803), he left his estates in trust to his eldest son, before he could have this legally recognized; but his wife obtained a royal licence to this effect for herself and their five children the following year.[2]

Waring Maxwell, who had a minor interest in Down Tory politics, got up an anti-Catholic petition at Inch in April 1819.[3] He offered, on the interest of Lord de Clifford, for the open and venal householder borough of Downpatrick, where he had his estates, at the general election of 1820. After seeing off challenges from other local gentlemen, including his brother-in-law David Ker*, he defeated the radical Edward Ruthven* by 42 votes.[4] In the Commons he voted 'in general' with the Liverpool administration, but was sometimes wayward, which makes it likely that he was occasionally confused with John Maxwell, Whig Member for Renfrewshire.[5] As 'W. Maxwell', he voted for inquiry into military expenditure, 16 May 1820, and against dockyard expenses and the ordnance estimates, 7, 14 May 1821. No doubt hostile to Queen Caroline, he divided in defence of ministers' conduct towards her, 6 Feb. 1821.[6] He was probably not the 'John Maxwell' who voted for more extensive tax reductions to relieve distress, 21 Feb., or abolition of one of the joint-postmasterships, 2 May 1822, but he did apparently divide with opposition for parliamentary reform, 25 Apr.[7] He divided against the Catholic peers bill, 30 Apr. He blamed Irish distress on the tithe system, 20 May, and voted for inquiry into this, 19 June.[8] He was credited with votes in favour of repealing the salt and window taxes, 28 June, 2 July 1822. He divided against the repeal of £2,000,000 of taxes, 3 Mar., and of the assessed taxes, 18 Mar. 1823. He voted for inquiries into the legal proceedings against the Dublin Orange rioters, 22 Apr., and the state of Ireland, 12 May. He apparently voted to condemn the conduct of the lord advocate in the Borthwick case, 3 June, but the 'W. Maxwell' who divided for the Scottish juries bill,

20 June 1823, was probably Sir William Maxwell, Member for Wigtownshire. No trace of parliamentary activity has been found during the 1824 session. He voted for the Irish unlawful societies bill, 25 Feb., and against Catholic relief, 1 Mar., and brought up the hostile Downpatrick petition, 9 Mar. 1825. On 22 Mar. he insisted that his support for committing the relief bill did not amount to a change of heart, but he announced his conversion to the cause, 21 Apr., when he voted for the second reading.[9] Yet he was again listed in the hostile minority on the third reading, 10 May 1825, and thereafter remained an opponent of emancipation. If he was not the Maxwell who spoke for retaining a metallic currency and for tax reductions, 26 May 1826, he made no parliamentary contributions that session. He was returned unopposed for Downpatrick at the general election of 1826.[10]

Waring Maxwell, who signed the anti-Catholic petition from the noblemen and gentlemen of Ireland in February 1827, got up another hostile petition from Inch early that year.[11] He was thanked (including at a dinner in May) for his condemnation of the pro-Catholic petition from Bangor, which was presented on 2 Mar., and brought up a hostile petition from there, 5 Mar.[12] He was listed in the majority against Catholic relief, 6 Mar. 1827, but was absent from the division the following session, during which he was inactive. He was again toasted at a dinner of Bangor Protestants, 8 May, and, having joined the Irish Brunswick Club, he became president of the Downpatrick branch on 14 Nov. 1828.[13] In February 1829 Planta, the Wellington ministry's patronage secretary, classified him as 'opposed to the principle' of Catholic emancipation, but he missed all the divisions in March through illness. He had been entrusted with more hostile petitions from Down, but it was apparently his kinsman Henry Maxwell, Member for Cavan, who brought up the one from Downpatrick, 30 Mar.[14] Yet it was surely he, not Sir William Maxwell, who presented the petition of the North Down militia staff against the reductions in their establishment, 15 May, and he certainly voted against Daniel O'Connell being allowed to take his seat unimpeded, 18 May 1829. He was again said to be unwell during the following session, although he was listed in the minority for transferring East Retford's seats to Birmingham, 5 Mar. 1830.[15]

Facing a contest with Ruthven, Waring Maxwell withdrew at the dissolution in 1830, claiming that he had long been in 'very delicate and uncertain' health.[16] In March 1831 he signed the requisition for the Down county meeting against agitating repeal of the Union.[17] An anti-reformer, he played no part in the

Downpatrick election that year, but was well enough to chair a meeting in defence of the Protestant interest at Inch in January 1832.[18] Described by one radical paper as 'that old Tory hack', he was re-elected unopposed for Downpatrick at the general election of 1832, when Ruthven won a seat at Dublin and another reformer failed to show up.[19] He retired two years later, making way for Ker, but remained an active and 'decided Tory' in local affairs. He died childless in December 1869, leaving the bulk of his estate to his nephew Robert Perceval (1813-1905) of Groomsport, Down, who took the additional surname of Maxwell in 1839.[20]

[1] *Belfast News Letter*, 29 Aug. 1817. [2] PRO NI, Perceval-Maxwell mss D3244/F/2/1; F/23; *Burke Irish Fam. Recs.* (1976) sub (Perceval-) Maxwell, co. Down; *Index to Prerogative Wills of Ireland* ed. Sir A. Vicars, 321; *Hist. Irish Parl.* v. 222-3; vi. 501-2. [3] PRO NI, Castlereagh mss D3030/M/40; Perceval-Maxwell mss G/1/45. [4] *Belfast News Letter*, 28 Mar. 1820; PRO NI, Ker mss D2651/3/36. [5] *Session of Parl. 1825*, p. 476. [6] Perceval-Maxwell mss G/1/9, 10. [7] *Black Bk.* (1823), 177. [8] *The Times*, 21 May 1822. [9] Ibid. 10, 23 Mar. 1825. [10] *Belfast Commercial Chron.* 3, 7, 17 June 1826. [11] Add. 40392, f. 5; Perceval-Maxwell mss G/1/42-5; *Belfast News Letter*, 2 Mar. 1827. [12] Perceval-Maxwell mss G/1/40, 41, 48, 49, 54; *Belfast News Letter*, 19 Jan., 13 Apr., 8 June; *The Times*, 6 Mar. 1827. [13] *Belfast Guardian*, 13 May; *Belfast News Letter*, 18 Nov. 1828; Perceval-Maxwell mss G/1/55. [14] Perceval-Maxwell mss E/7/31, 44; G/1/59. [15] Ibid. E/7/48, 51. [16] Ibid. G/1/65-70; *Belfast News Letter*, 16, 20 July 1830. [17] *Newry Commercial Telegraph*, 18 Mar. 1831. [18] Perceval-Maxwell mss G/1/74, 74A, 75; *Belfast News Letter*, 27 Jan. 1832. [19] *Belfast News Letter*, 11, 18 Dec.; *Newry Examiner*, 15 Dec. 1832. [20] *Downpatrick Recorder*, 24 Dec. 1869; Perceval-Maxwell mss E/58/2.

S.M.F.

WARRE, John Ashley (1787–1860), of West Newton Manor, nr. Taunton, Som.; West Cliff House, Ramsgate, Kent, and 71 Belgrave Square, Mdx.

LOSTWITHIEL	1812–1818
TAUNTON	1820–1826
HASTINGS	1831–1834
RIPON	1857–18 Nov. 1860

b. 5 Oct. 1787, 1st s. of John Henry Warre of Queen Square, Bloomsbury, Mdx. and Belmont Lodge,[1] Herts. and Brathwaite, da. of John Ashley of Barbados. *educ.* Harrow 1796-1804; Christ Church, Oxf. 1804. *m.* (1) 2 Mar. 1819, Susan (*d.* 4 July 1820), da. of John Cornwall of Hendon, Mdx., 1s. *d.v.p.*; (2) 9 June 1823, Florence Catherine (*d.* 17 Sept. 1837), da. of Richard Magenis*, 5s. (2 *d.v.p.*) 1da.; (3) 30 Jan. 1839, Caroline, da. of Pascoe Grenfell*, *s.p. suc.* fa. 1801; uncle Thomas to West Newton and West Cliff 1824. *d.* 18 Nov. 1860
   Charity commr. 1835-7.
   Sheriff, Kent 1848-9.
   Maj. W. Som. militia 1811.

Warre came from an old Somerset family who were settled by about 1400 at Hestercombe, near Taunton, where they remained until the eighteenth century.[2] They had recently prospered through involvement in various branches of foreign and colonial trade, notably port wine, and Warre's father had married a West Indian heiress. Warre had first entered Parliament in 1812 for Lord Mount Edgcumbe's borough of Lostwithiel, but his growing opposition proclivities (he joined Brooks's Club, 7 May 1816) presumably caused his withdrawal from this seat in 1818, when he unsuccessfully contested Weymouth. He came forward on the independent interest at Taunton in 1820, describing himself as 'a warm supporter of the principle of civil and religious liberty' and 'a strenuous advocate for the most rigid economy in every branch of the public service'. He denounced the Six Acts as an 'utterly unnecessary' infringement of popular liberties and argued that their easy passage demonstrated the need for parliamentary reform, which he had previously opposed. However, he did not 'pretend to say in what mode the House of Commons could be amended' and would not 'lend himself to wild, extravagant and dangerous views'. He was returned in second place, five votes ahead of his Tory opponent, and a subsequent scrutiny increased his majority to nine; the contest was said to have involved him in a 'heavy expense'.[3]

He was a regular attender, serving on various committees, and an active figure in the Whig opposition to Lord Liverpool's ministry on most issues, including parliamentary reform, 9, 31 May 1821, 25 Apr., 24 June 1822, 20 Feb., 24 Apr. 1823, 26 Feb. 1824, 13, 27 Apr., 26 May 1826. He voted for Catholic relief, 28 Feb. 1821, 1 Mar., 21 Apr., 10 May 1825. While disclaiming any hostility to 'the splendour of royalty', he complained that the civil list committee did not have adequate powers, 8 May 1820; he was a minority teller for the amendment to defer consideration of its report. He supported the Grampound disfranchisement bill, urging the House not to miss an opportunity to deal with a specific case for reform, 19 May. He was granted one month's leave owing to ill health, 25 May, and another three weeks because of a near relative's illness, 27 June 1820. He made brief interventions during the debates on the address, criticizing the home secretary Lord Sidmouth's selection of addresses for presentation to the king, 23 Jan., and pressing the foreign secretary Lord Castlereagh for information concerning British naval assistance to the king of Naples, 24 Jan. 1821. He inquired as to ministerial intentions regarding coastal patrols to prevent smuggling, arguing that the employment of naval officers for this purpose was 'injurious' to their character, 14 Feb. He spoke briefly in support of a motion concerning fatalities in Sussex arising from the patrols, 22 Mar., and supported a petition for the supply of new life-saving equipment to protect the men thus engaged, 4 June.[4] He moved for inquiry into the imprisonment of the Bowditch family, but withdrew when new facts came to light during the debate, 15 Feb. He maintained that 'the Protestant mind and ... Protestant feeling of this country had ... much changed' on the question of Catholic relief, 12 Mar.[5] He supported a Taunton petition for revision of the criminal law, 29 Mar.[6] He doubted whether the petition from Robert Thorpe complaining of unfair dismissal as chief justice of Sierra Leone was worthy of consideration, 25 May.[7] He backed inquiry into the game laws, 'the source of much crime', 5 Apr. He warned against the 'dangerous precedent' of encouraging petitions against the abolition of offices when ministers proposed it, 19 Apr.[8] He expressed relief at ministerial assurances that Russian troops were not being sent to assist Austria, 7 May, and during the debate on the Austrian loan convention, 22 June, he declared that 'the faith of Austria was not to be depended on'. He was surprised that ministers had offered no explanation concerning the conduct of the Constitutional Association in Ireland, 30 May. He supported the ill treatment of horses bill, arguing that the present law was 'defective', 1 June. He called for more information regarding the claim for compensation by General Desfourneaux, 8 June, thought there was not the 'slightest probability' that it was just, 15 June, and spoke in favour of a greatly reduced grant, 28 June, when he was a majority teller.[9] He successfully moved that the Liverpool extra post bill, which he considered impracticable, be referred to a select committee, 13 June.[10] He spoke four times that day in the debate on the slave trade, to condemn the conduct of foreign powers and demand more vigorous action by British authorities overseas.[11] He voted with ministers against the omission of arrears from the grant to the duke of Clarence, 18 June 1821.

During the discussion on the petition concerning the treatment of the radical agitator Henry Hunt* in Ilchester gaol, 27 Feb. 1822, he argued that a distinction should be made between criminals and those confined for political offences, and warned ministers of the danger of Hunt being 'hailed by the people as a martyr'. He supported inquiry into the prison laws, urging the need to consider the problems arising from the conflict between corporate and local jurisdictions, 5 Mar.[12] He presented a Taunton inhabitants' petition for revision of the criminal code, 25 Mar. He spoke against Hume's motion to cut the army by 10,000 men,

suggesting that the reductions already implemented were 'sufficient', 4 Mar. He argued that public servants' salaries should be the whole of their remuneration, 11 Mar. On 16 May he moved to reduce the cost of the embassy to the Swiss cantons to its 1792 level, which was apparently brought on 'faute de mieux' after other opposition Members had declined to act. It had been postponed two days earlier, ostensibly until the outcome of Barrett Lennard's motion (15 May) for inquiry into diplomatic expenditure was known, but possibly because a heavy defeat was feared after ministers threatened to resign unless they received reliable support from backbenchers. It was reported on the 15th that 'while those Members who voted for Lennard's motion were out on the division, Warre addressed them in the lobby and, having stated his fixed resolution to bring on ... his motion ... requested the attendance of the friends of economy. His communication was received with loud cheers'. Ministers responded by taking vigorous steps to ensure a good turnout by their supporters, and although Warre was studiously careful to avoid any personal criticism of the ambassador, the Grenvillite Henry Williams Wynn†, concentrating instead on the argument that Switzerland was less important than when Britain had been at war with France, his motion attracted little support from beyond the ranks of the regular opposition and was defeated by 247-141; he was a minority teller.[13] He presented a Somerset petition for a small debts recovery bill, 15 Mar., and petitions from the owners of silk mills in Taunton against the navigation laws, 31 May, and silk weavers against the warehousing bill, 17 June. He spoke and was a majority teller for Canning's Catholic peers bill, 30 Apr. On a petition from individuals arrested under the revenue laws and impressed into the navy, 8 July 1822, he indicated that he would have raised the matter himself had it not been placed in other hands.[14]

He inquired, 'in a low tone of voice', as to the conclusions reached by the foreign trade committee on the wine duties, 17 Feb. 1823.[15] Next day he seconded a motion for inquiry into the recovery of small debts.[16] He spoke against bringing up the report on the National Debt Reduction Acts, 6 Mar.[17] He approved of the profane swearing bill, 18 Mar. He asked Canning, the foreign secretary, whether anything had been agreed at the Congress of Aix La Chapelle beyond confirmation of the treaties of 1815, 26 Mar. He hoped that official papers would show that ministers had protested against interference by the Allies in Spain's affairs, 27 Mar. In a partially inaudible speech, 22 Apr. 1823, he pressed Canning to state whether the Congress of Verona had agreed anything to justify French intervention in Spain.[18] He asked whether ministers intended to continue the preventive force against smuggling in its present form, 16 Feb. 1824. He presented a Taunton petition for repeal of the coal duties, 18 Feb. He argued that reduction of the wine duties should be viewed not as a means of relief to the consumer, but as a way to increase consumption to benefit the revenue, 22 Mar. He inquired as to the truth of reports that the docks at Sherness and Chatham were too small to accommodate first-class ships, 23 Feb.[19] He made more observations on the Austrian loan convention, doubting that the emperor was a man of 'strict honour and fine feeling', 24 Feb. He criticized the grant for the completion of work on the Caledonian Canal, 'a useless speculation', 1 Mar., and moved the rejection of the Bristol and Taunton Canal bill, 30 Mar., acting as a minority teller.[20] He presented a petition from Taunton silk throwsters against the proposed regulations affecting their trade, 11 Mar. He blamed the conduct of the continental autocracies for the refugee problem, 23 Mar., 2, 12 Apr. He supported the grant for building new churches, 12 Apr., arguing that many people in the large towns would attend services if sufficient places were available and denying that he was motivated by hostility to Nonconformists; he acted purely out of 'reverence to the church in which he was bred'. He believed that the uninformed sections of society ought not to be exposed to the doctrines of atheists, 3 June. During the debate on a petition against the Catholic Association, 31 May, he denied that the bulk of the Catholic population were indifferent to emancipation, but 'regretted that Catholics of birth, character, and influence did not unite to place the cause under their own guidance'. On a petition condemning the prosecution of the Methodist missionary John Smith in Demerara, 10 June 1824, he pointed to the wider issue of the 'wanton cruelty' towards black prisoners. That day he favoured an inquiry into the 'untenable' system of naval impressment.

He advised against suppressing the Catholic Association, 11 Feb. 1825, as it would only be revived in some other form while it represented 'the feelings and sentiments of six millions of people' who were in an 'anomalous and irreconcilable state'. He presented petitions from Watchet against the coal duty, 17 Feb., and Taunton for equalization of the land tax, 23 Feb. He once more supported the introduction of the ill treatment of animals bill, though professing himself unfamiliar with its details, 24 Mar. He supported the motion for papers regarding the state of the Indian army, a matter on which 'it was time to feel alarm and adopt inquiry', 25 Mar. He moved the rejection of the

duke of Cumberland's annuity bill and was a minority teller, 9 June 1825. He opposed an inquiry into the state of the silk trade, 24 Feb. 1826, rejecting any suggestion of a return to the system of prohibition and measures which might 'tend to impede the march of principles which he felt perfectly convinced were for the public good'. He approved of the government's promissory notes bill, 27 Feb., observing that 'the lower classes, particularly, had no choice ... but to take this trash'. He supported the bill for a more effectual execution of the law in local jurisdictions in Ireland, arguing that it should be extended to England, 9 Mar. In the debate on the electoral bribery bill, 14 Mar., he contended that the existing law was sufficient to deal with corruption and that the Commons needed more time for hearing petitions; it was necessary to reform the electors as well as the elected. He lamented that 'the existence of the most gross and criminal corruption was notorious and undenied', 26 May. He now spoke against the cruelty to cattle bill, believing that enough legislation had been enacted in this area, 16 Mar.; yet he presented next day a petition from clergy and inhabitants of London for measures to prevent cruelty to animals. He expressed sympathy for the West Indian planters, who had been unjustly attacked by abolitionists, 29 Apr., declaring that he was 'no enemy to the cause of negro improvement, when temperately and properly conducted, but he felt deeply the difficulties of the question'. He presented a petition from inhabitants of Dominica and St. Vincent urging that no legislation regarding slavery be carried without prior inquiry, 17 May 1826.

In the summer of 1825 Warre and his Whig colleague Alexander Baring came under intense pressure at Taunton, owing to their support for Catholic relief. Warre issued a public letter in August, expressing the hope that he would be supported at the next general election, but the following month Baring announced his intention of standing down and Warre subsequently informed the electors that he was unwilling to engage in a contest which must 'entail upon me an expense which, for private reasons, I do not wish to incur'; he duly retired at the dissolution in 1826.[21] Shortly before the general election of 1830 he was pressed by the Taunton Whigs for an immediate decision on whether he would stand again, but he declined to do so, apparently on the ground of expense; it was later alleged that the object of the approach had been to elicit a refusal from him in order to smooth the path for another candidate.[22] He offered instead for Hastings, where he was adopted by the Reform Association which was seeking to liberate the borough from corporation control. He failed on this occasion but was returned unopposed at the general election of 1831, following a compromise between the reformers and the corporation.[23]

Warre defended the Grey ministry's decision not to prosecute Daniel O'Connell, given the paramount importance of carrying its reform bill, 27 June 1831. He divided for the second reading of the reintroduced bill, 6 July, and voted steadily for its details. He protested at the language used by Hunt towards the Lancashire Member Heywood, 8 July, declaring that 'nothing can be more injurious to the people than to pledge a Member to whatever might take place at a public election', and ridiculing Hunt's assertion that there had been a long term trend towards the disfranchisement of the people. He supported the enfranchisement of new boroughs, 3 Aug., arguing that they would return 'men of talents and integrity' rather than demagogues, and having no fears about the ability of county Members to defend their constituents' interests. He spoke against allowing 40s. freeholders to vote in boroughs, 20 Aug., as this would cause 'considerable inconvenience and injury', making many boroughs too unwieldy and introducing a potentially corrupt element into them. He voted for the bill's passage, 21 Sept., and for Lord Ebrington's confidence motion, 10 Oct. On the vote to defray the expenses incurred in supporting negroes liberated from the slave trade, 18 July, he urged government to consider whether this should be continued when other countries, lacking Britain's 'moral feeling' on the subject, gave no assistance. He divided with ministers to punish only those guilty of bribery at the Dublin election, 23 Aug. On 7 Sept. he observed that the debate on the wine duties bill was reminiscent of earlier ones, 'when we first endeavoured to emancipate ourselves from the trammels of our old commercial code', and that the dire predictions made then had been falsified. He voted for the second reading of the revised reform bill, 17 Dec. 1831, and for its details, although local interest prompted him to support a Ramsgate petition for its union with Sandwich, 14 Mar. 1832. He divided for the third reading, 22 Mar., and for Ebrington's motion for an address asking the king to appoint only ministers committed to carry an unimpaired measure, 10 May. After the bill's passage, he asked whether tenants whose landlords neglected to pay over their rates would be eligible to vote, 13 July. He voted with ministers on the Russian-Dutch loan, 26 Jan., 12, 16 July, relations with Portugal, 9 Feb., and the navy civil departments bill, 6 Apr., but was in the minority for a tax on absentee Irish landlords, 19 June. He voted to make coroners' inquests public, 20 June 1832.

Warre was again returned for Hastings as a 'reformer' at the general election of 1832, but retired in 1834. He stood there unsuccessfully in 1847 and 1852 before being returned for Ripon as a Liberal in 1857.[24] He died in November 1860 and left his estates to his eldest son, John Henry Warre (1825-94).

[1] Sold after his death to John Kingston† (J. Cass, *East Barnet*, 148). [2] J. Collinson, *Som.* (1791), iii. 259-63; *VCH Som.* iv. 44. [3] *Taunton Courier*, 16 Feb., 15 Mar., 5 Apr.; Grey mss, Tierney to Grey, 22 Mar. 1820. [4] *The Times*, 23 Mar., 5 June 1821. [5] Ibid. 13 Mar. 1821. [6] Ibid. 30 Mar. 1821. [7] Ibid. 26 May 1821. [8] Ibid. 20 Apr. 1821. [9] Ibid. 9, 16, 29 June 1821. [10] Ibid. 14 June 1821. [11] Ibid. 14 June 1821. [12] Ibid. 6 Mar. 1822. [13] Add. 75939, Lady to Lord Spencer, 13 May; NLW mss 2794 D, Sir W. to H. Williams Wynn, 15 May; *The Times*, 15, 16 May 1822; Buckingham, *Mems. Geo. IV*, i. 327; A. Mitchell, *Whigs in Opposition*, 165-6. [14] *The Times*, 9 July 1822. [15] Ibid. 18 Feb. 1823. [16] Ibid. 19 Feb. 1823. [17] Ibid. 7 Mar. 1823. [18] Ibid. 27 Mar., 23 Apr. 1823. [19] Ibid. 24 Feb. 1824. [20] Ibid. 31 Mar. 1824. [21] *Bristol Mirror*, 4 June, 27 Aug.; *Taunton Courier*, 24 Aug., 21 Sept. 1825. [22] *Taunton Courier*, 18, 25 Aug. 1830. [23] *The Times*, 2 Aug. 1830, 3 May 1831. [24] *Dod's Parl. Companion* (1833), 173; (1857), 297.

T.A.J.

WARREN, Charles (1764–1829), of 15 Bedford Square, Mdx. and Sundridge, Kent.

DORCHESTER   18 June 1819–1826

b. 19 Mar. 1764, 3rd but 2nd surv. s. of Richard Warren (*d.* 1797), MD, physician in ordinary to George III, and Elizabeth, da. of Peter Shaw, MD, physician in ordinary to George II and George III. *educ.* Westminster 1774; Jesus, Camb. 1782, fellow 1786-1813; L. Inn 1781, called 1790. *m.* 9 July 1813, Amelia, da. of Charles Sloper of Sundridge, *s.p. d.* 12 Aug. 1829.

Commr. of bankrupts 1790-1816; chan. diocese of Bangor 1797-d.; KC 8 Mar. 1816; att.-gen. to prince of Wales May 1819-Jan. 1820; c.j. Chester circuit June 1819-d.

Bencher, L. Inn 1816, treas. 1821, librarian 1822.

Warren, whose father and maternal grandfather were noted royal physicians, was initially an advanced Whig and enjoyed a successful practice, at 4 Stone Buildings, Lincoln's Inn, as a counsel in election cases; he acted, for instance, on behalf of the opponents of the Grosvenor interest at Chester in 1818.[1] Yet his cynical decision to throw in his lot with Lord Liverpool's ministry in 1819, by accepting a Welsh judgeship, with a salary of about £1,000, destroyed his career and resulted in his public humiliation.[2] As Sir George Philips* recounted in the mid-1840s:

Warren was the best and most leading counsel in parliamentary committees of that day. The same preference was given to him as is now given to [Charles] Austin.

His political opinions were democratical to an extreme. They went far beyond those of most Ultra Whigs. Lord Castlereagh* having conceived a high notion of his talents, thought him worth bribing, and he was ready enough to be bribed. The report of what was going on between them was soon circulated. One of the leading members of the Whig party (Creevey*) saw him early one morning at Lord Castlereagh's door, and going up to him, said 'I have caught you in the fact'. Castlereagh made him chief justice of Chester, meaning to advance him, as he might have opportunities of doing. He seemed however to have lost his talents with his principles, for no man ever proved himself in my time so incompetent a judge. He could not even state the evidence correctly in his charges to the jury, and the counsel on both sides were obliged to point out to him his unintentional omissions and misrepresentations. Lord Castlereagh afterwards called him 'my bad bargain'.[3]

Having been provided with a seat for Dorchester by the ministerialist Lord Shaftesbury in June 1819, when he became a freeman of the borough, Warren defended the government's repressive policies and was taunted for his desertion of opposition.[4] He was returned unopposed for Dorchester at the general election of 1820.

Following an (ultimately unsuccessful) application in king's bench, 22 Apr. 1820, for a retrial in the case of the king v. Sir Charles Wolseley and Joseph Harrison, whom Warren had found guilty of seditious activity at a meeting in Stockport the previous summer, the Whig James Macdonald* wrote to Edward Davies Davenport* on the 24th that

the rat Warren is likely to receive such a set down as no man in a judicial character ever yet has. A new trial is likely to be granted on account of his most flagrant and iniquitous summing up at Chester. This will be followed by a motion in Parliament to exclude the Welsh judges from the House of Commons.[5]

Warren vindicated the Welsh judicature on a motion for inquiry, 1 June, when he attacked Lord John Russell for apparently having stated (in the debate on the civil list, 8 May) that being dependent on government for promotion he would support their measures, however unconstitutional; he concluded by boasting that 'he could, even from his practice before committees above stairs, soon contrive to earn enough to purchase a moiety of the fee simple of the salary which that office afforded'. The anomalous position of his judicial appointment being compatible with a seat in Parliament was criticized by Creevey, who said that for 20 years Sir Francis Burdett* had been 'uniformly the subject of his most fervent panegyric', and Russell, who declared that if Warren 'actually thought his character stood higher in the country in consequence

of his recent change, he should only say, that he wished the learned gentleman joy of his taste and judgement'. Condemnation was swift and universal, because, as Philips put it, he showed 'such a low and sordid character of mind in his mode of venerating himself, that even his new friends could not fail to be disgusted with him'. Charles Williams Wynn* reported to his wife that 'Warren was certainly well roasted and made as angry, as vain and as bad a speech as ever I heard'; and, according to Sir James Mackintosh*, Warren 'made a wretched figure ... He struggled ineffectually to conceal his agitation under the appearance of a gross and vulgar buffoonery which much resembled a total indifference to character'.[6] Warren, who was portrayed in one satire blacking George IV's jackboots and was denounced in a radical publication as 'a notorious RAT', thereafter lacked any political credibility.[7]

He spoke in favour of the king's bench proceedings bill, 20 June 1820. He seconded the treasury secretary Stephen Rumbold Lushington's motion to recommit the marriage bill and was a teller for the minority, 30 June. He was added to the select committee on election polls, 3 July. He called Phillimore's resolution declaring illegal the paying of out-voters at Grantham 'crude and ill-digested', 12 July 1820, when he was a teller for the hostile minority, and the following day he commented on the offences at sea bill.[8] He divided against condemning ministers' conduct towards Queen Caroline, 6 Feb. 1821. He was granted leave to go the Chester circuit, 23 Mar., and for a fortnight on account of ill health, 2 May 1821. He voted against more extensive tax reductions to relieve distress, 11 Feb., abolition of one of the joint-postmasterships, 13 Mar., and inquiry into the conduct of the lord advocate relative to the press in Scotland, 25 June; and for the aliens bill, 29 July, and the grant for government proclamations in the Irish newspapers, 22 July 1822. He divided against parliamentary reform, 20 Feb., and alteration of the Scottish representative system, 2 June 1823. He sided with ministers against rescinding the tax on houses valued under £5, 10 Mar., and limiting the sinking fund to the real surplus of revenue, 13 Mar. He divided against repeal of the Foreign Enlistment Act, 16 Apr., and inquiry into chancery administration, 5 June 1823. No evidence of parliamentary activity has been traced for the 1824 session. He voted for the Irish unlawful societies bill, 25 Feb., and against Catholic relief, 1 Mar. 1825. He divided in favour of the duke of Cumberland's annuity bill, 6, 10 June 1825. His only other known vote was against condemning the Jamaican slave trials, 2 Mar. 1826.

Liverpool had envisaged the possibility of Warren leaving the House in January 1824, but he did not retire until the dissolution in 1826.[9] Later that year the barrister John Campbell II* noted the opinion of John Copley*, the new master of the rolls, on his failure in the Commons in 1820: 'poor Warren, he did not know how to carry it off. He defended himself instead of attacking his accusers'. To this Campbell was tempted to reply, '*Ille crucem sceleris*, etc. You have a crown and he has a cross'. Elderly and in poor health, his official duties were largely taken over by the second judge Thomas Jervis[†], and it was he, not Warren, who gave written evidence to the common law commissioners, whose first report was published in February 1829. He was the last chief justice of Chester, none being appointed to replace him before the court of session there was abolished under the Administration of Justice Act of 1830.[10] Warren died at Sundridge in August 1829.[11] Philips, who commented that 'what makes Charles Warren's case the worse is, that all his family were virtuous and excellent people', believed that he

> proved as worthless in private as he had done in public life. He robbed his nephews and nieces, of whom he was the guardian, of a great part, if not the whole, of their fortunes. I have been told that he also defrauded his widow.[12]

By his will, dated 17 Dec. 1825, Warren left his wife his entire estate, which included personalty sworn under £14,000 (resworn under £16,000 in 1831), 'knowing she will be kind to such of my relations as may require her assistance and to those persons who have been dependent on me'. He bequeathed a Gainsborough portrait of his father to his brother, the society doctor Pelham Warren (1778-1835).[13]

[1] *Report of Committee on Late Controverted Election for Chester* (1819), 18; J. Hemingway, *Hist. Chester* (1831), ii. 417. [2] *Extraordinary Red Bk.* (1821), 237; *Black Bk.* (1823), 376; *PP* (1822), iv. 349 gives £900 in 1821. [3] Warws. RO MI 247, Philips mems. i. 396-7. [4] C.H. Mayo, *Municipal Recs. of Dorchester*, 434; *HP Commons, 1790-1820*, v. 491. [5] *The Times*, 12, 13, 24 Apr., 13, 16 May 1820; JRL, Bromley Davenport mss. [6] Philips mems. i. 397, 400; NLW, Coedymaen mss 939; Add. 52444, f. 125. [7] M.D. George, *Cat. of Pol. and Personal Satires*, x. 14217; *Black Bk.* (1823), 201. [8] *The Times*, 14 July 1820. [9] Add. 40304, f. 214. [10] *PP* (1829), ix. 211-12; Sir W. Holdsworth, *Hist. English Law* (1856), i. 131-2; W.R. Williams, *Hist. Great Sessions in Wales*, 54-55. [11] *Gent. Mag.* (1829), ii. 188. [12] Philips mems. i. 395-6, 400-2. [13] PROB 8/222; 11/1764/742.

S.M.F.

WARRENDER, Sir George, 4th bt. (1782–1849), of Lochend, Dunbar, Haddington; Cliveden, Bucks., and Bruntsfield House, Edinburgh.

HADDINGTON BURGHS	1807–1812
TRURO	1812–1818
SANDWICH	1818–1826
WESTBURY	1826–1830
HONITON	1830–1832

b. 5 Dec. 1782, 1st s. of Sir Patrick Warrender[†], 3rd bt., of Lochend and Helen, da. of James Blair of Dunbar.[1] *educ.* Christ Church, Oxf. 1799; Trinity Coll. Camb. 1811. *m.* 3 Oct. 1810, Hon. Evelyn Boscawen, da. of George Evelyn, 3rd Visct. Falmouth, *s.p. suc.* fa. as 4th bt. 14 June 1799; cos. Hugh Warrender, writer to signet, to Bruntsfield 1820. *d.* 21 Feb. 1849.

Ld. of admiralty Oct. 1812-Feb. 1822; commr. bd. of control Feb. 1822-Feb. 1828; PC 4 Feb. 1822.

Dir. (extraordinary) Bank of Scotland 1822-8.

Lt.-col. Berwick, Haddington, Linlithgow and Peebles militia 1805.

Warrender, a former Grenvillite Whig who had defected to take junior office in the Liverpool ministry in 1812 and so branded himself as a 'rat', often cut a preposterous figure. A fat, garrulous and rather stupid man, he was pompous, quick-tempered and coarse.[2] Despite his ancestry, title and inherited property in Haddingtonshire there was, so Lady Gower thought, a '*parvenu*-feeling' about him;[3] and Luttrell the wag pronounced that 'the two most disgusting things in the world, because you cannot deny them, are Warrender's wealth, and John Croker's* talents'.[4] His frequent and lavish dinner parties earned him the sobriquet of 'Sir Gorgeous Provender'.[5] His marriage was a bad one, as his wife admitted to Croker in 1819, when she formally separated from him and went to live abroad.[6]

At the general election of 1820 Warrender was again returned unopposed for Sandwich on the government interest, having turned down Lord Falmouth's offer to bring him in for his former seat at Truro.[7] He assured his admiralty chief Lord Melville, the government's Scottish manager, that he had 'done everything I could to ensure the return' of the ministerialist Sir James Grant Suttie for Haddingtonshire, where he encountered 'hostility' to his own pretensions to the county, in which Melville had 'encouraged' him.[8] He was named to the select committees on Scottish burgh reform, 4 May 1820, 16 Feb. 1821. He handled the navy estimates, 17 May, 9 June, when he boasted of a reduction of £114,000 and replied to Hume's criticisms of the grant for naval shipbuilding.[9] On 12 June he was given three weeks' leave on account of the illness of his father's first cousin Hugh Warrender, deputy keeper of the signet and crown agent in Scotland. He had in fact died four days earlier, having bequeathed all his property, which included the 'gloomy, but comfortable and dignified' Edinburgh mansion of Bruntsfield and a smaller house at 625 Castle Hill, to Warrender; the residual personal estate was calculated at almost £74,000.[10] Warrender voted with his colleagues against economies in revenue collection, 4 July. In December 1820 Sir William Rae*, the lord advocate, told Melville that he 'would not be a desirable candidate' for Haddington Burghs in the event of a vacancy.[11]

In a debate on Scottish petitions in support of Queen Caroline, 31 Jan. 1821, Warrender admitted her popularity among those 'least informed', but declared that 'the great mass of the persons of landed property in Scotland were decidedly friendly to ministers'. He was hounded by Creevey, Hume and others when he presented the navy estimates, 2 Feb.; and according to Creevey he 'was so cursed sore upon my fire into him ... that he did nothing but bluster and vow vengeance upon me ... at White's, telling everyone that the first opportunity, he would blow me up sky high in the House of Commons'. Creevey decided to 'anticipate his shot', and on 14 Feb. attacked Warrender as 'a sinecure and sham lord' of the admiralty, 'once himself a tip-top patriot ... who combatted much for retrenchment'. Warrender, he later wrote, 'looked like the damnest idiot you ever saw, and could not produce a single word in reply'; but the following day Warrender demanded a private apology through Lord Binning* who, with Creevey's representative General Ronald Ferguson*, reached 'a settlement' after four hours' negotiation.[12] For the first time since 1813, Warrender voted for Catholic relief, 28 Feb. 1821. He again clashed with Hume and other critics of the navy estimates, 4 May, when the radical Whig Henry Grey Bennet* dismissed his speech as 'weak, flippant, bad', and 7 May, when he defeated a proposed inquiry into dockyard expenditure by 82-27.[13] He presented a Dumfriesshire landowners' petition against the Scottish juries bill, 9 May 1821.[14] By the end of the year it was known that he wished to leave the admiralty, and in February 1822, as part of the reshuffle which took in his quondam friends the Grenvillites, he was moved to the less demanding India board.[15] Opposing reduction of the number of junior admiralty lords, 1 Mar., he recalled his own heavy workload, which had kept him in London for five consecutive summers. To general hilarity he blundered on:

In fact, the duties of the office so much interfered with his private pursuits, arrangements and interests, that it had formed one strong ground with him relinquishing a situation he had long held, and with so much satisfaction.

(Robert Hay, Melville's private secretary, 1812-23, told Greville in 1830 that in his experience Warrender ranked second only to Sir George Murray* for total inefficiency in office.)[16]

Warrender played host to an eclectic range of guests during the king's visit to Edinburgh in August 1822, when he was supposed to be in unrequited love with the young widow, the Vicomtesse de Noailles.[17] His younger brother John's marriage to a daughter of the earl of Lauderdale the following year gave him the chance to be 'very magnificent'. To the 'great amusement' of Edward Ellice*, he was seated next to Creevey at a private London dinner, 10 Feb. 1824. Creevey, who never tired of baiting him, boasted that 'I cracked my jokes with such success that Old Rat Warrender was compelled to ask me to drink wine with him, though he was infernally annoyed all the time, and made a most precipitate retreat after dinner'.[18] He was not conspicuous in the House in these years. He presented a Berwickshire petition for repeal of the duties on foreign wool, 25 Mar. 1824.[19] By the end of that year he had bought the attractive estate of Cliveden, near Maidenhead, where he carried out a 'substantial repair' to the old and fire damaged house.[20] He had attached himself politically to Canning, the foreign secretary, whom he dined 'very often'.[21] He voted for Catholic relief, 1 Mar., 21 Apr., 10 May 1825. He presented Haddingtonshire and Roxburghshire petitions against alteration of the corn laws, 28 Apr.[22] On 6 June 1825 he defended the duke of Cumberland's annuity, provoking derisive laughter with his observation that he and his duchess were 'at present enjoying the highest degree of domestic happiness and comfort'. He presented petitions against interference with the Scottish banking system, 28 Feb., 15 Mar., 10 Apr., 9 May, and one from Jedburgh for the abolition of slavery, 5 May 1826.[23]

At the general election that summer Warrender abandoned Sandwich, pleading 'the state of my health', and came in unopposed for Westbury with its patron, Sir Manasseh Masseh Lopes.[24] He voted for Catholic relief, 6 Mar., and for the spring guns bill, 23 Mar. 1827. On the formation of Canning's ministry in April a joke, attributed to Lady Morley, became current that Warrender, one of 'Canning's toads', was to 'share the office of privy seal with [Lord] Dudley; Warrender to be the privy'.[25] He kept his place at the India board and in the House, 3 May, deplored the breakdown of 'neutrality' on the Catholic question, which had 'very nearly lost him his election' (Masseh Lopes was anti-Catholic.) He pledged his 'most zealous aid' to the new ministry in defiance of the 'factious course' pursued by Canning's erstwhile colleagues, particularly Peel. Canning told the king that this was 'a sentiment only important from the manner in which it was generally received'.[26] The following day Peel's brother William made fun of Warrender for being 'ready even to sacrifice his dinner' to support Canning. Warrender replied that he was, but that 'there seemed to be a little too much soreness among some Members ... for the loss of places to allow them fully to enjoy themselves'. Edward Littleton* later claimed that he and Warrender were the only personal friends of Canning to whom no favours were offered.[27] Warrender welcomed Williams Wynn's proposal to consolidate the regulations for dealing with controverted elections, 8 May, and spoke against an amendment to the Dunbar harbour bill, 15 June 1827; he was a teller for the majority.[28]

In October 1826 Warrender had written to Melville on the subject of a 'considerable' balance of money allegedly owed by the treasury to the estate of Hugh Warrender on account of his 'secret and confidential services' as crown agent. He evidently got no satisfaction, and in July 1827 voiced his grievance to Melville's kinsman William Johnstone Hope*, who reported to the Scottish solicitor-general John Hope that he

> talked a great deal of nonsense. At the same time, he talked of the ill usage he had met with from Lord Melville, but I own I could not discover in what he had been injured. But he held out a *threat*, that I think you ought to know and perhaps would be glad to put out of his power to execute. It was, 'that it was lucky for the Melville interest in Scotland that he was an *honourable* man, as he had in his possession ... all the accounts of the secret service money that was disbursed in Scotland for the whole time Hugh Warrender was crown agent, and that he could a tale unfold'.

Johnstone Hope was inclined to buy him off, but John Hope, who thought 'Warrender's jaw is so loose that one cannot rely on there being even the pretext of a foundation for what he says', was prepared to call his bluff; and Melville declared that 'he might have advertised ... [the vouchers] in all the newspapers, as far as I cared, either on my father's or my own account'.[29] That was presumably the end of the matter. After Canning's death Warrender told Huskisson, his political heir, that he would act with him, but that he could not 'have any kind of feeling in common' with the former Tory ministers who had hounded Canning to the grave.[30] It

was reported in November that Warrender, possibly under the influence of Lauderdale, seemed 'inclined to go against [Lord Goderich's] government';[31] and Huskisson, unwilling to credit a story that he had 'become a *frondeur*', asked Lord Binning* if he had noticed 'any symptoms of this disease coming upon him before he left Scotland'. Binning replied, 2 Dec. 1827:

> Warrender's language when I saw him ... was rather tending to despondency than *fronde*, and he quoted certainly pretty high authority for some of the gloomy views he took. With respect to Scotland he has been a *frondeur* from the beginning, taking always as I thought, very unsound views of the real interests of ... [Canning] and his government ... But I suppose he must have been haranguing while he was in London, for I received a letter from him from thence in which he says that he concludes he shall be supposed to be a *frondeur* ... I believe that let him talk as he will, he is desirous to uphold the present government, and to act with the friends of Canning. He always speaks of you with real interest and regard. He is, as old Dean Jackson used to tell him, 'a *strange* creature'.[32]

On the collapse of the Goderich ministry and the duke of Wellington's accession to power Warrender, though professedly not upset by Huskisson's acceptance of office, resigned his place at the India board; he told Melville, the new president, that he had asked Goderich the previous September not to include him in any future commission.[33]

Warrender disapproved the reference in the king's speech to Navarino as an 'untoward' event, 31 Jan. 1828. On 18 Feb. he defended Huskisson against charges of inconsistency, but said he could not give 'entire confidence' to the new ministry because of its 'decided opposition to the Catholic question'. He presented petitions for repeal of the Test Acts, 22 Feb., and voted thus, 26 Feb. When Peel flounced out of the chamber in pique with a phalanx of ministerialists during the debate on the formal resolution for repeal two days later, Warrender 'poured a violent philippic' on him. The Whig Lord Milton* thought his speech 'admirable' but, like the Canningite Lord George Cavendish Bentinck*, considered its effect was ruined when Warrender 'ate up his words as fast as he had uttered them' on being told that Peel, who returned to hear the end of his attack, had left merely to avoid the division.[34] On Williams Wynn's scheme to improve election committee procedure, 3 Apr., Warrender suggested the appointment of an assessor to advise on legal technicalities. He brought up the report on the Aberdeen harbour bill, 5 May, and was a teller for the minority in the subsequent division. He voted for Catholic relief, 12 May. After the Huskissonites' resignation from the ministry he praised Wellington's military services but expressed 'apprehensions in respect of the continuance of his civil career', 30 May. He was one of 'the ejected liberals as mustered in [the] House of Commons', 3 June, and voted against government for inquiry into the Irish church, 24 June, and reduction of the salary of the lieutenant-general of the ordnance, 4 July 1828.[35] The following month he speculated that Huskisson, reportedly depressed and ill in Switzerland, had regrets about 'his mode of leaving office' and, in a change of tune, avowed that Wellington was 'the only man in England' who could settle the Irish problem.[36] Many years later Littleton wrote that Warrender did much socially to promote the views of the Huskissonite group and accomplished a great deal 'towards cementing the confederacy' against Wellington.[37] Warrender disputed Lord Chandos's assertion that majority opinion in Buckinghamshire was hostile to Catholic relief, 16 Feb. 1829, and the following day forecast that emancipation would pacify Ireland. He voted for it, 6, 30 Mar., but, as he explained on 17 Mar., he could not, as one 'opposed to parliamentary reform', accept the Irish 40s. freeholders bill. He was in the small minorities against it, 19, 20 Mar., and on the 26th argued that the proposed criterion of value would give landlords too much knowledge of their tenants' financial circumstances. He supported the militia suspension bill, 23 Mar., but, 'as a representative of the people', he joined Huskisson in opposing the proposed increase in Scottish judicial salaries, 21 May 1829.

He voted for the amendment to the address, 4 Feb., and, from the government side of the House, 12 Feb. 1830, praised the Whig Sir James Graham's speech advocating retrenchment. He voted for the transfer of East Retford's seats to Birmingham, 11 Feb., 5 Mar., and for inquiry into alleged electoral malpractice at Newark by the duke of Newcastle; but he divided against Lord Blandford's reform scheme, 18 Feb., and the enfranchisement of Birmingham, Leeds and Manchester, 23 Feb. He supported the navy estimates, 1 Mar., though he agreed with some of Hume's detailed criticisms. He also questioned the accuracy of Hume's statement of the extent of distress, yet on 15 Mar. he insisted that it was so bad in Perthshire that he could not raise 'a farthing of rent' on his local estates. He was in the opposition minorities on British involvement in Portugal, 10 Mar., and the Terceira incident, 28 Apr. He spoke and voted for Graham's unsuccessful motion to subsume the treasurership of the navy in another office, 12 Mar., but opposed Smith's bid to reduce its salary by £1,200, 22 Mar., blaming the House and not the government, in which he now professed to have 'the greatest confidence', for the rejec-

tion of the earlier proposal. He voted for a revision of taxation, 25 Mar., and to do away with the post of lieutenant-general of the ordnance, 29 Mar.; but he opposed an attempt to reduce the salary of the chief treasury clerk because it was 'mistaken economy to attempt to pare down the salaries of efficient public officers', 10 May. That day he presented Scottish petitions against any increase in spirit duty and to extend jury trial to the provincial courts. He voted against government for abolition of the Irish lord lieutenancy, 11 May, information on privy councillors' emoluments, 14 May, and against the grant for consular services, 11 June. On 18 June he called for the Scottish court of session bill to be postponed and got ministers to admit that it was intended as a foundation for increases in judges' salaries. He threatened to divide the House against its third reading, 21 June, but when it came on, 23 June, he agreed not to do so in return for being allowed to rehearse his objections to it, which no one could understand. At the same time he tried to discomfit Rae by pointing out that he had been passed over for the post of chief baron of the exchequer in favour of the renegade Whig James Abercromby*, elevated by the very men who had denounced him for joining Canning's ministry as judge advocate. Warrender's prediction that the measure would be substantially amended in the Lords proved inaccurate. He voted against the increase in recognizances required by the libel law bill, 9 July 1830.

At the subsequent general election Warrender came in unopposed for the venal borough of Honiton and was 'a happy witness' of the return of the Whig Ferguson for Nottingham. He took a prominent part in the Haddingtonshire contest, supporting George Grant Suttie, one of the county's 'great landed proprietors', in unavailing opposition to the ministerialist outsider Lord John Hay. In a controversial speech he referred to his own pledge of 1820 'never to trouble the county' as a candidate and deplored the 'somewhat new and extraordinary' degree of government interference there and elsewhere:

> He would tell ministers ... such was the view taken by the public of their interference, that they would lose all the counties and great towns in England, though they might gain by it in the rotten boroughs and in Scotland ... He did not wish it to be supposed that he had become a convert to any wild scheme of parliamentary reform. He had always uniformly voted against it, because he had always considered that the elective franchise was wisely distributed and fairly exercised; but from what he had recently seen he doubted very much whether at the end of this general election he might continue of the same opinion.

Hay asked him what property he had at Honiton.[38] Ministers listed Warrender as one of 'the Huskisson party' and Brougham counted his return as a gain for opposition. After Huskisson's death he told Graham that he hoped to see a junction between the Whigs and the Huskissonite rump; and on 6 Oct. 1830 he wrote to Littleton:

> I anxiously hope nothing may arise to break up our little society in the House of Commons. We are all so well together and there is nothing so delightful ... as a small and united party who command general respect both in the House and in the country, and who avoid the extremes to which others go.

He was hostile to 'a second junction with Peel and the duke', but considered some of Brougham's recent speeches on reform to have been 'quite wild'.[39] On the eve of the new session he told Sir John Hamilton Dalrymple[†] of his pleasure that the Huskissonite leaders, with whom he enjoyed 'cordial union and consultation', would have no truck with the beleagured government and that 'although co-operating with, we are not joined to the Whigs'. As for the expected showdown on reform, he had 'not decided what I shall do', having 'never yet voted for reform in any shape' and 'differed from my friends on it last year and voted with ministers against Huskisson and all the rest'.[40]

Warrender voted against the ministry on the civil list, 15 Nov. 1830. Soon afterwards he informed Hay that as 'a strong anti-reformer' he had 'written to some of his friends in the north to get up petitions against any degree of reform'.[41] He applauded the Grey government, in which his associates Charles Grant*, Lord Melbourne and Lord Palmerston* took office, for their good start in implementing measures of economy, 6 Dec. He also made a suggestion concerning the proposed select committee on the reduction of public salaries, to which he was named, 9 Dec. Two days later, speaking from the opposition benches, he denied that successive governments had neglected Ireland, approved the pension granted to Rae's wife after his removal from office, but again noticed his failure to become lord chief baron, and, praising Lord Althorp's* honesty, announced that he was 'disposed to watch the government, but ... in a spirit of perfect confidence'. He threatened to propose a deduction of 27 per cent in tax from all pensions and sinecures except those conferred for distinguished services, 16 Dec. At the same time, he refuted 'the imputations that are most unjustly cast on the whole aristocracy of this country, as grasping at and retaining all that they can obtain': 'efficient public service' was not 'overpaid, but the inefficient must be cut down and ultimately abolished'. As a freeman

of Evesham, though 'not unfriendly to reform', he objected to Lord Chandos's attempt to supersede its writ and deal with bribery there, 16 Dec. According to Sir George Clerk*, he was 'so much alarmed' by the unruly mood of the House in this debate that 'he went to some of the ministers, urging them to dissolve'.[42] He endorsed the sentiments of the Middlesex petition presented by Hume as far as retrenchment went, but warned ministers against the more lunatic radical nostrums, 21 Dec. 1830. On reform, he argued that the 'majority of the persons of property and education' were hostile to it and that the defeat of the Irish secretary Smith Stanley by Hunt at Preston did not augur well for any reformed system. Later that evening he rebutted Tennyson's comment that he was wilfully blinding himself to the strength of pro-reform feeling in the country, reminding him that he had supported his attempts to enfranchise Birmingham. He tried to clarify his earlier pronouncement on reform:

> I said that if I could be convinced that the majority of the middle classes and the reasonable part of the community were desirous of reform, I did not know that I might not change my opinions. I should be sorry to be so misrepresented to the public, as to be understood to be decidedly hostile to every plan of reform, for that is not the case.

Warrender was willing to support the transfer of Evesham's seats to Birmingham if a case could be made out, 18 Feb. 1831, but he feared that the impending ministerial reform scheme would be 'too extensive'. He thought Hume's advocacy of the confiscation of church property showed that 'the state is in danger', 26 Feb., and said that naval lords of the admiralty should be allowed to keep their allowances, 28 Feb. He condemned the reform bills as 'a violation of ancient charters and sacred rights', 7 Mar., but criticized preceding Tory governments for resisting the enfranchisement of large manufacturing towns, which he now claimed consistently to have supported. With mounting fury, he predicted that 'a large portion of the intelligence and property of Scotland' would oppose reform, forecast that all surviving boroughs would be under treasury influence and professed contempt for recent attacks on him in the national press. He voted against the second reading of the English bill, 22 Mar. He supported the civil list grant, even though he considered it inadequate, 25, 28 Mar., when he deplored the proposed disfranchisement of the Anstruther district of burghs but said he would support 'a just, proper and moderate reform'. He denied that the salaries committee had made an invidious distinction between the army and the navy and did not consider ministers pledged to accept its recommendations on pensions, 30 Mar. He welcomed the abolition of the office of lieutenant-general of the ordnance, 13 Apr., but opposed Hume's attempt to reduce the civil list allowances for the royal dukes, 14 Apr. That day he admitted that in the light of communications from Scotland he had changed his mind on reform there, and now believed that 'a popular system of election' was desirable, though he remained hostile to all disfranchisement. He therefore spoke and voted against Gascoyne's wrecking amendment to the English reform bill, 19 Apr. 1831, contending that if its proposed veto on any reduction in the number of English Members was carried, the 'general wealth and intelligence of Scotland', notably in Aberdeen, Dundee, Edinburgh and Glasgow, would have no chance of adequate representation. The reformers John Fazakerley and Thomas Spring Rice reacted favourably to his 'good speech', which they hoped would have a beneficial effect on the Scottish Members; but the Tory Lord Ellenborough thought he had 'behaved shabbily'.[43] Warrender was returned for Honiton after a contest at the ensuing general election; one newspaper attributed his success to the 'constitutional and antirepublican sentiments of the inhabitants'.[44] At the Haddingtonshire election his brother John, who had declared his opposition to the reform bill, supported the successful Tory James Balfour on Warrender's principle that the Member should have 'a considerable stake' in the county.[45]

Warrender voted against the second reading of the reintroduced reform bill, 6 July, but on 12 July 1831 he expressed his approval of some of its details, while advising ministers against wholesale disfranchisement. He presented a Jedburgh petition for all existing Scottish electors to be allowed to retain the franchise for their lives, 14 July. He dissented from the prayer of an anti-Maynooth petition from Glasgow, 19 July. He presented one from the inhabitants of Chelsea asking to be allotted a separate Member, though he condemned the plan to create metropolitan district constituencies, 27 July, when he voted against the partial disfranchisement of Chippenham. Next day he put in a word for Honiton which, though scheduled to lose a Member, had over 300 £10 houses and 550 resident electors, and attacked schedule B as the worst feature of the bill, threatening to move at the report stage that no borough with over 400 resident electors should be disfranchised. Later, responding to a personal attack by Denman, the attorney-general, he said that 'to destroy a decayed borough is intelligible', but to deprive 'considerable towns' of ancient rights was 'founded on nothing but a reckless spirit of innovation'. He delivered 'a short funeral oration' on

Honiton, 29 July, but did not divide the House, which had become 'a court of injustice to convict innocent and unoffending boroughs'. On 11 Aug. he opposed printing the Waterford petition for disarming the Irish yeomanry in the aftermath of the Newtownbarry massacre, wishing to 'establish the welfare and tranquillity of Ireland' by assuaging 'violent religious and party feelings'. He voted with ministers for the division of counties, 11 Aug., said he would welcome any scheme to give two Members to the more populous Scottish counties, 16 Aug., and spoke and voted against the censure of government's alleged interference in the Dublin election, 23 Aug., observing that 'some degree of undue influence is proved', but 'unless the exercise of some influence is allowed, the business of government cannot be conducted'. Explaining that he had abandoned his motion to preserve boroughs with over 400 resident electors in order to avoid a charge of offering 'vexatious opposition' to the bill, 1 Sept., he addressed 'some young Members' on his own side of the House who 'look upon me as a suspicious character': as 'an independent Member', he did 'not seek to please them, but to do my duty'. On the government's concession of additional Members for some Welsh counties, 14 Sept., he urged them to do the same for Scotland; and the following day he again attacked the 'gross injustice' of schedule B and of 'the whole of this bill', though he conceded that 'a very considerable and extensive reform is necessary'. He voted against the passage of the bill, 21 Sept. On 23 Sept. he approved the idea of Scottish university representation and supported the second reading of the Scottish reform bill, although he cavilled at some of its details and wanted at least five more Members; he acknowledged that 'I now stand in a situation in which I shall get credit with neither party'. He admitted that he had concurred in the salaries committee's recommendation of a reduction for the president of the India board, 29 Sept., and supported the government amendment to Hobhouse's vestries bill, 30 Sept. He backed Murray's unsuccessful bid to secure eight additional Scottish county Members, 4 Oct. He saw no reason to ban the appointment of non-residents as lord lieutenants of Irish counties, 6 Oct., but objected to the government's Scottish exchequer court bill, 6, 7 Oct. He thanked Peel for his work in setting up the metropolitan police force, 11 Oct. He dissociated himself from Wetherell's charge that ministers had connived in the disturbances provoked by the loss of the reform bill in the Lords, 12 Oct., and spoke for suspension of the Liverpool writ on account of the 'mass of corruption' revealed there. He supported the sugar refinery bill and Brougham's reform of bankruptcy jurisdiction, 15 Oct. 1831.

In November 1831 Littleton had 'excellent fun' at dinner with Warrender, who

> we discovered, had written and printed a letter to his constituents at Honiton expressing his regret that his avocations and *the state of his health* (robust) would not allow of him going down to them this winter, and sending them a printed copy of his speech on the case of Honiton ... Quite clear from the tone of the letter that friend Warrender finds that his anti-reform votes are putting him in the wrong box in their estimations.

A few days later he made Warrender 'very angry' by describing him as 'a Zephyr *entre deux Flores*' when seated between his own wife and the pretty Mrs. Twiss.[46] Warrender, who voted for the grant to improve Buckingham House, 9 Dec., 'triumphed for the immaculate Honiton' by welcoming 'the spirit of conciliation' exhibited in the revised reform bill, which restored the borough to full status, 12 Dec.; his speech was one of a number seen as Tory rebukes for Peel.[47] He drew attention to himself as a 'convert' by voting for the second reading, 17 Dec. 1831.[48] He voiced strong objections to Campbell's general register bill, 17 Jan., and was in the government majorities on the Russian-Dutch loan, 26 Jan., and relations with Portugal, 9 Feb. 1832. On the introduction of the new Scottish reform bill, 19 Jan., he expressed disappointment that no increase in representation was offered, though he disclaimed any 'hostile feeling' towards government. He was again at pains to justify his vote against Gascoyne's amendment. He spoke in support of the opposition amendment to schedule B and in explanation of his vote for the second reading of the English bill, 23 Jan.: he had cast it to promote 'the peace, tranquillity and security of the country', which depended on the speedy passage of a 'practicable, conciliatory and safe' measure of reform. While he agreed that thriving manufacturing and commercial centres should be enfranchised, he still disliked the schedule B disfranchisements, which he suggested could be avoided by abandoning the London districts and the three Member counties; he called for concessions on both sides. He voted against the third reading of the bill, 22 Mar. Clerk's motion to add him to the committee on the exchequer court bill, of which he claimed to have no prior knowledge, was defeated by 100-56, 2 Feb. He supported calls for British intervention on behalf of Poland, 18 Apr., 28 June. In yet another change of mind, he gave his 'most cordial support' to the second reading of the Scottish reform bill as 'a final measure', 21 May, when he admitted that he was no longer anxious to obtain additional Members, being now satisfied that the English boroughs would continue to provide Scots with an alternative route to

Parliament. Accordingly, he opposed Murray's motion to increase the Scottish representation, 1 June, though he used the curious argument that if carried it would entitle Ireland to 50 new Members. While he had no objection to allowing superiorities to continue providing county votes, if only because in practice they would prove too expensive to keep up, he told the bill's opponents that if their extinction was indeed 'a spoliation', it was 'one for the public benefit, and must be submitted to'. He had some qualms about the proposed arbitration procedure for disputed voting claims, 5 June, and dispensing with the property qualification oath, 27 June; but he looked askance at Johnstone's attempt to bar the Scottish clergy from voting, 6 June, and was a teller for the majority against it. He deplored party squabbles over the corn laws and professed his willingness, for all his own vested interest in agriculture, to back any measure 'calculated to produce permanent cheap food', 1 June. He supported the inclusion of Protestant scripture instruction in the Irish education scheme, 8 June, and favoured the establishment of a tribunal to deal with financial claims on the East India Company, 14 June. On 2 July he said that his previous vote on the Russian-Dutch loan did not bind him for the future, when the separation of Belgium and Holland had been effected; and he paired with the opposition minority on the issue, 12 July. Later that day he had a sharp exchange with Peel's brother-in-law George Dawson on the subject of ministerial salaries but, after mutual apologies, said he was 'determined to avoid being nettled at any remarks that may be made in this House'. He sought and received an assurance that the dissolution would not take place until registration had been completed, 15 Aug. 1832.

Warrender decided not to stand at the 1832 general election because of 'the state of my health, and the determination of passing several winters out of England'.[49] For all this, he was in London in late January 1833.[50] John Hobhouse* visited him at Lochend in September 1834:

> Warrender was very kind and hospitable, and had a great deal to say, particularly about the men with whom he had lived, Canning being the chief: but he verged on the absurd and talked too much of himself, and how he was employed and treated by Canning.[51]

A year earlier Warrender had brought an action in the court of session for divorce on the ground of adultery by his wife, then living in France. She entered objections, based essentially on a claim that a Scottish court could not dissolve a marriage contracted in England between a resident Englishwoman and a domiciled Scotsman. They were dismissed in an interlocutor of 28 June 1834, but Lady Warrender appealed to the Lords and Warrender's attempts to have the appeal disallowed were unsuccessful. After several delays, the Lords heard counsel on the case in May 1835; and on 27 Aug. 1835 Brougham and Lyndhurst, arguing that in law a wife's domicile became that of her husband, upheld the interlocutor of the lower court. It does not appear, however, that Warrender subsequently proceeded with the case in Scotland.[52] He died at his London house at 63 Upper Berkeley Street in February 1849, having on 19 June 1821 devised all his property to his brother John (1786-1867), his successor in the baronetcy. By a codicil of 8 Jan. 1847 he left an annuity of £100 to one Rosa Phillicory. His personalty within the province of Canterbury was sworn under £12,000, but his Scottish personal estate was rated for duty at £24,968 in August 1871.[53]

[1] They were married on 26 Nov. 1780 (IGI). [2] Hatherton diary, 24 Nov. [1831]; Creevey's Life and Times, 258. [3] Howard Sisters, 227. [4] Disraeli Letters, i. 146. [5] Wellington and Friends, 36; N. Gash, Sir Robert Peel, 666. [6] Croker Pprs. i. 153. [7] Kentish Chron. 11, 25 Feb., 14 Mar. 1820; Add. 38282, f. 89; 38458, f. 227. [8] NAS GD51/1/198/9/28. [9] The Times, 18 May 1820. [10] Gent. Mag. (1820), i. 573; Cockburn Jnl. ii.142; PROB 11/1632/450; IR26/847/591; Bk. of Old Edinburgh Club, x. 24-26; Warrender Letters (Scottish Hist. Soc. ser. 3, xxv), pp. xiv-xxii. [11] NAS GD51/1/198/8/8. [12] Creevey's Life and Times, 139; HLRO, Hist. Coll. 379, Grey Bennet diary, 20, 37. [13] Grey Bennet diary, 68; The Times, 18 May 1821. [14] The Times, 9 May 1821. [15] Buckingham, Mems. Geo. IV, i. 266; Christ Church, Oxf. Phillimore mss, Phillimore to Buckingham, 23 Dec. 1821. [16] Greville Mems. ii. 11. [17] Fox Jnl. 141-3. [18] Creevey Pprs. ii. 60, 74. [19] The Times, 26 Mar. 1824. [20] G. Lipscomb, Bucks. iii. 297; Von Neumann Diary, i.190; ii. 306; Dyott's Diary, ii. 139; Geo. IV Letters, iii. 1530. [21] Buckingham, ii. 157. [22] The Times, 29 Apr. 1825. [23] Ibid. 1, 16 Mar., 11, Apr., 6, 10 May 1826. [24] Kentish Chron. 23 May; Salisbury Jnl. 12 June 1826. [25] Keele Univ. Lib. Sneyd mss SC12/79; Bagot, Canning and Friends, ii. 390; Canning's Ministry, 108, 132. [26] Geo. IV Letters, iii. 1323. [27] Hatherton diary, 12 July [1840]. [28] The Times, 9 May, 16 June 1827. [29] NLS mss 1057, ff. 196-204. [30] Add. 38750, ff. 119, 192. [31] Add. 51590, Agar Ellis to Lady Holland, 19 Nov. 1827. [32] Add. 38752, ff. 85, 177. [33] Add. 38754, f. 114; Wellington mss WP1/899/9; NLS mss 1074, f. 188. [34] Fitzwilliam mss, Milton to sister, 29 Feb.; Harewood mss, Cavendish Bentinck to Lady Canning, 3 Mar. 1828; Gash, Secretary Peel, 463-4. [35] Palmerston Letters, 205-6. [36] Hatherton mss, Warrender to Littleton, 31 Aug. 1828. [37] A. Aspinall, 'Last of Canningites', EHR, l (1935), 650, 659. [38] Edinburgh Evening Courant, 12 Aug.; Stair mss (History of Parliament Aspinall transcripts), Murray to Dalrymple [10 Aug. 1830]; NLS mss 2, ff. 149, 151; Add. 56554, f. 133. [39] Parker, Graham, i. 88-89; Hatherton mss. [40] Stair mss. [41] NLS mss 14441, f. 82. [42] Three Diaries, 36. [43] Add. 51573, Rice to Holland [19 Apr.]; 51576, Fazakerley to same [19 Apr. 1831]; Three Diaries, 86. [44] Exeter and Plymouth Gazette, 7 May; Western Luminary,10 May 1831. [45] Edinburgh Evening Courant, 4 Apr., 12 May 1831. [46] Hatherton diary, 20, 24 Nov. [1831]. [47] Ibid. 12 Dec; Add. 51573, Rice to Lady Holland [12 Dec. 1831]. [48] TNA GD30/29, Seaford to Granville, 23 Dec. 1831. [49] Devonshire Chron. 11 Nov.; The Times, 10 Nov. 1832. [50] Three Diaries, 291. [51] Broughton, Recollections, iv. 16. [52] Greville Mems. iii. 210; LJ, lxvi. 782, 783, 833, 945, 955; lxvii. 17, 19, 25, 27, 28, 141, 145, 149, 604, 620; Edinburgh Evening Courant, 3 Sept. 1835. [53] PROB 11/2090/240; 11/2097/557; IR26/1853/133, 202.

D.R.F.

WASON, **Peter Rigby** (1797–1875), of Cable Street, Liverpool, Lancs. and 49 Lincoln's Inn Fields, Mdx.

IPSWICH	1831–1834
IPSWICH	19 June 1835–1837
IPSWICH	1841–25 Apr. 1842

b. 12 Apr. 1797, 2nd s. of John James Wason (d. 1810), merchant and ironmonger, of Berkeley Square, Bristol, Glos. and Catherine, da. of Peter Rigby, merchant and iron founder, of Liverpool. educ. M. Temple 1818, called 1824. m. c.1843, Euphemia Douglas, da. of Peter McTier, yeoman, of Corwar and Knockglass, Ayr, 4s. (1 d.v.p.) 1da. d. 24 July 1875.[1]

Wason's family had benefited from the growth of the iron industry in West Derby, Lancashire, and reciprocal toll exemptions available to Bristol and Liverpool freemen. His maternal grandfather Peter Rigby (d. 1794) was mayor of Liverpool, 1774-5, when the corporation negotiated the purchase of a reversionary interest in the lordship of Liverpool from the 1st earl of Sefton; and in February 1777 he himself bought the reversion of properties in Lord Street for less than £7,000.[2] Rigby's business interests and fortune passed to his sons (the eldest of whom, Peter, was detained in the Fleet prison for debt, 1812-20), but Wason's mother (Rigby's only daughter) and her issue had equal rights to the reverted properties and ground rents; she also inherited the toll revenue from Black Rock lighthouse.[3] Wason's father left under £1,500 in trust for his children, but bequeathed his Bristol property, trading interests and a house in Cable Street, Liverpool, to his widow, who made it her home.[4] From the age of 21 Wason, who had probably acquired mercantile experience previously, trained as an equity draughtsman and barrister, which brought him into contact with Elizabeth Hart, daughter of Sir Anthony, the lord chancellor of Ireland. He proposed marriage to her in 1822 but was deemed not to have 'enough money', and when, as a barrister on the western circuit, in 1827 he renewed his suit and offered to settle £1,200 on her, Hart had his financial affairs investigated and rejected him. Wason, in turn, challenged Hart's attorney to a duel, for which he was prosecuted in the court of king's bench for a libel with intent to provoke a breach of the peace.[5] He was appointed soon afterwards to the sessions at Bristol, where his cousin James Wason was a solicitor, and retained close ties with Liverpool, where his younger brothers Eugene Edmund Wason (d. 1836) and Edward Sidney Wason (d. 1841) became attorneys.[6] Wason was not a Liverpool freeman, but 'Wason

Buildings' was a popular venue for meetings and he was an interested observer at the November 1830 by-election contest between John Evelyn Denison* and William Ewart*. Amid the furore and bribery allegations which followed, he took it upon himself, with possible encouragement from John Gladstone*, as whose 'tool' he was denigrated, to petition Parliament for 'measures to prevent the recurrence of such scandalous proceedings', and, encouraged by the *Liverpool Chronicle*, he requested the common council, who resented his intervention, 'to aid him in his attempt to purify the system of voting' and prevent bribery.[7] Squibs bemoaned the loss of public revenue 'by having a parcel of drones pensioned on [the lighthouse]', and a mob stoned his mother's house after the parliamentary committee chaired by John Benett found Ewart guilty of bribery, 26 Mar. 1831.[8] Eugene Wason, however, was appointed solicitor for the Liverpool disfranchisement bill. Wason's conduct before the election committee brought him to the attention of lord chancellor Brougham and led to his candidature in the reform interest at Ipswich, where he was returned with the reformer James Morrison at the general election in May, at a personal cost of £1,200.[9] An Ipswich contemporary described him as 'a tall gaunt gentleman with a cast in one of his eyes ... called by some of his opponents "two yards of bad stuff"'.[10] A parliamentary commentator recalled him as 'well known and much esteemed on both sides of the House ... bearded, tall and well formed ... his grave expression ... would have well become the pulpit' and classified him as a 'stock still speaker'.

> He speaks with some rapidity and is usually fluent enough in his utterance, but at times he hesitates a little. His language is unpolished ... but his style is correct. He is not wordy; he expresses himself with great conciseness, and is always clear, were he sufficiently audible in his statements and arguments. He is not a man of superior intellect but he has a sound judgement ... [and is] exemplary in his attention to his parliamentary duties.[11]

Wason's particular interests in 1831-2 lay in supporting reform and the bill to prevent bribery and treating at Liverpool, opposing the anatomy bill, promoting the Westminster improvement scheme and re-establishing Ipswich's right to hold the assizes. He was praised by *The Times* when, on 29 June 1831, the paymaster general and architect of the reform bill Lord John Russell wrote conceding his request that half-yearly rate payments should not be a prerequisite for qualification as £10 voters.[12] He was prevented from making his maiden speech that day, as the House became inquorate, and one of the Liverpool reform-

ers, the Rev. William Shepherd, was informed by Ewart, 5 July:

> You would be amused at the issue of Benett's resolutions. Wason came into the House with all the pomp and circumstance of a judge about to record the final sentence of disfranchisement against the freemen. He was armed with a large black book in mourning for the carpenters and other victims of his legislative justice. Great was his wrath when John Wood so promptly put an end to the proceedings; and he seemed well disposed to quarrel with me. This I shall avoid as much as I should his acquaintance.[13]

He voted for the second reading of the reintroduced reform bill, 6 July. Opposing the issue of a new Liverpool writ, he made his first speech on the prevalence of bribery and corruption there, 8 July, when he urged Members not to take pity on the borough merely because it was a large, populous town.[14] The *Manchester Herald* attributed the motion's defeat (by 117-99), despite government backing, to Wason's descriptions of on-going treating, to which he referred again, 14 July.[15] He informed *The Times* that he had not missed a single division on the motions to adjourn proceedings on the reform bill, 12 July; and he generally divided for its details and campaigned and spoke out against any he opposed.[16] On 27 July he proposed making all schedule B boroughs contributory because they

> contribute only £32,151 in taxes and contain only 50,000 inhabitants ... 12,000 voters would return a sixth of the Members of this House. Looking to these facts, I say that it is impossible that schedule B should remain a final measure in a reformed Parliament. The only way I see by which we can prevent the rediscussion of it, is to make the boroughs in that schedule contributory boroughs; and instead of returning 39 Members, to return only 16, giving to each borough a constituency of about 800 voters.

Claiming that he was not 'bound hand and foot to the bill', he voted in the minority for awarding Stoke-on-Trent two Members, 4 Aug., and suggested doing the same for all towns in schedule D because of their large numbers of £10 houses. He made a point, when Whitehaven was considered, 6 Aug., of asking the anti-reformer John Croker if he would seek separate representation for neighbouring Workington, Harrington and Bissington, and proposed enfranchising Toxteth Park independently of Liverpool. He withdrew the motion for want of government support, but his speech, drawing parallels with Gateshead, to which the bill accorded separate representation from Newcastle-upon-Tyne, was extensively reported in the Liverpool press.[17] He cast wayward votes for the separate representation of Merthyr, 10 Aug., against the division of counties, 11 Aug., to permit borough voters to vote in county elections, 17 Aug., and for the enfranchisement of £50 tenants-at-will, 18 Aug. His suggestion that sheriffs be liable to penalties for non-performance of duties if a returning officer proved unsatisfactory was received in uproar, 19 Aug. He called in vain for freeholders in boroughs and corporate counties to be given the right to chose whether to vote in the borough or the county, 20 Aug. Using Liverpool as his example and backed by Nicolson Calvert, he secured an amendment enabling £10 occupiers to qualify as £10 voters in districts where landlords compounded with parishes for rates and charged tenants a neat rent, 26 Aug. He voted for the bill's third reading and passage, 19, 21 Sept., and for Lord Ebrington's confidence motion, 10 Oct. Arguing that the reform bill was inadequate to 'meet so gross a case of corruption as that at Liverpool', he called for the postponement of the writ and claimed that the select committee appointed to investigate corruption there was dominated by Members sympathetic to the freemen and willing to suppress evidence, 29 Aug. He was a majority teller for Benett's amendment for including a reference to bribery at the last election in the order for the Liverpool writ, and was appointed with him to bring in the Liverpool franchise bill, 5 Sept. He failed by 93-67 on 12 Oct. 1831 with an amendment deferring the writ until 14 days after the opening of the next parliamentary session, a calculated concession following the reform bill's defeat in the Lords.[18] He was paraded through the streets and docks of Liverpool in effigy during the corporation elections that month.[19]

He divided for the second reading of the revised reform bill, 17 Dec. 1831, and for its details. Referring to Ipswich, which had 'only 800 persons assessed to the rates at £10 and upwards ... but about 1,800 who occupy houses of the value of £10 and upwards', 3 Feb. 1832, he opposed Denison's amendment settling the £10 householder qualification on particular properties in each borough, and another raising the qualification to £15 in boroughs where the number of £10 houses exceeded 500; but he now conceded that £10 was 'too low a franchise for Liverpool', where rents were high, properties frequently subdivided and poor rate assessments 'fiddled' to prevent large families becoming chargeable on the parish. His amendment clarifying the residence qualification of freeman voters retaining their franchise under the bill was deemed 'advantageous and proper to be adopted', 7 Feb. Another preventing metropolitan police officers from voting until 12 months after retirement was rejected outright, 8 Feb.; and one limiting polling to one day in constituen-

cies with electorates below 1,000 was defeated by 95-1, 15 Feb. He recommended sorting voters 'by alphabet' rather than 'by district' in Liverpool, 15 Feb., thought Totnes should take Dartmouth's place in schedule B, 23 Feb., and, in a renewed call for the enfranchisement of Toxteth Park, 28 Feb., he asked for maps of Bath, Bristol and Liverpool to be made available for scrutiny before the House divided on the separate enfranchisement of Gateshead and Salford. He explained that unlike last year, when there were 30 'vacancies', there were now none, and he therefore wished to combine Salford with Manchester and Gateshead with Newcastle; he spoke and voted against awarding a Member to Gateshead, 5 Mar. At the bill's third reading, 22 Mar., when he divided in the government majority, he reaffirmed his commitment to it, despite his opposition to separating Gateshead and Newcastle and to particular clauses. He spoke in passing of his support for Sadler's bill to regulate child labour. Later in the debate, he repudiated a suggestion by the antireformer Sugden that ministers had enfranchised £10 householders who paid rent quarterly in order to pacify the political unions, and explained that he himself had secured the concession, two days before the unions had raised the problem, by bringing to the attention of ministers the case of 'a property belonging to my family and myself situated in the best part of Liverpool, and amounting to £10,000 per annum, for which not a single tenant would have had the right of voting, all the rents being paid quarterly'. He voted for the address calling on the king to appoint only ministers who would carry the reform bill unimpaired, 10 May, and against a Conservative amendment to the Scottish measure, 1 June. He said he would vote to retain the proposed £300 property qualification for parliamentary candidates in the Scottish districts of burghs, 22 June 1832.

The editor of the *Albion* had speculated from the outset 'whether his motive is actuated by private pique or by public principle', and by 1832 it was rumoured at Westminster that Wason's agent had admitted that he was promoting the Liverpool disfranchisement bill so that he could subsequently take legal action against individuals to recover penalties.[20] As announced, 3 Feb., he produced a letter from his agent denying the charge, 8 Feb.[21] He spoke against the Liverpool revenue buildings bill that day, and was a majority teller for the second reading of the disfranchisement bill, 23 May. Seconding Benett's motion to proceed with it in committee, 4 July, he criticized Liverpool's sitting Members Lord Sandon and Ewart for attempting to kill the bill by adjournment and spoke of the franchise as a 'trust', which 'if an individual chooses to sell that trust to the highest bidder, he cannot complain that it should be taken away from himself and consequently from his children'. He dismissed Alexander Baring's electoral bribery bill as 'a piece of waste paper compared with the effect that would have been produced by the passing of the Liverpool disfranchisement bill, which it seems has been dropped' (on 13 July), and proposed moving an amendment in the next Parliament making it retrospective, 30 July. As in his subsequent correspondence, publications and speeches, he argued that as malpractice was the work of agents not candidates, it was impossible to frame an effective bribery oath.[22] He divided with government on the Russian-Dutch loan, 26 Jan., 16 July, relations with Portugal, 9 Feb., and the navy civil departments bill, 6 Apr. 1832.

Wason's liberalism generally 'stopped short of radicalism',[23] but he voted in radical minorities for inquiry into the conduct of the magistrates of Winchester towards Thomas and Caroline Deacle, 27 Sept. 1831, and military punishments, 16 Feb. 1832. He voted against the Vestry Act amendment bill, 23 Jan., for inquiry into the glove trade, which concerned his colleague Morrison, 31 Jan., 3 Apr., and to reduce the sugar duties, 7 Mar., and urged that strict attention be paid to all judicial appointments in the colonies, 13 Apr. He voted to tax absentee landlords to provide for the Irish poor, 19 June, and for inquiry into the Inns of Court, 17 July; but he supported ministers when Sugden, in a thinly veiled attack on the appointment of William Brougham* as a master in chancery by his brother the lord chancellor, criticized their failure to abolish chancery sinecures, 25 July. Wason was opposed in principle to the sale of bodies, but not to dissection at licensed medical schools, and he strenuously opposed the anatomy bill, 27 Feb., objecting to 11 of the first 15 clauses on inspectors and contracting parties and listing seven points which he wished to see included. In committee, he vainly tried to secure amendments to prevent body-snatching, dissection at surgeons' residences and the sale of bodies by innkeepers and workhouses, 30 Mar., 11, 13, 18 Apr. He called for the bill to be recommitted 'to place my amendments on the records of the House', 8 May, and suggested sarcastically at its third reading, 11 May, that as the 'whole purpose of the bill is to regulate dissection at private residences of surgeons', its title should reflect this; but his amendment to this effect was rejected with another making the sale of bodies illegal, and he now failed to delay the bill by adjournment. He voted to make coroners' inquests public, 20 June. He moved successfully for and was appointed to a select committee on Bardwell's plan to improve the approaches to the House, the law courts and the 'immediate neighbourhood of Buckingham Palace', 6 June; and objected to but failed (by 48-22) to secure a reduction in the grant for new barracks at Birdcage Walk, which jeopardized it, 2 July. He said he would continue to 'report from time to time' on the Westminster improvements committee's work, 29 June, and had their minutes of evidence printed, 18 July, but he failed to prevent the report's deferral, 31 July.[24] Drawing parallels with the 'injustice' to Liverpool and Manchester of holding the Lancashire assizes at Lancaster, Wason supported the bill making Norwich Norfolk's sole assizes town, 3 Apr., and was a seconder and majority teller at its second reading, 23 May.[25] He presented and endorsed Ipswich's petition for the right to hold the assizes alternately with Bury St. Edmunds, 2 June, and, acknowledging that it exposed him to taunts of electioneering, obtained leave to introduce a bill to this effect, 3 July. His speech described how previous attempts to transfer the sessions to Ipswich had been blocked by the duke of Grafton and the marquess of Bristol, whose sons shared the representation of Bury St. Edmunds. He raised no objections to the bill's deferral at the request of Bristol's heir Lord Jermyn while the opinion of the county was taken, and presented a favourable petition from the magistrates, grand jury and yeomanry of East Suffolk, 13 July, but he failed to prevent the measure being deferred for that session, 23 July 1832.

Wason was returned for Ipswich as a Liberal at the general election of 1832, petitioned successfully following his defeat there in 1835 by Fitzroy Kelly, who challenged him to a duel, and was re-elected at the ensuing by-election. His 'match extraordinary' in 1837 with Kelly, commemorated in MacLean's cartoon 'Cock-a-doodle-do practising the bar', left them both without seats. Wason topped the poll at Ipswich in 1841, but was unseated on petition, and he did not stand for Parliament again. He remained a member of the Reform Club, 'ever conspicuous and attractive on the hustings'.[26] He now moved permanently to Ayrshire, where his brother Eugene had died in 1836, living at Kildonnan, before building a mansion at Drumlamford, which he purchased from his brother-in-law Thomas Dickason Rotch, and sold to purchase the Corwar estate.[27] He retained a taste for litigation, wrote regularly to the newspapers and published pamphlets on land reclamation at Corwar, bribery at elections, the route of the railway, Hope and Napier's plan for London sewage, the 1866 parliamentary reform proposals, usury, monetary panics and the currency, on which, as an anti-bullionist, he disagreed passionately with William Ewart Gladstone†; he was bitterly disappointed not to be invited to speak before the Liverpool Chamber of Commerce.[28] He died of angina at Corwar in July 1875 and was buried with both Free and Established Church rites in the mausoleum he had built at Barrhill.[29] An agreement of 1832 with his mother and brothers had made him the major shareholder in their Liverpool estate, which, as he had willed, was retained by his family and Corwar sold. He had provided for his widow and daughter and divided his real estate and the residue equally between his three surviving sons. Two became well-known parliamentarians: Eugene Wason (1846-1927), Liberal Member for Ayrshire South, 1885-6, 1892-5, and Clackmannan and Kinross, 1899-1918; and John Cathcart Wason (1848-1921), Liberal Member for Orkney and Shetland, 1900-21.[30]

[1] Mr. M.S. Wason of Highfield Lodge, Church Hill, Totland Bay, I.o.W. (in 1991) supplied information on Wason's date of birth and marriage and McTier's residence. He points out that the assumption that Wason married Euphemia, some 28 years his junior, in 1843 is not confirmed by the following entry for 1844 in the Colmonell par. reg.: 'son to Rigby Wason and Fanny Mactier, Kildonnan, born 17 July and baptized 11 August, but not lawful wedlock'. The date of birth matches that of Wason's eldest son Rigby (d. 1870). [2] J. Touzeau, *Rise and Progress of Liverpool*, 559-60; *Liverpool Vestries Bk.* ii. 205, 212, 298, 394; R. Brooke, *Liverpool During Last Quarter of 18th Cent.* 195, 212-3. [3] *Gent. Mag.* (1794), ii. 1209; PROB 11/1255/471; *Caledonian Mercury*, 27 Apr. 1820. [4] *Gent. Mag.* (1810), i. 676; PROB 8/203; 11/1515/483. [5] *The Times*, 18 June 1827, 19, 20 May 1828; R. Gatty, *Portrait of a Merchant Prince, James Morrison, 1789-1857*, p. 124. [6] *Gent. Mag.* (1836), i. 102; (1841), ii. 665. [7] *The Times*, 7, 11 Oct., 29 Nov., 2, 9, 14, 21 Dec.; *Liverpool Chron.* 25 Dec. 1830, 1 Jan. 1831; *CJ*, lxxxvi. 103; Brougham mss, W. Shepherd to Brougham [n.d.]. [8] *Albion*, 20, 27 Dec. 1830, 3 Jan., 21, 28 Mar.; *Liverpool Mercury*, 28 Jan., 1 Apr.; St. Deiniol's Lib. Glynne-Gladstone mss 103, Denison to J. Gladstone, 12 Mar.; 197, T. Gladstone to same, 18 Mar., 21 Apr.; *Liverpool Chron.* 2 Apr. 1831; J. Picton, *Memorials of Liverpool* (1875), i. 429. [9] *Liverpool Mercury*, 15 Apr.; *Ipswich Jnl.* 7 May 1831; R. Wason, *Short and Sure Way of Preventing Bribery at Elections*, 3, 4. [10] Suff. RO (Ipswich), J. Glyde, 'Materials for Parl. Hist. Ipswich', f. 211. [11] [J. Grant], *Random Recollections of Commons* (1838), ii. 61-66. [12] *The Times*, 30 June 1831. [13] Manchester New Coll. Oxf., William Shepherd mss VII, f. 53. [14] Ibid.; *Liverpool Mercury*, 15 July 1831. [15] *Manchester Herald*, 13 July 1831. [16] *The Times*, 18 July 1831. [17] *Liverpool Mercury*, 12 Aug. 1831. [18] Picton, i. 448-9. [19] *Manchester Herald*, 26 Oct. 1831 [20] *Albion*, 27 Dec. 1830, 3 Jan. 1831; [21] Glynne-Gladstone mss 199, T. to J. Gladstone, 6, 9, 11 Feb. 1832. [22] Brougham mss, Wason to Brougham, 10 July 1847; Wason, *Short and Sure Way* and *Extension of the Franchise* (1866). [23] Grant, ii. 62. [24] *Gent. Mag.* (1832), i. 646. [25] *Bury and Norwich Post*, 2, 30 May 1832. [26] Glyde, ff. 123-45, 214; Suff. RO (Ipswich) HD12/2747/3; Add. 40503, ff. 98-104. [27] *Gent. Mag.* (1836), i. 102; J.L. McDevitt, *House of Rotch*, 562. [28] Wason, *Monetary Panics Rendered Impossible* (1867), 3-13 and app. [29] *Ayr Advertiser*, 29 July; *Galloway Advertiser*, 5 Aug. 1875; *Solicitors' Jnl.* (1875), xix. 713, [30] *Liverpool Mercury*, 28 July 1875; PROB 11/1882/577; IR26/2941/913; 3383/1208.

M.M.E.

WATERPARK, 3rd Bar. [I] *see* **CAVENDISH, Henry Manners**

WATSON, Hon. Richard (1800–1852).

CANTERBURY	1830–1834
PETERBOROUGH	1852–26 July 1852

b. 6 Jan. 1800, 4th s. of Lewis Thomas Watson[†], 2nd Bar. Sondes (*d.* 1806), and Mary Elizabeth, da. and h. of Richard Milles[†] of North Elmham, Norf. and Nackington, Kent. *educ.* Eton 1808. *m.* 21 Dec. 1839, Lavinia Jane, da. of Lord George Quin, 3s. 2da. (1 *d.v.p.*). *suc.* bro. Hon. and Rev. Henry Watson to Northants. estates 1849. *d.* 26 July 1852.

Cornet 10 Drag. 1817, lt. 1820, capt. 1825; half-pay 1830-48; brevet maj. 32 Ft. 1848.

Watson, whose maternal grandfather sat for Canterbury, 1761-80, as did his uncle George Watson from 1800 to 1806, was the youngest brother of the 3rd Baron Sondes, who held considerable landed property at Rockingham Castle, Northamptonshire, and Lees Court, Faversham, Kent, and used his electoral interests in the Whig cause.[1] He served with the army in Portugal in the mid-1820s, but during election speculation in late 1825 an approach was made to Sondes by a group of Canterbury freemen who were interested in supporting an independent candidate against the sitting Members.[2] Watson gave up any thought of the seat and hoped instead to be returned for one of Lord Fitzwilliam's boroughs.[3] Yet John Chalk Claris, editor of the Whig *Kent Herald*, wrote on 17 Apr. 1826 to urge him to stand on principles of liberty and reform, in order to be returned with Lord Clifton*. Although the Tory *Kentish Gazette* thought he would be frightened off by the expense, and despite his being absent with his regiment, a meeting in Canterbury resolved to support him and an election committee was established.[4] He came a distant third, amid allegations that his candidacy had only succeeded in weakening Whig support for Clifton, at the general election that summer. Arriving just as the poll closed, he stated that 'though nominated entirely without the concurrence of himself or his family, he felt highly flattered by the spontaneous act of those who had brought him forward and those who voted for him'.[5] On rumours that the sitting Member Stephen Rumbold Lushington had accepted an Indian governorship, Claris advised Watson, 29 Nov., that if he immediately declared his candidacy all opposition would be quashed and his interest permanently established. He declined, perhaps because of a difference of opinion with his brother, as he apparently accused Sondes of failing to support him. Sondes angrily replied, 8 Dec. 1826, that he had never offered any assistance:

You pretty plainly accuse me of having taken an active part for you during the last election at Canterbury which always was furthest from my thoughts and to which I never gave the smallest encouragement, always giving a negative to every application ... I never used the expression (in your letter) 'you was determined to spare no expense to bring me in'.[6]

Though privately informed by Claris of Watson's decision, his name was brought forward in April 1827 and a requisition was sent to him in Portugal. He again refused, and was annoyed with Claris for having caused a good deal of needless speculation and public embarrassment.[7] Expectations were again raised when Watson returned to England early the following year. He attended a dinner in favour of greater religious liberty at Maidstone, 22 Dec. 1828.[8]

Another approach was made to Sondes, 1 Mar. 1830, to elicit Watson's candidature.[9] In an undated letter to his brother, he stated that he would scotch rumours of his standing, but added as a postscript that

the above was written this morning. I have since been told that it is fully expected at Canterbury that I am going to stand and that no opposition of any consequence is likely to be offered. I can scarcely believe it, but confess that it revives all my former wishes on the subject. It appears to be an opportunity that one might lament hereafter having lost. My own property has been embarked in regimental commissions and I have literally *nothing* at this moment. Consequently if the sum *exceeded* what you mentioned in a former letter, I should be left in a *disgraceful* state, *not able to pay*.[10]

They must have come to an arrangement, since Watson declared his candidacy, 3 July. He maintained that he was unconnected with any party, supporting Whig demands for retrenchment and reform, but disclaiming any hostility towards the duke of Wellington's government.[11] The initial speculation was that, in the continued absence of Lushington, Watson and Clifton would unite their interests and be returned together. But Watson refused any overt collusion with Lord Fordwich*, who replaced Clifton as the main Whig candidate. Fordwich's mother, Lady Cowper, was worried by this indifference, but was satisfied with a letter, obtained from Sondes by Lord Holland, in which it was denied that Watson would join the Tories.[12] Yet Watson did seek an accommodation with the government, making a private arrangement with the Tory candidate Henry Bingham Baring*, who condemned Fordwich for attempting to split votes with Watson and, at the same time, told Watson that he would find 'my London committee *every* way disposed to assist you in any *quiet* way you may wish'.[13] Watson's conduct was ridiculed in the press:

A laughable shifting and uncertainty attended the hues of Mr. Watson's insignia. They changed like the chameleon with the passing hour: first blue [Whig], which after a time changed to blue and pink; then came blushingly a tinge of purple (the church colour) [Tory], which by the way roused a furious schism among his many-coloured partisans and was withdrawn, when pink (the neutral) was finally declared to be the distinguishing colour of the mutable candidate.[14]

However, his careful positioning allowed him to obtain mainstream Whig support and a substantial element of the Tory interest, in the form of split votes with both other candidates. Elected a freeman, 21 July, he was returned at the head of the poll ten days later, with what he boasted was the highest number of votes ever recorded at Canterbury. According to his accounts, the election cost him £4,500.[15] In fulfilment of an election pledge not to neglect his constituents, he resigned from active service in the army, 10 Sept. 1830.[16]

Watson, who had been elected to Brooks's, 31 Mar. 1830, was listed by ministers among the 'doubtful doubtfuls' that autumn. He later recorded that he had been inclined to support the administration, but, after Wellington's anti-reform speech on 2 Nov., was proud to have voted against it on the civil list, 15 Nov.[17] He presented anti-slavery petitions from Canterbury, 3 Nov., 7 Dec.[18] He spoke briefly for repeal of the partial and unjust coal duties, 21 Dec. 1830, when presenting a petition to that effect from the corporation of Canterbury. He was closely involved in the preparation of the Herne Bay pier bill in February 1831.[19] He expressed his perfect concurrence with the pro-reform petition of Henry Cooper, mayor of Canterbury, which was presented by Fordwich, 4 Feb. When bringing up a similar one from the city's inhabitants, 7 Mar., he said that he would support ministers over their bill, and that 'the measure is not what it has been characterized, revolutionary and radical, but ... is conservative and constitutional in its principle and necessary to the salvation of the country'. He praised the corporation of Canterbury for offering to surrender their privileges on presenting its petition, 10 Mar. He was given a fortnight's leave of absence because of illness after having served on an election committee, 10 Mar., but returned to the House to vote for the second reading of the reform bill, 22 Mar. He defended it at a county meeting at Maidstone, 24 Mar., and proposed a petition to the Lords in its favour. For his support of the bill, he was publicly applauded when he attended the theatre at Canterbury, 9 Apr.[20] Having voted against Gascoyne's wrecking amendment, 19 Apr., he stood again at the ensuing general election, explaining that he had supported reform only after deliberate and mature reflection had convinced him that, despite its minor defects, the bill was 'founded upon the principles of the constitution and calculated to give securities to the liberties of the people'. He also called for the alleviation of distress, attention to the interests of agriculture and the gradual emancipation of slaves. Baring declined to enter another expensive contest, so Watson and Fordwich were returned unopposed, each claiming to be the more popular candidate.[21] Watson only incurred about £700 in expenses.[22] He nominated Thomas Law Hodges* at the Kent election, 11 May 1831, stating that the county was split on the subject of reform, but that Hodges was firmly in its favour.[23]

Watson divided for the second reading of the reintroduced reform bill, 6 July, and usually for its details, though he voted against the proposed division of counties, 11 Aug., to preserve the rights of freemen, 30 Aug., and for the total disfranchisement of Aldborough, 14 Sept. 1831. He voted for the passage of the bill, 21 Sept., and for the second reading of the Scottish bill, 23 Sept., when he was thanked by the Canterbury freemen for supporting the cause of reform.[24] He attended another Kent meeting in favour of reform, 30 Sept., and voted for Lord Ebrington's confidence motion, 10 Oct.[25] He voted against the grant for the Society for the Propagation of the Gospels, 25 July; the *Kentish Chronicle* commented that in denouncing such a job, he had done himself infinite credit, as 'this one act is better than fifty flummery speeches'.[26] He divided to postpone the Dublin writ, 8 Aug., and for printing the Waterford petition for disarming the Irish yeomanry, 11 Aug. He presented a petition from the landowners of east Kent against the use of molasses in breweries and distilleries, 10 Aug. He voted for the second reading of the revised reform bill, 17 Dec. 1831, and its committal, 20 Jan. 1832. He generally sided with government on its details, but went with opposition on allowing borough freeholders to vote in county elections, 1 Feb., and against the enfranchisement of Tower Hamlets, 28 Feb. He voted for the third reading of the bill, 22 Mar., for Ebrington's motion for an address calling on the king to appoint only ministers who would carry it unimpaired, 10 May, and against increasing the Scottish representation, 1 June. He was in opposition minorities on the Russian-Dutch loan, 26 Jan., and inquiry into distress in the glove trade, 31 Jan., but in government majorities on relations with Portugal, 9 Feb., and military punishments, 16 Feb. He reversed his earlier vote by dividing with ministers on the Russian-Dutch loan, 12, 20 July, but cast a hostile one on the Greek loan, 6 Aug. He received the thanks of a court of burghmote at Gravesend, 6 July,

for his assistance with its pier bill.[27] He was named as a steward for the east Kent celebration of reform dinner, 26 July 1832, but was unable to attend because of his duties in the House.[28]

As early as June 1831 it had been rumoured that Watson would contest the county at the next election. In May he accepted an invitation to stand for Kent East, but he agreed to continue at Canterbury at the request of a common hall, held on 6 June 1832, and so dropped his candidature for the county.[29] He was returned as a Liberal for Canterbury at the general election that year, but was so incensed that the freemen should entertain the candidacy of the lunatic John Thom, who went by the name of Sir William Courtenay, that he refused to stand thereafter. He inherited Sondes's Northamptonshire estates on the death of another brother in 1849, but he had made his home at Rockingham Castle since 1836. He instituted local improvements, including the Rockingham Flower Show, and was highly respected for his benevolence and piety.[30] After an interval of 18 years, he was again returned to Parliament in July 1852, but he died suddenly less than three weeks later, being succeeded by his eldest son, George Lewis Watson (1841-99).

[1] For his family background, see T. Hay, *Lees Court* (Faversham Pprs. lvii). [2] *Kentish Chron.* 1, 8 Nov. 1825. [3] Fitzwilliam mss 124/2, 3. [4] Watson mss WR 757; *Kentish Chron.* 2, 9 June; *Kentish Gazette*, 2, 6 June 1826; *Canterbury Pollbook* (1826), p. iv. [5] *The Times*, 12 June; *Kentish Chron.* 13 June; *Kentish Gazette*, 13 June 1826. [6] Watson mss WR 757. [7] Ibid. WR 757, Mathers to Watson, 7 Apr., 17 May, Claris to same, 26 June; WR 763, Watson to Claris, 20 July; *Kentish Chron.* 6, 10 Apr., 4, 25, 29 May, 26 June; *Kentish Gazette*, 10 Apr., 25, 29 May, 26 June 1827. [8] *Kentish Chron.* 19 Feb., 30 Dec. 1828. [9] Ibid. 9 Mar.; Cent. Kent. Stud. Harris mss U624 C242, Sondes to Harris [?3 Mar., 1830]. [10] Watson mss WR 763. [11] *Kentish Chron.* 25 May, 6, 27 July, 3 Aug.; *Kentish Gazette*, 25 June, 6, 27, 30 July; *The Times*, 30 July, 1830; *Canterbury Pollbook* (1830), 13-23; Watson mss WR 758, notes for an address [n.d.]. [12] *Kentish Chron.* 27 July; *Kentish Gazette*, 27 July; Add. 51599A, Lady Cowper to Holland, Thurs., Sat., Thurs. [July 1830]. [13] Watson mss WR 761, Baring to Watson, Thurs. [22 July]; WR 763, Peel to Seymour, Tues., Tisdall to Watson, misdated Mon. 4 Oct. 1830. [14] *Kentish Gazette*, 6 Aug. 1830. [15] Watson mss WR 758, Warren to Watson, 21 July, notes for a speech [n.d.], Watson's election expenses, 1830. [16] Ibid. WR 795, Wyndham to Watson, 4 July; *Kentish Gazette*, 14 Sept. 1830. [17] *Kentish Chron.* 3 May 1831. [18] Ibid. 9 Nov.; Watson mss WR 758, Blomfield to Watson, 26 Oct. 1830. [19] *Kentish Chron.* 22 Feb. 1831. [20] Ibid. 29 Mar., 19 Apr.; *Kentish Gazette*, 29 Mar., 12 Apr. 1831. [21] *Kentish Chron.* 26 Apr., 3 May; *Kentish Gazette*, 26 Apr., 3, 7 May 1831. [22] Watson mss WR 759, second election of Watson, accts. 1831. [23] *The Times*, 12 May; *Kentish Chron.* 17 May; *Kentish Gazette*, 13 May 1831. [24] *Kentish Chron.* 27 Sept. 1831. [25] Ibid. 4 Oct. 1831. [26] Ibid. 2 Aug. 1831. [27] Watson mss WR 760, Matthews to Watson, 6 July 1832. [28] *Kentish Chron.* 24, 31 July; *Kentish Gazette*, 24, 27 July 1832. [29] *Kentish Chron.* 3 June 1831, 8 May, 5, 12 June; *Kentish Gazette*, 8, 12 June; Watson mss 760, Freeholders of Kent to Watson, 27 May 1832. [30] *Gent. Mag.* (1852), ii. 307; T. Madge, *Perpetuity of God's Word* (1852); C. Wise, *Rockingham Castle and the Watsons*, 115-16.

S.M.F.

WATSON TAYLOR, **George** (1771–1841), of Cavendish Square, Mdx. and Erlestoke Park, nr. Devizes, Wilts.[1]

NEWPORT I.O.W.	15 Apr. 1816–1818
SEAFORD	1818–1820
EAST LOOE	1820–23 Feb. 1826
DEVIZES	1 Mar. 1826–1832

bap. 12 May 1771,[2] 4th s. of George Watson of Saul's River, Jamaica and Isabella, da. of Thomas Stevenson. *educ.* L. Inn 1788; St. Mary Hall, Oxf. 1791. *m.* 6 Mar. 1810, Anna Susanna, da. of Sir John Taylor, 1st bt., of Lyssons, Jamaica, 4s. (1 *d.v.p.*) 1da. Took additional name of Taylor by royal lic. 19 June 1815, his w. having suc. her bro. Sir Simon Richard Brissett Taylor, 2nd bt., 18 May 1815. *d.* 6 June 1841.

Dep. teller of exch.; commr. of excise 1805-15; capt. Excise Office vols. 1806.

Watson Taylor, whose father was a West India planter, may briefly have practised as a barrister, and in early life made a name for himself as an author. His historical play *England Preserved* was performed, at the request of George III, at the Theatre Royal, Covent Garden in February 1795 and was applauded for its anti-Gallic spirit.[3] Several of his poems were printed, as were his *Cross-Bath Guide* (1815), under the pseudonym of 'Sir Joseph Cheakill', and a comedy, *The Profligate* (1820).[4] He wrote the lines of 'Croppies lie down', which, according to Tom Moore, was a 'song to the tune of which more blood has been shed than often falls to the lot of more lyrical productions'.[5] In his pamphlet *Thoughts on Government* (1799), he praised Britain's mixed monarchy, but warned that 'if not properly restrained, the superior influence of the people will swallow up the power of the crown'. Something of an antiquarian, he arranged the letters of the countess of Suffolk, which were published by John Wilson Croker* in 1824, and edited the *Poems, written in English, by the duke of Orleans* (1827).[6]

He was appointed private secretary to the 1st Marquess Camden during his lord lieutenancy of Ireland from 1795 to 1798, and subsequently held an office there, probably as an assistant to Lord Castlereagh*, the chief secretary. He witnessed the atrocities of 1798 and warned of the threat of a French invasion in late 1801.[7] On a visit to Camden at Bayham Abbey in January 1802 he thanked Lord Auckland, another of Pitt's ministers, for his flattering interest in his poem *The Old Hag* (1801), and added that 'I am happy in this opportunity of assuring you how strongly I shall always feel your lordship's kindness to me when

I first commenced politician'.[8] He apparently followed Castlereagh to the India board in 1802 as his private secretary, but gave that up in May 1804, to resume his old connection with Camden on his appointment as colonial secretary. He subsequently worked again for Castlereagh, who replaced Camden in 1805, and he probably stayed in place under the Grenville ministry, since Camden informed Lord Bathurst, 10 Dec. 1806, that the 'prince is certainly very ill and in a bad way. You know that through Watson I have means of knowing this circumstance'.[9] It was no doubt at the instigation of Camden, the teller of the exchequer, that Watson was appointed to a deputy tellership and a commissionership of excise, which gave him a combined salary of about £2,200.[10]

Although it was acknowledged that he 'bears a most excellent character, and is much esteemed by all his relations and friends', his lack of a private fortune initially stood in the way of his marriage to Anna Susanna Taylor, the niece of the wealthy Jamaican proprietor, Simon Taylor. The match was allowed to proceed, however, on the understanding that a favourable settlement was made on her and any future children.[11] According to Lady Nugent, Simon Taylor was 'the richest man in the island, and piques himself upon making his nephew, Sir Simon [Richard Brissett] Taylor ... the richest commoner in England, which he says he shall be at *his* death'. He died, 14 Apr. 1813, when he owned the estates of Lyssons, Holland, Llanrhumney and Haughton Court, and personal property valued at nearly £740,000, which together brought in an estimated yearly income of £47,000.[12] His heir, who himself had had ambitions to enter Parliament, died, aged only 30 and unmarried, 18 May 1815, and his property, including personal wealth sworn under £100,000, then passed to his elder sister.[13] Watson took the additional name of Taylor, was said to have refused a baronetcy and other honours, and set about establishing his position in high society. Lady Charlotte Bury commented:

> What a wonderful change of fortunes for these persons! – from having had an income of two to three thousand a year, with tastes far beyond such limits, to almost boundless and unequalled riches! It is said they are full of projects of splendour and enjoyment.[14]

Negotiations for the purchase of Houghton from Lord Cholmondeley eventually fell through, but in 1819 Watson Taylor bought Erlestoke for £200,000 from the executors of Joshua Smith, a former Member for Devizes.[15] Regarded as an extremely fine mansion, even the normally critical William Cobbett† described it as a 'very pretty seat', and it was often the scene of society fêtes and royal visits.[16] He also obtained other property in the area and began to cultivate an interest there, becoming a regular attender at meetings of the Devizes Bear Club and the Wiltshire Society. He continued to be listed in the London directories as resident at a number of different places, but he purchased a house in Cavendish Square in 1819 for £20,000, and spent £48,000 on its decoration. Philipp von Neumann, dining there with ministers in March 1821, wrote that the 'splendour of the house equals that of those belonging to the greatest nobles'.[17] Joseph Jekyll[†] remarked at this time that '*Dives* Watson Taylor' was 'an unassuming man of some talents and makes a good use of riches'.[18] Noting his position as 'the entertainer of the fashionable world, and the host of princes', *The Times* observed, 16 Aug. 1831, that 'bred as a dependent in office, as a point of honour, he seems to have adopted the principles of his superiors, and he firmly maintains them'.

In October 1815 Watson Taylor informed his rich Jamaican agent and friend, John Shand, that

it is my intention to go into Parliament at the first convenient opportunity and accustomed to public life, it is possible I may be induced to take a part in the discussion, which may there arise, upon West India concerns.

The following year he bought a seat at Newport, Isle of Wight, transferring to Seaford at the 1818 general election, but he failed to find one for Shand.[19] He was added to the standing committee of the West India Planters and Merchants' Committee, 19 Jan. 1816, and was a steady attender at its meetings throughout that year. Thereafter he was seldom present, but because of his management of his wife's Jamaican estates, he took a close interest in their affairs. As he reported to Shand, 19 Feb. 1816, 'from my long habits of friendship with Lord Castlereagh, I have ready access to him', and he used this private channel to raise sensitive colonial matters with the foreign secretary. He respected his wife's desire that her slaves should be treated with considerations of 'pure humanity, benevolence, justice and liberality', but opposed the abolitionists' campaigns for their emancipation. He was sanguine of success, noting in early 1819 that 'ministers may from time to time temporise, but they dare not concede ultimately to visionaries, that, for which they are struggling, and which all parties know would be the forerunner of the destruction of our colonies'. He occasionally raised West Indian issues in the House, where he was otherwise largely inactive.[20]

At the general election of 1820 he was returned for East Looe by Sir Edward Buller[†], who made way for him because of illness, and who informed Lord Liverpool, the prime minister, that he would find him a 'most strenuous supporter of those principles which have invariably guided my actions through life, and equally disposed towards the government'.[21] It was reported that Watson Taylor's town house was 'superbly illuminated' on the acquittal of Queen Caroline in November 1820, but he did not vote in the division on the opposition's censure motion, 6 Feb. 1821.[22] He witnessed the petition from the Jamaican House of Assembly for relief being presented to the king, 23 Feb.[23] He voted against Catholic claims, 28 Feb. 1821, and the Catholic peers bill, 30 Apr. 1822. He explained to the House, 30 June 1821, that the duke of Clarence had previously declined to accept so low a grant as £6,000 because he had been advised that it would have made his former award appear excessive. He voted against more extensive tax reductions to relieve distress, 11 Feb. 1822, abolition of one of the joint-postmasterships, 13 Mar., and inquiry into the conduct of the lord advocate relative to the Scottish press, 25 June. On 22 May 1822 he advised Peel, the home secretary, that several hundred Irish refugees were making their way from the west country to London.[24] He divided against condemning chancery delays, 5 June 1823, and, according to Lord Colchester, he regretted, 'as a *parliamentary Protestant*', that the lord chancellor had blocked his motion in the Lords, 18 July, for a return of all Catholic churches and institutions.[25]

At the Planters and Merchants' Committee meeting, 10 Feb. 1824, Watson Taylor spoke against any discussion of the abolition of slavery on the ground that it was a subject which ought first to be decided by the colonial legislatures.[26] In the House he objected to the way in which itinerant adventurers had collected signatures for anti-slavery petitions by inflaming the passions of the people, 15 Mar., and made clear that 'it was the abuse, and not the use' of the right of petitioning to which he objected. The following day he boasted that he had spent £140,000 over eight years in attempting to ameliorate the condition of his slaves, and that 'no consideration of equal weight, with regard to the management of his property, had pressed upon his mind'. He said he was reassured by Canning's speech, which was 'remarkable for its temperance and for its moderation', expressed his hope that eventual emancipation would be accompanied by compensation for the proprietors, and excused the conduct of the Jamaican assembly, as it had to act in the midst of 'fearful dangers'. On 13 May he justified the pensions received by government clerks, 'a very deserving class of persons'. He did not vote in the division on the opposition motion condemning the trial of the

Methodist missionary John Smith in Demerara, 11 June. He spoke in defence of colonial interests at the Devizes Bear Club dinner, 27 Aug. 1824.[27] Watson Taylor wrote to Peel, 2 Feb. 1825, to offer him a copy of Castlereagh's paper on the Catholic question and the reply of Lord Rosslyn, who, he thought, had acted beneficially in poisoning George III's ear against concessions to the Catholics. He added that

if now, or at any time during the session, *you* should foresee the want of an independent vote, let me know quietly and I will run up, from my plantings and my road makings, and house alterings and all my other country gentleman pursuits.

Peel thanked him for the papers, and asked for his attendance on 10 Feb. for the Irish unlawful societies bill. He divided in favour of the third reading, 25 Feb., and against Catholic relief, 1 Mar. Asking Peel to attend the Wiltshire Society dinner, which he was due to chair, 10 Apr., he wrote jocosely that 'I shall be with you on the second reading. NB this is not meant as a bribe'.[28] He duly voted against the second, 21 Apr., and third reading of the relief bill, 10 May, and the Irish franchise bill, 26 Apr. 1825.

He attended the dinners for the new mayor of Devizes in 1824 and 1825, speaking on both occasions of his attachment to the town and his hopes for cordial relations between its inhabitants and Erlestoke. He subscribed £500 to the costs of the local improvement bill in 1825, and in January 1826 he qualified as a magistrate for the county.[29] He was thus placed in an excellent position to stand when Thomas Grimston Bucknall Estcourt resigned his seat in February 1826, vacating East Looe for this purpose. Bolstered by his connections in the corporation, he saw off a challenge from another local candidate and was elected as a self-styled independent, who 'recognized no political leader' and 'had no favourite party'.[30] He was not present in the House to vote in the division on Denman's motion condemning the Jamaican slave trials, 2 Mar., and no trace of parliamentary activity has been found for that session. He contributed a further £500 to the town's improvements and was returned with his colleague John Pearse, amid popular celebrations, at the general election. On the hustings, 9 June, he admitted he had not committed himself on certain issues, but argued for a reconciliation between the agricultural and commercial interests, and against Catholic relief.[31] He spoke in praise of Camden's eldest son Lord Brecknock and Lord John Thynne, the newly elected Members for Bath, at a dinner there, 29 June 1826.[32] He was elected a free burgess of Devizes, 23 Jan., and sworn, 4 June 1827, when he declared that

he would have no fear of standing again even if every householder had the vote.[33]

He promised Peel that he would attend on the first day of the 1827 session, and voted against Catholic claims, 6 Mar. He warned Peel, 7 May, that

in consequence of a remark I heard yesterday from an able and warm supporter of the [Canningite-Whig] coalition, I suspect that they hope you will tonight commit yourself *warmly*, and that they may make out a disagreement between your line of argument now, and that when you were in office, and manfully shared any blame which might be placed solely to the account [of William] Huskisson.*

He also informed Peel that the Dissenters intended to petition in large numbers for repeal of the Test Acts; he himself presented two from those resident in Devizes, 30 May 1827, 18 Feb. 1828.[34] In January he pledged his support for the duke of Wellington's administration. He voted against repeal of the Test Acts, 26 Feb., and Catholic relief, 12 May 1828.[35] In February 1829 he was listed by Planta, the patronage secretary, as one of the 'opposition or doubtful men, who, we think, will vote with the government on this question', but he divided against emancipation throughout March. In October he was listed by Sir Richard Vyvyan*, the Ultra leader, among the 'Tories strongly opposed to the present government', and on 4 Dec. 1829 Lord Lansdowne described him to Lord Holland as one of those who were 'quite malignants' in their attitude to the ministry.[36] He voted against Jewish emancipation, 17 May 1830. He told the House that he would follow Lord Chandos if he pushed his motion for lower duties on West Indian sugar to a division, 14 June, so he probably voted in the minority of 23. At the Planters and Merchants' Committee, 10 July 1830, he seconded the vote of thanks to Chandos for his defence of their interests.[37]

On one of his incognito rambles, 20 July 1830, William IV met Watson Taylor in Pall Mall, and, surrounded by a mob, they walked together up St. James's.[38] He spoke in praise of the king during the general election, when he again offered for Devizes. He acknowledged that he had attempted to defend the endangered rights of the church, but promised to support ministers over the revolution in France. He argued against excessive expenditure and pointed out that he had retired without a pension or a sinecure. He was elected unopposed.[39] He attended the Wiltshire meeting to congratulate the king on his accession, 17 Aug., and in Devizes, 29 Sept., he commented on the value of independent Members such as himself, by whom 'the balance was sustained between ministerial profligacy on the one side and factious revolutionary principles on the other'.[40] He was listed by ministers among their 'friends', and voted with them on the civil list, 15 Nov. He was given a month's leave on account of the disturbed state of his neighbourhood, 30 Nov. 1830, when he made himself popular on his own estate by increasing wages, reducing rents and ending the preservation of game.[41] Watson Taylor voted against the second reading of the Grey ministry's reform bill, 22 Mar. 1831. He acknowledged that he might risk his popularity in Devizes, but declared that he would 'continue to oppose it in all its future stages', 18 Apr., when he denied that his seat was in the nomination of Lord Sidmouth. He voted for Gascoyne's wrecking amendment the following day. He was, indeed, attacked in the local press during the subsequent general election, when he gave a long defence of his independence and claimed that the measure was revolutionary rather than ameliorative and 'a *disfranchising* rather than an *enfranchising* bill'. He was, however, again returned by the corporation.[42] He voted against the second reading of the reintroduced bill, 6 July, at least once for adjourning debate on it, 12 July, and for postponing consideration of the partial disfranchisement of Chippenham, 27 July. He justified the grant for Princess Victoria, 3, 10 Aug. He signed the Wiltshire declaration against reform.[43] He voted against the third reading of the bill, 19 Sept., paired against its passage, 21 Sept., and divided against the second reading of the Scottish bill, 23 Sept. He voted against the second reading of the revised bill, 17 Dec. 1831, going into committee on it, 20 Jan 1832, the enfranchisement of Tower Hamlets, 28 Feb., and the third reading, 22 Mar. He was in the majority against Wason's amendment to limit polling in boroughs with less than 1,200 voters to one day, 15 Feb. He voted against government on the Russian-Dutch loan, 26 Jan., but was listed as an absentee from the division of 12 July 1832.

According to John Macarthur, writing in May 1821, Watson Taylor was

> sadly out of spirits respecting his West India property. I do not believe it produces one third of what it was when he succeeded to the estate. Unlike other West Indians, however, he has an English estate to fall back on.[44]

According to Hudson Gurney*, he faced financial disaster late the following year, 'occasioned by the total failure of his West India remittances'.[45] In 1823 he raised over £30,000 from sales of his books and paintings, and two years later he had to part with the furniture and sculpture from Cavendish Square, many of the finest pieces being bought by the king.[46] His financial problems worsened over the next decade,

exacerbated by his reckless purchases, and when the collapse came in mid-1832, he brought down many of his dependants with him. As the local newspaper commented, after his possessions had been put up for auction

> notwithstanding Mr. Watson Taylor was surrounded by a degree of splendour, which it has been well said, might have excited the envy of royalty itself, his mind was scarcely for a moment at ease – he appeared to have an insatiable thirst for something he did not possess ... He could not for a moment have thought of the money he was expending.[47]

By the autumn he was reported to have taken up residence in Holland. Nothing was heard of his retaining his seat at Devizes, and he left the House at the dissolution in December 1832. He was not formally declared bankrupt, but in 1839 he was still reckoned to owe over £60,000. The Erlestoke and Jamaican estates were, however, settled on his wife, who continued to control them until her death in 1853.[48] Watson Taylor died in Edinburgh in June 1841. No will, administration or entry in the death duty register has been found. His eldest son Simon (1811-1902), who had been elected a member of the standing committee of the Planters and Merchants' Committee, 8 Feb. 1832, restored his family's standing and was Liberal Member for Devizes, 1857-9.[49]

[1] See also I. Ide, 'A Very Pretty Seat: Erlestoke Park', *Wilts. Arch. Mag.* xciii (2000), 9-19. [2] IGI (London). [3] *The Times*, 23 Feb. 1795; H. Bull and J. Waylen, *Hist. Devizes*, 527. [4] *Allibone's Dict. of Eng. Literature* (1871), iii. 2343-4. [5] *Moore Mems.* v. 314. [6] Add. 34569, f. 62; Add. 22625-9; BL, Harl. ms 782. [7] Cent. Kent. Stud. Camden mss U840 C90/3; C134 (NRA 8410); *Colchester Diary*, i. 365-6. [8] Add. 34455, f. 476. [9] Add. 13446, f. 81; *R. Kalendar* (1805), 132; (1806), 131; *HMC Bathurst*, 54. [10] Inst. of Commonwealth Stud. Simon Taylor mss VI/A/84. [11] Ibid. VI/A/84, 87, 91, 92; I/J/2, 3, 6, 14. [12] R. B. Sheridan, 'Simon Taylor, Sugar Tycoon of Jamaica', *Agricultural Hist.* xlv (1971), 287, 289-95. [13] Simon Taylor mss VI/A/44, 50, 81; IR26/657/490. [14] *Lady in Waiting*, 181-2. [15] Simon Taylor mss VIII/B/14, 28, 35; D/20; *VCH Wilts.* vii. 84; Wellington mss WP1/634/10; J. Waylen, *Annals of Devizes*, 25. [16] Wilts. RO, Poore mss 1915/60/2, *sub* 10 Aug. 1829; *Cobbett's Rural Rides* ed. G.D.H. and M. Cole, ii. 400; *Devizes Gazette*, 4 Aug., 4 Oct. 1820; *Keenes' Bath Jnl.* 7 Dec. 1829, 1 Nov. 1830. [17] *Von Neumann Diary*, i. 56; *Arbuthnot Jnl.* i. 84; *Devizes Gazette*, 8 May 1823. [18] Dorset RO, Bond mss D/BOH C16, Jekyll to Bond, 20 Mar. 1821. [19] Simon Taylor mss VIII/A/2, 8, 9, 12; B/21, 25, 36; C/1-3; *HP Commons, 1790-1820*, v. 497. [20] Simon Taylor mss VIII/A/3, 6, 12; B/14; D/2, 4, 5, 8, 10-12, 18; Inst. of Commonwealth Stud. M915/3, 4. [21] Add. 38283, f. 228; *West Briton*, 10 Mar. 1820. [22] *Devizes Gazette*, 16 Nov. 1820. [23] L.J. Ragatz, *Guide for Study of Brit. Caribbean Hist.* 145. [24] Add. 40347, f. 133. [25] *Colchester Diary*, iii. 297. [26] *The Times*, 11 Feb. 1824. [27] *Devizes Gazette*, 2 Sept. 1824. [28] Ibid. 12 May 1825; Add. 43073, ff. 18, 22; 40374, f. 40; 40376, f. 65. [29] *Devizes Gazette*, 30 Sept. 1824, 6 Oct., 17 Nov. 1825; *Salisbury Jnl.* 16 Jan. 1826. [30] *Devizes Gazette*, 9 Feb., 2 Mar. 1826. [31] Ibid. 15 June; *Salisbury Jnl.* 1 May 1826; Add. 40387, f. 111. [32] *Keenes' Bath Jnl.* 3 July 1826. [33] Wilts. RO, Devizes borough recs. G20/1/22; *Devizes*

Gazette, 7 June 1827. [34] Add. 40394, f. 111; *The Times*, 31 May 1827. [35] Add. 40395, f. 80; Wellington mss WP1/915/43. [36] Add. 51687. [37] Inst. of Commonwealth Stud. M915/4. [38] *Ellenborough Diary*, ii. 319; *Greville Mems.* ii. 9. [39] *Devizes Gazette*, 5 Aug. 1830. [40] Ibid. 30 Sept.; *Salisbury Jnl.* 23 Aug. 1830. [41] *Devizes Gazette*, 9 Dec.; *Keenes' Bath Jnl.* 13 Dec. 1830. [42] *Devizes Gazette*, 31 Mar., 14 Apr., 5 May 1831. [43] Ibid. 11 Aug. 1831. [44] Mitchell Lib. Sydney, Macarthur mss ML A 2911, f. 39. [45] Trinity Coll. Camb. Dawson Turner mss DT2/K3/13, Gurney to Dawson Turner, 4 Dec. 1822. [46] S. de Ricci, *English Collectors*, 95; *Cat. of Collection of Watson Taylor* (1823); *The Times*, 19 June 1823; H. Roberts, '"Quite Appropriate for Windsor Castle": Geo. IV and Watson Taylor', *Furniture Hist.* xxxvi (2000), 115-21. [47] *Devizes Gazette*, 21, 28 June 1832; *Cat. of Property at Erlestoke Mansion* (1832); *Raikes Jnl.* i. 26. [48] *Salisbury Jnl.* 1 Oct. 1832; *The Times*, 25 Feb. 1839; Simon Taylor mss VII/B; PROB 11/2169/234. [49] Inst. of Commonwealth Stud. M915/4; *The Times*, 12 June 1841, 26 Dec. 1902.

S.M.F.

WATTS RUSSELL, Jesse (1786–1875), of Ilam Hall, Staffs.

GATTON   1820–1826

b. 6 May 1786, 2nd s. of Jesse Russell (*d.* 1820), soap boiler, of Goodman's Yard, Minories, London and Walthamstow, Essex and Elizabeth, da. of Thomas Noble of Boroughbridge, Yorks. *educ.* Worcester Coll. Oxf. 1804-8. *m.* (1) 29 Jan. 1811, Mary (*d.* 8 July 1840), da. and h. of David Pike Watts, wine merchant, of Portland Place, Mdx., 4s. 4da. (1 *d.v.p.*); (2) 20 June 1843, Maria (*d.* 30 Oct. 1844), da. of Peter Barker of Bedford, 1s.; (3) 22 Nov. 1862, Martha, da. of John Leach of Wexford, *s.p.* Took name of Watts before Russell by royal lic. 28 Mar. 1817. *d.* 26 Mar. 1875.

Sheriff, Staffs. 1819-20.

Though described by an obituarist as 'a venerable country gentleman',[1] Watts Russell was in fact a land-owning *parvenu*, the son of an East End soap manu-facturer. He was educated at Oxford and there is no evidence that he took part in his father's business. He was established at his Staffordshire seat by the time of his advantageous marriage in 1811 to the heiress of a wealthy wine merchant, who died five years later and whose surname he subsequently adopted.[2] On his father's death in 1820 he received a half-share of estates in Essex and a third-share of the residue of personalty sworn under £500,000.[3] At the general election that year he was returned for Gatton, presum-ably as a paying guest of the patron Sir Mark Wood†.

He was a fairly regular attender who gave silent support to Lord Liverpool's ministry (his father had signed the London merchants' declaration of loyalty in 1795)[4]. He was granted a fortnight's leave on account of his father's illness, 21 June 1820. He voted in defence of ministers' conduct towards Queen Caroline, 6 Feb. 1821. He divided against Catholic

relief, 28 Feb. He voted against Maberly's resolution on the state of the revenue, 6 Mar., repeal of the addi-tional malt duty, 3 Apr., and Hume's economy and retrenchment motion, 27 June. He divided against the disfranchisement of civil officers of the ordnance, 12 Apr., parliamentary reform, 23 May, and the forgery punishment mitigation bill, 23 May 1821. He voted against more extensive tax reductions, 11 Feb., aboli-tion of one of the joint-postmasterships, 13 Mar., and repeal of the salt duties, 28 June 1822. He divided against relieving Catholic peers of their disabilities, 30 Apr. 1822. He was one of the ministerialist ren-egades who voted with the majority for inquiry into the prosecution of the Dublin Orange rioters, 22 Apr. 1823. He divided for repeal of the usury laws, 27 Feb., and against the motion condemning the trial of the Methodist missionary John Smith in Demerara, 11 June 1824. He was granted a month's leave for urgent private business, 24 Feb., paired against Catholic relief, 21 Apr.,[5] and voted against it, 10 May 1825. He retired at the dissolution in 1826.

He apparently made no attempt to return to the House until the general election of 1832, when he stood unsuccessfully as a Conservative for North Staffordshire. The diarist William Dyott commented that while 'not an orator', Watts Russell seemed 'a worthy and most excellent man', and Sir Robert Peel 'spoke warmly' of him. He became a vice-president of the Staffordshire Conservative Association on its foundation in 1835. Three years later Robert Plumer Ward* remarked that he was one of those Staffordshire landowners 'with no blood, but immensely rich', but that he 'bears his faculties so meekly, that he is deservedly popular'. He declined an invitation at that time to offer again for North Staffordshire.[6] He died in March 1875 and left Ilam Hall, which he had had rebuilt 'in the Gothic style' in the 1820s, and which Dyott deemed 'most magnificent' and 'splendidly furnished', together with estates in Derbyshire and Northamptonshire, to his eldest son, Jesse David Watts Russell (1812-79), Conservative Member for North Staffordshire, 1841-7. Known as a patron of the arts, he left a sizeable collection of paintings 'chiefly of the English School', which were auctioned at Christie's.[7]

[1] *The Times*, 1 Apr. 1875. [2] *Gent. Mag.* (1816), ii. 182-3; PROB 11/1583/473; IR26/694/545. The personalty was sworn under £160,000. [3] PROB 11/1632/437; IR26/836/679. [4] *Gent. Mag.* (1820), i. 639. [5] *The Times*, 26 Apr. 1825. [6] *Dyott's Diary*, ii. 133-5, 149, 196-7; P.G. Patmore, *Friends and Acquaintances*, ii. 103; Keele Univ. Lib. Sneyd mss 3031. [7] N. Pevsner, *Buildings of England: Staffs.* 152; *Dyott's Diary*, ii. 181; *Cat. of Pictures of Jesse Watts Russell* (1875).

H.J.S.

WEBB, Edward (1779–1839), of Adwell, nr. Tetsworth, Glos. and 181 Piccadilly, Mdx.

GLOUCESTER   1 Oct. 1816–1832

b. 30 Jan. 1779, 2nd s. of John Webb[†] (*d.* 1795) of Cote House, nr. Bristol, Glos. and Arabella, da. of Thomas Bushell of Sevinbroke, Oxon. *educ.* Elmore Court, Glos. c. 1793.[1] *m.* 22 July 1807,[2] Jane Mary Catherine, da. of Sir John Guise, 1st bt., of Highnam Court, Glos., 1da. *d.* 18 Sept. 1839.

Writer, E.I. Co. (Bengal) 1795; asst. to office of Persian translator to bd. of revenue 1795; asst. to registrar of sadar diwani and nizamat adalat 1796; asst. to collector of Dinajpur 1796; res. 1801.

Capt. N. Glos. militia 1803; lt.-col. 1 R. East Glos. militia 1809.

Webb had succeeded to most of his father's property through the wills of his elder brother John in 1797 and of his mother in 1801.[3] He was first returned for Gloucester at a by-election in 1816 after an expensive contest, supported by the Whig corporation and the Gloucestershire Constitutional Whig Club, in which his brother-in-law, Sir Berkeley William Guise*, the county Member, was prominent.[4] He was returned unopposed with his Tory colleague Cooper at the general election of 1820, after proclaiming his support for 'the just prerogatives of the crown' and opposition to 'all such measures as tended to subvert our valued rights and privileges'.[5] He continued to vote with the Whig opposition to Lord Liverpool's ministry on most major issues, including parliamentary reform, 9, 10, 31 May 1821, 25 Apr., 3 June 1822, 24 Apr., 2 June 1823, 26 Feb. 1824, 13, 27 Apr. 1826. However, he was one of the few Whigs who divided against Catholic claims, 28 Feb. 1821.[6] He rarely spoke in debate, but reportedly denied that the burden of local rates was light, 15 Mar. 1821.[7] He voted to go into committee on the usury laws repeal bill, 17 June 1823, but turned against this measure, 27 Feb. 1824, 17 Feb. 1825. He divided with the minority for inquiry into the state of Ireland, 11 May, but with ministers for the Irish insurrection bill, 14 June 1824. He voted against the Irish unlawful societies bill, 21, 25 Feb., but also against Catholic claims, 1 Mar., 21 Apr., 10 May, and the Irish franchise bill, 9 May 1825. At the annual meeting of the Constitutional Whig Club, 24 Jan. 1826, he acknowledged that his anti-Catholic stance was contrary to the views of many of his constituents, but claimed that he acted from conscience and declared his intention of standing at the next general election.[8] He voted in the protectionist minority against the corn bill, 11 May 1826. At the general election that summer he was again returned unopposed with Cooper, after a threatened intervention by a local Whig, John Phillpotts*, failed to materialize. He affirmed his commitment to the abolition of sinecures, the repeal of taxes bearing heavily on the poorest classes and parliamentary reform.[9]

He divided against the Clarence annuity bill, 2 Mar., for information on the Barrackpoor mutiny, 22 Mar., and for inquiry into the Irish miscellaneous estimates, 5 Apr. 1827. He again voted against Catholic relief, 6 Mar., and the corn bill, 2 Apr. He was granted a week's leave for urgent private business, having served on an election committee, 5 Apr. He divided against Canning's ministry to remove bankruptcy jurisdiction from chancery, 22 May, to disfranchise Penryn, 28 May, and against the grant to improve water communications in Canada, 12 June 1827. He presented petitions for repeal of the Test Acts, 21, 25 Feb., and voted in that sense, 26 Feb., but he paired against Catholic claims, 12 May 1828. He voted against extending East Retford's franchise to Bassetlaw freeholders, 21 Mar., and for a lower pivot price for the corn duties, 22 Apr. He divided against the financial provision for Canning's family, 13 May, and the grant for the Society for Propagation of the Gospels in the Colonies, 6 June, and to reduce civil list pensions, 10 June, condemn the misapplication of public money for work on Buckingham House, 23 June, cut the salary of the lieutenant-general of the ordnance, 4 July, and delete the grant for North American fortifications, 7 July 1828. In February 1829 Planta, the Wellington ministry's patronage secretary, predicted that Webb would side 'with government' for Catholic emancipation, despite his previous opposition. He presented an anti-Catholic petition from the Gloucestershire rural dean and clergy, 23 Feb., and testified to the respectability of the signatories to a similar petition from Gloucester, 2 Mar., but indeed voted for emancipation, 6, 30 Mar. He divided for an amendment to the Irish franchise bill to allow reregistration, 20 Mar., and for Lord Blandford's reform scheme, 2 June 1829. He voted for Hume's tax cutting amendment, 15 Feb., and inquiry into the revision of taxation, 25 Mar. 1830, and steadily in the revived opposition campaign for retrenchment that session. He again divided for Blandford's reform scheme, 18 Feb., and against the East Retford disfranchisement bill, 15 Mar. He presented a Gloucester corporation petition against renewal of the East India Company's charter, 29 Mar. He voted against ministers on the affair at Terceira, 28 Apr., the civil government of Canada, 25 May, and to abolish the Irish lord lieutenancy, 11 May. He divided against Jewish emancipation, 17 May. He paired for abolition of the death penalty for forgery, 7 June, and voted against the administration of justice bill,

18 June, and to prohibit sales for on-consumption in beer houses, 21 June 1830. He offered again for Gloucester at the general election that summer, when he faced a challenge from Phillpotts but was helped by the decision of another Whig candidate, Frederick Berkeley*, to withdraw rather than jeopardize his chances. In his address, Webb stressed his voting record on retrenchment and tax cuts and advocated measures to 'ameliorate the condition of my fellow creatures', including 'the abolition of slavery and the removal of punishment too severe to be inflicted'. He was returned at the head of the poll.[10]

He voted against Wellington's ministry, who of course had listed him among their 'foes', in the crucial civil list division, 15 Nov. 1830. He presented a Gloucester corporation petition in favour of parliamentary reform, 26 Feb., and petitions supporting the Grey ministry's bill from the same body, 16 Mar., and the inhabitants of Gloucester, 19 Mar. 1831. He divided for the bill's second reading, 22 Mar., and against Gascoyne's wrecking amendment, 19 Apr. 1831. Next day he stated that the freemen of Gloucester, many of whom faced disfranchisement, were nevertheless 'entirely satisfied' with the measure. At the ensuing dissolution he was persuaded not to retire, in accordance with a promise made to Berkeley at the previous election, and to stand in conjunction with him. He trusted that there would be a 'triumphant majority' for the bill and that 'the whole horde of borough-mongers might in a very few months be driven from their strongholds'. He wished to see 'the just rights of the people exercised and the privileges of voting extended to those who contributed to the burthens of the state'. He was returned in second place behind Berkeley, but comfortably ahead of Phillpotts.[11]

Webb divided for the second reading of the reintroduced reform bill, 6 July 1831, and generally supported its details. However, he voted against the disfranchisement of Downton, 21 July, which caused 'great offence' in Gloucester and led to his effigy being burned in the streets,[12] and the proposed division of counties, 11 Aug., and for the Chandos amendment to enfranchise £50 tenants-at-will, 18 Aug., and the preservation of the rights of non-resident freemen, 30 Aug. He divided for the bill's third reading, 19 Sept., its passage, 21 Sept., the second reading of the Scottish bill, 23 Sept., and Lord Ebrington's confidence motion, 10 Oct. He attended the unofficial county meeting in Gloucester to petition the Lords for reform, 28 Sept., when he declared that 'he had always supported the bill and never was absent from

any of its stages'.[13] He voted to punish only those guilty of bribery at the Dublin election and against the censure motion on the Irish administration, 23 Aug. He divided for the second reading of the revised bill, 17 Dec. 1831, and generally supported its details, but he voted against the enfranchisement of Gateshead, 5 Mar. 1832. He divided for the third reading, 22 Mar., and Ebrington's motion for an address asking the king to appoint only ministers committed to carrying an unimpaired measure, 10 May. He voted against ministers on the Russian-Dutch loan, 26 Jan., but was absent from the divisions on this issue in July. He divided with the minority for inquiry into the glove trade, 31 Jan., but with government on relations with Portugal, 9 Feb. He voted to recommit the Irish registry of deeds bill, 9 Apr. He was in the minorities for the abolition of slavery, 24 May, and permanent provision for Irish paupers from a tax on absentees, 19 June. He voted to make coroners' inquests public, 20 June 1832. That summer he was requisitioned to offer again for Gloucester at the impending general election, but announced that he would not do so on the ground that his candidature might jeopardize Berkeley's return, adding that in any case 'if a seat ... is only to be obtained by an enormous sacrifice of money and anxiety of mind, I am not ambitious of seeking it on those terms'.[14] He made an unsuccessful attempt to regain his seat, in the Liberal interest, at a by-election in May 1838. He died in New York in September 1839, after being taken ill on a visit to Niagara Falls.[15] He left the residue of his estate, including land in four counties, to his only child Elizabeth Frances Webb; his personalty was sworn under £25,000.[16]

[1] Diary of a Cotswold Parson ed. D. Verey, 59. [2] Gent. Mag. (1807), ii. 779. [3] PROB 11/1258/221; 1291/382; 1362/564; IR26/9/250; 54/146. [4] G. Goodman, 'Pre-Reform Elections in Gloucester City, 1789-1831', Bristol and Glos. Arch. Soc. Trans. lxxxiv (1965), 148-50. [5] Gloucester Jnl. 28 Feb.; Cheltenham Chron. 16 Mar. 1820. [6] A. Mitchell, Whigs in Opposition, 14. [7] The Times, 16 Mar. 1821. [8] Gloucester Jnl. 30 Jan. 1826. [9] Ibid. 5, 12 June 1826. [10] Ibid. 3, 31 July, 7 Aug. 1830. [11] Ibid. 30 Apr., 7 May 1831. [12] Ibid. 30 July 1831. [13] Ibid. 1 Oct. 1831. [14] Ibid. 14 July, 11 Aug. 1832. [15] Gent. Mag. (1840), i. 94. [16] PROB 11/1920/790; IR26/1536/637.

T.A.J.

WELBY, Glynne Earle (1806–1875), of Denton Hall, nr. Grantham, Lincs.

GRANTHAM 1830–1857

b. 26 June 1806, 1st s. of Sir William Earle Welby†, 2nd bt., of Denton and Wilhelmina, da. and h. of William Spry, gov. Barbados. educ. Rugby 1820; Oriel, Oxf. 1824. m. 6 Mar. 1828, Frances, da. of Sir Montague

Cholmeley*, 1st bt., 7s. (2 *d.v.p.*) 4da. (2 *d.v.p.*). *suc.* fa. as 3rd bt. 3 Nov. 1852; took additional name of Gregory by royal lic. 5 July 1861. *d.* 23 Aug. 1875.

Capt. Royal S. Lincs. militia 1847, maj. 1852, lt.-col. 1852-4.

Sheriff, Lincs. 1860-1.

Originally from the area of Wellibi, near Grantham, the Welbys could trace their ancestry back to the Conquest. William Welby† (*d.* 1657), who was elected as a Parliamentarian but prevented from taking his seat by Cromwell, acquired the manor of Denton, near the Leicestershire border, in 1648. This Member's grandfather represented Grantham, 1802-6, as did his father, who headed the local Red interest, 1807-20, and his father-in-law Sir Montague Cholmeley, who was returned at a by-election, 1820-6. At the 1830 general election Welby came forward on the family interest in place of his brother-in-law Montague Cholmeley, who had assured him that he intended to stand down. It was rumoured that he would be returned unopposed, but Cholmeley's decision to offer again forced a contest. During his campaign he declared his principles to be those of his father, citing his 'attachment to church and state', but refused to give 'any pledge as to my future conduct'. He topped the four-day poll and was returned with Cholmeley.[1]

He was listed by the Wellington ministry among their 'friends', but he voted against them in the crucial division on the civil list, 15 Nov. 1830. Yet he divided against the second reading of the Grey ministry's reform bill, 22 Mar., and for Gascoyne's wrecking amendment, 19 Apr. 1831. On account of these votes, the local press did not expect him to offer again at the ensuing general election, but he returned to Denton and immediately offered an unrepentant address, 24 Apr.[2] Canvassing next day, he told the electors that he 'could not consent to assist' in depriving so many voters 'of their rights and privileges ... for no other fault than that of being poor'. His effigy was burnt in the town, but with the support of the London out-voters he topped the three-day poll. At the declaration he regretted being at odds with some of his constituents on reform, which he believed 'would endanger our best and dearest institutions, which it had taken centuries to perfect'. A few stones were thrown at him during his chairing but caused no injury.[3] Welby was evidently a lax attender in the new Parliament. He voted against the second reading of the reintroduced reform bill, 6 July, its passage, 21 Sept., and against ministers on the Dublin election controversy, 23 Aug. 1831. He paired against the second reading of the revised reform bill, 17 Dec. 1831,[4] and voted against the enfranchisement

of Tower Hamlets, 28 Feb., and the third reading of the reform bill, 22 Mar. 1832. He divided against ministers on the Russian-Dutch loan, 26 Jan., 12 July. He presented a Grantham petition against the general register bill, 8 Mar. 1832. He is not known to have spoken in debate in this period.

At the 1832 general election he successfully contested Grantham, where he sat as a Conservative until his retirement in 1857, when he was replaced by his eldest son William (1829-98). In compliance with the will of Gregory Gregory of Harlaxton, near Grantham, he added the name of Gregory to his own in 1861. He died at Denton in August 1875. By his will, dated 18 Oct. 1873, he left his wife his leasehold London house in Upper Belgrave Street and an annuity of £1,000. He gave £22,000 to each of his four surviving younger sons and £5,000 to each of his two daughters in addition to their 'ample' marriage settlements. The residue and family estates passed to William, his successor in the baronetcy, who was Conservative Member for Grantham, 1857-68, and South Lincolnshire, 1868-84.

[1] *Grantham Pollbook* (Storr, 1830), *passim.*; *Drakard's Stamford News*, 6 Aug. 1830. [2] *Boston Gazette*, 26 Apr. 1831. [3] Ibid. 3 May 1831; *Grantham Pollbook* (Ridge, 1831), *passim.* [4] *The Times*, 22 Dec. 1831.

M.P.J.C./P.J.S.

WELD FORESTER, Hon. George Cecil Weld (1807–1886), of Willey Park, Salop and 14 Stanhope Street, Mdx.

WENLOCK 17 June 1828–10 Oct. 1874

b. 10 May 1807, 2nd s. of Cecil Forester (afterwards Weld Forester†) (*d.* 1828) of Ross Hall, nr. Shrewsbury and Lady Katherine Mary Manners, da. of Charles, 4th duke of Rutland; bro. of Hon. John George Weld Weld Forester*. *educ.* Westminster 1818-22. *m.* 8 Nov. 1862, Hon. Mary Anne Jervis, da. of Edward, 2nd Visct. St. Vincent, wid. of David Ochterlony Dyce Sombré†, h. to the Begum Sumroo, *s.p. suc.* bro. as 3rd Bar. Forester 10 Oct. 1874. *d.* 14 Feb. 1886.

Cornet R. Horse. Gds. 1824, lt. 1826, capt. 1832, brevet maj. 1846, maj. and lt.-col. 1848, half-pay 1859; maj.-gen. 1863; lt.-gen. 1871; gen. 1877.

Groom of bedchamber Feb. 1830-Feb. 1831; comptroller of household Feb. 1852-Jan. 1853, Mar. 1858-June 1859; PC 27 Feb. 1852.

Cecil, or 'Cis' Forester as he was generally known, was, like his elder brother George, a godson of George IV. He was intended for the army, and in May 1822 his father Lord Forester, a coronation peer, asked the duke of Wellington to recommend him 'for a cornetcy in the Blues'. This the duke agreed to do, and to 'give him leave of absence afterwards for as long a period as you please to enable him to finish his education'.[1] The Shropshire Member Rowland Hill's cornetcy in the Blues was purchased for him, 27 May 1824.[2] When on leave, Forester was a popular guest at balls and house parties and a hunting and gambling companion of Robert Myddelton Biddulph*, to whom his sister Isabella, who afterwards married George Anson*, was briefly engaged.[3] His coming of age in May 1828 was clouded by the death of his gout-ridden father, who 'fell off a pony'; and on 24 June he took his seat as Member for Wenlock in place of George, who had succeeded to the peerage.[4]

Weld Forester, who soon complained that attending the Commons curtailed his hunting,[5] divided with the Wellington administration against ordnance reductions, 4 July, and on the silk duties, 14 July 1828. His uncle, the Rev. Townshend Forester, a stalwart of the Shropshire Brunswick Club, encouraged anti-Catholic petitioning,[6] and the patronage secretary Planta's February 1829 prediction that Weld Forester would vote 'with government' for emancipation proved incorrect, for he divided resolutely against the measure, 6, 18, 30 Mar. 1829, although his brother gave Wellington his proxy.[7] He voted against transferring East Retford's seats to Birmingham, 11 Feb. 1830. His re-election following his appointment as groom of the bedchamber that month passed without incident and it soon became his duty to issue bulletins on the king's deteriorating health.[8] The only votes recorded for him before the dissolution precipitated by George IV's death were against Jewish emancipation, 5 Apr., 17 May. He presented his constituents' petition for lower duties on bricks, tiles and slates, 9 July 1830. Nothing came of a proposed challenge at Wenlock, which returned him unopposed at the general election.[9]

Weld Forester retained his place at court under William IV, and was naturally counted among the ministry's 'friends'; but he was absent from the division on the civil list which brought them down, 15 Nov. 1830. He presented an anti-slavery petition from the Baptists of Broseley, 10 Nov. 1830. The king was said to have considered his resignation, 23 Feb., before the details of the Grey ministry's reform bill were announced, precipitate;[10] but it left him free to vote against the bill at its second reading, 22 Mar., and for Gascoyne's wrecking amendment, 19 Apr. 1831. His brother also opposed it, and his return for Wenlock at the ensuing general election was never in doubt.[11] During the contest for the county, he created a stir by rowing daily

up the River Severn to Shrewsbury to campaign for Hill and the anti-reformers.[12] The defeated reformer William Lloyd, a family friend, now dubbed him 'the most noisy fool I ever met with'.[13] In June a report circulated that 'Cecil Forester was obliged to abscond his country for misdemeanour in gambling'.[14] He divided against the reintroduced reform bill at its second reading, 6 July, and for adjournment, 12 July, to use the 1831 census to determine English borough disfranchisements, 19 July, and against taking a Member from Chippenham, 27 July 1831. He voted against the bill's passage, 21 Sept., and the second reading of the Scottish measure, 23 Sept. He divided against the revised reform bill at its second reading, 17 Dec. 1831, and committal, 20 Jan., against enfranchising Tower Hamlets, 28 Feb., and the third reading, 22 Mar. 1832. He voted against the second reading of the Irish measure, 25 May, and for the Liverpool disfranchisement bill, 23 May. He divided with opposition on the Russian-Dutch loan, 26 Jan., 12 July 1832. In October the *Spectator* described him as 'a Tory after the duke of Wellington's own heart. He votes regularly, speaks not at all, and manifests a strong repugnance to be of the slightest public service to his fellow man'.[15]

Despite a sharp contest, during which he was pelted with mud and stones, Weld Forester's return for Wenlock as a Conservative in December 1832 was assured and he remained one of its Members until he succeeded to the peerage in 1874, when he was 'Father of the House'.[16] Peel passed him over for preferment in 1835, 1839 and 1841, but in 1837 Lord Granville Somerset* considered him a possible 'whipper-in'.[17] A confirmed protectionist, he opposed repeal of the corn laws in 1846, and was appointed a privy councillor and comptroller of the household by Lord Derby as premier in 1852.[18] He remained an army officer, and both before and after his late marriage to the wealthy widow Mary Anne Dyce Sombré, whose dowry and eccentric late husband (Member for Sudbury, 1841-2) were the subject of much gossip, he spent part of each year in Hamburg, visiting Shropshire for occasional shooting parties. He died a general in the army in February 1886, a month after injuring himself on a hurdle, and was buried at Willey. Obituarists recalled his 'winning charm', which made him 'for many years one of the best known figures in London society'.[19] His will confirmed previous settlements and ensured that all his papers passed to his widow (*d.* 1895), whom he directed to 'look them over and destroy such as she considers necessary or desirable'. Being childless, he was succeeded in his titles and estates by his brother, the Rev. Orlando Watkin Weld Forester (1813-94), rector of Gedling, Nottinghamshire, and chancellor of York.[20]

[1] Salop Archives, Weld-Forester mss 1224/332/105. [2] Wellington mss WP1/793/30. [3] NLW, Aston Hall mss C.323-4; Weld-Forester mss 37/215-236; 332/194. [4] Weld-Forester mss 332/159; *Salopian Jnl.* 28 May, 11, 18, 25 June; *Gent. Mag.* (1828), ii. 82. [5] Aston Hall mss C.327. [6] Weld-Forester mss 332/180; *Salopian Jnl.* 7 Jan., 11 Feb. 1829. [7] See WELD FORESTER, John George. [8] Wellington mss WP1/1094/11; 1098/33; *Wolverhampton Chron.* 17 Feb., 3 Mar. 1830; Salop Archives 1634/21; *Von Neumann Diary* i. 209. [9] *Salopian Jnl.* 14, 21, 28 July, 4 Aug.; *Wolverhampton Chron.* 21 July, 4 Aug. 1830. [10] *Greville Mems.* ii. 120. [11] *Salopian Jnl.* 27 Apr.; *Wolverhampton Chron.* 4 May 1831. [12] *Salopian Jnl.* 6, 13, 20 May; *Wolverhampton Chron.* 18 May 1831. [13] Aston Hall mss C.5329. [14] Salop Archives 1649, Alderman Jones's diary, 12 June 1831. [15] *Spectator*, 27 Oct.; *Shrewsbury Chron.* 2 Nov. 1831. [16] Alderman Jones's diary, 2 Nov.-26 Dec.; *Shrewsbury Chron.* 14 Dec. 1832. [17] Add. 40411, ff. 62, 177; 40413, ff. 175, 185, 187; 40424, f. 47; 40426, f. 291; 40486, f. 247; 40487, f. 324. [18] Add. 40584, ff. 428-38; *Gladstone Diaries*, vi. 479. [19] *Gent. Mag.* (1851), ii. 201-2; *Shropshire Guardian*, 20, 27 Feb.; *Illustrated London News*, 20 Feb. 1886; *Oxford DNB sub* Dyce-Sombré. [20] Salop Archives, wills 1886/345.

M.M.E.

WELD FORESTER, Hon. John George Weld (1801-1874).

WENLOCK   1826-23 May 1828

b. 9 Aug. 1801, 1st s. of Cecil Forester (afterwards Weld Forester†) of Ross Hall, nr. Shrewsbury and Lady Katherine Mary Manners, da. of Charles, 4th duke of Rutland; bro. of Hon. George Cecil Weld Weld Forester*. *educ.* Westminster 1814-18; Christ Church, Oxf. 1820. *m.* 10 June 1856, Countess Alexandrina Julia Theresa Wihelmina Sophia, da. of Joachim Carl Ludwig Mortimer, Count Von Maltzan, wid. of Frederick James Lamb, 3rd Visct. Melbourne [I], 1s. *d.v.p. suc.* fa. as 2nd Bar. Forester 23 May 1828. *d.* 10 Oct. 1874.
Capt. of gentlemen at arms 1841-6; PC 14 Sept. 1841.

George Forester, as he was known, the heir to the Weld Foresters' prestigious Shropshire estates of Dothill, Ross Hall and Willey, spent his early life in London and at Belvoir Castle, Leicestershire, the seat of his maternal uncle, the 5th duke of Rutland. He had been baptized at St. James's, Westminster, 7 Sept. 1801, but at the age of six and with the prince of Wales as their godfather, he was christened again in Shrewsbury with his younger brother Cecil. Their father, a celebrated sportsman, retired as Member for the family borough of Wenlock in 1820 in anticipation of a peerage, and felt so 'ill used' on being denied the Wenlock barony and created Baron Forester in 1821 that he and his wife, who lamented the lack of rank which 'Lord Fagend' brought her, determined to stay away from the coronation.[1] Weld Forester's coming-of-age the following August was the first great celebration at their new mansion at Willey, with its 'extremely fine' vestibule.[2] He received a quarterly allowance of

£125,[3] took his freedom at Wenlock,[4] indulged the passion for hunting he had acquired at Oxford, and formed a lifelong attachment to Mrs. Lane Fox, the wife of his friend George, Member for Beverley.[5]

As Member for Wenlock, where he was substituted for his uncle Francis Forester at the general election of 1826,[6] Weld Forester acquired a reputation for indolence and was among those criticized by the patronage secretary Planta in March 1828 for failing to give the Wellington ministry reliable support despite the public money their families received.[7] He divided against Catholic relief, 6 Mar. 1827, 12 May 1828, and the provision for Canning's family, 13 May 1828. He presented Shropshire petitions for repeal of the Test Acts, 9 June 1827. He travelled through the Low Countries that summer with his future brother-in-law George Anson* and their friends, and in November became a founder member of the Crown Club, exclusive to Members, government ministers and East India Company personnel.[8]

Removed to the Lords by his father's death in May 1828, he made his proxy available to Wellington whenever he was away hunting, and surprised many in Shropshire by supporting Catholic emancipation in 1829.[9] Family papers reveal that he was highly supportive of his mother and ten young siblings, who were otherwise poorly provided for.[10] Acknowledging his 'great kindness', his mother, who died, 1 May 1829, entreated him 'constantly to receive the sacrament, examine yourself', and to remove the '*one* blot in your life' by marrying 'a sensible girl' and settling 'in your own country where you will always be looked up to'.[11] Friends observed that he was then too '*sentimental*' about Mrs. Lane Fox to do so.[12] Following discussions with Wellington, he opposed reform in 1831 and 1832, for which his coach was ransacked by the London mob and his guns stolen, and became an early member of the Carlton Club.[13] A lifelong Conservative and friend of Benjamin Disraeli†, his request to be made captain of the gentlemen at arms in 1841 instead of master of the queen's hounds, as first proposed, was readily granted as premier by Sir Robert Peel.[14] He died in October 1874, recalled as an able master of the Belvoir Hunt, 1830-58, and for his 'Wenlock programme', which brought competitive athletics to Shropshire.[15] The only child of his late marriage to the daughter of the Prussian envoy (Lord Melbourne's young widow) was a stillborn son;[16] and the barony and estates, which benefited through his promotion of the Severn Valley Railway, agricultural improvements and careful management of iron and coal deposits, passed to Cecil.[17] His widow (*d.* 1894), sister Lady Bradford, four surviving brothers, niece Isabella Curzon and Mrs. Lane Fox were the principal beneficiaries of his will, which was proved at Shrewsbury, 21 Jan. 1875.[18]

[1] *VCH Salop*, iii. 296-7; J.D. Nichol, 'Wynnstay, Willey and Wenlock', *Trans. Salop Arch. Soc.* lviii (1965-8), 222, 230-1; Salop Archives, Weld-Forester mss 1224/332/159; *HP Commons, 1790-1820*, iii. 790-1. [2] NLW, Aston Hall mss C.5717; *Gent. Mag.* (1822), ii. 306; *Von Neumann Diary*, ii. 192. [3] Weld-Forester mss 37/112. [4] Ibid. box 337, Procs. at Wenlock, 29 Sept. 1823. [5] Essex RO, Gunnis mss D/Gu C6/1/9, K. Forester to Louisa Lloyd, 30 Sept. 1820; Add. 52017, J.R. Townshend to H.E. Fox, 6 Aug. 1825. [6] Weld-Forester mss 37/161; Salop Archives, Blakemore mss 604, box 8, Lord Forester's letterbk. pp. 113-22; *Salopian Jnl.* 17 May, 14 June; *The Times*, 23 May 1826. [7] *Arbuthnot Jnl.* ii. 176. [8] Weld-Forester mss 37/81A, 160, 166. [9] Wellington mss WP1/1006/21; 1094/36; 1098/36; 1101/14; 1105/8, 23; Aston Hall mss C.5723; Add. 40427, f. 125. [10] PROB 11/1745/535; Weld-Forester mss, boxes 331 and 332; NLW ms 2796 D, Sir W. to H. Williams Wynn, 27 May 1828. [11] Weld-Forester mss 37/124-7; 332/192. [12] Aston Hall mss C.5298-9; *Greville Mems.* ii. 50. [13] Wellington mss WP1/1187/20; *Three Diaries*, 94; Aston Hall mss C.2115a. [14] Add. 40486, f. 247; 40487, ff. 324-6; 40489, f. 295; 40531, ff. 167-8; 40554, ff. 82, 85. [15] *VCH Salop*, ii. 175, 193, 449, 454; xi. 278-82; *Wellington Jnl.* 17, 24 Oct. 1874. [16] *Gent. Mag.* (1859), i. 86. [17] *Illustrated London News*, 17 Oct. 1874. [18] Salop Archives, wills 1875/52.

M.M.E.

WELLESLEY, Arthur Richard, mq. of Douro (1807–1884).

ALDEBURGH	27 Feb. 1829–1832
NORWICH	1837–1852

b. 3 Feb. 1807, 1st s. of Arthur Wellesley†, 1st duke of Wellington, and Hon. Catherine Sarah Dorothea Pakenham, da. of Edward Michael, 2nd Bar. Longford [I]. *educ.* Eton 1820-3, Christ Church, Oxf. 1824; Trinity Coll. Camb. 1825. *m.* 18 Apr. 1839, Lady Elizabeth Hay, da. of George, 8th mq. of Tweeddale [S], *s.p. styled* Lord Douro 1812-14, mq. of Douro 1814-52; *suc.* fa. as 2nd duke of Wellington 14 Sept. 1852; KG 25 Mar. 1858; *suc.* cos. William Richard Arthur Pole Tylney Long Wellesley as 6th earl of Mornington [I] 25 July 1863. *d.* 13 Aug. 1884.

Ensign 81 Ft. 1823, 71 Ft. 1825; cornet R. Horse Gds. 1825, lt. 1827; capt. 60 Rifle Corps 1828; maj. (army) 1830, Rifle Brigade 1831, lt.-col. (half-pay) 1834; a.d.c. to fa. as c.-in-c. army 1842-52; brevet col. 1846; lt.-col. Victoria Rifle Corps 1853-70; maj.-gen. 1854; lt.-gen. 1862; ret. 1863.

PC 7 Feb. 1853; master of horse Jan. 1853-Feb. 1858. Ld. lt. Mdx. 1868-*d.*

Douro, who was destined to be '*une lune bien pâle auprès de son père*', spent his early life with his mother and younger brother Charles, while his father acquired fame through military successes in the war against Buonaparte and ennoblement as duke of Wellington.

His parents' marriage was unhappy and the brothers, who were not considered close to the duke, accompanied each other to Eton and to university and embarked on army careers simultaneously. Describing their situation in his diary in June 1832, following a conversation with Lord Charles, Edward John Littleton* noted:

> The duke is fond of his sons, but I never saw them riding or walking together in my life and I believe they seldom converse. He seems to like that he and his sons should live independently of each other. But he allows them [to] treat Apsley House as a barrack and to use his table when he dines there.[1]

Wellington's appointment as premier in 1828 brought offers to seat his sons from supporters seeking patronage, and Douro's candidature was sought by a deputation from Weymouth in January and the duke of Rutland in July – the latter offering a seat for Cambridge in return for employment for the Member Frederick William Trench.[2] Wellington, however, accepted an offer from the 3rd marquess of Hertford, who wanted preferment for Horace Beauchamp Seymour*, and Douro's return for Aldeburgh, where the Ultra Wyndham Lewis was made to resign, was effected by Hertford's former steward John Wilson Croker*, 27 Feb 1829.[3] Douro and his brother were then touring the continent, where, in March, Hertford, who immediately asked a favour for an Aldeburgh corporator, found him in Genoa looking thinner and better because 'some foreign princess has drawn him fine'.[4] He took his seat, 4 Feb. 1830. Thomas Creevey*, seeing him for the first time, wrote to Miss Ord:

> His teeth are the only feature in which he resembles his father, and altogether he is very homely in his air. Do you know he is engaged to be married to a daughter of Hume, the duke's doctor? It seems she has stayed a good deal with the duchess, which has led to the youth proposing to her. When it was told to the duke, all he said was – 'Ah! Rather young, Douro, are you not, to be married? Suppose you stay till the year is out and if then you are in the same mind, it's all very well'.[5]

A silent vote with government against Jewish emancipation, 17 May, is the only one recorded for him before the dissolution in July 1830. His father declined a requisition from Berkshire on his behalf that month, and at the general election he resumed the representation of Aldeburgh, which he visited for the first time with Croker.[6] Before Parliament commenced, his father, who had received flattering reports of his progress as a soldier from the commander-in-chief Lord Hill, paid Greenwoods £1,400 to procure him an unattached majority.[7]

Douro was in London and conspicuously absent from the division on the civil list by which his father's ministry was brought down, 15 Nov. 1830.[8] General Sir William Napier, whom he sought out afterwards and asked to accompany him to Stratfield Saye in December observed:

His politics are decidedly adverse to his father's and he is for a thorough reform. He dislikes London society for its heartlessness, and as good as told me Sir John Moore was as great a man as his father: this shows how keen he is in observation. What he liked best in Sir John Moore was his kindness of disposition.[9]

A bitter disagreement with Wellington, which the latter's confidante Mrs. Arbuthnot failed to resolve, ensued; but eventually, in the charged atmosphere of his mother's final illness, he reluctantly agreed to defer politically to his father.[10] He voted against the Grey ministry's reform bill, by which Aldeburgh was to be disfranchised, at its second reading, 22 Mar., and for Gascoyne's wrecking amendment, 19 Apr. 1831, and retained his seat at the general election that month.[11] He voted against the reintroduced reform bill at its second reading, 6 July 1831, to postpone its committal, 12 July, and make the 1831 census the criterion for English borough disfranchisements, 19 July, against the bill's passage, 21 Sept., and the second reading of the Scottish bill, 23 Sept. He voted against the revised reform bill at its second reading, 17 Dec. 1831, against enfranchising Tower Hamlets, 28 Feb., and the third reading, 22 Mar., and against the second reading of the Irish measure, 25 May 1832. He divided against government on the Russian-Dutch loan, 26 Jan., 12 July 1832.

Douro's main interest now lay with his regiment at Dover, and he was 'not inclined to become a Member of the next Parliament'.[12] However, after turning down requisitions from Dublin University and county Antrim, he agreed to stand on 'home ground' for Hampshire North, where predictions that the reformers would defeat the Conservatives by two to one proved correct.[13] He declared on the hustings that 'he had opposed the reform bill, but ... not voted against the *whole* bill' and expressed support for the enfranchisement of £50 tenants-at-will.[14] Lord Rosslyn fawningly described his defeat as 'an excellent opportunity for the display of activity and talent which must rate him high in the public estimation and act as a powerful excitement to useful exertion'.[15] He refused to stand there on his return from a mission to Russia in 1835, but represented Norwich as a Conservative from 1837 until his defeat at the general election of 1852, shortly before he succeeded as 2nd duke of Wellington.[16] Thereafter he combined his official duties as master of the horse in the

Aberdeen and Palmerston ministries, and as a soldier, with management of his Stratfield Saye and Clermont estates and his role as vice-chancellor of Wellington College. The loss of an eye through infection and his old fashioned clothes gave him a 'rather grotesque appearance', but he remained active and a renowned wit to the last.[17] When he died suddenly on the platform at Brighton station in August 1884, Lord Lytton commented that 'he had bravely won his last painless moment'. He was succeeded in his titles and estates by his nephew Henry Charles Wellesley (1846-1900), Conservative Member for Andover, 1874-80.[18]

[1] Hatherton diary, 17 June 1832. [2] Lonsdale mss, Lowther to Lonsdale, 26 Jan. 1828; Wellington mss WP1/914/32, 41; 943/27. [3] Wellington mss WP1/967/13; 1002/9; Add. 60288, ff. 22, 25, 29-30, 101, 125, 133; Croker Pprs. ii. 11. [4] Wellington mss WP1/1097/6; 1010/5; Add. 60288, f. 133. [5] Creevey Pprs. ii. 209. [6] Wellington mss WP1/1123/12; Suff. Chron. 31 July 1830. [7] Wellington mss WP1/1144/23; 1148/46. [8] Add. 40401, f. 292. [9] Life of Napier ed. H.A. Bruce (1864), i. 333. [10] Arbuthnot Corresp. 142, 143. [11] Wellington mss WP1/1179/32. [12] Ibid. WP1/1234/1,2. [13] The Times, 8 Nov. 1832; Add. 60289, f. 70; Wellington mss WP1/1239/10, 22, 26, 27, 38; 1241/9. [14] The Times, 15 Dec. 1832. [15] Wellington mss WP1/1239/35. [16] Wellington Pol. Corresp. ii. 347, 489, 529, 532. [17] Redesdale Mems. ed. Lord Redesdale (1915), ii. 612. [18] The Times, 14, 15, 19, 20 Aug. 1884; Life and Letters of Lady Dorothy Neville ed. R. Neville, 227, 229.

M.M.E.

WELLESLEY, Richard (1787–1831).

QUEENBOROUGH	1 June 1810–Dec. 1811
EAST GRINSTEAD	11 Jan. 1812–27 Feb. 1812
YARMOUTH I.o.W.	1812–3 Feb. 1817
ENNIS	29 June 1820–1826

b. 22 Apr. 1787, 1st illegit. s. of Richard Colley Wellesley[†], 1st Mq. Wellesley (*d.* 1842), and Hyacinthe Gabrielle, illegit. da. of Christopher Fagan, chevalier in the French service[1] (whom he *m.* 1794, *s.p.* legit.). *educ.* Mr. Roberts's sch. Mitcham, Surr.; Eton 1800; Christ Church, Oxf. 1805. *m.* c. June 1821,[2] Jane Eliza, da. of George Chambers[†] of Hartford, nr. Huntingdon, 4s. 1da. *d.v.p.* 1 Mar. 1831.

Ld. of treasury Jan.-June 1812; commr. of stamp duties 1826-*d.*

At the age of 21 Wellesley, taking his first step in public life, assured his father that 'if I can ever forget myself I shall never forget my father. I hope to share his fortune with his toils'. His letter was later endorsed with this comment:

Alas! His youthful feelings and expectations of future fortune and happiness were not to be realized and all his future life was blighted by that very father he cherished.

Lord Wellesley, the most self-centred of men, was initially keen for his first-born son to succeed, but only on terms of obedience which made it impossible for Richard, too weak to rebel, to stand on his own feet. The vagaries of the marquess's politics and his insistence on submission to them cost Richard his seat in Parliament, along with junior office, in 1812 and again in 1817, when he complained to his brother Gerald:

The quarrel between my father and the proprietor of ... [Yarmouth] rendered it impossible for me to vote with him in opposition; and my own sense of honour prevented me from keeping it and voting against him with the government ... It was no trifling misfortune to be thrown out of Parliament at the best age for exertion ... but in vain did I write to him repeatedly on the subject ... I did not receive a word of regret or of interest, of blame or of praise.

Additionally harried by poor health and lack of money, he became the victim of Lord Wellesley's rancour against his late wife in a wrangle over the execution of her will. In 1818 his uncle the duke of Wellington managed to effect an improvement in Lord Wellesley's relations with his offspring; but the marquess had lost interest in Richard and his attitude towards him rarely went beyond amiable indifference.[3]

Soon after vacating his seat in 1817 Wellesley became a member of Brooks's, and he was suspected of masquerading as a supporter of the Liverpool ministry in his fruitless search for a seat the following year. His real wish was for a position of genuine independence in the House, but this eluded him. Early in 1820 it was rumoured that he was to be appointed a lord of the treasury: he denied it, but it was thought that 'something of this sort has certainly been projected for him by others'.[4] Lord Bath mentioned him to Lord Liverpool as 'a person of abilities who would be of service to government', whom he would be willing to return for Weobley, though he was 'not certain as to his political opinions', beyond his sympathy for Catholic relief. Liverpool discounted him, saying that he had already arranged his return, but he did not come in at the general election.[5] His exclusion, according to his sister Hyacinthe and her husband Edward Littleton*, was 'his own fault', for he refused Wellington's offer of a seat 'free of expense', having the 'folly' to insist on 'only coming in upon *independent* ground'. His father, too, 'could have procured him to be brought in, but not on those terms'.[6] At the end of June 1820 he was returned on a vacancy for Ennis, which was controlled by the ministerialist Fitzgeralds of Inchicronan.

He immediately voted against the aliens bill, 7 July 1820, but this was his last independent gesture. He soon lapsed into illness and depression. His father commanded him to 'exert your manly spirit to subdue all nervous despondency, the inseparable companion of bilious disorder'.[7] More sympathetically, his sister wrote to Gerald Wellesley, 20 Apr. 1821:

I wish he would get some official employment: it would do him more good than anything else, as he would then feel himself bound to work hard. I suspect that he frets at finding although life advances, he does not get on.[8]

He was present to vote against parliamentary reform, 9 May, and for the forgery punishment mitigation bill, 4 June 1821. At the end of the year his father was appointed lord lieutenant of Ireland. Lord Bathurst, asking if it were true that Richard was to go with him 'in some court place', thought he had recently 'looked much more like a man going to his last home. I was quite hurt to see him such a wreck'.[9]

From this point Wellesley, enjoying improved health, voted consistently and regularly with government. He opposed tax reductions, 11, 21, 28 Feb., abolition of one of the joint-postmasterships, 13 Mar., and the Whig attack on the lord advocate, 25 June 1822. In April he told his father that his regime in Ireland enjoyed 'the universal confidence of the House of Commons'. On a personal note, he continued:

I am very glad that the improvement of my health enables me to attend these debates ... and it is certainly not from want of interest that I do not take any part in them, but I believe from those mixed and painful feelings which have often prevented me from exerting whatever portion of ability I may possess to my own honour and advantage. In the summer and autumn I suffered most severely from illness, not only in health but in spirits and therefore in mind; and I am convinced that the greater part of those sufferings may be ascribed to the want of a regular and compulsory or rather responsible occupation; but I am so far recovered at present that I hope to make Parliament a substitute for this want, and by a salutary system to preserve the health I have been able to acquire.[10]

Soon afterwards he surprised his relatives by disclosing that he had been married for some time (perhaps as long as a year) to the 'very pretty' Jane Chambers. His sister, who fairly described her parents as 'good for nothing', attributed his secrecy to his 'dreadful shyness'. He had probably feared his father's disapproval of the match, which brought him no money; but the marquess sent him an affable, if lifeless letter of congratulation, to which Wellesley replied with obsequious relief. The marriage proved reasonably happy, but the regular production of children only increased his financial problems.[11] In October 1822 Lord John Russell* wondered why George Canning* had 'never thought of' Wellesley as his under-secretary on his recent appointment to the foreign office: 'To be sure he is undecided ... but he is an amiable and well-informed man'.[12] He divided with ministers against repeal of the assessed taxes, 10, 18 Mar., on the sinking fund, 13 Mar., against attacks on the legal proceedings following the Dublin Orange theatre riot aimed at his father, 24 Mar., 22 Apr., for the grant for Irish glebe houses, 11 Apr., and against reform of the Scottish county representation, 2 June 1823. By an Act of the following month (4 Geo. IV, c. 70), his father's sinecure post of remembrancer of the Irish court of exchequer, to which he held the reversion, worth £3,700 a year, was made an efficient office. A compensatory annuity was provided for Lord Wellesley and for Richard after his death. He is not known to have spoken in debate in this period, but was credited with the presentation of a petition from Inverness for repeal of the barilla duties, 16 July 1823.[13] He was in the government majorities against reform of Edinburgh's representation, 26 Feb., in defence of the conviction of the Methodist missionary John Smith in Demerara, 11 June, and for the Irish insurrection bill, 14 June 1824. On 17 Dec. 1824 he attended a non-party London meeting called to raise money to assist 'the unhappy Spanish and Italian refugees'.[14] He voted for repeal of the usury laws, 8 Feb., and the Irish unlawful societies bill, 15, 25 Feb. 1825. He was a defaulter, 28 Feb., but was in his place next day to vote for Catholic relief, as he did again, 21 Apr, 10 May. He voted steadily for the duke of Cumberland's grant in May and June 1825. His last recorded votes were in defence of the Jamaican slave trials, 2 Mar., for the proposal to give the president of the board of trade a ministerial salary, 10 Apr., and against reform of Edinburgh's representation, 13 Apr. 1826.

Wellesley was hurt not to receive '*one word*' from his father about his second marriage in October 1825, but could see in it no threat to the interests of his own family, beyond the slight chance that it might produce a son who would succeed to the title from which he himself was debarred by illegitimacy. More importantly, with a growing family and an income of 'scarcely £700 a year', he was facing penury; and in 1826, swallowing his 'scruples', he threw himself on the mercy of ministers in a quest for 'a public employment'. He failed to find a seat in the new Parliament and at the dissolution wrote *The Last Will and Testament of an Expiring Member of Parliament*:

Of mind and memory sound (at least in sense
Of Parliament) my goods I thus dispense.
To Hume my silence and my modest fears;
My voice to Pelham, *Eldon* all my tears;
To Country Gents, my *independent votes*;
To Maiden Speakers, all my Folio notes
Of still-born periods and of embryo jokes.[15]

His sister wrote:

It grieves me to see poor Richard thrown out for want of money and kind friends to bring him in again. However, if he gets some situation under government that will be *lucrative*, it will be better for him than being in Parliament, and we have some hopes that ere long this object will be attained ... [His] health has been his greatest enemy through life. It has always deprived him of the power of availing himself of the advantages he possessed as to situation or friends and he is now so shy and nervous that his great wish in life is to avoid his friends instead of seeking them and benefitting by their assistance.[16]

His father intervened with Liverpool and Wellington to help secure his appointment as a commissioner of stamp duties: as he later wrote, though it was 'contrary to the habits and feelings of my earlier life, the very subsistence of my family obliges me to adhere to it'.[17]

Wellesley remained a tragic figure, dogged by worsening health, which disrupted his attendance at his office, and living beyond his means on borrowed money.[18] His father's recall from Ireland and exclusion from Wellington's administration were further blows to his hopes, and when he applied to Wellington for a more lucrative office which would allow him to maintain his position as a gentleman and provide for his children, the duke replied that there was no possibility of being able to oblige him.[19] His father took household office in the Grey ministry in November 1830, but by then Richard was near his end. He spent his last days at Brighton (transported there 'almost without consciousness') in a pitiful state, as his wife reported to John Fazakerley*, 25 Jan. 1831:

Wellesley ... still remains dangerously ill; his life has been despaired of by all his physicians. He is reduced to the appearance of death, from total lack of sleep and refusal of all nourishment for the past month ... I have never left him day or night now for nearly one month, expecting and dreading every moment to have the horror of seeing him lost to his poor children and me for ever ... Lord Wellesley has ... during this awful calamity been everything I could have wished. He has sent the best physicians from London, his own servant, and writes every day; and he is not satisfied without daily and hourly accounts. Everyone here have [sic] been most kind, including the king and queen; and from his universal popularity his door has been thronged from morning to night with anxious enquiries, but all now is of no avail to him ... He has had so much to contend with, and no friend to assist him in any way in his endeavours for independence for himself and poor children; and feeling it impossible to ask for places, disgusted with the horrid stamp office, so different to all his father had brought him up to expect, and with such a mind and education as his, his mind was unable to bear up against his sufferings any longer ... He is reduced to a perfect skeleton. He has not the least trace of his former appearance.[20]

Lord Wellesley told Robert Wilmot Horton* that Richard was 'in a state of insane hypochondria'; and he was twice thwarted in suicide attempts.[21] Lord Dudley (soon himself to go incurably mad) lamented the impending loss of 'a very amiable and accomplished man', which took place at the beginning of March 1831.[22] Both his body and his finances were found to have been in ruins: the reversion was lost with him and his pregnant widow, who was accused by the Wellesleys of extravagance, was left in dire straits.[23]

---

[1] She was adopted as his da. by Pierre Roland, banker, of Paris (Iris Butler, *The Eldest Brother*, 50). [2] TNA FO 352/10A/3, Planta to S. Canning, 18 June 1822 suggests that the marriage may have taken place c. Mar. 1822. [3] Butler, 487-99. [4] Add. 51659, Whishaw to Lady Holland, 15 Jan. 1820. [5] Add. 38283, f. 104; 38458, f. 285. [6] Hatherton diary, 31 Mar.; Hatherton mss, Hyacinthe Littleton to Gerald Wellesley, 11 June 1820. [7] Butler, 520. [8] Hatherton mss. [9] *HMC Bathurst*, 526. [10] Add. 37315, ff. 267, 271. [11] TNA FO352/8/4, Planta to Canning, 18 June 1822; Hatherton mss, Hyacinthe to Gerald, 10 July 1822, 26 May 1823; Butler, 517-18. [12] Add. 51679, Russell to Lady Holland [Oct. 1822]. [13] *The Times*, 17 July 1823. [14] Northants. RO, Agar Ellis diary. [15] Butler, 520-1, 524; Add. 38301, f. 204. [16] Hatherton mss, Hyacinthe to Gerald, 16 June 1826. [17] Wellington mss WP1/855/26; 936/18; *Wellesley Pprs*. ii. 222. [18] Wellington mss WP1/925/54; 939/23; Hatherton mss, Hyacinthe to Gerald, 26 June, 9 Dec.1827. [19] Hatherton mss, Hyacinthe to Gerald, 27 Mar. 1829; Add. 40396, f. 104; Wellington mss WP1/1054/66. [20] Duke Univ. Lib. Fazakerley mss. [21] Add. 61937, f. 123; Butler, 536. [22] Ward, *Letters to 'Ivy'*, 368. [23] Butler, 536-7; Hatherton mss, Hyacinthe to Gerald, 7 Mar., 23 Apr. 1831; Add. 40880, f. 515.

D.R.F.

WELLESLEY *see also* **POLE TYLNEY LONG WELLESLEY**

WELLESLEY POLE, Hon. William (1763–1845), of 3 Savile Row, Mdx.

EAST LOOE	1790–12 Mar. 1795
QUEEN'S CO.	28 Dec. 1801–17 July 1821

b. 20 May 1763, 2nd s. of Garret Wesley, 1st earl of Mornington [I] (*d.* 1781), and Hon. Anne Hill, da. of Arthur, 1st Visct. Dungannon [I]; bro. of Sir Arthur Wellesley[†], Hon. Henry Wellesley[†] and Richard Colley Wellesley, 2nd earl of Mornington [I][†]. *educ.* Eton

1774-6. *m.* 17 May 1784, Katherine Elizabeth, da. and coh. of Adm. John Forbes, MP [I], of Castle Forbes, co. Longford, 1s. 3da. (1 *d.v.p.*). *suc.* cos. William Pole of Ballyfin, Queen's Co. 1781 and took additional name of Pole; *cr.* Bar. Maryborough [UK] 17 July 1821; GCH 1830; *suc.* bro. Richard as 3rd earl of Mornington [I] 26 Sept. 1842. *d.* 22 Feb. 1845.

MP [I] 1783-90.

Midshipman RN 1778-82.

Jt.-remembrancer of exch. [I] 1797; clerk of ordnance July 1802-Feb. 1806, Mar.-July 1807; sec. to admiralty June 1807-Oct. 1809; PC [GB] 18 Oct. 1809 and [I] 24 Oct. 1809; chief sec. to ld. lt. [I] Oct. 1809-Aug. 1812; commr. of treasury [I] 1810-11 and [GB] Jan.-June 1812, Nov.-Dec. 1834; chan. of exch. [I] July 1811-Aug. 1812; master of mint Sept. 1814-Sept. 1823; master of buckhounds Sept. 1823-Nov. 1830; postmaster-gen. Dec. 1834-May 1835.

Gov. Queen's Co. 1783,[1] custos rot. 1823; capt. Deal Castle 1838-43.

Capt. Ballyfin inf. 1796, Mdx. yeomanry 1803.

Throughout his long political career Wellesley Pole was overshadowed by his celebrated brothers Lord Wellesley and the duke of Wellington, who secured his admission to Lord Liverpool's cabinet as master of the mint in 1814. This office handsomely supplemented his income from his Irish sinecure.[2] In January 1820 his colleague Robert Ward* found him nursing a cold 'in his library – candles lighted, a roaring fire, and his reading-desk, most like a statesmen, but his book was *Ivanhoe* ... We laughed, but immediately fell upon other business'. His conversation revealed his satisfaction at the recent rout of radicalism and the discomfiture of the Whig opposition.[3] At the general election a few weeks later he faced his second contest for Queen's County in under two years. He topped the poll, but could ill afford the expense, which sharpened his desire, keen since 1816, to effect his removal from the Commons through a United Kingdom peerage.[4] Shortly before the new Parliament met he complained 'as usual' to Ward of Lord Liverpool's 'want of warmth' and ignorance of 'the arts of party government', which left individual ministers to sink or swim.[5] He spoke against abolition of the Irish lord lieutenancy, 17 May, and inquiry into Irish unrest, 28 June. In the debate on the aliens bill, 10 July 1820, he replied to Scarlett's attack on the ministry with a vehemence which the Speaker considered unseemly. By then he anticipated imminent escape from the Commons by means of a coronation peerage, which, he assured Liverpool, when rejecting a late attempt to fob him off with the reversion of Lord Wellesley's barony, was the 'greatest object' of his life. Yet the peerage, which his detractors attributed to 'a decided and very natural wish on the part of ministers to get rid of him out of the House of Commons' and was said to have 'mortally' offended Wellesley, was snatched from him when the necessity of dealing with Queen Caroline forced government to postpone the coronation. 'I do not believe it can take place till next summer', he told his son-in-law Sir Charles Bagot: 'This is a cruel blow to me, for I am afraid that no peers will be made till just before the ceremony and that I shall have another House of Commons session to encounter'.[6]

Wellesley Pole made a spirited defence of ministers' conduct towards the queen in the adjournment debate, 17 Oct. 1820. Next day he 'complained strongly' to Ward of Canning for leaving his colleagues in the lurch. He felt that they were bound to proceed against Caroline, but a fortnight later he

> thought everything very bad ... and what was more, no prospect of getting right – all ties were loosened. Insolence and insubordination out of doors, weakness and wickedness within. The Whigs ... were already half Radicals, and would be entirely so, if we did not give way.

He was 'inclined to an honourable *mezzo termine*, if it could be found', but considered this unlikely.[7] He regarded it as a blessing in disguise when the bill of pains and penalties had to be abandoned, for he had all along dreaded its reaching the Commons, where he feared it would be defeated. As it was he thought the queen was 'clearly found guilty' and opposition, for all their momentary jubilation, had received 'a positive death blow to their hopes of removing the administration'. He was confident of obtaining 'a very large majority for whatever we may think it proper to propose about the queen' in the next session.[8] When Canning resigned from the India board in December 1820 it was rumoured that Wellesley Pole would replace him, but nothing came of this.[9]

He defended Wellington against allegations that he had denigrated the Hampshire county meeting in support of the queen, 26 Jan. 1821. There were divided opinions on his combative speech against the opposition censure motion, 6 Feb.: his brother's friend Mrs. Arbuthnot thought he performed 'powerfully and well', but in Whig circles it was reckoned that he 'spoke very ill', though the 'Mountaineer' Henry Grey Bennet thought he 'made the best speech I ever heard from him, not ... much to the purpose, but a gay good humoured and sharp attack upon the Whigs'.[10] Later that month the king subjected him to a three-hour vilification of Liverpool which, at Wellington's prompting, he relayed to the premier.[11] He voted for Catholic relief, 28 Feb. After a short illness in March he spoke on the Irish barracks accounts, 6 Apr., and the cash payments bill, 11

Apr., and had a tart exchange with Brougham over the government's dealings with spies, 16 Apr. 1821.

On 17 May 1821 he told Bagot:

> No power on earth shall induce me to sit another session in the House of Commons. It is worth no man's while to do so after he passes fifty, if he can find means of living without it. It is killing us all by inches, or rather by *feet*.[12]

Yet when Wellington, commissioned by Liverpool, asked him whether, in return for a peerage, he would surrender his cabinet office to accommodate Peel or Canning, he became 'quite frantic', according to Mrs. Arbuthnot:

> He abused the duke furiously, said that he ought not to have allowed such a proposal to be made to him, that he never in his life had done anything for him; in short, was quite beside himself, positively refused to listen to the proposal and burst out of the room after declaring that the duke owed his advancement in life to him!

Wellington was 'excessively indignant' and told Mrs. Arbuthnot that 'he never again would do anything good natured' for his brother.[13] Wellesley Pole had his way, retaining his office and cabinet place when he was raised to the British peerage at the end of the 1821 session.[14] He again reacted 'like a madman' when a renewed attempt was made to shift him in January 1823. Later that year Liverpool enlisted the king to persuade him to leave the cabinet and go 'to the dogs' as master of the buckhounds. Gloating reports of his 'bitter anger' at his demotion may have been exaggerated.[15] The next few years of his life were blighted by the sordid public antics of his scapegrace son William Pole Tylney Long Wellesley*, whose finances and marriage he tried to save from ruin before his patience ran out. He left office with Wellington in November 1830, but returned briefly to power in Peel's first administration. Ten days short of his 76th birthday, and feeling that 'I have some years work left in me', he offered his services to Peel on his abortive attempt to form a ministry in 1839. No room was found for him in 1841.[16] He died in February 1845, three weeks after his daughter Lady Bagot.[17]

Wellesley Pole accomplished some sound departmental work at the mint, where he oversaw renewal of the entire coinage, but his political reputation was modest.[18] An anonymous obituarist wrote:

> In his own bustling, active, practical way, he contrived to do a good deal of public business, to make a great many speeches, to enjoy no small quantity of patronage, influence, and even emolument ... At no period of his life did he manifest parliamentary talents of a high order; though in the House of Commons he was accustomed to display unbounded confidence in his own judgement; and this habit, combined with other peculiarities, rendered his

speeches anything but acceptable ... [He] was simply angry – angry at all times, with every person, and about everything; his sharp, shrill, loud voice grating on the ear as if nature had never intended it to be used for the purpose of giving expression to any agreeable sentiment, or any conciliatory tone ... Wellesley Pole was an undignified, ineffective speaker, an indiscreet politician, and a man by no means skilful in the conduct of official transactions, although he was not deficient in that sort of practical activity which sometimes obtains for men in high office the reputation of being men of business.[19]

Edward Littleton* considered that Wellesley Pole

would never have obtained any distinction if his brothers had not reflected it upon him ... He was not without some talent, and had great energy and perseverance, but he was very choleric, and of most crabbed and ungracious manner. He had however some excellent qualities. He was a very kind father to his children, and attached to his friends, and exceedingly hospitable ... He shared the great besetting sin of his family – a dreadful selfishness in everything that touched their ambition: no liberality for a competitor, no allowance for any obligation of duty in political opponents.[20]

[1] Add. 37416, f. 167. [2] *The Times*, 21 Feb. 1821. [3] Phipps, *Plumer Ward Mems.* ii. 46-47. [4] Cent. Kent. Stud. Stanhope mss U1590 C199/2, Stanhope to Wellesley Pole, 10 Mar. 1820; *HP Commons, 1790-1820*, v. 515. [5] Phipps, ii. 52-53. [6] Add. 38285, ff. 140, 168; Bucks. RO, Fremantle mss, Buckingham to Fremantle, 20 July 1820; Buckingham, *Mems. Geo. IV*, i. 51; Bagot, *Canning and Friends*, ii. 96-97. [7] Phipps, ii. 60-63, 70-72, 78-79. [8] Bagot, ii. 104-6; Bagot mss (History of Parliament Aspinall transcripts), Wellesley Pole to Bagot, 12 Nov. 1820. [9] *Croker Pprs.* i. 184; Lonsdale mss, Beckett to Lonsdale, 19 Dec. 1820. [10] *Arbuthnot Jnl.* i. 69; Buckingham, i. 143; HLRO, Hist. Coll. 379, Grey Bennet diary, 14a. [11] *Hobhouse Diary*, 50; *Arbuthnot Jnl.* i. 75. [12] Bagot mss. [13] *Arbuthnot Jnl.* i. 94-96, 99. [14] NLW mss 2793 D5, C. to H. Williams Wynn [12 June 1821]. [15] *Arbuthnot Jnl.* i. 205, 208, 210, 254-5; Add. 38291, f. 395; 38568, f. 122; *Arbuthnot Corresp.* 39-41; Bagot, ii. 192-3; *Geo. IV Letters*, iii. 1079, 1080, 1110; Buckingham, i. 488-9, 494; ii. 7; *HMC Bathurst*, 542; *Hobhouse Diary*, 105-6; Add. 51586, Tierney to Lady Holland, 24 Aug. 1823. [16] Add. 40406, ff. 133, 135; 40426, f. 353. [17] *Gent. Mag.* (1845), i. 666; PROB 11/2014/226. [18] *Oxford DNB*. [19] *The Times*, 24 Feb. 1845. [20] Hatherton diary, 25 Feb. 1845.

D.R.F.

WELLS, John (1761–1848), of 24 Lombard Street, London and Bickley Hall, Bromley, Kent.

MAIDSTONE   1820-1830

b. 1761, 3rd but 2nd surv. s. of William Wells (*d.* 1805), shipbuilder, of Deptford and Susanna, da. of James Neave of London and Walthamstow, Essex. *m.* 3 Sept. 1796, Esther Puget of Wickham,[1] 3s. (2 *d.v.p.*) 5da. (at least 2 *d.v.p.*). *d.* 22 Nov. 1848.

Sheriff, Kent 1812-13.

Wells came from a family of shipwrights which had been established in business at Deptford since the seventeenth century. His grandfather, Abraham Wells, who was in partnership with a Mr. Brunsdon, died in 1752. His two sons purchased the Howland Great Dock from the 4th duke of Bedford in 1763 and constructed many ships for the East India Company and the navy. The elder, John, rebuilt Bickley Hall and died, 'an eminent shipbuilder', in June 1794. The younger, William, lived at the family home of Canister House, Chislehurst, acquired Holmewood, Huntingdonshire, from his brother-in-law, Sir Richard Neave, and inherited Bickley from his brother. John Wells was the second surviving son of William and became, like his youngest brother William (1768-1847), a partner in the family firm, which moved to Blackwall, Poplar, in about 1805. When his father died in November 1805 he was left £14,000 outright, and he later received a share from the trust established for his mother, who died in 1810.[2] His elder brother, Thomas, vice-admiral of the white, settled at Holmewood and sold Bickley to Wells, who made it his permanent home. He became a magistrate, was appointed sheriff of Kent in 1812, being called in to hear Philip Nicholson's confession to the brutal murder of his master Thomson Bonar and his wife in 1813.[3] He seems to have left the family firm, then known as Wells, Wigrams and Green, in about 1814. In 1821 he became a partner in the London banking house which was thenceforth known as Whitmore, Wells and Whitmore, whose senior partner was Thomas Whitmore*.

Wells's first known venture into politics was at Maidstone at the general election of 1818. He was brought forward on the day before the poll to oppose the Whig George Longman[†], but was forced to retire when it became clear that Longman and a new Whig candidate, Abraham Robarts*, were ahead. In an address of 20 June 1818, Wells claimed that he would have succeeded if circumstances had allowed him to be introduced earlier and he promised to offer again 'upon the British principles of loyalty and independence'.[4] His chance came at the general election of 1820, when it was rumoured that he would stand on the ministerial interest. Despite being staunchly anti-Catholic, he initially withdrew his pretensions when his supporters in the corporation insisted that he pledge himself to vote against emancipation, and he only agreed to re-enter the field after having made it clear that he did so '*unshackled and unrestrained*'.[5] He stood against Robarts and another Whig, Richard Sharp*, but received popular support and was returned in second place behind Robarts. In an address of thanks, 13 Mar. 1820, he promised to discharge his constituents' trust, 'neither influenced by party nor intimidated by faction', and to assist in the alleviation of distress caused by the war.[6] A petition against him lapsed owing to a failure to enter recognizances.

Although Wells was broadly sympathetic to the Liverpool ministry, he took an increasingly independent line, particularly on issues of economy and taxation. He moved the third reading of the bill to prevent frauds in the delivery of coal in places adjacent to the Thames, 30 June 1820.[7] He voted with government on Hume's motion for economies in revenue collection, 4 July, but divided against receiving the report of the barrack agreement bill, 17 July 1820. He was entrusted with the address calling on the king to dismiss ministers because of the prevailing agrarian distress, which was agreed by a meeting in Maidstone, 1 Jan. 1821, and his concern over the issue was shown by his forgiving one of his tenants a debt of £350.[8] In the House, 2 Feb., he stated that he had signed the London merchants' declaration of loyalty to the king agreed at the *London Tavern*, and rebutted John Smith's allegations that this had been a clandestine meeting not truly representative of mercantile opinion in the City. He voted in defence of ministers' conduct towards Queen Caroline, 6 Feb. He divided against Catholic claims, 28 Feb. 1821, and allowing Catholic peers to sit in the Lords, 30 Apr. 1822. He voted with government on the state of the revenue, 6 Mar., and Hume's motion for economy and retrenchment, 27 June, but against them on the additional malt duty repeal bill, 3 Apr., the timber duties, 5 Apr., the war office grant, 6 Apr., and the omission of arrears from the duke of Clarence's grant, 18 June 1821. He divided against parliamentary reform, 9 May. He presented a petition from Maidstone for reform of the criminal law, 17 May, but voted against the forgery punishment mitigation bill, 23 May.[9] He was appointed to the select committee on poor returns, 28 May 1821, as he was every year until 1827. He was listed as voting against more extensive tax reductions to relieve distress, 11 Feb., but for this, 21 Feb. 1822. He voted for gradual reduction of the salt duties, 28 Feb., and abolition of one of the joint-postmasterships, 13 Mar., 2 May. He divided for Lethbridge's motion for a fixed 40s. duty on corn, 8 May, and against the new corn duties, 9 May 1822.

Wells was given ten days' sick leave, 17 Feb., but was present to vote against the appointment of Lord Beresford as lieutenant-general of the ordnance in peacetime, 19 Feb. 1823. He voted for papers on the plot to murder the lord lieutenant of Ireland, 24 Mar., and inquiry into the legal proceedings against the Dublin Orange rioters, 22 Apr. He divided for abolition of the death penalty for larceny, 21 May, and

inquiry into chancery administration, 5 June. He voted for Whitmore's motion to equalize the duties on East and West Indian sugar, 22 May, and was listed in both the majority and minority on inquiry into the currency, 12 June. He divided against the grant for a new London Bridge, 16 June, the beer duties bill, 17 June, and the reciprocity of duties bill, 4 July. On 30 June he stated that Hume, in making accusations of persecution against the Catholics, had charged Joseph Butterworth* 'with matters as far from the fact as any can be'.[10] During the session he assisted in obtaining the bill to light Maidstone with gas, including reporting from committee, 5 May 1823. The following year, he was involved in the passage of the bill to erect new markets there, and reported to the House, 18 Mar. 1824, that delays had been caused by the need to arrange a court of burghmote, but that leave should be given. He voted to end flogging in the army, 5 Mar., and for postponing the grant for repairs to Windsor Castle, 5 Apr. He divided for repeal of the leather tax, 18 May, and against lifting the prohibition on the exportation of long wool, 21 May. He voted against the beer bill, 24 May, stating that it 'would not only be ruinous to a numerous class of tradesmen, but of no advantage to the public', and the practice of plurality among Irish clergy, 29 May. Wells, 'whose urbanity and kindness of heart gave zest to the proceedings of the day', spoke at the mayoral dinner in Maidstone, 8 Dec. 1824, concluding 'by a hearty assurance that, as he felt it to be his bounden and conscientious duty, for the safety and happiness of Great Britain, so would he strenuously oppose every attempt at Catholic emancipation'.[11] He duly voted with ministers for the Irish unlawful societies bill, 25 Feb., and against Catholic claims, 1 Mar., 21 Apr., 10 May 1825. He brought up a hostile Maidstone petition, 26 Apr., when he divided against the Irish franchise bill. He voted against the duke of Cumberland's annuity bill, 9, 10 June 1825, and for a select committee on the silk trade petitions, 24 Feb. 1826. On 17 Mar., when he commented that slavery was inimical to the liberty of the subject and ought to be abolished, he remarked that in his visits to France he had attempted to persuade the minister, Villèle, of the need to empower their navy to stop the trade.[12] He urged the Bank of England to take greater precautions against the circulation of forged notes, 21 Mar. His only other known vote in this Parliament was against reform of the representation of Edinburgh, 13 Apr. 1826.

The local Tory newspaper reported that as a result of his anti-slavery speech, the 'thinking part of our townsmen are resolutely determined to support Mr. Wells to the uttermost at the general election'. Indeed, a meeting in his favour, attended by over 200 freemen, 26 May 1826, revealed the extent of his popularity.[13] He expressed his gratitude for their support in his address, in which he also stressed his independence of party. On the eve of the poll the following month, he confirmed his stance against Catholic relief and slavery. He also opined that the price of bread 'ought to be as low as it possibly can be, consistent with the safety and protection of the farmer', and that ministers had acted wrongly in trying to alter the corn laws. On the hustings, he professed 'neither to be Whig nor Tory, but my principles are those which were established in this country in 1688', and he denied the partisan slurs which were cast against him. The acknowledged Tory candidate, Wyndham Lewis*, whose own canvassing lists revealed Wells's strength among the jurats and common councilmen, failed to gain his expected support and was easily defeated by Wells and Robarts.[14] Wells, who became increasingly alienated from official Toryism, spoke and voted against Clarence's annuity bill, 2 Mar. 1827. He presented an anti-Catholic petition from the corporation of Maidstone, 5 Mar., when his observations could not be heard above the coughing and cries of 'question', and he voted against relief the following day.[15] He divided for information on the mutiny at Barrackpoor, 22 Mar., and to consider separating bankruptcy jurisdiction from chancery, 22 May. He voted against the second reading of the corn bill, 2 Apr. He declared that a 'great proportion of the Protestant Dissenters among his constituents were adverse to the Catholic claims', 22 May, and opposed concessions to Catholics, 6 June, observing that he would vote for ministers to stay neutral on the question. On 8 June he made some inaudible comments in reply to Robarts's denial that most Dissenters were against relief.[16] He praised the non-partisan work of the Church Missionary Society in Kent, at its meeting in Maidstone, 4 July 1827.[17]

He presented a Dissenters' petition against the Test Acts, 22 Feb., and voted for their repeal, 26 Feb. 1828. He likewise brought up an anti-Catholic one from Beckenham, 1 May, and divided against relief, 12 May. He voted against provision for Canning's family, 13 May, and reduction of the salary of the lieutenant-general of the ordnance, 4 July. At the request of a court of burghmote, 23 May, he presented Maidstone corporation's petition against the alehouses licensing bill, 30 May.[18] At a meeting of the Kent Auxiliary to the British Reformation Society at Maidstone, 5 June, he blamed Irish distress on the Catholic church and supported the extension of Protestantism there.[19] He promised Lord Winchilsea, the leader of the anti-Catholic campaign in Kent, that he would attend a

meeting in Maidstone to form a Brunswick Club that autumn.[20] He duly endorsed its principle, 16 Sept., 'for that constitution which we so justly love and revere would not be handed down to our children inviolable, unless the Protestant ascendancy was maintained'. He mentioned the Catholic threat to 'lick the Protestants', and received immense applause when he added that 'I am now an old man, but if ever that time should come, my frame would be invigorated with youthful strength and I would fight up to my knees in blood in defence of Protestantism'. He attended the stormy county meeting on Penenden Heath as a Brunswicker, 24 Oct. 1828, but did not speak.[21] At the end of the year he acknowledged the thanks of the Maidstone freemen belonging to the Purple Single Vote Society for his anti-Catholic votes, but mentioned that he did not intend to offer himself for re-election.[22] He was, of course, listed by Planta, the Wellington ministry's patronage secretary, in February 1829 as 'opposed to the principle' of Catholic emancipation, against which he voiced his opposition on the 12th. On presenting hostile Maidstone petitions, 26 Feb., he acknowledged his fear of the intolerant spirit of the Catholics and the influence which 60 Catholic Members might hold in the House, affirmed that he would oppose 'Stuart' attempts to endanger the Protestant constitution and again quarrelled with Robarts over the balance of opinion in their constituency. He voted against relief, 6 Mar., and called Stephen Lushington's attack on the likeminded Sir Robert Inglis, 9 Mar., 'altogether unmerited'. In a major speech, 16 Mar., he criticized ministers for changing their policy, pledged himself once more to follow his constituents' wishes and claimed that 'I have attended in this House and voted on every occasion against the progress of these bills'. He ended with a peroration on the country's obligations to 'the family of Brunswick', and when John Martin criticized him for having incited agitation the previous September, he answered that he deplored violence and that his 'foolish expression' had merely been intended as a riposte to Catholic threats. He voted against the second reading of the relief bill, 18 Mar., receiving the report, 27 Mar., and the third reading, 30 Mar. He divided against the silk trade bill, 1 May, arguing that it did too little to safeguard protection for manufacturers and so alleviate the distress which they blamed on free trade, and he again spoke against it, 7, 8 May. On 7 May 1829 he stated that it was the newly introduced system of free trade, not protection, which had caused economic depression.

Like Sir Edward Knatchbull, the county Member, Wells was listed by Sir Richard Vyvyan*, the Ultra leader, among the 'Tories strongly opposed to the present government' in October 1829. He was a steward at the dinner to thank Knatchbull for his anti-Catholic activities, 13 Nov. 1829, when he spoke in praise of his conduct in Parliament and of Winchilsea's on Penenden Heath.[23] He duly voted for Knatchbull's amendment to the address on distress, 4 Feb. 1830. He divided for transferring East Retford's seats to Birmingham, and against the bill to prevent bribery there, 11 Feb., for which he received the praise of the Whig *Maidstone Gazette*, 16 Feb., as 'one of the few independent men who support the marquess of Blandford in his patriotic though we fear unavailing endeavours to redress the grievances of the people'. He sided with opposition against granting supplies, 11 Feb. He presented a Tonbridge petition for repeal of the beer duties, 23 Feb., and, endorsing it, commented on the very great and widespread distress which he blamed on free trade and government's refusal to act. He divided in favour of Blandford's reform scheme, 18 Feb., and enfranchising Birmingham, Leeds and Manchester, 23 Feb. Having again voted for transferring East Retford's seats to Birmingham, 5 Mar., he was in the minorities against the third reading of the East Retford disfranchisement bill and for O'Connell's proposal to include the ballot in its provisions, 15 Mar. He sided with opposition against the admiralty grant, 22 Mar., the Bathurst and Dundas pensions, 26 Mar., and the salary of the lieutenant-general of the ordnance, 29 Mar., and for returns of the emoluments of privy councillors, 14 May. When Knatchbull presented the Kent petition complaining of distress, 29 Mar., Wells supported its call for relief and its secondary request that Parliament reform itself in order to be more responsive to the demands of the people. He eschewed visionary political schemes, but warned ministers of the threat of enforced changes:

> These principles of free trade and altered currency have extensively connected themselves with the causes of distress of the agriculturalist, the manufacturer and the shopkeeper; as long as these important classes are depreciated, all under them must of course suffer and it will be in vain to hope for an improvement of the national resources.

When Honywood, the other county Member, expressed surprise at his change of heart on reform, Wells replied that he was 'mistaken: I always wished to see abuses remedied'. He presented and endorsed petitions from the licensed victuallers of Maidstone and Aylesford against the beer bill, and voted against it, 4 May. On 1 July he stated that it would be injurious to the peace of the country, as 'numbers of houses are already fitting up in contemplation of it, which

will of course be mere pot-houses and tend greatly to demoralize the lower classes'; he voted for postponing for two years permission to sell beer for consumption on the premises that day. Partly through his identification with the disaffected landowning Tories, Wells had become increasingly separated from the mainstream of the party, and, in addition to his consistent stance against financial extravagance, his conversion to reform had made him in practice almost indistinguishable from the Whigs by 1830. As expected, he retired at the dissolution that year, pleading that his age did not allow him to pay sufficient attention to his parliamentary duties.[24] However, he continued to play a local political role, and in February 1831, for instance, he chaired a meeting of agriculturists in Bromley to petition Parliament. He was briefly considered as a possible candidate for Maidstone at the general election of 1831.[25] He plumped for the Whig Thomas Law Hodges* for Kent West at the general election of 1837.[26] He probably suffered heavy financial losses when his bank failed in July 1841, and some time later he left Bickley and moved to 53 Cambridge Terrace, Hyde Park.[27] He died there, only two weeks after his wife, in November 1848, aged 87, leaving his entire estate to his only surviving son, John Joseph (*b.* 1804).[28] His great-nephew, another William Wells, was Liberal Member for Beverley, 1852-7, and Peterborough, 1868-74.[29]

[1] IGI (Kent); *Gent. Mag.* (1796), ii. 789 gives 2 Sept. [2] *Gent. Mag.* (1794), ii. 672; (1805), ii. 1087; (1810), i. 496; PROB 11/1434/810; IR26/105/216; E.L.S. Horsburgh, *Bromley, Kent*, 203-4; P. Banbury, *Shipbuilders of Thames and Medway*, 139-42; *Oxford DNB sub* William Wells (1729-1805). [3] *Gent. Mag.* (1813), i. 583. [4] *Maidstone Jnl.* 23 June 1818. [5] Ibid. 15, 29 Feb., 7 Mar. 1820, 13 June 1826. [6] Ibid. 14 Mar. 1820. [7] *The Times*, 1 July 1820. [8] *Maidstone Jnl.* 2 Jan., 13 Mar. 1821. [9] *The Times*, 18 May 1821. [10] Ibid. 1 July 1823. [11] *Maidstone Jnl.* 14 Dec. 1824. [12] Ibid. 21 Mar. 1826. [13] Ibid.; *The Times*, 2, 9 June 1826. [14] *Maidstone Jnl.* 6, 13 June 1826; Bodl. Hughenden Dep. D/II/C/13c. [15] *The Times*, 6 Mar. 1827. [16] Ibid. 23 May, 7, 9 June 1827. [17] *Maidstone Jnl.* 10 July 1827. [18] Cent. Kent. Stud. Maidstone borough recs. Md/ACp17. [19] *Maidstone Jnl.* 10 June 1828. [20] Northants. RO, Finch Hatton mss FH 4605. [21] *Maidstone Jnl.* 23 Sept.; *Kentish Chron.* 28 Oct. 1828. [22] *Kentish Gazette*, 5 Dec. 1828. [23] Finch Hatton mss FH 4641; *Maidstone Jnl.* 17 Nov. 1829. [24] J. Phillips, *Great Reform Bill in Boroughs*, 111; *Maidstone Gazette*, 25 May; *Maidstone Jnl.* 6 July 1830. [25] *Maidstone Jnl.* 8 Feb., 26 Apr. 1831. [26] *Kent W. Pollbook* (1837), 4. [27] *The Times*, 3 July 1841; Horsburgh, 204. [28] *Gent. Mag.* (1849), i. 103. [29] *Oxford DNB sub* William Wells (1818-89).

S.M.F.

WEMYSS, James Erskine (1789–1854), of Wemyss, Fife.

FIFESHIRE	1820–1831
FIFESHIRE	1832–1847

b. 9 July 1789, 1st. s. of William Wemyss† of Wemyss and Frances, da. of Sir William Erskine, 1st bt., of Torrie. *m.* 8 Aug. 1826, Lady Emma Hay, da. of William, 17th earl of Erroll [S], 2s. 2da. (1 *d.v.p.*) *suc.* fa. 1822; to Torrie by right of his mother 1841. *d.* 3 Apr. 1854.
Entered RN 1801, midshipman 1804, lt. 1808, cdr. 1812, capt. 1814, half-pay 1814, r.-adm. 1850.
Ld. lt. Fife 1840-*d.*

Wemyss gained a reputation in this period as a formidable electioneer whose speeches and addresses were 'those of a jolly mariner, rough, homespun, full of a sort of ready raillery, blunt, off hand and ready witted, such as were sure to draw cheers from a crowd'.[1] The well-connected heir to valuable Fifeshire estates, he had joined the navy in 1801, three years after his mother's death, as a first class volunteer on his uncle Charles Wemyss's ship *Unicorn*. He transferred to Sir Edward Pellew's† crew off Ferrol the following year and served in several ships in the East Indies, the Mediterranean, the North Sea and on the home station. Pellew, after whom he was to name his second son, made him his flag lieutenant in 1808 after the *Victor*, in which he was acting lieutenant, suffered heavy losses. Admiral Josias Rowley* praised his contribution to the reduction of Genoa as commander of the *Éclair* at the battle of Port d'Anzo in April 1814. In July that year, after captaining the *Rainbow* on her return voyage to England, he went on half-pay and was awarded an additional £100 a year for bravery.[2] His father, the ailing Member for Fifeshire, was thwarted in his ambition of making way for him at the general election of 1818, but, with government acquiescence, they effected the transfer in 1820 after an expensive contest.[3] In notices, speeches and his letters to the Liverpool ministry's Scottish manager Lord Melville, who acknowledged his popularity but privately doubted his competence, Wemyss professed allegiance to the 'principles which actuated the late Mr. Pitt' and declared that 'so long as the present government continue to entertain such, they will be steadily supported by me in all their great questions'.[4] His complaint early in the new Parliament that his Tory rival Sir John Oswald of Dunnikier claimed the right to control Fifeshire patronage brought reassurance from Melville that the government had not intervened at the late election and he hinted at future support for Wemyss as their sitting Member.[5]

He divided against Catholic relief, 28 Feb. 1821, 30 Apr. 1822, 21 Apr. 1825, and the Irish franchise bill, 26 Apr. 1825, and against parliamentary reform, including changes in the Scottish representation, 9, 10 May 1821, 20 Feb., 2 June 1823, 13 Apr. 1826. Assertions in radical publications that he 'always' voted with ministers were, however, inaccurate.[6] He made a point of attending county meetings and dealing personally with petitions, and his support for administration was tempered by his readiness to represent local interests. At the Fifeshire meeting of 28 Dec. 1820 he spoke in favour of adopting a loyal address to the king and against a hostile Whig amendment defending the freedom of the press.[7] He divided with government in 1821 on the Queen Caroline affair, 6 Feb., the revenue, 6 Mar., and retrenchment, 27 June, but against them on the additional malt duty, 21 Mar., 3 Apr., which he declared when presenting hostile petitions, 12, 21 Mar., 17 May, that it was the duty of every Scottish Member to oppose.[8] He voted against committing the printer of *John Bull* to Newgate for an alleged libel on Henry Grey Bennet*, 11 May, and against making forgery a non-capital offence, 23 May 1821. Having delayed his return to Westminster on account of his father's death, 4 Feb. 1822, he presented petitions for repeal of the leather tax, 1 May, the malt tax and excise duties, 6 May, and repeated the arguments voiced at their adoption in Fifeshire, which the chancellor of the exchequer Vansittart had difficulty in countering, 6 May. He divided with Lethbridge and the agriculturists against the government's relief proposals, 8 May.[9] He voted against inquiring into Irish tithes, 19 June, and the lord advocate's treatment of the Scottish press, 25 June 1822. He voted in Whitmore's minority for a gradual reduction to 60s. in the corn pivot price, 26 Feb., and against government for inquiry into the prosecution of the Dublin Orange rioters, 22 Apr., but with them on chancery delays, 5 June 1823. He presented petitions on the laws regulating the trades in tallow and linen, 7, 21 May 1823, and one against slavery from the convocation of Fife, 7 May 1824, but he voted against condemning the indictment in Demerara of the Methodist missionary John Smith, 11 June 1824.[10] At the Fifeshire head court, 5 Oct. 1824, he said that he had opposed the introduction of the Scottish judicature bill late that session on account of its timing and 'without regard to the merits of the measure itself' and 'would have opposed any other bill of consequence prepared at the same period'.[11] His success in obtaining the living of Cupar for Dr. Adamson in January 1825 was marred by allegations of jobbing and the difficulties with the corporation and heritors which it generated.[12] He presented several petitions against corn law reform, 28 Apr. He condemned the Leith docks bill as a 'gross job' and voted to kill it, 20 May. He voted against increasing the duke of Cumberland's award, 27 May, but for the annuity bill, 10 June 1825. He presented and endorsed Auchtermuchty's petition against altering the Scottish banking system, 7 Apr., and several against slavery, 16, 17 Apr. 1826.[13] Although injured in a fall during his passage by steamboat from London, Wemyss chaired the county meeting on the Forth ferries, 5 May 1826. He stayed on to convalesce and canvass and came in unopposed at the general election in June. On the hustings he explained that he had generally supported ministers hitherto 'because he thought them right', but because he deplored the president of the board of trade Huskisson's decision to repeal the navigation laws and their recent 'vacillating conduct on the corn laws', he intended voting in future 'as he saw fit'.[14] He spoke similarly at Melville's installation as rector of St. Andrews University in October and candidly acknowledged that his conduct as a Member was not 'free from mistakes'.[15] His local influence was boosted by his marriage in August 1826 to Lord Erroll's daughter Emma (whose sister Isabel had married his brother William in 1820) and by his only sister Frances's marriage in October 1826 to Lord Loughborough*.

Wemyss presented Fifeshire petitions for and against corn law revision, 26 Feb., and divided against the Liverpool ministry's corn bill, 2 Apr. 1827. He voted against Catholic relief, 6 Mar., and for the grant to the duke of Clarence, 16 Mar., and the spring guns bill, 23 Mar. 1827.[16] Responding on 5 Feb. 1828 to a summons from Peel as home secretary and leader of the House in the duke of Wellington's ministry, he congratulated him on his return to office, apologized for his late arrival that session and cautioned that he would oppose the colonial secretary Huskisson's measures, 'which regard I owe to myself, as well as to my constituents'.[17] He welcomed Wellington's decision to appoint Loughborough's father the earl of Rosslyn lord lieutenant of Fifeshire that month.[18] He presented a petition for facilitating anatomical dissection, 2 May, and vehemently opposed the Aberdeen harbour bill, 5 May, but his anti-Catholic vote, 12 May, was the only one reported that session. Drawn during the recess into the controversy concerning the appointment of a convener for Fifeshire, he informed Oswald, 26 Aug. 1828:

I came to the resolution of supporting General Balfour from no political motive, but from being well advised that he was the only man likely to secure *unanimity* amongst all parties. As Member for the county it is rather against my feelings to interfere in this matter beyond a vote, par-

ticularly as I have such a respect for General Durham and *personally* I care not who is convener, but as long as I am Member, it is my bounden duty to keep the county and the commissioners of supply in good humour, and heal, if possible, the recent wounds that have been *so industriously inflicted* on our peace.[19]

The patronage secretary Planta predicted that he would vote 'with government' for Catholic emancipation in 1829, but he divided against the measure, 6, 18, 30 Mar., and presented and endorsed hostile petitions from Fifeshire and Inverary, 11 Feb., 26 Mar., and defended the decision of the Associate Synod of Kirkcaldy to petition similarly in the name of their president Thomas Grey, 30 Mar. He did not vote on distress in 1830, but he referred to it when presenting petitions against the proposed additional duty on corn spirits from Fifeshire and elsewhere 3, 17 May. He also brought up petitions that day against taxing Scottish probate inventories and against the East India Company's trading monopoly. He cast a rare vote with the revived Whig opposition for abolishing the Irish lord lieutenant, 11 May, and voted to amend the sale of beer bill's provisions for on-consumption, 21 June. He secured an uncontested return for Fifeshire at the 1830 general election. His notices highlighted local issues, and when pressed on the hustings to explain his parliamentary conduct, he declared that 'since the break-up of Lord Liverpool's administration, he had voted for no particular party' and 'had he ... adhered to every successive administration ... his conduct must have been like a fool's coat – of many colours'. He insisted that his vote on the Irish lord lieutenancy was, like the office itself, of no consequence, as 'there might as well be a lord lieutenant of Edinburgh', defended his stance on the beer bill and refused, when challenged, to make pledges on reform.[20] He probably interfered at St. Andrews at the burgh elections at Michaelmas.[21]

Ministers counted Wemyss among their 'friends', but he was absent from the division on the civil list when they were brought down, 15 Nov. 1830. He presented a petition for parliamentary reform from Cupar, 19 Mar., and divided for the Grey ministry's English reform bill at its second reading, 22 Mar. 1831.[22] In a major speech on the 25th, which the pro-reform *Fife Herald* edited and printed, he countered claims made by Hume and Sir Michael Shaw Stewart on behalf of the Scottish reformers and tempered contradictory ones by the anti-reformer James Lindsay, whose father Lord Balcarres was intriguing in Fifeshire with a view to returning Lindsay and accused Wemyss of jobbing to promote his own interests under the proposed Leven navigation bill. A proposal in the Scottish reform bill to disfranchise the Anstruther Easter Burghs was widely resented, and the reformers had been refused a county meeting.[23] Wemyss's speech stated that he supported the English bill only so far as it 'relates to the out-voters and dependent boroughs. Further I cannot go, for I do not pretend to understand the measure'. He acknowledged the shortcomings of the Scottish system but added:

I am one of those who think that real property should be entitled to a proper share in the representation, even if it went only as far as £20; but when the franchise is attempted to be placed in the hands of the manufacturing and agricultural classes of Scotland, I fear that the interests of the people will be continually at war with each other and think that the result of such a measure would be to produce a continual political warfare ... We should have one party petitioning for a corn bill and another ... for no corn bill and so on ... With regard to the alteration of the boroughs, that I admit is good in principle, but requires some alteration in the details. It is a great anomaly to disfranchise one borough, and without a good, or indeed any reasons being assigned, to allow another to remain in its existing state ... I know there is a feeling in favour of reform, but it is a silent feeling as yet: for the petitions I have hitherto received came from those who are under the influence of others, and do not embrace the intelligence and respectability of all the counties ... I have reason to believe that many of my constituents in the county of Fife are alarmed at the proposed alteration in the franchise.

He issued notices countering reports that he would make way for Lindsay, 17 Apr., and voted against Gascoyne's wrecking amendment to the reform bill, 19 Apr.[24] Assisted by his 1820 Whig opponent Robert Ferguson* of Raith, he contested the ensuing general election as a reformer, but lost by 85-68 to Lindsay.[25] He attributed his defeat to his pro-reform votes and maintained at the election meeting that

it had been well known, at the treasury, during the duke of Wellington's administration, that he was friendly to reform. The only reason why he had never before voted for that measure was that he thought it improper to agitate a question involving so many interests till it should be brought forward by the government and the country and not by an individual.

He also signalled his intention of standing again, when the county should 'be inclined to support a candidate who had no fortune to spend on canvassing, and no East India interest to offer'.[26] His political loss was followed by a personal one in July 1831, when his eldest daughter was stillborn.[27]

Now regarded as a 'semi-liberal',[28] Wemyss obliged Lindsay to make way for him without a contest at the general election of 1832, defeated him in 1835 and made the Fifeshire seat a 'hopeless' one for the Conservatives during his lifetime.[29] He retired at the dissolution of 1847, having been appointed lord lieutenant six years previously and ensured the succession of his heirs to the Erskine estates by a private Act of 1841. He died in April 1854 at Wemyss Castle, to which with Torrie he was succeeded by his elder son James Henry Erskine Wemyss (d. 1864), Liberal Member for Fifeshire, 1859-64.[30]

[1] Fifeshire Jnl. 6 Apr. 1854. [2] Ibid.; W.R. O'Byrne, Naval Biog. iii. 1268-9. [3] NAS GD51/1/198/10/70,75. [4] NAS GD51/1/198/10/76-87; Caledonian Mercury, 7 Feb., 9, 23 Mar.; Scotsman, 25 Mar. 1820. [5] NAS GD51/1/198/10/88, 89; Oswald of Dunnikier mss VIA/2, election speeches 1820. [6] Extraordinary Red Bk. (1821), 240; Black Bk. (1823), 201. [7] Caledonian Mercury, 1 Jan. 1821. [8] The Times, 13, 22 Mar., 18 May 1821. [9] Ibid. 2, 7 May 1822. [10] Ibid. 8, 22 May 1823, 8 May 1824. [11] Caledonian Mercury, 7 Oct. 1824. [12] Add. 40370, ff. 235-8; 40371, ff. 53, 59; 40372, ff. 43, 45, 170-84. [13] The Times, 8, 18, 27 Apr. 1826. [14] NAS GD164/1799/11, 12, 15; Edinburgh Evening Courant, 8, 12 June; Scotsman, 1 July 1826. [15] Edinburgh Evening Courant, 30 Oct. 1826. [16] The Times, 27 Feb. 1827. [17] Add. 40395, f. 194. [18] NLS mss 2, f. 125. [19] Oswald of Dunnikier mss VIA/2, Wemyss to Oswald, 26 Aug. and passim, 1828. [20] Fife Herald, 8, 29 July, 12 Aug.; Scotsman, 14 Aug. 1830. [21] NAS GD16/34/387/7, F.W. Drummond to Airlie, 7 Sept. 1830. [22] The Times, 24 Mar. 1831. [23] Fife Herald, 4 Nov., 9, 23 Dec. 1830, 20, 27 Jan., 10, 31 Mar., 7 Apr. 1831; Oswald of Dunnikier mss VIA/2, G. Campbell to Oswald, 28, 31 Dec. 1830. [24] Edinburgh Evening Courant, 23 Apr. 1831. [25] Fife Herald, 28 Apr., 12 May; Caledonian Mercury, 7 May; Scotsman, 28 May 1831. [26] Fifeshire Herald, 2 June 1831. [27] Edinburgh Evening Courant, 21 July 1831. [28] The Times, 25 Aug. 1831. [29] Fife Herald, 21 June, 13, 20 Dec. 1832; Scottish Electoral Politics, 252, 274-5. [30] Gent. Mag. (1854), i. 192.

M.M.E.

WEST, Frederick Richard (1799–1862), of Ruthin Castle, Denb.[1]

DENBIGH BOROUGHS	30 Mar. 1827–1830
EAST GRINSTEAD	1830–1832
DENBIGH BOROUGHS	1847–1857

b. 6 Feb. 1799, o.s. of Hon. Frederick William West[†] of Chirk Castle, Denb. and Culham Court, Berks. and 2nd w. Maria, da. of Richard Myddelton[†] of Chirk Castle. educ. Eton 1811; Christ Church, Oxf. 1818. m. (1) 14 Nov. 1820, Lady Georgiana Stanhope (d. 14 Aug. 1824), da. of Philip, 5th earl of Chesterfield, s.p.; (2) 11 Sept. 1827, Theresa Cornwallis, da. of Capt. John Whitby, RN, 3s. (1 d.v.p.) 3da. suc. mother 1843; fa. 1852. d. 1 May 1862. Steward, Ruthin 1820; mayor, Holt 1822.

West, whose father was the placeman son of the courtier John, 2nd Earl De La Warr, was brought up at Chirk Castle and in London. His father, a Tory, had represented Denbigh Boroughs on his wife's

Myddelton interest in the 1802 Parliament and had hoped to make the seat his own, but he was defeated there in 1806 by his sister-in-law's husband, the Foxite Whig Robert Myddelton Biddulph, who had also taken up residence at Chirk Castle.[2] Litigation between them was eventually settled in 1819, when chancery apportioned Llangollen to Mrs. West, and Chirk Castle and Ruthin Castle to her sisters, Mrs. Biddulph and Miss Myddelton; but their dispute, which had strong political overtones, continued.[3] West's father had meanwhile reached agreement with his cousins over their Hampshire and Sussex estates and had decided that his son should try to recapture Denbigh Boroughs at the earliest opportunity. Burgesses were created at Ruthin in his interest in 1819, and he was the symbolic choice to chair celebrations there when Miss Myddelton took formal possession of her estate, 30 Nov.[4] He was newly of age and contested Denbigh Boroughs at the general election of 1820. His bilingual notices stressed his lineage and projected him as a 'church and state' Tory. His inexperience, the De La Warr connection, doubts concerning the legality of recent burgess creations and his father's reputation for turning out tenants who resisted him marred his prospects, and he conceded defeat to the sitting Whig, the recorder of Denbigh John Wynne Griffith, after a two-day poll and promised to stand again at the first opportunity.[5]

West's marriage in November 1820 was widely celebrated, and the lavish dinner with which he marked the coronation in 1821 encouraged speculation that he was about to be raised to the peerage.[6] His friends failed to take control of Holt in 1820, but succeeded there in 1821, paving the way for his election as mayor. He was thought to be 'in a decline and his young wife very little likely to survive him' in 1822, but he recovered and made Blythe Hall in Staffordshire his country home until he was widowed in 1824, residing thereafter at Ruthin and Pentre Pant, near Oswestry.[7] At the 1826 general election his party controlled the Denbigh Boroughs writ and fixed the nomination for 13 June, a week before his cousin and rival Robert Myddelton Biddulph* came of age. The bitter contest against Biddulph's locum Joseph Ablett ended in a double return and reputedly cost West £40,000.[8] After petitioning, he was declared elected, 29 Mar. 1827. He took his seat the following day and was probably the 'M. West' who voted against the spring guns bill, 30 Mar.[9] A sporadic attender who made few speeches, in May 1827 he was added to and testified before the select committee on borough polls. His second wife (d. 1868), whom he married in September 1827, was an heiress of Admiral Cornwallis, 'pretty and pleasing

and sings marvellously well, having learned in Italy'. They divided their time between his Welsh homes, De La Warr's Arnwood and her Newlands estate in Hampshire.[10] He voted against repeal of the Test Acts, 26 Feb., and Catholic relief, 12 May 1828, and presented Denbigh's petitions for repeal of the Malt Act, 21 Feb., and of the Promissory Notes Act, 20 June. His first-born son died in December 1828, when barely three months old.[11] West and his political ally Lord Kenyon presented most Denbighshire anti-Catholic petitions.[12] Doing so, 9 Feb. 1829, West praised Peel as home secretary and leader of the House, stated that his 'conversion' surprised him, and requested further information on securities. He declared that 'till the absolute necessity of the case is proved, and till proper securities are given, I shall be the last man to allow any additional concessions to be made to the Roman Catholics'. He presented further hostile petitions, 16, 20 Feb., 4, 30 Mar. As the patronage secretary Planta had predicted in February, he divided against emancipation, 6, 27, 30 Mar., and paired, 18, 23 Mar. 1829. He voted against the army estimates, 19 Feb., the sale of beer bill, 4 May, and Jewish emancipation, 17 May 1830. Despite the strength of anti-Catholicism in North Wales, West had made little headway in Denbigh, where the Catholic banker William Sankey and others took steps to prevent him acquiring borough property during sales and land exchanges with the Biddulphs.[13] He stood down there to avoid defeat at the 1830 general election and was brought in by his cousin De La Warr for East Grinstead.[14]

The Wellington ministry counted West among their 'friends', and he divided with them on the civil list when they were brought down, 15 Nov. 1830. He was granted a fortnight's leave 'on account of the disturbed state of his neighbourhood', 30 Nov. 1830, a time of unrest in the Wrexham area, Hampshire and Sussex. He voted against the Grey ministry's reform bill at its second reading, 22 Mar., and for Gascoyne's wrecking amendment, 19 Apr. 1831. At the ensuing general election East Grinstead, which was set to lose a Member under the bill, returned him unopposed, amid pro-reform demonstrations.[15] He divided against the reintroduced reform bill at its second reading, 6 July, and voted to adjourn its consideration, 12 July, to make the 1831 census the criterion for English borough disfranchisements, 19 July, and against depriving Chippenham of a Member, 27 July 1831. He divided against the bill's passage, 21 Sept. He was granted three weeks' leave on account of ill health, 30 Sept. He refrained from voting on the second reading of the revised reform bill, 17 Dec. 1831, but voted against considering it in committee, 20 Jan., and its third reading, 22 Mar. 1832. He failed to defend East Grinstead, 20 Feb., but voted for Waldo Sibthorp's amendment concerning Lincoln freeholders, 23 Mar., and recommended enfranchising rural voters in the boroughs of Arundel, 8 June, and Newry, 9 July. He divided against government on the Russian-Dutch loan, 26 Jan. 1832.

West's interest in Denbigh Boroughs was enhanced through the addition of Wrexham to the constituency, but he declined requisitions to stand there or for Denbighshire at the 1832 general election. He remained out of Parliament until 1847, when he profited from local differences over the corn laws and church rates to come in unopposed for Denbigh Boroughs as a Liberal Conservative. He retained the seat, with one contest, until 1857, initially looking to Peel for patronage.[16] Already in poor health, he retired to Ruthin, where he died in May 1862 and was buried in a new family vault in St. Peter's church.[17] His will confirmed the settlement of his Welsh estates in 1851 on his eldest son Frederick Myddelton West (1830-68) and was proved in St. Asaph, 9 Aug. 1862. He left mortgage incomes and shares to his daughters and bequeathed his Hampshire estates in trust to his second son William Cornwallis West (1835-1917), who in 1869 succeeded his brother to Ruthin Castle.

[1] Generally known as Frederick Myddelton West. [2] HP Commons, 1790-1820, ii. 495; v. 517-18. [3] NLW, Chirk Castle mss F/11402-6; Private Act 59 Geo. III, c. 4; The Times, 15 Apr. 1819. [4] Chester Chron. 19 Nov., 10 Dec. 1819, 14 Jan. 1820; NLW, Garn mss (1956), W. Hughes to J.W. Griffith, 19 Feb. 1819, W. Shipley to same, 2 Jan. 1820. [5] Chester Chron. 11, 18, 25 Feb., 3, 17 Mar.; Shrewsbury Chron. 18 Feb.; Cambrian, 26 Feb.; The Times, 1 Mar.; N. Wales Gazette, 23 Mar. 1820; Chirk Castle mss C/78-85. [6] Chester Chron. 24 Nov., 1 Dec. 1820, 20 July 1821; Shrewsbury Chron. 17, 24 Nov., 8 Dec. 1820. [7] Chester Chron. 7 Apr., 30 June 1820, 12 Oct. 1821; NLW ms 2794 D, Lady Williams Wynn to H. Williams Wynn, 13 Aug. 1822, J. Powell, Holt, 52-53. [8] Chester Courant, 11, 18, 25 Apr., 2 May, 20, 27 June, 4 July; N. Wales Gazette, 13, 20, 27 Apr., 8, 29 June; The Times, 19, 26 Apr., 9 June; Cambrian, 17 June, 1 July 1826. [9] N. Wales Chron. 22 Feb., 22 Mar. 1827; CJ, lxxxii. 370, 375. [10] NLW ms 2795 D, ? to H. Williams Wynn, 28 Nov. 1826. [11] Shrewsbury Chron. 26 Sept.; Cambrian, 27 Dec. 1828. [12] Chester Courant, 13 Jan. 1829. [13] N. Wales Chron. 15 Oct. 1829. [14] NLW ms 2797 D, Lady Williams Wynn to H. Williams Wynn, 13 July; Chester Courant, 13 July; Chester Chron. 16 July 1830. [15] Brighton Gazette, 5 May 1831. [16] NLW ms 2797 D, Sir W. to H. Williams Wynn, 10 July 1832; F. Price Jones, 'Politics in 19th Cent. Denb.' Trans. Denb. Hist. Soc. x (1961), 179-94; Add. 35793, f. 484; 35802, f. 464. [17] N. Wales Chron. 10 May; Caernarvon and Denbigh Herald, 17 May 1862.

M.M.E.

WESTENRA, Hon. Henry Robert (1792–1860), of Cortolvin Hills and Rossmore Park, co. Monaghan and The Dell, Windsor, Berks.

Co. Monaghan	1818–1830
Co. Monaghan	1831–1832
Co. Monaghan	17 May 1834–30 July 1834
Co. Monaghan	1835–10 Aug. 1842

b. 24 Aug. 1792, 1st s. of Warner William Westenra†, 2nd Bar. Rossmore [I], and 1st w. Mary Anne, da. of Charles Walsh of Walsh Park, co. Tipperary. educ. Westminster until 1806; Trinity, Dublin 1810. m. (1) 25 Jan. 1820, Anne Douglas Hamilton (d. 20 Aug. 1844), illegit. da. of Douglas, 8th duke of Hamilton [S], s.p.; (2) 19 May 1846, his cos. Josephine Julia Helen, da. of Henry Lloyd of Farrinrory, co. Tipperary, 4s. 4da. (2 d.v.p.). suc. fa. as 3rd Bar. Rossmore [I] and 2nd Bar. Rossmore [UK] 10 Aug. 1842. d. 1 Dec. 1860.
Ld. lt. co. Monaghan 1838-58.

The Westenras, who were Dutch in origin, settled in Ireland in the late seventeenth century and this Member's great-grandfather and grandfather sat in the Irish Parliament in the eighteenth. Westenra's father, who represented county Monaghan at the time of the Union, succeeded his uncle to the Irish barony of Rossmore in 1801, but, owing to a complicated inheritance, he did not come into full possession of the Monaghan estates until the 1820s and was largely an absentee. For much of this period, therefore, Rossmore Park was shared by the 2nd Baron's two surviving aunts, the redoubtable 'Queen Anne' and 'Queen Bess', who were occasionally joined by one of their male relatives.[1] Westenra, who shared a small house in Cortolvin Hills with his father on their visits to Ulster, also lived mostly in England. Although Rossmore had a significant interest in Monaghan, his son's unopposed return in 1818 was dependent on the backing of the largest proprietor, Lord Cremorne, a Whig. Yet Westenra, who had apparently favoured Catholic claims in 1813, was understood (despite his denials) to have pledged himself to oppose them when he first entered Parliament. In addition, he generally supported Lord Liverpool's administration, and this led him into political difficulties with Cremorne and therefore Rossmore, as is revealed in their extensive correspondence.[2] In January 1820 he married the bastard daughter of the actress Harriet Esten (née Hughes) and the duke of Hamilton, who had bequeathed her the family's alienable properties on his death in 1799.[3] On the basis of his enhanced status, notably owing to the electoral influence that his wife brought him in Renfrewshire, Westenra applied to Liverpool for the promise of government support for Rossmore at the next election of an Irish representative peer. However, the prime minister evidently disregarded his threat to go into open opposition and Rossmore remained outside Parliament.[4] Lord Melville, the ministerialist manager in Scotland, also refused to countenance Westenra's attempt to link the deployment of his electoral interest to the award of a baronetcy to his relative Thomas Darby Coventry.[5]

Westenra was almost entirely silent in the Commons, perhaps because of a bad stammer, an unfortunate family 'habit' which later led him to consult a specialist.[6] The surviving division lists show that he often sided with ministers, though he cast at least three wayward votes in the 1818 Parliament, during which he fulfilled his pledge to oppose Catholic relief. Cremorne was disappointed in his conduct, but at the general election of 1820 he agreed to back him, without stipulations, in order to secure their continued control of the seat; as Westenra later put it, 'general politics had nothing to do with our engagement: county politics had'.[7] Little evidence of parliamentary activity has been traced for the following session, but he evidently persisted with his independent line, as on 26 May 1820 he wrote to his father that

> I *will not* bow to Lord Cremorne's wish that I should oppose government upon every single measure they propose. I will not bow to anyone else's wish that I should link myself with government so close that I must go with them through everything.[8]

Later that year he differed with Cremorne over Queen Caroline, whom he deemed 'most maliciously guilty', and for a while quarrelled with Rossmore, to whom he offered to resign his seat under the pressure of his constant disapproval.[9]

He divided in defence of ministers' conduct towards the queen, 6 Feb., but for inquiry into the conduct of the sheriff of county Dublin on the meeting relating to the affair, 22 Feb. 1821, when (as on 3 July 1820) he was presumably in the minority against allowing the Irish master in chancery Thomas Ellis to continue as a Member.[10] He paired for repeal of the additional malt duty, 21 Mar. (although he was listed in the majority against it on 3 Apr.), and voted for Hume's motion for economy and retrenchment, 27 June. About the attempt to abolish the death penalty for forgery, for which he divided on 4 June, he afterwards boasted that 'I supported that bill through every stage of it, nor left the House for one moment until every clause of the bill was negatived and they began to call each other ugly names, when I instantly got up and left them to finish their dirty work together'.[11] Having

given Rossmore advice on how to bolster their interest in Monaghan, especially by establishing Rossmore Park as the rebuilt family headquarters,[12] between 28 Nov. 1821 and 20 Jan. 1822 he composed a lengthy vindication of his independent conduct and expressed his exasperation at the risk his father and Cremorne were running in intending to disturb the county and thereby jeopardizing his seat.[13] Westenra voted against more extensive tax reductions to relieve distress, 11 Feb., but for reducing the number of junior lords of the admiralty, 1 Mar., and to abolish one of the joint-postmasterships, 13 Mar. and (as a pair) 2 May 1822. He voted for reform of the criminal law, 4 June 1822, and, vaunting his independence despite fears of a future contest, he later related that he 'on many other occasions was present in the House for the purpose of supporting measures brought forward by opposition, but which were not pressed to a division'.[14] Anxious not to alienate his Protestant constituents or to disturb the delicate balance of interests, he angrily rebuffed his father's apparent request for him to support Plunket on the Catholic question in the spring of 1823.[15] His name appeared in both the majority and minority lists on the Foreign Enlistment Act, 16 Apr., but his correspondence makes clear that he divided for its repeal (having opposed its passage in 1819).[16] He voted for inquiry into the legal proceedings against the Dublin Orange rioters, 22 Apr., and for Buxton's amendment to recommit the silk manufacture bill, 9 June. He expressed his displeasure at his brother Richard's departure from Rossmore Park that year, but disliked the idea of taking up permanent residence himself and was censured for failing to attend the assizes; he did, however, voice his concerns about the importance of registering Catholic tenants in order to keep up the interest.[17] Amid further observations and cross words on their declining fortunes in Monaghan politics that autumn, he accused his father of bandying about his principles so as to humour the worthless Cremorne, who simply wished to claim him as his Member. Rather, as he insisted in November 1823, he did vote sometimes with opposition:

> Those some times were, I believe, nearly equal to my voting with the ministers. The public I do not care one bulrush about, whether they observed it or not. Their mind is swayed by faction, prejudice and envy. But it *was* observed by some of my constituents, and from those I have received as you know honourable testimony of their approbation. They treat me more justly than you do.[18]

Despite attempts to settle the family quarrel, his resentments continued to rankle into the new year.[19]

His wife's illness kept Westenra away from the spring assizes of 1824 and may have accounted for his parliamentary inactivity that session, although he did attend the debate on colonial slavery on 16 Mar. Largely agreeing with his father's assessment that he should stay on an 'independent track' for county purposes, he commented that there was little point in joining any political connection at Westminster:

> Parties in the House are at so very low an ebb at the moment, government, from the liberal views they are acting on, having swallowed up all the country gentlemen of any liberal or independent notions who are not pledged to either faction, and they have stopped the mouths of every man of character on the opposite side, that people do not now so much look after making an interest to stick by them always, as they did in the days of Fox and Pitt.[20]

He voted for Maberly's motion for an advance of capital to Ireland, 4 May, and favoured the proposed general measure to facilitate local improvements, especially as it could have been advantageously applied to Monaghan borough. Anxious for his father to come to some understanding with Cremorne, he prepared for the latter an abstract of his anti-government votes and in September he declined to join the committee of the Grand Orange Lodge, of which his uncle Colonel Henry Westenra was a member.[21] That autumn, when it looked as if Cremorne would withdraw his backing, he insisted that Rossmore should remind his patron that he had accepted that Westenra would oppose Catholic claims and was worthy of respect for his independent conduct. He also made strenuous efforts to deny that his statement in 1818 really amounted to a firm pledge against relief, explaining privately that he was 'no exclusionist', quite the reverse in fact, but could only support a measure which would guarantee that Protestants remained in control of the senior executive offices of state. By December 1824 his and Rossmore's approaches to Cremorne had evidently removed the immediate threat to their interest.[22]

One contemporary source described Westenra as having divided sometimes with and sometimes against ministers in the 1825 session.[23] However, he seems to have been taken up with his Irish concerns, which ranged from research on ancient burial customs to involvement in the establishment of the Ulster Canal, and his only known votes that year were for the Irish unlawful societies bill, 15, 25 Feb., and (as on 28 Feb. 1821 and 30 Apr. 1822) against Catholic relief, 1 Mar., 10 May.[24] His father, who signed the public declaration in favour of the Catholics, informed Cremorne in June 1825 that 'my eldest son had voted against Catholic claims, on his own conviction, founded (as he declares) on the arguments he heard in the House of Commons (I know the veto sticks in his throat)', and noted that his other sons Richard, an Orangeman, and John Westenra†, a pro-Catholic, had been suggested as candidates for Dublin and King's County, respectively.[25] Neither stood at the general election the following year, but Westenra, who voted against the emergency admission of foreign corn, 8, 11 May 1826, was early in the field in Monaghan and clearly counted on a mixture of support from Protestants and Catholics.[26] Although, as one of the sitting Members, he secured many promises, his position among the former was weakened by his public denial that he had ever been pledged to uphold the Protestant ascendancy indefinitely. However, despite his hostile voting record, his father's reputation, Daniel O'Connell's* endorsement and Cremorne's partial backing gave him a significant popularity among the Catholics, whose cause he thereafter agreed to advocate. Since his Orange colleague Leslie had allied himself to a powerful new candidate, Evelyn Shirley, ostensibly an advocate of emancipation, he also received widespread encouragement as the upholder of a nascent independent interest.[27] Silent on the hustings, 24 June 1826, when a mob attacked his opponents, he overtook Leslie to be elected with Shirley, in a signal success for the Catholics, and he defended his conduct in his subsequent address.[28] Following an altercation in the grand jury room between him and Colonel John Madden, Leslie's proposer, over the cause of the election riot, they fought a duel at Ardgonnell Bridge, on the border with Armagh, on 10 July 1826. His adversary was grazed on the shoulder, while, as Westenra light-heartedly related to Peel, Madden's

> ball struck the ground a little before and a little to the right of me and off that cushion (do you play billiards?) made a beautiful losing hazard into my ankle, and after a pleasing tour round the bone of the leg, between it and the tendon, was taken out on the opposite side, leaving behind it (as travellers generally do) marks of where it had been – gravel, etc. – which however has all come out since.[29]

The brouhaha did not end there, for Rossmore sued the *Dublin Evening Mail* for libel and Colonel Westenra was himself forced to fight a duel to vindicate his nephew's honour.[30]

Westenra divided for the first time for Catholic claims, 6 Mar. 1827; his only other known vote that year was against the Coventry magistracy bill, 18 June. His notes on the proceedings attest to his presence on the Ludlow election committee in early May, and on 6 June he was appointed to the select committee on Irish grand jury presentments, about which, in an attempt to revive the old practice of Members sending communications to their constituents, he informed the magistrates of county Monaghan by letter, 26 July 1827.[31] At a local dinner in April 1828 for Rossmore, now one of the leading pro-Catholic Whig peers in Ireland, a message was read explaining that his son had missed the division on the repeal of the Test Acts because of illness.[32] He did, however, vote again for Catholic relief, 12 May, and sided with opposition for ordnance reductions, 4 July. In October 1828 he declined to play any part in the formation of the county's Brunswick Club, whose activities he condemned as belligerent and divisive.[33] Listed by Planta, the Wellington ministry's patronage secretary, as 'opposed to securities', he voted for Catholic emancipation, 6, 30 Mar., and brought up local petitions in its favour, 16 Mar. 1829. Yet, mindful of their role in his return at the previous election, he dedicated to the Monaghan 40s. freeholders a pamphlet in their defence, and on 19 and 20 Mar. he divided against the Irish franchise bill, by which they were to lose their voting rights.[34] He was listed in the minority for allowing O'Connell to take his seat unimpeded, 18 May. He took an interest in the question of the non-representative peers of Ireland and Scotland, about which Rossmore issued a circular letter in August 1829. He was also credited, probably wrongly, with the authorship of *Queries for the Consideration of the Government and the People of Great Britain and Ireland* (1830), a reply to his father's pamphlet on the subject.[35]

He voted for Knatchbull's amendment to the address on distress, 4 Feb. 1830. He divided for transferring East Retford's seats to Birmingham, 11 Feb., 5 Mar., the enfranchisement of Birmingham, Leeds and Manchester, 23 Feb., and parliamentary reform, 28 May. He sided with opposition to condemn the filling of the vacancy of treasurer of the navy, 12 Mar., to reduce the grant for public buildings, 3 May, and to make Irish first fruits revenues no longer nominal, 18 May. He voted for the abolition of capital punishment for forgery, 24 May, and against going into committee on the administration of justice bill, 18 June. He presented his county's petition against the increased Irish spirit and stamp duties, 7 July 1830, and in the run-up to the dissolution was praised in a local address as 'one of the few Irish Members that was always found at his post, when any question relating to his country was under discussion'.[36] Aware of the Protestant anger at the general election that summer, Westenra sought an alliance with Cadwallader Blayney, whose Tory father Lord Blayney usually acted with the family. Yet Blayney switched his allegiance to Shirley, who had opposed Catholic emancipation, and Westenra, whose recent conduct was defended on the hustings

by his uncle Henry, was humiliatingly defeated after a week-long poll.[37] The introduction of his brother John Westenra of Sharavogue, King's County, and the family's agent was evidently with a view to a petition, but none was forthcoming, perhaps because Westenra intended to offer on the vacancy to be caused by Lord Blayney's expected death that winter.[38]

Westenra, who gave no pledge on reform, came forward at the general election of 1831, when his brother was defeated in King's County. The family were optimistic, and Shirley withdrew in the face of his combined opponents, so allowing him and Blayney to be returned without a contest.[39] He voted for the second reading of the Grey ministry's reintroduced reform bill, 6 July, at least twice against adjourning proceedings on it, 12 July, and steadily for its details. Although he cast a wayward vote for the disfranchisement of Aldborough, 14 Sept., he divided for the third reading, 19 Sept., and passage of the bill, 21 Sept., the second reading of the Scottish bill, 23 Sept., and Lord Ebrington's confidence motion, 10 Oct. He sided with O'Connell for swearing in the original Dublin committee, 29 July, and postponing the issuing of a new writ, 8 Aug., but was listed in the two government majorities on the corrupt electoral proceedings there, 23 Aug. Stressing his support for government, he added to his father's requests to ministers for a United Kingdom peerage by stressing that 'we have stood three contested elections and turned out two contumacious Tories, but at an expense to ourselves of £20,000'. Rossmore was rewarded with the lord lieutenancy of Monaghan that autumn, but had to wait until 1838 to take his place in the Lords.[40]

Westenra voted for the second reading of the revised reform bill, 17 Dec. 1831, paired for its committal, 20 Jan., again usually divided for its details and voted for the third reading, 22 Mar. 1832. He sided with ministers for the Russian-Dutch loan, 26 Jan., 12, 16 July, and against producing information on Portugal, 9 Feb., but against them for printing the Woollen Grange petition urging the abolition of Irish tithes, 16 Feb. He divided for the address calling on the king to appoint only ministers who would carry reform unimpaired, 10 May, the second reading of the Irish bill, 25 May, and maintaining the size of the Scottish county representation, 1 June. He presented petitions from Monaghan parish against the plan for Irish national education and for a more extensive Irish reform bill, 3 July, and was in the minority for Sheil's amendment to the Irish tithes bill for wider reform, 24 July. He told O'Connell that 'I am proud to say *I do think* our family *deserve* Irish confidence', but his father's failure to appease the Monaghan Independent Club accounted for his defeat at the general election of 1832.[41] He blamed the ungrateful Catholic freeholders, but declined the offer of a seat for an English borough and (in addition to a brief spell in 1834) sat for the county as a Liberal from 1835, as did John Westenra for King's County.[42] He succeeded Rossmore as lord lieutenant of Monaghan in 1838 and inherited his father's titles and estates in August 1842.[43] Remembered by one of his sons as a charming, handsome man, whose pastimes included yachting, shooting, fishing and playing the bagpipes, he died in December 1860. He was buried in Monaghan churchyard, but his remains were moved to the family mausoleum which was consecrated in the grounds of Rossmore Park in 1874. He left his estates to his eldest son Henry Cairnes ('Rosie') Westenra (1851-74), who became the 4th Baron Rossmore and was succeeded as 5th Baron by his brother and fellow army officer, Derrick Warner William (1853-1921).[44]

[1] E.P. Shirley, *Hist. Co. Monaghan*, 214-15; *Hist. Irish Parl.* vi. 528-31; *Co. Monaghan Sources*, 122-3. [2] PRO NI, Rossmore mss T2929/3/1, 2, 79, 86, 120; *Co. Monaghan Sources*, 130-1. [3] Lord Rossmore, *Things I Can Tell* (1912), 6-8; *CP*, vi. 272-3; xi. 182. [4] Add. 38283, f. 75; 38574, f. 161; 40296, f. 65; *HP Commons, 1790-1820*, v. 518. [5] NLS mss 2, ff. 27, 34. [6] Rossmore, 2-3; Rossmore mss 3/14, 91, 92, 94, 98. [7] Rossmore mss 3/87. [8] Ibid. 3/3. [9] Ibid. 3/4, 7, 9. [10] Ibid. 3/8. [11] Ibid. 3/14, 56. [12] Ibid. 3/10-13. [13] Ibid. 3/14; *Co. Monaghan Sources*, 130. [14] *Black Bk.* (1823), 201; Rossmore mss 3/15-20, 24, 56. [15] Rossmore mss 3/25, 27, 29. [16] Ibid. 3/56. [17] Ibid. 3/25, 27-29, 31-33, 43; *Co. Monaghan Sources*, 131-2. [18] Rossmore mss 3/36-42. [19] Ibid. 3/44-46. [20] Ibid. 3/47-50. [21] Ibid. 3/54-56, 59, 64-65; PRO NI, Leslie mss MIC606/3/J/7/21/4. [22] Rossmore mss 3/69-71, 73-76, 78, 82, 84, 86-87, 90-91, 107, 121. [23] *Session of Parl. 1825*, p. 489. [24] Rossmore mss 3/110, 114. [25] Ibid. 9/8. [26] Leslie mss 3/J/7/14/35-36, 37-39, 41, 53-54. [27] Ibid. 3/J/7/14/81-82, 87-89, 104, 108-9, 111-12, 117-21, 130-1; PRO NI, Clogher Diocesan mss DIO (RC)1/6/2; Rossmore mss 10B/13-20; *Dublin Evening Post*, 8, 24, 29 June 1826. [28] *Newry Commercial Telegraph*, 30 June, 4 July; *Dublin Evening Post*, 11 July 1826; Rossmore mss 10B/14. [29] *The Times*, 15 July 1826; Add. 40388, f. 320. [30] *Enniskillen Chron.* 24 Aug., 16 Nov. 1826. [31] Rossmore mss 4/17; *Impartial Reporter*, 9 Aug. 1827. [32] *O'Connell Corresp.* iii. 1367-9; viii. 3410; *Enniskillen Chron.* 24 Apr., 1 May 1828. [33] Rossmore mss 9/17-19; 10B/5A; PRO NI, Barrett Lennard mss MIC170/3, handbill, 19 Oct., Westenra to Barrett Lennard, 2 Nov. 1828. [34] H.R. Westenra, *Case of Forty Shilling Freeholders of Ireland* (1829). [35] Rossmore mss 5/1, 70, 77; Lord Rossmore, *Appeal in Cause of Ex-Parliamentary Peers of Ireland and Scotland* (1830). [36] Clogher Diocesan mss 1/6/13. [37] Leslie mss 3/J/7/17/6-7, 9-10, 15-18, 20-21, 31-33, 35-36, 49-50, 55-56, 58-60; Barrett Lennard mss 3, Westenra to Barrett Lennard, 7, 9 July, 17 Aug., Ellis to same, 3, 28 Aug.; *Newry Commercial Telegraph*, 9 July, 17, 20, 24 Aug.; *Enniskillen Chron.* 19, 26 Aug. 1830. [38] Leslie mss 3/J/7/17/42, 44; Barrett Lennard mss 3, Ellis to Barrett Lennard, 28 Aug., 4 Nov. 1830. [39] Rossmore mss 4/31; *Newry Commercial Telegraph*, 29 Apr., 10, 17 May 1831. [40] Rossmore mss 6/1-2, 10-11; W. Suss. RO, Goodwood mss 1434, f. 248; Derby mss 920 Der (14) 122/2, Rossmore to Smith Stanley, 25 July, 20 Sept., 12 Oct. 1831, 5 Jan. 1832. [41] *O'Connell Corresp.* iv. 1940; *Newry Examiner*, 5 Sept., 22, 26 Dec. 1832, 5 Jan. 1833. [42] Rossmore mss 4/35, 36; 7/25. [43] Ibid. 12A/1. [44] Rossmore, *Things I Can Tell*, 18-20; *Northern Standard*, 8 Dec. 1860; Shirley, 313; Rossmore mss 41/5.

S.M.F.

WESTERN, Charles Callis (1767-1844), of Felix Hall, Kelvedon, Essex.

MALDON	1790-1806
MALDON	4 Feb. 1807-1812
ESSEX	1812-1832

b. 9 Aug. 1767, 1st s. of Charles Western of Rivenhall, Witham, Essex and Frances Shirley, da. and h. of William Bollan of Rivenhall, agent for the council of Massachusetts. *educ.* Newcome's, Hackney;[1] Felsted; Queens', Camb. 1784. *unm. suc.* fa. 1771; *cr.* Bar. Western 28 Jan. 1833. *d.* 4 Nov. 1844.

Capt. Kelvedon vols. 1798.

'Squire' Western, as his old friend Thomas Creevey* nicknamed him (he also featured as 'Stiff-rump' and 'The Turkey' in Creevey's menagerie), was a member of the Whig 'Mountain' and an outspoken champion of agricultural protection and currency reform, whose unreliable health disrupted his political activities.[2] As Member for Essex on the old Whig interest since 1812, he had refused to promote a county meeting to protest against the Peterloo massacre, arguing to his fellow Whig Thomas Barrett Lennard*, 15 Sept. 1819, that 'to *volunteer an attack* when defeat is *certain* is only to do *certain* mischief': 'our Essex men ... must be coaxed into Whiggism and care taken not to frighten them'.[3] He came forward again at the 1820 general election, despite stories of poor health, and was returned unopposed under the long-standing Whig-Tory compromise. After a personal attack on him at the nomination by the archdeacon of Essex, he defended his support for Catholic claims and contribution to the fund for victims of Peterloo (which he had publicized, together with an explanation of his aversion to potentially dangerous popular assemblies) and condemned the authorities' heavy-handed response to that meeting.[4]

When his health permitted, he remained steady in opposition to the Liverpool ministry, dividing with his Whig friends on most major issues and voting for Catholic relief (28 Feb. 1821, 10 May 1825) and, though perhaps without great enthusiasm, for parliamentary reform. He generally acted, when present, with Creevey, Henry Grey Bennet and the 'Mountaineers' who, with Joseph Hume, forced the pace in the campaign for economy, retrenchment and lower taxation. On 18 May 1820 Western asked ministers if they intended to reduce the inconvenient interval between the spring and summer circuits. He raised the matter again, 22 Feb. 1821, 27 Mar. 1822, 9 July 1823, 11 Feb. 1824, but to no avail.[5] He opposed the bill to divide the Essex sessions between Chelmsford and Colchester, 5, 10 June 1820, when he had it thrown out.[6] He was against Lord Milton's call for repeal of the duty on foreign wool imports, 26 May. 'Under the pressure of severe indisposition', he supported Holme Sumner's motion for inquiry into agricultural distress, 30 May, arguing that domestic corn producers required enhanced protection not to increase prices but to 'render this country independent of a foreign supply', and criticizing the 1819 Act for the resumption of cash payments.[7] He was named to the select committee next day, as he was to its revivals, 7 Mar. 1821, 18 Feb. 1822. He presented and endorsed the petition of distressed Essex agriculturists, 5 June 1820.[8] He silently supported Wilberforce's compromise resolution on the Queen Caroline affair, 22 June 1820, and on the 26th moved a wrecking amendment to the government motion for a secret committee on the evidence, hoping to 'promote a final and amicable adjustment'; he was defeated by 195-100.

'*Sighing* to get somewhere for benefit of my health' in early August 1820, he condemned to Creevey 'the extreme desire of office by the [Whig] leaders', especially Lord Grey, which had paralysed the party on the queen's case. He was in the Commons to protest against 'the erection of that House into a court of justice', 21 Aug., but by the end of the month was enjoying the 'baths and hills and bracing air' of Buxton, whence he railed to Creevey against the 'baseness, cowardice [and] folly' of the trial.[9] In late October he feared that 'we shall come to blows somewhere if ministers do not mind what they are about', felt that it was 'too much that the tranquillity of the country should be hazarded by such villainy of such men' and was determined when Parliament reconvened to do something towards 'striking at the conspiracy and punishing the perjured villains and removing or impeaching ministers'.[10] He was with Creevey at the lord mayor of London's dinner in November and took him thence to his home at Felix Hall where, to celebrate the abandonment of the bill of pains and penalties, he illuminated the house, staged a bonfire and supplied free beer for the inhabitants of Kelvedon, who marched to the Hall to burn a replica green bag. He witnessed the queen's thanksgiving visit to St. Paul's, 29 Nov.[11] His rumoured plan to promote a county meeting was scotched by the Tories, but he chaired a public celebration dinner at Colchester, 19 Dec. 1820.[12] He was keen to attempt 'a direct severe censure' on ministers, who were 'chargeable with the conspiracy, the perjury, the bribery, the beastliness of the associations, the malignity, the everything', for their 'most heinous' November prorogation; he had 'no reliance' on the party leaders 'being up to the mark'. This scheme was shelved when a precedent was unearthed.[13]

He demanded inquiry into the 'foul and abominable conspiracy' against the queen, 24, 31 Jan. 1821, when, in what Creevey considered a 'capital speech' and Grey Bennet a 'good and animated' one, he called also for 'extensive reductions' in public expenditure to help relieve distress.[14] He presented and endorsed a West Ham petition for restoration of the queen's name to the liturgy, 31 Jan., and next day complained that many Members seemed determined to besmirch her with 'a never-dying stigma'; he was at the Surrey meeting in her support, 2 Feb., and a member of the management committee of the public subscription for her.[15] He supported the prayer of the Birmingham merchants' distress petition, 8 Feb., and before dividing against renewal of the sugar duties next day said he was 'determined not to vote away any more of the public money until the agricultural distress had been fully taken into consideration'; he was in the minority of 22 against the malt tax, 14 Feb., and voted for repeal of the agricultural horse tax, 5 Mar. His private pronouncements on the subject of agricultural distress seemed to one observer to be tantamount to 'a declaration of war against the fundholders'.[16] He demanded improved protection and tax cuts, 2 Mar., presented Essex, Chelmsford and Romford distress petitions, 6 Mar., and, supporting renewal of the agricultural committee, 7 Mar., denounced the free traders' 'visionary project of feeding the country by the sale of its manufactures and hoped for inquiry into the effects of the 1819 Bank Act.[17] On 21 Mar., despite what Grey Bennet thought an 'indifferent' speech, he carried against ministers by 149-125 his motion for leave to introduce a bill to repeal the additional malt duty of 1819. Ministers threatened to resign and mustered their supporters to defeat its second reading by 242-144, 3 Apr., when Western presented favourable petitions.[18] He was in minorities of 29 and 27 for inquiry into the currency question, 30 Mar., 9 Apr. When supporting the distress and reform petition from the Suffolk county meeting, which he had attended, 17 Apr., he declared that he 'had no hope of seeing any alleviation of the public distress except through the means of such a reform in the representation as would give to the people a fair and legitimate influence over the proceedings of that House'.[19] Yet he was absent from the divisions on reform, 18 Apr., 9 May 1821, and only paired for it, 25 Apr., and otherwise divided for its application to Edinburgh, 26 Feb. 1824, 13 Apr. 1826. He presented and supported petitions for mitigation of the criminal code, 26 Mar., 17 May, and voted for the abolition of capital punishment for forgery offences, 23 May, 4 June 1821.[20] He thought Scarlett's proposals for poor law reform deserved a hearing, 8 May 1821.

At the annual Holkham sheep-shearing, 1 July 1821, Western confirmed his conversion to the belief that tax reductions rather than protection offered the only realistic hope of relief for agriculture.[21] The following month he led his tenantry to escort the queen's coffin through Essex.[22] After inspecting various prisons during his late summer tour of the Buxton area, he published in October 1821 *Remarks upon Prison Discipline*, in which, seeking an effective but humane regime, he advocated solitary confinement as the punishment for bad behaviour, single-occupancy of cells, use of the treadmill for hard labour and a more frugal diet than that supplied in Millbank penitentiary, which he considered 'an insult to honest industry'. The pamphlet, particularly its criticism of the Millbank experiment, generated some controversy.[23] Western was added to the select committee on prison regulations, 28 Mar. 1822, and named to it, 18 Mar. 1824. On the gaols bill, 5 Mar. 1824, he defended treadmills, as 'all punishment should be accompanied with a feeling of degradation'.

By early 1822 Western, who was kept away from Parliament by illness in the first two months of that session, had concluded that 'almost the sole cause' of agricultural distress was the Bank Act of 1819 which, by contracting the circulating medium had produced 'a *sudden revolution* in the whole property of the community' for the benefit of creditors, while doubling the national debt and the civil list and enhancing the value of salaries, sinecures and pensions.[24] He expounded this argument, which became thenceforward his constant, boring refrain, in an *Address to the Landowners of the United Empire* (Feb. 1822) and a *Supplement* (Apr. 1822). After voting in small minorities on the estimates, 25, 28 Mar., Western, claiming that agriculturists were 'on the brink of ruin' and that two-thirds of Essex farmers were technically bankrupt, put these views to the Commons, 1 Apr., when he presented a Waltham distress petition.[25] On 3 Apr. he defended the agriculture committee against the criticisms of Ellice, Member for Coventry, but in turn dismissed their recommendation of corn law revision and denounced the 1797 Bank Act as 'a breach of faith to the public creditor' and the 1819 measure as 'a breach of faith to the public debtor'. He said on 29 Apr. that ministers had at last acknowledged the 'baneful operation' of the resumption of cash payments. At the Essex county distress meeting, 8 May, he ranked this above 'overwhelming taxation' and 'an indifferent system of corn laws' as the main source of the problem.[26] In the House that day he spoke and voted in the minority of 37 for Wyvill's amendment to the government proposals to deal with distress, which demanded large

tax remissions. He argued that 'the present state of the currency' made it impossible to legislate on protection, 9 May, when he was in the minority of 24 for an 18*s.* bounty on wheat exports. He defended his currency views against Ricardo's attacks, 13 May, and presented the Essex distress petition, 17 May.[27] He acquiesced in the ministerial plan to allow the export of warehoused foreign corn ground as flour, 3 June, when he divided with Hume on the sinking fund and with Curwen for repeal of the salt tax. He presented three petitions for revision of the criminal code, 4 June.[28] On 11 June, speaking 'indifferently for three hours', according to the Whig George Agar Ellis*,[29] he moved for inquiry into the effects of the 1819 Act: his wish was, by devaluing the standard and adjusting dividends, debts, contracts and salaries, to achieve a 'system which should give to the products of industry of every description the same relative money price which they commanded during the suspension of cash payments, and secure a fair and reciprocal remuneration for the general industry of the country'. After an adjournment, his motion was crushed by 194-30 on 12 June.[30] On the 14th he deplored the home secretary Peel's 'consummate assurance' in condemning the language of the Kent reform petition. He said that 'excess of taxation' prevented British agriculturists from competing on equal terms with foreigners, 20 June. He was a steady opponent of the aliens bill that month and voted for repeal of the salt, 28 June, and window taxes, 2 July. On 10 July he moved a series of resolutions on the currency question, which were negatived at four the next morning after Ricardo had demolished them. He presented Essex petitions against the beer retail bill, 15 July 1822, but expressed his personal approval of its principle.[31] In a *Second Address to the Landowners* that autumn he rehearsed his currency views. To Creevey he explained that he had written privately to Lords Grey, Lansdowne and Holland on the subject:

> The *real* drift of the two latter particularly was to inform them that I thought they were turning their backs upon calamity *quite unprecedented* in the state of our country, to the infliction of which they had unknowingly been *instrumental*, and to each of them I said what I said to you, that I consider the question as quite unconnected with general politics.[32]

These arguments cut no ice with the Whig hierarchy, but Western, who thought that if Canning, the new foreign secretary, made war on France over Spain and repealed the 1819 Bank Act he would make himself 'more *popular* and more powerful ... than can be imagined', and in February 1823 did 'not feel confident yet in the soundness of the health and strength

I have got', received backing from the eccentric Lord Stanhope. He promoted a county meeting to consider agricultural distress, 20 Mar. 1823, when he successfully pleaded with Daniel Whittle Harvey, the Essex radical and former and future Member for Colchester, to drop his alternative petition calling for parliamentary reform and a wholesale revision of taxation. To Stanhope he reported that there had been 'strong indications of feeling right upon the currency subject, but by no means general or sufficiently so I think to hazard an attempt at a petition on that specific subject'. He deluded himself that if landowners resolutely petitioned for relief, ministers would realize that the currency problem was the key.[33] Appearing late in the Commons, he voted against the naval and military pensions bill, 11, 14 Apr., and paired for repeal of the Foreign Enlistment Act, 16 Apr. He opposed Maberly's motion to transfer the tax on beer to malt alone, 28 May, arguing that both imposts should be reduced. He moved at length for inquiry into the currency, 11 June, allowed Lord Folkestone to amend his motion to include an adjustment of contracts and saw it defeated by 96-27 on 12 June. He regretted Brougham's abandonment of his beer retail bill, 9 July, when he complained that 'in the taxes repealed this session, there had been an entire forgetfulness of the peculiar distress of the landed interest'. He voted for repeal of the usury laws, 27 June, and to end prison flogging, 7 July (and again, 15 Mar. 1824). On 19 June 1823 he got leave to introduce a bill to qualify the possessors of £400 in personal wealth for jury service. At Peel's request, he set it aside for the session, 9 July 1823. Peel consulted him and invited his comments on the subject during the recess; he did not think much of the home secretary's planned bill. He reintroduced his own, 26 Feb., but had reluctantly to abandon it, 4 June 1824. On 2 May 1825 he had a clause qualifying the owners of £400 added to Peel's current jurors bill and reserved for future consideration.[34]

On the address, 4 Feb. 1824, Western deplored the government's failure to intervene against France, but dropped his intended amendment after the threat of it had made Brougham take a firmer line.[35] He voted for a repeal of assessed taxes, 2 Mar., 10 May, and against grants for Windsor Castle repairs, 5 Apr., and new churches, 9 Apr. He presented petitions for repeal of the excise licence duty, 4 Mar., and against slavery, 5 Mar., but bouts of 'indisposition' seriously disrupted his attendance that session.[36] He was unhappy with the proposed duty on long wool exports but was appeased by the chancellor's explanation, 26 Mar. 1824. He paired for inquiry into the state of Ireland, 11 May 1824. Next session he seems not to have attended until

late April.[37] On 2 May 1825 he defended the corn laws. He was in minorities of 23 for repeal of the beer duties, 5 May, and of 29 for Brougham's attempt to make puisne judges immovable, 20 May. He voiced the alarm of barley growers over the plan to allow the rectification of rum into gin, 2 June, but his amendment of 13 June was lost by 81-43.[38] He voted in small minorities against naval flogging, 9 June, for inquiry into Ireland, 13 June, and for amendments to the combination bill, 27 June 1825. Poor health made him a virtual absentee during the 1826 session, when he presented petitions against interference with the corn laws, 13 Apr., and for the abolition of slavery, 20 Apr.[39] In mid-May 1826 he composed, with much 'fatigue and anxiety', a public *Letter to the Earl of Liverpool*, in which he dismissed the monetary measures of that session as 'palliatives ... not only futile but injurious', argued for a return to a paper currency and tried to distinguish between an extended circulation and excessive taxation as causes of high corn prices.[40] At the general election in June he was too ill to canvass or appear on the hustings, but his cousin Thomas Burch Western stood in for him and he was returned unopposed.[41]

Western refused to support Hume's amendment to the address, which offered a 'sweeping condemnation of the whole system of corn laws' and went too far in its demand for economies, 21 Nov. 1826. Next day, for the record, he moved but did not press an amendment drawing attention to the 'severe' agricultural distress, though he admitted that it was less damaging than in 1822. On 24 Nov. 1826 he said that ministers had been 'justified' in facilitating the emergency admission of foreign corn. He voted against the Clarences' grant, 16 Feb., paired for Catholic relief, 6 Mar., and was in the opposition minorities on the Barrackpoor mutiny, 22 Mar., the Lisburn Orange procession, 29 Mar., supply, 30 Mar., and chancery delays, 5 Apr. He divided for the spring guns bill, 23 Mar. He presented and endorsed petitions against relaxation of the corn laws, 16, 27 Feb., 19 Mar., 2 Apr., and vowed to 'oppose any material alteration.[42] He duly condemned the government's proposed corn bill, which he said would bring 'bankruptcy to the farmers' and leave the country at the mercy of foreign growers. On 2 Apr. he spoke and voted against the second reading. Presenting a protectionist petition from Suffolk, 17 May, he said that when, as he expected, the measure was rejected by the Lords, he would propose to bring the 1822 Act into immediate operation by reducing the prohibitive price of corn from 80s. to 70s., with a graduated import duty. He did this, 18 June, when the Canning ministry, not daring to meet him with a direct negative because they were pledged to revise the laws, countered with a proposal to allow the temporary admission of warehoused corn to the market; this was carried by 238-52.[43] Western voted for the disfranchisement of Penryn, 28 May, when he opposed the free import of foreign wool. As chairman of the East Retford election committee, he reported the need for further action to deal with corruption there, 11 June, but handed the problem over to Charles Tennyson. On 14 June he stood by his currency views and contended that 'the prosperity of the country would never be permanently restored until Parliament retraced its steps'. He presented many Essex petitions for repeal of the Test Acts, 6, 12, 18 June 1827, 26 Feb. 1828, when he voted for that measure.[44]

He presented and endorsed Maldon and Colchester protectionist petitions and one from Chelmsford maltsters against the Malt Act, 22 Apr. 1828. He objected to the Wellington government's planned revision of the corn duties, but conceded that the bill as a whole was 'a point gained' and evidence of the premier's sympathy for agriculturists, 25 Apr. He brought up and supported further hostile petitions, 28 Apr., when he failed by 99-43 to increase the duties on rye, peas, and beans. On the third reading, 23 May, he placed on record his belief in the 'considerable danger' involved in this 'experiment'. He denounced the bill by which Maldon's Tory corporation sought to levy river tolls, 24 Apr. He spoke and voted for Whittle Harvey's motion for more efficient control over crown excise prosecutions, 1 May, though he felt it went too far. He presented petitions for Catholic relief, and voted thus, 12 May. Next day he opposed the provision for Canning's widow, but Canning's nephew gave him credit for doing so fairly and without resorting to personal abuse.[45] He supported Davenport's plan to give petty felons the option of summary conviction by magistrates, 13 May, and his motion for an inquiry into prison discipline, 14 May. He supported a Flintshire miners' petition against reduction of the duty on foreign lead ore and the abolition of one pound notes, 22 May, presented and endorsed a Colchester petition against the restriction of small notes, 3 June, and was in the minority of 24 against the small notes bill, 16 June. He brought up several Essex anti-slavery petitions, 3, 13, 19, 23 June, 4 July. He voted against items in the miscellaneous estimates, 20, 23 June, and suggested that savings banks' interest rates should be increased in line with deposits, 3 July 1828. He voted for Catholic emancipation, 6, 30 Mar. 1829, and on 17 Mar., when he refuted his colleague Admiral Harvey's assertion that Essex opinion was hostile, expressed his pleasure at its concession by ministers. He voted to allow Daniel O'Connell to take his seat without

hindrance, 18 May. He supported Fyler's motion for inquiry into the silk industry, 14 Apr., but called for investigation of all distress, which he blamed on cash restriction. He liked the idea of Slaney's wages bill, but felt that it was too risky in the present economic conditions. He cautiously welcomed Davenport's juvenile offenders bill, 12 May. He was persuaded to drop his motion for repeal of the agricultural horse tax by a ministerial promise to revise all the assessed taxes next session. On 12 June 1829 he pressed for inquiry into the 'general calamity and distress' affecting industry.

At the end of the year he published *A Letter on the Present Distress of the Country addressed to his Constituents*, in which he repeated his familiar diatribe against cash payments. A *Second* and *Third Letter* followed in January 1830.[46] On the address, 4 Feb., he expressed 'indignation at the cold and unfeeling manner' in which ministers had alluded to 'the distress of the people', predicted 'a convulsion more terrible than any we have yet seen' if redress was not forthcoming, as 'men in the lower walks of life' were acquiring 'a knowledge of men and things', and advocated currency reform. The backbencher Hudson Gurney thought he 'spoke well'.[47] Western voted for the amendment. Next day he tried in vain to persuade Lord Blandford not to divide the House on parliamentary reform, which he now favoured. He was in the minority of 57 for Blandford's scheme, 18 Feb., and paired for the enfranchisement of Birmingham, Leeds and Manchester, 23 Feb.; but he was 'decidedly opposed' to the secret ballot, which he said would create 'eternal suspicion and hypocrisy', 5 Mar., and he did not vote for Russell's general reform motion, 28 May. At the Essex county meeting, 11 Feb., he opposed Whittle Harvey's successful radical amendment;[48] and when presenting the petition next day, he disavowed its advocacy of ecclesiastical reform, said that its language cast 'unjust aspersions upon the motives and conduct of the gentry and higher classes', read the original petition and traded insults with Whittle Harvey.[49] He felt that Hume's motion for large reductions in expenditure was too general, 15 Feb., stressed the need for currency reform and divided in the majority against the motion;[50] but on 19 Feb. he spoke and voted with Hume against the army estimates. He presented and supported agriculturists' distress petitions, 23 Feb., 9, 23 Mar., when he said that national distress was 'unexampled'. To Sir John Sinclair[†] he wrote, 4 Mar.:

I am sorry to say there is no disposition on the part of ministers or *Whigs* to give way upon currency, and the country is getting into a most *frightful* state. I never was an alarmist, but I confess at this moment the prospect is to me terrific. The people are (naturally enough) throwing off all respect for authority, and looking only to beat down institutions of every kind, to despoil property and to crush the higher ranks.[51]

On 25 Mar. he presented and endorsed an Essex millers' petition for permission to grind bonded wheat for export and opposed Poulett Thomson's motion for a revision of taxation as too vague; but next day he was in the opposition majority against the Bathurst and Dundas pensions. He supported distillers' petitions against the additional duty on corn spirits, 7 Apr., 4 May. He presented and endorsed a petition for abolition of the death penalty for forgery, 8 Apr., and voted to that effect, 24 May, 7 June, 20 July. He divided for economies in public expenditure, 3, 10 May, 7, 11, 14 June, for specific tax cuts, 13, 21 May, and for abolition of the Irish lord lieutenancy, 11 May, and, as one of O'Connell's minority of 17, for Irish vestry reform, 10 June. He paired for Jewish emancipation, 17 May. He generally approved the sale of beer bill, 21 May, 1 July, when he argued for an increase in licence fees to prevent the proliferation of 'obnoxious' alehouses. He supported a Colchester petition for higher duties on foreign flour, 28 May. He welcomed the new metropolitan police force, 15 June. He supported Hume's motion to reduce judges' salaries, 7 July, and voted against any increase in recognizances in libel cases, 9 July 1830. At the 1830 general election Western, who tried to promote a Whig challenge to the Tory domination of Ipswich, offered again for Essex, though he was again too weak to canvass in person.[52] At the nomination he rested on his past record, expressed 'firm reliance' on the 'honour and integrity' of Wellington and applauded events in France. In the contest promoted by Whittle Harvey in a bid to break the gentry's party compact, Western refused to endorse his candidate, the reformer William Long Wellesley*, and in effect coalesced with the Tory Tyrell to exclude him and save himself. He came second in the poll.[53]

He presented two dozen petitions against slavery, 11, 17 Nov. 1830. He was in the majority which voted the ministry out of office on the civil list, 15 Nov. On 21 Dec. he again blamed the 'ruinous change ... in the currency' for the current distress and disorder and defended the corn laws. Soon afterwards he had 'half an hour's conversation' with the new premier, Lord Grey, during which he 'pressed upon him with all the earnestness I felt, my *gloomy* opinion of the state of the country, which he said could not be more gloomy than

his own'. Reporting this to Grey's cabinet colleague Sir James Graham*, 26 Dec. 1830, Western wrote:

> I am sorry to say he appeared to me very much out of spirits ... What I fear over and above the rocks and quick sands which show destruction on every side, is the discordant sentiments of his officers. A measure ... to suit them all must be reached. He must play the *autocrat* ... I pressed upon him of course *the* subject, my long rooted conviction that we were going forward to inevitable destruction unless he had courage to retrieve the dreadful error of 1819, and my no less honest conviction that ... it was retrievable, even with ease.

He told Graham, who shared some of his views on the currency, that he was minded to write to Grey's son Lord Howick* 'in order to make a sort of record of the opinion I had expressed to Lord Grey':

> I am convinced ... that it is fear which keeps people back from speaking out sentiments very like our own upon currency. This fear arises from two causes, first that of being charged with a robbery of the public reduction and secondly the timidity that arises from a want of fully understanding of the subject.

He concluded with expressing his dislike of a proposal to 'prohibit' the cultivation in Ireland of tobacco, 'vegetable delightful to man, which the earth is ready to give abundantly for his use'.[54]

Like Tyrell, Western avoided the Essex reform meeting promoted by Whittle Harvey, 28 Feb. 1831, as he explained in the House that day; but he declared his support for 'efficient' and 'moderate reform'. Creevey told his stepdaughter, 3 Mar., that the scale of the Grey ministry's reform bill had initially taken him aback:

> If you would really like to see the effect of this reform bill upon the r-a-a-lly grave and reflecting mind, you should have seen your Squire Western with me yesterday. After having looked me through with *awe* for some minutes he said, 'Did you ever hear of such a plan of reform as this in the world?' 'Never'. 'It is quite impossible it can ever be carried, Creevey'. 'It is as sure to be carried as we are now in this room' ... He then said he did not know what to do, that Maldon was to lose a Member, that he *dare* not vote for that. In short, I never saw a man in a greater *quandary* in my life.[55]

Western swallowed his fears, warmly supported the bill at the Essex county meeting, 19 Mar., voted for the second reading, 22 Mar., and next day presented the county address to the king.[56] He brought up, without comment, a Walden petition for reform, commutation of tithes and a repeal of assessed taxes, 28 Mar., but when presenting the Essex reform petition, 13 Apr., he denounced the so-called 'friends of moderate reform' as its 'most insidious and dangerous enemies'. He voted against Gascoyne's wrecking amendment, 19 Apr. He would have no truck with Littleton's bill to end payment in kind, 12 Apr. 1831. At the ensuing general election, when Pole Wellesley and Tyrell also stood again, Western praised the reform bill, said that its 'whole spirit', if not all its details, must be preserved and damned 60 years of Tory misrule. A reform coalition with Long Wellesley saw them returned comfortably ahead of Tyrell; 'a slight indisposition' kept Western away near the end of the contest. At the celebration dinner, 24 May 1831, he advised the electors to resist 'the corruption of faction or the workings of popular excitement' and extolled the bill as 'a royal and a loyal and a popular measure, calculated to establish and preserve an exact equilibrium between the estates of the constitution'.[57]

He voted for the second reading of the reintroduced reform bill, 6 July 1831, but at the meeting of government supporters called to settle tactics for the committee stage five days later he aired his 'crotchet' of 'objecting to a division of counties'.[58] He gave generally steady support to the bill's details until the end of the third week in August, though he voted in minorities on the disfranchisement of Saltash, 26 July, and, as expected, the division of counties, 11 Aug. On the proposal to deprive Maldon, his former seat, of one Member, 29 July, he half-heartedly suggested combining it with Heybridge to return two, but concluded that it would be better off as 'a very respectable resident constituency'. On 17 Aug. he argued that Lord Milton's amendment to get rid of the county leaseholder franchise would 'divest nearly the whole tenantry of England of any share in the representation'; and next day he spoke and voted in the majority for the enfranchisement of £50 tenants-at-will. He voted for the passage of the bill, 21 Sept. He approved the grant for the Swan River settlement, 25 July; largely approved the game bill, but bridled at the powers it gave to magistrates, 8 Aug.; presented and endorsed Essex barley growers' petitions against distillation from molasses, 18 Aug., 19 Sept., when he announced with 'satisfaction' the decision of the select committee to prohibit this; opposed the introduction of poor laws to Ireland, 29 Aug., and took issue with Hume over his captious opposition to the navy estimates, 30 Sept. 1831.

Western was absent from the division on Lord Ebrington's confidence motion, 10 Oct., but at the annual dinner of the Maldon Independent Club, 21 Nov. 1831, he defied 'indisposition' to call for reformers' unity, praise the king and attack the 'vicious majority' of Tory peers and bishops who by reject-

ing the bill had 'thrown the cards into the hands of the demagogues'. He spoke in the same vein at the county meeting, 10 Dec., when he urged reformers to eschew 'melancholy division' and disavowed 'abstract rights of universal suffrage'.[59] Presenting the petition, 14 Dec., he condemned the conduct of the Lords as 'most extraordinary and calamitous in its consequences', declared his support for the essentials of the reform bill, but firmly dissociated himself from Whittle Harvey's attack on church revenues at the county meeting. Privately he felt that Whittle Harvey, who '*hates* the Whigs in his heart', was playing into the hands of the Essex Tories with his assault 'upon *landlords* and *property*'.[60] He divided for the second reading of the revised reform bill (which reprieved Maldon), 17 Dec. 1831, to go into committee on it, 20 Jan. 1832, and generally for its details. He did, however, support Barrett Lennard's unsuccessful bid to preserve the franchise of freemen by marriage, 7 Feb. He dismissed the Chelmsford petition seeking representation and criticizing the proposed division of Essex as an antireformers' attempt to obstruct the measure, 23 Feb. He voted for the third reading, 22 Mar. He divided with government on the Russian-Dutch loan, 26 Jan., and the affairs of Portugal, 9 Feb., but was in the minority for immediate inquiry into the glove trade, 31 Jan. He presented petitions for, 23 Feb., and against, 20 Mar., the factories regulation bill. He had been mentioned in September 1831 as a likely candidate for the peerage if creations became necessary to carry reform, and his name cropped up again in April 1832.[61] He was absent from the division on the address calling on the king to appoint ministers who would carry reform undiluted, 10 May, and only paired against a Conservative amendment to the Scottish reform bill, 1 June, when he tried to stop Milton advocating free trade in corn but was cut short by the Speaker. He paired with government on the Russian-Dutch loan, 16, 20 July 1832.

Despite worsening health ('at my age ... no joke') Western stood for North Essex at the 1832 general election, boasting of his support for reform and the agricultural interest and advocating the prompt abolition of slavery. He was beaten into third place by Tyrell and a wealthy Conservative arriviste who finished only 36 votes ahead of him. He partially blamed the illness which had handicapped his campaign, but refused to repent of his vote for the enfranchisement of tenants-at-will, which was thought by many observers to have strengthened the Conservatives. He promised to try again and declared that 'the continuance of the present administration in power is essential to the maintenance of our liberties and ... the liberties of every nation in Europe'.[62] The duke of Bedford strongly urged Holland to use his 'powerful influence with Grey' to have Western, 'a zealous and faithful servant in the Whig cause for 42 years', made a peer:

> Western has no son or heir. He is not a young man, and has very bad health. Let him at least have the satisfaction of ending his days a member of one branch of that legislature in which he has so long and so often fought the battles of the Whig cause.

Grey readily obliged, but some Conservatives scoffed at the notion of ennobling a man 'because he was rejected by a *reformed constituency*'.[63] In 1836 Western publicly praised Lord John Russell for his work as home secretary in the Melbourne administration; but when Russell came out for relaxation of the corn laws in 1839 Western took issue with him and defended protection.[64] He spent his last years in comparative retirement at Felix Hall, where he continued the agricultural experiments and improvements which fascinated him.[65] He died in November 1844. By his will, dated 27 Apr. 1844, he left all his real estate to Thomas Burch Western (1795-1873), who was created a baronet in 1864 and was Liberal Member for North Essex, 1865-8.[66]

---

[1] *Creevey's Life and Times*, 8. [2] Ibid. pp. xix, 121; B. Hilton, *Corn, Cash, Commerce*, 13, 30, 99-100, 134. [3] Essex RO, Barrett Lennard mss D/DL C60. [4] Ibid. C58/87; *Suff. Chron.* 11 Mar. 1820; *Procs. at Colchester and Essex Elections* (1820), 42-43, 46-48, 50-55. [5] *The Times*, 19 May 1820, 23 Feb. 1821, 12 Feb. 1824. [6] Ibid. 6, 21 June 1820. [7] Ibid. 31 May 1820. [8] Ibid. 6 June 1820. [9] Creevey mss, Western to Creevey, 6, 30 Aug. 1820; *Creevey Pprs.* i. 310, 313, 319. [10] Creevey mss, Western to Creevey, 26, 29 Oct. 1820; *Creevey Pprs.* i. 334. [11] *Creevey Pprs.* i. 339; *Creevey's Life and Times*, 133; *Suff. Chron.* 18 Nov.; Creevey mss, Western to Creevey, 30 Nov. 1820. [12] Add. 38288, f. 303; *The Times*, 21 Dec. 1820. [13] Creevey mss, Western to Creevey, 14 Jan. [1821]; *Creevey Pprs.* ii. 5. [14] *Creevey's Life and Times*, 137; HLRO, Hist. Coll. 379, Grey Bennet diary, 8. [15] *The Times*, 1 Feb. 1821; Grey Bennet diary, 10, 24. [16] Harrowby mss, Labouchere to Sandon, 12 Feb. 1821. [17] *The Times*, 3, 7 Mar. 1821; Grey Bennet diary, 32. [18] Grey Bennet diary, 41-42; Hilton, 137; *Three Diaries*, 320; Merthyr Mawr mss L/204/5; *The Times*, 4 Apr. 1821. [19] *The Times*, 18 Apr. 1821. [20] Ibid. 27 Mar., 18 May; *Colchester Gazette*, 26 May 1821. [21] Hilton, 142; *The Times*, 10, 14 July 1821. [22] Creevey mss, Western to Creevey, 14 Aug. 1821; *VCH Essex*, ii. 241. [23] *Edinburgh Rev.* xxxvi (1821-2), 353-73; *Thoughts on Prison Discipline* (1822); G.P. Holford, *Vindication of the Penitentiary at Millbank* (1822). [24] Hilton, 142-3. [25] *The Times*, 2 Apr. 1822. [26] Ibid. 9 May 1822. [27] Ibid. 18 May 1822. [28] Ibid. 4, 5 June 1822. [29] Northants. RO, Agar Ellis diary, 11 June 1822. [30] Hilton, 31-32, 92; JRL, Bromley Davenport mss, T. Attwood to E.D. Davenport, 27 Apr., 9 June 1822. [31] *The Times*, 16 July 1822. [32] Creevey mss, Western to Creevey, 14 Nov. 1822. [33] Ibid. Western to Creevey, 28 Feb.; Cent. Kent. Stud. Stanhope mss U1590 C 190/1, same to Stanhope, 4, 22 Mar.; *The Times*, 21 Mar. 1823. [34] Add. 40363, ff. 239, 241; 40378, f. 63; *The Times*, 27 Feb., 5 June 1824. [35] A. Mitchell, *Whigs in Opposition*, 175. [36] *The Times*, 5, 6 Mar. 1824; Add. 40363, f. 239; 40365, f. 87. [37] *The Times*, 29 Apr. 1825. [38] Ibid. 3, 14 June 1825. [39] Add. 40385, f. 271; *The Times*, 14, 21 Apr. 1826. [40] *Colchester Gazette*, 24 June 1826. [41] Ibid. 3, 17 June; Barrett Lennard mss C60, Western to Lennard, 12 June 1826. [42] *The*

Times, 17, 28 Feb., 20 Mar., 3 Apr. 1827. [43] Ibid. 18 May, 15 June 1827; *Canning's Ministry*, 391; *Arbuthnot Jnl.* ii. 126; *Geo. IV Letters*, iii. 1357; *Hobhouse Diary*, 137-8. [44] *The Times*, 7, 13, 19 June 1827. [45] Harewood mss, Lord G. Cavendish Bentinck to Lady Canning, 14 May 1828. [46] *The Times*, 2 Dec. 1829. [47] Gurney diary, 4 Feb. 1830. [48] *Colchester Gazette*, 13 Feb. 1830. [49] Grey mss, Howick jnl. 12 Feb. [1830]. [50] Ibid. 15 Feb. [1830]. [51] Rev. J. Sinclair, *Mems. Sir John Sinclair*, ii. 315. [52] Lincs. AO, Ancaster mss XIII/B/5q, t, v; *Colchester Gazette*, 24, 31 July 1830. [53] *Essex Co. Election* (1830), pp. x, 4-5, 12; *Essex Election, Aug. 1830*, pp. 23-24, 47-48, 50, 53-54, 159-60; *Greville Mems.* ii. 144. [54] Sir James Graham mss (IHR microfilm XR 80). [55] *Creevey's Life and Times*, 340. [56] *The Times*, 21 Mar.; *Colchester Gazette*, 26 Mar. 1831. [57] *The Times*, 27 Apr., 6, 11, 26 May; *Colchester Gazette*, 7, 14 May 1831. [58] Hatherton diary, 11 July [1831]. [59] *Colchester Gazette*, 26 Nov.; *The Times*, 12 Dec. 1831. [60] Barrett Lennard mss C60, Western to Lennard, 21 Dec. 1831. [61] *Creevey Pprs.* ii. 236; *Greville Mems.* ii. 283. [62] Barrett Lennard mss C60, May to Lennard, 9 Aug., Western to same, 12, 19 Aug.; *The Times*, 20, 24 Dec. 1832. [63] Add. 51664, Bedford to Holland [8 Jan.]; 51671, same to Lady Holland, 3 Jan. [1833]; *Creevey's Life and Times*, 359; *Greville Mems.* ii. 343; *Croker Pprs.* ii. 199. [64] Walpole, *Russell*, i. 261, 367; Western, *Maintenance of the Corn Laws* (1839). [65] *Oxford DNB*; C. Smith, 'Western Fam.' *Essex Rev.* x (1901), 76; *Gent. Mag.* (1844), ii. 645-6. [66] *Gent. Mag.* (1845), i. 662; PROB 11/2013/173; IR26/1724/89.

D.R.F.

WETHERELL, Charles (?1770–1846), of 5 Stone Buildings, Lincoln's Inn and 7 Whitehall Place, Mdx.

RYE	21 Dec. 1812–Feb. 1813
SHAFTESBURY	19 Feb. 1813–1818
OXFORD	1820–1826
HASTINGS	1826–Dec. 1826
PLYMPTON ERLE	16 Dec. 1826–1830
BOROUGHBRIDGE	1830–1832

b. ?1770, 3rd s. of Rev. Nathan Wetherell, DD (*d.* 1807), master of Univ. Coll. Oxf. and dean of Hereford, and Ricarda, da. of Alexander Croke of Studley Priory, Oxon.[1] *educ.* St. Paul's sch. 1783; Univ. Coll. Oxf. 14 Jan. 1786, aged 15; Magdalen, Oxf. 1788-91; I. Temple 1790, called 1794; L. Inn 1806. *m.* (1) 28 Dec. 1826, his cos. Jane Sarah Elizabeth (*d.* 21 Apr. 1831), da. of Sir Alexander Croke of Studley, 1s. *d.v.p.*; (2) 27 Nov. 1838, Harriet Elizabeth, da. of Col. Francis Warneford of Warneford Place, Wilts., *s.p.* kntd. 10 Mar. 1824. *d.* 17 Aug. 1846.

KC 25 Mar. 1816; bencher, I. Temple 1816, treas. 1825; solicitor-gen. Jan. 1824-Sept. 1826; att.-gen. Sept. 1826-Apr. 1827, Feb. 1828-Mar. 1829.

Counsel for Magdalen 1804, for Oxf. Univ. 1830-*d.*; recorder, Bristol 1827-*d.*; dep. steward, Oxf. Univ. 1846.

In 1820 Wetherell was 'a disappointed lawyer' without a seat. Despite the patronage of lord chancellor Eldon, his rise at the chancery bar had been slow. Above all, he fancied himself entitled to legal office in the Liverpool ministry, which, as a 'thorough Tory of the oldest school', he had supported in the 1812 Parliament.[2] He had undeniable talent and considerable learning, but damaged himself through his intemperance, prolixity and quixotism, which often betrayed him into buffoonery. The clownish aspect of his public persona was reinforced by his permanent state of dishevelment and his indifference to personal hygiene. One observer recalled that

> whilst strait-laced in his opinions, his ideas of dress were much the reverse, in fact he was one of the greatest slovens who ever walked, and it was a wonder when he did walk how his clothes and his body contrived to keep together.[3]

He could not, however, be ignored.

At the general election of 1820 he stood for his native city of Oxford, where he became involved in a contest with one of the sitting Members, standing on the Blenheim interest, and a barrister who had been turned out of the seat in 1818. In a canvassing speech, he praised the 'excellence' of the existing constitution. At the nomination, when he boasted of his 'growing reputation and fame in Westminster Hall', he denied being 'addicted to the purposes and intentions of the radical reformers' (an impression created by his successful defence of the radical James Watson in the treason trial of 1817, which he had undertaken purely to make a professional point), and tried to prove 'how incompatible the infatuated schemes of the radical reformers were with the sober genius and well-established foundations of the British constitution'. He comfortably topped the poll.[4] Echoing his conduct in 1817, he sought to make a name for himself by championing the cause of Queen Caroline. His attempt to secure action against the editor of the *Western Luminary* for a libel on her, 24, 25 July 1820, when he denied being her 'shadow or faggot', ended in near farce and failure. On 23 Jan. 1821 he insisted, despite having been ruled out of order, on moving for the production of copies of documents in anticipation of the Whig Lord Archibald Hamilton's motion on the omission of the queen's name from the liturgy. Ministers moved the previous question, which was carried by 260-169.[5] Wetherell was allowed to repeat the motion without hindrance the next day. Supporting Hamilton's motion, 26 Jan., he said that he had 'always been opposed to the principles of the radicals' and their 'wild and visionary schemes of reform', but argued that 'the whole course of the proceedings pursued by ministers, from the first introduction of the bill of pains and penalties, had been a series of monstrous and unjustifiable innovations on the constitution'. His

speech, which was loudly cheered, was considered by the Whig Members James Abercromby and Thomas Creevey as 'effective ... and very good' and 'a most triumphant, unanswerable legal argument ... supported with great ability'. George Howard*, a spectator in the gallery, thought it 'masterly and unanswerable ... only too lengthy in the end'.[6] The 'Mountaineer' Henry Grey Bennet described it as

> one of the most vigorous and able speeches I ever heard. It had rather too much of the *copia verbum* and was too long, with terrible repetitions; but for legal argument and clear and powerful illustrations, and above all, the claim for riveting attention, I hardly ever heard from anyone a speech of the same character.[7]

Wetherell, who got into more trouble with the Speaker for referring back to this debate, 31 Jan., voted for the opposition censure of ministers' conduct, 6 Feb., and for further motions on the liturgy question, 13, 15 Feb. He divided against government on the suppression of the liberal constitution in Naples, 21 Feb. He voted silently against Catholic relief, which was anathema to him, 28 Feb., and spoke against aspects of the relief bill, 23 Mar. (when, to the great private amusement of Canning, he minted the word 'posteriority'), 26, 27 Mar.[8] He voted with government against repeal of the additional malt duty, 3 Apr., and the disfranchisement of ordnance officials, 12 Apr. 1821.

He did likewise against more extensive tax reductions, 11, 21 Feb., and abolition of one of the jointpostmasterships, 13 Mar. 1822. He said that the bill to reduce the navy five per cents must be effected so as not to depreciate them in the event of war, 8 Mar., and upheld the royal prerogative to dismiss army officers and make articles of war, 12 Mar.[9] He denounced the Catholic peers bill as 'the acme and perfection of unrivalled singularity' and attributed dubious motives to Canning, its author, 30 Apr.; but 'the House grew so noisy and impatient' that he was 'obliged to stop before he had finished half of what he had prepared'.[10] On 10 May he moved an unsuccessful killing amendment against its second reading. He raised objections to details of the Marriage Act amendment bill, 'an unconstitutional innovation on the rights of property', 20 May, 12 July, when he was a teller for small minorities against the Lords' amendments to it. He said a 'few words', inaudible to the reporters, against Brougham's motion condemning the increasing influence of the crown, 24 June.[11] He spoke and voted against repeal of the salt duties, 28 June, observing that 'tax after tax could not, with safety to the country, be remitted'. He favoured investigation of the Calcutta bankers' financial claims, 4 July, and was a teller for the majority in the division. According to the Whig Henry Fox*, in his defence of the aliens bill, 19 July, Wetherell

> used some of the strangest words imaginable in a long tiresome speech. Somebody said to the chancellor [of the exchequer], 'what words Wetherell coins'. 'Oh!' said he, 'I should not mind the coinage, if it was not for the utterance'.[12]

He voted for the grant for the publication of government proclamations in Ireland, 22 July. At the annual Oxford mayoral feast, 30 Sept. 1822, he reviewed and explained his parliamentary conduct, 'much to the satisfaction of the assembly'.[13]

After describing the revised Marriage Act as 'an Arabia of rapine and confusion', Wetherell presented a petition from the archdeacon of Oxford against it, 14 Feb. 1823.[14] He voted against repeal of the house tax, 10 Mar., when his call for abolition of the tax on Oxford college grooms was deemed facetious by the chancellor. In the absence of the Members for Dublin he presented the petition of the grand jury complaining of aspersions cast on their conduct in the prosecution of the Orange theatre rioters, 11 Apr.; and he divided in the ministerial minority against inquiry into the affair, 22 Apr. In the committee in May he insisted that the Commons had the power to compel jurors called as witnesses to break their oaths of secrecy and objected to the Irish attorney-general being examined in a case which involved his professional character. He voted against repeal of the Foreign Enlistment Act, 16 Apr. He presented anti-Catholic petitions from the corporation and inhabitants of Oxford, 15, 17 Apr. He favoured an immediate, comprehensive grant to finance the erection of the new Westminster law courts, 18 Apr.[15] He called for the case against the judge O'Grady to be postponed, 16 May, 13, 17 June, opposed going into committee on it, 2 July, objected to the implication of criminality, 3 July, and supported the dropping of all charges, 9 July. On 16 May he denounced the principle of the Irish tithes composition bill, which 'deprived the clergy of their character of freeholders, and gave them a character of pensioners on the state'. He reiterated these views, 30 May, 6, 16 June, when he voted against going into committee on the measure. He opposed Lord Nugent's bill to place British Catholics on the same footing as Irish, which he considered as tantamount to a repeal of the Test Acts, 28 May, 18, 23 June. He spoke and voted in defence of Eldon and the existing chancery administration on Williams's motion for inquiry into delays, 5 June. He supported the bill setting up the Scottish law commission as 'a choice of considerable difficulties', 10 July 1823.

Charles Williams Wynn*, president of the board of control, ruled Wetherell out of consideration for the vacant puisne justiceship of Chester in September 1823 because his 'business is I apprehend too great to induce him to sacrifice a portion of it to this office'.[16] In the reshuffle in the legal hierarchy necessitated by death and retirement at the end of the year, he was an obvious candidate for the solicitor-generalship, if only, as the cynics said, 'to stop his mouth about the court of chancery in the House of Commons'.[17] As the Whig Sir James Mackintosh* observed:

> A connection with Wetherell is a difficulty for an administration. It is not desirable to drive him into opposition and it is impossible to place him in any conspicuous office that requires common sense. I thought they might have got out of the scrape (though not well) by withdrawing him into the exchequer.

His fellow Whig John Whishaw told Lady Holland that Wetherell 'is very anxious for office, but will assuredly be disappointed'.[18] In fact, Wetherell had the backing not only of Eldon but of Peel, the home secretary, who commented to the lord chancellor that

> on account of his general knowledge, of his attainments as a chancery lawyer, and his readiness in debate on all subjects, the attention which he has paid to ecclesiastical matters, and his zeal for the interests of the church, I think decidedly that he will be more useful to us in the House of Commons than any other man.

Privately, Peel confessed to his friend Goulburn, the Irish secretary, that he inclined to Wetherell 'partly because having an appetite for tithe bills (which appetite will be wonderfully sharpened by the preference of another candidate) he will be a most troublesome opponent'. The king was 'strongly for Wetherell, having a high opinion of his powers of abusing a foe'.[19] Williams Wynn, a pro-Catholic who considered Wetherell a 'bore', was

> not surprised the chancellor and Peel should support him, for he is as bigoted and furious No Popery as they could wish; but why Canning should, unless because he was one of the queen's friends, I cannot conceive. He is a good lawyer, but a most tedious House of Commons speaker, most uncouth in his manners.[20]

It was not quite plain sailing for Wetherell, because Lord Liverpool and Eldon agreed that it was essential to accompany the offer 'with some explanation as to particular measures likely to be brought before Parliament', especially the tithe question, and 'likewise (in order to obviate future embarrassment and misapprehension), with some reserve as to certain situations in the course of judicial succession'.[21] Eldon conducted the initial interview with Wetherell, who on 31 Dec. 1823 gave Liverpool the impression that he was 'perfectly tractable on the tithe question, and all other questions'. Later that day, however, he threw all into confusion by returning to Eldon and expressing his concern that Liverpool's 'reserve' on 'the matter of judicial succession' amounted to an unacceptable and degrading 'stipulation' that he was not to be considered for promotion to the higher ranks of the judiciary after he had become attorney-general, which he could expect to be whenever it proved possible to promote John Copley*. Liverpool, who professed merely to be keen to ensure that in future the law officers of the crown retained their places for longer periods than had been the case of late, was unwilling to give way, and it was left to Eldon to try to mollify Wetherell with assurances that no personal slight was intended and that, subject to the desirability of long service by the law officers, his professional pretensions to such vacancies as arose in the future would be given due weight. He was, however, pessimistic on 3 Jan. 1824, when he told Liverpool that

> the final tenor of his conversation was to the effect that his future condition would rest in such a state of uncertainty, as he understood the rule as exemplified by practice would leave him, that he felt not disposed to accept, and he intimated that I should receive a letter from him today, which from what he said, I expect will be a refusal ... I told him my opinion was that he was deciding wrong if he declined.

In the event, to Eldon's surprise, he meekly signified his acceptance without further demur.[22] Hobhouse of the home office reviewed the affair later in the month:

> The arguments in favour of Wetherell were that he is a man of undoubted talents, that he had brought himself for some years into Parliament, probably not without encouragement from the chancellor, and had with some rare exceptions supported the administration, that through his father he was connected both with Lord Liverpool and the chancellor, that he had already been twice disappointed in 1817 and 1819, and borne those disappointments ill, and if again foiled would probably become a desperate opponent in Parliament, and a grievous annoyance to the chancellor personally in the discussions respecting his court. The objections to him were, that he has an uncontrollable spirit and very strong passions and an ill-regulated mind, and an hereditary tendency to madness ... The chancellor from the first was a strong advocate for Wetherell, and prepossessed the king in his favour ... It may be doubted whether the chancellor in his selection of Wetherell were more actuated by fear or favour. Even the favoured person himself during his suspense expressed this sentiment. The chancellor flatters himself that W. being conciliated will follow his

advice. This may be doubtful even while he remains in his present office or that of attorney-general, but is scarcely to be looked for, when he shall be removed to one of the high judicial offices; and much less, if it should be deemed prudent to repel him from one of those offices, which may be expected to become vacant in a year or two.[23]

William Fremantle* alleged that the appointment was 'universally condemned'.[24]

Hobhouse underestimated Wetherell's loyalty and instinct for self-preservation, for he did not kick over the traces during his tenure of the post, the duties of which he apparently executed efficiently enough. His re-election for Oxford was undisturbed.[25] He voted against the production of information on Catholic office-holders, 19 Feb., and reform of Edinburgh's representation, 26 Feb. 1824. He objected to Hume's call for accounts bearing on the Austrian loan, 25 Feb., and opposed reception of a petition complaining of the conduct of Chetwynd, Member for Stafford, as chairman of quarter sessions, 27 Feb.[26] That day he divided against repeal of the usury laws. On 1 Mar., speaking 'humbly', he defended Eldon against a charge of breach of privilege and supported a further grant for the new law courts, although he 'approved of the buildings as little as any man could do';[27] he was named to the select committee on the cost of the undertaking, 23 Mar., having been appointed to that on the criminal laws, 16 Mar. He voted against abolishing flogging in the army, 5 Mar., and opposed Martin's bill to prevent the ill-treatment of cattle, 9 Mar.[28] He favoured compensation for officials of the courts who were made redundant by reforms, 26 Mar. He presented a claim for compensation from employees of the palace court, 14 Apr.[29] He was dismissive of George Lamb's scheme to allow defence by counsel in felony trials, 6 Apr., and saw no reason to change the existing regulations governing Catholic baptisms, marriages and burials, 13 Apr. He helped to see off Curteis's mariners' apprentices settlement bill, 18 May. He was in the ministerial majorities against inquiry into the prosecution of the Methodist missionary John Smith in Demerara, 11 June, and for the Irish insurrection bill, 14 June 1824.

Wetherell presented an Oxford parish petition for repeal of the house and window taxes, 8 Feb. 1825, but of course had nothing to do with the parliamentary campaign for that object. His statement that the chancery commissioners, of whom he was one, would make 'a partial report' very soon, 10 Feb., provoked derisive opposition laughter.[30] He moved a successful wrecking amendment against Onslow's usury laws repeal bill, which was 'unseasonable in time and pernicious in principle', 17 Feb. He spoke against hearing the Catholic Association against the bill to suppress it, 18 Feb., and, opposing consideration of Catholic claims, 28 Feb., argued that what had been 'denied to reason, argument, and quiet solicitation, ought never to be yielded to menace, terror, or intimidation'. He was a teller for the hostile minority, 1 Mar. He insisted that in opposing relief he was following 'his own unbiased opinion' rather than deferring to his constituents, 18 Apr. He voted silently against the relief bill, 21 Apr., and spoke and voted (as a teller) against it, 10 May. He voted against the disfranchisement of Irish 40s. freeholders, 21 Apr. He was wary of Fyshe Palmer's county transfer of land bill, 25 Apr., and, while admitting that the law concerning wrongous imprisonment in Scotland required 'improvement', urged John Grant to consult legal experts before proceeding with his proposed amendment bill, 5 May. He denied Hume's allegation that Eldon had it in his power to regulate fees, line his own pockets and generally profit from chancery delays, 27 May; and on 31 May denounced petitions on this sore point as 'unfair, false, fabricated, fallacious and deceptive'. He voted for the grant to the duke of Cumberland, 30 May, 6, 10 June. He was involved in talks with Peel and his colleague at Oxford about the universities police bill, which was unpopular in the city; but he supported it in the House, 20 June.[31] He objected to Denman's motion for the attendance of witnesses for the inquiry into the William Kenrick[†] affair, 21 June 1825.

By the end of the year Wetherell had apparently decided not to stand again for Oxford, where it was thought that in any case he would be 'turned out ... for parsimony' at the next general election.[32] When a vacancy occurred for Oxford University in January 1826 he offered himself, with the backing of his college, though it was reported that 'the feeling is strong against him', and he was extremely unpopular. Peel, the sitting Member, remained officially neutral, but privately told the dean of Christ Church that if he was 'a free man', he would vote for Wetherell (a 'strange fellow') or the eminent civilian Sir John Nicholl*, who was one of several men initially in the field: 'Wetherell is the most active and most unsafe. He is a bitter and a powerful enemy, if he is roused to exertion, but his capacity to serve is not equal to his power of injuring. At the same time he is very zealous'. It seemed for a while that Wetherell would come in by default, but his opponents put up a generally acceptable country gentlemen, Thomas Estcourt, and, aware that he faced the humiliation of being defeated for the University and failing to regain his city seat if he vacated it, he withdrew in mid-February 1826.[33] He spoke and voted in defence of the Jamaican slave trials,

2 Mar. 1826. He opposed Wilson's motion for a return of bankruptcy commissioners' tavern expenses, 15 Mar., and Martin's cruelty to cattle prevention bill the following day. He was in the government majorities on the salary of the president of the board of trade, 10 Apr., and against reform of Edinburgh's representation, 13 Apr., when he was also a teller for the majority against Hume's motion on Westminster Abbey. On 18 Apr. he deplored Hume's description of Eldon as a 'curse' on the country and was contemptuous of the 'far-fetched invective, gross calumny, and wanton falsehood' of the petition of a prisoner confined for contempt of chancery. Three days later he complained that 'there existed a systematic attempt to hunt down the lord chancellor'. He again opposed defence by counsel in felony trials, 25 Apr. On the government motion for a bill to implement the recommendations of the chancery commissioners, 18 May, he defended them against Williams's strictures. He protested against the use of arguments in favour of Catholic relief based on an alleged violation of the Treaty of Limerick, 28 Apr. Wetherell, whom Hudson Gurney*, his neighbour at a ministerial dinner, described at this time as 'the awkwardest hound at a *table* I ever saw',[34] was a government teller in the division on the corn law report, 8 May. He objected to inquiry into James Silk Buckingham's[†] petition concerning the freedom of the press in India, 11 May, and voted against Russell's resolution condemning electoral bribery, 26 May 1826.

At the general election the following month he duly abandoned Oxford and was returned unopposed for Hastings on the treasury interest.[35] When Copley was promoted to the vacant mastership of the rolls in September, he, Liverpool and Eldon finally agreed that for all their misgivings, it was impossible to pass over Wetherell for the attorney-generalship. Liverpool floated the notion of trying to fob him off with a judgeship, but Eldon

was quite sure that W. would receive that as an insult to him, and ... *I* certainly would not propose it to him ... I could see no determination, if he did not succeed Copley, which he could act upon, and that upon any such office as could be, or had been thought of, he would have no option but to retire without office to the bar. I am quite sure he would not take a judgeship. In all this Copley ... fully concurred. His emoluments at the bar were very considerable before he was solicitor. They have of course since (for such always happens with a solicitor-general) been less. But I have no doubt that if he quitted that office, such emoluments would be very considerable ... You should not discourage gentlemen from taking the office of solicitor by not allowing them to have the few advantages which vacancies of higher offices may offer ...

I have not the slightest doubt that W., with some friendly advice first given, would make a very good master of the rolls, to which he may be removed if Copley goes higher, and that removal cannot be distant if things remain as to politics as they probably now are. But I think there was no option between the attorney-generalship and retirement for W.

It was hoped that the highly regarded Nicholas Tindal*, who was to replace Wetherell as solicitor-general, would 'have considerable influence over him'; and following his acquiescence in certain 'explanations', he received his promotion.[36] In December 1826 he vacated Hastings and came in on the Mount Edgecumbe interest for Plympton.

He was a teller for the majority in the division on the Dover election petition recognizances, 13 Feb. 1827. On 21 Feb. he opposed inquiry into the allegations of electoral malpractice by Northampton corporation, though he claimed that he had no wish to 'screen delinquency'. He conceded that Catholics had a case in complaining of double exactions of land tax in certain instances, but foresaw difficulties in rectifying the matter, 26 Feb. He voted against Catholic relief, 6 Mar. He repelled renewed attacks on Eldon and chancery administration, 27 Feb., 13 Mar., 5 Apr., when he was a teller for the majority against the production of information. He voted for the spring guns bill, 23 Mar. He was dubious about Shadwell's writ of right bill, 27, 30 Mar., deprecating 'rash or hasty interference' with the laws of real property. He opposed inquiry into the state of debtors' gaols and the laws governing imprisonment for debt, 3 Apr., and expressed strong reservations over Hume's proposed bill to prevent frivolous arrests for debt on mesne process, 10 Apr. A week later he 'very handsomely' resigned with Peel, Eldon and the other Protestant ministers rather than serve in Canning's ministry, even though he would almost certainly have soon become master of the rolls or vice-chancellor had he remained in office. He opposed Lords' amendments to the spring guns bill, 17 May, and was a teller for the minority in two divisions. Opposing the Coventry magistracy bill, 8 June, he argued that the Commons 'ought rather to exercise a conservative power, for the preservation of charters, than lend itself to the uncalled for confiscation of them'. He was in the small minorities against the measure, 11, 18 June. He did not oppose the introduction of the bill to transfer East Retford's seats to Birmingham, 11 June, but said that its advocates must prove their case at the bar of the House; and he suggested that it would raise false expectations if it was given a second reading, 22 June. He opposed Smith's Dissenters' marriages bill, which 'placed the people of

this country, and of these times, under the revolutionary law of Cromwell', 18 June. He spoke against Lord Nugent's proposal for the registration of voters, 29 June 1827.[37]

In August 1827 the duke of Wellington was informed that lord chancellor Lyndhurst (as Copley had become) thought that in the event of the Protestant Tories' return to power, Wetherell, 'one of the bad bargains of the previous administration', might be 'easily satisfied' by appointing him chief baron of the exchequer in the room of Alexander, who was ready to 'retire when desired'. When Wellington formed his ministry in January 1828 he, Peel and other ministers would have preferred to retain the services as attorney-general of Sir James Scarlett*, the Whig who had replaced Wetherell in 1827. The king, too, was keen to keep Scarlett, so that he could take the lead in certain duchy of Cornwall law cases pending in king's bench in which he had a direct interest. Wetherell, who was reported to be 'very much depressed' at receiving no immediate approach, wrote to Wellington '*positively declining* all contingent offers'. In the event Scarlett, after consulting his close political connections, decided that he was too nearly associated with the Whigs to continue in the post, and it was offered to and accepted by Wetherell. Eldon, who was piqued at being himself disregarded for office, claimed to have been instrumental in persuading Wellington to restore Wetherell as fair reward for his political loyalty and personal sacrifice.[38] A delay ensued while Wellington, Lyndhurst and Eldon tried to cajole Wetherell into waiving his technical right as attorney-general to lead in the king's bench cases and give precedence to Scarlett. To their annoyance, and the great fury of the king, he refused to comply, insisting that his professional honour was at stake; but his appointment was eventually ratified, and he was quietly re-elected for Plympton.[39]

On 21 Feb. 1828 he was named to the select committee on parochial settlements, though he warned that he would be able to give only occasional attendance. He thought that Davies's proposed bill to limit the duration of borough polls would be of little benefit, and he opposed it, 3, 31 Mar., 2, 28 Apr., 6, 15 May. He still had reservations about the Catholic land tax bill, 21 Feb., and he criticized it in detail, 10 Mar., 18 Apr., and was appointed to the select committee on the problem, 1 May. He voted against repeal of the Test Acts, 26 Feb., and spoke at length and voted against Catholic relief, 12 May. He was willing to accept a commission of inquiry into the common law 'with limited objects and intelligible means', but not the comprehensive affair proposed by Brougham, 29 Feb. He encouraged

Kennedy to divide his bill to amend the Scottish law of entail into prospective and retrospective parts, 6 Mar., and was sceptical about Spring Rice's plans to amend the law concerning testators and executors, 2 Apr. He opposed Taylor's motion on chancery delays, 24 Apr., still unconvinced of the need for a fourth equity judge. He clashed with Williams Wynn and Littleton during the East Retford inquiry, 3, 4 Mar., and spoke and voted against the committal of a witness for prevarication, 7 Mar. He opposed Sykes's motion for inquiry into the parliamentary franchise in boroughs with county jurisdiction, 11 Mar., arguing that once one anomaly was corrected, 'you know not when you will be allowed to stop in your career of alteration'. He was hostile to the bill which Sykes introduced, 20 Mar., 23 May, when he complained that it had 'cost me a great deal of labour, and not a little inconvenience', but seemed to be of no interest to most Members. He thought Benett's tithes commutation bill was hopelessly flawed, 17 Mar. He had insurmountable objections to Lord Althorp's freeholders registration bill, 25 Mar. Leading the resistance to Harvey's motion for more efficient control over crown excise prosecutions, 1 May, he mocked the 'plausible idea, that it is possible to devise a petty system for the protection of a revenue of £43,000,000'. He was willing to accept Poulett Thomson's bill to amend the usury laws if it preserved their principle, 20 May, but warned that he would have no truck with repeal of the standard of interest. He defended the archbishop of Canterbury's bill, 5 June, commenting that opposition, with their 'great talent for multiplication', were guilty of exaggerating the registrar's income. He carried its third reading, 16 June, when he was a teller for the majority in two divisions. He was twice a teller for majorities in favour of the additional churches bill, 30 June. He opposed investigation of Baron de Bode's compensation claims and was a teller for the hostile majority, 1 July. He voted with his colleagues on the ordnance estimates, 4 July, and the customs bill, 14 July. On 17 July 1828 he denounced a petition attacking the conduct of Nicholl in the prerogative court as 'a gross, scandalous, and malicious libel'.

In late October 1828 Wellington and Peel considered the possibility of offering Wetherell a puisne judgeship and, if he refused to accept it, of forcing him to resign as attorney-general, to be replaced by Scarlett or Tindal. Neither thought he would take the offer, and on reflection they decided 'not to resort to extremities', for reasons which Peel explained:

> We *reappointed* Wetherell, therefore we thought him qualified ... at the beginning of the year. Since that time he has done his business at least as well as he ever did it, probably better ... He would not put his refusal of the puisne judgeship on any private or personal ground. He would say, 'I refuse, because acceptance in my case would be to lower the pretensions and dignity of the office of attorney-general' ... Whatever you and I may think of Wetherell's wrongheadedness in excluding Scarlett from the duchy of Cornwall cause, the bar would violently resent anything that had the appearance of a punishment inflicted for the assertion of a right. Then comes the Catholic question and political martyrdom added to the above considerations ... I would not offer the puisne judgeship ... unless you have reason to expect that he would accept.[40]

According to Lord Ellenborough, president of the board of control, Lyndhurst at the end of the year was determined in the event of the death of the master of the rolls to exclude Wetherell, for he would 'ruin the court of chancery and be a most mischievous man in the House of Commons, a great Tory and bigoted Protestant'. He contemplated making him chief baron in the room of Alexander, whom he earmarked for the rolls. When the cabinet decided in late January 1829 to concede Catholic emancipation, Ellenborough noted that Peel 'thought Wetherell would resign', though he also wondered whether 'the weak state of the master of the rolls' health might possibly induce *honest* Wetherell to profess his Protestantism'. John Croker*, observing the 'wry face' which he made at 'Peel's merriment' at the Speaker's eve of session dinner, also thought he might well resign.[41] In the House, Wetherell defended the bill to suppress the Catholic Association. On 22 Feb. Wellington reported to the cabinet on 'a long conference with Wetherell ... who does not so much seem to object to the [relief] bill as to being abused for supporting it'. The following day Wellington demanded a final answer from Wetherell as to whether he would help to prepare it; and Wetherell replied that 'without a sacrifice of opinion, which I think I ought not to make, I should be unable to give my individual support in Parliament to the proposed measure'. Wellington, to the frustration of Ellenborough, who considered Wetherell 'a discredit to the government', made no move to dismiss him. John Campbell II*, who thought that 'the opportunity would have been seized to get rid of an inefficient ... officer', reported that Wetherell 'says to his private friends that he will not resign, and that he will throw the onus of dismissing him upon the government'.[42] His silent vote against the measure, 6 Mar., increased the pressure on Wellington from Lyndhurst, Ellenborough and Mrs. Arbuthnot, among others, to act against him; but the duke was anxious not to alienate the Protestants permanently from his ministry.[43] Wetherell opposed Spring Rice's proposed bill to make better provision for the undisposed effects of testators, 10 Mar. He brought matters to a head on the Catholic question with his rabid rant against emancipation, 18 Mar., when he accused Peel of betraying the Protestant cause, claimed that he had only told him of the decision to concede it seven days before the opening of the session, and made a savage personal attack on Lyndhurst. Peel accused him of a breach of official confidence, to which he made a blustering but unconvincing retort, coolly dismissed by Peel. Wetherell's 'bitter but absurd' speech was wildly applauded in the anti-Catholic press, but even Lord Lowther*, a sympathizer, thought that he had given 'too much' vent to his feelings: 'if he had handled his subject he would have been more effective'. Hostile observers were astounded by the uncontrolled vehemence and sheer vulgarity of his performance; many supposed him to have been drunk. Althorp wrote that he had

> never heard such a speech ... He out-Heroded Herod. Its vulgarity and coarse buffoonery was beyond anything that ever was exhibited. His contortions were such that his braces broke, and his breeches were near coming down, so that his shirt appeared in large expanse between his waistcoat and them.

Henry Bankes* confirmed that 'his manner, countenance, grimace and gesture, and his variety and contortion of attitude were so excessively grotesque that the House was kept almost in a continued roar of laughter'. Greville, who described Wetherell as 'half mad, eccentric, ingenious, with great and varied information and a coarse, vulgar mind delighting in ribaldry and abuse, besides an enthusiast', recorded the Speaker's comment (which Ellenborough attributed to Horace Twiss*) that 'the only lucid interval he had was that between his waistcoat and his breeches'.[44] It was decided to dismiss him, 'not distinctly upon the Catholic question, but upon his conduct in abusing the chancellor, breaching confidence, etc.' There was some concern that the king might make difficulties, especially as Cumberland was said to be boasting that ministers would not dare to sack Wetherell; but he put up no serious resistance, and Wellington summarily gave Wetherell his marching orders on 22 Mar.[45] He voted silently against emancipation the following day. In the course of his frantic speech against the bill, 27 Mar., he accidentally hit George Bankes on the head with the copy which he was brandishing. On the third reading, 30 Mar., when Abercromby thought he was 'less mad and less entertaining' than before, he said that it 'may be sent as a covering for butter and cheese to ... shops

of green-grocers, but for any legislative or protective purpose, the bill is an utter waste of printing, ink and paper'.[46] He was suspicious of Smith Stanley's bill to amend the laws concerning the leasing power of Irish bishops and ecclesiastical corporations, 2 Apr. He did not think any significant improvement in the patent laws could be achieved, 9 Apr., and objected to Hume's proposal for the sale of admiralty advowsons in Northumberland, 14 Apr. When Wellington sought the king's permission to 'restore the resigners', 15 Apr., George, according to Ellenborough, 'just mentioned Wetherell's name as if he thought he was to be excepted from the restoration, but desired to be *certior factus*'. Peel reflected soon afterwards that Wetherell had 'lately made a wrong cast in politics'.[47]

In October 1829 the Ultra leader Sir Richard Vyvyan* listed him among the 'Tories strongly opposed to the present government', and it was with the Ultras that he was politically associated for the remainder of his parliamentary career. On 11 Dec. 1829 he had a furious row in the chancery court with Edward Sugden*, the solicitor-general, over a matter of etiquette, which might have ended in a duel if they had not been dragged before a magistrate and bound over to keep the peace.[48] Wetherell voted for Knatchbull's amendment to the address, 4 Feb., but against the transfer of East Retford's seats to Birmingham, 11 Feb. 1830. That day, when he approved the government's various bills to reform chancery procedure (he said on the 24th that he had all along contended that 'reforms in the law ... should not be undertaken by sweeping commissions, but by bills brought in to remedy particular evils') he made a savage personal attack on Hume, who had pilloried previous law officers and Eldon. He observed, 26 Feb., that the law officers were not the servile tools of administration and received no payment for supporting bills, and modestly noted that there were 'cases where the law officers have been independent enough to vote against and oppose the ministry'. He was willing to support Taylor's bill reforming lunacy regulations, on which he had been consulted, 2 Mar., provided it did not diminish the authority of the lord chancellor. Later that day, in what the Whig Member Lord Howick deemed a 'violent and tiresome' harangue of two-and-a-half hours, he moved for papers concerning the filing of an *ex-officio* prosecution for libel by Scarlett, who had replaced him as attorney-general, against Alexander of the Protestant *Morning Journal*. Harsh words were exchanged between him, Scarlett, Peel and John Hobhouse. Littleton reported that

Wetherell was glorious. The brute will sit next to me, when he has not a friend, but it is near the treasury bench. He stank so unutterably as he advanced in his argument, that he cleared a space round himself, like the upas tree.[49]

On 4 Mar. he supported Inglis's motion for the previous question to be moved against Newport's call for a commission on the Irish church, which ministers were ready to concede to a limited degree; he was not happy with Peel's attitude. He voted against government in the divisions on relations with Portugal, 10 Mar., the Bathurst and Dundas pensions, 26 Mar., and the ordnance estimates, 29 Mar. He supported Davenport's motion for inquiry into the state of the nation, 19 Mar., but saw no reason why it should dwell on the currency question. He clashed with Daniel O'Connell over demands for repeal of the Union, 22 Mar. He secured returns of information on chancery administration, 30 Mar., 8 Apr. He was not happy with Ellenborough's divorce bill, 1 Apr. He opposed Poulett Thomson's usury laws repeal bill, 26 Apr., 6 May, when he was a teller for the hostile minority, and 15 June. He challenged O'Connell to proceed with his threatened motion on the Cork conspiracy trials, 29 Apr., and thought his bill dealing with Catholic charitable bequests went too far, 4 May. He voted against ministers for the production of information on privy councillors' emoluments, 14 May. He divided against Jewish emancipation, 17 May. He protested against the notion that ministers could shelter behind the formal opinions of the law officers, 21 May, expressed misgivings about the House's handling of the inquiry into the Barrington case, 22 May, and voted against the amendments to the Galway franchise bill, 24 May. He failed to secure the addition of a clause to the king's signature bill making it a treasonable offence to forge royal stamps, 27 May. Later that day he condemned the administration of justice bill as a half-baked mess, which would do 'ten times more mischief than we pretend to reform'; and on 18 June, when he was a teller for the minority against going into committee on it, he said that majority opinion in Wales was hostile to it and that 'leave might as well have been given to bring in a blank sheet of paper', so incomprehensible was it. He asked for support from 'the Cambrian warriors' in his unsuccessful attempt to secure its postponement, 5 July. He opposed Phillimore's motion for inquiry into the divorce laws, 3 June, and was a teller for the majority against it. He also pressed Sadler to drop his motion for the introduction of a system of poor laws to Ireland. On 4 June he explained that having been prevented by the pressure of Commons business from bringing in a bill to regulate *ex-officio* prosecutions, he would move that the expenses incurred in the Alexander case be deducted from the supply unless ministers gave a satisfactory statement of intent; Peel mollified him. He gave notice of a motion for a bill, 10 June, but did not act on it. He spoke and voted against abolition of the death penalty for forgery, 7 June. On 10 June he moved for prior inquiry before sanctioning the proposed appointment of a fourth chancery judge. When the debate was resumed, 24 June, he argued that arrears were not sufficient to justify it; but the order of the day for the second reading of the justice in equity bill was carried against him by 133-96, and against an adjournment motion, for the division on which he was again a minority teller, by 118-77. He said that the House was not obliged to adopt the recommendations of the law commissioners, especially regarding a general register, 11 June. That day he voted against government on the grant for consular services. He voted for restrictive amendments to the sale of beer bill, 21 June, 1 July. On 30 June he called on Members not to adopt the address on the temporary provision for the public service after the death of George IV, which would leave ministers free to dissolve Parliament without dealing with the regency question. He opposed Hume's demand for a reduction in the salary of the chairman of ways and means, 7 July 1830.

At the general election of 1830 Wetherell was put up for Boroughbridge by the 4th duke of Newcastle and was returned with another Ultra after a contest forced by the duke's local rival. There had been approaches to him from Bristol, where he was recorder, and supposedly, though Croker could not credit it, from Protestant extremists in Dublin.[50] Ministers listed him as one of the 'violent Ultras'. He opposed abolition of the oath of abjuration as proposed by Williams Wynn, 4, 12 Nov. 1830 (and later explained, 4 Feb. 1831, that he wished it to be preserved 'as a kind of Protestant *momento*'). He was absent from the division on the civil list which brought down the ministry, 15 Nov. 1830. In discussions with their successors Knatchbull, the Ultras' spokesman, admitted to Lord Palmerston*, the foreign secretary, 'the difficulty of making anything of Wetherell'.[51] He opposed the production of information on churchwardens' accounts, 25 Nov., and on borough freemen, 7, 9 Dec., suspecting that in moving for the latter Hodgson had a political motive. He was named to the select committee on the reduction of salaries, 9 Dec. He wanted the regency bill to be made more specific about Princess Victoria's rights, 9 Dec. The following day he said that arguments for parliamentary reform were 'subversive of the constitution'. He seconded O'Connell's motion against the second reading of Scarlett's judgements in execution bill, 13 Dec., stated his hostility to Campbell's plan for a general registry and defended the practice of appointing solicitors to chancery secretaryships, 16 Dec. He was declaiming on the subject of chancery returns when the House was counted out, 20 Dec. 1830.

Wetherell deplored calls for repeal of the Union and supported the Grey ministry in their avowed determination to enforce the rule of law in Ireland, 8 Feb. 1831. He said that the laudable practice of allowing prisoners free communication with their attorneys was not confined to London gaols, as Wood suggested, 10 Feb. He supported Sugden's unsuccessful motion for a bill to extend the Mortmain Act of 1736 to Ireland, 22 Feb. On 3 Feb. he mischievously asked why, if the forthcoming reform bill was a government measure, it was to be brought in by Russell, who was not a member of the cabinet. He spoke briefly against the secret ballot, 9 Feb. He supported Lord Chandos's attempt to pre-empt the bill by investigating electoral corruption at Evesham, 17 Feb., when he was a teller for the majority against printing a petition alleging corrupt practices at Bridport, and the following day tried to get Graham, one of the ministers responsible for drafting the measure, to admit that he had threatened the House with dissolution if it was defeated. Unlike Vyvyan and Knatchbull, who were prepared to accept moderate changes, Wetherell and his closest associates were implacably opposed to all reform. Greville recorded that when Russell unveiled the ministerial scheme, 1 Mar., 'Wetherell, who began to take notes, as the plan was gradually developed, after sundry contortions and grimaces and flinging about his arms and legs, threw down his notes with a mixture of despair and ridicule and horror'. Thomas Gladstone* told his father that

> Wetherell's vociferations and contemptuous cheers, every now and then, when Lord John Russell announced some new sweep, were very amusing. He seemed to lose all control over himself and would toss the sheet of paper from his hand to the table, as much as to say 'this is absurd'.

Significantly, when Peel in his reply 'admitted that he would consent to some reform, Wetherell looked grave and desisted from cheering'.[52] Meetings of Ultras at his and Knatchbull's houses 'resolved ... not to divide at present' against the scheme.[53] He spoke against it, 2 Mar., rising as 'the dying Member for Boroughbridge' (which was to be disfranchised) to address the House for the last time. He said that the borough disfranchisement proposals were based on 'motives of partiality or conceived expediency', noticing particularly the retention of both Members by the cabinet min-

ister Lord Lansdowne's borough of Calne, deplored the reduction in the overall number of Members and likened 'Althorp and Company' to Cromwell and the Regicides. His main argument against the plan was that it amounted to nothing less than 'corporation robbery'. In a striking conclusion, he ranted:

> I will call this bill Russell's Purge of Parliament ... [It] is republican in its basis ... [and] destructive of all property, of all right, of all privilege ... The same arbitrary violence which expelled a majority of Members in the time of the Commonwealth, is now ... proceeding to expose the House of Commons again to the nauseous tyranny of a repetition of Pride's Purge.

The cheering when he sat down was 'immense', as Gladstone reported, while Greville commented that 'such loud and long cheering as everybody agreed had not been before heard in the House' was less a testimony to the merits of his 'long, rambling and amusing' speech than 'an indication of the disposition of the majority of the House'. Mackintosh thought it was one of 'his coarsest, but not his strongest speeches', and that the applause for it revealed 'the imbecility of the Tory party'.[54] On 3 Mar. he derided Russell's motion for the 1821 population returns for the schedule A boroughs as an attempt to 'legislate on posthumous information'. On 6 Mar. he had a 'long and full conference' with Newcastle, who

> told him that I quite approved of what he had done and that I strongly recommended him to *persevere* in the same line – to be forward in setting an example of what is right and to leave it to others to follow if they will, but by all means to avoid being led, as that is the only way to make good government.[55]

The following day he was called to order for trying to force Althorp to say what ministers intended to do if the threat of armed rebellion in the event of the defeat of the reform bill became reality. He said that it was 'highly problematical' whether Canning or Huskisson would have supported the measure, 9 Mar. He suggested that the freemen of Canterbury who petitioned for reform were in breach of their corporate oaths, 10 Mar., as were petitioners from Kinghorn and Dundee, 16 Mar., and criticized ministers for leaving their budget proposals in suspense on account of the reform bill, 11 Mar. He thought Newport's motion for a revaluation of Irish first fruits should be submitted directly to the law officers, 14 Mar. He stated some objections to Scarlett's examination of witnesses bill, 17 Mar. Supporting Inglis's motion alleging a breach of privilege by *The Times*, 21 Mar., he condemned Burdett's 'dictatorial' speech inviting the Members for condemned boroughs to leave the House. He voted against the second reading of the reform bill, 22 Mar., having been reported beforehand as being utterly confident of its defeat.[56] He also sought to embarrass Palmerston over his delay in presenting an anti-reform petition from his constituency of Cambridge University, and enraged O'Connell with a reference to a 'diplomatic approximation of amicable tendencies' between him and Smith Stanley, the Irish secretary, which hinted at bargaining with the authorities to secure his support for the Irish reform bill in return for concessions on Ireland. On 24 Mar., when he presented a petition against reform from Wootton Bassett, he alleged that the 'list of boroughs to be disfranchised is a stock in trade ministers have kept in their hands to job with, here and there, as may be convenient for the general purpose of carrying the measure'. He called for abandonment of the proposal to disfranchise freemen and noted that many of those Members now enthusiastic for reform had been 'the most staunch opponents' of inquiry into distress the previous year, 29 Mar. On the report of the salaries committee, 30 Mar., he said that its recommendations, along with the reform bill, formed part of 'a plan for striking at the just prerogatives of the crown'. He made humorous capital out of Palmerston's tardy presentation of the Cambridge University petition. In late February he, Eldon and Lord Mansfield, worried by 'the progress of disorganization' among the Tory opposition, had approached Wellington via Lord Burghersh for a rapprochement. At that time Wetherell and Peel were still not on speaking terms, and Peel gave an initially frosty reception to further peace overtures sent by him and Lord Stormont* at the end of the month. Soon afterwards, however, it was reported that he and Peel were 'reconciled', though the opposition remained in a fractured state.[57] He advised 'the utmost caution and care' in proceeding to reform real property law, as Campbell proposed, 14 Apr. The following day he had more to say on the subject of Calne. He repeated his warnings about the sweeping nature of O'Connell's Catholic charities bill, 18 Apr. He voted silently for Gascoyne's wrecking amendment to the reform bill, 19 Apr. 1831, and next day argued that it was not popular in Oxford, on account of its threat to freemen, and still less understood by the majority of the inhabitants. He presented a Boroughbridge petition against the measure and called for a favourable one from Staffordshire artisans to be withdrawn because it breached privilege.[58] It was reported on the eve of the dissolution that he had been authorized by Cumberland to spread the word that the king had promised not to sanction it.[59]

Wetherell, who lost his wife on 22 Apr. 1831 (their only child had died in infancy the previous year), was returned unopposed for Boroughbridge a week later. He and Thomas Sadler* were nominated for Norwich without their consent, and were heavily beaten by two reformers.[60] On the eve of the session Ellenborough met him at dinner and found him 'very reasonable' on the subject of relations between Peel and the Ultras, having 'no disinclination' to an 'approximation'.[61] On the address, which was 'a waste of words', 21 June, he complained of the lord mayor's having been party to the activities of the 'vitreo-faction' organizing the recent London illuminations, deplored the violence and intimidation exerted by reformers at the elections, and ridiculed the ministerial budget. It was observed that when speaking he 'jumps about like a kangaroo and spoils the effect of his wit, sarcasm and eloquence'.[62] He accused government of dropping the intended prosecution of O'Connell to avoid trouble in Ireland, 27 June, and complained of subversive doctrines published in the *Republican* and apparently endorsed by Hume, 29 June. He raved against the second reading of the reintroduced reform bill, 6 July, declaring that the effect of the £10 borough franchise would be to 'melt down the church, the monarchy, and the peerage', that 'the abolition of tithes, and the conversion of church property to the paying off the national debt' had been held out as corollaries of reform by irresponsible Members, and that the bill could in no way be final. Hudson Gurney wrote that in an insufferably hot House he was 'bothering beyond human endurance', while Spring Rice dismissed his performance as mere 'buffoonery'.[63] He duly voted against the bill. On 12 July he attacked ministers for bungling the borough schedules and predicted that in a reformed Parliament Members would be mere delegates. He took a prominent role in the ensuing farce, after Peel had left the House, of repeated divisions for an adjournment, insisting that opposition were merely trying to show that 'we are not to be put down by clamour'.[64] He claimed that the working classes, especially those likely to be affected by the disfranchisement of freemen by apprenticeship, were awakening to the defects of the bill, and objected to the extensive and arbitrary powers to be given to the boundary commissioners, 13 July. The following day he attacked ministers for their muddled thinking on the problem of disfranchisement according to population and refusal to hear evidence at the bar. On 19 July, when he voted for adoption of the 1831 census, he expressed horror at the prospect of 'a seraglio of these assembled beauties of St. Giles, Saffron Hill and the Tower Hamlets' sending Members to the House by 'Jacobin nomination'. Wetherell was one of the most persistent, indefatigable and irritating critics of the reform bill in committee, assuming, with a few others, the role largely abdicated by Peel. While his boorishness and clowning damaged his credibility, the bill, a flawed piece of legislation, gave ample scope for legal captiousness, and he was by no means a negligible opponent. From 20 July until 2 Aug. he was a frequent speaker on schedules A and B, pointing out their inconsistencies and anomalies: he referred to A as 'this schedule of irrational disparities', 26 July; held out the prospect of its rejection by the Lords, 27, 28 July, and lamented the 'military proscription and erasure of boroughs', 29 July, when he also claimed that as a result of opposition's detailed exposure of its shortcomings, 'the bill daily retrogrades in public opinion'. He was equally pertinacious in his opposition to the enfranchisement of new boroughs, 2-9 Aug. On the union of Rochester with Chatham, for example (9 Aug.), he said:

> If the political cranium of the framers of this bill were dissected by a skilful phrenologist, some disciple of Gall or Spurzheim would say that the organ of destructiveness was not only fully developed, but that it protruded marvellously. The organ of destructiveness would only be second in size to the organ of inconsistency.

He denounced the proposal for three Member counties, 13 Aug., saw merit in Hume's call for colonial representation, 16 Aug., welcomed the decision to give Parliament ultimate control over the boundary commissioners, 17 Aug., and objected to the appointment of returning officers by sheriffs, 19 Aug. When Peel went to the opposition headquarters to announce that he could not undertake to stay in London for much longer to continue the pointless struggle against the bill, 23 Aug., Wetherell was one of those 'dissatisfied with this and prepared to go on interminably on the present system'.[65] On the £10 householder franchise, which he abominated, 25 Aug., he pronounced that 'every large town ... will be democratized, sans-culottised, by the unconstitutional submission of the government to the Birmingham Union'. He foolishly and fatefully remarked, 27 Aug., that in Bristol 'reform fever' had 'a good deal abated'; and when Ellenborough a few days later 'complimented him on his useful exertions ... against the bill', he said that there had been 'a decided change in public opinion'. Ellenborough 'represented the inexpediency of raising that too much, as it would produce meetings in its favour'.[66] He spoke and voted for attempts to preserve the voting rights of non-resident freemen, 30 Aug., and the freeholder franchise in the four sluiced boroughs, 2 Sept. He made technical comments on the registration machinery, 3 Sept., when he said that

the bill was 'so much darned, stitched, mended, and remended, that like Sir John Cutler's stockings, not a thread of the original workmanship remains', 5, 6 Sept. On 4 Sept. he made a bantering reply to Tom Duncombe's proposal to transfer Newcastle's borough of Aldborough to schedule A. He was shut out of the unexpected division on the third reading of the bill, 19 Sept. Two days later he angrily accused Crampton, the Irish solicitor-general, of breaching privilege by threatening a dissolution and suspension of the writs for schedule A boroughs if the bill foundered in the Lords. He went on to speak against the passage of the measure, which 'necessarily lays the train for evils which those who introduced it can never have contemplated', and was 'calculated to subvert the throne, the monarchy, the church, and ultimately the liberties of the people'. The Tory Lord Worcester* thought he was 'very good and very amusing, but as he usually is, much too long'.[67] In a wrangle with Torrens, 23 Sept., Wetherell said that 'there was abroad a spirit of insolent threat ... [and] of unconstitutional terrorism, a spirit bordering on illegal threat, and actual violation of the law'. He detected 'some smell of patronage' in the arrangements for appeals on disputed votes under the Scottish reform bill, 4 Oct. According to Littleton, when he went to the Lords to listen to the debate on the English bill, 8 Oct., Wetherell, 'in order to escape the constant solicitation of ... the deputy serjeant to leave room for the entrance, or rather the exit of the peers ... walked straight into the House and stood there'.[68] He made a wild speech, following Macaulay's triumphant effort, against the motion of confidence in the government, 10 Oct. The young reformer John Hawkins reckoned it 'not better than his usual string of jokes and quibbles'. Wetherell was in an even more agitated state on 12 Oct., when he was called to order in the course of a denunciation of the recent reform riots, especially those in Nottingham, where Newcastle had been targeted. Threatening to move for the appointment of a special commission of inquiry (which he did the following day, to no avail), he said that he did 'not believe that ministers will boldly, manfully, and energetically use the constitutional powers in their hands to control and suppress these scandalous and anti-social outrages'. Hobhouse recalled:

> [Wetherell] so misbehaved himself that it was charitable to think him either drunk or crazy. He threw his legs on the bench, and called on Lord Althorp to speak up. We passed the word that no notice should be taken of his speech; but, as he had fallen foul of O'Connell, we could not prevent that gentleman from rising and giving Sir Charles his deserts. The castigation was most complete and most severe.

Hawkins told the same tale:

> Wetherell got well drubbed with his own weapons ...
> by Dan O'Connell. The castigation which the placid
> Althorp was provoked to bestow upon him, was in reply
> to his outrageous personal attack ... Some passages in
> Althorp's speech, which are not very intelligible in a
> newspaper report, were provoked by the disorderly and
> insolent *gesticulations* in which he indulged while Althorp
> was speaking, a demeanour which gave the House, at the
> time, the idea that the Old Buffoon was *inebriated*. This
> I believe was not the case. The opinion of his own party
> now is (seriously) that he is labouring under a temporary
> derangement on the subject of reform.

Hawkins thought that the effects of this 'double casti-
gation' were evident in Wetherell's 'improved behaviour and somewhat mitigated abuse' on 14 Oct. 1831.[69]

He expressed surprise at allegations that Irish
tithes could not be collected without the assistance
of the civil or military authorities, 12 July 1831. He
deemed William Pole Long Wellesley* to be guilty
of contempt of chancery, 18 July. He thought ministers should have been firmer with Brazil over acts
of piracy, 19 July, accused them of breaching the
Methuen Treaty concerning duty on foreign wines, 4
Aug., and was critical, though not censorious, of their
policy on Holland and Belgium, 12 Aug. That day he
seconded a wrecking amendment to the Irish judicial
officers bill. He favoured immediate payment of the
claims of Lescene and Escoffery, 22 Aug. The following day he spoke and voted against government on the
Dublin election controversy, and he voted to suspend
the Liverpool writ while bribery was investigated, 5
Sept. He thought the House would have to intervene if
the problem of the Irish master of the rolls's secretary
could not be amicably resolved, 16 Sept. He said that
the commissioners under the new lunacy bill should
be accountable to the home secretary rather than the
lord chancellor, 26 Sept, when he voted in the minority
to end the Maynooth grant. He opposed O'Connell's
motion for documents concerning alleged irregularities at the Cork trials, but favoured investigation of
the Deacles' charges against Hampshire magistrates,
27 Sept. He wanted changes under the vestry bill to
require the consent of at least two-thirds of ratepayers, 30 Sept. He spoke and was a teller for the minority
against the bill to reform the Scottish exchequer court,
7 Oct. He supported Sadler's motion for leave to introduce a bill to improve the condition of the labouring poor, 11 Oct. 'With half-a-dozen young chancery
lawyers at his back', he led an obstructive opposition
to lord chancellor Brougham's bill to reform bankruptcy administration.[70] He condemned it out of hand
and divided the House in a vain bid to have its second

reading deferred, 28 Sept., but was more successful,
30 Sept. He supported an attempt to have it referred
to a select committee, 12 Oct., and the following day
outlined his own alternative plan to reduce the number
of commissioners and give an appeal from the lower
courts to chancery. His amendment to have only one
puisne judge for the court of review was defeated by
71-19. He spoke in detail against the measure, 14,
15, 17 Oct., and on its third reading, 18 Oct. 1831,
described it as 'mischievous ... and unjust in the
extreme'. That day he opposed reception of a petition
calling for the exclusion of bishops from the Lords.

Wetherell's words on the waning enthusiasm for
reform in Bristol came back to haunt him on 29 Oct.
1831, when, as recorder, he processed into the town
to open the assizes, disregarding prior warnings of
trouble, which he considered it was the responsibility
of government to prevent. His appearance triggered a
riot and an attack on the Mansion House, from which
he barely escaped with his life by disguising himself
as a postilion and scrambling over the rooftops. (The
wags had it that 'he made his escape from the fury of
the mob in the disguise of a clean shirt and a pair of
braces'.) Aided by official timidity and military bungling, the mob remained in control of Bristol for three
days, at the end of which large parts of the town had
been destroyed and burnt and numerous people were
dead. Wetherell was widely condemned and pilloried
for having gone there, though in fairness it must be
said that Protheroe, one of the Members, had given
the home secretary assurances that there would be
no disturbance. As recorder, he would normally have
presided at the trial of the rioters, but ministers wisely
bypassed him by omitting him, without explanation,
from the special commission.[71]

On the address, 6 Dec. 1831, Wetherell denied
having been 'directly the author' of the riots and complained of his exclusion from the commission. He
welcomed the 'beneficial change' in the revised reform
bill regarding the freeman franchise, 12 Dec., but portrayed this and other modifications as admissions by
ministers of earlier errors rather than genuine concessions. He joined in criticism of ministerial conduct on
the Russian-Dutch loan, 'a flagrant violation of the
law', 16 Dec. The following day, after presenting and
endorsing a petition for reform of the system of poor
management in the southern counties, he opposed the
second reading of the reform bill, a defective measure
brought forward to 'satisfy people out of doors' and
'bottomed on the principle of radical equality'.
On 20 Jan. 1832 he spoke and voted against going
into committee on the bill, a 'new-fangled plan of a

constitution', with 'cooked up' borough schedules. Hawkins reported to his father:

> Wetherell, I think, promises more madly than ever. He seems more incoherent in his ideas, and less under command in his manner. If his gesticulations on so tame a subject as last night's discussion are a specimen of what may be expected when we arrive at more irritating topics, the House will not hold him.[72]

For the next two months he was indefatigable in his criticism of the details of the bill, taking particular notice of the inadequate information on which the borough disfranchising and enfranchising proposals were based and mocking the calculations of Drummond, 'the English Euclid'. On 19 Feb. he asserted that the creation of enough peers to carry the measure through the Lords would be 'illegal, unconstitutional, and unprecedented'. He was a teller for the minority against proceeding with the disfranchising schedules, 20 Feb., after complaining that 'we are committing political injustice at the expense of mathematical accuracy'. He voted against the enfranchisement of Tower Hamlets, 28 Feb., when he also objected to giving Manchester and Salford separate representation. At this time Croker noted that while 'the Ultra Tories are but a hollow support' to the opposition leaders, Wetherell was 'very cordial', indeed 'sincerely, actively and usefully so'. Hawkins dismissed his speech against the third reading, 20 Mar. 1832, when he attacked ministers on all fronts, as a 'grotesque rodomontade'.[73] He was in the minority two days later.

Wetherell was a steady opponent of Campbell's bill to establish a general registry, 17 Jan., 8, 22 Feb., 6 Mar.; he was added to the select committee on the subject, 27 Mar. 1832. Nor did he see any merit in his fines and recoveries bill, 20 Jan. On the bill to provide for the continuity of the work of the court of session in the event of the death of a judge, 24 Jan., he said that as his arguments against the appointment of extra bankruptcy judges had been vindicated by subsequent experience, the surplus men should be sent to Scotland; and he strongly objected to abolishing the Scottish court of exchequer without proper inquiry, 2 Feb. He voted against ministers on the Russian-Dutch loan, 26 Jan., and argued on 6 Feb. that it revealed their 'utter incapacity'. He was against the production of information on unenclosed lands and intestates' estates, 31 Jan. He supported the prayer of a petition for the restriction of childrens' hours in factories, 1 Feb. On 8 Feb. he welcomed Grey's statement that government were determined to uphold the rule of law to enforce tithe collection in Ireland, but he failed to goad Althorp into making a similar declaration.[74] He

supported the opposition motion for information on relations with Portugal, 9 Feb., and had more to say on the subject, 26 Mar. He was cautious about Baring's bill, which he was given a hand in preparing, to exclude insolvents and bankrupts from the Commons, 14 Feb. He disapproved of the way in which money was to be levied under the cholera prevention bill, 15 Feb. The following day he voted against Hunt's motion for information on military punishments. He approved of the principle of O'Connell's Irish witnesses in equity bill, 22 Feb. He supported a call for documents concerning Lord Plunket's alleged nepotism and corruption as Irish chancellor, 6 Mar. Next day he accused ministers of yielding to popular clamour in deciding to prosecute Bristol magistrates over the riots, and, opposing the sugar duties, said that 'the whole system of the present government may be termed anti-colonial'. On Irish tithes, 28 Mar., he admitted the need for reform, but would not accept their extinction; and he was severely critical of the ministerial proposals, which amounted to spoliation in response to 'a very extensive conspiracy', 2, 6 Apr. He doubted the utility of Warburton's anatomy bill, 11 Apr., and called for redress from Brazil for acts of piracy, 16 Apr. 1832.

Two days later, when he saw Campbell while filing a criminal information for a libel on Cumberland, he boasted that ministers were 'afraid to meet Parliament, and that this is the reason why the Easter recess is so unusually long'.[75] Opposing the address asking the king to appoint only ministers who would carry the reform bill unimpaired, 10 May, when he again followed Macaulay, he cracked what the Whig Member William Ord described as 'small, bad jokes'; and even Croker thought his 'flourish ... on the mode of presenting the address', which was answered by Althorp, was 'very foolish'. During the ensuing ministerial crisis, he let Ellenborough know that he would support a ministry formed by Wellington.[76] He contended that government were wrong not to prosecute in a recent case of libel on the king, 21 May, for 'the licentiousness of the press' had become intolerable. He supported their temporizing amendment to Fowell Buxton's motion for the abolition of slavery, 24 May. He voted against the second reading of the Irish reform bill the following day, and made technical comments on it, 25 June. He had remarks to make on various details of the boundaries bill, including one on Oxford, 7 June, when he wondered why two parishes had been 'capriciously' added: 'when the system of proscription is abandoned, there is established in its stead a system as anomalous and discrepant'. That day he reprimanded Paget for suggesting that the discretionary power of the crown to commute death sentences had not been generously exercised. He insisted that ministers had not expressed any leaning towards the immediate 'total extinction' of tithes, 14 June; but on the 29th he said that a petition for that object confirmed his view that they had been unwise to give that impression, and protested against O'Connell's plan to enforce a call of the House for the debate on the ministerial bill, 5 July. He also said that the reduction of the prescription period to 60 years was too drastic and that the whole measure was 'most awkwardly framed'. He had no truck with Sheil's argument that the House, being *defunctus officio* after the enactment of the reform bill, should not deal with the tithes problem. He thought it was too late to press on with the Indian juries bill, 18 June. That day (the anniversary of Waterloo), Wellington was harassed by a mob while on horseback in Holborn, and took refuge with Wetherell in Lincoln's Inn.[77] He raised this incident, and the recent attack on the king, in the House, 20 June, when he defended Peel's attempt to get Smith Stanley to say that 'the use of physical force was unjustifiable'. Later he deplored the haste with which Campbell's real property reform bills had been pushed through, having joined with leading equity lawyers of both parties in a signed protest to Brougham.[78] On the Scottish reform bill, 27 June, he said that in effectively abandoning the proposed property qualification for Members, ministers had tamely submitted to the Scottish unions and their 'radical republican principle'. He spoke and voted for Baring's bill to exclude bankrupts, though it did not entirely satisfy him. On 28 June he got the Speaker to confirm that a petition from London Poles complaining of the conduct of Russia was inadmissible, and on 7 Aug. he applauded ministers' resistance to De Lacy Evans's motion condemning Russia. He forced Wyse to defer his proposed bill to enable Irish tenants to raise mortgages for improvements, 28 June. He condemned Hume's 'unconstitutional' doctrine that soldiers should not be punished for 'a political offence', 3 July. He spoke and voted against ministers on the Russian-Dutch loan, 12 July, and spoke again on it, 16 July, when he seized on Hume's admission that he would 'vote black was white' to keep ministers in office. He was scornful of Hume's 'petty farthing economy' in calling for a reduction in the Bahamas establishment, 23 July. He stated his undiminished hostility to the general register scheme, 16 July, and spoke and was a teller for the minority of two against Harvey's motion to inquire into the Inns of Court, 17 July. He supported and vindicated Sugden in his attack on Brougham's allegedly corrupt disposal of chancery sinecures, 25, 26, 27 July.[79] He paid tribute to Manners Sutton on his retirement as Speaker, 30 July, and on 1 Aug. defended the

pension of £4,000 for him and his male heir against Hume's strictures. He said that the electoral bribery bill was 'an instrument of vexation and ... political intrigue', 30 July. He spoke against the 'most mischievous' proposal to abolish the death penalty for all forgery offences, 31 July, 2 Aug. He was in the minority against the crown colonies relief bill, 3 Aug. When Evans raised the problem of the possible disfranchisement of borough voters through failure to pay their rates in time, 9 Aug., Wetherell observed that it was clear that the enthusiasm to register fell far short of ministerial expectations. In his last reported intervention in Commons debates, 16 Aug. 1832, he secured the withdrawal of a Hull petition against government interference with Irish tithes.

Newcastle reported in mid-July 1832 that Wetherell had 'a short time since abandoned the idea of coming into the next Parliament, but he has since *revoked*', and wondered whether he might stand for Newark.[80] Nothing came of this, but at the general election in December he put himself forward for Oxford, where he had reduced the mayoral dinner in October to farce with a facetious speech mocking the reform bill as 'the feast of reason'. He tried to court popularity by carousing in the taverns, but he had little support in the city, trailed badly in the poll and withdrew before its close.[81] He declined an invitation to stand for Dover on a vacancy soon afterwards.[82] As counsel for Oxford University, he made 'an amusing speech', which he subsequently published, before the privy council in April 1834 in opposition to the London University petition for a charter. Greville noted that 'it is seldom that the sounds of merriment are heard within those walls, but he made the Lords laugh, and the gallery too'.[83] Having been loyal to Wellington in May 1832, he was a candidate for legal office when Peel formed his first ministry in December 1834. He was earmarked for the vice-chancellorship, but Lancelot Shadwell*, the incumbent, refused to take the Irish seals. With great misgivings, Peel and Lyndhurst offered him the attorney-generalship, and they were far from sorry when he declined it because 'it would appear to the world *supercession*'. Lyndhurst, who thought he hankered after the place of chief baron, and took upon himself 'entirely on political grounds the responsibility of not sending him to Ireland', concluded that he was 'satisfied that we did all we fairly could for him'.[84] Wetherell claimed to have turned down two free offers of seats from '*private individuals*' at the 1835 general election, and certainly rejected an approach from the Conservatives of Bandon Bridge.[85] In August 1835 he annoyed Peel by helping to work the Conservative peers 'into a frenzy' with a speech at the bar of the House against the municipal corporations bill.[86] He was nominated without his consent by desperate Birmingham Conservatives at the by-election of January 1840 and polled quite respectably, though he finished well behind the Liberal candidate.[87] He admitted that there were 'circumstances which prevent my coming forward at Oxford' at the 1841 general election, and he did not expect to be in the new Parliament.[88]

Wetherell died at Preston Hall, near Maidstone, Kent in August 1846, a week after suffering 'concussion of the brain' in a carriage accident nearby.[89] He had not made a will, and administration of his estate, which was sworn under £250,000, was granted to his second wife. There was also valuable real estate.[90] An obituarist commented that 'he never acquired any great influence with the House', where he was 'treated by both sides ... as a whimsical pedant'. Although his opposition to reform was deemed ultimately futile and 'exposed him to the effects of extreme unpopularity', it was reckoned that 'every one admired the learning, talent, enthusiasm, and even good humour and drollery' with which he conducted it.[91] As king of Hanover, Cumberland, to whom Wetherell had been devotedly attached for over 30 years, wrote of his sorrow at the death of

> that most excellent and deserving man ... No one knows his sterling merits or great qualities better than I do ... I never knew a man of keener sense or neater perspicacity, one who had the clearest insight into all going on, whose principles were the soundest both in church and state, and who had the courage not only boldly to declare them, but always acted up to them ... In private life ... he was one of the most agreeable companions that I have ever met.[92]

---

[1] *HP Commons, 1790-1820*, v. 521, following *Gent. Mag.* (1846), ii. 426, states that at his death Nathan Wetherell was 'worth £100,000'. In fact, his personalty was sworn under £3,500, though the residue was calculated for duty at £19,143. Charles Wetherell received an equal share with his five brothers in a trust fund of unknown value (IR26/131/379; PROB 11/1473/73). [2] *Colchester Diary*, iii. 201; W. Ballantine, *Some Experience of a Barrister's Life*, i. 148. [3] Ballantine, i. 148; *Gent. Mag.*(1846), ii. 428; M.D. George, *Cat. of Pol. and Personal Satires*, xi. 16836, 17194. [4] *Jackson's Oxford Jnl.* 19, 26 Feb., 4, 11 Mar. 1820. [5] Dorset RO D/BKL, Bankes jnl. 122; HLRO, Hist. Coll. 379, Grey Bennet diary, 2. [6] Add. 51574, Abercromby to Holland [26 Jan.]; *Creevey's Life and Times*, 136; Castle Howard mss, Howard to Lady Morpeth, 28 [Jan.1821.] [7] Grey Bennet diary, 5a. [8] Harewood mss, Canning to Miss Leigh, 24 Mar.; *The Times*, 27 Mar. 1821. [9] *The Times*, 9, 13 Mar. 1822. [10] Bankes jnl. 136. [11] *The Times*, 25 June 1822. [12] *Fox Jnl.* 136. [13] *Jackson's Oxford Jnl.* 5 Oct. 1822. [14] *The Times*, 15 Feb. 1823. [15] Ibid. 16, 18, 19 Apr. 1823. [16] Add. 38296, f. 356. [17] Grey mss, Ellice to Grey, 8 Dec. [1823]. [18] Add. 51654, Mackintosh to Lady Holland, 8 Nov.; 51659, Whishaw to same, 13 Nov. 1823. [19] Add. 40304, f. 197; 40315, f. 106; 40329, ff. 229, 247; 40359, f. 147. [20] Buckingham, *Mems. Geo. IV*,

ii. 17, 22. [21] Add. 38298, f. 103; 38576, f. 33; 40304, f. 204. [22] Add. 38298, ff. 101, 140, 147; 38302, f. 156; 38370, f. 134; 40259, f. 307. [23] *Hobhouse Diary*, 108-9. [24] Bucks. RO, Fremantle mss D/FR/138/14/9. [25] *Jackson's Oxford Jnl.* 7, 14 Feb. 1824. [26] *The Times*, 26 Feb. 1824. [27] Northants. RO, Agar Ellis diary, 1 Mar. [1824]. [28] *The Times*, 10 Mar. 1824 [29] Ibid. 15 Apr. 1824. [30] Ibid. 9, 11 Feb. 1825. [31] Add. 40379, f. 20; *The Times*, 21 June 1825. [32] Add. 40342, f. 297; 40383, f. 272. [33] *Colchester Diary*, 409; *Oxford University and City Herald*, 28 Jan., 18 Feb. 1826; Add. 40342, ff. 297, 303, 311, 315, 316; 40385, ff. 102, 111, 114, 116, 132, 151, 162, 168, 170, 173; 43231, f. 171; Wellington mss WP1/850/9. [34] Gurney diary, 7 May [1826]. [35] *Jackson's Oxford Jnl.* 10, 17 June 1826. [36] Add. 38302, f. 52; 40315, ff. 217, 268; *Geo. IV Letters*, iii. 1250. [37] *The Times*, 30 June 1827. [38] *Wellington Despatches*, iv. 216-17, 222; v. 179; Wellington mss WP1/913/1; 915/57; Add. 40307, f. 23; 40395, ff. 21, 129; Lonsdale mss, Lowther to Lonsdale, 18 Jan. 1828; *Life of Campbell*, i. 45; Twiss, iii. 27-28, 32. [39] *Geo. IV Letters*, iii. 1491, 1494-7, 1499, 1500; Wellington mss WP1/917/4, 13, 17, 27; 918/15; 920/18, 21, 36; 979/7. [40] *Wellington Despatches*, v. 179-80, 189-90, 192, 203-4, 217; Wellington mss WP1962/8; 964/24; 965/7; 968/17. [41] *Ellenborough Diary*, i. 284-5, 321; *Croker Pprs.* ii. 8; Bankes jnl. 166 [Feb. 1829]. [42] *Ellenborough Diary*, i. 355, 368; *Wellington Despatches*, v. 507-8; Wellington mss WP1/998/10; 1000/28; *Life of Campbell*, i. 462-3. [43] *Ellenborough Diary*, i. 382, 383, 385-6; *Arbuthnot Jnl.* ii. 250-1. [44] Broughton, *Recollections*, iii. 311; Agar Ellis diary, 18 Mar.; Bankes jnl. 166 [Mar.]; Lonsdale mss, Lowther to Lonsdale, 19 Mar.; Add. 76369, Althorp to Brougham, 19 Mar. 1829; *Greville Mems.* i. 274, 278; *Ellenborough Diary*, i. 399, 406. [45] *Ellenborough Diary*, i. 400-1, 404-8; *Arbuthnot Jnl.* ii. 256, 257; *Wellington Despatches*, v. 547-8; Wellington mss WP1/1004/18; 1007/30; Lonsdale mss, Lowther to Lonsdale, 23, 24 Mar. 1829. [46] *Croker Pprs.* ii. 12; Brougham mss, Abercromby to Brougham [31 Mar. 1829]. [47] *Ellenborough Diary*, ii. 15; Add. 40336, f. 266. [48] *The Times*, 12, 15 Dec. 1829; George, xi. 16020. [49] Grey mss, Howick jnl. 2 Mar.; Keele Univ. Lib. Sneyd mss, Littleton to Sneyd, 2 Mar. 1830. [50] Nottingham Univ. Lib. Newcastle mss Ne2 F3/1/245-6, 248; Add. 40320, f. 166. [51] Hatherton mss, Palmerston to Littleton, 17 Nov. 1830. [52] *Three Diaries*, 14, 49; *Greville Mems.* ii. 123; St. Deiniol's Lib. Glynne-Gladstone mss 197, T. to J. Gladstone, 2 Mar. 1831. [53] TCD, Jebb mss 6397/427. [54] George, xi. 16602; Glynne-Gladstone mss 197, T. to J. Gladstone, 3 Mar.; *Greville Mems.* ii. 124; Broughton, iv. 89; Add. 51655, Mackintosh to Lady Holland [3 Mar. 1831]. [55] Newcastle mss Ne2 F3/1/327. [56] *Creevey Pprs.* ii. 224. [57] *Greville Mems.* ii. 126; *Arbuthnot Jnl.* ii. 416; *Wellington Despatches*, vii. 408; Wellington mss WP1/1176/23; *Arbuthnot Corresp.* 145; *Three Diaries*, p. xxxix; Lonsdale mss, Lowther to Lonsdale, 3 Apr. 1831. [58] Newcastle mss NeC 6982. [59] Le Marchant, *Althorp*, 306. [60] Notts. Archives, Tallents mss, Newcastle to Tallents, 23 Apr.; *The Times*, 5 May 1831. [61] *Three Diaries*, 94. [62] Glos. RO, Hyatt mss 26/F32/13. [63] Gurney diary, 6 July; Add. 51573, Rice to Lady Holland [6 July 1831]. [64] Hatherton diary, 13 July [1831]; *Greville Mems.* ii. 165. [65] *Peel Letters*, 134. [66] *Three Diaries*, 126. [67] Badminton mun. Fm M 4/1/19. [68] Hatherton diary, 8 Oct. [1831]. [69] Cornw. RO, Hawkins mss 10/2171, 2172, 2174; Broughton, iv. 141. [70] Hawkins mss 10/2172. [71] N. Gash, *Sir Robert Peel*, 23-24; M. Brock, *Great Reform Act*, 251-2; J. Cannon, *Parl. Reform*, 227; J. A. Phillips, *Great Reform Bill in Boroughs*, 65-71; Ballantine, i. 149; *Three Diaries*, 153; *Wellington Despatches*, viii. 26-29; Wellington mss WP1/1201/16; Cockburn *Letters*, 354; George, xi. 16824, 16836, 17194; *Holland House Diaries*, 87, 89. [72] Hawkins mss 10/2178. [73] *Croker Pprs.* ii. 151; Hawkins mss 10/2189. [74] *Three Diaries*, 191. [75] *Life of Campbell*, ii. 7. [76] Add. 51569, Ord to Lady Holland [10 May 1832]; *Croker Pprs.* ii. 157; *Three Diaries*, 257. [77] *Creevey Pprs.* ii. 248; *Von Neumann Diary*, i. 274. [78] Brougham mss, memo [June 1832]. [79] *Greville Mems.* ii. 314. [80] Tallents mss, Newcastle to Tallents, 17 July 1832. [81] *Jackson's Oxford Jnl.* 6, 13, 20, 27 Oct., 3, 10, 17, 24 Nov., 1, 8, 15 Dec. 1832; Add. 40403, f. 105. [82] *Wellington Pol. Corresp.* i. 14. [83] Ibid. i. 448, 460, 463, 465, 471-2, 476, 478, 479, 507, 509; *Greville Mems.* iii. 32, 35. [84] *Three Diaries*, 291, 312; *Arbuthnot Corresp.* 175;

Wellington Pol. Corresp. ii. 227; Add. 34571, f. 411; 40316, ff. 95, 97, 100, 104, 106; Durham CRO, Londonderry mss D/Lo/C115 (8). [85] Add. 34571, f. 411; 40409, f. 148. [86] Peel Letters, 153; Greville Mems. iii. 229; Torrens, Melbourne, ii. 152. [87] The Times, 24, 25, 27 Aug. 1840. [88] Add. 34581, f. 552. [89] The Times, 24, 25, 27 Aug. 1846. [90] PROB 6/222/330; Gent. Mag. (1846), ii. 430. [91] Gent. Mag. (1846), ii. 428-9. [92] Letters of King of Hanover to Lord Strangford ed. C. Whibley, 93-94.

D.R.F.

WEYLAND, John (1774–1854), of Woodrising Hall, Norf.

HINDON   1830–1832

b. 4 Dec. 1774, 1st s. of John Weyland of Woodrising and Woodeaton Hall, Oxon. and Elizabeth Johanna, da. of John Nourse of Woodeaton; bro. of Richard Weyland*. educ. Christ Church, Oxf. 1792; St. Mary Hall, Oxf. 1794; L. Inn 1794; I. Temple 1796, called 1800. m. 12 Mar. 1799, Elizabeth, da. of Whitshed Keene† of Richmond, Surr. and Hawthorn Hill, Berks., s.p. suc. fa. to Norf. and Suff. estates 1825. d. 8 May 1854.
    Lt. Bullington, Dorchester and Thame yeoman cav. 1798, W. Mdx. militia 1803.

Weyland was from an ancient Norfolk family, although since the seventeenth century some of its leading members had settled in London. Thus Mark Weyland (d. 1688) of St. Saviour's, Southwark, had a son, also called Mark (1661-1742), who was an eminent merchant and a director of the Bank of England. One of this man's sons, another Mark (d. 1797), was also a Bank director, while his eldest brother John (1713-67) lived at Woodrising Hall. John's son John, who was born in 1744, married, 31 Dec. 1772, the daughter and coheir of an Oxfordshire gentlemen, and it was she who brought the Woodeaton estate into the family. He was sheriff of Oxfordshire, 1777-8, and one of the most progressive farmers in that county.[1] His eldest son, John Weyland junior, was, as he later wrote, 'brought up from my earliest days within sight of an university of which I subsequently became an unworthy member'.[2] He initially studied for the bar at Lincoln's Inn, and then transferred to the Inner Temple, where in 1798 he was unable to keep a term because of illness.[3] By 1802, and for at least the following ten years, he was a London counsel, and was possibly employed by the duke of Clarence, since the Law Lists give his address as Bushey Park. In 1799 he had married the daughter and coheir of the Pittite Member for Montgomery, and it was perhaps through him that he established himself at Winkfield Lodge and, later, Hawthorn Hill, Berkshire, and became a proprietor of East India stock. A landowner and magistrate in Berkshire, Oxfordshire and Surrey, he con-

centrated his attention on the issues of poverty and employment.

Weyland's first major work, published in 1807, was A Short Inquiry into the Policy, Humanity and Past Effects of the Poor Laws, which he supplemented later that year with his much shorter Observations on Mr. Whitbread's Poor Bill. In these, as in his later writings, he empirically rebutted Malthus's theory of population. He also defended the existence of the poor laws, while admitting that they needed careful improvement if they were to continue to contribute to the economic strength and moral well-being of the country. His emphasis on the importance of education as a means of inculcating religious principles was further explored in his Letter to a Country Gentleman on the Education of the Lower Orders (1808). Three years later, as the barrister and author William Roberts recalled, Weyland

> being dissatisfied, as were the religious public generally, with the tone and spirit of the two popular reviews, resolved upon the bold enterprise of setting on foot a new critical journal, which, free from prejudice and party bias, should represent the opinions of that part of the public who view religion as a vital principle.

The British Review and London Critical Journal duly appeared for the first time in March 1811, and it continued to be published quarterly until November 1825, although after the first one or two issues Weyland resigned its editorship to Roberts.[4] He took an interest in Indian affairs and, despite his diffidence, he moved some resolutions relative to the renewal of the East India Company's charter in the court of proprietors, 19 Jan. 1813.[5] He also wrote a public Letter to Sir Hugh Inglis (1813), on the means of improving the state of religion in India, which was answered by John Scott Waring†. As a 'country gentleman, a proprietor of game', he was the author of a Letter on the Game Laws (1815) and a Second Letter (1817), in which he advocated their reform. By this time he was a friend of the agriculturist Arthur Young and an ordinary member of the board of agriculture, to which in 1815 he submitted a short statement on the corn laws.[6] That year he issued another defence of poor provision in his Principle of the English Poor Laws, which analyzed the evidence given by Scottish proprietors to the Lords select committee on corn.

Weyland is principally known for his second major work, The Principles of Population and Production, as they are affected by the Progress of Society, with a View to Moral and Political Consequences (1816). In it he boasted that his Short Inquiry was a 'publication which at the time attracted perhaps more notice than it deserved, but of which I may venture to say that I have not yet seen it fairly answered'. Seeking to draw together his various interests into a systematic treatise, he firmly believed that 'Christian morality is the very root and principle of the questions discussed' in his *Principles*. In its three books he argued that the population would not increase so as to press perniciously against the means of production; that there was no physical impossibility about maintaining the people in sufficient comfort, and that morality was essential to the salutary progress of mankind. He concluded that

the three books together may perhaps be allowed to exhibit something not far removed from a complete system of the elements of civil society, uniform in its tendency, agreeing with itself in all its parts, and strictly consonant with the revealed will of God, and with the moral laws thence derived. It shows that population may continue regularly increasing in numbers, wealth and happiness from the first step in the career of society up to the highest point of civilization, under the operation of the laws which God himself hath appointed for their introduction, checked by no impediments but those which arise out of wilful deviation from those laws; and above all unembarrassed by any principle of evil necessarily arising, not from their own propensity to vice, but from their obedience to the laws which God has given them to counteract it.[7]

Unsurprisingly, he was praised in his own journal, but his attack was answered by Malthus the following year in the fifth edition of his *Essay on the Principle of Population*.[8] By this time Weyland's career as an author had been largely completed.[9]

Described as a 'dull pamphleteer' by Lady Holland, he began to canvass Reading as a ministerialist and nominee of the corporation at the end of 1816. He was very active there in the months before the general election of 1818, and in one incident his donation of £5 to a bricklayer was censured as a bribe. He fared badly against the popular radical candidates, coming third in the poll, and lost the subsequent petition.[10] After an initial hesitation he offered again for Reading at the general election two years later. A local woman, Miss A.H. Trefusis, feared he would succeed:

I say *fear* because he will do more *harm* than good – for he is a good sort of man, who always boasts of his *independent* principles – and will *always* vote *against* you, when you want his support, and *with* you, when it is of no consequence.[11]

In his address, 28 Feb. 1820, he declared that 'I am not (as has been falsely asserted) devoted to ministers, nor am I ... devoted to opposition, for I have nothing to ask or expect of either party'. He expressed his wishes for

the improvement of laws and the situation of the industrious classes, and on the hustings he supported moderate reform, 'though he thought it should be in the morals of the people, before we could hope for political regeneration'. He eventually retired from the poll, narrowly finishing third, behind two advanced Whigs.[12]

Weyland's father died in late July 1825. By his will he confirmed the settlement of his Norfolk and Suffolk properties on his eldest son which he had made during his lifetime. The residue from his personal wealth, which was sworn under £50,000 (later resworn under £60,000), was divided between Weyland and his younger brother, Richard, an army officer, who inherited Woodeaton Hall.[13] Weyland then established himself in Norfolk, to the delight of Joseph John Gurney of Earlham Hall, who commented that 'one does love to see people heartily and without reserves disposed to do all the good they can, and I should think from Weyland's appearance and conversation he must be a person of talent'.[14] One of the chairmen of the quarter sessions, he attended the Norfolk county meeting on the malt tax, 16 Jan. 1830, and that year he became one of the first directors of the Norfolk and Norwich Friendly Society.[15] His *Thoughts Submitted to the Employers of Labour in the County of Norfolk* (1830), which argued in favour of economies and reduced taxation, the abolition of monopolies and an alteration of the currency, urged landlords to increase capital investment and wages in order to improve the material conditions of the poor. He was an acquaintance of the leading philanthropist Lord Calthorpe, to whom he had confided (in December 1827) his anxiety 'to see something substantial done on behalf of the labouring classes, who (in parishes where no peculiar advantages are offered) appear to get worse and worse every year; and sooner or later it must end in a *bellum servile*'.[16] On the retirement of his brother Arthur Gough Calthorpe at the dissolution in 1830, Calthorpe brought Weyland in unopposed for the vacant seat which he controlled at Hindon.

Weyland, who was listed by the Wellington ministry among the 'good doubtfuls', made his maiden speech, 3 Nov. 1830, when, as James Joseph Hope Vere* recorded, he 'sat down three times, not being able to get on', but 'the House good-naturedly cheered him on and he at last succeeded in giving birth to his speech'.[17] He complained that there was no mention in the address of poor labourers, and related his achievements at Woodrising:

I succeeded to a long neglected estate a few years ago, which I found in the usual condition of such estates. I had determined to make an experiment by placing myself in the position of an enlightened and benevolent legislature with respect to the people residing on it. I have taken from my own funds those sums which I calculated would have been in the hands of my tenants for investment or further improvement by labour, under a wholesome system of encouragement, by law, to productive industry, and I have invested them myself in the further improvement of my estate.

Robert Waithman complimented him in the House on his respectful manner and useful qualifications as a Member. Weyland obtained leave, 5 Nov., to introduce his settlement of the poor bill, which was designed to remove a legal loophole in the poor laws. He voted in the minority in favour of reducing the duty on wheat imported into the West Indies, 12 Nov. He divided against ministers on the civil list, 15 Nov. 1830; as he told the Commons, 11 Oct. 1831

what induced me as much as anything else to vote against the government of the duke of Wellington, nearly as much perhaps, as his refusal of reform, was, although I came here inclined to support him, the answer of ... [the home secretary, Peel]. When asked whether it was intended to institute any inquiry into the condition of the labouring classes, he answered that question by saying, that nothing could be done ... That was not the answer that ought to have been given.

Weyland again asserted, 2 Dec. 1830, that ministers could relieve distress: 'let them but repeal injudicious taxes, so as to extend the market at home – let them but open up fresh markets abroad by cutting away injudicious monopolies – and much, very much, may be done by them for the relief of the people'. His bill was given a postponed second reading, 10 Dec. 1830, and he oversaw the committee stages, 10, 11 Feb. 1831, when he reiterated that its purpose was to prevent confusion and litigation over who was eligible for poor relief; it received royal assent that session. He spoke in favour of the chancellor Lord Althorp's game bill, 15 Feb., arguing that opening the trade would end poaching and its attendant evils. He was granted ten days' leave on urgent private business, 11 Mar. He presented the Hindon anti-reform petition, 22 Mar., when he voted for the second reading of the Grey ministry's reform bill. He presented a settlement by apprenticeship bill, 25 Mar., which was lost at the dissolution. He voted against Gascoyne's wrecking amendment to the reform bill, 19 Apr. 1831.

Calthorpe again put him forward for Hindon at the general election of 1831, when he was opposed by a Tory, Horace Twiss*. Weyland later explained:

From the time when the bill was first proposed in the last Parliament, I avowed myself a moderate reformer;

and while parties were balanced so as to afford a hope of reasonable modifications, I uniformly voted for the bill. In consequence, at the general election, I had to sustain, in the borough which I represent, a contest against a strenuous and eloquent anti-reform Member ... On that occasion I fully stated my views to my constituents and pledged myself to support no measure which went beyond them. My constituents were satisfied and re-elected me.[18]

His brother Richard, who was returned for Oxfordshire at this time, proved to be a silent Whig, and although the *Mirror of Parliament* attributes many speeches to him, all were probably given by John, and are considered to be his in what follows. Unless it was in fact Richard, he obtained leave to introduce a settlement by hiring bill, 28 June, which was designed to improve the functioning of the poor laws by removing the impediments to the free circulation of labour in agricultural areas, and a liability of landlords bill. The former was favourably received, including by Althorp, but Weyland admitted that the doubts raised in the debate had shaken his confidence in the effectiveness of the measure. He did not vote in the division on the second reading of the reintroduced reform bill, 6 July, because (as he told the House, 22 July), at the recent contest

I had explained the nature of my [reform] vote to my constituents and I told them that, although I should at all times feel it to be my duty to support the principle of reform, I never would consent to their being totally disfranchised. I told them that, if they returned me to the present Parliament, I should hold myself at liberty to vote for the second reading of the bill, when it should be again proposed; and I should most undoubtedly have done so, had it not been for certain papers which were laid before the House and which convinced me that the measure proposed was not properly founded.

He presented and this time endorsed another anti-reform petition from Hindon, 13 July, when he also presented one from Norwich for the settlement by hiring bill. He seconded the amendment against the first clause of the reform bill, and argued that the schedule A boroughs ought for the sake of justice to be retained, which he claimed could be done by organizing them into districts. He was criticized over the details of this plan and for inconsistency by Althorp, but he presumably voted in the minority in favour of the amendment. He divided in favour of using the 1831 census to determine the boroughs in the disfranchisement schedules and against the inclusion of Appleby in schedule A, 19 July. He objected to the total disfranchisement of Hindon, 22 July 1831, when he declared that

I give my vote on this occasion as an independent Member of Parliament. I care not for my seat, but I hope that these £10 householders into whom these freemen are to be, as it were, transmigrated, will, in the exercise of their franchise, send to Parliament a more efficient Member than I have been. With respect to disfranchisement I am a thorough reformer, an enemy to every disfranchisement that is not necessary – unnecessary disfranchisement I look upon as the greatest injustice towards any party. When we come to the enfranchising clauses, I trust that I shall be able to show that a consolidation of boroughs, placing them on the principle of scot and lot, would be a much better plan of reform than that which is now proposed. It would more effectually prevent improper patronage, and give a more independent set of electors than the principle of disfranchising one body of men for the purpose of enfranchising others.

There is no evidence that he actually pursued this plan.

Weyland reiterated his objections to the £10 householder franchise, 4 Aug. 1831, arguing that a House returned by such electors would attempt to abolish the corn laws and undermine other essential elements in the constitution. He summed up the reform bill as one 'which I think sound in principle, but crude and hasty, and dangerous in its details'. He spoke, and probably voted, against the enfranchisement of Gateshead, 5 Aug. He made three interventions in favour of the game bill, 8 Aug., when he divided to postpone issuing the Dublin writ. He defended the poor laws and advocated their introduction to Ireland, 10 Aug. He answered queries about his settlement by hiring bill, 12 Aug., and, recognizing that there was insufficient time, withdrew it and the liability of landlords bill, 31 Aug. He voted for Lord Chandos's amendment to enfranchise £50 tenants-at-will, 18 Aug., and he spoke (and probably divided in the minorities) against allowing borough freeholders to vote for counties, 24 Aug., and for a higher than £10 franchise in more populous towns, 25 Aug. He seconded Sadler's motion for making legal provision for the Irish poor, 29 Aug., and voted in the minority for this, having stated that 'I am decidedly of opinion that the poor laws of England, although in some instances oppressive, have still been one of the chief causes of our present greatness'. He stated his opposition to overturning the right to vote of existing property holders and members of corporations, 30 Aug., but he divided with ministers against allowing all the non-resident freeholders of the hundreds of Aylesbury, Cricklade, East Retford and New Shoreham to retain the right of voting for their lives, 2 Sept., and he supported shortening the duration of the poll, 6 Sept. Among other speeches, he urged ministers to make better provision for the poor and to fulfil their promise to investigate the subject, 26, 29 Sept., 11 Oct. He was listed as absent from the division on the passage of the reform bill, 21 Sept., but as having voted for the second reading of the Scottish bill, 23 Sept. 1831.

He regretted that the address omitted the subject of distress, 6 Dec. 1831, claiming that the 'wretched state, moral and political, of the labouring classes, is the great canker which is eating out the vitals of the country', and he repeated his call for an inquiry into it (as he did again, 27 Jan., 1, 3 Feb. 1832). He asked ministers about their intentions towards the beer and glove trades, 9, 14 Dec. 1831, 19 Jan. 1832. If he divided on it at all, he almost certainly voted against the second reading of the revised reform bill, 17 Dec. 1831, as he did against going into committee on it, 20 Jan. 1832. He sided with opposition against the Russian-Dutch loan, 26 Jan. He approved of the division of counties, because it would free them from domination by a single family, but complained that the borough seats were unevenly distributed, 27 Jan., and he raised technical queries about the £10 qualification, 1 Feb., and the expenses of parish officers, 8 Feb. He objected to the funding of an Irish poor law from church property, and the non-collection of Irish tithes, 23 Jan., when he advocated throwing out the whole of schedule B of the reform bill and spoke and acted as a teller for the minority of 40 against Hobhouse's vestry bill. He seconded Perceval's motion for a general fast, 26 Jan., and supported the regulation of child labour in factories, 9 Feb. He spoke against the anatomy bill, 27 Feb., acting as a teller for the minorities of 13 and seven against its recommittal. He voted in the minority against the second reading of the malt drawback bill, 29 Feb. As part of a general desire to improve the economic prosperity of the country, he moved for leave to bring in an allotments bill, 15 Mar., which he said was preferable to the 'usually bad and politically insufficient' system of supplementing wages, because it would give people a share in the productive capacity of the soil. Althorp praised the depth of his knowledge, but indicated that he could not promise a good reception for the bill, which was read a first time, 20 Mar.; it passed that session. He voted against the third reading of the reform bill, 22 Mar., and for the second reading of the Liverpool disfranchisement bill, 23 May. He introduced a sale of beer bill, 22 May, but, after seconding Trevor's motion for leave for a similar bill, 31 May, he withdrew his own measure, 5 June, not being sure of government support. He was listed among the 'anti-reformers absent' on the Russian-Dutch loan, 12 July 1832, and made no other recorded votes in the House.

In mid-1832, facing the abolition of his seat at Hindon, Weyland offered for Norfolk East, 'as the advocate of moderate and impartial politics', a supporter of the corn laws, a proponent of repeal of the malt tax, a defender of the church, an opponent of slavery, and a friend to economies and peace abroad. He also explained his conduct on the reform bill, stating that

> I made every exertion, public and private, to obtain the modifications to which I stood pledged, and which I conscientiously thought necessary to render the bill safe, practicable and just. Failing in them all, I could not do otherwise than withdraw my support from the measure.

His candidature was briefly supported by the Conservative lord lieutenant John Wodehouse*, but nothing came of it, nor of a rumour that he might offer for Norfolk West.[19] He therefore left the House at the dissolution in December 1832, and he is not known to have sought another seat. He plumped for the Conservative William Bagge at the Norfolk West election in 1835, and split for Bagge and another Conservative William Lyde Wiggett Chute in 1837.[20] He died in May 1854, leaving his estate to his brother Richard.[21]

[1] *Oxon. Arch. Soc. Rep.* (1917), 114-15; *VCH Oxon.* v. 312, 315; *Gent. Mag.* (1797), i. 356. [2] J. Weyland, *Principles of Population and Production* (1816), p. vi. [3] *CITR*, v. 640. [4] *Life, Letters and Opinions of William Roberts* ed. A. Roberts, 37-38; *Biog. Dict. of Living Authors* (1816), 381. [5] *The Times*, 20 Jan. 1813. [6] Add. 35132, f. 19; 35133, f. 297; 35700, f. 506. [7] Weyland, pp. ix-xxiv, 484-7. [8] *British Rev.* viii (1816), 290; *Works of Malthus* ed. E.A. Wrigley and D. Souden, iii. 609-21. [9] He edited *Boyle's Occasional Reflections* (1808). *A Pat from the Lion's Paw ... by Leo Britannicus* (1815), and *A Remonstrance addressed to the Author of Two Letters to the Right Honourable Robert Peel* (1819) have been attributed to him in the Univ. of London Lib. cat. [10] *Horner Pprs.* 634; [W. Turner], *Reading 70 Years Ago* ed. P.H. Ditchfield, 61, 73, 75-79, 82-83; *HP Commons, 1790-1820*, ii. 15. [11] Add. 38458, f. 303. [12] *The Times*, 29 Feb., 3, 11, 17 Mar.; *Reading Mercury*, 6 Mar. 1820. [13] PROB 11/1703/463; IR26/1069/648. [14] Hants RO, Calthorpe mss 26M62/F/C 927. [15] *Norf. Chron.* 23 Jan., 26 June 1830. [16] Calthorpe mss F/C 386, 1132. [17] Hopetoun mss 167, f. 179. [18] *Devizes Gazette*, 5 May 1831; *Norf. Chron.* 14 July 1832. [19] *Norf. Chron.* 23 June, 14 July; *Bury Post*, 27 June, 4 July, 5 Sept. 1832. [20] *W. Norf. Pollbook* (1835), 103; (1837), 153. [21] *Gent. Mag.* (1854), i. 670; *DNB*; *Oxford DNB*.

S.M.F.

WEYLAND, Richard (1780–1864), of Woodeaton Hall, nr. Islip, Oxon.

OXFORDSHIRE 1831–1837

b. 25 Mar. 1780, 3rd but 2nd surv. s. of John Weyland of Woodrising Hall, Norf. and Woodeaton and Elizabeth Johanna, da. and coh. of John Nourse of Woodeaton; bro. of John Weyland*. *educ.* St. John's, Camb. 1798. *m.* 12

Sept. 1820, Charlotte, da. of Charles Gordon of Cluny, Aberdeen, wid. of Sir John Lowther Johnstone†, 6th bt., of Westerhall, Dumfries, 2s. 1da. *suc. fa.* to Woodeaton 1825; bro. to Woodrising 1854. *d.* 14 Oct. 1864.

Sheriff, Oxon. 1830-1.

Ensign 9 Ft. 1805, lt. 1806; lt. 16 Drag. 1807; capt. army July 1811, 16 Drag. Sept. 1811; maj. army 1819; ret. 1820.

Weyland belatedly entered the army in 1805, served with the cavalry throughout the Peninsular war, twice sustaining wounds, and was present at Waterloo. He sold out the month after his marriage to a wealthy Scottish widow in 1820.[1] On his father's death in 1825 he inherited his Oxfordshire property at Woodeaton Hall, five miles north-east of Oxford, and an equal share in the residue of substantial personalty with his elder brother John, a former barrister turned poor law pamphleteer, who took the family's Norfolk and Suffolk estates.[2] At the general election in Oxfordshire the following year, despite 'intolerable heat' and being, by his own admission, 'unused to public speaking', Weyland seconded the nomination of the sitting Member William Ashhurst, a near neighbour, who had generally voted with the Liverpool ministry. When Ashhurst declined to stand rather than face a contest, Weyland seconded Sir George Dashwood, who was brought forward in his room; but he was one of those who subsequently signed a declaration successfully calling on Ashhurst to persevere and promising financial support, and he again seconded him at the formal opening of the poll. He voted for him and Fane, the other sitting Member.[3] At that election he was also involved with his brother-in-law John Gordon* at Weymouth, where his wife's late husband had sat before his premature death in 1811 on the former Pulteney interest, and where the Johnstones were in dispute with one of the trustees of their Scottish property, Masterton Ure*. Gordon initially put himself forward, but a fortnight later he issued a joint address with Weyland declining to stand, ostensibly to avoid any appearance of coalition with Ure. Some electors invited Weyland to stand on the Johnstone interest, but he ruled himself out of the running for Gordon, who was returned after a protracted contest.[4] Weyland, assured of support at the next opening, continued to cultivate the borough; and on a vacancy in January 1828 he was first in the field. When a deputation was sent to London to secure the candidature of Lord Douro*, the premier the duke of Wellington's son, Weyland wrote to the duke stating his own pretensions and claiming that he intended to support his newly formed administration. Wellington sent down Edward Sugden*, a leading chancery barrister. Weyland persisted, stressing his connection with the Johnstones and professing himself to be 'a steady and inflexible supporter' of the constitution in church and state and 'a friend to the government', who would 'ever decidedly oppose any innovation which may be brought forward for innovation's sake'. He was beaten by 120 votes in a poll of 524.[5] The following year he asked the Whig lawyer Henry Brougham* for assistance in his legal struggle on behalf of his stepson Sir George Frederic Johnstone, a minor.[6] As sheriff of Oxfordshire, he presided over the contested county election of 1830, when his brother was returned for Hindon.[7]

At the general election of 1831 Weyland, whose brother had voted for the Grey ministry's reform bill, accepted a requisition to stand for Oxfordshire as a reformer, to be returned free of expense by public subscription. He and another reformer contested the county with one of the sitting Members, who had opposed the bill, but claimed to favour moderate change. Weyland pledged support for 'the bill, the whole bill, and nothing but the bill', giving assurances that he would accept no modifications to it which were not approved by ministers. On the day of the nomination news reached Oxford that he had been returned in absentia for Weymouth. Weyland, who, with his wife, had fallen out with his brother-in-law over management of the Johnstone interest and Gordon's alleged involvement with Sugden in secret deals, publicly renounced the Weymouth seat. During the Oxfordshire poll, he argued that the old 'borough-mongering system', far from working well, had seen the creation of a crippling national debt and a massive tax burden, the promotion of incompetent generals and diplomats and widespread abuses in legal administration. After his return in second place he promised to support economy and retrenchment and the abolition of unjustified pensions and sinecures; and at a celebration dinner he said that the promoters of the reform bill 'did not desire to overthrow, but to repair the constitution'.[8]

It has been assumed that the speeches attributed by the Mirror of Parliament to Weyland were in fact delivered by his brother, although it is possible that some of the minor interventions were his. He had developed strong reservations about certain aspects of the ministerial reform proposals; but, after dividing for the second reading of the reintroduced bill, 6 July, when John abstained, he proved to be a steady supporter of its details, though he voted, like his brother, for the enfranchisement of £50 tenants-at-will, 18 Aug. 1831. He divided for the passage of the bill, 21 Sept. (John

was an absentee), the second reading of the Scottish bill, 23 Sept., and the motion of confidence in the Grey ministry, 10 Oct. He was in O'Connell's minority for swearing the Dublin election committee, 29 July, but divided twice with ministers on the issues arising from its report, 23 Aug. He voted for the second reading of the revised reform bill, 17 Dec. 1831, when his brother probably opposed it, was absent from the divisions on the borough disfranchisement clauses, 20, 23 Jan. 1832, but subsequently voted reliably for its details and divided for its third reading, 22 Mar., when his brother voted the other way. They were also on opposite sides on 26 Jan., when Weyland voted with government on the Russian-Dutch loan, as he did on relations with Portugal, 9 Feb. He voted for the address asking the king to appoint only ministers who would carry the reform bill unimpaired, 10 May, and the second reading of the Irish bill, 25 May. His last recorded vote in this period was in favour of making coroners' inquests public, 20 June 1832.

Weyland was returned unopposed for Oxfordshire at the general elections of 1832 and 1835. His political views became increasingly conservative, and he supported Peel's first ministry.[9] He retired from Parliament at the dissolution in 1837. On the death of his brother without issue in 1854 he inherited the Norfolk and Suffolk estates, including Woodrising, where he took up residence, having made over Woodeaton to his elder son John Weyland (1821-1902).[10] He died at Woodrising, 'universally respected', in October 1864.[11] By his will, dated 14 July 1858, he left all his real estate, including leasehold properties in George Lane, Botolph Lane and Eastcheap, London, to his elder son. He bequeathed legacies of £5,000 and £500 respectively to his younger son Richard Henry and his daughter Elizabeth, countess of Verulam, and provided for the payment to his children of £20,000 to which he was entitled in lieu of arrears on annuities secured to his late wife on her first marriage settlement. The Weylands' Oxfordshire estates were sold in 1911.[12]

[1] Gent. Mag. (1864), ii. 801; Northumb. RO, Middleton mss ZMI/ S76/40/6, 38. [2] PROB 11/1703/463; IR26/1069/648. [3] Jackson's Oxford Jnl. 17 June; The Times, 19 June 1826; Oxon. Pollbook (1826), 26. [4] Dorset Co. Chron. 18 May, 1, 8, 15, 22, 29 June 1826; Middleton mss S76/52/2. [5] Dorset Co. Chron. 7, 14, 21 Feb.; The Times, 31 Jan., 2, 4, 5, 12, 22 Feb. 1828; Wellington mss WP1/914/41; 916/12. [6] Brougham mss, Weyland to Brougham, 4 May 1829. [7] Jackson's Oxford Jnl. 31 July 1830. [8] The Times, 7 Apr., 12-14 May; Dorset Co. Chron. 28 Apr., 5, 26 May; Oxford University, City, and County Herald, 7, 14 May, 4 June 1831. See WEYMOUTH AND MELCOME REGIS. [9] Gent. Mag. (1864), ii. 801. [10] PROB 11/2194/502; IR26/2016/262. [11] Gent. Mag. (1864), ii. 802. [12] Rep. of Oxon. Arch. Soc. (1917), 115.

D.R.F.

WHARTON, John (1765–1843), of Skelton Castle, nr. Guisborough, Yorks.

BEVERLEY   1790–1796
BEVERLEY   1802–1826

b. 21 June 1765, 1st s. of Joseph William Stevenson (formerly Hall) of Skelton and Ann, da. and h. of James Foster of Drumgoon, co. Fermanagh. *educ.* R. Sch. Armagh; Trinity, Dublin 1781; L. Inn 1784. *m.* 14 Oct. 1790, Susan Mary Anne, da. of Gen. John Lambton† of Lambton, co. Dur., 2da. *d.v.p. suc.* fa. 1786; took name of Wharton 3 May 1788 on *suc.* to estates of aunt Mrs. Mary Wharton. *d.* 29 May 1843.

Wharton, a well-connected Foxite Whig, the uncle of 'Radical Jack' Lambton* and a former Friend of the People, stood for the venal borough of Beverley for the eighth time in 1820. Politics aside, the severe financial embarrassments which had obliged him in 1816 to place his estates in the hands of trustees, who allowed him a dole, made a seat essential as a refuge from creditors. He deplored the Liverpool ministry's recent repressive legislation and failure to redeem their 'promises of economy and retrenchment', and was returned in second place.[1] He continued to vote with his friends in opposition, but was far from being a thick and thin attender in the 1820 Parliament. He divided against Wilberforce's compromise resolution on the Queen Caroline affair, 22 June, and steadily in support of the parliamentary campaign on her behalf in early 1821; he presented a Beverley petition for restoration of her name to the liturgy, 24 Jan. 1821.[2] He voted for economies in revenue collection, 4 July, and against the barrack agreement bill, 13 July 1820. On 20 Feb. 1821 he introduced a bill to amend the General Enclosure Act, which became law on 19 Apr. (1 & 2 Geo. IV, c. 23). He voted to condemn the Allies' suppression of liberalism in Naples, 21 Feb. He divided for Catholic relief, 28 Feb. 1821, 1 Mar., 21 Apr., 10 May 1825. He was in the minority for giving Leeds a ratepayer franchise if it received Grampound's seats, 2 Mar., and divided for parliamentary reform, 9 May 1821, 24 Apr. 1823, 27 Apr. 1826. He cast sporadic votes for economy and retrenchment, 6 Mar., 30 Apr., 4, 14, 21, 28 May, 1, 18 June 1821. He was given a month's leave on account of illness in his family, 12 Mar. 1821. He paired for repeal of the Blasphemous and Seditious Libels Act, 8 May, and divided with Burdett for inquiry into Peterloo, 16 May, having presented a petition from one of the wounded victims the previous day.[3] He paired for the forgery punishment mitigation bill, 23 May 1821. His only known votes in 1822 were for reduction of the army estimates, 4 Mar., and abolition of one of the joint-postmasterships and

inquiry into the board of control, 14 Mar. He voted against government on the sinking fund, 6, 13 Mar., the army estimates, 10 Mar., tax cuts, 17, 18 Mar., the deadweight pensions, 18 Apr., and repeal of the Foreign Enlistment Act, 16 Apr. 1823. He divided for inquiry into the prosecution of the Dublin Orange rioters, 22 Apr., and abolition of the death penalty for larceny, 21 May 1823. In 1824 he voted for inquiries into the reports of the Scottish judicial commissioners, 30 Mar., the state of Ireland, 11 May, and Irish first fruits revenues, 25 May; against the aliens bill, 2, 12 Apr., and the grant for new church building, 9, 12 Apr.; for allowing defence by counsel in felony cases, 6 Apr., and to condemn the prosecution of the Methodist missionary John Smith in Demerara, 11 June. On 24 May 1824 he brought up a Northallerton justices' petition against a clause of the gaols bill.[4] He was in the opposition minorities against the bill to suppress the Catholic Association, 18, 25 Feb. 1825. He voted for the production of information on the reorganization of the Indian army, 24 Mar., paired for repeal of the window tax, 17 May, and divided against the duke of Cumberland's annuity bill, 10 June, for inquiry into the cost of emigration schemes, 13 June, and to reduce judges' salaries, 17 June. He voted against the spring guns bill, 21 June 1825. He voted to reduce the army estimates, 6, 7 Mar., and in Hume's minorities of 47 for the abolition of army flogging, 10 Mar., and 51 for inquiry into the state of the nation, 4 May 1826. He was in the largely protectionist minority against the emergency admission of foreign corn, 8 May, and before dividing likewise, 11 May, he defended his fellow 'country gentlemen' against the charge that they had 'brought the country to its present state of distress by supporting the last war'. He voted for Russell's resolution outlawing electoral bribery, 26 May 1826.

At the general election the following month Wharton offered again for Beverley, but loss of support among the resident freemen and his shortage of money condemned him to defeat at the hands of two new candidates.[5] Lord Dundas commented that 'being out of Parliament may be very inconvenient to him', and he cast round desperately for an escape from his creditors.[6] In early December 1826 he wrote to Lord Fitzwilliam's son Lord Milton*:

> It would be a very great accommodation to me to have a seat ... for one year, and therefore I take the liberty of requesting you will have the goodness to get me brought in upon a double return, if the seat is not promised, or upon a vacancy when one occurs, and I pledge myself to vacate on the first day of the session of 1828 if required, or at any time I may be required after that day. I shall not

trouble you with my reasons for making this request, but assure you that if you comply you will confer on me an obligation that no length of time can efface.

Milton evidently advised him to petition against the return of one of his opponents at Beverley. He thought it was 'too late' for this (a petition in the names of two electors had already been presented, but it subsequently lapsed), and he asked Milton to secure his temporary return for Malton if the death of Lord Mulgrave removed one of the sitting Members to the Lords. This did not happen.[7] A year later Wharton was served with several writs for recovery of debts, and in January 1828 he was confined within the rules of king's bench prison.[8] From there he declared himself a candidate for Beverley at the 1830 general election, but 'his inability to discharge his pecuniary engagements' forced him to withdraw.[9] On 30 Aug. 1830 he wrote to Henry Brougham, who had been returned for both Yorkshire and Knaresborough, asking him to recommend him to the duke of Devonshire for the latter seat for the next session 'if I cannot get it for the entire Parliament, which if there is such quality as gratitude amongst politicians, I think myself entitled to expect from the party'; nothing came of this.[10] In February 1831 Brougham, now lord chancellor in the Grey ministry, told Lord Holland that at dinner their cabinet colleague Lord Durham (as Lambton had become) had

> quarrelled ... with Bear Ellice [the patronage secretary] and myself for not knowing he had a difference with his uncle J. Wharton, and calling him 'poor Peg', which God knows he is whether he quarrels with his nephew or no, but it turns out (I did not know it) that he is pressing ... [Durham] to pay him £15,000 under his father's will and that ... [Durham] don't much like it.[11]

(There is no such provision in Durham's father's will, but it left an annuity to Mrs. Wharton 'only until such time as the estates of her husband ... shall be so far liberated as to produce for her ... the clear sum of £2,000 per annum'.)[12] Wharton was still harbouring hopes of being able to stand again for Beverley as late as 1839, but he remained within the rules until his death from prostate cancer, at 3 Asylum Buildings, Westminster Road, Lambeth, in May 1843.[13] He had tried in his will to provide for his family, but an outstanding debt of £5,000 was claimed against his estate.[14]

[1] HP Commons, 1790-1820, v. 523; The Times, 7 Mar. 1820 [2] The Times, 25 Jan. 1821. [3] Ibid. 16 May 1821. [4] Ibid. 25 May 1825. [5] Hull Univ. Lib. Hotham mss DDHO/8/3, Hall to Hotham, 4 June; Hull Advertiser, 9 June 1826. [6] Fitzwilliam mss 125/2. [7] Ibid. Wharton to Milton, 4, 12 Dec. 1826. [8] TNA Pris 4/39/154. [9] Hull Advertiser, 16, 30 July 1830; Lincs. AO, Ancaster mss XIII/b/5b, j, k.

[10] Brougham mss. [11] Add. 51562, Brougham to Holland, Mon. [Feb. 1831]. [12] PROB 11/1308/420. [13] The Times, 31 May 1843; Gent. Mag. (1843), ii. 207. [14] PROB 11/1982/451; IR26/1661.

M.P.J.C.

WHITBREAD, Samuel Charles (1796–1879), of Grove House, Kensington Gore and 33 Maddox Street, Mdx.

MIDDLESEX   1820–1830

> b. 16 Feb. 1796, 3rd but 2nd surv. s. of Samuel Whitbread[†] (d. 1815) of Cardington and Southill, Beds. and Elizabeth, da. of Lt.-Gen. Sir Charles Grey of Falloden, Northumb.; bro. of William Henry Whitbread*. educ. by private tutor Richard Salmon 1802-7; Sunninghill, Berks. (Rev. Frederick Neve) 1807; Eton 1808; St. John's, Camb. 1814. m. (1) 28 June 1824, Juliana (d. 13 Oct. 1858), da. of Maj.-Gen. Henry Otway Trevor (afterwards Brand), 3s. (1 d.v.p.) 3da. (1 d.v.p.); (2) 18 Feb. 1868, Lady Mary Stephenson Keppel, da. of William Charles, 4th earl of Albemarle, wid. of Henry Frederick Stephenson*, s.p. suc. bro. to family estates 1867. d. 27 May 1879.
> Sheriff, Beds. 1831-2.

Whitbread, a member of the brewing dynasty, was raised in London and Bedfordshire, where his father, a leading Foxite Whig, inherited the family's recently purchased estate of Southill in 1796.[1] His parents' favourite, he was educated with his elder brother William and sent to Cambridge to prepare him for a career in the church or politics. Little is known of his reaction to his father's suicide in July 1815. His uncle Edward Ellice*, who now oversaw the Whitbreads' troubled finances, dismissed the brothers' private tutor Sam Reynolds, who 'goes about as an idle companion to the boys', and pressed their continued attendance at Cambridge.[2] Whitbread joined Brooks's, 22 May 1818, and became a trustee the following month of his father's will, by which he received £5,000 and £500 a year from the age of 21, £5,000 in lieu of the church livings of Southill and Purfleet (Essex) reserved for him, and was granted the right to reside at Cardington when the house fell vacant.[3] William came in for Bedford at the general election of 1818 and Samuel was now suggested for Westminster and Middlesex, where he nominated the Whig veteran George Byng* in a speech proclaiming his own credentials as a candidate-in-waiting.[4] Encouraged by his mother, who took a house in Kensington Gore after William came of age, he fostered his connections with the Westminster reformers, purchased a £10,000 stake in the brewery and in 1819 joined their controlling partnership, which was then worth £490,000 'on paper' and dominated by his father's partners Sir Benjamin Hobhouse[†],

William Wilshere of Hitchin and the Martineau and Yallowley families.[5] Maria Edgeworth, who now met Whitbread for the first time, described him as a 'good, but too meek looking ... youth'.[6]

Whitbread grasped the opportunity to contest Middlesex at the general election of 1820, when, backed by his relations, brewing partners, the Nonconformists and the Whig-radical coalition campaigning in Westminster (which he denied), he defeated the sitting Tory William Mellish in a 12-day poll to come in with Byng.[7] His lacklustre brother had shown none of their father's talent and energy, but Samuel impressed with his enthusiasm and appealed throughout to his father's reputation as a reformer and advocate of civil and religious liberty.[8] Ellice praised his common sense and popularity and surmised that Parliament 'may save him by throwing him into society and engaging him in politics, although possibly the situation he will occupy will be rather too prominent for either his abilities or experience'. He later informed Lord Grey:

> Sam has exceeded all our expectations ... He has on every occasion conducted himself with skill and feeling, and shown a quickness and talent, which I did not give him credit for, and if he will only apply himself with activity and industry to the business of the county, he may retain the seat as long as he pleases.[9]

He was caricatured as a phial of 'Whitbread's entire' – the blue to John Cam Hobhouse's* red in Sir Francis Burdett's* tricolour.[10] He declined attendance at the 'Westmorland' dinner at the *Mermaid Tavern*, Hackney, to fête Henry Brougham's* supporters, 17 Apr. 1820, and Ellice had to reassure Grey that they 'did not intend to enlist ourselves under Burdettite banners'.[11] As a main speaker with Hobhouse at the Middlesex 'Independence' dinner that Henry Grey Bennet* chaired at the *Freemasons' Tavern*, 3 June 1820, he reaffirmed his commitment to reform, praised the 'union of the friends of freedom and reform at the late election' and was commended by Burdett for his 'promising start' in the House.[12]

Except for occasional lapses to go hunting, Whitbread attended unstintingly until 1827, when he became seriously ill with scrofula, 'the Grey disease', from which his mother had suffered intermittently since 1798.[13] Demonstrating greater commitment than his brother, he voted with the main Whig opposition on most major issues and aligned with Hobhouse, Hume and the 'Mountain', in whose small minorities for retrenchment and lower taxes he was frequently listed. Attempting to take the House by storm, he made major contributions to the 1820-21 debates on the Queen

Caroline affair and reform. He left most constituency business to Byng, invariably defended Whitbreads in discussions on brewing, the Excise Acts and the licensing laws and could be relied on to criticize the game laws. He promoted Ellice's interests in the 1823-5 select committees on the London and Westminster gas light bills and resolutely opposed the 1824 and 1825 Equitable Loan bills, whose defeat contributed to the collapse of several 'bubble companies' and ruined his erstwhile political ally Peter Moore*. Whitbread presented and endorsed a petition for the restoration of Sligo's chartered privileges, 28 Apr., and another from the Thames watermen complaining that London Bridge was unsafe, 4 May 1820. He commented briefly on the Newington church bill, 19 May, and pressed the radical George Dewhurst's allegations of ill-treatment by his Lancaster gaolers, 31 May 1820.[14]

Queen Caroline visited Whitbread's mother directly she returned from the continent and, assuming his father's mantle, he became one of her staunchest partisans.[15] He voted against Wilberforce's compromise resolution, 22 June 1820, and seconded Western's adjournment motion on the 26th, when he argued that by requesting the queen to submit to a trial 'which must have the effect of degrading her for ever', ministers 'were endeavouring to delude the House into some sort of sanction of what they had done'. He addressed her Middlesex supporters, 8 Aug., and accompanied their delegation to Brandenburgh House on the 15th.[16] His attendance at the Paddington Green ladies' meeting, 11 Sept., together with false reports of his sisters' presence, prompted the Evangelical vicar of Harrow John Cunningham to write a pamphlet denouncing his conduct.[17] Whitbread countered that it had been his duty as a Member to attend and he highlighted errors in the newspaper reports cited by his absent critics.[18] Before voting in Hobhouse's minority of 12 for an immediate prorogation, 18 Sept., he spoke again of the 'calamitous consequences' of proceeding with the bill of pains and penalties and restricting inquiry to the queen's morals. Later that day the leader of the House Lord Castlereagh scotched his attempt to obtain detailed accounts of expenditure on her prosecution since 1814. He joined the queen's procession to St. Paul's, 29 Nov., for a service of thanksgiving when the proceedings were suspended, and pressed for county meetings in Bedfordshire and Middlesex to petition for reform and the restoration of her name to the liturgy.[19] He presented her supporters' petitions, 26 Jan., 13 Feb., and protested at the change in procedures that reduced the time accorded to them, 21 Feb. 1821.[20] On 18 June he presented and endorsed a St. Pancras reform petition deprecating 'new taxes' and urging the 'restoration of the queen to her rights'.[21] He divided for Catholic relief, 28 Feb. 1821, 1 Mar., 21 Apr., 10 May, and against the attendant Irish franchise bill, 26 Apr. 1825.

He voted for a scot and lot franchise for Leeds under the Grampound disfranchisement bill, 2 Mar., and to disqualify civil ordnance officers from voting in parliamentary elections, 12 Apr. 1821. Seconding Lambton's reform motion, 17 Apr., he testified to Middlesex's support for the scheme, including triennial parliaments, and compared the 'House, as present constituted ... [to] a woman of bad character, with whom you might take any liberty, but that of telling her of her frailty'. He denounced electoral abuses, 'contempt of the standing orders ... rotten boroughs ... corruption in the returns' and the sale of seats, and cited Parliament's indifference to distress petitions as 'the strongest argument in favour of reform'. He was a minority teller when the motion was rejected (55-43) in a snap division, 18 Apr., and warned of a possible backlash to its summary dismissal.[22] He divided again for reform, 9, 10 May 1821, 25 Apr. 1822, 20 Feb., 24 Apr., 2 June 1823, 13, 27 Apr. 1826. He spoke against considering the army estimates in committee, 9 Mar. 1821, presented petitions for inquiry into the Peterloo massacre, 15 Apr., and divided accordingly next day.[23] He voted to make forgery a non-capital offence, 23 May, 4 June. Targeting the Constitutional Association, and backed by petitions presented by Hobhouse and Colonel Davies, on 3 July 1821 he proposed an address praying that the king would 'order a *nollo prosequi* to be entered in every case where the Association were prosecutors'. This, Londonderry (as Castlereagh had become) informed the king, 'gave rise to a long debate in which the attorney and solicitor-general spoke with much ability in maintenance of the legality of the Association'.[24] The Mountain's spokesman Henry Grey Bennet commented: 'no division took place, but the "loyalists" were very roughly handled, and I hope shamed in some degree out of their scandalous proceedings'.[25] Henceforward 'Whitbread's entire' was used to caricature 'factious froth' and Whitbread kept a lower profile on radical causes.[26]

Representing local interests, he raised objections, 21 Mar., and presented petitions against the Stoke Newington select vestry bill, 14 May, and the metropolis road bill, 27 Mar., 9 May 1821.[27] He candidly acknowledged that the critics of the Middlesex court of requests, whose complaints were taken up by the Ipswich Member Barrett Lennard, had not consulted him, 19 June, and vainly opposed the Highgate Chapel bill promoted by Byng, 5 July 1822.[28] He presented the

silk weavers' petitions and argued against repealing the Spitalfields Acts on their behalf, 21 May, 2 June 1823.[29] He refrained from commenting on the reciprocity duties when presenting the Thames shipwrights' hostile petition, 1 July, so his declaration for them on the hustings in 1826 was something of a surprise.[30] He endorsed the petitions for the abolition of colonial slavery he presented, 23 May, 2 June 1823, 17 Mar. 1826, and voted in condemnation of the indictment in Demerara of the Methodist missionary John Smith, 11 June 1824, and of the Jamaican slave trials, 2 Mar. 1826.[31]

Whitbread's unexplained absence from the minorities against the Irish insurrection bill, 8 Feb. 1822, 'enraged' his mother, but he was soon forgiven, and in March he took a party of her friends to the ventilator to observe the debates.[32] In his only major speech that session, he defended Whitbreads' policy of discouraging tied houses, 6 May. He voted to consider criminal law reform, 4 June 1822. He hosted a grand dinner at the Chiswell Street brewery in May 1823, and divided with Maberly for alterations in the beer and malt duties, 28 May (and again, 15 Mar. 1824).[33] Pressing for major changes, he condemned the current game laws as 'a disgrace to the national character, and a great cause of the demoralization of the poorer classes' that encouraged the poaching they were calculated to suppress, 2 June 1823. He lent his support to measures promoted by Hume in opposition in 1824, but became increasingly preoccupied with changes proposed in the beer duties, on which he spoke as the unofficial representative of the licensed victuallers, 24 May. He also presented their petitions, 16, 27 Mar. 1824.[34] Tussles involving Ellice and Moore over the London and Westminster oil gas bill and the Equitable Loan Society bank bill compromised him personally and politically from 1824 to 1826. Assisting Ellice, he secured the committal of the oil gas bill (by 74-71), 12 Apr.,[35] but, despite support from Sir George Robinson, Burdett and Hobhouse, he failed by 52-12, 26 May, and by 40-32 and 44-5, 2 June 1824, to prevent the passage of the Equitable Loan bill, which later foundered in the Lords. (He presented petitions, 15 Mar., and was a minority teller against the third reading of the 1825 bill, 24 Mar.).[36] He voted against the Irish insurrection bill, 14 June, and funding new churches, 9 Apr., 14 June 1824. Acquaintances considered Juliana Brand, whom he married that month, pretty and good-natured, and although his mother did not immediately welcome the connection, she was soon reconciled to it.[37]

A radical publication noted that Whitbread 'attended constantly' in 1825 and 'voted with the opposition'.[38]

He brought up petitions against the St. Katharine's Docks bill, 16 Mar., 19 Apr., handled the abortive sea baths bill, 17 Mar., and the Hyde Park turnpike bill, 18 May, and supported the St. Olave (Hart Street) tithe bill on his constituents' behalf, 30 May. He brought up the shipwrights' hostile petition, 19 Apr., and voted in a minority of 15 against permitting factory masters who were magistrates from enforcing the provisions of the revised Combination Act, 27 June.[39] As chairman of the select committee on the reintroduced oil gas bill, he protested at length at the manner of its defeat on the floor of the House, by individuals who knew nothing of the bill or his committee's deliberations, 2 June 1825.[40] He presented a petition for a new corn market for his county, 21 Feb., and voted for corn law revision, 18 Apr. 1826.[41] He supported inquiry into the silk trade, 24 Feb., and voted against increasing Huskisson's board of trade salary, 7 Apr. Drawing on his recent experience of the oil gas, Equitable Loan, and metropolis road bills, he seconded Littleton's resolutions regulating the composition of select committees on private bills, 19 Apr. He voted for Hume's state of the nation motion, 4 May, and was in a minority of 13 for reducing the salaries of Irish prison inspectors, 5 May 1826. A campaign to unseat 'Solon' Whitbread had been under way since October 1825, but no suitable candidate was forthcoming and his return at the general election of 1826 was unopposed.[42] On the hustings, he criticized the government, spoke proudly of his opposition to 'jobbing' speculations in joint-stock companies, and maintained (untruthfully), when pressed, that he 'had supported ministers on every motion for the introduction of free trade', together with the tax reductions necessary to make it effective.[43]

Whitbread voted for Catholic relief, 6 Mar., and to disfranchise Penryn for corruption, 28 Mar. 1827, but otherwise kept a low profile pending the appointment of a successor to Lord Liverpool as premier. He presented petitions for repeal of the Test Acts, 6, 7 June.[44] He was caricatured with Matthew Wood* and Lord Lansdowne at 'the installation of the new deputy grand master of the most venerable order of the red halter', 10, 19 July, 1827.[45] He voted to repeal the Test Acts, 26 Feb., and paired for Catholic relief, 12 May 1828, but missed most of that session and the next following a life-threatening bout of scrofula. He had constantly ignored medical advice to conserve his strength.[46] His Bedfordshire neighbour and political ally Lord William Russell* commented that he had 'sacrificed his health to fox-hunting, and neglected his duty as Member for Middlesex'.[47] He divided for Catholic emancipation as expected, 6, 30 Mar., and voted to permit Daniel O'Connell to sit without taking the oath of supremacy,

18 May, and for the Ultra Lord Blandford's reform proposals, which most Whigs considered absurd, 2 June 1829. He presented a handful of petitions backing the Independent Gas Light Company bill, 12 May, for amending the East London waterworks bill, 14 May, and repeal of the window tax, 2 June 1829.

Whitbread delayed his return to Parliament in 1830 at Lord Tavistock's* request to attend to the affairs of the Oakley Hunt, of which he was secretary, and in particular their differences with its master Grant Berkley. These were essentially political and almost caused a duel between Berkley and Whitbread.[48] He divided with Hume for tax reductions, 15 Feb., and on the estimates, 22 Feb., voted for Blandford's reform scheme, 18 Feb., and paired for the enfranchisement of Birmingham, Leeds and Manchester, 23 Feb. He voted to transfer East Retford's seats to Birmingham, 5, 15 Mar. He divided against the Bathurst and Dundas pensions, 26 Mar., and fairly steadily with the revived Whig opposition until 13 July, including for Jewish emancipation, 5 Apr., 17 May, repeal of the Irish coal duties, 13 May, and to consider abolishing colonial slavery, 13 July. He introduced a petition against the watching and parishes bill, 5 Apr., but otherwise made no reported speeches that session. He had discussed his impending retirement at the general election with Hobhouse on 15 June and was prepared to support Hobhouse, Hume or Lord John Russell as his successor.[49] Nominating Byng, 5 Aug. 1830, before returning to Bedford to assist his brother, he spoke of his regrets on resigning and the poor health that had marred his performance.[50] He sponsored the successful candidate, the Whig lawyer William Baker, at the hotly contested Middlesex East coroner's election in September, when, countering criticism of his own parliamentary record, he insisted that he had not been 'driven out' of the county.[51]

Out of Parliament, Whitbread acted to combat the 'Swing' riots in Bedfordshire in December 1830, attended the Bedford reform meeting in January 1831, and addressed the Middlesex meeting at the *Mermaid* with Charles Shaw Lefevre*, 21 Mar. He declared for the Grey ministry's reform bill, notwithstanding the omission from it of the ballot.[52] As sheriff, he assisted his brother and the Bedford reformers in the county and borough at the May 1831 general election, when both constituencies were contested.[53] He continued to promote reform and the ministerial bill at district meetings in Middlesex, where he turned down a requisition to contest the new Tower Hamlets constituency at the 1832 general election.[54] A lifelong Liberal, Whitbread did not stand for Parliament again, but from 1852 took a keen interest in his son Samuel's political career as Member for Bedford. His health remained erratic, and he increasingly devoted his time to business and scientific pursuits. As a fellow since 1849 of the Royal Astronomical Society, and treasurer, 1857-78, he built the Howard observatory at Cardington (1850), and became a founder member that year of the British Meteorological Society and a fellow of the Royal Society in 1854. In 1867 he succeeded his childless brother William to the family estates and as head of the brewery and trusts, and in 1868, almost ten years after Juliana's death, he married into the Albermarle family, making Cardington available for Samuel, who had inherited his uncle's shares in Whitbreads'. He died in May 1879 at his town house in St. George's Square, survived by his second wife (*d.* 20 Sept. 1884) and four of his six children.[55] According to his obituary in the *Bedford Mercury*

> in the world at large, Mr. Whitbread did not figure greatly. He was fond of sport, but not to a base degree; his caution prevented him making rash ventures, which often end unhappily. As a walker he was rather famous; it was a matter of amusement to his friends to see how in the vigour of his manhood and even of late years he used to walk down interviewers who bored him ... The anecdotes of this species of pedestrianism are neither few nor far between, and the richest of them are those in which the bores were portly and ponderous to a degree. It may be imagined therefore that he was humorous; and so he was. He was good company everywhere. Political economists might have praised his habits of economy, for his chief fault was his desire never to waste anything.[56]

His will, dated 30 Nov. 1875, was proved in London, 24 July 1879. By it he confirmed Samuel's succession to the entailed estates and several family settlements, ensured that the non-entailed estates, including the brewery's Chiswell Street premises, passed to his younger son William, and provided generously for other family members.[57]

[1] *Inventories of Beds. County Houses* ed. J. Collett-White (*Beds. Hist. Rec. Soc.* lxxiv), 212-33. [2] Grey mss, Ellice to Grey, 3 Aug., 7 Sept., 27 Dec. 1815, 10, 26 Jan., 9 Aug., 8 Dec. 1816, 27 Jan. 1817. [3] Beds. RO, Whitbread mss W 3524; IR26/3157/761. [4] *The Times*, 26, 27 June 1818; A. Mitchell, *Whigs in Opposition*, 50, 54. [5] Whitbread mss 3525, 3526; LMA, Whitbread mss 4453/A/03/01; B12/022. [6] *Edgeworth Letters*, 180. [7] Grey mss, Tierney to Grey, 27 Feb., Ellice to same, 31 Mar., Whitbread to same, 5 May; Add. 56541, f. 17; *County Chron.* 28 Mar.; *The Times*, 8, 30 Mar.; *Morning Chron.* 1 Apr. 1820. [8] Grey mss, Tierney to Grey, 22 Mar. 1820; R. Fulford, *Samuel Whitbread*, 88-96. [9] Grey mss, Ellice to Grey, 16, 21 Mar. 1820. [10] M.D. George, *Cat. of Pol. and Personal Satires*, x. 13714. [11] Grey mss, Ellice to Grey, 17 Apr.; *The Times*, 19 Apr.; Brougham mss, Whitbread to J. Brougham, 20 Apr. 1820. [12] Add. 56541, f. 39; *The Times*, 5 June 1820. [13] *Russell Letters*, i. 159; D. Rapp, *Samuel Whitbread*, 51. [14] *The Times*, 29 Apr., 20 May 1820. [15] E. Parry, *Queen Caroline*, 196-205; E.A. Smith, *Queen on Trial*,

28. [16] *The Times*, 9, 15, 16 Aug. 1820. [17] *Ann. Reg.* (1820), Chron. pp. 417-20; *The Times*, 12, 15 Sept. 1820. [18] *The Times*, 18 Sept. 1820. [19] *Geo. IV Letters*, ii. 884; George, x. 13975; Add. 51662, Bedford to Holland [1820]; 51831, Whitbread to same, 17 Dec. 1820; *Cambridge and Hertford Independent Press*, 6, 20 Jan. 1821. [20] *The Times*, 27 Jan., 14 Feb. 1821; HLRO, Hist. Coll. 379, Grey Bennet diary, 25. [21] *The Times*, 19 June 1821. [22] Reid, *Lord Durham*, i. 149. [23] *The Times*, 16 Apr. 1821. [24] *Geo. IV Letters*, ii. 938. [25] Grey Bennet diary, 115. [26] George, x. 14193-4. [27] *The Times*, 22, 27 Mar., 10, 15 May 1821. [28] Ibid. 20 June, 6 July 1822. [29] Ibid. 21 May, 3 June 1823. [30] Ibid. 2 July 1823, 21 June 1826. [31] Ibid. 24 May, 3 June 1823, 18 Mar. 1826. [32] *Edgeworth Letters*, 346, 354, 369. [33] *Creevey Pprs.* ii. 71. [34] *The Times*, 16, 27 Mar. 1824. [35] Ibid. 13 Apr. 1824. [36] Ibid. 27 May, 3 June 1824, 16 Mar. 1825. [37] *Gent. Mag.* (1824), i. 636; Grey mss, Ellice to Grey, 25 Aug. 1824; Broughton, *Recollections*, iii. 161; *Edgeworth Letters*, 545. [38] *Session of Parl. 1825*, p. 490. [39] *The Times*, 16-18 Mar., 20 Apr., 19 May 1825. [40] Ibid. 23 Feb., 3 June 1825. [41] Ibid. 22 Feb. 1826. [42] Add. 51655, Mackintosh to Lady Holland, 6 Oct. 1825; *The Times*, 14 Feb.; *Courier*, 20 June; *Globe*, 20 June 1826. [43] *The Times*, 21 June 1826. [44] Ibid. 7, 8 June 1827. [45] George, x. 15422. [46] Grey mss, Ellice to Grey, 2, 6, 14 Apr. 1828. [47] *Russell Letters*, ii. 257-9. [48] *Herts Mercury*, 20 Feb. 1830; *Oakley Hunt* ed. J. Godber (*Beds. Hist. Rec. Soc.* xliv), 49-58, 73-76. [49] Broughton, iv. 28. [50] *Courier*, 6 Aug. 1830; C.T. Flick, 'The Bedford Election of 1830', *Beds. Hist. Rec. Soc.* xxxix. 160-170. [51] *The Times*, 10, 11, 16-18, 20, 21 Sept. 1830. [52] A.F. Cricket, *1830 Riots in Beds.* (*Beds. Hist. Rec. Soc.* lvii); *Russell Letters*, ii. 299; *County Herald*, 22 Jan.; *The Times*, 22 Mar. 1831. [53] *Cambridge and Hertford Independent Press*, 30 Apr., 7, 14, 21 May 1831. [54] *The Times*, 29 June 1832. [55] Ibid. 28 May; *Ann. Reg.* (1879), Chron. p. 81. [56] *Bedford Mercury*, 31 May 1879. [57] *The Times*, 15 Aug. 1879; IR26/3157/76.

M.M.E.

WHITBREAD, William Henry (1795–1867), of Southill, nr. Biggleswade, Beds.

BEDFORD   1818–1834

b. 4 Jan. 1795, 2nd but 1st surv. s. of Samuel Whitbread† of Southill and Elizabeth, da. of Lt.-Gen. Sir Charles Grey of Falloden, Northumb.; bro. of Samuel Charles Whitbread*. *educ.* Eton 1808; Trinity Coll. Camb. 1813. *m.* (1) 10 June 1819, Judith (*d.* 25 June 1845), da. of George Pigott of Cambridge, *s.p.*; (2) 6 Nov. 1845, Harriet, da. of Rev. Wettenhall Sneyd of Newchurch, I.o.W., wid. of Turner Macan of Carriff, co. Armagh, *s.p. suc.* fa. 1815. *d.* 21 June 1867.
Sheriff, Beds. 1837-8.

As head of the family from 1815, Whitbread owned landed property, which included over 12,000 contiguous acres in Bedfordshire, worth well in excess of £20,000 a year. At the same time, he had inherited very substantial debts, which required 'a plan' of 'management' to keep under control. Shortly before he came of age in January 1816, his uncle Edward Ellice*, the Whig man of business, wrote that 'he has an excellent heart, but like his father can be ... violent and obstinate in his opinions'.[1] In 1819, when he made what apparently turned out to be an unsatisfactory marriage, he joined the controlling partnership of the London brewery on which his grandfather had founded the family's fortunes, taking a personal capital share of £45,000.[2] Always overshadowed by his younger brother, his parents' favourite, he had none of his formidable father's talent and energy: he was, it seems, stolid and rather dim, though he was at least free from the inner demons which had tormented his father for much of his life.[3] Although he remained a staunch Whig, utterly loyal to his uncle Lord Grey, he made no significant mark in politics, which sometimes took second place to hunting and shooting. By the standards of many of his political associates, he was a poor attender of the House, where he is not known to have uttered a word in debate in this period.

He was again returned unopposed for Bedford on the long established family interest in 1820.[4] At the contested county election he nominated the Whig sitting Member, Lord Tavistock, the eldest son of the 6th duke of Bedford, the Whitbreads' ally in local politics, whose second son was the other borough Member. (There had been speculation earlier that he might himself be a candidate on the Whig interest.)[5] Whitbread voted against government on the civil list, 5, 8, 15, 16 May, Wilberforce's attempt to effect a compromise on the Queen Caroline affair, 22 June, and the barrack agreement bill, 17 July 1820. He was one of the signatories of the requisition for a county meeting in support of the queen, 14 Jan. 1821, when he seconded the resolutions.[6] He voted for the restoration of her name to the liturgy, 23, 26 Jan., 13 Feb., and for the opposition censure motion, 6 Feb. He voted, as ever, for Catholic relief, 28 Feb. His only known votes for economy, retrenchment and tax reductions that session were on the army estimates, 12 Mar., the additional malt duty, 21 Mar. (he paired for their repeal, 3 Apr.), and the ordnance extraordinaries, 21 May. He voted for the disqualification of ordnance officials from voting in parliamentary elections, 12 Apr. He was one of the Whig Members caught out at dinner by the unexpected division on Lambton's parliamentary reform motion, 18 Apr.;[7] but he was present to vote for Lord John Russell's scheme, 9 May, when he voted in condemnation of the delay in the commission of judicial inquiry. He divided for inquiries into the Peterloo massacre, 16 May, and the administration of justice in Tobago, 6 June, for abolition of the death penalty for forgery, 4 June (he had paired in the same sense, 23 May), and in the minority of 28 who censured the conduct of the Holy Alliance towards independent states, 20 June 1821. Perhaps mischievously, he made a claim to be allowed to act as an almoner at the coronation of George IV in August by virtue of his own-

ership of one third of the barony of Bedford; he was ignored.[8]

Whitbread voted for the amendment to the address, 5 Feb., and more extensive tax reductions to relieve distress, 11 Feb. 1822; but his only recorded votes of the session in that line were on the salt duties, 28 Feb., the lottery tax, 1 July, and the window tax, 2 July. He divided for cuts in the army estimates, 4 Mar., the ordnance estimates, 27 Mar., and diplomatic expenditure, 15, 16 May. He voted for investigation of the alleged attack on Alderman Waithman* at the queen's funeral, 28 Feb, remission of Henry Hunt's* gaol sentence, 24 Apr., inquiries into the government of the Ionian Isles, 14 May, and chancery administration, 26 June, and in protest at the increasing influence of the crown, 24 June. At the Bedfordshire county reform meeting, 20 Apr. 1822, he seconded the petition moved by Bedford, and declared that

reform was absolutely necessary, for the purpose of alleviating the present great and almost intolerable distress ... If to be an advocate for a thorough ... reform was to be a radical, he ... would feel proud to be called 'a thorough radical' ... The present profuse expenditure ... would work its own remedy ... Ministers would no longer be able to keep up the system, when the sources of that extravagant expenditure were exhausted ... It would make any honest man's heart ache to see the hard earnings of the industrious poor converted by a corrupt House of Commons to the use of a profligate administration.[9]

For all this stirring rhetoric, Whitbread evidently did not attend to support Russell's reform motion two days later, and neither does his name appear in the surviving list of those who paired for it.

He presented a petition from Bedford tradesmen for reform of the insolvency laws, 18 Feb. 1823, and the following day paired for abolition of the post of lieutenant-general of the ordnance in peacetime.[10] His only known votes that session were for repeal of the assessed taxes, 18 Mar., and of the Foreign Enlistment Act, 16 Apr., inquiries into the prosecution of the Dublin Orange rioters, 22 Apr., and the cost of the coronation, 19 June, and Russell's reform motion, 24 Apr. It is not clear whether it was he or his brother, Member for Middlesex (with whom he was a genial host of 'a most agreeable dinner' at the Chiswell Street brewery in May)[11] who voted against ministers on the beer and malt taxes, 28 May 1823. He was in a minority of eight for a substantial reduction of manpower in the army, 23 Feb. 1824. He voted with opposition on the complaint against the lord chancellor, 1 Mar., repeal of some assessed taxes, 2 Mar., 10 May, the Scottish judicial inquiry, 30 Mar., the aliens bill,

2 Apr., the grant for building new churches, 9 Apr., and the trial of the Methodist missionary John Smith in Demerara, 11 June. He was in the minority against proceeding with the beer duties bill, 24 May 1824. Whitbread voted against the legislation to suppress the Catholic Association, 15, 18, 21, 25 Feb. 1825. He divided for Catholic relief, 1 Mar., 21 Apr.,10 May. His only other known vote that session was for a repeal of assessed taxes, 3 Mar. In 1826 he voted against going into committee on the Bank Charter Acts, 13 Feb., and the ministerial salary of the president of the board of trade, 10 Apr., and for reform of Edinburgh's representation and Russell's general reform motion, 27 Apr. He handled the bill to revise the regulations governing the Harpur Charity in Bedford.[12] At the general election, when he and his colleague Lord George William Russell were unopposed there, he endorsed his colleague's hustings declarations in praise of recent liberal government policy, in support of reform and Catholic claims and in favour of adequate agricultural protection, and added the observation that 'after so long a period of peace as this country had enjoyed, we had a right to expect a much greater diminution of the public expenditure and consequent reduction of taxation than had yet taken place'. He again did the honours for Tavistock at the county nomination.[13]

The duke of Bedford heard that the electors of Bedford were disgruntled that neither of their Members had attended to vote against the duke of Clarence's grant, 16 Feb. 1827;[14] but Whitbread turned up to divide against his annuity bill, 2 Mar. He voted for Catholic relief, 6 Mar. He was in the majority for the spring guns bill, 23 Mar. He did not join Russell in attending the county meeting to petition the Lords to strengthen the protection afforded by the new corn bill, 23 May 1827.[15] He voted for repeal of the Test Acts, 26 Feb., paired for Catholic relief, 12 May, and voted in condemnation of the expense of improving Buckingham House, 23 June 1828. His only known votes in 1829 were for Catholic emancipation, 6, 30 Mar. He was rather more active in the lobbies in 1830, when he voted for the amendment to the address, 4 Feb., substantial tax reductions, 15 Feb., and various measures of economy and retrenchment, 22 Feb., 1, 12, 22 Mar., 3, 13 May, 14 June. He pleaded parliamentary attendance as his reason for not attending the county meeting to petition for repeal of the malt tax, 16 Feb.[16] He divided for Lord Blandford's reform plan, 18 Feb., the enfranchisement of Birmingham, Leeds and Manchester, 23 Feb., and general reform, 28 May. He was in the minority of 26 for preventing Members from voting in committee on measures in which they had a personal interest, 26 Feb.

He voted for Jewish emancipation, 5 Apr., 17 May. On 13 May he presented a petition from Bedford property owners against the appointment of commissioners for the northern roads scheme. The following day he voted for the production of information on privy councillors' emoluments, and he was in the opposition minorities on Irish first fruits, 18 May, and the commercial state of Ceylon, 27 May. He paired with them on the civil government of Canada, 25 May, as he did for Knatchbull's unsuccessful attempt to prohibit on-sales under the beer bill, 21 June 1830.

At the subsequent general election Whitbread became embroiled in a contest at Bedford, where the local Tories, masquerading as independents, mounted a strong challenge to the Russell interest, which had been damaged and made vulnerable by the persistent absenteeism of Lord George William, who was dropped by Bedford for his brother Lord John. There was some talk of Whitbread's stepping aside to avert a contest, in return for Russell support in the county, but nothing came of it.[17] On the hustings, he apparently said little on politics, beyond claiming to be 'independent' and to have supported the sale of beer bill, except on the on-sales provision, which posed a threat to country brewers. (A hostile newspaper had earlier credited him with unusually 'punctual attendance' to oppose it throughout.)[18] His seat was not in serious danger, and he topped the poll at the end of the bitter contest, which saw Russell beaten by one vote. He was said to have been 'most disinterested' and to have 'appeared more anxious for Lord John's success than his own'.[19] The Wellington ministry of course counted him among their 'foes', but he was one of the nine opposition Members who were at dinner when the House divided against them on the civil list, 15 Nov. 1830.[20] Next day he presented a Bedford petition for the abolition of slavery. At the borough reform meeting, 17 Jan. 1831, he called for support for his uncle's ministry, which was

composed of such men, who knew that the time is come when they have no longer to spend the public money to obtain patronage; that they are no longer to be dependent on peers of the realm; but that parliamentary reform is at hand, and all other good will follow in its train.[21]

He presented the meeting's petition, 8 Feb., and others from Ledbury and Bedford, 21 Mar., in support of the ministerial reform bill, for which he voted at its second reading, 22 Mar., and on Gascoyne's wrecking amendment, 19 Apr. 1831. At the subsequent general election he stood again for Bedford as 'a sincere supporter' of the measure 'in its most extended sense' and pledged himself 'not to be absent one hour from my duty, till we witness the defeat of the present corrupt system of representation'. He was returned without opposition. Nominating Tavistock for the county, he urged the freeholders to 'declare whether or not they considered a corrupt representation a bane, and whether they were anxious to be fairly represented'.[22]

Whitbread voted for the second reading of the reintroduced reform bill, 6 July, and against the adjournment, 12 July 1831. He was reasonably though not outstandingly assiduous in his attendance to support its details, and he is known to have paired for at least the divisions on Dorchester, 28 July, and Gateshead, 5 Aug. He voted for the passage of the bill, 21 Sept., and Lord Ebrington's confidence motion, 10 Oct. His only known votes on the revised bill were for the second reading, 17 Dec. 1831, going into committee, 20 Jan., the enfranchisement of Tower Hamlets, 28 Feb., and of Gateshead, 5 Mar., and the third reading, 22 Mar. 1832. He was initially listed as an absentee from the division on Ebrington's motion for an address calling on the king to appoint only ministers who would carry the bill unimpaired, 10 May; but it subsequently emerged that he had taken a pair.[23] He voted for the second reading of the Irish reform bill, 25 May, and paired for the Scottish measure, 1 June, and in support of government on the Russian-Dutch loan, 12, 16 July. At the Bedford dinner to celebrate the enactment of reform, 27 June 1832, he claimed to have 'invariably supported' the Grey ministry and denounced the 'nonsensical opposition' which had been raised to reform.[24]

Tavistock speculated in October 1832 that Whitbread might one day come in for the county, but he never did.[25] At the general election that year he was returned at the head of the poll for the borough. He was, however, defeated in 1835, and again in 1841. He died at Southill in June 1867 and was succeeded in the family estates by his brother. By his will, dated 9 Oct. 1863, he devised part of his personal share in the brewery, to the tune of £50,000, to his nephew Samuel Whitbread[†].

[1] R. Fulford, *Samuel Whitbread*, 88-96; D. Rapp, 'Social Mobility in 18th Cent.', *EcHR* (ser. 2), xxvii (1974), 383-4; Grey mss, Ellice to Grey, 3 Aug., 13 Sept., 27 Dec. 1815, 10, 26 Jan., 29 Aug., 8 Dec. 1816. [2] Blakiston, *Lord William Russell*, 146; P. Mathias, *Brewing Industry in England*, 311-12. [3] Fulford, 70-71. [4] *Cambridge and Hertford Independent Press*, 4, 11 Mar.; *Northampton Mercury*, 11 Mar. 1820. [5] *Cambridge and Hertford Independent Press*, 18 Mar. 1820; Beds. RO, Wrest mss L 30/11/20/13. [6] *Cambridge and Hertford Independent Press*, 6, 20 Jan. 1821. [7] *The Times*, 19 Apr. 1821. [8] *VCH Beds.* iii. 15; Fulford, 95-96. [9] *Cambridge and Hertford Independent Press*, 13, 27 Apr. 1822. [10] *The Times*, 19, 21 Feb. 1823. [11] *Creevey Pprs.* ii. 71. [12] *The Times*, 24, 25 Feb. 1826. [13] *Cambridge and Hertford Independent Press*, 17 June, 8 July 1826.

[14] *Russell Letters*, i. 86. [15] *Herts. Mercury*, 26 May 1827. [16] Ibid. 20 Feb. 1830. [17] Ibid. 17 July 1830. [18] R.M. Muggeridge, *Hist. of Late Contest for Bedford* (1830), 37; *Herts. Mercury*, 17 July 1830. [19] *Russell Letters*, ii. 267. [20] *The Times*, 19 Nov.; *Herts. Mercury*, 20 Nov. 1830. [21] *Cambridge and Hertford Independent Press*, 22 Jan. 1831. [22] Ibid. 30 Apr., 7 May 1831. [23] *The Times*, 14 May 1832. [24] *Cambridge and Hertford Independent Press*, 30 June 1832. [25] *Russell Letters*, i. 183.

D.R.F.

WHITE, Henry (1787–1873), of Hacketstown, co. Dublin.

Co. DUBLIN	11 Feb. 1823–1832
Co. LONGFORD	1837–1847
Co. LONGFORD	1857–June 1861

b. 1787,[1] 4th s. of Luke White* (*d.* 1824) of Woodlands, co. Dublin and 1st w. Elizabeth, da. of Andrew de la Maziere of Fleet Street, Dublin; bro. of Luke White[†] and Samuel White*. *educ.* Trinity, Dublin, aged 17⅓, 2 Oct. 1804. *m.* 3 Oct. 1828, Ellen, da. of William Soper Dempster of Skibo Castle, Sutherland, 6s. (4 *d.v.p.*) 2da. *suc.* bro. Luke to Woodlands and Rathcline, co. Longford 1854; *cr.* Bar. Annaly 19 Aug. 1863. *d.* 3 Sept. 1873.
  Ld. lt. co. Longford 1850-d.
  Cornet 14 Drag. 1811, lt. 1812, res. 1813.
  Lt.-col. co. Dublin militia; col. co. Longford militia 1837-d.

White, who saw action in the Peninsula and was awarded a medal with two clasps following the battles of Badajoz and Salamanca, was initially, like his brothers, brought forward for Parliament by his father Luke, a self-made man who had purchased a large estate near Dublin and gained a seat for Leitrim. Unexpectedly, when a vacancy arose for county Dublin in the winter of 1822 it was not his eldest brother and fellow militia officer Colonel Thomas White, who had fought contests there at the general elections of 1818 and 1820, nor his other brothers Samuel and Luke, who later represented Leitrim and Longford, but Henry who offered. Thomas was perceived to be ambivalent in his attitude to the Catholics, which may have been partly why he declined, but Henry, whose father was venerated locally, was considered their friend and rapidly gained popular support. In his address, 26 Dec. 1822, he exploited the recent Dublin theatre riot to emphasize his loyal but anti-Orange sentiments, and he moved the congratulatory address to the pro-Catholic lord lieutenant Lord Wellesley at a county meeting, 8 Jan. 1823. He claimed to be of no party on the hustings the following month, when he was enthusiastically endorsed by Daniel O'Connell*, and after a lengthy contest he triumphantly defeated his Tory opponent, despite the latter's extensive territorial interest.[2]

He voted to reduce taxes by £7,000,000, 28 Feb., and, unless it was his father, by £2,000,000, 3 Mar. 1823.[3] He divided for inquiries into the Irish church, 4 Mar., and the state of Ireland, 12 May. He voted for information on Inverness municipal elections, 26 Mar., parliamentary reform, 24 Apr., and alteration of the Scottish representative system, 2 June. He divided for inquiry into the legal proceedings against the Dublin Orange rioters, 22 Apr. He was in opposition minorities for abolition of the death penalty for larceny, 21 May, condemning the conduct of the lord advocate in the Borthwick case, 3 June, and inquiry into chancery administration, 5 June 1823. He criticized the taxes levied by Dublin corporation at a county meeting, 16 Feb. 1824, and apparently missed the start of the new session following the death that month of his father, under whose will he received £13,000 a year.[4] He voted for an advance of capital to Ireland, 4 May, inquiry into the state of Ireland, 11 May, and to condemn the trial of the Methodist missionary John Smith in Demerara, 11 June 1824. White, who that summer announced his intention of standing at the next election, was made a member of the Catholic Association in October 1824.[5] He divided steadily against the Irish unlawful societies bill in February 1825, and on the 23rd presented a petition from Rathmines against it, being convinced, as he wrote to the petition's sponsor, that 'the passing this bill, without another to emancipate the Catholics of Ireland, will have no other effect than to perpetuate the animosities which have so long distracted that country'.[6] He duly voted for Catholic relief, 1 Mar., 21 Apr., 10 May. He was admitted to Brooks's, 4 Mar., proposed by Lord Duncannon* and Sir John Newport*. He divided for repeal of the window tax, 17 May 1825, and regulation of the Irish first fruits fund 20 Mar. 1826. In February 1826 he attended the O'Connellite dinner for the friends of civil and religious liberty, signing the ensuing Protestant petition for Catholic relief, and another in Dublin in honour of Henry Villiers Stuart, the soon-to-be Member for county Waterford.[7]

Dwelling on his former victory, White stood again with his like-minded colleague Richard Wogan Talbot at the general election of 1826, when he was returned with Catholic support after another fierce contest against a local Protestant Tory landlord; he survived a petition.[8] Seemingly much less active in the new Parliament, he divided for inquiry into the allegations against the corporation of Leicester, 15 Mar., and, unless it was Samuel White, took three weeks' leave, 1

May 1827. He voted for Catholic emancipation, 6 Mar. 1827, 12 May 1828, 6, 30 Mar. 1829. He divided for O'Connell being allowed to take his seat unimpeded, 18 May 1829. He joined in the opposition's renewed campaign for economies and tax reductions, 9 Mar., 3, 10 May, 7 (when he voted against abolition of the death penalty for forgery) and 14 June 1830. In April he was a prominent requisitionist for the two county Dublin meetings against the increased Irish spirit and stamp duties.[9] His only other known votes that session were for Jewish emancipation, 17 May, to make Irish first fruits no longer nominal, 18 May, parliamentary reform, 28 May, and against the administration of justice bill, 18 June 1830.

Although it was at one point rumoured that he might retire at the dissolution of 1830, his paternal and personal claims and the withdrawal of Talbot led to his being returned in second place with the Whig Lord Brabazon against one of his former challengers. He had received the tacit support of the Wellington administration, but distanced himself from it at the end of the contest and at his election dinner.[10] Like Samuel, he was reckoned by Pierce Mahony[†] to be 'pro-government', but ministers listed him among the 'good doubtfuls', and he voted against them on the civil list, 15 Nov. 1830. He voted for the second reading of the Grey ministry's reform bill, 22 Mar., and against Gascoyne's wrecking amendment, 19 Apr. 1831. At the ensuing general election, when he advocated the introduction of poor laws to Ireland but objected to calls for repeal of the Union, he was returned unopposed as a reformer. In April he signed his county's address thanking the lord lieutenant Lord Anglesey for defending the Union and in June 1831 he was a requisitionist for the county reform meeting.[11]

White divided for the second reading of the reintroduced reform bill, 6 July, at least twice against adjourning proceedings on it, 12 July 1831, and generally for its details. He was named to the Dublin election committee, 28 July, but, when it was pointed out that he had voted (presumably for the reformers Robert Way Harty* and Louis Perrin*) in the city contest, the Speaker ruled that the ballot would have to be repeated. The following day O'Connell divided the House, but only mustered 82 (including Samuel, while Henry apparently abstained) against 100 for swearing him with the rest of the original committee.[12] Having registered a wayward vote with the minority for printing the Waterford petition for disarming the Irish yeomanry, 11 Aug., he sided with ministers for punishing those guilty of bribery in the Dublin election and against censuring the Irish government over it, 23 Aug.

He was absent from the division on the passage of the reform bill, 21 Sept., but voted for Lord Ebrington's confidence motion, 10 Oct. 1831. Forwarding an unsuccessful peerage application on his behalf later that year, Anglesey commented to Lord Grey that he was 'a very staunch supporter of your government, and has always advocated liberal politics, and the family is very affluent'.[13] White voted for the second reading of the revised reform bill, 17 Dec. 1831, again steadily for its details, and for the third reading, 22 Mar. 1832. He divided against the production of information on Portugal, 9 Feb., but was listed in the minority for Thomas Lefroy's amendment to recommit the Irish registry of deeds bill, 9 Apr. Having sided with ministers for Ebrington's motion for an address calling on the king to appoint only ministers who would carry the reform bill unimpaired, 10 May, he voted for the second reading of the Irish bill, 25 May, and against increasing the county representation of Scotland, 1 June, but he was in O'Connell's minority for extending the Irish franchise to £5 freeholders, 18 June. Apart from the one for making coroners' inquests public, 20 June, his only other known votes that session were in the government majorities for the Russian-Dutch loan, 16, 20 July, and in the small minorities for amendments to the Irish tithes composition bill, 1 Aug. Perhaps for reasons of ill health, he announced his resignation in an address, 20 July 1832, when he stated that his original success in establishing the county's independence had been consolidated by the passage of reform and now enabled him to pass on the seat to another Member on the same interest.[14]

White returned to Parliament in two spells as Member for county Longford, where he inherited substantial estates and held local office, and was awarded a peerage in 1863. On his death in September 1873, the title was inherited by his eldest son Luke (1829-88), who, like his younger brother Charles William (1838-90), enjoyed a short career in the Commons.[15]

[1] *Al. Dub.* 873, though *Burke PB* (1930), 119 gives 1789 and *CP*, i. 162 gives 1791. [2] *Dublin Evening Post*, 28 Dec. 1822, 9, 11, 14 Jan., 1, 4, 11, 13, 15, 18 Feb. 1823; *O'Connell Corresp.* ii. 996, 999. [3] Votes by 'Col. White' have been attributed to him throughout. [4] *Dublin Evening Post*, 17 Feb.; *Roscommon and Leitrim Gazette*, 10 Apr. 1824. [5] *Dublin Evening Post*, 17 Aug., 12 Oct. 1824. [6] *Morning Register*, 24 Feb.; *The Times*, 24 Feb. 1825. [7] *Dublin Evening Post*, 4, 21 Feb., 23 Mar. 1826. [8] Ibid. 8, 10, 13, 15, 24 June, 6, 11 July 1826. [9] Ibid. 22, 27, 29 Apr. 1830. [10] Ibid. 3, 8, 10, 15 July, 10, 17, 19, 28 Aug.; *Warder*, 17 July; NAI, Leveson Gower letter bks. Leveson Gower to Brabazon, 6 July 1830. [11] *Dublin Evening Post*, 5, 30 Apr.; 17 May, 16 June 1831. [12] *CJ*, lxxxvi. 706-9. [13] PRO NI, Anglesey mss D619/28C, pp. 206-8. [14] *Dublin Evening Post*, 19, 24 July 1832. [15] Ibid. 6 Sept. 1873.

S.M.F.

WHITE, Luke (c.1750–1824), of Woodlands, (formerly Luttrellstown), co. Dublin and Porters, Shenley, Herts.

CO. LEITRIM   1818–25 Feb. 1824

b. c.1750. *m.* (1) 6 Feb. 1781, Elizabeth, da. of Andrew de la Maziere of Fleet Street, Dublin, 4s. 4da. (1 *d.v.p.*); (2) 6 Jan. 1801, Arabella, da. of William Fortescue of Cork,[1] 1s. *d.* 25 Feb. 1824.
Sheriff, co. Dublin 1804-5, co. Longford 1806-7; gov. co. Leitrim 1817-*d.*

In 1803 Lady Hardwicke, the wife of the Irish viceroy, gave the following account of White, who had risen from obscurity as a bookseller to accumulate great wealth as a speculator and contractor for government loans:

He was the servant of an auctioneer of books (some say he first cried newspapers about the streets). As he rose in his finances, he sold a few pamphlets on his own account ... His talent for figures soon made him his master's clerk, and he afterwards was taken into a lottery office, where his calculations soon procured him a partnership. Good luck attended him in every speculation, and he knew how to profit by it, but *with the fairest fame*. He continued his trade in books on the great scale, and was equally successful in all the train of money transactions ... His next view was landed property to a great amount. Lord Carhampton* ... determined to sell his estate at Luttrellstown ... which place Mr. Luke White bought, to the great offence of all the aristocrats in Ireland ... As it was wished by Lord Hardwicke that some attention should be paid to this extraordinary man, I suggested ... that we should propose to come and see it, both Mr. White and his wife being too modest to invite us, without our previously intimating that we wished it. A breakfast was therefore settled for this day, and no doubt the loan, the lottery or the stocks never gave Mr. White half the trouble and perplexity of this party ... The day was excellent and we all proceeded in grand cavalcade to Woodlands, the name of the place being changed, some say at the desire of Lord Carhampton. Mr. White is a very well-looking man of fifty, and has a very fine countenance, sensible and penetrating ... Mrs. White is a very well-behaved little woman, without fuss or bustle. His manners I thought particularly good. There were about sixty people, with a magnificent breakfast, and the party afterwards walked or drove about the grounds, which are most extremely beautiful. We then returned to the house and found ices, etc., and after a little very good music we departed, much pleased with our day on our own account, and far more for our hosts, for it would have been very uncomfortable had there been any mishap or awkwardness that could have raised a smile on the saucy faces of Dublin.[2]

White, who also had parliamentary ambitions on his sons' accounts, retained his seat for county Leitrim without opposition at the general election of 1820, when his son Thomas was again the defeated candidate in county Dublin, but his son Luke did not persist in again contesting county Longford.[3] A 'decided reformer', as Daniel O'Connell* described him, White continued to oppose government when present.[4] He took a month's leave, 4 July 1820. He attended to vote against the omission of Queen Caroline's name from the liturgy, 23 Jan. 1821. He paired for further divisions on the queen, 26 Jan., 6, 13 Feb., but on one of these occasions evidently did so with Carhampton and each 'went comfortably off to bed, without finding out that they were on the same side'.[5] He condemned the conduct of the sheriff of Dublin in curtailing the pro-Caroline county meeting, and voted for inquiry into this in the House, 22 Feb.[6] He divided for Catholic relief, 28 Feb., when he thanked the pro-Catholic Irish secretary Charles Grant for his 'excellent and manly speech in behalf of his suffering country'. On 23 Mar. he denied allegations that Irish Catholics were hostile to the relief bill: they were 'most warmly engaged in its favour'.[7] He voted to make Leeds, scheduled for enfranchisement in place of Grampound, a scot and lot borough, 2 Mar., and for parliamentary reform, 18 Apr. He divided to end the duty on farm horses, 5 Mar., and paired for repeal of the additional malt duty, 3 Apr. 1821. He voted for more extensive tax reductions to relieve distress, 11 Feb. 1822, and for other economies that session. He divided for parliamentary reform, 25 Apr., and Brougham's condemnation of the influence of the crown, 24 June. He voted against the Irish constables bill, 7 June, and for tithe reform, 19 June 1822.

In January 1823 White spoke at the county Dublin meeting in support of the pro-Catholic viceroy Lord Wellesley after the Orange demonstration against him the previous year. His reputation as a resident and independent landlord helped secure the return of his son Henry for county Dublin at a by-election, which he attended, the following month.[8] Either he or Henry divided for repeal of £2,000,000 in taxes, 3 Mar. The next day White voted for inquiry into the Irish church establishment. Denying charges that Catholic priests had improperly influenced voters to secure his son's election, 17 Apr., he said:

> They were a most exemplary body of men. If people were better informed about Ireland, its population would not be maligned and calumniated. A concession of the claims was not so much a boon to the Catholics as a grant for the sake of the peace and security of the empire.

He spoke to the same effect, 22 Apr., and said a few 'inaudible' words on the Irish joint tenancy bill, 27

May.[9] He paired for parliamentary reform, 24 Apr., and voted for Scottish reform, 2 June. He divided against the silk bill, 9 June, to inquire into naval promotions, 19 June, and for the Scottish juries bill, 20 June 1823. His last recorded vote was for information on the government's attitude to the Franco-Spanish war, 17 Feb. 1824.

White, who was reputed to have 'realized the largest fortune ever made by trade in Ireland', died in February 1824.[10] On the 27th the duke of Bedford commented to Lady Holland: 'Old Luke White will *cut up well* and tallow richly on the kidneys. This is butcher's language and I dare say unintelligible to you, but in plain English he must have died immensely rich'.[11] So he did, leaving property amounting to at least £30,000 a year in real estate and £100,000 in cash and securities. In his will, dated 4 July 1823, he directed that his Hertfordshire property be sold and the proceeds added to his personal estate. He distributed his lands in eight Irish counties and his property in Dublin among his four sons with his first wife. He made handsome provision for his daughters, continued to his second wife for life the annuity of £1,000 which he had secured to her 'on our separation', and to his son with her, William White (1801-57), he gave £500 a year until he reached 25, when he became entitled to the sum of £10,000. White's eldest son Thomas (d. 1847), who never entered the Commons despite several attempts, fared relatively poorly, allegedly because he had refused to stand for county Dublin as a supporter of Catholic relief. His second son, Samuel, replaced him as Member for Leitrim; his third, Luke (d. 1854), who stood unsuccessfully for Leitrim in 1830 and Longford in 1831, came in for the latter as a Liberal after the passage of the Reform Act; and his fourth, Henry, who left the representation of county Dublin in 1832, also later represented Longford.[12]

[1] IGI. [2] A.J.C. Hare, *Two Noble Lives*, i. 13-17. [3] *HP Commons, 1790-1820*, v. 545-6; *Dublin Evening Post*, 29 Feb. 1820; Rosse mss D/7/107, 112 (NRA 25548). [4] *O'Connell Corresp.* ii. 996; *Black Bk.* (1823), 202. [5] Buckingham, *Mems. Geo. IV*, i. 122. [6] *Dublin Evening Post*, 9 Jan. 1821. [7] *The Times*, 24 Mar. 1821. [8] *Dublin Evening Post*, 9 Jan., 1, 4 1823; *O'Connell Corresp.* ii. 982. [9] *The Times*, 23 Apr. 1823. [10] *Ann. Reg.* (1854), Chron. p. 330. [11] Add. 51668. [12] PROB 11/1686/329; *Gent. Mag.* (1824), i. 642; *Roscommon and Leitrim Gazette*, 10 Apr. 1824.

D.R.F./S.M.F.

WHITE, Samuel (c.1784–1854), of Killakee, co. Dublin.

CO. LEITRIM   5 Apr. 1824–1847

b. c.1784, 2nd s. of Luke White* (*d.* 1824) of Woodlands, co. Dublin and 1st w. Elizabeth, da. of Andrew de la Maziere of Fleet Street, Dublin; bro. of Henry White* and Luke White†. *m.* 4 July 1821, Salisbury Anne, da. of George Rothe of Mount Rothe, co. Kilkenny, *s.p. d.* 29 May 1854.
    Sheriff, co. Leitrim 1809-10.

White may have served briefly in the army.[1] He received £7,000 a year under the will of his father Luke, the founder of the family's banking fortune, who died in February 1824. Offering to replace him as Member for Leitrim, he declared his principles to be those of his father, who he said 'loved Ireland and belonged to no party'. As nothing came of a threatened opposition, he was returned at the by-election in April and, although silent in the Commons, he emulated his brother Henry, Member for county Dublin (with whom his parliamentary conduct may sometimes have been confused), by attending frequently and voting with the Whig opposition to Lord Liverpool's ministry.[2] He divided for an advance of capital to Ireland, 4 May, inquiries into the Irish church establishment, 6 May, and the state of Ireland, 11 May, and against the Irish insurrection bill, 14 June 1824, when he also voted twice against the new churches bill. He was one of the Irish Members added to the select committee on the state of Ireland that was appointed on 17 Feb. 1825.[3] He voted against the Irish unlawful societies bill, 15, 18, 21, 25 Feb., and for Catholic relief, 1 Mar., 21 Apr., 10 May. He divided in minorities for repealing the assessed and window taxes, 3 Mar., 17 May 1825, and for Hume's attempt to add a clause to the promissory notes bill to enforce payment in specie, 27 Feb. 1826. Although criticized by his pro-Catholic supporters for supposedly allying with his Orangeman colleague John Clements, who in the end withdrew, he boasted of having followed his father's liberal and independent conduct on being returned unopposed, with the Whig Lord Clements, at the general election later that year.[4] He served as foreman of the Leitrim grand jury that summer, and again in 1830, and from early 1827 began to build a residence in the county.[5]

He voted for Catholic relief, 6 Mar., but was granted leave for a month on account of ill health, 14 Mar., and again (unless it was his brother) for three weeks after having served on an election committee, 1 May 1827. He again divided for emancipation, 12 May 1828, 6,

30 Mar. 1829. He was listed in the opposition majority against the Bathurst and Dundas pensions, 26 Mar., voted for Jewish emancipation, 5 Apr., 17 May, and divided in the minority against Lord Ellenborough's divorce bill, 6 Apr. 1830. If it was he, and not Henry, who was given a month's leave on urgent private business, 3 May, he was nevertheless present to vote for a return of privy councillors' emoluments, 14 May, and to make Irish first fruits revenues no longer nominal, 18 May. He sided with opposition for reducing the grants for South American missions, 7 June, and Nova Scotia and Prince Edward Island, 14 June. Forced to deny rumours that he would stand down at the general election, he was beaten into second place by John Clements, but, against expectations, narrowly defeated Lord Clements, to whose insulting remarks on the hustings he took grave exception.[6] He was considered by Pierce Mahony† to be 'pro-government', but ministers only reckoned him among the 'good doubtfuls' and he voted against them on the civil list, 15 Nov. 1830. He divided for the second reading of the Grey ministry's reform bill, 22 Mar., and against Gascoyne's wrecking amendment, 19 Apr. 1831. Despite having to travel to France for what he termed 'family circumstances', he was returned unopposed as a reformer at the ensuing general election.[7]

White voted for the second reading of the reintroduced reform bill, 6 July, at least twice against adjourning proceedings on it, 12 July 1831, and steadily (sometimes by pairing) for its details. On 29 July he divided for O'Connell's motion for swearing the original Dublin election committee, from which his brother Henry had been disqualified. He paired for the passage of the reform bill, 21 Sept., but attended to vote for the second reading of the Scottish bill, 23 Sept., and Lord Ebrington's confidence motion, 10 Oct. After pairing for the second reading of the revised reform bill, 17 Dec. 1831, he divided for the disfranchisement schedules, 20, 23 Jan., again usually for its details, and for the third reading, 22 Mar. 1832. He sided with government against producing information on Portugal, 3 Feb., and an amendment to the navy civil departments bill, 6 Apr., but was in minorities for printing the Woollen Grange petition for the abolition of Irish tithes, 16 Feb., and against the tithes bill, 13 July. An absentee from the division on Ebrington's motion for an address calling on the king to appoint only ministers who would carry the reform bill unimpaired, 10 May, he voted for the second reading of the Irish measure, 25 May, and against increasing the Scottish county representation, 1 June. He divided for making coroners' inquests public, 20 June. His only other known votes were with ministers for the Russian-

Dutch loan, 26 Jan., 12, 16, 20 July. Following what he described as a struggle 'of unexampled duration and difficulty', he called for further reforms at the general election of 1832, when he was returned as a Liberal for county Leitrim, where he now had a sizeable personal interest.[8] He died, childless, in May 1854, seven years after leaving Parliament and three months before the death of his brother Luke, former Member for county Longford.[9]

[1] According to the *Army Lists*, one Samuel White became cornet, 9 Drag. in 1801 and retired as capt. in 1808. [2] *Roscommon and Leitrim Gazette*, 6, 13, 27 Mar., 10 Apr. 1824; *Session of Parl. 1825*, p. 490. [3] Add. 40373, f. 187. [4] *Dublin Evening Post*, 25, 30 May; *Roscommon and Leitrim Gazette*, 10, 24 June, 15 July 1826. [5] A. Harrison, *Leitrim Sheriffs*, 10; *Roscommon and Leitrim Gazette*, 10 Mar. 1827. [6] *Roscommon and Leitrim Gazette*, 17 July, 14, 21 Aug.; *Dublin Evening Post*, 17 Aug. 1830; Add. 40338, f. 223. [7] *Roscommon and Leitrim Gazette*, 5, 21 May 1831. [8] Ibid. 17 Nov., 8, 22, 29 Dec. 1832. [9] Ibid. 3 June; *The Times*, 31 May 1854; *Gent. Mag.* (1854), ii. 393.

S.M.F.

WHITMORE, Thomas (1782–1846), of Apley Park, Salop.

BRIDGNORTH   1806–1831

b. 16 Nov. 1782, 1st s. of Thomas Whitmore[†] of Apley and 2nd w. Mary, da. of Capt. Thomas Foley, RN, of Stockton, Salop. *educ.* Eton 1796-9; Christ Church, Oxf. 1799. *m.* 19 July 1804, Catherine, da. and h. of Thomas Thomason, MD, of York, 3s. 3da. *suc.* fa. 1795. *d.* 6 Feb. 1846.
Recorder, Bridgnorth 1805-36; sheriff, Salop 1805-6.

A partner in the London bank of Chatteris, Whitmore and Company, Whitmore was responsible for rebuilding Apley Park, 'one of the most costly and splendid mansions in the county', and had represented nearby Bridgnorth, where he was the recorder and controlled at least one seat, since the first election after his coming of age.[1] He was an anti-Catholic Tory and silent supporter of Lord Liverpool's government, whose refusal to support the candidature of his fellow Wolverhampton Pitt Club member Ralph Benson* for Bridgnorth in 1820, so facilitating the return of his kinsman, the pro-Catholic Whig and political economist William Wolryche Whitmore, was strongly resisted and proved to be a great drain on his estate, then worth £20,000 a year.[2] Thereafter, although he continued to divide with administration, his reported parliamentary activities were prone to confusion with those of his much more active kinsman, and a radical publication of 1825 erroneously stated that he 'appeared to vote with opposition'.[3]

Whitmore joined his political allies in Shropshire, the 1st earl of Bradford, the Foresters of Willey Park and the 1st earl of Powis, in promoting a 'ministerialist' loyal address at the county meeting, 10 Jan., and he divided against censuring ministers' handling of Queen Caroline's case, 6 Feb. 1821.[4] Wayward votes credited to him for the restoration of her name to the liturgy, 26 Jan., reductions in the army, 15 Mar., and a return to 1797 salary levels, 30 Mar., can safely be attributed to Wolryche Whitmore.[5] He divided against Catholic relief, 28 Feb. 1821, 30 Apr. 1822, 1 Mar., 21 Apr. 1825, brought up hostile petitions from Bridgnorth, 15 Mar. 1821, 18 Apr. 1825, and was listed, probably erroneously, in the minority against the attendant Irish franchise bill, 26 Apr. 1825.[6] He distanced himself from the controversy which surrounded the Shropshire distress meeting, 25 Mar. 1822, and in November he chaired the committee which unsuccessfully promoted the return of the 'church and state' candidate William Lacon Childe* for the vacant county seat.[7] He voted against government for inquiry into the prosecution of the Dublin Orange rioters, 22 Apr. 1823, divided for the Irish unlawful societies bill, 25 Feb., and officiated at the Wolverhampton Pitt Club dinner, 29 May 1825.[8] Votes against the duke of Cumberland's grant credited to him, 6-10 June 1825, were almost certainly cast by Wolryche Whitmore. He claimed to represent both commercial and agricultural interests, but his views on his cousin's numerous motions for corn law reform are not known. A contest provoked by the late candidature of the anti-Catholic recorder of Bristol, Ebenezer Ludlow, made Whitmore's attendance at Bridgnorth at the 1826 general election essential despite 'severe indisposition' and cost him over £2,667 for hospitality without staunching opposition to the 'Whitmore pact'.[9]

As requested by the agriculturists at their meeting, 17 Feb., Whitmore presented Bridgnorth's petition for agricultural protection with another from Shifnal, 27 Feb. 1827.[10] He voted against Catholic relief, 6 Mar. 1827, 12 May 1828. Endorsing his application for an East India Company cadetship for a constituent in September 1828, the new president of the India board Lord Ellenborough informed the duke of Wellington, 'he is a Member, and a good friend, and this his first ask'.[11] He presided at the early meetings and dinners of the Shropshire Brunswick Club, which he declared to be 'entirely defensive' and calculated 'by every means to preserve unchanged our constitution in church and state', and he encouraged anti-Catholic petitioning.[12] Peel and Wellington's decision to concede emancipation dismayed him and, presenting a hostile Bridgnorth petition, 13 Feb. 1829, he said that 'whatever alteration had taken place in the opinion of others on the subject, his remained unchanged'. As the patronage secretary Planta predicted, he voted against the measure, 6, 18 Mar. (and paired, 30 Mar.) 1829. He divided against Jewish emancipation, 5 Apr., 17 May 1830. He probably voted against making forgery a non-capital offence, 7 June 1830. He topped the poll at Bridgnorth at the general election in August, when Richard Arkwright*, a stalwart of the Herefordshire Pitt Club, failed to oust Wolryche Whitmore, whose pro-Catholic votes, espousal of manufacturers' interests and campaign to end the East India Company's trading monopoly had proved divisive. When challenged over the latter, Whitmore declared that it was an issue on which he would choose not to vote.[13]

The Wellington ministry listed Whitmore among their 'friends', but he was absent from the division on the civil list which brought them down, 15 Nov. 1830. He refused to present Bridgnorth's petition endorsing the Grey ministry's reform bill, and voted against its second reading, 22 Mar., and for Gascoyne's wrecking amendment, 19 Apr. 1831.[14] He declared his candidature for Bridgnorth at the ensuing general election, 22 Apr., but his constituents accused him of 'upholding a system fraught with much venality and disgrace, as is evinced by the costly depravities of your own borough', evading window tax on his new mansion, and failing to represent their interests, and he stood down rather than risk defeat, 25 Apr. In his resignation address he defended his conduct and criticized the reform bill and Wolryche Whitmore, who came in unopposed with another reformer, the ironmaster James Foster. Denouncing the bill, he said that he trusted that the public would perceive

> its baneful effects before it is too late, and that they will not suffer themselves to be led away by the absurd and visionary schemes of the political economists and speculative theorists, but that this highly favoured country may soon be restored to that sound and healthy state which has for so long a period caused it to be the envy and admiration of the world.[15]

In the contest for Shropshire, he gave his interest to the sitting anti-reform Tory Rowland Hill, who topped the poll.[16]

A founder member of the Carlton Club, Whitmore declared early for the new Shropshire South seat at the general election of 1832, and was nominated at Church Stretton, 17 Dec. However, his hopes of an unopposed return were unexpectedly thwarted by the late nomination of Powis's second son Robert Henry Clive* following his defeat at Ludlow and, disappointed, he declined to proceed to a poll.[17] He refused to support the sitting Members at Bridgnorth, where he brought

in his son and heir Thomas Charlton Whitmore (1807-65), leaving the Pigot and Tracy families, whose ancient interests in the borough were boosted by the Reform Act, to contest the second seat.[18] Whitmore continued to finance and support Conservative candidates in Shropshire, but his patronage requests to Peel were ignored. He was also denied the peerage he coveted, and claimed in December 1834 that he had declined one offered to him in 1820.[19] Financially constrained in his later years, he raised £100,000 from land sales and left Apley Park, where he died in February 1846, encumbered by a £180,000 mortgage and settlements, which reduced its net annual income to under £5,000.[20] He was succeeded there by his eldest son, whose family were assured of £1,200 a year, but, bowing to financial pressure, his grandson Thomas Charles Douglas Whitmore sold out for £550,000 to James Foster's heir William Orme Foster[†] and purchased the Leicestershire estate of Gumley with the proceeds.[21]

[1] J.F.A. Mason, *Bridgnorth*, 28-30; C. Hulbert, *Hist. Salop*, ii. 173; *Von Neumann Diary*, ii. 192; *HP Commons, 1790-1820*, v. 548-9. [2] *Shrewsbury Chron.* 18, 25 Feb., 3 Mar.; *The Times*, 29 Feb.; *Wolverhampton Chron.* 1, 15 Mar.; *Wolverhampton Antiquary*, ii (1934), 10-25; Salop Archives, Weld-Forester mss 1224, box 337, J. Robins to J. Pritchard, 5, 6 Mar., Pritchard to C.W. Forester, 31 Mar.; Hatherton diary, 21 Mar 1820; *VCH Salop*, iv. 208. [3] *Session of Parl. 1825*, p. 490. [4] *Shrewsbury Chron.* 5 Jan.; *Salopian Jnl.* 17 Jan. 1821. [5] Lonsdale mss, Lowther to Lonsdale, 27 Jan. 1821. [6] *The Times*, 16 Mar. 1821, 4 Mar., 19 Apr. 1825. [7] Salop Archives 81/7; Salop Archives, Morris-Eyton mss 6003/3, Slaney jnl. 15 Nov.; *Shrewsbury Chron*, 15, 22 Nov.; *The Times*, 18 Nov. 1822. [8] *Wolverhampton Chron.* 17, 31 May 1825. [9] *John Bull*, 28 May; *The Times*, 29 May, 9 Oct.; *Wolverhampton Chron.* 14 June 1826; Salop Archives 4001/Admin, Bridgnorth Borough 7/49; 24/14; 26/14-17; 50, parl. returns; 3/6, common hall bk. pp. 148-208. [10] *Wolverhampton Chron.* 21, 28 Feb.; *The Times*, 28 Feb. 1827. [11] *Ellenborough Diary*, i. 223. [12] *Salopian Jnl.* 26 Nov. 1828, 14 Jan., 18 Feb. 1829. [13] *Wolverhampton Chron.* 14 July, 4, 11 Aug.; *Shrewsbury Chron.* 6 Aug. 1830. [14] *Shrewsbury Chron.* 18 Apr. 1831. [15] Ibid. 22, 29 Apr.; *Salopian Jnl.* 27 Apr., 4, 11 May 1831. [16] Salop Archives D45/1170/17. [17] *Wolverhampton Chron.* 13 June, 10 Oct., 26 Dec. 1832. [18] Ibid.; *Shrewsbury Chron.* 2 Nov. 1832. [19] Add. 40367, f. 13; 40406, f. 100; 40407, ff. 129-33; 40485, f. 181; 40570, f. 89. [20] V.J. Walsh, 'Diary of a Country Gentleman', *Trans. Salop Arch. Soc.* lix (1971-2), 145; *VCH Salop*, iv. 208. [21] PROB 11/2039/550; IR26/1757/361; *VCH Salop*, iii. 208, 215.

M.M.E.

WHITMORE, William Wolryche (1787–1858), of Dudmaston Hall, Quatt, Salop.[1]

BRIDGNORTH	1820–1832
WOLVERHAMPTON	1832–1834

bap. 16 Sept. 1787,[2] 1st s. of William Whitmore of Dudmaston and 1st w. Frances Barbara, da. of John Lyster of White Whitmore. *educ.* Shrewsbury 1799. *m.* 29 Jan. 1810, Hon. Lucy Elizabeth Georgiana Bridgman, da. of Orlando, 1st earl of Bradford, *s.p. suc.* fa. 1816. *d.* 11 Aug. 1858.
Ensign 1 Ft. Gds. 1804; lt.-col. 3 Salop militia 1808-15. Sheriff, Salop 1838-9.

Whitmore's father, a kinsman of the Whitmores of Apley, had succeeded to the Wolryche estate of Dudmaston on the death of Thomas Weld in 1774. The Wolryche baronetcy had been extinct since 1723, and though not required to take that name, he gave it to Whitmore as a baptismal one.[3] His mother died in 1792, and he spent his childhood in Shropshire with his nine sisters and a stepbrother and three step-sisters from his father's second marriage. He was bought a commission in the Grenadier Guards on leaving Shrewsbury, but promotion eluded him and, prompted by concern at his prolonged absence on active service in Sicily, his relations secured him a domestic appointment as second in command of his future father-in-law the 1st earl of Bradford's militia regiment, with which he served at Dover, Plymouth and in Ireland.[4] His wife Lucy (*d.* 17 Mar. 1840) had a jointure of £10,000 and, under a family set-tlement of 1 May 1809, land and valuable mineral rights in Leebotswood, Picklescote, Smethcote, and Woolstanson were transferred to Whitmore.[5] As his succession to Dudmaston, worth £3,000 a year, was assured, his father left him 'my love, and the late Colonel Weld's decorated Spanish gun' and made his sisters and half-brother John Henry (1797-1853), upon whom Chastleton, the Oxfordshire estate of their kinsman John Jones was settled (he assumed the name Jones after Whitmore, 14 Mar. 1829), the main benefi-ciaries of his will, which was proved under £30,000, 16 Jan. 1817. Afterwards, Whitmore authorized extensive alterations at Dudmaston and negotiated land sales and exchanges to consolidate his Shropshire holdings.[6]

He consistently 'refused to identify himself with the prescribed policy of any particular party', but his early political views were close to those of his wife's Whig cousin Lord John Russell*, with whom he trav-elled in Italy in 1814, and far removed from the anti-Catholic Toryism of Bradford and his cousin Thomas Whitmore of Apley, Member for Bridgnorth.[7] The

latter nevertheless tacitly endorsed his candidature for the vacant second seat there in 1820, when, profess-ing 'complete independence', he saw off his challeng-ers, the Tory Ralph Benson* and the anti-corporation candidate Edmund Lechmere Charlton† of Ludford.[8] Whitmore's early votes and minor speeches were regularly misattributed to Thomas Whitmore, unlike whom he generally divided with opposition and for Catholic relief, 28 Feb. 1821, 1 Mar., 21 Apr., 10 May 1825. He almost certainly voted against the attendant Irish franchise bill, 26 Apr. 1825 (a vote attributed to Thomas). He initially held aloof from the controversy surrounding Queen Caroline's case and joined his relations in supporting the contentious loyal address to the king adopted at the Shropshire meeting, 10 Jan. 1821,[9] but he nevertheless supported the parliamen-tary campaign on the queen's behalf. In a powerful and well-received maiden speech for the opposition censure motion, 6 Feb., delivered 'not as a party man' but 'from conviction', he maintained that 'nothing but danger to the succession of the crown, or injury to the moral character of the country could have justified' the Milan commission or green bag inquiry, and that the 'whole conduct of ministers had tended to sepa-rate the aristocracy from the body of the people'. He deplored the tendency to interpret loyal addresses, like the one he had signed, as endorsements of gov-ernment policy and warned that the current economic crisis caused by £850,000 of unredeemed public debt and artificially high wartime prices could only be resolved if all classes co-operated to rectify it.[10] He did not vote on the opposition motions on the revenue, 6 Mar., the agricultural horse tax, 5 Mar., the additional malt duty, 21 Mar., 3 Apr., and the conduct of foreign policy; but he divided with the radical Hume for the production of detailed ordnance estimates, 16 Feb., and in small minorities for reductions in military and admiralty spending, 14 Mar.-28 May. He also voted to restore 1797 salary levels, 30 Mar., and for inquiry into the currency, 9 Apr. When a committee on agri-cultural distress petitions was appointed, 7 Mar., he called for 'economy in all departments of state' and, citing wartime increases in rents and tithes, advocated the abrogation of all duties which restricted commerce 'except perhaps that on corn, where perhaps some protection was necessary for the English grower'. He was excluded from that committee, but drafted and presented the report from that on receivers general of taxes, 8 June.[11] Seconding Russell's reform resolu-tions in a speech which Henry Bankes* considered 'of better taste than that which he followed', 9 May, he

assured the House that he was an enemy to radical reform, whether in the shape of annual parliaments and universal suffrage, or in the milder form of it which proposed to give the right of voting to inhabitant householders, because it appeared to him to aim at the total overthrow of the constitution, and would make the House purely and entirely democratical.[12]

He praised Russell's plan, 'easy in its execution and safe in its future consequences', as a means of ending bribery and corruption and of enfranchising large towns.[13] He again divided for reform, 25 Apr 1822, 20 Feb., 24 Apr., 2 June 1823, 26 Feb. 1824, 13, 27 Apr. 1826. He voted to abolish the death penalty for forgery, 23 May, 4 June 1821, and for criminal law reform, 4 June 1822.

Disturbed by the opposition's response to the king's speech, 5 Feb. 1822, Whitmore requested an immediate interview with Huskisson, the minister who had drafted the 1821 agriculture committee's report

with a view to consider what steps would be most desirable to take in order to combat the doctrines propounded to the House last night by Mr. Brougham, doctrines not less, as you counselled, founded in error ... [and] pregnant with danger to the best interests of the country if generally adopted and acted upon. Subversive as I consider them of public credit, although I have not the honour of your acquaintance, I will not attempt to apologize for this intrusion, convinced that if the general advancement of the cause of truth and the welfare of the country do not induce you to excuse it, I have no other motive to urge. I have not the least wish to pry into the measures which may be in the contemplation of His Majesty's ministers in the present arduous crisis.[14]

Despite his misgivings, he divided for Brougham's general resolution for retrenchment and tax reductions, 11 Feb., but he opposed Lord Althorp's itemized proposals for more extensive relief than that announced by government in a speech which Hudson Gurney* summarized as 'taking a more encouraging view of agriculture, and supporting the sinking fund, ending, however, with an unhappy attempt at eloquence', 21 Feb.[15] Drawing on Malthus's works and population and price data, he warned of 'the danger of encouraging farmers to grow ... sufficient ... corn for the whole supply of the country' and of attributing distress solely to taxation, and suggested rent reductions as a remedial measure.[16] He was loudly cheered when he stated that 'the present distresses arose from a reaction of that extraordinary stimulus which agriculture had received in the last war', of which every landed gentlemen in the House had experience.[17] He repeated his views, which were discussed in his absence by the political economist David Ricardo* and others at the 25 Mar. Shropshire meeting and at

branch meetings of the General Agriculture Society in July, in *A Letter on the Present State and Future Prospects of Agriculture Addressed to the Agriculturists of Shropshire*.[18] His much postponed bill to amend the laws on the land and assessed taxes received royal assent, 29 June 1822.[19]

He divided for the production of detailed estimates, 27 Feb., reductions in the salt duties, 28 Feb., admiralty lordships, 1 Mar., and the victualling office grant, 18 Mar., and abolition of one of the joint-postmasterships, 2 May 1822. Before voting to finance naval and military pensions from the sinking fund, 3 May, he explained that

he had voted for preserving the sinking fund at the start of the session because a great financial project was then before the country, the payment of the five per cents, but now that object had been so easily effected it became the duty of the House to consider the best and speediest means of affording relief to the country ... [and] he voted for the amendment on the faith that whatever saving was made should go to the reduction of the national debt.[20]

He divided for a similar proposal, 3 June. He told Denis Le Marchant† that the proceedings of the agriculture committee, to which he was appointed, 18 Feb., were 'conducted with much warmth and bad temper'. He also recalled how his surprise when its chairman, Lord Londonderry, 'manfully stood up for the liberal principles enunciated by Mr. Huskisson, at the risk of offending some of his most zealous supporters', turned to dismay when the report was delayed and protectionist remedies were advocated.[21] In the House, he reiterated his belief that the problem was one of overproduction and his hostility to the 1815 corn law, complained that the sliding scale which Londonderry proposed in the corn importation bill was too high and voted in the minority of 25 for Ricardo's proposal for a 20s. fixed duty on wheat, 9 May.[22] Londonderry opposed his amendment lowering the pivot price from 70s. to 64s., which was defeated by 87-42, 3 June.[23] He voted to permit the export as flour of bonded corn admitted for grinding, 10 June. William Wilberforce*, who met him in Shropshire in November 1822, commented:

Our Whitmore loses nothing from a closer view, on the contrary, new features appear which are not often associated with the qualities for which at first sight he seems most distinguished. A kindness and generosity unassuming and great, and a modesty and humility truly delightful to witness in a man whose understanding is certainly good, and who has studied more than most of his own circle of relatives. Poor Lady Lucy was seriously indisposed, but the little we did see of her was quite enough to make us admire and love her, but ... I fear she is not long for this world, if I may use a common but significant expression.[24]

Whitmore welcomed Huskisson's transfer to the board of trade and the appointment of Robinson as chancellor of the exchequer in January 1823. As announced, 5 Feb., and supported by a petition from Keating, 21 Feb.,[25] he requested leave to introduce a bill to effect a gradual reduction to 60s. in the corn pivot price, which was refused (by 78-25), 26 Feb. His speech was peppered with statistics and citations from Cropper's recent publication and criticized from both sides of the House. He argued in favour of treating the corn and currency questions separately and highlighted flaws in the way in which corn was taxed, but conceded that free trade in corn remained impractical because of the 'peculiar burdens' which the land tax, tithes and poor rates placed on agriculture.[26] He reaffirmed his support for corn law revision when the Southampton distress petition was presented, 12 May.[27] Advocating equalization of the tariffs on East and West Indian sugars, he presented petitions from East Indian traders, 3 Mar., and Calcutta merchants disadvantaged by the current system, 22 May, but failed that day to have the matter referred to an investigative committee, by 161-34. He had estimated that the 'species of monopoly' enjoyed by the West Indian trade cost the country £2,000,000 annually and he praised the United Kingdom's achievement in importing raw cotton from India and selling back manufactured cloth at lower prices than native Indian producers.[28] He opposed sweeping cuts in taxation, 3, 18 Mar., and deliberately confirmed his support for retaining the sinking fund before voting to amend the national debt reduction bill, 17 Mar.[29] He voted in a minority of six for amending the merchant vessels apprenticeship bill, 24 Mar., divided against the military and naval pensions bill, 14 Apr., and for inquiry into the prosecution of the Dublin Orange rioters, 22 Apr., the Newfoundland fisheries, 14 May, and the taxes on beer and malt, 28 May. Warning that preparations for partitioning Portugal were afoot, he poured scorn on ministers' claim to be neutral arbitrators in the negotiations with Spain, 29 Apr., and cast a critical vote on the lord advocate's handling of the Borthwick case, 3 June 1823.

Whitmore thought Robinson had already done as much as was currently practicable to reduce taxation, and divided with administration against repealing the window tax, 2 Mar. 1824, having previously explained that corn law reform remained his priority and that he approved of the government's policy of keeping a surplus of income over expenditure and reducing tariffs.[30] He supported the proposed reduction in the

silk duties, 8 Mar., and when a hostile petition was received from the London trade, 18 Mar., he countered that Manchester's silk manufacturers supported the measure. His arguments against prohibiting wool exports were well received, 21 May.[31] Recommending him to lord chancellor Eldon as a possible commissioner to inquire into chancery administration, 22 Mar., the home secretary Peel described him as 'a clever and independent and gentlemanly man ... who might be serviceable as far as public impression is concerned', but nothing came of it.[32] He voted against the Welsh judicature bill, 11 Mar., and in favour of repealing the usury laws, 8 Apr. (and 19 June 1828.) He presented Bridgnorth's petitions against the coal duties, 8 Apr., and for repeal of the leather duties, 12 May.[33] On 3 May he was elected to the Political Economy Club, of which he remained a lifelong Member, nominated by Zachary Macaulay and Thomas Tooke.[34] When the details of the budget were announced, 7 May, Whitmore was dismayed by the decision to restore the tariff on wool exports to finance compensation payments for silk merchants, but welcomed that to retain the sinking fund.[35] Citing the case of the infamous South Sea Bubble, and Adam Smith's finding that each of the 55 joint-stock companies incorporated in Europe since 1680 had failed, he opposed the establishment of a West India Company, which he perceived as a monopolistic threat to 'the general interest of the sugar trade', 10 May. He had deferred his motion for inquiry into the drawback duties on sugar, 8, 19 Mar., lest the issue became too closely embroiled with the slavery question and the case of the Demerara Methodist missionary John Smith, and it was rejected without a division, 13 May.[36] He presented a petition from Bridgnorth, 1 June, and voted in condemnation of Smith's indictment, 11 June.[37] When Liverpool petitioned for changes in the corn laws, 24 May 1824, he promised to raise the whole grain issue, 'difficult as it was', next session, 'if no one else will'.[38]

Whitmore voted to hear the Catholic Association at the bar of the House, 18 Feb., and against the bill outlawing it, 25 Feb. 1825. Speaking on the financial state of the country, 28 Feb. (a speech which *The Times* erroneously attributed to Thomas Whitmore), he called for equalization of the sugar duties, stressed the commercial potential of the East Indies and, taking the 'monopoly' of port wine as his example, stated that he hoped to see the tariffs on wine equalized rather than lowered uniformly as proposed. Predictably, he claimed that the corn laws were 'the heaviest burden' under which people laboured, and promised to propose their reform should ministers fail to do so. He spoke similarly, 11 Mar., 25 Apr., adding that he had desisted only to make way for the Catholic relief bill.[39] He knew of the jibes against him in the press as a correspondent of Mack and Watson, but he was apparently unaware when he introduced his proposals for corn law reform, 28 Apr., that Huskisson, who opposed them, had already persuaded the cabinet to act.[40] His call for revision was preceded by supportive petitions and couched in a speech, which he later had printed, that demonstrated statistically that the law jeopardized reserve corn supplies and that farmers no longer needed protection from foreign competition. Gooch, speaking for the protectionists, denied this and Huskisson cautioned against 'letting the corn laws loose at present and so exciting speculation'. Although defeated, by 187-74, Whitmore promised to raise the issue 'annually until it was settled satisfactorily'. He claimed that ministers overestimated the potential of Canadian corn imports, called for lower duties under their warehoused corn bill, 13 May, 9 June, and voiced support for Edmond Wodehouse's alternative proposals, 2 June.[41] He was for amending the distillery bill, 13 June. Urging the appointment of an independent stipendiary magistracy, he warned of the additional power over their employees which employers who were magistrates in manufacturing districts would derive under the combination bill, and voted for abortive amendments relating to intimidation and trial by jury, 27 June. His announcement, two days later, that he would introduce similar proposals as resolutions yielded a late concession granting workers the right of appeal, 30 June.[42] He divided against the duke of Cumberland's grant, 27 May-10 June, and for inquiry into chancery arrears, 7 June 1825.

The omission of the corn laws from the 1826 king's speech prompted Whitmore to state that despite his 'confidence in the sincerity and good intentions of government', he perceived influences 'operating to postpone and avoid its discussion' which he promised to counter, 3 Feb.[43] He refused to be deterred by ministers and a hostile press and, backed by pro-repeal petitions, he introduced his motion, 18 Apr.[44] He supported his case for 'liberalisation' with statistics from parliamentary returns and citations from William Jacob's[†] *Report on the Trade in Corn and on the Agriculture of the North of Europe*, which government had sponsored; but Huskisson warned that discussion 'could only terminate in inconvenience and embarrassment', and the motion was rejected by 250-81.[45] He repeatedly endorsed the government's corn importation bill,[46] but, smarting from his defeat and misrepresentations of his views, on 5 May he reminded the House that

ministers had thrown in his teeth, that he had adopted a bad course by agitating the question, after they had decided against any alteration of the law during the present session; but the propositions now before the House bore ample testimony that the course which he had pursued was salutary and proper.[47]

He welcomed the promissory notes bill and, confining his comments to its committee stage, he recommended extending its provisions to £5 notes, pointed to the inflation generated by paper and argued for 'enlargement of the metallic base', 20 Feb. He had conceded the close connection between currency and corn law reform, but considered Ricardo's scheme for a corn-based bank impractical and suggested issuing mint notes against bullion. Insisting that he was acting 'disinterestedly', he again defended government policy, 28 May, when, setting aside his preference for legislating on the currency or raising funds directly through the Bank, he expressed qualified support for their scheme to finance public works by exchequer bills and criticized Attwood's counter-proposals as tending to national bankruptcy.[48] He presented anti-slavery petitions from Colne, 27 Feb., Oswestry, 28 Feb., and Warrington, 20 May, voted to condemn the Jamaican slave trials, 2 Mar., and was added to the select committee on the slave trade at Mauritius, 12 May 1826.[49] He overcame a late challenge from the 'No Popery' recorder of Bristol, Ebenezer Ludlow, to come in for Bridgnorth at the general election in June, after a costly five-day poll that demonstrated his vulnerability. When challenged on the hustings, he refused to modify his views on corn and Catholics.[50] At Michaelmas he strengthened the borough's 'manufacturing' vote by partisan burgess creations and published a pamphlet on the corn laws as *A Letter to the Electors of Bridgnorth*.[51] *The Times* considered it

a clear and able production, giving not merely the substance of recognized arguments against the continuance of these pernicious corn laws, but adding many sound and forcible reflections on the part of the author, and administering, in our judgement, a valuable accession of good sense and knowledge to the common stock of intelligence on a subject which will one day, we trust, be decided on grounds not wholly suggested by intemperance or gratuitous alarm with respect to their influence on the landlords of England.[52]

Corn remained Whitmore's preoccupation, and he revised his pamphlet in an attempt to answer his critics.[53] He condoned the government's decision to authorize imports of oats, oatmeal, rye, peas and beans during the recess by order in council; and, as a prelude to introducing his own proposals, he cited a list of 'recent infractions of the corn laws' to demonstrate their obsolescence, for which he was criticized by the late Londonderry's brother-in-law Thomas Wood, 24 Nov. 1826.[54] However, he welcomed comments made by Lord Milton as the presenter of Yorkshire petitions for corn law reform, 21 Feb. 1827. It is unclear which Whitmore presented Bridgnorth's petition for protection on the 27th.[55] Whitmore expressed 'qualified approval' of Canning's corn resolutions and was prevented from detailing his objections to them by 'loud and general coughing', 1 Mar. The 'House was so extremely impatient they would scarcely hear anybody' when he tried (and failed by 335-50) to secure a reduction from 60s. to 50s. in the corn pivot price, 9 Mar., and his warnings that 'capital would drain abroad' at the higher threshold and that greater price fluctuations would prove detrimental to agriculture were ignored. Lord Howick informed his father Lord Grey, 12 Mar, that Whitmore's was a 'good speech except his attack upon the landed interest, which was so gross that I could not vote with him without objecting to it'. Grey replied, 14 Mar., 'if Whitmore's plan had been carried, I am persuaded it would have ruined the country'.[56] His attempts to speak before voting against increasing the protection for barley, 12 Mar., were again opposed from both sides of the House and rendered inaudible by coughing.[57] He urged ministers to proceed with their original resolutions in view of the uncertainty generated by Liverpool's stroke, 19 Mar., and opposed Hume's amendment for the staggered introduction of a fixed 10s. duty, 27 Mar.[58] He voted to postpone the division on supply pending the appointment of a new administration, 30 Mar. He struggled to criticize Canning's corn bill, and declared that 'as he had no alternative except between it and the law of 1822, he should support the second reading', 2 Apr. The following day he was granted a fortnight's leave 'because of illness in his family'. He divided against the duke of Clarence grant, 2 Mar., and for Catholic relief, 6 Mar., inquiry into the allegations against Leicester corporation, 15 Mar., and the spring guns bill, 23 Mar. During Canning's ministry Whitmore introduced but withdrew his motion for inquiry into the India trade, 15 May, on the understanding that the president of the India board Charles Williams Wynn had the matter in hand.[59] He spoke of the harmful effects of the 1815 corn law, 15, 26 May. He protested at the Lords' rejection of Canning's measure, 18 June, and as Members scrambled from their seats to avoid hearing him repeat his marginal views, he expressed qualified support 'as a matter of expediency' for the premier's makeshift amendments to Western's proposals.[60] He objected to government spending on the national gallery, 11 May,

and the Canadian waterways, 14 May, 12 June,[61] and condemned their customs bill as a retrograde measure 'involving an essential departure from the liberal principles laid down early in the session' by Huskisson, 19 June.[62] In November 1827 Tierney, master of the mint in the Goderich ministry, included Whitmore in his list of possible members of the finance committee, but he was not appointed to it. Nothing came of his approaches to Goderich and his successor as premier the duke Wellington on behalf of his brother-in-law, the mathematician Charles Babbage, who sought government sponsorship for his calculating machine.[63]

Whitmore steered his salmon fisheries bill, which had strong Shropshire support, successfully through its first and second readings, 14, 19 Feb., and presented Bridgnorth's favourable petition, 12 Mar., but the ministry's chief commissioner of woods and forests Lord Lowther opposed the measure and killed it by adjournment (32-23), 20 Mar. 1828.[64] He presented petitions, 18 June 1827, 25 Feb. 1828, and voted for repeal of the Test Acts, 26 Feb., which he was glad to see carried.[65] Perceiving its advantages and difficulties, he prevaricated over whether to support the assisted emigration of the poor, 4 Mar., but he backed Slaney's poor rates bill and, endorsing his claim that poverty was locally rather than universally severe, insisted that it was impossible to formulate legislation to prevent pressure being placed on the means of subsistence, 17 Apr. On East Retford, he intervened briefly when the testimony of bribed voters was considered, 4 Mar., and divided against sluicing the franchise there, 21 Mar. He thought that the disfranchisement of Penryn would fail to conciliate the anti-reformers unless polling in Manchester, which hoped to receive its seats, was limited to 'two or three days at most', 24 Mar., and suggested making short polls obligatory under the cities and boroughs poll bill, 6 May 1828. The delay to the ministry's corn bill irritated him, 14, 28 Mar., and he took umbrage at its mover, the president of the board of trade Charles Grant's assessment of Canning's policy, criticized his decision to cluster the additional duties proposed around the pivot price as 'unwise' and 'complicated' and added, 31 Mar.:

> If corn be excluded except at high prices, I can see no difference between protection which results from duties and that which results from law. If this measure be, as it has been stated to be, a compromise between conflicting opinions, it is a compromise between conflicting opinions in the cabinet, not of conflicting opinions in the country.

Later that day, he announced that he would move for a fixed 10s. duty when prices ranged from 55s.-65s. a quarter, increasing as they fell below and decreasing as they rose above those levels. Citing 'Jacob's last excellent report', he criticized Benett's counter-resolutions 'framed upon the high restrictive system' as harmful to the 'interests of the country at large and of the agricultural class in particular', and asserted that although he had then been ridiculed, the principles on which he had based his doctrine of home supply in 1823 remained correct, 24 Apr. He countered the protectionists' arguments for a steeper tariff scale 28, 29 Apr., and, pointing to the need for cheap food in manufacturing areas, 9, 20 May, he persevered with his original amendment, which was rejected by 132-36, 20 May. He presented a Shropshire petition, 25 Apr., and voted for Catholic relief, 12 May. He criticized the government's expenditure proposals, 19 May, and divided against them, 20 June, having voted for details of civil list pensions, 20 May. He was against giving the archbishop of Canterbury control over the appointment of his registrar, 16 June. Supporting the bill restricting the circulation of Irish and Scottish bank notes that day, he declared that it was

> contrary to common sense to suppose that the Bank of England, or country banks, will, year after year keep a hoard of gold in their coffers when there is no demand for it, except in the event of a panic ... I am convinced we have surmounted the chief difficulties incident to a change in the currency, and that, at the present moment, there is in circulation and in the coffers of the bank, and of individuals an ample amount of gold to satisfy all the demands consequent upon the recall of the one pound notes. I therefore hope no consideration whatever will induce government to pause in the course it has commenced, or tamper with so important a matter as the currency.

He spoke, 6, 31 Mar., and presented petitions against colonial slavery, 9 June. Citing arguments previously used by Bishop Heber, he failed to carry his resolution for equalization of the sugar duties, 9 June. He refused to 'rush in' with a new motion, when the Calcutta merchants' petition urged it, but he spoke at length on the indigo trade and the condition of the natives, on which he had been briefed by his brother-in-law, the Calcutta judge Sir Edward Ryan, 16 June.[66] He ordered accounts of trade with the East Indies, China and Mauritius, and announced that he would seek inquiry early next session, 19 June 1828, but deferred doing so pending the passage of Catholic emancipation, for which he divided, 6, 30 Mar., voting also to permit Daniel O'Connell to sit without taking the oath of allegiance, 18 May 1829. Backed by petitions from the manufacturing districts, he urged inquiry into the India trade in a speech crammed with statistics from recent returns and accounts of the cotton, indigo, silk

and sugar trades and tried to demonstrate the advantages of encouraging 'secure settlers', expanding the 'stagnant' China trade and legislating to end the East India Company's monopoly, 14 May. He withdrew the motion, at ministers' request, and published an extended version of his speech, which was strongly criticized in letters to the press.[67] He presented a petition from Leith against renewing the Company's charter, 19 May, and raised the issue again when opposing the radical Waithman and the protectionist Benett's arguments for a return to a paper currency, 4 June. He praised William's Wynn's speech for the extension of jurors' rights to Muslims and Hindoos, 5 June. He voted to transfer East Retford's seats to Birmingham, 5 May, for Lord Blandford's reform resolutions, 2 June, and against additional expenditure on the marble arch, 25 May. He supported the sugar duties bill which Grant proposed from the opposition benches the same day. He addressed the Liverpool East India Association dinner chaired by James Cropper, 15 Sept., and at the bailiff's dinner at Bridgnorth, 29 Sept. 1829, he promised to devote his 'most strenuous endeavours' to the East India question and expressed his conviction that 'greater freedom in trade would act to revive the distressed state of the manufacturing trade and commerce'.[68]

Whitmore was one of 28 'opposition Members' who voted against Knatchbull's amendment to include reference to distress in the address, 4 Feb. 1830. He conceded, though few stayed to hear him, that he did so reluctantly as he believed distress to be general, and said that he could 'not vote for the establishment of a depreciated currency' or massive reductions in taxation.[69] Peel's announcement on the 9th of the appointment of a select committee to inquire into the East India Company's affairs deprived Whitmore, who was named to it, of his intended mission and, doubting the impartiality of government, 'or at least the cabinet', he repeatedly complained that the committee's judgement was distorted by overreliance on the testimony of Company officials. He called for the state of the law, the question of colonisation and the rights of half-castes to be added to the committee's remit, brought up and endorsed mercantile petitions against renewing the Company's charter and ordered returns and gave notice, preparatory to seeking inquiry into the China trade early in the next Parliament, 6 July. He presented a paper on the subject to the Political Economy Club, 1 Mar.[70] He divided for Blandford's reform proposals, 18 Feb., to transfer East Retford's seats to Birmingham, 11 Feb., 5, 15 Mar., and the enfranchisement of Birmingham, Leeds and Manchester, 23 Feb. He voted for tax reductions, 15 Feb., and divided with opposition on the estimates, 19, 22 Feb., 1, 9 Mar. Contributing to the debate on the state of the nation, 18 Mar., he refused to attribute the worsening distress to currency change in itself, and argued that cyclical factors, disruptions to supply markets and trade restrictions, including the East India Company's monopoly, were largely to blame. He pointed to the buoyant markets in silk and cotton as indicators that the situation would improve, and cautioned against replacing gold with a bimetallic or silver standard. He voted to reduce the admiralty grant, 22 Mar., and against the Bathurst and Dundas pensions, 26 Mar., and the salary of the lieutenant-general of the ordnance, 29 Mar. He regarded the ordnance department as an unjustifiable monopoly, 'a burden, not a saving' to the country and, opposing its award, 2 Apr., he embarrassed ministers by citing irrefutable evidence of its commercial inefficiency, supplied to him by connections in the Birmingham manufacturing trade. He continued to divide steadily with the revived Whig opposition until July, including for Jewish emancipation, 5 Apr., 17 May, and to end capital punishment for forgery, 24 May. He protested at the continuing differentiation in the levies on East and West Indian sugars when a general reduction was announced, 30 June. Having decided that it posed no threat to free trade, he belatedly declared his support for the labourers' wages bill 'with all its flaws', 3, 5 July, despite Bridgnorth's opposition to the measure. Announcing his candidature there, 1 July, he appealed to his parliamentary record:

> Economy in the public expenditure, a diminution as far as was practicable in the burden of taxation, and the advancement of the interests of trade and commerce have been the objects I have kept constantly in view, satisfied that I was thereby contributing what lay in my power to the prosperity of the agricultural and the augmentation of the wealth and power of the commercial part of the empire.[71]

With opposition certain, his political ally and business connection, the Stourbridge ironmaster James Foster*, encouraged manufacturers and East India Association members to rally publicly for Whitmore. His declared opponent Ludlow made way for the Tory Richard Arkwright*, who was supposedly backed by the East India Company but was soundly defeated.[72] Whitmore shared election costs of £7,700 with his cousin, but on the hustings he insisted that they were 'of the same name but not the same family', stressed their political differences as proof of his independence and claimed that he had secured the Bridgnorth interests of Sir Ferdinand Richard Acton of Aldenham and

Charles Hanbury Tracy*.[73] He and Babbage visited Liverpool at Foster's instigation, 13 Sept., and he used his speech at the Bridgnorth bailiff's dinner, 29 Sept. 1830, to quash reports that he had been requisitioned to stand for the vacancy there occasioned by Huskisson's death.[74]

Ministers of course listed Whitmore among their 'foes', and he divided against them on the proposed increases in the wheat duties, 12 Nov., and on the civil list when they were brought down, 15 Nov. 1830. He presented and endorsed anti-slavery petitions, 9, 12 Nov. 1830, 29 Mar. 1831, and deplored what he perceived as the revival of protection, 12, 16 Nov. 1830. When Grant, as president of the India board in Lord Grey's ministry, announced the reappointment of the East India committee, 4 Feb. 1831, Whitmore was named to it and immediately urged government to legislate to improve the condition of the Indian people. He added that he would proceed with his proposals on the China trade, and sought further information, 4, 9 Feb., but his motion was twice deferred and overtaken by the dissolution. Airing his arguments for free trade and corn law reform, 15 Feb., he cited the achievements of the Arkwrights, Peels and Watts to disprove Waithman's claim that machinery reduced the demand for labour. He welcomed Waithman's support for corn law revision but, having previously heard him 'dilate on the subject', insisted that he had failed to grasp the difference between real and official values. He criticized the government's plans to introduce a property tax and foster trade with Canada and disputed Irving's theory that tax cuts had a damping effect on profits, rents, and 'the means of the poor', so exacerbating distress, 15 Feb. He also made it known that he would oppose the colonial under-secretary Lord Howick's and any other emigration bill, 22 Feb. He endorsed Slaney's speech attributing distress to poor law abuse and an oversupply of labour, 22 Feb., repeated his call for free trade when the excise duties were considered, 28 Feb., 11, 15 Mar., and opposed the truck system, 12 Apr. He voted for the government's reform bill at its second reading, 22 Mar., and against Gascoyne's wrecking amendment, 19 Apr., having presented a favourable petition from Bridgnorth, 29 Mar.[75] He stressed his support for reform at the general election in May, when he and Foster were returned unopposed for Bridgnorth, where Thomas Whitmore retired and Acton desisted.[76] At the county election, Whitmore was almost alone among the Shropshire gentry in delivering a strong endorsement of and plumping for the defeated reformer, William Lloyd of Aston Hall.[77] Afterwards he published a pamphlet dedicated to Lord Althorp: *Britain Regenerated, or the National*

Debt shown capable of immediate redemption, with some Remarks on the Electioneering System. He was a steward at the Shrewsbury reform dinner, 1 June 1831, and was invited to stand for the new Kidderminster and Wolverhampton constituencies at the first post-reform election.[78]

Commercial issues remained Whitmore's preoccupation in the 1831 Parliament, and he was appointed to the East India committees, 28 June 1831, 27 Jan. 1832, and to that on steam power, 21 July 1831. He is not known to have spoken on reform, but he shelved his inquiry motion on the China trade to make way for it, 28 June. He voted for the second reading of the reintroduced bill, 6 July, and generally for its details. He probably cast wayward votes against disfranchising Saltash, which ministers no longer pressed, 26 July, and for the enfranchisement of £50 tenants-at-will, 18 Aug.[79] He divided for the bill's passage, 21 Sept., the second reading of the Scottish measure, 23 Sept., and Lord Ebrington's confidence motion, 10 Oct. His views on the establishment (in November 1831) of a branch of the Birmingham Political Union at Bridgnorth are not known, but he later wrote to Babbage:

> Speakers and cheerers at such meetings are ever loud and vehement and appear of course to be speaking the sense of the great body of the electors when perhaps they are stating those of a minor party. The more moderate rarely attend radical meetings and *their* voice would only be heard in the polling booth.[80]

He voted for the second reading of the revised reform bill, 17 Dec. 1831. Possibly heeding its likely impact on the reformed Bridgnorth electorate, he apparently voted for the amendment against enfranchising £50 tenants-at-will, which ministers had conceded, 1 Feb. 1832. Otherwise, he divided steadily for its details, the third reading, 22 Mar., and the address requesting the king to appoint only ministers who would carry it unimpaired, 10 May. He voted for the second reading of the Irish reform bill, 25 May, and against a Conservative amendment to the Scottish measure, 1 June 1832. He divided with government on the Dublin election controversy, 23 Aug. 1831, (but was absent from the division on the censure motion that day), and on relations with Portugal, 9 Feb. 1832. His failure to do so on the Russian-Dutch loan in July may have been attributable to 'a very sharp attack in my stomach', which kept him out of London for most of that month.[81] He voted for the immediate appointment of a select committee on colonial slavery, 24 May 1832.

He called again for an extension of the East India committee's powers and antagonized the Company by repeating his charge that the committee relied too heavily on evidence from their officials, 28 June 1831, presented petitions against the renewal of their charter, 20 July, and propounded the merits of free trade, ending the Company's monopoly and reforming the corn laws as means of fostering trade and alleviating distress, in correspondence and speeches within and without doors throughout the session.[82] Unlike other reformers with constituencies affected by the depression in the glove trade, he opposed the appointment of an investigative committee, 31 Jan. 1832. He criticized the proposed expenditure on the Swan River colony, developed 'only because a private individual wished to settle in part of Australia', 17 Feb., and warned of local opposition to the friendly societies bill, 15 Mar. Dismayed and taken aback by the decision to appoint a committee on the renewal of the Bank's 'monopolistic' charter too late in the session to permit a full review, he called for an interim measure and urged that the matter be held over to the next Parliament, 22 May. He similarly opposed the introduction of the government's abortive proposals on corn, arguing that to 'agitate' the question without a decisive settlement 'would only tend to throw the landed interests into a worse state of distress', 1 June 1832.

Reviewing Whitmore's parliamentary career that month, the *Parliamentary Drawing* praised him for sacrificing domestic comforts 'for the tedious acquisition of knowledge upon such subjects as the Bank of England and the East India charters', on which his 'perseverance and usefulness ... have deservedly gained him the gratitude of his country ... [so] ranking him among the public men'. It commended the 'plain, sensible language' and 'decision and fluency' of his speeches, but criticized his failure to hide the fact that they were prepared, and his 'habit of lifting his arms above his head *à la* Irving, which often gives a notion of solemnity not well suited to every day matters of business'.[83] Discussing the possibility of contesting Wolverhampton in a letter to the ironmaster Joseph Baker, 16-19 May, when Grey's threatened resignation and the king's overture to Wellington prompted talk of a dissolution, Whitmore gave his own assessment of his politics, political weight and attributes as a parliamentarian:

> First with respect to political sentiments. Those I possess are based on moderation, from a conviction that real liberty shuns violent extremes and that the best way to promote the main interests of the country, especially the great manufacturing interest upon which in my judgement everything connected with the prosperity of the country and the employment of the people turns, as upon a pivot, is by preserving the peace of the country,

securing the rights of property and of industry, upholding the laws and avoiding a policy the main feature of
which is repeated change. I have ever been anxious to
remove acknowledged abuse, but I like not change for
change's sake and being fully convinced that whatever
the frame of government may be, there will appertain to
it some of that evil which clings to every human institution, I do not consider it either sound policy or real
wisdom to quarrel with the institutions of the country,
merely because evils may be detected and then by a critical observer. I should, I confess, view with some alarm
the continuance and exertion of those Unions, which,
necessary perhaps to ensure the great measure of reform,
would, I fear if rendered permanent militate against good
government and prevent that free discussion and liberty
of opinion and judgement which upon all subjects, but
especially on the more delicate and intricate, ought to
belong to a representative of the people. He is responsible for every word he speaks and every vote he gives
and unless his sentiments are in the main in accordance
with those of a considerable majority of his constituents,
he ought not to be re-elected as their representative, but
subject to the account he must thus render, he ought in
my judgement to be a free agent, speaking his own sentiments and voting according to his honest conviction, not
shackled and pledged as to the line of conduct he is to
pursue ... With reference to expense, the system hitherto
of elections has been such that no individual of moderate
fortune cold come forward as a candidate for a popular
representation without entailing upon himself burdens
of a serious amount. For myself, I have on a recent occasion been aided in a manner so liberal that it would ill
become me to utter a complaint upon this head, but still
in looking forward I hope I shall not be considered over
cautious in pecuniary matters if I state that in a contest
conducted in the usual mode by employing professional
agents and keeping open houses I am in no condition
to enter, especially where the constituency is so large as
more to resemble a county than a borough. With regard
to ... personal weight ... I possess no abilities of a superior order. I have no turn naturally for public speaking.
I am therefore but ill-calculated to take a prominent part
in the discussion of great public questions. The possession of some common sense and common honesty with
an anxious desire to discharge conscientiously the duties
confided to me as a representative, are the sole qualifications I can pretend to. I am too of opinion that an individual so situated ought not frequently to obtrude his
sentiments in debate, the effect of which, if general,
would be to retard most inconveniently all public measures, indeed if all were to be speakers and upon all occasions to the business of the country delayed as it now is,
never could it be got through at all. Except then when
from previous study he may have real information to give
upon the subject under discussion, or where the interests of his constituents are more immediately involved,
it appears to me the duty of such an individual to abstain
from speaking in debate.

Whitmore retired at Bridgnorth, where the loss of the
Apley interest and changes under the Boundary Act
rendered his return in December 1832 unlikely, and,
thwarted at Kidderminster, he declined a late invitation from Birmingham and overcame Conservative and
radical opposition to come in for the new constituency
of Wolverhampton.[84] He did not seek re-election there
in 1835 and, tired of London society, in 1844 he gave
up the rooms he had occupied at the Babbages' since
1833.[85] As a committed political economist and occasional pamphleteer, he kept up his interest in science
and education and experimented with agricultural
innovations at Dudmaston, where he died in August
1858.[86] His wife and stepbrother predeceased him,[87]
and, as he had willed, his Shropshire estates, worth an
estimated £118,000, or £6,355 a year, and encumbered
with a £40,000 mortgage debt, were left to accumulate
for five years in trust before his nominated heir, his sister
Mary Dorothea's son, the Rev. Francis Henry Laing of
Forthampton, Gloucestershire, succeeded to them in
1864 and took the names of Wolryche and Whitmore.[88]

[1] Draws on the Dudmaston mss, seen by permission of the
National Trust at Dudmaston Hall. No biography of Whitmore has
been published, but his great-niece Mary Whitmore Jones's novel
The Grinding Mills (1903) is based on his life. [2] IGI (Salop). [3] Salop
Archives, Labouchere mss (deeds and papers relating to the
Dudmaston estate of the Wolryche fam.) 2922/12/14. [4] Salop
Archives, earl of Bradford's militia pprs. 190/331-8, 362, 369, 372,
403, 705, 813, 818, 820-4, 920, 926, 986, 1129-1130. [5] Labouchere
mss 2292/11/1/209/1-3; 11/1/215; 12/17. [6] PROB 11/1588/54;
IR26/727/27; Dudmaston mss DUD/25/5; Salop Archives
2292/11/1/215-216, 219; 14/9/16, 17. [7] *The Times*, 13 Aug.
1858; Dudmaston mss 12/14; Walpole, *Russell*, i. 74. [8] *Shrewsbury
Chron.* 18, 25 Feb., 3 Mar.; *The Times*, 29 Feb.; Salop Archives,
Bridgnorth Borough 4001/Admin/3/6, common hall bk. pp. 11-15;
Wolverhampton Chron. 1, 8, 15 Mar.; Salop Archives, Weld-Forester
mss 1224, box 337, J. Robins to J. Pritchard, 5, 6 Mar., Pritchard to
C.W. Forester, 31 Mar.; Hatherton diary, 21 Mar.; Salop Archives,
Morris-Eyton mss 6003/1, Slaney jnl. 5 Mar. 1820. [9] *Salopian Jnl.* 10,
17 Jan.; *The Times*, 13, 16 Jan. 1821. [10] HLRO, Hist. Coll. 379, Grey
Bennet diary, 12; *The Times*, 6 Feb. 1821. [11] *The Times*, 9 June 1821.
[12] Dorset RO, Bankes mss D/BKL, Bankes jnl. 128 (9 May 1821).
[13] Grey Bennet diary, 76; *The Times*, 10 May 1821. [14] Add. 38743,
f. 38. [15] Gurney diary, 21 Feb. 1822. [16] Le Marchant, *Althorp*, 205.
[17] *The Times*, 22 Feb. 1822. [18] *Shrewsbury Chron.* 29 Mar.; *Salopian
Jnl.* 10 July 1822; B. Hilton, *Corn, Cash, Commerce*, 150-2. [19] *The
Times*, 12 Feb., 10 May 1822; *CJ*, lxxvii. 73, 78, 82, 438, 471. [20] *The
Times*, 4 May 1822. [21] Le Marchant, 203-4. [22] *The Times*, 10 May
1822. [23] Ibid. 4 June 1822. [24] Hants RO, Calthorpe mss 26M62/F/
C87. [25] *The Times*, 6, 11 Feb. 1823. [26] Ibid. 27 Feb. 1823. [27] Ibid. 13
May 1823. [28] Ibid. 4, 20 Mar., 23 May 1823. [29] Ibid. 18 Mar. 1823.
[30] Ibid. 3 Mar. 1824. [31] Ibid. 22 May 1824. [32] Add. 40315, f. 135.
[33] *The Times*, 13 Apr., 13 May 1824. [34] *Pol. Economy Club: Minutes,
Members, Attendances and Questions, 1821-1880* (1882), ii. 62-65, 197.
[35] *The Times*, 8 May 1824. [36] Ibid. 9, 19 Mar., 14 May 1824. [37] *The
Times*, 2 June; Salop Archives, Longnor mss 1066/133, diary of
Katharine Plymley, 20 June 1824. [38] *CJ*, lxxix. 404; *The Times*, 25 May
1824. [39] *The Times*, 1 Mar. 1825. [40] Ibid. 27, 29 Apr. 1825; Dudmaston
mss O8/57; O8/59/50; Hilton, 272. [41] *The Times*, 3 June 1825.
[42] Ibid. 28, 30 June, 1 July 1825. [43] Ibid. 4 Feb. 1826. [44] Ibid. 7,
9, 21, 28 Feb., 2 Mar., 18 Apr. 1826. [45] Ibid. 17, 19 Apr. 1826;

Hobhouse Diary, 120; Hilton, 274-5. [46] The Times, 3, 9, 13 May 1826. [47] Parl. Deb. (n.s.), xv. 950. [48] The Times, 1 Mar. 1826; Hilton, 223-8. [49] The Times, 28 Feb., 2 Mar., 20 May 1826. [50] John Bull, 28 May; The Times, 29 May; Wolverhampton Chron. 14 June 1826; Bridgnorth Borough 7/49, 24/14, 26/14-17; box 50, parl. returns; common hall bk. pp. 148-96. [51] Salopian Jnl. 4 Oct.; The Times, 9 Oct.; Bridgnorth common hall bk. pp. 198-208. [52] The Times, 3, 4 Oct. 1826. [53] Hilton, 297-9; Cincennatus, Remarks on 'A letter to the Electors of Bridgnorth upon the Corn Laws' (1827); Observations on the Corn Laws addressed to Whitmore (1826-7); Anon, Remarks on the State of the Corn Question addressed to Whitmore (1826-7). [54] The Times, 25 Nov. 1826. [55] Ibid. 28 Feb.; Wolverhampton Chron. 21, 28 Feb., 7, 14 Mar. 1827. [56] Grey mss. [57] The Times, 2, 3, 10, 13 Mar. 1827. [58] Ibid. 17, 20 Mar. 1827. [59] Ibid. 15, 24 Mar., 16 May 1827. [60] Ibid. 27 May, 19 June 1827. [61] Ibid. 12 May, 13 June 1827. [62] Ibid. 20 June 1827. [63] Add. 37184, ff. 114, 299, 304, 306. [64] The Times, 13 Mar. 1828. [65] Add. 37184, f. 114. [66] Oxford DNB (Ryan); NRA 4482; Corresp. of Lord William Bentinck ed. C.H. Philips, i. 585. [67] Salopian Jnl. 20, 27 May 1829. [68] J. Picton, Memorials of Liverpool (1875), i. 416-7; Wolverhampton Chron. 7 Oct. 1829. [69] Grey mss, Howick jnl. 5 Feb. 1830. [70] Pol. Economy Club, ii. 97; C.H. Philips, E.I. Co. 288-9; Dudmaston mss 12/6-8. [71] Wolverhampton Chron. 7 July 1830. [72] NLW, Aston Hall mss C.599; VCH Salop, iii. 283; Salop Archives 840/443; Bridgnorth Borough 7/49; 24/450, box 50, squibs and handbills; common hall bk. pp. 329-76. Wolverhampton Chron. 14 July, 3, 11 Aug. 1830; Dudmaston mss 12/9. [73] Shrewsbury Chron. 6 Aug. 1830. [74] Add. 37185, f. 289; Wolverhampton Chron. 7 Oct. 1830. [75] Shrewsbury Chron. 18 Mar., 22 Apr. 1831. [76] Wolverhampton Chron. 27 Apr., 4 May; Salopian Jnl, 27 Apr.; Shrewsbury Chron. 6 May 1831; Bridgnorth common hall bk. pp. 403-4. [77] Liverpool RO, Parliament Office mss 328/PAR5/1. [78] Dudmaston mss 8/7; Shrewsbury Chron. 3 June 1831. [79] The Times, 19 Aug. 1831. [80] Shrewsbury Chron. 18 Nov. 1831; Wolverhampton Chron. 23 May 1832; Add. 37187, f. 203. [81] Add. 37187, f. 15. [82] Ibid. f. 38. [83] Wolverhampton Chron. 13 June 1832. [84] Dudmaston mss 8/8-17; 8/60/10-14; Add. 37187, ff. 150, 203, 253, 283, 291, 404; Wolverhampton Chron. 20 June, 26 Sept., 17 Oct., 5, 19 Dec. 1832, 11 Jan. 1833; Spectator, 27 Oct. 1832; J. Hardcastle, Old Wolverhampton, ch. 5. [85] Add. 37187, ff. 253, 283; 37193, f. 9. [86] Pol. Economy Club, ii. 146, 168.; Jacobus Veritas, Plea from the Poor (1841); Whitmore, Probable Price of Wheat on Repeal of Corn Laws (1842); Prospects of Agriculture Under Free Trade (1850); Wine Duties (1853); Add. 37021, ff. 599-605; 37189, f. 558; 37191, f. 203; Overstone Corresp. ii. 657-8, 864; VCH Salop, ii. 171; iii. 153; V.J. Walsh, 'Diary of a Country Gentleman', Trans. Salop Arch. Soc. lix (1971-2), 135-6, 158; VCH Salop, iv. 183, 217; Shrewsbury Chron. 13 Aug. 1858. [87] Add. 37191, f. 345; Warws. RO MI 247, Philips mems. ii. 128. [88] IR26/2157/705; Walsh, 135-6; Dudmaston mss 5/12-22; 8/64-70; 24/67, 68; VCH Salop, iv. 209.

M.M.E.

WIGRAM, Sir Robert (1773–1843), of Belmont Lodge, Malvern Wells, Worcs. and 10 Connaught Terrace, Mdx.

FOWEY	1806–1818
LOSTWITHIEL	1818–1826
WEXFORD	3 June 1829–15 Mar. 1830

b. 25 Sept. 1773, 1st s. of Robert Wigram† of Walthamstow House, Essex and 1st w. Catherine, da. of John Brodhurst of Mansfield, Notts.; bro. of William Wigram*. educ. privately. m. 3 Aug. 1812, Selina, da. of Sir John Macnamara Hayes, 1st bt., of co. Clare, 6s. 5da.

kntd. 7 May 1818; suc. fa. as 2nd bt. 6 Nov. 1830; took name of Fitzwygram instead of Wigram by royal lic. 22 Oct. 1832. d. 17 Dec. 1843.

Maj. 6 Loyal London vols. 1803.
Dir. Bank of England 1807-21.

Wigram, a silent supporter of the Liverpool ministry, continued to sit for Lostwithiel, where he was returned unopposed on the Mount Edgcumbe interest at the 1820 general election.[1] A very lax attender, he was granted a fortnight's leave on account of family illness, 3 July 1820.[2] He voted in defence of ministers' conduct towards Queen Caroline, 6 Feb., and against repeal of the additional malt duty, 3 Apr. 1821. He was absent from the division on Catholic relief, 28 Feb. 1821, but divided against it, 21 Apr., 10 May 1825. He voted against condemning the trial of the Methodist missionary John Smith for inciting slave riots in Demerara, 11 June 1824. At the 1826 dissolution he retired. In May 1829 he came forward for a vacancy at Wexford on the interest of his kinsman the 2nd marquess of Ely, who was challenging his former allies for control of the representation. After a 'furious family contest' Wigram was returned in absentia at the head of the poll, amidst allegations of 'corrupt practices' by his agents.[3] He cast no known votes before being unseated on petition, 15 Mar. 1830. In November that year he succeeded to the family estates and the 'enormous fortune' and baronetcy of his father, an East India merchant and ship's husband, whose will, dated 14 Sept. 1825, was proved under £400,000, 'besides freehold estates', 1 Dec. 1830.[4]

On 9 May 1839 Wigram, whose 'fanciful alteration' of his surname to Fitzwygram was widely regarded as 'not in good taste', wrote to Sir Robert Peel* about a position as 'maid of honour' for one of his daughters, explaining that 'with the great wealth in my family, rank is all we have to seek', and recalling that 'our revered parents were friends and since 1795 my family have uniformly supported Pitt principles, in and out of Parliament'.[5] He repeated his request, 11 Sept. 1841, adding that his brother James had recently been elected Conservative Member for Leominster and that he had been 'promised' an Irish peerage by the late duke of York, about which he had sent a 'memorial' to the duke of Wellington in 1830. Peel, now premier, replied that the queen's appointments were 'entirely' her 'personal act' and that he was 'unable to give any assurances' on the 'other points'. Undeterred, Wigram assured Peel that he had 'the power to make up the entailure' to 'half a million' and that his 'fortune should be dedicated to Conservative principles', 19 Jan., and on 23 Apr. 1842 requested promotion to 'the rank of a privy councillor', citing the 'recent elevation' of James to the vice-chancellorship, which had 'again reminded me of my long deferred hopes'.[6] Peel's unfavourable reply of 25 Apr. 'so disappointed' Wigram's 'expectations' of 'friendship after 40 years attachment' that on 13 June 1842 he wrote to complain that

I am about to enter my 70th year without receiving a single favour from any minister and I am naturally anxious that my wealthy son and heir should follow my Conservative principles and should you promote me ... to the rank of a privy councillor, you will find us most grateful. If not, I must submit to leave my son free. When I read over the list and see how many are made by favour of the late ministry, I consider you must have the power to oblige a large wealthy family.

Peel responded the same day, explaining that he could not comply and that

however great your wealth and estimable your private character, I do not consider that your nomination to be a privy councillor would be warranted ... With regard to your son's future course in political life, I will do him the justice of confidently believing that it will be ... influenced by higher considerations than my compliance or non-compliance with your request.[7]

A publication on 'eminent Conservatives' which appeared shortly afterwards remarked that Wigram was 'among commoners, wealthy without ostentation, and among senators, consistent without reward'.[8]

He died in Brighton in December 1843.[9] By his will, dated 21 Nov. 1843 and proved under £50,000, he made ample provision for his wife and divided the surplus between his younger children. The entailed estates passed to his eldest son and successor Robert (1813-73), who retained his original surname.[10]

[1] R. Cornw. Gazette, 16 Mar.; West Briton, 17 Mar. 1820. [2] Black Bk. (1823), 202; Session of Parl. 1825, p. 490. [3] Wexford Evening Post, 2, 5 June; Wexford Herald, 6 June 1829. [4] Wexford Independent, 11 Feb. 1831; PROB 11/1779/734; IR26/1246/561. [5] Gent. Mag. (1844), i. 317; Add. 40426, f. 289. [6] Add. 40488, ff. 219-22; 40507, ff. 66-68. [7] Add. 40510, ff. 143-5. [8] H.T. Ryall, Portraits of Eminent Conservatives (1841), ii. ch. 12. [9] Gent. Mag. (1844), i. 317. [10] PROB 11/1991/19; IR26/1672/5.

P.J.S.

WIGRAM, William (1780–1858), of 56 Upper Harley Street, Mdx. and Belmont Lodge, Worcs.

New Ross	1807–1812
Wexford	1820–1826
New Ross	1826–1830
Wexford	1830–21 Feb. 1831
New Ross	15 Aug. 1831–1832

b. 23 July 1780, 4th s. of Robert Wigram† (d. 1830) of Walthamstow House, Essex and 1st w. Catherine, da. of John Brodhurst of Mansfield, Notts.; bro. of Robert Wigram*. educ. at 'a good school at Holloway'.[1] unm. d. 8 Jan. 1858.

Dir. London Assurance Co. 1806-9; E.I. Co. 1809-54, dep. chairman 1822-3, Apr.-Oct. 1833, chairman 1823-4. Lt. Epping Forest vol. cav. 1804; maj. 2 R.E.I. vols. 1809, lt.-col. 1812, 1820.

Wigram, a 'shipping interest' director of the East India Company since 1809, was the favourite son of an opulent East India merchant and ship's husband, who lavished a 'large fortune' on his numerous children. On his father's retirement in 1819 Wigram took over the running of his business empire, which included docks and breweries.[2] At the 1820 general election he was returned unopposed for Wexford, where his father had sat, 1806-7, on the interest of their kinsman the 2nd marquess of Ely, who had alternate control of the representation.[3] An irregular attender, when present Wigram was reckoned to have voted 'always for ministers' by a radical commentary of 1823, but during this period he became hostile to their economic policies, especially with regard to the East India trade.[4] He voted in defence of their conduct towards Queen Caroline, 6 Feb. 1821, against repeal of the additional malt duty, 3 Apr., for raising money by lottery, 1 June, in support of the duke of Clarence's grant, 18 June, and against an opposition call for economy and retrenchment, 27 June 1821. He divided against Catholic relief, 28 Feb. 1821, 30 Apr. 1822, 1 Mar., 21 Apr. 1825. He voted against more extensive tax reductions, 11 Feb., but was in a largely Whig and radical minority of 36 against the new corn duties, 9 May 1822. He defended the East India Company against a Calcutta bankers' petition complaining of their handling of the debts of the nabob of Oude and was in the minority against a committee of inquiry, to which he was appointed, 4 July 1822. That summer he led a campaign by East India traders for equalization of the duty on East and West Indian sugars, in support of which he was one of the Company 'chairs' who unsuccessfully lobbied ministers. On 22 May 1823 he presented and endorsed a Company petition for equalization and was in the minority of 24 for inquiry.[5] He divided with opposition for ordnance reductions, 19 Feb., but with ministers against inquiry into the prosecution of the Dublin Orange rioters, 22 Apr. He was in minorities for inquiry into the malt and beer taxes, 28 May, and against the appointment of the London Bridge engineer by the treasury, 20 June. He divided against the usury laws repeal bill, 27 June, and for continuing the proceedings against chief baron O'Grady, 9 July 1823. On 27 Mar. 1824 Stephen Rumbold Lushington, secretary to the treasury, warned Lord Liverpool, the premier, that Wigram and 'some of the old directors' intended to oppose his appointment as governor of Madras as he had a 'repugnance to any person connected with the government', believing it to be

conducted by persons 'ignorant of the details of business, especially in the chancellor of [the] exchequer's department, as shown in the bad arrangements with regard to the silk and wool [duties], which had produced great discontent and injury to the respectable persons engaged in those trades ...' My impression is that he rejoices in the opportunity of showing his (brief) authority in conflict with the government; and that he rather hails the occasion of gratifying his resentment for the disappointment of the pretensions of his family to a peerage, recently more embittered by our silk arrangements.[6]

Writing in similar terms to Sir George Robinson*, another company director, next day, Lushington commented:

Wigram I find so hates the government because he cannot get a peerage for his father and because our silk arrangements are not agreeable to his friends ... His language though personally kind to me was very offensive as applied to the government and I am sure that ... the Company will have a good riddance when his time is out.[7]

Wigram and his supporters hatched a scheme to transfer Lord Elphinstone, the governor of Bombay, to Madras and to appoint Sir John Malcolm* in his place, thereby snubbing Lushington, who was 'exceedingly mortified both on my own account and for the government not to get through'. On the outbreak of the Burmese war in December 1824, however, the vacancy was put on hold.[8] Wigram voted for the Irish insurrection bill, 14 June 1824, and suppression of the Catholic Association, 15, 25 Feb. 1825. He opposed a motion by Hume for information on Indian military allowances and 'vindicated the conduct of the East India directors towards the army', 24 Mar. He divided for the duke of Cumberland's annuity bill, 6 June, and was in the minorities against the spring guns bill, 21

June 1825, and for relaxation of the corn laws, 18 Apr. 1826. He presented a Wexford petition against slavery, 20 Apr.[9] On 9 May 1826 he was appointed to the select committee on the petition of James Silk Buckingham[†] concerning curbs on press freedom in India.

At the 1826 general election Wigram retired from Wexford, where it was the other patron's turn to nominate, and was returned unopposed for New Ross on the interest of his brother-in-law Charles Tottenham*, whose family had alternate control of the representation.[10] He presented a New Ross petition against Catholic claims, 19 Mar., and voted thus, 6 Mar. 1827, 12 May 1828.[11] He divided against repeal of the Test Acts, 26 Feb. 1828. He was appointed to the committee on the East India prize money bill, 10 June, and defended the Company's power to restrict re-entry to India on the ground of 'character', 16 June 1828. He voted for the Wellington ministry's ordnance estimates, 4 July, but against their revision of the silk duties, 14 July 1828. In February 1829 Planta, the patronage secretary, predicted that Wigram would vote 'with government' for Catholic emancipation, but he divided against it, 18, 27, 30 Mar. He voted against allowing Daniel O'Connell to take his seat unhindered, 18 May. He presented a constituency petition against any alteration of the law prohibiting the cultivation of tobacco in Ireland, 13 Apr. He divided for the issue of a new writ for East Retford, 2 June 1829. He voted against Lord Blandford's parliamentary reform plan, 18 Feb., and the enfranchisement of Birmingham, Leeds and Manchester, 25 Feb., but was in the opposition minority for ordnance reductions, 29 Mar. 1830. He criticized the inclusion of the lord chancellor's libel costs in the supplies, arguing that as he had been 'attacked in his private capacity' he 'should defend himself in the same manner', 4 June. He voted for amendments to the sale of beer bill, 21 June, 1 July 1830, when he presented a New Ross petition complaining of distress.

At the 1830 general election Wigram stood again for Wexford, where his eldest brother Robert had recently been unseated on petition, saying that he was 'perfectly independent of all parties' and would 'vote for all necessary retrenchment in the public expenditure and reduction of taxes'. After a two-day contest he was returned three votes ahead of his brother's former rival Sir Edward Dering*, whose allegations of illegal conduct he denied. (His opponent later alleged on petition that he had 'offered to spend £2,000 in building a dock or sluice for vessels' and had 'made various promises of places in the East India Company's service'.) He attended a celebratory dinner of the town's Wigram Club, which had been established in 1825 to mark his father's birthday.[12] His return was reckoned a gain by the ministry, who listed him as one of their 'friends', but he was absent from the crucial division on the civil list, 15 Nov. He presented a Wexford petition for abolition of the sugar duties, 7 Dec. 1830. On 21 Feb. 1831 he was unseated on petition. He did not stand at the 1831 general election, and it is not clear what Lord Ellenborough, one of the Tory election managers, meant when he noted that 'Wigram goes with Hope to Norwich, a capital man', 25 Apr.[13] In August 1831 he offered for a vacancy at New Ross in the room of his nephew, apparently because his brother-in-law wanted to put in a 'more thorough-going Tory'. He was returned unopposed, whereupon Holmes, the Tory whip, advised Mrs. Arbuthnot that 'we have carried an anti for New Ross'.[14] He voted against the third reading of the Grey ministry's reintroduced reform bill, 19 Sept., and its passage, 21 Sept. He was absent from the division on the second reading of the revised bill, 17 Dec. 1831, but voted against going into committee on it, 20 Jan., the enfranchisement of Tower Hamlets, 28 Feb., and the third reading, 22 Mar. 1832. He divided against the second reading of the Irish measure, 25 May. He voted against ministers on the Russian-Dutch loan, 26 Jan., 12 July (as a pair). He was added to the select committee on the affairs of the East India Company, 2 Feb. He presented a petition from the East India merchants against the zemindar of Nozeed bill, which he considered 'highly injurious to the interests of certain individuals', 6 Mar. He was in the minority of 20 against inquiry into the relief of crown colonies, 3 Aug. 1832. At the 1832 dissolution he retired from Parliament. In October 1833 he resigned as a director of the East India Company in protest at the ministry's East India Charter Act.[15]

Wigram, who later acquired Bennington Park, near Stevenage, Hertfordshire, died at his London residence at 15a Grosvenor Square in January 1858.[16] By his will, dated 22 Jan. 1852, he left £10,000 to each of his 11 half-brothers, £2,000 to a half-sister and the children of a second who was deceased, and made ample provision for the families of his late brother Robert and late brother-in-law. His younger sister Maria was given an annuity of £1,000. Control of the substantial residue of his estate passed to his executors, his half-brothers Money Wigram, a director of the Bank of England, Ely Duodecimus Wigram, a retired colonel, Loftus Tottenham Wigram, Conservative Member for Cambridge University, 1850-9, and his nephew Unwin Heathcote.

[1] HP Commons, 1790-1820, v. 557. [2] Wexford Independent, 11 Feb. 1831. [3] Dublin Evening Post, 1 Apr. 1820. [4] Session of Parl. 1825,

p. 490; Black Bk. (1823), 202. [5] C.H. Philips, E.I. Co. 250-1; The Times, 23 May 1823. [6] Add. 38411, f. 233. [7] BL OIOC Robinson Coll. MSS. Eur. F. 142. 26 [8] Ibid. Lushington to Robinson, 20 Mar. 1824; Philips, 252-4; Wellington mss WP1/783/10. [9] The Times, 21 Apr. 1826. [10] Dublin Evening Post, 29 June; Wexford Evening Post, 30 June 1826. [11] The Times, 20 Mar. 1827. [12] Wexford Herald, 4, 7, 11 Aug., 1 Sept.; Kilkenny Moderator, 11 Aug. 1830; CJ, lxxxvi. 662. [13] Three Diaries, 88. [14] Wexford Herald, 17 Aug. 1831; Arbuthnot Corresp. 148. [15] See Philips, 286, 297. [16] Gent. Mag. (1858), i. 229.

P.J.S.

WILBERFORCE, William (1759–1833), of Gore House, Kensington, Mdx. and Markington, nr. Harrogate, Yorks.[1]

KINGSTON-UPON-HULL	1780–1784
YORKSHIRE	1784–1812
BRAMBER	1812–1 Mar. 1825

b. 24 Aug. 1759, o.s. of Robert Wilberforce, Baltic merchant, of Kingston-upon-Hull, Yorks. and Elizabeth, da. of Thomas Bird of Barton, Oxon. educ. Hull g.s. 1766; Chalmers's sch. Putney 1768-71; Pocklington g.s. 1771-6; St. John's, Camb. 1776. m. 30 May 1797, Barbara Ann, da. of Isaac Spooner, merchant banker, of Elmdon Hall, Warws., 4s. 2da. d.v.p. suc. fa. 1768. d. 29 July 1833. Dir. Sierra Leone Co. 1791; member, bd. of agriculture 1801.

In the opinion of the Quaker Joseph Gurney, Wilberforce, whose 'curved and diminutive person' quivered with restless energy, was remarkable for the 'rapid productiveness' of his mind, teeming with a 'cornucopia of thought and information' even in old age.[2] His social vivacity and personal charm (having on his religious conversion at the age of 26 successfully suppressed an unbecoming irritability) were undisputed: he himself regarded it as 'a fault to be silent; everyone is bound to present his contribution to the common stock of conversation and enjoyment'.[3] Charles Shore, who stayed with him at Bath in the autumn of 1820, later wrote:

> In person ... Wilberforce was slightly deformed ... [He] usually carried an inkstand in his coat pocket ... He invariably wore black clothes, sometimes till they became quite dingy, for he ignored his outer man, never, as his valet intimated ... making use of a glass ... He was quite unconscious of the notice which his personal appearance attracted ... Though seemingly physically little qualified for work – and in compliance with the advice of his medical advisers he had habitually since early youth taken a small but not increasing dose of opium – it was marvellous to observe his powers of endurance ... His ... discriminating knowledge of mankind was derived from the force of his sympathy and quick perception of peculiarity ... But for the extraordinary activity and elastic-

ity of his intellectual temperament, the irregularity of his habits would have cost him a much more exceeding waste of time ... Excessive candour proved an impediment to decision and dispatch ... Few men have been so little influenced by the distracting passions of ambition, avarice, vanity, and resentment ... The mainspring of his public and private acts ... [was] that steadfast independence which too often gains little credit because as little credence.[4]

The daughter of his friend William Smith* wrote that 'his rich talk flowed on incessantly, but not as if he wanted to be the object of the company, rather as if he could not help saying what was in him and as if he wanted everybody else to do the same'.[5] Wilberforce's scrupulous independence, unwavering Christian faith and application to political questions of the principles of the moderate Evangelicalism of the Clapham Sect, for which he received fresh inspiration in 1817 from the sermons of Thomas Chalmers, gave him a unique position in British public life, where his moral authority was strong.[6] In his private dialogue with God, however, he was, as William Lamb* remarked after reading his diaries, 'perpetually vexing himself because he amused himself too much and too well and had not religion enough'.[7] To some, of course, particularly those on the political left, he seemed a tiresome humbug. Hazlitt, while recognizing his many estimable qualities, observed:

His patriotism may be accused of being servile, his humanity ostentatious, his loyalty conditional, his religion a mixture of fashion and fanaticism ... He has two strings to his bow; he by no means neglects his worldly interests, while he expects a bright reversion in the skies ... [He] is far from being a hypocrite; but he is ... as fine a specimen of *moral equivocation* as can be found.

A radical commentator denounced him in 1823 as 'a strange compound of cant, weakness, selfishness and aristocracy'.[8]

By 1820 Wilberforce, just turned 60, was in unreliable health, which had been undermined by his addiction to opium. Prone to chest infections and a martyr to colitis, constipation and piles, he was plagued above all by rapidly worsening eyesight, which made him largely dependent on readers for information and entertainment. Yet his mental strength was scarcely impaired, and his awareness of what remained to be done to put an end to negro slavery, the cause to which he had dedicated his life for over 30 years, drove him on. To his fellow Evangelical Lord Calthorpe, on whose proprietary interest he had sat for Bramber since giving up the representation of Yorkshire in 1812, he confessed to misgivings about the suitability of such a seat for a man of his beliefs, but he set them aside to come in again at the general election of 1820:

For reasons nearly the same as yours, if not quite so, I believe that to retire from the representation of such places as you speak of, would not be at present the Christian path of duty, though I entirely concur with you as to the character of the proceedings, which you really with admirable force say, want that *noonday* simplicity and integrity which ought to characterize the conduct of a Christian either in politics or in any other line ... I hope I need not go down to Bramber ... My health is really a fair plea for non-residence during this severe weather ... I should feel strangely embarrassed in addressing my thanks personally to my constituents, though I have only feelings of gratitude in thanking you.[9]

Wilberforce, who wrote to Arguelles through Fox's nephew Lord Holland, a West Indian proprietor, on the subject of the continuing Spanish slave trade, and tried with Calthorpe to persuade Holland to resist Maxwell's proposed slaves removal bill, secured the production of the reports of the African naval commander on the state of affairs in Sierra Leone and the Gold Coast, 18 May 1820.[10]

He admired the 'spirit' of Queen Caroline, whom he considered to have been badly treated by her husband, though he had no doubt of her profligacy while abroad. Above all, he feared the damaging effects of an investigation, foreseeing dire consequences 'if the soldiery should take up her cause'. On 7 June 1820 he was persuaded by his friend and fellow 'Saint' Thomas Fowell Buxton*, who was apparently responding to pressure from the Whig Sir Robert Wilson*, to move, after concerting with the Grenvillite Charles Williams Wynn*, a two-day adjournment of the debate on the issue 'in order', as he privately recorded, 'to give the parties time to effect an amicable accommodation', and with the ultimate aim of preventing an inquiry into the contents of the green bag, which, he told Sir James Mackintosh*, was like Pandora's box 'without hope at the bottom'. Buxton reported that Wilberforce had 'wavered a good deal, but when he spoke, he spoke most beautifully'. The sense of the House, especially the country gentlemen, was overwhelmingly with him. Edward Littleton* noted that 'all parties hailed with joy his motion', and that 'this is exactly the kind of case in which Wilberforce will guide the House of Commons, if he can but make up his own mind'.[11] His subsequent letter to the king entreating him to concede the restoration of the queen's name to the liturgy went unanswered.[12] Mackintosh thought he spoke 'beautifully' in paying tribute on 14 June to Henry Grattan I*, who, he said, had shown that 'the love of liberty was never so substantially gratified as when it was gratified with a due observance of that proper rule and subordination without which the principles of civil society must immediately dissolve'.[13] Three days later Wilberforce was shown by Henry Brougham*, the queen's adviser, details of the negotiations with ministers. On the strength of this, and an apparent assurance by Brougham that Caroline would bow to an appeal from the Commons to give up the liturgy in return for a recommendation to any continental court and a recognition that her doing so would not be regarded as an admission of guilt, he gave notice on 20 June of a motion for an address to her, but refused to divulge its contents beyond saying that its object was to 'remove, as far as possible, all obstacles to an amicable arrangement'.[14] That night, however, he received an angry note from the queen (composed, he thought, by Brougham's rival Alderman Matthew Wood*) refusing to surrender the liturgy and asking him to drop his motion. This, as Mackintosh saw it, 'produced its full effect on the timidity and irresolution of Wilberforce', who, after consulting James Stuart Wortley, Member for Yorkshire, decided, 'against the advice of all my friends', to alter his motion and put it off for a day, to give the queen time to reconsider. When the Speaker called his name, 'in the fullest House ever seen', 21 June, there was no sign of him, and 'a general laugh' broke out. He eventually appeared almost an hour later when, to cries of protest, he secured a postponement to the following day. He noted privately that 'several of my friends pressed me strongly to make my motion a defence of ministry; but I saw all depended on my keeping to my point – no inquiry'.[15] That evening Brougham took Wilberforce another letter from the queen, which seemed to leave the question more open, and evidently promised to press her to give a firm pledge that when the address was presented she would give up her insistence on the liturgy. Wilberforce, unaware that Caroline was furious with Brougham, whom she suspected of betraying her, duly proposed his address, from the opposition benches, in a packed and 'very noisy and impatient' House, 22 June. He thought his reply, in which he denied the collusion with ministers with which many in opposition charged him, was better than his speech. Mackintosh considered it be 'the worst ... I ever heard him make', as did Littleton, who commented that 'his conscience is [in] its dotage and will not allow him to make up his mind on points'. John Hobhouse*, too, deemed it 'bad', and Henry Bankes* noted that he 'spoke less well than upon most other occasions'. A Whig amendment insisting on restoration of the queen's name to the liturgy was negatived without a division and the address carried

by 391-124.[16] When Wilberforce, Stuart Wortley, Bankes and Sir Thomas Dyke Acland* presented it to the queen at 22 Portman Square, 24 June, she summarily rejected it. They were hissed and barracked by an orchestrated mob, who denounced Wilberforce as 'Doctor Cantwell'; and when Stuart Wortley, with Wilberforce as his 'prompter', announced the outcome to the House that evening, they 'boggled and looked foolish', in the view of Hobhouse.[17] Wilberforce was initially 'very low and dispirited' over the failure of his mediation and remained fearful of the consequences of inquiry. Convinced by the wily Brougham that the queen had acted on her own initiative, he never publicly revealed the assurances he had been given of her compliance and bore stoically the popular abuse which he received, from William Cobbett[†] among others, for supposedly trifling with the Commons and conniving with ministers. In the House, 26 June, he denounced and voted against the opposition attempt to postpone the inquiry for six months, 'not meaning to vote for a secret committee at all ... but not being able at once to take a by-way of defeating a thing which might at any moment be revived'.[18] On 28 June he welcomed Brougham's scheme for the education of the poor. He defended the grant for the support of captured negro slaves against Hume, 6 July, commending the practice of enlisting them into black regiments.[19] He divided against the aliens bill, 7 July 1820.

He was appalled by the government's apparent indifference to 'the unrestrained licence with which bad men are permitted to diffuse their poison in frequent periodical doses throughout the great body of our people', and tried to prompt the authorities to bring on Mrs. Carlile's trial before the vacation. To Hannah More he wrote, 21 July, of

a turbid, fermenting mixture, which really at this day teems with as many nauseous ingredients as Macbeth's witches' cauldron ... while *green bag*, like the roll in the soup, floats in the midst of the mess, imparting its pungency and flavour to the whole composition ... We are in a sad state. I own it does greatly shock me to see our rulers, even such of them as we have reason to believe have some sense of religion, exhibiting no feeling of the necessity of our 'humbling ourselves under the mighty hand of God' ... My race is nearly run, though ... I am quite distressed when I contemplate the idea of retiring from public life, without even bringing forward more than one very important business, which I have long had in view ... I have wanted a little of your decision and alacrity.[20]

He contemplated appealing direct to the king to give up the proceedings, naively believing that he 'could write him a speech which without an abatement of dignity would get him out of the scrape, and all the rest of us also, and would make him universally popular with all but the absolute radicals – avowed enemies of God and man'. He talked privately of promoting county meetings to petition for an end to the business, but, as Lamb pointed out to him, apart from the fact that it was too late, there was no guarantee that the nobility and gentry would be able to control and restrain such gatherings.[21] At the end of July he joined his family at Weymouth. The appearance in *The Times* of 5 Aug. of a public letter from the Whig Lord John Russell* asking him, as the representative of majority independent backbench opinion, to intervene to avert the queen's trial, annoyed him, for it dished his plan of approaching the king as a neutral. Cobbett denounced the 'ridiculous exhibition' of 'the proud Whig crawling to the obsolete Saint'.[22] Wilberforce went to London on 13 Aug., 'partly out of a nervous fear of leaving any possible endeavour unattempted to extricate both Houses out of the sad scrape'. With his brother-in-law James Stephen, a master in chancery, he concocted a proposal, which seemed 'absurd' to those who got wind of it, for the evidence to be considered by a 'grand jury' of county Members and for the queen to be tried, if there was a case to answer, by a specially constituted lord steward's court under the master of the rolls. Some ministers, including Lord Castlereagh*, were by now resentful of Wilberforce's meddling, suspecting him of intriguing to remove them from office. (They had reason to be alarmed, for Wilberforce was urging the quartermaster general, Sir James Willoughby Gordon*, to impress on the king's brother, the duke of York, the desirability of a change of government.)[23] He was, however, granted an interview with Lord Liverpool and Castlereagh on 16 Aug., when the conversation proved 'very satisfactory' and they 'hoped he would be prevailed on not to embarrass their proceedings by any motion in the House of Commons'. Wilberforce, who was reported to have admitted privately that 'the act of his life which he most reproached himself with was not having moved [in June] to restore the queen to the liturgy', said nothing on the adjournment motion, 21 Aug. 1820, beyond repeating his denial that in seeking a settlement he had been trying to 'fortify ministers', predicting that if the bill of pains and penalties reached the Commons it would 'become an absolutely interminable proceeding' and opposing the opposition motion for a prorogation.[24]

A month later, as the queen's trial in the Lords progressed, he wrote to Bankes:

What is government about, to suffer such a multitude of poisoned fountains to be playing in the great city ... Surely we never were in such a scrape. The bulk of the people are I grant run mad; but then it was a species of insanity on which we might have reckoned, because we know their prejudices against foreigners; their being easily led away by appeals to their generous feelings ... I begin more and more to think that a change of ministers might afford the most probable way out of our present difficulties. Yet one must not be unfair to them; but, judging candidly, their conduct has been very ill-advised.[25]

The marquess of Buckingham, observing that the queen's guilt had been proved by 'the evidence of her being seen with her hand in *Bergami's* breeches', wondered how Wilberforce could, 'even indirectly, serve a woman who has been known to put her hand into a man's breeches. Mrs. W[ilberforce] never touched his sacred parts except with a pair of tongs'.[26] At this time he wrote to Liverpool complaining of the deliberate exclusion of Evangelical clergymen, most of whom, he argued, did not espouse the Calvinistic doctrines attributed to them, from church preferment:

Believing as I do most firmly that this country is in a state of extreme danger, of which the queen's affair, though constituting one of its chief elements now in action, is by no means the whole cause [and] ... that this danger is the consequence of a *moral disease* ... [and] believing this moral disease to be the result of an erroneous doctrinal system, producing a low and depraved practical system of religion, it is my decided opinion that this country ... can in no way be so essentially benefited as by endeavouring to promote among the people the prevalence not of formal but of true, honest practical Christianity. The men of property ... are naturally disposed to support the constitution and laws of their country when party spirit does not hurry them in a wrong direction ... But on what can we depend for preserving the loyalty ... in the lower orders, breathing as they do an atmosphere of falsehood, profaneness and insubordination, in consequence of the swarms of worse than Egyptian plagues which are poisoning and destroying the land from the seditious and irreligious press? ... Ultimately, I am persuaded, your only security will consist in *educating your people up to their circumstances* ... But this is a slow process ... Before the effects of this system can be obtained ... the true dependence must be on improving, by God's blessing, the moral character of your people, through the augmenting influence of true Christianity.[27]

At the end of October he told Stephen that he thought he had left five or six more years of useful public life, in which he would 'greatly like to lay a foundation for some future measures for the emancipation of the poor slaves, and also to diminish the evil of oaths': 'These things being done, how gladly should I retire! I am quite sick of the wear and tear of the House of Commons; of the envy, malice and all uncharitableness'.[28] He was favourably impressed by the personal conduct of Liverpool and lord chancellor Eldon during the trial, but, while he welcomed the abandonment of the bill after the narrow majority for its third reading, he reflected:

What a mess have ministers and the queen's advisers and the House of Lords ... made of this sad business ... How party does govern people in our days ... I can conceive people strongly impressed with a persuasion of the falsehood of Italian witnesses and therefore disposed to think the charges not clearly proved against her. But to hear some highly respectable individuals (I mean men who would not say what they would not believe) declare themselves clear that her innocence is established !!!

He confided to Stephen that if ministers did meet Parliament on 23 Nov., as had been originally arranged, he 'should not be sorry' to remain at Bath, where his wife's illness provided a sufficient excuse

because some violent motions for their censure, etc., may probably be moved, and I see no reasons why I should volunteer a service which may place me in situations awkward in themselves and perhaps in their consequences injurious to the cause we hold most dear ... The conduct of ministers in several parts of the late business ... was so very censurable that nothing would prevent me taking a strong part against it, but the fair consideration of the difficulties of their situation and of the way in which they were drawn into it.[29]

Ministers, in canvassing backbench opinion, were anxious to ascertain Wilberforce's views, and on 29 Nov. Liverpool wrote personally to him to explain that while fair financial provision, with no condition of residence abroad, would be made for the queen, he and his colleagues would resign if the Commons voted for restoration of her name to the liturgy.[30] Wilberforce merely acknowledged receipt of the letter, but Henry Beeke, a Bristol informant of the chancellor of the exchequer, who claimed to have inside knowledge of his conversations at Bath, initially reported that he considered the queen to have been in effect acquitted and that ministers must make concessions: 'he does not disguise how much he thinks himself courted by *both* parties ... and you must not mistake civil words for friendly intention, for depend upon it that the Whigs will be the successful suitors'. Beeke hoped to be able to persuade him through Acland to detail in the Commons the events leading up to his compromise resolution, and in particular to expose Brougham's conduct. Nothing came of this, and Beeke construed Wilberforce's evasion of an explanation to Liverpool and his reported new 'crotchet' of arguing that there was no reason for ministers to resign, even if beaten on

the liturgy question, as an indication that he had 'committed himself by declarations if not by promises'. In the same vein, Sir Henry Hardinge* informed Lady Londonderry, 28 Dec. 1820, that he had heard that Wilberforce now 'says the first thing at any sacrifice, even that of the present administration, is to get rid of the whole question, as he conceives ministers have [so] irreparably lost the confidence of the nation that they ought to go out'.[31]

On the eve of the 1821 session Wilberforce told his wife that the question was 'a choice of evils' and that 'I have a most painful route to travel whatever course I pursue'. According to his diary, he intended to vote for Hamilton's motion condemning the exclusion of the queen's name from the liturgy, 26 Jan., though 'had the division come on a few days before, I should have voted against it, on the ground of the queen's outrageously contumacious conduct'. In the event, he was 'forced to go home by illness' before the division; but William Huskisson*, a member of the government, interpreted his departure as an indication that he 'could not manage his little party in the House'.[32] He divided silently with ministers against the opposition censure motion, 6 Feb., after supporting Smith's call for papers on the continuation of the West African slave trade by France, Portugal and Spain. He told a correspondent that he

was very sorry to be unable to find a convenient opportunity of speaking ... my mind a little plainly on some topics, more especially on that system of party which now reigns with such avowed predominance. It is that, in my mind, which has done more harm than any other cause to the character of Parliament. It so tinctures and distorts the view of the best men, and so biases their judgements, as to make them act in ways which you would previously have thought impossible ... What else can render our old nobility blind to the efforts that are using with such mischievous industry to pull down the throne, and with it the church, and all that preserves the order and peace of society?[33]

On 13 Feb. he spoke and voted for restoration of the queen's name to the liturgy as an expedient means of tranquillizing the country, though he defended ministers, whose errors had been ones of 'judgement' and 'ought not to be imputed to incapacity, and still less to want of integrity'. He told his wife that 'it grieved me more than it ought to differ from so many dear friends, but I really could not in conscience forbear to support the motion'. He was 'extremely distressed, but was told I spoke well'. A disgusted Mrs. Arbuthnot noted that 'his principles of *right* and *wrong* yield to popular clamour'; and Williams Wynn considered it 'a remarkably feeble, vacillating speech'.[34]

Wilberforce supported as 'absolutely necessary' the ministerial bill to vest African forts in the crown, 20 Feb. 1821.[35] Next day, 'after considerable hesitation', he spoke and voted for Mackintosh's motion condemning the Allies' suppression of the liberal regime in Naples, calling at the same time for economy and retrenchment to help relieve distress, though he privately felt that 'it was very foolish in opposition to divide' and that he had failed to prepare properly, having 'as too common with me, expended nearly all my time over old accounts'.[36] He advocated and voted for army reductions, 15 Mar., and, after supporting compensation for American loyalists, divided for repeal of the additional malt duty, 21 Mar. He did not vote in the division on Catholic relief, 28 Feb., but on 16 Mar., having presented and dissented from Catholic petitions against concessions, he delivered what the Grenvillite William Fremantle* thought a 'very animated and eloquent' speech in favour of the second reading of the relief bill. Bankes described the effort as 'agreeable but desultory', while Lady Holland, a spectator, wrote that it was 'full of feeling, harmonious sentences, melodious voice'. Wilberforce himself noted that 'I was complimented on my speaking, though from turning away from the gallery said to be inaudible there'.[37] A fortnight later, shortly before he suffered a series of illnesses which kept him away from the House for several weeks, he reflected that 'day passes away after day so rapidly, that life is sliding away from me, yet little seems to be done. There is I hope no intentional misapplication of time ... but I must retire from business for which not especially fitted'. His brother-in-law William Spooner told Calthorpe, 17 May:

> I do not hear without pain the report from various quarters of the very ill looks of Mr. Wilberforce. He is very generally thought to be greatly aged of late, and much less adequate to parliamentary fatigues. My sister has kept him at Bath as long as she could, and nursed him, with early dinner and a time of repose after it; but she returns to London with many uneasy apprehensions, and her fears are certainly in accordance with the remarks of various friends who have seen him lately. I cannot but earnestly wish that the remnant of a life so valuable to his family ... might be preserved to him by some greater measure of retirement from public duties. Perhaps he *ought* to leave Parliament; and I almost question if, by employing his then greater leisure, in writing, he might not do more essential service to society, than by now retaining his seat, while he would also reserve for *domestic use* the portion of his taper, which otherwise may somewhat prematurely be consumed ... I am sure *you* will not be backward to throw in a word of advice of this kind, if on observation of his state you see that there is good

reason ... and your sentiments will have much weight with him.[38]

Wilberforce decided to soldier on, and was in the House to vote for Mackintosh's forgery punishment mitigation bill, 23 May, when he also gave notice of a motion on the continuance of the foreign slave trade.[39] The following day he wrote to Buxton, whose speech on the forgery bill he admired, asking him to consider their forming an 'alliance' so that Buxton could take over the slavery question if, as seemed likely, Wilberforce was unable to see it to a conclusion:

> From my time of life, and much more from the state of my constitution, and my inability to bear inclemencies of weather, and irregularities, which close attendance on the House of Commons often requires, I am reminded ... of my being in such a state that I ought not to look confidently to my being able to carry through any business of importance.

It was eighteen months before Buxton finally agreed.[40] Wilberforce presented and endorsed a Newfoundland petition for judicial reform, 28 May. He recommended acceptance of the Lords' amendments to the Grampound disfranchisement bill rather than have it wrecked by splitting hairs, 30 May.[41] Next day he spoke in favour of Stephen being heard at the bar of the House as the representative of slaves affected by Maxwell's removal bill, which he opposed on its second reading, 1 June.[42] He supported inquiry into the administration of justice in Tobago and again backed the just claims of American loyalists, 6 June, and endorsed Buxton's motion for information on suttee, a 'dreadful practice' which he wished to see eradicated by education rather than compulsion, 20 June. On 26 June he suggested that a small group of Members could investigate Owen's New Lanark project more effectively than a commission. He was dissatisfied with his speech later that day in support of his motion, in which government acquiesced, for an address urging them to renew their pressure on other European powers to put an end to the slave trade. On 28 June he carried an address for the better regulation, protection and education of apprenticed slaves, a subject on which he subsequently had discussions with ministers.[43] He defended the Constitutional Association, 3 July, and the Society for the Suppression of Vice, 10 July 1821.[44]

That month Wilberforce, whose financial position, with four sons to support, was becoming constrained, partly because he kept rents on his Yorkshire estates uneconomically low, sold his property in Kensington and leased a house at Marden Park, near Godstone, in

Surrey.[45] His continued private efforts, through correspondence, to expose the horrors of the European slave trade impeded his fanciful scheme to write 'both a religious and a political work, which would not be without value'.[46] In November 1821 Maria Edgeworth met him at Wycombe Abbey and was struck by

> his delightful conversation and ... the extent and variety of his abilities. He is not at all anxious to show himself off: he converses – he does not merely talk. His thoughts are wakened and set going by conversation and you see the *thoughts* living as they rise. They flow in such abundance and from so many sources that they often cross one another. He leaves many things half said and sometimes a *reporter* would be quite at a loss ... As he literally seems to speak *all* his thoughts as they occur, he produces what strikes him on both sides of any question. This often puzzles his hearers but to me this is a proof of candour and sincerity ... He is very lively – full of odd contortions ...[His] *indulgent* and benevolent temper has struck me particularly ... He made no pretension to superior sanctity or strictness.[47]

The death from consumption of his elder daughter Barbara at the end of 1821 was a severe blow to Wilberforce, who was advised by his doctors to attend the House 'very little' in the approaching session.[48]

In the first weeks of 1822, when he was 'on the sick list', he completed a public appeal to the tsar on the slave trade. As a witness of the disorder at the queen's funeral, he thought Wilson had been treated 'very harshly', though he would not have supported inquiry into his dismissal from the army, and he was 'glad' at the opposition majority in favour of admiralty reductions, 1 Mar.[49] He resumed attendance later that month, after interviews with Liverpool and Londonderry on the subject of slavery.[50] On the government's colonial trade bills, 1 Apr., he thanked the president of the board of trade for his support for abolition of the slave trade and acknowledged the extent of the West India planters' distress, but expressed his fear that the measures would, 'by increasing the intercourse of our colonies with other nations, facilitate the illicit importation of slaves'. He thought he spoke 'not well', and was 'out of spirits'. He had more talks with ministers, and on 17 May argued that it was desirable to connect with the bills a provision for the registration of slaves. All this formed part of what he described to Stephen as the essential task of 'enlightening ... the public mind on this subject'.[51] He 'half intended to speak' on Russell's parliamentary reform motion, 25 Apr., but in the event voted silently for it, subsequently regretting that he had not explained that he did so 'to put an end to the moral corruption of elections in the smaller towns, where drunkenness and bribery gain the day'.[52] Illness forced him to leave the House before the division on Canning's bill to relieve Catholic peers, of which he warmly approved, 30 Apr.[53] On 2 May Mackintosh found him 'provokingly desultory' in 'vexatious and unprofitable' talks with ministers about the objects of the African Institution.[54] Later that day he spoke and voted for abolition of one of the joint-postmasterships, asserting that the argument that its preservation was 'necessary for the influence of the crown ... seemed calculated to produce a bad impression on the public' at a critical time. Some derogatory remarks on men's motives for joining administrations were interpreted in the press as a slur on Williams Wynn, who had recently come in with the Grenvillites; but they amicably cleared the air, 10 May. Wilberforce, as Williams Wynn reported, 'made a point' of staying to vote in defence of his brother's embassy to Switzerland, 16 May. On 14 May Wilberforce, who sometimes 'felt unfit for public business', slept through the bulk of Hume's attack on the government of the Ionian Islands: 'I was not fit for undertaking to judge, so I retired and gave no vote'.[55] He presented a petition from Christian Separatists to be relieved of the obligation to take oaths, 5 June.[56] He saw no need to divide Yorkshire for electoral purposes as Williams Wynn proposed, 7 June. He agreed with Stephen to postpone the planned motion for the abolition of slavery until next year, as current distress had put the planters in a strong position. He again talked of handing over the lead to Buxton or William Woolryche Whitmore*, while he gave 'occasional assistance as my indifferent health and infirmities will allow': 'My spirits are low, and I feel quite unequal to the bustle and turmoil, which was nothing to me formerly'. He was however, set on bringing forward two addresses to pave the way for an abolition motion; and on 27 June, after hasty last minute preparations, he carried the first, which called for more efforts to stop the foreign slave trade: 'the temper of the House was clearly favourable to the proposal', he wrote, 'and we all came back in high spirits'. That day he voted for Bennet's public house licensing bill. He successfully moved his second address, which called on ministers to prevent the introduction of slavery into the British colonies in South Africa, 25 July, when he supported the appointment of a commission of inquiry into the Cape, Mauritius, Ceylon and the Leeward Islands.[57] Asked by Mackintosh to support the cause of the Greeks against Turkish persecution, 15 July 1822, Wilberforce, sitting on the ministerial side of the House, did so heartily, to the extent even of saying that war would be justified to rescue them from 'bondage and destruction'. Later that day he supported the Irish insurrection bill 'because ... the situation of Ireland demanded it. The want of social order which prevailed in that country was truly lamentable, and he should be most happy if some comprehensive measure could be introduced to remove the evil'.

The succession of his friend Canning to the foreign secretaryship in September 1822 raised Wilberforce's hopes of effective government action on slavery and the slave trade. Canning made him privy to confidential papers, but remained careful not to commit himself.[58] During a round of country house visits in the autumn Wilberforce left behind at Calthorpe's an essential item of equipment:

> Let me ask about a machine (wrapped up for decency's sake in a towel), a steel girdle cased in leather and an additional part to support the anus ... It fits me so much better than any other of the kind I ever used, that I should be very sorry to lose it. It must be handled carefully, the steel being so elastic as to be easily broken ... I constantly wear another of the same sort and had worn that individual machine too long because it answered its purpose better than any other. How gracious is God in giving us such mitigations and helps for our infirmities. But for a machine of this [sort] I must have given up public speaking and indeed public life near 30 years ago.

During his wanderings he was pleased to find confirmation of the 'manifest improvement in the moral (I mean religious) state of the country within the last few years'.[59] He was initially pleased with reports of the duke of Wellington's firmness at Verona on the subject of the slave trade. In December 1822 he wrote to Stephen:

> You little know how I reproach myself for not having expended wisely and economically the many more years of health than from my bodily frame I could reasonably have expected to be employed on earth on my Master's business. I do not mean that I essentially waste much time ... but I am sadly chargeable with the fault of not expending my time with judgement ... For many years it has been the fixed desire of my heart, to employ my faculties as well as I could, to the glory of God and the benefit of my fellow-creatures. But alas, I have been, and I still am, continually led into frittering away on comparatively speaking trifles, that time which ought to be doggedly reserved en masse for real work – solid, substantial, permanent work, vested labour ... and yet, in practice, the boundary lines between the trifles and the serious business are not always very clear.[60]

He lectured his son Samuel on the need to be

> diffident in our judgements of others, and to hold our own opinions with moderation ... The best preparation for being a good politician, as well as a superior man in every other line, is to be a truly religious man. For this

includes in it all those qualities which fit men to pass through life with benefit to others and with reputation to ourselves. Whatever is to be the effect produced by the subordinate machinery, the main-spring must be the desire to please God, which, in a Christian, implies faith in Christ and a grateful sense of the mercies of God through a Redeemer, and an aspiration after increasing holiness of heart and life.[61]

In January 1823 Wilberforce, who took a house at 32 St. James's Place for the new session, concerted plans with Buxton, now the leader, Zachary Macaulay and Smith for their campaign for the abolition of slavery. At the end of the month they formed the Anti-Slavery Society to promote its mitigation and eventual extinction. Wilberforce worked laboriously and fretfully on a 'manifesto' which aimed to 'impress on all religious and good men throughout the empire, that the West Indian slave system ... ought as soon as possible to be abolished; but at least that the subject ought to be duly investigated for the purpose of ascertaining, beyond dispute, the real state of facts, that we may adopt the right line of conduct'. It was published, as *An Appeal to the Religion, Justice, and Humanity of the Inhabitants of the British Empire, in behalf of the Negro Slaves in the West Indies*, in March 1823.[62] Wilberforce, who voted in the minority of 25 to lower the import price of corn to 60s., 26 Feb., wrote in secrecy to Holland and Brougham to enlist their aid for the amelioration campaign, observing to the latter that the basic aim should be to give the slaves 'hope ... one of the grand sweeteners of the cup of life'.[63] On 19 Mar. he presented and briefly endorsed the Quaker petition for the abolition of slavery throughout British territory; George Agar Ellis* thought he 'did not speak so well as usual'. Partly through his own admitted 'mismanagement' and partly through Canning's parliamentary cunning, he was outmanoeuvred and prevented from speaking at length on the motion to print the petition; he was severely 'vexed' and made sleepless by self-reproach.[64] Having been warned that Hume intended to attack the Society for the Suppression of Vice, 26 Mar., he replied to the strictures of Ricardo, whom he accused of seeking to introduce a free trade in morals.[65] In April a chest infection prevented him from attending for debates on the Franco-Spanish conflict and the attack on the Irish attorney-general Plunket's prosecution of the Dublin Orange rioters, which he would have opposed. He was present to vote silently for Russell's parliamentary reform motion, 24 Apr. He defended government against opposition criticism of their handling of the negotiations over Spain, 28 Apr., though he could have wished that their remonstrances to France had taken 'a higher moral tone'. Not wishing to vote, he left the House early, but was prevailed on by Canning to attend the adjourned debate, 30 Apr., only to leave the chamber in the small hours before the division because he was 'not satisfied' with the minister's explanation.[66] In the debate on Buxton's motion for the gradual and total abolition of slavery, 15 May, he found himself, as he told his son, 'in very embarrassing circumstances, from having at once, and without consultation, to decide on' Canning's alternative of resolutions committing Parliament and the government to amelioration. He acquiesced in them, while warning Canning to place no reliance on the co-operation of the colonial legislatures:

I thank God, I judged rightly that it would not be wise to press for more on that night. On the whole, we have done I trust good service, by getting Mr. Canning pledged to certain important reforms. I should speak of our gains in still stronger terms, but for Canning's chief friend [Charles Ellis*] being a West Indian.[67]

The following day he reluctantly stayed away from a public meeting in support of the Greeks on account of 'the danger of hindering our slavery cause, consciousness that I might offend others whose meetings I had declined, and ... feeling very weakly'. On 22 May he spoke and voted for inquiry into the equalization of the duties on East and West Indian sugars, pointing out that the falling slave population of the West Indies proved that there was a 'radical defect' in the system. He avoided the anniversary dinner of the Pitt Club, which had 'become a mere party affair'. On 4 June he pestered Lord Melville, the first lord of the admiralty, on the 'horrid indecencies in our ships of war', and Lord Bathurst, the colonial secretary, on Catholic restrictions on the circulation of bibles in Malta. He had a satisfactory interview with Canning on the slavery issue, 13 June, and that evening spoke 'well, but with little effect' in favour of the postponement of proceedings against chief baron O'Grady. He was alarmed at this time by the 'very violent' speeches of the Irish Catholic leaders, which he feared threatened to incite their followers to 'actual rebellion'.[68] He encouraged Buxton to persevere in his campaign against suttee, 18 June. On 20 June he presented a number of anti-slavery petitions, secured copies of the correspondence with foreign powers on the slave trade and voted for the Scottish juries bill.[69] He spoke and voted in the minority of 19 for Mackintosh's amendment to end capital punishment for privately stealing from shops attached to dwelling houses, 25 June.[70] On Hume's motion for free discussion of religious matters, 1 July, he defended the Constitutional Association and Society for the Suppression of Vice;

but his speech seemed to his own ears 'dry and barren'. He presented a Pershore anti-slavery petition, 2 July, and on the 4th tried unsuccessfully to prevent the exportation of slaves to Trinidad under the slave trade consolidation bill; Canning subsequently agreed to limit its operation to three years.[71] He voted against prison flogging and supported the introduction of jury trial to New South Wales. Wilberforce, who moved to a house in Brompton Grove at the beginning of July, presented the petition of the Rev. John Lempriere complaining of his dismissal from the mastership of Exeter grammar school, 7 July.[72] He gave notice of a motion, which he did not bring on, for inquiry into the condition of slaves in Honduras, 10 July, and presented a Selkirk church petition for the abolition of slavery, 11 July 1823.

Wilberforce was attacked in August by Cobbett for his solicitude for the blacks and indifference to the plight of British factory workers.[73] He sought Brougham's co-operation in stamping out the practice on the northern and other circuits of 'forcing every barrister, on the grand night as I believe it is called, to drink with an audible voice a certain obscene toast'.[74] He renewed his unsuccessful pressure on Melville over the 'shocking licentious practices' prevailing in the naval ports.[75] He largely blamed ministers for the Demerara slave uprising, which he thought had been provoked by their raising of false hopes by the ill-considered and unexplained abolition of the practice of whipping to work; and he told Macaulay in November that 'we should become the assailants'. Ministers were unimpressed with his suggestion at the turn of the year, when he was reported to be 'in good health' and not despondent about the cause, for the allocation of a specific sum in compensation to the planters for eventual abolition.[76] He emerged from an interview with Canning, 14 Feb. 1824, 'sadly disappointed' with the ministerial plan to restrict implementation of the amelioration resolutions to an order in council for Trinidad. He continued discussions with Canning thereafter. On 16 Feb. he told Agar Ellis that he considered the state of the West Indies 'very alarming, from the irritated temper of the negroes, who having been last year encouraged by the government to hope for an amelioration in their condition, are now told they have nothing of the kind to expect'. He attended the House, 1 Mar., expecting a debate on Martin's cruelty to animals bill, but was confronted with a Whig charge of breach of privilege against Eldon, for which he stayed to vote, despite suffering considerable pain.[77] On 16 Mar., when Canning detailed the ministerial plan, Wilberforce, feeling 'better voiced and better heard than usual', said that it was 'idle' to expect action from the colonial governments, attacked the planters for spurning all offers of conciliation and predicted that the 'dilatory and circuitous' scheme would 'incur the imminent risk of involving the colonies in confusion and misery'. He presented anti-slavery petitions from Helston and Montrose the following day.[78] Assessing the state of the abolitionist cause, he wrote to Buxton of

> the solid satisfaction with which I take a *sober estimate* of the progress which, through the goodness of Providence, we have already made, and the good hopes which we may justly indulge as to the future. To find two Houses of Parliament, each full of Members to the brim, consulting about the interests and comforts of those, who, not long ago, were scarcely rated above the level of ourang-outangs, is almost as sure an indication of our complete success ere long, as the streaks of morning light are of the fullness of meridian day.[79]

He thought that Canning easily got the better of Russell on the Spanish issue, 19 Mar. Soon afterwards he contracted pneumonia, which kept him at home for about eight weeks.[80] He attended on 1 June for the debate on the prosecution of the Methodist missionary John Smith in Demerara, which, as Members rushed from the chamber to watch Graham's balloon, was adjourned to the 11th. According to Creevey

> Wilberforce had given all his *serious* acquaintants notice that he meant to take leave of public life in his speech on this occasion, so that every hole and corner was crammed with saints and missionaries in expectation of this great event; when, lo and behold, this wicked aeronaut proved more attractive to the giddy Council of the Nation.

He remained determined to 'bear my testimony against the scandalous injustice exercised upon poor Smith', but when it came to it in the resumed debate he 'quite forgot my topics for a speech, and made sad work of it', reflecting that 'I greatly doubt if I had not better give up taking part in the House of Commons'. Yet Agar Ellis thought he 'spoke ... very eloquently'. In what proved to be his last speech there, 15 June 1824, he made the presentation of an anti-slavery petition from Carlow the pretext for condemning the government's 'fundamentally hopeless' policy on amelioration: 'if mischief happens', he noted privately, 'it will not be chargeable to me'.[81]

The 26th of June 1824 was a red letter day for the costive Wilberforce, who 'to my surprise felt bowels alive and had quite a loose motion'. Almost immediately afterwards he was taken badly ill, and on medical advice he spent some time at Bath, before returning to his latest family home, a cottage at Uxbridge, by the end of the year.[82] He dismissed the suggestion

of Sir John Sinclair† that he should solicit a peerage, which 'would have been carving for myself ... much more than a Christian ought to do'; but, having been warned by his doctor that anything more than very occasional attendance would endanger his life, he resolved to retire at the next dissolution. After further careful consideration, and under pressure from his wife, he decided at the beginning of February 1825 to go out immediately, though the formalities were not completed for about three weeks. He reasoned:

> I am not now much wanted in Parliament; our cause has powerful advocates, who have now taken their stations. The example of a man's retiring when he feels his bodily and mental powers beginning to fail him, might probably be useful. The public have been so long used to see persons turning a long-continued seat in Parliament to account for obtaining rank, etc., that the contrary example [is] the more needed, and it ought to be exhibited by one who professes to act on Christian principles.[83]

No corroboration has been found for the story recorded six years later at third hand by Greville that on his retirement Wilberforce offered Canning 'the lead and direction of his party (the Saints)', which Canning declined after three days' consideration.[84] Later in the year Wilberforce told Gurney that

> though I should not speak truly if I were to charge my parliamentary life with sins of commission (for I can call God to witness, so far as I can recollect, that I always spoke and voted according to the dictates of my conscience, for the public and not for the private interest) yet I am but too conscious of numerous and great sins of omission, many opportunities of doing good either not at all or very inadequately improved.[85]

In April 1825 he bought a cottage at Highwood Hill, Hendon, into which he moved a year later. He maintained his interest in the abolitionist cause, and occasionally chaired Anti-Slavery Society meetings.[86] He toured Yorkshire in 1827, when Sydney Smith told Holland that he 'looks like a little spirit running about without a body, or in a kind of undress without a body'.[87] Some time later Mackintosh wrote of him:

> If I were called upon to describe Wilberforce in one word, I should say he was the most 'amusable' man I ever met with ... Instead of having to think what subjects will interest him, it is perfectly impossible to hit on one that does not ... When he was in the House of Commons, he seemed to have the freshest mind of any man there. There was all the charm of youth about him. And he is quite as remarkable in this bright evening of his days as when I saw him in his glory many years ago.[88]

He suffered a devastating financial blow in March 1830 when the dairy business in which he had set up his eldest son William, a black sheep who had failed at Cambridge, ran into serious difficulties. The resultant expenditure, which he took on himself, forced him to leave and lease Highwood and to sell his birthplace in Hull and nearby land. On becoming aware of Wilberforce's plight, Brougham, lord chancellor in the Grey ministry (whose reform bill was a little too sweeping for Wilberforce's peace of mind), secured church preferment for two of his sons. Wilberforce, by now almost blind, became their lodger.[89] In 1832 he lost his recently married daughter Elizabeth and Stephen. He was well enough to speak at an antislavery meeting at Maidstone in April 1833, but soon afterwards went into terminal decline, rendered virtually immobile by swollen legs and a 'protrusion a posteriori', though he 'preserved his faculties to the very last, and his cheerfulness almost to the very last'. He died, hoping for eternal salvation and aware that the government's bill for the abolition of slavery was certain to become law, in the London house of his cousin Lucy Smith at 44 Cadogan Place in July 1833.[90] Tom Macaulay*, to whom he had shown great kindness in his early political career, told his sister that on his death bed Wilberforce

owned that he enjoyed life much, and that he had a great desire to live longer. Strange in a man who had, I should have said, so little to attach him to this world, and so firm a belief in another – in a man with a ruined fortune, a weak spine, a worn out stomach, a vixen wife, and a reprobate son ... Yesterday evening [30 July] I called at the house in Cadogan Place where the body is lying. It was deserted. Mrs. Wilberforce had gone into the country. Henry was out. Samuel was not yet come. And this great man, so popular, so much worshipped, was left to strangers and servants within thirty-six hours after his death.[91]

In his will of 11 Apr. 1831 he had expressed a wish to be buried 'without the smallest pomp which in such a case seems to me to be preposterous and unseemly' in the Stephen family vault in Stoke Newington churchyard; but in response to a requisition signed by many peers and Members of Parliament his family agreed to his interment in Westminster Abbey, near Pitt, Fox and Canning, on 3 Aug. 1833. He left his wife £300 and household goods, devised his real estate to William and divided his personal estate, which was sworn under £25,000 in the province of Canterbury and under £6,000 in that of York, equally among his three younger sons. There was no residue.[92] Wilberforce's eldest son William (1798-1879) was Conservative Member for Hull, 1837-8, and unsuccessfully contested Bradford and Taunton in 1841. The three younger, Robert Isaac (1802-57), Samuel (1805-73) and Henry William (1807-73) made careers in the

church, with 'Soapy Sam' becoming bishop of Oxford and Winchester. He was the only one to remain in the Church of England, for his three brothers converted to Roman Catholicism in the 1850s.[93]

Wilberforce was a great humanitarian reformer and a very skilled propagandist, whose life and career helped to shape the attitudes of a generation of public men by promoting belief in the possibility of changing human nature through practical Christianity.[94] Littleton observed in 1831 that like all 'truly great men', he had 'activity and energy of mind in its purest and most ethereal form'.[95] Brougham wrote after his death that he was

naturally a person of great quickness and even subtlety of mind, with a lively imagination, approaching a playfulness of fancy; and hence he had wit in an unmeasured abundance ... These qualities, however, he had so far disciplined his faculties as to keep in habitual restraint, lest he should ever offend against strict decorum ... His nature was mild and amiable beyond that of most men. His eloquence was of the highest order. It was persuasive and pathetic in an eminent degree; but it was occasionally bold and impassioned.[96]

Mackintosh said that 'I never saw anyone who touched life at so many points; and this is the more remarkable in a man who is supposed to live absorbed in the contemplation of a future state'.[97]

[1] Based principally on R.I. and S. Wilberforce, *Life of William Wilberforce* (1838) and the two deposits of Wilberforce mss in Bodl. The many current biographies include R. Furneaux, *William Wilberforce* (1974); J. Pollock, *William Wilberforce* (1977); P. Cormack, *Wilberforce* (1983); K.C. Belmonte, *Hero for Humanity* (2002); M. Pura, *Vital Christianity* (2002), and D.J. Vaughan, *Statesman and Saint* (2002). See also the bibliography by L.W. Cowie (1992). [2] Gurney, *Familiar Sketch of Wilberforce* (1838), 10, 13-14; *Gurney Mems.* ed. J.B. Braithwaite, i. 411-12, 493. [3] J.S. Harford, *Recollections*, 255, 262; *Life*, v. 51. [4] Lord Teignmouth, *Reminiscences*, i. 244-7, 253-5. [5] CUL, Smith mss Add. 7621/15, Julia Smith's recollections, 11. [6] Add. 38191, f. 272. See B. Hilton, *Age of Atonement*, 57-61; R.J. Hind, 'Wilberforce and Perceptions of British People', *HR*, lx (1987), 321-35. [7] *Life*, v. 54, for an e.g.; *Melbourne's Pprs.* 379. [8] Hazlitt, *Spirit of the Age* ed. E.D. Mackerness, 239-41; *Black Bk.* (1823), 202. [9] Hants RO, Calthorpe mss 26M62/F/C70-72. [10] *Wilberforce Corresp.* ii. 430; Add. 51820, Wilberforce to Holland, 27 May, 15 June; *The Times*, 19 May 1820. [11] *Life*, v. 54-55, 57; Add. 30123, f. 171; 52444, f. 138; NLW, Coedymaen mss 939; Bodl. (Rhodes House), Buxton mss ms Brit. Emp. s. 444, vol. 1, p. 247; Hatherton diary, 10 June 1820; *Greville Mems.* i. 95. [12] *Life*, v. 56. [13] Add. 52444, f. 151. [14] *Life*, v. 57-58; Hatherton diary, 19 June 1820; Buckingham, *Mems. Geo. IV*, i. 44-45. [15] Add. 52444, f. 165; 56541, f. 43; *Life*, v. 59; Hatherton diary, 21 June 1820. [16] *Life*, v. 59-60; Add. 52444, ff. 120, 168; 56541, ff. 44-45; Hatherton diary, 22 June; Grey mss, Grey to Lady Grey, 23 June 1820; Dorset RO D/BKL, Bankes jnl. 119; Pollock, 271-5. [17] *Life*, v. 61-62; *Greville Mems.* i. 99; *Von Neumann Diary*, i. 27; *Arbuthnot Jnl.* i. 25; Grey mss, Grey to Lady Grey, 24 June 1820; Add. 56541, f. 45. [18] E.M. Forster, *Marianne Thornton*, 19; *Life*, v. 62-68; Bodl. ms. Wilberforce c. 37, ff. 248, 250; d. 16, f. 114; Eg. 1964, f. 96. [19] *The*

Times, 7 July 1820. [20] Eg. 1964, f. 99; Life, v. 70-72. [21] Eg. 1964, f. 99; Pollock, 277; Wilberforce Corresp. ii. 433-5. [22] Life, v. 74-75; Walpole, Russell, i. 121; Bagot, Canning and Friends, ii. 99; Pol. Reg. 12 Aug. 1820. [23] Add. 49508, ff. 16-31. [24] ms. Wilberforce d. 16, f. 130; Life, v. 77; Creevey mss, Creevey to Miss Ord [16 Aug. 1820]; Buckingham, i. 70; Arbuthnot Jnl. i. 31-32; Creevey Pprs. i. 306; Hobhouse Diary, 35. [25] Life, v. 78-79. [26] Bucks. RO, Fremantle mss D/FR46/11/33/1. [27] Add. 38191, ff. 274, 280. [28] Life, v. 79-80; ms. Wilberforce d. 16, f. 122; Teignmouth, 258-9. [29] Life, v. 80-81; ms. Wilberforce d. 16, ff. 136, 145, 148. [30] Add. 38288, f. 209; Arbuthnot Corresp. 18. [31] Add. 31232, ff. 254, 260, 264-8; Cent. Kent. Stud. Camden mss U840/C530/6. [32] Life, v. 84-85; Add. 38742, f. 171. [33] Wilberforce Corresp. ii. 442-5. [34] Life, v. 86; Arbuthnot Jnl. i. 71; Buckingham, i. 122. [35] The Times, 21 Feb. 1821. [36] Life, v. 95. [37] The Times, 17 Mar. 1821; Bankes jnl. 126; Add. 58967, f. 138; Lady Holland to Son, 3; Life, v. 96. [38] Life, v. 96-97; Brougham mss, Wilberforce to Brougham, 23 Apr. 1821; Calthorpe mss F/C273; Pollock, 278-9. [39] The Times, 24 May 1821. [40] Life, v. 100; Buxton Mems. 117-19, 121, 123. [41] The Times, 31 May 1821. [42] Ibid. 1 June 1821. [43] Life, v. 101; Add. 40862, f. 60. [44] The Times, 11 July 1821. [45] Pollock, 277-8; Life, v. 102. [46] Life, v. 106-7; Wilberforce Corresp. ii. 453-4, 456. [47] Edgeworth Letters, 251-2. [48] Life, v. 109-16. [49] Ibid. v. 118-20; Add. 41266, f. 218. [50] Life, v. 121-2; Add. 41267A, f. 99. [51] The Times, 2 Apr. 1822; Life, v. 122-5. [52] Life, v. 125-6. [53] Wilberforce Corresp. ii. 459. [54] Add. 52445, ff. 84-85. [55] Life, v. 127; Buckingham, i. 326, 328-9. [56] The Times, 6 June 1822. [57] Life, v. 128-31; Eg. 1964, f. 107. [58] Life, v. 133-8; Wilberforce Corresp. ii. 466. [59] Calthorpe mss F/C86, 87. [60] Life, v. 154-5. [61] Wilberforce Priv. Pprs. 205-6. [62] Buxton Mems. 124; Life, v. 163-70; Wilberforce Corresp. ii. 473-4. [63] Add. 51820, Wilberforce to Holland, 25 Feb.; Brougham mss, same to Brougham, 20 Mar. 1823. [64] Northans. RO, Agar Ellis diary, 19 Mar. [1823]; Life, v. 170-1; Broughton, Recollections, iii. 17; Furneaux, 406-7. [65] Life, v. 172. [66] Ibid. v. 173-6. [67] Ibid. v. 177-9. [68] Ibid. v. 180-2. [69] The Times, 21 June 1823. [70] Ibid. 26 June 1823. [71] Ibid. 3, 5 July 1823; Life, v. 186. [72] Life, v. 187; The Times, 8 July; Brougham mss, Wilberforce to Brougham, 16 June, 5 July 1823. [73] Pol. Reg. 30 Aug. 1823. [74] Brougham mss, Wilberforce to Brougham, 3 Oct. 1823, 6 Mar., 31 July 1824. [75] Add. 41085, f. 47; ms. Wilberforce c. 39, f. 62. [76] Life, v. 201-2; Macaulay Letters, i. 194; Buxton Mems. 142; Wilberforce Corresp. ii. 477-8. [77] Life, 207-8, 213-15; Agar Ellis diary, 16 Feb. [1824]; ms. Wilberforce c. 39, ff. 61-62. [78] Life, v. 216; The Times, 18 Mar. 1824. [79] Buxton Mems. 149. [80] Life v. 217-21; ms. Wilberforce d. 55, 23 [May 1823]. [81] Creevey Pprs. ii. 76-77; Life, v. 221-3; Agar Ellis diary, 11 June; Brougham mss, Wilberforce to Brougham, 6 July 1824. [82] ms. Wilberforce c. 39, f. 64; Life, v. 225-7. [83] Life, v. 233-9; Buxton Mems. 151-2; Harford, 158-9; Gurney, 34-35; Brougham mss, Wilberforce to Brougham, 3 Feb.; ms. Wilberforce c. 1, f. 115; d. 55, 20 Feb. [1825]. [84] Greville Mems. ii. 126. [85] Life, v. 231. [86] Ibid. v. 248, 262-3, 272; Wilberforce Corresp. ii. 495-8, 524-7; Add. 52453, f. 176. [87] Smith Letters. i. 469. [88] Life, v. 315. [89] Pollock, 296, 302-6; Life, v. 326-7; Wilberforce Priv. Pprs. 264-5; Brougham mss, Wilberforce to Brougham, 28 Apr., 21 June, 19 Sept. 1831, 8 Feb. 1832; CUL, Thornton mss Add. 7674/1/H/11. [90] Life, v. 352, 373; Gurney Mems. i. 494-6; Gladstone Diaries, ii. 51; Wilberforce Corresp. ii. 527; Macaulay Letters, ii. 284-5; Gent. Mag. (1833), ii. 273-6. [91] Macaulay Letters, ii. 286. [92] PROB 11/1825/794; IR26/1342/665; Macaulay Letters, ii. 289-92; Gent. Mag. (1833), ii. 561. [93] See D. Newsome, The Parting of Friends. [94] Hind, 321, 329. [95] Three Diaries, 164. [96] Brougham, Hist. Sketches (1839), i. 269-71. [97] Life, v. 315.

D.R.F.

WILBRAHAM, George (1779–1852), of Delamere Lodge, nr. Northwich, Cheshire and Upper Seymour Street, Mdx.

STOCKBRIDGE	1826–1831
CHESHIRE	1831–1832
CHESHIRE SOUTH	1832–1841

b. 8 Mar. 1779, 1st surv. s. of George Wilbraham[†] of Delamere and Maria, da of William Harvey[†] of Chigwell, Essex. educ. Rugby 1787; Trinity Coll. Camb. 1796. m. 3 Sept. 1814, Lady Anne Fortescue, da. of Hugh Fortescue[†], 1st Earl Fortescue, 5s. suc. fa. 1813. d. 24 Jan. 1852.

Sheriff, Cheshire 1844-5.[1]

In 1784 Wilbraham's father, who could trace his Cheshire roots back to the thirteenth century, had moved the family from Townsend, Nantwich, their seat for the last 200 years, to Delamere Lodge, newly built to James Wyatt's design.[2] Wilbraham inherited it with the residue of his father's personal estate and took possession of the family's London house in Marylebone following his mother's death in a coaching accident in September 1822.[3] His father had made no impression in the House, but his uncle Roger Wilbraham[†] was a well-known Foxite and friend of Thomas Coke I*, and in 1821 Wilbraham recalled that 'from his earliest infancy, he had been taught to look to the example of Lord Crewe', Whig Member for Cheshire, 1768-1802, 'as a model for imitation'.[4] He or his father joined Brooks's, 12 June 1804.[5] His marriage to Lord Ebrington's* sister strengthened his ties with the Whig moderates and the Grenvillite Williams Wynns of Wynnstay, Denbighshire, although, as Lady Williams Wynn observed, the latter generally excluded the Wilbrahams and James Hamlyn Williams*, with whom they were similarly connected, from their guest lists, after the Grenvillites adhered to the Liverpool ministry in 1822.[6] Wilbraham had established himself among Cheshire's Whig coterie at the county meeting of 28 Feb. 1817, vainly attempted to include a condemnation of the proceedings against Queen Caroline in the Cheshire loyal address, 11 Jan. 1821, signed the ensuing protest at the conduct of the Tory sheriff, and became, in his own words, 'particularly active and zealous' in the foundation of the Cheshire Whig Club.[7] As vice-president at the inaugural dinner, 9 Oct. 1821, he condemned the 'harsh, unconstitutional and pernicious' tendency of recent government policy and urged continued pressure for parliamentary reform.[8] Addressing them in 1824, he maintained that the advance of Whig principles in government, through liberal Toryism, owed much to the mobilization of public opinion through organizations such as theirs, and called for a 'more conciliatory policy towards Ireland'.[9] In 1826 he contested Stockbridge successfully on the interest of the wealthy Cheshire Whig, the 2nd Earl Grosvenor, whom he had briefed on manoeuvring there by the former patron Joseph Foster Barham*.[10]

Wilbraham presided at the Cheshire Whig Club in October 1826.[11] He divided with opposition against the duke of Clarence's grant, 16 Feb. 1827. His attendance lapsed during the ministerial uncertainty created by Lord Liverpool's stroke and Canning's succession as premier, but he signalled his opposition to the duke of Wellington's ministry with a vote against the navy estimates, 11 Feb. 1828, he presented a petition from the Dissenters of Nantwich for repeal of the Test Acts, 19 Feb., and prefaced his vote for it, 26 Feb., with what the Whig George Agar Ellis* termed a 'good maiden speech' arguing that the union of church and state was an 'imagined necessity'.[12] He commended the abolition of flogging in the Indian army, and regretted that elsewhere 'the British soldier is still treated like a dog', 10 Mar. He voted against sluicing the franchise at East Retford, 21 Mar. Criticism of Cheshire's palatine jurisdiction and its association with the Welsh courts of great session revived with the appointment of an investigative commission that month, and Wilbraham asked its instigator, the Whig lawyer Henry Brougham and the Cheshire bench to endorse the superfluous inquiry motion by which he had the county's courts added to its remit, 22 Apr.[13] He voted for a reduction from 64s. to 60s. in the corn pivot price, 22 Apr., divided for inquiry into chancery delays, 24 Apr., and on the 28th presented and had an unfavourable Stockbridge petition referred to the select committee on the friendly societies bill, to which he had been appointed, 25 Mar. He divided for Catholic relief, 12 May, against the Canning family's pension, 13 May, for information on civil list pensions, 20 May, and against the proposed expenditure on the Society for the Propagation of the Gospels, 6 June, the barracks, 20 June, and Buckingham House, 23 June 1828. He denied that Cheshire's petition against Catholic emancipation represented general opinion in the county, 24 Feb., praised ministers for conceding the measure, and divided for it, 6, 30 Mar. 1829. Presenting a Nantwich petition for the removal of disabilities affecting Catholics, Quakers and Jews, 20 Mar., he cited the size of the force required to pacify Ireland as proof of the necessity of emancipation. He later implied (5 May) that he had deliberately refrained from voting against narrowing the Irish county franchise as a paving measure, 19 Mar., to safeguard the

relief bill. He spoke of the distressed Macclesfield silk trade, 26 Feb., and opposed the Cheshire constabulary bill as unnecessary, 13 Apr. Before voting to transfer East Retford's seats to Birmingham, 5 Mar., he urged ministers to seize such ready opportunities to enfranchise 'the middling, but now enlightened and valuable portion of the community', recalled his own consistent support for 'that now almost forgotten and ill starred cause of reform', blamed the concept of virtual representation for the loss of the American colonies, and praised the Canadian legislature's practice of granting representation to communities when they reached a certain size. According to *The Times*, he was shut out of the division on Lord Blandford's reform scheme, 2 June.[14] On 9 Oct. 1829, in his absence as chairman, the Cheshire Whig Club put itself into abeyance.[15]

Wilbraham declared that 'he could not approve of sending flattering messages to the duke of Wellington and his colleagues' and was appointed to the committee that drafted a compromise petition at the Cheshire distress meeting, 25 Jan. 1830. He presented a similar one from Stockbridge, 17 Mar.[16] He voted for tax concessions, 15 Feb., and ordered returns that day of public funds held by savings banks. He voted to transfer East Retford's seats to Birmingham, 11 Feb., 5, 15 Mar., and seconded the motion for the enfranchisement of Birmingham, Leeds and Manchester, as 'one step in the right road of practical reform' and a just extension of the influence of the manufacturing interest, 23 Feb. He voted for inquiry into Newark's petition of complaint against the duke of Newcastle's electoral interference, 1 Mar., and Lord John Russell's general reform proposals, 28 May, and divided steadily with the revived Whig opposition until 11 June, including for Jewish emancipation, 5 Apr., reform of the divorce laws, 3 June, and abolition of the death penalty for forgery, 7 June. He presented petitions against the Macclesfield water bill, 5 Apr., and criticizing proceedings in Chester's ecclesiastical court, 11, 30 June. As requested by the county magistrates, he spoke against the proposed abolition of Chester's exchequer court under the administration of justice bill, 27 May;[17] but he nevertheless endorsed the wider measure, which had Grosvenor's approval, after this concession was refused, 18 June. At the general election in July, he supported Grosvenor's heir Lord Belgrave* in Cheshire, where his own candidature had been broached, and retained his seat at Stockbridge after an ill-tempered contest.[18] Afterwards, he publicly disavowed an inflammatory victory address issued under his name by his opponent John Foster Barham*, and subscribed £10 to a relief fund for victims of the July revolution in Paris.[19]

The Wellington ministry naturally listed Wilbraham among their 'foes' and he divided against them on the civil list when they were brought down, 15 Nov. 1830. He presented a Nantwich petition in favour of election by ballot, 28 Feb. 1831, and announced his support for the Grey ministry's reform bill as a 'great healing and constitutional measure' in a letter read to the Cheshire meeting, 17 Mar.[20] He divided for the bill's second reading, 22 Mar. Opposing Gascoyne's wrecking amendment, 19 Apr., he observed that the gradualist approach to reform he had previously advocated had failed, denied that the bill was revolutionary, and asserted that the reduction in Members it proposed would 'cast out 160 drones and take in 115 working bees'. The pro-reform *Chester Chronicle* praised his speech, which with his vote that day (19 Apr. 1831) was deliberately misreported, as 'one of the best and most convincing'.[21] Announcing his candidature for Cheshire at the dissolution that month, he proclaimed his connection 'by birth and habit' with the county's landed interest and promised to 'foster and protect' the growing manufacturing sector.[22] The sitting Tory Wilbraham Egerton declined a contest and the anti-reformers Sir Philip de Malpas Grey Egerton* and Lord Henry Cholmondeley* eventually desisted, leaving Wilbraham, whom the Lancashire and Cheshire reformers had resolved to return free of charge, to come in unopposed with Belgrave. On the hustings he expressed concurrence with the 'leading principles' of the reform bill, cited the enfranchisement of tenant farmers as a desirable amendment to it, and declared against slavery, 'whether it be exercised over black men or over white'.[23]

He divided for the reintroduced reform bill at its second reading, 6 July, against adjournment, 12 July, and fairly steadily throughout August for its details, but despite his remarks on the hustings, he did not apparently vote on Lord Chandos's clause to enfranchise £50 tenants, 18 Aug. 1831. He cast a wayward vote for the complete disfranchisement of Aldborough, 14 Sept., and divided for the bill's passage, 21 Sept., the second reading of the Scottish measure, 23 Sept., and Lord Ebrington's confidence motion, 10 Oct. At the county reform meeting at Nantwich, where he was well received, 25 Oct., he announced that he would not allow his hostility to the proposed division of the county to compromise his support for the reform bill as a whole, and opposed Edward Davies Davenport's* abortive proposal urging that supplies be withheld pending its enactment.[24] He voted for the second reading of the revised reform bill, 17 Dec. 1831, and, except for a wayward vote against the division of counties, which he believed would 'overthrow old associations' and

increase the likelihood of county representation falling entirely under urban or oligarchic influence, 27 Jan. 1832, he divided consistently for its details. He maintained that Cheshire's anti-reform petition was a 'hole in corner' affair unrepresentative of majority opinion in the county, 19 Mar., and commended the bill that day as a 'charter of the middle classes' as great as that granted by King John to the barons. He divided for its third reading, 22 Mar., and the address requesting the king to appoint only ministers who would carry it unimpaired, 10 May. He presented a petition from Hyde for withholding supplies pending its passage, 23 May. He voted for the second reading of the Irish reform bill, 25 May, and against a Conservative amendment to the Scottish measure, 1 June 1832. He divided with government on the Dublin election controversy, 23 Aug. 1831, and the Russian-Dutch loan, 26 Jan., 12, 20 July 1832, but against them on the civil list grants, 18 July, to halve that to the Society for the Propagation of the Gospels in the colonies, 25 July 1831, and the appointment of a select committee on colonial slavery, 24 May 1832.

Attending to constituency business, Wilbraham presented petitions from Macclesfield for legislative control of child labour, 29 June, from Stockport against importing flour, 13 July, one hostile to the Warrington-Newton railway bill, 4 Aug., and several for amendment of the Sale of Beer Act, 4, 25 Aug., 19 Sept. 1831. He cautioned against giving credence to petitions against the imprisonment of the radicals Taylor, Carlile and Carpenter, 22 Sept. Drawing on statistics and a petition from the Macclesfield silk manufacturers, he illustrated the damaging effects of free trade in the Cheshire silk towns, 16 Dec. 1831, 1 Mar. 1832. He presented petitions on 5 Mar. against the general register bill, for amendment of the Lighting and Watching Act, and for and against the factories regulation bill, for which he expressed qualified support, 16 Mar., and he was named to the select committee on the measure that day at his own request.[25] On 2 July he revealed that some manufacturers, of whose good faith he had been certain, had compelled employees to sign petitions opposing the measure. He presented the Cheshire petition complaining of the maladministration of the Cheshire Constabulary Act and wanton expenditure of the magistracy, to which he added his own criticisms of the measure, 10 July 1832. This led to a spat with his colleague Lord Grosvenor (as Belgrave had become), who, irritated by Wilbraham's 'pompous manner', queried the legitimacy of the meeting at which the petition had been adopted. The Grosvenors had come to regard Wilbraham as an irksome upstart, whom they were pleased to upstage at the opening of the Dee Bridge in Chester in October 1832.[26]

When in December 1832 Wilbraham's candidature as a Liberal for the new Cheshire South constituency hazarded her husband's return, Lady Elizabeth Grosvenor observed that he had 'a great number of the people with him, but hardly six gentlemen, which, as he is very touchy, makes him extremely irascible and discontented'.[27] He declared for the existing corn laws, refused to discuss church establishment, and topped the poll.[28] He retained the seat until defeated by a Conservative in 1841, because, it was said, of his conversion to corn law reform.[29] He had long expressed concern at the effect on the Cheshire trade of the East India Company's salt monopoly and advocated its abolition in an 1847 pamphlet, *Thoughts on the Salt Monopoly in India*. He died in January 1852, recalled as 'a man of great firmness and sincerity, earnest in his convictions, and decided in their expression'.[30] His widow (*d.* 1866) retained a life interest in his London house in Lower Brook Street, Mayfair, and Delamere Lodge passed successively to his eldest son George Fortescue Wilbraham (1815-85) and second son Roger William Wilbraham (1817-97).[31]

[1] Cheshire and Chester RO QDA/12/13. [2] J. Hall, *Hist. Nantwich*, 424-5; *Bagshaw's Cheshire Dir.* (1850), 647. [3] PROB 11/1554/192; IR26/628/155; *The Times*, 21 Sept. 1822. [4] *HP Commons, 1754-90*, iii. 637-8; *HP Commons, 1790-1820*, v. 576; *The Times*, 13 Oct. 1821. [5] The admission is misattributed to his father. [6] *Williams Wynn Corresp.*, 317. [7] *The Times*, 5 Mar. 1817, 10, 13, 18 Jan.; NLW ms 2793 D, Mrs. H. to H. Williams Wynn, 17 Apr. 1821. [8] *Chester Chron.* 12 Oct.; *The Times*, 13 Oct. 1821. [9] *The Times*, 13 Oct. 1824. [10] Ibid. 15 May 1824; Grosvenor mss 9/13/53. See STOCKBRIDGE. [11] *Chester Chron.* 13 Oct. 1826. [12] Northants. RO, Agar Ellis diary, 26 Feb. 1828. [13] Brougham mss, Wilbraham to Brougham, 12 Mar.; *The Times*, 26, 29 Mar.; *Chester Chron.* 2, 9 May 1828. [14] *The Times*, 4 June 1829. [15] *Chester Chron.* 16 Oct. 1829. [16] Ibid. 29 Jan. 1830. [17] Cheshire and Chester RO QCX1/2. [18] Grosvenor mss 12/1,2,4; *Macclesfield Courier*, 3 July; *The Times*, 27 July, 6 Aug. 1830. [19] *Salisbury Jnl.* 9 Aug.; Bodl. Clarendon dep. c.369, bdle. 6; Brougham mss, Barham to J. Brougham [Aug. 1830]. [20] *Chester Chron.* 18 Mar.; *Chester Courant*, 5 Apr. 1831. [21] *The Times*, 25 Apr.; *Chester Courant*, 22 Apr. 1831. [22] Ibid. 29 Apr. 1831. [23] *The Times*, 29 Apr., 5 May; *Macclesfield Courier*, 30 Apr., 21 May; *Manchester Times*, 7 May 1831. [24] *Chester Chron.* 28 Oct. 1831; *The Times*, 27 Oct. 1831. [25] *The Times*, 19 Mar. 1832. [26] G. Huxley, *Lady Elizabeth and the Grosvenors*, 42. [27] Ibid. 102-5; *The Times*, 26 Sept. 1832. [28] *Chester Chron.* 14 Dec., *Chester Courant*, 25 Dec. 1832. [29] Huxley, 107-8, *The Times*, 3 June, 1, 19 July 1841. [30] *Chester Chron.* 31 Jan. 1852. [31] PROB 11/2155/534; IR26/1950/329.

H.J.S./M.M.E.

WILBRAHAM   BOOTLE   see   BOOTLE WILBRAHAM

WILDE, Thomas (1782–1855), of 7 King's Bench Walk, Inner Temple and 69 Guildford Street, Russell Square, Mdx.[1]

NEWARK	1831–1832
NEWARK	1835–1841
WORCESTER	1841–July 1846

b. 7 July 1782, 2nd s. of Thomas Wilde, attorney, of College Hill, London and Saffron Walden, Essex and w. Margaret Anne Knight. *educ.* St. Paul's 1785-96; I. Temple 1811, called 1817. *m.* (1) 12 Apr. 1813,[2] Mary (*d.* 13 June 1840), da. of William Wileman, wid. of William Devaynes[†], banker, of Pall Mall, Mdx., 3s. (1 *d.v.p.*) 1da.; (2) 13 Aug. 1845, Augusta Emma D'Este, illegit. da. of Augustus Frederick, duke of Sussex and Lady Augusta Murray, *s.p.* kntd. 19 Feb. 1840; *cr.* Bar. Truro 15 July 1850. *d.* 11 Nov. 1855.

Sjt.-at-law 13 May 1824; king's-sjt. 1827; solicitor-gen. Dec. 1839-July 1841; att.-gen. 3 July-Sept. 1841, 2-6 July 1846; PC 30 Oct. 1846; l.c.j.c.p. 7 July 1846-July 1850; ld. chan. July 1850-Feb. 1852.

Wilde, whose father was a prosperous London attorney, left school at 14 to enter the family firm. His elder brother John (1780-1859) went to Cambridge, was called to the bar in 1805 and was chief justice of the Cape, 1827-55. Wilde, a natural if laborious law student, was admitted attorney in 1805 and, declining a partnership, practised successfully on his own at 7 Castle Street, Falcon Square. Setting his sights on the bar, he enrolled at the Inner Temple in 1811, worked as a certificated special pleader from 1815 and was called in 1817, at the age of 35. His experience and connections, allied to technical ability and great industry, enabled him to rise rapidly and do well on the western circuit, despite his unprepossessing looks, a speech impediment and professional prejudice against his 'origin and manners', which still operated in 1834.[3] On the recommendation of Alderman Matthew Wood* he was retained in 1820 for the defence of Queen Caroline against the bill of pains and penalties. He soon dispelled the doubts of his seniors Brougham and Denman, and was 'extremely able and acute' in cross-examination.[4] As one of the queen's executors he was involved in the negotiations with ministers over her funeral arrangements in August 1821.[5] He subsequently developed an extensive common law practice and in May 1824 was made serjeant-at-law. Soon afterwards Crabb Robinson witnessed his defence in a libel case, when 'he spoke with vehemence and acuteness combined. His vehemence is not united to elegance, so that he is not an orator, but the acuteness was not petty. He will soon be at the head of the common pleas'.[6]

Appointed king's serjeant in 1827, he went on to lead the western circuit.

In February 1829 he was persuaded by professional colleagues to contest the Newark by-election on the independent Blue interest against the duke of Newcastle's anti-Catholic nominee Sadler. At the rowdy nomination he condemned Newcastle's electoral 'tyranny' over the borough, where recalcitrant tenants had been summarily evicted, and welcomed the Wellington ministry's concession of emancipation. He was beaten by 214 votes in a poll of 1,388.[7] He subsequently espoused and helped to promote the Blues' legal campaign against Newcastle's electoral interference and dictation.[8] At the general election of 1830 he was a rumoured candidate for Hull, but in the event he tried again at Newark, where he was beaten into third place.[9] He stood again on a vacancy in February 1831, when his campaign was handicapped by his absence at the trials of the 'Swing' rioters in Hampshire and he was easily beaten by a local man who had Newcastle's support.[10] In April 1831 the Grey ministry's patronage secretary Ellice told Brougham, now lord chancellor, that it might be possible to provide Wilde with a seat for £2,500, a price 'not too great for that desirable object'.[11] At the general election precipitated by the defeat of the reform bill he offered again for Newark, after turning down an invitation to stand for Poole.[12] He declared for reform and the ballot, condemned the undue influence exercised by Newcastle and said he would 'desert the Whigs the moment they deserted reform'. He topped the poll. At a celebration dinner he reiterated his commitment to reform, but argued that the best safeguard for the poor rested in the just influence of property in the hands of benevolent men. He said that he considered the proposed £10 English borough franchise to be too exclusive, but that he would waive his objection in order to secure the greater object.[13]

Wilde voted silently for the second reading of the reintroduced reform bill, having failed to catch the Speaker's eye, 6 July,[14] and against the adjournment, 12 July, and the proposal that the borough disfranchisement schedules should be determined by the 1831 census, 19 July; but he was absent (on the circuit) from the divisions on details, 26 July-9 Aug. 1831. On 17 Aug. he spoke and voted for allowing urban freeholders a county vote, and next day he was in the government minority against the enfranchisement of £50 tenants-at-will. He defended the provisions for returning officers, 19 Aug., and opposed Hunt's proposal for a general householder franchise, 24 Aug., when he called on reformers not to 'urge their exclusive views, as that would certainly tend to defeat the

measure' in the Lords. He tried to clarify the clause dealing with borough tenants' qualification, 26 Aug., and divided with ministers against preserving freemen's voting rights, 30 Aug., and permitting non-resident freeholders of the four sluiced boroughs to vote, 2 Sept. He praised the 'simplicity' of the registration procedure, 5 Sept. He voted for the third reading, 19 Sept., and passage of the bill, 21 Sept., after endorsing the Hertford petition complaining of Lord Salisbury's 'gross abuse of power', and for the second reading of the Scottish measure, 23 Sept. He denied Sir Abraham King's entitlement to compensation for surrendering his Irish patent office, 11, 18 July, when he acquiesced in the grant of £240,000 for the civil list, but called for future inquiry and asked Lord Althorp, the chancellor of the exchequer, to speak up when addressing the House. On 21 July he defended Henry Bingham Baring* and the Hampshire magistrates against the allegations of assault made by the Deacles; and when their petition for redress was brought up, 22 Aug., he refuted the accusation that he had traduced them. He gave up an important chancery brief and the first two days of the circuit in order to address the committee of privileges on the Wellesley Pole case, on which he was at odds with Brougham, 22 July. Edward Littleton* believed he was ambitious to become solicitor-general and therefore keen to make ministers 'feel his power'. According to Lord Holland, 'upon a hint' he 'backed out of it' and went the circuit.[15] On 22 Aug. he spoke in favour of the immediate compensation of Lescene and Escoffery for their expulsion from Jamaica. He divided with government on the Dublin election controversy, 23 Aug., but voted against the issue of a new writ for Liverpool, 5 Sept. He upheld the Irish master of the rolls's right to appoint his own secretary, 16 Sept., and criticized some of the Lords' amendments to the game bill, which 'invaded the rights of property', 30 Sept. He welcomed Brougham's bill to reform the 'most imperfect and inefficient' bankruptcy administration, 5 Oct., and supported the proposal to transfer the business of the Scottish exchequer court elsewhere, 7 Oct. He voted for Lord Ebrington's confidence motion, 10 Oct., and supported clauses of the bankruptcy bill, 14, 15, 17 Oct. 1831.

Wilde, who was reported to be a contender for the office of solicitor-general in December 1831,[16] voted for the second reading of the revised reform bill on the 17th, and divided steadily for its details. He approved the proposal that sheriffs should appoint borough returning officers, 24 Jan., and on 16 Feb. 1832 commended the clause which clarified prevailing election law. He was absent from the division on the third reading, 22 Mar. He was in the minority for

Hobhouse's vestry reform bill, 23 Jan., but divided with ministers on relations with Portugal, 9 Feb. He voted for the motion for an address calling on the king to appoint only ministers who would carry reform unimpaired, 10 May, and the second reading of the Irish reform bill, 25 May. He spoke and was a minority teller for Buxton's motion for the immediate abolition of slavery, 24 May.[17] He was named to the East India select committee, 25 May. He divided with government on the Russian-Dutch loan, 12, 16, 20 July 1832, when he presented a private petition against the bankruptcy bill and regretted that no opportunity had been given to discuss the measure.

At the general election of 1832 Wilde, who never joined Brooks's, was defeated at Newark by two Conservatives. He regained the seat in 1835. He was described in 1837 as 'an excellent speaker' and a 'stoutly and compactly formed' man with 'large' eyes 'full of fire and intelligence'.[18] Appointed solicitor-general by Lord Melbourne in 1839, he attained the pinnacle of his profession less than 11 years later. His judicial patience became a by-word. He died at his London home in Eaton Square in November 1855 and was succeeded in the peerage by his elder surviving son Charles Robert Claude (1816–91).[19]

[1] See J.B. Atlay, *Victorian Chancellors*, i. 417-55; *Oxford DNB*. [2] *The Times*, 15 Apr. 1813. [3] *Holland House Diaries*, 265. [4] Brougham, *Life and Times*, ii. 381; Arnould, *Denman*, 160-1. [5] *Creevey Pprs.* ii. 21-22, 24. [6] *Crabb Robinson Diary*, i. 406. [7] *The Times*, 27, 28 Feb., 2, 4-6, 8 Mar.; *Nottingham Jnl.* 7, 14 Mar. 1829. [8] *The Times*, 2, 7, 16 Oct. 1829. [9] *Lincoln and Stamford Mercury*, 9 July; *Nottingham Jnl.* 7, 14 Aug. 1830. [10] *Lincoln and Newark Times*, 23 Feb.; *Nottingham Jnl.* 26 Feb 1831. [11] Brougham mss. [12] *Dorset Co. Chron.* 14 Apr. 1831. [13] *Lincoln and Newark Times*, 4, 11, 25 May 1831. [14] *Life of Campbell*, ii. 518. [15] Hatherton diary, 20, 22 July 1831; *Holland House Diaries*, 15. [16] *Life of Campbell*, ii. 2. [17] Bodl. (Rhodes House) Buxton mss Brit. Emp. S. 444, vol. 2. p. 251, H. Buxton to F. and R. Cunningham [25 May 1832]. [18] [J. Grant], *Random Recollections of Commons* (1837), 309, 312. [19] *Gent. Mag.* (1855), ii. 664-5.

S.R.H.

WILDMAN, James Beckford (1788–1867), of Chilham Castle, Kent.

COLCHESTER   19 Feb. 1818–1826

b. 18 Oct. 1788,[1] 1st s. of James Wildman[†] of Chilham and Joanna, da. of J. Harper of Jamaica. *educ.* Winchester 1800-6; Christ Church, Oxf. 1808; L. Inn 1811. *m.* 9 Oct. 1820, Mary Anne, da. of Stephen Rumbold Lushington*, 2s. 5da. (1 *d.v.p.*). *suc.* fa. 1816. *d.* 25 May 1867.

In 1816 Wildman had inherited from his father a Kent estate near Canterbury and the Esher plantation in Jamaica, both the fruits of his father's and uncles'

profitable association with and exploitation of the eccentric wastrel William Beckford[†], together with the residue of personalty sworn under £30,000.[2] At the general election of 1820 he successfully contested Colchester for the second time in two years, on the True Blue interest of the corporation.[3] He continued to support the Liverpool ministry when present, but he was extremely lax in his attendance.[4] He introduced, 30 May, and defended on its second reading, 20 June 1820, a bill to establish quarter sessions at Colchester, but it was defeated by 118-55; he was a minority teller.[5] In the autumn he married a daughter of Lushington, the financial secretary to the treasury, who at Christmas, writing from a family gathering at Chilham, told Robert Peel* that he and Wildman, like 'all good Protestants', were keen to see him back in the cabinet as their 'bulwark'.[6] Wildman presented Colchester corporation's petition against Catholic relief before voting accordingly, 28 Feb. 1821.[7] He divided against Canning's bill to relieve Catholic peers, 30 Apr. 1822. He voted in defence of ministers' conduct towards Queen Caroline, 6 Feb., and against the omission of arrears from the duke of Clarence's grant, 18 June 1821. He chaired the anniversary dinner of the Colchester True Blue Club, 20 Nov. 1821.[8] He divided against more extensive tax remissions, 21 Feb. 1822. Despite his poor attendance record, he was chosen to second the address, 4 Feb. 1823, when he congratulated the House on 'the happy prospect of improvement held out to the country', hoped for continued exertions to eradicate the 'iniquitous traffic' of the slave trade and advised complaining agriculturists to diversify their crops. He presented Colchester corporation's anti-Catholic petition, 17 Apr. 1823.[9] At the end of the year he was in Jamaica 'for the purpose of protecting his West India property';[10] and no trace of parliamentary activity has been found for 1824. He presented a Colchester petition in favour of the St. Katharine's Docks bill, 11 Feb. 1825.[11] He defaulted on a call of the House, 28 Feb., but attended and was excused the following day, when he divided against Catholic relief. He presented hostile petitions from East Donyland and Colchester, 19 Apr.,[12] voted against the relief bill, 21 Apr., and paired against its third reading, 10 May. He voted against the Irish franchise bill, 26 Apr., when he gave suppers to about 200 members of the various Colchester loyal clubs. At the Loyal Association's celebration of the king's birthday next day, he declared that Catholic emancipation was 'not the nostrum to cure Ireland's disorders and that the followers of ... the Pope were ... as unfit for place and power in this Protestant country as ever'. He also indicated that he was 'decidedly opposed' to any alteration of the corn laws; he brought up an eastern Essex petition to that effect, 28 Apr. He extolled 'the Protestant ascendancy' at the Colchester True Blue Club, 22 Nov. 1825.[13] He presented a Colchester anti-slavery petition, 14 Feb. 1826.[14] His contests had reportedly cost him over £16,000, and 'pecuniary embarrassment' was the reason given for his retirement from Parliament at the 1826 dissolution.[15]

Wildman, who was a steward for the Kent dinner in honour of the Ultra Tory county Member Knatchbull in August 1831,[16] seems to have disposed of his Jamaican property during his lifetime. His grandiose plans for the improvement and enlargement of Chilham Castle were never implemented, but he founded a new village school there. He sold the estate in 1861 and bought Yotes Court, Mereworth, near Maidstone. He died there in May 1867.[17] By his will, dated 1 Mar. 1865, he provided through a trust fund for his wife and his six surviving children and their families.

[1] M.I. in Chilham church (C. Hardy, *Chilham Castle*, 36). [2] *Gent. Mag.* (1816), i. 375; PROB 11/1579/229; IR26/693/220; Heron, *Notes*, 264; *HP Commons, 1790-1820*, v. 577-8. [3] *Suff. Chron.* 26 Feb., 4, 11 Mar. 1820; *Procs. at Colchester and Essex Elections* (1820), 8-9, 25-8, 29, 37-38. [4] *Black Bk.* (1823), 202; *Session of Parl. 1825*, p. 490. [5] *CJ*, lxxv. 226, 249, 331; *The Times*, 31 May, 21 June 1820. [6] Add. 40344, f. 75. [7] *The Times*, 1 Mar.; *Colchester Gazette*, 3 Mar. 1821. [8] *Colchester Gazette*, 24 Nov. 1821. [9] *The Times*, 18 Apr. 1823. [10] *Colchester Gazette*, 22 Nov. 1823. [11] *The Times*, 12 Feb. 1825. [12] Ibid. 20 Apr. 1825. [13] Ibid. 29 Apr.; *Colchester Gazette*, 30 Apr., 26 Nov. 1825. [14] *The Times*, 15 Feb. 1826. [15] *Kent and Essex Mercury*, 14 Oct. 1823; *Colchester Gazette*, 27 May 1826; Bodl. MS. Eng. lett. c. 159, f. 38. [16] *Maidstone Jnl.* 19 July, 9 Aug. 1831. [17] Hardy, 15; *Gent. Mag.* (1867), ii. 119.

S.K./D.R.F.

WILKINS, Walter (1741–1828), of Maesllwch, Rad. and Wallsworth Hall, Glos.

RADNORSHIRE   1796–17 Mar. 1828

b. 14 or 15 Nov. 1741, 2nd. s. of John Wilkins (*d.* 1784),[1] attorney, of The Priory, Brecon and Sybil, da. of Walter Jeffreys of Llywel, Brec. *educ.* Christ Coll. Brecon; Winchester 1754-8; Reeves's acad., Bishopsgate Street, London 1758. *m.* 24 Feb. 1777, Catherine, da. and h. of Samuel Hayward of Wallsworth Hall, 1s. 1da. *d.* 17 Mar. 1828.

Writer, E.I. Co. (Bengal) 1758; resident, Lakhipur by 1768; sen. merchant and gov. Chittagong 1771; member, supreme council 1772; res. 1772.

Sheriff, Rad. 1774-5, Brec. 1778-9; lt.-col. commdt. Rad. vols. 1803; lt.-col. E. Brecon militia 1809.

Wilkins, a descendant of the de Wintons of Breconshire and Glamorgan, had used his East Indian wealth to buy one of Radnorshire's largest estates and invest in his family's Brecon bank and South Wales canals and iron works.[2] Seeking his seventh return for Radnorshire in 1820, he boasted:

> For the last 24 years ... I have diligently endeavoured to the best of my abilities to discharge the duties of an independent Member of Parliament. I have most conscientiously adopted every measure which I conceived best calculated to promote the true interests of our common country. I have always supported every proposition for a moderate reform in the House of Commons as likely to be highly advantageous to the public welfare, but I have been no advocate for those wild theories which, so intemperately urged by weak and wicked men, have afforded a pretext (which has been too eagerly seized upon) for abridging the ancient and dear bought rights and liberties of Britons. Gentlemen, on these principles I have uniformly acted, on these I shall continue to act.[3]

Initially his votes had been difficult to predict, but in the 1818 Parliament he had divided steadily with the Whig opposition to Lord Liverpool's ministry on retrenchment, civil liberties and legal and parliamentary reform, and he was a known opponent of corn law revision and supporter of Catholic relief. He attended the Radnorshire meeting that sent addresses of condolence and congratulations to George IV, 14 Mar., and was returned unopposed at Presteigne, 17 Mar. 1820. At the Breconshire elections he was represented by his only son Walter Wilkins (1777-1830), the unsuccessful candidate in Brecon in 1818.[4]

Wilkins divided steadily with the main Whig opposition on most major issues and with the 'Mountain' for economy and retrenchment in the 1820 Parliament. He supported the parliamentary and extra-parliamentary campaigns on behalf of Queen Caroline in 1820 and 1821,[5] and chaired the Brecon county meeting of 20 Jan. 1821 which petitioned for parliamentary reform and urged the king to dismiss his ministers.[6] He paired for Catholic relief, 28 Feb. 1821, and voted for it, 1 Mar., 21 Apr. 1825. He divided for parliamentary reform, 25 Apr. 1822, 13 Apr. 1826. *Seren Gomer* lauded Wilkins as the only Welsh Member to vote for Brougham's motion on the distressed state of the country, 11 Feb. 1822, and he divided consistently for economies that session, including a gradual reduction of the salt duties, 28 Feb. He presented and endorsed the Radnorshire distress petition, 26 Apr. 1822.[7] According to *The Times*, 21 Feb. 1823, he paired in condemnation of the peacetime appointment of a lieutenant-general of the ordnance, 19 Feb., but that session he was dogged by ill health, for which he was granted a month's leave, 14 Apr. 1823. He divided for

information on Catholic burials, 6 Feb., and the negotiations with France and Spain, 17 Feb., and steadily with opposition until 5 Apr. He presented and
endorsed anti-slavery petitions, 2, 4, 26 Mar. 1824.[8]
Though named to bring in the Radnor, Hereford and
Meirioneth roads bill, 12 Mar. 1824, he clearly delegated doing so to others.[9] As he freely admitted, age
and infirmity made it impossible for him to attend to
much parliamentary business, and henceforward his
known votes were paired. Even so, a radical publication of 1825 gave the impression that he 'attended frequently and voted with opposition'.[10] *The Times* added
Wilkins's name to its list of Members paired against
receiving the report on the salary of the president of
the board of trade, 10 Apr. 1826.[11] His son deputized
for him and Sir Harford Jones Brydges was his spokesman at Presteigne when he was returned *in absentia* at
the 1826 general election. His printed notices praised
opposition, but expressed indifference 'as to the source
of measures provided they are good'.[12]

Wilkins paired for Catholic relief, 6 Mar. 1827, and
repeal of the Test Acts, 26 Feb. 1828. He was named
as hitherto to sponsor local legislation in 1826-8.[13]
Despite his advanced age and infirmity, his sudden
death at his London home in March 1828 took his
business associates by surprise and caused problems
for the Brecon Bank, in which he had remained a
partner.[14] Thomas Frankland Lewis, his successor as
Member for Radnorshire, thought he 'had been useful
rather in obstructing what he thought to be wrong
than in forwarding or providing measures of a contrary tendency'.[15] By his will, dated 24 May 1823 and
proved under £250,000, he entrusted his Breconshire,
Glamorgan and Radnorshire estates to his nephews,
the Rev. Walter Wilkins of Hay and Thomas Maybery
of the Brecon Bank, making Walter, who in September
1828 separated from his wife, life-tenant. He left annuities and cash sums to other relatives and servants. His
executors, who controlled £267,139 6s. 7d. in capital
and investments, called in £38,285 of the £61,982
lent by Wilkins in mortgages.[16] Walter's son Walter
Wilkins (1809-40), Liberal Member for Radnorshire
from 1835 until his death, reassumed the name de
Winton by royal license, 6 July 1839.[17]

[1] Powys RO MP3/2 (10 May 1784). [2] D.R. Ll. Adams, 'Parl. Rep.
Rad. 1536-1832' (Univ. of Wales M.A. thesis, 1969), 674-5; NLW,
Maybery mss 125, 341, 4019; *Modern S. Wales.* ed. C. Baber and
J.G. Williams, 33, 66-67; R.O. Roberts, 'Brecon Old Bank, 1778-
1890', *Brycheiniog*, vii (1961), 56-70. [3] *Hereford Jnl.* 16 Feb. 1820.
[4] Ibid. 8, 22, 29 Mar. 1820. [5] Ibid. 22 Nov. 1820. [6] *The Times*, 24
Jan., 15 Feb.; *Cambrian*, 27 Jan. 1821. [7] *Seren Gomer*, v (1822), 91,
124, 187. [8] *The Times*, 3, 5 Mar., 6 Apr. 1824. [9] *CJ*, lxxix. 154, 191,
247. [10] *Session of Parl.1825*, p. 490. [11] *The Times*, 12, 15 Apr.; *Hereford
Jnl.* 14 June 1826. [12] NLW, Harpton Court mss C/397, 595; *Hereford*

Jnl. 28 June 1826. [13] *Hereford Jnl.* 20 Sept. 1826, 17 Jan. 1827; *CJ*,
lxxxiii. 35. [14] Maybery mss 3595-6. [15] *Cambrian*, 19 Apr. 1828.
[16] PROB 11/1742/394; IR26/1181/307; Maybery mss 4019-72;
NLW, D.T.M. Jones mss 1769. [17] Powys digital archives project,
Maesllwch 3.

M.M.E.

WILKS, John I (c.1776–1854), of 3 Finsbury Square,
London.

BOSTON 1830–1837

b. c. 1776, s. of Rev. Matthew Wilks (*d.* 1829), wholesale
stationer and pastor, of Old Street Road, London and
Elizabeth, da. of John Shenstone of Halesowen, Staffs.
m. (1) Mary (*d.* 26 Feb. 1814), 2s. 3da.[1]; (2) 2 Sept. 1829,
Isabella Sarah Stubbs (*d.* 18 Jan. 1846), *s.p.*[2] *d.* 25 Aug.
1854.

A cradle radical and Dissenter raised in Hoxton,
where he later became a trustee of the academy, Wilks
was one of seven children (probably the eldest) born
to 'the eccentric but useful minister of Whitfield's
Tabernacle in Moorfields' Matthew Wilks and his
wife, a cousin of the poet William Shenstone.[3] He
became a founder member with his father in 1798
of the Missionary Society, drafted and published
their *Apology* in 1799, and qualified as an attorney
in 1800 after being articled to Philip Morshead of
Biliter Square, London. He acquired political prominence and employment through his father's sponsorship of the Village Itinerancy Society and the Royal
Institution for the Education of the Poor, and by
establishing the Protestant Society for the Protection
of Religious Liberty (1811) to lobby for Test Acts
repeal and Dissenters' rights. As their secretary for the
next 25 years, he corresponded regularly with ministers, the Whig hierarchy and the Dissenting deputies.[4]
In 1809, at the third attempt, he became vestry clerk
and acquired for his legal practice the business of the
populous Middlesex parish of St. Luke, Old Street,
where his tenure remained unchallenged until 1826,
despite complaints about St. Luke's strong support
for the Protestant Society's petitioning campaigns and
unease at the conduct of Wilks's sons by his first marriage, John Wilks II* and Rowland Wilks, who had
been articled to him.[5] Assisted by Rowland and the
Dissenters, whose opposition to Henry Brougham's
1820 education bill and support for the 1823-6 anti-
slavery campaign and the Spanish Liberals he had
orchestrated, Wilks belatedly contested Boston,
where he polled a good third on the 'Blue' or radical
interest at the general election of 1826.[6] He deliberately held aloof from the 'bubble' ventures and candidature for Sudbury of John Wilks II and devoted

the summer to drafting and depositing *Crynhodeb o'r Weithred*, the administrative conventions of the Welsh Calvinistic Methodists, but failed to escape suspicion that 'they were both rogues alike' when the 'bubble' burst in October 1826.[7] His 'discrediting' in 1829 by the vestry of St. Luke's, who thwarted his attempt to transfer the clerkship to Rowland, had him prosecuted for malpractice and embezzlement (Whitmore and another *v.* John Wilks) and encouraged the government 'spy' Richmond to sue him for libel, coincided with invitations to Wilks to contest Queenborough and Colchester on the anti-corporation interests.[8] However, it was Boston, where he financed trial borings for water in the market place in 1826 and 1828 at an estimated cost of £2,000, which returned him in 1830, when he succeeded the Norwich Member William Smith as the parliamentary spokesman of Dissent.[9] He made slavery, civil and religious liberty, reform and the corruption of the corporation the election issues and was arraigned as 'an old vestry clerk of canting notoriety', dependent on St. Luke's and the London Alderman Matthew Wood* for character references.[10] Brougham, with whom he had liaised on behalf of the Protestant Society to secure Test Acts repeal in 1828 and Catholic emancipation in 1829, and whose return for Yorkshire he now applauded, predicted that Wilks, who promised 'at least by my votes to maintain the principles which certainly promote the honour and happiness of man', would divide regularly with opposition.[11] Though 'defective in pronouncing the letter "R"', he proved to be a fluent, frequent and effective parliamentary speaker, described by a commentator in 1837 as 'of middle size ... slenderly formed ... [and] venerable appearance. His face is angular. His nose is prominent and his eyes are large. His complexion is florid and his hair a dark brown. The crown ... partially bald'.[12]

The Wellington ministry counted Wilks among their 'foes', and he divided against them when they were brought down on the civil list, 15 Nov. 1830. He commended the Dissenters on bringing up their numerous anti-slavery petitions, 4, 10, 11, 12 Nov., and urged Robert Grant to reintroduce his Jewish emancipation bill on their behalf, 11 Nov., but he had to concede that day that the Wesleyan Methodists remained reluctant to entrust petitions to him. He presented over 75 anti-slavery petitions on eight further occasions between 17 Nov. 1830 and 29 Mar. 1831. During the same period he ordered returns, 23 Nov., and promised legislation to reduce Dissenters' liabilities for church rates, 25 Nov., which neither the new Grey ministry nor the anti-reformers in opposition were prepared to support, and endorsed petitions and

pressed the case for civil registration, 22 Nov., 16 Dec., open vestries, 16 Dec. 1830, and tithe reform, 29 Mar. 1831. East India Company interests ensured that his calls for the abolition of the pilgrim tax, 30 Dec. 1830, 3 Feb., 29 Mar. 1831, and Hindoo immolation, 23 Dec. 1830, 3 Feb. 1831, were rejected. He raised objections on behalf of the Middlesex parishes opposed to the metropolitan police levy, 18, 30 Nov., 7, 8, 21 Dec. 1830, and ordered returns with a view to securing its reduction, 30 Mar. 1831, presented petitions and endorsed Boston's opposition to the tax on the coastal coal trade, 8 Dec. 1830, and made representations on behalf of the 8,000 or so small friendly societies, representing two million 'of the industrious population', that remained unregistered under the 1829 Act, 8 Feb. 1831.

Although critical of their spending on ambassadors' salaries, Wilks declared for the Grey administration, stating that he expected them to promote freedom and reform and reduce expenditure, 13 Dec. 1830. He presented Boston's petition for retrenchment and reform, 16 Dec., ordered detailed returns of taxable houses in all counties and franchised and unfranchised boroughs, 21 Dec. 1830 (delivered, 17 Mar. 1831) and presented and endorsed further pro-reform petitions, 28 Feb., 17, 19, 29 Mar. 1831, including one for the ballot, 28 Feb. He said that he looked to the ministerial bill as a means of reducing the influence of closed corporations, 17 Mar., endorsed the parishioners of St. Luke's petition in its favour, 19 Mar., and voted for its second reading, 22 Mar., and against Gascoyne's wrecking amendment, 19 Apr. 1831. He had rallied with the London radicals and Dissenters at the *Crown and Anchor* in March to denounce Russian aggression in Poland, and wrote to the Lincolnshire newspapers to publicize his great activity in the House as a reformer.[13] Proclaiming that 'the churchman has not withheld his approbation from a Dissenter, and all Dissenters have united in the great cause of reform', he polled second at Boston at the 1831 general election to his fellow reformer Heathcote.[14]

He voted for the second reading of the reintroduced reform bill, 6 July, presented a favourable Boston petition, 14 July 1831, and generally divided silently and steadily for its details. He spoke out against any which he deemed unadvisable, and refused to align with the bill's radical detractors such as Hunt.[15] He voted for the total disfranchisement of Saltash, which ministers no longer urged, 26 July, and in the minorities for the separate enfranchisement of Merthyr Tydfil, which Welsh Members advocated, 10 Aug., against the proposed division of counties, 11 Aug., and to transfer

Aldborough from Schedule B to A, 14 Sept. He protested that the arrangements for appointing returning officers for the new metropolitan constituencies were ill defined, 10 Aug., 6 Sept. To Heathcote's annoyance, he echoed the Lincolnshire Members' opposition to dividing their county, 10, 11, 12 Aug., 14 Sept., and highlighted anomalies in the proposed urban ratepayer franchise, 19, 25, 26 Aug., 13 Sept. He presented petitions from freemen whose enfranchisement by marriage the bill abolished, 27, 30 Aug., 2 Sept., but voted with the majority against preserving all freemen's rights, 30 Aug. He deliberately eschewed his personal preference for a longer interval between the nomination and poll, 2 Sept., and for triennial parliaments and a poor rate based franchise, 6, 13 Sept., lest by seeking amendment he should jeopardize the bill. He voted for its passage, 21 Sept., and Lord Ebrington's confidence motion, 10 Oct. 1831. His parliamentary conduct was commended by the Middlesex reform meeting at Hackney, 27 Sept., where he called for addresses to the king from every parish in the kingdom should the bill be defeated in the Lords.[16] He divided for the second reading of the revised reform bill, 17 Dec. 1831, its details, 20, 23 Jan., 28 Feb., and third reading, 22 Mar. 1832, intervening only to criticize its provisions for Lincolnshire, 20, 23, 24 Jan., and Stamford, 19, 23 Mar., which, with the changes to neutralize Lord Lonsdale's influence in Whitehaven, he opposed as a minority teller against the boundary bill, 22 June. He voted for the address calling on the king to appoint only ministers who would carry the bill unimpaired, 10 May, for the second reading of the Irish measure, 25 May, and against a Conservative amendment to the Scottish bill, 1 June, but was in O'Connell's minority for extending the franchise to £5 Irish freeholders, 18 June. He reiterated his support for triennial parliaments on presenting Boston's petition for amendment of the bribery bill, 30 July, and proposed legislating for it in the next Parliament, 6 Aug. 1832. He voted in the minority for appointing 11 of its original members to the reconstituted Dublin election committee, 29 July, with ministers against censuring the Irish government for electoral interference, 23 Aug., against Benett's 'time-wasting' Liverpool franchise bill, 5 Sept. 1831, and in the government majorities on the Russian-Dutch loan, 26 Jan., and the navy and civil departments bill, 6 Apr. 1832.

Wilks's radicalism was more pronounced in the 1831-2 Parliament and he was expected to 'cordially unite with such men as O'Connell, Hume, Colonel Evans, Warburton ... [and] Whittle Harvey, and ... take a firmer stand in the contest for popular rights'.[17] He voted in small minorities on the grant for professors'

salaries, 8 July 1831, 13 Apr. 1832, and the civil list, 18 July 1831, which he again criticized before voting against the award for the Society for the Propagation of the Gospels, 25 July. He cast a hostile vote for printing the Waterford petition for disarming the Irish yeomanry, 11 Aug. He presented and endorsed petitions for inquiry into the Deacles' case, 16, 19 Sept., and seconded, 22 Sept., and voted, 27 Sept., for motions advocating it. He voted in Hume's minorities of 12 against expenditure on the royal palaces, 28 Sept. 1831, and of ten for receiving a petition for the repeal of Irish tithes, 2 Aug. 1832, with Hunt for inquiry into the Peterloo massacre, 15 Mar., and for inquiry into smuggling in the glove trade, 3 Apr. 1832. He presented petitions from the Protestant Society for a reduction in official oath taking, 12 July, 17 Oct. 1831, and called for toleration towards those declining to take them on grounds of 'Christian conscience', 4 Oct., and an end to restrictions whereby (as in Boston) borough officers could be elected only in a parish church, 20 July 1831, and Dissenting clergy denied access to capital offenders, 16 Aug. 1832. He considered Sabbath observance a matter of conscience, provided local legislation was adequately enforced, and refused to be goaded into giving indiscriminate support to all petitions on the subject, 2, 14 Sept., 12 Oct. 1831, 6, 16 Aug. 1832. He advocated a civil registration system similar to the French one, 2 Sept., condoned the locally unpopular general register bill as a consultative measure 4, 12 Oct. 1831, and seconded Lord Nugent's motion for civil registration of baptisms, 23 Feb. 1832. He called for repeal of the newspaper duties, 12 Aug., and changes to the game laws, 3, 8 Aug., and the highways bill favourable to the agricultural poor, 3 Aug. 1831. Citing their current maladministration in England, he spoke against extending the provisions of the poor laws to Ireland, 26 Sept., and criticized and ordered returns to demonstrate the preponderance of squarson magistrates in the shires, 28 Sept. He defended the bankruptcy bill on behalf of its author lord chancellor Brougham, 17 Oct., but pointed out that chancery folios contained 90 words, not 72, as stated. He continued to press for abolition of the pilgrim tax, 14, 17 Oct., and reform of church rates, 21 July 1831, 9 Aug. 1832, and reacted swiftly to reports of maltreatment of Catholics and Nonconformists in Canada and Jamaica, when matters relating to the two colonies came before the House, 25 July, 14 Oct. 1831, 13, 18 Apr. 1832. He favoured alternatives to the death penalty in forgery cases, 14 June, and abolition of tithes in Ireland, 9 Mar., 2, 6, 16 Aug., and strenuously supported the cruelty to animals bill, 24, 30 May, 5 July 1832. His second wife Isabella was an active member of the Society for the Prevention of Cruelty to Animals, and Wilks became a fellow of the London Zoological Society.[18] Being anxious to restrict the poor's consumption of 'spiritous liquors', he pragmatically conceded the merits of the Beer Act and presented petitions in this vein, 17, 23 Aug., 5 Sept., 13 Oct. 1831. He also sought to increase the number of societies registered under the 1829 Friendly Societies Act by simplifying procedures and extending the registration period from three to five years, 6 Oct., and presented petitions accordingly, 6, 13, 14 Oct. As Edward Berkeley Portman and Robert Slaney ascertained, 12 Dec. 1831, 2 Mar. 1832, however, progress towards the bill which he introduced, 15 Mar., trailed by further petitions, 8, 14, 15 Mar., was slow. Although favourable petitioning continued, 20 Mar., 24 May, 6 July, 2 Aug. 1832, it was timed out that Parliament. He was a majority teller for amending the Highbury Place road bill, 3 Apr., assisted with the Gravesend pier and Exeter improvement bills, 10 Apr., 30 May, 13 June, and was instrumental with George Byng in preventing the passage of the Golden Lane burial ground bill, 8 June 1832. He presented anti-slavery petitions, 15 July 1831, 18 Apr., 24 May 1832, strenuously supported Buxton's abolition motion that day, and urged the passage of the West India relief bill unamended so that decisions concerning its implementation could be left to the commissioners, 15 Aug. 1832. He presented petitions and steadfastly opposed the bill founding Durham University on the ground that non-Anglicans would not benefit thereby, 22, 25 June 1832.

Standing as a Liberal, 'a real reformer not a mere conformer', Wilks topped the poll at Boston at the 1832 general election, pressed for municipal reform as a means of redressing religious grievances and retained his seat until 1837, when he made way for Alderman Sir James Duke.[19] He continued to work for the Dissenters in an honorary and a professional capacity, campaigned strenuously against church rates and, deeming the Whig reforms inadequate, contested St. Albans as a Conservative in 1847. He died at his home in Finsbury Square in August 1854, predeceased by his wives and sons, and cared for by his only unmarried daughter Sophia.[20] His estate included a 'collection of autograph letters, manuscripts and curiosities of literature': the Shenstone papers, original works by Southey, a collection of Queen Caroline's correspondence and notes by many radicals.[21] Reviewing his career, the *Evangelical Magazine* commented: 'His greatest contribution ... was towards the cause of religious liberty, by teaching, we might almost say compelling, Nonconformists to fight their own battles'.[22]

[1] IGI (Mdx., Staffs.); *Gent. Mag.* (1814), i. 412. *Oxford DNB* erroneously omits Wilks's first marriage (probably to Mary Mullis at Chesham, 5 May 1797). [2] LMA P76/LUK; *Gent. Mag.* (1846), 329; PROB 11/1752/120; 2040/552; 2198/108. [3] *Evangelical Mag.* (1829), 89-91; (1854) 590-1; T. Jackson, *Faithful Pastor*; G. Collison, *Pastor's Tomb*; *Bunhill Memorials* ed. J.A. Jones (1849), 318. [4] J. Wilks, *Apology for the Missionary Soc.*; TNA IND1/4569/8833; 4584/175; DWL, New College Collection, mss 41/82-87; 42/23; 43/8; *Recs. Protestant Society for the Protection of Religious Liberty*, 38, 193-4, 196, 198, 203; Add. 38246, f. 341; 38247, ff. 50, 61, 68, 187, 201, 221; 38251, f. 245; 38253, f. 83; 38281, ff. 227, 229, 319, 322; 38286, f. 214; 38328, f. 35; 38379, f. 3; 38410, ff. 68, 240, 263; R.G. Cowherd, *Politics of English Dissent* (1959), 17, 29. [5] *Gent. Mag.* (1827), i. 457; (1854), ii. 629; *Morning Chron.* 18 Mar. 1820; Finsbury Pub. Lib. vestry mins. St. Luke, Old Street (1808-22), pp. 4-14, 45-50, 96-97, 109, 113-18, 175, 223, 264, 367, 397, 420, 444, 464, 491, 514; (1822-31), pp. 8, 46, 66, 84-86, 105-6, 143-52; *The Times*, 29 Mar. 1826. [6] J. Bennet, *Hist. Dissenters* (1839), 54-59; Add. 51832, Wilks to Holland, 28 May 1823; *The Times*, 27 May, 5 June; Lincs. AO, Tennyson d'Eyncourt mss, Herries to Tennyson, 31 May; *Lincoln, Rutland and Stamford Mercury*, 9, 16 June 1826. [7] NLW, Fronheulog mss 146-72; Add. 51663, Bedford to Holland, 6 Oct. [1826]. [8] Vestry mins. St. Luke, Old Street (1822-31), pp. 105-6, 203-9, 234-51; *Morning Herald*, 6, 7 Dec. 1827; *The Times*, 9, 20 Jan., 9 Feb., 7 Apr., 6 July 1829, 24 Nov. 1830, 28 June 1831. [9] P. Thompson, *Boston* (1856), 672, 787; *Lincoln, Rutland and Stamford Mercury*, 20 June, 25 July, 22 Aug. 1828; Lincs. RO, Ancaster mss, Garfit to Heathcote, T. Hopkins to same, 10, 17, 31 July 1830; Cowherd, 76. [10] *Sketch of Boston Election* (1830), 20, 23, 36-37, 39-42, 44, 46-47, 67 and *passim.*; *Lincoln, Louth, Newark, Stamford and Rutland Champion*, 13, 20 July, 3 Aug. 1830. [11] Brougham mss, Wilks to Brougham, 19 May 1828, 25 Aug., Brougham to Denman [3 Sept. 1830]. [12] [J. Grant], *Random Recollections of Commons* (1837), 358-9. [13] *The Times*, 10 Mar.; *Stamford Champion*, 22 Mar., 19, 26 Apr.; *Boston Gazette*, 31 Mar., 5, 19 Apr. 1831; R.W. Davis, *Dissent in Politics, 1780-1830*, pp. 250-1. [14] Ancaster mss, T. Hopkins to Heathcote, 9 Apr.; *Boston Gazette*, 26 Apr., 3 May 1831. [15] Cowherd, 79. [16] *The Times*, 28 Sept.; *Bury and Norwich Post*, 5 Oct. 1831. [17] *Poor Man's Guardian*, 28 Jan. 1832. [18] *Gent. Mag.* (1854), ii. 629; PROB 11/2040/552. [19] *The Times*, 27 July, 15, 17 Dec.; *Stamford Champion*, 7, 14, 21 Dec. 1832. [20] *Gent. Mag.* (1846), i. 329, 649; (1854), ii. 629; DWL mss 38, 194, 204; L52/3/89; Cowherd, 84, 91. [21] *Cat. Residue of Coll. ... formed by late John Wilks*; PROB 11/2198/108; IR26/2017/505. [22] *Evangelical Mag.* (1854), 590-1.

M.M.E.

WILKS, John II (c.1793–1846), of Littlesbur, Mill Hill, Mdx. and 36 New Broad Street, London.

SUDBURY   1826–2 Apr. 1828

b. c. 1793, 1st s. of John Wilks I* (*d.* 1854), attorney, of London and 1st w. Mary[1]. *m.* 1 June 1820, Cordelia, da. of Rev. George Townsend, Dissenting minister of Ramsgate, Kent, ?*s.p. d.v.p.* 24 Jan. 1846.

No record of Wilks's birth has been found, but other evidence indicates that he was the eldest of five children born to the attorney (and parish clerk of St. Luke's, Finsbury) John Wilks and his first wife.[2] He was raised in Dissenting circles in Hoxton, where his paternal grandfather Matthew Wilks, a minister at Whitfield's Tabernacle and Tottenham Court chapels, had property, and moved in 1814 to Finsbury Square, where from 1815 to 1820 he was articled to his father.[3] On qualifying as an attorney, he married the daughter of a Dissenting minister who had trained with his grandfather at Trevecca. The couple had many relatives in holy orders and close connections with the Missionary Society and the Society for the Protection of Religious Liberty.[4] Through them Wilks, who also assisted Matthew Wilks with the *Evangelical Magazine*, published his first works, *A Christian Biographical Dictionary* (1821) and *Memoirs of Queen Caroline* (1822). A novella, *Bianca: A Fragment* (1823) is also attributed to him.[5] His legal partnership with Robert Griffith, 24 June 1822-24 Feb. 1824, meanwhile languished: Griffiths successfully prosecuted him in January 1827 for non-payment of his pension.[6] After his first venture, an appeal to Protestants to found a joint-stock company to finance a campaign to enforce Tudor legislation on Sabbath observance, failed, Wilks and a new legal partner Charles Verbecke made a career of exploiting the repeal of the Bubble Act. Their London firm in Broad Street acted for the British Annuity Company and the Kentish Railway Company, and by 1825 Wilks was solicitor to the Equitable Loan Bank Company, which listed nine Members among its 11 vice-presidents and four more among its directors. The Welch Slate Company, the Welch Iron and Coal Company and the Cornwall and Devon Mining Company (founded in 1825 to exploit the duke of Cleveland's mineral rights) were served by Wilks and had directors in common and many shareholders in the House.[7] The secretary at war Lord Palmerston*, an investor in the last three, commented: 'I am sure [Wilks] is a bit of a rogue if nature writes a legible hand; at the same time he is a clever fellow and as long as his interest goes hand in hand with ours will probably do well by us'.[8]

Wilks displayed his new-found wealth at entertainments at his mansions at Mill Hill and Ramsgate, but fearing his eventual bankruptcy, he canvassed the venal borough of Sudbury when a dissolution was anticipated in the autumn of 1825, with a view to securing parliamentary privilege.[9] Casting a political 'net calculated to catch all sorts of fish' – pro-Catholics, anti-Catholics, Dissenters and Anglicans – the 'red-hot demagogue' professed himself to be 'not a Tory, a Whig or a radical' but an independent 'constitutional Briton' and 'friend of the poor'. He stated that Tories regarded people as 'mere ciphers', all Whigs were 'place hunters' and radicals made 'people everything'.[10] Known as 'plum pudding Wilks' or 'plum pudding Jack' on account of his largesse, he topped the Sudbury poll at the 1826 general election at a personal cost of £3,000.[11] He had recently offered a seat

to the Liverpool ministry for £5,000; and refusing it, Palmerston added the private comment, a 'thorough paced Jew'.[12] *The Times* portrayed the collapse of the canopy at Wilks's chairing as a portent of business failures and, taking up *John Bull*'s refrain, observed:

> We are not surprised that *John Bull* should have taken him for a Methodist, and his manner and delivery are so completely those of a Methodist preacher, that we are sure the House ... will be startled if he should ever (as he has promised he will) raise his voice within the walls.[13]

Wilks's Provincial Bank for England and Wales and recent promotions had attracted little investment, and with others, notably the Welch Slate Company and the Devon and Cornwall Mining Company foundering, the bubble had burst for the 'rogue', whose wrongdoings were widely publicized and lampooned before Parliament met.[14] His 'character was so well known that he seldom showed his face' in the House, but he voted against Catholic relief, 6 Mar., and for the duke of Clarence's annuity bill, 17 Mar. 1827. He was detained by the serjeant-at-arms for non-attendance, 29 Mar., released, 5 Apr., and was present when investors in the Devon and Cornwall Mining Company petitioned blaming him and its chairmen Samuel Moulton Barratt* and Peter Moore* for its collapse, 9 Apr.[15] It now emerged that Wilks's purchase of the mines for £78,000 had been conditional on his success in floating a joint-stock company to fund it. He had apparently achieved this, but there was 'no written agreement between the company and Wilks for the purchase', and fraud arose through the reservation of 2,750 undeclared shares for the directors, who had advanced Wilks £20,000 prematurely and paid brokers inflated prices for shares to attract further investment.[16] Making his maiden speech, Wilks proclaimed that the petition was 'one of the most impudent attempts to deceive the legislature ... ever made' and complained that it was deliberately presented shortly before litigation against him commenced. He stated that only £54,000 of the required £121,000 had been realized. His comments were given credence and a motion referring the petition to a select committee was withdrawn, 15 May. The Quaker banker Hudson Gurney* noted in his diary that day that Wilks was a 'great rogue but clear, vulgar speaker'.[17] He voted to remove bankruptcy cases from the court of chancery, in which, in view of recent litigation, he might be said to have had a vested interest, 22 May 1827.[18] Chancery and king's bench had rejected his pleas for compelling the directors of the Welch Iron and Coal Company to pay him £40,000.[19] *The Times* commented that the company was 'his Waterloo and

William Clark [its secretary] ... his Wellington. His parliamentary phalanx was broken'.[20] He also faced prosecution at Stafford assizes that month for conspiracy to induce 'several of the inhabitants of Stafford to surrender their premises'; released on bail, he fled to North Wales and thence to Bruges to avoid his creditors.[21] There, for £100, he provided an agent for John Norman Macleod* with a letter relinquishing the representation of Sudbury.[22]

In Paris, where his uncle Mark Wilks was a minister and assisted him, Wilks established himself as the correspondent of the *Standard*, contributed regularly to the London press under the pseudonym *O.P.Q.*, and was 'considered "a savoury vessel" by all the English Saints' on account of his piety.[23] His occasional letters with information for Peel and the duke of Wellington were well received, but he failed to secure employment as a confidential agent.[24] His business ventures, the *London and Paris Courier*, *La Revue Protestante* and his Paris Parcel Delivery Company, all failed, and he was denounced for spreading false rumours on the Paris *bourse*.[25] Returning to London, where his *Tory Baronet* (1841), a political satire, and *The Boot* (1842), published by Richard Bentley, were highly acclaimed,[26] he failed to find a backer for the *Church and State Gazette* which he proposed, but established two subscription agencies, the Author's Institute in Surrey Street and a Clerical Registry in the Strand, both of which defrauded their members without enriching Wilks. His sudden death *v.p.* of tonsillitis, a few days after that of his stepmother, in January 1846 left many at a financial loss. According to his death certificate, he was 'approximately 52 years' old. His obituarist denounced his misuse of his great abilities and wrote: 'If there were two ways of arriving at the same point, a right and a wrong one ... Wilks was certain to choose the latter, even if it were the more difficult'.[27] Probate on effects up to £1,000 was granted to his widow, 4 May 1846.[28]

[1] *Oxford DNB* erroneously states that Wilks's mother was his fa.'s 2nd wife Isabella. [2] *N and Q* (ser. 5), vii. 180; *Gent. Mag.* (1814), i. 412. [3] T. Jackson, *Faithful Pastor*, 16-42; TNA IND1/4571/18915. [4] *Gent. Mag.* (1820), i. 562; A.J. Bevis, *Rev. George Townsend*; G. Collison, *Pastor's Tomb*, 26-33. [5] *Cat. of Residue Coll. of late John Wilks of Finsbury Square*. [6] *The Times*, 11 Jan. 1827. [7] R. Harris, 'Political economy, interest groups, legal institutions and repeal of the Bubble Act in 1825', *EcHR*, l (1997), 675-96; H. English, *Complete View of Joint-Stock Companies* (1827). [8] *Palmerston-Sulivan Letters*, 175. [9] *Colchester Gazette*, 15, 22 Oct.; *Ipswich Jnl.* 19, 26 Nov. 1825; *The Times*, 27 Mar. 1828. [10] *The Times*, 6, 9, 14, 15 June 1826; NLW, Ormathwaite mss FG/1/5, pp. 76-77. [11] 'Sudbury Borough' (ms penes A.T. Copsey in 1991). [12] Southampton Univ. Lib. Broadlands mss PP/GC/WI/7-8. [13] *The Times*, 19 June 1826. [14] Gwynedd Archives (Caernarfon) XD/8/2/210; *Palmerston-Sulivan Letters*, 166; Add. 40385, ff. 273-5;

51663, Bedford to Holland, 6 Oct.; *The Times*, 20, 27, 28 Sept. 1826. [15] *The Times*, 10 Apr. 1827. [16] Brougham mss, Powlett to Brougham, 2 Feb. 1827; K. Bourne, *Palmerston*, 263-4. [17] Gurney diary. [18] *The Times*, 23 Jan., 8 Mar., 28 Apr. 1827. [19] Ibid. 28 Apr., 1 May 1827. [20] Ibid. 27 Mar. 1828. [21] Ibid. 17, 20 Mar.; *Sun*, 20 Mar. 1828. [22] *Sun*, 27 Mar.; *The Times*, 27 Mar. 1828; Macleod mss 1062/7, 9, 10. [23] *Weekly Dispatch*, 15 Feb. 1846. [24] Add. 40310, f. 42b; 40404, f. 296; 40411, f. 292; 40413, f. 224; Wellington mss WP2/24/61; 27/114; 28/55-57. [25] *Gent. Mag.* (1846), i. 649. [26] Add. 46614, f. 40; 46650, f. 220, 228. [27] *The Times*, 20 Jan.; *Weekly Dispatch*, 15 Feb. 1846. [28] PROB 6/222/290. M.M.E.

M.M.E.

WILLIAMS, John (1777-1846), of 3 Stone Buildings, Lincoln's Inn and 28 Grovsenor Square, Mdx.

LINCOLN	23 Mar. 1822-1826
ILCHESTER	1826-22 Feb. 1827
WINCHELSEA	15 Feb. 1830-1832

bap. 10 Feb. 1777, o.s. of Rev. William Williams, vic. of Bunbury, Cheshire, and Esther, da. of John Richardson of Beeston. *educ.* Manchester g.s. 1787-94; Trinity Coll. Camb. 1794, BA 1798, fellow 1800, MA 1801; I. Temple 1797, called 1804. *m.* 8 Sept. 1825, Harriet Catherine, da. of Davies Davenport*, *s.p. suc.* fa. 1813; kntd. 16 Apr. 1834. *d.* 14 Sept. 1846.[1]

KC 1827; solicitor-gen. to Queen Adelaide July-Nov. 1830, att.-gen. Nov. 1830-May 1832; sjt.-at-law 28 Feb. 1834; puisne bar. of exch. Feb.-Apr. 1834; puisne judge, k.b. Apr. 1834-*d.*

Williams's family had its roots in Merioneth, and he was always fiercely proud of his Welsh ancestry. He was an outstanding Greek scholar and achieved his great early ambition of a Cambridge fellowship, which he prized above all his subsequent attainments. He defeated his friend Francis Howes, whose abilities he considered superior to his own; and, with characteristic generosity, he later provided Howes with an annuity of £100 and remembered his children in his will. In January 1820 Williams contributed an article to the *Edinburgh Review* (xxxiii. 226-46) on his hero and model Demosthenes, 'the greatest orator whom the world has ever produced'.[2] After his call to the bar he went the northern circuit, where he got 'a very respectable amount of business' and established a reputation for diligence and acuteness, especially in cross-examination. He became very friendly with his contemporaries Henry Brougham* and Thomas Denman*, whose liberal politics he shared, and he was admitted to Brooks's Club, 1 Feb. 1818.[3] At the general election later that year he was introduced by the Chester independents as a token partner for their candidate in a contest against the Grosvenor interest. Williams, who was billed as 'a strenuous advocate for the freedom of election', was in Cornwall on election business, possibly for Lord Darlington, and only appeared in Chester on the fifth day, when the cause was already lost. A subsequent petition was unsuccessful.[4] At the general election of 1820 he offered on the Whig interest for Preston against the Derby-Horrocks coalition. He shared a large number of votes with the radical orator Henry Hunt* and finished in third place, only 124 behind the second Tory.[5]

Williams first came significantly to public notice later in 1820, when he acted as junior counsel to Brougham and Denman in defence of Queen Caroline. Brougham ranked his 'most able and effectual' cross-examination of Louise Demont as second in importance only to his own demolition of Majocchi's evidence. On 4 Oct. he confronted the difficult task, from which he had been 'most anxious to be excused', of following Brougham's brilliant closing speech. Inevitably his effort suffered by comparison and Lord Grey, for one, complained of the 'tone and slang' of 'this tiresome little lawyer'. Yet he largely redeemed himself when he resumed the next day, and Denman reckoned that he 'argued that part of the case closely, powerfully, and ingeniously'. Like Brougham and Denman he suffered professionally for his part in this affair, being 'especially high in Eldon's hatred', and did not obtain his silk gown until the Liverpool ministry had collapsed.[6] On 21 Dec. 1821 he was one of five Whigs who attended a public meeting to concert action in support of the Greek liberals.[7] When a vacancy occurred for the open borough of Lincoln during the circuit early in 1822 Denman and Brougham, who had been pestering Darlington to bring Williams into Parliament, persuaded him to stand. Williams was prepared to give way to his 'most intimate friend' Edward Davies Davenport*, but Davenport stepped aside for him and Brougham thwarted a bid from Holland House to insinuate John Nicholas Fazakerley*. Williams walked over the course and resumed the circuit at Lancaster.[8]

His first recorded vote was for abolition of one of the joint-postmasterships, 2 May 1822. He delivered his maiden speech in favour of tax remissions to relieve agricultural distress, 8 May, when he also declared himself a supporter of parliamentary reform, for which he voted, 3 June. He voted against the naval and military pensions bill, 3, 24 May, 3 June, and in the minority against the revised corn duties, 9 May. He called for inquiry into the government of the Ionian Islands, 14 May, lamenting that 'the freemen of England' seemed 'destined for the avocation of repressing the liberties of struggling nations', and

supported cuts in diplomatic expenditure, 15, 16 May. He voted for repeal of the salt duties, 3 June, and said a few words for it, 24 June, 8 July.[9] He opposed the aliens bill, 14 June, 1 July, when he argued that 'the proper course was, not to give ministers credit for what they would do, but to prevent them from doing what they by possibility might do'. The Whig Sir James Mackintosh* 'watched him closely' as 'a man of talent whom I never heard before':

> His language is correct and terse but I think too much condensed for public speaking. Some part of his argument was very close and pressing, but he must open more and give himself more up to impulse before he can be a considerable speaker. His manner has neither warmth nor dignity, but it is firm and collected.[10]

He voted in condemnation of the influence of the crown, 24 June, and of the lord advocate's dealings with the Scottish press, 25 June. Next day he spoke briefly for Michael Taylor's motion for reform of chancery administration and was a teller for the minority. He voted for abolition of the lottery tax, 1 July, and was in two small minorities on the Irish insurrection bill, 8 July 1822.

Williams condemned the laws on debt, 10 Feb., and was named to the select committee on small debts, 18 Feb. 1823.[11] He spoke and voted against the appointment of a lieutenant-general of the ordnance in peacetime, 19 Feb., voted for parliamentary reform, 20 Feb., and took leave to go the circuit, 27 Mar. On his return he voted for inquiry into the legal proceedings against the Dublin Orange rioters, 22 Apr., and he later took a prominent role in the examination of witnesses before it. He divided for parliamentary reform, 24 Apr., 2 June, called for 'complete revision' of the game laws, 25 Apr., and spoke at length in protest at the government's failure to remonstrate more vigorously against the French invasion of Spain, 29 Apr. On 2 May he got leave to introduce a bill to make Quakers' affirmations admissible in criminal cases, but it failed to get a second reading. He voted against the Irish insurrection bill, 12 May, 24 June, and for inquiry into Catholic grievances over the administration of justice in Ireland, 26 June. He favoured abolition of the death penalty for larceny, 21 May, 25 June, deplored the nomination of special juries by the crown office, 28 May, supported the Scottish juries bill, 20 June, and voted for an end to prison flogging, 7 July. He divided with opposition on the malt and beer taxes, 28 May, the lord advocate's conduct, 3 June, the silk bill, 9 June, the coronation expenses, 9, 19 June, and naval promotions, 19 June, and was not prepared to drop the proceedings against chief baron O'Grady, 9 July 1823.

In this session Williams took over from Taylor the parliamentary leadership of the campaign for chancery reform. On 4 June 1823 he moved for inquiry, combining a detailed attack on the notorious and ruinous delays and arrears with severe criticism of lord chancellor Eldon's 'learned doubtfulness'. His speech, George Tierney* thought, was 'most powerful and able', but the motion was beaten by 174-89.[12] He welcomed the bill to facilitate inquiry into the forms of process in Scottish appeals, 10 July 1823, but announced that he would pursue the question of chancery reform early next session. After the summer circuit he accompanied Brougham and Denman to Scotland 'to preach the word of rebellion among the faithful'.[13] He voted for the production of information on Catholic burials, 6 Feb., and the criminal jurisdiction of the Isle of Man, 18 Feb., and on 24 Feb. 1824 renewed his call for inquiry into chancery delays. Williams, who seemed to Eldon 'as savage as the Dey of Algiers', was a far more formidable opponent than Taylor, and the home secretary Peel, anxious to shield Eldon from criticism, yet to institute some form of effective inquiry, had persuaded the chancellor to agree to the appointment of a commission nominated by government. He duly countered the motion with this proposal which Williams, on the advice of Brougham and others, reluctantly accepted, though he suspected that it was an attempt to screen abuses and would prove to be 'nothing else than mockery and deception'.[14] The Tory Henry Bankes* thought his speech was 'long and tiresome', but the Whig George Agar Ellis* reckoned that he 'spoke clearly and well for two and a quarter hours, and made out a most frightful case of the injury accruing to individuals from the chancellor's doubting and delay'.[15] Williams failed to get satisfactory answers to his questions as to whether the commission would submit its evidence to the Commons, 4, 7 May 1824.[16]

He voted for reform of Edinburgh's representation, 26 Feb., and against the grant for Irish Protestant charter schools, 15 Mar. 1824. After the circuit he again raised the issue of Quakers' affirmations, 6 May, when he voted for inquiry into the Irish church establishment. He favoured repeal of the assessed taxes, 10 May, and inquiry into the state of Ireland, 11 May. He presented a petition against the combination laws, 12 May, and on 3 June welcomed the repeal bill, which swept away 'cruel and vexatious statutes'.[17] He denounced Lord Althorp's county courts bill as a threat to the independence of the bar, 24 May, and tried in vain to secure the exemption of the Lancaster court of requests.[18] He was a teller for the majority in favour of the Scottish juries bill later that day. He

presented petitions against slavery, 12 May, and, as Brougham recalled, made a distinguished contribution to the debate on the case of the Methodist missionary John Smith, 11 June, when he denounced slavery as 'a bitter sarcasm upon the vaunted civilization of modern times'. Agar Ellis and Panton Corbett* wrote at the time that Williams performed well.[19] He was in a minority of 14 against the Irish insurrection bill, 18 June 1824.

In January 1825 Williams replied in the *Edinburgh Review* (xli. 410-27) to a defence of Eldon in the *Quarterly*, and cast further doubt on the efficacy of the commission of inquiry.[20] His questions in the House as to its progress, 10 Feb., 25 Apr., received evasive answers.[21] He attacked the 'vicious' Irish unlawful societies bill, 10 Feb., voted against it, 15, 18 Feb., and after spells of circuit leave, 21 Feb. and 15 Apr., supported Catholic relief, 21 Apr., 10 May. He voted for relaxation of the corn laws, 28 Apr., and repeal of the window tax, 17 May. He argued against reinstatement of the Combination Acts, 4 May, and was in small minorities in favour of amendments to the repeal bill, 27 June. He criticized the government's proposals to regulate and augment judicial salaries, 16 May, and on 2 June successfully proposed an increase in retirement pensions to encourage 'a judge to retire from the bench before he retired to the grave'. He spoke and voted against the third reading of the enabling bill, 17 June. He steadily opposed the duke of Cumberland's annuity in May and June. When presenting petitions complaining of chancery delays, 31 May, he attributed the dilatoriness of the commission to 'the great degree of patience which some men were known to exercise with respect to the sufferings of others' and restated the case for reform. He was a teller for the minority in favour of Burdett's call for the production of the commission's findings, 7 June. He regretted the failure of the writs of error bill to deal with sham pleas, 20 June 1825. Lord John Russell* told Lady Holland, 25 Aug. 1825, that Williams, 'our Demosthenes', was shortly to marry Edward Davenport's sister, 'a very clever, sensible girl, but mortal ugly'. They were well matched, for Williams was not a handsome man, being 'about five feet high' with 'a red face and a hook nose'. The marriage involved a settlement worth £40,000 and added considerably to Williams's already substantial wealth, derived from a steady professional income and a useful inheritance from his father.[22]

He opposed the referral of Members' complaints of their being fined for non-attendance as jurymen to the committee of privileges, 20 Feb. 1826. He presented petitions against the importation of foreign silks,

23 Feb., and later that day seconded a motion for inquiry into the distress prevalent in the silk industry. He savaged Huskisson, president of the board of trade, for dogmatic application of free trade theory without reference to circumstances, and was not prepared to see 500,000 people 'sacrificed to abstract principles, however pure those principles might be'. Huskisson's cabinet colleague Canning replied in kind the following evening.[23] Williams supported George Lamb's attempts to allow counsel for defendants in cases of felony to address the jury on the evidence, 25 Feb., 25 Apr. He divided against government on the Jamaican slave trials, 2 Mar., the army establishment, 3 Mar., the president of the board of trade's salary, 10 Apr., and the state of the nation, 4 May. He voted for parliamentary reform, 13, 27 Apr. He condemned the chancery commission's report as facile, 18 Apr., and had no expectation of benefit from the government's bill to effect its recommendations, which would amount to 'legislating in the dark', 18 May. He spoke and voted for inquiry into agricultural distress, 2 May 1826, being unwilling to let ministers 'take the command of the corn laws' through their proposed temporary measures.

At the general election of 1826 Williams abandoned Lincoln and was returned on Darlington's interest for Ilchester, after a contest. He was in a minority of 24 for Hume's amendment to the address, 21 Nov. 1826. He seconded Harvey's motion for information on conveyancing fees, 29 Nov., established that ministers intended to reintroduce their chancery reform bill, 6 Dec., and gave notice of a motion for returns on the subject, 12 Dec. 1826.[24] He protested against the length of the adjournment the following day. He was in the minority on the Leominster election petition, 9 Feb., and presented an Oldham sawyers' petition for a tax on machinery, 21 Feb. 1827.[25] Next day he was unseated on his Ilchester opponents' petition, and the ministerialist Lord Lowther* rejoiced that 'we shall be relieved from some long speeches on the chancery business'.[26] In the summer of 1827 Williams declined repeated invitations from the Carlisle Whigs to contest a vacancy for the borough.[27] He re-entered the House early in 1830 when Lord Cleveland (as Darlington had become) returned him for Winchelsea in place of Brougham who, not wishing to be hampered by Cleveland's recently declared adhesion to the Wellington ministry, accepted the offer of a seat on the duke of Devonshire's interest. Brougham was reported to be 'charmed at his protégé ... succeeding him'; but the Whigs James Abercromby* and Edward Ellice* thought Cleveland's choice of Williams was a 'strange' one, which implied that he 'expected that the government would be conducted on liberal

principles'.[28] The Whig duke of Bedford inferred that Williams was 'satisfied' with lord chancellor Lyndhurst's plans for chancery reform.[29] Williams took his seat on 17 Feb. and, before leaving for the circuit, voted for the enfranchisement of Birmingham, Leeds and Manchester, 23 Feb. 1830. He spoke for the abolition of capital punishment for forgery, 4, 13 May. On 27 May he welcomed the ministry's bill for the reorganization of the judiciary as 'an abandonment of patronage by ministers to a greater extent than ever was resigned by any ministers, either by compulsion, or by voluntary act, since the Revolution'. Their suits in equity bill, which involved the appointment of an additional chancery judge, and was one of a group of measures intended to improve equity administration, also won his approval, 24 June:

> This is the first time within my recollection that any attempt at a series of legal reforms has been made by a ministry, and it is not because everything is not done ... that we should reject this measure ... though it is not all I could wish ... I will not be found one of those who offer opposition to it.

Later in the debate Brougham, who objected to the extra judge, chided Williams for his eagerness to accept it for the sake of what were very modest reforms. Brougham's pleasure at Williams's return for Winchelsea had turned sour; and many years afterwards he reflected:

> Williams ... very improperly (the only wrong thing, public or private, I have ever known him to do in a long and intimate acquaintance) left us when ... Cleveland seceded in 1830. This desertion of Williams was partly owing to a grudge on account of silk, political economy, Huskisson, and Canning; but it was very bad, for he took the worst form of desertion – viz., that of leaving us on his own chancery reform question.[30]

Williams was appointed solicitor-general to Queen Adelaide in July 1830 and became her attorney-general the following November. After the general election, when Cleveland again returned him for Winchelsea, ministers counted him among their 'friends', but he was absent from the division on the civil list which brought them down, 15 Nov. 1830. He was on the circuit when the Grey ministry introduced its reform bill and missed the division on its second reading, 22 Mar. 1831. Yet, as he wrote to Brougham, now lord chancellor, he was an unequivocal supporter of the measure (as was Cleveland, despite its disfranchisement of his pocket boroughs), and he attended to vote against Gascoyne's wrecking amendment, 19 Apr. 1831. On the subject of Brougham's plans to reform local courts he said:

I, of course, will not attempt to oppose anything, but I am not very anxious. In truth, I feel myself like a horse in a mill, who does not probably care much whether he is whipped round a circle of larger or smaller diameter.[31]

Williams came in again for Winchelsea at the 1831 general election and voted for the second reading of the reintroduced reform bill, 6 July. He took leave for the summer circuit, 18 July, but arranged to pair for at least one division on the bill in committee, 26 July. He voted for clause 22, 30 Aug., supported the new legal apparatus for the revision of electoral registers, 3 Sept., and divided for the third reading, 19, and passage of the bill, 21 Sept., after declaring that he had 'from first to last, been a steady, though a silent supporter of this measure', which would effect 'an equal representation of the people'. He voted for the second reading of the Scottish reform bill, 23 Sept., and Lord Ebrington's motion of confidence in the ministry, 10 Oct. He spoke at length in 'hearty' support of Brougham's bill to reform the bankruptcy jurisdiction, 5 Oct. 1831, when he was a teller for the majority in favour of the bill to abolish truck payments.

Williams voted for the second reading of the revised reform bill, 17 Dec. 1831, and for a number of its details in committee, but he was on the circuit at the time of its third reading, for which he paired, 22 Mar. 1832. He was in the government majorities on the Russian-Dutch loan, 26 Jan., and relations with Portugal, 9 Feb. He voted for the address asking the king to appoint only ministers who would carry undiluted reform, 10 May, and resigned as the queen's attorney-general. When his friends resumed office he found that William Taddy had been appointed in his place, on the ground that it had been decided that the post should no longer be tenable with a seat in the House. He disapproved proceeding against the press for alleged libels on the royal family, 21 May, voted for the second reading of the Irish reform bill, 25 May, and paired against a Conservative amendment to the Scottish measure, 1 June. He opposed Harvey's motion to open the Inns of Court and the bar to merit, 14 June, and was a teller for the majority against it. His last known vote was with government on the Russian-Dutch loan, 16 July 1832.

With Winchelsea doomed, Williams had no obvious prospect of a seat in the first reformed Parliament, and a notion that he might stand for Rye came to nothing.[32] His lack of a seat was partly responsible for his being passed over for John Campbell II* for the post of solicitor-general in November 1832 but, by Brougham's later account, there was more to

it than that. Brougham would personally have preferred Williams but, having got his own way over the appointment of Denman as lord chief justice, felt it would be 'clearly wrong' to force Williams's elevation on reluctant colleagues, who had not forgotten his 'desertion' in 1830. Early in 1834 Brougham compensated him by making him a baron of exchequer, but after only a term he was transferred to king's bench because, according to Greville, Brougham found that he 'would not do in the exchequer'.[33]

As a judge Williams, who resembled 'Punch in ermine', was not of the highest calibre, but he was painstaking and fair-minded and very popular with the bar.[34] One of its members, Frederick Pollock*, recalled:

John Williams went the northern circuit for the first time as a judge of assize in the summer of 1838, and ... previously entertained a large party of the bar of his old circuit at dinner at his house in London – a residence of which he used to say, 'I live in Grosvenor Square; but I am d—d if I know where the other judges live' – being one of the last of those in his position who occasionally garnished their conversation with somewhat profane expletives ... Lady Williams and himself had their separate sets of friends and acquaintances – his chiefly legal, hers chiefly fashionable; and they gave separate entertainments accordingly.[35]

Macaulay dined with Lady Williams in Rome, 1 Dec. 1838, but 'liked neither the house nor the woman nor the dinner nor the company'.[36] Williams remained a devotee of classical literature and in 1839 published some of his accomplished verses in *Literary Trifles, Chiefly Greek*.[37] He died suddenly at his then residence at Livermere, near Bury St. Edmunds in September 1846.[38] He had earlier invested in an estate at Dowsby, Lincolnshire, which brought in £1,200 per annum. The chief beneficiary of his will was his widow, who died abroad in 1861.[39] Brougham paid tribute to Williams as a man

who ... passed through life without a single enemy ... No one had more clear and decided opinions ... or acted more on his own convictions; few were less cautious in expressing an unpopular opinion, or took less care to conceal his unfavourable impressions of others ... He was ... a good hater, but in the better sense of the phrase. For when he differed with you, he left no room to fancy he did so from the spirit of contradiction; and when he pronounced his condemnation of either a doctrine, or a person, or a class, there was no doubt that he did so conscientiously, for the sake of truth, and not vainly from the love of singularity, while in all he said, there prevailed a kindly nature, and appeared an honest purpose.[40]

¹ *The Times*, 17 Sept. 1846; IR26/1758/538. *Oxford DNB* erroneously gives 15 Sept. ² *Gent. Mag.* (1846), ii. 537-8; *Law Mag.* vi (1847), 60; *Oxford DNB*; PROB 11/2042/698. ³ *Law Mag.* vi. 61-62; *Law Rev.* v (1846-7), 185; *Smith Letters*, i. 347. ⁴ *Late Elections* (1818), 677-69; *Hist. Chester Election, 1818*, pp. 32, 35, 37, 39, 44, 53, 69, 73. ⁵ Lancs. RO, Whittaker of Simonstone mss DDWh/4/99; *The Times*, 20 Mar. 1820. ⁶ *Law Rev.* v. 186-7; Arnould, *Denman*, i. 144, 164, 170, 197; Brougham, *Life and Times*, ii. 386, 461; iii. 27; *Geo. IV Letters*, ii. 833, 847, 851; iii. 1334; Grey mss, Grey to wife, 4 Oct.; JRL, Bromley Davenport mss, Macdonald to Davenport, 4 Oct. 1820. ⁷ Add. 36459, f. 183. ⁸ Bessborough mss, Brougham to Duncannon [14 Mar.]; Add. 51562, Brougham to Holland [14, 21 Mar.]; *The Times*, 23, 29, 30 Mar. 1822. ⁹ *The Times*, 25 June, 9 July 1822. ¹⁰ Add. 52445, f. 90. ¹¹ *The Times*, 11 Feb. 1823. ¹² Add. 51586, Tierney to Lady Holland, 6 June 1823. ¹³ Add. 51564, Brougham to Lady Holland, 31 July 1823. ¹⁴ Twiss, *Eldon*, ii. 487-8; N. Gash, *Secretary Peel*, 321-6; Parker, *Peel*, i. 360-1. ¹⁵ Dorset RO D/BKL, Bankes jnl. 148; Northants. RO, Agar Ellis diary, 24 Feb. [1824]. ¹⁶ *The Times*, 5, 8 May 1824. ¹⁷ Ibid. 13 May, 4 June 1824. ¹⁸ Ibid. 25 May 1824. ¹⁹ *Law Rev.* v. 188; Agar Ellis diary, 11 June; Salop RO, Plymley diary 1066/133 [20 June 1824]. ²⁰ E.B. Sugden, *Letter to John Williams* (1825), 3-4. ²¹ *The Times*, 11 Feb. 1825. ²² Add. 51679; *Hist. Chester Election, 1818*, p. 69; *Gent. Mag.* (1846), ii. 539; *Law Mag.* vi. 64, 71. ²³ Agar Ellis diary, 24 Feb. [1826]. ²⁴ *The Times*, 30 Nov., 7, 13 Dec. 1826. ²⁵ Ibid. 10, 22 Feb. 1827. ²⁶ *Geo. IV Letters*, iii. 1289. ²⁷ Lonsdale mss, Lowther to Lonsdale, 21 July, 3 Aug. 1827. ²⁸ Brougham, iii. 22-33; Grey mss, Ellice to Grey [Feb.]; Bessborough mss, Abercromby to Duncannon, 16 Feb. 1830. ²⁹ Add. 51670, Bedford to Lady Holland [9 Feb. 1830]. ³⁰ Brougham, iii. 228. ³¹ Brougham mss, Williams to Brougham [14 Mar.], Sunday [1831]. ³² E. Suss. RO, Rye corporation recs. 141/7. ³³ *Life of Campbell*, ii. 18; Brougham, iii. 227-8; *Greville Mems.* iii. 24. ³⁴ Arnould, ii. 17-18; *Oxford DNB*. ³⁵ Pollock, *Personal Remembrances*, i. 116-17. ³⁶ *Macaulay Letters*, iv. 69. ³⁷ Add. 37312, f. 321; 37313, f. 129. ³⁸ *Gent. Mag.* (1846), ii. 539. ³⁹ PROB 11/2042/698; IR26/1758/538. ⁴⁰ *Law Rev.* v. 183.

D.R.F.

WILLIAMS, Owen (1764–1832), of Temple House, Bisham, Berks. and Craig-y-Don, Anglesey.

GREAT MARLOW   1796–23 Feb. 1832

bap. 19 July 1764,¹ 1st s. of Thomas Williams† of Llanidan, Anglesey and Temple House and Catherine, da. of John Lloyd, attorney, of Caerwys, Flints. *educ.* Westminster 1776. *m.* 18 July 1792, Margaret, da. of Rev. Edward Hughes of Kinmel Park, Denb., 2s. *suc.* fa. 1802. *d.* 23 Feb. 1832.
    Recvr.-gen. Anglesey to 1796.
    Capt. S. Bucks. vols. 1803.

At the general election of 1820 Williams again returned himself on the well-established family interest for Great Marlow, which lay across the Thames from his Berkshire residence. He gave the other seat to his elder son, Thomas Peers Williams, having set aside Pascoe Grenfell*, his colleague of 17 years and his partner in the copper processing business on which his substantial fortune was based. By 1829 he had fallen out with Grenfell and completely withdrawn from the enterprise.² Williams, who had joined Brooks's in 1806,

began this period as a conservative member of the Whig opposition to the Liverpool ministry; but he was a very poor attender, partly because of worsening health, and by the end of 1830 he had gravitated to the Tories.

He paired with opposition on the Queen Caroline affair, 26 Jan., 6 Feb. 1821. He was given three weeks' leave on account of illness, 12 Mar., but was in Hume's minority of 29 for a revision of public salaries, 30 Mar. He got a fortnight's leave to deal with urgent private business, 7 May. He was present to vote in a minority of 14 against the duke of Clarence's annuity bill, 25 June, and for Hume's call for economy and retrenchment, 27 June 1821. He divided for abolition of one of the joint-postmasterships, 13 Mar., 2 May, and for inquiries into the board of control, 14 Mar., and the government of the Ionian Islands, 14 May, and was in small minorities to reduce the navy estimates, 18 Mar., and adjourn proceedings on the aliens bill, 14 June 1822. His only recorded votes in the next two sessions were for repeal of the assessed taxes, 18 Mar., in a minority of 37 for the abolition of whipping as a punishment, 30 Apr. 1823, and to postpone consideration of the grant for Windsor Castle repairs, 5 Apr. 1824. He paired on the government side against inquiry into the prosecution of the Methodist missionary John Smith in Demerara, 11 June 1824. After defaulting on a call of the House, 28 Feb., he voted for Catholic relief, 10 May, and against the duke of Cumberland's annuity, 10 June 1825. He divided against giving the president of the board of trade a separate ministerial salary, 7 Apr. 1826.

At the general election two months later Williams encountered a challenge to his control of Marlow from resentful independents, who took up James Morrison*, a wealthy London silk merchant of advanced liberal views. He topped the poll and brought his son safely in with him, but Morrison polled respectably, and in 1827 and 1828 Williams vengefully evicted those of his borough tenants who had cast a hostile vote.³ A report in January 1827 that 'age and infirmities' had brought him to the verge of retirement came to nothing;⁴ but his only known vote in the first two sessions of the 1826 Parliament was for the Whig opposition's motion for a suspension of supply until the ministerial crisis had been resolved, 30 Mar. 1827. Yet his inclusion by Planta, the Wellington ministry's patronage secretary, in a list of Members expected to vote 'with government' for Catholic emancipation in 1829, indicates that he (and his son) were no longer seen as part of the regular opposition. He apparently broke a 32-year silence in debate to express his 'entire confidence' in the government's decision to concede emancipation, 12 Feb., before voting for it, 6, 30 Mar. On 12 May 1829 he complained of the irresponsible and unchecked expenditure of public money by the office of woods and forests. 'Severe illness' prevented him from attending Parliament in the early weeks of the 1830 session, and on 9 Mar. he was given a month's sick leave.[5] He attended to vote against Jewish emancipation, 5 Apr., 17 May. As the owner of an estate in Anglesey (where he supported the Pagets' Plas Newydd interest), he condemned the plan to reorganize the Welsh judicial system, 27 Apr.; he voted in a minority of 30 against the measure, 18 June. He divided for a reduction in the grant for public buildings, 3 May, but to pay that for South American missions, 7 June, when he paired against the forgery punishment mitigation bill. He voted against the sale of beer bill, 4 May, 1 July 1830. This added to his increasing unpopularity with a significant portion of his constituents; and at the general election of 1830 he and his son were hard and expensively pressed by the independents, whose new candidate was the son of a Berkshire baronet and former Member for Marlow.[6]

Williams was initially placed among the 'good doubtfuls' by ministers, but he was subsequently deemed to be a 'friend'; he was in their minority in the decisive division on the civil list, 15 Nov. 1830. He voted against the second reading of the Grey ministry's reform bill, 22 Mar., and for Gascoyne's wrecking amendment, 19 Apr. 1831, and that month tried unsuccessfully to block a Marlow meeting in its support. At the general election called after the bill's defeat he and his son were only narrowly returned ahead of their opponent of 1830. Williams was absent throughout 'in consequence of a dangerous indisposition', which was thought likely to carry him off.[7] He is not known to have voted in the first session of the new Parliament and he defaulted on a call of the House, 10 Oct. 1831. He was able to divide against the second reading of the revised reform bill, 17 Dec. 1831, and going into committee on it, 20 Jan., and against government on the Russian-Dutch loan, 26 Jan. 1832; but he died at his London house in Berkeley Square a month later.[8] By his brief will, dated 11 Aug. 1825, he left £35,000 to his younger son Owen Edward and all his real estate and the residue (calculated for duty at £25,723) of his personal estate to his elder son. His personalty as a whole was sworn under £120,000.[9]

[1] J.E. Griffith, *Peds. Anglesey Fams.* 68. [2] *HP Commons, 1790-1820*, v. 541-2, 585-6; J.R. Harris, *Copper King*, 182-3; Add. 58977, f. 165; NLW, Vivian mss 1120. [3] *Bucks. Chron.* 10, 17 June 1826, 24 Mar., 13 Oct. 1827, 26 Jan. 1828; R.W. Davis, *Political Change and Continuity*, 25. [4] *Bucks. Chron.* 27 Jan. 1827. [5] *The Times*, 27 Feb. 1830. [6] *Reading Mercury*, 5 July, 9, 16 Aug.; *Bucks Gazette*, 28 Aug. 1830. [7] *Reading Mercury*, 18 Apr.; *The Times*, 6, 12 May; *Bucks Gazette*, 28 May 1831. [8] *Gent. Mag.* (1832), i. 366. [9] PROB 11/1800/337; IR26/1307/158.

D.R.F.

WILLIAMS, Robert (1767-1847), of Bridehead, nr. Dorchester, Dorset; Moor Park, Herts.; 36 Grovesnor Square, Mdx., and 20 Birchin Lane, London.

WOOTTON BASSETT	1802-1807
GRAMPOUND	17 Mar. 1808-10 May 1808
KILKENNY	4 Feb. 1809-1812
DORCHESTER	1812-1834

b. 11 Feb. 1767, 1st s. of Robert Williams[†] of Bridehead and Moor Park and Jane, da. of Francis Chassereau of Marylebone, Mdx.; bro. of William Williams*. *m.* 28 Aug. 1794, Frances, da. of John Turner of Putney, Surr., 1s. 1da. *suc.* fa. 1814. *d.* 10 Mar. 1847. Alderman, London 1796-1801, sheriff 1797-8; prime warden, Goldsmiths' Co. 1810-11; dir. Hope Assurance Co. 1820, chairman 1822-45. Capt. Cornhill vols. 1797, maj. commdt. 1798; lt.-col. commdt. 1799; vol. London and Westminster light horse 1803-7.

Williams's father and namesake, a self-made man, was descended from a cadet branch of the Williams family of Herringston, Dorset, and married the daughter of a French Huguenot refugee. He became a leading London banker and a director of the East India Company, purchased estates in Dorset and Hertfordshire and secured a seat at Dorchester in 1807. This Member, the elder of his two sons, had a brief spell on the corporation of London and in 1802 entered the Commons, where he was an almost silent supporter of successive Tory administrations.[1] He was the principal beneficiary under his father's will, succeeding in 1814 to his landed property, bank and three per cent stocks, and personalty sworn above £500,000.[2] He also became senior partner in the family bank in Birchin Lane, which was then known as Williams, Moffatt and Company; it went through several changes of name in the following years.[3] He had replaced his father as Member for Dorchester in 1812, when he was made a freeman of the town, and his acquisition of numerous properties there secured his unchallenged position as patron of one of the seats, which he continued to occupy himself.[4] His brother William, who joined him in the House as Member for Weymouth in 1818, sided with opposition, but Robert, who was again returned unopposed for Dorchester at the general election of 1820, was later said to have voted 'always with ministers'.[5]

Williams voted against economies in revenue collection, 4 July 1820. He divided in defence of ministers' conduct towards Queen Caroline, 6 Feb. 1821. He is unlikely to have been the 'R. Williams' who was listed as voting for revision of official salaries, 30 Mar.; he divided against repeal of the additional malt duty, 3 Apr., and Hume's motion for economy and retrenchment, 27 June 1821. He voted against more extensive tax reductions to relieve distress, 11, 21 Feb., and abolition of one of the joint-postmasterships, 13 Mar., but was credited with dividing for inquiry into the duties of the officers of the board of control, 14 Mar. 1822. He wrote offering his backing at the forthcoming Dorset by-election to the Tory Henry Bankes*, 10 Feb. 1823.[6] His only recorded vote that year was against repeal of the Foreign Enlistment Act, 16 Apr. 1823, and no parliamentary activity has been traced during the 1824 session. As he had on 28 Feb. 1821 and 30 Apr. 1822, he voted against Catholic relief, 1 Mar., 10 May, pairing in the same sense on 21 Apr. 1825. His bank suffered a temporary suspension during the financial crisis at the end of that year.[7] He appears to have been inactive during the 1826 session, but was re-elected for Dorchester that summer, when he explained that he opposed relief because of the remaining political power of the Catholics.[8]

The following week he wrote from Bridehead to Peel, the home secretary:

I find a great inconvenience in having two large places in the country, without time to be as much at either as I should wish, and have therefore thought of parting with one. *This* is my native county, and a favourite residence to myself and family, and, having lately added much to its extent by a large purchase and opportunity occurring of more, I have made up my mind to sell Moor Park and its appendages, which are, an estate in a ring-fence of about £5,000 per annum, exclusive of the park (500 acres), a large farm in hand and some fine woodlands. The house is very magnificent, fit for *any* man's residence ... [and] 17 miles from Oxford Street.

Peel declined to make the purchase and it was soon afterwards sold to Lord Grosvenor.[9] Williams's name was among those proposed for baronetcies by the prime minister, Lord Goderich, in November 1827. George IV believed Robert to be 'a most respectable loyal man, and always supporting the king's government', who was 'not unworthy of such a mark of distinction'. Unfortunately, in his confusion, the king thought that the man being suggested was his radical brother William, and insisted that further inquiries should be made. Goderich therefore suggested that the matter be put off, and it was apparently not reconsidered.[10]

Williams voted against Catholic relief, 6 Mar. 1827. He may have been the 'Mr. Williams' who spoke in defence of the board of lunacy, 19 Feb. 1828. He divided against repeal of the Test Acts, 26 Feb., presented a Dorchester anti-Catholic petition, 24 Apr., and again voted against Catholic claims, 12 May. In February 1829 he was listed by Planta, the Wellington ministry's patronage secretary, as likely to be 'with government' on Catholic emancipation. In fact, he presented another anti-Catholic petition from his constituents, 3 Mar., and divided steadily against emancipation that month. He voted against Jewish emancipation, 5 Apr., 17 May 1830. He was returned unopposed for Dorchester, on the basis of his long service in defence of the principles of the constitution, at the general election that year.[11] He was listed by ministers among their 'friends', but was absent from the division on the civil list, 15 Nov. 1830, which led to their resignation. He voted against the second reading of the Grey ministry's reform bill, 22 Mar., and for Gascoyne's wrecking amendment, 19 Apr. 1831. He was returned unopposed for Dorchester with his anti-reform colleague Lord Ashley at the subsequent general election, when he condemned the bill for disfranchising so many voters and for depriving Dorchester of one of its seats. He signed the requisition to Bankes, and plumped for him in the Dorset contest that year.[12]

He voted against the second reading of the reintroduced reform bill, 6 July, and, despite being granted one month's leave because of a death in the family, 12 July, divided in favour of using the 1831 census to determine the boroughs in schedules A and B, 19 July, and for postponing consideration of the partial disfranchisement of Chippenham, 27 July 1831. He presented and endorsed a Dorchester petition for retention of both its seats, 28 July, when he admitted that at the time of his first election he had not owned a single house there. He divided against the passage of the bill, 21 Sept. He voted for Ashley in the Dorset by-election that autumn.[13] He was absent from the division on the second reading of the revised reform bill, 17 Dec. 1831, but divided against the enfranchisement of Tower Hamlets, 28 Feb., and the third reading of the bill, 22 Mar. 1832. He attended the Dorset dinner in Bankes's honour, 26 July, when he damned the intentions of what he dubbed '*inconsiderate* reformers, not to say *mad*, as I think them'. He was re-elected for Dorchester as a Conservative at the general election in December 1832.[14] Williams, who was treasurer of the Society for Promoting the Religious Principles of the Reformation, retired from the House at the dissolution in 1834, but remained at the head of the London bank, which from the 1840s was called Williams, Deacon and Company. He died in March 1847 and was buried in Little Bredy church, with his mother and wife (who had both died in 1841). He was succeeded by his banker son Robert (1811-90), Conservative Member for Dorchester, 1835-41, whose heir Robert (1848-1943), Conservative Member for West Dorset, 1895-1922, was awarded a baronetcy in 1915.[15]

[1] J. Hutchins, *Dorset*, ii. (1863), 187, 524-5; J.E. Cussans, *Herts.* Cashio, 127-8; *HP Commons, 1790-1820*, v. 583-4. [2] *Gent. Mag.* (1814), i. 202; PROB 11/1552/104; IR26/627/67. [3] F.G. Hilton Price, *Handbook of London Bankers* (1890-1), 177. [4] C.H. Mayo, *Municipal Recs. of Dorchester*, 434; Dorset RO, Williams of Bridehead mss D/WIB P1; Dorset RO, Dorchester borough recs. DC/DOB 26/12, 13; Dorset RO, q. sess. recs. D1/OE 1; Oldfield, *Key* (1820), 50; *Key to Both Houses* (1832), 318. [5] *Salisbury Jnl.* 13 Mar. 1820; *Black Bk.* (1823), 203. Some of his ministerial votes were wrongly attributed to Sir Robert Williams, Member for Caernarvonshire and Beaumaris. [6] Dorset RO, Bankes mss D/BKL. [7] *Dorset Co. Chron.* 15 Dec. 1825. [8] Ibid. 8, 15 June 1826. [9] Add. 40387, ff. 129, 133; Cussans, 128. [10] *Geo. IV Letters*, iii. 1422, 1423; Bucks. RO, Buckinghamshire mss O.100, Goderich to Geo. IV [Nov. 1827]. [11] *Dorset Co. Chron.* 29 July, 5 Aug. 1830. [12] Ibid. 5 May 1831; *Dorset Pollbook* (1831), 26. [13] *Dorset Pollbook* (Sept.-Oct. 1831), 44. [14] *Dorset Co. Chron.* 2 Aug., 13 Dec. 1832. [15] Ibid. 11, 18 Mar. 1847; Hutchins, ii. 187; *Gent. Mag.* (1847), i. 546-7; *The Times*, 13 June 1890, 17 Apr. 1943.

S.M.F.

WILLIAMS, Sir Robert, 9th bt. (1764–1830), of Friars, Anglesey and Plas y Nant, Caern.

CAERNARVONSHIRE	1790–1826
BEAUMARIS	1826–1 Dec. 1830

b. 20 July 1764, 1st s. of Sir Hugh Williams[†], 8th bt., of Plas y Nant and Emma, da. and h. of Thomas Rowlands of Caerau, Llanfair-yng-Nghornwy, Anglesey and Plas y Nant, wid. of James Bulkeley[†], 6th Visct. Bulkeley [I]. *educ.* Blackheath; Westminster 1774; Harrow 1776-80. *m.* 11 June 1799, Anne, da. of Rev. Edward Hughes of Kinmel Park, Denb., 3s. 7da. *suc.* mother 1770; fa. as 9th bt. 19 Aug. 1794. *d.* 1 Dec. 1830.

A.d.c. to ld. lt. [I] 1787-93.

Ensign 1 Ft. Gds. 1782, lt. and capt. 1789, capt. and lt.-col. 1794, ret. 1795. Snowdon rangers 1803; capt. Caern. militia 1808; maj. Anglesey militia 1809.

Mayor, Beaumaris 1800, 1804, 1807, 1811, 1815, recorder 1822-*d.*

Williams had been brought into Parliament for his native county in 1790 on the interest and largely at the expense of his half-brother Thomas James, Viscount Bulkeley[†], whose 1784 arrangement with the Pagets of Plas Newydd gave them control of the representation of Anglesey and Caernarvon Boroughs, while Bulkeley returned Williams for Caernarvonshire and the Member for Beaumaris. Williams had supported the Grenvillite third party with Bulkeley early in his parliamentary career, but he had recently gravitated towards the Whiggism of his brothers-in-law William Hughes* and Owen Williams*, joining Brooks's in June 1816, and declining to go over to administration with Bulkeley the following year or the rest of the party in December 1821.[1] His personal fortune and estates were not large and financial difficulties had led him to grant Thomas Farncombe a £720 life annuity chargeable on them to secure a £5,000 loan in January 1819.[2] His parliamentary attendance was at best erratic, but he was a powerful public speaker and presided at the meetings which adopted the customary addresses of condolence and congratulations to the new king from Anglesey, 3 Mar., and Caernarvonshire, 6 Mar. 1820. At his election, he declared his support for the constitution and the 'restrictive measures' adopted after Peterloo and claimed that he was 'always ashamed to act on the same side of the House as some of the radical visionaries', but said that as an advocate of retrenchment and lower taxes he would oppose any increases in civil list expenditure and all taxes 'which abridged the comforts of the lower orders'. In Beaumaris, 16 Mar., he nominated the marquess of Anglesey's eldest son, Lord Uxbridge, who replaced his uncle as Member for Anglesey.[3]

Williams presented Caernarvonshire's petition for measures to combat agricultural distress, 9 May, and divided with the Whig opposition on the civil list, 5, 8, and the recent appointment of an additional Scottish baron of exchequer, 15 May 1820.[4] He had been wounded at Valenciennes during the war against Buonaparte, and paid £600 to take his family on a tour of French and Low Countries battlefields in the summer of 1820, later renting a house near Paris, where they remained until 1822.[5] He was disappointed at the failure of his eldest son Richard Williams Bulkeley* to obtain a scholarship to Magdalene College, Cambridge in December 1820.[6] The Welsh language monthly magazine *Seren Gomer* reported that he was in the government majorities on the Queen Caroline case, 6 Feb., the additional malt duty, 3 Apr., and Hume's motion for economy and retrenchment, 27 June, and divided against Catholic relief, 28 Feb. 1821; but his name does not appear in the surviving lists, and these were a few of many instances when votes cast by Robert Williams, the Member for Dorchester, were misattributed to him in the provincial press.[7] On the eve of his return from France, 25 Mar. 1822, he asked the Tory chairman of Caernarvonshire quarter sessions, Colonel Richard Edwards of Nanhoron, to furnish him with petitions 'against the leather tax and salt tax, anything for the relief of the agricultural interest', adding:

I believe that the time is not far distant when the stock jobber and fund holder will get possession of the land. Ministers care not in whose hands the land may be placed, so that the interests of the debt may be paid and they may retain their places. Forgive me ... these observations on your friends, but are ministers the friends of the landed property? If you answer in the negative, then you must be pleased with my opposition.[8]

He also asked Charles Williams Wynn, president of the India Board and the Grenvillites Commons leader, if he intended 'to propose any measure respecting the administration of justice in Wales', 27 Mar., and hearing that he did not, promised to 'bring it under the consideration of the whole House ... soon after the vacation', but failed to do so.[9] He divided for reform, 25 Apr. 1822, 24 Apr. 1823, and Lord John Russell's resolutions to curb electoral bribery, 26 May 1826. He voted for remission of the remainder of Henry Hunt's* sentence, 24 Apr. 1822, and after presenting the Caernarvon and Caernarvonshire tanners' petition for repeal of the leather tax, 29 Apr., he wrote to Edwards:

> Since the Grenville party have been *bought over* they are held in the greatest abhorrence by all the world, and so Lord John Russell has told them to their face. This will assist that moderate reform in Parliament that he has so judiciously brought forward, and I never gave a vote with greater pleasure. *Tom* Smith (not old Assheton) swears he will attack me at the first county meeting. I shall be too happy to have an opportunity of defending myself if it is necessary. I trust we shall run them hard on the leather tax, but I doubt it. The salt tax will be the first to be given up.[10]

According to Bulkeley, Williams's vote to relieve Catholic peers of their disabilities, 30 Apr., provoked such hostility in Caernarvonshire that he felt compelled not to vote on it in the Lords 'to allay the storm'.[11] Williams divided for inquiry into the government of the Ionian Isles, 14 May, and reductions in ambassadorial expenditure, 15 May 1822.

He was a minority teller against the usury laws repeal bill, 17 June, and carried the amendment by which it was lost, 27 June. 1823.[12] He supported inquiry into the coronation expenses, 19 June, and Irish disturbances, 24 June, and voted to refer the Catholics' petition against the administration of justice in Ireland to the grand committee, 26 June 1823. Bulkeley had died the previous June, leaving his North Wales estates in trust for Richard and making Williams his trustee, but the controlling interest was Lady Bulkeley's.[13] In July 1823 he negotiated the release of the Farncombe annuity and a settlement making over all his debts to Richard as heir to his parents' estates and Baron Hill.[14]

He felt wronged by Bulkeley's will and his forced dependence on his son, but Lady Bulkeley observed: 'I never talk upon business with Sir R. Williams for he is quite *incapable* of understanding anything of the sort'.[15] He was instrumental in securing the enactment of the 1824 Porthdinllaen roads bill,[16] paired against a government amendment to Lord Althorp's motion for inquiry into the state of Ireland, 11 May, and presented the Hollywell tanners' petition against the hides and skins bill, 19 May. His vote in condemnation of the indictment in Demerara of the Methodist missionary John Smith, 11 June 1824, was commended in the Welsh press.[17] When in August Thomas Clarkson brought the Anti-Slavery Society's campaign to Wales, he was informed, 'Sir Robert Williams ... must be with us, being a man of extraordinary tenacity; and ... if we were to speak to him when in London, he would secure Beaumaris in our favour'.[18] Ill health, for which he received three weeks leave, 17 Feb., and a fortnight, 15 Apr., curtailed Williams's attendance in 1825, but he paired for Catholic relief, 10 May, and assisted with the Caernarvon-Llanllyfni railway bill, 14 Feb., and the abortive Ffestiniog railway bill, 18 Feb. He accused ministers with interests in rival concerns of mounting 'vexatious opposition' to the Caernarvon railway, 12 May, and was relieved to see it enacted, 20 May 1825.[19] He voted in a minority of 29 that day for making puisne judges immovable, and against the duke of Cumberland's annuity, 6, 9, 10 June, and he defended William Kenrick[†], a judge on the North Wales circuit whose conduct as a Surrey magistrate was criticized, 14 June.[20] It was rumoured in August 1825 that Williams planned to give up Friars.[21]

A dissolution seemed likely, and by September Lord Newborough* of Glynllifon, whose supporters included Bulkeley's successor as lord lieutenant of Caernarvonshire, Thomas Assheton Smith I*, was canvassing the county. Williams promptly defended himself, ensured that the Plas Newydd interest remained loyal and ignored Anglesey's intimation that he should withdraw because 'your political line of conduct is very generally disapproved of throughout the county'.[22] Assheton Smith informed Anglesey:

> Friends in Caernarvonshire must have thought me the most inconsistent of men if I had given my support to Sir Robert who has so constantly voted with every radical measure that has ever been proposed whenever *he has been in the House*.[23]

Williams was refused a face-saving compromise whereby he was to be returned unopposed and resign voluntarily in Newborough's favour before the next election.[24] He admitted that his health was 'so bad that

I am now obliged to give up attending the House of Commons' and that he stood for Parliament in 1826 against medical advice.[25] He presented a petition from Llangollen for the abolition of colonial slavery, 15 Mar., and divided for Hume's state of the nation motion, 4 May. Sparing little time for canvassing, he decided 'to try his strength in Caernarvonshire, but not to put himself to any expense', remaining in London and Brighton, where his daughter Harriet's wedding and his younger children's whooping cough kept him busy. However, he ordered freeholders' lists, and William Hughes vainly tried to negotiate a compromise with Newborough through Sir Coutts Trotter.[26] Lady Bulkeley's death, 23 Feb. 1826, had put Richard in control of Beaumaris, and 'to soften in a great degree the mortification of losing my seat for Caernarvonshire', Williams asked to be returned for Beaumaris, with reversion to Richard. Discussing Caernarvonshire with his Beaumaris agent, he wrote, 12 May:

> Colonel Hughes I believe understands with myself that I am to appear on the day of election and to be proposed and seconded ... and then to inform my friends that it is quite impossible for me to spend money, but to show them that I do not mean to desert them or fly my colours I will offer the Baron Hill interest which is all that I am in possession of.[27]

And on the 22nd:

> All I want to do is to face my enemies. I am not ashamed of any public act I ever did and I shall see how I am supported by the independent gentlemen. In case of need can you get a requisition by 12 respectable freeholders for a day of nomination?[28]

He attributed his late withdrawal to health and financial reasons, stayed away from the election, and defended his conduct and reputation in the correspondence columns of the *North Wales Gazette*, where his opponents made much of his 'posting from Versailles to Westminster at the fag end of the [1822] session to give his *conscientious* vote in favour of the vagabond Hunt'. He went to Beaumaris to be elected, 13 June, and commended his supporters in speeches that day and at the Anglesey nomination on the 16th.[29] Afterwards he insured Richard's life and negotiated a new mortgage for the Baron Hill, Caerau, Nant and Friars estates, 17 July 1826.[30]

Williams distanced himself from a flurry of controversial local legislation affecting Caernarvonshire in 1826-7. His health remained poor, and he received two months' leave, 6 Mar. 1827. He divided against the funding proposed for the Canadian waterways, 12 June

1827. The duke of Wellington as premier agreed to his second son Robert Griffith Williams obtaining a commission as an extra aide-de-camp to Anglesey as Irish lord lieutenant, and he remained in Dublin following Anglesey's dismissal in January 1829.[31] Reports that Williams voted against Catholic relief, 12 May, were false.[32] He reaffirmed his opposition to repealing the usury laws when certain London merchants, traders and bankers petitioned requesting it, 15 May, and promised 'to divide the House at every stage' should it be proposed. As was his custom when in town, he cast a handful of late session votes: against restricting the circulation of one and two pound bank notes, 5 June, for revision and reduction of civil list pensions, 10 June, and against the additional churches bill, 30 June, and the ordnance estimates, 4, 7 July 1828. He entertained the corporation of Beaumaris at Friars at Michaelmas, to celebrate Richard's birthday, and attended the Anglesey magistrates' meeting, which joined him in resisting any proposal to transfer assize business from Beaumaris to the mainland or abolish the Welsh courts of great sessions, 2 Dec. 1828.[33] In a futile attempt to stem local opposition to Catholic emancipation, he spoke at the Anglesey county meeting, 6 Jan. 1829, of the ignominy of his dismissal as Member for Caernarvonshire 'for voting for civil and religious liberty', and of the ingratitude and inconsistency of the Dissenters, who had benefited from the recent repeal of the Test Acts, in opposing Catholic relief. His amendment to delay petitioning until the details of the government's legislation were announced was soundly defeated.[34] He brought up a petition against militia reductions from corporals in the Anglesey regiment, 23 Feb. His recent attempts to enclose Beaumaris's prestigious green had soured his relations with his constituents.[35] Owen Williams commented:

> I have been all my life pretty much habituated to the vagaries of our friend, the Bart., but really this last piece of charity oversteps in *absurdity* almost anything I have ever known him before *gratuitously* to offer. I really never could have imagined I should find in a connection of mine a parallel for *Jonathan Martin* [the York Minster arsonist]!!! Firebrands both in their way, one moral and the other physical, with the difference only that the one is inextinguishable, but time and money will repair the other.[36]

The patronage secretary Planta predicted in late February that Williams would support Catholic emancipation without requiring additional securities, but ill health, for which he received a fortnight's leave, 4 Mar., prevented him from voting on the issue. Nevertheless, at the Caernarvonshire Protestant meeting, 11 Apr., he made a rousing speech in defence of Peel and

Wellington and drew attention to the absence that day of gentry who had hitherto opposed emancipation. As anticipated, he made little headway, but his personal standing remained high.[37] His only reported vote that session was for a reduction in the hemp duties, 1 June 1829. He was too ill to deal with parliamentary business in 1830. He was granted a month's leave, 26 Feb., and attended on 6 July, when, speaking against the regency bill, he stressed the 'great delicacy of the subject' and urged its deferral to the next Parliament.

He had 'no intention to move in Caernarvonshire' at the general election, gave his Caernarvon Boroughs interest to Sir Charles Paget* and was returned *in absentia* for Beaumaris.[38] Ministers naturally listed him among their 'foes', but he was too ill to oppose them, and died at Nice in December 1830, recalled as the last of the Williamses of Arianwst to represent Caernarvonshire in Parliament. His body was brought back for burial in the family vault at Llanfair-yng-Nghornwy, where the gentry and corporation of Beaumaris were in attendance and the inhabitants formed a long cortège.[39] Richard succeeded him in the baronetcy and representation of Beaumaris and to entailed estates over £30,000 in debt. Limited probate on personalty sworn under £3,000 (of which £1,200 was life insurance) was granted to his widow, 27 July 1831, after counsel's opinion had been obtained on his liabilities. He provided small annuities and gifts to his children, sons-in-law, servants and solicitors, asked to be commemorated by a fountain in Beaumaris, and left tokens to William Hughes, the Beaumaris attorney Owen Williams, and Assheton Smith (who had predeceased him in 1828) noting:

> Although I conceive that Mr. Assheton Smith acted most treacherously by me, nevertheless, I request that some token of remembrance may be offered to him as a mark of my entire forgiveness of whatever is past.[40]

[1] *HP Commons, 1790-1820*, ii. 483-4; v. 582-3; J.J. Sack, *Grenvillites*, 127, 164. [2] UCNW, Baron Hill mss 3404-9. [3] *N. Wales Gazette*, 17, 24 Feb., 2, 9, 16, 23 Mar. 1820. [4] *Seren Gomer*, iii (1820), 190. [5] Baron Hill mss 5358. [6] Add. 34585, ff. 57-60. [7] *Seren Gomer*, iv (1821), 93, 124, 154, 252. [8] Sack, 224; NLW, Nanhoron mss 823. [9] *The Times*, 28 Mar. 1822. [10] Nanhoron mss 824. [11] Buckingham, *Mems. Geo. IV*, ii. 334. [12] *N. Wales Gazette*, 2 July 1823. [13] Baron Hill mss 3399, 3421. [14] Ibid. 3436, 3437, 3452. [15] NLW, Llanfair and Brynodol mss C365. [16] *CJ*, lxxix. 54, 172, 467. [17] *Seren Gomer*, vii (1824), 224-5. [18] NLW ms 1498 A, ii. 45, 46. [19] *CJ*, lxxx. 35, 74, 411, 441; G.I.T. Machin, *Catholic Question in English Politics*, 75; *The Times*, 13, 14 May 1825. [20] *The Times*, 15 June 1825. [21] Llanfair and Brynodol mss C302. [22] Llanfair and Brynodol mss C345; *N. Wales Gazette*, 1, 8, 15, 22, 29 Sept., 6, 13 Oct.; Cheshire and Chester Archives, Stanley of Alderley mss DSA45 [W.O.] Stanley to mother, 25 Sept. 1825; Nanhoron mss 819; UCNW, Plas Newydd mss i. 213-18, 233, 238, 242. [23] Plas Newydd mss i. 224. [24] Ibid. 5173; Plas Newydd mss i. 213, 218-21, 226, 227,

232, 311. [25] Baron Hill mss 5173. [26] Ibid 5173; Gwynedd Archives, Caernarfon, Vaynol mss 2599; Plas Newydd mss i. 313. [27] Baron Hill mss 3399, 3421. [28] Ibid. 5173. [29] *N. Wales Gazette*, 1, 8, 15, 22, 29 June, 6, 13 July; *Shrewsbury Chron.* 2, 23, 30 June 1826. [30] Baron Hill mss 3442, 5173. [31] Wellington mss WP1/987/27; PRO NI, Anglesey mss D619/32/A/6. [32] *CJ*, lxxxiii. 67, 334; *Seren Gomer*, xi (1828), 188. [33] *N. Wales Chron.* 2 Oct. 1828; Plas Newydd mss i. 748, 752; *PP* (1829), ix. 411. [34] Plas Newydd mss vii. 2018; *N. Wales Chron.* 8 Jan. 1829. [35] UCNW, Henllys mss 435. [36] Ibid. 289. [37] *N. Wales Chron.* 12, 26 Mar., 16 Apr. 1829. [38] Plas Newydd mss i. 399, 401, 404, 405, 457; *Shrewsbury Chron.* 6 Aug.; *Chester Courant*, 10 Aug 1830. [39] *N. Wales Chron.* 16, 30 Dec. 1830. [40] Baron Hill mss 3452, 3453; PROB 11/1788/433; IR26/1276/342.

M.M.E.

WILLIAMS, Thomas Peers (1795–1875).

GREAT MARLOW   1820–1868

b. 27 Mar. 1795, 1st s. of Owen Williams* and Margaret, da. of Rev. Edward Hughes of Kinmel Park, Denb. *educ.* Westminster 1808-12; Christ Church, Oxf. 1813. *m.* 27 Aug. 1835, Emily, da. of Anthony Bacon of Elcott, Berks., 2s. 6da. *suc.* fa. 1832. *d.* 7 Sept. 1875.
  Capt. R. Anglesey militia by 1847, lt.-col. 1853.
  Mayor, Beaumaris 1827-8.

Williams, who may have joined Brooks's club on 11 May 1816, came in for Great Marlow on the dominant family interest in 1820.[1] He retained his seat at the next twelve general elections, eight of which were contested. Like his father, he acted initially with the Whig opposition to the Liverpool ministry, but ended this period as a Conservative. He was an indifferent attender, though he was less negligent of his parliamentary duties than was his father. He divided against government on the civil list, 5, 8 May, and for economies in revenue collection, 4 July 1820. He voted to deplore the omission of Queen Caroline's name from the liturgy, 26 Jan., and to censure ministers' prosecution of her, 6 Feb. 1821. He divided for Catholic relief, 28 Feb. He voted for reductions in the military estimates, 14 Mar., 14 May, and for abolition of the death penalty for forgery offences, 23 May 1821. In 1822 he voted for more extensive tax reductions, 11 Feb., relaxation of the salt duties, 28 Feb., when he also voted to condemn Sir Robert Wilson's* dismissal from the army, admiralty economies, 1 Mar., and abolition of one of the joint-postmasterships, 13 Mar., 2 May. He divided for large tax remissions, 28 Feb., ordnance cuts, 17 Mar., against the naval and military pensions bill, 11, 18 Apr., for inquiries into the prosecution of the Dublin Orange rioters, 22 Apr., and the cost of the coronation, 19 June, and for the abolition of punishment by whipping, 30 Apr. 1823. His only known votes in 1824 were against the aliens bill, 23 Mar., and for repeal of the assessed taxes, 10 May. He paired against Brougham's motion condemning the prosecution of the Methodist missionary John Smith in Demerara, 11 June 1824. He defaulted on a call of the House, 28 Feb., but appeared and was excused, 1 Mar. 1825, when he voted for Catholic relief; he did so again, 21 Apr., 10 May. He divided for repeal of the assessed taxes, 3 Mar., 17 May, and against the duke of Cumberland's grant, 30 May, 10 June 1825. He was in the opposition minorities against the president of the board of trade's separate salary, 1, 10 Apr., and divided for Lord John Russell's parliamentary reform motion, 27 Apr. 1826.

Williams was absent from the division on Catholic relief, 6 Mar. 1827. He voted to withhold supply until the ministerial crisis following Lord Liverpool's stroke had been resolved, 30 Mar. 1827. He presented a Marlow petition for repeal of the Test Acts, 19 Feb. 1828, and voted for that measure a week later. As expected by the Wellington ministry, who did not now regard him as being in regular opposition, he divided for Catholic emancipation, 6, 30 Mar. 1829. He may have voted for the amendment to the address, 4 Feb. 1830. He was credited with dividing for the transfer of East Retford's seats to Birmingham, 11 Feb., but against the enfranchisement of Birmingham, Leeds and Manchester, 23 Feb. With his father, he voted against the sale of beer bill, 4 May, 21 June. He moved unsuccessfully to adjourn the debate on the second reading of the bill to reorganize the Welsh judicial system, 27 Apr., and voted in a minority of 30 against it, 18 June. He divided against Jewish emancipation, 17 May 1830. In September Williams, like his father, was considered a 'friend' by the government, after being listed initially as one of the 'good doubtfuls'; but he was absent from the crucial division on the civil list, 15 Nov. 1830. He joined his father in voting against the second reading of the Grey ministry's reform bill, 22 Mar., and for Gascoyne's wrecking amendment, 19 Apr. 1831. He divided against the second reading of the reintroduced measure, 6 July, paired against combining Rochester with Chatham and Strood, 9 Aug., and voted to preserve freemen's rights, 30 Aug. On the proposal to deprive Marlow of one seat, 15 Sept., he argued that it deserved to retain both, like its neighbour Chipping Wycombe, a Whig stronghold towards which ministers had shown 'gross partiality'. He voted against the passage of the bill, 21 Sept. He took three weeks' leave to attend to urgent business, 6 Oct. He divided against the second reading of the revised reform bill (which reprieved Marlow), 17 Dec. 1831, but only paired against the third reading, 22 Mar. 1832, a month after succeeding his father in the family's Berkshire and Anglesey estates. He voted against the second reading of the Irish reform bill, 25 May,

and paired with opposition on the Russian-Dutch loan, 12 July 1832.

At the general election of 1832 Williams, 'a stubborn Conservative, stung by the loss of a seat for Marlow' to a reformer on his father's death, withdrew from the Pagets of Plas Newydd the support which his grandfather and father had given to their electoral interests in Anglesey and North Wales.[2] In 1840 his near neighbour Benjamin Disraeli[†] described him as 'a nincompoop', though they were 'friends enough'.[3] He opposed Peel's repeal of the corn laws in 1846 and supported Lord Derby's Conservative administrations of 1852, 1858-9 and 1866-8, retiring at the dissolution in 1868 after 48 years of unbroken and thoroughly undistinguished membership of the Commons.[4] He died 'after a painful illness' in September 1875.[5] He was succeeded in the family estates by his elder son Colonel Owen Lewis Cope Williams (1836-1904), Conservative Member for Marlow in the 1880 Parliament. Of his six daughters, three married peers, two the younger sons of peers and one a baronet.

[1] Add. 58977, f. 165. [2] UCNW, Plas Newydd mss iii. 3618, 3655. [3] *Disraeli Letters*, iii. 1089. [4] *Dod's Parl. Companion* (1847), 254; (1865), 308. [5] *The Times*, 9, 11 Sept. 1875.

D.R.F.

WILLIAMS, William (1774–1839), of Belmont House, South Lambeth, Surr. and 37 Portland Place, Mdx.

WEYMOUTH & MELCOMBE REGIS   1818–1826

b. 28 Mar. 1774, 2nd s. of Robert Williams[†] (*d.* 1814) of Bridehead, nr. Dorchester, Dorset and Moor Park, Herts. and Jane, da. of Francis Chassereau of Marylebone, Mdx.; bro. of Robert Williams*. *educ.* Wormley, Herts.; St. John's, Camb. 1791; I. Temple 1792, called 1798. *m.* 30 Nov. 1797, Anne, da. of John Rashleigh of Penquite, Cornw., 5s. (4 *d.v.p.*) 1da. *d.* 8 Feb. 1839.

Vol. London and Westminster light horse 1803-21.

The barrister William Williams, who in 1796 went on a walking tour in Wales, was installed as provincial grand master of Dorset in 1812 and three years later published a volume of masonic *Constitutions*.[1] He inherited £60,000 on the death of his father in 1814, and thereafter became a partner in the family bank in Birchin Lane, London, which was taken over by his elder brother Robert, Member for Dorchester. He was also a principal in the Dorchester bank of Williams and Company, and later held several directorships.[2] An advanced Whig, he was returned for Weymouth at his fifth attempt at the general election of 1818, when (with the social reformer Thomas Fowell Buxton*) he forced a compromise for the 'town' interest on Masterton Ure*, who represented the 'trustees' of the Johnstone family. Under this agreement he was re-elected unopposed at the general election two years later, when he stood on the same independent principles.[3] His refusal to fulfil the 'union' arrangement to purchase the fee farms in Weymouth created additional problems in 1820 for Ure and the other electoral managers, who were concerned that these properties would be threatened if Williams secured the passage of a bill, which had failed the previous year, to prevent the fraudulent splitting of votes.[4] He retained his early sympathies for radicalism, expressing to Sir Francis Burdett* his support for the cause of 'popular election' during the Westminster contest in 1820, and attending the trial of John Cartwright later that year.[5] He was active in the House and, although he never joined Brooks's, spoke and voted frequently with the Whig opposition on all major issues, notably on motions for economies and retrenchment in the early 1820s.[6]

Williams commented on the validity of Henry Ellis's election for Boston during his absence abroad, 25 May, spoke for inquiry into the practice of returning paupers to Ireland, 6 June, and said it was unjust that the Irish should pay a ten per cent duty on necessary commodities, 14 June 1820. He promised to consider the complaints made against the splitting of votes at Lichfield whenever he should reintroduce his bill on this subject, 16 June.[7] Stating that he had intended to frame a motion on the Queen Caroline affair, though not as a 'party man', 22 June, he urged the restoration of her name to the liturgy and voted against Wilberforce's compromise resolution that day. He argued that Thomas Ellis should not be allowed to take his seat for Dublin while continuing to serve as an Irish master in chancery, 30 June. He praised the East India Company's volunteers bill on the ground that a militia was 'the most constitutional force that could be used for the preservation of the public peace', 11 July, and objected to the law officers having a vote on the bill of pains and penalties if it reached the Commons, 12 July. During the general jubilation over Caroline's acquittal in November 1820, it was reported from Weymouth that 'Williams is here with his family but doing nothing to appearance'.[8] He spoke for revising the criminal laws at a meeting there, 20 Jan. 1821.[9] He presented petitions for reinstating the queen's name in the liturgy from Lambeth, 26 Jan., and Eye, 13 Feb., and voted for this, 23, 26 Jan., 14 Feb., and to censure ministers' conduct towards her, 6 Feb. He insisted that 'he would not be put down by a laugh or a cough' while supporting the reduction of the army by 10,000

men, 14 Mar. He was listed among the stewards of the Friends of Reform dinner in London on 4 Apr.[10] He divided to disqualify civil officers of the ordnance from voting in parliamentary elections, 12 Apr., stated that he had supported parliamentary reform 'from his earliest days' and that nomination boroughs gave ministers excessive influence in the Commons, 17 Apr., and voted for reform, 18 Apr., 9 May. He divided for the forgery punishment mitigation bill, 23 May, 4 June. He reintroduced his occasional votes bill, 24 May, which had its first reading the following day, but was then allowed to lapse.[11] He laid the foundation stone of the new Weymouth bridge 'with masonic form', 14 Sept. 1821.[12]

He voted for inquiry into the Scottish royal burghs, 20 Feb., and parliamentary reform, 25 Apr. 1822. He criticized the proposed alteration of the rates of return on navy five per cent stock and condemned government for mismanagement of the sinking fund, 25 Feb., 8, 11, 27 Mar. He expressed willingness to introduce measures to remove army officers from the Commons, 12 Mar., and to equalize county rates, 25 Mar.[13] He called for the creation of an effective sinking fund, 1, 24 May, and for the opening of the trade in sugar, 17 May, and abolition of the salt tax, 24 June 1822.[14] He again divided for parliamentary reform, 20 Feb., 24 Apr., and reform of the Scottish representative system, 2 June 1823. He was critical of government's attitude towards French aggression in Spain, 18 Mar., and explained on 30 Apr. that he could neither condone ministers' weak handling of the crisis nor vote for Macdonald's censure motion because he feared this would lead to hostilities. He suggested the introduction of an *ad valorem* tax on beer, 24 Mar. 1823. He strongly supported Abercromby's motion complaining of a breach of privilege by the lord chancellor, 1 Mar. 1824, when he objected to the cost of completing the new courts of justice. He attacked the West India Company bill as an obstacle to the abolition of slavery, 10 May 1824. He called the Catholic Association 'most inimical to the interests of the Catholics of Ireland' and gave his support to the Irish unlawful societies bill, 11 Feb. 1825, when he declared himself to be in favour of Catholic relief. He was not, however, listed in any of the majorities in its favour that session. He brought in a bill to enable the Cape of Good Hope Banking Company to be sued in the names of its secretary and governor, 30 Mar., and objected to sharp practices by the promoters of the Western Ship Canal bill, 3 June.[15] As a result of the banking crisis, Williams's establishment in Dorchester temporarily suspended trading in December 1825.[16] He voted for the bill to disfranchise non-resident voters in Irish boroughs, 9 Mar., and to abolish flogging in the army, 10 Mar. 1826. He retired from Parliament at the dissolution that summer. In a valedictory address on the hustings at Weymouth, 10 June 1826, he vindicated his conduct in the Commons and apparently gave expression to the anti-Catholic sentiments that the electors expected; that day and the next, when he proposed Buxton, he praised the independent interest.[17]

Williams was described by George IV in 1827 as 'one of the worst of radicals, invariably opposing the king and his government in every instance; in short one of the staunchest, bitterest and very worst of Whigs, a friend of [Henry] Hunt's*, etc., etc., etc.'[18] Williams, who made no further attempt to gain a seat in Parliament,[19] again nominated Buxton for Weymouth at the general election of 1830.[20] During the 'Swing' riots that autumn he led a group of special constables from Cerne Abbas, near his residence at Castle Hill, Dorset.[21] In Weymouth, 3 May 1831, he complained of having been silenced at a meeting of the inhabitants on 17 Mar. and again spoke in favour of Buxton as a reformer; he added that in the House 'he had made himself a slave to his duty, but now, after he had tasted the happiness of a quiet and retired life, not all the wealth of India should induce him to come forward as a parliamentary candidate'.[22] He voted for the reformers Edward Portman* and John Calcraft* in the Dorset contest that month, and for William Ponsonby* in the county by-election in late 1831.[23] Williams died in February 1839, leaving two surviving children, and was buried in Little Bredy church, where a commemorative tablet was erected by his masonic brethren.[24]

[1] E.R. Sykes, 'A Walking Tour in Wales in 1796', *Procs. Dorset Nat. Hist. and Arch. Soc.* lxiv (1942), 84-91; H.P. Smith, *Hist. Lodge of Amity no. 137, Poole*, 202; William Williams, *Constitutions of Antient Fraternity of Free and Accepted Masons*, pt. 2 (1815). [2] PROB 11/1552/104; IR26/627/67; *Gent. Mag.* (1814), i. 202; *The Times*, 7 Feb. 1825. [3] *HP Commons, 1790-1820*, v. 586-7; *Western Flying Post*, 28 Feb., 13 Mar. 1820. [4] Northumb. RO, Middleton mss ZMI/S76/40/2, 5. [5] Add. 47222, f. 23; *Life and Corresp. of Cartwright* ed. F.D. Cartwright, ii. 186. [6] *Black Bk.* (1823), 203; *Session of Parl. 1825*, p. 491. [7] *The Times*, 17 June 1820; Hatherton diary. [8] Middleton mss S76/40/38. [9] *Salisbury Jnl.* 29 Jan. 1821. [10] *The Times*, 14 Feb., 15 Mar., 4 Apr. 1821. [11] *CJ*, lxxvi. 376, 378, 413, 423. [12] *Salisbury Jnl.* 17 Sept. 1821. [13] *The Times*, 12, 26 Mar. 1822. [14] Ibid. 25 June 1822. [15] Ibid. 31 Mar. 1825. [16] *Dorset Co. Chron.* 15, 29 Dec. 1825. [17] Ibid. 8, 15 June 1826. [18] *Geo. IV Letters*, iii. 1422. [19] The defeated candidate at Seaford in 1830 was William Williams of Aberpergwm, Glam. Another namesake, the son of Thomas Williams of Llanpumsent, Caern., was Liberal Member for Coventry, 1835-47, and Lambeth, 1850-65. [20] *Dorset Co. Chron.* 5 Aug. 1830. [21] B. Kerr, *Bound to the Soil*, 114. [22] *Dorset Co. Chron.* 24 Mar., 5 May 1831. [23] *Dorset Pollbooks* (1831), 34; (Sept.-Oct. 1831), 46. [24] *Dorset Co. Chron.* 14, 21 Feb. 1839; *Gent. Mag.* (1839), i. 661-2; J. Hutchins, *Dorset*, ii. (1863), 187.

S.M.F.

WILLIAMS *see also* **HAMLYN WILLIAMS**

WILLIAMS BULKELEY, Sir Richard Bulkeley, 10th bt. (1801–1875), of Baron Hill, Anglesey.

BEAUMARIS	8 Feb. 1831–1832
ANGLESEY	1832–Jan. 1837
FLINT BOROUGHS	1841–1847
ANGLESEY	1847–1868

b. 23 Sept. 1801, 1st s. of Sir Robert Williams*, 9th bt., of Plas y Nant, Caern. and Friars, Anglesey and Anne, da. of Rev. Edward Hughes of Kinmel Park, Denb. *educ.* Westminster 1815-19; Christ Church, Oxf. 1820. *m.* (1) 27 May 1828, his cos. Charlotte Mary (*d.* 11 May 1829), da. of William Lewis Hughes*; (2) 20 Aug. 1830, Maria Frances, da. of Sir Thomas Stanley Massey Stanley of Hooton, Cheshire, 4s. (1 *d.v.p.*) *suc.* to estates of uncle Thomas James Bulkeley†, 7th Visct. Bulkeley [I] and 1st Bar. Bulkeley [UK], 3 June 1822; fa. as 10th bt. 1 Dec. 1830. Took name and arms of Bulkeley and assumed the style Sir Richard Bulkeley by royal lic. 26 June 1827. *d.* 28 Aug. 1875.

Mayor, Beaumaris 1824-5, 1830-1; recorder 1831-5.

Sheriff, Caern. 1838-9; ld. lt. Caern. 1851-66; sheriff, Anglesey 1870.

Williams, as he was first known, could trace his ancestry to Ednyfed Fychan. More recently, his family had profited from the development of Anglesey's copper mines, in which his maternal uncles William Lewis Hughes, the future Lord Dinorben, and Owen Williams* held an interest, and also through their connection with his father's half-brother, Lord Bulkeley of Baron Hill. The latter returned the Member for Beaumaris, and since 1784 they had controlled the representation of Caernarvonshire by arrangement with the Pagets of Plas Newydd in return for their support for a Paget in Anglesey. Bulkeley was childless and early versions of his will reflected his concern for the manner in which 'Sir Robert's son' should be groomed to succeed him. He was to attend Westminster School and 'Christ Church or other eminent college at Oxford', not Cambridge, and 'have a tutor while he remains in college'.[1] He entered Christ Church from Westminster in 1820 with Bulkeley's godson Lord Newborough* of Glynllifon; but only after Magdalene College, Cambridge had refused him a scholarship on Dr. Millington's foundation because he 'left school so ill informed as to the first principles of grammar'. Nothing had come of Bulkeley's late suggestion that he try Peterhouse, Cambridge.[2]

Williams was almost 21 when Bulkeley died, 3 June 1822, and was not destined to inherit Baron Hill, of which his father was the trustee and in which Lady Bulkeley retained a controlling interest, until his 25th birthday. However, in 1823 he signed agreements pledging future estate income to settle family debts.[3] Lady Bulkeley judged her nephew to be 'much improved in appearance and manner' from residence in France with his family, 1820-2, and considered returning him for Beaumaris, but wrote that 'he has *more* of the *father* than one could wish'.[4] Her death left Williams in control of Beaumaris at the 1826 general election when, declining to return the sitting Member, Thomas Frankland Lewis, he made the seat available to his father, to dissuade him from proceeding with an expensive contest against Newborough in Caernarvonshire. This, and his readiness to ease his family's financial predicaments, led his father to comment, 'My boy is acting so honourable a part I can refuse him nothing'.[5] He was a personable man and an able public speaker, who participated readily at Beaumaris hunt week and county occasions, and there was great rejoicing on his marriage to his cousin Charlotte in 1828 and sorrow at her premature death the following year.[6] As stipulated in Bulkeley's will, he took that surname in 1827 and adopted the style of Sir Richard Bulkeley. He was in Cadiz at the dissolution in 1830 and reputedly not interested in coming into Parliament when Beaumaris again returned his father.[7] His father's death in Nice, 1 Dec. 1830, left Bulkeley, who failed to arrive in time to see him, in possession of about 36,000 acres in Anglesey and Caernarvonshire, with over £30,000 to clear in bond debts and annuities averaging £17,000 drawn on Baron Hill, which rarely yielded over £14,000.[8] He was returned *in absentia* for Beaumaris without the customary celebrations, 8 Feb. 1831.[9]

Bulkeley, who is not known to have spoken in debate in this period, was granted a week's leave to attend to urgent private business after serving on the Dunbartonshire election committee, 14 Mar. He divided for the Grey ministry's reform bill at its second reading, 22 Mar., and against Gascoyne's wrecking amendment, 19 Apr. The bill proposed making Holyhead, where the Stanleys of Alderley and Penrhos were in control, a contributory of Beaumaris, and arrangements were also in hand for the enfranchisement of Amlwch and Llangefni, where Anglesey, Hughes and Bulkeley were the largest landlords.[10] Bodley's Librarian, Dr. Bulkeley Bandinel, advised him and Beaumaris corporation that the bill would 'only act as a prelude to much more and much worse';[11] but in circulars and at his election for Beaumaris following its defeat, Bulkeley confirmed his support for reform, describing it as 'the renovation of the constitution, not a revolution', and he cautioned the corporation against putting their private interests first. He canvassed actively with Anglesey's son and heir Lord Uxbridge for Sir Charles Paget in Caernarvon Boroughs, and as he had been injured in a clash with William Ormsby Gore's* supporters, his brother Robert Griffith Williams deputized for him at Uxbridge's election for Anglesey.[12] Uxbridge expected to be elevated to the peerage and Bulkeley hoped to come in for Anglesey at the first post-reform election. To facilitate it he offered his interest in Beaumaris to a Paget. However, resisting, Anglesey, then lord lieutenant of Ireland, warned from Dublin, 17 June 1831, 'if Sir B. Williams ever gets in, there he will stay'.[13]

The reintroduced reform bill provided for the enfranchisement of Amlwch, Holyhead and Llangefni with Beaumaris, and Bulkeley divided for it at its second reading, 6 July, sparingly for its details, 26, 27 July, 5, 9 Aug., and for its passage, 21 Sept. 1831. His support for the revised reform bill was erratic. He was absent from the division on its second reading, 17 Dec. 1831. He voted against an amendment for a £10 poor rate franchise, 3 Feb., and to leave Helston in schedule B, 23 Feb., but against the enfranchisement of Tower Hamlets, 28 Feb., and awarding Gateshead separate representation, 5 Mar. 1832 – a protest vote commonly cast by Welsh Members angered by the meagre provision for Merthyr Tydfil. He divided for the third reading, 22 Mar., but was out of town when the House divided on the address requesting the king to appoint only ministers who would carry it unimpaired, 10 May. He had little local legislation to attend to, but he presented Bangor's petition against the Caernarvonshire roads bill, 26 Feb., and was appointed to the select committee on communications between Great Britain and Ireland, 16 Mar. He divided with government on the Russian-Dutch loan, 26 Jan., 12, 16 July, and information on Portugal, 9 Feb. 1832.

His main interests were his racehorses, courtship of the Catholic heiress Maria Stanley, and the future representation of Anglesey. He handled negotiations for the latter astutely, heeding advice from Dinorben, and profiting from the uncertainty concerning Uxbridge's peerage and his own residence in Anglesey, where opposition from the Stanleys of Penrhos and Fuller Meyrick of Bodorgan was anticipated. Negotiations with Plas Newydd, however, languished until Robert, one of Anglesey's aides-de-camp, spoke 'openly and confidently' of the matter in Dublin in March 1832.[14] On 21 Apr. Uxbridge, Bulkeley, and the Plas Newydd agent John Sanderson agreed to form a coalition *'quietly ... respecting the county and borough'*, but Anglesey only approved the plan, under which

Bulkeley gave the Pagets his Conway and Beaumaris interests, after he paid him a personal visit in Dublin in November 1832, and quashed rumours that he might bring in his brother or one of the Stanleys of Penrhos for Beaumaris.[15] Despite Bulkeley's claim that 'love and business go d—d badly together', the close proximity in time of the celebration of his second marriage with Anglican and Catholic rites in August 1832, the Beaumaris eisteddfod and regatta, Princess Victoria's visit and the hunt week, served well to publicize his supremacy in Anglesey, which returned him unopposed as a Liberal in December 1832, despite resentment at the pact and rumblings of discontent from Tory squires.[16] A fire at Baron Hill increased his financial worries and he relinquished the county seat in 1837, but regained it without a contest in 1847, after representing Flint Boroughs for a single Parliament. Although a lifelong Liberal, he supported the Conservative Dawkins Pennant in Caernarvonshire in 1852 and his sons were staunch Conservatives. His retirement in 1868 was attributed to misgivings about the 1867 Reform Act, but he supported the Liberal Richard Davies in Anglesey in 1868 and 1874, when his eldest son Richard Mostyn Williams Bulkeley (1833-84), a captain in the Horse Guards, was the defeated candidate. Lord Melbourne and Lord John Russell as prime ministers rejected his requests for a peerage, and he died in August 1875, having dominated local government and politics in Anglesey for half a century. He was buried at Llanfaes and commemorated by a monument on Cremlyn Hill above Beaumaris.[17] He was succeeded in his estates by his eldest son as he had willed, 31 July 1862, but a codicil of 21 July 1865, drafted after the latter had divorced his wife, deprived him of all interest in the Snowdon Mine, and all horses, stock and agricultural and moveable farming effects at Baron Hill. These passed to his younger sons Thomas James (1840-81), the defeated Conservative at New Windsor in 1852, and Charles William (1841-92), who, with his widow (d. 1889), had equal shares in his personalty.

[1] UCNW Baron Hill mss 3399. [2] Add. 34585, ff. 57-60. [3] UCNW Baron Hill mss 3399, 3437; PROB 11/1663/561; IR26/895/1341. [4] NLW, Llanfair and Brynodol mss C365; Buckingham, Mems. Geo. IV. ii. 33. [5] UCNW Baron Hill mss 3442, 5173; N. Wales Gazette, 15 June 1826. [6] N. Wales Chron. 15 May, 5, 19 June, 2 Oct. 1828. [7] Plas Newydd mss i. 397, 404; Chester Courant, 10 Aug. 1830. [8] N. Wales Chron. 16, 30 Dec. 1830; PROB 8/224; 11/1788/443; IR26/1276/342; Baron Hill mss 3452, 3453, 4871-3. [9] Beaumaris mss v. 61; Caernarvon Herald, 12 Feb. 1831. [10] D.A. Wager, 'Welsh Politics and Parl. Reform, 1780-1832', WHR, vii (1974), 436-9; Plas Newydd mss vii. 282; Chester Courant, 12 Apr. 1831. [11] UCNW Baron Hill mss 3451. [12] Beaumaris mss v. 62; Caernarvon Herald, 7, 14 May 1831. [13] Plas Newydd mss i. 43-50; vii. 287; Ll. Jones, 'Edition of Corresp. of 1st mq. of Anglesey relating to

General Elections of 1830, 1831 and 1832 in Caern. and Anglesey' (Univ. of Liverpool M.A. thesis, 1956), 507. [14] Plas Newydd mss i. 50, 57, 61. [15] Ibid. i. 62-74, 78, 85, 89, 99-109, 112; iii. 3675, 3589-91; vii. 304-7; W. Suss. RO, Goodwood mss 1436, ff. 327-8. [16] Chester Courant, 11 Oct., 22 Nov., 20, 27 Dec. 1831, 28 Dec. 1832; N. Wales Chron. 7, 14 Aug., 4 Sept., 11, 18, 25 Dec. 1832; UCNW Baron Hill mss 5629-53; Plas Newydd mss i. 121. [17] E.A. Williams, Day Before Yesterday, 82-83, 85, 89, 93-94, 105, 312; Caernarvon and Denbigh Herald, 4 Sept. 1875.

M.M.E.

WILLIAMSON, Sir Hedworth, 7th bt. (1797–1861), of Whitburn Hall, nr. Sunderland, co. Dur.

DURHAM CO.	1831–1832
DURHAM NORTH	1832–1837
SUNDERLAND	22 Dec. 1847–1852

b. 1 Nov. 1797, 2nd. but 1st. surv. s. of Sir Hedworth Williamson, 6th bt., of Whitburn and Maria, da. of Sir James Hamilton of co. Monaghan. educ. St. John's, Camb. 1815. m. 18 Apr. 1826, Hon. Anne Elizabeth Liddell, da. of Thomas Henry Liddell[†], 1st Bar. Ravensworth, 4s. suc. fa. as 7th bt. 14 Mar. 1810. d. 24 Apr. 1861.
Sheriff, co. Dur. 1840-1; mayor, Sunderland 1841-2, 1847-8.

Williamson was a direct descendant of the Nottinghamshire Royalist baronet, Sir Thomas Williamson (1609-57), of East Markham, whose namesake son had acquired the Monkwearmouth estate on the Durham (north) bank of the River Wear through his marriage with the Northumberland heiress Dorothy Fenwick of Brinkburne. They intermarried afterwards with the Durham families of Hedworth, Hopper, Huddleston, Lambton and Liddell, settled at Whitburn and held the shrievalty without interruption from 1723 until the death of Williamson's father in 1810. His subsequent upbringing was entrusted to his mother and her co-trustees Ralph Lambton[†], the recorder of Newcastle Robert Hopper (Williamson), and the Durham attorney Richard Scruton. Williamson took control of the heavily encumbered Whitburn estate in 1819 and declined the shrievalty on financial grounds that year. As his father had directed, he provided £9,000 settlements for his sisters, Maria, wife of the banker David Barclay*, and Sophia, who in 1823 married the Whig Thomas Dundas* Following his own marriage in 1826 to his neighbour Lord Ravensworth's daughter, he economized by spending two years on the continent.[1] He had joined Brooks's, 11 May 1823, seconded the Whig John George Lambton's* nomination for the county in 1826 and headed the requisition for the county meeting of 7 May 1831, ostensibly called on 28 Apr. to thank the king for dissolving Parliament following the defeat of the Grey ministry's reform bill.[2] Lord Cleveland's son had been obliged (as an anti-reformer) to stand down, and a meeting of the 'select few' (all reformers) chaired by Lambton's (now Lord Durham's) brother Hedworth Lambton[†], 28 Apr., had resolved to put forward Williamson, who at the meeting declared for the reform bill, economy and retrenchment. He was returned unopposed, professing the same principles, with the sitting Whig William Russell at a cost of £1,000.[3]

Williamson voted for the reintroduced reform bill at its second reading, 6 July, and steadily for its details, casting wayward votes only for the total disfranchisement of Russell's borough of Saltash, which ministers no longer pressed, 26 July, and the transfer of Aldborough to schedule A, 14 Sept. 1831. He contradicted the anti-reformers' arguments against the separate enfranchisement of Gateshead, 5 Aug. 1831, 5 Mar. 1832. He divided for the reform bill's passage, 21 Sept., the second reading of the Scottish bill, 23 Sept., and Lord Ebrington's confidence motion, 10 Oct. 1831. When Sunderland (27 Oct.) and the county (31 Oct.) met to protest at the bill's defeat in the Lords, he defended the ministry and the bill, praised Durham as one of its authors and was thanked for supporting it.[4] He divided for the revised reform bill at its second reading, 17 Dec. 1831, and, excluding his vote against enfranchising £50 tenants-at-will, 1 Feb. 1832, voted consistently for its details. He divided for the bill's third reading, 22 Mar., and the address calling on the king to appoint only ministers who would carry it unimpaired, 10 May, and presented and endorsed petitions from Gateshead, Darlington and Malton for the withdrawal of supplies pending its enactment, 23 May. He voted for the Irish reform bill at its second reading, 25 May, and against a Conservative amendment to the Scottish measure, 1 June 1832. He divided with government on the Dublin election controversy, 23 Aug. 1831, the Russian-Dutch loan 12, 16, 20 July (as a pair), Portugal, 9 Feb., and the navy civil departments bill, 6 Apr. 1832.

Testifying to its local unpopularity, he presented petitions against the general register bill, 18 Oct. 1831, 31 Jan., and was added to the select committee on the measure, 27 Mar. 1832. He spoke in favour of amending the anatomy bill, 11 Apr. Williamson hoped to make his estate profitable by mining coal and building a railway and harbour at Sunderland, for which Brunel was the engineer, and he conducted constituency business along commercial rather than party lines. Backed by petitions from Sunderland and north Durham, he opposed the rival South Shields and Monkwearmouth railway bill, 14, 16 Feb., 6 Mar., and having failed to kill it (by 9-55),

14 Feb., he secured its referral to a committee of appeal (by 37-22), 26 Mar. Assisted by his Dundas relations, he led the opposition to the associated Sunderland (South Side) docks bill, backed by the corporation and the Durham Member William Chaytor, 27 Feb., and engineered its defeat in committee (by 10-7), 2 Apr. The publication of the division list by the *Durham Chronicle* became the subject of breach of privilege proceedings, 16 Apr., 7 May.[5] The supporters of the South Side bill defeated Williamson's Sunderland (North Side) docks bill (by 12-2) in the Lords, where it was entrusted to Ravensworth, 17 July 1832, and mounted a vigorous campaign to 'floor' him 'out of the county, or rather his seat in the county', where they 'erroneously' advertised his retirement.[6] He carried the Bishopwearmouth roads and the Clarence railway bills without incident. On 27 Sept. 1832 he fought a bloodless duel with his Conservative opponent Edward Braddyll over allegations of 'dock-jobbing' and collusion with Lord Durham to 'impose his brother-in-law Barclay' on the new Sunderland constituency. A bitter and acrimonious contest, during which he advocated freedom of voting and 'moderate protection', preceded his return for Durham North as a Liberal with Hedworth Lambton at the general election in December.[7] Williamson's precipitate retirement in 1837, ostensibly on health and financial grounds, left little time to find a Liberal replacement and enabled his brother-in-law Thomas Henry Liddell* to take the seat for the Conservatives. After living for a time in Bruges, when his North Dock proved unprofitable, he returned to take Barclay's place as Liberal Member for Sunderland in 1847. He retired at the next dissolution.[8] Williamson died at Whitburn in April 1861, survived by his wife and four sons, the eldest of whom, Hedworth Williamson (1827-1900), Liberal Member for Durham North, 1864-74, succeeded to the baronetcy and estates. His younger sons were the principal beneficiaries of his will proved at Durham, 14 Feb. 1862.[9]

[1] PROB 11/1511/285; IR26/159/430; T. Nossiter, *Influence, Opinion and Political Idioms in Reformed England*, 117; W.W. Bean, *Parl. Rep. Six Northern Counties*, 102. [2] *Durham Chron.* 17 June 1826, 30 Apr. 1831. [3] Durham CRO, Londonderry mss D/Lo/C86/17; *Durham Advertiser*, 29 Apr., 6, 13 May 1831; *Pprs. of Sir William Chaytor, 1771-1847* ed. M.Y. Ashcroft (N. Yorks. Co. RO Publications, 1 (1993 edn.)) [hereafter *Chaytor Pprs.*] 157. [4] *Tyne Mercury*, 1 Nov.; *Durham Advertiser*, 4 Nov. 1831; J. Sykes, *Local Recs.* ii. 333-4. [5] *Durham Chron.* 16, 30 Mar., 6, 13, 20 Apr. 1832. [6] *Chaytor Pprs.* 172-7; *John Bull*, 24 June 1832. [7] Derbys. RO, Gresley of Drakelow mss D77/36/8 (iii), Trevor to Gresley [undated]; *Diaries and Corresp. of James Losh* ed. E. Hughes (Surtees Soc. clxxiv), ii. 217-18; *Durham Chron.* 21 Dec.; *Durham Co. Advertiser*, 28 Dec. 1832. [8] Nossiter, 71-74, 108, 117. [9] *Gent. Mag.* (1861), i. 697, 706; *Durham Chron.* 26 Apr. 1861; Durham Univ. Lib. Durham Wills DPR 1862.

M.M.E.

WILLIAMS WYNN, Charles Watkin (1775–1850), of Llangedwyn, Denb.[1]

OLD SARUM	29 July 1797–Mar. 1799
MONTGOMERYSHIRE	14 Mar. 1799–2 Sept. 1850

b. 9 Oct. 1775, 2nd s. of Sir Watkin Williams Wynn, 4th bt.[†] (*d.* 1789), of Wynnstay and 2nd w. Charlotte, da. of George Grenville[†]; bro. of Sir Watkin Williams Wynn, 5th bt.* and Henry Watkin Williams Wynn[†]. *educ.* by Rev. Robert Nares 1779-83; Westminster 1784; Christ Church, Oxf. 1791; L. Inn 1795, called 1798. *m.* 9 Apr. 1806, Mary, da. of Sir Foster Cunliffe, 3rd bt., of Acton Park, Denb., 3s. (2 *d.v.p.*) 5 da. *d.* 2 Sept. 1850.

Under-sec. of state for home affairs Feb. 1806-Apr. 1807; pres. bd. of control (with a seat in the cabinet) Jan. 1822-Jan. 1828; PC 17 Jan. 1822; sec. at war Nov. 1830-Apr. 1831; chan. of duchy of Lancaster Dec. 1834-Apr. 1835; eccles. commr. 1835.

Recorder, Oswestry 1798-1835; bencher, L. Inn 1835.

Vol. London and Westminster light horse 1798-9, 1801-3; maj. Ruabon vols. 1798, lt.-col. commdt. 1803; lt.-col. commdt. Mont. vol. legion 1803-8; col. E. Denb. militia 1808; commdt. Mont. yeoman cav. 1808-28, 1831-44.

Following his defeat in the 1817 Speakership election, Williams Wynn, 'never strictly a Whig or a Conservative', but a committed advocate of humane reforms, had assumed the leadership in the Commons of the oligarchic third party of his uncle Lord Grenville.[2] A potential cabinet minister, he aspired to the political achievements of the Grenvilles, his paternal grandfather Sir Watkin Williams Wynn, 3rd bt.[†], who led the Tory opposition to the government of Sir Robert Walpole, and his great-great-grandfather Speaker William Williams. His expertise on procedural matters was already widely acknowledged, but his interventions on precedents often pre-empted the Speaker's and were shouted down; for although he was a frequent and fluent debater, his enunciation and high-pitched voice were ridiculed, and it was said of him that he 'may squeak, but never can speak so as to command attention or make effect'.[3] A parliamentary commentator described him in the early 1830s as

> of middle size, rather, if anything, inclined to corpulency. He has a round face, is of dark complexion and slightly pitted with the smallpox ... He often takes the common sense view of questions, not immediately bearing on party objects: but at other times he is quite unintelligible.[4]

His return in 1820 for Montgomeryshire, which he had represented since 1799 on the Wynnstay interest of his elder brother Sir Watkin, was unopposed, and he belatedly negotiated support at Wenlock for their kinsman by marriage Paul Beilby Lawley (Thompson)*.[5] On constituency matters, the brothers acted with Members controlled by Sir Watkin's father-in-law, the 1st earl of Powis, a Tory group headed by Powis's eldest son Viscount Clive*. Williams Wynn endeavoured to attend assizes and yeomanry exercises, patronized the hunt, and sought inclusion on locally important parliamentary select committees on asylums, gaols, militia expenses, the poor and turnpikes, on which his constituents initiated legislation, 1820-32.[6] He dined in the best circles and placed great store on displaying his Welshness if he thought it would bring him votes, for by 1820 he commanded no more than six Members. Their support for Lord Liverpool's Tory administration on the suspension of habeas corpus in 1817 had signalled the end of the Grenvillite coalition with the Foxite Whigs who had sustained them in office, 1806-7. Grenville's nephew, the 2nd marquess of Buckingham, their party's leader in the Lords, advocated open collaboration with the ministerial Tories; but Williams Wynn set greater store by political consistency and, unlike Buckingham, he (with their cousin Lord Ebrington*) had voted with the opposition Whigs in 1819 for Brougham's appointment to the secret committee on the Bank of England and against the grant to the duke of York.[7]

Unsure about the stance and tactics their party should adopt during pre-session negotiations, he stayed at Llangedwyn to entertain his friend Robert Southey* and corresponded with Joseph Phillimore*, Buckingham and their uncles, Grenville and Thomas Grenville[†]. To Phillimore, 25 Mar. 1820, he observed that 'opposition have gained on the whole six, but there may be many among the new Members some whose names and probable votes I do not know. I am very sorry for Lambton's triumph and also for Morpeth's defeat'.[8] He arrived in London, 2 May, resumed his place on the cross bench next day, but left early to avoid voting on the review of civil list expenditure 'which I really thought government had no ground whatever for resisting'. He intended abstaining on the opposition motion to have admiralty and crown droits treated as civil list revenue but, bowing to family pressure, he justified Lady Grenville's pension and announced that he would divide with administration, 5 May.[9] He accepted the Lords' amendments to the civil list, despite a clerical error, 30 May. He divided with opposition on the appointment of an additional Scottish baron of exchequer, 15 May, and on revenue collection, 4 July 1820.

Expounding on precedents and procedures enabled 'Squeaker' Williams Wynn, who chaired the select committee on privileges, 1820-5, to demonstrate his knowledge and avoid taking sides in debate. He declared against proceeding with Alderman Wood's motion on the case of George Edwards, implicated in the Cato Street conspiracy, 9 May, but wished he had 'said many things which I had intended and which escaped me'.[10] He thought the Aldborough election petition merited consideration and that extra time should be allowed for the receipt of recognizances from Drogheda, 25 May, and objected to discussing the Boston petition on the floor of the House instead of in committee, 26 May. He reported that day on the case of Robert Christie Burton[†], freed without authority from the Fleet prison, and welcomed the withdrawal of the petition against him, 31 May 1820. On his advice, the Boroughbridge election committee ruled that the franchise there was confined to resident 'boroughmen' [burgesses], 7 June.[11] Supporting its chairman Phillimore, he cited precedents justifying the Grantham election committee's decisions to summon Sir William Manners[†], 5 July, and request his committal to Newgate for non-attendance, 10 July, and endorsed calls for the release of Manners's servant, 12 July. He opposed clemency for the convicted boroughmonger Sir Manasseh Masseh Lopes*, 11 July 1820, and was a majority teller that day for Phillimore's motion for making compensation payments for loss of working time at elections illegal.

The 1817 select committee on the administration of justice in Wales had been Grenvillite in conception, and following its chairman George Ponsonby's death Williams Wynn had compiled and submitted their evidence. He welcomed and was appointed to the committees conceded to John Frederick Campbell (afterwards 2nd earl of Cawdor) in 1820 and 1821, but warned that measures barring judges from sitting in Parliament and practising as barristers, and for abolishing the Welsh courts of great sessions, 'could not all at once be effected, or effected with immediate advantage', 1 June 1820. Responding on 22 Mar. 1822 to a question from Sir Robert Williams, the erstwhile Grenvillite and patron of Beaumaris, whose assize town status was at risk, he explained that although he wanted the Welsh courts assimilated and their judicature abolished, he had no plans to legislate. He asked Cawdor's Member John Hensleigh Allen to withdraw resolutions to this effect, 23 May, and raised no objection to the rival remedial measure brought in with government's acquiescence by John Jones, whom he had refused to recommend for a puisne judgeship on the Chester circuit, and supported it until it became law, 24 June 1824.[12]

He had anticipated the financial and constitutional problems which bedevilled the Queen Caroline affair, on which 'all parties are got into an embarrassment'.[13] Realizing that 'both parties' considered Commons support vital, he wrote proudly to his wife, 9 June 1820, after his plea that the House should be deferred to was cheered: 'I really begin to be an important person and am appealed to on both sides on the present negotiation'.[14] Discussing the case's impact on party politics and negotiations to strengthen the ministry in which they expected to be involved, he observed to Grenville, 15 June:

> It is certainly true that the dearth of talent which has prevailed in the ... Commons for several years past and the weakness of the conduct of those who ought to have guided it have released it from all control and that there is no longer any means of ascertaining how the majority ... may vote upon any given question. I do not ... think it improbable that Lord Lansdowne might be willing to cooperate for this purpose with Lord Buckingham and the duke of Wellington, since he must be aware that the old opposition is incapable of making up an administration, particularly in the ... Commons, which could command any degree of confidence or support.[15]

When James Stuart Wortley and William Wilberforce sought his support for an address to the queen, 20 June, he refused to sanction anything stronger than a resolution, deeming it 'a step too degrading for us to take, much as [I] wish this abominable investigation at an end'. He did 'not at all like' that drafted by Wilberforce, 22 June, 'though perhaps one must at least swallow it' as 'an address in the form of a resolution', favourable to the queen 'in effect, though not in words'.[16] As the queen's reply left no alternative to proceeding 'through all the evils of this disgusting and protracted inquiry', he spoke against adjournment, 26 June, but contradicted Grenville and Phillimore by letting it be known that he doubted whether the Lords had the power to proceed with the investigation before the Commons, as there was no precedent for instigating a bill of pains and penalties in the Upper House.[17] Despite his preference for impeachment, he affirmed in debate, 6 July, that 'the public, not the king, was the suitor' and expressed 'full confidence' in the Lords' proceedings. As usual, when his views differed from those of his colleagues, he confined his observations to procedural points, 12 July. When Buckingham and Lord Grenville resolved to offer the king and ministers 'consistent parliamentary support', he informed Thomas Grenville[†], 27 Aug., that he could not approve a bill, which, 'without any clause for divorce', was 'a mere measure of degradation and punishment', and being first considered by the Lords, 'seems to me subversive of every principle of our political system'.[18] However, in October, after studying it, he informed Buckingham, their uncles and Phillimore that he would support it despite his doubts.[19] He warned:

> You offer as a *bribe* to reconcile me to this course that through a bill of pains and penalties the Commons exercise those judicial functions which the general practice of the constitution vests exclusively in the Peers. Now this really is among my strongest objections, for under existing circumstances I feel even more dread of our encroaching upon functions and privileges which do not belong to us, than of our losing those which do. The judicial character is that of all others which from our number and from the limitation of our powers we can exercise with least advantage, and which therefore when not absolutely forced upon us, we ought to avoid, and it is on this account, among others, that I *dread*, as a Member of the ... Commons, seeing myself obliged to act as a final judge instead of sending up a case for the decision of a tribunal with higher powers and less biased by popular clamour.[20]

In fact, he expected it to fail, sparing him 'the necessity of declaring my difference from my uncles and most of my political connection', and he was preparing for the 'prorogation and censure motions' he was sure would follow.[21] His relief at its withdrawal, 10 Nov., was tempered by misgivings over the likely 'popular commotion' and a summons to Stowe, where Buckingham hoped for an invitation to join the government. Williams Wynn, trusting to 'the usual and never failing effect of office in making them vehement anti-radicals', would have preferred an arrangement with the Whigs.[22] He also thought ministers would gain more 'at this juncture' by replacing the president of the India board Canning with Robert Peel and the chancellor Nicholas Vansittart with Charles Grant. He informed Grenville, 12 Nov:

> I really do not see what prospect a junction with the present ministers or any large proportion of them could afford us but degradation to our own character, distrust, and desertion. Much as I object to the conduct of the opposite party, I feel at least a greater confidence in their sincerity and integrity, though I am aware that in all probability there is such a difference of opinion with respect to the internal policy of this country as must raise an insurmountable barrier between us. Altogether, I am best satisfied with the hope that it is most probable that no such proposition will be made to us. If the Whigs come into undivided possession of power they must bring in so large a proportion of radicals that I fear nothing could check the progress of revolution, and if the present ministers continue, their weakness and disunion will still combine to make the same result more certain and probably less distant.[23]

The clamour for Grenville persisted, but he turned down the king's invitation to form a ministry, as Williams Wynn had anticipated.[24] He genuinely regretted the 'injudicious' omission of the queen's name from the liturgy, but was 'averse to the ... Commons expressing any opinion upon [it] ... or the grant of a palace to the queen', and informed Grenville, 26 Dec. 1820, that he would 'support ministers against every proposition' except ending the £50,000 annuity which formed part of her marriage settlement.[25] Indeed, his endeavours to further his brother Henry's diplomatic career, his few known votes despite regular attendance, his active membership of committees and frequent interventions in debate when Parliament reassembled, have been interpreted as indications that he no longer actively sought realignment with the Whigs.[26] William Fremantle* and his patron Buckingham complained repeatedly that Williams Wynn followed 'his own whim', taking Phillimore with him, 'at all times on the alert to catch an opportunity of attacking the government', yet he consulted Buckingham and Lord Grenville throughout and voted against the opposition censure motion, 6 Feb. 1821. Even Buckingham acknowledged that his speech against restoring the queen's name to the liturgy, 13 Feb., was 'a very good one', although 'you stated stronger than I should have done the misdeeds of ministers'.[27] He opposed attempts by the queen's partisans to have the Nottingham petition for the impeachment of ministers received, 20 Feb., and proceedings at the Cheshire and Dublin meetings investigated, 20, 22 Feb. 1821.[28]

On the Grampound disfranchisement bill, 12 Feb. 1821, he reaffirmed the Grenvillites' opposition to sweeping parliamentary reform and suggested transferring the seats to Yorkshire, divided so that the West Riding returned two and the North and East Ridings one Member each, instead of two to Leeds. He failed to secure alterations in the Lords' amendments, 30 May, but obtained leave for a bill to divide the Yorkshire constituency, 3 July 1821. (It was considered, 2, 3 Apr., 2 May and killed by adjournment, 7 June 1822.) He voted against reform, 9 May 1821, 20 Feb., 2, June 1823, 26 Feb. 1824. He failed to stall an opposition inquiry motion into the Holy Alliance's treatment of Naples, 21 Feb., but he carried new standing orders governing the business of the House, 22 Feb., 14 Mar. 1821. He judged several petitions inadmissible, including those against legal judgements in the cases of Thomas Davison, 23 Feb., 7 Mar., and Nathan Broadhurst, 7 Mar., and for naval half-pay, 2 July. Despite the Speaker's reservations, he had a petition from Lower Canada rejected because it was in French, 16 Mar. He helped to delay and destroy the contentious Stoke

Newington select vestry bill on procedural points, 16 Feb., 21 Mar., 6 Apr. Preferring withdrawal to defeat, 19 Feb., he raised several points of order before voting to consider Catholic relief, 28 Feb. Liaising with William Plunket* and Buckingham, he worked with Lord Londonderry* and Thomas Spring Rice* on the measure, which they failed to amend to include provision for Catholic clergy and oath-taking, 2, 27, 29 Mar., 2 Apr. They co-operated again on the case of the absentee Irish chief baron O'Grady and reform of the Irish judicial system, 5 Mar., 2, 6 Apr., 9 May, 22 June, 3 July 1821, and resolved to instigate future Catholic legislation in the Lords.[29]

He 'showed by the proceeding of the House on the Westminster case in 1745' that the use of military force at the Carlisle election had been irregular, 15 Mar., and testified to the impartiality of the committee which found it 'impossible not to disapprove' of the use of regular troops there despite the inadequate civil force, 3 Apr. 1821.[30] He explained that the privileges committee was not empowered to consider Lyme Regis's petition for restoration of its ancient electoral rights, 12 Apr. On 11 May, after failing to secure his committal, he demanded a harsh sentence for Robert Thomas Weaver, the printer of *John Bull* found guilty of libelling Henry Grey Bennet by misreporting parliamentary debates.[31] On 30 May he deemed Stuart Wortley's motion to indemnify Christie Burton's creditors superfluous, and was equally dismissive of private prosecutions brought against the Constitutional Association. To Williams Wynn, who chaired the 1821 select committee, 'nothing short of absolute necessity, the safety of the state and the preservation of society could justify' capital punishment for forgery, 23 May, 4 June. On slavery, he remained abolitionist in principle but dreaded precipitate action and wanted the slave removal bill postponed pending the receipt of further evidence, 31 May, 1 June. He voted in his cousin Lord Nugent's minority for inquiry into the administration of justice in Tobago, 6 June, and backed William Courtenay's abortive call that day for an address to the king on behalf of uncompensated American loyalists. He divided with government against omitting arrears from the duke of Clarence's grant, 18 June 1821. During the recess he promoted the candidature of Richard Heber* for Oxford University, where Lord Grenville was vice-chancellor.

Acting through the duke of Wellington and Fremantle, on 10 June 1821 Liverpool had authorized a formal approach to the Grenvilles and suggested offering Williams Wynn, who had little knowledge of Asia, the presidency of the India board with a seat in the cabinet.[32] Buckingham made his appointment a *sine qua non* of acceptance, but refused to include the Lansdowne Whigs in the arrangement as Williams Wynn had wished, and complained of 'the difficulties which I have to encounter in managing the *half-Whig* principles of Charles, encouraged as they are by the very different but *chilling* feelings of my uncles':

> Everything that is told him passes immediately through the sieve of every possible uncle and aunt, and not only gets all over London, but is submitted to the question of their individual imprimatur, the consequence of which is that I am thwarted in all my views.[33]

Williams Wynn saw little prospect of success without ousting Lord Harrowby as president of the council, removing Vansittart and securing 'the assistance of Canning or Peel, if not both', and predicted correctly, 12 June, that the reshuffle would be delayed 'till after the session, then till after the coronation, then till the return [of the king] from Ireland'. Buckingham quipped to Fremantle that 'Charles the sulky is now changed into Charles the impatient ... *he wants to make his arrangement and get out of town*'.[34] When negotiations resumed, 21 Nov., Buckingham accepted a proffered dukedom, and after Londonderry and the new pro-Catholic Irish viceroy Lord Wellesley, whom he met, 5, 8 Dec., had convinced him that the king would not attempt to bring in the Whigs, Williams Wynn agreed, despite his own and his uncles' dismay at the continued anti-Catholic majority in the cabinet, to take the presidency of the India board. Reports that he and Buckingham would be sent to Ireland proved unfounded, and although he was briefly considered for the secretaryship at war, he was not offered it.[35] Before formally accepting office, he took the unprecedented step of writing to Liverpool from Dropmore, 11 Dec. 1821, expressing approval of Plunket's appointment as Irish attorney-general and Wellesley's as lord lieutenant, concern at that of the anti-Catholic Henry Goulburn* as Irish secretary, and claiming 'perfect liberty' to speak and act as he saw fit for the Catholic cause, whose success, he wrote, was his 'principal inducement to accept of office'. Liverpool, already briefed by Londonderry, acquiesced.[36] Henry Williams Wynn was promised the Swiss embassy with £4,000 a year, and his friend Peter Elmsley preferment in the church. Phillimore and Fremantle remained unplaced, and Lord Northland was not offered the British peerage Grenville had promised him until 1825.[37] The elder Grenvilles declined to approve the arrangement and distanced themselves from the 'dispersal' of their party.[38] Lord Eldon, Harrowby, Huskisson and their followers thought 'the Squeaker' had risen 'much beyond his pretensions' and that government had gained nothing.[39] The Whig Lord Althorp* feared that Williams Wynn placed too much store by Plunket's and Wellesley's appointments and warned:

> In my opinion the step you have taken will not add one title to the probability of the Catholic concessions being carried; and ... the system of compromise and balance with regard to this most important subject to which you have lent yourself, is of the most mischievous and unconstitutional character.[40]

Southey, who understood Williams Wynn's disappointment at failing to get Ireland or the home office, observed that 'the voluminous documents with which you must become acquainted will not be so appalling or irksome to you as they would be to most persons'.[41] Williams Wynn broke his journey to Wales for the Christmas recess to discuss Irish affairs with Wellesley at Dropmore, and he was quick to seek patronage and press Phillimore's claims to become a judge. However, he found Liverpool 'cool', and Phillimore, like Fremantle, had to settle for a place on the India board, adding to Grenville's disappointment.[42] Williams Wynn's voice, his brother's posting and the strong Grenvillite presence on his board attracted lampoons and hostile comment, and testing motions were expected when Parliament reassembled.[43]

Grenville hinted, 5 Feb. 1822, that Williams Wynn should resign over the nature and paucity of the government's relief package to alleviate agricultural distress, but he did not do so, and he divided with his colleagues against Althorp's critical resolutions, 21 Feb.[44] At his re-election in Montgomery, 18 Feb., he had claimed that retrenchment and recent currency reforms had enabled him to support government without changing his opinions and that it was idle to think that precipitate tax reductions were possible or parliamentary reform 'by principle and application' necessary.[45] Though clearly embarrassed by Calcraft's motion for a reduction in the salt tax, which the Grenvillites had long advocated, he decided to take consolation from Vansittart's intimation that something might be possible the following year and voted against reduction, 28 Feb., and repeal, 23 June.[46] His criticism of John Maberly's resolutions for massive tax cuts, 4 Mar., caused a disappointed North Wales landowner to comment: 'Our new cabinet minister Charles Williams Wynn seems quite as ignorant as any of them'.[47] He assisted with the Superannuation Act amendment bill, 11 Mar., 25 July. Pre-empting criticism of nepotism and inconsistency preoccupied Williams Wynn in the Commons. He had to justify his vote against abolishing one of the joint-postmas-

terships, 13 Mar., after supporting similar measures in 1812 and 1813.[48] Not content with Canning's 'expert defence of the board and demolition of Creevey', who couched his attack on the Grenvillites and the cost to the exchequer of their party's adhesion to government, by seeking inquiry into the duties of the India board, 'a peg on which to hang his remarks against me',[49] Williams Wynn repeated the 'wretched personal' defence he had delivered in Montgomery, 14 Mar.[50] He interpreted Lord John Russell's reform proposals, 25 Apr., as a fresh attack on the Grenvillites, and was drawn to disclose that he favoured repeal of the salt tax, supported Catholic relief and would always oppose general motions for reform. However, he also stressed his previous differences with opposition over reform and the Six Acts. Countering charges of bringing his friends to the India board, he expressed regret at William Sturges Bourne's* removal. Grenville was glad that 'an opportunity has been afforded you ... to vindicate your character and conduct and that you have done so in manner satisfactory to your own feelings'.[51] Discouraged by lack of support from Liverpool and cabinet colleagues, he faced further difficult debates and divisions on the aliens bill, which he had previously opposed, and from which he now absented himself at ministers' behest. He spoke as planned against an opposition motion for reductions in diplomatic expenditure that concentrated on Henry's appointment, 15 May. He supported Grey Bennet's attempt to legislate to amend the manslaughter laws, 17 Apr., and, having failed to secure the withdrawal of Mackintosh's motion for criminal law reform, which he advocated, he annoyed Buckingham but pleased Grenville by apparently voting for it, 4 July.[52] Writing to Liverpool when Buckingham threatened a breach with government in June 1822, he sought confirmation that he had been free to do so.[53]

He conferred and corresponded regularly with Grant, Grenville, Sir John Newport*, Sir Henry Parnell*, Phillimore, Plunket, Tierney, Wellesley and Buckingham (with whom relations were now strained) on the best strategy to adopt to secure Catholic relief, and despite his regrets at its introduction 'without consultation', he spoke for Canning's bill to emancipate Catholic peers, 10 May 1822, and praised Phillimore's speech.[54] He spoke for the Irish constables bill, 21 June, defended the grant to the Cork Institution, 17 July, and presented Mitford's petition on the O'Grady case, 23 July. He had failed to prevent the production of colonial accounts, 6 Mar., and was annoyed to see how debts had accumulated at the India office under Lord Bathurst and Canning, whose nomination to succeed Lord Hastings as governor-general he bemoaned because of the loss to domestic politics.[55] When Liverpool East India merchants petitioned for the removal of restrictions on trade with China, 31 May, he said nothing could be done until the Company's charter was renewed. His bill to consolidate the East India Trade Acts was repeatedly deferred and timed out that session.[56] He was hard pressed to justify East India Company policy and the deployment of their revenues, 1 July, and suggested delaying the sugar bill until the board of trade had reported and commodity quality could be taken into account, 25 July. When the select committee on the Calcutta bankers' petition (of which he was a member) reported, 29 July, he endorsed Canning's arguments for a declaratory Act and agreed to refer the matter to the attorney and solicitor-general and East India Company counsel. He stalled Hume's attempt to secure information on prisoners taken after the Persian Gulf expedition, 30 July 1822.

Assisting government colleagues, he argued against treating interference with Members' mail as a breach of privilege, 25 Feb., 15 Mar., opposed an appeal to the royal prerogative to secure Henry Hunt's* early release from Ilchester gaol, 4 Mar., the receipt of pro-Hunt petitions from Leeds, 14 Mar., and Newcastle, 22 Mar., and remission of his sentence, 24 Apr. 1822. He upheld the crown's sole right to grant military rewards and distinctions, 22 Mar., and denied that there was any understanding that government would take up the Masseh Lopes case, 24 Apr. He advocated adjournment to hear Abercromby's testimony before summoning the *Courier*'s printers for breach of privilege, but was overruled, 9, 12 July, and when the printers were examined, 17 July, he accepted that the case against them was proven. The rapid growth in petitioning alarmed him, and he commented on Maidenhead's petition for licensing individual beer sellers instead of their premises, 17 Apr., objected to receiving those for remission of the Bowditches' sentences, as an underhand attack on Justice Best, 24 May, and spoke against receiving the radical Greenhoe petition linking distress and parliamentary reform, 'a menace and an insult to the House', 3 June. Even so he insisted that he would never recommend rejecting a petition merely because of particular expressions or words. He spoke against receiving the 4,000-signature petition in favour of the Middlesex county court bill, which was backed by Huskisson and accepted, 19 June, and commented on those from Wood, 26 June, William Murray Borthwick, 28 June, and against packing juries, 22 July. He was in favour of authorizing a complete printed edition of 'the ancient histories of this realm, without any splendour', 24 July. Londonderry's suicide in August 1822 deprived

Williams Wynn of his 'best support in cabinet' at a time when plotting to oust the Grenvillites was rife.[57] John Croker*, having heard from Huskisson, who hoped to profit by Williams Wynn's removal, informed Peel, 25 Aug.:

Wynn is a man of good sense and fair character; but he is extremely unpopular and his parliamentary oratory is almost ludicrous from his voice and manner. He will do very well for a short speech, but, even when at the head of a floating party the House never bore him for a long one such as a minister must occasionally make on what poor Londonderry used to call his *field days* ... I cannot better explain to you the estimation in which his weight and talents as a minister in the House ... are held than by this fact, that, except in Huskisson's hint, I have never heard his name mentioned as one to whom the future leader was to look for support.[58]

Williams Wynn consulted Buckingham, Frederick Robinson* and Wellington, and readily accepted the need to have Canning as leader of the Commons. He was considered for the Indian governorship, a lucrative post which, with a family of seven and annual income, out of office, of no more than £1,500, Buckingham and Fremantle thought he should accept '*if it were offered him*'.[59] Aware that Canning's real intention was to remove him to make way for Huskisson, he prevaricated; but it mattered little, for the East India Company 'would not *hear*' of his appointment.[60] Ministers considered sending out Charles Manners Sutton and backing Williams Wynn's nomination for the Speakership in return for continued Grenvillite support, and Canning discussed this with Grenville, 22 Sept. When it was put to Williams Wynn, 23 Sept., Grenville reminded him that it arose from pressure to promote Huskisson and left him free to decide.[61] Buckingham hoped for cabinet office through Williams Wynn's removal and advised him to go, but changed his mind on learning that his departure would leave them unrepresented in the cabinet.[62] By 4 Oct., he had decided to refuse, conscious that his acceptance would deprive Fremantle and Phillimore of their places and alienate him from many of his former supporters.[63] Manners Sutton's conduct during the Cambridge University by-election, 'the most stupid and unpardonable mess at Cambridge made by anyone', brought fresh reports of the Speakership or the chancellorship of the duchy of Lancaster being offered to Williams Wynn, who, at Grenville's request, had canvassed on behalf of Lord Bristol's son Lord Hervey*.[64] The 3rd marquess of Hertford quipped: 'Had Wynn unluckily had still a penchant for the Chair, he would have let Sutton take the hundreds, but it seems as if he just permitted him to bestir himself and then tendered *the* *paper* [his resignation]'.[65] George Dawson* informed his brother-in-law Peel:

> It is said ... that both ... Liverpool and ... Canning were most anxious to induce Wynn to vacate his seat in the cabinet for the Speaker's chair, but that he steadily refused giving up the certain place, for the uncertain honour. Perhaps he was right, but the Speaker thinks that his prospects should not have been allowed to depend upon Wynn's choice.[66]

Similar rumours circulated when Vansittart was removed from the exchequer in January 1823, but Williams Wynn kept his cabinet post despite his reputed unpopularity.[67] He and his family were summoned to Dropmore that month to help Grenville entertain Liverpool and his wife, but Grenville suffered a stroke and the visit was postponed.[68]

Despite his uncles' reassurances, he disapproved of the decision to send Henry to Stuttgart instead of Stockholm, as originally proposed, and remained convinced that Canning sought his removal.[69] He anticipated a stormy session on Irish business, but was broadly satisfied with the king's speech and taxation policy.[70] On the O'Grady case, which saw the Grenvillites in the minority against the 'whitewashing', he supported Spring Rice's motion to have the latest papers printed, 12 Feb. 1823, and thought it would be better dealt with by a private Member than by government. When he brought up the select committee report on fees charged in Irish law courts, 16 May, Abercromby asserted that it was indeed a government matter, and Canning had to come to his defence. He wanted O'Grady's case referred back to the committee, 13, 17, 27 June, and for him to testify at the bar of the House, but he had to proceed with the report without him, 2, 4, 9 July. He welcomed O'Grady's resignation as chief baron, 4 Oct.[71] After much deliberation and consultation he voted against producing information on, 24 Mar., and inquiry into the prosecution of the Dublin Orange rioters, 22 Apr. He divided for the Irish churches grant, 11 Apr., and, according to Buckingham, cut a 'wretched figure' when he spoke against repealing the Foreign Enlistment Act, 16 Apr.[72] The following day, during a rowdy debate on Catholic claims, for which he had tried to ensure that Plunket had strong support, he refused to second Henry Bankes's motion to have Canning and Brougham taken into custody for their derogatory comments on the Lords, whereupon Tierney accused him of 'inconsistency'. His 'indiscreet' defence, 'that his great object in coming into office had been to serve the interests of the Catholic body', coupled with the impression he gave that all Irish governments before

Wellesley's had been partial, was interpreted as a slur on Peel's conduct as Irish secretary and generated a public exchange of letters between them. Assisted by Charles Grant, he made a clarificatory declaration, which might have provoked further disagreement had not the Speaker intervened, 22 Apr.[73] Liverpool warned Wellington before the Irish Insurrection Act was considered, 12 May 1823, that it was

> the policy of opposition to endeavour to provoke Wynn to state again his differences with the government on questions relating to Ireland. I am quite of opinion that he ought not to suffer himself to be goaded by our enemies and his own, and if he falls into the trap he will only provoke a reply from Peel which must have the very worst effects. I am led, however, particularly to notice this at the present moment, as I heard he had expressed some intention of reading the letter he addressed to me upon the occasion of his taking office, and I am persuaded that if he does this it will lead to a dissolution of the government ... It is a step to which he ought not to resort, but in the last extremity, and certainly not because he is attacked by the opposition ... give him a *hint* as to his proceeding. He might take it better from you than from me.[74]

Having remained silent hitherto, he was drawn by Sir Abraham Bradley King's testimony on the Dublin prosecutions to disagree with his colleagues, who on the advice of Canning, Goulburn and Peel had excluded him from their deliberations, and he urged Bradley King to disclose information, notwithstanding his oath as an Orangeman, 23 May, certain that the House was empowered to compel him to do so though he now doubted its expediency, 26 May. Annoyed at the 'unmerited and uncalled for reserve and disinclination manifested toward Charles Wynn and myself by Mr. Canning since his return to office', Buckingham asked Wellington to discuss Williams Wynn's treatment with Liverpool, 28 May.[75] Wellington replied that Williams Wynn's conduct in cabinet was satisfactory.[76] He spoke against amending the Irish tithes composition bill, 30 May, and pressed for ample compensation payments, 16 June. He intervened when Colonel Allen's petition complaining of the loss of his commission was presented, 6 Mar., testified to the 'excellent conduct and discipline' of the Montgomeryshire yeomanry when the grant was voted, 7 Mar., challenged Hume's assertion that the mutiny bill did not authorize the king to dismiss an officer and vainly tried to halt the ensuing spat between Colonel Davies and Lord Palmerston, 14 Mar. 1823. Claiming that government had the matter in hand, he had a private Member's bill to repeal the Insolvent Debtors Act withdrawn, 18 Mar. He opposed the receipt on the 24th of the Arundel election petition and defended Sir Thomas Maitland's[†] conduct as governor of the Ionian Islands. Stating that a libel had been proved, he clashed with Hume over Mary Ann Carlile's petition for release from Dorchester gaol, 26 Mar. 1823.

His correspondence with Buckingham, whom he defended against accusations of unfair prosecution under the game laws, 23 Apr. 1823, was chiefly devoted to the likely conflict between France and Spain, and although Buckingham did not share Grenville's admiration for Canning's foreign policy, they agreed to adhere to the government line.[77] Opposition pressure forced Williams Wynn to seek adjournment of the debate on the negotiations with Spain, 29 Apr., and his understanding of the monarchical principle was savagely criticized by Hobhouse before they carried the division, 30 Apr. Drawn late into the debate on Whitbread's motion for inquiry into the duties on East and West Indian sugars, 22 May, he refused to confirm or deny reports that ministers would concede one and maintained that Vansittart had wished to restrict inquiry to the 15s. additional duty on clayed sugars. He introduced the Indian mutiny bill, 22 May, and it was enacted, 18 July. He had been denied leave to introduce the East India half-pay bill (announced, 12 June) on a point of order, 27 June, and though the Commons passed it, 11 July, he was hard pressed to refute Courtenay and Bright's criticisms, 3 July.[78] He defended Lord Hastings's handling of the James Silk Buckingham[†] case in the Commons, 10 July; but writing on 12 Aug. to Wellington, whom he consulted regularly and embarrassed by pursuing Wellesley's claim to an East India Company grant, he blamed Hastings for

> the very injudicious encouragement of the licence of the press [and] the hazard to which he has brought the security and tranquillity of India in order to gratify a foolish vanity and acquire an ephemeral popularity among the newspaper writers, but there is also a more serious charge which may possibly affect even his personal character, which arises out of the loans from the House of Palmer and Company to the nizam, illegally sanctioned by him. These have excited such general attention and suspicion that I should not be at all surprised if they became the subject of parliamentary investigation.[79]

He abhorred Hindu immolation and infanticide and had no qualms about releasing copies of relevant departmental correspondence, but he opposed legislative interference, preferring to delegate the matter to local authorities lest force should prove ineffective, 18 June 1823, 6 June 1825.[80] He voted against inquiry into the currency, 12 June, and to receive the report on the usury laws repeal bill, 27 June 1823, and, citing the

works of Bentham and Adam Smith, supported similar measures, 27 Feb., 8 Apr. 1824, 8, 17 Feb. 1825, claiming on the last occasion, and in their absence, that it had the approval of the chancellor and the president of the board of trade. He projected the 1826 bill as a boon to the landed interest, 15 Feb., and on 15 Mar. carried an amendment to it, restricting inquiry into bankruptcy expenses to cases under the 1824 Act. Deeming it a matter for the courts, he had petitions charging James Crosbie* with bribery to secure his son-in-law a place in the excise thrown out, 26 June, 1 July 1823. Like 'all Grenvilles', his absence from the divisions on the Crosbie case, 1 July, and the Irish reciprocities bill, 4 July, was 'much commented upon and considered as a retaliation for the desertion of Plunket in the House of Commons'.[81] He spoke against permitting bills to be engrossed in 'Italian' [Latin] instead of old script, 3 July. He was ready to accept the Lords' amendments to the Scottish juries bill, 18 July. He and his wife attended Liverpool's end of session dinner at Carlton House, and when ministerial changes were contemplated in August, he encouraged Buckingham to press his claim for 'official responsibility', hoping it would strengthen the 'lukewarm and hollow' Catholic party in the cabinet and end his own isolation.[82] He cautioned: 'Canning knows not where to look for support but is afraid that by joining himself with us, who seem his natural allies, he would increase the indisposition of the king and the duke of York, which he would make any sacrifice to deprecate'. He thought Buckingham would need the support of Wellington, who looked only to his fellow Protestants Peel and Goulburn, and that Robinson, with whom he had discussed possible changes, 'confines himself to his own business';[83] but Buckingham's overtures to Wellington in September 1823 conflicted with plans to bring in Huskisson and threatened to increase Williams Wynn's isolation.[84] He thus remained in place, unable to secure patronage at Buckingham's request, dealt with by Peel 'only as much as necessary to avoid any public rupture', ever conscious of the loss of Londonderry and his own exclusion from the inner cabinet of Bathurst, Canning and Wellington, who regularly shadowed his brief.[85]

Before Parliament reassembled, Williams Wynn discussed draft legislation to increase the number of Catholic office-holders with Plunket and Buckingham and was delegated by the cabinet to enlist Plunket's assistance to ensure that Newport's contentious Catholic burials bill failed.[86] Assisted by Canning, he had a petition sponsored by opposition complaining of George Chetwynd's* conduct as chairman of Staffordshire quarter sessions withdrawn as a matter for king's bench, 27 Feb., and refuted Abercromby's allegations of a breach of privilege by Eldon, 1 Mar. 1824. He voted against a radical motion to end military flogging, 5 Mar. Drawn that day into the discussion on the depressed silk trade by Haldimand's criticism of the India board and the East India Company, and on the 22nd by the 7,000-signature Bethnal Green petition, he laid the blame on the Company's charter, which could not yet be altered. Opposition also goaded him over the Alien Act renewal bill, which he privately considered 'useless and unnecessary', but, as agreed in cabinet and with Buckingham, he declared for it, stating that its mode of enforcement over the last eight years had 'quieted' his fears, 23 Mar.[87] He felt confident of government backing on Indian issues, but lamented their encroachment on time he wished to devote to Ireland.[88] He declined to comment on the Silk Buckingham petition and the treaty with the Netherlands, for the endorsement of which by the House he was responsible, 30 Mar., 14 Apr. He insisted that the cattle ill-treatment bill, 9 Mar., admission charges at Westminster Abbey, 9 Apr., and legislation on horse slaughter, 4 June, were not Parliament's business, and halted discussion of the liberty of the Indian press, 'incidentally introduced and when the House was unprepared', 25 May. He refused to delay his East India trade bill and claimed it would operate to the advantage of the colonies rather than the Company, 12 June, and on the 17th defended the East India possessions bill, enacted on the 24th.[89] He voiced support for Peel's unsuccessful jury laws consolidation bill, 18 June. Though aware of Court hostility towards Robert Waithman* and the City as former supporters of the queen, Williams Wynn warned Buckingham, 17 Apr., that he intended going to the lord mayor's dinner, at which a South American delegation was expected to promote their campaign for diplomatic recognition independent of Spain, 'partly because I think Canning right in going, though none of his other *confrères* go, and partly because Waithman is a Welshman'.[90] A letter attached to the king's formal protest at Canning's attendance stated: 'I have not mentioned Mr. Wynn's name, for he is quite contemptible and below my notice'.[91] Williams Wynn presented Merioneth's petition criticizing the treatment of the Methodist missionary John Smith, indicted for inciting slaves to riot in Demerara, 2 June, and planned to speak and vote accordingly, 11 June, 'but the lawyers spoke too long', and Canning's speech 'approached sufficiently to my opinions to cover my vote tolerably satisfactorily'.[92] His interventions that day helped to secure the withdrawal of petitions of complaint against the Middlesex magistrate Cockerell and the continued detention of Robert Gourlay for assaulting Brougham. He wel-

comed the decision to set up an investigative committee on the disturbed districts in Ireland preparatory to renewing the Insurrection Act, was appointed to it, 11 May, and judged it 'well selected'. Although disappointed that the renewal bill was first introduced in the Lords, he was happy to remain in London to vote for it, 14 June 1824.[93] Speculation that Liverpool would retire proved premature but brought fresh reports of plots to oust the Grenvillites, Canning's personal hostility to Williams Wynn and plans to send him to India. His own preference was for a ministry with Robinson as foreign secretary with a seat in the Lords and Canning as prime minister and chancellor, but he realized that the strength of the duke of York and the anti-Catholics would make it unworkable.[94] Sir Thomas Munro's resignation as governor of Madras gave him the difficult task of assessing the rival claims of Lords Combermere, Mountstuart and Elphinstone, Stephen Rumbold Lushington* and Sir John Malcolm* to succeed him.[95] Lord Granville, writing in May, reported that the East India Company Directors disapproved of Lushington

and Squeaker Wynn seems disposed to compromise with them and find out a person who may not be objectionable either to the Court of Directors or government. If he does so, all the patronage of this government in India will infallibly be lost, and having gained this point they will certainly attempt to nominate the next governor-general.[96]

Acting with discretion throughout,[97] he postponed his departure for a continental holiday until September, but the matter remained unresolved when he returned in October, and was further complicated by the Bengal mutiny, disagreements over Amherst and Sir Edward Paget's[†] handling of the Burmese war, and differing interpretations of the duties of Indian governors. After consulting Liverpool and Wellington, Williams Wynn set aside his preferences and agreed to fight for Lushington. He advised the king to appoint Combermere rather than Malcolm as commander-in-chief in the East Indies, Elphinstone to Bombay and Lushington to Madras. In November 1824, news of Munro's decision to stay on (until 1827) brought temporary relief, and Williams Wynn thought his own position improved by Lord Sidmouth's retirement from the cabinet.[98]

Parliament's recall brought the expected pleas for information on Amherst and the war, and Williams Wynn, whose work was now shadowed by Buckingham and Wellington, promised to comment as soon as practicable, 4 Feb. 1825.[99] On 24 Mar., after news arrived of the previous autumn's troubles in Bengal, he rejected a request for particular papers, claiming it was 'a peg on which to hang' charges against the absent Amherst, who had been forced into war by Burma. He affirmed that 'much government' had to be left to the direction of the governor, whom he praised, refused to divulge more until a full statement could be issued to replace 'those exaggerated and ... garbled accounts which had been received from private quarters', and defeated the motion by 58-5.[100] He steadfastly opposed combining the offices of governor-general and commander-in-chief.[101] He laid copies of recent treaties with native powers before the House, 21 Apr., and when Sir Charles Forbes called for dispatches allegedly received in the secret department, he had to concede that there had been delays in producing information on Bengal, 1 July. Opposition interest in the Silk Buckingham case continued. Hume carried a slightly amended motion for papers on deportations, 24 Feb., and Williams Wynn was repeatedly obliged to defend the independence of the Indian judicature, before his East India judges bill received royal assent, 5 July.[102] He agreed to produce returns of prisoners detained without trial and of half-caste jurors, 7 June 1825, but denied the existence of Hastings's 1817 council minute on the appointment of Indo-Britons and resisted endeavours to authorize the appointment of half-castes in Bombay and Madras.

Liverpool had sought his opinion on the 'explosive' state of Ireland, where he feared a union of radicals and emancipationists and considered the organization of the Catholic Association formidable, 'not from the amount of its funds ... but from its correspondence with a regular rent collector in every part'.[103] Briefed by Plunket and Thomas Frankland Lewis*, whose communications he circulated, he shared his uncles' and Plunket's preference for non-intervention, and differed from Buckingham by welcoming the promise in the king's speech to confine inquiry to facts.[104] Addressing the House, 11 Feb. 1825, he said that he thought the Irish unlawful societies bill was unlikely to pacify Ireland unless combined with emancipation and denounced the Association for the harm it had done to the Catholic cause. He added that he had always disliked Orange Associations 'not so much from a fear of the mischief which they did in themselves, as the formation of such bodies as the Catholic Association' in retaliation, which their very existence encouraged. Fremantle thought his declaration 'manly, and quite right in his situation, and he was better heard than usual'.[105] He was appointed to the select committee on Ireland, 17 Feb., and objected to hearing counsel for the Catholic Association at the bar of the House, 18 Feb. Co-operating with Canning, Huskisson and

Robinson, he intervened on a point of order when the Irish franchise bill was considered, 22 Apr., voted for Catholic relief, 1 Mar., 21 Apr., 10 May, and endorsed the franchise bill, 29 Apr.[106] Buckingham, who had been expected to introduce the Catholic clergy bill in the Lords, tried to insist on Williams Wynn's resignation over the duke of Cumberland's anti-Catholic speech, 25 Apr. Disagreeing, Grenville thought Buckingham and Canning should resolve the matter between them. Williams Wynn and Canning meanwhile agreed to do nothing which might force a dissolution, and negotiated through Spring Rice to hold back petitioning. Thus 'neglected', Buckingham refused to return Phillimore again for St. Mawes.[107] Williams Wynn cautioned against introducing a rule preventing Members from voting on questions in which they had a pecuniary interest, 10 Mar., and joined Phillimore in opposing the production of returns on clergymen holding corporate office, 17 Mar., preferring wider inquiry into the eligibility of the clergy for civil office. After errors in the Ipswich returns were disclosed, he recommended withdrawing all similar requests, 17 Mar. He voted for the Cumberland annuity bill, 30 May, 2, 6, 10 June, having first declared, 27 May, that there was no inconsistency with his hostile votes in 1815 and 1818, when there had been no children to consider. He took up the cause of the Welsh judge and recorder of Dover William Kenrick†, charged as a Surrey magistrate with felony against a poor man, John Franks, 29 May, 14, 17, 21 June, but conceded that there had been 'some haste and intemperance in Mr. Kenrick's conduct' and that the matter would have to be held over, 18 June 1825. He failed to prevent the appointment of a committee of inquiry, 17 Feb., and despite his efforts Kenrick's petition against his treatment was rejected, 20 Feb., and the charge against him remained, 21 Feb. 1826.[108]

Amid speculation that Amherst would be recalled, Williams Wynn wrote to Liverpool, 7 Aug. 1825:

> Should a vacancy arise, I am by no means blind to the strong objections which may oppose themselves to the nomination of the duke of Buckingham, but I should very much prefer not being called upon to form a decision where I have so natural and obvious a bias and would therefore, if possible, wish to leave the question wholly to the determination of Canning and yourself.[109]

Newspaper reports that Buckingham was preparing to leave ensured that the king raised the matter with Canning and Williams Wynn at their audiences in September, and afterwards Williams Wynn informed Buckingham, whom he had briefed on India throughout, despite suspicions that he was intriguing against Amherst, that he would be proposed. He denied this directly he realized that Buckingham was prepared to withdraw his support from government over the issue.[110] He and Phillimore failed to placate Buckingham, 4 Oct., and before leaving for yeomanry duty and the Montgomeryshire assizes that day Williams Wynn notified Liverpool of his 'mistake', attributed it to his having misunderstood Canning, and asked government to act without delay. Liverpool, finding 'the whole Indian question is in a very disturbed state, from a course having been followed decidedly at variance with what I understood had been settled', consulted Wellington, who advised that Amherst was not to blame for the Barrackpoor mutiny and should not be removed, 11 Oct.[111] On the 13th Liverpool asked Williams Wynn to make Buckingham accept that he would never be appointed and to resolve the Amherst problem, a task that Buckingham and his son Lord Chandos* made almost impossible.[112] Piqued, Williams Wynn informed Liverpool, 19 Oct., and again after an acrimonious meeting with Fremantle and Chandos, 1 Nov.:

> You know I never had any confidence in Lord Amherst as a public man, and the experience we have had of him in India more than ever convinces me that we require a much more able governor-general.[113]

Confirming his preference for 'a new governor-general', in a detailed report to Wellington, 27 Oct., he suggested Lord William Cavendish Bentinck* or Munro. He told his wife that he would propose Buckingham, certain that he would be rejected and, not anticipating the East India Company's continued insistence on Amherst's recall, he informed Buckingham, 3 Nov., that there was now no vacancy. Difficult secret meetings with the Court of Directors, with which Wellington assisted, followed, 16, 24 Nov.[114] Suspecting 'some intrigue against me in which Canning is endeavouring to hook in Lord Liverpool, and Charles Wynn is frightened out of his wits', Buckingham denounced Williams Wynn as 'a perfectly incapable and inefficient representative in cabinet: he can neither speak nor act without inviting attack'.[115] Hurt to see his dismissal urged as the 'only obstacle' to Buckingham's appointment and Fremantle's reassurances of his good intentions ignored, Williams Wynn again looked to the cabinet to resolve the issue, and despite his professed dread of 'exposure to the abuse of a general court' on 21 Dec. 1825, professed himself 'completely indifferent' to the outcome.[116] Cabinet's decision not to recall Amherst displeased Buckingham and the Court of Directors, and Williams Wynn's situation became even more uncomfortable when, at

Buckingham's behest, the king ordered an inquiry into this alleged conspiracy by Canning, which Williams Wynn's report of 15 Feb. 1826 duly denied.[117] Lady Williams Wynn thought the episode 'leaves my dear Charles, however, with a lesson on the danger of unreserved confidence and communication which he has bought too dearly soon to forget'.[118]

Charged with 'indifference' during the debate on the address, 3 Feb. 1826, Williams Wynn defended the principle and conduct of the Burmese war, but refused to make private correspondence available and left the defence of Amherst to others. Securing leave on 22 Feb. for his Indian juries bill (enacted on 5 May after a difficult passage, 6, 20 Mar., 7 Apr.), he pointed out that although jury service would be widened to include half-castes, Christians would always be tried by Christians. He insisted, 16 Mar., that his East India Company writers bill, which received royal assent, 26 May, was a reaction to a shortage and implied no dissatisfaction with the training offered by Haileybury College. He had already sponsored a writership competition at Westminster.[119] Knowing that the slightest reference to Amherst and Buckingham would make Chandos disclose everything, he resisted Hume's call for information on the Barrackpoor mutiny and Burmese war, 23 Feb., and again when his bill to fund an additional naval force for the East Indies (which received royal assent, 26 May) passed its first reading, 26 Apr.[120] He voted against the immediate abolition of West Indian slavery, 2 Mar., and presented an anti-slavery petition from Llangollen, 6 Mar. He defended the £10,180 cost of indexing the *Commons Journals*, 10 Mar. He supported the spring guns bill, and Goulburn's amendment restricting their use, 26 Apr. On privilege, he considered Members exempt from jury service during parliamentary sittings, 20, 21 Feb. He agreed with Russell that 'any practice tending to defeat [the] fairness and purity with which elections ought to be conducted' should be opposed, 1 Mar., but rejected his electoral bribery bill, 14 Mar., 28 Apr., and declaratory resolutions, 26 May, claiming that prosecutions brought under existing legislation were sufficient. He voted against reforming the representation of Edinburgh, 13 Apr., and on the 26th said that it was too late to bring in a bill on the rights of electors in counties corporate that Parliament. Sykes, who did so, blamed Williams Wynn for delaying his bill. An opponent of the 1825 bill, he spoke against receiving petitions on the St. Olave tithes, 25 Apr., 18 May. His objections to the strong opposition presence on the select committee on the Silk Buckingham case were heeded, 9 May, and ten ministerialists, including the Grenvillite Sir Edward Hyde East, were added, 11 May. However, delaying tactics deployed by Hume ensured that they failed to report before the dissolution.[121] Williams Wynn was returned without incident at the general election in June 1826, having negotiated a compromise of sorts with Buckingham in which their uncles would have no part.[122] He viewed the results solely according to Members' views on the Catholic question:

> I am happy to say that although in this part of the world 99 out of 100 are anti-Catholic in their inclinations, poor Sir R. Williams [who, facing defeat in Caernarvonshire, came in for Beaumaris] is the only candidate whose election has been affected by it. There were new candidates who started at Bridgnorth and at Shrewsbury on the cry of 'No Popery', but failed in both instances. We lose, however, two by the change, one at Denbigh, the other in the borough of Caernarvon ... To the crowd I would still hold confident language, but as far as I can judge of the returns I certainly expect that we shall lose sufficient to turn the majority against us, at least in the first session, on the Catholic question. I think, however, that the result of a dissolution in the autumn would have been still more unsatisfactory.[123]

He discussed this with Spring Rice before Parliament met, and corresponded with Huskisson, Peel and Wellington on controverted elections and Indian affairs, including equalization of the three Indian armies, which Williams Wynn advocated and Wellington opposed. He passed September in Spa with his wife.[124] Buckingham excluded him from the new arrangement he suggested to Canning, 13 Nov., but offered to co-operate with him provided he paid his 'debt of honour' by acknowledging his claim to the Indian governorship, 15 Nov. 1826. Williams Wynn declined, and their uncles refused to intervene.[125]

Williams Wynn congratulated Manners Sutton on his re-election as Speaker and proposed the customary adjournment, 14 Nov. 1826. His objections to readopting Russell's bribery resolutions, 22 Nov., were assumed to be government's. He made many useful procedural points and appeals to precedent when the returns for Athlone, Denbigh Boroughs, Dundalk, Galway, Leicester, Leominster, Penryn, Reading and Tregony were considered that session. Arguing that existing legislation was adequate, he successfully opposed Althorp's motion for a standing committee on election petitions, 26 Feb. 1827. Lord Howick* wrote:

> The debate ... was very interesting though it ended in a most unsatisfactory manner ... I was very much provoked at Hobhouse and a few more being so completely taken in by the resolution proposed by Wynn and preventing Ld. Milton from dividing on the original one. Wynn's as one might expect is likely to do a great deal more harm

than good as without making the corporations of small boroughs at all more honest, it will prevent money being brought into competition with places and favours from government ... merely exchang[ing] one kind of corrupt influence for another.[126]

Williams Wynn (who was included on the select committees, 15 Mar., 5 Apr.) found Althorp's inquiry motion on county polls difficult to counter, 15 Mar., and merely regretted its timing and referred to his dislike of staggered polls and making land tax returns serve as electoral registers. His arguments against treating petitions against the Arigna Iron and Coal Company, in which Sir William Congreve* was implicated, as parliamentary matters prevailed, 28 Nov., 5, 7 Dec., and he spoke effectively against Littleton's resolutions on committees on private bills, 28 Nov., and foiled an attempt by Waithman to introduce general legislation on joint-stock companies, 30 Nov. 1826. However, he failed to prevent the receipt of a petition against the Devon and Cornwall Mining Company, which had many Members on its board, 9 Apr. 1827. He divided for Catholic relief, 6 Mar., and to consider the Clarence annuity, 16 Mar., and spring guns bills, 23 Mar., to which he gave his 'most cordial support, 26 Mar. 1827.

Amherst's decision to return rekindled Buckingham's false optimism and renewed the pressure on Williams Wynn, who had successfully moved the vote of thanks to the victorious troops in India, 27 Nov. 1826, corresponded regularly with Wellington, Canning, Combermere and Malcolm, and supplied Peel with information to counter Hume's East India House motion on Barrackpoor, 13 Feb. 1827.[127] He pointed out factual errors in Hume's speech, on opposing production of Sir Edward Paget's report on the Burmese war, 22 Mar., when the motion was defeated 'most satisfactorily by a majority of four to one', but realized it was fortunate that Hume had changed his tactics.[128] Insisting that Williams Wynn 'does not speak my sentiments', Buckingham approached Wellington and Canning during the ministerial negotiations which followed Liverpool's stroke and doggedly pressed his futile claim to be governor-general, which, according to Fremantle, Williams Wynn unfairly undermined. Canning of course would have none of it and the breach with Buckingham became complete.[129] Buckingham informed Wellington, 2 Apr.:

> I owe it to myself to state distinctly that Mr. Williams Wynn, from circumstances which it is not necessary for me to detail, is no longer considered by me as my representative in the cabinet now to be formed, and I am authorized to say that no part of the support of my friends

will attach itself to him in that situation or through him to government.[130]

Wellington replied, 4 Apr.:

I may have used the term your *representative* in the cabinet as applied to Mr. Wynn. I knew that he was in the cabinet for the two reasons because he was one of your family and because he possessed the qualifications to entitle him to look to high office in this country. You have the full right to withdraw your confidence from him and to announce to the minister that you have done so, but I beg you to decline to charge myself with the delicacy of the message.[131]

Williams Wynn monitored Robinson and Lansdowne's reactions, corresponded closely with his uncles while Canning formed his ministry and probably benefited from their friendship with him.[132] He kept his place at the India board, hosted a cabinet dinner for Canning, 11 Apr., so revealing the extent of the Tory resignations, and moved the writ for his re-election to opposition cheering the next day.[133] Though not considered for the home office, to which he always aspired as a means of influencing Irish decisions, he concluded:

I am inclined to think that I am better where I am, as besides all the disadvantages of comparison with Peel, I should have to encounter that of my going beyond most of my colleagues in my impression of the urgency of the Catholic question, and besides, I conceive myself to be personally more unacceptable to the king.[134]

He had declined Canning's offer of the Indian governorship, which 'would indeed be, in my opinion, for myself and my children, "to sell for gold what gold can never buy"'.[135] His mother wrote:

We have personally every reason to be satisfied with the situation in which it all leaves Charles, who, without having been mixed up in any intrigue or cabal, stands more on his own ground, steadily adhering to the support of those measures to which he has repeatedly pledged himself.

His period in office under Canning was reputedly his happiest.[136] Nevertheless, Wellington's resignation and anti-Catholic speech dismayed him. He considered the subsequent departure from the India board of William Peel* and Lord Salisbury inevitable, 10 May 1827.[137]

Seconded by Hume, he proposed the promised vote of thanks to the troops in India, 8 May 1827, endorsed the decisions made by officers and apologized for the 'accidental' omission of the naval commander in the original address. He also now announced the deferral of his bill to consolidate election law until next session and expressed support for Althorp's election expenses regulation bill, which was enacted, 21 June.[138] He refused to condemn Penryn, where the extent of corruption was not determined, though its existence was not in doubt, criticized the witnesses examined, and secured an adjournment, 18 May. Convinced that bribery there was systematic, he backed Canning and voted with the minority against its disfranchisement, 28 May.[139] He agreed that a *prima facie* case for disfranchisement had been established for East Retford, but refused to give 'any opinion as to the place to which the franchise should be transferred', 11, 22 June.[140] He persuaded Wolrych Whitmore and Cutlar Fergusson to withdraw motions for inquiry into trade with, 15 May, and land ownership in India, 21 June, claiming that investigations were already under way, 29 June. He welcomed Peel's criminal justice bill enacted that session, and the different provisions he suggested for genuine mutes and those deliberately exercising their right to silence were widely approved, 18 May. He supported the Coventry magistracy bill, 18 June, and urged postponement that day of Hume's resolutions on private bills. He assisted government on supply, 25 May, 12 June, and presented petitions from Montgomeryshire for repeal of the Test Acts, 8 June 1827.

Following Canning's death in August 1827, when Robinson, as Lord Goderich, formed his administration, Williams Wynn was 'decidedly against remaining if the Whigs are forced out' and unnerved by the appointment of the anti-Catholic John Herries* as chancellor of the exchequer. Heeding his uncles' pleas for caution, he stayed on in London, where he consulted Althorp, Sturges Bourne, Huskisson, Frankland Lewis and Tierney, and accepted the India board with an assured pension of £3,600 a year.[141] He informed his wife:

Nothing can be more satisfactory than the footing on which I find myself with my colleagues, *reste à voir* how it may last, but at present my situation is far more comfortable than it has been.[142]

His brother Henry welcomed the new arrangement.[143] By December, ill with rheumatism and influenza, and neglected by cabinet colleagues, he realized that his department had hardly been consulted over Navarino or Lord Combermere's future as commander of the Indian army.[144] He complained to Huskisson of Wellington:

I cannot help being struck by the general tone which he has taken on this occasion, and the want of attention in writing letters as being so decidedly contrary to the course he has adopted with respect to all former communications from me.[145]

Sturges Bourne tried to keep him abreast of developments, but even so his situation deteriorated, and when Wellington became prime minister in January 1828 he was ousted.[146] He wrote:

> I must fairly say that from the way in which things have been going on ever since Canning's death I have seen such frequent reasons to expect it, that it does not prove any disappointment to me; and that I only rejoice that I have for so long been able to retain my office honourably, indeed far longer than I originally thought there was any chance of.[147]

Southey, with whom he was editing Bishop Heber's letters, had warned him in September 1827 to 'look to another plank in the State-vessel start ere long', as 'men in office' found him 'one of the most impracticable persons to deal with, taking crotchets in his head and holding to them with invincible pertinacity'.[148] Writing to Phillimore from Plymouth for clarification, Fremantle asked 'Does Wynn stick to the Whigs, and is the government quite settled?'[149] He was particularly dismayed to find Phillimore and their friends all thrown out.[150] Faced with a drop in annual income from £5,800 to £1,800, he pursued the promised pension, assisted by Goderich and Lord Grenville; but, as it had not been authorized before Goderich resigned, the decision became Wellington's, who knew that the king, although ready to grant audiences to Goderich and Williams Wynn, would only award the pension as a personal favour to him.[151] Williams Wynn regarded the pension as a reward for past not future services, and, 'surprised' and saddened by Wellington's neglect, he did not reapply.[152]

According to Palmerston, Williams Wynn, who saw parallels between Wellington's coalition ministry and that of the earl of Chatham, 1766-8, thought that the Canningites in and out of office should likewise be seated together and conduct themselves as a distinct group in the Commons, and seek out contentious policy issues to exploit to their own advantage.[153] He placed little credence in current rumours that he would be offered the Speakership and decided to 'hold back and keep guard at present, connecting myself with no one, but supporting the course of policy pursued by the late administration'. He confided to Henry that he was not yet ready to 're-embark with the Whigs or even to join company with Lord Lansdowne', as their uncles favoured.[154] His family had always lived up to their means, and to economize he let their house in Whitehall Place to Sir Richard Vyvyan* for the season for £650 and took one in Clarges Street for £315 before settling in Jermyn Street.[155] His mother wrote:

> The one object with them all is to be able to afford to keep a home in London ... some place he must find a permanent deposit for his books and papers which he really could not stow at Llangedwyn and if he could he would be miserable to be separated from them for so long as he continues a regular attender on the House of Commons. Great are the political storms at this moment and never was there a union so widely disunited as that of the present administration, but nothing I fear can arise to our advantage out of the jars and squabbles ... Our late premier has certainly proved himself not equal even to be *dernier*, and has with the best intentions towards Charles, done him a mischief which I fear will be long irreparable.[156]

From Naples, Buckingham, who had given Goderich his proxy, expressed sorrow at Williams Wynn's plight, and regret 'that prudence did not remind him that having kicked away the ladder upon which he had mounted, he was not likely to find another support to maintain him in his position or break his fall'.[157] Williams Wynn rejected his proffered reconciliation.[158] He continued to receive private dispatches from India and retained an interest in the administration of justice in its presidencies.[159] He defended his former department, 7 Feb., 21 Feb. 1828, when, backed by Sturges Bourne, he repeatedly denied Herries's charge that he had known of impending ministerial changes before 9 Jan. He dismissed allegations that the East India Company had embezzled the estate of the late Myles O'Reilly, 18 Apr. Reminded by Hume of his promises to introduce legislation to improve the administration of criminal justice and relieve insolvent debtors in the East Indies, 22 May, he brought in both bills, 4 June, and secured their passage, 10 July; they were enacted later that month. He waived his earlier objections to Fergusson's real property in India bill, which was also passed that session. Demonstrating his command of departmental detail, he denied that Britain ruled India for her own benefit and successfully opposed the referral of the Calcutta petition against stamp duty to a select committee, 17 June. He drew parallels with Calcutta when endorsing Huskisson's New South Wales bill, 20 June. Being eager to extend free trade to India, he found it 'impossible' to keep silent at the third reading of the customs bill, 14 July 1828, and declared for Fergusson's amendment.

He presented petitions, 25 Feb., voted, 26 Feb., and spoke, 28 Feb. 1828, for repeal of the Test Acts, believing that Dissenters would accept nothing less and would petition until it was granted. He saw no need for securities, nor did he oppose the declaration proposed by Peel, 18 Mar., but on 5 May he said he feared that by permitting Quakers and Moravians to affirm rather than swear an oath, the law of evidence bill (which received royal assent, 27 June) would establish an unworkable precedent. Drawing on the work of his 1827 select committee, he steered the pauper lunatic regulation bills successfully through the Commons, 17 Mar. On 5 May he criticized the failure of the government's offences against the person bill to provide for Britons fighting duels abroad, 'intent to murder', trying lesser offences with a capital charge to facilitate conviction, and for divorce following conviction for bigamy. He divided for Catholic relief, 12 May, and after the Lords had rejected it, expressed regret, praised Peel and called for moderation, 12 June. The House took his advice that the Kilkenny petition against charity abuse was a private rather than a parliamentary matter, 20 June. He had the third reading of the archbishop of Canterbury's bill deferred pending the production of papers on the office of his registrar, 5 June, but apart from Sir Watkin and Phillimore, he could find little support for a compromise clause, and he voted with the minority against giving the archbishop control over the appointment, 16 June. He divided with government against reductions in ordnance salaries, 4 July 1828.

On East Retford, the attorney general Wetherell remarked that 'all the store of knowledge of [Williams Wynn]... will not enable him to produce a precedent like the present case', 3 Mar. 1828. His hopes of securing a postponement that day were dashed, but he successfully countered Littleton's assertion that witnesses' testimony before Commons select committees could be cited in a court of law without the House's consent, 4 Mar., and intervened effectively when witnesses were examined, 7 Mar. He was against summoning the entrepreneur Samuel Crompton to testify, 10 Mar., but acknowledged that his objections were not those commonly held and cited Colonel Wardle's case in 1782 to substantiate his claim that there were not 'sufficient grounds for the delay which would result from Crompton's examination'. He also committed himself to opposing 'any motion which has the effect of placing any person in a situation to criminate him unless it is absolutely unavoidable for the ends of justice'. He explained that he was against sluicing the franchise at East Retford, 21 Mar., but at the same time affirmed his retrospective support for the adoption of this course at Aylesbury, Cricklade and New Shoreham. On 19 May, replying to Peel, he suggested allocating the East Retford franchise 'alternately to a borough and to a great town', sending up both bills and letting the Lords decide; and, protesting that the case had not been fairly tried, he voted with Smith Stanley and the Whigs to transfer the seats to Birmingham (which was rejected by 146-128).[160] He

was in the minority against the bill's recommittal, 27 June, when, citing the case of Bishop's Castle, he again called for a proper investigation of corruption and delaying the writ. He opposed the candidature of the returning officer at Penryn, 28 Mar., and endorsed Phillimore's witnesses indemnity bill, 2, 3 Apr., which received royal assent, 18 Apr. He remained against general reform of Parliament, arguing that the system as a whole was strengthened by its anomalies, 11 Mar., but he welcomed attempts to improve efficiency and suggested extra booths, shorter polls, and awarding magistrates the right to choose county polling places, 31 Mar. He defended and commended the borough polls bill, 15 May, which received royal assent, 15 July. As Southey had hoped, his controverted elections bill was well supported, 3 Apr., 5 May, and after it was assented to, 23 May, he chaired the committee which amended the standing orders and brought up their resolutions, 14 July. Its object was to ensure that a Parliament heard all relevant election petitions in its first session, to prevent sitting Members dithering over whether to defend their returns, to stop nominees sitting on election committees, and to restrict membership to 11 of 33 Members balloted instead of 15 of 49 as hitherto.[161] He supported Littleton's bill exempting turnpike legislation from renewal fees, 21 Apr. He advocated piecemeal reform of the corn laws, and having welcomed the lowering of the pivot price in 1826, he voted similarly to reduce it to 60s., 22 Apr.[162] However, on 25 Apr., when it was carried by 140-50, he declared for the measure. Despite his dislike of protection, he presented Montgomeryshire petitions for duties on imported wool and repeal of the 1827 Malt Act, 29 Apr., dissenting only from their petition for repeal of the Small Notes Act, 17 June 1828.

Williams Wynn had renewed contact with Lords Holland and Lansdowne and was not considered for office during the May and August 1828 reshuffles, when his only recorded meeting with Wellington was on Asiatic Society business.[163] He spent part of the recess in Ireland executing Lord Carysfort's will, and while there predicted that the 'stalemate' on the Catholic question would continue.[164] His letters to Holland and Henry Williams Wynn from Llangedwyn, 17 Sept., were cautiously optimistic, and by November, having heard again from Spring Rice and Goderich, he surmised that Wellington might carry emancipation. Informing Holland, 27 Dec. 1828, he observed: 'It is more than I expected of him'.[165] As was customary, he and his family celebrated twelfth night at Wynnstay, and he returned to London in January 1829 from Llangedwyn, after studying schemes for codification of the laws and penal reform.[166] He was saddened by

Lord Anglesey's dismissal as Irish viceroy, which he realized had little to do with his letter to Dr. Curtis, and was delighted by the cabinet's decision to concede emancipation.[167] When Peel resigned his Oxford University seat, Williams Wynn expected to be offered it 'notwithstanding my Papistical principles', and informed Henry, 11 Feb., 'I shall of course decline, but if there were anyone of the family at liberty and of an age to hold Montgomeryshire, I certainly should come to a different decision'. He campaigned strenuously for Peel at the by-election, chaired the meeting of his Oxford supporters, and was hurt when Peel neglected to thank him during their joint deliberations over the relief bill.[168] In the Commons, he praised Peel and disputed Cooper's claim that if the bill were passed the title of the House of Brunswick would be impaired, 13 Feb. He had failed to stem the anti-Catholic tide at Oswestry, and he presented and dissented from Montgomeryshire's anti-Catholic petition, 4 Mar., describing it as genuine but misguided. With Sir Watkin he adopted a high profile at the London St. David's Day celebrations, and both were named as defaulters, 5 Mar. He divided for the relief bill, 6, 30 Mar., raised procedural points in committee, 17, 18, 30 Mar., and declared that he only backed the 'defective' Irish 40s. freeholders bill, 19 Mar., and a modified oath, 23 Mar., to avoid jeopardizing emancipation. He saw its passage by the Lords as the 'accomplishment of the great object of our labours during my political life', and soon accepted that it could only have been carried by its former opponents.[169] He confirmed that it would not open India and Madras to Catholics, 24 Mar., and equated the power of the general council with that of the Council of Trent, 27 Mar. Despite the precedents he cited, his advice that Daniel O'Connell be permitted to state his case against taking the oath of supremacy at the table or bar of the House was ignored, as was his proposal for a Declaratory Act, 15 May. He voted to permit O'Connell to sit without taking the oaths, 18 May, and spoke against issuing a new writ for county Clare, where 40 days had not passed since freeholder registration, 19 May. By moving 'that Mr. O'Connell, not having taken the oath of supremacy is disqualified from sitting and voting', 21 May, he contrived to avoid creating an incorrect precedent. Spring Rice assured him that O'Connell would be returned quietly.[170] He said that he saw nothing new in the Irish Catholic bishops' petition for a national education system based on the commissioners' report, 9 Apr. 1829.

Citing precedents, he confirmed that a by-election at Canterbury was necessary following Lushington's appointment as governor of Madras, 19 Mar., and raised the issue again, 22 May 1829, when he was named to the select committee. He defended the India board's handling of the Bencoolen compensation claims, 6 Apr., and was added to the select committee on the registrar at Madras, 7 May. He had to concede that he was no longer on the investigative committee when Whitmore's East India Company resolutions were considered, 14 May, and privately expected government to concede committees, but postpone the charter question 'for a year or two longer'. On 16 June he wrote to Sir John Malcolm:

> Of news of this country it is scarcely sending any as it consists solely of reports which vary from day to day. The internal political situation is totally unlike anything which I can recollect as the whole pack of cards has been so comprehensively shuffled that no one can tell what will be played next. There seems to be a strong expectation of the introduction of Edward Stanley into the cabinet, of which I shall be glad as I think he is *facillime primus* among the rising generation in the ... Commons, but I am not disposed to give now credit to that more than the other reports. At the same time it does appear almost impossible that the persons I have mentioned should meet Parliament without some acquisition of strength and I know not where the duke is to get this but from the Whigs. He would prefer the old Tories, but they can supply him with no parliamentary talent, and his unabated hostility to Huskisson and the rest of Canning's friends render it highly improbable that he will ask their assistance. The next session must at all events be a peculiarly busy and interesting one as all the business of this year has been deferred.[171]

Presenting Calcutta's petition requesting that Muslims and Hindus be permitted to hold office and serve as jurors under the 1826 Act, 5 July 1829, he said he did so knowing that Cavendish Bentinck, Munro, Elphinstone and Heber had advocated it.

His assertion that the circumstances of the Dover election petition were covered by the Grenville Act was ruled incorrect, 26 Mar., and he arranged next day for it to be heard on 28 Apr. 1829. On East Retford, 'a judicial question which should not have been mixed up with political considerations', 5 May, he said he had formerly thought corruption proven and favoured 'absolute disfranchisement'; but in view of the problem of reconciling the rival claims of the landed interest in Bassetlaw and the commercial interest in Birmingham, he would now vote to transfer the franchise to the latter. He presented Oswestry's petition for a change in the law on small debts, 22 May. He opposed additional expenditure on the marble arch sculpture, 27 May. As agreed by Welsh Members and peers at Sir Watkin's house, 16 May, he headed a delegation to Peel, 19 May, to protest against the proposed partitioning of counties to form new assize districts when the Welsh courts of great sessions were abolished.[172] During the recess the brothers failed to persuade Denbighshire to adopt the *pro-forma* petition agreed in London (16 May), requesting the introduction of the English assize system, but leaving the existing county assize structure intact, 15 Sept. 1829.[173] Afterwards, Williams Wynn went to Dublin, where his sister Henrietta's case against Hamerton was heard, staying on to observe the effects of emancipation, which he dutifully reported to his uncles. His assessment of the political system on the mainland was unchanged.[174]

He now believed that he had gained more by leaving office in January 1828 than 'the other remains of Canning's cabinet' ousted in May, and expected and obtained nothing from Wellington's reshuffle in January 1830, when he 'lingered' in Wales, 'not sorry' to miss the debate on the omission of distress from the king's speech.[175] He informed Phillimore:

> Believing, as I do, the general distress to arise from causes which Parliament could not remedy or control, I should not have wished to excite fallacious hopes and strengthen the anti-currency, anti-free traders by supporting an amendment, the adoption of which I was not prepared to follow up by forcing any measure upon government. The only real object in amendment to an address is either to drive ministers out or to compel them to do something they are not inclined to. My objection to the present administration is, I must fairly avow, rather to men than to measures.[176]

Over the following months, he repeatedly expressed his reluctance 'to see the management of affairs taken out of the hands of the duke and of Peel', preferring to see their administration broadened to remove the 'ever present danger of a government in minority'. In June 1830 Wellington included him on his list of party leaders 'more anxious to and ready to support and join the government than any other party acting in opposition'.[177] Returning to London as planned for the inquiry motion on the East India Company,[178] he was appointed to the investigating committee, 9 Feb., and had a petition from Woodhouse for free trade in India and China referred to it, 5 Apr.[179] He voted against Lord Blandford's reform motion, 18 Feb. Opposing the enfranchisement of Birmingham, Leeds and Manchester, 23 Feb., he said that he feared it would establish a precedent for increasing Commons Membership and explained that he was now sorry he had not supported Grey's call for disfranchisements to be made before permitting the influx of Irish Members in 1801.[180] Feeling obliged to comment on East Retford, he continued:

> I think it much safer when a borough shall be convicted of corruption that the franchise shall be given to a great town than to a hundred, which has no recommendation but that of its vicinity to the disfranchised borough. If the amendment ... shall be pressed to a division, I will certainly vote for it. I oppose the [present] motion ... because the principle which it would establish would inevitably lead to an indefinite increase of the number of Members in this House and would totally change the character of its representation and would render it most tumultuous and less adapted for business than it is at present.

He opposed Littleton's parliamentary agency bill, 26 Feb., and confined his observations on the Rye election petition to procedural points, 25 Mar. He was against treating Galway's Catholic and Protestant traders equally because it took rights away from Protestants instead of conferring them on Catholics, 4 Mar., but was for proceeding with the Galway franchise bill, 26 Apr. He spoke and voted for inquiry into the Bombay judicature, 8 Mar., stressing at the same time that he did not consider the dispute between Sir John Peter Grant* and Malcolm one on which the House should rule: both men had acted conscientiously and from the best motives. Lord Ellenborough as president of the India board vainly hoped that the Calcutta petition for better status for half-castes would not be presented by Williams Wynn,[181] who on doing so supported it and moved successfully for a copy of Munro's 1824 minute on the Fort St. George presidency, 4 May 1830.

One of the cases which interested him that session was that of Sir Jonah Barrington, the Irish admiralty judge accused of peculation. He failed to prevent its deferral, 4, 6, 10 May, but he succeeded in having Barrington's petition printed, 13 May, and his testimony heard by counsel, 18 May. When the resolutions against Barrington were passed, 22 May, he suggested and cited precedents for proceeding otherwise, but to no avail. He objected to the Commons being 'made a sort of court of appeal for the reconsideration of cases which have been already decided by those who had competent jurisdiction' in the case of the dismissed Irish excise officer James Kelly, 18 May, and spoke to little effect the same day on the Dean Forest bill and Birmingham-London Junction Canal bill. When the latter was considered, 20 May, he accused its solicitor Eyre Lee of a breach of privilege. He also took up the case of Dumbarton corporation, represented by its provost Jacob Dixon, against the Clyde navigation bill, 26 May. He had Dixon's petition referred to a committee of appeal, 28 May, reported their finding against the bill, 7 June, and prevented its recommittal and speedy passage, 10 June. Speaking for Phillimore's abortive motion for a commission of inquiry into the divorce laws, 3 June, he tried to counter Dr. Lushington's objections that it was a matter for the ecclesiastical courts and cited the increase in bigamy as proof that civil legislation was necessary. Not wishing to act as a 'factious opponent' of administration or to align with the revived Whig opposition, he informed Phillimore and announced in debate, 29 Mar., that as in 1823 and 1828, he would vote against combining the offices of lieutenant and master-general of the ordnance.[182] He divided, 5 Apr., and paired, 17 May, for Jewish emancipation, voted to make forgery a non-capital offence, 24 May, 7 June, and cited statistics undermining the case for its retention and the strong petitioning campaign for its abolition to strengthen his case against accepting the Lords' amendment that undermined the bill, 20 July, when he blamed the Upper House for the 'critical' delay by which the measure was lost. When the king was dying, Williams Wynn, supporting attempts by Peel and Brougham to reschedule public business to deal with the legislative backlog, 15 June, suggested introducing additional Wednesday and Saturday sittings in order to rush though the Madras registrar bill which he promoted, 15, 19 June. He spoke in favour of retaining the metropolitan police despite the additional cost and his dislike of a military police force, 15 June 1830, and later that day defended the usury bill which he asserted would not affect the Annuity Act or inconvenience trustees.

When the administration of justice bill that abolished the Welsh judicature and great sessions was introduced, 9 Mar. 1830, he lauded the advantages of assimilation, but predicted incorrectly that despite recent hostile petitions the measure would become popular in Wales, now the proposed division of counties was largely abandoned (this was not confirmed until 27 May). He had its second reading deferred so that opinion could be sounded at the assizes and quarter sessions, and duly commended it to the House, 27 Apr., but privately he considered the measure

> incorrectly and loosely drawn ... The outline of the proposed plan of circuits ought to be detailed subject to the subsequent modification of the privy council. My own wish is that the Oxford circuit should be divided combining the Chester and North Wales circuits with Worcester, Stafford and Shrewsbury and the South West circuits with the remainder of Oxford. One judge only on each of the former Welsh circuits, so that the Montgomeryshire and Merioneth assizes would be contemporaneous. Denbigh and Flint, Caernarvon and Anglesey to be respectively united ... Or Oxfordshire might be added to the first of the two if it were thought preferable.[183]

As most petitions indicated that the Welsh were satisfied with their courts, he colluded with the barrister

William Owen to procure a petition favouring their abolition from Montgomeryshire, but he declined attendance at the county meeting, 27 Apr., on account of Madras business and the debate on the 'bungled' Terceira affair, 28 Apr., when he divided with the opposition.[184] Presenting the Montgomeryshire petition, 4 May, he emphasized its prayer for English jurisdiction and made light of its other demands.[185] He defended the bill in committee 18, 19, 27 May, 18 June, 5 July, but complained when the Lords returned it amended, 22 July, that improved modes of proceeding were being sacrificed to its rapid passage. Peel now denied him the Lords' conference he requested and his confidence that corrective legislation would soon follow proved misplaced.[186] He had had little to say on the continuation of offices bill, 10 May, but when George IV died he deferred his measure to repeal the oath of abjuration, 28 June, and urged the House to adopt an address of condolence, 29 June, and to proceed with the civil list, 30 June. He considered the enactment of a regency bill before the dissolution 'essential' and was sorry to see it made a party issue, for which he blamed Brougham. In a speech packed with precedents he supported and was a minority teller for Robert Grant's motion for an address pressing William IV for immediate clarification on the regency, 6 July 1830.[187] He faced no opposition in Montgomeryshire at the ensuing general election, and mediated successfully between Edward Clive and Edmund Lechmere Charlton[†] at Ludlow.[188]

Williams Wynn made his customary plea for early consideration of election petitions in the new Parliament, pointing out that the reduction he had achieved in committee size made it possible to consider four daily instead of two, 3 Nov. 1830. He later intervened with limited success when those from Calne, Carrickfergus, Perth Burghs, Queenborough, St. Mawes, Rye and Wigan were considered.[189] He scorned Hume's 'useless' suggestion that a minister should be present whenever the House was sitting, 3 Nov., and gave notice that day of his oaths in Parliament bill, which he introduced with Sturges Bourne, carrying its first and second readings, 9, 12 Nov. Fergusson, Lord Nugent and Robert Palmer supported it, but for O'Connell it did not go far enough, and Peel, like Wetherell, was against repealing the abjuration oath and would only assent to it 'with reservations'. He prevented Sir Harcourt Lees's petition against it being printed, 23 Dec., but was obliged to defer its committal until 4 Feb., when he split it to concentrate on the less contentious oaths before the lord steward bill, which encountered opposition, 11 Feb., 20 Apr. 1831, and was timed out. The ministry had classified him in

September 1830 as one of their 'foes', and he divided against them on the wheat import duties, 12 Nov., and on the civil list when they were brought down, 15 Nov. 1830. Advocating inquiry, he cited precedents from Burke's time onwards and drew on his experience of the 1820 committee when the 'indelicacy' of the royal couple's situation had complicated the issue. Sir John Walsh* described him that day as a 'Canningite'.[190] When Lord Grey as premier considered him for office he did not want to return to the India board, hoped for the home office, and negotiated, with Palmerston and Brougham as intermediaries, for freedom of action on reform. He also vainly tried to secure ministerial backing for the Speakership, 'my whole object ... which *must* be vacant soon'. After accepting the proffered post of secretary at war, without cabinet, and at only £2,480 a year, which he conceded was 'not brilliant', he confided to Brougham, 25 Nov.:

> At present I cannot flatter myself that my acceptance of a department of mere detail of which I am wholly ignorant can be of advantage to the government or afford me opportunity of rendering myself more useful than in my private capacity as a Member ... actively supporting it.[191]

To ensure the arrangement was 'clearly understood', Grey, who believed he might refuse and held Lord Sandon* in reserve, wrote to Williams Wynn, 24 Nov., acknowledging his 'qualification' to be Speaker, but refusing to commit his government to supporting him. He also warned that on reform, 'I probably may feel it necessary to go to a greater extent than you would approve in the suppression of what are called the rotten boroughs ... You can be under no obligation to resign your office'. Lord Anglesey thought ministers would find Williams Wynn 'eminently useful in all reform discussions', and Grey promised him 'an opportunity hereafter of fully considering the measure before it is finally determined upon and brought forward'.[192] With fees of £157 payable on appointment, Williams Wynn calculated: 'If I remain in office less than three months, as may very possibly be the case, I shall be the loser'.[193] Henry Williams Wynn wrote:

> I am disappointed that in the formation of a new administration in direct opposition to the last you should find yourself in the same situation, that of being between two stools. Independence is the most desirable line, in the same manner that *being a gentleman* is the best profession, but this is a sacrifice which such as you and I with large families must in some degree make.[194]

The ailing Grenville, who had not been consulted until a late stage in negotiations, shared his dismay at seeing ministers disposed to favour Littleton for the Speakership during Manners Sutton's illness

that winter.[195] Palmerston intimated that Williams Wynn had threatened resignation, but that his bluff was called.[196] His attempts to secure something for Phillimore failed.[197] A strong Powis Castle and Wynnstay presence at Machynlleth gave him 'a most triumphant re-election' in December 1830 despite 'the baiting we had at a county meeting on reform', which 'certainly was by no means agreeable'.[198] Although he categorically refused to declare for reform, ministers expected him to divide with them and were not alarmed that support for it was minimal.[199] He quickly perceived a link between reform meetings and unrest which proved difficult to quell in Montgomeryshire and neighbouring counties.[200]

In office, Williams Wynn laboured to master the army estimates, which he moved successfully, 21 Feb., 14 Mar. 1831, despite increases in colonial expenditure and voluble opposition from Hume and Davies, who failed to restrict payments to a single quarter.[201] His constant 'dread of ... splitting from the concern on the reform question' intensified when he learnt of the bill's details. After discussing it with Grey and Russell, 21 Feb., he consulted Grenville, who, troubled by speculation in *The Times* over his sinecure exchequer auditorship, declined to take responsibility for 'one of the most important decisions of your life'.[202] Presenting a reform petition, 1 Mar., he generated 'a roar of laughter throughout the House from the circumstance of having the whole of the front of his hat covered with a leek which he wore in commemoration of St. David's Day'.[203] He considered remaining silent and supporting the second reading of the government's bill 'with an expression of hope of such alterations being made in committee as might relieve if not remove my objections', but decided against doing so, lest his motives be misconstrued.[204] He informed Henry, 5 Mar.:

> The measure proposed goes so much further than anything I could have anticipated that I shall tonight declare my utter inability to support it without great and essential modification, more than I can reasonably expect will now be consented to by its authors. I regret this extremely, not so much as it must be followed by going out of office, for I think that there is no probability of the bill passing or the administration remaining in office, as because it will again leave me isolated and unconnected and because [of] the excitement and ferment and party violence which I must look forward to encounter. Still, after much consideration I thought I had no other course to adopt, and have just notified it to ... Grey.[205]

In a widely reported speech expected to damage government, he drew parallels between the importance of reform and Catholic emancipation and stressed his readiness to disfranchise boroughs found guilty of corruption and transfer Helston's franchise to Yorkshire in 1813. He endorsed the ministry's policy on peace and retrenchment. He explained that as he had not been in the cabinet, he had had no opportunity to discuss the bill's details at an early stage and learnt of its contents only a week before it was published. He endorsed its proposals to restrict the borough franchise to resident freemen and replace non-residents with £10 householders, and approved the proposed extension of the county franchise and all regulatory provisions except that 'authorizing the crown to appoint a committee of privy councillors to divide counties into districts and determine what adjoining parishes shall be added to such boroughs as shall not contain a sufficient number of £10 householders'. This he considered a task for Parliament. Concluding, he upheld Parliament's right to legislate for reform and expressed approval of it in principle, but added that the bill proposed greater change than he could agree to and would have to be altered before he could support it.[206] His resignation on 'a point of conscience' pleased his uncles. Goderich and Brougham, who had hoped he would support the bill, respected his decision, but Lord Holland did not 'think Squeaker Wynn behaves well in deferring his resignation till after the plan had been opened'. He stayed on at the war office until his successor was appointed.[207] On 15 Mar. 1831, convinced that the bill, which he condemned for starting with disfranchisement, would be 'cut to pieces' and eventually fail, he joined William Ormsby Gore in deploring the use made of anti-Catholic sentiments in reform petitions from Caernarvon and Oswestry that he refused to present, and ordered returns of population and houses rated above £10 in the Welsh contributory boroughs (schedule F).[208] His vote for the bill at its second reading, 22 Mar., surprised former colleagues and attracted much comment.[209] A Montgomeryshire reformer observed:

I see our Member has drawn in his horns. He has done wisely. He would otherwise have had an opposition at the next election. His transfiguration will probably save him.[210]

Buckingham thought any prospect of an accommodation between Grenville and Wellington was over and wrote to the duke: 'As to Mr. Wynn's conduct it is too disgusting to allow of a thought. It would be contamination again to come near him'.[211] In the Commons, 24 Mar., Williams Wynn explained that he had divided for the bill to ensure that it was considered in committee, where he hoped to modify it and would immediately move to postpone or omit the disfranchisement clause. He conceded privately that he had

acted at the entreaty of Sir Watkin, who was anxious to please their disgruntled constituents. This at least placated Buckingham, who had hoped for reconciliation between them before the anticipated dissolution.[212] Grenville opposed reform, but when Williams Wynn asked him whether they should introduce their own bill or take a lead in opposing the government's, he urged caution:

You are of all men in the House, the most unfit to put yourself forward in the very first (or indeed in any) discussion of the bill as the *leader* of any mode or plan of resistance and it is quite clear to me that unless you mean to make yourself responsible to the House or country for the whole cause, details and consequences of any modified plan of reform, you have in common prudence (I had almost said *with reference to your particular situation* in common decorum) nothing else to do in any part of this discussion but to await the proposals and motions of others for or against the bill and to speak for or against *them* as you shall honestly judge them beneficial or harmful to the country ... It is well worth your observance how strongly Peel, though not under half your difficulties of situation, evidently feels the impolicy of taking this sort of lead. He plainly waits, and so undoubtedly should you to follow, or oppose, as the case may be, the proposals or motions of country gentlemen and others, not avowed and seasoned politicians, like himself and you, both men in the line of office whether at this moment in or out.[213]

Apparently heeding this advice, Williams Wynn confined his remarks to procedures until the debate on Gascoyne's wrecking amendment, 19 Apr., when he reiterated his reasons for voting for the second reading, confirmed his support for the bill's committal and mentioned among its anomalies the incorporation of population totals for enfranchised towns in county figures, awarding Glamorganshire (population, 101,000) two borough and two county Members, but leaving Carmarthenshire (population, 90,000) with two single Member constituencies, and the enfranchisement as £10 householders of the 'delinquent' electors of Aylesbury, Cricklade, East Retford and New Shoreham. He suggested withdrawing the bill for redrafting and resubmission, making the 1831 census the criterion for determining borough representation, classifying the disfranchised boroughs, and, as Spring Rice observed, 'nearly, though not explicitly promised his vote for Gascoyne' by declaring against a proportionate increase in Irish representation. Countering, the Irish secretary Smith Stanley, who, with Sir Edward Pryce Lloyd had been requisitioned to oppose him in Montgomeryshire, referred to Williams Wynn's early briefing on the bill's details and constituency pressure to support it. Williams Wynn conceded this and claimed to be confident of electoral success. He divided for the amendment, 19 Apr. 1831.[214] Portraying himself as a supporter of limited reform, he made no effort to disguise his annoyance at being forced to a five-day poll by the reformer Joseph Hayes Lyon at the ensuing general election.[215] His speech on the hustings encouraged speculation that he would introduce an alternative reform bill.[216]

Williams Wynn nominated the Speaker in the new Parliament and was complemented on his own expertise, 'constant attendance' and 'unwearied attention to all questions affecting or connected with the privileges, orders, and proceedings of the House', 14 June 1831. He raised his usual points on election petitions, 22 June, and on 20 July carried his oaths before the lord steward bill, which received royal assent on the 30th. As a member of the East India committee, he joined Goulburn in opposing a reduction from £5,000 to £3,500 in the salary of the president of the India board, arguing that the attendant patronage, which was expected to supply the deficit, was no substitute for emolument, 28 June. He declined to present an Oxford University anti-reform petition, and, as he had warned a disappointed Grenville, but to the king's surprise, he and his brother divided for the reintroduced reform bill at its second reading, 6 July.[217] Their decision was apparently dictated by local factors and, after the division, Williams Wynn considered himself free to oppose the bill as he wished.[218] He met Croker, Peel and 20 others to discuss tactics, 11 July. With them, he urged that counsel be heard on the Appleby petition and voted to adjourn the bill's committal, 12 July.[219] Next day he carried a referral motion for all petitions, accounts, returns and papers on reform, but failed to have the disfranchisement clause deferred. He also objected to giving the boundary commissioners legislative powers and to the 'magic 2,000' population threshold for continued borough representation, preferring multiple borough constituencies and adhering to 'the combined principles of population, property and situation'. He endorsed a petition for continued enfranchisement from the Clives' borough of Bishop's Castle, 14 July. Arguing that abolishing nomination boroughs would not improve county representation, he repeated his case for contributories, 15 July, but conceded that there was no scope for considering this until the disfranchisements had been dealt with. He voted to use the 1831 census to determine English borough representation, 19 July, and against disfranchising Appleby, 19 July, and Downton, 21 July, and criticized government plans for rushing the bill through committee, 21 July. Althorp, whom he privately warned of likely defeats unless a separate committee on county

representation was appointed,[220] agreed that reform committees should start at five o'clock. Williams Wynn defended his erstwhile patron Lord Camelford's management of Old Sarum and divided against disfranchising St. Germans, 26 July. He was against taking a Member from Chippenham on 'a parish officer's error', 27 July, argued that corruption at Malmesbury should be proved and Sudbury's case reconsidered, 30 July, and made useful interventions on scheduling and the use of Saturday sittings, 29 July. He confided to Grenville, 2 Aug., that he expected the bill to lose support as 'clauses of *construction*' replaced 'the work of *destruction*'.[221] In debate that day he objected to the notion of the bill as a step to further reform and portrayed it as threat to ancient chartered rights and privileges. He stressed the dangers of electorate control, radicalism and unrest in populous constituencies, 3, 4 Aug., but he did not vote on the enfranchisement of Greenwich, 3 Aug., and agreed that Stoke-on-Trent should be awarded two Members, 4 Aug. He privately considered further opposition in the Commons futile, although 'perseverance may produce some effect out of doors and may at all events encourage the Lords to resist the attempts to overawe them', and confessed that he was 'grievously sick' of the bill and Saturday sittings, which prevented him from joining his family at Cowes.[222] He spoke against combining Chatham with Rochester and Strood, 9 Aug. Later that day, when Schedule F boroughs were considered, he restated the case for increased Welsh representation, bemoaned the 'harsh treatment' of Merthyr, and suggested that Caernarvonshire, Carmarthenshire, Denbighshire, Merioneth, Montgomeryshire and Pembrokeshire merited two Members. Wynnstay's preferred boundaries for newly enfranchised Wrexham were acceded to, 10 Aug. Endorsing the division of counties, 11 Aug., he commended his Yorkshire plan, urged the exclusion of enfranchised borough populations from county totals, and suggested restricting the annuitant franchise. He failed to have the whole bill recommitted or consideration of the Welsh counties deferred, 12, 13 Aug.; but his suggestions elicited little response until taken up on the 18th by the Ultra Lloyd Kenyon, who was to stand for Denbighshire in 1832. Williams Wynn observed:

> To my great surprise, Althorp showed a disposition in some degree at least to concede. Personally, I rather wish that he would not, as I think that the alteration may produce more frequent contests in the counties than we have hitherto been exposed to.[223]

He is not known to have voted on Chandos's clause enfranchising £50 tenants-at-will, 18 Aug., but, encouraged by this sign of government's vulnerability, he exploited errors and anomalies in the provisions for returning officers as signs that 'the bill was brought forward in a hurried and undigested form', 19, 20 Aug., but refused to endorse Hume's criticism of the government's scheduling policy, 27 Aug. He repeatedly criticized the householder franchise, 24-27 Aug., suggesting that a universal £10 qualification would prove as easy to manipulate as scot and lot, and calling for a qualification period of six months instead of six weeks after rates were paid, to limit landlord influence.[224] He opposed the reception of a petition from Arundel for election by ballot, 19 Aug., and voted to defeat an opposition amendment to preserve freemen's voting rights, 30 Aug. On learning that the boundary commissioners would report to Parliament, he waived his objections to them, 1 Sept.; but, anticipating problems where boundaries were disputed and petitioned against, he proposed adding a clause to prevent the Act taking effect 'before completion of these final steps', in the event of a dissolution. Early in September he joined his family at Cowes.[225] Returning to hear the bill reported, 13, 14 Sept., he failed to have it recommitted or amended to include the second Members promised to Carmarthenshire and Denbighshire. His objections to the £10 franchise and suggestions for polling by parish and allowing extra time for allocating booths were ignored, but his advice on registration courts was heeded, and a clause covering dissolution was added as a rider to the bill at its third reading, 19 Sept. He approved it in principle and in part, leaving Peel and others to highlight its shortcomings. Before voting against its passage, 21 Sept., he defended the powers of amendment held by the Lords, denounced large towns as centres of corruption and explained:

I have repeatedly been in the minority when motions have been made to direct prosecutions in cases of bribery. I voted for the second reading of the bill and for its being committed that it might be fairly considered, and so improved and amended as to render it a proper and beneficial measure ... It is still calculated to effect too great a change, and I therefore feel bound to oppose it.

He repeated his objections to its unnecessary disfranchisements and uniform £10 franchise, defended small boroughs for affording opportunities to men of talent and direct representation for East and West Indian interests, and ended with a pledge 'to be healthily negative to this bill, but ready as ever to support a moderate measure'. Writing to Thomas Grenville, 22 Sept., he welcomed the recent damage inflicted on the bill and praised Croker, Peel and Thomas Pemberton's speeches.[226] Before leaving for yeomanry

duties, the quarter sessions and a round of post-election dinners and celebrations in Montgomeryshire, for which he had been granted three weeks' leave, 26 Sept. 1831, he wrote to Grenville of his regret at seeing their kinsman Lord Ebrington 'at the head of the party who have united to urge ministers forward to measures of violence', and the Glynnes and others 'of my connections and relations' supporting reform, 'when Lord Brougham has so prudently held back from committing himself'.[227] He had expressed support for administration on supply, 8 July, and the secret service estimates, 18 July, and was appointed to the select committees on civil list expenditure, 12 Aug., and the coronation 6 Sept.[228] He raised many points of order and procedure on railway and other private bills, 6, 18, 25 July, 4, 9, 19 Aug.; and, though moved by the *Rothsay Castle* disaster, said he thought Parliament could do little to protect steamboat passengers except legislate against overloading, 19 Aug., 20 Sept. He denounced liberty of the press as an 'absurd doctrine', 28 June. He intervened on behalf of the sitting Member Sir John Owen when the Pembrokeshire election petition was considered, 8 July, 23 Sept., and had Richard Gurney's petition against the Tregony election committee's decision rejected, 12 Sept. On the Dublin election controversy, he sought to delay summoning William Gossett*, 20 Aug., and was a minority teller for Gordon's censure motion, 23 Aug. 1831, but spoke highly of the Irish lord lieutenant Anglesey.[229]

While he was in Wales on yeomanry duty, Frankland Lewis briefed him as arranged on the Dorset by-election and the reform bill's progress in the Lords, where he had anticipated its defeat.[230] He wrote to Southey, 27 Oct. 1831:

The late division in the Lords has had the effect of awakening many of those who, conceiving their position past remedy, had like the Indians folded their arms and lain down in the canoe, but what is wanted to afford us a hope of deliverance is the inspiriting voice of some man of courage and eloquence fitted to seize the command of the vessel, such as providence has in like emergencies frequently raised up, but such as we have now nothing approaching to. There are many who have done their duty morally and honestly and with great effect, but there is no head that commands public confidence. Peel is decidedly the best, but he is too cautious, too rich and too much at his ease for active ambition to excite him and he is too cold, reserved and unconfiding ever to attach warm and zealous friends.[231]

Sturges Bourne wrote that day asking 'what course' he 'and the few others with whom I have acted in and out of office' would now take. Williams Wynn was expected back in London for the round of pre-session dinners and meetings, but politics now depressed him, and after prevaricating he 'determined to remain in Wales till after the recess unless something more pressing should arrive'.[232] Early in December Lord Harrowby, using Lord Clive and Thomas Grenville as intermediaries, asked him to return, and Grenville reminded him that his position in the Commons could only be 'maintained as it has been created, by attendance'.[233] He attributed his failure to do so to 'a lame leg', the cost and family commitments, but added:

> I should have little hope of being of service in communicating with Ld. P[almerston]. In truth he is a person in whom I have no kind of confidence and I had much rather discuss any subject of the kind with Brougham, Graham or Ld. John [Russell] rather than any of my *ci-devant* colleagues except perhaps Ld. Lansdowne, and he has voluntarily shelved himself.[234]

Like the Clives, Barings, Frankland Lewis and others associated with Harrowby, he hoped for an alliance of moderates from both sides without an immediate change of government, and deliberately avoided voting on the revised reform bill at its second reading, 17 Dec. 1831, but he subsequently regretted this division on 'diminished [reduced] numbers'.[235] He claimed that constituency pressure had played no part in his decision, and informed Thomas Grenville that

> as at present advised, I am disposed to follow the same course in the committee on this bill as I did on the last, and point out all the mistakes and blunders which seem to me nearly as numerous though different. The great objection to the £10 qualification in large towns and to the suburban Members continue and the number of Members from the sinks of radicalism and sedition such as Oldham, Bradford, Blackburn and Stockport are increased. The provisions for the registration of county votes are rendered still more impracticable than ever.[236]

He remained 'most anxious to act in concert' with Harrowby, Baring and Clive, but without the 'previous engagement to government' they had offered, and he perceived correctly that there was little prospect of Grey compromising.[237]

He returned to London after the Christmas festivities at Wynnstay, and opposing the bill's committal, 20 Jan., he condemned it as vague and full of faults, and advised the House to 'keep the power of altering the number of boroughs in its own hands', 21 Jan. 1832. He complained that the designation of returning officers was flawed, 24 Jan., and criticized the proposed county divisions, 27 Jan., and methods of determining county copyhold, freehold and leasehold franchises, 1 Feb. Co-operating with opposition, he helped to delay the bill's progress, 2, 3, 16, 21 Feb.,

2 Mar. On 28 Feb. he successfully proposed the high constable as returning officer for Greenwich and voted against enfranchising Tower Hamlets. He kept aloof from the debate on Merthyr, 5 Mar.; but on the 14th he exposed irregularities in the disfranchisement in 1728 of Montgomery's former contributories and protested at the bill's failure to restore fully their 'ancient rights' prior to re-enfranchisement. He presented supportive petitions prepared by Powis Castle retainers, 19 Mar., but to no purpose.[238] He divided against the bill's third reading, 22 Mar. Following its defeat in the Lords, and using Buckingham as go-between, Wellington summoned Williams Wynn and asked him to join his projected administration, bringing with him Alexander Baring and Frankland Lewis, but he had many misgivings and had not replied when the plan was abandoned and Grey reinstated.[239] His acceptance seems unlikely. He did not divide on Ebrington's motion for an address calling on the king to appoint only ministers who would pass the bill unimpaired, 10 May, and was privately convinced that 'as it must pass, it should be passed by those ministers who introduced it'. He thought the Whigs would achieve this without creating further peers, a precondition of his acting with Wellington, whom he likened to a 'military dictator'. He considered that a Conservative-sponsored bill would cause more damage than the current one, which he did not think irreparable 'should a talented administration arise', and favoured one headed by Peel, Smith Stanley and Brougham.[240] His brother Watkin thought the 'one good consequence from these discussions' was an improvement in their relations with Buckingham.[241] Williams Wynn asked questions on the incorporation of new boroughs and their designated returning officers, 4 June, and made several useful interventions on the boundaries bill, 7, 8 June, the Scottish reform bill, 27 June, and the Liverpool franchise bill, 4 July. Inclined by 'experience' to oppose Baring's electoral bribery bill, he suggested its postponement, 6 May, voted for its committal, although he doubted whether it could be made to operate beneficially, so that he could support it, 27 June, but belatedly endorsed it, 9 Aug. He referred that day to France's occupation of the Low Countries as evidence of Britain's 'total want of influence, in itself a serious charge against an administration', and predicted that they would forfeit the support of the Irish Members directly the reform bill was enacted. He spoke and voted against government on the Russian-Dutch loan, 26 Jan., 12 July,[242] but with them on the civil list and chancery sinecures, 9 Aug. 1832. Concerned at the slenderness of the 'barrier' between Whigs and radicals and the likely succession of weak ministries, he wrote after the

January division:

> The ministry exists by the [reform] bill … In short we are still in the situation in which the breaking up of Lord Liverpool's government in 1827 left us: split, subdivided into parties which the course of events inevitably unites upon some question to beat the minister.[243]

Ever the champion of procedures and precedents, on 17 Feb. 1832 he defended Beresford's conduct of the Portuguese campaigns and upheld his own decision, as secretary at war, not to means test the pensions of army widows. He made further points on army matters, 6, 28 Mar., breach of privilege, 7 May, 1 June, petitions and procedures 8, 30 May; but his opinion was of insufficient weight to procure amendment of the London-Birmingham railway bill for the Clives, 18 June. His interventions on the coroners bill achieved little, 20 June, and he failed to impede the progress of Kenyon's labourers' employment bill, 27 June. He presented Montgomeryshire's petition for changes in the highways bill, 13 June. Although he was for amending the laws on slavery and capital punishment, in neither case was he a true abolitionist, and the high profile and popular appeal of both issues as the dissolution approached troubled him.[244] He suggested and obtained a conference with the Lords when their amendments virtually wrecked the punishment of death abolition bill, 5, 6 July; and did the same for the lunatic asylums bill he had worked hard for, 9, 10 Aug. After 24 years' campaigning he said that he would rather accept the amendments than lose the asylums bill, which received royal assent, 11 Aug. 1832.

It had been a difficult period in Williams Wynn's personal life. His mother's illness and death in October 1832 followed closely on those of his wife's brother, the reformer Foster Cunliffe Offley*, his mother-in-law and his elder son Watkin, who, as he had been warned in March, failed to recover from an inflammation of the lungs.[245] The 'one bright point amid the gloom' was his acquisition of a son-in-law 'with a passion for the House quite equal to his own' in James Milnes Gaskell, who, assisted by him, contested Wenlock successfully at the 1832 general election.[246] His campaign for the Speakership, for which his rival was Littleton, was unsuccessful. Liaising with Peel, who, possibly because of Wellington's reservations, proved slow to rally, he eventually secured Conservative support, possibly, as Lord Granville Somerset's* memorandum to Peel suggested, 11 Nov. 1832, 'because Wynn had better be the vanquished man than Goulburn'.[247] He found the canvassing, with which his nephew Charles Shipley Conway assisted, difficult and irksome and 'Members in

general extremely unwilling to commit themselves'. Buckingham and his relations backed him, and so did the 'reformers' Ebrington, Newton Fellowes, Sir Stephen Glynne and James Hamlyn Williams, '*a tribe of Welshmen*', joined out of hostility to Littleton by Edward Bolton Clive, Sir Edward Foley and Sir Matthew White Ridley. General election results were inauspicious for the Conservatives, and Manners Sutton's decision to stay on left Williams Wynn 'happy to be relieved from a pursuit which I consider as quite hopeless'.[248] His return for Montgomeryshire passed off smoothly and he retained the seat unchallenged for life.[249] Already 57, he considered his health 'still apparently equal to the exertion' of being Speaker, but, being prone to rheumatism, he surmised that it might not long continue so and he reluctantly agreed with Peel, when Manners Sutton retired in 1834, that the opportunity had come too late for him, and became chancellor of the duchy of Lancaster.[250] He was not included in Peel's 1841 cabinet and declined the commissionership of Greenwich Hospital he was then offered.[251] He died in September 1850, recalled as a scholarly and 'sterling advocate of social reforms', and was buried at St. George's, Hanover Square, alongside his wife and son. By his will Llangedwyn, his town house and his mother's Grenville bequests passed in trust to his son Charles (1822-96), Conservative Member for Montgomeryshire, 1862-80, and there were small annuities for his married and unmarried daughters.[252] His nephew Herbert Watkin Williams Wynn (1822-62) succeeded him as Conservative Member for Montgomeryshire.

[1] Reference was made to unpublished work by Gwyneth Evans, 'Charles Watkin Williams Wynn, 1775-1850' (Univ. of Wales M.A. thesis, 1935), which treats the subject chronologically; M.A. Whittle, 'Charles Watkin Williams Wynn (1775-1850): a political biography' (Univ. of Wales M.A. thesis, 1984), which treats it thematically; and A.W. Williams Wynn, 'Mem. of Charles Watkin Williams Wynn, 1796-1850' (1936), held at NLW. There is no published biography of note. [2] A.D. Harvey, *Britain in Early 19th Cent.* 10; T.G. Davies, 'Welsh Contribution to Mental Health Legislation in 19th Cent.' *WHR*, xviii (1996), 40-62, esp. 41-50. [3] J.J. Sack, 'The Decline of the Grenvillite Faction under the First Duke of Buckingham and Chandos, 1817-1829', *JBS*, xv (1975), 112-19; PRO NI, Castlereagh mss D3030/P/194; *Oxford DNB*. [4] [J. Grant], *Random Recollections of Lords and Commons*, ii (1838), 139-40. [5] Salop RO. Weld-Forester mss box 337, C.W. Forester to Emery, 2 Mar., P. Acton to C.W. Forester, 2 Mar.; *Shrewsbury Chron.* 17, 24 Mar. 1820. [6] See DENBIGHSHIRE, MONTGOMERYSHIRE, SHROPSHIRE and WENLOCK. [7] *HP Commons, 1790-1820*, v. 587-94; W.A. Hay, *The Whig Revival*, 94; J.J. Sack, *Grenvillites*, 176-184; A.D. Harvey, 'The Ministry of All the Talents', *HJ*, xv (1972), 619-48. [8] *Life and Corresp. of Southey* ed. C.C. Southey (1850), v. 36-39; Buckingham, *Mems. George IV*, i. 33-34; NLW, Coedymaen mss 578; bdle. 29, Williams Wynn to Phillimore, 25 Mar., 10 Apr. 1820; Sack, *Grenvillites*, 183. [9] Coedymaen mss 579. [10] Ibid. 935. [11] *CJ*, lxxv. 264, 284-5; Coedymaen mss 938. [12] Buckingham, i. 428; Add. 38296, ff. 356-8; M. Escott, 'How Wales lost its judicature: the making of the 1830 Act for the

Abolition of the Courts of Great Sessions', *Trans. Hon. Soc. of Cymmrodorion* (2006), 135-59. [13] Coedymaen mss 576, 598, 600. [14] Ibid. 937, 939, 940, 943. [15] Ibid. 581. [16] Coedymaen mss 588-602, 944. [17] Ibid. 582-3, 945; Buckingham, i. 48-49. [18] Buckingham, i. 57-58; Sack, *Grenvillites*, 184-5; Coedymaen mss 183, 585. [19] Buckingham, i. 57-58; Coedymaen mss 184, 592. [20] Coedymaen mss bdle. 29, Williams Wynn to Phillimore [9 Oct. 1820]. [21] NLW ms 2793 D, Williams Wynn to H. Williams Wynn, 31 Aug.; 4816 D, same to same, 9 Oct.; Coedymaen mss bdle. 29, same to Phillimore 12, 18 Oct., 2 Nov. 1820. [22] Buckingham, i. 77-78. [23] Ibid. i. 102; Coedymaen mss 594, 595. [24] Sack, *Grenvillites*, 185 and *JBS*, xv. 119-20; Coedymaen mss bdle. 29, Williams Wynn to Phillimore, 19, 30 Dec.; TNA, Dacres Adams mss, T.P. Courtenay to Adams, 21 Dec.; Lonsdale mss, Ward to Lonsdale, 27 Dec. 1820; Cent. Kent. Stud. Camden mss U840 C530/6; Add. 58963, f. 46; Hay, 120-1. [25] Coedymaen mss 596; bdle. 29, Williams Wynn to Phillimore, 21 Dec. 1820. [26] NLW ms 2793 D, Buckingham to H. Williams Wynn, 9, 18, 29 Mar., H. Williams Wynn to wife, 21 May 1821; Coedymaen mss bdle. 21, *passim*; Buckingham, i. 125-7, 130-2; Sack, *Grenvillites*, 186. [27] Bucks. RO, Fremantle mss D/FR/46/11/45; 46/12/36; Christ Church, Oxf. Phillimore mss, Buckingham to Phillimore, 3 Feb. 1821; Coedymaen mss 348, 603, 605, 611; Buckingham, i. 111-17, 119-23, 162-6. [28] HLRO, Hist. Coll. 379, Grey Bennet diary, 25. [29] *The Times*, 20 Feb., 3, 8 Mar. 1821; Coedymaen mss 606, 607; bdle. 17, Plunkett to Williams Wynn, 4 Apr.,tt 2, 11 May; bdle. 21, Buckingham to same, 11, 18 Mar. [24 Apr.]; NLW ms 2793 D, Williams Wynn to H. Williams Wynn [29 June] 1821. [30] Grey Bennet diary, 37 [31] Ibid. 77, 79. [32] Coedymaen mss 586, 944; bdle. 21, Buckingham to Williams Wynn, 9 Mar., 5, 10 [undated], June; Add. 38289, f. 169. [33] Fremantle mss 46/12/29, 30; Buckingham, i. 166-7, 175-9, 197-9. [34] Fremantle mss 51/5/14. [35] Add. 38370, f. 57; 38743, ff. 31, 56; 51574, Abercromby to Holland [1821]; Buckingham, i. 227-8, 232-6, 243-5; Add. 69044, Buckingham to Grenville, 30 Nov., 2, 6, 7 [10] Dec.; Add. 69044, Williams Wynn to same, 4, 5, Dec.; Fremantle mss 46/11/58, 59; 46/12/25; Castlereagh mss P/193; Coedymaen mss 350, 352, 353; *Geo. IV Letters*, ii. 971, 973; Aberdeen Univ. Lib. Arbuthnot mss, Londonderry to Wellington [9 Dec.] 1821; Sack, *Grenvillites*, 189, 190. [36] Add. 38290, ff. 143-5, 155, 191-9, 210; Coedymaen mss 946; bdle. 21, Buckingham to Williams Wynn, 8, 30 Dec.; Buckingham, i. 241-3, 247-54; Harrowby mss, Bathurst to Harrowby, 12 Dec. 1821. [37] Add. 38290, ff. 210-16; NLW ms 2793 D, H. Williams Wynn to wife, 18 Dec. 1821. [38] Coedymaen mss 350-2; Add. 69044, Buckingham to Grenville, 30 Nov. [1821]. [39] Add. 38743, f. 77; Castlereagh mss P/194; Lonsdale mss, Long to Lonsdale, 21 Dec; Grey mss, Tierney to Grey, 30 Dec. 1821; Buckingham, i. 265. [40] Coedymaen mss 501. [41] *Southey Letters* ed. J.W. Warter, iii. 290. [42] Add. 38290, ff. 176, 222-4; Coedymaen mss 355, 610, 613-18; Buckingham, i. 262-4, 272-3, 275, 279, 281-2; Sack, *Grenvillites*, 192. [43] Grey mss, Tierney to Grey, 23 Jan.; Hatherton mss, R. Smith to Littleton, 29 Jan. 1822; Buckingham, i. 275-6, 281-2, 284-5; Sack, *Grenvillites*, 194. [44] Coedymaen mss 360. [45] *Shrewsbury Chron.* 22 Feb. 1822; Coedymaen mss 626. [46] Coedymaen mss 363, 621. [47] Flint RO, Leeswood mss D/LE/1352. [48] Fremantle mss 46/10/19. [49] *The Times*, 15 Mar. 1822. [50] Gurney diary, 14 Mar. 1822. [51] Coedymaen mss 370, 624. [52] *Arbuthnot Jnl.* i. 162; Whittle, 82; Coedymaen mss 373, 632, 642; *CJ*, lxxvii. 273; Leeswood mss 1352; NLW ms 2794 D, Sir W. to H. Williams Wynn, 14, 15 May 1822; Coedymaen mss 46/12/77. [53] Add. 40373, f. 196; Fremantle mss 46/12/77, 78. [54] Add. 37298, f. 342; 51586, Tierney to Lady Holland, 15/16 Apr.; Buckingham, i. 304, 306, 309-10, 313-19, 323; Fremantle mss 46/10/20, 25, 29, 56; Coedymaen mss 368-8, 630-3, 640; bdle. 17, Plunket to Williams Wynn, 5 Feb., 6 Apr.; *The Times*, 11 May; Phillimore mss, Buckingham to Phillimore [12 May 1822]. [55] Coedymaen mss 364, 625, 629, 637, 640; Add. 37398, f. 342; Buckingham, i. 273-5. [56] *CJ*, lxxvii. 327, 347, 352. [57] Buckingham, i. 350-1, 354-6. [58] Add. 40319, f. 57. [59] Coedymaen mss 185, 647, 1021; Buckingham, i. 369-72, 375, 379, 380; Fremantle mss 46/11/64; 46/12/76; 51/5/16; Add. 51586, Tierney to Lady Holland [4 Sept.] 1822. [60] Buckingham, i. 381; Add. 38743, f. 215. [61] Powis mss (History

of Parliament Aspinall transcripts), Palmerston to Lord Clive, 13 Sept.; Harewood mss WYL 250/8/83, Liverpool to Canning, 15 Sept.; Grey mss, Ellice to Grey, 24 Sept. 1822; Add. 38732, f. 211; Coedymaen mss 187, 377. [62] Fremantle mss 46/10/43/1. [63] TNA 30/29/9/5/16; Add. 38743, ff. 217, 227, 236; 51578, Morpeth to Holland, 2 Oct.; Add. 69044, Grenville to Buckingham, 1, 3 Oct.; Harewood mss 8/83, Williams Wynn to Canning, 5 Oct., reply, 6 Oct.; Fremantle mss 46/12/72, 73; Lonsdale mss, Lowther to Lonsdale, 11 Oct. 1822; Coedymaen mss 188. [64] Buckingham, i. 390-3; Fremantle mss 46/11/66; Coedymaen mss 378, 379, 653. [65] Add. 60286, f. 283. [66] Add. 40352, ff. 27-28. [67] Buckingham, i. 408, 411-12, 417-19; *Greville Mems.* i. 136; Add. 38193, f. 171; 38291, f. 270; NLW ms 2794 D, Buckingham to H. Williams Wynn, 5 Jan., Sir W. Williams Wynn to same, 12 Jan. 1823. [68] Coedymaen mss 385. [69] Buckingham, i. 406-7, 409-10. [70] Coedymaen mss 384; bdle. 17, Williams Wynn to Plunket, 4 Dec., replies, 29 Dec. 1822, 28 Jan. 1823. [71] Add 40358, f. 229. [72] Buckingham, i. 427-44, 446-50; Fremantle mss 46/11/84/3. [73] Buckingham, i. 454-7; Add. 40355, ff. 307-12; *The Times*, 23 Apr. 1823, N. Gash, *Secretary Peel*, 401. [74] Wellington mss WP1/7623/13. [75] Ibid. WP1/7623/24. [76] Buckingham, i. 458. [77] Fremantle mss 51/5/17; Wellington mss WP1/760/11; Buckingham, i. 452-5, 466-7, 473, 477. [78] Buckingham, i. 474. [79] Wellington mss WP1/760/2, 8; 762/18; 769/8; 770/8. [80] NLW ms 4815 D, Williams Wynn to Southey, 25 July 1823. [81] Buckingham, i. 477-8. [82] Fremantle mss 46/11/84/3. [83] Buckingham, i. 491; Coedymaen mss 1022. [84] Fremantle mss 51/5/19; Wellington mss WP1/771/8, 15; 773/6; 774/2. [85] Buckingham, i. 338-9, 458, 474, 494; ii. 9-12, 18; Harewood mss 8/83, Canning to Williams Wynn, 1, 7 Apr., reply, 7 Apr. 1823. [86] Buckingham, ii. 11-23, 32, 36-39, 46-47, 55, 56; Coedymaen mss bdle. 17, Williams Wynn to Plunket, 1 Nov., replies, 18 Nov., 28 Jan.; *The Times*, 7 Feb. 1824. [87] Buckingham, ii. 49. [88] Ibid. ii. 35-36, 85-86. [89] *CJ*, lxxix. 520, 536. [90] W. Hinde, *Canning*, 361-2; Buckingham, ii. 361-2; Whittle, 64-67. [91] Wellington mss WP1/790/32. [92] Buckingham, ii. 85. [93] Ibid. ii. 69-71, 80-81, 86. [94] Ibid. ii. 85-86, 91, 106. [95] Wellington mss WP1/790/1; Buckingham, ii. 207, 210, 214. [96] TNA 30/29/6/7/53. [97] Fremantle mss 46/11/106/2. [98] Buckingham, ii. 112, 114-15, 120, 121, 145, 147, 161-2, 169-71; Add. 38411, ff. 238-40, 247; 40371, ff. 245, 269; 40372, f. 77; Wellington mss WP1/799/7; 805/5, 14, 20-25; 806/23, 29, 31, 34, 35; 807/22, 24; 810/5; 812/18; 815/6, 16, 21; Fremantle mss 46/11/111/3. [99] Fremantle mss 46/11/111/3; Buckingham, ii. 164-5, 197. [100] Buckingham. ii. 228-32. [101] Ibid. ii. 232-3. [102] *CJ*, lxxx. 626. [103] Buckingham, ii. 164-6, 171. [104] NLW, Harpton Court mss C/589; Coedymaen mss 410, 414; Buckingham, ii. 200-3, 205-6, 215. [105] Buckingham, ii. 211. [106] Ibid. ii. 240, 242-3; Coedymaen mss bdle. 18, Fremantle to Williams Wynn [1825]; N. Gash, *Secretary Peel*, 417. [107] Fremantle mss 46/11/116, 117; 138/16/18; Coedymaen mss 416, 418, 420, 994-1001; bdle. 18, Fremantle to Williams Wynn, 28 Aug. 1825; Buckingham, ii. 241-2, 244-7, 257-63, 265; G.I.T. Machin, *Catholic Question in English Politics*, 68. [108] *CJ*, lxxx. 536-7, 582, 600, 602, 606-7, 612; lxxxi. 16, 44, 76, 82, 88. [109] Add. 38412, ff. 14-17; Buckingham, ii. 272, 274-5. [110] Add. 38576, f. 72; Fremantle mss 46/12/64; Coedymaen mss 947; Buckingham, ii. 276-81. [111] Phillimore mss, Fremantle to Phillimore, 5 Oct.; Add. 38412, ff. 24-27, 59-60; Wellington mss WP1/829/5, 6, 8, 16; 830/10-14, 18; 831/2, 9, 13, 22; 832/3; 833/5, 15; Fremantle mss 138/12/9b. [112] Add. 38412, ff. 47-52; 51679, Lord J. Russell to Lady Holland, 11 Oct. 1825; Fremantle mss 46/12/60-63; Coedymaen mss 948-51; Wellington mss WP1/832/4. [113] Add. 38412, ff. 74-81; Fremantle mss 46/12/47. [114] Add. 38412, ff. 95-96; Wellington mss WP1/829/16; 831/3; 831/7/21; 832/16; Coedymaen mss 952-5; Buckingham, ii. 283-4. [115] Fremantle mss 46/12/48, 55, 56. [116] Coedymaen mss 957-61, 969; bdle. 18, Fremantle to Williams Wynn, 2 Dec. 1825; Add. 40331, f. 243; Buckingham, ii. 288. [117] Coedymaen mss 964, 967, 968; Fremantle mss 46/11/128; 46/12/46-56, 65; 138/12/2, 3; Add. 38576, f. 95; Wellington mss WP1/834/13, 850/2. [118] NLW ms 2795 D, Lady Williams Wynn to H. Williams Wynn, 28 Mar. 1826. [119] *CJ*, lxxxi. 92, 130, 183, 189, 219, 225, 324, 376. [120] Fremantle mss 51/8/1; *CJ*, lxxxi. 292, 376. [121] *CJ*, lxxxi. 346; NLW ms 10804 D, letterbk. 3, Williams Wynn to Amherst,

29 May 1826. [122] Fremantle mss 46/11/135, 136; 46/12/82-85, 90, 92; 51/5/25; 138/16/15a; Buckingham, ii. 300-1. [123] NLW ms 10804 D, letterbk. 2, Williams Wynn to Buckingham, 24 June 1826. [124] Coedymaen mss 997, 1002, 1004; Add. 38748, ff. 163-7, 171-81; 40387, f. 290, 292; 40388, ff. 48, 51, 77; Wellington mss WP1/858/27; 859/6, 17; 860/12; 861/4, 6; 866/4; NLW ms 2797 D, Lady Williams Wynn to H. Williams Wynn, 19 Sept. 1826. [125] Harewood mss 8/87, Canning to Warrender, 13 Nov.; Fremantle mss 46/11/168, 149; Fremantle mss 49/1/24; Coedymaen mss bdle. 18, Williams Wynn to Fremantle, 21 Nov. 1826. [126] Grey mss, Howick to Grey, 2 Mar. 1827. [127] Fremantle mss 46/11/152; Add. 40391, f. 312; Wellington mss WP1/897/9, 11, 13, 20; 880/3; 881/5; 882/5, 11; 885/21; 886/16. [128] NLW ms 10804 D, letterbk. 3, Williams Wynn to Amherst, 23 Mar. 1827. [129] Wellington mss WP1/883/4; 886/12; 887/3, 4, 6, 9; Canning's Ministry, 15, 92, 93, 106, 122-3; Fremantle mss 46/11/153; 46/12/100-4; 138/21/1/8, 9; Sack, Grenvillites, 210-12. [130] Wellington mss WP1/888/1. [131] Ibid. WP1/888/2. [132] Coedymaen mss 190-7; Greville Mems. i. 172; Sack, Grenvillites, 210. [133] Creevey Pprs. ii. 113; Canning's Ministry, 91, 94, 98, 102, 124, 269. [134] Coedymaen mss 191. [135] Canning's Ministry, 246; NLW ms 4817 D, Williams Wynn to H. Williams Wynn, 4 May 1827; Hatherton diary, 19 Aug. 1831. [136] NLW ms 2795 D, Lady Williams Wynn to Mrs. H. Williams Wynn, 30 Apr., F. to H. Williams Wynn, 25 May, Charlotte Shipley to same, 5 Oct. 1827. [137] Coedymaen mss 192; Wellington mss WP1/889/7, 10; 890/4, 8; NLW ms 2795 D, Brook Taylor to H. Williams Wynn, 23 Mar., 24 Apr., Buckingham to same, 13 Apr. 1827. [138] CJ, lxxxii. 502, 587. [139] Geo. IV Letters, iii. 1337. [140] Coedymaen mss 436. [141] Ibid. 198-204, 437, 712, 715, 716, 719-22, 729, 730, 1023; Lonsdale mss, Croker to Lowther, 11 Aug. 1827; Greville Mems. i. 184; NLW, Harpton Court mss C/621; Add. 38750, f. 126; 40340, f. 200; 40394, f. 210; Buckingham, ii. 260-1. [142] Coedymaen mss 970. [143] NLW ms 2803 D, H. Williams Wynn to Williams Wynn, 30 Oct. 1827. [144] Wellington mss WP1/899/2; 901/3, 6, 13; 903/14; 908/8. [145] Add. 38752, f. 169. [146] Coedymaen mss 252-5, 972; NLW ms 4817 D, Williams Wynn to H. Williams Wynn, 11 Jan. 1828; Wellington mss WP1/914/4; 915/36. [147] Coedymaen mss 973. [148] New Letters of Southey (1965) ed. K. Curry, ii. 325, 349-53; iv. 132. [149] Phillimore mss, Fremantle to Phillimore, 22 Jan. 1828. [150] NLW ms 4815 D, Williams Wynn to Southey, 9 Feb. 1828. [151] Add. 38754, f. 240; 40395, f. 275; Wellington mss WP1/914/48; 915/36, 65; 917/6, 13; 918/7, 17; 919/9; 920/31, 32, 36, 65, 79; NLW ms 4817 D, Williams Wynn to H. Williams Wynn, 15, 18, 22 Jan.; Devon RO, Sidmouth mss, H.U. Addington to Sidmouth, 23 Jan. 1828; Coedymaen mss 488; Geo IV Letters, iii. 1466, 1498, 1499, 1506, 1507, 1509. [152] NLW ms 4817 D, Williams Wynn to H. Williams Wynn, 18, 25 Jan., 12 Feb. 1828; Buckingham, ii. 369-70. [153] Southampton Univ. Lib. Broadlands mss BR23AA/5/1. [154] NLW ms 4817 D, Williams Wynn to H. Williams Wynn, 25 Jan., 1, 29 Feb., 14 Mar. 1828. [155] Coedymaen mss 737; NLW ms 4817 D, Williams Wynn to H. Williams Wynn, 1 Feb., 4 July; NLW ms 2795 D, F. Williams Wynn to same, 7 Feb., Lady Williams Wynn to same, 25 Feb.; NLW ms 2796 D, same to same 18 July 1828. [156] NLW ms 2796 D, Lady Williams Wynn to H. Williams Wynn, 19 Feb. 1828. [157] Fremantle mss 51/5/35; Buckingham, ii. 362. [158] NLW ms 2796 D, Lady Delamere to H. Williams Wynn, 3 May 1828. [159] NLW ms 10804 D, letterbk. 3, passim, esp. Williams Wynn to Malcolm, 14 Apr. 1828. [160] Derby mss 920 Der (14) 2/3, parl. proceedings, 19 May 1828. [161] Southey Letters, iv. 65, 85; CJ, lxxxiii. 375, 532. [162] NLW ms 10804 D, letterbk. 2, Williams Wynn to Buckingham, 7 May 1828. [163] NLW ms 2796 D, Sir W. to H. Williams Wynn, 21 July 1828; Coedymaen mss 205. [164] NLW ms 4817 D, Williams Wynn to H. Williams Wynn, 4 July, 17 Aug. 1828; Coedymaen mss 206. [165] Add. 51834; NLW ms 4817 D, Williams Wynn to H. Williams Wynn, 17, 19 Sept., 26 Oct., 2 Nov. 1828; Coedymaen mss 1003, 1005. [166] Coedymaen mss 207; Add. 51580, Carlisle to Lady Williams, 18 Jan. 1829. [167] PRO NI, Anglesey mss D619/32A/3/5; Coedymaen mss 1006; NLW ms 4817 D, Williams Wynn to H. Williams Wynn, 11 Jan., 3 Feb. 1829. [168] NLW ms 4817 D, Williams Wynn to H. Williams Wynn, 10, 11 Feb., 3, 17 Mar., 30 Apr.; Lonsdale mss, Lowther to Lonsdale, 16 Feb. 1829; Add. 40396, f. 55; 40399, ff. 66, 195. [169] NLW

ms 4817 D, Williams Wynn to H. Williams Wynn, 3 Apr.; NLW ms 10804 D, letterbk. 1, Williams Wynn to Whateley, 23 July 1829. [170] Coedymaen mss 1007. [171] NLW ms 10804 D, letterbk, iii, Williams Wynn to Malcolm, 16 June 1829. [172] NLW, Glansevern mss 905; Chester Courant, 26 May 1829. [173] Cambrian Quarterly Mag. i (1829), 260; Chester Courant, 7 Sept.; Shrewsbury Chron. 25 Sept. 1829; Glansevern mss 905; NLW, Garn mss (1956), J. Edwards to J.W. Griffith, 11 Sept., J. Copner Williams to same, 13 Sept. 1829. [174] Coedymaen mss 210-12, 974, 975. [175] NLW ms 10804 D, letterbk. i, Williams Wynn to Whateley, 29 July 1829; Coedymaen mss 212, 213, 976; NLW ms 4817 D, Williams Wynn to Southey, 8 Feb. 1830. [176] Coedymaen mss bdle. 29, Williams Wynn to Phillimore, 6 Feb. 1830. [177] Ibid. Williams Wynn to Phillimore [Apr.]; NLW ms 4815 D, same to Southey, 8 Feb. 1830; Wellington mss WP1/1166/8. [178] NLW ms 4817 D, Williams Wynn to Southey, 8 Feb. 1830. [179] N. Wales Chron. 4, 11, 18 Mar. 1830. [180] Geo IV. Letters, iii. 1579. [181] Wellington mss WP1/1104/10. [182] Coedymaen mss bdle. 29, Williams Wynn to Phillimore [Apr. 1830]. [183] Glansevern mss 8419. [184] Escott, 150-53. [185] Glansevern mss 1435, 8491. [186] Escott, 153-9; Brougham mss, same to Brougham, 24 Jan. 1832. [187] NLW ms 4817 D, Williams Wynn to H. Williams Wynn, 11 May, 25 June, 1, 9 July 1830. [188] NLW, Aston Hall mss C.599; Greville Mems. ii. 16. [189] St. Deiniol's Lib. Glynne-Gladstone mss 197, T. to J. Gladstone, 11 Feb. 1831. [190] NLW, Ormathwaite mss F/G/1/5, p. 133. [191] NLW ms 4815 D, Williams Wynn to Southey, 8 Feb. 1830; 4817 D, same to H. Williams Wynn, 19, 26 Nov. 1830; Brougham mss, same to Brougham, 25 Nov.; Coedymaen mss 258, 756; Harrowby mss, Sandon to Harrowby, 25 Nov.; Powis mss, Holmes to Powis [Nov]; Hatherton mss, Littleton to R. Wellesley, 26 Nov. 1830. [192] Grey mss, Grey to Williams Wynn 24 Nov., replies 24, 25 Nov.; Add. 51568, Anglesey to Holland [21 Nov.] 1830. [193] Coedymaen mss 978. [194] NLW ms 2803 D, H. Williams Wynn to Williams Wynn, 27 Nov. 1830. [195] Coedymaen mss 464, 756-8; Hatherton mss, Littleton to Grey and reply, 6 Dec. 1830; NLW ms 4817 D, Williams Wynn to H. Williams Wynn, 14 Jan., 4 Feb.; Brougham mss, Williams Wynn to Brougham, 22 Jan. 1831. [196] Hatherton mss, Palmerston to Littleton [Dec. 1830]. [197] NLW ms 4817 D, Williams Wynn to H. Williams Wynn, 4 Feb. 1831. [198] Coedymaen mss 758-8; Glansevern mss 3798; NLW ms 4817 D, Williams Wynn to H. Williams Wynn, 21 Dec.; Shrewsbury Chron. 17 Dec. 1830. [199] Add. 56555, f. 77; TNA 30/12/7/6. [200] NLW ms 2797 D, Lady Delamere to H. Williams Wynn [23 Jan.], Lady Harriet to F. Williams Wynn, 11 Feb.; 4817 D, Williams Wynn to H. Williams Wynn, 11, 14 Jan., 22 Feb. 1831. [201] NLW ms 4817 D, Williams Wynn to H. Williams Wynn, 22 Feb. 1831. [202] Ibid. Williams Wynn to H. Williams Wynn, 4 Feb.; The Times, 17 Feb. 1831; Coedymaen mss 471, 472, 763. [203] Shrewsbury Chron. 4 Mar. 1831. [204] Brougham mss, Williams Wynn to Brougham, 5 Mar. 1831. [205] NLW ms 4817 D, Williams Wynn to H. Williams Wynn, 5 Mar. 1831. [206] Salopian Jnl. 9 Mar.; Shrewsbury Chron. 11 Mar; Add. 51576, Fazakerley to Holland [4 Mar.]; Grey mss, Grey to Holland [c. 4 Mar. 1831]. [207] Coedymaen mss 473, 764, 1029; Grey mss, Holland to Grey, 5 Mar.; NLW ms 4817 D, Williams Wynn to H. Williams Wynn, 11 Mar. 1831; Greville Mems. ii. 125. [208] NLW ms 4815 D, Williams Wynn to Southey, 15 Mar.; 4817 D, same to H. Williams Wynn, 15 Mar. 1831. [209] Greville Mems. iii. 133. [210] Glansevern mss 2421. [211] Wellington mss WP1/1179/13; Coedymaen mss 473-5. [212] Coedymaen mss 765-9; NLW ms 4817 D, Williams Wynn to H. Williams Wynn, 25 Mar. 1831; Wellington mss WP1/1197/19; Fremantle mss 139/20/9. [213] Coedymaen mss 476, 477. [214] Ibid. 239, 240, 478, 479; Glynne-Gladstone mss 198, T. to J. Gladstone, 20 Apr.; Add. 51573, Rice to Holland [19 Apr.]; NLW ms 4817 D, Williams Wynn to H. Williams Wynn, 22 Apr.; Spectator, 23 Apr. 1831. [215] Glansevern mss 1099, 1103, 1407, 2423-7, 8279, 8452; Coedymaen mss 221, 239-51, 770, 979; NLW ms 4817 D, Williams Wynn to H. Williams Wynn, 15 Apr., 20 May; Shrewsbury Chron. 29 Apr., 6, 13 May; Salopian Jnl. 4, 11 May, 26 Oct, 9, 30 Nov.; The Times, 10 May; N. Wales Chron. 14 May; Chester Courant, 6 Dec.; NLW ms 2797 D, F. to H. Williams Wynn, 9 May 1831; B. Ellis, 'Parl. Rep. Mont. 1728-1868', Mont. Colls. lxiii (1973) 79-84. [216] Keele Univ. Lib. Sneyd mss SC17/58;

Wellington mss WP1/1186/21. [217] Wilts. RO, Pembroke mss 2057/85/15; Coedymaen mss 481; Grey mss, Taylor to Grey, 7 July 1831. [218] Coedymaen mss 772. [219] Lonsdale mss, Croker to Lowther, 11 July; Hatherton diary, 13 July 1831. [220] Hatherton diary, 24 July 1831. [221] Coedymaen mss 214. [222] Ibid. 215; NLW ms 4817 D, Williams Wynn to H. Williams Wynn, 5 Aug. 1831. [223] Coedymaen mss 217. [224] Ibid. [225] Ibid. 218. [226] Ibid. 220. [227] Ibid. 221; NLW ms 4815 D, Williams Wynn to Southey [Sept. 1831]. [228] Coedymaen mss 218. [229] Ibid. 217. [230] NLW, Harpton Court mss C/590; Coedymaen mss 219, 1014-20. [231] NLW ms 4815 D, Williams Wynn to Southey, 27 Oct. 1831. [232] Coedymaen mss 222, 256; NLW ms 4817 D, Williams Wynn to H. Williams Wynn, 9, 18, Oct., 2 Nov. 1831. [233] Coedymaen mss 223; bdle. 19, Clive to Williams Wynn, 9 Dec. 1831. [234] Coedymaen mss 223. [235] Ibid. 224; bdle. 19, Clive to Williams Wynn, 23 Dec.; Powis mss, Williams Wynn to Clive, 20 Dec. 1831. [236] Coedymaen mss 224. [237] Powis mss, Williams Wynn to Clive, 25 Dec. 1831; Coedymaen mss 226. [238] PP (1831-2), xli. 131, 133, 145; (1838), xxxv. 255-65, 307-20, 361-7; UCNW, Mostyn of Mostyn mss 265, E.M.Ll. Mostyn to fa. 9, 28 Mar. [1832]. [239] Wellington mss WP1/1224/2, 3; Coedymaen mss 795. [240] NLW ms 4815 D, Williams Wynn to Southey, 17 Mar.; Glynne-Gladstone mss 199, T. to J. Gladstone, 19/20 Apr. 1832; Coedymaen mss 227. [241] NLW ms 2797 D, Sir W. to H. Williams Wynn, 18 May 1832. [242] Coedymaen mss 216. [243] NLW ms 4815 D, Williams Wynn to Southey, 31 Jan. 1832. [244] Ibid. D, Williams Wynn to Southey, 31 Jan., 17 Mar. 1832. [245] NLW ms 4817 D, Williams Wynn to H. Williams Wynn, 15 Sept. 1830; 4815 D, same to Southey, 17 Mar.; 2797 D, F. to H. Williams Wynn, 17 Apr., 10 July, 5 Oct., 7 Nov.; Sir W. to same, 10 July 1832. [246] NLW ms 2797 D, F. to H. Williams Wynn, 15 June, 7 Nov., Sir W. to same, 21 Nov.; 4815 D, Williams Wynn to Southey, 24 Apr. 1832; Salop Archives, Aston mss 1093/248-9; Coedymaen mss 230. [247] Add. 40403, ff. 85, 105-9; Wellington mss WP1/1236/16; Add. 61937, Littleton to Fazakerley, 2 Nov. 1832; Coedymaen mss 231-3. [248] Mostyn of Mostyn mss 8422; Coedymaen mss 234-6; bdle. 28, Buckingham to Williams Wynn, 22, 27 Dec.; bdle. 29, Williams Wynn to Phillimore, 28 Nov., [Dec]; NLW ms 4817 D, Williams Wynn to H. Williams Wynn, 23 Dec. 1832. [249] N. Wales Chron. 1 Jan. 1833; Coedymaen mss bdle. 29, Williams Wynn to Phillimore [Dec. 1832]. [250] Coedymaen mss 229; A.W. Williams Wynn, 87, 93-7. [251] A.W. Williams Wynn, 98-101. [252] PROB 8/243; 11/2120/713; 11/2128/185; Illustrated London News, 7 Sept. 1850.

M.M.E.

WILLIAMS WYNN, Sir Watkin, 5th bt. (1772–1840), of Wynnstay, Ruabon, Denb. and St. James's Square, Mdx.

BEAUMARIS	20 Oct. 1794–1796
DENBIGHSHIRE	1796–6 Jan. 1840

b. 26 Oct. 1772, 1st s. of Sir Watkin Williams Wynn, 4th bt.[†], of Wynnstay and 2nd w. Charlotte, da. of George Grenville[†]; bro. of Charles Watkin Williams Wynn* and Henry Watkin Williams Wynn[†]. educ. by Rev. Robert Nares; Westminster 1784-9; Christ Church, Oxf. 1789-90; European tour (Brussels to St. Petersburg) 1792. m. 4 Feb. 1817, Lady Henrietta Antonia Clive, da. of Edward Clive[†], 1st earl of Powis, 2s. 1da. suc. fa. as 5th bt. 29 July 1789. d. 6 Jan. 1840.
   Ld. lt. Merion. 1793-d., Denb. 1795-d.
   Steward, Cyfeiliog 1794-d., Bromfield and Yale 1796-d.; mayor, Oswestry 1800, 1831, Chester 1813.

Col. Ancient British Drag. 1794-1800; col. Denbigh militia 1797; lt.-col. commdt. 3rd batt. militia for service in France Mar.-June 1814; col. commdt. Denbigh yeoman cav. 1820; a.d.c. Welsh militia 1830-d.
   Pres. Soc. of Ancient Britons.
   Member, bd. of agriculture 1796.

The Grenville connection, succession to Wynnstay, whose estates and influence ranged over seven counties in North Wales and the Marches, and the excesses of his youth had made Williams Wynn 'a person of great weight in every sense of the word'. Called 'the prince of Wales', he presided over the Society of Ancient Britons, chaired the Honourable Society of Cymmrodorion on its revival in 1820, patronized London's Welsh charity school and eisteddfodau, and was expected, like his grandfather, to make his town house in St. James's Square the focus of the Welsh elite in London, as Wynnstay remained in North Wales. His marriage alliance with the Clives of Powis Castle, who supported Lord Liverpool's administration, worked to his financial and electoral advantage, and has been noted as a step towards the subsequent Grenvillite rapprochement with government.[1] Williams Wynn had joined Brooks's and entered Parliament at the first available opportunity, but, in contrast to his brother Charles, his Member for Montgomeryshire, who led the Grenvillite third party in the Commons, Sir Watkin 'stood outside the political whirligig'.[2] An erratic attender committed to supporting Catholic relief, he had rarely voted against his brother, but only occasionally with him and had latterly confined his votes and remarks to agricultural and militia matters. On these, being an improving landlord, fond of country sports and military exercises, he was well able to comment, though hampered by the much-lampooned impediment of an overlarge tongue.[3] Fearing unrest and radical reform after Peterloo, he had summoned the Denbighshire lieutenancy and donated £300 to augment the yeomanry.[4] He officiated at the proclamation of George IV in Montgomeryshire and Denbighshire, where his canvassing addresses and speeches made no mention of politics and his return at the 1820 general election cost him £1,171 11s. 10d.[5] He proposed the unsuccessful candidate, his kinsman by marriage Paul Beilby Lawley (afterwards Thompson*), at Wenlock.[6]

In the House, where he sat under the gallery, Williams Wynn divided against government on the appointment of an additional Scottish exchequer baron, 15 May, and the barrack bill, 17 July 1820. He was named to the select committee on agricultural distress, 31 May, and informed it, as a witness, that the Wrexham corn returns were unreliable because most corn was sold by sample, 26 June.[7] As a member of the 1817 select committee, he had been in favour of abolishing the Welsh courts of great sessions and barring Welsh judges from sitting in Parliament and practising as barristers, and he was appointed to the 1820 and 1821 select committees which considered their report. A swollen knee kept him away from the yeomanry training in October 1820, but he recovered to entertain the home office under-secretary Henry Clive* at Wynnstay, where there was great rejoicing in November at the baptism of his heir. He marked the occasion by renouncing claims to rent arrears from his poorer tenants.[8] Charles Williams Wynn's misgivings about the queen's case were well known, and Sir Watkin's apparent failure to vote on the matter or arrange a loyal address from Denbighshire caused comment.[9] He divided for Catholic relief, 28 Feb. 1821, 1 Mar., 21 Apr., 10 May 1825. He divided with opposition for repeal of the additional malt duty, 21 Mar., 3 Apr. 1821, and was expected to support Curwen's motion for repeal of the agricultural horse tax, 5 Apr., when his expressed regret that it was brought forward before the agriculture committee (to which he had been added, 9 Mar.) could report, caused the motion to be withdrawn. When it was reintroduced, 14 June, he decided to vote for it as a means 'of relieving the landed interest', but *The Times* reporter could barely catch what he said.[10] He voted to make forgery a non-capital offence, 23 May 1821. His friends were 'very glad' to see him refurbishing Wynnstay in anticipation of a royal visit in late 1821; but according to Thomas Creevey*, he decided against receiving the royal party, when they returned prematurely from Ireland in September following the queen's death, because his wife disapproved of the king's 'ladies'.[11] Negotiations prior to the Grenvillite accession to administration in January 1822 brought the usual rumours that Sir Watkin would be made a peer. Charles became president of the India board with a seat in the cabinet and their brother Henry accepted diplomatic missions to Berne and Stuttgart.[12]

Sir Watkin's request that his wife be privileged to ride in her carriage through Hyde Park before and after her confinement in April 1822 was immediately granted.[13] He divided with government against abolition of one of the joint-postmasterships, 13 Mar. Slow to grasp that the inquiry that opposition sought into the duties of India board commissioners was intended as an attack on the Grenvillites for defecting to government, he entertained colleagues with cries of 'Hear, Hear' when his father was referred to, 14 Mar.[14] According to Sir James Mackintosh's* diary,

'Sir W. Wynn seemed for a moment to be mad. His explosion was perfect frenzy. But he soon subsided into his natural state and nodded for an hour in spite of the splendour of Canning's speech' in defence of Charles.[15] As a member (since 27 Feb.) of the select committee, he spoke authoritatively on agriculture and distress, favouring reductions in interest rates, a mortgage transfer tax, 1 Apr., and protective duties on grain, 6, 8, 13 May. He also confirmed on 13 May his opposition to taxes on salt, soap, candles and hides, whose repeal Charles still sought but voted against because of the constraints of office.[16] He forwarded detailed reports to Henry of the opposition motions criticizing the cost of his diplomatic post, 15, 16 May.[17] He divided with government against inquiring into the lord advocate's treatment of the Scottish press, 25 June, but said he would vote against spending government money on a public monument to commemorate the king's visit to Scotland, 15 July 1822.[18]

Liverpool's new Welsh church and the Denbigh dispensary benefited from Wynnstay's generosity and there was a 'grand christening for Herbert Watkin on Saturday [8 June 1822] and the house [Wynnstay] was as much admired as in its first days'.[19] However, Sir Watkin had serious financial problems and there was trouble at Wenlock, where he had negotiated a new arrangement with his co-patron, Lord Forester, with a view to returning Beilby Thompson at the next election.[20] He decided to take his family abroad to cut costs, but his mother complained: 'He has no intention of stopping up any one of his ruinous drains of stables, garden or farm. At least not one of the blood suckers who belong to each of those departments are I believe to be parted with'.[21] The Williams Wynns spent August on the Rhine, reached Milan and Verona in November, celebrated Christmas and new year in Rome, and planned a spring tour to Switzerland unless 'the Catholic question or any other may oblige me to be in town directly after Easter'.[22] His next reported vote was against inquiry into chancery delays, 5 June 1823.[23] Finding that Forester had 'endeavoured to fly off from the engagement', he went to Wenlock for the corporation elections that Michaelmas, accompanied by Charles and his brothers-in-law, the Clives, the guarantors of the agreement, and was 'conceded every material point'.[24] He wintered on the continent, returning 'to make a very quiet London season'.[25] He divided against producing papers on Catholic office-holders, 21 Feb. 1824. He presented Denbighshire petitions against the beer bill, 13 May, and the treatment in Demerara of the Methodist missionary John Smith, 10 June 1824.[26] Speculation, fuelled by his absences, had encouraged rival interests in

Denbighshire, and to counter them he made his birthday that October a great occasion, with dinner for 104 at Wynnstay, despite his continued need to economize. His mother still hoped he would 'give up the very uncreditable and still more unprofitable farce of sending horses all round the country to be beaten by every hack' and noted that he preferred to 'cut the 1st of March [St. David's Day celebrations in London] (*malgré* Charles's earnest remonstrances)' and to remain at Wynnstay 'until Easter, which certainly on many accounts I cannot help thinking far more eligible for him than opening his London and Boodle's campaign'.[27] He divided for the Irish unlawful societies bill, 25 Feb. 1825. Presenting Wrexham's anti-Catholic petition, 26 Apr., he dissented from its prayer and called for the issue to be settled quickly 'lest ... the country ... be placed in the painful and dangerous situation of finding the sovereign directly opposed to the two Houses of Parliament on one of the most important questions that could agitate the public mind'. He chaired the Cymmrodorion's May eisteddfod, attended to enclosure, estate and public business in Denbighshire, Merioneth and Montgomeryshire, and, possibly encouraged by Charles, who had virtually destroyed what remained of their party by refusing to resign over his failure to have their cousin the duke of Buckingham, the leader of their party in the Lords, sent to India as governor-general, he oversaw the refurbishment of his London mansion, where in April 1826 a 'grand assembly' was held for over 300 '*haut de ton*'.[28] He divided with administration against condemning the Jamaican slave trials, 2 Mar. 1826. He welcomed the proposal to release bonded corn, 5 May, and though initially opposed to the corn importation bill, he recognized its merits as a means of alleviating distress and decided to reserve his criticism until its committee stage, 11 May. His comments on the proposed resolutions governing consideration of private bills could not be reported, 20 Apr.[29] Interest focused on the bitter and costly contest for Denbigh Boroughs at the general election in June 1826, when the county returned him unopposed at a cost of £134 1s. 2d.[30] He regained a seat at Wenlock for Wynnstay, but was threatened with firecrackers in Chester, where he voted for the Grosvenors.[31]

Williams Wynn suffered severely from erysipelas and hearing problems in the winter of 1826-7.[32] He divided for Catholic relief, 6 Mar. During the ministerial uncertainty that followed Lord Liverpool's stroke, he declared for Canning's corn resolutions, 2 Apr., and, stressing that he 'belonged to neither party', he refuted the anti-Catholic protectionist Gooch's allegations that the corn bill had been 'proposed by ministers

and carried by their friends aided by the votes of opposition'. During the short-lived Canning and Goderich ministries, which Charles adhered to, he made a 'few remarks' on church briefs, 7 June, and presented petitions from North Wales for repeal of the Test Acts, 15, 21 June 1827.[33] He did so again, 25 Feb., and voted for their repeal, 26 Feb. 1828, although the duke of Wellington's new administration then opposed it. Of this and the ministry, from which Charles had been excluded, he wrote to Henry, 18 Mar.:

> I believe the repeal of the Test and Corporation Acts will pass; but that a declaration that nothing shall be done to the detriment of the established church will be substituted for the sacramental test upon entering into corporations. The government jog on quietly and I believe will stand. People like a prime minister instead of a government of departments which has been more or less the case ever since Lord Grenville.[34]

He had predicted and regretted ministerial differences over free trade, and expected government to encounter 'a good deal of trouble ... on the corn question' following publication of Huskisson's letter to his Liverpool constituents. He wrote: 'As I dread the *Lords upon the Catholic question*, I have full confidence in their protection on corn'.[35] Charles being out of office, Sir Watkin was prevailed on to preside over St. David's Day celebrations, of which he wrote:

> I may meet a parcel of Welsh shopkeepers in London on the 1st, but it is three or four years since I have attended and Charles makes such bother about it, I suppose partly from the hope of getting a stray vote upon an important question in the ... Commons, where certainly the attendance is very slack at that time of year. In such case ... I think I must go up.[36]

He presented a petition for repeal of the malt duties from Wrexham, 5 Mar., but was ill with 'a slight attack of erysipelas' when the corn resolutions were announced.[37] From newspaper reports, he concluded that

> there is little change from the proposal of last year excepting that when corn is below 60s. the duty will not be so high as was formerly proposed and that when it is above that point it will be higher. I do not see any reason for this change, but do not think that it will be a sufficient cause for opposing the bill.[38]

He cast a minority vote to lower the corn pivot price from 64s. to 60s., 22 Apr., went afterwards to Audley End and Newmarket for the racing and returned to vote for Catholic relief, 12 May, on his way to 'Chester races and to fix the place for my lodge' at Wynnstay.[39] By 27 May he was back in London, whence, at Charles's request, he wrote to inform Henry of Forester's death, Lord Chandos's* denunciation of Canning and ministerial changes following the Huskissonite exodus.[40] He voted against the indefinite appointment of a registrar to the archbishop of Canterbury, 16 June. Before dividing against the additional churches bill, 30 June 1828, he explained that he did so because it had been introduced too late in the session, and that he would not necessarily take the same line in future. In August, when floods caused severe damage to the grounds at Wynnstay, he was at Glanllyn, his Merionethshire mansion on the shore of Bala Lake.[41] There was great concern about his health in the winter of 1828-9, following a feverish bilious complaint.[42]

Now rarely acting independently of Charles in the Commons, he divided for Catholic emancipation, 6, 30 Mar., as ministers had predicted, voting also to permit Daniel O'Connell to sit without swearing the oath of supremacy, 18 May, and against additional expenditure on the marble arch, 27 May. He endorsed his corps's petition against recent militia cuts, 23 Feb., and they continued to serve without government funding. He presided over the London eisteddfod in the Argyll Rooms, 6 Mar.[43] On 16 May 1829 he hosted a London meeting of Members and peers with Welsh interests that organized opposition to the law commissioners' controversial proposals to partition and amalgamate counties and reorganize assize districts when the Welsh judicature and courts of great sessions were abolished.[44] Their *pro-forma* petition, approving assimilation into the English assize system, but opposing county divisions and joining English and Welsh counties, was rejected when he proposed it to the Denbighshire grand jury in July; and he and Charles failed to carry it at a county meeting, 15 Sept.[45] He stayed away when Denbighshire adopted a petition against the administration of justice bill through which the proposals were enacted, 15 Apr. 1830. Presenting it, with another from Pembrokeshire, 27 Apr., he dissented from their prayer.[46] He declined attendance at the Denbighshire distress meeting of 2 Mar., and his comments on presenting their petition, 25 Mar., were not reported.[47] A 'Society for reducing the expenses attending the office of sheriff of Flint, Denbigh and Montgomery' was subsequently formed.[48] He voted to enfranchise Birmingham, Leeds and Manchester, 23 Feb., and to transfer East Retford's seats to Birmingham, 5 Mar. He cast a critical vote with the revived Whig opposition on the Terceira affair, 28 Apr., and divided for Jewish emancipation, 17 May, to abolish capital punishment for forgery offences, 24 May, 20 July, and to reform the divorce laws, 3 June 1830. William IV, on his accession, appointed him his

militia aide-de-camp in Wales. He hurried to counter opposition in Wenlock at the ensuing general election.[49] At his own return in Wrexham, he spoke of the 'welcome' slight improvement in the local economy, his support for repeal of the Test Acts, and Catholic relief, whose benefits he had witnessed during his visit to the marquess of Anglesey in Ireland in October 1829, and admitted that the administration of justice bill he had recently supported had been 'completed in a slovenly manner'.[50]

Ministers listed Sir Watkin, who remained on friendly terms with Buckingham, among their 'foes', and he divided against them when they were brought down on the civil list, 15 Nov. 1830, and welcomed Charles's appointment as secretary at war in the Grey ministry.[51] He presented Ruabon's petition against truck shops, 2 Dec., and slept through most of the proceedings the following week.[52] Little was reported of what he said publicly when he accompanied Charles to Machynlleth for his re-election and addressed the reformers in Welshpool, 13 Dec., but he convinced them that he was a defender of rotten boroughs and they encouraged the Denbighshire reformers to campaign against him.[53] When disturbances broke out in the North Wales coalfield later that month, he mobilized the yeomanry, sheltered agents targeted by the mob at Wynnstay, and negotiated an agreement between the employers and colliers, the 'more orderly' of whom he enlisted as special constables to apprehend the agitators.[54] Charles resigned over the reform bill, and Sir Watkin, who now stayed away from reform meetings, presented a favourable petition from Wrexham, whose enfranchisement he welcomed, 18 Mar., but neglected to present the Denbighshire petition. His vote for the bill at its second reading, 22 Mar., caused surprise.[55] He had become 'nearly totally deaf' and, according to his sister Fanny, 'so beautifully patient under the heavy visitation that he is quite an example to all around him'. Medical advice and cures sought in London and Brighton had little immediate effect, and at the general election in May he attributed his failure to realize that his vote on 19 Apr. for Gascoyne's amendment might wreck the bill to deafness.[56] Privately he wrote:

> The government plan of reform goes in my opinion too far, but it has been so received all over the country that I doubt its being *possible were it expedient* to resist it. Add to which those who like myself are for moderate reform are so disjointed and separated that I fear no moderate plan will be brought forward.[57]

Opponents stressed his failure to present the Denbighshire reform petition, and at Ruthin he was burnt in an effigy bearing the caption 'I am opposed to reform, to the king, and the people; I am a friend to borough mongers and a snug place for my brother Charles'. He had to canvass in person, and narrowly avoided a poll against John Madocks of Glan-y-wern by promising to pay greater heed to his constituents' wishes on reform.[58] Thomas Gladstone* observed: 'Sir Watkin has pledged himself to support the bill as the price of his seat! Poor man! He must indeed value being in Parliament. His brother will act very differently'.[59] His hearing had improved, and before dining his supporters at Ruthin, 14 May 1831, he accompanied Charles to Montgomeryshire, where he defeated the reformer Joseph Hayes Lyon of Vaynor Park.[60]

Presenting the Denbighshire reform petition, 22 June, he categorically denied that he was pledged to support the reintroduced reform bill, but to the king's surprise, and possibly heeding constituency interests, the Williams Wynns divided for its second reading, 6 July 1831.[61] In committee, and generally with Charles, he voted to make the 1831 census the criterion for English borough disfranchisements, 19 July, against taking both seats from Appleby, 19 July, Downton, 21 July, and St. Germans, 26 July, and one from Chippenham, 27 July, and Sudbury, 2 Aug. Despite Waithman's objections, ministers accepted his advice that Wrexham's franchise should be confined to the townships of Wrexham Abbot and Wrexham Regis, 10 Aug. He voted against preserving freemen's voting rights, 30 Aug., after pairing off for a week from the 17th.[62] He divided against the bill's passage, 21 Sept. On 3 Oct. he was granted a month's leave 'on the public service', during which he oversaw militia training, was installed as mayor of Oswestry, and celebrated his birthday with a grand dinner and ball at Wynnstay, 26 Oct.[63] Denbighshire had belatedly been promised a second county Member, Robert Myddelton Biddulph* had declared his candidature and Wynnstay's May election bills remained unpaid.[64] Williams Wynn presided with Charles at post-election dinners and balls in Montgomeryshire in November; but family celebrations at Wynnstay that Christmas were marred by Lady Harriet's illness, and Charles observed: 'His deafness is particularly unfortunate as nothing can be worse for her than any attempt to exert her voice so as to be heard by him'.[65] They had deliberately avoided voting on the revised reform bill at its second reading, 17 Dec., of which he wrote to Henry:

You will see the amendments in the reform bill of which as far as they go I approve. I had paired with Lord Grosvenor but have withdrawn it, not wishing to be treated as being opposed to the second reading of the bill though I may vote for amendments in the commit-

tee, which I fear will call me to town early in January, and I may perhaps vote against the third reading, though I fear that it is now too late, and that the wisest plan will be to submit quietly and hope and endeavour to stop it here and not to let it be a stepping stone for further changes or reformations as they may be called. I was surprised at Chandos's speech, which is much more temperate and sensible than I should have expected from him.[66]

He voted against enfranchising Tower Hamlets, 28 Feb., and the third reading, 22 Mar. 1832. He paired against government on the Russian-Dutch loan, 12 July 1832. He thought the reform bill had brought Charles politically closer to Buckingham.[67]

At the general election in December 1832, he gave his interest at Wenlock to Charles's son-in-law John Milnes Gaskell[†], was annoyed by his co-patron Lord Clive's tardy announcement of a candidate for Montgomery Boroughs, and was sorry to see the Conservatives John Cotes[†] and William Ormsby Gore* contesting Shropshire North. He refused to endorse the Liberal Myddelton Biddulph or the Conservative Lloyd Kenyon* of Gredington for Denbighshire's second seat and topped the poll there, supported by all except 'a few who are either violent reformers or violent for the immediate abolition of slavery'.[68] At subsequent elections he endorsed Conservative candidates.[69] Though in declining health, his death at Wynnstay in January 1840, a few days after presiding at the quarter sessions, was unexpected; his heir Sir Watkin (1820-85), the 6th baronet, was still a minor.[70] His will gave his medical attendants 'full liberty to make any dissection and any preparation from my remains that they may wish', and was proved under £80,000 (adjusted to £41,489 9s.), and administered by Charles, whose £500 annuity was continued for life. His request for a private family funeral was overruled to safeguard Wynnstay's political interest at the ensuing by-election, when Denbighshire returned his Conservative nephew, Hugh Cholmondeley (1811-97), and his burial at Ruabon, 15 Jan. 1840, became a public pageant for the Wynnstay tenantry and inhabitants of the surrounding villages.[71]

[1] Denb. RO DD/WY/6580; *Chester Chron.* 28 July 1820; J.J. Sack, *Grenvillites*, 183. [2] *HP Commons, 1790-1820,* v. 594-6; *Williams Wynn Corresp.* 260. [3] T. Pritchard, 'Wynnstay', *Trans. Denb. Hist. Soc.* xxx (1981), 23-43. [4] *Chester Chron.* 29 Oct., 19 Nov., 24 Dec. 1819; *Cambrian,* 6 Nov. 1819, 22 Jan. 1820. [5] *Shrewsbury Chron.* 10 Feb., 24 Mar.; *Chester Chron.* 3 Mar.; *Salopian Jnl.* 8 Mar; *N. Wales Gazette,* 23 Mar. 1820; NLW, Wynnstay mss L/1323. [6] Salop Archives, Weld-Forester mss 1224, box 337, Procs. at Wenlock election. [7] *CJ,* lxxv. 331; *PP* (1820), ii. 160-1. [8] NLW, Coedymaen mss 592; NLW ms 2793 D, Lady Williams Wynn to H. Williams Wynn, 9 Oct.; *Chester Chron.* 3 Nov.; *Cambrian,* 4, 18 Nov. 1820. [9] NLW ms 2793 D, C. to H. Williams Wynn, 31 Aug.; *N. Wales Gazette,* 7

Dec. 1820. [10] *The Times*, 6 Apr., 15 June 1821; NLW ms 2793 D, H. Williams Wynn to wife, 21 May 1821. [11] NLW ms 2793 D, C. to H. Williams Wynn [12 June 1821]; *Heber Letters*, 288. [12] *Chester Chron.* 6 July 1821. [13] Add. 40245, ff. 209-11. [14] Bucks. RO, Fremantle mss D/FR/46/10/20. [15] Add. 52445, f. 66. [16] *The Times*, 7 May 1822. [17] NLW ms 2794 D, Sir W. to H. Williams Wynn, 14 May 1822. [18] *The Times*, 16 July 1822. [19] *Chester Courant*, 14 May; NLW ms 2794 D, Lady Williams Wynn to H. Williams Wynn, 11 June 1822. [20] J.D. Nichol, 'Wynnstay, Willey and Wenlock', *Trans. Salop Arch. Soc.* lviii (1965-8), 220-34. [21] NLW ms 2794 D, Lady Williams Wynn to H. Williams Wynn, 18 June, Sir W. to same, 28 June 1822. [22] Ibid., Lady Williams Wynn to H. Williams Wynn, 13 Aug., Sir W. to same, 7, 25 Nov., 24 Dec. 1822, 12 Jan. 1823. [23] *CJ*, lxxviii. 152, 334. [24] NLW ms 2794 D, Sir W. to H. Williams Wynn, 1 Oct. 1823; Weld-Forester mss, box 337, 'Wenlock Borough, 1822-3'. [25] NLW ms 2794 D, Mrs. H. to H. Williams Wynn, 18 May 1824. [26] *Chester Chron.* 7 May; *The Times*, 14 May, 11 June 1824. [27] NLW ms 2794 D, Lady Williams Wynn to H. Williams Wynn, 9, 27 Oct., 19 Dec., R. Smith to same, 15 Nov. 1824. [28] *The Times*, 23 May; *Chester Chron.* 25 Nov. 1825; Coedymaen mss 949, 965; *N. Wales Gazette*, 12 Jan., 23 Feb., 20 Apr. 1826. [29] *The Times*, 20 Apr. 1826. [30] *Chester Chron.* 9, 16, 23 June 1826; Wynnstay mss L/868. [31] See CHESTER and WENLOCK. [32] NLW ms 2795 D, F. to H. Williams Wynn, 3 Jan., Lady Delamere to same, 25 May 1827. [33] *The Times*, 8, 16, 22 June 1827. [34] NLW ms 2796 D, Sir W. to H. Williams Wynn, 18 Mar. 1828. [35] Ibid. Sir W. to H. Williams Wynn, 28 Jan. 1828. [36] *Shrewsbury Chron.* 7 Mar.; NLW ms 2796 D, Sir W. to H. Williams Wynn, 16 Jan. 1828. [37] NLW ms 2796 D, F. to H. Williams Wynn, 25 Mar. 1828. [38] Ibid. Sir W. to H. Williams Wynn, 1 Apr. 1828. [39] Ibid. same to same, 25 Apr. 1828. [40] Ibid. same to same, 27 May 1828. [41] Ibid. same to same, 10 Aug., Lady Williams Wynn to same, 17 Aug. 1828. [42] Coedymaen mss 207. [43] *Chester Courant*, 13 Jan., 3 Feb.; *Chester Chron.* 13 Feb.; *Shrewsbury Chron.* 6 Mar. 1829; Denb. RO DD/WY/6705; D.J.V. Jones, *Before Rebecca*, 183. [44] NLW, Glansevern mss 905; TNA HO43/37, pp. 258-9. [45] *Chester Courant*, 22 Sept.; *Shrewsbury Chron.* 25 Sept. 1829. [46] *Chester Courant*, 20 Apr.; *Salopian Jnl.* 21 Apr.; *Shrewsbury Chron.* 14 May 1830. [47] Coedymaen mss 213; *N. Wales Chron.* 11 Mar.; *Cambrian*, 12 Mar. 1830. [48] *Shrewsbury Chron.* 26 Feb. 1831. [49] NLW ms 2797 D, Lady Williams Wynn to H. Williams Wynn, 13 July 1830. [50] *Chester Chron.* 16 July, 13 Aug.; NLW ms 2797 D, Lady Williams Wynn to H. Williams Wynn, 17 Aug.; *Salopian Jnl.* 18 Aug. 1830. [51] NLW ms 2797 D, Sir W. to H. Williams Wynn, 5 Nov. 1830. [52] Hopetoun mss 167, f. 206. [53] *Shrewsbury Chron.* 17 Dec. 1830; NLW, Garn mss (1956), W. Owen to J.W. Griffith, 1 Jan. 1831. [54] Jones, 118-20, 183; *Salopian Jnl.* 5, 12 Jan. 2; *Shrewsbury Chron.* 7, 14, 21 Jan.; NLW ms 2797 D, Lady Delamere to H. Williams Wynn [23 Jan.], Lady Harriet to F. Williams Wynn, 1 Feb., C. Williams Wynn to Grenville, 21 Feb.; *Chester Courant*, 15 Mar. 1831; Coedymaen mss 763. [55] Coedymaen mss 764-9; *Chester Chron.* 25 Mar., 8, 22 Apr., 6, 13 May 1831. [56] NLW ms 2797 D, F. to H. Williams Wynn, 19 Mar., Sir W. to same, 11 Apr. 1831. [57] Ibid. Sir W. to H. Williams Wynn, 11 Apr. 1831. [58] *Chester Courant*, 22, 29 Mar., 4 Apr., 3, 10 May; *Chester Chron.* 25 Mar., 29 Apr., 6, 13 May; *Shrewsbury Chron.* 29 Apr., 6, 13 May; *Spectator*, 30 Apr., 7 May; *Morning Chron.* 3, 5 May; *Salopian Jnl.* 4 May; *Caernarvon Herald*, 7 May; *The Times*, 10 May; Garn mss (1956), J. Madocks to J.W. Griffith, 4, 7, 9 May; NLW ms 2797 D, F. to H. Williams Wynn, 9 May 1831; Wynnstay mss L/932-3; *Y Gwyliedydd*, viii (1831), 190-1. [59] St. Deiniol's Lib. Glynne Gladstone mss 198, T. to J. Gladstone, 8 May 1831. [60] *Salopian Jnl.* 18 May; *Shrewsbury Chron.* 19 May; *N. Wales Chron.* 24 May; NLW ms 2797 D, Lady Delamere to H. Williams Wynn, 20 May 1831. [61] Grey mss, Sir H. Taylor to Grey, 7 July 1831; Coedymaen mss 772. [62] Coedymaen mss 217. [63] *Chester Courant*, 11 Oct.; *Salopian Jnl.* 26 Oct. 1831; Coedymaen mss 221, 256. [64] Wynnstay mss L/934-6; *Caernarvon Herald*, 27 Sept. 1831. [65] *Chester Courant*, 2, 9, 30 Nov.; *Salopian Jnl.* 6 Dec. 1831; Coedymaen mss 222, 225. [66] NLW ms 2797 D, Sir W. to H. Williams Wynn, 18 Dec. 1831. [67] Glynne-Gladstone

mss GG37, S. to Mary Glynne 4 Apr.; NLW ms 2797 D, Sir W. to H. Williams Wynn, 18 May 1832. [68] NLW ms 2797D, same to same, 15 Jan., 10 July, 7, 21 Nov.; Coedymaen mss 231, 234; bdle. 28, C.W. Williams Wynn to Phillimore, 28 Nov., Dec. 1832; Wynnstay mss L/889, 936-45, 957, 965-70, 975, 1040; *Chester Chron.* 17 Aug., 26 Oct., 28 Dec.; *Salopian Jnl.* 7 Nov. 5, 26 Dec. 1832. [69] UCNW, Mostyn of Mostyn mss 7882; *Caernarvon Herald*, 3 Jan. 1835; F. Price Jones, 'Politics in 19th Cent. Denb.' *Trans. Denb. Hist. Soc.* x (1961), 183-90. [70] Add. 40404, f. 62; Broughton, *Recollections*, v. 118; *Chester Chron.* 10 Jan. 1840. [71] PROB 11/1926/297; IR26/1566/220; Denb. RO DD/WY/6662; *Chester Chron.* 17 Jan.; *The Times*, 27 Jan. 1840; *Ann. Reg.* (1840), Chron. p. 149.

M.M.E.

WILLOUGHBY, Henry (1780–1849), of Birdsall and Settrington, nr. Malton, Yorks.

NEWARK 8 Feb. 1805–29 Jan. 1831

b. 15 Dec. 1780, 3rd but o. surv. s. of Rev. James Willoughby, rect. of Guiseley, and Eleanor, da. and coh. of James Hobson of Kirby Moorside. *educ.* Rugby 1795; Christ's, Camb. 1799; L. Inn 1802, called 1808. *m.* 20 June 1815, Charlotte, da. of the Ven. John Eyre, adn. of Nottingham, 4s. (1 *d.v.p.*) 3da. (1 *d.v.p.*). *suc.* fa. 1816. *d.* 20 Nov. 1849.

Capt. York vol. inf. 1803; capt.-lt. N. regt. W. Riding yeoman cav. 1810, capt. 1814; capt. commdt. Wollaton vols. 1817; lt.-col. S. Notts. yeoman cav. 1826-35.

Willoughby's re-election for Newark on the interest of his cousin the 6th Baron Middleton in 1820 was uncontested. He continued to support the Liverpool ministry when present, but he was a very lax attender.[1] He was given leave of absence on account of ill health, 23 June 1820 and 18 Feb. 1825. He divided against more extensive tax reductions, 11, 21 Feb., and abolition of one of the joint-postmasterships, 13 Mar. 1822. He voted against relieving Catholic peers of their disabilities, 30 Apr. 1822, and against Catholic claims, 1 Mar., 21 Apr., 10 May 1825. He chaired the Nottingham Pitt Club dinner in May 1822.[2] He voted against repeal of the Foreign Enlistment Act, 16 Apr.,[3] and inquiry into the prosecution of the Dublin Orange rioters, 22 Apr. 1823. He presented Newark corporation's anti-slavery petition, 27 Feb. 1826. He topped the poll there at the general election in June. He presented a constituency petition against Catholic relief, 5 Mar. 1827, and voted thus the following day. He took three weeks' leave on account of a family illness, 23 Mar., and was again granted leave, having served on an election committee, 14 May 1827. He voted against repeal of the Test Acts, 26 Feb., and Catholic relief, 12 May 1828. In the debate on corruption at East Retford, 6 Mar., he endorsed the petition of Jonathan Fox, who had been committed to Newgate for withholding evidence at the bar of the House, and called for his release. Planta, the Wellington ministry's patronage secretary, was 'doubtful' as to how he would vote on Catholic emancipation in February 1829, but in the event he proved to be one of its diehard opponents in the lobbies. He presented hostile petitions from Nottinghamshire, 17 Mar. He voted against the transfer of East Retford's seats to Birmingham, 5 May 1829. At the Newark dinner to celebrate the return of the anti-Catholic Sadler, 24 July 1829, Willoughby justified his hostility to emancipation on the ground that Catholicism was 'diametrically opposed to the British constitution', argued that education and a resident gentry were the only reliable means of dispelling 'the mists of ignorance, error and superstition' in Ireland and denounced the liberal economic policies of Huskisson.[4] In October 1829 Sir Richard Vyvyan*, the Ultra leader, listed him as one of the 'Tories strongly opposed to the present government'. He voted with them against the transfer of East Retford's seats to Birmingham, 11 Feb., and the enfranchisement of Birmingham, Leeds and Manchester, 23 Feb., but divided to cut military expenditure, 19 Feb. 1830. He presented a Newark petition against the sale of beer bill, 5 Apr., and voted against its second reading, 4 May 1830. Criticized at the general election that summer for neglecting his parliamentary duties, he admitted to 'a temporary absence' on account of family bereavement and appealed to the finer feelings of his constituents. He was returned with Sadler after a contest.[5] Ministers classed him as one of the 'moderate Ultras', and he voted against them in the division on the civil list which brought them down, 15 Nov. 1830. Early the following year he retired from Parliament on the pretext of 'particular circumstances connected with my family'.[6]

Willoughby, who was heir presumptive to the 7th Baron Middleton, died at Apsley Hall, Nottinghamshire in November 1849.[7] By his will, dated 1 Dec. 1837, he provided for his youngest children and devised his estates to his eldest son Henry Willoughby (1817-77), who succeeded as 8th Baron Middleton in 1856. His personalty was sworn under £5,000, with residue of £1,718.[8]

[1] *Black Bk.* (1823), 203; *Session of Parl. 1825*, p. 491. [2] *Nottingham Jnl.* 1 June 1822. [3] *The Times*, 21 Apr. 1823. [4] *Full Report of Newark Dinner, 24 July 1829*, pp. 4-5. [5] *Nottingham Jnl.* 7, 14 Aug. 1830. [6] *Lincoln and Newark Times*, 9 Feb. 1831. [7] *Gent. Mag.* (1850), i. 541. [8] PROB 11/2109/180; IR26/1885/147.

S.R.H.

WILLOUGHBY, Sir Henry Pollard, 3rd bt. (1796–1865), of Baldon House, Oxon. and 20 Cork Street, London.

YARMOUTH I.o.W.	1831–1832
NEWCASTLE-UNDER-LYME	1832–1834
EVESHAM	1847–23 Mar. 1865

b. 17 Nov. 1796, 2nd s. of Sir Christopher Willoughby, 1st bt. (*d.* 1808), of Baldon and 2nd w. Martha, da. of Maurice Evans of St. James's, Westminster, Mdx. *educ.* Eton 1808; Christ Church, Oxf. 1814. *unm. suc.* bro. Sir Christopher William Willoughby, 2nd bt., as 3rd bt. 24 June 1813. *d.* 23 Mar. 1865.

Willoughby came from Bristol mercantile stock, but could trace descent from the medieval barons Willoughby d'Eresby. One ancestor, John Willoughby (*b.* c.1616), served as treasurer and master of the Society of Merchant Venturers and, as mayor of Bristol, gained notoriety for sentencing women to punishment by public ducking. His grandson Christopher Willoughby (c.1700-73) of Prince Street, Bristol and Berwick Lodge, Gloucestershire, also held office in the Merchant Venturers.[1] In 1754 he rented the manor of Baldon, formerly in the possession of the Pollard family, which, when subsequently purchased, became the site for the farming experiments of his son Christopher Willoughby (1748-1808), this Member's father.[2] An indefatigable agricultural improver, he promoted the cultivation of swedes in elaborate crop rotations, innovatory methods of tillage and, unfashionably, the use of open fields for growing corn. His endeavours brought him a baronetcy in 1794 and later, from Arthur Young, secretary to the board of agriculture, a commendation as a 'very attentive and reflecting proprietor'.[3] It is probable that his father-in-law (and this Member's maternal grandfather) was Maurice Evans, the mercer of 64 Cheapside, London, whose will was proved, 21 Mar. 1782.[4]

Willoughby succeeded to the baronetcy as a minor, after the death of his elder brother at Corpus Christi, Oxford in 1813, from a blow sustained whilst playing cricket. He went up to Oxford himself the following year. On coming of age, he succeeded to the family estates, which comprised 2,882 acres in Oxfordshire, Gloucestershire, Surrey and Berkshire in 1872, and the £30,390 residue of his father's will.[5] He does not appear to have inherited his enthusiasm for farming and leased Baldon in 1848. In 1821 he pressed the authorities of Queen's College, Oxford, the other main local landowner, to agree to a general enclosure on the pretext that it was no longer possible to find tenants 'of skill and capital' who were prepared to cultivate in a 'barbarous mode'. An Act was finally obtained in 1827 and applied ten years later, when the Willougby estate consisted of 596 acres enclosed and 426 open.[6] In his *Apology of an English Landowner* (1827), addressed to his fellow Oxfordshire proprietors, he argued that the landed interest's heavy tax burden entitled them to a degree of economic protection and warned that the 'great improvement' effected by the 1822 corn law could be nullified by the fluctuations of a paper currency. On 11 Mar. 1826 he announced his candidacy for his local borough of Wallingford at the anticipated general election, promising to maintain the constitution 'inviolate and unimpaired' and oppose Catholic relief. After a canvass, however, he withdrew, criticizing the notoriously venal electors in his parting comment that 'my honest exertions are insufficient to secure the cause of your independence', 21 Mar.[7] At the 1830 general election the same disinclination to spend dissuaded him from contesting Beverley.[8] Instead he offered a quixotic challenge to the established Holdsworth interest at Dartmouth, where he and his colleague polled no votes from the *bona fide* freemen and saw their petition seeking to widen the franchise rejected by the Commons, 30 Nov. 1830.[9]

At the 1831 general election he was returned for Yarmouth, Isle of Wight, where the 2nd Baron Yarborough held a controlling interest and returned Members friendly to the Grey ministry. He duly voted for the second reading of the reintroduced reform bill, 6 July, at least twice against adjourning the debates, 12 July, and gave generally steady support to its details, though he was in the minorities against the disfranchisement of Appleby, 19 July, Downton, 21 July, and St. Germans and Saltash, 26 July, and for an amendment to withhold the vote from weekly tenants and lodgers, 25 Aug. 1831. When the fate of his own borough was considered, 26 July, he drew attention to an inhabitants' petition, of which no record has been found. He divided with ministers on the Dublin election controversy, 23 Aug. He voted for the reform bill's passage, 21 Sept., the second reading of the Scottish measure, 23 Sept., and for Lord Ebrington's confidence motion, 10 Oct. 1831. He divided for the second reading of the revised reform bill, 17 Dec. 1831, when he suggested that the more viable national constituency produced by the enfranchisement schedules would provide a more effective check on public expenditure, denied that close boroughs were a necessary buttress of the constitution, and hoped that their abolition might be linked to ending the requirement for those appointed to office to seek re-election. On a note of caution he added that in the metropolitan districts the £10 franchise qualification might prove

'too low'. He voted for going into committee on the bill, 20 Jan., and supported some of its details, but was in the minorities for excluding urban freeholders from the county electorate, 1 Feb., the enfranchisement of all persons rated to the poor at £10, 3 Feb., and against the inclusion of Helston in schedule B, 23 Feb., Tower Hamlets in schedule C, 28 Feb., and Gateshead in schedule D, 5 Mar. 1832.[10] On 21 Feb. he brought up and endorsed an inhabitants' petition against the partial disfranchisement of Dartmouth, having obtained returns on its trade and shipping, 16 Dec. 1831, and its assessed taxes, 16 Feb. 1832. As these had only just been presented to the House, he was able to secure a postponement of the decision on the borough's fate, contending that the returns of its houses and taxes were incorrect and did not accurately reflect the town's importance. To Mackworth Praed's retort that he should not, therefore, have supported the second reading, he replied that 'it was not my wish to vote against the principle of the bill'. On 28 Mar. Lord John Russell indicated a desire to placate him by inviting him to state his objections to proceeding with discussions on schedule B. He offered none, but on 2 Mar. divided the House against the inclusion of Dartmouth, which he lost 106-205, despite his insistence that the crucial figures had been corrupted by the 'abominable conduct of a tax collector'. This he attempted to prove with 'unquestionable documents', 14 Mar., but ministers remained unimpressed. He divided for the third reading of the bill, 22 Mar., but was absent from the division on the motion for an address calling on the king to appoint only ministers who would carry it unimpaired, 10 May, and subsequently appeared in a recriminatory list of Members supposedly present, 'who might have voted if they had thought proper'.[11] He was in the minority to preserve the rights of freemen in Irish boroughs, 2 July. Speaking against the Liverpool disfranchisement bill, he considered that the city would be adequately 'sluiced' by the provisions of the reform bill, but recommended prosecuting those accused of bribery at the late election, 4 July 1832.

Willoughby was in the majority against the second reading of the Vestry Act amendment bill, 23 Jan. 1832. He voted with ministers on the Russian-Dutch loan, 26 Jan., 12, 16, 20 July, and relations with Portugal, 9 Feb. On 31 Jan. he was in the minority for inquiry into distress in the glove trade. He divided to go into committee on Baring's bill to exclude insolvent debtors from Parliament, 27 June. On 1 Aug. he argued that tithes should be commuted to a fixed charge, especially in Ireland, but denied that the amount appropriated by the Irish clergy had been generally excessive and warned that the anti-tithe movement was the first step towards anarchy. On this issue he could draw on personal experience, having quarrelled with the rector of Marsh Baldon, his half-brother Hugh Pollard Willoughby, over tithe apportionment the previous year, since when he had retained the sums collected for his own use.[12] It is possible that this state of affairs had some bearing on his presence in the minority of 12 against applying a retrospective provision to the ecclesiastical courts contempts bill, which removed Members' immunity from their jurisdiction, 3 Aug. 1832.

At the 1832 general election Willoughby contested Newcastle-under-Lyme as a 'moderate and constitutional reformer' and displaced Edmund Peel, a brother of Sir Robert. In the House he veered towards the Conservatives on such issues as reforming the Irish church and the new poor law, but he lost to Peel at the next general election.[13] He stood unsuccessfully as a Conservative at Poole in 1837 and Northampton in 1841, and was returned as such for Evesham in 1847, a seat he held for life. Latterly he was described as a supporter of free trade and gained a reputation as a dogged scrutinizer of government finances, notably the alleged misappropriation of funds from savings banks. In 1857 he published *A few words on the question whether there is by law any effective control over the public expenditure*, which called for the comptroller-general of the exchequer to be given sufficient power to act as a proper watchdog. Willoughby died suddenly in March 1865 at his London residence at 63 Lower Brook Street.[14] A brief will, dated 18 Oct. 1861, directed that his personal estate should be invested in landed property. Administration was granted on 12 July to his brother John Pollard Willoughby, the sole legatee and heir to the baronetcy. Willoughby requested to be buried in the family plot at Marsh Baldon church, of which parish, ironically, he had been accused of 'neglect and indifference' in an 1854 church report.[15]

[1] IGI (Glos.); J. Latimer, *Annals of Bristol in 18th Cent.* 312; *Soc. of Merchant Venturers*, 327, 329, 334-5; PROB 11/992/453. [2] *VCH Oxon.* v. 32-33, 35; IGI (Glos.) [3] *VCH Oxon.* v. 35, 40-41: A. Young, *Gen. View of Agriculture of Oxon.* (1813), 33-34, 105, 109, 130-1, 149, 158, 167, 173, 176, 262, 264-5. [4] PROB 11/1088/128. [5] J. Bateman, *Great Landowners* (1883), 480; IR26/133/429. [6] *VCH Oxon.* v. 35, 41. [7] Berks. RO, Wallingford borough recs. W/AEp 8, election handbills. [8] Hull Univ. Lib. Hotham mss DDHO/8/4, Hall to Hotham, 4, 11 July 1830. [9] *The Times*, 14, 16 Aug. 1830; *CJ*, lxxxvi. 13-14, 134. [10] *The Times*, 4, 24, 29 Feb., 6 Mar. 1832. [11] Ibid. 14 May 1832. [12] *VCH Oxon.* v. 45. [13] J.C. Wedgwood, *Staffs. Parl. Hist.* iii. 75-78, 81, 87; *Language, Print and Electoral Politics, 1790-1832. Newcastle-under-Lyme Broadsides* ed. H. Barker and D. Vincent, 329-33. [14] *Dod's Parl. Companion* (1847), 255; *Gent. Mag.* (1865), i. 663; (1866), ii. 690-1. [15] *VCH Oxon.* v. 45.

H.J.S./P.J.S.

WILMOT, **Robert John** (1784–1841), of Osmaston, Derbys. and Sudbrook Park, Petersham, Surr.

NEWCASTLE-UNDER-LYME	1818–1830

b. 21 Dec. 1784, o.s. of Sir Robert Wilmot, 2nd bt., of Osmaston and 1st w. Juliana Elizabeth, da. of Adm. John Byron, wid. of Hon. William Byron†. *educ.* Eton 1802; Christ Church, Oxf. 1803. *m.* 6 Sept. 1806,[1] Anne Beatrix, da. and coh. of Eusebius Horton of Catton, Derbys., 4s. 3da. (1 *d.v.p.*). Took additional name of Horton by royal lic. 8 May 1823 in accordance with will of his fa.-in-law. kntd. 8 June 1831; GCH 22 June 1831; *suc.* fa. as 3rd bt. 23 July 1834. *d.* 31 May 1841.

Under-sec. of state for war and colonies Dec. 1821-Jan. 1828; PC 23 May 1827; gov. and c.-in-c. Ceylon 1831-7. Capt. Staffs. militia 1805.

Wilmot, who admitted 'without reserve the *object* of ultimately holding *high* political situation', had sat since 1818 for Newcastle-under-Lyme, where he gave very little 'personal attention' to his constituents, relying instead on the declining electoral influence of Lord Stafford and the corporation, with whom he had continued to act following his initial defeat in 1815.[2] He 'maintained stoutly' that 'the surer and earlier road to high political office' was not 'to oppose diligently and malignantly', but 'to support energetically and uncompromisingly *any* government'.[3] A frequent speaker and attender, who took an insatiable interest in the affairs of his own department, his rhetorical skills frequently drew adverse comment, particularly on occasions when, as the radical Whig Henry Grey Bennet put it, 27 June 1821, he gave 'a very poor speech, and, as usual, ended by a long quotation which, this evening, was in Latin'.[4] An assiduous correspondent, guilty of a 'frightful prolixity' which 'I cannot cure', Wilmot was in regular but not necessarily reciprocal contact with most of the leading political figures of the day, on questions of political economy, currency reform, Catholic emancipation, slavery and emigration.[5] His memoranda, pamphlets and printed speeches were legion, but mostly consisted of revised drafts of earlier items. A member of the Political Economy Club from 1829 until 1831, who dubbed Joseph Hume* his 'natural enemy', 18 Feb. 1828, he lost no opportunity to attack those who believed that the distresses of the country could be relieved by tax reductions, arguing instead for 'applying public money specifically to the relief of that distress, under such novel conditions as are in keeping with the *soundest views* of political economy'.[6] His increasing obsession with schemes of pauper emigration, which he saw as the main remedy for distress, along with his outspoken views on Catholic relief and slavery, placed him increasingly at odds with his colleagues and constituents.

At the 1820 general election Wilmot offered again for Newcastle, defending his support for the Liverpool ministry and Catholic claims and refuting the 'atrocious falsehoods' circulated by his opponents that he placed his own ambitions above the interests of the constituency and was opposed to the education of the poor, whom he wished to remove to the 'barren soil of a foreign land'. After a spiteful contest he was returned in second place with a much reduced majority.[7] He seconded the address, 27 Apr. 1820, when he inveighed against any 'sweeping alteration of the constitution', which was 'the most perfect of any age or country'. 'If the inferior orders, in the manufacturing districts, were once convinced of its benefits', he declared, 'much of the power of the agitators would be destroyed forever'. John Hobhouse, radical Whig Member for Westminster, called it 'a miserable performance indeed'.[8] Arguing against too rigid an approach to agricultural distress, 31 May, Wilmot stressed limits to David Ricardo's* methods in the formulation of policy, contending that 'the principles of political economy serve as beacons to enable us to direct our course, but as in mechanics allowance must be made for friction and resistance, so in legislation reference must be had to the actual situation of affairs'.[9] He 'could see no reason why the Irish should pay ten per cent on imported articles manufactured in this country', and was in the minority for inquiry into Anglo-Irish trade, 14 June. Defending the government's conduct towards Queen Caroline, 22 June, he argued that 'nothing had been more frequently ridiculed than the introduction of so many names of the royal progeny into the liturgy' and that her omission was 'no degradation'. He was a government teller on the issue the following day and spoke again in their support, 6, 13 Feb. 1821. He divided with ministers against economies in revenue collection, 4 July 1820, but was in the minority for repeal of the malt tax next day. Attacking misleading press reports that had 'done him considerable injury at the last general election', he insisted that 'he had always been a warm friend to the education of the poor', 7 July 1820.[10] On 12 Feb. 1821 Wilmot recommended giving Grampound's seats to Leeds, but urged the House not to 'mix up this subject with the general question of parliamentary reform'. Discussion of this issue, he added, 17 Apr., was 'dangerous' and 'subversive of the real and tried constitution', and had become erroneously linked to 'the pecuniary difficulties under which the country now labours'. He duly divided against parliamentary reform, 9 May. He voted for Catholic relief, 28 Feb. 1821, 1 Mar., 21 Apr., 10 May 1825. On 15 May 1821 he spoke against Burdett's motion for inquiry

into Peterloo, which would be 'attended by the most prejudicial consequences'. His defence of the magistrates was heavily criticized during an exchange with Burdett the following day. He divided for the forgery punishment mitigation bill, 23 May, 4 June, when he spoke briefly in its favour. He argued and voted against Hume's motion for economy and retrenchment, 27 June 1821.

In the government reshuffle of December 1821 Wilmot accepted the under-secretaryship at the colonial office, which Huskisson described as 'a very pleasant' post, rendered 'more important by the principal not being in the House of Commons'.[11] 'As it does not vacate a seat it will be very convenient to him', noted the secretary of state, Lord Bathurst, who believed himself 'mistaken' in apprehending that Wilmot 'might be through his friendship with Lord Granville be a devoted to Canning, to which there might be an objection'.[12] Mrs. Arbuthnot, however, later related how Bathurst suspected that 'Wilmot repeated everything to the Canning party', adding that the duke of Wellington had warned her to 'be very much on my guard, and take care what I said, for ... there was a system of espionage and of repeating every word that was said before the Canning party to their chief'.[13] Wilmot, who regularly fielded questions on colonial issues and acted as a ministerial teller, argued against more extensive tax reductions to relieve distress, 21 Feb. 1822. On 4 Mar. he opposed any 'further military reduction' in the colonies and 'entreated the House to consult petty savings less than the real and prospective advantage of the nation'. The following day Hume suggested that his 'being a few weeks in office had produced such an effect ... as to make him conceive the saving of half a million a petty, paltry saving', but Wilmot denied that he had 'made use of the expressions' and exposed flaws in Hume's own calculations. He opposed the reception of a petition blaming distress in Lower Canada on 'acts of the British legislature', 13 Mar. On 10 May he welcomed Canning's Catholic peers bill, which 'would conciliate the people of Ireland', but acknowledged that on this issue he 'had the misfortune to differ with a large and respectable body of his constituents'. Introducing the Canada government and trade bill unifying its two legislatures, 20 June, he asserted that 'consent' by the 'people of the provinces' to the measure was unnecessary 'since their present constitution was derived from an Act of the British legislature'. He spoke at length in the bill's support, 18 July, when the Whig Sir James Mackintosh referred in the House to his 'very able and perspicacious speech'. On slavery at the Cape, 25 July, he argued that 'the remedy for it, to be safe, must be gradual' and that 'anything like a sudden and general manumission would be ruinous not only to the master, but to the parties it was intended to benefit'. He secured the appointment of a commission of inquiry into the settlements there, and in Mauritius and Ceylon, and successfully resisted calls for the inclusion of Trinidad, 26 July 1822. He refuted Hume's assertion that the 'colonies were rather a burden than a benefit to the country', 26 Feb., and declared that in all of them 'government had united practical economy with the most extended views of general policy', 18 Mar. 1823. He defended the governor of Upper Canada, 24 Mar., and the union of Cape Breton with Nova Scotia, 25 Mar. He brought in the Newfoundland laws bill that day, and opposed inquiry into the colony, 14 May. He argued against introducing trial by jury into the penal settlement of New South Wales, 2 July 1823. He voted for repeal of the usury laws, 27 Feb., 8 Apr. 1824, 17 Feb. 1825. He again dealt with departmental questions, 4, 12 Mar. 1824, when he praised 'the value which the country derived from its colonies', 2 Apr., 10, 21 May 1824. On 13 Apr. he stated 'his firm belief' that 'on some points' the House 'had been grossly deceived' over the case of the Methodist missionary John Smith, prosecuted for inciting slaves to rebel in Demerara. In a long speech judged 'very ill' by the Whig Member Agar Ellis, 1 June, he contended that Smith's conduct 'had all the attributes of criminality' and that he was 'unequivocally ... guilty of misprision of treason'.[14] He fielded opposition questions on the affair, 3 June, and on Barbados, 15 June 1824.

Wilmot, who had been 'offended' at being discouraged by the foreign secretary Canning from speaking in debates on slavery during 1824, with the proviso that 'if I did I had better confine himself to one point', bridled at further attempts to keep him silent the following year.[15] In a letter to Robinson, chancellor of the exchequer, 22 Mar. 1825, he complained:

> I feel and have felt very considerable annoyance at the disposition which exists to prevent my saying anything in Parliament on subjects concerned with the colonies ... I am not conscious of ever having got the government, in any single instance, into a single scrape.

Writing again, 5 Apr., he protested against 'leaving the sole management of one of the most important departments' to an under-secretary 'whose tongue is tied, I will not say at the discretion of his superiors, but by their caprice or their impatience to get the business of the day over'. Citing the slavery issue, which Canning 'took out of my hands', he asked, 'Is it fitting that that question should rest entirely in his hands, at a time when he is necessarily ignorant of

every one of the details belonging to it?'[16] He justified military increases, citing 'the increased population of our colonial dependencies', 7, 11 Mar. He introduced the Canada wastelands bill, which was 'calculated to improve the condition and strength of our colonies in North America', 15 Mar.[17] On 15 Apr. he defended the proposed government grant of £30,000 to aid emigration from Southern Ireland to Canada as 'an experiment' of 'national importance', which would 'place settlers in such a situation as to enable them to support themselves by their own industry'. He supported bills on warehoused corn and quarantine, 13 May, and the West India Company, 16 May, when he argued that 'as the profits of the master increased, so would the condition of the slave under him be ameliorated'. He moved the second reading of the Mauritius trade bill for equalizing sugar duties, 3 June. He opposed inquiries into the deportation of two persons of colour from Jamaica by its governor, 16 June, and the expulsion from Barbados of a missionary whose actions had 'given offence' and appeared 'dangerous to those ... involved in the possession of slaves', 23 June. He announced that government intended to hold an inquiry into emigration in the next session, 18 June.[18] On 5 July he argued against allowing a petitioner to return to the Cape of Good Hope in order to collect further evidence against its governor, Lord Charles Henry Somerset†, whose conduct he defended, 8 May 1826. He was 'splenetic' at Liverpool's initial refusal to appoint a second departmental permanent secretary and bet Lord Granville 'a thousand pounds' that Robert Hay, who was 'at last appointed', 6 July 1825, would find 'his half, without Parliament quite as much as he will have time and spirits to manage'.[19] He commended the government's improvements to 'the condition of the slaves in our West Indian colonies', but cautioned against further 'legislative interference' in Jamaica, 1 Mar. 1826. He answered questions on slavery, 3 Mar., 20, 25 Apr., 9, 19 May, when he spoke against Brougham's motion for ameliorating the condition of the slaves. 'Though much shorter', observed Agar Ellis, his speech was 'infinitely more tedious'.[20] Replying to Hume's criticism of costs at Sierra Leone, 10 Mar., he complained of the great expense of printing the papers which he and other opposition Members persistently requested. He secured the appointment of a select committee on emigration, which he chaired, 14 Mar. He expressed support for the spring guns bill, provided it led to a law 'legalizing the sale of game', 28 Apr. 1826.

At the 1826 general election Wilmot offered again for Newcastle, where, during the rumours of a dissolution the previous autumn, he had promised to 'give every person within the borough' the 'means of judging for himself' on the Catholic question, which his opponents had 'raised against' him, 4 Oct. 1825.[21] 'This pledge', he later explained to Granville, 'induced me to write the letter to the duke of Norfolk calling upon the Catholics for "a Declaration"'.[22] His *Letter to the Electors of Newcastle-under-Lyme* (1826) 'made as much effort as any man ever has, to bring the subject calmly and argumentatively before my constituents', who he trusted would 'not be led away by any general declamation against the course which I, in common with some of the first and best men in the country ... have felt it my duty to pursue'.[23] In a controversial arrangement, he persuaded his colleague John Denison to withdraw at the last moment, arguing that 'the proper course to be pursued' was 'for each party to return one Member', and was returned unopposed alongside the popular independent candidate. On the hustings he promised 'strenuously' to 'support the enlightened and liberal policy of the present administration' and defended himself against taunts of 'No Popery' and 'No slavery', a subject to which 'he had devoted days and nights and weeks and months'.[24] On 3 June 1826 Wilmot, who had frequently complained of overwork at the colonial office, confided to Stephen Rumbold Lushington* that his 'health and spirits were breaking down under the accumulated pressure' of being the only representative of the department in the Commons, where he 'had to direct *all* the details, as well as do *all* the duty'.[25] 'I ought not either in rank or emoluments to be *necessarily limited* by the analogy of the [other] under-secretaries, who are not ... called upon for such acts of responsibility and duty', he complained to Granville, 13 Aug.[26] Granville concurred, later observing, 'I marvel how you find time to be under-secretary of a felonious department and be the most voluminous contributor to a review, and the author of pamphlets upon all the interesting questions of the day, and to be the chairman of committees in the House of Commons ... and at the same time *faire la crux aux dames*'.[27] Writing to Huskisson, 10 Nov. 1826, Wilmot argued against continuing 'the present standard of gold unchanged' and in favour of Robert Torrens's* system of 'concurrent paper and metallic circulation'.[28] In the House, 5 Dec., he defended the colonial office against charges of corruption in granting mining concessions in New South Wales. He presented a Glasgow petition in favour of emigration, 7 Dec. 1826. His growing interest in pauper emigration, which he claimed to have studied 'privately with great assiduity' since 1822, had increasingly placed him at odds with his ministerial colleagues, whom he lost no 'opportunities of endeavouring to convert'.[29] In a letter

to Wilmot, 25 Mar. 1826, Robinson had advised that 'an extensive emigration effected by the government' was 'unnecessary and impracticable'; but Wilmot was convinced that although 'the government are, I believe, all against me' and 'Goulburn considers it farcical', he had the support of '*all* the leading political economists'.[30] Moving the renewal of the emigration committee, 15 Feb. 1827, in what Denison described as 'a bad speech', he urged the case for a national scheme of emigration funded from the poor rates, as he did again, 26 Feb., 18 May.[31] His suggestion to the committee that some of the costs might be defrayed from the sinking fund prompted an angry response from Peel, who wrote to Robinson, 12 Mar. 1827, asking, 'how can an under-secretary of state in a matter immediately relating to his own department, strip himself of his *official* capacity?' Robinson concurred:

> I was as much astonished as you were at seeing appended to a private memorandum submitted by Wilmot to the emigration committee ... a suggestion that the guarantee of the government might be made a charge upon the sinking fund. I lost no time in seeing Wilmot, and protested in the strongest manner against any such principle.[32]

Wilmot introduced a bill authorizing the sale of clergy reserves in Canada, 20 Feb., and answered questions on colonial slavery, 21 Feb., 13 Mar. 1827. Commenting to Huskisson on the 'difficulties' facing the government over Catholic relief, 2 Mar., he advocated a middle course 'between the two extremes of unqualified concession and unqualified rejection of the Catholic claims', believing that there was 'a portion of the Catholic gentry, both English and Irish, who would accept ... a statutory enactment that they should be for ever disqualified from voting in either House ... upon any point deemed ... to affect ... the Protestant church', and that 'such securities' might reconcile the anti-Catholic members of the cabinet to the measure.[33] He spoke in favour of relief that day, and divided accordingly, 6 Mar. 1827.

On 6 May 1827 Canning, the new premier, renewed Wilmot's 'present office with the sanction of privy councillor', which John Croker* later said was given 'as a salve to his wounded honour in not being promoted'.[34] According to Lord Colchester, he had 'expected to be chief secretary for Ireland', but as Edward Littleton* informed Wilmot, 20 Oct., Canning had vetoed this on account of his having 'spoilt himself for Ireland by his publications'.[35] In disclosing this information, Littleton was 'anxious' to demonstrate 'the injury you were doing yourself by *constantly striking your ideas off at a heat, and disseminating them by publications and writings*'; but an indignant Wilmot was convinced that Canning had 'felt he must offer up some victims to suspicious Protestantism, and thought that I should make a very convenient one'. 'I followed him to his grave', he complained, 'but in this and other matters I shall ever think he treated me unfairly and unkindly'.[36] Wilmot defended his support for Lord Charles Somerset against remarks in a pamphlet recently published by Sir Rufane Donkin, 17 May, 8, 29 June, when, in a veiled attack on Hume, he denounced the 'extreme expense' which had been incurred in investigating the charges, none of which had been 'in the slightest degree substantiated'. On 12 June 1827 he argued against giving 'people of colour in the West Indies' the 'privileges of British citizens', as 'time was necessary to remove an evil which centuries had completed'. He spent much of July in Ireland, where, as he informed Colonel Shawe, he became convinced that 'the most efficient remedy for the moral ills of Ireland' was 'the settlement of the Catholic question' and 'for the physical evils emigration'.[37] Whilst away he complained that Lord Goderich, the new colonial secretary, '*never* communicated with me on departmental business, though there were several important points on which I wrote to him, nor did he ever write me a single line during Canning's illness'.[38] As Canning's successor, Goderich broached the difficulty of what to offer Wilmot with Croker, 11 Aug., who responded that 'if the great points of a union with the duke [of Wellington] and Peel could be arranged, all the rest was trash and lumber which might easily be disposed of'.[39] Three days later Goderich suggested to Huskisson that Wilmot 'would wish to make some change in his post', and proposed either Lord Francis Leveson Gower* or Edward Smith Stanley* to replace him.[40] As Thomas Frankland Lewis* explained:

Goderich vacates the colonial office by taking the treasury and it is wished that Huskisson should fill that office and lead the House of Commons. Only two under-secretaries of state can sit in the Commons, and as Canning's death would leave the House without anyone to speak on foreign affairs, Lord Dudley must have an under-secretary and I expect Stanley will be the man, but this makes it necessary to remove Wilmot and he will succeed [Charles] Grant, who will be promoted to the first seat at the board of trade.[41]

Goderich duly offered Wilmot the vice-presidency of that board, 16 Aug., which he initially appeared '*most happy* to take', providing he 'could have a government seat' and so avoid 'the risk of a contest at Newcastle' where, according to James Macdonald*, he was 'in great jeopardy', three candidates having 'announced themselves against him ... one on anti-Catholic, one on anti-slavery and another on anti-emigration

grounds'.[42] Privately, however, he was unenthusiastic, later admitting that there was 'nothing in the situation of the vice-president of the board, with the president *in* the House of Commons, which could at all make the situation abstractedly desirable'.[43] Huskisson was informed of a 'report' that he was about to resign, 19 Aug., but to Granville he wrote:

If Huskisson *accepts* the colonial department and if he *personally* wished me to remain as under-secretary notwithstanding he as chief secretary was in the House of Commons, to *oblige* him I would do it, under the fair understanding that I should not lose *caste* by that decision, and also its being publicly understood that I remained where I was to accommodate him. But very probably Huskisson may wish to have an under-secretary of his own, who may not have all the opinions and impressions which six years' connection with the department has necessarily imbued me with.[44]

From 16 to 23 Aug. Wilmot heard nothing from Goderich, to whom he had considered himself 'more *connected* ... than with any other man', and during 'the latter part of this period' became '*very angry*', attributing 'this total change of system with me' to John Herries*, the new chancellor of the exchequer, who he suspected had counselled Goderich 'not to have any communication with me'. 'I have long known Herries' indisposition towards me', he told Granville, 'and I fancy that his jealousy at my being made a privy councillor was unmeasured in feeling and unrestrained in expression'.[45] Wilmot, who was succeeded by Smith Stanley at the colonial office, successfully proposed to Huskisson that he might

remain as under-secretary of state, retaining the West India department, till the 5th January, when, under any circumstances, I should retire from the colonial office. I also propose that Stanley's *salary* should commence *from* the 5th January. I think he is much better off acting as under-secretary for two and a half months without a salary, than attending as an *amateur* during that period ... If I *did now* accept the vice-presidency of the board of trade, I might involve the government in a serious difficulty, for having *entirely decided* not to stand a contest at Newcastle, should such a contest be altogether unavoidable, I should be obliged to remain out of Parliament altogether *unless a quiet seat* could *be found for me*.[46]

In subsequent explanations of his actions he continued to cite the hazard of 'a re-election at Newcastle', claiming that 'there was a proposition of finding me a seat elsewhere, but the opportunity of executing it never arrived'. An 'offer of Hastings *vice* Newcastle, on the payment on my part of £1,000', however, was eventually forthcoming, but he turned it down.[47] Sensing that 'promotion was clearly stopped with respect to me *at home*', he now began to 'apply for it abroad', and his name was laid 'before the king for the civil government of Canada'.[48] On 7 Nov. 1827 Huskisson told Goderich:

> Wilmot Horton has set his heart upon going to Canada ... He considered himself, as far as your consent, tolerably sure of success, till you mentioned to him yesterday the king's wishes about Burton. I am afraid if the king has a strong feeling in favour of the latter, that it will be impossible to contend against it, upon the ground of preference to Wilmot, though I have no objection to try what can be done.[49]

His appointment was, as he informed Littleton, 27 Nov. 1827, 'refused *graciously* in consequence of the claims and application of another party, but Jamaica was proposed for me, and my *present position* is that of an accepted or rather accep*ting* candidate'.[50] Nothing came of this, however, probably on account of his outspoken views on slavery.

Wilmot retired as arranged, 5 Jan. 1828, having, as he subsequently notified Peel, who regretted that he 'had not been found in office' when Wellington and he came to power two weeks earlier, 'received full salary, and continued to exercise more or less the functions of the situation up to that day'. Having thus 'inferred' that 'the being found in office had furnished a sort of rule for applications being made', he wrote to ask Peel

> whether Huskisson mentioned me and my peculiar position and views to the duke of Wellington? A person called on me the other day, to inform me that ... as I had not made any application to the duke of Wellington respecting coming into office, it could not be expected that any application would be made to me. I told my informant that as Mr. Huskisson was entirely acquainted with my views and feelings, etc., I could not mark my distrust in him, by volunteering a separate communication upon the subject.[51]

In reply Peel explained that he was unaware 'of the particular arrangement ... with respect to your ceasing to hold the situation of under-secretary', having 'fancied that you had long since resigned that office', and ignorant of what had 'passed between the duke of Wellington and Huskisson respecting your position'.[52] In private Wilmot protested that he could 'not in the *slightest* degree understand Huskisson's conduct to me', but publicly he professed himself 'very glad to be out', informing Granville that although he had 'not the slightest intention of Whiggifying myself', there were 'two or three *leading* questions on which I am much committed by overactivity', and 'until they are more or less settled ... my *belonging* to a government would be embarrassing to them, and possibly irksome to

myself'. 'In addition', he declared, 'I have no taste for *scrub* office'.[53] On 18 Feb. Wellington warned Peel that they could not 'consider' him among their 'friends' on the finance committee, to which he had been appointed three days before with other Huskissonites.[54] He clarified certain points regarding Herries's role in the collapse of Goderich's administration, 18 Feb. He divided for repeal of the Test Acts, 26 Feb., and spoke against all laws imposing 'political penalties on account of religious belief' two days later. On 27 Feb. he hinted at Hume's involvement in 'a gross breach of confidence' following the publication of secret correspondence between the duke of Manchester, governor of Jamaica, and the colonial office regarding its slave population. Hume denied any wrong-doing, but was ridiculed by Wilmot the following day during a debate on the metropolitan police. He spoke, 9 May, and divided for Catholic relief, 12 May. After a long speech on emigration to an inattentive House, 4 Mar., he postponed his motion to bring in a bill enabling parishes 'to mortgage their poor rates for the purpose of assisting voluntary emigration'. That day he introduced a bill to revise the Passengers Act, which he guided through the House and received royal assent, 23 May (9 Geo. IV, c. 21). He obtained papers on slavery, 5, 6 Mar., when he spoke of 'the difficulty and delicacy' of reconciling 'the progressive emancipation of the slave' with respect for 'the rights of private property' and advocated 'some middle course'. The abolitionist Member Fowell Buxton, who considered Wilmot 'a leading member of the West India body', remarked that it was an 'extremely able' speech, which he 'listened to ... with feelings of real distress'.[55] Wilmot supported the East Retford disfranchisement bill, 21 Mar., but warned of 'the danger' that it would be rejected by the Lords. Forced to postpone his motion for an emigration bill a second time on account of the 'limited attendance' of the House, 25 Mar., he complained bitterly of the 'manifest indisposition' of Members 'to attend to the subject'. Instead he presented various petitions for 'aid to emigrate', 27 Mar., 6 May, on each occasion speaking on the issue, as he did in debates on the poor, 1, 17 Apr., when he brought in his postponed bill enabling parishes to raise funds for emigration. It went no further. He urged Members 'to devote their serious attention to the subject', 24 June, when Peel retorted that 'no part of the empire calls for this mode of relief'. He spoke on issues affecting New South Wales and Canada, 18 Apr., 2 May, 20 June, 7, 14 July. He voted with ministers on delays in chancery, 24 Apr. He presented petitions from the Presbyterian Church of Upper Canada for equal treatment with the Church of Scotland, 6 May, and from Lower Canada for a legislative assembly, 12 May. Speaking against naval cuts, 16 May 1828, he declared that it was 'unworthy of a great nation to reduce its necessary establishments on account of the pressure on its resources in any one particular year'.

Following the resignation of Huskisson and his associates from the government, Wilmot was described by Wellington in a draft memorandum as one those 'whose assistance it is very desirable to attain', 25 May 1828.[56] Croker was 'willing to make way' for him at the admiralty in the event of his being unable to 'vacate' Newcastle, and there were plans to give him the Irish secretaryship. Mrs. Arbuthnot, however, considered him

> without any exception, the most unfit man that can be thought of. He is a very violent partisan of the Catholics and has not one grain of judgement or calm sense. He has talent and speaks well, and this latter qualification makes Mr. Peel (*the furious Protestant*) wish for him.[57]

Lord Ellenborough agreed, describing him as 'a bore full of fancies' and advising the duke against his plan to appoint him as 'secretary at war, not in the cabinet', even though he was 'very anxious to have all he could in the Commons', 28 May.[58] Next day, however, Wilmot took the unusual step of writing to pre-empt 'any specific proposition' which it might have been Wellington's 'intention to make', saying he 'could not in honour or consistency accept office' under the duke, who in reply regretted 'very much ... that I had not the pleasure of seeing you, as I think I could have convinced you'.[59] Wilmot 'behaved in true Canning style', remarked Mrs. Arbuthnot, for 'he refused, and immediately sent off copies of the duke's letter and his answer to all his friends!'.[60] In a subsequent memorandum, Wilmot stated that 'the independent opinions which I entertained upon ... the Catholic question, the West India question and emigration made a secession from office *advisable*, until I had had an opportunity of placing those opinions fairly before Parliament'.[61] Yet Mrs. Arbuthnot recorded hearing that he was 'in despair at not being in office', and he later admitted to her that he had been 'wrong in not having spoken instead of sending a letter when the duke requested to see me', although he defended his refusal of office, 'a course which I *abjure* for the remaining term of my natural life', on the grounds of his belief that Wellington would be unable to settle the Catholic question, to which he was 'pledged more than deeply'.[62] He was twice listed in June as one of the 'Huskisson party'. On 4 July he voted against the finance committee's recommendation to abolish the office of lieutenant-general of the ordnance, which

was an attempt to 'procure popularity ... out of doors by pretending to relieve the burdens of the country by the farce of reducing an office, the expense of which is only £1,200 a year'. He argued against cuts in superannuation allowances, 14 July. That day he was in the minority against amendments to the silk duties. He agreed to withdraw his motions on Ireland and slavery 'for the present', 8, 25 July 1828.

Over the next six months Wilmot travelled to Paris and Rome and became heavily involved in negotiations on Catholic relief and securities, writing pamphlets, meeting representatives of the Vatican, and corresponding regularly with leading government figures.[63] In the House, 12 Feb. 1829, he commended the bill to suppress the Catholic Association as 'just and politic' in view of 'the measure of conciliation which was to succeed it', which was widely rumoured to be modelled on his own scheme of relief.[64] As Greville noted, 5 Feb., 'many people expect that Wilmot's plan will be adopted, restraining the Catholics from voting in matters concerning the church, which I do not believe, for Wilmot is at a discount and his plan is absurd and impracticable'.[65] That month he was listed by Planta, the patronage secretary, among 'opposition or doubtful men' who would 'vote with the government' for the concession of emancipation, which he duly did, 6, 30 Mar. He spoke in its support, 18, 24, 27 Mar., 21 May, when he saw 'no objection' to Daniel O'Connell being allowed to take his seat without swearing the oath of supremacy. He presented favourable petitions from Tutbury, Rolleston and Marston-upon-Dove, 17 Mar., and Newcastle, 26 Mar. He presented a petition for emigration from the Paisley Friendly Society, 10 Apr., when he again pressed for its discussion. Called to order by the Speaker after protesting at the 'scandalous manner' in which Sadler, Ultra Member for Newark, had allegedly misrepresented his opinions on the subject, 13 Apr., he apologized but pleaded 'some excuse for the warmth with which I have expressed myself'. He presented petitions from the Irish Friendly Emigration Society of Paisley and 13 Glasgow emigration societies, 7 May 1829, when he advocated emigration as 'the only remedy for pauperism' during a debate on the poor laws and clashed again with Sadler. Resuming a debate on the currency, 4 June, he derided 'certain pseudo-philosophers and their absurd projects' and strained the patience of the House with a lengthy lecture on poverty. He divided for the transfer of East Retford's seats to Birmingham, 5 May 1829, 5 Mar. 1830, when he spoke in its support. He urged the necessity of treating Canadian colonists 'with greater liberality', 5 June 1829.

Wilmot again attacked the notion of using tax reductions to deal with distress, 19 Feb. 1830. On 4 Mar. he refused Palmerston's request to postpone his motion for a committee on the poor, which was scheduled for 9 Mar., when he spoke at length of his plans for pauper 'colonization'. 'Went for a short time to the House in the evening', noted Agar Ellis, 'and found Wilmot Horton prosing away'.[66] He voted with opposition for information on the role of British troops in the internal affairs of Portugal, 10 Mar. On 16 Mar. he sarcastically opposed the reception of a petition for assisted emigration, observing that as 'all hope of relief on this hand seems to be abandoned by the House, the people ought not to be encouraged to look ... to it as a means of relief', but should instead 'look to the measure ... last night proposed for ... a reduction of the duty on beer; which no doubt will be an effectual remedy for all their distresses'. He presented petitions from Newcastle against the truck system that day, and against the East India Company's monopoly, 8 Apr. He objected to the appointment of a committee on the currency but not on colonization, 19 Mar., and stated his intention of introducing an emigration bill, 23 Mar. He supported the principle of separating families in receipt of poor relief, 26 Apr. He was appointed to select committees on civil superannuations the same day, and manufacturing employment, 13 May. He obtained leave to bring in his poor rate annuities bill enabling parishes 'to raise money for certain purposes', 4 May, which was presented, 22 May, but deferred, 24 June, and went no further. Speaking on colonial matters, 10 May, he defended himself against charges of 'being devoted to slavery' which had appeared in a pamphlet 'by a Member of this House', and again, 21, 24, 25 May, 11, 14 June, 8 July. He divided for Jewish emancipation, 17 May, and abolition of the death penalty for forgery, 24 May, 7 June. Presenting a petition from Frome for 'aid to emigrate', 15 June, he again dilated on the subject, providing details of a successful pauper emigration scheme in Benenden, Kent, from which 'every rate-payer' had gained. In his last known speeches in the Commons, 13 July 1830, Wilmot defiantly returned to the themes which had become his trademark, observing that although emigration had 'not met with that support in this House upon which I think I ought to have reckoned', he would continue 'to pursue, out of doors, those exertions for the success of this measure', which was 'a plain and simple remedy' for poverty. The same day he appealed to the House 'to avoid irritating the West Indians':

> Whatever may be the inherent guilt of slavery, whatever may be its atrocities, it has been fostered and patronised by the British nation for its own purposes; and it is most

unjust to visit on the accidental present holders of that property those inconveniences which ought to be shared by the nation at large, if we are prepared to offer a tardy expiation for our original injustice.

At the 1830 dissolution Wilmot retired from 'that *villainous* Newcastle' and apparently sought no other seat.[67] Financial difficulties may have been partly to blame. Principal shareholder in a large South American pearl fishing venture, described as a 'fraudulent transaction' by the duke of Bedford in 1825, three years later Wilmot was privately rescheduling his debts to Sir William Call, explaining that he had 'not been able to find a banker prepared to supply that accommodation'.[68] He was a rumoured candidate for the Liverpool by-election, where he had been approached as a successor to Huskisson in 1827, but he did not stand.[69] He was nevertheless considered for office by Peel, who was advised by Charles Arbuthnot*, 14 July 1830, to 'reflect a great deal about the cabinet for Wilmot', as the duke 'certainly doubts whether it would not be going too quick'.[70] Ellenborough, who thought that Wilmot was neither 'of cabinet calibre' nor 'a gentleman', noted that Sir Henry Hardinge* preferred him to 'Frankland Lewis as his successor at the war office' and that Bathurst 'rather wished to have Wilmot in office'.[71] According to Mrs. Arbuthnot, 8 Aug., William Vesey Fitzgerald* thought that Wilmot 'would be very useful in a privy councillor's office out of the cabinet if Peel would only instruct him and encourage him to speak instead of preventing it'.[72] On 17 Sept. Arbuthnot reported that the duke

> would not like the cabinet for Wilmot Horton because he thinks him so unsteady, and that he must be sobered down before he can be admitted with any safety into your councils. The duke, however, would be most anxious to get office for him out of the cabinet.[73]

Peel was still considering Wilmot for office, 23 Oct., but Thomas Gladstone* reported that he was 'on the continent, or at all accounts has retired from Parliament for the present'.[74] He was 'extremely annoyed' at 'being *omitted* altogether in the list of those private friends of poor Huskisson who were privately informed of the details of his funeral', but confessed to Granville 'that the stream has been running against me, and that the folly and irrationality of my views have been the theme of the regret and criticism of many of *his* friends', 21 Oct.[75] His misgivings, however, quickly evaporated with the impending collapse of the Wellington ministry, Lady Granville remarking, 9 Nov., that he had 'turned up' for breakfast 'like small fish in a storm' and 'must think himself lucky in having kept aloof'.[76] 'Every *succeeding* hour convinces me that the new government will be *obliged* to adopt my views', he wrote to Granville, 2 Dec., but 'what are they to do with me?':

All home situations *are filled up* ... I will not accept a subordinate situation *here*. If a scheme as comprehensive as mine, the result of so much labour, the subject of so much *praise* from scientific authorities ... is to be adopted by a reluctant government, its author is worthy of a place in the cabinet if he is worthy of any reward. But I have been too much *disgusted* to look at home office with any degree of zeal and satisfaction, even if such *could be* offered to me as I could take, and *none such exists*.[77]

His lectures to the Mechanics' Institute, subsequently published in a revised form, 'on the general theory of labour', the 'general theory of taxation' and 'of course the efficacy of his own plan of emigration' were, commented Greville, 23 Dec. 1830, 'full of zeal and animation, but so totally without method and arrangement that he is hardly intelligible'.[78] His pamphlets on 'negro slavery' of the same year attacked 'the abolitionists out of their own mouths', but 'it would have been well', commented Gladstone, 'if he had abstained from ... throwing ridicule upon them'.[79]

Wilmot was 'delighted' at being offered the governorship of Ceylon, which other contending parties were not aware had become vacant, by the Grey ministry in January 1831.[80] He accepted it 'with perfect satisfaction', but was reported to be 'vexed beyond measure at the *Age* having said that he was going there as a pauper emigrant'.[81] He consoled himself with the '*firm* opinion' that 'before I have been twelve months in Ceylon, the government, of whatever consistency, will adopt all my views', finding 'that nothing *can be done* in the way of relief from retrenchment and reduction' and 'that extensive reductions of army and navy would only tend to throw fresh labourers on a glutted market'. 'The most contended exile', who succeeded to his father's baronetcy and estates in 1834, he remained in Ceylon for six years, continuing to campaign for emigration and commencing a project to collate all his papers with his deputy private secretary, George Lee. After his return, he wrote prolifically on Canada, Ireland, taxation and parliamentary reform.[82] He had been party to the destruction of the manuscript 'memoirs' of his cousin Lord Byron, which were considered 'unfit' for publication, and the compensation of their publisher, John Murray, 1824-5.[83] Wilmot died in May 1841 at Sudbrook Park, Surrey, leaving behind an extensive personal archive, which has become much decayed.[84] By his will, dated 21 Sept. 1838, his personalty passed to his wife who, under a

codicil of 19 Jan. 1839, was named as sole executrix. A second codicil of 12 July 1839 left £3,000 to friends and provided for the education of his godson, Robert Morris of Ceylon, at the Blue Coat School. The baronetcy and entailed Derbyshire estates passed to his eldest son Robert Edward (1808-80).[85]

[1] IGI (Derbys.). *HP Commons, 1790-1820*, iv. 599 erroneously gives 1 Sept. [2] TNA 30/29/9/6/42; Derbys. RO, Catton mss D3155 WH2932, Wilmot to Goderich, 18 Oct. 1827; S. M. Hardy and R. C. Baily, 'Downfall of Gower Interest in Staffs. Boroughs', *Colls. Hist. Staffs.* (1950-1), 271-8. [3] Hatherton mss, Wilmot to Huskisson, 22 Jan. 1828; Add. 38751, f. 325. [4] HLRO, Hist. Coll. 379, Grey Bennet diary, 108. [5] TNA 30/29/9/6/41. [6] Hatherton mss, Wilmot to Littleton, 17 Aug. 1830. [7] *Language, Print and Electoral Politics* ed. H. Barker and D. Vincent, 232-40; *Staffs. Advertiser*, 11, 18 Mar.; *Birmingham Chron.* 9 Mar. 1820. [8] Broughton, *Recollections*, ii. 126. [9] *Pol. Econ. Club Minutes* (1921), 359; B. Gordon, *Political Economy* (1976), 85, 207. [10] *The Times*, 15 June, 6, 8 July 1820. [11] TNA 30/29/9/3/9. [12] Harrowby mss, Bathurst to Harrowby, 28, 29 Nov. 1821. [13] *Arbuthnot Jnl.* i. 210-11. [14] Northants. RO, Agar Ellis diary, 1 June 1824. [15] TNA 30/29/9/6/18. [16] Catton mss WH2932. [17] *The Times*, 12, 16 Mar. 1825. [18] Ibid. 19, 27 May, 4, 7, 14, 17, 20 June 1825. [19] TNA 30/29/6/32. [20] Agar Ellis diary, 19 May 1826. [21] Bodl. G. Pamph. 2736 (13), *Speech by Robert Wilmot Horton ... in the Town Hall of Newcastle-under-Lyme, on the occasion of his attending the Election of the Mayor* (1825), 3-4. [22] TNA 30/29/9/5/41; Bodl. 26.494, *Letter to Duke of Norfolk on Catholic Question* (1826). [23] Catton mss WH3027/1912 and Bodl. 26.493, *Letter to Electors* (1826), 3-4, 15. [24] *Staffs. Advertiser*, 3, 10 June; Nottingham Univ. Lib. Acc. 636, Denison diary, 6 June 1826; TNA 30/29/9/6/59; Catton mss WH2932, Wilmot to Goderich, 18 Oct. 1827. [25] Catton mss WH2932. [26] TNA 30/29/9/6/40. [27] Catton mss WH3029, Granville to Wilmot, 26 Jan. 1827. [28] Ibid. WH3027, Wilmot to Huskisson, 10 Nov. 1826. [29] TNA 30/29/9/6/41. [30] Catton mss WH2796, Robinson to Wilmot, 25 Mar.; WH3027/1968, Wilmot to Blake, 10 June 1826. [31] Denison diary, 15 Feb. 1827. [32] Add. 40392, ff. 267-9. [33] *Canning's Ministry*, 38. [34] Catton mss WH2760; Add. 40320, f. 49. [35] *Colchester Diary*, iii. 486; Catton mss WH2932. [36] Catton mss WH2932, Wilmot to Littleton, 23, 27 Nov. 1827. [37] Catton mss WH2932, Wilmot to Col. Shawe, 22 July 1827. [38] TNA 30/29/9/6/54. [39] *Croker Pprs.* i. 384. [40] Add. 38750, f. 22. [41] NLW, Harpton Court mss C/621, Frankland Lewis to wife, 20 Aug. 1827. [42] TNA 30/29/9/6/51; Lansdowne mss, Macdonald to Lansdowne, 21 Oct. 1827. [43] Catton mss WH2932, Wilmot to Granville, 11 Dec. 1827. [44] Add. 38750 f. 36; TNA 30/29/9/6/51. [45] TNA 30/29/9/6/54. [46] Catton mss WH2932. [47] Ibid. Wilmot's memorandum, 6 July 1828; TNA 30/29/9/6/59. [48] Catton mss WH2932, Wilmot to Littleton, 27 Nov. 1827. [49] Add. 38752 f. 38. [50] Catton mss WH2932. [51] Ibid. Wilmot to Peel, 28 Jan. 1828. [52] Add. 40395 f. 148. [53] Hatherton mss, Wilmot to Littleton, 22 Jan.; TNA 30/29/9/6/65. [54] Add. 40307 f. 50; B. Hilton, *Corn, Cash, Commerce*, 247. [55] *Buxton Mems.* 202-3. [56] Wellington mss WP1/980/30. [57] *Croker Pprs.* i. 420; *Arbuthnot Jnl.* ii. 190. [58] *Ellenborough Diary*, i. 122-4; Wellington mss WP1/980/30. [59] Catton mss WH2932, Wilmot to Wellington, 29 May 1828; Wellington mss WP1/934/18; 935/59. [60] *Arbuthnot Jnl.* ii. 190. [61] Catton mss WH2932, memo. 6 July 1828. [62] *Arbuthnot Jnl.* ii. 194; Aberdeen Univ. Lib. Arbuthnot mss, Wilmot to Mrs. Arbuthnot, 18 June 1829. [63] Bodl. 28.292, *Protestant Securities Suggested* (1828); 29.524, *Protestant Safety compatible with the Remission of the Civil Disabilities of Roman Catholics*, (1829); TNA 30/29/9/6/69; Add. 38757 f. 160; Wellington mss WP1/992/18; Cent. Kent. Stud. Stanhope mss U190 C355, Pusey to Mahon, 2 Jan. 1829. [64] Grey mss, Durham to Grey, 3 Feb. 1829. [65] *Greville Mems.* i. 247. [66] Agar Ellis diary, 9 Mar. 1830. [67] Hatherton mss, Wilmot to Littleton, 17 Aug. 1830. [68] Add. 51668, Bedford to Lady Holland, 27 Jan.; Hatherton

diary [Mar. 1825]; Catton mss WH2932, Wilmot to Call, 17 July 1828. [69] TNA 30/29/9/6/70; Lonsdale mss, Lowther to Lonsdale, 1 Nov. 1830. [70] Add. 40340, f. 228. [71] *Ellenborough Diary*, ii. 297-9, 306. [72] *Arbuthnot Jnl.* ii. 378. [73] Add. 40340, f. 236. [74] *Arbuthnot Jnl.* ii. 393; St. Deiniol's Lib. Glynne-Gladstone mss 196, T. to J. Gladstone, 18 Sept. 1830. [75] TNA 30/29/9/6/70. [76] *Countess Granville Letters*, ii. 65. [77] TNA 30/29/9/6/71. [78] Catton mss WH2932, Wilmot to Brougham, 11 Dec. 1830; *Greville Mems.* ii. 95-98. [79] Glynne-Gladstone mss 196, T. to J. Gladstone, 18 Sept. 1830. [80] *Three Diaries*, 43. [81] Add. 61937, f. 123; *Edgeworth Letters*, 524. [82] For example, *Exposition and defence of Earl Bathurst's administration of … Canada* (1838); *Ireland and Canada* (1839); *Correspondence … upon … Ireland and Canada* (1839); *Reform in 1839, and reform in 1831* (1839); *Observations upon Taxation* (1840). [83] Broughton, *Recollections*, iii. 334; TNA 30/29/9/6/73; Catton mss WH2828-2829, 2949-52, 2960; Add. 31037, ff. 47-60. [84] *Oxford DNB* erroneously gives 8 June. [85] *Gent. Mag.* (1841), ii. 90-91; PROB 8/234; 11/1947/425.

P.J.S.

WILSON, James (*d.* 1830), of Sneaton Castle, Whitby, Yorks. and 3 Brunswick Place, Mdx.

YORK   1826–1830

m. 1da. *d.* 7 Sept. 1830.

Wilson is an enigmatic figure: according to George Strickland* of Boynton, Yorkshire, he was 'a man risen from nothing, partly by a relation leaving him a West India property',[1] and he himself told the House, 23 Mar. 1830, that 'at the age of 15 I began to serve my country with brown bess on my shoulder as a common soldier'. Throughout the brief documented period of his life he was referred to as 'Colonel Wilson', but no reliable record has been found to confirm his entitlement to this, or any other rank. It seems certain, given his military background, that the identification of him as the only son of James Wilson of Horton, Buckinghamshire and Jamaica, who was a fellow of King's College, Cambridge, 1797-1806, is erroneous.[2] He is known to have been the proprietor of the Cane Grove estate on St. Vincent, which employed 231 negroes in 1827, and he may have been, at one time, a member of the legislative council of that island.[3] There is no other known trace of his life before 1820, when he purchased Sneaton Manor, which he subsequently rebuilt as Sneaton Castle, a castellated mansion house with a commanding view over Whitby. In 1823 he completely rebuilt the church of St. Hilda at Sneaton.[4] John Beckett*, who visited Wilson in October 1825, noted that his wife, like him, was 'as orange as her own locks'.[5] Early in 1826 he agreed to offer for York at the forthcoming general election on behalf of the Tories, or Blues, who were informed that he was 'a gentleman of great respectability, property and influence' and 'decidedly opposed to any further concessions to Catholics'. Sensitive to Whig attacks

on him as a plantation owner, he declared that 'long experience has fully convinced my mind that a gradual improvement of the slave population of the colonies, both in mind and morals, is best calculated to promote the true interests of all parties', and that he would work towards this object 'whenever it can be effected with safety and without infringing upon the vested rights and acknowledged claims of the West Indian proprietors'. In the event, divisions amongst the Whigs meant that he and the sitting Whig Member were returned unopposed at the election that summer.[6]

In the House, whether because of his accent or his manner, Wilson appears to have become a figure of fun; an obituarist recalled how he 'attracted some notice by the bluntness and singularity of his speeches on the Catholic question'.[7] He presented anti-Catholic petitions from York and Boston, 5 Mar. 1827, and divided against relief the next day. He voted in the minorities against the spring guns bill, 2 Apr., and the Coventry magistracy bill, 18 June 1827. That day he presented a petition from a resident of St. Vincent complaining of the loss of slaves and the deterioration of his lands as a result of the existing law. He divided against repeal of the Test Acts, 26 Feb., and Catholic relief, 12 May 1828. In his first known speech, 6 Mar., he complained of the 'foul aspersions and groundless insinuations' made against West India proprietors, and accused his 'compassionate brethren' the Whigs of 'seeking to bestow their benevolence everywhere but in those places where it is most wanted'; he suggested they turn their attention to Ireland and Scotland. He advised that emancipation be allowed to 'grow up from the seedling, like an oak from an acorn', and dismissed calls for the immediate liberation of slaves, arguing that 'subordination is necessary' and warning that 'property would be destroyed' and 'bloodshed and murder … take place' if the process was hurried. He presented 16 petitions from various places in the North Riding calling for greater protection for agricultural producers, 22 Apr., and concurred in their request for restrictions to the bonding system. On 23 May, claiming to have 12 similar petitions in his possession, he moved an amendment to the corn bill to enforce the payment of import duty, in order to 'do away with that system of speculation in corn', that 'fatal monopoly' which 'the opulent importer and corn factor keep up between them'. However, in the face of opposition, he withdrew the amendment. He voiced his approval of the alehouses licensing bill, 25 June. He voted with the duke of Wellington's ministry against reduction of the salary of the lieutenant-general of the ordnance, 7 July. On behalf of the residents of Whitby he appealed to the chancellor of the exchequer, Goulburn, to delay the savings banks bill, 10 July 1828, and when this was refused he moved a hostile amendment, which was negatived. That day he objected to the 'unjust' and 'unnecessary' corporate funds bill, 'an unauthorized and unconstitutional interference with the rights and property of others', and insisted that the means to punish corporations for the misapplication of funds already existed in common law. His condemnation was greeted with hoots of derision, and his hostile amendment was defeated by 35-10. In February 1829 Planta, the patronage secretary, listed him among those who were 'opposed to the principle' of Catholic emancipation. When presenting a hostile petition from Hull, 26 Feb., he expressed regret at being forced to 'differ on any subject from the government of my royal master', but believed that 'I should act as a traitor to my constituents ... my country ... [and] my own conscience if I did not oppose them on this'. Amidst whoops of laughter, he reiterated his loyalty to the king and said he cared not who were ministers as long as they acted for the welfare of the country. He pressed on, maintaining that he had no personal animosity to Catholics, and he predicted that emancipation would prove useless in curing the ills of Ireland. He brought the House down with his statement that Daniel O'Connell*, who 'acts as I like ... plainly, openly and manfully', was 'one of the finest fellows I met in my life' and that 'I wish to God we had some O'Connells on this side' of the chamber. This was too much for the Whigs, and to a chorus of derision he thundered that he was 'glad to find that my ... opponents, who call themselves the friends of liberal principles, are obliged to resort to such baseness of opposition as this'. After praising George Canning* as a 'great Protestant leader', he concluded with the couplet

> Whilst I can handle stick or stone,
> I will support the church and throne.

One junior minister described this as 'a most laughable speech ... full of repetitions and mispronunciations appearing like those of a drunken man'.[8] He presented further petitions from Stockton-on-Tees and York, 2, 4 Mar., and voted against the government's emancipation bill, 6, 18, 23, 30 Mar. On 11 Mar. he gave the House the benefit of his thoughts on how to solve the problems of Ireland, declaring that he would 'give the colony of Sierra Leone to the Pope ... send there all the mischievous Popish priests of Ireland ... and ... make all the discontented agitators follow them'. He also favoured compelling Irish landowners to be resident for six months of each year and providing all labouring families with half-an-acre of land. He pre-sented a petition from the Whitby Oil and Gas Light Company against the bill to extend Crosley's patent on gas apparatus, which he said he would oppose 'inch by inch', 10 Apr. He repeated his opposition to the bill when presenting a petition from the York Gas Light Company, 1 May. He seconded a motion for continuation of the fishery bounties, 2 June, and warned the House that their withdrawal, at a time of distress, would be 'unwise' and might put an end to fishing on the east coast. In August 1829 he was mentioned as one of those who had offered to help bail out the troubled Protestant newspaper, the *Morning Journal*.[9] That autumn the Ultra Tory leader, Sir Richard Vyvyan*, listed him among 'Tories' who were 'strongly opposed' to the present government.

He voted against the enfranchisement of Birmingham, Leeds and Manchester, 23 Feb. 1830. Speaking in support of the Whitby petition complaining of distress in the shipping industry, 5 Mar., he condemned the system of free trade, which had been 'the ruin' of both the shipping and the agricultural interests. He again encountered a volley of guffaws, which provoked him into declaring that if he could have his way, 'I would have a call of the House every week'. The laughter did not subside, but he was undeterred, remarking that the only class who were exempt from distress were 'that privileged class [who] enjoy the protection of the justice of the country ... who share the dividends and who never pay sixpence to the general expenses, but let the whole weight of it fall on the land'. He accused the House of 'dilly-dally' in endless debate over 'a few men more or less in the army', while ignoring the real problem of distress. On 23 Mar. he offered his own remedy, declaring that if he was prime minister he would 'without consultation have thrown the assessed taxes overboard' and introduced an 'equitable and well regulated property tax framed in such a way as to bring in all absentees'. He attacked the Reciprocity Act as harmful to the shipping interest and a cause of distress, 6 May. He attended the London meeting of West India proprietors, 2 June, which resolved to support the government's proposals regarding the duty on rum but to seek a large reduction in the duty on sugar imported into Ireland.[10] He divided against Jewish emancipation, 5 Apr., and paired against it, 17 May. However, he introduced his own relief bill, 17 June, which proposed to 'enable British and Irish born Jews to inherit property of every description' and 'render them eligible to the corporate and elective franchise'. He believed that the Jews had been 'unfairly and unjustly treated', but qualified the liberality of his measure by explaining that they would still be prevented from sitting in

Parliament or holding any ministerial or judicial office. He hoped that his bill would 'open the door to the Jews and encourage them to emigrate towards the Christian religion', but finally agreed to withdraw it because of opposition. In presenting a petition from the brewers and publicans of York against the sale of beer bill, 6 May, he expressed concern about its potential impact on the lower orders. His attempt to move an amendment, 3 June, was ruled out of order, but he explained that its aim was to prevent the entire country from becoming a 'tippling shop' and warned that without some such restriction, 'every pickpocket in the country will become a beer seller'. He moved his amendment the next day but withdrew it, on the understanding that Sir Edward Knatchbull would move a similar one at the report stage. He duly voted for Knatchbull's proposed clause to prohibit on-consumption in beer houses, 21 June, and to postpone on-consumption for two years, 1 July. He divided in the minority against amendments to the Galway franchise bill, 24 May. On the second reading of the northern roads bill, 3 June, he said that unless it was withdrawn he would move a wrecking amendment. Yet he presented and endorsed a York petition in favour of the bill, 2 July, and explained that his previous opposition had been based on a misunderstanding that the new road would not pass through York. He paired against abolition of the death penalty for forgery, 7 June. He presented a Whitby petition against compulsory contributions by seamen for the upkeep of Greenwich Hospital, 10 June. In response to a petition objecting to soldiers being required to attend Greek and Catholic church services while on duty in the Mediterranean, 17 June, he observed that it was 'part of their duty only' and 'on no account [did it] bind them in a conscientious view'. He voted with government against a reduction in judges' salaries, 7 July 1830. That summer he delayed the announcement of his intention to offer again for York until after George IV's death and put off his election canvass until after the funeral. When he finally entered the contest, he realized that he had late it too late and withdrew before the poll.[11]

Wilson died in September 1830 and was buried at St. Hilda's, Sneaton; his coffin was enclosed in 'a mahogany case ornamented with 32 guns ... made some time ago in pursuance of the Colonel's own orders'.[12] He left Sneaton Castle to his daughter Mary, who married Joseph Barker Richardson of Fieldhouse Whitby in 1849, but such was the scale of his debts that the Cane Grove estate and his personalty, which was sworn under £4,000, were absorbed in repayments.[13]

[1] Brougham mss, Strickland to James Brougham [1826]. [2] Gerrit P. Judd, *Members of Parl. 1734-1832*, p. 379. [3] C. Shepherd, *Hist. St. Vincent*, pp. xvi, lxi; *Gent. Mag.* (1830), ii. 283. [4] *VCH Yorks. (N. Riding)*, ii. 513; N. Pevsner, *Buildings of England: Yorks. (N. Riding)*, 399. [5] Lonsdale mss, Beckett to Lowther, 15 Oct. 1825. [6] *Yorks. Gazette*, 18, 25 Mar., 15 Apr.; *The Times*, 8 June 1826. [7] *Gent. Mag.* (1830), ii. 283. [8] Add. 36465, f. 80. [9] Hatfield House mss, 1829-30 bundle, Rev. John Litton Crosby to Salisbury, 6 Aug. 1829. [10] Inst. of Commonwealth Stud. M915/11. [11] W.W. Bean, *Parl. Rep. Six Northern Counties*, 117. [12] *Yorks. Gazette*, 25 Sept. 1830. [13] PROB 11/1781/53; IR26/1275/31; *VCH Yorks. (N. Riding)*, ii. 513.

M.P.J.C.

WILSON, Sir Robert Thomas (1777–1849), of Charles Street, Berkeley Square, Mdx.[1]

SOUTHWARK   1818–1831

b. 17 Aug. 1777, 3rd *s.* of Benjamin Wilson (*d.* 1788), serjeant painter to the king, of Great Russell Street, Mdx. and *w.* Jane *née* Hetherington. *educ.* Westminster 1786-7; Winchester 1787-8; by a clergyman, Tottenham Court Road. *m.* 8 July 1797, at Gretna Green, and again, 10 Mar. 1798, Jemima, da. of Col. William Belford of Harbledown, Kent, 7s. (4 *d.v.p.*) 6da. (4 *d.v.p.*). kt. of order of Maria Theresa of Austria, sanctioned by George III 2 June 1801. *d.* 9 May 1849.

Cornet 15 Drag. 1794, lt. 1794, capt. 1796; a.d.c. to Gen. St. John in Ireland 1798; maj. Hompesch's mounted riflemen 1800, lt.-col. 1802, half-pay 1802; insp. yeoman cav. Som., Devon and Cornw. 1802-4; lt.-col. 19 Drag. 1804, 20 Drag. 1805; brevet col. and a.d.c. to the king 1810; lt.-col. 22 Drag. 1812; maj.-gen. 1813, dismissed 1821, restored as lt.-gen. 1830, with effect from 1825; col. 15 Drag. 1835; gen. 1841.

Gov. and c.-in-c. Gibraltar 1842-9.

Wilson had enjoyed a distinguished and eventful military career before entering the House in 1818. His 'incredible stories of his battles with serpents in the East' captivated Henry Edward Fox*, who thought that 'with a tartan and a claymore' he would make 'an admirable character' for a Scott novel. Fox added that 'there is something about him ... that makes it impossible to see and hear him without having an admiration for his high spirit and enterprise, and at the same time great contempt for his understanding and judgement'.[2] For all his undoubted charm and charisma, Wilson's political talents indeed proved to be limited. His frequent interventions in debate during his first Parliament had earned him a reputation as a bore, his attempts to effect a Whig-radical rapprochement achieved nothing, and he confessed to John Cam Hobhouse* in 1820 that he was 'disgusted with the little figure he has made in the House'.[3] Although he enjoyed the confidence of Lord Grey, the latter's view of him as 'one of the ablest men in Europe' was cited as evidence of the Whig leader's own failings by both John Croker* and Charles Greville. Lord Holland voiced the sentiment of many in 1823 when he contrasted one of Wilson's occasional successes as a conciliator with his 'common want of judgement and discretion'.[4] At the general election of 1820 he offered again for the populous metropolitan constituency of Southwark. He ominously compared the condition of the country with that of France before the revolution and characterized the Six Acts as the commencement of tyranny. He called for a reduction in taxes, repeal of the Foreign Enlistment Act, inquiry into Peterloo and a measure of parliamentary reform, 'extending the ... franchise to all who pay taxes, abolishing rotten boroughs and shortening the duration of Parliaments'. However, he was careful to avoid giving a direct pledge on Catholic relief. He finished comfortably ahead of a Tory challenger after a four-day poll.[5]

He continued to be an assiduous attender who voted with the Whig opposition to Lord Liverpool's ministry on all major issues, including parliamentary reform, 9 May 1821, 25 Apr. 1822, 20 Feb. 1823, 13, 27 Apr., 26 May 1826. He divided for Catholic relief, 28 Feb. 1821, 1 Mar., 21 Apr., 10 May 1825. Early in May 1820 he was reportedly disgusted at Henry Brougham's part in opposing Wood's motion on the role of the government informer Edwards in the Cato Street conspiracy.[6] He pressed for an inquiry into this matter, 9 May, when his intervention to soften a 'sharp skirmish' between George Canning and Sir Francis Burdett earned him a 'very handsome' letter of thanks from the former, who wrote that his interposition was 'as judicious ... as it was kindly intended'. Wilson's reply, in which he affirmed that he had acted from 'personal as well as public feeling', was early evidence of his warm regard for Canning.[7] On 17 Oct. he inquired about the release of one Franklin, who had been charged with producing treasonable placards, implying that he was an *agent provocateur*. In supporting Brougham's motion on the droits of the crown and admiralty, 5 May, he condemned the seizure of foreign vessels. He accepted that the expense of maintaining British embassies abroad did not permit of any savings, 18 May. He opposed the Newington church bill, 19, 26 May, when he joined in criticisms of the neglect of St. Paul's Cathedral.[8] He was a minority teller against Holme Sumner's motion for a select committee on agricultural distress, 30 May. He opposed the Aliens Act as unnecessary and pointed to outrages committed in its name, 1 June. Sir James Mackintosh, who attended this debate 'at Wilson's desire', regretted afterwards that 'he would not ... let me answer Castlereagh [the leader of the Commons]

but began the debate very injudiciously with the cases of the Buonopartists, which were sure to excite all the prejudices and apprehensions most favourable to the [Act]'.[9] Wilson was twice a minority teller against the continuation bill, 7, 12 July, when he disapproved of modifying clauses, thinking it better that 'the bill should pass with all its obnoxiousness about it'. He complained about the cession of the island of Parga to Turkey, 29 June 1820.

Early in 1820 Wilson had tried to convince Grey that George IV's desire for a divorce from his wife might precipitate a political crisis of such magnitude as to drive the government from office. He expressed to Grey in May his 'firm belief' that ministers would resign if Queen Caroline came to England, and he protested in the House against attempts to prevent her from landing in the country, 6 June.[10] In July it was reportedly his view that the queen should accept a financial settlement and retire abroad, and when her counsel Stephen Lushington* asked him to go to Italy to gather evidence in her favour, Wilson declined, citing his wife's health and his former friendship with the king.[11] However, his zeal in the queen's cause was roused by the progress of the bill of pains and penalties, which he observed from the gallery in the Lords. His conviction that the bill would not pass was thought foolish by Thomas Creevey*, but showed uncharacteristic political foresight.[12] He declared to the Commons, 18 Sept., that there was 'no resistance, no obstacle ... which the wit of man could devise, or perseverance apply', that he would not use to impede the proceedings against the queen, which he denounced as 'a foul and infamous conspiracy'. Determined to defend the queen against 'perjured witnesses and a partial tribunal', he sought to embarrass Lord Castlereagh over the discovery of forged banknotes in the possession of a courier employed by the Milan commission. The same day he was a minority teller for Hobhouse's motion for an address asking the king to prorogue Parliament. One government supporter suspected that Wilson was 'about to make himself *perfectly* intolerable', and he reiterated his belief in the queen's innocence at meetings in Southwark, 24 Oct., 22 Nov., when he also called for the dismissal of ministers.[13] His allies were also wary of his activities: Grey was dismayed by his participation in the queen's 'processionary cavalcade' to celebrate her acquittal, 29 Nov., and early the following month entreated him, 'as a friend, and for the sake of your family', to do nothing 'that public duty does not require' and 'not to act offensively so as to furnish those, who would be only too willing to avail themselves of it, with a pretence for depriving you of your commission'. Undeterred, Wilson replied with his thoughts on the legislative programme of the Whig administration that he expected to take office shortly. This included repeal of the Six Acts and the Aliens Act, tax cuts financed by reduced expenditure on civil and military administration in the colonies, a return to triennial parliaments and an extended franchise. He remained equivocal on Catholic relief, advising against a pledge, and acknowledged that 'the state of agriculture and the resumption of cash payments are replete with difficulties'.[14] Following Canning's resignation from the government, Wilson congratulated himself on his prescience and wrote to John George Lambton* that

> I think you and Lord Grey will find yourselves in the wrong about change of ministry. I am more and more satisfied there will be a break-up. It is impossible these men can go on unsupported as they are even by their vassals when meeting to frame ultra loyal addresses. They have lingered to try their fortunes. They have drawn a blank and must now withdraw all pretensions.[15]

At a meeting in Southwark, 18 Jan. 1821, he accused the Austrian government of complicity in assembling evidence against the queen and identified the restoration of her name to the liturgy as 'a point of honour'.[16] In presenting the resulting petition to the Commons, 31 Jan., he railed against ministerial obstinacy. That day he indiscreetly informed the Tory patronage secretary Charles Arbuthnot* of plans to raise a subscription to sustain the campaign on the queen's behalf, and admitted that if it failed 'our game is gone'.[17] He reopened the debate on the censure of ministers, 6 Feb., when he asserted that their intransigence 'menaced the country with more danger than had ever yet been threatened by any subversive power'. Henry Grey Bennet* described this as 'a long artificial speech', and noted that Wilson 'read several documents of evidence in favour of the queen from witnesses who might have been called or who came too late'. Brougham had 'entreated him not to do so, but proceed he would and the result was that he let in Castlereagh in his speech to comment on the evidence of the trial.[18] Wilson denied that the queen had squandered money on public demonstrations in her favour, 9 Feb. Four days later he presented a petition from Southwark mechanics which was so long that it rolled along the floor of the House: this inspired him to predict the eventual triumph of the queen's cause. However, much to the amusement of ministerialists, he was shut out of the division in her favour that day, having been away at supper.[19] He maintained that the government's flouting of public opinion justified the refusal of a vote of supply, 14 Feb. In supporting the printing of the Nottingham petition

for their impeachment, 20 Feb. 1821, he recalled the events of Peterloo.

Wilson frequently assailed the government on foreign policy issues during the 1821 session, though his often convoluted queries were generally treated with disdain by Castlereagh, who would not be drawn on ministers' attitude to the formation of a constitutional government in Naples, 24 Jan., or their likely response to any threat of invasion by the Holy Alliance, 13 Feb.[20] Yet in the debate on Mackintosh's motion condemning the conduct of the Allies towards Naples, 21 Feb., Wilson made what Grey Bennet reckoned to be 'the best [speech] he has ever done and was very much cheered', as he stung Castlereagh into issuing a denial that Britain had connived in placing the Neapolitan king on trial; he was a teller for the minority.[21] His own motion that day for the production of papers was defeated by 144-125, and he was induced to withdraw a similar one, 20 Mar., when he declared that 'the knell of despotism had been rung' by the Neapolitan patriots. His protests at Buonaparte's confinement on St. Helena were met with a laugh, 29 Mar. (His attitude to the former French emperor had softened to the extent that he now played host to exiled Buonapartists.)[22] He told ministers that they were 'so entangled with the confederate tyrants' that 'it was impossible for them to follow the true policy of this country, even if it were their inclination', 4 May. Having characterized the restored monarchical constitution of Naples as a 'select vestry appointed', 20 June, he denied that a policy of non-intervention in foreign conflicts was sustainable, 21 June 1821.[23]

With the Whig opposition in a disorganized state, Wilson was mentioned by Joseph Planta* early in 1821 as one the 'guerillas' who carried on 'the warfare' against ministers and were determined to 'give all the trouble they can'.[24] In presenting petitions from London ropemakers and leather manufacturers complaining of distress, 12 Feb., 7 May 1821, Wilson advocated the taxation of machinery.[25] He opposed Scarlett's poor relief bill, 8 May, suggesting that the burden of taxation rather than the poor rates was to blame for economic distress. He was a minority teller against the malt duties bill, 14 Feb., and opposed the prohibition on the sale of roasted grain as a coffee substitute, 21 Feb., 12 Mar., 2 July.[26] While he 'deprecated any sudden diminution of the military force of the country', 9 Mar., he nevertheless found much to speak and vote against that session in the minutiae of the army estimates. He made various observations regarding the funding and deployment of the armed services, 14 Mar., 18 Apr., 2 May, but was obliged to modify the language of his protest that the proposed grant for army volunteer forces 'would make rebellion a duty', 16 Apr. On the other hand, his vote with ministers for the payment of arrears in the duke of Clarence's grant, 18 June, led to him being called to account at the annual meeting of his supporters in Southwark four days later. He explained that 'from personal feeling he was peculiarly bound to act with liberality towards the royal family', but this did not satisfy many of those present, including Burdett, who thought his vote had been 'a mistake'. Grey Bennet noted that he had 'nearly lost all support in Southwark' and that 'if an election was now to take place, he would not be returned again'.[27] Wilson favoured the enfranchisement of Leeds as a scot and lot borough in place of Grampound, 2 Mar., on the principle that 'representation should be coextensive with taxation'. He attended the *London Tavern* meeting of the friends of reform, 4 Apr.[28] He told the House that he supported a general measure of reform 'in compliance with the wishes of 2,000 of my constituents', 17 May. In what Grey Bennet described as 'a long and dull speech', he condemned as 'utterly unjust and unwarrantable' the proposal to create a select vestry at Newington, 5 Mar.[29] He successfully moved for the standing orders committee to inquire into the proceedings on this bill, 6 Apr. He stated that if his vote for Catholic relief earlier that session did not meet with the satisfaction of his constituents, he would willingly relinquish his seat, 26 Mar., 2 Apr.[30] He denounced the system of slavery in the West Indies as 'cruel and atrocious', 4 May, and quizzed ministers about an alleged increase in the number of slaves in Barbados, 24, 28 June.[31] He defended his friend Grey Bennet for pursuing a case of breach of privilege against the *John Bull* newspaper, 17 May. He spoke against renewal of the Aliens Act, 3 July 1821.[32]

Shortly after the end of the session Wilson left for Paris, where he received a letter from Queen Caroline avowing her determination to attend the coronation; she failed to heed the advice contained in his temperate reply 'to avoid any proceeding which may be the subject of future regrets'.[33] On receiving news of her death, he returned for the funeral, 14 Aug. 1821. Afterwards, he found himself at the centre of the row over disturbances on the processional route, which had resulted in its diversion through the City of London, to the intense annoyance of the government and the king. Wilson had attended the funeral with Brougham and, from his subsequent account in the House, first made himself conspicuous at Kensington Gore, where he suggested to the commanding officer of the guard of honour that, to avoid trouble, the proces-

sion should be allowed to pass through the City. Here he also persuaded the crowd to release a kidnapped baggage wagon bound for Windsor. At Cumberland Gate his instinct for interference surfaced again, as he hastened towards the sound of gunfire and strongly remonstrated with the Life Guards for firing on an unruly crowd. He asked the commanding officer, Major Oakes, whether he had given orders to do so: Oakes replied in the negative, and subsequently confirmed this in writing.[34] Calm was eventually restored, but whether this was owing to Wilson's intervention is not impartially clear. Oakes reported Wilson's actions to his seniors, who regarded his behaviour as a serious breach of military discipline (neither his parliamentary speeches against corporal punishment, nor his part in the rescue of Lavalette in 1816, had endeared him to the military hierarchy). The commander-in-chief, the duke of York, was 'not sorry that he has at last given a fair opportunity of freeing the army of a person who has long been a disgrace to it', and the duke of Wellington, the second in command, later defined Wilson's actions as mutinous, informing Mrs. Arbuthnot that only the difficulty of obtaining witnesses had prevented his arraignment for the treasonable offence of obstructing the king's highway. Wellington was 'quite sure' that Wilson had been personally responsible for the disturbances at the funeral, a reference to his supposed attendance at a meeting beforehand in Hammersmith to plan its disruption.[35] This charge was demonstrably untrue, but in the fever of the times other stories were in circulation telling how Wilson had regaled the mob with beer, incited them to pull up paving stones to throw at the troops, and drunk a toast of damnation to the king.[36] All the evidence indicates that these tales were fabricated by informers, but ministers needed no further encouragement to make a scapegoat of one of their most dedicated political adversaries. Sensible of royal disfavour, Liverpool fully appreciated the 'political advantages' of offering up Wilson's head on a platter to the king, and resolved that his conduct at the funeral should be 'the very first business' laid before the monarch on his return from Ireland. Lord Sidmouth, the home secretary, gloated that 'it seems ... impossible that Sir R. can entirely escape'.[37] Wilson realized that he was 'in a scrape and wished to be advised how to get out of it', but Grey, while counselling him to lie low, offered the unfortunate suggestion of 'a formal manifesto in the shape of a memorial to the king'; Wilson duly sent this via Lord Donoughmore. On reading this document, the king's reported reaction was to ask 'why was Sir Robert Wilson there at all?'[38] The failure of this 'most irregular and improper' approach was welcomed by Liverpool, who, on receiving assurances from Wellington about the reliability of the soldier witnesses, sought his approval for invoking the royal prerogative to summarily dismiss Wilson from the army. Wellington concurred, warning that 'considering who and what the man is, and the persons who will probably try him', a general court martial would probably result in an acquittal, or else 'some very lenient censure'.[39] The matter was discussed in cabinet, 14 Sept., and the order for Wilson's dismissal was signed by the king the next day and gazetted on 18 Sept. 1821. Wilson learned of this in Paris and wrote twice to the duke of York in tones of measured outrage, but this drew a rebuff, as did his attempts to ascertain from Sidmouth the exact nature of the charges against him.[40] This denial of a hearing won him much sympathy, and a subscription was raised to compensate him for the loss of his commissions, which he accepted with some reluctance. Few subscribed from outside the circle of his Whig friends, a point noted with regret by Mackintosh but with relish by Mrs. Arbuthnot, who also rejoiced that the existence of such an indemnity fund would further irritate the king and so put an end to any chance of the Whigs kissing hands.[41]

Wilson brought the matter before the Commons with a motion for inquiry into his dismissal, 13 Feb. 1822. In a lengthy speech of exculpation he sought to establish that his actions at the funeral had been motivated only by a wish to prevent bloodshed and disorder, and he attempted to refute some of the more fantastic allegations about his conduct. He produced and read copies of his correspondence with Sidmouth and key witnesses, which was published in *The Times* two days later. The independent Member Hudson Gurney regarded his defence as 'perfect', and it appears that even Castlereagh (now Lord Londonderry) privately 'expressed surprise at the good taste with which Wilson stated his case'. A Tory Member acknowledged that 'what he said was certainly done in the most judicious manner, with great moderation and good sense, so as to leave a very favourable impression upon many who were by no means predisposed to think well of him', and Lady Holland claimed that 'several who went down determined to vote against him were convinced'.[42] However, the crux of Wilson's argument was a denial of the king's prerogative right of dismissal from the army, which was unlikely to have persuaded many. Lord Palmerston replied for the government in a sarcastic vein for which he was widely reprobated, and the motion was lost by 199-97; Grey commented that the result was 'better than I expected'.[43] Turning to the privations of the radical agitator Henry Hunt*, Wilson presented several petitions for remission of

his prison sentence and protested against the conditions of his incarceration at Ilchester, 1, 14 Mar.[44] On 6 Mar. he asked ministers if it was intended to continue prosecutions for selling roasted wheat as a coffee substitute, a law of which Hunt had also fallen foul. He presented petitions from other individuals affected, 27 Mar., 14 June, and moved for relevant papers, 29 Mar., 25 Apr. The government obliged by introducing the vegetable powder bill, though his request that its provisions be made retrospective, 4, 28 June, were not accepted.[45] He supported the Newcastle petition in Hunt's favour, 22 Mar., and used the occasion to launch a general attack on ministers' use of stipendiary offices to reward their friends. He recited the prayer of a Bethnal Green petition protesting at the government's reliance on placemen in the Commons, 28 Mar., and spoke in favour of receiving the Greenhoe reform petition, 3 June, when he challenged Londonderry 'as a man of honour' to deny that seats were routinely bought and sold. On other issues that session, he condemned interference with Members' mail, 25 Feb., and opposed the granting of licenses to public houses owned by brewers, 17 Apr. He called for a broad consideration of the corn laws, 6 May.[46] Two days later, concerned that discontent arising from agricultural distress would lead to 'coercive government', he recommended a large reduction of taxation. He welcomed the remissions granted, but not the plan to finance military and naval pensions from the sinking fund, 24 May. He approved the principle of the poor removal bill, 31 May. His attendance record was praised at a meeting of his Southwark supporters, 18 June, when he expressed little sympathy for the sufferings of the landed interest, given their previous record of support for the ministry.[47] He protested 'in the most unqualified terms' against the Irish insurrection bill, 2 July, and bore witness to the severity of distress in Ireland, 8 July, when his motion for inquiry was lost by 135-17. He considered expenditure on a Scottish national monument to be 'most indecent in the present state of Ireland', 16 July. In opposing renewal of the Aliens Act, 5 June, he accused Londonderry of having 'disgraced this country by connecting us with the police establishments of the continent'. He called for repeal of the Foreign Enlistment Act, so that Britons could legally fight in the cause of Greek independence, 15 July, and was assured by Londonderry of Britain's dispassionate attitude towards the newly independent South American republics, 23 July. After he had deprecated the cheers from government benches which greeted the testimony of John Hope, the Scottish judge found guilty of a breach of privilege, 17 July, Lord Binning sarcastically referred to Wilson as 'that pattern of orderly behaviour and decorum'.[48] The following month Lord Cochrane[†] endeavoured to persuade him to go to South America to fight for the cause of the new republics, and it took Donoughmore to persuade him that he was too old. Instead he opted to go to France to canvass support for the republics, only to be deported in October 1822. In a printed address to his constituents, he claimed to have been informed that his Napoleonic connections had made him 'in spite of myself ... a ... rallying point for the opponents of the French government', and he described his deportation as 'unconstitutional'.[49]

He welcomed the condemnation of the Holy Alliance contained in the king's speech, 5 Feb. 1823, but was disappointed in the profession of neutrality in the Franco-Spanish conflict, believing that early British intervention might deter French aggression. He issued a fierce denunciation of foreign despotism at a Southwark meeting on parliamentary reform, 11 Feb., and presented the resulting petition, 19 Feb.[50] He raised the case of a Briton imprisoned in France, 27 Feb. He likened French aggression towards Spain to that of 'tyrants, fanatics and bigots against the rights of free nations', 18 Mar., and added that he hoped Britons would 'go over in crowds' to assist the Spanish, in spite of the Foreign Enlistment Act. He expressed the hope that ministers would repeal the Six Acts and reduce taxes, 24 Feb. He believed that corporal punishment in the army was 'wholly unnecessary' and 'ought to be put an end to', 6 Mar. He reported that a Southwark meeting had evinced no desire for reform of the law on insolvent debtors, 18 Mar. In presenting an anti-slavery petition, 27 Mar., he expatiated about the sufferings of the slaves. On 17 Apr. 1823 he intervened to defuse a row between Canning and Brougham, with what Creevey regarded as 'a speech of very great merit'.[51] That day he was one of a squad of opposition Members who left the chamber as Plunket introduced his motion on Catholic relief, in order (so he told the House, 15 Feb. 1825) to avoid exciting unrealistic expectations of concession.

Defying the Foreign Enlistment Act, Wilson sailed to fight for Spain, 22 Apr. 1823, and remained abroad until the autumn. The vote recorded in his name against the Scottish juries bill, 20 June, is clearly an error. One of his correspondents wondered if his prolonged absence might cause resentment in Southwark, but none was in evidence at the meeting of his supporters, 26 June, and constituency business was dealt with by Lambton.[52] In Spain Wilson was met with garlands, but he failed to galvanize his hosts into active resistance against the French, while his efforts to recruit in

England had little effect other than to annoy the king.[53] A foray into Portugal in June ended in humiliation: the constitutional government had just been toppled, and after his refusal to drink a toast to absolute monarchy almost cost him his life, he was unceremoniously deported. Returning to Spain, he was wounded in the thigh at the siege of Corunna in mid-July, and withdrew to Gibraltar to recuperate. Here his ham-fisted attempts to involve Britain in mediation, after a private conversation with the British envoy Sir William A'Court[†], led the latter to inform him in peremptory fashion that he had never entertained 'the slightest intentions of making him the channel of his communication with the Spanish government'; the offended tone of Wilson's reply suggests that he had believed otherwise.[54] He was given the doomed command of the besieged city of Cadiz, where he received news of the death of his wife in August. In October 1823 he returned to England via Gibraltar, from what one biographer has termed 'the sorriest escapade of his whole life'.[55] As a result of it, he was stripped of the decorations previously conferred by the members of the Holy Alliance, including his Austrian knighthood, though a Turkish honour permitted him to continue to use the same style.[56] Fears that he might be prosecuted under the Foreign Enlistment Act proved unfounded, though Wellington subsequently claimed that government would have proceeded against him but for the difficulty of securing hard evidence.[57] In the Commons, 18 Mar. 1824, Wilson lamented that no show of British naval strength had been made and attested to the bravery he had encountered in Cadiz. He then thanked Canning for securing an apology from the French government for his daughters' detention and maltreatment at Calais two months earlier. The foreign secretary chided him for the diplomatic embarrassment he had caused, but other Members were unreserved in praising his courage; the Whig Agar Ellis recorded that he 'spoke well and modestly, in vindicating himself'.[58] Wilson defended Hume's use of the word 'despots' to describe Britain's former continental allies, 2 Apr. At a meeting of his supporters in Southwark, 22 June, he gave an account of his adventures in Spain and called for recognition of the South American republics; his parliamentary conduct was eulogized. Nevertheless, one of his friends could 'not see that there is any object for you to remain in Parliament ... You can do no good'.[59] He advocated reform of the usury laws, 27 Feb., when he supported the admission of a petition complaining of the conduct of George Chetwynd[*] as a Staffordshire magistrate, asking: 'were the doors of the House ... to be closed against the peoples of England?' He spoke against flogging in the army, 5 Mar., and naval impressment, 18 Mar., 10 June. He supported the London common councilmen's petition for parliamentary reform, 17 May, and a Yorkshire petition complaining of restrictions on freedom of speech, 3 June 1824.[60] That day he inquired about the evidence concerning the prosecution of the Methodist missionary John Smith in Demerara.

Though he did not exempt the Catholic Association from criticism, Wilson opposed the Irish unlawful societies bill 15, 22 Feb. 1825, wondering why, since it was admitted to be a short-term expedient, the government did not simply enact Catholic emancipation. He expressed implacable opposition to the disfranchisement of Irish 40s. freeholders, 28 Mar., 22 Apr. He favoured repeal of the assessed taxes, 3 Mar., but next day defended the army estimates, given the international situation, and hotly disputed Hume's assertion that the existing defences at Gibraltar were adequate. In the discussion on the quarantine laws, 13 Apr., he drew on his own experience in Egypt to support the contention that plague was not contagious, but he admitted that public apprehensions, 'however ill grounded', must be soothed. He successfully moved a wrecking amendment to the Southwark paving bill, over which he faced out his colleague Calvert in the lobbies, 15 Apr.[61] He offered his 'warmest thanks' to Canning for concluding treaties of recognition with the South American republics, with whom he anticipated a fruitful trading relationship, 16 May.[62] His hopes for reinstatement in the army may account for his absence from the divisions on the annuity for the duke of Cumberland. James Abercromby drew Wilson's case to the House's attention, 12 June, when ten other Members attested to his military achievements. From the government benches, Sir George Murray hoped that Wilson would in future 'confine his talents and abilities within their proper channels'. No division was taken, and the discussion did not advance Wilson's cause, as Wellington was firmly opposed to any amnesty. The duke wrote to Liverpool, 16 June, recalling the rescue of Lavalette, the queen's funeral and the Spanish episode, and observed that while 'I disclaim the character of enemy to Sir Robert ... I must say that as one of the king's servants I cannot forget these transactions ... particularly the last'.[63] At a meeting in Southwark, 21 June, when thanks were voted to the home secretary Peel for his 'excellent' juries bill, Wilson reasserted the need for parliamentary reform, 'notwithstanding the liberal course pursued by the present ministry'.[64] He asked questions during the investigation into the conduct of the Welsh magistrate William Kenrick[†], 24 June. He approved the principle of the combination bill but thought the

penalties too harsh, 27 June.[65] On 1 July 1825 he wondered aloud if foreign pressure might explain the non-admission of a South American minister to a levee and protested against the continued French presence in Spain.[66] He enquired about existing provision for the punishment of bear-baiting and dog-fighting, 21 Feb. 1826. He favoured a proposal to enforce payments in specie, on the ground that it would restore confidence in country bank notes, 27 Feb., and he supported compulsory returns on the number of notes issued, 7 Mar. Grey's wife observed at this juncture that Wilson, with Brougham and Lord Lansdowne, sided with ministers on the issue of small notes; this portended the later schism in the opposition ranks.[67] Wilson believed that the governor of Jamaica deserved censure for his acquiescence in the slave trials, 2 Mar., and he called on ministers to make effectual efforts to enforce treaties against the slave trade, 10 Mar.[68] His support for swingeing cuts in the army estimates, 3, 7 Mar., represented a shift in his position from the previous session. He wondered if English regiments stationed at the Cape might become self-supporting, as their Dutch predecessors had, 6 Mar. He again spoke for the abolition of flogging in the army, 10 Mar. As an advocate of free trade he criticized those landowners who were unwilling to contemplate any revision of the corn laws, 6 Mar. He approved of Peel's consolidation of the criminal law, 9 Mar., but wanted child stealing made a specific offence. Next day he asked Canning about the promised French evacuation of Spain. He moved for an account of the 'enormous and illegal' expenses of bankruptcy commissioners, 15 Mar. He claimed that provisions for the registration of aliens had been abused, 20 Apr. Having evidently been involved with the London Greek committee, he spoke on behalf of the Greek cause in the House, 19 May. However, that summer Hobhouse gave the Greek deputies a less than glowing reference for Wilson as their prospective military commander, noting that he had 'a brave heart and a weak head' but was 'better than nobody'; he was not offered the post.[69] He was present at the inaugural meeting of the Southwark Mechanics' Institute, 22 May 1826, but declined to subscribe to it, recommending self-help.[70] Around this time he wrote to the king, at Wellington's suggestion, seeking the restoration of his army rank, but to no avail.[71] At the general election that summer he faced a challenge from an anti-Catholic opponent. He declared his commitment to civil and religious liberty and his opposition to slavery and the corn laws. He was returned in second place, after a seven-day poll.[72]

While he voted for Hume's amendment to the address, 21 Nov. 1826, Wilson distanced himself from some of his cavils on expenditure. He also warned that Catholic emancipation was 'a measure which, if long delayed, must be ultimately wrested by ... violence', and praised Canning for having raised Britain's international reputation from 'a low state of obloquy to a very high degree of estimation'. He welcomed the government's announcement of its intention to stand by Portugal in the face of Spanish aggression, 11, 12 Dec. 1826, and gratefully withdrew his planned motion on the subject, assuring Canning that he had not sought to air the issue from party motives. Though he eulogized the late duke of York for the improvements he had made in the organization and discipline of the army, 12 Feb. 1827, he recognized, in a thinly veiled reference to his own case, that the duke had been a stern taskmaster. He hoped that Wellington's appointment as commander-in-chief might improve prospects for the abolition of corporal punishment, 12 Mar. He divided for Catholic relief, 6 Mar., but declined to support repeal of the Test Acts as a separate measure, 23 Mar., 14 May, as he believed Dissenters should link their cause to that of the Catholics. With government approval, he introduced an amending bill to the Distresses for Rent Act, 23 Mar., to make the regulations governing seizures for unpaid rent apply to rates, tithes and taxes; it gained royal assent, 28 May (7 & 8 Geo. IV, c. 17).[73] He voted to reduce the price threshold for the importation of corn to 50s., 9 Mar., but for increased protection for barley, 12 Mar. 1827.

On 21 Feb. 1827 Wilson informed Grey that Liverpool's stroke had prompted an 'indefinite number of speculations', but 'Canning's friends feel confident that either he will be premier of a concordant cabinet or ... there will be a total break-up and [a] new combination'.[74] Grey refused to deal with Canning and never forgave Wilson for the leading part he played in the negotiations, which drew a section of the Whigs into avowed support for the coalition government. Wilson's account of what was easily his most significant contribution to politics was subsequently edited and published by his son-in-law.[75] At the Whig meeting at Lansdowne House in late March, he was among those who urged opposition to the Tory Sir Thomas Lethbridge's motion hostile to a Canning premiership.[76] Behind the scenes he was the main conduit for negotiations between Canning, Brougham (absent on the circuit) and Lansdowne, who had to be persuaded not to make official adoption of Catholic emancipation a condition of his entering the cabinet. Brougham needed to be soothed into not insisting on an office as the price of his support, and Wilson tactfully suppressed the more indiscreet passages of the correspondence on this point that passed through his

hands. From his own account, Wilson 'continued to render the most zealous aid to Mr. Canning, and had a variety of occasions to be eminently useful, particularly in allaying heats and correcting misunderstandings'. To those members of his own party who had stayed on the opposition benches he was less generous, and he apparently took to referring to Grey as an 'old woman'.[77] He joined the procession of Whigs across the floor of the House, 1 May. On 31 May he maintained that he had 'come with the colours of liberal principles flying, to support a ministry formed for the purpose of uniting the prerogative of the king with the liberty of the people'. That day he was unable to let Peel's eulogy of Londonderry pass without comment, and he declined to support Hume's motion for repeal of the Blasphemous and Seditious Libels Act, which he regarded as rocking the ministerial boat. He persuaded Hume not to pursue a motion for repeal of the newspaper stamp duty, which had been brought forward at the behest of Francis Place, who accordingly condemned Wilson as 'a sneaking hound'.[78] He protested at the time wasted by Lethbridge's efforts to uncover details of the formation of the ministry, 21 May.[79] He voted for the disfranchisement of Penryn, 28 May, when he spoke in favour of banning election ribbons. Canning's death in August was a devastating blow to Wilson, who 'considered his life essential to the interests of mankind'. It was also a personal setback as Palmerston, the secretary at war, had privately admitted only a week earlier that Wilson's exclusion from the army was 'a political transaction continued by the arbitrary notions and obstinate character of the duke of York'. Wilson had evidently not pressed his claims on Canning, nor did he accede to Brougham's suggestion that he should make his reinstatement a condition of his support for Lord Goderich's administration, to which he promised 'zealous and truly disinterested support'. He welcomed Lansdowne's adhesion and put out a feeler to Lambton, stating his 'too painful sense of schisms among friends'.[80] In September 1827 he was confident that Goderich 'aims only at honest objects', and at the beginning of 1828 he informed Scarlett of his conviction that much support existed for the government amongst 'the intellectual as well as the popular body'. He suggested that a liberal momentum should be maintained, by 'the repeal of invidious laws, which though dead letters in the statute book, still offend'.[81] Within weeks, however, Goderich had ignominiously given up his office.

Wilson divided for repeal of the Test Acts, 22 Feb., and Catholic relief, 12 May 1828. He thought the House should insist on answers from witnesses in the inquiry into electoral corruption at East Retford,

3, 4 Mar., and opposed the extension of its franchise to the neighbouring hundred, 21 Mar. He called for an immediate prohibition on the flogging of female slaves, 5 Mar. He quizzed Wellington's ministry on details of its policy towards Greece, 7, 24 Mar., 9 Apr., 19 May, and Portugal, 26 June. On 28 Apr. Lord Strangford reported that Wilson had informed him of his intention to 'make a furious attack on me this evening in the House ... for my libellous assertions respecting the South American republics'; evidently nothing came of this.[82] He voted for a 15s. corn duty, 29 Apr. With a tribute to Canning, he voted to make financial provision for his family, 13 May, having reportedly spent 'all evening going about conciliating the ultra Whigs to support the motion'.[83] He favoured the opening of select vestries, as they 'sanction the principle of taxation without representation and without responsibility, which is contrary to the principle of all free government', 9 June. He damned the voters' registration bill as one of 'disfranchisement', 19 June. He voted that day for reform of the usury laws, and for inquiry into the Irish church, 24 June. Though sensible of its imperfections, he supported the sale of game bill *faute de mieux*, 24, 27 June. He spoke and voted against the introduction of excise licenses for cider vendors, 26 June, and described the chancellor of the exchequer Goulburn's attempt to present it as a measure of moral reform as 'cant ... of the very worst species'. He opposed the additional churches bill by speech and vote, 30 June. In renewing his attack on the Foreign Enlistment Act he clashed angrily with Charles Williams Wynn, 3 July. Next day he was upbraided by Mackintosh for his failure to pay attention during a debate on trade. He opposed the retrospective provision in the superannuation allowances bill, 14 July. With an anecdote about a military corps drawn from the indigenous peoples of the Cape, he supported Fowell Buxton's attempt to secure their release from slavery, 15 July 1828. That day he helpfully suggested that holders of bonds issued by the deposed Spanish government should address their claims to France. Early in February 1829 Lambton, now Lord Durham, reported to Grey that Wilson had been in 'high excitement' at the possibility of his reinstatement in the army, but that Wellington had 'thrown him over, as I suspected, saying "why did not his friend Mr. Canning do it"'.[84] In the House, Wilson joined in the discussion arising from Bristol petitions for and against Catholic emancipation, 26 Feb., and voted for the government's bill, 6, 30 Mar. Observing that 'some price must be paid for every political boon', he reluctantly accepted the disfranchisement of Irish 40s. freeholders, 20 Mar; he made copious notes on

this debate, the purpose of which is unclear.[85] While he agreed in principle with the clauses of the emancipation bill dealing with the Jesuits, he thought them too inflexible, 24 Mar. He divided in the minority against obliging Daniel O'Connell to swear the oath of supremacy, 18 May. He was unsympathetic towards petitioners against the London Bridge bill, 8 Apr., 8 May. He suggested that a remonstrance from the chancellor of the exchequer might persuade the Spanish government to honour its commitments to holders of bonds issued by its predecessor, 15 Apr., 19 June. He divided for the transfer of East Retford's seats to Birmingham, 5 May, and Lord Blandford's reform resolutions, 2 June. He voted in the minority for a fixed duty on corn imports, 19 May, when he scorned provincial opponents of the metropolis police bill and spoke in favour of an extension to the grounds of the Zoological Society in Regent's Park. He was impatient with tardy objections to opening the vestry of St. James, Westminster, 21 May, and voted for Hume's proposed additional clause to the ecclesiastical courts bill, 5 June. He suggested that commissioners sent to report on the condition of slaves in the colonies should be allowed to continue their work, 25 May. His claim to be an oracle on international affairs suffered as a result of his failure to foretell Russia's defeat of the Turks in September; Hobhouse relished being 'able to laugh at Bob Wilson', but he was unabashed. Greville recorded in December 1829 that Wilson had 'written to the sultan a letter full of advice and ... says the Turks will be more powerful than ever', adding that he 'is always full of opinions and facts; the former are wild and extravagant, the latter generally false'.[86]

Wilson divided for Knatchbull's amendment to the address on distress, 4 Feb. 1830. He acted with the revived Whig opposition on most major issues that session. He voted for the transfer of East Retford's seats to Birmingham, 11 Feb., but favoured extending the franchise to Bassetlaw freeholders on the principle that 'half a loaf is better than no bread', 15 Mar. He was a majority teller against O'Connell's proposal to institute vote by ballot in the enlarged borough, explaining that 'there is something in the privacy, in the concealment of vote by ballot ... that is ... contrary to the feelings of Englishmen'. He voted for Lord Blandford's reform plan, 18 Feb., but emphasized that he 'never was authorized by my constituents to vote for any measure which could affect the security of property'. He divided for the enfranchisement of Birmingham, Leeds and Manchester, 23 Feb., and Russell's reform resolutions, 28 May. He expressed suitable outrage at the duke of Newcastle's treatment of recalcitrant tenants in Newark and supported referral of their petition to a select committee, 1 Mar. He asserted that Canning's failure to repeal the Test Acts had arisen from a desire to carry the measure in conjunction with Catholic emancipation, 8 Feb. He voted for Jewish emancipation, 5 Apr., 17 May, when he declared that he 'should be glad to see the Jew, the Christian and the Unitarian all sitting together in the House'. He divided for abolition of the death penalty for forgery, 24 May, and, despite the Lords' amendments, criticized the 'neck or nothing' approach of those opposition Members who opposed the bill, 20 July. He called for the East India Company to contribute to the funding of home-based Indian regiments, 19 Feb. Though he was generally supportive of economy motions, he apparently 'voted with ministers' against delaying the army estimates, 19 Feb.,[87] avowed his intention of voting with them against a reduction in the size of the navy, 1 Mar., and hoped there were no plans to close the Royal Military Academy at Woolwich, 30 Apr. He reportedly voted with government on the sugar duties, 21 June.[88] He cited commercial interests as a reason for British intervention in the conflict between Spain and her former colonies of Mexico and Colombia, 1 Mar., 20, 24 May. He supported the right of Barrington, the judge of the Irish court of admiralty accused of embezzlement, to be heard at the bar of the House, 22 May, and recommended that leniency be shown to a stranger who had thrown papers into the chamber. He spoke against the charitable institutions bill, which would have exempted Bethlehem Hospital from paying poor rates, 24 May. He regarded Sadler's attempt to ameliorate the condition of the labouring poor as 'most desirable', 3 June, and called for the withdrawal of the Scottish and Irish paupers removal bill the next day. He supported the labourers' wages bill, which aimed to abolish the truck system, 5 July. He thought the sale of beer bill did the government 'the highest credit', 3 June. For reasons of military discipline he did not believe that British troops serving abroad could expect to be excused from participation in Catholic ceremonial, 17 June. Following the death of George IV Wilson renewed his plea for reinstatement in the army, and William IV gratified his wish at a levee on 28 July; his lieutenant-general's commission was dated 1 Dec. 1830 (backdated to 27 May 1825). Lord Ellenborough, the president of the board of control, wrote that this 'pleases everybody', although Mrs. Arbuthnot claimed that Wellington had still been 'violent against it' earlier in the year.[89] Prior to the dissolution that summer it was suggested that Grey's son, Lord Howick*, might be invited to offer for Southwark, as Wilson's former supporters were

'very much disgusted with him ... and are anxious to have some one for a candidate who had voted regularly and well'. But Grey advised against such a move and 'seemed averse to being the person directly to oppose Wilson, however much he may have deserved it'.[90] At the general election Wilson faced a challenge from a local candidate apparently put up by the licensed victuallers, who were angered by his support for the sale of beer bill. He answered criticism of his inattention to local interests and defended his stance on the bill, exclaiming that 'he thanked God ... it was sometimes possible to support ministers'. He spoke out forcefully against universal suffrage, the ballot and annual parliaments. Recovering from a poor start, he was returned in second place behind the newcomer, ousting Calvert. At a celebration dinner he anticipated that the force of public opinion would ensure the triumph of reform.[91]

The ministry listed Wilson as one of the 'bad doubtfuls', and he was an unexplained absentee from the crucial division on the civil list, 15 Nov. 1830. He lost no time in pressing his claims for preferment on Lord Grey's new government, bemoaning to lord chancellor Brougham the financial loss caused by the enforced break in his army career.[92] He presented a Surrey petition against the metropolitan police force, 18 Nov., but did not share the petitioners' fear that it might become the tool of a despotic government. He was a majority teller against the reintroduced charitable institutions bill, 7 Dec. He endeavoured to demonstrate the inefficacy of the ballot in countries where it had been adopted, 9, 21 Dec., and dramatically warned that its introduction to Britain would lead to the 'overthrow [of] the monarchy', to which he would be 'no party'. He painted a grim picture of the condition of Ireland before the Act of Union and opposed O'Connell's call for its repeal, 11 Dec. 1830. He opined that the introduction of a poor law to Ireland was both desirable and inevitable, 30 Mar. 1831. He declared himself willing to support a property tax in lieu of existing assessed taxes, which pressed 'too heavily on the industrious classes', 14 Dec. 1830. Evidently he spent January 1831 in Paris, where he was informed by the leader of the Commons, Lord Althorp, of the date of Parliament's reassembly.[93] He presented a Southwark petition for reform and repeal of the window tax, 10 Feb., and supported another in favour of the ministry's reform bill, which had his 'most cordial approbation and shall have my warmest support', 14 Mar. He duly divided for the bill's second reading, 22 Mar. The House had therefore no inkling of the bombshell he was to drop on 19 Apr., when he rose 'under the most painful circumstances of embarrassment' to announce his concurrence in Gascoyne's amendment to retain the existing number of English Members. In a contorted argument, he claimed to have been given assurances that the amendment was not a wrecking device, and maintained that ministers had previously told him the question was not 'vital or essential'. Yet it was with apparent recognition of the threat to the whole measure that he said he would abstain from the division. He concluded with a valedictory statement of the purity of his motives, and indicated his willingness to give up his seat. The next speaker, the Irish secretary Smith Stanley, expressed 'pain' and 'surprise' at what he had heard, and reckoned that the electors of Southwark would be 'astonished at the course which he has taken' and 'will not be disposed to forgive him'. Wilson must have anticipated this reaction, and in an undated note to Brougham he made the hopeful suggestion that 'if you were to make me quartermaster general ... I should have an honourable political retreat from the borough and your brother [William Brougham*] would be my successor infallibly'.[94] A meeting of his constituents summoned for 22 Apr. 1831 was postponed until the following day at his request, but even then he sent only a letter signifying his intention of retiring. Words like 'hypocrite' and 'imposter' were freely used, and there was criticism of his abstention on the civil list vote. Some detected early signs of his ratting in his arguments against the ballot, and there were demands for the return of subscription monies.[95] A mob smashed his windows, and government supporters queued up to denounce him: 'a puffed up bubble burst and gone to nothing', was Lady Bute's verdict, while Hobhouse described his final Commons speech as 'the most disgraceful exposure that ever closed a life of pretended patriotism'.[96]

Wilson's subsequent reflections on the affair, published posthumously, centred on the importance of preserving the number of English Members, and showed that his self-satisfaction knew no bounds:

> I did not let my personal interests prevail over my sense of duty to the country, and ... I contributed to save 60 Members to the English representation. If every Member of the ministerial side had acted as fearlessly and honestly, the bill would never have passed the Commons in the state that it did ... There never was such venal and servile voting as in this Parliament on this measure.

But it is plain that his objection to the bill was general, not specific: as early as 3 Mar. 1831 he had recorded in his private journal that he considered it 'an initiatory measure of republican government'. The clear shift in his politics can be measured in the Tory language he employed to explain himself to the poetess Sibella Elizabeth Hatfield, a recently acquired confidante:

> I have ever been too proud of our exemplified history, too sensible of the blessings we enjoy, and too well acquainted with the generous envy we have excited in all the nations of the earth, to promote any subversive change and democratic novelties.[97]

Shortly after his departure from the Commons, he abandoned Brooks's Club for White's, where he consorted with such Tories as Croker and Arbuthnot, who helped him to establish friendly relations with Wellington. This created a new audience for his endless prognostications: in December 1832, for example, he pontificated in typical fashion about the conflict in Belgium.[98] He continued to press the Grey government for some domestic recognition of his military services, and in June 1831 complained to Brougham, his remaining friend in office, of the promotion of officers inferior to him in precedence. Grey assured Brougham of his 'kind disposition' towards Wilson, 'notwithstanding our political separation', and recalled that on entering office he had expressed an 'anxiety to see a regiment given to him'. Nothing had happened by February 1833, when Wilson admitted to Brougham that in the prevailing political climate he was 'worse than a fish out of water'; discounting any prospect of a return to the Commons, he expressed a desire to go abroad. Nearly four years were to pass before he was given command of a regiment. In 1841 his foreign military honours were restored, and his wish for a posting abroad was gratified the following year by his appointment as governor of Gibraltar. The prime minister Peel's assessment of him at this time indicated that nothing but his politics had changed: 'he is one of those who live on ... speculations, and are never easy unless they can make you believe you are on the eve of some miraculous explosion'.[99]

Wilson died on a visit to England in May 1849 and was buried in Westminster Abbey. He had made provision for his five surviving children in his marriage settlement and his will; property in Kent acquired through his marriage passed to his daughter Rosabella Stanhope Randolph. Of his sons, only Belford Hinton Wilson (1804-58) achieved any prominence, serving as a senior diplomat in Peru, Bolivia and Venezuela. With an eye to posterity, he instructed that 'the publication of all private letters, many of which are of great interest, must ... undergo ... careful revision', and he enjoined 'the decorous observation of social propriety'.[100] His son-in-law, the Rev. Herbert Randolph, obliged with an hagiographical *Life of Sir Robert Wilson*, covering his early career, which was published in 1862. Since then, Wilson's quixotic heroism as a soldier has attracted the interest of three biographers, but none has ventured to portray him as a successful politician.

¹ This article draws on three biographies of Wilson: G. Costigan, *Sir Robert Wilson: A Soldier of Fortune in the Napoleonic Wars* (1932) gives the most detailed coverage of his political career; M. Glover, *A Very Slippery Fellow* (1978) is predominantly a military study; I. Samuel, *An Astonishing Fellow* (1985) takes a more sympathetic view of Wilson. ² *Fox Jnl.* 50-51. ³ Costigan, 224-6; Broughton, *Recollections*, ii. 118-19. ⁴ *Greville Mems.* ii. 81; *Croker Pprs.* ii. 104; Lord Ilchester, *Chrons. Holland House*, 33. ⁵ *The Times*, 8, 9, 11 Mar. 1820. ⁶ Broughton, ii. 127. ⁷ Add. 30115, ff. 17, 19; 30213, f. 153. ⁸ *The Times*, 20, 27 May 1820. ⁹ Add. 52444, f. 125. ¹⁰ Add. 30123, ff. 123, 151. ¹¹ *Hobhouse Diary*, 30-31; Add. 30103, ff. 24-28, 30, 109, 120. ¹² *Creevey Pprs.* ii. 315. ¹³ Sheffield Archives, Wharncliffe mss, Seymour Bathurst to Lady Stuart Wortley, 20 Sept.; *The Times*, 25 Oct., 23 Nov. 1820. ¹⁴ Add. 30109, ff. 140-2; 30123, ff. 219-22, 227. ¹⁵ Add. 30123, f. 232; Lambton mss, Wilson to Lambton, 29 Dec. 1820. ¹⁶ *The Times*, 20 Jan. 1821. ¹⁷ *Arbuthnot Jnl.* i. 67-68. ¹⁸ HLRO, Hist. Coll. 379, Grey Bennet diary, 14. ¹⁹ *The Times*, 14 Feb. 1821; Buckingham, *Mems. Geo. IV*, i. 122; Grey Bennet diary, 19. ²⁰ *The Times*, 14 Feb. 1821. ²¹ Grey Bennet diary, 26. ²² *Creevey Pprs.* ii. 26. ²³ *The Times*, 21, 22 June 1821. ²⁴ TNA FO352/8/4, Planta to Stratford Canning, 15 Mar. 1821. ²⁵ *The Times*, 8 May 1821. ²⁶ Ibid. 22 Feb., 13 Mar., 3 July 1821. ²⁷ Ibid. 23 June 1821; Grey Bennet diary, 113. ²⁸ Grey Bennet diary, 50. ²⁹ Ibid. 82; *The Times*, 6 Mar. 1821. ³⁰ *The Times*, 27 Mar., 3 Apr. 1821. ³¹ Ibid. 25, 29 June 1821. ³² Ibid. 4 July 1821. ³³ Add. 30103, ff. 19-23; 30109, f. 199. ³⁴ Add. 30109, f. 240. ³⁵ *HMC Bathurst*, 514; *Arbuthnot Jnl.* i. 119; Wellington mss WP1/822/13. ³⁶ Add. 30109, ff. 260, 296, 300; Wellington mss WP1/1076/27. ³⁷ Wellington mss WP1/679/3; *HMC Bathurst*, 514-15. ³⁸ Colchester Diary, iii. 236; Add. 30125, ff. 102-6. ³⁹ *HMC Bathurst*, 515-16; Wellington mss WP1/679/3; 680/4, 6. ⁴⁰ *Hobhouse Diary*, 74; Add. 30109, ff. 223-4, 278, 284, 296, 307; 30113, ff. 145, 148, 150. ⁴¹ Add. 51654, Mackintosh to Holland, 21 Dec. 1822; *Arbuthnot Jnl.* i. 102. ⁴² *Gurney Diary*, 13 Feb.; Add. 52445, f. 43; Dorset RO D/BKL, Bankes jnl. 133 (13 Feb. 1822); *Lady Holland to Son*, 1. ⁴³ Add. 30110, f. 20. ⁴⁴ *The Times*, 5, 14, 15 Mar. 1822. ⁴⁵ Ibid. 7, 30 Mar., 26 Apr., 5, 15, 29 June 1822; J. Belcham, *'Orator' Hunt*, 139-40. ⁴⁶ *The Times*, 7 May 1822. ⁴⁷ Ibid. 19 June 1822. ⁴⁸ NLS mss 3895, f. 28. ⁴⁹ Add. 30110, ff. 56, 70, 74, 97; 30125, f. 35; *The Times*, 28 Oct. 1822. ⁵⁰ *The Times*, 12, 20 Feb. 1823. ⁵¹ *Creevey Pprs.* ii. 68; C. New, *Brougham*, 220. ⁵² Add. 30110, f. 120; *The Times*, 27 June 1823. ⁵³ *Arbuthnot Jnl.* i. 247. ⁵⁴ Add. 30111, ff. 62, 72-73. ⁵⁵ Costigan, 217; Add. 30103, ff. 64-214 and 30137, *passim* give Wilson's own account of this episode. ⁵⁶ *The Times*, 6, 9 Sept., 7 Dec. 1823; Glover, 185. ⁵⁷ Wellington mss WP1/784/18; 786/13; 822/13. ⁵⁸ Northants. RO, Agar Ellis diary, 18 Mar. 1824. ⁵⁹ *The Times*, 23 June 1824; Add. 30126, f. 10. ⁶⁰ *The Times*, 18 May, 4 June 1824. ⁶¹ Ibid. 16 Apr. 1825. ⁶² Ibid. 17 May 1825. ⁶³ Wellington mss WP1/822/13. ⁶⁴ *The Times*, 22 June 1825. ⁶⁵ Ibid. 28 June 1825. ⁶⁶ Ibid. 2 July 1825. ⁶⁷ *Creevey Pprs.* ii. 95. ⁶⁸ *The Times*, 11 Mar. 1826. ⁶⁹ Add. 30110, f. 148; Broughton, iii. 115. ⁷⁰ *The Times*, 23 May 1826. ⁷¹ *Arbuthnot Jnl.* ii. 25. ⁷² *The Times*, 7, 8, 15, 27 June 1826. ⁷³ Ibid. 24 Mar. 1827. ⁷⁴ Add. 30124, f. 252. ⁷⁵ *Canning's Administration: Narrative of Formation, with Correspondence* ed. Rev. H. Randolph (1872), on which the following account is based. ⁷⁶ Castle Howard mss, Holland to Carlisle [Mar. 1827]. ⁷⁷ Broughton, iii. 195. ⁷⁸ D. Miles, *Francis Place*, 175-6. ⁷⁹ *The Times*, 22 May 1827. ⁸⁰ *Canning's Administration*, pp. vi, 33-35; Lambton mss, Wilson to Lambton, 12 Aug. 1827. ⁸¹ Add. 30111, f. 314; 51617, Wilson to Holland, 15 Sept. 1827. ⁸² Cent. Kent. Stud. Stanhope mss U1590 C138/1, Strangford to Stanhope, 28 Apr. 1828. ⁸³ Harewood mss, Lord George Cavendish Bentinck to Lady Canning, 13 May 1828. ⁸⁴ Grey mss, Durham to Grey, 4 Feb. 1829. ⁸⁵ Add. 30142, ff. 91-121. ⁸⁶ Add. 51569, Hobhouse to Holland, 25 Sept. 1829; *Greville Mems.* i. 336-7. ⁸⁷ Add. 56554, f. 66. ⁸⁸ Grey mss, Howick jnl. 21 June 1830. ⁸⁹ Add. 30128, f.

27; *Ellenborough Diary*, ii. 273, 324; *Arbuthnot Jnl.* ii. 339-40. ⁹⁰ Howick jnl. 26-27 June 1830. ⁹¹ *The Times*, 31 July, 13 Aug. 1830. ⁹² Brougham mss, Wilson to Brougham, 22 Nov. 1830. ⁹³ Add. 30112, ff. 133, 142. ⁹⁴ Brougham mss, Wilson to Brougham n.d. [Apr. 1831]. ⁹⁵ *The Times*, 23, 25 Apr. 1831; G. Gleig, *Personal Rems. of Duke of Wellington*, 258. ⁹⁶ Buckingham, *Mems. William IV*, i. 294; Harrowby mss 22, f. 212; Broughton, iii. 102. ⁹⁷ *Canning's Administration*, pp. vii-x. ⁹⁸ Costigan, 260-2; Lonsdale mss, Beckett to Lowther, 4 Dec. 1832. ⁹⁹ Brougham mss, Wilson to Brougham, 20 June 1831, Feb. 1833, Grey to same, 24 June 1831; Parker, *Peel*, ii. 449. ¹⁰⁰ PROB 11/2094/407; IR26/1854/250.

H.J.S.

WILSON, Thomas (?1767–1852), of 4 Jeffery's Square, St. Mary Axe, London and Hackney, Mdx.

LONDON 1818–1826

b. ?1767, s. of Robert Wilson (*d.* 1807) of Wood House, East Ham, Essex and his w. (*d.* wid. 17 May 1818).¹ *m.* 23 Nov. 1796,² Anne Mary Sabina Chenebie, da. of John Francis Blache of Homerton, Mdx. (formerly of Vevey, Switzerland), 4s. 3da. *d.* 10 Oct. 1852.

Member, Spectaclemakers' Co.; dir. Phoenix Assurance Co. 1811-*d.*, East Country Dock Co. 1817.

Cornet London and Westminster light horse 1796.

Wilson's father died intestate at his home at East Ham, 25 Mar. 1807, 'aged 67, in consequence of an apoplectic and paralytic attack on the 21st'. Administration of his estate, which was sworn under £3,500, was granted on 10 Apr. 1807 to Wilson, who was by then about 40 years old and established as a prominent and prosperous London merchant.³ His firm of Wilson and Blanshard (previously Wilson, Agassiz and Company) operated from 4 Jeffery's Square. He had at one time been in Grenada, had an interest in the Atlantic trade and was a long-serving chairman of the Society of Merchants trading to the continent.⁴

After his return for London with three opposition Members in 1818 the duke of Wellington asked Thomas Creevey*, 'Who is Wilson that is come in for the City, and what side is he of?'⁵ The answer proved to be that of the Liverpool ministry, generally speaking, though he readily took an independent line on specific issues, particularly those on which his constituents had strong feelings. When he stood again at the general election of 1820, some leading aldermen complained of his persistent refusal to join their body; but at his adoption meeting, when he was promoted as the spokesman for the City's shipping and mercantile interests and as 'a very sensible speaker' listened to by ministers, he repeated his view that aldermanic and parliamentary duties were incompatible. In his address, he declared his 'firm attachment to an unrivalled constitution', and on the hustings stated that 'his opinions, generally, had inclined rather to the support of the present government than to the other side, but he had acted ... honestly and independently'. After his return in second place he announced that for all the 'bias of his own mind in favour of the administration of the country, in whose hands soever it might be', he would never 'suffer any measures to pass ... which he conceived to be unjust or ill-advised, without ... rising upon the ministerial benches to oppose them'.[6]

Wilson, who took the oaths on 28 Apr., secured a return of wool imports, 2 May 1820, when he voted against government on the civil list accounts, and next day he presented and endorsed a London wool manufacturers and merchants' petition against the previous year's 'unwise and impolitic' duty on foreign wool.[7] He seconded the Whig Lord Milton's attempt to have it repealed, 26 May, and was a teller for the minority. Yet he thought that the restrictions on trade of which London merchants complained, 8 May, 'could not be entirely removed while the taxes remained the same'. He declined to be named to the select committee on agricultural distress, 31 May,[8] but was appointed to that on foreign trade (as he was in the next four years), 5 June, when he presented and supported a London ship owners' petition against relaxation of the duties on Baltic timber to the detriment of the Canadian trade. He defended the profits of the Bank of England, 13 June. In response to an opposition attack on the barracks grant, 16 June, he deplored their determination to attribute 'all the evils of the country to the government'. However, he complained of the expenditure of money on new public buildings at a time of distress, 19 June.[9] He criticized opposition for taking up the cause of Queen Caroline for party purposes, 3 July, and when taken to task by Grey Bennet replied that 'his standing in that House was not such as bound him to support ministers'.[10] He proved his point next day by voting for economies in revenue collection, and he opposed the plan for a new barracks in Regent's Park as 'exorbitant', 12, 13, 14, 17 July 1820, when he was a teller for the minority.

Wilson sided with ministers on the queen's case and signed the London merchants' loyal declaration of 11 Jan. 1821.[11] He vouched for the 'respectability' of the signatories of a West Ham loyal address and asserted that 'when ministers gave good reasons for their measures, they deserved support', 31 Jan. 1821.[12] He denied an allegation that the 'tumult' at the London merchants' meeting in favour of Caroline was provoked by a loyalist 'conspiracy', 2 Feb. He voted against the opposition censure motion, 6 Feb., and on the 13th,

when one of his colleagues presented a queenite petition from the corporation of London, he defended Lord Liverpool and his colleagues and said that 'though ... [Caroline] had peace on her tongue, there was war in her heart'. He presented a Montreal petition for continued protection of the Canadian timber trade, 9 Feb., and one from London Russia merchants against proposed changes in the mode of collecting the duties on foreign timber, 19 Feb.[13] He approved the Grampound disfranchisement bill 'because it went to remedy a practical evil' and represented 'the only way in which parliamentary reform could safely take place', 12 Feb.; but on 18 Apr. he opposed Lambton's general reform scheme, which would give electors 'too much control over their representatives', and he voted against Russell's motion, 9 May. He divided against Catholic relief, 28 Feb. He voted with ministers on the state of the revenue, 6 Mar., but next day supported inquiry into agricultural distress, arguing that 'a rise in the price of corn would enable the landlord to pay his labourer better, and keep him out of the workhouse'. He supported the bill to eradicate fraud in the compilation of the corn averages, 29 Mar., 2 Apr.[14] According to Grey Bennet, Wilson was one of the 'few' Members whom opposition 'gained ... from the government' for a motion to reduce the army by 5,000 men, 14 Mar.[15] He opposed Hume's call for a revision of public salaries, 30 Mar.,[16] but spoke and voted for a variety of army economies, 6, 11, 30 Apr. He supported the Blackfriars Bridge bill, 3 Apr., and presented a London corn merchants' petition for revision of the corn laws, 9 Apr., and one from Thameside traders against the London wharves bill, 21 May.[17] He disputed Ricardo's assertion that 'it was a matter of indifference whether the return for foreign timber was made in goods or specie', 5 Apr., arguing that the former were infinitely preferable. On 9 Apr. he attacked the duty on foreign wool and spoke and voted, in a minority of 27, for inquiry into the currency. He defended the Bank's directors, 13 Apr., when he saw no reason to reduce the salaries of commissioners of stamps.[18] He divided for admiralty and dockyards economies, 4, 7 May, and on the 24th suggested that distress could best be relieved by reducing taxes in proportion to inflation. That day he voted against the forgery punishment mitigation bill, and he presented and endorsed a London merchants' and bankers' hostile petition, 4 June.[19] He voted with opposition on the Barbados pension fund, 24 May, with government for the barracks grant, 28 May, but with Hume against the miscellaneous services grant later that day. On behalf of interested constituents, he opposed the clover seeds bill, 13, 22 June.[20] He was in a minority of

11 against the tobacco duties bill, 21 June, and on the 25th voiced misgivings over the extent to which ministers seemed prepared to go to relax the Navigation Acts. He voted with them against Hume's call for economy and retrenchment, 27 June. He denounced the extra post bill as 'prejudicial and unfair' and was a teller for the minority against it, 29 June 1821.[21]

Wilson voted with government against more extensive tax reductions, 11, 21 Feb. 1822, when he suggested that their planned £1,500,000 of remissions should be used to buy corn in order to raise prices. He voiced worries about the effects of the navy five per cents bill on investors, 25 Feb., 4 Mar., but pronounced in its favour, 11 Mar.[22] He approved the principle of repealing the salt tax, 28 Feb., but felt that Calcraft's motion to that effect was 'far from wise at this moment'; he spoke, 11 June, and voted, 28 June, against repeal.[23] He voted in a majority against government for admiralty reductions, 1 Mar. Defending the Bank again, 8 Mar., he observed that if the 1797 cash restrictions had not been enforced, the war could not have been won and some of the whining Whigs would not have enjoyed such high rents. He voted with ministers against abolition of one of the joint-postmasterships, 13 Mar., but supported that of a 'confessedly useless' clerical job at Woolwich dockyard, 18 Mar.[24] As 'a friend to free trade', he objected to Curwen's plan to increase the duties on tallow and repeal that on candles, which would alienate Russia, 20 Mar. He presented a corn factors' petition for compensation for losses sustained through the deterioration of warehoused corn, 25 Mar.[25] On the presentation of the London livery's reform petition, which he had been publicly and privately pressed to support, 2 Apr., he refused to apologize for having avoided the meeting of 28 Mar. which had promoted it:

> When he was called upon to support a prayer for retrenchment and economy and reform, he felt it difficult to ascertain where he ought to stop. It might be expected by some, that he ought to vote for all the reductions proposed by ... [Hume], but he did not attribute such sentiments to his constituents. They did not wish to impose ties on their representatives.

He did back Hume's criticism of the British consul in Brazil for dereliction of duty, 22 Apr. He asserted that the City could not afford to build the new London Bridge unless government made a significant contribution, 29 Apr.[26] Next day he voted against Canning's bill to relieve Catholic peers. He supported the ministerial plan to contract for the naval and military pensions fund, 1, 3 May. He presented a London sugar refiners' petition expressing alarm at free trade proposals, 2

May, and one from curriers and tanners against repeal of the leather tax, 16 May, when he voted against government on the cost of the embassy to Switzerland.[27] On 6 May he was almost alone in his enthusiasm for their proposal to advance £1,000,000 for the purchase of corn, which the agriculturists scouted. He said that Wyvill's scheme for large tax remissions would be 'productive of infinite mischief', 8 May, and he disputed Attwood's currency theories and supported the government's revised plan to relieve agricultural distress, 13 May. But he opposed the colonial trade bill, 17 May, and saw little merit in the navigation bill, 20 May; he presented London silk merchants' petitions against the latter, 23, 30 May.[28] He was persuaded to withdraw his motion for leave to introduce a bill to regulate the carrying of precious metals, 21 May.[29] He 'thought there was something more ... than met the eye' in Canning's amendment to the corn bill concerning the grinding of foreign wheat, 10 June. He accused Whig opponents of the resumption of cash payments of political opportunism, 14 June, and on the Irish butter trade, 20 June, said that Ricardo's free trade principles were 'not applicable to the present state of this country'. He divided with government in defence of the lord advocate's dealings with the Scottish press, 25 June, and supported the grant for colonial agents, 5 July, but he opposed that for a national monument in Edinburgh, 15 July. He presented a London publicans' petition against the beer retail bill, 17 July. He spoke and voted in the minority of 14 against the Canada bill, 18 July, but he was in the ministerial majorities for the aliens bill, 19 July, and the grant for Irish proclamations, 22 July, when he was a teller for the majority for an amendment to the orphans' fund bill.[30] He thought government should pay all the late queen's debts, 24 July, called for inquiry into the state of Trinidad, 25 July, and approved the chancellor's modification of the barilla duties bill, 29 July 1822.[31]

On 12 Feb. 1823 Wilson assured Wallace, vice-president of the board of trade, that London merchants appreciated his efforts to liberalize commerce.[32] He said that he would be 'in his place at every discussion of reform, and would give his opinion to the best of his ability', 14 Feb.; but he cast silent votes against inquiry into the franchise, 20 Feb., and Scottish reform, 2 June. Although the shipping industry was 'labouring under considerable embarrassment', he rejected Hume's tax reduction proposals, 21 Feb., preferring the relief measures outlined by ministers. He accordingly supported their sinking fund adjustment and voted against the tax remissions advocated by opposition, 3 Mar. In common council, 27 Feb., he promised to give his 'best attention' to their petition for a revision of London tithes and approved the 'conciliatory' manner in which the subject had been broached.[33] Though not convinced that British shipping in the West Indies had been adequately protected from piracy, he backed the admiralty in their dispute with Lloyd's, 4 Mar. He welcomed the merchant vessels apprenticeship bill, which would 'create ... a nursery of active and able seamen at the least possible expense', 13 Mar. Endorsing ministers' stance on the Franco-Spanish conflict, 18 Mar., he said that he was 'not afraid of being charged with a dastardly spirit' for wishing to avoid war; and on 28 Apr. he seconded at some length an amendment approving the government's 'adherence to the principles of honest neutrality'. On the warehousing bill, 21 Mar., he called for wool to be given the same exemption as linen and silk; and he presented a London merchants' petition against the wool duty, 21 Apr., and endorsed one from Leeds, 4 June.[34] He now voted for a reduction in the grant for colonial agents, 24 Mar. He supported a London merchants' petition for changes in the Insolvent Debtors Act and one from Marylebone for repeal of the coastwise coal duties, 27 Mar. He presented and urged the merits of a petition from London silk manufacturers for repeal of the restrictive Spitalfields Acts, 9 May. He commended this as the best remedy for distress, 9 June, but in the meantime favoured proceeding with the silk bill. He argued that the West Indian colonies deserved preferential treatment on the sugar duties, 22 May.[35] He divided with administration against inquiries into chancery arrears, 5 June, and the currency, 12 June. He had reservations about the reciprocity of duties bill, 6 June, and spoke and voted against increasing the barilla duties, 13 June, when he was in another small minority against the beer duties bill. He repeated this vote on 17 June and, not without qualms, divided for repeal of the usury laws, as he did again, 27 June. He was a teller for the minority against a clause of the London Bridge bill which curbed the corporation's powers, 20 June, when he voted against the Scottish juries bill. He condemned the 'oppressive conduct' of the victualling board towards Cochrane, 24 June, and next day voted for Mackintosh's attempt to abolish capital punishment for certain larcenies. He opposed printing the Christian ministers' petition in favour of free discussion presented by Hume, 1 July: 'the minds of the people had been poisoned by the blasphemous publications which had been spread abroad. The lower orders would eagerly imbibe the poison, but would not seek the antidote'. On 2 July 1823 he presented a London ship-owners' petition complaining of the way in which the committee on the reciprocity bill had taken evidence, and he was in a

minority of 15 against the measure's third reading the following day.

Wilson presented London petitions for repeal of the duties on coal, 6 Feb., foreign wines, 19 Feb., and the 'utterly indefensible' impost on wool, 20 Feb. 1824.[36] 'Very much staggered' by arguments advanced against repeal of the usury laws, 27 Feb., he now voted to preserve them, as he did again, 17 Feb. 1825, when he said that their abolition would 'unhinge all the existing pecuniary relations of the country'. It is not clear whether he was the 'T.C Wilson' who voted in support of a complaint of breach of privilege against lord chancellor Eldon, 1 Mar. 1824. He divided against the abolition of flogging, 5 Mar. That day he praised ministers 'for the manly and candid manner in which they had brought forward their measures' to deal with distress in the silk trade, but doubted their 'propriety or expediency':

> Until, by an alteration of the corn laws, the people of this country should be enabled to eat their bread as cheap as the people of foreign countries, the repeal of the duties on silk would fail of the end it was intended to accomplish.

Yet on 8 Mar. he conceded that ministers had shown 'so much good will and such a spirit of conciliation' that it was only fair to withdraw opposition and 'trust to their considerate mode of conduct for some relief as to the duties already paid for stock in hand'. That day he presented an Aldgate victuallers' petition against excise licences. On 11 Mar. he secured referral of a Norwich merchants' petition for lower wine duties to the foreign trade committee, and he presented more petitions to the same effect, 22 Mar.[37] He defended the grant for the Society for the Propagation of the Gospels, 12 Mar. On a call for amelioration of the condition of slaves in the West Indies, 16 Mar., he stated that when in Grenada he had 'seen none of those scenes of wretchedness' described by the abolitionists and gave his 'cordial support' to the government's gradualist approach. He objected to Fowell Buxton's motion for information on the West Indian colonies, 13 Apr., defended the West India Company bill, 10 May, and voted against Brougham's motion condemning the prosecution of the Methodist missionary John Smith in Demerara, 11 June. He supported a London mercers' petition for drawback to be extended to cut silk, 19 Mar. He presented petitions against the Tower suspension bridge, 23, 29 Mar., and in favour of the St. Katharine's Docks bill, 31 Mar, 2 Apr.[38] He was in the minority in favour of allowing defence by counsel in felony trials, 6 Apr. He supported the grant for building new churches because those erected in the past were 'built for the rich and not for the poor', 12 Apr. He spoke in favour of the enabling bill, 14 June, but was credited, presumably in error, with two votes against its passage that day.[39] He supported the wheat warehousing bill, 4 May, but sought modifications to it, 17 May.[40] He presented a London licensed victuallers' petition against the beer duties bill, 7 May, and spoke and voted against the measure, 24 May. On 13 May he announced that he would take 'his share of the odium' now attached to the reorganization of the superannuation fund, which he had supported in good faith; and he endorsed the bill to regulate it, 12 June.[41] On the London corporation reform petition, 17 May, he said that he 'could never promise his support to any measure of parliamentary reform until brought forward in a tangible shape, by way of complaint against some stated grievance or abuse'. Later that day he opposed the marine insurance bill, which on 28 May he described as 'invading vested rights upon theoretic speculations'; he was a teller for small minorities against it, 7, 14 June.[42] He got leave to introduce a measure to prevent frauds in the Irish butter trade, 27 May, but it foundered after its second reading.[43] He concurred in the prayer of the London merchants' and ship-owners' petition against naval impressment, 10 June, and on 15 June 1824 thanked Mackintosh for his 'masterly' presentation of their petition for recognition of the independence of the new South American states.

Wilson presented a petition in favour of the St. Katharine's Docks project, 11 Feb. 1825, and on the 14th one from the East Country Dock Company, of which he was a director, for permission to amend their regulating Act. He obtained leave to introduce this measure, the Rotherhithe Dock bill, 21 Feb.; it received royal assent on 20 May.[44] He presented a Cornhill ward petition for repeal of the house and window taxes, 25 Feb., when he voted for the Irish unlawful societies bill.[45] He voted against Catholic relief, 1 Mar., and paired likewise, 10 May. He applauded the government's budget proposals, 28 Feb.,[46] but expressed 'astonishment' at their scheme for dealing with the sinking fund, 3 Mar. He defended the Metropolitan Fish Company bill, and demanded inquiry into the Irish butter trade, 15 Mar. As one of the Members involved in bringing in the Peruvian Mining Company bill, he upheld it as 'a fair and bona fide speculation', 16 Mar. He endorsed the grant for the Irish linen board, 18 Mar., though he was normally 'decidedly opposed to all shackles upon trade'. He presented petitions against the Metropolitan Water and Thames Quay bills, 22 Mar.[47] He 'approved of the principle' of the ministerial proposals for relaxation of customs duties, 25 Mar., but 'thought it would be advisable to begin the reduction at a higher point, and come down by degrees', in case

'this system should leave the produce and manufactures of the country open to loss and detriment from the want of sufficient protection'.[48] On 28 Mar., when he supported the grant for the improvement of the chief government office buildings, he asserted that the corn laws could no longer be left untouched. At the London merchants' meeting to petition for their alteration, 13 Apr., when he said that he was there 'to hear the opinions, and receive the instructions of his constituents', he stressed the universal benefits of lower corn prices.[49] Presenting the petition, 25 Apr., he argued at some length for the imposition of a fixed duty, with due regard for the 'fair protection' to which domestic growers were entitled. He professed 'satisfaction' with ministerial explanations of their intentions, but on 28 Apr., when he supported the London corporation petition for relaxation of the laws, he spoke and voted for Wolryche Whitmore's motion to that effect.[50] He presented constituency petitions against alteration of the 1824 Combination Act and the Dissenters' marriages bill, 22 Apr.[51] Supporting the West India Company bill, 16 May, he maintained that it would 'afford relief to the distressed planters ... and contribute to the improvement of the condition of the negroes'. Later that day he said that £6,000 was too high a salary for a puisne judge. On 20 May he spoke and voted against the Leith Docks bill and supported a London ship owners' petition against the deduction from seamen's wages of contributions to Greenwich Hospital. He approved the proposed grant of £6,000 for the education of Princess Victoria, but had doubts about the same provision for the duke of Cumberland's son, 27 May. On the 30th, however, he voted for it 'on the ground of confidence in the government', as he explained on 6 June, when he complained of Brougham's unwarranted attack on its backbench supporters and divided for Cumberland's annuity bill, as he did again, 10 June. He called for reform of private bill committee proceedings and endorsed a London merchants' petition for revision of the law of merchant and factor, 2 June; he supported the bill dealing with this, 28 June. He voted for the St. Olave tithe bill, 6 June, and against the spring guns bill, 21 June. He applauded the work of the board of trade and approved the proposal to enhance the salaries of its president and vice-president, 14 June.[52] On 17 June he welcomed the government's modification of the customs consolidation bill:

> He had not, perhaps, adopted the ideas of free trade quite so rapidly as some ... but he felt confident that, by surrendering some apparent advantages, we should ultimately derive solid benefit from the course of policy which the government was pursuing.

He wanted the 'beneficial' Scottish partnerships bill to be extended to England, 22 June. On 29 June 1825 he deplored 'inflammatory' language on the combination laws and supported the ministerial legislation 'because it tended to protect the workers from themselves'.[53]

At a non-party Mansion House meeting of City merchants and bankers, 14 Dec. 1825, Wilson, who attributed the current finical crisis to 'an excess of riches', proposed the resolution pledging the participants to mutual trust and confidence.[54] On the address, 2 Feb. 1826, he urged protection for the distressed silk trade. The ministry's proposals for dealing with the commercial crisis dissatisfied Wilson and soured his relations with them. On 13 Feb., when he presented a London petition for reduction of the tobacco duties, he attacked the planned restriction on the issue of small notes, endorsed Baring's scheme for a bimetallic currency and voted in the minority of 39 against going into committee on the Bank Charter Acts.[55] On the promissory notes bill, 20 Feb., he supported the government amendment authorizing the Bank to stamp small notes until 10 October; but he opposed their proposal to inquire into Scottish small notes issue, which was 'tantamount to giving a dog a bad name', 16 Mar. Reporting that distress and panic were daily increasing in the City, 14 Feb., he objected to the government's blaming the crisis on the merchants' speculation which they had themselves encouraged, and demanded a substantial measure of relief. When he said that ministers, whom he had 'hitherto always felt proud and happy to support', had been 'excellent pilots' in calm weather, but 'did not know how to steer the boat ... during the raging of the storm', Robinson, the chancellor of the exchequer, remarked that 'he ought not to have contributed to support them in the management of the boat during the fair weather'. Wilson retorted that 'when he spoke of his confidence being lessened in ministers, he was not speaking of his confidence in the wisdom of their general policy, but ... in their wisdom as to this particular measure'. He wanted a direct issue of exchequer bills by government, as in 1793 and 1811, and, like most mercantile men, was unhappy with their plan for the Bank to buy the bills, as he explained in the House, 15 Feb., and at a merchants' meeting which petitioned to that effect, 23 Feb.[56] When he presented the petition later that day, he 'left his usual place behind the treasury bench, and took a neutral position'. There was widespread backbench ministerial support for his plea for an issue of exchequer bills and attack on ministerial indifference to the distress which their inflationary policy had 'superinduced'; and the motion of which he gave notice for 28 Feb., for the appointment of a select committee of inquiry, threatened to

embarrass ministers. In covert negotiations, they persuaded the Bank to lend £3,000,000 to distressed merchants on the security of their goods; and on the 28th Wilson grudgingly withdrew his motion, after eliciting a statement from Robinson. Later in the debate, however, he registered his protest 'against the tone in which ministers had treated both the applicants for relief and Parliament in general'.[57] In a discussion of anti-slavery petitions, 1 Mar., he 'declared himself hostile to any measure which should have for its object to set the slaves free at the expense of their masters' and demanded adequate compensation for the planters. He supported the West India merchants' petition for compensation, 20 Apr., when he urged government to disregard 'popular clamour' and to 'proceed upon a sound, temperate, and deliberate view of what the real interests of the country demanded'. He called for revision of the corn laws, 6 Mar., and voted in the minority for that, 18 Apr. He opposed the London corn exchange bill as an infraction of 'private rights', 17 Apr. He gave guarded approval to the government's proposed modification of the laws, 1 May, but pressed for 'pecuniary aid' to create employment in the manufacturing districts; he attended a London meeting to open a relief fund, 2 May.[58] He went to the House, 5 May, intent on opposing the plan to release warehoused corn, but was persuaded to swallow it by the 'great' alteration which ministers had made to it. He defended corn dealers, 12 May. He now took a dim view of the proposal to give the president of the board of trade a separate ministerial salary: he said that it 'went unnecessarily to increase the patronage of the crown', 6 Apr. He divided to postpone the decision and spoke and voted for Hume's amendment for inquiry into the duties of the treasurer of the navy, 7 Apr., and was again in the hostile minority, 10 Apr. After the statement by Huskisson, the president, of ministerial plans for further relaxation of the Navigation Acts, 13 May, Wilson insisted that ministers rather than merchants were responsible for the recent 'over-trading' and expressed his fear of too much advantage being conceded to foreign competitors. On 26 May 1826 he presented a petition from Cork ship owners against these changes; spoke and voted against Lord John Russell's resolution condemning electoral bribery, which he said was unheard of in the City, and asserted that it had been 'entirely wrong' of government to interfere with the power of English country bankers to issue notes.

In March 1826 Wilson was expected to stand again for London at the approaching general election, having changed his mind since the previous autumn, but he announced his retirement at the end of April and gave his support to the Bank director William Ward*.[59]

His business, which became known as Wilson, Wilson and Company, continued at Jeffery's Square.[60] At the general election of 1835 he stood jointly for London with two other Conservatives as supporters of Peel's fledgling first ministry. In his address, he stated that he wished to 'arrest the effect of that disloyalty towards our king, enmity towards the church and opposition to the great prerogative of the crown, which have been lately made manifest'; and at the nomination he professed willingness to 'reform every proved abuse'. Unable to gain a hearing from the hustings after the first day's polling, he doffed his hat, proclaimed 'the constitution and king, God bless him', and departed. He finished bottom of the poll as the four Liberals swept the board.[61] In March 1843, when he was 75, he solicited from Peel church preferment for his third son Robert Francis, 'a poor curate at £130 per annum', citing his parliamentary services and his unsuccessful candidacy in 1835, since when he had been 'by purse and in person a zealous and constant supporter of Conservative principles at the City and Middlesex elections'. Peel could do nothing for him.[62] Wilson died at Hackney, 'aged 85', in October 1852.[63] By his will, dated 23 Feb. 1852, he confirmed the terms of his marriage settlement and additional provision since made for his seven children, to the tune of £13,000. He left his freehold and copyhold property at East Ham and Little Ilford to his eldest son Francis, his residuary legatee, who also received £16,000 and 30 shares in the capital stock of the Phoenix Fire Office. He made Francis and Robert Francis trustees of his marshlands in Plaistow Level and created a trust fund of £17,000 to provide for his three daughters and their children.[64] The Jeffery's Square business seems to have gone out of existence soon after Wilson's death.

[1] *Gent. Mag.* (1818), i. 639. [2] Par. reg. St. John's, Hackney. *Gent. Mag.* (1796), ii. 965 incorrectly gives 21st. [3] *Gent. Mag.* (1807), i. 385; PROB 6/183. [4] *The Times*, 18 Feb.1820; Add. 40507, f. 175; 40571, f. 166. [5] *Creevey Pprs.* i. 278. [6] *The Times*, 7, 12, 18 Feb., 4, 8, 16, 17 Mar. 1820. [7] Ibid. 29 Apr., 3 May 1820. [8] Ibid. 1 June 1820. [9] Ibid. 20 June 1820. [10] Ibid. 4 July 1820. [11] Ibid. 12 Jan. 1821. [12] Ibid. 1 Feb. 1821. [13] Ibid. 20 Feb. 1821. [14] Ibid. 30 Mar., 3 Apr. 1821. [15] HLRO Hist. Coll. 379, Grey Bennet diary, 37. [16] *The Times*, 31 Mar. 1821. [17] Ibid. 4, 10 Apr., 22 May 1821. [18] Ibid. 14 Apr. 1821. [19] Ibid. 5 June 1821. [20] Ibid. 14, 23 June 1821. [21] Ibid. 30 June 1821. [22] Ibid. 5, 12 Mar. 1822. [23] Ibid. 12 June 1822. [24] Ibid. 19 Mar. 1822. [25] Ibid. 26 Mar. 1822. [26] Ibid. 30 Apr. 1822. [27] Ibid. 3, 17 May 1822. [28] Ibid. 24, 31 May 1822. [29] Ibid. 22 May 1822. [30] Ibid. 6, 16, 18, 19 July 1822. [31] Ibid. 25, 26, 30 July 1822. [32] Ibid. 13 Feb. 1823. [33] Ibid. 28 Feb. 1823. [34] Ibid. 22 Apr., 5 June 1823. [35] Ibid. 23 May 1823. [36] Ibid. 7 Feb. 1824. [37] Ibid. 9, 12, 23 Mar. 1824. [38] Ibid. 24, 30 Mar., 1 Apr. 1824. [39] Ibid. 15 June 1824. [40] Ibid. 5 May 1824. [41] Ibid. 14 June 1824. [42] Ibid. 29 May 1824. [43] Ibid. 28 May 1824; *CJ*, lxxix. 423, 429, 447, 484. [44] *The Times*, 12, 15 Feb., 8 Mar. 1825; *CJ*, lxxx. 101, 122, 167, 353, 441. [45] *The Times*, 26 Feb. 1825. [46] Ibid. 1 Mar. 1825. [47] Ibid. 23 Mar. 1825. [48] Ibid. 26 Mar. 1825. [49] Ibid. 14 Apr. 1825. [50] Ibid. 29 Apr. 1825. [51] Ibid. 23 Apr. 1825. [52] Ibid. 15 June 1825. [53] Ibid. 30 June 1825.

[54] Ibid. 15 Dec. 1825; B. Hilton, *Corn, Cash, Commerce*, 216-17. [55] *The Times*, 14 Feb. 1826. [56] Ibid. 24 Feb. 1826. [57] Add. 51584, Tierney to Holland, 23 [Feb.]; Nottingham Univ. Lib. Denison diary, 23 [Feb. 1826]; *Croker Pprs.* i. 314-17; *Wellington Despatches*, iii. 116-17; Hilton, 225-6. [58] *The Times*, 3 May 1826. [59] Ibid. 10 Mar., 13 May 1826. [60] It did not, as erroneously stated in *HP Commons, 1790-1820*, v. 607, move in about 1834 to 6 Warnford Court, Throgmorton Street: the Thomas Wilson who had been running that concern since about 1814 was another man. [61] *The Times*, 3, 5-9 Jan. 1835. [62] Add. 40536, ff. 427-31. [63] *Gent. Mag.* (1852), ii. 637. [64] PROB 11/2162/; IR26/1952/639.

D.R.F.

WILSON, **William Wilson Carus** (1764–1851), of Casterton Hall, Kirkby Lonsdale, Westmld.

COCKERMOUTH   21 July 1821–1 Feb. 1827

b. 24 July 1764, o.s. of William Carus of Kirkby Lonsdale and Elizabeth, da. of Roger Wilson of Casterton. *educ.* Queen Elizabeth's g.s. Kirkby Lonsdale;[1] Trinity Coll. Camb. 1782. *m.* 10 Sept. 1787, Margaret, da. and h. of Benjamin Shippard of Narland, 7s. (4 *d.v.p.*) 3da. *d.v.p. suc.* fa. 1768; aunt Anne Place to Casterton and took name of Wilson by sign manual 1 Mar. 1793. *d.* 11 Feb. 1851.

Carus, as he was first known, was of Westmorland stock, being one of the Wilsons of Dallam Tower and Casterton and heir to the Carus family's Lancashire estates of Arkholme, Melling, Whittington and Wrayton, near Kirkby Lonsdale. His father died when he was four and he was brought up by his mother at Casterton and educated at nearby Kirkby Lonsdale and at Cambridge, where he was one of the early followers of the Evangelical Charles Simeon and graduated in mathematics in 1786. He assumed control of the Carus estates and was married in 1787 to Margaret Shippard, a local heiress who shared his religious beliefs. They settled at Heversham, moving in 1793 to Casterton, left to him by his mother's sister Anne, the widow of the Rev. Marwood Place, in compliance with whose will he assumed the name of Wilson.[2] As befitted his standing, he built a new mansion at Casterton and became a magistrate in Lancashire, Yorkshire and Westmorland, where he was foreman of the grand jury. With his brother-in-law Edward Hassell of Dalemain, near Penrith, and Daniel Wilson of Dallam Tower he supported the Tory Lowther or Yellow interest at the Westmorland elections of 1818 and 1820, when they defeated the Whig Henry Brougham*. He was also the author of the Westmorland loyal addresses of 1819 and 1820.[3] In July 1821, by arrangement with Daniel Wilson, the Lowthers returned him on a vacancy for their borough of Cockermouth. On the hustings Wilson promised to support church, state and Westmorland interests.[4] According to Henry Elliott, who put him up at Clapham and arranged for him to be briefed on 'probable business' and 'his new duties' by Frederick Gough Calthorpe*

> Mr. Carus Wilson feels rather doubtful whether he has done well in leaving his duties in the country, which were certainly of a very extensive and beneficial kind and entering upon the untried and to a man of his great modesty, the dreaded office of an MP.[5]

He divided against Catholic relief, 30 Apr. 1822, 1 Mar., 21 Apr. 10 May 1825, and parliamentary reform, 20 Feb., 2 June 1823, and fairly steadily for the Liverpool government with the Lowthers. His few wayward votes reflected local concerns and his commitment to the penal and poor law reforms promoted by the Tory Evangelicals, especially his son William, rector of Whittington, whose Cowen Bridge school for clergymen's daughters he endowed. (The Bronte sisters, who maligned it, were early pupils.)[6] His maiden speech against treating interference with Members' mail as a breach of privilege, 25 Feb. 1822, was 'inaudible in the gallery', but he became a regular contributor to debates and select committees, where his experience of local administration and stance on humanitarian issues were widely respected.[7] He divided with ministers against more extensive tax reductions, 21 Feb., and abolition of one of the joint-postmasterships, 13 Mar., but he cast a wayward vote for repeal of the salt tax, 28 June 1822. On 28 Mar. he received a month's leave on account of the illness of his daughter Elizabeth, an invalid since 1818.[8] He condemned the Salford small debts bill as a deliberate means of transferring 'from £4,000 to £8,000 a year' to the court of record for the benefit of Lord Sefton*, and was a minority teller against it, 13 May. He testified to the integrity of the current Welsh judges, but supported the assimilation of the courts of great sessions which ministers were not yet ready to concede, 23 May, and presented and endorsed Blackburn's petition complaining of the severity of the penal code, 4 June.[9] He voted against inquiring into Irish tithes, 19 June, and the lord advocate's treatment of the Scottish press, 25 June, and opposed the lottery, 1 July. He divided with government on the national debt reduction bill, 12 Mar., and taxation, 10, 18 Mar. 1823. When Peter Moore moved in vain that day to repeal the Insolvent Debtors Act, Wilson called for an *amicus curiae* to assist county magistrates with insolvency cases, and expressed support afterwards for Phillimore's proposals to amend the profane swearing bill. He voted against repealing the Foreign Enlistment Act, 16 Apr., and was in the government minority against inquiry into the prosecution of the Dublin Orange rioters, 22 Apr. During it he challenged attempts by

Brougham and Lord Stanley to force disclosure of the Orangemen's secret oath, 26 May.[10] He divided with Hume for inquiry into the Newfoundland fisheries, 14 May, and was for abolishing the death penalty for larceny, 21 May. He presented Cockermouth's petition for the abolition of West Indian slavery the next day.[11] He voted to inquire into chancery arrears, 5 June 1823.

Wilson voted with the Lowthers against reforming Edinburgh's representation, 26 Feb., but they found his votes of conscience for the motion of complaint against lord chancellor Eldon, 1 Mar., and in condemnation of the trial in Demerara of the Methodist missionary John Smith, 11 June 1824, 'very provoking'.[12] He seconded the adjournment motion by which the mariners' apprentices settlement bill was lost, 11 May, spoke for the new churches bill, 4 June, and secured a late amendment to the vagrants bill (as a member of the committee), 5 June.[13] His criminal lunatics bill received royal assent, 17 June 1824.[14] During the recess he consulted the home secretary Peel about the Millthorpe murder.[15] He endured an arduous journey in appalling weather to return to London for the 1825 session.[16] He voted for the Irish unlawful societies bill, 25 Feb., staunchly defended the anti-Catholic clergy of Cambridge University, 15 Mar., and other hostile petitioners, 21 Apr., and pressed for the deferral of the Catholic question until after the spring assizes, 23 Mar.[17] Speaking as an Irish landlord, he condemned the planned disfranchisement of the lower classes by the franchise bill, 26 Apr., 9 May. He advocated reform of the game laws, 7 Mar., and spoke, 11 Mar., and was a minority teller for the ill-treatment of animals bill, 24 Mar. He would 'not give any opinion' on Grattan's Irish poor relief bill, 22 Mar., but testified to the beneficial effect of the Irish Vagrants Act in northern England and explained that he objected to the poor rates because of abuses in their administration and not on account of the amounts levied. He called for the extension of the Factory Act to children in all manufactories, 5 May, and was probably the 'C. Wilson' who paired for repeal of the window tax, 14 May. He divided for the duke of Cumberland's award, 30 May, 2, 10 June, and was 'perfectly satisfied' with the proposed increases in judges' salaries, 2 June.[18] He was a majority teller for the church land exchange bill, 21 June, and recommended classifying offenders under the cattle ill-treatment bill as miscreants rather than felons that day.[19] He also wanted bear-baiting and dog-fighting made illegal and disputed claims that 'the pleasures of the poor' would thereby be diminished, 21 Feb. 1826. In the wake of the 1825-6 banking crisis, he said he would support any measure making country bank notes payable on demand at the place of issue, 27

Feb., and pointed to the stability of the Cumberland and Westmorland banks administered in this way. He also urged better safeguards to prevent forgery of Bank of England pound notes, 7 Mar. He welcomed Peel's proposals to consolidate the criminal laws, 9 Mar. He voted to condemn the Jamaican slave trials, 2 Mar. (was later named to the select committee on the trade in Mauritius, 9 May), and had 'no hesitation' in granting the award for Sierra Leone, 10 Mar. He introduced and endorsed a petition from Preston, where his son Roger was the incumbent, for abolishing West Indian slavery, 15 Mar.[20] He objected to funding 'any system of education' in Ireland from which the Scriptures were excluded, 14 Apr. Perceiving agriculture and industry as interdependent, 6 Mar., he considered the temporary release of bonded corn to alleviate distress 'vital', suspended judgement on Wolryche Whitmore's scheme, 5 May, and endorsed the government's proposals, 8 May 1826.[21] He chaired the Lowthers' Westmorland committee at the general election in June, when they secured a decisive majority against Brougham, and they returned him for Cockermouth on their interest.[22] That summer he faced prosecution by his neighbour Alexander Nowell*, whose candidature for Lancashire he had opposed, for cattle trespass, and resolved to resign his seat on health grounds. Lord Lowther* attributed his decision to his unwillingness 'to sanction the introduction of foreign corn under any scale of duties'.[23]

Wilson remained loyal to the Lowthers and agreed to be brought forward belatedly by them for Westmorland in 1831 to thwart a challenge by a second reformer with Nowell, but he did not proceed to a poll.[24] He declared for them again at personal cost when the Dallam Tower Wilsons defected in 1832.[25] He was deeply affected by the death of his wife that year and also by lengthy bankruptcy and libel proceedings involving his son Charles, a London attorney and the defendant in the case of Le Sueur v. Gross.[26] He entertained Queen Adelaide at Casterton in 1840 and died there in February 1851, shortly after presiding at an anti-Catholic meeting at Kendal. He was buried in Kirkby Lonsdale.[27] He left his estates to William (1791-1859), and directed him to pay £3,000 to Charles and lesser sums to his younger children and grandchildren, except his son Edward Carus Wilson (1795-1860), whom he had provided for on his marriage in 1835 and again on his retirement as vicar of Crosby Ravensworth, Westmorland, in 1848.[28]

[1] J. Ewbank, *Life and Works of Rev. William Carus Wilson*, 2. Reference in *Al. Cant.* to his attendance at the King's School, Chester is not confirmed by the school lists. [2] Ewbank, 2-3; Cumbria

RO (Kendal), Carus Wilson mss WD/CAT/Acc. 2364. [3] *Wordsworth Letters* ed. M. Moorman and A.G. Hill (1970 edn.), ii. 563; *Westmld. Gazette*, 26 Feb. 1820. [4] R.S. Ferguson, *Cumb. and Westmld. MPs*, 244, 453; *Cumb. Pacquet*, 23 July 1821. [5] Hants RO, Calthorpe mss 26M62/F/C/122. [6] Ewbank, *passim*; Carus Wilson mss WD/CAT/Acc. 2364; Rev. W. Carus Wilson, *Tracts* (1824). [7] *The Times*, 26 Feb. 1822. [8] Rev. W.C. Wilson, *Mem. of a Beloved Sister* (1832). [9] *The Times*, 5 June 1822. [10] Ibid. 27 May 1823. [11] Ibid. 23 May 1823. [12] Lonsdale mss, Lowther to Lonsdale, 9 Mar. 1824. [13] *CJ*, lxxix. 382, 462, 465; *The Times*, 7 June 1824. [14] *The Times*, 7, 9 Apr. 1824; *CJ*, lxxix. 260, 264, 276, 367, 378, 389, 502. [15] Carus Wilson mss WD/CW misc. [16] Wilson, *Mem. of a Beloved Sister*, 296. [17] *The Times*, 16, 24 Mar. 1825. [18] Ibid. 3 June 1825. [19] Ibid. 22 June 1825. [20] Ibid. 16 Mar. 1826. [21] Ibid. 7 Mar. 1826. [22] *Cumb. Pacquet*, 13 June; Lonsdale mss, Wilson to Lowther, 15 June; *The Times*, 26 June, 13 July 1826. [23] Carus Wilson mss WD/CAT/Acc. 2364; WD/CW; Lonsdale mss, Lowther to Lonsdale, 18, 27 Nov. 1826. [24] Brougham mss, J. to H. Brougham, 4 May 1831; *Westmld. Advertiser*, 7 May; *The Times*, 10 May 1831. [25] Brougham mss, J. Brougham to Atkinson, 15 Nov. 1832. [26] *The Times*, 1 Oct. 1828, 30 Sept. 1844; Ewbank, 8. [27] *Gent. Mag.* (1851), i. 453. [28] PROB 11/2130/255; IR26/1917/190.

M.M.E.

WILSON *see also* **WRIGHT WILSON**

WILSON PATTEN (formerly **WILSON**), **John** (1802–1892), of Bank Hall, Warrington, Lancs. and 24 Hill Street, Mdx.

LANCASHIRE	1830–1831
LANCASHIRE NORTH	1832–1874

b. 26 Apr. 1802, 2nd but 1st surv s. of Thomas Patten Wilson of Bank Hall and Elizabeth, da. of Nathan Hyde of Ardwick, Lancs. *educ.* Eton 1817; Magdalen, Oxf. 1821. *m.* 15 Apr. 1828, his cos. Anna Maria, da. and coh. of Peter Patten Bold[†] of Bold Hall, Lancs., 2s. *d.v.p.* 4da. (2 *d.v.p.*). *suc.* fa. 1827; took additional name of Patten 1823; *cr.* Bar. Winmarleigh 22 Mar. 1874. *d.* 11 July 1892.

Chairman of ways and means 1852-3; chan. of duchy of Lancaster June 1867-Sept. 1868; PC [GB] 26 June 1867, [I] 15 Oct. 1868; chief sec. to ld. lt. [I] Sept.-Dec. 1868.

Commr. on common law 1856-7; militia 1858-9; army recruitment 1866; international coinage 1868; cts. martial 1868.

Col. 3 R. Lancs. militia 1841-72; a.d.c. to Queen Victoria Mar. 1857-d.; hon. col. army 1872-d.

Constable, Lancaster Castle 1879-d.

By the sudden death in Italy in 1819 of his elder brother Thomas, Wilson, who was then at Eton and intended for the army or the church, became heir to the industrial wealth and church livings of Warrington and 5,338 acres in Lancashire (4,200 acres), Cheshire and Staffordshire.[1] After leaving Oxford, he travelled on the continent, where, as at Eton, he was the close companion of the Whig 12th earl of Derby's grandson Edward George Geoffrey Smith Stanley*. No longer bound by the testamentary injunction of the Rev. Thomas Wilson, by which his father had acquired the estates of his great-uncle, the bishop of Sodor and Man, when he came of age in 1823 he adopted the name of Wilson Patten. He took control of and added to the estates following his father's death in December 1827 and became a partner in the family firm, the patent roller manufacturers John Wilson Patten and Company of Oakmoor Mills, Cheadle.[2] His marriage in 1828 to his cousin Anna Maria Bold (*d.* 1846), daughter and coheir of the former Tory Member for Newton and Lancaster, continued the family's trend of consolidating their interests by fortuitous marriages with their Bold, Blackburne, Patten and Wilson kinswomen and boosted his prospects of representing Lancashire.[3] He promoted anti-Catholic petitions in 1829 with the Tory county Member Blackburne's son and heir, John Ireland Blackburne[†], and declared his candidature as Blackburne's successor directly his intended retirement at the dissolution was announced in November 1829.[4] At the general election of 1830 his kinsman and likely rival Peter Hesketh was disqualified as sheriff from standing, attempts to bring forward alternative candidates failed, and he came in with the sitting Whig, Smith Stanley's father Lord Stanley.[5] On the hustings, where the Ultras and radicals quizzed him closely, he stated that there was 'no turning back' on Catholic emancipation, made retrenchment the '*sine qua non*' of his support for the duke of Wellington's administration, expressed qualified support for opening the East India trade and reserved the right to vote for any alteration of the corn laws he perceived as necessary and 'calculated to promote ... agricultural, manufacturing and commercial interests'. On reform, he declared for the enfranchisement of certain large towns and against the ballot.[6]

Ministers listed him as one of the 'moderate Ultras'. He sat next to Sir John Walsh on the left hand in entering under the gallery, and divided against them when they were brought down on the civil list, 15 Nov. 1830.[7] He presented petitions for the abolition of colonial slavery from Lancashire and Shrewsbury, 22 Nov., 9, 17 Dec., and briefly seconded Littleton's motion for a labourers' wages bill in his maiden speech, 18 Dec., having previously presented favourable petitions, 14 Dec.[8] A committed and eventually successful campaigner for repeal of the duty on calicoes and raw cottons, he brought up petitions from Manchester and the manufacturing towns, 17 Dec. 1830, 8, 9, 10, 25 Feb., criticized the drawbacks proposed in the Grey ministry's budget and suggested instead making wholesale reductions to end the uncertainty and prevarication over stock in hand, 16, 28 Feb. 1831.[9] He brought up

further petitions and resolutely defended his stance, 9 Mar., 12 Apr., when he also testified to the 'desperate circumstances' of cotton workers earning 4*s*. 6*d*. to 5*s*. a week. He waited on the prime minister Lord Grey with the East India delegation, 29 Jan., and presented Wigan's petition for ending the Company's monopoly, 16 Mar.[10] He opposed the ballot on his constituents' behalf, 26 Feb., and refused to endorse a plea for it in the Warrington reform petition he introduced, 16 Mar. He remained undecided how to vote on the ministerial reform bill to the last, divided for its second reading, 22 Mar., brought up favourable, 23 Mar., and hostile petitions, 12 Apr., and voted for Gascoyne's wrecking amendment, 19 Apr.[11] He had won widespread support through his select committee work, especially the facility with which he handled the numerous local and transport bills during that Parliament, and a deputation headed by the Manchester Whig industrialist Richard Hyde Gregg[†] tried in vain to persuade him to declare unequivocally for the reform bill before organizing opposition to him at the ensuing general election.[12] Supported by the *Manchester Chronicle*, the *Manchester Herald* and the *Lancaster Gazette*, he declared 'limited support for the bill', namely 'the disfranchisement of the nomination boroughs, and for giving representatives to the large towns' and promised to explain his vote in Gascoyne's majority on the hustings.[13] However, his hostile reception, reputation as an anti-reformer and an unstoppable campaign to return the Manchester banker Benjamin Heywood made his position untenable and prompted his retirement, 3 May.[14] The anti-reformer Lord Salisbury had heard from his Lancashire agent Leigh the previous day that Wilson Patten's £5-6,000 a year was insufficient to support a full-scale contest.[15] At the election dinner Lord Stanley and Heywood and their sponsors paid tribute to him as a Member, 10 May 1831.[16]

Wilson Patten announced his candidature for the first post-reform election, 4 June 1831, and was fêted with Lord Stanley at the calico printers' dinner that month.[17] He declared for Lancashire North directly the reform bill became law and came in there unopposed with Edward Smith Stanley in December 1832, having given his interest in the new Warrington constituency to John Ireland Blackburne.[18] A staunch Conservative who supported labour reforms irrespective of party, he retained his seat until his elevation to the peerage in March 1874, having chaired the committee of ways and means during Lord Derby's (Smith Stanley's) administration and served briefly as chancellor of the duchy of Lancaster and as Irish secretary, which 'thoroughly disgusted him', under Derby and Benjamin Disraeli[†], 1867-8. He was also considered for the Speakership.[19] Deterred from living at Bank Hall by encroaching industrialization, in 1871 he built a new mansion at Winmarleigh near Garstang, where he died in July 1892, predeceased by his wife, both sons, Eustace (1836-73) and Arthur (1840-66), two of his three daughters and his only grandson. He was recalled as a career politician who commanded his regiment at Gibraltar during the Crimean War and as a prominent member of the cotton famine relief fund committee during the American Civil War.[20]

[1] Lancs. RO, Wilson Patten mss DDSb1/1, 5, 6. [2] Ibid. 3/26, 27; Staffs. RO D953; M.J. Turner, *Reform and Respectability*, 290. [3] I. Sellers, *Early Modern Warrington*, 219. [4] *Lancaster Gazette*, 14, 21 Nov. 1829. [5] Ibid. 3, 24, 31 July, 7 Aug.; *Blackburn Gazette*, 7, 14 July; Hatfield House mss, bdle. 3, Leigh to Salisbury, 9 July; *Manchester Guardian*, 17, 24 July 1830; Turner, 293. [6] *Manchester Guardian*, 7 Aug.; *Blackburn Gazette*, 11 Aug. 1830. [7] NLW, Ormathwaite mss FG1/5, pp. 118, 121. [8] St. Deiniol's Lib. Glynne-Gladstone mss 196, T. to J. Gladstone, 18 Dec. 1830. [9] A. Howe, *The Cotton Masters*, 93-94. [10] *Manchester Herald*, 9 Feb. 1831. [11] Glynne-Gladstone mss 197, T. to J. Gladstone, 11, 19 Mar. 1831. [12] *Manchester Guardian*, 23, 30 Apr., 7 May; Derby mss 920 Der (14) 116/6, Winstanley to Smith Stanley, 25 Apr.; Hatfield House mss, bdle. 4, Leigh to Salisbury, 27, 30 Apr.; Brougham mss, Shepherd to Brougham [1831]. [13] *Manchester Chron.* 12, 26 Mar., 2, 23, 30 Apr.; *Manchester Herald*, 30 Apr. 1831. [14] *Manchester Guardian*, 30 Apr.; TNA 30/29/9/5/80; *Lancaster Herald*, 7 May 1831; Turner, 306-7. [15] Hatfield House mss, bdle. 4. [16] *Manchester Guardian*, 14 May; *Manchester Herald*, 18 May 1831; *Arbuthnot Jnl.* ii. 421. [17] *Manchester Herald*, 1, 8 June; *Manchester Guardian*, 18 June 1831. [18] *Lancaster Gazette*, 23, 30 June, 22 Dec. 1832; HLRO, Greene mss GRE/4/20. [19] Wilson Patten mss 1/20-27; *Gladstone Diaries*, ii. 21; iv. 456-7; *Disraeli Letters*, vol. iv. 2360, 2378; *Disraeli, Derby and the Conservative Party* ed. J. Vincent, 340. [20] *Manchester Guardian*, 12 July; *The Times*, 12 July 1892; Wilson Patten mss 1/8-11.

M.M.E.

WINCHESTER, Henry (1777–1838), of 12 Buckingham Street, Mdx. and Oakfield Lodge, Hawkhurst, Kent.

MAIDSTONE   1830–1831

b. 5 Jan. 1777, 1st s. of William Winchester, stationer, of 61 Strand, Mdx. and w. Sarah Clarke of Hereford. *m.* 24 Nov. 1803, Elizabeth, da. and h. of John Ayerst of Hawkhurst, 3s. (2 *d.v.p.*) 5da. (3 *d.v.p.*). *suc.* fa. 1820.[1] *d.* 8 Mar. 1838.

Sheriff, London 1826-7, alderman 1826-d., ld. mayor 1834-5; master, Cutlers' Co. 1829-30; pres. St. Thomas's Hosp. 1835-d.

Winchester was an irascible and cantankerous man who carried the seeds of discontent into all his spheres of endeavour. The origins of his father, William Winchester, are obscure, although he probably came from a family resident in Westminster, where he

married, 2 July 1774.[2] He lived in the Strand, where he ran the stationery firm of Winchester, Kirkham, Yockney, Harris and Company, but later moved to Cecil Street and Acre Hill, Malden, Surrey. By 1794 he was listed in the directories as the sole proprietor of the business, and it was there that Winchester received his first employment. He was admitted to the freedom of the Cutlers' Company, by apprenticeship, 26 May 1800, and to the livery, 30 May 1801, and he served as steward, 1803-4.[3] He entered a partnership with his father in 1803. They seem to have expanded their business by establishing a small press at 20 Villiers Street in 1804 with their kinsman, William Clowes, who purchased their property at 6 Northumberland Court in 1815 for £576. By 1819 they had taken in a third partner, Arthur Varnham.[4] On his father's death, 5 Jan. 1820, Winchester inherited his share of the business and part of his personalty, which was sworn under £50,000, though not without a quarrel with his brother-in-law, William Blew.[5] He was living in Buckingham Street by 1826, and he also rebuilt the house at Hawkhurst, Kent, which he inherited from his father-in-law.

Winchester led Sir Murray Maxwell's campaign in the parish of St. Martin-in-the-Fields at the fiercely contested Westminster election of 1818, plumping for him at the poll.[6] As he wrote to Lord Liverpool, the prime minister, in 1823:

> During that arduous contest, in which I incurred great personal danger, I exerted myself as chairman of the committee to the utmost of my ability, sparing neither expense nor trouble individually, in order to promote the object that was so much desired, the election of a government candidate for this city; and it was some consolation to find that, during the contest, my endeavours met the unqualified approbation of His Majesty's government.

After Sir Samuel Romilly's[†] suicide later in 1818, he was informed that it was

> intended again to propose Sir Murray Maxwell for Westminster and that I had *carte blanche* to do as I considered most advisable for the attainment of that object, having been given to understand that ample funds (*not public*) by individual subscription would be forthcoming whenever I should require them.

He reconvened the committee and had already begun to canvass for Maxwell before it was decided to abandon his candidacy. He found that the subscriptions had been returned, and so, as he later recorded, 'feeling my own honour, and that of the government, in a great degree at stake, I determined paying the demands myself, and which I accordingly did, but to this moment I have not been reimbursed one penny, nor do I wish to be'.[7] Until a treasury minute reorganizing the stationery office was issued, 21 Mar. 1823, Winchester had held contracts to supply various government departments. In high dudgeon, he wrote a lengthy letter of complaint to Liverpool, 15 Apr., which stated that the new arrangement 'completely deprives me of the *few* advantages which I possessed of a public nature, in the line of my business'. Although Thomas Creevey* alleged in 1835 that Winchester, 'having been employed by a Tory government for supply of the treasury, was formally dismissed by the same government, for *cheating*, that was all', the decision was no doubt motivated by financial considerations. Winchester, however, felt betrayed by ministers, who had promised him their protection in return for his former exertions in Westminster; hence his outburst to Liverpool.[8] Nevertheless, he continued to enjoy certain contracts in the years that followed. He was one of the earliest proprietors of the *Mirror of Parliament*, of which the three volumes covering the debates of the 1828 session were published under the imprint 'Winchester and Varnham'; but he had to meet most of the £7,000 losses made at its commencement that year, and soon backed out in favour of Frederick Gye*.[9]

He was elected one of the sheriffs of the City of London, 29 Sept. 1826, and was satirized in a print depicting George IV's refusal to receive the address of the common council congratulating him on the change of ministers in April 1827.[10] He was first in the field on the morning of Christopher Magnay's death, 27 Oct. 1826, in the contest to replace him as alderman for Vintry. His principal opponent, Edward Archer Wilde, claimed that Winchester had promised to withdraw if a respectable candidate presented himself, and that he could not be returned while holding the allegedly incompatible office of sheriff. After a heated election and a subsequent scrutiny, Winchester was declared the winner by 26-23, 28 Nov. 1826.[11] On the presentation of a petition against his return, the court of aldermen declared the election void and, after another lengthy contest, a scrutiny decided in favour of Wilde by 38-35, 25 Jan. 1827.[12] The aldermen objected to Winchester's instituting legal proceedings against them as an infringement of their right of adjudication, and on several occasions in 1827 party divisions in the court prevented either man being sworn.[13] Deliberations continued in the court of king's bench, at a cost to the corporation of £6,000, until Lord Tenterden ruled in favour of Winchester, subject to arbitration on certain disputed votes, 23 Jan. 1829. William Webb Follett† declared a victory

for Winchester by 27-24, 18 Sept. 1829, and he was finally seated four days later.[14] He was also involved in a case brought by his son-in-law, William Row, of 5 Suffolk Street, possibly over the marriage settlement of his eldest daughter, Sarah.[15] Having joined the court of the Cutlers' Company, 13 Sept. 1826, he served consecutively as junior and senior warden, and became master in 1829.[16] On the withdrawal of the Ultra John Wells* from Maidstone at the dissolution in 1830, Winchester offered in his place and received the backing of the Wellington government as an anti-reformer. He opposed the Whig sitting Member, Abraham Wildey Robarts, but had no other challengers until two independents intervened. At a meeting of the non-resident freemen in London, 13 July, he declared his support for the constitution as a Protestant, 'which faith he had derived from his father, whose firm and revered precepts he hoped and felt he should ever follow and maintain so long as he had memory and energy to assist him'.[17] He reiterated these sentiments on the eve of the poll, 29 July, but also stated his opposition to all imposts and restrictions on agriculture and commerce. The next day he argued for reduced expenditure and pledged himself to act as an apt scholar in a new school, but refused to say whether he would vote for reform or the ballot. He was, however, comfortably returned in second place behind Robarts.[18] A petition alleging that he was a contractor and guilty of corruption was presented, 11 Nov. 1830, but these claims were dismissed, 16 Mar. 1831, on the ground that his contracts for supplying the navy commissioners with sheet paper had been transferred to his partner just prior to the election.[19]

Winchester was, of course, listed by ministers among their 'friends', and he duly voted with them on the civil list, 15 Nov. 1830. His brief spell in Parliament revealed his concern for charities, such as St. Thomas's Hospital, of which he was a governor. He urged that, as it already provided its own lighting and watchmen, it should be exempted from the payment of rates in Southwark, 7 Dec. 1830, and was a teller for the minority against the postponement of a bill to this effect. He presented and endorsed a petition from the common council and inhabitants of Vintry against the duty on seaborne coal in the port of London, 4 Feb. 1831, and raised the issue again, 17 Feb. He urged postponement of Hobhouse's select vestries bill, 14 Feb., and presented a petition against it from the vicar, churchwardens and vestrymen (of which he was one) of St. Martin-in-the-Fields, 17 Feb., arguing that there was 'no reason whatever for the interference', which would 'unsettle not only all the institutions of that parish, but of every other similarly situated in the kingdom'. He opposed it again, 21 Feb., especially over the proposed alteration in the elective franchise of his parish where

> there is a scale as to the right of voting, and property has its proper influence, but in this bill that point so essential to the welfare and good government of any parish is annihilated, and one nearly approaching to universal suffrage substituted in its place.

He offered not to divide the House provided he could introduce a protecting clause for St. Martin's, as he did again, 28 Feb. He asked the attorney-general to prevent vexatious and expensive law suits against the trustees of charities coming under the operation of the new charity commission, 10 Mar. On 21 Mar. he brought up a Vintry petition in favour of parliamentary reform, though he did 'not approve' of the Grey ministry's bill, and one against it from the inhabitants of Maidstone, who objected to the loss of their privileges. He voted against the second reading of the bill, 22 Mar. He opined that allowing employers to oblige their employees to take meals at work, 'having the profit of procuring them', would render the truck bill inoperative, 12 Apr. On the presentation of the Sussex reform petition, 18 Apr., he stated that he had refused to sign it, and asked what concessions ministers would make to opposition views. He voted for Gascoyne's wrecking amendment, 19 Apr. 1831, which precipitated a dissolution.

It also led to his own departure from the Commons. On 5 Apr. the Whiggish *Kentish Chronicle* had asked if there was 'a man in all England that can explain what miracle induced the people of Maidstone to send Winchester the stationer into Parliament?' He offered again, 23 Apr., but Charles James Barnett* emerged as a reformer to unite with Robarts, and the candidacy of the former Member, George Simson, did nothing to prevent Winchester being insulted during the campaign.[20] On the hustings, 3 May 1831, he was criticized by the electors for not fulfilling their wishes, and was shouted down when he tried to explain that he was in favour of the enfranchisement of large towns, but not of the destruction of vested rights. Trailing badly behind the reformers, he withdrew at the end of the first day and apparently never attempted to re-enter Parliament.[21] He was one of the four aldermen who voted against the reappointment of Sir John Key†, the pro-reform lord mayor, at all three elections that year, and he supported George Lyall† at the general election of 1832 in London.[22] He dissolved his partnership with Varnham, who took over their premises in the Strand, 31 Dec. 1833.[23]

Winchester became lord mayor of London by rotation, being formally elected, 29 Sept. 1834. At his inaugural dinner, 8 Nov., he eulogized Wellington as 'the great captain of the age', but the corporation was predominantly Whig, and he twice had to present addresses to the king (against the change of ministers in late 1834 and in favour of their dismissal in April 1835) with which he disagreed. He made himself very unpopular by his refusal to allow Guildhall to be used for public meetings, after having given a specific promise to the contrary.[24] He frequently differed with the aldermen and common councilmen, as over the police committee, the number of sessional dinners, the opening of their proceedings to the public and the costs of his mayoralty.[25] Their biggest dispute was over a committee report on municipal reform which proposed limiting the tenure of aldermen to seven year terms. By peremptorily adjourning the court, Winchester repeatedly denied it a hearing, or the possibility of its making any submission to Parliament. On one occasion he spoke of the 'similarity between the proceedings of the common council in the days of Cromwell and those of the committee'. At the end of his period in office he was given the customary vote of thanks by the court of aldermen, but the common council passed a censure motion against him, by 99-35, 26 Nov.[26] During his period in office, Benjamin Rotch†, chairman of the Middlesex quarter sessions, objected to Winchester's dismissal of his criticisms of the corporation's management of Newgate gaol as 'this scandalous matter', and challenged him to a duel. Declining it, Winchester took action against him for attempted breach of the peace, and the affair was dropped only after Rotch had apologized.[27] This was just one of the episodes exploited in a publication which purported to be the *Memorandums of My Mayoralty* by 'Lord Winchester'. It portrayed him as a blustering simpleton, and the laughing-stock of the ministers with whom he claimed great friendship. It also ridiculed his general dishonesty, his attacks on radicals and their newspaper, the *True Son*, and his ambitions for an hereditary mayoralty or a seat in the Lords as 'Baron Foolscap'.[28]

Winchester remained loyal to the Conservatives, voting for them at Kent West and Westminster elections in 1835 and 1837.[29] He became president of St. Thomas's, 11 Feb. 1835, and was also a vice-president of the Society for the Promotion of Arts, Manufactures and Commerce, and treasurer of the Printers' Pension Society.[30] His personal affairs, which were known to be unhappy, were worsened by the deaths of his children, including that of his youngest son at the Mansion House, 17 June 1835. However, even the *Memorandums* drew a veil, having 'Winchester' write that 'I shall not, for very obvious reasons, touch upon what may be called my private life'.[31] His business dealings had been encumbered for some time, and he was officially ordered to surrender as a bankrupt on 1 Mar. 1838. He died a week later 'at a lunatic asylum, to which he had been removed, having unhappily brooded with such intense melancholy on his domestic calamities as to have been bereft of his senses'.[32] No will or grant of administration has been found. He was succeeded by his second, but only surviving son, William (b. 1815).

[1] W. Berry, *Kent Genealogies*, 80. [2] IGI (London). [3] *Ex. inf.* Worshipful Co. of Cutlers. [4] W.B. Todd, *Directory of Printers*, 40, 215; *Survey of London*, xviii. 19-20. [5] PROB 11/1626/114; IR26/845/90. [6] *Westminster Pollbook* (1818), 129. [7] Add. 38293, f. 349. [8] Ibid.; *PP* (1823), xiv. 579-86; *Creevey Pprs.* ii. 380. [9] J. Grant, *Great Metropolis*, ser. 2, ii. 217. [10] M.D. George, *Cat. of Pol. and Personal Satires*, x. 15408. [11] *The Times*, 30 Oct., 3, 4, 7, 13, 29 Nov. 1826; A.B. Beaven, *Aldermen of London*, i. 215. [12] *The Times*, 2-5, 26 Jan. 1827. [13] Ibid. 25 May, 8, 13, 16 June, 5, 18 July, 18 Oct. 1827. [14] Ibid. 24 Jan. 1829; Beaven, i. 214, 215; *Gent. Mag.* (1838), i. 662. [15] *The Times*, 24 Jan. 1829. [16] *Ex. inf.* Worshipful Co. of Cutlers. [17] *Maidstone Gazette*, 6, 13, 20 July 1830. [18] *Maidstone Jnl.* 3 Aug. 1830. [19] *Maidstone Gazette*, 30 Nov. 1830; *The Times*, 17 Mar. 1831. [20] *Maidstone Jnl.* 26 Apr., 3 May 1831. [21] Ibid. 10 May 1831. [22] Beaven, i. 293; ii. p. lviii. [23] *London Gazette*, 3 Jan. 1834. [24] *The Times*, 30 Sept., 11, 27 Nov. 1834, 8 Aug. 1835. [25] Ibid. 5 Jan., 4 Feb., 29 Apr., 28 May, 28 Sept. 1835. [26] Ibid. 6 Apr., 12, 20, 23 May, 25, 27 Nov. 1835; C. Welch, *Hist. Cutlers' Co.* 249-50; I.G. Doolittle, *City of London and its Livery Cos.* 28; Beaven, ii. 204. [27] *The Times*, 28 Oct., 3 Nov. 1835, 23 Jan. 1836. [28] *Mems.* (1835), 11-15, 17, 21-23, 33-37, 42-49. [29] *Kent W. Pollbooks* (1835), 54; (1837), 50; *Westminster Pollbook* (1837), 17. [30] *The Times*, 12 Feb. 1835; *Gent. Mag.* (1838), i. 662. [31] *Gent. Mag.* (1835), ii. 218; *Mems.* 3. [32] *Gent. Mag.* (1838), i. 662; *The Times*, 21 Feb., 10 Mar. 1838.

S.M.F.

WINN *see* **ALLANSON WINN**

WINNINGTON, **Sir Thomas Edward**, 3rd bt. (1779–1839), of Stanford Court, Worcs.

DROITWICH	1807–19 Mar. 1816
WORCESTERSHIRE	1820–1830
DROITWICH	1831–1832
BEWDLEY	1832–1837

bap. 14 Apr. 1779,[1] 1st s. of Sir Edward Winnington†, 2nd bt., of Stanford Court and Hon. Anne Foley, da. of Thomas Foley†, 1st Bar. Foley. *educ.* Eton 1793; Christ Church, Oxf. 1798. *m.* 11 Nov. 1810, Joanna, da. of John Taylor of Moseley Hall, Worcs., 3s. 4da. (2 *d.v.p.*). *suc.* fa. as 3rd bt. 9 Jan. 1805. *d.* 24 Sept. 1839.
Sheriff, Worcs. 1806-7.

The Winnington family's traditional seat at Droitwich, which had been lost to the Foleys, had been regained by Winnington's father with the support of his brother-in-law, the 2nd Baron Foley, in 1777. Two years after his father's death Winnington was returned on the same interest, headed since 1793 by his first cousin, the 3rd Baron. Winnington retired from Droitwich in 1816 and at the 1820 general election came forward as Foley's nominee for Worcestershire, where he was returned unopposed.[2] A regular attender, who like his father is not known to have spoken in debate, he voted with the Whig opposition to the Liverpool ministry on most major issues, including economy, retrenchment and reduced taxation.[3] He presented Kidderminster petitions complaining of the 'atrocious conspiracy' against Queen Caroline, 31 Jan. 1821, and for criminal law reform, 29 Apr. 1822.[4] He was absent from the division on Catholic relief, 28 Feb. 1821, but voted for it, 1 Mar., 21 Apr., 10 May 1825. He was also absent from the division on parliamentary reform, 9 May 1821, for which he divided, 20 Feb., 24 Apr. 1823. He rejoined Brooks's, his earlier membership having apparently lapsed, sponsored by Lords Foley and Fitzwilliam, 12 May 1821. On 8 Feb. 1822 he attended a Worcestershire county meeting called to petition for agricultural relief and parliamentary reform.[5] Writing to Sir Thomas Phillipps, 15 Feb., he described a bill for improving the road between the Worcester and Stratford-Upon-Avon turnpikes as 'a great misery to Broadway and its neighbours' and promised to 'do all I can to oppose it'.[6] (The bill received royal assent, 12 Apr. 1824.) He voted for inquiry into an alleged affray by soldiers of the Knightsbridge barracks, under the command of his Tory colleague for Worcestershire, Colonel Lygon, 28 Feb. 1822. He presented a constituency petition against the hop duties, 12 June 1822.[7] He presented constituency petitions for the abolition of slavery, 18 Apr. 1826.[8]

At the 1826 general election Winnington offered again, promising to perform 'his duty as hitherto'. Rumours of a third candidate came to nothing and he was returned unopposed.[9] He voted in the minority of 24 for Hume's amendment to the address, 21 Nov. 1826, and against the grant to the duke of Clarence, 16 Feb. 1827. He divided for Catholic claims, 6 Mar. 1827, but was absent from the division of 12 May 1828. On 8 Mar. 1827 he was granted a month's leave on account of the death of his daughter Caroline. He presented constituency petitions for repeal of the Test Acts from Worcestershire, 1, 9 June 1827, but did not vote on the issue, 26 Feb. 1828. He divided for the Wellington ministry's concession of Catholic emancipation, 6, 30 Mar. 1829. In October of that year he was listed by Sir Richard Vyvyan*, leader of the Ultras, as one of the pro-Catholic Members whose sentiments regarding a putative coalition ministry were 'unknown'. He voted for the transfer of East Retford's seats to Birmingham, 5, 15 Mar. 1830. He presented petitions against the truck system from the ironworkers of Cradley, 10 Mar., and the tradesmen and shopkeepers of Dudley, 15 Mar. In his only other known votes of 1830, he paired against the appointment of a navy treasurer, 12 Mar., and voted for naval reductions, 22 Mar. That day he presented a petition from the parishes of Claines and St. Peter against the Worcester suburbs improvement bill. He brought up a Worcestershire petition complaining of distress and calling for currency and parliamentary reform, 25 Mar. On 11 May 1830 he was granted a fortnight's leave on account of illness in his family.

At the 1830 general election Winnington made way for his cousin's heir Thomas Foley, who had recently come of age, citing his 'health and other circumstances' that 'imperiously call upon me to retire into private life'. Thoughts of standing elsewhere were, according to the Dowager Lady Gresley, also tempered by the fact that within the last 'few years' it had become 'quite impossible for the baronet to stand a contest, as I know he is not *too* rich, and it requires many thousands to do this, for any place'.[10] In March 1831 he assisted Lord Foley in getting up a Worcestershire petition in favour of the Grey ministry's reform bill. At the 1831 general election his replacement on the Foley interest at Droitwich, Lord Sefton, made way for him and he was returned unopposed. He presided at the dinner held to celebrate the return of two reformers for the county, 16 May 1831.[11]

Winnington voted for the second reading of the reintroduced reform bill, 6 July, against the adjournment, 12 July 1831, and gave general support to the bill's details. He was in the minority for the disfranchisement of Saltash, 26 July, when the government offered no clear lead. He divided for the bill's passage, 21 Sept., Lord Ebrington's confidence motion, 10 Oct., and the second reading of the revised bill, 17 Dec. 1831. He voted to go into committee on it, 20 Feb., again supported its details, and divided for the third reading, 22 Mar. 1832. He voted for the address calling on the king to appoint only ministers who would carry the measure unimpaired, 10 May, and paired for the second reading of the Irish reform bill, 25 May. No other votes by him have been found for 1832. At that year's general election he retired from Droitwich, which lost one Member by the Reform Act, and came in unopposed for Bewdley, where the enfranchisement of £10 householders had opened the representation. He sat undisturbed as a reformer until 1837, when he made way for his eldest son and namesake (1811-72),

Liberal Member, 1837-47, 1852-68. Winnington died in September 1839. By his will, dated 18 Mar. 1838 and proved under £12,000, all his property passed to his son and successor in the baronetcy.[12]

[1] IGI. [2] W.R. Williams, *Parl. Hist. Worcs.* 136; Bodl. MS Phillipps-Robinson c. 408, f. 262, Winnington to Sir T. Phillipps, 21 Feb.; *Berrow's Worcester Jnl.* 24 Feb., 2 Mar. 1820. [3] *Black Bk.* (1823), 203; *Session of Parl. 1825*, p. 491. [4] *The Times*, 1 Feb. 1821, 30 Apr. 1822. [5] Ibid. 11 Feb. 1822. [6] MS Phillipps-Robinson b.113, f. 201. [7] *The Times*, 13 June 1822. [8] Ibid. 19 Apr. 1826. [9] Ibid. 5, 20 June; *Worcester Herald*, 10, 17 June 1826. [10] *Worcester Herald*, 10 July; Worcs. RO, Lechmere mss, Lady Gresley to Sir A. Lechmere, 11 July 1830. [11] Worcs. RO BA 3762 b.899:31, Foley Scrapbk. vol. 4, pp. 172-8; *Worcester Herald*, 21 May 1831. [12] *Gent. Mag.* (1839), ii. 649; PROB 11/1925/219; IR26/1565/153.

P.J.S.

WODEHOUSE, Edmond (1784–1855), of Sennowe Lodge, Norf.

NORFOLK	24 May 1817–1830
NORFOLK EAST	1835–9 July 1855[1]

b. 26 June 1784, 1st s. of Thomas Wodehouse, barrister and gent. of privy chamber, of Sennowe and Sarah, da. of Pryse Campbell† of Stackpole Court, Pemb. *educ.* Harrow 1796-1800; Corpus, Oxf. 1801. *m.* 26 June 1809, his cos. Lucy, da. of Rev. Philip Wodehouse of Hingham, Norf., 5s. 4da. (2 *d.v.p.*). *suc.* fa. 1805. *d.* 21 Aug. 1855.[2]

Lt. E. Dereham yeoman cav. 1802; capt. E. Norf. militia 1803, maj. 1808; lt.-col commdt. 2 regt. W. Norf. militia 1808-13; capt. and lt.-col. W. Norf. yeoman cav. 1813.

Wodehouse was a nephew of the leading Norfolk high church Tory, the 1st Baron Wodehouse of Kimberley, whose family the Quaker Joseph John Gurney of Earlham deemed 'remarkable for never keeping up the heat of party after a battle is over, and for never bearing malice'.[3] First returned for the county on their interest at the severely contested by-election of 1817, when his twice defeated cousin John Wodehouse* declined to stand, he had proved to be a 'frank, open [and] intrepid' public speaker, defended Lord Liverpool's administration at county meetings after Peterloo, but voted against them on matters which he considered contrary to the public interest such as charity abuse, the awards to the royal dukes and the malt tax.[4] At the general election of 1820 the prospect of a Whig challenge to him evaporated and he came in unopposed with the veteran Foxite Thomas William Coke.[5]

As a busy and forthright representative of a large corn-growing county, Wodehouse's parliamentary conduct was closely watched, and his wayward vote against the appointment of an additional Scottish baron of exchequer, 15 May 1820, attracted comment.[6] He presented the Norfolk growers' petition for higher tariffs on imported corn, 16 May. His observations when a select committee on agricultural distress was proposed 'were inaudible in the gallery', 30 May, but in a major speech when it was conceded, 31 May, he referred to the great regional variation in corn prices, warned of the frauds operating via Hamburg and called for government action to 'suppress that dreadful system of gambling' affecting corn.[7] As chairman of the Grantham election committee, he moved the warrant for the detention of Sir William Manners[†] and others who had failed to testify before it, 5 July, and presented the report, 11 July.[8] He opposed the adoption of a radical address supporting Queen Caroline at the Norfolk county meeting, 19 Aug.;[9] but the patronage secretary Arbuthnot found him reluctant to declare his backing for government over her exclusion from the liturgy and informed Liverpool that Wodehouse was 'always *queerish*' and 'I suppose does not choose to commit himself till he knows what others think', 26 Dec. 1820.[10] He criticized the queen's partisans for assuming that all government supporters were their servile dependants and that freedom of speech was exclusive to opposition, 23 Jan., and divided against censuring ministers' handling of her case, 6 Feb. 1821. He presented a hostile petition from the Norwich diocese and voted against Catholic relief, 28 Feb., but when their pro-Catholic petition was presented, 16 Mar., he expressed regret at use of the term 'bigotry' by both sides.[11] He presented six Norfolk agricultural distress petitions, 1 Mar.[12] On being named to the subsequent select committee, 7 Mar., he described himself as a sincere advocate of retrenchment and attributed his voted with government on the revenue, 6 Mar., to his wish to see relief applied equally to all classes of the community. He considered the additional duty on malt the 'most objectionable of all … in a moral and political point of view', and presented petitions, 13 Mar., and divided for its repeal, 21 Mar.; but, 'guarding himself … against any implied censure of … government', he voted to defeat the proposal at their request, 3 Apr.[13] He supported the inquiry into the currency proposed by the Whig banker Alexander Baring as an amendment to the bank cash payments bill, 9 Apr., and voted against the adjutant general's grant, 11 Apr. He divided against parliamentary reform, 9 May 1821, 2 June 1823, and voted to make forgery a non-capital offence, 23 May 1821. He obtained leave to introduce a bill to amend the 1808 Lunatic Act, 24 May, but apparently failed to do so.[14] On 9 June the Tory *Norfolk Chronicle* countered

speculation that the party would replace Wodehouse during the shrievalty of the prospective Whig candidate Sir Jacob Astley[†] on account of his political lapses. He divided with government on public expenditure, 27 June 1821.

When the county met to petition for action against agricultural distress, 12 Jan. 1822, Wodehouse delivered what *The Times* termed a 'kind of *peccavi* speech' that irked both the Whigs and his Tory critics. In it he endorsed the call for lower taxes on malt, salt, leather, soap and candles, cautioned that the resolution for a £5,000,000 cut in taxation was 'too violent to do any good' and said he could not support reform. He attributed distress to 'various factors, of which the alteration in the currency was the chief', but he conceded that repeal of the 1819 Act that had brought it about was unlikely. He spoke against imposing higher duties on foreign corn and condemned the agriculture committee's 1821 report drafted by the minister Huskisson, which he had voted against, for its 'stupidity and absurdity, and for its chaotic confusion of ideas'.[15] He expressed qualified support for the petition when Coke presented it and called for 'an immediate reduction in the civil list' and repeal of the malt tax as conciliatory measures, 7 Feb., but divided with government against more extensive tax reductions, 11 Feb. He presented and endorsed several moderate Norfolk petitions for relief, 12 Feb., and criticized the doctrines of George Webb Hall, apparent in the Lewes petition, 13 Feb.[16] On being appointed to the agriculture select committee chaired by Lord Londonderry, 18 Feb., he said that he had no doubt that its proposals would be generally beneficial; but he also emphasized the agriculturists' debt to the Whig Members Henry Brougham and Lord John Russell in opposition and warned against 'rekindling the corn war'. To ministers' relief, he divided with them on taxation, 21 Feb., and the salt duties, 28 Feb.;[17] but he voted to abolish one of the joint-postmasterships, 13 Mar., 2 May 1822. Wodehouse disputed the home secretary Peel's use of poor rate returns, 20 Feb., pointing out that they were 'so incorporated with the labour of the poor, that they could not be detached', and he was appointed to the select committee which considered them, 23 Apr. 1822, and annually subsequently.[18] When Coke, as presenter of the radical petition from the hundred of Earsham, vented his spleen against Londonderry, 29 Apr., Wodehouse rallied to his defence, but he admitted that ministers had underestimated the scale of the distress, that the agriculture committee's report was unsatisfactory and that protection for domestic corn growers was inadequate. To opposition cheers, he added that 'the best and most effectual relief … would be a reduction of the pressure of the public burdens', and, conscious of his own inconsistency, he explained that he had voted to retain the sinking fund 'as he did not know how the public credit might be injured by its abolition', against repealing the salt duties, as government could not afford further concessions, and against reductions in the army, as he saw no point in sending men home to rot. He also maintained that distress and William Cobbett's† visits had been factors in the recent unrest in Norfolk and Suffolk.[19] He presented and endorsed petitions against Londonderry's resolutions based on the agriculture committee's report, 7 May.[20] To cries of 'salt, salt', he vainly opposed the adoption of a petition for reform at the Norfolk distress meeting, 11 May.[21] Huskisson now held Wodehouse and Sir Edward Knatchbull personally responsible for encouraging hostility to him within and without doors as author of the contentious 1821 agriculture committee report, and protested to Londonderry in writing, 12 May.[22] In committee on the government's corn bill, 3 June, Wodehouse proposed an amendment raising the pivot price from 70s. to 75s., which he withdrew directly Wolryche Whitmore's attempt to lower it to 64s. failed.[23] He cast wayward votes against the Irish constables bill and on the currency, 12 June, but divided with government against inquiry into the lord advocate's dealings with the Scottish press, 25 June, and against retaining 'the wretched remnant of a tax' on salt, 28 June.[24] He presented hostile petitions, 1, 15, 17 July, and received leave for a bill to amend the Excise Licenses Act, 2 July 1822, but, thwarted by John Maberly's proposals and the ministerial measure, he opposed both, 28 May, 13 June 1823. Following Londonderry's suicide, he paid tribute to him in a speech at the Norwich Pitt Club dinner, 17 Oct. 1822, but, reporting it, *The Times*, blamed him and his colleagues for failing to 'force economy upon the ministers whom they panegyrize':

> Mr. W.'s private worth no one disputes, but we think he has woefully embarrassed himself in politics. He will adhere, as much as he can or dares, to the old corrupt, extravagant system, and yet, he cannot help feeling for the miseries which it has created, and which he now sees around him.[25]

At the riotous Norfolk meeting of 3 Jan. 1823, Wodehouse praised the government's tax concessions, reiterated his views on the currency and criticized the 'loose' Whig petition and Cobbett's violent one, which superseded it.[26] In the House, he accused the chancellor Robinson of doing nothing in his budget to reduce the disproportionate tax burden which the county, highway and poor rates placed on the landed interest,

21 Feb., and criticized the currency change, 26 Feb. Later that day, in a speech peppered with statistics and citations from Sir Claude Scott and Jolly's testimony to the 1814 select committee on corn, he opposed Whitmore's proposals for a gradual reduction to 60s. in the pivot price, dismissed the import prices which he gave as 'fallacious' and accused his own detractors of misrepresenting him as a critic of Huskisson 'solely' on account of his vote against the 1821 agriculture committee's report. He presented an anti-Catholic petition from the clergy of Norwich, 16 Feb., endorsed others against the malt duties, 18 Apr., and joined its presenter Coke in denouncing the county's Cobbettite petition, 24 Apr.[27] He voted to abolish punishment by whipping, 30 Apr., and backed the Limerick corporation bill introduced to remedy the abuses he had noted as chairman of the 1820 election committee, 6 May.[28] He gave a cautious welcome to the chancellor's conditional offer to repeal the duty on foreign wool, 4 June.[29] Before voting for inquiry into the currency, 13 June 1823, he acknowledged that he was responsible for coining the phrase 'equitable adjustment', adding that he had first used it in a Pitt Club speech, when speculating how Pitt might have resolved the currency question. He surmised that Pitt would have retained part of the property tax, altered the monetary standard or done both, and he attributed the current distress to ministers' failure to do either. Praising Peel, he dismissed the theories of Davis Ricardo* and the political economists as 'utterly incomprehensible', commended those of the philosophers David Hume and John Locke and cautioned against rejecting a silver standard 'from a false regard to parliamentary consistency'. During the recess, he commanded yeomanry exercises at Bylaugh.[30]

Wodehouse presented petitions from Norfolk and elsewhere for repeal of the coastwise coal duties, 12, 18, 19, 23 Feb. 1824.[31] He supported Peel's juries bill, 19 Feb., and warned against carrying military reductions too far at the behest of Hume, 20 Feb. He postponed his intended motion for equalization of the duties on malt and beer and, clashing frequently with Maberly, against whose rival motion he was a majority teller, 15 Mar., he expressed qualified support for the government's measure, 24 May. He presented a petition complaining of the prohibitive tax on salt-cake for cattle, 31 Mar., and astounded colleagues by ordering returns and announcing a motion against the anticipated expiry of the salt tax, 6 Apr. His argument that to do so would release funds for more pressing reductions carried little weight and the proposal, which *The Times* condemned as 'a connivance to relieve the chancellor from his solemn obligation to end the tax', was rejected,

13 May.[32] He voted to postpone the Windsor Castle grant, 5 Apr., and in condemnation of the indictment in Demerara of the Methodist missionary John Smith, 11 June. He supported the Norfolk magistrates' campaign to transfer the spring assizes from Thetford to Norwich but, deferring to ministers, he withdrew his motion for a select committee on the matter, 15 June 1824. He was a minority teller when government secured its rejection (by 72-21), 24 Feb. 1825.[33] He supported the warehoused wheat bill, 17 May 1824.

Wodehouse engaged in financial dealings with his friends the Hoares and voted against repealing the usury laws, 17 Feb. 1825. As expected, he divided for the Irish unlawful societies bill, 25 Feb., and his votes for Catholic relief, 1 Mar., 21 Apr., 10 May, and endorsement of 'the spirit of toleration' in the Norwich archdeaconry's favourable petition, 19 Apr., surprised its advocates, set him apart from his relations and incensed his erstwhile supporters.[34] He backed the attendant Irish franchise bill, 22, 26 Apr. A contemporaneous radical publication correctly observed that he 'attended frequently and appeared to vote sometimes with and sometimes against ministers'.[35] He postponed his motion on corn averages, 22 Feb., presented protectionist petitions, 28 Feb., and called for the corn question to be discussed 'with firmness but with temper', 22 Apr. He dissented from the London petition for a fixed duty, 24 Apr., and, stating that he had 'always supported the average system, from his conviction of its being the best', he opposed major change, 28 Apr. However, he conceded that some revision was necessary and spoke of the 'mischievous fallacy' of using atypical Danzig prices.[36] He spoke in favour of Ridley's amendment to the ministerial bill, proposing a reduction from 10s. to 7s. in the tariff on corn imports, and stated 'on behalf of the agriculturists' that they had 'no objection to the foreign corn being taken out of bond free of duty altogether', 31 May. He sought further information through the foreign office with a view to improving the statistical base for the averages, 2 June.[37] He spoke against repealing the beer duties, 5 May, and presented the French Brandy Company's petition for changes in the laws affecting distilling, 14 June.[38] He divided with government for the duke of Cumberland's grant, 6, 10 June. He presented petitions for repeal of the coastwise coal duty, 24 Feb., and offered to support the Tyne and Weardale railway bill as a means of bypassing it, 4 Mar.[39] Unlike his cousin, Member for Great Bedwyn, Wodehouse openly supported the campaign against colonial slavery, but he criticized the vehemence of the 3rd Baron Suffield and Thomas Fowell Buxton's* abolitionist speeches at the Norfolk county meeting, 20 Oct. 1825, and ensured

that the resulting petition expressed concurrence with Canning's resolutions of 1823.[40] He voted against condemning the Jamaican slave trials, 2 Mar., was named to the select committee on slave trading in Mauritius, 9 May 1826, and subsequently endorsed Buxton's claim that it was not too late to press charges against the island's governor, Sir Robert Townsend Farquhar*, 3 June 1829.

Warning of local currency shortages resulting from the 1825-6 banking crisis, Wodehouse voted in a minority of seven for retaining Bank of England small notes, 13 Feb. 1826. He opposed the usury laws repeal bill as 'badly timed' and 'because he thought it impossible to calculate the effect which it would have on the landed interest', 15 Feb. His bill, introduced on 22 Feb., permitting the sale and disposal of prisons, received royal assent, 10 Apr.[41] He secured returns on foreign corn imports, 3 Mar., and poor rates, 14 Mar., when, using statistics for Norfolk, where 31,451 families employed in agriculture contributed £224,977, and 23,084 families employed in trade £41,295 towards parochial relief, he reiterated his complaint that 'the great burden of parochial relief rested upon the landed interest' and called for further inquiry. He helped to defeat Whitmore's corn bill, 18 Apr., and acquiesced in the ministerial measure, 1, 11 May, notwithstanding his condemnation of William Jacob's† 'biased' *Report on the Trade in Corn and on the Agriculture of the North of Europe* as its statistical base, 2 May, which he said he hoped to improve by using statistics from embassies and consuls abroad, 18 May.[42] He voted against Russell's resolutions denouncing electoral bribery, 26 May 1826. He came in unopposed but with reduced support at the general election in June, backed by his relations (partly because of the reluctance of John Wodehouse's son Henry to stand), tolerated by the Whigs, criticized for opposing the Norwich and Lowestoft navigation bill and vilified and physically attacked by the anti-Catholic mob.[43]

He approved the ministry's decision to implement the Corn Importation Acts by order in council, 24 Nov., but his dissatisfaction with Jacob's statistics persisted and he pressed for further returns, 28 Nov., 2, 4, 5 Dec. 1826.[44] He presented protectionist petitions, 8, 29 Mar., 2 Apr., and opposed the government's corn bill, 8 Mar., 2 Apr., having failed to secure concessions on oats, 12 Mar., or rye, peas and beans, 19 Mar. 1827.[45] He endorsed the Norfolk clergy's proCatholic petition, 5 Mar., and voted for relief, 6 Mar. He presented and endorsed a petition that day against the double land tax charged to Catholics, and carried a remedial bill, 23 May, 29 June 1827, which was lost in the Lords; he was named to the committee of inquiry, 1 Mar. 1828.[46] He had written privately to Huskisson, 6 May 1827, suggesting that the new Canning ministry should test support generally and opinion on the Catholic question in particular by means of a debate on the state of the nation; and, conscious of the damage caused to his reputation by the letter's disclosure, he retaliated, from the opposition benches, by reading out Huskisson's 'private' reply, 11 May.[47] He belatedly declined to support Gascoyne's motion for inquiry into the depressed shipping industry, 8 May.[48] He presented petitions for increases in coroners' fees, 4 May, changes in the game laws, 4 May, and the malt duties, 20 June, for Test Act repeal, 6 June, and action to combat distress, 18 June.[49] His bill limiting constables' presentments received royal assent, 21 June 1827.[50] Following his appointment to the select committee on the licensing laws, 14 May, he assisted the maltsters in their campaign against the 1827 Act, and he engaged in an acrimonious public correspondence with the vice-president of the board of trade, Frankland Lewis, when their representations were rejected.[51] He presented petitions for the Act's repeal, 15 Feb. 1828.

With the London bankers Sir Peter Pole and Company, Hoares, Everett Walker and Company and others, Wodehouse had stood surety in 1822 for the discredited Middlesex county treasurer George Boulton Mainwaring's[†] debts, and he was almost bankrupted in 1828 when the magistrates redeemed his personal bond.[52] He abandoned his parochial accounts bill, announced on 25 Apr., directly a committee of inquiry was conceded, 15 May, voted for Catholic relief, 12 May, and became increasingly preoccupied with the Wellington administration's corn bill, to which he gave qualified support. Considering 'the question of wheat ... satisfactorily settled', he opposed Benett's counter resolutions, 25 Apr., and sought ministerial backing for his own amendments to include returns from Irish and Scottish towns in the averages and to afford further protection for oat and barley growers.[53] Peel and Frankland Lewis ensured that his proposals were rejected, 28 Apr., 20 May. Urging the Sussex Member Curteis to withdraw his amendment governing warehousing, he added, 23 May:

I never knew a measure to have been more fairly discussed or considered, but I entertain very serious apprehensions that any good which might be expected from the measure will be destroyed by the proceeding which government has in contemplation for the contraction of the currency.

He voted against their small notes bill, 5, 16, 27 June, but divided with them against ordnance reduc-

tions, 4 July. He presented anti-slavery petitions, 13 June, 24 July. At the opening of the new Norwich corn exchange, 28 Nov., he praised the 1828 Corn Importation Act as the best that could have been passed for the good of agriculture.[54]

As expected, Wodehouse divided 'with government' for Catholic emancipation, 6, 30 Mar. 1829. He endorsed the Norfolk clergy's favourable petition, 12 Mar., but conceded the continued strength of the Norfolk anti-Catholics, whose petitions he silently presented the same day. He brought up a second pro-emancipation petition from the Norfolk clergy and drew attention to the unauthorized use of the dean of Hereford's signature in the hostile Hereford one, 24 Mar. He voted to permit Daniel O'Connell to sit without taking the oaths of allegiance, 18 May. He obtained returns, 17 Feb., 27 Mar., 11 May, but failed to persuade the chief excise officers to discuss the failings of the 1827 Act with the maltsters' delegation, 21 May. On the 15th he joined the Norfolk growers, whose hostile petition he presented, 6 May, in opposing the abortive Smithfield market bill. Utilizing information available to him as a member of the 1825 and 1827 select committees, he spoke against the friendly societies bill and the labourers' wages bill, 15 May, describing the latter as a 'hazardous experiment' whose impact on the poor laws could not be predicted. He ordered further corn returns with a view to replacing Jacob's statistics, 27 Mar., and criticized the currency change, the averages, the use of statistics for the atypical war years and the doctrines of free trade in his speech against the fixed duty proposed by Hume, whom he challenged, as a fellow Norfolk landowner, to put his arguments with him to the weavers of Norwich, 19 May. He proudly persisted in speaking out against the currency change as 'a public duty', 1, 4 June. The sudden death on 21 June 1829 of his wife, with whom he had 14 children, affected him deeply, and soon afterwards he let his mansion at Sennowe, which his brother Thomas later occupied, and rented another at Thorpe, near Norwich.[55]

Addressing the county meeting requisitioned by the yeomanry to petition for the repeal of the malt duties to alleviate distress, 16 Jan. 1830, Wodehouse maintained that the time for pleading 'parliamentary consistency' was over. He stated that he was prepared to disagree openly with the government and proposed an amendment adding reductions in the taxes on tea, sugar, coal and candles, commodities 'equally applicable to the poorer and industrious classes', to the petition's demands, together with resolutions attributing distress to the currency change and high taxes;

his proposals were rejected outright in favour of the single tax petition.[56] He divided with opposition in protest at the omission of distress from the king's speech, 4 Feb., and for the transfer of East Retford's seats to Birmingham, 11 Feb. He presented but dissented from distress petitions advocating corn law repeal, 12 Feb., and abolition of the malt tax, 15 Mar. He had read Baring's testimony of 26 Apr. 1828 to the privy council on a silver currency, and after vainly urging ministers to produce it, 9, 10 Feb., 10 Mar., he obtained information from the mint and parliamentary committees in lieu, 5 Mar., 8 Apr., with a view to raising the issue himself. He announced the postponement of Davenport's state of the nation motion, in a speech that also pleaded for fewer restraints on banking when the Bank Charter Acts expired, 15 Feb., and stated afterwards in committee of supply:

> Is it not delusion, and worse than delusion, to talk of a gold standard existing for ten years? Those years have been years of grinding oppression, and that oppression has been caused by the Act of this House. You may send me to Newgate for speaking thus boldly; but for that I care not. I know the House has absolute power, and that it also pretends absolute wisdom. The reduction of taxation is all that is left for us; it is here my confidence rests, for my confidence in ... ministers is gone, utterly gone. All the great names, every great authority that has been or can be referred to on this subject, differ from ... [Peel] and his colleagues.

Liaising with Suffield, who was to assist him in the Lords, and Robert Slaney, he obtained returns, 11, 17 Feb., 5 Mar., 7 Apr., and sought to legislate to transfer poor rate liability from the occupiers to the owners of cottages rated at or below £5, but nothing came of it.[57] He presented and endorsed petitions for abolition of the coastwise coal duty, 16, 17, 18 Feb., 17 Mar., 28 May, 30 June, but postponed his repeal motion, 14 May, after the Irish bill, which he also supported, failed, 13 May. He requested returns on corn averages, 11 Mar., and import prices, 22 Mar., but he now acknowledged that he had undervalued Jacob's work and explained:

> I believe the representations of Mr. Jacob on foreign corn to have been made the organ of mischievous falsehood; while, at the same time, I must add that he is the author of various pamphlets on this subject, and I must believe that his intentions are of the best kind.

Attending to local concerns, he steered the Sekforde's Almshouse bill successfully through the Commons and was a majority teller with the Suffolk Member Gooch for the contentious Southwood Haven bill, by which Gooch's son Edward stood to profit, 3 May.[58] He

suggested that the West India interest would benefit by a reduced tariff on sugar, 7 Apr., and presented and endorsed Norfolk petitions for equalization of the duties on corn spirits and rum, 28 May, 3 June. He presented petitions against the sale of beer bill, 13 May, and opposed its provisions for on-consumption from a conviction that government had acted shortsightedly and that the change would do great harm, 21 June, 1 July. He voted for Jewish emancipation, 5 Apr., 17 May, and to abolish the death penalty for forgery, 1 June 1830.

Wodehouse announced his candidature at the general election, 8 July 1830, knowing that that his pro-emancipation votes and criticisms of government had cost him the backing of most high church Tories. He canvassed assiduously and sought support from Suffield, one of the few who had condoned his 16 Jan. speech.[59] Whigs anxious to avoid the expense of a contest and sympathetic to his 'liberal' views were prepared to acquiesce in his return, but the yeomen refused to forgive his inconsistencies and his stance on malt and put forward the Whig Sir William Browne Ffolkes. Coke condoned their conduct, 3 Aug., and Wodehouse stood down the following day on his cousin's advice.[60] The Whig 4th earl of Albemarle interpreted his defeat as a 'warning to any Tory who might henceforward be disposed to liberal principles'.[61] Countering a favourable review of Wodehouse's parliamentary career by 'Norfolkiensis', who had reached a similar conclusion, a correspondent informed *The Times*:

> It is perfectly true that all parties give Mr. Wodehouse credit for most assiduous regard to the private parliamentary interests of his constituents, and for absolute integrity in his public conduct; but as this conduct appears the result only of incipient dissatisfaction with his original opinions, it wants the stability and decision of confirmed principle, and leaves all parties utterly incapable of divining, by the laws of consistency, what course, in the exercise of his judgement, he would on any future occasion pursue.[62]

Wodehouse kept a low profile during the reform era, but he remained an active magistrate and lobbied for 'any measure for the employment and relief of the poor'.[63] He declined to stand for Norfolk East or Norfolk West in 1832, but contested Norfolk East successfully as a Conservative in 1835 and remained its Member for twenty years, loyal to Peel on all issues which did not compromise his protectionist principles. He retired on health grounds shortly before he died in August 1855, and was recalled as a handsome, bold and conscientious 'politician of conviction, rather than eminence', and for personal generosity beyond his means.[64] Limited administration of his personal estate and effects, worth under £50, was granted in London to Sir Samuel Bignold on behalf of his insurers the Norwich Union Life Insurance Society, 9 July 1858, 11 Nov. 1867. A further grant, under £20, was awarded to his cousin Admiral George Wodehouse (1811-1900), 23 Nov. 1870. His eldest son, Sir Philip Edmond Wodehouse (1811-87), was governor of British Guiana, 1854-8.[65]

[1] *CJ*, cx. 364. [2] Not 1853, as stated in *HP Commons, 1790-1820*, v. 640. [3] Brougham mss, Buxton to Brougham with enclosure from Gurney, 24 Dec. 1832. [4] *HP Commons, 1790-1820*, v. 639-40; *The Times*, 25, 29 Oct., 2, 26 Nov. 1819. [5] Hants RO, Calthorpe mss 26M62/F/C219; Essex RO, Barrett Lennard mss D/DL C60, G. Keppel to Barrett Lennard, 14 Mar.; *Norf. Chron.* 5, 12, 26 Feb., 11, 18 Mar.; *Bury and Norwich Post*, 15 Mar. 1820. [6] *Bury and Norwich Post*, 24 May 1820. [7] *The Times*, 31 May, 1 June 1820; B. Hilton, *Corn, Cash, Commerce*, 103. [8] *CJ*, lxxv. 338, 383; *The Times*, 6 July 1820. [9] *The Times*, 21 Aug.; *Bury and Norwich Post*, 23 Aug. 1820. [10] Add. 38574, f. 232. [11] *The Times*, 1, 17 Mar. 1821. [12] Ibid. 2 Mar. 1821. [13] Ibid. 4 Apr. 1821. [14] Ibid. 25 May 1821. [15] Ibid. 14, 15 Jan.; *County Herald*, 19 Jan. 1822; R.M. Bacon, *Mems. Baron Suffield*, 161. [16] *The Times*, 13, 14 Feb. 1822. [17] Gurney diary, 28 Feb. 1822. [18] *The Times*, 21 Feb. 1822. [19] Ibid. 30 Apr. 1822. [20] Ibid. 8 May 1822. [21] Ibid. 15 May; *Norf. Chron.* 18 May 1822. [22] Add. 38743, f. 148. [23] *The Times*, 4 June 1822. [24] Ibid. 29 June 1822. [25] *Norf. Chron.* 19 Oct.; *The Times*, 22 Oct. 1822. [26] *Norf. Chron.* 4, 11 Jan.; *The Times*, 6 Jan. 1823. [27] *The Times*, 17, 18, 25 Apr. 1823. [28] Ibid. 7 May 1823; *CJ*, lxxv. 393, 435. [29] *The Times*, 5 June 1823. [30] J.R. Harvey, *Recs. Norf. Yeoman Cav.* 217. [31] *The Times*, 13, 19, 20, 24 Feb. 1824. [32] Ibid. 1, 7 Apr., 6, 14 May 1824. [33] Ibid. 12, 16 June 1824. [34] Buckingham, *Mems. Geo. IV*, ii. 217; TNA 30/29/6/3/93; Gurney diary, 1 Mar.; *The Times*, 20 Apr.; *Norf. Chron.* 23 Apr. 1825. [35] *Session of Parl. 1825*, p. 491. [36] *The Times*, 23 Feb., 1 Mar., 26, 29 Apr. 1825. [37] Ibid. 3 June 1825. [38] Ibid. 15 June 1825. [39] Ibid. 25 Feb., 5 Mar. 1825. [40] *Norwich Mercury*, 15, 22, 29 Oct.; *The Times*, 24 Oct. 1825; Bacon, 229-38. [41] *The Times*, 23, 24 Feb. 1826; *CJ*, lxxxi. 92, 97, 116, 121, 126, 137, 227. [42] *The Times*, 4, 15 Mar., 29 Apr., 19 May 1826. [43] Wilts. RO, Ailesbury mss 9/34/30; *Norwich Mercury*, 6 May; *The Times*, 25 May; *Norf. Chron.* 10, 24 June, 1 July 1826. [44] *The Times*, 29 Nov., 3, 5, 6 Dec. 1826. [45] Ibid. 9, 30 Mar., 3 Apr. 1827. [46] Ibid. 6, 7 Mar.; *Norf. Chron.* 17 Mar. 1827; *CJ*, lxxxii. 487, 607. [47] *The Times*, 12 May 1827. [48] St. Deiniol's Lib. Glynne-Gladstone mss 123, Gascoyne to J. Gladstone, 9 May 1827. [49] *The Times*, 5 May, 7, 19, 21 June 1827. [50] *CJ*, lxxxii. 465, 487, 535, 553, 587. [51] *The Times*, 21 June; *Morning Chron.* 24 Oct. 1827. [52] *The Times*, 18 Jan., 29 Feb. 18 Apr. 1828. [53] Wellington mss WP1/929/7; 931/11. [54] *Bury and Norwich Post*, 3 Dec. 1828. [55] Ibid. 24 June; *Gent. Mag.* (1829), ii. 648. [56] *Norwich Mercury*, 16, 23 Jan.; *The Times*, 19 Jan. 1830; Bacon, 291. [57] Norf. RO, Gunton mss 1/31, Wodehouse to Suffield, 5 Mar. 1830; Bacon, 293-301. [58] *CJ*, lxxxv. 343, 356; *Suff. Chron.* 7 Aug. 1830. [59] Gunton mss 1/23, Wodehouse to Suffield, 8 July; *Norwich Mercury*, 10 July; *Bury and Norwich Post*, 7 Aug. 1830. [60] Staffs. RO, Stafford Jerningham mss D641/3/P/3/14/57; Norf. RO, Hamond of Westacre mss HMN 5/121/3; Gunton mss 31/2, Wodehouse to Suffield, 28 July; Norf. RO NRS 8741; *The Times*, 5, 9 Aug.; *Norwich Mercury*, 7, 14 Aug. 1830. [61] Gunton mss 1/31, Albemarle to Suffield, 12 Aug. 1830. [62] *The Times*, 17, 20 Aug. 1830. [63] Ibid. 26 Dec. 1831; Brougham mss, Wodehouse to Brougham [1832]. [64] *The Times*, 27 Aug. 1832; 16 July 1844, 19 Jan., 2 Feb. 1846, 22 Aug.; *East Anglian*, 7 July; *Norf. Chron.* 25 Aug.; *Gent. Mag.* (1855), ii. 435-6. [65] Oxford *DNB sub* Sir Philip Edmond Wodehouse.

M.M.E.

WODEHOUSE, Hon. John (1771–1846), of Witton Park, nr. North Walsham, Norf.

GREAT BEDWYN	1796–1802
MARLBOROUGH	1818–1826

b. 11 Jan. 1771, 1st s. of John Wodehouse†, 1st Bar. Wodehouse, and Sophia, da. and h. of Hon. Charles Berkeley of Bruton Abbey, Som. *educ.* Westminster 1783; Christ Church, Oxf. 1787. *m.* 18 Nov. 1796, Charlotte Laura, da. and h. of John Norris of Witton and Witchingham, 6s. (2 *d.v.p.*) 5da. (1 *d.v.p.*). *suc.* fa. as 2nd Bar. Wodehouse 29 May 1834. *d.* 29 May 1846.

Ld. lt. Norf. 1822-*d.*

Lt. and capt. E. Norf. militia 1793, col. 1798.

Wodehouse, 'a strong, burly man, six feet in height', was heir to the head of Norfolk's leading Tory family, whose ancestral estates centred on Kimberley House, Wymondham, though he lived at Witton from the time of his marriage in 1796. He was elected for Great Bedwyn that year, on the interest of the 1st earl of Ailesbury, and followed the same political line as his father, who, having succeeded as 6th baronet in 1777 and served as ministerialist Member for his native county since 1784, was rewarded with a peerage by Pitt in 1797.[1] Wodehouse was a colonel of militia, for which he received £1,000 a year.[2] He twice failed to gain a seat for Norfolk, where he sided with the Tory interest, and in 1817 he acquiesced in the election of his like-minded first cousin Edmond Wodehouse. He returned to the House at the general election the following year, being brought in by the 2nd earl of Ailesbury for his family's other pocket borough, Marlborough. He gave general and usually silent support to Lord Liverpool's administration, but his activities in Parliament thereafter are not always readily distinguishable from those of his much more active cousin.[3] He moved the Tory address of condolence to the prince regent on the death of Queen Charlotte at the Norfolk county meeting in December 1818, and, having attended another on Peterloo a year later, signed the declaration deploring the fact that it had been called.[4] At the general election of 1820 he was again returned unopposed for Marlborough. He attended the Norfolk election and, at the Pitt Club dinner in Norwich, 29 May, spoke in favour of loyal and constitutional principles, praised Lord Grenville's speech justifying the actions of the militia in Manchester, and denied that agricultural distress gave legitimate grounds for political agitation.[5]

Wodehouse divided against economies in revenue collection, 4 July 1820, the censure motion on ministers' conduct towards Queen Caroline, 6 Feb., omitting the arrears from the grant to the duke of Clarence, 18 June, and economy and retrenchment, 27 June 1821. He voted against Catholic relief, 28 Feb. 1821, and the Catholic peers bill, 30 Apr. 1822. In August 1821 he successfully solicited Liverpool for the lord lieutenancy of Norfolk, arguing that his father (whom he was expected soon to succeed) was of too advanced an age to undertake the position, and that it would be due reward for his family's having engaged in four severe contests for the county.[6] He was officially sworn, 28 Mar. 1822. He divided against more extensive tax reductions to relieve distress, 11, 21 Feb., and inquiry into the conduct of the lord advocate relative to the Scottish press, 25 June. At the Norfolk and Norwich Pitt Club dinner, 17 Oct. 1822, he again extolled the virtues of Pitt's moderate political principles and condemned the undue concentration on reform at the recent county meeting on agricultural distress.[7] He objected to complaints against placing clergymen on commissions of the peace, 28 Apr. 1823. He voted against inquiry into the legal proceedings against the Dublin Orange rioters, 22 Apr., reform of the Scottish representative system, 2 June, and criticizing chancery administration, 5 June 1823. He was possibly the 'Col. Wodehouse' who said that he would give no opposition to the warehoused wheat bill, 17 May 1824, but added that 'with reference to the whole question of the corn laws, he trusted the House would exercise the greatest caution, and that it would not, from any quarter, take opinions upon trust'. Having previously brought the matter to the attention of ministers and called a local meeting on it, he presented a petition from the magistrates of Norfolk requesting that the spring assizes be moved from Thetford to Norwich, 10 June.[8] He divided with ministers against condemning the trial of the Methodist missionary John Smith in Demerara, 11 June 1824.

Wodehouse paired with Hudson Gurney against the motion for hearing the Catholic Association at the bar of the House, 18 Feb. 1825.[9] He voted for the third reading of the Irish unlawful societies bill, 25 Feb., but was absent from the call of the House, 28 Feb., although he was present to make his excuses and to vote against Catholic relief, 1 Mar. Since he remained a staunch anti-Catholic, it was presumably his cousin (who did not) who presented and endorsed the pro-Catholic petition of the clergy of the archdeaconry of Norwich, 19 Apr. He voted against the third reading of the relief bill, 10 May. He divided in favour of the duke of Cumberland's grant, 2 June, had something to say on the possible restoration of Sir Robert Wilson* to the army, 17 June, and voted in the majority for the spring guns bill, 21 June. He refused to sign the requisition for a Norfolk meeting to petition against

slavery, but attended it, 20 Oct. 1825, when he argued that a moderate approach, which did not encourage acts of rebellion, was the best policy. It was, however, probably he who presented a Southwold anti-slavery petition, 14 Mar. 1826, the last known evidence of his activity in the Commons. By August 1825 he had 'expressed an inclination to retire rather than to continue in Parliament', and he duly left the House at the dissolution in 1826.[10]

Wodehouse attended the Norfolk election, 19 June 1826, and, at a dinner that evening, spoke in praise of his re-elected cousin, though he made clear that he differed 'most widely and decidedly' with him on making concessions to the Catholics, whom he could not support because of their 'divided allegiance'.[11] As lord lieutenant he naturally played an important part in Norfolk politics, though he did not invariably attend county meetings. In 1830 he became the first president of the Norfolk and Norwich Friendly Society. He was active on behalf of Edmond Wodehouse at the general election that year, but, as he explained in an address and on the hustings, had advised him to retire in the face of the unpopularity caused by his pro-Catholic votes, in order to preserve the peace of the county.[12] He was active in the suppression of the 'Swing' riots in late 1830, and, according to one local newspaper, 'it is on his decision of character, no less than on his vigour of conduct, that the county may and will repose its fullest confidence'.[13] He apparently kept a low profile in the general election of 1831, when two reformers were again returned for Norfolk, but he signalled his hostility to parliamentary reform by signing the county declaration against the Grey ministry's reform bill in late 1831, and the address to the king in May 1832 to preserve the existing constitution.[14] Before the dissolution later that year, he initially threw his weight behind John Weyland* as candidate for Norfolk East, but soon transferred his support to the preferred Conservatives, Nathaniel William Peach* and Lord William Henry Hugh Cholmondeley.* Chairing a dinner in their honour, 19 Oct., he stated that he had

> opposed every measure of reform because the country had flourished under the old system, and that he believed the constitution would be destroyed unless a considerable portion of the Conservatives found their way into the new Parliament to counteract the effects of that 'political murder' which had been perpetrated by the Whigs and the Radicals.

Chairman of their committee, he probably attended the election in December 1832, when they were defeated.[15] He succeeded his father as 2nd Baron Wodehouse in May 1834. No doubt he contributed his influence to the Conservative cause, which regained both county seats at the general election of 1835, but despite his strong partisanship he was a widely respected lord lieutenant. He died, after a long illness, at the end of May 1846. Political to the last, his proxy was given in the Lords in favour of the second reading of the bill to repeal the corn laws on the night of 28-29 May, so that 'ere the ink was dry which recorded his name on the roll of the converts to those principles, his lordship was no more'. He was succeeded as 3rd Baron Wodehouse by his grandson John (1826-1902), who was created earl of Kimberley in 1866 and served in high office under William Gladstone†.[16]

[1] Earl of Kimberley, *Wodehouses of Kimberley* (1887), 55-58, 65-66. [2] *Full View of Commons* (1821), i. [3] *HP Commons, 1790-1820*, v. 640-1; *Black Bk.* (1823), 204. [4] *Norf. Chron.* 2, 16 Jan., 30 Oct., 6 Nov. 1819. [5] Ibid. 18 Mar., 3 June 1820. [6] Devon RO, Sidmouth mss, Wodehouse to Liverpool, 2 Aug., latter to Sidmouth, 2 Aug. 1821; Add. 38290, f. 6. [7] *Norf. Chron.* 19 Oct. 1822. [8] *The Times*, 26 Feb., 11 June 1824; Add. 40360, ff. 172-3; 40365, f. 207; 40366, f. 33. [9] Gurney diary. [10] Wilts. RO, Ailesbury mss 9/34/34, Wodehouse to Ailesbury, 9 Aug. 1825. [11] *Norf. Chron.* 24 June 1826. [12] Ibid. 26 June, 31 July, 7, 14 Aug. 1830. [13] Ibid. 4 Dec. 1830; Norf. RO, Kimberley mss KIM 6/38; LLC/1/1-17. [14] *Norf. Chron.* 3 Dec. 1831, 26 May 1832. [15] Ibid. 14, 21 July, 15 Dec.; *Bury Post*, 27 June, 4 July, 24 Oct., 14 Nov.; *The Times*, 24 Oct. 1832. [16] *The Times*, 11 Dec. 1839, 2, 16 June; *Norf. Chron.* 6 June 1846; *Gent. Mag.* (1846), ii. 92.

S.M.F.

WOOD, Charles (1800–1885), of Hemsworth, nr. Pontefract, and Hickleton, nr. Doncaster, Yorks. and 22 Charles Street, Mdx.

GREAT GRIMSBY	1826–1831
WAREHAM	1831–1832
HALIFAX	1832–1865
RIPON	1865–Feb. 1866

b. 20 Dec. 1800, 1st s. of Sir Francis Lindley Wood, 2nd bt., of Hemsworth and Anne, da. and coh. of Samuel Buck of New Grange, recorder of Leeds. *educ.* Eton 1817; Oriel, Oxf. 1818; L. Inn 1822. *m.* 29 July 1829, Lady Mary Grey, da. of Charles Grey†, 2nd Earl Grey, 4s. 4da. (1 *d.v.p.*). *suc.* fa. as 3rd bt. 31 Dec. 1846; GCB 19 June 1856; *cr.* Visct. Halifax 11 Feb. 1866. *d.* 8 Aug. 1885. Priv. sec. to first ld. of treasury Nov. 1830-Aug. 1832; sec. to treasury Aug. 1832-Nov. 1834; sec. of admiralty Apr. 1835-Sept. 1839; PC 6 July 1846; chan. of exch. July 1846-Feb. 1852; pres. bd. of control Dec. 1852-Feb. 1855; first ld. of admiralty Feb. 1855-Feb. 1858; sec. of state for India June 1859-Feb. 1866; ld. privy seal July 1870-Feb. 1874.

Wood was descended from George Wood, who had purchased Monk Bretton, near Barnsley, in the reign of James I. His grandfather and namesake was a captain in the navy, while his great-uncle Sir Francis, the first baronet, was a wealthy East India merchant and friend of the 2nd marquess of Rockingham.[1] On his death in 1795 he was succeeded by his nephew, this Member's father, Sir Francis Lindley Wood of Hemsworth, who maintained the connection with Rockingham's descendants and was a close friend and confidant of the 2nd Earl Fitzwilliam and his son Lord Milton*. Sir Francis passed up a number of opportunities to become a Member himself, preferring to be one of the leading Whig activists in Yorkshire politics. Wood attended a prep school at Everton before going to Eton, where he was said to have been 'the most promising young man in every respect they have had for some time'.[2] At Oxford his tutor Edward Hawkins considered him 'the cleverest person he had ever had as a pupil'. He took a double first in classics and mathematics, and became friendly with George Grey† and Francis Thornhill Baring*, subsequently colleagues in Lord John Russell's* first administration. Although one of his examiners at Oriel was John Keble, unlike his brother Samuel and later his own son, he was never drawn into the developing religious movements of Oxford.[3] After Oxford he undertook the grand tour with Thomas Henry Bucknall Estcourt* before returning to study the law. During the rumours of a dissolution in October 1825, his father wrote to Fitzwilliam seeking an opening for him. Fitzwilliam replied that Lord Yarborough was looking for a second Whig for his Blue party at Great Grimsby, where the cost would be £4,000. Sir Francis accepted these terms and asked Fitzwilliam to secure the seat, adding:

My son has shown a creditable show of industry at least by his degree at Oxford and by his unremitting attention for two years to the study of law which he determines not to follow as a profession ... I have not the slightest doubt of his fulfilling his own resolution of attending consistently and unremittingly to his duties.

Yarborough duly approved of Wood as a candidate.[4] At Yarborough's instigation, he canvassed Great Grimsby in March 1826 with his colleague George Heneage.[5] On 20 Mar. he informed Estcourt that they had

dined, drank toasts, speechified from five till one in the morning, canvassed for five days, and have secured such a majority as, we trust, renders us quite secure ... I trust that the business is settled, and unless an opposition ... should unexpectedly start up, I hope that I shall have nothing more to do till a dissolution, the speedy arrival of which I pray for.[6]

Wood again returned to Great Grimsby after reports that an agent had been there trying to secure a ministerial candidate.[7] At the general election Sir Thomas Phillipps of Middle Hill Hall, Worcestershire provoked a contest, but the two Whigs easily defeated him, Wood topping the poll.[8] 'My own election was easy enough', he told Estcourt, 27 June 1826, 'and since that I have been busy in Yorkshire where we had fears of a contest up to the day before the election'.[9]

Wood fulfilled his father's expectations as a parliamentarian, attending regularly and taking an active part in proceedings. He voted against the grant to the duke of Clarence, 16 Feb. 1827. He joined Brooks's on the 18th, sponsored by Milton and John Ramsden*. He divided for Catholic relief, 6 Mar., and inquiry into Leicester corporation, 15 Mar., and against going into committee on the spring guns bill, 23 Mar. When the latter returned from the Lords, 17 May, *The Times* reporter believed it to be Wood (making his first known intervention) who voiced support for their amendments.[10] He was in the minorities for information on the Dublin Orange procession and the Lisburn magistrates, 29 Mar., and chancery delays, 5 Apr. He voted to disfranchise Penryn, 28 May. He was a member of the committee on the Coventry magistracy bill and defended its report, 8 June, insisting that they were 'not fit to be entrusted with the preservation of peace' during elections, and was a majority teller for the ensuing bill, 15, 18 June. He divided for the grant to improve water communications in Canada, 12 June 1827. He was appointed to the select committee to consider the consolidation of the Acts concerning the treatment of lunatics the following day, and was one of the Members authorized to bring in the county lunatic asylums and madhouses regulation bills, 19 Feb. 1828. He defended the former's clause forbidding the medical officer of an establishment from being one of its inspecting commissioners, not as a slur on the medical profession, but merely as a wise precaution, 17 Mar. He voted for repeal of the Test Acts, 26 Feb., and Catholic claims, 12 May. He thought the Wakefield and Ferrybridge canal bill ought to be proceeded with sometime that session, notwithstanding the preference which had been given to the Aire and Calder scheme, 3 Mar. However, despite his amendment to postpone its second reading, the Wakefield bill was thrown out that day. He voted against extending East Retford into the neighbouring hundred, 21 Mar., and spoke in the same sense, 2 June, when he advocated transferring its seats to 'some large and populous town', or to Yorkshire, if this was impractical. However, when Lord Howick proposed that option, 27 June, he rejected it, saying the majority opinion

in the county was hostile. He voted against the East Retford disfranchisement bill that day. He presented a Rotherham petition against the Malt Act, 21 May, and claimed that it operated unequally on barley producers in different parts of the country, 23 May. On 21 May he welcomed the alehouses licensing bill, which would remove many of the evils of the present system and give county magistrates 'a concurrent jurisdiction in certain cases'. He defended the bill and argued that all public houses should have the same closing time, 19 June, but objected to the proposals in the perry and cider excise licences bill, 26 June, as being 'of a contrary principle' to those enacted for alehouses. On 6 June he and John Stuart Wortley were ordered to prepare a bill to alter the game laws. He explained that its purpose was not to suppress poaching, which could 'never be effectually done', but to 'encourage, as much as possible, a legal sale of game', 13 June, and protested that if the House imposed conditions based on the amount of land owned before granting the right to kill game on it, 'they would restore all the anomalies which it was the object of the bill to remove', 26 June. He voted against the appointment of a registrar to the archbishop of Canterbury, 16 June, the use of public money for renovating Buckingham House, 23 June, and the additional churches bill, 27 June. He voted for a reduction in the salary of the lieutenant-general of the ordnance, 4 July, and against the grant for North American fortifications, 7 July 1828.

Wood voted for the Wellington ministry's concession of Catholic emancipation, 6, 30 Mar. 1829. He expressed his hope that the labourers' wages bill would go to a committee, 4 May. Next day he was a minority teller for the transfer of East Retford's seats to Birmingham. He divided against an additional grant for the marble arch, 25 May 1829. That summer he married a daughter of the Whig leader Lord Grey, a politically fortuitous union which presaged his steady rise in the party. During the honeymoon, which was spent touring the continent in the late autumn, Wood fell dangerously ill shortly after leaving Genoa. Fortunately a Dr. Heath, travelling with Lord Bessborough, was at hand to minister to him. For a time there was great concern for his life, and Grey resolved to send out his son Frederick to assist, but before his departure news arrived of Wood's recovery.[11] During October there was great anxiety about Fitzwilliam's health, and it seemed likely that Milton would soon succeed him, creating a vacancy for Yorkshire. George Strickland* of Hildenley, one of the county's leading Whigs, informed Wood's father, 10 Oct. 1829, that he had heard Wood's name mentioned, but, admitting his concern at the likely expense, suggested that Lord Morpeth* should probably be the Whigs' choice.[12] In the event Fitzwilliam rallied.

Wood voted for the Ultra Knatchbull's amendment to the address, 4 Feb. 1830. Before dividing for Hume's motion for tax reductions, 15 Feb., he called for 'a considerable reduction of public burdens', warned that a return to a paper currency would 'increase and aggravate all the evils we at present endure', and added that there was great dissatisfaction in the country at ministers' inadequate response to distress. Informing his father of the defeat of the motion that day, he observed:

> You cannot think what an altered loose state all politics are in. Nobody knows what his neighbour thinks and the government is in talent weaker than is conceivable. All the debate on every question and each side of it is carried on by our side and the opposite benches never more have to decide. Goulburn is inefficient most lamentably, Herries ditto in debate and character, ditto ditto of everybody but Peel.[13]

He divided against the army estimates, 19 Feb., and voted steadily with the revived opposition for economy and reduced taxation from March onwards. On 22 Mar. he proposed abolishing the vacant treasurership of the navy, but withdrew his amendment in favour of Vernon Smith's proposal for a reduction of £1,200 in the salary. He moved another to reduce the salary of the assistant secretary to the treasury, which he condemned as 'an unjustifiable violation of the treasury minute' stating that the salary should not exceed £2,000, which was defeated by 178-106. He divided for repeal of the Irish coal duties, 13 May. Before voting for a reduction in consular services, 11 June, he complained that 'such a system of lavish expenditure was scarcely ever before submitted to this House'. He divided to transfer East Retford's seats to Birmingham, 11 Feb., 5 Mar. (as a pair), 15 Mar. He voted for the enfranchisement of Birmingham, Leeds and Manchester, 23 Feb., inquiry into the Newark electors' petition against the duke of Newcastle, 1 Mar., and for Russell's parliamentary reform motion, 28 May. He divided for information on the interference by British troops in the affairs of Portugal, 10 Mar., and declared that the government had not 'a shadow of defence' for the intervention at Terceira, before voting for the critical resolutions, 28 Apr. He thought the poor law amendment bill was 'calculated to produce much good', 26 Apr. He voted for Jewish emancipation, 17 May, and abolition of the death penalty for forgery, 24 May, 7 June (as a pair). He was a majority teller for the third reading of the Galway

franchise bill, 25 May. On the sale of beer bill, 4 June, he said that because adulteration was impossible to stop, caused no harm to the public, and would not deprive the revenue of duty, there was no longer any need to outlaw it. The renewed cohesion of the Whig opposition after the death of George IV led Wood to become more closely involved with some of the party's leaders, and on 29 June he attended the meeting at Brooks's which resolved to call for an adjournment of 24 hours on ministers' notice for a temporary supply.[14] Reporting the ensuing debate to his father, 3 July, he observed:

> We had such a night as seldom occurs, [Henry] Brougham raging mad, utterly unamenable to any sort of reason ... After all we had a very fair division, but so far as the debate went it was an ill managed matter, and I suppose that we shall have another session of the present ministry, bad and inefficient as they are.[15]

He voted against increased recognizances in the libel law amendment bill, 9 July 1830.

Before the 1830 general election, Wood had considered offering for Yorkshire, having been advised that 'such an opportunity never before existed of success on cheap grounds'. After conferring with Morpeth, who was undecided about his own candidacy, he resolved to 'think about' this 'tempting prospect'. In the event, however, he felt that while it might be possible to secure the county seat for less than the £4,000 that Great Grimsby would cost, it was improbable without the backing of the manufacturers.[16] He therefore started for Great Grimsby on the same terms as previously. Reporting on his canvass, 12 July, he told his wife, 'I am quite safe, the popular candidate and in high favour, they cannot find anything to say against me'.[17] Next day he added:

> I have talked myself quite hoarse, besides being obliged to taste and swallow diverse sorts of villainous compounds called punch, etc., etc. Heavens! what a disgusting operation it is. What would I give for a quiet snug seat of my own.[18]

The following day two ministerial or 'Red' candidates arrived, but Wood dismissed their chances and shortly afterwards left Great Grimsby to attend the Whig meeting in York, which was to decide on candidates for the county.[19] It was generally agreed that Morpeth would be one, but the second was still open to debate. Rumours that the manufacturers wanted Brougham led the country gentlemen to panic, and many, including Wood, declared their willingness to stand before the meeting opened. Morpeth was soon approved, but the proposal of Brougham caused uproar, and Wood alleged that there was a stronger feeling against than for him. After a rapid conference, the country gentlemen agreed to set aside their own aspirations in favour of Ramsden, whom Wood formally proposed. Deadlock ensued, and many urged Wood to withdraw Ramsden's nomination, which at length he agreed to do, though with some ill grace. He said that he reserved the right to nominate another at a later date, but Brougham was eventually adopted.[20] Wood returned to Great Grimsby, and after addressing the freemen, assured his wife, 'I shall have more votes than enough and more than I care for', 28 July.[21] Next day he reported, 'I am the best of friends with my opponents ... I was dragged, all in a friendly way, into a room full of Reds, had my sherry, made 'em a speech, was cheered three times three, and came out again'.[22] He was returned in first place. As a member of the Whig election committee he subsequently went to York, where he seconded Morpeth's nomination for the county. 'I am quite contented and pleased', he informed his wife, 6 Aug., 'all the world congratulate me on my speech ... [and] folks are kind enough to say that I played a difficult game very well, so I am highly gratified'.[23]

He voted against the ministry, who had of course listed him as one of their 'foes', in the crucial division on the civil list, 15 Nov. 1830. When the result was known, he and his close friend and brother-in-law Lord Howick dashed to a reception in Berkeley Square that their kinsman Lord Durham was attending and 'rushed into the room, calling out in great excitement, "We've beat them; they're done for"'.[24] On 18 Nov. Wood reported to his father that the construction of the incoming Grey ministry was 'going smoothly':

The Whigs, Huskissonians, with perhaps a sprinkling of Tories, those once called Ultras, will form the new government. They are now become good reformers, and certainly gave most effectual assistance in turning out the late administration ... I think it very possible now that I shall not be able to leave town for any time this winter; at present I am to act as Lord Grey's private secretary.[25]

He was one of six close relations whom Grey immediately appointed to office.[26] When Brougham was charged by William Duncombe with abandoning his Yorkshire constituents by accepting office as lord chancellor, 23 Nov. 1830, Wood retorted that he was 'running away a little too hastily as to the opinion of the people of Yorkshire', who he believed would welcome Brougham's elevation. Advising his father of the Irish situation, 10 Jan. 1831, he commented:

In my opinion Ireland will never be at peace till we pay the Catholic priesthood, and if I was dictator I would

suppress two-thirds of the Irish bishops and deans, and so form a fund, and sooner or later that must be done, though it would be cutting one's throat, perhaps, to say so now.

On 21 Jan. he reported that everything was going well in Ireland, and that the tribute to Daniel O'Connell* was 'a failure entirely'.[27] Towards the end of that month he advised Thomas Creevey* that provided the king would give his support, Grey would dissolve Parliament if it rejected the ministerial reform bill.[28] On 1 Feb. he confided to his father, 'The cabinet is unanimous on the plan of reform, and the *king* !!!! highly approves, so that it will be hard if king and country do not beat the Parliament'. Writing again, 3 Mar., he observed:

the reform is an efficient, substantial, anti-democratic, pro-property measure, but it sweeps away rotten boroughs and of course disgusts their proprietors. The main hope therefore of carrying it, is by the voice of the country, thus operating by deciding all wavering votes ... The radicals, for which heaven be praised, support us ... A strong demonstration in Yorkshire would rivet Bethell [the liberal Tory Member], and *perhaps* decide Duncombe [the Ultra Tory Member]; but county meetings now if you can, without a moment's delay. We stand well as yet, but boroughmongers are numerous.[29]

Thereafter Wood kept his father regularly informed of the progress of the bill, for which he voted at its second reading, 22 Mar. According to Tom Macaulay*, on learning the result of the division, 'Wood who stood near the door, jumped on a bench and cried out, "They are only three hundred and one". We set up a shout that you might have heard to Charing Cross'.[30] Next day Wood told his father, 'we must, I take for granted, reckon upon a dissolution'.[31] When George Dawson criticized the bill for unfairly giving representatives to Gateshead, South Shields and Sunderland, while unrepresented towns and parishes in Lancashire had larger populations, 25 Mar., Wood replied that his argument was invalid because it was not intended to enfranchise districts. He divided against Gascoyne's wrecking amendment, 19 Apr. As a member of the Liverpool election committee, he rejected Gascoyne's complaint that their finding of gross corruption at the last election was based on the testimony of a single witness, but absolved Gascoyne himself of involvement in bribery, 21 Apr. That day, when Lord Althorp realized that the ordnance estimates would not pass, he sent Wood and Howick to inform the cabinet of his wish for an immediate dissolution.[32] Wood told his father, 24 Apr. 1831, that 'there never was a more successful coup'.[33]

At the ensuing general election Wood abandoned Great Grimsby, where the proposed abolition of one of its seats was unpopular, and sought a safer berth. Having asked Milton 'for a seat which he cannot give me', and declined an approach from the reformers of Pontefract, he was returned for John Calcraft's* pocket borough of Wareham, probably as a paying guest.[34] This enabled him to remain in London, where he helped to collate the election returns and calculate their probable consequences for the prospects of the reform bill. In early May he reported that the elections were going 'à merveille' and on their conclusion declared, 'if we do not let our bill be damaged in committee, we shall have it safe enough through the Lords, black and sulky though they look'.[35] On 23 May he asked Lord Holland to use his influence to secure the attendance of Lords Oxford, Suffolk and Waldegrave 'as early as they can in the next session'.[36]

Wood voted for the second reading of the reintroduced reform bill, 6 July 1831, and though not actually on the payroll vote, was an assiduous supporter of its details, casting not one wayward vote. On the presentation of an Appleby petition complaining of a mistake in the census returns and asking for the case to be heard at the bar of the House, 12 July, he denied the assumption that ministers were determined to disfranchise the borough without inquiry. He added that he might be put in a similar situation with respect to Wareham, where there was also a mistake in the return, though if he did appeal to the House, it would be 'to its justice, not to its passions'. He was a majority teller against the petitioners' request. On 14 July he contended that the opposition attempt to substitute the 1831 census for that of 1821 was simply a delaying tactic. That month he declined an approach from Halifax to stand there at the first post-reform election, explaining that his 'constant occupation in London would prevent my making myself acquainted with my future constituency in the manner which I should feel it my duty to do'.[37] During discussion of Gateshead's enfranchisement, 5 Aug., he rejected comparisons of its relationship to Newcastle with that of Hull to Sculcoates, pointing out that the former were separate towns in different counties, while the latter were essentially the same town, under one jurisdiction. He divided with ministers on the Dublin election controversy, 23 Aug. He was a majority teller for the passage of the reform bill, 21 Sept., and divided for the second reading of the Scottish measure, 23 Sept., and Lord Ebrington's motion of confidence in the government, 10 Oct. On 8 Nov. 1831 Lord Palmerston*, the foreign secretary, informed the duke of Richmond that Wood was one of those who thought that the bill ought now to be made more extensive and radical.[38]

Wood voted for the second reading of the revised bill, 17 Dec. 1831. On 26 Jan. 1832 he confided to Denis Le Marchant† that the 'crux in the cabinet' was Grey and Althorp's disagreement over the need to create peers to carry the bill.[39] Again a consistent supporter of the bill's details, he was a majority teller to go into committee on it, 20 Jan., and divided for its third reading, 22 Mar. In early April he was assigned the task of getting Charles Greville to try to persuade Lord Harrowby, one of the leading 'Waverers', of the necessity of securing the second reading of the bill in the Lords, and to approve the number of boroughs in schedule A.[40] Their negotiations continued for almost two weeks, although Wood predicted to Francis Thornhill Baring, 5 Apr., that the bill would have a majority of 'seven undoubted, twelve certain, and fifteen sure, and should not wonder if it were carried by seventeen to twenty'.[41] Revising his opinion, he told Grey to expect nine, 10 Apr., which proved to be the actual majority, 14 Apr.[42] He voted for the address calling on the king to appoint only ministers who would carry the bill unimpaired, 10 May, and the second reading of the Irish reform bill, 25 May, and paired against a Conservative amendment to increase the Scottish county representation, 1 June. He divided with government on the Russian-Dutch loan, 26 Jan., 12, 16, 20 July, and relations with Portugal, 9 Feb. He was a majority teller for the Greek convention, 6 Aug., and the bill to restrain party processions in Ireland, 8 Aug. 1832.

Edward Ellice*, secretary to the treasury and Grey's brother-in-law, wanted to resign after the reform bill had passed, but Wood advised Grey, 3 July 1832, that he was 'indispensable'.[43] On 19 July Wood notified his father that *John Bull*, 'that most veracious of papers' and, 'as being conducted by [John] Croker*, the *best informed* of our intentions, announced my promotion to the office of secretary to the treasury. Ergo, the Tory would believe it: what more is to be said?'[44] When Ellice's wife died later that month he resigned and on his recommendation Wood replaced him. As such he chaired the government's management committee for the 1832 general election, when, notwithstanding his earlier reservations, he was returned for Halifax after a contest.[45] He represented the borough for next 33 years and progressed steadily through the ranks of the Liberal party. At the admiralty he distinguished himself with his defence of the navy estimates in 1839, but, like Howick, he resigned out of loyalty to Grey later that year. He spent an unhappy time as Russell's chancellor of the exchequer, but appeared to find his niche at the board of control under Lord Aberdeen and later as secretary of state for India under Palmerston. He suffered from a speech impediment, which earned him an unenviable reputation as a Commons bore. Greville recalled:

> He was a deplorable speaker ... His utterances [were] so unintelligible that they might almost as well have been spoken in a foreign language ... [One] speech of five hours was the dullest that was ever heard. The Speaker told Charles Villiers that it was the very worst speech he had ever heard since he had sat in the House.[46]

Grenville Fletcher wrote of him in 1862:

> Of ... strong party feeling there does not sit in the House a man of more decided character ... [His] political creed appears to be, that the reins of government are theirs by right of birth and of position ... I have always considered [him] to be one of its most shining lights, shining by his indisputable ability, shining by his staunch Whig opinions, and still more brightly by his undeviating and unwearied attachment to his Whig connections.[47]

Wood fell from his horse while hunting in November 1865 and suffered concussion. He used this as a pretext for resigning from Russell's ministry the following February, and a few days later he was elevated to the peerage. He subsequently served in Gladstone's first ministry.[48] He died in August 1885. By his will, dated 12 Apr. 1880, he left all his property to his wife, but as she had predeceased him in 1884, everything passed to his eldest son and successor in the peerage, Charles Lindley Wood (1839-1934), a leading Anglo-Catholic.

[1] R.J. Moore, *Sir Charles Wood's Indian Policy*, i.   [2] J.G. Lockhart, *Charles Lindley, Visct. Halifax*, i. 11.   [3] Moore, i. [4] Borthwick, Halifax archive, Fitzwilliam to Sir F.L. Wood, 18 Oct., reply, 21 Oct., Milton to Sir F.L. Wood, 11 Dec. 1825. [5] Ibid. Yarborough to Wood, 18 Feb. 1826. [6] Glos. RO, Sotheron Estcourt mss F365/1571. [7] Halifax archive, Yarborough to Wood, 27 Mar. 1826. [8] *Lincs., Rutland, and Stamford Mercury*, 9 June 1826. [9] Sotheron Estcourt mss F365/1571. [10] *The Times*, 18 May 1827. [11] Halifax archive, Lady Grey to Georgiana Grey [?9], 17 Dec., Grey to Sir F.L. Wood, 16 Dec. 1829. [12] Halifax archive. [13] Ibid. C. to Sir F.L. Wood [16/17 Feb. 1830]. [14] A. Mitchell, *Whigs in Opposition*, 229. [15] Halifax archive. [16] Ibid. C. to Sir. F.L. Wood, 3 July. [17] Halifax archive. [18] Ibid. [19] Ibid. Wood to wife, 14 July 1830. [20] *Leeds Mercury*, 24 July 1830. [21] Halifax archive. [22] Ibid. Wood to wife. [23] Ibid. [24] Reid, *Lord Durham*, i. 215. [25] Halifax archive. [26] *Three Diaries*, 25. [27] Halifax archive. [28] *Creevey Pprs.* ii. 216. [29] Halifax archive. [30] *Macaulay Letters*, ii. 10. [31] Halifax archive. [32] E.A. Wasson, *Whig Renaissance*, 212. [33] Halifax archive. [34] Ibid. C. to Sir F.L. Wood, 24 Apr.; *Leeds Mercury*, 30 Apr 1831. [35] Halifax archive, C. to Sir F.L. Wood, 4, 27 May, 25 June 1831. [36] Add. 51569. [37] Halifax archive, C. Wood to R. Briggs, 16 July 1831. [38] Southampton Univ. Lib. Broadlands mss, PP/GC/RI/11. [39] *Three Diaries*, 186. [40] *Greville Mems.* ii. 286, 288, 289, 294. [41] *Baring Jnls.* i. 93. [42] *Three Diaries*, 222. [43] G.M. Trevelyan, *Lord Grey*, 384. [44] Halifax archive, C. to Sir F.L. Wood, 19 July 1832. [45] I. Newbould, *Whiggery and Reform*, 26, 30. [46] *Greville Mems.* vii. 289. [47] G. Fletcher, *Parl. Portraits*, iii. 120. [48] *The Times*, 7 Feb. 1866; *Oxford DNB*.

M.P.J.C./P.J.S.

WOOD, John (1789–1856), of Edge Hill, Liverpool, Lancs.; Scoreby, Yorks., and Tanfield Court, Inner Temple, Mdx.[1]

PRESTON   1826–1832

b. 4 Nov. 1789, 1st surv. s. of Ottiwell Wood, fustian manufacturer, of Manchester and Grace, da. of John Grundy, woollen manufacturer, of Bury, Lancs. *educ.* by Rev. William Shepherd at Gateacre, Lancs.; Glasgow Univ. 1806; I. Temple 1820, called 1825.[2] *m.* 9 Dec. 1828, Elizabeth, da. of Rev. James Serjeantson, rect. of Kirkby Knowle, Yorks., 2da. *suc.* fa. to Scoreby 1847. *d.* 10 Oct. 1856.

Chairman, bd. of stamps and taxes 1833-8, bd. of revenue 1838-49, bd. of inland revenue 1849-d.

Recorder, York 1832-3.

A cradle radical of Lancashire freeholder stock, Wood was baptized on 19 Nov. 1789 at Moseley Street Unitarian Chapel in Manchester, where his father Ottiwell Wood (1759-1847), a prosperous manufacturer and lifelong advocate of liberal ideas, had a house in Oldham Street.[3] He was a founding trustee of Manchester Academy (1786) and treasurer (1803-8) during its transfer to York, where in 1808, when he also 'retired' to Liverpool, he purchased the 1,281-acre Scoreby estate, five miles south of the city, by which Wood later qualified as an East Riding magistrate.[4] His mother was a great-great-granddaughter of John Grundy of Mathers (*d.* 1728), the progenitor of the Bury manufacturing dynasty and a co-founder in 1719 of Bank Street Presbyterian Chapel, Bolton, the source of many petitions that Wood presented.[5]

Intended for the Unitarian ministry, which his brother Samuel (1797-1849) entered in 1819, Wood left Glasgow University in 1808 without taking his degree and went into business at the Liverpool counting house of William and Edgar Corrie, preparatory to trading as a sugar refiner in partnership with his fellow Dissenter William Thornhill.[6] A leading member with his father and brothers of the Liverpool Concentric Club, he seconded the nomination of the reformer William Ramsden Fawkes[†] for Lancashire in 1818, and canvassed for the radical Dr. Peter Crompton at Preston that year and Liverpool at the general election of 1820.[7] Possibly for health reasons, he had recently (at the age of 30) embarked on a career in the law, and by 1826, when, at his father's instigation, he contested Preston on the anti-corporation interest of Crompton's former backers, he was a barrister on the Northern circuit and a successful practitioner at the bar of the Commons.[8] Assisted by his Liverpool friends and wealthy Manchester liberal Dissenters

(Edward Baxter[†], Joseph Brotherton[†], Mark Philips[†], Richard Potter[†], Thomas Potter, John Shuttleworth[†] and J.E. Taylor) and their newspapers (the *Liverpool Mercury*, *Manchester Guardian* and *Manchester Gazette*), he defeated the radical William Cobbett[†] and the 'No Popery' candidate Robert Smith Barrie and came in with the Whig 12th earl of Derby's grandson Edward George Geoffrey Smith Stanley after a riotous 15-day poll. During it, he left Preston briefly on account of his mother's death and was detained as a precaution after Barrie's henchman Captain Samuel Martin Colquhitt challenged him to a duel for allegedly insulting the royal ensign.[9] Mocked throughout as a 'sugar baker' and rabid Deist, 'half-merchant, half-lawyer', he advocated parliamentary reform, lower taxes and free trade, including repeal of the corn laws or a fixed duty. He also called for civil and religious liberty, the abolition of West Indian slavery, education for 'the lower orders', and temperance.[10]

Recalling the 1826 Parliament, in 1832 Edward Davies Davenport named Wood as one of the three 'most willing' members of the opposition 'virtually' led by Hume.[11] A regular seconder and teller, his interventions in debate were frequent, wide-ranging and interrupted only by his regular absences on the circuit, for which he received leave, 9 Mar. 1827, 13 Mar. 1828, 1 Mar. 1830. He spoke for peace and toleration and combined the constitutional Whigs' commitment to retrenchment, remedying distress and checking corruption with the radicals' demands for an extended suffrage, the ballot, shorter parliaments, and ending military flogging. Though proficient, he did not excel as an orator: Brotherton, who observed him in 1828, noted that he was impossible to hear in a rowdy House.[12] He voted in Hume's minority on the address, 21 Nov. 1826, and seconded him against Canning on war with Portugal, 12 Dec., denouncing it as a harbinger of high property taxes and currency restrictions. His maiden speech, 7 Dec. 1826, delivered on presenting three Bradford distress petitions, described the sorry plight of the Lancashire weavers and labourers and was the first of his many tirades against agricultural monopolists and pleas for corn law and currency reform that session (22 Feb., 12 Mar., 21 May 1827).[13] He voted in Whitmore's minority for a 50s. corn pivot price, 9 Mar., and against increased protection for barley, 12 Mar. He opposed the duke of Clarence's annuity bill, 16, 26 Feb., 2 Mar., and the proposed expenditure on garrisons, 20 Feb., and Canadian waterways, 12 June. His objections to the purchase of York House for use as a national art gallery focused on the building's unsuitability and were easily dismissed by government, 11 May.[14] He voted to consider removing bankruptcy jurisdiction from chancery, 22 May, and in a minority of ten for repeal of the Blasphemous and Seditious Libels Act, 31 May. Like the Unitarian leader William Smith, Wood sought to distance himself from the weavers' radical petitions for wage regulation while expressing sympathy for their plight and supporting inquiry, 30 May 1827, 30 Apr., 1 May, 2 June 1828.

He divided for Catholic relief, 6 Mar., and presented petitions he had solicited from congregations in Lancashire and elsewhere for repeal of the Test Acts, 23, 25, 30, 31 May, 6, 7, 8, 12 June 1827. On 7 June he described and stressed the practical difficulties faced by the Nonconformist merchants of 'immense wealth ... shut out from all influence in the corporation of Liverpool'.[15] The Smith Stanleys and others expected him to promote the enfranchisement of Manchester and electoral reform in Preston, and he was added to the committee on the borough polls bill, 3 May, and voted to restrict election expenditure, 28 May 1827.[16] He divided for the Penryn disfranchisement bill that day, but made his support for it conditional on the rejection of sluicing, saying that he viewed the proprietorial influence of aristocratic landowners 'with as much contempt as he did these corrupt boroughs'. He recommended the controversial Preston poll bill drafted by Derby's attorneys, 14 June, and introduced it on the 18th, for printing and circulation.[17] His inclusion on the select committee on the alehouse licensing bill and endorsement on 15 June 1827 of a Preston petition for modification of the 1824 ('Tom and Jerry') Act were severely criticized by the corporation and the Tory *Preston Pilot*.[18]

Opposing the duke of Wellington's administration, he rallied to Hume on the estimates and tried in vain to expose and exploit the political differences between the home secretary Peel and the beleaguered colonial secretary Huskisson, 11, 12 Feb. 1828. He urged repeal of the Test Acts on presenting favourable petitions, 15, 20, 25 Feb., 5 Mar., and voted thus, 26 Feb. On 20 Feb., as a self-professed spokesman for the Dissenters, he made a personal plea for the repeal bill's prompt enactment and also Catholic emancipation. He warned that the Dissenters' 35-year silence was over and that defeat in the Lords (which he anticipated) would inevitably unleash a 'grand and powerful union' countrywide for religious toleration. He commended the Irish Catholics for petitioning for Test Acts repeal, when the Unitarians reciprocated, 24 Apr., 6 May, and divided for Catholic relief, 12 May. Wood questioned East Retford witnesses, 3, 4 Mar., and voted to find one of them guilty of perjury, 7 Mar. He voted against the disqualification bill, 24 June, and objected (as committee chairman) to changes proposed by Peel to the revived disfranchisement bill, before dividing against it, 27 June. He voted to lower the corn pivot price, 22 Apr., and for the gradual introduction of a fixed 10s. duty, 29 Apr. 1828, 19 May 1829. He divided for inquiry into chancery administration, 24 Apr., and took charge of the bankrupt laws amendment bill, 16, 23 May 1828. On the 28th he attended the Westminster reform dinner.[19] Perceiving that his motive for opposing the Canning family's pension, 13 May, was 'perhaps different to that of others' in the minority, he explained that it derived solely from Canning's 'uncompromising' opposition to parliamentary reform, praised his 'talents and genius' and criticized the Tories' 'factious conduct which had embittered the latter years of his life', 14 May. He joined in the criticism of the finance committee, its chairman Sir Mathew White Ridley and the estimates, 16 May, voted (as subsequently) against the grant to the Society for the Propagation of the Gospels, 6 June, and echoed Hume's objections to civil list pensions, 20 May, 10 June. He voted for the usury laws repeal bill, 19 June, and retrenchment, 20 June. He criticized the proposed Buckingham House expenditure, 23 June, and divided for inquiry into the Irish church, 24 June, and ordnance reductions, 4, 7 July. He considered the church establishment 'overgrown' and opposed the additional churches bill from conviction, 20 June. After failing to kill it by forcing four time-wasting divisions, 30 June 1828, he presented a barrage of hostile petitions from Unitarian congregations countrywide over the next ten days.

Addressing Lancashire concerns, and after prior consultation with the Smith Stanleys, on 12 Feb. 1828 Wood postponed the Preston poll bill, which the corporation now opposed, and sought to realize its principal objectives through the borough polls bill, on which committee he sat. He was a spokesman for it, 28 Apr.[20] His detailed account of Liverpool's electoral corruption failed to convince the House that a franchise bill was justified, 9 June, and his attempts (3, 4, 12, 26 June) to secure changes that Derby's agents sought in the turnpike bill were also unavailing.[21] He persisted in his bid to amend the 1824 Licensing Act (30 Apr., 19, 26, 27 June, 10 July), notwithstanding Preston corporation's objections.[22] His success, as counsel with George William Wood[†], in resolving local differences over voter qualification facilitated the passage of the 1828 Manchester Police Act, which in July (after hopes that it would assist the transfer of Penryn's seats to Manchester had been dashed) was celebrated as a tribute to his 'sound judgement ... steady, consistent

and inflexible adherence to liberal principles' and growing influence.[23] At Kirkby Knowle in December he married Elizabeth Serjeantson (d. 1887), whose brother Peter was a Liverpool broker. A pre-nuptial settlement gave them £6,000 and £550 a year charged to Scoreby.[24]

Wood welcomed the concession of Catholic emancipation in 1829 despite the 'bitter pill' of the attendant Irish disfranchisements. Before going the circuit he presented and endorsed favourable petitions from Lancashire's Dissenters, 6, 11, 16, 23, 27 Feb., 2, 3, 4 Mar., ridiculed Preston's anti-Catholic petition as the Ultra Isaac Gascoyne's bantling, 4 Mar., and divided for emancipation, 6 Mar.[25] He attended a dinner at Preston's *Bull Inn* to celebrate its passage, 28 Apr., but refused to make common cause with its radical supporters at the *Black Bull*.[26] He was for permitting Daniel O'Connell to sit without swearing the oath of supremacy, 18 May. His interventions (on 11, 12, 25 May, 19 June) helped to revive the controversy over Nash's role in the costly Buckingham House refurbishment and contributed to the baiting of the anti-Catholic Lord Lowther*, whose office as commissioner of woods and forests had been in abeyance. Having first criticized Lord Blandford's opposition to the proposal, he voted to transfer East Retford's seats to Birmingham, 5 May (as again, 11 Feb. 1830). He refused to vote for a new East Retford writ, 2 June, but divided for Blandford's reform resolutions that day. As one of Hume's key spokesmen against the ecclesiastical courts bill, which drew support from both sides of the House, he deliberately faulted its details and late introduction, so engaging its author, the dean of the court of arches Sir John Nicholl, in debate and forcing ministers to intervene, 3, 5 June. He had opposed the 1828 friendly societies bill on his constituents' behalf and he ensured that they received copies of the 1829 bill, to which he secured minor alterations, 15 May. In December 1829 the corporation of York made him their counsel, and he took a house there in Tower Street.[27]

Wood was not in the Commons, 4 Feb. 1830, and maintained next day that had he been, he would have 'felt at a loss' how to vote on Knatchbull's amendment regretting the omission of distress from the address, for although he shared the Ultras' disappointment and hoped retrenchment and concessions on corn would alleviate the weavers' plight, he could not align with them in opposition. Later that month, signalling a hardening of opinion, he refused to endorse distress petitions from Salford, 17 Feb., and Preston, 26 Feb., stating that he now saw no point in cutting taxes while

Parliament remained unreformed. He spoke similarly of the need to put reform first when presenting a petition against the East India Company's trading monopoly, 4 June. He voted for Blandford's scheme, 18 Feb., to enfranchise Birmingham, Leeds and Manchester, 23 Feb., and for Russell's moderate and O'Connell's radical reform proposals, 28 May. He had endorsed resolutions similar to O'Connell's on the 12th as the presenter of a Preston petition. He continued to support Hume and also divided fairly steadily with the revived Whig opposition on most issues, including Jewish emancipation, 17 May, on which he brought up favourable petitions, 20 May, 4 June, and abolition of the death penalty for forgery, 24 May (paired), 7 June. He voted in O'Connell's small minorities on the Doneraile conspiracy, 12 May, for universal suffrage, 28 May, and for reform of the Irish Vestry Acts, 10 June 1830 (and again, 23 Jan. 1832).

With George IV's death and a dissolution in prospect, he paid greater attention to local legislation (30 Apr., 12, 20 May, 4 June 1830). He had a petition criticizing Lancashire's 'close' grand jury printed, despite the Smith Stanleys' objections, 24 May, and opposed the administration of justice bill with Hume and O'Connell to the last, having on 4 June presented and supported hostile petitions from Cheshire, whose separate jurisdiction it abolished. He pressed in vain for inquiry into the management of the London parish of St. Luke's by the church commissioners, 8, 17 June. He had yet to act on a promise (made in debate, 19 May 1829) to amend the Sugar Acts on behalf of the refiners, when Huskisson proposed a further reduction in the duty on West Indian sugars, 14 June. Opposing this, he criticized ministers, pleaded for deregulation and warned that 'this silly idea of protecting the West Indian interest' had resulted in a shortfall in raw sugar, harming the refiners and driving business abroad. Glancing at Huskisson, he added: 'it is of no use to enter into commercial treaties with foreign powers with respect to refined sugar, for it is not a market our refiners want'. He rightly surmised that a three-cornered contest at Preston at the general election, when the radical Henry Hunt* made Smith Stanley's seat his target, would not jeopardize his return, and he secured it at a cost of only £450; but his failure to spend deprived him of his early lead in the poll and dented his popularity. He paid tribute to Smith Stanley in his closing speech and argued against intervention on the continent to assist the deposed French king.[28] Before Parliament assembled he was fêted in the manufacturing towns and as a guest at the opening of the Liverpool-Manchester railway.[29]

The Wellington ministry naturally listed Wood among their 'foes'. Opposing them on the address, 3, 5 Nov. 1830, he reserved particular criticism for the facility with which it sanctioned intervention in the Netherlands, Poland and Portugal, and the absence of any pledge on reform or measures to assist the labourers and the agricultural poor. He divided against them on the civil list, 12 Nov., and again on the 15th, when they were brought down. Addressing the House for the first time after Lord Grey succeeded Wellington as premier, 22 Nov., he promised to scrutinize the new ministry closely, expressed admiration for the Tories Sir Robert Peel and Lowther and explained that he would continue to sit with opposition as a 'private individual', yet would back the government on reform and taxation and support them in the event of an early dissolution. As 'one of the no-party', he criticized the 'spoiling' tactics resorted to by Peel in opposition, 7 Dec. 1830, 15 Feb. 1831, over the chancellor Lord Althorp's game bill. He was appointed to the select committee on the East India Company's charter, 4 Feb., and was an effective lobbyist against the calico duties, 28 Feb., 8 Mar. 1831. Making reform, including the ballot, his priority, he presented and endorsed favourable petitions from the manufacturing towns, 7 Dec. 1830, 21, 26, 28 Feb. 1831. Countering allegations by the anti-reformers and his colleague Hunt, who had defeated Smith Stanley at the December 1830 by-election, he described Lancashire as 'overwhelmingly' pro-reform, criticized Liverpool's 'narrow franchise' and urged ministers to concede separate representation to Salford and to extend Wigan's franchise, 26 Feb. Two days later he spoke similarly of York, 'a great town in which there is merely a pretence of representation', and, anticipating that the ministerial bill would disappoint the radicals, he projected it as an 'essential benefit' and 'important step' towards reform which 'neither I nor those with whom I act will oppose'. Claiming support for it from 'all Northern England and the manufacturing towns', he defended it at length, 7 Mar., disputed counter claims made by Gascoyne as the presenter of Liverpool's 'moderate reform' petition, 14 Mar., and brought up favourable ones, 16, 19 Mar. He voted for the bill at its second reading, 22 Mar., and against Gascoyne's wrecking amendment, 19 Apr. Presenting heavily signed favourable petitions from Manchester and Preston in Hunt's absence, 20 Apr., he drew on them to dispute Hunt's claim that Lancashire had tired of reform. Most of the mass of anti-slavery petitions he presented during that Parliament (4, 10, 12, 17, 25 Nov., 6 Dec. 1830, 14 Apr. 1831) were from Lancashire's Dissenters, whose petitions against church rates,

25 Nov. 1830, and for tithe reform, 19 Mar. 1831, he also endorsed. On the locally divisive issue of the factory bill, he was named to the select committee, 14 Mar., and presented petitions from both sides, 19 Mar., 18 Apr., but declined to speak. At the 1831 general election he canvassed for reformers at Liverpool and in the county and only narrowly avoided a contest at Preston, which returned him with Hunt after intrigues against him failed. On the hustings, where he defended the reform bill, while reaffirming his support for shorter parliaments, a wider franchise and the ballot, he was (wrongly) accused of poor attendance and criticized for neglecting corn law reform and failing to defer to Hunt's political leadership on 'matters affecting the working classes'.[30]

William Ewart* recalled that on 5 July 1831, on the 'important issue' of the Liverpool writ and the anti-reformer John Benett's attempt to disfranchise the borough for corruption

> Rigby Wason came into the House with all the pomp and circumstance of a judge about to record the final sentence of disfranchisement against the freemen. He was armed with a large black book in mourning for the carpenters and other victims of his legislative justice. Great was his wrath when John Wood so promptly put an end to the proceedings.[31]

He divided for the reintroduced reform bill at its second reading, 6 July, and gave it steady support in committee. Commenting, 14 July, 8 Aug., on several petitions entrusted to him advocating amendments, he stated, to taunts from Hunt, that although he was sympathetic towards their demands, supporting the ministerial bill remained his priority. He defended the decision to retain the 1821 census as the standard for English borough disfranchisements, 14 July, and the provision made for Yorkshire, 10 Aug. When on 4 Aug. a second seat for Stoke-on-Trent was proposed, he stated his preference for single Member constituencies and conceding a Member to Ashton-under-Lyne (which was afterwards awarded). He voted for the bill's third reading, 19 Sept., and was a majority teller for its passage, 21 Sept. He voted for the second reading of the Scottish reform bill, 23 Sept., and Lord Ebrington's confidence motion, 10 Oct. He divided for the revised reform bill at its second reading, 17 Dec. 1831, and consistently for its details, intervening only to ascertain how the registration clause would operate in Preston, 20 Feb. 1832. He paired for the bill's third reading, 22 Mar., and voted for the address calling on the king to appoint only ministers who would carry it unimpaired, 10 May. Next day, as directed by the meeting, he presented and endorsed a Manchester

petition requesting that supplies be withheld pending its passage, which had had been rushed to him by Richard Potter, Fielden and Shuttleworth.[32] On 17 and 24 May he cited the 'large number' of similar petitions he had received as proof of the continued popularity of the measure.[33] He divided against a Conservative amendment to the Scottish reform bill, 1 June. He wanted the proposed boundaries for Whitehaven altered to neutralize Lord Lonsdale's influence there and to amend the provisions for Stamford, 22 June 1832. He cast a minority vote for appointing 11 of its original members to the reconstituted Dublin election committee, 29 July, but divided with government on the controversy, 23 Aug. 1831, having first equated the motion to Benett's 'time-wasting' Liverpool franchise bill (that he had opposed, 21 Apr. 1831) and condemned both. He divided with administration on the Russian-Dutch loan, 26 Jan., 12, 16, 20 July, and relations with Portugal, 9 Feb. 1832.

Wood's pragmatism extended beyond reform, although he generally remained true to his original beliefs. He took pride in his select committee work on private and public bills, and his competence as a lawyer and businessman was recognized in appointments to the select committees on the East India Company, 28 June 1831, 27 Jan. 1832, and the West Indies, 6 Oct., 15 Dec. 1831. The demands they placed on him prevented him going the circuit.[34] He defended the bankruptcy bill on behalf of its author lord chancellor Brougham, 14 Oct. 1831, 20 July 1832. Continuing to sit with opposition, he voted in small minorities against the grant for Cambridge professors' salaries, 8 July 1831, 13 Apr. 1832, and the civil list, 18 July, whose provisions he again criticized, 25 July, 10 Aug. 1831. He spoke in favour of printing the Waterford petition for disarming the Irish yeomanry, 11 Aug., and inquiry into Thomas and Caroline Deacle's case, which had a popular following in Preston, 27 Sept. However, he refused to let 'irritation at past extravagance' sway his votes on expenditure on the royal palaces, 28 Sept., 9 Dec. Preferring a fixed duty, he gave only qualified support to Hunt's campaign for corn law repeal, 24 June, 13 Aug. His absence when the Preston petition was brought up, 12 Aug., was severely criticized in the radical press.[35] Although pressed by Hunt and the magistracy to advocate repeal of the 1830 Sale of Beer Act, he was prepared to concede its merits and agreed with Althorp that change should be limited to making licensing hours uniform, 30 June. He brought up petitions requesting this, 14 June, 23 Aug., 7 Oct. 1831, 7 May 1832. As a member of the select committee, he defended their recommendation permitting the use of molasses in distilling, 20 July 1831. He apparently did not vote when party strength was tested on the sugar refinery bill, 12 Sept., but, clashing frequently with the West India planters' spokesmen William Burge and Keith Douglas, he stated the refiners' case for reviving the Act, 28 Sept., when government conceded inquiry to avoid defeat, and again, 7, 13 Oct., when it was carried. Wood had appeared ill at ease when dealing with petitions from Richard Carlile, 3, 24 Aug., and the Deist William Taylor, 15, 30 Aug. 1831, and the reference to 'Divine Providence' in the preamble to the cholera bill, which he voted to omit, 16 Feb. 1832, infuriated him. He was also drawn to speak against church rates, 7 Mar. He presented petitions for the immediate abolition of colonial slavery, 24 May 1832, but he is not known to have voted on Buxton's motion that day. He voted to suspend military flogging, 19 June. His 'clever words' on the Peterloo massacre, 10 Feb., equivocal stance on the locally unpopular general register bill, 2, 22 Feb., and the factory regulation bill, 9, 10 Feb., 14 Mar. 1832, together with the generally silent support he gave to the anatomy bill, which Hunt vehemently opposed, won him few friends, and the weekly propaganda sheets of Hunt's 3,730 voters exploited them as further evidence of his betrayal, incompetence and neglect.[36] In June 1832, the corporation of York, which in January had commended him for clarifying their election laws, made him their recorder.[37]

With no prospect of a fourth return for Preston, Wood announced his retirement directly the reform bill became law. At the 1832 general election he campaigned for the Liberals Charles Poulett Thomson* and Sir George Philips* in Manchester and George William Wood in Lancashire South, and reported regularly to ministers on their candidates' prospects in Northern England.[38] Appointed by Grey in 1833 to chair the board of stamps and taxes, he relinquished the recordership of York for an administrative career, heading the revenue board under successive Liberal and Conservative governments. In June 1854 he turned down the knighthood offered to him by Lord Aberdeen's ministry in recognition of his service.[39] His commitment to education was a lifelong one. A committee member since 1832 of the Society for the Diffusion of Useful Knowledge, he frequently deputized for Lord Brougham at meetings. He resigned as their treasurer over policy differences in 1844 and subsequently played an active part in the development of University College, London, where he was a member of the council (1835-d.), chaired the management committee (1845-56), and instituted scholarships and tuition for recruits to the Inland Revenue.[40] He died at Bath in 1856, survived by his wife (d. 1887) and two

daughters. His will, dated 13 Dec. 1828, confirmed a pre-nuptial settlement in their favour.[41]

[1] Draws on obituaries in *Preston Chron.* 18, 25 Oct.; *Manchester Guardian*, 22 Oct.; *Inquirer*, 25 Oct. 1856; *Christian Reformer*, xii (1856), 757; *Univ. Coll. London Ann. Report* (1857), 13-14. [2] I. Temple Archives Adm/4/9; BAR/4/1. [3] IGI (Lancs.). Wood was not, as commonly stated, baptized in Cross Street chapel. [4] Ibid.; *Albion*, 8 Mar. 1847; V.D. Davies, *Hist. Manchester Coll.* 72; *VCH Yorks. E. Riding*, iii. 161; *VCH Lancs.* v. 137, 142; PROB 11/2055/371. [5] M. Gray, *Hist. Bury*, 44; E.D. Priestly Evans, *Hist. Presbyterian Chapel, Bank Street, Bury*, 179-80, 425-8. [6] *The Times*, 31 Dec. 1822. [7] J. Picton, *Memorials of Liverpool* (1875), i. 341; *Manchester Mercury*, 14 Mar. 1820; *Preston Election Addresses* (1826), 44-45, 122. [8] *The Times*, 11 May; *Liverpool Mercury*, 12 May 1826. [9] *Manchester Guardian*, 13 May, 10, 17 June, 1 July; *Billinge's Liverpool Advertiser*, 20, 27 June, 4 July 1826. [10] *Preston Election Addresses* (1826), 24, 44-45, 111-16; *Manchester Guardian*, 3 June; *Preston Pilot*, 1 July 1826; M.J. Turner, *Reform and Respectability*, 175. [11] JRL, Bromley Davenport mss, Davenport mem. [12] LSE Lib. Archives Division, Coll. Misc. 0146, Potter mss xii, Brotherto to R. Potter, 23 Apr. 1828. [13] *The Times*, 8 Dec. 1826, 23 Feb., 22 May 1827. [14] Ibid. 12 May 1827. [15] Ibid. 24, 26, 31 May, 1, 7, 8, 9, 13 June 1827; *Inquirer*, 25 Oct. 1856. [16] *Preston Pilot*, 17 Feb., 3 Mar.; Potter mss xiiia, ff. 181-2; Derby mss 920 Der (13) 2, Lord Stanley's letterbk. iii, Birley to Stanley, 18 June 1827 and *passim*. [17] *The Times*, 15, 19 June; *Preston Pilot*, 30 June 1827. [18] *The Times*, 15, 16 June; *Preston Pilot*, 16, 23, 30 June, 7, 14, 21 July 1827. [19] Add. 56552, f. 101. [20] Derby mss (14) 61/1, Wood to Smith Stanley, 14, 27 Dec. 1827; 62, same to same, 7 Mar., Palmer to same, 8 Mar. 1828; *Preston Pilot*, 15 Dec. 1827. [21] Derby mss (14) 62, Haydock to Smith Stanley, 3 May 1828. [22] Ibid. Palmer to Smith Stanley, 22 Feb. 1828. [23] Potter mss xii, ff. 136-203; M.J. Turner, 'Manchester Reformers and the Penryn Seats', *Northern Hist.* xxx (1994), 139-60; *Billinge's Liverpool Advertiser*, 29 July 1828. [24] *Liverpool Advertiser*, 16 Dec.; *Gent. Mag.* (1828), ii. 638; PROB 11/2075/371; 2242/881. [25] Potter mss xii, f. 63. [26] *Preston Pilot*, 2 May 1829. [27] *The Times*, 7 Dec. 1829; *Preston Pilot*, 6 Feb. 1830. [28] *Preston Pilot*, 3, 14 July, 7 Aug.; Derby Local Stud. Lib. Strutt mss, Strutt to wife, 13 July; Brougham mss, Shepherd to Brougham, 15 Aug.; Derby mss (14) 116/6, Winstanley to Smith Stanley, 18 Nov. 1830. [29] Potter mss vi, almanac, 8 Sept.; *Preston Pilot*, 18 Sept. 1830. [30] Derby mss (14) 116/6, Winstanley to Smith Stanley 24 Apr.; Hatfield House mss, bdle. 4, Leigh to Salisbury, 30 Apr.; *Preston Chron.* 30 Apr., 7 May; Brougham mss, Shepherd to Brougham [1831]; W. Proctor, 'Orator Hunt', *Trans. Hist. Soc. Lancs. and Cheshire*, cxiv (1962), 148-9. [31] Manchester New Coll. Oxf. William Shepherd mss vii, f. 53. [32] *Manchester Guardian*, 12 May; *The Times*, 12 May; *Manchester Herald*, 14 May 1832; *Diaries of Absalom Watkin, a Manchester Man* ed. M. Goffin, 145. [33] *Wheeler's Manchester Courier*, 19 May 1832. [34] William Shepherd mss vii, f. 87. [35] H.N.B. Morgan, 'Social and Political Leadership in Preston, 1820-60' (Lancaster Univ. M. Litt. thesis, 1980), 101. [36] Lancs. RO, 'Letters from the 3,730', Jan.-June 1832, *passim*. [37] *York Chron.* 19 Jan., 7 June 1832. [38] *Preston Chron.* 30 June, 14 July; *Manchester Herald*, 28 Nov. 1832; Add. 37949, f. 285. [39] Add. 40401, f. 119; W. Griffith, *Hundred Years: The Board of Revenue, 1848-1949*, pp. 7, 204. [40] SDUK pprs. [BL 739.d.5.; 818.m.10.]; UCL archives, SDUK archives, 1832-44; college corresp. 1828-49. [41] *Gent. Mag.* (1856), ii. 662; PROB 11/2242/881; IR26/2085/889.

M.M.E.

WOOD, Matthew (1768–1843), of 77 South Audley Street and Little Strawberry Hill, Mdx.

b. 2 June 1768, 1st s. of William Wood, serge manufacturer, of Tiverton, Devon and w. Catherine *née* Cluse. *educ.* Southgate Street, Exeter; Blundell's, Tiverton. *m.* 5 Nov. 1795, Maria, da. of John Page, surgeon and apothecary, of Woodbridge, Suff., 4s. (1 *d.v.p.*) 2da. *suc.* fa. 1809; James Wood, banker, of Gloucester to Down Hatherley, Glos. 1836; *cr.* bt. 11 Nov. 1837. *d.* 25 Sept. 1843.

Common councilman, London 1802-7, alderman 1807-*d.*, sheriff 1809-10, ld. mayor 1815-17.

Prime warden, Fishmongers' Co. 1834-6; gov. Irish Soc. of London 1835-*d.*

Dir. British Herring Fishing Co. 1812.

Maj. 8 Loyal London vols. 1803.

Wood, a popular former lord mayor of London and enthusiastic promoter of civic improvements, was a committed radical reformer with a taste for rabble-rousing. He earned his living as a hop merchant, in partnership with Edward Wigan. In about 1820 the business moved from Falcon Square, Cripplegate (Wood's aldermanic ward) across the Thames to St. Margaret's Hill, Southwark. By 1825 Wigan had left and Wood's brothers Benjamin and Philip and youngest son Western became variously involved in the concern, which by 1832, as Wood, Field and Wood, was back in the City at 25 Mark Lane. Wood had also held a substantial stake in the Cornish Wheal Crennis copper mine since 1812, but it had run into difficulties and at the start of this period was the subject of a chancery suit.[1] At the general election of 1820 Wood, who in late 1819 had sided with his fellow radical alderman and City Member Robert Waithman* in the corporation's internal squabbles over Peterloo and its aftermath, offered again for London.[2] At the nomination, mindful no doubt of the City alarmism provoked by Peterloo and the Cato Street conspiracy, he declared that

> liberal as his political sentiments were, he was certain that nobody would accuse him of a desire to overturn the constitution; he was ready to check all mobs; and to do everything which a magistrate ought to do, to preserve the public peace.

He narrowly topped the poll, but Waithman and the Whig sitting Member Thorp were beaten. Tierney, the Whig leader in the Commons, partly blamed Wood's selfishness (which Wood himself denied), while a Tory observer lamented that the livery were 'still too much attached' to such a 'vain, foolish busybody'.[3] Wood, who in the House, 11 Feb. 1828,

described himself as a 'disciple' of Joseph Hume*, continued to act steadily with the extreme left wing of opposition, voting remorselessly, often in tiny minorities, for economy, retrenchment and reduced taxation, and dividing against the Liverpool ministry on most major party issues. He was a frequent but pedestrian speaker ('plain' was his own word for it), and was keenly attentive to the interests of his constituents.[4]

He made an immediate impact in the new Parliament by raising the case of George Edwards, the government informer involved in the Cato Street affair, on which he had obtained information in his capacity as a magistrate. Having failed to persuade Lord Sidmouth, the home secretary, to prosecute Edwards for treason and been frustrated in his bid to interrogate the condemned conspirators in Newgate, he shouted questions at Thistlewood on the scaffold, 1 May. Next day he moved that Edwards be brought to the bar, treating the matter as one of breach of privilege, but he was talked out of it by the Whig lawyer Henry Brougham. On 9 May, after detailing his correspondence with the home office, he moved for the appointment of a secret committee, but the sense of the House was overwhelmingly hostile to what the Whig Lord Althorp considered an 'absurd' proposition. Charles Williams Wynn* reported that Canning, for government, had 'drubbed and exposed' Wood and his few backers, and the backbencher Hudson Gurney agreed, though he thought that Canning had overdone his 'demolition' of Wood, who was 'proved a very foolish meddler, but I believe an *honest gull*'. The Tory Member Henry Bankes, who dismissed Wood as 'a meddling, busy and mischievous man', was outraged by the 'folly' of his motion.[5] Wood was amenable to an investigation of the supposedly decrepit state of London Bridge, 4 and 12 May, and defended the planned City improvements, including the new post office, 11 May.[6]

He had been corresponding with Queen Caroline (whom he had championed as princess of Wales in 1813) in Italy since mid-April 1820, and his eldest son, the Rev. John Page Wood, met her at Geneva. To the alarm of Brougham, her attorney-general, who denounced him as a 'Jack Ass' and a 'jobbing fool', alleging that he hoped to persuade her to buy the late duke of Kent's villa near Ealing to relieve himself of some of the responsibility, as a trustee, for the duke's debts, and to secure places in her household for his supporters in the livery, Wood went to France at the end of May.[7] At St. Omer he stole a march on Brougham, who presented Caroline with the government's offer to buy her off, and his coadjutor Lord Hutchinson, who condemned him to the king as an 'enlightened mountebank'. He enticed Caroline, with assurances of popular acclaim, which he had orchestrated in advance, to disregard their advice and return to England with him.[8] They arrived in London on 6 June, with Wood, whose 'vulgarity' shocked the establishment, sitting beside the queen in an open carriage and acknowledging the cheers of the crowds lining the route. Satirized as 'Mother Wood', a notorious brothel-keeper and procuress, but also lauded as the 'Foe to Oppression', he accommodated her in his house in South Audley Street for two months before she moved to Brandenburgh House, Hammersmith, where he became one of her motley court and won William Cobbett's[†] support for the cause.[9] In the Commons, 7 June, Brougham, who had come close to washing his hands of the queen's case on account of Wood's interference, raised a laugh at his expense by referring to him as 'Absolute Wisdom'.[10] Wood voted against government on the affair, 22, 26 June, and endorsed London corporation's petition in her support, 17 July, but kept out of her trial, to Brougham's relief.[11] He tried in vain to amend Althorp's insolvency bill, 16 June, welcomed Littleton's truck bill, 22 June, and presented inadmissible parliamentary reform petitions from Birmingham, 24, 25 July 1820.[12]

Delighted by the abandonment of the bill of pains and penalties in November, he helped to organize the City's celebrations and calls for restitution, attended Caroline's thanksgiving at St. Paul's and was one of the minority who opposed the court of aldermen's loyal address to the king, 5 Dec. 1820.[13] At the opening of the 1821 session he presented petitions for the restoration of her name to the liturgy, repeatedly denied that she was deep in debt and voted steadily in her support. He spoke in the same sense at the livery meeting of 29 Jan. and presented and endorsed its petition, 13 Feb.[14] He divided for Catholic relief, 28 Feb., as he did again, 1 Mar., 21 Apr., 10 May 1825. Having personally inspected conditions in Ilchester gaol, which housed the demagogue Henry Hunt* (who had engineered Wood's first return for London in 1817), he raised the issue in the House, 9, 12 Mar., 11 Apr. 1821, when he moved for a select committee of inquiry but was forced by ministers to settle for a commission. He was in the minority for the production of the visiting magistrates' report, 21 June 1821, when his own motion on the subject of the dubious Llanllechid slate quarry leases was lost by 90-19.[15] He took up Hunt's case for an early release in the 1822 session, and voted for Burdett's motion, 24 Apr.[16] At the *City Tavern* reform dinner, 5 Apr. 1821, he called for unanimity among reformers to thwart the ministerial 'game' of fomenting divisions 'in order to succeed

in their profligate expenditure'.[17] He voted for reform, 9 May 1821, 25 Apr., 3 June 1822, 24 Feb., 24 Apr., 2 June 1823, 9 Mar., 27 Apr. 1826, presented the livery's reform petition, 2 Apr. 1822, endorsed the corporation's petitions, 17 Feb. 1823, 17 May 1824, and presented a Halifax petition for reform on Major Cartwright's plan, 22 Apr. 1823.[18] Soon after the inconclusive outcome of the chancery suit brought by his former Cornish mining partner Rowe for the enterprise to be removed from Wood's possession and placed in receivership (the lord chancellor rejected this but advised the disputants to come to terms), he called for Cornwall to be exempted from Taylor's bill to regulate steam engines, 18, 30 Apr., 7 May. 1821.[19] He presented petitions from wounded victims of Peterloo, 15 May, and voted for inquiry into the incident next day.[20] On 23 May he attended the Westminster purity of election anniversary dinner and proposed the toast to the Member, Sir Francis Burdett.[21] He had secured the appointment of a select committee on the condition of London Bridge, 12 Feb., and on 25 May he brought up its report. He was involved in subsequent legislation to repair and improve the structure.[22] He supported atttempts to curb cruelty to animals, 1, 14 June 1821.[23] On 18 June, when he voted three times against the duke of Clarence's grant, he condemned ministers' meanness to the queen; and on 10 July 1821 he refuted Butterworth's allegation that her credit and popularity were gone.[24] Yet he was apparently 'hooted' when he appeared with her in her futile attempt to gain admittance to the coronation. Supposedly disappointed at not being mentioned in her will on account of his financial problems over the Cornish mine, he was depicted immediately after her death as a smashed 'Humpty Dumpty'. He was involved in the organization of her funeral procession.[25]

On 8 Feb. 1822, when he voted in small minorities against coercive legislation for Ireland, he had printed the City corporation's petition complaining of an assault by troops on Waithman, as sheriff of London, at Knightsbridge the previous August. His motion for inquiry, which was contemptuously seconded by his Tory colleague Curtis, was defeated by 184-56, 28 Feb. On 22 July he tried unsuccessfully to amend the contentious bill to regulate the London orphans' fund coal duties.[26] He welcomed the 'very salutary' vagrant laws amendment bill and was named to the committee on it, 29 Mar. (as he was to that on a new measure, 6 May 1824). He failed by 75-33 to postpone consideration of the grant for public building works.[27] He was in the minority of 36 against the revised corn duties, 9 May 1822. He presented petitions against Bennet's alehouses licensing bill, 3 June, but warmly supported the measure, 27 June.[28] He failed by 55-54 to carry an amendment to the prisons bill, 21 June, and complained of the effect on small maltsters of the Excise Licences Act, 1 July. He backed Hume's objections to the receivers general bill, 9 July, but did not divide the House on it, 18 July, on the understanding that salaries would not exceed £2,000. He presented publicans' petitions against Brougham's beer retail bill, 17 July 1822, and attacked it on their behalf next day.[29] He was again one of the publican's spokesmen against the bill on its reintroduction in 1823, when he also opposed the government's beer duties proposals, 24 Mar., 13, 17 June, and spoke and voted for inquiry into transferring the tax from beer to malt, 28 May.[30] He had secured a return of information on this subject, 25 Feb., and on 26 Mar. he endorsed the London merchants' petition for repeal of the Insolvent Debtors Act.[31] He voted to lower the import price for corn, 26 Feb. At a City meeting the following day he expressed his support for a reform of London tithes.[32] He laughed at the notion of erecting a statue of Dr. Jenner at public expense, 19 Mar. He spoke and voted for the abolition of punishment by whipping in gaols, 30 Apr. He voted for inquiry into the currency, 12 June, and for repeal of the usury laws, 17 June 1823, 27 Feb. 1824, 17 Feb. 1825. He was an advocate outside the House of financial support for Greek and Spanish liberals in June 1823.[33] He divided in the minority of 15 against the reciprocity bill, 4 July 1823.

Wood saw nothing wrong with the judicious use of treadmills in prisons, 19 Feb., though he did not wish women to be so punished, 5 Mar. 1824. He called for repeal of the wool tax, 20 Feb. Having on the 12th promoted a corporation petition for repeal of the coal duties, he pressed this matter when presenting other London petitions, 20, 23, 27 Feb., 8, 29 Mar., 12 Apr.[34] He welcomed the proposed reductions, 1 Apr. He advocated abolition of the duty on excise licences, 1, 10, 11, 30 Mar.[35] He presented anti-slavery petitions from Cripplegate, 2 Mar., and Brentwood, 15 Mar.[36] He credited ministers with good intentions towards the silk industry, 9 Mar., but urged them to allow drawback on cut goods for the sake of the smaller dealers, 10, 19, 22 Mar. He wanted relaxation of the regulations governing the processing of hides and skins, 18 Mar., 3, 7 May.[37] He jocularly called for the inspector-general of gas companies to examine the gasometer at Mansion House, 'over which he had slept for two years', 2 Apr. He presented a London brass-founders' petition for repeal of the Combination Acts, 5 Apr., and demanded a reduction of the rum duties, 8 Apr.[38] He again attacked the beer duties proposals on behalf of the 'deserving' publicans, 6 Apr., 7, 19,

24 May, when he voted in the minority of 32.[39] On 10 May he brought in bills to enable London corporation to borrow money to discharge debts on the coal exchange, Thames navigation and the orphans' fund. The first two became law that session, but the last was defeated on its third reading by 35-30, 9 June.[40] He opposed the marine insurance bill, 28 May, 11 June, when he was a teller for the hostile minority. He was in those of 15 against the new churches bill, 14 June, and of 14 against the Irish insurrection bill, 18 June. In October 1824 he was granted the freedom of Gloucester, where a sister of the eccentric local banker James Wood had befriended him and left him a house in recognition of his championship of the late queen.[41]

Wood was described by Daniel O'Connell* on their first acquaintance in February 1825 as having 'the air of an honest man, cordial and frank'.[42] He endorsed the City corporation's petition for a revision of London tithes, 14 Feb., and presented parish petitions to the same effect, 17 Feb. 1825. On 21 Mar. he introduced a London tithes bill, but ministers ensured its rejection on its second reading, 17 May. He supported the St. Olave tithe bill, 6 June.[43] He endorsed the corporation's petition for a repeal of assessed taxes, 25 Feb., spoke and voted in that sense, 3 Mar., presented petitions, 17 Mar., 19 Apr., and divided for repeal of the window tax, 17 May.[44] He supported corporation petitions against the Metropolitan Waterworks and Equitable Loan Bank bills, 11 Mar., and joined in criticism of the Fish Company bill, 15, 16 Mar.[45] In common council, 7 Apr., and at a public meeting, 13 Apr., he spoke in favour of revision of the corn laws,[46] as he did in the House, 25, 28 Apr., when he applauded ministers' general relaxation of commercial restrictions but urged them to follow suit on corn; he was in the minority that day. He presented petitions against re-enactment of the combination laws, 3, 10 May.[47] Supporting Maberly's motion for repeal of the beer duties, 5 May, he complained that in the current session 'not one shilling had been taken from the taxes that pressed immediately upon the poor', while the 'rich duke and the opulent commoner' had benefited from reductions in the wine duties. He had been added to the committee on the county courts bill, 17 Feb., and on 19 May he secured the City's exemption from its provisions. On behalf of Cornish miners, he called for a reduction of the duty on soap and tallow candles, 7 June, reminding ministers that the £6,000 a year which they were about to 'throw away' on the grant to the duke of Cumberland was taken from 'the pockets of the labouring classes'. Before voting in a minority of 37 for inquiry into the Irish church, 14 June 1825, he said that its proposer Hume 'did not wish to despoil the church, but for a more equal distribution of its amazing wealth'.

On the address, 3 Feb. 1826, Wood declared that the proposed relief would not assuage the 'suffering of his constituents': repeal of the corn laws and tax remissions were essential. He spoke in the same terms in common council on the 8th.[48] He presented a Coggeshall silk manufactures' petition for protection against French imports, 10 Feb.,[49] and voted for inquiry into the trade, 24 Feb. Of the government's emergency financial legislation, which he resolutely opposed, he observed on 14 Feb. that 'if ministers did not get many cheers, they got what they liked much better, a vast majority'. He assured Wilmot Horton that there were plenty of distressed Londoners who would leap at subsidized emigration, 14 Mar.[50] He divided for inquiry into the Jamaican slave trials, 2 Mar., and presented an abolitionist petition, 15 Mar.[51] Next day he chided Martin the animal protector for failing to vote for an end to the flogging of 'his own species' on the 10th. He was twice a teller for tiny minorities against items in the Irish estimates, 23 Mar. On 17 Apr. he spoke and was a teller for the minority against the London corn exchange bill and endorsed the corporation's petition for revision of the corn laws, for which he voted the following day. The bill which he had introduced on 10 Mar. to provide public funds for the rebuilding of London Bridge became law on 5 May; but he had to abandon his measure to regulate the employment of Thames watermen.[52] When supporting Russell's resolution condemning electoral bribery, 26 May 1826, he boasted that in his three elections for the City he had 'never paid either in meal or in malt' or 'expended a single shilling in coach hire' for out-voters. In the House, 21 Apr. 1825, he had declared that he would vote for Catholic relief even if doing so alienated his constituents and cost him his seat. At the general election of 1826, when he admitted publicly that he 'had no claims to the character of an orator', his support for Catholic claims damaged him enough to leave him only in fourth place in the poll; he resented that he 'should have been selected as a sort of popular mark'.[53]

At a common hall, 19 Oct. 1826, Wood acquiesced in the call for revision of the corn laws, but pointed out that without an immediate reduction of extravagant expenditure it would be nugatory.[54] He duly spoke, 1, 12 Mar., when he divided the House against the proposals for barley, and voted, 9, 22 Mar. 1827, for lower protection. He supported and was a minority teller for Hume's amendment to the address, 21 Nov. 1826. He pressed for a reform of bankruptcy administration, 8

Dec. 1826,[55] and the regulation of naval impressment, 13 Feb. 1827. Wood, who voted for Catholic relief, 6 Mar., was in the opposition minorities on the army estimates, 20 Feb.; the Clarence annuity bill, 2, 16 Mar., when he told 'the vociferators' who tried to shout him down that he would not be silenced by 'the intolerant spirit of the landed faction'; the conduct of Leicester corporation, 15 Mar.; the Barrackpoor mutiny, 22 Mar, and the Lisburn Orange procession, 29 Mar. He did not, however, vote next day for the motion to withhold supplies until the ministerial crisis had been resolved. He demanded inquiry into and improvement of the Fleet debtors' gaol, 14 Mar., 3 Apr., 22 May.[56] He voted for the spring guns bill, 23 Mar. He divided with opposition for inquiries into the Irish miscellaneous estimates and chancery delays, 5 Apr. On Althorp's proposed elections regulation bill, 8 May, he argued for the retention of nominees to safeguard the interests of petitioners. At a common council meeting next day to petition for repeal of the Test Acts (for which he presented petitions, 23, 31 May, 7, 8, 19 June), he observed that although Canning, the new premier, had 'avowed his determination to oppose ... repeal and ... reform', he was 'now surrounded by a large number of men who were pledged to support these measures'.[57] In the House on the 11th he told Canning that 'a large number of his constituents were satisfied with his government' and that 'though he continued in his former seat, he would support the ministry as far as he could'. Yet he felt bound to denounce the grant for a national gallery that day,[58] and he voted against government on bankruptcy jurisdiction, 22 May, the disfranchisement of Penryn, 28 May, repeal of the Blasphemous and Seditious Libels Act, 31 May (when he was a teller for the minority of ten), and the grant for Canadian canals, 12 June. He reintroduced his Thames watermen bill, 5 Apr., and saw it through to the statute book on 14 June 1827.[59]

Peel, back in office as home secretary in the duke of Wellington's ministry, was warned in late January 1828 that 'some foolish fellow' such as Wood might create parliamentary difficulties over the duke's concurrent appointments as premier and commander-in-chief, but nothing came of this.[60] In common council, 24 Jan., he promised 'hearty support' for their petition for repeal of the Test Acts.[61] He duly endorsed it, 11 Feb., urging Dissenting electors to 'use their best endeavours to control the opinion of their representatives on a point of so much importance'; and he presented other petitions, 23, 26 Feb., when he voted for repeal. He divided for Catholic relief, 12 May. He spoke and voted, in Hume's minority of 15, for navy economies, 11 Feb., and was in a minority of eight the next day. He presented petitions from Gloucester and Gloucestershire maltsters for repeal of the 'almost inoperative' Malt Act, 18 Feb. He was named to the select committees on the police of the metropolis, 28 Feb., after assuring Peel, who gently mocked him, that the City authorities had confidence in their own arrangements. (He was named to the revived select committee, 15 Apr. 1829.) He pressed for London freeholders to be enfranchised, 11 Mar., supported the transfer of East Retford's seats to Birmingham, 21 Mar., 27 June, and endorsed Davies's bill to limit borough polls to six days, 6, 15 May 1828. He wanted reform of St. Marylebone vestry, 31 Mar., and he presented numerous petitions against the friendly societies bill, 3, 21, 24, 25 Apr. He voted for relaxation of the corn laws, 22, 29 Apr., and inquiry into chancery delays, 24 Apr. He supported London corporation's petition for partial repeal of the stamp duty on receipts, 28 Apr., and presented ones from Sunderland against the coal owners' monopoly, 9 May, and from Warminster manufacturers for an end to truck payments, 20 May. He welcomed the government's church briefs abolition bill and plan to facilitate the recovery of small debts, 22 May. He presented a Ramsgate anti-slavery petition, 30 May, and one from Gloucester against the restriction of the circulation of small bank notes, 2 June; he voted against this bill, 5, 16 June. He opposed any increase in the duties on foreign wool, 3 June, and was in small minorities for economies, 6, 10 June. He defended London corporation's stand on Smithfield meat market, 12, 13 June, drew attention to the parlous state of the City militia, 20 June, and, as instructed, endorsed the livery's petition on abuses in the secondaries office, 23 June, when he divided against government on the refurbishment of Buckingham House. He voted for repeal of the usury laws, 19 June. He spoke and voted in a minority of ten against the cider retail bill, 26 June. On the 30th he attacked the additional churches bill as 'an odious measure, that would wring money out of the hands of industrious poor people', and was a teller for the minority. He voted against administration on the ordnance estimates, 7 July, and the silk duties, 14 July 1828, and next day dismissed the Irish butter trade bill as 'absurd'.

Wood divided for Catholic emancipation, 6, 30 Mar., endorsed London corporation's favourable petition, 9 Mar., presented one from Pendlebury Dissenters, 18 Mar., and questioned the validity of signatures on the London and Westminster anti-Catholic petition, 19 Mar. 1829. That session he introduced bills to extend the scope of the St. Katharine's Docks Act, to improve the approaches of London Bridge (which he defended,

23 Mar., 6 May), to give estate purchasing powers to the board of the London Workhouse, to improve Smithfield market and to start the East London railway. Only the two last failed to become law: the Smithfield bill, which he tried to save, 15 May, was thrown out by 54-31.[62] He approved the ministerial bill to reform the management of Greenwich Hospital, 9 Apr., but was a critic of the West India Dock bill, 14 Apr. He voted for the transfer of East Retford's seats to Birmingham, 5 May, and Lord Blandford's reform scheme, 2 June, for O'Connell to be allowed to take his seat unimpeded, 18 May, and in minorities of 12 for a fixed duty on corn, 19 May, and seven against the ecclesiastical courts bill, 5 June 1829.

Wood divided against the address, 4 Feb. 1830. He voted as before on East Retford, 11 Feb., 15 Mar., again for Blandford's reform plan, 18 Feb., and for the enfranchisement of Birmingham, Leeds and Manchester, 23 Feb., and in support of the Newark petition complaining of the duke of Newcastle's electoral interference, 1 Mar. He was in the minorities for O'Connell's radical reform scheme, as well as for Russell's more moderate proposals, 28 May, when he reiterated his approval of the enfranchisement of City freeholders. He voted for tax reductions, 15 Feb., and presented and approved petitions to that effect from his ward, 16 Feb., 15 Mar. He divided steadily for economies and reduced taxation throughout the session. Although he supported the prayer of the London merchants' distress and reform petition, 12 Mar., he reckoned that few in the City shared Waithman's reservations about free trade. In common hall, 5 Apr., when Hunt proposed a string of resolutions calling for radical reform to relieve distress, Wood ascribed this to 'the enormous amount of taxation' and advocated a property tax to permit other remissions. He saw 'no near prospect' of reform, but he duly presented and supported the petition, 17 May.[63] He was named to the select committee on the sale of beer, 4 Mar., endorsed a London licensed victuallers' petition against the subsequent bill, 11 Mar. (when he also secured the appointment of a an inquiry into the London coal trade, which he chaired); he expressed his objections to the proposals for on-sales, 4 May, and voted in this sense, 21 June, 1 July. He presented a Finsbury Dissenters' petition for mitigation of the criminal code, 25 Mar., and voted for abolition of the death penalty for forgery offences, 24 May, 7 June. He spoke and voted in a minority of 16 against Lord Ellenborough's divorce bill, 6 Apr., and divided for reform of the laws, 3 June. He voted for Jewish emancipation, 5 Apr., 17 May. He introduced and carried a bill to make further provision for funding redevelopment of the approaches to London Bridge.[64] He voted for abolition of the Irish lord lieutenancy, 11 May, and was in O'Connell's small minority for Irish vestry reform, 10 June. He spoke in favour of allowing the Irish judge Barrington to be heard in his own defence at the bar and was a minority teller, 22 May. He endorsed London corporation's petition against the Irish and Scottish vagrants removal bill, 24 May, and opposed the measure, 26, 27 May, 3 June. That day he gave notice of a motion for a reduction of public salaries to 1797 levels (as he had been instructed to do by the livery, under Hunt's direction, in April),[65] but the dissolution after the king's death intervened. On 10 June he secured leave to introduce a bill to curb the spread of canine rabies by increasing magistrates' powers, but on Peel's advice he referred it to a committee upstairs, 15 June. He supported the City corporation's petition for the abolition of superfluous oaths, 5 July 1830.

At the ensuing general election Wood, who declared his undiminished support for 'the reform of abuses' and hostility to 'extravagant expenditure', and bragged about his dedicated attendance, was returned unopposed for London.[66] Ministers of course numbered him as one of their 'foes', but 'severe indisposition' made him an unwilling absentee from the division on the civil list which brought them down, 15 Nov. 1830, when he also missed the common council reform meeting.[67] He approved of its petition when it was presented next day, observing that Wellington's anti-reform declaration and decision to put off the new king's visit to the City had convinced him that 'it was time for the government to be changed'. He supported the corporation's petition for repeal of the coastwise coal duties, 14 Dec. 1830, and presented ward petitions for this, 3, 7, 10, 11 Feb. 1831. He welcomed Hobhouse's plan for vestry reform as an essential adjunct to parliamentary reform, 16 Dec. 1830, and brought up favourable petitions, 11, 14 Feb. 1831. On 3 Feb. he gave notice of his motion on public salaries, but events again overtook it. He presented a ward petition for repeal of the house and window taxes, but dissented from its advocacy of a tax on luxuries, 7 Feb., arguing that if the Grey ministry kept their promises no new taxes would be required. He reintroduced his rabies bill, 10 Feb., and secured its second reading on the 23rd, but it made no further progress that session.[68] His measure to extend the scope of the 1830 London Bridge Act (20 Dec. 1830) became law on 11 Mar. 1831. He presented a petition from St. Giles, Cripplegate for tithe relief, 11 Feb.; called for the exemption of Scotland from the proposed tax on steamboat passengers and for an end to the 'dead robbery' of the drawback on malt used in Scottish distilleries, 17 Feb.; endorsed the City corporation's petition for bankruptcy reform, 21 Feb., and approved Slaney's 'very good' liability of landlords bill, 23 Feb. He presented a 'singular' petition for 'radical reform' from 15 electors of the 'snug borough' of Malmesbury, 11 Feb., and one from his ward for more frequent parliaments and the secret ballot, 28 Feb. On 4 Mar. he supported London corporation's petition in favour of the ministerial reform bill, which he said would 'save' the country. He spoke for it in common hall and in the House, 7 Mar., chaired a Cripplegate meeting to approve it, 8 Mar., and presented its and other favourable ward petitions, 16 Mar., when he proclaimed that 'the present administration stands higher with the country than any administration ever has done' and denied Tory allegations that the bill's threat to the livery's votes was an issue with them. He presented more ward petitions, 19, 22 Mar., when he divided for the second reading. As a veteran reformer, he applauded the measure at a merchants' Mansion House meeting, 25 Mar.,[69] and he endorsed their petition, 18 Apr. On 29 Mar. he clashed with the anti-reformer Wetherell over the strength of reforming sentiment in Cornwall, claiming that he had once employed about 1,200 people there and admitting that he had 'paid one bill for £7,000 arising out of proceedings' in chancery. Wood, who, with Waithman and other radicals, had not crossed the House on the change on ministry and sat among the Tories for the rest of this period,[70] defended the alterations made to the bill and ridiculed the opposition's attempts 'to get back into office', 13 Apr. Next day, however, he felt compelled to join Hume in resisting the grant for civil list pensions. He largely favoured Evans's corporate funds bill that day. He welcomed the ministerial measures to regulate Tower Hamlets militia, 10 Mar., and the coal trade, 28 Mar. He voted against Gascoyne's wrecking amendment to the reform bill, 19 Apr. 1831. At the ensuing general election he came in again unopposed for London on the united reform platform, promising to 'continue a reformer for the rest of his life' and asserting that 'if they had had a reformed Parliament 30 years ago, they would not now have that enormous load of debt which was hanging about them'. At the livery dinner, 9 May 1831, he announced that 'though he was satisfied with the bill [he] would go further if necessary, even to the extent of vote by ballot'.[71]

On 28 June 1831 Wood, who was nettled by smirks from ministers and some new Members, secured leave to reintroduce his rabies bill, threatening if necessary to divide the House 'in order to see whether it cares more for its dogs than for the human species'.

He presented it next day, but it made no further progress.[72] On 30 June he moved his resolution for a reduction of public salaries, complaining that it was 'a robbery to transfer the public money to the pockets of those who perform no actual service in return', but ministers treated it as a question of confidence and it was crushed by 216-13.[73] He called for repeal of the duty on tiles and found fault with the former Tory chancellor Goulburn's new concern for the poor, 1 July, though he admitted when pressed that his repeal of the beer and leather taxes had been beneficial. He said that Millbank penitentiary was the useless 'hobby of gentlemen who like to try experiments in prison discipline' and opposed the National Gallery grant on behalf of his 'thousands' of philistine constituents, 8 July. Advocating the construction of a new road from Waterloo Bridge to the New (Euston) Road, 11 July, he remarked that he had 'been often charged with having a hand in every job about the town where improvement is concerned, but I am still ready to bear all the weight of this charge'. He was in the minority against the civil list grant, 18 July. He voted for the second reading of the reintroduced reform bill, 6 July, and at least twice against the adjournment, 12 July, and exchanged angry words with some of his Tory neighbours over opposition's obstructive tactics, 14 July. He gave the measure steady general support in committee. In common council, 7 Sept., when he dismissed some extremists' criticism of his preference for a scot and lot over the £10 householder franchise, he boasted that he had 'sat in the House every night until two and three in the morning, always giving his best attention to the interests of the bill, and voting with the government in every division':[74] in fact, he spoke and voted for separate representation for Merthyr Tydfil, 10 Aug. He made an uneasy defence of the livery's reprimand of and dictation to his colleague Thompson over a wayward vote, 3 Aug. Next day he welcomed the enfranchisement of Tower Hamlets. Although he divided with ministers against the enfranchisement of £50 tenants-at-will, 18 Aug., he admitted that he rather liked the idea, 24 Aug., when he also said that he was at odds with some of the livery over the proposal to allow City freeholders to vote in London, which he approved. He was anxious to ensure that those who only rented offices in City counting houses should not be allowed to vote, 26 Aug. He saw no reason why the expenses of revising barristers should not be met by the constituencies, 5 Sept. He secured the addition to the bill of a clause compelling the livery companies to make a return of the members claiming the vote, 14 Sept. In the last speech before the division on the passage of the bill, 21 Sept., when he was of course in

the majority, he refuted Hunt's allegation that enthusiasm for it had cooled among the livery, having spoken in the same sense at the common hall to petition the Upper House in its favour, 19 Sept.[75] He voted for the second reading of the Scottish bill, 23 Sept., and for the motion of confidence in the government, 10 Oct., and attended the City meeting to address the king, 13 Oct.[76] Wood voted in O'Connell's minority on the composition of the Dublin election committee, 29 July, and to postpone issuing the Dublin writ, 8 Aug., but with government on the Dublin election controversy, 23 Aug. He was in the minorities against issuing the Liverpool writ, 5 Sept., and against the quarantine duties next day. On 11 Aug. he brought in, on the recommendation of City magistrates, a bill to regulate the speed of steam vessels in the port of London. It ran into strong opposition and on 5 Sept. he withdrew it, but he secured the appointment of a select committee on the subject the following day. He welcomed lord chancellor Brougham's bankruptcy reform bill, 13 Oct. 1831.

Wood voted for the second reading of the revised reform bill, 17 Dec.1831. He again gave general support to its details, though he was in Hunt's minority of 11 for a tax-paying householder franchise, 2 Feb. 1832. He voted for the third reading, 22 Mar. He divided with ministers on the Russian-Dutch loan, 26 Jan., 12, 16, 20 July, relations with Portugal, 9 Feb., and the navy civil departments bill, 6 Apr.; but he was in the minority for information on military punishments, 16 Feb. On 17 Jan. he brought in a new London steam vessels bill, but, to his great annoyance, it was got rid of when his back was turned, 30 July.[77] He carried through another London Bridge bill, commenting on 13 Feb. that if it was rejected 'the city will be deprived of a great and noble street opening from the river into the heart of the town'.[78] As requested, he supported a London silk weavers' petition for inquiry into their plight, 21 Feb., but he said nothing about their demands for protection. He presented a Clerkenwell petition in favour of Sadler's factories regulation bill, 7 Mar., but noted that it would not be applicable to woollen mills, where children were not employed. He again pressed for the removal of all drawback on Scottish distillery malt, 30 Mar., endorsed London corporation's anti-slavery petition, 4 Apr., and supported the Gravesend pier bill for the recreational benefit of poor Londoners, 10 Apr. In common council next day he approved the ministerial plan for Irish education and denounced Protestant 'fanatics'.[79] He liked the principle of Warburton's anatomy bill, but would have no truck with the proposed payment of money for corpses, 11, 18 Apr. He was named to the secret committee on renewal of the Bank's charter, 22 May. A 'domestic calamity' prevented him from attending the common council meeting which petitioned for supplies to be withheld until reform had been secured, 10 May; but in the House later that day he supported the petition and voted for the motion for an address requesting the king to appoint only ministers who would carry the bill unimpaired. At the livery meeting on the 11th he promised that in such 'awful times' he 'would never desert' his 'post'.[80] He gave 'cordial support' to the Manchester supplies petition that day, presented the livery's petition, 14 May, and brought up several others from City wards and parishes, 18, 24 May. On the 25th he voted for the second reading of the Irish reform bill, but he was in O'Connell's minority for the enfranchisement of £5 freeholders, 18 June. He voted against a Conservative amendment to the Scottish bill, 1 June; failed in his attempt to 'make some excitement' by interrupting the committee on it in order to receive the English bill back from the Lords, 4 June;[81] and endorsed the City corporation's petition for the principles of the English to be extended to the Scottish measure, 4 July. He presented petitions against the cruelty to animals bill in so far as it infringed the Smithfield Act, 30, 31 May. He voted against Alexander Baring's bill to exclude insolvent debtors from the House, 6 June, divided with Hunt for the suspension of flogging, 19 June, and with Hume for liberalizing amendments to the coroners bill, 20 June. He was in the minority against ministers on the proposed boundaries of Whitehaven constituency, 22 June. On 2 July he denounced and voted in the minority of 22 against the grant for the Waltham Abbey ordnance establishment. He presented and endorsed City ward and parish petitions against the Scottish and Irish poor removal bill, 5, 9 July. He approved the plan to supply the capital with water at public expense, 6 July, and agreed with government that men made redundant by the Irish coal trade bill should be compensated, 24 July. He presented an Irish petition for the abolition of tithes, 31 July, and on 6 Aug. 1832, with a view to registration, secured a return of the number of rated inhabitants of the City and of those who had now paid their dues.

In October 1831 the patronage secretary Ellice had told Lord Grey that 'our friend' Alderman Wood

> was deeply grieved at no offer of a baronetcy being made to him, when you gave that distinction to his less worthy brother, Alderman Heygate*. If he could get a baronetcy conferred upon his namesake and relation ... [James] Wood of Gloucester, with remainder to the alderman and his heirs, he would obtain a more substantial advantage with it, and the settlement of a million of money on his

family, to *enable them to support the dignity*. He calls Mr. Wood his relation. I believe he would have some difficulty in tracing the connection, but the object of the alderman's ambition is to revive the dignity of baronet in his own person, which formerly belonged to a branch of his family. If that could be done through the alderman's influence, the other consequences would flow from it. This would be barely an act of justice for poor Wood's political conduct and adherence to the party, and a great act of kindness on your part.

On Ellice's advice, Wood laid his case before Grey at the turn of the year; but the king had personal objections to him, and nothing came of the scheme.[82]

Wood was returned in second place for London at the general election of 1832 and came in again at the next three elections.[83] In 1836 he benefited handsomely from the will of James Wood, who left him his county estate at Down Hatherley and a share worth at least £1,000,000 in his personal fortune. The following year Queen Victoria, in a gesture of personal friendship in memory of her father, made him a baronet.[84] Wood died at Matson House, near Gloucester, the home of his son-in-law Edwin Maddy, in September 1843. He was acknowledged to have been an 'honest and consistent' man, who left a lasting physical mark on the City.[85] By his will, dated 7 July 1843, he directed his executors to sell all his real estate in Gloucestershire, Middlesex, Surrey, London and Southwark and to combine the proceeds with the residue of his personal estate to provide a life annuity of £1,500 for his wife. He left £20,000 to his eldest son and successor in the baronetcy, John Page Wood (1796-1866), rector of St. Peter's, Cornhill, together with an equal share with his four surviving siblings in the residuary estate.[86] His second son, William Page Wood (1801-81), a successful barrister, was Liberal Member for Oxford, 1847-52, vice-chancellor, 1853-68, and lord chancellor, as Baron Hatherley, 1868-72. His third son, Western Wood (1804-63), carried on the Mark Lane business and was Liberal Member for London, 1861-3.[87]

[1] *The Times*, 12 Mar. 1821. [2] Ibid. 13 Oct., 8 Nov., 8 Dec. 1819, 12, 18 Feb. 1820. [3] Ibid. 22 Feb., 2, 7, 16, 17 Mar.; Grey mss, Tierney to Grey, 17 Mar. 1820; *Colchester Diary*, iii. 121. [4] J.R. Dinwiddy, *Radicalism and Reform*, 64; *The Times*, 27 Apr. 1826. [5] J.A. Hone, *For the Cause of Truth*, 347; *The Times*, 2, 25 May; Broughton, *Recollections*, ii. 127; *Althorp Letters*, 107; NLW, Coedymaen mss 935; Gurney diary, 9 May; Dorset RO D/BKL, Bankes jnl. 117 (9 May); 118 (5 June 1820). [6] *The Times*, 13 May 1820. [7] C. New, *Brougham*, 238; Add. 38284, ff. 141, 227, 306; 52444, ff. 141-2; Brougham mss, Brougham to Lady C. Lindsay [28 May 1820]; *Mem. Bar. Hatherley*, i. 33, 39-40. [8] New, 239-41; *Geo. IV Letters*, ii. 821, 822, 847; Brougham, *Life and Times*, ii. 357-65; *Von Neumann Diary*, i. 24; *Arbuthnot Jnl.* i. 21; *Creevey's Life and Times*, 128-9; *London in the Age of Reform* ed. J. Stevenson, 120-1. [9] Brougham, ii. 366; New, 242; *Greville Mems.* i. 94-95; *Hobhouse Diary*, 24;

Creevey Pprs. i. 302; *Farington Diary*, xvi. 5513; *Lady Palmerston Letters*, 34, 43; Hatherton diary, 10 June 1820; *Colchester Diary*, iii. 141; M.D. George, *Cat. of Pol. and Personal Satires*, x. 13736, 13749, 13852; *London in Age of Reform*, 123; R.R. Sharpe, *London and the Kingdom*, iii. 318. ¹⁰Add. 52444, f. 135; George, x. 13899, 14146; New, 243. ¹¹*Greville Mems.* i. 195. ¹²*The Times*, 17 June, 25 July 1820. ¹³George, x. 13989; D. Miles, *Francis Place*, 159; *Geo. IV Letters*, iii. 884; *Ann. Reg.* (1820), Chron. pp. 499-500; *The Times*, 15, 17 Nov., 6, 15 Dec.1820. ¹⁴*The Times*, 25, 27, 30 Jan., 14 Feb. 1821; *Hobhouse Diary*, 49. ¹⁵*The Times*, 13 Mar., 12 Apr., 3 May, 22 June 1821. ¹⁶Ibid. 9, 19, 26 Feb., 2, 15, 21, 29 Mar., 6, 14 June 1822. ¹⁷Ibid. 5 Apr. 1821. ¹⁸Ibid. 3 Apr. 1822, 23 Apr. 1823. ¹⁹Ibid. 12, 14, 16, 19, 23 Mar., 1 May 1821. ²⁰Ibid. 16 May 1821. ²¹Add. 56542, f. 29; *The Times*, 24 May 1821. ²²*The Times*, 26 May 1821, 6, 14 Mar. 1822, 7, 17 June 1823. ²³Ibid. 2, 15 June 1821. ²⁴HLRO, Hist. Coll.379, Grey Bennet diary, 116. ²⁵*Creevey Pprs.* ii. 17-18; *Croker Pprs.* i. 197, 201; Nottingham Univ. Lib. Portland mss PwH 87; George, x. 14247-8; *London in Age of Reform*, 138. ²⁶*The Times*, 23 July 1823. ²⁷Ibid. 30 Mar. 1822. ²⁸Ibid. 4 June 1822. ²⁹Ibid. 22 June, 2, 10, 18 July 1822. ³⁰Ibid. 4, 25 Mar., 14, 24 June 1823. ³¹Ibid. 26 Feb., 27 Mar. 1823. ³²Ibid. 28 Feb. 1823. ³³Ibid. 11, 14 June 1823. ³⁴Ibid. 21, 28 Feb., 9 Mar., 13 Apr. 1824. ³⁵Ibid. 2, 11, 12, 31 Mar. 1824. ³⁶Ibid. 3, 16 Mar. 1824. ³⁷Ibid. 19 Mar., 4, 8 May 1824. ³⁸Ibid. 6, 9 Apr. 1824. ³⁹Ibid. 20 May 1824. ⁴⁰Ibid. 11, 15 May, 10 June 1824; *CJ*, lxxix. 340, 502, 525. ⁴¹*The Times*, 19 Oct. 1824; *Mem. Bar. Hatherley*, i. 67; *Gent. Mag.* (1843), ii. 542; *Oxford DNB*. ⁴²O'Connell *Corresp.* iii. 1169. ⁴³*The Times*, 15, 18 Feb., 22 Mar., 18 May, 7 June 1825; *CJ*, lxxx. 230, 425. ⁴⁴*The Times*, 18 Mar., 20 Apr. 1825. ⁴⁵Ibid. 12, 17 Mar. 1825. ⁴⁶Ibid. 8, 14 Apr. 1825. ⁴⁷Ibid. 4, 11 May 1825. ⁴⁸Ibid. 9 Feb. 1826. ⁴⁹Ibid. 11 Feb. 1826. ⁵⁰Ibid. 15 Mar. 1826. ⁵¹Ibid. 16 Mar. 1826. ⁵²*CJ*, lxxxi. 149, 312, 324; *The Times*, 19, 26 Apr., 5, 12 May 1826. ⁵³*The Times*, 10 Mar., 27 Apr., 10, 17, 20 June, 20 July 1826; George, x. 15138. ⁵⁴*The Times*, 20 Oct. 1826. ⁵⁵Ibid. 9 Dec. 1826. ⁵⁶Ibid. 15 Mar., 23 May 1827. ⁵⁷Ibid. 10, 24 May, 1, 8, 9, 20, 22, 30 June 1827. ⁵⁸Ibid. 12 May 1827. ⁵⁹*CJ*, lxxxii. 348, 387, 396, 475, 558; *The Times*, 6 Apr., 22 May 1827. ⁶⁰Add. 40395, f. 132. ⁶¹*The Times*, 25 Jan. 1828. ⁶²*CJ*, lxxxiv. 26, 101, 129, 136, 158, 304, 416. ⁶³*The Times*, 6 Apr. 1830. ⁶⁴*CJ*, lxxxv. 58, 500. ⁶⁵*The Times*, 6 Apr. 1830. ⁶⁶Ibid. 27, 31 July 1830. ⁶⁷Ibid. 16 Nov. 1830. ⁶⁸*CJ*, lxxxvi. 223, 229, 297, 484. ⁶⁹*The Times*, 26 Mar. 1831. ⁷⁰Add. 40403, f. 167. ⁷¹*The Times*, 25, 28, 30 Apr., 10 May 1831. ⁷²*CJ*, lxxxvi. 583, 589. ⁷³Le Marchant, *Althorp*, 325-6. ⁷⁴*The Times*, 8 Sept. 1831. ⁷⁵Ibid. 20 Sept. 1831. ⁷⁶Ibid. 14 Oct. 1831. ⁷⁷*CJ*, lxxxvii. 33, 178, 495, 531. ⁷⁸Ibid. 78, 85, 95, 183, 199, 226, 234, 244. ⁷⁹*The Times*, 12 Apr. 1832. ⁸⁰Ibid. 11, 12 May 1832. ⁸¹Hatherton diary, 4 June 1832. ⁸²Grey mss, Ellice to Grey, Wed. [Oct. 1831], Sun. [Jan. 1832], Wood to Ellice, 31 Dec. 1831. ⁸³*The Times*, 26 Oct., 20 Nov., 10-13 Dec. 1832. ⁸⁴*Oxford DNB*; *Mem. Bar. Hatherley*, i. 66-72. ⁸⁵*Gent. Mag.* (1843), ii. 541-3. ⁸⁶PROB 11/1987/723; 8/236 (27 Oct. 1843). ⁸⁷*Oxford DNB*; *Mem. Bar. Hatherley*.

D.R.F.

WOOD, Thomas (1777–1860), of Gwernyfed Park, Three Cocks, Brec. and Littleton Park, nr. Staines, Mdx.

BRECONSHIRE	1806–1847

b. 21 Apr. 1777, 1st s. of Thomas Wood of Littleton Park and Mary, da. and h. of Sir Edward Williams, 5th bt., of Gwernyfed. *educ.* Harrow 1788-95; Oriel, Oxf. 1796. *m.* 23 Dec. 1801, Lady Caroline Stewart, da. of Robert Stewart, MP [I], 1st mq. of Londonderry [I], and 2nd w. Lady Frances Pratt, da. of Charles Pratt†, 1st Earl

Camden, 7s. 3da. *suc.* mother 1820; fa. 1835. *d.* 26 Jan. 1860.

Sheriff, Brec. 1809-10.

Lt.-col. E. Mdx. militia 1798, col. 1803; militia a.d.c. to William IV 1831.

Wood, the heir to Gwernyfed, Littleton and his father's East India Company shares, was an active Middlesex magistrate and militia commander. A personal friend and future executor of the duke of Clarence, he was also a brother-in-law of Edward Law†, 2nd Baron Ellenborough, Sir Henry Hardinge* and the Liverpool ministry's foreign secretary Lord Castlereagh*, whose pro-Catholic Toryism he espoused.¹ Since 1806 he had represented Breconshire on the Gwernyfed interest, allied to that of his kinsman John Jeffreys Pratt†, Marquess Camden, whose seat, The Priory, he used when at Brecon socially or on county business. He had defeated the heir to Y Dderw and Tredegar Charles Morgan Robinson Morgan* to retain his seat in 1818, but to do so he had been obliged to give a public pledge to oppose Catholic relief. His victory speech in Abergavenny had been interpreted as an invitation to Monmouthshire to rise against the Morgans, and he anticipated a further challenge from that quarter.² None materialized in 1820, and he came in unopposed, promising attention to local interests.³

Wood was a forthright Member whose conduct was carefully monitored on account of his government connections. He remained a ready defender of the Liverpool ministry and the corn and poor laws in the 1820 Parliament, advocated game law reform, spoke on military and militia matters, and attended closely to local legislation, particularly for roads and tramways, in which he regularly invested. A prominent member of the 1820 and 1821 select committees on turnpikes, he proved to be a busy promoter of bills for Middlesex and South Wales trusts throughout his parliamentary career.⁴ Hitherto he had opposed the abolition of the Welsh judicature and courts of great session, of which he wrote to his Breconshire agent, John Jones of Glan Honddu, before the 1820 dissolution:

A few modifications may improve it, but we must on no account part with it, and if the Member for Carmarthen [John Frederick Campbell] does not know what is good for the Principality and would for the sake of a party question forget he is a Welshman, the Member for Breconshire does, and will do his best to preserve it ... I think all things considered I had better be without a vote for Carmarthen.⁵

When Campbell (afterwards 1st earl of Cawdor) sought inquiry with a view to abolition, 1 June 1820, Wood claimed that the Welsh would be 'much dissatisfied if their judicature was ever altered', and cited the poor roads and widespread use of the Welsh language as evidence of the Principality's backwardness and as current obstacles to change. His prediction that the end of the language was nigh and progress thus assured prompted a furious backlash 'without doors', while in the House John Hensleigh Allen, Campbell's Member for Pembroke Boroughs, pointed to Wood's non-residence and questioned his right to speak as a Welshman. Charles Williams Wynn* informed his wife: 'Wood is one of the South Wales Members, a very good natured very silly brother in law of ... Castlereagh, who resides but little in Wales but has a great love for speechifying'.[6] Criticizing him for denigrating the language while defending the people, the Nonconformist periodical *Seren Gomer* commented that a thorough knowledge of the language would make Wood better qualified to represent a Welsh county.[7]

As regular member of select committees on issues affecting the poor, Wood condemned the labourers' wages bill as a 'restrictive' measure, 23 June 1820. Fraternising with the South Wales industrialists, he warned the ironmaster Samuel Homfray†, a kinsman by marriage of the Morgans and his putative opponent in Breconshire in 1806, that the Grand Junction Canal Company wanted to incorporate a clause authorizing high tolls on iron in the 1820 Western Union Canal bill, and he entertained Lewis Weston Dillwyn† of Penlle'rgaer in the Commons, when legislation against smoke and noxious emissions was broached, 6 July 1820.[8] Amid strong constituency support for Queen Caroline, he avoided declaring his views, but declined to present addresses to her. He distanced himself from the Breconshire meeting of 20 Jan. 1821, which attached parliamentary reform and distress to her cause, and petitioned urging the dismissal of ministers.[9] Instead, with Camden and the lord lieutenant, the 6th duke of Beaufort, he procured and publicized a loyal address attributing distress and unrest to 'inflammatory declamations at public meetings' and 'the increasing activity and unrestrained operation of a licentious, disloyal and perverted press'.[10] He presented but dissented from the Breconshire petition, confident that 'the tide is turned' and 'honour, virtue and loyalty triumphant', 14 Feb., having divided against censuring ministers' handling of the queen's case, 6 Feb. 1821.[11] Afterwards, he consulted his fellow Middlesex magistrates on relevant points of law and steered the 1821 Breconshire Bridges Act through the Commons.[12] He criticized the reductions proposed by the opposition 'Mountain' and defended the proposed expenditure on the cavalry, the militia and

the Royal Military Academy, 20 Feb., 14, 30 Mar., 30 Apr. 1821. Opposing the malt duty repeal bill, 3 Apr., he acknowledged that the tax 'pressed hard on the poor', but accused the Whigs of trying to undermine the government's resources through a systematic assault on all taxes. Nevertheless, he declared that he would be prepared to consider lowering the tax on malt, should the 'great error' of repealing the property tax be reversed. His well-publicized campaign to extend the tax exemption for husbandry horses to ponies used in the South Wales iron industry failed, 18, 21 June. He again claimed to be representing South Wales interests when opposing the steam engines bill, 7 May, and the Wolverhampton petition against itinerant traders, 'without whom his part of the country would be imperfectly supplied with necessary articles', 21 June.[13] Advocating reform of the game laws, 'an evil which filled our gaols with peasantry and laid the foundation of so many crimes', he attributed the recent upsurge in offences to the failure of the 1810 select committee to endorse his recommendations, 5 Apr. 1821. In September, the courtier Lord Graves* complimented him on the arrangements made for receiving George IV at Brecon, where he broke his journey from Ireland to London following the queen's death.[14] At Monmouth the following month Wood lent his support to Beaufort and his partisans.[15]

Wood divided with government on distress and taxation, 11, 21 Feb., including against abolition of one of the joint-postmasterships, 13 Mar. 1822.[16] He thought that transferring the tax on tallow would 'materially benefit' the depressed cattle trade, 22 Feb., and suggested that the proposed duty on malt 'would teach the public to brew their own beer', 16 Mar. Although he had advocated lowering the salt tax since 1817, he refused to commit himself on the issue in February 1822 and explained that he would divide with government, 28 June, as 'I always vote upon principle against isolated motions for repeal of taxes'. He reaffirmed his opposition to military reductions, 4, 20 Mar., and supported the mutiny bill, 12 Mar., but moved unsuccessfully for a £10,000 reduction in the grant to barrack masters, 29 Mar. He seconded the vagrancy laws amendment bill, which he claimed would relieve the country of the expense of passing vagrants from parish to parish, 31 May, and promised to support Scarlett's poor removal bill that day. Convinced that 'locking up' the poor in parishes increased their demoralization while distorting the labour market, he announced his own resolutions on settlement, 23 July, but they had to be held over as the House was poorly attended, 30 July. He pressed successfully with John Calcraft for the withdrawal of a clause in the alehouse licensing bill, authorizing appeals to quarter sessions against petty sessions decisions, 27 June. Backed by Williams Wynn, now president of the India board, Wood resisted inquiry into the Middlesex court of requests in view of the lateness of the session and because the Middlesex Members had not presented the petition advocating it, 19 June 1822. However, in 1824 he failed to prevent the prosecution of the court's clerk Heath, and his deputy Dubois, who were found guilty of taking excessive fees.[17] Wood was deeply distressed by the suicide of Lord Londonderry (Castlereagh) in August 1822, 'an awful lesson', which, writing to his eldest son Thomas Wood (1804-72), the future Middlesex Member, he attributed to 'incessant labour' and failure to keep the Sabbath as a day of rest. It was an ordnance Wood always observed and cautioned his sons against breaking, whatever career they should pursue.[18]

As his brother-in-law the 3rd marquess of Londonderry had predicted, Wood decided against jeopardizing Tom's Horse Guards career by voting for the amendment to the address, condemning the peacetime appointment of Canning's ally Beresford as lieutenant-general of the ordnance, 4 Feb. 1823.[19] He criticized Wolryche Whitmore's corn law proposals as likely to 'unsettle the mind of the country' and encourage unrest, 26 Feb., and denounced Nolan's proposed bill for the employment and maintenance of the poor as a coercive measure, 4 Mar., but failed to proceed with his own resolutions until 4 June, when, despite some encouragement from the Whig Lord Althorp and Scarlett, the sliding scale he suggested (leading to guaranteed settlement after 15 years residence) proved so unpopular with Members representing the industrial North, that on the home secretary Peel's advice he withdrew them and circulated a draft bill for consideration the following session. He opposed the tax cuts sought by opposition, 3 Mar., but deemed the sinking fund 'unnecessary' and criticized the national debt reduction bill, 6, 13 Mar. He declined attendance at the Breconshire distress meeting, 11 Apr., but presented their petition, 29 Apr., and one from Staines for repeal of the corn duties, 5 May.[20] He disagreed with the chancellor of the exchequer Robinson's decision to reduce the price of beer, 25 Apr., succeeded by 45-16 with an amendment raising the tax on strong beer from 27s. to 30s. a barrel, and opposed the proposed reduction in the price of malt, 28 May, maintaining that it would have little effect on beer prices and cause great suffering to farmers. He voted against reforming the Scottish representative system, 2 June. When Allen, his colleague on the 1820 and 1821 committees, moved for reform of the Welsh judicature, 23

May, Wood, unlike ministers, supported him, declaring that he had changed his mind 'from conviction' as a result of Wales's increased prosperity. He voted in the minority for recommitting Fowell Buxton's silk manufacture bill, 9 June, at the behest of Spitalfields weavers who had served his militia regiment well. He presented Breconshire anti-slavery petitions, 26 June 1823. When in July Camden and Londonderry considered a political alliance, the latter predicted that Wood 'will be as little the follower of you as of me'.[21]

In view of constituency opposition to funding alterations required under the 1823 Consolidated Gaol Act, Wood called on Beaufort on his way to the Brecon October assizes, and in December took advice from colleagues on the Middlesex bench.[22] In the House, 19 Feb. 1824, he asked Peel to exempt Wales from certain clauses in the Act, citing the cases of Radnorshire, where the gaol had only two cells and one prisoner, and Breconshire, where the estimated cost of a treadmill and alterations was '£3,000, or the amount of four county rates'. The Glamorganshire Member Sir Christopher Cole supported him, but Peel thought 'the difficulty might be met by three or four Welsh counties combining to erect a prison for themselves' and no concession was granted. Giving his customary endorsement of military flogging, 5 Mar., Wood expressed regret that the 1823 Act permitted the use of treadmills in 'common gaols' for imprisoned soldiers.[23] He objected to a clause in Stuart Wortley's game bill depriving landlords and lessees or manor lords of their shooting rights, supported an amendment safeguarding them, and strongly opposed the punishment proposed for night poachers (which was later withdrawn), 12 Apr. Nevertheless, he spoke and was a minority teller with Stuart Wortley against postponing the bill's recommittal, 31 May. Wood presented the Radnorshire sheep farmers' petition for drawbacks on imported wool, 25 Mar. He considered Althorp's settlement bill unsatisfactory 'as an isolated measure' and proposed amending it by adding a clause giving settlement 'to all persons who paid poor rates in the parish in which they had paid them' 30 Mar. He conceded that the opposition of the large manufacturing towns made the passage of his own measure impossible and bemoaned the facility with which young people from agricultural parishes were 'enticed away' and young women returned pregnant, to become 'encumbrances upon their former parishes'. Resisting change, he argued that the capital of the British farmer was still in very poor condition despite high corn prices, and suggested postponing the president of the board of trade Huskisson's warehoused wheat bill until the state of the next harvest was known, 17

May. He presented Minehead's petition for repeal of the duty on coal carried coastwise, 16 Feb. When the London (Middlesex) coal duties were considered, 1 Apr. 1824, he complained that the debate was deliberately confined to the rival monopolistic claims of the Staffordshire and Northern coal owners and objected to any system of pithead tolls. He added that he preferred light to fire and, cautioning against pressing the chancellor too far, he suggested repealing the window tax or 'some tax of more general and impartial operation ... the abolition of which would have been more consonant with the principles of free trade'. That autumn he took his family to Wales, where George Rice Trevor* sought to dissuade him from taking his wife canvassing lest his bride should have to do the same.[24]

He confirmed his preference for qualification by 'a mixed calculation of property and rating' when a new settlement bill was proposed, 22 Mar. 1825. Breconshire and Glamorganshire entrusted their petitions for the free movement of fish to him for presentation, as a member of the 1824 and 1825 select committees, 29 Mar. He divided for the Irish unlawful societies bill, 25 Feb., but refrained from voting on Catholic relief in deference to his constituents, and presented a hostile petition from the hundred of Brennig, 18 Apr. 1825. Opposing corn law revision, 28 Apr., he asserted that its detractors confused the achievements of the 1815 Act with those of the 1822 agriculture committee, and that the 'fraudulent practice of returning fictitious averages ought not to be laid upon the present system'. He objected to a fixed duty on principle, preferring a 70s. or 65s. pivot price and a 17s. tariff. He used similar protectionist arguments against admitting Canadian grains, 2 May 1825. He travelled to Brecon for the assizes when a dissolution was anticipated in September and stayed on to steward the October race meeting.[25] Wood seconded an unsuccessful amendment against proceeding with the case against the Welsh judge and Surrey magistrate William Kenrick†, 17 Feb. 1826. The Warwick lion fight induced him to support legislation against cruel sports, 21 Feb. He voiced his customary support for expenditure on the barracks and Royal Military College, 6 Mar., and presented a petition for restoration of the 8s. daily allowance to retired militia adjutants, 22 Mar. 1826, (and another, 6 June 1827). He presented Breconshire anti-slavery petitions, 8, 22 Mar. 1826. Opposing the Welsh Mining Company bill later that day with the Staffordshire Member Littleton, he described it as a 'great evil', likely to 'increase the competition to a mischievous extent', and unnecessary, because of the abundance

of iron. He was not convinced that changes to the Corn Importation Act, introduced in the wake of the London petition for a fixed duty, would alleviate distress, and instead suggested appointing a select committee to settle the corn question 'at once', 2 May. He added that provided this was done he had no objection to lowering the pivot price to 70s. or 65s. and releasing bonded corn at a 12s. duty. The Whig Lord Milton opposed his suggestion. Peel and Canning countered his objections to the government's corn importation bill, 8, 11 May, when Canning challenged him to deny that he had agreed to a 65s. pivot price. He was prevailed upon to vote for the bill's second reading that day, but resolutely maintained that 'a free trade with a fixed duty ... [was] extremely objectionable', a graduated scale inefficient, and a fixed duty no more than a short-term solution. In committee, 12 May, he suggested, but did not proceed with an amendment for a 65s. pivot price. He thought that the information Edmond Wodehouse sought from the foreign office with a view to improving the statistical base for the averages should be qualified with details of production costs, 18 May. He left for Breconshire, where he was in dispute with Sir Charles Morgan over the rights to Llangors Pool, directly Parliament was dissolved in June 1826.[26] His return that month was unopposed and his speech at Brecon largely devoted to describing his work as a Member.[27] At the Brecon eisteddfod in September he endeavoured to reassure supporters of the Welsh language that the Breconshire aristocracy were not against its cultivation.[28]

He approved the ministry's decision to implement the Corn Importation Acts by order in council and urged the House to put an end to 'the aggravating attempts of the press to dissever the manufacturing and agricultural interests', 24 Nov. 1826. Saddened and angered by Whig-led opposition to Clarence's grant, Wood spoke, 16 Feb., and voted in favour of the award, 14 Mar. 1827. He reiterated his protectionist principles in the corn debates that month, following Lord Liverpool's stroke. He said that he was inclined to support the import scale proposed in the government's corn bill although he considered the prices too low, 1 Mar., objected to the use of the Winchester bushel for taking averages, 8 Mar., spoke out against taking the price of peas, beans, and rye into account, 19 Mar., and called for averages to be taken over six weeks not one, 26 Mar. He divided for the bill, 2 Apr., hoping to amend it in committee, but had to withdraw his amendment extending the prohibition on imports, 6 Apr. He had earlier been denied a hearing amid the clamour that greeted reports of Canning's likely succession as premier. He called for protection by 'prohibitions rather than regulation' when the Canning ministry's warehoused corn bill was committed, 21 June, and approved their resolution for a 70s. corn pivot price, 18 June.[29] During Canning's ministry Wood also assisted with the passage of the Glamorgan roads bill, which emulated the Breconshire system by establishing a single countywide trust, served on the Ludlow election committee and objected to the receipt of Edmund Lechmere Charlton's[†] petition against its findings, 14 May, and defended the award to the national vaccine establishment, 14 May. He introduced his game laws suspension bill, 17 May, and, supported by Milton and Wodehouse, carried its second reading on the 30th by 56-2, and secured its committal, despite objections from Sir Gilbert Heathcote and supporters of a rival bill introduced in the Lords, 7 June; but the report was deferred, 20 June, and it was timed out. He endorsed Robert Gordon's call for a select committee on provisions for pauper lunatics in Middlesex and was appointed to it, 13 June 1827.

During the first supply debate of the duke of Wellington's ministry, in which Hardinge was clerk of the ordnance, 18 Feb. 1828, Wood refuted Lord Normanby's claim that Canning had openly attributed his South American policy to Castlereagh and expressed confidence in the government. He called for an end to

> all such contrasts and such expressions as 'that Mr. Canning's party is scattered to the winds' ... The grave should be a protection against such expressions ... I will only add, that, after hearing all I have heard about the blowing up, as it has been termed, of the late administration, I think the House had better cease to look backward and turn their eyes toward the present administration.

He condemned the practice of supplementing wages from the poor rates and sought a wider brief for the select committee on parochial settlement he was appointed to, 21 Feb., adding that if no one 'better qualified ... could be found', he would move to have the 'question of the poor laws generally' referred to it. He agreed with Burdett that assisting the emigration of the Irish poor was as important an Anglo-Irish issue as the Catholic question or free trade and cited the Harrow labour auction as proof of the degradation the poor laws created, 4 Mar. He had little to say on Macqueen's abortive bill to end settlement by hiring, 29 Apr., but he ordered returns of removal orders and of quarter session appeals, and was added to the select committee on the poor laws, 3 June. Wood presented his constituents' petitions for repeal of the Test Acts, 25 Feb., and published denials after being listed in the government minority against it, 26 Feb.

1828.[30] He disapproved of spending on Irish education and the commission's work, 28 Feb., and was named to the committee that considered their reports, 11 Mar. As in 1822 and 1829, he was appointed to the select committee on policing the metropolis, 28 Feb., when, commenting on the state of Newgate and other prisons, he called for individual cells, separate prisons for commitment and correction, and an end to the Middlesex-Westminster rivalry, which precluded sharing resources, although the authorities had many magistrates in common. On 10 Mar., goaded by Lord Nugent, he denied ever arguing that the 'salutary effects' of flogging would benefit grown men as well as schoolboys, and spoke of its importance to the army as a deterrent, which, when applied as an early punishment, had saved at least two young men under his command from vice. He was in favour of limiting the duration of tithe commutation agreements (a contentious issue in his manor of Glasbury and the hundred of Builth), 17 Mar., and presented and endorsed Breconshire's petition for amendment of the 1827 Malt Act, to permit earlier wetting of corn, 20 Mar. On behalf of Spitalfields weavers, he seconded and was a minority teller for ending the prohibition on the use of ribbons at elections, a 'harmless demonstration of public feeling'. He suggested that if the House was serious about curbing election costs it should restrict the franchise to residents. He recommended postponing Althorp's freeholders registration bill, 25 Mar., and said that he would oppose its second reading, because it would increase election costs and did not provide for simultaneous polling by district. Challenged by Hume, he said he did not consider the government's corn resolutions a party matter, 31 Mar., but he was confident that their bill would 'protect the interests of agriculture' and that the proposed 58s. pivot price would 'turn out to be a prohibitory duty', 25 Apr. He presented Breconshire petitions against concessions to Catholics, 28 Apr., and for protective tariffs on wool, 16 May.[31] Assisting Hardinge, on whose select committee he had served, he said he was confident that the government's decision to implement militia reductions was correct and well founded, 20 June. When goaded, he defended the reputation of his 1,200 Middlesex troops and pressed for continued recruitment by ballot. Supporting ministers, he gave a detailed technical explanation of why the post of lieutenant-general of the ordnance should be retained, 4 July 1828. He had recently assisted at the Durham by-election necessitated by Hardinge's appointment as secretary at war, and he became an intermediary during the recess between Wellington, the king and Clarence, who had to resign as lord high admiral.[32]

Wood sent Wellington a draft oath designed to protect 'the Protestant church establishment', and the patronage secretary Planta predicted in February 1829 that he would divide 'with government' for Catholic emancipation.[33] Asked to support the borough of Brecon's hostile petition, he endorsed it as respectably signed and 'temperate and conciliatory' in language, 3 Mar., but reserved 'the opportunity of delivering my opinions' on the measure.[34] He did not vote on the introduction of the relief bill, 6 Mar., but he summarized it and the securities offered at a predominantly anti-Catholic county meeting in Brecon on the 9th. He also reaffirmed his commitment to representing their views and supporting the hostile petition adopted.[35] Referring to it on presenting another from the hundred of Pencelli, 16 Mar., he explained that he could no longer be 'strictly neutral' and was 'bound' to oppose emancipation. He acknowledged that

some ... may consider it unconstitutional and wrong on my part to have given such a pledge, but, having had the benefit of it for some years, I cannot do otherwise now than fulfil what I consider to be an honourable engagement with my constituents.

He divided against the bill, 18 Mar., but reminded the Ultra Sir Edward Knatchbull that he did so 'reluctantly in obedience to his constituents'. He delayed presenting the Breconshire petition until 26 Mar., when it could be received with the county's pro-emancipation petition entrusted to the Whig Edward Smith Stanley, who, as Wood had been forewarned, questioned the provenance of the anti-Catholic petition.[36] The recorder of Brecon Hugh Bold, who liaised with Wood and Smith Stanley, wrote to the latter, 4 Apr., 'poor Wood had not a word to say in answer. I cannot bring myself to pity a person who sits for this county [except] to voting according to his conscience'.[37]

Wood called for game sales to be made legal and an end to differential treatment of the rich and poor under the game laws, 6 Apr., and defended spending on the militia, 4 May. He pressed for the recommittal of the labourers' wages bill, 15 May, commended it as the work of the 1828 committee and argued that by attempting to end magistrates' wage scales and payments from poor rates, it separated the poor laws, of which he approved, from 'the evils ... grafted on them'. He suggested raising the proposed householder rating threshold from £6 to £10, helped to secure the withdrawal of a clause permitting parish overseers to contract for the employment of the poor, and carried an amendment making owners (not occupiers) of tenements rated at £10-£12 liable for rate payments. His objections to proceeding with the anatomy regula-

tion bill that day were ignored. He attended the Pitt dinner as Lord Mansfield's guest, 28 May.[38] In July Wellington refused to make his brother a metropolitan police commissioner.[39] Wood had informed the 1828 justice commission that he and his constituents supported abolition of the Welsh courts of great session and judicature; but he realized when their report also recommended partitioning and amalgamating counties to form new circuits, that this would be strongly resisted, particularly in Breconshire, where, under the tripartite county division proposed, Brecon forfeited its assize town status.[40] When Brougham urged Peel to introduce a bill based on the report that session, 4 May 1829, Wood predicted that Breconshire would petition against it, accused the commissioners of reporting 'without having any notion of the localities', and prevailed on Peel to pre-empt opposition by circulating a draft bill and letting it 'mature' preparatory to legislating the following session.[41] He shared Thomas Frankland Lewis's distaste for a union of Breconshire and Radnorshire, and in a bid to avoid it sought support from the 2nd marquess of Bute, as lord lieutenant of Glamorgan, for uniting that county with Breconshire and holding assizes alternately at Brecon and Cardiff.[42] He also met the leading abolitionists Dillwyn and Cawdor in London to discuss strategy, and chaired the September assizes at Brecon, where he dissuaded the magistrates from petitioning.[43]

Wood acknowledged that suffering was rife, but suggested that the time of the House would be better spent seeking remedies for distress than discussing an amendment protesting at its omission from the address, which served only to highlight party differences, 4 Feb. 1830. To cries of 'Where?', he claimed that distress was already on the wane, when the revived Whig opposition cited it as a reason for abolishing the office of lieutenant-general of the ordnance, which he voted to retain, 29 Mar. He divided against Lord Blandford's reform scheme, 18 Feb., and the enfranchisement of Birmingham, Leeds and Manchester, 23 Feb. He presented private petitions against the Brechfa road and Swansea gas bills, 17, 18 Mar., and another on the 23rd for extending the provisions of the Breconshire roads bill.[44] Speaking on assisted emigration for the poor that day, he repeated that 'a great part of the evils attributed to the poor laws arise from their maladministration' and cited regional variations to prove his point. He supported the Scottish and Irish poor removal bill, 26 May, and when its opponents pointed to the threat it posed to Middlesex and the metropolis, he cited the lack of legislation for Welsh migrants as proof that none was necessary. He voted against Jewish emancipation, 5 Apr., 17 May. He spoke highly of Ellenborough and was a majority teller for his divorce bill, 6 Apr. 1830. 'As a Welsh Member' Wood strenuously supported the 1830 administration of justice bill, by whose enactment the courts of great sessions and Welsh judicature were abolished. He acknowledged the bill's inherent weakness, 27 Apr., but claimed that all opposition to it would cease if judges appointed by the lord chancellor were sent to hear the assizes in every county town, and reminded ministers that uniting English and Welsh counties was perceived as an even greater evil than combining Welsh ones. Drawing parallels with an Englishman facing trial in France, he also stressed the need for juries to be Welsh, 'not out of prejudice', but because 'most of the evidence given by the lower classes of the people on criminal trials is given in Welsh'. He repeated his objections to the proposed division and consolidation of counties, 27 May, 18 June, and defended the rights of court officials to compensation, 5 July. The Carmarthen reformer George Thomas held Wood personally responsible for securing the late government amendment that left the existing assize structure almost intact when the bill was hurriedly enacted immediately before the dissolution precipitated by George IV's death.[45] During the king's illness, his family and ministers had drawn on Wood's connection with Hardinge and Clarence to obtain information on the latter's political sentiments. Meanwhile he had echoed ministers' opposition to the continuation of offices bill, 10 May, and cutting the grant for South American missions, 7 June, and voted against abolishing the death penalty for forgery.[46] His return at the 1830 general election was never in doubt. Addressing the freeholders afterwards he explained that William IV favoured economy, retrenchment and reform, while he disliked reform 'in any shape or form' and regarded election by ballot as 'poking beans into boxes'.[47]

The Wellington ministry naturally listed Wood among their 'friends' and he divided with them on the civil list when they were brought down, 15 Nov. 1830. He blamed Parliament for permitting the 1830 game bill to lapse and remained as anxious as ever to see legislation enacted that permitted game sales, applied to all classes, and enabled property owners to permit whomever they pleased to sport on their land. He accordingly welcomed Lord Chandos's game bill, although he conceded that it was hopelessly encumbered with detail, 7 Dec. He presented several Breconshire antislavery petitions the same day. Commenting on the budget, 11 Feb. 1831, he said he had to agree with the radical Henry Hunt that a reduction in malt duty would be of greater benefit to the poor than cuts in the tobacco tax, adding that it would also serve as a deter-

rent to illicit brewing and distilling mixtures of barley and malt. Following the introduction of the Grey ministry's reform bill, which he did not expect to pass 'in its present form', Wood corresponded regularly at length with his Breconshire agent John Jones of Glan Honddu, in order to ascertain his constituents' views and to ensure that his own were not misrepresented. He was granted five days' leave on account of ill health (an attack of gout), 16 Mar.[48] He divided for the bill at its second reading, 22 Mar., and explained when the Cambridge University petition urging moderation was presented, 30 Mar., that he had done so, that the House 'might proceed with caution and circumspection', and because he did not think it right to cut short the progress of so important a bill. Breconshire reformers welcomed his vote, but complained that his speech was 'bob ochr' (two sided) and called a county meeting to petition for the bill and warn Wood that half-hearted support for reform would not do.[49] 'Not a little mortified' to find his contribution to carrying the bill by a single vote 'so little appreciated', and 'because every gentleman must see that a representative so shackled is no longer a free agent and can no longer be a Member of a *deliberative* body, calmly and constitutionally considering the welfare and the interests of his constituents',[50] he informed his Breconshire friends that he would oppose any reduction in the number of English Members, and left them to address the county on his behalf:[51]

You may make them quite easy on the state of their own borough [Brecon], for the opening of which, and all other boroughs, I shall most decidedly give my vote. But I am quite sure they are not aware of the details of the proposed bill, and I believe there is scarce a man all round this part of the country that is not of opinion that the bill must be materially amended. The bill as at present drawn ... *extinguishes 70* English representatives and *adds to the number of Irish Members. This I never will vote for.* Ireland and its present Members with Mr. O'Connell at their head gives us trouble sufficient already. This is a mill stone round our necks and keeps us in an eternal state of expense and anxiety and pays almost nothing to the taxes. Last year, when the chancellor of the exchequer of the day [Goulburn] tried to make a more equitable arrangement, the whole 100 Irish Members united to resist them, and they would unite again at this moment if a modified property tax was proposed ... [and] make England pay the whole of that burden. As long as this is the feeling of Irishmen I am quite sure we ought not to add to their power in the ... Commons by reducing the number of English representatives. I will vote for a full, fair and efficient measure of reform. Every borough that shall continue to send Members to Parliament after the passing of the bill shall no longer be closed as it is at present ... I will not consent to rob freemen of their birthrights ... All that part of the bill which goes to the register of votes and the annual circuits of our assessors would be useless and would inflict on all counties very heavy annual expense ... When the bill gets into committee I will do my best to render it an efficient measure and to divest it of its several inconsistencies. I will also, previous to its being committed, state fully in the House my view of the whole of the arrangement, but I must say if every word I am *reported* to have said is to be productive of a county meeting it is not much encouragement to say anything, or much incitement to the active performance of one's public duties ... None of the papers that I have seen ... accurately reported what I did say on the Cambridge petition ... What I did say was certainly cheered *by both sides of the House*, giving as I thought general satisfaction. Thus, if I cannot open my mouth without sending a written report of my speech to the papers I will cease to speak at all, for I cannot believe that is a very creditable way of making my opinions known to the public ... The constant study of my life has been to do my duty by those who have done me the honour for so many years to send me to Parliament, and my sole object and wish is to be considered by them a faithful, honest and independent representative.[52]

He received the Breconshire petition, 18 Apr., but failed to secure an opportunity to present it.[53] Supporting Gascoyne's wrecking amendment that day, he tried to explain, amid great clamour, that he had voted for the bill, with all its shortcomings, at its second reading 'because I conscientiously believe that the time is arrived when some reform is rendered absolutely necessary', but that he felt compelled 'as an independent English Member to vote against the reduction of any one [English] representative'. Next day he sent offprints of his speech from the *Mirror of Parliament* to Brecon for circulation, and divided for the amendment.[54] Deeming it 'best to be prepared for war', by the 23rd he had sent canvassing notices to the printer, engaged counsel, issued retainers, and directed his agent 'to fix the day of election as *early as possible*'. A declaration of satisfaction with his conduct as a Member was also in train.[55] The contest, a two-day poll which kept him from Littleton when his father's life was feared for and put him to great trouble and expense, was not, as anticipated, against his erstwhile proposer Penry Williams of Penypont, but his brother Charles's brother-in-law, John Lloyd Vaughan Watkins[†] of Penoyre, who started too late to have a reasonable prospect of success, but was supported by the Merthyr Tydfil reformers.[56] *The Times* accused Wood of trying to get rid of reform 'by a side wind' and attributed his success to Beaufort, Camden and Sir Charles Morgan's agents.[57] Complimenting John Jones on carrying 'the Colonel through his dif-

ficulties', the Merthyr ironmaster John Josiah Guest[*] added: 'I was decidedly against him upon principle, but should have been really sorry to have *voted* against him. Nothing but the casting vote and sincerity would have induced me to do so'.[58]

Wood declined a household appointment in order to sit unfettered, though he took a militia post and Lady Caroline became a lady-in-waiting to the queen. As the king expected, he voted for the reintroduced reform bill at its second reading, 6 July.[59] The reformers persisted with their Breconshire canvass, erroneously believing that Wood would be made a coronation peer. Adhering to his 'bob ochr' strategy, he was one of ten critics of the bill who voted to proceed with it committee and to hear counsel on the Appleby petition, 12 July.[60] He informed Jones, 13 July:

> I shall vote for the transfer of all the weak and decayed boroughs to populous places, but *we must ascertain that they are so*. Appleby, about which we debated last night, has in the returns not only one of its townships omitted, but it is a burgage tenure borough and the *court house* and *several of the burgage houses* are situated in the parish that is thus omitted and the population of 1821 not 1831 amounted to 2,650 ... The taking away *one seat* from a class of boroughs and giving one seat to a class of towns, I decidedly oppose. Lord Milton has given notice of a motion for each place having two Members and so it ought; if it is otherwise instead of one boon to a place we should plant in every town a bone of election contention that would prove the greatest curse that could be inflicted on them. The right of voting in towns I think had better be for long lease £10 owners and £20 occupiers in England and £8 owners and £12 occupiers in Wales. Col. Davies has also given notice of a motion that all the freeholders of the towns should vote for the boroughs, which I think is desirable. I shall certainly propose that long holders should be enfranchised down to 40s. This is my idea of reform and this I firmly believe will be satisfactory to the country. I am sure it ought to be so. We had last night a second vote of time on the question of adjournment. From two until seven this morn the contest went on. I did all I could to bring them to terms without success. I voted with the ministers against the adjournments. If I could have got an opportunity I was anxious to have stated my opinion on the bill but there are so many speakers I did not succeed and now I shall not do so until we get into committee.[61]

He made several of these points in his speech that day against starting with the disfranchisement clause, 'one of the most objectionable in the whole bill, which, by ending the freeman, scot and lot and householder vote, left the lower orders without any means of enfranchisement', drawing 'a broad line through society which did not exist before', and explained that he disagreed 'on principle' with the creation of one and three Member constituencies. He voted to make the 1831 census the determinant of English borough disfranchisements, 19 July, against including Downton, 21 July, and St. Germans, 26 July in schedule A, and consistently against the schedule B disfranchisements. When these had been carried, he suggested using 'those 112 seats at our disposal' to give two Members to towns with populations above 12,000 and to 'increase the representation of populous counties', 2 Aug. He expressed concern that day at the way government was forcing though 'the whole bill', and his formal protest that the creation of metropolitan boroughs violated the principle of the bill paved the way for the anti-reformers' trial of strength on the enfranchisement of Greenwich, 3 Aug., which ministers carried by 295-188. He had proposed making Middlesex a six Member county with a 40s. copyhold and freehold franchise, three divisions and Tower Hamlets, Brentford and Hackney as polling towns, and suggested similar arrangements for Kent and Surrey to avoid enfranchising Greenwich, Deptford and Lambeth. He had decided by 8 July to curry local support by campaigning for the separate enfranchisement of Merthyr Tydfil, a contributory designate of Cardiff, which extended into Breconshire at Cefn-Coed-y-Cymer.[62] As announced, 5, 6, 9 Aug., when Welsh contributory boroughs were considered on the 10th, he moved to exclude Merthyr Tydfil from the Cardiff group, but was defeated by 164-123. South Wales Members of all parties supported him. Fearing that his speech would be misreported, he again sent copies of the *Mirror of Parliament* to Brecon.[63] He spoke and voted against three Member counties, 1, 12 Aug., but in favour of dividing counties, 11 Aug. He moved unsuccessfully for a 40s. county copyholder franchise as a means of encouraging the 'lower classes to aim at independence', 17 Aug., and, to Lord Chandos's annoyance, he countered his amendment for the enfranchisement of £50 tenants-at will, 18 Aug., by calling for all occupiers of farms worth £50 a year to be given the vote. He criticized the registration clauses, particularly the provisions for non-resident voters, 19, 25, 27 Aug., 2, 5 Sept., and was in the small minority on clause 27, governing polling arrangements, 2 Sept., having earlier created a stir by suggesting a system linked to the poor rate assessments. He divided against the bill's passage, 21 Sept. The bells were rung when, to counter local opposition, he and his family arrived in Brecon, 8 Oct. 1831. After presiding at the sessions, he hosted a Brecon dinner at which he justified his recent parliamentary conduct, taking care as previously to send local newspapers copies of his speech.[64]

Wood had 'no problem voting for the second reading' of the revised reform bill, 17 Dec. 1831, though he still found it 'clogged with complicated details that will, I fear, very much impede its passage into law'. He restated his objections to altering the quotas of English, Irish and Scottish Members, settling disfranchisement before enfranchisement, metropolitan districts, single Members English boroughs and 'lump sum votes on each Schedule'. As amendments, he suggested a separate registration bill, using Lieutenant Drummond's disfranchisement scale, confining the urban franchise to residents while preserving the rights of freeman, scot and lot, and householder voters, and replacing the £10 land tax with the £10 poor rate qualification.[65] Acting independently of others pressing Merthyr Tydfil's claim, he promised to raise it again, 23 Jan. 1832. He disapproved of the late decision to award a third Member to Monmouthshire, when its boroughs had only one, 27 Jan., and repeated his criticisms of the proposed franchise qualifications, 1, 3, 8, 10, 11, 20 Feb. He voted against introducing single-day polling in boroughs with under 1,200 voters, 15 Feb., and against enfranchising Tower Hamlets, 28 Feb. Co-operating with Lord Granville Somerset and Bute's brother Lord James Crichton Stuart, he presented Merthyr Tydfil's petition for separate representation, 20 Feb., and tried to have it substituted for Gateshead in Schedule D, 5 Mar.[66] Government hostility ensured failure (by 214-167), but the compelling demographic and economic arguments he cited and his references to the role of the chapels in curbing political union activity after the 1831 riots contributed to the government's awkward decision to award it the additional Member intended for Monmouthshire, 14 Mar. He voted to enfranchise Merthyr Tydfil, but protested that he had been made 'a scapegoat'. He was also a minority teller against depriving Monmouthshire of a third Member, 14 Mar.[67] In a speech intended for both the House and his constituents, 20 Mar. (which the *Mirror of Parliament* corrected to coincide with the report in the *Morning Herald*), he said he was disappointed with the amendments made to the bill and would vote against its third reading because of the threat it posed to the country and constitution through the schedule B disfranchisements and its provisions for metropolitan districts. He supported the rotten borough disfranchisements, enfranchising large towns and extending the suffrage, and said that he had been against taking its third Member from Monmouthshire 'because he thought the interests of agriculture in that county ought not to be diminished'. His elderly father and Lady Caroline were both seriously ill, rendering Commons attendance difficult, and he was listed in both the absentee and minority lists on the bill's third reading, 22 Mar. 1832.[68] He divided against government on the Russian-Dutch loan, 12 July 1832. In August the colonial secretary Lord Goderich rejected his patronage requests.[69]

Standing as a Conservative and assisted by his sons, Wood pledged support for the established church and Sabbatarianism, advocated the abolition of slavery, factory regulation and an equitable composition of tithes and came in for Breconshire unopposed in December 1832.[70] He retained the seat until he retired to avoid defeat in 1847, after supporting Peel's decision to repeal the corn laws.[71] He afterwards published pamphlets outlining his views on free trade, pauper settlement and the poor laws.[72] He had inherited an estimated £88,000 on succeeding his father to Littleton in 1835, and correctly turned down William IV's offer to make him a knight of the Guelphic Order that year, because he had never served abroad with his regiment.[73] He died at Littleton in January 1860 and was succeeded there by Tom. His will, proved in 1860 and 1861, honoured and extended family settlements made in favour of his wife and descendents, who, after Littleton was destroyed by fire in 1874, settled at Gwernyfed.[74]

[1] PROB 11/1848/399; IR26/1404/284; *Gent. Mag.* (1837), ii. 199; LMA ACC/1302, Schedule, p. 2; T. Jones, *Hist. Brec.* iv. 275-6; E. Wood, *Thomas Wood*, passim. [2] NLW, Tredegar mss 45/1506; 121/792, 852, 854; 135/764, 765, 768, 775, 777; P.D.G. Thomas, 'Parl. Elections in Brec. 1689-1832', *Brycheiniog*, vi (1960), 99-113; E.G. Parry, 'County Election of 1818', *Brycheiniog*, xxvii (1994-5), 79-109; *HP Commons, 1790-1820*, ii. 482-3. [3] *Cambrian*, 26 Feb., 4, 11, 18 Mar. 1820. [4] *HP Commons, 1790-1820*, v. 648-50; D. Jones, *Brecknock Historian*, 11; NLW, Gwernyfed mss, parcel 36, passim. [5] NLW, Maybery mss 6906. Arrangements for Wood to receive his Carmarthen franchise were completed in September 1824 (ibid. 6556). [6] NLW, Coedymaen mss 939. [7] *Seren Gomer*, iii (1820), 219-21. [8] *HP Commons, 1790-1820*, iv. 219-20; Tredegar mss 45/1520; *Diary of Lewis Weston Dillwyn* ed. H.J. Randall and W. Rees (S. Wales and Mon. Rec. Soc. v), 41. [9] *Cambrian*, 28 Oct., 4 Nov. 1820; *Hereford Jnl.* 10, 17, 24 Jan.; *Seren Gomer*, iv (1821), 61-62. [10] Maybery mss 6545, 6547-6548, 6550, 6822-6823, 6862-6863, 6919; *Courier*, 20, 31 Jan. 1821. [11] *The Times*, 15 Feb.; Maybery mss 6920. [12] Maybery mss 6544, 6922; *Brecknock Historian*, 29, 39. [13] *The Times*, 19, 22 June; *Seren Gomer*, iv (1821), 222. [14] LMA ACC/1302/108, 199, 200. [15] *Bristol Mercury*, 20 Oct. 1821. [16] *Seren Gomer*, v (1822), 91, 124. [17] *The Times*, 9 Jan., 10, 13 Feb., 14 May 1824. [18] LMA ACC/1302/201; E. Wood, 'Col. Thomas Wood', *Brecon and Radnor Express*, 4 July 1974. [19] Norf. RO, Blickling Hall mss, Lord to Lady Londonderry, 14, 29 Dec. 1822, Hardinge to Londonderry, 24 Jan. 1823. [20] *The Times*, 14, 30 Apr. 1823. [21] Londonderry mss (Aspinall transcripts), Londonderry to Camden, 18 July 1823. [22] Maybery mss 6553-5. [23] Ibid. 6557. [24] NLW ms 21674 C, Rice Trevor to Lady Frances Fitzroy, 26, 31 Aug. [Sept.] 1824. [25] Maybery mss 6558; *Cambrian*, 1, 8 Oct. 1825. [26] Tredegar mss 137/314-315; Maybery mss 6916. [27] *Cambrian*, 3, 10, 24 June; *Hereford Jnl.* 14, 21 June 1826. [28] *Cambrian*, 30 Sept. 1826. [29] *Geo. IV Letters*, iii. 1357. [30] *Cambrian*, 1, 15 Mar.; *Hereford*

Jnl. 12 Mar. 1828. [31] *Cambrian*, 23 May 1828. [32] Durham CRO, Londonderry mss D/Lo/C83 (180); Wellington mss WP1/957/14; *Arbuthnot Corresp.* 110. [33] Wellington mss WP1/1069/26. [34] *Hereford Jnl.* 18 Feb.; *Cambrian*, 21, 28 Feb. 1829. [35] *Hereford Jnl.* 4, 18 Mar.; *Cambrian*, 14 Mar. 1829. [36] Lonsdale mss, Lowther to Lonsdale, 17 Mar.; *Ellenborough Diary*, i. 399; *Cambrian*, 28 Mar., 4 Apr. 1829. [37] Derby mss 920 DER (14) 63. [38] *Ellenborough Diary*, ii. 33-34. [39] Wellington mss WP1/1029/23. [40] *Hereford Jnl.* 22 Apr.; *Cambrian*, 25 Apr. 1829. [41] *PP* (1829), ix. 381; *Hereford Jnl.* 22, 29 Apr.; *Cambrian*, 25 Apr. 1829. [42] Glam. RO D/DA15/27. [43] NRA 34425, ii. 95; *Hereford Jnl.* 9 Sept. 1829. [44] Maybery mss 6564. [45] *Cambrian*, 31 July 1830. [46] *Ellenborough Diary*, ii. 242, 247; *Arbuthnot Jnl.* ii. 356, 359, 363-4. [47] *Cambrian*, 10, 17, 24 July; *Hereford Jnl.* 14 July, 4, 11 Aug. 1830. [48] Maybery mss 6566, 6567. [49] *Cambrian*, 26 Mar., 16, 23 Apr.; *Hereford Jnl.* 16 Mar., 11 Apr.; *Carmarthen Jnl.* 22 Apr. 1831. [50] Maybery mss 6929. [51] Ibid. 6930. [52] Ibid. 6568. [54] Ibid. 6568, 6751-6752; *Cambrian*, 23 Apr.; *Hereford Jnl.* 27 Apr. *Mon. Merlin* of 23 Apr. 1831 incorrectly included Wood in the minority. [55] Maybery mss 6569-72, 6582-6583; 6753-7; *Carmarthen Jnl.* 29 Apr. *Cambrian* 30 Apr.; *Hereford Jnl.* 4 May 1831. [56] Maybery mss 6574-6, 6931; Londonderry mss C83 (33); NLW, mân adnau 1341 A; NLW, Gwernyfed mss, bdle. 36, Wood to J. Jones, 4 July 1832; *Carmarthen Jnl.* 6, 13 May; *Cambrian*, 7, 14 May; *Mon. Merlin*, 7, 14 May 1831; G. Williams, *Merthyr Rising*, 97-99. [57] *The Times*, 26 Apr., 12 May 1831. [58] Maybery mss 2318. [59] Grey mss, Taylor to Grey, 7 July 1831. [60] Maybery mss 6580-6581. [61] Ibid. 6584. [62] Ibid. 6580-6581. [63] Ibid. 6585; *Mon. Merlin*, 13 Aug. 1831. [64] *Cambrian*, 22 Oct.; *Mon. Merlin*, 22 Oct.; *Hereford Jnl.* 26 Oct. 1831. [65] *Carmarthen Jnl.* 30 Dec. 1831. [66] M. Elsas, *Iron in the Making*, 219-20; NLW, Bute mss L75/16, 23. [67] Maybery mss 6590; *Carmarthen Jnl.* 9 Mar.; *Mon. Merlin*, 10 Mar. 1832; *Cambrian*, 17, 24 Mar. 1832. [68] Maybery mss 6591, 6592, 6935; *Mon. Merlin*, 24 Mar. 1832; LMA ACC/1302/202. [69] Add. 40880, f. 534. [70] Maybery mss 6597, 6601, 6603; *Cambrian*, 8 Dec.; *Carmarthen Jnl.* 21 Dec. 1832; *Pol. Tracts*, 'Speeches of Mr. Gordon and Colonel Wood' (1833). [71] Tredegar mss 84/810; Add. 40485, f.230; *Silurian*, 4 July 1846. [72] *Croker Pprs.* iii. 101; Wood, *Letter to Lord John Russell from a Member of the 1817 Committee*; E. Poole, *Hist. Brec.* 403. [73] LMA ACC/1302/136-8; IR26/1404/284. [74] *Gent. Mag.* (1860), i. 411; *Ann. Reg.* (1860), Chron. pp. 511-12.

M.M.E.

WORCESTER, mq. of *see* **SOMERSET**, Henry

WORSLEY HOLMES, Sir Leonard Thomas, 9th bt. (1787-1825), of Westover, Calbourne, I.o.W.[1]

NEWPORT I.o.W.   7 Apr. 1809-10 Jan. 1825

b. 16 July 1787, 1st s. of Rev. Sir Henry Worsley, 8th bt., of Pidford (who took the additional name of Holmes, 1804) and Elizabeth, da. and coh. of Rev. Leonard Troughear Holmes (formerly Troughear), 1st Bar. Holmes [I], wid. of Edward Meux Worsley† of Gatcombe, Hants. *educ.* Eton 1802-5; Christ Church, Oxf. 1805. *m.* 5 June 1813, Anne Redstone, da. and h. of John Delgarno† of Newport, I.o.W., 3 da. (1 *d.v.p.*) *suc.* fa. as 9th bt. 7 Apr. 1811. *d.* 10 Jan. 1825.

Recorder, Newport 1816-*d.*[2]

Maj. Newport loyal vol. inf. 1805; lt.-col. N. Hants militia 1811-12; capt. commdt. I.o.W. (or Vectis) yeoman cav. 1817.

Worsley Holmes's family had been connected with the Isle of Wight since the sixteenth century and included several governors of the island and Members of Parliament for its boroughs.[3] On his father's death in 1811 he had inherited about £15,000, property at Westover (built by his maternal grandfather as a hunting lodge), and effective powers of nomination over the Members for Newport and Yarmouth.[4] A post-1814 memorandum indicates that he also coveted the island's other borough of Newtown, though he never secured a controlling stake.[5] His marriage to his second cousin brought him additional land in Ireland, chiefly around Ardagh, in county Limerick.[6] For a time Worsley Holmes had placed his considerable influence at the disposal of the 1st Marquess Wellesley, an unsuccessful contender for the premiership in 1812, allegedly in the hope of reviving his grandfather's peerage. He was retrospectively listed by Greville as part of the Wellesley-Canning connection, 22 Mar. 1820.[7]

At the 1820 general election he was again returned unopposed for Newport, where he thanked the compliant corporators for their 'unbounded confidence, in once more entrusting to him the selection of a colleague'. He had earlier canvassed the inhabitants on behalf of his friend John Fleming II*, an aspirant to the county representation, and pronounced himself flattered by the response.[8] A very lax attender, who is not known to have spoken in debate, he was inaccurately assumed to have voted 'for ministers always' by a radical commentary of 1823, this being the line he had pursued, 1815-20.[9] He was granted a week's leave on urgent private business, 3 July 1820. That September he supervised the annual training of his yeomanry troop.[10] On 26 Jan. 1821 he divided with opposition against the omission of Queen Caroline's name from the liturgy. He arrived on the Isle of Wight, 5 Feb. 1821, and paired against the forgery punishment mitigation bill, 23 May.[11] On 28 July 1821 he provided the inhabitants of Newport with the means to celebrate the king's coronation.[12] According to a correction in *The Times*, he voted in the minority for a gradual reduction of the salt duties, 28 Feb. 1822.[13] He was in Newport on 9 July 1822 for the visit of the bishop of Winchester, and his gifts to the poor of meat and blankets in the winter of 1822-3 were the subject of laudatory press notices.[14] Next spring he was again preoccupied with a mustering of the yeomanry, whose exemplary discipline was said to reflect 'the highest possible credit on their worthy commander'.[15] No trace of parliamentary activity has been found for 1823 or 1824. In February 1824 he chaired a meeting of a savings bank in Newport, but that September it was noted by his auditor that his 'continued indisposition' prevented his attendance even to local affairs.[16]

Worsley Holmes died at his mother's house in January 1825. Posthumous confirmation of his continued attachment to ministers came from his friend and executor William Mount*, who informed Liverpool, 20 Jan.:

> The health of Sir Leonard had been declining for some months, and it was his intention ... to have made your lordship acquainted with his inability to attend Parliament and have offered his seat to your lordship for any friend you might wish to succeed him for the remainder of the present session.[17]

Obituaries paid tribute to his 'benevolence' and at his funeral a cortège nearly a mile in length followed his coffin to its interment in the family vault at Arreton.[18] His surviving accounts reveal benefactions to schools, hospitals, evening lectures in Newport church, the Isle of Wight Institution, and the Society for the Promotion of Christian Knowledge. He also subscribed to the Vectis lodge of freemasons and the Hampshire hunt. In the financial year 1820-1, when his Isle of Wight property gave him a rental income of £8,110 and his lands in Limerick, Wicklow and Waterford produced £2,608, his charitable donations totalled £170, but in 1823-4, when his income fell to £4,481 and £2,000 respectively, his subscriptions were reduced to £94.[19] By the terms of his will, dated 27 Nov. 1824, his landed property passed to his eldest daughter Elizabeth, then a minor. (The trustees were Mount, his distant cousins the 2nd Baron Yarborough and the Rev. Henry Worsley of Godshill, the Newport solicitors Thomas Sewell and William Hearn, and Robert Clark of Carisbrooke.) His younger daughter Anne Emily received legacies worth £30,000, charged on his real and personal estate, while his widow, who had been provided with a marriage settlement, was named as residuary legatee. In 1833 Elizabeth Holmes married Sir William Henry Ashe A'Court (1809-91), who, in accordance with his father-in-law's will, took the name of Holmes after his own.[20] He sat as a Conservative for the Isle of Wight, 1837-47, and succeeded as 2nd Baron Heytesbury in 1860. A bas-relief marble monument to Worsley Holmes was completed in 1829 and placed over his tomb the following year.[21]

[1] Pidford House, the address given in *HP Commons, 1790-1820*, v. 651, was the residence of his mother. [2] D. Herapath, 'Holmes and Leigh Fams. of I.o.W.', *Blackmansbury*, v (1968), pt. iii, p. 83. [3] W. Berry, *Hants Genealogies*, 134, 136-9, 350-3. [4] *VCH Hants*, v. 218; PROB 11/1522/231; IR26/171/120. [5] I.o.W. RO, Heytesbury mss JER/HBY/232/15. [6] Ibid. 112/1; 121/2. [7] Grey mss, Goodwin to Grey, 24 Dec. 1812; *Greville Mems*. i. 92. [8] *Hants Telegraph*, 20, 27

Mar.; *Hants Chron.* 27 Mar. 1820. [9] *Black Bk.* (1823), 164. [10] *Hants Telegraph*, 18 Sept. 1820. [11] Ibid. 5 Feb. 1821. [12] Ibid. 30 July 1821. [13] *The Times*, 4 Mar. 1822. [14] *Southampton Co. Chron.* 11 July 1822, 9, 30 Jan. 1823. [15] Ibid. 20 Mar., 10 Apr. 1823. [16] *Hants Chron.* 9 Feb. 1824; Heytesbury mss 232/18. [17] Berks. RO, Mount mss D/EMt F14. [18] *The Times*, 14 Jan.; *Hants Chron.* 17 Jan. 1825; *Gent Mag.* (1825), i. 182-3. [19] Heytesbury mss 139/1-9. [20] PROB 11/1702/430; IR26/1046/781; Heytesbury mss 121/2. [21] *Hants Chron.* 11 May 1829, 11 Oct. 1830.

H.J.S./P.J.S.

WORTLEY see STUART WORTLEY

WRANGHAM, Digby Cayley (1805–1863), of Wilton Crescent, Mdx.

SUDBURY   1831–1832

b. 16 June 1805, 2nd s. of Rev. Francis Wrangham (*d.* 1842), rect. of Hunmanby, Yorks. and adn. of Yorks. (E. Riding), and 2nd. w. Dorothy, da. and coh. of Rev. Digby Cayley of Thormanby, Yorks. *educ.* Ripon; private tutor 1819-22; Brasenose, Oxf. 1822; G. Inn 1828, called 1831. *m.* 8 Dec. 1828, Amelia, da. of Walter Ramsden Fawkes[†] of Farnley Hall, Yorks., 2s. 2da. *d.* 10 Mar. 1863.

Asst. jun. clerk, foreign office Apr. 1827-Apr.1831; priv. sec. to Lords Dudley and Aberdeen as foreign secs. Apr. 1827-Nov. 1830.

Sjt.-at-law 1840; patent of precedence 1843; queen's sjt. 1857-*d.*

Wrangham, whose paternal grandfather and uncle kept a large stationer's shop in London's Bond Street, was intended from an early age for the law. He spent his childhood at Hunmanby, near Scarborough, where his father, a prolific writer and bibliophile, was rector. His mother, a North Riding heiress with an annual income of £700, claimed decent from King Edward I and Eleanor of Castile. An ardent pro-Catholic emancipation Whig and excellent manager of clergy, Francis Wrangham's successful career as a churchman and scholar is well documented, as is his advocacy of Joseph Lancaster's teaching methods and the delight he took in educating his six children. 'A six month reading at home' and two years in the care of 'Mr. Brass, a pupil of Tate's', near St. Neots, preceded Wrangham's admission to Oxford, where he was president of the debating society and the union and gained a double first in mathematics and classics in 1826.[1] This brought him to the notice of John William Ward*, Lord Dudley, who on becoming Canning's foreign secretary in April 1827 secured him a junior clerkship in the foreign office and made him his personal private secretary at £400 a year. Contrary to the usual practice, Wrangham was retained as private secretary by Lord Aberdeen, Dudley's successor following the

Huskissonite exodus from the duke of Wellington's ministry in May 1828.[2] His marriage in December that year to Amelia Fawkes surprised at least one of his colleagues, who dismissed her as 'a dowdy little body, with a very moderate portion, not likely either to fascinate and turn his head, or to be a *bon parti* in any way'.[3] The ministerial changes of November 1830 left Wrangham with little more than his £130 foreign office salary to support his young family pending his call to the bar, 8 June 1831. However, his connections within the Tory opposition and their management committee in Charles Street were impeccable. He resigned from the foreign office directly the defeat of the Grey ministry's reform bill in April 1831 precipitated a dissolution and vainly canvassed Hindon on the recommendation of Horace Twiss*. In response to an urgent plea for a second man from their partisan Sir John Benn Walsh*, William Holmes* sent him to the venal borough of Sudbury, which was scheduled to lose a Member under the bill. Drawing on the support of the corporation and the London freemen and on his father's reputation as archdeacon of the East Riding, he overcame a challenge by the reformer Admiral William Windham after a two-day poll.[4] Taking the credit for his return, Aberdeen recommended him to Wellington as 'a very clever young man, and there is every hope that he will go well in the House of Commons'.[5]

As a party man, Wrangham was privy to the political manoeuvring, meetings and private dinners that accompanied opposition policy-making and the eventual formation of the Carlton Club in 1831-2. He was also instrumental in bringing the younger opposition Members, including Walsh, to the attention of Aberdeen and the party hierarchy.[6] A certain jealousy, however, developed between Wrangham and Walsh over the former's high connections and dependence on party funds to pay his electioneering costs, and the latter's prior claim to corporation patronage in Sudbury.[7] In the House, Wrangham took an active part in debate from the outset, defending and justifying the Wellington ministry's policies and promoting the case against parliamentary reform in speeches and interventions that demonstrated his familiarity with departmental briefs and his mastery of legal niceties. Opposing the reintroduced reform bill at its second reading in his maiden speech, 6 July 1831, he countered the case made by his fellow barrister John Campbell for equating political power and property. He conceded that the enfranchisement of the great towns was necessary and overdue, but argued that the bill would 'narrow the basis of the constitution' and compared its likely impact with the effects of introducing a paper currency. (He voiced similar arguments before voting to amend it to perpetuate the voting rights of current freemen, 27, 30 Aug.) He voted for an adjournment, 12 July, to make the 1831 census the criterion for English borough disfranchisements, 19 July, and to postpone consideration of the partial disfranchisement of Chippenham, 27 July. He protested against the postponement of the Sudbury clause 'from a full to a thin House' at ministers' convenience, 29, 30 July.[8] On 2 Aug., drawing parallels with other towns separated from their suburbs by rivers, he used extracts of Paving Acts and parish and legal documents discovered by Walsh to present a strong case for including Ballingdon in the Sudbury constituency, which, if accepted, rendered arguments for depriving it of a Member on the ground of population untenable. They lost the division by 157-108. He pressed for separate representation for Kingston-upon-Hull and Sculcoates, 9 Aug., ten Members instead of six for Yorkshire, 10 Aug., and cautioned against authorizing the boundary commissioners, as political appointees, to determine county divisions and polling places, 1 Sept. He maintained that two-day polls would be unmanageable and too short, 5 Sept. Deferring to Peel and the party managers in Charles Street, who considered the bill's detention in the Commons pointless, he abandoned his intention of reopening Sudbury's case the following week.[9] He divided against the bill's third reading, 19 Sept., and passage, 21 Sept., and against the second reading of the Scottish bill, 23 Sept. He voted to deal with bribery at Liverpool, 5 Sept., and spoke against issuing the by-election writ because of the proven corruption there, 12 Oct. 1831. On the 21st he accompanied Walsh to Sudbury, where the corporation marked the reform bill's defeat in the Lords with a celebration dinner.[10] He also actively assisted the Tory Philip Yorke's London committee during the Cambridgeshire by-election.[11]

Wrangham briefly justified spending on diplomatic messengers when Hume queried the practice, 8 July 1831. He defended the Wellington ministry when Dixon, representing the merchants affected, ordered papers on the Brazilian capture of British ships, 19 July, but he failed to extract information on the Belgian insurrection from the foreign secretary Lord Palmerston, 9 Aug. He presented a Sudbury petition against permitting the use of molasses in brewing and distilling, 3 Sept., and voted against the sugar refinery bill and the truck bill, 12 Sept. He expressed support for amending the bankruptcy court bill, 13 Oct. As a principal speaker against its third reading, 18 Oct., he criticized those who attributed his opposition to 'factious motives', and argued against separating the administration of bankruptcy from the chancery

court. He nevertheless conceded that the current system was severely overloaded and recommended replacing it with one that dispensed with the part-time commissioners and replaced them with full-time judges sitting daily; he suggested one chief and three puisine judges. He also proposed creating a separate review court for appeals. Appraising him later that month, Walsh observed in his journal:

> Wrangham will never, in my opinion, make an effective speaker in the House of Commons. He is too lengthy and round about ... [He] is certainly a man of talent, but he has an overweening ambition and conceit, which runs away with him. He is deficient in that rarest of all gifts to an Englishman, tact.[12]

Wrangham was surprised to see Parliament recalled before Christmas and privately speculated that it was on account of the unrest caused by the political unions and differences within the cabinet over Lord Grey's negotiations with Lord Wharncliffe and the prospect of a modified and moderate reform bill.[13] The revised bill restored its second Member to Sudbury, which duly rewarded him with its freedom.[14] As they had agreed at a strategy meeting at Peel's, 5 Dec.,[15] he voted against its second reading, 17 Dec. 1831, and committal, 20 Jan., and divided against enfranchising Tower Hamlets, 28 Feb., and the third reading, 22 Mar. 1832. He quibbled only briefly over the omission of Northallerton as a North Riding polling town, 24 Jan., and the provisions for Huddersfield, 5 Mar., and Lincoln, 9 Mar. He presented Great Grimsby's petition pleading to retain two Members, 21 Feb. The popular reform petitions prompted by a further Lords defeat and the king's abortive invitation to Wellington to form a government riled him, and he vainly raised points of order when the Manchester one was brought up, 11 May. He insisted that his opposition to Baring's 'ill-advised and most injudicious' bill to exclude insolvent debtors from Parliament was one of principle and not personal, but freely admitted that his small fortune made him vulnerable to such an imputation, 6 June. On the boundary bill, he contributed to the discussions on the addition of Corfe Castle to Wareham and the parish of St. Martin to Stamford, 22 June, and thanked the commissioners for including Ballingdon in the redrawn Sudbury constituency. He pointed to anomalies and double standards in the Scottish freeholder voting qualification, 27 June 1832.

Wrangham divided with opposition on the Russian-Dutch loan, 26 Jan. 1832. Walking home with Lord Ellenborough afterwards, he described the government's 'miserable' showing, O'Connell's effort to save them by sending away 'seven or eight Liberal

Irish Members', Palmerston's good speech spoilt by his bad temper and how Peel had sacrificed '15 votes by intimating that the payment, although contrary to law, might yet be fit to be made in equity'.[16] As previously trailed in asides and anonymous paragraphs in the press, when opposition tested their strength with a motion for information on Portugal, 9 Feb., Wrangham gave a 'long and forcible' defence of Dudley and Aberdeen's policies towards Dom Miguel, in a speech that according to *The Times* (whose editor Barnes was one of his personal friends) was well received.[17] He now claimed that he had been professionally but never politically involved with the 1827-30 administrations and could consequently take a balanced overview of events. Brandishing correspondence deliberately selected to counter letters 'leaked' to the *Edinburgh Review*, he read extracts from Aberdeen's November 1830 dispatches to prove that the Wellington ministry had had the situation under control before they were brought down, and that it was therefore the Grey ministry who should have acted earlier and interfered more rigorously to prevent the detention of ships on suspicion of involvement in Dom Pedro's expedition. Gally Knight countered that Wrangham had failed to establish his case. The ensuing 274-139 division was perceived as a disappointing one for opposition.[18] Wrangham divided silently against government on the Russian-Dutch loan, 12 July 1832.

Walsh had repeatedly sought and grudgingly received confirmation from Wrangham of his superior claim to the corporation and Conservative vote in Sudbury. This encouraged Wrangham to test the ground in York in the summer of 1832, but considering his Sudbury prospects better, he resumed his canvass there in late October and finished in third place behind Walsh and the Whig veteran Michael Angelo Taylor at the general election in December.[19] Reappraising him that month Walsh wrote:

> He was not particularly well received by the House, and his one or two speeches were rather considered failures. To these particulars of his previous history I may add that he has the advantage of a very elegant *distingué* appearance and particularly gentlemanlike manners, that he has a certain easy assurance which seems to stand his friend in all societies, and *qu'il s'empare beaucoup de la conversation*. He has a delicate consumptive constitution, and a great want of natural flow of animal spirits, though his conversation is occasionally enlivened with anecdote, yet the serious is his style. He is thoroughly ambitious, aspiring, and actively pushing ... There was more of the special pleader, or the diplomatist in Wrangham's conduct, than of perfect candour and fair dealing with me.[20]

Wrangham did not stand for Parliament again although his legal appointments did not disqualify him from doing so. Poor health impaired his progress on the northern circuit, but he developed an enviable practice at the parliamentary bar, where he was counsel for the disfranchisement of Sudbury in 1844. He signed the invitation to Peel to stand for the chancellorship of the university of Oxford in 1834, appealed to him as prime minister in 1841 and to Aberdeen in 1842 for 'a mastership in chancery or any appointment of that class' and was accorded the rank of a queen's counsellor by patent of precedence in 1843.[21] His appointment as queen's serjeant in 1857 was among the last made before the office fell into abeyance. He died, recalled as an exemplary legal practitioner and formidable opponent in court, at his Gloucestershire home, 'The Rocks', Marshfield, near Bath in March 1863.[22] His Gloucestershire and Wiltshire property and his reversionary interest in the North Riding estate of his mother (*d.* 1860) passed to his sons Digby Strangeways Wrangham and Walter Francis Wrangham.

[1] *Oxford DNB*; M. Sadleir, *Archdeacon Francis Wrangham*, 4-26 and *passim*.   [2] C.R. Middleton, *Administration of British Foreign Policy, 1782-1846*, pp. 207-8; Add. 43245, f. 232.   [3] NLW, Ormathwaite mss F/G/1/5, p. 178.   [4] Ibid. pp. 178-80; *Ipswich Jnl.* 30 Apr.; *Bury and Norwich Post*, 4 May; *Suff. Chron.* 7 May 1831.   [5] Wellington mss WP1/1184/25.   [6] Ormathwaite mss FG/1/5, pp. 183-4, 192.   [7] Ibid. FG/1/6, pp. 175-86.   [8] *The Times*, 30 July 1831.   [9] Ormathwaite mss G39, f. 84.   [10] Ibid. FG/1/5, pp. 211-3.   [11] Wellington mss WP1/1199/13.   [12] Ormathwaite mss FG/1/5, pp. 213-4.   [13] Ibid. pp. 225-7.   [14] Suff. RO (Bury St. Edmunds), Sudbury Cockett bk. p. 112;   [15] Ormathwaite mss FG/1/5, pp. 233-4.   [16] *Three Diaries*, 184.   [17] Grey mss, Ellice to Grey Nov. 1831; *The Times*, 10 Feb. 1832.   [18] *The Times*, 12 Feb. 1832.   [19] Ormathwaite mss FG/1/6, pp. 97, 104, 153-4, 159, 163, 167, 170, 172; *The Times*, 3, 14 Dec. 1832.   [20] Ormathwaite mss FG/1/6, pp. 179, 185.   [21] Add. 40453, ff. 216-17; 40601, ff. 22, 29; 40488, ff. 351-5.   [22] J.H. Baker, *Order of Serjeants at Law*, 61-62, 235, 545; *PP* (1842), vii. 847; (1843), vi. 503, 547; *The Times*, 16 Mar.; *Gent. Mag.* (1863), i. 532.

M.M.E.

WRIGHTSON, William Battie (1789–1879), of Cusworth Hall, Doncaster, Yorks. and 22 Upper Brook Street, Mdx.

East Retford	1826–1 May 1827
Kingston-upon-Hull	1830–1832
Northallerton	1835–1865

b. 6 Oct. 1789, 1st s. of William Wrightson† of Cusworth Hall and 2nd w. Henrietta, da. and coh. of Richard Heber of Marton Hall, Yorks. *educ.* Trinity Coll. Camb. 1812; L. Inn 1811, called 1815. *m.* 24 Mar. 1821, Georgiana, da. of Inigo Freeman Thomas† of Ratton Park, Suss., *s.p. suc.* fa. 1827. *d.* 10 Feb. 1879.

When Joshua Walker* withdrew as a candidate for the venal borough of East Retford in 1825, Henry Savile Foljambe, the banker, took advantage of the vacuum and Lord Fitzwilliam's disillusionment with opponents among the aldermen to introduce Wrightson, who had 'long desired a seat in Parliament'. Wrightson's father, Member for Aylesbury, 1784-90, held an account with Foljambe's Doncaster bank and was resident nearby. Backed by Fitzwilliam, who sought to establish an interest there, he offered the freemen security against his son's not paying. Wrightson was well received during his canvass that September, but his pro-Catholic views were not popular.[1] He played them down at the 1826 general election, when he was returned second on the poll after a violent contest. The defeated candidate lodged a petition against the result.[2]

He joined Brooks's, sponsored by Fitzwilliam and Lord Milton*, 3 Mar., and voted for Catholic relief, 6 Mar. 1827. He was in the minorities against increased protection for barley, 12 Mar., and for inquiry into Leicester corporation, 15 Mar. He divided for the duke of Clarence's annuity bill, 16 Mar., and the spring guns bill, 23 Mar. On 1 May 1827 he was unseated by an election committee, though personally exonerated from any wrong doing. He apparently intended to offer again, but no writ for a new election was issued that Parliament. Shortly before the 1830 general election he was invited to come forward on Fitzwilliam's interest for Kingston-upon-Hull, where his father had stood briefly in 1802. A requisition was started to invite him formally, which, after some hesitation, he accepted. In his address he cited his support for retrenchment, repeal of the corn laws, the abolition of slavery, removal of all monopolies and measures that would 'extend [Hull's] trade and benefit its shipping'. After an acrimonious contest, in which he criticized navy impressment and the merchant seamen's contributions to Greenwich Hospital, he was returned in second place. His chairing was marred by violence, including a blow to his head from a stone, which the local press blamed on his refusal 'to offer himself on the *accustomed* terms of expense'.[3]

Wrightson presented and endorsed a petition for revision of the corn laws, 3 Nov., and was in the minority of 39 to reduce West Indian wheat import duties, 12 Nov. 1830. He presented and supported petitions from Hull's ship owners for repeal of the coal duties, 11, 19 Nov. He was listed by the Wellington ministry as one of their 'foes' and he voted against them in the crucial division on the civil list, 15 Nov. 1830. He presented Hull petitions for the abolition of slavery that

day, and for repeal of the window tax, with which he did not fully concur, 2 Dec. 1830. He was appointed to the select committee on the East India Company's monopoly, 4 Feb. 1831. He brought up and supported constituency petitions for parliamentary reform, 9 Feb., 19 Mar. On 16 Mar. he seconded Sykes's motion for leave to introduce a sea apprentices settlements bill, which he was ordered to help prepare. He divided for the second reading of the Grey ministry's reform bill, 22 Mar., and against Gascoyne's wrecking amendment, 19 Apr. 1831. At the ensuing general election he offered again as a supporter of reform and government, which he believed would improve the conditions for trade in the empire. He was returned unopposed.[4] He was reappointed to the East India select committee, 28 June 1831, 1 Feb. 1832. He voted for the second reading of the reintroduced reform bill, 6 July, at least twice against adjournment, 12 July, and gave steady support to its details, although he was in the minority for an amendment to withhold the vote from tenants and lodgers who paid weekly, 25 Aug. 1831. He brought up but dissented from a Sculcoates petition for its own representation, 9 Aug., when he indicated that he would welcome an increase of Hull's Members to three. On 11 July he introduced a bill to prevent the practice of paying the house rents of able-bodied labourers out of the poor rates, but withdrew it from lack of support. He called for an overhaul of the game laws, 8 Aug. That month he received letters from Hull's guardians of the poor thanking him for forwarding to them a draft of the proposed poor law settlement bill, and requests that he would support Slaney's poor relief bill, which he apparently ignored, and oppose the tax on steam packets and the length of quarantine imposed on ships in the Humber, on which he presented a petition, 28 Sept.[5] He voted for the reform bill's passage, 21 Sept. On the 26th he contended that the introduction of poor laws to Ireland would cause 'as much distress in one quarter as they remove in another'. He was appointed to the select committee on the subject that day. He divided for Lord Ebrington's confidence motion, 10 Oct. 1831.

Wrightson voted for the second reading of the revised reform bill, 17 Dec. 1831, again supported its details, and divided for the third reading, 22 Mar. 1832. He voted with ministers on the Russian-Dutch loan, 26 Jan., 20 July, relations with Portugal, 9 Feb., and the navy civil departments bill, 6 Apr. He divided for the motion for an address calling on the king to appoint only ministers who would carry the reform bill unimpaired, 10 May, and presented a constituency petition for supplies to be withheld until it passed, 24 May. He was in the minority of ten against the Liverpool disfranchisement bill, 23 May. He voted for the second reading of the Irish reform bill, 25 May, and against a Conservative amendment to increase Scottish county representation, 1 June. He brought up a Hull petition supporting the new plan of Irish education, 27 July 1832.

At the 1832 general election Wrightson retired from Hull and contested Northallerton, where his wife had inherited an interest, as a Liberal.[6] He failed, but came in at the election of 1835 and remained Member until 1865. He was the author of a short work on the corn laws, based on a speech he gave in the House, 11 May 1845. Wrightson, 'a Whig of old principles', died at his London home in February 1879.[7] Cusworth Hall passed to his brother Richard.

[1] *Nottingham Jnl.* 26 Sept., 10 Dec. 1825. [2] *Nottingham Rev.* 23 June 1826. [3] Lincs. AO, Ancaster mss, D. Sykes to G. Heathcote, 26 July; X111/B/5h, same to same, 27 July; *Hull Advertiser*, 30 July, 6 Aug. 1830; W.A. Gunnell, *Hull Celebrities*, 437. [4] *Hull Rockingham*, 16, 30 Apr. 1831. [5] Hull RO, Battie Wrightson mss DMX8/11. [6] *Hull Advertiser*, 6 July, 3 Aug. 1832. [7] *Dod's Parl. Companion* (1847), 256.

M.P.J.C.

WRIGHT WILSON, Sir Henry (c.1760–1832), of Chelsea Park, Mdx.; Crofton Hall, nr. Wakefield, Yorks., and Drayton Lodge, Barton Stacey, Hants.

ST. ALBANS   9 Jan. 1821–1826

b. c. 1760, 1st s. of Joshua Wilson of Pontefract and Crofton and w. the h. of Stevens of Glam. *m.* (1) 2 Aug. 1780, Jane, da. of William Chaloner of Guisborough, *s.p.*; (2) 17 Sept. 1799,[1] Lady Frances Brudenell Bruce, da. of Thomas, 1st earl of Ailesbury, *s.p.* kntd. 23 July 1794; *suc.* fa. 1797; took name of Wright before Wilson by royal lic. 10 Dec. 1814. *d.* 3 Dec. 1832.
   Ensign 2 Ft. 1778, lt. 1780; lt. 6 Drag. 1780; capt. army 1793; capt. 1 Life Gds. 1793, ret. 1798.

Wilson shared a common ancestor with Richard Fountayne Wilson*, namely Richard Wilson (1625-88), a Leeds merchant, the son of Thomas Wilson of Leeds. While Fountayne Wilson was descended from Richard's first son, this Member belonged to the branch founded by his second, Joshua Wilson (*d.* 1693), a Danzig merchant, who married Eva Schmidt of that place. His grandson Joshua Wilson (1705-78) lived at Pontefract, married Anne Clifton of Houghton and purchased the estate of Crofton, about six miles from Pontefract and three from Wakefield.[2] His eldest son and namesake was born in 1731 and became recorder of Pontefract and a magistrate of the West Riding: in the latter capacity, according to

an obituarist, he was 'prudent, temperate and decisive'. An amateur scientist and enthusiastic collector of fossils, he improved and tastefully embellished the mansion house at Crofton.[3]

With his wife, whose precise identity remains unknown, he had two sons, Henry and Edward, both of whom entered the army. Henry Wilson's first marriage made him brother-in-law to Edward Lascelles[†] (1740-1820), later 1st Baron and 1st earl of Harewood. In 1794, when he was a captain in the Life Guards, he was knighted. His brother Edward, a cavalry officer, fathered an illegitimate daughter, Mary, with one Ann Hardwick in about 1791. On 28 June 1795, when he was a captain in the newly formed 29th Hussars, Edward composed a brief will, in which he made Mary Hardwick his universal heiress and commended her to the care and protection of his father. He went with the regiment to the West Indies and was dead of yellow fever by early 1797.[4] His father had no time to prove Edward's will before he too died, in the summer of 1797, at Doncaster, on his way to Buxton 'for the recovery of his health'. By his own will, dated 10 Mar. 1797, Joshua Wilson, whose personalty was sworn under £5,000, left the Crofton estate, his Pontefract house and other property there to Henry, his residuary legatee and sole executor. He also directed that his leasehold estate at Kilham in the East Riding should be sold for Henry's benefit. He enjoined Henry to 'make a proper provision' for Mary Hardwick, to whose mother and aunt Hannah he left annuities of £12 and £20 respectively. Henry Wilson proved his father's and brother's wills together and took his niece, who now became known as Mary Wilson, under his own roof.[5]

He retired from the army soon after coming into his inheritance. It is not clear for how long he had been a widower, but in 1799 he made another socially prestigious marriage, to the daughter of the 1st earl of Ailesbury, a lord of the bedchamber. At some time in the first decade of the nineteenth century he acquired a 'pleasant habitation' at Chelsea Park in the western suburbs of London, a 'capital mansion, surrounded with extensive pleasure grounds'.[6] In December 1812 he submitted to Lord Liverpool, the new prime minister, a scheme for the establishment of asylums to take in the sons of paupers and orphaned and abandoned boys and train them for the army and navy; nothing came of it.[7] Fourteen months later Wilson and his wife had a windfall from a totally unexpected source. The eccentric William Wright (*b.* ?1731), a graduate of Cambridge and former student of the Inner Temple, died at his 'obscure lodging' in Pimlico, 14 Feb. 1814.

It emerged that by a will made on 5 Aug. 1800, he had devised his extensive landed property in the Andover area of Hampshire, which included the house of Drayton Lodge, estates in Essex (near Braintree), Buckinghamshire and Oxfordshire, and £5,000, to Lady Frances Wilson, whom he did not know, but whom he had long admired from a distance before her marriage. After overcoming her initial incredulity, Lady Frances went to view Wright's corpse, and recognized him as a man who had years ago discomfited her by staring at her in her box at the opera. (In seven codicils to his will, Wright left substantial legacies to Lords Eldon and Sidmouth, Lady Rosslyn, and Charles Abbot, Speaker of the Commons, with none of whom he had the remotest personal acquaintance.) Lady Frances, the residuary legatee, proved the will with Abbot, the other executor, 3 Oct. 1814, when Wright's personalty was sworn under £45,000. The residue alone was calculated for duty at £38,250, and the real estate was thought to be worth over £30,000 a year. It was supposed that Sir Berkeley William Guise*, the heir-at-law, might contest the will, but he apparently did not do so; and at the end of the year Wilson and his wife added Wright's name to their own 'out of respect' to his memory.[8]

At the general election of 1820 Wright Wilson stood for the venal and open borough of St. Albans, but he finished a distant third. The suddenly deteriorating health of one of the successful candidates, the Whig Robarts, encouraged him to continue cultivating the borough; and by the time of Robarts's death in early December 1820 he had the start over his two rivals for the vacant seat, though in the event his victory at the fiercely contested by-election was a narrow one. In the view of a hostile observer, he owed his success almost entirely to the length of his purse, and deviously secured promises of support 'from persons of opposite principles and of none':

> To some he hinted the necessity of reform, to others he represented himself as the friend of the queen, and talked of the independence of the borough; while, by a more palpable species of argumentation, he gained over a large number of the poorest voters to his interest. Since then ... [he] has thrown off the mask, and proclaimed the queen from the hustings to be a *common prostitute*.[9]

Wright Wilson, who made no mark in the House, duly voted in defence of the Liverpool ministry's conduct towards the queen, 6 Feb. 1821, and he went on to give them general but apparently silent support. He voted against Catholic claims, 28 Feb. 1821, and Canning's bill for the relief of Catholic peers, 30 Apr. 1822. He was in the minority for repeal of the tax on

agricultural horses, 6 Mar., but he divided with government on the revenue the following day, and did likewise on repeal of the additional malt duty, 3 Apr., the army estimates, 11 Apr., and economy and retrenchment, 27 June 1821. He voted against more extensive tax reductions, 11, 21 Feb., and abolition of one of the joint-postmasterships, 13 Mar. 1822, but (perhaps bearing a grudge over the rejection of his own military asylum scheme) divided with Hume to reduce the grant for the Royal Military College, 20 Mar. 1822, 10 Mar. 1823. He sided with ministers on the sinking fund, 3 Mar., the assessed taxes, 10, 18 Mar., and against repeal of the Foreign Enlistment Act, 16 Apr., inquiry into the prosecution of the Dublin Orange rioters, 22 Apr., and Scottish parliamentary reform, 2 June 1823. Soon afterwards he successfully applied to the duke of Wellington, the lord lieutenant, to be placed on the commission of the peace for Hampshire.[10] His only known parliamentary activity in the 1824 session was the presentation of a St. Albans petition for reform of the licensing laws, 11 May.[11] A defaulter on a call of the House, 28 Feb., he was ordered to be taken into custody after failing to attend, 2 Mar. 1825. Two days later the Speaker notified the House that Lady Frances had informed him that Wright Wilson was detained in the country by illness, and the order was discharged. He voted against Catholic relief, 21 Apr., 10 May, and the Irish franchise bill, 26 Apr., 9 May. His last known vote was for the duke of Cumberland's grant, 30 May 1825. It was thought at St. Albans in September 1825 that Wright Wilson intended to take 'final leave' of the borough at the next dissolution.[12] Two months later he was introduced to East Retford by the recently formed True Blue Club to challenge the two candidates who had declared themselves for the next general election on the Fitzwilliam interest. In a blatant appeal to anti-Catholic feeling, Wright Wilson and his supporters kept the borough in turmoil with a spate of 'No Popery' propaganda as they canvassed during the winter. When Wright Wilson made what he described as a 'triumphal' entry to East Retford in February 1826, there were serious disturbances, and the Fitzwilliam candidates were forced to abandon their canvass and flee the town. Wright Wilson then visited the duke of Newcastle, whose rump of supporters on the corporation had originally inspired the anti-Fitzwilliam agitation, and who connived in their activities by turning a blind eye. He accepted the duke's invitation to stay the night, and left him convinced that he was 'decidedly the favourite and will ultimately, so I hope and expect, succeed in his election'.[13] He duly came forward at the general election later in the year, but on the first day of polling, which was marked by drunkenness and violence, he trailed a distant third. The disorder escalated into a riot, in which the Fitzwilliam candidates were attacked, and troops were called in to restore order. Wright Wilson was said to have made things worse by delivering an inflammatory rant against military intervention to an already agitated crowd. The next day, though he claimed to have many votes not yet polled, he declined to proceed further, ostensibly because of the threat from the army, and made it clear that he would petition against the return of his opponents. It seems certain that Wright Wilson and his allies had all along been aiming at a petition; and there is a strong suspicion that they deliberately provoked the introduction of troops to furnish a pretext for lodging one. Wright Wilson and four aldermen petitioned for a void election, 4 Dec. 1826, alleging partiality by the returning officers, the unconstitutional intervention of the military and bribery and treating. Shortly before the ballot for the election committee, 3 Apr. 1827, Wright Wilson solicited support for his cause from Peel, home secretary in the disintegrating Liverpool ministry, on the ground that he had 'always been a true friend to the administration'; Peel made his excuses.[14] The committee declared the election void, but directed the attention of the House to the evidence of systematic corruption which it had uncovered. The case of East Retford became a bone of political contention for three years, and no new writ was issued before the dissolution of 1830.[15]

Wright Wilson died at Chelsea Park in December 1832. By his will, made on 4 July that year, he left his wife £2,000 in cash, and £4,000 in three per cent consols, and confirmed the terms of their marriage settlement. He devised his Yorkshire and Chelsea estates and recent acquisitions in Hampshire and Essex to her for her life, and thereafter to his niece Mary, to whom he also left £2,000, his London house at 24 Grosvenor Street and his shares in the Wakefield Assembly Rooms. His personalty was sworn under £50,000 within the province of Canterbury.[16] On the death of Lady Frances Wilson in 1836, Crofton passed to Mary, who married John Henniker. On her death without issue in 1866, it went to her kinsman Henry Wilson (1806-69), Sir Henry's godson and the son of his cousin Christopher Wilson. The Hampshire property went after Lady Frances's death to Christopher Wilson's daughter Frances Elizabeth, who married Sir Michael McCreagh.

[1] *Gent. Mag.* (1799), ii. 812. [2] The fullest pedigree of this Member's branch of the family is in the 8th edn. of *Burke LG* (1894). There is a defective one of the whole Wilson of Leeds family in J. Foster, *Peds. Yorks. Fams.* [3] *Gent. Mag.* (1797), ii. 619. [4] PROB

11/1295/580. [5] *Gent. Mag.* (1797), ii. 619; PROB 8/190 (22 Aug. 1797); 11/1295/580. [6] *London and Its Environs* (1820), 55; T. Faulkner, *Hist. Chelsea* (1829), i. 151. [7] Add. 38378, ff. 295-300. [8] *The Times*, 28 Feb. 1814; *Gent. Mag.* (1814), i. 308; PROB 11/1561/591; IR26/630/606. [9] *The Times*, 6, 15, 18 Jan. 1821. [10] Wellington mss WP1/765/9. [11] *The Times*, 12 May 1824. [12] Add. 76036, J. Harrison to Spencer, 22 Sept. 1825. [13] Nottingham Univ. Lib. Newcastle mss Ne2 F2/1/99. [14] Add. 40393, f. 114. [15] See EAST RETFORD. [16] *Gent. Mag.* (1833), i. 283; PROB 11/1813/196; IR26/1339/102.

D.R.F.

WRIXON BECHER, **William** (1780–1850), of Ballygiblin, Mallow, co. Cork.

MALLOW   1818–1826

b. 31 July 1780, 1st s. of William Wrixon of Cecilstown and Mary, da. of John Townsend Becher of Annisgrove. *educ.* Magdalen, Oxf. 1796. *m.* 18 Dec. 1819, Elizabeth, da. of John O'Neill, actor-manager, of Drogheda, co. Louth, 3s. 2da. Took additional name of Becher by sign manual 29 Sept. 1831; *cr.* bt. 30 Sept. 1831. *d.* 23 Oct. 1850.

Wrixon Becher (as he seems to have been known throughout this period) had been returned unopposed for Mallow on the independent Catholic interest in 1818, ousting his anti-Catholic cousin James Lawrence Cotter, and had joined Brooks's, sponsored by Lord George Cavendish* and Lord Duncannon*, 19 May 1819. At the 1820 general election he offered again, refuting charges of absenteeism brought against him by his opponent Charles Jephson*, whom he accused of trying to 'close the borough', and stressing his independence from party, for although 'he generally voted in opposition' to the Liverpool ministry, it 'was when he considered them wrong'. Daniel O'Connell*, who had agreed to be his agent, considered his election speech 'one of the best I ever heard ... full of excellent principle and admirably well delivered', and recorded 'going out to his house to dinner ... principally to see' Wrixon Becher's wife, the celebrated actress Elizabeth O'Neill, 'on a new stage'. Wrixon Becher was returned after a four-day contest.[1] An irregular attender, when present he continued to vote with the Whig opposition on most major issues, including economy, retrenchment and reduced taxation.[2] He endorsed a petition to the king for a pension from the mother and sister of the late General William Hume, deputy assistant commissary in Demerara, 4 Apr. 1820.[3] On 14 June he paid tribute to Henry Grattan I*, who had dictated a 'dying exhortation' to 'his Catholic countrymen', which he proceeded to read. Sir James Mackintosh* thought he delivered it 'very well', but the reporters could only collect an 'imperfect' account as he 'read the document so rapidly'.[4] He was granted six weeks' leave on urgent private business, 16 June 1820. At a county meeting on the Queen Caroline affair in January 1821 he helped to defeat attempts by 'ministerialists' to resist calls for 'discussion'.[5] He voted for Catholic claims, 28 Feb. 1821, 1 Mar., 21 Apr., 10 May 1825, arguing that it would end the 'unmerited sufferings of the Irish nation', 23 Mar. 1821. Next month Henry Edward Fox* remarked that 'Becher's speech at the Theatrical Fund Dinner was very good indeed, full of feeling and good taste, and besides beautifully delivered. He speaks well, I believe, in Parliament'.[6] He voted for parliamentary reform, 9 May 1821, 25 Apr. 1822, 20 Feb., 24 Apr. 1823. On 16 May 1821 he refuted assertions that he and other Members who had 'hitherto given a silent vote' for inquiry into the Peterloo massacre 'necessarily approved of the principles of those who had convened the meeting'. He was in the minorities for the equalization of interest rates on Irish treasury and exchequer bills, 30 May, and against the grant for Irish glebe houses, 18 June. He objected to the inclusion of arrears in the duke of Clarence's grant and voted thus, 18, 29 June, 2 July, when he protested that it was 'inconsistent' with ministerial 'professions of economy'.[7] He welcomed the attention drawn to Irish education by the report of the commissioners, 10 July 1821.[8] On 29 Apr. 1822 he warned of widespread distress in Ireland, where 'in a very short time, even the scanty subsistence now on hand would be altogether expended'. He was in the minority of 22 for a 20s. duty on wheat, 9 May. On the 15th he defended the conduct of Irish landlords, saying it was the tithe proctors who 'inflicted oppression upon the people' and ought to be 'investigated'. He welcomed measures for the employment of the Irish poor but asserted that if they had been implemented earlier, 'much of the present distress ... might have been avoided', 17 May. He voted for inquiry into the Irish church, 4 Mar. 1823, 6 May 1824. On 23 Apr. 1823 he complained that Protestant petitions against Catholic claims kept Ireland in a perpetual 'state of irritation'. He supported one for an increase in Irish coroners' salaries, 2 May.[9] He felt 'bound to support' the Irish Insurrection Act, 'bad as it was', for 'necessary protection', but voted for inquiry into the causes of unrest prior to its renewal, 12 May 1823, expressing his belief that a 'reduction of rents and a commutation of tithes' were also 'indispensable'. He endorsed a county Cork petition against repeal of the Irish linen duties, 6 May 1824.[10] He divided for inquiry into the state of Ireland and was appointed to the ensuing select committee, 11 May. Called to give evidence as one of its members, 22 May, he admitted the utility of the Irish Insurrection Act but urged the necessity of

Catholic relief, adding that in his work for the Society for the Improvement of the Irish Peasantry he and his brother had discovered that the 'most miserable' habitations in their parish were those let 'upon a yearly holding', where it was 'not the interest of a tenant to lay out money', and noting the 'good effects' of emigration in removing 'persons who have been brought up in turbulent and irregular habits'.[11] He voted for proper use of Irish first fruit revenues, 25 May, and against Irish church pluralities, 27 May. Testifying to the respectability of a county Cork petition for Catholic claims, 10 June 1824, he enquired, 'What would be the conduct of the people of England, if the major part of the population laboured under the same disabilities as the Catholics of Ireland?' He voted to hear the Catholic Association at the bar of the House, 18 Feb., and against its suppression, 25 Feb. 1825. He was appointed to the select committee on the state of Ireland, 17 Feb. He welcomed the Irish franchise bill, observing that 'whatever objection there might be to it in theory, it would ... in its practical results ... favour purity of election' and facilitate 'the great measure' of emancipation, 9, 12 May 1825. He agreed to attend the Association dinner for the 'friends of civil and religious liberty', 2 Feb. 1826.[12] He divided against the emergency admission of foreign corn, 8, 11 May 1826.

At the 1826 general election Wrixon Becher retired from Mallow in favour of Jephson after an 'unsuccessful canvass', hoping that he had 'proved useful' in securing the independence of the borough and 'in defeating the hopes of any candidate not pledged to support' emancipation. Meetings of the independents paid tribute to his talents and efficiency.[13] He was spoken of as a 'fitting' successor to his first cousin Richard Hare, Viscount Ennismore, at the 1827 county Cork by-election, 'possessing talents of no common order' and 'competent in every way', but he 'could not be induced ... to quit ... private life'.[14] In November 1828 he signed a county Cork Protestant declaration in support of Catholic emancipation.[15] He proposed the Member Robert King for that county at the general elections of 1830 and 1831, when he welcomed the Grey ministry's reform bill as a 'bold but prudent measure', observing that the Whigs had 'been ahead of their opponents in the cause of reason and right, fully half a century', but objected to demands for King to pledge support for the 'whole bill', as it would 'debar an honourable mind from exercising ... discretion upon minor points'. At Mallow he spoke in similar terms of the necessity of re-electing Jephson 'without trouble or expense'.[16] Later that year he received a baronetcy. He spoke at a Cork county meeting to celebrate the passage of the Reform Act in August 1832.[17] That November he signed a county declaration in support of the Union and a complete reformation of Irish tithes and the Irish church.[18] As foreman of the county's grand jury in the 1840s he corresponded with Peel, the premier, about Cork's harbour and constabulary expenses. On 11 Feb. 1848 he thanked Charles Babbage for a copy of his *Thoughts on the Principles of Taxation*, hoping that 'at present, when an income or property tax seems impending ... we shall have your valuable assistance in fighting it off'.[19] He died in October 1850 and was succeeded by his eldest son Henry (1826-93).

[1] *Dublin Evening Post*, 21, 25, 30 Mar. 1820; *O'Connell Corresp.* ii. 823. [2] *Black Bk.* (1823), 139; *Session of Parl. 1825*, p. 450. [3] Add. 38380, f. 148. [4] Add. 52444, f. 151. [5] *The Times*, 30 Jan. 1821. [6] *Fox Jnl.* 66. [7] *The Times*, 19 June, 3 July 1821. [8] Ibid. 11 July 1821. [9] Ibid. 23 Apr., 3 May 1823. [10] Ibid. 7 May 1824. [11] *PP* (1825), vii. 178-89. [12] *O'Connell Corresp.* iii. 1278. [13] *Southern Reporter*, 6, 8, 13, 15 June 1826. [14] Ibid. 2, 4 Oct. 1827. [15] Ibid. 13 Nov. 1828. [16] Ibid. 7, 12 May 1831. [17] I. D'Alton, *Protestant Society and Politics in Cork*, 216. [18] *The Times*, 13 Nov. 1832. [19] Add. 37194, f. 117; 40542, f. 92; 40563, f. 48.

P.J.S.

WROTTESLEY, Henry (1772–1825), of 10 New Square, Lincoln's Inn, Mdx.

BRACKLEY   28 Dec. 1810–17 Feb. 1825

b. 25 or 26 Oct. 1772, 2nd s. of Sir John Wrottesley[†], 8th bt. (*d.* 1787), of Wrottesley, Staffs. and Hon. Frances Courtenay, da. of William Courtenay[†], 1st Visct. Courtenay; bro. of Sir John Wrottesley, 9th bt.* *educ.* Westminster 1786; Christ Church, Oxf. 1791; L. Inn 1793, called 1798. *unm. d.* 17 Feb. 1825.
Cursitor in chancery 1795-*d.*; commr. of bankrupts 1799-*d.*; solicitor to bd. of control 1806-11.
Capt. St. James's vols. 1798; Staffs. militia 1803, maj. 1809.

Wrottesley continued to sit for the pocket borough of Brackley as the nominee of the 2nd marquess of Stafford, whom he had followed into supporting the Liverpool ministry by 1817. A regular attender, he was described as one of the 'treasury phalanx' by a radical commentary of 1823, though he occasionally took an independent line, notably on legal issues.[1] On 5 May 1820 he brought up a petition challenging the return at Petersfield.[2] He defended the recommendations of the select committee on the administration of Welsh justice, on which he had served, urging partial reform of the Welsh judicature, 1 June. That day he welcomed the labourers' wages bill. He successfully proposed an amendment to the marriage bill concern-

ing the marriage of minors, 2 June. A commissioner of bankrupts (on a salary of £350 a year), he was critical of the insolvent debtors bill, which he contended would only work if three commissioners were retained to administer it, but admitted that it was an improvement on recent legislation, 5 June. In the first half of 1821 he repeatedly tried to introduce his own reform of debtors law, transferring the surrendering of bankrupts from the London Guildhall to the new bankruptcy court, but his proposals never got beyond a first reading.[3] On 14 June 1820 he secured leave for a bill to tighten up the rules governing access to specifications of patents, telling Hume, who had protested that the proposal was anti-liberal, that it was primarily a legal and not a political matter. It went no further. He opposed the bill preventing Irish masters in chancery from sitting at Westminster, warning that it could set a precedent for legislation against any Member who, owing to other commitments, could not attend regularly, 30 June. He spoke against the commital to Newgate of Sir William Manners[†] for absconding after a warrant had been issued for his arrest in connection with malpractices in the Grantham election, 10 July, and took issue with Dr. Phillimore's contention that the payment of out-voters for loss of time was 'highly illegal', arguing that it was not 'decidedly against the law', 12 July 1820.[4] He voted in defence of ministers' conduct towards Queen Caroline, 6 Feb., and against repeal of the additional malt duty, 7 Apr. 1821. On 27 Feb. he presented and sympathized with a petition from Northamptonshire complaining of agricultural distress, but doubted the efficacy of legislation to cure the problem.[5] He divided against parliamentary reform, 9 May, the omission of arrears from the duke of Clarence's grant, 18 June, and an opposition motion for economy and retrenchment, 27 June. On 29 June 1821 he was a majority teller for the third reading of a bill to prevent cruel and improper treatment of cattle. He voted against more extensive tax reductions, 21 Feb., and secured returns of the quantity of country bank notes in circulation between October 1819 and October 1821, 3 Apr. 1822.[6]

Wrottesley died unmarried in February 1825. 'He was a easy and fluent speaker', observed the family historian, but 'confined himself to speaking only on questions with which he was well acquainted, such as legal matters'.[7] In his will, dated 25 July 1822 but not proved until 7 Feb. 1831, his elder brother and executor Sir John Wrottesley was instructed to pay off his debts. The residue of his personal estate, which was sworn under a meagre £200, was bequeathed to one Anna Maria Douglas of John Street, Berkeley Square, Middlesex.[8]

[1] *Black Bk.* (1823), 206. [2] *The Times*, 6 May 1820. [3] Ibid. 20 Feb., 6, 14 Mar., 29 May, 7 June 1821. [4] Ibid. 11 July 1820. [5] Ibid. 28 Feb. 1821. [6] Ibid. 4 Apr. 1822. [7] G. Wrottesley, *Hist. Fam. Wrottesley of Wrottesley* (1903), 361-2. [8] PROB 11/1782/120; IR26/1275/40.

S.K./P.J.S.

WROTTESLEY, Sir John, 9th bt (1771–1841), of Wrottesley Hall, Staffs. and 13 St. George's Street, Mdx.

LICHFIELD	2 Mar. 1799–1806
STAFFORDSHIRE	23 July 1823–1832
STAFFORDSHIRE SOUTH	1832–1837

b. 25 Oct. 1771, 1st s. of Sir John Wrottesley, 8th bt.[†], of Wrottesley and Hon. Frances Courtenay, da. of William Courtenay[†], 1st Visct. Courtenay; bro. of Henry Wrottesley*. *educ.* Westminster 1782; Angers mil. acad. 1787. *m.* (1) 23 June 1795, Lady Caroline Bennet (*d.* 7 Mar. 1818), da. of Charles, 4th earl of Tankerville, 5s. (2 *d.v.p.*) 5da. (4 *d.v.p.*); (2) 19 May 1819, Julia, da. of John Conyers of Copt Hall, Essex, wid. of Hon. John Astley Bennet (bro. of Wrottesley's 1st w.), *s.p. suc.* fa. as 9th bt. 23 Apr. 1787; *cr.* Bar. Wrottesley 11 July 1838. *d.* 16 Mar. 1841.

Ensign 35 Ft. 1787; lt. 19 Ft. 1790, 29 Ft. 1790; capt. 16 Drag. 1793; maj. 32 Ft. 1794, ret. 1795; lt.-col. commdt. W. Staffs. militia 1809, lt.-col. 1835-*d.*

Wrottesley, an East India proprietor, agricultural improver and Wolverhampton banker, who had abandoned the Lichfield seat of his Tory patron Lord Stafford in 1806 in order to obtain his independence, aspired to sit for Staffordshire like his father. Following an abortive attempt in 1812, when he had secured the backing of the Whig Lord Anson, he offered again for the county at the 1823 by-election, allegedly supported by the united interests of Stafford and Anson, acting together in 'an odd combination'. He was eulogized by local Whigs as 'the enemy of extravagance and corruption, and the friend of reform', but the Tories were less enthusiastic, his county neighbour William Dyott, who described him as 'a man of good understanding, rather austere in manner', being unable to 'recollect an event that appeared to give such general disapprobation'. Attempts to get up an opposition came to nothing, however, and he was returned unopposed.[1]

Wrottesley, who was regarded by his colleague Edward Littleton as 'one of the best Members', voted with the Whig opposition to the Liverpool ministry on most major issues, notably economy, retrenchment and reduced taxation, on which he spoke regularly, and campaigned steadily for 'throwing open the banking trade'.[2] He divided for information on Catholic

burials, 6 Feb. 1824. He obtained a return of the value of silver and gold coinage in circulation, 9 Feb.[3] He spoke against abolition of the usury laws, which had 'greatly benefited' the country, 16 Feb., and moved an amendment (which he later withdrew) for delaying their repeal by one year, 8 Apr. He pledged his support for remission of the wool tax if the 'remaining sixpence' of malt duty were also repealed, 20 Feb. Citing his constituents' concern at the proposed reforms of the coal duties, he enquired whether the Grand Junction Canal would be permitted to transport coals to London and what 'amount of duty they would be subjected to', 25 Feb., and recommended giving 'every facility to the inland coalowners' against 'the northern owners', 1 Apr. On 25 Feb. he moved for inquiry into adapting 'the coin of the realm' to 'a decimal scale', and proposed that the 'present denominations' should be replaced by 'pounds, double shillings, and farthings', where '100 farthings would make a double shilling, and ten double shillings, or 1,000 farthings, would amount to a pound'. He abandoned the motion, but hoped that younger Members 'would live to see his measure carried into effect'. He divided for reform of Edinburgh's representation, 26 Feb. 1824, 13 Apr. 1825, parliamentary reform, 27 Apr., and curbing electoral bribery, 26 May 1826. On 27 Feb. 1824 he spoke in defence of George Chetwynd, Member for Stafford, accused by a petitioner of a 'gross abuse of magisterial authority', and stated that he had 'signed the resolution of the magistrates passed in [his] approbation'. He suggested that abolition of the window tax might be effected 'by retaining the duties on coals' and by 'abandoning' plans to appropriate '£800,000 to the decoration of Windsor Castle, and the building of new churches', 5 Mar. 1824, when he presented an individual's petition against the importation of foreign silks and spoke against the proposed lowering of duties.[4] He brought up a Buxton petition against slavery, 12 Mar.[5] He argued for retention of 'the permissive rights which landowners at present possessed of appointing game keepers', 25 Mar., and spoke against the game laws amendment bill, 1 Apr. He presented a Wolverhampton petition against the combination laws, 30 Mar.[6] He called for remission of the salt duties, 6 Apr. He denounced the 'scandalous extortion' of charging for admission to Westminster Abbey, 9 Apr. 1824, 13 Apr. 1826, when he was a minority teller on the issue. He argued that the 'greatest mischief connected with the trade in corn was the constant tampering with the laws by which it was regulated', 4 May 1824. The following day he presented a petition from the licensed victuallers of Wolverhampton against the beer duties.[7] He voted for inquiry into the state of

Ireland, 11 May, and against Irish church pluralities, 27 May. He was a majority teller for an amendment to the county courts bill, 24 May. He presented constituency petitions against the prosecution in Demerara of the Methodist missionary John Smith, 25, 26, 31 May 1824.[8]

Wrottesley divided against the Irish unlawful societies bill, 15 Feb. 1825. He was granted a fortnight's leave on account of the death of a relation, 17 Feb. He voted for Catholic claims, 1 Mar., 21 Apr., when he presented a favourable petition from the Midland counties, and 10 May.[9] The previous day he had contended that emancipation was necessary for 'the solid union of the kingdoms', and condemned the proposed disfranchisement of 200,000 Irish freeholders by the Irish franchise bill. He presented a Wolverhampton petition in favour of assigning its county court a concurrent jurisdiction with the court of requests, 26 Apr.[10] He enquired about proposals to alter the regulations respecting flour, 28 Apr., and doubted that the importation of American corn was as 'difficult' as had been represented, 13 May.[11] He argued that '£6,000 a year was too much for the puisne judges', condemned 'the disgraceful practice' of their 'making money' out of their offices, and proposed an amendment 'to substitute £5,000', which was negatived, 16 May.[12] He recommended delaying the distillery bill, 2 June, and presented a petition against it from Wolverhampton the following day.[13] He hoped that Hume 'had inquired well' before presenting a petition complaining of country bank notes not being paid in gold, as it would have 'a tendency to effect the credit of a mercantile establishment in a very important point', 22 June. He argued for proceeding with the case of William Kenrick[†] at Canfor in order to preserve 'the honour of the magistracy', 24 June 1825.

Wrottesley contended that bankrupt country banks were 'rather the victims of the speculations of others, than speculators themselves', 9 Feb. 1826. In a speech described as 'unbearable' by George Agar Ellis*, which he prefaced by announcing that 'he was an interested man, a banker' 13 Feb., Wrottesley repudiated assertions that country banks had 'over issued' small notes and argued at length against inquiry into the Bank Charter and Promissory Note Acts, on which he 'persisted in dividing' the House and was a teller for the minority of 39. 'But for the obstinacy of Sir John', griped Agar Ellis, 'we would have been unanimous, which would have had a good effect in the country'.[14] Speaking against the promissory notes bill, 17 Feb., he accused ministers of having succumbed to the 'novel and extraordinary' theories of 'friends of the

Philosophic Club', and warned against 'taking away country bank notes, which were seldom forged, and suffering the reissue of Bank of England notes, which were easily forged'. He spoke in similar terms, 24, 27 Feb. He voted for a select committee on silk trade petitions, 24 Feb. He welcomed government plans to alleviate distress, 1 May, called for the corn duties to be applied 'to the benefit of the distressed manufacturers', 5 May, and asserted that 'if the currency had not been interfered with, the present distress would not have existed', 12 May 1826.

At the 1826 general election Wrottesley offered again, boasting of his 'independence'. (Littleton's belief that he would have 'considerable difficulty in getting a good proposer', since there were 'but few Whig *landowners* in the county' who were not his own 'personal friends and well-wishers', proved inaccurate.) Pressed on the progress of tax reductions at the nomination, 12 June 1826, Wrottesley observed that 'in the abolition of tax, greater difficulties had arisen than in the imposition of it', 'dwelt at considerable length on the distress of the manufacturing districts and the currency question', for which 'ministers were highly culpable', and called for their 'ruinous measures' to be 'speedily abrogated'. After his unopposed return he ordered 'six barrels of ale to be distributed among the population of Wolverhampton'.[15] He attacked the extent of promotion in the navy, especially the practice of men being 'made captain without any ship to command', 13 Feb. 1827. He divided against the duke of Clarence's grant, 16 Feb. He criticized the scale of duties proposed for barley and oats, 1 Mar., and the 'inconvenience' arising from changes to the corn laws, 23 Mar. He paired in favour of Catholic relief, 6 Mar. 1827, and voted for it, 12 May 1828. He recommended that in county elections 'the poll should be taken first in one hundred, and that the sheriff should then proceed to others', 15 Mar. 1827. On the 26th he resumed his campaign for economical reforms, arguing at length that ministers should 'get rid of the delusion of a sinking fund, and employ that surplus in relieving the country from a portion of its burdens'. He endorsed a Wolverhampton petition presented by Littleton against the game laws, and demanded 'a bill to legalize the sale of game', 28 Mar. Following his chairmanship of the Coventry election committee, for which he was granted a fortnight's leave, 30 Mar., he introduced a bill giving the Warwickshire magistrates 'a concurrent jurisdiction with those of the city of Coventry in regulating the affairs of the elections', 22 May, which he 'warmly defended', 8 June. He was a majority teller for its various stages until it was defeated, 19 June. He divided for the disfranchisement of Penryn, 28 May. He defended the issue of £1 notes by country banks and moved for inquiry into their treatment by the Bank of England (which he later withdrew), 1 June. He divided for a grant to improve the water communications of Canada, 12 June 1827.

Wrottesley was one of the 'reformers' whom the Wellington ministry considered but did not appoint to the finance committee, 10 Feb. 1828.[16] Next day he predicted that the committee 'would be used as scapegoats' for 'the imposition of fresh taxes on the people' and demanded further naval reductions. On 12 Feb., however, he appeared to accept the admiralty's statement that 30,000 seamen and marines were 'necessary', although he otherwise concurred in 'a great deal' of what Hume had said. He continued to harass the government on exchequer bills, successfully moving for their accounts, 15 Feb. He presented petitions against the Malt Act, 18, 21 Feb., 4 June, when he pressed ministers about their intentions on the matter. He called for 'a better system' of dealing with Irish and Scottish vagrants, citing the cost to Staffordshire of £1,256 in a single year, 19 Feb., was appointed to the select committee on it, 12 Mar., and again urged reform, 14 Mar. He presented petitions against the Test Acts, 20, 21 Feb., and paired for their repeal, 26 Feb. That month he was part of a deputation to the duke of Wellington, the premier, and Peel, the home secretary, for transferring East Retford's seats to Birmingham rather than extending its franchise to the freeholders of Bassetlaw, against which he spoke, 7 Mar., and voted, 21 Mar.[17] On 6 Mar. he blamed recent increases in crime on 'Peel's Act', which had 'strongly tended to encourage prosecutions' by 'holding out the temptation of reward'. Asserting that military provisions 'could always be procured cheaper than through the commissariat', he pressed for its abolition, 10 Mar. He was appointed to the select committee on the poor laws, 22 Mar. On 24 Mar. he resumed his criticism of the sinking fund, which 'if persisted in, must be productive of the most disastrous and ruinous effects'. He opposed plans outlined by Wilmot Horton, former colonial under-secretary, to relieve distress through emigration, 27 Mar., observing that before 'any plan for sending any part of the population out of the country' was pursued, 'they ought to try every possible experiment to remedy the evils of the country'. He presented a petition against the friendly societies bill from Maidstone Friendly Society, 17 Apr. He voted for setting the pivot price of corn at 60s. not 64s., 22 Apr. That day he presented a petition against Catholic relief from Black Ladies, Wolverhampton. He brought up one in favour from the Catholics of Tixall, 25 Apr. He divided for more efficient recovery of customs

penalties, 1 May. He secured copies of the country bankers' memorial, 9 May. On 15 May he defended the usury laws, insisting that the 'present state of the money market does not call for any alteration'. He seconded the motion to adjourn the debates on the small notes bill, 3 June, and recommended a 'continuation of the one pound notes, for an indefinite period', 5 June, when he voted for inquiry. He denounced the prohibition of Scottish bank notes 'outside that country' as 'quite absurd', and divided thus, 16 June. On 26 June, however, he resisted Hume's motion for returns of the number of notes in circulation, observing that since the banks were 'preparing for small notes withdrawal', it would merely produce an 'erroneous view of the proper circulation of the country'. He opposed the introduction of legislation for the suppression of bull-baiting, which he thought would greatly increase the evil rather than diminish it, 6 June. That day he voted against a grant for propagating the gospels in the colonies. He spoke against the county bridges bill, 9 June, arguing that they should 'be repaired under the turnpike trusts like any other parts of a road'. He opposed a clause in the licensing bill limiting opening times, 19 June, remarking that 'where ironworks are carried on, there is as much labour performed by night as by day' and that it would be unfair to 'prevent persons so employed from obtaining refreshment during the night'. On the army estimates, 20 June, he declared that pensions should only be 'bestowed upon those who really deserve them' and demanded measures to render the militia 'more effective'. He condemned a grant of £25,000 for the education of the Irish poor as 'worse than wasted', 26 June. He promised to 'make the most desperate attempts to oppose' the additional churches bill and divided for adjourning the debates, 30 June. He spoke in support of Colonel Bradley's case against the war office, 3 July 1828.

Wrottesley continued to campaign against exchequer bills, 16 Feb., and the manner of their funding, 8, 11 May 1829. He argued that the game laws amendment bill should be confined solely to the sale of game, 17 Feb. He voted for the Wellington ministry's concession of Catholic emancipation, 6, 30 Mar., and dismissed a hostile Wolverhampton petition as unrepresentative, 6 Mar., saying that he knew of a counter-petition signed by 2,760 adults 'of intelligence and information', which he duly presented, 11 Mar., along with one from Albrighton, Shropshire. He brought up favourable petitions from the Protestant Dissenters of Burton-upon-Trent, Coseley and Cotton, 16 Mar. He expressed dismay at the number of hostile petitions received by the House, and hoped that in the aftermath of emancipation 'peace and charity will soon knit together, in bonds of indissoluble amity, all sects and classes', 19 Mar. He was in the minorities for the transfer of East Retford's seats to Birmingham, 5 May 1829, 5, 15 Mar. 1830, and protested that 'giving this franchise to Bassetlaw' would be 'a retrograde step', 7 May 1829. He welcomed the justices of the peace bill, 11 May, and inquiry into the collection of malt and beer duties the following day. On 28 May 1829 he presented a petition signed by 'almost every' Wolverhampton merchant and manufacturer against the monopoly of the East India Company, which he asked the government to take 'into the earliest and most serious consideration'. Wrottesley blamed the increasing distress of the country on 'the course adopted by this House in the year 1826, with respect to the currency', 12 Feb. 1830. Presenting a Bilston petition against the truck system, 18 Feb., he urged ministers to 'repeal the measure of 1826', as the withdrawal of small notes had rendered the 'payment of wages in goods ... the rule, and the payment of wages in money ... the exception'. He presented similar petitions from various places, 3, 10, 16 Mar. He voted for parliamentary reform, 18 Feb., 28 May (as a pair), and the enfranchisement of Birmingham, Leeds and Manchester, 23 Feb. On 3 Mar. he was one of 27 opposition Members who met at the Albany and agreed to act under Lord Althorp's Commons leadership to seek reductions of expenditure and taxation.[18] He was in a minority of 15 for information on the Bombay judicature, 8 Mar. He defended the solicitor of the London and Birmingham Canal Company who was charged by Benson, Member for Stafford, with having submitted a fraudulent list of subscribers to the House, 11 Mar., 20, 21 May. He presented constituency petitions against the Walsall road bill, 18 Mar., slavery, 23 Mar., 21 May, and complaining of distress, 25 Mar. He was a minority teller for limiting ordnance salaries, 2 Apr., when he complained that by 'employing itself in its own manufactures', the government 'damps that ardour and inquisitiveness by which the public, when competition is common in the market, derive the benefit of improved skill and cheapened price'. On the same issue, 6 Apr., he agreed with Hume that 'the system of manufacturing by government is anything but one of economy', and cited the example of arms 'made for the East India Company at our manufactory at Enfield', which 'might have been obtained much cheaper at Birmingham'. He presented a petition from the magistrates of Stafford against the beer bill, which would be 'productive of serious injury to a deserving class of the community', 28 Apr., and another from Uttoxeter, 4 June. He contended that the cadets of Woolwich Military Academy should 'pay for their education', 30 Apr. He was appointed to select

committees on the labourers' wages bill, 3 May, manufacturing employment, 13 May, and, following his own motion for inquiry, the Hackney coach service, 13 May. He argued that Jews should only 'enjoy all the rights of British born subjects so far as relates to their trade and commerce' and that the 'power of obtaining a seat in this House' should not be placed 'in the hands of any one not of the Christian religion', but nevertheless voted for their emancipation, 17 May. On 24 May he divided for abolition of the death penalty for forgery. He defended the Scottish and Irish poor removal bill, which was not intended 'to burden the metropolis, but to relieve distant counties from a heavy burden', 26 May 1830.

At the 1830 general election Wrottesley stood again, stressing his support for tax reductions and claiming that the 'removal of beer duties' would be 'a source of considerable relief and comfort to the poor man', who 'would be able to drink three pints of beer for what two would now cost him'. Although he had 'never, upon any occasion, pledged himself to adopt any course', he would 'upon this occasion give one pledge, namely that if anything should arise likely to benefit the agriculture and commerce of the kingdom, it should have his honest support'. Rumours of an opposition came to nothing and he was returned unopposed.[19] He was of course listed by the Wellington ministry as one of their 'foes', and he divided against them on the civil list, 15 Nov. 1830. He presented constituency petitions for the abolition of slavery, 9, 17 Nov. 1830, 10 Mar. 1831. On 9 Nov. 1830 he demanded more 'effectual measures' against popular disturbances, but also urged inquiry into the causes of distress. He protested that there was 'a monopoly so firmly established among the coal-owners of the North, as would prevent the public from deriving the smallest benefit from the remission of the duty' on seaborne coals, 12 Nov. He endorsed a petition from the Staffordshire potteries against the East India Company's monopoly, 18 Nov., and presented another from the same place, signed by 10,000 artisans, against the truck system, 14 Dec. 1830. He welcomed the register of deeds bill, which would lessen the 'insecurity and expense of conveyancing', 9 Feb. 1831. He commended the Grey ministry's budget, 11 Feb., asserting that their proposals to repeal taxes on coal, candles and tobacco 'amply redeemed their pledges to the country'. He was appointed to the public accounts committee, 17 Feb. On 14 Mar. he argued for improved public access to the British Museum, particularly on Saturdays when it was 'invariably closed'. Next day he defended the Birmingham Grammar School bill, denying that it was biased 'exclusively to the education of the children of the rich'. Wrottesley presented constituency petitions for reform, 3 Feb., when he observed that it was a cause that he had 'long advocated', 10, 19, 29 Mar. Rebutting Tory statements that bribery was common in all constituencies, 17 Feb., he argued that 'county Members are not generally returned by the influence of bribery, whether in the shape of money or patronage'. He drew attention to the large number of reform petitions awaiting presentation, 7 Mar., and refuted claims made by Miller, Tory Member for Newcastle-under-Lyme, that they were being 'got up' improperly, asserting that 'in Staffordshire there is not an individual who is not enthusiastic in the cause', 19 Mar. He hoped the Grey ministry's reform bill would 'be thrown out altogether, rather than not carried to its full extent', and warned against sacrificing 'any detail which will risk the principle of the measure', 21 Mar. He paired for its second reading the following day and divided against Gascoyne's wrecking amendment, 19 Apr. 1831. At the ensuing general election he offered again, promising to support economy, retrenchment and reform. 'So far from being revolutionary', he declared, the reform bill was 'a moderate' measure which would 'tend to unite all classes, and correct and modify public opinion'. Talk of an opposition promoted by Peel came to nothing and he was re-elected unopposed.[20]

Wrottesley urged ministers to 'institute a full inquiry' into military accounts, 27 June 1831. He voted for the second reading of the reintroduced reform bill, 6 July, at least twice against the adjournment, 12 July, and gave generally steady support to its details, although he was in the minority against the inclusion of Downton in schedule A, 21 July, and spoke and divided for giving two Members to Stoke, the omission of which he deemed a 'striking inconsistency' given that the two Member boroughs of Sunderland and Devonport had smaller populations, 4 Aug. He was also in the majority for Lord Chandos's clause to enfranchise £50 tenants-at-will, 18 Aug. He condemned the anti-reform speeches of the Tory opposition as 'a merciless waste of time', 5 Aug., protesting that 'Members should not be detained in town at this season of the year' and that 'the sooner the bill is passed the better it will be for all parties'. On 11 Aug. he argued against retaining the annuitant franchise in cities such as Lichfield which were counties of themselves, as 'a person of large property, by cutting it up into annuities, may acquire such influence as to turn the place into a close borough'. He denied opposition charges of political bias in the appointment of the boundary commissioners, 11 Sept. He divided for the reform bill's passage, 21 Sept., and Lord Ebrington's

confidence motion, 10 Oct. He had Wetherell called to order for naming 'Tavistock Abbey, Althorp and Chatsworth' as places likely 'to be the objects of popular fury' over the £10 householder clause, 12 Oct. He called for more time to enable the sheriff to answer charges arising from the Pembrokeshire election, 8 July. On 11 July he denied that 'much advantage' was 'derived by the public' from the widening of London streets. He was appointed to the select committee on the House of Commons buildings, 12 Aug., but protested that the 'alterations' they were considering 'would cost considerably more than the building of a new House', 11 Oct. He cautioned against 'acting hastily' over the delayed election return of Great Grimsby, 16 Aug., and voted with ministers on the Dublin election controversy, 23 Aug. He was a majority teller against an amendment to the labourers' wages bill, 13 Sept. 1831.

Wrottesley voted for the second reading of the revised reform bill, 17 Dec. 1831, and for going into committee on it, 20 Jan., 20 Feb. 1832, and again gave general support to its details. He dismissed concerns about the expense of the proposed registration system, insisting that the shilling to be charged would 'be more than ample ... and there will be a surplus to go to the poor rates', 20 Feb. Deputizing for Littleton, he refuted attacks by Croker on the boundary proposals, 9 Mar., when, in Littleton's opinion, he spoke 'remarkably well' in defence of the new constituency arrangements for Staffordshire and 'the claims of Walsall to one representative', as he did again, 7 June.[21] He divided for the reform bill's third reading, 22 Mar., and the address calling on the king to appoint only ministers who would carry it unimpaired, 10 May. On 17 May he gave notice of a Wolverhampton petition signed by 12,000 inhabitants and political unionists for withholding the supplies until the bill became law, which he duly presented, 22 May. He voted for the second reading of the Irish reform bill, 25 May, and against a Conservative amendment to the Scottish bill, 1 June. He divided with government on the Russian-Dutch loan, 26 Jan., 12, 20 July, and relations with Portugal, 9 Feb. He voted for information on military punishments, 16 Feb. He presented a Wolverhampton petition in support of the London and Birmingham railway bill, 14 May, and opposed inquiry into alleged irregularities in its standing orders, 18 June. He warned that if measures against distress were 'not speedily taken', many people would 'be thrown out of employment, and under the stimulus of privation, may have recourse to violence', 17 May. He was appointed to the committee of secrecy on the Bank of England charter, 23 May. He drew attention to the 'impropriety' of using the word 'extinction' in the Irish tithes bill when 'commutation' was actually intended, 29 June 1832.

At the 1832 general election Wrottesley was returned unopposed for the new division of Staffordshire South, where he sat until his defeat at the general election of 1837. It was his motion for a call of the whole House to consider the fate in the Lords of the Irish church bill which unexpectedly led to a humiliating defeat for the Grey ministry and split the cabinet, 15 July 1833.[22] Raised to the peerage in 1838, he retired to farming on his model demesne of 800 acres, which was noted for its agricultural improvements, particularly in turnip growing, but by 1840 Dyott considered that 'his days are numbered'. Wrottesley died 'after long suffering' in March the following year.[23] By his will, dated 30 June 1835 and proved under £45,000, he left legacies of £6,000 to each of the four surviving children of his first marriage and three step-children by his second. The residue and entailed estates passed to his eldest son and successor in the barony John Wrottesley (1798-1867), an astronomer.[24]

[1] Staffs. Advertiser, 5, 12, 19, 26 July; Lichfield Mercury, 11 July 1823; Dyott's Diary, i. 350, ii. 148. [2] Hatherton mss, Littleton to Leigh, 16 May 1829; Dod's Parl. Companion (1833), 177. [3] The Times, 10 Feb. 1824. [4] Ibid. 6 Mar. 1824. [5] Ibid. 13 Mar. 1824. [6] Ibid. 31 Mar. 1824. [7] Ibid. 5, 6 May 1824. [8] Ibid. 26, 27 May, 1 June 1824. [9] Ibid. 22 Apr. 1825. [10] Ibid. 27 Apr. 1825. [11] Ibid. 29 Apr. 1825. [12] Ibid. 16 May 1825. [13] Ibid. 31 May, 3, 4 June 1825. [14] Keele Univ. Lib. Sneyd mss SC8/79; Broughton, Recollections, iii. 125; Northants. RO, Agar Ellis diary, 13 Feb. 1826. [15] Staffs. Advertiser, 10, 17, 24 June; Hatherton mss, Littleton to Leigh, 13, 15 May, 2 June 1826. [16] Add. 38761, f. 269; 40395, f. 221. [17] Lincs. AO, Tennyson d'Eyncourt mss 2 Td'E M85/9, C. to G. Tennyson, 27 Feb. 1828. [18] Castle Howard mss, Graham to Morpeth, 3 Mar. 1830. [19] Staffs. Advertiser, 17, 24, 31 July, 7, 14 Aug. 1830. [20] Ibid. 30 Apr., 7 May 1831. [21] Hatherton diary, 9 Mar. 1832. [22] Three Diaries, 362. [23] Dyott's Diary, ii. 146, 328, 336; Gent. Mag. (1841), i. 650-1. [24] PROB 11/1948/463; IR26/1594/351; Oxford DNB.

P.J.S.

WYNDHAM, Wadham (1773–1843), of St. Edmund's College, Salisbury, Wilts.

SALISBURY	1818–6 May 1833
SALISBURY	1835–23 Oct. 1843

b. 16 Oct. 1773, 2nd but 1st surv. s. of Henry Penruddocke Wyndham† of St. Edmund's College and Caroline, da. and h. of Edward Hearst of The Close, Salisbury.[1] educ. Warminster sch. 1787; Eton 1793. m. 1 Mar. 1821, Anne Eliza, da. of Lt.-Gen. Sir John Slade, 1st bt., of Maunsell House, Som., s.p. suc. fa. 1819. d. 23 Oct. 1843.
    Cornet Wilts. yeomanry 1794; capt. Wilts. militia 1796, maj. 1805.
    Mayor, Wilton 1825-6.

In 1819 Wyndham succeeded his father, who was Member for Wiltshire, 1795-1812, to the bulk of an estate comprising land in Wiltshire and Hampshire, a medieval college in Salisbury and personal wealth sworn under £18,000.[2] A 'country squire of an old Tory family', he was active in local government and landed society. After an abortive attempt in 1813, when he was made a freeman of the city, he was returned for his native borough at the general election of 1818.[3] This was understood to be on the interest of the corporation, and with the tacit approval of the Tory 2nd earl of Radnor, who nominated his eldest son, Lord Folkestone, for the other seat. Unlike his colleague, he was a supporter of the Liverpool administration and an opponent of Catholic relief.[4] He signed a protest in November 1819 against any Wiltshire meeting taking place over Peterloo, and the requisition in March 1820 for a meeting of freeholders to promote a loyal address to George IV. In the expectation of another contest for the county, he chaired a meeting, 3 Mar. 1820, when it was agreed to raise a subscription of £20,000 to ensure the success of John Benett.* He was again returned unopposed for Salisbury at the general election that month.[5]

He divided for production of the civil list revenue accounts, 3 May 1820, but was not listed as siding with opposition on any other motions for retrenchment and lower taxation in the early 1820s, and, indeed, voted against economies in revenue collection, 4 July 1820. He divided against censuring ministers' conduct towards Queen Caroline, 6 Feb., disqualifying civil officers of the ordnance from voting in parliamentary elections, 12 Apr., and the forgery punishment mitigation bill, 23 May 1821. He was in majorities against abolishing one of the joint-postmasterships, 13 Mar., and inquiry into Irish tithes, 19 June 1822. In accordance with the mayor's request, he forwarded to the corporation a copy of the petition from the inhabitants of Salisbury against the severity of Henry Hunt's* gaol sentence, which was presented to the House by Benett, 24 Apr. 1822.[6] He voted against reform of the Scottish representative system, 2 June 1823. No other trace of parliamentary activity has been found for that and the following year. As he had on 28 Feb. 1821, he divided against Catholic relief, 1 Mar., 21 Apr., 10 May, and the related Irish franchise bill, 26 Apr. 1825. He was publicly fêted on his return to Salisbury, 29 June, when he stated that

respecting the Catholic question, I assure you that my vote was not lightly given, nor until after the most mature deliberation on the important subject; for conscientiously differing from the opinion of many valued friends on this point, it demanded and received my most serious consideration; and the more I weighed the question in my mind, the more I felt convinced of the necessity of opposing the measure; for depend upon it, should the bill ever pass into a law, that sooner or later, consequences *must* arise that will endanger the safety of our present constitution.[7]

His name headed the requisition for a local meeting on slavery, 1 Feb., when he supported a petition for its abolition, which he presented to the Commons, 9 Feb. 1826.[8]

In giving thanks for his unopposed return at the general election of 1826, Wyndham trusted 'that you will never have to accuse me of deviating from a manly independence, and that I shall ever evince an unshaken loyalty to my sovereign and a firm attachment to our excellent constitution'.[9] Having been elected a burgess in 1819, he became mayor of Wilton, Lord Pembroke's borough, in the autumn of 1825, but he was presumably not present to oversee the election of his distant relation, John Hungerford Penruddocke, and his fellow militia officer, Edward Baker, 12 June 1826, because his name is not among the signatories on the return.[10] He divided against Catholic claims, 6 Mar. 1827. He voted against the second reading of the corn bill, 2 Apr., the disfranchisement of Penryn, 28 May, and the third reading of the Penryn election bill, 7 June 1827. Nothing came of attempts in early 1828 by Lord Chandos* to secure a place from the duke of Wellington, the new prime minister, for Wyndham, who Chandos claimed had recently sustained heavy losses.[11] He voted against repeal of the Test Acts, 26 Feb., and Catholic relief, 12 May. He presented a petition from the corporation of Salisbury against the alehouses' licensing bill, 6 June 1828. He brought up an anti-Catholic one from the archdeaconry and clergy of the diocese of Sarum, 26 Feb. 1829, and, in his only known speech in Parliament, commented that 'no petition from that quarter, and on that subject, had ever been more numerously or respectably subscribed'. He was listed by Planta, the patronage secretary, among those 'opposed to the principle' of the emancipation bill, and he signed the hostile Wiltshire declaration and voted against the measure, 6, 18, 30 Mar.[12] He divided against the grant for the marble arch, 25 May. Perhaps it was partly because of his hostile votes that Peel, the home secretary, refused to appoint him to the receivership of police in London in July 1829, despite his experience of local business and his 'integrity and high respectability'.[13] Wellington offered him a position the following year, but what it was, or whether he accepted it, is not known.[14] He was granted a week's leave on urgent private business, 15 Mar. 1830. He

paired against Jewish emancipation, 17 May. He presented a Salisbury petition against the sale of beer for on-consumption, 14 May, and voted for Knatchbull's amendment to this effect, 21 June 1830.

At the general election of 1830 Wyndham was returned with Duncombe Pleydell Bouverie, who was a reformer, like his brother Folkestone, now 3rd earl of Radnor. He entertained Princess Victoria to lunch on her visit to Salisbury in October that year.[15] He was listed by ministers among their 'friends', but was absent from the division on the civil list, 15 Nov. He was present the following day to hear the end of Wellington's administration announced, and wrote to an unknown friend that 'I can give no particulars further, and what will become of us God only knows'.[16] He presented an anti-slavery petition from the Independents of Salisbury, 17 Nov. In late November and early December 1830 he saw service with militia units attempting to disperse rioters in the vicinity of Salisbury and at the attack on Benett at Pythouse.[17] He voted against the second reading of the Grey ministry's reform bill, 22 Mar., and for Gascoyne's wrecking amendment, 19 Apr. 1831. At the ensuing general election, he was spotted canvassing for Chandos at Chipping Wycombe.[18] He himself faced a challenge at Salisbury and was barely given a hearing, 30 Apr., when he justified his vote against the reform bill as one cast conscientiously, and turned the attack on his opponent William Bird Brodie† by accusing him of inconsistency in now advocating the reforms he had once condemned. Brodie retaliated, and stressed that he had acted fairly by Wyndham in calling upon him to warn him of his plans and to persuade him to support reform, but that he had only received the answer

that the question was one involved in difficulty; that he dared not think for himself on it; and that Sir Robert Peel was the person, above all others, in whose opinion he generally placed the highest confidence; and that he should probably be guided by him.[19]

Wyndham, who informed a correspondent that 'ministers are under some alarm, and by all accounts plunged into difficulty, by reason of their judicious measure and the excitement existing abroad', believed that he had had the better of the argument. As expected, he was elected in second place, narrowly behind Pleydell Bouverie and, after rowdy scenes, he 'got off as fast as he could, but did not escape being hustled' in returning home.[20] Brodie and Pleydell Bouverie offered again almost immediately, and Wyndham was therefore forced to issue an address himself, 4 June 1831, though he had to apologize to Radnor for inadvertently casting a slur on his brother's conduct.[21]

He voted against the second reading of the reintroduced reform bill, 6 July, and for using the 1831 census to determine the boroughs in the disfranchisement schedules, 19 July 1831. He was listed as absent on the partial disfranchisement of Chippenham, 27 July. He divided in the majority against the second reading of the Irish union of parishes bill, 19 Aug. He voted against the passage of the reform bill, 21 Sept., and was named as a defaulter, 10 Oct., the day of Lord Ebrington's confidence motion. He voted against the second reading of the revised bill, 17 Dec. 1831, the enfranchisement of Tower Hamlets, 28 Feb., and the third reading, 22 Mar. 1832. He attended the Commons on the resignation of the Grey cabinet, 9 May, and commented that 'there is less *fever* in the House than could have been expected, and from the different speeches I calculate affairs will proceed in a quiet way'.[22] His only other known votes were in the minority against the second reading of the malt drawback bill, 29 Feb., and against the Grey government on the Russian-Dutch loan, 26 Jan., 12 July 1832. It was probably after the former occasion that he reported that

> ministers were sadly put to shifts this morning at half-past three, and the only reason why they were not left in a minority on Herries's motion was their friends observing they were so mauled and beaten down, that they did not afterwards wish to trample upon them, and quitted the House without voting.[23]

Edward Hinxman of Little Durnford House wrote publicly to Wyndham, 21 June 1832:

> Nothing could have been easier for you than to have followed that path, to have voted for a measure which in your conscience you believed dangerous to the country, and kept your seat in peace! But you pursued a nobler course, you sacrificed your interest to your principles.[24]

He was, in fact, re-elected at the general election of 1832 and, having been unseated in 1833, sat from 1835 until his death in October 1843. Remembered for his integrity and the strictness of his Conservative principles, the 'unostentation in his generosity, sincerity in his friendships, true hospitality and a love of the invigorating sports of the field combined to make his character completely defined in the brief expression "a fine old English gentleman"'. He was succeeded by his sister Caroline Frances (?1769-1845), the wife of John Campbell (1771-1846) of Dunoon, Argyll and Blunham, Bedfordshire, and by their only son, John Henry Campbell (1798-1869) of Corhampton House, Hampshire, who was Member for Salisbury, 1843-7, and took the additional name of Wyndham in 1844.[25]

[1] Sir R.C. Hoare, *Wilts. Salisbury*, 815; PROB 11/933/417. [2] PROB 11/1617/302; IR26/806/475. [3] C. Haskins, *Charter of Hen. III and Hist. St. Edmund's Coll.* 40, 47; *The Times*, 16 Aug. 1831. [4] *HP Commons, 1790-1820*, v. 660-1. [5] *Devizes Gazette*, 4 Nov. 1819, 9, 16 Mar.; *Salisbury Jnl.* 13 Mar. 1820. [6] Wilts. RO, Salisbury borough recs. G23/1/7. [7] *Salisbury Jnl.* 4 July 1825. [8] Ibid. 30 Jan., 6 Feb.; *The Times*, 10 Feb. 1826. [9] *Salisbury Jnl.* 12 June 1826. [10] Wilts. RO, Wilton borough recs. G25/1/22, ff. 296, 312, 314. [11] Wellington mss WP1/915/74; 918/6; 920/43; 939/1. [12] Glos. RO, Sotheron Estcourt mss D1571 X114, Long to Bucknall Estcourt, Feb. 1829. [13] Add. 40399, ff. 281, 285; N. Gash, *Secretary Peel*, 500. [14] Wellington mss WP1/1110/13. [15] *Salisbury Jnl.* 2 Aug., 1 Nov. 1830. [16] Wilts. RO, Wilts. Arch. Soc. mss 1553/10. [17] *Salisbury Jnl.* 29 Nov., 6 Dec. 1830. [18] *Three Diaries*, 88. [19] *Salisbury Jnl.* 18, 25 Apr., 2, 9 May 1831. [20] Wilts. Arch. Soc. mss 10; Wilts. RO, Radnor mss 490/1375, Boucher to Radnor, 24, 25, 30 Apr., Pleydell Bouverie to same, 24, 26, 27, 30 Apr. 1831. [21] Radnor mss 490/1375, Boucher to Radnor, 3, 5 May, Wyndham to same, 6, 8, 10 June; *Salisbury Jnl.* 23 May, 6 June 1831. [22] Wilts. Arch. Soc. mss 10, Wyndham to unknown [?9 May 1832]. [23] Ibid. Wyndham to unknown [27 Jan. 1832]. [24] *Salisbury Jnl.* 25 June 1832. [25] *Devizes Gazette*, 26 Oct.; *Salisbury Herald*, 28 Oct. 1843; *Gent. Mag.* (1844), ii. 93-94; (1846), i. 109, 543-4; H.A. Wyndham, *A Fam. Hist. 1688-1837*, pp. 230, 348, 355.

S.M.F.

WYNN, Thomas John, 2nd Bar. Newborough [I] (1802–1832), of Glynllifon, Caern.

CAERNARVONSHIRE	1826–1830

b. 3 Apr. 1802, 1st surv. s. of Thomas Wynn†, 1st Bar. Newborough [I], of Glynllifon and 2nd w. Maria Stella Petronilla, da. of Lorenzo Chiappini, constable of Modigliana, *styled* Marchesina de Modigliana. *educ.* Rugby 1816-18; Christ Church, Oxf. 1820. *unm. suc.* fa. as 2nd Baron Newborough [I] 12 Oct. 1807. *d.* 15 Nov. 1832.

Mayor, Nefyn 1824-*d.*

Thomas John, the elder of two sons born to the 1st Lord Newborough and his Florentine child bride, was not conceived until his half-brother John, the only child of his father's marriage to Lady Catherine Perceval, had died without issue. The family's fortunes had declined and they had lost the Caernarvonshire seat in 1774, the county lieutenancy in 1781 and Caernarvon Boroughs in 1790 to the Bulkeleys of Baron Hill and the Pagets of Plas Newydd.[1] They could nevertheless appeal to strong Welsh and parliamentary pedigrees and retained land and influence in 36 Caernarvonshire parishes and the boroughs of Caernarvon, Pwllheli and Nefyn. Indeed, Bulkeley saw fit to compensate Newborough's father by returning him for Beaumaris from 1796 until he died in 1807, leaving a widow and sons aged five and four.[2] His will established a trust administered by Spencer Perceval†, Edward Majoribanks, Thomas Atkinson and Sir Coutts Trotter, and settled the 22,941-acre estates, which included quarries in Dyffryn Nantlle and Ffestiniog, on Thomas John, a godson of Lord Bulkeley, with provision for his minority. Under its terms, Lady Newborough, who married the Russian baron, Ungern Sternberg, 11 Sept. 1810, thereby forfeited the guardianship of her sons to David Hughes, principal of Jesus College, Oxford. He placed them in the care of their cousin Thomas Edward Wynn Belasyse for four years before sending them to Rugby, which Newborough left in March 1818 when the headmaster recommended that the brothers be separated.[3] Hughes's widow subsequently cared for the boys at her home in Whitchurch, near Pangbourne, Berkshire, where their behaviour caused problems. Their tutor John Slater advised Coutts Trotter, 29 Feb. 1819:

> From my experience of ... [Newborough's] opinions and disposition, I cannot but think the most beneficial plan which can be adopted for his future education would be either to send him immediately to Christ Church if possible (and perhaps a single admission for a nobleman might be obtained) or adopt some line of proceeding by which he may be entitled to see more of the world, and thus learn to conform to the practices of society in general.[4]

He was sent to the continent for a year with the Rev. William Phillips, who became his Oxford tutor. The trustees, whom his mother threatened with prosecution, expended £29,650 during his minority and made several applications to chancery for additional funds.[5] Newborough was estimated to be worth £113,000 when he came of age in 1823. Rents on the Abbey, Bodfean and Glynllifon estates grossing £13,718 a year were £20,300 in arrears, and a further £2,500 was outstanding from Denbighshire and Merioneth estates worth £2,156 a year. He had £5,600 in chancery, a £4,000 mortgage, dilapidated mansions, and realizable income of just under £11,000 a year. His visits to Glynllifon, the Caernarvon eisteddfod and Pwllheli hunt in 1821 had attracted much attention, and his coming of age was celebrated with dinners for his tenantry and doles to the poor of Caernarvon, Conway, Ffestiniog, Pwllheli and Nefyn. However, he had little experience of Wales or estate matters.[6] Glyn Griffith of Bodegroes, whom he appointed 'general agent', let it be known that 'it was not the intention of Lord Newborough either to disturb the county or borough of Caernarvon ... though he would never lose sight of either'.[7]

Bulkeley had died in 1822 and his successor as lord lieutenant, Thomas Assheton Smith I* of Vaenol, encouraged Newborough to oppose the return of Bulkeley's pro-Catholic half-brother Sir Robert Williams for Caernarvonshire at the first opportu-

nity. Disappointed at the failure of the Ffestiniog railway bill and shortcomings in the 1825 Caernarvon-Llanllyfni Railway Act, he announced his candidature when a dissolution was anticipated that September. He denied making any pledge not to oppose Williams and raised the 'No Popery' cry. Williams was outraged that after 'living on the most friendly terms with all my family', he should behave thus.[8] Adopting a high public profile, and with a view to opposing the Pagets in Caernarvon Boroughs, he had also become mayor of Nefyn (11 Sept. 1824), leased Conway corporation farm, and taken his freedom (29 Sept. 1825) at Caernarvon, where he and Assheton Smith were the major property owners and the candidature of his brother Spencer Bulkeley Wynn (1803-88) was mooted.[9] Williams's pre-poll resignation left him unopposed in Caernarvonshire at the general election in June 1826, when his brother refrained from opposition in the Boroughs and spent £5,120. He confirmed his anti-Catholic politics at his election dinner.[10] Afterwards, he borrowed £15,000 to cover his costs, improvements at Glynllifon, and land acquired from Richard Garnons of Plas Llanwnda.[11]

By the time he took his seat in November, his agents and supporters had made the necessary local preparations for bills to fund the Nantlle Railway Company and enclose Landwrog and Llanwnda to further Glynllifon's agricultural and quarrying interests. Petitions for both bills were presented, 24 Nov. 1826, and Newborough was given leave to bring them in.[12] He spent Christmas and New Year hunting in Dorset, returning to London for the duke of York's funeral, of which he sent a long account to his Pwllheli agent; it was marked by a gun salute and tolling of bells at Glynllifon.[13] He secured the enactment of the Nantlle bill, 21 Mar. 1827;[14] but the Llanwnda and Llandwrog enclosure was repeatedly postponed and he had to withdraw it, 21 May, after a successful parliamentary campaign against it led by Williams's brother-in-law, William Hughes of Kinmel. Locally, petitioning was accompanied by organized violence by Rhostryfan cottagers threatened with eviction.[15] The contentious Caernarvon improvement bill which failed that month had also been entrusted to him.[16] He divided against Catholic relief, 6 Mar., presented Caernarvon's unfavourable petition, 22 Mar. 1827,[17] and voted against repealing the Test Acts, 26 Feb., and Catholic relief, 12 May 1828. His application to the duke of Wellington, 14 May, for the county lieutenancy, vacant through Assheton Smith's death, was turned down.[18] That summer, he and his brother visited Marseilles and stayed briefly in Paris where his mother, who was pursuing her case to prove she was the daughter of Louis Égalité, Comte de Joinville and heiress to the Orléans fortune, had fallen victim to the swindler John Mills. A bishop's court in Faenza had confirmed her noble parentage in 1824, and she made much of her sons' physical resemblance to Louis XVI.[19] In Caernarvonshire, Newborough faced costly litigation over the Glynrhonwy quarries and Llanberis road, the Llanbeblig evictions and the lease of Caernarvon customs house.[20] Ministers considered him as a possible mover or seconder of the 1829 address and expected him to vote with them for Catholic emancipation.[21] Reports of proceedings in the House when he presented anti-Catholic petitions from Bangor, Caernarvonshire's Welsh Calvinistic Methodists, Llannor and Pwllheli, 12 Feb., differed so much that he inserted a an explanatory notice and compilation of newspaper reports in the anti-Catholic *North Wales Chronicle*, 19 Feb. He claimed he had stated, 12 Feb., that

> whatever measures ... ministers may think proper to bring before this House, for securing the peace and happiness of Ireland, for remedying the dreadful evils that now exist – and above all for healing the religious animosities between Catholic and Protestant – I shall give my most cordial support, provided they are accompanied by those *solid securities which are likely to tranquillize the just fears of His Majesty's Protestant subjects*. Without those safeguards ... I consider it would be an extravagant extension of confidence to yield anything like unconditional submission to their claims. Should such be attempted by ... ministers, which I am sure they will not do, I shall conceive it my duty to give my most determined opposition to the measure.

The paper's editor remained dissatisfied.[22] Glynllifon withdrew its subscription to the *North Wales Chronicle*, which published calls for Newborough's resignation for not adhering to his election pledge. It reported that he had voted for Catholic relief, 6 Mar., when he did not vote at all, and the clamour for his resignation continued at north-west Wales Protestant meetings throughout March.[23] He divided against the relief bill, 18 Mar., and presented a hostile petition from Beddgelert, 25 Mar., but did not vote on the bill's third reading, 30 Mar. 1829. At Shropshire assizes in August, Caernarvon corporation lost their case against him over the customs house lease. His defence cost £347 8s.[24] He no longer paid attention to his parliamentary duties. His health problems, a weak lung and skin disorder, were genuine, and he went to the south of France in search of a cure. Work on the mausoleum in which he proposed to be buried had commenced in 1826.[25] He was convalescing in Marseilles, and contactable only through Coutts Trotter, when the general

election was called in 1830, which made the outcome of a possible contest in Caernarvon Boroughs, where Thomas Assheton Smith II* was invited to stand or nominate, hard to predict.[26] 'Lord Newborough's absence and silence' encouraged his agents, particularly Rumsey Williams's brother-in-law George Bettiss, to support the anti-Paget faction.[27] In the county, Assheton Smith hoped to bring in his cousin Charles Wynne Griffith Wynne* of Cefnamlwch, Newborough's 1826 proposer.[28] The slate industry was depressed, and Newborough, who was known not to be ready to stand a contest, adopted a passive approach, making no move to announce his retirement through ill health until 10 July 1830.[29]

A slight improvement in his condition enabled him to return and campaign actively for repeal of the slate duties in 1831. Presiding at the county meeting, 15 Jan., he condemned that tax which 'prevents the flow of capital, fetters the spirit of enterprise, and creates distress and dissatisfaction among the industrious and labouring classes of the community'. He also promised 'to come forward with my heart, as well as my purse, to promote every cause which has for its object the welfare of the town and the county of Caernarvon'.[30] Caernarvon harbour trustees had prosecuted him in November 1830 for erecting a wharf on the Seiont, but he staunched opposition by becoming their chairman in February 1831 and appointing his brother a trustee.[31] His support was again assiduously cultivated at the 1831 general election, when the reformer Sir Charles Paget narrowly defeated William Ormsby Gore* in Caernarvon Boroughs; and he seconded the nomination of the anti-reformer Griffith Wynne for the county.[32] Arguing that the same restrictions applied to Irish as English peers, Paget's counsel prevented him from voting for Ormsby Gore and had notices informing Glynllifon tenants of their landlord's allegiance removed.[33] Spencer Wynn voted for Paget.[34] As a magistrate, Newborough tried those accused of misdemeanour following disturbances at the election.[35]

Glynllifon's influence in the Boroughs increased under the Reform Act, but neither Newborough nor his brother agreed to stand for Parliament, and by September 1832 both had declared their support for the Tory candidates in the Boroughs and county.[36] Newborough died of consumption in November and was buried with great ceremony and mourning at Llandwrog. His funeral sermon was preached on the text, 'the liberal deviseth liberal things, and by liberal things shall he stand'. His will, dated 24 Aug. 1830, and proved, 15 Mar. 1833, revoked one he had made in 1822 in favour of his trustees and settled everything on his brother, who also succeeded him as 3rd Baron Newborough.[37]

[1] *HP Commons, 1754-90*, i. 460-1; iii. 669-71. [2] G. Roberts, *Aspects of Welsh Hist.* 160-71; Maria Wynn, *Mems. of Maria Stella* trans. M.H.M. Capes (1914), 88-94; UCNW, Beaumaris mss iv. 318. [3] PROB 11/1471/893; Gwynedd Archives, Caernarfon, Glynllifon mss 4352, 4361, 4367-9, 5725; *Mems. of Maria Stella*, 97-99; D. Williams, 'Maria Stella, Lady Newborough', *Trans. Caern. Hist. Soc.* xv (1954), 24-48. [4] Glynllifon mss 4665 [5] Ibid. 4625, 4654, 4658-71, 4681, 4725, 5724-6. [6] Ibid. 4665, 5736-8, 8360-7; *N. Wales Gazette*, 6, 13, 20 Sept., 18 Oct. 1821; *Shrewsbury Chron.* 4 Apr. 1823. [7] UCNW, Plas Coch mss 3770; Plas Newydd mss i. 215. [8] Plas Newydd mss i. 211, 213, 215, 218, 223, 224, 226, 227, 231, 241; J.I.C. Boyd, *Ffestiniog Railway*, i. 20-22; *N. Wales Gazette*, 22, 29 Sept., 6, 13 Oct. 1825; UCNW, Porth yr Aur mss 12533, 12663E. [9] *N. Wales Gazette*, 13 Jan., 1 Sept. 1825; *PP* (1838), xxxv. 241-2, 324; Plas Newydd mss i. 223, 226, 231, 238, 245, 265, 281; Gwynedd Archives, Caernarfon, Caernarvon borough recs. 12. [10] *N. Wales Gazette*, 8, 15, 23 June 1826; Glynllifon mss 4238-42, 6061. [11] Glynllifon mss 4440, 4570. [12] *N. Wales Gazette*, 12 Oct., 2 Nov. 1826; *CJ*, lxxxii. 30, 46. [13] Gwynedd Archives, Caernarfon XD2/Temp/2139 [Bodfean 36], Newborough to D. Williams, 20 Jan.; *N. Wales Gazette*, 25 Jan. 1827. [14] *CJ*, lxxxii. 122, 212, 252, 338. [15] *N. Wales Gazette*, 26 Apr., 7, 14, 21 June; *The Times*, 21 May 1827; Glynllifon mss 6063; D.J.V. Jones, *Before Rebecca*, 50, 63; *CJ*, lxxxii. 332, 341, 424, 437, 442, 477. [16] *CJ*, lxxxii. 252; *N. Wales Gazette*, 12 Apr. 1827. [17] *N. Wales Gazette*, 8, 22 Mar. 1827. [18] Wellington mss WP1/932/9; 935/22. [19] *Mems. of Maria Stella*, 16, 230, 236; Glynllifon mss 4156, 4681; *Gent. Mag.* (1833), i. 82. [20] Glynllifon mss 5891-3; NLW, Henry Rumsey Williams mss 23, 25. [21] Add. 40398, f. 86. [22] *The Times*; *Morning Chronicle*; *Courier*; *Morning Herald*; *Morning Post*; *Morning Standard*; *St. James's Chronicle*, 13 Feb.; *N. Wales Chron.* 19 Feb. 1829. [23] *N. Wales Chron.* 26 Feb., 12, 26 Mar., 2 Apr. 1829. [24] Glynllifon mss 5897, 6068. [25] *Mems. of Maria Stella*, 94, 238; Plas Coch mss 3770; Roberts, 175. [26] Glynllifon mss 4883; Plas Newydd mss i. 378, 389, 381-3, 403, 404, 410, 423, 479, 484; Gwynedd Archives, Caernarfon, Poole mss 5434. [27] Plas Newydd mss i. 445, 461, 475, 479. [28] Ibid. i. 380, 383, 393, 486, 490; Poole mss 5459. [29] Plas Newydd mss i. 383, 393, 404, 432; A.H. Dodd. *Industrial Revolution in N. Wales* (1990), 214-18; *N. Wales Chron.* 15 July 1830. [30] *Caernarvon Herald*, 8, 22 Jan., 19 Feb. 1831. [31] Glynllifon mss 5898; *Caernarvon Herald*, 1 Feb., 5 Mar. 1831. [32] Plas Newydd mss i. 555, 558, 567; *Caernarvon Herald*, 7, 14 May 1831. [33] Plas Newydd mss i. 604; vii. 291; Ll. Jones, 'Edition of Corresp. of 1st mq. of Anglesey relating to General Elections of 1830, 1831 and 1832 in Caern. and Anglesey' (Univ. of Liverpool M.A. thesis, 1956) 508, 512; Porth yr Aur mss 12570, 12577; *The Times*, 12 May 1831. [34] Plas Newydd mss i. 583; K. Evans, 'Caernarvon Borough', *Trans. Caern. Hist. Soc.* viii (1947), 62. [35] *Chester Courant*, 5 July 1831. [36] Plas Newydd mss i. 73, 551, 554, 629; ii. 3601, 3602, 3612, 3614-7. [37] *Caernarvon Herald*, 17 Nov., 1 Dec.; *Chester Courant*, 4 Dec.; *N. Wales Chron.* 4 Dec. 1832; PROB 8/226; PROB 11/1813/176; Glynllifon mss 4102, 4371, 4372, 4374, 4443.

M.M.E.

WYNN *see also* **WILLIAMS WYNN**

WYNNE, John Arthur (1801–1865), of Hazelwood, co. Sligo.

SLIGO	1830–1832
SLIGO	8 Mar. 1856–1857
SLIGO	31 July 1857–July 1860

b. 20 Apr. 1801, 2nd but 1st surv. s. of Owen Wynne* of Hazelwood and Lady Sarah Elizabeth Cole, da. of William, 1st earl of Enniskillen [I]. *educ.* Winchester 1816-19; Christ Church, Oxf. 1820. *m.* 7 Apr. 1838, Lady Anne Wandesford Butler, da. of James Wandesford Butler*, 1st mq. of Ormonde [I], 2s. (1 *d.v.p.*) 2da. *suc.* fa. 1841. *d.* 19 June 1865.

Under-sec. to ld. lt. [I] Feb.-Dec. 1852; PC [I] 1852; member, R. commn. on tenure of land [I] 1843.

Sheriff, co. Leitrim 1834-5.

In August 1828 Wynne and his younger brother William attended a Sligo Protestant dinner at which toasts were drunk to the former Tory lord chancellor Eldon and their father, patron of the pocket borough and its Member, who they declared had 'never deserted the Protestant cause' and 'never will'.[1] At the 1830 general election Wynne replaced his father at Sligo, probably on account of his mother's declining health, and was returned unopposed.[2] He was listed by the Wellington ministry as one of their 'friends', but was absent from the crucial division on the civil list, 15 Nov. He presented petitions for the abolition of slavery, 23 Nov., 2, 6, 23 Dec. 1830, and one to increase the grant to the Kildare Place Society, 14 Apr. 1831. He divided against the second reading of the Grey ministry's reform bill, 22 Mar., and insisted that the Protestants of Sligo were 'decidedly hostile' to it, 18 Apr., when he objected to allusions to his family's boroughmongering and the 'fact of my being the representative of this particular borough' having subjected him to 'personal attack'. He divided for Gascoyne's wrecking amendment, 19 Apr. At the ensuing general election he stood as an opponent of reform and was returned unopposed.[3] He voted against the second reading of the reintroduced reform bill, 6 July, at least three times to adjourn the debates, 12 July, for use of the 1831 census to determine the disfranchisement schedules, 19 July, to postpone consideration of the inclusion of Chippenham in B, 27 July, and against the bill's passage, 21 Sept. 1831. On 5 Aug. he presented a petition for the continuance of the grant to the Kildare Place Society. He divided against ministers on the Dublin election controversy, 23 Aug. He was in the minority of 47 to end the Maynooth grant, 26 Sept. On 12 Oct. 1831 he presented a Sligo petition against Protestants holding civil and military positions abroad being compelled to attend local Catholic services. He voted against the second reading of the revised reform bill, 17 Dec. 1831, the enfranchisement of Tower Hamlets, 28 Feb., and the third reading, 22 Mar. 1832. He divided against ministers on the Russian-Dutch loan, 26 Jan., 12 July. On 9 Apr. he called for legislation to enable 'all to read the entire word of God', for which petitions would be presented 'from all parts' of Ireland 'if the influence of the Catholic hierarchy could be withdrawn for a few months'. He presented a Protestant petition against the new plan of Irish education, 16 Apr. He was absent from the division on the second reading of the Irish reform bill, 25 May 1832.

At the 1832 general election he stood unsuccessfully as a Conservative for Sligo, where the Reform Act had weakened his family's control. In 1843 he was appointed a member of the commission of inquiry into Irish land tenure, in which he took an 'active and prominent' part. He served as under-secretary to the Irish viceroy Lord Eglington in the first Derby administration of 1852 and sat again for Sligo as a Conservative, 1856-60. Wynne, who was 'well versed in Irish antiquarian knowledge' and an 'indefatigable field botanist', died at the palace of the archbishop of Tuam, where he had gone on a visit, in June 1865. He was succeeded by his eldest son Owen (1843-1910).[4]

¹ *Sligo Jnl.* 30 Aug. 1828. ² Ibid. 6 Aug. 1830. ³ Ibid. 13 May 1831. ⁴ *Gent. Mag.* (1865), ii. 245-6; *Dod's Parl. Companion* (1859), 314.

P.J.S.

WYNNE, Owen (c.1756–1841), of Hazelwood, co. Sligo.

SLIGO	1801–June 1806
SLIGO	1820–1830

b. c. 1756, 1st. s. of Owen Wynne, MP [I], of Hazelwood and Hon. Anne Maxwell, da. of John, 1st Bar. Farnham [I]. *m.* 20 Jan. 1790, Lady Sarah Elizabeth Cole, da. of William, 1st earl of Enniskillen [I], 3s. (1 *d.v.p.*) 4da. *suc.* fa. 1789. *d.* 12 Dec. 1841.
   MP [I] 1776-1790, 1791-1800.
   Collector, Sligo 1784-1801; gov. and custos rot. co. Sligo 1789-*d.*; sheriff 1819-20, 1833-4.
   Trustee, linen board [I] 1795-1824.
   Capt. Carbery vol. cav. 1796.

Wynne, the patron of the pocket borough of Sligo, resumed the seat he had vacated in 1806 at the 1820 general election. A silent Member who 'attended seldom', when present he generally supported the Liverpool ministry, who listed him as seeking pro-

motion for a Henry Philips in the tax department and noted the appointment of his nephew as collector of customs in Sligo.¹ He was granted six weeks' leave on urgent private business 12 Feb., but was present to vote against Catholic claims, 28 Feb. 1821, as he did again, 1 Mar., 21 Apr., 10 May 1825. At the 1822 county Sligo by-election he backed the unsuccessful Tory Alexander Perceval*, and at a dinner of his supporters 'laid aside his usual frigidity, and favoured the company with some excellent songs during the night, particularly one written *extempore* for the occasion', and 'made a neat and appropriate speech'.² He divided against repeal of the Foreign Enlistment Act, 16 Apr., but with opposition for inquiry into the prosecution of the Dublin Orange rioters, 22 Apr. 1823. He divided for suppression of the Catholic Association, 15 Feb. 1825.

At the 1826 general election he was again returned unopposed.³ He signed the petition of Irish landed proprietors against Catholic claims in February 1827 and voted thus, 6 Mar. 1827, 12 May 1828.⁴ He was granted three weeks' leave on urgent business, 23 Mar. 1827. In a letter to Peel, the home secretary, welcoming the recent 'happy change' of government, 20 Apr. 1828, he hoped that the duke of Wellington, the premier, and Peel would 'protect us from the speculative legislation of some of the opposition Members' and complained about the 'grossly unjust' parish rates payments bill:

> One great object of a resident gentleman is to improve his estate. How does this projected law operate? Every improvement induces a higher valuation and imposes an additional annual tax upon him and it is therefore his interest to prevent instead of encouraging and paying for the improvement of his farms ... It really would not surprise me to see a bill to enable vestries to levy money to build Catholic chapels ... This country (at least this part of it) is certainly improving and will I trust continue to improve if we are only suffered to go on without too much legislative interference, and if we could be rescued from the government of the Catholic Association, which is doing more mischief than you can be aware of.

Peel referred the matter to Goulburn, the chancellor of the exchequer, and promised to give it his 'very serious' and 'unprejudiced consideration'.⁵ In February 1829 Wynne was listed by Planta, the patronage secretary, as 'opposed' to Catholic emancipation, though likely to support securities when the principle was carried. He duly voted against emancipation, 18, 23, 26, 27, 30 Mar., but was in the minority of 16 to raise the new minimum county freehold qualification from £10 to £20, 27 Mar. In August 1829 he applied to Peel for promotion in the church for his son William, which

Peel recommended be given to 'one of the most valuable and respectable country gentlemen in Ireland', citing 'his support of the government and forbearance in asking favours'. The duke of Northumberland, the Irish viceroy, and Leveson Gower, the Irish secretary, both agreed to assist.[6] He was granted two months' leave on account of family illness, 15 Mar. 1830. There is no record of any parliamentary activity that session.

At the 1830 dissolution Wynne made way for his eldest son John at Sligo, probably on account of his wife's declining health. He assisted the return of a local Tory against a reformer in the county election, and at the declaration welcomed the 'triumph of the aristocracy' over 'modern liberalism' and refuted charges that he operated a 'system of oppression' or had threatened to 'make the grass grow on the streets of Sligo':

> I have been in Parliament longer than any man in this kingdom now alive ... It has been asserted that I am not in the habit of making speeches in Parliament, but a man who attends to the superior information of others may ... give a better vote and be more useful than gentlemen who are fond of pronouncing pieces of oratory ... Such bad taste have I seen in the House of Commons that ... I have frequently seen the unfortunate orator, who, at the commencement of his speech had a crowded House, left speaking to empty benches.[7]

At the 1831 county Sligo nomination he spoke against the Grey ministry's 'impracticable' reform bill, denounced the Whigs as 'factious anarchists' and warned the electors, 'Do not break down what you know to be good, adhere to the constitution you have'.[8]

Wynne, who was 'constantly resident' in county Sligo, died in December 1841 in 'his 86th year', when an obituarist claimed he was 'amongst the first to introduce improvements in the system of agriculture', but incorrectly named him 'the oldest living representative of the Irish Parliament'.[9]

[1] *Black Bk.* (1823), 207; *Session of Parl. 1825*, p. 492. [2] NLI, O'Hara mss 20316. [3] *Dublin Evening Post*, 22 June 1826. [4] Add. 40392, f. 5. [5] Add. 40396, ff. 159, 162. [6] Add. 40327, f. 53; 40337, f. 185; NAI, Leveson Gower letterbks. M. 737/93, Leveson Gower to Peel, 31 Aug. 1829. [7] *Sligo Jnl.* 6 Aug. 1830. [8] Ibid. 20 May 1831. [9] Add. 40502, f. 57; *Gent. Mag.* (1842), i. 329.

P.J.S.

WYNNE PENDARVES, Edward William (1775–1853), of Pendarves, nr. Camborne, Cornw. and 36 Eaton Place, Belgrave Square, Mdx.

Cornwall	1826–1832
Cornwall West	1832–26 June 1853

b. 6 Apr. 1775,[1] 2nd but o. surv. s. of John Stackhouse of Pendarves and Susanna, da. and h. of Edward Acton of Acton Scott, Salop. *educ.* Harrow 1790-3; Trinity, Oxf. 1793; fellow, All Souls 1796. *m.* 5 July 1804, Tryphena, da. and h. of Rev. Browse Twist of Bowden, Devon, *s.p. suc.* cos. Rev. Luttrell Wynne 1814; fa. 1819; took additional name of Wynne by royal sign manual 4 Jan. 1815 and Pendarves in lieu of Stackhouse 28 Feb. 1815. *d.* 26 June 1853.

Dep. warden of stannaries 1852.

Lt.-col. Cornw. yeomanry corps 1816.

Wynne Pendarves, who had taken the surname Wynne after inheriting the estates in Cornwall and elsewhere of his maternal cousin in 1814,[2] apparently chose to adopt the name of the old Cornish family of Pendarves, whose estates in the west of the county had passed to his father through the female line and were duly inherited by him in 1819.[3] However, his financial circumstances were 'considerably narrowed' in the early 1820s as a result of the failure of the North Cornwall Bank, and for a time he 'discharged his servants, laid down his carriage, sold his horses and abridged the extent of his hospitalities'.[4] Since 1809 he had taken a prominent part in the Cornish reform movement, attending the meeting of the friends of reform at the *Freemasons' Tavern*, London, in June 1811, and chairing several county meetings, including those of November 1819 which called for inquiry into the Peterloo massacre, and of March 1821 which supported Queen Caroline and demanded retrenchment and parliamentary reform. The Tory lord lieutenant, Lord Mount Edgcumbe, expressed regret that 'a man of such pleasing manners in society and otherwise so respectable should have taken such an unfortunate line in politics'.[5] He declined to be nominated at the by-election for the county in January 1825, but he came forward as promised at the general election of 1826 as the champion of the independent yeomanry against aristocratic dictation. He declared that he had been 'bred in Whig principles, which were confirmed by long habit', and advocated an unspecified measure of parliamentary reform, retrenchment and tax reductions, and the gradual abolition of slavery with compensation to the owners. In the face of strong pressure he had modified his position on the Catholic question, emphasizing that he was a 'Protestant by education, habit and conviction' who would support no relief measure that did not provide 'sufficient security for the established church', and merely pledging to 'sedulously attend to the arguments ... and give a conscientious vote' when the issue was raised in Parliament. He believed that the corn laws operated in a detrimental way, resulting in price fluctuations, but he still favoured 'an adequate protective duty'. He said he approved of much that had been done by Lord Liverpool's government, and if it took up reform it would be 'the least objectionable ministry the country had possessed for many years'. He was returned unopposed with the Tory Sir Richard Vyvyan, after the liberal Tory John Hearle Tremayne* retired from the contest.[6] He joined Brooks's Club, 12 May 1827.

According to Vyvyan's account, after Sir Francis Burdett had given notice, 9 Feb. 1827, of a call of the House before the debate on Catholic relief, he 'left ... *followed by Pendarves*'. Vyvyan was confident that 'upon the Catholic question our friend must give a decided vote, and he will most probably overset himself on the corn laws'.[7] He indeed divided for Catholic relief, 6 Mar. 1827, 12 May 1828. He presented, without comment, a petition from owners and occupiers of land in Cornwall to maintain the corn laws, 12 Feb. 1827.[8] He voted against the garrisons grant, 20 Feb., and condemned the 'most indecent ... expenditure of ... public money' on the Clarence grant, 16 Mar., arguing that 'now ... the currency was restored to a proper standard' the sums granted to members of the royal family went 'much beyond, in actual value, what would have been voted'. He divided with Canning's coalition ministry for the grant to improve water communications in Canada, 12 June. He was allowed a month's leave on account of family illness, 19 Mar. In May he joined a deputation of Members from Cornwall and Devon to the president of the board of trade, Huskisson, to press the case for maintaining the export bounty on pilchards.[9] He predicted that the free importation of copper ore from South America would have injurious consequences for the Cornish mines, 15 June 1827.[10] He presented various Cornish petitions for repeal of the Test Acts, 21, 25 Feb., and voted accordingly, 26 Feb. 1828. In presenting a Redruth petition against the coastwise coal duty, 6 Mar., he observed that it 'pressed very heavily on his constituents, as Cornwall did not afford fuel of any other description'. He divided for a 60s. rather than a 64s. pivot price in the corn law schedule, 22 Apr. He warned that 'there are few lead mines in England which can stand against' the free importation of lead ore, 15 July, and argued that 'a really protecting duty' was needed. He opposed the duke of

Wellington's ministry by voting to withdraw the grant to the Society for the Propagation of the Gospels in the colonies, 6 June, reduce that for the Royal Cork Institution, 20 June, condemn the misapplication of public money for building work at Buckingham House, 23 June, abolish the salary of the lieutenant-general of the ordnance, 4 July, and omit the grant for North American fortifications, 7 July. He presented several petitions against the small notes bill, 20, 22 May, 3 June, when he informed the House that 'this subject excited the most serious apprehensions in Cornwall'; he voted for inquiry, 5 June, and against the third reading, 27 June. He divided against extending East Retford's franchise to Bassetlaw freeholders, 21 Mar., but presented and approved a Redruth petition to extend Penryn's franchise to the hundreds of Penwith and Kerrier, 24 Mar., explaining that this was an 'extremely populous' area whose 'peculiar interests ... connected with the fishery trade were not proportionally represented' in the Commons. He voted to condemn delays in chancery, 24 Apr., and was against the additional churches bill, 30 June, and the corporate funds bill, 10 July. He presented several Cornish anti-slavery petitions in June 1828.

He contradicted Vyvyan's assertion that anti-Catholic petitions from Cornwall were representative of public opinion, 24 Feb. 1829, and expressed his 'firm conviction' that 'the intelligence and property of the county are directly in favour' of relief. He criticized the way in which some of the meetings had been organized and signatures collected, and maintained that 'if the people of Cornwall were not excited by fanatical preachers or by inflammatory books or pictures, they would be very well satisfied to leave the settlement of this question to Parliament'. He expressed 'sincere thanks' to the government for taking the initiative and was sure that emancipation was 'the only thing that will quiet Ireland'; he later presented three pro-Catholic petitions. He duly divided for emancipation, 6, 30 Mar., and to allow Daniel O'Connell to take his seat without swearing the oath of supremacy, 18 May. He defended himself from the strictures made against him in the Upper House by Lord Falmouth and saw 'no reason to believe' that he had forfeited the confidence of his constituents, 11 Mar. He voted to transfer East Retford's seats to Birmingham, 5 May, and for Lord Blandford's reform resolutions, 2 June. He presented Cornish petitions for the continuation of the export bounty on pilchards, 13 May, and confirmed that 'great distress prevails' in that industry, 2 June, when he reminded the House that 'the coast of Cornwall ... furnishes a very good description of sailors to the navy' and cautioned against 'weakening our maritime power'. He voted against the additional grant for the sculpture of the marble arch, 25 May, and to reduce the hemp duty, 1 June 1829. However, he divided against Knatchbull's amendment to the address on distress, 4 Feb. 1830. A few days later Lord Howick* consulted him about his forthcoming resolutions on the disfranchisement of East Retford.[11] While he voted for Blandford's reform plan, 18 Feb., he admitted that there was 'much ... I condemn in the detail' and said he would have preferred a 'simple and efficient' measure based on Burdett's resolutions of 1809. He wanted 'all who were subject to direct taxation' to be enfranchised, counties divided, all elections held on the same day and parliaments 'brought back to a constitutional duration', preferably three years. He maintained that Cornwall received 'no benefit' from its 'disproportionate' representation, as only seven of its Members were Cornishmen, and pointed out that 'the mines and the fisheries ... impose additional duties on its Members which can be only fully appreciated by Cornishmen'. He was 'satisfied that the House must shortly yield to the wishes of the people'. He voted to enfranchise Birmingham, Leeds and Manchester, 23 Feb., refer the Newark petition against the duke of Newcastle to a select committee, 1 Mar., and transfer East Retford's seats to Birmingham, 5, 15 Mar. He divided for Russell's reform motion, 28 May. He presented a Cornwall petition for relief from distress and reform, which derived from a meeting held in March but which 'from some unaccountable delay ... did not reach me until this morning', 14 June. In early March he was one of the three county Members who sought to revive the 'old Whig opposition' by asking Lord Althorp to assume the Commons leadership.[12] Thereafter he took a regular part in the opposition campaign on all major issues, particularly retrenchment and tax reductions. He welcomed the government's proposal to reduce the duty on coastwise coal, 16 Mar., but thought it 'would not be asking a very great boon' to have it repealed, as there was 'no tax more oppressive or unequal'. He made suggestions for 'saving ... no small amount' in the naval estimates by making changes to the Falmouth packet service, 5 Apr. On the other hand, he feared that the withdrawal of fish bounties would 'do great injury to a most deserving body', 28 May. He paired for Jewish emancipation, 5 Apr., and divided for it, 17 May. He voted for abolition of the death penalty for forgery, 24 May, 7 June. He seconded Sir Matthew White Ridley's merchant seamen bill, 17 June 1830, in the belief that 'a more suitable provision' of hospitals was required. At the general election that summer he offered as 'an enemy to all corrupt or unnecessary expenditure' and

'a friend to constitutional government and reform'. He claimed that he had given 'constant and unremitted attention' to parliamentary business, but had seldom been reported as he had no 'peculiar talent for public speaking'. In a review of recent history, he thought it was 'unfortunate for this country' that Canning's life had been cut short and argued that there had been 'more danger ... from refusing than granting' Catholic emancipation, although he admitted having felt 'difficulties' on this subject. He explained that he had opposed Knatchbull's motion on distress because its 'real object' was the removal of Wellington's government, when there was 'no prospect' of its being replaced by a better one, but he pointed out that he had subsequently supported Davenport's motion for inquiry into the state of the nation. He praised the government's Beer Act, which would 'do more to discourage the pernicious and too prevalent practice of dram drinking than all the proclamations against vice', and welcomed the repeal of certain taxes, although he wished this had been taken further. He rejoiced that the 'atrocious attempt to overthrow the liberties of France' had been defeated and looked forward to a 'speedy and ... complete revolution' there, leading to the creation of a liberal monarchy. After being returned unopposed with Vyvyan, he declared that he was 'bound to no party'.[13]

In September ministers listed Wynne Pendarves among their 'foes', and he voted against them in the crucial civil list division, 15 Nov. 1830. He presented numerous Cornish anti-slavery petitions, particularly from Protestant Dissenters, in November 1830 and March 1831. He attended the county meeting on reform, 19 Jan. 1831, and declared that it testified to the 'progress [of] liberal opinions'. He argued that 'they had seen the deplorable consequences of a defective state of the representation in the increasing distress and discontent of the country', and maintained that there was 'scarcely a man of intelligence amongst the middle classes' who did not now support reform. He recommended support for Lord Grey's 'enlightened and ... honest administration' and presented the resulting petition, 14 Feb.[14] He presented further petitions from parliamentary boroughs and unrepresented towns, 26 Feb., 19, 28 Mar. He gave his 'unqualified approbation' to the government's reform bill, 21 Mar., and hoped ministers would not 'sacrifice any part of the principle', although 'some slight alterations may be necessary in the details'. He felt that Cornwall's representation had been 'reduced a little too low, considering the population and wealth of the county and its various interests of mines and fisheries', and 'considering also the unrepresented towns of Falmouth and Penzance', but he had 'no hesitation in saying that its local interests are likely to be as well if not better protected by the ... allotted number of real representatives, as by the nominal representatives under the present system'. He rejected the argument that close corporations formed 'a part of the settled institutions of the country', pointing out that popular chartered rights had often been 'usurped' by the corporations which had 'bartered their franchise for a valuable consideration'; he was confident that 'men of superior talent will ... readily find their way' into the House through a 'more legitimate and independent channel'. He divided for the second reading, 22 Mar., and against Gascoyne's wrecking amendment, 19 Apr. 1831. At the ensuing general election he was involved in a major struggle between Whigs and Tories for control of Cornwall. He described himself as a 'uniform and zealous supporter' of the reform bill, which 'united the principles of population and property, and secured all the interests of the state by conferring the franchise on the middle classes of society', and would thus 'prevent revolution'. He also advocated a 'fair and equitable commutation' of tithes and was 'anxious' for the abolition of the 'monstrous evil' of slavery. He was returned at the head of the poll, with another Whig, after a contest lasting five days.[15]

He divided for the second reading of the reintroduced reform bill, 6 July 1831, and steadily for its details. He saw no compelling reason for enfranchising Penzance 'in preference to other places in ... Cornwall', 6 Aug., and had 'every reason to believe that ... the respectable portion of the inhabitants' did not want it. He voted for the bill's passage, 21 Sept., the second reading of the Scottish bill, 23 Sept., and Lord Ebrington's confidence motion, 10 Oct. Following the Lords' rejection of the reform bill he attended a county meeting, 26 Oct., when he expressed confidence that 'ministers would not propose a measure less efficacious than the last' and that the peers would 'see it right to concede to the wishes of the people'. He looked forward to a reformed Parliament in which 'fewer pensions' would be granted, 'wars would be of shorter duration, if they would not occur more seldom', and 'less taxes' would be required. At a subsequent dinner, he asserted that the agricultural interest would be 'more adequately represented' after the bill was carried and would obtain 'a due share of protection'.[16] He divided with the minority to print the Waterford petition for disarming the Irish yeomanry, 11 Aug. He voted to punish only those guilty of bribery at the Dublin election and against the censure motion on the Irish administration's conduct, 23 Aug. He divided for the second reading of the revised reform

bill, 17 Dec. 1831, steadily for its details and for the third reading, 22 Mar. 1832, after which he paired off until early May to attend the assizes and quarter sessions.[17] On 9 May, following the resignation of Grey's ministry, he attended a meeting at Brooks's where he was one of the 'country gentlemen' who favoured allowing Wellington to form a government 'without serious opposition', thus leaving it to the country to decide who was 'best entitled to public confidence'.[18] He voted next day for the motion for an address asking the king to appoint only ministers committed to carrying an unimpaired measure. He paired for the second reading of the Irish bill, 25 May,[19] and voted against the Conservative amendment for increased Scottish county representation, 1 June. He divided with the minorities for the Vestry Act amendment bill, 23 Jan., information regarding military punishments, 16 Feb., the immediate abolition of slavery, 24 May, and reduction of the barracks grant, 2 July. He voted with ministers on the Russian-Dutch loan, 26 Jan., 12, 16 July, and relations with Portugal, 9 Feb. After the debate on Irish tithes, 9 Mar., he reportedly told Althorp that it had been 'a brilliant night';[20] he presented four Cornish petitions for commutation, 16 July 1832.

At the general election of 1832 Wynne Pendarves was returned unopposed for West Cornwall as an advocate of 'Whig principles' and supporter of 'all ... measures of rational reform'.[21] He sat until his death in June 1853, when he left all his estates in Cornwall, Herefordshire and Shropshire to his great-nephew, William Cole Wood (1841-1929), who assumed the name Pendarves.[22]

[1] *Ex. inf.* Stephen Lees. [2] He was the residuary legatee of the personal estate, which was sworn under £30,000 (PROB 11/1563/685; IR26/630/783). [3] The personalty was sworn under £10,000, but he was not the residuary legatee (PROB 11/1624/39; IR26/839/20). [4] *R. Cornw. Gazette*, 18 Dec. 1824. [5] E. Jaggard, *Cornw. Politics in Age of Reform*, 32-40; *West Briton*, 26 Nov. 1819, 9 Mar. 1821; Carew Pole mss CC/N/58, Mount Edgcumbe to Pole Carew, 20 Dec. 1824. [6] *West Briton*, 28 Jan. 1825, 16, 23 June 1826. [7] Carew Pole mss CC/N/60, Vyvyan to Pole Carew, 10 Feb. 1827. [8] *The Times*, 13 Feb. 1827. [9] *West Briton*, 1 June 1827. [10] *The Times*, 16 June 1827. [11] Grey mss, Howick jnl. 7 Feb. 1830. [12] A. Mitchell, *Whigs in Opposition*, 226-7; Le Marchant, *Althorp*, 243-4. [13] *West Briton*, 9 July, 13 Aug. 1830. [14] Ibid. 21 Jan. 1831. [15] Ibid. 29 Apr., 6, 13, 20 May 1831. [16] Ibid. 28 Oct., 4 Nov. 1831. [17] Ibid. 30 Mar., 4 May 1832. [18] *Three Diaries*, 253. [19] *The Times*, 29 May 1832. [20] *Three Diaries*, 211. [21] *R. Cornw. Gazette*, 25 Aug., 22 Dec. 1832; *Dod's Parl. Companion* (1833), 149. [22] PROB 11/2177/624; IR26/1976/681; *Gent. Mag.* (1853), ii. 417-18.

T.A.J.

WYSE, Thomas (1791–1862), of the Manor of St. John, co. Waterford.[1]

Co. TIPPERARY	1830–1832
WATERFORD	1835–1841
WATERFORD	13 June 1842–1847

b. 9 Dec. 1791, 1st. s. of Thomas Wyse of the Manor of St. John and Frances Maria, da. and h. of George Bagge of Dromore. *educ.* by Michael Quin of Cashel 1797; Stonyhurst 1800; Trinity, Dublin 1809; L. Inn 1813. *m.* 4 Mar. 1821, at Canino, Letitia Christine, da. of Lucien Buonaparte, prince of Canino (bro. of Napoleon I), 2s. CB 1 Mar. 1851; KCB 27 Mar. 1857. *d.* 15 Apr. 1862.
    Ld. of treasury Aug. 1839-Sept. 1841; sec. to bd. of control July 1846-Jan. 1849; PC [I] 13 Feb. 1849; minister plenip. to Greece 1849-*d.*

Wyse came from an old Anglo-Norman family who had acquired the monastic manor of St. John on its dissolution by Henry VIII and been prominent in the politics of Waterford corporation prior to their exclusion as Catholics. His great-grandfather and namesake had helped found the first Catholic Association in 1760. In 1800 he and his younger brother George entered the Jesuit college of Stonyhurst, where he was a 'serious' and 'conscientious' student and his contemporaries included John Talbot, later 16th earl of Shrewsbury, and his distant kinsman and life-long associate Richard Sheil*. Wyse and Sheil experienced remarkably similar political careers, though Sheil clearly considered himself the superior speaker, as is evident from his later satirical portrait of Wyse in the *New Monthly Magazine*:

> His person is small and rather below the middle size ... However ... he holds himself erect, and seems a little animated by a consciousness that he belongs to an ancient family and is the owner of the manor of St. John. He is exceedingly graceful ... and at once conveys the impression of his having lived in the best society ... [He] is eminently accomplished; a master of several languages; a poet; a painter; versed in antiquities, and a traveller in the East ... His eloquence, however, is perhaps a little too rotund and full, and he is too wholesale a dealer in abstractions and too lofty an intonator of high-sounding diction: but it flows out of a copious and abundant fountain, and runs through a broad channel, amidst all the rich investings of highly decorated phrase. What he mainly wants is simplicity and directness ... He gives his hearer credit for more velocity in following him than he is entitled to, and forgets that when he arrives himself *per saltum* at a conclusion, full many an auditor may not be able to leap with the same agility to his consequences as himself.[2]

In 1809 Wyse was admitted to Trinity, where he won prizes in Greek and Latin composition and became noted for his oratory as an active member of its Historical Society. After graduating he received an annual allowance of £600 from his father, an Irish absentee landlord, and read for the bar, but on the cessation of hostilities in 1815 he decamped to the continent. There he remained for the next ten years, travelling widely and spending long periods in Italy, where he became a frequent guest of Lucien Buonaparte, prince of Canino, a younger brother of Napoleon I. Encouraged by Sheil, he agreed to Lucien's offer of marriage to his 16-year-old daughter Letitia and, after a lengthy legal wrangle with his father, which resulted in contradictory settlements based on English and Roman law, the couple were married in 1821. His first son was born the following year but thereafter the marriage deteriorated into mutual hatred. They separated in 1828, by when it had become a 'matter of notoriety' that their 'happiness had not been uniform or uninterrupted'. Thereafter Wyse, by all accounts an indifferent father, became increasingly estranged from his two sons, who remained devoted to their mother.[3]

In August 1825 Wyse and his family returned to Waterford, where, in an attempt to ease his financial difficulties, he threw himself into travel writing, contributing articles to the *New Monthly Magazine* and preparing a book, *The Continental Traveller's Oracle, or, Maxims for Foreign Locomotion* (1828), for which he received an advance of £150. During the rumours of a dissolution in October 1825 he became chairman of the county Waterford election committee for Henry Villiers Stuart*, a Protestant member of the Catholic Association. At the 1826 general election he presided over Villiers Stuart's successful campaign against the sitting Member Lord George Thomas Beresford, directing the local management of committees and travelling around with a Catholic priest, who translated his speeches into Irish. He later established the Protecting Association of Waterford to provide relief for persecuted tenants who had voted against Beresford, for which he secured funds from the Association.[4] On 7 Apr. 1827, at an aggregate meeting of the Catholics of county Waterford, he proposed the appointment of a committee to draw up the rules for a county Liberal Club.[5] Hearing in early February 1828 that his wife had 'received an invitation from Lady Holland to spend some time with her in London', he advised Lord Holland, 'She has left this country and her family in defiance of my express prohibition and consequently I cannot consider myself responsible for her future conduct or pecuniary engagements'.[6] That month he secured the support of the Association for the publication of a common manual to 'direct the popular mind' and help unite the 'scattered and divergent impulses' in the Catholic movement. His *Political Catechism*, explaining 'the constitutional rights and civil disabilities of the Catholics of Ireland', appeared shortly before the passage of emancipation the following year.[7]

Following the election of Daniel O'Connell for county Clare in 1828, Wyse urged Edward Dwyer, the Association's secretary, to establish a 'uniform' and 'permanent' network of county and parochial clubs headed by the Association across the 'entire nation', 30 July. 'By such a system', he contended, 'the Catholic or rather independent constituency of Ireland will be completely disciplined' and 'every county in a few months, will naturally and almost of itself become a Clare or Waterford'. He later asserted that within a few months, 'in every county in Munster and in most counties in Leinster and Connaught, Liberal Clubs were established', providing the Association with 'a more visible supremacy' and 'a much more manageable description of power'.[8] That summer he reorganized the city of Waterford club and established a county club, of which he became secretary. He also launched a campaign to open the closed corporation of Waterford, to which he was admitted as a freemen in June 1829.[9] At a Munster provincial meeting chaired by his kinsman James Scully of Tipperary, 25 Aug. 1828, he denied assertions by John Hely Hutchinson, Member for county Tipperary, that the Association's activities were 'reckless' and 'prejudicial' to the final settlement of the Catholic question or that 'they should stand in the surliness of despondency, leaving it to the march of events to right their cause', and demanded that England, as the 'perverter of the ways of providence and the interceptor of all those blessings which were meant for Ireland', immediately redress 'a despotism unexampled for its length and iniquity amongst the civilised nations of the earth'. Next day he seconded a motion for the establishment of a Tipperary Liberal Club on the Waterford model, and at the ensuing dinner argued in favour of forming committees for the purpose of 'detecting municipal abuses and ascertaining the rights and franchises of corporations ... in close boroughs'.[10] At the club's first meeting that October he was toasted as its founder.[11] On 4 Nov. 1828 a dinner attended by over 150 persons was held for him in the city of Waterford under the chairmanship of Robert Carew, Member for county Wexford.[12] Next month he successfully opposed O'Connell's proposed mission to England to plead the cause of emancipation.[13] He was a founding member of the non-sectarian Society of the Friends of Civil and Religious Liberty established in Dublin,

21 Jan. 1829. 'Wyse and others of the Catholics ... felt as we all do how much harm to the cause the violent members of the Association do, and how impossible it is to control them unless the Protestants come forward', an informant explained to Lord Downshire, 5 Feb. 1829.[14] Writing next day from England, where he had gone to witness the Wellington ministry's concession of emancipation, Wyse informed Dwyer that 'the great event is about to take place' and urged the immediate dissolution of the Association, observing that 'it will be a glorious precedent in our history'. It was dissolved on a motion made in his absence, 13 Feb.[15] On 13 Apr. 1829 he recorded in his diary:

> The relief bill had just received the royal assent. This is the most memorable legislative event for two successive centuries, the Magna Carta of modern times, a real revolution ... Everything is accomplished, we are *free* ... Another era begins, the Union is at last sealed as well as signed. We are no longer the chained galley slave, rejoicing in the wreck of the vessel which was his prison, but a band of free fellow sailors, determined ... to sink or swim with the country.[16]

Next month it was reported that he had started for an anticipated vacancy at Waterford city, which did not occur.[17] His *Historical Sketch of the Late Catholic Association*, containing a 'frank and candid' account of the inner workings of the Association and a 'mass of useful' documents relating to the struggle over the previous 60 years, was published to wide acclaim at the end of that year.[18]

At the 1830 general election it was expected that he would offer for Waterford city, but in the event he came forward for the county, where he was joined by Beresford and, to his dismay, O'Connell, who had accepted an invitation from the independents. After an ill-humoured public exchange he withdrew on the second day of the poll, conceding that only one 'popular' candidate could succeed, 13 Aug.[19] Later that day he was solicited to stand for county Tipperary, where there was a last minute opening on the independent interest. After a short delay, during which O'Connell remonstrated with him that 'in the present state of public affairs it is the duty of every man of intellect ... to lead and not check the public sentiment', 15 Aug., he agreed to accept. In his address he declared his support for 'constitutional reform' and opposition to 'every encroachment on popular rights', including Irish tithes, the Irish Vestry Subletting Acts and the 'flagrant abuses' of corporations. Following a seven-day poll, in which he was widely 'applauded' for 'resigning in favour of the Liberator', he was narrowly returned in second place, amidst allegations of wholesale intimidation by his supporters and comparisons with the earlier Catholic victories in county Waterford and Clare. A petition was presented against his return but not pursued.[20] Congratulating him, 26 Aug., the Whig Lord Lansdowne observed, 'I had no expectation of seeing your name represented ... perceiving that some sort of understanding between O'Connell and the Beresfords had excluded you from the county. That a proportion of Catholic Members should enter into the representation ... was a great public object, but it is even greater that Ireland should be represented by persons like yourself'.[21] 'My county Tipperary comrades have done their duty', observed another correspondent, adding, 'O'Connell 'tis true was worthy of any county in Ireland ... but ... Waterford was your native right'.[22] In October 1830 a county Waterford meeting was 'marked by clashes' between him and local supporters of O'Connell's campaign for repeal of the Union.[23]

Wyse voted for O'Connell's motion for repeal of the Irish Subletting Act, 11 Nov., when, in a maiden speech said to be in the 'style and language of the late Henry Grattan*', he welcomed government plans for its amendment but argued that repeal would be 'preferable' and advocated 'other remedial measures', including the abolition of the monopolies of grand juries and corporations and the provision of loans for the employment of the Irish poor. 'Though moderate ... I approve', noted his agent and kinsman Edmund Scully.[24] 'A few ... find fault that you did not support O'Connell when attacked', wrote James Scully, 'but you must ... best judge how to act'.[25] He was appointed to the select committee on the Irish poor that day. He divided for reduction of West Indian wheat import duties, 12 Nov. He had been listed by the Irish agent Pierce Mahony† as a 'neutral', but as 'opposed to government' by Henry Brougham* and one of its 'foes' by ministers, and he voted against them in the crucial division on the civil list, 15 Nov. Next day he presented a repeal petition from Carrick-on-Suir and, in remarks that were evidently inaudible in the gallery and not 'fairly reported', called on O'Connell 'to fix an early date for the discussion of the repeal question', as he later recounted.[26] 'Your call upon O'Connell relative to ... the repeal of the Union has given a great deal of dissatisfaction', the Catholic bishop of Waterford warned him, 27 Nov. In a similar vein, Edmund Scully told George Wyse, 'I regret much your brother put the question to O'Connell as to the time he would bring forward the repeal of the Union so soon after Doherty asked him the same, as it has made great noise here'.[27] That month Stephen Coppinger, a former secretary of the Association, reported that at a repeal meeting

in Dublin a 'severe attack' had been made on Wyse's parliamentary conduct.[28] 'They were ... severe on you because you did not at once declare in favour of ... repeal ... and go hand in hand with O'Connell', explained an observer.[29] Wyse brought up further repeal petitions, 22 Nov., 17 Dec., when he announced his disinclination to comment further on the issue, and 18 Dec. He explained his silence to the promoter of the latter petition:

I have already declared in the House that I should abstain from all discussion of so important a question in presenting petitions and should reserve whatever may be my opinions, until such time as it should come in a regular and practical shape before the House. I professed on the hustings the greatest readiness to represent the wishes of my constituents ... A question which during a period of such excitement did not appear of sufficient importance to produce a single observation from a single freeholder, much less a distinct demand on the candidate to support, must at least be new to the public mind and as such would appear to ... require a little more investigation and deliberation ... before we proceed to an irrevocable decision.[30]

He gave notice of a motion to reform the funding of Irish education, 16 Nov., and endorsed a petition against the 'intolerable abuses' of Irish charter schools, 16 Dec. He argued that the metropolitan police should be financed from local rather than national taxation, 18 Nov. He presented and endorsed a petition against the 'oppressive' Irish seaborne coals tax, 22 Nov. He denied that distress in Ireland arising from high agricultural rents was owing to the 'exorbitancy of landlords', contending that the 'absence of manufactures and other outlets' caused an 'unnatural and pernicious competition', which could only by remedied by enabling the 'enterprising and industrious to take advantage of government capital', 23 Nov. He presented petitions for the equalization of the Galway franchise that day, 16 Dec., when he called for the penalties against Catholic electors to be remedied 'as speedily as possible'. Writing to Edmund Scully following the accession of the Grey ministry, 2 Dec., he declared:

A new impulse has been given, the old rubbish swept away. Education, employment, retrenchment, reform are the order of the day and honest men need no longer despair of the redemption of their country. With these hopes so full upon me ... how calmly I can look down on the misrepresentations which have been heaped on my parliamentary conduct. My great offence is not having *stood* by O'Connell when attacked by the treasury bench ... In presenting the Carrick petition, it is true I called on O'Connell to fix an early day for the discussion ... I echoed the wish of many of my constituents; in their petition they call for 'an immediate discussion' also ...

O'Connell I shall always *ardently* support, whenever I think him *right*, but not one little bit further. This I have told him in public ... The assumption of leadership either in the House or out ... I utterly spurn. I never endured it from any man and never will.[31]

He secured returns of Irish county freeholders in order to determine how the disfranchisement bill had worked, 2 Dec., presented and endorsed a petition for the enfranchisement of Irish chattel leaseholders, citing the 'preponderance of town voters over the rustic constituency', and argued that Irish commercial towns such as Belfast, Limerick and Waterford had as good a claim to additional representatives as the 'numerous insignificant boroughs in the south of England', 16 Dec. On 7 Dec. it was reported to the new viceroy Lord Anglesey that Wyse had quarrelled publicly with O'Connell over repeal.[32] That month Lord Melbourne, the home secretary, informed Anglesey that Parnell, Member for Queen's County, was confident that O'Connell could be brought into government, having 'conversed with Wyse' who 'knows O'Connell well', but cautioned that 'he is in his heart not friendly to him, and may perhaps entertain of him a worse and lower opinion than he deserves'.[33] On 20 Dec. Anglesey contemplated using Wyse, whom he believed to be 'honest', as a possible go-between in ministers' abortive attempt to offer O'Connell the office of master of the rolls. Four days later, however, he was warned that O'Connell had 'made a ferocious attack on Mahony, Sheil, Wyse and others'.[34] On 29 Dec. 1830 James Scully reassured Wyse that he had dined with a large party in Tipperary, who 'all agreed that nothing could be better than your conduct in Parliament, and that if you allowed yourself to be made the follower of *any man*, right or wrong, you would not deserve the place you have'.[35]

Defending his stance on repeal at a constituency meeting in early February 1831, Wyse explained that 'should my judgement be convinced by fair debate, I will willingly vote for the measure' and, in a thinly disguised attack on O'Connell, declared:

Of what use is it to invite argument if, in the next breath, I declare to my antagonist that if he dares to argue against me, I will treat him as my foe, brand him as a monster, refuse to deal with him, and hold him up to popular execration? ... A just cause requires no such weapons: a man truly imbued with what liberty ought to be, will and ought to despise them.[36]

To the accompaniment of 'loud cheers' in the House, 8 Feb., Wyse denied the existence of 'universal support' for repeal, spoke of its 'dangerous effects' and of the many popular fallacies to which its agitation was attrib-

utable and demanded that O'Connell bring the question before the Commons for a 'proper examination'.[37] 'I was cheered vehemently throughout from both sides ... and next day warmly congratulated by friend and foe', he observed in an undated but surely related letter to his brother Francis, adding, 'My position in that House is henceforth certain, I hope I can now afford to be utterly indifferent to the ignorance and malignity of the coteries at Waterford'.[38] 'Wyse has by his manly conduct deserved well of us all. Would he now like a baronetcy? If he would, might he not have it?', Lord Holland told Anglesey, 9 Feb.[39] He presented petitions against the grant to the Kildare Place Society, 14 Feb., 4, 29, 30 Mar., and endorsed one for repeal of the Irish Vestry Act, 16 Feb. Informing him that a constituency repeal petition had been sent to O'Connell, a correspondent explained that 'they would not have gone out of their own county for a person to present it' had they 'supposed that you would have pressed ... the petition on the attention of the House in a forcible manner'.[40] He welcomed the ministry's plan of reform, but complained that Ireland had a 'claim to a considerably greater number' of Members, 9 Mar., and after 'measuring fairly the extent, population and revenue' of each country argued that it should receive 132, England and Wales 467 and Scotland 59, 20 Apr. On 19 Mar. he presented a favourable constituency petition and conceded that reform 'would do more than anything else to promote the tranquillity of Ireland'. He deferred his motion for a bill to establish a board of public works for the employment of the Irish poor, 22 Mar., explaining that he was 'much gratified' that government was to adopt a 'portion' of his intended scheme, 30 Mar. Advocating the replacement of Irish grand juries with elected boards that day, he declared, 'I am for domestic legislatures' and 'would bring them to every man's door', for 'the elector to a county board would soon understand the duties of an elector to an Imperial Parliament. It would do more good than gaols or bayonets to bind the poor to the rich, and Ireland to England'. He spoke and voted for the second reading of the English reform bill, 22 Mar., and divided against Gascoyne's wrecking amendment, 19 Apr.[41] On 21 Apr. 1831 he contended that by making a 'concession in time' and 'being liberal, whilst yet you may, revolution may yet be quenched by reform', but 'wait a little longer, temporize, modify, delay', and 'events marching rapidly will be beyond your control'.

At the 1831 general election he offered again for county Tipperary as a reformer, amidst reports that a 'strong feeling' had been got up against him by O'Connell, who it was rumoured would also stand.[42] On 2 May James Scully advised him to retaliate and 'either really stand for Waterford county ... or else appear to do so in a manner that may alarm O'Connell for his safety there', adding 'What would you think of stating that if the reformed Parliament does not do full justice to Ireland speedily, that you would then either support any measure generally recommended by your constituents or ... resign ... I do not think it could be fairly called cringing to the repealers at this critical period'.[43] He spoke accordingly on the hustings, stressing his support for reform, which 'unless ... carried' would promote 'a scene of blood and slaughter', and calling for additional Members to be given to such Irish counties as Tipperary. A contest was narrowly averted at the last minute and he was returned unopposed.[44] On 15 June he invited James Emerson to comment on a plan which he had 'extensively circulated ... for the creation of a sort of local government in Ireland. It is intended to supply the want of that able administration ... and to effect a radical correction of the innumerable abuses of our church, grand jury and corporation systems'.[45] He welcomed the announcement of a £500,000 grant for the new Irish board of public works and secured clarification from Smith Stanley, the Irish secretary, that its commissioners would be based in Dublin rather than London, 30 June. He protested that the Irish arms regulation bill 'would ripen the very discontent it was intended to check' and urged ministers to 'subdue Ireland' by 'other measures such as reform', 1 July. He spoke in support of the bill to prevent corporate funds being applied to electioneering purposes, saying he knew of instances in which their charitable funds been 'shamefully abused', 4 July. He voted for the second reading of the reintroduced reform bill, 6 July, at least twice against the adjournment, 12 July, and gave general support to its details, though he was in the minority for the disfranchisement of Saltash, 26 July, and divided against the division of English counties, 11 Aug. He voted for the bill's passage, 21 Sept., the second reading of the Scottish bill, 23 Sept., and Lord Ebrington's confidence motion, 10 Oct. On 14 July he condemned the grant to the Kildare Place Society 'sect' and spoke in favour of establishing a system of education for Ireland which was non-sectarian and 'acceptable to the entire nation'. He campaigned steadily against grants to 'proselytizing societies' and for a national system thereafter, citing his desire to 'unite Catholics and Protestants and remove the religious animosities which at present exist', 2 Aug., and obtaining leave for a bill to establish parochial schools accountable to a board in Dublin, 8 Aug. 1831, which was introduced but went no further. ('Much of it was put into practical operation by the government in the month following', he explained, 20 July 1832.)

He endorsed a petition for the establishment of non-sectarian scholarships to Dublin University, 19 Aug. 1831. On 29 Aug. he opposed the grant to the Dublin Society on account of its 'exclusive character', but defended that to the Belfast Academical Institution, whose leaders had 'paid great attention to the various systems of education' and 'tried on a small scale the systems of Pestalozzi and Fellenberg': he called for the foundation of a university 'along similar lines' at Cork. On 9 Sept. 1831 he welcomed Smith Stanley's new plan of education, declaring, 'the great point is at last conceded ... Ireland is to have a system of national education' without reference to 'any particular party or sect', and urging the appointment of 'both Catholic and Protestant inspectors'.

Wyse voted against the grant for the Society for the Propagation of the Gospels in the colonies, 25 July 1831. He warned that the 'imposition' of tithes had begun to promote a 'spirit of insubordination' in Ireland, 2 Aug. He divided against the issue of the Dublin writ, 8 Aug., but with ministers on the election controversy, 23 Aug. He argued and voted in favour of printing the Waterford petition for disarming the Irish yeomanry, whose 'bayonets' had 'only added exasperation to discontent and bloodshed to tumult', 11 Aug., and protested that the 'power entrusted to them' had 'been abused', 3 Oct. He welcomed the Irish public works bill, 15 Aug., noting the similarity to his intended bill next day, when he spoke in support of establishing an elected board, or Irish domestic legislature, to control trade, agriculture, charities, gaols and police, and public education. He introduced the Galway franchise bill removing impediments to Catholic electors, 24 Aug., which was read a third time, 26 Sept., and received royal assent, 15 Oct. (1 & 2 Gul. IV, c. 49). That August he was one of the deputation of Irish Members which threatened Lord Grey with 'opposing the government' if 'their views of the policy fit to be pursued' in Ireland were not adopted.[46] He defended their actions and denied the use of 'threats', 26 Aug. A few days later Holland noted that Parnell, the war secretary, was in 'earnest to procure offices of trust for some Catholics such as Sheil, Wyse and others'.[47] He voted for legal provision for the Irish poor, 29 Aug. On 31 Aug. he declared that the Irish church was 'nothing more than a corporation' and asked:

> Is it to continue the only one, amongst all the corporations, unaltered by the necessities and habits of the people of the present day? ... By the reform bill vested and corporate rights are swept away with a resolute and wise hand for the good of the community ... If that justification is admitted in one case, I cannot see why it should be disallowed in another.

He welcomed the government's bill to reform the Irish grand jury system, 16 Sept., but on hearing its details told Smith Stanley it would prove insufficient to placate the Irish people, 29 Sept. 1831.

Wyse spoke at a county Tipperary meeting in support of reform in November.[48] He paired for the second reading of the revised bill, 17 Dec. 1831, and again generally supported its details, though he was in the minority of 32 against the enfranchisement of £50 tenants-at-will, 1 Feb. 1832. He voted for the third reading, 22 Mar., and paired for Ebrington's motion for an address calling on the king to appoint only ministers who would carry it unimpaired, 10 May. He voted for the second reading of the Irish bill, 25 May, but complained that it was not 'such an efficient reform as they had a right to expect', protested at the different treatment of England and Ireland and called for the re-enfranchisement of the Irish 40s. freeholders, without which there would be an 'unreformed and a reformed' House 'under the same roof', 13 June. He was in the minorities for a Conservative amendment to increase Scottish county representation, 1 June, and for a system of representation for New South Wales, 28 June. He commended O'Connell's plan to extend the Irish county franchise to £5 freeholders and voted accordingly, 18 June. He presented and endorsed petitions for an extension of the Irish bill and the enfranchisement of Carrick-on-Suir, 5 July. On 18 July he demanded abolition of the Irish registration oath, observing that it was 'a most abominable and insulting thing to require a man to swear that he does not believe that the Pope possesses the power to order subjects to murder their sovereigns'. He voted for the Irish Vestry Act amendment bill, 23 Jan. Next day he warned that the non-payment of tithes was spreading 'over every part' of Ireland and that it was 'an opprobrium on the legislature to leave the matter as it stands'. He condemned the absurdity of the Irish tithes committee making its report before hearing 'the whole of the evidence' and argued and was a minority teller for printing the Woollen Grange petition for the abolition of tithes, 16 Feb. He presented others in similar terms, 13, 19, 30 Mar., 6, 10, 11 Apr., 5 July, and spoke and voted to print that from Preston, 3 Aug. He divided against the Irish tithes bill, 8 Mar., and opposed it steadily thereafter, complaining that Irish Members had a 'right' to a 'longer discussion' of the subject when they had sat 'night after night' listening to 'details of the boundaries of villages of which they knew nothing', 28 Mar., and urging Smith Stanley to abandon a measure which was merely 'coercive' without having any remedy attached to it, 30 Mar., 10 July, 2 Aug. 1832.

Wyse divided with government on the Russian-Dutch loan, 26 Jan., 12, 16, 20 July, and relations with Portugal, 9 Feb. 1832. On 13 Feb. he objected to Protestant demands 'for the full use of the Bible' under the new plan of Irish education, observing, 'Are there not in that volume passages unfit for youth and for the female eyes especially?' Thereafter he presented numerous petitions and spoke regularly in defence of the new plan, clashing repeatedly with the Protestant proselytiser James Edward Gordon over his scheme to put the Bible in the hands of every child. On 20 July he called for the 'ordonnance du jour' establishing the new plan to be replaced by 'permanent' legislation following the passage of reform, to 'which this education question was constantly made auxiliary', adding that this had been the intention of his abandoned parochial schools bill. He recommended inquiry into a national system of secondary schools for the 'education of the professional and middle classes', 26 July. On 4 Aug. he urged the 'absolute necessity' of establishing a 'good system for the instruction' of Irish teachers. He was in a minority of 13 against the recommittal of the anatomy bill, 27 Feb. He called for a complete revision of the Irish grand jury system and controls on their expenditure, 5 Mar. He presented and endorsed a Galway petition against the unfair admission charges levied on Catholic freemen since the passage of his Act, 13 Mar., and brought in a bill to remedy the situation which was read a first time, 24 July, but went no further. He voted with ministers for the navy civil departments bill, 6 Apr., but against the Irish registry of deeds bill, 9 Apr., and was in a minority of four against Alexander Baring's bill to exclude insolvent debtors from Parliament, 30 May. Next day he cautioned against legislative interference to suppress disturbances in Queen's County, where the magistrates should be allowed to 'do their duty', and successfully moved an amendment limiting inquiry to 'the immediate causes' of unrest; he was appointed to the select committee that day.[49] On 5 June he postponed a tabled motion for inquiry into the state of Irish diocesan schools in order not to impede the reform bills, 'the most important measures ever introduced in this country since 1688'. He advocated delaying inquiry into the introduction of Irish poor laws for similar reasons, 19 June. On 28 June he urged ministers to condemn the invasion of Poland by Russia, whereby 'sworn charters have been violated, a gallant people laid in bondage, women and children massacred, and a high-spirited and intelligent nation ... blotted out from the map of Europe'. He ridiculed the appointment of a select committee on the better observance of the Sabbath, arguing that the only effect of any 'restraints' would be to 'produce hypocrisy and not religion', 3 July. He called for an extension of the forgery bill to Ireland, 6 July, and welcomed this, 31 July. He defended Dublin University's proposed £2 admission charge to a Masters degree conferring the vote as it would 'fund two professorships', 9 July. Next day he obtained leave for a bill to enable tenants for life to raise money by mortgage which would 'facilitate the raising of capital in Ireland'. On 2 Aug. he called on the House to 'strongly express its disapprobation' of the Diet of Frankfurt for issuing decrees that 'have violated not only the rights of man, and of civilized Europe, but its own previous engagements'. He presented a petition for abolition of the death penalty for forgery, 4 Aug. In September 1832 he published a scheme for a reorganisation of Ireland under three heads:

1) Total alteration of the ecclesiastical system, including the abolition of all sinecures.

2) Total alteration of the legislative system, as a result of which subordinate parliaments would be set up in England, Scotland, Wales and Ireland.

3) Total alteration of the municipal system, and the extension of the principles of local government in every way possible.[50]

At the 1832 general election Wyse retired from county Tipperary, was rumoured to have started for county Carlow, but in the event came forward as a Liberal for the city of Waterford, where he was defeated in fourth place on account of his refusal to take O'Connell's repeal pledge.[51] He devoted the next two years to preparing his most widely read book, *Education Reform, or, The Necessity of a National System of Education* (1836), and nurturing the Waterford constituency, for which he was returned in first place in 1835 and sat until his defeat in 1847. (He was defeated in 1841 but seated on petition the following year.) He continued to campaign steadily on education issues, earning himself the sobriquet 'the Member for education', and was an 'able but dilatory' member of numerous select committees and the royal commission on fine arts, which oversaw the decoration of the new Houses of Parliament. Like Sheil's, his political career faded away into second class ministerial office in the Liberal administrations of Melbourne and Russell, by whom he was appointed British plenipotentiary to Greece in 1849. Wyse died in harness of heart failure in April 1862 and was given a public funeral on the orders of the king of Greece. By his will, dated 12 Mar. 1862, he left his Waterford estates to his niece Winifrede Mary Wyse, who posthumously edited his *An Excursion in the Peloponnesus in the Year 1858* (1865) and *Impressions of Greece ... and Letters to Friends at Home* (1871). Following a legal challenge,

however, the estates reverted to his estranged son and heir-at-law Napoleon Alfred Bonaparte-Wyse (1822-95), who during his lifetime passed them to his brother William Charles Bonaparte-Wyse (1826-92).[52]

[1] See J.J. Auchmuty, *Sir Thomas Wyse* (1939). [2] R. Sheil, *Sketches, Legal and Political* ed. M.W. Savage, ii. 339-40. [3] Auchmuty, 2-47; *The Times*, 27 June 1828. [4] Auchmuty, 81-96; T. Wyse, *Hist. Catholic Association*, i. 262-7, 342; *Waterford Chron.* 1 July, 2 Nov. 1826. [5] *Dublin Evening Post*, 19 Apr. 1827; F. O'Ferrall, *Catholic Emancipation*, 170. [6] Add. 51834, Wyse to Holland, 5 Feb. 1828. [7] O'Ferrall, 173-4; Auchmuty, 115. [8] Wyse, i. 342; ii. pp. clxv-cliv; O'Ferrall, 215. [9] O'Ferrall, 221-3. [10] Wyse, ii. p. clvii; *Dublin Evening Post*, 28 Aug., 2 Sept.; *Waterford Chron.* 1 Sept.; *Tipperary Free Press*, 3 Sept. 1828. [11] *Tipperary Free Press*, 11 Oct. 1828. [12] Ibid. 8 Nov. 1828. [13] Wyse, i. 424. [14] PRO NI, Downshire mss D671/C/12/379. [15] Wyse, ii. pp. cclii, cclxvi, ccxcvii. [16] Auchmuty, 118. [17] PRO NI, Pack-Beresford mss D664/A/56. [18] *The Times*, 30 Dec. 1829. [19] Pack-Beresford mss A/149; *Waterford Chron.* 14 Aug. 1830; *O'Connell Corresp.* iv. 1711. [20] NLI, Wyse mss 15024 (7), Hayes to Wyse, 13 Aug.; (9), Dwyer to Wyse, 16 Aug.; (6), Stephen Coppinger to Wyse, 28 Aug.; Auchmuty, 126; *Tipperary Free Press*, 18, 21, 25 Aug. 1830. [21] Wyse mss (7). [22] Ibid. (6), Osborne to Wyse, 26 Aug. 1830. [23] *O'Connell Corresp.* iv. 1716. [24] Wyse mss (2), E. Scully to Wyse, 16, 19 Nov. 1830. [25] Ibid. J. Scully to Wyse, 26 Nov. 1830. [26] *The Times*, 17 Nov. 1830; Wyse mss (1), Slattery to Wyse, 27 Nov., Wyse to Slattery, 19 Dec. 1830. [27] Wyse mss (2), E. Scully to G. Wyse, 30 Nov. 1830. [28] Ibid. (1), Coppinger to Wyse, 26 Nov. 1830. [29] Ibid. (2), R. Scully to Wyse, 30 Nov. 1830. [30] Ibid. (10), Wyse to Grene, 31 Dec. 1830. [31] Ibid. (1). [32] PRO NI, Anglesey mss D619/32A/3/1/254. [33] *Melbourne Pprs.* 168. [34] Anglesey mss 29B/4-7; 32A/3/1/258. [35] Wyse mss (2). [36] *The Times*, 8 Feb. 1831. [37] Ibid. 9 Feb. 1831. [38] Cited in Auchmuty, 138, where the letter is connected with his unreported speech of 16 Nov. 1830. [39] Anglesey mss 27A/101. [40] Wyse mss (3), Cooke to Wyse, 20 Feb. 1831. [41] *The Times*, 21 Apr. 1831. [42] *Tipperary Free Press*, 4, 7 May; Wyse mss (13), Maher to Wyse, 4 May 1831. [43] Wyse mss (6). [44] *Clonmel Herald*, 14 May; *Tipperary Free Press*, 14 May 1831. [45] PRO NI, Emerson Tennant mss D2922/C/1A/5. [46] *O'Connell Corresp.* iv. 1832; Anglesey mss 28A-B/71. [47] *Holland House Diaries*, 41. [48] *The Times*, 29 Nov. 1831. [49] *O'Connell Corresp.* iv. 1899. [50] *Freeman's Journal*, 20 Sept. 1832, cited in Auchmuty, 141. [51] *O'Connell Corresp.* iv. 1929; v. 2032; *The Times*, 8 Dec. 1832. [52] *Oxford DNB*; W.A. Munford, *William Ewart*, 117; *The Times*, 23 Apr., 11 Sept., 19 Nov. 1862.

P.J.S.

WYVILL, Marmaduke (1791–1872), of Constable Burton, nr. Richmond, Yorks.

YORK 1820–1830

b. 14 Feb. 1791, 1st s. of Rev. Christopher Wyvill of Constable Burton and 2nd w. Sarah Codling. *educ.* Eton 1805-8; Trinity Coll. Camb. 1808. *m.* 13 Dec. 1813, Rachel, da. of Richard Slater Milnes† of Fryston Hall, Yorks., 3s. 4da. (2 *d.v.p.*). *suc.* fa. 1822. *d.* 9 Dec. 1872.

Wyvill was descended from an old parliamentary family who had resided at Constable Burton since the sixteenth century. His father was the celebrated campaigner for parliamentary reform, through the Yorkshire Association, and a tireless advocate of Catholic relief.[1] As a young man, he encountered the financial problems that were to plague him throughout his life: whether gambling caused his early debts is unknown, but he certainly became a regular client of the bookmakers. He borrowed £780 in 1812 and was taken to court the following year for failing to repay it. He ran up another debt of £300 with a 'money lending Jew' and was negotiating for a further £700 before his father, who described him as 'my rash, but not I hope obstinately ill-disposed young man', stopped him and paid off the initial loan.[2] He shared his father's Whiggish politics and joined Brooks's Club, 11 May 1816. In October 1819 he signed the requisition for a Yorkshire county meeting to discuss the Peterloo incident, and he subsequently resigned his commission in the yeomanry as a gesture of solidarity with Lord Fitzwilliam, who had been removed from the lord lieutenancy.[3] In 1820 he offered for York with the backing of the local Whig Club and the approval of Fitzwilliam and the corporation. He stood in coalition with Lawrence Dundas, Fitzwilliam's kinsman, and stipulated that his election was to cost him nothing; Fitzwilliam agreed to foot the bill. In his published address he advocated 'retrenchment of the enormous public expenditure' and pledged to 'uphold the rights and liberties of the people'. On the hustings he attacked the Tories for their 'infringements of all those rights which the [Whig] party had gained' and declared his support for a 'radical reform' of Parliament, 'not to overthrow the constitution, but to repair it ... defend it and ... keep it in good order'. He was returned in second place ahead of a Tory.[4]

He was an assiduous attender who voted with the opposition to Lord Liverpool's ministry on all major issues, including parliamentary reform, 9 May 1821, 25 Apr. 1822, 13, 27 Apr. 1826. He divided for Catholic relief, 28 Feb. 1821, 1 Mar., 21 Apr., 10 May 1825. He was granted a fortnight's leave on account of illness in his family, 19 June 1820, but was present three days later to vote against Wilberforce's motion urging Queen Caroline to compromise her stance. When presenting a York petition calling for the restoration of her name to the liturgy, 26 Jan. 1821, he protested at the conduct of ministers, which showed that neither they nor the king were 'aware of the irritation which prevailed throughout the country on this subject'. He presented petitions for parliamentary reform from York and the West Riding, 31 Jan., 26 Feb., when he predicted that 'sooner or later the House must comply with [their] prayer'.[5] On 14 July Harriet Arbuthnot recorded a recent incident involving Wyvill:

In a committee upstairs one day, the clerk made a mistake and put down the majority to have been on the radical side, when it had, in reality, been on the other. Lord Lowther, who was the teller, said it must be altered. Mr. Wyvill, a radical, said it should not and tried to snatch the paper from Lowther's hand, who, however, held it tight. Mr. Wyvill then seized him by the collar and a general scuffle ensued.[6]

In December 1821 he chaired the annual dinner of the York Whig Club, which he declared had been 'the means of rousing public spirit' and defeating 'the Tory faction'. He believed that in the quest for public freedom and liberty of the press, other places would do well to establish similar associations.[7] Presenting a North Riding petition for relief from agricultural distress, 15 Feb. 1822, he told the House that 'taxation ought to be reduced [by] at least ten millions'. He moved an amendment on the subject, 8 May, when he argued that a £20 million reduction of taxes was required to provide 'permanent relief'; he was defeated by 120-37. He expressed 'his earnest hope' that the House would accede to Lambton's reform motion, 18 Apr. 1822, but like many of his colleagues he failed to vote for it when the division was unexpectedly called after a foreshortened debate. On his father's death that spring he inherited the family estates and was the residuary legatee of personalty which was resworn under £3,000.[8] In the summer of 1825 the threat of opposition from 'a more decided reformer' at York prompted him to announce his intention of retiring at the next general election, but he was persuaded to reconsider his decision by a requisition from the electors and an address from the Whig Club, which praised his 'firm and consistent support of civil and religious freedom'. A hostile local newspaper nevertheless tried to discredit him, describing him as a 'notoriously incompetent' Member who induced the 'laughter and derision of his compeers' whenever he spoke in the House, and who took more interest in the Turf than in the welfare of York.[9] At the dissolution in the summer of 1826 he initially intended to stand in conjunction with Thomas Dundas*, the son of his former colleague, but disagreements over the apportionment of the expenses caused Dundas to withdraw, and Wyvill was returned unopposed with the Tory James Wilson. During the election he reaffirmed his support for reform and Catholic relief, declared himself an enemy of slavery, blamed 'excessive tax' as the 'primary cause' of distress and said that the corn laws had 'no other tendency than to oppress the working classes and render exorbitantly dear the prime necessity of life'.[10] Despite the comparatively cheap cost of his re-election, he appears to have borrowed an unknown amount of money about this time.[11]

He was a less frequent attender in the 1826 Parliament, though his principles remained unchanged. He voted for Hume's amendment to the address, 21 Nov. 1826. He divided for Catholic relief, 6 Mar., and presented a York petition in its favour, 7 May 1827.[12] He voted for a lower import duty on wheat, 9 Mar., and against increased protection for barley, 12 Mar. He supported the Wakefield and Ferrybridge canal bill, 15 Mar.[13] He was granted a month's leave owing to illness in his family, 19 Mar. 1827. In his only recorded activities in the next session he voted for repeal of the Test Acts, 26 Feb., and paired for Catholic relief, 12 May 1828. He presented a petition from the Catholics of York for their relief, 'the first that had been agreed to since the recommendation from the throne', 24 Feb. 1829. When Wilson presented a hostile petition from the city, 4 Mar., Wyvill criticized the method used to collect signatures and claimed that majority opinion was in favour of the Catholic cause. He divided for the Wellington ministry's emancipation bill, 6, 30 Mar. He presented a York anti-slavery petition, 11 May 1829. He divided for Knatchbull's amendment to the address on distress, 4 Feb. 1830, and acted with the revived Whig opposition on all major issues that session. He voted to transfer East Retford's seats to Birmingham, 11 Feb., Lord Blandford's reform motion, 18 Feb., and the enfranchisement of Birmingham, Leeds and Manchester, 23 Feb. On 28 May he divided for O'Connell's motion for radical reform as well as for Lord John Russell's more conventional reform motion. He voted for Jewish emancipation, 17 May, and paired for abolition of the death penalty for forgery, 24 May 1830. Shortly before the dissolution that summer it was announced that he would not offer again for York. No explanation was given, but the Whig Club was by now in steep decline, the Fitzwilliam-corporation interest was keen to reassert its position and Wyvill was again facing pecuniary difficulties; he was due to pay back interest on his earlier borrowings about this time.[14] He chaired the meeting of Yorkshire Whigs, 23 July 1830, which adopted Henry Brougham* as a candidate for the county, and that of April 1831 to organize support for the candidacy of four Whigs.[15]

Wyvill had tried unsuccessfully to revive the family baronetcy in 1825, and in October 1831 he failed in his application to Lord Grey for a peerage. However, that December he successfully lobbied Grey's ministry to have his brother Christopher promoted to the rank of captain in the navy.[16] His financial problems caught up with him in the years immediately after he left the House, and by 1833 he was living abroad, mostly in Germany, on an annual allowance of £750

from Christopher, who appears to have taken over the running of the family estates. Sales of land, farms and other possessions occurred in these years to cover his debts.[17] In 1841 he was invited to stand as a Liberal for Richmond, which was still under the influence of the Dundas family, but replied that he had 'resolved not to engage again in parliamentary life'.[18] He died in December 1872. Constable Burton passed to his son Marmaduke Wyvill (1815-96), Liberal Member for Richmond, 1847-65, 1866-8.

[1] Oxford DNB sub Rev. Christopher Wyvill. [2] N. Yorks. RO, Wyvill mss ZFW/7/1; 10/297. [3] The Times, 5 Oct. 1819; Althorp Letters, 92; P. Brett, Rise and Fall of York Whig Club, 16. [4] Yorks. Gazette, 4, 11 Mar.; York Herald, 4, 18 Mar. 1820. [5] The Times, 27 Feb. 1821. [6] Arbuthnot Jnl. i. 85-86. [7] The Times, 7 Dec. 1821. [8] IR26/937/1233. [9] York Herald, 28 May, 20 Aug.; Yorks. Gazette, 20 Aug. 1825, 2 May, 9 June 1826. [10] York Herald, 3, 10 June; York Courant, 23 June 1826. [11] Wyvill mss 1699/335, 764. [12] The Times, 8 May 1827. [13] Ibid. 16 Mar. 1827. [14] Yorks. Gazette, 26 June 1830; Wyvill mss 1699/765. [15] Yorks. Gazette, 31 July 1830; York Herald, 30 Apr. 1831. [16] Wyvill mss 1699/316, 352, 355. [17] Ibid. 1699/502-10, 766. [18] Ibid. 1699/5236-40.

M.P.J.C.

YARMOUTH, earl of *see* **SEYMOUR CONWAY, Francis Charles**

YORKE, Charles Philip (1799–1873), of Sydney Lodge, nr. Southampton, Hants.

REIGATE	13 July 1831–22 Oct. 1831
REIGATE	15 Dec. 1831–1832
CAMBRIDGESHIRE	1832–18 Nov. 1834

b. 2 Apr. 1799, 1st s. of Sir Joseph Sydney Yorke* and 1st w. Elizabeth Weake, da. of James Rattray of Atherston, Perth. *educ.* Harrow 1810; RN Coll. 1813. *m.* 14 Oct. 1833, Hon. Susan Liddell, da. of Thomas Henry Liddell†, 1st Bar. Ravensworth, 5s. (1 *d.v.p.*) 3da. *suc.* fa. 1831; uncle Philip Yorke† as 4th earl of Hardwicke 18 Nov. 1834. *d.* 17 Sept. 1873.

Midshipman RN 1815, lt. 1819, cdr. 1822, capt. 1825, r.-adm. (reserve) 1854, v.-adm. 1858, adm. 1863.

Ld. in waiting Sept. 1841-July 1846; councillor to duchy of Lancaster 1847; PC 27 Feb. 1852; postmaster-gen. Mar.-Dec. 1852; ld. privy seal Feb. 1858-June 1859.

Ld. lt. Cambs. 1834-*d.*; pres. R. Agricultural Soc. 1843.

Yorke, like his father, followed a naval career. His first posting was in the Mediterranean, where he was commended by his captain for his 'active, spirited and highly meritorious' conduct during the siege of Algiers in August 1817.[1] After a tour of duty on the North American station at Halifax, from 1817 to 1822, he returned to a Mediterranean command, 1822-6 and

1829-31, in which he was chiefly engaged in policing the Turkish-Greek conflict; in the intervening period he made a tour of Scandinavia. His journals and letters home chart the development of his conservative political outlook and demonstrate much of the bluff asceticism of his father, with whom he shared an intense suspicion of France.[2] While on an off-duty visit to that country in 1823, he observed: 'there are parts of their form of government which ... must always be unpleasant to every Englishman'.[3] He was broadly sympathetic to the Greeks' struggle for independence, but disavowed all sentimentality in their cause, writing in March 1824:

> English notions must be abolished, so must all romance of liberty and the children of the ancient Greeks struggling to shake off the yoke of the bloody Turk. Lord Byron knows all this, and is in fact the only man that has ever come out to them who understands the people.

With Byron, whom he met at this time, he enjoyed a useful rapport, and the poet sprang to his defence when his firm handling of a recalcitrant Greek leader brought accusations of bullying from Colonel Leicester Stanhope, envoy of the London Greek committee. Yorke generally regarded the committee's efforts as misdirected, and Stanhope, he sourly noted, had 'come out with Jeremy Bentham under his arm to give the Greeks a constitution'. By 1830 he had reached the conclusion that 'though the Greeks love liberty, they love money better'.[4] He was called away from this arena by the accidental death of his father in May 1831, which created a vacancy for Reigate that his uncle, Lord Hardwicke, invited him to fill. His reluctance to leave the navy and the 'politically disagreeable' intelligence which he had received from England meant that he contemplated a parliamentary career with no great relish:

> What part in the play am I to act? I wish my mind were made up on this cursed reform question. It will be carried, but I should like to do what I think right and honourable towards myself, that is, act and vote as I really think. We must become republican England as well as republican France (damn France, she is the root of all evil and the branch of no good): it matters little how, whether by reform which will produce national bankruptcy, or by a starving population, which will produce rebellion and civil war.

He landed at Falmouth on 30 June 1831 and was returned for Reigate a fortnight later, after an expected opposition failed to materialize.[5]

In the House he followed his instincts, as well as the views of Hardwicke and his father, by opposing the Grey ministry's reintroduced reform bill, which proposed to partially disfranchise Reigate. Either he or his colleague Joseph Yorke denied that it was a rotten borough, 20, 30 July 1831; the air of resignation about the bill's passage, evident in the latter speech, was certainly redolent of this Member's earlier ruminations. He voted against the partial disfranchisement of Chippenham, 27 July, for the amendment to make borough voting rights conditional on the proven payment of rent, 25 Aug., and against the bill's passage, 21 Sept. On 10 Oct. he was absent from the call of the House prior to the division on Lord Ebrington's confidence motion. Shortly afterwards he resigned his seat in order to contest a vacancy for Cambridgeshire, where Hardwicke had a leading interest. In a bullish hustings speech he declared that the reform bill was 'pregnant with ruin and destruction for the agricultural interest' and warned that protection would not survive in a Parliament dominated, as he anticipated, by northern manufacturing interests. He therefore welcomed the adoption of the Chandos clause enfranchising £50 tenants-at-will in the counties. He compared the government's record on retrenchment unfavourably with that of the duke of Wellington's, and disclaimed the Tory label fixed on him by his opponents. One speaker approvingly observed that he 'swore so that it would do their hearts good to hear him', and another supporter claimed that such was the impression he created that he had 'received numerous offers from ladies (not professional) soliciting his favours for one night'. Nevertheless, he was defeated by a reformer after a four-day poll, in what was widely seen as an important test of opinion.[6] He was subsequently re-elected for Reigate. He divided against the second reading of the revised reform bill, 17 Dec. 1831, and entering into committee, 20 Jan. 1832. He clashed with the Cambridgeshire Member Adeane when presenting a hostile petition from that county, 15 Feb., and warned that the £10 householder franchise in the boroughs would reduce Members to mere delegates. He voted against the enfranchisement of Tower Hamlets, 28 Feb., acted as a minority teller against the bill at the report stage, 14 Mar., and voted against the third reading, 22 Mar., and the second reading of the Irish bill, 25 May. He divided against Hobhouse's Vestry Act amendment bill, 23 Jan. He questioned the arrangement with France regarding the mutual right to search ships, 24 Jan. Taking up his father's favourite subject of naval expenditure, he advised that the future allocation of resources should anticipate the triumph of steam over sail, 13 Feb., and spoke against the merger of the admiralty and navy boards, 14 Feb., 6 Apr. While professing himself friendly to the principle of economy in the service, 16 Mar., he set his face against substantial reductions, particularly in the marines. He voted against ministers on the Russian-Dutch loan, 26 Jan., and paired against them, 12 July 1832.

In October 1832 Yorke recorded in his briefly resumed journal that the state of the country was 'tranquil (except as always Ireland)' and that his return for Cambridgeshire at the forthcoming general election was 'finally secure'. However, he took a gloomy view of the political prospect, observing that 'in Ireland the return is fought between Catholic and Protestant, in England between high and low church, and in Scotland between aristocrat and democrat'; he predicted that the reformed House of Commons would 'consist of 300 Whigs, 200 Tories and 150 Radicals'.[7] He comfortably topped the poll in Cambridgeshire. Two years later he succeeded his uncle as 4th earl of Hardwicke. He served as a lord in waiting during Peel's second ministry, before resigning over the repeal of the corn laws, and, after briefly returning to active service at Genoa in 1849, he held cabinet office in Lord Derby's minority governments of the 1850s. In spirit, though, he never left the navy, and he was devastated that his services were not required in the Crimean conflict. He chaired a royal commission on manning in the navy in 1858, but his own preference for reviving the press gang found few supporters.[8] He died in September 1873.[9] His title and main estate at Wimpole, Cambridgeshire, passed to his eldest son Charles Philip Yorke (1836-97), Conservative Member for the county since 1865; his younger son Eliot Charles Yorke then filled the seat until his death in 1879.

[1] E.P. Biddulph, *Mem. 4th earl of Hardwicke*, 29-47. [2] Ibid. 48-152, *passim*. [3] Bodl. mss Eng. lett. c. 60, f. 115. [4] Biddulph, 68, 73-74, 90, 146; Sir H. Nicholson, *Byron: the Last Journey*, 207. [5] Surr. Hist. Cent. 171/5/1e; Biddulph, 150-2. [6] *The Times*, 27-31 Oct., 1, 3 Nov. 1831; Norf. RO, Ketton-Cremer mss WKC 6/236. [7] Add. 36261, ff. 294-5. [8] Biddulph, 162-206, 220-91. [9] Ibid. 300-2; *The Times*, 18 Sept. 1873.

H.J.S.

YORKE, Joseph (1807–1889), of Forthampton Court, Tewkesbury, Glos.

REIGATE   1831–1832

b. 11 Jan. 1807, 1st s. of Joseph Yorke of Forthampton and Catherine, da. of James Cocks, banker, of London. *educ.* Eton 1823; St. John's, Camb. 1825. *m.* 31 Dec. 1834, Frances Antonia, da. of Reginald Pole Carew[†] of Antony, Cornw., 1s. *suc.* fa. 1830. *d.* 4 Feb. 1889.
Sheriff, Glos 1844-5.

Yorke was the great-grandson of the 1st earl of Hardwicke, lord chancellor under Walpole, and the grandson of James Yorke (1730-1808), successively bishop of St. Davids, Gloucester and Ely, who had acquired the Forthampton estate in Gloucestershire through marriage.[1] He inherited Forthampton on his father's death in December 1830.[2] He was related to both the patrons for Reigate, the 3rd earl of Hardwicke and the 1st Earl Somers, and it was on the latter's interest that he was returned unopposed at the general election of 1831. He appears to have attended only occasionally during his brief and undistinguished parliamentary career. He divided against the second reading of the Grey ministry's reintroduced reform bill, which proposed to partially disfranchise Reigate, 6 July 1831. His only known vote in committee was for use of the 1831 census in determining the disfranchisement schedules, 19 July. Either he or his colleague Charles Philip Yorke denied the imputation that patronal influence at Reigate had been corruptly exercised or sold, 20, 30 July. He voted against the bill's third reading, 19 Sept., and its passage, 21 Sept. He was in the minority of seven who backed Waldo Sibthorp's complaint of inaccurate parliamentary reporting by *The Times*, 12 Sept. Although Lord Somers subsequently changed his position and supported reform, Yorke divided against the second and third readings of the revised bill, 17 Dec. 1831, 22 Mar., and the second reading of the Irish bill, 25 May 1832. His only other recorded vote was in the minority for information on military punishments, 16 Feb. 1832.

The surviving seat at Reigate was required for Somers's son at the general election of 1832, and Yorke never returned to the Commons. A magistrate in Gloucestershire and Worcestershire, he maintained his family's philanthropic traditions on his border estate. His wife's aunt Lady Lyttelton encountered the Yorkes in 1847 and found them 'as usual, totally unchanged'.[3] He was a director and major shareholder in the Gloucestershire Steam Plough Company, a venture in agricultural mechanization which failed in 1862.[4] He died in February 1889 and left Forthampton to his only son John Reginald Yorke (1836-1912), Conservative Member for Tewkesbury, 1864-8, East Gloucestershire, 1872-85, and the Tewkesbury division, 1885-6.

[1] *VCH Glos.* viii. 201, 206, 208. [2] The personalty was sworn under £16,000 (PROB 11/1485/729; IR26/1275/1). [3] *The Times*, 11 Feb. 1889; *VCH Glos.* viii. 208; *Lady Lyttelton Corresp.* 366. [4] C. Miller, 'Glos. Steam Plough Co.', *Trans. Bristol and Glos. Arch. Soc.* xcix (1982), 141-56.

H.J.S.

YORKE, Sir Joseph Sydney (1768–1831), of Sydney
Lodge, nr. Southampton, Hants.

REIGATE	1790–1806
ST. GERMANS	1806–16 Apr. 1810
WEST LOOE	17 Jan. 1812–1812
SANDWICH	1812–1818
REIGATE	1818–5 May 1831

b. 6 June 1768, 3rd s. of Charles Yorke† (*d.* 1770) of
Tittenhanger, Herts. and 2nd w. Agneta, da. and coh. of
Henry Johnston of Great Berkhampstead, Herts. *educ.*
Harrow 1779-80. *m.* (1) 29 Mar. 1798, Elizabeth Weake
(*d.* 29 Jan. 1812), da. of James Rattray of Atherston,
Perth, 4s. 1da.; (2) 22 May 1813, Lady Urania Anne
Paulet, da. of George Paulet†, 12th mq. of Winchester,
wid. of Henry, 1st mq. of Clanricarde [I], and of Col.
Peter Kingston, *s.p.* kntd. 21 Apr. 1805; KCB 2 Jan. 1815.
d. 5 May 1831.
   Midshipman RN 1780, lt. 1789, cdr. 1790, capt. 1793,
r.-adm. 1810, v.-adm. 1814, half-pay 1818, adm. 1830.
   Ld. of admiralty July 1810-Apr. 1818.
   Dir. Greenwich Hosp. 1818.

Yorke was again returned for Reigate in 1820 on the
interest of his half-brother, the 3rd earl of Hardwicke.
He was a fairly regular attender who continued to
profess his support for Lord Liverpool's ministry,
but, being under no obligation to them since his swift
exit from the admiralty in 1818, he displayed a marked
streak of independence, particularly in his often irrev-
erent interventions in debate. His chief concerns
were for cost-effective naval defences, on which he
freely offered ministers advice, and for general public
economies. A naval biography of 1828, which was
frank enough to admit that there were 'differences of
opinion' about his professional worth, noted that while

> his parliamentary speeches have not been remarkable
> either for length or profundity, they have been for a vein
> of facetiousness which has almost invariably run through
> them ... Though his speeches are generally off hand,
> he has the merit of seizing a strong point in debate, and
> placing it in so clear a light as to bring conviction to the
> plainest understanding.[1]

His threat of a hostile vote on the civil list, 5 May
1820, proved to be an empty one. He tempered his
'opposition speech' for naval economies, 9 June, with
praise for the comptroller of the service, Sir Thomas
Byam Martin*. With a sneer at Elizabeth Fry, he condemned the penitentiary system and recommended
transportation instead, 16 June; three days later he
opposed the grant for the Millbank establishment.
Though apparently favourable to mitigation of the

penal code for shoplifters, 30 June, he wanted punishments to be specified. He denied that punishments at
sea were unduly harsh, 13 July.[2] On the move to remit
Sir Manasseh Masseh Lopes's* prison sentence for
electoral corruption, 11 July 1820, he cited the case of
Henry Swann* as a more deserving one. His distaste
for lawyers was evident in his opposition to allowing
defendants the right of counsel in all capital cases, 30
Mar. 1821. He divided with ministers against repeal
of the additional malt duty, 3 Apr. His vote for admiralty economies, 4 May, was accompanied with a
warning that 'the great ships *Britannia*, *Caledonia*
and *Hibernia*, if ... not completely waterlogged, had
at least six feet [of] water in their holds'. Dismissing
the admiralty secretary Croker's accusation of disloyalty, he advocated a reduction of the junior lords from
seven to five. He made more suggestions for savings,
notably in ship repairs, 7 May, but defended the grant
for Sheerness dockyard, in the development of which
he took an active interest.[3] He voted against the grant
for ordnance repairs at Barbados, 21 May, and to
reduce that for the medical establishment, 21 May, and
queried the army estimates, 25 May. He spoke, 8 June,
and voted, 18 June 1821, for the omission of arrears
from the duke of Clarence's grant, and was insistent that no provision should yet be made for Princess
Victoria, as the duke and duchess were not too old
for 'procreation'. He divided against more extensive
tax reductions, 11 Feb. 1822. He had harsh words for
Hume's proposed naval economies, 18 Feb., but produced his own list of detailed queries when the estimates were discussed, 18, 22 Mar.[4] He spoke and voted
for abolition of one of the joint-postmasterships,
13 Mar. He doubted that brewers would pass on the
saving arising from repeal of the malt duty, 15 Mar.[5]
He welcomed the reduction in the salt duties, 28 June
1822, but said he did not believe in remitting taxes by
halves and therefore voted for their repeal.[6]

   At the opening of the next session, 4 Feb. 1823, he
initiated his practice of commenting on the address.
He applauded ministers for adopting a neutral stance
on the burgeoning conflict between France and Spain,
but recognized that intervention might become inevitable. He was granted a fortnight's leave for urgent
private business, 12 Feb. His observations on the naval
estimates were chiefly in their defence, 14 Mar., though
he strongly disputed an assertion that the service was
underfunded.[7] He voted to deduct a grant for colonial
agents from the army estimates, 24 Mar., and against
the military and naval pensions bill, 14, 18 Apr. He
regarded repeal of the Foreign Enlistment Act as a step
prejudicial to British neutrality and a danger to naval
recruitment, 16 Apr. He was a minority teller against

the second reading of the Southwark court of requests bill, 2 May. He recommended abandonment of the inquiry into the prosecution of the Dublin Orange rioters, 27 May, and made a suggestion for the display of the Elgin marbles, 1 July 1823. He concurred in calls for the reduction of duties on malt, coals and candles, 25 Mar., and spoke and voted for repeal of the leather tax, 18 May 1824, though he wondered if the benefits would reach the public. He presented a petition against the beer bill, which he quipped had caused 'a fermentation throughout the country', 11 May.[8] He was a minority teller against the second reading of the St. Katharine's Docks bill, 2 Apr. He advised against following the caprices of architectural fashion in the alterations to Windsor Castle, 5 Apr., and supported Sir John Soane's petition protesting at changes made to his design for the law courts, 21 May. While urging ministers to ignore protests at the salary reductions meted out to clerks in government offices, 13 May,[9] he thought abolition of the public officers' superannuation fund was too trifling a saving to be concerned with, 21 June. He spoke and voted in condemnation of the trial of the Methodist missionary John Smith in Demerara, 11 June 1824, describing Canning's speech on this occasion as a 'mere brilliant apology'. In the course of his regular scrutiny of the navy estimates, 14, 24 Feb. 1825, he questioned the reduction in sailors' grog allowances and appeared contrite at his earlier advocacy of the removal of two admiralty lords, given the negligible savings achieved in other areas.[10] He thought the proposed western ship canal would be prejudicial to the coastal trade, 'a nursery for seamen', 3, 11 Mar.[11] Observing that Ireland 'would never be quiet until it had been 24 hours under water', he promised to support the suppression of the Catholic Association, 18 Feb., and he divided against Catholic relief, 1 Mar., 21 Apr., 10 May. His general hostility to 'speculations' was evident in his scorn for Trench's plan for the Thames quay, 18 Feb., and in his opposition to docks bills, 22 Feb., 23 Mar. He presented an anti-slavery petition, 10 Apr. 1825.[12] He maintained that he would 'rather at once cut away the deadweight, of which he formed himself a distinguished part', than 'diminish ... one single effective man of the army or navy', 6 Mar. 1826. He subsequently suffered from illness, which restricted his activity for the remainder of that session. On 21 May he informed Hardwicke that he hoped to return to London, 'to resume my usual habits and occupations, without fear of relapse'.[13] He voted against Russell's resolutions to curb electoral bribery, 26 May 1826. He was again returned for Reigate at the general election that summer.

In welcoming the re-election of the speaker, Manners Sutton, 14 Nov., Yorke apparently made an unreported charge that James Brogden had used his position as chairman of ways and means to further his business interest; this was strongly denied, 21 Nov. 1826. That day he said he had hoped to find more 'earnests of economy' in the king's speech, but Canning noted that he was one of those who voted against an amendment to it.[14] He maintained that the navy estimates were 'as low as was consistent with the honour and safety of the country', 12 Feb. 1827, and expressed the hope that impressment could be abandoned. He was granted ten days' leave for urgent business, 26 Feb. He betrayed hostility to the East India Company when supporting inquiry into the Barrackpoor mutiny, 22 Mar., and he supported the vote of thanks to the army in India, 8 May. On the formation of Canning's ministry he joined Peel on the opposition benches, but he hinted at a softening of his attitude towards Catholic relief, 11 May; Canning thought this intimation of qualified support worthy of mention to the king.[15] He voiced doubts about Huskisson's free trade doctrines when urging an inquiry into the shipping interest, 7 May. Four days later he replied to an attack on Soane's buildings by George Bankes, the design of whose Dorset residence he derided as 'the very worst he had ever seen'.[16] He spoke against the grant for the national vaccine establishment, 14 May, and presented petitions from the Royal College of Surgeons to facilitate a supply of bodies for dissection, 20 June 1827. He was indignant at the abrupt end of the ministry of his cousin Lord Goderich, 'so happy a mixture of Whigs and Tories', 28 Jan. 1828, and disapproved of the tone of the address regarding the battle of Navarino, being marginally pro-Turkish. He dissented from the view that the duke of Wellington's military background suited him for the premiership, believing rather the opposite, 4 Feb. He made plain his disgust at the recriminations following the demise of Goderich's administration, 21 Feb. However, four days later, when pressing for a thorough scrutiny of the navy estimates, he assured Wellington's ministry that 'they have not a more sincere friend, nor a more faithful servant'. His jibes at Goulburn, the chancellor of the exchequer, were taken in good humour, 24 Mar., when he supported Hume's proposal to divide the finance committee. However, his bluff manner did not find favour with Huskisson, who took offence at what were intended to be supportive comments following his resignation from the government, 24 June. He divided against repeal of the Test Acts, 26 Feb., and Catholic relief, 12 May, but his speech on the latter issue, 12 June, appeared to be favourable, although he dwelt on the need for securities. He proclaimed his commitment to a 'moderate and practical' reform of Parliament, 24 Mar., and favoured the transfer of Penryn's seats to an unrepresented town. He questioned the size of the food allowance in prisons, 14 May, but reckoned that as Millbank penitentiary was 'now built and paid for we had better make the best of it', 23 May. He scorned proposals to cut expenditure on the coast blockade, 16 May, and pointed to the shipbuilding programme as his preferred candidate for economies, 19 May. He wanted the Longitude Acts to remain in place as an incentive for further exploration of uncharted waters, 28 June. He thought the ordnance survey a waste of money, 7 July, but could not swallow Hume's proposed reduction of ordnance spending to 1822 levels; his own suggestion to finance military expenditure by cutting fundholders' dividends was so outlandish as to suggest to several listeners that he was drunk. He advocated repeal of the glass duty, 12 June, and spoke and voted against the archbishop of Canterbury's bill, 16 June. He disavowed any personal interest in the discussion on London water companies, 30 June 1828, declaring that he was 'no joint-stock baronet' and that he had 'only one little share in Waterloo Bridge'.

Yorke's speech directly after the seconding of the address, 5 Feb. 1829, though dismissed as buffoonery by John Cam Hobhouse*, was important for its announcement that he would support Catholic emancipation.[17] He defended Peel, the leader of the Commons, against accusations of inconsistency, 9 Feb., and indicated next day that he would support measures to suppress the Catholic Association. He divided for emancipation, 6, 30 Mar. As a director of Greenwich Hospital, he objected to the bill brought in for its better management, 9 Apr., 4 May, but could find no reply to the glaring examples of maladministration cited. He thought the transfer of East Retford's seats to Birmingham 'a judicious reform', 5 May. Linking the proposed increase in Scottish judges' salaries to the revision of the sugar duties, 21 May, he likened Peel (who viewed his comment indulgently) to 'the man who stopped up the spiggot, and let the liquor run out at the bung hole'. He voted against the grant for the sculpture of the marble arch, 25 May, when he questioned the integrity of John Nash. He opposed the development of Hampstead Heath, 19 June 1829. In welcoming the address, 5 Feb. 1830, he ridiculed the lurid depictions of economic distress by some opposition Members. He was granted two weeks' leave on account of ill health, 1 Mar. He presented, but dissented from, a petition for abolition of the death penalty for forgery, 27 Apr., and aligned himself with

Peel against this measure, 24 May. He supported plans for a new feeder road for Waterloo Bridge, 6, 10 May (he was chairman of the Bridge Company at the time of his death)[18]. He spoke and voted for abolition of the Irish lord lieutenancy, 11 May. He also divided against ministers for a return of privy councillors' emoluments, 14 May, and reduction of the grant for South American missions, 7 June. He voted against Jewish emancipation, 17 May. He raised the question of compensation for slave owners, 20 July 1830. Prior to the dissolution that summer it was suggested that he might offer for Cambridgeshire, where his half-brother was a major landowner, but Hardwicke found he was 'not very keen on the subject ... says he is just turned of 62, is very comfortable at Reigate and desires nothing better'; his wish was granted.[19]

In the autumn of 1830 the ministry listed him as one of the 'good doubtfuls'. He had words of praise for the Speaker, 26 Oct. In lending his support to the address, 2 Nov., he described Lord Blandford's amendment as 'a tough and long yarn' and turned his sarcasm on Wellington's profligate nephew, William Pole Tylney Long Wellesley, while also warning of the possibility of revived French expansionism. One observer thought Yorke's reply to these Members was 'most complete'.[20] Yet he was absent from the crucial division on the civil list, 15 Nov. He pointed to the outgoing ministry's failure to deal with venal boroughs, 22 Nov., and, while regretting that Lord Grey's government included no members of the old cabinet, he promised his support if they acted as pledged. On 13 Dec. 1830, however, he confessed himself 'lamentably disappointed' with their initial measures of retrenchment, although in the context of the 'Swing' disturbances he believed Hume's proposals for military economies made him 'a candidate for a straight waistcoat'. He opposed Hunt's call for a general amnesty for the rioters, 8 Feb. 1831, and boldly predicted his imminent conversion to high Toryism; a vision which inspired the satirists.[21] He welcomed the withdrawal of Lord Althorp's budget proposal to tax transfers of stock, 14 Feb., but expressed concern at the extent of the tax reductions planned. He bashfully added that he hoped he had 'not said anything which is offensive', as he was 'anxious, if I can', to support the government. When calling for the maintenance of military expenditure, at a time of continental instability, 18 Feb., he was again supportive of ministers. Nevertheless, he could not stomach their 'extraordinary' and 'unjust' reform bill, 8 Mar., despite his professed antipathy to the aristocracy's domination of the Commons. He specifically objected to the arbitrary means used to determine the sweeping borough disfranchisements, and amused the

House by quoting another Member's aside that, had he been allowed nine month's notice of his borough's demise, he could have made good the shortfall in population. Set to lose his own seat, he divided against the bill's second reading, 22 Mar. To his eldest son, he glumly predicted that the family's *metier* could be as 'hewers of wood and drawers of water', if the measure passed as it stood. He contended that

> it cannot be denied that it must give a preponderating bias to that class, namely the £10 householder, which are by far the most numerous, active and republican class; who by living in towns, can be collected for any political purpose at a moment's notice; who are shopkeepers, citizens, manufacturers, possessing great intelligence and spirit, and whose business it will be to have the chief government, and bring down the interests of the funds. This will, of course, straiten most severely all those who at present derive any income therefrom ... It will totally ruin a great many.

He was optimistic that the bill would be 'greatly modified', but continued to worry about the influence of the recent French revolution in all parts of Europe.[22] He expressed concern that increased Irish representation in a reformed Parliament would give undue weight to Catholic interests, 18 Apr. He did not vote on Gascoyne's wrecking amendment the next day. He welcomed the changes made in the means for coastal defence, 25 Mar. 1831, and made suggestions for naval economies, which he regarded as preferable to Hume's proposal to contract out services.

Yorke was returned again for Reigate at the subsequent general election, but did not live to take his seat. On 5 May 1831 he was aboard a small pleasure craft which sank with all hands in Southampton Water, off Netley Abbey, apparently after being struck by lightning. His sudden death was widely lamented: one obituarist, writing from an anti-reform perspective, mourned the passing of 'a valuable ally to the cause of national freedom, and the menaced institutions of his native land', while the Whig duke of Bedford observed that 'he was, though eccentric and "rude in speech", a very good man'.[23] His personal estate, which was sworn under £40,000, was divided equally between his five children. Sydney Lodge passed to his widow and then to his eldest son, Charles Philip Yorke, who also succeeded to his parliamentary seat.[24] Another son, Eliot Thomas Yorke (1805-85), was Conservative Member for Cambridgeshire, 1835-65.

[1] J. Ralfe, *Naval Biog.* iii. 108-13. [2] *The Times*, 14 July 1820. [3] Ibid. 8 May 1821; Add. 45046, f. 22. [4] *The Times*, 19 Mar. 1822. [5] Ibid. 16 Mar. 1822. [6] Ibid. 29 June 1822. [7] Ibid. 15 Mar. 1823. [8] Ibid. 12 May 1824. [9] Ibid. 14 May 1824. [10] Ibid. 25 Feb. 1825. [11] Ibid. 4, 12 Mar.

1825. [12] Ibid. 11 Apr. 1825. [13] Add. 35395, f. 342. [14] *Geo. IV Letters*, iii. 1271. [15] Ibid. iii. 1238. [16] *The Times*, 12 May 1827. [17] Broughton, *Recollections*, iii. 301-2. [18] *Gent. Mag.* (1831), i. 561. [19] Herts. Archives, Caledon mss D/E Cd/E167, Hardwicke to Parkinson, 23 June 1830. [20] Hopetoun mss 167, f. 177. [21] M.D. George, *Cat. of Pol. and Personal Satires*, xi. 16579. [22] E.P. Biddulph, *Mem. 4th earl of Hardwicke*, 154-6. [23] *Gent. Mag.* (1831), i. 477, 559-61; *Victoria Letters* (ser. 1), i. 483; Add. 51670, Bedford to Lady Holland, 12 May 1831. [24] PROB 11/1787/373; IR26/1276/237.

H.J.S.

YOUNG, John (1807–1876), of Bailieborough Castle, co. Cavan.

Co. Cavan	1831–Mar. 1855

b. 31 Aug. 1807, in Bombay, 1st s. of Maj. Sir William Young, 1st bt., of E.I. Co. Service (Bombay) and Lucy, da. of Lt.-Col. Charles Frederick of E.I. Co. Service (Bombay). *educ.* Eton 1823; Corpus, Oxf. 1825; L. Inn 1829, called 1834. *m.* 8 Apr. 1835, Adelaide Annabella, da. of Edward Tuite Dalton of Fennor, co. Meath, *s.p. suc.* fa. as 2nd bt. 10 Mar. 1848; GCMG 16 May 1855; KCB 4 Feb. 1859; GCB 13 Nov. 1868; *cr.* Bar. Lisgar 16 Oct. 1870. *d.* 6 Oct. 1876.

Ld. of treasury Sept. 1841-May 1844, sec. May 1844-July 1846; PC 28 Dec. 1852, PC [I] 28 Jan. 1853; chief sec. to ld. lt. [I] Jan. 1853-Mar. 1855; ld. high commr. Ionian Islands 1855-9; gov. New S. Wales 1861-7; gov.-gen. Canada and gov. Prince Edward Island 1869-72.

Ld. lt. and custos rot. co. Cavan 1871-*d.*

Young's father, the second son of the Rev. John Young of Eden, county Armagh, joined the infantry of the Bombay army as a cadet in 1788 and rose steadily through the ranks. On 20 Sept. 1806 he married the daughter of a fellow officer Charles Frederick (*d.* 1791), whose father, Sir Charles Frederick, was Member for New Shoreham, 1741-54, and Queenborough, 1754-82. Having obtained the rank of lieutenant-colonel in 1809, Young retired in 1813 and earned plaudits for his military career, including his contributions to the recruitment and supply systems of the Company's forces.[1] He settled in Cavan, where he purchased Bailieborough Castle in 1815 from Thomas Corry, Member for Monaghan, and in London, where he had residences at 15 Bishopsgate and 24 Upper Wimpole Street. He was awarded a baronetcy on 28 Aug. 1821. Described by John Maxwell Barry, in a letter recommending him for an East Indian directorship, as 'a powerful constituent of mine' in Cavan, he backed the leading Orangeman Henry Maxwell* to succeed Barry (on his becoming Lord Farnham) in the summer of 1823, but expressed the hope that he might find a close borough for himself in order to promote his ambitions within the Company.[2] He did not in the end offer for the county at the general election of 1826, when he seconded Maxwell.[3] He was elected a director of the East India Company in 1829.

Although he does not seem to have participated in the Protestant activities there towards the end of the decade, Sir William Young unsuccessfully stood against the other sitting Cavan Member, the now pro-Catholic Alexander Saunderson, at the general election of 1830, when it was thought that he could only have won by bribing the Farnham tenants into giving him their second votes.[4] It was at this contest that John Young, who graduated from Oxford and began his legal training in 1829, first made his mark with his highly promising closing speech in vindication of his absent father.[5] Following the dissolution in April 1831 it was he, not the baronet, who took advantage of Saunderson's resignation to offer in conjunction with Maxwell and he was duly returned as an anti-reformer at the general election, defeating a pro-Catholic radical in a four-day contest.[6] It had been understood that Young's father would be assisted with his expenses by a grant from Tory funds, but his demand for £1,200 was considered ill-timed and excessive.[7]

Young divided against the second reading of the Grey ministry's reintroduced reform bill, 6 July, at least four times for adjourning the proceedings on it, 12 July, against the disfranchisement of St. Germans, 26 July, and for postponing consideration of the partial disfranchisement of Chippenham, 27 July 1831. He voted to censure the Irish government over the Dublin election, 23 Aug., against issuing the Liverpool writ, 5 Sept., and for inquiry into the effects of the renewal of the Sugar Refinery Act on the West India interest, 12 Sept. He spoke against the disbandment of the Irish yeomanry, 9 Sept., and defended Maxwell's comments on the Newtownbarry affray, 3 Oct. He voted against the passage of the reform bill, 21 Sept., and the second reading of the Scottish bill, 23 Sept. He divided against the Maynooth grant, 26 Sept., and condemned the partisan appointments of often non-resident lord lieutenants in Irish counties, 6 Oct. He attended Protestant gatherings in Dublin, 7 Dec. 1831, and Cavan, 13 Jan. 1832.[8] He divided against the second reading, 17 Dec. 1831 (unless this was Joseph Yorke, Member for Reigate), and the third reading, 22 Mar. 1832, of the revised reform bill. He was granted two weeks' leave to attend the assizes, 27 Feb. He urged the continuation of the grant to the Kildare Place Society, 18 Mar., and voted against one for Irish national education, 23 July. He was listed in the minority against Crampton's amendment to the Irish tithes bill, 9 Apr., but in the majority against postponing it to

the next session, 13 July. He voted against the second reading of the Irish reform bill, 25 May, and, claiming to have done likewise on a former occasion, divided for Daniel O'Connell's motion to restore the 40s. freehold in Irish counties, 13 June. His only other known votes that session were with opposition against the Russian-Dutch loan, 26 Jan., 12 July 1832.

A founder member of the Carlton Club that year, Young was again returned for Cavan as a Conservative at the general election of 1832. He served as Sir Robert Peel's* chief whip in the mid-1840s and, having succeeded to the title and estates of his recently disgraced father in March 1848, was Irish secretary under Lord Aberdeen in the early 1850s. He left the Commons in March 1855, on being appointed to the first of a series of overseas postings, but he obtained a seat in the Lords 15 years later. He died in October 1876, when the barony of Lisgar became extinct, and was succeeded as 3rd baronet by his nephew, William Muston Need Young (1847-1934), an official in the Indian telegraph department. Lady Lisgar subsequently married her late husband's former private secretary, Sir Francis Charles Fortescue Turville of Bosworth Hall, Leicestershire.[9]

[1] Gent. Mag. (1848), i. 660. [2] Add. 40357, f. 195; NLI, Farnham mss 18602 (1), Young to Farnham, 16 Aug. 1823. [3] PRO NI, Richardson mss D2002/C/27/3; Farnham mss 18602 (18), Young to Maxwell, 10 June; Newry Commercial Telegraph, 23 June 1826. [4] Newry Commercial Telegraph, 6, 9, 13, 23, 30 July, 3, 17, 20 Aug.; Farnham mss 18602 (41), Saunderson to Maxwell [14 Aug.] 1830. [5] Enniskillener, 1 Sept. 1830. [6] Dublin Evening Post, 3, 24 May; Enniskillen Chron. 19, 26 May; Farnham mss 18602 (45), Headfort to Maxwell, 7 May 1831. [7] Farnham mss 18606 (1), Arbuthnot to Maxwell, 7 May, 15 June; Wellington mss, same to Wellington, 10, 17 Aug. 1831. [8] Belfast Guardian, 16 Dec. 1831; Ballyshannon Herald, 20 Jan. 1832. [9] The Times, 13 Mar. 1848, 9 Oct. 1876; Ann. Reg. (1876), Chron. p. 157; DNB; Oxford DNB.

S.M.F.